Frommer's®

W9-BMS-717

USA

10th Edition

Here's what the critics say about Frommer's:

"Amazingly easy to use. Very portable, very complete."

—*Booklist*

"Detailed, accurate, and easy-to-read information for all price ranges."
—*Glamour Magazine*

"Hotel information is close to encyclopedic."

—*Des Moines Sunday Register*

"Frommer's Guides have a way of giving you a real feel for a place."
—*Knight Ridder Newspapers*

BICENTENNIAL
1807
WILEY
2007
BICENTENNIAL

Wiley Publishing, Inc.

Published by:

Wiley Publishing, Inc.
111 River St.
Hoboken, NJ 07030-5774

ISBN: 978-0-470-04726-2

Editor: Naomi P. Kraus
with Mike Kelly and Anuja Madar
Production Editor: Ian Skinnari
Cartographer: Guy Ruggiero
Photo Editor: Richard Fox
Anniversary Logo Design: Richard Pacifico
Production by Wiley Indianapolis Composition Services

Front cover photo: Cowboy training a horse in New Mexico
Back cover photo: Farm in Vermont

Contents

4 The Southeast   214

5 Florida   332

6 The Gulf South   412

7 The Midwest   453

8 The Northern Rockies & Great Plains   557

9 Texas   615

10 Colorado & Utah   664

11 The Southwest   728

12 California   824

13 The Pacific Northwest   933

14 Alaska & Hawaii   987

Appendix A: The Best of the Rest   1024

List of Maps

Acknowledgments

This book has been created from dozens of Frommer's guides covering the United States, and it simply couldn't exist without the tireless efforts of our many talented writers. They deserve special recognition for spending countless hours hitting the pavement, inspecting hotels, sampling restaurants, chasing down information, and visiting attractions so they can offer you the best logistical tips.

Thanks for a job well done year in and year out to: Lesley Abravanel, David Baird, Harry Basch, Rich Beattie, Elizabeth Canning Blackwell, Shane Christensen, Victor Fiorillo, Elise Ford, Jeanette Foster, Bill Goodwin, Mary Herczog, Mark Hiss, Edie Jarolim, Paul Karr, Lesley King, Don and Barbara Laine, Erika Lenkert, Herbert Bailey Livesey, Laura Miller, Marie Morris, Eric Peterson, Matthew Poole, Darwin Porter and Danforth Prince, Laura Reckford, Kurt Repanshek, Linda Romine, Karl Samson and Jane Aukshunas, Neil Schlecht, Brian Silverman, Karen Snyder, David Swanson, Mary K. Tilghman, and Charles Wohlforth.

Special thanks also go to another group of contributors, who covered destinations especially for this guide: **Amy Donohue** (Atlantic City and Cape May), **Victor Fiorillo** (Philadelphia), **Karen Snyder** (Atlanta), **Darwin Porter** and **Danforth Prince** (Carolinas and Georgia), **Linda Romine** (Cleveland, Cincinnati, Kentucky, Tennessee, Alabama, and Mississippi), **Amy Eckert** (Pittsburgh, Michigan, Wisconsin, Minneapolis, and St. Paul), **Beth Reiber** (St. Louis, Kansas City, Branson, Oklahoma City, and Omaha), **David Baird** (Texas), **Karl Samson** (Oregon), **Matthew Poole** (Reno), **Harry Basch** (South Dakota), and **Bill McRae** (Idaho).

Major kudos to on-staff contributors **Christine Ryan, Ian Skinnari, Heather Wilcox, Katie Robinson, Jon Scott, David Lytle, Melinda Quintero,** and **Naomi Kraus.** Special thanks to editorial intern **Megan Murray** for her assistance.

This book also owes much to our on-staff cartographers: **Roberta Stockwell, Elizabeth Puhl, Guy Ruggiero, Andrew Murphy,** and **Andrew Dolan.**

An Invitation to the Reader

In researching this book, we discovered many wonderful places—hotels, restaurants, shops, and more. We're sure you'll find others. Please tell us about them, so we can share the information with your fellow travelers in upcoming editions. If you were disappointed with a recommendation, we'd love to know that, too. Please write to:

Frommer's USA, 10th Edition
Wiley Publishing, Inc. • 111 River St. • Hoboken, NJ 07030-5774

An Additional Note

Please be advised that travel information is subject to change at any time—and this is especially true of prices. We therefore suggest that you write or call ahead for confirmation when making your travel plans. The authors, editors, and publisher cannot be held responsible for the experiences of readers while traveling. Your safety is important to us, however, so we encourage you to stay alert and be aware of your surroundings. Keep a close eye on cameras, purses, and wallets, all favorite targets of thieves and pickpockets.

Frommer's Icons & Abbreviations

This book uses **three feature icons** that point you to the great deals, family-friendly options, and top experiences that separate travelers from tourists. Throughout the book, look for:

Kids   Best bets for kids and advice for the whole family

Value   Great values—where to get the best deals

Best   The best hotel, restaurant, or attraction in the city or region

The following **abbreviations** are used for credit cards:

AE American Express	DISC Discover	V Visa
DC Diners Club	MC MasterCard	

Frommers.com

Now that you have this guidebook to help you plan a great trip, visit our website at **www.frommers.com** for additional travel information on more than 3,500 destinations. We update features regularly to give you instant access to the most current trip-planning information available. At Frommers.com, you'll find scoops on the best airfares, lodging rates, and car rental bargains. You can even book your travel online through our reliable travel booking partners. Other popular features include:

- Online updates of our most popular guidebooks
- Vacation sweepstakes and contest giveaways
- Newsletters highlighting the hottest travel trends
- Online travel message boards with featured travel discussions

Planning Your Trip to the USA

If the United States has one defining quality, it's variety. This vast area of some 3.6 million square miles—it's 2,500 miles from New York to Los Angeles, and that again to Hawaii—has something for everyone.

Although TV, suburban sprawl, strip malls, and chain restaurants have a homogenizing effect, America hasn't yet become a monolithic place. Each region still speaks with its own accent, enjoys its own favorite foods, and has its own political and social attitudes. Indeed, you sometimes wonder if we aren't one nation but an amalgam of 50 little countries. We've seen New Yorkers floored by the laid-back pace of the West Coast (but ultimately thrilled by the "enforced" relaxation), and southerners slightly frazzled by the Big Apple's breakneck pace (but totally enthused by the vast number of shopping and dining opportunities in the space of a few square miles). Whatever you want to see, do, or eat, you're likely to find it within the vast and diverse confines of the United States of America.

WHAT'S HERE & WHAT'S NOT

It's not easy to boil down the essence of such a huge, varied, complicated country. No doubt, some of you will look at the table of contents and raise an eyebrow at what's missing. That's sure to be the case with any guide professing to cover the entire United States.

This book doesn't pretend to be comprehensive. It's simply not possible to cover every great destination in the country in one usable volume. We did, however, concentrate on a select group of destinations that will appeal to a wide cross section of domestic travelers, be they road-trippers, business travelers, outdoor enthusiasts, history buffs, or museum lovers. This way, rather than glossing over lots of destinations with coverage that's broad but an inch deep, we've been able to offer you in-depth, practical coverage you can really use.

Take, for example, Martha's Vineyard and Nantucket: We'd love to cover both islands, but we chose to focus on Martha's Vineyard instead. Few travelers have time to visit both, so we used the space to include more detailed and useful information on the Vineyard, which is larger and easier to reach. We've applied the same sort of logic to our destination choices throughout. In the end, we've come up with a list of destinations that's representative of the very best America has to offer—cities, national parks, beaches, resort areas, and more.

And because we recognize the diversity of American travelers and their interests, you will find at least some information on every single state in the Union inside these pages. In appendix A, we highlight the best offerings of five states that would otherwise get the (undeserved) short end of the stick.

We hope you'll discover your own America as you hit the road and start exploring. If you'd like more coverage of

The USA—Major Interstate Routes

the destinations covered here, or if any of them prompt you to explore further—if you want to see Nantucket, say, after the Vineyard has charmed you—chances are good that we have a more dedicated, in-depth guidebook for you; see the complete list of destinations covered by Frommer's guides at the end of this book. Happy trails!

Note: International visitors, be sure to check out appendix C as well for planning information tailored exclusively to you.

1 When to Go

Climate differences are dramatic across the United States. When it's shivering cold in New England, the upper central states, and Alaska, it's sunny and warm in Florida, California, and Hawaii. When it's raining cats and dogs along the Northwest coast, it's dry as a bone in the Southwest desert. It can be a pleasant 75°F (24°C) on the beaches of Southern California in summer, yet 120°F (49°C) just a few miles inland.

And there isn't a nationwide high or low season. In summer, room rates are highest on the Northeast and mid-Atlantic beaches but lowest on the sands of hot-and-humid Florida (though not in Central Florida, where rates can reach sky-high proportions) and in the sticky climes of the Gulf South. Winter snows virtually close the great Rocky Mountain national parks and the major tourism centers of the northern Great Plains, but they bring crowds to the nearby ski slopes. Alaska is usually well below freezing until summer, when the midnight sun smiles down on warm days, and higher hotel rates greet the tourist crowds. Hawaii is warm year-round, but winter brings massive amounts of rain—and higher prices.

The Northeast and mid-Atlantic states have their summer beach season from June to Labor Day and their great fall foliage in September and October. Climate can vary wildly in these regions: One day can be warm and lovely, the next muggy and miserable. Winter storms are not an infrequent occurrence in these regions—New England is practically famous for its nor'easters—though some mid-Atlantic winters in the not-too-distant past have been remarkably mild (and others have been frigid—the unpredictability of the weather in this region is always a safe topic of discussion).

Summer can be brutally hot and humid in the Southeast (and is also prime hurricane season), but spring and fall last longer there, and winter is mild—with snow the exception rather than the rule. The Gulf South summers are often exceptionally sticky and hot, though winters (except in the mountain areas) are generally mild, if rainy. Southern Florida's best season is from January to April, though cold snaps can turn it nippy for a few days. The central states see harsh winters and scorching summers. Southwest weather varies from east Texas's hot, humid summers and mild winters to Arizona's dry, 110°F (43°C) summers and pleasant, dry winters. Nevada is similar, though it tends to get a bit chillier in winter. The mountains of Colorado, Utah, and the Northwest have dry, moderately hot summers and cold, snowy winters. The California coast is fine all year except early spring, when it rains; the Northwest coast is wet most of the time except July.

The long and the short of it: Late spring and early fall are the best times to visit most of the country. See "Special Events & Festivals" in all of the chapters that follow for more dates around which to plan your trip.

2 Money Matters

ATMS

Nationwide, the easiest and best way to get cash away from home is from an ATM (automated teller machine), sometimes referred to as a "cash machine," or "cashpoint." The **Cirrus** (℃ **800/424-7787**; www.mastercard.com) and **PLUS** (℃ **800/843-7587**; www.visa.com) networks span the country; you can find them even in remote regions. Look at the back of your bank card to see which network you're on, then call or check online for ATM locations at your destination. Be sure you know your personal identification number (PIN) and daily withdrawal limit before you depart. *Note:* Remember that many banks impose a fee every time you use a card at another bank's ATM, and that fee can be higher for international transactions (up to $5 or more) than for domestic ones (where they're rarely more than $2). In addition, the bank from which you withdraw cash may charge its own fee. To compare banks' ATM fees within the U.S., use **www.bankrate.com**. For international withdrawal fees, ask your bank.

CREDIT CARDS & DEBIT CARDS

Credit cards are the most widely used form of payment in the United States: **Visa** (Barclaycard in Britain), **MasterCard** (Eurocard in Europe, Access in Britain, Chargex in Canada), **American Express, Diners Club,** and **Discover.** They also provide a convenient record of all your expenses, and they generally offer relatively good exchange rates. You can withdraw cash advances from your credit cards at banks or ATMs, provided you know your PIN.

Visitors from outside the U.S. should inquire whether their bank assesses a 1% to 3% fee on charges incurred abroad.

It's highly recommended that you travel with at least one major credit card.

You must have one to rent a car, and hotels and airlines usually require a credit card imprint as a deposit against expenses. (*Note:* Businesses in some U.S. cities may require a minimum purchase, usually around $10, before letting you use a credit card.)

ATM cards with major credit card backing, known as **"debit cards,"** are now a commonly acceptable form of payment in most stores and restaurants. Debit cards draw money directly from your checking account. Some stores enable you to receive "cash back" on your debit-card purchases as well. The same is true at most U.S. post offices.

TRAVELER'S CHECKS

Traveler's checks are usually accepted in the U.S., but foreign visitors should make sure that they're denominated in U.S. dollars; foreign-currency checks are often difficult to exchange.

You can buy traveler's checks at most banks. Most are offered in denominations of $20, $50, $100, $500, and sometimes $1,000. Generally, you'll pay a service charge ranging from 1% to 4%.

The most popular traveler's checks are offered by **American Express** (℃ **800/807-6233**, or 800/221-7282 for card holders—this number accepts collect calls, offers service in several foreign languages, and exempts Amex gold and platinum cardholders from the 1% fee.); **Visa** (℃ **800/732-1322**)—AAA members can obtain Visa checks for a $9.95 fee (for checks up to $1,500) at most AAA offices or by calling ℃ **866/339-3378**; and **MasterCard** (℃ **800/223-9920**).

If you do choose to carry traveler's checks, keep a record of their serial numbers separate from your checks in the event that they are stolen or lost. You'll get a refund faster if you know the numbers.

3 Travel Insurance

The cost of travel insurance varies widely, depending on the cost and length of your trip, your age and health, and the type of trip you're taking, but expect to pay between 5% and 8% of the vacation itself. You can get estimates from various providers through **InsureMyTrip.com**. Enter your trip cost and dates, your age, and other information, for prices from more than a dozen companies.

Note: Many tour operators, particularly those offering trips to remote or high-risk areas, include insurance in the cost of the trip or can arrange insurance policies through a partnering provider, a convenient and often cost-effective way for the traveler to obtain insurance. Make sure the tour company is a reputable one, however: Some experts suggest you avoid buying insurance from the tour or cruise company you're traveling with, saying it's better to buy from a "third party" insurer than to put all your money in one place.

TRIP-CANCELLATION INSURANCE

Trip-cancellation insurance will help retrieve your money if you have to back out of a trip or depart early, or if your travel supplier goes bankrupt. Permissible reasons for trip cancellation can range from sickness to natural disasters to the State Department declaring a destination unsafe for travel.

For more information, contact one of the following recommended insurers:

Access America (© 866/807-3982; www.accessamerica.com); **Travel Guard International** (© 800/826-4919; www.travelguard.com); **Travel Insured International** (© 800/243-3174; www.travelinsured.com); and **Travelex Insurance Services** (© 888/457-4602; www.travelex-insurance.com).

MEDICAL INSURANCE

Although it's not required of travelers, health insurance is highly recommended. Most health insurance policies cover you if you get sick away from home—but verify that you're covered before you depart, particularly if you're insured by an HMO.

LOST-LUGGAGE INSURANCE

On flights within the U.S., checked baggage is covered up to $2,500 per ticketed passenger. If you plan to check items more valuable than what's covered by the standard liability, see if your homeowner's policy covers your valuables, get baggage insurance as part of your comprehensive travel-insurance package, or buy Travel Guard's "BagTrak" product.

If your luggage is lost, immediately file a lost-luggage claim at the airport, detailing the luggage contents. Most airlines require that you report delayed, damaged, or lost baggage within 4 hours of arrival. The airlines are required to deliver luggage, once found, directly to your house or destination free of charge.

Travel in the Age of Bankruptcy

Airlines go bankrupt, so protect yourself by **buying your tickets with a credit card.** The Fair Credit Billing Act guarantees that you can get your money back from the credit card company if a travel supplier goes under (and if you request the refund within 60 days of the bankruptcy). **Travel insurance** can also help, but make sure it covers against "carrier default" for your specific travel provider. And be aware that if a U.S. airline goes bust midtrip, a 2001 federal law requires other carriers to take you to your destination (albeit on a space-available basis) for a fee of no more than $25, provided you rebook within 60 days of the cancellation.

4 Health & Safety

HEALTH

The United States doesn't present any unusual health hazards, provided travelers take reasonable precautions. **Lyme Disease,** carried by deer ticks, is a growing concern in the woodlands of the Northeast and mid-Atlantic, but you can seriously minimize your risk by using insect repellent and by covering up when hiking in the deep woods. Should you get bitten by a tick or notice a bull's-eye-shaped rash after hiking or camping, consult a doctor immediately. Another insect-related illness that's become a nationwide issue is **West Nile Virus,** spread by mosquitoes. Again, use insect repellent and avoid swampy areas during the summer mosquito season, and you should encounter no problems. To keep from contracting **rabies,** avoid contact with wild animals, no matter how cute or friendly they appear. If you even think you may have been exposed, see a doctor at once.

In the Rocky Mountain states and the high elevations of the Southwest, one of the biggest health concerns is **altitude sickness.** Don't arrive in Denver planning to tackle the Rocky Mountains on the same day—the only thing that will happen is that you'll end up short of breath, exhausted, or worse. The best way to avoid this is to ease your transition into high altitude climates, drink lots of water, and get plenty of rest; if you have breathing difficulties, your doctor may be able to prescribe medication to ease any difficulties.

If you plan on visiting some of the country's sun-soaked spots, limit the time you spend in direct sunlight and bring sunscreen with a high protection factor (at least 25). Apply it liberally—and often. This advice goes double if you're climbing at high altitudes, where the air is thinner and it's far easier to get a serious burn (even if the climate is actually cold).

Skin cancer is one of the fastest-growing illnesses in the United States and it doesn't take much time in the sun to do serious damage. Remember that children need more protection than adults do.

The other natural hazards for outdoor enthusiasts include **poison ivy** (learn to recognize and avoid it) and **hazardous wildlife** (never approach a wild animal or feed it). To minimize risks, never hike alone, notify someone of your planned hiking route, always carry a first-aid kit, and check in with park rangers to get the lowdown on possible hazards in the area in which you're hiking. If you're hiking in forested areas during hunting season, be sure to wear brightly colored clothing.

If you plan to head into the great outdoors, keep in mind that injuries often occur when people fail to follow instructions. Believe the experts who tell you to stay on the established ski trails and hike only in designated areas. Follow the marine charts if you're piloting your own boat. If you're rafting, wear a life jacket. If you're biking or rock climbing, be sure to use appropriate safety gear. Mountain weather can be fickle at any time of the year, so carry rain gear and pack a few warm layers. Watch out for summer thunderstorms that can leave you drenched or send bolts of lightning your way. In the Southwest, a summer storm can easily cause a flash flood, so be cautious and keep your wits about you.

When camping, always inquire if campfires are allowed in the area in which you are traveling. Some of the country's worst forest fires in recent years were started by careless campers who didn't follow proper safety protocols.

Tap water is safe to drink throughout the country, though you can get bottled water pretty much everywhere if you prefer it. Water in the wild should always be treated or boiled before drinking it.

The United States **Centers for Disease Control and Prevention** (© 800/311-3435; www.cdc.gov) provides up-to-date information on health hazards by region and offers tips on food safety.

If you suffer from a chronic illness, consult your doctor before your departure. For conditions like epilepsy, diabetes, or heart problems, wear a **MedicAlert identification tag** (© 888/633-4298; www.medic alert.org), which will immediately alert doctors to your condition and give them access to your records through MedicAlert's 24-hour hot line. If you have dental problems, a nationwide referral service known as **1-800-DENTIST** (© 800/336-8478) can give you the name of a nearby dentist or clinic.

Pack **prescription medications** in your carry-on luggage, and carry them in their original containers, with pharmacy labels—otherwise they won't make it through airport security. Also bring along copies of your prescriptions in case you lose your pills or run out. Don't forget an extra pair of contact lenses or prescription glasses.

SAFETY

Although tourist areas are generally safe, U.S. urban areas have their fair share of crime. You should always stay alert; this is particularly true of large cities. If you're in doubt about which neighborhoods are safe, don't hesitate to inquire at the hotel's front desk or at the local tourist office.

Avoid deserted areas, especially at night, and don't go into public parks after dark unless there's a concert or similar occasion that will attract a crowd.

Avoid carrying valuables with you on the street, and keep expensive cameras or electronic equipment bagged up or covered when not in use. If you're using a map, try to consult it inconspicuously—or better yet, study it before you leave your room. Hold on to your pocketbook, and place your billfold in an inside pocket. In theaters, restaurants, and other public places, keep your possessions in sight.

Always lock your room door—don't assume that once you're inside the hotel you are automatically safe and no longer need to be aware of your surroundings. Hotels are open to the public, and in a large hotel, security may not be able to screen everyone who enters.

DRIVING SAFETY Driving safety is important too, and carjacking is not unprecedented. Question your rental agency about personal safety, and ask for a traveler-safety brochure when you pick up your car. Obtain written directions—or a map with the route clearly marked—from the agency showing how to get to your destination. And, if possible, arrive and depart during daylight hours.

If you drive off a highway and end up in a dodgy-looking neighborhood, leave the area as quickly as possible. If you have an accident, even on the highway, stay in your car with the doors locked until you assess the situation or until the police arrive. If you're bumped from behind on the street or are involved in a minor accident with no injuries, and the situation appears to be suspicious, motion to the other driver to follow you. Never get out of your car in such situations. Go directly to the nearest police precinct, well-lit service station, or 24-hour store. You may want to look into renting a cellphone on a short-term basis. One recommended wireless rental company is **InTouch USA** (© 800/872-7626; www.intouchusa.com).

Park in well-lit and well-traveled areas whenever possible. Always keep your car doors locked, whether the vehicle is attended or unattended. Never leave any packages or valuables in sight. If someone attempts to rob you or steal your car, don't try to resist the thief/carjacker. Report the incident to the police department immediately by calling © **911.**

5 Specialized Travel Resources

TRAVELERS WITH DISABILITIES

Most disabilities shouldn't stop anyone from traveling in the U.S. There are more options and resources out there than ever before.

The **Golden Access Passport** gives visually impaired or permanently disabled persons (regardless of age) free lifetime entrance to all properties administered by the National Park Service, the U.S. Fish and Wildlife Service, the U.S. Forest Service, the U.S. Army Corps of Engineers, the Bureau of Land Management, and the Tennessee Valley Authority. This may include national parks, monuments, historic sites, recreation areas, and national wildlife refuges.

You may pick up a Golden Access Passport at any NPS entrance fee area by showing proof of medically determined disability and eligibility for benefits under federal law. Besides free entry, the Golden Access Passport also offers a 50% discount on federal-use fees charged for such facilities as camping, swimming, parking, boat launching, and tours. For more information, go to www.nps.gov/fees_passes.htm or call © 888/467-2757.

Many travel agencies offer customized tours and itineraries for travelers with disabilities. Among them are **Flying Wheels Travel** (© 507/451-5005; www.flyingwheelstravel.com); **Access-Able Travel Source** (© 303/232-2979; www.access-able.com); and **Accessible Journeys** (© 800/846-4537 or 610/521-0339; www.disabilitytravel.com). **Avis Rent a Car** has an "Avis Access" program that offers such services as a dedicated 24-hour toll-free number (© 888/879-4273) for customers with special travel needs; special car features such as swivel seats, spinner knobs, and hand controls; and accessible bus service.

Organizations that offer assistance to travelers with disabilities include **MossRehab** (www.mossresourcenet.org); the **American Foundation for the Blind (AFB)** (© 800/232-5463; www.afb.org); and **SATH** (Society for Accessible Travel & Hospitality) (© 212/447-7284; www.sath.org). **AirAmbulanceCard.com** is now partnered with SATH and allows you to preselect top-notch hospitals in case of an emergency.

The community website **iCan** (www.icanonline.net/channels/travel) has destination guides and several regular columns on accessible travel. Also check out the quarterly magazine *Emerging Horizons* (www.emerginghorizons.com); and *Open World* magazine, published by SATH.

GAY & LESBIAN TRAVELERS

The International Gay and Lesbian Travel Association (IGLTA) (© 800/448-8550 or 954/776-2626; www.iglta.org) is the trade association for the gay and lesbian travel industry, and offers an online directory of gay- and lesbian-friendly travel businesses; go to their website and click on "Members."

Many agencies offer tours and travel itineraries specifically for gay and lesbian travelers. Among them are **Above and Beyond Tours** (© 800/397-2681; www.abovebeyondtours.com); **Now, Voyager** (© 800/255-6951; www.nowvoyager.com); and **Olivia Cruises & Resorts** (© 800/631-6277; www.olivia.com).

Gay.com Travel (© 800/929-2268 or 415/644-8044; www.gay.com/travel or www.outandabout.com), is an excellent online successor to the popular *Out & About* print magazine. It provides regularly updated information about gay-owned, gay-oriented, and gay-friendly lodging, dining, sightseeing, nightlife, and shopping establishments in every important destination worldwide.

The following travel guides are available at many bookstores, or you can order them from any online bookseller: *Spartacus International Gay Guide* (Bruno Gmünder Verlag; www.spartacusworld.com/gayguide) and *Odysseus: The International Gay Travel Planner* (Odysseus Enterprises Ltd.); and the *Damron* guides (www.damron.com), with separate, annual books for gay men and lesbians.

SENIOR TRAVEL

Mention the fact that you're a senior when you make your travel reservations. Many hotels offer discounts for seniors. In most cities, people over the age of 60 qualify for reduced admission to theaters, museums, and other attractions, as well as discounted fares on public transportation.

Members of **AARP** (formerly known as the American Association of Retired Persons), 601 E St. NW, Washington, DC 20049 (© **888/687-2277;** www.aarp.org), get discounts on hotels, airfares, and car rentals. AARP offers members a wide range of benefits, including *AARP: The Magazine* and a monthly newsletter. Anyone over 50 can join.

The **U.S. National Park Service** offers a **Golden Age Passport** that gives seniors 62 years or older lifetime entrance to all properties administered by the National Park Service—national parks, monuments, historic sites, recreation areas, and national wildlife refuges—for a one-time processing fee of $10, which must be purchased in person at any NPS facility that charges an entrance fee. Besides free entry, a Golden Age Passport also offers a 50% discount on federal-use fees charged for such facilities as camping, swimming, parking, boat launching, and tours. For more information, go to www.nps.gov/fees_passes.htm or call © **888/467-2757.**

Many reliable agencies and organizations target the 50-plus market. **Elderhostel** (© **877/426-8056;** www.elderhostel.org) arranges study programs for those aged 55 and over. **ElderTreks** (© **800/741-7956;** www.eldertreks.com) offers small-group tours to off-the-beaten-path or adventure-travel locations, restricted to travelers 50 and older. **INTRAV** (© **800/456-8100;** www.intrav.com) is a high-end tour operator that caters to the mature, discerning traveler (not specifically seniors), with trips that include guided safaris, private-jet adventures, and small-boat cruises.

Recommended publications offering travel resources and discounts for seniors include: the quarterly magazine *Travel 50 & Beyond* (www.travel50andbeyond.com); *Travel Unlimited: Uncommon Adventures for the Mature Traveler* (Avalon); *101 Tips for Mature Travelers,* available from Grand Circle Travel (© **800/221-2610** or 617/350-7500; www.gct.com); and *Unbelievably Good Deals and Great Adventures That You Absolutely Can't Get Unless You're Over 50* (McGraw-Hill), by Joann Rattner Heilman.

FAMILY TRAVEL

To locate accommodations, restaurants, and attractions that are particularly kid-friendly, refer to the "Kids" icon throughout this guide.

Familyhostel (© **800/733-9753;** www.learn.unh.edu/familyhostel) takes the whole family, including kids ages 8 to 15, on moderately priced U.S. and international learning vacations. Lectures, field trips, and sightseeing are guided by a team of academics.

Recommended family travel websites include **Family Travel Forum** (www.familytravelforum.com), a comprehensive site that offers customized trip planning; **Family Travel Network** (www.familytravelnetwork.com), an award-winning site that offers travel features, deals, and tips; **Traveling Internationally with**

Your Kids (www.travelwithyourkids. com), a comprehensive site offering sound advice for long-distance and international travel with children; and **Family Travel Files** (www.thefamilytravelfiles.com), which offers an online magazine and a directory of off-the-beaten-path tours and tour operators for families.

Frommer's and the Unofficial Guides both publish a "With Kids" series that features some of the major tourist destinations in the United States.

WOMEN TRAVELERS

More and more hotels in the United States are ratcheting up security measures for women traveling alone on business or for pleasure. Some are even offering secure "women only" floors, with the added perk of spa services.

Check out the award-winning website **Journeywoman** (www.journeywoman. com), a "real life" women's travel-information network where you can sign up for a free e-mail newsletter and get advice on everything from etiquette and dress to safety; or the travel guide *Safety and Security for Women Who Travel* by Sheila Swan and Peter Laufer (Travelers' Tales, Inc.), offering common-sense tips on safe travel.

AFRICAN-AMERICAN TRAVELERS

Black Travel Online (www.blacktravel online.com) posts news on upcoming events and includes links to articles and travel-booking sites. **Soul of America** (www.soulofamerica.com) is a comprehensive website, with travel tips, event and family-reunion postings, and sections on historically black beach resorts and active vacations.

Agencies and organizations that provide resources for black travelers include: **Rodgers Travel** (© 800/825-1775; www.rodgerstravel.com); the **African American Association of Innkeepers International** (© 877/422-5777; www. africanamericaninns.com); and **Henderson Travel & Tours** (© 800/327-2309 or 301/650-5700; www.hendersontravel. com), which has specialized in trips to Africa since 1957. For more information, check out the following collections and guides: *Go Girl: The Black Woman's Guide to Travel & Adventure* (Eighth Mountain Press), a compilation of travel essays by writers including Jill Nelson and Audre Lorde; *The African American Travel Guide* by Wayne Robinson (Hunter Publishing; www. hunterpublishing.com); *Steppin' Out* by

On Your Own or with a Furry Friend

Prefer to do your traveling alone? So long as you avoid all-inclusive resorts and vacation packages (which base their prices on double occupancy), you likely won't face the dreaded "single supplement," a penalty added to the base price of a room or package. For more information, Eleanor Berman's latest edition of *Traveling Solo: Advice and Ideas for More Than 250 Great Vacations* (Globe Pequot), a guide with advice on traveling alone, either solo or as part of a group tour.

If, like John Steinbeck, you want to take your dog (or cat, or whatever) with you for companionship on your travels, many hotels across the U.S. (for example, all Motel 6 properties) will be happy to roll out the welcome mat for your pet. For travel tips and advice on traveling with Fido or Fluffy, head online to **www.petswelcome.com, www.pettravel.com,** and **www.travelpets.com.**

Carla Labat (Avalon); *Travel and Enjoy Magazine* (© 866/266-6211; www.travelandenjoy.com); and *Pathfinders Magazine* (© 877/977-PATH; www.pathfinderstravel.com), which includes articles on everything from Rio de Janeiro to Ghana as well as information on upcoming ski, diving, golf, and tennis trips.

6 Planning Your Trip Online

SURFING FOR AIRFARE

The most popular online travel agencies are **Travelocity** (**www.travelocity.com** or www.travelocity.co.uk); **Expedia** (**www.expedia.com**, www.expedia.co.uk, or www.expedia.ca); and **Orbitz** (**www.orbitz.com**).

In addition, most airlines now offer online-only fares that even their phone agents know nothing about. For the websites of airlines that fly to and within the United States, go to appendix D.

Other helpful websites for booking airline tickets online include:

- www.biddingfortravel.com
- www.cheapflights.com
- www.hotwire.com
- www.kayak.com
- www.lastminutetravel.com
- www.opodo.co.uk
- www.priceline.com
- www.sidestep.com
- www.site59.com
- www.smartertravel.com

SURFING FOR HOTELS

In addition to **Travelocity, Expedia, Orbitz, Priceline,** and **Hotwire** (see above), the following websites will help you with booking hotel rooms online:

- www.hotels.com
- www.quickbook.com
- www.travelaxe.net
- www.travelweb.com
- www.tripadvisor.com

Of the sites listed above, we really like Travelaxe. It's an excellent free program that can help you search multiple hotel sites at once, even ones you may never have heard of—and conveniently lists the total price of the room, including the taxes and service charges.

If you plan on bidding for a hotel room on Priceline, be sure to visit the **BiddingForTravel** website (www.biddingfortravel.com) before placing the bid; it features a fairly up-to-date list of hotels in the U.S. that Priceline uses in major cities and you'll get a fairly good idea of how much to bid for a hotel in your selected area. The downside is that the site does not offer information on Hotwire hotels—for help in getting a good hotel room on that site, try **www.betterbidding.com**.

It's always a good idea to **get a confirmation number** and **make a printout** of any online booking transaction.

And keep in mind that hotels at the top of a site's listing may be there for no other reason than that they paid money to get the placement.

SURFING FOR RENTAL CARS

For booking rental cars online, the best deals are usually found at rental-car company websites, although all the major online travel agencies also offer rental-car reservations services. Priceline and Hotwire work well for rental cars, too; the only "mystery" is which major rental company you get, and for most travelers the difference between Hertz, Avis, and Budget is negligible.

TRAVEL BLOGS & TRAVELOGUES

To read a few blogs about destinations within the United States, try:

- www.gridskipper.com
- www.salon.com/wanderlust
- www.travelblog.com
- www.travelblog.org
- www.worldhum.com
- www.writtenroad.com

Frommers.com: The Complete Travel Resource

For an excellent travel-planning resource, we highly recommend **Frommers. com** (www.frommers.com), voted Best Travel Site by *PC Magazine*. We're a little biased, of course, but we guarantee that you'll find the travel tips, reviews, monthly vacation giveaways, bookstore, and online-booking capabilities thoroughly indispensable. Among the special features are our popular **Destinations** section, where you'll get expert travel tips, hotel and dining recommendations, and advice on the sights to see for more than 3,500 destinations around the globe; the **Frommers.com Newsletter,** with the latest deals, travel trends, and money-saving secrets; our **Community** area featuring **Message Boards,** where Frommer's readers post queries and share advice (sometimes even our authors show up to answer questions); and our **Photo Center,** where you can post and share vacation tips. When your research is done, the **Online Reservations System** (www.frommers. com/book_a_trip) takes you to Frommer's preferred online partners for booking your vacation at affordable prices.

7 The 21st-Century Traveler

INTERNET ACCESS AWAY FROM HOME
WITHOUT YOUR OWN COMPUTER

It's hard nowadays to find a city that *doesn't* have a few cybercafes. Although there's no definitive directory for cybercafes—these are independent businesses, after all—two places to start looking are at **www.cybercaptive.com** and **www. cybercafe.com**.

Aside from formal cybercafes, most **public libraries** in the United States offer Internet access free or for a small charge. Avoid **hotel business centers** unless you're willing to pay exorbitant rates.

WITH YOUR OWN COMPUTER

More and more hotels, cafes, and retailers are signing on as Wi-Fi (wireless fidelity) "hotspots." Mac owners have their own networking technology, Apple AirPort. **T-Mobile Hotspot** (www.t-mobile.com/hotspot) has wireless connections at more than 1,000 Starbucks coffee shops nationwide. **Boingo** (www.boingo.com)

and **Wayport** (www.wayport.com) have set up networks in airports and high-class hotel lobbies. IPass providers (see below) also give you access to a few hundred wireless hotel lobby setups. To locate other hotspots that provide **free wireless networks** in cities around the world, go to **www.personaltelco.net/index.cgi/WirelessCommunities**.

For dial-up access, most business-class hotels in the U.S. offer dataports for laptop modems, and a few thousand hotels in the U.S. and Europe now offer free high-speed Internet access. In addition, major Internet service providers (ISPs) have **local access numbers** around the world, allowing you to go online by placing a local call. The **iPass** network also has dial-up numbers around the world. You'll have to sign up with an iPass provider, who will then tell you how to set up your computer for your destination(s). For a list of iPass providers, go to **www.ipass.com** and click on "Individuals Buy Now." One solid provider is

Online Traveler's Toolbox

Veteran travelers usually carry some essential items to make their trips easier. Following is a selection of handy online tools to bookmark and use.

- **Airplane Food** (www.airlinemeals.net)
- **Airplane Seating** (www.seatguru.com; www.airlinequality.com)
- **Maps** (www.mapquest.com)
- **Subway Navigator** (www.subwaynavigator.com)
- **Time and Date** (www.timeanddate.com)
- **Travel Warnings** (http://travel.state.gov; www.fco.gov.uk/travel; www.voyage.gc.ca; www.dfat.gov.au/consular/advice)
- **Universal Currency Converter** (www.xe.com/ucc)
- **Visa ATM Locator** (www.visa.com)
- **MasterCard ATM Locator** (www.mastercard.com)
- **Weather** (www.intellicast.com; www.weather.com)

i2roam (www.i2roam.com; © **866/811-6209** or 920/235-0475).

Wherever you go, bring a **connection kit** of the right power and phone adapters, a spare phone cord, and a spare Ethernet network cable—or find out whether your hotel supplies them to guests.

USING A CELLPHONE

Just because your cellphone works at home doesn't mean it'll work everywhere in the U.S. (thanks to our nation's fragmented cellphone system). It's a good bet that your phone will work in major cities, but take a look at your wireless company's coverage map on its website before heading out; T-Mobile, Sprint, and Nextel are particularly weak in rural areas. If you need to stay in touch at a destination where you know your phone won't work,

rent a phone that does from **InTouch USA** (© **800/872-7626**; www.intouch global.com) or a rental car location, but beware that you'll pay $1 a minute or more for airtime.

If you're venturing deep into national parks, you may want to consider renting a **satellite phone ("satphone").** It's different from a cellphone in that it connects to satellites rather than ground-based towers. Unfortunately, you'll pay at least $2 per minute to use the phone, and it only works where you can see the horizon (i.e., usually not indoors). In North America, you can rent Iridium satellite phones from **RoadPost** (www.roadpost.com; © **888/290-1606** or 905/272-5665). InTouch USA (see above) offers a wider range of satphones but at higher rates.

8 Getting Around the United States

BY PLANE

For long-distance trips, the most efficient way to get around the United States is by plane, even in these days of increased security and poor airline service. See appendix D at the end of this book for a

list of airlines, with their toll-free numbers and websites.

GETTING THROUGH THE AIRPORT

- Arrive at the airport 1 hour before a domestic flight and 2 hours before an international flight; if you show up late, tell an airline employee and he or she will probably whisk you to the front of the line.

- Beat the ticket-counter lines by using airport electronic kiosks or even online check-in from your home computer, from where you can print out boarding passes in advance. Curbside check-in is also a good way to avoid lines.

- Bring a current, government-issued photo ID such as a driver's license or passport. Children under 18 do not need government-issued photo IDs for flights within the U.S., but they do for international flights.

- Speed up security by removing your jacket and shoes before you're screened. In addition, remove metal objects such as big belt buckles. If you've got metallic body parts, a note from your doctor can prevent a long chat with the security screeners.

- Use a TSA-approved lock for your checked luggage. Look for Travel Sentry certified locks at luggage or travel shops and Brookstone stores (or online at **www.brookstone.com**).

FLYING FOR LESS: TIPS FOR GETTING THE BEST AIRFARE

- Passengers who can book their ticket either **long in advance or at the last minute,** or who **fly midweek** or at **less-trafficked hours** may pay a fraction of the full fare. If your schedule is flexible, say so, and ask if you can secure a cheaper fare by changing your flight plans.

- Search **the Internet** for cheap fares (see "Planning Your Trip Online," above).

- Keep an eye on local newspapers for **promotional specials** or **fare wars,** when airlines lower prices on their most popular routes. You rarely see fare wars offered for peak travel times, but if you can travel in the off-months, you may snag a bargain.

- Join **frequent-flier clubs.** Frequent-flier membership doesn't cost a cent, but it does entitle you to better seats, faster response to phone inquiries, and

---

(*Tips*) Coping with Jet Lag

Jet lag is a pitfall of traveling across time zones. If you're flying north-south and you feel sluggish when you touch down, your symptoms will be the result of dehydration and the general stress of air travel. When you travel east-west or vice versa, however, your body becomes thoroughly confused about what time it is, and everything from your digestive system to your brain is knocked for a loop. Traveling east, say from San Francisco to Boston, is more difficult on your internal clock than traveling west, say from Atlanta to Hawaii, because most peoples' bodies are more inclined to stay up late than fall asleep early.

Here are some tips for combating jet lag:

- **Reset your watch** to your destination time before you board the plane.
- **Drink lots of water** before, during, and after your flight. Avoid alcohol.
- **Exercise and sleep well** for a few days before your trip.
- If you have trouble sleeping on planes, **fly eastward on morning flights.**
- **Daylight** is the key to resetting your body clock. At the website for **Outside In (www.bodyclock.com),** you can get a customized plan of when to seek and avoid light.

Tips for Digital Travel Photography

- **Take along a spare camera—or two.** Even if you've been anointed the "official" photographer of your travel group, encourage others in your party to carry their own cameras and provide fresh perspectives—and backup. Your photographic "second unit" may include you in a few shots so you're not the invisible person of the trip.

- **Stock up on digital film cards.** At home, it's easy to copy pictures from your memory cards to your computer as they fill up. During your travels, cards seem to fill up more quickly. Take along enough digital film for your entire trip or, at a minimum, enough for at least a few days' of shooting. At intervals, you can copy images to CDs. Many camera stores and souvenir shops offer this service, and a growing number of mass merchandisers have walk-up kiosks you can use to make prints or create CDs while you travel.

- **Share and share alike.** No need to wait until you get home to share your photos. You can upload a gallery's worth to an online photo sharing service. Just find an Internet cafe where the computers have card readers, or connect your camera to the computer with a cable. You can find online photo sharing services that cost little or nothing at **www.click herefree.com**. You can also use America Online's Your Pictures service, or commercial enterprises that give you free or low-cost photo sharing: Kodak's EasyShare gallery **(www.kodak.com)**, Yahoo! Photos **(www. photos.yahoo.com)**, Snapfish **(www.snapfish.com)**, or Shutterfly **(www. shutterfly.com)**.

- **Add voice annotations to your photos.** Many digital cameras allow you to add voice annotations to your shots after they're taken. These serve as excellent reminders and documentation. One castle or cathedral may look like another after a long tour; your voice notes will help you distinguish them.

- **Experiment!** Travel is a great time to try out new techniques. Take photos at night, resting your camera on a handy wall or other support as your self-timer trips the shutter for a long exposure. Try close-ups of flowers, crafts, wildlife, or maybe the exotic cuisine you're about to consume. Discover action photography—shoot the countryside from trains, buses, or cars. With a digital camera, you can experiment and then erase your mistakes.

—From Travel Photography Digital Field Guide, *1st Edition*
(John Wiley & Sons, 2006)

prompter service if your luggage is stolen or your flight is canceled or delayed, or if you want to change your seat. And you don't have to fly to earn points; **frequent-flier credit cards** can earn you thousands of miles for doing your everyday shopping. With more than 70 mileage awards programs are on the market, consumers have never had more options. Investigate the program details of your favorite airlines before you sink points into any one. Consider which airlines have hubs in the airport nearest you, and, of those carriers, which have the most advantageous alliances, given your most common routes. To play the frequent-flier game to your best advantage, consult Randy Petersen's **Inside Flyer** (www.insideflyer.com). Petersen and friends review all the programs in detail and post regular updates on changes in policies and trends.

BY CAR

Usually, the most cost-effective, convenient, and comfortable way to travel around the United States is by car. Many highlights of the country just can't be seen any other way.

The interstate highway system connects cities and towns all over the country; in addition to these high-speed, limited-access roadways, there's an extensive network of federal, state, and local highways and roads. *Note:* To help you plan your driving routes, check out "The USA— Major Interstate Routes" map at the beginning of this chapter

If you plan on driving your own car over a long distance, then automobile-association membership is recommended. **AAA,** the **American Automobile Association** (✆ **800/222-4357;** www.aaa.com), is the country's largest auto club and supplies its members with maps, insurance, and most important, emergency road service. The cost of joining is $58 for a single member.

If your destination is too far from home to drive, but will require a car once you arrive, see appendix D at the end of this book for a list of car-rental agencies, with their toll-free numbers and websites. These national companies have offices at most airports and in many cities. You must have a valid credit card to rent a vehicle. Most also require a minimum age,

ranging from 19 to 25 (some companies that will rent to the under-25 crowd will nevertheless assess underage driving fees of up to $25 per day extra), and some also set maximum ages. Others deny cars to anyone with a bad driving record. Ask about rental requirements and restrictions when you book to avoid problems later.

Car-rental rates vary even more than airfares. The price you pay depends on the size of the car, where and when you pick it up and drop it off, the length of the rental period, where and how far you drive it, whether you purchase insurance, and a host of other factors. A few key questions could save you hundreds of dollars; you should comparison-shop and be persistent because reservations agents don't often volunteer money-saving strategies.

- Is a weekly rate cheaper than the daily rate? If you need to keep the car for 4 days, it may be cheaper to keep it for 5, even if you don't need it that long.
- Does the agency assess a drop-off charge if you do not return the car to the same location where you picked it up? Is it cheaper to pick up the car at the airport instead of a downtown location?
- How much tax will be added to the rental bill? Local tax? State use tax? Some state's rental-car taxes can top 25% of the base rate, so be sure you know exactly how much you'll be paying in total before making a decision. Recently, many online booking sites have begun posting the total rental price of a car instead of just the base rates.
- What is the cost of adding an additional driver's name to the contract?

Before you drive off in a rental car, be sure you're insured. Hasty assumptions about your personal auto insurance or a rental agency's additional coverage could end up costing you tens of thousands of dollars—even if you're involved in an accident that was clearly the fault of another driver.

If you already hold a private auto insurance policy, you are most likely covered for loss of or damage to a rental car, and liability in case of injury to any other party involved in an accident. Be sure to ask whether your policy extends to all persons who will be driving the rental car, how much liability is covered in case an outside party is injured in an accident, and whether the type of vehicle you are renting is included under your contract.

The basic insurance coverage offered by most car-rental companies, known as the **Loss/Damage Waiver (LDW)** or **Collision Damage Waiver (CDW),** can cost as much as $20 per day. It usually covers the full value of the vehicle with no deductible if an outside party causes an accident or other damage to the rental car. In many states, you will probably be covered in case of theft as well (ask before making any assumptions). **Liability coverage** varies according to the company policy and state law, but the minimum is usually at least $15,000. If you are at fault in an accident, however, you will be covered for the full replacement value of the car but not for liability. Some states allow you to buy additional liability coverage for such cases. Most rental companies require a police report to process any claims you file, but your private insurer is not notified of the accident.

Most major credit cards offer some degree of coverage as well—if they were used to pay for the rental. Terms vary widely, however, so be sure to call your credit card company directly before you rent.

If you're uninsured, your credit card provides primary coverage as long as you decline the rental agency's insurance. That means the credit card will cover damage or theft of a rental car for the full cost of the vehicle. (In a few states, however, theft is not covered; ask specifically about state law where you will be renting and driving.) If you already have insurance, your credit card will provide secondary coverage—which basically covers your deductible.

Credit cards will not cover liability, the cost of injury to an outside party, and/or damage to an outside party's vehicle. If you do not hold an insurance policy, you may seriously want to consider purchasing additional liability insurance from your rental company, even if you decline collision coverage. Be sure to check the terms, however: Some rental agencies cover liability only if the renter is not at fault; even then, the rental company's obligation varies from state to state.

BY TRAIN

Long-distance trains in the United States are operated by **Amtrak** (© **800/USA-RAIL;** www.amtrak.com), the national

---

Other Transportation Options

Traveling the U.S. in a **recreational vehicle (RV)** is an increasingly popular way of seeing the country. One good RV-rental agency with locations all over the country is **Cruise America (www.cruiseamerica.com)**. It would take dozens of pages to thoroughly discuss the ins and outs of RV travel, so if you're thinking of hitting the road this way, check out *Frommer's Exploring America by RV.*

If you're more of the *Easy Rider* sort and have dreams of cruising the country on a **motorcycle,** know that you'll need a special motorcycle license and that almost every state also requires that riders wear a helmet. The best outfit for renting a bike nationwide is **EagleRider** (© **888/900-9901;** www.eaglerider.com).

rail passenger corporation. Be aware, however, that with a few notable exceptions (for instance, the Northeast Corridor line between Boston and Washington, D.C.), intercity service is not particularly fabulous. Delays are common, routes are limited and often infrequently served, and fares are seldom much lower than discount airfares. That said, if time isn't an issue, train travel can be a very scenic method of traveling the country. If you choose to travel by train, do it for the experience, not for the convenience.

There are discount rail passes sold to U.S. residents who want to see the country by rail though you'll need quite a bit of time on your hands to make the pass worth your while. Rail travelers can buy a **North America Rail Pass,** good for up to 30 days of unlimited travel in economy class on Amtrak (© **800/USA-RAIL;** www.amtrak.com) in the U.S. and Canada, except on the Acela Express trains and the Auto Train that run on the East Coast. There's also a peculiar quirk—you must travel at least one segment of your journey in Canada. Meals and sleeping accommodations are extra. Reservations are generally required and should be made for each part of your trip as early as possible. For full details and prices on this pass and on regional rail passes (in California and Florida), call Amtrak or check its website.

Amtrak also offers rail/fly packages that allow travelers to fly to their destination in one direction and to take the train in another.

BY BUS

Bus travel is often the most economical form of public transit for short hops between U.S. cities, but it can also be slow and uncomfortable—certainly not an option for everyone (particularly when Amtrak, which is far more luxurious, offers similar rates). **Greyhound/Trailways** (© **800/231-2222;** www.greyhound. com), the sole nationwide bus line, offers several pass and discount options geared to domestic travelers.

9 Special-Interest Vacation Planner

Here's a sampling of companies that offer escorted adventures and tours, and some suggestions on where to go to enjoy your favorite activities. For information on the individual states mentioned below, see the appropriate destination chapter in the book.

ADVENTURE-TRAVEL COMPANIES

Scores of "soft" and "hard" adventure-travel companies have sprung up in recent years. Most travel agents have catalogs that list upcoming trips. More than 500 different tour operators are represented in the **Specialty Travel Index Online** at www.specialtytravel.com. Another good source of up-to-date information is the monthly *Outside* magazine, available on newsstands throughout the country, or online at **http://outside mag.com.**

Mountain Travel—Sobek (© **888/ 687-6235** or 510/594-6000; www.mt sobek.com) is perhaps the granddaddy of adventure-travel companies, guiding its own trips and acting as an agent for other outfitters. It began with river rafting, which is still its strong suit. **Backroads** (© **800/462-2848** or 510/527-1555; www.backroads.com) originally sold bicycle tours, but now has walking, hiking, cross-country skiing, trail running, and other trips. It's especially noteworthy for having options catering to adults traveling solo. **Bicycle Adventures** (© **800/443- 6060** or 360/786-0989; www.bicycle adventures.com) offers biking, hiking, and cross-country skiing, as well as other multisport options in the West Coast states, the Rocky Mountain states, and Hawaii. Tours are tailored to ability levels; some are designed for families, others for solo travelers. The venerable **Sierra Club** (© **415/977-5522;** www.sierraclub.com) offers a number of trips each year.

These and other operators plan their adventures at least a year ahead of time, so ask them or your travel agent for their schedules and catalogs as far in advance as possible.

WHERE SHOULD I GO FOR . . . ?

BEACHES Miami (chapter 5) and Southern California (chapter 12) have the best beaches in the continental United States, though they all pale in comparison to the spectacular sands on all the islands of Hawaii (chapter 14).

The entire **Atlantic** is lined with sand where you can sun and swim in the summer, and you'll find no shortage of resorts and beach motels. If you try hard enough, you can even find a little undeveloped solitude at the **Cape Cod National Seashore** near Provincetown, Massachusetts (p. 57) and at **Cape Hatteras National Seashore** on North Carolina's Outer Banks (p. 285).

The **Maine coast** (chapter 2) is gorgeous, but too cold for actual swimming. The same goes for the lovely, dramatic scenery in **Northern California** (chapter 12) and along the **Oregon coast** (chapter 13).

BIKING Biking is a great way to see the country up close and personal. Except for the interstate highways, you can bike on most roads in the United States. Among the best are the **Maine coast, Cape Cod,** and the hills of **New England**—especially Vermont (chapter 2); Virginia's rolling **Shenandoah Valley** (chapter 4); the combined **Skyline Drive** and **Blue Ridge Parkway** in Virginia and North Carolina (chapter 4); the **Outer**

Banks of North Carolina (chapter 4); the dramatic **California coast** (chapter 12); the **Oregon coast** (chapter 13); the **San Juan Islands** near Seattle (p. 952); and the road circling the **Big Island** of Hawaii (p. 1018). Exceptional mountain biking is also available in most of **West Virginia's state parks** (p. 1036). Biking is an excellent way to see some of the national parks, especially **Shenandoah** (p. 233), **Yosemite** (p. 877), **Yellowstone** (p. 585), **Grand Tetons** (p. 576), and **Glacier** (p. 567).

An ongoing nationwide program is converting some 50,000 miles of abandoned railroad beds into biking-and-walking paths. For a list, contact the **Rails-to-Trails Conservancy,** 1100 17th St. NW, 10th Floor, Washington, DC 20005 (© **202/331-9696;** www.rail trails.org), which celebrated its 20th anniversary in 2006.

Several companies and organizations offer escorted bike excursions, including **Backroads** and **Bicycle Adventures** (see "Adventure-Travel Companies," above). **American Youth Hostels** (© **301/495-1240;** www.hiayh.org) has trips for its members. **CrossRoads Cycling Adventures** (© **800/971-2453;** www.crossroads cycling.com) offers nationwide excursions, including California to Massachusetts and Maine to Florida.

BIRDING The entire East Coast is on the Atlantic Flyway for migrating water birds and waterfowl. You can see them all the way from the Maine coast (chapter 2), particularly **Monhegan and Machias islands,** to the **Wellfleet Wildlife Sanctuary** on Cape Cod, and on south to Maryland's eastern shore, where **Chincoteague National Wildlife Refuge** on the Maryland-Virginia line is the best bet (© **757/336-6122**).

Shorebirds also migrate along the Pacific side of the country, with good viewing anywhere along the Washington and Oregon coasts but especially in **Malheur National Wildlife Refuge** in southeastern Oregon.

Once endangered, the **bald eagle** is now widespread across the country. Dozens make their winter home at **Lake Cachuma** near Santa Barbara in California. In January they flock to the **Skagit River** north of Seattle to feast on salmon, and you can even spot them while riding a Washington State ferry through the **San Juan Islands** (p. 952). In September, look for them along **Alaska's southeastern coast** (chapter 14). Alaska also has many other birds not found in the lower 48 states.

In the Arizona (chapter 11) desert, **Ramsey Canyon Preserve** is internationally known as home to 14 species of **hummingbird,** more than anywhere else in the United States. **San Pedro Riparian National Conservation Area** is another good spot in Arizona, with more than 300 species.

For tropical species, head to **Florida** (chapter 5), especially to **Everglades National Park** (p. 386).

Hawaii's (chapter 14) tropical birds are found nowhere else on earth, including the rare **o'o,** whose yellow feathers Hawaiians once plucked to make royal capes. Large colonies of seabirds nest at **Kilauea National Wildlife Preserve** and along the **Na Pali Coast** on Kauai; and **Molokai's Kamakou Preserve** is home to the Molokai thrust and Molokai creeper, found nowhere else.

For information about escorted birdwatching trips, contact **Field Guides** (*©* **800/728-4953** or 512/263-4795; www.fieldguides.com) or **Victor Emanual Nature Tours** (*©* **800/328-8368** or 512/328-5221; www.ventbird.com). The **National Audubon Society** (*©* **212/ 979-3000;** www.audubon.org) runs superb bird-watching programs for both aspiring and experienced naturalists.

CANOEING & KAYAKING There's a wide variety of rivers, streams, lakes, and sounds for canoeing and kayaking enthusiasts. In fact, most cities with rivers running through them now have a contingent of outfitters.

Out in the hinterlands, some of the best paddling takes place along **Maine's coast** (chapter 2) or through its 92-mile **Allagash Wilderness Waterway,** a series of remote rivers, lakes, and ponds.

In summer, it's hot and humid in **Florida's Everglades National Park** (p. 386), but winter offers great opportunities along a maze of well-marked trails. You can rent canoes at the main park center at **Flamingo.**

The peaceful lakes of Minnesota's **Boundary Waters Canoe Area** north of Minneapolis are another good choice.

Puget Sound's **San Juan Islands** (p. 952) near Seattle are enchanting when seen by canoe or kayak. **San Juan Kayak Expeditions** (*©* **360/378-4436;** www.sanjuankayak.com) and **Shearwater Adventures** (*©* **360/376-4699;** www.shearwaterkayaks.com) both have multiday trips to the islands, and biologists and naturalists lead educational expeditions sponsored by the nonprofit **Sea Quest Expeditions** (*©* **888/549-4253** or 360/ 378-5767; www.sea-quest-kayak.com).

For a truly unique kayaking experience, you can paddle among the humpback whales taking their winter break in Hawaii. Contact **South Pacific Kayaks** (*©* **800/776-2326** or 808/661-8400; www.southpacifickayaks.com).

For general information, contact the **American Canoe Association,** 7432 Alban Station Blvd., Suite B226, Springfield, VA 22150 (*©* **703/451-0141;** www.acanet.org), the nation's largest organization, for lists of trips and local clubs.

CIVIL WAR BATTLEFIELDS The Civil War started in 1861 at **Fort Sumter**

in Charleston, South Carolina (p. 271). Battles raged all over the South during the next 4 years. Gen. Ulysses S. Grant took **Vicksburg,** Mississippi (p. 431), after a long siege, and Gen. William Tecumseh Sherman burned **Atlanta** (p. 240), but the most famous fighting took place within 100 miles of **Washington, D.C.** (p. 191). This area has more national battlefield parks than any other part of the country.

It won't be in chronological order, but you can tour them by starting at the battles of **Fredericksburg, Chancellorsville,** and **The Wilderness** in and near Fredericksburg, Virginia (chapter 4). Proceed north to the two **Battles of Manassas** (or Bull Run) southwest of Washington, then north across the Potomac River to the **Battle of Antietam** at Sharpsburg, Maryland. From there, go northwest through Harpers Ferry, West Virginia, to the **Battle of Gettysburg** (p. 173), the turning point of the war, in south-central Pennsylvania. Gettysburg is perhaps the most moving and well preserved of the battlegrounds. You'll also pass several battlefields driving through the **Shenandoah Valley** (chapter 4).

FALL FOLIAGE   Fall in **New England** (chapter 2) is one of the great natural spectacles on earth, with rolling hills blanketed in brilliant reds and stunning oranges. The colors start to peak in mid-September in the **Green and White mountains** of Vermont and New Hampshire, and then bleed down into the **Berkshires** of Massachusetts. The colors move progressively south down the East Coast, through New York's **Hudson River Valley** (p. 132), into October, when bumper-to-bumper traffic jams **Virginia's Skyline Drive** through Shenandoah National Park (p. 233). The precise dates for prime viewing vary from year to year, depending on temperatures and rainfall, but the local newspapers and TV stations closely track the coloration.

Fall is also quite spectacular in the Rockies, especially in **Colorado** (chapter 10); in **West Virginia's mountains** (p. 1036); and in the **Wisconsin Dells** (p. 519).

Tauck World Discovery (© 800/788-7885; www.tauck.com), **Maupintour** (© 800/255-4266 or 913/843-1211; www.maupintour.com), and several other escorted tour operators have foliage tours; see your travel agent.

FISHING   The United States can boast of record-setting catches and has every type of fishing invented—from surf-casting off **Cape Cod** or **Cape Hatteras** to flicking a fly in **Maine** or **Montana.**

Fly-fishing camps are as prolific as fish in the Maine woods. **Grant's Kennebago Camps** in Oquossoc has 18 of them, built on Kennebago Lake in 1905. Over in Vermont, **Orvis** (© 800/548-9548; www.orvis.com) runs one of the top fly-fishing schools in the country. See chapter 2 for more on New England fishing.

The nation's other great fly-fishing area is in the Montana and Wyoming mountains near **Yellowstone National Park** (p. 585), made famous by *A River Runs Through It.* The top river out here is Montana's **Madison,** with headquarters starting in the park, but cutthroat trout make the **Snake River** over in Wyoming almost as good—and the resort of **Jackson Hole** offers luxury relief within casting distance (see chapter 8).

Most ports along the nation's seaboards have deep-sea charter-fishing fleets and less expensive party boats (all you have to do is show up for the latter). The best tropical strikes are in the **Florida Keys** (p. 388) and off the **Kona coast** of the **Big Island** in Hawaii (p. 1018). **Alaska** (chapter 14) is famous for summertime salmon and halibut fishing, with the biggest in the **Kenai River** and on **Kodiak Island,** which has the state's best roadside salmon fishing.

FLOWERS & GARDENS Flower lovers have many opportunities to stop and smell the roses, especially in **Portland, Oregon** (p. 965), which calls itself the City of Roses. Many other cities have gardens of note, including **Atlanta, Boston** (p. 29), **Denver** (p. 666), **New Orleans** (p. 438), **New York** (p. 103), **Seattle** (p. 933), and **Tucson** (p. 766). **Longwood Gardens** in the **Brandywine Valley** (p. 172) is noted for its greenhouses as well as its grounds. The **Biltmore Estate** in Asheville, North Carolina (p. 294), has a walled English garden on its 25 acres. **Magnolia Plantation** near Charleston, South Carolina (p. 271), is famed for its azaleas, camellias, and 60-acre cypress swamp. If you like gardens from the Elizabethan era, head for **Colonial Williamsburg,** Virginia (p. 222).

It's also a spectacular sight to see the commercial flower farms of **Washington State's Skagit Valley.** In the spring, tulips and daffodils carpet the farmlands surrounding the town of **La Conner** with great swaths of red, yellow, and white. In March and April, the town hosts an annual Tulip Festival; the countryside erupts with color in a display that matches the legendary flower fields of the Netherlands. See chapter 13 for more on Washington.

You may also be interested in seeing wildflowers in bloom out West. Springtime brings glorious color to the **Texas Hill Country** (p. 660), just north of San Antonio. The **deserts of New Mexico, Arizona, and Southern California** (chapters 11 and 12) are also magical in the spring. Two of California's prettiest viewing areas are **Anza-Borrego Desert State Park,** near San Diego, and the **Antelope Valley Poppy Reserve,** in the high desert near L.A. There are also beautiful spring blooms in the Washington Cascades, especially in **Olympic National Park** (p. 956) and throughout the **Rocky Mountains** (chapter 10).

A few travel companies have escorted tours of gardens, others include them on their general sightseeing excursions, and still others organize trips for local botanical gardens or gardening and horticultural groups. Check with those in your hometown for upcoming trips, or try **Maupintour** (📞 **800/255-4266** or 913/843-1211; www.maupintour.com).

GOLF & TENNIS You can play golf and tennis almost anywhere in the country, although the southern tier of states, where the outdoor seasons are longest, offer the best opportunities. In the Southeast, top golfing destinations are **Pinehurst,** North Carolina; **Hilton Head Island** and **Myrtle Beach,** South Carolina (chapter 4); and almost anywhere in **Florida** (chapter 5). You can get information about most Florida courses, including current greens fees, and reserve tee times through **Tee Times USA** (📞 **888/465-3356** or 904/439-0001; www.teetimesusa.com). This company also publishes a vacation guide that includes many stay-and-play golf packages.

In the Southwest, the twin desert cities of **Phoenix** and **Scottsdale,** Arizona (p. 754), have some of the country's most luxurious golf resorts. The same can be said of **Palm Springs** and the **Monterey coast** in California (chapter 12).

And **Hawaii** (chapter 14) has some of the most famous and most unique courses in the world.

Most of the nation's top golf resorts also have excellent **tennis** facilities. For the top 50 tennis resorts, see *Tennis* magazine's rankings each November. Good choices include the **Ritz-Carlton Key Biscayne** in Key Biscayne, Florida (p. 382), Tampa's **Saddlebrook Resort—Tampa** (p. 409), and **Sea Pines Plantation** on Hilton Head, South Carolina (p. 267).

MOUNTAIN BIKING If mountain bikes are your thing, you'll find plenty of dirt roads and backcountry pathways to explore. Many national parks and forests have a good selection of trails—**Acadia National Park**'s (p. 98) carriage roads, for example, are unique. You can also take guided tours through 60 miles of connected trails in the **Sebago Lake area,** near the New Hampshire border, with **Back Country Excursions (**© **207/ 625-8189;** www.bikebackcountry.com).

Out in Colorado (chapter 10), ski areas often open their lifts to bikers in the summer. **Winter Park** is considered the state's mountain-bike capital (© **800/ 903-PARK** or 970/726-4118). The state's single best route, the 30-mile **Tipperary Creek Trail,** ends at Winter Park. Another popular area is the **Bryce, Zion,** and **Canyonlands** regions of southern Utah (chapter 10). Contact **Rim Tours** (© **800/626-7335;** www.rimtours.com) or **Escape Adventures** (© **800/596-2953;** www.kaibabtours.com), based in the town of Moab.

West Virginia (p. 1036) is a top destination for mountain biking; especially good spots are **Canaan Valley Resort** and **Backwater Falls State Park.**

The companies mentioned under "Biking," above, also offer mountain-biking expeditions throughout the country and abroad.

NATURE & ECOLOGY TOURS Not just for bird-watchers, the **National Audubon Society** (© **212/979-3000;** www.audubon.org) has its Ecology Camp on Hog Island off the Maine coast and another in the Grand Tetons of Wyoming, and it sponsors ecology excursions to such places as California's Death Valley. The **Sierra Club** maintains base camps in the Rockies and sponsors a wide variety of nature- and conservation-oriented trips (© **415/977-5500;** www.sierraclub.com). On a tour sponsored by a conservation association, you'll learn more about our national parks than you could just by driving through them. To find out what's available, contact the individual park you plan on visiting.

RIVER RAFTING The most famous place to run the rapids is the **Grand Canyon** (p. 782), with steep walls that tower above you as you race down the **Colorado River.** It's also the most popular spot, with bumper-to-bumper rafts in summer.

You may have less unwanted company on the Colorado upstream in **Utah**— which also has good rafting on the **Green River.** Call the **Utah Travel Council** (© **800/200-1160** or 801/538-1030; www.utah.com) and ask for a copy of *Raft Utah.* The **Snake River** south of Yellowstone National Park near Jackson Hole, Wyoming, is also a best bet. The Snake River flows into Idaho, where its wild Hells Canyon offers exciting rides— as do the Salmon and Middle Fork rivers. For more information, see chapter 8.

The **New River** cuts a dramatic, 2,000-foot-deep gorge through the Appalachian Mountains inside **New River Gorge National River Recreation Area** (p. 1039), near the town of Beckley, West Virginia, making it the most scenic rapids route in the east.

SCENIC DRIVES There are so many wonderful driving tours that it's impossible to offer anything like a comprehensive list, but here are just a few favorites.

In New England (chapter 2), the dramatic **Kancamagus Highway** (N.H. 112) cuts through New Hampshire's White Mountains between Lincoln and Conway. Nearby is the privately owned **Mount Washington Auto Road,** to the top of one of the tallest peaks in the east. The loop road in Maine's **Acadia National Park** is another beauty.

In the Southeast (chapter 4), you can't beat Virginia's **Skyline Drive** and the **Blue Ridge Parkway,** which continues south to North Carolina's Great Smoky Mountains near Asheville.

You'll traverse a wild and undeveloped portion of Monongahela National Forest on the **Highland Scenic Highway** in West Virginia (appendix A), a drive that's especially beautiful during fall foliage season.

The **Historic Coastal Highway** stretches along the eastern coast of Florida, offering up prime ocean views and lots of wildlife.

In the Gulf South (chapter 6), the **Natchez Trace Parkway** winds through forested beauty in the states of Mississippi, Tennessee, and Alabama on the way from Natchez to Nashville. Another good option in this region is the stunning beauty (including trees, rock formations, and waterfalls) along the **Red River Gorge Highway** in Kentucky. For picture-perfect views of marshlands and their accompanying wildlife, look no further than the **Creole Nature Trail** in Louisiana.

In the Great Plains (chapter 8), a driving tour of Glacier Country in Montana puts you on **Going-to-the-Sun Road** through Glacier National Park, one of the great summertime drives in the country. Over the border in Wyoming, the **Beartooth Scenic Byway** (U.S. 212) from the northern part of Yellowstone National Park east to Red Lodge climbs over 10,947-foot **Beartooth Pass,** from where you can see mile upon mile of Wyoming and Montana mountains. Custer State Park in the **South Dakota Badlands** offers not one, but three scenic auto routes, though if you have time for only one, make it **Iron Mountain Road.**

In Colorado, a driving tour of the Western Slope follows the **Million Dollar Highway** (U.S. 550) across 11,008-foot **Red Mountain Pass,** an unforgettable drive. The **San Juan Skyway,** a 236-mile circuit that crosses five mountain passes, takes in the magnificent scenery of the San Juan Mountains,

including some wonderful Old West towns. And visitors to Rocky Mountain National Park should not pass up a drive on the exceptionally scenic **Trail Ridge Road,** especially in spring when the wildflowers are in bloom and wildlife is out in force.

In the Southwest (chapter 11), the **Kaibab Plateau—North Rim Parkway** winds itself through the trees of Kaibab National Forest before landing at the scenic northern edge of the Grand Canyon. In the **Arizona desert,** the drive from Phoenix through Prescott and Sedona includes huge red rocks and the cool oasis of Oak Creek Canyon. The desert's most spectacular scenery is in **Monument Valley** on the Arizona–Utah border in Navajo and Hopi country and the nearby **Canyonlands.**

Out in California and the Pacific Northwest (chapters 12 and 13), driving doesn't get any more dramatic than it is along the **California** and **Oregon coasts.**

Up in Alaska (chapter 14), one of the world's great drives begins in Anchorage and leads roughly 50 miles south on the **Seward Highway** to Portage Glacier; chipped from the rocky Chugach Mountains, the **Turnagain Arm** provides a platform for viewing an untouched landscape full of wildlife.

Out in Hawaii (chapter 14), the drive from Honolulu to Oahu's Windward coast on **Highway 61** offers an unparalleled view down from the near-vertical Pali cliff. The narrow, winding **Hana Road** on Maui will reward your driving skills with wonderful seascapes.

For a comprehensive list of the major scenic byways and roads in the U.S., check out the U.S. Department of Transportation's **America's Byways** website at **www.byways.org**; while you're online, be sure to request their free *America's Byways* map.

SKIING New England may have started downhill skiing in the United States, but for the best, forget about the East altogether and head for the deep powder out West.

Colorado (chapter 10) is endowed with more than two dozen ski resorts, including world-renowned Aspen, Vail, Breckenridge, and Wolf Creek; **Utah** (chapter 10) is home to Alta, Beaver Mountain, Snowbasin, Park City, and Deer Valley; and **Taos** (p. 815) in New Mexico has well-known slopes. In California's Sierras, **Lake Tahoe** (p. 870) is home to Alpine Meadows, Heavenly Resort, and the famous Squaw Valley USA. And there's **Jackson Hole** (p. 576) in Wyoming, plus the Big Mountain and Big Sky resorts nearby in Montana (chapter 8).

New England (chapter 2) does have good cross-country skiing, especially at the **Trapp Family Lodge Cross-Country Ski Center** (© 800/826-7000 or 802/ 253-8511; www.trappfamily.com) in Stowe, Vermont, and the entire village of Jackson, New Hampshire, which is laced with a network of ski trails maintained by the **Jackson Ski Touring Foundation** (© 800/927-6697; www.jacksonxc.org). Moving south along the East Coast, you'll find good options in Lake Placid, New York (chapter 3) and Snowshoe in West Virginia (appendix A). Out West, many of the downhill resorts mentioned above have cross-country trails as well. The best are in **Yosemite** (p. 233), **Yellowstone** (p. 585), and **Glacier** (p. 567) national parks. The rims of the **Grand Canyon** (p. 782) and **Bryce Canyon** (p. 721) national parks also present some unusual skiing venues.

WHALE- & WILDLIFE WATCHING The best whale- watching on the East Coast leaves from **Provincetown** on Cape Cod (p. 56), where some boats sight humpbacks and finbacks with a 99% success rate from April to November.

On the West Coast, you can see Pacific gray whales during their spring and fall migrations from **Point Reyes National Seashore** north of San Francisco; **Depoe Bay** and other points on the Oregon coast; and the **San Juan Islands** near Seattle, which also have orcas. See chapters 12 and 13 for more information on these areas.

The port of **Sitka** (p. 992) in southeastern Alaska, **Kenai Fjords National Park,** and nearby **Seward** are great spots to watch humpbacks feeding in summer— plus a profusion of seals, otters, and other marine mammals.

For many humpbacks, the fall migration takes them south to sunny Hawaii (chapter 14), where they frolic in the warm waters from December to May. They are best seen here from **Maui's west coast.**

For wildlife watching, you can see moose in **Rocky Mountain National Park** (p. 680) in Colorado, maybe a bear in the **Great Smoky Mountains** (p. 298), or alligators and other critters in **Florida's Everglades** (p. 388). But the best places to spot a variety of animals are undoubtedly the national parks out west and in Alaska. Without question, **Yellowstone** (p. 585) offers some of the top opportunities, with an abundance of elk and bison. Some of them will walk right up to your car. **Glacier** (p. 567) has this and more—mountain elk and the occasional grizzly bear. Alaska's **Denali** (p. 998) national park offers visitors a great chance to see grizzlies and other types of bears.

10 Tips on Accommodations

The United States has a wide range of accommodations: from roadside chain motels, to park lodges, to rental condos, to mammoth themed resorts, to historic inns (where George Washington really did sleep!). And there are tons of excellent campgrounds located all over the country.

For a list of the major hotel and motel chains' telephone numbers and websites, see appendix D. In the individual chapters in this book, we also provide information on local reservation services, if available. Most state tourism offices put out directories or other information on available accommodations—contact them and they'll be happy to send you the information. Much of the information is also available on the states' tourism websites. A list of all 50 state tourism bureaus is available in appendix B.

If you prefer the intimacy and character of a bed-and-breakfast, there are several reservation agencies and online websites that deal solely with B&Bs. A few of these B&B-only websites include **Inntravels.com, Bed & Breakfast Inns Online** (www.bbonline.com), **North American Bed & Breakfast Directory** (www.bbdirectory.com), and **Bedand Breakfast.com**.

For historic lodging in the United States, look no further than the **Historic Hotels of America** (© 800/678-8946; www.historichotels.org), operated in conjunction with the National Trust for Historic Preservation. We've noted several hotels rich in American history throughout the book.

For information on campgrounds and RV parks in the United States, pick up the comprehensive *Frommer's RV & Tent Campgrounds in the U.S.A.* You can also contact the **National Association of RV Parks and Campgrounds (www.go campingamerica.com);** or **KOA** (© 406/ 248-7444; www.koa.com), which operates numerous campgrounds and RV parks all over the country.

SAVING ON YOUR HOTEL ROOM

The **rack rate** is the maximum rate that a hotel charges for a room. Hardly anybody pays this price, however, except in high season or on holidays. To lower the cost of your room:

- **Ask about special rates or other discounts.** You may qualify for corporate, student, military, senior, frequent flier, trade union, or other discounts.
- **Dial direct.** When booking a room in a chain hotel, you'll often get a better deal by calling the individual hotel's reservation desk rather than the chain's main number.
- **Book online.** Many hotels offer Internet-only discounts, or supply rooms to Priceline, Hotwire, or Expedia at rates much lower than the ones you can get through the hotel.
- **Remember the law of supply and demand.** Resort hotels are most crowded and therefore most expensive on weekends, so discounts are usually available for midweek stays. Business hotels in downtown locations are busiest during the week, so you can expect big discounts over the weekend. Many hotels have high-season and low-season prices, and booking even one day after high season ends can mean big discounts.
- **Look into group or long-stay discounts.** If you come as part of a large group, you should be able to negotiate a bargain rate. Likewise, if you're planning a long stay (at least 5 days), you might qualify for a discount. As a general rule, expect 1 night free after a 7-night stay.
- **Avoid excess charges and hidden costs.** When you book a room, ask whether the hotel charges for parking. Use a cellphone, pay phones, or prepaid phone cards instead of dialing direct from hotel phones, which usually have exorbitant rates. Don't be tempted by the room's minibar offerings: Most hotels overcharge for water, soda, and snacks. Finally, ask

about local taxes and service charges, which can increase the cost of a room by 15% or more.

- **Book an efficiency.** A room with a kitchenette allows you to shop for groceries and cook your own meals. This is a big money saver, especially for families on long stays.
- **Consider enrolling in hotel "frequent-stay" programs**, which are upping the ante lately to win the loyalty of repeat customers. Frequent guests can now accumulate points or credits to earn free hotel nights, airline miles, in-room amenities, merchandise, tickets to concerts and events, discounts on sporting facilities—and even credit toward stock in the participating hotel, in the case of the Jameson Inn hotel group. Perks are awarded not only by many chain hotels and motels (Hilton HHonors, Marriott Rewards, Wyndham ByRequest, to name a few), but individual inns and B&Bs. Many chain hotels partner with other hotel chains, car-rental firms, airlines, and credit card companies to give consumers additional incentive to do repeat business.

LANDING THE BEST ROOM

Somebody has to get the best room in the house. It might as well be you. You can start by joining the hotel's frequent-guest program, which may make you eligible for upgrades. A hotel-branded credit card usually gives its owner "silver" or "gold" status in frequent-guest programs for free. Always ask about a corner room. They're often larger and quieter, with more windows and light, and they often cost the same as standard rooms. When you make your reservation, ask if the hotel is renovating; if it is, request a room away from the construction. Ask about nonsmoking rooms, rooms with views, rooms with twin, queen- or king-size beds. If you're a light sleeper, request a quiet room away from vending machines, elevators, restaurants, bars, and discos. Ask for a room that has been most recently renovated or redecorated.

If you aren't happy with your room when you arrive, ask for another one. Most lodgings will be willing to accommodate you.

In resort areas, particularly in warm climates, ask the following questions before you book a room:

- What's the view like? Cost-conscious travelers may be willing to pay less for a back room facing the parking lot, especially if they don't plan to spend much time in their room. If, on the other hand, you can't do without that view of the ocean, the skyline, the Strip, whatever, then be prepared to pay extra for it.
- What's included in the price? Your room may be moderately priced, but if you're charged for beach chairs, towels, sports equipment, and other amenities, you could end up spending more than you bargained for.
- Is there a resort fee? These are recent and particularly heinous schemes (anywhere from $5–$20 per day!) dreamed up by hotel executives trying to make an extra dime off travelers. They ostensibly cover items (local calls, a bottle of water, a newspaper, the electricity in your room) that used to be free, but that you're now being charged for. And these extra charges are *never* included in the quoted rate. You'll find this sort of gouging mostly at resorts in the major resort destinations such as Florida and Hawaii, but we've seen even small chain hotels in some of these areas assessing this fee.

New England

One of the greatest challenges of traveling in New England is choosing from an abundance of superb restaurants, accommodations, and attractions. Do you want the mountains or the beach? Shining cities or quiet vistas? In this chapter, we give you an overview of one of the most historic regions of the United States, and still one of the most vital. We start in Massachusetts with Boston; go out to Cape Cod and Martha's Vineyard; swing through the Mystic seaport in Connecticut and then around to Rhode Island's glamorous Newport and revitalized Providence; and return to Massachusetts to the Berkshires. We head inland to the natural glories of southern Vermont and New Hampshire's White Mountains, then up the rocky, majestic Maine coast.

1 Boston & Cambridge

Boston embodies contrasts and contradictions—it's blue blood and blue collar, Yankee and Irish, home to budget-conscious graduate students and free-spending computer wizards (still!). Rich in Colonial history and 21st-century technology, it's a living landmark whose unofficial mascot is the construction worker. A new highway, a dramatic new bridge, and new buildings of all sizes are altering the landscape of eastern Massachusetts.

Take a few days (or weeks) to get to know the Boston area, or use it as a gateway to the rest of New England. Here's hoping your experience is memorable and delightful.

ESSENTIALS

GETTING THERE **By Plane** Most major domestic carriers and many international carriers serve Boston's **Logan International Airport** (© 800/23-LOGAN; www.massport.com/logan), across the harbor from downtown. Access to the city is by subway (the "T"), cab, and boat. The **subway** is fast and cheap—10 minutes to Government Center and a one-way fare of $1.25. Free **shuttle buses** run from each terminal to the Airport station on the Blue Line of the T daily from 5:30am to 1am. The Blue Line stops at State Street and Government Center, downtown points where you can exit or transfer (free) to the other lines. A **cab** from the airport to downtown or the Back Bay costs about $22 to $30. The ride into town takes 10 to 45 minutes, depending on traffic and the time of day.

The trip to the downtown waterfront (near cabstands and several hotels) in a weather-protected **boat** takes 7 minutes and costs $10 one-way. The free no. 66 shuttle bus connects all terminals to the Logan ferry dock. **Harbor Express** (© 617/222-6999; www.harborexpress.com) runs to Long Wharf, behind the Marriott Long Wharf hotel. It operates every 20 minutes on weekdays from 7am to 8pm (Fri until 11pm), and every 30 minutes from 10am to 6pm on weekends. Hours are shorter in the winter.

By Train   Amtrak (© **800/USA-RAIL** or 617/482-3660; www.amtrak.com) serves all three of Boston's three rail centers: **South Station,** on Atlantic Avenue; **Back Bay Station,** on Dartmouth Street across from the Copley Place mall; and **North Station,** on Causeway Street near the TD Banknorth Garden. Each train station is also a **rapid-transit** station (© **800/392-6100** outside Massachusetts, or 617/222-3200; www.mbta.com). A **commuter rail** serves Ipswich, Rockport, and Fitchburg from North Station, and points south and west of Boston, including Plymouth, from South Station.

By Car   Boston is 218 miles from New York; driving time is about 4½ hours. From Washington, it takes about 8 hours to cover the 468 miles; the 992-mile drive from Chicago takes around 21 hours. Driving to Boston is not difficult, but if you're think-ing of using the car to get around town, you won't need one to explore Boston and Cambridge.

The major highways are **I-90,** the Massachusetts Turnpike ("Mass. Pike"), an east-west toll road that leads to the New York State Thruway; **I-93/U.S. 1,** which extends north to Canada; and **I-93/Route 3,** the Southeast Expressway, which connects with the south, including Cape Cod. **I-95** (Mass. Rte. 128) is a beltway about 11 miles from downtown that connects to I-93 and to highways in Rhode Island, Connecticut, and New York to the south, and New Hampshire and Maine to the north. The **Mass. Pike** extends into the city and connects with the **Central Artery** (the John F. Fitzger-ald Expwy.).

VISITOR INFORMATION   Contact the **Greater Boston Convention & Visitors Bureau,** 2 Copley Place, Suite 105, Boston (© **888/SEE-BOSTON** or 617/536-4100, or 0171/431-3434 in the U.K.; www.bostonusa.com). It offers a comprehensive infor-mation kit ($10) with a planner, guidebook, map, and coupon book; and a *Kids Love Boston* guide ($5). Free smaller planners for specific seasons or events are often available.

The **Cambridge Office for Tourism,** 4 Brattle St., Suite 208, Cambridge (© **800/ 862-5678** or 617/441-2884; www.cambridge-usa.org), distributes information about Cambridge. The **Massachusetts Office of Travel and Tourism,** 10 Park Plaza, Suite 4510, Boston (© **800/227-6277** or 617/973-8500; www.massvacation.com), distrib-utes the *Getaway Guide,* a free magazine with information on attractions and lodgings, a map, and a seasonal calendar.

The **Boston National Historical Park Visitor Center,** 15 State St. (© **617/ 242-5642;** www.nps.gov/bost), across the street from the Old State House and the State Street T, is a good place to start exploring. National Park Service rangers staff the center and lead free tours of the Freedom Trail. The audiovisual show provides basic information on 16 historic sites on the trail. The center is wheelchair accessible and has restrooms. It's open daily from 9am to 5pm.

The Freedom Trail begins at the **Boston Common Information Center,** 146 Tremont St., on the Common. The center is open Monday through Saturday from 8:30am to 5pm, Sunday from 9am to 5pm. The **Prudential Information Center,** on the main level of the Prudential Center, is open Monday through Friday from 8:30am to 6pm, Saturday and Sunday from 10am to 6pm. The **Greater Boston Convention & Visitors Bureau** (© **888/SEE-BOSTON** or 617/536-4100) operates both centers.

GETTING AROUND   When you reach your hotel, leave your car in the garage and walk or use public transportation. Free maps of downtown Boston and the transit sys-tem are available at visitor centers around the city. If you must drive in town, ask at

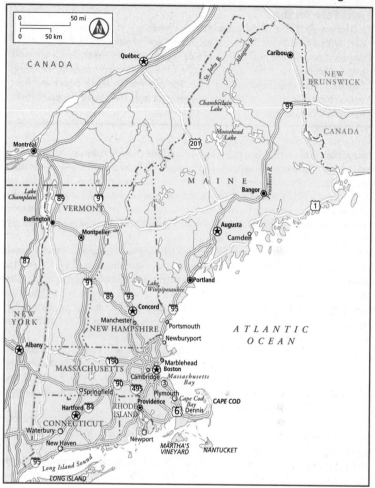

the front desk for the quickest route (which may not be obvious from a map or mapping website).

By Public Transportation   The Massachusetts Bay Transportation Authority, or **MBTA** (© **800/392-6100** or 617/222-3200; www.mbta.com), is known as the "T," and its logo is that letter in a circle. It runs subways, trolleys, buses, and ferries in Boston and many suburbs, as well as the commuter rail. Its website includes maps, schedules, and other information.

Newer stations on the Red, Blue, and Orange lines are wheelchair accessible; the Green Line is being converted. All T buses have lifts or kneelers; call © **800/LIFT-BUS** for information. To learn more, call the **Office for Transportation Access** (© **617/222-5438** or TTY 617/222-5854).

All's Fare on the T

In January 2007, the MBTA completed its conversion to automated fare collection, with a concurrent fare increase. Tokens are no longer accepted; the three payment options are now cash, a pre-paid paper **CharlieTicket,** and a pre-paid plastic **CharlieCard.** The CharlieCard offers the greatest cost savings, including free transfers between subway and bus. For information about where and how to purchase a CharlieCard, check the website or quiz the phone representatives for details before your trip.

Red, Blue, and Orange line trains and Green Line trolleys make up the **subway** system, which runs partly aboveground. The fare is $2 cash, or $1.70 with the CharlieCard. Transfers within these lines are free, however, bus transfers are an additional $1.50 for cash riders (free for CharlieCard customers). Route and fare information and timetables are available through the website and at centrally located stations. Service begins around 5:15am and ends around 12:30am. A sign on in every station gives the time of the last train in either direction.

T buses and **"trackless trolleys"** (buses with electric antennae) provide service around town and to and around the suburbs. The local bus fare is $1.50, or $1.25 with the CharlieCard; express buses are $3.50 and up ($2.80 and up with the CharlieCard). Exact change is required. Important local routes include **no. 1** (Mass. Ave. from Dudley Sq. in Roxbury through the Back Bay and Cambridge to Harvard Sq.), **nos. 92** and **93** (between Haymarket and Charlestown), and **no. 77** (Mass. Ave. from Harvard Sq. north to Porter Sq. and Arlington).

The MBTA Inner Harbor ferry connects **Long Wharf** (near the New England Aquarium) with the **Charlestown Navy Yard**—it's a good way to get back downtown from "Old Ironsides" and the Bunker Hill Monument. The fare is $1.70 (at press time, the CharlieCard was not yet available for ferry service). Visit **www.mbta.com** or call ℂ **617/227-4321** for information.

Taxis are expensive and not always easy to flag—find a cabstand or call a dispatcher. To call ahead, try the **Independent Taxi Operators Association** (ℂ **617/426-8700**) or **Boston Cab** (ℂ **617/262-2227**). Boston Cab can dispatch a wheelchair-accessible vehicle; advance notice is recommended. In Cambridge, call **Ambassador Brattle** (ℂ **617/492-1100**) or **Yellow Cab** (ℂ **617/547-3000**).

FAST FACTS   If you need medical attention, your hotel concierge should be able to help you. Hospital referral services include **Brigham and Women's** (ℂ **800/294-9999**), **Massachusetts General** (ℂ **800/711-4-MGH**), and **Tufts New England Medical Center** (ℂ **617/636-9700**). An affiliate of Mass. General, **MGH Back Bay,** 388 Comm. Ave. (ℂ **617/267-7171**), offers walk-in service and honors most insurance plans.

Downtown Boston has no 24-hour **drugstore.** The **CVS** at 155–157 Charles St. (ℂ **617/523-1028**), next to the Charles/MGH Red Line T stop, is open until midnight. The **CVS** at the Porter Square Shopping Center, off Mass. Ave. in Cambridge (ℂ **617/876-5519**), is open 24 hours.

On the whole, Boston and Cambridge are safe cities for walking. As in any urban area, stay out of parks (including Boston Common, the Public Garden, and the Esplanade) at night unless you're in a crowd. Areas to avoid at night include Boylston

Street between Tremont and Washington, and Tremont Street from Stuart to Boylston. Try not to walk alone late at night in the Theater District and around North Station. Public transportation is busy and safe, but service stops between 12:30 and 1am.

The 5% **sales tax** does not apply to food, prescription drugs, newspapers, or clothing that costs less than $175; the tax on meals and takeout food is 5%. The **lodging tax** in Boston and Cambridge is 12.45%.

SPECIAL EVENTS & FESTIVALS   Every March 17, a 5-mile parade salutes both **St. Patrick's Day** and the day British troops left Boston in 1776 (© **800/888-5515**). **Patriot's Day,** the third Monday in April, features reenactments of the events of April 18 and 19, 1775, which signified the start of the Revolutionary War, as well as the running of the **Boston Marathon;** call the Boston Athletic Association (© **617/ 236-1652;** www.bostonmarathon.org). The **Boston Pops Concert and Fireworks Display,** held at Hatch Memorial Shell on the Esplanade during Boston, Massachusetts, Independence Week, culminates in the famous Boston Pops's **Fourth of July** concert. The program includes Tchaikovsky's *1812 Overture* with actual cannon fire that segues into the fireworks. On the Web, head to **www.july4th.org**.

WHAT TO SEE & DO IN BOSTON

CityPass (© **888/330-5008;** www.citypass.com) is a booklet of tickets to the Harvard Museum of Natural History, Kennedy Library, Museum of Fine Arts, Museum of Science, New England Aquarium, and Prudential Center Skywalk. The price (at press time, $39 for adults, $21 for children 3–11) represents a 50% savings for adults who visit all six attractions, and having a ticket means you can go straight to the entrance without waiting in line. The passes are on sale at participating attractions, from the website, and through the **Greater Boston Convention & Visitors Bureau** (© **800/SEE-BOSTON;** www.bostonusa.com).

CityPass's main competition is the **Explorer Pass,** a spinoff of the **Go Boston Card** (© **800/887-9103** or 617/742-5950; www.gobostoncard.com) that covers its own list of attractions. The Explorer Pass (www.explorerpass.com) is good for 2 days and costs $39 for adults, $29 for children—a deal, but fitting in all 10 destinations to score the full savings takes serious planning. The original Go Boston card includes admission to more than 60 Boston-area and New England attractions, dining and shopping discounts, a guidebook, and a 2-day trolley pass. If you strategize wisely, it's a great value. Prices range from $49 for 1 day to $159 for 7 days, with discounts for children and winter travelers. Purchase through the website; at the office in the Ferry Terminal behind the Boston Harbor Hotel, Rowes Wharf (off Atlantic Ave.); or from the Bostix booths in Faneuil Hall Marketplace (closed Mon) and Copley Square.

THE TOP ATTRACTIONS

Faneuil Hall Marketplace *Kids*   Since Boston's most popular attraction opened in 1976, cities all over the country have imitated the "festival market" concept. The complex of shops, food counters, restaurants, bars, and public spaces is a magnet for tourists and suburbanites. The five-structure complex sits on brick-and-stone plazas that teem with crowds shopping, eating, performing, viewing performers, and people-watching. **Quincy Market** is the central Greek Revival–style building; its central corridor is an enormous food court. On either side, glass canopies cover full-service restaurants as well as pushcarts that hold everything from crafts created by New England artisans to hokey souvenirs. In the plaza between the **South Canopy** and the

Boston

ACCOMMODATIONS ■
Boston Harbor Hotel **10**
Chandler Inn Hotel **16**
Charlesmark Hotel **19**
The Fairmont Copley
 Plaza Hotel **18**
Four Seasons Hotel **13**
Harborside Inn **9**
Jurys Boston Hotel **15**
The MidTown Hotel **22**
Omni Parker House **11**

DINING ◆
Billy Tse Restaurant **6**
Buddha's Delight **12**
Café Jaffa **20**
Dalí **2**
Durgin-Park **8**
Hamersley's Bistro **17**
The Helmand **3**
L' Espalier **21**
La Summa **5**
Legal Sea Foods **14**
Mr. Bartley's Burger Cottage **1**
Pizzeria Regina **4**
Ye Olde Union Oyster House **7**

To Central Square
and Harvard Square

Longfellow Bridge

CAMBRIDGE

Ames St.   Amherst St.

3rd St.   2nd St.   1st St.

CHARLES
RIVER
RESERVATION

Vassar St.

Massachusetts Institute
of Technology

Memorial Drive

Hatch Memorial
She

Charles River Basin

Amherst Alley

Harvard Bridge

BOSTON CITY LIMITS

MASSACHUSETTS
★ Boston

James J. Storrow Memorial Embankment

Berkeley St.

James J. Storrow
Bay State Road   Memorial Drive

Back St.   Beacon St.

Marlborough St.

Clarendon St.

Boston
Univ. ⊠

Deerfield St.   Raleigh St.

Charlesgate W.

Charlesgate E.

Hereford St.   Gloucester St.

Fairfield St.   Exeter St.   Dartmouth St.

Commonwealth Ave.

Newbury St.

COPLEY Ⓣ Copley
Square
St. James Ave.

Ⓣ KENMORE
Kenmore
Square

21 20

Newbury St. Ⓣ

BACK BAY

HYNES/ICA

Boylston St.   19

⊠

18

ⓘ P

Stuart St.

Tunnel

← To Brookline

Fenway
Park

Ipswich St.

Newbury St. Ⓣ

90   MASS. TPK.

P

Harcourt St.

P

BACK BAY/SOUTH END   Ⓣ

Yawkey Way   Van Ness St.

Boylston St.

Back Bay
Fens

Muddy River

Massachusetts Ave.

Dalton St.

Norway St. ⊠

Burbank St.

PRUDENTIAL
Ⓣ

Huntington Ave.

Garrison St.

Yarmouth St.
Canton St.
Holyoke St.

Braddock Pk.

Columbus Ave.

Warren Ave.
W. Cant
W. Brookline
Pembroke St.
Rutland St.
Concord St.
W. Newton St.

Peterborough St.

Queensberry St.

Agassiz Rd.

Westland Ave.

Symphony Rd.

SYMPHONY
Ⓣ

Cumberland

22

Greenwich
Albemarle St.
Claremont
Pkwy.
Wellington

W. Newton St.
W. Springfield St.
Worcester St.
W. Concord St.

Tremont St.
W. Haven St.
Newland Pl.
Clinton

Park Dr.

Gainsborough St.

Massachusetts Ave.

Fenway

Hemenway St.
Forsyth Way
Spear St. Pl.

NORTHEASTERN
Ⓣ

Huntington Ave.

Museum of
Fine Arts

MUSEUM

Northeastern
University

Wm. E. Carter
Playground

MASSACHUSETTS
AVE.   Ⓣ

Northampton
St.

Camden
St.

South Market building is an **information kiosk. Faneuil Hall** itself—nicknamed the "Cradle of Liberty"—sometimes gets overlooked, but it's worth a visit. National Park Service rangers give free 20-minute talks every half-hour from 9am to 5pm in the auditorium.

Between North, Congress, and State sts. and I-93. ⓒ **617/523-1300.** www.faneuilhallmarketplace.com. Marketplace Mon–Sat 10am–9pm; Sun noon–6pm. Food court opens earlier; some restaurants close later. T: Green or Blue Line to Government Center, Orange Line to Haymarket, or Blue Line to Aquarium or State.

Isabella Stewart Gardner Museum Isabella Stewart Gardner (1840–1924) designed her exquisite home in the style of a 15th-century Venetian palace and filled it with European, American, and Asian painting and sculpture. You'll see works by Titian, Botticelli, Raphael, Rembrandt, Matisse, and Mrs. Gardner's friends James McNeill Whistler and John Singer Sargent. The building holds a hodgepodge of furniture and architectural details imported from European churches and palaces. The *pièce de résistance* is the magnificent courtyard, filled year-round with fresh flowers from the museum greenhouse.

280 The Fenway. ⓒ **617/566-1401.** www.gardnermuseum.org. Admission $12 adults, $10 seniors, $5 college students; free for children under 18 and adults named Isabella with ID. Tues–Sun and some Mon holidays 11am–5pm. T: Green Line E to Museum.

John F. Kennedy Library and Museum *Kids* The Kennedy era springs to life at this dramatic library, museum, and research complex overlooking Dorchester Bay. It captures the 35th president's accomplishments in sound and video recordings as well as fascinating displays of memorabilia and photos. A visit begins with a 17-minute film about Kennedy's early life. The exhibits start with the 1960 campaign and end with a tribute to Kennedy's legacy. There's a film about the Cuban Missile Crisis, along with displays on Attorney Gen. Robert F. Kennedy, the civil rights movement, the Peace Corps, the space program, First Lady Jacqueline Bouvier Kennedy, and the Kennedy family.

Columbia Point. ⓒ **877/616-4599** or 617/929-4500. www.jfklibrary.org. Admission $10 adults, $8 seniors and college students, $7 youths 13–17; free for children under 13. Surcharges may apply for special exhibitions. Daily 9am–5pm (last film at 3:55pm). T: Red Line to JFK/UMass, then free no. 2 shuttle bus, which runs every 20 min. By car, take Southeast Expwy. (I-93/Rte. 3) south to Exit 15 (Morrissey Blvd./JFK Library), turn left onto Columbia Rd., and follow signs to free parking lot.

Museum of Fine Arts *Best* One of the world's great museums, the MFA works constantly to become even more accessible and interesting and is especially noted for its **Impressionist paintings** (including 43 Monets—the largest collection outside Paris), Asian and Old Kingdom Egyptian collections, classical art, Buddhist temple, and medieval sculpture and tapestries. The American and European paintings and sculpture are a remarkable assemblage of timeless works. Pick up a floor plan at the information desk, or take a free **guided tour** (weekdays except Mon holidays at 10:30am and 1:30pm; Wed at 6:15pm; and Sat at 10:30am and 1pm). Note that the MFA's admission fees are among the highest in the country. A Boston CityPass is a great deal if you plan to visit enough of the other included attractions.

465 Huntington Ave. ⓒ **617/267-9300.** www.mfa.org. Admission $15 adults, $13 seniors and students when entire museum is open ($13 and $11, respectively, when only West Wing is open); $6.50 children under 18 on school days before 3pm, otherwise free. Admission good for 2 visits within 10 days. Voluntary contribution ($15 suggested) Wed 4–9:45pm. Surcharges may apply for special exhibitions. Free admission for museum shop, library, restaurants, and auditoriums. Entire museum Sat–Tues 10am–4:45pm; Wed 10am–9:45pm; Thurs–Fri 10am–5pm. West Wing only Thurs–Fri 5–9:45pm. T: Green Line E to Museum or Orange Line to Ruggles.

Museum of Science *(Kids)*   Among the 600-plus exhibits, you might meet an iguana or a dinosaur, find out how much you'd weigh on the moon, or climb into a space module. Activity centers focus on fields of interest—natural history (with live animals), light and optics, computers, and the human body—as well as interdisciplinary approaches. The separate-admission theaters are worth planning for, even if you skip the exhibits. Buy all your tickets at once, not only because it's cheaper but also because shows sometimes sell out. Tickets are for sale in person and, subject to a service charge, over the phone and online (www.tickets.mos.org). The **Mugar Omni Theater,** which shows IMAX movies on a five-story screen, is an intense experience. The **Charles Hayden Planetarium** takes you into space with daily star shows as well as shows on special topics that change several times a year.

Science Park, off O'Brien Hwy. on bridge between Boston and Cambridge. ℂ 617/723-2500. www.mos.org. Admission to exhibit halls $16 adults, $14 seniors, $13 children 3–11. Mugar Omni Theater, Hayden Planetarium, or laser shows $9 adults, $8 seniors, $7 children 3–11. Discounted combination tickets available. July 5 to Labor Day Sat–Thurs 9am–7pm, Fri 9am–9pm; day after Labor Day to July 4 Sat–Thurs 9am–5pm, Fri 9am–9pm. T: Green Line to Science Park.

New England Aquarium   This entertaining complex is home to more than 7,000 fish and aquatic mammals. You'll want to spend at least half a day here, and afternoon crowds can make getting around painfully slow. A Boston CityPass allows you to skip the ticket line, which can be uncomfortably long. The worthwhile **Simons IMAX Theatre,** which has its own hours and admission fees, shows 3-D films that concentrate on the natural world. The focal point of the main building is the four-story, 200,000-gallon **Giant Ocean Tank.** Other exhibits focus on freshwater and tropical specimens, sea otters, the Aquarium Medical Center, denizens of the Amazon, and the ecology of Boston Harbor. The hands-on **Edge of the Sea** exhibit contains a tide pool with resident sea stars, sea urchins, and horseshoe crabs.

Central Wharf. ℂ 617/973-5200. www.newenglandaquarium.org. Admission $18 adults, $15 seniors, $10 children 3–11. Free admission for outdoor exhibits, cafe, and gift shop. July to Labor Day Mon–Thurs 9am–6pm, Fri–Sun and holidays 9am–7pm; day after Labor Day to June Mon–Fri 9am–5pm, Sat–Sun and holidays 9am–6pm. Simons IMAX Theatre: ℂ 866/815-4629 or 617/973-5206. Tickets $10 adults, $8 seniors and children 3–11. Daily 10am–9pm. T: Blue Line to Aquarium.

THE FREEDOM TRAIL

A line of red paint or red brick on the sidewalk, the 3-mile **Freedom Trail** links 16 historic sights. Markers identify the stops, and plaques point the way from one to the next. The trail begins at **Boston Common,** where the Information Center, 146 Tremont St., distributes pamphlets that describe a self-guided tour. For a preview, visit the Freedom Trail Foundation's website at **www.thefreedomtrail.org**.

You can also explore the **Black Heritage Trail.** Stops include stations on the underground railroad and homes of famous citizens as well as the African Meeting House, the oldest standing black church in the country. A 2-hour guided tour starts at the visitor center at 46 Joy St. (ℂ 617/742-5415; www.nps.gov/boaf), daily in summer and by request at other times.

As you follow the Freedom Trail, you'll come to the **Boston National Historic Park Visitor Center,** 15 State St. (ℂ 617/242-5642; www.nps.gov/bost). From here, rangers lead free tours of the heart of the trail. An audiovisual show provides basic information on the stops. The wheelchair-accessible center has restrooms and a bookstore. It's open daily from 9am to 5pm.

The hard-core history fiend who peers at every artifact and reads every plaque along the trail will wind up at Bunker Hill some 4 hours later. The family with restless children will appreciate the efficiency of the 90-minute ranger-led tour.

The highlights of the trail include **Boston Common;** the **Massachusetts State House** (© 617/727-3676; www.sec.state.ma.us/trs); the **Old Granary Burying Ground,** which contains the graves of Samuel Adams, Paul Revere, and John Hancock; the **First Public School;** the **Old South Meeting House** (© 617/482-6439; www.oldsouthmeetinghouse.org), the starting point of the Boston Tea Party; the **Boston Massacre Site;** the **Paul Revere House** (© 617/523-2338; www.paulreverehouse.org); **Old North Church** (© 617/523-6676; www.oldnorth.com), where Revere saw a signal in the steeple and set out on his "midnight ride"; the **USS *Constitution*** (© 617/242-5670; www.oldironsides.com), where active-duty sailors in 1812 dress uniforms give free tours of "Old Ironsides"; and the **Bunker Hill Monument** (© 617/242-5641; www.nps.gov/bost), the 221-foot granite obelisk that honors the memory of the men who died in the Battle of Bunker Hill on June 17, 1775.

The best-known **park** in Boston is the **Public Garden,** bordered by Arlington, Boylston, Charles, and Beacon streets. Something lovely is in bloom at least half of the year. For 5 months, the lagoon is home to the celebrated **swan boats** (© 617/522-1966; www.swanboats.com). The pedal-powered vessels—the attendants pedal, not the passengers—come out of hibernation on the Saturday before Patriot's Day (the third Mon of Apr). The 15-minute ride costs $2.75 for adults, $2 for seniors, and $1.25 for children under 16.

ORGANIZED TOURS

From May to October, the **Boston by Foot** ✦✦ (© 617/367-2345, or 617/367-3766 for recorded info; www.bostonbyfoot.com), conducts historical and architectural walking tours that focus on neighborhoods or themes. Buy tickets ($12 adults, $8 children 6–12; Boston Underfoot $14 per person) from the guide; reservations are not required. The 90-minute tours take place rain or shine. The **Boston Park Rangers** (© 617/635-7383; www.ci.boston.ma.us/parks) offer free guided walking tours. The best-known focus is the **Emerald Necklace,** a loop of green spaces designed by pioneering landscape architect Frederick Law Olmsted. Call for schedules. The nonprofit **Boston History Collaborative** (© 617/350-0358; www.bostonhistorycollaborative.org) coordinates several heritage trail tours focusing on maritime history, immigration, literary history, and inventions.

The most unusual way to see Boston is with **Boston Duck Tours** (© 800/226-7442 or 617/267-DUCK; www.bostonducktours.com). From April to November, sightseers board a "duck," a reconditioned World War II amphibious landing craft, on the Boylston Street side of the Prudential Center (the Pru). The 80-minute narrated tour begins with a quick but comprehensive jaunt around the city. Then the duck lumbers down a ramp, splashes into the Charles River, and takes a spin around the basin. Tickets cost $26 for adults, $23 for seniors and students, $17 for children 3 to 11, and $3 for children under 3.

The **sightseeing cruise** season runs from April to October, with spring and fall offerings often restricted to weekends. **Boston Harbor Cruises,** 1 Long Wharf (© 877/733-9425 or 617/227-4321; www.bostonharborcruises.com), is the largest company. Ninety-minute historic sightseeing cruises, which tour the Inner and Outer harbors, depart daily at 11am, 1pm, 3pm, and 6 or 7pm (the sunset cruise), with extra excursions at busy times. Tickets are $19 for adults, $17 for seniors, and $15 for children 4 to 12; sunset-cruise tickets are $1 more.

EXPLORING CAMBRIDGE

Harvard Square is a people-watching paradise of students, instructors, commuters, and sightseers. Restaurants and stores pack the three streets that radiate from the center of the square and the streets that intersect them.

Harvard University is the oldest college in the country. Free student-led tours of the main campus leave from the **Events & Information Center,** in Holyoke Center, 1350 Mass. Ave. (© **617/495-1573**), during the school year twice a day Monday through Friday and once on Saturday (except during vacations), and during the summer four times a day Monday through Saturday and twice on Sunday. The Events & Information Center has maps, illustrated booklets, and self-guided walking-tour directions.

Note: The **Boston Tea Party Ship & Museum** (© **617/338-1773;** www.bostonteapartyship.com) closed after a fire in late 2001. It's currently renovating, expanding, and planning to reopen in spring 2008. It makes an entertaining stop on the way to or from the Children's Museum.

Harvard Museum of Natural History and Peabody Museum of Archaeology & Ethnology *(Kids* These museums house the university's collections of items and artifacts related to the natural world. The **Botanical Museum** displays the **Glass Flowers,** 3,000 models of more than 840 plant species devised by Leopold and Rudolph Blaschka. Children love the **Museum of Comparative Zoology,** where dinosaurs share space with preserved and stuffed insects and animals that range in size from butterflies to giraffes. Young visitors enjoy the dollhouselike "Worlds in Miniature" display at the **Peabody Museum,** which represents people from all over the world in scaled-down homes. The Peabody also boasts the **Hall of the North American Indian,** where 500 artifacts representing 10 cultures are on display.

Museum of Natural History: 26 Oxford St. © 617/495-3045. www.hmnh.harvard.edu. Peabody Museum: 11 Divinity Ave. © 617/496-1027. www.peabody.harvard.edu. Admission to both $9 adults, $7 seniors and students, $6 children 3–18; free to all Sun until noon year-round and Wed 3–5pm Sept–May. Daily 9am–5pm. T: Red Line to Harvard. Cross Harvard Yard, keeping John Harvard statue on right, and turn right at Science Center. First left is Oxford St.

Harvard University Art Museums   The **Fogg Art Museum,** 32 Quincy St., near Broadway, offers a broad range of items—17th-century Dutch and Flemish landscapes, 19th-century British and American paintings and drawings, French paintings and drawings from the 18th century through the Impressionist period, contemporary sculpture, and changing exhibits. The **Busch-Reisinger Museum,** in Werner Otto Hall (enter through the Fogg), is the only museum in North America devoted to the art of northern and central Europe. The early-20th-century collections include works by Kandinsky and other Bauhaus artists. The **Arthur M. Sackler Museum,** 485 Broadway, at Quincy Street, houses the university's collections of Asian, ancient, and Islamic art.

32 Quincy St. and 485 Broadway. © 617/495-9400. www.artmuseums.harvard.edu. Admission to all 3 museums $9 adults, $7 seniors, $6 students, free for children under 18; free to all until noon Sat. Mon–Sat 10am–5pm; Sun 1–5pm. T: Red Line to Harvard. Cross Harvard Yard diagonally from the T station and cross Quincy St.

Longfellow National Historic Site   The books and furniture inside the yellow mansion have remained intact since the poet Henry Wadsworth Longfellow died here in 1882. During the siege of Boston in 1775 and 1776, the house served as the

(*Best*) **Take Me Out to the Ballgame . . .**

Football and basketball's TV ratings may be higher, but they've never succeeded in wresting baseball's position as America's national pastime. Millions worship at the sport's cathedrals each year hoping to catch a home run or celebrate a win over a hated rival. Here are our picks for the best places to watch the Boys of Summer duke it out:

1. Cubs fans have been crying "Maybe next year" since **Wrigley Field** opened in 1914, but it's the champ of baseball stadiums (even if it's suffering the effects of old age, we love underdogs!). From its famous Bleacher Bums and numerous day games to its old-fashioned scoreboard and classic seventh-inning stretch rendition of "Take Me Out to the Ballgame" (which has lost only a little luster since the passing of legendary announcer Harry Carey), Wrigley is the class of the field. And a 2005 expansion added more than 1,800 bleacher seats and spruced things up, giving it a further leg up on the competition.

2. The oldest in the majors—it opened in 1912—**Fenway Park** in Beantown is loaded with history and atmosphere. It's a national treasure and we were genuinely torn when we gave it second place behind Wrigley. Sure it's cramped and the sightlines can get iffy, but it's still a beauty, the fans are both knowledgeable and nice (provided you aren't sporting Yankee pinstripes), the hand-operated scoreboard is still used, and the seats atop the famous Green Monster are the best in baseball. And the Red Sox's 2004 World Series victory ended the team's infamous 86-year losing streak. Take that, Babe Ruth!

headquarters of Gen. George Washington, with whom Longfellow was fascinated. On the absorbing tour—the only way to see the house—you'll learn about the history of the building and its famous occupants.

105 Brattle St. © 617/876-4491. www.nps.gov/long. Guided tours $3 adults, free for children under 17. Call ahead to confirm hours and tour times. June–Oct Wed–Sun 10am–4:30pm. Tours 10:30am, 11:30am, 1, 2, 3, and 4pm. Closed Nov–Mar. T: Red Line to Harvard, then follow Brattle St. about 7 blocks; house is on the right.

SPECTATOR SPORTS

No other experience in sports matches watching the **Boston Red Sox** play at **Fenway Park.** The Fenway Park **ticket office** (© 877/RED-SOX-9; www.redsox.com) is at 4 Yawkey Way, off Brookline Avenue. Tickets go on sale in January, and prices start at $23. **Tours** (© 617/236-6666) start on the hour from 9am to 4pm (or 3 hr. before game time, whichever is earlier) daily, year-round. There are no tours on holidays or before day games. The cost is $12 for adults, $11 for seniors, and $10 for children under 15.

Every year on Patriot's Day (the third Mon in Apr), the **Boston Marathon** rules the roads from Hopkinton to Copley Square in Boston. For information about qualifying, contact the **Boston Athletic Association** (© 617/236-1652; www.boston marathon.org).

3. Opened in 1992, **Oriole Park at Camden Yards** was the pioneer that inspired the building of many a classic baseball park throughout the country and for that alone it deserves a standing O. Architecturally and comfortwise this beauty's still arguably tops in the country. And it offers some of the best eats in baseball. Even better (though not for Baltimore), because the Orioles haven't had much to sing about lately, it's not that tough to get a very affordable seat to a game.

4. One of the most famous shrines in Sportsdom, **Yankee Stadium** opened with a bang (okay, a three-run homer) by the Babe in 1923. The House that Ruth Built would earns its place on this list merely due to its history—no other stadium comes close on that score (check out Monument Park inside the stadium if you doubt us). Alas, the aging stadium lacks a lot of creature comforts (and it just doesn't have that homey Wrigley vibe to combat the shabby feeling), and the neighborhood's borderline at best (the food could be described that way, too). Fanwise, as long as you root for the home team, you'll be in excellent company.

5. We argued long and hard over this last choice before finally settling on gorgeous **Coors Field** in Denver. Why? Because the home run rules in America and the thin air here means lots of tearful pitchers (who says there's no crying in baseball?), who get hammered in this park like no other. Watching batting practice here is a blast (or three or eight). Tack on the friendly crowds, the views of the Rocky Mountains, and good food, and this one's a winner.

SHOPPING

The Back Bay is the area's premier shopping district. If you're passionate about art, set aside a couple of hours for a stroll along Newbury Street, a world-famous destination with dozens of galleries, shops, and boutiques. Besides being a prime location for upscale boutiques, it boasts an infinite variety of styles and media in the dozens of art galleries at street level and on the higher floors. (Remember to look up.) Pick up a copy of the free monthly *Gallery Guide* at businesses along Newbury Street. Nearby, a weatherproof walkway across Huntington Avenue links upscale **Copley Place** (© 617/375-4400) and the **Shops at Prudential Center** (© 800/SHOP-PRU).

Downtown, **Faneuil Hall Marketplace** (© 617/523-1300) is the busiest attraction in Boston not only for its smorgasbord of food outlets, but also for its shops, boutiques, and pushcarts. If the hubbub here is too much for you, stroll over to **Charles Street,** at the foot of Beacon Hill. A short but commercially dense (and picturesque) street, it's home to perhaps the best assortment of gift and antiques shops in the city. One of Boston's oldest shopping areas is **Downtown Crossing.** Now a traffic-free pedestrian mall along Washington, Winter, and Summer streets near Boston Common, it's home to two major department stores (**Filene's Basement** and **Macy's**); tons of smaller clothing, shoe, and music stores; and food and merchandise pushcarts.

In **Cambridge** the bookstores, boutiques, and T-shirt shops of **Harvard Square** lie about 15 minutes from downtown Boston by subway. You'll find a mix of national and regional outlets, and more than a few persistent independent retailers. For a less generic experience, walk along **Mass. Ave.** in either direction to the next T stop. The stroll takes about an hour. Bookworms flock to Cambridge; Harvard Square in particular caters to general and specific audiences. Check out the basement of the **Harvard Book Store,** 1256 Mass. Ave. (© **800/542-READ** outside the 617 area code, or 617/661-1515; www.harvard.com), for great deals on remainders and used books.

WHERE TO STAY

Boston has one of the busiest hotel markets in the country, with some of the highest prices. Rates at most downtown hotels are lower on weekends than on weeknights; leisure hotels offer discounts during the week. It's always a good idea to make a reservation, especially during foliage season and around college graduation time. The Convention & Visitors Bureau **Hotel Hot Line** (© **800/777-6001**) can help make reservations even at the busiest times. It's staffed Monday through Friday until 8pm, Saturday and Sunday until 4pm.

B&Bs are a popular form of lodging in the area. The following organizations can help you find a B&B (most require a minimum stay of at least 2 nights): **Bed & Breakfast Agency of Boston** (© **800/248-9262** or 617/720-3540, or 0800/89-5128 in the U.K.; www.boston-bnbagency.com); **Host Homes of Boston** (© **800/600-1308** or 617/244-1308; www.hosthomesofboston.com); **Bed & Breakfast Reservations North Shore/Greater Boston/Cape Cod** (© **800/832-2632** outside MA, 617/964-1606, or 978/281-9505; www.bbreserve.com); and **Bed and Breakfast Associates Bay Colony** (© **888/486-6018** or 781/449-5302, or 08/234-7113 in the U.K.; www.bnbboston.com).

Boston Harbor Hotel The Boston Harbor Hotel is one of the finest in town, an excellent choice for both business and leisure travelers. The 16-story brick building is within walking distance of downtown and the waterfront attractions; the Airport Water Shuttle stops behind the hotel. Each guest room is a luxurious combination of bedroom and living room, with mahogany furnishings. Rooms with city views are less expensive than those that face the harbor. The best units are suites with private terraces and dazzling water vistas.

Rowes Wharf (entrance on Atlantic Ave.), Boston, MA 02110. © 800/752-7077 or 617/439-7000. Fax 617/330-9450. www.bhh.com. 230 units. $295–$595 double; from $455 suite. Extra person $50. Children under 18 stay free in parent's room. Weekend packages available. AE, DC, DISC, MC, V. Valet parking $25–$34; self-parking $20–$30. T: Red Line to South Station or Blue Line to Aquarium. Pets accepted. **Amenities:** Restaurant; cafe; indoor lap pool; health club; spa.

Chandler Inn Hotel *Value* The comfortable, unpretentious Chandler Inn is a bargain for its location, just 2 blocks from the Back Bay. Guest rooms have individual climate control and tasteful contemporary-style furniture. Each unit holds a queen-size or double bed or two twin beds, without enough room to squeeze in a cot. Bathrooms are tiny. This is a gay-friendly hotel—**Fritz,** the bar next to the lobby, is a neighborhood hangout—that books up early for foliage season and events such as the Marathon and Boston Pride March.

26 Chandler St. (at Berkeley St.), Boston, MA 02116. © 800/842-3450 or 617/482-3450. Fax 617/542-3428. www.chandlerinn.com. 56 units. Apr–Dec $139–$169 double; Jan–Mar $129–$139 double. Children under 12 stay free in parent's room. AE, DC, DISC, MC, V. No parking. T: Orange Line to Back Bay. Pets under 25 lb. accepted with prior approval.

The Charles Hotel This nine-story brick hotel a block from Harvard Square has been *the* place for business and leisure travelers in Cambridge since it opened in 1985. Much of its fame derives from its excellent restaurants, jazz bar, and day spa; the service is equally impeccable. In the posh guest rooms, which were renovated in 2006, the style is contemporary country, with custom adaptations of Shaker furniture. The austere design contrasts with the indulgent amenities, which include down quilts and Bose Wave radios; bathrooms contain telephones and TVs.

1 Bennett St., Cambridge, MA 02138. © **800/882-1818** or 617/864-1200. Fax 617/864-5715. www.charleshotel. com. 293 units. $259–$599 double; $309–$4,000 suite. Extra person $20. Packages available. AE, DC, MC, V. Valet or self-parking $28. T: Red Line to Harvard. Pets under 25 lb. accepted; $50 fee. **Amenities:** 2 restaurants; access to adjacent health club and spa.

Charlesmark Hotel *(Value)*

In an excellent location overlooking the Boston Marathon finish line, the Charlesmark has a boutique feel and great prices. It's both luxurious and—literally, not figuratively—no frills. The contemporary design evokes a yacht, using custom furnishings to pack plenty of comfort into compact spaces. Rooms have pillow-top mattresses and enough room to hold a comfortable chair. The amenities don't challenge the perks of the large hotels in this neighborhood, but they're more than sufficient for most business or leisure travelers—rates include continental breakfast, access to a computer in the lobby, and local phone calls.

655 Boylston St. (between Dartmouth and Exeter sts.), Boston, MA 02116. © **617/247-1212.** Fax 617/247-1224. www.thecharlesmark.com. 33 units (most with shower only). $99–$249 double. Rates include continental breakfast. Children under 12 stay free in parent's room. AE, DC, DISC, MC, V. Self-parking $32 in nearby garage. T: Green Line to Copley. Pets accepted with prior approval. *In room:* Minifridge.

The Fairmont Copley Plaza Hotel

The "grande dame of Boston" is a true grand hotel with a well-earned reputation for service. Built in 1912, the six-story Renaissance Revival building faces Copley Square. The spacious guest rooms have a residential feel, thanks largely to a $34-million overhaul completed in 2004. The custom-made traditional furnishings reflect the elegance of the opulent public spaces. Rooms that face the lovely square afford better views than those that overlook busy Dartmouth Street.

138 St. James Ave., Boston, MA 02116. © **800/441-1414** or 617/267-5300. Fax 617/247-6681. www.fairmont.com/ copleyplaza. 383 units. From $259 double; from $699 suite. Extra person $30. Packages available. AE, DC, MC, V. Valet parking $32. T: Green Line to Copley, or Orange Line to Back Bay. Pets accepted; $25 per day. **Amenities:** Restaurant; exercise room.

Four Seasons Hotel *(Best)*

Many hotels offer exquisite service, a beautiful location, elegant guest rooms and public areas, a terrific health club, and wonderful restaurants. But no other hotel in Boston—indeed, in New England—combines every element of a luxury hotel as seamlessly as the Four Seasons. The 16-story brick-and-glass building (the hotel occupies eight floors) blends traditional and contemporary style. The best units overlook the Public Garden; city views from the back of the hotel aren't as desirable. Children receive bedtime snacks and toys, and can ask at the concierge desk for duck food to take to the Public Garden. Small pets even enjoy a special menu and amenities.

200 Boylston St., Boston, MA 02116. © **800/332-3442** or 617/338-4400. Fax 617/423-0154. www.fourseasons.com/ boston. 272 units. $425–$650 double; from $695 1-bedroom suite; from $2,200 2-bedroom suite. Packages available. AE, DC, DISC, MC, V. Valet parking $37. T: Green Line to Arlington. Pets under 15 lb. accepted. **Amenities:** Restaurant; pool; health club; spa.

Harborside Inn

The Harborside Inn offers a good combination of location and (for this neighborhood) value. The renovated 1858 warehouse is near Faneuil Hall Marketplace, the harbor, the Financial District, and the Big Dig. The guest rooms have hardwood floors, Oriental rugs, and Victorian-style furniture. They surround a sky-lit atrium; city-view units are more expensive but can be noisier. Still, they're preferable to the interior rooms, whose windows open only to the atrium. Units on the top floors have lower ceilings but better views.

185 State St. (between Atlantic Ave. and the Custom House Tower), Boston, MA 02109. $\textcircled{C}$ **888/723-7565** or 617/723-7500. Fax 617/670-6015. www.harborsideinnboston.com. 54 units. $120–$210 double; $235–$310 suite. Extra person $15. Packages and long-term rates available. Rates may be higher during special events. AE, DC, DISC, MC, V. Off-site parking $20; reservation required. T: Blue Line to Aquarium or Orange Line to State. **Amenities:** Restaurant.

Harvard Square Hotel   The Harvard economics department could use this hotel to illustrate supply and demand: At busy times, including almost every night in the fall, rates seem high for such modest accommodations (supply)—but you can't beat the location (demand). Smack in the middle of Harvard Square, the six-story brick hotel is a favorite with visiting parents and budget-conscious business travelers. The unpretentious guest rooms are relatively small but comfortable; they were renovated in 2006.

110 Mount Auburn St., Cambridge, MA 02138. $\textcircled{C}$ **800/458-5886** or 617/864-5200. Fax 617/864-2409. www. harvardsquarehotel.com. 73 units. $99–$269 double. Extra person $10. Children under 17 stay free in parent's room. Corporate rates and AAA and AARP discounts available. AE, DC, DISC, MC, V. Parking $27. T: Red Line to Harvard. **Amenities:** Dining privileges at the Harvard Faculty Club. *In room:* Fridge.

Jurys Boston Hotel   In the former Boston Police Headquarters building, the Irish chain caters to both business and leisure travelers. The 1925 limestone-and-brick structure now holds dramatic public areas and plush accommodations. The luxurious guest rooms have nice touches such as a work area with an ergonomic chair, good-size bathrooms, and windows that open but also muffle street noise. Still, light sleepers will want to face away from busy Berkeley Street. Opened in 2004, this is Jurys Doyle's first U.S. property outside Washington, D.C.

350 Stuart St. (at Berkeley St.), Boston, MA 02116. $\textcircled{C}$ **866/JD-HOTELS** or 617/266-7200. Fax 617/266-7203. www.jurysdoyle.com. 225 units (some with shower only). $155–$435 double; $275–$575 1-bedroom suite; from $1,150 2-bedroom suite. Children under 16 stay free in parent's room. Extra person $20. Packages from $155 per night. AE, DC, DISC, MC, V. Valet parking $36. T: Orange Line to Back Bay or Green Line to Arlington or Copley. **Amenities:** Restaurant; exercise room. *In room:* Fridge.

The MidTown Hotel *(Kids)*   Even without free parking and an outdoor pool, this centrally located hotel would be a good deal for families and budget-conscious businesspeople. It's on a busy street within walking distance of Symphony Hall and the Museum of Fine Arts. The well-maintained rooms are large, bright, and attractively outfitted, although bathrooms are on the small side. Some units have connecting doors that allow families to spread out. The best rooms are on the side of the building that faces away from Huntington Avenue.

220 Huntington Ave., Boston, MA 02115. $\textcircled{C}$ **800/343-1177** or 617/262-1000. Fax 617/262-8739. www.midtown hotel.com. 159 units. $119–$259 double; $139–$279 suite. Extra person $15. Children under 18 stay free in parent's room. Packages and AAA, AARP, and government employee discount available, subject to availability. AE, DC, DISC, MC, V. Free parking (1 car per room). T: Green Line E to Prudential, or Orange Line to Mass. Ave. **Amenities:** Restaurant; heated pool.

Omni Parker House   The Parker House offers a great combination of over 150 years of history (since 1855!) and extensive renovations. Regular renovation (most recently, $5 million-plus in updates just in 2005 and 2006) keeps the property in excellent shape. Guest rooms, a patchwork of more than 50 configurations, aren't huge, but they are thoughtfully laid out and nicely appointed. Business travelers can book a room with an expanded work area, while sightseers can economize by requesting a smaller, less expensive unit.

60 School St., Boston, MA 02108. © **800/THE-OMNI** or 617/227-8600. Fax 617/742-5729. www.omnihotels.com. 552 units (some with shower only). $189–$289 double; $249–$399 suite. Children under 18 stay free in parent's room. Packages and AARP discount available. AE, DC, DISC, MC, V. Valet parking $36. T: Green or Blue Line to Government Center, or Red Line to Park St. Pets accepted; deposit required. **Amenities:** Restaurant; exercise room.

WHERE TO DINE

Travelers from around the world relish the variety of skillfully prepared seafood available in the Boston area. Lunch is an excellent, economical way to check out a fancy restaurant without breaking the bank. For those who like to dine alfresco, the **food court** at Faneuil Hall Marketplace is a great place to pick up picnic fare.

Billy Tse Restaurant CHINESE/PAN-ASIAN/SUSHI
This casual and non-touristy spot on the edge of the Italian North End serves excellent renditions of the usual Chinese dishes and good fresh seafood. The Pan-Asian selections and sushi are just as enjoyable as the Chinese classics. Be sure to ask about the daily specials—bitter Chinese broccoli, when it's available, is deftly prepared. Lunch specials, served until 4pm, include vegetable fried rice or vegetable lo mein.

240 Commercial St. © **617/227-9990.** www.billytserestaurant.com. Reservations recommended at dinner on weekends. Main courses $7–$33 (most items less than $17); lunch specials $6–$8; sushi from $3.75. AE, DC, DISC, MC, V. Mon–Thurs 11:30am–11:30pm; Fri–Sat 11:30am–midnight; Sun 11:30am–11pm. Closed 1 week in Feb. T: Green or Orange Line to Haymarket, or Blue Line to Aquarium.

Buddha's Delight (Value) VEGETARIAN/VIETNAMESE
Fresh and healthful intersect with cheap and filling here. The menu lists "chicken," "pork," and even "lobster"—in quotes because the chefs substitute fried and barbecued tofu and gluten for meat, poultry, fish, or dairy (some beverages have condensed milk) to create more-than-reasonable facsimiles of traditional dishes. Between trying to figure out how they do it and savoring Vietnamese cuisine's strong, clear flavors, you might not miss your usual protein.

3 Beach St., 2nd floor. © **617/451-2395.** Main courses $5.50–$13; lunch specials $6.50. MC, V. Sun–Thurs 11am–9:30pm; Fri–Sat 11am–10:30pm. T: Orange Line to Chinatown.

Café Jaffa MIDDLE EASTERN
A narrow brick room with a glass front, Café Jaffa looks more like a snazzy pizza place than the excellent Middle Eastern restaurant it is. Reasonable prices, high quality, and large portions draw hordes of people for traditional dishes such as falafel, baba ghanouj, and hummus, as well as burgers and steak tips. For dessert, try the baklava if it's fresh (give it a pass if not). There is a short list of beer and wine, and many fancy coffee offerings.

48 Gloucester St. © **617/536-0230.** Main courses $5–$16. AE, DC, DISC, MC, V. Mon–Thurs 11am–10:30pm; Fri–Sat 11am–11pm; Sun noon–10pm. T: Green Line B, C, or D to Hynes/ICA.

Dalí SPANISH
The bar at this festive restaurant fills with people cheerfully waiting an hour or more for a table. The payoff is authentic Spanish food, notably tapas. Entrees include excellent paella, but most people come in a group and explore the three dozen or more tapas offerings. They include delectable garlic potatoes, salmon balls with not-too-salty caper sauce, pork tenderloin with blue goat cheese, and delicious sausages. The staff sometimes seems rushed, but never fails to supply bread for sopping up juices, and sangria for washing it all down. Finish with "ubiquitous flan" or the luscious *tarta de chocolates*.

415 Washington St., Somerville. © **617/661-3254.** www.dalirestaurant.com. Reservations not accepted. Tapas $4.50–$9.50; main courses $19–$25. AE, DC, MC, V. Daily 5:30–11pm. T: Red Line to Harvard, then follow Kirkland St. to intersection of Washington and Beacon sts. (20-min. walk or $5 cab ride).

Durgin-Park (Kids) NEW ENGLAND
For huge portions of delicious food, a rowdy atmosphere where CEOs share tables with students, and famously cranky waitresses,

Bostonians have flocked to Durgin-Park since 1827. They come for prime rib the size of a hubcap, piles of fried seafood, fish dinners broiled to order, and bounteous portions of roast turkey. Steaks and chops are broiled on an open fire over wood charcoal. Boston baked beans are a signature dish, and this is the best place to try them. For dessert, the strawberry shortcake is justly celebrated.

340 Faneuil Hall Marketplace. © 617/227-2038. www.durgin-park.com. Reservations accepted only for parties of 15 or more. Main courses $7–$11 at lunch, $10–$25 at dinner; specials $19–$40. Children's menu $8–$9. AE, DC, DISC, MC, V. Mon–Sat 11:30am–10pm, Sun 11:30am–9pm; lunch menu daily until 2:30pm. Validated parking available. T: Green or Blue Line to Government Center, Green or Orange Line to Haymarket, or Blue Line to Aquarium.

Hamersley's Bistro FRENCH/AMERICAN   This is the place that put the South End on Boston's culinary map, a pioneering restaurant that's both classic and contemporary. It's one of the most beloved special-occasion restaurants in the Boston area yet somehow manages to feel like a neighborhood hangout. The seasonal menu offers entrees noted for their emphasis on local ingredients and classic techniques. Cassoulet with pork, duck confit, and garlic sausage is a gorgeously executed combination of flavors and textures. The kitchen also has a way with fish—perhaps salmon au poivre with sorrel, leeks, and fingerling potatoes. The wine list is excellent.

553 Tremont St. © 617/423-2700. www.hamersleysbistro.com. Reservations recommended. Main courses $26–$40; tasting menu varies. AE, DISC, MC, V. Mon–Fri 6–10pm; Sat 5:30–10:30pm; Sun 5:30–9:30pm. Closed Jan 1–10. Valet parking available. T: Orange Line to Back Bay.

The Helmand AFGHAN   The Helmand enjoyed a burst of publicity when the manager's brother took over the provisional government of Afghanistan, and it's hardly had a slow night since. Unusual cuisine, an elegant setting, and reasonable prices had already made this spot near the CambridgeSide Galleria mall a favorite. Afghan food is vegetarian friendly; many non-veggie dishes use meat as one element rather than the centerpiece. *Aushak,* pasta pockets filled with leeks or potatoes and topped with split-pea-and-carrot sauce, also comes with meat sauce. For dessert, don't miss the Afghan version of baklava.

143 First St. © 617/492-4646. Reservations recommended. Main courses $12–$20. AE, MC, V. Sun–Thurs 5–10pm; Fri–Sat 5–11pm. T: Green Line to Lechmere.

L'Espalier *(Best)* NEW ENGLAND/FRENCH   Chef-owner Frank McClelland presides over one of Boston's favorite special-occasion destinations, which consists of three dining rooms on the second floor of an 1886 town house. The space is formal yet inviting, the service excellent, the food magnificent. The imaginative kitchen uses classic techniques to turn the freshest and most interesting ingredients available— many from small New England purveyors of everything from seafood to game to organic produce—into unforgettable dishes. The breads, sorbets, ice creams, and alarmingly good desserts (many adapted from the family's heirloom cookbooks) are made in-house. Dining here is a special and unique experience.

30 Gloucester St. © 617/262-3023. www.lespalier.com. Reservations recommended. Prix fixe (3 courses) $75; menu degustation (7 courses) $94. AE, DC, DISC, MC, V. Mon–Sat 5:30–10pm; Sat 2–3pm (tea). Valet parking available. T: Green Line B, C, or D to Hynes/ICA.

La Summa SOUTHERN ITALIAN   La Summa maintains a neighborhood atmosphere in the North End. Unlike some neighborhood places, it's friendly to outsiders— you'll feel welcome even if your server doesn't greet you by name. It's worth seeking out for homemade pasta and desserts; the more elaborate entrees are scrumptious, too. Try any seafood special, lobster ravioli, *pappardelle e melanzane* (eggplant strips tossed with ethereal fresh pasta), or the house special—veal, chicken, sausage, shrimp, artichokes, pepperoncini, olives, and mushrooms in white-wine sauce. Desserts are terrific.

30 Fleet St. ✆ 617/523-9503. Reservations recommended on weekends. Main courses $11–$24. AE, DC, DISC, MC, V. Sun–Fri 4:30–10:30pm; Sat 4:30–11pm. T: Green or Orange Line to Haymarket.

Legal Sea Foods SEAFOOD   This family-owned business enjoys an international reputation for serving only the freshest, best-quality fish and shellfish, which it processes at its own state-of-the-art plant. The menu includes regular selections (scrod, haddock, bluefish, salmon, shrimp, calamari, and lobster, among others) plus whatever was at the market that morning, prepared in every imaginable way, and it's all splendid. The wide-ranging, reasonably priced wine list is exceptional. And the whole chain (there are numerous branches sprinkled throughout the city) recently started accepting reservations. Can you feel the love?

255 State St. ✆ 617/227-3115. www.legalseafoods.com. Reservations recommended. Main courses $11–$19 at lunch, $14–$35 at dinner. AE, DC, DISC, MC, V. Mon–Thurs 11am–10pm; Fri–Sat 11am–11pm; Sun noon–10pm. T: Blue Line to Aquarium.

Mr. Bartley's Burger Cottage *(Value)* AMERICAN   Great burgers and the best onion rings in the world make Bartley's a perennial favorite with a cross section of Cambridge. The 40-year-old family business is a high-ceilinged, crowded room plastered with signs and posters. Anything you can think of to put on ground beef is available, from American cheese to grilled pineapple. There are also some good dishes that don't involve meat, notably veggie burgers and creamy, garlicky hummus.

1246 Mass. Ave. ✆ 617/354-6559. Burgers $8–$13; main courses, salads, and sandwiches $5–$9. No credit cards. Mon–Sat 11am–9pm. Closed Memorial Day, July 4, Labor Day, and Dec 25–Jan 1. T: Red Line to Harvard.

Pizzeria Regina PIZZA   Regina's looks like a movie set, but it's the real thing. Busy waitresses weave through the boisterous dining room, delivering peerless pizza hot from the brick oven. The list of toppings includes nouveau ingredients such as sun-dried tomatoes, but that's not authentic. House-made sausage, maybe some pepperoni, and a couple of beers—now, *that's* authentic.

11½ Thacher St. ✆ 617/227-0765. www.pizzeriaregina.com. Reservations not accepted. Pizza $10–$17. No credit cards. Mon–Thurs 11am–11:30pm; Fri–Sat 11am–midnight; Sun noon–11pm. T: Green or Orange Line to Haymarket.

Ye Olde Union Oyster House NEW ENGLAND/SEAFOOD   Wise guys sneer about all the tourists, but the Union Oyster House is a local favorite for a reason—the locals eat there, too. The unbeatable combination of historic atmosphere and traditional food has drawn crowds since 1826. After just a few minutes of gobbling fresh seafood and being hypnotized by the shuckers, you might feel sorry for the people who wound up with the pearls instead of the oysters. A "shore dinner" (chowder, steamers, lobster, corn, and dessert) is an excellent introduction to local favorites.

41 Union St. (between North and Hanover sts.). ✆ 617/227-2750. www.unionoysterhouse.com. Reservations recommended. Main courses $8–$22 at lunch, $17–$29 at dinner; lobster market price. Children's menu $5–$12. AE, DC, DISC, MC, V. Sun–Thurs 11am–9:30pm (lunch menu until 5pm); Fri–Sat 11am–10pm (lunch until 6pm). Union Bar daily 11am–midnight (lunch until 3pm, late supper until 11pm). Validated and valet parking available. T: Green or Orange Line to Haymarket.

BOSTON & CAMBRIDGE AFTER DARK
For up-to-date entertainment listings, consult the "Sidekick" section of the daily *Boston Globe,* the "Edge" section of the Friday *Boston Herald,* or the Sunday arts sections of both papers. Three free publications, available at newspaper boxes around

town, publish nightlife listings: the *Boston Phoenix,* the *Stuff@Night* (a *Phoenix* off-shoot), and the *Improper Bostonian.* The *Phoenix* website (**www.bostonphoenix.com**) archives the paper's season preview issues; especially before a summer or fall visit, it's a worthwhile planning tool.

Gay- and lesbian-specific events and venues list what's happening in *Bay Windows* (**www.baywindows.com**), available at newsstands and at Glad Day Bookstore, 673 Boylston St., Back Bay (© 617/267-3010; T: Copley).

Visit a **BosTix** (© 617/482-2849; www.bostix.org) booth at Faneuil Hall Market-place (on the south side of Faneuil Hall) or in Copley Square (at the corner of Boyl-ston and Dartmouth sts.). Same-day tickets to musical and theatrical performances are half price, subject to availability. Credit cards are not accepted, and there are no refunds or exchanges. Check the board or the website for the day's offerings. The booths, which are also Ticketmaster outlets, are open Tuesday through Saturday from 10am to 6pm (half-price tickets go on sale at 11am), Sunday from 11am to 4pm. The Copley Square location is also open Monday from 10am to 6pm.

THE PERFORMING ARTS   The Boston Symphony Orchestra, one of the world's greatest, performs at Symphony Hall, 301 Mass. Ave. (© 617/266-1492; www.bso.org; T: Green Line E to Symphony, or Orange Line to Mass. Ave.). The sea-son runs from October to April. From May to July, members of the BSO lighten up. Tables and chairs replace the floor seats at Symphony Hall, and drinks and light refreshments are served. The famed **Boston Pops** (same contact info as the BSO) play a range of music from light classical to show tunes to popular music, sometimes with celebrity guest stars.

The **Boston Ballet**'s reputation seems to jump a notch every time someone says, "So it's not just *The Nutcracker.*" The country's fourth-largest dance company per-forms the holiday staple from Thanksgiving to New Year's. During the rest of the sea-son (Oct–May), it presents an eclectic mix of classic ballets and contemporary work. Call © 617/695-6955 or check out **www.bostonballet.com**. Performances are held at the Wang Theatre, 270 Tremont St. (T: Green Line to Boylston).

The excellent local theater scene boasts the **Huntington Theatre Company,** which performs at the Boston University Theatre, 264 Huntington Ave. (© 617/266-0800; www.huntington.org); and the **American Repertory Theatre,** which makes its home at Harvard University's Loeb Drama Center, 64 Brattle St., Cambridge (© 617/547-8300; www.amrep.org).

You'll find most of the shows headed to or coming from Broadway in the **Theater District.** The promoter often is **Broadway Across America** (© 866/523-7469; www.broadwayacrossamerica.com).

THE CLUB SCENE   The Boston-area club scene changes constantly, and some-where out there is a good time for everyone. Bars close at 1am, clubs at 2am. The sub-way shuts down between 12:30 and 1am; Night Owl bus service operates until 2:30am on Friday and Saturday. Be prepared to show ID if you appear to be younger than 35 or so.

For **dancing,** try **Avalon,** 15 Lansdowne St. (© 617/262-2424; www.avalon boston.com; T: Green lines B, C, or D to Kenmore), a cavernous space divided into several levels. When the stage isn't in use, DJs spin for the crowd of 20- and 30-some-things. The dress code calls for jackets and shirts with collars, and no jeans or athletic wear. Avalon is open Thursday (international night) through Sunday (gay night). **The Roxy,** in the Tremont Boston hotel, 279 Tremont St. (© 617/338-7699;

www.roxyplex.com; T: Green Line to Boylston), boasts excellent DJs and live music, a huge dance floor, a stage, and a balcony. Occasional concerts and boxing cards take good advantage of the sightlines. No jeans or athletic shoes. The Roxy is open Thursday through Saturday, plus some Wednesdays and Sundays.

FOLK & ECLECTIC   Legendary coffeehouse **Club Passim** at 47 Palmer St., Cambridge (℅ **617/492-7679;** www.clubpassim.org; T: Red Line to Harvard), is where Joan Baez, Suzanne Vega, and Tom Rush started out. There's live music nightly, and coffee and food (no alcohol is served) until 10pm. Cover is $5 to $25; most shows $15 or less. It's open nightly.

JAZZ & BLUES   On summer Thursdays at 6pm, the **Boston Harbor Hotel** (℅ **617/439-7000**) stages performances on the "Blues Barge," which floats in the water behind the hotel. The lineup of local and international artists at the **Regattabar**, 1 Bennett St., Cambridge (℅ **617/661-5000;** www.regattabarjazz.com), is often considered the best in the area, though the stellar (and somewhat less noisy) **Sculler's Jazz Club,** 400 Soldiers Field Rd. (℅ **617/562-4111;** www.scullersjazz.com) might dispute that contention.

   Wally's Café, 427 Mass. Ave. (℅ **617/424-1408;** www.wallyscafe.com; T: Orange Line to Mass. Ave.), is a Boston institution. Opened in 1947 in the South End, it draws a diverse crowd—black, white, straight, gay, affluent, indigent—and features nightly live music.

ROCK & ALTERNATIVE   Big-name rock and pop artists play **TD Banknorth Garden,** 100 Legends Way (Causeway St.; ℅ **617/624-1000;** www.tdbanknorthgarden. com), when it's not in use by the Bruins (hockey), the Celtics (basketball), the circus (in Oct), and touring ice shows.

   The Middle East, the best club in town, books an impressive variety of progressive and alternative acts upstairs and downstairs every night at 472–480 Mass. Ave., Central Square, Cambridge (℅ **617/864-EAST;** www.mideastclub.com; T: Red Line to Central). Cover is $7 to $15. Other good venues are the **Paradise Rock Club** near Boston University, which draws enthusiastic crowds for top local and national performers at 967 Comm. Ave. (℅ **617/562-8800,** or 617/423-NEXT for tickets; www.dlclive.com; T: Green Line B to Pleasant St.); and **T. T. the Bear's,** 10 Brookline St., Cambridge (℅ **617/492-0082;** www.ttthebears.com; T: Red Line to Central), a no-frills spot with bookings ranging from alternative rock to ska to up-and-coming pop acts.

BARS & LOUNGES   If you want to go "where everybody knows your name," you have two choices: There's **Cheers,** 84 Beacon St. (℅ **617/227-9605;** www.cheers boston.com; T: Green Line to Arlington), the inspiration for the television show *Cheers.* It looks nothing like the bar on TV. It really is a neighborhood bar with good pub grub, but it's far better known for attracting legions of out-of-towners. Then there's **Cheers,** a bar that replicates the set of the TV show at Faneuil Hall Marketplace (℅ **617/227-0150;** www.cheersboston.com; T: Green or Blue lines to Government Center, or Orange Line to Haymarket).

   At **The Black Rose,** 160 State St. (℅ **617/742-2286;** www.irishconnection.com; T: Orange or Blue lines to State), an always jampacked pub and restaurant, you can sing along with the entertainment. An excellent jukebox, excellent food, and excellent eavesdropping make **Casablanca,** 40 Brattle St., Cambridge (℅ **617/876-0999;** T: Red Line to Harvard), a legendary Harvard Square watering hole that's always jammed with students and professors. At **Top of the Hub,** 800 Boylston St. (✆ 617/ 536-1775; T: Green Line E to Prudential), the 52nd-story view of greater Boston from this appealing lounge atop the Prudential Center is lovely at sunset. There's music and dancing nightly. Dress is casual but neat.

A SIDE TRIP TO CONCORD

Concord revels in its legacy as a center of groundbreaking thought and its role in the country's political and intellectual history. For an excellent overview of town history, start your explorations at the **Concord Museum.**

After just a little time in this lovely town, you may find yourself adopting the local attitude toward two of its most famous residents: Ralph Waldo Emerson, who comes across as a well-respected uncle figure; and Henry David Thoreau, everyone's favorite eccentric cousin. The first official battle of the Revolutionary War took place at the North Bridge, now part of Minute Man National Historical Park. By the middle of the 19th century, Concord was the center of the Transcendentalist movement. Homes of Emerson, Thoreau, Nathaniel Hawthorne, and Louisa May Alcott are open to visitors.

GETTING THERE   From Boston by **car** (30–40 min.), take Route 2 into Lincoln and stay in the right lane. Where the main road makes a sharp left, go straight onto Cambridge Turnpike, and follow signs to HISTORIC CONCORD. To go directly to Walden Pond, use the left lane, take Route 2/2A another mile or so, and turn left onto Route 126. There's parking throughout town.

The **commuter rail** (✆ 800/392-6100 outside Massachusetts, or 617/222-3200; www.mbta.com) takes about 45 minutes from North Station in Boston, with a stop in Cambridge. The round-trip fare is $10.

VISITOR INFORMATION   The **Chamber of Commerce,** 15 Walden St., Suite 7 (✆ 978/369-3120; www.concordmachamber.org), maintains a visitor center at 58 Main St., next to Middlesex Savings Bank, 1 block south of Monument Square. It's open daily 9:30am to 4:30pm from April through October; public restrooms in the same building are open year-round. Guided walking tours are available. Weekday and group tours are available by appointment. The community (**www.concordma.com**) and town (**www.concordnet.org**) websites include visitor information. You can also contact the **Greater Merrimack Valley Convention & Visitors Bureau** (✆ 800/ 443-3332 or 978/459-6150; www.merrimackvalley.org).

WHAT TO SEE & DO

Concord Museum *Kids*   This is a great place to start your visit. The **History Galleries** explore the question "Why Concord?" Artifacts, murals, films, maps, documents, and other presentations illustrate the town's role as a Native American settlement, Revolutionary War battleground, 19th-century intellectual center, and focal point of the 20th-century historic preservation movement. You'll also see the contents of Ralph Waldo Emerson's study and a collection of Henry David Thoreau's belongings. Pick up a **family activity pack** as you enter and use the games and reproduction artifacts (including a quill pen and powder horn) to give the kids a hands-on feel for life in the past.

Cambridge Tpk. at Lexington Rd. ✆ 978/369-9609 for recorded info, or 978/369-9763. www.concordmuseum.org. Admission $8 adults, $7 seniors and students, $5 children under 16. June–Aug daily 9am–5pm; Apr–May and Sept–Dec Mon–Sat 9am–5pm, Sun noon–5pm; Jan–Mar Mon–Sat 11am–4pm, Sun 1–4pm.

The Old Manse   The history of this home touches on the military and the literary, but it's mostly the story of a family. The Rev. William Emerson built The Old Manse in 1770 and watched the Battle of Concord from his yard. For almost 170 years, the house was home to his descendants and to two famous friends. In 1842, Nathaniel Hawthorne and his bride, Sophia Peabody, moved in and stayed for 3 years. As a wedding present, Henry David Thoreau sowed the vegetable garden for them. This is also where William's grandson Ralph Waldo Emerson wrote the essay "Nature." Today, you'll see mementos and memorabilia of the Emerson and Ripley families and of the Hawthornes.

269 Monument St. (at North Bridge). ℭ **978/369-3909.** www.oldmanse.org. Guided tour $8 adults, $7 seniors and students, $5 children 6–12, $25 families. Mid-Apr to Oct Mon–Sat 10am–5pm; Sun and holidays noon–5pm (last tour at 4:30pm). Closed Nov to mid-Apr.

Orchard House (Best   *Little Women* (1868), Louisa May Alcott's most popular work, was written and set at Orchard House. Seeing the family home brings the Alcotts to life for legions of visitors. Fans won't want to miss the tour, illustrated with heirlooms. Check in advance for information on holiday programs and other special events. Louisa's father, Amos Bronson Alcott, created Orchard House by joining and restoring two homes. The family lived here from 1858 to 1877. Her mother, Abigail May Alcott, frequently assumed the role of breadwinner—Bronson, Louisa wrote in her journal, had "no gift for money making." *Note:* Call before visiting; an extensive preservation project is underway.

399 Lexington Rd. ℭ **978/369-4118.** www.louisamayalcott.org. Guided tour $8 adults, $7 seniors and students, $5 children 6–17, $20 families. Apr–Oct Mon–Sat 10am–4:30pm, Sun 1–4:30pm; Nov–Mar Mon–Fri 11am–2:45pm, Sat 10am–4:30pm, Sun 1–4:30pm. Closed Jan 1–15.

Ralph Waldo Emerson House   Emerson, also an essayist and poet, lived here from 1835 until his death in 1882. He moved here after marrying his second wife, Lydia Jackson, whom he called "Lydian"; she called him "Mr. Emerson," as the staff still does. The tour gives a good look at his personal side and at the fashionably ornate interior decoration of the time. You'll see original furnishings and some of Emerson's personal effects.

28 Cambridge Tpk. ℭ **978/369-2236.** Guided tours $7 adults, $5 seniors and students. Call to arrange group tours (10 people or more). Mid-Apr to Oct Thurs–Sat 10am–4:30pm; Sun 1–4:30pm. Closed Nov to mid-Apr.

Sleepy Hollow Cemetery   Follow the signs for AUTHOR'S RIDGE to the graves of some of the town's literary lights. Emerson's grave is marked by an uncarved quartz boulder. Thoreau's grave is nearby; at his funeral in 1862, Emerson concluded his eulogy with these words: "wherever there is knowledge, wherever there is virtue, wherever there is beauty, he will find a home."

Entrance on Rte. 62 W. ℭ **978/318-3233.** www.concordnet.org. Daily 7am–dusk, weather permitting. Call ahead for wheelchair access. No buses allowed.

The Wayside   The Wayside was Nathaniel Hawthorne's home from 1852 until his death in 1864. The Wayside is part of Minute Man National Historical Park, and the fascinating 45-minute ranger-led tour illuminates the occupants' lives and the house's crazy-quilt architecture. The exhibit in the barn (free admission) consists of audio presentations and figures of the authors.

455 Lexington Rd. ℭ **978/369-6975.** www.nps.gov/mima/wayside. Guided tour $4 adults, free for children under 17. May–Oct; open days and hours vary. Closed Nov–Apr.

MINUTE MAN NATIONAL HISTORICAL PARK

This 900-acre park preserves the scene of the first Revolutionary War battle, which took place on April 19, 1775. Encouraged by their victory at Lexington, the British continued to Concord in search of stockpiled arms (which the colonists had already moved). Warned of the advance, the Minutemen crossed the North Bridge, evading the "regulars" standing guard, and awaited reinforcements on a hilltop. The British searched nearby homes and burned any guns they found, and the Minutemen, seeing the smoke, mistakenly thought the soldiers were burning the town. The gunfire that ensued, the opening salvo of the Revolution, is remembered as "the shot heard round the world."

The park is open daily year-round. A visit can take as little as half an hour—for a jaunt to the North Bridge—or as long as half a day (or more), if you stop at both visitor centers and participate in a ranger-led program. To reach the bridge from Concord Center, follow Monument Street until you see the parking lot on the right. On one side of the bridge is a plaque commemorating the British soldiers who died in the Revolutionary War. On the other side is Daniel Chester French's *Minute Man* statue, engraved with a stanza of the poem Emerson wrote for the dedication ceremony in 1876.

You can also start at the **North Bridge Visitor Center,** 174 Liberty St., off Monument Street (© **978/369-6993;** www.nps.gov/mima), which overlooks the Concord River and the bridge. A diorama and video illustrate the Battle of Concord; exhibits include uniforms, weapons, and tools of Colonial and British soldiers. Park rangers lead programs and answer questions. Outside, picnicking is allowed, and the scenery (especially the fall foliage) is lovely. The center is open daily from 9am to 5pm (until 4pm in winter).

At the Lexington end of the park, the **Minute Man Visitor Center** (© **781/ 862-7753;** www.nps.gov/mima), off Route 2A, about ½ mile west of I-95, Exit 30B, is open daily from 9am to 5pm (until 4pm in winter). You'll see a multimedia program on the Revolution, displays, and a 40-foot mural illustrating the battle. On summer weekends, rangers lead tours—call ahead for times. The **Battle Road Trail,** a 5.5-mile interpretive path, carries pedestrian, wheelchair, and bicycle traffic. Panels and granite markers display information about the area's history.

Also on the park grounds, on Old Bedford Road, is the **Hartwell Tavern.** Costumed interpreters demonstrate daily life on a farm and in a tavern in Colonial days. It's open from 9:30am to 5pm, daily June through August and weekends only in April, May, September, and October. Admission is free.

WILDERNESS RETREATS

Henry David Thoreau's first published works can serve as starting points: *A Week on the Concord and Merrimack Rivers* (1849) and *Walden* (1854).

To see the area from water level, rent a **canoe** at the **South Bridge Boathouse,** 496 Main St. (© **978/369-9438**), about ⅔ mile west of the center of town, and paddle to the North Bridge and back. Rates are about $12 per hour on weekends, less on weekdays.

At the **Walden Pond State Reservation,** 915 Walden St., Route 126 (© **978/ 369-3254;** www.mass.gov/dcr), a pile of stones marks the site of the cabin where Thoreau lived from 1845 to 1847. Today the picturesque reservation is an extremely popular destination for walking (a path circles the pond), swimming, and fishing. Although crowded, it's well preserved and insulated from development, making it less difficult than you might expect to imagine Thoreau's experience. Call for the schedule of interpretive programs. No dogs or bikes are allowed. Parking costs $5. Call before setting out, because the rangers turn away visitors if the park has reached capacity (1,000). From Concord Center, take Walden Street (Rte. 126) south, cross Route 2, and follow signs to the parking lot.

2 Cape Cod

Curling some 70 miles into the Atlantic, Cape Cod offers miles of beaches, freshwater ponds, and richly historic New England villages; it's a popular summer destination, with plenty of activities after the sun goes down as well.

ESSENTIALS

GETTING THERE   **By Car**   From Providence and New York, cross the Cape Cod Canal on the Bourne Bridge; from Boston, cross on the Sagamore Bridge. Head east on **Route 6.** Exits are marked for all major destinations. Traffic can be a nightmare on peak weekends, so plan accordingly.

By Plane   The Cape's major hub is **Barnstable Municipal Airport,** Hyannis (© 508/775-2020), served by US Airways (© 800/428-4322; www.usair.com) and smaller airlines from Boston's Logan Airport and New York's LaGuardia and Newark. **Provincetown Airport** (© 508/487-0241) is served by **Cape Air** (© 800/352-0714; www.flycapeair.com) from Boston.

By Boat   Bay State Cruises (© 617/748-1428; www.baystatecruisecompany.com) runs a ferry to Provincetown from Boston, in addition to a daily round-trip passenger ferry late June through Labor Day and on weekends late May to late September.

HYANNIS

Hectic Hyannis has a diverse selection of restaurants, bars, and nightclubs. But if you were to confine your visit to this one town, you'd get a warped view of the Cape. Along routes 132 and 28, you could be visiting Anywhere, USA. The roads are lined with the standard chain stores and mired with maddening traffic. It's a rainy-day destination, or a place to go if you need something from a mall.

Don't even bother trying to track down the Kennedy Compound in Hyannisport; it's effectively screened from view. You'll see more at the **John F. Kennedy Hyannis Museum,** 397 Main St. (© 508/790-3077; www.hyannis.com/JFKMuseum.asp), with a multimedia display capturing the Kennedys during their glory days from 1934 to 1963. Admission is $5 adults, $2.50 for children ages 10 to 16. The museum is open April to October Monday to Saturday 9am to 4:30pm, Sunday and holidays noon to 4:30pm; last admission is at 3:30pm.

BREWSTER

With miles of placid Cape Cod Bay beach and acres of state park, Brewster is an attractive place for families. Brewster's Main Street houses a bevy of B&Bs, restaurants, and the Cape's finest **antiques** shops. Brewster also welcomes tens of thousands of campers and day-trippers headed for Nickerson State Park.

VISITOR INFORMATION   Contact the **Brewster Chamber of Commerce Visitor Center** behind Brewster Town Hall, 2198 Main St./Rte. 6A, Brewster (© 508/896-3500; www.brewstercapecod.org).

Brewster's eight bay **beaches** have minimal facilities. When the tide is out, the beach extends as much as 2 miles, leaving behind tidal pools to splash in. On a clear day, you can see the whole curve of the Cape, from Sandwich to Provincetown. Purchase a beach parking sticker ($15 per day, $40 per week) at the **Visitor Center.**

The **Cape Cod Rail Trail** intersects with the 8-mile **Nickerson State Park** trail system at the park entrance, where there's plenty of free parking; you could follow the Rail Trail back to Dennis (about 12 miles) or toward Wellfleet (13 miles). In season, **Idle Times** (© **508/255-8281**) provides rentals within the park. About ½ mile south of Route 6A, you'll find **Brewster Bicycle Rental,** 442 Underpass Rd. (© **508/896-8149**); and **Brewster Express,** which makes sandwiches to go. Just up the hill is **Rail Trail Bike & Blade,** 302 Underpass Rd. (© **508/896-8200**). Both shops offer free parking. Bicycle rentals start at around $14 for 4 hours and go up to about $22 for 24 hours.

Noted naturalist John Hay helped found the **Cape Cod Museum of Natural History,** 869 Rte. 6A (© **800/479-3867** in eastern Massachusetts, or 508/896-3867; www.ccmnh.org), dedicated to preserving Cape Cod's unique landscape. Children's exhibits include a "live hive"—like an ant farm, only with busy bees—and marineroom tanks. The bulk of the museum is outdoors. There's an on-site archaeology lab on Wing Island. Admission is $8 adults, $7 seniors, $3.50 children 5 to 12.

WHERE TO STAY & DINE

The mint-green 1866 Victorian known as **Captain Freeman Inn,** 15 Breakwater Rd., off Route 6A, in the town center (© **800/843-4664** or 508/896-7481; www.captain freemaninn.com), has a terrific location, right next to the Brewster Store and within walking distance of a pretty bay beach. The reasonably priced, large historic **Old Sea Pines Inn** is a great spot for families. The inn's former days as the Sea Pines School of Charm and Personality for Young Women can still be seen in the handful of rather minuscule boarding-school-scale rooms on the second floor. These bargain rooms share bathrooms and are the only ones in the house without air-conditioning, but at $95 per night in season, who cares!

One of the best restaurants on Cape Cod, the **Bramble Inn Restaurant,** 2019 Main St. (© **508/896-7544**), is also one of the most expensive—but worth it. To get the gist of the expression "chow down," just observe the early-evening crowd happily doing so at the **Brewster Inn & Chowder House,** 1993 Rte. 6A (© **508/896-7771**), a century-old restaurant where the draw is hearty staples at prices geared to ordinary people.

CHATHAM

Chatham (say *Chatt*-um) is small-town America the way Norman Rockwell imagined it. Roses climb white picket fences in front of Cape cottages within a stone's throw of the ocean. Visit the **Chatham Chamber of Commerce,** 533 Main St., Chatham, MA 02633 (© **800/715-5567** or 508/945-5199; www.chathaminfo.com); or the new **Chatham Chamber booth** at the intersection of routes 137 and 28 (no phone).

BEACHES & OUTDOOR PURSUITS

Chatham has an unusual array of **beaches,** from the peaceful shores of Nantucket Sound to the shifting shoals along the Atlantic. For beach stickers ($15 per day, $60 per week), call the **Permit Department** on George Ryder Road in West Chatham (© **508/945-5180**). Among the beaches are **Cockle Cove Beach, Ridgevale Beach,** and **Hardings Beach;** lined up along the sound, each at the end of its namesake road south of Route 28, these family-pleasing beaches offer gentle surf and full facilities. **Oyster Pond Beach,** off Route 28, is only a block from Chatham's Main Street. This sheltered saltwater pond (with restrooms) swarms with children. **North Beach** extends all the way south from Orleans. This 5-mile barrier beach is accessible from Chatham only by boat; you can take the **Beachcomber** (© 508/945-5265), a water taxi, which leaves from the fish pier. The round-trip costs $12 for adults, $8 for children 12 and under.

Though Chatham has no separate recreational paths per se, a demarcated **biking/skating** lane makes a scenic 8-mile circuit of town, heading south onto "The Neck," east to the Chatham Light, up Shore Road all the way to north Chatham, and back to the center of town. A brochure prepared by the **chamber of commerce** (© 800/715-5567 or 508/945-5199) shows the route. Rentals are available at **Bikes & Blades,** 195 Crowell Rd. (© 508/945-7600).

Chatham has five ponds and lakes that permit **fishing.** For saltwater fishing sans boat, try the fishing bridge on Bridge Street at the south end of Mill Pond. First, get a license at **Town Hall,** 549 Main St. (© 508/945-5101). If you hear the deep sea calling, sign on with the *Booby Hatch* (© 508/430-2312; www.capecodfishingcharters. com) or the *Banshee* (© 508/945-0403). Shellfishing licenses are available at the **Permit Department,** on George Ryder Road in west Chatham (© 508/945-5180).

Heading southeast from the Hardings Beach parking lot, the 2-mile round-trip **Seaside Trail** offers beautiful parallel panoramas of Nantucket Sound and Oyster Pond River. Access to 40-acre Morris Island, southwest of the Chatham Light, is easy: Walk or drive across and start right in on a marked .75-mile trail.

The *Beachcomber* (© 508/945-5265) runs seal-watching cruises out of Stage Harbor. Parking is behind the former Main Street School just on the left before the rotary. The cruises cost $20 for adults, $14 for children 3 to 15.

Uninhabited **Monomoy Island,** 2,750 acres of brush-covered sand favored by some 285 species of migrating birds, is the perfect pit stop along the Atlantic flyway. Harbor and gray seals carpet the coastline from late November to May. Both the **Wellfleet Bay Wildlife Sanctuary,** operated by the Audubon Society (© 508/349-2615), and Brewster's **Cape Cod Museum of Natural History** (© 508/896-3867) offer guided trips.

Seaworthy vessels, from surfboards to Sunfish, can be rented from **Monomoy Sail and Cycle,** 275 Rte. 28, north Chatham (© 508/945-0811). Pleasant Bay is the best place to play for those with sufficient experience; if the winds don't seem to be going your way, try Forest Beach on the south Chatham shore.

WHERE TO STAY

For those allergic to inns, Chatham has several decent motels. The basic **Hawthorne,** 196 Shore Rd. (© 508/945-0372; www.thehawthorne.com), is on the water, with views of Chatham Harbor, Pleasant Bay, and the Atlantic. The **Seafarer of Chatham,** 2079 Rte. 28, about ½ mile east of Route 137 in west Chatham (© 800/786-2772 or 508/432-1739; www.chathamseafarer.com), lacks a pool, but is close to Ridgevale Beach.

Set above the beach in Chatham with commanding views, the grand old **Chatham Bars Inn,** Shore Road (© 800/527-4884 or 508/945-0096; www.chathambarsinn. com), is the premier hotel on Cape Cod. The colonnaded 1914 brick building is surrounded by 26 shingled cottages. Take in the sweeping views on the breezy veranda. Amenities include an outdoor heated pool; putting green; public 9-hole golf course next door; tennis courts; basic fitness room; summer children's programs; shuffleboard; croquet; volleyball; and a complimentary launch to Nauset Beach. Cottage rooms are cheery with painted furniture and Waverly fabrics. Guests can take meals in **The Main Dining Room,** the **Tavern,** or the seasonal **Beach House Grill** right on the private beach.

The Captain's House Inn, 369–377 Old Harbor Rd. (© **800/315-0728** or 508/945-0127; www.captainshouseinn.com), is an 1839 Greek Revival house, along with a cottage and carriage house, a shining example of 19th-century style. Bedrooms are richly furnished with canopied four-posters, beamed ceilings, and, in some cases, brick hearths and Jacuzzis. Rates include full breakfast and afternoon tea. There are bikes for the guests to use, and many rooms have minifridges.

Across the street from Pleasant Bay, a few minutes' walk from a bay beach, **Pleasant Bay Village,** 1191 Orleans Rd./Rte. 28 (© **800/547-1011** or 508/945-1133; www.pleasantbayvillage.com), is one fancy motel. It's a Zen paradise, where waterfalls cascade through colorful rock gardens into a stone-edged pool surrounded by whimsical Oriental gardens. Many bathrooms in the lovely guest rooms feature marble countertops and stone floors. The suites have fully equipped kitchens, including microwave ovens. In summer, the restaurant serves three meals a day. You can order lunch from the grill without having to leave your place at the heated pool.

WHERE TO DINE

We highly recommend **The Main Dining Room** at the Chatham Bars Inn (see above for location). This is not delicate food, but it is delicious—and the chowder may be the best on Cape Cod.

The Chatham Wayside Inn, 512 Main St. (© **508/945-5550**), is a good spot for a reasonably priced meal in town. Specialties include crab cakes, rack of lamb, and pesto cod. For something a little different, try the Portuguese-style chowder, with double-smoked bacon, fresh quahogs, and red bliss potatoes.

A major renovation has turned **28 Atlantic,** 2173 Rte. 28 at the Wequasett Inn, about 5 miles northwest of Chatham center, on Pleasant Bay (© **508/430-3000;** www.wequasett.com), into one of the top places to eat on Cape Cod. The elegant, spacious dining room overlooks Pleasant Bay through immense floor-to-ceiling glass panels. And the food stands out as superb, from the *amuse bouche* (a little taste teaser), to the exceptional desserts. Menu items use local provender as much as possible, but there are also delicacies from around the world.

CHATHAM AFTER DARK

Chatham's free **band concerts** attract crowds in the thousands. This is small-town America at its most nostalgic, as the band plays old standards that never go out of style. Held in Kate Gould Park (off Chatham Bars Ave.) from July to early September, they kick off at 8pm every Friday. Call © **508/945-5199** for information.

A great leveler, the **Chatham Squire,** 487 Main St. (© **508/945-0942**), attracts CEOs, seafarers, and collegians alike. Great pub grub, too! The piano bar **Upstairs at Christian's,** 443 Main St. (© **508/945-3362**), has the air of a vintage frat house with scuffed leather couches and movie posters. Live music is offered nightly in season and weekends year-round.

PROVINCETOWN

You've made it all the way to the end of the Cape, to one of the most interesting spots on the eastern seaboard. Charles Hawthorne, the painter who "discovered" this near-derelict fishing town in the late 1890s and introduced it to the Greenwich Village intelligentsia, was besotted by this "jumble of color in the intense sunlight accentuated by the brilliant blue of the harbor."

The whole town, in fact, is dedicated to creative expression, both visual and verbal. That same open-mindedness may account for Provincetown's ascendancy as a gay and lesbian resort. The street life also includes families, art lovers, and gourmands. In short, Provincetown has something for just about everyone.

Contact the **Provincetown Chamber of Commerce,** 307 Commercial St., Provincetown, MA 02657 (℃ **508/487-3424;** www.ptownchamber.com), or the gay-oriented **Provincetown Business Guild,** 115 Bradford St., P.O. Box 421, Provincetown, MA 02657 (℃ **800/637-8696** or 508/487-2313; www.ptown.org).

BEACHES & OUTDOOR PURSUITS

BEACHES   With nine-tenths of its territory protected by the Cape Cod National Seashore, Provincetown has miles of beaches. The 3-mile bay beach that lines the harbor, though certainly swimmable, is not all that inviting compared to the ocean beaches overseen by the National Seashore. The two official access areas tend to be crowded; however, you can always find a less densely populated stretch if you're willing to hike down the beach a bit.

BICYCLING   North of town is one of the more spectacular bike paths in New England, the 7-mile **Province Lands Trail,** a heady swirl of steep dunes anchored by wind-stunted scrub pines. With its free parking, the **Province Lands Visitor Center** (℃ **508/487-1256**) is a good place to start. Rentals are offered in season by **Nelson's Bike Shop,** 43 Race Point Rd. (℃ **508/487-8849**). In town, rentals are available at **Ptown Bikes,** 42 Bradford St. (℃ **508/487-8735**); reserve several days in advance.

BOATING   **Flyer's Boat Rental,** 131 Commercial St., in the West End (℃ **508/487-0898**), offers all sorts of craft, from kayaks to sailboats; lessons and fishing-gear rentals are available.

MUSEUMS   Anywhere you go in town, the **Pilgrim Monument & Provincetown Museum** on High Pole Hill Road (℃ **508/487-1310;** www.pilgrim-monument.org) looms. Climb the 60 gradual ramps interspersed with 116 steps and you'll get a gargoyle's-eye view of the spiraling coast and Boston against a backdrop of New Hampshire's mountains. Admission is $7 adults, $3.50 children 4 to 14. It's closed December to March. The **Provincetown Art Association & Museum,** 460 Commercial St. (℃ **508/487-1750;** www.paam.org), is an extraordinary cache of 20th-century American art begun by Charles Hawthorne. Founded in 1914, the museum was the site of innumerable "space wars," as classicists and modernists vied for square footage. Admission is $2 adults, free for children under 12.

TOURS   **Art's Dune Tours** is at the corner of Commercial and Standish streets (℃ **800/894-1951** or 508/487-1950; www.artsdunetours.com). In 1946, Art Costa started driving sightseers out to ogle the "dune shacks" where Eugene O'Neill, Jack Kerouac, and Jackson Pollock found their respective muses. The tours typically take 1 to 1½ hours. Tickets are $18 to $26 for adults, $13 to $16 for children 6 to 11. Additional tours offered include a sunset clambake dune tour ($66), and a barbecue tour ($56).

WHALE-WATCHING   Stellwagen Bank, 8 miles off Provincetown, is a feeding ground for whales. The **Dolphin Fleet** at MacMillan Wharf (℃ **800/826-9300** or 508/349-1900) was the first, and by most accounts is still the best, outfitter running whale-watching trips to Stellwagen. Tickets for the 3½-hour trips are $28 for adults,

$26 for seniors, and $22 for children 7 to 12. Call to reserve. Closed November through March.

WHERE TO STAY

The Brass Key Guesthouse, 67 Bradford St. (© **800/842-9858** or 508/487-9005; www.brasskey.com), is the fanciest place in town. The innkeepers have thought of everything: down pillows, jetted showers, and iced tea and lemonade delivered poolside. Rooms in the 1828 Federal-style Captain's House and the Gatehouse are outfitted in a country style, while the Victorian-era building is elegant. Most deluxe rooms have gas fireplaces and whirlpool tubs. Rates include continental breakfast and afternoon wine and cheese. There's a heated outdoor pool, a Jacuzzi, and fridges and safes in the rooms. No children under 18.

Carpe Diem, 12 Johnson St. (© **800/487-0132** or 508/487-4242; www.carpe diemguesthouse.com), is a stylish 1884 house on a quiet side street that suits most P-town habitués to a T. Guest rooms are outfitted with antiques, down comforters, robes, and (most rooms) refrigerators. Two deluxe garden suites boast private entrances, Jacuzzis, and fireplaces. The cottage has a two-person whirlpool and a wet bar. The full breakfast features homemade pastries served at the dining-room table. On clear days, sun worshippers prefer the patio. Rates include continental breakfast.

The Masthead, 31–41 Commercial St. (© **800/395-5095** or 508/487-0523; www.themasthead.com), is one of the few places in town, other than the impersonal motels, that actively welcomes families, and the placid 450-foot private beach will delight young splashers. The cottages are fun, some with wicker furniture and antiques. In the water-view rooms perched above the surf, with their 7-foot picture windows overlooking the bay and Long Point, you may feel as though you're onboard a ship. All rooms have fridges; two share a bathroom.

Look for the house with the bright yellow door in the East End; it's the very embodiment of Provincetown's bohemian mystique: the **White Horse Inn,** 500 Commercial St. (© **508/487-1790**). Frank Schaefer has been tinkering with this late-18th-century house since 1963; a number of his fellow artists helped him out in cobbling together the studio apartments out of salvage. Some units have shared bathrooms; there are no televisions or phones in the room, adding to the serenity.

WHERE TO DINE

Spiritus, 190 Commercial St. (© **508/487-2808**), is an extravagant pizza parlor open until 2am. Peruse the scrumptious meat pies and pastries at the **Provincetown Portuguese Bakery,** 299 Commercial St. (© **508/487-1803**). Both establishments are closed November through March.

Martin House, 157 Commercial St. (© **508/487-1327**; www.themartinhouse. com), is easily one of the most charming restaurants on the Cape. The chef favors local delicacies, such as the littlenecks that appear in a kafir-lime-tamarind broth with Asian noodles. Main courses might include grilled rack of pork with mango salsa and cactus-pear demi-glace on spicy masa.

Bubala's by the Bay, 183 Commercial St. (© **508/487-0773**), promises "serious food at sensible prices." And that's what it delivers: from buttermilk waffles to creative focaccia sandwiches to fajitas, Cajun calamari, and pad Thai. The huge patio facing Commercial Street is particularly popular in the morning. **Cafe Heaven,** 199 Commercial St. (© **508/487-9639**), is prized for its leisurely country breakfasts. The modern storefront also turns out substantial sandwiches, such as avocado and goat cheese on a French baguette.

The best gourmet takeout shop is **Angel Foods,** 467 Commercial St., in the East End (✆ **508/487-6666**), which offers Italian specialties and other prepared foods. The "rollwiches"—pita bread packed with a wide range of fillings—at **Box Lunch,** 353 Commercial St. (✆ **508/487-6026**), are ideal for a strolling lunch.

PROVINCETOWN AFTER DARK

To order tickets for any of the shows at Provincetown's nightclubs and cabarets, call **Ptown Tix** (✆ **508/487-9793**; www.ptowntix.com).

An on-again, off-again contender for hottest club in town is **Club Euro,** 258 Commercial St., 2nd floor, beside Town Hall (✆ **508/487-8800**), the current home of "Two Fags and a Drag" and the ever-popular all-star musical comedy drag revue "Big Boned Barbies," starring Kandi Kane. Closed October to May.

Perhaps the nation's premier gay bar, the **Atlantic House,** 6 Masonic Place, off Commercial Street (✆ **508/487-3821**), is open year-round. The "A-house" welcomes straight folks, except in the leather-oriented Macho Bar upstairs. Come late afternoon; it's a safe bet that the crowds are at the gay-lesbian tea dance held daily in season from 3:30 to 6:30pm on the pool deck at the **Boatslip Beach Club,** 161 Commercial St. (✆ **508/487-1669**). The action then shifts to the **Pied,** 193A Commercial St. (✆ **508/ 487-1527;** www.thepied.com), for its After Tea T-Dance from 5 to 10pm.

The women's bar **Vixen,** at the Pilgrim House, 336 Commercial St. (✆ **508/ 487-6424**), occupies the lower floors of a former hotel. On the roster are jazz, blues, and comedy. There are also pool tables.

3 Martha's Vineyard

With 100 square miles, Martha's Vineyard is New England's largest island, yet each of its six communities is blessed with endearing small-town charm. Admire the sea captains' homes in **Edgartown.** Stroll down Circuit Avenue in **Oak Bluffs,** then ride the Flying Horses Carousel, said to be the oldest working carousel in the nation. Check out the cheerful "gingerbread" cottages behind Circuit Avenue. Then journey "up-island" to marvel at the red-clay cliffs of **Aquinnah.** Or bike the country roads of **West Tisbury** and **Chilmark.** Buy a lobster roll in the fishing village of **Menemsha.**

ESSENTIALS

GETTING THERE   By Ferry   Most visitors take ferries from the mainland to the Vineyard. It's easy to get a passenger ticket on almost any of the ferries, but space for cars is limited. We advise you to leave your car on the mainland. It's easy to take the shuttle buses from town to town or bike around.

From **Falmouth, The Steamship Authority** (✆ **508/477-8600;** www.islandferry. com) operates daily year-round, weather permitting. These ferries make the 45-minute trip to Vineyard Haven throughout the year; some boats go to Oak Bluffs from late May to late October. You can take your car on the ferry (though most visitors don't) or park your car in Woods Hole or Falmouth for $10 per day (arrive at least 45 min. ahead of time if you're leaving your car on the mainland). Free buses run regularly to the ferry terminal. The cost of a round-trip passenger ferry ticket is $14 for adults and $8 for children 5 to 12. Bringing a bike costs an extra $6 round-trip. You do not need a ferry reservation if you're traveling without a car.

From **Falmouth Inner Harbor,** you can board the *Island Queen* (© 508/548-4800; www.islandqueen.com) for a 35-minute cruise to Oak Bluffs (passengers only). The **Falmouth–Edgartown Ferry Service,** 278 Scranton Ave. (© 508/548-9400; www.falmouthferry.com), operates a 1-hour passenger ferry, called the *Pied Piper,* from Falmouth Inner Harbor to Edgartown. The boat runs from late May to mid-October; reservations are required. From **Hyannis,** May through October, **Hy-Line** (© 508/778-2600; www.hy-linecruises.com) operates from the Ocean Street Dock to Oak Bluffs on Martha's Vineyard.

A fast ferry from Rhode Island to Oak Bluffs makes the trip in 90 minutes and avoids Cape Cod traffic jams. **Vineyard Fast Ferry Company** (© 401/295-4040; www.vineyardfastferry.com) runs this seasonal high-speed catamaran, called *Millennium,* which leaves from Quonset Point in **North Kingston.** The round-trip cost is $72 for adults and $54 for children. Parking next to the ferry port is $8 per day.

Another option for Vineyard vacationers is a high-speed ferry from **New Bedford** to the island. A ticket costs $29 one-way and $58 round-trip for adults; free for children under 13 traveling with a parent. Contact New England Fast Ferry for details (© 866/683-3779; www.nefastferry.com).

By Plane   You can fly into **Martha's Vineyard Airport** (© 508/693-7022; www.mvyairport.com), in West Tisbury, about 5 miles outside Edgartown.

Airlines serving the Vineyard include **Cape Air/Nantucket Airlines** (© 800/352-0714 or 508/771-6944) from Boston, Hyannis, Nantucket, and New Bedford; and **US Airways** (© 800/428-4322), which has regular service from Boston and seasonal weekend service from LaGuardia.

By Bus   Bonanza Bus Lines (© 888/751-8800 or 508/548-7588; www.bonanzabus.com) connects the Woods Hole ferry port with Boston (from South Station and Logan Airport), New York City, and Providence, Rhode Island. Fares range from $30 to $93 round-trip, depending on your departure point.

GETTING AROUND   By Bicycle & Moped   The best way to explore the Vineyard is on two wheels. There's a little of everything for cyclists, from paved paths to hilly country roads. You need a driver's license to rent a moped.

Bike-, scooter-, and moped-rental shops are clustered throughout all three down-island towns. Bike rentals cost about $20 a day, scooters and mopeds $46 to $85. In Vineyard Haven, try **Strictly Bikes,** Union Street (© 508/693-0782). In Edgartown, you'll find **Wheel Happy,** 204 Upper Main St. and 8 S. Water St. (© 508/627-5928), which rents only bikes.

By Shuttle Bus   In season, shuttle buses certainly run often enough to make them a practical means of getting around. They are also cheap, dependable, and easy. The **Martha's Vineyard Regional Transit Authority** (© 508/693-9440; www.vineyardtransit.com) operates shuttle buses year-round on about a dozen routes around the island. The buses, which are white with purple logos, cost about $2 to $5 depending on distance. The formula is $1 per town. For example, Vineyard Haven to Oak Bluffs is $2, but Vineyard Haven to Edgartown (passing through Oak Bluffs) is $3. A 1-day pass is $6; a 3-day pass is $15.

For bus tours of the island, call **Island Transport** (© 508/693-0058) or hop on one of the Island Transport buses that are stationed at the ferry terminals in Vineyard Haven and Oak Bluffs in the summer.

Martha's Vineyard

By Taxi You'll find taxis at all ferry terminals and the airport, as well as taxi stands in Oak Bluffs (at the Flying Horses Carousel) and Edgartown (next to the Town Wharf). Most taxi companies operate vans for larger groups and travelers with bikes. Cab companies on the island include **Accurate Cab** (🕿 **888/557-9798** or 508/627-9798; the only 24-hr. service), and **All Island Taxi** (🕿 **800/693-TAXI** or 508/693-2929). In summer, rates from town to town are generally flat fees based on distance and the number of passengers. Late-night revelers should keep in mind that rates double from midnight until 7am.

VISITOR INFORMATION Contact the **Martha's Vineyard Chamber of Commerce,** Beach Road, in Vineyard Haven (🕿 **508/693-0085;** www.mvy.com). There are also information booths at the ferry terminal in Vineyard Haven, across from the Flying Horses Carousel in Oak Bluffs, and on Church Street in Edgartown. For information on current events, check the newspapers *Vineyard Gazette* (www.mvgazette.com) and the *Martha's Vineyard Times* (www.mvtimes.com).

BEACHES & OUTDOOR PURSUITS

Most down-island **beaches** in Vineyard Haven, Oak Bluffs, and Edgartown are open to the public and just a walk or a short bike ride from town. In season, shuttle buses make stops at **State Beach,** between Oak Buffs and Edgartown. Most of the Vineyard's magnificent up-island shoreline is privately owned or restricted to residents, and thus off-limits to visitors. Renters in up-island communities can obtain a beach sticker (around $35–$50 for a season sticker) for those private beaches by applying for a lease at the relevant town hall.

The party boat *Skipper* (© 508/693-1238) offers half-day **fishing** trips out of Oak Bluffs Harbor in season. Deep-sea excursions can be arranged aboard **Big Eye Charters** (© 508/627-3649) out of Edgartown, or with **Summer's Lease** (© 508/693-2880) out of Oak Bluffs.

About a fifth of the Vineyard's landmass has been set aside for conservation, and it's accessible to **bikers** and **hikers.** The **West Chop Woods,** off Franklin Street in Vineyard Haven, comprise 85 acres with marked trails. Midway between Vineyard Haven and Edgartown, the **Felix Neck Wildlife Sanctuary** includes a 6-mile network of trails over varying terrain.

The 633-acre **Long Point Wildlife Refuge,** off Waldron's Bottom Road in West Tisbury (© 508/693-7392 for gatehouse), offers heath and dunes, freshwater ponds, a beach, and interpretive nature walks for children.

Some remarkable botanical surprises can be found at the 20-acre **Polly Hill Arboretum,** 809 State Rd., West Tisbury (© 508/693-9426). Horticulturist Polly Hill has developed this property over the past 40 years and allows the public to wander the grounds Thursday through Tuesday from 7am until 7pm. There's a requested donation of $5 for adults and $3 for children under 12.

Wind's Up, 199 Beach Rd., Vineyard Haven (© 508/693-4252), rents canoes, kayaks, and various sailing craft, including windsurfers, and offers instruction on a placid pond. Canoes and kayaks rent for $20 per hour.

WHERE TO STAY

After a fire destroyed the 200-year-old Tisbury Inn in Vineyard Haven in 2001, the fate of the property was uncertain. But the three-story building has reopened as the **Mansion House Inn,** 9 Main St., Vineyard Haven (© 800/332-4112 or 508/693-2200; http://mvmansionhouse.com), a luxury 32-room inn that's a community hub with a restaurant, health club, and shops. The rooms range in size from cozy to spacious; many have kitchenettes, plasma-screen TVs, and extralarge bathtubs.

Linked by formal gardens, each of the 18th- and 19th-century houses at the **Charlotte Inn,** 27 S. Summer St., Edgartown (© 508/627-4751), has a distinctive look and feel, though the predominant mode is English country. It's the best inn on the island. All but one of the rooms at this Relais & Châteaux property have TVs, but none have phones. Some of the luxurious bathrooms are bigger than those of most standard hotel rooms. The inn's restaurant, **L'étoile,** is one of the island's finest. Rates include continental breakfast; full breakfast is offered for $15 extra. No children under 14.

With its graceful wraparound colonnaded front porch, the **Jonathan Munroe House,** 100 Main St., Edgartown (© 877/468-6763 or 508/627-5536; www.jonathanmunroe.com), stands out from the other inns and captains' homes on this stretch of upper Main Street. Guest rooms are immaculate, antiques-filled, and dotted with clever details. Many units have fireplaces. At breakfast (included in room rates, along with an afternoon wine hour), don't miss the homemade waffles and pancakes. No children under 12 are permitted.

Do you long to stay at a reasonably priced inn that's bigger than a B&B but smaller than a Marriott? **The Victorian Inn,** 24 S. Water St., Edgartown (© 508/627-4784; www.thevic.com), is a freshened-up version of those old-style hotels that used to exist in every New England town. With three floors of long, graceful corridors, the Victorian could serve as a stage set for a 1930s romance. Several units have canopy beds and balconies. Rates include full breakfast and afternoon tea. Dogs are welcome. There are no phones in the rooms.

The Edgartown Inn, 56 N. Water St. (© **508/627-4794;** www.edgartowninn.com), offers perhaps the best value on the island. It's a lovely 1798 Federal manse. Rooms are no-frills but traditional; some have TVs and harbor views. Modernists may prefer the cathedral-ceilinged quarters in the annex. Service is excellent. The inn does not accept credit cards, and there are no phones in the rooms.

WHERE TO DINE

Outside Oak Bluffs and Edgartown, all of Martha's Vineyard (including Vineyard Haven) is "dry," so bring your own bottle; some restaurants charge a small fee for uncorking.

Alchemy is a spiffy restaurant that's a little slice of Paris on 71 Main St. (© **508/627-9999**). There's also a large selection of cocktails, liqueurs, and wines. In addition to lunch and dinner, a bar menu is served from 2:30 to 11pm.

Everything's appealing at **Among the Flowers Cafe** on Mayhew Lane (© **508/627-3233**) near the dock. The breakfasts are the best around, and the comfort-food dinners are among the most affordable options in this pricey town.

At **The Newes from America,** 23 Kelly St. (© **508/627-4397**), a subterranean tavern built in 1742, beers are a specialty: Try a rack of five brews, or let your choice of food—from a wood-smoked oyster "Island Poor Boy" sandwich to a porterhouse steak—dictate your draft.

The **Black Dog Tavern,** at the Beach Street Extension on the harbor (© **508/693-9223**), is a national icon (with cool T-shirts). Soon after Robert Douglas decided in 1971 that this port could use a good restaurant, vacationers waiting for the ferry began to wander into this saltbox to tide themselves over with a bit of "blackout cake" or peanut-butter pie. The food is still home-cooking good. Come early, when it first opens, and sit on the porch, where the views are perfect.

MARTHA'S VINEYARD AFTER DARK

All towns except for Oak Bluffs and Edgartown are dry, and last call at bars and clubs is at midnight. Hit Oak Bluffs for the rowdiest bar scene and best nighttime street life. In Edgartown, you may have to hop around before you find the evening's most happening spot.

Young and loud are the buzzwords at the **Lamppost** and the **Rare Duck,** 111 Circuit Ave., Oak Bluffs (© **508/696-9352**), a pair of clubs in the center of town. The Lamppost features live bands and a dance floor; the Rare Duck, acoustic acts. This is where the young folk go, and the performers could be playing blues, reggae, R&B, or '80s. The cover is $1 to $5.

4 The Berkshires

More than hills but less than mountains, the Taconic and Hoosac ranges that define this region at the western end of Massachusetts go by the collective name "The Berkshires." Mohawks and Mohegans lived and hunted here. Farmers, drawn to fertile flood plains of the Housatonic, were supplanted in the 19th century by manufacturers. Artists and writers came for the mild summers and seclusion offered by these hills and lakes. Nathaniel Hawthorne, Herman Melville, and Edith Wharton were among those who put down temporary roots. By the 1930s, theater, dance, and music performances had established themselves as regular summer fixtures. Tanglewood, Jacob's Pillow, and the Berkshire and Williamstown Theatre festivals draw tens of thousands of visitors every summer.

ESSENTIALS

GETTING THERE   The Massachusetts Turnpike **(I-90)** runs east-west from Boston to the Berkshires, with an exit near Lee and Stockbridge. From New York City, the scenic Taconic State Parkway connects with I-90 not far from Pittsfield.

Amtrak (© **800/USA-RAIL;** www.northeast.amtrak.com) operates several trains daily between Boston and Chicago, stopping in Pittsfield each way.

VISITOR INFORMATION   The **Berkshire Visitors Bureau,** Berkshire Common (off South St., near the entrance to the Hilton), Pittsfield (© **800/237-5747** or 413/443-9186), can assist with questions and lodging reservations. Also check out **www.berkshires.org**.

SHEFFIELD

Sheffield, known as the "Antiques Capital of the Berkshires," occupies a flood plain beside the Housatonic River, 11 miles south of Great Barrington. The canny, knowledgeable dealers know exactly what they have, so expect high quality and few bargains.

There are more than two dozen antiques dealers along Route 7. Most of them stock the **free directory** of the Berkshire County Antiques Dealers Association, which lists dealers from Sheffield to Cheshire and across the border in Connecticut and New York. Look, too, for the pamphlet called *The Antique Hunter's Guide to Route 7.*

GREAT BARRINGTON

Even with a population barely over 7,500, this pleasant retail center, 7 miles south of Stockbridge, is the largest town in the southernmost part of the county. Great Barrington has no sights of particular significance, leaving time to browse its many antiques galleries and specialty shops. Convenient as a home base for excursions to such nearby attractions as Monument Mountain, Bash-Bish Falls, Butternut Basin, Tanglewood concerts, and Stockbridge, it has a number of adequate motels north of the center along or near Route 7 that tend to fill up more slowly on weekends than the better-known inns in the area. It is something of a dining destination, too, with 55 eating places, including, at last count, *four* sushi bars! *Note:* The local board of health has banned smoking in *any* public space in town.

The **Southern Berkshire Chamber of Commerce** maintains an information booth at 362 Main St. (© **413/528-1510;** www.southernberkshires.com), near the town hall. It's open Tuesday through Sunday from 10am to 5pm.

Head straight for Railroad Street. Start on the corner with Main Street, at **T. P. Saddle Blanket & Trading Co.** (© **413/528-6500**). An unlikely emporium that looks lifted whole from the Rockies, it's packed with boots, hats, Indian jewelry, blankets, and jars of salsa. **Mistral's,** 6 Railroad St. (© **413/528-1618**), stocks Gallic tableware, linens, fancy foods, and furniture. **The Chef's Shop,** 31 Railroad St. (© **413/528-0135**), still features a bounty of gadgets and cookbooks as well as cooking classes. At the north end of town, just before Route 7 turns right across a short bridge, Route 41 goes straight, toward the village of Housatonic. In about 4 miles you'll see a shed that houses the kiln of **Great Barrington Pottery** (© **413/274-6259**). Owner Richard Bennett has been throwing pots according to Japanese techniques for more than 30 years.

WHERE TO STAY & DINE

There are several acceptable motels north of town on Route 7, the most desirable being the **Holiday Inn Express,** 415 Stockbridge Rd. (© **413/528-1810;** www.hiexgb.com), which has an indoor pool and whirlpool, and rooms with Jacuzzis and/or fireplaces; rates include breakfast. The **chamber of commerce** operates a lodging hot line at © **800/269-4825** or 413/528-4006.

The Old Inn on the Green on Route 57, New Marlborough (© **413/229-7924;** www.oldinn.com), comprised of a former 1760 tavern/general store and the adjacent 18th-century Thayer House, are under new management. The most desirable rooms are in Thayer House, some with fireplaces and all with air-conditioning, VCRs, and whirlpool tubs. All five intimate dining rooms serve sophisticated cuisine and have fireplaces; reservations are strongly advised. Rates ($205–$365 double) include breakfast, and there is a courtyard pool at Thayer House.

A roadside lodging built in the middle of the last century in Federal style, **The Windflower Inn,** 684 S. Egremont Rd. (© **800/992-1993** or 413/528-2720; www.windflowerinn.com), commands a large plot of land opposite the Egremont Country Club. Six rooms have fireplaces; four have canopy beds. Rates ($100–$225 double) at the entirely smoke-free property include breakfast and afternoon tea. There's an outdoor pool.

The Castle Street Cafe, 10 Castle St. (© **413/528-5244**), is a storefront bistro that has ruled the Great Barrington roost for some time now, and has expanded into the next building. While a Francophilic inclination is apparent in the main room, what with duck breast with potato galette and steak au poivre, it isn't overpowering. An award-winning wine list is another reason to stop in. Main courses cost $20 to $28.

STOCKBRIDGE

Stockbridge's ready accessibility to Boston and New York (about 2½ hr. from each and reachable by rail since the mid–19th c.) transformed the frontier settlement into a Gilded Age summer retreat for the rich. The town has long been popular with artists and writers.

Stockbridge lies 7 miles north of Great Barrington and 6 miles south of Lenox. The **Stockbridge Chamber of Commerce** (© **413/298-5200;** www.stockbridgechamber. org) maintains an information booth opposite the row of stores depicted by Rockwell. It's open May through October.

WHAT TO SEE & DO

From June to August, the **Berkshire Theatre Festival,** Main Street (© **413/ 298-5576;** www.berkshiretheatre.org), holds its season of classic and new plays, often with marquee names starring or directing. Kevin Kline and Al Pacino have been participants. Its venue is a "casino" built in 1887 to plans by architect Stanford White.

The striking **Norman Rockwell Museum,** Route 183 (© **413/298-4100;** www.nrm.org), opened in 1993 to house the works of Stockbridge's favorite son. The illustrator used both his neighbors and the town to tell stories about an America now rapidly fading from memory. Most of Rockwell's paintings adorned covers of the *Saturday Evening Post:* warm and often humorous depictions of homecomings, first proms, and visits to the doctor. He addressed serious concerns, too, notably with his poignant portrait of a little African-American girl being escorted by U.S. marshals into a previously segregated school. The lovely 36-acre grounds also contain Rockwell's last studio (closed Nov–Apr). Admission is $13 adults, $7 students, free for children 18 and under.

WHERE TO STAY

The Inn at Stockbridge, 30 East St. (✆ **888/466-7865** or 413/298-3337; www.stockbridgeinn.com), is a 1906 building with a grandly columned porch. It's set well back from the road on 12 acres. The innkeepers are eager to please, serving full breakfasts by candlelight and afternoon spreads of wine and cheese. Several bedrooms have fireplaces and whirlpools. There's an outdoor pool. No children under 12. Doubles run $140 to $345.

So well known that it serves as a symbol of the Berkshires, **The Red Lion Inn,** Main Street (✆ **413/298-5545;** www.redlioninn.com), had its origins as a stagecoach tavern in 1773. The rocking chairs on the porch are the perfect place to while away an hour. An ancient birdcage elevator carries guests up to halls and rooms filled with antiques ranging in styles of over 2 centuries. Six satellite buildings have been added, all within 3 miles of the inn. Jackets are required for men in the main dining room, but not in the casual **Widow Bingham Tavern** nor, in good weather, in the courtyard out back. The wine cellar has been recognized with important awards. **The Lion's Den** has nightly live entertainment, usually of the folk-rock variety. There's also an outdoor pool and an exercise room. Rooms cost $110 to $220 double.

LEE & JACOB'S PILLOW

While Stockbridge and Lenox were developing into luxurious recreational centers, Lee was a thriving paper-mill town and thus remained essentially a town of workers and merchants. The town's contribution to the Berkshire cultural calendar is the Jacob's Pillow Dance Festival, which first thrived as "Denishawn," a fabled alliance between founders Ruth St. Denis and Ted Shawn.

Lee is 5 miles southeast of Lenox. In summer and early fall, the **Lee Chamber of Commerce** (✆ **413/243-0852;** www.leechamber.org) operates an **information center** on the town common, Route 20 (✆ **413/243-4929**).

The Jacob's Pillow Dance Festival, George Carter Road, Becket (✆ **413/243-0745;** www.jacobspillow.org), began in 1933 when Ted Shawn decided to put on a show in the barn. Jacob's Pillow is now to dance what Tanglewood is to classical music. The theater has long welcomed troupes of international reputation, including the Mark Morris Dance Group, Twyla Tharp, and the Paul Taylor Dance Company. The season runs from mid-June to late August, and tickets go on sale April 1. The growing campus includes a store, pub, dining room, tent restaurant, and exhibition space. Picnic lunches can be pre-ordered 24 hours in advance.

WHERE TO STAY

On the road to Lenox, the lakeside **Best Western Black Swan Inn,** 435 Laurel St./Rte. 20 (✆ **800/876-7926** or 413/243-2700; www.bestwestern.com), has a pool and restaurant; some of the 52 rooms have fireplaces.

Applegate, 279 W. Park St. (✆ **800/691-9012** or 413/243-4451; www.applegateinn.com), utilizes a gracious 1920s Georgian Colonial manse to full advantage. The top unit has a canopy bed, Queen Anne reproductions, a steam shower, and a fireplace (with real wood). Some rooms have Jacuzzis and/or gas fireplaces. Chocolates and brandy await guests at bedside. Breakfast is by candlelight, and the innkeepers set out wine and cheese in the afternoon. They are "flexible" on children. Rates run $120 to $350.

The Chambéry Inn, 199 Main St. (✆ **413/243-2221;** www.berkshireinns.com), was the Berkshires' first parochial school (1885), named for the French hometown of the nuns who ran it. The extra-large bedrooms were formerly classrooms. Six of them, with 13-foot ceilings and the original woodwork and blackboards, are equipped with whirlpool tubs and gas fireplaces. Some rooms have TV/VCRs, CD players, and fridges. A breakfast basket is delivered to your door each morning. No children under 18. Rooms cost $75 to $239.

LENOX & TANGLEWOOD

Stately homes and fabulous mansions mushroomed in this former agricultural settlement, and Lenox remains a repository of extravagant domestic architecture surpassed only in such resorts as Newport and Palm Beach. And because many of the cottages have been converted into inns and hotels, it is possible to get inside some of these beautiful buildings, if only for a cocktail or a meal.

The reason for so many lodgings in a town with a population of barely 5,000 is Tanglewood, a nearby estate where a series of concerts by the Boston Symphony Orchestra is held every summer.

Lenox lies 7 miles south of Pittsfield. The **Lenox Chamber of Commerce** (© 413/ 637-3646; www.lenox.org) provides visitor information and lodging referrals.

TANGLEWOOD MUSIC FESTIVAL

Lenox is filled with music every summer, and the undisputed headliner is the **Boston Symphony Orchestra (BSO).** Concerts are given at Tanglewood estate, beginning in July, ending the weekend before Labor Day. The estate is on West Street (actually in Stockbridge township). From Lenox, take Route 183 1½ miles southwest of town.

The program features a menagerie of other performers and musical idioms. These run the gamut from popular artists (such as James Taylor and Bonnie Raitt) and jazz musicians (including Dave Brubeck and Wynton Marsalis) to such guest soloists as Itzhak Perlman and Yo-Yo Ma.

The **Koussevitzky Music Shed** is an open auditorium that seats 5,000, surrounded by a lawn where an audience lounges on folding chairs and blankets. Chamber groups and soloists appear in the smaller **Ozawa Hall.** Major performances are on Friday and Saturday nights and Sunday afternoons.

Tentative programs are available after January 1; the schedule is usually locked in by March. Tickets can sell out quickly, so get yours as far in advance as possible. If you decide to go at the last minute, take a blanket or lawn chair and get tickets for lawn seating, which is almost always available. You can also attend open rehearsals during the week, as well as the rehearsal for the Sunday concert on Saturday morning.

The estate itself (© 413/637-5165 June–Aug), with over 500 acres of lawns and gardens, was put together starting in 1849 by William Aspinwall Tappan. Admission to the grounds is free when concerts aren't scheduled. In 1851, a structure on the property called the Little Red Shanty was rented to Nathaniel Hawthorne, who stayed here long enough to write a children's book, *Tanglewood Tales,* and meet Herman Melville, who lived in nearby Dalton. The existing Hawthorne Cottage is a replica (and isn't open to the public). On the grounds is the original Tappan mansion, with fine views.

For recorded information, call © 617/266-1492 from September to June 10 (information on Tanglewood concerts is not available until the program is announced in Mar or Apr). Children under 5 are not allowed in the Shed or Ozawa Hall. To order tickets by mail before June, write the Tanglewood Ticket Office at Symphony Hall, 301 Mass. Ave., Boston, MA 02115. After June 1, write the Tanglewood Ticket Office, 297 West St., Lenox, MA 01240. Tickets can be charged to a credit card through **Symphony Charge** (© **888/266-1200** outside Boston, or 617/266-1200; www.bso.org).

OTHER ATTRACTIONS

The Mount, 2 Plunkett St. (© **413/637-1899;** www.edithwharton.org), was the home of Edith Wharton, a member of the upper classes of the Gilded Age who won a Pulitzer for her novel detailing the strata of high society, *The Age of Innocence.* Wharton had her villa built on this 130-acre property in 1902 and lived here for 10 years. She took an active hand in its creation—one of the few designated National Historic Landmarks designed by a woman. A $25-million restoration campaign continues, with work so far completed on the terrace and greenhouse and continuing on the interior and gardens. Admission costs $18 adults; free for children under 12.

The repertory theater group **Shakespeare & Company,** 70 Kemble St. (© **413/ 637-3353;** www.shakespeare.org), has long used buildings and amphitheaters on the grounds of the Mount to stage its May-to-October season of plays by the Bard, works by Edith Wharton and George Bernard Shaw, and works by new American playwrights. With the construction of a Founder's Theatre, the Spring Lawn Theatre, the tented Rose Footprint Theatre, an administration building, and planned rehabilitation of other existing buildings, the Company now enjoys its very own campus devoted to the dramatic arts. Walking trails have been developed at the north end of the grounds and a cafe in the theater lobby serves drinks and light fare. Free outdoor performances are staged before evening curtain times.

WHERE TO STAY

The list of lodgings below is only partial, and most can accommodate only small numbers of guests. The Tanglewood concert season is a powerful draw, so prices are highest in summer as well as during the foliage season. Minimum 2- or 3-night stays are usually required during the Tanglewood weeks, foliage season, weekends, and holidays. Reserve well in advance for Tanglewood! Note that some lodgings are so crabby and rule-ridden, we say good riddance; others are open only 6 or 7 months a year and charge the world for a bed or a meal.

If all the area's inns are booked or if you want to be assured the full quota of 21st-century conveniences, routes 7 and 20 north and south of town harbor a number of motels, including the **Mayflower Motor Inn** (© **413/443-4468**), the **Days Inn** (© **413/637-3560**), the **Lenox Motel** (© **413/499-0324**), and the **Comfort Inn** (© **413/443-4714**).

Blantyre, 16 Blantyre Rd. (© **413/637-3556;** www.blantyre.com), is a Relais & Châteaux property ensconced in a 1902 Tudor-Norman mansion that used to be open only in the warmer months. Now it cossets its guests year-round in its undeniably luxurious public rooms, dining areas, and bedchambers. If any place is worth breathtaking tariffs, it's this one. Rates are $450 to $750 double, up to $1,050 for the top suite.

The Canyon Ranch in the Berkshires, 165 Kemble St. (© **800/742-9000** or 413/637-4100; www.canyonranch.com), is a one-of-a-kind spa/resort, with its core the 1897 mansion modeled after Le Petit Trianon at Versailles. Sweat away the pounds in the spa complex, with 40 exercise classes a day, weights, an indoor track, racquetball, squash, and all the equipment you might want. Canoeing and hiking are added possibilities. Guest rooms are in contemporary New England style, with every hotel convenience except minibars. After you've been steamed, exhausted, pummeled, and showered, the big events of each day are mealtimes: "nutritionally balanced gourmet," naturally. All-inclusive 3- to 7-night packages run from $1,580 to $5,290 double.

Harley Procter hitched up with a man called Gamble and made a bundle. In 1912, he built the current home of the totally smoke-free **Gateways Inn,** 51 Walker St., Lenox (✆ **888/492-9466** or 413/637-2532; www.gatewaysinn.com). The stunning staircase that winds down into the lobby is just the thing for a grand entrance. Eight rooms have working fireplaces. Dining here is one of Lenox's greater pleasures. The bar features 130 single-malt scotches and 55 grappas. Also, a terrace has been added for after-concert light meals and desserts. Rates run $100 to $295 double.

An inn off and on since 1775, **The Village Inn,** 16 Church St. (✆ **800/253-0917** or 413/637-0020; www.villageinn-lenox.com) hasn't a whiff of pretense. Its smoke-free rooms (all have VCRs) come in considerable variety. You'll find four-posters in the high-end rooms, some of which have fireplaces and/or Jacuzzis, and constricted quarters with double beds at the lower end. Claw-foot tubs are common. Ask about rooms on the renovated third floor. Afternoon tea and dinner are served in the restaurant, where prices are lower than the town average. Doubles run $109 to $269, including breakfast.

WHERE TO DINE

See also "Where to Stay," above, as many inns have dining rooms. In particular, **Blantyre** (✆ **413/637-3556**) is worth a splurge. In high season, **Spigalina,** 80 Main St. (✆ **413/637-4455**), serves imaginative Mediterranean cooking. Note that the restaurants recommended below serve lunch, in a region where most of the better restaurants don't open until evening.

The Church Street Café, 65 Church St. (✆ **413/637-2745**), is the most popular place in town, delivering combinations that please the eye and pique the taste buds. Menus change with the seasons, but past options have included fried oysters with a lemony rémoulade sauce and sake-soy marinated shrimp with crabmeat wontons. Lunch is a busy time, with crab-cake sandwiches among the favorites. Main courses run about $19 to $30.

Dish, 37 Church St. (✆ **413/637-1800**), is a narrow storefront eatery that was packed from the day it opened. Since the decor is negligible and the accommodations cramped, the principal discernible reason for its furious popularity is the food. It comes from the kitchen in stuttering intervals, the uncertainty easily compensated by the startlingly high quality of what the creative chef-owner sends forth. At dinner, the charbroiled rainbow trout and herb-roasted baby rack of lamb au jus are stars. Another reason the locals like it—they don't need a bank loan to eat here. A main course will set you back $18 to $28.

WILLIAMSTOWN

This community and its prestigious college were named for Col. Ephraim Williams, killed in 1755 in the French and Indian War. He bequeathed the land for creation of a school and a town. Over the town's long history, buildings have been erected in several styles of the times. That makes Main Street a virtual museum of institutional architecture, with representatives of the Georgian, Federal, Gothic Revival, Romanesque, and Victorian modes, as well as a few yet to be labeled.

A free weekly newspaper, the *Advocate* (✆ **413/664-7900**), produces useful guides to both the northern and southern Berkshires. For a copy, write to the *Advocate,* 87 Marshall St., North Adams, MA 01267. An **information booth,** at North Street (Rte. 7) and Main Street (Rte. 2), has an abundance of pamphlets and brochures free for the taking.

WHAT TO SEE & DO

The Sterling and Francine Clark Art Institute, 225 South St. (© **413/458-2303;** www.clarkart.edu), is a gem with canvases by Renoir (34 of them), and the Degas sculpture *Little Dancer.* There are also works by 15th- and 16th-century Dutch portraitists, European genre and landscape painters, and Americans Sargent and Homer, as well as porcelain, silver, and antiques. Adults pay $10 admission (kids enter free) mid-June to October; the museum is free to all on Tuesday and from November to June. It's open July to August daily 10am to 5pm, closed Monday the rest of the year.

The Williams College Museum of Art, 15 Lawrence Hall Dr. (© **413/597-2429;** www.williams.edu/WCMA), is the second leg of Williamstown's two prominent art repositories. It exists in large part thanks to the college's collection of almost 400 paintings by the American modernists Maurice and Charles Prendergast. The museum also has works by Gris, Léger, Whistler, Picasso, Warhol, and Hopper. Admission is free. The museum is open Tuesday through Saturday (and some Mon holidays) from 10am to 5pm, Sunday from 1 to 5pm.

Williamstown has long hosted one of The Berkshires' premier summer attractions, the **Williamstown Theatre Festival** (© **413/597-3400;** www.wtfestival.org), and now it has a facility that provides a proper showcase: **The '62 Center for Theatre and Dance,** 1000 Main St. (© **413/597-2425** for box office; www.williams.edu/go/62center). This ambitious center opened in the fall of 2005 and hosts dramatic productions, as well as dance, music, and related cultural events, involving students and alumni as well as professionals. The schedule is usually announced by April. Tickets to the Festival itself range from about $20 to $55, while admission to other events is often free, and no more than $10.

5 Mystic

The spirit and texture of the maritime life and history of New England are captured in many ports along its indented coast, but nowhere more cogently than beside the Mystic River estuary and its harbor. The town is home to one of New England's most singular attractions, the Mystic Seaport museum village.

GETTING THERE By **car** from New York or Boston, take **I-95** to Exit 90 at Mystic. **Amtrak** (© **800/USA-RAIL**) serves Mystic with several **trains** daily from New York (trip time: 3¼ hr.) and Boston (1¾ hr.).

VISITOR INFORMATION Two helpful sources of information are **Mystic & More** (© **800/873-6569;** www.mysticmore.com) and **Mystic Coast & Country** (© **800/692-6278;** www.mycoast.com). A **visitor center** is in Building 1D of the Olde Mistick Village shopping center, at Route 27 and Coogan Boulevard, near the Interstate (© **860/536-1641**).

EXPORING MYSTIC SEAPORT

The village of **Mystic Seaport,** 75 Greenmanville Ave., Route 27 (© **888/9-SEA-PORT** or 860/572-5315; www.visitmysticseaport.org), encompasses an entire waterfront settlement, more than 60 buildings on and near a 17-acre peninsula. A useful map guide is available at the ticket counter in the **visitor center** in the building opposite the museum stores (which stay open later than the village most of the year, so make them your last stop).

Exit the visitor center and bear right along the path between the Galley Restaurant and the village green. It bends to the left, intersecting with a street of shops, public buildings, and houses. At that corner is an 1870s hardware and dry-goods store. Turning right here, you'll pass a schoolhouse, a chapel, and an 1830s home. Stop at the **children's museum,** which invites youngsters to play games characteristic of the seafaring era. It faces a small square that is the starting point for **horse-drawn wagon tours.**

From here, the three-masted barque *Charles W. Morgan,* built in 1841, one of the proudest possessions of the Seaport fleet of over 400 craft, is a few steps away.

If you're a fan of scrimshaw and ship models, continue along the waterfront until you reach the **Stillman Building,** which contains fascinating exhibits of both. Otherwise, head left toward the lighthouse. Along the way, you'll encounter a tavern, an 1833 bank, a cooperage, and other shops and services that did business with the whalers and clipper ships that put in at ports such as this.

The friendly docents in the village are highly competent at the crafts they demonstrate and always ready to impart information. The fact that they aren't dressed in period costumes enhances the village's feeling of authenticity by avoiding the contrived air of many such enterprises.

The next vessel is the iron-hulled square-rigger *Joseph Conrad,* which dates from 1881. Up ahead is a **lighthouse,** which looks out across the water toward the riverside houses that line the opposite shore. Round the horn, go past the boat sheds, the fishing shacks, and the ketches and sloops moored here in season until you come to the dock for the 1908 **SS Sabino.** This working ship gives half-hour river rides from mid-May to early October, daily from 11am to 4pm, and 1½-hour evening excursions. A few steps away is the 1921 fishing schooner *L. A. Dunton.*

A few steps south is the **Henry B. Du Pont Preservation Shipyard,** where the boats are painstakingly restored. One recent project was the re-creation of the schooner *Amistad,* which inspired an exhibit exploring the historical incident.

Also on the grounds are the **Galley Restaurant,** which serves fish and chips, fried clam strips, and lobster rolls; and **Sprouter's Tavern,** which offers snacks and sandwiches. When you exit for the day, ask the gatekeeper to validate your ticket so you can come back the next day for free.

Across the courtyard with the giant anchor is a building containing several **museum stores** as well as an art gallery. These superior shops stock books, kitchenware, fresh-baked goods, nautical prints and paintings, and ship models.

Admission to the shipyard is $17 adults, $9 for children 6 to 12 (second day included with validation). The ships and exhibits are open from April to October daily from 9am to 5pm, November to March daily from 10am to 4pm; the grounds are open 9am to 5pm.

While you're in town, check out the **Mystic Aquarium,** 55 Coogan Blvd. at Exit 90 off I-95 (✆ **860/572-5955;** www.mysticaquarium.org). The 15-minute marine show here illuminates as it entertains. It features alternating dolphins, sea lions, and orcas. And there are a host of other exhibits featuring marine mammals and other creatures of the deep that will occupy at least another hour of your time. In the outdoor "Alaskan Coast," see five beluga whales squeal and twirl and otherwise perform for their trainers at feeding time. Next door is a facsimile of the Bering Strait's Pribilof Islands, home to fur seals and endangered Steller sea lions, and out back are African black-footed penguins, with underwater viewing windows. There's also a new re-creation of a Louisiana bayou stocked with "Swamp Things:" frogs, turtles, carp, largemouth bass, and small alligators. Elsewhere, visitors are eye to eye with such creatures as sea horses, jellyfish, and the pugnacious yellow-head jaw fish, which spends its hours digging fortifications in the sand. Dozens of rays flutter like butterflies and

A Casino in the Woods

What has been wrought in the woodlands north of the Mystic coast in the last decade is astonishing. There was little but trees here when the Mashantucket Pequot tribe received clearance to open a gambling casino on their ancestral lands in rural Ledyard. Virtually overnight, the tribal bingo parlor was expanded into a full-fledged casino, and a hotel was built.

That was in 1992. Within 3 years, **Foxwoods Resort & Casino** (© 800/369-9003; www.foxwoods.com), had become the single most profitable gambling operation in the world, with a reported 40,000 visitors a day. Money cascaded over the Pequot (pronounced *Pee*-kwat) in a seemingly endless torrent. Expansion was immediate—another hotel, then a third, more casinos, golf courses, and the $139-million **Mashantucket Pequot Museum and Research Center**, devoted to Native American arts and culture. The tribe bought up adjacent lands and at least four nearby inns and hotels, and then opened a ship works to build high-speed ferries. All that hasn't sopped up the cascades of money, and the tribe has made major contributions to the Mystic Aquarium and Smithsonian Museum of the American Indian.

And that isn't the end of it. The Mashantucket Pequot Tribal Nation has announced a new $700-million project, scheduled for completion in mid-2008. Included will be a fourth high-rise hotel, another parking garage, two new golf courses, and more shops, restaurants, and gambling spaces.

All this prosperity came to a tribe of fewer than 520 acknowledged members, nearly all of them of mixed ethnicity. Residents of surrounding communities were ambivalent, to put the best face on it. When it was learned that one of the tribe's corporate entities was to be called Two Trees Limited Partnership, a predictable query was, "Is that all you're going to leave us? Two trees?" But while there is a continuing danger of damage to the fragile character of this authentically picturesque corner of Connecticut, it is also a

translucent jellyfish billow and flex in slow-motion dance, a hypnotic display. Admission to the aquarium is $18 adults, $13 children 3 to 12; the museum is open daily except Christmas and New Year's.

WHERE TO STAY & DINE

Mystic's most appealing lodging is **The Steamboat Inn,** 73 Steamboat Wharf (© **860/536-8300;** www.steamboatinnmystic.com), a yellow-clapboard structure that has apartment-size downstairs bedrooms, with Jacuzzis and wet bars, while the upstairs units have wood-burning fireplaces. Every room is decorated uniquely and has a fridge; all but one have water views. The inn commissioned the 97-foot yacht, *Valiant,* that is moored at its dock. The staterooms can be rented when the yacht isn't chartered. Rates ($140–$300 double) include breakfast. Children over 9 are welcome.

There are plenty of adequate area motels. Pick of the litter may be the **Best Western Sovereign,** north of Exit 90 (© **860/536-4281**), with a pool and restaurant. Nearby fact that because of the recent development, thousands of non-Pequots have found employment in their various enterprises.

The complex is reached through forested countryside of quiet hamlets that give little hint of the behemoth rising above the trees in Ledyard Township. There are no signs screaming FOXWOODS. Instead, watch for plaques with the symbols of tree, wolf, and fire above the word RESERVATION. As you enter the property, platoons of attendants point the way to parking and hotels. Ongoing construction surrounds the glassy, turquoise-and-violet towers of the hotels and casino. Though bustling, it doesn't look like Vegas from the outside—happily, there are no sphinxes, no fake volcanoes, and no neon palm trees.

Inside, the glitz gap narrows, but it is still relatively restrained, as such temples to chance go. The gambling rooms have windows, for example, even though the prevailing wisdom among casino designers is that they should not give customers any idea of what time of day or night it is.

And no one is allowed to forget that this whole eye-popping affair is owned and operated by Native Americans. Prominently placed around the main buildings are larger-than-life sculptures by artists of Chiricahua and Chippewa descent, depicting Amerindians in a variety of poses and artistic styles. One other Indian-oriented display is *The Rainmaker*, a glass statue of an archer shooting an arrow into the air. Every hour on the hour, he is the focus of artificial thunder, wind-whipped rain, and lasers pretending to be lightning bolts, the action described in murky prose by a booming voice-of-Manitou narrator. That's as close as the chest thumping gets to going over-the-top.

Two dozen bus companies provide daily service to Foxwoods from numerous cities in the northeast and mid-Atlantic regions, including Boston, Providence, New York, and Philadelphia, among many other cities. For information on transit from particular destinations, call © 860/885-3000.

competitors are the **Comfort Inn** (© 860/572-8531), **Days Inn** (© 860/572-0574), and **Residence Inn** (© 860/536-5150).

For dining, **Abbott's Lobster in the Rough,** 117 Pearl St., Noank (© 860/536-7719), is a nitty-gritty lobster shack with plenty of picnic tables. The classic shore dinner rules. That means clam chowder, boiled shrimp, mussels, and a lobster, with coleslaw, chips, and drawn butter. Bring your own beer. Main courses run $16 to $34.

Similarly, **Kitchen Little** on Route 27, 1 mile south of I-95 (© 860/536-2122), is not much more than a shack by the water, but the menu offers 45 distinct breakfast choices and some of the coast's tastiest clam and scallop dishes. At lunch, you must have the definitive clear broth clam chowder, maybe the whole belly clam rolls, and absolutely the fried scallop sandwich. Try to snare a table out back, in view of the tall ships. Main courses cost $4 to $13.

6 Newport

Newport occupies the southern tip of Aquidneck Island in Narragansett Bay, and is connected to the mainland by three bridges and a ferry. Wealthy industrialists, railroad tycoons, coal magnates, financiers, and robber barons were drawn to the area in the 19th century. They bought up property at the ocean's rim to build what they called summer "cottages"—patterned after European palaces.

But despite Newport's prevailing image as a collection of ornate mansions and regattas, the city is, for the most part, middle class and moderately priced. Scores of inns and B&Bs assure lodging even during festival weeks, at rates and fixtures from budget to luxury level. In almost every respect, this is the "First Resort" of the New England coast.

GETTING THERE   From New York City, take **I-95** to the third Newport exit, picking up **Route 138** heading east (which joins briefly with Rte. 4) and crossing the Newport toll bridge slightly north of the downtown district. From Boston, take **Route 24** through Fall River, picking up **Route 114** into town.

T. F. **Green/Providence Airport** (© 401/737-8222; www.pvdairport.com) in Warwick, south of Providence (Exit 13, I-95), handles national flights into the state on several major carriers. A few of the larger Newport hotels provide shuttle service, as does **Cozy Cab** (© 401/846-2500).

VISITOR INFORMATION   For advance information available 24 hours, call **visitor information** (© 800/976-5122 outside Rhode Island, or 800/556-2484; www. goNewport.com). In town, stop by the excellent **Newport Gateway Visitor Center,** 23 America's Cup Ave. (© 800/326-6030 or 401/849-8048). Open daily from 9am to 5pm (until 6pm Fri–Sat).

GETTING AROUND   Most of Newport's attractions, except for the mansions, can be reached on foot. If you'd prefer not to hoof it, the **Rhode Island Public Transit Authority,** or **RIPTA** (© 800/244-0444 or 401/781-9400; www.ripta.com), has a free shuttle bus that follows a roughly circular route through town, making stops at major sights.

SPECIAL EVENTS   Arrive any day in summer and expect to find at least a half-dozen festivals, competitions, or other events; for a comprehensive listing of the city's best waterfront festivals, check out **www.newportfestivals.com**. In the off season, there's the 2-week **Christmas in Newport** (© 401/849-6454; www.christmasin newport.org) festival, when candlelight tours of the city's magnificent homes are offered. In June, there's **Great Chowder Cook-Off** (© 401/846-1600), where 30 of the country's best chefs compete. During the middle 2 weeks in July, the **Newport Music Festival** (© 401/849-0700; www.newportmusic.org), offers classical concerts daily at various venues. August brings the **Dunkin' Donuts Newport Folk Festival** (www.newportfolk.com) and the 4-day **JVC Jazz Festival—Newport** (© 866/ 468-7619; www.festivalproductions.net), both held at Fort Adams State Park.

THE COTTAGES

That's what wealthy summer people called the sumptuous mansions they built in Newport. We suggest you visit only one or two per day: The sheer opulence can soon become numbing. Each residence requires 45 minutes to an hour for its guided tour. If at all possible, go during the week to avoid crowds and traffic.

Newport

Newport Bridge (Toll)

East Passage

Coasters Harbor Island

Adm. Kalbfus Rd.

Miantonomi

Bliss Mine Rd.

Narragansett Bay

Third St.

Van Zandt Ave.

Bliss Rd.

Broadway

Rhode Island Ave.

Kay St.

Causeway ①

America's Cup Ave.

✡ Touro Synagogue

✉

Easton's Pond

† Church
ⓘ Information
--- Ferry Routes
✉ Post Office
✡ Synagogue

Ferry to Providence

Goat Island

Trinity Church
Mill St.
②

Old Beach Rd.

→ To Middletown

Memorial Blvd.
④

③

Conanicut Island

Newport Harbor

Fort Adams State Park

Thames St.

Spring St.

⑤

⑥

Annandale Rd.

Ferry to Block Island

Fort Adams Rd.

Narragansett Ave.

Harrison Ave.

Wickham Rd.

Ruggles Ave.

Bellevue Ave.

†

⑦

⑧

Cliff Walk

Ridge Rd.

Moorland Rd.

Hazard Rd.

Lily Pond

Ocean Dr.

Almy Pond

⑨

⑩

⑪

Easton Bay

Castle Hill Ave.

Harrison Ave.

Ocean Dr.

⑫

⑬

Brenton Point State Park

ATLANTIC OCEAN

Providence ★

RHODE ISLAND

Newport ○

Six of the mansions are maintained by the **Preservation Society of Newport County,** 424 Bellevue Ave. (℗ **401/847-1000;** www.newportmansions.org), which also operates the 1748 Hunter House, the 1860 Italianate Chepstow villa, the 1883 Isaac Bell House, and the Green Animals Topiary Gardens in Portsmouth. The Society sells a **combination ticket,** good for a year, to five of its properties; the cost is $31 for adults, $10 for children 6 to 17. Individual tickets for The Breakers are $15 for adults, $4 for children, and for Hunter House $25 for adults, $4 for children. Individual tickets for Kingscote, The Elms, Chateau-sur-mer, Marble House, and Rosecliff are $10 for adults, $4 for children. They can be purchased at any of the properties. Credit cards are accepted at most, but not all, of the cottages.

Mansions that aren't operated by the Preservation Society but are open to the public are **Belcourt Castle, Beechwood,** and **Rough Point.**

The cottages include **Kingscote** on Bowery Street (west of Bellevue Ave.), built in 1839, considered one of the Newport Cottages because it was acquired in 1864 by the sea merchant William Henry King, who furnished it with porcelains and textiles accumulated in the China trade. Architect Richard Upjohn designed the mansion in the same Gothic Revival style he used for Trinity Church in New York. The firm of McKim, Mead & White was commissioned to design the 1881 dining room, notable for its Tiffany glass panels.

Architect Horace Trumbauer is said to have been inspired by the Château d'Asnieres outside Paris, and a first look at the dining room of **The Elms,** on Bellevue Avenue, buttresses that claim. So, too, do the sunken gardens, laid out and maintained in the formal French manner. Trumbauer completed the cottage in 1901 and filled it with genuine Louis XIV and XV furniture as well as paintings and accessories true to the late 18th century. Visitors can opt for a self-guided audio tour.

If you have time to see only one cottage, make it **The Breakers** on Ochre Point Avenue. Architect Richard Morris Hunt was commissioned to create this replica of a Florentine Renaissance palazzo. The high iron entrance gates alone weigh over 7 tons. The 50×50-foot great hall has 50-foot-high ceilings, forming a giant cube, and is sheathed in marble. Such mind-numbing extravagance shouldn't really be surprising—Hunt's patron was Cornelius Vanderbilt II, grandson of railroad tycoon Commodore Vanderbilt. The mansion's foundation is approximately the size of a football field, and the Breakers took nearly 3 years to build (1892–95). Platoons of artisans were imported from Europe to apply gold leaf, carve wood and marble, and provide mural-size baroque paintings. The furnishings on view are original.

From the Breakers, return to Bellevue Avenue and turn left (south); **Rosecliff** is on the left. Stanford White thought the Grand Trianon of Louis XVI at Versailles a suitable model for this 1902 commission for heiress Tessie Fair Oelrichs. It has the largest ballroom of all the cottages, not to mention a storied heart-shaped grand staircase. It was used as a setting for some scenes in the Robert Redford movie of F. Scott Fitzgerald's *The Great Gatsby* (1974). On a humid summer day, keep in mind that this mansion is air-conditioned.

Mrs. William Backhouse Astor—*the* Mrs. Astor—was the arbiter of who constituted New York and Newport society. "The 400" list of socially acceptable folk was influenced or perhaps even drawn up by her. Being invited to **The Astors' Beechwood,** 580 Bellevue Ave. (℗ **401/846-3772;** www.astors-beechwood.com), was a coveted prize. Rebuilt in 1857 after a fire destroyed the original version, the mansion isn't as large or impressive as some of its neighbors. But it provides a little theatrical pizazz with a corps of actors who pretend to be friends, children, and servants of Mrs.

Astor. In set pieces, they share details about life in the late Victorian era. Admission is $18 to $30 for adults, $8 to $15 for children 6 to 12, $45 per family.

OUTDOOR PURSUITS: THE BEACH & BEYOND

Fort Adams State Park, Harrison Avenue (© **401/841-0707;** www.fortadams.org), is on the thumb of land that partially encloses Newport Harbor. It can be seen from the downtown docks and reached by driving or biking south on Thames Street and west on Wellington Avenue (a section of Ocean Dr., which becomes Harrison Ave.). Boating, ocean swimming, fishing, and sailing are all possible in the park's 105 acres. The park is open from Memorial Day to Labor Day.

Farther along Ocean Drive is **Brenton Point State Park,** a scenic preserve that borders the Atlantic, with nothing to impede the waves rolling in and collapsing on the rock-strewn beach. Scuba divers are often seen surfacing offshore, anglers enjoy casting from the long breakwater, and on a windy day the sky is dotted with colorful kites.

On Ocean Drive, less than 2 miles from the south end of Bellevue Avenue, is **Gooseberry Beach,** which is privately owned but open to the public. Parking costs $8 Monday through Friday, $12 Saturday and Sunday.

Cliff Walk skirts the edge of the southern section of town where most of the cottages were built, and provides better views of many of them than can be seen from the street. The walk is open from 9am to 9pm.

Biking is one of the best ways to get around town, especially out to the mansions and along **Ocean Drive.** Among several rental shops are **Firehouse Bicycle,** 25 Mill St. (© **401/847-5700**); **Ten Speed Spokes,** 18 Elm St. (© **401/847-5609**); and **Scooters,** 411 Thames St. (© **401/619-0573**).

Adventure Sports Rentals, at the Inn on Long Wharf, 142 Long Wharf (© **401/849-4820**), rents not only bikes and mopeds, but also outboard boats, kayaks, and sailboats; parasailing outings can be arranged.

ORGANIZED TOURS   Several organizations conduct tours of the mansions and the downtown historic district. Between May 15 and October 15, the **Newport Historical Society,** 82 Touro St. (© **401/846-0813**), offers a few different itineraries of considerable variety and length. Tickets cost as little as $4 and as much as $12. They can be purchased at the Society or at the Gateway Visitor Center. **Viking Tours,** based at the Gateway Visitor Center, 23 America's Cup Ave. (© **401/847-6921**), has narrated bus tours of the mansions and harbor cruises on the excursion boat *Viking Queen.* Bus tours—daily in summer, Saturdays from November to March—are 1½ to 4 hours and cost $22 to $47 for adults, $13 to $21 for children 5 to 11. Boat tours, from late May to early October, are 1 hour in length and cost $12 for adults, and $6 for kids.

The *Spirit of Newport* ⚓, 2 Bowen's Wharf (© **401/849-3575**), offers daily 1½-hour cruises of the bay and harbor from May 1 to Columbus Day; Fares are $13 for adults, $7 for children ages 4 to 12. The **Newport Touring Company,** 19 America's Cup Ave. (© **800/398-7427** or 401/841-8700; www.newportdinnertrain.com), features 90-minute round-trip excursions in vintage railroad trains along the edge of the bay. Fares are $15 for adults; kids 10 and under are free, but only one per paying adult; additional kids are charged $7.95.

SHOPPING

For nautical shopping, try the shops along **Lower Thames Street.** For example, **J. T.'s Ship Chandlery** (no. 364) outfits recreational sailors with sea chests, ship lanterns, and foul-weather gear. **Aardvark Antiques** (no. 475) specializes in salvaged architectural components. **Spring Street** is noted for its antiques shops and purveyors of crafts, jewelry, and folk art. Antique boat models are displayed along with marine paintings and navigational instruments at **North Star Gallery** (no. 105). **The Drawing Room/The Zsolnay Store** (nos. 152–154) stocks estate furnishings and specializes in Hungarian Zsolnay ceramics. Folk art and furniture are the primary goods at **Liberty Tree** (no. 104).

WHERE TO STAY

The **Gateway Visitor Center** (© 800/976-5122 or 401/849-8040; www.gonewport. com) lists vacancies in motels, hotels, and inns. Most can be called from free direct-line phones located nearby. Less impulsive travelers should reserve in advance, especially on weekends (2 months ahead for weekends from Memorial Day to Labor Day). **Bed & Breakfast Newport, Ltd.** (© 800/800-8765 or 401/846-5408; www.bb newport.com) claims to offer 350 choices of accommodations.

Many of the better motels are located in Middletown, about 2 miles north of downtown Newport. Possibilities include the **Courtyard by Marriott,** 9 Commerce Dr. (© 401/849-8000); **Newport Ramada Inn,** 936 W. Main Rd. (© 401/846-7600); **Newport Gateway Hotel,** 31 W. Main Rd. (© 401/847-2735); and **Howard Johnson,** 351 W. Main Rd. (© 401/849-2000). Newport itself has a **Marriott,** 25 America's Cup Ave. (© 401/849-1000).

The innkeepers and hoteliers of Newport keep topping themselves, but it will be a long while before they can best **The Chanler,** 117 Memorial Blvd. (© 401/847-1300; wwwthechanler.com). A boutique hotel with only 20 units, the main structure dates from 1873. It stands above the northern end of the Cliff Walk, overlooking the surf that rolls through the bay and onto Eaton's Beach. All rooms are decorated in theme—Mediterranean, Renaissance, Tudor—and have DVD and CD players, gas fireplaces, two TVs (some are plasma), separate sitting areas, and, except for one suite, double Jacuzzis, supplemented by multinozzled shower stalls. Rates run $350 to $1,195 double.

At the **Francis Malbone House,** 392 Thames St. (© 800/846-0392 or 401/846-0392; www.malbone.com), several modern rooms were added in a wing attached to the original 1760 Colonial house. They are nice, with reproductions of period furniture and CD players. Given a choice, take a room in the old section, where antiques outnumber repros, Oriental rugs adorn buffed wide-board floors, and silks and linens are deployed unsparingly. Rates include breakfast and afternoon tea. No children under 12. Rates range from $99 to $345 double.

Mill Street Inn, 75 Mill St., 2 blocks east of Thames (© 800/392-1316 or 401/849-9500; www.millstreetinn.com), is a 19th-century sawmill that was scooped out and rebuilt from the walls in. Apart from exposed expanses of brick and an occasional wood beam, all of it is new. An all-suite facility, even the smallest unit has a queen-size bed and a sofa bed. The duplexes have private balconies, but everyone can use the rooftop decks, where breakfast is served on warm days. Rates are $119 to $199 double.

WHERE TO DINE

There are far too many restaurants in Newport to give full treatment even to the best among them. Equal in many ways to those recommended below are **Canfield House,** 5 Memorial Blvd. (© 401/847-0416); **Yesterday's & the Place,** 28 Washington Sq. (© 401/847-0116); **The Bistro,** 41 Bowen's Wharf (© 401/849-7778); and **The**

West Deck, 1 Waites Wharf (© **401/847-3610**). And for bargain dining in pricey Newport, the bountiful pastas of **Salas,** 343 Thames St. (© **401/845-8772**), are a perfect choice for hungry families.

Winter hours and days of operations vary considerably. Call ahead to avoid disappointment.

Asterix, 599 Lower Thames St. (© **401/841-8833**), is a cheerful place that offers classic Gallic bistro dishes. Come and discover how delectable a near-perfect roast herbed chicken or sole meunière can be. Sunday dinners are served to live jazz from 7pm. Excellent breads are provided by the chef/owner's **Boulangerie,** 382 Spring St. (© **401/846-3377**). Main courses cost $21 to $33.

Still going strong after almost 330 years, the **White Horse Tavern,** 25 Marlborough St. (© **401/849-3600**), makes a credible claim of being the oldest tavern in America. On the ground floor are a bar and two dining rooms. The food is quite good, from the daily lunch specials to the spice-rubbed venison with pears poached with rosemary. About a third of the dishes involve seafood. Prices are significantly lower on the Pub menu ($10–$24 for entrees) available from 5pm Sunday through Thursday. Otherwise, main courses run $28 to $40. At **Scales & Shells,** 527 Lower Thames St. (© **401/846-3474**), the graceless name reflects the uncompromising character of this clangorous fish house. Diners who insist on a modicum of elegance should head for the upstairs room, called **Upscales** (© **401/847-2000**). Myriad fish and shellfish, listed on the blackboard, are offered in guileless preparations that allow the natural flavors to prevail. Main courses downstairs cost $11 to $21, at Upscales it's $16 to $29.

NEWPORT AFTER DARK

The most likely places to spend an evening lie along **Thames Street.** One of the most obvious possibilities, **The Red Parrot,** 348 Thames St., near Memorial Boulevard (© **401/847-3140**), has the look of an Irish saloon and features jazz combos Thursday through Sunday. **One Pelham East,** at Thames and Pelham streets (© **401/847-9460**), has a cafe, a small dance floor, a pool table, and another bar upstairs, with mostly college-age patrons attending to rockers on the stage at front. Free pizza is served some evenings.

A full schedule of live music is featured at the **Newport Blues Café,** 286 Thames St., at Green Street (© **401/841-5510**), plus a Sunday gospel brunch. With its fireplace, dark wood, and massive steel back door that used to guard the safe of this former bank, the cafe has a lot more class than most of the town's bars. Meals are available nightly in summer, Thursday through Sunday nights off season.

7 Providence

Providence delights in its sobriquet, "Renaissance City." No question, this city is moving on up, counter to the trend of so many small and midsize New England cities. *Money* magazine even declared it the "Best Place to Live in the East." Revival is in the air and prosperity is returning, evident in the resurgent "downcity" business district. Rivers have been uncovered to form canals and waterside walkways; distressed buildings of the last century have been reclaimed; and continued construction has added a new hotel behind Union Station as well as Providence Place, a monster mall that brings national department stores to town for the first time. Adjacent to downcity is the Downtown Arts District, newly designated to the National Register of Historic Places, attracting restaurants, shops, a new boutique hotel, and several theater and repertory companies.

GETTING THERE   **By Air**   **T. F. Green/Providence Airport** (© 888/268-7222 or 401/737-8222; www.pvdairport.com) in Warwick, south of Providence (Exit 13, I-95), is served by major airlines. The Rhode Island Public Transit Authority (RIPTA) provides transportation between the airport and the city center. Taxis are also available, costing about $20 for the 20-minute trip.

By Train   **Amtrak** (© 800/USA-RAIL; www.amtrak.com) runs several trains daily between Boston and New York, stopping at the attractive station at 100 Gaspee St., near the State House.

By Car   **I-95,** which connects Boston and New York, runs right through the city. From Cape Cod, pick up **I-195 West.**

VISITOR INFORMATION   For advance information, contact the **Providence Warwick Convention & Visitors Bureau,** 1 West Exchange St. (© 800/233-1636 or 401/274-1636; www.providencecvb.com). In town, consult the new visitor center in the Rhode Island Convention Center, 1 Sabin St. (© 800/233-1636 or 401/751-1177), or check with the helpful park rangers at the visitor center of the Roger Williams National Park, at the corner of Smith and North Main streets, open daily from 9am to 4:30pm.

EXPLORING PROVIDENCE
STROLLING THE HISTORIC NEIGHBORHOODS

This is a city of manageable size—the population is about 170,000—that can easily occupy 2 or 3 days of a Rhode Island vacation. Two leisurely walks, one short, another longer, pass most of the prominent attractions and offer up a sense of the city's evolution from a colony of dissidents to a contemporary center of commerce and government.

Downtown, chart a route from the 1878 City Hall on Kennedy Plaza along Dorrance Street 1 block to Westminster. Turn left, then right in 1 block, past The Arcade, then left on Weybosset.

To extend this into a longer walk, follow Weybosset until it joins Westminster and continue across the Providence River. Turn right on the other side, walking along South Water Street as far as James Street, just before the I-195 overpass. Turn left, cross South Main, and then turn left on Benefit Street. This is the start of the so-called **Mile of History.** Lined with 18th- and 19th-century houses, it is enhanced by gas streetlamps and sections of brick herringbone sidewalks. Along the way are opportunities to visit, in sequence, the 1786 **John Brown House,** the **First Unitarian Church** (1816), the **Providence Athenaeum,** and the **Museum of Art, Rhode Island School of Design** (see below).

The **Rhode Island Historical Society** (© 401/438-0463; www.rihs.org) offers 90-minute guided tours of four different neighborhoods of interest.

Boosters are understandably proud of their **Waterplace Park & Riverwalk,** which encircles a tidal basin and borders the Woonasquatucket River down past where it joins the Moshassuck to become the Providence River. It incorporates an amphitheater, boat landings, landscaped walkways, and vaguely Venetian bridges that cross to the East Side. Summer concerts and other events are held here, among them the enormously popular **WaterFires** (© 401/272-3111), when 97 bonfires are set ablaze in the basin of Waterplace Park and along the river on New Year's Eve and on more than 20 other dates July through October, their roar accentuated by amplified music.

Nearby, in Kennedy Plaza, the **Fleet Skating Center** has an ice rink twice the size of the one in New York's Rockefeller Center, fully utilized almost every winter evening. Skate rentals, lockers, and a snack bar are available.

The prestigious **Museum of Art, Rhode Island School of Design,** 224 Benefit St., between Waterman and College streets (© **401/454-6500;** www.risd.edu/museum.cfm), is an ingratiating center of fine and decorative arts that ranks near the top of New England's many fine university museums because of the sheer breadth of its collection. Those holdings include Chinese terra cotta, Greek statuary, French Impressionist paintings, works by masters such as Rodin and Picasso, and a wing containing paintings by American artists such as Gilbert Stuart and John Singer Sargent. The Gorham silver collection alone is nearly worth the admission ($8 adults, $2 children 5–18).

Constructed of Georgian marble that blazes in the sun, the **Rhode Island State House,** 82 Smith St. (© **401/277-2357**), dominates the city center. This near-flawless example of neoclassical governmental architecture boasts one of the largest self-supported domes in the world. The gilded figure on top represents "Independent Man," the state symbol. Inside, a portrait of George Washington by native Rhode Islander Gilbert Stuart is given pride of place. Guided tours are available on weekday mornings by prior appointment only.

Situated in a 430-acre park that also contains a museum of natural history and a planetarium, the **Roger Williams Park Zoo,** 1000 Elmwood Ave., at Exit 17 off I-95 (© **401/785-3510;** www.rogerwilliamsparkzoo.org), is divided into three principal habitats: Tropical America, the Farmyard, and the Plains of Africa. A newer exhibit is devoted to Australia, with the zoo's first saltwater aquarium. A walk-through aviary and underwater viewing areas with polar bears, sea lions, and harbor seals are additional attractions. The facility has looked a bit bedraggled of late, but not enough to deter visits. Admission is $12 adults, $6 kids 3 to 12.

WHERE TO STAY & DINE

The clusters of motels around most of the exits from I-95 and I-195 offer decent value. Among these possibilities are the **Days Hotel,** 220 India St. (© **401/272-5577**), and the **Ramada Inn,** 940 Fall River Ave., Seekonk, MA (© **508/336-7300**). *Note:* Rates at most area inns and motels go up on alumni and parents' weekends and during graduation weeks.

At the **Providence Biltmore,** 11 Dorrance St. (© **800/294-7709** or 401/421-0700; www.providencebiltmore.com), a grand staircase beneath the stunning Art Deco bronze ceiling dates the centrally located building from the 1920s, and a plaque in the lobby shows the nearly 7-foot-high water level of the villainous 1938 hurricane. From the lobby, the dramatic glass elevator literally shoots skyward, exiting outdoors to scoot up the side of the building. Most guest rooms are large and some of the 20 suites have kitchenettes. An Elizabeth Arden Red Door Spa should be open by the time you read this. Rates run $249 to $289 double.

Easily the city's best hotel, the **Westin Providence,** 1 W. Exchange St. (© **800/ 937-8461** or 401/598-8000; www.westin.com), has a luxurious interior and a central downtown location. Skyways connect the hotel with the new Providence Place mall and the convention center. The architectural grandeur of the lobby rotunda and other public spaces is only enhanced by the sunny dispositions of the staff. Rooms are equipped with Westin's signature "Heavenly Bed." Rooms run $199 to $339 double. **Agora,** the main dining room, gets excellent reviews from critics.

Providence has a sturdy Italian heritage, resulting in a profusion of tomato-sauce and pizza joints, especially on Federal Hill, the district west of downtown and I-95. Because they are so obvious, the suggestions below focus on restaurants that break away from the red-gravy imperative.

One fruitful strip to explore for lower-cost dining options is that part of **Thayer Street** that borders the Brown University campus. It counts Thai, Tex-Mex, barbecue, and Indian restaurants among its possibilities.

The very steady **Cafe Nuovo,** 1 Citizens Plaza (access is from the Steeple St. bridge; ✆ 401/421-2525), occupies a spacious room of glass, marble, and burnished wood on the ground floor of a downtown office tower that overlooks the confluence of the Moshassuck and Woonasquatucket rivers. The kitchen here impresses with every course, from dazzling appetizers to stunning pastries. The fare is grounded in the Italian repertoire, but skips lightly among other inspirations, too—Thai, Greek, and Portuguese among them. There's music on weekends and outdoor dining in warm weather. Main courses cost $22 to $32.

XO Café, 125 N. Main St. (✆ 401/273-9090), draws a young, casual crowd, which keeps the staff moving at a fast evening-long pace. Behind the copper-topped bar are female mixologists in clothes not meant to conceal their gender, though they serve almost as many meals as drinks. A note at the top of the varied menu insists "Life is short, order dessert first" and some diners happily take the advice (whatever you do, don't skip dessert). Slaves to tradition can order the "Pre Fixe"—their spelling—which on one occasion listed seared foie gras in brioche with candied shallots and citrus-honey glaze. Main courses cost $20 to $31.

Providence claims the invention of the diner, starting with a horse-drawn wagon transporting food down Westminster Street in 1872. The tradition is carried forward by the likes of the **Seaplane Diner,** 307 Allens Ave. (✆ 401/941-9547), a silver-sided classic with tableside jukeboxes; and **Richard's Diner,** 377 Richmond St. (✆ 401/331-8541), so small you can walk across it in six strides.

8 Southern Vermont

ARLINGTON & MANCHESTER

Southwestern Vermont is the turf of Ethan Allen, Robert Frost, Grandma Moses, and Norman Rockwell. The rolling Green Mountains are rarely out of view from this region. And in midsummer, the lush green hereabouts gives Ireland a good run for its money—verdant hues are found in the forests blanketing the hills, the valley meadows, and the mosses along the tumbling streams, making it obvious how these mountains earned their name.

These Vermont villages make an ideal destination for romantic getaways, antiquing, and outlet shopping. **Arlington** has a town center that borders on microscopic; with its auto-body shops and redemption center (remnants of a time when the main highway artery passed through town), it gleams a bit less than its sibling towns to the north.

To the north, **Manchester** and **Manchester Center** share a town line, but maintain distinct characters. The more southerly Manchester has an old-world elegance with a campuslike town centered around the Equinox Hotel. Just to the north, Manchester Center is a major mercantile center with dozens of national outlets offering discounts on brand-name clothing, accessories, and housewares.

ESSENTIALS

GETTING THERE   From **I-91** at Brattleboro, take **Route 9 west.** Arlington, Manchester, and Manchester Center are north of Bennington on Historic Route 7A, which runs parallel to and west of **Route 7. Vermont Transit** (✆ **800/552-8737;** www.vermonttransit.com) provides bus service to Manchester.

VISITOR INFORMATION   The **Manchester and the Mountains Chamber of Commerce** (𝄞 800/362-4144 or 802/362-2100; www.manchestervermont.net) maintains a year-round information center at 5080 Main St. (Rte. 7A) beside the small village green in Manchester Center. Hours are Monday through Saturday from 10am to 5pm; from Memorial Day weekend through October, it's also open Sundays from 10am to 5pm, and to 7pm Fridays and Saturdays.

For information on outdoor recreation, the **Green Mountain National Forest** maintains a district ranger office (𝄞 **802/362-2307**) in Manchester on routes 11 and 30 east of Route 7. It's open Monday through Friday from 8am to 4:30pm.

EXPLORING THE AREA

Arlington has long been associated with illustrator Norman Rockwell, who lived here from 1939 to 1953. Its residents were regularly featured in Rockwell covers for the *Saturday Evening Post.* "Moving to Arlington had given my work a terrific boost. I'd met one or two hundred people I wanted to paint . . . the sincere, honest, homespun types that I love to paint," Rockwell wrote. At press time, the small **Norman Rockwell Exhibition** (𝄞 802/375-6423) was up for sale and its status was in doubt.

Manchester has long been one of Vermont's moneyed resorts, attracting prominent summer residents. This town is worth visiting to wander its quiet streets, bordered by distinguished homes dating from the early Federal period. Be sure to note the sidewalks made of irregular marble slabs. The town is said to have 17 miles of such sidewalks, composed of the castoffs from Vermont's marble quarries.

Hildene, Route 7A (𝄞 **802/362-1788;** www.hildene.org), was built by Robert Todd Lincoln, the only son of Abraham and Mary Todd Lincoln to survive to maturity. Lincoln summered in this 24-room Georgian Revival mansion between 1905 and 1926 and delighted in showing off its features, including a sweeping staircase and a 1908 Aeolian organ with 1,000 pipes. Lincoln had formal gardens designed after the patterns in a stained-glass window and planted on a gentle promontory with outstanding views of the flanking mountains. The home is viewed on group tours that start at the visitor center; allow time following the tour to explore the grounds. Admission is $12 adults, $4 children 6 to 14. Tours are given from mid-May to October daily from 9:30am to 4pm; grounds close at 5:30pm.

Skiers head to **Bromley Mountain Ski Resort** in Manchester Center (𝄞 **800/865-4786** for lodging, or 802/824-5522; www.bromley.com) to learn to ski. Gentle and forgiving, the mountain also features long, looping intermediate runs tremendously popular with families. **Stratton** (𝄞 **800/STRATTON** for lodging, or 802/297-4000; www.stratton.com) is another popular resort, where new owners have added $25 million in improvements in recent years, mostly in snowmaking, with coverage now up over 80%. The slopes are especially popular for snowboarding, a sport invented here. Expert skiers should seek out Upper Middlebrook, a fine, twisting run off the summit.

WHERE TO STAY & DINE

Owned and managed by the upscale Rockresorts, **The Equinox,** Route 7A, Manchester Village (𝄞 **800/362-4747** or 802/362-4700; www.equinoxresort.com), is a blueblood favorite, with acres of white clapboard behind a long row of stately columns that define lovely Manchester Village. Its roots extend back to 1769, but don't be misled by its lineage: The Equinox is a full-blown modern resort, complete with the full-service spa. You'll find extensive sports facilities scattered about its 2,300 acres, four dining rooms, scheduled events (such as guided hikes up Mount Equinox), and a sense of settled graciousness. The rooms are tastefully appointed, though not terribly large. Rates run $279 to $449 double.

The Arlington Inn, Route 7A (© **800/443-9442** or 802/375-6532; www.arlington inn.com), is an 1848 Greek Revival that would be at home in the Virginia countryside. But it anchors this village well, on a lawn bordered with sturdy maples. Inside, unique wooden ceilings adorn the first-floor rooms and a tavern that borrows its atmosphere from an English hunt club. If you prefer modern comforts, ask for a room in the 1830 parsonage next door, where you'll find phones and TVs. The quietest units are in the detached carriage house. There's also a tennis court. Rates ($95–$315 double) include breakfast.

If you're looking for a bit of history with your lodging but are shell-shocked by area rates, consider the **Barnstead Inn,** Route 30, Manchester Center (© **800/331-1619** or 802/362-1619; www.barnsteadinn.com), a congenial place within walking distance of Manchester. All but two of the guest rooms are in an 1830s barn; many are decorated in a rustic style, some with exposed beams. Expect vinyl bathroom floors, industrial carpeting, and a mix of motel-modern and antique furniture. Among the more desirable units are room B, which is the largest, and the two rooms (nos. 12 and 13) above the office, each with original round beams. Children over 12 are welcome. In the summer, there's a heated pool. Rates run $90 to $229 double.

If you like superbly prepared Continental fare but are put off by the stuffiness of highbrow restaurants, **Chantecleer** on Route 7A, 3½ miles north of Manchester Center (© **802/362-1616**), is the place for you. Rustic elegance is the best description for this century-old dairy barn. Chef Michel Baumann specializes in game and might feature veal with a roasted garlic, sage, and balsamic demi-glace. Especially good is the whole Dover sole, filleted tableside. Main courses cost $26 to $35.

The Little Rooster Café, Route 7A South, Manchester Center (© **802/362-3496**), is the best choice in town for breakfast or lunch. Start the day with flapjacks, a Cajun omelet, or a luscious corned-beef hash. Lunches feature a creative sandwich selection, such as a commendable roast beef with pickled red cabbage and a horseradish dill sauce. Menu items run from $4.50 to $6.75 at breakfast to a high of $8.25 at lunch.

THE SOUTHERN GREEN MOUNTAINS

The southern Green Mountains are New England writ large. If you've developed a notion in your head of what New England looks like, this may be the place you've envisioned. This region is known for its pristine, historic villages. Stop for a spell in Brattleboro to stock up on supplies, then head for the southern Green Mountains and continue your explorations on foot or by bike. In winter, you can plumb the snowy hills by cross-country ski or snowshoe.

NEWFANE & TOWNSHEND

These two villages, about 5 miles apart on Route 30, are the epitome of Vermont. Both are set within the serpentine West River Valley and built around open town greens. Both consist of impressive white-clapboard houses and public buildings that share the grace and scale of the surrounding homes. Both boast striking examples of Early American architecture, notably Greek Revival.

For visitors, inactivity is often the activity of choice. Guests find an inn or lodge that suits their temperament, then spend the days strolling, driving the back roads, soaking in a mountain stream, hunting for antiques, or striking off on foot for one of the rounded, wooded peaks that overlook villages and valleys.

ESSENTIALS

GETTING THERE   Newfane and Townshend are located on **Route 30** northwest of Brattleboro. The nearest interstate access is off Exit 3 from **I-91.**

VISITOR INFORMATION   No formal information center serves these towns. Brochures are available at the **state visitor center** (© 802/254-4593) on I-91 in Guilford, south of Brattleboro. The website **www.newfanevermontusa.com** provides good local information.

WHAT TO SEE & DO

Newfane was originally founded on a hill a few miles from the current village in 1774; in 1825, it was moved to its present location on a valley floor. Some of the original buildings were dismantled and rebuilt, but most date from the early to mid–19th century. The **National Historic District** comprises some 60 buildings around the green and on nearby side streets. You'll find styles ranging from Federal to Colonial Revival, although Greek Revival appears to carry the day. For more information on area buildings, get a copy of the free walking-tour brochure at the Moore Free Library on West Street or at the Historical Society.

Newfane's history is explored at the **Historical Society of Windham County,** on Route 30 across from the village common, in a 1930s Colonial Revival brick building. There's an assemblage of local artifacts (dolls, melodeons, rail ephemera), along with changing exhibits. It's open from late May to mid-October, Wednesday through Sunday from noon to 5pm; admission is by donation.

More than two dozen **antiques shops** are on or near Route 30 in the West River Valley. They provide good grazing and are a fine resource for collectors. At any of the shops, look for the brochure *Antiquing in the West River Valley.* Treasure hunters should time their visit to coincide with the **Newfane Flea Market** (© 802/365-7771), which features 100-plus tables of assorted stuff, including some of the 12-tube-socks-for-8-bucks variety. The flea market is held on Sundays from May through October on Route 30 just north of Newfane Village.

On Route 30 between Townshend and Jamaica, you'll pass the **Scott Covered Bridge** below the Townshend Dam (closed to car traffic). It dates from 1870 and is an example of a Towne lattice-style bridge, with an added arch. At 166 feet long, it is the longest single-span bridge in the state.

WHERE TO STAY & DINE

You can't help but notice the **Four Columns Inn,** West Street, Newfane (© 800/787-6633 or 802/365-7713; www.fourcolumnsinn.com). It's the regal white-clapboard building with four Ionic columns just off the green. Rooms in the Main House and Garden Wing are larger (and more expensive) than those above the restaurant. Four units have been made over as luxury suites. The best choice in the house is room no. 12, with a Jacuzzi, skylight, gas fireplace, and private deck with a view of a small pond. Low beams and white damask tablecloths characterize the inn's dining room, which features creative New American cooking. Rates include continental breakfast. There's an outdoor pool and hiking trails. Rates ($160–$225 double) include continental breakfast.

The Windham Hill Inn, Windham Hill Road, West Townshend (© 800/944-4080 or 802/874-4080; www.windhamhill.com), is about as good as it gets in this region. Situated on 160 acres at the end of a dirt road in a high upland valley, it was built in 1823 as a farmhouse. The guest rooms are appointed in an elegant country style; six have

Jacuzzis or soaking tubs, nine have balconies or decks, 13 have gas fireplaces, and all have views. The dining room features creative cooking with a strong emphasis on local ingredients. Rates ($245–$435) include breakfast. There's a heated pool, tennis court, and 6 miles of cross-country ski trails in winter. Children over 12 are welcome.

WOODSTOCK

For more than a century, the resort community of Woodstock has been considered one of New England's most exquisite villages. The downtown is compact and neat, populated largely by galleries and boutiques. The village green is surrounded by handsome homes, creating what amounts to a comprehensive review of architectural styles of the 19th and early 20th centuries.

It was first settled in 1765, rose to some prominence as a publishing center in the mid–19th century, and began to attract wealthy families who summered here in the late 19th century. Much of the town is on the National Register of Historic Places, and the Rockefeller family has deeded 500 acres surrounding Mount Tom to the National Park Service.

ESSENTIALS

GETTING THERE   Woodstock is 13 miles west of White River Junction on **Route 4** (take Exit 1 off I-89). From the west, Woodstock is 20 miles east of Killington on Route 4. **Vermont Transit** (© 800/451-3292; www.vermonttransit.com) provides bus service to Boston and Burlington.

VISITOR INFORMATION   The **Woodstock Area Chamber of Commerce,** 18 Central St. (© 888/496-6378 or 802/457-3555; www.woodstockvt.com), staffs an information booth on the green, open June through October daily from 9:30am to 5:30pm.

EXPLORING THE AREA

The heart of the town is the shady, elliptical green. To put local history in perspective, stop by the **Woodstock Historical Society,** 26 Elm St. (© 802/457-1822). Housed in the beautiful 1807 Charles Dana House, it has rooms furnished in Federal, Empire, and Victorian styles. It's open from late May to October, plus weekends in December. Hours are Monday through Saturday from 10am to 5pm and Sunday from noon to 4pm. Admission is $5.

The **Billings Farm and Museum** on Elm Street, about a half-mile north of town on Route 12 (© 802/457-2355; www.billingsfarm.org), was the creation of Frederick Billings, who is credited with completing the Northern Pacific Railroad. The 19th-century dairy farm was once renowned for its scientific breeding of Jersey cows and its fine architecture, especially the gabled 1890 Victorian farmhouse. A tour includes hands-on demonstrations of farm activities, exhibits of farm life, a look at an heirloom kitchen garden, and a visit to active milking barns. Admission is $10 adults, $8 children 13 to 17, $6 children 5 to 12, and $3 children 3 to 4.

The Billings Farm and the National Park Service have teamed up to manage the **Marsh-Billings-Rockefeller National Historic Park** (© 802/457-3368; www.nps.gov/mabi), focusing on the history of conservation. Visitors can tour the elaborate Victorian mansion, walk the carriage roads surrounding Mount Tom, and view one of the oldest professionally managed woodlands in the nation.

Admission to the grounds is free; mansion tours cost $6 adults, $3 children 16 and under. Advance reservations are recommended for mansion tours.

A Little Mountain Music

The **Marlboro Music Festival** offers classical concerts by accomplished masters as well as talented younger musicians from mid-July to mid-August in Marlboro, in the foothills of southeastern Vermont on Route 9. The retreat was founded in 1951 and has hosted countless musicians, including Pablo Casals, who participated between 1960 and 1973.

Concerts are in the 700-seat auditorium at Marlboro College, and advance ticket purchases are recommended. Between September and June, contact the festival's winter office at Marlboro Music, 135 S. 18th St., Philadelphia, PA 19103 (© **215/569-4690**). In summer, write Marlboro Music, Marlboro, VT 05344; or call the box office (© **802/254-2394;** www.marlboromusic.org). Marlboro's about a 4-hour drive from New York City and 2½ hours from Boston.

OUTDOOR PURSUITS

The rolling, hilly terrain around Woodstock is ideal for exploring by **bike.** Few roads don't lead to great rides; just grab a map and go. Mountain bikes are available for rent at **Woodstock Sports,** 30 Central St. (© **802/457-1568**).

Mount Tom is the prominent hill overlooking Woodstock, and its low summit has great views over the village and to the Green Mountains to the west. You can ascend the mountain right from the village: Start at Faulkner Park. To reach the trail head from the green, cross Middle Covered Bridge and continue straight on Mountain Avenue. The road soon arrives at the park at the base of Mount Tom.

The area's best **cross-country skiing** is at the **Woodstock Ski Touring Center** (© **800/448-7900** or 802/457-6674), at the Woodstock Country Club, just south of town on Route 106. The center maintains 36 miles of trails, including 12 miles of trails groomed for skate-skiing. The full-day trail fee is $14 for adults.

WHERE TO STAY & DINE

Jackson House Inn, 114–3 Senior Lane (© **800/448-1890** or 802/457-2065; www.jacksonhouse.com), was built in 1890 by a lumber baron who hoarded the best wood for himself; the cherry and maple floors are so beautiful you'll feel guilty for not taking off your shoes. The guest rooms are well appointed with antiques, although some of the older rooms are rather small. A well-executed addition (1997) created four suites with fireplaces and Jacuzzis. The inn welcomes guests with complimentary evening hors d'oeuvres and champagne, and a 3-acre backyard with formal English gardens. Rates ($195–$260 double) include breakfast. Children 14 and over are welcome. The **Dining Room** (3-course prix-fixe dinner about $55) offers Continental fare in a modern addition to the original inn. Its centerpiece is a 16-foot-high stone fireplace, and it boasts soaring windows with views of the gardens. Men may feel most comfortable in a sports coat, though a jacket is not required.

The **Shire Motel,** 46 Pleasant St. (© **802/457-2211;** www.shiremotel.com), is within walking distance of the green and with its Colonial decor is better appointed than your average motel. The rooms are bright, with most facing the river that runs behind the property; all have fridges. (The downside: thin sheets and some scuffed walls.) Off a second-floor porch is an outdoor kitchen where you can sit on rockers overlooking the river and enjoy a cup of coffee. The yellow-clapboard house next door has three modern suites, all with gas fireplaces and Jacuzzis. Rates run $78 to $315 double.

The Woodstock Inn & Resort, 14 The Green (© **800/448-7900** or 802/457-1100; www.woodstockinn.com), is central Vermont's best full-scale resort. The inn appears to be a venerable and long-established institution at first glance. But it's not—it wasn't built until 1969, but adopted a dignified Colonial Revival look well suited for Woodstock. Guest rooms are decorated in either country pine or a Shaker-inspired style. The best units, in a wing built in 1991, feature plush carpeting, fridges, and fireplaces. There are two restaurants; indoor and outdoor pools; a Robert Trent Jones–designed golf course (at the inn-owned Woodstock Country Club); tennis courts; a free shuttle to a fitness center; bike rental; and cross-country ski trails. Rates run $149 to $434 double.

On the dining front, **The Prince and the Pauper,** 24 Elm St. (© **802/457-1818;** www.princeandpauper.com), takes a bit of sleuthing to find (located down Dana Alley, next to the Woodstock Historical Society's Dana House), but it's worth the effort. This is one of Woodstock's more inviting restaurants, with an intimate but informal setting. Ease into the evening with a libation in the taproom, then move over to the rustic but elegant dining room. The menu changes often; the house specialty is a boneless rack of lamb baked in puff pastry with spinach and mushroom duxelles. The fixed-price dinner (appetizer, salad, entree) is $43.

The setting of the **Simon Pearce Restaurant,** the Mill, Quechee (© **802/295-1470;** www.simonpearce.com), can't be beat. Housed in a restored 19th-century woolen mill with wonderful views of a waterfall (spotlighted at night), Simon Pearce is a collage of exposed brick, pine floorboards, and handsome wooden tables and chairs. Meals are served on Simon Pearce pottery and glassware—if you like your place setting, you can buy it afterward at the sprawling retail shop in the mill. The atmosphere is a wonderful concoction of formal and informal. At dinner, look for entrees such as roast duck with mango chutney, and pan-roasted wild salmon. Main courses cost $22 to $28.

KILLINGTON

Killington is not the Vermont pictured on calendars and place mats. But the region around the mountain boasts Vermont's most active winter scene. Those most content here are skiers, singles in search of mingling, and travelers who want a wide selection of amenities.

ESSENTIALS

GETTING THERE   Killington Road extends southward from **routes 4** and **100** (marked on some maps as Sherburne). It's about 12 miles east of Rutland on Route 4. Many inns offer shuttles to the Rutland airport. **Amtrak** (© **800/USA-RAIL;** www.amtrak.com) offers service from New York to Rutland, with connecting shuttles to the mountain and various resorts. The **Marble Valley Regional Transit District** (© **802/773-3244;** www.thebus.com) operates the **Skibus,** with $2 shuttle rides service between Rutland and Killington daily in winter.

VISITOR INFORMATION   The **Killington Chamber of Commerce** (© **800/773-4181** or 802/773-4181; www.killington-chamber.org) has information on lodging and travel packages, and staffs an information booth on Route 4 at the base of the access road, open Monday through Friday from 9am to 5pm, and Saturday through Sunday from 10am to 2pm. For information on accommodations in the area and travel to Killington, contact the **Killington Lodging and Travel Service** (© **877/4-K-TIMES**).

SKIING & MORE

Killington (© **877/4-K-TIMES** for lodging, or 800/734-9435; www.killington.com) is New England's largest ski area, offering greater vertical drop than any other New

England mountain. You'll find the broadest selection of slopes, with trails ranging from long, narrow, old-fashioned runs to killer bumps high on its flanks. Thanks to this diversity, it has long been the destination of choice for serious skiers. That said, it's also a huge operation run with efficiency and not much of a personal touch. To avoid getting lost, ask about the free tours of the mountain, led by the ski ambassadors based at Snowshed. If you're looking for the big mountain experience, with lots of evening activities and plenty of challenging terrain, it's a good choice. Lift-ticket prices vary through the season, but they average around $70 adults, and $50 for kids and seniors.

Nearest to the downhill ski area (just east of Killington Rd. on Rte. 100/Rte. 4) is **Mountain Meadows Cross Country Ski Resort** (© **800/221-0598** or 802/775-7077; www.xcskiing.net), with 34 miles of trails groomed for both skating and classic skiing. The trails are largely divided into three pods, with beginner trails closest to the lodge, an intermediate area a bit farther along, and an advanced 6-mile loop farthest away. Rentals and lessons are available. A 1-day pass is $18, a half-day pass (after 1pm) $15. The intricate network of trails at **Mountain Top Inn** (© **802/483-6089**) has long had a loyal local following. The 66-mile trail network offers pastoral views through mixed terrain groomed for traditional and skate skiing. Adults pay $19 for 1-day trail passes, $16 for half-day passes (after 1pm). With more challenging and picturesque terrain, Mountain Top is the better value of the two options.

WHERE TO STAY

Skiers headed to Killington for a week or so should consider the condo option. A number of condo developments spill down the hillside and along the low ridges flanking the access road. These vary in elegance, convenience, and size. **Highridge** features units with saunas and Jacuzzis, along with access to a compact health club. **Sunrise Village** has a more remote setting, along with a health club and access to the Bear Mountain lifts. **The Woods at Killington** is farthest from the slopes (free shuttle) but offers access to the finest health club and the best restaurant. Rates fluctuate, depending on time of year, number of guest rooms, and length of stay. But figure on prices ranging from around $100 to $130 and up per person per day, including lift tickets. You can line up a vacation—or request more information—by contacting the **Killington Lodging and Travel Bureau** (© **888/4-K-TIMES;** www.killington.com), which also arranges stays at area inns and motels.

The **Blueberry Hill Inn,** Goshen–Ripton Road, Goshen (© **800/448-0707** or 802/247-6735; www.blueberryhillinn.com), is along a quiet road about 45 minutes northwest of Killington. It's an extraordinary destination for those inclined toward spending time outdoors. The inn dates to 1813; one graceful addition is the greenhouse walkway, which leads to the cozy guest rooms. Family-style meals are served in a rustic dining room, with a great stone fireplace and homegrown herbs drying from the wooden beams. Rates ($110–$190 double) include breakfast and dinner. There's lake swimming nearby, a sauna, bike rental, and cross-country ski trails. There are no phones in the rooms.

WHERE TO DINE

It's our impression that *every* Killington restaurant serves up chicken wings, and plenty of them. If you love wings, especially free wings, you'll be in heaven. Most restaurants are okay spots to carbo-load for a day on the slopes, and if you're with a group of friends, you may not mind the middling quality—but for the most part, don't expect much of a dining adventure.

One of the locally favored spots for consistently good, unpretentious fare is **Choices Restaurant and Rotisserie,** Killington Road at Glazebook Center (𝄐 **802/ 422-40300**), located on the access road across from the Outback. Full dinners come complete with salad or soup and bread and will amply restore calories lost on the slopes or the trail. Fresh pastas are a specialty (try the Cajun green-peppercorn fettuc-cine); other inviting entrees include meats from the rotisserie. The atmosphere is nothing to write home about and the prices are higher than at nearby burger joints, but the high quality of the food and the care in preparation make up for that. Main courses run $13 to $22.

Hemingway's, 4988 Rte. 4, between Route 100 North and Route 100 South (𝄐 **802/422-3886;** www.hemingwaysrestaurant.com), is an elegant spot—and one that ranks among the best restaurants in New England. Located in the 1860 Asa Briggs House, a former stagecoach stop, Hemingway's seats guests in three formal areas. The two upstairs rooms are sophisticatedly appointed with damask linen, crys-tal goblets, and fresh flowers. Diners tend to dress casually but neatly (no shorts or T-shirts). The three- or four-course dinners are offered at a price (fixed-price menu $42–$60) that turns out to be rather reasonable given the quality of the kitchen and the unassailable service. The menu changes often to reflect available stock.

9 The White Mountains of New Hampshire

The White Mountains are northern New England's outdoor-recreation capital. This cluster of ancient mountains is a sprawling, rugged playground that attracts kayakers, mountaineers, rock climbers, skiers, mountain bikers, bird-watchers, and especially hikers.

The **White Mountain National Forest** encompasses some 773,000 acres of rocky, forested terrain, more than 100 waterfalls, dozens of remote backcountry lakes, and miles of clear brooks and cascading streams. The center of the White Mountains—in spirit if not in geography—is its highest point: 6,288-foot **Mount Washington,** an ominous, brooding peak that's often cloud-capped and mantled with snow both early and late in the season.

JACKSON & MOUNT WASHINGTON

Jackson is a village in a picturesque valley just off Route 16, about 15 minutes north of North Conway. The village center, approached on a single-lane covered bridge, is tiny, but touches of old-world elegance remain—vestiges of a time when Jackson was a favored destination for the East Coast upper middle class.

ESSENTIALS

GETTING THERE   Jackson is off **Route 16** about 11 miles north of North Con-way. Look for the covered bridge on the right when heading north.

VISITOR INFORMATION   The **Jackson Chamber of Commerce** (𝄐 **800/ 866-3334** or 603/383-9356; www.jacksonnh.com), based in offices at the Jackson Falls Marketplace, can answer questions about area attractions and make lodging reservations.

WHAT TO SEE & DO

Mount Washington, just north of Jackson, is the highest mountain in the Northeast at 6,288 feet. It's also got some of the worst winter weather in the northeast: It holds the world's record for the highest surface wind speed ever recorded—231 mph, in 1934.

Mount Washington may also be the mountain with the most options for getting to the top. Visitors can ascend by cog railroad, by car, by guide-driven van, or on foot.

Despite the raw power of the weather, Mount Washington's summit is not the best destination for those seeking wilderness wild and untamed. The summit is home to a train platform, a snack bar, a gift shop, a museum, and a handful of outbuildings, some of which house the weather observatory. And there are the crowds, which can be thick on a clear day. Then again, on a clear day the views can't be beat, with vistas extending into four states and to the Atlantic Ocean.

The best place to learn about Mount Washington is rustic **Pinkham Notch Visitor Center** (✆ 603/466-2721), operated by the Appalachian Mountain Club. At the crest of Route 16 between Jackson and Gorham, Pinkham Notch offers overnight accommodations and meals, maps, and advice from the helpful staff. A number of hiking trails depart from Pinkham Notch.

The **Mount Washington Auto Road** (✆ 603/466-3988; www.mountwashington autoroad.com) opened in 1861 as a carriage road, and has since remained one of the most popular White Mountain attractions. The steep, winding, 8-mile road (with an average grade of 12%) is partially paved and incredibly dramatic. The ascent will test your iron will; the descent will test your car's brakes. The trip's not worth doing if the summit is in the clouds.

Van tours also ascend throughout the day, allowing you to relax, enjoy the views, and learn about the mountain from informed guides. The Auto Road, which is on Route 16 north of Pinkham Notch, is open from mid-May to late October from 7:30am to 6pm (limited hours early and late in the season). The cost is $20 for car and driver, $7 for each additional adult ($5 for children 5–12). The fee includes audiocassette narration pointing out sights along the way. Management has imposed some curious restrictions on cars; for instance, Acuras and Jaguars with automatic transmissions must show a "1" on the shifter to be allowed on the road; call or check the website for details before heading out.

One additional note: The average temperature atop the mountain is 30°F (–1°C). The record low was –43°F (–42°C), and the warmest temperature ever recorded atop the mountain, in August, was 72°F (22°C). Even in summer, visitors should come prepared for blustery, cold conditions.

WHERE TO STAY & DINE

The Covered Bridge Motor Lodge, Route 16 (✆ 800/634-2911 or 602/383-9151; www.jacksoncoveredbridge.com), is a pleasant motel on 5 acres between Route 16 and the river next to Jackson's covered bridge. While pretty basic, the lodge features lovely gardens and other appealing touches that make it a good value. The best rooms have balconies that overlook the river. Ask about the two-bedroom apartments with kitchen and fireplace. Rates ($79–$139 double) include continental breakfast. There's an outdoor pool and a tennis court.

The **Inn at Thorn Hill,** Thorn Hill Road (✆ 603/383-4242; www.innatthorn hill.com), is a great choice for a romantic getaway. Built in 1895, the inn sits outside the village center surrounded by hills. Inside, there's a Victorian feel and luxuriously appointed guest rooms. A favorite is Catherine's Suite, with a fireplace and two-person Jacuzzi. The hospitality is warm and top-notch, and the meals are among the best in the valley. The romantic **Inn at Thorn Hill Restaurant** is a great choice for a memorable meal. The candlelit dining room faces the forested hill behind the inn. Start with a glass of wine (the restaurant has won the *Wine Spectator* award of excellence), then browse the menu selections, which change weekly but often feature Asian accents. Rooms run $60 to $410 double, and rates include breakfast and dinner.

Thompson House Eatery, Route 16A, Jackson, near north intersection with Route 16 (© **603/383-9341**), a friendly, old-fashioned spot in a 19th-century farmhouse at the edge of Jackson's golf course, attracts crowds not only for its well-prepared fare but also for its reasonable prices. Dining is indoors and out, offering both lunch and dinner. Main courses cost $19 to $25.

For basic family dining, **Wilfred's,** 117 Main St. (© **603/466-2380**), serves steaks, chops, and a variety of seafood. The **Moonbeam Café,** 19 Exchange St. (© **603/ 466-5549**), has hearty meals such as potato pancakes and cups of coffee; a visit to the antique bathroom (complete with pull-chain) is mandatory. **Libby's Bistro,** at 115 Main St. (© **603/466-5330**), is in a handsomely renovated bank and serves dinners better than any place in North Conway.

CRAWFORD NOTCH

Crawford Notch is a wild, rugged mountain valley that angles through the heart of the White Mountains. **Route 302** (which is wide and speedy on the lower sections) runs through it, becoming steeper as it approaches the narrow defile of the notch itself. The views up the cliffs from the road can be spectacular on a clear day; on an overcast or drizzly day, the effect is nicely foreboding.

The **Twin Mountain Chamber of Commerce** (© **800/245-8946;** www.twin mountain.org) offers general information and lodging referrals at its booth near the intersection of routes 302 and 3.

WHAT TO SEE & DO

Much of the land flanking Route 302 falls under the jurisdiction of **Crawford Notch State Park,** established in 1911 to preserve land that elsewhere had been decimated by logging. The headwaters of the Saco River form in the notch, and what's generally regarded as the first permanent trail up Mount Washington also departs from here. The trail network on both sides of Crawford Notch is extensive; consult the *AMC White Mountain Guide* or *White Mountains Map Book* for detailed information.

The **Mount Washington Cog Railway,** Route 302, Bretton Woods (© **800/ 922-8825** or 603/846-5404; www.thecog.com), was a marvel of engineering when it opened in 1869. Part moving museum, part slow-motion roller-coaster ride, the cog railway steams to the summit at about 4 mph. Passengers enjoy the expanding view on this 3-hour round-trip. (There are stops to add water to the steam engine, to check the track switches, and to allow other trains to ascend or descend.) There's also a 20-minute stop at the summit. Be aware that the ride is noisy and sulfurous. Dress warmly and expect to acquire a patina of cinder and soot. The fare costs $57 adults, $37 children 6 to 12.

WHERE TO STAY & DINE

The Mount Washington Resort, Route 302, Bretton Woods (© **800/258-0330** or 603/278-1000; www.mtwashington.com), was built in 1902. In its heyday, it attracted luminaries like Babe Ruth and Thomas Edison. Guest rooms vary in size and decor (not too lavish, though innkeepers are making improvements); many have grand views of the mountains and countryside. A 900-foot veranda makes for relaxing afternoons. Meals are enjoyed in an impressive octagonal dining room. Rates ($145–$525 double) include breakfast and dinner. This remains one of our favorite spots in the mountains, partly for the sheer improbability of it all, and partly for its direct link to a lost era.

Located off Route 302 in a wild section of Crawford Notch, **Notchland Inn,** Route 302, Hart's Location (© **800/866-6131** or 603/374-6131; www.notchland.com), would fit quite well in a Sir Walter Scott novel. Built of hand-cut granite in the mid-1800s, Notchland is classy yet informal, perfectly situated for exploring the wilds of the White Mountains. Guest rooms are outfitted with antiques, wood-burning fireplaces, high ceilings, and individual thermostats. All but three rooms have air-conditioning. The inn is also home to affable Bernese mountain dogs and llamas. You may want to add the five-course dinner to your plan ($30 per person). It's not just good value—the closest restaurant is a long, dark drive away. Rates ($245 double) include breakfast.

FRANCONIA NOTCH

Franconia Notch is rugged New Hampshire writ large. Most of the notch is included in a well-managed state park. Those seeking the sublime should plan on a leisurely trip through the notch, allowing enough time to get out of the car and explore forests and craggy peaks.

ESSENTIALS

GETTING THERE   **I-93** runs through Franconia Notch, gearing down from four lanes to two (where it becomes the Franconia Notch Pkwy.) in the most scenic and sensitive areas of the park. Several roadside turnoffs dot the route.

VISITOR INFORMATION   Information on the park and surrounding area is available at the **Flume Information Center** (© **603/745-8391**), at Exit 1 off the parkway. It's open in summer daily from 9am to 4:30pm. North of the notch, the **Franconia Notch Chamber of Commerce** (© **603/823-5661;** www.franconianotch. org) on Main Street next to town hall is open spring through fall, Tuesday through Sunday from 10am to 5pm (days and hours often vary).

EXPLORING FRANCONIA NOTCH STATE PARK

Franconia Notch State Park's 8,000 acres, nestled within the surrounding White Mountain National Forest, hosts an array of scenic attractions easily accessible from I-93 and the Franconia Notch Parkway. For information on any of the following, contact the park offices (© **603/745-8391**).

The Flume is a rugged gorge through which the Flume Brook tumbles. The gorge, a popular attraction in the mid–19th century, is 800 feet long, 90 feet deep, and as narrow as 20 feet at the bottom; visitors explore it on a 2-mile walk through a network of boardwalks and bridges. It's open May through October; admission is $8 for adults, $5 for children 6 to 12.

Echo Lake is a picturesquely situated recreation area, with a 28-acre lake, a handsome swimming beach, and picnic tables scattered within view of Cannon Mountain on one side and Mount Lafayette on the other. A bike path runs alongside the lake and meanders up and down the notch for a total of 8 miles. Mountain bikes, canoes, and paddle boats can be rented for $10 per hour. Admission to the park is $3 for all visitors over age 12, $1 for visitors under 12. It's open from mid-June through Labor Day only.

Robert Frost lived in New Hampshire from the time he was 10 until he was 45. This humble farmhouse on Ridge Road (© **603/823-5510;** www.frostplace.org) is where Frost lived with his family. Wandering the grounds, it's not hard to see how his granite-edged poetry evolved at the fringes of the White Mountains. First editions of Frost's works are on display; a nature trail in the woods nearby is posted with excerpts from his poems. Admission costs $4 for adults, $2 for children 6 to 12.

WHERE TO STAY & DINE

Sugar Hill Inn, Route 117, Franconia (© **800/548-4748** or 603/823-5621; www. sugarhillinn.com), is a classic inn, with wraparound porch and sweeping mountain panoramas occupying 16 acres on lovely Sugar Hill. This welcoming, comfortable spot is a great base for exploring the western White Mountains. Rooms are graciously appointed in antique country style, some influenced by Shaker sensibility. Most have gas Vermont Castings stoves for heat and atmosphere. The restaurant, one of the area's best, features upscale regional fare. Rates ($140–$290 double) include breakfast.

10 The Maine Coast

Maine's southern coast runs roughly for 60 miles from the state line at Kittery to Portland, and is the destination of most travelers to the state (including many day-trippers from the Boston area). While it takes some doing to find privacy and remoteness here, you'll find at least two excellent reasons for a detour: long, sandy beaches, the region's hallmark; and a sense of history in some of the coastal villages. It's not hard to find a relaxing sandy spot, whether you prefer dunes and the lulling sound of the surf or the carnival-like atmosphere of a festive beach town. Waves depend on the weather—during a good Northeast blow (especially prevalent in spring and fall), they pound the shores and threaten beach houses built decades ago. During balmy midsummer days, the ocean can be as gentle as a farm pond, barely audible waves lapping timidly at the shore.

One thing all beaches share in common: a season that is generally brief and intense, running from July 4th to Labor Day. While an increasing number of beach towns see visitors well into the fall, shorefront communities tend to adopt a slower, more somnolent pace after Labor Day.

KITTERY & THE YORKS

Kittery is the first town you'll come to if you're driving to Maine from the south on **I-95** or **Route 1.** Kittery was once famous for its naval yard, but regionally it's now better known for its dozens of factory outlets.

"The Yorks," to the north, are three towns that share a name but little else. In fact, it's rare to find three such well-defined and diverse New England archetypes in such a compact area. **York Village** is full of early (17th-c.) American history and architecture. **York Harbor** reached its zenith during America's Victorian era, when wealthy urbanites built cottages at the ocean's edge. **York Beach** has an early-20th-century beach-town feel, with loud amusements, taffy shops, and summer homes in crowded enclaves near the beach.

The **Kittery Information Center** (© **207/439-1319**) is at a well-marked rest area on I-95. It's open daily from 8am to 6pm in summer, from 9am to 5:30pm the rest of the year. The **York Chamber of Commerce** (© **207/363-4422**) operates an information center at 571 Rte. 1. It's open in summer daily from 9am to 5pm (until 6pm Fri), limited days and hours the rest of the year.

FUN ON & OFF THE BEACH

Kittery's consumer mecca is 4 miles south of York on Route 1. Some 120 **factory outlets** flank the highway, including Dansk, Eddie Bauer, Calvin Klein, and Polo/Ralph Lauren.

In summer, navigating the area can be frustrating. (A free shuttle bus links the outlets and lessens some of the frustration.) The selection of outlets is more diverse than in Freeport an hour north, which is more clothing oriented. But Freeport's quaint village setting is more appealing. Information on current outlets is available from the **Kittery Outlet Association** (℡ **888/KITTERY;** www.thekitteryoutlets.com).

Learn about the area at the **Old York Historical Society,** 5 Lindsay Rd., York (℡ **207/363-4974**). First settled in 1624, York Village has several early buildings open to the public. A good place to start is **Jefferds Tavern,** across from the handsome old burying ground. Changing exhibits here document various facets of early life. Next door is the **School House,** furnished as it might have been in the last century. A 10-minute walk along Lindsay Road will bring you to **Hancock Wharf,** which is next door to the **George Marshall Store.** Also nearby is the **Elizabeth Perkins House,** with its well-preserved Colonial Revival interiors. The one don't-miss structure is the intriguing **Old Gaol,** built in 1719 with musty dungeons for criminals. (The jail is the oldest surviving public building in the U.S.) Just down the knoll is the **Emerson-Wilcox House,** built in the mid-1700s. Added to periodically over the years, it's a virtual catalog of architectural styles and early decorative arts. Admission to the village costs $10 adults, $5 children 4 to 16.

York Beach consists of two beaches—**Long Sands Beach** and **Short Sands Beach**—separated by a rocky headland and a small island capped by scenic **Nubble Light.** Both offer plenty of room when the tide is out. When the tide is in, they're both cramped. Short Sands fronts the town of York Beach, with its candlepin bowling and video arcades. It's the better bet for families with kids. Long Sands runs along Route 1A, across from a profusion of motels and convenience stores. Changing rooms, restrooms, and parking (50¢ per hour) are available at both beaches.

WHERE TO STAY & DINE

York Beach has a number of motels facing Long Sands Beach. Reserve ahead during high season. Among those with simple accommodations on or near the beach are the **Anchorage Inn** (℡ **207/363-5112**) and **Sea Latch** (℡ **800/441-2993** or 207/363-4400).

Dockside Guest Quarters in York (℡ **888/860-7428** or 207/363-2868; www.docksidegq.com) was established by David and Harriet Lusty in 1954, and recent additions haven't changed the maritime flavor of the place. Situated on a 7-acre peninsula, the inn occupies grounds shaded with maples and white pines. Five rooms are in the main house (1885), but most of the accommodations are in small, modern, town house–style cottages. These are bright and airy, and all have private decks that overlook the entrance to York Harbor. Several rooms also have woodstoves and/or kitchenettes. Rates run $95 to $190.

Chauncey Creek Lobster Pier, on Chauncey Creek Road between Kittery Point and York off Route 103, Kittery Point (℡ **207/439-1030**), is one of the best lobster pounds in the state, not least because the Spinney family, which has been selling lobsters here since the 1950s, takes such pride in the place. You reach the pound by walking down a wooden ramp to a broad deck on a tidal inlet, where some 42 festively painted picnic tables await. Lobster (served at market price) is the specialty, of course, but steamed mussels (in wine and garlic) and clams are also available. It's BYOB. Menu items run $1.50 to $9.

The Goldenrod Restaurant, Railroad Road and Ocean Avenue, York Beach (© 207/363-2621; www.thegoldenrod.com), has been an institution in York Beach since 1896. Visitors gawk at the ancient machines churning out taffy in volumes. Behind the taffy and fudge operation is the restaurant, short on gourmet fare but long on atmosphere. Diners sit around a stone fireplace or at the antique soda fountain. The meals are basic and filling; expect waffles, griddlecakes, club sandwiches, and deviled egg and bacon sandwiches. Nothing on the menu costs more than $8.

THE KENNEBUNKS

"The Kennebunks" are the villages of **Kennebunk** and **Kennebunkport,** situated along the shores of small rivers, both claiming a portion of rocky coast. The region was settled in the mid-1600s and flourished after the American Revolution, when ship captains, boat builders, and merchants constructed imposing, solid homes.

The **Kennebunk-Kennebunkport Chamber of Commerce,** 17 Western Ave. (P.O. Box 740), Kennebunk, ME 04043 (© 800/982-4421 or 207/967-0857), can answer your questions year-round by phone or at its offices on Route 9 next to Meserve's Market. The **Kennebunkport Information Center** (© 207/967-8600), operated by an association of local businesses, is off Dock Square (next to Ben & Jerry's) and is open daily throughout the summer and fall.

A local "trolley" service (© 207/967-3686; www.intowntrolley.com)—actually, it's a bus with a tour narrator—makes stops in and around Kennebunkport and also serves the beaches. The fare, a day pass costing $11 per adult or $6 per child ages 3 to 14, includes unlimited trips.

FUN ON & OFF THE BEACH

Kennebunkport is the summer home of Pres. George Bush the Elder, whose family has summered here for decades. As such, it's possessed of the tweedy, upper-crust feel that you might expect. The tiny downtown, whose streets were laid out during days of travel by boat and horse, is subject to traffic jams. If the municipal lot off the square is full, head north on North Street to the free long-term lot and catch the trolley back into town. Or go about on foot—it's a pleasant walk of about 10 to 15 minutes from the satellite lot to Dock Square.

Dock Square has an architecturally eclectic wharflike feel to it, with low buildings of mixed vintages and styles, but the flavor is mostly clapboard and shingles. Kennebunkport's deeper appeal is found in the surrounding blocks, where the side streets are lined with Federal-style homes.

For a clear view of the coast, sign up for a 2-hour sail aboard the *Schooner Eleanor* (at the Arundel Wharf Restaurant, Kennebunkport; © 207/967-8809), a 55-foot gaff-rigged schooner, built in Kennebunkport in 1999 after a classic Herreshoff design. If the weather's willing, you'll have a perfect view of the Bush compound and Cape Porpoise. Fare is $38 per person.

A bit farther afield, in the neighborhood around the Colony Hotel (about 1 mile east of Dock Sq. on Ocean Ave.), is a collection of homes of the uniquely American shingle style. Ocean Drive from Dock Square to **Walkers Point** and beyond is lined with summer homes overlooking surf and rocky shore. You'll likely recognize the former president's home at Walkers Point when you arrive (look for the shingle-style Secret Service booth). There's nothing to do here but park for a minute, take a picture of the house, then push on.

The Seashore Trolley Museum, 95 Log Cabin Rd. (© 207/967-2800; www.trolley museum.org), is a local marvel: a scrap yard masquerading as a museum. Founded in 1939 to preserve a disappearing way of life, today it contains one of the largest collections in the world—more than 200 trolleys, including specimens from Glasgow, Moscow, San Francisco, and Rome. (Naturally, there's a streetcar named "Desire.") About 40 cars still operate, and admission includes rides on a 2-mile track. Admission is $8 adults, $5.50 children 6 to 16.

The area around Kennebunkport is home to several of the state's best **beaches.** Across the river are **Gooch's Beach** and **Kennebunk Beach. Goose Rocks Beach** is north of Kennebunkport off Route 9 (watch for signs), and is a good destination for those who like their crowds light. Offshore is a narrow barrier reef that has historically attracted flocks of geese. No restrooms are available here.

WHERE TO STAY & DINE

Housed in a Federal-style home that peers down a shady lawn toward the river, **The Captain Lord Mansion,** Pleasant and Green streets (© **800/522-3141** or 207/967-3141), is one of New England's most architecturally distinguished inns. Check out the grandfather clocks and Chippendale highboys in the front hall. Guest rooms are furnished with antiques, and all feature gas fireplaces; there's not a single unappealing room. Among our favorites: Excelsior, a corner unit with a massive four-poster and a two-person Jacuzzi; and Hesper, the best of the lower-priced rooms. Children 12 and over are welcome. Rates ($248–$419 double) include breakfast.

One of the few resorts that have preserved intact the classic New England vacation experience, **The Colony Hotel,** 140 Ocean Ave. (© **800/552-2363** or 207/967-3331; www.thecolonyhotel.com/maine), is a mammoth Georgian Revival (1914) that lords over the ocean and the mouth of the Kennebunk River. All the bright and cheery rooms in the main inn have been renovated, though few have air-conditioning or TV. Rooms in two of the three outbuildings carry over the rustic elegance of the main hotel; the exception is the East House, a 1950s-era building with 20 uninteresting motel-style rooms. Staff encourages guests to socialize in the evening downstairs in the lobby, on the porch, or at the shuffleboard court, which is lighted for nighttime play. Rates ($145–$545 double) include breakfast.

The Franciscan Guest House, Beach Street (© **207/967-4865;** www.franciscan guesthouse.com), on the grounds of St. Anthony's Monastery, is a unique budget choice. The rooms are institutional, basic, and clean, with private bathrooms; guests can stroll the very attractive riverside grounds or walk to Dock Square, about 10 minutes away. It's not nearly as inexpensive as it used to be, but the place is still an outstanding bargain, especially given the fine walking trails. Rates run $50 to $144 double; credit cards are not accepted.

Prices for lobster in the rough tend to be a bit more expensive around Kennebunkport than farther up the coast. But if you can't wait, **Nunan's Lobster Hut,** on Route 9 north of Kennebunkport at Cape Porpoise (© **207/967-4362**), is a good choice.

Grissini, 27 Western Ave. (© **207/967-2211;** www.restaurantgrissini.com), is a handsome trattoria that offers good value. The mood is elegant but rustic. Italian advertising posters line the walls of the soaring, barnlike space, while the stone fireplace takes the chill off a cool evening. The menu includes a wide range of pastas and pizza, served with considerable flair. Expect an exceedingly pleasant experience. Main courses run $3 to $14.

ACADIA NATIONAL PARK

It's not hard to fathom why Acadia is one of the biggest draws in the U.S. national park system. The park, located on Mount Desert Island, offers a rich tapestry of rugged cliffs, restless ocean, and quiet woods.

The park's more recent roots can be traced back to the 1840s, when Hudson River School painter Thomas Cole packed his sketchbooks and easels for a trip to this remote island, then home to a small number of fishermen and boat builders.

By the early 1900s, the popularity and growing development of the island began to concern its most ardent supporters. Boston textile heir and conservationist George Dorr and Harvard president Charles Eliot, aided by the largesse of John D. Rockefeller, Jr., started acquiring large tracts for the public's enjoyment. These parcels were donated to the government, and in 1919 the land was designated Lafayette National Park. Renamed Acadia in 1929, the park has grown to encompass nearly half the island.

ESSENTIALS

GETTING THERE   Acadia National Park is reached from the town of Ellsworth via **Route 3.** If you're driving from southern Maine, avoid the coastal congestion along **Route 1** by taking the Maine Turnpike to Bangor, picking up **I-395** to **Route 1A,** then continuing south on Route 1A to Ellsworth. It's the quickest route in summer.

Daily flights from Boston to the airport in Trenton, just across the causeway from Mount Desert Island, are offered year-round by US Airways affiliate **Colgan Air** (✆ **207/667-7171;** www.colganair.com). In summer, **Concord Trailways** (✆ **800/ 639-3317** or 207/945-5000; www.concordtrailways.com) offers van service between Bangor (including an airport stop), Ellsworth, and Bar Harbor; reservations are required.

GETTING AROUND   A wonderful, free **shuttle bus** service known as the *Island Explorer* (**www.exploreacadia.com**) was inaugurated as part of an experiment to reduce the number of cars on island roads. It's working. The propane-powered buses, equipped with racks for bikes, serve seven routes that cover nearly the entire island and will stop anywhere you request outside the village centers, including trail heads, ferries, villages, and campgrounds. All routes begin or end at the Village Green in Bar Harbor, but you're encouraged to pick up the bus wherever you're staying, whether motel or campground, to minimize the number of cars in town. Route 3 goes from Bar Harbor along much of the Park Loop, offering easy access to some of the park's best hiking trails. The buses operate from late June to mid-October.

VISITOR INFORMATION   The **Thompson Island Information Center,** on Route 3 (✆ **207/288-3411**), is maintained by the local chambers of commerce; park personnel are usually on hand to answer inquiries. It's the best stop for lodging and restaurant information. The center is open from mid-May to mid-October. For more detailed information, continue on Route 3 to the National Park Service's **Hulls Cove Visitor Center,** about 7½ miles beyond Thompson Island. This stone-walled center includes displays and a short film. You can request brochures on trails and carriage roads, or purchase guidebooks. The center is open from mid-April to October. Information is also available year-round, by phone or in person, from the park's **headquarters** ✆ **207/288-3338;** www.nps.gov/acad), on Route 233 between Bar Harbor and Somesville.

ENTRY POINTS & FEES   A 1-week park pass, which includes unlimited trips on Park Loop Road (which closes in winter), now costs $20 per car, $10 in the off season; there's no additional charge per passenger. Pedestrians, cyclists, and others traveling without a vehicle (basically, motorcyclists and stowaways) must pay a $5 per person fee.

Best Staying & Dining at the White Barn

Part of the exclusive Relais & Châteaux group, Kennebunkport's **White Barn Inn**, Beach Avenue (© **207/967-2321**; www.whitebarninn.com), pampers its guests like no other in Maine. The atmosphere is distinctly European, with an emphasis on service. The rooms are individually decorated in an upscale country style and offer many unexpected niceties, such as robes and fresh flowers in the rooms. Nearly half the rooms have wood-burning fireplaces, while the suites are truly spectacular; each is themed with a separate color, and most have plasma TVs, whirlpools, or similar perks. Guests can avail themselves of the inn's free bikes, or take a cruise on its Hinckley charter yacht. You might also lounge around the beautiful outdoor pool. In 2003, the inn acquired a handful of cottages on the Kennebunk River. The wonderful cottages are cozy, are nicely equipped with modern kitchens and bathrooms, and will continue to see future upgrades; an adjacent "friendship cottage" is stocked at all times with snacks, wine, and the like. Rates ($280–$540 double; $565–$785 suite) include continental breakfast and afternoon tea.

The restaurant here is just as noteworthy as the accommodations, attracting gourmands from New York and Boston and was selected as one of America's top inn restaurants by readers of *Travel + Leisure*. Housed in a rustic barn with a soaring interior and a collection of country antiques displayed in a hayloft, it's pricey but worth it. The setting is magical, the service is attentive, and the kitchen rarely produces a flawed dish. You might start with a lobster spring roll, then graduate to roasted pheasant breast with butternut squash. Anticipate a meal to remember. The fixed-price dinner is $89; a tasting menu costs $105 per person.

The main point of entry to Park Loop Road is the visitor center at **Hulls Cove**. Mount Desert Island consists of an interwoven network of park and town roads, allowing visitors to enter the park at numerous points. A glance at a park map (available free at the visitor center) will make these access points self-evident. The entry fee is collected at a tollbooth on Park Loop Road ½ mile north of Sand Beach.

OUTDOOR PURSUITS

CAMPING   The national park offers no overnight accommodations other than two campgrounds. Both are extremely popular; in July and August, expect them to fill by early to mid-morning.

Blackwoods (© **207/288-3274**) tends to fill first. It has a better location—bikers and pedestrians are just off the Park Loop Road and the rocky shore via a short trail—and, more important, it's the only one of the two that accepts reservations (required from mid-May to mid-Sept). Blackwoods is open year-round; late fall through spring, sites are easy to come by. You can reserve up to 5 months in advance by calling © **800/365-2267**. (This is a national reservations service whose contract is reviewed from time to time by the Park Service; if the number doesn't work, call the campground directly to ask for the current toll-free reservation number.) Reservations may also be made online, between 10am and 10pm only, at **http://reservations.nps.gov**. Fees are $20 per night.

First-come, first-served **Seawall** (✆ **207/244-3600**) is on the quieter western half of the island, near the fishing village of Bass Harbor. This is a good base for road biking, and several short coastal hikes are within easy striking distance. Drive-in RV sites are available, but none have hookups. The campground is open from late May to September. In general, if you get here by 9 or 10am, you'll have little trouble securing a site, even in midsummer. No showers are on-site, but they're available nearby. Fees are $20 for a site with vehicle, $14 for walk-ins.

CARRIAGE RIDES   Carriage rides are offered by **Wildwood Stables** (✆ **207/276-3622**; www.acadia.net/wildwood), a park concessionaire located half a mile south of Jordan Pond House. The 1-hour trip departs three times daily and takes in sweeping ocean views; it costs $14 for adults, $7 for children 6 to 12, and $4 for children 2 to 5. Longer tours are available, as is a special carriage designed to accommodate disabled passengers.

DRIVING THE PARK LOOP ROAD   The 20-mile Park Loop Road is the park's premier attraction. This remarkable roadway starts near the Hulls Cove Visitor Center and follows the high ridges above Bar Harbor before dropping down along the rocky coast. Here, the spires of spruce and fir cap dark granite, and the earthy tones contrast sharply with the frothy white surf and the steely blue sea. After following the picturesque coast and touching on several coves, the road loops back inland along Jordan Pond and Eagle Lake, with a detour to the summit of the island's highest peak.

From about 10am to 4pm in July and August, anticipate large crowds along the Park Loop Road, at least on those days when the sun is shining. Parking lots may fill at some of the more popular destinations, including Sand Beach, Thunder Hole, and the Cadillac Mountain summit. Make the best of wet days by donning rain gear and letting the weather work to your advantage. You'll discover that you have the place to yourself.

HIKING   Acadia National Park has 120 miles of hiking trails, plus 57 miles of carriage roads suitable for walking. The park is studded with low "mountains" (called hills elsewhere), and almost all have trails with superb views of the ocean. Many pathways were crafted by stonemasons and others with high aesthetic intent, and thus the routes aren't the most direct—but they're often the most scenic, taking advantage of fractures in the rocks, picturesque ledges, and sudden vistas.

The Hulls Cove Visitor Center has a brief chart of area hikes; combined with the park map, this is all you'll need to explore the well-maintained, well-marked trails. It's not hard to cobble together loop hikes to make your trips more varied. Coordinate your hiking with the weather; if it's damp or foggy, you'll stay drier and warmer strolling the carriage roads. If it's clear and dry, head for the highest peaks with the best views.

MOUNTAIN BIKING   The 57 miles of **carriage roads** built by John D. Rockefeller, Jr., are among the park's most extraordinary hidden treasures. These were maintained by Rockefeller until his death in 1960, after which they became shaggy and overgrown. A major restoration effort was launched in 1990, and today the roads are superbly restored and maintained. With their wide hard-packed surfaces, gentle grades, and extensive directional signs, they make for very smooth biking. Note that bikes are also allowed on the island's free shuttle buses (see "Getting Around," above).

A useful map of the roads is available free at visitor centers; more detailed guides may be purchased at area bookshops, but aren't necessary. Where carriage roads cross private land (generally between Seal Harbor and Northeast Harbor), they're closed to mountain bikes, which are also banned from hiking trails.

Mountain bikes can be rented along Cottage Street in Bar Harbor, with rates around $17 to $18 for a full day, $12 to $13 for a half-day (which is actually only 4 hr. in the bike-rental universe). Most bike shops include locks and helmets as basic equipment, but ask what's included before you rent. Also ask about closing times, since you'll be able to get in a couple of extra hours with a late-closing shop. **Bar Harbor Bicycle Shop** (© 207/288-3886), at 141 Cottage St., gets my vote for the most convenient and friendliest; you could also try **Acadia Outfitters** (© 207/288-8118), at 106 Cottage St., or **Acadia Bike & Canoe** (© 800/526-8615 or 207/288-9605), at 48 Cottage St.

SEA KAYAKING   Sea kayaking has boomed around Mount Desert Island over the past decade. Experienced kayakers arrive in droves with their own boats. Novices sign up for guided tours that are offered by several outfitters. Many new paddlers have found their inaugural experiences gratifying; others have complained that the quantity of paddlers on quick tours in peak season makes the experience a little too much like a cattle drive to truly enjoy.

A variety of options can be found on the island, ranging from a 2½-hour harbor tour to a 7-hour excursion. Details are available from the following outfitters: **Acadia Outfitters,** 106 Cottage St. (© 207/288-8118); **Coastal Kayaking Tours,** 48 Cottage St. (© 800/526-8615 or 207/288-9605); and **National Park Sea Kayak Tours,** 39 Cottage St. (© 800/347-0940 or 207/288-0342). Rates range from approximately $40 to $50 per person for a 2- to 3-hour harbor or sunset tour, up to $75 for a 1-day excursion.

Sea-kayak rentals are available from **Loon Bay Kayaks,** which is located in summer at Barcadia Campground at the junction of routes 3 and 102 (© 888/786-0676 or 207/288-0099), and which will deliver a boat to you; and from **Aquaterra Adventures,** 1 West St., Bar Harbor (© 207/288-0007). Solo kayaks rent for $25 to $40 per day. With unpredictable weather and squirrelly tides, kayakers are advised to have some prior experience before attempting to set out on their own.

WHERE TO DINE IN THE PARK

Jordan Pond House, on Park Loop Road near Seal Harbor (© 207/276-3316; www.jordanpond.com), is the only full-service restaurant within park boundaries, on a grassy lawn looking northward up Jordan Pond. Afternoon tea with popovers is a hallowed tradition. Ladies who lunch sit next to bikers, and everyone feasts on tasty popovers and strawberry jam served with tea or lemonade. The lobster and crab rolls are abundant and filling; the lobster stew is expensive but good. Dinners include classic resort fare like prime rib and baked scallops. Main courses range from $13 to $19; afternoon tea costs $8.50.

BAR HARBOR
WHERE TO STAY

After a period of quiet decay, Bar Harbor has been revived and rediscovered by both visitors and entrepreneurs. Its history, distinguished architecture, and beautiful location along Frenchman Bay make it a desirable base for exploring the rest of the island, and it offers the most varied selection of lodging, meals, supplies, and services.

Reputable motels in or near town that have some rooms under $100 in peak season include the conveniently located **Villager Motel,** 207 Main St. (© 207/288-3211); the in-town, pet-friendly **Rockhurst Motel,** 68 Mount Desert St. (© 207/288-3140); and the smoke-free **Highbrook Motel,** 94 Eden St. (© 800/338-9688 or

207/288-3591). About 4 miles west of Bar Harbor on Route 3 is **Hanscom's Motel and Cottages** (© **207/288-3744;** www.hanscomsmotel.com), an old-fashioned motor court with 12 units (some two bedrooms) that have been well maintained. Its rates range from $86 to $120 in summer; from $68 off season.

The Bar Harbor Inn, Newport Drive (© **800/248-3351** or 207/288-3351; www. barharborinn.com), is a handsome combination of inn and motel that has the best location of any lodging in Bar Harbor. The rambling, shingled inn on shady waterfront grounds dates back to the turn of the 20th century, and offers convenience and charm. Guest rooms in the Oceanfront and Main Inn feature sweeping views of the bay, and many have private balconies; the less expensive Newport building lacks views but is comfortable and up-to-date. There's a formal dining room and outdoor grill, heated outdoor pool, and fitness room. Rates ($79–$369 double) include continental breakfast.

The handsome pale-green and maroon Victorian stick-style **Primrose Inn,** 73 Mt. Desert St. (© **877/846-3424** or 207/288-4031; www.primroseinn.com), was built in 1878. Comfortable and furnished with functional antiques and more modern reproductions, many rooms have a floral theme and thick carpets. It's not a stuffy place—it has a distinctly informal air that encourages guests to mingle and relax in the common room, equipped with a piano. Two guest rooms feature whirlpools or fireplaces. The suites in the rear are spacious and comfortable, and the efficiencies offer a kitchen (they rent by the week only). Daily rates ($95–$215 double) include breakfast; efficiencies cost $650 to $1,200 per week.

WHERE TO DINE

If you're needing a light bite or breakfast, our local favorite is **Cottage Street Bakery and Deli** (© **207/388-1010**) at 59 Cottage St. Egg dishes, omelets, blueberry pancakes, and baked goods are all well done, and there are plenty of coffee drinks; I also like the outdoor patio. The kids' menu is fun and welcome.

Café This Way, 14½ Mount Desert St. (© **207/288-4483;** www.cafethisway.com), has the feel of a hip coffeehouse; bookshelves line one wall, and there's a bar tucked into a nook. The breakfasts are excellent and mildly sinful, with offerings such as eggs Benedict with spinach, artichoke, and tomato. The robust coffee requires two creamers to lighten it. Dinners are equally appetizing, with tasty dishes such as filet mignon grilled with fresh basil. Main courses cost $14 to $23.

Right across the street from the bay, chef Mark Rampacek operates Bar Harbor's only vegetarian eatery, **Eden Vegetarian Café,** 78 West St. (© **207/288-4422;** www. barharborvegetarian.com), bringing high culinary flair and atmosphere to the cause; most dishes here use organic and/or locally grown ingredients, and you might want to dress up a bit if you dine here. The menu changes daily. There's a full range of coffees and teas, and a full bar. Main courses cost $9 to $17.

For more than 2 decades, **George's,** 7 Stephens Lane (© **207/288-4505;** www. georgesbarharbor.com), has been a Bar Harbor classic, offering fine dining in elegant yet informal surroundings. The place captures the joyous feel of summer with four smallish dining rooms and plenty of open windows, plus additional seating on the terrace outside—the best place to watch the gentle dusk settle over town. The service is upbeat, the meals wonderfully prepared. All entrees sell for one price, which includes salad, vegetable, and potato or rice. The house specialty is lamb in its many incarnations. Entrees cost $25; a three-course meal runs $37 to $40.

3

The Mid-Atlantic

Part of the thrill of visiting the mid-Atlantic states is following in the footsteps of George Washington, John D. Rockefeller, Franklin D. Roosevelt, Robert E. Lee, and many others who cut wide paths through American history. In New York City, pay your respects to Lady Liberty overlooking the city's famous harbor or stroll the Brooklyn Bridge, still one of the country's most famous architectural achievements. Then head off to the Hudson River Valley, the playground of such famous names as Rockefeller, Vanderbilt, and Roosevelt. In Philadelphia, you can see where the Founding Fathers crafted the U.S. Constitution. In Baltimore, you can dine on Chesapeake Bay crabs near where Francis Scott Key wrote the words to "The Star-Spangled Banner." In Washington, D.C., you can see the flag that inspired Key to write his famous words at the famous Smithsonian Institution, arguably the greatest museum in the world. Then it's off to explore such American icons as the White House, the Capitol, and the Supreme Court.

Today New York City, Philadelphia, Baltimore, and Washington are part of the great East Coast megalopolis running south from Boston, but you can easily escape to broad bays, wide rivers, rolling piedmont, gentle mountains, and quaint small towns that make this region lovely and charming. Few places are as charming as the Brandywine Valley, loaded with both natural beauty and historical significance.

Whether it's the hubbub of New York City and Washington, D.C., or the quiet charm of Lancaster County and the Adirondacks, the mid-Atlantic really does have something for everyone.

1 New York City

New York City is the nerve center of world finance and trade; the international hub of advertising, publishing, entertainment, and fashion; and the creative core for the arts. Just about every language and any dialect is spoken here, from Mandarin to Brooklynese, and no other dot on the map is quite so ethnically, culturally, socially, and economically diverse. This is a city that is in a constant state of flux, and it is this ebb and flow that keeps New Yorkers from leaving despite the high rents, the noise, the crowds, the cabdrivers who don't know Lincoln Center from the Lower East Side, and the more stark realities of high-security-alert days and living in the shadow of great tragedy. Nowhere else is the challenge so tough, the pace so relentless, the stimuli so ever-changing and insistent—and the payoff so rewarding. It is why the city goes on and the residents proudly persist in living their vibrant lives.

ESSENTIALS
GETTING THERE
BY PLANE   Three major airports serve New York City: **John F. Kennedy International Airport** (© 718/244-4444) in Queens, about 15 miles from Midtown Manhattan; **LaGuardia Airport** (© 718/533-3400), also in Queens, about 8 miles from

The Mid-Atlantic

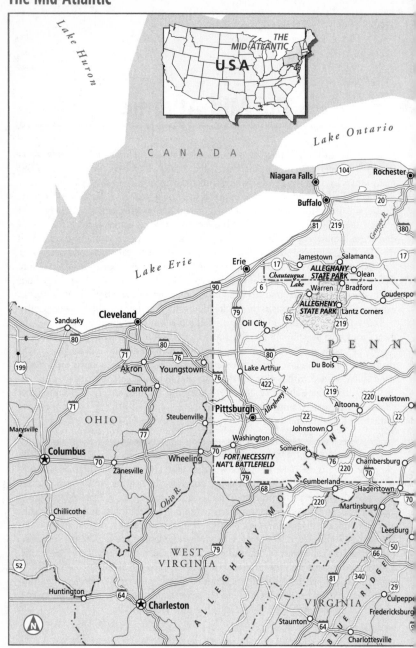

THE MID-ATLANTIC

USA

Lake Huron

Lake Ontario

CANADA

Niagara Falls   104   Rochester

Buffalo   81   219   20   380

Genesee R.

Lake Erie   Erie   17   Jamestown   Salamanca   17

Chautauqua Lake   ALLEGHANY STATE PARK   Olean

90   6   Warren   Bradford

Coudersport

ALLEGHENY STATE PARK   Lantz Corners

Sandusky   79   Oil City   62   219

Cleveland   PENN

6   80   80   Du Bois

199   71   76   Lake Arthur   219   220   Lewistown

Akron   Youngstown   76   422   Altoona   22

Canton   Allegheny R.   Pittsburgh   22

OHIO   Steubenville   Johnstown

Marysville   77   Washington   Somerset   76   Chambersburg

Columbus   70   Wheeling   70   FORT NECESSITY NAT'L BATTLEFIELD   220

Zanesville   79   Cumberland   70

68   Hagerstown

Chillicothe   220   Martinsburg   70

Ohio R.   Leesburg

52   WEST VIRGINIA   79   50

66

Huntington   64   81   340   29

52   ALLEGHENY MOUNTAINS   VIRGINIA   Culpeper

Charleston   Fredericksburg

N   Staunton   64   BLUE RIDGE

Charlottesville

Midtown; and **Newark International Airport** (© **973/961-6000**) in nearby New Jersey, about 16 miles from Midtown. Almost every major domestic carrier serves at least one of the New York–area airports; most serve two or all three. Information about all three airports is available online at **www.panynj.gov**.

For complete transportation information for all three airports, call **Air-Ride** (© **800/247-7433**), which offers 24-hour recorded details on bus and shuttle companies and private car services registered with the New York and New Jersey Port Authority. Similar information is available at **www.panynj.gov/airports**; just click on the airport at which you'll be arriving. Generally, travel time between the airports and Midtown Manhattan by taxi or car is 45 to 60 minutes for JFK, 20 to 35 minutes for LaGuardia, and 35 to 50 minutes for Newark. Always allow extra time, though, especially during rush hour, during peak holiday travel times, and if you're taking a bus.

SuperShuttle (© **212/258-3826;** www.supershuttle.com) serves all three airports. One-way fares average $13 to $22 depending on the airport, with discounts available for prepaid round-trips or large parties. You don't need to reserve your airport-to-Manhattan ride, though you will need to schedule pickup to return to the airport.

New York Airport Service (© **718/875-8200;** www.nyairportservice.com) buses travel from JFK and LaGuardia to the Port Authority Bus Terminal (42nd St. and Eighth Ave.), Grand Central Terminal (Park Ave. between 41st and 42nd sts.), and to select Midtown hotels between 27th and 59th streets, plus the Jamaica LIRR Station in Queens, where you can pick up a train for Long Island. One-way fare for JFK is $15, $27 round-trip; to LaGuardia it's $12 one-way and $21 round-trip. **Olympia Airport Express** (© **212/964-6233;** www.olympiabus.com) provides service every 15 to 30 minutes from Newark Airport to Penn Station (34th St. and Eighth Ave), the Port Authority Bus Terminal, and Grand Central Terminal. Call for the exact schedule for your return trip to the airport. The one-way fare runs $13, $22 round-trip; seniors and passengers with disabilities ride for $6.

The shuttle services are our favorite option for getting to and from the airports during peak travel times because the drivers take local streets that end up getting you there faster than a taxi. And taxis from all three airports can be a very expensive proposition (despite flat-rate fares, you can run up a $60 bill when you toss in tolls and tip).

BY TRAIN Amtrak (© **800/USA-RAIL;** www.amtrak.com) runs frequent service to New York City's **Penn Station,** on Seventh Avenue between 31st and 33rd streets. If you're traveling along Amtrak's Northeast Corridor—to or from Boston, Philadelphia, Baltimore, or Washington, D.C.—Amtrak may be your best travel bet. The **Acela Express** trains cut travel time from D.C. down to 2½ hours, and travel time from Boston to a lightning-quick 3 hours.

BY BUS Buses arrive at the **Port Authority Terminal** (© **212/564-8484;** www.ny. com/transportation/port_authority.html), on Eighth Avenue between 40th and 42nd streets. The fares up and down the East Coast are usually cheaper than the train fares, and if you get an express bus, they don't take much longer. Call **Greyhound Bus Lines** (© **800/231-2222;** www.greyhound.com).

VISITOR INFORMATION

For information before you leave home, your best source (besides this book, of course) is **NYC & Company,** the organization that fronts the New York Convention & Visitors Bureau (NYCVB), 810 Seventh Ave., New York, NY 10019. You can call © **800/ NYC-VISIT** to order the **Official NYC Visitor Kit,** which contains the *Official NYC*

Guide detailing hotels, restaurants, theaters, attractions, events, and more; a foldout map; a decent newsletter on the latest goings-on in the city; and brochures on attractions and services. It costs $5.95 to receive the packet (payable by credit card) in 7 to 10 days, $9.95 for rush delivery (3–4 business days) to U.S. addresses and international orders. (***Note:*** I have received complaints that packages don't always strictly adhere to these time frames.)

You can also find a wealth of free information on the bureau's website, **www.nyc visit.com**. To speak with a travel counselor who can answer specific questions, call ℂ **212/484-1222,** which is staffed weekdays from 8:30am to 6pm EST, weekends from 9am to 5pm EST.

GETTING AROUND
Do not even think of driving in Manhattan. Traffic is horrendous, and you don't know the rules of the road or the arcane alternate-side-of-the-street parking regulations. If you do arrive in New York City by car, park it in a garage (expect to pay at least $25–$45 per day) and leave it there for the duration of your stay.

For the most part, you can get where you're going in Manhattan pretty quickly and easily using some combination of subways, buses, and cabs; this section will tell you how to do just that. But between traffic gridlock and subway delays, sometimes you just can't get there from here—unless you walk. During rush hours, you'll easily beat car traffic on foot. You'll also just see a whole lot more by walking than you will if you ride beneath the street in the subway or fly by in a cab. So pack your most comfortable shoes and hit the pavement—it's the best, cheapest, and most appealing way to experience the city. ***Tip:*** *Never take your walking cues from the locals.* Wait for walk signals and always use crosswalks—don't cross in the middle of the block. Do otherwise and you could quickly end up as a flattened statistic.

BY SUBWAY   Run by the **Metropolitan Transit Authority (MTA),** the much-maligned subway system is actually the fastest way to travel around New York, especially during rush hours. The subway is quick, inexpensive, relatively safe, and pretty efficient, as well as being a genuine New York experience.

The **subway** runs 24 hours a day, 7 days a week. The rush-hour crushes are roughly from 8 to 9:30am and from 5 to 6:30pm on weekdays; the rest of the time the trains are much more manageable.

Less expensive than taxis and more pleasant than subways (they provide a mobile sightseeing window on Manhattan), **MTA buses** are a good transportation option, especially of you're going crosstown or a short distance (take the subway for longer trips). Their very big drawback: They can get stuck in traffic, sometimes making it quicker to walk. For long distances, the subway is your best bet; but for short distances or traveling crosstown, try the bus.

Paying Your Way   Subway and bus fares are $2 (half price for seniors and those with disabilities), and children under 44 inches tall ride free (up to three per adult).

You pay your fare with a **MetroCard,** a magnetically encoded card that debits the fare when swiped through the turnstile (or the fare box on any city bus). Once you're in the system, you can transfer freely to any subway line that you can reach without exiting your station. MetroCards also allow you **free transfers** between the bus and subway within a 2-hour period.

MetroCards can be purchased from each station's staffed token booth, where you can only pay with cash; at the ATM-style vending machines now located in just about

Subway Service Alert

On almost every weekend, and throughout the year, changes in normal subway service tend to occur. We strongly recommend you check with the **Metropolitan Transit Authority** at ✆ **718/330-1234** or **www.mta.nyc.ny.us** before you plan your travel routes; your hotel concierge or any token booth clerk should also be able to assist you. Riders with disabilities should direct inquiries to ✆ **718/596-8585**; hearing-impaired riders can call ✆ **718/596-8273**.

every subway station in the city, which accept cash, credit cards, and debit cards; from a MetroCard merchant, such as most Rite Aid drugstores or Hudson News at Penn Station and Grand Central Terminal; or at the MTA information desk at the Times Square Visitor Center, 1560 Broadway, between 46th and 47th streets.

MetroCards come in a few different configurations:

Pay-Per-Ride MetroCards can be used for up to four people by swiping up to four times (bring the whole family). You can put any amount from $4 (two rides) to $80 on your card. Every time you put $10 or $20 on your Pay-Per-Ride MetroCard, it's automatically credited 20%—that's one free ride for every $10, or five trips. You can refill your card at any time until the expiration date on the card, usually about a year from the date of purchase, at any subway station.

Unlimited-Ride MetroCards, which can't be used for more than one person at a time or more frequently than 18-minute intervals, are available in three values: the **daily Fun Pass,** which allows you a day's worth of unlimited subway and bus rides for $7; the **7-Day MetroCard,** for $24; and the **30-Day MetroCard,** for $76. Seven- and 30-day Unlimited-Ride MetroCards can be purchased at any subway station or from a MetroCard merchant. Fun Passes, however, can only be bought at a MetroCard vending machine; from a MetroCard merchant; or at the MTA information desk at the Times Square Visitor Center. Unlimited-Ride MetroCards go into effect the first time you *use* them—so if you buy a card on Monday and don't begin to use it until Wednesday, Wednesday is when the clock starts ticking on your MetroCard. A Fun Pass is good from the first time you use it until 3am the next day, while 7- and 30-day MetroCards run out at midnight on the last day. These MetroCards cannot be refilled; throw them out once they've been used up and buy a new one.

For MetroCard questions, call ✆ **800/METROCARD** or 212/METROCARD (212/638-7622) Monday through Friday between 7am and 11pm, Saturday and Sunday from 9am to 5pm. Or go online to **www.mta.nyc.ny.us/metrocard**, which can give you a full rundown of MetroCard merchants in the tristate area.

BY TAXI If you don't want to deal with public transportation, then take a taxi. The biggest advantages are, of course, that cabs can be hailed on any street (providing you find an empty one—often simple, yet at other times nearly impossible) and will take you right to your destination. We find they're best used at night when there's little traffic to keep them from speeding you to your destination and when the subway may seem a little daunting.

Official New York City taxis, licensed by the Taxi and Limousine Commission (TLC), are yellow, with the rates printed on the door and a light with a medallion number on the roof. You can hail a taxi on any street. *Never* accept a ride from any other car except an official city yellow cab (private livery cars are not allowed to pick up fares on the street). The cost is 40¢ for every ⅕ mile or 40¢ per minute in stopped or very slow-moving traffic. You must pay bridge or tunnel tolls. You'll also pay a $1 surcharge between 4 and 8pm and a 50¢ surcharge after 8pm and before 6am. A 15% to 20% tip is customary.

Always make sure the meter is turned on at the start of the ride. You'll see the red LED readout register the base fare of $2.50 and start calculating the fare as you go. We've witnessed unscrupulous drivers buzzing unsuspecting visitors around the city with the meter off, and then overcharging them at drop-off time. Be sure to ask for a receipt when you get out of the cab—it'll come in handy if you need to make a complaint or accidentally leave something behind in the cab. For driver complaints and lost property, call the 24-hour Consumer Hotline at ✆ 212/NYC-TAXI. For further taxi information, point your browser to **www.ci.nyc.ny.us/taxi**.

FAST FACTS

Walk-in service for non-emergency illnesses is available from **DOCS at New York Healthcare**, 55 E. 34th St., between Park and Madison avenues (✆ 212/252-6001; subway: 6 to 33rd St.). Hospitals with emergency rooms include **Beth Israel Medical Center**, First Avenue and 16th Street (✆ 212/420-2000; subway: L to First Ave.); **New York University Medical Center**, 560 First Ave., at 33rd Street (✆ 212/263-7300; subway: 6 to 33rd St.); and many others. There are several 24-hour pharmacies, including **Duane Reade** at Broadway and 57th Street (✆ 212/541-9708; subway: A, B, C, D, 1, or 9 to 59th St./Columbus Circle). **Sales tax** is 8.625% on meals, most goods, and some services. **Hotel tax** is 13.25% plus $2 per room per night (including sales tax). **Parking garage tax** is 18.25%.

SPECIAL EVENTS & FESTIVALS

For a complete New York City events schedule, point your browser to **www.nycvisit. com** and click on "Calendar of Events." Here are some favorites:

The ultimate purebred pooch fest and one of the oldest events in the nation (129 years and counting), **Westminster Kennel Club Dog Show** takes place in mid-February inside **Madison Square Garden.** Some 30,000 dog fanciers from all over the world show up at this "World Series of Dogdom."

More than 150,000 marchers participate in the **St. Patrick's Day Parade** March 17, as Fifth Avenue from 44th to 86th streets rings with the sounds of bands and bagpipes. The parade usually starts at 11am, but go extra early if you want a good spot.

The U.S. Open Tennis Championships, the final grand slam event on the tennis calendar, are held at the Arthur Ashe Stadium at the USTA National Tennis Center, the largest public tennis center in the world, at **Flushing Meadows Park** in Queens around Labor Day.

The Greenwich Village Halloween Parade is Halloween at its most outrageous. It's on October 31, of course. The **New York City Marathon** features some 30,000 hopefuls from around the world; more than a million fans will cheer them on as they follow a route that touches on all five New York boroughs and finishes at Central Park.

Macy's Thanksgiving Day Parade that proceeds from Central Park West and 77th Street and down Broadway to Herald Square at 34th Street continues to be a national tradition. The night before, you can usually see the big blow-up on Central Park West at 79th Street. On **New Year's Eve,** the biggest party of them all happens in **Times Square,** where thousands of raucous revelers count down in unison the year's final seconds until the new lighted ball drops at midnight.

WHAT TO SEE & DO
SOME TOP ATTRACTIONS

In addition to the choices below, don't forget about **Central Park,** the great green swath that is, just by virtue of its existence, Manhattan's greatest marvel.

American Folk Art Museum   This gorgeous, ultramodern boutique museum is not only a stunning structure, but also heralds American folk art's entry into the top echelon of museum-worthy art. The modified open-plan interior features an extraordinary collection of traditional works from the 18th century to the self-taught artists and craftspeople of the present, reflecting the breadth and vitality of the American folk-art tradition. A splendid variety of quilts, in particular, makes the textiles collection the museum's most popular.

45 W. 53rd St. (between Fifth and Sixth aves.). © **212/265-1040.** www.folkartmuseum.org. Admission $9 adults, $7 seniors and students, free for children under 12, free to all Fri 5:30–8pm. Tues–Thurs and Sat–Sun 10:30am–5:30pm; Fri 10:30am–7:30pm. Subway: E or V to Fifth Ave.

American Museum of Natural History   This is one of the hottest museum tickets in town, thanks to the **Rose Center for Earth and Space,** whose planetarium sphere hosts the Space Show, "Are We Alone?" The diversity of the museum's holdings is astounding: some 36 million specimens ranging from microscopic organisms to the world's largest cut gem, the Brazilian Princess Topaz (21,005 carats). Rose Center aside, it would take you all day to see the entire museum, and then you *still* wouldn't get to everything. If you don't have a lot of time, you can see the best of the best on free **highlights tours** offered daily every hour at 15 minutes after the hour from 10:15am to 3:15pm. If you only see one exhibit, see the **dinosaurs,** which take up the entire fourth floor. The magical **Butterfly Conservatory,** a walk-in enclosure housing nearly 500 free-flying tropical butterflies, has developed into a can't-miss fixture from October through May; check to see if it's in the house while you're in town.

Central Park West (between 77th and 81st sts.). © **212/769-5100** for information, or 212/769-5200 for tickets (tickets can also be ordered online). www.amnh.org. Suggested admission $14 adults, $11 seniors and students, $8 children 2–12; Space Show and museum admission $30 adults, $23 seniors and students, $19 children under 12. Additional charges for IMAX movies and some special exhibitions. Daily 10am–5:45pm; Rose Center open 1st Fri of every month until 8:45pm. Subway: B or C to 81st St.; 1 to 79th St.

Bronx Zoo Wildlife Conservation Park *Kids*   Founded in 1899, the Bronx Zoo is the largest metropolitan animal park in the United States, with more than 4,000 animals living on 265 acres. One of the most impressive exhibits is the **Wild Asia Complex,** where you'll find an indoor re-creation of Asian forests, with birds, lizards, gibbons, and leopards; and the **Bengali Express Monorail** (open May–Oct), which takes you on a narrated ride high above free-roaming Siberian tigers, Asian elephants, Indian rhinoceroses, and other nonnative New Yorkers. The **Himalayan Highlands** is home to some 17 extremely rare snow leopards, as well as red pandas and white-naped cranes. The **Children's Zoo** (open Apr–Oct) allows young humans to learn about their wildlife counterparts.

Fordham Rd. and Bronx River Pkwy., the Bronx. © **718/367-1010.** www.bronxzoo.com. Admission $11 adults, $8 seniors and children 2–12; discounted admission Nov–Mar; free Wed year-round. There may be nominal additional charges for some exhibits. Nov–Mar daily 10am–4:30pm (extended hours for Holiday Lights late Nov to early Jan); Apr–Oct Mon–Fri 10am–5pm, Sat–Sun 10am–5:30pm. Transportation: See "Getting There," above.

Brooklyn Bridge *Value*   Its Gothic-inspired stone pylons and intricate steel-cable webs have moved poets like Walt Whitman and Hart Crane to sing the praises of this

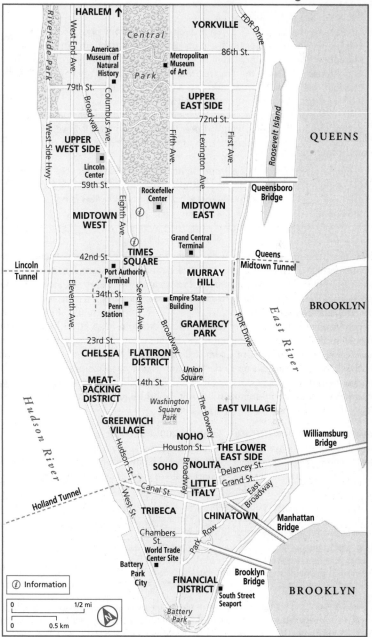

Manhattan Neighborhoods

HARLEM ↑

Central Park

YORKVILLE

FDR Drive

American Museum of Natural History

Metropolitan Museum of Art

86th St.

West End Ave.

Riverside Park

79th St.

Columbus Ave.

Broadway

West Side Hwy.

UPPER WEST SIDE

Lincoln Center

59th St.

Eighth Ave.

UPPER EAST SIDE

72nd St.

Fifth Ave.

Lexington Ave.

First Ave.

Roosevelt Island

QUEENS

Rockefeller Center

MIDTOWN WEST

MIDTOWN EAST

Queensboro Bridge

42nd St.

TIMES SQUARE

Port Authority Terminal

Grand Central Terminal

Queens Midtown Tunnel

Lincoln Tunnel

34th St.

Penn Station

Eleventh Ave.

Seventh Ave.

MURRAY HILL

Empire State Building

BROOKLYN

Broadway

GRAMERCY PARK

FDR Drive

East River

23rd St.

CHELSEA

FLATIRON DISTRICT

MEAT-PACKING DISTRICT

14th St.

Union Square

GREENWICH VILLAGE

Washington Square Park

EAST VILLAGE

Hudson River

NOHO

Houston St.

The Bowery

Williamsburg Bridge

SOHO

NOLITA

THE LOWER EAST SIDE

Delancey St.

Hudson St.

Broadway

LITTLE ITALY

Grand St.

Canal St.

West St.

TRIBECA

CHINATOWN

East Broadway

Manhattan Bridge

Holland Tunnel

Chambers St.

Park Row

World Trade Center Site

Battery Park City

Brooklyn Bridge

ⓘ Information

FINANCIAL DISTRICT

South Street Seaport

BROOKLYN

0   1/2 mi

0   0.5 km

N

Battery Park

Money- & Time-Saving Tip

CityPass may be New York's best sightseeing deal. Pay one price ($63, or $46 for kids 12–17) for admission to six major Big Apple attractions: The American Museum of Natural History (admission only; does not include Space Show), the Guggenheim Museum, the Empire State Building, the *Intrepid* Sea-Air-Space Museum, the Museum of Modern Art, and a 2-hour Circle Line harbor cruise. Individual tickets would cost more than twice as much.

More important, CityPass is not a coupon book. It contains actual admission tickets, so you can bypass lengthy ticket lines. This can literally save you hours of time, because popular sights such as the Empire State Building often have ticket lines of an hour or more.

CityPass is good for 9 days from the first time you use it. It's sold at all participating attractions and online at **http://citypass.com**. For more information, call CityPass at ✆ **208/787-4300** (note, however, that CityPass is not sold over the phone).

great span, completed in 1883. Walking the Brooklyn Bridge is one of our all-time favorite New York activities, although there's no doubt that the Lower Manhattan views from the bridge now have a painful resonance as well as a joyous spirit. A wide wood-plank pedestrian walkway is elevated above the traffic, making it a relatively peaceful, and popular, walk.

For Manhattan skyline views, take an A or C train to High Street, one stop into Brooklyn. From there, you'll be on the bridge in no time: Come aboveground, then walk through the little park to Cadman Plaza East and head downslope (left) to the stairwell that will take you up to the footpath. (Following Prospect Place under the bridge, then turning right onto Cadman Plaza E., will also take you directly to the stairwell.) It's a 20- to 40-minute stroll over the bridge to Manhattan.

Subway: A or C to High St.; 4, 5, or 6 to Brooklyn Bridge–City Hall.

Center for Jewish History This 125,000-square-foot complex is the largest repository of Jewish history, art, and literature in the Diaspora. The collection includes 100 million archival documents, 500,000 books, and tens of thousands of objects of art and ephemera, ranging from Thomas Jefferson's letter denouncing anti-Semitism to memorabilia of famous Jewish athletes. The main gallery space is the Yeshiva Museum, which comprises four galleries, a genealogical research facility, an outdoor sculpture garden, and a children's workshop; a range of exhibits also showcase various holdings belonging to the other institutions as well.

15 W. 16th St. (between Fifth and Sixth aves.). ✆ 212/294-8301. www.cjh.org. Admission to Yeshiva University Museum $8 adults, $6 seniors and students; free admission to all other facilities. Yeshiva University Museum Sun and Tues–Thurs 11am–5pm. Reading Room and Genealogy Institute Mon–Thurs 9:30am–5pm; Fri by appt. All other exhibition galleries Mon–Thurs 9am–5pm; Fri 9am–4pm. Subway: L, N, R, 4, 5, or 6 to 14th St./Union Sq.; F or V to 14th St.

The Cloisters This remote yet lovely spot is devoted to the art and architecture of medieval Europe. Atop a cliff overlooking the Hudson River, you'll find a 12th-century chapter house, parts of five cloisters from medieval monasteries, a Romanesque chapel, and a 12th-century Spanish apse brought intact from Europe. Surrounded by peaceful gardens, this is the one place on the island that can even approximate the kind of solitude suitable to such a collection. Inside you'll find extraordinary works that include the famed unicorn tapestries, sculpture, illuminated manuscripts, stained glass, ivory, and precious metalwork.

At the north end of Fort Tryon Park. ℂ **212/923-3700**. www.metmuseum.org. Suggested admission (includes same-day entrance to the Metropolitan Museum of Art) $15 adults, $10 seniors, $7 students, free for children under 12. Nov–Feb Tues–Sun 9:30am–4:45pm; Mar–Oct Tues–Sun 9:30am–5:15pm. Subway: A to 190th St., then a 10-min. walk north along Margaret Corbin Dr., or pick up the M4 bus at the station (1 stop to Cloisters). Bus: M4 Madison Ave. (Fort Tryon Park–The Cloisters).

Ellis Island   Roughly 40% of Americans can trace their heritage back to an ancestor who came through Ellis Island. For the 62 years when it was America's main entry point for immigrants (1892–1954), Ellis Island processed some 12 million people. The **Immigration Museum** relates the story of immigration in America by placing the emphasis on personal experience. What might be the most poignant exhibit is *Treasures from Home,* 1,000 objects and photos donated by descendants of immigrants, including family heirlooms, religious articles, and rare clothing and jewelry. Outside, the **American Immigrant Wall of Honor** commemorates more than 500,000 immigrants and their families. *Touring tips:* Ferries run daily to Ellis Island and Liberty Island from Battery Park and Liberty State Park at frequent intervals; see the Statue of Liberty listing (p. 115) for details.

In New York Harbor. ℂ **212/363-3200** (general info), or 212/269-5755 (ticket/ferry info). www.nps.gov/elis or www.ellisisland.org. Free admission (ferry ticket charge). Daily 9:30am–5:15pm (last ferry departs around 3:30pm). For subway and ferry details, see the Statue of Liberty listing on p. 115 (ferry trip includes stops at both sights).

Empire State Building   It took 60,000 tons of steel, 10 million bricks, 2½ million feet of electrical wire, 120 miles of pipe, and 7 million worker-hours to build. On September 11, 2001, it once again regained its status as New York City's tallest building. And through it all, the Empire State Building has remained one of the city's favorite landmarks, and its signature high-rise. Completed in 1931, the limestone-and-stainless-steel streamline Deco dazzler climbs 102 stories (1,454 ft.); it harbors the offices of fashion firms and, in its upper reaches, a jumble of broadcast equipment. It glows every night, bathed in colored floodlights to commemorate events of significance—red, white, and blue for Independence Day, and so forth. The familiar silver spire can be seen from all over the city. But the views that keep nearly three million visitors coming every year are the ones from the 86th- and 102nd-floor **observatories.** The lower one is best; the higher observation deck is glass-enclosed and cramped.

350 Fifth Ave. (at 34th St.). ℂ **212/736-3100**. www.esbnyc.com. Observatory admission $16 adults, $14 seniors and children 12–17, $10 children 6–11, free for children under 6. Daily 8am–midnight; last elevator at 11:15pm. Subway: B, D, F, N, R, Q, V, or W to 34th St.; 6 to 33rd St.

The Frick Collection   This museum, housed in an 18th-century French-style mansion (1914)—one of the most beautiful remaining on Fifth Avenue—is a living testament to New York's vanished Gilded Age. Come here to see the classics by some of the world's most famous painters: Titian, Bellini, Rembrandt, Turner, Vermeer, and El Greco, to name a few. A highlight of the collection is the **Fragonard Room,** graced with the sensual rococo series *The Progress of Love.* Included in the price of admission, the audio tour is particularly useful because it allows you to follow your own path rather than a prescribed route.

1 E. 70th St. (at Fifth Ave.). ℂ **212/288-0700**. www.frick.org. Admission $15 adults, $10 seniors, $5 students. Children under 10 not admitted; children under 16 must be accompanied by an adult. Tues–Sat 10am–6pm; Sun 11am–5pm. Closed all major holidays. Subway: 6 to 68th St./Hunter College.

Grand Central Terminal   The 1913 landmark has been reborn as one of the most magnificent public spaces in the country. Its restoration is an utter triumph, putting the "grand" back into Grand Central. The greatest visual impact comes when you enter the vast **main concourse.** The high windows once again allow sunlight to penetrate the space, glinting off the half-acre Tennessee marble floor. The masterful **sky ceiling,** again a brilliant greenish blue, depicts the constellations of the winter sky above New York. They're lit with 59 stars, surrounded by 24-carat gold and emitting light fed through fiber-optic cables, their intensities roughly replicating the magnitude of the actual stars as seen from earth. The **Municipal Art Society** (© **212/935-3960;** www.mas.org) offers a walking tour of Grand Central Terminal on Wednesday at 12:30pm, which meets at the information booth on the Grand Concourse (there is a $10 "suggested donation" for the tour).

42nd St. at Park Ave. © 212/340-2210 (events hot line). www.grandcentralterminal.com. Subway: S, 4, 5, 6, or 7 to 42nd St./Grand Central.

Metropolitan Museum of Art *Best*   Home of blockbuster after blockbuster exhibition, the Metropolitan Museum of Art attracts some five million people a year, more than any other spot in New York City. This is the largest museum in the Western Hemisphere. Nearly all the world's cultures are on display through the ages—from Egyptian mummies to ancient Greek statuary to Islamic carvings to Renaissance paintings to Native American masks to 20th-century decorative arts—and masterpieces are the rule. Unless you plan on spending your entire vacation in the museum, you cannot see the entire collection. Our recommendation is to give it a good day—or better yet, 2 half-days so you don't burn out. One good way to get an overview is to take advantage of the **Museum Highlights Tour,** offered every day at various times throughout the day (usually 10:15am–3:15pm). The least overwhelming way to see the Met on your own is to pick up a map at the round desk in the entry hall and choose to concentrate on what you like, whether it's 17th-century paintings, American furniture, or the art of the South Pacific. Don't forget the marvelous **special exhibitions,** which can range from "Orazio and Artemisia Gentileschi: Father and Daughter Painters in Baroque Italy" to "Mother of Pearl: A Tradition in Asian Lacquer."

Fifth Ave. at 82nd St. © 212/535-7710. www.metmuseum.org. Admission (includes same-day entrance to the Cloisters) $15 adults, $10 seniors and students, free for children under 12 when accompanied by an adult. Sun, holiday Mon (Memorial Day, Labor Day, and so on), and Tues–Thurs 9:30am–5:30pm; Fri–Sat 9:30am–9pm. Strollers are permitted in most areas—inquire at Information Desks for gallery limitations. Oversize and jogging strollers are prohibited. Subway: 4, 5, or 6 to 86th St.

Museum of Modern Art   After 2 years of temporary exile in Queens, MoMA returned to its original Manhattan location in late 2004. Its 630,000-square-foot quarters, designed by Yoshio Taniguchi, highlight space and light, with open rooms, high ceilings, and gardens—a beautiful work of architecture and a perfect complement to the art that resides within. This is where you'll find van Gogh's *Starry Night,* Cézanne's *Bather,* Picasso's *Les Demoiselles d'Avignon,* and the great sculpture by Rodin, *Monument to Balzac.* We like to browse the fun "Architecture and Design" department, with examples of design for appliances, furniture, and even sports cars. But the heart of the museum remains the **Abby Aldrich Rockefeller Sculpture Garden.** Our big complaint: The *very* high ($20) admission charge for adults.

11 W. 53rd St. (between Fifth and Sixth aves.). © 212/708-9400. www.moma.org. Admission $20 adults, $16 seniors, $12 students, children under 16 free accompanied by an adult. Free admission Fri 4–8pm. Sat–Mon and Wed–Thurs 10:30am–5:30pm; Fri 10:30am–8pm. Subway: E or V to Fifth Ave.; B, D, or E to Seventh Ave.

Rockefeller Center   A streamlined modern masterpiece, Rockefeller Center is one of New York's central gathering spots for visitors and New Yorkers alike. A prime example of the city's skyscraper spirit and historical sense of optimism, it was erected mainly in the 1930s, when the city was deep in the Depression as well as its most passionate Art Deco phase. The **Rink at Rockefeller Center** (© 212/332-7654; www.rockefellercenter.com) is tiny but romantic, especially during the holidays, when the giant Christmas tree's multicolored lights twinkle from above. **NBC** television maintains studios throughout the complex, and the 70-minute **NBC Studio Tour** (© 212/664-3700; www.nbcsuperstore.com) will take you behind the scenes at the Peacock network. **Radio City Music Hall,** 1260 Sixth Ave., at 50th Street (© 212/247-4777; www.radiocity.com), is perhaps the most impressive architectural feat of the complex. Designed by Donald Deskey and opened in 1932, it's one of the largest indoor theaters, with 6,200 seats. But its true grandeur derives from its magnificent Art Deco appointments. The crowning touch is the stage's great proscenium arch, which evokes a faraway sun setting on the horizon of the sea. The theater hosts the annual **Christmas Spectacular,** starring the Rockettes. The 1-hour **Stage Door Tour** is offered Monday through Saturday from 10am to 5pm, Sunday from 11am to 5pm; tickets are $16 for adults, $10 for children under 12.

Between 48th and 50th sts., from Fifth to Sixth aves. © **212/332-6868**. www.rockefellercenter.com. Subway: B, D, F, or V to 47th–50th sts./Rockefeller Center.

Solomon R. Guggenheim Museum   It's been called a bun, a snail, a concrete tornado, and a giant wedding cake. Whatever description you choose to apply, Frank Lloyd Wright's only New York building, completed in 1959, is a brilliant work of architecture. Inside, a spiraling rotunda circles over a slowly inclined ramp that leads you past changing exhibits. Permanent exhibits of 19th- and 20th-century art, including strong holdings of Kandinsky, Klee, Picasso, and French Impressionists, occupy a stark annex called the **Tower Galleries.**

1071 Fifth Ave. (at 89th St.). © **212/423-3500**. www.guggenheim.org. Admission $18 adults, $15 seniors and students, free for children under 12, pay what you wish Fri 6–8pm. Sat–Wed 10am–5:45pm; Fri 10am–8pm. Subway: 4, 5, or 6 to 86th St.

Staten Island Ferry *(Value)*   Here's New York's best freebie—especially if you just want to glimpse the Statue of Liberty and not climb its steps. You get an enthralling hour-long excursion (round-trip) into the world's biggest harbor. The old orange-and-green boats usually have open decks along the sides or at the bow and stern. Grab a seat on the right side of the boat for the best view. On the way out of Manhattan, you'll pass the Statue of Liberty, Ellis Island, Governor's Island, and the Verrazano Narrows Bridge spanning the distance from Brooklyn to Staten Island in the distance.

Departs from the Whitehall Ferry Terminal at the southern tip of Manhattan. © **718/727-2508**. www.ci.nyc.ny.us/html/dot. Free admission. 24 hr.; every 20–30 min. weekdays, less frequently during off-peak and weekend hours. Subway: R or W to Whitehall St.; 4 or 5 to Bowling Green; 1 to South Ferry (ride in one of the 1st 5 cars).

Statue of Liberty *(Kids)*   For the millions who first came by ship to America in the last century, Lady Liberty, standing in the Upper Bay, was their first glimpse of America. The statue was designed by sculptor Frédéric-Auguste Bartholdi and unveiled on October 28, 1886. After nearly 100 years of wind, rain, and exposure to the harsh sea air, Lady Liberty received a resoundingly successful $150-million face-lift in time for her centennial celebration on July 4, 1986.

Touring tips: Ferries leave daily every half-hour to 45 minutes from 9am to about 3:30pm (their clock), with more frequent ferries in the morning and extended hours in summer. Try to go early on a weekday to avoid the crowds that swarm in the afternoon, on weekends, and on holidays. You can **buy ferry tickets in advance** via **www. statuereservations.com**, which will allow you to board the boat without standing in the sometimes-long ticket line; however, there is an additional service charge.

After September 11, 2001, access to the base of the statue was prohibited, but in the summer of 2004, access, albeit still somewhat limited (you can't climb to the statue's crown), was once again allowed. Now you can explore the Statue of Liberty Museum, peer into the inner structure through a glass ceiling near the base of the statue, and enjoy views from the observation deck on top of a 16-story pedestal.

On Liberty Island in New York Harbor. ☏ 212/363-3200 general info., or 212/269-5755 ticket/ferry info. www.nps. gov/stli or www.circlelinedowntown.com. Free admission; ferry ticket to Statue of Liberty and Ellis Island $12 adults, $9.50 seniors, $4.50 children 3–17. Daily 9am–5pm (last ferry departs around 4pm); extended hours in summer. Subway: 4 or 5 to Bowling Green; 1 to South Ferry. Walk south through Battery Park to Castle Clinton, the fort housing the ferry ticket booth.

United Nations   The UN headquarters occupies 18 acres of international territory—neither the city nor the United States has jurisdiction here—along the East River from 42nd to 48th streets. The complex along the East River weds the 39-story glass-slab Secretariat with the free-form General Assembly on beautifully landscaped grounds. **Guided tours** leave every half-hour or so and last 45 minutes to an hour. Your guide will take you to the General Assembly Hall and the Security Council Chamber and introduce the history and activities of the United Nations and its related organizations. Along the tour you'll see donated objects and artwork, including charred artifacts that survived the atomic bombs at Hiroshima and Nagasaki, stained-glass windows by Chagall, a replica of the first *Sputnik,* and a colorful mosaic called *The Golden Rule,* based on a Norman Rockwell drawing, which was a gift from the United States in 1985.

At First Ave. and 46th St. ☏ 212/963-8687. www.un.org/tours. Guided tours $12 adults, $8.50 seniors, $8 high school and college students, $6.50 children 5–14. Children under 5 not permitted. Daily tours every half-hour 9:30am–4:45pm; closed weekends Jan–Feb; limited schedule may be in effect during the general debate (late Sept to mid-Oct). Subway: S, 4, 5, 6, or 7 to 42nd St./Grand Central.

World Trade Center Site (Ground Zero)   Do you call a place where over 3,000 people lost their lives on September 11, 2001, an "attraction"? Or do you now call it a shrine? This is the quandary of the World Trade Center site. As you read this book, it is still just a site, and though ground was broken for rebuilding in the summer of 2004, there is still controversy over what actually will be built on the site. So don't expect to see much more than a big open hole for years to come. Now they are saying that the planned "Freedom Tower" will be built by 2011. Don't hold your breath. In the meantime, you can see the site through a viewing wall on the Church Street side of the site; on that **"Wall of Heroes"** are the names of those who lost their lives that day along with the history of the site, including photos of the construction of the World Trade Center in the late 1960s and how, after it opened in 1972, it changed the New York skyline and downtown. A walk along the Wall of Heroes remains a painfully moving experience.

Bounded by Church, Barclay, Liberty, and West sts. ☏ 212/484-1222. www.nycvisit.com or www.southstseaport.org for viewing information, or www.downtowny.com for lower-Manhattan area information and rebuilding updates. Subway: C or E to World Trade Center; N or R to Cortlandt St.

ORGANIZED SIGHTSEEING TOURS

Double-decker bus tours are one of the best ways to get an overview of Manhattan. Among the operators who offer tours narrated by a guide are **Gray Line New York Tours** (🕿 **800/669-0051** or 212/445-0848; www.graylinenewyork.com), which has hop-on/hop-off privileges on tours day and night, uptown, downtown, and all around the town for about $49 adults, $39 children 5 to 11.

You can see New York Harbor aboard **Bateaux New York** (🕿 **212/727-7735;** www.bateauxnewyork.com). They offer evening dinner cruises complete with live music, departing from Pier 61, Chelsea Piers, West 23rd Street and Twelfth Avenue, with 2-hour lunch cruises $46; 3-hour dinner cruises $88 to $117.

The Circle Line (🕿 **212/563-3200;** www.circleline42.com, www.ridethebeast. com, or www.seaportmusiccruises.com) circumnavigates the entire 35 miles around Manhattan. The panorama is riveting, and the commentary isn't bad. The big boats are basic, with lots of deck room. Snacks, soft drinks, coffee, and beer are available onboard. They depart from Pier 83, at West 42nd Street and Twelfth Avenue, and from Pier 16 at South Street Seaport. Sightseeing cruises range from $12 to $28 adults, $15 to $23 seniors, $10 to $15 children 12 and under.

WALKING TOURS

The **Municipal Art Society** (🕿 **212/439-1049** or 212/935-3960; www.mas.org) offers historical and architectural walking tours aimed at individualistic travelers, not the mass market. Highly qualified guides give insights into the significance of buildings, neighborhoods, and history. Weekday walking tours are $12, weekend tours are $15. Reservations are required on some tours, so call ahead.

All tours from **Joyce Gold History Tours of New York** (🕿 **212/242-5762;** www. nyctours.com) are offered by Gold herself, an instructor of Manhattan history at New York University and the New School for Social Research, who has been conducting history walks around New York since 1975. Joyce is full of fascinating stories about the city. Tours are offered on most weekends from March to December and cost $12 per person.

TOP SHOPPING STREETS & NEIGHBORHOODS

DOWNTOWN   Lower Manhattan continues to shine in the discount department. **Century 21,** the king of discount department stores, is across the street from the World Trade Center site. In **Chinatown, Canal Street** and **Mott Street,** between Pell Street and Chatham Square, boast the most interesting shopping. On **The Lower East Side,** there's the **Historic Orchard Street Shopping District** where prices on leather bags, shoes, luggage, and fabrics on the bolt are still quite good.

Take Me Out to the Ballgame

The world-famous **Yankees** play at Yankee Stadium (subway: C, D, or 4 to 161st St./Yankee Stadium). For tickets ($12–$115 in 2006), call **Ticketmaster** (🕿 **212/ 307-1212** or 212/307-7171; www.ticketmaster.com) or **Yankee Stadium** (🕿 **718/ 293-6000;** www.yankees.com). Bleacher seats ($8) are sold only on the day of the game. The **Mets** play at **Shea Stadium** in Queens (subway: 7 to Willets Point/Shea Stadium). For tickets (which ran $5–$70 in the 2006 season) and information, call the **Mets Ticket Office** at 🕿 **718/507-TIXX** or visit **www.mets.com.**

People love to complain about **SoHo**—it's become too trendy, too tony, too Mall of America. But it is still one of the best shopping 'hoods in the city—and few are more fun to browse. It's the epicenter of cutting-edge fashion and boasts plenty of unique boutiques.

Elizabeth Street is the star of the neighborhood known as **Nolita.** Its boutiques are largely the province of sophisticated shopkeepers specializing in high-quality, fashion-forward products and design.

The **East Village** personifies bohemian hip. **East 9th Street** between Second Avenue and Avenue A has become one of our favorite shopping strips. Up-and-coming designers sell excellent-quality and affordably priced original fashions for women here. If it's strange, illegal, or funky, it's probably available on **St. Marks Place,** which takes over for 8th Street, running east from Third Avenue to Avenue A.

Lafayette Street has grown into a full-fledged Antiques Row, especially strong in mid-20th-century furniture. Prices are high, but so is quality. The **West Village** is great for browsing and gift shopping. Specialty book- and record stores, antiques and crafts shops, and gourmet food markets dominate.

West Chelsea has been transformed into the **Chelsea Art District,** where more than 200 galleries have sprouted up in a once-moribund enclave of repair shops and warehouses. The hottest shopping/eating/hanging-out neighborhood in the city may be **Union Square**. The **Flatiron District** off Sixth Avenue is the city's discount shopping center, with superstores and off-pricers filling up the renovated spaces.

MIDTOWN Herald Square—where 34th Street, Sixth Avenue, and Broadway converge—is dominated by **Macy's,** the self-proclaimed world's biggest department store. At Sixth Avenue and 33rd Street is the **Manhattan Mall** (✆ **212/465-0500;** www.manhattanmallny.com).

Times Square and the **Theatre District** have become increasingly family oriented with a **Virgin Megastore; Toys "R" Us** has its own Ferris wheel. West 47th Street between Fifth and Sixth avenues is the city's famous **Diamond District.**

The heart of Manhattan retail is the corner of **Fifth Avenue and 57th Street.** **Tiffany & Co.** has long reigned supreme here, near **Niketown** and the **NBA Store.** In addition, a good number of mainstream retailers have flagships along Fifth. Still, you will find a number of big-name, big-ticket designers radiating from the crossroads, including **Versace, Chanel, Dior,** and **Cartier.** You'll also find big-name jewelers along here, as well as chichi department stores such as **Bergdorf Goodman, Henri Bendel,** and **Saks Fifth Avenue.**

UPTOWN Madison Avenue from 57th to 79th streets has usurped Fifth Avenue as *the* tony shopping street in the city. This strip is home to the most luxurious designer boutiques in the world—particularly in the high 60s—with **Barneys New York** as the anchor.

The **Upper West Side**'s best shopping street is **Columbus Avenue.** Small shops catering to the neighborhood's mix of young hipsters and families line both sides of the pleasant avenue from 66th Street to about 86th Street. You won't lack for good browsing along here.

Boutiques also dot Amsterdam Avenue, but **Broadway** is most notable for its terrific gourmet edibles at **Zabar's,** 2445 Broadway, at 80th Street (✆ **212/787-2000;** www.zabars.com), and **Fairway,** 2127 Broadway, at 74th Street (✆ **212/595-1888;** www.fairwaymarket.com) markets.

THE TRAVELOCITY GUARANTEE

...THAT SAYS EVERYTHING YOU BOOK WILL BE RIGHT, OR WE'LL WORK WITH OUR TRAVEL PARTNERS TO MAKE IT RIGHT, RIGHT AWAY.

*To drive home the point,
we're going to use the word "right" in every single sentence.*

Let's get right to it. Right to the meat! Only Travelocity guarantees everything about your booking will be right, or we'll work with our travel partners to make it right, right away. Right on!

Here's a picture taken smack dab right in the middle of Antigua, where the Guarantee also covers you.

The Guarantee covers all but one of the items pictured to the right.

For example, what if the ocean view you booked actually looks out at a downright ugly parking lot? You'd be right to call – we're there for you. And no one in their right mind would be pleased to learn the rental car place has closed and left them stranded. Call Travelocity and we'll help get you back on the right track.

Now, you may be thinking, "Yeah, right, I'm so sure." That's OK; you have the right to remain skeptical. That is until we mention help is always right around the corner. Call us right off the bat, knowing our customer service reps are there for you 24/7. Righting wrongs. Left and right.

Now if you're guessing there are some things we can't control, like the weather, well you're right. But we can help you with most things – to get all the details in righting,* visit travelocity.com/guarantee.

Sorry, spelling things right is one of the few things not covered under the Guarantee.

I'd give my right arm for a guarantee like this, although I'm glad I don't have to.

* travelocity
You'll never roam alone.™

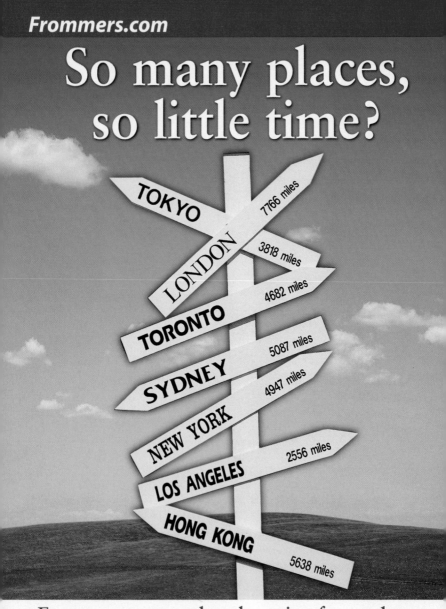

WHERE TO STAY

New York hotel rooms give everybody a whole new perspective on "small." Space is the city's biggest asset, and getting space costs money (New York's rates are the highest in the United States). If you're traveling on a budget, don't be surprised if your room isn't much bigger than the bed that's in it and your cramped bathroom has a sink so small that it looks like it was manufactured for the Keebler elves. Even expensive rooms can be on the small side, or lack closet space, or have smallish bathrooms.

We've given you a choice of chain hotels and independent properties, traditional and avant-garde, in neighborhoods from fast-paced to quiet (well, for New York).

The Benjamin   When you enter the high-ceilinged marble lobby at The Benjamin, it's as if you've suddenly stepped into the jazz era of 1920s New York. But once you get to your spacious and luxurious room and notice the numerous amenities, such as Bose Wave radios, Web TV, and ergonomic chairs and you will know you are most definitely in the 21st century. How many hotels can claim a "sleep concierge" (choose from 11 pillow designs) or *guarantee* a good night's sleep? Bathrooms feature Frette robes, TV speakers, and water pressure from the shower head strong enough to make you think you've just experienced a deep-tissue massage. The hotel also features the Woodstock Spa and Wellness Center. *Tip:* If you are a light sleeper, book a room off Lexington Avenue.

125 E. 50th St. (at Lexington Ave.), New York, NY 10022. ☏ **888/4-BENJAMIN,** 212/320-8002, or 212/715-2500. Fax 212/715-2525. www.thebenjamin.com. 209 units. From $459 superior double; from $499 deluxe studio; from $559 suite. Call or check website for special weekend-stay offers. AE, DC, DISC, MC, V. Parking $45. Subway: 6 to 51st St.; E or F to Lexington Ave. **Amenities:** Restaurant; exercise room; full-service spa. *In room:* Kitchenette.

The Blakely New York   After a major renovation, The Blakely now has a clubby yet modern feel to it and is an excellent small-Midtown-hotel option. The rooms are all generously sized; some have views of the City Center dome across the street. The dark cherrywood furniture helps perpetuate the clubhouse aura that is contrasted, happily, by modern amenities such as flatscreen TVs and Wi-Fi in all the rooms. Marble bathrooms are well sized and appointed; bathroom suites have separate tubs and showers. The lobby, though redesigned, remains small and can get hectic at times, but the staff is helpful and efficient.

136 W. 55th St. (between Sixth and Seventh aves.), New York, NY 10019. ☏ **212/245-1800.** Fax 212/582-8332. www.blakelynewyork.com. 120 units. $260–$365 double; $275–$385 suite. Check the website for packages and seasonal specials. AE, DISC, MC, V. Parking $33. Subway: N or R to 57th St. **Amenities:** Restaurant; access to nearby health club. *In room:* Fridge, microwave.

The Carlyle: A Rosewood Hotel   This 34-story grande dame perfectly epitomizes the old-world, moneyed neighborhood where it stands. Service is white-glove (literally); many celebrities and dignitaries sip tea in the hotel's cozy Gallery. The recently renovated lobby offers marble floors and columns, Baccarat light fixtures, a new reception desk, and an expanded concierge space. Guest rooms range from singles to seven-room suites. All have marble bathrooms with whirlpool tubs and all the amenities you'd expect from a hotel of this caliber. The English manor–style decor is luxurious but not excessive, creating the comfortably elegant ambience of an Upper East Side apartment. Many apartments have breathtaking views of either downtown or the West Side and Central Park.

35 E. 76th St. (at Madison Ave.), New York, NY 10021. ☏ **800/227-5737** or 212/744-1600. Fax 212/717-4682. www.thecarlyle.com. 180 units. $650–$950 double; from $950 1- or 2-bedroom suite. AE, DC, MC, V. Parking $50.

New York City: Midtown Accommodations & Dining

ACCOMMODATIONS ■

The Carlyle: A Rosewood Hotel **3**

Casablanca Hotel **6**

Hotel Metro **13**

Le Parker Meridien **7**

The Lucerne **1**

Red Roof Inn **14**

Ritz-Carlton New York,
  Central Park **8**

Waldorf-Astoria and the Waldorf
  Towers **12**

DINING ◆

Aquavit **9**

The Benjamin **11**

The Blakely New York **5**

Café Boulud **2**

City Bakery **15**

Katz's Delicatessen **16**

Oceana **10**

Sapporo **4**

UPPER WEST SIDE

Lincoln Center

CENTRA

West End Ave.

Amsterdam Ave.

Columbus Ave.

Central Park

West Drive

W. 64th St.
W. 63rd St.
W. 62nd St.
W. 61st St.
W. 60th St.
W. 59th St.
W. 58th St.

Central Park S.
Columbus Circle

W. 57th St.
W. 56th St.
W. 55th St.
W. 54th St.
W. 53rd St.
W. 52nd St.
W. 51st St.

Carnegie Hall

Tenth Ave.
Ninth Ave.

DeWitt Clinton Park

THEATER DISTRICT

W. 50th St.
W. 49th St.
W. 48th St.
W. 47th St.
W. 46th St.
W. 45th St.
W. 44th St.
W. 43rd St.
W. 42nd St.
W. 41st St.
W. 40th St.

Broadway

MIDTOWN WEST

Twelfth Ave.
Eleventh Ave.
Tenth Ave.
Eighth Ave.
Seventh Ave.

TIMES SQUARE

Port Authority

Lincoln Tunnel

Javits Convention Center

W. 39th St.
W. 38th St.
W. 37th St.
W. 36th St.
W. 35th St.
W. 34th St.
W. 33rd St.

GARMEN DISTRIC

Ninth Ave.

W 32nd St.

Tunnel Entrance

Penn Station/
Madison Square
Garden

W 32nd

W. 31st St.
W. 30th St.
W. 29th St.
W. 28th St.

Chelsea Park

W. 27th St.

W. 26th St.
W. 25th St.

Eleventh Ave.
Tenth Ave.

W. 24th St.
W. 23rd St.

CHELSEA

West Side Hwy.

W. 22nd St.

Chelsea Piers Sports & Entertainment Complex

W. 21st St.
W. 20th St.
W. 19th St.

Hudson River

Chelsea Piers

W. 18th St.
W. 17th St.
W. 16th St.
W. 15th St.
W. 14th St.
W. 13th St.

Ninth Ave.
Eighth Ave.
Seventh Ave.

MEAT-PACKING DISTRICT

Upper Manhattan

Uptown

Midtown

Downtown

Subway: 6 to 77th St. Pets accepted. **Amenities:** 3 restaurants; high-tech fitness room; spa. *In room:* Pantry kitchenette or full kitchen (in some).

Casablanca Hotel (Value)

Who wouldn't want a desert oasis in the middle of all the Times Square mayhem? And that's what the Casablanca Hotel really is: a calming refuge where you can escape from the noise and crowds. In the hotel's homey guest lounge, you can sit by a fire, read a paper, check your e-mail, watch television on the gargantuan-size screen, or sip a cappuccino from the serve-yourself cappuccino/espresso machine. Or you can just retreat to your well-outfitted room, which includes a ceiling fan, bathrobes, free bottles of water, and beautifully tiled bathrooms. Service is top-notch. Because of its location, moderate prices, and size, the Casablanca is in high demand, so book early.

147 W. 43rd St. (just east of Broadway), New York, NY 10036. *(C)* **888/922-7225** or 212/869-1212. Fax 212/391-7585. www.casablancahotel.com. 48 units. $199–$299 double; from $299 suite. Rates include continental breakfast, all-day cappuccino, and weekday wine and cheese. Check website for Internet rates and other special deals. AE, DC, MC, V. Parking $25 next door. Subway: N, R, 1, 2, 3, or 9 to 42nd St./Times Sq. **Amenities:** Access to New York Sports Club.

Cosmopolitan Hotel—Tribeca (Value)

This is one of the best hotel deals in Manhattan for budget travelers who insist on a private bathroom. Everything is strictly budget, but nice. Beds are comfy, and sheets and towels are of good quality. Rooms are small but make the most of the limited space, and the place is pristine. The two-level minilofts have lots of character, but expect to duck on the second level. Management does a great job of keeping everything fresh. Services are kept at a bare minimum to keep costs down, so you must be a low-maintenance guest to be happy here.

95 W. Broadway (at Chambers St.), New York, NY 10007. *(C)* **888/895-9400** or 212/566-1900. Fax 212/566-6909. www.cosmohotel.com. 105 units. $129–$189 double. AE, DC, MC, V. Parking $20, 1 block away. Subway: 1, 2, or 3 to Chambers St.

Hotel Metro (Value) (Kids)

The Metro is the best choice in Midtown for those who don't want to sacrifice either style or comfort for affordability. This Art Deco–style jewel's large rooms are outfitted with retro furnishings, refrigerators, and marble bathrooms. Only about half the bathrooms have tubs, but the others have shower stalls big enough for two (junior suites have whirlpool tubs). The "family room" is a two-room suite that has a second bedroom in lieu of a sitting area. The comfy library/lounge area off the lobby, where complimentary buffet breakfast is laid out and the coffeepot's on all day, is a popular hangout. The rooftop terrace boasts a breathtaking view of the Empire State Building.

45 W. 35th St. (between Fifth and Sixth aves.), New York, NY 10001. *(C)* **800/356-3870** or 212/947-2500. Fax 212/279-1310. www.hotelmetronyc.com. 179 units. $175–$355 double; $195–$355 triple or quad; $225–$425 family room; $275–$475 suite. Extra person $25. 1 child under 14 stays free in parent's room. Rates include continental breakfast. Check with airlines and other package operators for great-value package deals. AE, DC, MC, V. Parking $20 nearby. Subway: B, D, F, V, N, or R to 34th St. **Amenities:** Restaurant; fitness room. *In room:* Fridge.

Le Parker Meridien (Kids)

A stay at Le Parker Meridien is a New York experience in itself. Not many hotels in New York can rival the attributes of this hotel: Its location on 57th Street is practically perfect; the 17,000 square-foot state-of-the-art fitness center features a basketball and a racquetball court, a spa, and a rooftop pool; a gorgeous, bustling lobby that also serves as a public space; and elevators with televisions that continuously show cartoons and Charlie Chaplin shorts that are a wonder for the kids. The spacious hotel rooms, though a bit on the Ikea side, have a fun feel to them.

Rooms have wood platform beds with feather beds; built-ins that include large work desks, stylish Aeron chairs, and 32-inch flatscreen televisions with VCR/CD and DVD players. The slate-and-limestone bathrooms are large, but unfortunately come only with shower.

118 W. 57th St. (between Sixth and Seventh aves.), New York, NY 10019. © **800/543-4300** or 212/245-5000. Fax 212/307-1776. www.parkermeridien.com. 731 units. $600–$800 double; from $780 suite. Extra person $30. Excellent packages and weekend rates often available (as low as $225 at press time). AE, DC, DISC, MC, V. Parking $45. Subway: F, N, Q, or R to 57th St. Pets accepted. **Amenities:** 3 restaurants; indoor pool, fitness center; spa.

The Lucerne   This magnificent 1903 landmark building on the Upper West Side (it was once a dormitory) has been transformed into a luxury boutique hotel, and that transformation has been a triumph on many levels. Service here is impeccable, especially for a moderately priced hotel; everything is fresh and immaculate. The rooms are all spacious and comfortable, with attractive bathrooms complete with travertine counters. Some of the rooms have views of the Hudson River. The suites are extra special here and include a kitchenette and a sitting room with a sofa and extra television.

201 W. 79th St. (at Amsterdam Ave.), New York, NY 10024. © **800/492-8122** or 212/875-1000. Fax 212/579-2408. www.newyorkhotel.com. 250 units. $140–$270 double or queen; $180–$330 king or junior suite; $220–$410 1-bedroom suite. Extra person $20. Children under 16 stay free in parent's room. Continental breakfast additional $5 per person. AAA discounts offered; check website for special Internet deals. AE, DC, DISC, MC, V. Parking $25 nearby. Subway: 1 to 79th St. **Amenities:** Restaurant; fitness center. *In room:* Kitchenette (in suites only).

Red Roof Inn *(Value*   Manhattan's first, and only, Red Roof Inn offers welcome relief from Midtown's high-priced hotel scene. The hotel occupies a former office building that was gutted and laid out fresh, allowing for more spacious rooms than you'll usually find in this price category. The high-ceilinged lobby feels smarter than most in this price range, and elevators are quiet and efficient. What's more, in-room amenities (including Wi-Fi) are better than most competitors', and furnishings are new and comfortable. The location—just a stone's throw from the Empire State Building and Herald Square—is excellent. A complimentary continental breakfast adds to the good value.

6 W. 32nd St. (between Broadway and Fifth Ave.), New York, NY 10001. © **800/567-7720**, 800/RED-ROOF, or 212/643-7100. Fax 212/643-7101. www.applecorehotels.com or www.redroof.com. 171 units. $89–$329 double (usually less than $189). Rates include continental breakfast. Children under 14 stay free in parent's room. AE, DC, DISC, MC, V. Parking $24. Subway: B, D, F, N, R, or V to 34th St. **Amenities:** Exercise room. *In room:* Fridge.

Ritz-Carlton New York, Central Park *(Best (Kids*   This hotel features an enviable location overlooking Central Park, impeccable and personable service, and luxury galore—but it still manages to maintain a homey elegance. Rooms are spacious and decorated in traditional, English-countryside style. Suites are larger than most New York City apartments. Rooms facing Central Park come with telescopes, and all have flatscreen TVs with DVD players. The marble bathrooms are also oversize and feature bathrobes and Frederic Fekkai bath amenities. For families who can afford the very steep prices, the hotel is extremely kid-friendly. Children are given in-room cookies and milk. The Switzerland-based La Prairie Spa offers loads of pampering.

50 Central Park South (at Sixth Ave.), New York, NY 10019. © **212/308-9100**. Fax 212/207-8831. www.ritzcarlton.com. 273 units. $650–$1,075 double; from $1,295 suite. Package and weekend rates available. AE, DC, DISC, MC, V. Parking $50. Subway: N, Q, or R to 57th St. Pets under 60 lb. accepted. **Amenities:** Restaurant; fitness center; La Prairie spa and facial center.

Waldorf=Astoria and the Waldorf Towers   If you are looking for the epitome of old-school elegance, you can't do better than this Art Deco masterpiece—a genuine

New York City landmark. No two rooms are exactly alike, yet all are airy, with high ceilings, traditional decor, comfortable linens and beds, and spacious marble bathrooms. If you crave more luxury, book a room on the **Astoria** level, which features huge suites, deluxe bathroom amenities, access to the clubby Astoria Lounge for breakfast or afternoon hors d'oeuvres, and free entry to the hotel's fitness club (other guests pay a fee). For even more opulence, try a suite in the **Waldorf Towers,** where most rooms are bigger than most New York City apartments.

301 Park Ave. (between 49th and 50th sts.), New York, NY 10022. (C) 800/WALDORF, 800/774-1500, or 212/355-3000. Fax 212/872-7272 (Astoria) or 212/872-4799 (Towers). www.waldorfastoria.com or www.waldorf-towers.com. 1,245 units (180 in the Towers). Waldorf=Astoria $229–$485 double; from $349 suite. Waldorf Towers $329–$739 double; from $515 suite. Extra person $40. Children under 18 stay free in parent's room. Corporate, senior, seasonal, and weekend discounts may be available, as well as attractive package deals. AE, DC, DISC, MC, V. Parking $45. Subway: 6 to 51st St. **Amenities:** 3 restaurants; fitness center, spa. *In room:* Kitchenette or wet bar with fridge (in some).

WHERE TO DINE

Reservations (where taken) are always a good idea in New York, and a virtual necessity if your party is bigger than two or you want a special meal at a top restaurant. Do yourself a favor and call ahead as a rule of thumb so you won't be disappointed.

Besides the restaurants listed below, also consider the legendary Central Park restaurant **Tavern on the Green,** Central Park West and West 67th Street ((C) **212/873-3200**). Food takes a back seat to dining in one of the city's best settings. Views over the park are wonderful; in good weather, try for a seat in the outdoor garden, with its whimsical topiary shrubs and Japanese lanterns. It's also a great place to visit during the holidays.

For nonvegetarians and the non-health-minded, consider the cheapest, yet in some ways, most comforting indulgence: **Gray's Papaya,** 2090 Broadway, at 72nd Street ((C) **212/799-0243**). This 24-hour hot-dog stand is a New York institution. The "Recession Special"—two hot dogs and a drink (overly sweetened papaya, piña colada, or orange juice)—is a whopping $2.45.

Note: Smoking is forbidden in every restaurant in the city. Tipping, however, is a must—do as locals do and tip double the sales tax on your meal.

Aquavit SCANDINAVIAN   This first-rate restaurant is designed in sleek Scandinavian style with modernist furniture. In the front of the restaurant is an informal and less expensive cafe, while past a long bar is the dining room. The smoked fish—really all the fish—is prepared perfectly. I often daydream about the herring plate: four types of herring accompanied by a tiny glass of Aquavit, distilled liquor not unlike vodka flavored with fruit and spices, and a frosty Carlsberg beer. The hot smoked arctic char on the main a la carte menu, served with clams and bean purée in a mustard green broth, is also a winner. Most fixed-price menus offer a well-chosen beverage accompaniment option.

65 E. 55th St. (between Park and Madison aves.). (C) 212/307-7311. www.aquavit.org. Reservations recommended. Cafe main courses $9–$32; 3-course fixed-price meal $20 at lunch, $35 at dinner. Main dining room fixed-price meal $35 at lunch, $78 at dinner ($39 for vegetarians); 3-course pretheater dinner (5:30–6:15pm) $55; tasting menus $48 at lunch, $100 at dinner ($58 for vegetarians); supplement for paired wines $30 at lunch, $75 at dinner. AE, DC, MC, V. Mon–Fri noon–2:30pm; Sun–Thurs 5:30–10:30pm; Fri–Sat 5:30–10:45pm. Subway: E or F to Fifth Ave.

Big Wong King ✿ CHINESE/CANTONESE   For over 30 years, Big Wong has been an institution for workers from the nearby courthouses and Chinese families who come to feast on congee (rice porridge) and fried crullers for breakfast. They also come for the superb roasted meats, the pork and duck seen hanging in the window, the comforting noodle soups, and the terrific barbecued ribs. This is simple, down-home Cantonese food—lo mein, chow fun, bok choy in oyster sauce—cooked lovingly, and so cheap. If you don't mind sharing a table, Big Wong is a must at any time of day.

67 Mott St. (between Canal and Bayard sts.). ✆ 212/964-0540. Appetizers $1.50–$5; congee $1.50–$6; soups $3–$5; Cantonese noodles $5.25–$11. No credit cards. Daily 8:30am–9pm. Subway: N or R.

Café Boulud *(Value)* FRENCH   Here's a chance to sample the stellar cuisine of Daniel Boulud, New York's best French chef, at a less than hefty price tag. Four menus are offered, featuring either Boulud's signature French-country classics; a vegetarian menu; seasonal dishes; or a monthly globe-hopping menu highlighting Tuscany, Thailand, or somewhere in between. The experimental nature of the wide-ranging menus makes choosing a thrill, and even the most inventive dishes tend to dazzle the palate. The poached Dover sole with baby leeks and sauce vin blanc is truly memorable. All in all, a first-rate dining experience at more palatable prices than cuisine this memorable usually costs. Don't be in a rush, though, especially at lunch.

20 E. 76th St. (between Madison and Fifth aves.). ✆ 212/772-2600. www.danielnyc.com. Reservations recommended. Main courses $33–$40 at lunch, $26–$43 at dinner; 2- or 3-course prix-fixe lunch $29–$36. AE, DC, MC, V. Daily 5:45–11pm; Tues–Sat noon–2:30pm (no lunch Sat July–Aug). Subway: 6 to 77th St.

Chanterelle *(Best)* CONTEMPORARY FRENCH   This West Village spot is our favorite special-occasion restaurant (you don't dine here on the cheap). The dining room is a charmer, with widely spaced tables (a rarity in New York City), and gorgeous floral displays. Your server will work with you on your choices, paring items that go best together. The French-themed menu is seasonal and changes every few weeks, but one signature dish appears on almost every menu: a marvelous grilled seafood sausage. Cheese lovers should opt for a cheese course—the presentation and selection can't be beat. The wine list is superlative but expensive.

2 Harrison St. (at Hudson St.). ✆ 212/966-6960. www.chanterellenyc.com. Reservations recommended well in advance. Fixed-price lunch $42; a la carte lunch $22–$30; 3-course fixed-price dinner $95; tasting menu $125. AE, DC, DISC, MC, V. Mon 5:30–10:30pm; Tues–Sat noon–2:30pm and 5:30–11pm. Subway: 1 to Franklin St.

City Bakery *(Kids)* ORGANIC AMERICAN   City Bakery offers comfort food that manages to be delicious, nutritious, *and* eco-friendly. Its salad bar is unlike any other in the city, where the integrity of the ingredients is as important as the taste. This is health food, all right—roasted beets with walnuts, glistening sautéed greens, lavender eggplant tossed in miso—but with heart and soul, offering such classic favorites as French toast with artisanal bacon, flavorful mac 'n cheese, fried chicken, tortilla pie, even smoked salmon with all the trimmings on Sunday. The "bakery" in the name refers to the plethora of sinful desserts; kids love the spinning wheel of chocolate and the homemade marshmallows. *One caveat:* It's a bit pricey for a salad bar, but oh, what good eats.

3 W. 18th St. (between Fifth and Sixth aves.). ✆ 212/366-1414. Salad bar $12 per pound; soups $4–$7; sandwiches $5–$10. AE, MC, V. Mon–Fri 7:30am–7pm; Sat 7:30am–6:30pm; Sun 9am–6pm. Subway: N, R, Q, 4, 5, or 6 to Union Sq.

Katz's Delicatessen *(Value)* JEWISH DELI   Arguably the city's best Jewish deli. The motto is "There's Nothing More New York Than Katz's," and it's spot-on. Founded in 1888, this cavernous, brightly lit place is suitably Noo Yawk, with dill pickles, Dr. Brown's cream soda, and old-world attitude to spare. But one word of caution: Katz's is a serious tourist destination so if you see a big tour bus parked in front, you might

For the Perfect Pizza

Patsy's Pizzeria, 2287 First Ave., between 117th and 118th streets (☎ **212/534-9783**), is our favorite pizzeria in the city, and was also the favorite of Frank Sinatra, who liked it so much he had pies packed and flown out to Las Vegas. The coal oven here has been burning since 1932, and though the neighborhood in East Harlem where it is located has had its ups and downs, the quality of pizza at Patsy's has never wavered. Try the marinara pizza, a pie with fresh marinara sauce but no cheese that's so good you won't miss the mozzarella. Don't be fooled by imitators using Patsy's name; this is the original and the best.

be in for a long wait. (And remember to tip your carver, who gives you a plate with a sample of the succulent pastrami or corned beef as he prepares your sandwich!)

205 E. Houston St. (at Ludlow St.). ☎ 212/254-2246. Reservations not accepted. Sandwiches $2.15–$10; other main courses $5–$18. AE, MC, V ($20 minimum). Sun–Tues 8am–10pm; Wed 8am–11pm; Thurs 8am–midnight; Fri–Sat 8am–3am. Subway: F to Second Ave.

Lupa *Value* ROMAN ITALIAN   Since it first opened in late 1999, this Roman-style osteria has remained a hot ticket. Co-owned by Mario Batali, the Food TV "Iron Chef," it offers high-quality food at good value—you can eat well here and not max out your credit card. Though the food is consistently tasty and you won't starve, don't expect big portions. The menu is thoughtful and creative, focusing on lusty Roman fare like ricotta gnocchi with sausage and fennel, or pork saltimbocca. Wines, too, have been thoughtfully chosen. The service hits just the right notes: Servers are both warm and supremely knowledgeable. Make a reservation, or go early to snag one of the tables set aside for walk-ins.

170 Thompson St. (between Houston and Bleecker sts.). ☎ 212/982-5089. www.luparestaurant.com. Reservations recommended. *Primi* $9–$16; *secondi* $16–$20. AE, MC, V. Mon–Fri noon–3pm and 5–11:30pm; Sat–Sun noon–2:45pm and 4:45–11:30pm. Subway: B, D, F, Q, A, C, or E to W. 4th St.

Maremma ITALIAN/WESTERN   Maremma is the name of the rocky, rough coastal region of Tuscany where Italian cowboys roam the land and the menu at New York's only Italian/Western restaurant is an unlikely mix of Tuscan and cowboy cuisine. Here you'll find small plates on the menu such as a spin on the traditional sloppy Joe called "sloppy Giuseppe," made with tender pieces of shredded beef over thick-crusted Tuscan bread. The addition of chocolate to the wild-boar ragout that covers the fresh pappardelle is a nod to the West, while a touch of bourbon Westernizes the tomato-and-*grana-padano* sauce served over artisanal pasta. The Tuscan fries, traditional fries but with herbs and garlic sprinkled on them, are an addictive revelation.

228 W. 10th St. (between Bleecker and Hudson sts.). ☎ 212/645-0200. Reservations recommended. Small plates $9–$12; big plates $16–$28. AE, DC, DISC, MC, V. Mon–Wed 5:30–11pm; Thurs–Sat 5:30pm–midnight. Subway: 1 to Christopher St.

Oceana SEAFOOD   When you enter Oceana, the nautical themes are obvious. But this is no seafood shack—it's more like a luxury ocean liner. Standouts include tartare of yellowfin tuna with daikon radish, black cardamom, and horseradish sorbet; striped bass wrapped in a ham croissant; and stuffed artichoke and Icelandic cod basted in butter and herbs. Dishes look so good on the plate you might not want to eat them, but this artwork is extremely edible. Oceana also features an excellent wine list and your waiter will help pair wines with your dishes if you desire. The atmosphere is relaxed and the service is personable.

55 E. 54th St. (between Park and Madison aves.). © 212/759-5941. www.oceanarestaurant.com. Reservations recommended. AE, DISC, MC, V. 3-course prix fixe $48 lunch, $78 dinner. AE, DISC, MC, V. Mon–Fri noon–2:30pm and 5:30–10:30pm; Sat 5–10:30pm. Subway: E or F to Fifth Ave.

Peter Luger Steakhouse STEAKHOUSE   If you love steak, then book a table here and hop a cab to Williamsburg in Brooklyn. Expect loads of attitude and nothing in the way of decor or atmosphere (beer hall is the theme)—but this century-old institution is porterhouse heaven. The first-rate cuts—the only ones this 114-year-old institution serves—are dry-aged on the premises and come off the grill dripping with fat and butter, crusty on the outside and tender pink within. It's the best steak in the five boroughs, bar none. The $5.95 Peter Luger burger is a little-known treasure. *Note:* Bring wads of cash because this place is expensive, but doesn't take credit cards.

178 Broadway (at Driggs Ave.), Williamsburg, Brooklyn. © 718/387-7400. www.peterluger.com. Reservations essential; call a month in advance for weekend bookings. Main courses $5–$20 at lunch, $20–$32 at dinner. No credit cards (Peter Luger accounts only). Mon–Thurs 11:45am–9:45pm; Fri–Sat 11:45am–10:45pm; Sun 12:45–9:45pm. Subway: J, M, or Z to Marcy Ave. (or take a cab).

Sapporo ⟨*Value*⟩ JAPANESE NOODLES   If the mostly Japanese clientele at this longtime Theater District noodle shop doesn't convince you of Sapporo's authenticity, the constant din of satisfied diners slurping at huge bowls of steaming ramen (noodle soup with meat and vegetables) surely will. And though the ramen is Sapporo's well-deserved specialty, the *gyoza* (Japanese dumplings) and the *donburi* (pork or chicken over rice with soy-flavored sauce) are also terrific. Best of all, nothing on the menu is over $10, and that's not easy to accomplish in the oft-overpriced Theater District.

152 W. 49th St. (between Sixth and Seventh aves.). © 212/869-8972. Reservations not accepted. Main courses $6–$9. No credit cards. Mon–Sat 11am–11pm; Sun 11am–10pm. Subway: N or R to 49th St.

NEW YORK CITY AFTER DARK

For the latest, most comprehensive nightlife listings, the magazine *Time Out New York* (www.timeoutny.com) is our favorite weekly source; it comes out every Thursday. The free weekly *Village Voice's* (www.villagevoice.com) arts and entertainment coverage is extensive, and just about every live-music venue advertises here. The *New York Times* (www.nytoday.com) features terrific entertainment coverage, particularly in the two-part Friday "Weekend" section. *New York* magazine's **www.nymetro.com** site is an excellent online source.

THE THEATER SCENE

We can't tell you precisely what will be on while you're in town, so check the publications listed above for specifics. Another good source is the **Broadway Line** (© 888/ BROADWAY; www.livebroadway.com), where you can obtain details and descriptions on current Broadway shows, and choose to be transferred to TeleCharge or Ticketmaster. There's also **NYC/Onstage** (© 212/768-1818; www.tdf.org), a recorded service providing complete schedules, descriptions, and other details on theater and the performing arts.

   Ticket prices vary dramatically. Expect to pay for good seats; the high end for any given show is likely to be between $60 and $100 (though it can be a lot more). Off-Broadway and Off-Off-Broadway shows tend to be cheaper, with tickets often as low as $10 or $15, though seats for the most established shows can command prices as high as $50 to $75.

TICKET-BUYING TIPS   Phone ahead or go online for tickets to the most popular shows as far in advance as you can. You need only call such general numbers as **TeleCharge** (© 212/239-6200; www.telecharge.com) or **Ticketmaster** (© 212/307-4100;** www.ticketmaster.com).

Theatre Direct International (TDI) is a ticket broker (minimum service charge of $15) that sells tickets to select Broadway and Off-Broadway shows. Check to see if they have seats to the shows you're interested in by calling © **800/BROADWAY** or 212/541-8457; you can also order tickets via its website, **www.broadway.com**.

Three competing sites—**Broadway.com (www.broadway.com)**, **Playbill Online (www.playbill.com** or www.playbillclub.com), and **TheaterMania (www.theater mania.com)**—offer information on Broadway and Off-Broadway shows, with links to the ticket-buying agencies. Each offers an **online theater club** that's free to join and can yield substantial savings—as much as 50%—on advance-purchase theater tickets for select Broadway and Off-Broadway shows.

You should also try the **Broadway Ticket Center,** run by the League of American Theatres and Producers at the Times Square Visitors Center, 1560 Broadway, between 46th and 47th streets (open Mon–Sat 10am–6pm; Sun 10am–3pm). They often have tickets available for otherwise sold-out shows, both for advance and same-day purchase, and only charge about $5 extra per ticket.

Even if saving money isn't an issue for you, check the boards at the **TKTS Booth** in Times Square (open 3–8pm for evening performances, 10am–2pm for Wed and Sat matinees, 11am–8pm on Sun for all performances), for same-day discounted tickets. Tickets for the day's performances are usually offered at half-price, with a few reduced only 25%, plus a $2.50-per-ticket service charge. Boards outside the ticket windows list available shows. Only cash and traveler's checks are accepted (no credit cards). There's often a huge line, so show up early for the best availability and be prepared to wait—but frankly, the crowd is all part of the fun. Visit **www.tdf.org** or call **NYC/ Onstage** at © 212/768-1818 and press "8" for the latest TKTS information.

THE PERFORMING ARTS

In addition to the listings below, see what's happening at **Carnegie Hall,** 881 Seventh Ave. (© **212/247-7800;** www.carnegiehall.org; subway: N, R, or W to 57th St.); and at the **92nd Street Y,** 1395 Lexington Ave., at 92nd Street (© **212/415-5500;** www. 92ndsty.org), which offers many excellent cultural events.

LINCOLN CENTER FOR THE PERFORMING ARTS   New York is the world's premier performing arts city, and **Lincoln Center,** at Broadway and 64th Street (© **212/546-2656** or 212/875-5456; www.lincolncenter.org; subway: 1 or 9 to 6th St.), is its premier institution.

Resident companies include **The Chamber Music Society of Lincoln Center** (© **212/875-5788;** www.chambermusicsociety.org); **The Film Society of Lincoln Center** (© **212/875-5600;** www.filmlinc.com), which shows films at the Walter Reade Theater; **Jazz at Lincoln Center** (© **212/258-9800;** www.jalc.org), led by Wynton Marsalis; and **Lincoln Center Theater** (© **212/362-7600;** www.lct.org), with the Vivian Beaumont Theater, a home to Broadway shows and the Mitzi E. Newhouse Theater, an Off-Broadway house.

Other renowned tenants are the **Metropolitan Opera** (© **212/362-6000;** www. metopera.org), **New York City Opera** (© **212/870-5570;** www.nycopera.com), **New York City Ballet** (© **212/870-5570;** www.nycballet.com), **New York Philharmonic**

Value Park It! Shakespeare, Music & Other Free Fun

As the weather warms, New York culture comes outdoors to play.

Shakespeare in the Park, held at Central Park's Delacorte Theater, is by far the city's most famous alfresco arts event. The schedule consists of one or two summertime productions, usually of the Bard's plays. Productions often feature big names and range from traditional to avant-garde interpretations. The theater itself, next to Belvedere Castle near 79th Street and West Drive, is a dream—on a beautiful starry night, there's no better stage in town. Tickets are given out free on a first-come, first-served basis (two per person), at 1pm on the day of the performance at the theater. The Delacorte might have 1,881 seats, but each is a hot commodity, so people generally line up on the baseball field next to the theater about 2 to 3 hours in advance (even earlier if a big box-office name is involved). You can also pick up same-day tickets between 1 and 3pm at the Public Theater, at 425 Lafayette St., where the Shakespeare Festival continues throughout the year. For more information, call the Public Theater at ☎ **212/539-8500** or the Delacorte at ☎ **212/861-7277,** or visit **www.publictheater.org**.

With summer also comes the sound of music to Central Park, where the **New York Philharmonic** and the **Metropolitan Opera** regularly entertain beneath the stars. For schedules, call the Philharmonic at ☎ **212/875-5656,** the Metropolitan Opera at ☎ **212/362-6000,** or visit **www.lincolncenter.org**.

The most active music stage in the park is **SummerStage,** at Rumsey Playfield, midpark around 72nd Street. The season usually lasts from mid-June to early August. While some big-name shows charge admission, tickets aren't usually required; donations are warmly accepted, however. For the latest performance info, call the SummerStage hot line at ☎ **212/360-2777** or visit **www.summerstage.org**.

Central Park may be the most happening park in town, but the calendar of free events heats up throughout the city's parks in summertime. You can find out what's happening by calling the **Parks and Recreation Special Events Hot Line** at ☎ **888/NY-PARKS** or 212/360-3456 or pointing your browser to **www.nycgovparks.org**.

(☎ **212/875-5656;** www.newyorkphilharmonic.org), and **American Ballet Theatre (www.abt.org).**

Most of the companies' **major seasons** run from about September or October to April, May, or June. **Tickets** for all performances at Avery Fisher and Alice Tully halls can be purchased through **CenterCharge** (☎ **212/721-6500**) or online at **www.lincolncenter.org** (click on "Event Calendar"). Tickets for all Lincoln Center Theater performances can be purchased thorough **TeleCharge** (☎ **212/239-6200;** www.telecharge.com). Tickets for New York State Theater productions (New York City Opera and Ballet companies) are available through **Ticketmaster** (☎ **212/307-4100;** www.ticketmaster.com), while tickets for films showing at the Walter Reade Theater can be bought up to 7 days in advance by calling ☎ **212/496-3809.**

OTHER CONCERT HALLS & VENUES   Modern dance takes center stage at **City Center,** 131 W. 55th St. between Sixth and Seventh avenues (© **212/247-0430** or 212/581-1212; www.citycenter.org.; subway: F, N, Q, R, or W to 57th St.; B, D, or E to Seventh Ave.); and at the **Joyce Theater,** one of the world's greatest modern dance institutions, located at 175 Eighth Ave., at 19th Street (© **212/242-0800;** www.joyce.org.; subway: C or E to 23rd St.; 1 or 9 to 18th St.).

The **Apollo Theatre,** 253 W. 125th St., between Adam Clayton Powell and Frederick Douglass boulevards (© **212/531-5300** or 212/531-5301; www.apollotheater. com; subway: 1 or 9 to 125th St.), is internationally renowned for its African-American acts of all musical genres and is in the middle of a major restoration project. The **Brooklyn Academy of Music** presents cutting-edge theater, opera, dance, and music at 30 Lafayette Ave., off Flatbush Avenue, Brooklyn (© **718/636-4100;** www.bam.org; subway: 2, 3, 4, 5, M, N, Q, R, or W to Pacific St./Atlantic Ave.).

LIVE POPULAR MUSIC

A midsize venue for national acts is **The Bowery Ballroom,** 6 Delancey St., at the Bowery (© **212/533-2111;** www.boweryballroom.com), an atmospheric general admission space that holds about 500. Its slightly bigger brother, **Irving Plaza,** is another old hall near Union Square at 17 Irving Place (© **212/777-1224;** www.irving plaza.com; subway: L, N, R, 4, 5, or 6 to 14th St.–Union Sq.).

B. B. King Blues Club & Grill anchors Times Square's "new" 42nd Street with pop, funk, and rock names, mainly from the past (© **212/997-4144,** or 212/307-7171 for tickets; www.bbkingblues.com; subway: A, C, E, Q, W, 1, 2, 3, 7, or 9 to 42nd St.). **The Knitting Factory,** at 74 Leonard St., between Broadway and Church Street (© **212/219-3132;** www.knittingfactory.com; subway: 1 or 9 to Franklin St.), is the city's premier avant-garde music venue. Folk rock's legendary **Bitter End,** 147 Bleecker St., between Thompson and LaGuardia streets (© **212/673-7030;** www. bitterend.com), is still going strong.

JAZZ   **Birdland** has an excellent sound system and a top-notch talent roster at 315 W. 44th St., between Eighth and Ninth avenues (© **212/581-3080;** www.birdland jazz.com; subway: A, C, or E to 42nd St.). Prices are astronomical, but the **Blue Note** attracts the biggest names in jazz to its intimate setting at 131 W. 3rd St., at Sixth Avenue (© **212/475-8592;** www.bluenote.net; subway: A, C, E, F, or V to W. 4th St.). **The Lenox Lounge** (© **212/427-0253;** www.lenoxlounge.com; subway: 2 or 3 to 125th St.) is Harlem's best jazz club at 288 Malcolm X Blvd. (Lenox Ave.; between 124th and 125th sts.).

CABARET   Cabaret doesn't get any better than at the **Cafe Carlyle.** It's at The Carlyle hotel, 781 Madison Ave., at 76th Street (© **212/744-1600;** subway: 6 to 77th St.). Closed from July to August. **Joe's Pub** is a popular cabaret and supper club at the Joseph Papp Public Theater, 425 Lafayette St., between Astor Place and 4th Street (© **212/539-8777;** www.joespub.com; subway: 6 to Astor Place).

COMEDY   **Carolines on Broadway** presents today's headliners in its Theater District showroom at 1626 Broadway, between 49th and 50th streets (© **212/757-4100;** www.carolines.com; subway: N or R to 49th St.; 1 or 9 to 50th St.). The **Comedy Cellar** is the club of choice for stand-up fans in the know at 117 MacDougal St., between Bleecker and West 3rd streets (© **212/254-3480;** www.comedycellar.com; subway: A, C, E, F, V, or S to W. 4th St., use 3rd St. exit).

BARS & COCKTAIL LOUNGES

In TriBeCa, **Bubble Lounge** at 228 W. Broadway, between Franklin and White streets (*©* **212/431-3443;** www.bubblelounge), is dedicated to the bubbly with more than 300 champagnes and sparkling wines. No jeans, sneakers, or baseball caps. Chinatown's **Double Happiness** at 173 Mott St., between Grand and Broome streets (*©* **212/941-1282;** subway: 6 to Spring St.), is a speak-easy-ish lounge with artistic nods to the neighborhood throughout. Don't miss the green tea martini.

On the Lower East Side, **Barramundi,** 147 Ludlow St., between Stanton and Rivington streets (*©* **212/569-6900;** subway: F to Second Ave.), is notable for its outdoor garden and friendly staff.

In the West Village, **Chumley's** (*©* **212/675-4449**) dates back to Prohibition and offers a good selection of on-taps and microbrews at 86 Bedford St., at Barrow Street (subway: 1 or 9 to Christopher St.).

Near Gramercy Park, **Pete's Tavern,** 129 E. 18th St., at Irving Place (*©* **212/473-7676;** www.petestavern.com; subway: L, N, R, 4, 5, or 6 to 14th St./Union Sq.), opened while Lincoln was still president. There's Guinness on tap and a terrific happy hour.

On the West Side, at the **Oak Room at the Algonquin,** 59 W. 44th St., between Fifth and Sixth avenues (*©* **212/840-6800;** subway: B, D, F, or V to 42nd St.), you can feel the spirit of Dorothy Parker and the legendary Algonquin Round Table. It's the comfiest hotel bar in town. The **Russian Vodka Room,** at 265 W. 52nd St., between Broadway and Eighth Avenue (*©* **212/307-5835;** subway: C, E, 1, or 9 to 50th St.) is a Theater District find, with more than 50 vodkas plus the RVR's own miraculous infusions.

On the East Side, **The Campbell Apartment** in Grand Central Terminal, 15 Vanderbilt Ave. (*©* **212/953-0409;** subway: S, 4, 5, 6, 7 to 42nd St./Grand Central), is a high-ceilinged room restored to its full Florentine glory, and serves wines and champagnes by the glass, single-malt Scotches, fine stogies, and haute noshies to a well-heeled commuting crowd. There's a dress code.

The **All State Cafe,** 250 W. 72nd St., between Broadway and West End Avenue (*©* **212/874-1883;** subway: 1, 2, 3, or 9 to 72nd St.), is a subterranean pub that's one of Manhattan's undiscovered treasures—the quintessential neighborhood "snugger."

On the Upper East Side, **Bemelmans Bar** at The Carlyle hotel, 35 E. 76th St. at Madison Avenue (*©* **212/744-1600;** subway: 6 to 77th St.), is a luxurious spot for cocktails and the best hotel bar in the city. **Elaine's,** at 1703 Second Ave., between 88th and 89th streets (*©* **212/534-8103;** subway: 4, 5, or 6 to 86th St.), is where the glittering literati still come for dinner and book parties.

DANCE/NIGHTCLUBS

Baktun, 418 W. 14th St., between Ninth Avenue and Washington Street (*©* **212/206-1590;** www.baktun.com; subway: A, C, E, or L to 14th St.), has been hot, hot, hot since the word go. The music tends toward electronica, with some live acts in the mix. Your odds of getting into **crobar,** 530 W. 28th St., between Tenth and Eleventh avenues (*©* **212/629-9000;** www.crobar.com; subway: C or E to 23rd St.), are pretty fair. The venue holds up to 3,000 people and offers a fab sound system and great DJs.

Swing is a nightly affair at **Swing 46.** Music is live nightly except Monday and runs the gamut from big band to boogie-woogie to jump blues. Even first-timers can join in, as free swing lessons are offered Wednesday through Saturday at 9:15pm. No jeans or sneakers. It's at 349 W. 46th St., between Eighth and Ninth avenues (© **212/262-9554;** www.swing46.com; subway: C or E to 50th St.).

THE GAY & LESBIAN SCENE

To get a thorough, up-to-date take on what's happening in gay and lesbian nightlife, pick up copies of *HX* (www.hx.com), *Gay City News* (www.gaycitynews.com), the *New York Blade* (www.nyblade.com), or *Next.* They're available for free in bars and clubs all around town or at the **Lesbian and Gay Community Center,** at 208 W. 13th St., between Seventh and Eighth avenues (© **212/620-7310;** www.gaycenter. org). These days, many bars, clubs, cabarets, and cocktail lounges are neither gay nor straight but a bit of both, either catering to a mixed crowd or to varying orientations on different nights of the week.

Highlights of the GLBT bar scene include Chelsea's **Barracuda** (© **212/645-8613;** subway: C, E, 1, or 9 to 23rd St.), a trendy, loungey place that's regularly voted "Best Bar" by the readers of *HX.* Look for the regular drag shows at 275 W. 22nd St., between Seventh and Eighth avenues. **The Stonewall Bar** (© **212/463-0950;** subway: 1 or 9 to Christopher St.) is where it all started. A mixed gay and lesbian crowd makes this an easy place to begin. At least pop in to relive a defining moment in queer history at 53 Christopher St., east of Seventh Avenue. In the East Village, **The Boiler Room,** 86 E. 4th St., between First and Second avenues (© **212/254-7536;** subway: F to Second Ave.) is everybody's favorite gay dive. Despite the mixed guy-girl crowd, it's a serious cruising scene for beautiful boys and a fine hangout for those who'd rather play pool.

2 Historic Highlights of the Hudson River Valley

Just over 300 miles long, the **Hudson River Valley** spans eight counties along the east and west banks of the river, from Albany down to Yonkers. The entire valley is a National Heritage Area and one of the most beautiful regions in the eastern United States. The river valley's extraordinary landscapes gave birth to America's first art school, the Hudson River School of Painters, and writers such as Edith Wharton and Washington Irving set their stories and novels along the banks of the Hudson. And it was here that America's most legendary families—among them, the Livingstons, Vanderbilts, Roosevelts, and Rockefellers—shaped the face of American industry and politics, leaving legacies of grand country estates and the towns that grew up around them. When it comes to history, few areas can rival the Hudson.

ESSENTIALS

GETTING THERE   Most visitors traveling by air fly into one of the New York City area's three major airports. For information on those, see p. 103. Major rental car companies (a car is by far the best way to tour the region) have representatives at all the major airports.

The Lower Hudson Valley begins just north of New York City, on either side of the river; take either **I-87** (New York State Thruway) north or the **Taconic State Parkway.** From Albany south, take I-87 south to 9W or **I-90** south to Route 9. Heading either east or west, the most direct route is along **I-84.**

Amtrak (© **800/USA-RAIL;** www.amtrak.com) has service to the Hudson Valley from New York City. The commuter **Metro-North Railroad** (© **800/638-7646;** www.mta.nyc.ny.us/mnr) travels up and down the Hudson out of Grand Central

Station in New York City. The trip hugging the river on the east side is one of the prettier train trips in the U.S.

VISITOR INFORMATION   General tourist information is available by calling Hudson Valley Tourism, Inc. (© **800/232-4782**); visit the organization's website, **www.travelhudsonvalley.org**, for links to the very informative sites maintained by each of the eight counties that touch upon the Hudson River Valley. For fall foliage reports, visit **www.empire.state.ny.us/tourism/foliage**.

FAMOUS HISTORIC ESTATES & SITES

The Lower Hudson Valley is lined with grand manor houses, but none compares to **Kykuit** (pronounced *kye*-cut), in Sleepy Hollow (© **914/631-9491;** www.hudson valley.org/web/kyku-main.html). John D. Rockefeller built his estate in its present classical Greek-Roman style in 1913. Take the guided tour of the lovely mansion, which is loaded with priceless Chinese ceramics and a fabulous collection of 20th-century modern art, including an outstanding series of tapestries executed by Pablo Picasso. The gardens (which boast a magnificent view of the Hudson) are loaded with works by Alexander Calder, Henry Moore, and Constantin Brancusi. The estate's coach barn features horse-drawn vehicles and classic automobiles from the family's collection. *Note:* Tours to the estate actually leave from another spot worth touring— **Phillipsburg Manor** (© **914/631-3992;** www.hudsonvalley.org/web/phil-main. html), which transports visitors to a complicated time in history, when this estate functioned as one of the largest slave plantations in the North. The site still functions as a working farm, with horses and sheep, wool spinning, milling of flour, and harvesting of rye in June and July. It's a great educational outing for families.

   Sunnyside, West Sunnyside Lane, Tarrytown (© **914/591-8763;** www.hudson valley.org/web/sunn-main.html), was the home of Washington Irving, the author who made Sleepy Hollow a household name and introduced the world to Rip van Winkle. Sunnyside, with its mélange of historical and architectural styles, including a Dutch stepped-gable roofline, a Spanish tower, and a master bedroom modeled after a Paris apartment, was Irving's personal retreat, a place to write and retire. Today the charming pastoral villa, swathed in vines and wisteria and nestled into the grounds along the Hudson, remains as he left it, with his books and writing papers in the study.

   Farther up the Hudson, in the town of Garrison, lies **Boscobel Restoration,** 1601 Rte. 9D (© **845/265-3638;** www.boscobel.org), which features one of the best collections of Federal-period furnishings and decorative arts in the United States. The mansion, built in 1804 by a British Loyalist, is a neoclassical Georgian masterpiece that was rescued from government destruction (it was sold at auction for $35 in the 1950s), and moved piece by piece to its current location. For a truly breathtaking view of the Hudson, head through the lovely rose garden to the front of the mansion, in the direction of the river. The **Hudson Valley Shakespeare Festival** (advance reservations required; **www.hvshakespeare.org**) is held here in the summer.

   One sight you'll see off to the right if you glance down the Hudson from Boscobel is the **U.S. Military Academy at West Point,** Route 218, Highland Falls (© **845/ 446-4724;** www.usma.ed or www.westpointtours.com), the nation's oldest and foremost military college—which celebrated its 200th anniversary in 2002 and is the Hudson Valley's most popular attraction. The only way to visit is by organized 1- or 2-hour tour on a bus that, among other spots, stops at the famous Cadet Chapel, which possesses stained-glass windows and the largest church organ in the world, with more than 21,000 pipes. The massive campus, with its Gothic Revival buildings perched on the west side above the Hudson River, is undeniably handsome, especially in fall. Tickets for all tours must be purchased at the Visitor's Center.

Heading north into the middle section of the valley, you'll arrive in Hyde Park, site of several of the region's best attractions. First up is the **Vanderbilt Mansion National Historic Site** (② 845/229-9115; www.nps.gov/vama). Frederick Vanderbilt's lavish 54-room country palace (actually the smallest of the Vanderbilt mansions) in Hyde Park, built in 1898, is a no-holds-barred gem that epitomized the Gilded Age's nouveau riche. French in every respect, from Louise's Versailles-like bedroom to the grand dining room and Frederick's glittering master bedroom, it's impressively decorated in grand style and should not be missed. Nearby is the **Franklin Delano Roosevelt Presidential Library and Museum/FDR Home** (② 800/FDR-VISIT or 845/229-8114; www.nps.gov/hofr and www.fdrlibrary.marist.edu). FDR adored the Hudson River Valley and designed his own presidential library, the nation's first, while still in his second term; he built it next to his lifelong home in Hyde Park. It is the only presidential library to have been used by a sitting president. See his cluttered White House desk (left as it was the last day of his presidency), and exhibits on the FDR presidency and times. Two wings added in memory of his wife, Eleanor Roosevelt, make this the only presidential library to have a section devoted to a first lady. FDR and Eleanor are buried in the rose garden on the grounds. Also in the area is the **Eleanor Roosevelt National Historic Site (Val-Kill Cottage) & Top Cottage** (② 845/229-9115; www.nps.gov/elro), where you can visit the country retreats used by the Roosevelts to get away from it all and to entertain important guests (such as Winston Churchill and the queen of England). *Tip:* The National Park Service sells a pass to all three Hyde Park sites that offers a good discount off the regular single admission price (and those with valid National Parks passes can enter all three sites for free).

The best estate in the Upper Hudson area is the **Olana State Historic Site,** Route 9G, Hudson (② 518/828-0135; www.olana.org), the unique home of the accomplished Hudson River School painter Frederick Church (1826–1900), who designed both the building and the surrounding landscape. Named for a Persian treasure house, the home reflects Church's interest in Moorish design and is loaded with the knick-knacks, furniture, tapestries, rugs, bronzes, paintings, sculptures, and the other objets d'art collected by Church during his travels. Everything you see looks exactly as it did when Church died in 1900, down to the position of the paintbrushes in his studio. You can see the house only by guided tour; the docents here are especially knowledgeable and entertaining.

WHERE TO STAY & DINE

Most of the sites above can be visited as day trips out of New York City, but why not do as New Yorkers do and spend a night or a weekend at one of the region's many charming and romantic inns? What follows are two great places to stay in the region and one exceptional place to dine; contact Hudson Valley Tourism (see above) for more info on accommodations in the area.

Castle on the Hudson, 400 Benedict Ave., Tarrytown (② 914/631-1980; www.castleonthehudson.com), is a Relais & Châteaux property that offers some of the most extravagant accommodations along the Hudson Valley in a grand 45-room castle built in 1910 on a bluff overlooking the river. Even if you're not staying here, it's well worth dining at its restaurant for a special four-course prix-fixe meal or one of the periodic wine-tasting dinners.

In the Middle Hudson region, for unrestrained luxury in a country inn setting, nothing comes close to the **Belvedere Mansion,** Route 9, Staatsburgh (© **845/889-8000;** www.belvederemansion.com). The elegant interiors feature 18th-century antiques, silk fabrics, rich colors, luxurious linens, and marble bathrooms fit for a prince. The seven main-house rooms are the biggest and most expensive; several have fantastic river views and such details as claw-foot tubs and canopied beds. Stick to the main building or the rooms in the new Hunting Lodge (these have fireplaces) for the best experience. The restaurant in the inn offers exquisitely prepared cuisine in a refined setting (try to reserve the private dining nook just up the main staircase for an especially romantic meal—many a proposal's been tendered there).

If you have a chance, while in Hyde Park, try to have at least one meal at the legendary **Culinary Institute of America,** 1946 Campus Dr., off Route 9, Hyde Park (© **845/471-6608;** www.ciachef.edu). The nation's foremost culinary arts college has four on-campus restaurants and a bakery cafe that are open to the public (reserve online well in advance!). No matter where you eat, you're guaranteed to have a meal worth savoring.

3 Upstate New York Highlights

THE ADIRONDACKS

The 'dacks (as locals know them) is an area you simply can't ignore. Its 600 million acres hold some 2,000 peaks, 100 of them taller than 3,000 feet. Nearly half of the park is forest preserve: vast forests of pine, maple, and birch. The park supports 500,000 acres of old-growth forest, 200,000 acres of which have never been logged. And water? You'll find some 2,500 lakes and ponds, along with more than 30,000 miles of rivers and streams. Ralph Waldo Emerson and other thinkers found refuge here in the mid–19th century, forming philosopher's camps and using the woods for inspiration. And the park formed the exploratory dreams of Theodore Roosevelt, who canoed in the St. Regis Wilderness Canoe Area at the age of 12 and often returned to seek refuge.

Make no mistake: Though the peaks of the Adirondacks don't have the rugged, jagged look of, say, the Rockies, this can be harsh territory. But if you prepare well, it can be some of the most beautiful land to travel in. The region is well stocked with hotels, restaurants, and campsites, so you can get as much or as little civilization as you please.

ESSENTIALS

GETTING THERE   The Adirondack region is best appreciated by car. The New York State Thruway, **I-87,** a toll road from New York City to Albany, becomes the scenic, toll-free Adirondack Northway. It hugs the region's eastern border, with exits to Lake George (about 4 hr. from the Big Apple), Blue Mountain Lake, Ticonderoga, Lake Placid, and other areas of interest, eventually reaching Canada. The western side of the Adirondacks can be accessed from either **I-81** north at Watertown to **Route 3** or by following **I-90** east through Utica to **routes 8** and **12.** Inside the park, a sparse network of roads squeezes between mountain ranges and tunnel into dense forests. **Route 73,** which begins at Exit 30 of the Northway and ends in Lake Placid, provides a particularly picturesque tour through the High Peaks region.

VISITOR INFORMATION   The **Adirondack Regional Tourism Council** (© **518/846-8016;** www.adk.org) has an information center on I-87 southbound between exits 41 and 40 that's open from the end of June to Labor Day daily from 8am to 8pm. For information on Lake George, contact **Warren County Tourism, Municipal Center,** 1340 State Rte. 9, Lake George (© **800/365-1050** or 518/761-6366; www.visitlakegeorge.com). For info on Lake Placid, contact the **Lake Placid/ Essex County Visitors Bureau,** Olympic Center, 216 Main St., Lake Placid (© **800/ 447-5224** or 518/523-2445; www.lakeplacid.com). Other good sources of information are **www.adirondacks.com** or **www.adirondacklife.com**.

EXPLORING THE ADIRONDACKS

As an all-season destination, the Adirondack region has its highlights and its hazards. Icy roads and winter storms can make driving precarious, so call ahead to check road conditions. Visitors planning an outdoor excursion should anticipate unpredictable dips in temperature and unexpected precipitation year-round. For workshops on outdoor skills, such as paddling or mountain climbing, contact the **Adirondack Mountain Club** (© **800/395-8080** or 518/668-4447; www.adk.org).

THE OLYMPIC SIGHTS   The 1932 Winter Olympics put Lake Placid in the international spotlight; hosting the Games again in 1980 cemented its legacy. You can see some of the sites where legends were made, including the "Miracle on Ice" hockey victory of the Americans over the Russians. **The Olympic Regional Development Authority** (© **518/523-1655;** www.orda.org) handles it all.

Skip the Olympic Training Center, at 421 Old Military Rd.; there's not much open to the public. For downhill skiing on **Whiteface,** see below. You can see all of the following in 1 day. Start off at the **Verizon Sports Complex,** Route 73 (© **518/523-2811**), 20 minutes west of Lake Placid, for cross-country skiing. In the same complex—and definitely something you should not miss—is the **bobsled/luge/skeleton track,** where you'll watch athletes bomb down on and in crazy machinery. You can even strap yourself into a bobsled and race down the half-mile track with a guide and brakeman ($40)—you'll never watch the Olympics the same way. The sleds are on wheels in summer, but they go much faster on the winter ice. Then drive 10 minutes back toward town and you'll see the towering presence of the ski jump towers at the **MacKenzie-Intervale Ski Jumping Complex,** Route 73 (© **518/523-2202**). December through March and June through October, watch athletes soar off these ramps. Ride the lift alongside it and take the 26-story elevator to the top of the 394-foot tower ($9) to get the skiers' terrifying perspective. From June to October you can watch them jump, too—into a 750,000-gallon pool at the adjacent **Kodak Sports Park.** Drive back into town and spend a half-hour in the **Winter Olympic Museum** (© **518/523-1655**) at the **Olympic Center;** it's $4 to check out a good history of the Games in Placid and tons of memorabilia. While there, go skating on the rinks where such legends as Sonja Henie and Eric Heiden made history.

Whiteface, Route 86, Wilmington (© **518/946-2223;** www.whiteface.com), is the east's only Olympic mountain (elevation 4,400 ft.), and it has the best skiing in the state. With the greatest vertical drop in the east (3,430 ft.), there's a variety of terrain that will appeal to all levels. In fact, 35% of the trails are rated for novices. There are 65 trails and 11 lifts in all. A 1-day lift ticket costs $59.

TOURING LAKE CHAMPLAIN   Lake Champlain doesn't offer much in the way of hotels or recreation, but it does have one must-see attraction.

Fort Ticonderoga, Route 74, Ticonderoga (© **518/585-2821;** www.fort-ticonderoga.org), was once a grimy, bloody stage for battle during the French and

Indian War and the American Revolution. Military history buffs will be in heaven at this fort set right on Lake Champlain. Built by the French beginning in 1755, the fort protected this narrow strip of water from its high perch, and since 1909 it's been open to the public, detailing the military history of the Lake Champlain and Lake George valleys. The collection is anything but dry; on view are nearly 1,000 muskets, bayonets, pistols, and swords from the 18th century, as well as a unique collection of uniforms. Not interested in the military stuff? There are gorgeous gardens for wandering. Allow 2 to 4 hours. Admission is $12 for adults, $6 for children 7 to 12, free for children under 7.

CENTRAL ADIRONDACKS   The wilderness in the heart of this region drew the likes of J. P. Morgan, Andrew Carnegie, and the Vanderbilts, who built elaborate rustic retreats, some accessible only by rail, during the Gilded Age. The Vanderbilts' estate, **Great Camp Sagamore,** 4 miles south of Raquette Lake (© 315/354-5311; www.sagamore.org), is open to the public and is a spectacular achievement in rustic craftsmanship. Their 27-building summer retreat for more than 50 years even included a bowling alley.

Just about everything there is to learn about the Adirondacks can be absorbed at **The Adirondack Museum,** Route 30, Blue Mountain Lake, off routes 28 and 30 (© 518/352-7311; www.adirondackmuseum.org). History buffs will eat up the extensive collection that traces the transportation, tourism, and personal past of the region, as well as a rundown of its flora and fauna. A couple of odd items—a canoe big enough to camp in, a bark-covered outhouse—will appeal to everyone, and the setting, overlooking the lovely **Blue Mountain Lake,** is spectacular. Allow 3 hours to see the exhibits and grounds, and bring a picnic lunch to enjoy the view. Admission is $14 adults, $7 children 7 to 17. It's open from Memorial Day weekend to mid-October.

THE SOUTHEASTERN REGION   James Fenimore Cooper had Lake George and environs in mind when he penned *Last of the Mohicans.* This area, once a battle zone, then a busy 18th-century port, and later a getaway for the elite, is now a lively, family-friendly vacation spot in summer and a sleepy, though lovely, destination in winter. There's historic Fort William Henry, kitschy arcades, minigolf courses, a local rodeo, an amusement park, and accommodations galore. Lake George village hosts a range of events, such as Americade (a huge biker rally), the Adirondack Balloon Festival, and Jazz Fest.

For lake excursions, nothing beats **Lake George Steamboat Company,** Steel Pier, Lake George (© 800/553-BOAT or 518/668-5777; www.lakegeorgesteamboat.com), where you can choose from 1- to 4-hour narrated cruises with or without a meal on their steamship paddle-wheeler or one of the other two old-time ships. Lake George is also a gorgeous place to paddle, with crystal-clear, spring-fed waters and a wealth of islands and small bays; at 32 miles long, you'd be better off in a sea kayak if you want to do some serious exploring. Get your canoe or kayak from **Mountainman Outdoor Supply Company,** Route 28 in both Inlet and Old Forge (© 877/CANOE-NY or 315/357-6672; www.mountainmanoutdoors.com).

Lovers of kitschy minigolf shouldn't miss **Around the World Golf,** Route 9 (© 518/668-3223), where you can choose to putt around the U.S. (complete with graffiti under the Brooklyn Bridge) or the world (with the Egyptian pyramids and a Japanese garden). Outside Lake George, the **Wild West Ranch and Western Town,** Bloody Pond Road (© 518/668-2121), offers trail rides, gold panning, and a petting zoo.

WHERE TO STAY

In addition to the numerous hotels, B&Bs, and motels in the Adirondacks, the Department of Environmental Conservation maintains roughly 40 state campgrounds in the park. For information on sleeping alfresco, call © **518/457-2500** or visit **www. dec.state.ny.us**.

The exclusive **Lake Placid Lodge,** Whiteface Inn Road (© **877/523-2700** or 518/ 523-2700; www.lakeplacidlodge.com), is a Relais & Châteaux member set right on Lake Placid, with an upscale rustic look (*very* Adirondack) and lots of privacy. It's the kind of place that could get away with an air of snootiness, but there's none—you're in the woods, after all. The service is helpful and friendly, and staffers will bend over backwards to make your stay perfect. Birch branches are everywhere, from the hallway ceilings to the cozy bar to the funky, woodsy furnishings in the (nonsmoking) guest rooms. In fact, all the furniture, made by local artists, is for sale. Rooms and bathrooms are large, luxurious, and comfortable, but the cabins afford the ultimate in privacy—most are set right on the lake's shore, with stone fireplaces, sitting areas, and picture windows. Rates run $400 to $475 double. Children under 12 are not permitted.

Well-heeled travelers have been drawn to **The Sagamore,** 110 Sagamore Rd. (© **800/358-3585** or 518/644-9400; www.thesagamore.com), since 1883. Drive onto its personal 72-acre island and up to its Colonial-style main building and you'll immediately see why: peace, quiet, and luxury. Jutting out into Lake George, this private getaway serves up a wealth of water activities, a great golf course, a full spa, and lakeside lounging. The common-area decor is more formal than comfy; luckily, that stuffiness doesn't carry over to the helpful staff. The restored main-building rooms—done in flowery patterns and muted tones—have the same formal furniture, but bathrooms give you plenty of room to navigate. Suites, with two full rooms and some with views in two directions, are well worth the extra money. There are several buildings and price options. The contemporary "lodge" rooms are not actually in the lodge, but with balconies and fireplaces, offer the best bang for the buck. An eye-popping, privately owned castle is also for rent. All rooms are nonsmoking. Rates run $149 to $330 double.

Far from the madness of Lake Placid and set back in the woods on the shores of Saranac Lake, the **Wawbeek,** Panther Mountain Road, Route 30, Tupper Lake (© **800/ 953-2656** or 518/359-2656; www.wawbeek.com), is a dying breed—a homey, secluded, luxurious camp on the water. In its earlier manifestations it was a great camp—Rockefellers and du Ponts stayed here—and it's easy to see what drew them: walk the 40 acres, the 1,500 feet of shoreline, and the nature trail, and you'll find your own private slice of the 'dacks. Or just kick back in the gorgeous main lodge and read. The nonsmoking rooms and cottages are spread out and tucked deep in the woods, with several rooms overlooking the mountains. Rooms are generally large (though with smallish bathrooms) and come decked out in Adirondack-style furniture and some of the world's most comfortable beds. For more privacy, grab one of the log cabins, which boast full kitchens, decks, and views. None of the rooms have phones. Rates run $100 to $495 double and include breakfast.

The gorgeous 1870 Victorian that's home to **The Lake Champlain Inn,** 428 County Rte. 3, Ticonderoga (© **518/547-9942;** www.tlcinn.com), has a prime location right on Lake Champlain, and its rooms offer views of the lake, the Adirondacks, and even Vermont's Green Mountains. You're also just 2 miles from the northern end of Lake George. While rooms aren't the biggest, their views are among the best in the park. And they boast nice touches like wrought-iron beds, claw-foot tubs, and original woodwork. The one suite gives you two adjoining rooms. You'll also find a house

Cooperstown: Checking Out Baseball's Best Moments

For aficionados of America's national pastime, a pilgrimage to the **Baseball Hall of Fame** in the charming town of Cooperstown, a 5-hour drive north of New York City, is a must; for everyone else—it's still worth a trip. Yes, you'll find plenty of statistics-spouting baseball fanatics walking around the Hall. But this museum isn't just for passionate lovers of the game or its coveted collectibles. After all, this *is* America's pastime, and a walk through the 30,000 exhibits shows just how important this sport has been to America's past and present. The hall collected its first artifact in 1937, and now you can find baseballs, bats, uniforms, ballpark artifacts, priceless trading cards, and a microcosm of American history. You'll learn about the Negro Leagues and the integration of baseball, find out the president who established the tradition of throwing out the first pitch on opening day, and, of course, see some of the greatest moments of the greatest players ever.

A 3-year, $20-million renovation was completed in 2005, adding 10,000 square feet of exhibit space and new technology, so depending on how big a fan you are, you could spend anywhere from an hour to a full day (or more) browsing, learning, and loving the game.

For more information on the hall, call ℂ **888/HALL-OF-FAME** or 607/547-7200, or surf the Internet to **www.baseballhalloffame.org**. Admission to the hall costs $15 adults, $5 for kids ages 7 to 12.

Cooperstown is easiest to get to by car. From the New York State Thruway, take Exit 30 at Herkimer and go south on State Highway 28 or State Highway 80—both will take you to Cooperstown. The hall is located at 25 Main St.

---

with two rooms, called the Schoolhouse, a large modern Victorian-style house that's very modern inside and sits on 130 acres. The adjacent state land is perfect for hiking or cross-country skiing. The entire property is nonsmoking and none of the rooms have phones. Rates include full breakfast and run $85 to $135 double.

CORNING

Corning is a charming destination in New York's southern tier, surrounded by the natural beauty of the Finger Lakes region. Quite literally, it's the town that Corning built; the company, the original makers of Corningware, Pyrex, and now high-tech materials such as fiber optics, has employed as many as half the town's population. Corning was once known as "crystal city" for its concentration of glassworks and today glass is at the center of the town's attractions, at the world-renowned Corning Museum of Glass.

ESSENTIALS

GETTING THERE   Easily accessible by car from most points in the northeast, Corning is directly off **Route 17/I-86** and a straight shot along **Route 414** south of Watkins Glen; from the south, take **Route 15.**

VISITOR INFORMATION   The **Steuben County Conference & Visitors Bureau** is located at 5 W. Market St. (Baron Steuben Building, 2nd floor), Corning (ℂ **866/946-3386** or 607/936-6544; www.corningfingerlakes.com).

EXPLORING CORNING

The **Corning Museum of Glass,** I-86, Exit 46 (© **607/937-5371;** www.cmog.org), is the premier and most comprehensive collection of historical and art glass in the world. It is quite literally dazzling. On view are 35,000 glass pieces representing 35 centuries of glass craftsmanship, beginning with a piece dating from 1411 B.C. There is also a gallery of glass sculpture and a glass innovation center, with ingeniously designed exhibits that depict the use of glass in technology. The museum is anything but static; it offers hot-glass demonstrations, glass-making workshops, and some of the best shopping to be found, with a sprawling array of shops dealing in glass, crystal, and jewelry. The museum is especially well designed for children, who usually can't get enough of the interactive science exhibits and opportunities to handle telescopes and peer out a periscope that "sees" from the building's roof. A walk-in glass workshop allows visitors to make their very own glass souvenirs. The museum is open daily. Admission is $12 for adults, free for children under 17. A $16 combination ticket for adults includes admission to CMoG and the Rockwell Museum (see below). The museum also operates a free shuttle service from the museum to Market Street, downtown.

The **Rockwell Museum of Western Art,** 111 Cedar St. (© **607/937-5386;** www. rockwellmuseum.org), which occupies the former city hall, maintains an excellent collection of both historical and contemporary Western and Native American art. An inviting design of bold colors and gorgeous woods inside the shell of a neo-Romanesque building, the museum features daring juxtapositions that work surprisingly well, including a number of fantastic pieces by Native Americans. A neat idea for children is the color-coded "art backpacks," which come equipped with games and lesson and drawing books, making the museum an especially interactive place. The museum is open daily. Admission is $6.50 for adults, $4.50 for children 6 to 17, and free for children under 6. Allow an hour or two.

WHERE TO STAY

The best accommodations in town are at the **Hillcrest Manor Bed and Breakfast,** 227 Cedar St. (© **607/936-4548;** www.corninghillcrestmanor.com), one of the finest B&Bs we've seen anywhere. The impressively grand 1890 Greek Revival mansion, with massive pillars, porches, and terraces, sits in a quiet residential neighborhood up the hill from downtown Corning. Rooms are huge and impeccably decorated with great, luxurious taste. The house features stately parlors, an elegant candlelit dining room, and a palatial cedar stairway. Some rooms have fireplaces and immense tubs; all offer excellent value for the money. We could relax here for days. Rates include full breakfast and run $125 to $165 double; credit cards are not accepted.

The large and well-run **Radisson Hotel Corning,** 125 Denison Pkwy. (© **800/ 333-3333** or 607/962-5000; www.radisson.com/corningny), is the only full-service hotel in downtown Corning, a reason for its popularity with business travelers, though its pool and on-site restaurant also make it a good place for families and other leisure travelers. Rooms are spacious and attractively appointed. Rates run $89 to $130 double.

4 Highlights of the New Jersey Shore: Atlantic City & Cape May

ATLANTIC CITY

One of America's oldest seaside resorts, Atlantic City is most famous these days as a weekend gambler's mecca. It's the East Coast's answer to Las Vegas, and home to many of the same names: Caesars, Bally's, Sands, the Tropicana. Tourists come by the millions (more than 35 million of them, to be exact) to try their luck at the city's 12 casinos, 9 of which line the world's first oceanfront boardwalk, opened in 1870. The city itself began life in 1854 and celebrated its 150th anniversary in 2004 with a lot of fanfare.

Despite its historic pedigree, Atlantic City went to seed in the years following World War II, abandoned in the wake of cheap and easy air travel to Florida and the Caribbean. In the 1970s, in a last-ditch effort to reinvigorate this once-proud Victorian vacation resort, the state of New Jersey instituted casino gambling—and the unconventional urban-renewal plan has been something of a success, though not quite the bonanza that organizers might have hoped for. Still, when you consider that Atlantic City is within easy reach of New York City, Philadelphia, and most of the major Midwest and mid-Atlantic metropolitan areas, its status as a vacation destination seems assured.

The city is in the midst of a multibillion-dollar renewal plan that has already resulted in sparkling new convention and visitor centers, new bus and train terminals, a new outlet mall complex, and a generally more cleaned-up appearance. The opening of the Borgata in the Marina District in 2003, and its recent addition of a second tower, added quite a bit of luster to the city's revitalization efforts. In addition, in 2004, the Tropicana launched The Quarter, an Old Havana–themed complex consisting of added hotel space, restaurants, retail venues, and an IMAX theater. Meanwhile, Caesars has just debuted The Pier at Caesars, a multimillion-dollar retail and entertainment complex featuring fabulous Louis Vuitton and Tiffany & Co. boutiques.

Most important of all is a change in attitude. Atlantic City clearly has Vegas aspirations: It hopes to reemerge as a luxe playground catering to adults, and has already succeeded in ratcheting up its cool factor enormously. We couldn't help but notice all of the signs in the casino hotels politely but firmly telling kids who aren't guests to get lost (we also couldn't help but wonder at the irony of that given all the kid-friendly stuff going on at the Boardwalk just outside the casino hotels' doorsteps). We doubt the Boardwalk is going to be as successful as Sin City in this regard (and, indeed, plenty of families do take advantage of the beach), but we must note that few kids are to be found in the Marina District and the vacationing couples there seemed to be all the happier for it.

Still, this isn't Vegas. First of all, there's not a lot to do beyond the casino hotels and the beach, and though the neighborhood in the immediate vicinity of the Boardwalk is looking better nowadays, we still don't recommend walking around that area after dark. If you're looking for relaxation, and you aren't a gambling fan or don't want to catch a show or hit a late-night club, Cape May is a better option: It's cleaner and quieter, and the beaches are nicer. Second, while some of the casinos are on par with their desert counterparts in sophistication if not in scale (the lone exception being the Borgata, which we can imagine in Vegas), the Boardwalk still has some growing up to do before it will ever compete with the Vegas Strip.

ESSENTIALS

GETTING THERE   By Plane   You can fly into **Atlantic City International Airport** (© **609/645-7895;** www.acairport.com), 10 miles from downtown. **Atlantic City Airport Taxi** (© **877/LOU-TAXI** or 609/383-1457; www.actaxi.com) can whisk you to your hotel from the terminal for $25; another good option is **Yellow Van** (© **800/224-9945**). There are also several car-rental agencies with desks at the airport.

By Car   Atlantic City is on the southern New Jersey shoreline, 60 miles southeast of Philadelphia and 120 miles south of New York City. From Philadelphia, take **I-76** to

Atlantic City

THE CASINOS

Atlantic City Hilton **2**

Bally's **14**

Bally's Wild Wild West
Casino **13**

Borgata Casino Hotel
& Spa **22**

Caesars **12**

Harrah's **21**

Resorts **19**

Tropicana **7**

Trump Marina **23**

Trump Plaza **11**

Trump Taj Mahal **20**

OTHER ACCOMMODATIONS ■

Comfort Inn Boardwalk **15**

Days Inn on the Boardwalk **6**

Holiday Inn Boardwalk **5**

Quality Inn Beach Block **17**

DINING ◆

Babalu Grill **10**

Bacchanal **12**

Boby Flay Steak **22**

Capriccio **19**

Cuba Libre **7**

Girasole **4**

Irish Pub & Inn **16**

Knife & Fork Inn **2**

Lefty's 1200 Club **18**

Mexico **1**

MIXX **22**

mur.mur **22**

Old Homestead **22**

The Palm **7**

State Road 42, which connects to the Atlantic City Expressway. From Manhattan, take the Lincoln or Holland tunnels or the George Washington Bridge to the New Jersey Turnpike (**I-95**) south; pick up the **Garden State Parkway** at Perth Amboy and follow it south to Exit 38, which connects to the **Atlantic City Expressway.**

By Bus   A car isn't necessary in Atlantic City, so if you prefer not to drive, bus service is available from Philadelphia and New York (trip time: about 1½ hr. from Philly, 2 hr. from New York) via **Greyhound** (© **800/229-9424;** www.greyhound.com) and **NJ Transit** (© **800/772-2222** or 973/762-5100; www.njtransit.com). Buses arrive at the safe and relatively new bus station adjacent to the Convention Center at Atlantic and Michigan avenues, 2 blocks from the Boardwalk. **Academy Bus Lines** (© **800/ 442-7272** or 800/992-0451; www.academybus.com) offers direct service from New York's Port Authority to a number of Boardwalk casinos.

Most Atlantic City casinos offer **bus packages,** which often include such value-added premiums as $20 in coins or free meals, from major northeast cities—including New York, Philadelphia, Baltimore, Washington, D.C., and Pittsburgh—aboard casino-direct charters. They generally cater to day visitors who want to come in to gamble for 12 hours or so without the expense of a hotel room. Call the casinos directly or check your local paper to learn about current offers (see "The Casinos," below).

By Train NJ Transit's Atlantic City line (© **800/772-2222** or 973/762-5100; www.njtransit.com) offers frequent service from Philadelphia (trip time: 1½ hr.). There's a free shuttle bus from the station to the casinos.

VISITOR INFORMATION Contact the **Atlantic City Convention & Visitors Authority** (© **888/AC-VISIT** or 609/449-7130; www.atlanticcitynj.com) and request its free visitor's guide. Their newly redesigned website is easy to navigate and helpful in planning a trip.

The **Atlantic City Visitor Welcome Center,** right on the Atlantic City Expressway, makes an ideal first stop. You can't miss this state-of-the-art resource center at the city's gateway, open from 9am to 5pm daily and from 9am to 8pm summer weekends. Another welcome center is located on the Boardwalk right next to Boardwalk Hall at Mississippi Avenue. The staff at the centers can give you a good map, brochures, and answers to specific questions.

GETTING AROUND If you don't want to walk from casino to casino along the mile-long stretch of the Boardwalk where most of the action is, you can catch a ride in an old-fashioned **rolling chair.** These shaded surreys are rolled up and down the length of the Boardwalk by experienced guides, who are out soliciting riders day and night. The fee is based on the distance traveled, but expect a minimum fare of $5 plus tip.

You can also travel between the casinos along Pacific Avenue, which runs parallel to the Boardwalk 1 block inland, aboard the **Atlantic City Jitney** (© **609/344-8642; www.jitneys.net**), a fleet of minibuses that run 24 hours a day; the fare is $1.50. The baby-blue or green versions run to the Marina section of the city, where the Trump Marina and Harrah's casinos are located.

THE CASINOS

The casino hotels are Atlantic City's big draw, luring visitors to spend nearly $5 billion in 2005. First on the Boardwalk was **Resorts,** at Pennsylvania Avenue (© **888/ 336-6378** or 609/344-6000; www.resortsac.com), which boasts a sharp new look thanks to a stylish $50-million renovation. It's bright, casual, and colorful, with a beachy vibe and an active showroom with top-flight rock, country, and pop headliners. Next door is *The Apprentice*'s honcho Donald Trump's **Trump Taj Mahal,** at Virginia Avenue (© **800/825-8888** or 609/449-1000; www.trumptaj.com). Done in a loose *Arabian Nights* theme, the Taj is the most glamorous and attractive of the Boardwalk casinos though the rooms need better upkeep. (Nonsmokers, take note: It has the best ventilation on the Boardwalk, and Atlantic City is a smoker's haven; in fact, the casinos are exempt from the ban on smoking that exists in New Jersey's bars and restaurants.)

> **Do Not Pass Go . . .**
> Monopoly was created in 1933 by Pennsylvanian Charles Darrow, who used the streets of Atlantic City as the basis for his game board.

Clustered around the Boardwalk's midpoint are a number of notable casinos. A massive expansion has put **Caesars,** at Arkansas Avenue (© **800/443-0104** or 609/ 348-4411; www.caesars.com), in league with its landmark Vegas counterpart, and it has some of the best rooms in town (in the Centurion Tower). The casino is appropriately glitzy and the staff is still the best costumed in town. Expect headliners such as David Copperfield. The casino offers excellent packages and special promotions, too. Next door is **Bally's,** at Michigan Avenue (© **888/537-0007** or 609/340-2000; www. ballys.com), a fun, festive casino with inviting gaming tables and lots of dollar slots. On the second floor is the Gateway mall, connecting to the Claridge next door, and also to Bally's **Wild Wild West Casino,** Atlantic City's best themed casino. The casino is very well done in a Disneyesque style, with faux red rocks and audio-animatronic figures that offer a fun change of pace from the standard glitz (though we have to wonder about its obvious kid-appeal given the casino's stance on discouraging kids from entering).

Nearby at Indiana Avenue is **Sands** (© **800/AC-SANDS** or 609/441-4000; www. acsands.com), best known for its great package rates and state-of-the-art spa. Rooms were remodeled only a couple of years ago and are still in good shape. All that glitters isn't gold at **Trump Plaza,** at Mississippi Avenue (© **800/677-7378** or 609/441-6000; www.trumpplaza.com), but it sure is shiny. Behind the glitz, this is an Everyman's casino, though the hotel needs work. The showroom often showcases big-name stars.

The **Tropicana,** at Brighton and the Boardwalk (© **800/THE-TROP;** www. tropicana.net), has undergone a revitalization with its "Quarter at Tropicana" addition. This glossy new shopping and dining complex with an Old Havana theme even has an IMAX theater (and a bluemercury Spa!). The addition added 500 new hotel rooms, and some of the casino's old rooms have been updated.

Best A Vegas Resort in Atlantic City

The multibillion-dollar **Borgata Hotel Casino & Spa,** One Borgata Way
(© **866/692-6742;** www.theborgata.com), which debuted to great acclaim
in summer 2003 is the undisputed champ of the city's casino hotels. Perhaps
the best compliment we can give this superlative property—a joint venture
of Boyd Gaming and MGM MIRAGE—is that it's the first in Atlantic City to
remind us of a Vegas resort. The decor is sleek and beautiful: With an exceptional European-style spa (couples with big bucks should definitely indulge
in its ultraromantic couples' treatment room); a magnificent lobby with
Dale Chihuly chandeliers and a lovely "Living Room" seating area for guests
to relax in; full-scale fitness center; indoor pool; classic barbershop;
immense casino with reasonable table limits; and multiple retail, entertainment, and dining venues, you won't want to leave (our major complaint—
Atlantic City's hottest property doesn't exactly make you want to venture
out into the rest of the city). The large rooms ($129–$509 double) are luxurious, by far the nicest in town: Think Egyptian cotton sheets on the comfy
beds; plenty of lighting; designer toiletries; fridges; and immense marble
bathrooms with lots of counter space, a separately enclosed toilet, and a
huge, two-person temperature-controlled shower encased entirely in marble. The suites ($209–$620) are even more luxurious.

Dining here is the best of the casino hotels as well (you'll need to reserve
well in advance to get in on the weekends). Here you'll find not one but
two establishments run by famed chef Luke Palladino: **Specchio,** which features modern Italian cuisine in an upscale dining room loaded with cherrywood and the chef's antique mirror collection; and **Ombra,** a fabulous wine
bar (over 14,000 bottles) with a vaulted Italian brick ceiling. Noted Philly
legend Susannah Foo runs **Suilan,** a romantic restaurant featuring Foo's signature French-Asian cuisine. If beef is more your thing, head to the branch
of New York's famous **Old Homestead,** where superb steaks are served amid
modern ambience, accompanied by a superb selection of Scotch. Three
brand-new restaurants include chic **SeaBlue,** designed by Adam Tihany as a
backdrop for chef Michael Mina's superb seafood menu (including 2-lb.
Maine lobster pot-pie); **Wolfgang Puck's American Grille,** where the celebrated celebrity chef produces his signature Spago-style gourmet pizzas as
well as an excellent grilled steak with bleu cheese; and **Bobby Flay Steak,**
where classic chopped salads and gigantic rib-eyes are as excellent as you
would expect from the Food Network star. For style-conscious dining, head
to **MIXX,** a trendy restaurant/nightclub where the food is Latin-Asian fusion
and the music is hip (and where you might see Jessica or Ashlee Simpson);
for late-night partying, there's new **mur.mur,** a sleek lounge with pricey bottle service starting at 10pm and lasting until morning, of course. (This is a
casino, after all.)

Farther down, at the cleanest and quietest end of the Boardwalk, is the **Atlantic City Hilton** (© 800/257-8677 or 609/347-7111; www.hiltonac.com). The Hilton does what Atlantic City's other casino hotels don't dare (lest you leave the casino, of course): It provides full beach services to their guests, including beach chairs, cabanas, kayaks, on-the-sand volleyball, and more. It also features a headliner showroom and some surprisingly comfy rooms. It's hands-down the best choice in town for those who'd like to play at the beach and/or bring the kids, before returning to high-quality rooms.

At Farley State Marina, a quick drive from the Boardwalk via Brigantine Boulevard (Rte. 87), are three more casinos. With an '80s teal color scheme and oldies tunes playing over the sound system, **Harrah's** (© 800/HARRAHS or 609/441-5000; www.harrahs.com) draws a generally older crowd to its ultrafriendly casino. **Trump Marina** (© 800/777-8477 or 609/441-2000; www.trumpmarina.com) targets a younger crowd with rock-'n'-roll Muzak and headliners, but it otherwise seems like just another glittery Trump property. The best of the bunch is the brand-new **Borgata Casino Hotel & Spa** (see the box "A Vegas Resort in Atlantic City," below).

IN THE SHOWROOMS   On any given night, Atlantic City's showrooms are peopled with acts ranging from Chris Rock to Tony Bennett to Aerosmith to Alicia Keys to Ringo Starr's All-Starr Band—and the quality just keeps getting better. Check with the visitor bureau at © 888/AC-VISIT or www.atlanticcitynj.com, or contact the casinos directly for current schedules. You can also find out what's on and buy tickets through **Ticketmaster** (© 856/338-9000; www.ticketmaster.com).

MORE TO SEE & DO

The city has the usual tourist traps, but there are a number of places worth your time (alas, the Steel Pier is no longer one of them—it closed for good in 2006). At Gardner's Basin, at the top end of New Hampshire Avenue, is the **Ocean Life Center** (© 609/348-2880; www.oceanlifecenter.com), with eight giant aquariums (including a touch tank), shipwreck artifacts, and more marine-themed fun for the kids. You can't miss the **Absecon Lighthouse,** 31 S. Rhode Island Ave. (© 609/449-1360; www.absconlighthouse.org), which was built in 1857 and is the tallest in New Jersey. On a clear day, it's worth climbing the 228 steps to the top to get a magnificent view of the Jersey shoreline. The free **Atlantic City Historical Museum,** New Jersey Avenue and the Boardwalk (© 609/344-1943; www.acmuseum.net), offers some interesting insights into the city's history through various exhibits and artifacts (including a larger-than life Mr. Peanut!). Do check out the interesting video that plays continuously in the museum. Another hard-to-miss attraction is in nearby Margate: **Lucy the Elephant,** 9200 Atlantic Ave. (© 609/823-6473; www.lucytheelephant.org), is a 65-ton building built to look like—yep, you guessed it—an elephant. Built in 1881 and listed on the National Register of Historic Places, this is one of those curious pieces of Americana that you just don't see too much of anymore, so go ahead and take the 30-minute tour of its interior.

If shopping is more your thing, you'll find plenty of tacky souvenir shops on the Boardwalk, and expensive boutiques in many of the casino hotels; there are also some affordable but chic stores such as **White House/Black Market** in the Quarter at Tropicana.

Die-hard fashionistas will want to head straight to **The Pier at Caesar's** (www.the pieratcaesars.com), a just-opened retail mecca far more glamorous than could have been imagined here even 5 years ago. Here, you'll find the jewels of **Tiffany & Co.,** the handbags and gorgeous luggage at **Louis Vuitton,** and men's and women's clothing and accessories at **Burberry. It's Sugar** is a wonderland of a candy store where there's even a replica of Lucy the Elephant made of millions of jelly beans.

Check out the Atlantic City Outlets—The Walk, at Michigan and Arctic avenues (© **609/343-0387;** www.acoutlets.com), the city's latest shopping, dining, and entertainment venue. For the city's famous saltwater taffy (discovered here in 1883 after an ocean storm flooded a candy store), head straight to **James Salt Water Taffy,** 1519 Boardwalk (© **609/344-1519;** www.jamescandy.com), which has been in business since 1880; those whose tastes run more to chocolate should make a beeline for **Steel's Fudge,** 1633 Boardwalk (© **888/783-3571;** www.steelsfudge.com), the oldest continually operated fudge company in the world.

WHERE TO STAY

There's no useful way to quote exact room rates at Atlantic City's casino hotels (see "The Casinos," above). Doubles vary from a low of about $95 to a high of $375, and the hotels stay generally competitive across-the-board. Rates are usually highest on summer weekends and lowest midweek in winter, but they can go through the roof during certain events, or if there's a major convention in town. Always ask about packages and special promotions, which may be able to save you big bucks. And, if you plan to visit again, sign up for the casino hotel's free slot clubs—members often get special rates and packages.

If the big hotels are too expensive for you, you have some non-casino options. A few good motels are located right on or just off the Boardwalk—although these well-located options can be subject to similarly dramatic pricing, with rates fluctuating between $64 and $310 depending on the dates and property; again, always ask about packages. Near the very nice Hilton end of the Boardwalk is the **Holiday Inn Boardwalk,** at Chelsea Avenue (© **800/548-3030** or 609/348-2200; www.atlanticcity. holiday-inn.com), which also offers some amazingly cheap casino packages with the Hilton that include all meals and gambling tokens. The **Days Inn on the Boardwalk,** 1 block over at Morris Avenue (© **800/325-2525** or 609/344-6101; www.atlanticcity daysinn.com), even has rooms with ocean views. Just off the Boardwalk, near the Sands, is the **Comfort Inn Boardwalk,** 154 S. Kentucky Ave. (© **800/228-5150** or 609/348-4000; www.comfortinn.com), whose well-kept rooms feature Jacuzzi tubs.

WHERE TO DINE

If you're looking for something more sophisticated than theme restaurants (they are all over the Boardwalk and we can't say they serve exceptional cuisine), take heart. At chic, Tuscan-inspired, and critically lauded **Girasole,** in the Ocean Club Condos, 3108 Pacific Ave., at Montpelier Avenue (© **609/345-5554;** www.girasoleac.com), the creative kitchen has a welcoming light touch with wood oven–baked pizzas, excellent carpaccios, pastas, and seafood. Under new ownership, the **Knife & Fork Inn,** Atlantic and Pacific avenues (© **609/344-1133;** www.knifeandforkinn.com), in its revamped, iconic Tudor brick structure that once housed a men's club, has a glam charm again, and where better to indulge in old-A.C. classics such as lobster Thermidor?

For a romantic night out with Atlantic City flavor, head to **Lefty's 1200 Club** (© **609/348-5677**), an old-style supper club featuring terrific Italian cuisine, seafood, and steaks served by a friendly staff. Housed in a historic 19th-century building, the club sports an elegant Renaissance theme and features live music in the nightclub in back.

The casual **Tun Tavern Brewing Company,** at the corner of Baltic and Michigan avenues (© **609/347-7800;** www.tuntavern.com), serves upscale pub grub and first-rate microbrews in a festive, modern setting. For the city's best Mexican food, head to the appropriately named **Mexico,** 3810 Ventnor Ave. (© **609/344-0366**), which features a stellar seviche, reasonable prices, a colorful dining room, and several Mexican beers on tap.

The best casino dining is unquestionably at the **Borgata Hotel Casino & Spa** in the Marina District (see the box, "A Vegas Resort in Atlantic City," above, for the low-down on the hotel's best restaurants). A few other standouts are also worth mentioning. **Cuba Libre** (© **609/348-6700;** www.cubalibrerestaurant.com) in the Quarter at Tropicana combines a cool old-Havana decor with spicy seviche, guava BBQ ribs, gaucho steak, *camarones* (shrimp) enchiladas, and the most refreshing mojitos this side of Miami; there's even salsa dancing to work off the flan. **The Palm** (© **609/344-7256;** www.thepalm.com), also in the Quarter, draws a high-rolling, high-heeled, Armani-wearing crowd who like their caricatures on the walls—and consistently great porter-houses the size of a Louis Vuitton handbag. **Capriccio,** the Italian jewel at Resorts (© **609/344-6000**), has received Zagat's award of excellence for its array of pastas, seafood, and specialties such as *osso buco.* The dining room is particularly romantic and offers views of the Atlantic.

The **Irish Pub & Inn,** just off the Boardwalk at 164 St. James Place (© **609/344-9063;** www.theirishpub.com), is a true Atlantic City gem. It's appealingly old-fashioned, with friendly service and hearty fare that's the best cheap eats in town (nothing over $6.75). Rooms above the pub are also a steal: Rates range from $25 to $80 a night. And no Atlantic City visit is complete without a visit to the famous **White House Sub Shop,** 2301 Arctic Ave. (© **609/345-8599**), where you will stand in line (so worth it!) for one of its legendary and immense sandwiches—you will be in good company, as everyone from presidents to celebrities has sought out these yummy creations.

CAPE MAY

At the southern tip of the Garden State is the jewel of the Jersey shore: Cape May, a beautifully preserved Victorian beach resort that's popular with romance-seeking couples drawn by the impeccably restored inns and quaint vibe, and families that like the town's easygoing nature and fine collection of affordable beachfront motels. Visiting Cape May is like taking a step back in time to the glory days of the Jersey shore, before frenetic amusement piers and summer-break college crowds overtook the scene. Even at the height of the summer season, the town stays relaxed and friendly; after a lazy day at the beach, most folks' big activity is to retire to a wide veranda, glass of iced tea in hand, to sit back and watch the world stroll by.

ESSENTIALS
GETTING THERE & GETTING AROUND Cape May, a spit stretching 20 miles offshore between the Atlantic Ocean and Delaware Bay, is at the southern tip of New Jersey, about 40 miles south of the Atlantic City Toll Plaza at the end of the Garden State Parkway. **NJ Transit** buses (© **800/772-2222** or 973/762-5100; www.nj transit.com) arrive from Philadelphia and Atlantic City year-round, and from New York City in summer. If you're arriving from points south, you can take the 70-minute

Cape May–Lewes Ferry (© 800/64-FERRY; www.capemaylewesferry.com), which carries passengers and vehicles between Lewes, Delaware, and Cape May daily year-round (car fare costs $23–$29 one-way; passengers pay $7–$9.50).

Cape May can become quite traffic-congested and parking is hard to come by, particularly in summer, so most visitors park their cars for the length of their stay and walk or trolley around town. If you'd like to rent a bike or a four-wheeled surrey for two or for the entire family, stop into **Shields' Bike Rentals,** 11 Gurney St., just inland from Beach Drive (© 609/884-1818), or the **Village Bicycle Shop,** 605 Lafayette St. (© 609/884-8500). You can reserve in advance from **Cape Island Bicycle Center,** at Beach and Howard streets (© 609/898-7368; www.capeislandbike rentals.com). Rentals start at $10 a day for a single-speed bicycle.

VISITOR INFORMATION   For more information, contact the **Chamber of Commerce of Greater Cape May** (© 609/884-5508; www.capemaychamber.com), or the **Cape May County Chamber of Commerce** (© 609/465-5017; www.cape maycountychamber.com). Information is also available online at **www.capemay.com**. For events information, your best source is **www.capemaymac.org**. A staffed **information center** is at the Ocean View Plaza Rest Area, 1½ miles beyond the Garden State Parkway's Cape May Toll Plaza. The chamber of commerce runs an excellent **visitor center** a few minutes' drive south, at Exit 11 (on the right side of the road after the traffic light).

SPECIAL EVENTS & FESTIVALS   Highlights include the **Cape May Music Festival,** which draws distinguished classical performers from around the globe over 6 weeks in May and June; the **Cape May Food & Wine Festival,** where open-house food samplings at dozens of participating restaurants consume the better part of a week in late September; hugely popular **Victorian Week** in mid-October, celebrating the town's heritage with historic house tours and other nostalgic events; and **Christmas in Cape May,** a whole host of holiday-themed events (including special candle-light house tours) that start in mid-November. For more information on all of these events, call © 609/884-5404 or head online to **www.capemaymac.org**.

EXPLORING CAPE MAY

One of the best ways to explore Cape May is to take one of the many **trolley tours** offered by the **Mid-Atlantic Center for the Arts (MAC),** Cape May's premier preservation organization (© 800/275-4278 or 609/884-5404; www.capemaymac.org). You can buy tickets at the booth at the entrance to the Washington Street Mall, at Ocean Street; tours generally run a half-hour to 45 minutes and concentrate on a specific area of town, so you may want to take more than one. They cost $9 for adults, $4.50 for children 3 to 12. MAC also offers **walking tours, train tours,** and **self-guided audio tours.**

Cape May's top attraction is the **Emlen Physick Estate,** 1048 Washington St. (© 609/884-5404), a beautifully restored Victorian house museum. You can see the entire house on the wonderful 45-minute living history tour, which can be combined with a trolley tour. Housed in the carriage house on the estate is the **Twinings Tearoom,** serving lunch and elegant afternoon tea. Afternoon tea costs $15 per person. Call MAC for reservations.

The **Cape May Carriage Co.** (© 609/884-4466; www.capemaycarriage.com) offers half-hour guided tours ($10 adults; $4 kids 4–11) in old-fashioned horse-drawn carriages that leave from Ocean Street and Washington Mall.

At the heart of town is the **Washington Street Mall,** 401 Washington St. (© 609/
884-0555; www.washingtonstreetmall.com), a 3-block-long pedestrian mall lined
with clothing and gift boutiques. A block over from the mall is **Caroline,** 400 Carpenters Lane (© **609/884-5055**), a first-rate clothing boutique for women. Another
top shopping stop is **39 Degrees,** 251 Beach Ave. (© **609/884-6677**), in the Congress Hall hotel, which offers great casual dresses by Lilly Pulitzer, plus hip clothes for
men. For a list of local antiques dealers, go online to **www.capemay.com**, or stop by
one of the visitor centers listed above and ask for the *Antique Shops of Cape May* map.

No visit to Cape May is complete without a sporting round of minigolf. The best
of the local courses is **Cape May Miniature Golf,** between Jackson and Perry streets
(© **609/884-2222**).

BEACHES & NATURAL ATTRACTIONS   The big draws in summer are Cape
May's calm waters and wide, white sandy beaches. The beach is accessible all along
Beach Drive, with concessions and public restrooms available midbeach near Convention Hall (at Stockton Place) and at various points along the Promenade. In summer, **beach tags** are required on all Cape May beaches; virtually all inns and motels
will provide beach tags (currently $4 per day, $13 per week) to their guests.

Locals usually head to **Sunset Beach** at Cape May Point (take W. Perry St. to Sunset Blvd.), which has a nice swimming cove, easy parking, and a beach grill. It's worth
visiting any time of year to see the *Atlantus,* 1 of 12 experimental concrete ships built
during World War I. Needless to say, this was not a good idea; the curious ship ran
aground in 1926, and its remains poke through the waves just offshore.

The area's best beach is 2 miles south of town, at **Cape May Point State Park**
(© **609/884-2159**; www.state.nj.us/dep/parksandforests), also accessible via Sunset
Boulevard (turn left on Lighthouse Ave.). The quiet, noncommercial crescent of white
sand has restrooms but no concessions, so pack a picnic. You can climb to the top of
Cape May Lighthouse (© **609/884-5404**; www.capemaymac.org), the second-
tallest operating lighthouse in the United States, for breathtaking coastline views. It's
a grueling 199 steps (about 14½ stories), but exhibits give you an excuse to rest at various points along the way. Admission costs $5 for adults, $2 for children under 12.
The park also has 3 miles of **hiking trails** through wetlands (some wheelchair accessible), which are great for birders.

Avid birders will want to visit the **Cape May Migratory Bird Refuge,** just before
the park turnoff on Sunset Boulevard. This 212-acre refuge is one of the East Coast's
premier birding areas. Call the New Jersey Audubon Society's **Cape May Bird Observatory** (© **609/884-2736**) for more information.

WHERE TO STAY
Cape May has dozens of wonderful places to stay, ranging from small, lovely inns to
grand hotels. Rates tend to fluctuate dramatically, even for different rooms in the same
inn, so it's worth calling around and asking questions. Rates are generally lowest in
winter and highest over holiday and summer weekends. Most include both breakfast
and afternoon tea. Many establishments require minimum stays in season, and book
up far in advance for the summer months.

Many of Cape May's historic homes have been wonderfully restored and converted
into B&Bs. The **Mainstay Inn,** 635 Columbia Ave. (© **609/884-8690;** www.mainstay
inn.com), housed in an immaculate 1872 Italianate villa, is widely regarded as the
town's finest inn. Rates run from $155 to $425 double. Nonguests can visit the main
house by self-guided tour; call for details.

Best Simple, Relaxed Luxury

The most stylishly modernized of the Cape May grand hotels is **Congress Hall,** 251 Beach Ave. (© **888/941-1816** or 609/884-8421; www.congresshall. com). Its motto, "simple, relaxed luxury," is apparent everywhere from the chic lobby with its yellow walls, sisal carpet, and black wicker furnishings, to its sunny guest rooms with gaily striped carpets and snowy Frette linens. In winter or summer, its zebra-carpeted Brown Room lounge is a perfect setting for a glass of wine and a good book (or a flirtation), and its pool and beachfront setting make the hotel the most desirable place for both couples and families. A huge colonnaded porch overlooks the lawn and ocean, and many rooms have balconies. Rooms range from $100 to $450 double.

The **Fairthorne,** 111 Ocean St. (© **800/438-8742** or 609/884-8791; www. fairthorne.com), is our absolute favorite. This gorgeous Colonial Revival–style old sailing captain's home is impeccable without being too frilly or formal, and hosts Diane and Ed Hutchinson couldn't be more welcoming. Doubles run $214 to $249; a suite goes for $280. Around the corner is the **John F. Craig House,** 609 Columbia Ave. (© **877/544-0314** or 609/884-0100; www.johnfcraig.com), a beautifully restored Carpenter Gothic inn with a cozy, homey vibe. (*Warning:* Some rooms have tiny bathrooms.) Doubles cost $115 to $230.

If you like your lodgings to have a little personality but consider B&Bs too personal (or too expensive), consider the small, chic **Virginia Hotel,** 25 Jackson St. (© **800/ 732-4236** or 609/884-5700; www.virginiahotel.com), a full-service hotel since 1879. Fresh off a complete renovation, rooms sport such luxurious amenities as Bvlgari toiletries, CD players, and bathrobes; doubles run $125 to $425. Or opt for the attractive and well-outfitted 32-unit, four-building complex known as **The Queen Victoria Bed & Breakfast,** 102 Ocean St. (© **609/884-8702;** www.queenshotel.com), whose innkeepers emphasize privacy and keep rates ($115–$225 double) low.

Beach Drive is lined with value-priced motels—all with pools—that are ideal for those who prefer to avoid the fussiness of historic properties. Our favorite of a very good bunch is the **Sandpiper Beach Inn,** 11 Beach Dr. (© **609/884-4256;** www. capemaysandpiper.com), a lovely gray-and-white clapboard across from an excellent stretch of beach at the quietest end of Beach Drive. The rooms are mostly spacious, like-new suites with nice furnishings and modern kitchenettes. Note that the Sandpiper caters mainly to adults. Rates run $78 to $234 double. Another good choice is **La Mer Beachfront Motor Inn,** 1317 Beach Dr. (© **609/884-9000;** www.lamer motorinn.com), whose new addition features very comfortable rooms ($76–$369) that are big enough for budget-minded families. The rooms in the older building are cheaper but not nearly as spiffy. One floor is set aside solely for adults—a good choice for couples looking for peace and quiet.

WHERE TO DINE

Cape May boasts an excellent, if pricey, collection of restaurants. The best Cape May seafood joint is the rollicking, indoor-outdoor **Lobster House,** Fisherman's Wharf, Route 109 (© **609/884-8296**), where you dine on a dock overlooking the harbor on fresh steamed clams, crab cakes, or "port and starboard" (surf and turf), and have cocktails on the restaurant's own schooner, the *America*. Very highly regarded is the **Water's Edge,** at Beach Drive and Pittsburgh Avenue (© **609/884-1717**), a contemporary dining room with an ever-changing but consistently excellent chops-and-seafood menu and marvelous ocean views. There's an excellent wine list and a good selection of Scotches as well.

If you're a seafood lover, drop your anchor at the much-acclaimed **Axelsson's Blue Claw Restaurant,** 991 Ocean Dr. (© **609/884-5878;** www.blueclawrestaurant.com), with its sophisticated decor, nautical-style bar, and ocean views. The restaurant offers some great grilled meat selections, but it's the fresh seafood (crab cakes, lobster tail, Chilean sea bass) that draws diners. Start your meal off with one of the many martini options and cap it with one of the excellent desserts and specialty coffees.

Among Cape May's finest is the elegant **Washington Inn,** 801 Washington St., at Jefferson Street (© **609/884-5697;** www.washingtoninn.com), whose winning New American cuisine includes such classics as rack of lamb and filet mignon complemented by faultless service and a super-romantic setting. Its 10,000-bottle wine list is the largest in the region. Every Monday at 8pm, the chefs prepare a seven-course tasting menu with five wine pairings for $140 per person. It's perfect for celebrating a special occasion.

For classics such as clams casino, shrimp cocktail, and thick-cut steaks, head to the **Merion Inn,** 106 Decatur St., at Columbia Avenue (© **609/884-8363;** www.merion inn.com), somewhat less expensive than the Washington Inn but no less romantic. This dimly lit, old-world restaurant features several theme dining rooms (we like the porch ones best), and also has an excellent mahogany bar with a jazz pianist in summer.

For more affordable eats, a distinctive yellow striped awning signals the **Mad Batter,** 19 Jackson St., just off Carpenters Lane (© **609/884-5970;** www.madbatter.com), a comfortable, casual restaurant specializing in made-from-scratch breakfasts (their specialty); fresh, leafy salads at lunch; and unfussy European-style entrees at dinner (Mediterranean shrimp pasta, for example). Several vegetarian options are always offered, and there's a sizeable selection of moderately priced wines (several available by the glass).

If you want a quick, inexpensive lunch, your best bet is the **Depot Market Cafe,** 409 Elmira St., next to the Village Bike Shop on Ocean Street (© **609/884-8030**), an ultracasual sandwich shop with homemade everything and a pleasing alfresco patio.

Overlooking the beach action is **McGlade's on the Pier,** on the Promenade at Convention Hall (© **609/884-2614**), where the stars of the otherwise-average burgers-and-seafood menu are the stellar crab cakes and omelets. Next door is **Henry's on the Beach** (© **609/884-8826;** www.henrysonthebeach.com), serving up a similar all-day menu in a friendly laid-back atmosphere.

5 Philadelphia

It was in Philadelphia that the United States declared its independence on July 4, 1776, and where the Founding Fathers managed the Revolutionary War, wrote the U.S. Constitution, and governed the country until Washington, D.C., was built. Today, the Liberty Bell that proclaimed America's freedom from Great Britain, Independence Hall in which it all took place, and dozens of other historic treasures are preserved here in the largest Colonial district in the country, which also features the glossy National Constitution Center.

But you'll find a lot more than history in Philadelphia. Its smart Center City core is a stroller's paradise and a working urban environment, with restored Georgian and Federal structures integrated with sleek shops and chic restaurants along Walnut Street. Broad Street south of City Hall has been reconstituted as a first-class "Avenue of the Arts," anchored by the Philadelphia Orchestra's home, the Kimmel Center for the Performing Arts. With two gleaming sports stadiums in South Philadelphia, this is a city filled with art, music, and sports for every age and taste.

ESSENTIALS

GETTING THERE   By Plane   Philadelphia International Airport (✆ 215/ 937-6937; www.phl.org) is at the southwest corner of the city. For up-to-the-minute flight information, call ✆ **800/PHL-GATE.** Thirty airlines are spread throughout seven terminals, with a shopping mall and food court between Terminals B and C. You can pick up taxis and shuttles outside each terminal.

A **taxi** from the airport to Center City takes about 20 minutes and costs a flat rate of $26 plus tip, usually with a maximum of three passengers.

Airport limousine and shuttle services are provided by **Philadelphia Airport Shuttle** (✆ **215/333-1441**), **Lady Liberty** (✆ **215/724-8888**), or **Deluxe Limo** (✆ **215/ 463-8787**). Shuttles charge from $8 to $20 from the airport to Center City. Philadelphia Airport Shuttle charges $175 from the airport to Atlantic City, New Jersey (p. 141).

By Train   Amtrak (✆ **800/USA-RAIL;** www.amtrak.com) serves Philadelphia's 30th Street Station, about 15 blocks from City Hall. There's frequent service from New York (trip time: 1½ hr.), Washington (1¾–2 hr.), and Boston (5½–7 hr.).

SEPTA commuter trains (✆ **215/580-7800;** www.septa.org) connect 30th Street Station and several Center City stations to Trenton, New Jersey; and Delaware. **New Jersey Transit** (✆ **800/772-2222;** www.njtransit.com) operates commuter trains from New York and Newark to Trenton, where you can switch to the Philadelphia-bound SEPTA train.

SEPTA also runs a **high-speed rail link** (R1), offering direct service between the airport and Center City; trains depart daily every 30 minutes from 5:09am to 12:09am from raised pedestrian bridges at the terminals. Trains to the airport depart from Market East (near the Convention Center), Suburban Station at 16th Street, and 30th Street Station. The 30-minute trip costs $5.50 for adults, $1.50 weekdays and 75¢ weekends for children ages 5 to 11, free for children under 5, and $17 for families (off-peak hours and holidays only).

By Car   Philadelphia is some 300 miles (about 6 hr.) from Boston, and 100 miles (2 hr.) from New York City. If you think of Center City as a rectangle, **I-95** whizzes by its bottom and right sides; **I-276,** the Pennsylvania Turnpike, is the top edge; and **I-76** splits off and snakes along the Schuylkill River along the left side into town. **I-676** traverses Center City under Vine Street, connecting I-76 to adjacent Camden, New Jersey, via the Ben Franklin Bridge ($3 inbound only) over the Delaware River. The "Blue Route" of **I-476** forms a left edge for the suburbs, about 15 miles west of town, connecting I-276 and I-76 at its northern end with I-95 to the south.

VISITOR INFORMATION   The **Independence Visitor Center,** at 6th and Market streets in the heart of historical Philadelphia (✆ **800/537-7676** or 215/965-7676; www.independencevisitorcenter.com), pulls together information on over 500 attractions in the city and region. It also offers publications and wonderful orientation exhibitions, as well as a number of package tours combining special museum exhibitions, concerts, or sporting events with discount hotel prices, free city transit passes, and Amtrak discounts. Many city bus tours, historic trolley rides, and walking tours begin here. The center is open 8:30am to 7pm daily during summer and until 5pm the rest of the year.

GETTING AROUND Philadelphia is very pedestrian-friendly, so we advise leaving your car in a garage. Center City is easily explored on foot or by taxi, and traffic, particularly around City Hall and near Rittenhouse Square, can be very congested. Many hotels offer reduced-rate parking to guests.

SEPTA (© 215/580-7800; www.septa.org) operates a complicated and extensive network of trolleys, buses, commuter trains, and subways. The fare for any bus, trolley, or subway route is $2 cash or $1.30 by token, plus 60¢ for a transfer; exact change or tokens are required. A $5.50 **DayPass** is valid for buses, subways, trolleys, and a one-way trip on the commuter lines to most destinations, including the airport; an $19 weekly **TransPass** is good from Monday to the following Sunday and includes limited commuter train access on weekdays but unrestricted access on weekends and holidays.

Two **subway** lines crisscross the city, intersecting under City Hall. The Broad Street line connects directly to sporting events and concerts in the south. The Market–Frankford line stops at many popular destinations and stretches to the west and northeast. In addition, the Subway-Surface trolleys connect City Hall and 30th Street Station, stopping at 19th and 22nd streets along the way. West of 30th Street, the trolleys branch out to the north and south, moving aboveground.

Several **commuter trains,** known as the Regional Rail lines, service most suburban areas, including the posh Main Line area west of the city. Regional Rail trains depart Center City from 30th Street Station, Suburban Station at 16th Street and John F. Kennedy Boulevard, and the Market East station at 10th and Market streets. Fares vary from $3 to $7, based on destination and time of day. Tickets should be purchased in advance at the station to avoid surcharges.

The **PATCO** rail line (© 215/922-4600; www.drpa.org) begins at Locust and 16th streets, connects with SEPTA at 8th and Market, and crosses the Ben Franklin Bridge to New Jersey's Walter Rand Transportation Center in Camden for the bargain fare of $1.15. From there, you can take New Jersey Transit's River LINE (© 800/772-2222; www.riverline.com) to the nearby Adventure Aquarium.

Philadelphia has 1,600 licensed cabs; try **Olde City Taxi** (© 215/338-0838) or **Quaker City** (© 215/728-8000). Fares are $2.70 for the first ½ mile and 30¢ for each additional ⅓ mile or minute of the motor running.

Most tourist destinations—from the waterfront and Independence Park in the east to the Museum of Art in the west—are also serviced by **PHLASH,** a purple bus that loops around the city from March through November, 10am to 6pm. Fares are $1 for adults; children under 5 and seniors ride free. Discounted passes and maps are available at the Independence Visitor Center.

FAST FACTS Call the **Philadelphia County Medical Society** (© 215/563-5343) for a doctor referral, or © 215/925-6050 in a dental emergency. Major hospitals include **Children's Hospital of Philadelphia,** 34th Street and Civic Center Boulevard (© 215/590-1000); **University of Pennsylvania Hospital,** 3400 Spruce St. (© 215/662-4000); and **Thomas Jefferson,** 11th and Walnut streets (© 215/955-6000).

The only 24-hour pharmacy downtown is the **CVS** at 1826 Chestnut St., at the corner of 19th Street (© **215/972-0909**).

Philadelphia is generally safe if you concentrate on major tourist destinations, but stay alert, be aware of your immediate surroundings, and keep a close eye on your possessions. Be especially careful at night and around college campuses in West Philadelphia.

Within city limits, there is a 7% **sales tax** on general sales and restaurant meals, but not on clothing. Liquor, including wine, beer and hard liquor, is taxed at 10%. Lodging charges incur a 14% tax.

SPECIAL EVENTS & FESTIVALS   The all-day **Mummers Parade** (© **215/336-3050**), held on New Year's Day, attracts 15,000 spangled strutters marching in feathered outfits while strumming banjos. You can line up on Broad Street between Oregon Avenue and City Hall to watch; the most exotically appointed groups, known as the Fancy Brigades, perform indoors at the Convention Center.

The **Philadelphia Flower Show** (© **215/988-8800;** www.theflowershow.com) is the largest and most prestigious indoor exhibition of its kind. Acres of gardens, including exotic orchid displays and rustic settings, occupy the Convention Center in late February or early March.

Each March, **The Book and the Cook** festival (© **215/545-4543;** www.thebook andthecook.com), combines the love of reading and eating. Eminent food critics, cookbook authors, celebrity chefs, and restaurateurs create and serve special menus at the city's best restaurants; food samplings and wine- and beer-tastings are held all over town. The list of participating restaurants is published in January, and many get booked quickly.

In the week leading up to the Fourth of July, the whole town turns out for the **Welcome America!** festival (© **215/683-2200;** www.americasbirthday.com) to celebrate. There are dozens of free events, and the 4th brings special ceremonies to Independence Square, including a reading of the Declaration of Independence, and fireworks at the Philadelphia Museum of Art following a spectacular evening parade and concert on the Benjamin Franklin Parkway.

WHAT TO SEE & DO

The city's top attraction is **Independence National Historical Park** (SEPTA: buses or Market-Frankford Line to 5th St.), America's most historic square mile, centered at Independence Hall on Chestnut Street between 5th and 6th streets. The Declaration of Independence and U.S. Constitution were written here in the late 1700s, and the city served as the nation's capital for 10 years during the construction of the new capital in Washington, D.C.

The park is composed of 40 buildings on 45 acres of Center City real estate, including original sites such as **Independence Hall;** reconstructions such as **City Tavern** and **Declaration House;** and contemporary structures such as the **Liberty Bell Center** and the **National Constitution Center,** on the north side of the mall. Hours for most buildings are from 9am to 5pm (the Visitor Center opens at 8:30am, the Constitution Center at 9:30am). Visitors to most historical attractions must pass through a security screening. You will need free timed tickets to enter Independence Hall.

Make your first stop the **Independence Visitor Center,** 6th and Market streets (© **800/537-7676** or 215/965-7676), where you can pick up a map of the area; get tickets to tour Independence Hall; and reserve a spot on one of the frequent ranger-led tours of the Second Bank of the United States, Bishop White House, and Todd House.

Philadelphia

ACCOMMODATIONS ■
Embassy Suites Hotel Philadelphia-City Center **7**
Four Seasons Hotel **8**
Omni Hotel at Independence Park **12**
Penn's View Hotel **15**
Philadelphia Marriott and Philadelphia Downtown Courtyard Marriott **11**
Rittenhouse Hotel **1**
Rittenhouse 1715 **2**
Sofitel Philadelphia **6**
Ritz-Carlton **10**
Sheraton Philadelphia City Center **9**

DINING ◆
Buddakan **13**
Fork **14**
Lacroix **1**
La Famiglia **16**
Le Bec-Fin **5**
Monk's **3**
Striped Bass **4**

Barnes Foundation   The magnificent Barnes Foundation will stun you, if you are one of the lucky few who are able to get inside this quirky art gallery and education facility. In the 1920s, eccentric millionaire Albert Barnes crammed his French Provincial mansion with more than 1,000 masterpieces—180 Renoirs, 69 Cézannes, innumerable Impressionists and post-Impressionists, and a generous sampling of European art from the Italian primitives onward. Local zoning restricts the museum to only 1,200 visitors per week, so reserve months in advance. After a lengthy citywide debate and a couple of lawsuits, the collection will move to a central Philadelphia location, possibly as early as 2008. For now, the gallery resides in a leafy, upscale Main Line neighborhood.

300 N. Latches Lane, Merion Station. 🕐 610/667-0290. www.barnesfoundation.org. Admission $10; audio tour $7. On-site parking $10. Reserve at least 2 months in advance by telephone. July–Aug Wed–Fri 9:30am–5pm; all other months Fri–Sun 9:30am–5pm. SEPTA: R5 (Paoli local train) to Merion; from station, turn right and walk up Merion Rd., turn left onto N. Latches Lane. Bus: 44 to the intersection of Old Lancaster Rd. and Latches Lane.

Betsy Ross House   Elizabeth (Betsy) Ross was a Quaker needlewoman; some historians believe she sewed the original American flag of 13 stars and 13 stripes. Her tiny house takes only few minutes to walk through; it's a great picture of average Colonial life, from the low ceilings to the cellar kitchen and the model working areas for upholstering, making musket balls, and the like.

239 Arch St. 🕐 215/686-1252. www.betsyrosshouse.org. Suggested contribution $3 adults, $2 children. Daily 10am–5pm (Oct–Mar closed Mon, except legal holidays). SEPTA: Market-Frankford 2nd St. Bus: 9, 17, 21, 32, 24, 48, 57, or PHLASH.

Christ Church _Value_   This is the most beautiful Colonial building (1727–54) in Old City; its spire gleams white and can be seen from almost anywhere in the neighborhood. The interior spans one large arch, with galleries above the sides as demanded by the Anglican Church. The massive Palladian window behind the altar was the wonder of worshipers and probably the model for the one in Independence Hall. Seating is by pew—Washington's seat is marked with a plaque—and it's impossible to ignore the history etched in the church's stones and memorials.

2nd St. (a half-block north of Market St.). 🕐 215/922-1695. Free admission; donations welcome. Mon–Sat 9am–5pm; Sun 1–5pm; Sun services at 9 and 11am. Closed Jan–Feb Mon–Tues. SEPTA: Market-Frankford 2nd St. Bus: 9, 17, 21, 32, 24, 48, 57, or PHLASH.

Elfreth's Alley   The modern Benjamin Franklin Bridge shadows Elfreth's Alley, the oldest continuously inhabited street in the United States. Most of Colonial Philadelphia looked like this block does: cobblestone lanes between the major thoroughfares, small two-story homes, and pent eaves over doors and windows—a local trademark. A diverse population made this a miniature melting pot in the 18th and 19th centuries. Number 126, the 1755 **Mantua Maker's House** (cape maker), now serves as a museum. There is a gift shop with free brochures and information at no. 124.

Off 2nd St. (between Arch and Race sts.). 🕐 215/574-0560. Street is public; Mantua Maker's House suggested admission $3 adults, $1 children ages 6–18, free for children under 6. Tues–Sat 10am–5pm; Sun noon–5pm. SEPTA: Market-Frankford 2nd St. Bus: 9, 17, 21, 32, 24, 48, 57, or PHLASH.

Franklin Court _Value_   This imaginative, informative, and downright fun museum was designed under and around the site of Ben Franklin's home and is run by the National Park Service. The exhibits reflect Franklin's wide interests as scientist, inventor, statesman, printer, politician, and diplomat. Enter through arched passages from either Market or Chestnut streets; the Market entrance adjoins Franklin's reconstructed and fully operational post office, where employees still hand-stamp the marks.

Chestnut St. (between 3rd and 4th sts.), with another entrance at 316–318 Market St. Free admission, including the post office and postal museum. Daily 9am–5pm. SEPTA: Market-Frankford 2nd or 5th St. Bus: 21, 42, or PHLASH.

Franklin Institute Science Museum *(Kids)*   Set in an imposing, pillar-fronted limestone building, this museum explores the influence of science on our lives with an imaginative flair. It's a great spot for those traveling with kids. The complex includes a memorial to Ben Franklin; exhibitions such as a gigantic walk-through heart and antique airplanes; an imaginative outdoor science park; a newly renovated planetarium; and an IMAX theater.

222 North 20th St. ℂ 215/448-1200. www.fi.edu. Sci-Pass (includes admission and 1 planetarium show) $14 adults, $11 children and seniors; Sci-Pass plus 1 IMAX movie $19 adults, $11 children and seniors. Daily 9:30am–5pm; Tuttleman IMAX Theater until 9pm Fri–Sat. Bus: 33 or PHLASH.

Independence Seaport Museum   This user-friendly maritime museum is the star of the city's waterfront. It's beautifully laid out, blending a first-class maritime collection with interactive exhibits for a trip through time that engages all ages. The **Workshop on the Water** lets you watch classes and amateurs undertake traditional wooden boat building and restoration throughout the year. The **Historic Ship Zone** includes the USS *Becuna,* a guppy-size submarine which served in Admiral Halsey's South Pacific fleet; and the USS *Olympia,* the only ship from the Spanish-American War still in existence.

Penn's Landing, at 211 S. Columbus Blvd. ℂ 215/925-5439. www.phillyseaport.org. Admission $9 adults, $8 seniors, $6 children, free to all Sun 10am–noon. Daily 10am–5pm except major holidays. SEPTA: Market-Frankford 2nd St. Bus: 5,17, 21, 33, 42, 48, or PHLASH.

Liberty Bell Center *(Best)*   America's symbol of independence was commissioned in 1751 and hung in Independence Hall to "proclaim liberty throughout the land" as the Declaration of Independence was read aloud to the country's citizens (the quote engraved on the bell is from the Bible, not the Declaration). At some point in the 19th Century, the bell cracked, and no one knows why. The bell's roomy new home, an interactive pavilion run by the National Park Service, is only 300 feet from its former glass pavilion, but moving the 2,080-pound bell required a team of engineers and a special steel cart.

501 Market St. ℂ 215/965-7676. www.nps.gov/inde. Free admission. Daily 9am–5pm. SEPTA: Market-Frankford 5th St. Bus: 38, 44, 48, 121, or PHLASH.

National Constitution Center   A sprawling, dramatic, and unexpectedly modern steel-and-glass temple to the U.S. Constitution, the center at first seems rather unapproachable. But a multimedia theatrical show, *Freedom Rising,* which kicks off each visit, rallies adults and children into the right patriotic mindset for the more than 100 interactive exhibits that line this vast 160,000-square-foot building. Go ahead, take the Presidential Oath of Office, or test out a bench on the Supreme Court (without the Congressional hearings!). *Tip:* Reserve your tickets by phone or on the website before you visit to avoid long waits in line.

525 Arch St. ℂ 866/917-1787 or 215/409-6600. www.constitutioncenter.org. Admission $9 adults, $7 seniors and children, free for children under 4. Sun–Fri 9:30am–5pm; Sat 9:30am–6pm. SEPTA: Market-Frankford 5th St. Bus: 38, 44, 48, 121, or PHLASH.

Philadelphia Museum of Art   The third-largest art museum in the country is a resplendent Greco-Roman temple on a hill—approached, of course, by the *"Rocky* steps," made famous by the Oscar-winning film. It houses one of the finest decorative arts collections in the country, featuring many American arts and crafts, including Philadelphia-made furniture and silver. Upstairs, spread over dozens of galleries, is a chronological sweep of European art from medieval times through 1900. The 19th- and 20th century galleries highlight Cézanne's *The Large Bathers* and Marcel Duchamp's *Nude Descending a Staircase*—the museum is internationally renowned for its Duchamp collection. There are also many works by Philadelphia's Thomas Eakins.

26th St. and Ben Franklin Pkwy. *©* 215/763-8100, or 215/684-7500 for 24-hr. information. www.philamuseum.org. Admission $12 adults, $9 seniors, $8 students, seniors, and children 13–18, free for children under 13; on Sun, all ages pay what you wish. Tues–Sun 10am–5pm (until 8:45pm Fri). Bus: 7, 32, 38, 43, 48, or PHLASH.

Philadelphia Zoo *Kids*   This 42-acre zoo, opened in 1874, was the nation's first and remains a leader, with 1,600-plus animals (including adorable snow leopard cubs and other endangered cats in the brand-new Big Cat Falls). Other options include a Car- nivore Kingdom (starring a white-nosed coatis); a renovated Reptile House (Gaboon viper); a restored Primate Reserve (lowland gorillas); and the helium-filled Zoobal- loon, which carries you 400 feet in the air, with incredible views as far away as the New York skyline.

34th St. and Girard Ave. *©* 215/243-1100. www.phillyzoo.org. Admission $17 adults, $14 children 2–11; free for children under 2. Parking $10. Mar–Nov daily 10am–5pm; Dec–Feb daily 10am–4pm. Bus: 32, 38, or PHLASH. Trol- ley: 15.

ORGANIZED TOURS

Philadelphia Trolley Works (*©* 215/389-TOUR; www.phillytour.com) operates double-decker buses and buses decked out like old-fashioned trolleys. Guided tours of historic areas (all-day pass with unlimited on-and-off privileges: $27 adults, $25 sen- iors, $10 kids) leave from 5th and Chestnut streets in front of the Bourse building.

To get the feel of Philadelphia as it once was, try a narrated horse-drawn carriage ride. Operated daily by Philadelphia Trolley Works sister tour operator, the **76 Car- riage Co.** (*©* 215/923-8516; www.phillytour.com), tours begin at 5th and Chestnut streets in front of Independence Hall from 10am to around 3:30pm, with later hours in summer. Reservations are not necessary. There are three tour options: The short tour is 15 to 20 minutes and costs $30; 35 minutes is $40; and an hour is $80. Prices include up to four passengers.

From May to October, **Centipede Tours,** 1315 Walnut St. (*©* 215/735-3123), leads Saturday-evening candlelit strolls of the historic area; costumed guides leave from Welcome Park at Second and Walnut streets at 6:30pm. Tours of Society Hill cost $5 per person. Call for reservations or customized tours. Also from May to Octo- ber, the **Greater Philadelphia Tourism Marketing Corp.** (www.gophila.com) hosts tours of neighborhoods such as Chinatown and the Italian Market. Tours leave from the "ticket trolley" at 5th and Market streets (*©* 215/389-TOUR). Tours cost $27 for adults, $20 for students, seniors, and kids 8 to 12 (the organizers do not recommend the 3-hr. tours for kids under 8).

SHOPPING

The best places to look for high fashion and designer goods are the specialty shops around **Liberty Place** and **Rittenhouse Square.** The **Shops at Liberty Place,** 1625 Chestnut St., between 16th and 17th streets (*©* 215/851-9055), houses more than 60 quality stores and stalls in a handsome, 60-story tower. Luxury lovers should visit the **Shops at the Bellevue,** at Broad and Walnut streets (*©* 215/875-8350), which include Tiffany & Co., Polo Ralph Lauren, Nicole Miller, and Williams-Sonoma. The once-funky area on **South Street,** set between South Philadelphia and the downtown area, has turned into big business. Restaurants and nightlife now line South Street from Front to 8th streets, with many of the 180 stores here open well into the evening and offering goods ranging from the gentrified to the somewhat grotesque. The crowd tends to be young, pierced, and loud.

Pine Street from 9th to 12th streets is "Antiques Row," and also has a crop of charming new home stores filled with modern furniture and accessories, while **Sansom Street** from 7th to 9th streets is "Jeweler's Row." **Old City,** the city's trendiest area, on either side of Market Street between Front and 8th streets, contains former warehouses-turned-art-galleries, with chic loft apartments now occupying most of the old industrial spaces. This is a great area in which to discover an independent record store, sip espresso at a cafe, or browse for glossy Art Deco antiques at **Moderne Gallery,** 111 N. 3rd St. (© **215/923-8536;** www.modernegallery.com). **Manayunk** (www.manayunk.com), a neighborhood at the northwestern corner of the city, is known for contemporary crafts and clothing stores such as **Bias** and **Chico's.**

Reading Terminal Market, 12th and Arch streets (© **215/922-2317;** www.reading terminalmarket.org), is a 115-year-old landmark with a gastronomic bazaar of restaurants and greengrocers, snack shops, bakeries, butchers, fish markets, and more. You can still see the Amish in the big city Wednesday through Saturday, and you can buy sticky buns at **Beiler's Bakery,** soft pretzels at **Fisher's,** and chicken potpies and oversize apple dumplings at **The Dutch Eating Place.** The market is closed on Sunday.

While touring South Street or South Philadelphia, stop by the **Italian Market,** centered around 9th Street between Christian and Wharton streets. It feels straight out of another era: gritty, colorful, and redolent of garlic and just-baked bread, with pushcarts and open stalls selling fresh produce, cheese, pasta, and other culinary delights. Pick up a cannoli, a unique Italian pastry filled with sweet vanilla cream, then stroll by the stands selling live chickens, and white-coated butchers carving filets and T-bones out of massive sides of beef.

For a truly unique way to tour the Art Museum area, call **I Glide Tours** (© **877/ GLIDE-81** or 215/735-1700; www.iglidetours.com). They'll have you whizzing around the Benjamin Franklin Parkway and along the Schuylkill River on a Segway Human Transporter. Tours range from 1½ to 2½ hours, including a half-hour Segway class, and cost $49 to $69.

WHERE TO STAY

Center City has more than 10,000 hotel rooms, and packages and discounts abound; be sure to inquire. State and city surcharges will tack on an additional 14% to your lodging bill.

The **Independence Visitor Center,** 6th and Market streets (© **800/537-7676** or 215/965-7676), can help with any questions. For information on B&Bs, try **Bed & Breakfast Connections of Philadelphia** (© **800/448-3619** or 610/687-3565; www.bnbphiladelphia.com).

Many of the city's more affordable options are chain hotels, including the **Best Western Independence Park Hotel,** 235 Chestnut St. (© **800/624-2988** or 215/ 922-4443; www.independenceparkhotel.com); and the **Comfort Inn Downtown/ Historic Area,** 100 N. Columbus Blvd. (© **800/228-5150** or 215/627-7900; www. comfortinn.com).

Hotel options near the airport include the **Sheraton Suites Hotel at the Philadelphia Airport,** 4101 Island Ave. (© **800/325-3535** or 215/365-6600; www.sheraton. com); and the **Comfort Inn Airport,** 53 Industrial Hwy., Essington (© **800/228-5150** or 610/521-9800; www.comfortinn.com).

Embassy Suites Hotel Philadelphia—Center City *Value*
This 28-story cylinder of marble and glass, designed to house luxury apartments, looks dated, but the all-suite format actually works quite well. Fresh-air fans will enjoy the sliding doors that open onto small balconies with great Parkway views. Patience is required—while the rooms are a treat, the elevators and lobby weren't built to handle hotel-style volume. Weekend packages make this hotel very affordable.

1776 Benjamin Franklin Pkwy., Philadelphia, PA 19103. © **800/362-2779** or 215/561-1776. Fax 215/561-1850. www.philadelphiacentercity.embsuites.com. 288 units. From $159 double. Children under 18 stay free in parent's room. Rates include full breakfast buffet and lobby social hour. AE, DC, DISC, MC, V. Valet parking $24. Bus: 33. **Amenities:** Restaurant; fitness center. *In room:* Kitchenette.

Four Seasons Hotel
This refined, luxurious property sets the bar for hotel sophistication in Philadelphia, and it's perfect for weekday business or romantic weekend getaways. The just-refurbished elegant rooms have windows that open, or private balconies (on the seventh floor) boasting marvelous views of Logan Circle's Swann Fountain or the interior courtyard. Amenities include marble bathrooms with bathrobes and thick towels; hypoallergenic pillows are available, as is in-room exercise equipment. The Fountain, under head chef Martin Hamann, is one of Philadelphia's best restaurants, with its inventive, French-accented American menu and seamless service—come for the fabulous Sunday brunch.

One Logan Sq., Philadelphia, PA 19103. © **800/332-3442** or 215/963-1500. Fax 215/963-9506. www.fourseasons. com/philadelphia. 364 units. $280–$360 double; $425–$535 suite. Children under 18 stay free in parent's room. Weekend rates and discount packages available. AE, DC, MC, V. Valet parking $35; self-parking $24. Bus: 33. Pets under 15 lb. permitted. **Amenities:** 2 restaurants; indoor pool; health club; spa.

Omni Hotel at Independence Park
This polished hotel has a terrific location in the middle of Independence National Historical Park, and near Old City's gallery district. All units were renovated in 2001 and have park views; you can watch horse-drawn carriages clip-clopping by, or walk a half-block to trendy bars and restaurants. The classic lobby features current newspapers, huge vases of flowers, and a jazz trio on weekends. Rooms are cheery, and equipped with opulent marble bathrooms and state-of-the-art conveniences. There's also a brand-new spa, Balance Spa & Fitness. You can catch an after-dinner flick at the Ritz Five movie theater tucked into the hotel's back corner.

401 Chestnut St., Philadelphia, PA 19106. © **800/843-6664** or 215/925-0000. Fax 215/931-1263. www.omnihotels. com. 150 units. $169–$299 double; from $600 suite. Children under 10 stay free in parent's room. Weekend rates available. AE, DC, DISC, MC, V. Valet parking $28; self-parking $20. SEPTA: 5th St. **Amenities:** Restaurant; indoor pool; health club; spa.

Penn's View Hotel
Tucked behind the Market Street ramp to I-95 in a renovated 1856 warehouse, this small, pretty hotel offers roomy guest rooms with Chippendale-style furniture and modern amenities. The main concern is traffic noise, but rooms are well insulated; some offer fireplaces and Jacuzzi tubs. The hotel was developed by the Sena family, which runs La Famiglia—one of the city's best Italian restaurants (see "Where to Dine," below)—a couple of blocks away.

Front and Market sts., Philadelphia, PA 19106. © **800/331-7634** or 215/922-7600. Fax 215/922-7642. 51 units. $180–$255 double. Rates include European continental breakfast. Weekend rates and discount packages available. AE, MC, V. Parking $18 at adjacent lot. SEPTA: 2nd St. **Amenities:** Restaurant.

Philadelphia Marriott and Philadelphia Downtown Courtyard Marriott
The biggest hotel in Pennsylvania, linked by a sky bridge to the Convention Center, got even bigger in 1999 when Marriott converted the historic City Hall Annex across 13th Street into a 498-room Courtyard by Marriott. Setbacks and terraces provide plenty of natural light and views from the rooms on floors 6 to 23, and the courtyard property has sensitively restored bronze and copper details throughout. Although tastefully outfitted and equipped with spacious bathrooms, the rooms are slightly less elegant than those at the top hotels. Service is impeccable, thanks to the well-trained, knowledgeable staff.

1201 Market St. (at 12th St.) and 21 N. Juniper St., Philadelphia, PA 19107. ✆ 800/228-9290 or 215/625-2900. Fax 215/625-6000. www.marriott.com. Marriott: 1,408 units. From $389 double. Weekend rates available. Courtyard by Marriott: 498 units. From $269 double. Weekend rates available. AE, DC, DISC, MC, V. Valet parking $35. SEPTA: Direct internal connection to 11th St.–Market E. or 13th St. **Amenities:** 4 restaurants; pool; health club; spa.

Rittenhouse 1715: A Boutique Hotel   Steps from Rittenhouse Square, a pristine park ringed by million-dollar apartments and mansions, this is the city's best incarnation of a small, European-style luxury hotel. Set in two early-20th-century town houses on a leafy street 1 block from Walnut Street shopping, and 10 minutes' walk to the Convention Center, the hotel exudes modernized, haute-British style, with Frette linens, Berber carpets, and surprisingly large guest rooms and suites with excellent marble bathrooms. Sip wine in the lobby each evening, and enjoy a lavish continental breakfast, but forget about bringing along children under 12 or smoking.

1715 Rittenhouse Sq., Philadelphia, PA 19103. ✆ 877/791-6500 or 215/546-6500. Fax 215/546-8787. www.rittenhouse1715.com. 16 units. $209 double; $259 suite. Rates include complimentary continental breakfast and nightly wine reception. AE, DC, DISC, MC, V. SEPTA: 17th St. Children under 12 not permitted. **Amenities:** Smoking not permitted.

Rittenhouse Hotel *(Best*   Among Philadelphia's luxury hotels, the Rittenhouse has the fewest and largest rooms, dramatic views of the flowers and trees in Rittenhouse Square, and a franchise on hosting movie stars: Tom Hanks, Mel Gibson, and Denzel Washington have all roosted here while filming in Philly. Built in 1989, it's a jagged concrete-and-glass high-rise; the lobby is a peaceful oasis, with inlaid marble floors and frosted-glass chandeliers. The guest rooms have bay windows, reinforced walls, and VCRs. And everything you need for a wonderful vacation is on-premises: amenities include Lacroix, a world-class French restaurant (see below); an outpost of the renowned Smith & Wollensky steakhouses; and the luxe Adolf Biecker spa, salon, and gym.

210 W. Rittenhouse Sq., Philadelphia, PA 19103. ✆ 800/635-1042 or 215/546-9000. Fax 215/732-3364. www.rittenhousehotel.com. 98 units. $299–$480 double; $640–$780 suite. Discounts and packages available. AE, DC, MC, V. Valet parking $26. SEPTA: 19th St. Pets permitted. **Amenities:** 4 restaurants; indoor pool; health club; spa.

Ritz-Carlton Hotel   Philadelphia's newest luxury hotel is set inside a historic Broad Street bank building (itself designed to resemble the Pantheon in Rome) with a 140-foot-high, white marble lobby and some of the city's loveliest rooms and suites. Rooms are generously sized and traditionally decorated with exceptional city views and gorgeous marble bathrooms; some overlook City Hall next door. Splurge on one of the "club floors," and you'll be treated to champagne, brie, and a lavish breakfast in a paneled, 30th-floor former boardroom. The spa offers a full complement of treatments, The Grill restaurant features Georges Perrier alum Kevin Sbraga, and the Vault Cigar Bar and the grand Rotunda Bar are popular spots for after-work drinks.

10 Ave. of the Arts, Philadelphia, PA 19102. ℂ **800/241-3333** or 215/523-8000. Fax 215/568-0942. www.ritz carlton.com. 331 units. From $279 double. Weekend packages available. AE, DC, DISC, MC, V. Valet parking $34. Dogs permitted under certain conditions for a $75 surcharge. **Amenities:** 2 restaurants; health club; spa.

Sheraton Philadelphia City Center   The Sheraton is popular with business travelers, but rooms were recently renovated to appeal to the leisure crowd as well. The complex's lobby, lounge, and restaurants lie under a dramatic 70-foot glass roof. Request a west view above the 19th floor for an unobstructed peek at the Parkway, but be forewarned that the cathedral bells below ring at 7am daily. A fee of $15 gets you all-day access to racquetball, squash, outdoor handball, and tennis.

17th and Race sts., Philadelphia, PA 19103. ℂ **800/325-3535** or 215/448-2000. Fax 215/448-2864. www.sheraton. com. 758 units. From $160 double. Children 18 and under stay free in parent's room. Excellent weekend rates available. AE, DC, MC, V. Valet parking $32. SEPTA: 19th St. Bus: 33. Pets under 50 lb. permitted for $50 nonrefundable fee. **Amenities:** 3 restaurants; indoor pool; health club; spa.

Sofitel Philadelphia   This hotel is as smart and chic as the European guests who sip martinis in its popular lobby bar. Downstairs, the decor is all marble and tall windows softened by thoughtful details such as exquisite flower arrangements and modern, comfortable velvet sofas. The roomy guest rooms, with huge travertine marble bathrooms, dark wood accents, and Art Deco–style modern furniture are softened by sleek mirrors and luxe linens. All rooms have wireless Internet access. The Sofitel, an anchor of Sansom Street's "French district," is a Manolo Blahnik's throw from shopping along Walnut Street, and restaurants such as Striped Bass, Rouge, and Le Bec Fin.

120 S. 17th St., Philadelphia, PA 19103. ℂ **800/763-4835** or 215/569-8300. www.sofitel.com. 306 units. From $205 double. AE, DC, DISC, MC, V. Valet parking $29. SEPTA: 17th St. Pets up to 25 lb. permitted for $50 surcharge. **Amenities:** Restaurant; health club.

WHERE TO DINE

In addition to the choices below, you might want to head to South Philly for its numerous southern and central Italian restaurants. Try **The Saloon,** 750 S. 7th St. (ℂ **215/627-1811**), a dignified, *Sopranos*-worthy place for the best veal chops in town; or the red-sauce-perfumed **Villa di Roma,** 932 S. 9th St. (ℂ **215/592-1295**). Also noteworthy are restaurants in the Northern Liberties section of town, just north of Old City. Try the upscale tavern food and great local beers at **Standard Tap,** 901 N. 2nd St. (ℂ **215/238-0630**) and **North 3rd,** 801 N. 3rd St. (ℂ **215/413-3666**).

Buddakan ASIAN   With its high ceilings, mod dining room, giant golden Buddha statue overlooking sleek tables of trendy couples and extended families, Buddakan could coast on its good looks. But its stellar made-for-sharing Pan-Asian cuisine—"angry lobster," wok-seared and served with lobster mashed potatoes; and grilled lamb chops with Thai basil pesto, among other dishes—make it more than just a pretty place to dine.

325 Chestnut St. ℂ 215/574-9440. www.buddakan.com. Reservations recommended. Main courses $16–$28. AE, DC, MC, V. Mon–Fri 11:30am–2:30pm; Sun–Thurs 5–11pm; Fri–Sat 5pm–midnight. SEPTA: 2nd St. or 5th St.

Fork CONTINENTAL   This Old City stylish bistro is set in a historic brick warehouse that's been renovated into a warm, 68-seat restaurant with tall banquettes, a hip circular bar, open kitchen, and glorious lighting. Most of the ingredients used by the chefs come from organic farms and Amish purveyors; the menu changes daily. The signature dishes here are pan-seared miso-ginger salmon with coconut sushi rice, and a chimichurri-laced hanger steak with matchstick-thin yucca frites. The Sunday brunch is very popular with couples.

306 Market St. ⓒ **215/625-9425.** www.forkrestaurant.com. Reservations recommended. Main courses $14–$26. AE, DC, DISC, MC, V. Mon–Thurs 11:30am–10:30pm; Fri 11:30am–11:30pm; Sat 5–11:30pm; Sun 11am–3pm and 5–10:30pm. Late bar menu Thurs 10:30pm–midnight; Fri–Sat 11:30pm–1am. SEPTA: 2nd St. or 5th St.

Lacroix FRENCH *Esquire* named this restaurant on the second floor of the Rittenhouse Hotel the best new restaurant in the entire country in 2003. The setting is ethereal but unstuffy, with deep emerald-green armchairs and lovely limestone accents, and the menu of interchangeable courses (choose from three to five dishes) might feature sautéed Virginia squab on pine leaves with bluefoot-mushroom torte. The $26 prix-fixe business lunch is an exceptional deal.

210 W. Rittenhouse Sq. ⓒ **215/790-2533.** www.rittenhousehotel.com/lacroix.cfm. Reservations recommended. A la carte dinner entrees from $26; prix-fixe $26 lunch, $69–$85 dinner; brunch $52. AE, DC, DISC, MC, V. Daily 6am–2:30pm; Sun–Thurs 5:30–10pm; Fri–Sat 5:30–10:30pm.

La Famiglia ITALIAN *La Famiglia* refers to both the proprietors and the clientele of this refined spot. The Neapolitan Sena family aims for elegant dining, service, and presentation. The restaurant seats 60 in a private, warm setting of hand-hammered Venetian chandeliers and majolica tiles. Most of the pasta is homemade; you might try the *gnocchi al basilico,* which incorporates basil and sweet red-pepper sauce. The award-winning wine cellar here is legendary. For dessert, try a *mille foglie,* the Italian version of the napoleon, or profiteroles in chocolate sauce. People often stay here well after the closing hour, lingering over sambuca while arias play in the background.

8 S. Front St. ⓒ **215/922-2803.** www.lafamiglia.com. Reservations recommended. Main courses $28–$43. AE, DC, DISC MC, V. Tues–Fri noon–2:30pm; Mon–Thurs 5:30–9:30pm; Fri–Sat 5:30–10pm. SEPTA: 2nd St.

Le Bec-Fin *(Best* FRENCH For those who love jewel-box surroundings and lengthy, multicourse meals, Le Bec-Fin is the premiere restaurant in Philadelphia. Owner-chef Georges Perrier hails from Lyon, France's gastronomic capital, and commands the respect of restaurateurs on two continents. In this superbly elegant dining room, you'll enjoy a leisurely waltz through hors d'oeuvres, a fish course, a main course, a salad, cheese, a dessert, and coffee with petits fours. The dessert cart, laden with tortes and opera cakes, is exquisite. The basement **Le Bar Lyonnais,** with just four tables and bar stools, offers more affordable snacking and champagne toasts.

1523 Walnut St. ⓒ **215/567-1000.** www.georgesperriergroup.com. Reservations required a week ahead for weeknights, months ahead for Fri–Sat. Fixed-price lunch $54; fixed-price dinner $138. AE, DC, DISC MC, V. Lunch seatings Wed–Fri at 11:30am and 1:30pm; dinner seatings Mon–Thurs 6pm and 9pm, Fri–Sat 6pm and 9:30pm. Bar Lyonnais downstairs serves food and drink in a more casual setting. SEPTA: Walnut–Locust.

Monk's BELGIAN It's the mussels—generous bowls of dark-shelled little beauties dressed in five sauces, from spicy Thai to classic white wine and garlic—that Monk's legions of regulars dream about. Or is it the nearly 20 artisan beers on tap, and dozens of interesting European bottled brews, such as fruity Chimay made by Trappist monks? This is a no-nonsense tavern serving excellent hamburgers, fries with bourbon mayonnaise, or hearty salads, for when you crave comfort food in a no-attitude setting. The kitchen is open until 1am.

264 S. 16th St. ⓒ **215/545-7005.** www.monkscafe.com. No reservations. Main courses $12–$28. AE, DC, DISC, MC, V. Daily 11:30am–2am. SEPTA: Locust St.

Striped Bass SEAFOOD The setting of this renowned seafood restaurant is a lofty, 100-year-old former brokerage house, transformed into the most glamorous restaurant in Philly. Under the direction of chef Christopher Lee, the kitchen delivers creative preparations of seafood (and some meats and pastas for landlubbers), with an emphasis on fresh herbs and clean flavors: try the wild striped bass seviche, followed by the roasted Canadian lobster with *hon shimeji* mushrooms and rhubarb-lemon garlic butter. With its sleek banquettes, dramatic triple-story velvet curtains, and crystal light fixtures, Striped Bass is more modern-cool (and affordable) than Le Bec-Fin, but the experience is no less grand.

1500 Walnut St. (© 215/732-4444. www.stripedbassrestaurant.com. Reservations necessary. Main courses $28–$42. AE, MC, V. Sun 5–9pm; Mon–Thurs 5–10pm; Fri–Sat 5–11pm. SEPTA: Walnut–Locust.

PHILADELPHIA AFTER DARK

The best sources for what's going on are the "Weekend" supplement of the Friday *Philadelphia Inquirer,* and the free *City Paper* and *Philadelphia Weekly* (www.philly weekly.com), which you can find in free boxes on corners throughout Center City. The visitor center is also an excellent information source. You might also consult *Philadelphia* magazine's website, www.phillymag.com.

Event tickets may be purchased through the following vendors: **Upstages** (© 215/ 569-9700), which specializes in local theater; **Ticket Philadelphia** (© 215/893-1999; www.ticketphiladelphia.org) for larger cultural events; and **Ticketmaster** (© 215/336-2000; www.ticketmaster.com), primarily for rock concerts.

Lights of Liberty, Chestnut and 6th streets (© 215/542-3789; www.lightsof liberty.org; SEPTA: 5th St.), is a surprisingly entertaining, high-tech dramatized American Revolution tour that starts at dusk and winds through Society Hill from April to October. A 3-D sound system accessible through wireless headsets and five-story images projected on a historic building in Independence Park are synchronized with a musical score and the voices of Walter Cronkite and Whoopi Goldberg among others, as you follow the path of the story. Admission is $20 adults, $17 students and seniors, $13 children 12 and under.

THE PERFORMING ARTS Broad Street south of City Hall has been named "Avenue of the Arts," because it is home to several theaters and performing arts halls. The **Philadelphia Orchestra** (www.philorch.org), one of the "Big Five" American orchestras, performs at the recently built, glass enclosed **Kimmel Center,** Broad and Spruce streets (© 215/893-1999 for tickets; www.kimmelcenter.org; SEPTA: Walnut–Locust). The regular season runs from September to May. In summer, the orchestra moves to the **Mann Music Center** near 52nd Street and Parkside Avenue (© 215/ 893-1999 for tickets; www.manncenter.org). The **Curtis Institute,** 1726 Locust St. (© 215/893-5252, or 215/893-5261 for schedule; www.curtis.edu; SEPTA: Walnut–Locust), a world-famous conservatory, presents many free concerts, operas, and recitals during the school year.

The **Opera Company of Philadelphia** (© 215/928-2110; www.operaphilly.com), performs at the gorgeous Academy of Music (1420 Locust St.), which was built in 1857. It features internationally renowned opera singers. The **Pennsylvania Ballet** (© 215/551-7014; www.paballet.org) performs at the Academy of Music, Kimmel Center, and elsewhere from September to June.

Philadelphia is an attentive theater town. The acclaimed **Wilma Theater** stages modern plays in a state-of-the-art space at Broad and Spruce streets (© 215/546-7824; www.wilmatheater.org; SEPTA: Walnut–Locust). The popular **Arden Theatre Company,** 40 N. 2nd St. (© 215/922-8900; www.ardentheatre.org; SEPTA: 2nd St.), presents diverse productions in an intimate setting. **Philadelphia Theatre Company,** 1714 Delancey St. (© 215/985-0420 for tickets; www.phillytheatreco.com;

SEPTA: 15th–16th sts.), combines fine regional talent with Tony Award–winning actors and directors, and often stages contemporary plays that have recently enjoyed a run on Broadway.

Founded in 1809, the **Walnut Street Theatre,** 9th and Walnut streets (© **215/ 574-3550;** www.wstonline.org; SEPTA: 8th–Market), stages large-scale plays and musicals ranging from classics to recent hits. The **Prince Music Theater** (© **215/569- 9700** for tickets; www.princemusictheater.org) presents opera, musical comedy, cabaret, and experimental theater at a dramatically renovated movie palace at 1412 Chestnut St. (SEPTA: City Hall or 15th St.). The 2,000-seat, 1930s-built **Merriam Theater** (© **215/732-5446**) hosts major touring Broadway productions.

THE CLUB & MUSIC SCENE   The best nightlife areas are **Old City,** for young types in low-rise jeans sipping complicated cocktails; **Walnut Street** between 15th and 18th streets and around **Rittenhouse Square,** for sophisticated bars and lounges; and, for a more dressed down night out, **Northern Liberties.**

Zanzibar Blue, 200 S. Broad St. (© **215/732-4500;** www.zanzibarblue.com; SEPTA: Walnut–Locust), downstairs at the Park Hyatt at the Bellevue, features prominent jazz and R&B performers, such as Stanley Jordan and Roy Ayers, in a fancy setting. For a low key evening of good jazz and cheap drinks, opt for the slightly out-of-the-way **Ortlieb's Jazzhaus,** 847 N. 3rd St. (© **215/922-1035;** www.ortliebs jazzhaus.com).

Check out the **Khyber,** 56 S. 2nd St. (© **215/238-5888;** www.thekhyber.com; SEPTA: 2nd St.), or **Johnny Brenda's,** 1201 Frankford Ave. (© **215/731-9684;** www. johnnybrendas.com; SEPTA: Girard) for loud, local bands and great beer selections.

THE BAR SCENE   From lunchtime until 2am, the who's who of Philadelphia comes to Rittenhouse Square's **Rouge,** 205 S. 18th St. (© **215/732-6622**), to drink martinis and Bellinis and to gawk and be gawked at. Celebs such as Mick Jagger and Cameron Diaz wander in from time to time. Another popular setting for cocktails and hors d'oeuvres is the roomy bar at **Brasserie Perrier,** 1619 Walnut St. (© **215/568- 3000;** www.georgesperriergroup.com), a contemporary, colorful spot co-owned by Le Bec-Fin's Georges Perrier. In warmer months, vast yuppie crowds gather in the out-door courtyard of **Marathon Grill Commerce Square,** 2001 Market St. (© **215/ 568-7766;** www.marathongrill.com), for networking and canoodling.

One eternally cool spot in fickle Old City is the **Continental Restaurant & Martini Bar,** 138 Market St. (© **215/923-6069;** SEPTA: 2nd St.), a vintage diner that was transformed in the mid-1990s into a hip *Swingers*-style lounge. Late-night action can be found at intimate, trendy **32 Degrees** nightclub, 32 S. 2nd St. (© **215/627- 3132;** www.32lounge.com), and, uptown, at **Denim Lounge,** 1710 Walnut St. (© **215/735-6700**), which resembles Miami's Delano Hotel with its eclectic, mini-malist decor—one area is all white and lit by candles, another intimate space boasts a massive crystal chandelier. If you're looking for more of a "dive bar" experience, visit **Bob & Barbara's,** 1509 South St. (© **215/545-4511**) for Ping-Pong, drag shows, live jazz, and Bingo (all on different nights, of course). Be sure to order a $3 "special"—a can of Pabst Blue Ribbon and a shot of Jim Beam.

For a proper drink—say, a brandy or an old-fashioned—try the **Rotunda Bar** or **Vault Cigar Bar** at the Ritz-Carlton or the **Swann Lounge** at Four Seasons (see above for contact information).

THE GAY & LESBIAN SCENE   To find out what's happening, visit the so-called "Gayborhood," from 10th through 13th streets between Walnut and Pine (SEPTA:

Walnut–Locust). Check out the free weeklies or the *Philadelphia Gay News* (www. epgn.com), available at **Giovanni's Room,** 345 S. 12th St. (© **215/923-2960;** www. giovannisroom.com). Perennially popular **Woody's,** 202 S. 13th St. (© **215/545-1893**), has a downstairs bar and an always-fun upstairs dance floor. There's something for everyone at **12th Air Command,** 254 S. 12th St. (© **215/545-8088;** www.12th air.com)—a lounge, a game room, a disco, and a pub menu. Women gather at **Sisters,** 1320 Chancellor St. (© **215/735-0735;** www.sistersnightclub.com), a restaurant/bar/ nightclub near City Hall.

6 Side Trips from Philadelphia: The Amish Country, the Brandywine Valley & More

THE AMISH COUNTRY

Fifty miles west of Philadelphia is a quietly beautiful region of rolling hills, winding creeks, neatly cultivated farms, covered bridges, and towns with picturesque names such as Paradise and Bird-in-Hand. The Amish community, which steadfastly retains a life of agrarian simplicity centered on religious worship and family cohesiveness, numbers 18,000. The preservation of their world evokes feelings of curiosity, nostalgia, amazement, and respect.

The area is relatively small, with good roads for motorist and bicyclist alike. The attention to the Amish has spurred lots of interesting facsimiles and even some authentic pathways into Amish life, although you have to sift through them if you want to avoid overt religious messages. Tourism has promoted excellence in quilting, antiques, and farm-based crafts. There are historical sites, pretzel and chocolate factories, covered bridges, and wonderful farmers' markets, as well as modern diversions such as movie theaters, amusement parks, and great outlet-mall shopping. And, of course, the family-style, all-you-can-eat or gourmet Pennsylvania Dutch restaurants offer unique dining experiences as well as meals.

ESSENTIALS

GETTING THERE Lancaster County is 57 miles or a 90-minute drive west of Philadelphia, directly on Route 30. **From the Northeast,** take I-95 south from New York City onto the New Jersey Turnpike, then take Exit 6 onto the Pennsylvania Turnpike (I-76), turning south to Lancaster City via exits 266 or 286 (trip time: 2¼ hr.). **From the south,** follow I-83 north for 90 minutes from Baltimore, then head east on Route 30 from York into the county. **Amtrak** provides frequent service from 30th Street Station in Philadelphia to the great old Lancaster station (trip time: 70 min.).

VISITOR INFORMATION The **Pennsylvania Dutch Convention & Visitors Bureau,** 501 Greenfield Rd., Lancaster, PA 17601 (© **800/PA-DUTCH;** www.pa dutchcountry.com), provides an excellent map and visitors' guide, along with answers to specific questions and interests. The office itself (off the Rte. 30 Bypass east of Lancaster) offers direct telephone links to many local hotels and an overview slide show. Many towns such as Intercourse, Strasburg, and Lancaster have local information centers.

WHAT TO SEE & DO

The suggestive name of **Intercourse** refers to the intersection of two old roads, the King's Highway (now Rte. 340 or Old Philadelphia Pike) and Newport Road (now Rte. 772). It's now the center of Amish life, set in the midst of the wedge of country east of Lancaster; unfortunately, the number of commercial attractions, ranging from

All Things Chocolate

Hershey (www.hersheypa.com), the adorable village founded by Milton Hershey in 1903 as his candy empire's company town, literally *smells* of chocolate. It bills itself as "the sweetest place on earth," and offers great golf, gardens, rolling farmland, and lots of chocolate-related fun. Though it's best to visit here in summer, the town has a huge holiday spirit. Beginning in mid-November, more than one million holiday "Sweet Lights" are draped around town (including on the Kiss-shaped street lanterns); there's also Santa, reindeer, music shows, and a Teddy Bear Jubilee.

The big attraction here is the kid-friendly amusement park **HERSHEYPARK.** The 110-acre park sports 10 roller coasters (some of them, such as the Storm Runner, are among the best in the country) and a host of water and kiddie rides. Oh, and lots and lots of chocolate! Live "candy characters" parade around daily, offering kids the chance to get a hug from some real Kisses and Hugs. Admission is $44 adults, $25 kids 3 to 8 and seniors 55 to 69, and $18 seniors 70-plus.

Just outside the theme park is the free **Chocolate World** visitor center, where you can see how your Reese's Peanut Butter Cups and Mr. Goodbars are made (and get a free sample!). *Tip:* Ignore the 3-D film that costs extra; it's not worth the price.

The town offers several accommodations options, but the best is the national historic landmark **Hotel Hershey** (© **800/HERSHEY**), a Mediterranean-style luxury hotel (ca. 1933) where you're greeted with kisses. Chocolate Kisses, of course. The hotel's formal Circular Dining Room is top-notch and the cozy Iberian Lounge offers chocolate martinis. The hotel's luxurious $7-million **Spa at the Hotel Hershey** overlooks a formal rose garden (Milton's wife, Catherine, loved roses) and incorporates chocolate in its treatments; soak in the Whipped Cocoa Bath or get a Chocolate Bean Polish.

Note: Guests staying at a Hershey resort can breakfast with larger-than-life Hershey's product characters and then get early admittance to some family-friendly rides in the amusement park with the Breakfast in the Park package.

Hershey, off Route 322, is a 2-hour drive from Philly (3 hr. from New York City) via I-76. For more information about the town, the theme park, and dining and accommodations options in Hershey, as well as detailed directions and maps, call © **800/HERSHEY** or head online to **www.hersheypa.com**.

schlock to good quality, about equals the places of genuine interest along Route 340. One not-to-miss spot is **The People's Place,** 3518 Old Philadelphia Pike (© **800/ 390-8436** or 717/768-7171), a bookshop and interpretive center with as much information on the Amish as you can handle. Of the commercial developments, try **Kitchen Kettle Village** (© **800/732-3538** or 717/768-8261), where over 30 stores selling crafts from decoys to fudge are grouped around the Burnleys' 1954 jam and relish kitchen.

Ephrata, near Exit 286 off I-76, combines a historic 18th-century Moravian religious site with some pleasant country and the area's largest farmers' market and auction center. **Ephrata Cloister,** 632 W. Main St. (© 717/733-6600; www.ephrata cloister.org), near the junction of routes 222 and 322, was one of America's earliest communal societies, and is an interesting group of medieval-style structures that includes a museum shop. The main street of Ephrata is pleasant for strolling, including an old rail car where the train line used to run. **Doneckers,** 318–324 N. State St. (© 717/738-9500; www.doneckers.com), is a complex consisting of a hotel, sophisticated furniture and clothing boutiques, and a fine dining restaurant run by a former Le Bec-Fin chef de cuisine (the boutiques and restaurant are closed Wed and Sun). Just outside of town is the wonderful **Green Dragon Market** (© 717/738-1117; www.greendragonmarket.com), open Friday from 9am to 9pm. You might see goats and cows changing hands here. Summer brings fresh corn, fruit, and melons, which is one reason why chefs such as Greg Gable of Doneckers shop for produce here.

Other charming towns in the region include **Lititz,** with its pretzel factory and a lovely park adjoining a purely 18th-century main street; **Strasburg,** with rides on its preserved iron steam locomotive and assorted rail-related attractions; and **Bird-in-Hand,** known for its farmers' market (Fri–Sat year-round, plus Wed Apr–Nov and Thurs July–Oct) and homemade ice cream. For antiquing, the Sunday fairs in **Adamstown,** 2 miles east of Exit 286 off I-76, bring thousands of vendors to their enormous sites. The largest are **Stoudt's Black Angus Antiques Mall** (www.stoudts-beer.com), with more than 350 permanent dealers (and a great on-site brewery and restaurant); and **Renningers Antique and Collectors Market** (www.renningers.com), with 375 permanent dealers.

There's less to do in the city of **Lancaster** itself than in the surrounding area, though this is slowly changing. In town, the one visitor highlight is **Central Market,** erected in 1889 just off Penn Square but operating since the 1730s as the nation's oldest farmers' market, with more than 80 stalls. You can savor regional produce and foods, from sweet bologna and scrapple to egg noodles and shoofly pie (Tues and Fri 6am–4:30pm; Sat 6am–2pm). Don't miss the brand-new **Clipper Magazine Stadium** for minor league baseball featuring the **Lancaster Barnstormers** (© 717/509-HITS; www.lancasterbarnstormers.com). To the city's east on Route 30, the outlet centers of **Rockvale Square** (www.rockvalesquareoutlets.com) and **Tanger Outlets** (www.tanger outlet.com) offer dozens of top brands.

WHERE TO STAY & DINE

You're more apt to find solid, value-oriented quality than elegance in food and lodging in this family-oriented landscape. The **Best Western Eden Resort Inn & Suites,** 222 Eden Rd., routes 30 and 272 in Lancaster (© 800/528-1234 or 717/569-6444; www.bestwestern.com), is a cut above, with three pools (one indoor and one children's wading pool), a tropically landscaped atrium, and kitchenettes in 40 of the 276 rooms (others come with fridges). Doubles run $99 to $159. **Country Inn of Lancaster,** 2133 Lincoln Hwy. E. (Rte. 30), Lancaster (© 877/393-3413 or 717/393-3413; www.countryinnoflancaster.com), is a 125-room hotel that lets you rock away on your back porch overlooking beautiful Amish farmland, with a heated pool, free breakfast, and refrigerators in the deluxe rooms. Doubles from $100. The Convention & Visitors Bureau (see above) or the website **www.authenticbandb.com** will provide information on dozens of bed-and-breakfasts and a scattering of working farms taking in lodgers.

Pennsylvania Dutch meals or smorgasbords include German-style meats and pot-pies, starchy noodle dishes, boiled vegetables, and sweet desserts. Among the smorgasbords and family-style restaurants open Monday through Saturday, try **Miller's Smorgasbord,** Route 30 at Ronks Road, 5 miles east of Lancaster (℗ **800/669-3568** or 717/687-6621; www.millerssmorgasbord.com), which has served millions since 1929. In downtown Lancaster, try the premium homemade brews and great bar food at **Lancaster Brewing Company,** Walnut and Plum streets (℗ **717/391-6258;** www.lancasterbrewing.com).

VALLEY FORGE

Only 30 minutes from central Philadelphia today, Valley Forge was hours of frozen trails away in the winter of 1777–78. The Revolutionary forces had just lost the battles of Brandywine and Germantown. While the British occupied Philadelphia, Washington's forces repaired to winter quarters near an iron forge where the Schuylkill met Valley Creek, 18 miles northwest. A sawmill and gristmill were supposed to help provide basic requirements, but the British had destroyed them. Some 12,000 men and boys straggled into the encampment, setting up quarters and lines of defense.

Unfortunately, the winter turned bitter. Critical shortages of food and clothing, along with damp shelters, left nearly 4,000 men diseased and unfit for duty. Almost 2,000 perished, and many others deserted. Congress, which had left Philadelphia hurriedly, couldn't persuade the colonies to give money to alleviate the conditions. Nevertheless, the forces slowly gained strength and confidence, thanks in part to the Prussian army veteran Baron von Steuben, appointed by Washington to retrain the Continental Army under his revised and distinctly American "Manual of Arms." By springtime the Continentals were an army on which their new allies, the French, could rely. Replicas of their huts, some of the officers' actual lodgings, and later memorials dot the park today.

Admission to the park is free. Start your visit at the **National Historical Park Visitors Center,** at the junction of Pa. 23 and North Gulph Road (℗ **610/783-1077**). A 15-minute film depicting the encampment is shown at the visitor center every half-hour. Also at the visitor center is a museum containing Washington's tent, an extensive collection of Revolutionary War artifacts, and a bookstore.

Highlights in the park include the **National Memorial Arch;** an 1865 covered bridge; the **Isaac Potts House** (1770), which Washington commandeered as his headquarters; and the 1993 Monument to Patriots of African Descent. Admission to Washington's headquarters is $3 for adults, $2 for children from April to November. A 1903 Gothic **Washington Memorial Chapel** is free, with Sunday carillon recitals in the bell tower at 2pm. A private-public partnership is working on an extensive **National Center for the American Revolution**—don't look for completion before the late-2000s, though. A brand-new innovative "Cell Phone Tour" is available for free, offering information on the park's attractions through a cellular phone call.

The park's facilities are open daily from 9am to 5pm, later in summer.

GETTING THERE   From Philadelphia, access is from Exit 327, the Mall Boulevard exit, of the Pennsylvania Turnpike (I-76) to North Gulph Road. Follow the signs.

TWO PREMIER ATTRACTIONS IN THE BRANDYWINE VALLEY

The Brandywine Valley, bridging Pennsylvania and Delaware, is beautiful rolling country filled with Americana from Colonial days through the Gilded Age. Many of the farms that kept the Revolutionary troops fed have survived to this day. There are

15 covered bridges and scores of antiques stores in Chester County, with miles of country roads and horse trails between them. Though the area is filled with things to see and do, two particular attractions stand out.

Tip: For more information on the region and its attractions, contact the **Brandywine Conference and Visitors Bureau (CVB)** (© **610/565-3679;** www.brandywinecvb.org) and request its free visitor's guide; the CVB also offers information on discounted weekend packages, including hotel and attractions tickets. Or try the **Chester County Conference and Visitors Bureau** (© **800/228-9933** or 610/719-1730; www.brandywine valley.com) and ask for its official tourist guide.

LONGWOOD GARDENS   A scion of the wealthy du Pont family (who created the DuPont Engineering Company), Pierre S. du Pont devoted his life to horticulture, and after purchasing a 19th-century arboretum in 1906, du Pont spent more than 45 years creating the country's ultimate estate garden on a total of 1,050 acres. **Longwood Gardens,** one of the world's greatest garden displays, is on Route 1, 30 miles southwest of Philadelphia and just west of the junction with Pa. 52 (© **610/388-1000;** www.longwoodgardens.org).

No matter when you come here, you will be sure to find something in bloom in the 40 different gardens on the estate. Upon entering, most people head to the left, toward the **Main Fountain Garden,** with special fluid fireworks shows on various dates from May to September, usually preceded by hour-long garden concerts. (There are some 800 events held here each year, from Christmas shows to gardening demonstrations.) A topiary garden of closely pruned shrubs surrounds a 37-foot sundial. If you prefer your plants indoors, 4 acres of massive bronze-and-glass conservatories are among the finest and largest in the United States. African violets, bonsai trees up to 400 years old, hibiscus, orchids, and tropical plants are among the specialties, but expect anything from Easter lilies to scarlet begonias. In May 2001, a 62-bell carillon was installed in the Chimes Tower, and live performances are scheduled in summer.

Note: Longwood Gardens is in the midst of extensive renovations and is expanding its exquisite network of greenhouses. Though its magnificent 10,000-pipe organ will be out of commission until 2008, most displays and attractions remain open.

Admission most of the year is $14 adults, $6 ages 16 to 20, $2 ages 6 to 15, free for children under 6, with prices for adults at $15 during the holiday season and $12 the rest of the winter. Hours vary significantly throughout the seasons. Consult the website for more information.

WINTERTHUR   Winterthur, a du Pont country estate, provides the setting for America's best native collection of decorative arts. **Winterthur Museum & Country Estate** (© **800/448-3883** or 302/888-4600; www.winterthur.org) is 6 miles northwest of Wilmington, Delaware, on Route 52. Henry Francis du Pont (1880–1969), a great-grandson of industrialist E. I. du Pont, was a connoisseur of European antiques, whose attention turned to American pieces in 1923 after realizing that no study had ever explored how the concepts of beauty and taste differed in Europe and America. Henry collected American furniture, followed by native decorative objects, and then the interior woodwork of entire homes built between 1640 and 1840. By the time he was finished, he had to add more than 150 rooms to the family estate in order to display all of his collection; because the museum started out as a private home, the rooms have a unique richness and intimacy.

The **Main Museum,** open for specific guided tours, displays the bulk of the collection and includes complete interiors from every eastern seaboard colony. Special landmarks include the famous Montmorenci Stair Hall, two Shaker Rooms, fine examples of Pennsylvania Dutch decorative arts, and the du Pont dining room. The Campbell Soup Tureen collection, with 125 items currently on display, is housed in the Dorrance Gallery, between the museum and research building. In the Touch-It Room, children can dress up in Colonial costumes and get hands on with artifacts.

In spring, the extensive **Winterthur Gardens** explode into an abundance of cherry and crabapple blossoms, rhododendrons, Virginia bluebells, and azaleas. The lush, carefully planned gardens are well worth viewing any season. Garden tram rides through the grounds are offered when weather permits and are included in the admission fee. There are also two superb gift shops selling a selection of licensed reproductions, gifts, books, jewelry, and plants.

The **Garden & Galleries Pass** ($15 adults, $13 seniors and students, $5 children 2–11), available year-round and good for 2 consecutive days, includes the Galleries, the Dorrance Gallery, the Touch-It Room, a self-guided garden walk, and the garden tram. We highly recommend opting for the **Winterthur Experience** ($20 adults, $18 seniors and students, $10 children 2–11), which adds on one of the museum's wonderful guided tours, which are highly educational and entertaining. Other tours are available as add-ons for another $5 to $10; see the website for all touring options, including a new iPod tour. Winterthur is open Tuesday through Sunday from 10am to 5pm, closed most major holidays.

WHERE TO STAY & DINE   Accommodations are few and on the precious side in du Pont country. The **Brandywine River Hotel,** routes 1 and 100 in Chadds Ford (© **610/388-1200;** www.brandywineriverhotel.com), has adapted and expanded a historic inn. Doubles from $125. The **Mendenhall Inn** on Route 52, Mendenhall (© **610/388-2100;** www.mendenhallinn.com), is well located, near all Brandywine and du Pont attractions; some of the buildings date back to the Colonial era. Doubles from $129, including breakfast.

You can dine well at the **Gables,** 423 Baltimore Pike, nearby (© **610/388-7800**), with its extensive—and expensive—Continental menu; or, for more casual fare, Hank's Place, routes 1 and 100, in Chadds Ford (© **610/388-7061**). The strawberry pie is divine.

GETTYSBURG

The battle that took place at this small university town (about a 2-hr. drive from Philadelphia) in 1863 was the turning point of the Civil War. Over 3 broiling hot days in July, Gen. Robert E. Lee's 75,000-man Confederate Army of Northern Virginia clashed thrice with Gen. George Meade's 83,000-strong Union troops, each time failing to deliver the decisive blow that would convince President Lincoln to end the war. Over the 3 days, more than 51,000 men died and more than 40,000 others were wounded, making this the bloodiest battle in American history. The war didn't end until 2 years later, but after Gen. George E. Pickett's ill-fated charge up Cemetery Ridge on July 3, Lee realized he was beaten, and began his retreat south.

Lincoln traveled to Gettysburg 4 months after the battle to dedicate the cemetery that held 3,706 casualties, a third of them unknown. "Four score and seven years ago," Lincoln began his brief address—the most famous speech by any American president.

The battle and Lincoln's address are commemorated at **Gettysburg National Military Park,** the country's premier battlefield shrine, with a monument to just about every company that served here (more than 1,000 in all) spread out along 40 scenic miles. Start at the **visitor center,** 97 Taneytown Rd. (© **717/334-1124;** www.nps. gov/gett), where you can sit in on the **Electric Map** presentation that provides a hokey but informative overview of the 3-day battle, and visit the highly regarded museum covering the Civil War. A number of tours start here, including bus tours, licensed guide tours, and ranger walks. Rangers are glad to answer questions and provide maps of the hiking trails and the 18-mile self-guided auto tour, which hits all the major sites.

Note: In fall 2007, a new center and museum will open ⅔ mile away, at 1195 Baltimore Pike; the old visitor center will be removed.

Admission to Gettysburg National Military Park is free. The cost of the Electric Map presentation is $4. The battlefield is open daily year-round from 6am to 10pm April through October, and from 6am to 7pm November through March. The visitor center is open daily from 8am to 5pm (until 6pm in summer), except Thanksgiving, December 25, and January 1. The cemetery is open from dawn to dusk.

For information about accommodations, restaurants, shopping, and other local attractions, contact the **Gettysburg Convention and Visitors Bureau,** 89 Steinwehr Ave., Gettysburg, PA 17325 (© **717/334-2100;** www.gettysburg.com).

WHERE TO STAY   Gettysburg has two fine chain-hotel options within walking distance of the visitor center. The 109-room **Quality Inn Gettysburg Motor Lodge,** 380 Steinwehr Ave. (© **800/228-5151** or 717/334-1103; www.gettysburgqualityinn. com or www.qualityinn.com), just behind the visitor center, has doubles for $50 to $149. The rates at the 111-room **Holiday Inn Gettysburg,** 516 Baltimore St., at Pennsylvania Route 97 and Business Route 15 (© **800/315-2621** or 717/334-6211; www.ichotelsgroup.com), are $80 to $200 double.

If you'd like to sleep in a bit of history, the **Best Western Gettysburg Hotel,** 1 Lincoln Sq. (© **800/528-1234** or 717/337-2000; www.gettysburg-hotel.com), is right on the town square and charges $94 to $350 double. Just down the street is the small **James Gettys Hotel,** 27 Chambersburg St. (© **888/900-5275** or 717/337-1334; www.jamesgettyshotel.com), with 12 suites for $135 to $250.

GETTING THERE   Gettysburg is about 125 miles west of Philadelphia, 180 miles east of Pittsburgh, and about 36 miles southwest of Harrisburg. Take **I-76** (Pennsylvania Tpk.) west from Philadelphia or east from Pittsburgh to Harrisburg, then **U.S. 15** south to Gettysburg. From Lancaster and Amish Country, take **U.S. 30** west about 53 miles to Gettysburg.

7 Pittsburgh & Western Pennsylvania

PITTSBURGH

In the heart of Station Square, one of Pittsburgh's newest shopping and entertainment districts, stands a Bessemer converter, the remains of an old steel blast furnace. Once an integral cog in the works of the Steel City, the furnace now serves as a piece of art, right next to the Square's dancing fountain that shoots jets of multicolored water in time to the music of Christina Aguilera and ABBA.

How times have changed in Pittsburgh. Modern glass office towers, contemporary sculptures, and theaters are more the norm in the Steel City these days than are the belching mills for which the city is famous. Pittsburgh's natural beauty is also unmistakable. The city's hilly landscape is sliced by the Ohio, Allegheny, and Monongahela rivers, visible at every turn and crisscrossed by more bridges than any other city in the world. Add to all of this some of the nation's friendliest residents, and you've got the ideal place to get away and relax.

ESSENTIALS

GETTING THERE   By Plane   Pittsburgh International Airport (© 412/472-3525; www.pitairport.com) is 15 miles west of downtown. **US Airways** is the dominant carrier. To get downtown from the airport, take the public **28X Airport Flyer bus** (© 412/442-2000; www.ridegold.com) for $2.25, or a cab ride for $30. Car rentals are inexpensive in Pittsburgh, and more than 1,500 color-coded signs point the way to highways and attractions, making it easy to drive to and around town. The airport is a 20-minute drive (45 min. during rush hour) from downtown.

By Train   Amtrak (© 800/USA-RAIL or 412/471-6172; www.amtrak.com) provides daily service from Philadelphia (trip time: 7½ hr.), Washington, D.C. (8 hr.), Cleveland (2½ hr.), and Chicago (10 hr.) to its station at 1100 Liberty Ave.

By Car Major routes into the belt roads around Pittsburgh are **I-76** from the northwest (Cleveland) and east (Philadelphia), **I-70** from the west (Columbus) and southeast (Baltimore), and **I-79** from the north (Erie, PA) and south (Charleston, WV).

VISITOR INFORMATION The **Greater Pittsburgh Convention & Visitors Bureau,** 425 6th Ave. (© 800/359-0758 or 412/281-7711; www.visitpittsburgh.com), operates several **Visitor Information Centers:** downtown, Liberty Avenue next to the Gateway Center, Monday through Friday from 9am to 5pm, Saturday 9am to 3pm; at the Airport Landside, Monday through Saturday from 10am to 5pm; and at the Senator John Heinz Pittsburgh Regional History Center in the Strip District daily 10am to 5pm.

GETTING AROUND The **Port Authority of Allegheny County** (© 412/442-2000; www.ridegold.com) operates subways and buses throughout the city as well as the "T" Light Rail. Fares are free within the Golden Triangle downtown; prices vary outside that area, but are generally less than $2.

FAST FACTS For **medical services,** call **Allegheny General Hospital** near downtown at © 412/359-3131; in the Oakland area the major local hospital is **UPMC Presbyterian,** 200 Lothrop St. (© 412/647-2345). The 7% city sales tax is not assessed on clothing, groceries, or prescriptions; hotel taxes total 14%.

WHAT TO SEE & DO

From the **Mount Washington Overlook** (Grandview Ave.) you can see how Pittsburgh became a crucial junction of transportation and commerce, sitting at the confluence of three major rivers. History aside, the city's arching bridges, sparkling rivers, and Golden Triangle create a lovely panorama best enjoyed from one of many lookouts, restaurants, and bars atop Mount Washington. Hundred-year-old cable cars ferry passengers up Mount Washington. Visit either the **Duquesne Incline,** 1220 Grandview Ave. (© 412/381-1665; www.incline.cc), where the fares are $3.75 for adults and $1.70 for children; or the **Monongahela Incline,** 8 Grandview Ave. (© 412/442-2000; www.ridegold.com), with fares of $2 for adults, $1 for children.

Pittsburgh's compact and walkable downtown is called the **Golden Triangle,** where the Allegheny and Monongahela rivers converge flowing west into the Ohio. Here you'll find **Point State Park** (© 412/471-0235), the historic site of Fort Pitt and home to Pittsburgh's landmark 150-foot fountain. Entrance is free to the park and the adjoining **Allegheny Riverfront Park;** both are popular for a picnic or pleasant stroll.

Many of Pittsburgh's cultural institutions bear the names of American industrial barons who amassed their fortunes in Pittsburgh and said thanks with the endowments of concert halls, museums, and libraries. In 1895, Andrew Carnegie endowed the **Carnegie Museums** (www.carnegiemuseums.org), which today include the city's finest: **Carnegie Museum of Art,** 4400 Forbes Ave., Oakland (© **412/622-3131;** www.cmoa.org), with contemporary exhibitions and Impressionist and post-Impressionist masterpieces; the **Carnegie Museum of Natural History,** 4400 Forbes Ave., Oakland (© **412/622-3131;** www.carnegiemnh.org), renowned for its Dinosaur Hall; the **Carnegie Science Center,** 1 Allegheny Ave. (© **412/237-3400;** www.carnegiesciencecenter.org), where kids experience hands-on science and the interactive SportsWorks next door; and **The Andy Warhol Museum,** 117 Sandusky St. (© **412/237-8300;** www.warhol.org), devoted to the life and work of Pittsburgh's most fabulous native artist.

Unassociated with the Carnegie Museums but just as dynamic is the **Mattress Factory,** 500 Sampsonia Way (© **412/231-3169;** www.mattress.org), a museum of site-specific artworks by the likes of James Turrell. **Clayton,** the former home of Henry Clay Frick, shares a 6-acre site with the **Frick Art & Historical Center,** 7227 Reynolds St. (© **412/371-0600;** www.frickart.org), which has museums featuring artistic masterpieces and classic cars, as well as a floral conservatory. Many guests round out an afternoon of free chamber music with a formal high tea on the grounds. Among the city's most unusual sights are the **Nationality Rooms** in the 42-story Cathedral of Learning on the University of Pittsburgh's campus (© **412/624-6000;** www.pitt.edu/~natrooms). Twenty-four classrooms reflect the customs and architectural styles of Pittsburgh's diverse immigrant groups.

Pittsburghers love their sports teams, especially the Steelers. Spend an autumn day taking in a football game at **Heinz Field,** North Shore Dr. at Allegheny Ave. (© **412/323-1200;** www.steelers.com). **PNC Park,** 115 Federal St. (© **800/BUY-BUCS;** www.pirateball.com), home of the Pittsburgh Pirates, sits on the shore of the Allegheny River and offers terrific views of the city skyline as a backdrop to the action on the field. The Pittsburgh Penguins play at **Mellon Arena,** 66 Mario Lemieux Place (© **800/642-7367;** www.pittsburghpenguins.com), right off I-579.

The **Pittsburgh Zoo & Aquarium,** 1 Wild Place, at Baker Street (© **800/474-4966;** www.pittsburghzoo.com), set atop a hill in Pittsburgh's Shadyside neighborhood, is known for its large children's zoo. Other highlights include a walk-through bat flyaway, a rare Komodo dragon, and a well-stocked African savanna. Another family favorite is **Kennywood,** 4800 Kennywood Blvd. (© **412/461-0500;** www.kennywood.com), a traditional amusement park 10 miles southeast of Pittsburgh in West Mifflin. The park features steel and wooden roller coasters, water rides, and dozens of spinning, twirling attractions for all ages.

The Strip District, a warehouse district bounded roughly by 16th and 31st streets between Smallman Street and Liberty Avenue, is Pittsburgh's historic waterfront market. Today the Strip draws locals and visitors to its ethnic grocery stores; fresh produce, meat, and fish markets; bakeries; and specialty foods stores. Here you'll also find the **Senator John Heinz Pittsburgh Regional History Center,** 1212 Smallman St. (© **412/454-6000;** www.pghhistory.org), housed in a massive renovated 1898 icehouse. A highlight is the Heinz 57 exhibit, featuring the pickled relishes, ketchup, and mustards made famous by the Pittsburgh-born Heinz family.

WHERE TO STAY & DINE

The landmark **Omni William Penn,** 530 William Penn Place (© **888/444-6664** or 421/281-7100; www.omniwilliampenn.com), is Pittsburgh's historic grande dame.

Most guests at this downtown hotel are drawn to the crystalline lobby and the romantic, luxurious guest rooms. Rates start at $169 double. Another romantic downtown favorite is the **Renaissance Pittsburgh Hotel,** 107 6th St. (© **866/454-4400** or 412/562-1200; www.renaissancepittsburgh.com), a 14-story copper-clad hotel known for its 30-foot glass atrium, marble lobby, upscale rooms, and fabulous views. Doubles begin at $199. A $12-million renovation and a great location attract business and leisure travelers to the **Doubletree Hotel,** 1 Bigelow Sq. (© **800/225-5858** or 412/281-5800; www.doubletree.com), adjacent to Mellon Arena and within blocks of the David Lawrence Convention Center. Doubles begin at $139. The **Holiday Inn Select,** 100 Lytton Ave. (© **888/465-4329** or 412/682-6200), with doubles starting at $149, offers pleasant affordable accommodations within blocks of Carnegie Mellon, the University of Pittsburgh, and the Carnegie Museums of Art and Natural History.

For upscale dining within walking distance of the theater district and Heinz Hall, try **Opus,** inside the Renaissance Pittsburgh Hotel at 107 6th St. (© **412/992-2005**). The warm, intimate restaurant features a menu with Mediterranean and Middle Eastern influences and a very impressive wine list. On the Strip, **Lidia's,** 1400 Smallman St. (© **412/552-0150;** www.lidiasitaly.com), serves homemade pasta and northern Italian specialties created by Lidia Bastianich, hostess of the PBS cooking show "Lidia's Italian Table." For excellent German beer and food, visit Deutschtown's **Penn Brewery,** 800 Vinial St. (© **412/237-9402;** www.pennbrew.com). The Pastorius family, descendants of the oldest German family in America, brews award-winning beers and serves them alongside bratwurst and sauerbraten in a fun beer-hall atmosphere appropriate for the whole family.

Don't miss Pittsburgh's culinary gem, **Primanti Brothers,** a 70-year-old institution famous for putting the fries and coleslaw in their sandwiches along with the chopped meat, cheese, and sliced tomato. (It's a mess, but delicious.) The restaurant still churns out sandwiches in its original location in the Strip at 46 18th St. (© **412/263-2142;** www.primantibros.com), but you'll also find Primanti's at 10 other locations across town, including PNC Park and Heinz Field.

PITTSBURGH AFTER DARK

PERFORMING ARTS   Gilded and plush with red velvet, Italian marble, and Viennese crystal chandeliers, **Heinz Hall,** 600 Penn Ave. (© **412/392-4900;** www.pittsburghsymphony.org), endowed by Henry John Heinz, is the elegantly opulent home of the renowned **Pittsburgh Symphony.** The nearby **Benedum Center,** 719 Liberty Ave., is home to the **Pittsburgh Ballet Theatre** (© **412/281-0360;** www.pbt.org), **Pittsburgh Opera** (© **412/281-0912;** www.pittsburghopera.org), and **Pittsburgh CLO** (© **412/456-6666;** www.pittsburghclo.org), which produces a summer season of musicals. Pittsburgh is also home to several theater companies, including **PNC Broadway,** 719 Liberty Ave. (© **412/456-1390;** www.pgharts.org); **Pittsburgh Public Theatre,** 621 Penn Ave. (© **412/316-1600;** www.ppt.org); and **Pittsburgh City Theatre,** 1300 Bingham St. (© **412/431-2489;** www.citytheatrecompany.org).

THE BAR & CLUB SCENE   A good place to check out the nightlife is the **Strip District,** which becomes a club scene after dark. **Déjà Vu Lounge,** 2106 Penn Ave. (© **412/434-1144**), features alternating live music, karaoke, and DJs, and serves drinks and food. **Station Square** (© **800/859-8959;** www.stationsquare.com), across the Smithfield Street or Fort Pitt Bridges from downtown, is home to several after-hours restaurants and bars with nice city views.

OUTSIDE PITTSBURGH

The Laurel Highlands, 60 miles to the southeast, boasts historic sites and a wealth of outdoor activities, all set in some of Pennsylvania's loveliest countryside. The **Laurel Highlands Visitors Bureau** (© 800/333-5661 or 724/238-5661; www.laurel highlands.org) can provide details about the entire area.

Active outdoor enthusiasts generally head to **Ohiopyle State Park,** just east of Pa. 381 (© 888/PA-PARKS or 724/329-8591; www.dcnr.state.pa.us), home of the Ohiopyle Falls and more than 19,000 acres of unspoiled wilderness bordering the Youghiogheny River gorge. Popular activities include hiking, biking, camping, fishing, and serious white-water rafting down the "Yough" (pronounced *yawk*).

Nearby, just off U.S. 40, is the **Fort Necessity National Battlefield** (© 724/329-5512; www.nps.gov/fone), where George Washington had his first major test during the French and Indian War in 1754. The 900-acre site includes a visitor center, the battlefield, the reconstructed Fort Necessity, and the Mount Washington Tavern.

For some childish good fun, spend a day at **Idlewild Park** in Ligonier (© 724/238-3666; www.idlewild.com). Idlewild doesn't have America's sleekest, fastest rides; it's simply a great old amusement park, with a fresh new Soak Zone waterpark and Storybook Forest for younger kids. Little ones will enjoy the park's Mister Rogers' Neighborhood of Make-Believe, inspired by the late Fred Rogers, who lived close by.

Fallingwater, Pa. 381, Mill Run (© 724/329-8501; www.paconserve.org), Frank Lloyd Wright's 1936 architectural masterpiece, is another prime draw. Three cantilevered house levels extend from the side of a hill, allowing the namesake waterfall to run through the building's exterior and causing the house to appear carved out of the hillside rather than appended to it. When Wright first designed the house for Pittsburgh department store magnate Edgar Kaufmann, most engineers said it wouldn't stand. They were partly right; after more than 60 years a major effort to reinforce the building's foundation and floors with steel girders was needed to prevent Fallingwater from gradually rejoining the river that runs through it. But it remains one of the nation's most important architectural gems, named by the American Institute of Architects "the most important building of the 20th century."

The Western Pennsylvania Conservancy offers tours of **Fallingwater,** highlighting the house itself, the furniture Wright designed specifically for it, the teeny-tiny bedrooms he insisted on, and the low ceilings that never bothered the 5-foot 5-inch architect. With the exceptions of Mondays and major holidays, tours run every day from mid-March to Thanksgiving weekend; December weekends; and the week between Christmas and New Year's (weather permitting). Advance reservations are required. Standard 1-hour tours cost $16 adults, $10 kids 6 to 12; children under 6 are prohibited. A 2-hour in-depth tour, which includes many more interior rooms and extended interpretation, costs $55; children under 9 are prohibited. Nature tours and sunset tours are also available by reservation.

When I. N. Hagan saw Wright's Fallingwater, he commissioned the famous architect to construct **Kentuck Knob** (© 724/329-1901; www.kentuckknob.com), a home that's smaller and less pivotal in architectural history. But true Wright fans will find the half-hour side trip from Fallingwater worthwhile. Kentuck Knob is on Kentuck Knob Road, just north of Chalk Hill. Guided tours are available March through December daily 9am to 4pm; May through August with extended Saturday hours to 6pm; January through February daily 11am to 3pm, weather permitting. Standard 1-hour tours cost $15 adults, $8 kids under 18. In-depth 2-hour tours are given daily at 8:30am and 2:15pm, and cost $50. Kentuck Knob recommends guests be ages 6 or older. Advance reservations are recommended for all tours; reservations and a deposit are required for in-depth tours.

WHERE TO STAY   Greensburg is your best bet for affordable lodging near Idlewild. **Four Points by Sheraton,** U.S. 30 East (© 800/909-2918 or 724/836-6060; www.greensburgpa4points.com), offers an indoor pool; doubles begin at $100. The closest places to stay near Ohiopyle State Park, Fallingwater, and Kentuck Knob are in the tiny village of Farmington, home to two upscale resorts. The **Historic Summit Inn,** 101 Skyline Dr. (© 800/433-8594 or 724/438-8594; www.summitinn resort.com), is open April through November and offers doubles beginning at $110. **Nemacolin Woodlands Resort and Spa,** 1001 LaFayette Dr. (© 800/422-2736 or 724/329-8555; www.nemacolin.com), has town houses starting at $150 and lodge rooms beginning at $200. Both resorts include restaurants, pools, tennis courts, golf courses, health clubs, and spas. In the slightly larger burg of Uniontown, 10 miles away, the **Holiday Inn,** 700 W. Main St. (© 888/465-4329 or 724/437-2816; www. uniontownpa.holiday-inn.com), has an indoor pool; doubles start at $109.

GETTING THERE   To get to Idlewild from Pittsburgh, follow U.S. 30 east. To get to Fallingwater, Ohiopyle State Park, Farmington, and Chalk Hill, take I-76 east to Exit 91. From there take Pa. 31 east, then Pa. 381 south.

8 Baltimore

A combination of interesting tourist attractions, historical sites, and friendly people in such picturesque old neighborhoods as Fells Point, Mount Vernon, Canton, and Federal Hill makes Baltimore an ever-more-popular tourist destination. "Charm City" has welcomed visitors since 1729. It was founded as a shipping and ship-building town, so manufacturing has always been a big part of this city. General Motors and Bethlehem Steel have been a part of the east Baltimore landscape for decades. Domino Sugar's sign dominates the Inner Harbor. More recently, Baltimore has welcomed a new wave of service industries and nonprofits. And baseball fans flock to Camden Yards, Baltimore's beautiful ballpark, which has been instrumental in revitalizing the city's downtown area. Tourism plays an ever-increasing role in the city's economy, and a laid-back population welcomes its visitors with a friendly "Hello, hon!" in the unique Bawlamer accent.

ESSENTIALS
GETTING THERE   By Plane   Baltimore–Washington International Airport (© 800/I-FLY-BWI or 410/859-7111; www.bwiairport.com) is 10 miles south of downtown Baltimore, off I-295 (the Baltimore–Washington Pkwy.). It's a major domestic and international hub. To drive to downtown Baltimore from the airport, take I-195 west to Route 295 North. **SuperShuttle** (© 800/258-3826; www.super shuttle.com) operates vans between the airport and all major downtown hotels. Departures are scheduled every 30 minutes between 5:45am and 11:15pm, and the cost is $11 per person one-way. The **Light Rail** also connects the airport with downtown Baltimore and the Amtrak stations at BWI and at Penn Station.

By Car   I-95 provides the easiest routes to Baltimore from the north and south. Take I-95 south to **I-395** (Exit 53), and follow signs to the Inner Harbor. If you're driving in from the north, you'll have to pass through the **Fort McHenry Tunnel** ($2 toll).

From the west, take **I-70** east to Exit 91, I-695 South (the **Baltimore Beltway**) heading toward Glen Burnie. Take Exit 11A, I-95 to I-395, north to downtown.

Once you arrive, you'll find lots of parking garages, as well as metered on-street parking throughout the downtown district. Garages charge about $18 a day, or $5 to $8 for special events or evening visits. Parking meters must be fed $1 an hour (in quarters only).

By Train   Baltimore is a stop on **Amtrak**'s (© **800/872-7245;** www.amtrak.com) Northeast Corridor, between Wilmington, Delaware, and Washington, D.C. Trains arrive at and depart from Pennsylvania Station, 1500 N. Charles St. (north of the Inner Harbor), and BWI Airport Rail station, off Route 170 about 1½ miles from the airport (© **410/672-6169**). In addition, the **Maryland Area Rail Commuter Service** (**MARC;** © **800/325-RAIL;** www.mtamaryland.com) provides rail service on two routes from Washington, D.C., stopping at BWI en route. One ends at Camden Station, closest to the Inner Harbor, and the other ends at Penn Station about 20 blocks north.

VISITOR INFORMATION   Contact the **Baltimore Area Convention and Visitors Association** at 100 Light St., Baltimore, MD 21202 (© **877/BALTIMORE;** www.Baltimore.org), for maps, brochures, and water taxi schedules. In town, check out the new visitor center located between Harborplace and the Maryland Science Center. You can also pick up a copy of the *Baltimore Quick Guide,* a purse-size guide to what's happening in and around the city.

GETTING AROUND   Because so many of Baltimore's major attractions are clustered around the Inner Harbor, walking is often the easiest way to get around.

Baltimore's **Mass Transit Administration (MTA)** operates **Light Rail,** a 27-mile trolley system that travels north-south from the northern suburb of Timonium to Glen Burnie in the south, with a spur to Penn Station. The key stop within the city is Camden Station, next to the Orioles' ballpark. The Light Rail is the ideal way to get to a game or to travel within the downtown area between Camden Yards and the Inner Harbor to Lexington Market and the area around Mount Vernon Place. Tickets are $1.60 one-way and are dispensed at machines at each stop. Better yet, get a day pass covering all MTA transport for $3.50. Trains run Monday through Friday between 6am and 11pm, Saturday between 7am and 11pm, and Sunday between 11am and 7pm.

Baltimore's MTA also operates **Metro,** a subway system that connects downtown with the northwest suburbs, and an extensive **bus** system. The base fare is $1.60, and exact change is necessary, or you can buy a day pass for $3.50. For information and schedules for all MTA services, call © **800/543-9809** or 410/539-5000, or visit the MTA website at **www.mtamaryland.com.**

All taxis in the city are metered; two reputable companies are **Yellow Checker Cab** (© **410/841-5573**) and **Arrow Cab** (© **410/261-0000**). For airport trips, call **SuperShuttle** (© **410/258-3826**).

A ride on a water taxi is a pleasant way to visit Baltimore's attractions, or even to go to dinner. Two companies operate water taxi service and both have different stops. But you can use either to get within walking distance of your waterfront destination. **Ed Kane's Water Taxi & Trolley** (© **800/658-8947** or 410/563-3901) runs a continual service between about a dozen Inner Harbor locations including Harborplace, Fells Point, and Fort McHenry. The main stop at Harborplace is on the corner between the two pavilions. Tell the mate where you want to go; not all taxis stop at every destination.

Downtown Baltimore

0   1/4 mi
0   0.25 km

MOUNT VERNON

LEXINGTON MARKET

Greyhound/
Trailways terminal

Baltimore Arena

Convention Center

Oriole Park at Camden Yards

Inner Harbor

Harborplace

Northwest Branch

Shot Tower

M&T Bank Stadium

FEDERAL HILL PARK

FEDERAL HILL

(i) **Visitor Center**

(i) Information
L— Light Rail
▪ ▪ ▪ ▪ Mono
✉ Post Office

MARYLAND
Baltimore
Washington, D.C.
Annapolis

BALTIMORE
Area of detail

ACCOMMODATIONS ▪
Days Inn Inner Harbor **5**
Harbor Court Hotel **9**
Holiday Inn Baltimore
  Inner Harbor **4**
Hyatt Regency
  Baltimore **6**
Pier 5 Hotel **10**
Renaissance Harborplace
  Hotel **8**

DINING ◆
Brass Elephant **1**
Charleston **11**
Pisces **7**
Prime Rib **2**
Windows **8**
Woman's Industrial
  Exchange Restaurant **3**

The cost is $8 for adults and $4 for children 10 and under for a full day's unlimited use of the water taxi and trolley to Fort McHenry.

FAST FACTS   City hospitals include **Johns Hopkins Hospital,** 600 N. Wolfe St. (© 410/955-5000); **University of Maryland Medical Center,** 22 S. Greene St. (© 410/328-8667); and **Mercy Medical Center,** 301 St. Paul Place (© 410/332-9000). There's a **Rite Aid** at 17 W. Baltimore St. (© 410/539-0838). **Walgreens** is at 19 E. Fayette St. (© 410/625-1179). The state sales tax is 5%. The hotel tax is an additional 7.5%.

Baltimore has a nagging problem with property and violent crime. More police, along with the Downtown Partnership's safety guides, are doing a pretty good job of keeping the Inner Harbor and Mount Vernon areas fairly safe. But be alert and use common-sense precautions.

SPECIAL EVENTS   The biggest and best-known event in Baltimore is the **Preakness Celebration (www.preaknesscelebration.com),** a weeklong, citywide party leading up to the Preakness Stakes, the middle jewel of horse-racing's Triple Crown, held at Pimlico Racecourse in mid-May. Events include a 5K run, a music festival, hot-air balloon races, a golf tournament, and much more. For tickets to the horse race (they go on sale Jan 1—and they go fast), call © **410/542-9400** or go on the Internet to **www.marylandracing.com**.

WHAT TO SEE & DO

The city's focal point for tourism is the **Inner Harbor,** home of the Baltimore Convention Center and Festival Hall Exhibit Center, the Harborplace shopping pavilions, the National Aquarium and other museums, Oriole Park at Camden Yards, M&T Bank Stadium, and the Pier 6 Concert Pavilion.

American Visionary Art Museum   Look for the "Whirligig," a 55-foot multicolored, wind-powered sculpture at the front of this curvaceous building housing some of the most interesting art you're bound to see. Visionary art is made by people who aren't trained as artists but feel compelled to draw, paint, or create something in an unusual medium. A 10-foot model of the *Lusitania* made from 193,000 matchsticks dominates a first-floor gallery. All the exhibits are fascinating, but some are disturbing and certainly too strong for children (alerts are posted). Other exhibits are a joy that children would love. AVAM added new exhibit space and a sculpture garden in 2004.

800 Key Hwy. © **410/244-1900.** www.avam.org. Admission $12 adults, $8 seniors and students, free for children under 4. Tues–Sun 10am–6pm. Closed Thanksgiving and Dec 25.

Babe Ruth Birthplace and Museum/Baltimore Orioles Museum   George Herman "Babe" Ruth was born in this row house. Two rooms are re-created as they would have looked when the Sultan of Swat was a boy. Other exhibits include a wall enumerating all his home runs, and memorabilia from his Major League career as well as from his days at St. Mary's Industrial School in southwest Baltimore, where he learned to play the game. The Orioles and gone-but-not-forgotten Colts have their own exhibits here as well, and the museum opened a new gallery inside Camden Station in May 2005 so they could expand their exhibits on the Orioles.

216 Emory St. © **410/727-1539.** Fax 410/727-1652. www.baberuthmuseum.com. Admission $6 adults, $4 seniors, $6.50 ages 3–12. Apr–Oct daily 10am–5pm (until 7pm on Orioles home game days); Nov–Mar daily 10am–4pm (until 8pm on days of Ravens home games). Closed Jan 1, Thanksgiving, and Dec 25.

Baltimore Museum of Art   The largest museum in Maryland, the BMA boasts galleries dedicated to modern and contemporary art; European sculpture and painting; American painting and decorative arts; prints and photographs; arts of Africa, Asia, the Americas, and Oceania; and a 2¾-acre sculpture garden. The BMA is famous for the Matisse collection, housed in the $4-million Cone Wing, which also showcases other Impressionist paintings by Cézanne, Gauguin, van Gogh, and Renoir. The Jacobs Wing, a collection of 15th- to 19th-century European art beautifully displayed in rich jewel-toned rooms, reopened in 2003 after major renovations. Other highlights include the 35,000-square-foot West Wing for Contemporary Art and a wonderful gallery of miniature rooms.

10 Art Museum Dr. (at N. Charles and 31st sts.). ✆ 410/396-7100. www.artbma.org. Admission $10 adults, $8 seniors, $6 students with ID, free for ages 18 and under, free to all 1st Thurs of the month. Wed–Fri 11am–5pm; Sat–Sun 11am–6pm. Bus: 3 or 11.

Edgar Allan Poe's Grave Site and Memorial   Three modest memorials in this small old graveyard recall the poet who wrote "The Tell-Tale Heart" and "The Raven" (the only poem to inspire an NFL team's name). The main memorial features a bas-relief bust of Poe; a small gravestone adorned with a raven can be found at Poe's original burial lot; and there's also a plaque placed by the French, who, thanks to the poet Baudelaire, enjoy some of the best translations of Poe's works. The poet is remembered on his birthday every January when a mysterious visitor leaves half a bottle of cognac and roses at the grave. On the weekend closest to Poe's birthday, a party is held in his honor. A Halloween tour is also scheduled each year.

Westminster Cemetery, southeast corner of Fayette and Greene sts. ✆ 410/706-2072 (answered by a University of Maryland Law School staffer). Daily 8am–dusk. Closed major holidays.

Fort McHenry   The flag that flies at Fort McHenry is 30×42 feet, big enough for Francis Scott Key to see by the dawn's early light and write "The Star-Spangled Banner." The star-shaped fort, now a national park, looks much as it did in 1814, the year of the British attack. Its buildings, repaired in the days following that attack, still stand. Exhibits recall Baltimore under siege during the War of 1812, the fort's Civil War service, and its use as an army hospital during World War I. Visitors are invited to take part in the daily changing of the flag, so stop by at 9:30am or 4:30pm (7:30pm June–Aug) to join in. A visit takes about 90 minutes.

Fort McHenry National Monument, E. Fort Ave. ✆ 410/962-4290. www.nps.gov/fomc. Admission $5, free for children under age 16. Sept–May daily 8am–5pm; June to Labor Day daily 8am–8pm. Water taxi stop.

Maryland Historical Society Museum *(Kids)*   The collections here represent some part of Maryland's 350-plus years of history in a sprawling museum that takes up a city block. Francis Scott Key's manuscript of the "Star-Spangled Banner" is the centerpiece of an exhibit, "Looking For Liberty," which includes artifacts that recall Maryland's past. Another permanent exhibit, "Maryland Through the Artist's Eye," features the society's enormous art collection. You can also find all kinds of stuff here: Cal Ripken's bat, Baltimore painted furniture, Stieff silver, and mementos of the Duchess of Windsor (a local girl). Don't miss the gift shop. Allow at least a couple of hours to see everything.

201 W. Monument St. ✆ 410/685-3750. www.mdhs.org. Admission $8 adults, $6 seniors and ages 13–17, $4 ages 3–12. Pass for Maryland Historical Society Museum, Baltimore Civil War Museum—President St. Station, and Fells Point Maritime Museum $12 adults, $10 students and seniors, $4 ages 3–12. Wed–Sun 10am–5pm. Open until 8pm 1st Thurs of every month, when admission is free. Light rail: Centre St.

> ⌒Value⌒ **Money-Saving Harbor Pass**
>
> Baltimore's top tourism spots have teamed up with a **Harbor Pass**. For $46, adults can visit the National Aquarium, the Science Center, Port Discovery, and the Top of the World Observation Level—and ride Ed Kane's Water Taxi all day. The passes are good for 3 consecutive days but only one visit per location. Kids' passes are $30. The passes are also good for discounts at a few hotels and restaurants, an Orioles game, and other Inner Harbor attractions. Call ℭ **877/ BALTIMORE** or visit **www.baltimore.org**. Passes are also available at the Inner Harbor visitor center.

Maryland Science Center *Kids*   This museum's three floors of exhibits include the popular Outer Space Place, home of the Hubble Space Telescope National Visitor Center. Sometimes the exhibits are too crowded or have limited interest, but the IMAX theater and planetarium are always worth a visit. The IMAX theater presents shows as diverse as *Beauty and the Beast* and *Space Station 3D*. IMAX is so popular, extra screenings are available Friday and Saturday evenings. The stars are on display at the David Planetarium and The Crosby Ramsey Memorial Observatory; the latter is free to the public on Friday nights, weather permitting (call for hours).

601 Light St. (south side of the Inner Harbor). ℭ 410/685-5225. www.mdsci.org. Admission varies according to special exhibits; core experience with planetarium $15 adults, $10 children 4–12; core experience with planetarium and IMAX film $19 adults, $14 children 4–12; core experience with traveling exhibit $20 adult, $14 children 4–12; admission to everything $24 adult, $18 children 4–12. Memorial Day to Labor Day Thurs–Sat 10am–8pm, Sun–Wed 10am–6pm; rest of year Tues–Fri 10am–5pm, Sat 10am–6pm, Sun 11am–5pm. Call ahead, as hours change with some exhibits. Water taxi stop.

Maryland Zoo in Baltimore *Kids*   The third-oldest zoo in the United States is home to some 2,000 animals, including a beloved polar bear, prairie dogs, and tigers. Several exhibits are newly renovated, including the Polar Bear Watch, Chimpanzee Forest, Leopard Lair, and African Watering Hole. The children's zoo is a must-see with its lily pads, tree slide, farm animals, and Maryland wilderness exhibit. Plan to spend a few hours here.

Druid Hill Park. ℭ 410/366-LION. www.marylandzoo.org. Admission $15 adults, $12 seniors, $10 children 2–11. Daily 10am–4:30pm. Closed Jan–Feb, 2nd Fri in June, Thanksgiving, and Dec 25.

National Aquarium in Baltimore *Best*   Visitors can walk into a room surrounded by patrolling sharks, wander among the coral reefs, follow the yearly migration of fish, and visit a rainforest on the roof at one of best aquariums in the country. In addition to the watery denizens, exhibits include a popular puffin display; *Maryland: Mountains to the Sea;* and an Amazon River Forest filled with plants and animals as well as fish. The sharks are a main attraction, as is a dolphins exhibit/performance. **The Marine Mammal Pavilion** is where you'll find the dolphins: three generations from one family. Don't miss the presentations; reserve a seat when you get your tickets at no additional fee. The newest exhibit, **Animal Planet Australia: Wild Extremes,** set in a 120-foot-tall glass cube at the front of the aquarium takes visitors to the floor of an Australian river gorge— there are 1,800 animals in all, as well as plants native to Australia.

Insider tip: The aquarium draws huge crowds in summer. The best way to beat the crush is to buy timed tickets in person or through the website. Nonpeak visiting hours are weekday mornings, Friday evenings, or any day after 3pm.

501 E. Pratt St. (on the harbor). ℂ **410/576-3800.** www.aqua.org. Admission $22 adults, $21 seniors, $13 ages 3–11. Mar–June and Sept–Oct daily 9am–5pm; Nov–Feb daily 10am–5pm; July–Aug daily 9am–5pm. Year-round Fri until 8pm. Hours subject to change; call ahead. Exhibits are open 2 hr. after last ticket is sold.

USS Constellation *Kids*   You can't miss the *Constellation,* docked for years at the Inner Harbor (predating Harborplace). A stunning triple-masted sloop-of-war launched in 1854, the *Constellation* is the last Civil War–era vessel afloat. Tour her gun decks, visit the wardrooms, see a cannon demonstration, and learn about the life of a sailor. Demonstrations begin with the raising of the colors at 10:30am and continue on the hour.

Pier 1, 301 E. Pratt St. ℂ **410/539-1797.** www.constellation.org. Admission (including audio tour) $8.75 adults, $7.50 seniors, $4.75 ages 6–14. Apr–Oct daily 10am–5:30pm (extended hours June–Aug); Nov–Mar daily 10am–4:30pm. Closed Thanksgiving, Dec 25, and Jan 1.

Walters Art Museum *Value*   The Walters, with its collections of ancient art, medieval armor, and French 19th-century painting, has always been one of Baltimore's great attractions. And a renovation completed in 2001 has only made it better. Walk through the galleries of sculpture, paintings, gold jewelry, mummies, and sarcophagi and see the progress of fine art through 50 centuries. The exhibits finish with objects from the Middle Ages in the Knight's Hall, with tapestries, furnishings, and suits of armor. The Egyptian collection is one of the best in the United States. New exhibits include French paintings, architecture, quilts, and glass. The cafe serves light fare.

600 N. Charles St. ℂ **410/547-9000.** www.thewalters.org. Admission $10 adults, $8 seniors, $6 students with ID, $2 children 6–17. Free admission to permanent collections 1st Thurs of every month and every Sat 10am–noon. Wed–Sun 10am–5pm. Closed July 4, Thanksgiving Day, and Dec 24–25. Extended hours Dec 26–Jan 1. Bus: 3, 11, 31, 61, or 64. Light Rail: Centre St.

WHERE TO STAY

The city caters to business travelers and it can be hard to find a double in Baltimore for under $100 during the week; but that also means that some hotels offer weekend rates and packages that represent savings of 35% to 50% off normal Sunday through Thursday tariffs. So don't be scared off by midweek rates—come on a weekend instead. *Note:* Every hotel listed in this section is accessible to travelers with disabilities, although specific amenities vary from place to place.

Admiral Fell Inn   Updated and expanded over the years, this charming inn sits just a block from the harbor in the heart of Fells Point. It spans eight buildings, built between 1790 and 1996 and blending Victorian and Federal-style architecture. The inn features an antiques-filled lobby and library and guest rooms individually decorated with Federal period furnishings (and offering luxe touches such as bottled water and bathrobes). Some have canopy beds and some have Jacuzzis. A more rustic loft room has sloping ceilings that tall guests might not like, but its three dormer windows offer some of the best views in the inn. There's a complimentary shuttle to downtown.

888 S. Broadway, Baltimore, MD 21231. ℂ **866/583-4162** or 410/522-7377. Fax 410/522-0707. www.harbor magic.com. 80 units. $199–$399 double. Rates include breakfast. AE, DC, DISC, MC, V. Valet parking $20. Located across the street from a water taxi stop. Pets welcome. **Amenities:** Restaurant; access to health club at nearby Brookshire Suite.

Celie's Waterfront Inn   This 18th-century town house is one of only a few bed-and-breakfasts in Baltimore and it's delightful. Each of the rooms has its own charms: Two have a fireplace and whirlpool and harbor views. Two inside rooms are particularly quiet, as they overlook the courtyard filled with flowers in summer. New owners have added two suites (with living and dining rooms and full kitchens), which can accommodate four and six comfortably. Have breakfast in your room, on the deck, or in the garden. Furnishings throughout were chosen with comfort in mind, with big beds, private bathroom with bathrobes, and a homey parlor.

1714 Thames St., Fells Point, Baltimore, MD 21231. © **800/432-0184** or 410/522-2323. www.celieswaterfront.com. 9 units. $139–$239 double; $299–$349 suite. Rates include hearty continental breakfast. 2- or 3-night minimum may be required on weekends or holidays. AE, DISC, MC, V. On water taxi route. *In room:* Kitchen (in 2 suites only), portable phones upon request.

Days Inn Inner Harbor *Value*

If you're willing to give up proximity to the harbor (by 2 or 3 blocks), you can get a great deal at this modern nine-story hotel. It is located between the arena and convention center, and only 3 blocks from Camden Yards. "Work zone" rooms for business travelers offer large desks, a kitchenette, and plenty of room, but all rooms have the comfort you expect from this chain. Guest rooms offer standard chain-motel furnishings. Many rooms received fresh updates in 2005.

100 Hopkins Place (between Lombard and Pratt sts.), Baltimore, MD 21202. © **800/DAYS-INN** or 410/576-1000. Fax 410/576-9437. www.daysinnerharbor.com. 250 units. $99–$189 double. Children under 17 stay free in parent's room. AE, DC, DISC, MC, V. Parking $15. **Amenities:** Restaurant; pool; health club. *In room:* Kitchenette (in some rooms only).

Harbor Court Hotel

The Harbor Court strives for quiet dignity, refinement, and graciousness. It's a treat to walk in the door, and if you spend the night, prepare to be pampered. Rooms are exquisitely furnished, from suites with hand-painted decor, marble bathrooms, kitchenettes, and canopy beds to large standard rooms outfitted in fine furnishings and CD players. The hotel overlooks the harbor but only a few rooms have a clear harbor view. Dining options include the first-rate **Hampton's.** The Explorer's Lounge features music every night, and is popular with locals as well as hotel guests.

550 Light St., Baltimore, MD 21202. © **800/824-0076** or 410/234-0550. Fax 410/659-5925. www.harborcourt.com. 195 units. $275–$305 double; $450–$3,800 suite. AE, DC, DISC, MC, V. Valet parking $29; self–parking $21. **Amenities:** 3 restaurants; indoor pool; tennis courts; fitness center.

Holiday Inn Baltimore Inner Harbor *Value Kids*

For value and location, it's hard to beat this old-timer, the first major chain property in Baltimore. Located a block away from Oriole Park and 3 blocks from Harborplace, it has an executive tower with 175 rooms geared to business travelers and has been updated and renovated regularly (there's now free Wi-Fi access in the lobby). Guest rooms are decorated in bright colors with traditional furniture including a desk, brass fixtures, and wide windows offering views of the city skyline.

301 W. Lombard St., Baltimore, MD 21201. © **800/HOLIDAY** or 410/685-3500. Fax 410/727-6169. www.holiday-inn. com/bal-downtown. 375 units. $129–$189 double; $285 suite. Children under 18 stay free in parent's room. AE, DC, DISC, MC, V. Self–parking $15. **Amenities:** Restaurant; indoor pool; health club.

Hyatt Regency Baltimore *Best*

The eye-catching all-glass Hyatt was the Inner Harbor's first hotel 20 years ago, and it's still the best. The prime location is just across a skywalk from the Inner Harbor and the convention center, and it's only a few blocks to the stadiums. Rooms are standard hotel chain, but have breathtaking harbor views and terrific amenities. It's often busy but not too noisy. Staff here couldn't be nicer.

300 Light St., Baltimore, MD 21202. © **800/233-1234** or 410/528-1234. Fax 410/685-3362. www.baltimore.hyatt. com. 486 units. $199–$359 double. Ask for packages and discounts. Children under 18 stay free in parent's room. AE,

DC, DISC, MC, V. Valet parking $25; self-parking $19. **Amenities:** 2 restaurants; putting green; pool; 2 tennis courts; health club.

Pier 5 Hotel Be prepared for something wild when you walk into the lobby of the Pier 5. It's bright and airy, and it's fun to settle back into those offbeat sofas. The rooms continue the lobby's purple, red, and yellow color scheme, though much quieter and more refined. Standard rooms are quite comfortable and have lots of conveniences, including bathrobes and bottled water. Suites are luxurious with one, two, or even three tiny balconies overlooking the harbor or the National Aquarium next door. Just about every room has a water view. They offer lots of discount packages for both families and couples.

711 Eastern Ave. (at the end of Pier 5), Baltimore, MD 21202. ⓒ 866/583-4162 or 410/539-2000. Fax 410/783-1787. www.harbormagic.com. 65 units. $149–$399 double; $329–$1,500 suite. AE, DC, DISC, MC, V. Valet parking $28; self-parking $21. Located on a water taxi stop. Pets welcome. **Amenities:** 3 restaurants; access to exercise room at Berkshire Suites. *In room:* Fridge.

Renaissance Harborplace Hotel The Renaissance is right in the middle of everything. It's part of The Gallery at Harborplace, five floors of shops and a food court topped by an office tower. Rooms are the biggest in Baltimore with comfortable furniture, bathrobes, and wide windows that really open overlooking the Inner Harbor. It was renovated in 2003, and the lighter colors make the huge rooms seem even more spacious. Its views are good, especially on the upper floors. Special suites connect bedrooms to living room, dining room, and kitchenette. Some even have Murphy beds for extra guests.

202 E. Pratt St., Baltimore, MD 21202. ⓒ 800/HOTELS-1 or 410/547-1200. Fax 410/783-9676. www.renaissance harborplace.com. 622 units. $259–$309 double; $500–$5,000 suite. Children under 17 stay free in parent's room. AE, DC, DISC, MC, V. Valet parking $28; self-parking $21. **Amenities:** Restaurant; indoor pool; exercise room.

WHERE TO DINE

"Crabtown" has always been known for good seafood, but Baltimore is also home to an increasing variety of ethnic and regional cuisines. There are plenty of good restaurants in Baltimore's main tourist area, with excellent choices in nearby Little Italy, Fells Point, and Mount Vernon. A note for your wallet: Restaurant prices are creeping up, especially dinner prices, at $25 for an entree—unheard of in recent years—becoming more common.

Black Olive GREEK/SEAFOOD This Greek taverna, just beyond the busier streets of Fells Point, is creating its own traffic. The combination of Greek fare and fresh seafood has made this place a standout. Choose whatever the catch of the day is and trust the chef to make it wonderful. The restaurant has four intimate dining rooms, so small that reservations are a must. The service here is smooth but friendly. Tea fans should try the iced tea made with Greek flowers—it's fragrant and spicy.

814 S. Bond St. ⓒ 410/276-7141. www.theblackolive.com. Reservations required for dinner. Main courses $12–$28 lunch, $25–$36 dinner. AE, MC, V. Daily noon–2:30pm and 5–10pm.

Brass Elephant *Value* CONTINENTAL The Brass Elephant prides itself on well-prepared food in an elegant setting for reasonable prices. You can count on rockfish or soft-shell crabs in season, or hearty American dishes such as stuffed pork chops. And all of this comes in one of Baltimore's most elegant restaurant settings, an 1861 town house with fireplace, chandeliers, and gold-leaf trim. (Summer is a particularly good time to eat here, as they often roll the prices back even further.)

924 N. Charles St. ⓒ 410/547-8480. www.brasselephant.com. Reservations recommended. Main courses $18–$28. AE, DC, DISC, MC, V. Mon–Thurs 5:30–9:30pm; Fri–Sat 5:30–11pm; Sun 4:30–8:30pm.

Charleston ⓑₑₛₜ AMERICAN/SOUTHERN   With a beautiful setting and imaginative menu, the Charleston is a top choice for a special night out and has the best food in Baltimore. The menu changes every day, but might include pan-fried rockfish or bacon-wrapped tenderloin with seasonal vegetables. The cheese course, with about a dozen artisanal cheeses, remains popular. Portions aren't so big you can't enjoy one of the great desserts. Charleston also offers an outstanding three-course dinner for $64 a person and a six-course dinner for $102 a person (wine is extra). There's a selection of 500 bottles of wine to choose from. The lounge has its own menu of small plates ($10–$15), cocktails, and wines by the glass.

1000 Lancaster St. ⓒ 410/332-7373. www.charlestonrestaurant.com. Reservations recommended. Prix-fixe dinners $64–$102. AE, DC, DISC, MC, V. Mon–Sat 5:30–10pm.

Obrycki's SEAFOOD   Fells Point, the neighborhood where Baltimore began, is one of the city's best areas for seafood, and the benchmark of all the eateries here is Obrycki's. Foodies Craig Claiborne and George Lang rave about this place. The decor is charming, with stained-glass windows and brick archways. But the big attraction is the fresh seafood, especially crabs. There's crab soup, crab cocktail, crab balls, crab cakes, crab imperial, and soft-shell crabs. The rest of the menu is just as tempting—shrimp, lobster, scallops, haddock, flounder, and steaks. The service is extremely attentive. Note that Obrycki's is only open during the local crab season.

1727 E. Pratt St. ⓒ 410/732-6399. www.obryckis.com. Reservations recommended, but accepted only until 7pm Mon–Fri, 6pm Sat–Sun. Main courses $15–$29; lunch and light fare $6.50–$15. AE, DC, DISC, MC, V. Mon–Fri 11:30am–10pm; Sat 11:30am–11pm; Sun 11:30am–9:30pm. Closed late Nov to mid-Mar.

Pisces SEAFOOD   In a city where lots of restaurants have good views, this one tops them all. Overlooking the Inner Harbor, Camden Yards, and the downtown skyline, this two-tiered rooftop restaurant spreads the city before you. The interior is sleek and modern, the menu small but intriguing. Soups can range from cream of crab to grilled seafood miso, while entrees are mostly seafood in creative sauces and seasonings. Though the dining area is not particularly large, the well-spaced tables offer a pleasantly intimate dining experience. The waitstaff is quite knowledgeable, and service is anything but hurried. There's live jazz Friday and Saturday night and at Sunday brunch.

At the Hyatt Regency Hotel, 300 Light St., 15th floor. ⓒ 410/528-1234. Reservations recommended. Main courses $18–$38; Sun brunch $40. AE, DC, DISC, MC, V. Mon–Thurs 5:30–10:30pm; Sat 5:30–11pm; Sun 10am–2pm.

Prime Rib STEAKHOUSE   In the heart of Mount Vernon, this popular restaurant—a standout for fine beef since 1965—serves the best prime rib around. In fact, it could spoil you for all other steaks. The pork chops are huge and the lobster bisque is rich and creamy. If you want seafood, there are crab cakes and a variety of fish dishes. Tables are squeezed together and intimate conversation is impossible, but people come here for the food, not to talk.

1101 N. Calvert St. (between Biddle and Chase sts.). ⓒ 410/539-1804. www.theprimerib.com. Reservations recommended. Main courses $25–$45. AE, DC, DISC, MC, V. Mon–Sat 5–11pm; Sun 4–10pm.

Sabatino's ITALIAN   Sabatino's still stands out for its exceptional Italian cuisine at reasonable prices. Everyone will tell you to get the house salad with the house dressing—it's thick and garlicky. Simple pasta dishes come in very large portions. The menu also has some seafood and meat dishes with pasta on the side. Dining rooms fill three floors of this narrow building. It's worth the wait to be seated upstairs where it's quieter. This is a particularly good late-night dining spot, a good place to people-watch after the bars have closed.

901 Fawn St. (at High St.). ℂ 410/727-9414. www.sabatinos.com. Reservations recommended. Main courses $8–$15 lunch, $9.25–$28 dinner. AE, DC, DISC, MC, V. Sun–Thurs 11:30am–midnight; Fri–Sat 11:30am–3am.

Vaccaro's ITALIAN PASTRIES AND DESSERTS   To top off a perfect day, stop at Vaccaro's, the always-busy restaurant, for Italian desserts, coffee, and cappuccino. In addition to cannoli, rum cake, and tiramisu, it serves huge portions of decadently rich gelato. (Can't decide on a flavor? Ask the waitress for a sampler and you'll get three different flavors.) Coffee is a standout here, too, plain or scented with cinnamon or vanilla. They don't take reservations, but the wait is never too long. There's also a location at the Light Street Pavilion in Harborplace (ℂ **410/547-7169**).

222 Albemarle St. ℂ **410/685-4905**. www.vaccarospastry.com. Reservations not accepted. Desserts $2.95–$9.50. AE, MC, V. Mon 9am–10pm; Tues–Thurs 9am–11pm; Fri–Sat 9am–1am; Sun 9am–11pm.

Windows NEW AMERICAN   The sweeping views of the Inner Harbor are only the beginning at this fifth-floor restaurant. Using fresh seasonal ingredients, particularly Maryland produce and seafood, the chef has created a delightful menu. Entrees recently included wonderful rockfish and lump crab grilled with charred tomato vinaigrette, as well as pecan-crusted cod and filet mignon with savory potato hash. Lunchtime is just as adventurous, and breakfast is an occasion here.

At the Renaissance Harbor Hotel, 202 E. Pratt St. ℂ **410/685-8439**. Reservations recommended. Main courses $8.95–$18 lunch, $16–$39 dinner. AE, DC, DISC, MC, V. Daily 6:30am–11pm.

Woman's Industrial Exchange Restaurant AMERICAN   Housed in an 1815 brick building, where you're greeted by a gracious doorman, this restaurant, along with its craft shop, has been helping women help themselves since post–Civil War days. The waitresses, wearing big white bows around their blue uniforms, serve up delicious breakfasts and lunches. (The restaurant and its waitresses were featured in the movie *Sleepless in Seattle.*) The menu is simple, with homemade soups, salads, sandwiches, omelets, meat or fish platters, and luscious desserts (charlotte russe is a specialty). The chicken salad is terrific. Afterward, take time to browse in the shop.

333 N. Charles St. ℂ **410/685-2433**. Main courses $5.95–$12. MC, V. Mon–Fri 7am–3pm.

BALTIMORE AFTER DARK

Baltimore used to be very quiet after dark. Fells Point's bars always drew a crowd, and the streets were busy when a concert or play was scheduled. Now, however, the Inner Harbor, Federal Hill, Canton, Fells Point, and Mount Vernon have all developed lives after dark.

For major events, check the arts and entertainment sections of the *Baltimore Sun* and the *Washington Post.* The *City Paper,* a free Baltimore weekly, has very complete listings down to the smallest local bars and clubs. On the Web, try **www.baltimore funguide.com.**

Tickets for most major venues are available at the individual box offices and at **Ticketmaster** (ℂ **410/547-SEAT;** www.ticketmaster.com).

THE PERFORMING ARTS   The world-class **Baltimore Symphony Orchestra (BSO)** (ℂ **410/783-8000;** www.baltimoresymphony.org) performs several concerts a week at the Joseph Meyerhoff Symphony Hall September through June. Each season brings classical and pops concerts. In the summertime, you'll find the BSO outside at Oregon Ridge Park, north of the city off I-83. Their Fourth of July concerts are terrific fun.

Everyman Theatre, 1727 N Charles St., us earning rave reviews for its local productions of classics and new works (© **410/752-2208;** www.everymantheatre.org).

Located at 45 W Preston St., the **Theatre Project** is the city's professional company. Theatergoers can expect experimental and avant-garde work (© **410/752-8558;** www.theatreproject.org).

Center Stage, 700 N. Calvert St. (© **410/332-0033;** www.centerstage.org), Maryland's state theater, has been presenting new and classic works since 1963. The theater has two spaces, one a traditional proscenium stage and the other offering directors more flexibility in set design and staging.

For entertainment by local professional actors at affordable prices, check out these area theaters: The **Fells Point Corner Theater,** 251 S. Ann St. (© **410/276-7837;** www.fpct.org), presents eight productions a year. The **Vagabond Players,** 806 S. Broadway (© **410/563-9135**), presents a variety of classics, contemporary comedies, and dramas. The city's prominent African-American theater company **Arena Players,** 801 McCulloh St., off Martin Luther King Boulevard (© **410/728-6500**), presents contemporary plays and romantic comedies.

THE CLUB & MUSIC SCENE National acts come to the **1st Mariner Arena** near the Inner Harbor and to the **Pier Six Concert Pavilion** at the Inner Harbor. A number of smaller, local clubs welcome smaller touring acts and local performers, from rock to jazz to folk. Music venues include **Bertha's,** 734 S. Broadway (© **410/327-5795**), a great venue for live jazz and blues every day of the week; the **Cat's Eye Pub,** 1730 Thames St. (© **410/276-9085;** www.catseyepub.com), which features nightly live music ranging from traditional Irish music to bluegrass, zydeco, and jazz; and **Eight by Ten,** 8–10 E Cross St. (© **410/625-2000;** www.the8x10.com), where blues, funk, and rock groups play regularly.

Two top dance clubs are **Baja Beach Club,** 55 Market Place, at East Lombard Street, Inner Harbor (© **410/727-0468**), which is popular with locals and draws a crowd of energetic 20-somethings; and **The Depot,** 1728 N. Charles St. (© **410/685-3013**), which draws a mostly young crowd with its house and retro music.

THE BAR SCENE Baltimore locals like nothing better than to relax over a cold beer. The best drinking spots include the **Havana Club,** 600 Water St., upstairs from Ruth's Chris Steak House (© **410/468-0022;** www.serioussteaks.com), a sophisticated spot, offering tapas, appetizers, desserts, cigars; the cigar-friendly **Max's Tap Room,** 737 S. Broadway (© **410/675-MAXS;** www.maxs.com), a Baltimore institution known for its tremendous beer selection; and **Wharf Rat,** 206 W. Pratt St., at Hanover Street across from the convention center (© **410/244-8900**), a small brewpub with excellent stouts and ales.

Sports fans can stroll into any of a dozen bars near Camden Yards for lively game conversation, but try **Downtown Sports Exchange (DSX),** 200 W. Pratt St. (© **410/659-5844**); **Pickles Pub,** 520 Washington Blvd. (© **410/752-1784**); or **Orioles Bar,** in the Sheraton Inner Harbor (© **410/962-8300**).

THE GAY & LESBIAN SCENE For a complete listing of nightspots, check out *Gay Life,* published by the **Gay, Lesbian, Bisexual & Transgender Community**

Center of Baltimore (© 410/837-5445; www.baltimorepride.org), and **www.outin baltimore.com**. The gay scene centers around Charles Street in Mount Vernon. The popular disco **Hippo,** 1 W. Eager St. (© 410/547-0069; www.clubhippo.com), is a Baltimore mainstay. **Grand Central,** 1001 N. Charles St. (© 410/752-7133; www. centralstationpub.com), offers jazz, drag, karaoke, and other theme nights. Women gather at the comfy and friendly **Coconuts Café,** 311 W. Madison St., at Linden Avenue (© 410/383-6064; www.coconutscafe.com). The **Creative Alliance** (© 410/ 276-3206; www.creativealliance.org) hosts the Charm City Kitty Club, a troupe of lesbian, bi, and transgender performers. See the website for a schedule and ticket prices.

9 Washington, D.C.

The nation's capital fully commands center stage. The terrorists who crashed a plane into the Pentagon on September 11, 2001, did nothing to diminish Washington's place in the world—quite the contrary. Their acts served only to rally the city itself, strengthen the nation's federal government, and renew the country's commitment to democratic ideals, for all the world to see. Although security is tighter and additional safeguards have been put into place, Washington continues to offer its own special brand of excitement. You can still listen to Senate debates and hear the Supreme Court in session. Find inspiration in magnificent monuments to the greatest American presidents, and check out the palatial digs of the current chief executive. Wander the vast museums of the Smithsonian Institution. In short, you can see firsthand just how the government of the United States works, as well as visit some of the most important museums in the country.

ESSENTIALS

GETTING THERE   By Plane   Washington is served by three major airports. **Ronald Reagan Washington National Airport** (© 703/417-8000; www.metwash airports.com) is just across the Potomac River in Virginia and a 15-minute drive from downtown. Approximately 14 major airlines and shuttles serve this airport, which has flights to 69 U.S. cities. Climate-controlled pedestrian bridges connect the terminal directly to a Metro station, whose Blue and Yellow lines stop here. The trip downtown via Metro takes about 20 minutes.

   Washington Dulles International Airport (© 703/572-2700; www.metwash airports.com) is also in Virginia, about 45 minutes west of downtown. It's a big discount airline hub. The **Washington Flyer Express Bus** runs every 30 minutes between Dulles and the West Falls Church Metro station, where you can board a train for D.C. Buses cost $9 one-way. More convenient is the hourly Metrobus service that runs between Dulles and the L'Enfant Plaza Metro station, located near Capitol Hill and within walking distance of the National Mall. The bus departs hourly, daily, costs only $3, and takes about 45 to 60 minutes.

   Baltimore–Washington International Thurgood Marshall Airport (BWI) (© 800/435-9294; www.bwiairport.com) is northeast of the city near Baltimore, about 45 minutes from downtown. One factor especially recommends BWI to travelers: Southwest Airlines, with its bargain fares, commands a major presence here, pulling in nearly half of BWI's business. Both **Amtrak** (© 800/872-7245; www. amtrak.com; $13–$38 fare) and **Maryland Rural Commuter** (MARC; © 800/325-7245; $6 fare; weekdays only) trains link BWI to Washington's Union Station, about a 30-minute ride.

Washington, D.C.

Devonshire Pl.
Hawthorne NATIONAL
ZOOLOGICAL PARK
Kilbourne Pl.
Kenyon St.
Mt. Pleasant St.
Park Rd.
Park Hiatt St.

Klingle Rd.
Cathedral Ave.
Cortland Pl.
Irving St.
Hobart St.

Columbia Heights
Green Line

Garfield St.
Garfield Terr.
Harvard St.

Fulton St.
31st Pl.
Cleveland Ave.
Woodley Pl.
Ontario Rd. Pl.
Lanier Pl.
Columbia Rd.

Woodley Park-Zoo/
Adams Morgan
Red Line

ADAMS
MORGAN

Woodland Dr.
Edmunds St.
Davis St.
Calvert St.

Euclid St.
Belmont St.

EMBASSY
ROW

Observatory Circle

U.S. Naval
Observatory

McGill Terr.

ROCK CREEK
PARK

Belmont
Kalorama
Wyoming Ave
California Ave.
Vernon St.
U St.

Florida W. St.
V. St.

Massachusetts Ave.

Rock Creek

Belmont Rd.
Kalorama Rd.

2

Wyoming Ave.
Tracy Pl.
California St.
Bancroft Pl.

Florida Ave.
Swann St.

U St.

DUMBARTON
OAKS PARK

MONTROSE
PARK

R St.

T. St.
S St.
R St.

S St.
Decatur Pl.
R. St.

Riggs Pl.
New Hampshire Ave.

S St.
R St.
Q St.

Reservoir Rd.

Dent Pl.
Q St.
Volta Pl.

Q St.

Dupont
Circle
Red Line

Church St.

DUPONT
CIRCLE

Georgetown
University

P St.
O St.

P. St.
O. St.

N St.

Dumbarton St.
N St.

3
Dupont
Circle

P. St.
Loc Cir

Scott Circle
11

Thom Circle

GEORGETOWN
Prospect St.
M St.

4
5

8

Farragut North
Red Line

10

L St.

McPh Squar
Blue
Oran
Lines

Rock Creek and Potomac Pkwy

Whitehurst Fwy.

29
Washington Circle

7

L St.
K St.

Farragut
Square

12

Francis Scott Key Bridge

66

Georgetown Channel

Foggy
Bottom-GWU
Blue &
Orange Lines

6
George
Washington
University

H St.
G St.

Farragut
West
Blue &
Orange Lines

Pennsylvania Ave.

13

Theodore
Roosevelt
Island

N. Lynn St.
Wilson Blvd

Little River

Kennedy
Center

Virginia Ave.

F St.
E St.

White
House

George Washington Memorial Pkwy

Rosslyn
Blue &
Orange Lines

Theodore Roosevelt Mem. Bridge

FOGGY
BOTTOM

C St.

THE
ELLIPSE

17th St.
15th St.

1 50

Constitution Ave.

Vietnam Veterans
Memorial

Lincoln
Memorial

Reflecting Pool

WWII
Memorial

Washington
Monument

VIRGINIA

LADY BIRD
JOHNSON
PARK

Arlington Mem. Bridge

WEST POTOMAC PARK

50 Independence Ave.

Ohio Dr. W.

Potomac River

FDR
Memorial

Tidal Basin

Cherry Trees

Arlington
Cemetery
Blue Line

Jefferson Davis Hwy

Washington Blvd

ARLINGTON

NATIONAL

CEMETERY

Jefferson
Memorial

ACCOMMODATIONS ■
Embassy Suites Hotel Downtown 4
Hotel George 21
Hotel Monaco Washington DC 19
Hotel Washington 13
The Jefferson Hotel 11
Jurys Normandy Inn 2
Morrison-Clark Historic Inn 16
The Quincy 9
Renaissance Mayflower 10
The Ritz-Carlton, Washington, D.C. 5
Willard Inter-Continental 14

DINING ◆
Ben's Chili Bowl 15
Bombay Club 13
Café Atlantico 18
Cashion's Eat Place 1
Galileo 8
Jaleo 20
Kinkead's 6
Pizzeria Paradiso 3
The Prime Rib 7
Tosca 17

SuperShuttle (© 800/258-3826; www.supershuttle.com) offers shared-ride, door-to-door van service between National, Dulles, and BWI airports and your destination downtown or in the Maryland or Virginia suburbs. Expect to pay anywhere from $12 to $32, depending on distance. **Taxi** fares are $10 to $20 from National to downtown, $50 to $60 from Dulles, and $63 from BWI.

By Train Amtrak (© 800/872-7245; www.amtrak.com) serves **Union Station,** 50 Massachusetts Ave. NE (© 202/371-9441; www.unionstationdc.com), a turn-of-the-20th-century Beaux Arts masterpiece conveniently located near the Capitol; it now houses shops and restaurants. There's daily service from New York (trip time: 2¾–3½ hr.), Philadelphia (1¾–2 hr.), Boston (7–8 hr.), and Chicago (19 hr.). Amtrak also offers daily service from several points in the South, including Raleigh, Charlotte, Atlanta, cities in Florida, and New Orleans.

By Car Major highways approach Washington, D.C., from all parts of the country. Specifically, these are **I-270, I-95,** and **I-295** from the north; **I-95** and **I-395, Route 1,** and **Route 301** from the south; **Route 50/301** and **Route 450** from the east; and **Route 7, Route 50, I-66,** and **Route 29/211** from the west.

No matter which road you take, there's a good chance you will have to navigate some portion of the **Capital Beltway** (I-495 and I-95) to gain entry to D.C. The Beltway girds the city, 66 miles around, with 56 interchanges or exits, and is nearly always congested, but especially during weekday morning and evening rush hours, roughly 6 to 9:30am and 3 to 7pm. Commuter traffic on the Beltway now rivals that of major L.A. freeways, and drivers can get a little crazy, weaving in and out of traffic.

VISITOR INFORMATION Contact the **Washington, DC Convention & Tourism Corporation (WCTC),** 901 7th St. NW, Washington, DC 20001-3719 (© 800/422-8644 or 202/789-7000; www.washington.org), and ask for a free copy of the *Washington, D.C., Visitors Guide,* which details hotels, restaurants, sights, shops, and more, and is updated twice yearly. Consult the WCTC website for latest information, including upcoming exhibits at the museums and anticipated closings of tourist attractions.

The **Smithsonian Information Center,** in the "Castle," 1000 Jefferson Dr. SW (© 202/633-1000, or TTY 202/357-1729; www.si.edu), is open every day but Christmas from 8:30am to 5:30pm. Call or check the website for a free copy of the Smithsonian's "My Smithsonian," which is full of valuable tips, or stop at the Castle for a copy.

GETTING AROUND If you're thinking about driving, bear in mind that traffic is thick during the week, parking spaces are sparse, and parking lots will cost you. Street signs and parking information are often confusing and illegible. We can't recommend using a car within the city. Metrorail is definitely the easiest way to go.

By Metro Metrorail's 86 stations include locations at or near almost every sightseeing attraction and extend to suburban Maryland and northern Virginia. There are five lines in operation—Red, Blue, Orange, Yellow, and Green. When entering a Metro station for the first time, go to the kiosk and ask for a free *Metro System Pocket Guide.*

To enter or exit a Metro station, you need a computerized **farecard,** available at vending machines near the entrance. Charts posted near the farecard machines explain the fares, which at press time started at $1.35. If you plan to take several Metrorail trips during your stay, put more value on the farecard to avoid having to buy a new card each time you ride. Discount passes include the **7-Day Fast Pass,** for $33 per person, which allows you unlimited travel, and the **1-Day Rail Pass,** for $6.50 per person, allowing you unlimited passage for the day, after 9:30am weekdays, and all day on Saturday, Sunday, and holidays. Passes are available for purchase at all Metro stations.

Metrorail opens at 5:30am weekdays and 7am Saturday and Sunday, operating until midnight Sunday through Thursday, and until 3am Friday and Saturday. Call *©* **202/637-7000,** or visit **www.wmata.com** for information.

By Taxi   Taxis are plentiful, and you can hail them right off the street. Fares are based on a zone system rather than meters. The base fare in Zone 1 (extending from the U.S. Capitol through most of downtown) starts at $6.50 (during non–rush hour) for one person, but there's a $1 charge for each additional passenger, plus surcharges for trips at rush hour ($1), for large pieces of luggage (from 50¢ to $2 per piece, depending on size), and for arranging a pickup by phone ($3). Try **Diamond Cab Company** (*©* **202/387-6200**) or **Yellow Cab** (*©* **202/544-1212**).

FAST FACTS   Emergency-room treatment is available at **Children's Hospital National Medical Center,** 111 Michigan Ave. NW (*©* **202/884-5000**); and at **Georgetown University Medical Center,** 4000 Reservoir Rd. NW (*©* **202/444-3111**). The **CVS** drugstore chain has two 24-hour locations—in the West End, at 2240 M Street NW (*©* **202/296-9877**), and at Dupont Circle (*©* **202/785-1466**). The sales tax on merchandise in the District is 5.75%, the tax on restaurant meals is 10%, and you pay a 14.5% hotel tax.

SPECIAL EVENTS & FESTIVALS   For more information, call *©* **202/789-7000** or go to **www.washington.org**.

In early April, the 3,700 Japanese cherry trees by the Tidal Basin in Potomac Park burst into spectacular bloom. The **Cherry Blossom Festival** features a major parade with floats, concerts, celebrity guests, and more. For information, call *©* **202/547-1500** or go to **www.nps.gov/nacc/cherry**.

The **White House Easter Egg Roll** takes place on Easter Monday. Entertainment on the White House South Lawn and the Ellipse might include clog dancers, clowns, puppet and magic shows, military drill teams, an egg-rolling contest, and a hunt for 1,000 or so wooden eggs, many of them signed by celebrities, astronauts, or the president. Call *©* **202/208-1631** for details.

At 11am on **Memorial Day,** a wreath-laying ceremony takes place at the Tomb of the Unknowns in Arlington National Cemetery, followed by military band music, a service, and an address by a high-ranking government official; call *©* **703/607-8000** for details. Activities also take place at the city's other military memorials. **Fourth of July** festivities include a massive parade down Constitution Avenue. A morning program in front of the National Archives includes military demonstrations, period music, and a reading of the Declaration of Independence. In the evening, the National Symphony Orchestra plays on the west steps of the Capitol. Big-name entertainment precedes the fabulous fireworks display behind the Washington Monument. Consult the *Washington Post* or call *©* **202/789-7000** for details. In early December, at the northern end of the Ellipse, the president lights the **national Christmas tree** to the accompaniment of orchestral and choral music. The lighting inaugurates the 4-week Pageant of Peace, a tremendous holiday celebration with seasonal music, caroling, a nativity scene, 50 state trees, and a burning Yule log. Call *©* **202/208-1631** for details.

WHAT TO SEE & DO

Nearly 6 years after September 11, 2001, Washington, D.C., has a firm handle on workable security precautions, and for visitors that means standing in line at attractions—security clearances, no matter how efficient, do take time. At many tourist sites, like the Smithsonian's National Air and Space Museum and National Museum of Natural History, and at most government buildings, staff search handbags, briefcases, and backpacks and you must walk past metal detectors, which means that during the busy spring and summer seasons, you may be queuing outside as you wait your turn to pass through security. So pack your patience, but otherwise carry as little as possible, and certainly no sharp objects. Museums and public buildings rarely offer the use of lockers.

Here's a crucial piece of advice: Call the places you plan to tour each day before you set out. Many of Washington's government buildings, museums, memorials, and monuments are open to the general public nearly all the time—except when they're not. Because buildings like the Capitol, the Supreme Court, and the White House are offices as well as tourist destinations, the business of the day always poses the potential for closing one of those sites, or at least sections, to sightseers. (The White House is probably most vulnerable to this situation.) This caveat is even more important in the wake of the terrorist attack on the Pentagon; touring procedures change and then change again in response to the perceived need for security measures. Want to avoid frustration and disappointment? Call ahead.

THE TOP SIGHTS

Arlington National Cemetery   Since the Civil War, these 612 wooded acres on a ridge overlooking the Potomac River and Washington have been a cherished shrine to members of the U.S. armed forces. Upon arrival, head over to the **Visitor Center,** where you can view exhibits, pick up a detailed map, use the restrooms (there are no others until you get to Arlington House), and purchase a **Tourmobile ticket** ($6 per adult, $3 for children 3–11), which allows you to stop at all major sites in the cemetery and then reboard whenever you like.

Your first stop should be the **Women in Military Service for America Memorial** (🕿 **800/222-2294** or 703/533-1155; www.womensmemorial.org), which honors the more than two million women who have served in the armed forces from the American Revolution to the present. High atop a hill at the center of the cemetery is **Arlington House** (🕿 **703/235-1530;** www.nps.gov/arho), once the home of Robert E. Lee, who left here in 1861 to take command of the Confederate army (to spite him, the Union army buried its dead in his front yard). You can tour the house on your own. Below Arlington House is the **Gravesite of John Fitzgerald Kennedy.** Jacqueline Kennedy Onassis is buried next to her first husband, and Robert Kennedy is buried close by. America's most distinguished honor guard watches over the **Tomb of the Unknowns,** which contains the unidentified remains of service members from both world wars and the Korean War, and honors all Americans who gave their lives in war. Plan to see the changing of the guard, which takes place every half-hour April to September, every hour on the hour October to March, and every hour at night.

Just across the Memorial Bridge from the base of the Lincoln Memorial. 🕿 703/607-8000. www.arlingtoncemetery. org. Free admission. Apr–Sept daily 8am–7pm; Oct–Mar daily 8am–5pm. Metro: Arlington National Cemetery. If you come by car, parking is $1.25 an hour for the 1st 3 hr., $2 per hour thereafter. The cemetery is also accessible via Tourmobile.

Openings & Closings in D.C.

Much is happening in D.C. in 2007, a lot of it to do with construction and renovation. Until at least 2009, the **Smithsonian's National Museum of American History** and the **Arts and Industries Building** are closed for renovation. Scheduled for a 2008 opening is a new **Martin Luther King, Jr., National Memorial** on the northwest corner of the Tidal Basin. Scheduled to reopen in 2007 after thorough remodeling is the **FBI Building.** The new **Newseum** and the **Capitol Visitors Center** are both scheduled to open in 2007. Check **www.washington. org** in order to determine the status of any attraction you may wish to visit.

The Capitol *(Best* The U.S. Congress has met here since 1800. The hub of the building is the **Rotunda,** under the soaring 180-foot-high Capitol dome. The adjoining **National Statuary Hall** was originally the House chamber. The Senate used to meet in the **Old Supreme Court Chamber,** now beautifully restored. You can obtain free tickets to the **House and Senate galleries** by contacting the office of your senator or representative. (Visitors who are not citizens can obtain a gallery pass by presenting a passport at the Senate or House appointments desk.) Check the weekday "Today in Congress" column in the *Washington Post* for details on times of the House and Senate sessions and committee hearings.

Important note: Since a new underground Capitol Visitor Center (to be completed in 2007) is being constructed directly beneath the plaza where people traditionally line up for tours on the east side of the Capitol, touring procedures have changed. Call ahead (℃ **202/225-6827**) to find out the new procedures and whether any parts of the building will be temporarily closed. At this time, the only way to tour the Capitol Building is in groups of 40. A Capitol Guide Service guide conducts each tour, which is free and lasts about 30 minutes. Organized groups of no more than 40 can arrange tours in advance by contacting their congressional office. If you're on your own, get to the Capitol by 7:30am, to stand in line for one of the limited timed tickets distributed daily, starting at 9am.

At the east end of the Mall, entrance on E. Capitol St. and 1st St. NW. ℃ 202/225-6827. www.aoc.gov, www.house. gov, or www.senate.gov. Free admission. Year-round Mon–Sat 9am–4:30pm, with 1st tour starting at 9:30am and last tour starting at 3:30pm. Closed for tours Jan 1, Thanksgiving, and Dec 25. Parking at Union Station or on neighborhood streets. Metro: Union Station or Capitol South.

Corcoran Gallery of Art The first art museum in Washington, the Corcoran occupies a Beaux Arts building just west of the White House. The collection spans American art from 18th-century portraiture to works by 20th-century moderns such as Nevelson, Warhol, and Rothko. There's also an eclectic grouping of works by Dutch and Flemish masters and French Impressionists, plus Delft porcelains and a Louis XVI *salon doré* transported complete from Paris. Allow an hour for touring the collection.

500 17th St. NW (between E St. and New York Ave.). ℃ 202/639-1700. www.corcoran.org. $8 adults, $6 seniors, $4 students 12–18, children under 12 free; pay as you wish Thurs after 5pm. Wed–Sun 10am–5pm (Thurs until 9pm). Open certain Mon following holidays (see list on website). Free walk-in tours Wed–Sun at noon, as well as at 7:30pm Thurs and 2:30pm Sat–Sun. Closed Jan 1 and Dec 25. Metro: Farragut West or Farragut North.

Franklin Delano Roosevelt Memorial The FDR Memorial has become the most popular of the presidential memorials since it opened in 1997. Set amid waterfalls and quiet pools, "outdoor rooms" are devoted to each of Roosevelt's four terms in office (1933–45). Ten bronze sculptures honor Franklin and wife Eleanor and memorialize the struggles of the Great Depression and America's rise to world leadership. If you don't see a posting of tour times, look for a park ranger and request a tour; the rangers are happy to oblige. Thirty minutes is sufficient time to allot here.

In W. Potomac Park, about midway between the Lincoln and Jefferson memorials, on the west shore of the Tidal Basin. ℭ **202/426-6841.** www.nps.gov/fdrm. Free admission. Ranger on duty daily 8:30am–11:30pm, except for Dec 25. Metro: Smithsonian, with a 30-min. walk; or take the Tourmobile.

International Spy Museum   Try to pace yourself through this 68,000-square-foot museum, immensely popular ever since its mid-2002 opening. Interactive and video exhibits offer a fun indoctrination into "Tricks of the Trade." Learn about the use of codes and code-breaking in spying, with one room of the museum devoted to the Enigma cipher machine used by the Germans (whose "unbreakable" codes the Allied cryptanalysts succeeded in deciphering) in World War II. An actual Enigma machine is displayed. Much more follows, including a re-created tunnel beneath the divided city of Berlin during the Cold War, the intelligence-gathering stories of those behind enemy lines and of those involved in planning D-day in World War II, and an exhibit on escape and evasion techniques in wartime. This is the largest collection of international espionage artifacts ever put on public display.

800 F St. NW (at 8th St. NW). ℭ **866/779-6873** or 202/393-7798. www.spymuseum.org. Admission $15 adults (ages 12–64), $14 for seniors, $12 for children ages 5–11. Open daily, but hours vary; generally, hours are from 9 or 10am–5:30pm, staying open until 8pm in peak season. Check website for details. Closed Thanksgiving, Dec 25, and Jan 1. Metro: Gallery Place/Chinatown or Archives–Navy Memorial.

Jefferson Memorial   The domed interior of this beautiful columned rotunda in the style of the Pantheon in Rome contains a 19-foot bronze statue of Thomas Jefferson, the third U.S. president, who also served as ambassador to France, secretary of state, and vice president—and still found time to pen the Declaration of Independence, create the University of Virginia, and pursue wide-ranging interests, including architecture, astronomy, anthropology, music, and farming. A gift shop, a small museum, and a bookstore are located on the bottom floor of the memorial. Rangers present 20- to 30-minute programs throughout the day as time permits.

South of the Washington Monument on Ohio Dr. SW (at the south shore of the Tidal Basin). ℭ **202/426-6841.** www.nps.gov/thje. Free admission. Ranger on duty daily 8:30am–11:30pm, except Dec 25. Closed Dec 25. Metro: Smithsonian, with a 20- to 30-min. walk; or take the Tourmobile.

Lincoln Memorial   This beautiful neoclassical templelike structure, similar in design to the Parthenon in Greece, is a moving testament to the great Civil War president. Visitors are silently awed in the presence of Daniel Chester French's 19-foot-high seated statue of Lincoln in deep contemplation. Lincoln's enormously powerful Gettysburg Address is engraved on the interior walls. Especially at night, the view from the steps, across the Reflecting Pool to the Washington Monument and the Capitol beyond, is one of the city's most beautiful. An information booth, a small museum, and a bookstore are on the premises. Rangers present 20- to 30-minute programs as time permits throughout the day.

Directly west of the Mall in Potomac Park (at 23rd St. NW, between Constitution and Independence aves.). ℭ **202/426-6842.** www.nps.gov/linc. Free admission. Ranger on duty daily 8:30am–11:30pm except Dec 25. Metro: Foggy Bottom, then a 30-min. walk; or take the Tourmobile.

National Air and Space Museum *Kids*   A hit with kids of all ages, this museum chronicles the story of man's mastery of flight, from Kitty Hawk to outer space, including the Wright Brothers' first plane, Charles Lindbergh's *Spirit of St. Louis,* and the Apollo moon ships. Arrive before 10am to make a rush for the film-ticket line—the **IMAX films** are not to be missed (tickets are $8.50 adults, $7.50 seniors, $7 ages 2–12). One highlight is the *How Things Fly* gallery, which includes wind and smoke tunnels, a boardable Cessna 150 airplane, and dozens of interactive exhibits that demonstrate principles of flight, aerodynamics, and propulsion. You'll also need tickets ($8.50 adults, $7.50 seniors, $7 ages 2–12) to attend a show at the **Albert Einstein Planetarium,** where projectors display blended space imagery upon a 70-foot diameter dome, making you feel as if you're traveling in 3-D through the cosmos.

Note: In December 2003, the museum opened the **Steven F. Udvar-Hazy Center** in Washington Dulles Airport, which displays aviation and space artifacts. You can drive (call ℂ **202/786-2122** for directions, or go to the website), or you can take a shuttle bus from the Air and Space Museum on the Mall ($7 per person).

On Independence Ave. SW, between 4th and 7th sts., on the south side of the Mall, with entrances on Jefferson Dr. or Independence Ave. ℂ **202/633-1000** (for both locations), or 877/932-4629 for IMAX ticket information. www. nasm.si.edu. Free admission. Both locations daily 10am–5:30pm. The mall museum often opens at 9am in summer, but call to confirm. Free 1½-hr. highlight tours daily at 10:30am and 1pm. Closed Dec 25. Metro: L'Enfant Plaza (Smithsonian Museums/Maryland Ave. exit) or Smithsonian. The Udvar-Hazy Center is located at 14390 Air and Space Museum Pkwy., Chantilly, VA. Parking at the center costs $12.

National Archives

After a major restoration completed in 2004, visitors can now get a marvelous look at the nation's three most important documents—the *Declaration of Independence,* the *Constitution of the United States,* and the *Bill of Rights.* Exhibits in the newly renovated **Public Vaults** feature interactive technology and displays of documents and artifacts to explain our country's development in the use of records, from Indian treaties to presidential websites. A theater continually runs dramatic films during the day illustrating the relationship between records and democracy in the lives of real people, and at night serves as a premier documentary film venue for the city. Anyone is welcome to use the National Archives center for genealogical research—this is where Alex Haley began his work on *Roots*—and it's all available for the perusal of anyone age 16 or over (call for details). The building itself is an impressive example of the Beaux Arts style, with 72 columns on each of the four facades.

700 Pennsylvania Ave. NW (between 7th and 9th sts. NW; tourists enter on Constitution Ave., researchers on Pennsylvania Ave.). ℂ **202/357-5000.** www.archives.gov. Free admission. Daily 10am–7pm Apr 1 to Fri before Memorial Day; 10am–9pm Memorial Day weekend to Labor Day; and 10am–5:30pm day after Labor Day to Mar 31. Call for research hours. Closed Dec 25. Metro: Archives–Navy Memorial.

National Gallery of Art

Housing one of the world's foremost collections of Western painting, sculpture, and graphic arts from the Middle Ages through the 20th century, the National Gallery has a dual personality. You'll find the masters in the original **West Building,** a neoclassical marble masterpiece with a domed rotunda. This is your chance to see the works of the old masters, including several renowned Raphaels; about 1,000 paintings are on display at any one time. The ultramodern **East Building** appropriately houses an important collection of 20th-century art, including masterpieces by Picasso, Miró, Matisse, Pollock, and Rothko. Other exhibitions feature the decorative arts, drawings, and prints. The **National Gallery Sculpture Garden,** just across from the West Wing, features open lawns, a central pool with a spouting fountain (the pool is converted into an ice rink in winter), and an exquisite, glassed-in pavilion housing a cafe and an impressive sculpture garden. Allow a leisurely 2 hours to see everything here.

On Constitution Ave. NW between 3rd and 7th sts. NW, on the north side of the Mall. ℰ **202/737-4215.** www.
nga.gov. Free admission. Gallery: Mon–Sat 10am–5pm; Sun 11am–6pm; Sculpture Garden: late May to mid-Sept
Mon–Thurs and Sat 10am–7pm, Fri 10am–9:30pm, Sun 11am–7pm; mid-Sept to late May Mon–Sat 10am–5pm, Sun
11am–6pm. Closed Jan 1 and Dec 25. Metro: Archives–Navy Memorial, Judiciary Square, or Smithsonian.

National Museum of Natural History *Kids*   Another hit with kids, this fascinating museum contains more than 120 million artifacts and specimens—it's the largest
museum of its kind in the world. Exhibits include everything from one of the largest
African elephants to the infamous Hope Diamond. Before you enter the museum,
stop on the Ninth Street side of the building to visit the lovely butterfly garden. Inside,
dinosaurs loom large, including a life-size model of the pterosaur, which had a 40-foot
wingspan. Don't miss the **Discovery Center,** funded by the Discovery Channel, featuring the Johnson **IMAX theater** with a six-story-high screen for 2-D and 3-D
movies. Purchase tickets as early as possible; the box office opens at 9:45am. Ticket
prices are $8.50 for adults, $7.50 for seniors, and $7 for children (2–12). *Note:* The
museum is in the middle of an extensive renovation, including the creation of a brand-
new, 22,000-square-foot **Ocean Hall** (scheduled to open Sept 2008).

On Constitution Ave. NW., between 9th and 12th sts., on the north side of the Mall, with entrances on Madison Dr.
and Constitution Ave. ℰ **202/633-1000,** or 202/633-4629 for information about IMAX films. www.mnh.si.edu. Free
admission. Daily 10am–5:30pm. In summer the museum often stays open until 8pm, but call to confirm. Closed Dec
25. Free highlight tours Feb–July Tues–Fri 10:30am and 1:30pm. Metro: Smithsonian or Federal Triangle.

National Museum of the American Indian *Kids*   This $219-million museum
took 5 years to build before finally opening in September 2004. Very much a "living"
museum, the museum has performances, events, and exhibits that aim at giving
Native peoples the chance to tell their own stories. Exhibits explore Native life and history and specific themes, and showcase works of individual artists. Most importantly,
the museum is a giant display case for a collection of precious objects representing
1,000 Native communities. About 8,000 of the collection's 800,000 pieces, including
wood and stone carvings, masks, pottery, feather bonnets, and so on are on display at
any given time. The museum uses a timed-pass admission procedure. You should
arrive no later than 10am to stand in line to obtain a free pass, which will be printed
with the time you will be able to enter the museum.

4th St. and Independence Ave. SW. ℰ **202/633-1000.** www.nmai.si.edu. Free admission. Daily 10am–5:30pm.
Closed Dec 25. Metro: Federal Center Southwest or L'Enfant Plaza.

National World War II Memorial   Thousands of World War II veterans and their
families turned out when this memorial was dedicated on May 29, 2004. The 7½-acre
memorial funded mostly by private donations features 56 granite pillars, each one 17
feet high, representing each state and territory standing to either side of a central plaza
and the Rainbow Pool. Likewise, 24 bas-relief panels illustrate seminal scenes from the
war years as they relate to the Pacific and Atlantic theaters: Pearl Harbor, Normandy
Beach, the Battle of the Bulge, and so on. Beyond the center Rainbow Pool is a wall
of 4,000 gold stars, one star for every 100 soldiers who died in World War II. People
often leave photos and mementos everywhere around the memorial, which the
National Park Service gathers up daily. From the 17th Street entrance, walk south
around the perimeter of the memorial to reach a ranger station, where there are
brochures and registry kiosks, the latter for looking up names of veterans. Better information and faster service is available online at the memorial's website.

17th St. and Constitution Ave. NW. (C) **800/639-4WW2** or 202/426-6841. www.wwiimemorial.com. Free admission. Rangers on duty daily 8:30am–11:30pm, except Dec 25. Limited parking. Metro: Farragut West, Federal Triangle, or Smithsonian, with 20–25 min. walk, or take Tourmobile.

Phillips Collection   In an elegant 1890s Georgian Revival mansion (plus an added wing) is the exquisite collection of Duncan and Marjorie Phillips, avid collectors and proselytizers of modernism. The original building was once the Phillipses' elegant abode, and it still has the warmth of a home. Among the highlights: superb Daumier, Dove, and Bonnard paintings; some splendid small Vuillards; five van Goghs; Renoir's *Luncheon of the Boating Party;* seven Cézannes; and six works by Georgia O'Keeffe. It's a collection no art lover should miss.

Note: The Phillips Collection's admission structure is a little confusing: You may tour the permanent collection for free on weekdays. To tour the permanent collection on weekends, and to tour whatever special exhibit is currently running, whatever day of the week you are there, you pay the admission fee established for that special exhibition. This fee can vary, anywhere from $8 to $14 per person. The Phillips almost always has a special exhibition on view. You may order tickets in advance at the Phillips, or through Ticketmaster at (C) **800/551-SEAT** or online at www.ticketmaster.com.

1600 21st St. NW (at Q St.). (C) **202/387-2151.** www.phillipscollection.org. Admission: See information in the note above. Tues–Sat 10am–5pm year-round (Thurs until 8:30pm); Sun noon–7pm, June–Sept noon–5pm. Free tours Wed and Sat 2pm. Closed federal holidays. Metro: Dupont Circle (Q St. exit).

The Supreme Court of the United States   The Supreme Court hears and decides its cases in this stately Corinthian marble temple Monday through Wednesday from 10am to noon and from 1 to 2pm or 3pm, starting the first Monday in October through late April. From mid-May to late June, you can attend brief sessions (about 15 min.) at 10am on Monday, when the justices release orders and opinions. Find out what cases are on the docket by calling the Supreme Court ((C) **202/479-3211)** or, better yet, by going to the court's website, where the argument calendar and the "Merits Briefs" (case descriptions) are posted. Arrive at least 90 minutes early— and as early as 3 hours ahead in March and April, when schools are often on spring break and students lengthen the line—to line up for the 150 seats allotted to the general public. If the court is not in session, you can attend a **free lecture,** given every hour on the half-hour from 9:30am to 3:30pm. After the talk, explore the Great Hall and go down a flight of steps to see the **24-minute film** on the workings of the Court.

One 1st St. NE (between E. Capitol St. and Maryland Ave. NE). (C) **202/479-3000.** www.supremecourtus.gov. Free admission. Mon–Fri 9am–4:30pm. Closed all federal holidays. Metro: Capitol South or Union Station.

United States Holocaust Memorial Museum   This extraordinarily powerful museum (it remains one of the city's top draws, sometimes hosting up to 10,000 visitors in 1 day) reminds us of what can happen when civilization goes awry. An outer wall is reminiscent of an extermination camp's exterior brickwork, and towers evoke the guard towers of Auschwitz. A reconstructed Auschwitz barracks, the yellow stars that Jews were forced to wear, instruments of genocide, and a gas-chamber door are among the artifacts on display. As you enter, you'll be given the identity card of a real person living in Europe in the 1930s; at the end of your visit, you'll learn that person's fate. A highlight is a 30-minute film called *Testimony,* in which Holocaust survivors tell their own stories. Do not bring children under 11 to this museum. Timed tickets are required; reserve them via **Tickets.com** ((C) **800/400-9373;** www.tickets.com) for a small service fee. You can also get them at the museum box office; get in line around

8am. Note that same-day tickets are limited, and one person may obtain a maximum of four.

100 Raoul Wallenberg Place SW (formerly 15th St. SW; near Independence Ave., just off the Mall). © **202/488-0400.** www.ushmm.org. Free admission. Daily 10am–5:30pm (mid-Apr to mid-June Tues and Thurs until 8pm). Closed Yom Kippur and Dec 25. Metro: Smithsonian.

Vietnam Veterans Memorial The Vietnam Veterans Memorial is possibly the most poignant sight in Washington. Even if no one close to you died in Vietnam, it's wrenching to watch visitors grimly studying the directories at either end of this 492-foot-long, sunken black granite wall inscribed with the names of the nearly 60,000 American men and women who gave their lives, or remain missing, in the longest war in U.S. history. The names are inscribed in chronological order, documenting an epoch in American history as a series of individual sacrifices from the date of the first casualty in 1959 to the last death in 1975. Ask one of the very knowledgeable park rangers milling about if you have any questions. Allow about 20 to 30 minutes here.

Just across from the Lincoln Memorial (east of Henry Bacon Dr. between 21st and 22nd sts. NW). © **202/426-6841.** www.nps.gov/vive. Free admission. Rangers on duty daily 8:30am–11:30pm, except Dec 25. Limited parking. Metro: Foggy Bottom, with 25-min. walk, or take Tourmobile.

Washington Monument The 555-foot stark marble obelisk glowing under flood-lights at night is the city's most visible landmark. You can't climb or descend the 897 steps, but a large elevator whisks visitors to the top in just 70 seconds. The 360-degree views are spectacular. You can get free same-day tour tickets at 15th Street Northwest between Independence and Constitution avenues (arrive by 7:30 or 8am, especially in peak season). If you want to get them in advance, contact the **National Park Reservation Service** (© **800/967-2283;** http://reservations.nps.gov); you'll pay $1.50 per ticket plus a 50¢ service charge. To make sure that you get tickets for your desired date, reserve these tickets at least 2 weeks in advance.

Directly south of the White House (at 15th St. and Constitution Ave. NW). © **202/426-6841.** www.nps.gov/wash. Free admission. Daily 9am–4:45pm. Last elevators depart 15 min. before closing (arrive earlier). Closed Dec 25; July 4 open until noon. Metro: Smithsonian, then a 10-min. walk, or take Tourmobile.

The White House The White House is the only private residence of a head of state that has opened its doors to the public for free tours. It was Thomas Jefferson who started this practice, which is stopped only during wartime. After closing in 2002 due to the war on terrorism, the White House is once again open for public tours, though not walkup tours (you'll need to reserve space on a tour—minimum 10 people—at least 4 months in advance). The procedures for reserving a tour are complicated; consult the website or contact your congressperson for details. If you do get a reservation, be sure on the day of your White House tour to call © **202/456-7041** to make sure that the White House is still open that day to the public.

The White House is a repository of art and furnishings. Tours of the public areas include the gold-and-white **East Room,** scene of gala receptions and other dazzling events; the **Green Room,** used as a sitting room; the **Oval Blue Room,** where presidents and first ladies officially receive guests; the **Red Room,** used as a reception room and for afternoon teas; and the **State Dining Room,** a superb setting for state dinners and luncheons. There are no public restrooms or telephones in the White House, and picture-taking and videotaping are prohibited. Best advice: Leave everything but your wallet back at the hotel.

1600 Pennsylvania Ave. NW (visitor entrance gate at E St. and E. Executive Ave.). ℂ **202/456-7041** or 202/ 208-1631. www.whitehouse.gov. Free admission. Tours for groups of 10 or more, who have arranged the tour through their congressional offices. Metro: Federal Triangle.

AN ORGANIZED TOUR

Tourmobile Sightseeing (ℂ **888/868-7707** or 202/554-5100; www.tourmobile. com) provides open-air sightseeing trams that travel to as many as 24 attractions, including Arlington National Cemetery (the company changes its schedule and number of stops, depending on whether sites are open for public tours). It's the only narrated sightseeing shuttle tour authorized by the National Park Service. You can get on and off as often as you like throughout the day; buses serve each stop about every 15 to 30 minutes. You pay the driver when you first board the bus (you can also buy a ticket at the booth at the Washington Monument or inside the Arlington National Cemetery Visitor Center, or, for a small surcharge, order your ticket in advance from **Ticketmaster** at ℂ **800/551-SEAT**). The charge for its comprehensive American Heritage Tour (up to 24 sites visited, including Arlington Cemetery) is $20 for anyone 12 and older, $10 for children 3 to 11. For Arlington Cemetery only, those 12 and older pay $6, children 3 to 12 pay $3.

PARKS, GARDENS & THE NATIONAL ZOO

For the sight of lush, breathtakingly beautiful greenery and flowers year-round, stop in at the **United States Botanic Garden,** 100 Maryland Ave., at First Street SW, at the east end of the Mall (ℂ **202/225-8333;** www.usbg.gov), located at the foot of the Capitol, next door to the National Museum of the American Indian. The grand conservatory devotes half of its space to exhibits that focus on the importance of plants to people, and half to exhibits that focus on ecology and the evolutionary biology of plants. The new National Garden outside the conservatory includes a First Ladies Water Garden, formal rose garden, and lawn terrace. Admission is free; open daily from 10am to 5pm.

   West and East Potomac Parks, their 720 riverside acres divided by the Tidal Basin, are most famous for their spring display of cherry blossoms and all the hoopla that goes with it (check out **www.nps.gov/nacc/cherry** for info on the blossoms). West Potomac Park also encompasses Constitution Gardens; the Vietnam, Korean, Lincoln, Jefferson, and FDR memorials; a small island where ducks live; and the Reflecting Pool.

   Rock Creek Park (www.nps/gov.rocr), a 1,750-acre valley within the District of Columbia, extends 12 miles from the Potomac River to the Maryland border. It's one of the biggest and finest city parks in the nation. Adjacent to Rock Creek Park is the Smithsonian Institution's **National Zoological Park,** with its main entrance in the 3000 block of Connecticut Avenue NW (ℂ **202/673-4800** or 202/673-4717; www. si.edu/natzoo). It's home to several thousand animals of some 500 species, many of them rare or endangered (including a pair of pandas). The zoo animals live in large, open enclosures—simulations of their natural habitats—along two easy-to-follow numbered paths: Olmsted Walk and the Valley Trail. Free admission; open daily.

SHOPPING HIGHLIGHTS

D.C. isn't a serious shopper's town, but it does have outstanding museum shops. The **National Gallery of Art** shop sells printed reproductions, stationery, and jewelry whose designs are based on works in the gallery's collections. It also has one of the largest selections of books on art history and architecture in the country. The largest museum shop is at the **National Air and Space Museum** (three floors!).

The city also has many notable outdoor markets. The **Georgetown Flea Market,** Wisconsin Avenue, between S and T streets NW (✆ **202/775-FLEA;** www. georgetownfleamarket.com), is frequented by all types of Washingtonians looking for a good deal—they often get it—on antiques, painted furniture, vintage clothing, and decorative garden urns. In continuous operation since 1873, **Eastern Market,** 225 7th St. SE (✆ **202/544-0083;** www.easternmarket.net), a Capitol Hill institution, holds an inside bazaar Tuesday through Sunday, where greengrocers, butchers, bakers, farmers, artists, craftspeople, florists, and other merchants sell their wares. Saturday morning is the best time to go. Check **www.freshfarmmarkets.org** for locations, dates, and times of farmers' markets in the city.

One of the most popular tourist attractions in the Washington area (it attracts more visitors than any other site) is **Potomac Mills Mall** (✆ **703-496-9301;** www.potomac mills.com), a collection of 220-plus outlet and discount stores 30 miles south of Washington on I-95. Call ✆ **703/551-1050** for information about shuttle service from the city.

WHERE TO STAY

Washington, D.C., has just about every type of accommodations you can imagine. For ease in booking a reservation, try contacting one of two well-established local reservation services: **Capitol Reservations** (✆ **800/847-4832** or 202/452-1270; www.hotelsdc.com) or **Washington D.C. Accommodations** (✆ **800/503-3330** or 202/289-2220; www.dcaccommodations.com). Both services are free. Another free service is **Bed & Breakfast Accommodations, Ltd.** (✆ **877/893-3233** or 413/582-9888; www.bnbaccom.com), which works with more than 30 homes, inns, guest-houses, and unhosted furnished apartments to find visitors lodging.

Embassy Suites Hotel Downtown (Value) (Kids)   This hotel offers unbelievable value and a convenient location, within walking distance of Foggy Bottom, Georgetown, and Dupont Circle. In 2005, the hotel completed a $5.8-million renovation to give the entire property an "urban-modern, but not chichi" look. You enter a tropical and glassy eight-story atrium where two waterfalls are constantly running. The accommodations are nicer than your average hotel room; every unit is a two-room suite, with a kitchenette and separate living room. It's worth requesting one of the eighth- or ninth-floor suites with views as far as Washington National Cathedral.

1250 22nd St. NW (between M and N sts.), Washington, DC 20037. ✆ **800/EMBASSY** or 202/857-3388. Fax 202/293-3173. www.washingtondc.embassysuites.com. 318 suites. $149–$309 double. Extra person $20 weekdays. Children 18 and under stay free in parent's room. Rates include full breakfast and evening reception. AE, DC, DISC, MC, V. Parking $20. Metro: Foggy Bottom. **Amenities:** Restaurant; indoor pool; fitness center. *In room:* Kitchenette.

Hotel George   This capital establishment is one of the hippest in town and caters to celebs. The oversize guest rooms sport a minimalist look, all creamy white and modern. Fluffy vanilla-colored comforters rest on oversize beds. A speaker in the spacious, mirrored, marble and black granite bathroom broadcasts sounds from the 32-inch plasma-screen TV in the other room. Other in-room amenities include cordless phones, umbrellas, spa robes, and yoga essentials (mat, strap, and block, and instructional videos on a free TV channel). Lobbyists are often found wheeling and dealing in the hotel's French bistro.

15 E St. NW (at N. Capitol St.), Washington, DC 20001. ℂ **800/576-8331** or 202/347-4200. Fax 202/347-4213. www.hotelgeorge.com. 139 units. $169–$429 double; $950 suite. Extra person $25. Children under 18 stay free in parent's room. AE, DC, DISC, MC, V. Parking $35. Metro: Union Station. **Amenities:** Restaurant; fitness center.

Hotel Monaco Washington DC *(Best)*

The magnificent Monaco has been winning awards ever since it opened in 2002, and this is where we'd stay if we were visiting D.C. Museum-like in appearance, the hotel occupies a four-story, all marble, mid-19th-century building, half of which was designed by Robert Mills, the architect for the Washington Monument, and the other half by Thomas Walter, one of the architects for the U.S. Capitol. The spacious guest rooms combine historic and hip. Their vaulted ceilings are high (12–18 ft.) and windows are long; rooms are decorated in eclectic color and furniture schemes. The hotel gives you a complimentary goldfish at check-in (if you so request), and guest pets are welcomed with VIP treatment of their own—registration cards at check-in, maps of neighborhood fire hydrants and parks, and gourmet puppy and kitty treats. For tall guests, it offers specially designed "Tall Rooms" with 18-foot-high ceilings, 96-inch-long beds, and raised showerheads. Go to the hotel's website or call the hotel directly to obtain the lowest available rates.

700 F St. NW (at 7th St.), Washington, DC 20004. ℂ **800/649-1202** or 202/628-7177. Fax 202/628-7277. www. monaco-dc.com. 184 units. Weekdays $309–$429 double, $409–$958 suite; weekends $189–$349 double, $289–$798 suite. Extra person $20. Children under 18 stay free in parent's room. Rates include complimentary organic coffee in morning and wine receptions in evening. AE, DC, DISC, MC, V. Parking $30. Metro: Gallery Place. **Amenities:** Restaurant; spacious fitness center with flatscreen TVs.

Hotel Washington ✦

Built in 1918, this hotel is the oldest continuously operating hotel in Washington. Renovations throughout the years have played up the historic angle, including one completed in 2005 that spruced up the small guest rooms with new carpeting, wallpaper, and drapes, but didn't change the overall style. From its corner perch, the 12-story hotel surveys the avenue, monuments, the Capitol, and the White House. Ask for a room facing Pennsylvania Avenue for your own private view of the Washington Monument and the White House. No other hotel in town provides the panoramic spectacle of the Hotel Washington's rooftop Sky Terrace, which is open April through October; drinks and light fare are served.

515 15th St. NW (at Pennsylvania Ave. NW), Washington, DC 20004. ℂ **800/424-9540** or 202/638-5900. Fax 202/638-4275. www.hotelwashington.com. 345 units. Weekdays $195–$325 double; weekends $155–$285 double; $495–$800 suite. Family and other discount packages available. Extra person $20. Children under 12 stay free in parent's room. AE, DC, MC, V. Parking $28. Metro: Metro Center. **Amenities:** 2 restaurants; fitness center. *In room:* Fridge.

The Jefferson Hotel

Opened in 1923 just 4 blocks from the White House, the intimate Jefferson offers superb service, an acclaimed restaurant, sophisticated but comfortable accommodations, inviting public rooms (should you want to hang out), and proximity to attractions and restaurants (should you not want to hang out). A fine art collection, including original documents signed by Thomas Jefferson, graces the public areas. Guest rooms are decorated with antiques and lovely fabrics, evoking a European feel. In-room amenities include VCRs, CD players, and robes. A marvelous high tea is served in the paneled pub/lounge. A renovation in 2004 restored antiques, added sleeper sofas to all of the suites, and installed Wi-Fi access in the public areas.

1200 16th St. NW (at M St.), Washington, DC 20036. ℂ **866/270-8102** or 202/347-2200. Fax 202/331-7982. www.thejeffersonwashingtondc.com. 100 units. Peak season weekdays $489–$3,500; weekends $329–$3,500. Off-peak weekdays starting at $389; weekends starting at $329. Extra person $25. Children under 12 stay free in parent's room. AE, DC, DISC, MC, V. Parking $28. Metro: Farragut North. **Amenities:** Restaurant; 24-hr. fitness room.

Jurys Normandy Inn (*Value*)   This gracious hotel is a gem—a small gem, but a gem nonetheless. Situated in a neighborhood of architecturally impressive embassies, the six-floor hotel has small but pretty guest rooms (all remodeled in 2003), with tapestry-upholstered mahogany and cherrywood furnishings in 18th-century style, and pretty floral-print bedspreads covering firm beds. The Normandy is an easy walk from both Adams-Morgan and Dupont Circle, where many restaurants and shops await you. Complimentary wine and cheese are served from the antique oak sideboard on Tuesday evenings. In nice weather, you can lounge on the garden patio.

2118 Wyoming Ave. NW (at Connecticut Ave.), Washington, DC 20008. (© 800/424-3729 or 202/483-1350. Fax 202/387-8241. www.jurysdoyle.com. 75 units. $89–$185 double. Extra person $10. Children under 12 stay free in parent's room. AE, DC, DISC, MC, V. Parking $15. Metro: Dupont Circle. **Amenities:** Access to the neighboring Courtyard by Marriott Northwest's pool and exercise room. *In room:* Fridge.

Morrison–Clark Historic Inn   This magnificent property, refurbished in 2003, offers the homey ambience and personable service of an inn, coupled with hotel amenities. The inn, occupying twin 1865 Victorian town houses, is listed on the National Register of Historic Places. The high-ceilinged guest rooms are individually decorated and feature original artworks, sumptuous fabrics, luxe amenities, and antique or reproduction 19th-century furnishings. Most popular are the grand Victorian-style rooms, with new chandeliers and bedspreads; four have private porches, while many others have plant-filled balconies. All rooms are equipped with free wireless Internet access. Come the warm weather, the inn hosts Big Easy cocktail receptions every Thursday from 5:30 to 7:30pm.

1015 L St. NW (at 11th St. and Massachusetts Ave. NW), Washington, DC 20001. (© **800/332-7898** or 202/898-1200. Fax 202/371-0377. www.morrisonclark.com. 54 units. Weekdays $189–$329 double; weekends $129–$249 double. Extra person $20. Children under 16 stay free in parent's room. AE, DC, DISC, MC, V. Parking $26. Metro: Metro Center or Mt. Vernon Sq. **Amenities:** Restaurant; fitness center.

The Quincy (*Kids*)   Big changes are in the works at this hotel, formerly known as the good-value property, Lincoln Suites, located in the heart of downtown, near Metro stops, restaurants, and the White House. The Quincy is going upscale, adding pillow-top mattresses, flatscreen TVs, complimentary high-speed Internet access, and double-paned windows to all rooms by the end of 2007. The top-to-bottom renovation is also altering the decor to "conservative contemporary," replacing all the furniture, appliances, carpeting, and wall coverings. Key elements remain: Suites are large and comfortable, with about 28 offering full kitchens, while the rest have wet bars (minifridge, microwave, and coffeemaker); complimentary milk and homemade cookies are still put out each evening; and breakfast (fruit, pastries, muffins, cereals, and sometimes waffles) is still a fine freebie, served daily in the breakfast room.

1823 L St. NW, Washington, DC 20036. (© **800/424-2970** or 202/223-4320. Fax 202/293-4977. www.quincysuites. com. 99 suites. Weekdays $189–$269; weekends $139–$189 year-round. Rates include deluxe continental breakfast. Children under 16 stay free in parent's room. AE, DC, DISC, MC, V. Parking $30 (in adjoining garage). Metro: Farragut North or Farragut West. Pets under 25 lb. accepted, 2nd floor only, for $15 a day. **Amenities:** Restaurant; free passes to the well-equipped Bally's Holiday Spa nearby. *In room:* Fridge, microwave.

Renaissance Mayflower   Superbly located in the heart of downtown, the Mayflower is a celeb favorite and is steeped in history. When it opened in 1925, it was the site of Calvin Coolidge's inaugural ball. President-elect FDR and family lived in room nos. 776 and 781 while waiting to move into the White House, and this is where he penned the words "The only thing we have to fear is fear itself." In 2004, the hotel completed a $10-million, top-to-bottom renovation that transformed the guest rooms into individual refuges of pretty elegance. Each room has its own marble foyer, high ceiling, mahogany reproduction furnishings, and Italian marble bathroom with bathrobes. The clubby, mahogany-paneled Town and Country Lounge is always jumping.

1127 Connecticut Ave. NW (between L and M sts.), Washington, DC 20036. © 800/228-7697 or 202/347-3000. Fax 202/776-9182. www.renaissancehotels.com/WASSH. 657 units. Weekdays $199–$419 double, from $399 suite; weekends $179–$299 double, from $399 suite. Rates include complimentary coffee service with wake-up call. AE, DC, DISC, MC, V. Parking $28. Metro: Farragut North. **Amenities:** Restaurant; fitness center.

The Ritz-Carlton, Washington, D.C. *(Best)*   This Ritz-Carlton surpasses all other Washington hotels in service and amenities. The hotel is built around a multitiered Japanese garden and courtyard with reflecting pools and cascading waterfall. Standard rooms are very large and richly furnished with decorative inlaid wooden furniture and very pretty artwork. The marble bathrooms are immense, with long counter space and a separate bathtub and shower stall. Other nice touches include an umbrella, bathrobes, CD players, and windows that open. Don't pass up the evening turn-down—the maid places a warm, freshly baked brownie upon your pillow instead of the usual mint. Guests enjoy free use of the hotel's fitness center, the two-level, 100,000-square-foot **Sports Club/LA,** which leaves all other hotel health clubs and spas in the dust. A pianist plays in the Ritz's bar and lounge every day.

1150 22nd St. NW (at M St.), Washington, DC 20037. © 800/241-3333 or 202/835-0500. Fax 202/835-1588. www.ritzcarlton.com/hotels/washington_dc. 300 units. $499 double; from $649 suite. AE, DC, DISC, MC, V. Valet parking $28. Metro: Foggy Bottom or Dupont Circle. Pets accepted and pampered (no fee). **Amenities:** Restaurant; health club; spa. *In room:* Fridge.

Willard InterContinental Washington   The classy Willard is a stone's throw from the White House and the Smithsonian museums, down the block from the National Theater, and down the avenue from the Capitol. Rooms in this National Historic Landmark are handsome, if staid, and furnished with Edwardian- and Federal-style reproductions; amenities include bathrobes in the wonderful bathrooms. Those with the best views are the oval suites overlooking Pennsylvania Avenue to the Capitol. Stop in at the Round Robin Bar to hear bartender and manager Jim Hewes spin tales about the incredible history of the 1901 Willard and its predecessor, the City Hotel, built on this site in 1815.

1401 Pennsylvania Ave. NW (at 14th St.), Washington, DC 20004. © 800/827-1747 or 202/628-9100. Fax 202/637-7326. www.washington.interconti.com. 341 units. $269–$610 double; $500–$4,200 suite. AE, DC, DISC, MC, V. Parking $28. Metro: Metro Center. **Amenities:** Restaurant; fitness center; spa.

WHERE TO DINE

If a restaurant sounds irresistible, call ahead for **reservations,** especially for Saturday night. A number of restaurants are affiliated with an online reservation service called **www.opentable.com,** so if you've got Internet access, you might reserve your table online.

Ben's Chili Bowl AMERICAN   Ben's is a veritable institution, a mom-and-pop place, where everything looks, tastes, and probably even costs the same as when the restaurant opened in 1958. It was only one of four chosen by the 2004 James Beard Foundation Awards as an "America's Classic." Formica counters, red bar stools, and a jukebox plays Motown and reggae tunes. Ben's continues as a gathering place for black Washington (Bill Cosby's a longtime customer), though everyone's welcome—even the late-nighters who come streaming out of nearby nightclubs at 2 or 3 in the morning on the weekend. Of course, the chili, cheese fries, and half-smokes are great, but so are breakfast items.

1213 U St. NW. ✆ 202/667-0909. www.benschilibowl.com. Reservations not accepted. Main courses $2.50–$7.40. No credit cards. Mon–Thurs 6am–2am; Fri–Sat 6am–4am; Sun noon–8pm. Metro: U St.–Cardozo.

Bombay Club INDIAN   The Bombay Club is a pleasure, sure to please patrons who know their Indian food as well as those who've never tried it. Dishes present an easy introduction to Indian food for the uninitiated, and are sensitive to varying tolerances for spiciness. The menu ranges from fiery green-chile chicken ("not for the fainthearted," the menu warns) to the delicately prepared lobster Malabar, a popular favorite. The waitstaff seems straight out of *Jewel in the Crown*, attending to your every whim. This is one place where you can linger over a meal as long as you like.

815 Connecticut Ave. NW. ✆ 202/659-3727. www.bombayclubdc.com. Reservations recommended. Main courses $7.50–$24; Sun brunch $20. AE, DC, MC, V. Mon–Fri and Sun brunch 11:30am–2:30pm; Mon–Thurs 6–10:30pm; Fri–Sat 6–11pm; Sun 5:30–9pm. Metro: Farragut West.

Café Atlántico LATIN AMERICAN   This place rocks on weekend nights, a favorite hot spot in Washington's still-burgeoning downtown. The colorful, three-tiered restaurant throbs with Latin, calypso, and reggae music. If the place is packed, try to snag a seat at the second-level bar, where you can sample a *caipirinha,* made of limes, sugar, and *cachacha* (sugar-cane liqueur). Another treat for you is to sit at the bar and watch the waiter make fresh guacamole right before your eyes. As for the main dishes, you can't get a more elaborate meal for the price. The duck confit and seared Ecuadorean scallops are standouts. Take a gander at the remarkable, award-winning wine list, too—it boasts 110 selections, mostly from South America, with many bottles priced under $30.

405 8th St. NW, at D St. NW. ✆ 202/393-0812. www.cafeatlantico.com. Reservations recommended. Lunch main courses $8–$16; dinner main courses $18–$28; pretheater menu $28 (nightly 5–6:30pm); Latino dim sum: you can choose a la carte ($2–$9 each) items, or pay $25 for a vegetarian all-you-can-eat meal, or $35 for a deluxe version. AE, DC, DISC, MC, V. Mon–Fri 11:30am–2:30pm; Sat–Sun brunch 11:30am–2:30pm; Sun–Thurs 5–10pm; Fri–Sat 5–11pm. The bar stays open late on weekends. Metro: Archives–Navy Memorial and Gallery Place/Verizon Center.

Cashion's Eat Place AMERICAN   Owner/chef Ann Cashion continues to rack up culinary awards (in 2004, Cashion was named "Best Chef/MidAtlantic" by the James Beard Foundation) as easily as she pleases her patrons. Her menu changes daily and features about eight entrees, split between seafood and meat: sample entrees include rabbit stuffed with ham and truffles, *fritto misto* of whole jumbo shrimp and black sea bass filet, served with onion rings and house-made tartar sauce, and pork loin with garlic sauce. Save room for chocolate cinnamon mousse or coconut layer cake with huckleberries. In warm weather, the glass-fronted Cashion's opens to the sidewalk.

1819 Columbia Rd. NW. ✆ 202/797-1819. www.cashionseatplace.com. Reservations recommended. Brunch $8.95–$12; dinner main courses $19–$30. MC, V. Tues 5:30–10:30pm; Wed–Sat 5:30–11pm; Sun 11:30am–2:30pm and 5:30–10:30pm.

Galileo *(Best* ITALIAN   Galileo has been hailed as one of the best Italian restaurants in the country. Whether your menu features Neapolitan or Piedmontese dishes, you will have the choice of ordering a la carte, or relishing a 10- to 12-course tasting menu with about 25 other lucky diners at the **Laboratorio del Galileo** (✆ **202/331-0880**), a private dining area and kitchen enclosed by glass. Typical entrees include a roasted rack of lamb served with a porcini mushroom tart in a black olive sauce; homemade raviolis filled with buffalo ricotta, ham, and mozzarella in a meat ragout; and Mediterranean dorade fish baked in foil with mussels. The cellar boasts more than 400 vintages of Italian wine. The atmosphere is relaxed; some diners are dressed in jeans, others in suits. Waiters can be supercilious, though. Galileo also has a terrace for warm-weather dining. *Tip:* If you can't afford a dinner here, reserve a seat at **Osteria del Galileo** for lunch and enjoy something stupendous, say lasagna Bolognese or a bowl of fusilli tossed with asparagus, provolone, and prosciutto, for only $4 to $12.

1110 21st St. NW. ℂ 202/293-7191. www.galileodc.com. Reservations recommended. Galileo Lunch main courses $15–$20; dinner main courses $25–$35; Osteria lunch and dinner main courses $4–$12; Laboratorio $110 per person weekdays, $125 per person weekends. AE, MC, V. Mon–Fri 11:30am–2:15pm; Mon–Thurs 5:30–10:30pm; Fri–Sat 5:30–10:30pm; Sun 5–10pm. Metro: Foggy Bottom.

Jaleo SPANISH   This restaurant may be credited with initiating the tapas craze in Washington. It gets very crowded in theater season according to the schedule of the Shakespeare Theater next door. Tapas choices include savory warm goat cheese served with toast points, and a delicious mushroom tart served with roasted red-pepper sauce. Paella is among the few heartier entrees listed. The casual-chic interior focuses on a large mural of a flamenco dancer inspired by John Singer Sargent's painting *Jaleo*. On Wednesday at 7:45pm and 8:45pm, sevillana dancers perform.

480 7th St. NW (at E St.). ℂ 202/628-7949. www.jaleo.com. Reservations accepted at lunch and for dinner until 6:30pm. Dinner main courses $16–$18; tapas $3.95–$9.95. AE, DC, DISC, MC, V. Sun–Mon 11:30am–10pm; Tues–Thurs 11:30am–11:30pm; Fri–Sat 11:30am–midnight. Metro: Archives–Navy Memorial or Gallery Place.

Kinkead's AMERICAN/SEAFOOD   When a restaurant has been as roundly praised as Kinkead's, it's hard to live up to the hype—but Kinkead's is that good. After a brief closure in early 2004 for a remodeling of the dining room and a revamping of the menu, Kinkead's re-opened with even more pleasing items on the menu. Award-winning chef/owner Bob Kinkead is the star at this 220-seat restaurant, where booths and tables neatly fill the nooks and alcoves of the former town house. It's one of the best places in town for seafood. The signature dish, pepita-crusted salmon with shrimp, crab, and chiles, provides a nice hot crunch before melting in your mouth. If you're hungry but not ravenous in the late afternoon, stop in for some delicious light fare: fish and chips, lobster roll, soups, and salads. *Beware:* If the waiter tries to seat you in the "atrium," you'll be stuck at a table mall-side, just outside the doors of the restaurant.

2000 Pennsylvania Ave. NW. ℂ 202/296-7700. www.kinkead.com. Reservations recommended. Lunch and dinner main courses $22–$37; light fare $6–$25. AE, DC, DISC, MC, V. Sun–Fri 11:30am–2:30pm; Sun–Thurs 5:30–10pm; Fri–Sat 5:30–10:30pm (light fare served weekdays 2:30–5:30pm). Metro: Foggy Bottom.

Pizzeria Paradiso ITALIAN   This is the best pizza place in the city, no contest. Master chef Peter Pastan owns this classy, often crowded, pizzeria, with both table and counter seating. An oak-burning oven at one end of the charming room produces exceptionally doughy but light pizza crusts. Pizzas range from the plain Paradiso, which offers chunks of tomatoes covered in melted mozzarella, to the robust Siciliano, a blend of nine ingredients, including eggplant and red onion. Also popular are the panini of homemade focaccia stuffed with marinated roasted lamb and vegetables and other fillings. *Note:* Pizzeria Paradiso has another location at 3282 M St. NW (ℂ 202/337-1245), in Georgetown, right next door to Dean & Deluca.

2029 P St. NW. ℂ 202/223-1245. www.eatyourpizza.com. Pizzas $9.50–$17; sandwiches and salads $4.95–$7.95. DC, MC, V. Mon–Thurs 11:30am–11pm; Fri–Sat 11:30am–midnight; Sun noon–10pm. Metro: Dupont Circle.

The Prime Rib STEAK/SEAFOOD   The Prime Rib has plenty of competition now, but beef lovers still consider this The Place. It's got a definite men's club feel about it, with brass-trimmed black walls, leopard-skin carpeting, and comfortable black-leather chairs and banquettes. The meat is from the best grain-fed steers and has been aged for 4 to 5 weeks. Steaks and cuts of roast beef are thick, tender, and juicy. In case you had any doubt, The Prime Rib's prime rib is the best item on the menu, juicy and thick, top-quality meat. For less carnivorous diners, there are about a dozen seafood entrees, including an excellent crab imperial. We recommend the hot cottage fries.

2020 K St. NW. ✆ 202/466-8811. www.theprimerib.com. Reservations recommended. Jacket and tie required for men. Lunch main courses $12–$25; dinner main courses $27–$49. AE, DC, MC, V. Mon–Thurs 11:30am–3pm and 5–11pm; Fri 11:30am–3pm and 5–11:30pm; Sat 5–11:30pm. Metro: Farragut West.

Tosca NORTHERN ITALIAN   Washington probably has more Italian restaurants than any other kind of ethnic eatery, but Tosca remains the standout fine *ristorante italiano* between Capitol Hill and the White House, a range of at least 20 blocks. Tosca's interior design of pale pastels in the thick carpeting and heavy drapes creates a hushed atmosphere, a suitable foil to the rich food. The menu emphasizes the cooking of the Lake Como region of Italy. Tosca has something for everyone, including simply grilled fish accompanied by organic vegetables for the health conscious, tiramisu and citrus cannoli for those with a sweet tooth. The restaurant is always full, but even when there's a crowd, Tosca doesn't get too noisy—the restaurant's designers kept acoustics in mind.

1112 F St. NW. ✆ 202/367-1990. www.toscadc.com. Reservations recommended. Lunch main courses $11–$22; dinner main courses $12–$40. AE, DC, MC, V. Mon–Fri 11:30am–2:30pm; Sun–Thurs 5:30–10:30pm; Fri–Sat 5:30–11pm. Metro: Metro Center.

WASHINGTON AFTER DARK

To find out who's playing when you're in town, check the Friday "Weekend" section of the *Washington Post.* The *City Paper,* available free at restaurants, bookstores, and other places around town, and online at **www.washingtoncitypaper.com**, is another good source.

   TICKETplace (✆ **202/842-5387** for information; www.ticketplace.org), Washington's discount, day-of-show ticket outlet, has one location: at 407 7th St. NW, between D and E streets (Metro: Gallery Place/Verizon Center or Archives–Navy Memorial). Hours are Tuesday through Friday from 11am to 6pm and Saturday from 10am to 5pm; half-price tickets for Sunday and Monday shows are sold on Saturday. You can buy full-price tickets for most performances in town through **Ticketmaster** (✆ **800/ 551-7328;** www.ticketmaster.com) if you're willing to pay a hefty service charge. Another similar ticket outlet is **Tickets.com** (✆ **800/955-5566;** www.tickets.com).

THE KENNEDY CENTER   America's national performing-arts center, the hub of Washington's cultural and entertainment scene, is the **John F. Kennedy Center for the Performing Arts,** at the southern end of New Hampshire Avenue NW and Rock Creek Parkway (✆ **800/444-1324** or 202/467-4600; www.kennedy-center.org).

   The center is actually made up of six different theaters: the Opera House, the Concert Hall, the Terrace Theater, the Eisenhower Theater, the Theater Lab, and the Family Theater. After a major renovation of the Opera House, the **Washington National Opera** (www.dc-opera.org), under the direction of Placido Domingo, returned here in 2004. The **National Symphony Orchestra,** under the direction of Leonard Slatkin, presents concerts in the Concert Hall from September to June. The **Theater**

Lab continues by day as Washington's premier stage for children's theater and by night as a cabaret.

You should also know about the Kennedy Center's very popular free concert series: Known as the **"Millennium Stage"** (www.kennedy-center.org/millennium), the series features daily performances by national and local musicians, each evening at 6pm in the center's Grand Foyer.

Discounted tickets are usually offered to students, seniors, people with permanent disabilities, enlisted military personnel, and people with fixed low incomes (call ℂ **202/416-8340** for details).

THE THEATER SCENE   D.C.'s theatrical productions are first-rate and varied. Almost anything on Broadway has been tried out here or will eventually come here. The city also has several nationally acclaimed repertory companies and two companies specializing in Shakespearean productions. Check the *Washington Post* or the *City Paper* for specific listings of what's going on. Among the best are: **Arena Stage** (ℂ **202/488-3300;** www.arenastage.org), **Ford's Theatre** (ℂ **202/347-4833;** www. fordstheatre.org), the **National Theatre** (ℂ **800/447-7400** or 202/628-6161; www. nationaltheatre.org), and the **Shakespeare Theatre Company** (ℂ **202/547-1122;** www.shakespearetheatre.org).

The Shakespeare Theatre Company is set to move into its new Harman Center for the Arts (comprised of the existing Lansburgh Theater and the new Sidney Harman Hall) in 2007. Expansion at Arena Stage includes a third theater, schedule for a 2009 opening. Both companies do, however, remain in production throughout the various phases of construction.

THE CLUB & MUSIC SCENE   The best nightlife districts are Adams-Morgan; the U Street Corridor, 12th to 15th streets northwest, a still developing district that's in a somewhat dangerous part of town; the Seventh Street northwest corridor near Chinatown and the MCI Center; and Georgetown.

Latin jazz is popular in Washington, and one of the best places to salsa and merengue is **Habana Village,** 1834 Columbia Rd. NW (ℂ **202/462-6310**), a fun three-story nightclub in Adams-Morgan. Another option is **Chi-Cha Lounge,** also in Adams-Morgan at 1624 U St. NW (ℂ **202/234-8400**).

If you're in a dancing mood, stop in at **Eighteenth Street Lounge,** 1212 18th St. NW (ℂ **202/466-3922**), for a mix of DJ tunes that includes acid jazz, hip-hop, reggae, or Latin jazz; or **Madam's Organ Restaurant and Bar,** 2461 18th St. NW (ℂ **202/667-5370;** www.madamsorgan.com), if live jazz, blues, or R&B turns you on.

And if you like to mingle with an international crowd, stop by **Zanzibar on the Waterfront,** 700 Water St. SW (ℂ **202/554-9100;** www.zanzibar-otw.com), where you can dine well, dance to live music, lounge, sip and listen, or sip and talk; the club features a different kind of music every night.

Blues Alley, 1073 Wisconsin Ave. NW, in an alley below M Street (ℂ **202/337-4141;** www.bluesalley.com), in Georgetown, has been Washington's top jazz club since 1965.

Clubs hosting a combination of big names and up-and-coming bands for live rock include **DC 9,** 1940 9th St. NW (ℂ **202/483-5000;** www.dcnine.com); **Black Cat,** 1811 14th St. NW, between S and T streets (ℂ **202/667-7960;** www.blackcatdc. com); and the **9:30 Club,** 815 V St. NW, at Vermont Avenue (ℂ **202/393-0930;** www.930.com). Many of these clubs have DJs on nights when live acts aren't playing.

THE BAR SCENE   Washington has a thriving and varied bar scene. But just when you think you know all the hot spots, a spate of new ones pop up. Travel the triangle formed by the intersections of Connecticut Avenue, 18th Street, and M Street, in Dupont Circle, and you'll find the latest bunch. The **Big Hunt,** 1345 Connecticut Ave. NW, between N Street and Dupont Circle (© **202/785-2333;** www.thebighunt dc.com), is a casual and comfy hangout for the 20- to 30-something crowd, with a kind of *Raiders of the Lost Ark* jungle theme. If you like beer and you like choices, head for **Brickskeller,** 1523 22nd St. NW (© **202/293-1885**), which has been around for about 50 years and offers more than 1,000 beers from all over the world. With 200 televisions tuned to sporting events, **The ESPN Zone,** 555 12th St. NW (© **202/ 783-3776;** www.espnzone.com), is sure to have the big game on. Capitol Hill staffers and their bosses, apparently at ease in dive surroundings, have been coming to the **Tune Inn,** 33½ Pennsylvania Ave. SE (© **202/543-2725**), since 1955. For a sophisticated setting, the clubby, mahogany-paneled **Town and Country Lounge,** in the Renaissance Mayflower Hotel, 1127 Connecticut Ave. NW (© **202/347-3000**), is where personable bartender Sambonn Lek mixes drinks, performs magic tricks, and plays matchmaker.

Gay nightlife centers around **Dupont Circle,** with at least 10 gay bars within easy walking distance of one another. Younger men pack **J. R.'s Bar and Grill,** 1519 17th St. NW (© **202/328-0090**).

SIDE TRIPS TO MOUNT VERNON & OLD TOWN ALEXANDRIA
MOUNT VERNON

Mount Vernon, George Washington's stunning southern plantation, dates from a 1674 land grant given to his great-grandfather. The restoration by the Mount Vernon Ladies' Association is an unmarred beauty; many of the furnishings are original pieces acquired by Washington, and the rooms have been repainted in the original colors favored by George and Martha. There are a number of family portraits, and the rooms are appointed as if actually in day-to-day use. After leaving the house, you can tour the kitchen, slave quarters, storeroom, smokehouse, overseer's quarters, coach house, stables, and a 4-acre exhibit area called "George Washington, Pioneer Farmer." Explore the grounds to see the wharf, the slave burial ground, the greenhouse and gardens, and the tomb containing George and Martha Washington's sarcophagi. There's no formal tour of the plantation, but attendants stationed throughout the house and grounds provide brief orientations and answer questions.

In 2006, the estate opened an orientation and an education center, both just inside the main entrance, and much of it underground so as not to take away from the estate's pastoral setting. A 15-minute film in the orientation center fills you in on the life and character of George Washington. The education center's 23 galleries and theater presentations inform you further about Washington's military and presidential careers.

Admission is $13 for adults, $6 for children 6 to 11. The house and grounds are open April to August, daily from 8am to 5pm; March, September, and October, daily from 9am to 5pm; and November to February, daily from 9am to 4pm. For more information, call © **703/780-2000** or go to www.mountvernon.org.

GETTING THERE   Mount Vernon is 16 miles south of Washington via the George Washington Memorial Parkway (Va. 400). **Gray Line Buses** (© **800/862-1400** or 202/289-1995; www.graylinedc.com) go to Mount Vernon daily (except Christmas,

Thanksgiving, and New Year's Day), leaving from the bus's terminal at Union Station at 8:30am and returning by 1:30pm. The cost is $37 per adult and $18 per child. You can also get here with the **Spirit of Washington Cruises** (© **202/554-8000;** www. spiritcruises.com).

OLD TOWN ALEXANDRIA

Founded by a group of Scottish tobacco merchants, the seaport town of Alexandria came into being in 1749. Today, the original 60 acres of lots in the hometown of George Washington and Robert E. Lee are the heart of Old Town, a multimillion-dollar urban-renewal historic district. An abundance of quaint shops, boutiques, art galleries, and restaurants cater to tourists who come in search of a taste of Colonial times.

Your first stop should be the **Alexandria Convention and Visitors Association,** located at Ramsay House, 221 King St., at Fairfax Street (© **800/388-9119** or 703/838-4200; www.funside.com), open daily from 9am to 5pm (closed Jan 1, Thanksgiving, and Dec 25). Here you can get a free 1-day parking permit and discount attractions passes. *Note:* Many Alexandria attractions are closed on Monday.

The **Lee-Fendall House Museum,** 614 Oronoco St., at Washington Street (© **703/548-1789;** www.leefendallhouse.org), is a veritable Lee family museum of furniture, heirlooms, and documents. The **Carlyle House,** 121 N. Fairfax St., between Cameron and King streets (© **703/549-2997;** www.carlylehouse.org), is one of Virginia's most architecturally impressive 18th-century homes. **Christ Church,** 118 N. Washington St., at Cameron Street (© **703/549-1450;** www.historicchristchurch. org), has been in continuous use since 1773. The **Torpedo Factory,** 105 N. Union St., between King and Cameron streets on the waterfront (© **703/838-4565;** www. torpedofactory.org), is a block-long, three-story, former torpedo shell–case factory, which now accommodates some 160 professional artists and craftspeople who create and sell their own works on the premises.

For a fun time in a pubby setting, head to the **Union Street Public House,** 121 S. Union St. (© **703/548-1785;** www.unionstpub.com), where you can choose from burgers, poor-boys, oysters, fried calamari, salads, and other simple fare. Or try authentic Colonial grub at **Gadsby's Tavern,** 138 N. Royal St., at Cameron Street (© **703/548-1288**).

GETTING THERE   Old Town Alexandria is about 8 miles south of Washington. Take the George Washington Memorial Parkway south, which becomes Washington Street in Old Town Alexandria. Washington Street intersects with King Street, Alexandria's main thoroughfare. The easiest way to make the trip is to take the Metro's Yellow and Blue lines to the King Street station. From the King Street station, you can catch an eastbound AT2 or AT5 blue-and-gold DASH bus (© **703/370-DASH;** www.dashbus.com), marked either "Old Town" or "Braddock Metro," which will take you up King Street. Ask to be dropped at the corner of Fairfax and King streets. The fare is $1 most of the time, but it's free on weekends, from Friday evening through Sunday night.

4

The Southeast

The six states of the Southeast—Virginia, North and South Carolina, Kentucky, Tennessee, and Georgia—encompass a region that is among the most geographically diverse in the country. Topography ranges from the plains of Georgia and the gorgeous beaches of the Outer Banks to the misty peaks of the Great Smoky Mountains and the Bluegrass Country of Kentucky.

And the sights, tastes, and touring opportunities in this large region are just as varied. You history buffs can swing by Thomas Jefferson's Monticello on your way to Colonial Williamsburg, or you can head farther south to the famed historic port cities of Savannah and Charleston, or the Civil Rights District in the otherwise very metropolitan Atlanta. Outdoors enthusiasts will find opportunities to indulge in just about every form of recreation. Sports nuts will feel right at home in sports-crazy Atlanta, which hosted the 1996 Summer Olympics, or in horse-crazy Lexington, where the oldest continuous sports event in the country—the Kentucky Derby—still attracts hordes in May. If music moves you, then you owe it to yourself to make a trip out to Tennessee's Memphis and Nashville, where country music and the blues rule, and The King still reigns supreme. And if your tastes run more in the culinary direction, don't head home before you've had some down-home Carolina barbecue or a slice of Virginia ham (naturally washed down with bourbon, Jack Daniel's, or a mint julep). You name it, you'll likely find it; it's no wonder visitors have been increasingly making their way here over the past few years.

1 Jefferson's Virginia: Charlottesville & Monticello

It was in Charlottesville that Thomas Jefferson built his famous mountaintop home, Monticello; selected the site for and helped plan James Monroe's Ash Lawn–Highland house near Monticello; designed his "academical village," the University of Virginia; and died at home. "All my wishes end where I hope my days will end," he wrote, "at Monticello." Charlottesville today is a growing cosmopolitan center, attracting an increasing number of rich and famous folks—author John Grisham, for one. But its prime attractions are still Thomas Jefferson and his magnificent creations.

ESSENTIALS

GETTING THERE **By Plane** US Airways, Delta, and United fly commuter planes to **Charlottesville-Albemarle Airport,** 201 Bowen Loop (② **434/973-8341;** www.gocho.com), north of town off U.S. 29.

By Train The **Amtrak** station is at 810 W. Main St. (② **800/872-7245;** www.amtrak. com), about halfway between the town's commercial district and the University of Virginia.

By Car   Charlottesville is on **I-64** from the east or west and **U.S. 29** from the north or south. I-64 connects with **I-81** at Staunton and with **I-95** at Richmond.

VISITOR INFORMATION   For information, contact the **Charlottesville/ Albemarle Convention and Visitors Bureau,** P.O. Box 178, Charlottesville, VA 22902 (© **877/386-1102** or 434/977-1783; www.soveryvirginia.org). The bureau has two visitor centers. One is in the **Monticello Visitors Center,** on Va. 20 at Exit 121 off I-64, near Thomas Jefferson's home. The other is at 100 5th St., NE, on the second level of the Market Street parking garage on the northeastern edge of the Downtown Mall. The Monticello center is open March through October daily from 9am to 5:30pm; the rest of the year, daily until 5pm. The downtown center is open Monday to Saturday from 10am to 5pm, Sunday 11am to 3pm. Both are closed New Year's Day, Thanksgiving, and Christmas. The centers sell block tickets to Monticello and other attractions (see "What to See & Do," below). It also provides maps and literature about local and state attractions, and can make same-day, discounted hotel/ motel reservations for you.

WHAT TO SEE & DO

The Monticello Visitors Center (see above) sells a **Presidents' Pass,** a discount block ticket combining admission to Monticello, Michie Tavern, and Ash Lawn–Highland. It costs $26 for all ages. The three attractions are within 2 miles of each other on the southeastern outskirts of town. Allow at least a day to see them all.

Thomas Jefferson's architectural masterpiece, **Monticello** (© **434/984-9822** or 434/984-9800; www.monticello.org), is one of the highlights of any visit to Virginia. Jefferson designed it himself, combining the 16th-century Italian style of Andrea Palladio with features of the Parisian buildings that he knew and admired during his stint as U.S. minister (ambassador) to France.

Today the house has been restored as closely as possible to its appearance during Jefferson's retirement years. He or his family owned nearly all its furniture and other household objects. The garden has been extended to its original 1,000-foot length, and Mulberry Row—where slaves and free artisans lived and labored in light industrial shops such as a joinery, smokehouse-dairy, blacksmith shop-nailery, and carpenter's shop—has been excavated. Jefferson's grave is in the family burial ground, which is still in use. After visiting the graveyard, you can take a shuttle bus back to the visitor parking lot or walk through the woods via a delightful path.

Admission is $14 adults, $6 children 6 to 11, free for children under 6. You must take a 30-minute guided tour in order to go inside the house. These run March through October daily from 8am to 5pm, and November through February daily from 9am to 4:30pm. Expect long lines on spring and summer weekends and every day during the October "leaf season," so plan to get here when it opens in the morning. Timed passes are given out when the wait exceeds 45 minutes (these are given only to people standing in line, not at the ticket booth); you can spend the time exploring the gardens and outbuildings on your own.

Ash Lawn–Highland, on C.R. 795 (James Monroe Pkwy.), 2½ miles past Monticello (© **434/293-9539;** www.ashlawnhighland.org), was the estate of America's fifth president, James Monroe. Today Monroe's 535-acre estate is owned and maintained as a working farm by his alma mater, the College of William and Mary. Livestock, vegetable and herb gardens, and Colonial crafts demonstrations recall daily life on the Monroes' plantation. Horses, sheep, and cattle graze in the fields, while peacocks roam

The Southeast

Another Nearby Presidential Home

Twenty-five miles east of Charlottesville is **Montpelier,** 11407 Constitution
Hwy. (Va. 20), Montpelier Station (© **540/672-2728;** www.montpelier.org),
a 2,700-acre estate facing the Blue Ridge Mountains that was home to President James Madison and his wife, Dolley. They are buried here in the family cemetery. Two structures remain from their time: the main house and the
"Ice House Temple" (built over a well and used to store ice). William du
Pont, Sr., bought the estate in 1900; he enlarged the mansion and added
barns, staff houses, a sawmill, a blacksmith shop, a train station, a dairy, and
greenhouses, and his wife created a 22-acre formal garden. The National
Trust for Historic Preservation acquired the property following her death in
1984, and in 2003 launched a major, multiyear restoration, which will rip
away the du Ponts' additions to the mansion, reducing it from 55 rooms to
the 22-room version the Madisons occupied in the 1820s. The house is open
to the public during the project, with 30-minute tours explaining the near-
archaeological aspects of the work.

Admission is $11 adults, $10 seniors, $6 children ages 6 to 11. Open April
through October daily from 9:30am to 5:30pm, November through March
daily from 9:30am to 4:30pm. Call ahead for a schedule of special events,
such as birthday celebrations for James (Mar 16) and Dolley (May 20). To get
there from Charlottesville, go north on U.S. 29 to U.S. 33 at Ruckersville and
head east; at Barboursville, turn left (north) onto Va. 20.

the boxwood gardens. Five of the original rooms remain, along with the basement
kitchen, the overseer's cottage, restored slave quarters, and the old smokehouse.

On the mandatory 30-minute house tour, you'll see some of the family's original
furnishings and artifacts and learn a great deal about the fifth president. Admission is
$9 adults, $8 seniors, $5 children 6 to 11. The estate is open April through October
daily from 9am to 6pm; November through March daily from 11am to 5pm. Many
special events take place at Ash Lawn–Highland. The outdoor **Ash Lawn Opera Festival** features opera and contemporary music performances; and a major Colonial arts
festival, **Plantation Days,** which takes place in July, showcases dozens of 18th-century
crafts, historical reenactments, period music performances, and dressage.

Unless you're picnicking at Monticello, plan to have a Colonial-style lunch at
Michie Tavern ca. 1784, 683 Thomas Jefferson Pkwy. (© **434/977-1234;** www.
michietavern.com), which was built in 1784 and has been painstakingly reconstructed. Behind the tavern are reproductions of the "dependencies"—log kitchen,
dairy, smokehouse, icehouse, root cellar, and "necessary" (note the not-so-soft corn-
cobs). The re-created general store houses an excellent crafts shop. Mandatory 30-
minute tavern-museum tours depart as needed from April to October (self-guided
tours with recorded narratives are available other months). Admission is $8 adults, $7
seniors, $3 children 6 to 11. Meals cost $15 for adults, $7.25 for children. The
museum is open daily from 9am to 5pm (last tour 4:20pm). The restaurant serves
food daily from 11:30am to 3pm.

The **University of Virginia** (© **434/982-3200**), designed by Thomas Jefferson himself, is graced with spacious lawns, serpentine-walled gardens, colonnaded pavilions, and a classical rotunda inspired by the Pantheon in Rome. Jefferson was in every sense the university's father, since he conceived it, wrote its charter, raised money for its construction, drew the plans, selected the site, laid the cornerstone in 1817, supervised construction, served as the first rector, selected the faculty, and created the curriculum. His good friends Monroe and Madison sat with him on the first board. The focal point of the university is the **Rotunda** (at Rugby Rd.), today restored as Jefferson designed it. Some 600 feet of tree-dotted lawn extends from the south portico of the Rotunda to what is now Cabell Hall, designed at the turn of the 20th century by Stanford White. The room Edgar Allan Poe occupied when he was a student here is furnished as it would have been in 1826 and is open to visitors.

When school is in session, students usually lead 45-minute **campus tours** from the Rotunda daily at 10 and 11am and 2, 3, and 4pm, but call © **434/982-3200** to confirm. Self-guided walking tour brochures are available from the university's **Visitor Information Center** (© **434/924-7166**), which is located not on campus but in the University Police Headquarters, on Ivy Road (U.S. 250 Business) just east of the U.S. 29/U.S. 250 Bypass. The visitor center is open 24 hours a day. *Note:* The university is closed 3 weeks around Christmas.

WHERE TO STAY & DINE

Standing beside a picturesque lake, **The Boar's Head Inn,** 200 Ednam Dr. (© **800/476-1988** or 434/296-2181; www.boarsheadinn.com), is a university-owned property that's one of the best all-around resorts in Virginia. The focal point is a 19th-century gristmill that is loaded with antiques and art, and its plank flooring and huge old ceiling beams give ancient charm to the **Old Mill Room,** the resort's signature restaurant offering fine dining accompanied by an excellent selection of Virginia wines. The innlike guest rooms upstairs in the mill are charming and romantic, but if you want more space and a balcony, opt for a unit in one of the other lakeside structures. Guest quarters throughout are furnished with Colonial reproductions, and some units have kitchenettes. In addition to the full-service spa and the resort's own tennis courts, guests can use the adjacent Boar's Head Sports Club and the university's Birdwood Golf Course nearby. Rates run $150 to $325 double.

Also luxurious (and pricey) but slightly more formal is the 48-room **Keswick Hall at Monticello,** 701 Country Club Dr., in nearby Keswick (© **800/274-5391** or 804/979-3440; www.keswick.com). Many of the 1912 vintage Italianate rooms and suites have fireplaces, claw-foot tubs, and views over a golf course redesigned by Arnold Palmer. Dining here is gourmet all the way, and guests can also enjoy swimming pools, a fitness center, and tennis courts. Rates run $365 to $465 double and include afternoon tea.

Not as expensive, although still plenty upscale, are the **Silver Thatch Inn,** 3001 Hollymead Dr., Charlottesville (© **800/261-0720** or 434/978-4686; www.silverthatch.com; $145–$185 double); and **The Inn at Monticello,** 1188 Scottsville Rd. (Va. 20), Charlottesville (© **434/979-3593;** www.innatmonticello.com; $110–$220 double).

On the affordable end of the scale, one of Charlottesville's most reliable places is the **Hampton Inn & Suites,** 900 W. Main St., at 10th Street (© **800/HAMPTON** or 434/923-8600; www.hamptonsuites.com). Rates are $105 to $145 double. The commercial strip along U.S. 29 north of the U.S. 250 Bypass has an abundance of chain motels.

Guesthouses Reservation Service, Inc., P.O. Box 5737, Charlottesville, VA 22905 (© **434/979-7264;** www.va-guesthouses.com), handles bed-and-breakfast accommodations in elegant homes and private cottages. You can write or visit the website for information on the properties, but reservations must be made by phone. The office is open Monday through Friday from noon to 5pm.

Charlottesville has more than 200 restaurants—an enormous number for such a small city. For a complete rundown, pick up a copy of *Bites,* a free restaurant guide at the Monticello Visitor Center. There are also lists and reviews in *C-Ville* (www.c-ville. com) and *The Hook* (www.readthehook.com), the two free newspapers found in boxes all over town.

Some of the area's finest dining is at the country inns, such as **The Boar's Head Inn** and the **Silver Thatch Inn** (see above). Another favorite is the **C&O Restaurant,** 515 E. Water St. (© **434/971-7044**), whose excellent menu ranges across the globe— from France to Thailand, from New Mexico to Louisiana. One of Charlottesville's most popular dining spots is **Northern Exposure,** 1202 W. Main St., at 12th Street (© **434/977-6002**), offering both traditional and inventive Italian-accented cuisine.

2 Richmond

Now a sprawling metropolitan area flanking the James River in the center of the state, Richmond supplanted the more militarily vulnerable Williamsburg as Virginia's capital in 1780, and it has been the scene of much of the state's history ever since. It was here in St. John's Church that Patrick Henry concluded his address to the second Virginia Convention with the stirring words, "Give me liberty, or give me death!" But Richmond really made its mark on American history during the Civil War. This is where Jefferson Davis presided over the Confederate Congress, and Robert E. Lee accepted command of Virginia's armed forces.

ESSENTIALS

GETTING THERE   By Plane   Richmond International Airport, Airport Drive off I-64, I-295, and Williamsburg Road (U.S. 60; © **804/226-3052;** www.flyrichmond. com), known locally as Byrd Field, is about 15 minutes east of downtown. Several domestic carriers service the airport, and the major car-rental companies all have desks here.

By Train   Several daily **Amtrak** trains pull into the station at 7519 Staples Mill Rd., north of Exit 185 off I-64 (© **800/872-7245;** www.amtrak.com).

By Car   Richmond is at the junction of **I-64,** traveling east-west, and **I-95,** traveling north-south. **I-295** bypasses the city on its east and north sides. **U.S. 60** (east-west) and **U.S. 1** and **U.S. 301** (north-south) are other major arteries.

VISITOR INFORMATION   The **Richmond Visitors Center,** 401 N. 3rd St., at Clay Street, Richmond, VA 23219 (© **888/742-4666;** www.visit.richmond.com), provides information and operates a hotel reservation service. It's open daily from 9am to 5pm. In addition, the **Richmond International Airport Visitors Center** (© **804/ 236-3260**) is open Monday through Friday from 9:30am to 4:30pm. It will make same-day hotel reservations.

EXPLORING RICHMOND

Richmond was probably the most important city in the South during the Civil War, and was therefore a prime military target. The key sites are preserved by the **Richmond**

National Battlefield Park (© 804/226-1981; www.nps.gov/rich), whose visitor center is in the Tredegar Iron Works, Tredegar and 5th streets, at the western end of the city's **Riverfront Canal Walk,** a promenade running along the tow path of the old James River and Kanawha Canal. Rangers can give information on and driving directions to the several Civil War battlefields that lie on the city's eastern suburbs. The **Museum and White House of the Confederacy,** 1201 E. Clay St. (© **804/649-1861;** www.moc.org), houses the largest collection of Confederate objects in the country, many of them contributed by veterans and their descendants. Both the White House and museum are open Monday through Saturday from 10am to 5pm and Sunday from noon to 5pm. A combined ticket for the museum and White House is $10 adults, $9 seniors, and $5 children 7 to 18.

But Richmond's history goes back even farther than the Civil War. **St. John's Episcopal Church,** 2401 E. Broad St. (© **804/648-5015;** www.historicstjohnschurch.org), dates from 1741 and was the site of the second Virginia Convention in 1775, with Thomas Jefferson, George Washington, and Richard Henry Lee in attendance. In support of a bill to assemble and train a militia to oppose Great Britain, Patrick Henry stood up and delivered his famous speech: "I know not what course others may take, but as for me, give me liberty or give me death!" Admission is free, but 20-minute tours are available for $5 adults, $4 seniors, and $3 children 7 to 18. Tours run Monday through Saturday from 10am to 3:30pm and Sunday from 1 to 3:30pm.

Designed by Thomas Jefferson, the **Virginia State Capitol,** 9th and Grace streets (© **804/698-1788;** http://legis.state.va.us), has been in continuous use since 1788. Jefferson modeled it on the Maison Carrée, a Roman temple built in Nîmes during the 1st century A.D. Admission is free; 45-minute grounds tours depart continuously Monday through Friday from 9am to 4:30pm, Saturday from 10am to 4:15pm, and Sunday from 12:30 to 4:15pm.

History buffs should also visit the **John Marshall House,** 818 E. Marshall St., at 9th Street (© **804/648-7998;** www.apva.org/marshall), the restored home of the first chief justice of the United States. It's open Tuesday through Saturday from 10am to 4:30pm and Sunday from noon to 5pm. Admission is $10 adults, $7 seniors and students.

A Side Trip to Petersburg

The nearby town of Petersburg, 23 miles south of Richmond on I-95, offers an excellent excursion for history buffs. Petersburg was the site of the siege that ended in the Civil War's last great battle, which resulted in Robert E. Lee's surrender. When you arrive, take Washington Street (Exit 52) west and follow the Petersburg Tour signs to the **visitor center** at 425 Cockade Alley (© **800/368-3595** or 804/733-2400; www.petersburg-va.org), where you can get maps and literature, and buy a block ticket to local museums. The center is open daily from 9am to 5pm.

Petersburg's Old Town holds many interesting historic sights and museums, all within a short walk of the visitor center. Ringing the eastern and southern outskirts of town, the impressive 2,600-acre-plus **Petersburg National Battlefield** (© 804/732-3531; www.nps.gov/pete) preserves the key sites of the protracted siege that ended the war. The battlefield's visitor center is 2½ miles east of downtown on East Washington Street (Va. 36).

In addition, Richmond is home to the **Virginia Museum of Fine Arts,** Boulevard and Grove Avenue (© **804/340-1400;** www.vmfa.state.va.us), noted for the largest public Fabergé collection outside Russia—more than 300 objets d'art created at the turn of the 20th century for czars Alexander III and Nicholas II. Other highlights include the Goya portrait *General Nicholas Guye,* a rare life-size marble statue of Roman emperor Caligula, and Monet's *Iris by the Pond.* The museum is open Wednesday through Sunday from 11am to 5pm; admission is free.

A great place to take the kids is **Paramount's Kings Dominion** (© **804/876-5000;** www.kingsdominion.com), north of the city in Doswell (take I-95 to Va. 30). This family-oriented theme park, one of the most popular in the east, offers a variety of rides and entertainment, mostly based on themes from Paramount movies and TV shows. Check the website for the park's ever-changing hours and admission costs.

WHERE TO STAY

The **Richmond Visitors Center** (see above) operates a free hotel reservation service. Top hotels in Richmond include the magnificent **Jefferson Hotel,** Franklin and Adams streets (© **800/484-8014** or 804/788-8000; www.jefferson-hotel.com), a stunning Beaux Arts sightseeing attraction in its own right (check out the rotunda in the lobby!), which has hosted countless presidents and celebrities over the years. Rates run $265 to $315 double.

Other options include the intimate, upscale **The Berkeley Hotel,** 1200 E. Cary St. (© **888/780-4422** or 804/780-1300; www.berkeleyhotel.com; $190–$675 double); and the more moderately priced **Linden Row Inn,** 100 E. Franklin St. (© **800/348-7424** or 804/783-7000; www.lindenrowinn.com; $99–$149 double), which is comprised of a row of seven small, separate 140-year-old Greek Revival town houses and their garden dependencies.

Chain motels are scattered throughout the suburbs. The Executive Center area, on West Broad Street (U.S. 33/250) at I-64 (Exit 183), about 5 miles west of downtown, is a campuslike area convenient to the major attractions. The best of its hotels is the redwood-and-brick **Sheraton Richmond** (© **800/325-3535** or 804/285-1234).

WHERE TO DINE

East Cary Street between 12th and 15th streets is Richmond's premier dining mecca, with a bevy of good-to-excellent restaurants. Consistently popular with young professionals as a watering hole, **Siné Irish Pub & Restaurant,** 1327 E. Cary St. (© **804/649-7767**), is anything but a typical Irish pub, offering a wide selection of seafood, steaks, and chicken in addition to the usual corned beef and cabbage. In warm weather you can dine and drink on the deck out back. In the Jefferson Hotel downtown, **Lemaire,** 101 W. Franklin St. (© **804/649-2822**), is one of Virginia's finest hotel dining rooms, presenting a French-inspired cuisine that relies heavily on local produce. Up on Church Hill, **Millie's Diner,** 2603 E. Main St. (© **804/643-5512**), looks like the diner it used to be but now serves as a noisy temple of creative cuisine.

For picnic fare, head to **Coppola's Delicatessen,** in the Carytown section at 2900 W. Cary St. (© **804/359-NYNY**), with its aromatic clutter of cheeses, sausages, olives, pickles, and things marinated.

3 Williamsburg & Colonial Virginia

The narrow peninsula between the James and York rivers saw the very beginnings of Colonial America and the rebellion that eventually created the United States. Visitors today can get an extensive history lesson in the beautifully restored 18th-century town of Colonial Williamsburg, see the earliest permanent English settlement in North America at Jamestown, and walk the Yorktown ramparts where Washington decisively defeated Cornwallis, thus turning the colonists' dream of a new nation into a reality.

More than history, however, makes this one of America's family vacation meccas. There's also the Busch Gardens Williamsburg theme park with entertainment and rides, world-class shopping in the factory outlet stores near Williamsburg, and golf on some of Virginia's finest courses.

ESSENTIALS

GETTING THERE   By Plane   Several domestic carriers serve **Newport News/ Williamsburg Airport** (© 757/877-0221; www.nnwairport.com), 14 miles east of Williamsburg. More flights (and certainly more jets) arrive at **Richmond International Airport** (see "Essentials" under "Richmond," above), about 45 miles west of town via I-64.

By Train   Amtrak trains (© 800/USA-RAIL; www.amtrak.com) serve the Transportation Center, 468 N. Boundary St., at Lafayette Street (© 757/229-8750), within walking distance of the historic area.

By Car   **I-64** passes Williamsburg on its way between Richmond and Norfolk. For the historic area, take Exit 238 (Va. 143) off I-64 and follow the signs. The **Colonial Parkway,** one of Virginia's most scenic routes, connects Williamsburg to Jamestown and Yorktown (it runs through a tunnel under the Historic Area).

VISITOR INFORMATION   You and a few other million persons who come here every year will begin your visit at the **Colonial Williamsburg Visitor Center,** off the U.S. 60 Bypass, just east of Va. 132 (© **800/HISTORY** or 757/220-7645; www.colonial williamsburg.com). You can't miss it; bright green signs point the way from all access roads to Williamsburg. This is where you buy your tickets for the dozens of attractions that make up Colonial Williamsburg. The center is open daily 9am to 5pm. Parking is free.

The best source for general information about the hotels, restaurants, and activities not operated by the foundation is the **Greater Williamsburg Chamber & Tourism Alliance,** 421 N. Boundary St., Williamsburg, VA 23187 (© **800/368-6511** or 757/ 229-6511; www.visitwilliamsburg.com), open Monday through Friday from 8:30am to 5pm.

GETTING AROUND   Since few cars are allowed into the Historic Area from 8am to 10pm daily, you must park elsewhere. The visitor center has ample parking and operates a **shuttle bus** to and from the Historic Area. It's free for holders of tickets to the Historic Area attractions. There's also a footpath from the visitor center to the Historic Area.

The easiest way to get around outside the Historic Area is by public bus service operated by **Williamsburg Area Transport** (© 757/259-4093; www.williamsburg transport.com). Buses run Monday through Saturday, about every hour from 6am to 8pm, to 10pm during the summer months. Fare is $1.25 for adults, 50¢ for seniors, free for children under 6. Exact fare is required. The buses follow U.S. 60 from the Williamsburg Pottery Factory in the west to Busch Gardens Williamsburg in the east, with a detour to the Bypass Road hotels.

The land is flat here, so getting around via bicycle is a great idea. **Bike and stroller rentals** are available from Easter through October at the **Woodlands Hotel & Suites,** at the Colonial Williamsburg Visitor Center (✆ **757/229-1000;** see "Visitor Information," above). For a taxi, call **Yellow Cab** (✆ **757/722-1111**) or **Williamsburg Taxi** (✆ **757/566-3009**).

TICKETS   It costs nothing to stroll the streets of the Historic Area, and perhaps debate revolutionary politics with the actors playing Thomas Jefferson or Patrick Henry. However, you will need a **ticket** to enter the key buildings and all the museums, see the 35-minute orientation film at the visitor center, use the Historic Area shuttle bus, and take a 30-minute Orientation Walk through the restored village (reservations required).

The Colonial Williamsburg Foundation is notorious for frequently changing its system of tickets and passes, so what follows may be outdated by the time you arrive. You should *definitely* call the visitor center or check the Colonial Williamsburg website (www.colonialwilliamsburg.com) for the latest information. With that caveat, this was the pass structure at press time.

A 1-day **Capital City Pass** allows access to many Historic Area attractions, including walking tours and interpretive programs, but not to the Governor's Palace, Bassett Hall, and the museums. It costs $34 for adults, $15 for children 6 to 17, free for children 5 and younger. It is good for the day you buy it, regardless of the time you purchased it.

Much more useful is the **Governor's Key-to-the-City Pass,** which includes everything you're likely to see and is good for 2 consecutive days. It goes for $48 adults, $24 children 6 to 17. You can add a third consecutive day for just $6.

For longer stays, it's worth paying $59 per adult and $29 for children 6 to 17 for a **Freedom Pass,** which is good for 1 year and includes a 50% discount on the nighttime performances.

Tickets are available at the Colonial Williamsburg Visitor Center, a **ticket booth** at the Merchants Square shops on Henry Street at Duke of Gloucester Street, and **Lumber House** on Duke of Gloucester Street opposite the Palace Green.

American Express, Diners Club, MasterCard, and Visa credit cards are accepted at Colonial Williamsburg ticket outlets, attractions, hotels, and taverns.

WHAT TO SEE & DO

In addition to the sights below, look for the numerous 18th-century crafts demonstrations on view throughout the Historic Area. You can stroll the Historic Area streets anytime, but in general, its attractions are open from April to October daily from 9am to 5pm, to 6pm Memorial Day to Labor Day. Some places are closed on specific days, and hours can vary, so check with the visitor center for current information.

THE COLONIAL BUILDINGS

Brush-Everard House   The Brush-Everard House was occupied without interruption from 1717—when Public Armorer and master gunsmith John Brush built it as a residence-cum-shop—to 1946. Its most distinguished owner was Thomas Everard, clerk of York County from 1745 to 1771 and two-time mayor of Williamsburg. Today the home is restored and furnished to its Everard-era appearance. The smokehouse and kitchen out back are original. Special programs here focus on African-American life in the 18th century.

The Capitol   Virginia legislators met in the Capitol at the eastern end of Duke of Gloucester Street from 1704 to 1780. The House of Burgesses became a training

ATTRACTIONS●

Abby Aldrich Rockefeller
Folk Art Museum **10**
Bassett Hall **14**
Brush-Everard House **5**
The Capitol **13**
Carter's Grove **15**
The Courthouse **8**
De Witt Wallace Decorative
Arts Gallery **2**

George Wythe House **3**
Governor's Palace **4**
James Geddy House
& Silversmith Shop **7**
Magazine & Guardhouse **9**
Peyton Randolph House **6**
Public Gaol **12**
Public Hospital **1**
Raleigh Tavern **11**

Waller St.

York St.

Blair St.

Francis St.

Botetourt St.

Colonial St.

Printer &
Post Office

Queen St.

Colonial Parkway

North England St.

Nicholson St.

Market
Square

South England St.

Williamsburg
Lodge

Palace Green

Palace
Bus Stop

Gateway
Bldg.

To Visitor Center ↑

Colonial Parkway

Bruton Parish
Church

Duke of Gloucester St.

Nassau St.

Williamsburg
Inn

Lafayette St.

North Henry St.

Scotland St.

Fife & Drum
Inn

Prince George St.

Merchants

Square

South Henry St.

Governor's
Inn

Amtrak
& Bus
Depot

North Boundary St.

South Boundary St.

Information ⓘ
Pedestrian Mall

Williamsburg
VIRGINIA

1/10 mile

100 meters

ground for patriots and future governors such as George Washington, Thomas Jefferson, Richard Henry Lee, and Patrick Henry. The original Capitol burned down in 1747, was rebuilt in 1753, and succumbed to fire again in 1832. The reconstruction is of the 1704 building, complete with Queen Anne's coat of arms adorning the tower and the Great Union flag flying overhead. You must take a 30-minute **tour** to get inside the Capitol.

The Courthouse An intriguing window on the criminal justice system of Colonial life is offered in the courthouse, which dominates Market Square. An original building, the courthouse was the scene of widely varying proceedings, ranging from dramatic criminal trials to the prosaic issuance of licenses. Visitors can participate in the administration of Colonial justice at the courthouse by sitting on a jury or acting as a defendant.

George Wythe House On the west side of the Palace Green is the elegant restored brick home of George Wythe (pronounced *With*), the first Virginia signer of the Declaration of Independence. On principle, Wythe did not sign the Constitution, however, because it did not contain a bill of rights or antislavery provisions. This house, in which he lived with his second wife, was Washington's headquarters before the siege of Yorktown and Rochambeau's after the surrender of Cornwallis. Open-hearth cooking is demonstrated in the outbuilding.

Governor's Palace This building is a meticulous reconstruction of the Georgian mansion that was the residence and official headquarters of royal governors from 1714 until Lord Dunmore fled before dawn in the face of armed resistance in 1775, thus ending British rule in Virginia. The sumptuous surroundings, nobly proportioned halls and rooms, 10 acres of formal gardens and greens, and vast wine cellars all evoke splendor. **Tours,** given continuously throughout the day, wind up in the gardens, where you can explore at your leisure the elaborate geometric parterres, topiary work, bowling green, pleached *allées,* and a holly maze patterned after the one at Hampton Court. Plan at least 30 minutes to wander the stunning grounds and to visit the kitchen and stable yards.

James Geddy House & Foundry This two-story L-shaped 1762 home (with attached shops) is an original building. Here visitors can see how a comfortably situated middle-class family lived in the 18th century. Unlike the fancier abodes you'll visit, the Geddy House has no wallpaper or oil paintings; a mirror and spinet from England, however, indicate relative affluence. At a foundry on the premises, craftsmen cast silver, pewter, bronze, and brass items at a forge.

Hitting the Beach

A great antidote to an overdose of Colonial history is to head over to **Virginia Beach,** about 60 miles southwest of Williamsburg (take I-64 to I-264 East). Summertime vacationers flock to this resort area to enjoy over 20 miles of unbroken sand and surf, as well as the popular Virginia Marine Science Museum. A great choice for lodging is the **Cavalier Hotel,** oceanfront at 42nd Street, Virginia Beach (© **800/446-8199** or 757/425-8555; www.cavalierhotel.com). All but a few of the major chains are present here too, including Sheraton, Ramada, Comfort Inn, and Holiday Inn (see appendix D for their toll-free numbers).

The Magazine & Guardhouse The magazine is a sturdy octagonal brick building constructed in 1715 to house ammunition and arms for the defense of the British colony. It has survived intact to the present day. Today, the building is stocked with 18th-century equipment—British-made flintlock muskets, cannons and cannonballs, barrels of powder, bayonets, and drums, the latter for communication purposes. Children can join the militia here during the summer.

Peyton Randolph House The Randolphs were one of the most prominent—and wealthy—families in Colonial Virginia. This house (actually two connected homes) dates to 1715. Robertson's Windmill, in back of the house, is a post mill of a type popular in the early 18th century.

The Public Gaol Imprisonment was not the usual punishment for crime in Colonial times, but people awaiting trial (at the Capitol in Williamsburg) and runaway slaves sometimes spent months in the Public Gaol. Beds were rudimentary piles of straw; leg irons, shackles, and chains were used frequently; and the daily diet consisted of "salt beef damaged, and Indian meal." This thick-walled red-brick building served as the Williamsburg city jail until 1910. The building today is restored to its 1720s appearance.

The Public Hospital Opened in 1773, the "Public Hospital for Persons of Insane and Disordered Minds" was America's first "lunatic asylum." On a self-guided tour you'll see a 1773 cell—with a filthy straw-filled mattress on the floor, ragged blanket, and manacles—as well as rooms from later periods.

Raleigh Tavern This most famous of Williamsburg taverns was named for Sir Walter Raleigh. After the Governor's Palace, it was the social and political hub of the town. Regular clients included George Washington and Thomas Jefferson, who met here in 1774 with Patrick Henry, Richard Henry Lee, and Francis Lightfoot Lee to plot revolution.

THE MUSEUMS

Note: Plans were afoot at press time to combine Colonial Williamsburg's two museums—the Abby Aldrich Rockefeller Folk Art Museum and the DeWitt Wallace Decorative Arts Museum—into one facility occupied at present by the Wallace museum. They will maintain their separate identities but collectively will be known as The Museums at Colonial Williamsburg.

Abby Aldrich Rockefeller Folk Art Center This delightful museum—which was scheduled to reopen in a new location in late 2006—contains more than 2,600 folk-art paintings, sculptures, and art objects. The collection includes household ornaments and useful wares, mourning pictures, shop signs, carvings, whittled toys, calligraphic drawings, weavings, quilts, and paintings of scenes from daily life.

Bassett Hall Though Colonial in origin (built 1753–66), Bassett Hall was the mid-1930s residence of Mr. and Mrs. John D. Rockefeller, Jr., and it's been restored and furnished to reflect their era. Much of the furniture is 18th- and 19th-century American in the Chippendale, Federal, and Empire styles. Hundreds of pieces of ceramic and china are on display, as are collections of 18th- and 19th-century American and English glass, Canton enamelware, and folk art. Reservations are required; make them at the Special Programs desk at the visitor center.

DeWitt Wallace Decorative Arts Gallery The Public Hospital serves as entrance to this museum housing some 10,000 17th- to 19th-century English and American decorative art objects. In its galleries, you'll see period furnishings, ceramics, textiles, paintings, prints, silver, pewter, clocks, scientific instruments, mechanical devices, and weapons.

THEME PARK THRILLS

At some point you'll want to take a break from history, especially if you have kids in tow, and there's no better place here than **Busch Gardens Williamsburg,** 1 Busch Gardens Blvd. (© **800/343-9746;** www.buschgardens.com), on U.S. 60 about 3 miles east of the Historic Area. Here you can get a peek at European history, albeit fanciful, in authentically detailed 17th-century hamlets from England, Scotland, France, Germany, and Italy—but little mental effort is required to enjoy all the attractions you'll find here. Each village here has its own shops, crafts demonstrations, restaurants, rides, shows, and other entertainment. The sights are connected by trains pulled by reproductions of European steam locomotives, so you can easily skip around.

Admission and hours vary from year to year and season to season, so call ahead, check the website, or pick up a brochure at the visitor centers. Admission is at least $52 adults, $45 children 3 to 6, free for children under 3. Tickets include unlimited rides, shows, and attractions.

SHOPPING

Duke of Gloucester Street, in the Historic Area, is the center for 18th-century wares created by craftspeople plying the trades of American forefathers. You'll find hand-wrought silver jewelry, hats, hand-woven linens, leather-bound books, gingerbread cakes, and much more.

Don't miss **Craft House,** also run by Colonial Williamsburg, on Duke of Gloucester Street at Henry Street in Merchants Square. Featured at Craft House are exquisite works by master craftspeople and authentic reproductions of Colonial furnishings. There are also reproduction wallpapers, china, toys, games, maps, books, prints, and souvenirs aplenty.

Shopping in the Historic Area is fun, but the biggest merchandising draws are the outlets along **Richmond Road** (U.S. 60) between Williamsburg and Lightfoot, an area 5 to 7 miles west of the Historic Area.

WHERE TO STAY
IN COLONIAL WILLIAMSBURG

The Colonial Williamsburg Foundation operates four hotels in the Historic Area, in all price categories. For advance reservations or information on all four hotels, call the **Visitor Center reservations service** (© **800/447-8679;** www.colonialwilliamsburg. com). You also can make walk-in reservations at the Colonial Williamsburg Visitor Center. Parking at all four properties is free for guests. Another advantage to staying at one of these four hotels is the option to purchase discounted Colonial Williamsburg Hotel Guest Tickets valid for the length of their stay (recently $29 adults, $15 children 6–17).

One of the nation's most distinguished hotels, the rambling white-brick Regency-style **Williamsburg Inn,** at 136 Francis St., has played host to 17 heads of state over its lifetime. All the large accommodations (last renovated in 2001) have marble bathrooms with separate tubs and showers. All are exquisitely furnished with reproductions, books, and photos of famous prior guests. The Regency Dining Room features classic American cuisine (coats and ties required after 6pm) and a view of one of the inn's three top-flight golf courses. Rates in the main inn run $339 to $499 double.

Rooms in a modern building called **Providence Hall,** adjacent to the inn, are furnished in a contemporary blend of 18th-century and Asian style, with balconies or patios. Rates in this building range from $300 to $359. The Inn's fitness center is in Providence Hall. A full-service spa was scheduled to open here in 2006.

Across the street from the Williamsburg Inn, the foundation's second-best hotel, the **Williamsburg Lodge,** South England Street, remains open during extensive renovations that were scheduled for completion by the end of 2006. During the renovation, reception is in a building next to the Williamsburg Inn, and guests are treated to continental breakfast each morning in a hallway of the existing Tazewell Wing, which is being retained. Its rooms have balconies facing landscaped courtyards, which those in the other wings do not. New, more luxurious rooms already have opened in Colonial-style "Guest Houses" between the Tazewell Wing and the main building. The new units are notable for their Colonial Williamsburg–designed furniture and their retro 1930s bathrooms. In the meantime, you can stay here and take advantage of the Williamsburg Inn's facilities. Rates run $179 to $235 double.

The **Williamsburg Woodlands Hotel & Suites,** 105 Visitors Center Dr., is the foundation's newest and third-best hotel. A separate building with a peaked roof and skylights holds the lodgelike lobby, where guests are treated to a free continental breakfast in a room with a fireplace. All of the moderately spacious rooms have Colonial-style pine furniture and photos of the Historic Area on their walls. The more expensive suites have separate living and sleeping rooms divided by the bathroom and a wet bar, fridge, and microwave oven. There's plenty to keep kids occupied here, and when you couple that with the pullout sofa beds in the suites, it's a good choice for families of moderate means. Rates range from $99 to $149 double.

Least expensive of the foundation's hotels, the **Governor's Inn,** 506 Henry St. (Va. 132), at Lafayette Street, is a two- and three-story brick motel surrounded by parking lots. Natural wood furniture brightens the standard motel-style rooms, which have been spiffed up recently. There's a small outdoor pool for cooling off. It's near the visitor center on the northwest edge of the Historic Area. Some rooms are "pet friendly." Rates include a free continental breakfast and run $69 to $109 double. *Note:* The Governor's Inn is near the Transportation Center, which means that trains come by during the night.

The foundation also has 77 rooms in the Historic Area in its **Colonial Houses.** Tastefully furnished with 18th-century antiques and reproductions, they all are variously equipped with canopied beds, kitchens, living rooms, fireplaces, and/or sizable gardens. Many of these are former laundries, workshops, small homes, and stand-alone kitchens that have been converted into one- and two-bedroom bungalows. Others are rooms in taverns, some of which have as many as 16 units. Some rooms are tiny; tell the reservation clerk precisely what size room and what bed configuration you want. Some units are close to Francis Street, whose traffic noise can easily penetrate the non-insulated walls. Rates run $179 to $420 double.

OTHER AREA ACCOMMODATIONS

The area has more than 80 hotels and motels, including many chain options. You should be able to find a room on short notice except during the peak holiday periods.

One of the best of the chain entries is the 151-room **Courtyard By Marriott,** 470 McLaws Circle (© **800/321-2211** or 757/221-0700; www.courtyard.com), which enjoys an attractively landscaped setting of trees and shrubs on the eastern side of town near Busch Gardens. Rates run $119 to $169 double. A family-friendly choice is the 303-room **Crowne Plaza Williamsburg at Fort Magruder,** 6545 Pocahontas Trail (U.S. 60; ℂ **877/227-6963** or 757/220-2250; www.crowneplaza.com), with a convenient location right between the Historic Area and Busch Gardens. Rates run $89 to $169 double.

The **Fife & Drum Inn,** 441 Prince George St. (ℂ **888/838-1783** or 757/345-1776; www.fifeanddruminn.com), is a relaxed and interesting charmer that offers the only privately owned accommodations in the Historic Area. A sky-lit hallway with faux brick floor and clapboard siding leads to the B&B's seven medium-size rooms and two suites, some of which have dormer windows. Smokers need to look elsewhere. Rates include full breakfast and free parking; they run $155 to $175 double.

Nestled in a peaceful setting on beautifully landscaped grounds beside the James River, the luxurious, country-club-like **Kingsmill Resort,** 1010 Kingsmill Rd. (ℂ **800/832-5665** or 757/253-1703; www.kingsmill.com), is one of Virginia's most complete resorts, offering three golf courses (the River Course is the highlight), a sports complex with 15 tennis courts, and the Williamsburg area's only full-service spa. Accommodations consist of standard guest rooms, and one-, two-, and three-bedroom individually decorated suites with full kitchens and fireplaces. Kingsmill's main dining room offers fine cuisine with a terrific view of the James. Guests can take a complimentary shuttle to Colonial Williamsburg and Busch Gardens Williamsburg. Rates run $139 to $299 double.

WHERE TO DINE

The Colonial Williamsburg Foundation runs four popular reconstructed Colonial taverns: **Christiana Campbell's Tavern,** on Waller Street; and **Josiah Chowning's Tavern, Kings Arms Tavern,** and **Shields Tavern,** all on Duke of Gloucester Street. All are reconstructed 18th-century *ordinaries,* or taverns, and aim at authenticity in fare, ambience, and costuming of the staff. Although relatively expensive, dinner at one of the taverns is a necessary ingredient of the Williamsburg experience. Advance reservations for dinner at the taverns are essential during the summer and on spring and fall weekends. Except at Josiah Chowning's Tavern, which does not accept reservations, you can book tables up to 60 days in advance by dropping by or calling the visitor center (ℂ **800/TAVERNS** or 757/229-2141). Lunch reservations are only accepted for major holidays.

There are benches throughout the restored area (lots of grass, too) if you feel like a picnic, and if you have a car you can drive to nearby scenic overlooks along Colonial Parkway (the parking areas along the James and York rivers are best, but they don't have picnic tables or other facilities). **The Cheese Shop,** 424 Prince George St., in Merchants Square (ℂ **757/220-0298**), is a good place to purchase takeout sandwiches and other fixings.

Berret's Seafood Restaurant & Tap House Grill, 199 S. Boundary St., at Francis Street (ℂ **757/253-1847;** www.berrets.com), is a congenial, casual place, with a dining room that features Canvas sailcloth shades, blue-trimmed china, and marine artifacts—an appropriate backdrop for excellent seafood. The Tap House is the best place in town to slake a thirst after schlepping around the Historic Area all day and also serves light fare. Main courses in the main dining room cost $22 to $30.

Executive chef Marcel Desaulniers has brought national recognition to **The Trellis,** Duke of Gloucester Street between Henry and Boundary streets (ℂ **757/229-8610;** www.thetrellis.com), whose decor evokes California's wine country. The menu changes seasonally and combines the best in foods from different regions of the United States.

If it's offered, try the exciting combination of grilled fish, thinly sliced Virginia country ham, pine nuts, and zinfandel-soaked raisins. And don't skip the sinful Death by Chocolate for dessert. If the weather is fine, you might dine alfresco on the planter-bordered brick terrace. Main courses cost $16 to $32; a complete, fixed-price dinner for $28 is a steal.

One of the great places to sample traditional, down-home Virginia cooking, the **Old Chickahominy House,** 1211 Jamestown Rd., at Va. 199 (© 757/229-4689), is a reconstructed 18th-century house with mantels from old Gloucester homes and wainscoting from Carter's Grove. The entire effect is extremely cozy and charming, from the rocking chairs on the front porch to the blazing fireplaces within. This is the best place in town for hearty southern plantation food. It's open only for breakfast and lunch; main courses run $3 to $8.50.

A SIDE TRIP TO JAMESTOWN

You are in for a treat if you are traveling to Virginia in 2007, the 400th birthday of Jamestown, the first permanent English-speaking colony in North America. Plans were still in the works when we went to press, but you can be sure there will be some big bashes in this region, known as "the Peninsula."

Except for the partial remains of a brick church, little remains of the riverside settlement. But its story is documented here in museum exhibits and living-history interpretations. Archaeologists have excavated more than 100 building frames, evidence of manufacturing ventures (pottery, winemaking, brick making, and glass blowing), early wells, and old roads, as well as scores of artifacts of everyday life.

Allow a full day for your visit and consider packing a lunch. Other than a cafe at Jamestown Settlement, there are no restaurants, so you may want to take advantage of the picnic areas at the National Park Service site.

GETTING THERE   The scenic way here from Williamsburg is via the picturesque Colonial Parkway, or you can take Jamestown Road (Va. 31).

HISTORIC JAMESTOWNE

Jointly administered by the National Park Service and the Association for the Preservation of Virginia Antiquities (APVA; www.apva.org), **Historic Jamestowne** (© 757/898-2410 or 757/229-1773; www.nps.gov/colo) is the site of the actual colony. It was an island then; now an isthmus separates it from the mainland. At the Ranger Station entrance gate, you'll pay $8 for each person over 15 years old; admission is good for 7 days. You can buy a joint Jamestown–Yorktown Passport for $10 per person over 15, which will admit you for 7 days both here and to the Yorktown National Battlefield (see "A Side Trip to Yorktown," below). The gate is open daily from 8:30am to 4:30pm in summer. You can stay on the grounds until dusk.

After entering the park, stop first at the reconstructed **Glasshouse,** where costumed interpreters make glass in the ancient way used by the colonists in 1608 during their first attempt to create an industry (it failed). Then stop in at the **visitor center** before following the footpaths to the actual site of **"James Cittie,"** where rubbly brick foundations of 17th-century homes, taverns, shops, and statehouses are enhanced by artists' renderings, text, and audio stations. A fascinating **5-mile loop drive** begins at the visitor center parking lot and winds through 1,500 wilderness acres of woodland and marsh that have been allowed to return to their natural state in order to approximate the landscape as 17th-century settlers found it. Illustrative markers interpret aspects of daily activities and industries of the colonists—tobacco growing, lumbering, silk and wine production, pottery making, farming, and so on.

JAMESTOWN SETTLEMENT

Operated by the Commonwealth of Virginia, **Jamestown Settlement** (© **888/593-4682** or 757/253-4838; www.historyisfun.org), an indoor/outdoor museum, is open daily from 9am to 5pm (until 6pm June 15–Aug 15). Built in 1957 to celebrate Jamestown's 350th anniversary, this living history will be a major focus of the 400th anniversary events in 2007, beginning with "The World of 1607," a major exhibit featuring rare treasures of the time. Admission is $12 adults, $5.75 children 6 to 12, free for children under 6; or you can buy a combination ticket with Yorktown Victory Center (see "A Side Trip to Yorktown," below) for $17 adults, $8.25 children 6 to 12, free for kids under 6.

After purchasing tickets, you can watch a 15-minute film that gives you an introduction to Jamestown. Beyond the theater, three large permanent galleries feature artifacts and dioramas relating to the Jamestown period. Leaving the museum complex, you'll come directly into the **Powhatan Indian Village,** representing the culture and technology of a highly organized chiefdom of 32 tribes that inhabited coastal Virginia in the early 17th century. There are several mat-covered lodges, or longhouses, which are furnished as dwellings, as well as a garden and a ceremonial dance circle. Historical interpreters tend gardens, tan animal hides, and make bone and stone tools and pottery. Triangular **James Fort** is a re-creation of the one constructed by the Jamestown colonists on their arrival in the spring of 1607. Interpreters are engaged in activities typical of early-17th-century life, such as agriculture, animal care, carpentry, blacksmithing, and meal preparation. A short walk from James Fort are reproductions of the three **ships,** the *Susan Constant, Godspeed,* and *Discovery,* which transported 104 colonists to Virginia in 1607. *Tip:* Exhibits here are hands-on and interactive, making them more enjoyable for kids than those at Historic Jamestowne.

A SIDE TRIP TO YORKTOWN

Yorktown, the setting for the last major battle of the American Revolution, is about 14 miles northeast of Williamsburg. Today, the battlefield is a national park, and the Commonwealth of Virginia has built an interpretive museum explaining the road to revolution, the war itself, and the building of a new nation afterward. The old town of Yorktown itself is also worth seeing. For lunch, consider a picnic in a large tree-shaded area at the Victory Center or at a riverside picnic area with tables and grills on Water Street at the foot of Comte de Grasse Street.

GETTING THERE   From Williamsburg, drive to the eastern end of the Colonial Parkway. From Norfolk, take I-64 West to U.S. 17 North.

YORKTOWN NATIONAL BATTLEFIELD

The **National Park Service Visitor Center** (© **757/898-2410** or 757/898-3400; www.nps.gov/colo) displays Washington's actual military headquarters tent, a replica (which you can board and explore) of the quarterdeck of HMS *Charon,* additional objects recovered from the York River in the excavations, exhibits about Cornwallis's surrender and the events leading up to it, and dioramas detailing the siege. Upstairs, an "on-the-scene" account of the Battle of Yorktown is given by a 13-year-old soldier in the Revolutionary army, his taped narrative accompanied by a sound-and-light show. National Park Service rangers are on hand to answer questions; they also give **free tours** of the British inner defense line.

The Park Service visitor center is the starting point for the 7-mile **Battlefield route** and the 10-mile **Encampment route** auto tours of the battlefield. You'll be given a map indicating both routes and detailing major sites. At each stop there are explanatory historical markers (sometimes taped narratives as well), but for the most interesting experience, rent a cassette player and tape at the visitor center. If you can do only one, make it the Battlefield route.

The center is open daily from 9am to 5pm, with extended hours from spring to fall. Admission is $5 per person age 16 and older, good for 7 days. Or you can buy a joint Jamestown–Yorktown Passport for $10 per person age 16 and older, which will admit you for 7 days here and at Jamestown Island. Audiotape tours cost $4; audio CD tours cost $5. National Park Service passports are accepted.

YORKTOWN VICTORY CENTRE
Set on 21 acres overlooking part of the battlefield of 1781, the state-owned **Yorktown Victory Center** (© **888/593-4682** or 757/253-4838; www.historyisfun.org) offers an excellent orientation to Yorktown, including a film, a living-history program, and museum exhibits. In the outdoor Continental army encampment, costumed interpreters re-create the lives of men and women who took part in the American Revolution. Admission is $8.25 adults, $4 children 6 to 12; **combination tickets** for this site and Jamestown Settlement are also available (see above). It's open daily from 9am to 5pm.

4 The Shenandoah Valley

Native Americans called the 200-mile-long valley in northwestern Virginia *Shenandoah,* meaning "Daughter of the Stars." Today the Shenandoah National Park offers spectacular landscapes and a plethora of hiking and riding trails, and protects the beauty and peace of the Blue Ridge Mountains along the eastern boundary of the valley. Along the Blue Ridge crest, the 105-mile-long Skyline Drive—one of America's great scenic drives—runs the full length of the park and connects directly with the Blue Ridge Parkway, which continues south into North Carolina. Pioneers moved west from the Tidewater in the early 1700s to found picturesque small towns on the rolling valley floor, which was later to play a major role in the Civil War.

SHENANDOAH NATIONAL PARK
Running for 105 miles down the spine of the Blue Ridge Mountains, Shenandoah National Park is a haven for plants and wildlife. Although long and skinny, the park encompasses some 300 square miles of mountains, forests, waterfalls, and rock formations. It has more than 60 mountain peaks higher than 2,000 feet, with Hawksbill and Stony Man exceeding 4,000 feet. From overlooks along the road through the park, called the Skyline Drive, you can see many of the park's wonders and enjoy panoramic views over the Piedmont to the east and the Shenandoah Valley to the west. The drive gives you access to the park's visitor facilities and to more than 500 miles of glorious hiking and horse trails, including the Appalachian Trail. Animals such as deer, bear, bobcat, and turkey live here; the park also boasts more than 100 species of trees.

ESSENTIALS
ENTRANCES & ORIENTATION   The park and its Skyline Drive have four entrances. Northernmost is at **Front Royal** on U.S. 340 near the junction of I-81 and

I-66, about 1 mile south of Front Royal and 90 miles west of Washington, D.C. The two middle entrances are at **Thornton Gap,** 33 miles south of Front Royal on U.S. 211 between Sperryville and Luray, and at **Swift Run Gap,** 68 miles south of Front Royal on U.S. 33 between Standardsville and Elkton. The southern gate is at **Rockfish Gap,** 105 miles south of Front Royal at I-64 and U.S. 250, some 21 miles west of Charlottesville and 18 miles east of Staunton.

The Skyline Drive is marked with **Mile Posts,** starting at zero at the Front Royal entrance and increasing as you go south, with Rockfish Gap on the southern end at Mile 105.

VISITOR INFORMATION   For free information, call or write Superintendent, **Shenandoah National Park,** 3655 U.S. Hwy. 211 East, Luray, VA 22835 (© **540/999-3500;** www.nps.gov/shen). The headquarters is 4 miles west of Thornton Gap and 5 miles east of Luray on U.S. 211. The **Shenandoah National Park Association** (© **540/999-3582;** www.snpbooks.org) is the best source of maps, guidebooks, and other publications about the park's cultural and natural history. It has a bookstore at park headquarters, and many of its publications are available at the visitor centers. Aramark Virginia Sky-Line Co., the park's major concessionaire, maintains an informative website at **www.visitshenandoah.com.**

FEES, REGULATIONS & BACKCOUNTRY PERMITS   Entrance permits good for 7 consecutive days are $10 per car, $5 for each pedestrian or bicyclist. An annual pass ($30) is good for 1 year. Park entrance is free to holders of National Park Service's Golden Eagle ($50), Golden Access (free for U.S. citizens with disabilities), and Golden Age ($10 for U.S. citizens 62 or older) passports.

Speed limit on the Skyline Drive is 35 mph, although given the number of camper vans and rubberneckers creeping along this two-lane road, you'll be lucky to go that fast.

Plants and animals are protected; all hunting is prohibited. Pets must be kept on leashes at all times and are not allowed on some trails. Wood fires are permitted only in fireplaces in developed areas. The Skyline Drive is a great bike route, but neither bicycles nor motor vehicles of any sort are allowed on the trails.

Most of the park is open to backcountry camping. Permits, which are free, are required; get them at the entrance gates, at the visitor centers, or by mail from park headquarters (see "Visitor Information," above). Campers are required to leave no trace of their presence. No permits are necessary for backcountry hiking, but the same "no-trace" rule applies.

VISITOR CENTERS   There are two park visitor centers, **Dickey Ridge Visitor Center,** at Mile 4.6, and **Byrd Visitor Center,** at Mile 51 in Big Meadows. Both are open daily 8:30am to 5pm mid-April through October (to 6pm July 4 to Labor Day) and on an intermittent schedule through Thanksgiving weekend in late November. Both provide information, maps of nearby hiking trails, interpretive exhibits, films, slide shows, and nature walks.

In addition, the privately run **Rockfish Gap Information Center,** on U.S. 211 outside the park's southern gate (© **540/943-5187**), has a terrific room-size topographical map of the region. It's open daily from 9am to 5pm except Thanksgiving and Christmas.

SEASONS   The park is most popular from mid- to late October, when the fall foliage peaks and weekend traffic on the Skyline Drive can be bumper-to-bumper. Days also tend to be clearer in fall than in summer, when lingering haze can obscure the views. In spring, the green of leafing trees moves up the ridge at the rate of about 100 feet a day. Wildflowers begin to bloom in April, and by late May the azaleas are brilliant and the dogwood is putting on a show. Nesting birds abound, and the normally modest waterfalls are at their highest during spring, when warm rains melt the highland snows. You'll find the clearest views across the distant mountains during winter, but many facilities are closed then, and snow and ice can shut down the Skyline Drive. Also, parts of the drive are closed at night during Virginia's hunting season from mid-November to early January.

SEEING THE HIGHLIGHTS

Unless you're caught in heavy traffic on fall foliage weekends, you can drive the entire length of the **Skyline Drive** in about 3 hours without stopping. But why rush? Give yourself at least a day for this drive and its 75 designated scenic overlooks. Better yet, get out of your car and take at least a short hike down one of the hollows to a waterfall.

If you have only a day, head directly to the **Central District** between Thornton Gap and Swift Run Gap, the most developed but also most interesting part of the park. It has the highest mountains, the best views, nearly half of the park's 500 miles of hiking trails, and the park's only stables and overnight accommodations. Most visitors make Big Meadows or Skyland their base of operations for stays of more than a day, but if you plan to do this, place your lodge reservations early (see "Where to Camp & Stay," below).

Among the more interesting of the 75 designated overlooks along the drive are the **Shenandoah Valley Overlook** (Mile 2.8), with views west to the Signal Knob of Massanutten Mountain across the south fork of the river; **Range View Overlook** (Mile 17.1; elevation 2,800 ft.), providing fine views of the central section of the park, looking south; **Stony Man Overlook** (Mile 38.6), offering panoramas of Stony Man Cliffs, the valley, and the Alleghenies; **Thoroughfare Mountain Overlook** (Mile 40.5; elevation 3,595 ft.), one of the highest, with views from Hogback Mountain south to cone-shaped Robertson Mountain and the rocky face of Old Rag Mountain; **Old Rag View Overlook** (Mile 46.5), dominated by Old Rag, sitting all by itself in an eastern extremity of the park; **Franklin Cliffs Overlook** (Mile 49), offering a view of the cliffs and the Shenandoah Valley and Massanutten Mountain beyond; and **Big Run Overlook** (Mile 81.2), which looks down on rocky peaks and the largest watershed in the park.

HIKING

The number-one outdoor activity here is hiking. The park's 112 hiking trails total more than 500 miles, varying in length from short walks to a 101-mile segment of the Appalachian Trail running the entire length of the park. Access to the trails is marked along the Skyline Drive. There are parking lots at the major trail heads, but they fill quickly on weekends.

Free maps of many trails are available at the visitor centers, which also sell topographic maps published by the Potomac Appalachian Trail Conference, as well as a one-sheet map of all of the park's walks published by Trails Illustrated. See "Visitor Information," above, for addresses and phone numbers.

Try to take at least one of the short hikes on trails at Dickey Ridge Visitor Center (Mile 4.6), Byrd Visitor Center/Big Meadows (Mile 51), and Loft Mountain (Mile 79.5). There's an excellent 1.6-mile hike at Stony Man (Mile 41.7). The following are a few of the more popular trails:

Limberlost Accessible Trail   At Mile 43 south of Skyland, Limberlost is accessible to visitors in wheelchairs. The 1.3-mile loop runs through an old-growth forest of ancient hemlocks. The trail has a 5-foot-wide, hard-packed surface; crosses a 65-foot bridge; and includes a 150-foot boardwalk.

White Oak Canyon   Beginning at Mile 42.6 just south of Skyland, this steep gorge is the park's scenic gem. The 7.3-mile trail goes through an area of wild beauty, passing no less than six waterfalls and cascades. The upper reaches to the first falls are relatively easy, but farther down the track can be rough and rocky. Total climb is about 2,160 feet, so allow 6 hours.

Dark Hollow Falls   One of the park's most popular hikes is the 1.4-mile walk to Dark Hollow Falls, the closest cascade to the Skyline Drive. The trail begins at Mile 50.7 near the Byrd Visitor Center. Allow 1¼ hours for the round-trip.

Camp Hoover/Mill Prong   Starting at the Milam Gap parking area (Mile 52.8), this 4-mile round-trip hike drops down the Mill Prong to the Rapidan River, where Pres. Herbert Hoover, an avid fisherman, had a camp during his administration (sort of the Camp David of his day). The total climb is 850 feet. Allow 4 hours.

South River Falls   Third-highest in the park, South River Falls drops a total of 83 feet in two stages. From the parking lot at South River Overlook (Mile 62.7), the trail is a moderately easy 2.6 miles round-trip, with a total climb of about 850 feet. Allow 2½ hours.

Access points to the Appalachian Trail are well marked at overlooks along the Skyline Drive. Along the trail, five backcountry shelters for day use each offer only a table, fireplace, pit toilet, and water. The **Potomac Appalachian Trail Club** (© **703/242-0693;** www.patc.net) maintains seven huts and six fully enclosed cabins that can accommodate up to 12 people. Use of the huts is free, but they are intended for long-distance hikers only. Cabins cost $10 to $20 on weekdays, $15 to $40 on weekends, and must be reserved in advance through the park or by contacting PATC Monday through Thursday between 7 and 9pm, Thursday and Friday from noon to 2pm, Eastern time (*only* during these hours).

WHERE TO CAMP & STAY

The park has four campgrounds with tent and trailer sites (but no hookups anywhere): **Big Meadows** (Mile 51.2), **Mathews Arm** (Mile 22.2), **Lewis Mountain** (Mile 57.5), and **Loft Mountain** (Mile 79.5). The latter three are on a first-come, first-served basis at $19 per site per night. They are open from mid-May to late October.

Big Meadows Lodge and **Skyland Lodge** (see below) are the only hotels in the park. They are managed by the park concessionaire, **Aramark Virginia Sky-Line Co.** (© **800/999-4714** or 540/743-5108; www.visitshenandoah.com), which also operates food and other services for park visitors. Lodge reservations should be made well in advance—up to a year ahead for the peak fall season. In addition, cottages are available at Lewis Mountain.

Big Meadows Lodge *(Value)*   Accommodations at Big Meadows, built near a grassy meadow where deer like to graze, consist of rooms in the main lodge and in rustic cabins, and multiunit lodges with suites. Many of them have great views; some have fireplaces and balconies or terraces. You'll have a private bathroom but no other modern amenities in your room. Big Meadows is a major recreational center; many hiking trails start here, and it's also the site of the Byrd Visitor Center. The dining room features traditional regional dishes such as fried chicken and mountain trout. Live entertainment keeps the taproom busy in season.

P.O. Box 727, Luray, VA 22835 (on Skyline Dr. at Mile 51.2). ℂ **800/999-4714** or 540/999-2221. Fax 540/999-2011. www.visitshenandoah.com. 97 units. $67–$130 double main lodge; $85–$121 double motel; $124–$156 suite; $85–$99 cabin. Highest rates charged weekends and Oct. Packages available. AE, DISC, MC, V. Closed Nov to early May. **Amenities:** Restaurant. *In room:* No phone.

Skyland Lodge   Naturalist George Freeman Pollock built Skyland in 1894 as a summer retreat atop the highest point on the Skyline Drive. Encompassing 52 forested acres, the resort offers rustic wood-paneled cabins as well as motel-type accommodations with wonderful views (ask for a room with a view), but no major modern amenities. The central building has a lobby with a huge stone fireplace, seating areas, and a TV. Complete breakfast, lunch, and dinner menus are offered at reasonable prices. There's a fully stocked taproom.

P.O. Box 727, Luray, VA 22835 (on Skyline Dr. at Mile 41.8). ℂ **800/999-4714** or 540/999-2211. Fax 540/999-2231. www.visitshenandoah.com. 177 units. $85–$135 double lodge; $62–$260 double cabin; $119–$184 suite. Highest rates charged weekends and Oct. Packages available. AE, DISC, MC, V. Closed Nov to early May. **Amenities:** Restaurant. *In room:* No phone.

LEXINGTON

A lively college atmosphere prevails in Lexington, which consistently ranks as one of America's best small towns. Fine old homes line tree-shaded streets, among them the house where Stonewall Jackson lived when he taught at Virginia Military Institute (VMI). A beautifully restored downtown looks much like it did in the 1800s. Besides VMI, the town is also home to Washington and Lee University, which has one of the oldest and most beautiful campuses in the country.

ESSENTIALS
GETTING THERE   Lexington lies about 60 miles south and west of the southern end of the Skyline Drive. From Washington, D.C., take I-66 West, then I-81 South. From Richmond, take I-64 West.

VISITOR INFORMATION   The **Lexington & Rockbridge Area Visitor Center,** 106 E. Washington St., Lexington, VA 24450 (ℂ **877/453-9822** or 540/463-3777; www.lexingtonvirginia.com), is a block east of Main Street. It offers museum-like displays about the town's history and distributes free walking-tour brochures (you can park in the center's lot while touring the town). Be sure to see the engrossing slide show on Lexington's history. It's open daily from 8:30am to 6pm June through August, from 9am to 5pm the rest of the year.

WHAT TO SEE & DO
The **Lee Chapel and Museum,** near Letcher Avenue on the Washington and Lee University campus (ℂ **540/458-8768;** http://leechapel.wlu.edu), is a magnificent Victorian-Gothic chapel of brick and native limestone, built in 1867 at the request of General Lee. Lee's remains are in a crypt below the chapel. His office was in the lower level of the building, now part of the chapel museum and preserved just as he left it on September 28, 1870. His beloved horse, Traveller, is buried in a plot outside the office. Admission is free, and it's open Monday to Saturday 9am to 5pm (closes at 4pm Nov–Mar), Sunday 1 to 5pm.

The fine **Virginia Military Institute Museum,** in the basement of Jackson Memorial Hall, VMI Campus (ℂ **540/464-7232;** www.vmi.edu/museum), displays uniforms, weapons, and memorabilia from cadets who attended the college and fought in numerous wars. Of special note is the bullet-pierced raincoat Stonewall Jackson was wearing when accidentally shot by his own men at Chancellorsville, and also, thanks to taxidermy, Jackson's unflappable war horse, Little Sorrel. Admission is free. The museum is open daily 9am to 5pm.

Also on the VMI campus is the **George C. Marshall Museum and Research Library** (© 540/463-7103; www.marshallfoundation.org), with the archives and research library of General of the Army George C. Marshall, a 1901 graduate of VMI who served as army chief of staff during World War II and as secretary of state and secretary of defense under President Truman. He is best remembered for the Marshall Plan, which fostered the economic recovery of Europe after the war. For his role in promoting peace, he became the first career soldier to be awarded the Nobel Peace Prize. In contrast to the many Civil War shrines here, this is an excellent World War II museum. Admission is $3 adults, $2 seniors. The museum is open daily 9am to 5pm.

The **Stonewall Jackson House,** 8 E. Washington St. (between Main and Randolph sts.; © 540/463-2552; www.stonewalljackson.org), is where the legendary Confederate general lived from early 1859 until he answered General Lee's summons to Richmond in 1861. Appropriate period furnishings duplicate the items on the inventory of Jackson's estate made shortly after he died near Chancellorsville in 1863. His body was returned to Lexington and buried in **Stonewall Jackson Memorial Cemetery** on South Main Street. Admission is $6 adults, $3 children 6 to 17. The house is open Monday to Saturday from 9am to 6pm, Sunday 1 to 6pm.

An impressive attraction nearby is the **Natural Bridge** (© 800/533-1410 or 540/291-2121; www.naturalbridgeva.com), a limestone formation that Thomas Jefferson called "the most sublime of nature's works . . . so beautiful an arch, so elevated, so light and springing, as it were, up to heaven." This geological oddity rises 215 feet above Cedar Creek; its span is 90 feet long and spreads at its widest to 150 feet. The Monocan Indian tribes worshiped it as "the bridge of God" (the **Monacan Indian Living History Village** included in your admission price is definitely worth seeing). Today it is also the bridge of man, as U.S. 11 passes over it. The Natural Bridge is now a small tourist-industry enclave, with a cavern, department-store-size souvenir shop, restaurant, hotel, campground, wax museum, and zoo. The bridge is 12 miles south of Lexington on U.S. 11 (take Exit 175 off I-81). Admission to the bridge is $12 for adults, $6 for children 5 to 12.

Lexington's charming 19th-century downtown offers many interesting shops, most of them on Main and Washington streets. **Artists in Cahoots,** in the Alexander-Witherow House, at the corner of Main and Washington (© 540/464-1147), features an outstanding selection of arts and crafts. Antiques hunters will find fascinating browsing at the **Lexington Antique & Craft Mall** (© 540/463-9511), in which 250 dealers occupy 40,000 square feet of space in the Kroger Shopping Center on U.S. 11, about half a mile north of downtown.

The Maury River, which runs through Lexington, provides some of Virginia's best **white-water rafting** and **kayaking,** especially through the Goshen Pass, on Va. 39 northwest of town. The visitor center has information about several put-in spots, or you can rent equipment or go on expeditions on the Maury and James rivers with **James River Basin Canoe Livery** (© 540/261-7334; www.canoevirginia.com).

Two linear parks connect to offer hikers and joggers nearly 10 miles of gorgeous trail between Lexington and Buena Vista, a railroad town 7 miles to the southeast. The

A Side Trip to Warm Springs & Hot Springs

A scenic drive 42 miles from Lexington will bring you to the towns of Warm Springs and Hot Springs, famous for their thermal springs. The most famous are the **Jefferson Pools** (℡ 540/839-5346), which sit in a grove of trees at the intersection of U.S. 220 and Va. 39. Opened in 1761, they're still covered by the octagonal white clapboard bathhouses built in the 19th century, so the only luxuries you'll get are a clean towel and a rudimentary changing room. Use of the pools costs $15 an hour. Reservations aren't taken; just walk in. The pools are open from June to October, daily from 10am to 7pm. Call for winter hours.

In the tiny town of Hot Springs is the acclaimed and pricey **Homestead** (℡ 800/838-1766 or 540/839-1776; www.thehomestead.com; $155–$295 double per person, per night), a famous spa and golf resort that has hosted everyone from FDR to John D. Rockefeller. The Homestead's historic Dining Room is a lush palm court, in which an orchestra performs every evening during six-course dinners. The resort boasts three outstanding golf courses, indoor and outdoor pools, a spa with full health club facilities, 12 tennis courts, hiking trails, horseback and carriage rides, ice-skating on an Olympic-size rink, and much more. *Note:* Nonguests can pay to use all of the Homestead's facilities.

There are several B&B inns in the area as well as the **Roseloe Motel** (℡ 540/839-5373; www.roseloe.netfirms.com; $60–$70 double), an inexpensive, family-run motel on U.S. 220 between Warm Springs and Hot Springs. It's near the **Garth Newel Music Center** (℡ 877/558-1689 or 540/839-5018; www.garthnewel.org), whose summer-long chamber music festival has been drawing critical acclaim since the early 1970s.

For more information, contact the **Bath County Chamber of Commerce** (℡ 800/628-8092 or 540/839-5409; www.discoverbath.com), whose visitor center is 2 miles south of Hot Springs on U.S. 220.

major link is the **Chessie Nature Trail,** which follows an old railroad bed along the Maury River between Lexington and Buena Vista. No vehicles (including bicycles) are allowed, but you can cross-country ski the trail during winter. The Chessie trail connects with a walking path in **Woods Creek Park,** which starts at the Waddell School on Jordan Street and runs down to the banks of the Maury. Both trails are open from dawn to dusk. The visitor center has maps and brochures.

There are excellent hiking, mountain-biking, and horseback-riding trails in the **George Washington National Forest,** which encompasses much of the Blue Ridge Mountains east of Lexington. Small children might not be able to make it, but the rest of the family will enjoy the 3-mile trail up to **Crabtree Falls,** a series of cascades tumbling 1,200 feet down the mountain (the highest waterfall in Virginia). Crabtree Falls is on Va. 56 east of the Blue Ridge Parkway; from Lexington, go north on I-81 to Steeles Tavern (Exit 205), then east on Va. 56.

WHERE TO STAY & DINE

In town and just outside are three lovely and historic country inns: **Alexander-With-row House** and **McCampbell Inn,** both at 11 N. Main St. (rates $60–$140 double); and **Maple Hall,** which lies 6 miles north of town on U.S. 11 (rates $105–$140 double). Make reservations for all three through **Historic Country Inns** (© **877/283-9680** or 540/463-2044; www.lexingtonhistoricinns.com).

Another good lodging choice is the **Hampton Inn Col Alto,** 401 E. Nelson St. (© **800/426-7866** or 540/463-2223; www.hamptoninnlexington.com), situated in an 1827 manor house with 10 bedrooms (rates $180–$255 double) built on a plantation that was then on the outskirts of town. Motel-style rooms are in a new, L-shaped wing next door (rates $90–$139 double).

Lexington has several chain motels, especially at the intersection of U.S. 11 and I-64 (Exit 55), 1½ miles north of downtown. The 100-unit **Best Western Inn at Hunt Ridge,** 25 Willow Springs Rd./Va. 39 (© **800/780-7234** or 540/464-1500; www.bestwestern.com/innathuntridge), is the only full-service hotel among them, offering a restaurant, indoor-outdoor pool, and fine mountain views. Try to get one of its six rooms with balconies. Rates are $100 to $130 double.

While you're walking around town, stop in at Lexington's famous **Sweet Things,** 106 W. Washington St., between Jefferson Street and Lee Avenue (© **540/463-6055**), for a cone or cup of "designer" ice cream or frozen yogurt. For more substantial fare, head to **Willson-Walker House Restaurant,** 30 N. Main St. (between Washington and Henry sts.; © **540/463-3020**), which offers some of the valley's finest cuisine. At lunch, the $5 chef's special includes choice of soup or salad, entree, homemade muffins and rolls, and beverage. Changing seasonally, the dinner menu offers such tempting main courses as potato-crusted North Carolina rainbow trout. The best of Virginia wines are available by the glass or bottle. Main courses run $19 to $27.

5 Atlanta

With its international flavor and something-for-everyone reputation, Atlanta continues to redefine the South. It is the city of Martin Luther King, Jr., father of one of the country's most important social revolutions, and of Ted Turner, who brought the world a revolution of another sort. The dramatic downtown skyline, with its gleaming skyscrapers, is testimony to Atlanta's inability to sit still—even for a minute.

Consistently ranked as one of the best cities in the world in which to do business, Atlanta is third in the nation for the number of Fortune 500 companies headquartered here—16, including Home Depot, United Parcel Service, and Coca-Cola. The metro area is vast and sprawling. With a population of 4.8 million and counting, the only limit to its growth appears to be interminable traffic congestion.

But commerce and development are not the only things that characterize this bustling metropolis. You'll still hear gentle southern accents here, though at least half of Atlanta's citizens were born outside the South, with 1 of every 10 foreign-born. Those transplants, though, find themselves bending to the local customs, waving to strangers, saying "hey" and "ma'am" and holding doors open for each other.

ESSENTIALS

GETTING THERE   By Plane   Hartsfield-Jackson Atlanta International Airport (www.atlanta-airport.com), 10 miles south of downtown, is the world's busiest passenger airport and transfer hub, accommodating 85.9 million passengers a year.

Despite its size, Hartsfield is well planned and easy to negotiate. A recent $5.4-billion expansion has helped to relieve congestion, adding a fifth runway, upgrading the international concourse and terminal, and consolidating rental car terminals. Delta, which is based at Hartsfield, is the major carrier, but most other major domestic and several international airlines serve the airport.

A taxi from the airport to a downtown hotel costs $30 for one passenger, $32 for two, and $10 each for three or more. The ride should take about half an hour. To midtown hotels, the fare is $32 for one passenger, $34 for two or more. To Buckhead hotels, the fare is $38 for one passenger, $40 for two or more. *Warning:* Be sure the taxi driver knows how to get to where you want to go before you leave the airport.

Several of the larger hotels offer free shuttle buses from the airport. **MARTA** (Metropolitan Atlanta Rapid Transit Authority; ✆ **404/848-4711;** www.itsmarta.com) rapid-rail trains run from a station inside the airport weekdays from 5am to 1am and weekends from 6am to midnight, with a one-way fare of $1.75.

By Train Amtrak (✆ **800/USA-RAIL;** www.amtrak.com) serves **Brookwood Station,** 1688 Peachtree Rd., providing daily service from Washington (trip time: 14 hr.), New York (18 hr.), and New Orleans (11 hr.).

By Car Major routes into Atlanta are **I-75** from the northwest (Chattanooga) and south (Miami), **I-85** from the northeast (Charlotte) and southwest (Montgomery, AL), and **I-20** from the east (Columbia, SC) and west (Birmingham, AL).

VISITOR INFORMATION Contact the **Atlanta Convention & Visitors Bureau (ACVB),** 233 Peachtree St. NE, Suite 100, Atlanta, GA 30303 (✆ **404/521-6600;** www.atlanta.net), weekdays from 8:30am to 5:30pm. Once in town, you can visit ACVB information centers at the airport; Underground Atlanta, 65 Upper Alabama St.; the Georgia World Congress Center, 285 International Blvd.; and Lenox Square Shopping Center, 3393 Peachtree Rd.

GETTING AROUND It's possible to reach most major Atlanta sites by transit system (MARTA), but despite the growing problem of traffic jams, a car is preferable.

The **Metropolitan Atlanta Rapid Transit Authority (MARTA;** ✆ **404/848-5000;** www.itsmarta.com) operates subways and buses daily from about 5am to 1am. Regular fare is $1.75. Vending machines for the MARTA Breeze Card and Breeze Ticket passes are located at all stations, and transfers are free. A convenient feature on MARTA's website is a list of popular attractions, followed by the rail stations and buses necessary to get to each spot. Go to **www.itsmarta.com**, click on "Exploring Atlanta," then click on "Popular Destinations."

It's not possible to step outside anywhere and hail a cab. There are, however, always cabs outside the airport, major hotels, Underground Atlanta, and most MARTA stations, except those downtown. Taxis charge a flat rate based on travel between city zones. If you need to call for a taxi, try **Yellow Cab** (✆ **404/521-0200**), **Checker Cab** (✆ **404/351-1111**), or **Buckhead Safety Cab** (✆ **404/233-1152**). *Warning:* Many Atlanta taxis are dirty, mechanically suspect, and operated by drivers not familiar with the city. Be sure the fare is settled before setting off.

FAST FACTS Major downtown hospitals are **Atlanta Medical Center,** 303 Parkway Dr. NE (✆ **404/265-4000;** www.atlantamedcenter.com); and **Grady Memorial Hospital,** 80 Butler St. SE (✆ **404/616-1000;** www.gradyhealthsystem.org). **CVS Pharmacy** has two centrally located pharmacies open 24 hours daily, at 1943 Peachtree Rd. (✆ **404/351-4932;** www.cvs.com), across from Piedmont Hospital

A Note on Area Codes
In metro Atlanta, you must dial the area code (**404, 770,** or **678**) and the seven-digit telephone number, even if you are calling a number within the same area code. It is not, however, necessary to dial "1" before calling a different area code in metro Atlanta.

between downtown and Buckhead; and at 2350 Cheshire Bridge Rd. NE (© **404/ 486-7289**), near Midtown, Buckhead, and Virginia-Highland.

In addition to the 7% city sales tax, there is a 7% hotel and motel tax.

SPECIAL EVENTS & FESTIVALS The second week of January is King Week, honoring the late Rev. Martin Luther King, Jr., an Atlanta native. The week includes a variety of religious services, concerts, speeches, volunteer opportunities, and a parade. For details, contact the **King Center** (© **404/526-8900;** www.theking center.com).

Early February brings the **Southeastern Flower Show** (© **404/351-1074;** www. flowershow.org), followed in mid-April by the **Atlanta Dogwood Festival** (© **404/ 817-6642;** www.dogwood.org). Also beginning in April and running for 7 weekends is the **Georgia Renaissance Festival** (© **770/964-8575;** www.garenfest.com), a re-creation of a 16th-century English country fair with a birds-of-prey show, jousting knights, jugglers, giant stilt-walkers, minstrels, and magicians.

WHAT TO SEE & DO
Atlanta Botanical Garden This delightful garden, occupying 30 acres in Piedmont Park, includes a tranquil moon-gated Japanese garden, a rose garden, a fern glade, an orchid center, a camellia garden, a children's garden featuring a three-story treehouse, gurgling streams, beautiful statuary, and more. The Fuqua Conservatory houses rare and endangered tropical and desert plants—and a fascinating exhibit of carnivorous plants and poisonous dart frogs. Allow 2 to 3 hours.

1345 Piedmont Ave. NE (in Piedmont Park at Piedmont Ave. and The Prado). © **404/876-5859.** www.atlantabotanical garden.org. Admission $12 adults, $9 seniors, $7 students, free for children under 3. Tues–Sun 9am–7pm (until 5pm during daylight saving time); open same hours on holiday Mon. Closed Thanksgiving, Christmas, and New Year's Day.

Atlanta History Center From the prehistory of the area that became Atlanta to the present, it's all here in vivid display in this vast museum. In addition to traveling exhibits, permanent exhibits focus on the Civil War, folk art, golf legend and Atlanta native Bobby Jones, and the Atlanta Braves baseball team. On the grounds is recently renovated Swan House and Gardens, the finest residential design of architect Philip Trammel Schutze. This classical home—listed on the National Register of Historic Places—was constructed in 1928 by the Edward H. Inman family, heirs to a cotton fortune. Also on the grounds is a "plantation plain" home built around 1840, the Tullie Smith Farm. Here you can see how most Georgia farmers really lived. The grounds include two children's playhouses and 33 acres of gardens and nature trails. Allow 2 to 3 hours.

130 W. Paces Ferry Rd. (at Slaton Dr.). © **404/814-4000.** www.atlhist.org. Admission $15 adults, $12 seniors and students 13 and up, $10 children 4–12, free for children under 3. Mon–Sat 10am–5:30pm; Sun noon–5:30pm. Ticket sales stop at 4:30pm. MARTA: Lenox or Arts Center; then bus 23 to Peachtree St. and W. Paces Ferry Rd., then a 3-block walk.

Birth Home of Martin Luther King, Jr.   This Queen Anne–style house is where King was born on January 15, 1929. He was the eldest son of a Baptist minister and music teacher. The future civil rights leader lived at this modest house until he was 12. It has been restored to its appearance when young Martin lived here. A great deal of King memorabilia is displayed. *Note:* In summer, tickets to the house often run out because of the crowds. Plan to visit the nearby Ebenezer Baptist Church and Martin Luther King, Jr., Center for Nonviolent Social Change while you're here. For all, allow 2 to 3 hours.

501 Auburn Ave. 🕐 404/331-6922. www.nps.gov/malu. Free admission (obtain tickets at 449 Auburn Ave.). Daily 9am–5pm (mid-June to mid-Aug until 6pm). Closed major holidays. MARTA: King Memorial or Five Points, then bus 3 to Auburn Ave.

Centennial Olympic Park   This is a living monument to the 1996 Olympic Summer Games. A 21-acre swath of green space and bricks, the park was carved out of a blighted downtown area. It's an oasis of rolling lawns crisscrossed by brick pathways and punctuated by artwork, rock gardens, pools, and fountains, and it often hosts festivals, artists' markets, concerts, and other performances. The best part of the park is the fountain in the shape of five interlocking Olympic Rings. If you're here in summer, you and the kids can frolic in the fountain. Allow 1 hour.

Andrew Young International Blvd. NW at Techwood Dr. 🕐 404/222-PARK. www.centennialpark.com. Free admission. Daily 7am–11pm. MARTA: Philips Arena/Come/GWCC station, then walk 1 block (past CNN Center).

CNN Center   This building anchors the city's dynamic entertainment, news, sports, and business core and is adjacent to the Georgia Dome and the Georgia World Congress Center and near the Georgia Aquarium and Centennial Olympic Park. It houses the CNN, Headline News, and CNN International studios and offers guided, 50-minute tours of these facilities daily. *Note:* Reservations are highly recommended, and should be made at least 1 day in advance. Allow 2 hours.

One CNN Center (Marietta St. at Techwood Dr.). 🕐 877/4CNN-TOUR. www.cnn.com/tour/atlanta. Admission $12 adults, $11 seniors, $9 children 4–18. **Note:** Children under 4 not permitted. Tours daily every 10 min. 9am–5pm. MARTA: Philips Arena/Dome/GWCC station.

Cyclorama   For a panorama of the Battle of Atlanta, go see the world's largest oil painting, a 42-foot-high, 356-foot-circumference, 1880s painting with a three-dimensional foreground and special lighting, music, and sound effects. When you see the monumental work, you'll know why Union Gen. William Sherman, who burned Atlanta to the ground, said, "War is hell." One of only three cycloramas in the United States, it's an artistic and historical treasure that many visitors to Atlanta miss, erroneously thinking it's "strictly for kids." Allow 1 hour.

800 Cherokee Ave. in Grant Park. 🕐 404/624-1071. www.webguide.com/cyclorama.html. Admission $7 adults, $6 seniors, $5 children 6–12, free for children under 6. Daily 9:20am–4:30pm. Closed major holidays. Shows begin every half-hour, starting at 9:30am. MARTA: Five Points; then bus 97 (Grant Park). Zoo Atlanta is next door.

Ebenezer Baptist Church   From 1960 to 1968, this Gothic Revival–style church, founded in 1886 and completed in 1922, became a center of world attention. Martin Luther King, Jr., served as co-pastor of the church during the civil rights struggle. Martin Luther King, Sr., a civil rights leader before his son, was the pastor. A taped historical message and a 10-minute guided tour are available. Most church services are now conducted in a modern annex across the street. While here, visit the nearby Martin Luther King, Jr., Center for Nonviolent Social Change and the King Birth Home. Allow 2 to 3 hours total.

407 Auburn Ave. NE. © 404/688-7263. www.nps.gov/malu. Free admission (donations appreciated). Mon–Sat 9am–5pm; Sun 1–5pm; until 6pm during summer months. MARTA: King Memorial Station, then a long, 8-block walk; or Five Points, then bus 3 to Auburn Ave.

Fernbank Museum of Natural History   This is the largest natural science museum in the Southeast, a $43-million complex featuring "Giants of the Mesozoic," which includes skeletons of the world's largest meat- and plant-eating dinosaurs. It was recently gifted with a priceless collection of over one million artifacts that retell the story of human habitation in Georgia as it unfolded on St. Catherine's Island, the best-understood aboriginal landscape in the American Southeast. In addition to other permanent and rotating exhibits, the museum has an IMAX Theater with a six-story screen and a cafe with great prices. Allow 2 hours.

767 Clifton Rd. NE (off Ponce de Leon Ave.). © 404/929-6300. www.fernbank.edu. Admission to museum $12 adults, $11 students and seniors, $10 children 3–12, free for under 2. Admission to IMAX Theater $10 adults, $9 students and seniors, $8 children, free for under 2. Combined museum and theater admission $17 adults, $15 seniors and students, $13 children. Mon–Sat 10am–5pm; Sun noon–5pm. IMAX open Fri until 10pm. MARTA: North Ave. station, then bus 2. Ask the driver to drop you at the corner of Clifton Rd. Walk down Clifton; Fernbank Museum is the 1st driveway on the right.

Fox Theatre   This Moorish-Egyptian extravaganza began life as a Shriners' temple. It became a movie theater when movie mogul William Fox threw open its doors to the public. Its exotic lobby was decorated with lush carpeting; in the auditorium itself, a skyscape was transformed to sunrise, sunset, or starry night scenes as the occasion demanded, and a striped Bedouin canopy overhung the balcony. By the 1970s, the Fox was slated for demolition, but Atlantans raised $1.8 million to save their treasured movie palace. Restored to its former glory, it now thrives as a venue for live entertainment. Allow 1 hour.

660 Peachtree St. NE (at Ponce de Leon Ave.). © 404/688-3353. www.foxtheatre.org. Tours $10 adults, $5 students and seniors. The Atlanta Preservation Center conducts walking tours of the Fox Theatre and surrounding area Mon and Wed–Thurs 10am, Sat 10 and 11am. Meet in Fox Theatre arcade for tickets and tour. Tours can be canceled based on production/performance schedules. MARTA: North Ave., then walk 2 blocks east.

Georgia Aquarium *Kids*   Opened to constant massive crowds in late 2005, Atlanta is abuzz about the world's largest aquarium, boasting 8 million gallons of fresh and marine water, and more than 100,000 animals representing 500 species from around the globe. The aquarium includes five stunning exhibits—Cold Water Quest, Georgia Explorer, Ocean Voyager, River Scout, and Tropical Diver—each featuring inhabitants of those environments. Crowds have been so big that tickets are issued based on your preferred time to enter the aquarium. The 4-D Theater features 3-D film, live action, and interactive seats. For an additional $50 above general admission, visitors can experience an hour-long behind-the-scenes tour. Advanced booking online is highly recommended. The on-site Café Aquaria features burgers, sandwiches, and pizza.

225 Baker St. © 404/581-4000. www.georgiaaquarium.org. Admission $23 adults, $20 seniors, $17 children ages 3–12; 4-D Theater $5.50 adults, $4 children ages 3–12. Daily 9am–6pm; open certain dates until 8pm; spring and summer open 8am. MARTA: Omni/Dome/GWCC.

High Museum of Art   Having just undergone an impressive $85-million expansion project, this dazzling white porcelain-tiled building has an equally pristine white interior that houses four floors of galleries featuring more than 10,000 pieces. Among them is a significant group of 19th- and 20th-century American paintings that feature work of the Hudson River School. There's also an extensive sub-Saharan African art collection and the Virginia Carroll Crawford Collection of American Decorative Arts, covering changing tastes from 1825 to 1917. Friday Jazz is held the third Friday of each month from 5 to 10pm. An unprecedented Louvre exhibit will run fall 2006 to fall 2009. Allow 2 hours.

1280 Peachtree St. NE, at 16th St., part of the Woodruff Arts Center. 𝄢 404/733-4400. www.high.org. Admission $15 adults, $12 seniors and students, $10 children 6–17, free for children under 6. Tues–Sat 10am–5pm (until 8pm Thurs); Sun noon–5pm. MARTA: Arts Center.

Jimmy Carter Library and Museum

Set on 35 acres of gardens, lakes, and waterfalls 2 miles east of the center of downtown Atlanta, the library-museum is part of the Carter Presidential Center. The library-museum houses Carter's Nobel Peace Prize as well as millions of documents, photographs, and videotapes from Jimmy Carter's White House years. You'll see an exact replica of the Oval Office during Carter's presidency, enhanced by a recording of Carter speaking about his experiences in that office. Allow 1 to 2 hours.

441 Freedom Pkwy. 𝄢 404/865-7100. www.jimmycarterlibrary.org. Admission $8 adults, $6 seniors, military, and students, free for children 16 and under. Mon–Sat 9am–4:45pm; Sun noon–4:45pm. MARTA: Five Points station, then bus 16 Noble.

Margaret Mitchell House and Museum

Restoration has saved the Tudor Revival apartment house (the birthplace of *Gone With the Wind*) where Margaret Mitchell, who called the place "The Dump," wrote most of her epic novel and lived from 1925 to 1932. Tours, which last about an hour, feature a 17-minute film, a visit to the apartment, and an exhibit that celebrates Mitchell's life and examines the impact of her book and the subsequent movie. A museum shop offers all things *Gone With the Wind*. Allow 1 to 2 hours.

999 Peachtree St. (at 10th St.). 𝄢 404/249-7015. www.gwtw.org. Admission $12 adults, $9 seniors and students, $5 children 6–17, free for children under 6. Daily 9:30am–5pm. MARTA: Midtown station.

Martin Luther King, Jr., Center for Nonviolent Social Change *(Best*

The Nobel Prize winner's commitment to nonviolent social change lives on at this memorial and educational center. The self-guided tour includes the Freedom Hall complex, and several related sites nearby: Ebenezer Baptist Church, the King Birth Home, and the National Park Service Visitor's Center. The Freedom Hall portion includes memorabilia of King and the civil rights movement, including his Bible and clerical robe, a handwritten sermon, a photographic essay on his life and work, and, on a grim note, the suit he was wearing when a deranged woman stabbed him in New York City, as well as the key to his room at the Lorraine Motel in Memphis, Tennessee, where he was assassinated. In an alcove off the main exhibit area is a video display on King's life and work. There are other exhibits honoring Rosa Parks and Mahatma Gandhi. Outside in Freedom Plaza, Dr. King's white marble crypt rests surrounded by a five-tiered reflecting pool. An eternal flame burns in a small circular pavilion directly in front of the crypt. Allow 2 to 3 hours for all.

449 Auburn Ave. (between Boulevard and Jackson St.). 𝄢 404/524-1956. www.thekingcenter.com. Free admission. Daily 9am–5pm. MARTA: King Memorial or Five Points, then bus 3 to Auburn Ave.

Michael C. Carlos Museum of Emory University

Four human mummies and a wealth of funerary art from ancient Egypt, beautiful objects from the ancient Mediterranean, stunning art from Africa, and pre-Columbian art are among this museum's rich collections. There are also special shows mounted from the museum's vast holdings, including exquisite drawings—some from the 1600s. There's nothing in Georgia to equal this collection. The 1916 Beaux Arts building housing the museum is a National Historic Landmark. Allow 1 to 2 hours.

571 S. Kilgo St. (near the intersection of Oxford and N. Decatur roads on the main quadrangle of campus). (C) 404/ 727-4282. http://carlos.emory.edu. Admission $7. Tues–Sat 10am–5pm; Sun noon–5pm. MARTA: Candler Park or Lindbergh station, then bus 6 Emory; or Avondale or Arts Center station, then bus 36 N. Decatur.

Oakland Cemetery   Margaret Mitchell, author of *Gone With the Wind*, is buried here; perhaps she's swapping stories after dark with the 50,000 Union and Confederate soldiers who share this 88-acre site. The cemetery opened 10 years before the Civil War and has become an outdoor museum of funerary architecture, including classic and Gothic Revival mausoleums. Many other notable Georgians are buried here, including golfing legend Bobby Jones, 25 Atlanta mayors, and 6 Georgia governors. The cemetery, covered with a canopy of old oaks, is actually a beautiful city park. People often bring picnic lunches and eat ham sandwiches among the dead. Allow 1 to 2 hours.

248 Oakland Ave. SE; main entrance at Oakland Ave. and Martin Luther King, Jr., Dr. (C) 404/688-2107. http://oakland cemetery.com. Free admission; self-guided tour maps $1. Daily dawn–dusk. Visitor center Mon–Sat 9am–5pm; Sun 1–5pm. Guided weekend tours Mar–Nov Sat 10am and 2pm, Sun 2pm; Apr–Oct Sat–Sun 6:30pm: $10 adults, $5 children, and $3 seniors. MARTA: King Memorial station.

Stone Mountain Park   The world's largest granite outcropping, carved with a massive monument to the Confederacy, Stone Mountain is the focal point of a recreation area that covers 3,200 acres of lakes and beautiful wooded parkland. Over half a century in the making, Stone Mountain's neoclassical carving (90 ft. high and 190 ft. wide) depicts Confederate leaders Jefferson Davis, Robert E. Lee, and Stonewall Jackson galloping on horseback. Although the best view of the mountain is from below, the vistas from the top are spectacular. Visitors who are part mountain goat can take a walking trail up and down its moss-covered slopes, especially lovely in spring when they're blanketed in wildflowers. From the top, which you can also reach by cable car, you have an incredible view of Atlanta and the Appalachian Mountains. Other major park attractions include **Crossroads,** a re-creation of an 1870s southern village plus a 3-D theater; the **Great Barn,** which offers four stories of children's activities such as rope nets to climb and the chance to play a character in a computer game; the **Stone Mountain Scenic Railroad,** which chugs around the 5-mile base of Stone Mountain and features a staged train robbery; the *Scarlett O'Hara,* a paddle-wheel riverboat that cruises the 363-acre Stone Mountain lake; the **Antique Car and Treasure Museum; the Antebellum Plantation and Farmyard;** a 36-hole golf course; miniature golf; 16 tennis courts built for the 1996 Summer Olympics; and a sandy lakefront beach with water slides, carillon concerts, boating, bicycle rental, fishing, hiking, picnicking, and more. Allow at least 4 hours.

6867 Memorial Dr., Stone Mountain, 16 miles east of downtown on U.S. 78. (C) 800/317-2006. www.stonemountain park.com. $22 adults, $18 children 3–11, free for children under 3. Daily parking pass $8. Year-round gates open 6am–midnight. Major attractions fall and winter 10am–5pm; spring and summer 10am–8pm. MARTA: Train to Avondale station, then bus 120 to Stone Mountain.

The World of Coca-Cola   A three-floor pavilion exhibits memorabilia of what's been called "the world's most popular product," including endorsements by fabled stars of yesterday, ranging from Clark Gable to the Supremes. The pavilion boasts what has to be one of the most innovative outdoor neon signs ever created: an 11-ton extravaganza hanging 18 feet above its entrance. In all, there are more than 1,000 exhibits, including a 1930s soda fountain, complete with a soda jerk. A new facility is currently under construction and is scheduled to open summer 2007. Allow 1 to 2 hours.

55 Martin Luther King, Jr., Dr. SW (at Central Ave., across from Underground Atlanta). © 770/578-4325, ext. 1465. www.woccatlanta.com. Admission $9 adults, $8 seniors, $5 children 4–11, free for children under 6. Mon–Sat 9am–5pm, Sun 11am–5pm; June–Aug Mon–Sat until 6pm. Closed major holidays. MARTA: Five Points station.

SHOPPING

The stamping ground of well-to-do Atlanta, **Buckhead** is the ultimate shopping area, with two major malls and lots of little boutiques, antiques shops, and galleries. Start at the corner of Peachtree and Lenox roads, where two major malls—**Phipps Plaza** (www.phippsplaza.com) and **Lenox Square** (www.lenox-square.com)—face off against each other. If you have more time and are interested in art, antiques, or decorative accessories, head straight to **Bennett Street** (www.buckhead.org/bennettstreet), where you'll find a healthy concentration of stores in a 2-block strip. There are also many shops in the **Buckhead West Village** (www.buckhead.org/westvillage), near the intersection of Peachtree and West Paces Ferry roads, but there are many more establishments up and down Peachtree and scattered along smaller side streets.

The charming area of **Virginia-Highland,** centered on North Highland Avenue between University Drive and Ponce de Leon Avenue, boasts antiques shops, trendy boutiques, and art galleries. There are three major concentrations: on North Highland just south of University Drive; at the intersection of North Highland and Virginia avenues; and just north of Ponce de Leon around St. Charles Place. From one end to the other, it's about 1½ miles, but it's a nice walk and there are cafes where you can stop and take a break. For more info, check out **www.virginiahighland.com**.

An area similar to Virginia-Highland, but a lot funkier and much rougher around the edges, **Little Five Points** (www.l5p.com) is as much a happening as an offbeat shopping area. There are still authentic hippies here and enough young people with wildly colored hair and pierced body parts to give you a '60s flashback. Also in this area, but not nearly as funky, is **Underground Atlanta,** on Alabama Street between Peachtree Street and Central Avenue (© **404/523-2311;** www.underground-atlanta. com). This 12-acre mix of shops, nightclubs, and restaurants is not as vibrant as it was a few years ago, but it still can be fun to browse.

WHERE TO STAY

Many of the hotels are quite full during the business week, but they're usually not sold out on the weekend. Most of the major hotels that cater to business travelers, especially those downtown, offer reduced weekend rates.

Bed & Breakfast Atlanta, 1001 St. Charles Ave., Atlanta, GA 30306 (© **800/967-3224** or 404/875-0525; www.bedandbreakfastatlanta.com), can book you into more than 30 carefully screened homes and inns.

Ansley Inn   This former stately home in the prestigious Ansley Park neighborhood mimics many of the trappings of an exclusive, small-scale European inn. In 1995, nine rooms were added to the back of the house in distinguished style. Those in the front of the house retain a semi-antique flair. Wine and cheese socials are offered 5 to 7pm daily. Full breakfast is served in a formal dining room.

253 15th St. NE (at Lafayette Dr., between Piedmont Ave. and Peachtree St.), Atlanta, GA 30309. © **800/446-5416** or 404/872-9000. Fax 404/892-2318. www.ansleyinn.com. 22 units. $160–$250 double main house; $120–$175 Ansley Wing. Extra person $50, although no extra charge for small children in parent's room. Rates include full southern breakfast. AE, DC, DISC, MC, V. Free parking. MARTA: Arts Center.

Four Seasons Hotel *(Best)* Soaring 19 floors above midtown Atlanta, the Four Seasons has the most attentive and sophisticated staff and the most impressive and dramatic lobby of any hotel in Georgia. Accommodations are as plush as you'd expect from this top-notch chain, each with ultracomfortable chaise longues, deep mattresses, and bathrobes.

75 14th St. (between Peachtree and W. Peachtree sts.), Atlanta, GA 30309. © **800/332-3442** or 404/881-9898. Fax 404/873-4692. www.fourseasons.com/atlanta. 244 units. $445–$475 double; from $750 suite. Children stay free in parent's room. Weekend packages and other special offers often available. AE, DC, DISC, MC, V. Valet parking $26. MARTA: Arts Center. Pets up to 25 lb. accepted at no charge. **Amenities:** Restaurant; indoor pool; health club.

Gaslight Inn This 1913 Craftsman-style house is one of the most appealing B&Bs in Virginia-Highland—not to mention one of the most guest-friendly in the city. The accommodations, especially the suites, are exquisitely decorated; some have four-poster beds, while others have whirlpool tubs. Three of the seven units have full kitchens; the rest have microwaves and refrigerators. The breakfast—named one of the best in the Southeast—is served in the formal dining room or outside on the front porch.

1001 St. Charles Ave. (between Frederica St. and N. Highland Ave.), Atlanta, GA 30306. © **404/875-1001.** Fax 404/876-1001. www.gaslightinn.com. 8 units. $115–$215 double. Rates include breakfast. AE, DC, DISC, MC, V. Free parking. MARTA: North Ave. station, then bus 2 Ponce to Frederica St. *In room:* Fridge, microwave.

Holiday Inn Express and Suites *(Kids)* This is a good choice if you're looking for a great Buckhead location at less than the usual Buckhead price. It's within walking distance of several fine restaurants (Pricci is across the street and the Atlanta Fish Market is a few blocks away), and close to Buckhead nightlife. There's also good shopping in the area, and a park nearby for the kids. Accommodations include spacious one- or two-bedroom suites with queen-size beds, a separate living room, and a full kitchen. The complimentary full breakfast is served buffet-style in a bright room next to the lobby.

505 Pharr Rd. (about a block off Piedmont Rd.), Atlanta, GA 30305. © **888/465-4329** or 404/262-7880. Fax 404/262-3734. www.hiexpress.com. 88 units. $117 1-bedroom suite; $159 2-bedroom suite; $179 trio with 2 bathrooms. Rates include full breakfast. AE, DISC, MC, V. Free parking. MARTA: Bus 5 from Lindbergh Station stops at the corner of Pharr and Piedmont roads, about a block away. **Amenities:** Outdoor pool; exercise room.

Hotel Indigo *(Value)* This fun and funky boutique hotel opened in 2004 in a space that formerly housed the Days Inn Peachtree. Rooms have a welcoming foyer, hardwood floors, and beds with oversize pillows in funky color combinations. Also oversize are the Adirondack lobby chairs, sporting more funky pillows. The spa-style showers are the perfect treat after a long day of sightseeing, but the bathrooms are teeny tiny. Two rooms have bathtubs. This is the most pet-friendly place in town—no weight limit and no fee. The hotel is right across the street from the Fox Theatre, so you can just roll up into bed after attending a performance.

683 Peachtree St. (between Third St. and Ponce de Leon Ave.), Atlanta, GA 30308. © **404/874-9200.** Fax 404/873-4245. www.hotelindigo.com. 139 units. $149 double. Rates may be higher during conventions and special events. AE, DC, DISC, MC, V. Self-parking $18. MARTA: North Ave. **Amenities:** Fitness center.

Ritz-Carlton Atlanta Downtown Atlanta's finest hotel is a bastion of luxury filled with antiques and fine art. The rooms are restful refuges decorated in traditional style, with bay windows, CD players, bathrobes, and fresh flowers. Bathrooms are as large and luxurious as you'd expect. And the service is impeccable—you'll be cosseted as never before.

181 Peachtree St. NE (at Ellis St.), Atlanta, GA 30303. © **800/241-3333** or 404/659-0400. Fax 404/688-0400. www.ritzcarlton.com/hotels/atlanta_downtown. 444 units. From $289 double; $359 club level; $389–$1,500 suite. Rates

include up to 4 people. Weekend packages available. AE, DC, DISC, MC, V. Valet parking $24. MARTA: Peachtree Center. **Amenities:** Restaurant; health club.

Ritz-Carlton Buckhead   A 22-story tower soaring above Buckhead, the elegant Ritz-Carlton has been likened to Claridges in London. Located between Lenox Square and Phipps Plaza, it's a convenient way station for "shop-'til-you-drop" guests, with a lavish afternoon tea to revive your flagging energy. The guest rooms are large, yet manage to feel cozy; amenities include bathrobes, CD players in some rooms, and large bathrooms.

3434 Peachtree Rd. NE (at Lenox Rd.), Atlanta, GA 30326. ℂ **800/241-3333** or 404/237-2700. Fax 404/233-5168. www.ritzcarlton.com/hotels/atlanta_buckhead. 553 units. From $289 double; $359 club level; $389–$1,500 suite. Rates include up to 4 people. Weekend packages available. AE, DC, DISC, MC, V. Valet parking $25; self-parking $15. MARTA: Buckhead or Lenox stations, then a short walk. **Amenities:** 2 restaurants; indoor pool; health club.

Westin Peachtree Plaza   Atlanta's most famous contemporary hotel is also the tallest, with 73 soaring floors. A bank of 18 elevators will carry you to the roof with its revolving restaurant, a grand spectacle for a special evening on the town. The hotel is in tiptop shape. The elegant guest rooms are comfortably large, with all the expected luxuries, including Westin's famous Heavenly Bed, bathrobes, and roomy marble bathrooms. Ask for a room on a higher floor for a more panoramic view.

210 Peachtree St. NW (at International Blvd.), Atlanta, GA 30303. ℂ **800/228-3000** or 404/659-1400. Fax 404/589-7591. www.westin.com. 1,116 units. $209–$289 double; from $325 suite. Children 17 and under stay free in parent's room. AE, DISC, MC, V. Valet parking $22; no self-parking. **Amenities:** 2 restaurants; indoor pool; fitness center.

WHERE TO DINE

Atlanta Fish Market *(Best)* SEAFOOD   This place serves up a great mix of whimsy (there's a three-story copper fish outside the entrance) and really good food. The main dining area has been compared to an old southern train station; the Geechee Crab Lounge manages to be both upscale and comfortable. The seared sea scallops, with crab cake ravioli, asparagus, spinach, and more, are highly recommended. The extensive menu changes daily and you can buy fresh seafood from their market to take home.

265 Pharr Rd. (between Peachtree and Piedmont roads). ℂ **404/262-3165.** www.buckheadrestaurants.com. Reservations recommended. Main courses $11–$26 lunch (served until 3pm), $20–$39 dinner. AE, DC, DISC, MC, V. Mon–Thurs 11:30am–11pm; Fri–Sat 11:30am–midnight; Sun 4–10pm. MARTA: Buckhead.

Bacchanalia INTERNATIONAL   Posh and upscale, this establishment combines a stylish and sought-after restaurant with a boutique-style gourmet food shop. The setting is in a former 1920s meatpacking plant, on an unlikely looking drab commercial stretch at the edge of midtown. Menus change seasonally, but the unusual fruit-and-cheese pairings are hard to resist any time of the year. Wines are offered by the half-bottle.

1198 Howell Mill Rd. ℂ **404/365-0410,** ext. 22. www.starprovisions.com. Reservations recommended. Fixed-price dinner $68. AE, DISC, MC, V. Mon–Sat dinner starts at 6pm. MARTA: 10th St.

Bone's STEAK/SEAFOOD   In an atmosphere one food critic called "boardroom frat house," this is just the place to get that juicy rib-eye steak weighing in at 22 ounces. Fresh Maine lobster is flown in daily, and the corn-fed beef is cut into steaks on the premises. Locals favor cheese grits fritters. A cigar humidor can be brought to your table at your request after dinner.

3130 Piedmont Rd. NE (a half-block past Peachtree Rd.). ℂ **404/237-2663.** Reservations required. Main courses $12–$40 lunch, $25–$40 dinner; all extras a la carte. AE, DISC, MC, V. Mon–Fri 11:30am–2:30pm; Sun–Fri 5:30–10pm; Sat 5:30–11pm. MARTA: Buckhead.

Buckhead Diner AMERICAN   Even though this place sounds like a hash house for truckers, this award-winner is decidedly upscale. A highly theatrical venture, the interior is designed to look like the interior of the famed Orient Express's rail cars, and it has a gleaming stainless-steel exterior adorned with neon. Inside, the fare is contemporary: the veal and wild mushroom meatloaf, for example, or Granny Smith apple pie with a candied pecan crust. Be sure to leave room for the white chocolate banana-cream pie.

3073 Piedmont Rd. (at E. Paces Ferry Rd.). © 404/262-3336. www.buckheadrestaurants.com. Reservations not accepted, but you can call just before you go for "priority seating." Main courses $10–$20 lunch, $18–$24 dinner. AE, DC, DISC, MC, V. Mon–Sat 11am–midnight; Sun 10am–10pm. MARTA: Buckhead.

City Grill AMERICAN   One of Atlanta's most opulent restaurants, City Grill is a mecca for power-lunchers and couples seeking a special night out. The setting is the 1912 Hurt Building (originally a Federal Reserve Bank), with its rotunda lined in marble with a gold-leaf dome. The frequently changing menu incorporates many southern standards such as "Sunday" chicken with oyster dressing, pork loin chop, or quail. A South Georgia dairy farm provides the choices for the nighttime cheese plates. The selection of French and California wines is about as good as Atlanta gets.

50 Hurt Plaza (at Edgewood Ave.). © 404/524-2489. www.greathospitalityrestaurants.com. Reservations strongly recommended. Main courses $9–$19 lunch, $14–$32 dinner. AE, DC, DISC, MC, V. Mon–Fri 11:30am–2pm; Mon–Sat 6–10pm. MARTA: Peachtree Center.

The Colonnade SOUTHERN   An Atlanta favorite since 1927, this friendly joint offers great value, stiff drinks, and an authentic southern-style meat-and-three. Inexpensively priced steaks, chops, seafood, and the inevitable southern fried chicken round out the menu. Don't miss the yeast rolls.

1879 Cheshire Bridge Rd. NE, between Wellborne Dr. and Manchester St. © 404/874-5642. Reservations not accepted. Main courses $8–$10 lunch, slightly higher at dinner. No credit cards, but out-of-town personal checks accepted. Wed–Sat 11:30am–4pm; Mon–Thurs 5–9pm; Fri–Sat 5–10pm; Sun 11:30am–9pm.

Floataway Café COUNTRY FRENCH/ITALIAN   Mediterranean-inspired and innovative, this airy restaurant's menu features top-quality ingredients. Hand-cut pastas are wonderful; locals also rave about the hanger steak with pommes frites, and a salad of beets and avocados topped with a citrus dressing. You really can't get here using MARTA; if the cabdriver pulls up to an old warehouse, don't worry—you're in the right place. Get out and follow the crowd. If the inside is too noisy, move to one of the outdoor tables.

1123 Zonolite Rd. NE (between Briarcliff and Lenox roads, near Emory University). © 404/892-1414. www.star provisions.com. Reservations recommended. Main courses $14–$24. AE, MC, V. Tues–Sat from 6pm.

Horseradish Grill SOUTHERN   This restaurant began life as a country store, then a horse barn, and retains much of that simple style. Eat in the romantic main dining room or on the patio outside. Organic vegetables and wildflowers are grown in a backyard garden, and everything is made from scratch, including the ice cream. The menu is upscale southern, simply prepared. Start with the corn-bread-crusted Georgia mountain trout or jumbo shrimp and grits, and end with the Kentucky oatmeal spice cake topped with caramel ice cream.

4320 Powers Ferry Rd. (at W. Wieuca Rd.). © 404/255-7277. www.horseradishgrill.com. Reservations recommended. Main courses $9–$14 lunch, $22–$25 dinner. AE, DC, DISC, MC, V. Mon–Fri 11:30am–2:30pm; Mon–Thurs 5:30–9pm; Fri–Sat 5–10pm; Sun 5–9pm; Sun brunch 11am–2:30pm. MARTA: Buckhead.

Sotto Sotto TUSCAN   The best and most appealing restaurant in Inman Park occupies a former row of brick-fronted stores built around 1900. We recommend the excellent wood-roasted whole fish or the seafood risotto. A favorite pasta is *tortelli di Michelangelo,* stuffed with minced veal, pork, and chicken, served with brown butter and sage sauce. Portions are generous and the service friendly. Chocolate lovers *must* save room for the chocolate soup. If the wait is too long (and it can be 45 min., even with a reservation), get a Neapolitan pizza at next-door sister restaurant Fritti Fritti. *Note:* The restaurant's name may mean "Hush Hush" in Italian, but the noise level here can climb to unbearable levels. If you're looking for an intimate, romantic meal, head elsewhere.

313 N. Highland Ave. © 404/523-6678. www.sottosottorestaurant.com. Reservations recommended. Main courses $31–$50. AE, DC, MC, V. Mon–Thurs 5:30–11pm; Fri–Sat 5:30pm–midnight.

The Varsity AMERICAN   Some 16,000 people dine daily at this Atlanta institution, 30,000 if there's a home football game at nearby Georgia Tech. This is the world's largest drive-in, opened in 1928. Service is fast both car-side and inside, with seats and stand-up eating counters; the food is good and prices are definitely low. Ordering can be an adventure; counter workers greet you with a rapid-fire, "Whaddya have? Whaddya have?" Hot dogs are called "dawgs," and hamburgers are "steaks." *Tip:* If you want a cheeseburger, be sure to ask for pimento cheese. True, it's a mess, but you've never had anything like it.

For visitors staying closer to Buckhead or Virginia-Highland, there's a **Varsity Jr.** at 185 Lindbergh Dr. (© **404/261-8843**).

61 North Ave. (at Spring St.). © **404/881-1706.** www.thevarsity.com. All burgers and sandwiches under $5. No credit cards. Sun–Thurs 10am–11:30pm; Fri–Sat 10am–12:30am. MARTA: North Ave.

ATLANTA AFTER DARK

The biggest concentration of clubs and bars is in **Buckhead** (near the intersection of Peachtree and E. Paces Ferry roads); in **Virginia-Highland** (at the intersection of Virginia and N. Highland aves., on **North Highland** just north of Ponce de Leon Ave.); in **Little Five Points** (near the intersection of Moreland and Euclid aves.); and downtown near Peachtree Center. The Buckhead scene, for the most part, is like a huge frat party, especially on weekends. (*Warning:* Serious crime, including hit-and-run fatalities and high-profile murders, has risen here in recent years as the club scene grows.) Virginia-Highland is full of professional 20- and 30-somethings. Little Five Points is an eclectic mix of wildly, weirdly dressed folks and neighborhood regulars. Downtown has a large proportion of out-of-town visitors and convention-goers.

To find out what's going on, consult the *Atlanta Journal-Constitution*'s Thursday "Big 'A' List" pullout section. Or pick up a free copy of *Creative Loafing,* available all over town.

THE PERFORMING ARTS   See "What to See & Do," earlier in this section, for details on the Fox Theatre, which hosts all kinds of performances.

The oldest continuously operating ballet company in the United States, the **Atlanta Ballet,** performs in the Fox Theatre (© **404/892-3303;** www.atlantaballet.com).

The Atlanta Symphony Orchestra, Woodruff Arts, 1280 Peachtree St. NE, at 15th Street (© **404/733-5000;** www.atlantasymphony.org), is complemented by the 200-voice Atlanta Symphony Orchestra Chorus, enabling performances of large-scale symphonic/choral works. The season runs from September to May, plus summer concerts in Chastain Park Amphitheatre in Buckhead.

The Alliance Theatre Company, Woodruff Arts (© 404/733-5000; www.alliance theatre.org), is the largest regional theater in the Southeast, but there are many other excellent companies, with performances ranging from experimental to classic. Watch each summer for performances by the **Georgia Shakespeare Festival** (© 404/264-0020; www.gashakespeare.org).

THE CLUB & MUSIC SCENE   Atlanta's club scene is ephemeral; there's a good chance that the packed venue you visited on your last visit has since closed and reopened as something entirely different. Still, there are a few old reliables.

In Buckhead, **Johnny's Hideaway,** 3771 Roswell Rd., 2 blocks north of Piedmont Road (© 404/233-8026; www.johnnyshideaway.com), has been one of Atlanta's top nightspots for more than 2 decades. The music sweeps through the decades, from the big-band era to the '80s, attracting a crowd of all ages. Original owner Johnny Esposito, who retired for health reasons in 1999 and then un-retired due to boredom, opened a new club in June 2002 near his original. His new one, **Johnny's Side Door,** is compared to a 1940s martini bar and is part of the Landmark Diner, 3652 Roswell Rd., in Buckhead (© 404/844-0408). An elegant cocktail lounge/dance club, **Tongue & Groove,** 3055 Peachtree Rd. (© 404/261-2325; www.tongueandgroove online.com), attracts a chic crowd (there's a dress code). The DJ spins dance music with a different theme every night.

On the east side, closer to Emory, **Eddie's Attic,** 515-B N. McDonough St., Decatur (© 404/377-4976; www.eddiesattic.com), is Atlanta's most popular venue for acoustic singer/songwriters. The Indigo Girls, Billy Pilgrim, and Shawn Mullins started their careers here.

In Virginia-Highland, the **Dark Horse Tavern,** 816 N. Highland Ave. (© 404/873-3607; www.darkhorseatlanta.com), is known as the place for young professionals to meet. Those more interested in local bands than romance can visit 10 High Club in the Dark Horse basement.

East Atlanta Village, a newer, rougher version of Little Five Points but farther east at the intersection of Flat Shoals and Glenwood avenues, is home to several clubs featuring independent and underground acts. **The Earl,** 488 Flat Shoals Ave. SE (© 404/522-3950; www.badearl.com); and **Eastside Lounge,** 485 Flat Shoals Ave. (© 404/522-7841; www.eastsidelounge.net), are among the better known.

THE BAR & CAFE SCENE   Atlanta's quintessential sports bar is **Jocks & Jills Midtown,** 112 Tenth St. NE (© 404/873-5405; www.jocks-frankies.com), whose more than 70 TVs will ensure you don't miss a minute of the big game. **Mumbo Jumbo,** 89 Park Place NE, at Woodruff Park (© 404/523-0330), is a restaurant/bar that's the place to see and be seen.

Fadó, 3035 Peachtree Rd. NE, at the corner of Buckhead Avenue, just south of East Paces Ferry Road (© 404/841-0066; www.fadoirishpub.com), is divided into five pub areas: a cottage pub with a peat-burning fireplace, a Victorian pub with dark wood and stained glass, and so on. There's often traditional Irish or Celtic music. It's a good place to watch televised soccer.

Not far from Virginia-Highland and Little Five Points is **Manuel's Tavern,** 602 N. Highland Ave. NE, at North Avenue (© 404/525-3447; www.manuelstavern.com), a regular watering hole for journalists, politicos, cops, students, and writers. Jimmy Carter often drops by with the Secret Service when he's in town. It's lots of fun to watch a Braves game on TV here.

A classic San Francisco–style coffeehouse, the **RedLight Cafe,** 553 W. Amsterdam Ave., between Monroe Drive and Piedmont Park (℗ **404/874-7828;** www.redlight cafe.com), is a cybercafe with tables and comfy sofas, offering a mix of art, music, conversation, and beverages.

6 Savannah

Savannah's free spirit and hint of decadence give it more kinship with Key West or New Orleans than with the Bible Belt down-home interior of Georgia. Savannah—pronounce it with a drawl—conjures up all the clichéd images of the deep South: live oaks dripping with Spanish moss, stately antebellum mansions, and mint juleps sipped on the veranda. Old Savannah is beautifully restored and is the largest urban National Historic Landmark District in the country. *Forrest Gump* first put Savannah on the tourist map, but nothing changed the face of Savannah more than the 1994 publication of John Berendt's *Midnight in the Garden of Good and Evil.* It long ago disappeared from the bestseller lists but is still credited with launching mass tourism to this antebellum city.

ESSENTIALS

GETTING THERE   **By Plane**   **Savannah/Hilton Head International Airport** (℗ **912/964-0514;** www.savannahairport.com) is about 8 miles west of downtown just off I-16. It's served by American, Delta, United, and US Airways, and all major car-rental agencies have desks here. Pre-arranged limousine service to downtown locations (℗ **800/845-5582**) costs about $25. Taxi fare is about $25 for one person and $10 for each extra passenger.

By Train   **Amtrak** (℗ **800/USA-RAIL;** www.amtrak.com) provides service from Charleston (trip time: 1¾ hr.), Washington, D.C. (11 hr.), Jacksonville (2¼ hr.), and Miami (12 hr.) to its station at 2611 Seaboard Coastline Dr., some 4 miles southwest of downtown. Cab fare into the city is around $7.

By Car   Major routes into Savannah are **I-95** from the north (Richmond, Virginia) and south (Jacksonville), and **I-16** from the west (Atlanta).

VISITOR INFORMATION   The **Savannah Information Visitor Center,** 301 Martin Luther King, Jr., Blvd., Savannah, GA 31401 (℗ **912/944-0455;** www.savannah-visit.com), is open Monday through Friday from 8:30am to 5pm and Saturday and Sunday from 9am to 5pm. It offers organized tours and self-guided walking, driving, or bike tours with excellent maps.

GETTING AROUND   The grid-shaped Historic District is best seen on foot; the real point of your visit is to take leisurely strolls with frequent stops in the many squares.

You can reach many points of interest outside the Historic District by bus, but your own wheels will be much more convenient, and they're absolutely essential for sightseeing outside the city proper.

The base rate for taxis is $1.50, with a $1.50 additional charge for each mile. For 24-hour taxi service, call **Yellow Cab Co.** at ℗ **912/236-1133.**

FAST FACTS   There are 24-hour emergency-room services at **Candler General Hospital,** 5353 Reynolds St. (℗ **912/692-6637**), and at the **Memorial Medical Center,** 4700 Waters Ave. (℗ **912/350-8390**). The sales tax rate in Savannah is 6%; lodging sales taxes add an additional 6% to your bill.

Savannah

Savannah River

ACCOMMODATIONS ■
DINING ◆

W. River St.
Factors' Walk
E. River St.
W. Bay St.
E. Bay St.
EMMET PARK
W. Bryan St.
Franklin Square
Ellis Square
Johnson Square
Reynolds Square
Warren Square
Washington Square
E. Bryan St.
W. Congress St.
E. Congress St.
W. Broughton St.
Telfair Mansion & Art Museum
Owens-Thomas House & Musuem
Davenport House Museum
E. Broughton St.
W. State St.
President
Telfair Square
Wright Square
Oglethorpe Square
Columbia Square
Greene Square
E. State St.
Zulby St.
W. York St.
E. York St.
Greyhound Station
W. Oglethorpe Ave.
E. Oglethorpe Ave.
Houston St.
East Broad St.
Visitors Center
Elbert Square
Civic Center
Orleans Square
Chippewa Square
COLONIAL PARK CEMETERY
Crawford Square
W. Hull St.
E. Hull St.
Savannah History Museum
W. Perry St.
E. Perry
Perry La.
St.
W. Liberty St.
E. Liberty St.
Louisville Rd.
To Bonaventure → Cemetery
Green-Meldrim House
Hamilton-Turner House & Ghost House
Price St.
W. Harris St.
Pulaski Square
Madison Square
Lafayette Square
Flannery O'Connor Home
Troup Square
E. Harris St.
W. Charlton St.
Andrew Low House
E. Charlton St.
Whitaker St.
Bull St.
Barnard St.
Jefferson St.
Montgomery St.
Drayton St.
Abercorn St.
Lincoln St.
Habersham St.
W. Jones St.
E. Jones St.
Selma St.
W. Taylor St.
E. Taylor St.
Chatham Square
Monterrey Square
Calhoun Square
Whitfield Square
W. Gordon St.
E. Gordon St.
Mercer House
W. Gaston St.
E. Gaston St.
FORSYTH PARK

ACCOMMODATIONS ■
The Ballastone **10**
Bed and Breakfast Inn **14**
Eliza Thompson House **12**
The Gastonian **15**
Hampton Inn **4**
The Kehoe House **8**
The Marshall House **7**
River Street Inn **3**
17 Hundred 90 **9**

DINING ◆
Clary's Café **13**
45 South at the Pirate's House **5**
Huey's **2**
The Lady and Sons **1**
Mrs. Wilkes' Dining Room **11**
The Olde Pink House Restaurant **6**

★ Atlanta
Savannah ●
GEORGIA

Although it's reasonably safe to explore the Historic and Victorian districts during the day, the situation changes at night. The clubs, bars, and restaurants along the very touristy water riverfront seem reasonably safe, but muggings and robberies are frequently reported in some of the rougher neighborhoods. The usual discretion is always advised.

SPECIAL EVENTS & FESTIVALS   In mid-September, there's the **Savannah Jazz Festival,** featuring national and local jazz and blues legends. Contact Host South at (C) **912/232-2222** or see **www.savannahjazzfestival.org** for details. December is especially festive, with the **Festival of Trees** at the Marriott Riverfront Hotel; **Christmas 1864,** a dramatic re-creation of the Civil War evacuation of Fort Jackson; and the **Annual Holiday Tour of Homes** ((C) **912/236-8362**).

WHAT TO SEE & DO

Virtually every tour group in town offers tours of the *Midnight* sites, many of which are included on their regular agenda. Reactions from readers vary, some complaining that the Berendt book "is a tired cliché," others proclaiming that touring the *Midnight* sites "was the highlight of my visit to Savannah."

One way to see Savannah is by horse-drawn carriage. An authentic antique carriage carries you over cobblestone streets as the coachman spins a tale of the town's history. The 1-hour tour ($20 adults, $10 children 6–12) covers 15 of the city's 20 squares. Reservations are required, so contact **Carriage Tours of Savannah** ((C) **912/236-6756;** www.savannahgeorgia.com/carriagetours).

Old Town Trolley Tours ((C) **912/233-0083;** www.oldtowntrolley.com) operates tours of the Historic District, with pickups at most downtown inns and hotels ($21 adults, $9 children 4–12), as well as a 1½-hour **Haunted History** tour detailing Savannah's ghostly past (and present). Call to reserve for all tours.

Savannah Riverboat Cruises are offered aboard the *Savannah River Queen,* operated by the River Street Riverboat Co., 9 E. River St. ((C) **800/786-6404** or 912/232-6404; www.savannah-riverboat.com). The fare for adults is $18, children $10. More expensive dinner cruises are available, too.

Andrew Low House   After her marriage, Juliette Low lived in this 1848 house, and it was here that she founded the Girl Scouts. She died on the premises in 1927. The classic mid-19th-century house facing Lafayette Square is of stucco over brick with elaborate ironwork, shuttered piazzas, carved woodwork, and crystal chandeliers. William Makepeace Thackeray visited here twice, and Robert E. Lee was entertained at a gala reception in the double parlors in 1870. Guided tours are offered every half-hour.

329 Abercorn St. (C) **912/233-6854.** www.andrewlowhouse.com. Admission $8 adults; $4.50 students, children 6–12, and Girl Scouts; free for children under 6. Mon–Wed and Fri 10am–4:30pm; Sat–Sun noon–4:30pm.

Davenport House Museum   This is where seven determined women started the whole Savannah restoration movement in 1954. They raised $22,500 and purchased the house, saving it from demolition. Constructed between 1815 and 1820 by master builder Isaiah Davenport, this is one of the truly great Federal-style houses in the United States, with delicate ironwork and a handsome elliptical stairway. Give yourself about an hour to explore.

324 E. State St. (C) **912/236-8097.** www.davenporthousemuseum.org. Admission $8 adults, $5 children 6–17, free for children under 6. Mon–Sat 10am–4pm; Sun 1–4pm.

Fort Jackson Georgia's oldest standing fort, with a 9-foot-deep tidal moat around its brick walls, was begun in 1808 and staffed during the War of 1812. It was enlarged and strengthened between 1845 and 1860 and saw its greatest use as headquarters for the Confederate river defenses during the Civil War. Its arched rooms, designed to support the weight of heavy cannons mounted above, hold 13 exhibit areas. Allow 1 hour.

1 Fort Jackson Rd. (about 2½ miles east of Savannah via the Islands Expwy.). ℭ 912/232-3945. www.chsgeorgia.org/jackson. Admission $4.25 adults, $3.75 seniors and children 7–18, free for children under 7. Daily 9am–5pm.

Fort McAllister On the banks of the Great Ogeechee River stood this Confederate earthwork fortification. Constructed from 1861 to 1862, it withstood nearly 2 years of bombardment before it finally fell on December 13, 1864, in a bayonet charge that ended General Sherman's "March to the Sea." There's a visitor center with historical exhibits and also walking trails and campsites. A visit takes 45 minutes.

Richmond Hill, 10 miles southwest on U.S. 17. ℭ 912/727-2339. www.fortmcallister.org. Admission $2.50 adults, $1.50 children. Daily 8am–5pm.

Fort Pulaski It cost $1 million and took 25 tons of brick and 18 years of toil to finish this fortress at the mouth of the Savannah River. Yet this National Monument was captured in just 30 hours by Union forces. Completed in 1847 with walls 7½ feet thick, it was taken by Georgia forces at the beginning of the war. However, on April 11, 1862, defense strategy changed worldwide when Union cannons, firing from more than a mile away on Tybee Island, overcame a masonry fortification. The effectiveness of rifled artillery (firing a bullet-shaped projectile with great accuracy at long range) was clearly demonstrated. The new Union weapon marked the end of the era of masonry fortifications. You can still find shells from 1862 imbedded in the walls. Visits average 45 minutes.

15 miles east of Savannah off U.S. 80 on Cockspur and McQueen islands. ℭ 912/786-5787. www.nps.gov/fopu. Admission $3 adults, free for under 16. Daily 9am–5pm.

Green-Meldrim Home This impressive house was built on Madison Square for cotton merchant Charleston Green, but its moment in history came as the Savannah headquarters of Gen. William Tecumseh Sherman at the end of his 1864 "March to the Sea." It was from this Gothic-style house that the general sent a telegram to President Lincoln, offering him the city as a Christmas gift. Now the Parish House for St. John's Episcopal Church, the house is open to the public. A good look takes 30 minutes.

14 W. Macon St. ℭ 912/233-3845. Admission $5 adults, $3 children. Tues and Thurs–Fri 10am–4pm; Sat 10am–1pm.

Owen-Thomas House & Museum Famed as a place where Lafayette spent the night in 1825, this jewel box of a house evokes the heyday of Savannah's golden age. It was designed in 1816 by English architect William Jay, who instilled in it the grace of Georgian Bath in England and the splendor of Regency London. You can visit the bedchambers, kitchen, drawing and dining rooms, and garden in about 45 minutes.

124 Abercorn St. ℭ 912/233-9743. Admission $8 adults, $7 seniors, $4 students, $2 children 6–12, free for children under 6. Mon noon–5pm; Tues–Sat 10am–5pm; Sun 1–5pm.

Savannah History Museum Housed in the restored train shed of the old Central Georgia Railway station, this museum is a good introduction to the city. In the theater, *The Siege of Savannah* is replayed. In addition to theatrics, there's an exhibition hall displaying memorabilia from every era of Savannah's history. Allow 1 hour.

303 Martin Luther King, Jr., Blvd. ⓒ **912/651-6825.** www.chsgeorgia.org/shm. Admission $4.25 adults; $3.75 seniors, students, and children 11 and older; $3 children 6–11; free for children under 6. Mon–Fri 8:30am–5pm; Sat–Sun 9am–5pm.

Telfair Mansion and Art Museum   The oldest public art museum in the South, housing both American and European paintings, was designed and built in 1818 by William Jay, a young English architect noted for introducing the Regency style to America. A sculpture gallery and rotunda were added in 1883, and Jefferson Davis attended the formal opening in 1886. William Jay's period rooms have been restored, and the Octagon Room and Dining Room are particularly outstanding. Visits last 45 minutes.

121 Bernard St. ⓒ **912/232-1177.** www.telfair.org. Admission $9 adults, $8 seniors, $6 students, $4 children 5–12, free for children under 5. Mon noon–5pm; Tues–Sat 10am–5pm; Sun 1–5pm.

LITERARY LANDMARKS

Long before John Berendt's *Midnight in the Garden of Good and Evil,* other writers were associated with Savannah.

Chief of them was **Flannery O'Connor** (1924–64), one of the South's greatest writers. Between October and May, an association dedicated to her offers readings, films, and lectures about her and other southern writers. You can visit the **Flannery O'Connor Childhood Home** at 207 E. Charlton St. (ⓒ **912/233-6014**). The house is open Saturday and Sunday from 1 to 4pm. Free admission.

Conrad Aiken (1889–1973), the American poet, critic, writer, and Pulitzer Prize winner, was also born in Savannah. He lived at 228 and later at 230 E. Oglethorpe Ave.

Mercer House, 429 Bull St. (ⓒ **912/236-6352;** www.mercerhouse.com), used in *Midnight in the Garden of Good and Evil,* is open to the public, following a complete restoration. Currently, it is the star attraction of the city. The house is so spectacular it's been called "the envy of Savannah," and thousands of visitors stop by to photograph it. It was here in May 1981 that wealthy antiques dealer Jim Williams fatally shot his lover/assistant, that blond "walking streak of sex," Danny Hansford, age 21. Mercer House is also where Williams gave his legendary Christmas parties each year. In January 1990, Jim Williams died of a heart attack at 59, in the same room where he'd killed Hansford. (And, no, Johnny Mercer never lived in this house, but it was built by his great-grandfather.) The house is sumptuously furnished with antiques, paintings, and *objets d'art.* It is still lived in by Dr. Dorothy Kingery, sister of the late Jim Williams, a distinguished academician. Open Monday through Saturday from 10:30am to 3:40pm and Sunday 12:30 to 4pm. Admission is $13 for adults and $8 for children and students (college-age students need ID).

All fans of The Book must pay a visit to **Bonaventure Cemetery,** filled with obelisks and columns and dense shrubbery and moss-draped trees. Bonaventure is open daily from 8am to 5pm. Take Wheaton Street east from downtown to Bonaventure Road. This cemetery lies on the grounds of what was once a great oak-shaded plantation. It was at the cemetery that John Berendt had martinis in silver goblets with Miss Harty, while they sat on the bench-gravestone of Conrad Aiken. Songwriter Johnny Mercer is buried in plot H-48.

SHOPPING

River Street is a shopper's delight, with some 9 blocks (including Riverfront Plaza) of interesting shops, offering everything from crafts to clothing to souvenirs. The **City Market,** between Ellis and Franklin squares on West St. Julian Street, boasts art galleries, boutiques, and sidewalk cafes along with horse-and-carriage rides. Bookstores, boutiques, and antiques shops are located between Wright Square and Forsyth Park.

J. D. Weed & Co., 102 W. Victory Dr. (© 912/234-8540), is one of our favorite antiques dealers. **Memory Lane,** 220 W. Bay St. (© 912/232-0975), offers more than 8,000 square feet of collectibles.

The leading galleries include **Gallery 209,** 209 E. River St. (© 912/236-4583); **John Tucker Gallery,** 5 W. Charlton St. (© 912/231-8161); **Morning Star Gallery,** 8 E. Liberty St. (© 912/233-4307); and the **Village Craftsmen,** 223 W. River St. (© 912/236-7280).

WHERE TO STAY

Because many of Savannah's historic inns are in former converted residences, price ranges can vary greatly. A very expensive hotel might also have some smaller and more moderately priced units—so it pays to ask.

The Ballastone _(Best)_ This glamorous, award-winning B&B is a celeb favorite and occupies a dignified 1838 building separated from the Juliette Gordon Low House by a well-tended formal garden; it's richly decorated with hardwoods, elaborate draperies, and antiques and is ideal for romantic couples. There's an elevator, unusual for Savannah B&Bs, but no closets (they were taxed as extra rooms in the old days). All rooms offer bathrobes, deluxe toiletries, and VCRs; some have Jacuzzi tubs. The four suites are in a clapboard town house that's a 5-minute walk away from the main building and is staffed with its own live-in receptionists. A very good breakfast is served, as are afternoon tea and evening hors d'oeuvres.

14 E. Oglethorpe Ave., Savannah, GA 31401. © 800/822-4553 or 912/236-1484. Fax 912/236-4626. www.ballastone. com. 16 units. $215–$355 double; $395 suite. Rates include full breakfast, afternoon tea, and evening hors d'oeuvres. AE, MC, V. Free parking. Pets accepted for $50 fee (under 25 lb. permitted). No children under the age of 16. **Amenities:** Free passes to local health club; smoking not permitted.

Bed and Breakfast Inn In the oldest part of historic Savannah, this is a dignified stone-fronted town house built in 1853, and is a suitable address for both families and couples. You climb a gracefully curved front stoop to reach the cool high-ceilinged interior, outfitted with a combination of antique and reproduction furniture. Most rooms offer four-poster beds.

117 W. Gordon St. (at Chatham Sq.), Savannah, GA 31401. © 888/230-0518 or 912/238-0518. Fax 912/233-2537. www.savannahbnb.com. 18 units. $129–$199 double. Children up to age 12 stay in parent's room for $15. Rates include full breakfast and afternoon tea. DISC, MC, V. Free parking. **Amenities:** Smoking not permitted.

Eliza Thompson House The rooms of this stately home, attracting families and couples, are equally divided between the original 1847 building and a converted carriage house. Steve and Carol Day have completely redecorated, using original Savannah colors, beautiful antiques, and Oriental carpets. You'll find comfortable cotton robes, fine linens, and well-kept, elegant bathrooms. The inn is also graced with one of the most beautiful courtyards in the city. Breakfast is a lavish affair, usually served outdoors.

5 W. Jones St., Savannah, GA 31401. © 800/348-9378 or 912/236-3620. Fax 912/238-1920. www.elizathompson house.com. 25 units. $189–$249 double. Children under 12 stay free in parent's room. Rates include full breakfast and evening hors d'oeuvres. AE, DC, DISC, MC, V. Free parking. **Amenities:** Smoking not permitted.

The Gastonian One of the most posh B&Bs in Savannah, this Relais & Châteaux property, catering mainly to adults, incorporates a pair of Italianate Regency buildings constructed in 1868. Today everything is a testimonial to Victorian charm, except for a skillfully crafted serpentine bridge connecting the two buildings and curving above a verdant semitropical garden. Rooms are appropriately plush, comfortable, cozy, and beautifully furnished; some rooms have whirlpool tubs, others have working fireplaces. Afternoon tea is served in a formal drawing room.

220 E. Gaston St., Savannah, GA 31401. ℭ 800/322-6603 or 912/232-2869. Fax 912/232-0710. www.gastonian. com. 17 units. $205–$295 double; from $395 suite. Discount packages available. Rates include full breakfast and afternoon tea. AE, DISC, MC, V. Free parking. No children under 12.

Hampton Inn *(Value* *(Kids*   Opened in 1997, this family favorite rises above busy Bay Street, across from Savannah's Riverwalk and some of the city's most hopping nightclubs. Its lobby was designed to mimic an 18th-century Savannah salon, thanks to heart-of-pine flooring and antique Savannah bricks. Rooms are simple yet comfortable, with wall-to-wall carpeting and medium-size bathrooms.

201 E. Bay St., Savannah, GA. ℭ 800/576-4945 or 912/231-9700. Fax 912/231-0040. www.hotelsavannah.com. 144 units. Sun–Thurs $155 double; Fri–Sat $159–$189 double. Children 18 and under stay free in parent's room. Rates include continental breakfast. AE, DC, DISC, MC, V. Parking $8. **Amenities:** Pool; fitness room; smoking not permitted. *In room:* Fridge (in some), microwave (in some).

The Kehoe House   This is a spectacularly opulent B&B set in an 1892 mansion, with a museum-quality collection of fabrics and furniture, although it might be too flawless and formal for some tastes. Tom Hanks stayed in room no. 301 during the filming of *Forrest Gump*. Rooms are spacious, with 12-foot ceilings, and each is tastefully furnished in English period antiques. All units have well-kept bathrooms with plush bathrobes; some offer balconies.

123 Habersham St., Savannah, GA 31401. ℭ 800/820-1020 or 912/232-1020. Fax 912/231-0208. www.kehoe house.com. 13 units. $279–$429 double. Children 12 and under stay free in parent's room. Rates include full breakfast, afternoon tea, and evening hors d'oeuvres. AE, DISC, MC, V. Free parking. **Amenities:** Smoking not permitted.

The Marshall House   After a $12-million renovation, this landmark antebellum hotel, having closed in the early 1960s, is once again a favorite. A luxurious decor, great iron verandas, and original features such as claw-foot tubs await guests, who range from business execs to families and couples. All the midsize-to-spacious bedrooms are modernized but still retain an aura of the 19th century with pinewood floors and rocking chairs resting under ceiling fans. Nice touches include bathrobes, Bath & Bodyworks toiletries, and bottled water.

123 E. Broughton St., Savannah, GA 31401. ℭ 912/644-7896. Fax 800/589-6304 or 912/234-3334. www.marshall house.com. 68 units. $129–$199 double; $199–$229 suite. Children 12 and under stay free in parent's room. Rates include breakfast. AE, DC, DISC, MC, V. Parking $10. **Amenities:** Restaurant; free membership in nearby health club.

River Street Inn   This restored former cotton warehouse now has a dash of Colonial pizazz in its public areas, and the building's warren of brick-lined storerooms have been converted into some of the most comfortable and well-maintained rooms in town. All rooms offer a view of the Savannah River and bathrobes; some have four-poster beds. You'll be near tons of bars, restaurants, and nightclubs. A wine-and-cheese reception is held in the evening Monday through Saturday.

115 E. River St., Savannah, GA 31401. ℭ 800/253-4229 or 912/234-6400. Fax 912/234-1478. www.riverstreet inn.com. 86 units. $159–$229 double; $275 suite. Children under 12 stay free in parent's room. AE, DC, MC, V. Parking $6. **Amenities:** Smoking not permitted. *In room:* Fridge.

17 Hundred 90   The oldest inn in Savannah is located in a small clapboard house that was built in the year that gave the establishment its name. It's reminiscent of the kind of sea captain's house you might see emulated in a well-appointed private home. Eleven of the 13 smallish but charming guest rooms have fireplaces. There's a basement-level restaurant with a beamed ceiling and exposed original brickwork where locals come to eat and drink.

307 E. President St., Savannah, GA 31401. ☎ 877/468-1200 or 912/238-1200. Fax 912/236-2184. www.17hundred 90.com. 14 units. $149–$189 double. AE, DC, DISC, MC, V. **Amenities:** Smoking not permitted.

WHERE TO DINE

Clary's Café AMERICAN   Clary's, serving breakfast and lunch, has been a Savannah tradition since 1903, though the ambience today is decidedly 1950s. The place was famous long before it was featured in *Midnight in the Garden of Good and Evil.* John Berendt is still a frequent patron, as is the fabled drag diva Lady Chablis. Begin your day with the classic Hoppel Poppel (scrambled eggs with chunks of kosher salami, potatoes, onions, and green peppers), or drop in for fresh salads, stir-fries, homemade chicken soup, or flame-broiled burgers.

404 Abercorn St. (at Jones St.). ☎ 912/233-0402. Breakfast $3.95–$8.95; main courses $5.95–$7.95. AE, DC, DISC, MC, V. Mon–Thurs 7am–4pm; Fri 7am–5pm; Sat 8am–5pm; Sun 8am–4pm.

Elizabeth on 37th *(Best)* MODERN SOUTHERN   This restaurant is the most glamorous and upscale in town, and is the best choice for a romantic night out. It's housed in a palatial neoclassical-style 1900 villa ringed with semitropical landscaping and cascades of Spanish moss. Menu items change with the season and manage to retain their gutsy originality despite an elegant presentation. Their signature dish is grouper Celeste (sesame and almond-crusted grouper in a peanut sauce). The desserts are the best in Savannah.

105 E. 37th St. ☎ 912/236-5547. www.elizabethon37th.com. Reservations required. Main courses $24–$34. AE, DC, DISC, MC, V. Daily 6–10pm.

45 South at the Pirate's House INTERNATIONAL/SEAFOOD   Recommended by *Food & Wine, Southern Living,* and even *Playboy,* this ritzy restaurant has an ever-changing menu that might feature smoked North Carolina trout and other contemporary American food, including some of the best seafood caught off the Carolina coasts. The food has been called "gourmet southern." The setting is softly lit with elegantly set tables and a cozy bar; the service is impeccable.

20 E. Broad St. ☎ 912/233-1881. www.45south.net. Reservations required. Jacket or tie preferred for men. Main courses $22–$36. AE, MC, V. Mon–Thurs 6–9pm; Fri–Sat 6–9:30pm.

Huey's *(Kids)* CAJUN/CREOLE   This casual place overlooking the Savannah River even manages to please visitors from New Orleans—and that's saying a lot. It's usually packed with folks, especially families, enjoying dishes such as an oyster poor-boy, jambalaya with andouille sausage, crawfish étouffée, and crab-and-shrimp au gratin. The soups are homemade and the appetizers distinctive. Service is hectic but efficient.

Under the River Street Inn, 115 E. River St. ☎ 912/234-7385. Reservations not accepted. Main courses $12–$25; sandwiches $6–$10. AE, DISC, MC, V. Mon–Thurs and Sun 7am–10pm; Fri–Sat 7am–11pm.

Johnny Harris Restaurant AMERICAN   Started as a roadside diner in 1924, Johnny Harris is Savannah's oldest continuously operated restaurant. The place has a lingering aura of the 1950s and features all that great food so beloved back in the days of Elvis and Marilyn: barbecue, charbroiled steaks, and seafood. The barbecued pork is especially savory, and the prime rib is tender. Colonel Sanders never came anywhere close to equaling the fried chicken here. Guests can dine in the "kitchen" or in the main dining room, where you can dance under the "stars."

1651 E. Victory Dr. (Hwy. 80). © 912/354-7810. Reservations recommended. Lunch items $7–$10; dinner main courses $10–$20. AE, DC, DISC, MC, V. Mon–Thurs 11:30am–9:30pm; Fri–Sat 11:30am–10:30pm.

The Lady & Sons *Value* SOUTHERN   Paula Deen started this place in 1989 with $200; today she runs one of Savannah's most celebrated restaurants, a temple to greens and grits. The wonderful crab cakes and amazing chicken potpie topped with puff pastry best exhibit her style. The locals love her buffets, which are very southern—with fried chicken, meatloaf, collard greens, and macaroni and cheese. Lunches are busy with a loyal following; dinners are casual and inventive. Deen has numerous best-selling cookbooks in print and also hosts a top-rated cooking show, *Paula's Home Cooking,* on the Food Network.

102 W. Congress St. © 912/233-2600. www.ladyandsons.com. Reservations not accepted. Main courses $19–$25; all-you-can-eat buffet $17; Sun buffet $15. AE, DISC, MC, V. Mon–Sat 11am–3pm; Mon–Sat 5–9pm; Sun 11am–5pm (buffet only).

Mrs. Wilkes' Dining Room *Value* SOUTHERN   Remember the days of the board-inghouse, when everybody sat together and belly-busting food was served in big dishes at the center of the table? The late Sema Wilkes launched this former boardinghouse, now a restaurant, in the 1940s, and it's still going strong. You won't find a sign, but you probably will find a long line of people patiently waiting for a seat. The cooks believe in freshness, and will fill you and your family with fried or barbecued chicken, red rice and sausage, corn on the cob, squash and yams, corn bread, collard greens, and other down-home favorites.

107 W. Jones St. (west of Bull St.). © 912/232-5997. www.mrswilkes.com. Reservations not accepted. Lunch $13. No credit cards. Mon–Fri 11am–2pm.

The Olde Pink House Restaurant SEAFOOD/AMERICAN   Built in 1771 and painted pink, this house was once headquarters for one of Sherman's generals. Today its interior is severe and dignified, with stiff-backed chairs, bare wooden floors, and a Colonial ambience, ideal for a romantic night on the town. The cuisine is richly steeped in the traditions of the Low Country—heavy on collards, grits, and seafood, especially shrimp dishes. The chef's signature dish is crispy sautéed flounder in an apricot sauce. You can enjoy your meal in the candlelit dining rooms or in the base-ment-level piano bar.

23 Abercorn St. © 912/232-4286. Reservations recommended. Main courses $15–$29. AE, MC, V. Sun–Thurs 5:30–10:30pm; Fri 5:30–11pm.

SAVANNAH AFTER DARK

To find out what's what on the Savannah nightlife scene, check **www.savannah underground.com** on the Internet.

River Street, along the Savannah River, is the heart of the action. Many night owls stroll the waterfront until they hear the sound of music they like, and then follow their ears inside.

Savannah Civic Center's **Johnny Mercer Theater,** 301 W. Oglethorpe Ave. (© **800/ 351-7469** or 912/651-6656; www.savannahcivic.com), is home to ballet, musicals, and Broadway shows. Check locally to see what's on.

In summer, concerts of jazz, Big Band, and Dixieland music fill downtown **Johnson Square** with lots of foot-tapping sounds. Some of Savannah's finest musicians perform regularly.

Planters Tavern, in The Olde Pink House Restaurant, 23 Abercorn St. (© **912/ 232-4286**), is a beloved local spot, graced with a sprawling and convivial bar, a pair of fireplaces, and a decor of antique bricks and carefully polished hardwoods. You can listen to the melodies emanating from the sadder-but-wiser pianist, or perhaps you'll catch the endearingly elegant Gail Thurmond, one of Savannah's most legendary songstresses.

Most unpretentious is **Kevin Barry's Irish Pub,** 117 W. River St. (© **912/233-9626;** www.kevinbarrys.com), which is *the* place to be on St. Patrick's Day. **The Rail Pub,** 405 W. Congress St. (© **912/238-1311**), is sophisticated but low-key.

On your nightly pub crawl, check out such local fun spots as: **Mercury Lounge,** 125 W. Congress St. (© **912/447-6952**), with the biggest martinis in Savannah; the "high octane" **Monkey Bar,** 8 E. Broughton St. (© **912/232-0755**), with live music nightly, or the bar and grill; and **Bernies,** 115 E. River St. (© **912/236-1827**), lying along the waterfront in a pre–Civil War cotton warehouse, with all the ambience today of an old portside pub.

Savannah's leading gay club is **Club One,** 1 Jefferson St. (© **912/232-0200**), where you can catch a drag show, sometimes starring Lady Chablis.

7 Hilton Head

The largest sea island between New Jersey and Florida, Hilton Head offers broad, sandy beaches warmed by the Gulf Stream and fringed with palm trees and rolling dunes. The subtropical climate makes all this beauty the ideal setting for golf and saltwater fishing. Far more sophisticated and upscale than Myrtle Beach and the Grand Strand, Hilton Head feels like a luxurious planned community.

ESSENTIALS

GETTING THERE   It's easy to fly into Charleston, rent a car, and drive to Hilton Head (about 65 miles away). If you're driving from other points south or north, just take Exit 8 off I-95 to U.S. 278, which runs over the bridge to the island. It's 52 miles northeast of Savannah and located directly on the Intracoastal Waterway.

VISITOR INFORMATION   The **Island Visitors Information Center,** on 71 Pope Ave. (© **888/271-7666** or 843/341-9184; www.enjoyhiltonhead.com), can be found just before you cross over from the mainland. It's open daily 10am to 7pm.

Hilton Head Visitors and Convention Bureau, 1 Chamber Dr. (© **800/523-3373** or 843/785-3673; www.hiltonheadisland.org), offers a free vacation guide with golf and tennis tips and planning advice. It's open Monday through Friday from 8:30am to 5:30pm.

SPECIAL EVENTS & FESTIVALS   **Springfest,** a March festival, features seafood, live music, stage shows, and tennis and golf tournaments. Outstanding PGA golfers descend on the island in mid-April for the **Verizon Heritage** at the Harbour Town Golf Links. To herald fall, the **Hilton Head Celebrity Golf Tournament** is held on Labor Day weekend at several Island golf courses.

BEACHES, GOLF & OTHER OUTDOOR ACTIVITIES

BEACHES   Hilton Head's beaches possess extremely firm sand, providing a sound surface for biking, hiking, jogging, and beach games. In summer, watch for the endangered loggerhead turtles that lumber ashore at night to bury their eggs.

All beaches on Hilton Head are public, but do not necessarily offer easy public access; sometimes land bordering the beaches is private property and you can't enter the public land unless you're a private guest. Most beaches are safe, although there's sometimes an undertow at the northern end of the island. Lifeguards are posted only at major beaches, and concessions are available at which to rent beach chairs, umbrellas, and watersports equipment.

We recommend four public entrances to Hilton Head's beaches. **Coligny Beach** at Coligny Circle and Pope Avenue and South Forest Beach Drive is the island's busiest strip of sands and our favorite; it offers toilets, sand showers, a playground, and changing rooms. (*Note:* Locals sometimes call Coligny "North and South Forest Beach.") **Adler Lane,** entered along South Forest Beach Road at Alder Lane, offers parking and public toilets, and is less crowded. Off the William Hilton Parkway, **Dreissen Beach Park** at Bradley Beach Road has toilets, sand showers, and plenty of parking as well as a playground and picnic tables. On Starfish Road, **Folly Field Beach** has more limited parking but offers toilets and sand showers, and is our favorite of the beaches on the island's north side. The island also has a number of other less accessible and less desirable beaches.

BIKING   Hilton Head has 25 miles of bicycle paths. Some beaches are firm enough to support wheels, and every year cyclists seem to delight in dodging the waves or racing the fast-swimming dolphins in the nearby water.

Most hotels and resorts rent bikes to guests. If yours doesn't, try **Hilton Head Bicycle Company,** off Sea Pines Circle at 112 Arrow Rd. (© **800/995-4319** or 843/686-6888; www.hiltonheadbicycle.com). Rates start at around $27 weekly.

CRUISES   To explore Hilton Head's waters, contact **Adventure Cruises, Inc.,** Shelter Cove Harbour, Suite G, Harbourside III (© **843/785-4558;** www.hiltonheadisland.com/adventure/index.htm). Outings include a dolphin watch and a sport crabbing cruise. A 1¾-hour cruise costs $20 adults, $10 kids ages 3 to 12. **Calibogue Cruises,** Broad Creek Marina (© **843/342-8687**), offers boat transportation to Daufuskie Island for $35 per adult (includes golf cart), half price for children 12 and under.

FISHING   No license is needed for saltwater fishing, although freshwater licenses are required for the island's lakes and ponds. The season for fishing offshore is April to October. Inland fishing is good between September and December. Crabbing is also popular; these crustaceans are easy to catch in low water from docks, from boats, or right off a bank.

Off Hilton Head you can go deep-sea fishing for amberjack, barracuda, sharks, and king mackerel. **Harbour Town Yacht Basin,** Harbour Town Marina (© **843/671-4534;** www.harbourtown.com), can set you up with personal service and a small boat. A cheaper way to go—for only $47 per adult, $37 per child—is aboard *The Drifter* (© **843/363-2900**), a party boat that departs from the South Beach Marina Village.

GOLF   With 22 challenging golf courses on the island, this area is a mecca for golfers. For information on the area's various courses, consult **www.hiltonhead golf.com** online.

Many of Hilton Head's championship courses are open to the public, including the **George Fazio Course** at Palmetto Dunes Resort (✆ 843/785-1130), an 18-hole, 6,534-yard, par-70 course, named in the top 50 of *Golf Digest*'s "75 Best American Resort Courses." Greens fees are $59 to $75 depending on time of day.

Old South Golf Links, 50 Buckingham Plantation Dr., Bluffton (✆ 800/257-8997 or 843/785-5353), is an 18-hole, 6,772-yard, par-72 course, recognized by *Golf Digest* for its panoramic views and lovely setting. Greens fees are $50 to $80. The course lies on Highway 278, 1 mile before the bridge leading to Hilton Head.

Hilton Head National, Highway 278 (✆ 843/842-5900), is a Gary Player Signature Golf Course, an 18-hole, 6,779-yard, par-72 course with gorgeous scenery that evokes Scotland. Greens fees are $55 to $79.

Island West Golf Club, Highway 278 (✆ 843/689-6660), has a backdrop of oaks, elevated tees, and rolling fairways. It's a challenging but playable 18-hole, 6,803-yard, par-72 course. Greens fees are $37 to $57.

The **Robert Trent Jones Course** at the Palmetto Dunes Resort (✆ 843/785-1138) is an 18-hole, 6,710-yard, par-72 course with a winding lagoon system that comes into play on 11 holes. Greens fees are $89 to $105.

HORSEBACK RIDING Riding through beautiful maritime forests and nature preserves is reason enough to visit Hilton Head. We like **Lawton Fields Stables,** 190 Greenwood Dr., Sea Pines (✆ 843/671-2586), offering rides for both adults and kids (kids under 7 ride ponies) through the Sea Pines Forest Preserve. The cost is $50 per person for a ride lasting somewhat over an hour. Reservations are necessary.

NATURE PRESERVES The **Audubon-Newhall Preserve,** Palmetto Bay Road (✆ 843/689-2989), is a 50-acre preserve on the south end of the island. Here you can walk along marked trails to observe wildlife in its native habitat. Guided tours are available when plants are blooming. Open from sunrise to sunset; free admission.

Sea Pines Forest Preserve, Sea Pines Plantation (✆ 843/671-6486), is a 605-acre public wilderness with marked walking trails. Nearly all the birds and animals known to live on Hilton Head can be seen here (yes, there are alligators, but there are also less fearsome creatures, such as egrets, herons, osprey, and white-tailed deer). All trails lead to public picnic areas in the center of the forest. The preserve is open from sunrise to sunset year-round except during the Heritage Golf Classic in early April. Maps and toilets are available. There is a $5-per-car fee to enter the plantation.

TENNIS *Tennis* magazine has rated Hilton Head one of its "50 Greatest U.S. Tennis Resorts." No other domestic destination can boast such a concentration of tennis facilities, with more than 300 courts ideal for beginning, intermediate, and advanced players. The island has 19 tennis clubs, 7 of which are open to the public. A wide variety of tennis clinics and daily lessons is also found here, the academy of famed tennis guru Dennis van der Meer being just one of the instructional centers. The top tennis facility is the **Sea Pines Racquet Club** (✆ 843/363-4495), along with the **Port Royal Racquet Club** (✆ 843/686-8803), the **Hilton Head Island Beach and Tennis Resort** (✆ 843/842-4402), and the **Palmetto Dunes Tennis Center** (✆ 843/785-1152).

WHERE TO STAY

Villa rentals are available from two secluded enclaves of privately owned condos. The **Palmetto Dunes Resort** (✆ 800/845-6130 or 843/785-1161; www.palmettodunes. com) has a wide variety of units available for rental and offers golf packages. It's ideal for families, with kitchens, washer/dryers, and balconies or patios. Facilities include a huge tennis center, five golf courses, 3 miles of beach, 20 restaurants, a 10-mile lagoon ideal for canoeing, and a 200-slip marina. The **Sea Pines Resort** (✆ **888/807-6873** or 843/785-3333; www.seapines.com) is a huge development that's best for overnight stays; it attracts hordes of golfers since it's the home of the Verizon Heritage, a major stop on the PGA tour.

Moderately priced and affordable chain choices include the **Holiday Inn Oceanfront,** 1 S. Forest Beach Dr. (✆ **800/HOLIDAY** or 843/785-5126); **Fairfield Inn by Marriott,** 9 Marina Side Dr. (✆ **800/228-2800** or 843/842-4800); and **Hampton Inn,** 1 Dillon Rd. (✆ **800/HAMPTON** or 843/681-7900).

Crowne Plaza Resort
This five-story hotel, set on 800 landscaped acres, gives the Westin (see below) stiff competition, because of the sheer beauty of its landscaping, with a golf course praised by the National Audubon Society for its respect for local wildlife. Bedrooms don't quite match the style and comfort level of its competitor's, but they are neatly furnished and sport CD players. The attentive service is just another reason that a stay here is memorable.

130 Shipyard Dr., Shipyard Plantation, Hilton Head Island, SC 29928. ✆ **877/227-6963** or 843/842-2400. Fax 843/785-8463. www.crowneplaza.com. 338 units. $209–$406 double; $420–$615 suite. Children 17 and under stay free in parent's room. AE, DC, DISC, MC, V. Valet parking $10; free self-parking. **Amenities:** 2 restaurants; 2 pools (1 indoor); fitness center. *In room:* Fridge ($10 per night).

Disney Hilton Head Island Resort *(Kids)*
This family-friendly resort is on a 15-acre island that rises above Hilton Head's widest estuary, Broad Creek. About 20 woodsy-looking buildings are arranged in a compound. Expect lots of pine trees and fallen pine needles, garlands of Spanish moss, and plenty of kids. All accommodations contain kitchenettes, simple wooden furniture, and well-kept bathrooms. There are lots of summer camp–style activities (dolphin-watching cruises, eco-tours, canoeing lessons, marshmallow roasts), though the ambience is more low-key than what you'd expect from Disney.

22 Harbourside Lane, Hilton Head Island, SC 29928. ✆ **843/341-4100.** Fax 843/341-4130. www.dvcresorts.com. 123 units. $125–$285 studio; $165–$770 larger villas. Resort fee $9 per night. Children 17 and under stay free in parent's room. AE, DC, DISC, MC, V. Free parking. **Amenities:** 2 pools; fitness center; spa. *In room:* Kitchenette in studios, kitchen in villas.

Hilton Oceanfront Resort *(Kids)*
We like the Hilton because of its hideaway position, tucked at the end of the main road through Palmetto Dunes. Its low-rise design has hallways that open to sea breezes at either end. Rooms are some of the largest on the island, all with ocean views and well-kept bathrooms. All the studio suites have kitchenettes, making this resort a favorite of families, which also like the children's activities such as a kids' camp.

23 Ocean Lane, Hilton Head Island, SC 29938. ✆ **800/845-8001** or 843/842-8000. Fax 843/341-8033. www.hiltonheadhilton.com. 324 units. $205–$300 double; $399–$499 suite. Children 18 and under stay free in parent's room. AE, DC, DISC, MC, V. Parking $6. **Amenities:** 3 restaurants; 2 pools; fitness center. *In room:* Kitchenette.

Main Street Inn
Don't expect cozy Americana at this small, luxurious inn for adults—it's grander and more European than its name would imply. Designed like a small-scale villa that you might find in the south of France, it combines design elements from both New Orleans and Charleston, including cast-iron balustrades and a formal semi-tropical garden where guests are encouraged to indulge in afternoon tea. Inside, you'll find an artfully clipped topiary, French Provincial furnishings, and

accommodations that are more luxurious, and more richly appointed (marble bathrooms, bathrobes, the occasional fireplace), than any other hotel in Hilton Head.

2200 Main St., Hilton Head Island, SC 29926. ✆ **800/471-3001** or 843/681-3001. Fax 843/681-5541. www.mainstreet inn.com. 33 units. $159–$299 double. Rates include breakfast. AE, DISC, MC, V. Free parking. **Amenities:** Pool; spa.

South Beach Marina Inn *Value* Of the dozens of available accommodations in Sea Pines Plantation, this complex of marina-front buildings is the only place offering traditional hotel-style rooms by the night. With lots of charm, it meanders over a labyrinth of catwalks and stairways above a complex of shops and restaurants. The one- and two-bedroom units each have a kitchenette and at least one bathroom, and are cozily outfitted with country-style braided rugs and pine floors.

In the Sea Pines Plantation, 232 S. Sea Pines Dr., Hilton Head Island, SC 29938. ✆ **800/367-3909** or 843/671-6498. Fax 843/671-7495. www.southbeachvillage.com. 17 units. $65–$175 1-bedroom apt; $187–$210 2-bedroom apt. Children under 18 stay free in parent's room. AE, DISC, MC, V. Free parking. **Amenities:** Pool. *In room:* Kitchenette.

Westin Resort *Best* Set near the isolated northern end of Hilton Head Island on 24 landscaped acres, this opulent European-style hotel is rather formal, although suitable for families. Rooms, most with ocean views, are outfitted in Low Country Plantation style with touches of Asian art. Each room has a private balcony and Westin's signature Heavenly Bed; refrigerators are available. Suites toss in Jacuzzi tubs and sleeper sofas.

2 Grasslawn Ave., Hilton Head Island, SC 29928. ✆ **800/937-8461** or 843/681-4000. Fax 843/681-1087. www.westin.com. 412 units. $199–$459 double; $450–$1,900 suite. Resort fee $10 per night. Children under 17 stay free in parent's room; children under 5 eat free. Packages often available. AE, DC, DISC, MC, V. Valet parking $9.50; free self-parking. Pet fee $100 (under 30 lb. permitted). **Amenities:** 3 restaurants; 3 pools (2 indoor); 3 golf courses; 16 tennis courts; fitness center; spa. *In room:* Fridge ($10 per night).

WHERE TO DINE

Cafe Europa CONTINENTAL/SEAFOOD This fine European restaurant is at the base of the Harbour Town Lighthouse, opening onto a panoramic view of Calibogue Sound and Daufuskie Island. In an informal, cheerful atmosphere, you can order poached, grilled, baked, or fried fish. Specialty dishes include chicken Marsala, and baked shrimp Daufuskie. Fourteen omelets are perfectly prepared at breakfast, and the bloody mary is the island's best.

Harbour Town, Sea Pines Plantation. ✆ **843/671-3399.** www.cafeeuropahhi.com. Reservations recommended for dinner. Main courses $8–$13 lunch, $18–$28 dinner. AE, MC, V. Daily 9am–2:30pm and 5–10pm.

Charlie's L'Etoile Verte *Best* INTERNATIONAL/SEAFOOD Outfitted like a Parisian bistro, our favorite Hilton Head restaurant is also a favorite of Bill Clinton. The atmosphere is unpretentious but elegant, and it bursts with energy in an otherwise sleepy shopping center. Begin with roasted portabello and crab, and move on to tilapia sautéed in a Parmesan crust. The wine list is impressive and has won *Wine Spectator*'s Award of Excellence 10 years running.

8 New Orleans Rd. ✆ **843/785-9277.** www.charliesofhiltonhead.com. Reservations recommended. Main courses $23–$34. AE, DISC, MC, V. Tues–Sat 11:30am–2pm; Mon–Sat 6–9:30pm.

Hudson's Seafood House on the Docks SEAFOOD Built as a seafood-processing factory in 1912, this family-run restaurant still processes fish, clams, and oysters for local distribution—so you know everything is fresh. We recommend the crab cakes, the steamed shrimp, or the especially appealing blackened catch of the day. Before dinner, stroll on the docks past shrimp boats and enjoy the sunset view of the mainland and nearby Parris Island.

1 Hudson Rd. © 843/681-2772. www.hudsonsonthedocks.com. Reservations not accepted. Main courses $13–$22. AE, DC, MC, V. Daily 11am–2:30pm and 5–10pm. Go to Skull Creek just off Squire Pope Rd. (signposted from U.S. 278).

Scott's Fish Market *(Kids)* SEAFOOD/AMERICAN   The largest full-service outdoor dining area at Hilton Head, this family favorite is known for its fresh coastal seafood. In addition to fresh fish, a regular American menu of other dishes is also offered. Tables overlook the boats bobbing at anchor along the waterfront. The Hurricane Harry's Wharf Bar offers live entertainment if you want to make an evening of it.

Shelter Cove Harbour. © 843/785-7575. Reservations recommended. Main courses $16–$22; children's menu $4.95. AE, DC, DISC, MC, V. Mon–Sat 4:30–10pm. Closed Jan.

HILTON HEAD AFTER DARK
Nightlife starts with sunset cocktails and stays pretty mellow. There are lots of options in hotel bars and lounges. The **Quarterdeck,** Harbour Town, Sea Pines Plantation (© 843/671-2222), is our favorite waterfront lounge, the best place on the island to watch sunsets. There's dancing every night to beach music and Top-40 hits. Soft guitar music or the strains of Jimmy Buffett records usually set the scene at the **Salty Dog Cafe,** South Beach Marina Village, Sea Pines Plantation (© 843/363-2198; www. saltydogcafe.com), where you can enjoy your beer outdoors under a sycamore.

8 Charleston
If the Old South still lives all through South Carolina's Low Country—the term for the state's southern coastal communities—it positively thrives in Charleston. All romantic notions of antebellum days—stately homes, courtly manners, gracious hospitality, and above all, gentle dignity—are facts of everyday life in this old city. In spite of earthquakes, hurricanes, fires, and Yankee bombardments, Charleston remains one of the best-preserved cities in America. It boasts 73 pre-Revolutionary buildings, 136 from the late 18th century, and more than 600 built before the 1840s. With its cobblestone streets and horse-drawn carriages, Charleston is a place of visual images and sensory pleasures. Tea, jasmine, and wisteria fragrances fill the air; the aroma of she-crab soup (the local favorite) wafts from sidewalk cafes; and antebellum architecture graces the historic cityscape.

ESSENTIALS
GETTING THERE   By Plane   Charleston International Airport (www.chs-airport.com) is in north Charleston on I-26, about 12 miles west of the city. Taxi fare into the city runs from $25 to $29. If you're driving, follow the airport access road to I-26 into the heart of Charleston.

By Train   Amtrak (© **800/USA-RAIL;** www.amtrak.com) provides service from Savannah (trip time: 1¾ hr.) and Washington, D.C. (9 hr.), to its station at 4565 Gaynor Ave., north Charleston.

By Car   The main routes into Charleston are **I-26** from the northwest (Columbia, SC), and **U.S. 17** from the north (Myrtle Beach) and south (Savannah).

VISITOR INFORMATION   The **Charleston Visitor Reception & Transportation Center,** 375 Meeting St., Charleston, SC 29402 (© **800/774-0006** or 843/853-8000; www.charlestoncvb.com), provides maps and advice. Numerous tours depart hourly from here. It's open Monday through Friday from 8:30am to 5pm.

SOUTH CAROLINA

★ Columbia

Charleston ●

To Fort Sumter

| 0 | 1/4 mi |
| 0 | 0.25 km |

ACCOMMODATIONS ■

Anchorage Inn **18**
Andrew Pinckney Inn **14**
Ansonborough Inn **6**
Best Western King Charles Inn **5**
Charleston Place Hotel **11**
1837 Bed & Breakfast **4**
Francis Marion Hotel **3**
Hampton Inn Historic District **2**
Market Pavilion Hotel **16**
Planters Inn **9**

DINING ◆

Anson **13**
A. W. Shucks **19**
Charleston Grill **20**
Cypress **17**
82 Queen **15**
Hank's **12**
Hominy Grill **1**
Hyman's Seafood Company Restaurant **10**
McCrady's **7**
Peninsula Grill **8**
S.N.O.B. (Slightly North of Broad) **17**

GETTING AROUND   The **Downtown Area Shuttle (DASH;** ☎ **843/724-7420)** is the quickest way to get around the main downtown area daily. The fare is $1.25, and you'll need exact change. A pass good for the whole day costs $4 and can be bought on the bus. Leading taxi companies are **Yellow Cab** (☎ **843/577-6565)** and **Safety Cab** (☎ **843/722-4066)**; within the city, fares seldom exceed $5 to $12. You must call for a taxi—there are no pickups on the street. Don't try to drive around downtown; park your car and save it for day trips to outlying areas.

FAST FACTS   For a physician referral or 24-hour emergency-room treatment, contact **Charleston Memorial Hospital,** 326 Calhoun St. (☎ **843/792-2300).** Call **Doctor's Care** (☎ **843/556-5585)** for the names of walk-in clinics. Sales tax in Charleston is 6%; the hotel tax is also 6%.

SPECIAL EVENTS & FESTIVALS   Held from late May to early June, the **Spoleto Festival U.S.A.** (☎ **843/579-3100;** www.spoletousa.org) is the premier cultural event in the South. This famous international festival, the American counterpart to the equally celebrated one in Spoleto, Italy, showcases world-renowned performers in drama, dance, music, and art in various venues throughout the city.

During the mid-January **Low-Country Oyster Festival** (☎ **843/452-6068),** steamed buckets of oysters greet visitors at Boone Hall Plantation. Enjoy live music, oyster-shucking contests, and children's events. For nearly 50 years, people have been enjoying some of Charleston's most prestigious neighborhoods and private gardens in the **Festival of Houses and Gardens,** from mid-March to mid-April. Contact the **Historic Charleston Foundation** (☎ **843/722-3405;** www.historiccharleston.org) for details.

WHAT TO SEE & DO

We always head for the **Battery** (officially White Point Gardens) to get into the feel of this city. It's right on the end of the peninsula, facing the Cooper River and the harbor. There's a landscaped park, shaded by palmettos and live oaks, with walkways lined with old monuments and other war relics. The view toward the harbor goes out to Fort Sumter. We like to walk along the seawall on East Battery and Murray Boulevard and slowly absorb the Charleston ambience.

The **Old South Carriage Co.,** 14 Anson St. (☎ **843/723-9712;** www.oldsouth carriagetours.com), offers narrated horse-drawn carriage tours through the historic district daily from 9am to 5pm, at $20 for adults, and $12 for children 3 to 11.

Charleston Museum   Founded in 1773, this is the first and oldest museum in America. The full-scale replica of the famed Confederate submarine *Hunley* standing outside the museum is one of the most photographed subjects in the city. The museum has the city's largest silver collection, plus early crafts, historical relics, costumes and textiles, and hands-on exhibits for children.

360 Meeting St. ☎ 843/722-2996. www.charlestonmuseum.org. Admission $10 adults, $4 children 3–12. Combination ticket to the museum, Joseph Manigault House, and Heyward-Washington House (see below) $21. Mon–Sat 9am–5pm; Sun 1–5pm.

Charles Towne Landing   This 663-acre park is on the site of the city's first settlement (in 1670). There's a re-creation of a small village and a full-scale replica of a 17th-century trading ship. There's no flashy theme-park atmosphere: You'll walk under huge old oaks, past freshwater lagoons, and through the Animal Forest, seeing what those early settlers saw.

1500 Old Towne Rd. (S.C. 171, between U.S. 17 and I-126). © **843/852-4200**. www.southcarolinaparks.com. Admission $5 adults, $3.25 seniors, $3 children 6–15, free for travelers with disabilities and children under 6. Daily 9am–5pm.

Cypress Gardens
Giant cypress trees draped with Spanish moss provide an unforgettable setting as you glide along in a flat-bottomed boat. Footpaths in the garden wind through a profusion of azaleas, camellias, and daffodils. Visitors share the swamp with alligators, woodpeckers, wood ducks, otters, and barred owls. The gardens are worth a visit at any time of year, but they're at their most colorful in March and April. Other features include a butterfly house and a small freshwater aquarium.

U.S. 52 (24 miles north of Charleston), Moncks Corner. © **843/553-0515**. www.cypressgardens.info. Admission $10 adults, $9 seniors, $5 children 6–12. Daily 9am–5pm.

Edmondston-Alston House
This house, built in 1825, was one of the earliest constructed in the city in the late Federalist style; it was later modified in Greek Revival style. You can still see the Alston family's heirloom furnishings, silver, and paintings. At this house, in 1861, General Beauregard joined the Alstons to watch the bombardment of Fort Sumter. Robert E. Lee once found refuge here when his hotel uptown caught on fire.

21 E. Battery. © **843/722-7171**. www.middletonplace.org. Admission $10 adults, $5 children 7–15, free for children 6 and under. Guided tours Tues–Sat 10am–4:30pm; Sun–Mon 1:30–4:30pm.

Fort Sumter National Monument
It was here that the first shot of the Civil War was fired on April 12, 1861, as Confederate forces launched a 34-hour bombardment. Union forces eventually surrendered, and the Rebels' occupation became a symbol of southern resistance. This action led to a declaration of war in Washington. Amazingly, Confederate troops held onto Sumter for nearly 4 years, although it was almost continually bombarded. When evacuation finally came, the fort was nothing but a heap of rubble. Park rangers today are on hand to answer your questions, and you can explore gun emplacements and visit a small museum filled with artifacts related to the siege. Expect to spend about 2 hours. *Tip:* We recommend the tour of the fort and harbor offered by **Fort Sumter Tours**, 360 Concord St., Suite 201 (© **843/722-1691** or 843/881-7337). Sailing times change every month or so; call ahead.

In Charleston Harbor. © **843/883-3123**. www.nps.gov/fosu. Free admission to fort; boat trip $14 adults, $13 seniors, $8 children 6–11, free for children under 6. Daily 10am–5:30pm (in winter until 4pm).

Heyward-Washington House
In a district called "Cabbage Row," this 1772 house was built by Daniel Heyward, "the rice king," and was also home to Thomas Heyward, Jr., a signer of the Declaration of Independence. President George Washington bedded down here in 1791. Many of the fine period pieces in the house are the work of Thomas Elfe, one of America's most famous cabinetmakers. The restored 18th-century kitchen is the only historic kitchen in the city open to the public.

87 Church St. (between Tradd and Elliott sts.). © **843/722-0354**. www.charlestonmuseum.org. Admission $9 adults, $4 children 3–11. Mon–Sat 10am–5pm; Sun 1–5pm. Tours leave every half-hour until 4:30pm. Combination tickets with Charleston Museum available (see above).

Magnolia Plantation
Ten generations of the Drayton family have lived here continuously since the 1670s. They haven't had much luck keeping a roof over their heads: The first mansion burned just after the Revolution and the second was set afire by General Sherman. But you can't call its replacement "modern." A simple, pre-Revolutionary house was barged down from Summerville and set on the foundations of

its unfortunate predecessors. It's been furnished with museum-quality Early American furniture. The gardens of camellias and azaleas—among the most beautiful in America—reach their peak bloom in March and April but are colorful year-round. You can tour the house, the gardens, a petting zoo, and a waterfowl refuge, or walk or bike through wildlife trails. The **Audubon Swamp Garden,** also on the grounds, is an independently operated 60-acre cypress swamp offering a close look at wildlife, such as alligators, otters, turtles, and herons.

3550 Ashley River Rd. ℭ 800/367-3517 or 843/571-1266. www.magnoliaplantation.com. Admission to garden and grounds $14 adults, $13 seniors, $8 children 6–12. Tour of plantation house additional $7 for ages 6 and up; children under 6 not allowed to tour the house. Admission to Audubon Swamp Garden $7 adults, $6 seniors, $5 children 6–12. Summer daily 8am–5:30pm; winter daily 9am–5pm.

Middleton Place   This National Historic Landmark was the home of Henry Middleton, president of the First Continental Congress. Today it includes America's oldest landscaped gardens, where ornamental lakes, terraces, and plantings of camellias, azaleas, magnolias, and crape myrtle accent the grand design. The Middleton Place House itself was built in 1755, but in 1865 all but the south flank was ransacked and burned by Union troops. It was restored in the 1870s as a family residence and today houses fine silver, furniture, rare first editions, and portraits. In the stable yards, craftspeople demonstrate life on a plantation of yesteryear.

4300 Ashley River Rd. (14 miles northwest of Charleston). ℭ 843/556-6020. www.middletonplace.org. Admission $25 adults, $15 children 7–15, free for children under 6. Tour of house additional $10. Gardens and stable yards daily 9am–5pm. House Mon 1:30–4:30pm; Tues–Sat 10am–4:30pm.

Nathaniel Russell House   One of America's finest examples of Federal architecture, this 1808 house was completed by Nathaniel Russell, one of Charleston's richest merchants. It is celebrated for its "free-flying" staircase, spiraling unsupported for three floors. The interiors are ornate with period furnishings, especially the elegant music room with its golden harp and neoclassical-style sofa.

51 Meeting St. ℭ 843/805-6736. www.historiccharleston.org. Admission $10. Guided tours Mon–Sat 10am–5pm; Sun and holidays 2–5pm.

South Carolina Aquarium *Best Kids*   Visitors can explore southern aquatic life in an attraction filled with thousands of enchanting creatures and plants in amazing habitats, from five major regions of the Appalachian Watershed. Jutting out into the Charleston Harbor for 2,000 feet, the focal point is a 93,000-square-foot aquarium featuring a two-story Great Ocean Tank Exhibition. Contained within are some 800 animals, including deadly sharks but also sea turtles and stingrays. Every afternoon at 4pm the aquarium offers a dolphin program, when bottle-nosed dolphins can be viewed from an open-air terrace. A major exhibit exploring the aquatic life of the Amazon (including some piranha!) opened in 2004.

Adjacent to the aquarium is the **IMAX Theatre,** 360 Concord St. (ℭ 843/725-IMAX; www.charlestonimax.com), the only 3-D theater in South Carolina, which blasts you with great scenic images and puts you right into the action. It is open daily from 10am to 10pm.

100 Aquarium Wharf. ℭ 843/720-1990. www.scaquarium.org. Admission $15 adults (12–61), $13 seniors 62 and older, $8 children 3–11, free for children under 2. Aquarium and IMAX combination tickets $23 adults (12–61), $20 seniors 62 and older, $15 children 3–11. Apr 1–Aug 15 Mon–Sat 9am–6pm, Sun noon–6pm; Aug 16–Mar 31 Mon–Sat 9am–5pm, Sun noon–5pm.

BEACHES & OUTDOOR ACTIVITIES

BEACHES There are some great beaches within a 25-minute drive from Charleston. In the East Cooper area, both the **Isle of Palms** and **Sullivan's Island** offer miles of beaches, mostly bordered by beachfront homes. Windsurfing and jet-skiing are popular here. **Kiawah Island** has the area's most pristine beach at the **Beachwalker State Park,** on the southern end of the island. For more information on the beach scene, head online to **www.charlestonlowcountry.com/Beaches**.

GOLF Charleston is said to be the home of golf in America. **Wild Dunes Resort,** Isle of Palms (© **843/886-6000**), offers two championship golf courses designed by Tom Fazio. **The Links** is a 6,722-yard, par-72 layout ending with a pair of oceanfront holes once called "the greatest east of Pebble Beach." The course has been ranked in the top 100 in the world by *Golf Magazine.* **The Harbor Course** offers 6,402 yards of Low Country marsh and Intracoastal Waterway views. This par-70 layout chal-lenges players with 2 holes that play from one island to another across Morgan Creek. Greens fees at these courses can range from $70 to $200, depending on the season.

Your best deal if you'd like to play at any of the other Charleston-area golf courses is to contact **Charleston Golf Inc.** (© **800/774-4444;** www.charlestongolfguide. com), representing 20 golf courses and offering packages that include greens fees and accommodations. (They can also arrange rental cars and airfares.)

SHOPPING

King Street is lined with many specialty shops and boutiques.

Two of the leading galleries are the **Waterfront Gallery,** 215 E. Bay St., across from the Custom House (© **843/722-1155**); and the **Wells Gallery,** 103 Broad St. (© **843/853-3233**), both specializing in the works of local artists.

Charleston Crafts, 87 Hasell St. (© **843/723-2938**), offers locally made jewelry, basketry, leather, traditional crafts, and soaps. **Clown's Bazaar,** 56 Broad St. (© **843/723-9769**), features hand-carvings, silks, and pewter from exotic locales, with pro-ceeds going to benefit developing nations. Also supporting a good cause, **Historic Charleston Reproductions,** 105 Broad St. (© **843/723-8292**), aids local restoration projects. Licensed replica products range from furniture to jewelry. The pride of the store is its home furnishings collection, with most in lovely mahogany. It operates shops in several historic houses and runs the **Francis Edmunds Center Museum Shop** at 108 Meeting St. (© **843/724-8484**). A local company, **Charleston Gift Company,** 239½ King St. (© **843/577-7774**), specializes in all sorts of Charleston "things," including clothing, specialty gift baskets, handbags, and one-of-a-kind photo albums and frames.

WHERE TO STAY

For help with reservations, contact **Historic Charleston Bed & Breakfast** (© **800/743-3583** or 843/722-6606; www.historiccharlestonbedandbreakfast.com). During the major festivals, owners charge pretty much what the market will bear. Advance reservations are essential at those times.

Reliable moderately priced and affordable chain options include the **Hampton Inn Historic District,** 345 Meeting St. (© **800/HAMPTON** or 843/723-4000), across from the visitor center; and the **Best Western King Charles Inn,** 237 Meeting St. (© **866/546-4700** or 843/723-7451).

Anchorage Inn   Built in the 1840s as a cotton warehouse, this inn, a favorite of couples, boasts the only decorative theme of its type in Charleston: a mock-Tudor interior with lots of dark paneling; references to Olde England; canopied beds with matching tapestries; leaded casement windows; and, in some places, half-timbering. Modern conveniences include satellite TV and Neutrogena toiletries. Each room's shape is different from that of its neighbors, and the expensive ones have bona fide windows overlooking the street outside.

26 Vendue Range, Charleston, SC 29401. © **800/421-2952** or 843/723-8300. Fax 843/723-9543. www.anchorage ncharleston.com. 19 units. $109–$239 double; $159–$279 suite. Children under 12 stay free in parent's room. Rates include continental breakfast and afternoon tea. AE, MC, V. Parking $10. **Amenities:** Smoking not permitted.

Andrew Pinckney Inn   This nonsmoking boutique hotel—housed in a converted 18th-century stable—has old-world charm but is completely up-to-date with modern amenities. Its special feature is a three-story plant-filled atrium, along with a beautiful courtyard, plus a rooftop terrace overlooking the Market District and the French Quarter. The hotel is decorated in an elegant yet casual West Indian style. Its St. Philip's Suite is one of the best places in Charleston for a romantic getaway.

40 Pinckney St., Charleston, SC 29401. © **800/505-8983** or 843/937-8800. Fax 843/937-8810. www.andrewpinckney inn.com. 41 units. $99–$239 double; $149–$279 suite. Children under 12 stay free in parent's room. Rates include continental breakfast. AE, DC, MC, V. Parking $12. **Amenities:** Smoking not permitted. *In room:* Fridge, microwave (in some).

Ansonborough Inn   Once past the not-very-promising exterior, most visitors (it's popular with both couples and families) really like the unusual configuration of the suites here. Set close to the waterfront, this former warehouse has a lobby that features exposed timbers and a soaring atrium filled with plants. All accommodations are suites with ceilings of 14 to 16 feet and, in many cases, sleeping lofts; five have fireplaces. They're outfitted with copies of 18th-century furniture. There's a panoramic terrace with a bar on the rooftop.

21 Hassell St., Charleston, SC 29401. © **800/522-2073** or 843/723-1655. Fax 843/577-6888. www.ansonborough inn.com. 37 units. Mar–Nov $149–$379 double; off season $99–$379 double. Additional person $20 per night. Children under 12 stay free in parent's room. Rates include continental breakfast. AE, DISC, MC, V. Parking $10. **Amenities:** Smoking not permitted. *In room:* Kitchenette.

Charleston Place Hotel *(Best)*   Charleston's premier hotel is an eight-story landmark in the historic district that looks like a postmodern French château. It's big-time, glossy, and urban, with prices to match, and can be both a romantic getaway for couples or a good choice for well-heeled families. Rooms are among the most spacious and handsomely furnished in town—stately, modern, and state-of-the-art. All units have well-maintained marble bathrooms with upscale amenities. Dine in the highly recommended upscale Charleston Grill (see "Where to Dine," below), then swim off the calories in the hotel's heated indoor pool.

205 Meeting St., Charleston, SC 29401. © **800/611-5545** or 843/722-4900. Fax 843/722-0728. www.charleston placehotel.com. 440 units. $259–$639 double; $639–$1,900 suite. Children under 16 stay free in parent's room. Seasonal packages available. AE, DC, DISC, MC, V. Parking $10. Pet fee $75. **Amenities:** 2 restaurants; indoor pool; rooftop tennis court; fitness center; spa.

1837 Bed & Breakfast   Built in 1837 by a cotton planter, this place, which is best for couples, was restored and decorated by two artists. It's only a single room wide—which makes for some interesting room arrangements. Our favorite is no. 2 in the Carriage House, which has authentic designs, exposed brick walls, and a beamed ceiling. All the individually furnished rooms have separate entrances and canopied poster "rice beds." On one of the verandas (the piazza), you can sit under whirling ceiling fans and enjoy your breakfast or afternoon tea.

126 Wentworth St., Charleston, SC 29401. © **877/723-1827** or 843/723-7166. Fax 843/722-7179. www.1837bb. com. 9 units. $79–$175 double. Rates include full breakfast and afternoon tea. AE, DISC, MC, V. Free off-street parking. No children under age 7. **Amenities:** Smoking not permitted. *In room:* Fridge, no phone.

Francis Marion Hotel   A $14-million award-winning restoration has returned this historic hotel to its original 1920s elegance. Although the 12-story structure breaks from the standard Charleston decorative motif and has rooms furnished in traditional European style, it is not devoid of Charleston charm. Guest rooms feature a king-size, queen-size, or double bed, and the renovated bathrooms contain tub/shower combinations with brass fixtures. The hotel's restaurant, **Swamp Fox Restaurant & Bar,** serves breakfast, lunch, and dinner, and features classic southern cuisine.

387 King St., Charleston, SC 29403. © **877/756-2121** or 843/722-0600. Fax 843/723-4633. www.francismarion charleston.com. 226 units. $179–$249 standard double; $189–$289 deluxe double; $269–$339 suite. Children 11 and under stay free in parent's room. AE, DC, DISC, MC, V. Parking $10–$15. **Amenities:** Restaurant; spa.

Market Pavilion Hotel   In the Market District, this is Charleston's latest deluxe hotel. Its owners claim, with some degree of accuracy, that they are redefining the art of southern hospitality. You don't even have to leave the premises at night, as the Pavilion Bar atop the hotel is a popular nightspot, offering a topiary-framed skyline view. The midsize-to-spacious bedrooms are beautifully furnished with marble-clad bathrooms (with bathrobes and Hermès toiletries), mahogany furniture, and such luxe touches as Frette linens and cashmere blankets on the poster beds—most often occupied by couples seeking a romantic getaway. Some rooms have balconies and/or Jacuzzi tubs.

225 E. Bay St., Charleston, SC 29401. © **877/440-2250** or 843/723-0500. www.marketpavilion.com. 66 units. $209–$239 double; from $450 suite. Rates include continental breakfast. AE, DISC, MC, V. Valet parking $15. **Amenities:** Restaurant; pool. *In room:* Kitchenette in suite.

Planters Inn   For many years this distinguished brick-sided inn (a Relais & Châteaux member) next to the City Market was left to languish, but renovations have transformed it into a tasteful enclave of Colonial charm best suited to couples. The spacious rooms have an award-winning 18th-century decor, and a number of them overlook the hotel's garden courtyard. Some of the rooms have working fireplaces; others have whirlpool tubs. Afternoon tea is served in the lobby, and there's a well-recommended restaurant, the Peninsula Grill (see "Where to Dine," below).

112 N. Market St., Charleston, SC 29401. © **800/845-7082** or 843/722-2345. Fax 843/577-2125. www.planters inn.com. 62 units. $175–$475 double; $395–$750 suite. Children 15 and under stay free in parent's room. AE, DC, DISC, MC, V. Parking $16. Pet fee $75 (under 20 lb.). **Amenities:** Restaurant.

WHERE TO DINE

Anson LOW COUNTRY/MODERN AMERICAN   Anson is a hip, stylish place with a dash of Low Country charm, perfect for a romantic evening. The setting is a century-old brick-sided ice warehouse; the owners have added New Orleans–style iron balconies, Corinthian pilasters, and Victorian rococo. A well-trained staff offers sophisticated interpretations of traditional local dishes, including fried cornmeal oysters with potato cakes; and lobster, corn, and black-bean quesadillas. Our favorite is the crispy flounder.

12 Anson St. © 843/577-0551. www.ansonrestaurant.com. Reservations recommended. Main courses $15–$29. AE, DC, DISC, MC, V. Sun–Thurs 5–10pm; Fri–Sat 5–11pm.

A. W. Shucks SEAFOOD   This is a hearty oyster bar where thousands of crustaceans have been cracked open over the years. The menu highlights oysters and clams on the half-shell, tasty seafood chowders, deviled crab, shrimp Creole, and a selection of international beers. Nobody cares how you dress—just dig in.

70 State St. ℂ **843/723-1151.** www.a-w-shucks.com. Reservations not necessary. Main courses $15–$19. AE, DC, DISC, MC, V. Sun–Thurs 11am–10pm; Fri–Sat 11am–11pm.

Charleston Grill (Best) LOW COUNTRY/FRENCH   You'll be surprised how well French and Low Country cuisine are wed at this pocket of posh in the city's best hotel, a perfect place for a romantic evening. The decor makes no concessions to southern folksiness, with its marble floors, mahogany seating, and stained glass evoking the Gilded Age. In this old-world atmosphere, you dine on Charleston's most sophisticated cuisine, touted by everyone from the *New York Times* to *Wine Spectator*. Live jazz and Charleston's best cocktails help make this an enduring favorite.

In the Charleston Place Hotel, 224 King St. ℂ **843/577-4522.** www.charlestongrill.com. Reservations recommended. Main courses $29–$41. AE, DC, DISC, MC, V. Sun–Thurs 6–10pm; Fri–Sat 6–11pm.

Cypress LOW COUNTRY   Perhaps Charleston's trendiest dining spot, this place was deservedly hailed by local food critics for raising the bar for other eateries. One of South Carolina's best restaurants, it has also won the acclaim of *Wine Spectator* for its *carte*. Ideal for a romantic night out, Cypress offers a fresh modern take on classic Low Country cooking. From Carolina waters to its rich farmlands, the chefs pick the best products to turn into their distinctive and marvelous cuisine. A wood-burning grill is a feature in the dining room. What they do here with fresh oysters is reason enough to visit.

167 E. Bay St. ℂ **843/727-0111.** www.magnolias-blossom-cypress.com. Reservations required. Main courses $19–$36. AE, MC, V. Sun–Tues 5:30–10pm; Fri–Sat 5:30–11pm.

82 Queen LOW COUNTRY   Three 18th- and 19th-century houses are clustered around an ancient magnolia tree, with outdoor tables arranged in its shade. This is classic Charleston dining. Menu items filled with flavor and flair include an award-winning version of she-crab soup laced with sherry; a down-home barbecued shrimp-and-grits; and melt-in-the-mouth crab cakes. As one diner said, "We can't wait to tell the folks up north."

82 Queen St. ℂ **843/723-7591.** www.82queen.com. Reservations recommended for dinner. Main courses $22–$26. AE, DC, DISC, MC, V. Daily 11:30am–2:30pm and 5:30–10pm.

Hank's (Kids) SEAFOOD/LOW COUNTRY   If a movie producer were seeking a setting for a 1940s Charleston fish house, Hank's would be at the top of the list. In its old-fashioned saloon-style bar, crowds of locals and visitors mingle happily. Near the City Market, this family favorite occupies a 19th-century warehouse, with pine paneling and leather booths. Sometimes there's a big line waiting to get in to sample the chef's specialties such as Charleston oyster stew, Hank's crab cakes, or an assortment from the raw bar, the town's best.

10 Hayne St. ℂ **843/723-3474.** http://hanksseafoodrestaurant.com. Reservations recommended. Main courses $20–$25. AE, DC, DISC, MC, V. Sun–Thurs 5–10:30pm; Fri–Sat 5–11:30pm.

Hominy Grill (Kids) LOW COUNTRY   This family favorite features beautifully prepared dishes, served in a friendly environment inside an 1897 historic building. A devoted local following comes here to feast on barbecued chicken sandwiches; shrimp and grits; and—a brunch favorite—smothered or poached eggs on homemade biscuits with mushroom gravy. The catfish stew with corn bread at lunch is a temptation on a cold and rainy day, and the banana bread is worth writing home about. There's also outdoor patio seating.

207 Rutledge Ave. ℂ 843/937-0930. www.hominygrill.com. Reservations accepted for dinner only. Main courses $11–$19; brunch from $10. AE, MC, V. Mon–Fri 7:30–11am and 11:30am–2:30pm; Mon–Thurs 5:30–9:30pm; Fri–Sat 5:30–10pm; Sat–Sun 9am–2:30pm (brunch).

Hyman's Seafood Company Restaurant (Value (Kids SEAFOOD Hyman's was established a century ago and continues to be one of Charleston's all-time family favorites. It sprawls over most of a city block in the heart of Charleston's business district. Inside are at least six dining rooms and a take-away deli loaded with salmon, lox, and smoked herring. One sit-down section is devoted to deli-style sandwiches, chicken soup, and salads; another to a delectably messy choice of fish, shellfish, lobsters, and oysters.

215 Meeting St. ℂ 843/723-6000. www.hymanseafood.com. Reservations not accepted. Main courses $8–$23. AE, DC, DISC, MC, V. Daily 11am–11pm.

McCrady's AMERICAN/FRENCH In the historic district, Charleston's oldest eating establishment is where George Washington dined back in 1791. It is one of the finest kitchens in the Low Country. Entered from a mysterious-looking "Jack the Ripper alley," the restaurant—housed in the city's oldest tavern, built in 1778—looks like an elegant wine cellar with rough brick walls, exposed beams, and wide plank floors. Cooking times are unerringly accurate, and a certain charm and fragrance is given to every dish on the seasonally changing menu.

2 Unity Alley. ℂ 843/577-0025. www.mccradysrestaurant.com. Reservations required. Main courses $25–$34. AE, MC, V. Daily 5:30–10pm.

Peninsula Grill LOW COUNTRY/INTERNATIONAL The Peninsula Grill has caused quite a stir, though it's quaint and quiet, full of 19th-century charm. The multi-award winner (*Food & Wine* has consistently included it among its top-50 hotel restaurants in America) is a good place for a special evening out. The menu changes frequently. Start with the James Island clams with wild mushroom bruschetta, and follow with the duo of Low Country quail and shrimp with crab. Finish up with the exceptional coconut cake. The kitchen does a marvelous job of bringing new cuisine to an old city.

In the Planters Inn, 112 N. Market St. ℂ 843/723-0700. www.peninsulagrill.com. Reservations required. Main courses $22–$34. AE, DC, DISC, MC, V. Sun–Thurs 5:30–10pm; Fri–Sat 5:30–11pm.

S.N.O.B. (Slightly North of Broad) SOUTHERN There's an exposed kitchen, a high ceiling crisscrossed with ventilation ducts, and a smattering of wrought iron in this snazzy, rehabbed warehouse. The place was one of the first in town to put a sophisticated modern spin on traditional southern dishes. Main courses can be ordered in medium and large sizes. Try the grilled barbecue tuna or the maverick grits. For dessert, make it the chocolate pecan torte, the best in town. Wine is available by the glass or bottle.

192 E. Bay St. ℂ 843/723-3424. www.slightlynorthofbroad.net. Reservations recommended. Main courses $17–$34. AE, DC, DISC, MC, V. Mon–Fri 11:30am–3pm; Sun–Thurs 5:30–10pm; Fri–Sat 5:30–11pm.

CHARLESTON AFTER DARK

THE PERFORMING ARTS   Charleston's major cultural venue is the **Dock Street Theatre,** 135 Church St. (© **843/577-7183;** www.charlestonstage.com), a 463-seat theater that hosts various companies throughout the year, especially during the annual Spoleto Festival USA in May and June. The **Robert Ivey Ballet,** 1910 Savannah Hwy. (© **843/556-1343**), offers both classical and contemporary dance as well as children's ballet programs. The **Charleston Ballet Theatre,** 477 King St. (© **843/723-7334;** www.charlestonballet.com), is one of the South's best professional ballet companies. The **Charleston Symphony Orchestra,** 160 E. Bay St. (© **843/723-7528;** www. charlestonsymphony.com), performs throughout the state, but its main venues are the Gaillard Auditorium, Sottile Theater, and North Charleston Performing Arts Center. The season runs from September to May.

THE CLUB & MUSIC SCENE   Henry's, 54 N. Market St. (© **843/723-4363**), also presents bands playing a wide range of music from Sunday to Thursday. There also is music upstairs on Friday and Saturday starting at 10pm. In a restored warehouse in the City Market area, **Tommy Condon's Irish Pub,** 160 Church St. (© **843/577-3818;** www.tommycondons.com), features live Irish entertainment Wednesday through Sunday evenings. If your musical tastes run from the Delta blues to rock to reggae, head for **Cumberland's,** 301 King St. (© **843/577-9469;** www.cumberlands. net), where people of all ages lift a glass together; music is the common bond. The **Music Farm,** 32 Ann St. (© **843/722-8904;** www.musicfarm.com), covers nearly every taste in music from country to rock with a range of live acts.

THE BAR SCENE   Our favorite watering hole is the elegant and comfortable **First Shot Bar,** in the Mills House Hotel, 115 Meeting St. (© **843/577-2400**); if you get hungry, the kitchen will whip you up some shrimp and grits. **The Griffon,** 18 Vendue Range (© **843/723-1700**), is a popular place to share a pint. **Vickery's Bar & Grill,** 15 Beaufain (© **843/577-5300;** www.vickerysbarandgrill.com), is one of the most frequented gathering places in Charleston for the younger crowd.

9 Myrtle Beach & the Grand Strand

One of the most popular destinations along the East Coast, the Grand Strand area stretches south from the South Carolina state line at Little River to Georgetown. It's 98 miles north of Charleston, but a world away in ambience. Development, mostly in the form of theme parks, kiddie attractions, minigolf courses, and condos, has proceeded at a runaway pace.

The Grand Strand hosts more than twice as many visitors each year as Hawaii, mostly families and young singles from the Carolinas, who come year after year to enjoy the beach-party scene. It's become a rival to Branson and Nashville, with more than a dozen theaters offering "family-friendly" and country-music variety shows. The bustling resort city of Myrtle Beach is at the center of it all.

ESSENTIALS

GETTING THERE   The closest airport is **Myrtle Beach International Airport** (© **843/448-1589**). If you're driving, major routes into Myrtle Beach are **U.S. 17** from the north (Wilmington) and south (Charleston), and **U.S. 501** from the west (I-95).

VISITOR INFORMATION   The **Myrtle Beach Area Chamber of Commerce** is at 1200 N. Oak St., Myrtle Beach, SC 29578 (© **800/356-3016,** or 843/626-7444 to order literature only; www.mbchamber.com), open Monday through Friday from 8:30am to 5pm, and Saturday and Sunday from 9am to 5pm. Ask for their free *Stay & Play* guide (or order it in advance via the website).

THE BEACHES, THE LINKS & BEYOND

When you're ready to hit the beach, the main action is at Ocean Boulevard and Ninth Avenue North. For more seclusion, head north of 79th Avenue for several miles. The sands here are mostly hard-packed and the color of brown sugar. The beach has life-guards and plenty of fast-food joints, but amazingly, no public toilets. However, South Carolina law obligates hotels to allow beach buffs to use their facilities.

At the southern tier of the beach, **Myrtle Beach State Park** (© 843/238-5325; www.southcarolinaparks.com) offers 312 acres of pine woods and a sandy beach. Admission to the park is $4 adults, $2.50 seniors, $1.50 children 6 to 15. There are toilets, along with pavilions, picnic tables, and a nature center. It's possible to fish from the pier for $4.50 adults, $2.92 seniors, 11 and under free. The park is full of nature trails, and offers 350 campsites that rent quickly at $25 per site, so it's a good idea to book ahead.

Serious golfers will find plenty of places to play; the area has 120 golf courses. Many golf packages are available, including accommodations and greens fees; call **Golf Holiday** (© 800/845-4653; www.golfholiday.com). **Legends,** U.S. 501, Myrtle Beach (© 800/552-2660 or 843/236-9318), designed by Pete Dye and Tom Doak, is a 54-hole, par-72 course, charging greens fees of $113. We also like the following courses: **Arcadian Shores,** 701 Hilton Rd., Arcadian Shores (© 866/326-5275 or 843/449-5217), an 18-hole, par-72 course created by Rees Jones; **Azalea Sands,** 2100 U.S. 17, in North Myrtle Beach (© 800/253-2312 or 843/272-6191), an 18-hole course with white sand traps and blue lakes; and **Beachwood,** 1520 U.S. 17, Crescent Section, North Myrtle Beach (© 800/526-4889 or 843/272-6168), which annually hosts the Dupont World Amateur Handicap Championships.

Anglers can go out after mackerel, amberjack, barracuda, sea bass, grouper, and red snapper. You'll get great fishing aboard any boat of **Captain Dick's,** Business Highway 17, at Myrtle Beach South Strand and Murrells Inlet (© 866/557-3474 or 843/651-3676; www.captdicks.com), which provides half-day party boat outings that cost $41 for adults, $25 for kids 12 and under. There are also sailings that are strictly for sightseeing, offering stunning views of the Grand Strand.

You can spend a day at the **Myrtle Waves Water Park,** 10th Avenue at U.S. 17N Bypass (© 843/448-1026; www.myrtlewaves.com), enjoying the water slides, wave pool, children's play pool, video arcade, and tanning deck. Its Turbo-Twisters is the world's tallest water ride. Adults pay $25 and children ages 3 to 6 (and seniors 55 and older) are charged $16. The park is open daily from mid-May to mid-September, with varying days and hours.

WHERE TO STAY

In addition to the listings below, other solid, moderately priced and affordable choices include the **Holiday Inn Oceanfront,** 415 S. Ocean Blvd. (© 800/845-0313 or 843/448-4481); the **Landmark Resort,** 1501 S. Ocean Blvd. (© 843/448-9441); the **Coral Beach Hotel,** 1105 S. Ocean Blvd. (© 800/843-2684 or 843/448-8421); and **St. John's Inn,** 6803 N. Ocean Blvd. (© 800/845-0624 or 843/449-5251).

The Breakers Resort *(Kids)*   This longtime family favorite is better than ever. With one of the best north beachfront locations, it occupies both a multistory complex and a 19-floor North Tower 7 blocks away. The accommodations range from tastefully furnished rooms to efficiencies with kitchenettes, and even one- to three-bedroom suites. Many rooms have balconies and refrigerators; some have microwaves. A rooftop lounge features nightly entertainment.

2006 N. Ocean Blvd., Myrtle Beach, SC 29578. (©) 800/952-4507 or 843/626-5000. Fax 843/626-5001. www.breakers. com. 400 units. $45–$165 double; $60–$209 suite. Children 16 and under stay free in parent's room. Rates include breakfast. AE, DC, DISC, MC, V. Free parking. **Amenities:** Restaurant; 4 pools (2 indoor); fitness center. *In room:* Kitchenette in suite.

Kingston Plantation & The Embassy Suites at Kingston Plantation (Best) (Kids)

This is the top choice along the strip, a 20-story main building along with two other high-rises opening onto its own 145 acres of oceanfront property. Suites with beach views have living/dining areas, kitchens, balconies, and tasteful furnishings. In addition, the hotel has two 18-story oceanfront condos and town-house villas, all with fully equipped kitchens, beautiful bathrooms, living rooms, and balconies or decks; they're great for families.

9800 Lake Dr., Myrtle Beach, SC 29572. (©) 800/876-0010 or 843/449-0006. Fax 843/497-1110. www.kingston plantation.com. 255 suites, 595 condos and villas. $160–$379 suite; $89–$419 condo or villa. Children 12 and under stay free in parent's room. AE, DC, DISC, MC, V. Free parking. **Amenities:** 2 restaurants; 12 pools (4 indoor); 4 tennis courts; fitness center; spa. *In room:* Kitchen.

Ocean Creek Resort

One of the finest resorts along the beach, this first-class choice features studios and condos of varying sizes in half a dozen different complexes spread out on almost 57 acres. Units vary in size and are suitable for families or couples; all contain kitchenettes and well-kept bathrooms with tub/shower combinations. The Beach Club on the ocean operates in summer.

10600 N. Kings Hwy., Myrtle Beach, SC 29572. (©) 877/844-3800 or 843/272-7724. Fax 843/272-9627. www.ocean creek.com. 750 units. $60–$350 studio or condo. Resort fee $3 per night. Children 17 and under stay free in parent's room. AE, DC, DISC, MC, V. Free parking. **Amenities:** Restaurant; 8 pools (1 indoor); 6 tennis courts; fitness center. *In room:* Kitchenette.

Ocean Reef Resort

North of the bustling beach center, this 16-floor oceanfront resort is well maintained and better than most other moderately priced choices. All the rooms and efficiencies are well kept and tropically inspired. Most have two double beds, balconies, and kitchenettes, attracting both the family trade and couples.

7100 N. Ocean Blvd. (at 71st Ave. N.), Myrtle Beach, SC 29577. (©) 888/322-6411 or 843/449-4441. Fax 843/497-3041. www.oceanreefmyrtlebeach.com. 291 units. $140–$165 double; $150–$400 suite. Children 17 and under stay free in parent's room. AE, DC, DISC, MC, V. Free parking. **Amenities:** Restaurant; 9 pools (1 indoor); fitness center. *In room:* Kitchenette.

WHERE TO DINE

Murrells Inlet bills itself "The Seafood Capital of South Carolina." Just take U.S. 17 (Business) south 11 miles from Myrtle Beach, and prepare to dig in. Our favorite choices for a feast are the **Fisherman's Market** (©) **843/651-6440**) and **Drunken Jacks** (©) **843/651-3232**). Both of them are on U.S. 17 (Business), right along the water.

NASCAR Cafe AMERICAN   The most intriguing of Myrtle Beach's many theme restaurants, this one is set within a building that vaguely evokes a temple to some exotic high-tech god, and the dining room is prefaced with one of the most complete collections of NASCAR memorabilia in the world. The heavily American menu is relentlessly geared to the kind of fare you might expect at Indy on a superheated race day. Your waiter (who will identify him- or herself as a member of your "pit crew") will bring you heaping portions.

1808 21st Ave. N. © 843/946-7223. www.nascarcafe.com. Reservations not accepted. Sandwiches and platters $9–$20. AE, DC, DISC, MC, V. Daily 11am–10pm (Fri–Sat until 11pm).

Sea Captain's House AMERICAN   In a 1930s beachfront home 1½ miles north of the center, this family-run restaurant is loved by locals. A glassed-in patio affords an ocean view. She-crab soup is a specialty. The seafood platter includes five different types of seafood served with slaw, potatoes, and hush puppies; and there's a selection of succulent charcoal-broiled steaks, flavorful pork chops, and Mama's southern fried chicken.

3002 N. Ocean Blvd. © 843/448-8082. www.seacaptains.com. Reservations not accepted. Main courses $7.50–$28. AE, DISC, MC, V. Daily 6–10:30am, 11:30am–2:30pm, and 5–10pm.

Thoroughbreds *Best* SEAFOOD/CONTINENTAL   This, one of the few places along the Grand Strand that truly specializes in fine dining, has been a hit ever since it opened in 1988. Guests are seated in one of four handsomely appointed rooms (mahogany, leather, fireplaces, and so on); it also has a garden terrace and a piano bar. The staff is among the best trained in the area, but the food is what keeps people coming back for more. The steaks are among the juiciest and most tender along the Strand. The wine list is long and varied.

9706 N. Kings Hwy. © 843/497-2636. Reservations recommended. www.thoroughbredsrestaurant.com. Main courses $23–$30. AE, DC, DISC, MC, V. Daily 5–10pm.

THE GRAND STRAND AFTER DARK

Tickets for most of the following variety shows and revues begin at $30 for adults. You can catch Alabama and other top country stars, or a variety show, at the **Alabama Theatre,** Barefoot Landing, North Myrtle Beach (© 800/342-2262 or 843/272-1111; www.alabama-theatre.com), which is part of a waterside shopping complex. **The Carolina Opry,** North Kings Highway at U.S. 17 (© 800/843-6779 or 843/913-4000; http://carolinaopry.com), might host country, bluegrass, big band, or patriotic music, plus comedy. The Christmas show is so popular that it's often sold out by June. The **Dixie Stampede Dinner and Show,** North Kings Highway at U.S. 17 (© 800/433-4401 or 843/497-9700; www.dixiestampede.com), owned by Dolly Parton's Dollywood Productions, is one of the most entertaining shows at the beach. Catch it if you have to skip the rest. **Legends in Concert,** 301 U.S. 17, Surfside Beach (© 800/960-SHOW or 843/238-7827; www.legendsinconcertsc.com), features an array of celebrity impersonators. **The Palace Theatre at Myrtle Beach,** 1420 Celebrity Circle (© 800/905-4228 or 843/448-9224; www.palacetheatremyrtle beach.com), features "Le Grande Cirque," and a Dean Martin Tribute show.

   Medieval Times & Dinner Complex, 2904 Fantasy Way (© 888/WE-JOUST or 843/236-8080; www.medievaltimes.com), features falconry, sorcery, swordplay, and jousting, plus a four-course banquet (no utensils, of course). Catch this production only if you have nothing else to do.

   Barefoot Landing, Highway 17 South (www.bflanding.com), offers 13 restaurants, the Alabama Theater, an endlessly popular nightlife venue—the House of Blues—and a reptilian theme park known as Alligator Adventure. Everything about this place, frankly, is well-orchestrated except for parking, which can be very hard to come by. **Broadway at the Beach,** between 22nd and 29th boulevards (© 843/444-3200;

www.broadwayatthebeach.com), includes the Hard Rock Cafe, Ripley's Aquarium, and a collection of late-night bars and dance clubs that include everything from country-western line dancing to Latino salsa. The '50s live on at **Studebaker's,** 21st Avenue North and Highway 17 (© **843/448-9747;** www.studebakersclub.com), site of the National Shag Dance Championship held annually in March.

10 Wilmington & the Outer Banks

WILMINGTON & CAPE FEAR

As the chief port of North Carolina, Wilmington is a major retail, trade, and manufacturing center, but tourism is looming larger than ever in its economy. Boasting one of the largest districts listed in the National Register of Historic Places, Wilmington is known for its preservation efforts, reflected in the restored grandeur of its antebellum, Victorian, Georgian, and Italianate homes.

ESSENTIALS

GETTING THERE Wilmington International Airport, 1740 Airport Blvd. (© **910/341-4333**), is half a mile from the center of town. Taxis meet arriving planes. By car, Wilmington is reached via **I-40** from the north (Raleigh), and **U.S. 17** from the south (Charleston, SC). A cab into town costs $10 to $14, but to get around and explore this part of the state, a car is recommended. Several major rental-car agencies have desks at the airport.

VISITOR INFORMATION The **Cape Fear Coast Convention and Visitors Bureau,** 24 N. 3rd St., Wilmington, NC 28401 (© **877/406-2356** or 910/341-4030; www.cape-fear.nc.us), is inside the Hanover County Courthouse and is open Monday through Friday from 8:30am to 5pm, Saturday from 9am to 4pm, and Sunday from 1 to 4pm. Staffers provide free information, maps, and brochures on the area.

WHAT TO SEE & DO

To get an overview of the historic Wilmington waterfront, hop aboard the *Henrietta III* (© **910/343-1611**), which departs from the foot of Market Street for a 5-mile loop of the Cape Fear River. The 45-minute narrated cruise (which runs Memorial Day to Labor Day) stops at the dock for passengers who want to tour the battleship USS *North Carolina* (see below). Tours cost $14 adults, $5 kids ages 2 to 12.

The **Cotton Exchange** in the 300 block of North Front Street (© **910/343-9896;** www.shopcottonexchange.com), an in-town shopping center, is in the old exchange building with its 2-foot-thick brick walls and hurricane rods. The small shops and restaurants are a delight, and the wrought-iron lanterns and benches add to the setting's charm. It's right on the riverfront, and there's an ample parking deck next door.

In Historic Wilmington, the old residential area bounded roughly by Nun, Princess, Front, and 4th streets, the **Burgwin-Wright House,** 224 Market St. (© **910/762-0570**), was constructed in 1771 and used by British General Cornwallis as his headquarters in 1781. You can tour the interior Tuesday through Saturday from 10am to 4pm; $8 adults, $3 students, 5 and under free.

Arlie Gardens, Arlie Road off U.S. 76 (© **910/798-7700;** www.arliegardens.org), grace the grounds of what was once the plantation home of a wealthy rice planter. These huge lawns, serene lakes, and wooded gardens hold just about every kind of azalea in existence. Admission is $5 adults, $3 children 6 to 12, under 5 free.

The **USS** *North Carolina* **Battleship Memorial,** Eagle Island (© **910/251-5797;** www.battleshipnc.com), is a memorial to the state's World War II dead. You can tour most of the ship and an exhibit focusing on recollections of the battleship's former crew. Tours are $9 adults, $8 seniors, $4.50 children 6 to 11; open Memorial Day through Labor Day daily from 8am to 8pm, off season 8am to 5pm.

Fort Fisher State Historic Site, on U.S. 421, Kure Beach (© **910/458-5538**), one of the Confederacy's largest and most technically advanced forts, was the last stronghold of the Confederate Army. After withstanding two of the heaviest naval bombardments of the Civil War, the fort finally fell to Union forces in what was the largest land-sea battle in U.S. history until World War II. Costumed tour guides welcome visitors, and living-history events are held in summer. It's open April through September Monday to Saturday from 9am to 5pm and Sunday from 1 to 5pm; October through March Tuesday to Saturday 10am to 4pm. Free admission.

BEACHES & OUTDOOR ACTIVITIES

Everyone flocks to **Wrightsville Beach,** 6 miles east of Wilmington on U.S. 74/76. The island is separated from the mainland by a small drawbridge. This wide beach stretches for a mile, with beige sands set against a backdrop of sea oats. There's also **Carolina Beach State Park,** sprawling across 1,770 acres 10 miles north of Wilmington off U.S. 421. Flanked on one bank by the Cape Fear River and on the other by the Intracoastal Waterway, it lies at the northern edge of aptly named Pleasure Island. The beach here, however, is not for swimming; it's really for sunbathing and beach-combing. Facilities include toilets, a marina, a picnic area, hiking trails, and a family campground.

At the southern tip of Pleasure Island is the small, family-friendly community of **Kure Beach.** The white-sand beaches are generally uncrowded, the restaurants are informal, and the Kure Beach fishing pier is great for anglers. You can wander through the remains of Fort Fisher (see above).

The **Belvedere Plantation Golf & Country Club,** 2368 Country Club Dr., 14 miles from Wilmington in Hampstead (© **910/270-2703**), is one of the best courses, offering a par-71, 6,401-yard, 18-hole course. It charges greens fees of $25 to $40, depending on the season and the use of carts. Reservations are requested. For more information on golf in the area, contact the CVB or head online to **www.golfcarolina. com.**

WHERE TO STAY

The **Cape Fear Coast CVB** (see above) will send you its *Accommodations Guide* and can help find you an apartment or cottage to rent for a week or more if you contact them well in advance.

The smoke-free all-suite **The Wilmington,** 101 S. 2nd St. (© **800/525-0909** or 910/343-1800; www.thewilmingtonian.com), is Wilmington's premier inn. Some suites contain kitchenettes and washer/dryers. The "special occasion" suite—ideal for a honeymoon—has a fireplace, whirlpool tub, CD player, and VCR. There's an intimate dining room and a less formal bar and grill. Rates run $135 to $165 double.

In many ways, the **Graystone Inn,** 100 S. 3rd St. (© **888/763-4773** or 910/ 763-2000; www.graystoneinn.com), is the grandest of Wilmington's B&Bs. A neo-classical stone mansion from 1905, it offers 12- to 14-foot ceilings, Victorian period furnishings, and a grand staircase of hand-carved red oak. No children under 12 are allowed. Rooms run $159 to $210 double.

Other choices include the moderately priced **Coastline Inn,** 503 Nutt St. (© **910/763-2800;** www.coastlineinn.com), and **C. W. Worth House Bed & Breakfast,** a Queen Anne confection at 412 S. 3rd St. (© **800/340-8559** or 910/762-8562; www.worthhouse.com). Nearby Wrightsville Beach has the expensive 150-room **Blockade Runner Resort Hotel & Conference Center,** 275 Waynick Blvd. (© **800/541-1161** or 910/256-2251; www.blockade-runner.com), a full-service resort with ocean views and a fine restaurant.

WHERE TO DINE

The tiny town of **Calabash,** 35 miles south of Wilmington on U.S. 17, is renowned for its seafood restaurants—about 20 of them, vying with one another to serve the biggest platter of seafood at the lowest price. You can't miss, no matter which one you choose.

Moderately priced **Café Phoenix,** 9 S. Front St. (© **910/343-1395**), a block from the water in the center of town, is easily the best bistro in Wilmington. It has a light, open, and airy decor. Lunch choices include homemade soups, fresh salads, pasta, and sandwiches. Dinner becomes more elaborate, including spinach with prosciutto or chicken piccata. Many Wilmington artists dine here, and the place has a sizable gay following.

Elijah's, 2 Ann St., Chandler's Wharf (© **910/343-1448**), is installed in a renovated maritime museum offering outdoor dining and a view of the river. Lunches tend to emphasize sandwiches and simple platters that always include a fine version of crab cakes. Dinners are more elaborate, with classic and well-prepared dishes that include soft-shell crabs. Sunday brunch here is a tradition in Wilmington. A children's menu is featured.

On the Cape Fear River in the historic and restored Craig House, the **Pilot House,** 2 Ann St., Chandler's Wharf (© **910/343-0200**), is especially known for its Low Country specialties such as shrimp and grits or crunchy catfish. There are also prime cuts of beef. A children's menu is offered.

BEAUFORT

North Carolina's third-oldest town, Beaufort (pronounced *Bo*-fort) dates from 1713. Along its narrow streets are two 200-year-old houses, and some hundred houses more than a century old. Access is on U.S. 70 just over the Grayden Paul Bridge from Morehead City. From New Bern, take U.S. 70 east. The **Beaufort Historical Association,** 138 Turner St. (© **252/728-5225;** www.historicbeaufort.com), is open Monday through Saturday from 9:30am to 5pm.

The **Beaufort Historic Site** in the 100 block of Turner Street includes the 1767 Joseph Bell House, the 1825 Josiah Bell House, the 1796 Carteret County Courthouse, the 1829 county jail, the 1859 apothecary shop and doctor's office, and the 1778 Samuel Leffers House, home of the town's first schoolmaster. Tours are given Monday through Saturday at 10am, 11:30am, 1pm, and 3pm. Adults pay $6 for the tour, and children over age 5 are charged $4.

Divers are attracted to this area because of the many wrecks off the coast. If you want to get into this action, contact **Discovery Diving Co.,** 414 Orange St. (© **252/728-2265;** www.discoverydiving.com), whose staff knows the local waters best.

Our favorite local inns are the **Beaufort Inn,** 101 Ann St. (© **252/728-2600;** www.beaufort-inn.com); **The Cedars By the Sea,** 305 Front St. (© **252/728-7036;** www.

cedarsinn.com); the **Delamar Inn Bed & Breakfast,** 217 Turner St. (© **800/349-5823** or 252/728-4300; www.bbonline.com/nc/delamarinn); and the **Pecan Tree Inn Bed & Breakfast,** 116 Queen St. (© **252/728-6733;** www.pecantree.com).

CAPE HATTERAS NATIONAL SEASHORE

The Cape Hatteras National Seashore stretches 70 miles down the Outer Banks barrier islands. The drive along N.C. 12 (about 4½ hr.) takes you through a wildlife refuge and pleasant villages, past sandy beaches, and on to Buxton and the **Cape Hatteras Lighthouse** (www.nps.gov/caha), the tallest on the coast and a symbol of North Carolina. The light has stood here since 1870 as a beacon for ships passing through these treacherous waters that have claimed more than 1,500 victims of foul weather, strong rip currents, and shifting shoals. Preservation efforts have attempted to save the lighthouse, which is constantly battered by erosion.

From the little village of **Hatteras,** with its colorful fishing fleet and popular fishing pier, a car ferry crosses to **Ocracoke Island,** where more than 5,000 acres, including 16 miles of beach, are preserved by the National Park Service. **Pea Island Wildlife Refuge** (© **252/473-1131;** www.fws.gov/peaisland), on Hatteras Island (the northern part, south of Bonner Bridge), attracts birders from all over the country.

The National Seashore is best explored on an all-day trip, or on several half-day trips, from a Nags Head base (see "Nags Head & the Outer Banks," below, for lodging recommendations). Give yourself plenty of time for swimming, fishing, or just walking along the sand.

All along **N.C. 12,** you'll see places to pull off and park to reach the beaches, which are hidden from view by huge protective sand dunes. *Note: Don't* try to park anywhere else—the sand is very soft and it's easy to get stuck. Keep in mind that tides and currents along the Outer Banks are *very* strong, and ocean swimming can be dangerous at times.

NAGS HEAD & THE OUTER BANKS

Nags Head has been one of North Carolina's most popular beach resorts for more than a century. The town itself is a collection of nondescript beach houses and motels, but it has one of the finest beaches in the state. Toilets, showers, bathhouses, and picnic shelters line some 70 miles of beaches here. Ferocious tides, strong currents, and fickle, constantly changing winds alter the beach scene from day to day on the Outer Banks. These very conditions also make ocean swimming hazardous at certain periods. If you're with children, stick to the beaches along the northern banks that have lifeguard protection; they include Kitty Hawk, Kill Devil Hills, and Nags Head, all lying along Beach Road paralleling N.C. 12. Signs direct you to the parking lots.

From Virginia and points north, you can reach Nags Head via **U.S. 158;** from Raleigh, via **U.S. 64;** from Wilmington, via the Cedar Island ferry. **N.C. 12** runs the length of the Outer Banks, from Ocracoke to Duck. The nearest airport is 80 miles northwest in Norfolk, Virginia.

Contact the **Outer Banks Visitors Bureau,** in Manteo (© **877/629-4386** or 252/473-2138; www.outerbanks.org), for information about accommodations and outdoor activities. It's open Monday to Friday from 8am to 6pm, Saturday and Sunday from 10am to 4pm.

Jockey's Ridge, north of Nags Head, is the highest sand dune on the East Coast. Its smooth, sandy, 138-foot-high slopes are part of a state park. Also north of Nags Head at **Kill Devil Hills,** the Wright brothers made that historic first air flight back in 1903.

Learning to Fly

At Milepost 8 on U.S. 158 in Kill Devil Hills, you can visit the **Wright Brothers National Memorial** (© 252/441-7430; www.nps.gov/wrbr) for $3 per person; seniors and children 16 and under are admitted free. Both the hangar and Orville's and Wilbur's living quarters have been restored, and the visitor center holds a replica of that first airplane, as well as exhibits that tell the story of the two brothers who came here on vacation from their Dayton, Ohio, bicycle business to turn their dream into reality. The memorial is open daily from 9am to 6pm (to 5pm in winter). A park ranger gives tours at 11am and 3pm year-round.

From Whalebone Junction, U.S. 64/264 leads to Roanoke Island and the village of Manteo. Four miles west, you'll reach **Fort Raleigh National Historic Site,** where the old fort has been excavated and reconstructed just as it stood in 1585. The **visitor center** (© 252/473-5772; www.nps.gov/fora) is a first stop, with a museum and an audiovisual program to acquaint visitors with the park's story. Most people visit Roanoke Island to see a performance of Paul Green's moving drama, *The Lost Colony,* presented from mid-June to late August, Monday to Saturday at 8:30pm. It's the country's oldest outdoor drama, running since 1937. All seats are reserved (contact the **Waterside Theater** at © 866/468-7630 or 252/473-3414 to charge tickets). The nearby **Elizabethan Gardens** (www.elizabethangardens.org), as well as the Tudor-style auxiliary buildings, remind us that this was the first connection between Elizabethan England and what was to become the United States of America. The gardens charge an admission price of $8 adults, $7 seniors, and $5 for children ages 6 to 18; free for children under 6.

One of the top local golf courses is **Nags Head Golf Links,** 5615 S. Seachase Dr., Nags Head (© 252/441-8073; www.nagsheadgolflinks.com), which boasts an 18-hole, 6,130-yard, par-71 course. Greens fees start at $115. Reservations are required.

Kitty Hawk Water Sports Center, Bypass Highway, Milepost 16, Nags Head (© 252/441-2756), offers watersports equipment, including windsurfers and kayaks.

Our favorite accommodations in the area include the **Sanderling Inn Resort and Spa,** 1461 Duck Rd., Duck (© 877-650-4812 or 252/261-4111; www.thesanderling. com), the premier inn of the Outer Banks, bordering the 3,400-acre Pine Island National Audubon Sanctuary, where wild horses run free. Edenton's top choice is **The Lords Proprietors' Inn,** 300 N. Broad St. (© 888/394-6622 or 252/482-3641; www. edentoninn.com). Manteo has the lovely **Tranquil House Inn,** 405 Queen Elizabeth St. (© 800/458-7069 or 252/473-1404; www.tranquilinn.com). In Nags Head, we suggest the **First Colony Inn,** 6720 S. Virginia Dare Trail (© 800/368-9390 or 252/441-2343; www.firstcolonyinn.com); or the **Nags Head Inn,** 4701 S. Virginia Dare Trail (© 800/327-8881 or 252/441-0454; www.nagsheadinn.com).

11 Pinehurst: Where Golf Is King

Midland Road (N.C. 2), a highway divided by a stately 6-mile row of pine trees and bordered by lavish homes and gardens, sets the tone for this golf mecca. About a third of the area's more than 35 golf courses are accessible via this road. (Also on Midland Rd. you'll pass a rambling white building, Midland Crafters, a virtual survey of American crafts.) In addition to golf, this area offers some of America's best tennis facilities and programs, and it's also known for its equestrian competitions. Most of these events are free to spectators. *Horse Days,* a monthly publication about events, with calendar listings, is available locally at information offices.

U.S. 1 runs north and south through Southern Pines; **N.C. 211** runs east and west; **U.S. 15/501** reaches Pinehurst from the north; there's direct area access to I-95, I-85, and I-40. Raleigh/Durham is the nearest commercial airport. We strongly recommend that you call ahead to the **Pinehurst Area Convention and Visitors Bureau,** P.O. Box 2270, Southern Pines, NC 28388 (© **800/346-5362** or 910/692-3330; www. homeofgolf.com), to get information.

The town of Pinehurst has retained its New England village air, with a village green and shaded residential streets. Moderate temperatures mean color through all seasons—camellias, azaleas, wisteria, and dogwoods.

With its more than 35 superb championship golf courses, some of which are among the highest rated in the world, Pinehurst represents golf's grandest era. Legends were born and nurtured here, and some of the finest golf architects of the 20th century designed courses in the area, including Donald Ross, Ellis Maples, Robert Trent Jones, Jack Nicklaus, and Rees Jones.

There are too many courses here to list them all, but our favorites are **Longleaf Golf and Country Club** (© **800/542-0450** or 910/692-6100; www.longleafgolf. com); the **Legacy Golf Links,** U.S. 15/501 South, Aberdeen (© **800/344-8825** or 910/944-8825; www.legacypinehurst.com), the only public course to receive *Golf Digest's* four-star rating; the **Pine Needles Resort,** Southern Pines (© **910/692-7111;** www.pineneedles-midpines.com), a Donald Ross masterpiece built in 1927; and the **Pinehurst Hotel & Country Club,** Carolina Vista (© **800/ITS-GOLF** or 910/235-8507; www.pinehurst.com), a resort with eight courses that played host to golf's U.S. Open Championship in 1999 and 2005.

Tennis buffs will find nearly 100 public courts in the area (© **910/947-2504** for locations, hours, and fees), but most resorts have their own courts.

About an hour's drive to the northwest on U.S. 220 is the little town of **Seagrove** (www.tourseagrove.com), which has been turning out pottery for more than 200 years. Many of the potters work in or behind their homes, with only a small sign outside to identify their trade; just stop and ask—everybody does, so don't be shy. While you're there, inquire about **Jugtown,** a group of rustic, log-hewn buildings in a grove of pines where potters demonstrate their art Monday to Saturday. The **Museum of North Carolina Traditional Pottery** is at 250 East Ave., just off U.S. 220 and the intersection of N.C. 705 in Seagrove (© **336/873-7887**), or stop in at their visitor center at 120 Main St.

WHERE TO STAY

Pinehurst Hotel and Country Club, Carolina Vista (© **800/ITS-GOLF** or 910/235-8507; www.pinehurst.com), is one of America's premier golf and tennis resorts. Set on 10,000 acres of landscaped grounds, it's a white, four-story clapboard landmark, with porches lined with comfortable rocking chairs. Here the art of gracious living is still practiced, and service is superb. The resort's Carolina Dining Room is the finest in the area. The major attractions, of course, are the eight 18-hole golf courses, especially the world-famous No. 2, and the 24 tennis courts. Guests also enjoy trap and skeet fields; croquet and bowling lawns; bicycles; a huge pool and deck area; and 200 acres of fishing, boating, and swimming at Lake Pinehurst. Rates run $225 to $309 double.

Other hotels offer luxury and graciousness at more moderate prices. We like the intimate **Magnolia Inn,** 65 Magnolia Rd. (℃ **800/526-5562** or 910/295-6900; www.themagnoliainn.com); and the **Pine Crest Inn,** Dogwood Road (℃ **800/371-2545** or 910/295-6121; www.pinecrestinnpinehurst.com). For the ultimate golfer's haven, check into the **Carolina** hotel, Carolina Vista Drive, in the village of Pinehurst (℃ **800/ITS-GOLF** or 910/235-8507; www.pinehurst.com), a mecca for golfers with eight 18-hole courses designed by the sport's leading golf architects. In nearby Southern Pines, there's the lovely, old-fashioned, and affordable **Mid Pines Golf Club,** 1010 Midland Rd., Southern Pines (℃ **910/692-2114;** www.pineneedles-midpines. com), as well as several chain properties.

If there's a hotel in the area that *doesn't* arrange golf times for its guests, we couldn't find it.

12 Charlotte

The second-ranked financial center in the United States (behind New York City) is home to thriving banking, insurance, and transportation industries, and does more than $900 billion worth of business each year. Suburban sprawl continues to grow, with landscaped housing developments, skyscrapers, and enormous strip malls springing up in every direction. This is the New South, built squarely on the foundation of the Old South. Though 4.5 million visitors arrive here annually (and business travelers in droves), there's not much here for the casual tourist, though the city does feature some wonderful spots for those who make the trip.

ESSENTIALS

GETTING THERE   By Plane   Charlotte–Douglas International Airport (www. charlotteairport.com) is served by most major U.S. carriers (US Airways has its hub in Charlotte—and the lion's share of flights). Taxis found outside the terminal will get you into town for about $20. If you plan on doing much exploring outside of the city proper, however, we suggest you rent a car from one of the many agencies with desks at the airport.

By Train   Amtrak (℃ **800/USA-RAIL;** www.amtrak.com) provides daily service from Atlanta (trip time: 5½ hr.) and Washington, D.C. (8 hr.), to its station at 1914 N. Tryon St.

By Car   Major routes into Charlotte are **I-85** from the northeast (Greensboro, NC) and southwest (Atlanta), and **I-77** from the north (Charleston, WV) and south (Columbia, SC).

VISITOR INFORMATION   Contact the **Charlotte Convention & Visitors Bureau,** 500 S. College St., Suite 300, Charlotte, NC 28202 (℃ **800/722-1994** or 704/334-2282; www.charlottecvb.org), open Monday through Friday from 8:30am to 5pm. For walk-in visits to pick up brochures once you're here, stop by **Visit Charlotte,** at 330 S. Tryon Street.

GETTING AROUND   Those without rental cars can use the city's visitor-friendly **trolley system** (℃ **704/336-RIDE**), which runs across the city for a fare of $1. Trolleys operate Monday to Thursday 11am to 8pm, Friday and Saturday 10am to 11pm, and Sunday 11am to 6pm.

SPECIAL EVENTS   In late April, **Springfest** brings the streets alive with music and other entertainment, and street vendors dispense a wide variety of foods. In late October, the **Bank of America 500** (© 704/455-3200) packs 'em in at the Charlotte Motor Speedway. For 6 full days in mid-September, the **Festival in the Park** in Freedom Park celebrates regional arts and crafts.

WHAT TO SEE & DO

The stately **Mint Museum of Art,** 2730 Randolph Rd. (© 704/337-2000; www. mintmuseum.org), displays a fine survey of European and American art, as well as the internationally recognized Delhom Collection of porcelain and pottery. New galleries exhibit studio glass and pottery from North Carolina studios. Admission costs $6 adults, $5 students and seniors, $3 children ages 6 to 17. **Discovery Place,** 301 N. Tryon St. (© 800/935-0553 or 704/372-6261; www.discoveryplace.org), is one of the top hands-on science and technology museums in the region and also boasts an OMNIMAX theater. Admission is $10 adults (ages 14–59), $8 seniors and children 2 to 13. OMNIMAX tickets are $8 adults, $7 for seniors and children 2 to 13.

The **Wing Haven Gardens & Bird Sanctuary,** 248 Ridgewood Ave. (© 704/331-0664; www.winghavengardens.com), is a 3-acre enclosed area in the heart of a residential neighborhood. Some 142 winged species have been sighted in the walled garden. The gardens are at their most splendid in the spring, when birds are returning from their winter migration. Donations are accepted.

Charlotte is ringed by nature preserves and parks, including the nearly 1,000-acre **McDowell Park and Nature Preserve,** about 12 miles south of the center on N.C. 49, 15222 York Rd. (© 704/588-5224). Even bigger is **Latta Plantation Nature Preserve,** 5226 Sample Rd., Huntersville (© 704/875-1391), 12 miles northeast of the center. It's a favorite resting place for waterfowl. There are also stables where you can rent horses and ride along some 7 miles of trail. A nature center and picnic tables are available. Fishing is permitted, but there is no swimming. Admission to both preserves is free.

WHERE TO STAY & DINE

The modern 700-room **Westin Charlotte,** 601 S. College St. (© 704/375-2600; www.westin.com), offers exceedingly comfortable rooms, excellent service, and a location on the city's new trolley line. Other top hotels include the **Omni Charlotte Hotel,** 132 E. Trade St. (© 704/377-0400; www.omnihotels.com); the **Hyatt Charlotte,** 5501 Carnegie Blvd., opposite South Park Mall (© 888-591-1234 or 704/554-1234; www.hyatt.com); the luxurious **Park Hotel,** 2200 Rexford Rd. (© 800/228-9290 or 704/364-8220; www.marriott.com); and the more moderately priced **Residence Inn by Marriott,** 8503 N. Tryon St. (© 800/228-9290 or 704/547-1122; www.marriott.com).

The **Coffee Cup,** 914 S. Clarkson St. (© 704/375-8855), a local favorite open for breakfast and lunch, is a roadside joint where—as they say in the South—"all God's children got chicken grease on their fingers." The more formal **La Bibliothèque,** in the Morrison Office Building, 1901 Roxborough Rd. (© 704/365-5000; www.la bibliotheque.net), serves the city's finest French cuisine; dine on the patio in good weather. For the city's best Italian, head for **Bravo,** 555 S. McDowell St. (© 704/372-5440), in the Adams Mark hotel, complete with singing waiters and a savory Mediterranean menu.

CHARLOTTE AFTER DARK

The **Charlotte Symphony Orchestra** (© 704/972-2000; www.charlottesymphony. org) plays from September to July; **Opera Carolina** (© 704/332-7177; www.opera

carolina.org) performs from September to April; and the **Charlotte Pops** (© **704/ 972-2003**) gives outdoor concerts in Freedom Park on summer evenings. Classic plays are often performed by **Theatre Charlotte,** 501 Queens Rd. (© **704/376-3777;** www.theatrecharlotte.org). The immense **N.C. Blumenthal Performing Arts Center,** 130 N. Tryon St. (© **704/372-1000** for tickets; www.performingartsctr.org), presents headline acts, touring Broadway productions, and other theatrical performances.

Swing 1000, 1000 Central Ave. (© **704/334-4443**), is a nightclub/restaurant that's brought the neo-swing movement to town. The house band plays '30s and '40s big band, and the Continental cuisine is better than you'd expect. The same owners have another hot spot at 911 E. Morehead (© **704/347-4447**) called **The Big Chill,** featuring live R&B several nights a week. The venerable **Double Door Inn,** 218 E. Independence Blvd. (© **704/376-1446;** www.doubledoorinn.com), is a legendary place to hear the blues. The popular lesbian and gay nightclub **Scorpio,** 2301 Freedom Dr. (© **704/373-9124;** www.scorpios.com), has been going strong for years.

13 The Blue Ridge Parkway

One of America's most spectacular drives, the Blue Ridge Parkway takes up where Virginia's Skyline Drive leaves off, linking the southern end of Shenandoah National Park in Virginia with the eastern entrance of the Great Smoky Mountains National Park in North Carolina. It winds and twists along the mountain crests for 469 miles, offering panoramic views along the way. October brings incredible fall foliage that paints the valleys and slopes in vivid hues of scarlet, orange, and gold (expect big crowds and lots of traffic, though). At many overlooks you'll see a rifle-and-powder-horn symbol and the word TRAIL, which means there are marked walking trails through the woods.

There are frequent exits to nearby towns, plus 11 visitor centers, nine campgrounds (open May–Oct only; no reservations) with drinking water and comfort stations (but no shower or utility hookups), restaurants, and gas stations. Before you set out, get maps and detailed information from the Superintendent, **Blue Ridge Parkway Headquarters,** 199 Hemphill Knob Rd., Asheville, NC 28803 (© **828/271-4779;** www. nps.gov/blri).

Don't plan to hurry down the Blue Ridge: If you don't have time to amble and drink in the beauty, you'll only be frustrated. If you want to drive the entire length of the parkway, allow at least 2 or 3 days. On the first day, drive the Virginia half, then stop for the night at Boone, North Carolina, not far from the state border. The final two legs of the trip (from Boone to Asheville and from there to Fontana Village) can easily be accomplished in another day's drive.

You can veer off the parkway to see a number of attractions, including **Linville Falls,** with parking at Milepost 316 on the parkway. The falls plunge into the 2,000-foot-deep Linville Gorge. A 1-mile round-trip hike leads to the upper falls; other trails lead to more views. Another stop, **Linville Caverns,** lies at Milepost 382 on the parkway, just off U.S. 221 between Linville and Marion (© **828/756-4171**). The only caverns in North Carolina, these chilly tunnels go 2,000 feet underground.

TOWNS JUST OFF THE PARKWAY

BOONE Boone has been called "the coolest spot in the South," with average temperatures around 68°F (20°C) in summer. It's a great place for golf, swimming, fishing, skiing, mountain biking, canoeing, and white-water rafting. It lies an hour from **I-77, I-81,** and **I-40,** and is accessible by three major highways, **U.S. 321, U.S. 421,**

and **U.S. 221. N.C. 105** provides access from U.S. 221. The **Boone Area Convention and Visitors Bureau,** 208 Howard St., Boone, NC 28607 (✆ **800/852-9506** or 828/ 262-3516; www.visitboonenc.com), is open Monday through Friday from 9am to 4pm.

Kermit Hunter's *Horn in the West* is presented in the Daniel Boone Theatre, 591 Horn in the West Dr. (✆ **828/264-2120**), every night except Monday from late June to mid-August. It tells a vivid story of pioneer efforts to win freedom during the American Revolution. (Reserve tickets in advance.) Next door to the theater are the **Daniel Boone Native Gardens** (✆ **828/264-6390**) and the **Hickory Ridge Home-stead Museum** (✆ **828/264-2120**), an 18th-century living-history museum in a re-created log cabin.

The **Tweetsie Railroad Theme Park,** Blowing Rock Road, halfway between Boone and Blowing Rock (✆ **800/526-5740** or 828/264-9061; www.tweetsie.com), is hokey but fun for kids.

Boone Golf Club, U.S. 321/221 South, Blowing Rock Road (✆ **828/264-8760;** www.boonegolfclub.com), is the standard all High Country public courses are meas-ured against. Greens fees are $35 to $45.

Wahoo's Adventures, on U.S. 321 between Boone and the Tweetsie Railroad Theme Park (✆ **800/444-RAFT** or 828/262-5774; www.wahoosadventures.com), is the best all-around outfitter to get you out there white-water rafting, tubing, or fishing.

For overnight stays, we recommend the **Lovill House Inn,** 404 Old Bristol Rd. (✆ **800/849-9466** or 828/264-4204; www.lovillhouseinn.com). Families might pre-fer the **Holiday Inn Express,** 1943 Blowing Rock Rd. (✆ **800/HOLIDAY** or 828/ 264-2451), the best motel in the area.

BANNER ELK & GRANDFATHER MOUNTAIN The **Avery/Banner Elk Chamber of Commerce,** 4539 Tynecastle Hwy., no. 2 in the shops of Tynecastle (✆ **800/972-2183** or 828/898-5605; www.averycounty.com), is open Monday to Fri-day from 9am to 4pm, Saturday from 10am to 4pm, and Sunday from noon to 4pm.

Kilt-clad revelers gather here early in July for the annual **Highland Games and Gathering of the Clans.** Bagpipe music, dancing, wrestling, and tossing the caber make this a spectacle not to miss.

Grandfather Mountain, on U.S. 221 near Linville, a mile off the Blue Ridge Park-way (✆ **828/733-4337**), is the highest peak in the Blue Ridge. You can see as far as 100 miles from the **Mile High Swinging Bridge,** and the **Environmental Habitat** is home to Mildred the Bear and her black bear friends. Grandfather Mountain is open daily except Thanksgiving and Christmas; admission is $14 adults, $12 seniors, $6 children 4 to 12.

There's an excellent golf course at the **Hawksnest Golf & Ski Resort,** 2853 Skyland Dr., off N.C. 105, Seven Devils (✆ **800/822-4295** or 828/963-6561; www.hawksnest-resort.com); greens fees are $30 to $50, including cart.

Our favorite lodging in the area is the intimate **Banner Elk Inn Bed and Break-fast,** N.C. 407, Main Street East (✆ **828/898-6223;** www.bannerelkinn.com). Another recommended option is **Archers Mountain Inn,** 2489 Beech Mountain Pkwy., Beech Mountain (✆ **888/827-6155** or 828/898-9004; www.archersinn.com), which has an excellent restaurant, the Jackalope's View.

BLOWING ROCK Blowing Rock is filled with little B&Bs, inns, and galleries. To get here from Boone, take U.S. 321 South directly into Blowing Rock. The **Blowing Rock Chamber of Commerce,** 132 Park Ave. (✆ **800/295-7851** or 828/295-7851; www.blowingrock.com), is open Monday to Saturday from 9am to 5pm.

The area's biggest attraction is **Blowing Rock,** on U.S. 321, 2 miles south of town (© **828/295-7111**), rising 4,000 feet above John's River Gorge. Its strong updraft returns any light object (such as a handkerchief) thrown into the void. The observation tower, gazebos, and gardens offer panoramic views. Admission is $6 adults, $1 children 4 to 11.

Shoppers can check **Expressions Craft Guild & Gallery,** Main Street (© **828/ 295-7839**), a cooperative gallery featuring contemporary local crafts. The **Parkway Craft Center,** at Milepost 294 on the Bridge Ride Parkway in the Moses Cone Manor just off Route 221 (© **828/295-7938**), offers the finest quality mountain crafts.

For luxurious lodgings in a panoramic setting, there's the **Hound Ears Club,** off N.C. 105 South near Boone (© **828/963-4321;** www.houndears.com). We also like the timeworn charm of **Crippen's Country Inn,** 239 Sunset Dr. (© **828/295-3487;** www.crippens.com), a National Historic Landmark with a good restaurant.

14 Asheville

Asheville, once just a tiny mountain trading village at the confluence of the French Broad and Swannanoa rivers, has grown up and turned into a year-round resort, complete with architectural gems from several eras and a lively cultural scene.

ESSENTIALS

GETTING THERE The **Asheville Airport** (© **828/687-2226;** www.flyavl.com) is just off I-26. Major routes into Asheville are **I-40** from the east (Raleigh and Wilmington) and west (Knoxville), and **I-26** from the southeast (Charleston).

VISITOR INFORMATION The **Asheville Convention and Visitors Bureau,** 35 Montford Ave., Asheville, NC 28802 (© **800/257-1300** or 828/258-6101; www. ashevillechamber.org or www.exploreasheville.com), is open Monday to Friday from 8:30am to 5:30pm and Saturday and Sunday from 9am to 5pm.

SPECIAL EVENTS & FESTIVALS Special happenings at Biltmore Estate include a spring **Festival of Flowers.** Fiddlers, banjo pickers, and clog dancers entertain during the first weekend of August at the **Annual Mountain Dance and Folk Festival.** Most every Saturday night in summer, there's a **Shindig-on-the-Green** downtown, with mountain musicians and dancers having an old-fashioned wingding. In Brevard, 27 miles southwest of Asheville, a major music festival is held from late June to mid-August at the **Brevard Music Center** (© **888/384-8682** or 828/862-2140; www. brevardmusic.org), with symphony, chamber music, band, and choral concerts, as well as musical comedy and opera.

WHAT TO SEE & DO

Biltmore Village is a cluster of some 24 cottages housing boutiques, crafts shops, and restaurants. The best of them is the **New Morning Gallery,** 7 Boston Way (© **828/ 274-2831**), one of the South's largest galleries of arts and crafts. Asheville is also home to more than 50 other galleries around town. **The Kress Emporium,** 19 Patton Ave. (© **828/281-2252**), serves as a showcase for more than 80 local artists and craftspeople.

Some 5 miles east of downtown Asheville, at Milepost 382 on the Blue Ridge Parkway, the **Folk Art Center** (© **828/298-7928**) displays the finest handicrafts and runs a terrific crafts shop.

Thomas Wolfe, a native of Asheville, immortalized the town in *Look Homeward, Angel.* His mother's boardinghouse at 48 Spruce St. is maintained as a literary shrine

(© **828/253-8304** for information). An arsonist set the house on fire in 1998, but it has been restored. Wolfe lived here from 1906 to 1916 and celebrated it in his classic epics such as *Look Homeward, Angel.* Family furnishings and original manuscripts are on display. Both Wolfe and short-story writer **O. Henry** (William Sydney Porter) are buried in Riverside Cemetery (entrance on Birch St. off Pearson Dr.).

The rolling terrain around Asheville offers golfers hundreds of uncrowded fairways. Our favorite course, which opened in 1899, is at **The Grove Park Inn Resort & Spa,** 290 Macon Ave. (© **828/252-2711;** www.groveparkinn.com). The par-70 course was redesigned in 1924 by master golf architect Donald Ross. Seasonal greens fees range from $85 to $165. The Grove Park is also ranked one of the country's 50 greatest tennis resorts by *Tennis* magazine. Courts can be booked by the hour ($25 indoor, $20 outdoor).

Biltmore Estate *(Best)* This French Renaissance château, built by George W. Vanderbilt, has 250 rooms, and every inch of them is extraordinary. The largest private residence in the country, the National Historic Landmark is now owned by Vanderbilt's grandson. The elder Vanderbilt journeyed through Europe and Asia purchasing paintings, porcelains, bronzes, carpets, and antiques, along with artwork by Renoir, Sargent, and Whistler, and furniture by Chippendale and Sheraton. Vanderbilt also hired Frederick Law Olmsted to create one of the most lavish formal gardens you'll ever see, ablaze with more than 200 varieties of azaleas.

1 Approach Rd. (on U.S. 25, 2 blocks north of I-40). © **800/624-1575** or 828/225-1333. www.biltmore.com. House and gardens $38–$42 adults, $20 children 6–16. Jan–Mar daily 9am–4pm; Apr–Dec daily 8:30am–5pm.

WHERE TO STAY

In the heart of downtown, the elegant all-suite **Haywood Park Hotel,** 1 Battery Park Ave. (© **800/228-2522** or 828/252-2522; www.haywoodpark.com), is tops. Outstanding historic B&B choices include the **Beaufort House Victorian Inn,** 61 N. Liberty St. (© **800/261-2221** or 828/254-8334; www.beauforthouse.com); **The Lion and the Rose Bed & Breakfast,** 276 Montford Ave. (© **800/546-6988** or 828/255-7673; www.lion-rose.com); and the **Old Reynolds Mansion,** 100 Reynolds Heights (© **800/709-0496** or 828/254-0496; www.oldreynoldsmansion.com).

Cedar Crest Victorian Inn This Queen Anne mansion is one of the largest and most opulent residences surviving Asheville's 1890s boom. The mansion has a captain's walk, projecting turrets, and expansive verandas; inside it's a fantasy of leaded glass, ornately carved fireplaces, antiques, and a massive oak staircase. Rooms are romantic and whimsical; some sport canopy beds, ideal for couples. A few bathrooms have either claw-foot or whirlpool tubs.

674 Biltmore Ave., Asheville, NC 28803. © **800/252-0310** or 828/252-1389. Fax 828/253-7667. www.cedar crestinn.com/index.html. 12 units. $150–$255 double; $230–$300 suite. Rates include breakfast. AE, DC, DISC, MC, V. Free parking. No children under 10 allowed. *In room:* Shared kitchenettes in cottages.

The Greystone Inn Henry Ford and John D. Rockefeller once whiled away their summers here at this fabled all-inclusive inn that appeals to both couples and families. Set on a wooded peninsula along the lake, this Swiss Revival mansion is a National Historic Landmark. For dedicated do-nothings, there are wicker rocking chairs on the glassed-in sun porch overlooking the lake. The midsize rooms are beautifully maintained; some offer Jacuzzis and working fireplaces. Complimentary midafternoon tea is served with cakes.

Greystone Lane, Lake Toxaway, NC 28747. (C) **800/824-5766** or 828/966-4700. Fax 828/862-5689. www.greystor. inn.com. 33 units. Nov–Apr $280–$415 double, $465 suite. May–Oct Sun–Thurs $345–$485 double, $565 suite; Fri–Sat $390–$535 double, $615 suite. Children 3 and under stay free in parent's room, ages 4–7 additional $35, ages 7–10 additional $70, 11 years or older additional $95 per night. Rates include breakfast, dinner, champagne cruise, afternoon tea, and sports activities except golf. MC, V. Free parking. **Amenities:** Restaurant; pool; golf course; 6 tennis courts; fitness center; spa.

The Grove Park Inn Resort & Spa *(Best)* With panoramic views and old-world charm, this resort, built in 1913, is one of the oldest and most famous in the South, and our favorite choice in all of western North Carolina. A National Historic Landmark, it's hosted F. Scott Fitzgerald, Thomas Edison, Henry Ford, and a couple of presidents, and today shelters everybody from honeymooners to families. The large, recently refurbished guest rooms are bastions of luxury. **Horizons Restaurant** is the finest in the area and the **Blue Ridge Dining Room** has a legendary outdoor dining veranda.

290 Macon Ave., Asheville, NC 28804. (C) **800/438-5800** or 828/252-2711. Fax 828/253-7053. www.grovepark inn.com. 510 units. High season $325–$675 double, $1,300 suite; off season $265–$525 double, $750 suite. Children 16 and under stay free in parent's room. AE, DC, DISC, MC, V. Valet parking $15; free self-parking. **Amenities:** 3 restaurants (nonsmoking); 2 pools (1 indoor); golf course; 6 tennis courts; fitness center; spa. *In room:* Fridge, microwave.

Richmond Hill Inn This inn is Asheville's premier remaining example of Queen Anne–style architecture. The interior is graced with family heirloom portraits and original oak paneling. Rooms are charming, with balconies, canopied beds, refrigerators, fireplaces, and bathrooms containing showers and claw-foot tubs. Ideal for families, nine cottages, containing rooms and suites, all with small porches and rockers, are across the way. The inn has an exceptional restaurant, **Gabrielle's,** featuring American contemporary cuisine.

87 Richmond Hill Dr., Asheville, NC 28806. (C) **800/545-9238** or 828/252-7313. Fax 828/252-8726. www.richmond hillinn.com. 36 units. $195–$295 double; $275–$495 suite. Children 16 and under stay free in parent's room. Rates include full breakfast and afternoon tea. AE, MC, V. Free parking. **Amenities:** Restaurant; fitness center.

WHERE TO DINE

The **Richmond Hill Inn** and **The Grove Park Inn Resort** have outstanding restaurants; see above.

Charlotte St. Grill AMERICAN Downstairs is an authentic-looking English pub, and upstairs is a restaurant with a Victorian decor offering more intimate dining and suitable for families. The pub keeps the longest hours, and is noted for serving one of the best-value lunches in Asheville, including freshly made pastas and house salads that are meals in themselves. No matter where you eat, the food will be well prepared and based on fresh ingredients.

157 Charlotte St. (C) **828/253-5348**. Reservations recommended. Main courses $11–$24 dinner; pub lunches $7. AE, MC, V. Restaurant Mon–Thurs 11:30am–2pm and 5–9pm, Fri–Sat 5–10pm; pub daily 11:30am–2am.

The Market Place CONTINENTAL This upscale casual restaurant with candlelit tables—ideal for a romantic evening—offers impeccable service. The chef uses extra-fresh ingredients, and all herbs and vegetables are grown locally. Many dishes are nouvelle in style and preparation, and the staff is knowledgeable about the extensive wine list.

20 Wall St. (C) **828/252-4162**. Reservations recommended. Main courses $19–$31. AE, DC, MC, V. Mon–Sat 5:30–9:30pm.

Smoky Mountains National Park

...ky Mountains are the oldest mountains in the world, composed of
...range in elevation from 840 to 6,642 feet. The oval-shaped national park,
...sected by the North Carolina–Tennessee border, encompasses more than 520,000
acres of forests, streams, rivers, waterfalls, and hiking trails. More than 200 kinds of
birds and 70 species of mammals live in the park, including the lumbering black bear,
the white-tailed deer, groundhogs, wild turkeys, and bobcats. Abundant wildflowers
offer a kaleidoscope of colors in spring and early summer and a blanket of lush greenery in later summer.

See the section "Eastern Tennessee," later in this chapter, for information on
Gatlinburg, a convenient gateway town on the western side of the park.

CHEROKEE: THE NORTH CAROLINA GATEWAY TO THE PARK

From the southern end of the Blue Ridge Parkway and points south, U.S. 441 leads
to Cherokee; U.S. 19 runs east and west through the town. Asheville is 48 miles
southwest. The **Cherokee Visitor Center,** U.S. 441 North (© **800/438-1601** or
828/497-9195; www.cherokee-nc.com), is open daily from 8:15am to 5pm.

Oconaluftee Indian Village, U.S. 441 North (© **828/497-2315;** www.oconaluftee
village.com), is a living museum of the mid-1750s Cherokee people. You'll see men
and women shaping clay into pottery, chipping arrowheads, and firing blowguns. Lectures on all facets of Cherokee life are held at the Ceremonial Grounds and at the
Council House. Admission is $13 adults, $6 children; it's open from mid-May to mid-
October daily from 9am to 5:30pm.

Unto These Hills, the most popular outdoor drama in America, is staged in Cherokee each summer, relating the story of the Cherokees from 1540 until the "Trail of
Tears" exodus to Oklahoma in 1838, when thousands died. As you watch the first
encounter with Hernando de Soto, you'll hear voices echoing off the surrounding
mountainside, the very mountainside that became a hiding place for Cherokee determined to remain in their homeland instead of joining the long march to exile in Oklahoma. Performances are at the 2,800-seat **Mountainside Theater,** off U.S. 441
(© **828/497-4557;** www.untothesehills.com). Opening night is around June 10, and
the curtain goes down for the last time at August's end. Tickets cost $20 for reserved
seating or $16 for general admission; children are charged $8. No shows on Sunday.

The major outdoor pursuit on the reservation is fishing, with 30 miles of streams
stocked with 400,000 trout annually. A tribal permit is required.

Cherokee's major hotel, **Harrah's Cherokee Casino & Hotel,** 777 Casino Dr.
(© **800/HARRAHS** or 828/497-7777; www.harrahs.com), is a 576-room, 15-story
luxury hotel connecting directly to a casino. Local Indian crafts are on display on each
floor. Harrah's is under contract with the tribe to run the casino. When Tower II opens
during the lifetime of this edition, the number of rooms will be doubled.

Cherokee also has an abundance of motels, including the **Holiday Inn–Cherokee,**
U.S. 19 South (© **800/HOLIDAY** or 828/497-9181); the **Hampton Inn,** 185
Tsalagi Rd. (© **800/HAMPTON** or 828/497-3115); the **Newfound Lodge,** 34 U.S.
441 North (© **828/497-2746**); and the **Riverside Motel,** U.S. 441 South at Old
Route 441 (© **828/497-9311**).

PARK ESSENTIALS

ACCESS POINTS & ORIENTATION   Take I-40 from Asheville to U.S. 19, then U.S. 441 to the park's southern entrance near Cherokee, a distance of 50 miles west.

Although there are several side roads into the park, the best routes are through one of the three main entrances, two of which are on Newfound Gap Road, U.S. 441, a 33-mile road that stretches north-south through the park. The southern entrance is near Cherokee, North Carolina; the northern entrance is miles away near Gatlinburg, Tennessee (p. 310). The third main entrance is on the western side of the park at Townsend, Tennessee. Other access points are from the campgrounds at the edge of the park. The park is open year-round, and admission is free.

VISITOR CENTERS   At each of the three main entrances are visitor centers for the park. Each center offers information on road, weather, camping, and backcountry conditions. You'll also find books, maps, and first-aid information.

The **Sugarlands Visitor Center and Park Headquarters** (✆ **865/436-1291** for park headquarters and all three visitor centers; www.nps.gov/grsm) is at the northern entrance, near Gatlinburg, Tennessee. The smaller **Oconaluftee Visitor Center** is at the southern entrance. Both of these offer useful exhibits to help you understand what you're seeing.

The **Cades Cove Visitor Center,** at the western end of the park, on Laurel Creek Road about 12 miles southwest of Townsend, Tennessee, is set among a cluster of historic 19th-century farms and buildings (see "Seeing the Park's Highlights," below).

The visitor centers are open year-round.

WHEN TO GO   From late March to June, spring brings great bursts of color from the wildflowers, with mild daytime temperatures and cool evenings. As summer begins, the lush greenery comes into its full splendor and the weather gets warm and humid. Although the higher elevations offer milder temperatures, ranging from the low 50s (teens Celsius) to the mid-60s (late teens Celsius), the lower ones can bring on days that are in the 90s (30s Celsius). Around the beginning of October, elevations above a mile have seen the end of fall, but lower elevations are just coming into their own with brilliant reds, yellows, oranges, purples, and browns. The best time to experience this change is from mid- to late October.

Throughout the year, weather can change rapidly. During the course of a day, you can witness several thunderstorms with breaks of clear, bright skies while temperatures change from cool and comfortable to hot and humid. The wettest months are generally March and July.

The height of the tourist season lasts from late May to late August. As autumn approaches, the park is swamped on weekends, but the crowds are much more manageable during weekdays. Early-morning hours are always a good bet to avoid the hordes.

SEEING THE PARK'S HIGHLIGHTS

If you have only 2 days to see the park, start early in the morning to avoid the crowds. When crossing the park on the **Newfound Gap Road** (U.S. 441), you should allow, at the very least, 1 hour. The speed limit does not rise above 45 mph anywhere in the park. When ascending the mountain slopes, you can rarely go over 25 to 30 mph because of the winding roads. Pack a lunch—there are no restaurants in the park, but picnic sites abound.

Your best strategy is to visit the sights along the Newfound Gap Road. Begin at the Oconaluftee Visitor Center, where you can pick up park information and get a weather report. Today the **Oconaluftee Mountain Farm Museum,** a replica of a pioneer farmstead, operates here within a collection of original log buildings. Park staff, dressed in period costumes, make it a living-history farm from April to October. About half a mile north on the Newfound Gap Road is the Mingus Mill, constructed in 1886 and still grinding wheat and corn from mid-April to October.

As you travel north, you'll come to a turnoff for **Clingmans Dome,** the highest peak in the park, soaring 6,642 feet. Once you turn onto this road, you travel 7 miles southwest to a parking lot where you can walk a steep half-mile to a viewing platform featuring one of the park's best views. Next comes **Newfound Gap,** which, at 5,048 feet, is the center of the park. If the sky is clear, you can see for miles around; on other days you find yourself literally in the clouds.

The drive across the park leads you to the Sugarlands Visitor Center, where you can stroll through the nature exhibit, view a slide show, or browse through the gift shop. At this point, you can either head into Gatlinburg for the night or go west about 5 miles on Little River Road to Elkmont Campground. It's best to make reservations (accepted only mid-May to Nov).

On Day 2, continue your journey west on Little River Road to **Cades Cove,** where you'll find more pioneer structures than at any other location in the park. Plan to spend half a day exploring the many attractions along the 11-mile **Cades Cove Loop.** Stop at the visitor center for a pamphlet containing a key for the numbered sights. Founded in 1818, the cove was a thriving, self-supporting community for more than 100 years. Original homesites, smokehouses, and barns still stand today, giving visitors a glimpse into the lives of the original settlers. You'll also find cemeteries with such epitaphs as one from the Civil War that reads BAS SHAW—KILLED BY REBELS. Cades Cove offers several nature trails. *Note:* The loop is closed to cars and open to pedestrians and cyclists on select days from May to September.

Once you've completed the Cades Cove Loop, head toward the Sugarlands Visitor Center to the Newfound Gap Road to recross the park, this time taking advantage of the numerous pull-off areas dotting the roadside, all offering good photo opportunities. At most of them you'll find "Quiet Walkways," short paths created for moments of solitude to experience nature. Don't be discouraged if a pull-off is full, because another one will appear within a mile.

OUTDOOR ACTIVITIES IN THE PARK

FISHING   The park contains more than 700 miles of streams suitable for fishing. Anglers must have a valid North Carolina or Tennessee state fishing license, which can be purchased in the gateway towns at sporting goods stores. The optimum seasons are spring and fall. Popular fishing areas include Abrams Creek, Big Creek, Fontana Lake, and Little River.

HIKING   With more than 850 miles of trails, the park offers folks of all fitness levels a chance to experience the great outdoors firsthand. (Before setting out, make sure to check the weather forecast; carry rain gear, because sudden storms are common.)

Laurel Falls Trail, the most popular waterfall and dramatic trail in the park, is an easy, flat walk; it's 1.25 miles to the falls from the Laurel Falls parking area, a few miles from the Sugarlands Visitor Center. The **Abrams Falls Trail** has an elevation gain of 340 feet. You travel 2.5 miles from the Abrams Falls parking lot at the west end of

Cades Cove Loop Road to a 20-foot-high waterfall. The trail follows a clear stream and is relatively flat. The **Ramsay Cascades Trail** has a total elevation gain of 2,375 feet and is 8 miles long round-trip. This trail also leads to Ramsay Cascades, a 100-foot-high waterfall—the park's highest. From Greenbrier Cove, follow the signs to the trail head.

The famous **Appalachian Trail** stretches from Maine to Georgia and has 68 of its 2,100 miles situated in the park, following the Smokies' ridge line from east to west almost the entire length of the park. Access points are at Newfound Gap, Clingmans Dome, the end of Tenn. 32 just north of the Big Creek Campground, and the Fontana Dam. The most popular, if strenuous, section is from Newfound Gap to Charlies Bunion.

Self-guided nature trails offer even couch potatoes an opportunity to commune with nature. These trails are staked and keyed to pamphlets with descriptions of points of interest along the way. You can get a keyed pamphlet from one of the visitor centers or stands at the trail heads. There are about a dozen such trails ranging in length from .3 mile to 6 miles. All offer easy walks through peaceful surroundings.

HORSEBACK RIDING   The park offers some of the state's most beautiful scenery for equestrians. Off-trail and cross-country riding, as well as use of hiking trails, are prohibited. The following five drive-in horse camps offer easy access to designated horse trails: Anthony Creek, Big Creek, Cataloochee, Round Bottom, and Towstring. Reservations can be made 30 days in advance with the **Backcountry Reservations Office** by calling ✆ **865/436-1231.**

Horses can be rented for $20 an hour, from mid-March to late November. Ask for details at the individual concessions within the park at **Cades Cove** (✆ 865/448-6286); **Sugarlands Riding Stables** (✆ 865/436-3885); **Smokemont Campground** (✆ 828/497-2373); and **Smoky Mountains Riding Stables,** U.S. 321 (✆ 865/436-5634). The Park Service requires that a guide accompany all rental treks.

WHITE-WATER RAFTING   Starting at the Waterville Power Plant, a 5-mile stretch of the Big Pigeon River has 10 rapids and offers some of the most challenging white-water rafting in the South. **Rafting in the Smokies** (✆ **800/776-7238** or 865/436-5008; www.raftinginthesmokies.com) rafts the Big Pigeon, Nantahala, and Ocoee rivers. A trip on the Pigeon costs $39 per person, on the Nantahala $30, and on the Ocoee River $38 to $47.

WHERE TO CAMP

The park contains 10 campgrounds with picnic tables, fire grills, cold running water, and flush toilets, but no showers or water and electrical hookups. There are three major campgrounds. **Cades Cove,** 159 sites, features a camp store, bike rentals, a disposal station, wood for sale, and naturalist programs held in the small amphitheater. **Elkmont,** 220 sites, offers a disposal station, firewood for sale, vending machines, and a phone. **Smokemont,** 142 sites, has a disposal station and firewood for sale.

Reservations (✆ **800/365-CAMP**) can be made up to 5 months in advance. The campgrounds are full on weekends beginning in April, and daily from July to October. The busiest months are July and October, and you should make reservations at least 4 weeks in advance. From mid-May to October, there's a 7-day maximum stay; from November to mid-May, with limited sites available, the maximum stay is 14 days. The charge is $17 to $23 per day. The seven smaller campgrounds, open from mid-M October, are along the boundaries of the park and cost $14 to $23 per day

WHERE TO STAY

See also "Cherokee: The North Carolina Gateway to the Park," above, and the section, "Eastern Tennessee," later in this chapter, for information on Gatlinburg, Tennessee, which borders the other side of the park and also makes an excellent base.

Offering the only accommodations in the park itself, **LeConte Lodge** (© 865/429-5704; www.leconte-lodge.com), is on top of Mount LeConte, and it's very back-to-basics—no electricity, TV, phone, or indoor plumbing, although there are four flush toilets in outhouses. You have to hike in on a 4-mile one-way trip. Lodgings include private bedrooms in cabins with shared living rooms as well as private cabins. The rates include breakfast, dinner (served family-style), and lunch for those staying more than 1 night. There are seven rooms to rent, costing $93 per adult. A two-bedroom lodge rents for $496 for up to eight people, plus $31 extra per person for meals. Reservations are difficult to come by if you don't make them in October for the following year. It's open from the last week in March to late November. No credit cards.

In Bryson City, there's the highly recommended and moderately priced **Fryemont Inn,** Fryemont Road (© 800/845-4879 or 828/488-2159; www.fryemontinn.com). In Maggie Valley, the **Cataloochee Ranch,** Fie Top Road, 119 Ranch Dr. (© 800/868-1401 or 828/926-1401; www.cataloochee-ranch.com), is a 1,000-acre spread offering loads of activities.

16 Highlights of Kentucky

LEXINGTON & THE BLUEGRASS REGION

Often called the Heart of Kentucky, the centrally located Bluegrass region offers much of what Kentucky is all about—thoroughbred horses, bourbon, basketball, natural beauty, history, and southern hospitality.

Ringed by the stunning horse farms that give this area its reputation and personality is Lexington, the state's second-largest city and a growing urban area that has just the right mix of big city excitement and small town charm.

ESSENTIALS

GETTING THERE   By Plane   Major airlines fly into **Blue Grass Airport** (© 859/425-3100; www.bluegrassairport.com), 10 minutes from downtown. There's frequent service from most Midwest hubs. Most major car-rental agencies have desks at the airport.

By Car   The major routes into Lexington are I-75 from the north (Cincinnati) and south (Knoxville), and I-64 from the east (Charleston, WV) and west (Louisville).

VISITOR INFORMATION   Contact the **Lexington Convention and Visitors Bureau,** 301 E. Vine St., Lexington, KY 40507 (© 800/84-LEX-KY or 859/233-1221; www.visitlex.com).

EXPLORING THE AREA

Calumet Farms (www.calumetfarm.com) is the granddaddy of nine Kentucky Derby champions, including three Triple Crown rm Tours, 3429 Montavesta Rd., Lexington (© 859/268-2906), tours daily at 9am and 1pm, visiting at least two farms per tour met. Advance reservations, usually at least 10 days ahead, are at $25 per person.

Claiborne Farm, Winchester Road, Paris (© **859/233-4252;** www.claiborne farm.com), was the birthplace of Seabiscuit. It's also known in part for its association with Secretariat, the 1973 Triple Crown winner considered by many to be the greatest thoroughbred of all time. The horse once stood at stud at the farm and is buried here. Tour schedules vary, so call in advance to arrange an appointment. Tours are free, but tips for the guides are customary.

Triple Crown winner Seattle Slew (in 1977) once stood at stud at **Three Chimneys Farm,** Old Frankfort Parkway, Versailles (© **859/873-7053**). The farm's free tours fill up quickly, so call for schedule information and reservations (a must). No tours are offered December through February.

Part museum, part equestrian arena, the state-run **Kentucky Horse Park,** 4089 Iron Works Pike, Lexington (© **800/568-8813** or 859/233-4303; www.kyhorsepark. com), is a mecca for horse lovers, drawing more than 700,000 visitors yearly. A gravesite statue of Man o' War, who lost only one race in his career, welcomes visitors. Seasonal horse and pony rides please the kids. Open daily from 9am to 5pm (Nov–Mar closed Mon and Tues). Admission is $14 for adults, $7 for kids ages 7 to 12.

Keeneland, 4201 Versailles Rd., Lexington (© **800/456-3412** or 859/254-3412; www.keeneland.com), a meticulously manicured racetrack, may not be as famous as Churchill Downs, but most folks think it's one of the prettiest courses in America. Much of the film *Seabiscuit* was shot here. Races are held only 6 weeks a year: three in April, including the Blue Grass Stakes, a major Kentucky Derby tune-up, and three more in October. Post time is 1:10pm. A reserved seat in the grandstand costs $6 weekdays, $8 weekends. Order tickets in advance for major stakes races.

BOURBON DISTILLERY TOURS   Bourbon, a whiskey made from at least 51% corn, is distilled in several Bluegrass region towns, but ironically, none are in Bourbon County, which is dry. (You can, however, buy bourbon in Christian County.) A number of the distilleries within easy driving distance of Lexington offer tours. For general information, contact the **Kentucky Distillers Association** (© **859/336-9612;** www. kybourbon.com). One of the oldest and largest is the **Wild Turkey Distillery,** 1525 Tyrone Rd., Lawrenceburg (© **502/839-4544;** www.wildturkeybourbon.com). It's the closest to Lexington. Free tours are conducted weekdays at 9am, 10:30am, 12:30pm, and 2:30pm. The distillery is closed the first week of January and the last 2 weeks of July.

The producers of Evan Williams bourbon, **Heaven Hill Distilleries,** 1064 Loretto Rd., Bardstown (© **502/348-3921;** www.heaven-hill.com), bill themselves as "America's largest family-owned distillery." Learn all about their brands and the history of whiskey at the new, state-of-the-art **Heaven Hill Distilleries Bourbon Heritage Center** (© **502/337-1000;** www.bourbonheritagecenter.com). Photo murals, bourbon-making artifacts, antiques, handmade quilts, and other crafts are showcased. There's also a gift shop brimming with bourbon merchandise.

Family-owned **Maker's Mark Distillery,** 3350 Burks Spring Rd., Loretto (© **270/ 865-2099;** www.makersmark.com), a small-batch distillery (peak capacity is a mere 38 barrels), has attracted a devoted following. Its silky-smooth bourbon has garnered numerous awards. Free tours are offered on the half-hour from 10:30am to 3:30pm Monday through Saturday; closed Saturdays in January and February.

The oldest operating distillery in Kentucky is **Woodford Reserve Labrot & Graham Distillery** (© **859/879-1812;** www.labrot-graham.com), 7855 McCracken Pike, Versailles, in Woodford County, a short drive from Lexington. This picturesque distillery is located among lush, rolling horse farms. There's a lunchtime cafe with indoor and alfresco seating, offering lovely views of the grounds. Tours are held Tuesday through Saturday on the hour from 10am to 4pm, with a break at noon, and Sundays at 1, 2, and 3pm. As an added perk, visitors receive free tasting-size samples of bourbon and chocolate-covered bourbon balls.

In nearby Frankfort, a 25-minute drive from Lexington, is **Buffalo Trace Distillery,** 1001 Wilkinson Blvd., Franklin County (© **800/654-8471** or 502/223-7641; www.buffalotrace.com). Bourbon making on this 110-acre site dates from 1787. In the last decade the distillery has won more international awards than any other in North America. Free tours are held every day except Sunday and holidays.

MORE ATTRACTIONS   Downtown Lexington is home to several historic buildings. Maps for these as well as a self-driving tour of the area and horse farms are available at the visitor center, 301 E. Vine (© **800/845-3959**). **Mary Todd Lincoln House,** 578 W. Main St. (© **859/233-9999;** www.mlthouse.org), was the first American historic site restored to honor a First Lady. Tours are offered from April to mid-December Tuesday through Saturday from 10am to 4pm. Admission is $7 for adults, $4 for ages 6 to 12. **Ashland,** 120 Sycamore Rd. (© **859/266-8581;** www.henry clay.org), is the beautiful 20-acre estate of famous 19th-century statesman and emancipationist Henry Clay. It's open Tuesday through Saturday from 10am to 4:30pm, Sunday from 1 to 4:30pm; closed during January. Admission is $7 for adults and $3 for ages 6 to 18.

A scenic, 25-mile drive southwest of Lexington takes you to **Shaker Village of Pleasant Hill,** 3501 Lexington Rd., Harrodsburg (© **800/734-5611** or 859/734-5411; www.shakervillageky.org), the largest historic community of its kind in America. The National Historic Landmark features 33 original 19th-century buildings and 2,800 acres of farmland. Self-guided tours, horseback riding, and riverboat excursions are offered. Dining, lodging, and two crafts shops are also on the premises. It's open daily year-round except December 24 and 25. Admission for village tours is $14 for adults, $5 for children ages 6 to 11, and free for those 5 and under.

For a culturally rich retail therapy experience, be sure to stop by the impressive **Kentucky Artisan Center at Berea** (© **859/985-5448;** www.kentuckyartisancenter. ky.gov). Located about 40 miles south of Lexington off I-75 in Berea, the state's folk arts and crafts capital, this modern, museum-like center combines exhibits, artist demonstrations, and tourist services along with a world-class gift shop featuring fine Appalachian pottery, textiles, furniture, jewelry, and basketry. There's also a good selection of books and music by noted Kentucky authors, including Bobbie Ann Mason, Sue Grafton, Barbara Kingsolver, and the late Hunter S. Thompson. Admission is free. A sunny cafe features sandwiches as well as slow-cooked comfort foods. For more information, contact the Berea Tourism Center, 201 N. Broadway (© **800/ 598-5263** or 859/986-2540).

WHERE TO STAY

Marriott's Griffin Gate Resort and Golf Club, 1800 Newtown Pike, at the intersection of I-64 and I-75, Lexington (© **800/228-9290** or 859/231-5100; www.marriott. com), is a favorite of golf fanatics. In addition to an acclaimed 18-hole golf course, the resort boasts three lighted tennis courts, indoor and outdoor swimming pools, and a full-service health club. Four restaurants and three bars keep guests entertained any time of day or night. Doubles run $189 to $319.

Across the street, another popular property offering first-class service is the **Embassy Suites,** 1801 Newtown Pike (© **800/362-2779** or 859/455-5000; www. embassysuites.com). The upscale, 230-suite hotel offers amenities including a fitness center, lap pool, jogging track, and restaurant and lounge. Guests receive a complimentary breakfast and evening reception. Suites cost $189 to $289.

In downtown Lexington, you can't beat the luxurious **Gratz Park Inn,** 120 W. Second St. (© **800/752-4166** or 859/231-1777; www.gratzparkinn.com), for convenience or attentive service. Each room is individually decorated with antiques and other historic pieces. You'll get fresh flowers every morning, and there's limo service to downtown restaurants. Rates run $169 to $249 double.

You may be right next door to the Lexington Mall, but the wrought-iron furniture, live jazz performances on weekends, and Cajun restaurant in the lobby of the **Sheraton Suites,** 2601 Richmond Rd. (© **800/262-3774** or 859/268-0060), make you feel like you're in New Orleans. Each suite ($169–$199 double) offers a hot tub and refrigerator. There's also an outdoor pool and a fitness center.

If you just want a comfortable, affordable, chain hotel, the best options are the **Best Western Regency of Lexington,** 2241 Elkhorn Rd., Lexington (© **800/528-1234** or 859/293-2202); and **Holiday Inn South,** 5532 Athens-Boonesboro Rd., Lexington (© **800/HOLIDAY** or 859/263-5241), a family-style motel that's big on facilities and welcomes pets. Both have swimming pools. Rates at both hotels range between $70 and $170 double.

Prohibition ended Silver Springs Farm's life as a bourbon distillery in 1919, but the old springhouse still stands, providing water for the horses and garden at **Bed & Breakfast at Silver Springs Farm,** 3710 Leestown Pike, Lexington (© **877/255-1784** or 859/255-1784; www.bbsilverspringsfarm.com), an affordable ($139–$199 double) horse country B&B just 5 miles from downtown. Another cozy retreat, nestled on a secluded 300-acre organic farm southeast of Lexington, is **Snug Hollow Farm Bed and Breakfast,** 790 McSwain Branch, Irvine (© **606/723-4786;** www.snug hollow.com). Guests may stay in the antiques-filled two-story farmhouse or in the comfortably furnished and fully restored chestnut-log cabin. Hearty breakfasts and gourmet vegetarian meals are a specialty at Snug Hollow. Rates range from $100 to $195 double.

LOUISVILLE

Kentucky's largest city, Louisville (say it either *Loo*-uh-vul or *Looey*-ville) sits on the southeast bank of the Ohio River across from Indiana. It's about 100 miles west of Lexington.

Louisville is best known for hosting the Kentucky Derby, held on the first Saturday in May every year. It's all but impossible to get tickets to the Derby, but Churchill Downs is open other times of the year when it's not nearly as crowded.

ESSENTIALS
GETTING THERE   By Plane   Major airlines fly into **Louisville International Airport** (© **502/368-6524;** www.louintlairport.com), 10 minutes from downtown. There's frequent service from all major Midwest hubs. The flat rate for a taxi downtown is $16 (except during Derby week, when it runs about $35).

By Car   The major routes into Louisville are I-71 from the northeast (Cincinnati), I-65 from the north (Indianapolis) and south (Nashville), and I-64 from the east (Lexington) and west (St. Louis).

VISITOR INFORMATION   Contact the **Louisville and Jefferson County Convention and Visitors Bureau,** 400 S. First St., Louisville, KY 40202 (© **800/626-5646** or 502/584-2121; www.gotolouisville.com). There's also an **Information Booth** at the airport (© **502/367-4636**). To find out what's happening around town, go online to **The Louisville Scene** (www.louisvillescene.com), or pick up a copy of the *Courier-Journal* newspaper's free entertainment tabloid, *Velocity* (www.velocity weekly.com).

WHAT TO SEE & DO

Louisville celebrates its lazily idyllic waterfront with a 7-mile **RiverWalk** along the shore. Anchoring an ongoing downtown revitalization effort is the new **Muhammad Ali Center,** 144 N. Sixth St. (© **502-584-9254;** www.alicenter.org), a $60-million museum-like conflict-resolution center inspired by the life of boxing's "Greatest," Louisville native Ali. Brad Pitt and Angelina Jolie (she funded one of the galleries) were among the celebs who attended the star-studded grand opening in November 2005. Interactive displays (see any Ali fight on demand) and exhibits trace Ali's life, his boxing career, and his accomplishments as a peace activist and humanitarian. Admission is $9 for adults, $8 for seniors, $5 for students, and $4 for children. The center is open Monday through Saturday from 9:30am to 5pm, and Sunday from noon to 5pm.

   Churchill Downs, 700 Central Ave. (© **502/636-4400;** www.churchilldowns. com), has hosted the Kentucky Derby, which runs the first Saturday in May, since it was first run in 1875. The season runs from late April to early July and from late October to November; post times vary. General admission is $2 for adults, $1 for seniors, and free for children 12 and under. Parking is free in certain areas, $3 in a lot near Gate 17, or $5 for valet.

   On the same grounds is the **Kentucky Derby Museum** (© **502/637-1111;** www. derbymuseum.org), with photos, films, exhibits, and even a chance to sit on a saddle in a real starting gate. It's open year-round Monday through Saturday from 8am to 5pm, and Sunday from noon to 5pm. Admission is $9 for adults, $8 for seniors, and $4 for children ages 5 to 12; guided tours are available every half-hour.

   The **Six Flags Kentucky Kingdom Amusement Park,** 937 Phillips Lane, Kentucky Fair and Exposition Center (© **800/SCREAMS** or 502/366-2231; www.six flags.com), boasts one of the largest wooden roller coasters in the world and a 750,000-gallon wave pool among its 60-plus rides and attractions. Different parts of the park are open at different times of year, so call before you arrange to spend the entire day. It's open from April to October. Admission is $40 for adults, $25 for seniors and children shorter than 48 inches, free for children under 3.

   The **Louisville Slugger Museum and Factory,** 800 W. Main St. (© **502/588-7228;** www.sluggermuseum.org), offers fun for all ages. Look for the giant bat (the world's tallest) standing outside the door. Inside, you can see a bat used by Babe Ruth as well as miniature souvenir bats, and feel what it's like to stare down the stitches of a 90-mph fastball. The Hillerich & Bradsby factory here is where they turn out thousands of bats for Major Leaguers every year. It's open Monday through Saturday from 9am to 5pm and Sunday noon to 5pm, with 90-minute tours of the factory every 20 minutes from 9am to 3:30pm. Admission is $9 for adults, $8 for seniors, $4 for children ages 6 to 12, and free for children 5 and under.

   Gun enthusiasts and history buffs alike will find plenty to ponder at the new **Frazier Historical Arms Museum,** 829 W. Main St. (© **866/886-7103** or 502/412-2280;

www.frazierarmsmuseum.org). The interactive museum, which opened in spring 2004, features the largest collection of arms, armor, and related historical artifacts in the world. Hours are Monday through Saturday 9am to 5pm, and Sunday noon to 5pm. Admission, which includes an audio guide, is $9 for adults; $6 for seniors, students, and children under 14; and free for children 5 and under.

The **Belle of Louisville,** moored at Fourth Street and River Road (© 502/574-2355; www.belleoflouisville.org), is the oldest operating steamboat on the Mississippi River system. The stern-wheeler was built in 1914, and is now a National Historic Landmark. There's even an old-fashioned calliope on board. The *Belle* and a larger, more modern paddle-wheeler, *Spirit of Jefferson,* carry passengers along the Ohio River. Admission for a 2-hour sightseeing cruise is $14 for adults, $11 for seniors, and $6 for ages 3 to 12.

WHERE TO STAY & DINE

The two grande dames of Louisville hotels are the **Camberley Brown,** Fourth Street and West Broadway (© **502/583-1234;** www.thebrownhotel.com; $119–$225 double); and the **Seelbach Hilton,** 500 Fourth St. (© **502/585-3200;** www.seelbach hilton.com; $239–$284 double). The Seelbach opened in 1905, the Camberley Brown in 1923; both are downtown (within boasting distance of each other). Both also have top-flight formal restaurants: The English Grill at the Camberley Brown, and The Oakroom at the Seelbach Hilton.

Along the Ohio River, the gigantic **Galt House,** Fourth Street and River Road (© **800/626-1814** or 502/589-5200; www.galthouse.com; $135–$195 double), recently underwent a $50-million renovation. A few blocks away from the riverfront is the new full-service **Louisville Marriott Downtown,** a 616-room high-rise at 280 W. Jefferson St. (© **800/533-0127** or 502/627-5045; www.marriott.com; $139–$249 double).

The chic **21c Museum Hotel,** 700 W. Main (© **877/217-6400** or 502/217-6300; www.21chotel.com), is downtown Louisville's first cutting-edge boutique hotel, featuring a 9,000-square-foot contemporary art gallery and ultramodern furnishings in its 91 rooms. Rates range from $129 to $359 double. Proof on Main is the hotel's upscale restaurant, serving Tuscan-inspired American food, including Kentucky bison and various bourbon-spiked specialty dishes. Open daily for breakfast, lunch, and dinner; entrees start at $18.

Holiday Inn (© **800/HOLIDAY;** www.holiday-inn.com) alone has more than a dozen different properties in the Louisville area. **Best Western** can be found at 4805 Brownsboro Rd. (© **502/893-2551**), and at 1301 Kentucky Mills Dr. (© **502/267-8100**).

Everybody's favorite restaurant is **Lilly's,** 1147 Bardstown Rd., east of downtown (© **502/451-0447;** http://lillyslapeche.com). Owner-chef Kathy Cary, a frequent guest chef at New York's James Beard House, combines local meats and homegrown organic vegetables to create innovative cuisine that changes with the seasons. Main courses run from $10 to $15 for lunch, and $28 to $35 for dinner. **Lynn's Paradise Cafe,** 984 Barrett Ave. (© **502/583-3447;** www.lynnsparadisecafe.com), is considerably more downscale. Folks go here for the melt-in-your-mouth buttermilk biscuits and the famed breakfast burrito. Lunch and dinner are served Tuesday through Sunday. An entree costs about $15.

NORTHERN KENTUCKY

One of the fastest growing areas of Kentucky is the northern tip, across the Ohio River from Cincinnati. Its many riverfront restaurants and hotels provide spectacular views of the river and the Cincinnati skyline.

ESSENTIALS

GETTING THERE   See "Cincinnati" on p. 489.

VISITOR INFORMATION   Contact the **Northern Kentucky Convention and Visitors Bureau,** 50 E. River Center Blvd., Suite 40, Covington, KY 41011 (© **800/ STAYNKY;** www.nkycvb.com).

WHAT TO SEE & DO

One of the newest and most popular attractions is the **Newport Aquarium,** One Aquarium Way, Newport (© **800/406-3474** or 859/491-FINS; www.newportaquarium. com), located on the banks of the Ohio directly across from downtown Cincinnati. The aquarium displays 11,000 marine animals, including 50 sharks and 16 king penguins. It also offers 200 feet of clear, seamless tunnels that put visitors literally face-to-face with sharks and other creatures of the deep. The aquarium is open 365 days a year, from 10am to 7pm Memorial Day to Labor Day, from 10am to 6pm the rest of the year. Admission is $18 for adults, $16 for seniors, and $11 for children ages 3 to 12. Late afternoon and early evening are the best times to avoid crowds.

Leaving the aquarium, head west on Fourth Street, across the Licking River, and in about 2 miles you'll come to Main Street, Covington. A left turn takes you into **Main Strasse Village,** a neighborhood that recalls northern Kentucky's German heritage. Over several blocks, visitors will find an inviting and interesting collection of shops, antiques stores, restaurants, art galleries, pubs, and neighborhood taverns. It's rarely overcrowded and great for a late-afternoon stroll and window-shopping, followed by dinner in a local haunt.

BB Riverboats, 1 Madison Ave., Covington (© **800/261-8586** or 859/261-8500; www.bbriverboats.com), offers short afternoon and evening excursions up and down the Ohio River past the city's skyline, particularly beautiful from the water at night. Call or check the website for information on the numerous options and prices.

WHERE TO STAY

Northern Kentucky has become a popular alternative overnight destination for business and leisure travelers visiting Cincinnati. Most hotels offer shuttle buses to the city or other locations in northern Kentucky. The traffic is not as bad as Cincinnati's, and guests are close to nightlife and restaurants on the south side of the Ohio River.

The **Cincinnati Marriott at RiverCenter** (© **859/261-2900;** http://marriott. com) is a new high-rise hotel right on the river at the foot of Madison Avenue in Covington, directly across from the Northern Kentucky Convention Center. It's a favorite of business travelers; weekend packages are available for leisure visitors. Rates run $144 to $239 double.

A local landmark known for its circular style, the **Radisson Hotel Cincinnati Riverfront** (© **859/491-1200;** www.radisson.com/covingtonky) sits hard against I-75—the major north-south route through Ohio and Kentucky—along Covington's Fifth Street. Rooms cost $69 to $199 double. Other riverfront hotels include **Comfort Suites Hotel** (© **859/291-6700;** www.choicehotels.com) on Newport's Riverboat Row; **Embassy Suites** (© **888/EMBASSY** or 859/261-8400; www.embassy

suites.hilton.com) at Covington's RiverCenter; **Hampton Inn/Cincinnati River-front,** 200 Crescent Ave., Covington (② **800/HAMPTON** or 859/581-7800; www. hamptoninn.hilton.com); and **Holiday Inn/Riverfront,** 600 W. Third St., Covington (② **859/291-4300;** www.holidayinn.com).

Northern Kentucky's historic riverfront neighborhoods also offer some quaint bed-and-breakfasts. Two of the best are the **Amos Shinkle Townhouse B&B,** 215 Garrard St., Covington (② **859/431-2118;** www.amosshinkle.net), which is just 2 blocks from the river near the Mike Fink restaurant; and **Christopher's Bed and Breakfast,** 604 Poplar St., Bellevue (② **888/585-7085** or 859/491-9354; www.christophersbb. com), located in a restored turn-of-the-20th-century church that features the intriguing combination of whirlpool tubs and stained-glass windows in the guest rooms. Rates at both B&Bs run $99 to $169 double.

WHERE TO DINE

For great views of the Cincinnati skyline and the Ohio River, you can't beat the restaurants along the shorelines in Covington and Newport.

One of the best restaurants in Kentucky is found in Covington's Main Strasse. **Dee Felice Café,** Sixth and Main streets (② **859/261-2365;** www.deefelice.com), mixes live jazz and spicy New Orleans–style cuisine. Main courses cost $9 to $35.

Just upriver on the east side of the Roebling Suspension Bridge—a Civil War–era span that connects Kentucky with downtown Cincinnati—is **Mike Fink's** (② **859/ 261-4212;** www.mikefink.com). Named for a legendary riverman, the restaurant is housed in a paddle-wheeler replica at the foot of Greenup Street. Known for its seafood and raw bar, this is a fun place with moderate to expensive prices (main courses $19–$51).

Though it's not directly on the river, **Behle Street Café,** adjacent to the Embassy Suites Hotel just off the riverfront in Covington (② **859/291-4100**), offers the rare combination of good food and low prices (main courses $11–$24). This is a great place to hit for a quick meal or drink before a Reds game or other evening event.

Newport, just east of Covington across the Licking River, has a whole strip of restaurants along an area known as **Riverboat Row.** Most are family-friendly and offer outdoor docks and decks that provide wonderful views of the city and give the kids a chance to feed the ducks.

At Newport on the Levee, near the aquarium, we recommend **Fat Fish Blue** (② **859/261-4401;** www.fatfishblue.com), a hip Cajun eatery that features live blues and jazz. A few blocks away there's **Hofbrauhaus** (② **859/491-7200;** www.hofbrau hausnewport.com), a friendly German-American restaurant serving up hearty Bavarian favorites. Main courses run $9 to $13.

MAMMOTH CAVE NATIONAL PARK

This is the world's longest system of caves and one of America's most popular national parks, drawing almost two million visitors a year. They come not just for the miles and miles of underground exploring, but also for the 53,000 acres of pristine hardwood forest aboveground, where you can hike, ride horses, canoe, go boating, go birding, or camp.

The best way to see everything Mammoth Cave has to offer is by taking a cave tour and then hiking the surface afterward. The parks department runs several cave tours for all ability levels, including one that's open to visitors in wheelchairs. All tours sell out quickly, especially in summer, so reserve in advance.

Travel Tip

Dial ℂ **511** on your cellphone for tourist information throughout Kentucky. Friendly operators assist by answering questions and offering area travel suggestions.

ESSENTIALS

GETTING THERE Mammoth Cave is in western Kentucky, about 100 miles south of Louisville. From Louisville, take I-65 south to Cave City; from Lexington, take the Bluegrass Parkway to I-65, then I-65 south to Cave City. From Cave City, take Ky. 70 west to the East Entrance Road. From Nashville, take I-65 north to Park City, then Ky. 255 north to the South Entrance Road.

VISITOR INFORMATION Entrance to Mammoth Cave National Park (ℂ 270/ 758-2328; www.nps.gov/maca) is free. All entrances converge at the visitor center in the southeastern corner of the park. It's open year-round, usually from 8am to 5pm (from 9am Jan–Feb). Ranger-led tours of the caves leave from the visitor center at different times throughout the day.

CAVE TOURS

Rangers lead a host of different tours through the cave, varying in difficulty from a moderate walk to an all-day affair involving crawling on hands and knees. Call the park or check the website for a complete list. Reservations are strongly recommended for all cave tours. Tours range in price from $4 to $46.

OTHER ACTIVITIES IN THE PARK

A variety of hiking trails are available throughout the park. Pick up a hiking map and a schedule of ranger-led walks and campfire and evening programs at the visitor center. Mammoth Cave has more than 30 miles of canoeing along the Green and Nolin rivers. Pick up a map at the visitor center.

WHERE TO STAY

There are three campgrounds in the park, as well as a dozen backcountry campsites where you might not see another soul. Permits are required for both types of camping. Fees range from $5 to $20 for the campgrounds; backcountry permits are free. All campgrounds have toilets, grills, and drinking water.

The **Mammoth Cave Hotel** (ℂ 270/758-2225; www.mammothcavehotel.com) is the only lodging within the park boundaries. Accommodations run $36 for basic cabins with shared bathrooms to $89 for rooms with the usual modern conveniences. Cave City is the primary gateway to the park. It has a **Best Western Kentucky Inn** (ℂ 270/773-3161), a **Comfort Inn** (ℂ 270/773-2030), and a **Super 8 Motel** (ℂ 270/ 773-2500).

DANIEL BOONE NATIONAL FOREST & KENTUCKY STATE PARKS

When Daniel Boone first crossed into what is now Kentucky more than 200 years ago, he found a naturally beautiful yet rugged landscape: a place of deep forests, high mountains, steep cliffs, pristine lakes, lush valleys, and abundant wildlife. Today, these attributes draw millions of tourists each year. The antithesis of eastern Tennessee, with its traffic congestion and overdeveloped tourist traps, the southeastern highlands of

Kentucky are picturesque and unspoiled, marked by small towns and winding, two-lane roads dotted with old barns, country stores, and the occasional antiques shop.

The **Daniel Boone National Forest,** headquartered in Winchester, KY (© 859/745-3100; www.danielboonecountry.com), covers 21 Kentucky counties. Hiking, camping, rock climbing, fishing, caving, horseback riding, boating, exploring, and hunting are among the activities available to visitors. In addition to the 269-mile Sheltowee Trace National Recreation Trail, there are hundreds of shorter hiking trails to explore.

The park has several campgrounds (© 877/444-6777), but for lodges and cabins (as well as campsites), take advantage of the magnificent **Kentucky State Parks** (© 800/225-8747; www.parks.ky.gov), regarded as the nation's best. Resort parks such as **Cumberland Falls** (© 800/325-0063 or 606/528-4121) and **Pine Mountain** (© 606/337-3066) are revered for their scenic beauty, all-ages recreation, and ranger-led nature activities, as well as for clean, comfortable accommodations and lodge restaurants. Hiking is excellent in all state parks, where maps are available at each park's main Activities Center.

Another family-oriented attraction in the area is the **Big South Fork Scenic Railway** (© 800/462-5664 or 606-376-5330; www.bsfsry.com), located in the Big South Fork National River and Recreation Area along the south-central Kentucky and Tennessee border. The slow-moving, scenic train ride departs from the small-town depot at Stearns and takes passengers to an abandoned coal mining village and back. Tickets are $15 for adults, $14 for seniors, and $7.50 for children ages 3 to 12.

For detailed information about southern and eastern Kentucky, call © 877/TOUR-SEKY, or visit www.tourseky.com.

BLUEGRASS & COAL MINES

The **Kentucky Music Hall Of Fame and Museum** (© 877/356-3263 or 606/256-1000; www.kentuckymusicmuseum.com) in Renfro Valley (south of Lexington, along I-75) honors the rich history of Kentucky performers. The log-cabin-like venue showcases home-state natives from Rosemary Clooney and Ricky Skaggs to the Backstreet Boys. Hours are 10am to 6pm Tuesday through Saturday, and 9am to 5pm Sunday. Admission is $6 for adults, $5.50 for seniors, $4.50 for children.

Down-home music and variety shows are offered March through December at the nearby **Renfro Valley Entertainment Center** (© 800/765-7464; www.renfrovalley.com). Gospel, bluegrass, country, and comedy acts take the stage at the 1,500-seat New Barn Theater (open since 1990) and the weathered, 500-seat Old Barn Theater, where the barn dances began in 1939. (Ticket prices vary.) The area has an RV Park, restaurant, and gift shop, as well as several motels.

In the breathtaking highlands of southeastern Kentucky, along the Kingdom Come Scenic Parkway in the tiny town of Benham, lies the **Kentucky Coal Mining Museum,** 221 Main St. (© 606/848-1530; www.kingdomcome.org). Antiques and exhibits pack four levels in this historic commissary, offering a somber glimpse of life in this coal mining town around the 1940s. Kids can don lighted helmets to explore a simulated mine. Country music fans will lap up all the Loretta ("Coal Miner's Daughter") Lynn memorabilia, including a replica of Butcher Holler, the log cabin where she was raised. Hours are 10am to 5pm Monday through Saturday, and 1 to 4pm Sunday. Admission is $5 for adults, $4 for seniors, and $2 for students and children.

In the northwestern Kentucky river town of Owensboro, the state-of-the-art **International Bluegrass Music Museum,** 207 E. Second St. (© 270/926-7891; www.

bluegrass-museum.org), is a must-see for fans of the genre. Bill Monroe and other pioneers are honored through educational, interactive exhibits and artifacts. Hours are 10am to 5pm Tuesday through Friday, and 1 to 5pm Saturday and Sunday. Admission is $5 for adults, $2 for youths, and free to children 6 and under. For more information, contact the Owensboro Tourist Commission, 215 E. Second St. ((℃ **800/ 489-1131** or 270/926-1100; www.visitowensboro.com).

17 Eastern Tennessee

There's much to see and do on the outskirts of majestic Smoky Mountain National Park, where strip malls and fast-food joints compete with quaint historic towns. So when you tire of bargain shopping in Pigeon Forge's outlet malls or scaling the pedestrian-friendly cliffs of Rock City near Chattanooga, get out and explore the rural countryside, where time seems to stand still.

GATLINBURG

Just 7 miles south of Pigeon Forge on U.S. 321 is Gatlinburg, which borders the Great Smoky Mountains National Park. For more information, contact the **Department of Tourism** at 811 E. Parkway ((℃ **800/267-7088** or 865/436-2392; www.gatlinburg.com).

Gatlinburg is a great place to base yourself if you're interested in being near Great Smoky Mountains National Park (see above) and want to enjoy a wide range of outdoor activities. As for the town itself, well, despite an aerial tramway/amusement park calling itself **Ober Gatlinburg** ((℃ **865/436-5423;** www.obergatlinburg.com; admission $9.50 adults, $6.50 ages 7–11) with admittedly superb views of the surrounding mountains, this is no little Switzerland. Though not as strip-malled as Pigeon Forge, crowded Gatlinburg is still lined with hotels, restaurants, and other tourist traps.

Most of Gatlinburg's attractions line the Parkway (U.S. 441). In addition to the rides and views available at the Ober Gatlinburg amusement park, the **Space Needle Family Fun Center** ((℃ **865/436-4629;** www.gatlinburgspaceneedle.com) offers a great overview of the town and a fun trip for $6.75 adults, $4.50 seniors, and $2.50 children (free for under 6 with paid adult admission). Believe it or not, **Ripley's Aquarium of the Smokies** ((℃ **888/240-1358;** www.ripleysaquariumofthesmokies. com) offers an up-close-and-personal look at our fishy friends. One-day admission is $18 for ages 12 and up, $9.95 for children 6 to 11, and $3.95 for children ages 2 to 5. The museum is open 365 days a year.

Gatlinburg is packed with chain hotels and motels. All the big names, such as **Days Inn, Comfort Inn,** and **Fairfield Inn,** have links here. Or try the **Greystone Lodge,** 559 Parkway ((℃ **800/451-9202** or 865/436-5621; www.greystonelodgetn.com), where the standard motel rooms come with balconies overlooking a stream and free breakfast ($75–$145 double; 1- and 2-bedroom cottages $125–$225).

For more upscale accommodations with spectacular mountain views, book a room or suite at **The Lodge at Buckberry Creek,** 961 Campbell Lead Rd. ((℃ **865/430- 8030** or 866/30-LODGE; www.buckberrycreek.com). Dubbed "The Great Camp of the Smokies," this elegant, Adirondack-style retreat and restaurant opened in 2005. Rates range from $180 to $360.

For hearty traditional dishes, such as moonshine chicken and barbecue ribs, try **The Park Grill Restaurant,** 1100 Parkway ((℃ **865/436-2300;** www.parkgrillgatlinburg. com), where entrees run $14 to $39. Farmhouse-style comfort food—featuring fried ham, homemade biscuits, and apple butter—also fills the bill at the **Applewood**

Farmhouse Restaurants (www.applewoodfarmhouserestaurant.com). There are several locations, including two in Gatlinburg: Applewood @ the Park, 1151 Parkway (© 865/436-4665), and the Brass Lantern, 710 Parkway (© 865/436-4669).

PIGEON FORGE

The interactive **Pigeon Forge Welcome Center,** 1950 Parkway (© 800/251-9100 or 865/453-8574; www.mypigeonforge.com), is a good starting point for exploration in the area. Other tourist centers are at 2450 Parkway and 3107 Parkway.

Pigeon Forge is honky-tonk development run amok. What it lacks in charm and beauty, though, it makes up for with its shopping bargains. There are more than 200 stores in an array of outlet malls, offering discounts of up to 75% for popular brand names like Big Dog Sportswear, Nike, and Black & Decker, as well as Bibles, Christmas decorations, quilts, and cowboy boots.

For shopping that's more quaintly "Tennessee" in tone, check out The Old Mill at 160 Old Mill Ave. (© 888/453-6455 or 865/453-4628; www.old-mill.com). It may look out of place on Pigeon Forge's relentlessly overdeveloped strip, but it's a good place to pick up locally made gifts like jams and candy and stone-ground products for your own baking. Next door, the restaurant of the same name serves hearty southern meals at breakfast, lunch, and dinner.

No trip to this part of Tennessee would be complete without a visit to **Dollywood,** 1020 Dollywood Lane (© 865/428-9488; www.dollywood.com), the amusement park owned by Pigeon Forge's beloved daughter, Dolly Parton. The park has been credited with putting Pigeon Forge on the map as a major tourist attraction and almost single-handedly turning around the city's economy. The park's souvenir stands, rides, and cheesy attractions are redeemed somewhat by Dollywood's tribute to Appalachia and the singer's own origins. Demonstrations showcase regional crafts such as basket making, pottery making, and glass blowing, and shops provide an outlet for these traditional skills that might otherwise be lost. One-day park admission is $46 for ages 12 to 59, $43 seniors, and $35 ages 4 to 11. Closed January through March.

Nightlife in Pigeon Forge focuses on musical theater. Hot tickets include Louise Mandrell's singing and dancing at the **Louise Mandrell Theater,** 2046 Parkway (© 800/768-1170 or 865/453-3534; www.louisemandrell.com). It's open from April to December.

There's no shortage of places to stay in Pigeon Forge. All the major chains are represented. If you want to be in the thick of it all, try the **Best Western Plaza Inn,** 3755 Parkway (© 800/223-9715 or 865/453-5538). If you prefer to be a little farther away from the crowds, try **Mainstay Suites,** 410 Pine Mountain Rd. (© 888/428-8350 or 865/428-8350). Both hotels have indoor and outdoor pools, and rates (about $70 double at both hotels) include breakfast.

KNOXVILLE
ESSENTIALS
GETTING THERE   By Plane   You can fly directly into Knoxville's **McGhee Tyson Airport** (© 865/342-3000; www.tys.org).

By Car   Major routes into Knoxville are I-40 from the east (Winston-Salem, NC) and west (Nashville), I-75 from the north (Lexington, KY) and south (Chattanooga and Atlanta), and I-81 from the northeast.

VISITOR INFORMATION   For information on the region, visit the **Gateway Regional Visitor Center,** 900 Volunteer Landing Lane (© **800/727-8045;** www. knoxville.org). If you're interested in country music, pick up the "Cradle of Country Music" walking tour of downtown Knoxville; if you prefer your sights vintage, try the "Historic Homes" driving tour.

WHAT TO SEE & DO

Your one can't-miss attraction is the **Knoxville Zoo,** 3333 Woodbine Ave., off I-40, near Rutledge Pike, Exit 392 (© **865/637-5331;** www.knoxville-zoo.org). In particular, watch for the sweet-looking (but apparently ill-tempered) red pandas, and the otter exhibit, where you can see the otters swimming underwater. The zoo is justifiably popular, but unfortunately a little too close to the road; it's a little odd to watch a wrinkly baby rhino eating grass against a backdrop of whizzing cars. Admission is $15 adults, $11 seniors, and $6.95 children over 3. Parking is $3.

Fans of *Roots* will want to visit the larger-than-life-size **Alex Haley statue** at 1600 Dandridge Ave., in Morningside Park near downtown Knoxville. The writer was a native of Tennessee and adopted Knoxville as his home. The park is charming, and the seated figure provides a great photo op for those wanting to clamber into the storyteller's welcoming bronze lap.

If it's raining, head over to the **Knoxville Museum of Art,** 1050 World's Fair Park Dr. (© **865/525-6101;** www.knoxart.org). The museum features about 12 exhibitions a year, as well as a permanent collection that focuses on postmodern works. Admission is $5 adults and seniors, and free for children under 17.

Or, visit the new **Women's Basketball Hall of Fame,** 700 Hall of Fame Dr. (© **865/633-9000;** www.wbhof.com), downtown; just look for the world's biggest basketball, an orange orb that stands 30 feet tall and weighs 10 tons. Admission is $7.95 adults, $5.95 seniors and children ages 6 to 15.

WHERE TO STAY & DINE

Try to stay downtown, where you'll be close to all major attractions. The **Marriott Knoxville,** 500 Hill Ave. (© **800/836-8031** or 865/637-1234), is adjacent to the new Women's Basketball Hall of Fame. The hotel has an outdoor pool (necessary in summer), a restaurant, lounge, and small fitness center. Rates run $159 to $179 double. The **Holiday Inn Select Downtown,** 525 Henley St. (© **800/HOLIDAY** or 865/522-2800), has almost identical facilities, but its pool is indoors. Rooms cost $89 to $139 double.

CHATTANOOGA

Chattanooga is a great family destination, with historic districts, Civil War sites, and interactive museums, plus a whole range of outdoor activities.

ESSENTIALS

GETTING THERE   By Plane   Major airlines serve the **Chattanooga Metropolitan Airport** (© **423/855-2200;** www.chattairport.com) from Atlanta, Cincinnati, Memphis, and Charlotte. To reach the city center, take Highway 153 south to I-75, and then go west on I-24. Exits 1A, 1B, and 1C all get you downtown.

By Car   Major routes into Chattanooga are **I-75** from the north (Knoxville) and south (Atlanta), **I-24** from the northwest (Nashville), and **I-59** from the southwest (Birmingham, AL).

VISITOR INFORMATION   Start your visit at the **Chattanooga Visitors Center,** 2 Broad St. (© **800/322-3344** or 423/756-8687; www.chattanoogafun.com), open daily from 8:30am to 5:30pm, where you can pick up some helpful brochures and maps. Here you can buy discount ticket packages, which get you into several of Chattanooga's most popular attractions. A free electric shuttle from the visitor center makes touring downtown attractions a snap.

WHAT TO SEE & DO

Adjacent to the visitor center is the **Tennessee Aquarium,** 1 Broad St. (© **800/262-0695** or 423/265-0698; www.tnaqua.org), the world's largest freshwater aquarium, with exhibits designed to take you on a journey from the Tennessee River's source in the Appalachian high country, down through the Mississippi Delta. Should you tire of watching the 9,000 critters here busily swimming, flying, and crawling, you can check out the IMAX theater. Open daily from 10am to 6pm (to 8pm some summer evenings). Admission is $18 adults, $10 ages 3 to 12, free for children under 12. Tickets to the IMAX theater are an additional $7.75 adults, $5.25 children.

The **Creative Discovery Museum,** 321 Chestnut St. (© **423/756-2738;** www.cdmfun.org), just 2 blocks from the aquarium, caters to toddlers as young as 18 months while also enthralling the older set with such interactive exhibits as the Artist's and Musician's Studios and the Inventor's Workshop. Hours are daily from 10am to 6pm Memorial Day to Labor Day; otherwise, they are Tuesday through Sunday from 10am to 5pm, and Sunday from noon to 5pm. Admission is $7.95 adults (including children ages 13 and older), $6.95 children 2 to 12.

Culture vultures flock to the **Bluff View Art District** (© **423/265-5033;** www.bluffview.com), located just east of the Walnut Street Pedestrian Bridge. Spend some time ambling through the free Sculpture Garden, perched scenically on a bluff overlooking the Tennessee River. The **Houston Museum of Decorative Arts,** 201 High St. (© **423/267-7176**), houses an impressive glass collection. It's open Monday through Saturday from 9:30am to 4pm, summer Sundays from noon to 4pm. Admission is $7. Reopened in 2005 after a yearlong renovation, the **Hunter Museum of American Art,** 10 Bluff View (© **865/267-0968;** www.huntermuseum.org), showcases paintings, sculpture, decorative arts, and contemporary studio glass—not to mention spectacular river views. Just across the Walnut Street bridge is Coolidge Park, with its beautiful hand-carved carousel; and Frasier Street, where you'll find some funky shops and cafes.

EXPLORING AROUND LOOKOUT MOUNTAIN

From downtown, Lookout Mountain can be reached quickly and easily via Broad Street to Tenn. 58. Don't miss historic **Incline Railway,** 827 E. Brow Rd. (© **423/821-4224;** www.lookoutmountainattractions.com), the steepest passenger railway in the world with panoramic views of the city and the Great Smoky Mountains 100 miles away. Round-trips cost $12 adults and $6 ages 3 to 12. Open daily.

Also on Lookout Mountain is **Ruby Falls,** 1720 S. Scenic Hwy. (© **423/821-2544;** www.rubyfalls.com), a 145-foot waterfall located 1,100 feet inside the mountain. If you're at all claustrophobic, or simply don't want to be herded through a cave with a large group of people, skip it. Open daily at 8am. Admission is $15 adults and $7 ages 3 to 12.

Best among Lookout Mountain's main attractions is **Rock City Gardens,** 1 ′ Patten Rd. (© **706/820-2531** or 800-854-0675; www.seerockcity.com), where have a view of seven states on a clear day. Rock City's unique sandstone formations are striking, and younger kids will be fascinated by the displays based on classic fairy tales and nursery rhymes. Open daily year-round. Admission is $15 adults and $7.95 for ages 3 to 12.

Civil War buffs should check out **The Battles for Chattanooga Museum,** 1110 E. Brow Rd. (© **423/821-2812;** www.battlesforchattanooga.com). Just 3 blocks from the Incline Railroad's upper station at the entrance to **Point Park** (site of the "Battle above the Clouds" in 1863), this museum features a three-dimensional electronic battle map that presents details of major battles in Chattanooga's Civil War history. It's open daily; admission is $6.95 adults, $4.95 ages 3 to 12.

WHERE TO STAY & DINE

If the name *Chattanooga* makes you yearn for the days of leisurely train travel, there's no better place to stay than the **Chattanooga Choo Choo/Holiday Inn,** 1400 Market St. (© **800/TRACK-29** or 423/266-5000; www.choochoo.com), formerly Chattanooga's main railway terminal. Reserve the motel-issue rooms in the main building for all the comforts of a chain, or if you've got a sense of whimsy or are traveling with kids, try one of the converted train cars. Rates run $99 to $169 double. Alternatively, the Sheraton **Read House Hotel Chattanooga,** MLK Boulevard and Broad Street (© **800/333-3333** or 423/266-4121; www.readhousehotel.com), is a lovely National Historic Landmark. Rates run $139 to $289 double. Both hotels are on the shuttle route downtown.

After a day spent touring Lookout Mountain attractions, you can't go wrong with a meal at **Mount Vernon,** 3509 Broad St. (© **423/266-6591**), a family-friendly, white-tablecloth restaurant. Besides their signature fried green tomatoes, the locally owned landmark serves delicious salads along with steaks, seafood, and burgers. An entree will set you back about $10.

If you prefer a B&B atmosphere, head to the **Bluff View Inn,** 412 E. 2nd St. (© **423/265-5033**), in the Bluff View Arts District, where rooms are spread across three historic houses and rates run $105 to $240 double. There are several dining options in the district, including the **Back Inn Café,** which has a lovely outdoor patio overlooking the river. Other options are **Tony's Pasta Shop and Trattoria** and **Rembrandt's Coffee House** (try the hand-dipped chocolates or the lemon tarts).

18 Nashville

Nashville may be the capital of Tennessee, but it's better known as Music City USA, the country music capital of the world. At its epicenter, Nashville is still the city where unknown musicians can become overnight sensations, where the major record deals are cut and music-publishing fortunes are made, and where the *Grand Ole Opry* still takes center stage.

ESSENTIALS

GETTING THERE **By Plane** **Nashville International Airport** (© **615/275-**
...ed about 8 miles east of downtown Nashville and is just south of I-40. ...5 minutes to reach downtown Nashville from the airport. Many hotels ...t offer a complimentary shuttle service, while others slightly farther ...own fee shuttles; check with your hotel when you make your reserva-
...**Line Airport Express** (© **615/883-5555**) operates shuttles between

the airport and downtown and West End hotels. They run every 15 to 20 minutes daily between 5am and 11pm and will cost you $12 one-way and $18 round-trip.

By Car   Nashville is a hub city intersected by three interstate highways. **I-65** runs north to Louisville, Kentucky, and south to Birmingham, Alabama. **I-40** runs west to Memphis and east to Knoxville, Tennessee. **I-24** runs northwest toward St. Louis and southeast toward Atlanta.

VISITOR INFORMATION   Before heading to Music City, you can get more information on the city by contacting the **Nashville Convention & Visitors Bureau,** 211 Commerce St. (© **800/657-6910** or 615/259-4700; www.visitmusiccity.com).

GETTING AROUND   Because the city and its attractions are spread out, the best way to get around Nashville is by car.

Though it won't get you everywhere you need to go, Nashville is served by the Metropolitan Transit Authority (MTA) bus system (© **615/862-5950**). The MTA information center and ticket booth is on Deaderick Street at Fifth Avenue. Adult **bus fares** are $1.10 ($1.50 for express buses); children under 4 ride free. Exact change is required. You can purchase a weekly pass good for unlimited local rides from Sunday to Saturday for $15 per adult or $9 per youth age 19 and under; a picture ID is required. Seniors and riders with disabilities qualify for a 70¢ fare with an MTA Golden Age, Medicare, Tennesenior, or Special Service card. Call © **615/862-5950** to register for this discount.

For a quick way to get around downtown during weekdays, look for the Lunch-LINE shuttles. As a convenience to downtown workers, the Central Business Improvement District and Nashville Downtown Partnership offers a **free trolley** that loops through the heart of downtown weekdays from 11am to 1:30pm. Riders may hop on or off at any of the 15 stops. No tickets are required.

For quick cab service, call **American Music City Taxi** (© **615/262-0451**), **Checker Cab** (© **615/256-7000**), or **Allied Taxi** (© **615/244-7433**). The flag-drop rate is $3; after that it's $1.90 per mile.

WHAT TO SEE & DO

Country Music Hall of Fame and Museum *(Best)*   If you're a fan of country music, this is *the* museum in Nashville. Even if you aren't, almost anyone with an appreciation for American popular music will thrill to such sights as Bob Dylan's barely legible inscription scrawled across a lyric sheet; Emmylou Harris's petite, bejeweled cowboy boots; and Elvis's gold-leafed Cadillac (a gift from Priscilla). Savvy multimedia exhibits let visitors explore displays on bluegrass, cowboy music (a la Roy Rogers), country swing, rockabilly, Cajun, honky-tonk, and contemporary country music through personalized CD listening posts, interactive jukeboxes, and computer stations. Nashville resident Vince Gill is said to be a regular here, and other legends have been known to drop by for impromptu concerts.

222 5th Ave. S. (at Demonbreun). © **800/852-6437** or 615/416-2001. www.countrymusichalloffame.com. Admission $17 adults, $8.95 children 6–17. Daily 9am–5pm.

Grand Ole Opry Museum   Adjacent to the Grand Ole Opry House, these exhibits are tributes to the performers who have appeared on the famous radio show over the years: Patsy Cline, Hank Snow, George Jones, Jim Reeves, Marty Robbins, and other longtime stars of the show. There are also about a dozen other exhibits on more recent performers. These museums are best visited in conjunction with a night at the *Opry,*

Nashville

ACCOMMODATIONS ■

Embassy Suites Nashville **3**

The Hermitage Hotel **5**

The Millennium Maxwell House Hotel **6**

DINING ◆

Blackstone Restaurant & Brewery **2**

Bound'ry **1**

The Old Spaghetti Factory **7**

Noshville **4**

6

Harrison St.
5th Ave.
2nd Ave.
Main St.
Woodland St.

Nashville
Coliseum

Gay St.
Pearl St.
Charlotte
Ave.
Union St.
Church St.
3rd Ave.
7
Riverfront Park
Shelby Ave.
24
65

5

11th Ave.
12th Ave.
10th Ave.
8th Ave.
9th Ave.
Commerce St.
DOWN-TOWN
McGavock St.
1st Ave.
Cumberland River

40

i
6th Ave.
7th Ave.
4th Ave.
Shirley St.
Peabody St.
Rutledge St.
Hermitage Ave.

Broadway
Demonbreun St.
Bus Station
Lea Ave.
Lafayette St.
Lindsley Ave.

McGavock St.
17th Ave.
Music Row
Division St.
40
65
24
40

16th Ave.
Grand Ave.
12th Ave.
41
705

Edgehill Ave.
31
Fort Negley Park
City Cemetery
Murfreesboro Pike

Franklin Pike
4th Ave.

Ave.
65

Tennessee State Fairgrounds

Nolensville Pike

Nashville
24
65
265
MUSIC VALLEY
Area shown
THE DISTRICT
Cumberland River
DOWN-TOWN
THE WEST END
440
65
24
70
40
40

0   1/2 mi
0   0.5 km

so you might want to arrive early. Allow 20 to 30 minutes (just right for browsing before attending a performance of the *Grand Ole Opry*).

2804 Opryland Dr. ℂ 615/871-OPRY (6779). www.opry.com. Free admission. Daily 10am to varied closing hours depending on performance schedule. Closes for special events; call ahead. At the Grand Ole Opry House (it's within the same complex).

The Hermitage *(Kids)* Andrew Jackson, whose visage graces the $20 bill, built The Hermitage, a stately southern plantation home. Originally built in the Federal style in 1821, The Hermitage was expanded and remodeled in 1831, and acquired its current appearance in 1836. Recordings that describe each room and section of the grounds accompany tours through the mansion and around it. In addition to the main house, you'll also visit the kitchen, the smokehouse, the garden, Jackson's tomb, an original log cabin, the spring house (a cool storage house built over a spring), and, nearby, the Old Hermitage Church and Tulip Grove mansion. You can tour the museum and grounds in a few hours.

Old Hickory Blvd. ℂ **615/889-2941.** www.thehermitage.com. Admission $12 adults, $11 seniors, $5 children 6–12, free for children under 6. Daily 9am–5pm. Closed Thanksgiving, Dec 25, Jan 1, and 3rd week of Jan. Take I-40 east to Exit 221, then head north 4 miles.

The Parthenon This full-size replica of the Athens Parthenon was the centerpiece of the Tennessee Centennial Exposition of 1897. The original structure was only meant to be temporary but the city opted to reconstruct a permanent Parthenon in 1931. The building now duplicates the floor plan of the original Parthenon in Greece. Inside stands the 42-foot statue of Athena Parthenos, the goddess of wisdom, prudent warfare, and the arts. Newly gilded with 8 pounds of gold leaf, she is the tallest indoor sculpture in the country. A more recent renovation of the building included air-conditioning, which makes for pleasant viewing on muggy summer days.

Centennial Park, W. End Ave. (at W. End and 25th aves.). ℂ **615/862-8431.** www.parthenon.org. Admission $4 adults, $2.50 seniors and children. Oct–Mar Tues–Sat 9am–4:30pm; Apr–Sept Tues–Sat 9am–4:30pm, Sun 12:30–4:30pm. (Closed Sun after Labor Day.)

Ryman Auditorium & Museum The site of the *Grand Ole Opry* from 1943 to 1974, the Ryman Auditorium is known as the "Mother Church of Country Music," the single most historic site in the world of country music. Originally built in 1892, its stage has seen the likes of Enrico Caruso, Katharine Hepburn, Will Rogers, and Elvis Presley. The *Grand Ole Opry* began broadcasting from here in 1943 and hosted the most famous country music radio show in the world until 1974. Since its meticulous renovation in 1994, the Ryman has regained its prominence as a temple of bluegrass and country music. Allow at least an hour for a self-guided tour or opt for a live show instead.

116 5th Ave. N. (between Commerce and Broadway). ℂ **615/254-1445** or 615/889-3060. www.ryman.com. Admission $8 adults, $4 children 4–11, free for children under 4. Daily 9am–4pm. Closed Thanksgiving, Dec 25, and Jan 1.

WHERE TO STAY

National and regional chain motels in the area are increasing exponentially. Some of the newest properties include the following (see appendix D for toll-free reservation numbers): **Doubletree Guest Suites,** 2424 Atrium Way (ℂ **615/889-8889**), charging $89 to $179 for a double; **Homewood Suites,** 2640 Elm Hill Pike (ℂ **615/884-8111**), charging $79 to $134; and **Quality Inn and Suites,** 2521 Elm Hill Pike (ℂ **615/391-3919**), charging $90 to $120 for a double.

Embassy Suites Nashville *(Kids)*   This all-suite hotel makes a great choice and a good value for families, as well as business travelers. Not only do you get a two-room suite, but breakfast and evening cocktails are included in the rates. The centerpiece of the hotel is its large atrium, which is full of tropical plants, including palm trees. The casual restaurant is located amid the tropical plants in the atrium and serves moderately priced meals. Also in the atrium are the lounge where the evening manager's reception is held and a dining area where complimentary breakfast is served.

10 Century Blvd., Nashville, TN 37214. (✆) **800/EMBASSY** or 615/871-0033. Fax 615/883-9245. www.embassy-suites.com. 296 units. $99–$179 suite. Rates include cooked-to-order breakfast. AE, DC, DISC, MC, V. Free parking. **Amenities:** Restaurant; indoor pool; exercise room. *In room:* Fridge.

The Hermitage Hotel *(Best)*   This historic downtown hotel, built in 1910 in the classic Beaux Arts style, is Nashville's grand hotel. Reopened in 2003 after an $18-million restoration, this is the city's top choice if you crave both space and elegance. The lobby, with its marble columns, gilded plasterwork, and stained-glass ceiling, is the most magnificent in the city. Afternoon tea is served here Thursday through Saturday. Guest rooms (all of which are suites) are recently upgraded, spacious, and comfortable, with down-filled duvets and pillows on the beds. North-side rooms have good views of the capitol.

231 6th Ave. N., Nashville, TN 37219. (✆) **888/888-9414** or 615/244-3121. Fax 615/254-6909. www.thehermitage hotel.com. 123 suites. $299–$399 suite; $950 2-bedroom suite. AE, DC, DISC, MC, V. Valet parking $18 plus tax. Pets allowed ($25 daily fee). **Amenities:** Restaurant.

Holiday Inn Express Airport *(Value)*   Gone are the rustic mountain-lodge decorations that used to set this chain hotel apart from all the others. A recent renovation of the lobby replaced the folksy furnishings with sleek leather armchairs and marble-top tables. The guest rooms are all fairly spacious, with country-pine furniture and extralarge bathrooms. Many rooms have little balconies overlooking the courtyard gardens or the rolling hills of the surrounding office park.

1111 Airport Center Dr., Nashville, TN 37214. (✆) **800/HOLIDAY** or 615/883-1366. Fax 615/889-6867. www.holiday-inn. com. 212 units. $79–$99 double. Rates include continental breakfast and free local calls. AE, DC, DISC, MC, V. Free parking. **Amenities:** Pool.

The Millennium Maxwell House Hotel   So just why is a hotel named for a brand of coffee? The original Maxwell House, where President Theodore Roosevelt stayed, was in downtown Nashville. This modern-day successor is a 10-story hotel that sits north of downtown. The rooms are decorated in muted/earth tones, with your choice of full-size or king-size beds. Rather basic but relaxing and pleasant. South-side rooms on the upper floors of the hotel have a commanding view of the Nashville skyline and are well worth requesting. Glass elevators also take full advantage of the unobstructed outside views.

2025 Metro Center Blvd., Nashville, TN 37228-1505. (✆) **800/457-4460** or 615/259-4343. Fax 615/313-1327. www. millennium-hotels.com. 289 units. $80–$140 double; $175–$400 suite. AE, DC, DISC, MC, V. Free self-parking. **Amenities:** Restaurant; pool; nearby golf course; 2 lighted tennis courts; exercise room.

Opryland Hotel *(Kids)*   What Graceland is to Memphis, Opryland is to Nashville. Whether you're into country music or not, a tour of this palatial property with its 85-foot water fountains, tropical foliage, shops, restaurants, and winding "rivers" has become almost obligatory. The Opryland has the look and feel of a massive theme park and it does attract thousands of visitors daily (on top of the numbers who are actually staying at this massive hotel). Guest rooms, while modern and comfortable, don't quite live up to the promise of the public areas. There's something here for all tastes and budgets.

2800 Opryland Dr., Nashville, TN 37214-1297. (℃ **888/777-OPRY** or 615/889-1000. Fax 615/871-5728. www. gaylordhotels.com. 2,881 units. $189–$279 double; $319–$3,500 suite. AE, DC, DISC, MC, V. Valet parking $18 plus tax; self-parking $10 plus tax. **Amenities:** 7 restaurants; 3 pools (1 indoor); golf club; exercise room; salon/spa. *In room:* Kitchen or kitchenette (in suites).

Sheraton Music City Big, elegant, and set on 23 acres in a modern business park near the airport, this large convention hotel has a commanding vista of the surrounding area. In the elegant lobby, you'll find marble floors and burnished cherrywood paneling. Off to one side is a lounge with the feel of a conservatory. Following a recent $8-million renovation, all guest rooms have been updated with an eye toward the business traveler; each room has three phones, large work desks, and plenty of closet space, as well as a couple of comfortable chairs.

777 McGavock Pike, Nashville, TN 37214-3175. (℃ **800/325-3535** or 615/885-2200. Fax 615/231-1134. www.sheraton musiccity.com. 410 units. $99–$179 double; $150–$600 suite. AE, DC, DISC, MC, V. Valet parking $7; free self-parking. **Amenities:** Restaurant; 2 pools (1 indoor); tennis courts; health club.

WHERE TO DINE

When you just need a quick pick-me-up, a rich pastry, or some good rustic bread for a picnic, there are several good cafes, coffeehouses, and bakeries scattered around the city.

In hip Hillsboro Village, you'll find **Fido,** 1812 21st Ave. S. (℃ **615/385-7959**), a big place with an artsy, urban feel. No, it's not one of those upscale dog bakeries. Though the space used to be a pet shop, it is the friendliest coffeehouse in Nashville. Across the street, you'll find **Provence Breads & Café,** 1705 21st Ave. S. (℃ **615/ 386-0363;** www.provencebreads.com), which bakes the best breads and pastries in town and also serves sandwiches and salads. Provence also has a stylish bistro in the new downtown library, 601 Church St. (℃ **615/644-1150**).

In the downtown area, **Cibo,** 706 Church St. (℃ **615/726-2426**), is a cozy European cafe renowned for its pastries and baked goods as well as salads, sandwiches, and take-home entrees such as manicotti and chocolate cake.

Blackstone Restaurant & Brewery BURGERS/NEW AMERICAN   At this glitzy brewpub, brewing tanks in the front window silently crank out half a dozen different beers ranging from a pale ale to a dark porter. Whether you're looking for a quick bite of pub grub (pizzas, soups, pub-style burgers) or a more formal dinner (a meaty pork loin well complemented by apple chutney and a smidgen of rosemary, garlic, and juniper berries), you'll be satisfied with the food here, especially if you're into good microbrews.

1918 West End Ave. (℃ 615/327-9969. Sandwiches, pizza, and main courses $8–$20. AE, DC, DISC, MC, V. Mon–Thurs 11am–midnight; Fri–Sat 11am–1am; Sun noon–10pm.

Bound'ry *(Best)* NEW AMERICAN/NEW SOUTHERN   With its colorful murals and chaotic angles (seemingly inspired by Dr. Seuss), this Vanderbilt campus-area eatery is a fun yet sophisticated bastion of trendiness, popular with everyone from college students to families to businesspeople in suits. Add some jazz to the wild interior design and you have a very energetic atmosphere. In addition to signature salads such as the Bound'ry, which combines endive and radish relish with crispy ham, tomatoes, and black-eyed peas, "large platter" entrees include vegetarian dishes such as polenta stacked with eggplant, portobello mushrooms, and cheeses to meaty pork chops and steaks, including the 16-ounce porterhouse. Wine and beer choices are extensive.

911 20th Ave. S. ✆ 615/321-3043. www.pansouth.net. Reservations recommended, except Fri–Sat after 6:30pm when it's first-come, first-served. Tapas $4.75–$11; main courses $20–$30. AE, DC, DISC, MC, V. Restaurant daily 5pm–1am; bar daily 4pm–2:30am.

Cock of the Walk SOUTHERN   No, roosters aren't on the menu. The restaurant takes its unusual name from an old flatboatman's term for the top boatman. This big, barnlike eatery near the Opryland Hotel is well known around Nashville for having the best seafood in town. Like the catfish filets and dill pickles on the menu, the shrimp and chicken are fried in peanut oil. Rounding out the hearty platters are sides such as beans and turnip greens brought to the table in big pots.

2624 Music Valley Dr. ✆ 615/889-1930. www.cockofthewalkrestaurant.com. Reservations accepted for groups of 20 or more. Main courses $9–$12. AE, DISC, MC, V. Mon–Thurs 5–9pm; Fri–Sat 5–10pm; Sun 11am–9pm.

Harper's AMERICAN/SOUTHERN   If the thought of slow-simmered turnip greens, crispy fried chicken, tender sweet potatoes, and fluffy yeast rolls makes your mouth water, wipe off your chin and immediately head to the Jefferson Street district for Nashville's best soul food. Be sure to save room for a slice of pie or a heaping bowl of banana pudding. Popular with white-collar professionals and blue-collar laborers alike, Harper's attracts a friendly, diverse clientele. Unlike seamier soul-food haunts, this immaculate cafeteria accepts credit cards but (thankfully) does not allow smoking.

2610 Jefferson St. ✆ 615/329-1909. Main courses $4–$7. AE, DISC, MC, V. Mon–Fri 10am–8pm; Sat–Sun 11am–6pm.

Loveless Café SOUTHERN   For some of the best country cooking in the Nashville area, take a trip to this old-fashioned roadhouse and popular Nashville institution. People rave about the cooking here—and with good reason. Southern specialties are made just the way Granny used to make them back when the Loveless opened nearly 40 years ago. This restaurant may be a little out-of-the-way, but it's well worth it if you like down-home cookin'—and if you're prepared to endure a long wait to get one of the few available tables inside.

8400 Tenn. 100 (about 7½ miles south of Belle Meade and the turnoff from U.S. 70 S.). ✆ 615/646-9700. www. lovelesscafe.com. Reservations recommended. Breakfast $5.50–$9; dinner main courses $10–$14. AE, MC, V. Daily 7am–9pm.

Noshville DELICATESSEN   When the deli craving strikes in Nashville, head for Noshville. The deli cases in this big, bright, and antiseptic place are filled to overflowing with everything from beef tongue to pickled herring to corned beef to chopped liver. Make mama happy: Start your meal with some good matzo-ball soup. Then satisfy the kid inside you by splurging on a hefty, two-fisted chocolate-and-vanilla-iced shortbread cookie.

1918 Broadway. ✆ 615/329-NOSH. www.noshville.com. Main courses $6–$16. AE, DC, DISC, MC, V. Mon 6:30am–2:30pm; Tues–Thurs 6:30am–9pm; Fri 6:30am–10:30pm; Sat 7:30am–10:30pm; Sun 7:30am–9pm.

The Old Spaghetti Factory *(Kids)* ITALIAN   With its ornate Victorian elegance, you'd never guess that this restaurant was once a warehouse. Where boxes and bags were stacked, diners now sit surrounded by burnished wood. There's stained and beveled glass all around, antiques everywhere, and plush seating in the waiting area. The front of the restaurant is a large and very elegant bar. Now if they'd just do something about that trolley car someone parked in the middle of the dining room. A great spot to bring the family, this is one of the cheapest places to get a meal in The District.

160 2nd Ave. N. ℂ 615/254-9010. www.osf.com. Main courses $4.60–$10. DISC, MC, V. Mon–Fri 11:30am–2pm; Mon–Thurs 5–10pm; Sat noon–11pm; Sun noon–10pm.

Whitt's Barbecue *Value* BARBECUE   Walk in, drive up, or get it delivered. Whitt's serves some of the best barbecue in Nashville. There's no seating here, so take it back to your hotel or plan a picnic. You can buy barbecued pork, beef, and even turkey by the pound, or order sandwiches and plates with the extra fixins. The pork barbecue sandwiches, topped with zesty coleslaw, get my vote for the best in town. Among the many other locations are those at 2535 Lebanon Rd. (ℂ **615/883-6907**), and 114 Old Hickory Blvd. E. (ℂ **615/868-1369**).

5310 Harding Rd. ℂ 615/356-3435. www.whittsbarbecue.com. Meals $3–$8; barbecue $6.60 per pound. AE, DC, DISC, MC, V. Mon–Sat 10:30am–8pm.

NASHVILLE'S COUNTRY MUSIC SCENE

Nashville nightlife happens all around town but predominates in two main entertainment areas—The District and Music Valley. **The District,** an area of renovated warehouses and old bars, is the livelier of the two, whereas **Music Valley** offers a more family-oriented, suburban nightlife scene.

The *Nashville Scene* is the city's arts-and-entertainment weekly. It comes out on Thursday and is available at restaurants, clubs, convenience stores, and other locations. Just keep your eyes peeled. Every Friday, the *Tennessean,* Nashville's morning daily, publishes the *Opry* lineup, and on Sunday it publishes a guide to the coming week's entertainment. *Jazz & Blues News* is a free monthly newsletter featuring news and event listings of interest to music buffs of these genres. It can be found at local bookstores and cafes such as Café One Two Three.

The show that made Nashville famous, the *Grand Ole Opry,* 2804 Opryland Dr. (ℂ **800/SEE-OPRY** or 675-871-OPRY; www.opry.com), is the country's longest continuously running radio show and airs every weekend from this theater next to the Opryland Hotel. Over the decades, the Opry has featured nearly all the greats of country music. There's no telling who you might see, but the show's membership roster includes Vince Gill, Martina McBride, Garth Brooks, Loretta Lynn, Porter Wagoner, Ricky Skaggs, and many others. Nearly all performances sell out, and though it's often possible to get last-minute tickets, you should try to order tickets as far in advance of your trip as possible.

Once the home of the *Grand Ole Opry,* **Ryman Auditorium,** 116 5th Ave. N. (ℂ **615/254-1445** or 615/889-6611; www.ryman.com), was renovated a few years back and is once again hosting performances with a country-music slant. The schedule at the Ryman also usually includes a weekly bluegrass night in the summer and occasional Sunday-night gospel/Christian contemporary shows. You can also catch pop, rock, and classical concerts.

The **Texas Troubadour Theatre,** Music Valley Village, 2416 Music Valley Dr. (ℂ **615/889-2474**), is home to the Ernest Tubb Midnight Jamboree and the Sunday morning Cowboy Church.

The **Nashville Palace,** 2400 Music Valley Dr. (ℂ **615/884-3004**), is open nightly with live country-and-western music, a dance floor, and a full restaurant. This is where Randy Travis got his start.

The **Wildhorse Saloon,** 120 2nd Ave. N. (ℂ **615/251-1000;** www.wildhorse saloon.com), is a massive dance hall that's the hot spot for boot scooters, attracting everyone from country-music stars to line-dancing senior groups. Free line-dance lessons are available every hour.

The Bluebird Café, 4104 Hillsboro Rd. (© **615/383-1461;** www.bluebirdcafe. com), is Nashville's premier venue for both up-and-coming and established songwriters. Between 6 and 7pm, there is frequently music in the round, during which four singer-songwriters play some of their latest works. After 9pm, when more established acts take the stage, there's a cover charge. Reservations are recommended. The Bluebird's main competition is the **Douglas Corner Café,** 2106 8th Ave. S. (© **615/298-1688;** www.musicdigest.com/douglascorner). Though it has the look and feel of a neighborhood bar, this is one of Nashville's top places for songwriters trying to break into the big time. The club also has occasional shows by performers already established. It's located a few minutes south of downtown.

Tootsie's Orchid Lounge, 422 Broadway (© **615/726-0463;** www.tootsies.net), has been a Nashville tradition for decades, and still offers free live country music all day and all night.

SIDE TRIPS FROM NASHVILLE

To visit both the battlefield and the distillery described below, head south from Nashville on I-24.

On New Year's Eve 1862, what would become the bloodiest Civil War battle west of the Appalachian Mountains began just north of Murfreesboro along the Stones River. By the end of the first day of fighting the Confederates thought they were assured a victory, but Union reinforcements turned the tide against the Rebels. By January 3, the Confederates were in retreat and 23,000 soldiers lay dead or injured on the battlefield. Today, 351 acres of the site of the conflict are preserved in the **Stones River National Battlefield,** 3501 Old Nashville Hwy., Murfreesboro (© **615/893-9501**). The site includes a national cemetery and the Hazen Brigade Monument, which was erected in 1863 and is believed to be the oldest Civil War memorial in the United States. In the visitor center, you'll find a museum full of artifacts and details of the battle. Free admission; open daily from 8am to 5pm.

Old Jack Daniel (or Mr. Jack, as he was known hereabouts) didn't waste any time setting up his whiskey distillery after the Civil War came to an end. Founded in 1866, the **Jack Daniel's Distillery,** Tenn. 55, Lynchburg (© **931/759-4221;** www.jack daniels.com), is the oldest registered distillery in the United States and is on the National Register of Historic Places. After touring the distillery, you can glance into the office used by Mr. Jack and see the safe that did him in. Old Mr. Jack kicked that safe one day in a fit of anger and wound up getting gangrene for his troubles. If you want to take home a special bottle of Jack Daniel's, it can be purchased here at the distillery, but nowhere else in this county, which is another of Tennessee's dry counties. Free admission. It's open to the public daily except major holidays from 8am to 4:30pm, with tours at regular intervals throughout the day. No reservations.

19 Memphis

A trip to Memphis is a pilgrimage for Elvis fans and for music fans drawn to the birthplace of the most important musical styles of the 20th century—blues, soul, and rock 'n' roll. Memphis is where W. C. Handy put down on paper the first written blues music, where The King made his first recording, and where Otis Redding and Al Green expressed the music in their souls.

Memphis

ACCOMMODATIONS ■
French Quarter Suites Hotel **1**
Madison Hotel **7**
The Peabody Memphis **5**
Talbot Heirs Guesthouse **2**

DINING ◆
Automatic Slim's
 Tonga Club **3**
Chez Philippe **6**
Huey's **3**
Rendezvous **4**

Located at the far western end of Tennessee, Memphis sits on a bluff overlooking the Mississippi River, Arkansas and, a few miles to the south, Mississippi. With a metropolitan area of one million, it is a sprawling city, with high-rises sprouting in suburban neighborhoods. The wealthy live, do business, and shop in East Memphis, but in recent years Midtown, with its old homes and tree-lined streets, has been rediscovered and now blossoms with hip restaurants, boutiques, and nightlife.

But it was the renovation of Beale Street that succeeded in bringing business and people back downtown in the '90s. Beale Street was home to W. C. Handy, B. B. King, Muddy Waters, and others who merged the gospel singing and cotton-field word songs of the Mississippi delta into music called the blues.

Downtown Area

Madison Ave.

7

Monroe Ave.

Union Ave.

Gayoso Ave.

6

Bus
Station

Peabody 3 Pl.

2

4 5

Beale St.

Riverside Dr.

Wagner Pl.

Front St.

Main St.

Second St.

Third St.

Fourth St.

Linden Ave.

Church
Park

ⓘ

Jackson Ave.

**Rhodes
College**

North Pkwy.

Summer Ave.

Broad Ave.

Park Ave.

McLean Blvd.

Overton Park

Evergreen St.

Poplar Ave.

East Pkwy.

72

64 70 79 **OVERTON SQUARE**

1

Union Ave.

Chickasaw
Country Club
(Private)

Walnut Grove Rd.

Belvedere Blvd.

Cooper St.

277

*Frank J.
Tobey
Park*

*To East
Memphis →*

Central Ave.

*Mid-South
Fairgrounds*

Midland Ave.

*Memphis
Country
Club
(Private)*

Young Ave.

Southern Ave.

78

Church	�167
Post Office	✉
Monorail	- - - -
Information	ⓘ

ESSENTIALS

GETTING THERE   By Plane   The **Memphis International Airport** (✆ **901/
922-8000**) is located approximately 11 miles south of downtown Memphis and 9
miles from East Memphis, both off I-240. Generally, allow about 20 minutes for the
trip between the airport and downtown, and 15 minutes between the airport and East
Memphis—more during rush hour. A taxi from the airport to downtown Memphis
will cost about $25; to East Memphis it will cost about $20.

By Train   Amtrak (✆ **800/872-7245**) serves Memphis with a route that goes from
Chicago through Memphis to New Orleans on the *City of New Orleans,* stopping in
Memphis at **Central Station,** 545 S. Main St., near Calhoun Street (✆ **901/526-
0052**).

By Car   The main routes into Memphis include **I-40** from the east (Nashville) and west (Little Rock/Oklahoma City); **I-55** from the north (St. Louis/Chicago) and south (New Orleans).

VISITOR INFORMATION   For information on Memphis, contact the **Memphis Convention & Visitors Bureau,** 47 Union Ave., Memphis, TN 38103 (© **800/8-MEMPHIS** or 901/543-5300). You can also get information online at **www.memphis travel.com**.

GETTING AROUND   A car is nearly indispensable for traveling between downtown and East Memphis, yet traffic can make this trip take up to 45 minutes. East-west avenues and almost any road in East Memphis at rush hour are the most congested. When driving between downtown and East Memphis, you'll usually do better to take the interstate.

   If you want to take the bus, the best bet is to contact **Memphis Area Transit Authority** (**MATA**; © **901/274-6282**) or ask a bus driver for the latest schedule information. The standard fare is $1.25, and exact change is required.

   The **Main Street Trolley** (© **901/577-2640**) operates renovated 1920s trolley cars (and modern reproductions) on a circular route that includes Main Street from the Pyramid to the National Civil Rights Museum and Central Station and then follows Riverside Drive, passing the Tennessee State Visitors Center. The fare is $1 each way, with a special lunch-hour rate of 60¢ between 11am and 1:30pm. An all-day pass is $3.50; exact change is required, and passengers may board at any of the 20 stations along Main Street. Trolleys are wheelchair accessible.

   Taxi companies include **Yellow/Checker Cab** (© **901/577-7777**) and **City Wide Cab Company** (© **901/324-4202**).

WHAT TO SEE & DO

To blues fans, **Beale Street** is the most important street in America. The musical form know as the blues—with roots that stretch back to the African musical heritage of slaves brought to the United States—was born here. W. C. Handy was performing on Beale Street when he penned "Memphis Blues," the first published blues song. Shortly after the Civil War, Beale Street became one of the most important streets in the South for African Americans. Many of the most famous musicians in the blues world got their starts here; besides W. C. Handy, other greats include B. B. King, Furry Lewis, Rufus Thomas, Isaac Hayes, and Alberta Hunter.

   Today, Beale Street continues to draw fans of blues and popular music, and night-clubs line the blocks between Second and Fourth streets. The **Orpheum Theatre,** 203 S. Main St. (© **901/525-3000;** www.orpheum-memphis.com), once a vaudeville palace, is now the performance hall for Broadway road shows; and the **New Daisy Theatre,** 330 Beale St. (© **901/525-8981;** www.newdaisy.com), features perform-ances by up-and-coming bands and once-famous performers. Historic markers up and down the street relate the area's colorful past, and two statues commemorate the city's two most important musicians: W. C. Handy and Elvis Presley. In addition to the many clubs featuring nightly live music, check out the **W. C. Handy House Museum,** 352 Beale St., at 4th Avenue (© **901/527-3427**), and the museum-like **A. Schwab Dry Goods Store,** 163 Beale St. (© **901/523-9782**).

Dixon Gallery & Gardens   The South's finest collection of French and American Impressionist and post-Impressionist artworks is the highlight of this exquisite little museum. The museum, art collection, and surrounding 17 acres of formal and informal gardens once belonged to Margaret and Hugo Dixon, who were avid art collectors. After the deaths of the Dixons, their estate opened to the public as an art museum and has since become one of Memphis's most important museums. With strong local support, the museum frequently hosts temporary exhibits of international caliber. Allow an hour for the museum, and more time for the gardens.

4339 Park Ave. (C) **901/761-5250.** www.dixon.org. Admission $5 adults, $4 seniors, students and children free. Tues–Fri 10am–4pm; Sat 10am–5pm; Sun 1–5pm. Located adjacent to Audubon Park, off of Park Ave. at Cherry Rd. (between Getwell Rd. and Perkins Rd.).

Graceland (Kids)   It seems hard to believe, but Graceland, the former home of rock-'n'-roll legend Elvis Presley and annually the destination of tens of thousands of lovestruck pilgrims searching for the ghost of Elvis, is the second-most visited home in America. Only the White House receives more visitors each year. Purchased in the late 1950s for $100,000, Graceland today is Memphis's biggest attraction and resembles a small theme park or shopping mall in scope and design. There are his two personal jets (the *Lisa Marie* and the *Hound Dog II*), the Elvis Presley Automobile Museum, the Sincerely Elvis collection of Elvis's personal belongings, the *Walk a Mile in My Shoes* video, and, of course, guided tours of Graceland itself. If your time here is limited to only one thing, by all means, go for the mansion tour. It's the essence of the Big E. All the rest is just icing on Elvis's buttercream-frosted cake.

3734 Elvis Presley Blvd. (C) **800/238-2000** or 901/332-3322. www.elvis.com. Graceland Mansion Tour $22 adults, $20 seniors and students, $7 children 7–12. The Platinum Tour (includes admission to all Graceland attractions, including Elvis's Automobile Museum, tours of Elvis's custom jets [the *Lisa Marie* and *Hound Dog II*], and *Sincerely Elvis* film presentation) $28 adults, $25 seniors, $13 children 7–12. Tour reservations can be made 24 hr. in advance and are recommended if you have a tight schedule. Mar–Oct Mon–Sat 9am–5pm, Sun 10am–4pm; Nov–Feb daily 10am–4pm. (Dec–Feb mansion tour does not operate Tues.) Closed Thanksgiving, Dec 25, and Jan 1. Take Bellevue South (which turns into Elvis Presley Blvd.) south a few miles of downtown, past Winchester Ave. Graceland is on the left.

National Civil Rights Museum (Best)   On April 4, Dr. Martin Luther King stepped out onto the balcony outside his Lorraine Motel room and was shot dead by James Earl Ray. The assassination of King struck a horrible blow to the American civil rights movement and incited riots in cities across the country. Saved from demolition, the Lorraine Motel was remodeled and today serves as the nation's memorial to the civil rights movement. In evocative displays, the museum chronicles the struggle of African Americans from the time of slavery to the present: a public bus like the one Rosa Parks was riding when she refused to move to the back of the bus; a Greensboro, North Carolina, lunch counter; and the burned shell of a freedom-ride Greyhound bus. Allow 2 to 3 hours.

450 Mulberry St. (at Huling Ave.). (C) **901/521-9699.** www.civilrightsmuseum.org. Admission $12 adults, $8 seniors and students, $6.50 children 4–17, free for children under 4. Mon and Wed–Sat 9am–5pm; Sun 1–5pm; May–Aug until 6pm.

Sun Studio   Owner and recording engineer Sam Phillips first recorded, in the early 1950s, such local artists as Elvis Presley, Jerry Lee Lewis, Roy Orbison, and Carl Perkins, who together created a sound that would shortly become known as rock 'n' roll. Over the years Phillips also helped start the recording careers of the blues greats B. B. King and Howlin' Wolf and country giant Johnny Cash. By night, Sun Studio is still an active recording studio and has been used by such artists as U2, Spin Doctors, The Tractors, and Bonnie Raitt. The place has great vibes, and for those who know their music history, touching Elvis's microphone will be a thrill beyond measure. Allow an hour.

706 Union Ave. (at Marshall Ave.). © **800/441-6249** or 901/521-0664. www.sunstudio.com. Admission $9.50 adults, free for children under 12 accompanied by a parent. Daily 10am–6pm; closed some holidays.

WHERE TO STAY

In addition to the hotels listed below, national and regional motel chains in the area include the following (see also appendix D for toll-free reservation numbers): **AmeriSuites,** 1220 Primacy Pkwy. (© **901/680-9700**), charging $109 to $119 double; **La Quinta Inn & Suites,** 1236 Primacy Pkwy. (© **901/374-0330**), charging $60 to $89 double; **Red Roof Inn,** 6055 Shelby Oaks Dr. (© **901/388-6111**), charging $40 to $59 double; and **Super 8 Motel,** 6015 Macon Cove Rd. (© **901/373-4888**), charging $45 to $58 double.

Elvis Presley's Heartbreak Hotel–Graceland   If your visit to Memphis is a pilgrimage to Graceland, there should be no question as to where to stay. This hotel has a gate right into the Graceland parking lot. In the lobby, you'll find two big portraits of The King, and Graceland-esque decor. In the back courtyard, there's a smallish, heart-shaped outdoor pool. Indoors, four themed suites include the irresistibly named "*Burning Love* Suite." If you don't want to shell out big bucks for the entire suite, ask to split it and just rent a portion (or one room) of the suite. Many guests do this, we're told. If this place has one drawback, it's that there's no Internet access.

3677 Elvis Presley Blvd., Memphis, TN 38116. © **877/777-0606** or 901/332-1000. Fax 901/332-1636. www. elvis.com. 128 units. $104–$124 regular suite; $520 themed suite. AE, DC, DISC, MC, V. Free parking. **Amenities:** Pool.

French Quarter Suites Hotel   Its perch in the heart of Overton Square used to be a big plus, but just as this fledgling midtown entertainment district has been upstaged by a newly revitalized downtown, so have the few hotels here. Though this hotel looks charming enough with its French Quarter–style courtyards and balconies, the guest rooms and public areas suggest that the hotel has not been as well maintained as others in town.

2144 Madison Ave., Memphis, TN 38104. © **800/843-0353** or 901/728-4000. Fax 901/278-1262. www.memphis frenchquarter.com. 103 units. $109–$119 double. AE, DC, DISC, MC, V. Free parking. **Amenities:** Pool; exercise room.

Homewood Suites *Kids*   Homewood Suites offers some of the most attractive and spacious accommodations in Memphis. The suites, which are arranged around an attractively landscaped central courtyard with a swimming pool and basketball court, resemble an apartment complex rather than a hotel. The lobby has the feel of a mountain lodge and features pine furnishings, lots of natural-wood trim, and attractive decorations and artwork. Early American styling, with pine furnishings, sets the tone in the suites, many of which have wood-burning fireplaces and contemporary wrought-iron beds. There are two televisions (and a VCR) in every suite, as well as full kitchens and big bathrooms with plenty of counter space.

5811 Poplar Ave. (just off I-240), Memphis, TN 38119. © **800/CALL-HOME** or 901/763-0500. Fax 901/763-0132. www.homewood-suites.com. 140 units. $139–$169 double. Rates include breakfast. AE, DC, DISC, MC, V. Free parking. **Amenities:** Pool; exercise room. *In room:* Kitchen.

Madison Hotel *Best*   A member of the prestigious Small Luxury Hotels of the World, this sleek new hotel occupies the site of a former bank building. The graceful Beaux Arts architecture belies the bold, contemporary furnishings inside. From the elegant lobby, with its grand piano and musical instrument motif, to the rich, solid colors in the guest rooms, the Madison is a contrast between classic and modern. Whirlpool or jet tubs are available in many rooms. Nightly turndown and twice-daily housekeeping service keep guests feeling pampered. Take the elevator to the outdoor rooftop for breathtaking views of the Mississippi River and surrounding downtown.

79 Madison Ave., Memphis, TN 38103. © 866/44-MEMPHIS or 901/333-1200. Fax 901/333-1297. www.madison hotelmemphis.com. 110 units. $220–$260 double; from $330 suite. AE, DC, DISC, MC, V. Valet parking $10 (unlimited access). **Amenities:** Restaurant; indoor pool; fitness center. *In room:* Minibar.

The Peabody Memphis   For years, The Peabody enjoyed a reputation as one of the finest hotels in the South. A recent renovation has spiffed up room and public spaces, which exude genteel elegance. Marble columns, gilded mezzanine railings, hand-carved and burnished woodwork, and ornate gilded plasterwork on the ceiling give the lobby the air of a palace. The lobby's most prominent feature is its Romanesque fountain. Here, the famous Peabody ducks, one of Memphis's biggest attractions, while away each day.

149 Union Ave., Memphis, TN 38103. © 800/PEABODY or 901/529-4000. Fax 901/529-3677. www.peabody memphis.com. 468 units. $210–$345 double; from $380 suite. AE, DC, DISC, MC, V. Valet parking $17; self-parking $12. **Amenities:** 2 restaurants; athletic facility with small pool.

Talbot Heirs Guesthouse *(value)*   Trendy, contemporary styling is not something you often associate with the tradition-oriented South, which is what makes this upscale downtown B&B so unique. Each of the rooms is boldly decorated in a wide variety of styles. One room is done in bright solid colors (yellow walls and a fire engine–red tool chest for a bedside stand), while another is done in rich, subtle colors and has a neo-Victorian daybed. The rooms vary in size from large to huge; all have full kitchens—including a refrigerator stocked with milk, juice, and breakfast items.

99 S. 2nd St., Memphis, TN 38103. © 800/955-3956 or 901/527-9772. Fax 901/527-3700. www.talbothouse.com. 8 units. $175–$225 double. Rates include continental breakfast. AE, DC, DISC, MC, V. Self-parking $10. *In room:* Kitchen.

WHERE TO DINE

Automatic Slim's Tonga Club NEW AMERICAN   For relaxed artiness and creative food in downtown Memphis, try Automatic Slim's. The name "Automatic Slim" comes from an old blues song, and the Tonga Club was a local teen hangout popular in the early 1960s. Artists from New York and Memphis created the decor (they're credited on the menu), including zebra-print upholstered banquettes, slag-glass wall sconces, and colorfully upholstered bar stools. Be sure to try a cocktail with some of the vodka-soaked fruit. The food here is as creative as the atmosphere.

83 S. 2nd St. © 901/525-7948. Reservations recommended. Main courses $16–$25. AE, DC, MC, V. Mon–Fri 11am–2pm; Mon–Thurs 5–10pm; Fri–Sat 5–11pm.

Chez Philippe *(Best)* FRENCH/NEW SOUTHERN   Although Jose Gutierrez, the beloved French chef who first put Memphis on the culinary map, left Chez Philippe in mid-2005 after 2 decades (to open his own bistro, to be called **Encore,** 150 Peabody Place), the restaurant remains an opulent experience. The dining rooms are on three separate levels, with lacy New Orleans–style metalwork, wide marble columns, and sparkling chandeliers that give Chez Philippe a palatial atmosphere. On the menu, you'll find a mix of contemporary French and down-home New Southern dishes. Prices are steep, but expect to be pampered.

The Peabody Memphis Hotel, 149 Union Ave. © 901/529-4188. www.peabodymemphis.com. Reservations recommended. Main courses $21–$28. AE, DC, DISC, MC, V. Tues–Sat 6:30–9pm.

Corky's BARBECUE   Corky's is good-natured and boisterous, with rock-'n'-roll tunes piped both indoors and out. Aromatic barbecue permeates the air. An argument over which is the best barbecue restaurant in Memphis persists, but this one pretty much leads the pack when it comes to pulled pork shoulder barbecue, topped with tangy coleslaw. Photographs and letters from satisfied customers line the rough-paneled lobby, where you always have to wait for a table. Corky's even has a toll-free number (✆ **800/9-CORKYS**) to get their delicious ribs shipped "anywhere." A downtown location at 175 Peabody Place (✆ **901/529-9191**) is right around the corner from Beale Street. The suburbs have a Corky's at Dexter Road in Cordova (✆ **901/737-1988**).

5259 Poplar Ave. ✆ 901/685-9744. www.corkysbbq.com. Reservations not accepted. Main courses $3–$20. AE, DC, DISC, MC, V. Sun–Thurs 10:45am–9:30pm; Fri–Sat 10:45am–10pm.

Huey's AMERICAN   Ask Memphians where to get the best burger in town, and you'll invariably be directed to Huey's. This funky tavern also has one of the best beer selections in town. The original Huey's, at 1927 Madison Ave. (✆ **901/726-4372**), in the Overton Square area, is still in business. In recent years, suburban locations have also sprouted up in East Memphis and beyond, at 1771 N. Germantown Parkway, Cordova (✆ **901/754-3885**); and at 2130 W. Poplar at Hacks Cross, Collierville (✆ **901/854-4455**).

77 S. Second St. ✆ 901/527-2700. www.hueys.cc. Reservations not accepted. Main courses $5–$10. AE, DISC, MC, V. Daily 11am–2am.

Rendezvous BARBECUE   Rendezvous has been a downtown Memphis institution since 1948, and it has a well-deserved reputation for serving the best ribs in town. You can see the food being prepared in an old open kitchen as you walk in, but more important, your sense of smell will immediately perk up as the fragrance of hickory-smoked pork wafts past. You'll also likely be intrigued by all manner of strange objects displayed in this huge but cozy cellar. And when the waiter comes to take your order, there's no messin' around; you're expected to know what you want when you come in—an order of ribs.

52 S. 2nd St. ✆ 901/523-2746. www.hogsfly.com. Main plates $6.50–$17. AE, DC, DISC, MC, V. Tues–Thurs 4:30–10:30pm; Fri 11:30am–11pm; Sat noon–11pm.

MEMPHIS AFTER DARK

To find out about what's happening in the entertainment scene while you're in town, pick up a copy of the *Memphis Flyer,* Memphis's free arts-and-entertainment weekly, which comes out on Thursday. You'll find it in convenience, grocery, and music stores, some restaurants, and nightclubs. You could also pick up the Friday edition of the *Commercial Appeal,* Memphis's morning daily newspaper. The "Playbook" section of the paper has very thorough events listings.

BEALE STREET   This is the epicenter of Memphis's nightclub scene. This street, where the blues gained widespread recognition, is now the site of more than half a dozen nightclubs, plus a few other bars, restaurants, and theaters. For links to various clubs and other big businesses along Beale, click on **www.bealestreet.com**.

The "King of the Blues" does play occasionally, though not regularly, at **B. B. King's Blues Club,** 147 Beale St. (✆ **800/443-0972** or 901/524-5464). However, any night of the week you can catch blazing blues played by one of the best house bands in town here. Across the street, the **Blues City Café,** 138–140 Beale St. (© **901/ 526-3637**), takes up two old storefronts, with live blues wailing in one room (called the Band Box) and a restaurant serving steaks and barbecue in the other.

Dozens of autographed guitars, including ones signed by Cal Perkins, Stevie Ray Vaughan, Billie Gibbons of ZZ Top, Joe Walsh, George Thorogood, Albert Collins, and other rock and blues guitar wizards, hang from the ceiling at the **Rum Boogie Café & Mr. Handy's Blues Hall,** 182 Beale St. (© **901/528-0150**). There's live music nightly, with guest artists alternating with the house band, which plays everything from blues to country. Another good choice for live blues is **The Black Diamond,** 153 Beale St. (© **901/521-0800**).

Though actually 4 blocks south of Beale Street, **Earnestine & Hazel's,** 531 S. Main St. (© **901/523-9754**), is a downtown dive that has become one of Memphis's hottest nightspots. Things don't really get cookin' here until after midnight. The music is a mix of blues, R&B, and rock, and the clientele is equally mixed.

MORE MUSIC & DANCING   Retro coffeehouse **Java Cabana,** 2170 Young St. (© **901/272-7210**), has poetry readings and live acoustic music on different nights of the week. Although you can't get alcohol here, you can order an espresso.

Club 152, 152 Beale St. (© **901/544-7011;** www.bealestreet.com), is currently the hottest (but one of the few) dance clubs in town. Beale Street's best dance club is a favorite with energetic young adults who dance the night away on three floors. DJs such as Dave the Worm crank up techno, house, and alternative dance music for revelers who usually party until the early morning hours.

GAMBLING ON THE MISSISSIPPI   Just a few miles south of Memphis, across the Mississippi state line, casinos are sprouting like cotton plants in the spring. Near the town of Robinsonville, you'll find **Goldstrike Casino,** 1010 Casino Center Dr. (© **888/24K-PLAY** or 866/245-7511), and **Sheraton Casino,** 1107 Casino Center Dr. (© **800/391-3777** or 662/363-4900). Continuing south on U.S. 61 and then west on Miss. 304, you come to **Sam's Town Hotel and Gambling Hall,** 1477 Casino Strip Blvd. (© **800/456-0711** or 662/363-0711); **Fitzgerald's Casino,** 711 Lucky Lane (© **800/766-LUCK** or 662/363-5825); **Hollywood Casino,** 1150 Commerce Landing (© **800/871-0711** or 662/357-7700); and **Harrah's,** 1100 Casino Strip Blvd. (© **800/HARRAHS** or 662/363-7777). Continuing south on U.S. 61 to Tunica and then heading west on either Mhoon Landing Road or Miss. 4, you'll come to **Bally's Tunica,** 1450 Bally's Blvd. (© **800/38-BALLY**).

5

Florida

Florida is *the* most popular year-round family vacation destination in the United States. Every year millions escape bleak northern winters to bask in Florida's warmth, lured to the Sunshine State by the promise of clear skies and 800 miles of spectacular sandy beaches. And for those with children, there's the added bonus of numerous theme parks and kid-pleasers, from Busch Gardens to Walt Disney World, to add a dash of magic to your trip. It would take almost as many pages as this book to detail all that's available; we outline the major visitor highlights of Florida in this chapter, but for the works, we suggest getting a comprehensive guidebook such as *Frommer's Florida* or (if you're off to Disney World), *Frommer's Walt Disney World & Orlando.*

For general information, contact **Visit Florida,** P.O. Box 1100, Tallahassee, FL 32302-1100 (✆ **888/7-FLA-USA;** www.flausa.com). You can request a visitors' guide for the entire state in English, Spanish, German, or Portuguese.

1 Walt Disney World & Orlando

When Disney opened the Magic Kingdom in 1971, few imagined what Central Florida would be like 3 decades later. Today, it's bursting (and in some cases imploding) with newer, bigger, and better things for you to do. **Walt Disney World (WDW)** has four theme parks, dozens of smaller attractions, tens of thousands of hotel rooms, scores of restaurants, a ton of bars and clubs, and two cruise ships. Toss in **Universal Orlando**'s two theme parks, **SeaWorld**'s pair (soon to be trio), and the marginal players, and, well, it's safe to say that you won't have a problem finding something to do here.

GETTING THERE   By Plane   More than 33 million people fly into **Orlando International Airport** (✆ 407/825-2001; www.orlandoairports.net) each year. The airport, which just finished up a major expansion, is user-friendly, with centrally located information kiosks. The airport is 25 miles from Walt Disney World.

Mears Transportation (✆ 407/423-5566; www.mearstransportation.com) provides shuttle service to and from the airport. Vans run 24 hours a day, departing every 15 to 25 minutes. Round-trip fares are $26 to $42 for adults and $22 to $33 for children ages 4 to 11 (actual price depends on your destination); children 3 and under ride free.

By Train   Amtrak (✆ **800/USA-RAIL;** www.amtrak.com) provides daily service from Jacksonville (trip time: 3¾ hr.), Miami (5¼ hr.), and Washington, D.C. (18 hr.). Trains pull into stations in downtown Orlando (23 miles from Walt Disney World) and Kissimmee (15 miles from Disney).

Amtrak's **Auto Train** provides daily service from Lorton, Virginia, outside Washington, D.C., to Sanford, Florida, just 23 miles northeast of Orlando (17 hr.).

Florida

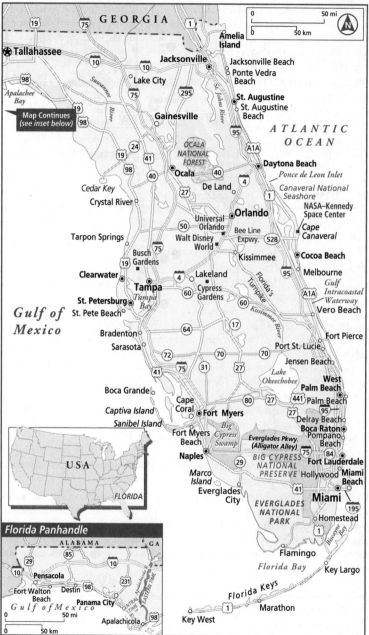

By Car   From Atlanta, take **I-75** south to the Florida Turnpike to **I-4** west. From the northeast, take **I-95** south to I-4 west. From Chicago, take **I-65** south to Nashville, **I-24** south to I-75, and then south to the Florida Turnpike to I-4 west. From Dallas, take **I-20** east to **I-49,** then south to **I-10,** east to I-75, and south to the Florida Turnpike to I-4 west.

VISITOR INFORMATION   The **Orlando/Orange County Convention & Visitors Bureau,** 8723 International Dr., Suite 101, Orlando, FL 32819 (🕾 **800/551-0181** or 407/363-5872; www.orlandoinfo.com), can answer questions and send maps and brochures, such as the *Official Visitors Guide* and *Official Accommodations Guide.* The packet should reach you in a couple of weeks and also includes the "Magicard," which is good for up to $500 in discounts on rooms, car rentals, attractions, and more.

For information about **Walt Disney World**—including vacation brochures and videos—contact Walt Disney World, Box 10000, Lake Buena Vista, FL 32830-1000 (🕾 **407/934-7639** or 407/824-2222; www.disneyworld.com). The website is an especially good bet. For information about **Universal Orlando,** call 🕾 **800/837-2273** or 407/363-8000; surf the Internet to **www.universalorlando.com**; or write to Universal Orlando, 1000 Universal Studios Plaza, Orlando, FL 32819. You can obtain Sea-World information online at **www.seaworld.com**.

GETTING AROUND   Although you can manage without a car, if you want to see attractions outside Walt Disney World or are staying at some of the outlying Disney resorts, a car is almost a must.

A thorough, free transportation network runs throughout the WDW complex. Disney resorts and official hotels offer unlimited free transportation via bus, monorail, ferry, or water taxi to all WDW parks and properties 14 to 18 hours a day. You can get to Universal and other attractions, too, but you'll have to pay extra. *The pluses:* The system is free; you can save on a rental car, insurance, and gas; and you don't have to pay for theme-park parking. *The minuses:* You're at the mercy of the system, which is often slow and *very* indirect.

Mears Transportation operates vans and buses that go to all of the theme parks, as well as Cypress Gardens, Kennedy Space Center, and Busch Gardens (yes, in Tampa), among others. Call 🕾 **407/423-5566** for rates.

Taxis gather at resorts, and smaller properties will call a cab for you. **Yellow Cab** (🕾 **407/699-9999**) and **Ace Metro** (🕾 **407/855-0564**) are both good choices and average $3.25 for the first mile and $1.75 per mile thereafter.

FAST FACTS   There are basic first-aid centers in all the major parks. **Doctors on Call** (🕾 **407/399-3627**) makes house and room calls in most of the Orlando area. **Walgreens,** 7650 W. Sand Lake Rd. (🕾 **407/345-9497;** www.walgreens.com), operates a 24-hour pharmacy. A 6.5% to 7% **sales tax** (depending on the local county you happen to be in) is charged on everything but groceries and medicines. **Hotel taxes** range from 10% to 12%.

A Note on Area Codes

If you're making a local call in Orlando, even to someone just across the street, *you must dial the 407 area code followed by the number you wish to call,* for a total of 10 digits.

TIPS FOR VISITING WALT DISNEY WORLD ATTRACTIONS

Walt Disney World, home to the four major theme parks of Magic Kingdom, Epcot, Disney–MGM Studios, and Animal Kingdom, welcomes around 43 million guests in a typical year. The quartet, along with California's Disneyland (p. 908), are the top-five theme parks in the United States in terms of attendance.

Besides its larger theme parks, Disney has an assortment of other venues, including Downtown Disney (Cirque du Soleil, DisneyQuest, and Pleasure Island), Blizzard Beach, and Typhoon Lagoon, just to name a few.

Avoiding the Crowds   There isn't really an off season in Orlando, but crowds are usually thinner from mid-January to March and from mid-September until the week before Thanksgiving. The busiest days at all theme parks are generally Saturday and Sunday, when the locals visit. Major holidays attract scores of visitors: From Christmas to New Year's is a frenzied time, and the weeks preceding and following Easter are similarly manic.

Note: Summer is the worst time: Crowds + heat + humidity = theme-park hell.

Arrive Early   Always arrive at the parks a good 30 to 45 minutes before opening time, thus avoiding a traffic jam entering the park and a long line at the gate. Early arrival also lets you experience one or two major attractions before big lines form. Once you get inside the parks, be sure to grab a park guide map! It not only tells you where the fun is but lists the daily entertainment schedule.

Parking   Cars, light trucks, and vans currently pay $10. Visitors with mobility impairments can park in special areas near the entrances; ask the parking-lot attendants or call © **407/934-7639.** *Don't forget* to write down where you parked (area and row number), because it's easy to get lost after a long day.

Operating Hours   Park hours vary and are influenced by special events and the economy. Not only will hours vary from park to park, but from week to week, and even day to day. So call ahead or go to **www.disneyworld.com** to check.

Tickets   Disney's Magic Your Way ticketing structure gives visitors who stay here for a few days far better deals than those who come for just a day. The following *don't include 6.5% sales tax* unless noted. *Note:* Changes are frequent occurrences, so call © **407/934-7639** or visit WDW's website (**www.disneyworld.com**) for up-to-the-minute fees. Note that some tickets can now be purchased in advance on the Web at a small discount.

1-day/1-park tickets, for admission to the Magic Kingdom, Epcot, Animal Kingdom, or Disney–MGM, are $67 for adults, $56 for children 3 to 9. (Ouch!) **Multi-day tickets** allow you to visit *one park per day.* A 7-day ticket costs $210 for adults ($30 a day), $173 for kids (about $25 a day).

A **Park Hopper** add-on ($45 *per ticket,* per person) allows visitors unlimited admission to the Magic Kingdom, Epcot, Animal Kingdom, and Disney–MGM Studios for the length of their ticket. A 1-day adult Park Hopper ticket costs $112, while the 7-day version costs $255—making the latter a far better deal.

The **Water Park Fun & More** add-on allows visitors their choice of two to six admissions to Typhoon Lagoon, Blizzard Beach, Pleasure Island, DisneyQuest, or Disney's Wide World of Sports. Prices range from an obscene $117 for a 1-day adult pass to $260 for a 7-day pass (a good deal).

A **1-day ticket to Typhoon Lagoon or Blizzard Beach** is $36 for adults, $30 for children 3 to 9. A **1-day ticket to Pleasure Island** is $22. Because this is primarily an 18-and-over entertainment complex, there's no bargain price for children.

FASTPASS

Don't want to stand in long lines? Disney parks use a free reservation system that lets you on the primo rides without having to spend too much time in line.

Hang onto your ticket stub when you enter, and head to the hottest ride of your choosing. If it's a FASTPASS attraction (they're noted in the guide map you get when you enter) and there's a line, feed your ticket stub into the waist-level ticket taker at the ride's entrance. Retrieve both your ticket stub and the FASTPASS stub that comes with it. Look at the two times stamped on the FASTPASS. Come back during that 1-hour window and you can enter the ride with almost no wait (up to 15 min. or less). In the interim, venture on out and experience another attraction or show.

Note: Early in the day, your window may begin as close as only 40 minutes after you feed the FASTPASS machine, but later in the day it could be hours. Initially, Disney allowed you to do this on only one ride at a time; however, now you can get a pass for a second attraction 2 hours after your first assigned time. Note, however, that the passes go quickly at times and the system can max out, sometimes by noon, so be sure to head to the rides most important to you earliest in the day.

THE MAGIC KINGDOM

The most enchanting theme park in Orlando, the Magic Kingdom offers a plethora of attractions, restaurants, and shops in a 107-acre package. Its symbol, Cinderella Castle, forms the hub of a wheel whose spokes reach to **seven "lands."**

MAIN STREET, USA   The gateway to the Kingdom, Main Street is designed to resemble a turn-of-the-20th-century American street. Don't dawdle here when you enter the park; leave it for the end of the day when you're heading back to your hotel. You can board the **Walt Disney World Railroad,** an authentic 1928 steam-powered railroad, for a 15-minute journey clockwise around the perimeter of the park, with stops in Frontierland and Mickey's Toontown Fair. At the end of Main Street, in the center of the park, you'll come to **Cinderella Castle,** 185 feet high, housing a restaurant and shops. Cinderella herself, dressed for the ball, often makes appearances in the lobby.

ADVENTURELAND   Stroll an exotic jungle of lush tropical foliage, thatch-roofed huts, and carved totems. Ascend a 50-foot banyan "tree" to wander the rooms of the ingenious **Swiss Family Treehouse.** Or sail through an African veldt, the Amazon rainforest, the Mekong River delta, and the Nile over the course of 10 minutes on the somewhat cheesy **Jungle Cruise.** Amid the cascading waterfalls and lush foliage are audio-animatronic zebras, lions, giraffes, crocodiles, tigers, even fluttering butterflies. Next up is the recently tweaked **Pirates of the Caribbean** (Johnny Depp has been added!), a WDW classic, where you sail past the adventures of a ragtag collection of yo-ho-hoing audio-animatronic mates as they raid, loot, chase wenches, and drink a bottle of rum or two. The **Enchanted Tiki Room Under New Management** is a cute show featuring a slew of tropical birds, chanting totem poles, and singing flowers that whistle, tweet, and warble. Finish up your exotic adventure on **The Magic Carpets of**

Aladdin, whose 16 four-passenger carpets delight wee ones as they spin and circle a giant genie's bottle while animatronic camels spit water at them.

FRONTIERLAND   Themed after *Song of the South,* **Splash Mountain** takes you on a leisurely journey in a hollowed-out log craft before your trip culminates in a breathtaking five-story splashdown at 40 mph. You *will* get wet! For more thrills, board **Big Thunder Mountain Railroad,** a mining disaster–themed roller coaster that derives its thrills from hairpin turns and descents in the dark. It's tailor-made for kids and grown-ups who want a thrill but aren't quite up to tackling the big coasters. If you've got kids along, the **Country Bear Jamboree** is a 15-minute show featuring a troupe of fiddlin', banjo-strummin' audio-animatronic bears belting out country tunes.

LIBERTY SQUARE   Liberty Square evokes 18th-century America with Georgian architecture and Colonial Williamsburg–type shops. In the red-brick Colonial **Hall of Presidents,** all American presidents are represented by extremely realistic audio-animatronic figures. If you look closely, you'll see them fidget and whisper. The **Haunted Mansion** is another WDW classic, replete with bizarre scenes and objects: a ghostly banquet and ball, luminous spiders, a talking head in a crystal ball, weird flying objects, and much more. It's more amusing than terrifying, so you can take small children.

FANTASYLAND   The attractions in this happy land are themed after Disney classics. In the **Mad Tea Party,** riders sit in oversize pink teacups on saucers that careen around a circular platform. **The Many Adventures of Winnie the Pooh** features the cute-and-cuddly fellow. **Cinderella's Golden Carousel** is a beauty, built by Italian wood-carvers in the Victorian tradition in 1917, and refurbished by Disney artists who added scenes from the Cinderella story. Riding in Captain Hook's ship, passengers careen through dark tunnels and over nighttime London into Never-Never Land while experiencing **Peter Pan's Flight.** It's fun, but the lines can be endless. The same can be said for **Snow White's Scary Adventures,** which aren't all that frightening. **Dumbo, the Flying Elephant,** is a very tame kiddie ride, but exciting for wee ones. Next up is **It's a Small World,** where you sail "around the world" through vast rooms designed to represent different countries. You know the song—and if you don't, you will. The ride is sickeningly cute, but it's almost a required rite of passage.

The must-see **Mickey's PhilharMagic** is an amazing 3-D film experience where Disney's most beloved characters make an appearance to help (or in some cases hinder) the attempts of Donald Duck to retrieve Mickey's magical sorcerer's hat.

MICKEY'S TOONTOWN FAIR   Head off those cries of "Where's Mickey?" by taking the kids to this 2-acre area where they can meet their favorite characters. Everything is brightly colored and kid-friendly in the best Disney tradition; there is even a kid-size roller coaster. There are also really long lines.

TOMORROWLAND   Tomorrowland depicts the future as a galactic, science fiction–inspired community inhabited by humans, aliens, and robots. There's also a vast state-of-the-art video-game arcade. **Space Mountain** is a cosmic roller coaster making thrilling hairpin turns and rapid plunges in the inky starlit blackness of outer space. In **Buzz Lightyear's Space Ranger Spin,** you'll pilot your own cruiser while shooting laser cannons at evil aliens as you spin through a world filled with gigantic toys. The **Tomorrowland Speedway** is a great thrill for kids who get to put the pedal to the metal, steer, and vroom down a speedway in an actual gas-powered sports car; adults and teens will find the slow speeds and choppy steering less than exhilarating. In the rather blah **Stitch's Great Escape,** riders help capture and contain the infamous "experiment 626," who is wreaking havoc on the galaxy.

PARADES, FIREWORKS & MORE   You'll get an *Entertainment Show Schedule* when you enter the park, which lists all kinds of special goings-on for the day.

SpectroMagic is a 20-minute production featuring fiber optics, holographic images, old-fashioned twinkling lights, and a soundtrack of classic Disney tunes. The parade runs on a *very limited basis.* Magic Kingdom's first new fireworks display in just over 30 years, **Wishes,** a precise mix of choreographed fireworks bursts, music, and story, is amazing and absolutely the best way to end your day in the park. The fireworks go off nightly during peak periods, but only on selected nights the rest of the year.

EPCOT

Epcot is an acronym for Experimental Prototype Community of Tomorrow, and it was Walt Disney's dream for a planned residential community. But, after his death, it opened in 1982 as Central Florida's second theme park.

The 260-acre park has two sections, **Future World** and **World Showcase.** It's so large that hiking World Showcase from tip to tip (1⅓ miles) can be exhausting. That's why some folks say Epcot really stands for "Every Person Comes Out Tired." Depending on how long you intend to linger at each of the 11 countries in World Showcase, this park can be seen in a day, but it's better over two.

FUTURE WORLD   Spaceship Earth, a massive, silvery geosphere, symbolizes Epcot, but all that awaits inside is a 15-minute yawn of a show/ride that takes you through the history of communications. *Tip:* Skip it.

Innoventions showcases cutting-edge technologies and future products. You'll get a chance to preview virtual reality, experience interactive television, and try out new computer programs and games.

The highlight of **The Living Seas** pavilion is a 5.7-million-gallon saltwater aquarium (complete with a coral reef) inhabited by thousands of sharks, barracudas, parrotfish, rays, and dolphins. Enjoy stunning close-up views of ocean denizens in a natural coral-reef habitat. It also features the delightful interactive film experience, **Turtle Talk with Crush.**

The Land, the largest of Future World's pavilions, highlights humankind's relation to food and nature. **Living with the Land** is a boat ride that takes you through a rainforest, an African desert, and windswept American plains. Combining spectacular live-action footage with animation, the excellent 15-minute motion picture called *Circle of Life* is a cautionary environmental tale featuring characters from *The Lion King.* Best of all is the new **Soarin',** which allows guests a bird's-eye view of the diverse California landscape from a 40-foot-high perspective. Sensory elements and gentle winds add realism to the experience.

The **Journey Into Imagination** pavilion has a show starring a park favorite: Figment the dinosaur. But the headliner here is **Honey, I Shrunk the Audience,** an attraction based on the Disney *Honey, I Shrunk the Kids* films. Dramatic 3-D action is enhanced by vibrating seats and creepy tactile effects.

Test Track puts guests in the driver's seat to experience the rigors of automobile testing. Six-passenger test cars travel upon what appears to be an actual roadway, accelerating on long straightaways, hugging hairpin turns, climbing steep hills, and braking abruptly. This ride is the best in the park and has the long lines to prove it.

Blast off to Mars on **Mission: Space.** Sophisticated technology launches you on an amazing simulated ride through space that feels a lot like the real deal (so some NASA astronauts have claimed, anyway). This one is definitely not for the faint of stomach.

Wonders of Life offers some of Future World's most engaging shows and attractions, including **Body Wars,** a motion simulator ride where you're miniaturized to the size of a single cell to take part in a medical rescue mission inside the immune system of a human body. **Cranium Command,** a hilarious multimedia attraction, features Buzzy, an audio-animatronic brain-pilot-in-training who's charged with the seemingly impossible task of controlling the brain of a typical 12-year-old boy. It's a must.

Universe of Energy, a 32-minute ride-through attraction with visitors seated in solar-powered "traveling theater" cars, aims to better our understanding of America's energy problems. **Ellen's Energy Adventure** features Ellen DeGeneres as an energy expert tutored to be a *Jeopardy!* contestant by Bill Nye, the Science Guy. The dinosaur section of this ride is better than ever.

WORLD SHOWCASE Surrounding a 40-acre lagoon at the park's southern end is a permanent community of 11 miniaturized nations, all with indigenous landmark architecture, landscaping, background music, restaurants, and shops.

Canada features an Inuit village, Rocky Mountains scenery, and stunning floral displays inspired by the Butchart Gardens in Victoria. The pavilion's highlight is *O Canada!,* a 360-degree CircleVision film that reveals Canada's scenic splendor.

United Kingdom evokes Merry Olde England. Four centuries of architecture are represented along quaint cobblestone streets; troubadours and minstrels entertain in front of a British pub; and there's a formal garden with a stereotypical red phone booth.

In **France,** a one-tenth replica of the Eiffel Tower looms above the *grands boulevards* and a park inspired by Seurat. Shown in a palatial (and mercifully a sit-down) theater a la Fontainebleau, *Impressions de France* is an entertaining 18-minute film journey through France, projected on a vast wraparound screen.

Exotic **Morocco** is heralded by a minaret. The Medina (old city), entered via a replica of an arched gateway in Fez, leads to Fez House (a traditional Moroccan home) and the narrow winding streets of the souk, a bustling marketplace where authentic handicrafts are on display.

Heralded by a flaming-red torii (gate of honor) and the graceful Goju No To pagoda, **Japan** features an exquisite Japanese garden. Exhibits ranging from 18th-century puppets to samurai armor are displayed in the moated White Heron Castle. The drums of **Matsuriza**—one of the best performances in the World Showcase—entertain guests daily.

Housed in a vast Georgian-style structure, **U.S.A.—The American Adventure** is a 29-minute dramatization of U.S. history using a 72-foot rear-projection screen, rousing music, and a large cast of lifelike audio-animatronic figures. You view Jefferson writing the Declaration of Independence, the Civil War, the attack on Pearl Harbor, and the Eagle heading toward the moon.

One of the prettiest World Showcase pavilions, **Italy** lures visitors over an arched stone footbridge to a central piazza enclosing a version of Bernini's Neptune Fountain. Mediterranean citrus, olive, and cypress trees frame a formal garden. Gondolas are moored on the lagoon.

Enclosed by towered castle walls, festive **Germany** is centered on a cobblestone *platz* (square). The pavilion's outdoor **Biergarten**—where it's Oktoberfest all year long—was inspired by medieval Rothenberg. Model-train enthusiasts shouldn't miss the detailed miniature German village.

Bounded by a serpentine wall, **China** is entered via a vast ceremonial gate inspired by the Temple of Heaven in Beijing. Gardens simulate those in Suzhou, with miniature waterfalls, fragrant lotus ponds, groves of bamboo, and weeping mulberry trees. The highlight is *Wonders of China,* a 360-degree CircleVision film that explores 6,000 years of history and the breathtaking diversity of the Chinese landscape.

In **Norway,** a replica of Oslo's 14th-century **Akershus Castle,** next to a cascading woodland waterfall, is the setting for the pavilion's featured restaurant. **Maelstrom,** a boat ride in a dragon-headed Viking vessel, traverses Norway's fjords and mythical forests to the music of *Peer Gynt,* while you're menaced by polar bears and trolls. You'll disembark in a 10th-century Viking village to view the 70mm film *Norway,* which documents 1,000 years of history.

You'll hear the music of marimba and mariachi bands as you approach **Mexico,** fronted by a towering Mayan pyramid. **El Rio del Tiempo (River of Time)** is a pleasant, 8-minute cruise through Mexico's history and culture.

SHOWS & SPECTACULARS   The **World Showcase Pavilion Shows** make up an important part of the Epcot experience. There are Chinese acrobats, German oompah bands, Moroccan belly dancers, Scottish pipers, and much more. Don't miss the nightly **IllumiNations,** a spectacular blend of fireworks, lasers, classical music, and fountains in a display that's signature Disney. The best places to see the show are the Crossroads of the World shopping arcade, the United Kingdom, and Canada.

DISNEY–MGM STUDIOS

You'll probably spy the Tower of Terror and the Earful Tower—a water tower outfitted with gigantic mouse ears—before you enter this park, which Disney bills as "the Hollywood that never was and always will be." Art Deco–style buildings accented with pastel colors and neon lights remember the golden age of Hollywood. This 110-acre park has some of the best street performing anywhere. It also has pulse-quickening rides and movie- and TV-themed shows.

The **Rock 'n' Roller Coaster** is a fast-and-furious coaster that blasts you from 0 to 60 mph in 2.8 seconds, and takes you on a wild ride (to an Aerosmith soundtrack) through a make-believe California freeway system in semidarkness. It's the best thrill ride at Disney. Or not. Many adrenaline junkies believe that **The Twilight Zone Tower of Terror,** a stomach-churning atmospheric journey to another dimension, is even better. Rod Serling narrates as you become the star in a special episode of *The Twilight Zone* that climaxes with a terrifying 13-story free-fall plunge!

At **The Magic of Disney Animation,** visitors can attempt their own Disney character drawings while under the supervision of a working animator. The 25-minute **Disney–MGM Studio Backlot Tour** takes you behind the scenes for a close-up look at props, costumes, sets, and special effects used in your favorite movies and TV shows. You'll also visit **Catastrophe Canyon,** where an earthquake causes canyon walls to rumble.

Voyage of *The Little Mermaid* is a charming musical spectacular based on the Disney feature film. The show combines live performers with more than 100 puppets, movie clips, and innovative special effects. A must for your little Ariel fan. Try to see it early in the day. **Beauty and the Beast Live On Stage** is a Broadway-style production of the Disney film. The sets and costumes are lavish, and the production numbers spectacular. Arrive early to get a good seat.

Sounds Dangerous, starring Drew Carey, is a fantastic attraction that allows you to experience sensational "3-D" sound effects that will have you squirming in your seat. **Jim Henson's MuppetVision 3-D** combines Jim Henson's puppets with Disney audio-animatronics and special-effects wizardry, 70mm film, and cutting-edge 3-D technology. The coming-at-you action includes flying Muppets, cream pies, cannonballs, fiber-optic fireworks, bubble showers, even an actual spray of water. Do not miss it!

Film footage and audio-animatronic replicas of movie stars take you on a nostalgic journey through some of the most famous scenes in Hollywood history on **The Great Movie Ride. Star Tours,** a galactic journey based on the original *Star Wars* trilogy (George Lucas collaborated on its conception), can't compete with the latest technology, but it's still plenty of fun. You'll board a 40-seat "spacecraft" for an otherworldly journey that includes sudden drops, violent crashes, and oncoming laser blasts.

Younger audiences (2–5) love **Playhouse Disney—Live on Stage!,** a 20-minute show where they meet characters from Bear in the Big Blue House, The Book of Pooh, and others. It encourages preschoolers to dance, sing, and play along with the cast.

At the **Indiana Jones Epic Stunt Spectacular,** visitors get an inside look at the world of movie stunts in a dramatic 30-minute show, which re-creates major scenes from the Indiana Jones series. The faster-paced **Lights, Motors, Action! Extreme Stunt Show** features high-flying, high-speed movie stunts full of pyrotechnic effects and more.

Based on Disney-owned ABC TV's game show, *Who Wants to Be a Millionaire—Play It!* allows contestants to win points used to buy prizes ranging from a collectible pin to a leather jacket to a 3-night Disney cruise (including airfare) for four. Games run continuously in the 600-seat studio. Audience members play along on keypads. The fastest to answer qualifying questions become contestants.

With more than 50 performers, more than 1 million gallons of water, a 32,000-pound dragon, a 59-foot-high mountain, laser lights, and pyrotechnics, **Fantasmic!** is one of the best nighttime shows in Disney World. It mixes special effects with classic movie clips projected on huge water screens and features Sorcerer Mickey and a host of other Disney favorites. Arrive at the theater at least 30 minutes early to get a seat.

ANIMAL KINGDOM

Disney's fourth major park combines animals, elaborate landscapes, and a handful of rides to create yet another reason that many guests don't venture outside this World.

DISCOVERY ISLAND   The 14-story **Tree of Life** is the park's central landmark. It is an intricately carved free-form representation of animals handcrafted by Disney artists (see how many you can spot). Inside, **It's Tough to Be a Bug!** is a 3-D attraction with creepy-crawly special effects and a special surprise ending that will send a real shiver up your spine. Tots may be frightened by the dark, cavelike atmosphere and the sometimes scary bugs. **The Discovery Island Trails** offer a leisurely stroll through the root system of The Tree of Life, where you might spot otters, flamingos, lemurs, tortoises, and colorful cockatoos.

DINOLAND U.S.A.   Enter by passing under "Olden Gate Bridge," a 40-foot-tall brachiosaurus reassembled from excavated fossils.

Ride past an array of snarling dinosaurs in **Dinosaur,** as you travel back in time to retrieve one of the creatures. The combination of height restrictions and realistic reptiles will probably keep youngsters from riding this one.

Disney introduced **Primeval Whirl,** a spinning, freestyle twin roller coaster in 2002, ostensibly for the young set, but it has a 48-inch height minimum, so it's hardly for little ones. Kids love the chance to slip, slither, slide, and crawl through **The Boneyard,** a giant playground and dig site.

CAMP MINNIE-MICKEY Head immediately for the best show in the park, **Festival of the Lion King,** which regularly draws enough people to fill the 1,000-seat pavilion. Based loosely on the animated movie, this stage show combines the pageantry of a parade with a tribal celebration. The **Character Greeting Pavilions** are a must for people traveling with children. The lines here can be excruciating as hundreds of kids line up to meet their favorite characters.

AFRICA Enter through the town of Harambe, a realistic representation of an African coastal village.

On the **Pangani Forest Exploration Trail,** there are no visible barriers between you and the animals as you watch a troop of African gorillas emerging from the reeds. Bathed in lush jungle foliage, this entire area is filled with exotic East African animals that range from toothy reptiles to brightly colored birds.

On **Kilimanjaro Safaris,** you might see black rhinos, hippos, antelopes, crocodiles, wildebeests, zebras, and lions as your vehicle moves through a simulated African landscape—as long as your timing is right. The animals are scarce at midday most times of year (in cooler months you may get lucky), so *ride this one as close to the park's opening or closing as you can.*

ASIA Disney's Imagineers did a good job of creating the mythical kingdom of **Anandapur.** The intricately painted artwork out front helps make the lines seem to move a tad faster.

On the **Kali River Rapids,** 12-person rafts plunge through a churning, turning waterway. The rainforest environments of Nepal, India, Thailand, and Indonesia are all represented on the **Maharajah Jungle Trek,** along with the species that call these tropical locales home. This is a great spot for viewing and photographing tigers, deer, and giant fruit bats. **Expedition Everest,** the newest and most impressive attraction in the park, transports guests to a meticulously detailed Himalayan village. Guests board the Anandapur Rail Service bound for Mount Everest; after passing bamboo forests and waterfalls, diving through fields of glaciers, and climbing snow-capped peaks, the train suddenly veers "out of control," sending riders careening down Mount Everest's rough and rugged terrain. And that's not the end—a close encounter with the legendary Yeti will have your hair standing on end before it's all over.

UNIVERSAL ORLANDO

Universal Orlando encompasses the original Universal Studios Florida park; its high-tech theme park, Islands of Adventure; the nighttime entertainment district, City-Walk; and three resort hotels.

Multiday tickets (see below) allow you to park-hop between Universal Studios Florida and Islands of Adventure. The cheapest way to see Universal, SeaWorld, *and* Wet 'n Wild is a FlexTicket, which allows you to pay one price to visit the participating parks during a 14-day period. A four-park pass to Universal Studios Florida, Islands of Adventure, Wet 'n Wild, and SeaWorld is $190 for adults and $156 for children 3 to 9. A five-park pass that adds admission to Busch Gardens (p. 400) is also available. The **FlexTicket** can be ordered through Universal (© **800/711-0080** or 407/363-8000; www.universalorlando.com) or the other participating parks.

UNIVERSAL STUDIOS FLORIDA

Universal Studios Florida (© **800/711-0080** or 407/363-8000; www.universalorlando. com) features a host of grown-up rides and fun moments for kids. And as a plus, it's a working motion-picture and TV studio, so occasionally there's filming being done at Nickelodeon's sound stages or elsewhere in the park.

A **1-day ticket** costs $67 (plus 6.5% sales tax) for adults, $56 for children 3 to 9. A 2-day, 2-park unlimited-access escape pass is $115 regardless of age. **Parking** costs $10 for cars, light trucks, and vans. *Note:* It's a long walk to the park from the garage and there is no tram service; parents of young children should bring strollers and those with mobility issues may want to rent a wheelchair or motor cart.

The park is open 365 days a year, usually at least from 9am to 6pm, though it's open as late as 8 or 9pm in summer and around holidays. And sometimes the park also closes early for special events, so your best bet is to call before you go so that you're not caught by surprise.

Major Attractions

A Day in the Park with Barney, set in a parklike theater-in-the-round, is a musical show starring the popular purple one. For young children, this could be the highlight of the day. For parents, our condolences. For a good dose of reality—reality TV, that is—be sure to catch *Fear Factor* **Live.** Audience members can sign up to be the stars of the show, but be prepared—the stunts, while toned down, are similarly challenging (and just as disgusting) as the ones on the TV show. On the **E.T. Adventure,** you'll soar with E.T. on a mission to save his ailing planet, through the forest and into space, aboard a star-bound bicycle. This one's good for the more timid members of your party.

Terminator 2: **3-D Battle Across Time** is the *best* 3-D live-action show in Orlando. The $60-million production features Arnold and other original cast members (on film) mixing with live actors to create some thrilling technical effects. On *Back to the Future:* **The Ride,** you blast through the space-time continuum in a flight simulator built to look like the movie's famous DeLorean.

In *Men in Black* **Alien Attack,** you board a six-passenger cruiser, buzz the streets of New York, and use your "zapper" to splatter up to 120 bug-eyed targets. Trouble is, you also have to battle environmental stimuli that can send you spinning out of control. Split-second decisions determine your fate, which ranges from a hero's welcome to being labeled bug bait.

You didn't *really* think it was safe to go back into the water, did you? A 3-ton, 32-foot-long great white shark tries to sink his teeth into passengers on *Jaws.* And that's not all. Before long, your boat is surrounded by a 30-foot wall of flame that lets you truly feel the heat. If the shark isn't enough to get your adrenaline pumping, **Revenge of the Mummy** will. The latest ride to debut at Universal is an indoor roller coaster that relies on speed, pyrotechnics, and robotics for its thrill factors as riders hurtle through Egyptian sets, passageways, and tombs in cars that move forward and in reverse.

For **Earthquake, the Big One,** you board a BART train in San Francisco for a peaceful subway ride and then an earthquake—8.3 on the Richter scale!—hits, and vast slabs of concrete collapse around you as the station floods (60,000 gal. of water cascade down the steps). Continuing the disaster theme, visitors from the twister-prone Midwest may find *Twister . . .* **Ride It Out** a little too close to the real thing. An ominous funnel cloud, five stories tall, is created by 2 million cubic feet of air per minute. It packs quite a wallop.

Buckle up for **Jimmy Neutron's Nicktoon Blast,** one of Universal's new rides. Jimmy's Rocket Pod hurtles you through hyperspace thanks to sophisticated computer graphics, state-of-the-art *ride* technology, animation, and programmable motion-based seats. Another new ride, ***Shrek* 4-D** is a 20-minute show that can be seen, heard, felt, and smelled thanks to motion simulator technology, OgreVision glasses, and special effects such as water spritzers. The theater's seats are pneumatic air-propulsion nodules that can turn and tilt.

Woody Woodpecker's Nuthouse Coaster is a kiddie coaster that will thrill some moms and dads, too. Although only 30 feet at its peak, it offers quick, banked turns. The ride lasts only about 60 seconds and waits can be 30 minutes or more, but few kids will want to miss the experience.

ISLANDS OF ADVENTURE

Universal's second theme park is 110 acres of adrenaline. Roller coasters roar above pedestrian walkways and water rides slice through the park. It is, bar none, *the* Orlando theme park for thrill-ride junkies.

A few words of caution: *Nine of the park's 14 major rides have height restrictions.* Though there are some rides for small ones, those with very young kids should think twice before coming here. And many of the same rides may not be suitable for those who are tall enough but are pregnant or have health problems, physical restrictions, or a tendency toward motion sickness.

Note: For information on ticket prices and parking, see "Universal Studios Florida," above. The park is open 365 days a year, generally from 9am to 6pm, though often later, especially in summer and around holidays, when it's sometimes open until 9pm.

Major Attractions

Seuss Landing, a 10-acre island, brings Dr. Seuss's world-famous characters and children's books to life. It's also the only "island" where a young child will feel totally at home. Six-passenger couches travel through 18 show scenes in **The Cat in the Hat.** The highlight is a revolving 24-foot tunnel that alters your perceptions and leaves your head spinning. On **One Fish, Two Fish, Red Fish, Blue Fish,** try to avoid getting sprayed as you guide your fish through the ride, taking directions from a Seussian rhyme. **If I Ran the Zoo** is an interactive play land for kids of all ages, with everything from flying water snakes to a chance to tickle the toes of a Seussian animal. And all ages will enjoy a ride on the whimsical **Caro-Seuss-El,** which sports Seussian characters instead of traditional horses.

Thrill junkies will love the twisting, turning, and stomach-churning rides on **Marvel Super Hero Island,** based on characters from Marvel Comics. **The Amazing Adventures of Spider-Man** combines a moving simulator ride with 3-D action and special effects, as guests find themselves in the midst of a battle between evil villains and Spider-Man. The high-tech ride, arguably the best in town, includes a simulated 400-foot drop that feels an awful lot like the real thing. You'll blast from 0 to 40 mph in 2 seconds, and spin upside down 100 feet from the ground on the **Incredible Hulk Coaster.** Coaster crazies love this 2-minute, 15-second ride that includes seven rollovers and two deep drops. On **Dr. Doom's Fearfall,** you're in for a rush as you drop, with feet dangling, down one of two 200-foot steel towers. **Storm Force Accelatron** is a spinning attraction in which guests help comic-book hero Storm harness weather to fight her archenemy, Magneto.

More than 150 life-size sculpted cartoon images let you know you have entered the **Toon Lagoon,** dedicated to your favorites from the Sunday funnies. **Dudley Do-Right's Ripsaw Falls** takes you around a 400,000-gallon lagoon in a flume before you hit a 75-foot drop at 50 mph. (You *will* get wet. Very wet.) **Popeye & Bluto's Bilge Rat Barges** are whirling 12-person rafts that bump and churn their way through a white-water ride. *Note:* You will get either very wet or completely soaked.

All the basics, and some of the high-tech wizardry, from Steven Spielberg's wildly successful movies are incorporated in a lushly landscaped tropical locale in **Jurassic Park.** On the exceptional **Jurassic Park River Adventure,** you come face to face with the living, breathing inhabitants of Jurassic Park. To escape, you take an 85-foot plunge straight down a very steep, very long descent. It's another chance to get completely soaked. In the **Triceratops Encounter,** pet a "living" dinosaur and learn from the trainers about the care and feeding of the 24-foot-long, 10-foot-high triceratops.

The **Lost Continent** section of the park blends the mysterious and the mythical, with components of Atlantis, Merlin, and Sinbad. **Poseidon's Fury** is a multimedia presentation that exposes you to torrents of waters, blasts of fire, and a 42-foot vortex of rushing water, as Poseidon, god of the sea, and Darkenon, an evil sorcerer, battle for supremacy, but it's not really worth the long lines. **Dueling Dragons** is a coaster crazy's fantasy that's not for the faint of heart. The rough-and-tumble ride is staged on intertwined tracks that hold you suspended with your legs dangling freely beneath you, like you're sitting on a jet-propelled swing. At times, riders of the dueling Fire and Ice coasters—zipping along between 60 mph and 65 mph—are just 12 inches apart. **The 8th Voyage of Sinbad** is a somewhat underwhelming stunt show that explores the next voyage of the mythical traveler and relies heavily on pyrotechnics for its thrill factor. **The Flying Unicorn,** a small roller coaster designed for kids, travels through a mythical forest. If you are traveling with kids, make sure to give the **Mystic Fountain** a hearty greeting—it will usually respond in kind.

SEAWORLD

This 200-acre marine-life park at 7007 Sea World Dr. (© **407/351-3600;** www.seaworld.com) explores the mysteries of the deep by combining conservation awareness with entertainment. The stars of the park are **Shamu,** a killer whale, and his ever-expanding family, which includes baby orcas. The pace is much more laid-back than either Universal or Disney, and is a good way to end a long week of trudging through the other parks. Be sure to budget some extra money to buy smelt to feed the animals—the close encounters offered at many wading and feeding pools are more than half the fun.

A **1-day ticket** costs $62 for ages 10 and over, $50 for children 3 to 9, plus 6.5% sales tax. See the Universal Studios Florida section above for information on the FlexTicket option. Parking is $10 for cars, light trucks, and vans. The park is usually open from 9am to 6pm and sometimes later, 365 days a year.

MAJOR ATTRACTIONS

Wild Arctic combines a high-definition adventure film with flight-simulator technology to display breathtaking arctic panoramas. After a hazardous flight over the frozen north, visitors enter an exhibit where you can see a playful polar bear or two, beautiful beluga whales, and walruses. **Shark Encounter** houses 220 specimens of venomous and otherwise scary sea creatures in a tropical-reef habitat. Immense acrylic tunnels provide close encounters with slithery eels, three dozen sharks, barracudas, lionfish, and poisonous puffer fish.

Taking a cue from Disney Imagineers, SeaWorld created a story to go with its $30-million water coaster, **Journey to Atlantis.** But what really matters is the drop—a wild plunge from 60 feet with lugelike curves. No hidden lessons here, just a splashy thrill. A thrill is also what you can expect on the **Kraken,** which features floorless and open-sided 32-passenger trains that plant you on a pedestal high above the track. When the monster breaks loose, you'll climb 151 feet, fall 144 feet, hit speeds of 65 mph, go underground three times (spraying bystanders with water), and make seven loops over a 4,177-foot track.

Today the Florida manatee is in danger of extinction, with as few as 2,000 remaining. Underwater viewing stations, innovative cinema techniques, and interactive displays in **Manatee Rescue** combine to teach visitors about the manatee and its fragile ecosystem. The **Penguin Encounter,** a rather superficial display of hundreds of penguins (including adorable babies) and puffins, also serves as a living laboratory for protecting and preserving polar life.

The Waterfront, SeaWorld's most recent expansion, is a wonderfully themed 5-acre Mediterranean seaport village featuring unique shops, a wide variety of desperately needed restaurants (each offering a very different atmosphere and menu), and, for entertainment, formal shows and street performances.

In **Clyde & Seamore Take Pirate Island,** a lovable sea lion-and-otter duo, with a supporting cast of walruses and harbor seals, appears in this fishy comedy with a swashbuckling conservation theme.

Everyone comes to SeaWorld to see Shamu and his friends—the stars of the impressively choreographed show *Believe.* An all-new set, spectacular special effects, and musical score add up to a great show. Be sure to heed the warnings, as those sitting in the first 14 rows are sure to get soaked with icy water more than once. Dolphins, acrobats, and exotic birds are the stars of *Blue Horizons,* a far cry from the ho-hum dolphin show it replaced.

And finally, parents can rest their weary feet while their offspring work off some energy at **Shamu's Happy Harbor,** a 3-acre play area that has a four-story net tower with a 35-foot-high crow's nest, water cannons, remote-controlled vehicles, nine slides, a submarine, and a water maze.

DISCOVERY COVE

Anheuser-Busch spent $100 million building SeaWorld's sister park, **Discovery Cove** (© 877/434-7268; www.discoverycove.com), which debuted in 2000. About 1,000 guests are admitted daily to this unique attraction, but you'll pay for the privilege of avoiding the crowds. Prices vary seasonally but range from $249 to $279 per person (plus 6.5% sales tax) for ages 6 and up if you want to swim with the dolphins, and $149 to $179 if you forego the experience. Double-check prices when you make your required reservations. The gate price includes a continental breakfast, lunch, all-day snacks and drinks, a towel, a locker, sunscreen, snorkeling gear (including a flotation vest), a souvenir photo, free parking, and 7 days of unlimited admission to SeaWorld or to Busch Gardens in Tampa (p. 400). For an additional $30 per person, you can upgrade that last option to 14 days of unlimited admission to both SeaWorld *and* Busch Gardens. Guests who choose the dolphin option will swim with, snorkel with, and feed dolphins; everyone can swim and snorkel with other aquatic life.

WHERE TO STAY

There are more than 114,000 rooms in the Orlando area with thousands added annually. Occupancy is generally high—as much as 90% at Disney—so if you plan to stay in one of Mickey's resorts, book as far ahead as possible. The lowest rates are usually available from September to November and from January to April. High season occurs during holidays and the summer months.

The rates below represent "rack rates," basic prices that should be used as a basis for comparison shopping only. You should be able to get a better deal, except during the busiest of times.

Important note: In addition to the accommodations described here, there are scores of chain hotels and motels. See appendix D at the end of this book for toll-free numbers and websites.

WALT DISNEY WORLD CENTRAL RESERVATIONS OFFICE   In addition to their proximity to the parks, rooms at Disney's resorts, villas, campgrounds, and official hotels offer additional advantages: complimentary transportation to and from the Disney parks (and the airport!); character breakfasts and/or dinners; a guest-services desk; use of the five Disney-owned golf courses and preferred tee times; and much more. Some of our favorite Disney resorts are listed in this section, as are our favorite hotels in Orlando. Keep in mind that non-Disney hotels tend to be far more favorably priced.

To reserve a room or book packages at Disney's resorts, campgrounds, and official hotels, contact the **Central Reservations Office (CRO),** P.O. Box 10000, Lake Buena Vista, FL 32830-1000 (© **407/934-7639;** www.disneyworld.com). They'll recommend accommodations to fit your price range and needs, such as proximity to your favorite park or to those with supervised child-care centers. While Disney reservations folks are very helpful and knowledgeable, they usually won't volunteer information about better deals or specials, so be sure to *ask.*

Comfort Suites Maingate East (Value)   This welcoming hotel is one of the nicest in the area. The lobby and accommodations—consisting of studio and one-bedroom suites—are bright and inviting. The main pool and the children's pool, with an umbrella fountain to keep everyone cool, are open round-the-clock. For entertainment, Old Town (a small-scale shopping, dining, and entertainment complex) is next door, and a great miniature-golf course is located just in front of the property.

2775 Florida Plaza Blvd., Kissimmee, FL 34746. © **888/782-9772** or 407/397-7848. Fax 407/396-7045. www. comfortsuitesfl.com. 198 units. $69–$175 double. Extra person $10. Rates include continental breakfast. Children 17 and under stay free in parent's room. AE, DC, DISC, MC, V. Free self-parking. **Amenities:** Heated pool; kids' pool; fitness center. *In room:* Fridge, microwave.

Disney's Grand Floridian Resort & Spa (Best)   From the moment you step into the opulent five-story domed lobby, you'll feel as if you've slipped back to an era when a guy named Gatsby was at the top of his game. High tea is served in the afternoon; later, a small band plays music from the 1940s. The Grand Floridian is the romantic choice for couples, especially honeymooners. Spend the day luxuriating in the first-class spa—the best in WDW. The Victorian-style rooms sleep at least four; virtually all overlook a garden, pool, courtyard, or the Seven Seas Lagoon. Located directly on the monorail system, it makes for a quick trip to the Magic Kingdom.

4401 Floridian Way (P.O. Box 10000), Lake Buena Vista, FL 32830-1000. ℃ **407/934-7639** or 407/824-3000. Fax 407/824-3186. www.disneyworld.com. 900 units. $359–$890 double; $940–$2,600 suite. Extra person $25. Children 17 and under stay free in parent's room. AE, DC, DISC, MC, V. Self-parking free; valet parking $7. Pets $9 per night. **Amenities:** 5 restaurants; heated pool; kids' pool; 2 lighted tennis courts; health club; spa. *In room:* Fridge, microwave.

Disney's Pop Century Resort ✓*Value*   Gigantic memorabilia from decades past—remember the 8-track and the Rubik's Cube?—mark the exteriors at Disney's newest value resort. While there might not be a lot of frills (think spartan '50s Holiday Inn), the price is right for families on a budget who want to bunk with Mickey. The guest rooms—just like Disney's similar All-Star properties—are tiny, and bathrooms are similarly cramped. That said, this is the cheapest you'll pay to bunk with Mickey. The resort is closest to the Wide World of Sports Complex.

1050 Century Dr. (off Oceola Pkwy.; P.O. Box 10000), Lake Buena Vista, FL 32830-1000. ℃ **407/938-4000** or 407/939-6000. Fax 407/938-4040. www.disneyworld.com. 2,880 units. $79–$137 double. Extra person $10. Children 17 and under stay free in parent's room. AE, DC, DISC, MC, V. Free parking. **Amenities:** Food court; 2 heated pools; kids' pool. *In room:* Fridge ($10 per day).

Disney's Port Orleans Resort ✓*Value*   Run as two separate resorts, each with a distinctive southern theme, the recently renovated Port Orleans has the best landscaping and coziest atmosphere of Disney's moderate resorts. The **French Quarter** reflects the charm of New Orleans at the turn of the 20th century, with accents of Mardi Gras, while **Riverside,** filled with grand mansions and back bayous, reflects the Old South. The dragon-themed Doubloon Lagoon pool, the Ol' Man Island swimming hole, and a nearby playground are a hit with kids. Guest rooms are large enough for four, but it'll be a tight fit. Its central location is just east of Epcot and MGM; there's boat service to Downtown Disney.

2201 Orleans Dr. (off Bonnet Creek Pkwy.; P.O. Box 10000), Lake Buena Vista, FL 32830-1000. ℃ **407/934-7639** or 407/934-5000. Fax 407/934-5353. www.disneyworld.com. 3,056 units. $133–$209 double. Extra person $15. Children 17 and under stay free in parent's room. AE, DC, DISC, MC, V. Free parking. Pets $9 per night. **Amenities:** 3 restaurants; 6 heated pools; 2 kids' pools. *In room:* Fridge (free upon request).

Disney's Wilderness Lodge   The surrounding tall timbers, spouting geyser and hot springs, mammoth stone hearth, and bunk beds for the kids give the Wilderness Lodge an old-time national park feel, making it a favorite of families and couples alike. Standard rooms sleep four, and if a view is important to you, those with woods views are the best. The decor is among Disney's best, and the restaurants offer some of the most spectacular views in WDW. While the nearest park is Magic Kingdom, the resort, in keeping with its theme, is in a fairly remote area.

901 W. Timberline Dr. (on the southwest shore of Bay Lake just east of the Magic Kingdom; P.O. Box 10000), Lake Buena Vista, FL 32830-1000. ℃ **407/934-7639** or 407/938-4300. Fax 407/824-3232. www.disneyworld.com. 909 units. $205–$575 lodge; $370–$500 concierge level; $380–$1,250 suite; $295–$1,040 villa. Extra person $25. Children 17 and under stay free in parent's room. AE, DC, DISC, MC, V. Free self-parking; valet parking $7. Pets $9 per night. **Amenities:** 2 restaurants; heated pool; kids' pool. *In room:* Fridge (free upon request).

Disney's Yacht Club Resort   The posh and nautically themed Yacht Club is geared more toward adults and families with older children, although young kids are catered to (this *is* Disney). It shares a 25-acre lake—Stormalong Bay—a first-class swimming area (including a life-size shipwreck with water slides and a sandy-bottomed pool), and magnificent landscaping with its sister property, the Beach Club. The theme is turn-of-the-20th-century New England. The comfortable rooms have space for up to five people, and most have balconies. Epcot is just a short walk away.

1700 Epcot Resorts Blvd. (off Buena Vista Dr.; P.O. Box 10000), Lake Buena Vista, FL 32830-1000. © **407/934-7639** or 407/934-7000. Fax 407/924-3450. www.disneyworld.com. 630 units. $305–$545 double; $555–$2,440 suite; $435–$695 concierge level. Extra person $25. Children 17 and under stay free in parent's room. AE, DC, DISC, MC, V. Self-parking free; valet parking $7. Pets $9 per night. **Amenities:** 4 restaurants; 2 heated pools; kids' pool; 2 lighted tennis courts. *In room:* Fridge (free upon request).

Fairfield Inn and Suites International Cove *(Value)*   If you're looking for I-Drive's best value, it's hard to beat the Fairfield. It offers a quiet location off the main drag, earthly rates, and a clean motel in one package. The rooms are very comfortable and there are a number of restaurants within walking distance.

7495 Canada Ave. (off International Dr. near Sand Lake Rd.), Orlando, FL 32819. © **407/351-7000.** Fax 407/351-0052. www.fairfieldinn.com. 200 units. $77–$119 for up to 4. Rates include continental breakfast. AE, DC, DISC, MC, V. Free self-parking. **Amenities:** Heated pool. *In room:* Fridge (some rooms), microwave (some rooms).

Hyatt Regency Grand Cypress   This getaway is a favorite of honeymooners and those seeking a luxurious adult oasis (though it's popular with families, too). Its lobby has lush foliage from which macaws greet passersby. The 18-story atrium has inner and outer glass elevators (ride the outers to the roof for a panoramic rush). The rooms are beautifully decorated and sleep four. The Hyatt has a golf club and school, a racquet club, and an equestrian center, and offers excellent packages aimed at the sports set. The Hyatt's half-acre, 800,000-gallon pool is one of the best in Orlando and features caves, grottoes, waterfalls, and a 45-foot water slide.

1 N. Jacaranda (off Hwy. 535), Orlando, FL 32836. © **800/233-1234** or 407/239-1234. Fax 407/239-3800. www.grandcypress.com. 750 units. $239–$585 double; $395–$5,750 suite. Optional $10 daily resort fee. Extra person $25. Children 17 and under stay free in parent's room. AE, DC, DISC, MC, V. Valet parking $12; free self-parking. **Amenities:** 4 restaurants; heated pool; 45 holes of golf; 12 tennis courts (5 lighted); health club; spa.

Marriott's Orlando World Center   Golf, tennis, and spa lovers find plenty to do at this 230-acre resort. The sports facilities are first-class, and the largest of its five pools has water slides and waterfalls. The location, only 2 miles from the Disney parks, is another plus. The large comfortable rooms sleep four, and the higher poolside floors offer views of Mickeyville.

8701 World Center Dr. (on Hwy. 536 between I-4 and Hwy. 535), Orlando, FL 32821. © **800/621-0638** or 407/239-4200. Fax 407/238-8777. www.marriottworldcenter.com. 2,111 units. $199–$329 for up to 5; $750–$1,600 suite. Children 17 and under stay free in parent's room. AE, DC, DISC, MC, V. Self-parking free; valet parking $16. **Amenities:** 4 restaurants; 4 heated pools (1 indoor); kids' pool; 18-hole golf course; 8 lighted tennis courts; health club; spa.

Nickelodeon Family Suites Resort *(Kids)*   This all-suite property is one of the best in the Orlando area for families. Its brightly colored Kid Suites feature second bedrooms for the kids (with either bunks or twin beds), mini-kitchens, and pullout sofas in the living areas. Three-bedroom suites include a second bathroom and a full kitchen. Nightly entertainment (including Studio Nick) has been added. Nickelodeon characters and color schemes (neon green and orange) run throughout the resort. The resort's two pool areas are veritable waterparks. "Nick After Dark," a supervised activity program for kids ages 5 to 12, allows parents to take a night off. Up to four kids eat free with a paying adult at the extensive breakfast buffet.

14500 Continental Gateway (off Hwy. 536), Lake Buena Vista, FL 32821. © **877/387-5437**, 407/387-5437, or 866/GO-2-NICK. Fax 407/387-1489. www.nickhotel.com. 789 units. $160–$275 suite. AE, DC, DISC, MC, V. Free self-parking. **Amenities:** Restaurant; 2 pools; fitness center. *In room:* Kitchen.

Peabody Orlando   The five mallards that march into a lobby fountain every morning at 11am and then back out at 5pm, accompanied by John Philip Sousa's *King Cotton March*, are just part of the appeal of this service-oriented hotel. If your budget allows for a splurge, you won't be disappointed with a stay here. Primarily a business and convention destination, the Peabody also appeals to adults looking for a classy hotel that provides top-of-the-line service, amenities, and atmosphere. Rooms sleep up to five, and are tastefully decorated and well appointed. Those on the west side (sixth floor and higher) offer a distant view of Disney and its fireworks displays.

9801 International Dr. (between Bee Line Expwy. and Sand Lake Rd.), Orlando, FL 32819. ✆ **800/732-2639** or 407/352-4000. Fax 407/354-1424. www.peabodyorlando.com. 891 units. $395–$490 standard room for up to 3; $550–$1,775 suite. Extra person $15. Children 17 and under stay free in parent's room. AE, DC, DISC, MC, V. Self-parking free; valet parking $14. **Amenities:** 3 restaurants; heated pool; kids' pool; 4 lighted tennis courts; fitness center; spa.

Royal Pacific Resort (Value) (Kids)   This Universal Orlando resort (run by Loews) has an open-air courtyard with an exquisite orchid garden, palm trees, and waterfalls. It doesn't quite succeed at creating a Polynesian paradise, but it's the best Universal resort in the theme department and the best for those traveling with young kids. The rooms, smaller than those at other Universal resorts, are attractively decorated with lovely wood accents and carvings. And the lagoon pool area—the largest in Orlando—is lovely. The big plus: Guests get no-line access to almost every ride at Universal Orlando, and seating privileges for shows and restaurants. The big minus—you have to pay for self-parking and the lot is far from the entrance.

6300 Hollywood Way, Orlando, FL 32819. ✆ **800/232-7827** or 407/503-3000. Fax 407/503-3202. www.loews hotels.com/hotels/orlando or www.universalorlando.com. 1,000 units. $199–$428 double; $325–$1,875 suite. Extra person $25. Children 17 and under stay free in parent's room. AE, DC, DISC, MC, V. Self-parking $10; valet parking $17. Small pets stay free. **Amenities:** 2 restaurants; heated pool; kids' pool.

Staybridge Suites Lake Buena Vista   Close to the theme park action, this property's one- and two-bedroom suites come with full kitchens. The suites' separate living areas are larger and more comfortable than similar ones at other all-suite hotels. A nicely landscaped inner courtyard is where you'll find the resort's pool, along with plenty of space to soak up the sun. A unique plus is the complimentary grocery service, which allows you to select supermarket items for delivery to your room.

8751 Suiteside Dr., Orlando FL 32836. ✆ **800/866-4549** or 407/238-0777. Fax 407/238-2640. www.sborlando.com. 150 units. $119–$199 1-bedroom suite (up to 4 people); $149–$269 2-bedroom suite (up to 8 people). Rates include continental breakfast. Rollaway beds and cribs available at no charge. AE, DC, DISC, MC, V. Free self-parking. **Amenities:** Deli; heated pool; kid's pool; 24-hr. fitness room. *In room:* Kitchen.

WHERE TO DINE

Artist Point   SEAFOOD/STEAKS   Enjoy a grand view of Disney's Wilderness Lodge in this rustically elegant establishment. Select from a seasonally changing menu that might include grilled buffalo sirloin with a sweet-potato-and-hazelnut gratin, or cedar plank–roasted Silver Bay salmon with maple-whiskey glaze. *Note:* Artist Point has a more relaxed atmosphere than some of the busier WDW resort restaurants.

901 W. Timberline Dr., in Disney's Wilderness Lodge. ✆ **407/939-3463** or 407/824-1081. www.disneyworld.com. Advanced Reservations recommended. Main courses $21–$49. AE, DC, DISC, MC, V. Daily 5:30–10pm. Free self- and valet parking.

Boma   INTERNATIONAL   One of the Animal Kingdom Lodge's signature restaurants, Boma offers a nice diversion from the usual Disney fare. In front of the open

How to Arrange Advance Reservations at Disney Restaurants

Advance Reservations *isn't* a reservation. It's a promise that you'll get the next available table once you arrive. There may be a wait, but if you don't use this system you may have a longer one (or not get in at all). To arrange for Advance Reservations at any WDW restaurant (in the parks or at the resorts), call ☎ **407/ 939-3463.** You can book as far as 180 days in advance of your arrival for most restaurants. If you're staying on Disney property, you can arrange Advance Reservations at your resort.

kitchen lies an incredible buffet of international cuisine featuring authentic African dishes from over 50 different countries alongside a few more familiar favorites— including dishes especially for kids. A family atmosphere, similar to an African marketplace, is enhanced by colorful fabrics draped from above. Everything is fresh and tasty. *Note:* An American buffet breakfast is served here daily.

2901 Osceola Pkwy., at Disney's Animal Kingdom Lodge. ☎ 407/938-3000. www.disneyworld.com. Advanced Reservations recommended. All-you-can-eat buffet $17–$26 for adults, $10–$12 for children 3–9. AE, DC, DISC, MC, V. Daily 7:30–11am and 5:30–10pm. Free self-parking.

Bubbaloo's Bodacious BBQ *Value* BARBECUE   This spot serves some of the best barbecue in Florida. Go for the full pork platter that comes with a heaping helping of pork and all the fixin's. The uninitiated should stay away from the "Killer" sauce, which produces a tongue buzz that's likely to last for hours; you might even taste-test the mild sauce before moving up to the hot.

15818 Conroy Rd. ☎ 407/423-1212. www.bubbalous.com. Reservations not accepted. Main courses $4–$13. AE, MC, V. Mon–Sat 10am–9pm.

California Grill CALIFORNIA   Make your way to the 15th floor of the Contemporary Resort and enjoy views of the Magic Kingdom while you drool over healthy options prepared in an exhibition kitchen. Headliners usually include wood-fired pizzas, smoked salmon, and grilled pork tenderloin with balsamic vinegar and crimini mushrooms. The Grill also features a sushi and sashimi menu. This is one of the few spots in WDW that isn't well suited to kids. It can be tough to get a table, so arrange Advance Reservations as far ahead as possible.

4600 N. World Dr., at Disney's Contemporary Resort. ☎ 407/939-3463 or 407/824-1576. www.disneyworld.com. Reservations required. Main courses $21–$34; sushi and sashimi $13–$24. AE, DC, DISC, MC, V. Daily 5:30–10pm. Free self-parking.

Dux INTERNATIONAL   Named for the Peabody's famous mallards (you won't find any version of duck on the menu), Dux offers a marvelous and oft-changing menu, as well as impeccable service. If it's there, try the succulent Alaskan Halibut with lobster mashed potatoes and lobster reduction or the tender veal chop marinated in apple cider and honey and served medium rare. The candlelit dining room provides a wonderful atmosphere, and Dux is best reserved for a very special night out or a meal on an expense account.

9801 International Dr., in the Peabody Orlando. ☎ 407/345-4550. www.peabodyorlando.com. Reservations recommended. Main courses $30–$50. AE, DC, DISC, MC, V. Mon–Sat 6–10pm. Free self- and validated valet parking.

Emeril's NEW ORLEANS   It's next to impossible to get short-term reservations for dinner unless you're willing to take your chances with no-shows, but most who wait say the Creole-inspired food is worth it. A good bet is the andouille-crusted redfish (a moist white fish with roasted pecan-vegetable relish and meunière sauce). If you want some *vino* with your meal, the back half of the building is a glass-walled 12,000-bottle aboveground cellar. Prices are high enough that Emeril can afford tons of legroom between tables. If you want a show, we recommend one of eight counter seats where you can watch chefs working their magic, but to get one, reservations are required *excruciatingly* early (2–3 months, at least).

6000 Universal Studios Blvd., in CityWalk. ℭ 407/224-2424. www.emerils.com/restaurants/index_orlando.htm. Reservations necessary. Main courses $18–$28 lunch, $18–$45 dinner. AE, DISC, MC, V. Daily 11:30am–2pm and 5:30–10pm (until 11pm Fri–Sat). Parking $9 (free after 6pm).

Pebbles Island Grill FLORIDIAN   If you want to dine like a gourmet without the hefty price, this is the restaurant for you. This local chain has a reputation for great food and creative appetizers. Its pleasant Key West style is casual and comfortable, and the generous portions are presented with artistic flair. The delicious Ybor Gold twin filets are seared, then bathed in the namesake lager and delivered with caramelized onions and three-cheese potatoes.

12551 Apopka-Vineland Rd., in the Crossroads Shopping Center. ℭ 407/827-1111. www.pebblesworldwide.com. Reservations not accepted. Main courses $8–$28. AE, DC, DISC, MC, V. Mon–Thurs 11am–11pm; Fri 11am–midnight; Sat noon–midnight; Sun noon–11pm. Free self-parking.

Siam Orchid THAI   Tim and Krissnee Martsching grow the mint, chiles, cilantro, lemon grass, and wild lime that go into their entrees. Star attractions include Pad Thai (noodles tossed with ground pork, garlic, shrimp, crab, and peanuts in a sweet sauce) and Royal Thai (chicken, potatoes, and onion in yellow curry sauce). Siam Orchid serves sake, plum wine, and Thai beers from a full bar.

7575 Universal Blvd. (between Sand Lake Rd. and Carrier Dr.). ℭ 407/351-0821. Reservations recommended. Main courses $12–$24. AE, DC, DISC, MC, V. Mon–Fri 11am–2pm; daily 5–11pm. Free self-parking.

Tchoup Chop PACIFIC RIM   Pronounced *chop chop*, Emeril Lagasse's second restaurant in Orlando is named for the location of his original restaurant, Tchoupitoulas Street in New Orleans. The service is impeccable and the relaxing atmosphere, stunning decor, and excellent food ensure that the experience is grand. The exhibition kitchen offers a look at chefs making Polynesian- and Asian-influenced entrees such as grilled rib-eye steak with garlic mashed potatoes, fried Maui onions, teriyaki sauce, and stir-fried vegetables.

6300 Hollywood Way, in Universal's Royal Pacific Hotel. ℭ 407/503-2467. www.emerils.com/restaurants/index_orlando.htm. Reservations strongly recommended. Main courses $13–$34. AE, DISC, MC, V. Daily 11:30am–2pm; Sun–Thurs 5:30–10pm; Fri–Sat 5:30–11pm. Valet parking $5.

Victoria & Albert's *Best* INTERNATIONAL   It's not often that dinner can be described as "an event," but Disney's most elegant restaurant earns that distinction. Dinner is next to perfect—if the portions seem small, we dare you to make it through all six courses. The setting is exceptionally romantic. Fare changes nightly, but you might find main events such as lamb seared with foie gras over brioche with Fuji apples, tamari-glazed blue-fin tuna over bok choy stir-fry, or Colorado lamb with corn risotto. The dining room is crowned by a domed, chapel-style ceiling; 20 exquisitely appointed tables are lit softly by Victorian lamps; and your servers (always named Victoria and Albert) provide service that will have you begging to take them home. There's an extensive wine list. We suggest splurging on the wine pairing.

The Chef's Table: Best Seat in the World

There's a special dining option at **Victoria & Albert's**. Reserve the **Chef's Table** (far, *far* in advance) and dine in a charming alcove at a candlelit table in the heart of the kitchen! Begin by sipping bubbly with the chef while discussing your food preferences for a menu (up to 13 courses) created especially for you. Diners get to tour the kitchen and observe the artistry of the chefs at work. The Chef's Table can accommodate up to 10 people a night. It's a leisurely affair, lasting 3 or 4 hours. The price is $150 per person without wine, $215 including five wines. This is so popular that Advance Reservations are a must, so reserve *early* by calling ℂ **407/939-3463**.

4401 Floridian Way, in Disney's Grand Floridian Resort & Spa. ℂ **407/939-3463**. www.disneyworld.com. Reservations required. Jackets required for men. Not recommended for children. Prix fixe $110 per person, $165 with wine pairing; $150 Chef's Table, $215 with wine. AE, DC, DISC, MC, V. 2 dinner seatings daily Sept–June, 5:45–6:30pm and 9–9:45pm; 1 seating July–Aug, 6:45–8pm. Chef's Table 6pm only. Valet parking $7.

Wolfgang Puck Café CALIFORNIA   The wait can be distressing and the sticker prices depressing, but the chefs turn out a mean menu of pizza, sushi, and froufrou food. Our favorite stop is the sushi bar, an artistic copper-and-terrazzo masterpiece that delivers some of the best sushi in Orlando. The upstairs room offers a more refined atmosphere—and a menu to match. Puck's is noisy, making conversation difficult. But after enough sake, who cares?

1482 Buena Vista Dr., at Disney's West Side. ℂ **407/938-9653**. www.wolfgangpuck.com/myrestaurants or www.levyrestaurants.com. Reservations not accepted on lower level; Advanced Reservations for upstairs dining room. Main courses upstairs $22–$37; main courses cafe $11–$36; pizza and sushi $11–$27; Express $9–$15. AE, DC, DISC, MC, V. Daily 11am–1am. Free self-parking.

EPCOT

WORLD SHOWCASE   The World Showcase has the best dining options inside the WDW theme parks, thanks to the cultural cuisine of its 11 nation pavilions. There are many options beyond the ones we list below; these are our favorites.

Le Cellier Steakhouse, in **Canada,** has a castlelike ambience accentuated by vaulted stone arches. Red-meat main events (all Midwest, corn-fed) include the usual range of cuts—filet, porterhouse, prime rib, sirloin, and so on. Wash down your meal with a Canadian ice wine or choose from a selection of Canadian beers.

The **United Kingdom**'s Tudor-beamed **Rose & Crown** is a cozy pub suggestive of Victorian England. Visitors from the U.K. flock to this spot, where folk music and sometimes-saucy servers entertain you as you feast on a short but joyfully traditional menu including steak-and-mushroom pie and fish and chips. The outdoor dining area overlooks the lagoon and is a good place to see IllumiNations.

Pricey **Les Chefs de France** has an impressive interior, agleam with mirrors and brass chandeliers. Three renowned French chefs take credit for the menu, which includes such entrees as Mediterranean seafood casserole (grouper, scallops, and shrimp dusted with saffron, then enrobed in a mild garlic sauce) and a leg of lamb braised in tomatoes and wine.

Of all the Epcot restaurants, **Morocco**'s **Marrakesh** best exemplifies the spirit of the park, yet a lot of guests ignore it because they're worried that the menu is too exotic. Expect belly dancers to entertain while you feast on such options as marinated beef shish kabob, braised chicken with green olives, and a medley of seafood, chicken, and lamb. The palatial restaurant—with handset mosaic tiles, latticed shutters, and a ceiling painted in elaborate Moorish motifs—represents 12 centuries of Arabic design.

If you've been to a Japanese steakhouse chain, you know the drill at **Japan**'s **Teppan-yaki:** Diners sit around grill tables while white-hatted chefs rapidly dice, slice, stir-fry, and sometimes launch the food onto your plate with amazing skill. Unfortunately, the culinary acrobatics here are better than the cuisine.

In **Italy,** and patterned after Alfredo De Lelio's celebrated ristorante in Rome, **L'Originale Alfredo di Roma** is Epcot's most popular restaurant. Nevertheless, critics say its pasta is overpriced and its servers are carefree. It's hard to take issue with the former when one meatless-pasta dish tops the $20 mark—the celebrated fettuccine.

When it comes to decor, **China**'s **Nine Dragons** shines with carved rosewood furnishings and a dragon-motif ceiling. Some windows overlook the lagoon outside. Main courses feature Mandarin, Cantonese, and Szechuan cuisine, but portions are small and the food isn't quite as glorious as the surroundings.

Akershus is a re-created 14th-century castle in **Norway** where you can sample a 40-item smorgasbord of *smavarmt* (hot) and *koldtbord* (cold) dishes. Norwegian beer and aquavit complement a list of French and California wines.

It's always night at **Mexico**'s **San Angel Inn,** where candlelit tables set the mood, and the menu delivers reasonably authentic food.

FUTURE WORLD   The only major sit-down restaurant in Future World is at the Living Seas pavilion. The mood is half the fun at the **Coral Reef,** where the tables circle a 5.6-million-gallon aquarium that has 4,000 denizens of the not-so-deep. Tiered seating ensures everyone a good view. Highlights include Florida mahimahi, yellowtail snapper, and salmon.

IN THE MAGIC KINGDOM

In addition to these restaurants, there are plenty of fast-food outlets located throughout the park. But you may find that a quiet, sit-down meal is an essential though brief getaway from the forced-march madness. Don't forget to make Advance Reservations arrangements, and bear in mind that no alcohol is served in the Magic Kingdom.

Romantics may find it hard to beat the ambience of eating at **Cinderella's Royal Table** in Cinderella Castle, the Magic Kingdom's icon. Servers treat you like a lord or lady while fetching you headliners such as spice-crusted salmon, New York strip, or roasted chicken.

The Liberty Tree Tavern's Colonial decor and mood are fun, but the food (including the evening character buffet) is basic. Expect roast turkey, marinated flank steak, and honey-mustard ham. The **Crystal Palace,** named for its beautiful glass exterior, is a favorite with families because of its all-you-can eat character buffets (where kids and adults can choose from a decent variety of meats, veggies, and desserts).

AT DISNEY–MGM STUDIOS

There are more than a dozen places to refuel in this Hollywood-style theme park. The ones listed below are the best of the bunch. Again, Advance Reservations are a must.

Modeled after the Los Angeles celebrity haunt where Louella Parsons and Hedda Hopper held court, the **Hollywood Brown Derby** offers a good time and pricey meal. On the lighter side, try a Cobb salad, invented in the 1930s by Bob Cobb, who owned

No Smoking!
Under Florida law, smoking in restaurants is prohibited, so forget about lighting up with your meal.

the restaurant in the other Hollywood. The Derby's signature dessert, grapefruit cake with cream-cheese icing, is a perfect meal-capper.

The **50's Prime Time Café** is like going home to Mom's kitchen for dinner—back in the 1950s. The atmosphere delivers with black-and-white TV sets showing *My Little Margie* and servers threatening to withhold dessert if you don't eat all your food. Although the desserts are good, the meatloaf and pot roast aren't quite as good as Mom used to make.

Take the above review for the 50's Prime Time Café, give it a science-fiction spin, and welcome to the **Sci-Fi Dine-In Theater Restaurant.** Diners sit in chrome-plated convertibles with the Hollywood Hills as a backdrop and are treated to newsreels, cartoons, and "B" horror flicks. Eating here is a bit pricey, but the really unique atmosphere is worth it.

The best bets at the casual **Mama Melrose's Ristorante Italiano** are the wood-fired and brick-baked specialties, including the flat breads (pepperoni, portobello mushroom, and four cheeses). The warm and welcoming atmosphere makes you feel like you're at a mom-and-pop-run restaurant.

IN THE ANIMAL KINGDOM
You'll find only a few dining options in the Animal Kingdom, and most of those are grab-and-go places. Nevertheless, there are two spots where you can park yourself.

Expect California fare with an island spin at the **Rainforest Cafe.** Menu offerings tend to be tasty and somewhat creative, but the prices tend to run on the high side for what you get. It is the atmosphere that attracts most guests to this establishment, with the sights and sounds of a tropical rainforest thoroughly surrounding and entertaining you while you dine.

The thatched-roof **Tusker House** in Harambe village offers fast food with a bit of flair. Options include a grilled chicken salad, rotisserie or fried chicken, a turkey wrap with corn chowder, roasted-vegetable sandwiches, and grilled salmon.

ONLY IN ORLANDO: DINING WITH DISNEY CHARACTERS
Dining with the Disney characters is a treat for almost any Disney fan, but it's a special one for those under the age of 10. The characters will greet, sign autographs, pose for photos, and interact with the entire family. These dining experiences are extremely popular, so make Advance Reservations arrangements (© **407/939-3463**) as early as possible, and call for schedules. Prices vary, but generally expect breakfast (most serve it) to be $17 to $32 for adults, and $11 to $22 for kids 3 to 9. Restaurants that serve dinner charge $28 to $40 for adults and $13 to $25 for kids.

Character meals open, close, and change at whim, but the top two meals in our book (and the most popular) are two veterans: **Chef Mickey's** at Disney's Contemporary Resort and **Cinderella's Royal Table** in Magic Kingdom's Cinderella Castle. For an up-to-date list of available character meals, check Disney's website at **www.disney world.com**.

ORLANDO AFTER DARK

The easiest way to find nighttime fun is to head for one of the massive entertainment complexes: **Pleasure Island, Disney's West Side** (both part of the Downtown Disney district), and **CityWalk.**

Pleasure Island, in Walt Disney World, adjacent to Walt Disney World Village (© 407/939-2648), is a 6-acre complex of nightclubs, restaurants, shops, and movie theaters; for a single admission price ($21 plus tax), you can enjoy a night of club-hopping until the wee hours. (If you arrive before 7pm, the entrance fee is waived if you just want to walk around and check out the shops and restaurants, but you can't get into the clubs without a paid admission.) The streets are festive with brightly colored lights and balloons. You'll be given a map and shown a schedule when you enter the park; take a look at it and plan your evening around shows that interest you. The on-premises clubs come and go, but expect to find a jazz club, a comedy club, an inter-active entertainment club, a few dance clubs, live bands, a tropical bar, a video arcade, shops, and more. And every night features a midnight New Year's Eve celebration with fireworks and confetti.

Just down the block is **Disney's West Side.** It includes the 1,500-seat **House of Blues,** a three-story concert hall that books big-name acts, from rappers to blues legends. Here you'll also find **Cirque du Soleil** (© 407/939-7600; www.cirquedusoleil.com). The international theater company known for combining acrobatics and elaborate avant-garde theatrics into a stage production has established a permanent venue here. Good seats at the $40-million stage production, dubbed *La Nouba,* cost $95 (including tax) for adults, $76 for children ages 3 to 9.

Universal's answer to Pleasure Island and Disney's West Side, the 12-acre entertainment complex **CityWalk** (© 407/363-8000; www.citywalk.com), is theme-restaurant heaven. Alcohol is prominently featured here, so an adult should accompany all teens, young children, and party-hearty peers. Venues here include the Down Beat Jazz Hall of Fame located in **City Jazz,** a tribute to reggae mon Bob Marley, and a 5,000-seat movie complex. Those desiring to dance the night away can refine their moves at **the groove,** or try out their South American steps at **Latin Quarter.** Parrot-heads can make their way to **Jimmy Buffet's Margaritaville.** Music lovers will flock to **Hard Rock Live Orlando,** a 2,200-capacity venue featuring performances by top music stars. Or down Hurricanes as you cheer on dueling pianos at a branch of New Orleans's **Pat O'Brien's.**

You can walk the district for free or visit clubs and pay their individual cover charges (usually under $6). CityWalk also offers two **party passes.** A pass to all clubs costs $10 plus tax. For $13 plus tax, you get a club pass and a movie at Universal Cineplex (© 407/354-5998). *Note:* Daytime parking in the Universal Orlando garages costs $9, but parking is free after 6pm. Universal also offers free club access to those who buy 2- and 3-day theme-park tickets (see "Universal Orlando," earlier in this chapter).

2 Highlights of Northeast Florida

COCOA BEACH, CAPE CANAVERAL & THE KENNEDY SPACE CENTER

The area around Cape Canaveral was once a sleepy place where city dwellers escaped the crowds from the exploding urban centers of Miami and Jacksonville. Then came the NASA space program. Today the region accommodates its own crowds, especially hordes of tourists who come to see where astronauts blast off into space.

ESSENTIALS

GETTING THERE   The nearest airport is **Melbourne International Airport** (© **321/723-6227;** www.mlbair.com), 22 miles south of Cocoa Beach. However, **Orlando International Airport,** about 35 miles to the west, is a much larger hub with more flight options and generally less expensive fares. A car is essential in this area, so rent one at whatever airport you arrive in, and hit the roads. By car, major routes into Cocoa Beach are **I-95** from the north (Daytona Beach and Jacksonville) and south (Miami), and **Fla. 528** (Bee Line Expwy.) from the west (Orlando).

VISITOR INFORMATION   For information about the area, contact the **Florida Space Coast Office of Tourism/Brevard County Tourist Development Council,** 8810 Astronaut Blvd., Suite 102, Cape Canaveral, FL 32920 (© **800/872-1969** or 321/868-1126; www.space-coast.com). The office is in the Sheldon Cove building, on Fla. A1A a block north of Central Boulevard, and is open Monday through Friday from 8am to 5pm.

EXPLORING THE AREA

The **Kennedy Space Center Visitor Complex,** on NASA Parkway (© **321/449-4444;** www.KennedySpaceCenter.com), is the best attraction in this neck of the woods. It features exhibits, rockets, IMAX movies, and several dining venues. From the center, bus tours (take an early one, as lines can be brutal) go to the massive Vehicle Assembly Building, the International Space Station Center, and the impressive Apollo/Saturn V Center. The latter includes artifacts, photos, interactive exhibits, and the 363-foot-high Saturn V, the most powerful rocket ever launched by the United States. Don't miss the **Astronaut Memorial,** a moving black-granite monument marked with the names of the U.S. astronauts who have died on missions or while in training.

Note: Kennedy Space Center acquired many of the exhibits from the **Astronaut Hall of Fame** and added them as a separate attraction at the KSC visitor center ($17 adults, $13 kids 3–11; or $37 adults and $27 kids for a 2-day Maximum Access Admission to the Center and the Hall of Fame). The attraction includes exhibits and tributes to the heroes of the Mercury, Gemini, and Apollo space programs. There's also a collection of spacecraft, including a Mercury 7 capsule, a Gemini training capsule, and an Apollo 14 command module. In "Simulator Station," guests can experience four times the force of gravity, ride a Rover across Mars, and land a Space Shuttle.

NASA originally took over much more land than it needed to launch rockets. Rather than sell off the unused portions, it turned them over to the **Cape Canaveral National Seashore** (© **321/867-4077,** or 321/867-0677 for recorded information; www.nps.gov/cana) and the **Merritt Island National Wildlife Refuge** (© **321/ 861-0667;** www.nbbd.com/godo/minwr), both on Fla. 402. Together they protect tidal marshes, a bay known as Mosquito Lagoon, and 13 miles of barrier island beach. This is a great area for bird-watching, and giant sea turtles nest here May through August.

Appearing rustic and slapped-together, the **Cocoa Beach Pier,** on Meade Avenue east of Fla. A1A (© **321/783-7549**), was built in 1962 and shortly thereafter became the East Coast's surfing capital. It has 842 feet of fishing, shopping, and food and drinks overlooking a wide, sandy beach.

You can go sailing and take deep-sea fishing expeditions from the south bank of **Port Canaveral,** a man-made harbor that also is home port to cruise ships bound for the Bahamas and the Caribbean.

WHERE TO STAY

The six-story **DoubleTree Cocoa Beach Oceanfront Hotel,** 2080 N. Atlantic Ave. (© **800/552-3224** or 321/783-9222; www.cocoabeachdoubletree.com), is the pick of the beachfront properties; all rooms have balconies with ocean views. Rates run $114 to $179 double. **The Inn at Cocoa Beach,** 4300 Ocean Blvd. (© **800/343-5307** or 321/799-3460; www.theinnatcocoabeach.com), is the most romantic place in town and draws many couples with its well-furnished rooms. Rates ($135–$325 double) include breakfast and afternoon tea.

Two good chain motels in this area are the **Hampton Inn Cocoa Beach,** 3425 Atlantic Blvd. (© **877/492-3224** or 321/799-4099; www.hamptoninncocoabeach. com); and **Courtyard by Marriott,** 3435 Atlantic Blvd. (© **800/321-2211** or 321/784-4800; www.marriott.com). They stand side-by-side and have access to the beach via a pathway through a condominium complex.

DAYTONA BEACH

Daytona Beach is the "World Center of Racing" and a mecca for spring breakers. Hundreds of thousands of race enthusiasts come here to see the Daytona 500, the Pepsi 400, and other races and to visit Daytona USA, a state-of-the-art motorsports entertainment attraction worth a visit even by non-racing fans. But you don't have to be a car aficionado to enjoy Daytona, for here you'll find hard-packed sand along 24 miles of beaches.

ESSENTIALS

GETTING THERE   Fly into the small, pleasant, and calm **Daytona Beach International Airport** (© **386/248-8030;** http://flydaytonafirst.com), 4 miles inland from the beach on International Speedway Boulevard (U.S. 92); or into **Orlando International Airport** (see "Walt Disney World & Orlando," earlier in this chapter), about an hour's drive away. **Daytona-Orlando Transit Service** (**DOTS;** © **800/231-1965** or 386/257-5411; www.dots-daytonabeach.com) provides transportation to and from Orlando International Airport ($28 for adults one-way; half-fare for children 11 and under).

If you fly directly into Daytona, be aware that there are no airport shuttles at the Daytona Airport, but major car-rental agencies do have desks here (and Daytona is a driver's town anyway, so it's best to rent a car). By car, the major route into Daytona Beach is **I-95** from the north (Jacksonville) and south (Miami), and **I-4** from the southwest (Orlando).

VISITOR INFORMATION   The **Daytona Beach Area Convention & Visitors Bureau,** 126 E. Orange Ave. (P.O. Box 910), Daytona Beach, FL 32115 (© **800/ 544-0415** or 386/255-0415; www.daytonabeach.com), can help you with information on attractions, accommodations, dining, and events. The office is on the mainland just west of the Memorial Bridge. The information area of the lobby is open daily from 9am to 5pm.

WHAT TO SEE & DO

You don't have to be a racing fan to enjoy a visit to the **Daytona International Speedway complex,** 1801 W. International Speedway Blvd. (© **386/253-7223** for race tickets and information; www.daytonaintlspeedway.com). Entertaining 30-minute guided tram tours ($7.50) of the facility (garage area, pit road, and so on) depart from the visitor center and are well worth taking. The visitor center houses the phenomenally popular **Daytona USA** (© **386/947-6800;** www.daytonausa.com), a state-of-the-art interactive attraction that costs $22 adults, $16 for kids 6 to 12. Here you can participate in a pit stop on a NASCAR Winston Cup stock car, see the actual winning Daytona 500 car still covered in track dust, talk via video with favorite competitors, and play radio or television announcer by calling the finish of a race. An action-packed IMAX film will put you in the winner's seat of a Daytona 500 race.

To really experience what it's like, you can actually make (for $134) three laps around the track in a stock car from May to October with the **Richard Petty Driving Experience Ride-Along Program** (© **800/237-3889;** www.1800bepetty.com). Professional drivers (sorry, none are named Petty) are at the wheel as you see and feel what it's like to travel an average 115 mph.

The bustling hub of beach activity is the **Main Street Pier.** You can drive and park directly on the sand along most of the beach, but watch for signs warning of sea turtles nesting. *And watch out for the tides.* If you park on an incoming tide and lose track of time, your vehicle may become an inadvertent rust bucket or artificial reef! There's a $5 vehicle access fee in most areas.

This is a popular zone for golfers, and there are more than 25 courses within 30 minutes of Daytona's beach. For course information online, go to **www.golf.com** and **www.floridagolfing.com**; or call the **Florida Sports Foundation** (© **850/488-8347**) or **Florida Golfing** (© **866/833-2663**).

WHERE TO STAY

The **Plaza Resort & Spa,** 600 N. Atlantic Ave. (© **800/874-7420** or 386/255-4471; www.plazaresortandspa.com), features some of Daytona Beach's best rooms (in a more tasteful atmosphere than many of the neighboring hotels)—provided you don't need a large bathroom. The choice units are the corner suites, which have balconies overlooking the Atlantic; some even have a Jacuzzi. All units have balconies and microwaves. Rates run $139 to $229 double.

The most unusual beachside property here, and a good inexpensive choice, **Old Salty's Inn,** 1921 S. Atlantic Ave. (© **800/417-1466** or 386/252-8090; www.old saltys.com), carries out a *Gilligan's Island* theme. Doubles cost $53 to $93. The refurbished **Shoreline All Suites Inn & Cabana Colony Cottages,** 2435 S. Atlantic Ave. (© **800/293-0653** or 386/252-1692; www.daytonashoreline.com), has both spacious motel suites and small beachside cottages. Rates run $79 to $350 for suites and cottages.

Thousands of rental condominiums line the beaches here. Among the most luxurious is the new, 150-unit condominium hotel **Ocean Walk Resort,** 300 N. Atlantic Ave., Daytona Beach, FL 32118 (© **800/649-3566** or 386/323-4800; www.ocean-walkresort.com). Near the Main Street Pier, it offers one- and two-bedroom apartments with fully equipped kitchens, washers and dryers, and all of the usual hotel amenities, plus a wondrous computer golf simulator, a "lazy river" in the outdoor pool, an island putting green, and much more.

JACKSONVILLE

The sprawling metropolis of Jacksonville—residents call it "Jax," from its airport abbreviation—is one of the South's insurance and banking capitals. Development is rampant throughout Duval County, with hotels, restaurants, attractions, and clubs rapidly springing up, especially in suburban areas near the interstate highways. The city recently got a boost when several major cruise lines began using its port as a base for some of their ships.

ESSENTIALS

GETTING THERE   By Plane   Several airlines fly into **Jacksonville International Airport,** on the city's north side about 12 miles from downtown (© 904/741-2000; www.jaxairports.org). The major car-rental firms (and you're best off with a rental car) have booths here. **Express Shuttle** (© 904/353-8880) and **Gator City Taxi** (© 904/741-0008** at the airport, or 904/355-8294 elsewhere) provide transportation to and from the airport.

By Train   Amtrak (© 800/USA-RAIL; www.amtrak.com) provides daily service from Orlando (trip time: 3¾ hr.), Tampa (4¾ hr.), and Miami (10 hr.) to its station at 3570 Clifford Lane.

By Car   Major routes into Jacksonville are **I-95** from the north (Savannah) and south (Miami), and **I-10** from the west (Tallahassee).

VISITOR INFORMATION   Contact the **Jacksonville and the Beaches Convention & Visitors Bureau,** 201 E. Adams St., Jacksonville, FL 32202 (© 800/733-2668 or 904/798-9111; www.jaxcvb.com), for maps, brochures, and advice. The bureau is open Monday through Friday from 8am to 5pm.

WHAT TO SEE & DO

Spanning the broad, curving St. Johns River, downtown Jacksonville is a hub of activity during weekdays and on weekend afternoons and evenings, when many locals return to the restaurants and bars of **The Jacksonville Landing (www.jacksonville landing.com)** and **Southbank Riverwalk,** two dining and entertainment complexes facing each other across the river. Like Baltimore's Inner Harbor, they have helped to revitalize downtown.

Also worth seeing here are the small but outstanding **Cummer Museum of Art & Gardens,** 829 Riverside Ave. (© 904/356-6857; www.cummer.org), especially for its American Impressionist paintings; the **Jacksonville Zoo,** 8605 Zoo Rd. (© 904/757-4462 or 904/757-4463; www.jaxzoo.org), whose main exhibits center on an extensive and growing collection of African wildlife; and the **Fort Caroline National Memorial,** on Fort Caroline Road (© 904/641-7155; www.nps.gov/timu), a two-thirds replica of a 16th-century fort built by French Huguenots who attempted to settle here. The fort serves as the main visitor center for the **Timucuan Ecological and Historic Preserve,** a new breed of national park that includes natural preserves as well as historic sites.

You can fish, swim, snorkel, sail, sunbathe, or stroll on the sand dunes (at least Mar–Nov, as winter can get downright chilly here). They're all just a 20- to 30-minute drive east of downtown in **Atlantic Beach, Neptune Beach, Jacksonville Beach,** and the ritzy enclave of **Ponte Vedra Beach.** At the beach end of Atlantic Boulevard (Fla. 10), which straddles Atlantic and Neptune beaches, **Town Center** is a quaint community with a number of shops, restaurants, pubs, and hotels. You won't need your car to hit the beach, shop, dine, or imbibe here.

WHERE TO STAY

Downtown on the Southbank Riverwalk, the 10-story **Hilton Jacksonville Riverfront,** 1201 Riverplace Blvd. (© **800/445-8667** or 904/398-8800; www.jacksonville-hilton.com), features the Elvis Presley Suite, where the King purportedly stayed half a dozen times (and, some say, still does). It and the other rooms have dark-wood furniture and smallish marble-tiled bathrooms.

A dozen modest chain hotels line Jacksonville Beach along the Atlantic Ocean, including the **Comfort Inn Oceanfront,** 1515 N. 1st St., 2 blocks east of Fla. A1A (© **800/654-8776** or 904/241-2311; www.comfortinnjaxbeach.com), one of the best-priced beachfront options. One of the anchors of quaint Town Center, the inexpensive **Sea Horse Oceanfront Inn,** 120 Atlantic Blvd. (© **800/881-2330** or 904/246-2175; www.seahorseoceanfrontinn.com), offers clean rooms with ocean views from balconies or patios. Also worth checking out in Town Center is the **Sea Turtle Inn,** 1 Ocean Blvd. (© **800/874-6000** or 904/249-7402; www.seaturtle.com), an older property that was completely gutted and restored in 2000.

In Ponte Vedra Beach, the upscale **Sawgrass Marriott Resort & Beach Club,** 1000 PGA Tour Blvd. (© **800/228-9290** or 904/285-7777; www.sawgrassmarriott.com), and **Ponte Vedra Inn & Club,** 200 Ponte Vedra Blvd. (© **800/234-7842** or 904/ 285-1111; www.pvresorts.com), are both built around championship golf courses and offer a variety of accommodations, from hotel rooms to luxury condos. Smaller and more intimate, **The Lodge & Club at Ponte Vedra Beach,** 607 Ponte Vedra Blvd. (© **800/243-4304** or 904/273-9500; www.pvresorts.com), is one of Florida's more romantic hotels and its rooms are the epitome of high-end luxury.

ST. AUGUSTINE

With its 17th-century fort, old city gates, horse-drawn carriages clip-clopping along narrow streets, historic buildings, and reconstructed 18th-century Spanish Quarter, St. Augustine seems more like a picturesque European village than a modern Floridian city. This is, after all, the oldest continuous European settlement in the United States (no, it wasn't Jamestown in 1607 or the Pilgrims at Plymouth Rock in 1620), originally established as a colony by Spain in 1562. Tourism is St. Augustine's main industry these days; but despite the daily invasion (with good reason—there are a plethora of interesting attractions), it's an exceptionally charming town, with good restaurants, a small-town nightlife, and shopping bargains. St. Augustine is one of those places that actually lives up to most of the sickly sweet and sentimental promotional literature written about it.

ESSENTIALS

GETTING THERE   The **Daytona Beach** airport (p. 358) is about an hour's drive south of St. Augustine, but services are more frequent—and fares usually lower—at **Jacksonville's International Airport** (see above), about the same distance north. Amtrak's nearest train station is in Jacksonville.

VISITOR INFORMATION   Before you go, contact the **St. Augustine, Ponte Vedra & The Beaches Visitors and Convention Bureau,** 88 Riberia St., Suite 400, St. Augustine, FL 32084 (© **800/653-2489** or 904/829-1711; www.visitoldcity.com), and request the *Visitor's Guide,* detailing attractions, events, restaurants, accommodations, shopping, and more. The **St. Augustine Visitor Information Center** is at 10

Castillo Dr., at San Marco Avenue, opposite the Castillo de San Marcos National Monument (© **904/825-1000**). There are numerous ways to see the city, depending on your interest and time, and this is a good place to make your plans. Check out the free 22-minute orientation video, which is helpful in planning your visit. The center is open daily from 8:30am to 5:30pm.

WHAT TO SEE & DO

Tip: Yes, the city is famed for being the supposed site of the Fountain of Youth, but that tourist trap is such a waste of time, we don't even bother covering it.

Parking is nonexistent in the historic district—where many of the best sights are located—which makes a decision to take one of the hop-on/hop-off trolley tours of the area that much easier. We like **St. Augustine Historical Sightseeing** (© **904/826-4218** or 904/829-3800), which operates green-and-white, open-air buses (and enclosed buses when it rains, a definite advantage). You can park your car at the headquarters (the Authentic Old Jail and the Florida Heritage Museum at the Authentic Old Jail, which are also stops on the tour—though admittedly, neither of these attractions are particularly outstanding). The bus tours cost $15 for adults, $5 for kids 6 to 12.

Do not think of leaving town without checking out the magnificent **Lightner Museum,** 75 King St. (© **904/824-2874;** www.lightnermuseum.org). Henry Flagler's opulent Spanish Renaissance–style Alcazar Hotel, built in 1889, closed during the Depression and stayed vacant until Chicago publishing magnate Otto C. Lightner bought the building in 1948 to house his vast collection of Victoriana. Both the building and the varied collection are must-sees. The imposing building across King Street was Henry Flagler's rival resort, the Ponce de León Hotel. It now houses **Flagler College,** which runs don't-miss-it 45-minute tours daily (at 10am and 2pm) of its magnificent Tiffany stained-glass windows, ornate Spanish Renaissance architecture, and gold-leafed Maynard murals ($5 adults, $1 kids under 12; call © **904/823-3378** or visit www.flagler.edu/news_events/tours.html for more information).

America's oldest and best-preserved masonry fortification, **Castillo de San Marcos National Monument,** East Castillo Drive (© **904/829-6506;** www.nps.gov/casa), is pretty cool. Today, the old bombproof storerooms surrounding the central plaza house exhibits documenting the history of the fort, a national monument since 1924. You can also tour the vaulted powder magazine, a dank prison cell (supposedly haunted), the chapel, and guard rooms. **The Colonial Spanish Quarter and Spanish Quarter Museum,** 33 St. George St. (© **904/825-6830;** www.historicstaugustine.com), is a re-created colonial Spanish village, complete with costumed folk doing things they used to do back in the 1700s. Watch as the blacksmiths, carpenters, leatherworkers, and homemakers demonstrate their skills and show you what life was like before the Internet. For an authentic historic experience, head to the **Old St. Augustine Village Museum,** 250 St. George St. (© **904/823-9722;** www.old-staug-village.com), which brings to life each period of the city's history, from Spanish colonial times to the early 20th century. The 10 restored homes here—built between 1790 and 1910—are original and on their original building sites.

For something a bit less historical, grab the kids and head out to the century-old **St. Augustine Alligator Farm and Zoological Park,** 999 Anastasia Blvd. (© **904/824-3337;** www.alligatorfarm.com), where more than 2,700 gators and crocodiles—including some rare white ones—are on display. In fact, it houses the world's only complete collection of all 22 species of crocodilians, a category that includes alligators, crocodiles, caimans, and gavials.

Passionate golf fans can easily spend a day at the **World Golf Hall of Fame,** at Exit 95a off I-95 (© **904/940-4123;** www.wgv.com), a state-of-the-art museum honoring professional golf, its great players, and the sport's famous supporters (including comedian Bob Hope and singer Dinah Shore). It's the centerpiece of **World Golf Village,** 21 World Golf Place (© **904/940-4000;** www.wgv.com), a complex of hotels, shops, and 18-hole golf courses. There's an IMAX screen next door.

WHERE TO STAY

There are plenty of moderate and inexpensive motels and hotels in St. Augustine. Most convenient to the historic district is the 40-room **Best Western Spanish Quarter Inn,** 6 Castillo Dr. (© **800/528-1234** or 904/824-4457; www.staugustinebest western.com), directly across the street from the visitor center. It's completely surrounded by an asphalt parking lot but does have a swimming pool and hot tub.

St. Augustine also has more than two dozen bed-and-breakfasts in restored historic homes. Contact **St. Augustine Historic Inns,** P.O. Box 5268, St. Augustine, FL 33085-5268 (no phone; www.staugustineinns.com), for descriptions of its member properties.

Originally built in 1888 by YMCA founder Franklin W. Smith, the restored Moorish-style **Casa Monica Hotel,** 95 Cordova St. (© **800/648-1888** or 904/827-1888; www.casamonica.com), is easily the best in town, with top-notch services and accommodations. Also built in 1888, the **Alexander Homestead,** 14 Sevilla St. (© **888/292-4147** or 904/826-4147; www.alexanderhomestead.com), is a restored Victorian beauty with antiques-laden rooms that offers a spectacular and romantic stay.

The 1897-vintage **Victorian House,** 11 Cadiz St. (© **877/703-0432** or 904/824-5214; www.victorianhouse-inn.com), is unusual for a St. Augustine B&B in that it accepts kids in its annex building (a former general store). Rooms in the main building offer more character, no kids, and no telephones or TVs.

3 Fort Lauderdale & Palm Beach

FORT LAUDERDALE

Fort Lauderdale, once infamous for its annual spring break mayhem, began discouraging partying college kids and marketing its charms to a more affluent crowd in the mid-'90s. In addition to beautiful wide beaches, the city includes more than 300 miles of navigable waterways and innumerable canals that permit thousands of residents to anchor boats in their backyards. Boating is not just a hobby here; it's a lifestyle. Huge cruise ships also take advantage of Florida's deepest harbor, Port Everglades. It is the second-busiest cruise-ship base in Florida (after Miami) and one of the top five in the world.

ESSENTIALS

GETTING THERE If you're driving from Miami, it's a straight shot north to Hollywood or Fort Lauderdale. Visitors on their way to or from Orlando should take the **Florida Turnpike** to Exit 53, 54, 58, or 62, depending on the location of your accommodations. The **Fort Lauderdale–Hollywood International Airport (www.broward. org/airport)** is undergoing a massive multiyear renovation, but is currently small, easy to negotiate, and located just 15 minutes from both of the downtown areas it services.

Amtrak (© **800/USA-RAIL;** www.amtrak.com) stations are at 200 SW 21st Terrace (Broward Blvd. and I-95), Fort Lauderdale (© **954/587-6692**); and at 3001 Hollywood Blvd., Hollywood (© **954/921-4517**).

VISITOR INFORMATION The **Greater Fort Lauderdale Convention & Visitors Bureau,** 1850 Eller Dr., Suite 303 (off I-95 and I-595 East), Fort Lauderdale, FL 33316 (© **954/765-4466;** www.sunny.org), is an excellent resource for area information. We highly recommend calling them in advance to request a free comprehensive guide covering events, accommodations, and sightseeing. Once you are in town, you can call a 24-hour **information line** (© **954/527-5600;** www.activityline.net) to get easy-to-follow directions, travel advice, and assistance.

FUN ON & OFF THE BEACH

The **Fort Lauderdale Beach Promenade** looks fantastic. Note, however, that this beach is hardly pristine; it is across the street from an uninterrupted stretch of hotels, bars, and retail outlets. The unusually clear waters are under the careful watch of lifeguards. Freshen up afterward in any of the clean showers and restrooms conveniently located along the strip. Also nearby, on Fla. A1A, midway between Las Olas and Sunrise boulevards, is **Beach Place,** a mega-retail and dining complex.

Fort Lauderdale provides ample opportunity for visitors to get on the water, either along the Intracoastal Waterway or out on the open ocean. **Aloha Watersports,** Marriott's Harbor Beach Resort, 3030 Holiday Dr., Fort Lauderdale (© **954/462-7245**), can outfit you with a variety of watercraft.

The **IGFA World Fishing Center** at 300 Gulf Stream Way (© **954/922-4212;** www.igfa.org) in Dania Beach is an angler's paradise. One of the highlights of this museum, library, and park is the virtual-reality fishing simulator, which allows visitors to actually reel in their own computer-generated catch. To get a list of local captains and guides, call IGFA headquarters and ask for the librarian (© **954/927-2628**). Admission is $6 for adults, $5 for children between 3 and 12. On the grounds is also **Bass Pro Outdoor World Store,** a huge multifloor retail complex situated on a 3-acre lake.

More than 50 golf courses in all price ranges compete for players. Some of the best include **Emerald Hills** at 4100 N. Hills Dr., Hollywood, just west of I-95 between Sterling Road and Sheridan Street **(www.theclubatemeraldhills.com).** This beauty consistently lands on "best of" lists of golf writers throughout the country. Greens fees start at $125. Call © **954/961-4000** for tee times. For one of Broward's best municipal challenges, try the 18-holer at the **Orangebrook Golf Course,** 400 Entrada Dr., in Hollywood (© **954/967-GOLF**), one of the area's best bargains. Morning and noon rates range from $17 to $22. After 2pm, you can play for about $15, including a cart. Men must wear collared shirts, and no spikes are allowed.

Plan to spend at least an afternoon or evening cruising Fort Lauderdale's 300 miles of waterways. The **Water Bus of Fort Lauderdale** (© **954/467-6677;** www.water taxi.com) is a trusty fleet of old-port boats that serve the dual purpose of transporting and entertaining visitors. Taxis operate on demand and along a fairly regular route and carry up to 48 passengers. Choose a hotel on the route so that you can take advantage of this convenient and inexpensive system. You can be picked up at your hotel, usually within 15 minutes of calling, and then be shuttled to any of the dozens of restaurants, bars, and attractions on or near the waterfront. Your afternoon of cruising might start with a tour of **Millionaires' Row,** where Lauderdale's largest yachts are dwarfed only by the homes at which they are docked. Starting daily at 8am, boats run until midnight 7 days a week, depending on the weather. Check their website for exact times of pickup. The cost is $5 for a day pass; $4 for a one-way trip; $10 for a 3-day pass; and $25 for a weeklong pass. Tickets are available on board; no credit cards are accepted.

If you are looking for unusual boutiques, especially art galleries, head to trendy **Las Olas Boulevard,** where there are literally hundreds of shops with alluring window decorations and intriguing merchandise. You may find kitchen utensils posing as modern art sculptures or mural-size oil paintings.

WHERE TO STAY

The Fort Lauderdale beach has a hotel or motel on nearly every block, and they range from the run-down to the luxurious. The **Lago Mar Resort and Club,** 1700 S. Ocean Lane, Fort Lauderdale (℃ **800/524-6627** or 954/523-6511; www.lagomar.com), is a casually elegant resort that occupies its own little island between Lake Mayan and the Atlantic. It's great for families, as most accommodations are suites with kitchenettes, and there are sports and facilities galore. Rates run $165 to $285 double.

A more moderately priced option is the **Banyan Marina Resort,** 111 Isle of Venice, Fort Lauderdale (℃ **954/524-4430;** www.banyanmarina.com). This hidden treasure is built around a dramatic 75-year-old banyan tree and is located directly on the active canals halfway between Fort Lauderdale's downtown and the beach. The recently renovated one- and two-bedroom apartments are comfortable and spacious, with full kitchens and living rooms. Rates run from $73 to $200 per apartment. Another magnificent find is the **Courtyard Villa on the Ocean,** 4312 El Mar Dr., Lauderdale-by-the-Sea (℃ **800/291-3560** or 954/776-1164; www.courtyardvilla.com), a small, eight-room historic hotel offering a romantic getaway right on the beach. It features spacious oceanfront efficiencies with private balconies, large suites overlooking the pool, and two-bedroom apartments. Rooms are plush, with carved four-poster beds, fully equipped kitchenettes, and tiled bathrooms. Relax in the hotel's unique heated pool/spa or on the second-floor sun deck. Rates run $115 to $272 double.

PALM BEACH & WEST PALM BEACH

Palm Beach has been the traditional winter home of America's aristocracy—the Kennedys, the Rockefellers, the Pulitzers, the Trumps, and plenty of CEOs. By contrast, West Palm Beach is a grittier workaday city. Recent renovations have made the metropolitan area a lively and affordable place to dine, shop, and hang out. In addition to good beaches, boating, and diving, you'll find great golf and tennis throughout the county.

ESSENTIALS

GETTING THERE   If you're driving up or down the Florida coast, you'll probably reach the Palm Beach area by **I-95.** Visitors on their way to or from Orlando or Miami should take the **Florida Turnpike,** a toll road.

All major **airlines** fly to **Palm Beach International Airport,** at Congress Avenue and Belvedere Road (℃ **561/471-7400**). Most major car-rental agencies (you'll need a rental) have desks at the airport. **Amtrak** (℃ **800/USA-RAIL;** www.amtrak.com) has a terminal in West Palm Beach, at 201 S. Tamarind Ave. (℃ **561/832-6169**).

VISITOR INFORMATION   The **Palm Beach County Convention and Visitors Bureau,** 1555 Palm Beach Lakes Blvd., Suite 204, West Palm Beach, FL 33401 (℃ **800/554-PALM** or 561/471-3995; www.palmbeachfl.com), distributes an informative brochure and will answer questions about visiting the Palm Beaches. Ask for a map as well as a copy of the *Arts and Attractions Calendar,* a day-to-day guide to art, music, stage, and other events in the county.

FUN ON & OFF THE BEACH

Most of the island's best beaches are fronted by private estates and inaccessible to the general public. However, there are a few notable exceptions, including **Midtown Beach** on Ocean Boulevard, between Royal Palm Way and Gulfstream Road. There are no restrooms or concessions here, although a lifeguard is on duty until sundown. This newly widened sandy coast is now a centerpiece and a natural oasis in a town dominated by commercial glitz. To the south is a less popular but better equipped beach at **Phipps Ocean Park.** On **Ocean Boulevard,** between the Southern Boulevard and Lake Avenue causeways, is a large and lively public beach encompassing more than 1,300 feet of groomed and guarded oceanfront. With picnic and recreation areas, as well as plenty of parking, the area is especially good for families.

One of the state's best golf courses is **Emerald Dunes Golf Course,** 2100 Emerald Dunes Dr., in West Palm Beach (© **561/687-1700**). Designed by Tom Fazio, this dramatic 7,006-yard, par-72 course was voted "One of the Best 10 You Can Play" by *Golf* magazine. It is just off the Florida Turnpike at Okeechobee Boulevard. Bookings are taken up to 30 days ahead. Fees are $45 to $135, including carts. The **Palm Beach Public Golf Course,** 2345 S. Ocean Blvd. (© **561/547-0598**), a popular public 18-hole course, is a par-54; the course is run on a first-come, first-served basis. Club rentals are available. Greens fees start at $16 to $35 per person.

The annual ritual of the ponies is played out each season at the posh **Palm Beach Polo and Country Club.** It is one of the world's premier polo grounds and hosts some of the sport's top-rated players. Matches are open to the public and are surprisingly affordable. Unless it is an opening game or some other special event, dress is casual. A navy or tweed blazer over jeans or khakis is a standard for men, while neat-looking jeans or a pantsuit is the norm for women. On warmer days, shorts and, of course, a polo shirt are fine, too. General admission is $10 to $20; box seats cost $75 to $100. Matches are held throughout the week. Schedules vary, but the big names usually compete on Sunday at 3:30pm January through April. The fields are at 11809 Polo Club Rd., Wellington, 10 miles west of the Forest Hill Boulevard exit of I-95. Call © **561/793-1440** or surf over to **www.palmbeachpolo.com** for more information.

The **Flagler Museum,** 1 Whitehall Way (at Coconut Row), Palm Beach (© **561/ 655-2833;** www.flaglermuseum.us), is a luxurious mansion commissioned by Henry Flagler, a co-founder of the Standard Oil Company. The must-see classically columned Edwardian-style mansion contains 55 rooms that include a Louis XIV music room and art gallery, a Louis XV ballroom, and 14 guest suites outfitted with original antique European furnishings. The **Norton Museum of Art,** 1451 S. Olive Ave., West Palm Beach (© **561/832-5196;** www.norton.org), is world famous for its prestigious collection, which includes works by American artists such as Georgia O'Keeffe and Jackson Pollock; works by French artists such as Monet, Picasso, and Renoir; and a number of Chinese bronzes, jades, and ceramics.

A great spot for families, the **Lion Country Safari,** Southern Boulevard West at S.R. 80, West Palm Beach (© **561/793-1084;** www.lioncountrysafari.com), has more than 1,300 animals wandering on its 500-acre preserve. The animals—lions, elephants, buffalo, watusi, pink flamingos, and more—wander the grassy landscape while visitors remain in the safety of their cars. Also on the premises are an amusement park, a carousel, and an animal nursery. Picnics are encouraged. Also cool for kids (especially the under-5 set) is the 17,000-square-foot **Playmobil Fun Park**, 8031 N. Military Trail, Palm Beach Gardens (© **800/351-8697** or 561/691-9880; www.playmobil.com), which is housed in a replica castle and loaded with themed areas for imaginative play: a medieval village, a Western town, a fantasy dollhouse, and more.

Known as "the Rodeo Drive of the South," **Worth Avenue** is a window-shopper's dream. No matter what your budget, don't miss the Worth Avenue experience. The 4 blocks between South Ocean Boulevard and Cocoanut Row—a stretch of more than 200 boutiques, posh shops, art galleries, and upscale restaurants—are home to Armani, Louis Vuitton, Cartier, Polo Ralph Lauren, and Chanel, among others.

City Place, Okeechobee Road, at 1-95, West Palm Beach (© **561/820-9716**), is a $550-million, Mediterranean-style shopping, dining, and entertainment complex that's responsible for revitalizing what was once a lifeless downtown West Palm Beach.

WHERE TO STAY

The Breakers, 1 S. County Rd., Palm Beach (© **800/833-3141,** 888/BREAKERS, or 561/655-6611; www.thebreakers.com) is what Palm Beach is all about. Elaborate, stately, and resplendent in all its Italian Renaissance–style glory, it's where old money mixes with new money, and the Old World gives way, albeit reluctantly, to a bit of modernity. The lush 140-acre grounds also sport Florida's oldest (though newly revamped) 18-hole golf course; a magnificent spa; a huge family entertainment center; and numerous top-notch restaurants. Doubles run $270 to $675.

For over-the-top pampering in a perfect location, the elegant **Four Seasons Resort Palm Beach,** 2800 S. Ocean Blvd., Palm Beach (© **800/432-2335** or 561/582-2800; www.fourseasons.com), is a favorite. The elegant marble lobby is replete with hand-carved European furnishings, grand oil paintings, tapestries, and dramatic flower arrangements. In addition to a host of services and sports facilities, there's a 6,000-square-foot spa and health club. Rates run $290 to $775 double. For a more intimate experience, try **The Chesterfield Palm Beach,** 363 Cocoanut Row, Palm Beach (© **800/243-7871** or 561/659-5800; www.redcarnationhotels.com), just 3 blocks from the beach. Reminiscent of an English country manor, it is a magnificent, charming hotel with lovely rooms and exceptional service. Rates run $230 to $500 double.

Looking for a bargain rather than a pricey resort? A special find is **Hibiscus House,** 501 30th St., West Palm Beach (© **800/203-4927** or 561/863-5633; www.hibiscus house.com), a 1920s-era B&B filled with handsome antiques. Every room here has its own private terrace or balcony. Rates run $95 to $210 double and include breakfast.

4 Miami

There's much more to South Florida than the neon-hued nostalgia of *Miami Vice* and pink flamingos. Beyond the whole glitzy, *Access-Hollywood*-meets-beach-blanket-bacchanalia-as-seen-on-TV, Miami has an endless number of sporting, cultural, and recreational activities to keep you entertained. Its sparkling beaches are beyond compare. Plus, there's excellent shopping and other nightlife activities that include ballet, theater, and opera.

ESSENTIALS

GETTING THERE   **Miami International Airport (MIA)** ranks 10th in the world for total passengers. Despite the heavy traffic, the airport is quite user-friendly and not as much of a hassle as you'd think. Visitor information is available 24 hours a day at the **Miami International Airport Main Visitor Counter,** Concourse E, second level (*©* **305/876-7000**). Information is also available at **www.miami-airport.com.** Miami International Airport is located about 6 miles west of downtown and about 10 miles from the beaches, so it's likely you can get from the plane to your hotel room in less than half an hour.

Note: Because MIA is the busiest airport in South Florida, travelers may want to consider flying into the less crowded **Fort Lauderdale Hollywood International Airport (FLL)** (*©* **954/359-1200**), which is closer to north Miami than MIA, or the **Palm Beach International Airport (PBI)** (*©* **561/471-7420**), which is about 1½ hours from Miami.

All the major car-rental firms operate off-site branches reached via shuttle from the terminals and we *strongly recommend that you rent a car* while in town. If you ignore our advice (don't!), **SuperShuttle** (*©* **305/871-2000;** www.supershuttle.com) is one of the largest airport shuttle operators, charging between $10 and $40 per person for a ride within the county. Its vans operate 24 hours a day and accept American Express, MasterCard, and Visa.

If you're driving to Miami, no matter where you start your journey, chances are you'll reach it by way of **I-95.** This north-south interstate is the city's lifeline, connecting all of Miami's different neighborhoods, the airport, and the beach, and it connects all of South Florida to the rest of America.

VISITOR INFORMATION   The most up-to-date information is provided by the **Greater Miami Convention and Visitor's Bureau,** 701 Brickell Ave., Suite 700, Miami, FL 33131 (*©* **800/933-8448** or 305/539-3000; fax 305/530-3113; www. tropicoolmiami.com). If you arrive at the Miami International Airport, you can pick up visitor information at the airport's main visitor counter on the second floor of Concourse E: It's open 24 hours a day.

GETTING AROUND   If you're counting on exploring the city, even to a modest degree, a car is essential. You can manage to get by without one only if you are spending your entire vacation at a resort or if you are here for a short stay centered in one area of the city, such as South Beach.

Every major rental-car agency is represented here, in the city and at the airport. A minimum age, generally 25, is usually required of renters, while some rental agencies have also set maximum ages! Many car-rental companies offer cellular phones or electronic map rentals. It might be wise to opt for these additional safety features (the phone will definitely come in handy if you get lost), although the cost can be exorbitant.

FAST FACTS   The Dade County Medical Association sponsors a **Physician Referral Service** (*©* **305/324-8717**) weekdays from 9am to 5pm. **Health South Doctors' Hospital,** 5000 University Dr., Coral Gables (*©* **305/666-2111**), is a 285-bed acute-care hospital with a 24-hour physician-staffed emergency department. **Walgreens Pharmacy (www.walgreens.com)** has dozens of locations all over town. The branch at 5731 Bird Rd. at SW 40th Street (*©* **305/666-0757**) is open 24 hours.

A 6.5% **sales tax** is added on at the register for all goods and services purchased in Miami. In addition, most municipalities levy **special taxes on restaurants and hotels.** In Miami Beach (including South Beach), it's 11.5%; and in the rest of Dade County, it's a whopping 12.5%.

SPECIAL EVENTS   March brings the **Calle Ocho Festival,** a salsa-filled blowout that marks the end of a 10-day extravaganza called Carnival Miami. It's one of the world's biggest block parties, held along 23 blocks of Little Havana's SW 8th Street between 4th and 27th avenues. Call © **305/644-8888** for more information.

New Year's Day is the date of the **Orange Bowl,** in which two of the year's top college football teams do battle at Pro Player Stadium. (Tickets to the game are available starting Mar 1 of the previous year through the Orange Bowl Committee at © **305/ 371-4600.**)

HITTING THE BEACH

Perhaps Miami's most popular attraction is its incredible 35-mile stretch of beachfront, which runs from the tip of South Beach north to Sunny Isles and circles Key Biscayne and the numerous other pristine islands dotting the Atlantic. Whatever type of beach vacation you're looking for, you'll find it in one of Miami's two distinct beach areas: Miami Beach and Key Biscayne.

IN MIAMI BEACH   Collins Avenue fronts more than a dozen miles of white-sand beach and blue-green waters from 1st to 192nd streets. Although most of this stretch is lined with a solid wall of hotels and condos, beach access is plentiful. There are lots of well-maintained public beaches here, complete with lifeguards, restroom facilities, concession stands, and metered parking (bring lots of quarters). Except for a thin strip close to the water, most of the sand is hard-packed—the result of a $10-million Army Corps of Engineers Beach Rebuilding Project meant to protect buildings from the effects of eroding sand.

In general, the beaches on this barrier island (all on the eastern, ocean side of the island) become less crowded the farther north you go. A wooden boardwalk runs along the hotel side of the beach from 21st to 46th streets—about 1½ miles—offering a terrific sun-and-surf experience without getting sand in your shoes. Miami's lifeguard-protected public beaches include 21st Street, at the beginning of the boardwalk; 35th Street, popular with an older crowd; 46th Street, next to the Fontainebleau Hilton; 53rd Street, a narrower, more sedate beach; 64th Street, one of the quietest strips around; and 72nd Street, a local old-timers' spot.

KEY BISCAYNE'S BEACHES   If Miami Beach doesn't provide the privacy you're looking for, try Virginia Key and Key Biscayne. Crossing the Rickenbacker Causeway ($1 toll), however, can be a lengthy process, especially on weekends, when beach bums and tanning addicts flock to the Key. The 5 miles of public beach there, however, are blessed with softer sand and are less developed and more laid-back than the hotel-laden strips to the north.

ACTIVE PURSUITS

BIKING   The cement promenade on the southern tip of the island is a great place to ride. Most of the big beach hotels rent bicycles, as does the **Miami Beach Bicycle Center,** 601 5th St., South Beach (© **305/674-0150**), which charges $8 per hour or $20 per day. It's open Monday through Saturday from 10am to 7pm, Sunday from 10am to 5pm.

Bikers can also enjoy more than 130 miles of paved paths throughout Miami. The beautiful and quiet streets of Coral Gables and Coconut Grove are great for bicyclists. Old trees form canopies over wide, flat roads lined with grand homes and quaint street markers. *Biking note:* Children under the age of 16 are required by Florida law to wear a helmet, which can be purchased at any bike store or retail outlet selling biking supplies.

BOATING & SAILING   Private rental outfits include **Boat Rental Plus,** 2400 Collins Ave., Miami Beach (℃ **305/534-4307**), where 50-horsepower, 18-foot powerboats rent for some of the best prices on the beach. There's a 2-hour minimum and rates go from $100 to $500, including taxes and gas. Renters must be over 21. The rental office is at 23rd Street, on the inland waterway in Miami Beach. It's open daily from 10am to sunset. If you want a specific type of boat, call ahead to reserve. Otherwise, show up and take what's available.

Sailboats of Key Biscayne Rentals and Sailing School, in the Crandon Marina (next to Sundays on the Bay), 4000 Crandon Blvd., Key Biscayne (℃ **305/361-0328** days, or 305/279-7424 evenings), can also get you out on the water. A 22-foot sailboat rents for $35 an hour or $110 for a half-day. A Cat-25 or J24 is available for $35 an hour or $110 for a half-day. They also offer sailing lessons.

GOLF   There are more than 50 private and public golf courses in the Miami area. Contact the **Greater Miami Convention and Visitor's Bureau** (℃ **800/933-8448;** www.miamiandbeaches.com) for a list of courses and costs.

Some of the area's best and most expensive are at the big resorts, many of which allow nonguests to play. Otherwise, the following represent some of the area's best public courses. **Crandon Park Golf Course,** 6700 Crandon Blvd., Key Biscayne (℃ **305/361-9129**), is the number-one-ranked municipal course in the state and one of the top five in the country. The park is situated on 200 bayfront acres and offers a pro shop, rentals, lessons, carts, and a lighted driving range. Greens fees (including cart) are $148 per person during the winter and $65 per person during the summer.

One of the most popular courses among real enthusiasts is the **Doral Park Golf and Country Club,** 5001 NW 104th Ave., West Miami (℃ **305/591-8800**); it's not related to the Doral Hotel or spa. Call to book in advance, since this challenging, semiprivate 18-holer is extremely popular with locals. Cart and greens fees vary, so call ℃ **305/592-2000,** ext. 2104, for information.

Known as one of the best in the city, the **Country Club of Miami,** 6801 Miami Gardens Dr., at NW 68th Avenue, North Miami (℃ **305/829-8456**), has three 18-hole courses of varying degrees of difficulty. You'll encounter lush fairways, rolling greens, and some history to boot. The west course is where Jack Nicklaus played his first professional tournament and Lee Trevino won his first professional championship. Cart and greens fees are $40 to $75 per person during the winter, and $20 to $34 per person during the summer.

SNORKELING & SCUBA DIVING   **Diver's Paradise** of Key Biscayne, 4000 Crandon Blvd. (℃ **305/361-3483**), offers one dive expedition per day during the week and two per day on the weekends to the more than 30 wrecks and artificial reefs

---

Par for the Course

You can get information about most Florida courses, including current greens fees, and reserve tee times, through **Tee Times USA,** P.O. Box 641, Flagler Beach, FL 32136 (℃ **800/374-8633,** 888/GOLF-FLO, or 386/439-0001; www.teetimesusa. com). This company also publishes a vacation guide that includes many stay-and-play golf packages.

0 1 mi
0 1 km

To Sunny Isles

BAL HARBOUR **1**

NE 125th St.   Miami Blvd.

Bay Harbor Islands

Broad Causeway

96th St. **2** **3**

BISCAYNE PARK

91st St / Surfside Blvd.

INDIAN CREEK VILLAGE

NE 103rd St.

Biscayne Bay

SURF-SIDE

Tallahassee

FLORIDA

Harbor Island

Normandy Isle

North Shore Dr.
South Shore Dr.
Normandy Dr.

77th St.

71st St.

Allison Island

Miami
Miami Beach

NE 79th St.   John F. Kennedy Causeway

934

North Bay Island   Treasure Island

La Gorce Island

W. 63rd St.

N. Bay Rd.

907

MIAMI BEACH

W. 51st St. **5**

Biscayne Bay

W. 47th St.

Alton Rd.

To Miami
Julia Tuttle Causeway

Arthur Godfrey Rd.

Sheridan Ave.
Pine Tree Dr.
Indian Creek Dr.

44th St.
41st St.

6

ACCOMMODATIONS ■

Beach House Bal Harbour **3**
Crest Hotel Suites **10**
Hotel Impala **15**
Hotel Shelley **16**
Indian Creek Hotel & Suites **7**
Pelican Hotel **17**
The Ritz-Carlton South Beach **11**

DINING ◆

Escopazzo **14**
Grillfish **12**
Joe Allen **9**
Jumbo's **4**
Mark's South Beach **13**
Nemo **18**
Nobu **8**
Sheldon's Drugs **3**
Shula's Steak House **5**
Wolfie Cohen's Rascal House **1**

Sunset Isles

Bay Rd.

7 30th St.
24th St.

8 23rd St.
COLLINS PARK

Rivo Alto Island

Belle Isle

W. 20th St. **9**

Venetian Causeway

CITY PARK

Lincoln Rd. Mall

10
11
12
FLAMINGO PARK
14th St.
13
11th St.
14
9th St.
7th St. **16**
15
17
LUMMUS PARK

ATLANTIC OCEAN

Star Island

SOUTH BEACH

Alton Rd.

A1A

MacArthur Causeway

5th St.
1st St.
Biscayne St.

41

Collins Ave.
Ocean Dr.

PIER PARK

18

Sams Island

SOUTH POINTE PARK

off the coast of Miami Beach and Key Biscayne. Call ahead for times and locations of dives.

South Beach Divers, 850 Washington Ave., Miami Beach (© **305/531-6110;** www.southbeachdivers.com), will also be happy to tell you where to go under the sea and will provide you with scuba rental equipment as well for $40. You can rent snorkel gear for $15. They also do dive trips to Key Largo three times a week and do dives off Miami on Sunday at $100 for a two-tank dive.

WHAT TO SEE & DO

Located in South Beach, the **Art Deco District** is a whole community made up of outrageous and fanciful 1920s and 1930s architecture. The district is roughly bounded by the Atlantic Ocean on the east, Alton Road on the west, 6th Street to the south, and Dade Boulevard (along the Collins Canal) to the north.

Most of the finest examples of the whimsical Art Deco style are concentrated along three parallel streets—Ocean Drive, Collins Avenue, and Washington Avenue—from about 6th to 23rd streets. Hundreds of new hotels, restaurants, and nightclubs have been renovated or are in the process, and South Beach is on the cutting edge of Miami's cultural and nightlife scene.

If you're touring this unique neighborhood on your own, start at the **Art Deco Welcome Center,** 1001 Ocean Dr. (© **305/531-3484**), which is run by The Miami Design Preservation League. The only beachside building across from the Clevelander Hotel and bar, they give away lots of informational material, including maps and pamphlets, and run guided tours about the neighborhood. The center is open Monday through Saturday from 9am to 6pm, sometimes later.

Take a stroll along **Ocean Drive** for the best view of sidewalk cafes, bars, colorful hotels, and even more colorful people. Another great place for a walk is **Lincoln Road,** which is lined with boutiques, large chain stores, cafes, and funky art and antiques stores.

Bass Museum of Art   World-renowned Japanese architect Arata Isozaki designed the Bass Museum of Art's magnificent facility, which features an outdoor sculpture terrace. The museum's permanent collection includes European paintings from the 15th to the early 20th centuries, with special emphasis on northern European art of the Renaissance and baroque periods, including Dutch and Flemish masters such as Rubens and Jordaens. Past exhibitions have included the works of Picasso, Frida Kahlo, and Francois Marie Banier.

2121 Park Ave. (1 block west of Collins Ave.), South Beach. © 305/673-7530. www.bassmuseum.org. Admission $8 adults, $6 students and seniors, free for children 6 and under. Free 2nd Thurs of the month 6–9pm. Tues–Wed and Fri–Sat 10am–5pm; Thurs 10am–9pm; Sun 11am–5pm. Closed Mon.

Miami Art Museum at the Miami-Dade Cultural Center   The Miami Art Museum (MAM) features an eclectic mix of modern and contemporary works by such artists as Eric Fischl, Max Beckmann, Jim Dine, and Stuart Davis. Rotating exhibitions span ages and styles, and often focus on Latin American or Caribbean artists. JAM at MAM is the museum's popular happy hour, which takes place the third Thursday of the month and is tied in to a particular exhibit. Almost as artistic as the works inside the museum is the composite sketch of the people—young and old—who attend these events.

101 W. Flagler St., Miami. © **305/375-3000**. www.miamiartmuseum.org. Admission $5 adults, $2.50 seniors and students, free for children under 12. Tues–Fri 10am–5pm; 3rd Thurs of each month 10am–9pm; Sat–Sun noon–5pm. Closed Mon and major holidays.

Miami Metrozoo *(Kids)*   This 290-acre complex is never really crowded and it's also completely cageless—animals are kept at bay by cleverly designed moats. This is a fantastic spot to take younger kids; there's a wonderful petting zoo and play area, and the zoo offers several daily programs designed to educate and entertain. Mufasa and Simba (of Disney fame) were modeled on a couple of Metrozoo's lions. Other highlights include two rare white Bengal tigers, a Komodo dragon, rare koala bears, a number of kangaroos, an African meerkat, a wonderful monorail tour, and an impressive aviary. *Note:* The distance between animal habitats can be great, so you'll be doing *a lot* of walking here.

12400 SW 152nd St., South Miami. © **305/251-0400**. www.miamimetrozoo.com. Admission $12 adults, $7 children 3–12. Daily 9:30am–5:30pm (ticket booth closes at 4pm). Free parking.

Miami Museum of Science and Space Transit Planetarium *(Kids)*   The Museum of Science features more than 140 hands-on exhibits that explore the mysteries of the universe. Live demonstrations and collections of rare natural-history specimens make a visit here fun and informative for adults and kids alike. A Wildlife Center holds more than 175 live reptiles and birds of prey. The adjacent Space Transit Planetarium projects astronomy and laser shows as well as interactive demonstrations of computer technology and cyberspace features. Call, or visit their website, for a list of upcoming exhibits and laser shows.

3280 S. Miami Ave. (just south of the Rickenbacker Causeway), Coconut Grove. © **305/646-4200** for general information. www.miamisci.org. $10 adults, $8 seniors and students, $6 children 3–12, free for children 2 and under; laser shows $7 adults, $4 seniors and children 3–12. $2 off admission for museum ticket holders. Call for laser show times. Tickets are half price after 4:30pm. 10% discount for AAA members. Tickets cover entrance to all museum galleries, planetarium shows, and the Wildlife Center. Museum of Science daily 10am–6pm; call for showtimes (last show is at 4pm weekdays and 5pm on weekends). Closed Thanksgiving and Christmas.

Museum of Contemporary Art (MOCA)   MOCA boasts an impressive collection of internationally acclaimed art with a local flavor. It is also known for its forward thinking and ability to discover and highlight new artists. A high-tech screening facility allows for film presentations to complement the exhibitions. You can see works by Jasper Johns, Roy Lichtenstein, Larry Rivers, Duane Michaels, and Claes Oldenberg, plus there are special exhibitions by such artists as Yoko Ono, Sigmar Polke, John Baldessari, and Goya.

770 NE 125th St., North Miami. © **305/893-6211**. Fax 305/891-1472. www.mocanomi.org. Admission $5 adults, $3 seniors and students with ID, free for children 12 and under. Tues by donation. Tues–Sat 11am–5pm; Sun noon–5pm. Closed Mon and major holidays.

Spanish Monastery Cloisters   Did you know that the alleged oldest building in the Western Hemisphere dates from 1133 and is located in Miami? The Spanish Monastery Cloisters were first erected in Segovia, Spain. Centuries later, newspaper magnate William Randolph Hearst purchased and brought them to America in pieces. The carefully numbered stones were quarantined for years until they were finally reassembled on the present site in 1954. It has often been used as a backdrop for movies and is a very popular tourist attraction.

16711 W. Dixie Hwy. (at NE 167th St.), North Miami Beach. ✆ **305/945-1461**. www.spanishmonastery.com. Admission $4.50 adults, $2.50 seniors and students with ID, $1 children 3–12. Mon–Fri 10am–4pm; Sun 1–5pm. Call ahead because the monastery closes for special events without being announced.

Venetian Pool *(Kids)*   Miami's most beautiful and unusual swimming pool, dating from 1924, is hidden behind pastel stucco walls and is honored with a listing in the National Register of Historic Places. Underground artesian wells feed the free-form lagoon, which is shaded by three-story Spanish porticos and features both fountains and waterfalls. During summer, the pool's 800,000 gallons of water are drained and refilled nightly thanks to an underground aquifer, ensuring a cool, *clean* swim. Visitors are free to swim and sunbathe here, just as Esther Williams and Johnny Weissmuller did decades ago. For a modest fee, you or your children can learn to swim during special summer programs.

2701 DeSoto Blvd. (at Toledo St.), Coral Gables. ✆ **305/460-5356**. www.venetianpool.com. Admission and hours vary seasonally. Nov–Mar $6.25 for those 13 and older, $3.25 children under 13; Apr–Oct $9.50 for those 13 and older, $5.25 children under 13. Children must be 3 years old and provide proof of age with birth certificate, or 38 in. tall to enter. Hours are at least 11am–4:30pm but are often longer. Call for more information.

The Vizcaya Museum and Gardens *(Best)*   Sometimes referred to as the "Hearst Castle of the East," this magnificent villa was built in 1916 as a winter retreat for James Deering, co-founder and former vice president of International Harvester. The industrialist was fascinated by 16th-century art and architecture; his ornate mansion, which took 1,000 artisans 5 years to build, became a celebration of that period. Most of the original furnishings, including dishes and paintings, are still intact. A free guided tour of the 34 furnished rooms on the first floor takes about 45 minutes. The second floor is open to tour on your own. Outside, lush formal gardens, accented with statuary, balustrades, and decorative urns, front an enormous swath of Biscayne Bay. Definitely take the villa tour, but immediately thereafter, wander and get lost in the resplendent gardens.

3251 S. Miami Ave. (just south of Rickenbacker Causeway), North Coconut Grove. ✆ **305/250-9133**. www.vizcaya museum.com. Admission $12 adults, $5 children 6–12, free for children 5 and under. Villa daily 9:30am–5pm (ticket booth closes at 4:30pm); gardens daily 9:30am–5:30pm.

Wolfsonian-Florida International University   Mitchell Wolfson, Jr., an eccentric millionaire, was the ultimate packrat. A premier collector of propaganda and advertising art, Wolfson bought a warehouse to house 70,000 of his items, from controversial Nazi propaganda to King Farouk of Egypt's match collection. Thrown in the eclectic mix are also zany works from great modernists such as Charles Eames and Marcel Duchamp. He then gave his incredibly diverse collection to Florida International University. The former 1927 storage facility has been transformed into a museum that is unquestionably fascinating and hosts lectures and rather swinging events surrounding particular exhibits.

1001 Washington Ave., South Beach. ✆ **305/531-1001**. www.wolfsonian.org. Admission $7 adults, $5 seniors, students with ID, and children 6–12. Mon–Tues and Fri–Sat 11am–6pm; Thurs 11am–9pm; Sun noon–5pm.

PRIME SHOPPING AREAS

Miami has earned a worldwide reputation as a shopping capital, especially among visitors from Latin America and the Caribbean. Take a quick glance around the airport, and you'll see more than a few departing passengers lugging refrigerator-size cardboard boxes and bulging suitcases. From exotic tropical fruits to high-tech electronics, fine art and Art Deco collectibles, Latin music and hand-rolled cigars, Miami has something for everyone.

AVENTURA   On Biscayne Boulevard between Miami Gardens Drive and the county line at Hallandale Beach Boulevard is a 2-mile stretch of major retail stores, including Best Buy, Borders, Circuit City, Linens N' Things, Marshalls, Sports Authority, and more. Also here is the mammoth **Aventura Mall,** housing a fabulous collection of shops and restaurants.

CALLE OCHO   For a taste of "Little Havana," take a walk down 8th Street between SW 27th Avenue and SW 12th Avenue, where you'll find some lively street life and many shops selling cigars, baked goods, shoes, and furniture, and record stores specializing in Latin music. For help, take your Spanish dictionary.

COCONUT GROVE   Downtown Coconut Grove, centered on Main Highway and Grand Avenue and branching onto the adjoining streets, is one of Miami's most pedestrian-friendly zones. The Grove's wide sidewalks, lined with cafes and boutiques, can provide hours of browsing pleasure. Coconut Grove is best known for its chain stores (Gap, Banana Republic, and others) and some funky holdovers from the days when the Grove was a bit more bohemian, plus excellent sidewalk cafes centered around CocoWalk and the Streets of Mayfair.

MIRACLE MILE (CORAL GABLES)   Actually only a half-mile long, this central shopping street was an integral part of George Merrick's original city plan. Today, the strip still enjoys popularity, especially for its bridal stores, ladies' shops, haberdashers, and gift shops. Recently, newer chain stores, like Barnes & Noble, Old Navy, and Starbucks, have been appearing on the Mile. **Merrick Park,** a mammoth, 850,000-square-foot upscale outdoor shopping complex between Ponce de León Boulevard and Le Jeune Road, just off the Mile, houses Nordstrom, Neiman Marcus, Armani, and Yves St. Laurent, to name a few.

DOWNTOWN MIAMI   If you're looking for discounts on all types of goods—especially watches, fabric, buttons, lace, shoes, luggage, and leather—**Flagler Street,** just west of Biscayne Boulevard, is the best place to start. I wouldn't necessarily recommend buying expensive items here, as many stores seem to be on the shady side and do not understand the word *warranty.* However, you can still have fun here as long as you are a savvy shopper and don't mind haggling with people who may not have the firmest grasp on the English language. Mary Brickell Village, a 192,000-square-foot urban entertainment center straddling South Miami Avenue between 9th and 10th streets downtown, is slated to open in late 2006. The $80-million complex will consist of a slew of trendy restaurants, boutiques, and the requisite Starbucks—a sure sign that a neighborhood has been revitalized.

SOUTH BEACH   South Beach has come into its own as far as shopping is concerned. While the requisite stores—Gap, Banana Republic, and so on—have anchored here, several higher-end stores have also opened on the southern blocks of **Collins Avenue.** For the hippest clothing boutiques (including Armani Exchange, Ralph Lauren, Versace, Benetton, Levi's, Kenneth Cole, and Nicole Miller, among others), stroll along this pretty strip of the Deco District.

For those who are interested in a little more fun with their shopping, consider South Beach's legendary **Lincoln Road.** This pedestrian mall, originally designed in 1957 by Morris Lapidus, recently underwent a multimillion-dollar renovation

Best Five Fabulous Historic Hotels

The U.S. is loaded with notable historic lodging (how many places can George Washington really have slept in?), but we've picked five that we are especially fond of from across the nation for those who like their accommodations to have a little history (or a lot). All of these National Historic Landmarks offer some unique features or a noteworthy background. For more information on these hotels and other historic properties, consult the **Historic Hotels of America** database (**www.historichotels.org**) maintained by the National Trust for Historic Preservation, or call ℂ **800/678-8946.**

1. **Hotel Del Coronado** (San Diego, California; p. 921): When the Del opened in 1888, it was the largest electrically lit building outside of New York City. In its 116-year history it's hosted 10 U.S. presidents (starting with Benjamin Harrison in 1891) and numerous foreign dignitaries (reportedly the Duke of Windsor met Wallis Simpson for the first time here). The property has been thoroughly modernized, but still retains its Victorian charm and is considered one of the loveliest resorts in the country.

2. **The Biltmore** (Miami, Florida; p. 378): This Mediterranean Revival masterpiece, with its signature tower modeled on Seville's La Giralda, debuted in 1926 and became *the* place to see and be seen in the 1930s. Everyone from Bing Crosby to Al Capone stayed here. Olympic swimmer (and future Tarzan star) Johnny Weissmuller once broke the world record in the hotel's exceptional 700,000-gallon pool. World War II saw the hotel transformed into an army hospital, which it remained until a $60-million restoration returned it to its place as one of the country's most elegant and upscale resorts in the late 1980s.

3. **The Greenbrier** (White Sulphur Springs, West Virginia; p. 1037). An inn was first built on the site of this top-rated resort in 1780, though the

restoring it to its former glory. Here, shoppers find an array of clothing, books, tchotchkes, and art as well as a menagerie of sidewalk cafes flanked on one end by a multiplex movie theater and on the other by the Atlantic Ocean.

WHERE TO STAY

Central Reservation Service (ℂ **800/950-0232** or 305/274-6832; www.reservation-services.com) works with many of Miami's hotels and can often secure discounts of up to 40%. It also gives advice on specific locales, especially in Miami Beach and downtown. During holiday time, there may be a minimum of a 3- to 5-day stay to use their services. Call for more information. For bed-and-breakfast information throughout the state, contact **Florida Bed and Breakfast Inns** (ℂ **800/524-1880;** www.florida-inns.com). For information on the ubiquitous boutique hotels, check out the Greater Miami Convention and Visitor's Bureau's new website, **www.miamiboutiquehotels.com.**

current white Georgian structure dates back to 1910. Robert E. Lee summered here in the years following the Civil War; presidents, royalty, and business tycoons have stayed here; and, in 1960, a top-secret bunker was constructed here to house Congress in case a nuclear warhead was launched on Washington, D.C., during the Cold War. The award-winning property has kept up with the times and is still one of the best resorts in the country.

4. Colonial Houses (Colonial Williamsburg, Virginia; p. 229). For an authentic historic experience, this is the top place to stay in the country. Accommodations are set in 28 restored, Colonial-era buildings (modernized plumbing, but forget high-tech) of various sizes and layouts (some as large as 16 rooms). Thomas Jefferson lived in the Market Square Tavern as a law student and John Tyler owned the Nicholas-Tyler Office, where, as vice president, he received the news he'd become America's 10th president upon the death of William Henry Harrison.

5. Brown Palace Hotel (Denver, Colorado; p. 671). Businessman Henry Cordes Brown commissioned architect Frank E. Edbrooke to design an "unprecedented" hotel in the popular Italian Renaissance style and Edbrooke came through—in spades. Still the best hotel in Denver (and among the best in the world), the Brown Palace opened its doors in 1892 as a triangular mass of red sandstone and granite, with an exquisite eight-story, stained-glass atrium lobby. The hotel has sheltered more than its fair share of famous guests: It was a favorite of Harry Truman, and Dwight D. Eisenhower used the hotel as his summer headquarters during his presidency.

South Florida's tourist season is well defined, beginning in mid-November and lasting until Easter. Hotel prices escalate until about March, after which they begin to decline. Off-season hotel rates are typically 30% to 50% lower than their winter highs.

Beach House Bal Harbour The Beach House Bal Harbour is comfortable, unpretentious, and luxurious, yet decidedly low-key. In place of an elaborate hotel lobby, the public spaces are divided into a series of intimate, homey environments, from the wicker-furnished screened-in porch to the Asian-inspired Bamboo Room. The 24-hour Pantry is packed with all the needs of the hotel's "unplugged" urban clientele. The ultraspacious rooms (those ending in 04 are the most spacious) are literally brimming with the comforts of home, including TV Web access, refrigerators, and stereo CD players. The 200-foot private beach, hammock grove, and topiary garden are incredibly lush.

9449 Collins Ave., Surfside, FL 33154. ℂ **800/327-6644** or 305/535-8606. Fax 305/535-8602. www.thebeachhouse
hotel.com. 170 units. Winter $150–$199 double, $209–$299 suite; off season $109–$124 double, $149–$199 suite.
AE, DC, DISC, MC, V. Valet parking $15. **Amenities:** Restaurant; heated pool; health club; spa. *In room:* Fridge.

The Biltmore Hotel A romantic sense of old-world glamour combined with a rich
history permeate The Biltmore as much as the pricey perfume of the guests who stay
here. Built in 1926, it's the oldest Coral Gables hotel and a National Historical Landmark. Rising above the Spanish-style estate is a majestic 300-foot copper-clad tower,
modeled after the Giralda bell tower in Seville and visible throughout the city. The
hotel is warm, welcoming, and extremely charming. It boasts large Moorish-style
rooms decorated with tasteful period reproductions and some high-tech amenities.
The enormous lobby, with its 45-foot vaulted ceilings, makes a bold statement of elegance. Always a popular destination for golfers, The Biltmore is situated on a lush,
rolling 18-hole course that is as challenging as it is beautiful. The spa is fantastic and
the enormous 21,000-square-foot winding pool (surrounded by arched walkways and
classical sculptures) is legendary—it's where a pre-*Tarzan* Johnny Weismuller broke
the world's swimming record. Even if you don't stay at The Biltmore Hotel, definitely
take a tour of it (call ℂ **305/445-1926** for more information) to learn about its fascinating history and mystery.

1200 Anastasia Ave., Coral Gables, FL 33134. ℂ **800/727-1926** or 305/445-1926. Fax 305/442-9496. www.biltmore
hotel.com. 276 units. Winter $294–$354 double; off season $254–$319 double; year-round $394–$2,850 specialty
suites. Additional person $20. Special packages available. AE, DC, DISC, MC, V. Overnight valet parking $16; free self-
parking. **Amenities:** 4 restaurants; pool; 18-hole golf course; 10 lighted tennis courts; state-of-the-art health club;
spa. *In room:* Kitchenette (in tower suites only).

Crest Hotel Suites *(Value* One of South Beach's best-kept secrets, the Crest Hotel is
located next to the pricier, trendier Albion Hotel (and around the corner from Lincoln Rd., in the heart of the Art Deco District) and features a quietly fashionable, contemporary, relaxed atmosphere with fantastic service. Built in 1939, the Crest was
restored to preserve its Art Deco architecture, but the interior of the hotel is thoroughly modern, with rooms resembling cosmopolitan apartments. All suites have a
living room/dining room area, kitchenette, and executive work space. An indoor/out-
door cafe with terrace and poolside dining isn't besieged with trendy locals, but does
attract a younger crowd.

1670 James Ave., Miami Beach, FL 33139. ℂ **800/531-3880** or 305/531-0321. Fax 305/531-8180. www.crestgroup
hotels.com/cresthotelsuites.htm. 64 units. Winter $155 double, $235 suite; off season $115 double, $175 suite.
Packages available and 10% discount offered if booked on website. AE, MC, V. **Amenities:** 2 restaurants; pool.
In room: Kitchenette (select units).

Fairmont Turnberry Isle Resort & Club One of Miami's classiest resorts, this
gorgeous 300-acre compound has every possible facility for active guests, particularly
golfers. The main attractions are two Trent Jones courses, available only to members
and guests of the hotel. Treat yourself to a visit at the exceptional (and recently renovated) Turnberry Spa, which offers numerous classes, treatments, and a juice bar.
Impeccable service from check-in to checkout consistently brings loyal fans back to
this resort for more. The higher-priced resort rooms are your best bet. The well-pro-
portioned rooms are gorgeously tiled to match the Mediterranean-style architecture
and have numerous amenities, including CD players. The huge bathrooms even have
a color TV mounted within reach of the whirlpool bathtubs and glass-walled showers.
The resort's location in North Miami Beach's Aventura section means you'll find

excellent shopping and some of the best dining in Miami right in the neighborhood. The only drawback to this hotel is that you'll need to take a shuttle to the beach.

19999 W. Country Club Dr., Aventura, FL 33180. ℭ **800/327-7028** or 305/936-2929. Fax 305/933-6560. www .turnberryisle.com. 392 units. Winter $459–$589 double, $609–$899 suite; off season $175–$275 double, $140–$409 suite; year-round $4,000 grand presidential suite. AE, DC, DISC, MC, V. Valet parking $12; free self-parking. **Amenities:** 6 restaurants; 2 pools; 2 golf courses; 2 tennis complexes; state-of-the-art spa. *In room:* Fridge (upon request).

Hotel Impala   This renovated Mediterranean inn is one of the area's best, and it's just beautiful, from the Greco-Roman frescoes and friezes to an intimate garden that is perfumed with the scents from carefully hung lilies and gardenias. Rooms are extremely comfortable, with supercushy sleigh beds, sisal floors, wrought-iron fixtures, imported Belgian cotton linens, wood furniture, stereo CD players, VCRs, and fabulous roomy bathrooms done up in stainless steel and coral rock. Enclaves like this one are rare on South Beach.

1228 Collins Ave., South Beach, FL 33139. ℭ **800/646-7252** or 305/673-2021. Fax 305/673-5984. www.hotel impalamiamibeach.com. 17 units. Winter $195–$425 double; off season $145–$325 double. AE, DC, MC, V. Valet parking $20. Small pets permitted. **Amenities:** Restaurant.

Hotel Place St. Michel   This European-style hotel in the heart of Coral Gables is one of the city's most romantic options. The accommodations and hospitality are straight out of old-world Europe, complete with dark-wood-paneled walls, cozy beds, beautiful antiques, and a quiet elegance that seems startlingly out of place in trendy Miami. One-of-a-kind furnishings make each room special. Bathrooms are on the smaller side but are hardly cramped. All have tub/shower combos except for two, which have either shower or tub. If you're picky, request your preference. Guests are treated to fresh fruit baskets upon arrival and enjoy perfect service throughout their stay. The exceptional Restaurant St. Michel is a very romantic dining choice.

162 Alcazar Ave., Coral Gables, FL 33134. ℭ **800/848-HOTEL** or 305/444-1666. Fax 305/529-0074. www.hotel placestmichel.com. 27 units. Winter $179 double, $200 suite; off season $129 double, $160 suite. Additional person $10. Rates include continental breakfast and fruit basket upon arrival. AE, DC, MC, V. Self-parking $7. **Amenities:** Restaurant.

Hotel Shelley *Value*   Newly renovated Hotel Shelley has a laid-back beach atmosphere, yet cutting-edge style. The architecturally sound boutique hotel built in 1931 in the heart of the Art Deco district in Miami Beach has reinvented itself with a complete $1.5-million renovation of its 49 guest rooms. Complete with Mascioni 300-thread-count linens, goose-down pillows and comforters, LCD plasma TVs, and custom-built cabinetry, the guest rooms at the Shelley allow you to chill out after a long day at the beach or rock out before a big night of partying. The subtle purple hues in the rooms and public areas lend to true Art Deco style. The bar in the lobby offers free drinks from 7 to 8pm every night and VIP passes to area nightclubs. There's also free airport pickup from Miami International.

844 Collins Ave., Miami Beach, Florida 33139 ℭ **305/531.3341.** Fax 305/535.9665. www.hotelshelley.com. 49 units. Winter $95–$225 double, $125–$245 king, $165–$300 minisuite; off season $75–$125 double, $95–$145 king, $115–$165 minisuite; during special events and holidays, rates are subject to change. Rates include complimentary continental breakfast and free cocktails in the lobby (7–8pm daily). AE, DC, MC, V. Parking $20.

Indian Creek Hotel & Suites   Located off the beaten path, the Indian Creek Hotel is a meticulously restored 1936 building featuring one of the beach's first operating elevators. It's also the most charming hotel in the area. Besides that, the service is impeccable. Because of its location facing the Indian Creek waterway and its lush landscaping, this place feels more like an old-fashioned Key West bed-and-breakfast than your typical Miami Beach Art Deco hotel. All of the rooms are outfitted in Art Deco furnishings, such as an antique writing desk, pretty tropical prints, and small but spotless bathrooms. The landscaped pool area is a great place to lounge in the sun. If you're looking for charm, friendly service, and peace and quiet, come here instead of South Beach.

2727 Indian Creek Dr. (1 block west of Collins Ave. and the ocean), Miami Beach, FL 33140. (*) **800/491-2772** or 305/531-2727. Fax 305/531-5651. www.indiancreekhotel.com. 61 units. Winter $69–$139 double, $269 suite; off season $69–$99 double, $179 suite. Additional person $25. Group packages and summer specials available. AE, DC, DISC, MC, V. **Amenities:** Restaurant; pool. *In room:* Fridge (in suites).

Mandarin Oriental, Miami *(Best)* Catering to business travelers, conventioneers, big-time celebrities (J-Lo, Will Smith, and so on), and the occasional leisure traveler who doesn't mind spending in excess of $500 a night for a room, the swank Mandarin Oriental features a waterfront location, residential-style rooms with Asian touches (most with balconies), and several upscale dining and bar facilities. The waterfront view of the city is the hotel's best asset, both priceless and absolutely stunning. The superattentive service is inspired. The 15,000-square-foot The Spa at Mandarin Oriental is your ticket to nirvana. The Mandarin Oriental Miami is home to a 20,000-foot white-sand beach club with a fabulous Friday-night happy hour, complete with beds with white cushions and canopies, beach butlers, and beachside cabana treatments, which is nice, considering that the hotel is 15 minutes from the beach.

500 Brickell Key Dr., Miami, FL 33131. (*) **305/913-8383.** Fax 305/913-8300. www.mandarinoriental.com. 327 units. Year-round $415–$860 double; $1,250–$5,500 suite. AE, DC, DISC, MC, V. Valet parking $24 plus tax. **Amenities:** 2 restaurants; pool; state-of-the-art fitness center; spa.

Pelican Hotel Owned by the same creative folks behind the Diesel Jeans company, the Pelican (whose brazen, albeit appropriate, motto is "A myth in its own limelight") is South Beach's only self-professed "toy-hotel," in which each of its 30 rooms and suites is decorated as outrageously as some of the area's more colorful drag queens. Each room has been designed daringly and rather wittily by Swedish interior decorator Magnus Ehrland, whose wild imagination has turned room no. 309, for instance, into the "Psychedelic(ate) Girl," and room no. 209 into the "Love, Peace, and Leaf-forest" room. But the most popular room is the tough-to-score room no. 215, or the "Best Whorehouse," which is said to have made even former Hollywood madam Heidi Fleiss red with envy. All rooms sport VCRs and CD players.

826 Ocean Dr., Miami Beach, FL 33139. (*) **800/7-PELICAN** or 305/673-3373. Fax 305/673-3255. www.pelican hotel.com. 30 units. Winter $180–$250 double, $270–$440 oceanfront suite; off season $155–$195 double, $230–$310 oceanfront suite. Valet parking $20. AE, DC, MC, V. **Amenities:** Restaurant. *In room:* Fridge.

Ritz-Carlton Key Biscayne *(Kids)* Described by some as an oceanfront mansion, the luxurious Ritz-Carlton has 44 acres of tropical gardens, a 20,000-square-foot European-style spa, and a world-class tennis center. Decorated in British colonial style, the hotel looks as if it came straight out of Bermuda. The Ritz Kids programs provide children ages 5 to 12 with fantastic activities, and the 1,200-foot beachfront offers everything from pure relaxation to fishing, boating, or windsurfing. Spacious and luxuriously appointed rooms are elegantly Floridian, featuring large balconies overlooking the ocean or the lush gardens. The best spa in Miami is also here, with 20,000 square feet of space that overlooks the Atlantic Ocean and features a plethora of treatment options.

455 Grand Bay Dr., Key Biscayne, FL 33149. © 800/241-3333 or 305/365-4500. Fax 305/365-4501. www.ritz carlton.com. 402 units. Winter $450–$590 double suite; off season $260–$490 double suite. AE, DC, DISC, MC, V. Valet parking (call for fees). **Amenities:** Restaurant; 2 heated pools; tennis center; fitness center; spa.

The Ritz-Carlton South Beach _Kids_   The luxe life comes to a congested and some-what seedy corner of South Beach. Debuting in fall 2003, this Ritz has restored the landmark 1950s DiLido Hotel to its original Art Moderne style and filled it with the hotel's signature five-star service. An impressive $2-million art collection consisting of original works by Joan Miró, among others, is on permanent loan to the hotel. Though South Beach is better known for its trendy boutique hotels, The Ritz-Carlton offers comfort to those who might prefer 100% cotton Frette sheets and goose-down pillows to high-style minimalism. The best rooms, by far, are the 72 poolside and oceanview lanai rooms. With impeccable service, an elevated pool that provides unobstructed views of the Atlantic, an impressive stretch of beach, an oceanfront Ritz Kids pavilion, and a world-class 13,000-square-foot spa and wellness center, The Ritz-Carlton kicks sand in the faces of some of the smaller hotels that think they're doing _you_ a favor by allowing you to sleep there.

1 Lincoln Rd., South Beach, FL 33139. © 800/241-3333 or 786/276-4000. Fax 786/276-4001. www.ritzcarlton.com. 375 units. Winter $450–$720 double suite; off season $245–$545 double suite. AE, DISC, MC, V. Valet parking $30. **Amenities:** 3 restaurants; heated pool; health club; spa.

WHERE TO DINE

With over 6,000 restaurants to choose from, dining out in Miami has become a pas-sionate pastime for locals and visitors alike. The biggest complaint when it comes to Miami dining isn't the haughtiness, but rather the dearth of truly moderately priced restaurants, especially in South Beach and Coral Gables. It's either really cheap or really expensive; the in-between somehow gets lost in the culinary shuffle. Quick-service diners don't really exist here as they do in other cosmopolitan areas. Budget accordingly.

Chef Allen's NEW WORLD CUISINE   Chef Allen Susser, winner of the esteemed James Beard Award for Best American Chef in the Southeast, is royalty in this town. This restaurant is his province, and foodies are his disciples. It is under chef Allen's magic that ordinary Key limes and mangos reappear in the form of succulent salsas and sauces. Whole yellowtail in coconut milk and curry sauce is a particularly spec-tacular entree. Unlike other restaurants where location is key, Chef Allen's, located in the rear of a strip mall, could be in the desert, and hordes of people would still make the trek.

19088 NE 29th Ave. (at Biscayne Blvd.), North Miami Beach. © 305/935-2900. Reservations recommended. Main courses $25–$40. AE, DC, MC, V. Sun–Thurs 6–10pm; Fri–Sat 6–11pm.

Escopazzo ITALIAN   _Escopazzo_ means "I'm going crazy" in Italian, but the only sign of insanity in this primo northern Italian eatery is the fact that it only seats 90. The wine bottles have it better—the restaurant's cellar holds 1,000 bottles of various vintages. Should you be so lucky as to score a table at this romantic local favorite, you'll have trouble deciding between dishes that will have you swearing off the Olive Garden with your first bite. The hand-rolled pastas and risotto are near perfection. Eating here is like dining with a big Italian family—it's never boring (the menu changes five or six times a year), the service is excellent, and nobody's happy until you are blissfully full.

1311 Washington Ave., South Beach. ☎ 305/674-9450. Reservations required. Main courses $18–$32. AE, MC, V. Mon–Fri 6pm–midnight; Sat 6pm–1am; Sun 6–11pm.

Grillfish SEAFOOD   From the beautiful Byzantine-style mural and the gleaming oak bar, you'd think you were eating in a much more expensive restaurant, but Grillfish manages to pay its South Beach rent with the help of a loyal local following who come for fresh, simple seafood in a relaxed but upscale atmosphere. The servers are friendly and know the menu well. The barroom seafood chowder is full of chunks of shellfish, as well as some fresh whitefish filets in a tomato broth. The small ear of corn, included with each entree, is about as close as you'll get to any type of vegetable offering besides the pedestrian salad. Still, at these prices, it's worth a visit to try some local fare, including mako, swordfish, tuna, marlin, and wahoo.

1444 Collins Ave. (corner of Española Way), South Beach. ☎ 305/538-9908. www.grillfish.com. Reservations for 6 or more only. Main courses $9–$26. AE, DC, DISC, MC, V. Daily 11:30am–4pm and 5:30pm–midnight.

Joe Allen AMERICAN   Located on the bay side of the beach, Joe Allen is nestled in an unassuming building in South Beach that is conspicuously devoid of neon lights, valet parkers, and fashionable pedestrians. Inside, however, you discover a hidden jewel: a stark yet elegant interior and no-nonsense, fairly priced, ample-portioned dishes such as meatloaf, pizza, fresh fish, and salads. The scene has a homey feel flavored by locals looking to escape the hype without compromising quality.

1787 Purdy Ave./Sunset Harbor Dr. (3 blocks west of Alton Rd.), South Beach. ☎ 305/531-7007. Reservations recommended, especially on weekends. Main courses $15–$25. MC, V. Daily 11:30am–11:30pm.

Jumbo's SOUL FOOD   Open 24 hours daily, this Miami institution (in a somewhat shady neighborhood) is the kind of place where you'll see everyone from Rastafarian musicians and cabdrivers to Lenny Kravitz. Family owned for over 50 years, Jumbo's is known for its world-famous fried shrimp, fried chicken, catfish fingers, and collard greens. The service is friendly and fun, and there's history here, too. Jimbo's is the first restaurant in Miami to integrate in 1966, and the first to hire African-American employees in 1967.

7501 NW 7th Ave., Miami. ☎ 305/751-1127. Main courses $5–$15. AE, DC, MC, V. Daily 24 hr.

Mark's South Beach NEW WORLD/MEDITERRANEAN   This cozy, contemporary restaurant—one of the best in Miami—is nestled in the basement of the quietly chic Hotel Nash. The New World and Mediterranean-influenced menu changes nightly. What doesn't change is the consistency and freshness of the restaurant's exquisite cuisine. The roasted rack of Colorado lamb with semolina gnocchi is exceptional and worth every bit of cholesterol it may have. Desserts here are outrageous, especially the pistachio cake with chocolate sorbet. Unlike many South Beach eating establishments, the knowledgeable servers are here because of their experience in the restaurant—not modeling—business.

In the Hotel Nash, 1120 Collins Ave., South Beach. ☎ 305/604-9050. Reservations recommended. Main courses $26–$41. AE, DC, DISC, MC, V. Wed–Sun 7–11am and noon–3pm; Wed–Sat 7pm–midnight; Sun 7–11pm.

Nemo PAN-ASIAN   Located on the quickly developing South Beach area known as SoFi (for "south of Fifth St."), Nemo is a funky, high-style eatery with an open kitchen and an outdoor courtyard canopied by trees and lined with an eclectic mix of model types and foodies. Among the reasons to eat here: grilled Indian-spiced pork chop; grilled local mahimahi with citrus and grilled sweet-onion salad, kimchi glaze, basil, and crispy potatoes; and an inspired dessert menu that's not for the faint of calories.

Seating inside is comfy-cozy but borders on cramped. On Sunday mornings, the open kitchen is converted into a buffet counter for the restaurant's unparalleled brunch. Be prepared for a long wait.

100 Collins Ave., South Beach. © **305/532-4550**. Reservations recommended. Main courses $22–$36; Sun brunch $29. AE, MC, V. Mon–Sat noon–3pm and 6:30pm–midnight; Sun 11am–3pm and 6–midnight. Valet parking $10 or $20 for curbside.

Nobu SUSHI   When Madonna ate here, no one really noticed. Not because people were purposely trying not to notice, but because the real star at Nobu is the sushi. The raw facts: Nobu has been hailed as one of the best sushi restaurants in the world, with always-packed eateries in New York, London, and Los Angeles. The Omakase, or Chef's Choice—a multicourse menu entirely up to the chef for $70 per person and up—gets consistent raves. And although you won't wait long for your food to be cooked, you will wait forever to score a table here.

At The Shore Club Hotel, 1901 Collins Ave., South Beach. © **305/695-3232**. Reservations for parties of 6 or more. Main courses $10–$30. AE, MC, V. Sun 7–11pm; Mon–Thurs 7pm–midnight; Fri–Sat 7pm–1am.

Norman's (Best NEW WORLD CUISINE   *Gourmet* magazine named Norman's the best restaurant in South Florida and it is here that chef and cookbook author Norman van Aken takes New World cuisine (which, along with chef Allen Susser, he helped create) to another plateau with dishes that have landed him on the wish lists of gourmands everywhere. The open kitchen invites you to marvel at the mastery that lands on your plate in the form of pan-roasted swordfish with black-bean *muneta;* or chargrilled New York strip steak with chimichurri sabayon, *pommes frites,* and Creole mustard–spiced caramelized red onions, just to name a few. The staff is adoring and professional, and the atmosphere is tasteful without being too formal. The portions are realistic, but still, be careful not to overdo it. You'll want to try some of the funky, fantastic desserts.

21 Almeria Ave. (between Douglas and Ponce de León), Coral Gables. © **305/446-6767**. Reservations highly recommended. Main courses $22–$38. AE, DC, MC, V. Mon–Thurs 6–10pm; Fri–Sat 6–10:30pm; closed Sun. Bar opens at 5:30pm.

Sheldon's Drugs (Value AMERICAN   This historic old-fashioned drugstore counter was a favorite breakfast spot of Isaac Bashevis Singer. Consider stopping by for a good piece of pie and a side of history. According to legend, the author was sitting at Sheldon's eating a bagel and eggs when his wife got the call in 1978 that he had won the Nobel prize for literature. The menu hasn't changed much since then. You can get eggs and oatmeal and a good tuna melt. A blue-plate special might be generic spaghetti and meatballs or grilled frankfurters. The food is pretty basic, but you can't beat the prices.

9501 Harding Ave., Surfside. © **305/866-6251**. Main courses $4–$8; soups and sandwiches $2–$7. AE, DISC, MC, V. Mon–Sat 7am–7pm; Sun 7am–4pm.

Shula's Steak House AMERICAN/STEAK   Climb a sweeping staircase in the Alexander All-Suite Luxury Hotel, go through the glass hallway, and you'll find yourself in this magnificent restaurant that has been acclaimed one of the greatest steakhouses in all of North America. If you're feeling adventurous, try the 48-ounce club (you can get your name engraved on a gold plaque if you can finish this absolutely *huge* piece of meat) or settle for the 20-ounce Kansas City strip or the 12-ounce filet mignon. Fresh seafood abounds when in season, and the oysters Rockefeller are a particularly good choice. The entertaining staff is very knowledgeable.

In the Alexander Hotel, 5225 Collins Ave., Miami Beach. ✆ 305/341-6565. Reservations recommended. Main courses $23–$78. AE, DISC, MC, V. Daily 11am–3:30pm and 6–11pm. Free valet parking.

Versailles CUBAN   Versailles is the meeting place of Miami's Cuban power brokers, who meet daily over *café con leche* to discuss the future of the exiles' fate. A glorified diner—and the place to come for *mucho* helpings of Cuban kitsch—the restaurant sparkles with glass, chandeliers, murals, and mirrors meant to evoke the French palace. There's nothing fancy here—nothing French, either—just straightforward food from the home country. The menu is a veritable survey of Cuban cooking and includes specialties such as Moors and Christians (flavorful black beans with white rice), *ropa vieja* (shredded beef stew), and fried whole fish. With its late hours, it's also the perfect place to come after spending your night in Little Havana.

3555 SW 8th St., Little Havana. ✆ 305/444-0240. Soup and salad $2–$10; main courses $5–$20. DC, DISC, MC, V. Mon–Thurs 8am–2am; Fri 8am–3am; Sat 8am–4:30am; Sun 9am–1am.

Wolfie Cohen's Rascal House DELI   Open since 1954 and still going strong, this historic, nostalgic culinary extravaganza is one of Miami Beach's greatest traditions. Scooch into one of the ancient vinyl booths—which have hosted many a notorious bottom, from Frank Sinatra to mob boss Sam Giancana—and review the huge menu that's loaded with authentic Jewish staples. Consider the classic corned beef sandwich, stuffed cabbage, brisket, or potato pancakes. If you're lucky, the waitress will give you a wax-paper doggy bag to wrap up the leftover rolls and Danish from your breadbasket.

17190 Collins Ave. (at 163rd St.), Sunny Isles. ✆ 305/947-4581. Main courses $8–$30. AE, MC, V. Sun–Thurs 6:30am–1am; Fri–Sat 6:30am–2am.

MIAMI AFTER DARK

For up-to-date listing information, and to make sure the club of the moment hasn't expired, check the *Miami Herald*'s "Weekend" section, which runs on Friday, or the more comprehensive listings in *New Times,* Miami's free alternative weekly, available each Wednesday; or visit **www.miami.citysearch.com online**.

THE PERFORMING ARTS   One of the most important and longest-running series is produced by the **Concert Association of Florida** (**CAF;** ✆ **877/433-3200**). Season after season, the schedules are punctuated by world-renowned dance companies and such seasoned virtuosi as Itzhak Perlman, Andre Watts, and Kathleen Battle. Since CAF does not have its own space, performances are usually scheduled in either the Miami–Dade County Auditorium or the Jackie Gleason Theater of the Performing Arts. The season lasts October through April, and ticket prices range from $20 to $70.

The artistically acclaimed and innovative **Miami City Ballet** (✆ **305/929-7000** or 305/929-7010) is directed by Edward Villella and features a repertoire of more than 60 ballets. The company's headquarters are located at the Ophelia and Juan, Jr., Roca Center at the Collins Park Cultural Center in Miami Beach. For a taste of local Latin flavor, see the **Ballet Flamenco La Rosa** (✆ **305/899-7729**) perform impressive flamenco and other styles of dance on various Miami stages.

South Florida's premier symphony orchestra, under the direction of James Judd, the **Florida Philharmonic Orchestra** (✆ **800/226-1812**) presents a full season of classical and pops programs interspersed with several children's and contemporary popular-music dates. The Philharmonic performs Downtown in the Gusman Center for the Performing Arts and at the Dade County Auditorium.

Over 60 years old, the **Florida Grand Opera** (© 800/741-1010; www.fgo.org) regularly features singers from top houses in both America and Europe. All productions are sung in their original language and staged with projected English supertitles. Tickets become scarce when Placido Domingo or Luciano Pavarotti (who made his American debut here in 1965) come to town. The opera's season runs roughly from November to April, with five performances each week. At press time, performances were taking place at the Miami–Dade County Auditorium and the Broward Center for the Performing Arts, about 40 minutes from downtown Miami.

LIVE MUSIC   Tobacco Road, 626 S. Miami Ave., over the Miami Avenue Bridge near Brickell Avenue, downtown (© 305/374-1198), is an institution that's been around since 1912 (Al Capone hung out here when it was a speak-easy). These days, you'll find locals flocking here to see local bands (and a few national acts) perform. It's small and gritty and meant to be that way.

Jazid, 1342 Washington Ave., South Beach (© 305/673-9372), is smoky, sultry, and illuminated by flickering candelabras. Music consists of live jazz (sometimes on acid), soul, and funk.

In Miami Beach, the elegant **Upstairs at the Van Dyke Cafe,** 846 Lincoln Rd. (© 305/534-3600), has live jazz 7 nights a week until midnight.

DANCE CLUBS   Clubs are as much a cottage industry in Miami as is, say, cheese in Wisconsin. Clubland, as it is known, is not just a nocturnal theme park but a way of life for some. Ask your hotel's concierge to get you on a club's guest list; you'll still have to wait to get in, but you won't need to fork over a ridiculous $20 to walk past the ropes. This is a fickle scene, but at press time, some of the hottest spots included **crobar,** 1445 Washington Ave., South Beach (© 305/531-8225; www.crobarmiami. com); **Mansion,** 1235 Washington Ave., South Beach (© 305/531-5535); **Club Space,** 34 NE 11th St., downtown (© 305/372-9378); **Opium Garden,** 136 Collins Ave., South Beach (© 305/531-5535); and **Bongo's Cuban Café,** 601 Biscayne Blvd., downtown (© 786/777-2100).

Tip: The club scene generally doesn't get started in Miami before 11pm.

LATIN CLUBS   Casa Panza, 1620 SW 8th St. (Calle Ocho), Miami (© 305/643-5343), is one of Little Havana's most happening nightspots. Make sure to catch the flamenco show here on Tuesday, Thursday, and Saturday nights.

If you want to dance to a funky, loud Brazilian beat until you drop, check out **Mango's Tropical Café,** 900 Ocean Dr., South Beach (© 305/673-4422), which features nightly live Brazilian and other Latin music on a little patio bar. One of the most popular spots on Ocean Drive, this outdoor enclave of Latin liveliness shakes with the intensity of a Richter-busting earthquake. The hottest Latin joint in the city is **La Covacha,** 10730 NW 25th St., at NW 107th Avenue, West Miami (© 305/594-3717). It's a hut in the middle of nowhere, but this shack really jumps on weekend nights when the place is open until 5am. Do not wear silk here, as you *will* sweat.

THE BAR SCENE   On the beach, you'd do best to walk along Ocean Drive and Washington Avenue to see what's hot. Just hold onto your bags. It's not dangerous, but, occasionally, a few shady types manage to slip into the crowd. Another very important tip when in a club: *Never put your drink down out of your sight*—there have been unfortunate incidents in which drinks have been spiked with illegal chemical substances. For a less hard-core, more collegiate nightlife, head to Coconut Grove.

The Clevelander, 1020 Ocean Dr., South Beach (© **305/531-3485**), is an old standby that's always crowded. It attracts a lively, sporty, adults-only crowd who have no interest in being part of a scene but are interested in the very revealing scenery. The **Rose Bar at the Delano,** 1685 Collins Ave., South Beach (© **305/672-2000**), is for amazing people-watching. The crowd here is full of the so-called glitterati, fabulatti, and other assorted poseurs who view life through (Italian-made) rose-colored glasses and down excruciatingly high-priced cocktails.

Standing on its own amid an oasis of trendiness, **Mac's Club Deuce,** 222 14th St., South Beach (© **305/673-9537**), is the quintessential dive bar, with cheap drinks and a cast of characters ranging from your typical barfly to your atypical drag queen. It's got a well-stocked jukebox, friendly bartenders, a pool table, and, best of all, it's an insomniac's dream, open daily from 8am to 5am. **Automatic Slim's,** 1216 Washington Ave., South Beach (© **305/695-0795**), is *the* bar where Ozzie and Harriet types become more like Ozzy and Sharon. As South Beach's most popular, unpretentious bar, Automatic Slim's packs people in thanks to an exhaustive list of cheap(er) drinks, lack of attitude, great rock music, and a decor that can only be described as white trash chic.

THE GAY & LESBIAN SCENE   The gay scene in Miami is outrageous, especially on South Beach. Still, most of the gay clubs welcome hetero visitors, too. And many of the normally "straight" clubs also have gay nights. Miami Beach is one of the major stops for circuit parties around the United States, though ever since South Beach got bit by the hip-hop bug, many of Miami's gays have been crossing county lines into Fort Lauderdale.

Score, 727 Lincoln Rd., South Beach (© **305/535-1111**), is a huge pickup scene and offers a multitude of bars, dance floors, loungelike areas, and outdoor tables in case you need to come up for air. One of the most popular cruise bars on South Beach is the recently expanded **Twist,** 1057 Washington Ave. (© **305/53-TWIST**). **O-Zone,** 6620 SW 57th Ave. (Red Rd.), South Miami (© **305/667-2888**), is the zone of choice for gay men with an aversion to South Beach's cruisy, scene-heavy vibes. It's known for a heavily Latin crowd and fantastic, outlandish drag shows on the weekends.

5 Everglades National Park

This vast and unusual ecosystem is actually a shallow, 40-mile-wide, slow-moving river. Rarely more than knee-deep, the water is the lifeblood of this wilderness, one of the few places where you can see dozens of endangered species in their natural habitat, including the swallowtail butterfly, American crocodile, leatherback turtle, southern bald eagle, West Indian manatee, and Florida panther. More than 350 species of birds make their homes in the Everglades. Tropical birds from the Caribbean and temperate species from North America can be found here, along with exotics that have blown in from more distant regions. The slow and subtle splendor of this exotic land may not be immediately appealing to kids, but they'll certainly remember the experience and no doubt thank you for it later. Meanwhile, you'll find plenty of dramatic fun around the park, like airboat rides, alligator wrestling, and biking, to keep the kids satisfied for at least a day.

Although the Everglades may seem overwhelmingly large and unapproachable, it's easy to get to the park's two main areas—the northern section, which is accessible via Shark Valley and Everglades City, or the southern section, accessible through the Ernest F. Coe Visitor Center, near Homestead and Florida City.

Shark Valley, a 15-mile paved road ending at an observation tower overlooking the pulsating heart of the Everglades, is the easiest and most scenic way to explore the Everglades. Shark Valley is best reached via the Tamiami Trail, South Florida's pre-Turnpike, two-lane road, which cuts across the southern part of the state along the park's northern border. Shark Valley is about an hour's drive from Miami. If you pick up State Road 29 and head south from the Tamiami Trail, you'll hit a modified version of civilization in the form of Everglades City (where the Everglades meets the Gulf of Mexico) and see another entrance to the park and the **Gulf Coast Visitor Center** (© **239/695-3311**). From Miami to Shark Valley: Go west on I-395 to State Road 821 South (the Florida Tpk.). Take the U.S. 41/SW 8th Street (Tamiami Trail) exit. The Shark Valley entrance is just 25 miles west. To get to Everglades City, continue west on the Tamiami Trail and head south on State Road 29.

If you're in a rush to hit the 'glades and don't care about the scenic route, the southern route is your best bet. Just southeast of Homestead and Florida City, off State Road 9336, the southern access to the park will bring you directly to the **Ernest F. Coe Visitor Center.** From Miami to the southern entrance: Go west on I-395 to State Road 821 South (Florida Tpk.). The Turnpike will end in Florida City. Take your first right turn through the center of town (you can't miss it) and follow the signs to the park entrance on State Road 9336. The Ernest F. Coe Visitor Center is about 1½ hours from Miami.

The **Royal Palm Visitor Center,** a small nature museum located 3 miles past the park's main entrance, is a smaller information center. The museum is not great (there are displays with recorded messages interpreting the park's ecosystem), but the center is the departure point for the popular Anhinga and Gumbo–Limbo trails (see below). Open daily from 8am to 4pm.

The **Flamingo Lodge, Marina, and Outpost Resort,** 1 Flamingo Lodge Hwy., Flamingo (© **800/600-3813** or 941/695-3101; www.flamingolodge.com), is the one-stop clearinghouse—and the only option—for in-park accommodations, equipment rentals, and tours. If you want to stay overnight, this is the number to call.

General inquiries and specific questions should be directed to **Everglades National Park Headquarters,** 40001 S.R. 9336, Homestead, FL 33034 (© **305/242-7700;** www.nps.gov/ever). Ask for a copy of *Parks and Preserves,* a free newspaper filled with up-to-date information about goings-on in the Everglades. Headquarters is staffed by helpful phone operators daily from 8:30am to 4:30pm.

Permits and passes can be purchased at the main park entrance, the Chekika entrance, or the Shark Valley entrance stations only. Even if you are just visiting the park for an afternoon, you'll need to buy a 7-day permit, which costs $10 per vehicle. Pedestrians and cyclists are charged $5 each.

There are two distinct seasons in the Everglades: high season and mosquito season. High season is also dry season and lasts from late November to May. Most winters here are warm, sunny, and breezy—a good combination for keeping the bugs away. This is the best time to visit because low water levels attract the largest variety of wading birds and their predators. As the dry season wanes, wildlife follows the receding water; and by the end of May, the only living things you are sure to spot will cause you to itch. The worst, called "no-see-ums," are not even swattable. If you choose to visit during the buggy season, be vigilant in applying bug spray. Also, realize that many establishments and operators either close or curtail offerings in the summer, so always call ahead to check schedules.

SEEING THE HIGHLIGHTS

Shark Valley offers a fine introduction to the wonder of the Everglades, but don't plan on spending more than a few hours here. Bicycling or taking a guided tram tour can be a satisfying experience, but neither fully captures the wonders of the park.

Stop first along the **Anhinga and Gumbo–Limbo trails,** which start right next to one another, 3 miles from the park's main entrance. These trails provide a thorough introduction to Everglades flora and fauna and are highly recommended to first-time visitors. Alligators, turtles, river otters, herons, egrets, and other animals abound, making it one of the best trails for seeing wildlife. Take your time—at least an hour is recommended. If you treat the trails and modern boardwalk as pathways to get through quickly, rather than destinations to experience and savor slowly, you'll miss out on the still beauty and hidden treasures that await.

Also, it's worth climbing the observation tower at the end of the quarter-mile-long **Pa-hay-okee Trail.** The panoramic view of undulating grass and seemingly endless vistas gives the impression of a semi-aquatic Serengeti. Flocks of tropical and semi-tropical birds traverse the landscape, alligators and fish stir the surface of the water, and small grottoes of trees thrust up from the sea of grass marking higher ground.

If you want to get closer to nature, a few hours in a **canoe** along any of the trails allows paddlers the chance to sense the park's fluid motion. Visitors who choose this option end up feeling more like explorers than merely observers. From a canoe, you'll get a closer look into the park's shallow estuaries where water birds, sea turtles, and endangered manatees make their homes. Everglades National Park's longest "trails" are designed for boat and canoe travel, and many are marked as clearly as walking trails. Park rangers can recommend trails that best suit your abilities, time limitations, and interests. You can rent a canoe at the Flamingo Lodge, Marina and Outpost Resort (see above); the concessionaire will shuttle your party to the trail head of your choice and pick you up afterward.

Shark Valley offers South Florida's most scenic **bicycle trail.** You can ride the 17-mile loop with no other traffic in sight. Instead, you'll share the flat paved road only with other bikers and a menagerie of wildlife. Don't be surprised to see a 'gator lounging in the sun or a deer munching on some grass. Otters, turtles, alligators, and snakes are common companions in the Shark Valley area. You can rent bikes at the Flamingo Lodge, Marina and Outpost Resort, or at **Shark Valley Tram Tours,** at the park's Shark Valley entrance (© **305/221-8455**).

6 The Keys & Key West

The islands of the Keys are strung out across the southern waters of Florida like cultured pearls, and each of the more than 400 islands that make up this 150-mile chain has a distinctive character. Some are crammed with strip malls and tacky shell shops, but most are filled with unusual species of tropical plants, birds, and reptiles. All are surrounded by calm blue waters, populated by stunning sea life, and graced by year-round warmth. This vibrant underwater habitat thrives on one of only two living tropical reefs in the entire North American continent (the other is off the coast of Belize). As a result, anglers, divers, snorkelers, and watersports enthusiasts of all kinds come to explore. The heavy traffic has taken its toll on this fragile ecoscape, but efforts are underway to protect it.

THE UPPER & MIDDLE KEYS: KEY LARGO TO MARATHON

This is the fishing and diving capital of America, and the swarms of outfitters and billboards never let you forget it. From Miami International Airport, take Le Jeune Road (NW 42nd Ave.) to **Route 836 West.** Follow signs to the Florida Turnpike south (about 7 miles). The turnpike extension connects with **U.S. 1** in Florida City. Continue south on U.S. 1.

Make sure you get your information from official, not-for-profit centers. The **Key Largo Chamber of Commerce,** U.S. 1 at MM 106, Key Largo, FL 33037 (𝒞 **800/ 822-1088** or 305/451-1414; www.keylargo.org), runs an excellent facility, with free direct-dial phones and plenty of brochures. Headquartered in a handsome clapboard house, the chamber operates as an information clearinghouse for all of the Keys and is open daily from 9am to 6pm.

Key Largo is the largest Key and is more developed than its neighbors to the south. Dozens of chain hotels, restaurants, and tourist information centers service the many water enthusiasts who come to explore the nation's first underwater state park, **John Pennekamp Coral Reef State Park,** on U.S. 1 at MM 102.5 (𝒞 **305/451-1202;** www.pennekamppark.com). It's a sanctuary for part of the only living coral reef in the continental United States. Because the water is extremely shallow, the 40 species of corals and more than 650 species of fish here are particularly accessible to divers, snorkelers, and glass-bottomed-boat passengers. Your first stop should be the visitor center, which is full of educational fish tanks and a mammoth 30,000-gallon saltwater aquarium that re-creates a reef ecosystem. At the adjacent dive shop, you can rent snorkeling and diving equipment and join one of the boat trips that depart for the reef throughout the day. Visitors can also rent motorboats, sailboats, windsurfers, and canoes. The 2-hour glass-bottomed-boat tour ($22 for adults, $15 for children 11 and under) is the best way to see the coral reefs if you refuse to get wet. Park admission is $3.50 per vehicle for one occupant; for two or more, it is $6 per vehicle, plus 50¢ per passenger; $1.50 per pedestrian or bicyclist.

The **Florida Keys Dive Center,** on U.S. 1 at MM 90.5, Tavernier (𝒞 **305/852-4599;** www.floridakeysdivectr.com), takes snorkelers and divers to the reefs of John Pennekamp Coral Reef State Park and environs every day. PADI (Professional Association of Diving Instructors) training courses are also available for the uninitiated. Tours leave at 8am and 12:30pm and cost $30 per person to snorkel (plus $9 rental fee for mask, snorkel, and fins) and $65 per person to dive (plus an extra $20 if you need to rent all the gear).

Islamorada, the unofficial capital of the Upper Keys, offers the area's best atmosphere, food, fishing, entertainment, and lodging. In these "purple isles," nature lovers can enjoy nature trails, historical explorations, and big-purse fishing tournaments. At **Robbie's Pier,** U.S. 1 at MM 77.5, Islamorada (𝒞 **305/664-9814**), the fierce steely tarpons have been gathering for the past 20 years. You may recognize these prehistoric-looking giants that grow up to 200 pounds; many are displayed as trophies and mounted on local restaurant walls. At Robbie's Pier, tens and sometimes hundreds of these behemoths circle the shallow waters waiting for you to feed them a bucket of fish ($2). **Robbie's Partyboats & Charters,** on U.S. 1 at MM 84.5, Islamorada (𝒞 **305/ 664-8070** or 305/664-4196), located at the south end of the Holiday Isle Docks, offers day and night deep-sea and reef-fishing trips aboard a 65-foot party boat. Big-game fishing charters are also available, and "splits" are arranged for solo fishers. Phone for information and reservations. No trip is complete without a stop at the **Tiki**

Bar at the Holiday Isle Resort, U.S. 1 at MM 84, Islamorada (© **800/327-7070** or 305/664-2321). It claims to have invented the rum runner drink and we have no reason to doubt that. Hundreds of revelers visit this ocean-side spot for drinks and dancing any time of day, but the live rock music starts at 8:30pm.

Marathon, smack in the middle of the chain of islands, is one of the most populated Keys. It is part fishing village, part tourist center, and part nature preserve. This area's highly developed infrastructure includes resort hotels, a commercial airport, and a highway that expands to four lanes. Thankfully, high-rises have yet to arrive. The best beach in the area is **Sombrero Beach,** in Marathon at the end of Sombrero Beach Road (near MM 50). More than 90 feet of sand is dotted with palms, Australian pines, and royal poincianas as well as with barbecue grills, clean bathrooms, and some brand-new Tiki huts for relaxing in the shade. Admission and parking at this little-known gem are free.

A stop at the **Seven-mile Bridge,** between MM 40 and 47 on U.S. 1, is a rewarding and relaxing break from the drive south. Built alongside the ruins of oil magnate Henry Flagler's incredible Overseas Railroad, the "new" bridge (between MM 40 and 47) is still considered an architectural feat. The wide arched span, completed in 1982 at a cost of more than $45 million, is impressive, its apex being the highest point in the Keys. The new bridge and especially its now-defunct neighbor provide excellent vantage points from which to view the stunning waters of the Keys.

WHERE TO STAY

U.S. 1 is lined with chain hotels in all price ranges. In the Upper Keys, the best moderately priced option is the **Key Largo Ramada,** off U.S. 1 at MM 100, Key Largo (© **800/THE-KEYS** or 305/451-3939), which has three pools and a casino boat, and is just 3 miles from John Pennekamp Coral Reef State Park. Another good Upper Keys option is **Days Inn Oceanfront Resort,** U.S. 1 at MM 82.5 (© **800/DAYS-INN** or 305/664-3681). In the Middle Keys, the **Wellesley Inn,** 13351 Overseas Hwy., MM 54 in Marathon (© **305/743-8550**), offers reasonably priced ocean-side rooms.

If you want moderate prices but not a standard chain hotel, try **Conch Key Cottages,** near U.S. 1 at MM 62.3, Marathon (© **800/330-1577** or 305/289-1377; www.conchkeycottages.com); or the **Kona Kai Resort & Gallery,** U.S. 1 at MM 97.8, Key Largo (© **800/365-7829** or 305/852-7200; www.konakairesort.com).

More luxurious choices include the recently renovated **Hawk's Cay Resort,** U.S. 1 at MM 61, Duck Key (© **888/814-9104** or 305/743-7000; www.hawkscay.com), which is located on its own 60-acre island just outside Marathon; it's a sprawling, impressive resort encompassing a marina and a saltwater lagoon that's home to a half-dozen dolphins. **The Moorings,** 123 Beach Rd. near MM 81.5 on the ocean side, Islamorada (© **305/664-4708;** www.themooringsvillage.com), offers romantic white-washed houses and a real sense that you've gotten away from it all, especially as you lounge on the 1,000-foot beach (one of the only real beaches around).

THE LOWER KEYS: BIG PINE KEY TO COPPITT KEY

The Lower Keys (farther south on U.S. 1, below the Seven-mile Bridge) are less developed and more tranquil than the Upper Keys. If you're looking for haute cuisine and happening nightlife, look elsewhere. But if you want to commune with nature or adventure in solitude, you've come to the right place.

Best Under the Sea

Snorkelers and divers should not miss the Keys' most dramatic reefs at the **Looe Key National Marine Sanctuary**. Here you'll see more than 150 varieties of hard and soft coral, some centuries old, as well as every type of tropical fish, including the gold and blue parrotfish, moray eels, barracudas, French angels, and tarpon. **Looe Key Dive Center**, U.S. 1 at MM 27.5, Ramrod Key (© **305/872-2215**), offers a mind-blowing 2½-hour tour aboard a 45-foot catamaran with two shallow 1-hour dives for snorkelers and scuba divers. Snorkelers pay $30, and divers with their own equipment pay $40. Good-quality rentals are available.

The **Big Pine and Lower Keys Chamber of Commerce,** ocean side of U.S. 1 at MM 31 (P.O. Box 430511), Big Pine Key, FL 33043 (© **800/872-3722** or 305/872-2411; www.lowerkeyschamber.com), is open Monday through Friday from 9am to 5pm and Saturday from 9am to 3pm. Call, write, or stop in for a comprehensive, detailed information packet.

Bahia Honda State Park, U.S. 1 at MM 37.5, Big Pine Key (© **305/872-2353;** www.bahiahondapark.com), has one of the most beautiful coastlines in South Florida. Bahia Honda (pronounced *Bah*-ya) is a great place for hiking, bird-watching, swimming, snorkeling, and fishing. The 524-acre park encompasses a wide variety of ecosystems, including coastal mangroves, beach dunes, and tropical hammocks. There are miles of trails packed with unusual plants and animals and a small white beach. Shaded seaside picnic areas are fitted with tables and grills. Although the beach is never wider than 5 feet even at low tide, this is the Lower Keys' best beach area. The park has relatively deep waters close to shore that are perfect for snorkeling and diving, with beautiful vibrant fish and coral. Admission to the park is $5 per vehicle (plus 50¢ per person), $1.50 per pedestrian or bicyclist, free for children 5 and under. If you are alone in a car, you'll pay only $2.50. Open daily from 8am to sunset.

The most famous residents of the Lower Keys are the tiny Key deer. Of the estimated 300 existing in the world, two-thirds live on Big Pine Key's **National Key Deer Refuge.** To get your bearings, stop by the rangers' office at the Winn-Dixie Shopping Plaza near MM 30.5 off U.S. 1. They'll give you an informative brochure and map of the area. It is open Monday through Friday from 8am to 5pm.

A stopping point for migratory birds on the Eastern Flyway, the Lower Keys are populated with many West Indian bird species, especially during spring and fall. The small vegetated islands of the Keys are the only nesting sites in the United States for the great white heron and the white-crowned pigeon. They're also some of the very few breeding places for the reddish egret, the roseate spoonbill, the mangrove cuckoo, and the black-whiskered vireo. Look for them on Bahia Honda and the many uninhabited islands nearby.

The Overseas Highway (U.S. 1) touches on only a few dozen of the many hundreds of islands that make up the Keys. To really see the Lower Keys, rent a kayak or canoe—perfect for these shallow waters. **Reflections Kayak Nature Tours,** operating out of Parmer's Resort, on U.S. 1 at MM 28.5, Little Torch Key (© **305/872-4668**), offers fully outfitted backcountry wildlife tours, either on your own or with an expert.

The expert, Mike Wedeking, a former U.S. Forest Service guide, keeps up an engaging discussion describing the area's fish, sponges, coral, osprey, hawks, eagles, alligators, raccoons, and deer. The 3-hour tours cost $50 per person and include spring water, fresh fruit, granola bars, and use of binoculars. Bring a towel and sea sandals or sneakers.

WHERE TO STAY

Exclusive **Little Palm Island Resort & Spa,** reached by launch at the ocean side of U.S. 1 at MM 28.5, Little Torch Key (© **800/343-8567** or 305/872-2524; www.little palmisland.com), offers pricey and posh thatch-roof bungalows on a private 5-acre island. Many villas have ocean views and private sun decks with rope hammocks. On the other end of the price scale is **Parmer's Resort,** near MM 28.5, Little Torch Key (© **305/872-2157;** www.palmersresort.com), offering 45 modest but comfortable cottages. Some are waterfront, many have kitchenettes, and others are just a bedroom. Parmer's, a fixture here for more than 20 years, is well known for its charming hospitality and helpful staff.

KEY WEST

There are two schools of thought on Key West—one is that it has become way too commercial, and the other is that it's still a place where you can go and not worry about being prim, proper, or even well groomed. It's probably a bizarre fusion of both—a fascinating look at small-town America in which people truly live by the (off)beat of their own drum, albeit one with a Banana Republic and Starbucks thrown in to bring you back to some reality. The locals, or "conchs" (pronounced *conks*), and the developers here have been at odds for years. This once low-key island has been thoroughly commercialized—there's a Hard Rock Cafe smack in the middle of Duval Street, and thousands of cruise-ship passengers descend on Mallory Square each day. It's definitely not the seedy town Hemingway and his cronies once called their own. Or is it?

The heart of town offers party people a good time. Here you'll find good restaurants, fun bars, live music, rickshaw rides, and lots of shopping. Don't bother with a watch or tie—this is the home of the perennial vacation.

ESSENTIALS

GETTING THERE If you're driving, continue south on **U.S. 1.** When entering Key West, stay in the far-right lane onto North Roosevelt Boulevard, which becomes Truman Avenue in Old Town. Continue for a few blocks, and you will find yourself on Duval Street, in the heart of the city.

Several regional airlines fly nonstop (about 55 min.) from Miami to Key West; fares are about $120 to $300 round-trip. Planes land at **Key West International Airport,** South Roosevelt Boulevard (© **305/296-5439**), on the southeastern corner of the island.

VISITOR INFORMATION The **Key West Chamber of Commerce,** 402 Wall St., Key West, FL 33040 (© **800/527-8539** or 305/294-2587; www.keywestchamber. com), offers both general and specialized information. The lobby is open daily from 8:30am to 6pm; phones are answered from 8am to 8pm. The **Key West Visitor Center** is the area's best for information on accommodations, events, and dining; the number is © **800/LAST-KEY.** It's open weekdays from 8am to 5:30pm and weekends from 8:30am to 5pm.

GETTING AROUND With limited parking, narrow streets, and congested traffic, driving in Old Town Key West is more of a pain than a convenience. Unless you're staying in one of the more remote accommodations, consider trading in the car for a bicycle. The island is small and as flat as a board, which makes it easy to negotiate, especially away from the crowded downtown. The **Bike Shop,** 1110 Truman Ave. (✆ **305/294-1073**), rents cruisers for $10 per day; a $150 deposit is required.

SPECIAL EVENTS The last week of October brings **Fantasy Fest,** Florida's Halloween version of Mardi Gras. Crazy costumes, wild parades, and even wilder revelers gather for an opportunity to do things Mom said not to. Definitely leave the kids at home! Call ✆ **305/296-1817.** Coinciding with Fantasy Fest is the **Goombay Festival,** in which you can sample Caribbean dishes and purchase art and ethnic clothing.

WHAT TO SEE & DO

The city's whole story is packed into a neat, 90-minute package on the **Conch Tour Train** (✆ **305/294-5161;** www.conchtourtrain.com), which covers the island and all its rich, raunchy history. Tours depart from both Mallory Square and the Welcome Center, near where U.S. 1 becomes North Roosevelt Boulevard, on the other side of the island. The cost is $25 for adults, $12 for children 4 to 12, and free for children 3 and under. Daily departures are every half-hour from 9am to 4:30pm.

The **Old Town Trolley** (✆ **305/296-6688**) is the choice in bad weather or if you are staying at one of the many hotels on its route. Humorous drivers maintain a running commentary as the enclosed tram loops around the island's streets past all the major sights. Trolleys depart from Mallory Square and other points around the island, including many area hotels. Tours are $22 for adults, $11 for children 4 to 12, and free for children 3 and under. Departures are daily every half-hour (though not always on the half-hour) from 9am to 4:45pm.

Dating from the early 19th century, the **Audubon House & Tropical Gardens,** 205 Whitehead St., between Greene and Caroline streets (✆ **305/294-2116;** www.audubonhouse.com), is a prime example of early Key West architecture. Named after the renowned painter and bird expert, John James Audubon, who was said to have visited the house in 1832, the graceful two-story home is a peaceful retreat from the bustle of Old Town. See rare Audubon prints, gorgeous antiques, historical photos, and lush tropical gardens. Admission is $10 for adults, $5 for children 6 to 12. Hours are daily from 9:30am to 5pm (last admission at 4:45pm).

Hemingway's particularly handsome stone Spanish Colonial house, now preserved as the **Ernest Hemingway Home and Museum,** 907 Whitehead St., between Truman Avenue and Olivia Street (✆ **305/294-1136;** www.hemingwayhome.com), was built in 1851. The author lived here from 1928 until 1940, along with about 50 cats, whose descendants still roam the premises. It was during those years that the Nobel Prize winner wrote *For Whom the Bell Tolls, A Farewell to Arms,* and *The Snows of Kilimanjaro.* Fans may want to take the optional half-hour tour. It's interesting and included in the price of admission, which is $11 for adults, $6 for children. It's open daily from 9am to 5pm.

Funky, picturesque **Key West Cemetery,** entrance at Margaret and Angela streets, perfectly captures the quintessential Key West attitude. Many tombs are stacked several high, condominium style—the rocky soil made digging 6 feet under nearly impossible for early settlers. I TOLD YOU I WAS SICK is one of the more famous epitaphs, as is the tongue-in-cheek widow's inscription AT LEAST I KNOW WHERE HE'S SLEEPING TONIGHT.

Best Going, Going, Gone . . . Sunset in Key West

A daily tradition in Key West, the Sunset Celebration is the best example of local flavor and the Jimmy Buffett–inspired attitude that prevails throughout the Florida Keys. Every evening, locals and visitors alike gather at the docks behind Mallory Square (at the western end of Whitehead St.) to celebrate the day gone by. Secure a spot on the docks about an hour before sundown for the full effect, complete with portrait artists, acrobats, food vendors, and animal acts.

If crowds aren't your thing, grab a seat at the Hilton's **Sunset Deck,** at the intersection of Front and Greene streets (© **305/294-4000**). From the calm of the bar, you can relax with a drink and look down on the mayhem. For the very best potent cocktails and great bar food on an outside patio or enclosed lounge, try **Pier House Resort and Caribbean Spa's Havana Docks** at 1 Duval St. (© **305/296-4600**). There's usually live music and a lively gathering of visitors enjoying this island's bounty. The bar is right on the water and is a prime sunset-viewing spot.

The **Mel Fisher Maritime Heritage Museum,** 200 Greene St. (© **305/294-2633;** www.melfisher.org), honors local hero Mel Fisher, who found a multimillion-dollar treasure-trove in 1985 aboard the wreck of the Spanish galleon *Nuestra Señora de Atocha.* The admission price is somewhat steep, but if you're into diving, pirates, and the mystery of sunken treasures, check out this small informative museum, full of doubloons, pieces of eight, emeralds, and solid-gold bars. Admission is $11 for adults; $6 for children ages 6 to 12. Open daily from 9:30am to 5pm.

Unlike the rest of the Keys, Key West actually has a few small beaches, although they don't compare to the state's wide natural wonders up the coast. Here are your options: **Smathers Beach,** off South Roosevelt Boulevard west of the airport; **Higgs Beach,** along Atlantic Boulevard between White Street and Reynolds Road; and **Fort Zachary Beach,** off the western end of Southard Boulevard. Although there is an entrance fee ($3.75 per car, plus more for each passenger), we recommend Fort Zachary, since it includes a great historical fort, a Civil War museum, shade trees, and a large picnic area with tables, barbecue grills, restrooms, and showers.

One of the area's largest scuba schools, **Dive Key West Inc.,** 3128 N. Roosevelt Blvd. (© **800/426-0707** or 305/296-3823; www.divekeywest.com), offers instruction on all levels and its dive boats take participants to scuba and snorkel sites on nearby reefs. Wreck dives and night dives are two of the special offerings of **Lost Reef Adventures,** 261 Margaret St. (© **800/952-2749** or 305/296-9737).

As any angler will tell you, there's no fishing like Keys fishing. Key West has it all: bonefish, tarpon, dolphin, tuna, grouper, cobia, and more. You'll find plenty of competition among the charter fishing boats in and around Mallory Square. However, you should know that the bookers from the kiosks in town generally take 20% of a captain's fee in addition to an extra monthly fee. So you can usually save yourself money by booking directly with a captain or going straight to one of the docks. You can negotiate a good deal at **Charter Boat Row,** 1801 N. Roosevelt Ave. (across from the Shell station), home to more than 30 charter fishing and party boats. Just show up to arrange your outing, or call **Garrison Bite Marina** (© **305/292-8167**) for details.

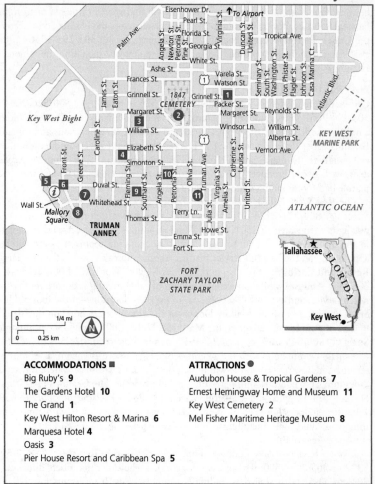

ACCOMMODATIONS ■
Big Ruby's **9**
The Gardens Hotel **10**
The Grand **1**
Key West Hilton Resort & Marina **6**
Marquesa Hotel **4**
Oasis **3**
Pier House Resort and Caribbean Spa **5**

ATTRACTIONS ●
Audubon House & Tropical Gardens **7**
Ernest Hemingway Home and Museum **11**
Key West Cemetery **2**
Mel Fisher Maritime Heritage Museum **8**

Serious anglers should consider the light-tackle boats that leave from **Oceanside Marina,** on Stock Island, at 5950 Peninsula Ave., 1½ miles off U.S. 1 (© **305/294-4676**). It's a 20-minute drive from Old Town on the Atlantic side. There are more than 30 light-tackle guides, which range from flatbed, backcountry skiffs to 28-foot open boats. There are also a few larger charters and a party boat that goes to the Dry Tortugas. Call for details. For a light-tackle outing with a very colorful Key West flair, call **Captain Bruce Cronin** at © **305/294-4929** or **Captain Kenny Harris** at © **305/294-8843,** two of the more famous (and pricey) captains working these docks for over 20 years. You'll pay from $650 for a full day, usually about 8am to 4pm, and from $450 for a half day.

Once the main industry of Key West, cigar making is enjoying renewed success at the handful of factories that survived the slow years. Stroll through **"Cigar Alley,"** between Front and Greene streets, where you will find *viejitos* (little old men) rolling fat stogies just as they used to do in their homeland across the Florida Straits. Stop at the **Conch Republic Cigar Factory,** at 512 Greene St. (© **305/295-9036**), for an excellent selection of imported and locally rolled smokes, including the famous El Hemingway.

WHERE TO STAY

Once a private residence, **The Gardens Hotel,** 526 Angela St. (© **800/526-2664** or 305/294-2661; www.gardenshotel.com), offers the best lodging in town and is hidden amid the exotic Peggy Mills tropical botanical gardens. It's a luxurious and romantic Bahamian-style hideaway featuring 17 luxuriously appointed accommodations in several buildings (the main one is a National Historic Landmark). The rooms are resplendent, with Aveda products, Jacuzzi bathtubs, hardwood floors, brass and iron beds, marble bathrooms, and a sense of serenity that words can't describe.

The **Key West Hilton Resort and Marina,** 245 Front St., at the end of Duval Street (© **800/221-2424** or 305/294-4000; www.keywestresort.hilton.com), which was lightly renovated in 2001, is Key West's only full-service resort, and it's situated in the middle of all of Old Town's action. The sparkling rooms are large and well appointed, and there's a full-service marina. Another upscale resort is the **Pier House Resort and Caribbean Spa,** 1 Duval St., near Mallory Docks (© **800/327-8340** or 305/296-4600; www.pierhouse.com), an oasis of calm offering luxurious rooms, top-notch service, and even a full-service spa. Its excellent location—at the foot of Duval Street and just steps from Mallory Docks—is the envy of every hotel on the island.

One of our absolute favorites, the **Marquesa Hotel,** 600 Fleming St., at Simonton Street (© **800/869-4631** or 305/292-1919; www.marquesa.com), offers all the charm of a small historic hotel with the amenities of a large resort. It encompasses four different buildings, two adjacent swimming pools, and a three-stage waterfall that cascades into a lily pond. Rooms have stunning, plush decor. **The Grand,** 1116 Grinnell St., between Virginia and Catherine streets (© **888/947-2630** or 305/294-0590; www.thegrandguesthouse.com), is an exceptionally run guesthouse with almost anything you could want, including a very moderate price tag. It's a well-kept secret and the best bargain in town.

If you're having trouble finding a room, contact **Vacation Key West** (© **800/595-5397** or 305/295-9500; www.vacationkw.com), a wholesaler that offers discounts of 20% to 30% and is skilled at finding last-minute deals. It represents mostly larger hotels and motels. The phones are answered weekdays from 9am to 6pm and Saturday from 11am to 2pm.

Gay travelers will want to call the **Key West Business Guild** (© **305/294-4603**), which represents more than 50 guesthouses and B&Bs in town, as well as many other gay-owned businesses. Be advised that most gay guesthouses have a clothing-optional policy. One of the most elegant and popular ones is **Big Ruby's,** at 409 Applerouth Lane, a little alley just off Duval Street (© **800/477-7829** or 305/296-2323). Rates start at $147 for a double during peak season and $102 during the off season. A low cluster of buildings surrounds a lushly landscaped courtyard where a hearty breakfast is served each morning and wine is poured at dusk. The mostly male guests hang out by a good-size pool, tanning in the buff. Also popular is **Oasis** at 823 Fleming St. (© **305/296-2131**), which is superclean and friendly, with a central location and a 14-seat hot tub. Rates are $169 to $229 in winter and $109 to $169 in summer.

KEY WEST AFTER DARK

Duval Street is the Bourbon Street of Florida. Amid the T-shirt shops and clothing boutiques, you'll find bar after bar serving neon-colored frozen drinks to revelers who bounce from one to the next from noon until dawn. Your best bet is to start at Truman Avenue and head up Duval to check them out for yourself. Cover charges are rare except in gay clubs, so stop into a dozen and see which you like.

Just around the corner from Duval's beaten path, **Captain Tony's Saloon,** 428 Greene St. (© **305/294-1838**), is a smoky old wooden bar, about as authentic as you'll find. **Durty Harry's,** 208 Duval St. (© **305/296-4890**), is a large entertainment complex that features live rock bands almost every night. You can wander to one of the many outdoor bars or head to Upstairs at Rick's, an indoor/outdoor dance club that gets going late. For the more racy singles or couples, there is also the Red Garter, a pocket-size strip club.

You'll have to stop into **Sloppy Joe's,** 201 Duval St. (© **305/294-5717;** www. sloppyjoes.com), just to say you did. Scholars and drunks debate whether this is the same Sloppy Joe's that Hemingway wrote about, but there's no argument that this classic bar's turn-of-the-20th-century wooden ceiling and cracked tile floors are Key West originals. There's live music most days and nights.

The best music and dancing can be found at the predominantly gay clubs. None of the spots mentioned here discriminate—anyone open-minded and fun is welcome. Cover varies, but is rarely more than $10. Two adjacent popular late-night spots are the **801 Bourbon Bar/Number One Saloon,** 801 Duval St. and 514 Petronia St. (© **305/294-9349** for both), featuring great drag and lots more disco. A mostly male clientele frequents this hot spot from 9pm until 4am. Another Duval Street favorite is **Aqua,** at 711 Duval St. (© **305/292-8500**), where you might catch drag queens belting out torch songs or judges voting on the best package in the wet jockey shorts contest. Better known around town as La-Te-Da, **La Terraza de Martí,** the former Key West home of Cuban exile José Martí, at 1125 Duval St. (© **305/296-6706**), is a great spot to gather poolside for the best martini in town—but don't bother with the food.

7 Tampa & St. Petersburg

Sitting on a large estuary midway down Florida's west coast, the city of Tampa is probably most renowned for Busch Gardens Tampa Bay, but there's so much more to it than a theme park. You can also see the sea life at The Florida Aquarium, stroll through the ornate, Moorish-style Henry B. Plant Museum, and experience exciting dining and nightlife in Ybor City, Tampa's historic Cuban enclave. Across the bay, St. Petersburg has one of the most picturesque and pleasant downtowns of any city in Florida, with a waterfront promenade, a famous pyramid-shaped pier, quality museums, interesting shops, and good restaurants. You'll find plenty of sun and sand on the 28 miles of slim barrier islands that skirt the gulf shore here. St. Pete Beach and Clearwater Beach are typical beach resort towns with towering hotels and condos, but this area also has protected some of the nation's finest beaches from development. From here, you can take a side trip south across the bay to affluent Sarasota, one of Florida's cultural centers.

Tampa, St. Petersburg, and the beaches are about 30- to 45-minute drives apart (longer in rush-hour traffic), so you should carefully plan your time here. Unless you're on business and need quick access to Tampa or downtown St. Petersburg, you may want to stay at the beaches.

Tampa & St. Petersburg

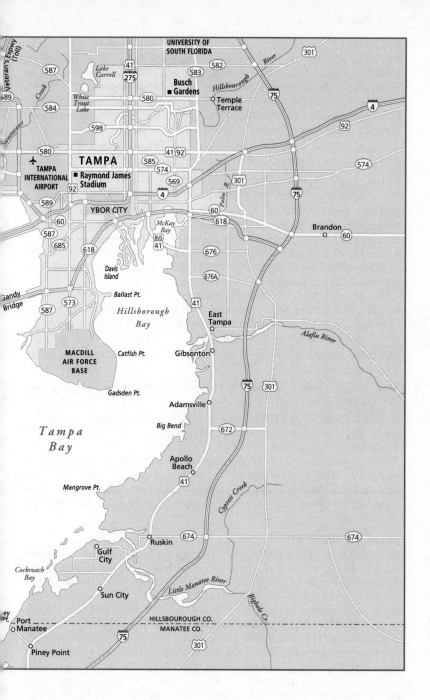

ESSENTIALS

GETTING THERE **By Plane** **Tampa International Airport** (© 813/870-8770; www.tampaairport.com), 5 miles northwest of downtown Tampa, is serviced by most major airlines. **St. Petersburg–Clearwater International Airport** (© 727/453-7800; www.fly2pie.com), on the western side of the bay, offers limited service. **The Limo/SuperShuttle** (© 800/282-6817 or 727/527-1111; www.supershuttle.com) operates van service between the airport and hotels throughout the Tampa Bay area.

By Train Amtrak trains arrive downtown at the **Tampa Amtrak Station,** 601 Nebraska Ave. N. (© **800/USA-RAIL;** www.amtrak.com).

By Car Major routes into Tampa are **I-75** from the north (Atlanta) and south (Fort Myers and Miami), and **I-4** from the east (Orlando).

VISITOR INFORMATION Contact the **Tampa Bay Convention & Visitors Bureau,** 400 N. Tampa St., Tampa, FL 33602-4706 (© **800/448-2672,** 800/368-2672, or 813/223-2752; www.visittampabay.com), for advance information. If you're downtown, you can head to the bureau's **visitor information center** at 400 N. Tampa St. (Channelside), Suite 2800 (© **813/223-1111**). It's open Monday through Saturday from 9:30am to 5:30pm.

For advance information about St. Petersburg and the beaches, contact the **St. Petersburg/Clearwater Area Convention & Visitors Bureau,** 14450 46th St. N., Clearwater, FL 34622 (© **800/345-6710,** or 727/464-7200 for hotel reservations; www.floridasbeach.com for information specific to the beaches).

GETTING AROUND You really need a car here. All major rental agencies have desks at the Tampa airport.

FAST FACTS **Tampa General Hospital,** 2 Columbia Dr. (© **813/251-7000;** www.tgh.org), offers 24-hour emergency service.

SPECIAL EVENTS & FESTIVALS In early February, hundreds of boats and rowdy "pirates" invade downtown Tampa during the **Gasparilla Pirate Fest** (© 813/353-8108; www.gasparillapiratefest.com). In mid-February, the **Florida State Fair** in Tampa displays the best of the state's agriculture and crafts (© **800/345-FAIR;** www.floridastatefair.com); it celebrated its 100th anniversary in 2004. Held on the last Saturday in October, Ybor City's Latin-style Halloween celebration **Guavaween** begins with the "Mama Guava Stumble," a wacky costume parade (© **813/248-0721;** www.ybor.org).

WHAT TO SEE & DO

Busch Gardens Tampa Bay *Best* *Kids* Although its heart-stopping thrill rides get much of the ink, this venerable theme park (it predates Disney World) ranks among the largest zoos in the country. It's a don't-miss attraction for children and adults, who can see, in person, all those wild beasts they've watched on the *Animal Planet*—and they'll get better views of them here than at Disney's Animal Kingdom in Orlando (p. 341). Busch Gardens has several thousand animals living in naturalistic environments that help carry out the park's overall African theme. Most authentic is the 80-acre plain, strongly reminiscent of the real Serengeti of Tanzania and Kenya, upon which zebras, giraffes, and other animals graze. Unlike the animals on the real Serengeti, however, the grazing animals have nothing to fear from lions, hyenas, crocodiles, and other predators, which are confined to enclosures—as are hippos and elephants. The park's sixth roller coaster, SheiKra, is the nation's first dive coaster that

(*Value* **Discounts for Busch Gardens**

You can save a few dollars and avoid waiting in long lines by buying your tickets to Busch Gardens Tampa Bay at the privately owned **Tampa Bay Visitors Information Center,** opposite the park at 3601 E. Busch Blvd., at North Ednam Place (© **813/985-3601;** www.hometown.aol.com\tpabayinfoctr). Owner Jim Boggs worked for the park for 13 years and gives expert advice on how to get the most out of your visit. He sells slightly discounted tickets to Busch Gardens, Adventure Island, and other attractions (buying here will also save you from standing in line to buy tickets at the parks), and he will book hotel rooms and car rentals for you, often at a discount. The center is open Monday through Saturday from 10am to 5:30pm, Sunday from 10am to 2pm, except Christmas.

Also, if you're going to Orlando, Busch Gardens Tampa Bay is included in the five-park version of the **FlexTicket,** a 14-day pass that also gives admission to Universal Studios Florida, SeaWorld, Islands of Adventure, and Wet 'n Wild for $235 for adults and $200 for children 3 to 9.

carries riders up 200 feet at 45 degrees and then hurtles them 70 mph back at a 45-degree angle. Yikes.

The park has eight areas, each of which has its own theme, animals, live entertainment, thrill rides, kiddie attractions, dining, and shopping. A Skyride cable car soars over the park, offering a bird's-eye view of it all. Turn left after the main gate and head to **Morocco,** a walled city with exotic architecture, crafts demonstrations, a sultan's tent with snake charmers, and an exhibit featuring alligators and turtles. The Moorish-style Moroccan Palace Theater features an ice show, which many families consider to be the park's best entertainment for both adults and children. Here you can also attend a song-and-dance show in the Marrakech Theater.

After watching the snake charmers, walk eastward past Anheuser-Busch's fabled Clydesdale horses to **Egypt,** where you can visit King Tut's tomb with its replicas of the real treasures and listen to comedian Martin Short narrate "Akbar's Adventure Tours," a wacky simulator that "transports" one and all across Egypt via camel, biplane, and mine car. The whole room moves on this ride, which lasts only 5 minutes—much less time than the usual wait to get inside. Youngsters can dig for their own ancient treasures in a sand area. Thrill-seekers can ride Montu, the tallest and longest inverted roller coaster in the world with seven upside-down loops. Your feet dangle loose on Montu, so make sure your shoes are tied tightly and your lunch has had time to digest.

From Egypt, walk to the **Edge of Africa,** the most unique of the park's eight areas, and the home of most of the large animals. Next stop is **Nairobi,** the most beautiful part of the park, where you can see gorillas and chimpanzees in the Myombe Reserve in a lush area that replicates their natural rainforest habitat. Nairobi also has a baby animal nursery, a petting zoo, turtle and reptile displays, an elephant exhibit (alas, the magnificent creatures seem to be bored to the point of madness), and Curiosity Caverns, where bats, reptiles, and small mammals that are active in the dark are kept in cages (it's the most traditional zoolike area here). The entry to Rhino Rally, the park's safari adventure, is at the western end of Nairobi.

Next, head to **The Congo,** highlighted by rare white Bengal tigers that live on Claw Island. The Congo is also home to two roller coasters: Kumba, the largest and fastest roller coaster in the southeastern United States; and The Python, which twists and turns for 1,200 feet. You will get drenched—and refreshed on a hot day—by riding the Congo River Rapids, where you're turned loose in round boats that float down the swiftly flowing "river." There are bumper cars and kiddie rides here, too.

From The Congo, walk south into **Stanleyville,** a prototype African village, with a shopping bazaar, orangutans living on an island, and the Stanleyville Theater, usually featuring shows for children. Two more water rides are here: the Tanganyika Tidal Wave, where you'll come to a very damp end; and the Stanley Falls Flume (an aquatic version of a roller coaster). Also, the picnic-style Stanleyville Smokehouse serves ribs and chicken that are among the best chow in the park.

Up next is **Land of the Dragons,** the most entertaining area for small children. They can spend an entire day enjoying a variety of play elements in a fairy-tale setting, plus just-for-kids rides. The area is dominated by Dumphrey, a whimsical dragon who interacts with visitors and guides children around a three-story treehouse with winding stairways, tall towers, steppingstones, illuminated water geysers, and an echo chamber.

The next stop is **Bird Gardens,** the park's original core, offering rich foliage, lagoons, and a free-flight aviary for hundreds of exotic birds, including American bald eagles. Be sure to see the Florida flamingos and Australian koalas.

Then you're off to take a break at the **Hospitality House,** which offers entertainment and free samples of Anheuser-Busch's famous beers. You must be 21 to imbibe (there's a limit of two free mugs), but soft drinks are also available.

If your stomach can take another hair-raising ride, try **Gwazi** (48-in. minimum), an adrenaline-pumping attraction where a pair of old-fashioned wooden roller coasters (named the Lion and the Tiger) start simultaneously and whiz within a few feet of each other six times as they roar along at 50 mph and rise to 90 feet. In Gwazi's "Water Wars," participants shoot water-filled balloons at each other with big slingshots. It's a soaking way to end your visit.

If you want to experience the park's fifth and final roller coaster, head to **Timbuktu** and climb aboard the **Scorpion,** a high-speed number with a 60-foot drop and 360-degree loop.

Recently added attractions include a 4-D multisensory R. L. Stine film in a new theater.

3000 E. Busch Blvd. (at McKinley Dr./N. 40th St.). © **888/800-5447** or 813/987-5283. www.buschgardens.com. **Note:** Admission and hours vary, so call ahead, check website, or get brochure at visitor centers. Admission single-day ticket $58 adults, $48 children 3–9, plus tax; free for children 2 and under. Daily 10am–6pm (extended hours to 7 and 8pm in summer and on holidays).

The Florida Aquarium (Kids   See more than 5,000 aquatic animals and plants that call Florida home at this entertaining and informative aquarium. Most impressive is a 43-foot-wide, 14-foot-tall panoramic window that lets you look out at schools of fish and lots of sharks and stingrays. Also worth visiting are the "Explore a Shore" playground to educate the kids, a deepwater exhibit, and a tank housing moray eels.

701 Channelside Dr. © 813/273-4000. www.flaquarium.net. Admission $18 adults, $15 seniors, $12 children 3–11, free for children under 3. Website sometimes offers discounts. Parking $5. Daily 9:30am–5pm. Dolphin Quest Mon–Fri 2pm; Sat–Sun 1 and 3pm. Eco Tour daily 2 and 4pm, plus Sat noon. Closed Thanksgiving and Christmas.

Henry B. Plant Museum Built as a hotel in 1891 by railroad tycoon Henry B. Plant, this ornate structure with 13 silver minarets and distinctive Moorish architecture is a National Historic Landmark and worth a visit. It's filled with art and furnishings from Europe and Asia; and exhibits that explain the hotel's role as a staging point for Teddy Roosevelt's Rough Riders during the Spanish-American War.

401 W. Kennedy Blvd. (between Hyde Park and Magnolia aves.). ℰ 813/254-1891. www.plantmuseum.com. Free admission; suggested donation $5 adults, $2 children 12 and under. Tues–Sat 10am–4pm; Sun noon–4pm. Closed Thanksgiving, Christmas Eve, and Christmas Day.

Museum of Fine Arts Resembling a Mediterranean villa on the waterfront, this museum houses a permanent collection of European, American, pre-Columbian, and Far Eastern art, with works by such artists as Fragonard, Monet, Renoir, and Gauguin. Other highlights include period rooms with antiques and historical furnishings, plus a gallery of Steuben crystal, a decorative-arts gallery, and world-class rotating exhibits. The best way to see it all is on a guided tour, which takes about 1 hour.

255 Beach Dr. NE (at 3rd Ave. N.). ℰ 727/896-2667. www.fine-arts.org. Admission $8 adults, $7 seniors 65 and over, $4 students with ID, free for children under 6 (special exhibits cost extra). Admission includes guided tour. Tues–Sat 10am–5pm; Sun 1–5pm. Guided tours Tues–Sat 11am and 1, 2, and 3pm; Sun 1 and 2pm. Closed New Year's Day, Martin Luther King, Jr., Day, Thanksgiving, and Christmas.

MOSI (Museum of Science and Industry) *Kids* A great place to take the kids, MOSI is the largest science center in the Southeast, with more than 450 interactive exhibits. Step into the Gulf Hurricane to experience 74-mph winds, explore the human body in "The Amazing You," and, if your heart is up to it, ride a bicycle across a 98-foot-long cable suspended 30 feet above the lobby (don't worry: you'll be harnessed to the bike). You can also watch stunning movies in Florida's first IMAX dome theater. Outside, trails wind through a nature preserve with a butterfly garden.

4801 E. Fowler Ave. (at N. 50th St.). ℰ 813/987-6100. www.mosi.org. Admission $20 adults, $18 seniors, $16 children 2–12, free for children under 2. Admission includes IMAX movies. Daily 9am–5pm or later.

The Pier *Kids* The Pier is a festive waterfront dining-and-shopping complex overlooking Tampa Bay. Originally built as a railroad pier in 1889, today it's capped by a spaceshiplike inverted pyramid offering five levels of shops, three restaurants, a tourist information desk, an observation deck, catwalks for fishing, boat docks, miniature golf, boat and watersports rentals, sightseeing boats, and a food court, plus an aquarium. Cruise boats often operate from The Pier during the winter months, and you can rent fishing gear and drop your line into the bay year-round. There's valet parking at the end of the pier, or you can park on land and ride a free trolley out to the complex.

800 2nd Ave. NE. ℰ 727/821-6443. www.stpete-pier.com. Free admission to all public areas and decks; donations welcome at the Pier Aquarium. Valet parking $6; self-parking $3. Pier Mon–Thurs 10am–9pm; Fri–Sat 10am–10pm; Sun 11am–7pm. Aquarium Mon–Sat 10am–8pm; Sun 11am–6pm.

Salvador Dalí Museum This starkly modern museum houses the world's largest collection of works by the renowned Spanish surrealist, including 94 oil paintings, more than 100 watercolors and drawings, and 1,300 graphics, plus posters, photos, sculptures, objets d'art, and a 5,000-volume library on Dalí and surrealism. Make sure to take one of the free docent-led tours to get the most out of the museum and its artwork.

1000 3rd St. S. (near 11th Ave. S.). ℰ 727/823-3767. www.salvadordalimuseum.org. Admission $15 adults, $14 seniors, $10 students, $4 children 5–9, free for children 4 and under; Thurs 5–8pm $5 for all. Mon–Wed and Fri–Sat 9:30am–5:30pm; Thurs 9:30am–8pm; Sun noon–5:30pm. Closed Thanksgiving and Christmas.

FUN ON & OFF THE BEACH

This entire stretch of coast is one long beach, but since hotels, condos, and private homes line much of it, you may want to sun and swim at one of the area's public parks. The best is **Caladesi Island State Park,** which boasts one of Florida's top beaches, a lovely, relatively secluded stretch with fine soft sand edged in sea grass and palmettos. You can get here by ferry from **Honeymoon Island State Recreation Area.** The two parks are open daily from 8am to sunset and are administered by Gulf Islands Geopark, 1 Causeway Blvd., Dunedin, FL 34698 (© **727/469-5918;** www.florida stateparks.org/caladesiisland and www.floridastateparks.org/honeymoonisland).

At the very mouth of Tampa Bay, **Fort DeSoto Park** (© **727/582-2267;** www.fort desoto.com) has a stunning white-sugar sand beach, a Spanish-American War–era fort, great fishing from piers, large playgrounds for kids, and 4 miles of trails winding through the park for in-line skaters, bicyclists, and joggers. The park's 230 gorgeous, bayside campsites usually are sold out, especially on weekends.

You can indulge in parasailing, boating, cruises, deep-sea fishing, wave running, sightseeing, dolphin watching, water-skiing, and just about any other waterborne diversion your heart could desire here. All you have to do is head to one of two beach locations: **Hubbard's Marina,** at John's Pass Village and Boardwalk (© **800/755-0677** or 727/393-1947; www.hubbardsmarina.com), in Madeira Beach on the southern tip of Sand Key; or **Clearwater Beach Marina,** at Coronado Drive and Causeway Boulevard (© **800/772-4479** or 727/461-3133), at the beach end of the causeway leading to downtown Clearwater. Agents in booths there will give you the schedules and prices, answer any questions you have, and make reservations if necessary. Expect to pay $35 to $45 for a half-day of fishing on a large party boat, $65 to $70 for a full day.

The Tampa Bay area has a wide range of golf courses, with greens fees ranging from about $30 to more than $100. Contact the tourist information offices for complete lists (see "Visitor Information," above). Call **Tee Times USA** (© **800/374-8633;** www.teetimesusa.com) to reserve times at all area courses. **The Westin Innisbrook Resort,** 36750 U.S. 19 (P.O. Box 1088), Tarpon Springs, FL 34688 (© **877/752-1480** or 727/942-2000; www.westin-innisbrook.com), is one of the country's best places to play (some golf magazines rank its Copperhead course, former home of the annual JCPenney Classic, as number one in Florida). St. Petersburg's **Mangrove Bay Golf Course,** 875 62nd Ave. NE (© **727/893-7800**), is one of the nation's top 50 municipal courses. To learn or sharpen your game, the **Arnold Palmer Golf Academy World Headquarters** is at Saddlebrook Resort, 5700 Saddlebrook Way, Wesley Chapel, 12 miles north of Tampa (© **800/729-8383** or 813/973-1111; www.saddle brookresort.com), though you'll have to stay at the resort in order to play.

SHOPPING

A terrific alternative to cookie-cutter suburban malls, Tampa's **Old Hyde Park Village,** 1507 W. Swann Ave., at South Dakota Avenue (© **813/251-3500;** www. oldhydeparkvillage.com), in a picturesque Victorian neighborhood, is a cluster of 50 upscale shops and boutiques, including some of the mall regulars. Tampa's Ybor City no longer is a major producer of hand-rolled cigars, but you can watch artisans making stogies at the **Gonzales y Martinez Cigar Factory,** 2025 7th Ave. (© **813/247-2469**), in The Columbia restaurant building. Gonzalez and Martinez are recent arrivals from Cuba and don't speak English, but the staff does at the adjoining **Columbia Cigar Store** (it's best to enter here). Rollers are on duty Monday through Saturday from 10am to 6pm.

In St. Petersburg, **Beach Drive** along the waterfront is the most fashionable downtown strolling and shopping venue. Be sure to check out the **Glass Canvas Gallery,** at 4th Avenue NE (© **727/821-6767**); and **Red Cloud** (© **727/821-5824**), an oasis for Native American crafts. Central Avenue is another shopping area, featuring the **Gas Plant Antique Arcade,** between 12th and 13th streets (© **727/895-0368**), the largest antiques mall on Florida's west coast, with more than 100 dealers displaying their wares.

WHERE TO STAY

Most vacationers elect to stay at the beaches and drive into Tampa and St. Petersburg to see the sights. If you're going to Busch Gardens, the nearest chain motel to the park is the **Safari Lodge at Busch Gardens Maingate,** 4139 E. Busch Blvd. (© **813/988-9191**), a motor lodge with very cheap rooms. A bit farther away, the 500-room **Embassy Suites Hotel and Conference Center,** 3705 Spectrum Blvd., facing Fowler Avenue (© **800/362-2779** or 813/977-7066), is the plushest and most expensive establishment near the park. Almost across the avenue stands **LaQuinta Inn & Suites,** 3701 E. Fowler Ave. (© **800/687-6667** or 813/910-7500). Just south of Fowler Avenue are side-by-side branches of **AmeriSuites,** 11408 N. 30th St. (© **800/833-1516** or 813/979-1922), and **DoubleTree Guest Suites,** 11310 N. 30th St. (© **800/222-8733** or 813/971-7690).

In downtown Tampa, the **Hyatt Regency Tampa,** 2 Tampa City Center (© **800/233-1234** or 813/225-1234; www.hyatt.com); the **Sheraton Tampa Riverwalk Hotel,** 200 N. Ashley St. (© **800/333-3333** or 813/223-2222; www.tampariverwalkhotel.com); and the **Tampa Marriott Waterside Hotel & Marina,** 710 N. Florida Ave. (© **800/228-9290** or 813/221-4900; www.marriott.com), all cater primarily to the corporate crowd.

St. Pete Beach and Clearwater Beach have national chain hotels and motels of every name and description. The **St. Petersburg/Clearwater Area Convention & Visitors Bureau** operates a free **reservations service** (© **800/345-6710**), through which you can book rooms at most hotels and motels in St. Petersburg and at the beaches.

Best Western All Suites Hotel *Value*   Enclosing a lush tropical courtyard with heated pool, hot tub, covered games area, and lively Tiki bar offering inexpensive barbecue, this all-suite hotel is the most beachlike vacation venue close to Busch Gardens. Great for kids, 11 "family suites" have bunk beds in one bedroom. All rooms have refrigerators. The bar can get noisy before closing, and ground-level units are musty, so ask for an upstairs suite away from the action.

Behind Busch Gardens, 3001 University Center Dr. (faces N. 30th St. between Busch Blvd. and Fowler Ave.), Tampa, FL 33612. (© **800/786-7446** or 813/971-8930. Fax 813/971-8935. www.thatparrotplace.com. 150 units. Winter $99–$159 suite for 2; off season $79–$99 suite for 2. Rates include hot and cold breakfast buffet. AE, DC, DISC, MC, V. **Amenities:** Restaurant; heated pool. *In room:* Fridge.

Don CeSar Beach Resort & Spa *Kids*   Dating from 1928, this romantic Moorish-style "Pink Palace"—listed on the National Register of Historic Places—ap[...] wide range of clientele, from groups to families to honeymooning couples. E[...] renovated in 2000, some of the 275 rooms under the minarets of the origi[...] ing may seem rather small by today's standards, but they have high window[...]

views of the gulf or Boca Ciega Bay. Some but not all of them have balconies. If you want more room but less charm, the resort has 70 spacious luxury condominiums in The Don CeSar Beach House, a mid-rise building ¾ mile to the north (there's 24-hr. complimentary transportation between the two). An excellent kids' program features supervised activities such as nighttime pizza parties and T-shirt decorating.

3400 Gulf Blvd. (at 34th Ave./Pinellas Byway), St. Pete Beach, FL 33706. © **866/728-2206** or 727/360-1881. Fax 727/367-6952. www.doncesar.com. 347 units. Winter $179–$428 double, $334–$1,731 suite; off season $209–$350 double, $269–$1,445 suite. $10 per person per day resort fee. Packages available. AE, DC, DISC, MC, V. Valet parking $10; free self-parking. **Amenities:** 4 restaurants; 2 heated pools; exercise room; spa.

The Heritage Holiday Inn
No ordinary Holiday Inn, the Heritage dates from the early 1920s, and although significantly updated, it retains the ambience of an old-fashioned hotel, with tall double-hung windows and hardwood floors that creak as you walk down the long central hallway. A lovely sweeping veranda, French doors, and a tropical courtyard help attract an eclectic clientele, from business travelers to seniors. The furnishings include period antiques. Some one-bedroom suites have sofa beds and two bathrooms.

234 3rd Ave. N. (between 2nd and 3rd sts.), St. Petersburg, FL 33701. © **800/283-7829** or 727/822-4814. Fax 727/823-1644. www.ichotelsgroup.com. 71 units. $100–$150 double. AE, DC, DISC, MC, V. **Amenities:** Restaurant; heated pool.

Hilton Garden Inn
This modern, four-story hotel stands just 2 blocks north of the heart of Ybor City's dining and entertainment district. A one-story brick structure in front houses the bright lobby, a comfy relaxation area with fireplace, and a small pantry selling beer, wine, soft drinks, and frozen dinners. You can heat up the dinners in your comfortable guest room's microwave oven or store them in your fridge. If you opt for a suite, you'll have a separate living room and a larger bathroom than in the regular units.

1700 E. 9th Ave. (between 17th and 18th sts.), Tampa, FL 33605. © **800/445-8667** or 813/769-9267. Fax 813/769-3299. www.hiltongardeninn.com. 95 units. $119–$289 double. AE, DC, DISC, MC, V. **Amenities:** Restaurant (breakfast only); heated pool; exercise room. *In room:* Fridge, microwave.

Island's End Resort *(Value*
A wonderful respite, and a great bargain to boot, this little all-cottage hideaway sits right on the southern tip of St. Pete Beach. You can step from the six contemporary cottages right onto the beach. And since the island curves sharply here, nothing blocks your view of the emerald bay. Linked by boardwalks, the comfortable one- or three-bedroom cottages have dining areas, living rooms, VCRs, and kitchens; the one three-bedroom unit has its own private beachside pool.

1 Pass-a-Grille Way (at 1st Ave.), St. Pete Beach, FL 33706. © **727/360-5023.** Fax 727/367-7890. www.islandsend.com. 6 units. Winter $155–$280 cottage; off season $125–$280 cottage. Weekly rates available. Complimentary breakfast served Tues, Thurs, and Sat. MC, V. *In room:* Kitchen.

Renaissance Vinoy Resort and Golf Club *(Best*
For the swankiest digs in the area, the Renaissance Vinoy is it. Built as the grand Vinoy Park in 1925, this elegant Spanish-style establishment has hosted everyone from Jimmy Stewart to Bill Clinton; it reopened in 1992 and landed on the National Register of Historic Places after a meticulous $93-million restoration that has made it the city's finest hotel. All the guest rooms, many of which enjoy lovely views of the bay front, offer the utmost in comfort and elegance. Some rooms in the original building have standing-room-only balconies; so if you need enough room to sit outside, request a balconied unit in the new ˜wer wing (some of these have whirlpool tubs, too).

501 5th Ave. NE (at Beach Dr.), St. Petersburg, FL 33701. ✆ 800/468-3571 or 727/894-1000. Fax 727/822-2785. www.renaissancehotels.com. 360 units. Winter $209–$429 double; off season $169–$369 double. Packages available. AE, DC, DISC, MC, V. Valet parking $13; self-parking $9. **Amenities:** 4 restaurants; 2 heated pools (connected by a waterfall); golf course; 12 tennis courts; health club; spa.

Saddlebrook Resort—Tampa *(Kids)*   Set on 480 acres, 30 minutes north of Tampa International Airport, this condominium development—renowned for its tennis and golf offerings—boasts two 18-hole championship golf courses and 45 tennis courts (hone your skills here at the Arnold Palmer Golf Academy or the Hopman Tennis Program), a 270-foot-long swimming pool, and a 7,000-square-foot luxury spa. Much more appealing than the standard rooms (all renovated to the tune of $8.5 million in 2005), the suites have kitchens and a patio or balcony overlooking lagoons and cypress and palm trees. There's an excellent kids' club with supervised, theme-oriented activities.

5700 Saddlebrook Way, Wesley Chapel, FL 33543. ✆ 800/729-8383 or 813/973-1111. Fax 813/973-4504. www. saddlebrookresort.com. 800 units. Winter $242–$402 per person; off season $147–$234 per person. Rates include breakfast and dinner. Packages available. AE, DC, DISC, MC, V. Valet parking $10 overnight; free self-parking. **Amenities:** 3 restaurants; heated pool; 2 golf courses; 45 grass, clay, and hard tennis courts; health club; spa. *In room:* Kitchen (suites only), fridge.

Safety Harbor Resort and Spa *(Value)*   You are in for some serious pampering at this venerable spa, a sprawling complex on 22 bayfront acres in Safety Harbor, a moss-draped town north of St. Petersburg. You may not recover your youth at this venerable spa, which has been in operation since 1926, but you will be rejuvenated by such services as massage, hydrotherapy, and a full menu of fitness classes, from boxing to yoga. Mineral springs enable the spa to offer acclaimed water-fitness programs. This is also a good place to work on your games at the Quinzi Golf Academy and the Phil Green Tennis Academy. The lush grounds make up for what the old-fogy-style rooms lack. Given the reasonable off-season room rates and special packages available, this is one of Florida's better spa values.

105 N. Bayshore Dr., Safety Harbor, FL 34695. ✆ 888/237-8772 or 727/726-1161. Fax 727/724-7749. www.safety harborspa.com. 189 units. Winter $205–$235 double; off season $129–$205 double; year-round from $325 suite. Packages available. AE, DC, DISC, MC, V. Valet parking $12; free self-parking. Pets accepted ($35 per night). **Amenities:** 2 restaurants; heated indoor and outdoor pools; golf course; 9 tennis courts; full-service spa.

Sheraton Sand Key Resort   Away from the honky-tonk of Clearwater, this nine-story Spanish-look hotel on 10 acres next to Sand Key Park is a big favorite with watersports enthusiasts and groups. It's only a 150-yard walk across the broad beach in front of the hotel to the water's edge. The moderately spacious guest rooms here all have traditional dark-wood furniture and balconies or patios with views of the gulf or the bay. The fitness center is on the top floor, rendering great workout views.

1160 Gulf Blvd., Clearwater Beach, FL 33767. ✆ 800/325-3535 or 727/595-1611. Fax 727/596-1117. www. sheratonsandkey.com. 390 units. Winter $165–$336 double; off season $165–$259 double. AE, DC, DISC, MC, V. **Amenities:** 2 restaurants; heated pool; 3 tennis courts; exercise room.

The Westin Innisbrook Resort   *Golf Digest, Golf,* and other magazines pick this as one of the country's best places to play (provided you stay here, of course). This 1,000-acre, all-condominium resort has 90 holes on championship courses (more challenging than those at the Saddlebrook), including the famed **Copperhead course.** If you want to learn, Innisbrook has the largest resort-owned and -operated golf school in North America, and it boasts a tennis center with instruction, too. A free shuttle runs around the property, and another goes to the beach three times a day. Ranging in size from suites to two-bedroom models, the quarters are privately owned condos spread all over the premises. The focal points are the golf and tennis clubhouses, all of which have restaurants and bars: This place is not for serious beachgoers.

36750 U.S. 19 N., Palm Harbor, FL 34684. ℂ **877/752-1480** or 727/942-2000. Fax 727/942-5576. www.westin-innisbrook.com. 700 units. Winter $229–$485 suite; off season $145–$289 suite. Golf packages available. AE, DC, DISC, MC, V. **Amenities:** 7 restaurants; 6 heated pools; 4 golf courses; 15 tennis courts; health club. *In room:* Kitchen.

WHERE TO DINE

Don't overlook the food court at St. Petersburg's **The Pier,** where the inexpensive chow is accompanied by a rich, but quite free, view of the bay. You can take a shopping break at **Old Hyde Park Village**'s trendy sidewalk bistros (see "Shopping," above).

Bella's Italian Cafe *Value* ITALIAN   Creative dishes and very reasonable prices make this sophisticated yet informal cafe one of the city's most popular neighborhood hangouts. Although you can order the wood-fired pizzas and homemade pasta under traditional Bolognese or Alfredo sauces, the stars here feature the tasty likes of blackened chicken in a creamy tomato sauce over fettuccine. Finish with the house version of tiramisu. Local professionals flock to the friendly bar during two-for-one happy hours nightly from 4 to 7pm and from 11pm until closing. The open kitchen provides only appetizers, salads, pizzas, and desserts after 11pm.

1413 S. Howard Ave. (at Mississippi Ave.). 813/254-3355. www.bellasitaliancafe.com Reservations not accepted. Main courses $12–$20; pizza $7–$10. AE, DC, DISC, MC, V. Mon–Tues 11:30am–11:30pm; Wed–Thurs 11:30am–12:30am; Fri 11am–1:30am; Sat 4pm–1:30am; Sun 4–11:30pm.

Bern's Steak House STEAKHOUSE   This famous steakhouse has eight ornate dining rooms with themes such as Rhone, Burgundy, and Irish Rebellion. They set an appropriately dark atmosphere for huge charcoal-grilled steaks (beef or buffalo). The phone book–size wine list—one of the restaurant's most famous attributes—offers more than 7,000 selections, with many available by the glass. The big surprise here is the dessert quarters upstairs, where 50 romantic booths can privately seat from 2 to 12 guests, who can select from a dessert menu offering almost 100 delicious selections and 1,400 after-dinner drinks.

1208 S. Howard Ave. (at Marjory Ave.). ℂ 813/251-2421. www.bernssteakhouse.com. Reservations recommended. Main courses $17–$59; sandwiches $9–$12. AE, DC, DISC, MC, V. Daily 5–11pm. Closed Christmas. Valet parking $5.

Carmine's Restaurant & Bar CUBAN/ITALIAN/AMERICAN   A great variety of loyal local patrons gather at this noisy corner cafe, one of Ybor's most popular hangouts, for genuine Cuban sandwiches—smoked ham, roast pork, Genoa salami, Swiss cheese, pickles, salad dressing, mustard, lettuce, and tomato on a crispy submarine roll. There's a vegetarian version, too, and the combination half sandwich and a choice of black beans and rice or a bowl of Spanish soup makes a hearty meal.

1802 E. 7th Ave. (at 18th St.). ℂ 813/248-3834. Reservations not accepted. Main courses $7–$17; sandwiches $4–$8. No credit cards. Mon–Tues 11am–11pm; Wed–Thurs 11am–1am; Fri–Sat 11am–3am; Sun 11am–6pm.

Chateau France CLASSICAL FRENCH   Chef Antoine Louro provides St. Petersburg's finest cuisine and most romantic setting in this charming pink Victorian house built in 1910. He specializes in French classics such as homemade pâté, Dover sole meunière, filet mignon au poivre, coq au vin, orange duck, and a rich seafood bouillabaisse. Fresh baby vegetables, Gruyère-cheese potatoes, and Antoine's special Eiffel

Tower salad accompany all main courses. The wine list is excellent, as are the bananas flambé and crêpes Suzette.

136 4th Ave. N. (between Bayshore Dr. and 1st St. N.). © 727/894-7163. Reservations recommended. Main courses $20–$38. AE, DC, DISC, MC, V. Daily 5–11pm.

Columbia *Best* SPANISH   Tourists flock to this famous hand-painted tile building, which celebrated its 100th anniversary in 2005. Here you can soak up Ybor City's Latin ambience and clap along during fire-belching Spanish flamenco floor shows Monday through Saturday at 7 and 9:30pm. You can't help coming back time after time for the famous Spanish bean soup and original "1905" salad. One of our favorites is *boliche* (eye of round stuffed with chorizo), accompanied by plantains and black beans and rice. All entrees come with a crispy hunk of Cuban bread with butter. Lighter appetites can choose from a limited menu of tapas.

2117 E. 7th Ave. (between 21st and 22nd sts.). © 813/248-4961. www.columbiarestaurant.com. Reservations recommended. Main courses $14–$28. AE, DC, DISC, MC, V. Mon–Thurs 11am–10pm; Fri–Sat 11am–11pm; Sun noon–9pm.

Fourth Street Shrimp Store *Value* SEAFOOD   If you're anywhere in the area, don't miss at least driving by to see the colorful, cartoonlike mural on the outside of this eclectic establishment just north of downtown. Inside, you'll pass a seafood market counter when you enter, from which comes the fresh namesake shrimp, the star here. You can also pick from grouper, clam strips, catfish, or oysters fried, broiled, or steamed, all served in heaping portions. This is the best and certainly the most interesting bargain in town.

1006 4th St. N. (at 10th Ave. N.). © 727/822-0325. Main courses $5–$14; sandwiches $2.50–$7. MC, V. Daily 11am–9pm.

Mise en Place ECLECTIC   This trendy and stylish bistro presents the freshest of ingredients, with a creative award-winning menu that changes daily. Main courses often include fascinating choices such as Creole-style mahimahi served with chili cheese grits and a ragout of black-eyed peas, andouille sausage, and rock shrimp.

In Grand Central Place, 442 W. Kennedy Blvd. (at S. Magnolia Ave., opposite the University of Tampa). © 813/254-5373. www.miseonline.com. Reservations recommended. Main courses $16–$35; tasting menu $53 with wine, $38 without. AE, DC, DISC, MC, V. Tues–Thurs 11:30am–2:30pm and 5:30–10pm; Fri 11:30am–2:30pm and 5:30–11pm; Sat 5–11pm.

The Salt Rock Grill SEAFOOD/STEAKS   Affluent professionals and other gorgeous folk make this high-powered waterfront restaurant *the* place to see and be seen on the beaches. In warm, fair weather you can dine out by the dock or slake your thirst at the lively Tiki bar (bands play out here on Sun during the summer). Anything from the wood-fired grill is excellent. Thick, aged steaks are the house specialties. Pan-seared peppered tuna and salmon cooked on a cedar board lead the seafood. You can avoid spending a fortune by showing up in time for the early-bird specials or by ordering the meatloaf topped with mashed potatoes and onion straws ($9) or the half-pound sirloin steak ($11).

19325 Gulf Blvd. (north of 193rd Ave.), Indian Shores. © 727/593-7625. www.saltrockgrill.com. Reservations strongly advised. Main courses $8–$40 (early-bird specials $8–$10). AE, DC, DISC, MC, V. Sun–Thurs 4–10pm; Fri–Sat 4–11pm (early-bird specials daily 4–5:30pm). Tiki bar open Sat 2pm–midnight (or later); Sun 2–10pm.

Ted Peters' Famous Smoked Fish *Value* SEAFOOD   This open-air eatery is an institution in these parts: Ted's has been around since the '50s. Some folks bring the fish they caught for the staff to smoke ($1.50 per pound); others figure fishing is a waste of time and come right to Ted's table for mullet, mackerel, salmon, and other fish slowly cooked over red oak. Enjoy the smell and sip a cold one while you wait for your order.

1530 Pasadena Ave. (just across St. Pete Beach Causeway), Pasadena. ℂ 727/381-7931. Main courses $8–$18. No credit cards. Wed–Mon 11am–7:30pm.

Wine Exchange MEDITERRANEAN   This Tampa hot spot is an oenophile's dream come true, in which each dish is paired with a particular wine available by the bottle or glass. While the menu is rather simple, featuring pizzas, pastas, salads, and sandwiches, the daily specials are more elaborate, including grilled Delmonico steak, blackened pork tenderloin, or Dijon-crusted salmon. The outdoor patio is a great place to sit, that is, if there's room. There's almost always a wait at this buzzworthy eatery.

1611 W. Swan Ave. ℂ 813/254-9463. Reservations not accepted. Main courses $10–$22. AE, DC, DISC, MC, V. Mon–Fri 11:30am–10pm; Sat 11am–11pm; Sun 11am–9pm; brunch Sat–Sun 11am–3pm.

TAMPA & ST. PETERSBURG AFTER DARK

The Tampa/Hillsborough Arts Council maintains an **Artsline** (ℂ 813/229-2787), a 24-hour information service providing the latest on current and upcoming cultural events. Racks in many restaurants and bars have copies of *Weekly Planet* (**www.weekly planet.com),** *Focus,* and *Accent on Tampa Bay,* three free publications detailing what's going on in the entire bay area. And you can also check the "Baylife" and "Friday Extra" sections of the *Tampa Tribune* (**www.tampatrib.com)** and the Thursday "Weekend" section of the *St. Petersburg Times* (**www.sptimes.com).**

THE PERFORMING ARTS   The four-theater **Tampa Bay Performing Arts Center,** 1010 N. MacInnes Place, next to the Tampa Museum of Art (ℂ 800/955-1045 or 813/229-7827; www.tampacenter.com), is the focal point of Tampa's performing-arts scene, presenting a wide range of Broadway plays, classical and pop concerts, operas, cabarets, improv, and special events. A sightseeing attraction in its own right, the restored **Tampa Theatre,** 711 Franklin St. (ℂ 813/274-8286; www. tampatheatre.org), between Zack and Polk streets, dates from 1926 and is on the National Register of Historic Places. It presents a varied program of classic, foreign, and alternative films, as well as concerts and special events.

THE CLUB & BAR SCENE   **Ybor City** is Tampa's favorite nighttime venue by far. All you have to do is stroll along 7th Avenue East between 15th and 20th streets to find a club or bar to your liking. The avenue is packed with people, a majority of them high schoolers and early-20-somethings, on Friday and Saturday from 9pm to 3am, but you'll also find something going on from Tuesday to Thursday and even on Sunday. You don't need addresses or phone numbers; your ears will guide you along 7th Avenue East. With all of the sidewalk seating, it's easy to judge what the clientele is like and make your choice from there.

In St. Petersburg, the Moorish-style **Coliseum Ballroom,** 535 4th Ave. N. (ℂ 727/892-5202; www.stpete.org/coliseum.htm), has been hosting dancing, big bands, boxing, and other events since 1924 (it even made an appearance in the 1985 movie *Cocoon*). The heart of downtown's nighttime scene is **BayWalk** (ℂ 727/895-9277; www.stpete.org/baywalk.htm), downtown's new shopping-dining-entertainment complex bordered by 1st and 2nd streets and 2nd and 3rd avenues North. There, a 20-screen cinema and several restaurants and bars will keep you busy.

At the beaches, the restored fishing community of **John's Pass Village and Boardwalk,** on Gulf Boulevard at John's Pass in Madeira Beach, has a handful of restaurants, bars, and shops to keep you occupied after the sun sets. Down south in Pass-a-Grille, there's the popular, always lively lounge in **Hurricane,** 807 Gulf Way, at 9th Avenue, opposite the public beach (© **727/360-9558**). In Clearwater Beach, the **Palm Pavilion Grill & Bar,** on the beach at 18 Bay Esplanade (© **727/446-2742**), has live music Tuesday through Sunday nights during winter and on weekends in the off season. Nearby, **Frenchy's Rockaway Grill,** at 7 Rockaway St. (© **727/446-4844;** www.frenchysonline.com/rockaway.html), is another popular hangout.

6

The Gulf South

In the popular mind, the South is still the Old South, a land of magnolias and Spanish moss, of plantation mansions, of racial tension, and the Civil War. But, unlike their stereotypical image, the Gulf South states are much more modern, and a good deal more ethnically diverse, ranging from the Cajuns and Catholics of Louisiana to the African-American descendants of slaves in Mississippi and Alabama.

True, you can find many remnants of the Old South in many places, especially in the region's historic cities, such as Natchez, Mississippi, where plantation homes are plentiful and blooming gardens abound. But though economic gaps still exist between whites and blacks in Dixie, desegregation and the civil rights movement have made long strides in alleviating the racial tension that marked the area for so long. And the states in the region have taken pains to document all of the struggles and preserve the historic moments that have taken place within their borders. This is the land of the Civil Rights Trail, the place where jazz and the blues were birthed, where battles between North and South hallowed many a field (Vicksburg), and where many literary giants (Faulkner and Welty, among others) penned their first works.

We'll take you through the highlights of the region in the pages that follow, from the pizazz of the French Quarter to the long stretches of the Mississippi Delta, making sure to stop off for the region's best music (from country to the blues to jazz to zydeco) and dining (from home-style barbecue and fried green tomatoes in Alabama to the decadent Creole cuisine of New Orleans).

Note: The catastrophic hurricane season of 2005, especially Hurricane Katrina, wreaked havoc on the Gulf South, tragically killing thousands, and destroying billions of dollars worth of property. The region is working very hard to return to (or even better) its old self, though recovery is very much an ongoing process. At press time, the information in this chapter was accurate, but we advise that you always call to confirm details before setting out anywhere.

Tip: For information on Arkansas, please see "appendix A: The Best of the Rest."

1 Birmingham

Birmingham has come a long way since the 1960s, when the civil rights struggles erupted in bombings, riots, and arrests that drew international attention to this city in north-central Alabama. The pioneer farm settlement of the mid-1850s expanded with the advent of railroads and influence of land barons that helped establish Birmingham as a city in 1871. Fueled by the area's coal, iron ore, and limestone resources, the city earned the nickname the "Magic City" for the rapidity with which Birmingham grew and prospered. Its fortunes waned with the Great Depression in the 1930s, even though the city was largely ruled by wealthy Northern industrialists.

The Gulf South

Racial tensions exploded throughout the South and in Alabama during the 1955 Montgomery Bus Boycott. In Birmingham, when the Ku Klux Klan bombed the Sixteenth Street Baptist Church on the Sunday morning of September 15, 1963, killing four innocent black girls, the city's reputation changed, earning it the derogatory nickname "Bombingham."

Today the city has preserved the painful lessons of the past in many attractions and landmarks that offer reconciliation and reflection. In addition to several important civil rights sites, this lovely city that hugs the foothills of the Appalachian Mountains boasts both a nationally renowned art museum and a motorsports park that racing enthusiasts revere as one of the best in the country.

ESSENTIALS

GETTING THERE By Plane Birmingham International Airport (© 205/595-0533; www.flybirmingham.com) is about 5 miles east of downtown. Major car-rental companies are housed at ground level on Concourse B, near baggage claim. It's an easy 10-minute drive into the city; take I-20/59 west into downtown.

If you're not renting, you can take the **E-Shuttle** (© 205/702-4566), which offers service between the airport and all Birmingham-area hotels and motels. Rates start at $25 per person. The **Birmingham Door-to-Door Shuttle Service** (© 205/591-5550) provides van service between the airport and points throughout Alabama. Reservations are required.

Taxis are available outside baggage claim; expect the fare to run about $20 into downtown.

By Train Amtrak (© 800/USA-RAIL; www.amtrak.com) runs trains from New York (trip time: 23 hr.) through Washington, D.C. (18 hr.) and Atlanta (4 hr.) to Birmingham's station at 1819 Morris Ave. (© 205/324-3033).

By Car The principal highway routes into Birmingham are **I-65** from the north (Nashville); **I-20** from the east (Atlanta); **I-59** from the northeast (Chattanooga, TN); I-20/59 from the southwest (Jackson, MS); and I-65 from the south (Montgomery, AL).

VISITOR INFORMATION To receive visitor information on the greater Birmingham area before your arrival, contact the **Greater Birmingham Convention and Visitors Bureau,** 2200 Ninth Ave. N., Birmingham, AL 35203-1100 (© 800/458-8085 or 205/458-8000; www.sweetbirmingham.com). Another useful resource is the **Alabama Bureau of Tourism and Travel** (© 800/ALABAMA; www.touralabama.org). In addition to its downtown location, the Greater Birmingham CVB has satellite locations at Riverchase Galleria, 2600 Riverchase Galleria (© 205/402-2663); and at Birmingham International Airport, lower level (© 205/458-8002).

GETTING AROUND For taxi service, call the **Yellow Cab Company of Greater Birmingham** (© 205/328-4444); the meter starts at $2.75 and runs $1.80 per mile.

FAST FACTS Emergency and urgent-care services are available at **University of Alabama Birmingham Hospital,** 619 19th St. S. (© 205/934-4011; www.health.uab.edu). A 24-hour **CVS Pharmacy** (© 205/942-7503) is located at 418 W. Valley Ave., in the suburb of Homewood. Sales tax is 9%; hotel tax is 14%.

WHAT TO SEE & DO

Many of Birmingham's major attractions are concentrated **Downtown,** where you'll find a handful of hotels, government buildings, and corporate headquarters, as well as all of the noted attractions in the Civil Rights District. **The Five Points South** area, just south of downtown, is a vibrant neighborhood that encompasses the University of Alabama at Birmingham campus and blocks teeming with upscale restaurants, boutiques, and apartments.

INSIDE THE CIVIL RIGHTS DISTRICT

The **Civil Rights District** is the heart and soul of Birmingham. Visitors from throughout the world travel here to remember the violent struggles for racial equality that shocked the nation in the 1950s and 1960s.

A good place to start exploring this important period in American history is at the **Birmingham Civil Rights Institute,** 520 16th St. N. (℃ **205/328-9696;** www.bcri. org). Allow at least half a day to tour this emotionally wrenching museum that takes visitors through the turbulent riots that erupted in Birmingham and throughout the South in the 1950s and 1960s. Deeply moving and ultimately inspiring, the museum's interactive displays take the viewer back to a harrowing place and time in our nation's history. With the hair-raising joyfulness of gospel choirs singing in the background, the museum journey culminates with a room-size mural that re-creates the March on Washington, D.C., when the Rev. Martin Luther King, Jr., delivered his electrifying "I Have a Dream" speech. Visitors of all ages are transfixed by the video of King's historic address, with many children reciting the pledge along with the slain civil rights leader. Other galleries address human rights issues throughout the world. In addition, the institute offers ongoing educational programs and houses a state-of-the-art library and research center. Admission costs $9 adults, $5 seniors, $4 college students, and is free to kids 17 and under. Admission is free on Sundays. The institute is closed on Mondays (except from Martin Luther King Day in Jan through the end of Feb) and national holidays.

Kelly Ingram Park, across the street from the Birmingham Civil Rights Institute and kitty-corner from the landmark 16th Street Baptist Church, has often been referred to as being at the threshold of the civil rights movement. Within the park, a paved Freedom Path features sculptures commemorating the riots that occurred here in the 1960s, when police turned attack dogs and fire hoses on men, women, and children protesting segregation. There are plaques recounting the importance of clergy in the movement, as well as an emotionally charged statue of children standing defiantly behind bars, in remembrance of those who went to jail for the cause of freedom. A placid water fountain flows in the center of the park, providing a shady spot for quiet reflection and contemplation. Hand-held electronic devices that provide audio tours of the park are available across the street at the Civil Rights Institute ticket office for a nominal fee. Using narrative and eyewitness accounts, the audio tours provide context and background for what visitors are seeing as they walk through the park.

From the park, walk back across the street to tour the historic **16th Street Baptist Church,** 1530 6th Ave. N. (℃ **205/251-9402**), where the infamous 1963 Klan bombing killed four adolescent girls—Cynthia Wesley, Addie Mae Collins, Carole Robertson, and Denise McNair—as they got ready for a Sunday School program. Tours begin in the resplendent sanctuary, where guides give an overview of the church's history before showing an interesting film tracing the devastating impact of the notorious hate crime, and the ensuing, decades-long legal trials that eventually brought the perpetrators to justice. In the church's basement and fellowship hall, a memorial to the girls contains enlarged black-and-white photographs of the chaos and aftermath of the bombing. Most chilling is the well-known photograph of the stained-glass window that remained undamaged except for the face of Jesus, which was blown away by the blast. Take some time to reflect on the wall clock that is frozen at the time the bombings occurred, 10:22am, and which remains a symbol of the church's defining moment. Allow at least 2 hours to see the church, where admission is by a suggested donation of $3.

In 2006 the church was designated as a national historic landmark. It is worth noting that the church is not merely a museum place but an ongoing, active congregation of some 600 members. Worship services usually begin at 11am on Sunday. Visiting tourists are warmly welcomed to participate.

COOL OPTIONS FOR KIDS

Families have various options for keeping the kids entertained. The **Birmingham Zoo,** 2630 Cahaba Rd. (© **205/879-0409;** www.birminghamzoo.com), is home to more than 800 animals, including bald eagles and Bengal tigers, red pandas and ring-tailed lemurs. A Children's Zoo area augments such other draws as a train ride and picnic areas. Admission is $11 adults, $6 children and seniors. Educational fun awaits at the hands-on **McWane Center,** 200 19th Street N. (© **205/714-8300;** www.mcwane. org), which features hands-on displays, discovery areas, and an IMAX theater. Admission to the exhibit halls and the IMAX theater is $14 adults, $12 kids 2 to 12.

Alabama Adventure (formerly known as Visionland) 4599 Visionland Parkway, Bessemer (© **205/481-4750;** www.alabamaadventure.com), is the Birmingham area's amusement park, located about 15 miles southwest of town. The park is home to The Rampage, one of America's favorite wooden roller coasters. Alabama Adventure also has a 600,000-gallon wave pool with sand beach at Splash Beach Water Park. Admission to both the theme park and water park costs $29.95 adults, $19.95 kids under 48 inches tall.

MUSEUMS

In downtown, the best cultural value around can be found at the brilliant **Birmingham Museum of Art,** 2000 Eighth Ave. N. (© **205/254-2565;** www.artsbma.org), regarded as one of the finest in the South. Besides its free admission, what makes this modern facility so outstanding is its impressive permanent collection of more than 21,000 works of art dating from antiquity to the present day, including a sculpture garden, the Kress Collection of Renaissance Art, and 18th-century French paintings and decorative arts. In addition to masterpieces by Claude Monet, John Singer Sargent, and many others, the museum has a popular children's gallery. Tentatively slated to open in October 2007 is "Pompeii: Tales from an Eruption," an exhibition of 500 objects from the ancient Italian city. Birmingham is one of only three U.S. venues for the exhibition (the other cities are Chicago and Houston).

Music lovers should not miss a chance to visit the **Alabama Jazz Music Hall of Fame Museum,** 1631 Fourth Ave. N. (© **205/254-2731;** www.jazzhall.com), which pays homage to musicians such as W. C. Handy, who was born in this state, and Erskine Hawkins, a noted local music educator who wrote Big Band leader Glenn Miller's hit song *Tuxedo Junction.* An entertaining, if rather outdated, film shown in the historic movie theater, now known as the Carver Center for the Performing Arts, begins the self-guided tour. In it, interviews and historical photos and voiceovers detail the state's contributions to the art form of jazz music. The bi-level museum exhibits costumes, musical instruments, records, and playbills recalling the glory days of jazz, primarily in the early part of the last century. Look for the display case devoted to Ella

Swinging into Birmingham

Alabama has been called a golfer's paradise, and the **Robert Trent Jones Golf Trail** that spans the state has become one of its top tourist attractions. When visiting the Birmingham area, golfers will find a challenging and scenic course at the **Oxmoor Valley Golf Club,** 100 Sunbelt Pkwy. (© **800/949-4444** or 205/942-1177; www.rtjgolf.com). The public, 54-hole course (greens fees $35–$57) is one of the trail's 11 courses and is only a few miles from downtown.

Fitzgerald (who had no other ties to Alabama other than once being hospitalized here for a brief illness), where the scat-singing diva's sequined dress is displayed along with her well-worn Neiman-Marcus credit card. It's closed on Monday. Admission is $3 for a guided tour or $2 for a self-guided tour.

Paying homage to pioneers of aviation is the **Southern Museum of Flight,** 4343 73rd St. N. (© **205/833-8226;** www.southernmuseumofflight.org), located 2 blocks east of Birmingham International Airport. More than 8 decades of aviation history are detailed in display and restoration projects being undertaken at the hangars. World War II bombers, biplanes, and an F14-Tomcat are among the vintage as well as experimental aircraft on display, along with ultralights and glider planes. Among aircraft from the Vietnam era are an A-12 Blackbird, a Huey UH-1 helicopter, and an F-4 Phantom jet fighter. A detailed history of the courageous Tuskegee Airmen is chronicled as part of the Alabama Aviation Hall of Fame gallery. The museum is closed Mondays. Admission is $3 for adults and $2 for seniors and students.

PARKS & OUTDOOR RECREATION

If you long to stretch your legs and let the kids run and explore, there's no better tourist attraction than **Vulcan Park,** 1701 Valley View Dr. (© **205/933-1409;** www.vulcanpark.org), site of the largest cast iron statue in the world. Created for the 1904 World's Fair in St. Louis, the imposing male statue depicts Vulcan, the god of forge. After a recent restoration, the statue once again dominates a 10-acre park atop Red Mountain. The grounds offer unparalleled views of the pretty Birmingham skyline—not to mention free Wi-Fi. A visitor center includes interactive exhibits and interpretive displays showcasing the city's rise to prominence as an iron-producing center at the turn of the 20th century, and traces the decline of industry during the Great Depression of the 1930s and beyond.

Tannehill Ironworks Historical State Park, 12632 Confederate Pkwy., McCalla (© **205/477-5711;** www.tannehill.org), is a 1,500-acre haven for hiking, camping, horseback riding, and other outdoor recreation. Artisans such as a blacksmith and miller ply their trades outside restored, 19th-century pioneer cabins to create a vision of a village from long ago. The ironworks give visitors a glimpse into life in the 1800s. The festive Tannehill Trade Days take place every third Saturday March through November. To reach the park from Birmingham, take I-59 south to Exit 100 and follow the signs.

Among other family-friendly recreation options are spectator sports, including minor league baseball's **Birmingham Barons,** 100 Ben Chapman Dr. (© **205/988-3200;** http://barons.com). The team, an AA Southern Class affiliate of the Chicago White Sox, plays at Hoover Metro Stadium, located about a mile off I-459 at Exit 10. Tickets are inexpensive, ranging from $6 to $10.

ATTRACTIONS NEAR BIRMINGHAM

Those in search of more testosterone-tested attractions should hit the road and head out to the rolling, wooded hills that surround the **Barber Vintage Motorsports Museum,** 6030 Barber Motorsports Pkwy. (© **205/699-7275;** www.barbermuseum. org). This one-of-a-kind museum, founded by a successful Birmingham businessman, showcases more than 800 motorcycles representing nearly 140 manufacturers. The venue's most-photographed chopper? The star-spangled replica of the Harley David-son Peter Fonda and Jack Nicholson rode in the film classic *Easy Rider.* The massive glass and concrete building reaches several stories high, with seamless displays that trace the evolution of motorized two-wheelers from the early 1900s to today's ultra-modern machines. Mechanically inclined visitors may want to visit the in-house restoration shop in the basement to watch as workers spiff up, shine, and fine-tune the antique cycles. Every bike in the museum is in working condition. Admission is $10 adults, $6 children. They're road-tested outside, along the awe-inspiring **Barber Motorsports Park,** a 2½-mile road course considered to be among the best in the U.S. Porsches also whiz along this winding ribbon of road during the **Porsche Driving Experience,** where, for a hefty fee, VIPs with advance reservations embark on a mul-tiday training course to learn to drive these quintessential sports cars. For more infor-mation on the school, call © **888/204-7474** (www.porschedriving.com).

And, of course, if you're in Birmingham, you can't be this close to Talladega and not take a day trip to see what NASCAR fanatics have labeled the world's biggest, fastest, and most competitive motorsports facility in the world. A short drive east of Birming-ham, the **Talladega Superspeedway,** off I-20 on Speedway Boulevard (© **800/G0-2-DEGA** or 256/362-9064; www.talladegasuperspeedway.com), is a shrine to speed that covers more than 2,000 acres and offers stadium seating capacity for more than 143,000 spectators. Tours of the 2¾-mile track are offered daily, except on race days. To attend an actual racing event, call well in advance to inquire about ticket availabil-ity. Next door to the track is the **International Motorsports Hall of Fame and Museum** (www.motorsportshalloffame.com), a must for racing fans of all ages. Admission to the museum costs $10 adults, $5 kids 7 to 17. Combination tickets that include guided bus tours of the racetrack cost $12 for adults, and $8 for kids. It's open daily, but the track is closed during and after racing events.

WHERE TO STAY

Downtown has several distinctive choices for travelers to lay down their weary heads. The **Historic Redmont,** 2101 Fifth Ave. N. (© **877/536-2085** or 205/324-2101; www.theredmont.com), is a modern high-rise that locals generally consider down-town's best choice. The rooms offer the usual business amenities. Doubles run about $115. Elsewhere downtown, the historic Wyndham-owned **Tutwiler,** 2021 Park Place N. (© **800/876-3426** or 205/322-2100), offers spacious rooms and turn-of-the-20th-century decor. A $7.2-million renovation in 2006 converted upper floor rooms to executive suites. Upon completion, the hotel will change its affiliation from a Wyn-dham to a Hampton Inn and Suites property, while retaining the Tutwiler brand name. Rates run $110 to $220 double.

The upscale and thoroughly modern **Birmingham Marriott,** 3590 Grandview Pkwy. (© **800/228-9290** or 205/968-3775; www.marriott.com), is an attractive alternative in which all rooms have large work desks and ottomans. Suites sport two bathrooms, including one with a Jacuzzi. In addition, the hotel offers an indoor pool and a health club. Rates run $120 to $190 double.

If you don't mind traveling along the interstate to the outskirts of town, and if you love to shop, there's no better place to stay than the luxurious **Wynfrey Hotel,** 1000 Riverchase Galleria (© **800/996-3739** or 205/987-1600; www.wynfrey.com). Package specials make weekend or shopping getaways to the Wynfrey surprisingly affordable, given the sumptuous elegance of its surroundings. The gleaming Italian-marble lobby is accented with fresh floral arrangements and French chandeliers. In each of the 15-story high-rise's 329 spacious rooms (including 12 suites) you'll find amenities such as beds with pillow-top mattresses and down comforters. All guest bathrooms were recently upgraded with Italian marble floors and fixtures. The Wynfrey has direct access into the massive Riverchase Galleria, a shopping paradise with hundreds of shops, restaurants, and one of the largest skylight-covered courtyards in the country. Doubles run $172 to $250.

WHERE TO DINE

When it comes to restaurants, Birmingham has many good choices. **Bottega Restaurant and Cafe,** 2242 Highland Ave. S. (© **205/939-1000;** www.bottegarestaurant. com), is an upscale Mediterranean- and Tuscan-style restaurant featuring a mixture of North African, Greek, and Italian cuisines. Noted local chef/restaurateur Frank Stitt's appetizers run the gamut from traditional carpaccio to exotic Spanish octopus. Varied preparations of monkfish, grouper, pastas, and veal dominate the menu. Pizzas and sandwiches also are available for takeout at the cafe next door, which is open daily except Sunday. Main courses cost $11 to $39.

Another local favorite is **Café Dupont,** 113 20th St. N. (© **205/322-1282;** www. birminghammenus.com). Chef/owner Chris Dupont draws raves as one of Birmingham's newest culinary stars. This casually elegant bistro makes a great place for a business lunch or a romantic dinner with its New Orleans–influenced menu. Start with a bowl of gumbo and then try the chorizo and crabmeat tart. Yes, just like the similarly named Café du Monde in the Big Easy (p. 448), beignets are on the dessert menu, along with more unusual treats such as brioche with sweet cream cheese and green grapes. Main courses cost $19 to $23. **Hot and Hot Fish Club,** 2180 11th Court S. (© **205/933-5474;** www.hotandhotfishclub.com), is up-and-coming chef Christopher Hasting's trendy eatery, housed in a former creamery turned '50s burger joint. Noted artisans have designed all the artwork, from paintings and sculptural details to the handmade pottery in which meals are served. The varied menu includes Asian-inspired seafood spring rolls with coconut-curry dipping sauce, as well as southern staples such as pork and beans with collard greens, cracklin' cornbread, and homemade chow-chow. For dessert, try the blackberry and white-chocolate bread pudding. Main courses cost $24 to $26.

Highlands Bar and Grill, 2011 11th Ave. S. (© **205/939-1400;** www.highlands barandgrill.com), is the darling of the Birmingham culinary scene at the moment. With raves from major food magazines and consistently good food and service, it's sometimes difficult to snare a reservation at this wildly popular place that combines the homey ambience of a French bistro with the familiarity of an American bar. The upscale crowd favors signature dishes such as fluffy baked grits with country ham and wild mushrooms. The seared tuna is succulent and flavorful, served rare over a bed of steamed vegetables. Quail, veal, poultry, and pasta dishes provide variety. The trio of homemade ice creams—butter pecan, coconut, and caramel—is sublime. Main courses cost $26 to $34.

G, 1820 Fourth Ave. N. (© **205/323-1820;** www.restaurantg.com), downtown's best fine-dining restaurant, is a sophisticated, multitiered space inside the One Federal Place building. Locally grown organic produce is one of the hallmarks of chef Geoffrey Slate's fresh, inventive cuisine. Heartier entrees include cornmeal-crusted rainbow trout with creamy crawfish hominy; and chargrilled five-spice Angus tenderloin with green-onion mashed potatoes in a hoisin broccoli stir-fry. With its gallery-like atmosphere, G is a favorite gathering spot for the martini set. Main courses cost $23 to $28.

A must for fans of the movie *Fried Green Tomatoes*—or for the batter-fried dish itself—is just a short ride out of town. **The Irondale Café,** 1906 1st Ave. N., Irondale (© **205/956-5258;** www.irondalecafe.com), is the nostalgic diner in the quaint suburb of Irondale that served as the inspiration for Alabama novelist Fannie Flagg's *Fried Green Tomatoes at the Whistle Stop Café.* Diners eat at red-and-white-checked tablecloths. Old-fashioned southern vegetables such as okra, sweet potatoes, and turnip greens accompany entrees of fried chicken, dumplings, and a multitude of other dishes that change daily. Don't miss the crispy, batter-fried green tomatoes or the rich macaroni and cheese. Peach cobbler and chocolate cream pie are dessert favorites. Entrees cost $5.50 to $11.

Another home-cooking restaurant that's a bit out-of-the-way but worth the trip is **Niki's West,** 233 Finley Ave. W. (© **205/252-5751**). Though the restaurant bills itself as a steak and seafood place, locals swarm here to stand in the cafeteria line for the knee-weakening array of old-fashioned meatloaf, fried fish, and chicken, and a rainbow of seasoned southern vegetables. Try the greens or macaroni and cheese, and don't miss the gooey, ultrasweet banana pudding for dessert. A platter of meat and three vegetables, plus drink and tax, costs about $10.

When you tire of southern fried foods, opt for the **Purple Onion Deli and Grill,** 1717 10th Ave. S. (© **205/933-2424**), a casual, locally owned chain restaurant that serves fresh quick sandwiches, salads, and side dishes in a fast-food-style atmosphere. Creamy hummus is served with pita wedges. Try the kabobs with charred chicken, lamb, and juicy vegetables. There are several locations scattered throughout the metropolitan Birmingham area. Entrees average $9 to $11 with all of the trimmings (rice, salad, and so on).

BIRMINGHAM AFTER DARK

Tickets for many local events are sold through **Ticketmaster** (© **205/715-6000;** www.ticketmaster.com).

THE PERFORMING ARTS   The **Alabama Ballet** (© **205/322-4300;** www.alabamaballet.org) performs a handful of programs each season, including a traditional holiday *Nutcracker* as well as performances featuring the classics and a more contemporary repertoire. Now in its 10th season, the **Alabama Symphony Orchestra** (© **205/251-7727;** http://alabamasymphony.org) offers a variety of classical, pops, and family programs at concert halls and outdoor venues such as the Birmingham Zoo. **Opera Birmingham** (© **205/975-2787;** www.operabirmingham.org) stages fall and spring productions, offering classics such as Puccini's *Madame Butterfly* and Verdi's *Rigoletto.* In addition, the company promotes up-and-coming vocal talents through competitions and recitals. One of the primary performing-arts venues is the **Alys Robinson Stephens Performing Arts Center,** 1200 10th Ave. S. (© **877/ART-TIKS** or 205/975-ARTS; www.alysstephens.org), a multiple-theater complex on the campus of the University of Alabama Birmingham. In addition to performances by local performing-arts organizations, the venue attracts a wide array of top-name entertainers and touring productions.

THE BAR & CLUB SCENE   To find out what's happening, pick up a copy of the *Birmingham News,* or check its website at **www.al.com**. There's always a big-name act coming to the **Verizon Wireless Music Center** (✆ **800/277-1700** or 205/985-4900; www.verizonwirelessmusiccenter.net) in the town of Pelham, a short drive south of Birmingham off I-65. Recent headliners have included John Fogerty, Willie Nelson, Bela Fleck, and Rascal Flatts.

Jazz lovers are on a first-name basis with **Ona's Music Room,** 423 20th St. S. (✆ **205/322-4662;** www.onasmusicroom.com), where swing, rhythm-and-blues, and contemporary jazz performances are held Thursday through Saturday nights. Another favored hangout is the **22nd Street Jazz and Blues Café,** 710 22nd St. S. (✆ **205/ 252-0407**). In the Five Points South area, **The Nick,** 2510 10th Ave. S. (✆ **205/ 252-3831;** www.thenickrocks.com), is the preeminent alternative rock venue, drawing heavily from the college crowd at nearby University of Alabama Birmingham. If you want to hear Cadillac Jones or the White Trash Messiahs, this is the place.

2 Montgomery

A small-town state capital, Montgomery is a pleasant city of surprising contrasts. There are museums devoted to local legends Rosa Parks and Hank Williams, as well as to F. Scott and Zelda Fitzgerald. The state capital also boasts such diverse pastimes as the Alabama Shakespeare Festival and Montgomery Biscuits minor-league baseball. As it slowly transforms its picturesque riverfront, Montgomery continues to attract thousands of visitors from all over the world to its historic civil rights sites. Meanwhile, Montgomery hums along at a refreshingly easygoing pace.

ESSENTIALS

GETTING THERE   By Plane   Most tourists flying into Montgomery do so via Birmingham (see p. 414 for airport information). By car, it is about 90 miles south along Interstate 65 from Birmingham to Montgomery. However, three carriers serve **Montgomery Regional Airport,** 4445 Selma Hwy. (✆ **334/281-5040;** www. montgomeryairport.org), located 15 minutes from downtown on U.S. Highway 80 West. **Northwest Airlink** (✆ **800/225-2525**) offers daily flights to Memphis; **Atlantic Southeast** (✆ **800/221-1212**) to Atlanta and Dallas/Fort Worth; and **US Airways Express** (✆ **800/428-4322**) to Charlotte, NC.

By Car   The major routes into Montgomery are I-65 from the north (Birmingham) and southwest (Mobile), and I-85 from the northeast (Atlanta).

VISITOR INFORMATION   Contact the **Montgomery Area Visitor Center,** 300 Water St., Montgomery, AL 36104 (✆ **800/240-9452** or 334/262-0013; www. visitingmontgomery.com).

GETTING AROUND   The nation's first electric streetcar system began in Montgomery in 1886. Motorized replicas of those cars (they're actually buses) make up the fleet of the **Lightning Route Trolley** (✆ **334/262-0013;** www.montgomerytransit. com), which provides daily service from the visitor center in Historic Union Station to major downtown points of interest, including Old Alabama Town, the Civil Rights

Memorial, and the Rosa Parks Museum. All-day passes cost $1. For exact hours, call the visitor center (see above).

If you want to explore outlying areas, such as the Alabama Shakespeare Festival or Montgomery Museum of Fine Arts, you will need a car.

FAST FACTS   A major local hospital is **Jackson Hospital,** 1725 Pine St. (© **334/ 293-8000**). Although there are no drugstores with 24-hour pharmacies in the metro area, there's a **CVS** pharmacy at 1525 Forest Ave. (© **334/263-9272**). In downtown, you'll find **Adams Drug,** 934 Adams Ave. (© **334/264-3496**). Sales tax is a whopping 10%; hotel tax is 12.5%.

SPECIAL EVENTS & FESTIVALS   The city's premier music festival, **Jubilee CityFest** (© **334/834-7220**), features nationally known entertainers on several stages throughout the downtown area each Memorial Day weekend.

WHAT TO SEE & DO

Montgomery is located in the flat south-central part of Alabama, perched along the banks of the lazily flowing Alabama River. All of the city's civil rights sites are located downtown. To see more of the area's cultural attractions, drive to lush Blount Cultural Park, located off I-85 North at Exit 6 (follow the signs). Old Cloverdale features several popular restaurants and boutiques. To get there, take Hull Street south out of downtown. It will take you straight into the district.

CIVIL RIGHTS SITES

If there is a single, don't-miss attraction in Montgomery, it is the wonderful **Rosa Parks Library and Museum and Children's Wing,** 252 Montgomery St. (© **334/ 241-8615;** http://montgomery.troy.edu/museum), at downtown's Troy State University. Through a series of stunning galleries, interactive displays help viewers empathize on a personal level with the black seamstress Rosa Parks, who sparked the Montgomery Bus Boycott in 1955 by refusing to give her seat on the bus to a white man. Her subsequent arrest made international headlines and led to a citywide boycott of public transportation, led by the Rev. Martin Luther King, Jr. An emotional highlight of the museum is the gallery that re-creates a 1955 street scene with a replica of the bus on which Parks rode. In a theatrical multimedia tableau, actors' dialogue is played over video images to bring alive that fateful encounter that sparked a long ride to freedom for the city's black population. In 2005 the library and museum expanded with a new children's wing, which provides computer stations where visitors may research historical documents and hear testimonials from those associated with the Montgomery Bus Boycott. Admission is $5.50 for those 13 and older and $3.50 for kids 12 and under. The museum is closed Sundays and holidays.

In keeping with the civil rights theme that pervades Montgomery, I highly recommend a visit to **Dexter Avenue King Memorial Baptist Church,** 454 Dexter Ave. (© **334/263-3970;** www.dexterkingmemorial.org). This National Historic Landmark is where the Rev. Martin Luther King, Jr., first preached as a young pastor, and it was from this pulpit that he rose to the challenge of leading the Montgomery bus boycott. In the basement of the church, a large, colorful, and intricate mural depicts King's civil rights crusade, which took him from Montgomery to Selma and, ultimately, to Memphis, where he was assassinated. Guided tours ($2 adults, $1 children) of the church are offered Monday and Thursday at 10am and 2pm. Self-guided walk-through tours

The Civil Rights Trail

The picturesque small town of Selma, Alabama, a leisurely hour's drive southwest of Montgomery, makes a good day trip for those who want to explore more civil rights history. The **National Voting Rights Museum,** 1012 Water Ave. (© **334/418-0800**), is a simple but moving collection of galleries and artifacts that detail the fight by black residents to obtain rights to vote.

Selma is best known for the aborted March 7, 1965, voting rights march, "Bloody Sunday," when civil rights protestors trying to march from Selma to Montgomery were brutalized by tear gas, cattle prods, and clubs at the hands of police, state troopers, and local vigilantes. The bloody riot took place on the **Edmund Pettus Bridge,** named for a Confederate hero who, after the Civil War, lost his seat in the state legislature to a black man. For a free *Black Heritage Guide* that includes information about prominent civil rights sites in various Alabama cities and towns, contact the **Alabama Bureau of Tourism and Travel** (© **800/ALABAMA**; www.800alabama.com).

are available on Friday, while Saturday tours are available by appointment only. Sunday tours are not conducted, but visitors are welcome to attend the worship service that usually begins at 10:30am.

In conjunction with a visit to Dr. King's church, Montgomery has just opened another site that explores the personal side of the slain civil rights leader. The newly restored **Dexter Parsonage Museum,** 309 S. Jackson St. (© **334/261-3270**; www.dakmf.org), is located a few blocks from the center of downtown. King lived in the parsonage from 1954 to 1960, while leading the Montgomery Bus Boycott. The humble bungalow with the wide front porch was built in the 1920s, but the interior has been restored to the mid-1950s, when King lived here with his new bride, Coretta Scott King, while he served as minister of Dexter Avenue Baptist Church. Tourists may enter the study where King read, studied, and typed his sermons, often while listening to music. Kids are usually amazed to see the small 1950s-era kitchen, which includes a tub-style washing machine, an old-fashioned Frigidaire "icebox," and a complete lack of modern conveniences such as a microwave. Furniture and furnishings actually used by the King family fill the home, including the dining room where the Kings entertained fellow church members and conducted business meetings. In chilling detail, a tour guide recounts the day when a bomb exploded in the parsonage's front window and destroyed much of the home, though the King family escaped injury. Admission costs $3 adults, $2 children under 12. *Note:* The Dexter church and parsonage are not within easy walking distance of each other; be prepared to drive.

Finally, outside the offices of the Southern Poverty Law Center downtown lies the city's most impressive monument. Designed by renowned architect Maya Lin (whose best-known work is the Vietnam Memorial in the nation's capital; p. 202), the **Civil Rights Memorial and Center,** 400 Washington Ave. (© **334/956-8200**; www.splcenter.org), is a simple yet stunning touchstone for absorbing the impact and meaning of the civil rights movement that tore apart this city and so much of the nation. The names of some of those who died during the struggle are inscribed in a circular, black granite table over which a gentle stream of water flows. Adjacent to the Memorial, the new **Civil Rights Memorial Center** provides an in-depth look at civil rights martyrs. Educational exhibits, a 69-seat theater, and a Wall of Tolerance are among the displays. Admission is $2 for adults and free to children 17 and under. The Center is closed Sundays. Civil War buffs should not miss the **First White House of the Confederacy,** 644 Washington Ave. (© **334/242-1861**), where Jefferson Davis and his family once lived. The Confederate White House contains period furnishings and many of Davis's personal belongings. It was here in Montgomery that Confederate President Davis gave the order to fire on Fort Sumter, which launched the Civil War. Closed weekends; admission is free.

MORE THINGS TO SEE & DO

The **Hank Williams Museum,** 118 Commerce St. (© **334/262-3600;** www.xaust. com/hank), is a labor of love for the venue's founder, who was a friend and a fan of the beloved country music singer/songwriter who shot to fame in the 1940s. The centerpiece of the museum is the baby-blue 1952 Cadillac in which Williams was riding when he collapsed and died in the back seat. Other galleries overflow with vinyl 78 records; many of Williams's personal belongings, costumes, and guitars; and an antique jukebox on which visitors can punch buttons to hear such classics as "Hey Good Lookin'" and "I'm So Lonesome I Could Cry." Williams is buried in Oakwood Cemetery Annex, 1304 Upper Wetumpka Rd., and there's a bronze statue of the lanky entertainer in the heart of downtown. If you're interested in seeing these, the museum offers directions on how to get to both sites. Admission is $7 adults, $3 children under 12.

Another fun-filled attraction in the downtown area is **Old Alabama Town,** 301 Columbus St. (© **888/240-1850** or 334/240-4500; www.oldalabamatown.com), a reconstruction of an Alabama village in the 19th and early 20th centuries. Among the collection of more than 40 restored structures are homes from the era, along with a tavern, drugstore, doctor's office, schoolhouse, cotton gin, and corner grocery. Self-guided walking tours are offered daily. Admission costs $8 adults, $4 children ages 6 to 18. Closed Sundays.

Set amid the verdant **Blount Cultural Park** just outside of downtown lies the **Montgomery Museum of Fine Arts,** 1 Museum Dr. (© **334/244-5700;** www.mmfa. org). The free museum features southern regional art as well as paintings and prints by the old masters. If the museum has a signature artwork, it is probably Edward Hicks's well-known *The Peaceable Kingdom* (ca. 1830). This magnificent building also houses Alabama's first interactive fine arts gallery for children, ARTWORKS. All activities are hands-on, giving children ample opportunity for creative exploration.

Literary enthusiasts should seek out the unassuming **F. Scott and Zelda Fitzgerald Museum,** 919 Felder Ave. (© **334/264-4222;** www.fitzgerald-museum.com). Fitzgerald, author of such 20th-century classic novels as *The Great Gatsby* and *Tender Is the Night,* lived here off and on during the early years of the couple's tempestuous relationship. F. Scott met Montgomery native Zelda while he was stationed in the city during World War I. After their marriage, the couple lived in this rambling old home that now houses a modest museum. Although it's not a heavily attended tourist attraction, it is the only museum in the world devoted to the author. After watching a video about the Fitzgeralds, guests may peruse handwritten love letters Zelda wrote to her husband, and admire her cigarette holder, a few pieces of jewelry, and other personal belongings, along with books and historical archives. Zelda's self-portraits and other paintings and drawings also fill the space, lending poignancy to the telling of her life story, in which she suffered from schizophrenia and teetered in and out of madness for most of her adult life. Admission is free but donations are accepted. The museum is open Wednesday through Friday from 10am to 2pm, Saturday and Sunday 1 to 5pm.

Newly minted in the spring of 2004 was the city's minor league baseball team, lovingly named the **Montgomery Biscuits,** 200 Coosa St. (C **334/323-2255;** www. biscuitsbaseball.com). An affiliate of the Tampa Bay Devil Rays, the team plays at downtown's Riverwalk Stadium, at the corner of Coosa and Tallapoosa streets. Stadium seats have excellent sightlines, and a picnic area makes a great place for families to spread out and enjoy a game. Concessions sold on-site include all the traditional game-day fare, as well as the eponymous southern biscuits and honey. There's also a playground, as well as lots of activities designed to appeal to all ages. Tickets range from $6 to $10.

Riverfront Amphitheater, 355 Coosa St. (C **334/240-4092;** www.funontheriver. net), is the latest addition to the Montgomery riverfront and ongoing Riverwalk development. This outdoor venue, with a white-columned pergola, overlooks the Alabama River in this shady setting for picnics, concerts, movies, and plays. A "splash pad" water feature cools off the kids. The park is free and open to the public year-round, though admission fees are charged for some amphitheater events.

WHERE TO STAY

Lodging choices are somewhat limited in downtown Montgomery, which has only a few reputable hotels and one excellent bed-and-breakfast, but all the familiar hotel-motel chains can be found near the interstate exits.

There is only one bed-and-breakfast in Montgomery, but it is one I can heartily recommend. **Red Bluff Cottage Bed and Breakfast,** 551 Clay St. (C **888/551-2529** or 334/264-0056; www.redbluffcottage.com), is an immaculate and cozy retreat for travelers who appreciate being pampered in homey surroundings. Four spacious guest rooms are beautifully furnished with quilts, antiques, and overstuffed furniture—as well as wireless Internet access, a rarity for most B&Bs. From the front porch, there are lovely views of the State Capitol and Alabama River. Perched in the quiet, Cottage Hill residential neighborhood, Red Bluff has easy interstate access and is just a few blocks from downtown attractions. Children are welcome. Doubles run from $99 to $120.

Downtown's newest and best full-service hotel is the **Embassy Suites Hotel Montgomery–Conference Center,** 300 Tallapoosa St. (C **334/269-5055;** www. embassysuites.com). Across the street from the visitor center and trolley stop, the all-suite hotel offers kitchenette-equipped suites, an indoor pool, and a fitness center. Rates ($119–$149) include breakfast. Despite its rather outdated exterior, the **Capitol Inn,** 205 N. Goldthwaite St. (C **866/471-9028** or 334/265-3844; www. capitolinnhotel.com), in the heart of downtown, is an excellent bargain for travelers on a budget. Rates are about $75 double. Rooms are tidy and basic, but the friendly staff and caring service create a welcoming atmosphere. There's also an outdoor pool. Foodies take note: Locals and in-the-know travelers alike storm the motel's restaurant at breakfast and lunch for old-fashioned southern cooking that locals brag is the best in town. If you're taking in a few plays at the Alabama Shakespeare Festival, the attractive, budget-priced **Fairfield Inn Montgomery,** 5601 Carmichael Rd. (C **334/270-0007;** www.marriott.com), located a mile from the theater, is convenient and comfortable. Free local calls and an outdoor pool are other perks. Fridges and microwaves are available in some rooms. Rates run $78, plus tax, double.

WHERE TO DINE

Montgomery has no shortage of good restaurants, many of which specialize in southern cooking. Since the 1940s, **Martin's Restaurant,** 1796 Carter Hill Rd. (© 334/ 265-1767), has been serving home-style cooking at various locations around town. Today Martin's sits in a modern shopping center near the local country club. The food is unpretentious, plentiful, and inexpensive. Did somebody say pies? They're legendary. Our weakness is the creamy coconut, piled with golden meringue. You may want to steer clear of Martin's on Sunday after church, when the place can become very crowded. Main courses range from $5 to $7. Downtown's newest restaurant, **Nobles,** 129 Montgomery St. (© **334/262-3326;** www.noblesandoliveroom.com), is a casually sophisticated lunch spot serving generous salads, seafood entrees, and southern staples such as fried pork chops. Sweet iced tea is the perfect accompaniment. The restaurant also has a full bar. Main courses cost $12 to $16.

One of the newest fine-dining restaurants in Montgomery is **Garrett's,** 7780 Atlanta Hwy. (© **334/396-9950**). Locally owned and operated by chef Gary Garner, the upscale eatery features Art Deco decor and a menu specializing in steaks and seafood. Reservations are recommended. Open for dinner only Tuesday to Saturday.

In the Old Cloverdale district, there are a couple of tempting dining options. Scores of young professionals dominate happy hour at **Sinclair's,** 1051 E. Fairview Ave. (© **334/834-7462;** www.sinclairsrestaurants.com), a locally owned bar and grill. The menu is varied, running from spaghetti pie made with lean turkey to Buffalo chicken wings, specialty burgers, and seafood. There's also a decent wine list. Eggs Benedict, along with shrimp and grits, are specialties at Sunday brunch. Service is unassuming and efficient. There are two other area Sinclair's locations, including one at 7847 Vaughn Rd. (© **334/271-7654**). Main courses cost $10 to $23. Across the street, pizzas made with traditional and whole-wheat dough are specialties of **Tomatino's Pizza and Bake Shop,** 1036 E. Fairview Ave. (© **334/264-4241**). The Italian eatery with an adjacent coffee and pastry shop offers an array of traditional pizza toppings, as well as premium choices such as fresh-leaf spinach, spicy tofu, and roasted garlic. Salads, breadsticks, cheese calzones, and focaccia are other options. A handful of wines, as well as imported and domestic beers, round out the menu. Main courses cost $7.50 to $23.

MONTGOMERY AFTER DARK

THE PERFORMING ARTS   The city's cultural pride and joy, the **Alabama Shakespeare Festival (ASF),** 1 Festival Dr. (© **800/841-4-ASF** or 334/271-5353; www.asf. net), is renowned throughout the nation for its high-caliber performances and ambitious programming. Originally located in an un-air-conditioned high school auditorium in Anniston, ASF moved to its new home—Montgomery's 250-acre Blount Cultural Park—in 1985. Performances are staged in two theaters within the $22-million Carolyn Blount Theatre complex. The ASU operates year-round, producing 14 world-class productions annually, including three works of William Shakespeare, as well as classics by such playwrights as George Bernard Shaw, Anton Chekhov, and Tennessee Williams. The ASF also commissions new works.

The city boasts two ballet companies, the professional **Montgomery Ballet** (© **334/409-0522;** www.montgomeryballet.com) and **Alabama Dance Theatre**

Cruise through Mobile

The gateway to southern Alabama's pristine beaches on the Gulf of Mexico is the bayside city of **Mobile**. In the fall of 2004, Mobile became a cruise port, when Carnival Cruise Lines' *Holiday* began launching 4- and 5-day cruises to Cozumel and the Yucatán out of the city's harbor. Although Hurricane Katrina in 2005 did minimal damage to the new port, the *Holiday* temporarily housed hurricane survivors. Cruises out of Mobile resumed on the *Holiday* in March 2006. For a pre- or postcruise stay, a convenient hotel is the **Radisson Admiral Semmes,** 251 Government St. (© **800/333-3333** or 251/432-8000; www.radisson.com/mobileal), downtown.

Attractions close to the port include the **Museum of Mobile,** 111 S. Royal St. (© **251/208-7569;** www.museumofmobile.com), an interesting spot detailing the city's 300-year-history. Admission is $5 adults, $4 seniors and $3 students. When you've worked up an appetite, great seafood awaits you at **Wintzell's Oyster House,** 605 Dauphin St. (© **251/432-4605;** www. wintzellsoysterhouse.com). For more information on the city and its cruise options, contact the **Mobile Bay Convention & Visitors Bureau,** 1 S. Water St. (© **800/5-MOBILE** or 251/208-2000; www.mobile.org).

(© **334/241-2590;** www.alabamadancetheatre.com), which stages traditional and contemporary works in two major performances annually. The 75-piece **Montgomery Symphony** (© **334/240-4004;** www.montgomerysymphony.org) performs 10 concerts a year. Its primary venue is the **Davis Theater for the Performing Arts,** 251 Montgomery St., at Troy State University. Built in 1941, the **Capri Theatre,** 1045 E. Fairview Ave. (© **334/262-4858;** www.capritheatre.org), was the city's first movie palace. Since being purchased by a grassroots community group in 1983, the venue has operated as a nonprofit cinema specializing in independent films. Call for features and showtimes.

One of the newest entertainment venues in Montgomery is **Faulkner University Dinner Theatre,** 5345 Atlanta Hwy. (© **334/386-7190;** www.faulkner.edu/campus life/dinnertheatre.asp), where Broadway-style family entertainment is offered in a Christian-based atmosphere.

3 Highlights of Mississippi

CLARKSDALE

An unmistakable vibe pervades the languid Mississippi Delta town of Clarksdale, about an hour's drive south of Memphis, Tennessee. It's by turns eerie and endearing, a flat landscape where fertile fields, endless railroad tracks, and run-down shacks are giving way to pockets of progress—an upscale restaurant, a strip mall full of dollar stores and fast-food drive-throughs, a museum celebrating the blues music that took root here in the early 20th century and changed the course of popular music.

This is a good place to begin a driving tour of legendary **Highway 61 (U.S. 61),** the two-lane road that took blues legends such as Muddy Waters, Robert Johnson, and B. B. King north from the impoverished cotton plantations of the south to the cities of Memphis and Chicago to the north. The long drive south will take you through the proverbial dusty Delta towns, and cities such as Greenville, Vicksburg and, finally, where Mississippi meets Louisiana in the southwest part of the state, historic Natchez.

ESSENTIALS

GETTING THERE   By Plane   Major airlines fly into Memphis International Airport (see "Oxford," below). Rent a car and head south on Highway 61, past the casinos in Tunica and on into Clarksdale.

By Car   The major route into Clarksdale is **Highway 61** from Memphis to the north.

VISITOR INFORMATION   Contact the **Clarksdale/Coahoma County Chamber of Commerce,** 1540 Desoto Ave., Clarksdale, MS 39614 (© **800/626-3764** or 662/627-7337; www.clarksdale.com).

WHAT TO SEE & DO

As you ease into town, your first stop should be at **The Crossroads,** at the intersection of highways 49 and 61. The site is legendary as the place where bluesman Robert Johnson is said to have sold his soul to the devil in exchange for the guitar prowess that has made him one of the most revered musicians of the past century. A guitar statue marks the spot.

From here, your next stop should be the **Delta Blues Museum,** 1 Blues Alley (© **662/672-6820;** www.deltabluesmuseum.org). Housed in a renovated train depot built in 1918, it includes a treasure-trove of old blues memorabilia, including the log cabin where Muddy Waters grew up, on a cotton plantation not far from here. There are displays, musical instruments, and costumes of some of the Mississippi-born greats, such as Albert King, James Cotton, and Son House. Admission is $6 adults, $3 children 6 to 12; it is open daily except Sunday. Bessie Smith fans can do a drive-by tour of the **Riverside Hotel,** 615 Sunflower Ave. (© **662/624-9163**), the former blacks-only hospital where the great blues singer died after a car crash in 1937. Blues legends Sonny Boy Williamson II, Ike Turner, Robert Nighthawk, and even politician Robert F. Kennedy once stayed here. Today it still operates as a motel, but most visitors see it only from their windshields.

While downtown, don't miss **Cathead Delta Blues & Folk Art,** 252 Delta Ave. (© **662/624-5992;** www.cathead.biz). The store sells new blues CDs, DVDs, and books as well as eye-catching—and affordable—folk and outsider art. The hepcat-cool hot spot also serves as a clearinghouse for what's going on around town. Check Cathead's chalkboard that tells of weekly music events and updates. The store also occasionally has book signings and special events. You'll likely find the owner chatting up tourists who've made the pilgrimage here for some serious blues sightseeing.

WHERE TO STAY & DINE

There's a pitiful lack of decent hotels in Clarksdale. Your best bet is to grab one of the inexpensive to moderately priced chain properties along State Street. Equally amenable are the Comfort Inn, 818 S. State St. (© **662/627-5122**), and the nearby Best Western, 710 S. State St. (© **662/627-9292**).

Hands-down the best restaurant in town is **Madidi,** 164 Delta Ave. (© **662/627-7770;** www.madidires.com), the upscale eatery and bar opened in 2001 by actor Morgan Freeman, who grew up in the area and is still seen around town from time to time. (He is also a partner in **Ground Zero Blues Club,** reminiscent of an old juke

Shacking Up

In the lodging category of too creepy for anyone but the most die-hard blues fan, there's the one-of-a-kind **Shack Up Inn,** 1 Commissary Circle (© 662/624-8329; www.shackupinn.com), on old Highway 49 south of Clarksdale. Billed as Mississippi's oldest B&B (and that stands for Bed and Beer), the property is on the site of a weedy rural cotton gin littered with rusting antique farming implements, old road signs, and crumbling sharecropper shacks that have been modernized enough to accommodate easy-to-please travelers in search of a good time and a place to crash—and great music at the on-premises Commissary club. Some shacks have kitchenettes. Rates range from $50 to $75 per room. There's a $5 additional fee per person, but hey—rates include tax *and* a Moon Pie on your pillow.

joint, in downtown.) Other popular venues are **Abe's Bar-B-Que,** 616 State St. (© 662/624-9947); and **Sarah's Kitchen,** 203 Sunflower Ave. (© 662/627-3239), which serves southern cooking.

VICKSBURG
ESSENTIALS
GETTING THERE   Vicksburg is located near the midpoint along the most famous stretch of Mississippi's fabled Highway 61, just north of Natchez and a few hours' drive south of Clarksdale.

VISITOR INFORMATION   Contact the **Vicksburg Convention and Visitors Bureau,** P.O. Box 110, Vicksburg, MS 39181 (© 800/221-3536 or 601/636-9421; www.visitvicksburg.com).

CIVIL WAR SITES
Vicksburg National Military Park, 3201 Clay St. (© 601/636-0583; www.nps.gov/vick), the city's best-known tourist attraction, operates under the auspices of the National Park Service. One of the oldest national parks in the country, it was established in 1899 and today draws more than one million visitors annually. Tours begin at the Visitors Center, where Confederate swords, uniforms, and other artifacts from the Siege of Vicksburg are on display. A tedious, 18-minute film may stir history buffs but will bore children as it recounts the campaign of Vicksburg. It does, however, set the stage for a driving tour of the park. Get in your vehicle and follow the 16-mile, self-guided trail that follows Union and Confederate siege lines. Tombstones and markers convey sobering statistics about the soldiers who suffered in the Civil War. The newest addition to the park is the **Mississippi African American Monument,** which was dedicated in February 2004 to honor the black soldiers who served during the Vicksburg Campaign. Aside from its rich history, the vast park is also popular for such outdoor pastimes as bird-watching, hiking, and bicycling. The Visitors Center is open daily from 8am to 5pm. Admission is $8 per car or $4 per person in vans.

   The Old Court House Museum-Eva W. Davis Memorial, 1008 Cherry St. (© 601/636-0741; www.oldcourthouse.org), is a National Historic Landmark. Built by slaves in 1858, the home has seen such noted figures as Ulysses S. Grant, Jefferson Davis, Booker T. Washington, and Theodore Roosevelt pass through its doors. Admission costs $5 adults, $3 children. In the historic downtown district, which civic leaders are hoping to revitalize, the **Biedenharn Museum of Coca-Cola Memorabilia,** 1107 Washington St. (© **601/638-6514**), is a gaudy, red-and-white shrine to all things Coke. It's housed in the building where Coke was first bottled in 1894. From billboards of Santa Claus sipping from ice-cold bottles to the ad-related merchandise of today, the soda shop is worth a quick peek. Admission costs $3 adults, $2 children under 12.

SHOPPING

Shopping enthusiasts, or those who aren't interested in historic homes or Civil War sites, will be thrilled to tackle the factory outlet mall here. **Vicksburg Factory Outlets,** 4000 S. Frontage Rd. (© **601/636-7434;** www.vicksburgfactoryoutlet.com), offers bargains on name-brand goods by Big Dogs, Claire, Gap, and Reebok, among others.

WHERE TO STAY & DINE

Sure, there are newer chain hotels on the interstates leading into Vicksburg, but to experience the true flavor of gracious southern living, consider staying in one of the city's many historic homes that also double as bed-and-breakfast properties.

The elegant eight-room **Anchuca,** 1010 First East St. (© **888/686-0111** or 601/661-0111; www.anchucamansion.com), a Greek Revival mansion built in 1830, features a year-round swimming pool. The lovely rooms are furnished with period antiques and fine linens; many sport canopy beds. Rates run from $95 for rooms in an adjacent carriage house to $175 for the romantic master suite. Children under 15 are not permitted. Built in 1840, **Cedar Grove Mansion-Inn,** 2200 Oak St. (© **800/862-1300** or 601/636-1000; www.cedargroveinn.com), sits on 4 acres overlooking the Mississippi River. There are 30 rooms $120 to $260 double, all with private bathrooms; some units sport Jacuzzi tubs, fireplaces, or canopy beds (Ulysses S. Grant once slept in one of them). **Annabelle,** 501 Speed St. (© **800/791-2000** or 601/638-2000; www.annabellebnb.com), is a Victorian Italianate home that dates back to 1868. The eight rooms, including a suite with a kitchen, are housed in the main mansion and an adjoining two-story building that overlooks an outdoor pool—a definite advantage during the hot summers. Rooms ($93–$115 double; $125–$160 suite) feature high ceilings, private bathrooms (one with a Jacuzzi), and period antiques.

Back out on the highways, there are several decent hotels and motels good for budget-minded travelers. Try the **Jameson Inn,** 3975 S. Frontage Rd. (© **800/526-3766** or 601/619-7799; www.jamesoninns.com); **Hampton Inn,** 3332 Clay St. (© **800/568-4044** or 601/636-6100; www.hamptoninn.com); or the aging but popular **Battlefield Inn,** 4137 I-20 Frontage Rd. (© **800/359-9363** or 601/638-5811; www.battlefieldinn.com). Rooms at any of these spots won't run you more than $75 double.

If you only have time to sample one meal in Vicksburg, make it **Walnut Hills Restaurant,** 1214 Adams St. (© **601/638-4910;** www.walnuthillsms.net). It looks like any other common, turn-of-the-20th-century house on the street of this leafy residential neighborhood—except for the long lines of families that curl across the wide front porch. Walnut Hills is a longtime local institution that serves sensational southern cooking family-style at oversize round tables. Fried chicken, shrimp, casseroles, green beans, mashed potatoes, and plenty of corn bread and sweet iced tea are always on tap. Main courses cost $10 to $20. Closed Saturday. The city's best locally owned seafood restaurant is **Rowdy's Family Catfish Shack,** at the intersection of Highway 27 and

Highway 80, I-20 Exit 5B (© **601/638-2375**). Order the platter, with coleslaw, fries, and hush puppies. Main courses cost $6 to $16. Another beloved eatery is **Goldie's Trail Bar-B-Que**, 4127 S. Washington St. (© **601/636-9839**), an informal place for pork and beef ribs, chicken, and all the trimmings. Main courses cost $5 to $15. Closed Sunday.

NATCHEZ

Boasting more antebellum homes than anywhere in the U.S., this charming small town on a bluff overlooking the Mississippi River is best visited in the spring and fall, when pilgrimages to historic houses are in full swing. With its semitropical climate, however, the city is pleasant year-round, though it can get quite muggy during the summer months.

ESSENTIALS

GETTING THERE   Fly into Jackson, Mississippi (see "Visiting Jackson," p. 432) and drive along U.S. 155 S. to Brookhaven (U.S. 94). Take U.S. 84 straight into Natchez. If you're driving in from New Orleans (trip time: 3½ hr.) in neighboring Louisiana, take I-10 West to I-55 North. Follow I-55 North to Highway 84 West and take the third McComb exit, which leads to Highway 61 and into Natchez.

VISITOR INFORMATION   One of the most attractive welcome centers in the South awaits travelers in the spacious **Natchez Visitor Reception Center**, 640 S. Canal St. (© **800/647-6724;** www.visitnatchez.com). An introductory film about the city's history provides an excellent overview for tourists about to embark on the area's Civil War–era attractions. Elsewhere in the visitor center, you'll find interactive exhibits, displays, and oversize maps as well as brochures, a gift shop, and a helpful staff.

In addition, advance information is available by contacting the **Natchez Convention and Visitors Bureau**, 211 Main St., Natchez, MS 39120 (© **800/647-6724** or 601/442-5880; www.visitnatchez.com). The staff is especially helpful to travelers looking for suggested itineraries or other tourist recommendations.

WHAT TO SEE & DO

Antebellum homes are everywhere in Natchez, the oldest permanent settlement on the Mississippi River. The **Natchez Spring Pilgrimage** (© **800/647-6742;** www.natchez pilgrimage.com), which occurs annually mid-March through mid-April, is an opportunity to visit all 32 of the city's antebellum homes, hosted by southern belles in hoop skirts and other period dress.

You will need several days to see all the homes, or you can pick and choose a few. Representative of most is **Rosalie,** 100 Orleans St. (© **601/446-5676**), which was built in the early 1820s and later purchased by the Daughters of the American Revolution, who operate it as a museum. The Federal-style mansion overlooks the Mississippi River, and its 4-acre gardens delight the senses with winding brick pathways and wrought-iron benches. Admission is $8 for adults and $4 for students. Atypical of the area's plantation homes is **Longwood,** 140 Lower Woodville Rd. (© **601/442-5193**), one of the most unusual mansions of Natchez. Designated as both a National Historic Landmark and a site on the Civil War Discovery Trail, it is a lavish octagonal home (the largest of its kind in the country) dating from 1859. The 32-room home has four floors and a solarium and observatory. It is crowned with a Byzantine dome. Construction on the interior of the home stopped during the Civil War and was never

Visiting Jackson

If you're driving through Mississippi, the capital city of Jackson—a pleasant if not particularly picturesque city of 184,000 people—makes a good home base for exploring sites in the southern half of the state. It's also your best alternative to flying into Memphis, Tennessee (p. 435), which is just a few miles over the border from the northwest corner of Mississippi.

Jackson is situated near the intersection of **Interstate 55,** which runs north and south, and **Interstate 20,** which runs east and west. Nine major air carriers including Delta, Northwest, and Southwest offer about 40 daily flights to **Jackson International Airport** (© 601/939-5631; www.jmaa.com) from such cities as Detroit, Baltimore/Washington, D.C., Atlanta, and Houston. All major car-rental agencies are located at the airport. **Amtrak,** 300 W. Capitol St. (© 800/872-7245 or 601/355-6350; www.amtrak.com), offers daily passenger rail service to New Orleans and Chicago.

Revered as Mississippi's oldest professional arts organization, the **Mississippi Museum of Art,** 201 E. Pascagoula St. (© 601/960-1515; www.ms museumart.org), includes everything from folk art and photography to pre-Columbian art and American landscapes.

Elsewhere in Jackson, a visit to the **Eudora Welty House and Garden,** 119 Pinehurst St. (© 601/353-7762; www.mdah.state.ms.us), is a must for literary fans. The late Eudora Welty (1909–2001) was one of Mississippi's most beloved writers and photographers. The Pulitzer Prize winner and her mother, Chestina, lived in the historic Belhaven neighborhood, where they cultivated a backyard flower garden bursting with camellias, roses, iris, jonquils, hyacinths, day lilies, and other perennials. The garden was restored and opened to the public in the spring of 2004; tours are offered on Wednesdays April through October by prior reservation only by calling © 601/353-7762. The house itself, listed on the National Register of Historic

completed, but Longwood is nevertheless a sight to behold. Admission is $10 for adults and $6 for students 6 to 17.

Aside from lavish mansions, there are other sites of historical importance in Natchez. Drive by **Holy Family Catholic Church,** 28 St. Catherine St. (© 601/445-5700), and admire the state's first African-American Catholic church. Built in 1894, the sanctuary is a beautifully preserved landmark where Masses are still held throughout the week. Tours are available by appointment only. Established in 1821, the **Natchez City Cemetery,** 2 Cemetery Rd. (© 601/445-4981), is a hauntingly beautiful green space dotted with tree-shaded graves dating back to the 1700s. Guests may drive through these hilly bluffs, which overlook the Mississippi River. If you'd like to know more about the cemetery, pick up a brochure at the Visitors Reception Area. It's open dawn to dusk.

WHERE TO STAY

If you want to live like a wealthy southern plantation owner, book a room at one of the area's luxurious plantation inns. **Dunleith Plantation,** 84 Homochitto St.

Places, is a two-story Tudor Revival–style residence built in 1924. It is set to open as a literary house museum in 2006, but it can be toured online before then.

Meanwhile, seasonal history buffs will want to see some of the city's old buildings downtown. The **Mississippi State Capitol,** 400 High St. (② **601/ 359-3114**), is a Beaux Arts beauty that resembles the nation's capitol in Washington, D.C. Free tours are conducted weekdays. Nearby, the **Mississippi Governor's Mansion,** 300 E. Capitol St. (② **601/359-6421**), is a fine example of Greek Revival architecture dating from 1841. Free tours of the National Historic Landmark are held Tuesday through Friday mornings.

For antiques shopping, gallery hopping, and myriad drinking and dining options, take State Street north from Woodrow Wilson to Meadowbrook Road to reach the lively **Fondren District,** 3318 N. State St. (② **601/981-9606;** www.fondren.org).

Hotels and motels in Jackson cater to a range of tastes and budgets. One of the nicest and most unique is the **Fairview Inn,** 734 Fairview St., Jackson, MS 39202 (② **601/948-3429;** www.fairviewinn.com), a grand white mansion with 18 luxurious rooms and formal gardens shaded by ancient magnolias. To reach the Fairview, which is located in a lovely residential neighborhood, take I-55 to Exit 98A. Dating from the 1920s, downtown's old standby is the venerable **Edison Walthall Hotel,** 225 E. Capitol St. (② **601/948-6161**), a good choice if you want to be within a few blocks of the art museum and other downtown sites. From I-55, take the Pearl Street exit.

For more information on the city, contact the **Jackson Convention & Visitors Bureau,** 921 N. President St. (② **800/354-7695** or 601/960-1891; www.visitjackson.com).

(② **800/433-2445** or 601/446-8500; www.dunleithplantation.com), is an august, 1856 Greek Revival mansion that dominates a massive 40-acre spread. The 26 rooms are decorated in period style and offer high ceilings and bathrobes, along with amenities such as an outdoor swimming pool. Rates range from $130 to $250 double and include full breakfast; children under 14 are not accepted. The much-acclaimed (and nonsmoking) **Monmouth Plantation,** 36 Melrose Ave. (② **800/828-4531** or 601/ 442-5852; www.monmouthplantation.com), has 30 lavish rooms in its 1818 mansion and modern, antiques-packed cottages nestled throughout the property's wooded and meticulously landscaped 26 acres. Several rooms offer canopy beds and/or Jacuzzi tubs. Rates range from $165 to $395 double and include full breakfast and evening canapés. Children under 14 are not accepted.

More modest in scope but elegant nonetheless is the **Natchez Eola Hotel,** 110 N. Pearl (② **866/445-3652** or 601/445-6000; www.natchezeola.com), a four-story red-brick hotel built in 1927. Located in the heart of downtown, the property has a grand but dark lobby dominated by marble, chandeliers, and oversize floral arrangements.

There's also a pleasant lounge and outdoor courtyard reminiscent of old New Orleans. Guest rooms are a bit more bright and cheerful, and contain all the basics travelers have come to expect. A bonus: All rooms have ceiling fans, important in the sweltering summer months, even on an air-conditioned property. Rates start at $101 double per night.

Natchez also has a wealth of wonderful bed-and-breakfast properties from which to choose. Overall, most are located in historic homes or bungalows and offer comfortable rooms and home-cooked breakfasts at very reasonable rates. The inn owners themselves are almost universally warm and gracious, seeming sincerely eager to extend old-fashioned southern hospitality to the thousands of tourists that are the backbone of Natchez's economy.

Theater lovers should try to book a room at **Myrtle Corner,** 600 State St. (© 601/ 455-5999; www.myrtlecorner.com), a crape-myrtle-shaded pink cottage downtown. Antiques and tasteful furnishings fill the four rooms, including a two-bedroom suite with fireplace and Jacuzzi. Rates run $110 to $330. *Note:* The inn's owners are two men who are actively involved in the **Natchez Little Theatre,** 319 Linton Ave., at Maple Street (© 601/442-2233; www.natchezlittletheatre.org), now in its 6th decade.

For privacy and spaciousness, consider **Arlington Heights,** 200 Arlington Ave. (© 601/446-7244; www.arlington-heights.net), a cozy 1890s home that has been recently converted to a bed-and-breakfast. The inn's owners live next door, leaving guests in the B&B's two large bedrooms to have the run of the house, including a cheerful library and comfy den. Children under 12 are not accepted, and smoking is not permitted. Rates are $125 double.

WHERE TO DINE

Located on the lush grounds of Stanton Hall, the **Carriage House Restaurant,** 401 High St. (© 601/445-5151), open since 1926, serves lunch daily and dinner only during pilgrimage tours. Sip a mint julep in the upscale dining room, where polished, pale wood furnishings are illuminated by lots of natural sunlight. The menu features burgers, salads, sandwiches, and southern staples such as fried chicken. Main courses run about $12.

Check your political correctness at the door if you want a peek at **Mammy's Cupboard,** 555 Hwy. 61 S. (© 601/445-8957), an eye-popping, lunchtime-only landmark known as much for its food (try the chicken salad) as for the unusual shape of its building. It's essentially a statue several stories high depicting the stereotypical Old South black "Mammy" figure; her hoop skirt forms a dome that houses the restaurant. This is one of those quirky places that you have to see to believe. Entrees run $5 to $8. For a potent combination of tangy, "knock-you-naked" margaritas and spicy tamales, head to another maternalistic favorite, **Fat Mama's Tamales,** 500 S. Canal St. (© 601/442-4548). Look for the cactus-bedecked log cabin aglow with orange neon. Nachos, chili, homemade sweet pickles, and Snickers pie round out the short menu. Nothing here costs over $8. In the downtown area, there are several notable diners, including **Pearl Street Pasta,** 104 A. Pearl St. (© 601/442-9284); and even the unexpected new **Thai Planet,** 112 N. Commerce St. (© 601/442-4220).

In the area along the river known as Natchez-Under-the-Hill, you'll find **Bowie's Tavern,** 100 Main St. (© 601/445-6627; www.bowiestavern.com). Spirits and pub

> ## Pull Over & into the Past
> If you're driving the lonely stretch of Highway 61 between Natchez and Vicksburg, take a restroom break or buy a Coke at the Old Country Store in the tiny burg of Lorman. The weathered wooden building used to be an old general store and gas station. Today it's a run-down but atmospheric flea market and souvenir shop that also offers a limited selection of hot soul food dishes prepared on the premises.

grub are dished out at this convivial nightspot that's part sports bar and part Old English–style tavern. Televisions carry live sporting events, and there's also occasional live music. Main courses run $9 to $14.

OXFORD

Home to the University of Mississippi, "Ole Miss," Oxford is a quaint small town where daily life revolves its 150-year-old Court Square. A popular weekend destination for out-of-towners and visiting alumni, Oxford offers an enticing array of great art galleries, bookstores, restaurants, and historic homes.

ESSENTIALS

GETTING THERE   **By Plane**   The easiest way to reach Oxford, as well as Clarksdale, is to fly into **Memphis International Airport** (© **901/922-8000;** www.memphisairport.org) and rent a car. It's about a 90-minute drive southwest to Oxford.

By Car   The major route into Oxford is **I-55** from both the north (Memphis) and south (Jackson).

VISITOR INFORMATION   Contact the **Oxford Tourism Council,** 107 Courthouse Sq., Suite 1, Oxford, MS 38655 (© **800/758-9177** or 662/234-4680; www.touroxfordms.com).

EXPLORING THE AREA

Oxford's favorite son is Nobel Prize–winning author William Faulkner, whose residence from 1930 until his death in 1963 was his beloved home, **Rowan Oak,** Old Taylor Road (© **662/234-3284**). A tour of the grounds, with its graceful magnolias and old farm buildings, is a trip back in time. Inside, literary enthusiasts can still marvel at the author's old manual typewriter, and read his handwritten outline for *A Fable,* which is scrawled on the wall of his study. It's closed Mondays and major holidays.

The most popular pastime in Oxford is simply strolling **The Square,** where travelers might spot former local residents, such as John Grisham, who have made guest appearances at **Square Books,** 160 Courthouse Sq. (© **662/236-2262;** www.squarebooks.com), in business since 1870 and regarded as one of the best independent bookstores in the country. Down the street is its bargain-priced annex, **Off Square Books,** 129 Courthouse Sq. (© **662/236-2828**), where thousands of discounted and remaindered books cram shelves and bins. It's also the site of Square Books' author signings and readings, as well as *Thacker Mountain Radio,* Oxford's original music and literature radio show. Best-selling authors such as Robert Olen Butler, Elmore Leonard, and Roy Blount, Jr., have read their works on the live show. Musical guests have run the gamut from Elvis Costello and Marty Stuart to the Del McCoury Band and the North Mississippi Allstars. The show is recorded live Thursdays from 5:30 to 6:30pm.

Next door, **Southside Gallery,** 150 Courthouse Sq. (© **662/234-9090**), is an always-interesting place that showcases everything from photography, painting, and sculpture to outsider art by the likes of Howard Finster.

WHERE TO STAY & DINE

Because of its proximity to Memphis, Oxford is a popular day-trip destination for many travelers. Perhaps as a result, there are only a handful of hotels and motels, most of them chains on the outskirts of town that cater to the parents of college kids and other travelers to the university.

Among the cleanest and most modern choices are the **Comfort Inn,** 1808 Jackson Ave. S. (© **662/234-6000**), which has a small outdoor pool; the larger **Days Inn,** 1101 Frontage Rd. (© **662/234-9500**); and **Holiday Inn Express and Suites,** 112 Heritage Rd. (© **800/465-4329** or 662/236-2500). Rates at the three range from about $55 to $80 double.

Call ahead and book early if you want to reserve a room at one of the city's bed-and-breakfast properties, which are often booked during weekends when Ole Miss has home football games or other major events. You won't see it advertised much because the place is always full, but try to book a stay at **Puddin' Place,** 1008 University Ave. (© **662/234-1250**), a spotless, cheerfully decorated 1892 house that has two large suites with private bathrooms. The owner is in the process of adding a private cottage in the tree-shaded backyard. Gourmet breakfasts are included in the room rates, which usually run $115 double (during Ole Miss football season it's $350 for the 2-night minimum weekend stay, and the hotel sells out these weekends months in advance).

For guests who don't mind rather simple furnishings and a lack of pizazz, try the **Oliver-Britt House Inn,** 512 Van Buren Ave. (© **662/234-8043**). The white-columned, red-brick structure has a welcoming front porch packed with potted plants and flowers. There are five guest rooms, all with private bathroom but no phone. Rates run $65 to $93 double; continental breakfast is available weekdays, and a full breakfast is served on weekends.

City Grocery, 152 Courthouse Sq. (© **662/232-8080;** www.citygroceryoxford. com), is one of the best restaurants in Mississippi. New Orleans–born chef John Currence finesses spicy cheese grits topped with plump shrimp, mushrooms, and smoked bacon, while offering an array of tempting gourmet salads, soups, and Cajun delicacies. Main courses cost $19 to $24. Reservations are recommended.

Doe's Eat Place, 1536 University Ave. (© **662/236-9003**), an offshoot of the legendary Greenville greasy spoon that offers steaks and hot tamales, is another noteworthy eatery. **Bottletree Bakery,** 923 Van Buren Ave. (© **662/236-5000**), is a must if you crave caffeine and the aroma of warm muffins being pulled from the oven. The cheery nook serves pastries and freshly baked breads as well as fine coffees, sandwiches, and salads. Oxford's favorite dive bar is **Proud Larry's,** 211 S. Lamar Blvd. (© **662/236-0050**), where live music and drink specials augment a simple menu of burgers, pasta, salads, and hand-tossed pizzas.

4 New Orleans

It may sound clichéd to call New Orleans magical and seductive, but it's the truth. Every one of your senses is engaged from the moment you arrive. Visually, the city is superb, from the lacy ironwork wrapped around the buildings of the French Quarter, to the stately, graceful old homes of the Garden District, to the giant oaks that drip

The French Quarter

ACCOMMODATIONS ■

Bourbon Orleans Hotel-A Wyndham
Historic Hotel **6**
Hotel Maison de Ville &
Audubon Cottages **5**
Hotel Monteleone **4**
Omni Royal Orleans **7**
Soniat House **11**

DINING ◆

Arnaud's **3**
Bayona **1**
Café du Monde **9**
Galatoire's **2**
Irene's Cuisine **10**
Johnny's Po' Boys **8**

with ghostly Spanish moss in City Park. But one cannot picture New Orleans anymore without recalling the devastation from the months following Hurricane Katrina. On August 29, 2005, New Orleans changed forever. In the wake of Hurricane Katrina, which was not quite as strong nor the direct hit originally predicted, at least three of the levees designed to keep the below-sea-level city safe from the waters of Lake Pontchartrain either broke or were breached. Eighty percent of one of the most historic and culturally rich cities in America was underwater. The water remained for weeks, months in certain places, and by the time it was gone, the landscape of New Orleans was permanently altered.

Today, recovery is ongoing, and fate of many citizens and establishments remains in question. Which prompts a question of your own, probably: Should I go?

Oh, yes.

Go, because New Orleans is not gone, not at all. Go, because the things you wanted—the beautiful architecture, the majestic oaks, the river wind, the quality of light that gives even the most mundane just a little bit of magic—all remain. New Orleans is a very user-friendly city, with most of what the average tourist would want to see concentrated in a few areas. As it happens, those areas were the least damaged by Katrina and the flooding aftermath. Go, because people are there, and as long as they are, there will be music, and food, and it will be some of the best of your life. Go, because perhaps you've wanted to help in any way you can, and now the best way you can is to help a historic city regain its economic feet. Go, because every brick in the French Quarter has a story to tell, and so does the damaged ground of the Ninth Ward, and you should bear witness. Go, because there is much to celebrate, and this is still the best place there is to do so.

"I want to be in that number," goes the song. I do indeed. I hope you do, too.

ESSENTIALS

GETTING THERE   By Plane   The city's **Louis Armstrong New Orleans International Airport** (www.flymsy.com) is served by most domestic major airlines. You'll find information booths scattered around the airport and in the baggage claim area, as well as a branch of the **Travelers Aid Society** (© 504/464-3522).

From the airport, you can reach the Central Business District by bus for $1.50 (exact change required). Buses run from 6am to 6:30pm. For more information, call the **Regional Transit Authority** (© 504/827-2600; www.norta.com). From the airport, you can get to your hotel on the **Airport Shuttle** (© 504/522-3500). For $13 per person (one-way), the van will take you directly to your hotel. There are Airport Shuttle information desks (staffed 24 hr.) in the airport. If you plan to take the Airport Shuttle *to* the airport when you depart, you must call a day in advance and let them know what time your flight is leaving.

A **taxi** from the airport to most hotels will cost about $29 for one to two persons; if there are three or more passengers, the fare is $12 per person plus a $1 gas surcharge.

By Train   Amtrak (© 800/USA-RAIL or 504/528-1610; www.amtrak.com) provides service to **Union Passenger Terminal,** 1001 Loyola Ave., in the Central Business District.

By Car   You can drive to New Orleans via **I-10, I-55, U.S. 90, U.S. 61,** or across the Lake Pontchartrain Causeway on **La. 25.** For the best roadside views, take U.S. 61 or La. 25, but only if you have time to spare. The larger roads are considerably faster.

VISITOR INFORMATION   Contact the extremely friendly and helpful **New Orleans Metropolitan Convention and Visitors Bureau,** 2020 St. Charles Ave., New Orleans, LA 70130 (© 800/672-6124 or 504/566-5011; www.neworleans cvb.com). Another source of information is the **New Orleans Multicultural Tourism Network,** 2020 St. Charles Ave., New Orleans, LA 70130 (© 800/725-5652 or 504/523-5652; www.soulofneworleans.com); you may be particularly interested in their self-directed tours of African-American landmarks.

SPECIAL EVENTS & FESTIVALS   Details on Mardi Gras and Jazz Fest, the city's two premier events, are found below.

From late March to early April is **Spring Fiesta,** with tours of many of the city's private homes, courtyards, and plantations. For the schedule, call the **Spring Fiesta**

Association (© **504/581-1367**). The mid-April **French Quarter Festival** kicks off with a parade down Bourbon Street. You can join people dancing in the streets, learn the history of jazz, visit historic homes, and take a ride on a riverboat. Many local restaurants set up booths in Jackson Square. For information, contact **French Quarter Festivals** (© **504/522-5730;** www.fqfi.org).

Halloween is celebrated citywide with events including Boo-at-the-Zoo for children, costume parties (including a Monster Bash), haunted houses (the best is in City Park), and the Moonlight Witches Run.

FAST FACTS If you need immediate medical assistance, go to the emergency room at **Ochsner Medical Institutions,** 1516 Jefferson Hwy. (© **504/842-3460**), or the **Tulane University Medical Center,** 1415 Tulane Ave. (© **504/588-5800**). The 24-hour pharmacy closest to the French Quarter is **Walgreens,** 1801 St. Charles Ave. (© **504/561-8458**).

You're allowed to drink on the street, but not from a glass or a bottle. Don't walk alone at night, and don't go into the cemeteries alone at any time during the day or night. Ask around locally about safety before you go anywhere. People will tell you if you should take a cab instead of walking or using public transportation.

The **sales tax** in New Orleans is 9%. An additional 4% tax is added to hotel bills, for a total of 13%

THE BIGGEST PARTIES OF 'EM ALL: MARDI GRAS & JAZZ FEST

MARDI GRAS The granddaddy of all New Orleans celebrations is Mardi Gras (French for "Fat Tuesday," the day before Ash Wednesday, when Lent begins). Two or 3 weeks before Mardi Gras itself, parades begin chugging through the streets with increasing frequency. If you want to experience Mardi Gras but don't want to face the full force of craziness, consider coming for the weekend 10 days before Fat Tuesday (the season officially begins the Fri of this weekend). You can count on 10 to 15 parades during the weekend by lesser-known *krewes* (sort of a social club) such as Cleopatra, Pontchartrain, Sparta, and Camelot.

Mardi Gras *krewe* Rex's King of Carnival arrives downtown from the Mississippi River on **Lundi Gras** the Monday night before Fat Tuesday. Festivities at the riverfront begin in the afternoon, with lots of drinking and live music leading up to the king's arrival around 6pm. Down the levee a few hundred feet, at Wolfenberg Park, the Zulu *krewe* has its own Lundi Gras celebration, with the king arriving around 5pm. That night, the Krewe of Orpheus holds their parade, with spectacular floats and a generous amount of trinkets and beads for parade-watchers.

The actual day of Mardi Gras starts with the two biggest parades, Zulu and Rex, which run back to back. Zulu starts near the Central Business District (CBD) at 8:30am; Rex starts Uptown at 10am. It will be early afternoon when Rex spills into the CBD. Nearby, at about this time, you can find some of the most elusive New Orleans figures, the Mardi Gras Indians, small communities of African Americans, and Creoles (some of whom have Native American ancestors), mostly from the inner city, decked out in elaborate beaded and feathered costumes.

After the parades, the action picks up in the French Quarter. The frat-party action is largely confined to Bourbon Street. The more interesting activity is in the lower Quarter and the Frenchmen section of the Faubourg Marigny.

Tips: Accommodations in the city and the nearby suburbs are booked solid during Mardi Gras, *so make your plans well ahead and book a room as early as possible.* Many people plan a year or more in advance. Prices are *much* higher during Mardi Gras, and most hotels and guesthouses impose minimum-stay requirements. Many, many cops are out, making the walk from Uptown to Downtown safer than at other times of year but, not surprisingly, the streets of New Orleans are a haven for pickpockets. Take precautions.

JAZZ FEST   The New Orleans Jazz & Heritage Festival, or simply Jazz Fest, is one of the best-attended, most-respected, and most musically comprehensive festivals in the world. Stand in the right place and, depending on which way the wind's blowing, you can catch as many as 10 musical styles from several continents and smell the tantalizing aromas of a dozen different food offerings.

Serious Jazz Fest aficionados eschew the big headliners and savor the lesser-known acts. They range from Mardi Gras Indians to old-time bluesmen who have never played outside the Delta, from Dixieland to avant-garde, from African artists making rare U.S. appearances to the top names in Cajun, zydeco, and, of course, jazz.

You must book hotels and flights months in advance, so you may have to schedule your visit around your own availability, not an appearance by a particular band. Just about every day at Jazz Fest is a good day, so this is not a hardship.

Try to purchase tickets as early as February. They're available by mail through **Ticketmaster** (© **504/522-5555;** www.ticketmaster.com). To order tickets by phone, or to get ticket information, call **New Orleans Jazz & Heritage Festival** (© **800/488-5252** or 504/522-4786; www.nojazzfest.com). Admission for adults is $20 to $30 in advance (depending on when you buy them) and $40 at the gate, $5 for children. Evening events and concerts (order tickets in advance for these events as well) can be attended at an additional cost—usually between $20 and $30.

Parking at the Fair Grounds is next to impossible. Take public transportation or one of the available shuttles. The **Regional Transit Authority** operates bus routes from various pickup points to the Fair Grounds. For schedules, contact © **504/827-7802** (www.norta.com).

WHAT TO SEE & DO
Audubon Aquarium of the Americas *Kids*
Still getting back up to speed after some devastating Katrina-related losses, this will once again be a world-class aquarium, highly entertaining and painlessly educational, with beautifully constructed exhibits. Kids love it, even those too impatient to read the graphics, but adults shouldn't overlook it, if for no other reason than it's a handy refuge from the rain.

Five major exhibit areas and dozens of smaller aquariums hold a veritable ocean of aquatic life native to the region and to the Americas. You can walk through the underwater tunnel in the Caribbean Reef exhibit, view a shark-filled re-creation of the Gulf of Mexico, or drop in to see the penguin exhibit. We particularly like the walk-through Waters of the Americas, where you wander in rainforests (complete with birds and piranhas) and see what goes on below the surface of swamps. The long-anticipated **Insectarium** (yep, a museum dedicated to the over 900,000 species of things that creep, crawl, and flutter) sustained a lot of damage, but fortunately, it will be opening in 2007. The Insectarium will be in the former U.S. Customs House, at 423 Canal St. The **IMAX theater** shows two or three films at regular intervals. Look for an astonishing Katrina documentary, showing the flooding and the rest of the devastation, to debut here in 2007. *Tip:* **Combination tickets** for the aquarium, the IMAX theater, the zoo, and a riverboat ride to the zoo are $41 for adults, $21 for children.

1 Canal St., at the river. ℭ **800/774-7394** or 504/581-4629. www.auduboninstitute.org. Aquarium $16 adults, $13 seniors, $9.50 children 2–12. IMAX $8 adults, $7 seniors, $5 children. Combination aquarium/IMAX tickets $20 adults, $17 seniors, $12 children. Aquarium Wed–Sun 10am–4pm; IMAX Wed–Sun 10am–5pm. Call for showtimes; advanced tickets recommended. Closed Mardi Gras and Christmas.

Audubon Zoo *(Kids)*

This is one of the country's best zoos. What's more, nearly perfectly planned and executed hurricane preparation meant the zoo virtually sailed through the catastrophe, with almost zero animal loss.

Here, in a setting of subtropical plants, waterfalls, and lagoons, some 1,800 animals (including rare and endangered species) live in natural habitats rather than cages. Don't miss the replica of a Louisiana swamp (complete with a rare white gator) or the "Butterflies in Flight" exhibit, where more than 1,000 butterflies live among lush, colorful vegetation. On hot and humid days, you should plan your visit for early or late in the day; otherwise, the animals will be sleeping off the heat.

6500 Magazine St. ℭ **504/581-4629.** www.auduboninstitute.org. Admission $12 adults, $9 seniors (over 64), $7 children 2–12. Tues–Fri 10am–4pm; Sat–Sun 10am–5pm. Last ticket sold 1 hr. before closing. Closed holidays.

The Cabildo

Constructed from 1795 to 1799 as the Spanish government seat in New Orleans, The Cabildo was the site of the signing of the Louisiana Purchase transfer. It is now the center of the Louisiana State Museum's facilities in the French Quarter. A multiroom exhibition informatively, entertainingly, and exhaustively traces the history of Louisiana from exploration through Reconstruction. Topics include antebellum music, mourning and burial customs, immigrants and how they fared here, and the changing roles of women in the South. Throughout are fabulous artifacts, including Napoleon's death mask.

701 Chartres St. ℭ **800/568-6968** or 504/568-6968. Fax 504/568-4995. http://lsm.crt.state.la.us/cabildo/cabildo.htm. Admission $6 adults, $5 students and seniors, free for children under 12. Tues–Sun 10am–4pm.

The Historic French Market *(Kids)*

Legend has it that the site of the French Market was originally used by Native Americans as a bartering market. It began to grow into an official market in 1812. Today, it's a mixed bag (and not nearly as colorful as its past). The Farmer's Market makes a fun amble as you admire everything from fresh produce and fish to more tourist-oriented items like hot sauces and Cajun and Creole mixes. Snacks like gator on a stick will amuse the kids. The Flea Market, a bit farther down from the Farmer's Market, is loaded with goods that are kind of junky: T-shirts, hats, purses, toys, and so on. Still, some good deals can be had. The flea market is open daily. *Note:* Renovations (planned before the storm) will be in progress until at least summer 2007. This should mostly affect only the Farmer's Market section, but be aware that some of the shops and stalls may be closed when you visit.

On Decatur St., toward Esplanade Ave. from Jackson Sq. ℭ 504/522-2621. www.frenchmarket.org. Daily roughly 9am–6pm (tends to start shutting down about an hour before closing).

Historic New Orleans Collection—Museum/Research Center

This museum of local and regional history is almost hidden away within a complex of historic French Quarter buildings. The oldest, constructed in the late 18th century, was one of the few structures to escape the disastrous fire of 1794. These buildings were owned by the collection's founders, Gen. and Mrs. L. Kemper Williams. Their former residence is open to the public for tours. There are also excellent tours of the Louisiana history galleries, with expertly preserved and displayed art, maps, and original documents like the transfer papers for the Louisiana Purchase of 1803. The Williams

Gallery, also on the site, is free to the public and presents changing exhibitions that focus on Louisiana's history and culture, including a terrific Katrina-related one.

533 Royal St., between St. Louis and Toulouse sts. ℭ **504/523-4662**. Fax 504/598-7108. www.hnoc.org. Free admission; tours $5. Tues–Sat 9:30am–4:30pm; tours Tues–Sat 10 and 11am, 2 and 3pm. Closed major holidays and Mardi Gras.

National D-Day Museum   Created by bestselling author (and *Saving Private Ryan* consultant) Stephen Ambrose, this unique museum tells the story of all 19 U.S. amphibious operations worldwide on that fateful day of June 6, 1944. A rich collection of artifacts (including some British Spitfire airplanes), plus top-of-the-line educational materials, make this museum one of the highlights of New Orleans. An expansion to be completed in 2009 will triple the museum's size and cover all the theaters and services in World War II, turning this already world-class facility into one of the major museums of the world. And they were recently declared the national WWII museum, expanding their scope and prestige.

945 Magazine St., in the Historic Warehouse District. ℭ **504/527-6012**. www.ddaymuseum.org. Admission $14 adults, $8 seniors, $6 military with ID and children ages 5–17, free for military in uniform and children under 5. Tues–Sun 9am–5pm (until 7pm on Thurs). Closed holidays.

New Orleans Museum of Art   NOMA, located in an idyllic section of City Park, is home to a 40,000-piece collection that includes pre-Columbian and Native American ethnographic art; 16th- to 20th-century European paintings, drawings, sculptures, and prints; Early American art; Asian art; and one of the largest decorative glass collections in the United States. Be sure to pick up a guide pamphlet from the information desk at the entrance. A great addition to the city's artistic offerings is the **Besthoff Sculpture Garden,** 5 acres of gardens, grass, and walkways that spotlight 50 modern sculptures. The garden has quickly become a New Orleans cultural highlight and is open Wednesday to Sunday 10am to 5pm, with free admission.

1 Collins Diboll Circle, at City Park and Esplanade. ℭ **504/658-4100**. www.noma.org. Admission $8 adults, $7 seniors (over 64) and students, $4 children 3–17, free to Louisiana residents. Wed–Sun 10am–4:30pm. Closed most major holidays.

The Ogden Museum of Southern Art   This museum may well be the premier collection of southern art in the United States. The new dramatic interior is a tad too short on space for art, and the fear is that certain exhibits may get short shrift and the breadth and range of southern artistry may be limited to outsider folk artists or photographers who specialize in old bluesmen (two of our favorite genres, we must admit). But we must also admit that the facility is wonderful, the artists are impressive, and the graphics are well designed. Though the hours at press time are limited, they have resumed their delightful Ogden After Hours, which includes a live band (anything from 1930s country to the New Orleans Klezmer All-Stars) playing in the atrium.

925 Camp St. ℭ **504/539-9600**. www.ogdenmuseum.org. Admission $10 adults, $8 seniors and students, $5 children 5–17. Thurs 6–8pm; Fri–Sun 11am–4pm.

The Presbytère   The Presbytère, part of the Louisiana State Museum, has turned the entire building into a smashing Mardi Gras museum. Five major themes (History, Masking, Parades, Balls, and the Courir du Mardi Gras) trace the history of this high-profile but frankly little-understood (outside of New Orleans) annual event. A re-creation of a float allows you to pretend you are throwing beads to a crowd on a screen in front of you. Heck, even some of the restrooms masquerade (appropriately) as the ubiquitous Fat Tuesday Porta Pottis! Allow a couple of hours to see it all.

751 Chartres St., Jackson Sq. © 800/568-6968 or 504/568-6968. Fax 504/568-4995. Admission $6 adults, $5 seniors and students, free for children under 13. Fri–Sun 10am–4pm.

ORGANIZED TOURS

Historic New Orleans Walking Tours (© 504/947-2120; www.tourneworleans. com) is the place to go for authenticity rather than sensationalism. Here, the tour guides are carefully chosen for their combination of knowledge and entertaining manner, and we cannot recommend the guides or the tours highly enough. The daily French Quarter tours ($12 adults) are the best straightforward, nonspecialized walking tours of this neighborhood. They also offer a Voodoo Tour, a Haunted Tour, and a Garden District Tour for $15 adults, $2 off on all tours for students and seniors.

Dr. Wagner's Honey Island Swamp Tours (© 985/641-1769 or 504/242-5877; www.honeyislandswamp.com) takes you by boat into the interior of Honey Island Swamp to view wildlife with native professional naturalist guides. Tours last approximately 2 hours. Prices are $23 for adults, $15 for children under 12 if you drive to the launch site yourself; the rate is $45 for adults, $25 for children if you want a narrated hotel pickup in New Orleans.

SHOPPING

Among the hunting grounds you may want to explore is the **Historic French Market** (see "What to See & Do," above).

Just across from Jackson Square at 600–620 Decatur St., the old **Jackson Brewery** building has been transformed into a jumble of shops (Cajun-Creole foodstuffs, souvenirs, fashion), cafes, and entertainment venues. For the best gallery-hopping, head straight to **Julia Street. Magazine Street** is the Garden District's premier shopping street. More than 140 shops (antiques, art galleries, boutiques, crafts, dolls) line the street in 19th-century brick storefronts and quaint cottagelike buildings. At the foot of Canal Street (365 Canal St.), where the street reaches the Mississippi River, **Canal Place** shopping center holds more than 50 shops, many of them branches of some of this country's most elegant retailers.

If you need a Mardi Gras costume, head for the **Little Shop of Fantasy,** 517 St. Louis (© 504/945-2435; www.littleshopoffantasy.com), where the owners sell the work of a number of local artists and more than 20 mask makers.

The **Louisiana Music Factory,** 210 Decatur St. (© 504/586-1094; www.louisiana musicfactory.com), carries a large selection of regional music.

WHERE TO STAY

Ashton's Bed & Breakfast   This charming guesthouse represents one of the gutsiest ventures in the city; post Katrina, their chimney collapsed and 5,000 bricks tore a gaping hole in their top story, causing all kinds of mayhem inside. And yet, it's been fully restored and is a fine and worthy alternative to some of its more costly compatriots. There's pretty custom paint treatments like shadow striping, on top of new molding and chandeliers, and other careful attention to detail. One room has a most inviting fluffy white bed, but its bathroom is contained in a curtained-off corner. Those with personal-space and privacy issues might want to head to room no. 3, which is most grand, with a four-poster bed and the nicest bathroom in the guesthouse, complete with a claw-foot tub. A full breakfast is served.

2023 Esplanade Ave., New Orleans, LA 70116. ℂ **800/725-4131** or 504/942-7048. Fax 504/947-9382. www.ashtonsbb.com. 8 units. $105–$170 double. Rates include full breakfast. AE, DISC, MC, V. Free parking.

Bourbon Orleans Hotel—A Wyndham Historic Hotel

The Bourbon Orleans takes up an entire block of prime real estate at the intersection of—guess where—Bourbon and Orleans streets. And, while many hotels *claim* to have an interesting history, this one actually does: The oldest part of the hotel is the Orleans Ballroom, constructed in 1815 as a venue for the city's masquerade, carnival, and quadroon balls. Today the hotel occupies three buildings but neither the lobby nor the French Regency–influenced rooms were hit by Katrina, which is a relief, since it had just gotten a handsome $16-million face-lift before the storm. The rooms for the mobility-impaired are well designed. Rooms in the 17s have views up Bourbon Street, but if you want to escape noisy street excitement, ask for an interior room. Small rooms are cozy but not unbearable. We are fond of the two-story town-house rooms, with exposed brickwork on the walls, and the beds upstairs in a romantic loft. Planned new additions include a blues bar featuring live local musicians, and a martini-and-wine bar—both done in contemporary styles.

717 Orleans St., New Orleans, LA 70116. ℂ **504/523-2222.** Fax 504/525-8166. www.bourbonorleans.com. 220 units. $139–$199 petite queen or twin; $189–$329 deluxe king or double; $239–$489 junior suite; $299–$599 town-house suite; $272–$482 town-house suite with balcony. Extra person $30. AE, DC, DISC, MC, V. Valet parking $25. **Amenities:** Restaurant; outdoor pool.

Chimes B&B

This is a real hidden gem, one that truly allows you to experience the city away from the typical tourist experience. The Chimes is in a less fashionable but more neighborhood-like portion of the Garden District, just 2 blocks off St. Charles Avenue. The Chimes reopened days after Katrina.

Rooms vary in size from a generous L-shape to a two-story loft type to some that are downright cozy. All have antiques but are so tastefully underdecorated, particularly in contrast to other B&Bs, that they are positively Zen. An ambitious continental breakfast is served in the hosts' house.

1146 Constantinople St., New Orleans, LA 70115. ℂ **504/899-2621,** or 504/453-2183 (owner's cellphone). Fax 504/899-9858. www.chimesneworleans.com. 5 units. $130–$155 double in season; $86–$140 off season. Rates include breakfast. Look for rates, availability, and featured specials online. AE, MC, V. Limited off-street free parking. Well-behaved pets accepted.

The 1896 O'Malley House

This (you guessed it) 1896 home flooded to a foot inside after Katrina, but has been so beautifully restored that you can't tell. It's one of the most smashing B&B's in the city, just a treasure inside, full of gorgeous antiques and repro furniture. The handsome, somewhat masculine (as opposed to frilly) rooms are each meticulously decorated, using clever touches such as vintage (at least appearing) oil paintings, Balinese puppets, and European art to set specific moods. Second-floor rooms are larger, and most have Jacuzzi tubs. The third floor is a clever use of design and space. These rooms are smaller and more garretlike. There is an expanded breakfast with eggs, waffles, and other fun. Although it's located on a dull stretch of street, and in a neighborhood only slowly returning post-flood (though soon there should be all kinds of newly restored Mid-City options close by), the B&B is also mere minutes from a nice section of Canal and a streetcar ride to the Quarter.

120 S. Pierce St., New Orleans, LA 70119. ℂ **866/226-1896** or 504/488-5896. www.1896omalleyhouse.com. 9 units. $99–$145 double; $175 special events. Rates include continental breakfast. AE, MC, V.

Hotel Maison de Ville & Audubon Cottages   A member of The Small Luxury Hotels of the World, the Maison de Ville is not quite as sterling as it has been, despite taking advantage of some storm damage to do some sprucing up in the form of new bedding, new paint, and replaced ceilings. Over all, it remains so romantic and charming that complaints only seem intermittently important. Most of the rooms surround an utterly charming courtyard (complete with fountain and banana trees). Rooms vary dramatically in size; however, some can be downright tiny, so ask when you reserve, as price is no indicator of size. Be careful you don't get a room overlooking the street—Bourbon is less than half a block away and makes its sorry presence known.

   The far more spacious **Audubon Cottages** (larger than many apartments, some with their own private courtyards), located a few blocks away and including a small, inviting pool, can go for less than the cramped queen rooms in the main hotel. All rooms are thoroughly lush, with nice touches such as feather beds, the service is helpful and courteous, and the continental breakfast disappointing. Overall, it's a romantic getaway—we just wish it wasn't so expensive.

727 Toulouse St., New Orleans, LA 70130. ℂ **800/634-1600** or 504/561-5858. Fax 504/528-9939. www.maison deville.com. 16 units, 7 cottages. $199–$249 double and queen; $219–$269 king; $329–$399 suite; $219–$399 1-bedroom cottage; $599–$699 2-bedroom cottage; $770–$960 3-bedroom cottage. Rates include continental breakfast. AE, DC, DISC, MC, V. Valet parking $30. **Amenities:** Restaurant; outdoor pool.

Hotel Monteleone   Opened in 1886, the Monteleone is the largest hotel in the French Quarter and it seems to keep getting bigger without losing a trace of its trademark charm. Everyone who stays here loves it, probably because it's a family hotel whose approach to their business is reflected by the staff, among the most helpful in town. One guest who stayed here with a child with disabilities raved about the facilities.

   All the rooms have been freshly renovated (Katrina winds broke windows) and look blandly pretty as a result, though there is still some difference in terms of size and style. Some have four-poster beds and Jacuzzis, others have no window. One of the city's best-kept secrets is the renovated rooftop pool, with unencumbered views of the city.

214 Royal St., New Orleans, LA 70130. ℂ **800/535-9595** or 504/523-3341. Fax 504/561-5803. www.hotel monteleone.com. 570 units. $199–$275 double; $360–$2,500 suite. Extra person $25. Children under 18 stay free in parent's room. Package rates available. AE, DC, DISC, MC, V. Valet parking $19 car, $25 small SUV. Pets allowed on certain floors, for a fee and deposit. **Amenities:** 3 restaurants; heated rooftop swimming pool (open year-round); fitness center (understocked but with fabulous views of the city and river).

The House on Bayou Road   If you want to stay in a rural and romantic plantation setting but still be near the French Quarter, try The House on Bayou Road, quite probably the most smashing guesthouse in town. Just off Esplanade Avenue, this intimate Creole plantation home, built in the late 1700s, has been restored by owner Cynthia Reeves, who oversees an operation of virtual perfection.

   Each room has its own charm and is individually decorated to a fare-thee-well—slightly cluttered, not quite fussy, but still lovingly done aesthetically. The Bayou St. John Room (the old library) holds a queen-size four-poster bed and has a working fireplace; the Bayou Delacroix has the same kind of bed and a wonderfully large bathtub. Unfortunately, a private cottage was destroyed post-Katrina and will need to be rebuilt.

   The unusually extensive grounds are beautifully manicured, despite losing about 22 trees to Katrina, and there's an outdoor pool, Jacuzzi, patio, and screened-in porch. Expect a hearty plantation-style breakfast.

2275 Bayou Rd., New Orleans, LA 70119. ⓒ **800/882-2968** or 504/945-0992. Fax 504/945-0993. www.house onbayouroad.com. 8 units, 2 cottages. $155–$320 double. Rates include full breakfast. AE, MC, V. Children over 12 welcome. Free off-street parking. **Amenities:** Outdoor pool; Jacuzzi.

International House　International House sets the local standard for modern hotels with its creative design and meticulous attention to detail. Record-company and film execs love it, but so should anyone who's had enough of Victorian sweetness and needs a palate cleanser. Here, a wonderful old Beaux Arts bank building has been transformed into a modern space that still pays tribute to its locale. Consequently, in the graceful lobby, classical pilasters stand next to modern wrought-iron chandeliers. Interiors are the embodiment of minimalist chic. Rooms are simple with muted, monochromatic (okay, beige) tones, tall ceilings and ceiling fans, up-to-the-minute bathroom fixtures, but also black-and-white photos of local musicians and characters, books about the city, plus some cushy amenities such as feather pillows, large TVs, your own private phone number in your room, and CD players with CDs.

221 Camp St., New Orleans, LA 70130. ⓒ **800/633-5770** or 504/553-9550. Fax 504/553-9560. www.ihhotel.com. 117 units. $149–$379 double; $369–$1,799 suite. AE, DC, DISC, MC, V. Valet parking $35. **Amenities:** Restaurant, health club.

The McKendrick-Breaux House　This is one of the best B&Bs in town. The rooms are done in impeccably good taste (barely storm touched—they reopened 3 weeks later, housing FEMA types!), with high-quality mattresses and pillows, and each has its own style; some modern with larger bathrooms, some with claw-foot tubs and (sadly nonworking) fireplaces, and others evoke classic garret quarters, with exposed brick walls and less traffic noise than others. A full breakfast has been added.

1474 Magazine St., New Orleans, LA 70130. ⓒ **888/570-1700** or 504/586-1700. Fax 504/522-7134. www. mckendrick-breaux.com. 9 units. $155–$235 double. Rates include tax and full breakfast. AE, DC, DISC, MC, V. Limited free off-street parking. **Amenities:** Jacuzzi in courtyard.

Omni Royal Orleans *Kids*　Despite being part of a chain, this is an elegant hotel that escapes feeling sterile and generic. This is only proper given that it is on the former site of the venerable 1836 St. Louis Exchange Hotel, one of the country's premier hostelries and a center of New Orleans social life until the final years of the Civil War. The hotel, which enjoys a prime location smack in the center of the Quarter, suffered no damage from Katrina. Furnishings in the guest rooms have grave good taste, full of muted tones and plush furniture, with windows that let you look dreamily out over the Quarter. Suites are vast, making this a good choice for families despite the fancy appearance. Service is swift and conscientious and there are more amenities available here than in comparable properties.

621 St. Louis St., New Orleans, LA 70140. ⓒ **800/THE-OMNI** in the U.S. and Canada, or 504/529-5333. Fax 504/529-7089. www.omniroyalorleans.com. 346 units. $169–$339 double; $339–$950 suite; $1,100–$1,500 penthouse. Children under 18 stay free in parent's room. AE, DC, DISC, MC, V. Valet parking $23. **Amenities:** Restaurant; heated outdoor pool; health club.

Soniat House　The recipient of endless tributes from various prestigious travel journals, the wonderful and romantic Soniat House lives up to the hype. Keeping a low profile behind a solid wood gate, it is classic Creole—the treasures are hidden off the street. Inside this nonsmoking property you will find a perfect little hideaway, an oasis of calm that seems impossible in the Quarter. The beyond-efficient staff will spoil you, and the sweet courtyards, candlelit at night, will soothe you.

Rooms do vary, if not in quality then at least in distinction. All have antiques, but if you want, say, high ceilings and really grand furniture, you are better off in the main house or the suite-filled annex across the street. The rooms in the old kitchen and other buildings are not quite as smashing by comparison. On the main property, bathrooms are small, though some rooms have their own private balconies, but across the street they gain size, not to mention Jacuzzi bathtubs, custom decor, and antique furnishings. Many rooms have nonworking fireplaces, and all are decorated in simple, elegant good taste, including original art on the walls. Our only real complaint is the extra charge ($13) for the admittedly delicious, but small, breakfast.

1133 Chartres St., New Orleans, LA 70116. (C) **800/544-8808** or 504/522-0570. Fax 504/522-7208. www.soniat house.com. 33 units. $265–$325 double; $395–$675 suite; $750 2-bedroom suite. AE, MC, V. Valet parking $25. No children under 12. **Amenities:** Access to nearby health club (for additional charge).

Windsor Court *(Best)*   Pre-Katrina, *Condé Nast Traveler* voted the Windsor Court the Best Hotel in North America And post? There likely is a finer hotel on the continent, but it can't be found in New Orleans. The unassuming, somewhat office-building exterior is camouflage for the quiet but posh delights found within. The accommodations are exceptionally spacious, with classy, not flashy, decor. Almost all are suites (either really big, or downright huge) featuring large bay windows or a private balcony overlooking the river or the city, a private foyer, a large living room, a bedroom with French doors, a large marble bathroom with particularly luxe amenities, two dressing rooms, and a "petite kitchen." You aren't going to get better traditional hotel accommodations anywhere else in New Orleans. The level of service is extraordinarily high.

300 Gravier St., New Orleans, LA 70130. (C) **800/262-2662** or 504/523-6000. Fax 504/596-4749. www.windsor courthotel.com. 324 units. $210–$350 standard double; $230–$400 junior suite; $355–$450 full suite; $525–$975 bedroom suite. Children under 12 stay free in parent's room. AE, DC, DISC, MC, V. Valet parking $28. **Amenities:** Restaurant; health club w/resort-size pool, hot tub.

WHERE TO DINE

Arnaud's CREOLE   You need to try at least one venerable, properly New Orleans atmospheric establishment, and that one should be Arnaud's, which post-Katrina is doing some of the best culinary work it has in years. Apart from the signature appetizer, shrimp Arnaud (boiled shrimp topped with a spicy rémoulade sauce), we love the crabmeat Ravigotte (generous amounts of sweet lump crabmeat tossed with a Creole mustard–based sauce, hearts of palm, and other veggies), and the newly added charbroiled oysters, all smoky and buttery flavor. Delicious fish dishes include snapper or trout Pontchartrain (topped with crabmeat). Any filet mignon entree is superb. In addition to the formal (and seriously New Orleans) dining room, there is the more casual jazz bistro, which features lovely lunches, with entertainment (and an extra cover charge) at night.

813 Bienville St. (C) **866/230-8892** or 504/523-5433. www.arnauds.com. Reservations requested. Business casual. Main courses $21–$36. AE, DC, DISC, MC, V. Daily 6–10pm; Sun brunch 10am–2:30pm.

Bayona INTERNATIONAL   Chef-owner Susan Spicer is a local treasure, and certainly her grit in reopening her business—she lost her house as did her co-manager, business manager, and assistant—has only increased that affection. Happily, Bayona's lovely courtyard came through the storm just fine, and was blooming like crazy by summer 2006.

Knockout entrees have included medallions of lamb loin with a lavender honey aioli (a mayonnaise-based sauce) and a zinfandel demi-glace, and a perfectly grilled pork

Whole Lotta Muffuletta Goin' On

Muffulettas are almost mythological sandwiches, enormous concoctions of round Italian bread, Italian cold cuts and cheeses, and olive salad. One person cannot eat a whole one—at least not in one sitting. Instead, share; a half makes a good meal. Judging from the line that forms at lunchtime, many others agree with us that **Central Grocery**, 923 Decatur St. (*Ⓒ* **504/523-1620**), makes the best muffuletta there is (about $10 for a whole sandwich).

chop with a stuffing of fontina cheese, fresh sage, and prosciutto. Entrees come with a nice selection of sides such as gnocchi, puréed butternut squash, or fresh sweet corn.

430 Dauphine St. *Ⓒ* **504/525-4455**. www.bayona.com. Reservations required at dinner, recommended at lunch. Main courses $9–$15 lunch, $22–$28 dinner. AE, DC, DISC, MC, V. Tues–Thurs 6–9:30pm; Fri–Sat 6–10pm; Wed–Fri 11:30am–2pm; Sat noon–3pm.

Brigtsen's CAJUN/CREOLE   There was some anxiety that Brigtsen's might not reopen post-storm, but it did, once again offering one of the loveliest evenings you'll spend in a Crescent City restaurant. Nestled in a converted 19th-century house at the Riverbend, it's warm, intimate, and romantic. Brigtsen has a special touch with rabbit; the rabbit and andouille gumbo is delicious. Save room for desserts such as banana bread pudding or a peanut butter mousse sandwich.

723 Dante St. *Ⓒ* **504/861-7610**. www.brigtsens.com. Reservations required. Main courses $21–$29. AE, DC, MC, V. Tues–Sat 5:30–10pm.

Café du Monde COFFEE   Since 1862 Café du Monde has been selling café au lait and beignets (and nothing but) on the edge of Jackson Square. And boy, was its reopening after Katrina one of those moments when the city knew it would be coming back. It's a must-stop on any trip to New Orleans. What's a beignet? (Say ben-*yay*, by the way.) A square French doughnut-type object, hot and covered in powdered sugar. You might be tempted to shake off some of the sugar. Don't. Trust us. Pour more on, even. You'll be glad you did. Wash them down with chicory coffee.

In the French Market, 800 Decatur St. *Ⓒ* **504/525-4544**. www.cafedumonde.com. 3 beignets for $1.60. No credit cards. Daily 24 hr. Closed Christmas.

Commander's Palace *Best* CREOLE   The much-beloved (and recently reopened) Commander's is perhaps *the* symbol of the New Orleans dining scene, and for good reason. The building has been a restaurant for a century, it's at the top (more or less) of the multibranched Brennan family restaurant tree, and its chefs have gone on to their own fame and household name status (Prudhomme and Emeril ring any bells?), plus they train and produce their own outstanding locals, so the tradition keeps spreading.

In a beautiful and now freshly renovated 1880s Victorian house, it has a nearly endless series of dining rooms, each more appealing and romantic than the last. We hope to see the return of the *petite couchon baton* ("little pig on a stick"), which consisted of a pork belly cooked in brown sugar and a fritter of pork *rillettes* impaled on a sugarcane baton. A daily gumbo of relatively exotic ingredients might convince even a committed Cajun cook to reconsider his own traditions. Try the Creole-mustard-crusted lamb or any of the Gulf fish preparations. We remain torn between the many incredible desserts such as bread pudding soufflé and the chocolate molten.

1403 Washington Ave. ✆ **504/899-8221.** www.commanderspalace.com. Reservations recommended. Main courses $26–$42. AE, DC, DISC, MC, V. Mon–Fri 11:30am–1:30pm; daily 6–9:30pm; Brunch Sat 11:30am–1pm and Sun 10:30am–1:30pm. Closed Christmas Day and Mardi Gras Day.

Cuvee CONTEMPORARY CREOLE Doing its darnedest to be considered the best restaurant in town, Cuvee is certainly the most innovative and interesting. Join local raving foodies in a romantic and cozy brick-lined room where you might get to sample—should the seasonally changing menu allow—the foie gras three ways (seared, tourchon topped with praline bacon on toast, and—wait for it—in crème brûlée, pretty much the best pork-and-egg dish you might ever have) or the hilarious and yet weirdly successful foie gras Twinkie. But it's the pork belly that keeps more than one local connoisseur coming back for more. Fittingly, desserts are equally witty.

322 Magazine St. ✆ **504/587-9001.** www.restaurantcuvee.com. Reservations highly recommended. Main courses $20–$30 dinner. AE, DC, MC, V. Mon–Sat 6–10pm.

Dooky Chase SOUL FOOD/CREOLE Owners Leah and husband Dooky Chase have served prominent African-American politicians, musicians, and business people Chef Leah's classic soul food as gloriously influenced by the city's French, Sicilian, and Italian traditions for decades. The restaurant had 2 feet of flooding and mold issues, and rebuilding has come along very slowly, but they expect to be reopened by the time you read this (plans are for Jan 2007). Longtime menu favorites include shrimp Clemenceau, an unlikely but successful casserole of sautéed shellfish, mushrooms, peas, and potatoes, not to mention exquisite fried chicken.

2301 Orleans Ave. ✆ **504/821-0600.** Reservations recommended at dinner.

Elizabeth's CREOLE The average tourist may not head over to the Bywater because, well, because it's not the Quarter. That's too bad—not only will they miss a true N'Awlins neighbahood, but they will also miss experiences like Elizabeth's. Here you eat, as they say, "Real Food, Done Real Good"—and, we add, real cheap. Food calling for health advisories, such as the praline bacon (topped with sugar and pecans—"pork candy" the shameless chef calls it; you must not miss this, but it's only served at breakfast time); or stuffed French toast (*pain perdu* piled high with cream cheese flavored with strawberries); or the breakfast po' boy. Dinner features specials such as pan-seared salmon with Dijon beurre blanc sauce and southern fried chicken livers with pepper jelly.

601 Gallier St. ✆ **504/944-9272.** www.elizabeths-restaurant.com. Breakfast and lunch, everything under $10; dinner $6.95–$16. MC, V. Tues–Fri 8am–2:30pm and 6–10pm; Sat 9am–2:30pm and 6–10pm; Sun 9am–2:30pm.

Emeril's CREOLE/NEW AMERICAN At press time, Emeril had reopened two of his restaurants and was working on the third. We can vouch for his first namesake restaurant. Although it may no longer be trend setting, it certainly isn't resting on its laurels in terms of quality, a remarkable feat given how long the place has been around. Since our last well-stuffed visit, the menu has been given an impressive overhaul, featuring many intriguing new dishes, and some old favorites.

For starters, try the barbecued shrimp, which is paired with charming little rosemary biscuits. Entree standouts include a precisely done Moroccan spice-crusted salmon with beluga lentils and andouille-crusted redfish. Save room for the notable banana cream pie. *Note:* This is a very popular place with suit-clad businessmen at lunch and other clear regulars who appear to get speedier service than more anonymous patrons.

800 Tchoupitoulas St. ℂ **504/528-9393**. www.emerils.com. Reservations highly recommended at dinner. Main courses $24–$39; menu degustation (tasting menu) only on weekends $65. AE, DC, DISC, MC, V. Sun–Thurs 6–10pm; Fri–Sat 6–10:30pm.

Galatoire's FRENCH   The venerable Galatoire's causes heated discussions among local foodies: the best restaurant in New Orleans or past its prime? This conversation was rendered almost irrelevant when it reopened after Katrina. But really, you don't come to Galatoire's for cutting-edge cuisine. You come to it to eat a nice piece of fish, perfectly sautéed or broiled, topped with fresh crabmeat. It was Tennessee Williams's favorite restaurant (his table is the one right behind the word RESTAURANT on the window). And the venerable James Beard Foundation must love it because it honored this restaurant with its Outstanding Restaurant Award in 2005. We love the lump crabmeat appetizer and the oysters Rockefeller. For an entree, get the red snapper or redfish topped with sautéed crabmeat meunière.

209 Bourbon St. ℂ **504/525-2021**. www.galatoires.com. Reservations accepted for upstairs. Jackets required for men after 5pm and all day Sun. Main courses $14–$27. AE, DC, DISC, MC, V. Tues–Sat 11am–10pm; Sun noon–10pm. Closed Memorial Day, July 4, Thanksgiving, and Christmas.

Irene's Cuisine FRENCH/ITALIAN   Waiting upward of 90 minutes for a table at Irene's is something you can count on. But locals feel the French Provincial and Italian food is worth it (you should have seen their faces when Irene's reopened in Oct 2005, wanting to be an oasis in the madness), and you may as well. Once you do enter, after being lured in from a block away by the potent smell of garlic, you will find a dark, cluttered tavern, not unromantic, with ultrafriendly waiters who seem delighted you came and who keep the crowds happy with prompt service. The menu is heavier on meats and fish than pasta; salads come with a tangy balsamic dressing; and soups can be intriguing combinations. Desserts, alas, are rather dull.

539 St. Philip St. ℂ **504/529-8811**. Reservations accepted only for parties of 5 or more, plus Christmas Eve, New Year's Eve, and Valentine's Day. Main courses $17–$26. AE, MC, V. Mon–Sat 5:30–10pm. Closed New Year's Day, July 4, Labor Day, Thanksgiving, and Christmas.

Johnny's Po' Boys SANDWICHES   For location (right near a busy part of the Quarter) and menu simplicity, you can't ask for much more than Johnny's, which returned to the culinary scene around December 2005. They put anything you could possibly imagine on huge hunks of French bread, including the archetypal fried seafood (add some Tabasco, we strongly advise), deli meats, cheese omelets, and the starch-o-rama that is a French Fry Po' Boy. You need to try it. *Really.*

511 St. Louis St. ℂ **504/524-8129**. Everything under $11. No credit cards. Daily 9am–3pm.

Liuzza's CREOLE/ITALIAN   This is a neighborhood institution since 1947 (it's humble, small, and often crowded with regulars), and when the waitress talks, you betcha you listen. The menu was somewhat limited at press time, though it included the famous deep-fried dill pickle slices and po' boys. By the time you read this, we hope they will have added back those specials, and all the hearty Italian and other comfort food that draws us to Liuzza's. Don't miss having a beer in the massive, frosted mugs that rode out Katrina safely in the fridge!

3636 Bienville St. ℂ **504/482-9120**. www.liuzzas.com. Main courses $3.95–$20 lunch, $7.50–$20 dinner. AE, DC, DISC, MC, V. Tues–Sat 11am–9pm.

Mandina's CREOLE/ITALIAN   In a city renowned for its small, funky, local joints as well as its fine-dining establishments, dis is da ultimate neighbahood N'Awlins restaurant. Tommy Mandina's family has owned and operated this restaurant and bar since the late 1800s, and the menu hasn't changed much in the last 50 years or so. This is a good thing. What will change when they reopen, which they should have by the time you read this, is the interior; Mandina's got hammered by the storm. Check the website for hours.

Standouts among the appetizers are the greasy but yummy fried onion rings, the excellent tangy shrimp rémoulade, and the crawfish cakes. Soups are always fine as well, especially seafood gumbo and turtle soup au sherry. Then go for the wonderful red beans and rice with Italian sausage, the trout meunière, or the grilled trout.

3800 Canal St. (C) **504/482-9179**. www.mandinas.com. Main courses $7.50–$23. AE, MC, V.

Mother's SANDWICHES/CREOLE   Perhaps the proudest of all restaurants when New Orleans was named Fattest City in the U.S. was Mother's, whose overstuffed, mountain-size po' boys absolutely helped contribute to the results. It has long lines and zero atmosphere, but who cares when faced with a Famous Ferdi Special—a giant roll filled with baked ham (the homemade house specialty), roast beef, gravy, and debris (the bits of beef that fall off when the roast is carved)? There's other food, including one of the best breakfasts in the city.

401 Poydras St. (C) **504/523-9656**. www.mothersrestaurant.net. Menu items $1.75–$20. AE, MC, V. Mon–Sat 7:30am–8pm.

Palace Café CONTEMPORARY CREOLE   This is where to go for low-key and non-intimidating romantic dining. Housed attractively in the historic Werlein's for Music building, this popular Brennan family restaurant, looking spiffy despite a whole lot of post-Katrina icky cleanup, is about to have the first sidewalk dining on Canal, thanks to some street renovations, which will be a treat on balmy nights. Be sure to order the crabmeat cheesecake appetizer, and possibly the escargots as well. As for main courses, they do fish especially well. For dessert, they invented the by-now-ubiquitous white-chocolate bread pudding, and no matter what others may claim, they have the best.

605 Canal St. (C) **504/523-1661**. www.palacecafe.com. Reservations recommended. Main courses $19–$27. AE, DC, DISC, MC, V. Tues–Fri 11:30am–2:30pm; Tues–Sat 5–9pm; Sun brunch 10:30am–2:30pm.

NEW ORLEANS AFTER DARK
JAZZ & BLUES CLUBS   **Donna's,** 800 N. Rampart St. ((C) **504/596-6914**),a corner bar at the very northern edge of the Quarter, has become one of the top spots for great local music, including the revival of the brass-band experience and a variety of jazz and blues traditions.

It doesn't get any more authentic than the jazz at **Preservation Hall,** 726 St. Peter St. ((C) **888/946-JAZZ** or 504/522-2841). With no seats, terrible sightlines, and constant crowds, you won't be able to see much, but you won't care because you will be having too fun and cheerfully sweaty a time. Even if you don't consider yourself interested in jazz, there is a seriously good time to be had here, and you very probably will come away with a new appreciation for the music.

If your idea of jazz extends beyond Dixieland and if you prefer a concert-type setting over a messy nightclub, head for **Snug Harbor,** 626 Frenchmen St. ((C) **504/ 949-0696**). On the fringes of the French Quarter (1 block beyond Esplanade Ave.), Snug Harbor is the city's premier showcase for contemporary jazz, with a few blues and R&B combos thrown in for good measure.

ZYDECO   Mid City Lanes Rock 'n' Bowl, 4133 S. Carrollton Ave. (© **504/482-3133**), is anything but an inauthentic tourist trap. The club is set in the middle of a bowling alley, which is itself set in the middle of a strip mall. Mid City bowling is nothing to write home about unless you like lanes that slope. But as a club, it's one of the finest and best experiences in New Orleans. Certainly it's the best place for zydeco. Mid City is not limited to just zydeco: It also features top New Orleans rock and R&B groups and some touring acts.

RHYTHM, ROCK & THE REST OF THE MUSIC SCENE   The Spotted Cat Cocktail Lounge, 623 Frenchmen St. (© **504/943-3887**), is our favorite live-music venue in New Orleans, but that's because of our particular New Orleans aesthetic bent; we are partial to cramped rooms where the band plays without much (if any) amplification, and what they play is usually fresh takes on classic and big-band jazz. This is the place on Frenchmen to go for late-night canoodling or an otherwise intimate evening, with chocolate martinis and local acts playing nightly.

House of Blues, 225 Decatur St. (© **504/529-2583**), is a little too Disney for New Orleans, but give them credit for adequate sightlines, good sound, and first-rate bookings, from local legends such as the Neville Brothers to such ace out-of-towners as Los Lobos, Marcia Ball, and Nanci Griffith.

The **Maple Leaf Bar,** 8316 Oak St. (© **504/866-9359**), is what a New Orleans club is all about and its reputation was only furthered when it became the very first live music venue to reopen, just weeks after Katrina, with an emotional, generator-powered performance by Walter "Wolfman" Washington. More often than not, the crowd spills onto the sidewalk and into the street to dance and drink. If Beausoleil or the ReBirth Brass Band is playing, do not miss it; go and dance 'til you drop.

THE BAR SCENE   At the Carousel Bar & Lounge in the Monteleone Hotel, 214 Royal St. (© **504/523-3341**), piano music is featured Wednesday through Saturday, but the real attraction is the bar itself—it really is a carousel, and it really does revolve. **Feelings Café,** 2600 Chartres St. (© **504/945-2222**), is a funky, low-key neighborhood restaurant and hangout, set around a classic New Orleans courtyard.

Pat O'Brien's, 718 St. Peter St. (© **504/525-4823**; www.patobriens.com), is a reliable, rowdy, and friendly introduction to New Orleans, though the wait to get in the door can be long. It's world famous for its gigantic, rum-based hurricane drink, served in signature 29-ounce glasses.

Lafitte's Blacksmith Shop, 941 Bourbon St. (© **504/593-9761**), dating from the 1770s, is the oldest building in the Quarter. In other towns, this would be a tourist trap. Here, it feels authentic and is totally worth a stop, even if you don't drink.

Outside the Quarter, **Circle Bar,** 1032 St. Charles Ave. (© **504/588-2616**), is a hip, happening place, with a quirky romantic mood. A sparkling and splendid new addition to the already terrific Frenchmen club scene is **Ray's Boom Boom Room,** 508 Frenchmen St. (© **504/248-0801**). The club is the epitome of New Orleans style and is partly owned by local music fave and staunch supporter Kermit Ruffins. Expect nightly music on two stages.

7

The Midwest

The midwestern states are America's heartland, where the ideal of small-town America and the values that go with it are epitomized. The area evokes images of neat farmlands, tree-lined small-town streets, and hardworking, industrialized cities.

This chapter concentrates on an area loosely composed of the states that originally made up the Northwest Territory: Illinois, Indiana, Michigan, Minnesota, Ohio, and Wisconsin, together with neighboring Missouri. America's richest farmland is found here as well as some of America's most important big cities, including the great metropolis of Chicago.

The ideal small town still exists, and as you travel through the area you'll discover that people really do seem more open, friendly, and down-to-earth—even the cities have a sense of community. Sports are a way of life here, from rooting for your baseball or basketball team—national or local—to hiking, skiing, or biking in gently rolling landscape or rugged terrain. And history is everywhere, reflecting the Midwest's Native American legacy and its immigrant heritage, the pioneers of every nationality who first came to settle this land.

1 Chicago

With all due respect to the late "Chairman of the Board," the city of Chicago is about as "toddlin'" as one of the Rat Pack's all-night blowouts. And don't call it the "Second City," either. It's certainly the first city of American architecture, not to mention its sizzling restaurant, music, and performing arts scenes. In fact, you could argue that Chicago is the quintessential American metropolis—not just the first great city carved from the young nation's western frontier, but an international capital of commerce and culture that somehow melds the urban swagger of New York with down-to-earth midwestern charm. "Toddlin'?" More like "struttin'."

ESSENTIALS
GETTING THERE   By Plane   O'Hare International Airport (© 773/686-2200; www.flychicago.com, online airport code ORD) has long battled with Atlanta's Hartsfield for the title of the world's busiest airport and is served by most domestic carriers and many international airlines. It's northwest of the city proper, about a 30-minute to an hour's drive from downtown; a cab costs $30 to $35. From the airport, the "El" (elevated train) takes you to the Loop for $2 (30- to 40-min. ride).

On the southwest side of the city is Chicago's other major airport, **Midway** (© 773/838-0600; www.flychicago.com, online airport code MDW), smaller than O'Hare and served by fewer airlines (but many of them are discount airlines, so fares into Midway can be cheaper). The "El" can take you to the Loop in about half an hour. A taxi into town will cost $25 to $30.

The Midwest

Continental Airport Express (☎ 888/2-THE-VAN; www.airportexpress.com) services most first-class hotels in Chicago; check with your bell captain. The cost is $25 one-way ($45 round-trip) to or from O'Hare and $20 one-way ($36 round-trip) to or from Midway.

By Train   Amtrak (☎ 800/USA-RAIL; www.amtrak.com) pulls into **Union Station,** 210 S. Canal St., between Adams and Jackson streets (☎ 312/655-2385; Subway/El: Clinton or Quincy; bus: 1, 60, 151, or 156). There's frequent service from Milwaukee (trip time: 1½ hr.) and Cleveland (6½ hr.); daily service from Detroit (6 hr.), Indianapolis (5½ hr.), St. Louis (5½ hr.), Kansas City (8 hr.), New York (20 hr.), Washington, D.C. (19 hr.), New Orleans (19½ hr.), Los Angeles (30 hr.), San Francisco (53 hr.), and Seattle (46 hr.).

By Car   The major routes into Chicago are **I-80/I-90** from the east (Cleveland), **I-80** and **I-88** from the west (Des Moines), **I-94** from the east (Detroit) and north (Milwaukee), **I-65** from the southeast (Indianapolis), and **I-55** from the southwest (Springfield, St. Louis). I-294 loops around the outer suburbs.

VISITOR INFORMATION   The **Chicago Office of Tourism,** Chicago Cultural Center, 78 E. Washington St., Chicago, IL 60602 (☎ 877/CHICAGO, or 866/710-0294 TTY; www.877chicago.com), will mail a packet of materials with information on upcoming events and attractions. The center itself has a phone that you can use to make hotel reservations, and several couches and a cafe where you can study maps and plan your itinerary. It's open Monday through Friday from 10am to 6pm, Saturday from 10am to 5pm, and Sunday from 11am to 5pm; it's closed on holidays.

The **Illinois Bureau of Tourism** (☎ 800/2-CONNECT, or 800/406-6418 TTY; www.enjoyillinois.com) can provide general and specific information about the city and other Illinois destinations 24 hours a day.

GETTING AROUND   By Public Transportation   The **CTA** (Chicago Transit Authority) operates a useful information service (☎ 836-7000, or 836-4949 TTY from any area code in the city and suburbs; www.transitchicago.com) that functions daily from 5am to 1am. Excellent CTA maps are usually available at subway or El stations, or by calling the CTA.

Fares for the bus, subway, and El are $2, with an additional 25¢ for a transfer that allows CTA riders to make two transfers on the bus or El within 2 hours of receipt. Children under 7 ride free, and those between the ages of 7 and 11 pay 85¢ (15¢ for transfers). Seniors can also receive the reduced fare if they have the appropriate reduced-fare permit (call ☎ 312/836-7000 for details on how to obtain one). The CTA uses credit card–size farecards that automatically deduct the exact fare each time you take a ride. The reusable cards can be purchased with a preset value already stored ($20 for 10 rides), or riders can obtain cards at vending machines located at all CTA train stations and charge them with whatever amount they choose (a minimum of $2 and up to $100). Note if you don't have a farecard when boarding a bus, you'll need $2 in exact change in coins and/or dollar bills.

By "El"/Subway   The rapid transit system operates five major lines. The "El" (elevated train) runs partly above ground and partly below ground, so it's known as both the "El" and the subway. While most trains run every 5 to 20 minutes, decreasing in frequency in the off-peak and overnight hours, some stations close after work hours (as early as 8:30pm) and remain closed on Saturday, Sunday, and holidays.

By Bus   A few buses that are particularly handy for many visitors are the **no. 146 Marine/Michigan,** an express bus from Belmont Avenue on the North Side that cruises down North Lake Shore Drive (and through Lincoln Park during nonpeak times) to North Michigan Avenue, State Street, and the Grant Park museum campus; the **no. 151 Sheridan,** which passes through Lincoln Park en route to inner Lake Shore Drive and then travels along Michigan Avenue as far south as Adams Street, where it turns west into the Loop (and stops at Union Station); and the **no. 156 LaSalle,** which goes through Lincoln Park and then into the Loop's financial district on LaSalle Street. To locate bus stops, look for the **blue-and-white signs** spaced about 2 blocks apart.

By Metra   The Metra commuter railroad (© **312/322-6777,** or 312/322-6774 TTY Mon–Fri 8am–5pm; www.metrarail.com) serves the six-county suburban area around Chicago with 12 train lines. Several terminals are located downtown, including **Union Station** at Adams and Canal streets, **LaSalle Street Station** at LaSalle and Van Buren streets, **North Western Station** at Madison and Canal streets, and **Randolph Street Station** at Randolph Street and Michigan Avenue. Commuter trains have graduated fare schedules based on the distance you ride.

By Taxi   The meter in Chicago cabs starts at $2.25 for the first mile and $1.80 for each additional mile, with a $1 surcharge for each additional rider ages 12 to 65 and 50¢ for each person after that. Taxis are easy to hail, but if you can't find one, try calling **Flash Cab** (© **773/561-1444**), **Yellow Cab** (© **312/TAXI-CAB**), or **Checker Cab** (© **312/CHECKER**).

FAST FACTS   The best hospital emergency room in Chicago is **Northwestern Memorial Hospital,** 251 E. Huron St. (© **312/926-2000;** www.nmh.org), with a state-of-the-art medical center right off North Michigan Avenue. The emergency department is located at 240 E. Erie St., near Fairbanks Court (© **312/926-5188,** or 312/944-2358 TTY). The hospital's **Physician Referral Service** can be reached at © **877/926-4664.** The local sales tax is 9%. Restaurants in the central part of the city, roughly the 312 area code, are taxed an additional 1%, for a total of 10%. The hotel room tax is 14.9%.

SPECIAL EVENTS & FESTIVALS   The **Mayor's Office of Special Events** operates a recorded hot line (© **312/744-3370**) listing current special events, festivals, and parades occurring throughout the city. The city of Chicago also maintains a 24-hour information line for those with hearing impairments; call © **312/744-8599.**

During the second week of June, you can catch the free **Chicago Blues Festival** at the Petrillo Music Shell, at Jackson and Columbus drives in Grant Park (© **312/744-3315**), with dozens of acts performing over 4 days. From June 29 to July 8, **The Taste of Chicago** (© **312/744-3315**) brings more than 10 days of feasting in the streets, when scores of Chicago restaurants cart their fare to food stands set up throughout Grant Park. Admission is free. The **Chicago Air & Water Show** (© **312/744-3315**) at North Avenue Beach is a hugely popular aquatic and aerial spectacular. In 2007, it takes place on August 18 and 19. On the Saturday before Thanksgiving, at the **Magnificent Mile Lights Festival** (© **312/642-3570**), a colorful parade of Disney characters makes its way south along Michigan Avenue, from Oak Street to the Chicago River, with lights being illuminated block by block as the procession passes.

WHAT TO SEE & DO
THE TOP ATTRACTIONS

Unless you have a lot of time and a ton of patience, we recommend skipping the view from Chicago's tallest landmark, the famed Sears Tower (no longer owned by Sears nor the tallest building in the world). The view from the 103rd-floor **Sears Tower Skydeck,** 233 S. Wacker Dr. (© **312/875-9696;** www.the-skydeck.com), is everything you'd expect it to be—once you get there. Unfortunately, you're usually stuck in a *very long,* very noisy line, so by the time you make it to the top (sometimes in 2 hr.), your patience could be as thin as the atmosphere up there. And the $12 admission price doesn't make it any more attractive.

Adler Planetarium and Astronomy Museum   The building—a zodiacal 12-sided structure at the end of ornamental Solidarity Drive—is historic, but some of the attractions here will captivate the most jaded video-game addict. The exhibit galleries feature a variety of displays and interactive activities designed to foster understanding of our solar system and more. The 60,000-square-foot **Sky Pavilion** features the must-do **StarRider Theater,** which takes you on a mind-blowing interactive virtual reality trip through the Milky Way and into deep space. The planetarium's signature exhibit, *From the Night Sky to the Big Bang,* traces changing views of the cosmos over 1,000 years and features artifacts from the planetarium's extensive collection of historical astronomical instruments. On the first Friday evening of the month, visitors can view dramatic close-ups of the moon, the planets, and distant galaxies through a closed-circuit monitor connected to the planetarium's Doane Observatory telescope. Allow 2 hours, more if you want to see more than one show.

1300 S. Lake Shore Dr. © **312/922-STAR.** www.adlerplanetarium.org. Admission (including 1 show) $16 adults, $15 seniors, $14 children 4–17, free for children under 4. Free admission Mon–Tues Sept–Feb only (except last 2 weeks of Dec). Memorial Day to Labor Day daily 9:30am–6pm; early Sept to late May daily 9:30am–4:30pm; 1st Fri of every month until 10pm. StarRider Theater and Sky Shows run throughout the day; call main number for current times. Bus: 12 or 146.

Art Institute of Chicago (Kids)   You can't (and shouldn't) miss the Art Institute, which features one of the world's major collections: Japanese *ukiyo-e* prints, ancient Egyptian bronzes and Greek vases, 19th-century British photography, masterpieces by most of the greatest names in 20th-century sculpture, and modern American textiles. Especially notable is the popular Impressionist collection (including one of the world's largest collections of Monet paintings), which boasts George Seurat's pointillist masterpiece *Sunday Afternoon on the Island of La Grande Jette.* Also worth seeing are the galleries of European and American contemporary art, ranging from paintings, sculptures, and mixed-media works by artists from Pablo Picasso and Salvador Dalí to Jackson Pollock and Andy Warhol. Don't miss Marc Chagall's stunning stained-glass windows. Allow 3 hours.

111 S. Michigan Ave. (at Adams St.). © **312/443-3600.** www.artic.edu. Admission $12 adults, $7 seniors and students with ID, free for children under 12. Additional cost for special exhibitions. Free admission Thurs 5–8pm. Mon–Fri 10:30am–5pm (Thurs until 8pm, until 9pm Thurs–Fri Memorial Day to Labor Day); Sat–Sun 10am–5pm. Closed Thanksgiving and Dec 25. Bus: 3, 4, 60, 145, 147, or 151. Subway/El: Green, Brown, Purple, or Orange line to Adams, or Red Line to Monroe/State or Jackson/State.

Auditorium Building and Theatre   A truly grand theater with historic landmark status, the auditorium is worth a visit to experience late-19th-century Chicago opulence. Designed and built in 1889 by Louis Sullivan and Dankmar Adler, the auditorium was a wonder of the world: the heaviest (110,000 tons) and most massive modern edifice on earth and the first large-scale building to be electrically lighted. The 4,000-seat theater is a marvel of visionary design and engineering with otherworldly acoustics and unobstructed sightlines. Don't miss the lobby fronting Michigan Avenue, with its faux ornamental marble columns, molded ceilings, mosaic floors, and Mexican onyx walls. The best way to see everything is to take a 1-hour guided tour, offered on Monday between 10am and 4pm (call ℂ **312/431-2389** to make reservations). Tours cost $6 for adults, $3 for seniors and students.

50 E. Congress Pkwy. ℂ **312/922-2110.** www.auditoriumtheatre.org. For ticket reservations or box-office information, call Ticketmaster: ℂ 312/902-1500. Bus: 145, 147, or 151. Subway/El: Brown, Green, Orange, or Purple line to Library/Van Buren, or Red Line to Jackson.

Chicago Children's Museum (Kids)
This popular museum has areas especially for preschoolers as well as for children up to age 10, and several permanent exhibits allow kids a maximum of hands-on fun. There are always creative temporary exhibitions on tap as well: A recent show on games included a larger-than-life chess set. Other exhibits explore such diverse topics as dinosaurs, water resources, prejudice, and more. There's also an **arts-and-crafts area** where visitors can create original artwork to take home. Allow 2 to 3 hours.

Navy Pier, 700 E. Grand Ave. ℂ **312/527-1000.** www.chichildrensmuseum.org. Admission $8 adults and children, $7 seniors. Free admission Thurs 5–8pm. Mon–Fri 10am–5pm (Thurs until 8pm); Sat 10am–8pm; Sun 10am–5pm. Closed Thanksgiving and Dec 25. Bus: 29, 65, or 66. Subway/El: Red Line to Grand; transfer to city bus or Navy Pier's free trolley bus.

Field Museum of Natural History (Best) (Kids)
You may recognize the museum as the very suitable home turf of the intrepid archaeologist and adventurer hero of the *Indiana Jones* movies. Spread over the museum's 9 acres of floor space are scores of permanent and temporary exhibitions—some interactive, but most requiring the old-fashioned skills of observation and imagination. Highlights include the largest, most complete *Tyrannosaurus rex* fossil ever unearthed—named **"Sue"** for the paleontologist who found it in 1990—an exhibit on Ancient Egypt, including 23 mummies; a kid-friendly Disneyesque insect exhibit; and a series of exhibits designed to re-create life in other cultures and areas of the world. Allow 3 hours.

Roosevelt Rd. and Lake Shore Dr. ℂ **312/922-9410,** or 312/341-9299 TTY. www.fieldmuseum.org. Admission $12 adults; $7 seniors, students with ID, and children 3–11; free for children under 3. Free admission Mon–Tues mid-Sept to Oct and Jan–Feb. Daily 9am–5pm. Closed Jan 1 and Dec 25. Bus: 6, 10, 12, 130, or 146.

John G. Shedd Aquarium
The Shedd is a city treasure and well deserving of its title as world's largest indoor aquarium, though we wish the admission price to all of the exhibits weren't so steep (though you really should pony up for all of them to truly experience the best the aquarium has to offer). The first thing you'll see as you enter is the **Caribbean Coral Reef** exhibit. This 90,000-gallon circular tank occupies the Beaux Arts–style central rotunda, entertaining spectators who press up against the glass to ogle divers feeding nurse sharks, barracudas, stingrays, and a hawksbill sea turtle. The 3-million-gallon saltwater **Oceanarium** is an indoor marine mammal pavilion that re-creates a Pacific Northwest coastal environment. As you follow a winding nature trail, you'll encounter beluga whales, white-sided dolphins, Alaskan sea otters, and harbor seals along the way. On a fixed performance schedule in a large pool flanked by an amphitheater, a crew of friendly trainers puts dolphins through their paces of leaping dives, breaches, and tail walking. The newest signature exhibit is *Wild Reef—Sharks at Shedd,* a series of 26 interconnected habitats that house a Philippine

coral reef patrolled by sharks and other predators. The floor-to-ceiling windows bring those toothy swimmers up close and personal. Allow 2 to 3 hours.

1200 S. Lake Shore Dr. (℃) **312/939-2438.** www.sheddaquarium.org. All-Access Pass (to all exhibits) $23 adults, $16 seniors and children 3–11, free for children under 3; admission to aquarium and Oceanarium $18 adults, $14 seniors and children; aquarium only $8 adults, $6 seniors and children. Free admission to aquarium Mon–Tues Oct–Feb (except the last 2 weeks of Dec). Memorial Day to Labor Day daily 9am–6pm; early Sept to late May Mon–Fri 9am–5pm, Sat–Sun 9am–6pm. Bus: 6 or 146.

Lincoln Park Zoo *Value* *Kids*   One of Chicago's don't-miss attractions; and because it's free, it's worth at least a quick stop during a stroll through Lincoln Park. The term "zoological gardens" truly fits here: Landmark Georgian Revival brick buildings and modern structures sit among gently rolling pathways, verdant lawns, and a kaleidoscopic profusion of flower gardens. The zoo has taken on an ambitious modernization campaign, and exhibits have been renovated and expanded to reflect natural habitats. The star attraction is the **Regenstein Center for African Apes,** which was completely rebuilt in 2004. **Regenstein African Journey** is home to elephants, giraffes, rhinos, and other large mammals; large glass-enclosed tanks allow visitors to go face-to-face with swimming pygmy hippos and Madagascar hissing cockroaches. The **Small Mammal–Reptile House** is a state-of-the-art facility, housing 200 species in a glass-enclosed walk-through ecosystem simulating river, savanna, and forest habitats. The popular **Sea Lion Pool** is home to harbor seals, gray seals, and California sea lions. The adjoining kids' zoo is very popular with little ones. Allow 2 to 3 hours.

2200 N. Cannon Dr. (at Fullerton Pkwy.). (℃) **312/742-2000.** www.lpzoo.com. Free admission. Buildings daily 10am–5pm (until 6:30pm Sat–Sun Memorial Day to Labor Day). Grounds Memorial Day to Labor Day daily 9am–7pm; Apr to late May and early Sept to Oct daily 9am–6pm; Nov–Mar daily 9am–5pm. Parking $12 per day in on-site lot. Free trolley service from area CTA stations and parking garages Sat–Sun and holidays 10am–6pm Memorial Day to Labor Day; visit the zoo website for route information and schedule.

Museum of Contemporary Art   The MCA claims to be the largest contemporary art museum in the country, emphasizing experimentation in a variety of media— painting, sculpture, photography, video and film, dance, music, and performance. You can see the MCA's highlights in about an hour, although art lovers will want more time to wander (especially if a high-profile exhibit is in town). The permanent collection highlights works created since 1945 by such artists as Alexander Calder, Sol LeWitt, and Bruce Nauman. For visitors who'd like a little guidance in making sense of the rather challenging works found here, there is an audio tour for rent as well as a free tour (1 and 6pm Tues; 1pm Wed–Fri; 11am, noon, 1, and 2pm Sat–Sun).

220 E. Chicago Ave. (1 block east of Michigan Ave.). (℃) **312/280-2660.** www.mcachicago.org. Admission $10 adults, $6 seniors and students with ID, free for children under 13. Free admission Tues. Tues 10am–8pm; Wed–Sun 10am–5pm. Bus: 3, 10, 66, 145, 146, or 151. Subway/El: Red Line to Chicago/State.

Museum of Science and Industry *Kids*   The massive Museum of Science and Industry is the granddaddy of interactive museums, with some 2,000 exhibits spread over 14 acres in 75 exhibition halls. A headline attraction is the **Henry Crown Space Center,** where the story of space exploration is documented. A favorite is the dark descent into a full-scale replica of an Illinois **coal mine.** From historic railroad trains to submarines (a real U-505 German World War II sub!) to space capsules, and from special effects to the mysteries of the human immune system, you'll find the object of your curiosity somewhere in this amazing place. The five-story OMNIMAX Theater offers double features on weekends (call for times). Allow at least 3 hours.

Value **Museums for Less**

If you plan to visit lots of Chicago museums, you should invest in a CityPass, a prepaid ticket that gets you into the biggest attractions (including the Art Institute, Field Museum of Natural History, Shedd Aquarium, Adler Planetarium, and Museum of Science and Industry). The cost at press time was $50 for adults and $39 for children, which is about 50% cheaper than paying all the museums' individual admission fees. You can buy a CityPass at any of the museums listed above, or purchase online before you get to town (**www.citypass.net**).

57th St. and Lake Shore Dr. © **800/468-6674** outside the Chicago area, 773/684-1414, or 773/684-3323 TTY; www. msichicago.org. Admission to museum only: $11 adults, $9 seniors, $7 children 3–11, free for children under 3. Free admission Mon–Tues mid-Sept to Nov and Jan–Feb. Combination museum and OMNIMAX Theater: $17 adults, $15 seniors, $12 children 3–11, free for children under 3 on an adult's lap. Memorial Day to Labor Day Mon–Sat 9:30am–5:30pm, Sun 11am–5:30pm; early Sept to late May Mon–Sat 9:30am–4pm, Sun 11am–4pm. Closed Dec 25. Bus: 6 or Metra Electric train to 57th St. and Lake Park Ave.

Navy Pier *(Kids)*   Built during World War I, this 3,000-foot-long pier has been transformed into Chicago's top attraction, with eight million visitors each year. A combination of carnival, food court, and boat dock, the pier makes a fun place to stroll (if you don't mind crowds), but you'll have to walk all the way to the end to get the best views back to the city. There's a winter garden, a 3-D IMAX theater, a concert stage, a space that holds an ice rink in winter and a merry-go-round in summer, and a giant 15-story Ferris wheel. Decorative arts fans shouldn't miss the free **Smith Museum of Stained Glass Windows** on the pier's ground floor. The pier is also home to many bland shops and several decent restaurants. During the summer there are fireworks on Wednesday and Saturday. Allow 1 hour.

600 E. Grand Ave. (at Lake Michigan). © **800/595-PIER** (outside 312 area code), or 312/595-PIER. www.navypier. com. Free admission. Summer Sun–Thurs 10am–10pm, Fri–Sat 10am–midnight; fall–spring Mon–Thurs 10am–8pm, Fri–Sat 10am–10pm, Sun 10am–7pm. Parking: Rates start at $14 for the 1st hr. and go up to $22 for up to 8 hr. Lots fill quickly. Subway/El: Red Line to Grand/State; transfer to city bus or board a free pier trolley bus. Bus: 29, 65, 66, 120, or 121.

Robie House   One of Frank Lloyd Wright's finest creations, Robie House is one of the great works of 20th-century American architecture. The open layout, linear geometry of form, and craftsmanship are typical of Wright's Prairie School design. Completed in 1909, the home is also notable for its exquisite leaded- and stained-glass doors and windows. The house is undergoing a massive, 10-year restoration and though it will be open throughout the process, your photos may include plenty of scaffolding. Recommended visiting time: 2 hours.

5757 S. Woodlawn Ave. (at 58th St.). © **773/834-1847**. www.wrightplus.org. Admission $12 adults, $10 seniors and children 7–18, free for children under 7. Mon–Fri tours at 11am, 1, and 3pm; Sat–Sun every half-hour 11am–3:30pm. Bookshop daily 10am–5pm. Bus: 6 or Metra Electric train to 57th St. and Lake Park Ave.

THE WRIGHT STUFF IN OAK PARK

The suburb of Oak Park has the highest concentration of houses or buildings anywhere designed and built by Frank Lloyd Wright, the dean of American architecture.

Oak Park is 10 miles west of downtown Chicago. By car, take the Eisenhower Expressway west (I-290) to Harlem Avenue (Ill. 43) and exit north. Continue on Harlem north to Lake Street. Take a right on Lake and continue to Forest Avenue.

Turn left here, and immediately on your right you'll see the **Oak Park Visitor Center,** 158 Forest Ave. (© **888/OAK-PARK;** www.visitoakpark.com), open daily from 10am to 5pm April through October and from 10am to 4pm November through March. Stop in for orientation, maps, and guidebooks. There's a parking lot next door. From here it's only a few blocks to the heart of the historic district and the Frank Lloyd Wright Home and Studio.

By public transportation, take the Green Line west to Harlem, roughly a 25-minute ride from downtown. Exit the station onto Harlem Avenue, and proceed north to Lake Street. Take a right on Lake to Forest Avenue, and then turn left.

Oak Park has, in all, 25 homes and buildings by Wright, constructed between the years 1892 and 1913, which constitute the core output of his Prairie School period. An extensive tour of the neighborhood surrounding the Frank Lloyd Wright Home and Studio leaves from the **Ginkgo Tree Bookshop,** 951 Chicago Ave., on weekends from 11am to 4pm. The tour lasts 1 hour and costs $12 for adults, $10 for seniors and children 7 to 18, and free for children under 7. At other times, you can follow a self-guided map and audiocassette tour of the historic district. Available at the Ginkgo Tree Bookshop from 10am to 3:30pm, the self-guided tour costs $12 for adults and $10 for seniors and children.

Frank Lloyd Wright Home and Studio For the first 20 years of Wright's career, this remarkable complex served as the sanctuary from which Wright was to design and execute more than 130 of an extraordinary output of 430 completed buildings. The home began as a simple shingled cottage that Wright built for his bride in 1889 at the age of 22, but it became a work in progress, as Wright remodeled it constantly until 1911 (he left there in 1909). The place has a certain whimsy even if it's not a masterpiece, and you should savor every room as an insight into the workings of a remarkable mind. Allow 2 hours.

951 Chicago Ave. © **708/848-1976.** www.wrightplus.org. Admission $12 adults, $10 seniors and children 7–18, free for children under 7. Combined admission for home and studio tour and guided or self-guided historic district tour $20 adults, $16 seniors and children 7–18. Admission to home and studio is by guided tour only; tours depart from bookshop Mon–Fri 11am, 1, and 3pm; Sat–Sun every 20 min. 11am–3:30pm. Closed Jan 1, last week in Jan, Thanksgiving, and Dec 25. Facilities for people with disabilities are limited; please call in advance.

Unity Temple In 1871, a community of Unitarian/Universalists settled near here and built a timber-framed house of worship typical of their native New England. Fire destroyed it around the turn of the 20th century. The congregation asked Frank Lloyd Wright, who was a member, to design an affordable replacement. Using poured concrete with metal reinforcements—a necessity owing to the project's small budget of $40,000—Wright created a building that seems as forbidding as a mausoleum on the outside. But inside, its details capture the tenets of the Prairie School that has made Wright's name immortal. His use of wood for trim and other decorative touches is exciting to behold; his sensitivity to grain and tone and placement was akin to that of an exceptionally gifted woodworker. Wright's stunning, almost minimalist use of form is what still sets him apart as a relevant and brilliant artist. Allow a half-hour.

875 Lake St. © **708/383-8873.** http://unitytemple-utrf.org. Self-guided tours $7 adults; $5 seniors, children 5–12, and students with ID. Tour price includes 45-min. guided tour (Sat–Sun on the hour 1–3pm). Mon–Fri 10:30am–4:30pm; Sat–Sun 1–4pm. Church events can alter schedule; call in advance.

ORGANIZED SIGHTSEEING TOURS

The **Chicago Trolley Company** (© **773/648-5000;** www.chicagotrolley.com) offers guided tours on a fleet of rubber-wheeled "San Francisco–style" trolleys that stop at a

It's a Beautiful Day, So Let's Play Two

Forget about all these new old-style ballparks being built all over the country. **Wrigley Field** (✆ **773/404-CUBS;** www.cubs.mlb.com), the home of the Cubs—with its ivy-covered outfield walls, its hand-operated scoreboard, and its "W" or "L" flag announcing the outcome of the game to the unfortunates who couldn't attend—is the real McCoy. To get here, simply take the Red Line to Addison. To order tickets in person, stop by the ticket windows Monday through Friday from 9am to 6pm, Saturday from 9am to 4pm, and game days. Or call ✆ **800/THE-CUBS** for tickets through **Tickets.com** (✆ **866/652-2827** outside of Illinois).

number of popular spots around the city. An all-day hop-on, hop-off pass costs $25 adults, $20 seniors, and $10 children 3 to 11.

Chicago is the first city of architecture, and the **Chicago Architecture Foundation (CAF),** 224 S. Michigan Ave. (✆ **312/922-3432,** or 312/922-TOUR for recorded information; www.architecture.org), offers first-rate guided programs, led by nearly 400 trained and enthusiastic docents. The foundation offers walking, bike, boat, and bus tours to more than 60 architectural sites and environments in and around Chicago.

We recommend CAF's popular 1½-hour **"Architecture River Cruise,"** which offers a unique perspective on some of Chicago's top buildings. The docents generally do a good job of making the cruise enjoyable for visitors with all levels of architectural knowledge. Tickets are $25 per person weekdays, $27 on weekends and holidays, and are scheduled hourly every day June through October. The trips are extremely popular, so purchase tickets in advance through **Ticketmaster** (✆ **312/902-1500;** www.ticketmaster.com/Illinois), or avoid the service charge and buy your tickets at one of the foundation's tour centers, 224 S. Michigan Ave. or the John Hancock Center, or from the boat launch on the southeast corner of Michigan Avenue and Wacker Drive.

SHOPPING

The **Magnificent Mile** refers to the roughly mile-long stretch of North Michigan Avenue between Oak Street and the Chicago River. The density of first-rate shopping is unmatched anywhere. Whether your passion is Tiffany diamonds, Chanel suits, or Gap jeans, you'll find it on this stretch of concrete. **Sony Gallery of Consumer Electronics,** 663 N. Michigan Ave. (✆ **312/943-3334**), is a haven for reluctant male shoppers where the latest high-tech gadgets are displayed in a museum-like setting. At the intersection of Michigan Avenue and Erie Street is a Chicago retail institution, the appropriately barrel-shaped flagship store of **Crate & Barrel,** 646 N. Michigan Ave. (✆ **312/787-5900**). Chicago's first—and still busiest—vertical mall is **Water Tower Place,** a block-size marble-sheathed building at 835 N. Michigan Ave., between East Pearson and East Chestnut streets (✆ **312/440-3165**).

In the State Street area, **Macy's** (formerly Marshall Field's), 111 N. State St., at Randolph (✆ **312/781-1000**), remains one of the world's largest department stores, occupying an entire city block and featuring the largest Tiffany glass mosaic dome in the United States. **Carson Pirie Scott & Co.,** 1 S. State St., at the corner of State and Madison (✆ **312/641-7000**), is a few blocks south. Both buildings are city landmarks and attractions in themselves.

Along with becoming Chicago's primary art gallery district, **River North**—the area west of the Magnificent Mile and north of the Chicago River—has attracted many interesting shops, concentrated on Wells Street from Kinzie Street to Chicago Avenue. **Manifesto,** 755 N. Wells St., at Chicago Avenue (© **312/664-0733**), offers custom-designed furniture, as well as imports from Italy and elsewhere in Europe; **Mig & Tig,** 540 N. Wells St., at Ohio Street (© **312/644-8277**), carries charming furniture and decorative accessories; and **Lightology,** 215 W. Chicago Ave., at Wells Street (© **312/944-1000**), boasts a mind-boggling array of lighting from more than 400 manufacturers.

The North Side neighborhood of **Lincoln Park** has a variety of unique specialty shops that make it easy to browse your way through this leafy, picturesque community. Shops are located on the primary commercial arteries running through the area, including Armitage Avenue, Webster Avenue, Halsted Street, Clark Street, and Lincoln Avenue.

WHERE TO STAY

For the annual *Illinois Hotel-Motel Directory,* which also provides information about weekend packages, call the **Illinois Bureau of Tourism** at © **800/2-CONNECT.** Discounted rooms at more than 30 downtown hotels are available through **Hot Rooms** (© **800/468-3500** or 773/468-7666; www.hotrooms.com). The 24-hour service is free, but if you cancel a reservation, you're assessed a $25 fee. A centralized reservations service called **At Home Inn Chicago** (© **800/375-7084** or 312/640-1050; www.athomeinnchicago.com) lists more than 70 accommodations in Chicago.

Chicago City Centre—A Holiday Inn Hotel *Value* *Kids*   Close to the Navy Pier, this nice surprise is a good bet for the budget-conscious family. Although the rooms are pretty basic, the amenities make this one of the best values in the city. Fitness devotees will rejoice because the hotel is located next door to the Lake Shore Athletic Club, where guests may enjoy the extensive facilities free of charge. The hotel also has its own spacious fifth-floor outdoor pool and sun deck. You might want to splurge on one of the "master suites," which boast large living-room areas with wet bars, along with a Jacuzzi-style tub and sauna in the bathroom. A massive AMC movie complex with 21 screens is next door. Children under 12 eat free in the hotel's restaurant.

300 E. Ohio St. (at Fairbanks Court), Chicago, IL 60611. © 800/HOLIDAY or 312/787-6100. Fax 312/787-6259. www.chicc.com. 500 units. $109–$270 double. AE, DC, DISC, MC, V. Self-parking $28. Subway/El: Red Line to Grand. **Amenities:** 3 restaurants; 2 pools (1 indoor); access to nearby health club.

Crowne Plaza Chicago—The Silversmith *Value*   This landmark building was built in 1897 to serve the jewelry and silver trade on Wabash Avenue, still known as Jeweler's Row. Rooms come in varying configurations, with 12-foot-high ceilings, 10-foot picture windows, Frank Lloyd Wright–inspired wrought-iron fixtures, armoires, and homey bedding; bathrooms are generously sized and some have whirlpool tubs. Natural light is limited in the rooms; those along the hotel's main corridor tend to be dark. And though windows are extra thick to muffle the noise of nearby "El" trains, you'll want to avoid the lower-level floors if you like things quiet; request a Wabash Avenue room on the 9th or 10th floor. Rooms don't book up as quickly as at other, hotter spots, so this is one place thrifty travelers can look for a good deal.

10 S. Wabash Ave. (at Madison St.), Chicago, IL 60603. © 800/2-CROWNE or 312/372-7696. Fax 312/372-7320. www.crowneplaza.com/silversmith. 143 units. $179–$359 double; from $289 suite; weekend rates available. AE, DC, DISC, MC, V. Valet parking $37 with in/out privileges. Subway/El: Brown, Green, or Orange line to Madison, or Red Line to Washington. **Amenities:** Restaurant; tiny fitness room.

The Drake Hotel   Fronting East Lake Shore Drive, this 1920 landmark building is more old-time glamour than glitz, but a $100-million renovation has streamlined its design and modernized the guest rooms. The typical room is spacious and furnished comfortably with a separate sitting area; some have two bathrooms. The lake-view rooms are lovely, though you'll pay more for them. All rooms have bathrobes. The Coq d'Or is one of Chicago's most atmospheric piano bars.

140 E. Walton Place (at Michigan Ave.), Chicago, IL 60611. © **800/55-DRAKE** or 312/787-2200. Fax 312/787-1431. www.thedrakehotel.com. 537 units. $179–$295 double; $239–$430 executive floor; from $545 suite. AE, DC, DISC, MC, V. Valet parking $32 with in/out privileges. Subway/El: Red Line to Chicago. **Amenities:** 3 restaurants; fitness center.

Four Seasons Hotel *(Best)* *(Kids)*   The Four Seasons—occupying a rarefied aerie between the 30th and 46th floors above the Mag Mile's most upscale vertical mall—offers an understated luxury that appeals to publicity-shy Hollywood stars and wealthy families. The beautiful rooms have English furnishings, custom-woven carpets and tapestries, and dark wood armoires. Each has a VCR and windows that open to let in the fresh air. Bathrooms boast such indulgences as a lighted makeup mirror, oversize towels and robes, scales, and Bulgari toiletries. Kid-friendly services include little robes, balloon animals, Nintendo, and milk and cookies. The hotel's elegant fitness center and spa exude the same upscale, old-money feel as the rest of the public areas.

120 E. Delaware Place (at Michigan Ave.), Chicago, IL 60611. © **800/332-3442** or 312/280-8800. Fax 312/280-1748. www.fourseasons.com. 343 units. $435–$535 double; $585–$3,500 suite; weekend rates from $305. AE, DC, DISC, MC, V. Valet parking $36 with in/out privileges; self-parking $26. Subway/El: Red Line to Chicago. Pets accepted. **Amenities:** 2 restaurants; indoor pool; fitness center and spa.

Hampton Inn & Suites Chicago Downtown *(Value)* *(Kids)*   This is a great choice for travelers on a budget, and caters mostly to families. You can book a room, a two-room suite, or a studio. Rooms are residential and warm, with coffeemakers, irons, hair dryers, and modestly sized bathrooms. The apartment-style suites feature galley kitchens with fridges, microwaves, dishwashers, and cooking utensils. Guests with children will appreciate the indoor pool and VCRs in every room for when the little ones need to chill out after a busy day.

33 W. Illinois St. (at Dearborn St.), Chicago, IL 60610. © **800/HAMPTON** or 312/832-0330. Fax 312/832-0333. www.hamptoninn.com. 230 units. $119–$199 double; $169–$259 suite. Children 17 and under stay free in parent's room. AE, DC, DISC, MC, V. Valet parking $38 with in/out privileges; self-parking $25 with no in/out privileges. Subway/El: Red Line to Grand. **Amenities:** Restaurant; indoor pool; exercise room.

Hotel Burnham   If you're looking for a spot with a sense of history with some modern style (but not extensive amenities), this is it. A $30-million restoration in 1999 of the historic Reliance Building—one of the first skyscrapers ever built and an architectural treasure—resulted in this intimate boutique hotel. The hallways recall the original office corridors with terrazzo tile floors, white marble wainscoting, and mahogany door and window frames. Rooms are clubby but glamorous, with plush beds, bathrobes, and Aveda toiletries. Ask for a room on a high floor in the northeast corner. The prime State Street location is right across from Macy's.

1 W. Washington St. (at State St.), Chicago, IL 60602. © **866/690-1986** or 312/782-1111. Fax 312/782-0899. www.burnhamhotel.com. 122 units. $179–$299 double; $229–$399 suite. AE, DC, DISC, MC, V. Valet parking $35 with in/out privileges. Subway: Red or Blue line to Washington. Pets allowed. **Amenities:** Restaurant; small fitness room.

House of Blues Hotel   The funky vibe here makes this a great choice for teenagers and anyone who wants a hotel to be an experience—not just a place to sleep. Blending

Chicago

Gothic, Moroccan, East Indian, and New Orleans influences, the House of Blues lobby is a riot of crimsons and deep blues (stop by to check it out even if you're not staying here), and the casually dressed staff is friendly. Banquettes and couches heaped with pillows invite lounging—grab a drink at the Kaz Bar and soak it all in. You can catch your breath in the lighter, whimsical rooms, which feature CD players, VCRs, and some of the most exciting southern folk art you'll ever see. One of the hotel's biggest selling points is its location in the entertainment-packed Marina Towers complex.

333 N. Dearborn St. (at the river), Chicago, IL 60610. © 800/235-6397 or 312/245-0333. Fax 312/923-2444. www.house ofblueshotel.com. 353 units. $159–$389 double; $500–$1,200 suite. AE, DC, DISC, MC, V. Valet parking $34 with in/out privileges. Subway/El: Brown Line to Clark/Lake or Red Line to Grand. Pets accepted. **Amenities:** Access to the very hip Crunch Health & Fitness Center for $15.

Majestic Hotel   Located on a charming tree-lined street (but convenient to the many restaurants and shops of Lincoln Park), this is a good choice for anyone who wants a quiet, bed-and-breakfast type of hotel stay. Some of the larger suites—the most appealing are those with sun porches—offer butlers' pantries with fridge, microwave, and wet bar. Avoid the claustrophobic single rooms with alley views. Guests receive a complimentary continental breakfast and afternoon tea in the lobby. *Tip:* The owners of this property also run the nearby **City Suites Hotel,** 933 W. Belmont Ave. at Sheffield Avenue (© **800/248-9108**), which offers excellent value in a somewhat noisy location.

528 W. Brompton St. (at Lake Shore Dr.), Chicago, IL 60657. © 800/727-5108 or 773/404-3499. Fax 773/404-3495. www.cityinns.com. 52 units. $99–$179 double; $129–$219 suite. Rates include continental breakfast. AE, DC, DISC, MC, V. Self-parking $19 in nearby garage with no in/out privileges. Subway/El: Red Line to Addison; walk several blocks east to Lake Shore Dr. and then 1 block south. **Amenities:** Exercise room. *In room:* Fridge and microwave (some suites only).

Park Hyatt Chicago   For those in search of chic modern luxury, the Park Hyatt is the coolest hotel in town. The property's best rooms are those that face east, overlooking the bustle of the Mag Mile and the lake in the distance. Luxury might be the watchword here, but the look is anything but stuffy: The lobby feels like a sleek modern art gallery and rooms feature Eames and Mies van der Rohe reproduction furniture and window banquettes with stunning city views (the windows actually open). The comfortable beds are well appointed with several plush pillows; and all rooms offer DVD players, CD players, and flatscreen TVs. The bathrooms are especially wonderful: Slide back the cherrywood wall for views of the city while you soak in the tub.

800 N. Michigan Ave., Chicago, IL 60611. © 800/233-1234 or 312/335-1234. Fax 312/239-4000. http://park.hyatt. com. 203 units. $375–$425 double; $695–$3,000 suite. AE, DC, DISC, MC, V. Valet parking $36 with in/out privileges. Subway/El: Red Line to Chicago. **Amenities:** Restaurant; indoor pool; health club and spa.

The Peninsula Chicago   The luxury Peninsula hotel group's first Midwest location wowed us, living up to its hype. Mixing an Art Deco sensibility with modern, top-of-the-line amenities, The Peninsula also features exceptional service. Rooms are average in size (and the "junior suites" are fairly small), but the hotel's in-room technology allows guests to control all the lights, curtains, and room temperature without getting out from under the covers. The marble-filled bathrooms have separate shower stalls and tubs, and vanities with plenty of room to sit. Add the flatscreen TVs and DVD players, and you have a classic hotel that's very much in tune with the present. The sultry hotel bar is already one of the city's top spots for romantic assignations. The bright, airy spa and fitness center fill the top two floors and make a lovely retreat (especially the outdoor deck).

108 E. Superior St. (at Michigan Ave.), Chicago, IL 60611. © 866/288-8889 or 312/337-2888. Fax 312/751-2888. http://chicago.peninsula.com. 339 units. $445–$455 double; $500–$4,500 suite. AE, DC, DISC, MC, V. Valet parking $36 with in/out privileges. Subway/El: Red Line to Chicago. Pets accepted. **Amenities:** 4 restaurants; indoor pool; free fitness center; spa.

Ritz-Carlton Chicago *(Kids)*   Top-notch service and an open, airy setting atop the Water Tower Palace make this one of Chicago's most welcoming hotels. The quality of the accommodations is of the highest caliber, although the standard rooms aren't very large. Doubles have space for a loveseat and desk but not much more; the bathrooms are elegant but not huge. Lake views cost more but are spectacular. The hotel also offers "allergy-sensitive" rooms that are cleaned with special nonirritating products and come stocked with hypoallergenic pillows and special bath products on request. Families will find this luxury crash pad quite welcoming. Every child receives a gift and can borrow toys and games from a stash kept by the concierge.

160 E. Pearson St., Chicago, IL 60611. © 800/621-6906 or 312/266-1000. Fax 312/266-1194. www.fourseasons. com. 435 units. $395–$535 double; $545–$4,000 suite; weekend rates from $310. AE, DC, DISC, MC, V. Valet parking $36 with in/out privileges; self-parking $25 with no in/out privileges. Subway/El: Red Line to Chicago. Pets accepted. **Amenities:** 4 restaurants; indoor pool; health club; spa.

Solis Chicago Hotel   The Solis (formerly Hotel 71) is similar to a timeshare property, where individual owners rent their rooms out when they're not in use. Rooms, which were renovated in 2006, are decorated in warm tones of brown, deep red, and yellow, and are filled with furniture that feels more residential than that at most chain hotels. Those on the north side of the hotel (overlooking the Chicago River) have the best views; if you can, snag one of the rooms on the west end of the building, which have views in two directions. Suites come with either a living room or meeting room and a bedroom down the hall (but the bathrooms are actually smaller than those in the regular rooms). You'll also be able to admire the skyline from the large fitness center and spa—which fills the entire fifth floor.

71 E. Wacker Dr. (at Wabash Ave.), Chicago, IL 60601. © 800/621-4005 or 312/346-7100. Fax 312/346-1721. www.solischicago.com. 454 units. $149–$349 double; from $250 suite. AE, DC, DISC, MC, V. Valet parking $39 with in/out privileges. Subway: Brown, Green, or Orange line to Randolph, or Red Line to Washington. **Amenities:** Restaurant; fitness center.

Talbott Hotel   The Talbott's cozy atmosphere and personal level of service appeal to visitors who don't mind forgoing extensive amenities in exchange for a hotel with the intimacy and atmosphere of a bed-and-breakfast. The wood-paneled lobby, decorated with leather sofas and velvety armchairs, two working fireplaces, tapestries, and numerous French horns used for fox hunts, is intimate and inviting. Although comfortable, the rooms aren't quite as distinctive; they also vary in size, so ask when making reservations. Suites and the hotel's "executive king" rooms have Jacuzzi tubs; suites also have separate sitting areas with sofa beds and dining tables.

20 E. Delaware Place (between Rush and State sts.), Chicago, IL 60611. © 800/TALBOTT or 312/944-4970. Fax 312/944-7241. www.talbotthotel.com. 149 units. $189–$449 double; from $319 suite. AE, DC, DISC, MC, V. Valet parking $36 with in/out privileges; self-parking $25. Subway/El: Red Line to Chicago. **Amenities:** Complimentary access to nearby health club.

W Chicago Lakeshore   The only hotel in Chicago with a location on the lake, this property prides itself on being a hip boutique hotel—but sophisticated travelers may feel like it's trying way too hard with dance music playing in the lobby and black-clad staff members doing their best to be eye candy. The compact rooms are decorated in deep red, black, and gray—a scheme that strikes some travelers as gloomy—and sport such high-tech amenities as VCRs and CD players. The Asian-inspired bathrooms are stylish, but the wooden shades that separate them from the bedroom don't make for much privacy. In W-speak, rooms and suites are "wonderful" (meaning standard, with a city view), which we prefer, or "spectacular" (meaning a lake view, for which you'll pay more). Unwind at the hotel's outpost of New York's popular Bliss Spa.

644 N. Lake Shore Dr. (at Ontario St.), Chicago, IL 60611. © **877/W-HOTELS** or 312/943-9200. Fax 312/255-4411. www.whotels.com. 520 units. $219–$429 double; from $399 suite. AE, DC, DISC, MC, V. Valet parking $39 with in/out privileges. Subway/El: Red Line to Grand. Pets accepted. **Amenities:** Restaurant; pool; exercise room; spa.

WHERE TO DINE

Ann Sather SWEDISH/AMERICAN This is a real Chicago institution, where you can enjoy Swedish meatballs with buttered noodles and brown gravy, or the Swedish sampler of duck breast with lingonberry glaze, meatball, potato-sausage dumpling, sauerkraut, and brown beans. All meals are full dinners, including appetizer, main course, vegetable, potato, and dessert. It's the sticky cinnamon rolls, though, that make addicts out of diners. Weekend brunch here can get frenzied, but the people-watching is priceless: a cross section of gay and straight, young and old, from club kids to elderly couples.

929 W. Belmont Ave. (between Clark St. and Sheffield Ave.). © **773/348-2378**. www.annsather.com. Reservations accepted for parties of 6 or more. Main courses $7–$12. AE, DC, MC, V. Mon–Tues 7am–3pm; Wed–Sun 7am–9pm. Free parking with validation. Subway/El: Brown or Red line to Belmont.

Bistrot Margot FRENCH BISTRO Bistrot Margot is not only one of the best restaurants in Old Town—it's also one of the city's better French bistros. It can get very busy and loud, and the tables are quite close together, but for many, that only adds to its charm. Start with out-of-this-world mussels in white wine with fresh herbs, then try one of the specials for the main course. The usual suspects (roasted chicken with garlic, lemon, herbs, and french fries or a terrific steak frites) are proof that when done right, it's hard to beat classic French cuisine. On warm summer nights, the restaurant sets about half a dozen tables on the sidewalk, which, on this colorful stretch of Wells Street, makes for a truly memorable meal.

1437 N. Wells St. (at W. Schiller St.). © **312/587-3660**. www.bistrotmargot.com. Reservations recommended. Main courses $14–$20. AE, DC, MC, V. Mon 11:30am–9pm; Tues–Thurs 11:30am–10pm; Fri 11:30am–11pm; Sat 10:30am–11pm; Sun 10:30am–9pm. Subway/El: Red Line to Clark/Division or Brown Line to Sedgwick.

Carson's *Value* AMERICAN/BARBECUE A true Chicago institution, Carson's calls itself "The Place for Ribs," and, boy, is it ever. The barbecue sauce is sweet and tangy, and the ribs are meaty. Included in the $20 price for a full slab of baby backs are coleslaw and one of four types of potatoes (the most decadent are au gratin), plus right-out-of-the-oven rolls. When you're seated at your table, tie on your plastic bib—and indulge. There are some selections for noncarnivores, but let's be honest, you don't go to a rib joint to have seafood. If by some remarkable feat you have room left after dinner, the candy-bar sundaes are a scrumptious finale to the meal. *Note:* There's often a wait for a table at dinnertime.

612 N. Wells St. (at Ontario St.). © **312/280-9200**. www.ribs.com. Reservations accepted for groups of 6 or more. Main courses $12–$25. AE, DC, DISC, MC, V. Mon–Thurs 11:30am–10:30pm; Fri 11:30am–11:30pm; Sat noon–11:30pm; Sun noon–10:30pm. Subway/El: Red Line to Grand.

Charlie Trotter's *Best* ECLECTIC Foodies flock to the namesake restaurant of celebrity chef Charlie Trotter, and it is an appropriate shrine of creative fine dining.

There is no a la carte menu, so this is not the place to come if you're a picky eater. Your choice of the vegetable ($115) or grand ($135) menu degustation (the extensive nonmeat choices make this an excellent spot for vegetarians with gourmet tastes) will feature an ever-changing lineup of exceptional dishes made with organic or free-range products (no guilt!). Recent menus featured ragout of leek confit, braised carrots, salsify, and cauliflower with Perigord black truffle emulsion; and black buck venison with Japanese kumai jasmine rice cake and red-wine Kalamata olive emulsion. The dining room is relatively formal, the staff highly professional but not intimidating. The wine list is extensive, and a sommelier is on hand to help match wines with each course. The entire restaurant is nonsmoking. For a taste of Trotter's gourmet fare without the high price tag, check out **Trotter's To Go,** his new gourmet food store in Lincoln Park at 1337 W. Fullerton Ave. (© 773/868-6510).

816 W. Armitage Ave. (at Halsted St.). © 773/248-6228. www.charlietrotters.com. Reservations required. Jackets required for men, ties requested. Fixed-price menus $115 and $135. AE, DC, DISC, MC, V. Tues–Thurs 6–9:30pm; Fri–Sat 5:30–9:30pm. Subway/El: Brown Line to Armitage.

Crofton on Wells CONTEMPORARY AMERICAN   Chef-owner Suzy Crofton has devoted herself to this critically acclaimed restaurant, a 70-seat River North storefront with a loyal following. Crofton's food is simply sophisticated and decidedly American, and the relatively spare dining room fits in with her no-attitude, midwestern aesthetic. The menu is based on seasonally available ingredients: You might start with a chilled cucumber and Vidalia onion soup with shrimp, melon, and avocado; then move on to grilled venison medallions, soaked in a red-wine sauce with cabbage, huckleberries, and arugula pesto. Entree selections always include a vegan choice. Close with a Granny Smith apple tart or bittersweet chocolate cake with espresso ice cream and black-peppercorn caramel sauce.

535 N. Wells St. (between Grand Ave. and Ohio St.). © 312/755-1790. www.croftononwells.com. Reservations recommended. Main courses $25–$32. AE, DC, MC, V. Mon–Thurs 5–10pm; Fri–Sat 5–11pm. Subway/El: Brown Line to Merchandise Mart.

ESPN Zone (Kids) AMERICAN   Sports fans, welcome to nirvana. This massive dining and entertainment complex features three components: the Studio Grill, designed with replicas of studio sets from the cable networks' shows (including *SportsCenter*); the Screening Room, a sports pub featuring a 16-foot screen and an armada of TV monitors and radio sets carrying live broadcasts of games; and the Sports Arena, a gaming area with interactive and competitive attractions. The food here is better-than-average tavern fare, including quite a few salads and upscale items. There's also a special kids' menu.

43 E. Ohio St. (at Wabash Ave.). © 312/644-3776. Reservations not accepted. Main courses $7.25–$20. AE, DC, MC, V. Sun–Thurs 11:30am–11pm; Fri–Sat 11:30am–midnight. Subway/El: Red Line to Grand.

Everest ALSATIAN/FRENCH   Forty stories above the Chicago Stock Exchange, the refined Everest features the best views of any restaurant in the city and four-star fine-dining civility. Its windows overlook the shimmering nightscape of downtown Chicago, and its culinary experience is one of the finest in town. Refined sensibilities, culinary imagination, and a focus on "noble" and "simple" ingredients enhance chef Jean Joho's appreciation of the earthy cookery of his native Alsace. While the menu changes frequently, you might find a starter of salmon soufflé followed by an entree of poached tenderloin of beef cooked *pot-au-feu* style and served with horseradish cream. Desserts are suitably sumptuous and the wine list offers some wonderful American and Alsatian selections.

440 S. LaSalle St., 40th floor (at Congress Pkwy.). 🕿 **312/663-8920**. www.everestrestaurant.com. Reservations required. Main courses $27–$46; menu degustation $89; 3-course pretheater dinner $49. AE, DC, DISC, MC, V. Tues–Thurs 5:30–9pm; Fri 5:30–9:30pm; Sat 5–10pm. Complimentary valet parking. Subway/El: Brown Line to LaSalle/Van Buren or Red Line to Adams.

Gino's East PIZZA   Gino's East was once the only Chicago restaurant where patrons would wait outside nightly—even in the dead of winter—for pizza. Now that the restaurant has moved into vast new digs, there are no more lines out front, though diners still sit in dark-stained booths, surrounded by paneled walls covered with graffiti. Many Chicagoans consider Gino's *the* quintessential deep-dish Chicago-style pizza. True to its reputation, the pizza is heavy (a small cheese pizza is enough for two), so work up an appetite before chowing down. Specialty pizzas include the supreme, with layers of cheese, sausage, onions, green pepper, and mushrooms; and the vegetarian, with cheese, onions, peppers, asparagus, summer squash, zucchini, and eggplant.

633 N. Wells St. (at Ontario St.). 🕿 **312/943-1124**. Reservations not accepted. Pizza $11–$28. AE, DC, DISC, MC, V. Sun–Thurs 11am–9pm; Fri–Sat 11am–11pm. Subway/El: Red Line to Grand.

Hot Chocolate AMERICAN   Mindy Segal's desserts got raves when she worked at the restaurant mk, so when she opened her own place in early 2005—with a dessert theme, no less—there were lines almost immediately. Stop by for a brioche and coffee in the morning, a Kobe beef steak sandwich at lunch, or a plate of glazed pork tenderloin in the evening. Don't leave without having dessert. Many, including the apple-cider potpie and the banana napoleon, with layers of caramelized bananas, banana coffeecake, graham crackers, and a topping of banana ice cream, use seasonal fruit, but chocoholics can get their fill, too, with dishes such as the rich chocolate soufflé with caramel ice cream or a flight of mini hot chocolates served with homemade marshmallows. Come on a weekday (for a late lunch or early dinner) to avoid a wait.

1747 N. Damen Ave. (at Willow St.). 🕿 **773/489-1747**. Reservations not accepted. Main courses $8–$15. AE, MC, V. Sun and Tues–Wed 9am–10pm; Thurs 9am–11pm; Fri–Sat 9am–midnight. Subway/El: Blue Line to Damen.

Morton's STEAK   The well-known Morton's chain is Chicago born and bred, and the original is still the king of the Chicago-style steakhouses. It holds its own against an onslaught of steakhouse competition with gargantuan portions of prime, wet-aged steaks, football-size baking potatoes, and trees of broccoli rolled out on a presentation cart. The restaurant is somewhat hidden in an undistinguished high-rise, and the decor hasn't changed in years. Neither has the menu: House specialties include the double filet mignon with sauce béarnaise, and classic cuts of porterhouse, New York strip, and rib-eye. This is a great place for a slice of carnivorous Chicago power dining—and a slice of Key lime pie or New York cheesecake.

1050 N. State St. (at Rush St.). 🕿 **312/266-4820**. www.mortons.com. Reservations recommended. Main courses $26–$44. AE, DC, DISC, MC, V. Mon–Sat 5:30–11pm; Sun 5–9:30pm. Subway/El: Red Line to Chicago.

North Pond AMERICAN   Tucked away in Lincoln Park, North Pond is a hidden treasure. The restaurant's Arts and Crafts–inspired interior blends perfectly with the park outside, and a recently added glass-enclosed addition lets you dine "outside" year-round. Chef Bruce Sherman emphasizes organic, locally grown ingredients and favors simple preparations—although the overall result is definitely upscale. One of the seasonal menu items might be grilled sea scallops with orange-Parmesan grain salad, glazed organic baby carrots, and spiced lobster sauce. For dessert, try mango "soup" with banana mousse and candied hazelnuts. To enjoy the restaurant's setting at a slightly lower price tag, try the fixed-price Sunday brunch ($30). The all-American wine list of 100 or so selections focuses on boutique vintners.

2610 N. Cannon Dr. (south of Diversey Pkwy.). ℂ 773/477-5845. www.northpondrestaurant.com. Reservations recommended. Main courses $28–$32. AE, DC, MC, V. Tues–Sat 5:30–10pm; Sun 11am–2pm and 5:30–10pm. Lunch served Tues–Sat 11:30am–2pm June–Sept. Bus: 151.

RoseAngelis (Value) NORTHERN ITALIAN   This is neighborhood dining at its best, a place with reliably good food and very reasonable prices. Tucked in a residential side street in Lincoln Park, the restaurant fills the ground floor of a former private home, with a charming series of cozy rooms and a garden patio. The menu emphasizes pasta (the rich lasagna is a favorite). RoseAngelis is vegetarian-friendly; there's no red meat on the menu, and many of the pastas are served with vegetables. Finish up with the deliciously decadent bread pudding with warm caramel sauce (it's big enough to share). Weeknights are your best bet; on weekends you'll wait up to 2 hours for a table.

1314 W. Wrightwood Ave. (at Lakewood Ave.). ℂ 773/296-0081. www.roseangelis.com. Reservations accepted for parties of 8 or more. Main courses $9.95–$15. DISC, MC, V. Tues–Thurs 5–10pm; Fri–Sat 5–11pm; Sun 4:30–9pm. Subway/El: Brown or Red line to Fullerton.

Spiaggia ITALIAN   Spiaggia is widely acknowledged as the best fine-dining Italian restaurant in the city. The dining room is bright, airy, and sophisticated (wear your jackets, gentlemen). Come here to linger over long lunches, romantic interludes, and celebrations of that big merger. You can order a la carte or try a seven-course degustation menu; entree choices change often and emphasize seasonal ingredients. For your starter, consider carpaccio of smoked Sicilian swordfish. The pasta roster tempts with pheasant-stuffed ravioli, and gnocchi with wild mushrooms. Entrees include classic zuppa di pesce, and grilled squab over lentils with foie gras. For dessert, the chilled mascarpone cheese torte with rich chocolate gelato and espresso sauce is a high point. Adjacent to the restaurant in a narrow, window-lined space is the informal, lower-priced **Café Spiaggia** (ℂ 312/280-2764), which serves Sunday brunch.

980 N. Michigan Ave. (at Oak St.). ℂ 312/280-2750. www.levyrestaurants.com. Reservations strongly suggested on weekends. Main courses $34–$41 dinner; menu degustation $95–$135. AE, DC, DISC, MC, V. Sun–Thurs 6–9:30pm; Fri–Sat 5:30–10:30pm. Subway/El: Red Line to Chicago.

Tru PROGRESSIVE FRENCH   The sense of humor of chefs Rick Tramonto and Gale Gand shines through the menu (which recently included Insane Black Truffle Soup and "Nut 'n Honey" Foie Gras), making Tru an approachable fine-dining experience. The menu is divided into a series of prix-fixe options. Appetizers include a visually sensational caviar staircase (caviars and fixin's climbing a glass spiral staircase). For your entree, the "surf, turf and turf" combines roasted lobster with sweetbreads and foie gras. Sate your sweet tooth with roasted pineapple carpaccio or a duet of chocolate and blood orange soufflés. The expansive wine list is a treat for oenophiles. The restaurant is nonsmoking.

676 N. St. Clair St. (at Huron St.). ℂ 312/202-0001. www.trurestaurant.com. Reservations required. Prix-fixe menu $80–$150. AE, DC, DISC, MC, V. Mon–Thurs 5:30–10pm; Fri–Sat 5:30–11pm. Subway/El: Red Line to Chicago.

Wishbone (Value) (Kids) SOUTHERN   Wishbone is a down-home, casual family spot that inspires intense loyalty (even if the food is only good rather than outstanding). Known for southern food and big-appetite breakfasts, Wishbone's extensive, reasonably priced menu blends hearty, home-style choices with healthful and vegetarian items. Brunch is the 'bone's claim to fame, when an eclectic crowd packs in for the plump and tasty salmon cakes and omelets. For a main course, try the "yardbird," a charbroiled chicken with sweet red-pepper sauce. The tart Key lime pie is one of the best desserts in the city. There's a newer location at 3300 N. Lincoln Ave. (© 773/ 549-2663), but the original has more character.

1001 Washington St. (at Morgan St.). © 312/850-2663. http://wishbone.epagecity.com. Reservations accepted except for weekend brunch. Main courses $5–$10 breakfast and lunch, $7–$14 dinner. AE, DC, DISC, MC, V. Mon–Fri 7am–3pm; Tues–Sat 5–10pm; Sat–Sun 8am–3pm.

CHICAGO AFTER DARK

For up-to-date entertainment listings, check the local newspapers and magazines, particularly the "Friday" and "Weekend Plus" sections of the two dailies, the *Chicago Tribune* and the *Chicago Sun-Times;* the *Chicago Reader* or *New City,* two free weekly tabloids with extensive listings; and the monthly *Chicago* magazine. The *Tribune's* entertainment-oriented website, **www.metromix.com**; the *Reader's* website, **www.chireader.com**; and the local Citysearch website, **http://chicago.citysearch.com**, are also excellent sources of information, with lots of opinionated reviews. For current listings of classical music concerts and opera, call the **Chicago Dance and Music Alliance** (© 312/987-1123; www.chicagoperformances.org).

THE PERFORMING ARTS   The world-class **Chicago Symphony Orchestra,** Orchestra Hall, Symphony Center, 220 S. Michigan Ave. (© **312/294-3000;** www. cso.org), was led by music director Daniel Barenboim (until the end of 2006), who introduced more modern works by 20th-century composers into the orchestra's traditional repertoire. Summertime visitors have an opportunity to hear a CSO performance at the delightful **Ravinia Festival** (© **847/266-5100**) in suburban Highland Park. It's also a tranquil setting for chamber music, world music, jazz and pop concerts, dance, and music study.

The **Lyric Opera of Chicago,** Civic Opera House, Madison Street and Wacker Drive (© **312/332-2244;** www.lyricopera.org), performs in the handsome 3,563-seat 1929 Art Deco Civic Opera House, the second-largest opera house in the country. It attracts top-notch singers from all over the world and has a strong commitment to new American works.

If you're going to see just one dance performance while you're in town, make it **Hubbard Street Dance Chicago** (© 312/850-9744; www.hubbardstreetdance.com), which seamlessly combines elements of jazz, modern, ballet, and theater dance. The **Joffrey Ballet of Chicago** (© 312/739-0120; www.joffrey.com), led by co-founder and artistic director Gerald Arpino, is committed to the classic works of the 20th century. It continues to draw crowds to its popular rock ballet, *Billboards,* set to the music of Prince, and tours internationally. The Joffrey and other noted dance and musical performers and touring Broadway shows take the stage at the landmark **Auditorium Theatre,** 50 E. Congress Pkwy., between Michigan and Wabash avenues (© 312/922-2110; www.auditoriumtheatre.org), which is reviewed earlier in this chapter.

THE THEATER SCENE   With more than 200 theaters, Chicago may have dozens of productions playing on any given weekend. It's one of the best theater cities in the country. To order tickets for many plays and events, call **Ticketmaster Arts Line** (© 312/902-1500), a centralized phone-reservation system that allows you to charge full-price tickets (with an additional service charge) for productions at more than 50 Chicago theaters. For half-price tickets on the day of the show (on Fri you can also purchase tickets for weekend performances), drop by one of the **Hot Tix** ticket centers

(© **312/977-1755;** www.hottix.org), located in the Loop at 72 E. Randolph St. (between Wabash and Michigan aves.); at the Water Works Visitor Center, 163 E. Pearson St.; and in Lincoln Park at Tower Records, 2301 N. Clark St. Tickets are not sold over the phone. The website lists what's on sale for that day beginning at 10am.

The dean of legitimate theaters in Chicago is the **Goodman,** Dearborn Street, between Randolph and Lake streets (© **312/443-3800;** www.goodman-theatre.org). You may not see anything revolutionary, but you'll get some of the best actors in the city and top-notch production values. The **Steppenwolf Theater Company,** 1650 N. Halsted St., at North Avenue (© **312/335-1650;** www.steppenwolf.org), is famous for launching the careers of luminaries such as John Malkovich and Gary Sinise. Unfortunately, it may be a victim of its own success. Though the acting is always high caliber, shows can be hit-or-miss, and unlike in the early days, you're certainly not guaranteed a thrilling theatrical experience. The home of the **Chicago Shakespeare Theatre** on Navy Pier, 800 E. Grand Ave. (© **312/595-5600;** www.chicagoshakes. com), opened in October 1999, and is a glittering glass-box complex that rises seven stories and cost $24 million. It features a 525-seat courtyard-style theater patterned loosely on the Swan Theatre in Stratford-upon-Avon. But what keeps loyal subscribers coming back is the talented company of actors, including some of the finest Shakespearean performers in the country.

COMEDY & IMPROV   Chicago continues to nurture young comics, drawn to Chicago for the chance to hone their improvisational skills. The **ImprovOlympic,** 3541 N. Clark St., at Addison Street (© **773/880-0199;** www.iochicago.net), offers a nightclub setting for a variety of unscripted nightly performances, from free-form shows to shows loosely based on concepts such as *Star Trek* or dating. **Second City,** 1616 N. Wells St., in the Pipers Alley complex at North Avenue (© **312/337-3992;** www.secondcity.com), remains the top comedy club in Chicago. You'll rarely see a weak or unfunny show—these actors are magicians at salvaging material that bombs with audiences.

LIVE MUSIC   Born in the Storyville section of New Orleans, **jazz** moved upriver to Chicago some 75 years ago, and it still has a home here. The **Green Mill,** 4802 N. Broadway (off Lawrence; © **773/878-5552;** Subway/El: Red Line to Lawrence), is a

I Got the Blues

With a few notable exceptions, Chicago's best and most popular blues showcases are located in the entertainment districts of the Near North Side. **B.L.U.E.S,** 2519 N. Halsted St., between Wrightwood and Fullerton avenues (© **773/528-1012;** www.chicagobluesbar.com; subway/El: Red/Brown lines to Fullerton), is a small joint for the serious blues aficionado—you won't miss a single move of the musicians standing on stage only yards away. Nearby, at 2548 N. Halsted St., between Wrightwood and Fullerton avenues, is **Kingston Mines** (© **773/477-4646;** www.kingstonmines.com; subway/El: Red/Brown lines to Fullerton), one of Chicago's premier blues bars, which celebrated its 35th anniversary in 2003. Kingston Mines is where musicians congregate after their own gigs to jam together and to socialize. There's also a kitchen open late serving up burgers and ribs.

Chicago treasure; get there early to claim one of the plush velvet booths. Still retaining its speak-easy flavor, it was a popular watering hole during the '20s and '30s, when Al Capone was a regular and the headliners included Sophie Tucker and Al Jolson. **Jazz Showcase,** 59 W. Grand St., at Clark Street (© **312/670-2473;** www.jazzshowcase. com; Subway/El: Red Line to Grand), in River North, is a spacious and handsome room with two shows a night.

The Bucktown/Wicker Park neighborhood is the center of the alternative rock movement. Scan the *Reader* or *New City* to see who's playing where. **Martyrs',** 3855 N. Lincoln Ave., between Berenice Avenue and Irving Park Road (© **773/404-9494;** www.martyrslive.com; Subway/El: Brown Line to Addison), presents a variety of local bands and the occasional performance by national touring acts. The low tables, high ceiling, and huge windows make Martyrs' one of the best places to catch a rock-'n'-roll show. **Metro,** 3730 N. Clark St., at Racine Avenue (© **773/549-0203;** www. metrochicago.com; subway/El: Red Line to Sheridan), in an old auditorium, is Chicago's premier venue for live alternative/rock acts on the verge of breaking into the big time. Everybody who is anybody has played here over the years, from REM to such local heroes as Smashing Pumpkins.

The **House of Blues,** 329 N. Dearborn St., at Kinzie Street (© **312/923-2000;** www.hob.com; subway/El: Red Line to Grand), is a massive complex, extravagantly decorated with 600 pieces of Mississippi Delta folk art. It isn't really a blues club as much as a showcase for rock, R&B, zydeco, reggae, and more, consistently booking top national acts. The popular Sunday gospel brunch, offering a southern-style buffet, brings a different Chicago gospel choir to the stage each week; get tickets in advance.

Country, folk, bluegrass, Latin, and Celtic—the **Old Town School of Folk Music** has it: 4544 N. Lincoln Ave., between Wilson and Montrose avenues (© **773/728-6000;** www.oldtownschool.org; subway/El: Brown Line to Western). The school has hosted everyone from the legendary Pete Seeger to bluegrass phenom Alison Krauss. Its pristine 425-seat concert hall in a former 1930s library in Lincoln Square is the world's largest facility dedicated to presenting traditional and contemporary folk music.

THE CLUB SCENE Chicago is the hallowed ground where house music was hatched in the 1980s, so it's no surprise to find a few big dance clubs pounding away the big beat. The **Funky Buddha Lounge,** 728 W. Grand Ave. (© **312/666-1695;** www.funkybuddha.com; subway/El: Blue Line to Grand), is one of the coolest temples of nightlife in the city, located west of the River North gallery district. The DJs flood the nice-size dance floor with a disco-tech mix infused with salsa, hip-hop, and soul. **Reserve,** 858 W. Lake St. (© **313/455-1111;** www.reserve-chicago.com; subway/ El: Green Line to Clinton), draws hordes of scenesters to the West Loop with its 5,000-square-foot club, downstairs lounge, and ultraexclusive VIP offerings. At **Le Passage,** One Oak Place, between Rush and State streets (© **312/255-0022;** www. lepassage.tv; subway/El: Red Line to Chicago), the beautiful, the rich, and the designer-suited are attracted by the lush loungey aesthetic; cool blend of house, dance, R&B, soul, and acid jazz music; and a stellar French/international fusion menu.

Rednofive, 440 N. Halsted St. (© **312/733-6699;** www.rednofive.com; subway/ El: Green Line to Clinton), has a sleek design and a tight lineup of local DJs spinning progressive and abstract house music, hip-hop, and pop, often accompanied by a percussionist on drums. **Transit,** 1431 W. Lake St. (© **312/491-8600;** www.transit

nightclubchicago.com; subway/El: Green Line to Ashland), is an excellent no-non-sense dance club that doesn't trick itself out under the auspices of any wacky theme.

THE BAR SCENE   The **Near North Side** has a few entertainment zones saturated with bright, upscale neighborhood bars. Around **Rush and Division streets** (subway/El: Red Line to Clark/Division) are what a bygone era called singles bars—attracting primarily a college-aged contingent.

Near the Magnificent Mile, the **Billy Goat Tavern,** 430 N. Michigan Ave. (✆ **312/222-1525;** subway/El: Red Line to Grand/State), has been a longtime hangout for newspaper reporters over the years, but it's the "cheezeborgers, cheezeborgers" served at the grill that gave inspiration to the famous *Saturday Night Live* sketch. In the Old Town 'hood, the family-run **Corcoran's,** 1615 N. Wells St. (✆ **312/440-0885;** subway/El: Brown Line to Sedgwick), is a cozy local hangout. At the top of any self-respecting Lincoln Park yuppie's list of meeting places is **Glascott's Groggery,** 2158 N. Halsted St., at Webster Avenue (✆ **773/281-1205;** subway/El: Brown Lines to Armitage), an Irish pub that's been in the same family since it opened in 1937.

In Wicker Park, hundreds of travel books and guides line the shelves of **The Map Room,** 1949 N. Hoyne Ave., at Armitage Avenue (✆ **773/252-7636;** subway/El: Blue Line to Damen). Peruse that tome on Fuji or Antarctica while sipping a pint of one of the 20-odd draft beers available. Located in the historic Flat Iron Building, **The Note,** 1565 N. Milwaukee Ave., at North Avenue (✆ **773/489-0011;** subway/El: Blue Line to Damen), is a great after-hours bar with pool tables and the right after-hours music: a jukebox exclusively devoted to blues and jazz and occasional live jazz.

THE GAY & LESBIAN SCENE   Most of Chicago's gay bars are conveniently clustered on a stretch of North Halsted Street in Lakeview, making it easy to sample many of them in a breezy walk. To find out what's happening, check out the weekly *Nightlines* and *Gab.*

Step into **Berlin,** 954 W. Belmont Ave., east of Sheffield Avenue (✆ **773/348-4975;** subway/El: Red/Brown lines to Belmont), where the disco tunes pulse, the clubby crowd chatters, and the lighting bathes everyone in a cool reddish glow. **Sidetrack,** 3349 N. Halsted St., at Roscoe Street (✆ **773/477-9189**), is a sleek video bar where TV monitors are never out of your field of vision, nor are the preppy professional patrons.

2 Cleveland

As fans of Drew Carey's former sitcom have long known, Cleveland rocks. But you don't need to take the TV comedian's word for it. Ask around. Over the past decade, Cleveland's tourism has doubled to more than nine million visitors annually, and its profile is shining more brightly than ever. Sprawling for 50 miles along the shores of Lake Erie, this former industrial hub of the heartland is on a roll.

George Washington once said that a great city would stand in the blessed spot where the Cuyahoga River met Lake Erie. Industrial success infused money into the city early on, as its steel and oil barons drew upon their vast fortunes to build a monumental downtown and a rich cultural legacy that includes the world-renowned Cleveland Museum of Art, Case Western Reserve University, and the Cleveland Orchestra. It was a solid foundation for the post-industrial urban vision, which took giant steps forward with the opening of Jacobs Field, the first of the nation's new wave of retro-modern Major League ballparks, at the gateway to downtown in 1994. A year later came I. M. Pei's splendid Rock & Roll Hall of Fame, which mirrors Pei's own Louvre expansion with its playful pyramid-shaped design. The latest high-profile tenant to take up anchor in downtown Cleveland is the House of Blues, a 1,000-seat club and restaurant at East Fourth Street at Euclid Avenue.

Although Cleveland's industrial foundation is very much in evidence, downtown's steel warehouses and tool-and-die factories now house trendy clubs and restaurants, and its many bridges lead to gentrified neighborhoods fueled by the optimism that comes with a measure of achievement. The city still has some rough edges, but the message couldn't be clearer: Cleveland is striving for global recognition, and the droves of American and international visitors flocking to the re-energized city indicate that success is in the air.

ESSENTIALS

GETTING THERE   By Plane   Cleveland Hopkins International Airport (© 216/265-6030; www.clevelandairport.com) is 10 miles south of downtown. Major car-rental companies are housed at a central off-site lot; pick up the shared shuttle bus, which stops just outside baggage claim. It's an easy 20-minute drive into the city; take I-480 to I-71 north to I-90 into downtown.

If you're not renting, you can take the **RTA Red Line** into the city from the main airport terminal for $1.50 per person. The ride takes about 25 minutes to downtown's Tower City Center and about 40 minutes to the University Circle section of town. Trains generally leave every 15 minutes at peak times, but not all trains stop at University Circle. For more information, see "Getting Around," below. **Taxis** are available outside baggage claim exit 2; expect the fare to run about $25 (plus tip) to downtown. For **limousine service** to downtown hotels, call **Hopkins Airport Limousine Service** (© **800/543-9912** or 216/267-8282; www.gohopkins.com); the per-person, one-way fare runs about $65.

By Train   Amtrak (© **800/USA-RAIL;** www.amtrak.com) provides daily service from Chicago (trip time: 7 hr.), New York (12 hr.), and Washington, D.C. (11 hr.) to its downtown station, 200 Cleveland Memorial Shoreway, across from the Great Lakes Science Center (© **216/696-5115**).

By Car   The principal highway routes into Cleveland are **I-77** from the south (Akron); **I-80** or **I-76** from the east (Youngstown and Pittsburgh, both connecting with I-77 north near Akron); **I-90** from the northeast (Buffalo); **I-71** from the southwest (Columbus); and I-80/90 from the west (Toledo). Both I-77 and I-90 will take you right into downtown Cleveland.

VISITOR INFORMATION   Contact the **Convention and Visitors Bureau of Greater Cleveland,** 3100 Terminal Tower, 50 Public Sq., Cleveland, OH 44113-2290 (© **800/321-1001**), or call the information hot line at © **800/321-1004** or 216/621-5555. The Cleveland arts and entertainment hot line (© **888/323-2787;** www.travelcleveland.com) is helpful. Other useful sites—especially for the latest arts and entertainment coverage—are **Visit Cleveland!** (www.cleveland.com), **Citysearch** (http://cleveland.citysearch.com), and **AOL City Guide** (www.cityguide.aol.com/cleveland).

The CVB's main **Visitor Information Center** is at Cleveland Hopkins International Airport, 5300 Riverside Dr. (© **216/265-3729**). Another location is at Terminal Tower, 50 Public Sq. (© **216/621-7981**). The helpful staff will answer your

Cleveland

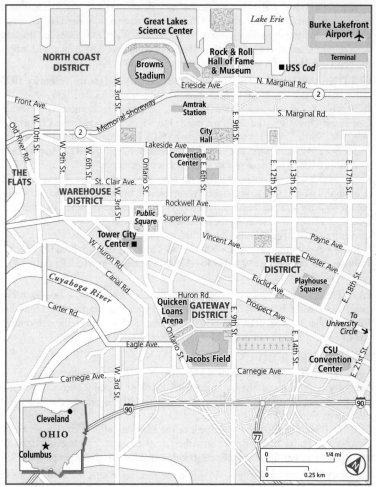

questions and can sell you discounted tickets to the city's main attractions, so this makes a great first stop.

ORIENTATION   Cleveland's major attractions are concentrated in two areas: **Downtown,** where you'll find most hotels, government buildings and corporate headquarters, the major sports arenas, and attractions such as the Rock & Roll Hall of Fame and Playhouse Square Center. **University Circle** is about 4½ miles east via Euclid Avenue; this leafy district is home to Case Western University (hence the name) and most of the city's major cultural institutions. Plans are underway to link the two enclaves via a redeveloped Euclid Avenue Corridor. Public transportation, tree-lined sidewalks, retail developments, and apartments are envisioned as part of this $325-million urban renewal project targeted for completion as this book goes to press.

The Gateway and Warehouse districts are an easy walk from Public Square. You can also walk to North Coast Harbor and down to the east bank of the Flats (as long as you don't mind the steep slope), or take the RTA rail's Waterfront Line. You'll want to drive or take a taxi to the west bank of the Flats. Ohio City has its own RTA stop on the Red Line. (For RTA information, see directly below.)

GETTING AROUND   The **Greater Cleveland Rapid Transit Authority (RTA) rail system** is not extensive. Visitors usually stick to the main Red Line, which travels between the airport and University Circle, with stops at downtown's Tower City Center and Ohio City; and the Waterfront Line, which connects Tower City with the Flats and North Coast Harbor. In addition, **RTA buses** cover five downtown loop routes from Public Square. For complete information, call the **RTA Answerline** at ℭ 216/621-9500, or check out its website at www.gcrta.org.

You don't need a car downtown, but it's convenient to have one if you'd really like to explore. The cost of taxis will negate what you save by not renting, and a 20- or 30-minute wait for a summoned cab is common, especially on evenings and weekends. Driving is also easier than using the RTA rail system to travel between downtown and University Circle. (See "Getting There," above, for car-rental information.)

If you still want to use a cab, try **Yellow Cab Company of Cleveland** (ℭ 216/623-1500) or **Ace Taxi Service** (ℭ 216/361-4700). The flag drops at $1.80 and it's $1.50 per mile thereafter.

FAST FACTS   Emergency and urgent-care services are available at **Lutheran Hospital,** 1730 W. 25th St. (ℭ 216/696-4300; www.lutheranhospital.org). A 24-hour **Rite Aid** pharmacy (ℭ 216/676-5561) is located 8 miles out of the city center at 15149 Snow Rd., in Brookpark. Sales tax is 8% and hotel tax is 15%.

WHAT TO SEE & DO

Lolly the Trolley (ℭ 800/848-0173 or 216/771-4484; www.lollytrolley.com) is a great way to get to know the lay of the land. Excellent 1- and 2-hour narrated tours take place aboard a fleet of replica trolley cars; the 1-hour version concentrates on downtown, skipping University Circle and the Lake Erie shoreline. Tours, which leave from the Powerhouse on the west bank of the Flats, are offered daily from May to October, on Friday and Saturday only the rest of the year. The fare is $10 or $15 adults, $9 or $14 seniors, and $7 or $10 kids 2 to 17; reservations are required.

Cleveland Botanical Garden   In spring and summer, 7 acres of lush blossoms and greenery abound at this oasis of nature at University Circle. Year-round, visitors are drawn to the tropical ecosystems housed in the stunning new Eleanor Armstrong Smith Glasshouse and Environmental Education Center. The crystal-like conservatory is home to hundreds of species of butterflies, birds, animals, and plant life of both Madagascar and a Costa Rican cloud forest.

11030 East Blvd., University Circle. ℭ 888/853-7091 or 216/721-1600. www.cbgarden.com. Admission $7.50 adults, $3 children 3–12. Apr 1–Nov 1 Mon–Sat 10am–5pm, Sun noon–5pm; open until 9pm Wed from Memorial Day to Labor Day. Closed Mon Nov–Mar; closed Thanksgiving, Dec 25, and Jan. 1.

Cleveland Metroparks Zoo   This well-maintained and well-organized zoo is a great place to spend half a day, especially if you're traveling with the kids. The standout attraction is the $30-million multilevel Rainforest exhibit. Don't miss the actual rainstorm inside this simulated biosphere, which boasts more than 600 animals and insects from all seven continents.

3900 Wildlife Way (off I-71, between W. 25th St. and Fulton Rd.). © 216/661-6500. www.clemetzoo.com. Admission $10 adults, $5 children 2–11. Daily 10am–5pm (summer Sat–Sun to 7pm). Closed Christmas and New Year's Day.

Cleveland Museum of Art (Value)

At presstime, the museum was undergoing a $258-million expansion, designed by internationally renowned architect Rafael Vinoly. Special exhibitions began showing again in October 2006, with *Barcelona & Modernity: Picasso, Gaudí, Miró, Dalí,* which was scheduled to run into January 2007. The permanent collections, which are scheduled to reopen in early 2007, include works by Titian, Holbein, Picasso, and Monet, among others. Other upcoming special exhibitions include *Monet in Normandy* February 18 to May 20, 2007, and *Artistic Luxury: Fabergé Tiffany Lalique,* February 1 to May 1, 2008.

11150 East Blvd., University Circle. © 216/421-7350, or 888/CMA-0033 for advance exhibition tickets. www.cleveland art.org. Free admission to museum (with fees for some special events and exhibitions). Tues, Thurs, and Sat–Sun 10am–5pm; Wed and Fri 10am–9pm.

Cleveland Museum of Natural History

Here's another fine University Circle museum that includes the state-of-the-art, sphere-shaped Shafran Planetarium. Among the museum's other draws are *Happlocanthosaurus,* a 70-foot-long plant-eating dinosaur; an excellent gem and jewels collection; a fascinating array of fossils and geological specimens, with a special emphasis on prehistoric Ohio; and a hands-on natural sciences Discovery Center for the little ones.

1 Wade Oval Dr., University Circle. © 800/317-9155 or 216/231-4600. www.cmnh.org. Admission $9.50 adults; $7.50 seniors, college students, and children 7–18; $6.50 children 3–6. Planetarium admission $4. Mon–Sat 10am–5pm; Sun noon–5pm; observatory hours Sept–May Wed 8–10pm.

Great Lakes Science Center (Kids)

More than 400 hands-on exhibits let kids and adults build their brain power. Daily live science demonstrations are offered at the museum, which includes a 3,000-square-foot interactive Great Lakes Environment and more than 320 hands-on science experiments. The six-story Cleveland Clinic OMNIMAX Theater shows larger-than-life features.

601 Erieside Ave., at North Coast Harbor between the Cleveland Browns Stadium and the Rock & Roll Hall of Fame & Museum. © 216/694-2000. www.GreatScience.com. Exhibit-only $8.95 adults, $7.95 seniors, $6.95 children 3–17. Combination ticket (with OMNIMAX movie) $13 adults, $11 seniors, $8.95 children. Daily 9:30am–5:30pm; call for OMNIMAX showtimes.

Rock & Roll Hall of Fame & Museum (Best)

If any one thing is most responsible for Cleveland's rebirth, this glass-and-porcelain pyramid is it. Designed by I. M. Pei, this temple to rock music is a high-concept, multimedia collection of exhibits, archives, and films that tell the story of rock from its bluesy roots through its post-grunge days. Fun for all ages, the museum offers the coolest collection of pop-culture memorabilia around. For an electrifying experience, check out the Jimi Hendrix Surround Sound Theater and Exhibit, where fans can revel in jaw-dropping videotaped performances and then peruse the legend's guitars, costumes, handwritten lyrics, and watercolor landscapes.

1 Key Plaza, downtown. © 888/764-ROCK or 216/781-7625. www.rockhall.com. Admission $20 adults, $14 seniors, $11 children 9–11, free for children 8 and under. Daily 10am–5:30pm (with extended evening hours Memorial Day to Labor Day Sat 10am–9pm). Closed Thanksgiving and Dec. 25.

World War II Submarine USS *Cod*

This World War II sub is credited with sinking more than 30,000 tons of Japanese shipping vessels. Completely intact and a designated National Historic Landmark, the *Cod* is particularly enlightening to tour because it has not been adapted for civilian access—visitors use the same vertical ladders and hatches that were used by the wartime crew.

1089 N. Marginal Dr. (just east of the Rock & Roll Hall of Fame). ℂ 216/566-8770. www.usscod.org. Admission $6 adults, $5 seniors, $3 students 5–12. May–Sept daily 10am–5pm.

MORE ATTRACTIONS

MUSEUMS Paying homage to Holocaust victims and recognizing the achievements of the area's significant Jewish population is the new **Milton and Tamar Maltz Jewish Heritage Museum,** 2929 Richmond Rd., Beachwood (ℂ **216/593-0575;** www.maltzjewishmuseum.org). The nonprofit museum, which opened in 2005, includes interactive exhibits and other displays, as well as traveling exhibitions. It is located next to the Temple-Tifereth Israel, 26000 Shaker Blvd., about a 30-minute drive from downtown Cleveland.

PARKS In the University Circle section of the city is **Rockefeller Park,** a 296-acre oasis between Lake Erie and Case Western Reserve University. Take 105th Street, Martin Luther King Jr. Drive, or East Boulevard for easiest park access. In adjoining **Wade Park** are the Cleveland Museum of Art, the Museum of Natural History, and the Cleveland Botanical Garden.

West of downtown is **Edgewater Park,** 6700 Memorial Shoreway, at West Boulevard (ℂ **216/881-8141**), one of the city's best swimming beaches, with bathhouses, concessions, fishing piers, and more. Beach access is free.

CRUISES The *Nautica Queen* (ℂ **800/837-0604** or 216/696-8888; www.nautica queen.com) offers lunch, brunch, and dinner cruises that also take in lake and river sights. Prices range from about $28 to $53 for adults, and $17 to $27 for kids, plus tax and gratuity. Cruises depart from the Nautica Entertainment Complex on the west bank of the Flats. Book ahead, as these hugely popular cruises regularly sell out in advance.

ATTRACTIONS NEAR CLEVELAND

Cedar Point Amusement Park Regularly named the best amusement park on the planet, lakefront Cedar Point boasts the world's biggest collection of rides (68) and

---

In the Grandstand

Cleveland is a monster sports town. Sentiments are heightened, no doubt, by the fact that all the city's pro teams play in first-rate venues within walking distance of one another in the heart of the city. When a game is on, downtown becomes electric with excitement (especially when the home team is winning).

Popularly known as "the Tribe," the Cleveland Indians play at state-of-the-art, 42,000-seat **Jacobs Field,** at Ontario Street and Carnegie Avenue (ℂ **216/420-4636;** www.indians.com), a retro-modern ballpark that's the envy of many a Major League owner. It's impossible to underestimate the effect that "The Jake" has had on the city's renaissance. Next door is **Quicken Loans Arena,** at Ontario Street and Huron Road (ℂ **216/420-2200;** www.theqarena.com), home to the NBA's Cleveland Cavaliers (ℂ **800/332-CAVS** or 216/420-CAVS; www.nba.com/cavs). The American Hockey League will have a new minor league team (no name had been determined at press time) to begin play in fall 2007 (ℂ **216/420-0000**). The NFL's Cleveland Browns play at **Cleveland Browns Stadium,** lakefront on Erieside Avenue (ℂ **440/891-5050;** www.clevelandbrowns.com).

The Gods of the Gridiron

True NFL fans shouldn't leave Ohio without visiting football's ultimate shrine, the **Pro Football Hall of Fame,** 2121 George Halas Drive NW, in the city of Canton (✆ **330/456-8207;** www.profootballhof.com). Just 60 miles south of Cleveland (an hour's drive) off I-77, the hall features exhibits on the history of the sport, loads of memorabilia, and, of course, monuments to the heroes of the game. Special events often feature former and current NFL greats. The annual Hall of Fame weekend (usually the end of July or beginning of Aug) kicks off the NFL pre-season and is when new members are enshrined.

General admission costs $15 adults, $8 kids under age 14; a family ticket is available for $45. The Hall is open daily 9am to 5pm; hours are extended in summer. For more information and event schedules, call or check the website.

more roller coasters (16) than any other park. Thrill-seekers love the **Top Thrill Dragster,** which reaches speeds of 120 mph in under 4 seconds. **Camp Snoopy** is an all-ages play land with its own kid-friendly coaster. Added in 2006, the $6-million **Skyhawk** is a giant swing ride that carries riders more than 125 feet into the air at speeds of more than 60 mph. Located in Frontiertown, Skyhawk is the tallest ride of its kind in the world. **Splash Zone,** a multistory interactive play area with more than 100 water gadgets, is located inside the 18-acre **Soak City** waterpark. **Castaway Bay** is a massive indoor waterpark resort that includes a wave pool and wave coaster as well as day-care and spa facilities.

1 Cedar Point Dr. (U.S. 250), Sandusky. ✆ **419/627-2350.** www.cedarpoint.com. Admission $40 for ages 3–61 or those 48 in. or taller, $9.95 those under 48 in. tall. age Additional admission charges for Soak City and selected rides apply. Multiple-day passes are also available. Daily May to Labor Day; weekends Sept–Oct. Call for exact operating schedule, which often changes. Cedar Point is 61 miles, or a 1¼-hr. drive, from Cleveland. Follow I-90 to I-71 south to I-480 west to I-80 west to Exit 118 (Sandusky); turn right onto U.S. 250. Parking $8.

Geauga Lake & Wildwater Kingdom   Formerly Six Flags World of Adventure, this local amusement park used to include SeaWorld Cleveland. That all changed at the start of the 2004 summer season, when Cedar Fair, L.P. (the same company that operates Cedar Point), purchased the historic property and reopened it with its original name, Geauga Lake. In 2005, the park constructed a new $24-million waterpark, called Wildwater Kingdom, on the 56 acres formerly operated by SeaWorld. In 2006, the park finished this expansion project with the addition of a new 30,000-square-foot wave pool called **Tidal Wave Bay.** The roller coaster **X-Flight,** which soars through eight loops, spins, and spirals at 51 mph, is a far cry from Geauga's first thrill ride, the **Big Dipper** roller coaster, which opened in 1926 (and is still in operation). Wildwater Kingdom, open Memorial Day through Labor Day, is included in the price of Geauga Lake admission.

1060 N. Aurora Rd., Aurora. ✆ **330/562-8303.** www.geaugalake.com. Admission $25 for those 48 in. and taller, $9.95 for those under 48 in., $9.95 seniors. Parking $9.

WHERE TO STAY

All of downtown's hotels also offer discounted weekend rates, and some feature attractive packages that can include such additional premiums as admission to the Rock & Roll Hall of Fame or weekend brunch.

Cleveland Marriott Downtown at Key Center One of downtown's top moderately priced choices, this comfortable 25-story high-rise has better in-room decor than the often pricier Renaissance (see below). The bright, spacious rooms feature the usual amenities found in a hotel of this class; request a room with lake and Rock Hall of Fame views at no extra cost. The hotel's 14 suites, or "lofts," each have a 42-inch HDTV in the living rooms.

127 Public Sq., Cleveland, OH 44114. (C) 800/228-9290 or 216/696-9200. Fax 216/696-0966. www.marriott.com. 410 units. $119–$199 double. Children 17 and under stay free in parent's room. Weekend rates as low as $119. AE, DC, DISC, MC, V. Valet parking $18; self-parking $12. **Amenities:** Restaurant; indoor pool. *In room:* Fridge.

Comfort Inn Downtown On the eastern edge of downtown, this motel is fine for budget travelers. Neatniks may have a few quibbles, but a VCR in every room, free video lending library, and complimentary continental breakfast fill the gaps. With such extras as a microwave, whirlpool tub, refrigerator, and pullout sofa in the sitting room, the suites—which you can usually nab for $109 or less—are the best deal in the house.

1800 Euclid Ave. (at E. 18th St.), Cleveland, OH 44115. (C) 800/228-5150 or 216/861-0001. www.comfortinn.com. 130 units. $89–$149 double; $109–$169 suite. Children 17 and under stay free in parent's room. Rates include continental breakfast. AE, DC, MC, V. Parking $6.50. *In room:* Fridge, microwave (suites only).

Glidden House Cleveland's best full-service boutique hotel (formerly a bed-and-breakfast) is housed in an elegant 1910 French Gothic mansion. After a $2-million renovation, the rooms and suites feature vibrant primary colors and such technological upgrades as plasma televisions and in-room Wi-Fi access. Situated in the leafy heart of University Circle, the location is tops for culture vultures, and a more intimate alternative than the nearby InterContinental Hotel and Conference Center.

1901 Ford Dr., Cleveland, OH 44106. (C) 800/759-8358 or 216/231-8900. Fax 216/231-2130. www.gliddenhouse. com. 60 units. $129–$179 double; $199–$299 suite. Rates include complimentary continental breakfast. AE, DC, DISC, MC, V. Free parking. **Amenities:** Restaurant.

Hampton Inn Cleveland—Downtown (Value) Here's Cleveland's best budget hotel. Rooms have a fresh, new feel and come with the kinds of amenities that usually cost more: coffeemakers, hair dryers, and irons and boards, plus sofas in some king rooms. Same-day valet service is available. The location is excellent, on a nice downtown block within walking distance of all major attractions.

1460 E. 9th St. (at Superior Ave.), Cleveland, OH 44114. (C) 800/HAMPTON or 216/241-6600. Fax 216/241-8811. www.hampton-inn.com. 194 units. $79–$149 double. Children 17 and under stay free in parent's room. Rates include hot breakfast. AE, DC, DISC, MC, V. Valet parking $18; self-parking $15. **Amenities:** Small fitness center.

Holiday Inn–City Center Lakeshore The prime advantage of this basic hotel is its location, within downtown's closest walking distance of the Rock Hall of Fame. The Browns' stadium, convention center, and the Flats are also accessible via courtesy shuttle—a nice plus. Rooms are basic but comfy. Don't expect more than a coffeemaker and a hair dryer in the bathroom, in addition to the standard motel decor.

1111 Lakeside Ave. (at E. 9th St.), Cleveland, OH 44114. (C) 888/425-3835 or 216/241-5100. Fax 216/241-7437. www.holiday-inn.com. 379 units. $99–$159 double. Children 17 and under stay free in parent's room. AE, DC, DISC, MC, V. Self-parking $16. **Amenities:** Restaurant; indoor pool.

InterContinental Hotel & Conference Center Cleveland Ohio's only five-diamond hotel is located on the campus of the world-renowned Cleveland Clinic and close to downtown museums and shopping. The modern, completely smoke-free facility features luxurious, elegant decor in public spaces, including the lobby with fireplaces and a grand staircase. Accommodations are designed for business travelers and equipped with such extras as bathrobes, scales, and Web TV.

9801 Carnegie Ave., Cleveland, OH 44106. ✆ 216/707-4100 or 877/707-8999. Fax 216/707-4101. www. cleveland.intercontinental.com. 323 units. $139–$189 double. AE, DC, DISC, MC, V. Valet parking $22. **Amenities:** 3 restaurants; smoking not permitted.

Radisson Hotel Cleveland–Gateway
This terrific, moderately priced hotel is perfect for sports fans, as both Jacobs Field and Quicken Loans (Q) Arena are just a block away (you may even see the visiting team in the halls). The plush, pretty Shaker-style rooms feature all the extras, plus video games. Complimentary cookies are served in the lobby every evening.

651 Huron Rd. (across from Jacob's Field/Quicken Loans Arena), Cleveland, OH 44115. ✆ 800/333-3333 or 216/377-9000. Fax 216/377-9001. www.radisson.com. 142 units. $119–$179 double; from $175 suite. Extra person $15. Children 17 and under stay free in parent's room. AE, DC, DISC, MC, V. Valet parking $18. **Amenities:** Restaurant.

Renaissance Cleveland Hotel
Conveniently attached to Tower City Center, this property, a member of Historic Hotels of America, looks more formal than it actually is. Don't be intimidated. The opulent lobby, with its marble floors and posh, oversize floral arrangements, makes a dramatic backdrop for an evening cocktail or special-occasion photo op. The Americana-style rooms are smaller than most in town due to the building's age, though suites are spacious and comfortable. Service is especially friendly and welcoming. The restaurant here is the best in town (see below).

At Tower City Center, 24 Public Sq., Cleveland, OH 44113. ✆ 800/696-6898 or 216/696-5600. Fax 216/696-0432. www.renaissancehotels.com. 491 units. $169–$249 double; from $269 suite. Extra person $20. AE, DC, DISC, MC, V. Valet parking $18. **Amenities:** 2 restaurants; indoor pool; fitness center.

The Ritz-Carlton, Cleveland *Best*
Within Tower City Center, the city's only Mobil four-star and AAA four-diamond winner is Cleveland's finest hotel. It offers the traditional Ritz-Carlton elegance and style, with expansive windows overlooking the Cuyahoga River and Lake Erie waterfront. Perfect for a romantic getaway, the hotel offers exceptional service in beautiful surroundings. In-room extras include oversize desks, European toiletries, bathroom scales, and plush terry or lightweight robes in every room. The fitness center and pool are free to guests and open 24 hours a day. The restaurant (see below) is top-notch.

At Tower City Center, 1515 W. 3rd St., Cleveland, OH 44113. ✆ 800/241-3333 or 216/623-1300. Fax 216/623-1491. www.ritz-carlton.com. 208 units. $229–$429 double; $359–$459 suite. Children 17 and under stay free in parent's room. AE, DC, DISC, MC, V. Valet parking $22. **Amenities:** Restaurant; indoor rooftop pool; spa; fitness center.

Wyndham Cleveland Hotel at Playhouse Square
This modern hotel, just a stone's throw from Jacobs Field and Playhouse Square, caters to both the business and leisure crowds. For theatergoers, the location is great, and guests staying here are quick to commend the friendly service. The stylish public spaces lead to rooms that are large, comfortable, and outfitted with all the extras.

1260 Euclid Ave. (at Huron Rd.), Cleveland, OH 44115. ✆ 800/WYNDHAM or 216/615-7500. Fax 216/615-3355. www.wyndham.com. 205 units. $169–$209 double. Children 17 and under stay free in parent's room. Inquire about packages. AE, DC, DISC, MC, V. Valet parking $20; self-parking $12. **Amenities:** Restaurant; indoor pool.

WHERE TO DINE
Cleveland's **Hard Rock Cafe** is at the Avenue mall at Tower City Center, 230 W. Huron Rd. (✆ **216/830-7625;** www.hardrock.com).

Alice Coopers'town AMERICAN   Feed your inner Frankenstein at pioneering shock-rocker (and native son) Alice Cooper's restaurant and sports bar. With a prime location across the street from Jacobs Field, the old brick warehouse is always packed on game days. The extensive menu ranges from hefty burgers to barbecued spareribs, plus pizzas, pasta dishes, and salads. As with the Hard Rock Cafes, the place is filled with loud music, eye-popping memorabilia, plus souvenirs for purchase.

2217 E. 9th St. ⓒ **216/566-8100.** www.alicecooperstowncleveland.com. Reservations accepted. Main courses $6.50–$20. AE, DC, MC, V. Daily 10am–1am.

Blue Point Grille SEAFOOD   This Warehouse District spot is Cleveland's hottest see-and-be-scene; don't be surprised if you spot a local sports hero or two among the stylish patrons. The kitchen excels at both creative and straightforward preparations of flown-in-daily fish, which can range from a masala-spiced sea bass to a simple seared sushi-grade ahi. The oysters are top-grade, natch, and steaks are on hand for non–fish eaters.

700 W. St. Clair Ave. (at W. 6th St.). ⓒ **216/875-7827.** www.bluepointgrille.com. Reservations highly recommended. Main courses $19–$50. AE, DC, DISC, MC, V. Mon–Thurs 11:30am–3pm and 5–10:30pm; Fri 11:30am–3pm and 4–11:30pm; Sat 4–11:30pm; Sun 5–10pm.

Century at the Ritz-Carlton AMERICAN/SEAFOOD   Cleveland's most sophisticated restaurant, this perennial award-winner combines sleek ambience with gourmet food and unexpected surprises. Named for the Twentieth Century Limited rail line, the sepia room has black-and-white photographs showcasing the city's turn-of-the-20th-century splendor. With impeccable service, Century features classics from filet mignon and grilled seafood to mouthwatering sushi. Desserts include expected pastries and soufflés as well as young-at-heart s'mores and cotton candy. Although indeed ritzy, business casual dress is the norm.

1515 W. 3rd St. ⓒ **216/623-1302.** www.ritzcarlton.com. Reservations highly recommended. Main courses $18–$38. AE, DC, DISC, MC, V. Daily 7–11am and 11:30am–2:30pm; Sun–Thurs 5:30–10pm; Fri–Sat 5:30–11pm.

Frank Sterle's Slovenian Country House *Value* CENTRAL/EASTERN EUROPEAN   This authentic central European beer hall has a large, open dining room with hand-hewn beams, a hearty old-world menu (Wiener schnitzel is a specialty), and late-night, weekend polka bands. At lunch, try the pirogi.

1401 E. 55th St. (off I-90). ⓒ **216/881-4181.** www.sterlescountryhouse.com. Reservations recommended for 5 or more. Main courses $6–$8 lunch, $11–$18 dinner. AE, MC, V. Mon–Wed 11:30am–2:30pm; Thurs–Fri 11:30am–9pm; Sat 4:30–9pm (with music and bar open until midnight); Sun 11:30am–7pm.

Great Lakes Brewing Company ECLECTIC PUB FOOD   When Drew Carey quaffed a beer on his (now long-gone) Cleveland-based TV show, it was usually Burning River Pale Ale, a crisp, full-bodied amber that's just one of Great Lakes' excellent brews. The only American brewery ever to win the coveted "Microbrewery of the Year" award is just a comfortable Ohio City pub with a long mahogany bar, big booths, and pleasant garden seating. The simple pub grub is fine accompaniment for the brews; look for such locally accented fare as beer-battered cod and bratwurst as well as satisfying burgers.

2516 Market Ave. (1 block north of Lorain Ave. at W. 26th St.). ⓒ **216/771-4404.** www.greatlakesbrewing.com. Reservations recommended. Main courses $15–$24. AE, DC, MC, V. Mon–Thurs 11:30am–midnight (kitchen closes at 10:30pm); Fri–Sat 11:30am–1am (kitchen to 11:30pm).

Lolita *(Best* MEDITERRANEAN   Celebrated chef Michael Symon, who has been lauded in *Bon Appétit* for his winningly inventive urban comfort food, opened this restaurant in 2005, just minutes from downtown in the still-gentrifying Tremont district. It replaced his Lola Bistro, which at press time was set to open in July 2006 next to House of Blues downtown. Lolita specializes in Greek-inspired small plates, a festive martini menu (try the margarita martini) and such popular entrees as roasted skate wing with almonds, olives, oven-dried tomatoes and arugula, and macaroni and cheese made with chicken and goat cheese. Service is excellent.

900 Literary Rd. *©* 216/771-5652. Reservations highly recommended. Main courses $17–$24. AE, DC, DISC, MC, V. Mon–Tues 5–11pm; Fri–Sat 5pm–1am; Sun 4–9pm.

Maxi's *(Kids* PIZZA   Close to University Circle's museums is this unassuming Little Italy bar and restaurant, which serves up excellent pizzas made from scratch with the freshest ingredients, including whole-clove garlic and garden-fresh mushrooms. Other Italian dishes, along with burgers, steaks, and seafood, round out the menu. Service is as friendly as can be. Down the street is **Mama Santa,** 12305 Mayfield Rd. (*©* **216/ 231-9567**), another local favorite that bakes a top-notch pie.

12113 Mayfield Rd. *©* 216/421-1500. www.maxisinlittleitaly.com. Reservations recommended. Pizzas $14–$18; pastas $14–$19. AE, DISC, MC, V. Mon–Thurs 11am–11pm; Fri 11am–midnight; Sat 5pm–midnight; Sun 5–10pm.

Sans Souci FRENCH/MEDITERRANEAN   Regularly touted as Cleveland's finest Continental restaurant, this lovely French-country dining room in the Renaissance Cleveland hotel is ideal for a special occasion. Sunny Provençal decor and a stone hearth provide a cozy setting for enjoying such classics as *osso buco* and roasted veal chops as well as a selection of Mediterranean-style pastas for lighter tastes (and wallets). Save room to savor the luscious dessert cart choices, or opt for a simple plate of ripe cherries, dates, and grapes.

In the Renaissance Cleveland Hotel, 24 Public Sq. *©* 216/902-4095. www.sanssoucicleveland.com. Reservations recommended. Main courses $12–$18 lunch, $20–$30 dinner. AE, DC, DISC, MC, V. Mon–Fri 11:30am–2:30pm; daily 5:30–10pm.

Sergio's BRAZILIAN   This University Circle restaurant bursts with Mondrian-ish primary colors and festive South American flavors. Nothing is too adventurous, so even timid palates will be pleased with such choices as Brazilian-style beef tenderloin (marinated in garlic, black pepper, and port). At lunch, there's a tropical-style patio for warm-weather dining and live Brazilian jazz, on occasion. (The restaurant offers room service to the Glidden House inn, next door.)

1903 Ford Dr. (next to Glidden House). *©* 216/231-1234. www.sergioscleveland.com. Reservations recommended. Main courses $16–$27. AE, DISC, MC, V. Mon–Thurs 5–9:30pm; Fri–Sat 5–11pm.

XO Prime Steaks NEW AMERICAN   The chic new steakhouse (formerly XO Restaurant and Bar) in the Warehouse District is awash in candlelight, white fabrics, and pale pink accents. Lobster, veal and lamb chops, salads, and soups are on the menu, but this is primarily a steakhouse. A choice of six house-made sauces (such as horseradish cream truffle or Hollandaise blue cheese) awaits your T-bones, rib-eyes, sirloins, filets, and New York strips. Sides include potatoes—and such unexpected options as three-cheese truffle macaroni with peas and prosciutto.

500 W. St. Clair Ave. (at W. 6th St.). *©* 216/861-1919. www.xoprimesteaks.com. Reservations recommended. Main courses $20–$40. AE, MC, V. Mon–Thurs 11am–3pm and 5–11pm; Fri 11am–3pm and 4pm–midnight; Sat 4pm–midnight; Sun 4–9pm.

CLEVELAND AFTER DARK

Tickets for many events are sold through **Ticketmaster** (© **216/241-5555;** www. ticketmaster.com). **Tickets.com** (© **800/766-6048** or 216/241-6000; www.tickets. com) sells tickets to events at Playhouse Square Center. Another great option is the online-only **Ctix** outlet (**www.ctix.org),** where budget culture vultures may purchase half-price, day-of-show theater tickets, and discounted movie tickets.

THE PERFORMING ARTS Considered by many to be the finest symphony orchestra in the U.S., the world-renowned **Cleveland Orchestra** (© **800/686-1141** or 216/231-1111; www.clevelandorch.com), under the leadership of music director Franz Welser-Most, performs at **Severance Hall,** 11001 Euclid Ave., at East Boulevard, in University Circle. The stately 1931 concert hall was greeted by rave reviews when it emerged from a massive renovation in early 2000. In summer, the orchestra takes up residence at the open-air **Blossom Music Center.** Blossom Music Center is located in Cuyahoga Falls, 34 miles south of the city off I-77.

The nation's second-largest performing arts center (after New York City's Lincoln Center) is **Playhouse Square Center,** 1501 Euclid Ave. (© **216/771-4444;** www. playhousesquare.com), a prime symbol of Cleveland's cultural renaissance. Four beautifully restored theaters present theatrical and musical performances of all kinds, including touring productions of Broadway shows. It's also home to such resident companies as the **Ohio Ballet** (www.ohioballet.org) and **DanceCleveland** (www. dancecleveland.org), which presents such renowned modern companies as Alvin Ailey Trinity Irish Dance Company; and the **Cleveland Opera** (www.clevelandopera.org), among others.

THE BAR & CLUB SCENE To find out what's happening, pick up one of the free weeklies, the *Cleveland Free Times* and the *Cleveland Scene,* which are available all over town.

Downtown's newest club is **House of Blues,** 308 Euclid Ave. (© **216/523-2583;** www.hob.com), which books live blues acts and serves a soul-stirring Sunday gospel brunch. The east bank of **the Flats** along Old River Road, between St. Clair Avenue and Front Street, is a former industrial district that used to boast loads of bars. Today the ragged area is in transition, with plans to revitalize it with housing and offices.

On the livelier west bank of the Flats (at Main Ave. and the river) is the waterfront **Nautica Entertainment Complex (www.nauticaflats.com),** where century-old smokestacks top the four-story warehouse now known as the **Powerhouse,** which is on the National Register of Historic Places and houses an array of clubs and restaurants. Among the complex's other after-dark attractions are the waterfront **Shooters** (© **216/861-6900;** www.shootersflats.com), a hulking behemoth of a restaurant and dance club that caters to young adults on the prowl and other revelers; the **Improv Comedy Club** (© **216/696-4677;** www.improvupcoming.com), featuring up-and-coming stand-up talent; and romantic dinner cruises aboard the *Nautica Queen* (see "More Attractions," earlier in this chapter).

A somewhat more sophisticated crowd gathers in the **Warehouse District,** mainly along West 6th Street between Superior and Lakeside avenues. Highlights include **Spy Bar,** 1261 W. 6th St. (© **216/621-7907;** www.spycleveland.com), an upscale lounge with a well-dressed crowd and a stylish vibe; hometown boy Trent Reznor celebrated here after a Nine Inch Nails show a few years ago. Young hipsters meet to relax in comfy chairs and play board games at lively **Liquid and Fusion,** 1212 W. 6th St.

(© **216/479-7717**). **Velvet Dog,** 1280 W. 6th St. (© **216/664-**
cleveland.com), is a high-style dance club with an excellent martini
DJs with a clue. Other trendy options for energetic bar-hoppers ¡
Blind Pig, 1228 W. 6th St. (© **216/621-0001;** www.theblindpig.-
upscale dance club **Tramp,** 1360 W. 9th St. (© **216/776-7777;** www.liquidliving.-

Elsewhere around town, jazz lovers flock to **Club Isabella,** 2025 University Hospital Dr. (© **216/229-1177;** www.clubisabella.com). In Cleveland Heights, **Night-
town,** 12387 Cedar Rd. (© **216/795-0550**), is a bar offering burgers and pub grub,
along with live jazz and world music.

Ohio City is great for those looking for an easygoing night on the town. The cozy,
candlelit **Market Avenue Wine Bar,** 2526 Market Ave., at West 26th Street (© **216/
696-9463;** http://marketavewinebar.com), boasts an extensive wine list and a pleasing
light-bites menu including cheeses, smoked salmon, and stuffed grape leaves. Next
door is the celebrated **Great Lakes Brewing Company** (see "Where to Dine," above).

3 Cincinnati

Located along the winding banks of the Ohio River and tucked amid rolling hills that
are home to its many historic and eclectic neighborhoods, Cincinnati is a major midwestern hub of commerce, art, family attractions, and entertainment. When it became
an important rail and river hub, Henry Wadsworth Longfellow pronounced it the
"Queen City of the West." Settled primarily by Germans in the 19th century, Cincinnati today remains a clean, attractive, and dynamic urban center, where life proceeds
at an unhurried pace.

ESSENTIALS
GETTING THERE   By Plane   Major airlines fly into **Cincinnati/Northern Kentucky International Airport** (© **859/767-3144;** www.cvgairport.com), one of the
fastest-growing airports in the world, which also serves as a gateway to northern Kentucky (p. 306). Look for the 14 Art Deco murals from Union Station before you leave
the airport. **Executive Transportation** (© **859/261-8841;** www.executivetranscincy.
com) provides regular service to downtown hotels for $15 one-way, $25 round-trip.
Cab fare is about $22.

By Train   Amtrak (© **800/USA-RAIL;** www.amtrak.com) serves Union Station,
1300 Western Ave. There's daily service from Chicago (trip time: 9 hr.), Indianapolis
(3½ hr.), and Washington, D.C. (16 hr.).

By Car   The major routes into Cincinnati are **I-75** from the north (Dayton) and
south (Lexington); **I-71** from the northeast (Columbus) and southwest (Louisville);
and I-74 from the northwest (Indianapolis).

VISITOR INFORMATION   Contact the **Greater Cincinnati Convention & Visitor Bureau,** 300 W. 6th St., Cincinnati, OH 45202 (© **800/543-2613** or 513/621-
2142; www.cincyusa.com).

GETTING AROUND   The **Queen City Metro** provides inexpensive bus service
(© **513/621-4455;** www.sorta.com). Exact change or token is required. On weekdays
the fare is $1; at rush hour it's 80¢. On weekends, the fare is 50¢. Transfers cost 25¢.

An odd city ordinance does not allow cabs to cruise downtown for fares; they must
park at taxi stands and wait for passengers. Cabs can usually be found on the west end
of Fifth Street, where the convention center and many hotels are located. You can also

a cab. **Yellow Community Cab** (📞 859/727-2900) charges $2.60 plus $1.60 per
.ıle.

FAST FACTS A major local hospital is **University Hospital,** 234 Goodman St.,
Clifton (📞 513/584-1000; www.medcenter.uc.edu). There's a 24-hour **CVS** pharmacy at 2520 Vine St. (📞 513/569-4301; www.cvs.com). Sales tax is 6.5% and hotel
tax is a whopping 17%.

SPECIAL EVENTS & FESTIVALS Fans of choral music fill Music Hall for the
internationally renowned **May Festival** (📞 513/381-3300; www.mayfestival.com),
an annual event since 1875. Summer officially kicks off downtown Memorial Day
weekend with the **Taste of Cincinnati,** when dozens of area restaurants sell small but
tasty portions of their best dishes. Summer closes with Labor Day weekend's **River-
fest,** featuring fireworks, entertainment, and food throughout the city's waterfront
parks. In mid-September, Fountain Square becomes a German *biergarten* for **Okto-
berfest-Zinzinnati,** with German music, dancing, food, and lots of beer.

WHAT TO SEE & DO

Cincinnati is built on hills overlooking the Ohio River. Take time to walk around the
city's colorful and historic neighborhoods. The **Over-the-Rhine** district just north of
downtown has the largest collection of 19th-century civic, religious, and residential
architecture in the U.S. It's home to Music Hall and historic **Findlay Market,** a year-
round, open-air fresh foods market that was recently expanded and renovated. The
narrow, winding streets of **Mount Adams** reveal stunning views of downtown and the
Ohio River. For attractions across the Ohio, see "Northern Kentucky," on p. 306.

Cincinnati Art Museum *(Best)* Perched atop a hill in a lush 19th-century park,
Cincinnati's Art Museum houses a rich collection of sculpture, photography, African
and Native American art, and decorative objects. A dazzling cobalt chandelier by
superstar glass artist Dale Chihuly glimmers in the museum's grand entryway. Paintings from Botticelli and Titian to Mary Cassatt, John Singer Sargent, Picasso, and
Andy Warhol adorn the galleries.

953 Eden Park Dr. 📞 513/721-5204. www.cincinnatiartmuseum.org. Free admission (special exhibition fees may
apply). Tues–Sun 11am–5pm (Wed until 9pm). Closed Thanksgiving and Dec 25.

Cincinnati Museum Center *(Kids)* The Cincinnati Museum Center is housed in
Union Terminal, built in 1931 and recently restored to its original Art Deco grandeur.
Inside you'll find three museums and the **Robert D. Lindner Family OMNIMAX
Theater.** In the **Museum of Natural History and Science,** exhibits immerse you in
different Ohio Valley environments. The **Cincinnati Historical Society Museum** has
one of the largest regional collections in the U.S. At the **Cinergy Children's Museum,**
you'll find nine interactive exhibits, including Waterworks, Energy Zone, Little Sprouts
Farm, and Kids at Work.

1300 Western Ave. 📞 800/733-2077 or 513/287-7000. www.cincymuseum.org. Single-attraction ticket prices:
$7.25 adults, $6.25 seniors, $5.25 children 3–12. Multiple-discount ticket combinations are also available. Mon–Sat
10am–5pm; Sun 11am–6pm. Closed Thanksgiving and Dec 25. Parking $3.

Cincinnati Zoo & Botanical Garden More than 125 years old, this 75-acre zoo
is America's second oldest and one of its best. More than 1 million people visit the
museum each year to see more than 500 animal and 3,000 plant species. Favorites
include the exotic collection of felines (including some white lions), the renovated
Sumatran rhino exhibit, the creatures of the evening in the Nocturnal House, and

exhibits focusing on elephants, manatees, polar bears, and more. There's also a Children's Zoo and a superb botanical garden.

3400 Vine St. ⓒ 800/94-HIPPO or 513/281-4700. www.cincinnatizoo.org. Admission $13 adults, $11 seniors, $7.95 children 2–12, free for children under 2. Memorial Day to Labor Day daily 9am–6pm (gates), until 8pm (grounds); other times daily 9am–5pm (gates), to dusk (grounds). Parking $6.50.

Contemporary Arts Center *Kids*　At the cutting edge of modern art for decades, this museum was one of the first in America to exhibit Picasso's savage *Guernica* in the 1940s and the controversial nude photographs of Robert Mapplethorpe in 1990. A noncollecting museum, the center showcases special exhibitions at its digs in the $28-million Lois and Richard Rosenthal Contemporary Arts Center. Opened in 2003, it was the first U.S. art museum designed by a woman, London-based Zaha Hadid, who won the prestigious Pritzker Prize for this design. The sixth floor of the museum, called the UnMuseum, is devoted to hands-on, interactive art experiences for children, families, and art lovers of all ages. Admission is free on Monday after 5pm.

44 E. Sixth St. ⓒ 513/345-8400. www.contemporaryartscenter.org. Admission $7.50 adults, $6.50 seniors, $5.50 students, $4.50 children 3–13. Sun, Tues–Wed, and Fri 11am–6pm; Mon and Thurs 11am–9pm; Sat noon–6pm.

National Underground Railroad Freedom Center　Opened in the summer of 2004, this $110-million museum traces 500 years of oppression and focuses on humanity's quest for freedom. The history of American slavery focuses on Africans' arrival in the New World through Colonial times and the Civil War, and the bravery of abolitionists involved in the underground railroad. Interactive displays in three pavilions include educational activities, films, and an old wooden slave pen that was recovered from nearby Kentucky and carefully reconstructed on-site.

50 E. Freedom Way. ⓒ 877/648-4838 or 513/333-7500. www.freedomcenter.org. Admission $12 adults, $10 seniors, $8 children 6–12. Tues–Sat 10am–5pm; Sun 11am–5pm. Closed major holidays.

Taft Museum　Reopened in 2004 after a $23-million expansion and renovation, the Taft is a true gem. The 1820 Federal-style mansion (one of the finest of its kind in the country) is furnished with period antiques and filled with paintings by Rembrandt, Hals, Turner, and Gainsborough, and with Chinese and Limoges porcelain (the Limoges enamel collection is among the best on the planet). Located in the heart of downtown, the museum serves sandwiches, soups, and desserts in its Tea Room and has an underground parking garage (rates vary).

316 Pike St. ⓒ 513/241-0343. www.taftmuseum.org. Admission $7 adults, $5 seniors and students over 18, free for students 18 and under, free on Wed. Tues–Wed and Fri 11am–5pm; Thurs 11am–8pm; Sat 10am–5pm; Sun noon–5pm.

MORE ATTRACTIONS

Professional baseball has been a favorite spring and summer pastime in Cincinnati since 1869. Since 2003, the **Cincinnati Reds,** featuring future Hall of Famer (and native son) Ken Griffey, Jr., have played at the **Great American Ballpark,** a nostalgic new facility that anchors the eastern edge of Cincinnati's famed riverfront. Tickets range from $5 to $60. Call Ticketmaster at ⓒ 800/829-5353 or 513/421-REDS; or go online to www.cincinnatireds.com.

Football fans were appeased in 2000 with the opening of the $400-million **Paul Brown Stadium,** another waterfront gem that has become a showcase for the NFL's **Cincinnati Bengals** (ⓒ 513/621-8383; www.bengals.com). Single ticket rates were unavailable at press time, though preseason tickets are $50.

Paramount's Kings Island (© **800/288-0808** or 513/754-5600; www.pki.com) is a roller-coaster rider's dream. Located off exits 24 and 25 on I-71 north of Cincinnati in Mason, Ohio, Kings Island boasts more than a dozen coasters, including the Son of Beast, the world's tallest and fastest roller coaster. New in 2006 was Nickelodeon Universe, with family-friendly rides and attractions. King's Island also boasts Boomerang Bay, a 15-acre waterpark resort that features 80 rides and attractions. All-day admission is $50 ages 7 to 59, $30 ages 3 to 6 and 60 and over, and $26 all ages after 5pm. Parking is $10. Multiple day passes also are available. Kings Island is open daily from Memorial Day to late August at 10am; closing times vary. Also open some weekends in April, May, September, and October.

Riverboat excursions on the Ohio, especially popular at night, leave from Covington, Kentucky, just across the river from downtown Cincinnati (see "Northern Kentucky," on p. 306).

WHERE TO STAY

Ask about weekend packages that include Cincinnati Reds games or discount tickets to sights. For accommodations across the Ohio River, see "Northern Kentucky" on p. 306.

Cincinnatian Hotel   The grande dame of the city's hotels is the elegant Cincinnatian, a AAA four-diamond winner for the past 19 consecutive years. Built in 1882, and on the National Register of Historic Places, it offers award-winning, round-the-clock service. Rooms have oversize tubs, dual-head showers, and bathrobes; some have whirlpools and fireplaces. In addition to its excellent Palace restaurant, the Cricket Lounge offers lighter fare, including afternoon tea.

601 Vine St., Cincinnati, OH 45202. © **800/942-9000** or 513/381-3000. www.cincinnatianhotel.com. 146 units. $139–$350 double. Children 17 and under stay free in parent's room. AE, DC, DISC, MC, V. Valet parking $25. **Amenities:** 2 restaurants; fitness center.

Hilton Cincinnati Netherland Plaza   Travelers looking for a splendid property in the heart of downtown need look no further than the Hilton Cincinnati Netherland Plaza, which has drawn raves for its French Art Deco styling since it opened in 1931. Listed on the National Register of Historic Places, the hotel is connected via skywalk to Tower Place, a four-story complex with shopping and restaurants. The elegant guest rooms have comfy "serenity" beds and offer Wi-Fi access.

35 W. 5th St., Cincinnati, OH 45202. © **800/445-8667** or 513/421-9100. www.hilton.com. 561 units. $144–$230 double. Children 17 and under stay free in parent's room. AE, DC, DISC, MC, V. Valet parking $18. **Amenities:** 2 restaurants; health club.

Millennium Hotel Cincinnati   Business travelers favor the Millennium, located in the city's business district just west of Fountain Square and connected by skywalk to the convention center. Club Level rooms include complimentary continental breakfast and evening hors d'oeuvres in the Club Lounge, as well as bathrobes and upgraded room amenities. Ask about seasonal specials at the hotel's revolving rooftop restaurant, Ventana's.

150 W. 5th St., Cincinnati, OH 45202. © **800/876-2100** or 513/352-2100. www.millennium-hotels.com. 872 units. $69–$229 double. Children 17 and under stay free in parent's room. AE, DC, DISC, MC, V. Valet parking $20. **Amenities:** Restaurant; outdoor pool; fitness room.

Westin Cincinnati *(Best*   Business and leisure travelers like the upscale Westin, a high-rise overlooking the Ohio River. A chic yet unpretentious property that draws an eclectic mix of families and business travelers, the hotel is a good choice for sports and culture fans. The city's major performing arts center, as well as its baseball and football fields, are all within a few blocks' walking distance. The comfortable guest rooms (which recently underwent a $7.1-million upgrade) have all the amenities associated with a hotel of this class, including heavenly soft beds and sumptuous linens.

21 E. 5th St., Cincinnati, OH 45202. ℂ **800/937-8461** or 513/621-7700. www.westin.com/cincinnati. 456 units. $309–$349 double; $400–$800 suite. Children 17 and under stay free in parent's room. AE, MC, V. Valet parking $24; self-parking $15. **Amenities:** 2 restaurants; indoor pool; fitness center.

WHERE TO DINE

For cheap eats, **Skyline Chili** has dozens of franchises in the city. Be forewarned, this "chili" may look to novices more like spaghetti than soup. For dining with a view of the downtown skyline from across the Ohio River, see "Northern Kentucky" on p. 306.

Jean-Ro *Best* FRENCH   When noted local chef Jean-Robert de Cavel opened this Parisian bistro downtown across the street from the Westin Hotel in 2004, it became an instant sensation. Boisterous gourmands pack the narrow room with its sunny yellow walls and butcher-paper-covered tables to sip wine and sample such quintessential dishes as chicken coq au vin, niçoise salad, or steak with french fries. Desserts span the decadent chocolate pots de crème to the delicate vanilla madeleines.

413 Vine St. ℂ **513/621-1465.** www.bistrojeanro.com. Reservations recommended. Main courses $17–$25. AE, DC, DISC, MC, V. Mon–Fri 11:30am–2pm; Mon–Thurs 5:30–9:30pm; Fri–Sat 5:30–10pm; Sun 5:30–9pm.

Palm Court AMERICAN/CONTINENTAL   Art Deco elegance and a bustling, upscale bar make the Palm Court a good choice for fine American/Continental cuisine. House favorites include the Caesar salad with grilled chicken and hefty steaks, as well as fresh seafood entrees and a few pasta dishes. Try the chocolate pear sensation for dessert.

In the Hilton-Cincinnati Netherland Plaza, 35 W. 5th St. ℂ **513/564-6465.** Reservations recommended. Main courses $13–$32. AE, DC, DISC, MC, V. Daily 11am–2pm and 5–10pm; Sun brunch 11:30am–1:30pm.

Rookwood Pottery Bistro *Kids* BURGERS   Although this casual, family-friendly restaurant and bar offers grilled entrees such as salmon and steaks, locals go for the oversize sandwiches and hamburgers. Try the Black and Bleu, a substantial blackened beef patty that encases a hunk of melting bleu cheese. Kids (and grown-ups) will love the castlelike wood-and-brick interior of this former pottery factory. You can even dine in a kiln. There's plenty of free parking on-site.

1077 Celestial St., Mt. Adams. ℂ **513/721-5456.** Main courses $8–$30. AE, DC, DISC, MC, V. Mon–Sat 11am–10pm; Sun 11am–9pm.

CINCINNATI AFTER DARK

THE PERFORMING ARTS   Music Hall, 1241 Elm St. (ℂ **513/721-8222**), is home of the fine **Cincinnati Symphony Orchestra** (ℂ **513/381-3300;** www.cincinnati symphony.org) and the **Cincinnati Opera** (ℂ **513/241-2742;** www.cincinnatiopera. com). The **Cincinnati Ballet** (ℂ **513/621-5219;** www.cincinnatiballet.com) performs at the Aronoff Center, 6th and Walnut (ℂ **513/621-2787**). Modern and classic plays and musicals are presented at **Playhouse in the Park,** Eden Park (ℂ **513/345-2242;** www.cincyplay.com), which won the 2004 Tony Award as best regional theater in the U.S.

THE BAR SCENE   Arnold's Bar and Grill, 210 E. 8th St., downtown between Main and Sycamore (ℂ **513/421-6234;** www.arnoldsbarandgrill.com), is Cincinnati's oldest tavern, with live Celtic, bluegrass, jazz, and swing music.

In the **Over-the-Rhine** district, along Main Street beyond Central Parkway, you'll find many bars, cafes, and microbreweries that offer entertainment. Along narrow cobblestone streets with excellent city views, **Mount Adams** has many bars that also offer entertainment. **The Incline Bar** at the fine-dining restaurant Celestial, 1071 Celestial St., Mount Adams (© **513/241-4455;** www.thecelestial.com), is a favorite of locals for weekend jazz (Fri–Sat starting at 8:30pm).

4 Indianapolis

Indianapolis is one serious sports town. The Indianapolis 500, Brickyard 400, and Formula One races attract hundreds of thousands of visitors to the city for each event. The city also justifiably bills itself as the "Amateur Sports Capital of the World," and boasts world-class sports facilities. Indy natives rally behind the city's pro franchises— the NBA's Pacers, the WNBA's Fever, the NFL's Colts, and the Indianapolis Indians, a minor league baseball club whose beautiful, cozy downtown stadium has been voted one of the "best small ballparks in America."

In its passion for sports, however, the city does not neglect the arts. In addition to a few notable art museums, Indianapolis also has neighborhoods worth exploring: the Lockerbie Square district downtown with renovated Victorian homes on cobblestone streets; the shops, restaurants, and art galleries along Massachusetts Avenue downtown; and Broad Ripple Village, a canal-side neighborhood with boutiques, restaurants, and nightlife.

ESSENTIALS

GETTING THERE By Plane Flights arrive at **Indianapolis International Airport** (© **317/487-9594;** www.indianapolisairport.com). Most major domestic airlines can get you there, although US Airways and Southwest have the most frequent service. There is no public transportation into town; taxis average $21 to downtown, but can go as high as $45 elsewhere. Share-a-ride car service through **Carey Indiana** (© **800/888-INDY** or 317/241-6700; www.careyindiana.com) costs $11 to downtown and around $20 to the north side. All major national car-rental agencies are represented at the airport. (Phone numbers and websites for all the major U.S. airlines and car-rental agencies can be found in appendix D.)

By Train Amtrak (© **800/USA-RAIL;** www.amtrak.com) has a station at 350 S. Illinois St. (© **317/263-0550**), with trains arriving from Chicago (trip time: 5½ hr.), Cincinnati (3½ hr.), and Washington, D.C. (18½ hr.). *Note:* Amtrak service to Indianapolis is spotty and often includes some time on a bus.

By Car Major routes into Indianapolis are **I-65** from the northwest (Chicago) and south (Louisville), **I-69** from the northeast (Detroit), **I-70** from the west (St. Louis) and east (Columbus, OH), and **I-74** from the southeast (Cincinnati).

VISITOR INFORMATION The **Indianapolis Convention & Visitor Bureau** is at One RCA Dome, Suite 100, Indianapolis, IN 46225 (© **800/323-INDY** or 317/ 639-4282; www.indy.org), and is open Monday through Friday from 8:30am to 5pm; its website offers video podcasts of what to see and do in the city. The **Indiana Tourism Hotline** is © **800/556-INDY.** Find local events online at www.indydt.com and www.indyarts.org.

GETTING AROUND **IndyGo buses** (© **317/635-3344;** www.indygo.net) run on heavily traveled routes; fares are $1.25. The popular **Blue Line Circulator** buses are **free** and run a continuous path circling downtown daily from 10am to 10pm. But you can't rely on public transportation to get everywhere you want to go, so you'll really need a car. Based on a grid system, the city is easy to negotiate. Parking is relatively easy in downtown Indy, which has numerous parking garages and surface parking lots. The Circle Centre mall lots are usually a good parking bet downtown, and it's only $1.50 for up to 3 hours; you can park there all day (6–12 hr.) for $12 (rates can be higher during special events).

Cabs usually line up at downtown hotels, or you can call a radio-dispatched taxi. Try **Yellow Cab** (© 317/487-7777).

FAST FACTS If you need a **doctor,** call **Methodist Hospital,** at I-65 and 21st Street (© 317/916-3525), for a referral. **Riley Children's Hospital,** 702 Barnhill Dr. (© 317/274-5000), is one of the nation's top children's hospitals.

A growing number of Walgreens and CVS locations have **24-hour pharmacies.** If you're staying downtown, the CVS at 1744 N. Illinois St. (© 317/923-1491) is convenient; otherwise check the Yellow Pages.

Downtown Indianapolis nearly empties out after the retail shopping spots close; although Indianapolis is fairly safe, be careful walking alone to your car in large outdoor parking lots.

SPECIAL EVENTS Seats for both the **Indianapolis 500** (run the day before Memorial Day) and the **Brickyard 400** (the first Sat in Aug) sell out very early, though you may be able to get bleacher or infield tickets at the last minute. Call the Indianapolis Motor Speedway ticket office at © 317/484-6700 at least 10 to 12 months in advance.

The **Indy Jazz Fest** (www.indyjazzfest.net) runs for a long weekend each June, and the **Indiana Black Expo** (© 317/925-2702; www.indianablackexpo.com) spans a full 10 days in July featuring speakers, live music, and more.

WHAT TO SEE & DO

The center of downtown Indianapolis is **Monument Circle,** with the Soldiers' and Sailors' Monument at its core. The monument is crowned by a statue of Victory, known as *Miss Indiana.* An observation deck offers a panoramic view. Lights strung from the top of the monument during the holidays make it the "world's largest Christmas tree."

In addition to the listings below, you might want to check out the **Indiana State Museum,** 650 W. Washington St. (© 317/232-1637; www.indianamuseum.org), which documents the history of Indiana since the pioneer era. Admission is $7 adults, $6.50 seniors, and $4 for children (IMAX films are extra). It's open Monday through Saturday from 9am to 5pm and Sunday from 11am to 5pm.

At the **NCAA Hall of Champions,** 700 W. Washington St., in White River State Park (© 800/735-NCAA; www.ncaahallofchampions.org), sports fanatics can see past collegiate sports highlights displayed on video monitors, as well as listen to university school songs on a push-and-play display. A 1920s gymnasium keeps the kids busy when not in use for educational programs. Admission is $3 adults, $2 students (free for children 5 and under); it's open from 10am to 5pm Monday through Saturday, from noon to 5pm Sunday.

Eagle Creek Park, 7840 W. 56th St. (© 317/327-7110; www.indyparks.org), is one of the largest municipal parks in the country, with 4,000 acres of wooded terrain for hiking, biking, and cross-country skiing, and a 1,300-acre reservoir. The main attraction of the 128-acre **Garfield Park Conservatory,** 2450 Shelby St. (© 317/327-7184), is a tropical greenhouse—complete with parrots and macaws, and waterfall-fed pools—planted with flora from around the world. Admission to the conservatory is free (donations welcome), though entrance to the park is $4 per vehicle; open daily from 10am to 6pm.

Children's Museum of Indianapolis *(Best (Kids)* This is one of the largest children's museums in the world, with interactive exhibits covering everything from archaeology to world cultures to biotechnology, plus extensive toy and dollhouse displays, a working antique carousel ($1 per ride), and a planetarium. Recent additions include Dinosphere, a $25-million multisensory exhibit that combines serious science (the largest collections of juvenile fossils in the world) with kid-friendly interactive exhibits (dressing up in a dinosaur costume), and *Fireworks of Glass,* a 43-foot-tall blown-glass sculpture by Dale Chihuly. If you have kids, this is the place to take them.

3000 N. Meridian St. © 317/334-3322. www.childrensmuseum.org. Admission $12 adults, $11 seniors, $7 children ages 2–17, free for children under 2. Additional charge for Dinosphere. Mar to early Sept daily 10am–5pm; early Sept to Feb Tues–Sun 10am–5pm.

Conner Prairie Pioneer Settlement *(Kids)* Located 30 miles northeast of downtown, this restored 19th-century village faithfully reproduces pioneer life between 1820 and 1840 with the help of 36 carefully restored buildings, crafts demonstrations, and reenactments of events on the frontier. In summer, you can pack a picnic and listen to a concert under the stars as part of the Indianapolis Symphony Orchestra's "Symphony on the Prairie" series.

13400 Allisonville Rd., Fishers. © 800/966-1836 or 317/776-6000. www.connerprairie.org. Admission $11 adults, $10 seniors, $7 children ages 5–12, free for children under 5. May–Oct Tues–Sat 9:30am–5pm, Sun 11am–5pm; reduced hours off season.

Eiteljorg Museum of American Indian and Western Art This impressive building—recently expanded to the tune of $20 million and an additional 45,000 square feet—houses the country's most notable collection of Native American and Western art. The "Art of the American West" collection includes works by Frederic Remington and Georgia O'Keeffe. The Native American artifacts include clothing, beadwork, and pottery from all over North America, as well as a special section focusing on the three main tribes of Indiana.

500 W. Washington St., White River State Park. © 317/636-9378. www.eiteljorg.org. Admission $8 adults, $7 seniors, $5 students and children 5–17, free for children under 5. Tues–Sat 10am–5pm, Sun noon–5pm; June–Aug also open Mon 10am–5pm. Free parking in the White River State Park garage with validation.

Indianapolis Motor Speedway Built in 1909, this is one of the most celebrated auto raceways in the world. Each May, more than 400,000 spectators throng to the 2.5-mile oval course to watch the Indianapolis 500, the largest single-day sporting event in the world, boasting the largest purse in motor racing. The Speedway also hosts the United States Grand Prix in June and the NASCAR Brickyard 400 in August.

The **Indianapolis Motor Speedway Hall of Fame Museum** (open daily 9am–5pm; $3 adults, $1 children 6–15) is within the track's oval. The 433-acre speedway also features **Brickyard Crossing,** an acclaimed golf course with 4 of its 18 holes inside the track.

4790 W. 16th St. © 317/481-8500, or 800/822-4639 or 317/484-6700 to charge tickets to events. www.brickyard. com. Daily 9am–5pm.

Indianapolis Museum of Art *(Value)* This world-class museum has notable paintings by El Greco, Rubens, American Impressionists, and European neo-Impressionists.

Other strengths include African art, Japanese Edo-period paintings, American furniture, textiles, costumes, and a superb collection of Turner works on paper. The museum's contemporary art collection includes Robert Indiana's famed *LOVE*. In summer, the museum hosts the Summer Nights concert and film series. Bring a picnic, find a spot on the lawn, and enjoy open-air performances or classic films. The museum's recent multimillion-dollar expansion made room for a new contemporary art gallery and a Wolfgang Puck restaurant, among other changes—one of which is that the museum now charges admission. Also on the grounds is the **Oldfields-Lilly House,** a historic 22-room mansion open to the public (admission $5 adults, $4 seniors, free kids 12 and under).

4000 Michigan Rd. (at 38th St.). © 317/923-1331. www.ima-art.org. Admission $7 adults, $5 seniors, free for kids 12 and under. Tues–Sun 10am–5pm (until 9pm Thurs).

Indianapolis Zoo *Kids*   This $64-million, 64-acre facility celebrated its 42nd anniversary in 2006 and features 2,000 animals roaming through simulated environments. Get up close with an armadillo, try your hand at feeding a giraffe, or catch a show at the huge new Marsh Dolphin Theater. The zoo is in the 250-acre **White River State Park,** 801 W. Washington St. (© 317/634-4567; www.inwhiteriver.com).

The **White River Botanical Gardens** are also located on the zoo grounds. Admission to the gardens is $7 adults, $6 seniors and children in summer; reduced admission in winter. The gardens are open from 9am to 4pm (longer hours in summer).

1200 W. Washington St. © 317/630-2001. www.indyzoo.com. Admission zoo $13 adults, $7.50 seniors and children 2–12; botanical gardens $7 adults, $6 seniors and children 2–12; combo ticket $14 adults, $8.50 seniors and children 2–12. Memorial Day to Labor Day daily 9am–6pm; late June to mid-Aug weekdays 9am–4pm, weekends 9am–5pm; Dec daily noon–9pm.

Morris-Butler House   Housed in an 1862 Victorian mansion, this three-story museum focuses on Victorian decorative arts such as fine silver, tapestries, and Belter & Meeks furniture.

1204 N. Park Ave. © 317/636-5409. www.historiclandmarks.org/what/mbhouse.html. Admission $5 adults, $4 seniors, $3 children 6–16. Tours Wed–Sat every half-hour 10am–3:30pm. Closed mid-Dec to Jan and legal holidays.

SHOPPING

The cornerstone of Indy's downtown shopping scene is **Circle Centre,** 49 W. Maryland St. (© 317/681-8000; www.circlecentre.com), with anchor stores Nordstrom and Parisian, 100 specialty shops, restaurants, nightclubs, a cinema, and the Artsgarden, a performance space suspended over a busy intersection and covered by a glass dome.

The **Fashion Mall at Keystone,** 86th Street and Keystone Avenue (© 317/574-4000; www.fashionmallatkeystone.com), is the city's other leading mall, with anchor stores Saks Fifth Avenue and Parisian, a number of national chain stores, and numerous specialty and designer boutiques. Recent additions include Crate & Barrel and Tiffany & Co. The **Castleton Square Mall,** 82nd Street just east of Allisonville Road (© 317/849-9993; www.simon.com), is larger than Keystone and has more choices for shoppers on a budget (such as JCPenney and Sears). Other department stores include Macy's and Von Maur, plus plenty of national chain stores.

For something different, head to **Broad Ripple,** a charming neighborhood 15 minutes north of downtown. For unique clothing and fun furnishings, check out **Girly Chic Boutique** at 841 E. Westfield Blvd. (© 317/217-1525). **Turandot,** 912 E. Westfield Blvd. (© 317/255-5969), features funky jewelry and gifts. Local independent chain **LUNA Music,** 5202 N. College Ave. (© 317/283-5862), sells CDs, vinyl, and posters, and hosts in-store live performances. LUNA Music also has stores downtown (431 Massachusetts Ave.) and on the north side (1315 W. 86th St.).

WHERE TO STAY

The more expensive hotels are downtown, but many moderate and budget hotels are in the surrounding area. Most downtown hotels offer weekend or theme packages. Throughout the city, chains dominate. In addition to the choices below, we recommend **Embassy Suites** (© **800/EMBASSY;** www.embassysuites.com): either the downtown location, with a sky bridge connection to Circle Centre, 110 W. Washington St. (© **317/236-1800**); or the one on the northwest side, off Michigan Road near I-465, 3912 Vincennes Rd. (© **317/872-7700**). Both feature suites with coffeemakers, wet bars, refrigerators, and microwaves. For a moderately priced downtown hotel, try **Hampton Inn Indianapolis—Downtown,** 105 S. Meridian St. (© **800/426-7866** or 317/261-1200). Housed in a 1920s National Historic Landmark building, this hotel offers two-room suites and king rooms with whirlpool tubs in addition to the usual doubles.

For a bed-and-breakfast alternative that's near downtown but sports a local charm, check into **The Villa Inn,** 1456 N Delaware St. (© **866/626-8500** or 317/916-8500; www.thevillainn.com). The property offers six rooms starting from $200 a night, a full spa, and a charming restaurant.

Near the airport, **Days Inn,** 5860 Fortune Circle W. (© **800/DAYS-INN** or 317/248-0621), is your standard budget motel, with a restaurant, bar, small workout room, and outdoor pool. A special park-and-fly program is available. Another good airport choice is the **Holiday Inn,** 2501 S. High School Rd. (© **800/465-4329** or 317/244-6861), right on the airport grounds and 10 minutes from downtown. The noted Chanteclair restaurant is here (a bit overpriced), along with a health club and indoor pool; some units have small terraces or whirlpools.

Brickyard Crossing Golf Resort & Inn   This conventional motel with standard rooms is noteworthy because of its location—outside turn two on the Indianapolis Speedway. But its location is really the only reason to stay here—unless you plan to spend all your time at the track, you're better off elsewhere. Refrigerators are available in king rooms for no extra charge.

4400 W. 16th St., Indianapolis, IN 46222. © 317/241-2500. Fax 317/492-2715. 108 units. $70–$200 double. AE, DC, DISC, MC, V. Free outdoor parking. Pets $25. **Amenities:** Restaurant; outdoor heated pool; 18-hole golf course. *In room:* Fridge (in some).

The Canterbury *(Best)*   This charming European-style hotel, with direct access into Circle Centre, sports "a bit of England" and is a registered historic landmark. This is where most celebrities stay when they're in Indianapolis, and it's still the best in town. Rooms are large, with four-poster beds, armoires, bathroom telephones, and refrigerators. Tea is served daily.

123 S. Illinois St. (north end of Circle Centre), Indianapolis, IN 46225. © 800/538-8186 or 317/634-3000. Fax 317/685-2519. www.canterburyhotel.com. 99 units. $189–$219 double; $399–$1,599 suite (lower rates on weekends). Extra person $25. Children stay free in parent's room. AE, DC, DISC, MC, V. Valet parking $20. **Amenities:** Restaurant; health club.

The Conrad   Only the fourth American branch of the global luxury chain, The Conrad commands a prime corner across from Circle Centre (it offers private access to guests) and lends a much-needed touch of swank to the downtown scene. Decor is simultaneously grand (lobby chandeliers rival the sun in shape and size) and subdued.

Luxury is the keyword with attention to details such as fresh flowers in every space. Biz travelers are indulged with in-room Wi-Fi and multiroomed suites for added privacy.

50 W. Washington St., Indianapolis, IN 46204. ✆ 800/CONRADS or 317/713-5000. Fax 317/638-3687. www.conrad indianapolis.com. 243 units. $299–$429 double; $699 suite (lower rates on weekends). AE, DC, DISC, MC, V. Valet parking $25. **Amenities:** 3 restaurants; indoor pool; health club; spa.

Courtyard by Marriott Downtown   This downtown chain hotel is nicely situated on the edge of White River State Park and across the street from the Eiteljorg Museum. The unusually clean and well-maintained rooms are bright and cheerful, and some have terraces. There's also a 24-hour exercise room.

501 W. Washington St., Indianapolis, IN 46204. ✆ 800/321-2211 or 317/635-4443. Fax 317/687-0029. www.marriott. com. 235 units. $159–$299 double. Children under 18 stay free in parent's room. AE, DC, DISC, MC, V. Free outdoor parking. **Amenities:** Restaurant; outdoor pool; exercise equipment.

Omni Severin Hotel *Kids*   This classy, beautifully restored 1913 hotel is directly across from Union Station. All of the comfortable guest rooms offer a range of amenities, including bathrobes, wireless Internet access, and Nintendo game systems. The hotel features an Omni Kids children's program. Some rooms have balconies; the "Get Fit" rooms have portable treadmills. *Tip:* The hotel's website often features great weekend deals.

40 W. Jackson Place, Indianapolis, IN 46225. ✆ 800/THE-OMNI or 317/634-6664. www.omnihotels.com. Fax 317 /687-3612. 424 units. $219 double; $279–$800 suite. Extra person $20. Children under 18 stay free in parent's room. AE, DC, DISC, MC, V. Valet parking $19; self-parking $8. Pets under 25 lb. $25. **Amenities:** 2 restaurants; indoor pool; fitness center.

University Place Conference Center and Hotel *Kids*   Located on the campus of Indiana University/Purdue University Indianapolis (IUPUI), this hotel offers well-furnished and functional rooms with refrigerators, coffeemakers, and hair dryers. Guests can use campus facilities, including the terrific NIFS indoor pool, fitness center, track-and-field stadium, and children's day-care center, making this a great choice for active families.

850 W. Michigan St., Indianapolis, IN 46202. ✆ 800/627-2700 or 317/269-9000. Fax 317/231-5168. www.university place.iupui.edu. 278 units. $139–$154 double; $199–$399 suite. Extra person $15. Children under 18 stay free in parent's room. AE, DISC, MC, V. Indoor parking $8. **Amenities:** 2 restaurants; indoor pool; fitness center.

Westin Hotel Indianapolis   This luxury hotel, connected via sky bridge to Circle Centre and the Convention Center/RCA Dome, is within convenient walking distance of Union Station and the downtown attractions. Guest rooms feature the usual array of deluxe amenities, including bathrobes. There are special rooms for fitness buffs (with yoga and Pilates equipment and an exercise bike) and for corporate types (fax, office supplies, and so forth). Some rooms offer wonderful views of the state's Capitol; ask when booking.

50 S. Capitol Ave., Indianapolis, IN 46204. ✆ 800/228-3000 or 317/262-8100. Fax 317/231-3928. www.starwood. com. 573 units. $319–$339 double; $369–$399 suite. Extra person $30. Children under 18 stay free in parent's room. AE, DC, DISC, MC, V. Valet parking $26. **Amenities:** 2 restaurants; indoor pool; fitness center.

WHERE TO DINE

In addition to the places listed below, you'll find many new dining options in the Circle Centre Mall. Chains such as **Palomino Euro Bistro** and the **Alcatraz Brewing Co.** are consistent with most of what you'll find in the downtown area. The old **City Market,** 222 E. Market St. (✆ 317/634-9266), has been revitalized with many new restaurants and food stands opening. It's a good place to grab breakfast or lunch if you're downtown. An outdoor farmers' market is open Wednesday from 10am to 1:30pm.

If you're heading to Broad Ripple Village for shopping or nightlife, you can't go wrong at **Bazbeaux Pizza,** 832 E. Westfield Blvd. (© **317/255-5711**), and 334 Mass. Ave., downtown (© **317/636-7662**), for gourmet pizza; **Mama Carolla's,** 1031 E. 54th St. (© **317/259-9412**), for neighborhood Italian in a renovated house; or **Yat's,** 5363 N. College Ave. (© **317/253-8817**), and 659 Mass. Ave., downtown (© **317/686 -6380**), for a heaping plate of cheap ($5–$6) Cajun food.

Café Patachou *(Kids)* NEW AMERICAN/FRENCH   After 19 years, this lunch and breakfast cafe maintains its popularity, mainly due to Bruce Steckler's consistent menu and owner Martha Hoover's keen sense of keeping the clients happy. Expect to pay New York prices ($2.75 for a cup of coffee that's frankly weak at best—for decent java, run across the street to local fave **Hubbard and Cravens**), but the food is truly worth it—as the Sunday brunch wait times bear out. The omelets are some of the best in town, and the turkey sandwich tastes like your mom cooked a bird and made you a sandwich immediately afterward—you can't beat that kind of freshness. There are three other locations throughout Indy: 8691 River Crossing Blvd.; 4733 E. 126th St.; and 225 W. Washington St.

4911 N. Pennsylvania. © **317/925-2823.** Omelets and sandwiches from $8.95. AE, MC, V. Mon–Fri 7am–3pm; Sat–Sun 8am–2pm.

Elements REGIONAL AMERICAN   Dropping in for dinner here is always a surprise because the menu changes daily. Chef Greg Hardesty keeps it fresh both figuratively and literally by structuring the offerings around whatever is currently in season and available—if it inspires him, you get to eat it. In summer, enjoy organically grown heirloom tomato salads, perhaps, with Hoosier melons and a dash of pine nuts and cheese. Ask the capable staff for a suggested pairing from the manageable and well selected wine list. Desserts are worthy of a visit unto themselves.

415 N. Alabama. © **317/634-8888.** www.elementsindy.com. Reservations recommended. Main courses $25–$30. AE, DC, MC, V. Tues–Thurs 5–9:30pm; Fri–Sat 5–10:30pm.

R bistro CONTEMPORARY AMERICAN   This casual but chic restaurant snuck onto the dining scene quietly, but has gained a local following. The airy atmosphere and fresh cuisine make it popular with the young and fashionable crowd. The chef generally sticks to fresh local produce, so the dinner menu changes weekly and lunchtime menu changes seasonally. Dishes can range from strip steaks to sesame-crusted salmon to peach cobbler.

888 Massachusetts Ave. © **317/423-0312.** www.rbistro.com. Reservations suggested. Main courses $13–$27. AE, DC, DISC, MC, V. Mon–Fri 11am–2:30pm; Wed–Sat 5–10pm.

Shalimar INDIAN   If you're looking to add a bit of spice to your Indianapolis dining experience, be sure to visit Shalimar, a local favorite. Whether you drop in for the popular lunch buffet or to unwind with one of the many dinner entrees after a day of window-shopping and people-watching in Broad Ripple, you're bound to find something that pleases your taste buds (and if you can't make up your mind, try one of the excellent prix-fixe dinners). Coupons are frequently found in *NUVO,* a local free paper, so be sure to pick up a copy before you go.

1043 Broad Ripple Ave. © **317/465-1100.** www.shalimarindianapolis.com. Lunch buffet $7; main courses $7.95–$13; fixed-price dinner $14–$15 (vegetarian or nonvegetarian). AE, DC, DISC, MC, V. Lunch buffet daily 11am–2:30pm; dinner Mon–Thurs 5–10pm, Fri 5–10:30pm, Sat 2:30–10pm, Sun 2:30–5:30pm.

St. Elmo Steak House *Best* AMERICAN/STEAK Popular with celebrities and politicians, this atmospheric National Historic Landmark is the city's premier steakhouse, and has been for the last 103 years. The restaurant's original tiger-oak back-bar is still in operation, and the decor is straight out of 1940s Chicago, with mahogany paneling and a tin ceiling; the ultraprofessional waiters even wear tuxedos. Start with the shrimp cocktail and then wash down your juicy prime rib or filet mignon with a selection from the award-winning 20,000-bottle wine cellar. *Note:* The congenial atmosphere is too boisterous for a romantic meal, so if you want a quiet evening out, this isn't the right pick.

127 S. Illinois St. (at the south edge of Circle Centre). ℂ 317/635-0636. www.stelmos.com. Reservations recommended. Main courses $25–$42. AE, DC, DISC, MC, V. Mon–Sat 4–10:30pm; Sun 4–9pm.

Taste Café & Marketplace NEW AMERICAN/DELI After heading the kitchen at L.A.'s Standard Hotel, chef Marc Urwand and partners set up shop here between downtown and Broad Ripple. Nearly everything on the premises is made fresh each day, and the fluffy overstuffed omelets, seasonal soups, and dense flaky cheddar biscuits stand out. If you can't dine in, check out the counter, where you can order breads, cheeses, pastries, jams, and more—all perfect for a picnic.

5164 N. College Ave. ℂ 317/925-2233. www.tastecafeandmarketplace.com. Omelets from $6.50; lunch entrees from $5.50. AE, DC, DISC, MC, V. Tues–Fri 7am–3pm; Sat–Sun 8am–3pm.

INDIANAPOLIS AFTER DARK
THE PERFORMING ARTS The **Indianapolis Symphony Orchestra** (ℂ 800/366-8457 or 317/639-4300; www.indyorch.org) has its home in the Hilbert Circle Theater, a vintage 1916 film palace on Monument Circle. **Clowes Memorial Hall,** 4600 Sunset Ave. (ℂ 800/732-0804, 317/940-6444, or 317/940-9696; www.clowes hall.org), a performing arts center on the campus of Butler University, is home to the **Indianapolis Opera, Butler Ballet,** and **Indianapolis Chamber Orchestra.** The professional **Indiana Repertory Theatre,** 140 W. Washington St. (ℂ 317/635-5277; www.indianarep.com), offers a September-to-May season.

The **Madame Walker Theatre Center,** 617 Indiana Ave. (ℂ 317/236-2099 for information and tickets; www.walkertheatre.com), is an ornate 1927 Art Deco theater offering jazz, gospel, drama, and dance performances. Every other Friday from 6 to 10pm, "Jazz on the Avenue" showcases local, regional, and national talent.

THE CLUB & BAR SCENE Indianapolis's nightlife is primarily located in the downtown area and in Broad Ripple Village, an artsy enclave of boutiques, bistros, and bungalows 15 minutes north of downtown.

For live jazz every night except Sunday, downtowners head to the cozy **Chatterbox Tavern,** 435 Massachusetts Ave. (ℂ 317/636-0584), where big-name acts playing in town sometimes stop by (Mick Jagger once dropped in after a Stones concert). Another downtown top spot for live music is the **Slippery Noodle Inn,** 372 S. Meridian St. (ℂ 317/631-6974), Indiana's oldest standing bar (established 1850; rumor has it that Hoosier hoodlum John Dillinger used the club's back wall for target practice) and *the* place in the city for blues. You can also check out the local scene at the friendly **Old Point Tavern,** 401 Massachusetts Ave. (ℂ 317/634-8943); in warm weather, the action spills onto an outside patio.

For dancing (or cruising), gay travelers shoot for **Greg's Indianapolis,** 231 E. 16th St. (ℂ 317/638-8138); or **Talbott Street,** 2145 N. Talbott St. (ℂ 317/931-1343)—the drag shows at Talbott Street are a must. Lesbians can hop over to mostly female dance club **The Ten,** 1218 N. Pennsylvania (📞 **317/638-5802**).

If you're not sure what you're in the mood for, check out **Jillian's,** 141 S. Meridian St. (📞 **317/822-9300**), a multistory complex that includes two restaurants, a game room, billiards, a dance club, and "multimedia" bowling (neon lanes, glow-in-the dark balls, and video walls).

Broad Ripple Village, an easy drive north of downtown straight up Meridian Street, is where the local yuppies, college students, *and* high school cool kids go for weekend fun. At **The Vogue,** 6259 N. College Ave. (📞 **317/259-7029;** www.thevogue.ws), local bands and big names (the Red Hot Chili Peppers, for one) perform in a renovated movie theater; when nobody's playing, it's a hot dance club. Other good bets are the casual **Broad Ripple Brew Pub,** 840 E. 65th St. (📞 **317/253-2739**); and the cigar/martini bar on the second floor of the **Broad Ripple Steak House,** 929 E. Westfield Blvd. (📞 **317/253-8101**). For a DJ and dancing with a younger crowd, head to **Rock Lobster,** 820 Broad Ripple Ave. (📞 **317/253-5844**). Mature audiences head to the **Jazz Kitchen,** 5377 N. College Ave. (📞 **317/253-4900;** www.thejazzkitchen.com), for live jazz Friday and Saturday.

On the north side, chic crowds gather for cocktails at the bar at **Lulu's** restaurant, 8487 Union Chapel Rd., near Keystone at the Crossing (📞 **317/251-5858**); and at the trendy **Vapour Lounge,** 5252 E. 82nd St. (📞 **317/579-9570**), complete with a 50-foot ice bar, pretentious "bottle-service only" area, and totally unnecessary, but free, valet parking. The new art house **Keystone Art Cinema and Indie Lounge** at The Fashion Mall (see "Shopping," above; 📞 **317/577-3009**) attracts north-siders with a full-service bar (live music on weekends) where you can stop before or after taking in the latest indie flick. Short on time? Pick up a cocktail to go and enjoy it during the show.

5 Detroit & Highlights of Michigan

DETROIT

Detroit rolled out the red carpet when Super Bowl XL came to town in January 2006, and the city's renaissance continues. Dozens of new restaurants and clubs dot the downtown landscape; abandoned buildings have been replaced with high-rise luxury condos; Campus Martius Park, in the heart of Detroit, draws crowds with open-air music stages in the summer and an outdoor ice rink in winter; and the city's riverfront has been beautified with a wooded Riverwalk. To be sure, Detroit's old favorites—the Henry Ford and Greenfield Village, the Motown Historical Museum and the Detroit Institute of Arts—are still worth visiting. But these days, visitors to the Motor City can't help but be impressed by all that's new.

ESSENTIALS

GETTING THERE   By Plane   The **Detroit Metropolitan Airport** (www.metro airport.com), 35 miles southwest of downtown, is a hub for **Northwest Airlines** (📞 **800/ 225-2525**). Cab service to downtown costs $39.

By Train   Amtrak (📞 **800/USA-RAIL;** www.amtrak.com) provides daily service from Chicago (trip time: 5½ hr.) and Ann Arbor (1 hr.) to its station at 11 W. Baltimore St. at Woodward Ave. Trains also stop at Amtrak stations in Dearborn, 16121 Michigan Ave.; Greenfield Village, 20900 Oakwood Blvd. Royal Oak, 201 S. Sherman Dr.; Birmingham, 449 S. Eton St.; and Pontiac, 1600 Wide Track Circle.

By Car   Major routes into Detroit are **I-75** from the south (Toledo) and north (Flint), **I-94** from the west (Chicago), and **Route 401** from the east (Toronto).

VISITOR INFORMATION   Contact the **Detroit Metro Convention & Visitors Bureau,** 211 W. Fort St., Suite 1000, Detroit, MI 48226 (© **800/DETROIT;** www. visitdetroit.com).

GETTING AROUND   They don't call Detroit the Motor City for nothing. There's little in the way of public transportation. The notable exception to that rule is the elevated **People Mover** train that loops around downtown, a convenient means of visiting the downtown tourist sites and Cobo Hall Convention Center for only 50¢ per ride. But unless you remain downtown, you'll need a car.

FAST FACTS   To find a physician, contact the **Detroit Medical Center** (© **888/ DMC-2500;** www.dmc.org). Medical assistance is available at **Detroit Receiving Hospital,** 4201 St. Antoine Blvd. (© **313/745-3000**). Sales tax in Michigan is 6%; hotel taxes in Detroit range between 13% and 15%, depending on the county.

SPECIAL EVENTS & FESTIVALS   The Motor City displays her best and newest at the annual **North American International Auto Show** (www.naias.com) in mid-January. In mid-August, '50s- and '60s-era muscle cars and street rods rule at the annual **Woodward Dream Cruise** (www.woodwarddreamcruise.com), a 16-mile parade of 40,000 vehicles along Woodward Avenue, the largest single-day car event in the world. The weeklong Windsor-Detroit **International Freedom Festival** celebrates Canada Day (July 1) and American Independence Day, ending with fireworks over the Ambassador Bridge.

WHAT TO SEE & DO

Detroit's rich cultural history comes alive in the **Cultural Center,** an area flanking Woodward Avenue 3 blocks south of I-94. Here you'll find a celebration of history, culture, and music at the Detroit Institute of Arts, the Detroit Historical Museum, the Charles H. Wright Museum of African American History, and the Detroit Science Center. The Detroit Public Library and Wayne State University also call the area home.

  Further explore Detroit's cultural offerings at one of the city's many fine galleries or on a downtown walking tour of public art. **Plum Tree Pottery,** 30435 W. 10-mile Rd. (© **248/476-4875;** www.plumtreepottery.com) in Farmington Hills sells the creations of master ceramist John Glick. Downtown, the **Sherry Washington Gallery**, 1274 Library St. (© **313/961-4500;** www.sherrywashingtongallery.com), and **G. R. N'Namdi Gallery,** 66 E. Forest St. (© **313/831-8700;** www.grnnamdigallery.com), feature works by some of the nation's preeminent African-American artists. Public art is easy to find on the **People Mover.** Each station along this landmark Detroit monorail features original paintings, mosaics, tilework, and sculptures. Other famous public artworks include **"Spirit of Detroit," "Monument to Joe Louis"** (often called "The Fist"), and the **"Pylon"** tower—all near the intersection of Woodward and Jefferson avenues.

Arab American National Museum   In 2005, America's first and only Arab-American museum opened its doors in the Detroit suburb of Dearborn. Permanent exhibits highlight Arab civilizations' contributions to mathematics, science, medicine, architecture, and the decorative arts; the history and diversity of Arab immigrants in the U.S.; and the impact that Arab Americans have had on American society and culture. Allow 1 to 2 hours.

13624 Michigan Ave., Dearborn. © **313/582-2266**. www.theaanm.org. Admission $6 adults, $3 seniors and students, free for children 5 and under. Free for all visitors on Sun. Wed and Fri–Sat 10am–6pm; Thurs 10am–8pm; Sun noon–5pm.

Detroit Historical Museum   Begin your exploration of Detroit with this repository of the city's history. You can walk a re-created cobblestone and brick street lined with 19th-century shops, and check out the two-story assembly line in the Motor City exhibit. Interactive displays entertain children of all ages. Allow 1 to 2 hours.

5401 Woodward Ave. © **313/833-1805**. www.detroithistorical.org. Admission $6 adults, $4 seniors and students 5–17, free for children under 5. Wed–Fri 9:30am–3pm; Sat 10am–5pm; Sun noon–5pm.

Detroit Institute of Arts   The DIA is undergoing a massive expansion that will leave portions of its collection off-limits until late 2007. Brave the sawdust anyway to see some of the world's great masters, including Rembrandt, Rubens, Caravaggio, van Gogh, Cézanne, Whistler, and Rothko. There are also impressive ancient Egyptian, African, Asian, and Native American collections, and Diego Rivera's *Detroit Industry* murals are must-sees. Friday nights at the DIA feature free music, tours, artists' demonstrations, and drop-in workshops for all ages. Allow 2 to 3 hours.

5200 Woodward Ave. © **313/833-7900**. www.dia.org. Suggested donation $6 adults, $3 children. Wed–Thurs 10am–4pm; Fri 10am–9pm; Sat–Sun 10am–5pm.

Detroit Zoo *Kids*   The Detroit Zoo is one of the finest in the nation, with all of the expected animals—elephants, giraffes, bears, lions, and more. The **Arctic Ring of Life** features the world's largest polar bear display. Visitors watch frolicking bears and seals from outside or through a 70-foot-long underwater Polar Passage. Other highlights include a butterfly and hummingbird garden, a free-flight aviary, and a great apes exhibit. Allow 3 hours.

8450 W. 10-mile Rd., Royal Oak. © **248/398-0900**. www.detroitzoo.org. Admission $11 adults, $9 seniors, $7 children 2–12, free for children under 2. Daily 10am–5pm.

Henry Ford Museum & Greenfield Village *Best*   The **Henry Ford Museum,** a 12-acre repository of Americana, holds something of interest for everyone. "Heroes of the Sky" features dozens of historic airplanes: Byrd's Arctic Fokker, a Sikorsky helicopter, and early commercial and barnstorming planes. But the museum's highlight is, not surprisingly, "The Automobile in American Life," exploring our nation's infatuation with cars. Look for the Rosa Parks Bus as well as Ford's 1901 Model-T, the Oscar Meyer Wienermobile, and a host of presidential cars, including the limousine in which Kennedy was shot. Facilities also include an IMAX theater. Allow 3 hours.

Greenfield Village encapsulates Ford's infatuation with history and the world's innovators. A hundred genuine 17th-, 18th-, and 19th-century homes were transported from throughout the U.S. and Europe to bring history to Detroit. The Wright brothers' bicycle shop, Edison's laboratory, and a collection of slave quarters are highlights. *Note:* The village is closed January through mid-April. Allow 2 hours.

The Henry Ford's newest addition is the **Ford Rouge Factory Tour.** Visitors view the production of Ford's most popular truck, the F-150, through the magic of virtual reality and an assembly plant walking tour. Tours begin in front of the Henry Ford Museum; reservations are strongly recommended. Allow 2 hours.

20900 Oakwood Blvd., Dearborn. © **313/271-1620**. www.hfmgv.org. Museum $14 adults, $13 seniors, $10 children 5–12, free for children under 5. Village $20 adults, $19 seniors, $14 children 5–12, free for children under 5. Factory tour $14 adults, $13 seniors, $10 children 3–12, free for children under 3. IMAX $10 adults, $9 seniors, $8.50

children under 13. 1-day combination: $26 adults, $24 seniors, $20 children 5–12; 2-day combination $48 adults, $46 seniors, $38 children 5–12, free for children under 5. Daily 9:30am–5pm; Village Fri–Sun only Nov–Dec, closed Jan to mid-Apr.; factory tours Mon–Sat 9:30am–5pm Sept to mid-Apr, daily 9:30am–5pm mid-Apr to Aug.

Motown Historical Museum   The Motown sound was born in two simple houses under the sign HITSVILLE U.S.A., and American music has never been the same. See the original control room and studio (with linoleum worn through by tapping feet) where the Supremes, the Temptations, Stevie Wonder, the Jackson 5, and many others made gold records from 1959 to 1972. Also on display are costumes worn by the famous performers; and Berry Gordy's apartment, left just the way it was in the 1960s when artists packed their records for shipment throughout the country. Allow 1 hour.

2648 W. Grand Blvd. © 313/875-2264. www.motownmuseum.com. Admission $8 adults, $5 children under 13. Tues–Sat 10am–6pm.

WHERE TO STAY

Best Western Sterling Inn *Kids*   The Sterling Inn offers great value for families— clean, comfortable rooms; a kid-friendly staff; and the hotel's chief draw: an indoor waterpark including a 5,000-square-foot pool, a three-story water slide, a lazy river, two large whirlpools, lots of squirting contraptions, and several lifeguards. More adult activities include an indoor running track and a very good fitness center.

34911 Van Dyke Ave., Sterling Heights, MI 48312. © 800/953-1400 or 586/979-1400. Fax 586/979-0430. www.best western.com. 240 units. $100–$250 double. Children under 18 stay free in parent's room. AE, DC, DISC, MC, V. **Amenities:** Restaurant; pool (indoor); fitness center.

The Dearborn Inn   The Dearborn Inn opened its doors in 1931 as the world's first airport hotel, located right across the street from Ford Airport. The airport has long since closed, but this historic inn remains popular, known for its Georgian elegance, first-class service, and business amenities. The 23 acres of meticulously landscaped grounds and gardens make this hotel feel worlds away from the big city. The Henry Ford Museum complex is within walking distance.

20301 Oakwood Blvd., Dearborn, MI 48124. © 800/228-9290 or 313/271-2700. Fax 313/271-7464. www.marriott hotels.com. 222 units. $129–$269 double. AE, DC, DISC, MC, V. Valet parking $10; free self-parking. **Amenities:** 3 restaurants; pool; fitness center.

Detroit Marriott at the Renaissance Center   Since the 1970s the Renaissance Center has served as General Motors' corporate headquarters, and the building recalls its automotive history in a ground-floor classic car museum. The Marriott on-site is popular with business travelers, but leisure guests love the hotel's downtown location, its People Mover station, and its proximity to the Joe Louis, Comerica Park, and Ford Field sports stadiums. The hotel's Wintergarden—a glass atrium meeting and retail center—is just the spot for casual dining, shopping, and riverfront views. Book an upper floor room for great views of the Detroit River and Windsor.

Renaissance Center (Jefferson Ave., between Brush St. and Beaubien), Detroit, MI 48243. © 800/228-9290 or 313/568-8000. Fax 313/568-8146. www.marriott.com. 1,298 units. $139–$259 double. AE, DC, DISC, MC, V. Valet parking $20; self-parking $15. Adjacent to "Renaissance Center" People Mover station. **Amenities:** 3 restaurants; health club.

The Inn on Ferry Street   The Inn on Ferry Street is actually a collection of four large 19th-century homes and their carriage houses. Once slated for demolition, the buildings were rescued and converted into a charming B&B complex, each with its own parlor with fireplace. The individually decorated rooms have the usual array of modern amenities and up-to-date private bathrooms. The inn is located in the heart of the Cultural Center, within easy walking distance of museums. Complimentary shuttle service is provided within a 5-mile radius.

84 E. Ferry St. (at Woodward Ave.), Detroit, MI 48202. © 313/871-6000. Fax 313/871-1473. http://innonferrystreet. com. 40 units. $124–$159 double; $169–$199 suite. Rates include deluxe continental breakfast. AE, DC, DISC, MC, V. Free parking.

The Townsend Hotel *(Best)* The gorgeous Townsend is one of Michigan's finest hotels, although it's about a 30-minute drive from downtown Detroit in Birmingham. You'll feel like a celebrity, and you just might see one—Hollywood's elite stay at the Townsend when they're in town. Rooms feature English-style decor and have Egyptian cotton linens, down comforters and pillows, deep marble tubs and terry robes. Suites sport full kitchens. The Rugby Grille serves award-winning Continental cuisine, and you can work off your meal in the hotel's state-of-the-art fitness center.

100 Townsend St., Birmingham, MI 48009. © 800/548-4172 or 248/642-7900. Fax 248/645-9061. www.townsend hotel.com. 150 units. $249–$365 double; $270–$2,000 suite. Children 18 and under stay free in parent's room. AE, DC, DISC, MC, V. Valet parking $24; self-parking $8. **Amenities:** 2 restaurants; fitness center. *In room:* Kitchen (suites only).

WHERE TO DINE

Cyprus Taverna GREEK Widely considered Greektown's best Greek restaurant, Cyprus Taverna serves up all the requisite Greek dishes—moussaka, *dolmathes* (stuffed grape leaves), and gyros—as well as a number of Cypriot specialties, vegetarian meals, and a selection of Greek beers and wines. Portions are hearty. Aegean fossils and Cypriot folk art decorate the walls.

579 Monroe St. © 313/961-1550. Reservations accepted. Main courses $8–$20. AE, DC, DISC, MC, V. Mon–Thurs 11am–2:30pm; Fri–Sat 11am–4am; Sun 11am–2:30am.

Detroit's Breakfast House & Grill SOUTHERN An orange, green, and white decor and east-facing windows give Detroit's Breakfast House the feeling of morning sunshine even on dismal winter days. This restaurant is the hip place to see and be seen, and its food won't disappoint either. Breakfast is the most popular meal, featuring bananas foster French toast, bacon pancakes, smoked salmon Benedict and New Orleans frittatas. Lunchtime specials include a fried chicken and waffle club sandwich, barbecued tuna salad, and catfish filets. Expect a wait, especially on weekends.

1241 Woodward Ave. © 313/961-1115. www.detroitbreakfasthouse.com. Main courses $8–$14. AE, DISC, MC, V. Mon–Fri 7am–3pm; Sat 7am–8pm; Sun 8am–5pm.

Seldom Blues AMERICAN Steaks and seafood dominate the menu at this hip fine dining and jazz restaurant located in Detroit's landmark Renaissance Center. Try the Blue-B-Q Bass on fresh thyme Vidalia onion hash; the Lobster Pontchartrain, two lobster tails dusted, baked, and finished with shrimp, lump crabmeat, and mushrooms; or the melt-in-your-mouth Steak Porcher (named for ex-Detroit Lion star turned restaurateur Robert Porcher). Live music is a mainstay at this restaurant. Expect blues, jazz, maybe a little big band from local and national acts every night of the week.

400 Renaissance Center. © 313/567-7301. www.seldomblues.com. Reservations accepted. Main courses $15–$39. AE, DISC, MC, V. Mon–Thurs 11:30am–10pm; Fri 11:30am–midnight; Sat 5pm–midnight; Sun 11:30am–4pm.

Small Plates TAPAS/PIZZA Always buzzing with conversation, Small Plates offers exactly what you'd expect—moderately priced, tapas-style entrees designed for sharing. But the restaurant also offers outstanding wood-fired pizzas and sandwiches for those who just aren't in a sharing mood. Favorite small-plate offerings include Spanish empanadas filled with chêvre and peppers; Pan-Asian lettuce wraps with a spicy chicken and vegetable stir-fry filling; and grilled chicken teriyaki skewers with Asian noodles.

1521 Broadway. ✆ 313/963-0497. www.smallplates.com. Small plates $4–$12; entrees $8–$13. AE, DC, DISC, MC, V. Mon–Thurs 11am–10pm; Fri 11am–1am; Sat noon–1am; Sun noon–8pm.

Tribute Restaurant *Best* FRENCH/ASIAN   Named one of the nation's best restaurants by the *New York Times, Gourmet,* and *Zagat* among others, Tribute serves up exceptional French cuisine enhanced with Asian flavors—try the grilled orange-anise glazed duck breast—and pairs it all with a choice of over 900 wines. The elegant food and decor—the theatrical dining room features stained glass, high ceilings, vivid murals, and orchids—make this *the* place for a special evening out.

31425 W. 12-mile Rd., Farmington Hills. ✆ 248/848-9393. www.tributerestaurant.com. Reservations required. Main courses $18–$39. AE, DC, DISC, MC, V. Tues–Sat 5:30–9:30pm.

DETROIT AFTER DARK

PERFORMING ARTS   The renowned **Detroit Symphony Orchestra** (✆ 313/576-5111; www.detroitsymphony.com) performs at Max M. Fisher Hall, 3711 Woodward Ave. **Michigan Opera Theatre** (✆ 313/961-3500; www.motopera.org) performs at the Detroit Opera House, 1526 Broadway. Touring Broadway shows play at the **Fox Theatre,** 2211 Woodward Ave. (✆ 313/471-3200); the **Fisher Theatre,** 3011 W. Grand Blvd. (✆ 313/872-1000); or the **Masonic Temple,** 500 Temple St. (✆ 313/832-7100).

THE BAR & CLUB SCENE   For over 70 years Detroiters have whiled away their evenings at **Baker's Keyboard Lounge,** 20510 Livernois (✆ 313/345-6300; www.bakerskeyboardlounge.com). Billing themselves as the "world's oldest jazz club," Baker's treats guests to the city's coolest live jazz and drinks every night of the week but Monday. Downtown, the Majestic Theater building, 4120 Woodward Ave. (✆ 313/833-9700; www.majesticdetroit.com), is home to two favorite music venues: **Garden Bowl,** a 16-lane glow-in-the-dark bowling alley accompanied by Detroit's hottest DJs; and **The Magic Stick** upstairs, a bar and billiards establishment widely known as the city's finest live music venue (the White Stripes got their start here).

It comes as no surprise that a sports-crazed town like Detroit is home to several great sports bars. **Nemo's,** 1384 Michigan Ave. (✆ 313/965-3180), is fun, friendly, and full of Detroit sports fans (the bar ranked number three on *Sports Illustrated*'s list of the "25 Best Sports Bars in America"); likewise, the **Post Bar,** 408 W. Congress (✆ 313/962-1293; www.postbars.com), is the place to be after Tigers and Red Wings games. No less fun—but certainly more upscale—is **Hockeytown Café,** 2301 Woodward Ave. (✆ 313/965-9500; www.hockeytowncafe.com). An ice-rink bar keeps drinks cold while Red Wings fans talk about the game; Red Wings paraphernalia covers the walls.

CASINOS   In 1999, casino gambling came to Detroit with the opening of the **MGM Grand Detroit,** U.S. 10 at Bagley Avenue (✆ 877/888-2121; detroit.mgmgrand.com); the **MotorCity Casino,** 2901 Grand River Ave. (✆ 877/777-0711; www.motorcitycasino.com); and **Greektown Casino,** 555 E. Lafayette (✆ 888/771-4386; www.greektowncasino.net). All casinos are open 24 hours daily, and have slots, table games, restaurants, entertainment, and secure parking. You must be 21 to enter.

WEST MICHIGAN BEACHES

Strung along the entire West Michigan shoreline, from Mackinaw City in the north to the Warren Dunes in the south, is a solid strip of sandy white beaches, the finest in the Midwest. A quick glance at any Michigan map reveals scores of sunning and swimming options. **State parks** provide inexpensive access ($6 per day, $24 per year for state residents; $8 per day, $29 per year for nonresidents). And the parks often feature great campgrounds. (Reserve your site *early*—a year in advance if possible.) You can get more information by calling ℂ **800/44-PARKS** or checking online at **www.michigan.gov/dnr**.

TRAVERSE CITY

Traverse City, in Michigan's northwestern Lower Peninsula, is known for boutique shopping, wineries, and a vibrant arts scene as well as its beaches. **Traverse City State Park,** 1132 U.S. 31 N. (ℂ **231/922-5270**), and **Bayside Park,** U.S. 31 North, 8 miles east in Acme, both offer great beaches, swimming, and picnicking. Twenty-five miles east, near Empire on M-22, **Sleeping Bear Dunes National Lakeshore** (ℂ **231/326-5134**; www.nps.gov/slbe) boasts some of the best beaches and dunes in the state. Contact the **Traverse City Convention & Visitors Bureau** (ℂ **800/TRAVERS**; www.mytraversecity.com) for information.

WHERE TO STAY & DINE   The Victorian-style **Bayshore Resort,** 833 E. Front St. (ℂ **800/634-4401** or 231/935-4400; www.bayshore-resort.com), has doubles beginning at $170. The **Grand Beach Resort Hotel,** 1683 U.S. 31 N. (ℂ **800/968-1992** or 231/938-4455; www.grandbeach.com), is a great family choice, with doubles starting at $139. Both hotels include continental breakfast and are right on the beach. For pampering, visit the **Grand Traverse Resort & Spa,** 100 Grand Traverse Blvd., Acme (off U.S. 31 North; ℂ **800/236-1577**; www.grandtraverseresort.com), which features newish guest rooms, a trio of 18-hole golf courses, shopping, dining, and a spa. Doubles begin at $155.

For dining out, head to Traverse City's Front Street downtown, where you'll find a wide array of choices. For a special evening out, try the contemporary Italian **Trattoria Stella,** 1200 W. 11th St. (ℂ **231/929-8989**; www.stellatc.com), a beautiful brick turn-of-the-20th-century manse on the wooded grounds of Grand Traverse Commons. Expect an extensive wine list and a changing menu based on the availability of fresh local ingredients and Atlantic and Pacific seafood.

LUDINGTON

It's worth a trip just to experience the pristine 8-mile dune drive along **Ludington's** shoreline. Wild dune vistas and superb swimming beaches are dotted with free parking, both in **Ludington City Park** (Lakeshore Dr.) and **Ludington State Park** (ℂ **231/843-2423**), on M-116. Both parks offer sugar sand beaches and "Big Lake" boating; the latter includes massive dunes, a lighthouse, and Hamlin Lake, a calmer (and warmer) inland option. For more information, contact the **Ludington Convention and Visitors Bureau** (ℂ **877/420-6618**; www.ludingtoncvb.com).

WHERE TO STAY & DINE   You'll find many chain hotels on U.S. 10 between U.S. 31 and Ludington. If you want to be near the beach, your best bet is **Snyder's Shoreline Inn,** 903 W. Ludington Ave. (ℂ **231/845-1261**; www.snydersshoreinn.com), across the street from the city beach. Doubles begin at $115. B&B choices include **The Lamplighter,** 602 E. Ludington Ave. (ℂ **800/301-9792** or 231/843-9792;

www.ludington-michigan.com), with doubles for $125 to $160; kids are not allowed. **The Inn at Ludington,** 701 E. Ludington Ave. (© 800/845-9170 or 231/845-7055; www.inn-ludington.com), offers doubles for $90 to $165; children under 10 stay free. Both properties include full breakfast and are within walking distance of Lake Michigan. **Ludington State Park** has three campgrounds.

Most restaurants are clustered along Ludington Avenue, but two good choices are **P. M. Steamers,** 502 W. Loomis St. (© 231/843-9555; www.pmsteamers.com), which features casual American fare and a waterfront view; and **Scotty's,** 5910 E. Ludington Ave. (© 231/843-4033), famous for its prime rib and seafood.

HOLLAND

Holland enjoys four great beaches: **Holland State Park,** 2215 Ottawa Beach Rd. (© 616/399-9390); **Oval Beach,** Oval Drive just off Perryman Street, Saugatuck; **Dunes State Park,** western end of 138th Avenue, Saugatuck (© 616/637-2788); and **Tunnel Park,** 66 Lakeshore Dr. (© 616/738-4810), named for the dune tunnel that connects the playground area to the beach. All four have picnic and playground facilities, but it's the huge, white beaches that attract thousands every year. For details, contact the **Holland Convention and Visitors Bureau** (© 800/506-1299; www.holland.org).

WHERE TO STAY & DINE   Holland's chain hotels cluster largely along U.S. 31. For a quieter, downtown location, try the **Haworth Inn,** 225 College Ave. (© 800/903-9142 or 616/395-7200; www.haworthinn.com), with doubles starting at $105, including continental breakfast. Want to stay near the beach? **Shaded Oaks B&B,** 444 Oak St. (© 616/399-4194; www.shadedoaks.com), offers a guesthouse and two lovely suites (one with a two-person soaking tub, the other with a fireplace) starting at $169, including full breakfast.

Several restaurants are located in downtown Holland on or near 8th Street. Favorites include **Alpenrose,** 4 E. 8th St. (© 616/393-2111; www.alpenroserestaurant.com), featuring German and Austrian fare; and **Butch's,** 44 E. 8th St. (© 616/396-8227; www.butchs.net), a deli and wine shop by day and fine-dining restaurant by night.

MACKINAC ISLAND

Set in the waters separating Michigan's upper and lower peninsulas, Mackinac (pronounced *Mack*-i-naw) Island is one of Michigan's loveliest and most romantic destinations. Cars are strictly prohibited; visitors get around the island on foot, bicycles, and horse-drawn carriages. The lack of modern transportation cultivates the sense of 19th-century nostalgia pervading the island, a veritable storehouse of beautifully restored Victorian homes. **Mackinac Island State Park** (© 906/847-3328; www.mackinacparks.com) constitutes 80% of the island. For more information, contact the **Mackinac Island Chamber of Commerce** (© 800/454-5227; www.mackinacisland.org).

The oldest structure in Michigan, and one of the few remaining Revolutionary War–era ruins in the nation, **Fort Mackinac** (© 906/436-4100; www.mackinacparks.com) looms high on a bluff overlooking the Straits of Mackinac. Originally a British outpost, Fort Mackinac was conquered by American soldiers 20 years after the Revolution. In addition to housing historic ruins, the Fort hosts Victorian children's games; bagpipe, bugle, and drum corps music; hourly rifle and cannon firings; and military reenactments performed by costumed interpreters.

Another prime vantage on the straits can be had from the porch at the **Grand Hotel** (© 906/847-3331), a National Historic Landmark. The veranda exudes romance and is a focal point on the world's largest summer hotel, built in 1887. For $10 you can tour this lovely landmark hotel (see below), drink cocktails, and take in the view. The price of your ticket will be deducted from any hotel restaurant meals.

If you like to bike, take a spin around the island, following an 8-mile circuit on **Mich. 185 (Lake Shore Rd).** The view of the straits is spellbinding from here and you can rubberneck without fear given the prohibition on motorized vehicles. Bike rentals ($4–$8 per hour for single speed, tandems and mountain bikes) are available throughout downtown. Ask about day rates and children's seats.

For an easier tour of the island, travel via horse and buggy with **Mackinac Island Carriage Tours** (© 906/847-3307; $19 adults, $8 children 5–12). Trips begin near the boat docks in the center of the shopping district and last about 2 hours. Sites include the Governor's Mansion, the Grand Hotel, Fort Mackinac and Arch Rock, a limestone formation that is among the island's most popular natural attractions.

Mackinac's newest attractions include two butterfly conservatories. The **Mackinac Island Butterfly House,** 1308 McGulpin St. (© 906/847-3972; $5 adults, $2 children 6–12); and the **Wings of Mackinac,** north of the Grand Hotel on Carriage Road (© 906/847-9464; $5.50 adults, $2.50 children 5–12). Downtown, a smattering of shops and galleries are worth an afternoon stroll. Don't leave the island without sampling its famous fudge—affectionately known as "fudgies." Many downtown shops sell the island's favorite confection to tourists.

WHERE TO STAY & DINE   Everyone should experience fine living at the **Grand Hotel** (© 800/33-GRAND or 906/847-3331; www.grandhotel.com) at least once. The comfortable rooms are each decorated individually, some with balconies and lake views. If money's no object, the suites are exceptionally luxurious; many are named and themed after famous figures, including six First Lady rooms. Resort grounds include tennis courts, a beautiful outdoor pool, an 18-hole golf course, and formal gardens. Doubles start at $345, including elaborate breakfast and dinner daily, horse-drawn shuttle service, and all tips. A great family resort is **Mission Point** (© 800/833-7711 or 906/847-3312; www.missionpoint.com), with 18 acres on the lakefront and a host of recreational facilities. Doubles begin at $194. Other moderately priced choices include the family-run **Hotel Iroquois,** Main Street (© 906/847-3321; www.iroquoishotel.com), a 100-year-old but thoroughly modernized inn. Doubles start at $160. Suites at the **Lilac Tree Hotel,** Main Street (© 866/847-6575; www.lilactree.com) include fridges and microwaves and start at $130.

For fine dining on the island, nothing surpasses the **Grand Hotel's Salle à Manger** (© 800/33-GRAND; www.grandhotel.com), known for its French-inspired entrees, decadent pecan ball dessert, and service fit for royalty. The hotel's **Jockey Club** and **Woods** restaurants offer casual meals—pasta, chicken, and steaks—at lower prices. The **Carriage House,** Main Street (© 906/847-3321; www.iroquoishotel.com), in the Hotel Iroquois, features local specialties such as broiled whitefish and pork tenderloin served with a chutney of Michigan apples and cherries. A nice family choice is **Dockside Inn,** near Star Line Ferry (© 906/847-3480), a casual restaurant serving local fish, chicken, ribs, wraps, and over 150 types of beer.

GETTING THERE   The major route to Mackinac Island is **I-75** from the south. From the lower peninsula, ferries depart from **Mackinaw City;** from the upper peninsula, ferries sail from **St. Ignace. Shepler's Ferry** (© 800/828-6157; www.sheplers ferry.com), **Arnold Transit Company** (© 800/542-8528; www.arnoldline.com), and **Star Line Ferry** (© 800/638-9892; www.mackinacferry.com) all service the island from both cities, and charge $20 adults, $10 children 5 to 12, free for children under 5. Bike transport is $7. You can also travel by plane from St. Ignace on **Great Lakes Air** (© **906/643-7165**).

PICTURED ROCKS NATIONAL LAKESHORE

On the north coast of Michigan's upper peninsula, rain, wind, and waves have sculpted 17 miles of multicolored sandstone cliffs into **Pictured Rocks,** one of the state's most scenic shores. The most spectacular cliffs extend from Munising to Grand Marais and soar to a height of 200 feet, varying from caves and arches to narrow columns and overlooks.

Highway 58 is a rough gravel road that runs parallel to the lakeshore between Munising on Route 28 and Grand Marais on Route 77. You'll find accommodations, restaurants, information, and camping supplies in both towns. For more information, contact **Grand Marais Chamber of Commerce** (© **906/494-2447;** www.grandmarais mi.com) or the park (© **906/387-2607;** www.nps.gov/piro).

There are many miles of hiking trails and roads, including the **North Country Trail,** that yield close-up views of the rocks. Many visitors prefer to see the shore on a 2-hour cruise. Boats dock at the **Munising City Pier,** Mich. 28 and Elm Avenue (© **906/387-2379;** www.picturedrocks.com). Adults pay $29, children 6 to 12 $12, and children under 6 ride free.

In the summer, lakeshore pastimes include hiking, picnicking, and swimming (if you can brave Lake Superior's frigid waters). In the winter, visitors enjoy snowshoeing, snowmobiling, or cross-country skiing on 21 miles of trails.

Near **Grand Marais,** the cliffs ease into **giant sand dunes,** which lumberjacks used as chutes to send forested timber into the lake below. Inland, you'll find waterfalls, forests, abundant wildlife, and fish swarming in lakes, ponds, and streams. At the base of the cliffs, a sand beach stretches for 12 miles.

After a rigorous day in the outdoors, replenish your energy without depleting your funds at **Sydney's,** Mich. 28, Munising (© **906/387-4067**). Grilled steaks or fresh Lake Superior fish are the specialties. Dine in or take out.

There are three drive-in campsites in the 40-mile Pictured Rocks National Lakeshore between Munising and Grand Marais. You can also hike into primitive campgrounds along the water. In Grand Marais, **North Shore Lodge,** Canal Street, 1 mile east of Mich. 77 (© **906/494-2361**), offers basic, affordable lodging on a stretch of private beach, an indoor pool, and a kids' play area.

GETTING THERE   To reach Pictured Rocks from the Mackinac Bridge (I-75), take **U.S. 2 west** immediately after the bridge, then **Mich. 77** north to Grand Marais. For Munising, turn west on **Mich. 28** at Seney.

ISLE ROYALE NATIONAL PARK

It's tough to get to **Isle Royale National Park** (© **906/482-0984;** www.nps.gov/isro), which is precisely its appeal. The remote, craggy islands are populated with hardwood forests, wildlife, lakes, and streams rather than lots of tourists and RVs. Cars are prohibited in this northern oasis, accessible only by boat and floatplane, 50 miles from Michigan's northwest coast and surrounded by Lake Superior's icy waters. The main island is the largest (45 miles wide×8 miles long) and most visited, but it is surrounded by 400 smaller islands. It's likely you'll have one all to yourself provided you can paddle there. And you can only do so mid-April through October; the park is closed to visitors the rest of the year.

A trip to Isle Royale takes careful planning. Ferries to the island return just a few hours after they dock; don't waste your time and money on the long voyage unless you plan to stay overnight. If you're traveling midsummer, it's probably wise to reserve space on a ferry in advance. The one-way, 2½-hour cruise from Grand Portage, Minnesota (on Hwy. 61 near Ontario) on *Wenonah* (© 715/392-2100; www.grand-isle-royale.com) costs $39 adults, $22 children under 12. The 3-hour, one-way trip from Copper Harbor, Michigan (on U.S. 41, on the Keweenaw Peninsula) on *The Isle Royale Queen* (© 906/289-4437; www.isleroyale.com) costs $60 adults, $30 children under 12. And the 6-hour trip from Houghton, Michigan (on U.S. 41, on the Keweenaw Peninsula) on *Ranger III* (© 906/482-0984; www.nps.gov/isro) costs $52 adults, $24 children under 12. The *Ranger III* is the only ferry large enough to transport boats; fees vary according to boat size. From Houghton you can also catch a **seaplane** (© 877/359-4753; www.royaleairservice.com) for $250 per person, round-trip. Visitors also need to pay a user fee of $4 per day for every person age 12 and over.

You'll encounter Isle Royale's sole inhabitants—200 bird species, foxes, beavers, wolves, and about 700 moose—along the park's 165 miles of foot trails. **Greenstone Ridge Trail,** the main artery, is strenuous, running east-west along the island—a 4- or 5-day trek even for fit hikers. Easier routes include the treks along the rugged bluffs of **Stoll Trail** and along **Tobin Harbor Trail** to Suzy's Cave; and up 880 feet to **Lookout Louise,** a more difficult climb that rewards with unsurpassed views. Even inexperienced paddlers can manage a canoe trip across **Hidden Lake,** where a natural salt lick attracts the local moose population.

Rock Harbor Lodge, Rock Harbor (© 906/337-4993 summer, 270/773-2191 winter; www.isleroyaleresort.com; open late May to mid-Sept), provides lodging and meals to those who need more comfort than a tent. Doubles include half-day canoe rentals and begin at $170 per night without meals or $276 per night with three meals. The lodge's surprisingly good dining room is open to all, or you can bring your own food and rent a cabin (with kitchenette) beginning at $165 a night. There are no grocery stores on Isle Royale. Sightseeing cruises depart Rock Harbor for a variety of island destinations beginning at $30 adults, $14 children under 12.

The campgrounds near Rock Harbor have three-sided wooden shelters, but they fill up fast because they are near the island's entry point. **Three Mile** and **Daisy Farm** are within a day's hike of Rock Harbor, west along the southern shore. **West Chickenbone** is a popular site, a 2- to 3-day hike from Rock Harbor, along the Greenstone Ridge Trail. *Note:* All campgrounds in the park have maximum-stay limits, usually 3 days.

For more information, call **Park Headquarters** at © 906/482-0984. **Ranger stations** are at Windigo, Rock Harbor, Malone Bay, and Amygdaloid.

6 Milwaukee & Highlights of Wisconsin

MILWAUKEE

If Milwaukee conjures up images of Harley-Davidsons and beer, you wouldn't be alone. But there's much more to this cosmopolitan Great Lake city. Milwaukee surprises many first-time visitors with its large, thriving, and well-supported arts community—just take a look at the spectacular Milwaukee Art Museum designed by renowned Spanish architect Santiago Calatrava. Fabulous waterfront summer festivals, great views of Lake Michigan and the Lake Express ferry to Michigan are just a few more reasons to visit. And then, of course, there are the Harleys and beer.

ESSENTIALS

GETTING THERE   By Plane   The **General Mitchell International Airport** (© **414/747-5300;** www.mitchellairport.com) is 10 miles south of downtown, a 15-minute drive on I-94 West to I-794 East. One-way transportation to downtown costs $11 via **Airport Connection** shuttle service (© **800/236-5450;** reservations recommended); $1.75 via the local Transit System (Rte. 80 serves the airport); $6 via Amtrak to its station at 433 W. St. Paul Ave.; and $25 via taxi.

By Train   Amtrak (© **800/USA-RAIL;** www.amtrak.com) provides service from Chicago (trip time: 1½ hr.) and Minneapolis/St. Paul (6¼ hr.) to its station at 433 W. St. Paul Ave.

By Car   Milwaukee is 90 miles from Chicago, a 1½-hour drive; and 80 miles from Madison, also a 1½-hour drive. Both cities are reached via **I-94.**

By Ferry   The **Lake Express Ferry** (© **866/914-1010;** www.lake-express.com) offers high-speed car and passenger service from Muskegon, Michigan (trip time: 2½ hr.). One-way fares are $55 for adults, $30 for children, $65 for autos.

VISITOR INFORMATION   Contact the **Milwaukee Convention and Visitors Bureau,** 400 W. Wisconsin Ave., Milwaukee, WI 53203 (© **800/554-1448** or 414/273-7222; www.officialmilwaukee.com).

GETTING AROUND   The **Milwaukee County Transit System** (© **414/344-6711;** www.ridemcts.com) offers service downtown and into the suburbs for $1.75. Downtown tourist attractions, restaurants, and hotels can be reached via the city's free **Trolley** system, which operates from May 31 to September 3. If you plan to venture outside the immediate downtown, it's best to drive; Milwaukee is easily navigated by car.

SPECIAL EVENTS & FESTIVALS   There are literally dozens of festivals held throughout the year in Milwaukee, sometimes called "The City of Festivals." The biggest and best include **Summerfest** (© **800/273-FEST;** www.summerfest.com), with world-class entertainment on a dozen waterfront stages throughout late June and early July; and **Irish Fest** (© **414/476-3378;** www.irishfest.com) in mid-August, the world's largest Irish culture festival. In early August, the **Wisconsin State Fair** (© **414/266-7000;** www.wistatefair.com) features entertainment, auto races, exhibits, fireworks, and more.

WHAT TO SEE & DO

Santiago Calatrava's redesign of the **Milwaukee Art Museum,** 700 N. Art Museum Dr. (at Michigan St. and Lincoln Memorial Dr.; © **414/224-3200;** www.mam.org), renders the museum itself as stunning as any of the works on display inside. The Burke Brise Soleil sunscreen on the roof opens and closes with the weather to resemble a large white gull. Inside, artworks range from ancient Greek to modern American, Asian, and African pieces; represented artists include Renoir, Monet, Kandinsky, and Miró. Admission is $8 for adults, $4 for students, and free for children under 13.

Milwaukee's hands-on science and technology museum, **Discovery World at Pier Wisconsin,** 500 N. Harbor Dr. (© **414/765-9966;** www.discoveryworld.org), reopened in 2006 in a new lakeshore location. Highlights include an aquarium and the tall ship S/V *Denis Sullivan,* a re-creation of a 19th-century Great Lakes schooner. Admission is $10 adults for the aquarium or the museum proper, or $16 adults for a combined ticket; $8 children for the aquarium or the museum, or $12 for both. Ship tours cost $5; public sails vary in price. Downtown, the **Milwaukee Public Museum,** 800 W.

Wells St. ((C) **414/278-2700;** www.mpm.edu), is home to a staggering array of re-created villages from around the world, a permanent live butterfly garden, dinosaur skeletons, a simulated rainforest, and an IMAX theater. A state-of-the-art planetarium opened November 2006. Museum admission is $11 adults, $6 children 3 to 15; planetarium fees are $8 adults, $5.50 children; IMAX films vary in price.

Mitchell Park Horticultural Conservatory, better known as **"The Domes,"** 524 S. Layton Blvd. ((C) **414/649-9800;** http://countyparks.com/horticulture), is a botanical garden housed in three seven-story, aluminum and glass domes. The Arid Dome features desert plants; a Tropical Dome houses rainforest plants, spices, nuts, and orchids; and a Show Dome includes seasonal botanical plantings. Admission is $5 adults, $3.50 children 6 to 17.

Miller Brewing Company, 4251 W. State St. ((C) **800/944-LITE** or 414/931-BEER; www.millerbrewing.com), operates one of the world's largest breweries. After a free 1-hour tour, visitors sample the product in the city's last remaining outdoor *biergarten*, weather permitting, or in the 19th-century Miller Inn the rest of the year. Another favorite factory tour is at the **Harley-Davidson Tour Center,** 11700 W. Capitol Dr., Wauwatosa ((C) **877/883-1450** or 414/343-7850; www.harley-davidson.com). The free hour-long tour allows visitors to see Harley powertrains in production. No children under 12.

A favorite for the kids is the **Milwaukee County Zoo,** 10001 W. Blue Mound Rd. ((C) **414/771-5500;** www.milwaukeezoo.org). All of the favorite exotic beasts are on hand, including elephants, bears, zebras, gorillas, and the big cats, but you'll also see raptor and sea lion shows and you can take a ride on a camel. Admission fees vary seasonally, but are generally around $10 adults, $7 children 3 to 12.

WHERE TO STAY & DINE

The **Hilton City Center,** 509 W. Wisconsin Ave. ((C) **800/HILTONS** or 414/271-7250; www.hiltonmilwaukee.com), is convenient to downtown and has a great restaurant (see below) and lounge. It's also home to the nation's first urban indoor waterpark, "Paradise Landing." Doubles begin at $135. Milwaukee's most historic hotel, the 102-year-old **Pfister,** 424 E. Wisconsin Ave. ((C) **800/472-4403** or 414/273-8222; www.thepfisterhotel.com), is centrally located and exudes old-style European elegance. Doubles start at $165 and go way up. The **Four Points by Sheraton Milwaukee Airport,** 4747 S. Howell Ave. ((C) **800/558-3862** or 414/481-8000; www.fourpointshotel.com), is the other leading upscale choice, with cozy rooms, two pools, a superb restaurant, and a location near the airport. Doubles begin at $105.

The **Milwaukee Chop House,** 633 N. 5th St., at the Hilton City Center ((C) **414/390-4562;** www.milwaukeechophouse.com), specializes in mouthwatering steaks and offers an extensive wine list. **Crawdaddy's,** west of town at 6414 W. Greenfield Ave., West Allis ((C) **414/778-2228;** www.foodspot.com/crawdaddys), is known for its Creole/Cajun seafood, although you'll find chicken and steak on the menu as well. Entrees run $13 to $30. **Water Street Brewery,** 1101 N. Water St. ((C) **414/272-1195;** www.waterstreetbrewery.com), brews its own beers and serves pasta, ribs, seafood, and sandwiches in a fun atmosphere.

A SIDE TRIP TO KOHLER & THE AMERICAN CLUB

One hour north of Milwaukee is the planned garden community of Kohler, its centerpiece the luxurious **American Club,** Highland Drive ((C) **800/344-2838;** www.destinationkohler.com). Built in 1918 to house employees of the Kohler plumbing factory, the grand Tudor-style American Club was converted into a hotel in 1981. It is now the Midwest's premier resort hotel, offering 236 luxurious guest rooms, each outfitted with fabulous bathroom fixtures. Also on-site is Kohler's Inn on Woodlake, a 110-room Arts and Crafts–style inn. The resort's extensive facilities include four Pete Dye–designed golf courses; a 500-acre wilderness preserve; a salon and day spa; health and racquet facilities; upscale boutiques; and the Kohler Design Center. The golf is the star attraction, though, and guests are encouraged to reserve tee times when they book their room—greens fees begin at $141. Double rooms at the American Club begin at $285 during golf season, $185 in the winter; doubles at the Inn cost $182 during golf season and $120 in the winter.

MADISON

For a small city, Madison has a lot of flair. Credit the presence of 41,000 university students, or perhaps the city's designation as Wisconsin's state capitol, or maybe its location between two scenic lakes. Whatever the reason, Madison boasts inexpensive entertainment, lots of city parks, and streets enlivened by bookstores, cafes, eclectic eateries, and funky boutiques. Madison's most bustling thoroughfare, **State Street,** and the downtown area, **Capitol Square,** are great places to shop and dine. And late April through early November, Capitol Square hosts a vibrant, open-air **Dane County Farmer's Market (www.dcfm.org)** on Saturday and Wednesday mornings, with produce vendors, arts and crafts booths, and street musicians.

VISITOR INFORMATION   For more information, contact the **Greater Madison Convention and Visitors Bureau,** 615 E. Washington Ave. (© **800/373-6376** or 608/255-2537; www.visitmadison.com).

WHAT TO SEE & DO

Madison's 100-year-old **State Capitol** (© **608/266-0382**) dominates the city center, topped by Daniel Chester French's gilded bronze statue *Wisconsin.* Hour-long tours are offered daily here and at **Monona Terrace,** just a few blocks away, 1 John Nolen Dr. (© **608/261-4000;** www.mononaterrace.com). Monona Terrace community and convention center was designed by Frank Lloyd Wright whose presence is richly felt in Madison and nearby Taliesin (see below). Tours examine the building's highlights and Wright's design philosophy. Enjoy superb lake and city views from the building's rooftop garden, a popular stop for lunchtime picnickers.

For more examples of Wright's legacy of Prairie School architecture, visit **First Unitarian Society,** 900 University Bay Rd. (© **608/233-9774**), which is open to the public, or drive past these private residences: **Airplane House** (1908), 120 Ely Place; **Dr. Arnold Jackson House** (1957), 3515 W. Beltline Hwy.; **Lamp House** (1899), 22 N. Butler St.; **J. C. Pew House** (1939), 3650 Lake Mendota Dr.; **Louis Sullivan Bradley's House,** 106 N. Prospect; and **"Jackobs I" House** (1937), 441 Toepfer Ave.

Madison enjoys more than its fair share of public green spaces, settled as it is on an isthmus between lakes Mendota and Monona. Of the city's more than 150 public parks, one of the most popular is the free **Henry Vilas Park Zoo,** 606 S. Randall Ave. (© **608/266-4733;** www.vilaszoo.org), where locals gather to picnic, feed ducks, and view more than 600 animals. **Olbrich Park,** on Atwood Avenue, sits on the northeastern shore of Lake Monona, with picnic tables and a swimming beach. Across the street **Olbrich Botanical Gardens** (© **608/246-4550;** www.olbrich.org) boasts 14 acres of outdoor flowering plants and a conservatory.

WHERE TO STAY & DINE

Head to the 1857 Romanesque Revival **Mansion Hill Inn,** 424 N. Pinckney St. (© **800/ 798-9070** or 608/255-3999; www.mansionhillinn.com), for luxurious and historic accommodations. Period antiques, original hardwood floors, marble fireplaces, and wrought-iron balconies assure a memorable romantic getaway. Doubles begin at $145 and include breakfast and afternoon wine service; kids under 13 not permitted. Downtown, the **Edgewater,** 666 Wisconsin Ave. (© **800/922-5512** or 608/256-9071; www.theedgewater.com), on Lake Mendota, boasts beautiful lakeside sunsets and a fine restaurant. Doubles begin at $119, $139 for lakefront rooms. The **Hilton Madison Monona Terrace,** 9 E. Wilson St. (© **608/255-5100;** www.hiltonmadison. com), is ideally located in central Madison, within a few blocks of the capitol, the university, and adjacent to Lake Monona and the Monona Terrace Convention Center. Doubles begin at $145 and include continental breakfast.

Madison claims to have more restaurants per capita than any other American city, including a rich array of ethnic eateries. You can't beat the fun atmosphere and great food at **Great Dane Pub & Brewing Co.,** 123 E. Doty St. (© **608/284-0000;** www. greatdanepub.com), serving up a dozen microbrewed beers alongside sandwiches, burgers, and dinners. Wisconsin comfort food comprises the menu at the **Old Fashioned,** 23 N. Pinckney St. (© **608/310-4545**); expect mac-n-cheese, walleye, and burgers in an upscale tavern. The menu at **Fitch's Chophouse & Spirits,** 5957 McKee Rd., Fitchburg (© **608/441-7070;** www.fitchschophouse.com), emphasizes premium aged steaks, which you can consume while surrounded by burnished woods and a fireplace.

SPRING GREEN & TALIESIN

Frank Lloyd Wright's former home, which he built and perfected over the course of 40 years, **Taliesin** (Tally-*es*-in), intersection of Highway 23 and County Highway C (© **877/588-7900** or 608/588-7900; www.taliesinpreservation.org), has been called the architect's "autobiography in wood and stone." Taliesin was also the architect's studio and laboratory. Located in south-central Wisconsin (an hour's drive west of Madison), the 600-acre National Historic Landmark is now a studio, farm, and architectural school for 40 undergraduates.

Welsh for "shining brow," Taliesin is built on the crest of a hill facing the Wisconsin River on land Wright's grandfather settled after immigrating from Wales. Wright built each of the grounds' five buildings during consecutive decades of his 50-year career. Visitors can purchase tickets to one of six Taliesin tours: the **Hillside Studio Tour** (1 hr., $16); the **Shuttle/Walking Tour** of the grounds (2 hr., $20); the **Highlights Tour** (2 hr., $50); **Wright's House Tour** (2 hr., $35–$45); the comprehensive **Estate Tour** (4 hr., $70–$75); and the **Sunset Tour** (3 hr., $80). The regular season runs May through October, but tour dates and hours vary widely. Reservations are strongly recommended; children are not permitted on certain tours.

South of town, the multilevel **House on the Rock,** Highway 23 (© **608/935-3639;** www.thehouseontherock.com), sits atop a 450-foot rock chimney. Built by Alexander Jordan, the stone house is an architectural curiosity, with massive fireplaces, trees, and pools of running water throughout the building. Views of the surrounding landscape are equally spectacular and easily visible through the house's 3,264 windows.

You can stay at **House on the Rock Resort,** 400 Springs Dr. (© **800/822-7774** or 608/588-7000; www.thehouseontherock.com), just a few miles from its famous namesake. The all-suite resort features private patios and balconies as well as a fine restaurant and 27 holes of championship golf. Doubles begin at $150. The **Silver Star Inn,** 3852 Limmex Hill Rd. (© **608/935-7297;** www.silverstarinn.com), is a modern log inn featuring fine art and photography and set on 350 wooded acres. Doubles begin at $95 and include a full breakfast.

For more information, contact the **Spring Green Chamber of Commerce,** 150 E. Jefferson St., Spring Green (© **800/588-2042** or 608/588-2054; www.springgreen.com).

THE WISCONSIN DELLS

The Wisconsin Dells draw thousands of tourists every year with man-made attractions—indoor waterparks, wax museums, and amusement parks—in spite of the Dells original attraction as a natural wonder: 15 miles of weathered sandstone cliffs and cool, wooded gullies. Ironically, few visitors to this most popular Wisconsin attraction ever see the Dells themselves.

You can observe the region's natural beauty from April to October on **Dells Boat Tours** (© **608/254-8555;** www.dellsboats.com), or aboard World War II amphibious "ducks" at **Original Wisconsin Ducks** (© **608/254-8751;** www.wisconsinduck tours.com). Both offer 2-hour tours of the sandstone gorges for $20 adults, $10 children. During the warm months you can also explore the gorgeous landscape on horseback with a guide at the **Beaver Springs Fishing Park, Riding Stables and Aquarium,** 600 Trout Rd., off Highway 13 (© **608/254-2707;** www.beaversprings fun.com). An hour's ride costs $23 adults, $8 children under 6 sharing a horse with an adult. Fifty-foot cliffs form the lakeshore of nearby **Mirror Lake State Park,** Fern Dell Road, off Highway 12 (© **608/254-2333;** www.mirrorlakewisconsin.com). A popular boating spot, the lake is surrounded by pine and oak woods where visitors can picnic and camp.

If man-made attractions suit your family, head to **Noah's Ark Waterpark,** 1410 Wisconsin Dells Pkwy. (© **608/254-6351;** www.noahsarkwaterpark.com), the nation's largest, with 41 water slides, two wave pools, two endless rivers, 4 children's water play areas, minigolf, and 12 restaurants and lounges. A day pass costs $30 adults, $24 children under 47 inches.

The popularity—and plethora—of indoor waterparks in the Dells has made the area a year-round family destination. Parks combine water slides, wave pools, and squirting toys with resort-style accommodations (sometimes including golf and spa facilities) under one roof, at an affordable price. **Great Wolf Lodge,** 1400 Great Wolf Dr. off Highway 12 (© **800/559-WOLF;** www.greatwolflodge.com), follows a North Woods log cabin theme and offers lots of children's activities. Room rates begin at $269. **Kalahari Resort,** 1305 Kalahari Dr. off Highway 12 (© **877/525-2427;** www.kalahariresort.com), also has a day spa on-site. Room rates begin at $129. The Dells' largest waterpark resort is **Wilderness Lodge,** 511 E. Adams St. (© **800/867-9453;** www.wildernessresort.com), with over seven football fields' worth of indoor and outdoor water-park fun as well as nearly 450 hotel rooms and condos and an 18-hole golf course and spa. Room rates begin at $99. *Note:* Rates for all of the above resorts include waterpark entry and double rooms occupied by up to four guests.

Wally's House of Embers, 935 Wisconsin Dells Pkwy., Lake Delton (© **608/253-6411;** www.houseofembers.com), has been a Dells institution since 1959. The friendly, family-owned restaurant specializes in ribs, but also serves fresh seafood and steaks. The romantic themed rooms are worth reserving for a special night out. Main courses run $19 to $34. For great burgers, check out the family-friendly **Monks Bar**

& Grill, 220 Broadway (© **608/254-2955;** www.monksbarandgrill.com), a local fixture with a friendly staff. Everything here costs less than $7.

The Dells—both the town and the geologic wonder—are 55 miles north of Madison; exits 85, 87, 89, and 92 off I-90/94 will deliver you here. For information, contact the **Wisconsin Dells Visitor and Convention Bureau,** 701 Superior St., Wisconsin Dells (© **800/223-3557;** www.wisdells.com).

DOOR COUNTY

Door County's rugged Lake Michigan coast, tiny fishing villages (now converted into tiny resort towns), and laid-back atmosphere draw scores of visitors looking for family and romantic getaways. With Green Bay to the west and Lake Michigan on three sides, Door County is a 75-mile-long strip of cliffs and unsullied beaches with 250 miles of limestone or dune coastline. No matter where you are on the peninsula, you're never more than 10 minutes from a water view.

Routes 57 and 42 circle the peninsula, passing through splendid natural scenery and inviting towns like the bayside villages of **Fish Creek, Sister Bay,** and **Ephraim,** each one charmingly different from the next. Tidy dairy farms and fruit orchards with ubiquitous red barns dot the landscape. Contact the **Door County Chamber of Commerce,** 1015 Green Bay Rd., Sturgeon Bay (© **800/527-3529** or 920/743-4456; www.doorcounty.com), for additional information.

Door County is home to several lovely state parks, each with miles of hiking and biking trails, fishing, sailing, camping, and swimming in the summer; beautiful fall leaf-peeping in the fall; and cross-country skiing and snowmobiling in the winter. **Peninsula State Park,** near Fish Creek (© **920/868-3258**), has all of that, a picturesque lighthouse, and 18 holes of championship golf. Ninety-foot dunes, jagged cliffs, and surf-carved caves lure visitors to **Whitefish Dunes State Park,** near Jacksonport (© **920/823-2400**). **Potawatomi State Park,** near Sturgeon Bay (© **920/746-2890**), has a nice observation tower offering sweeping views of Green Bay. State park campgrounds are popular—be sure to reserve a site early (© **888/947-2757**). A day pass to any state park costs $10; camping fees run $12 to $17. For online info on Wisconsin's state parks, see **www.dnr.state.wi.us/org/land/parks**.

Art galleries and crafts boutiques are located throughout Door County. Fish Creek, Egg Harbor, Sister Bay, and Ephraim have the best assortment; Ephraim is home to the finest and most eclectic art galleries.

French and Scandinavian fishermen settled the Door in the 17th century, and the surrounding waters are still a mother lode of walleye, northern pike, lake trout, and salmon. **Fish boils** are the stuff of ceremonial ritual here: Fresh whitefish, onions, and potatoes are tossed into a boiling cauldron, then finished off when a pint of kerosene is splashed onto the wood fire. This quintessential Door County dinner is available throughout the peninsula, with most restaurants charging about $18 per person, including Door County cherry pie. The **White Gull Inn,** 4225 Main St., Fish Creek (© **920/868-3517**), claims to have been boiling fish longer than anyone else on the peninsula. The **Square Rigger,** 6332 Hwy. 57, Jacksonport (© **877/347-4264**), serves their fish boil in their dining room rather than from a buffet line.

For an authentic Swedish breakfast of pancakes with lingonberry sauce, everyone heads to **Al Johnson's Swedish Restaurant,** Highway 42, Sister Bay (© **920/854-2626**); you'll recognize the building from its sod-covered roof (where you might see a grazing goat or two keeping the grass trimmed). **Wilson's Restaurant and Ice Cream**

Parlor, Route 42, Ephraim (© **920/854-2041**), has been serving sundaes, chocolate sodas, and burgers under its red-and-white awning since 1906.

Door County is known in part for its romantic B&Bs. **The Whistling Swan,** 4192 Main St., Fish Creek (© **888/277-4289** or 920/868-3442; www.whistlingswan.com), was built in mainland Wisconsin in 1887 and moved across the frozen Green Bay 20 years later to serve as an inn. It remains a charming B&B, furnished with antiques. Doubles start at $135 and rates include continental breakfast. Nearby is the elegant **White Gull Inn,** 4225 Main St. (© **888/364-9542** or 920/868-3517; www.white gullinn.com). Doubles begin at $140 and include a full, hot breakfast. **Edgewater Resort,** 10040 Water St., Ephraim (© **920/854-2734;** www.edge-waterresort.com), features spacious accommodations, most with water views and balconies, some with double whirlpool tubs and kitchens. Doubles begin at $110. An inexpensive but comfortable family favorite, the **Square Rigger Lodge,** 6332 Hwy. 57, Jacksonport (© **888/508-8008;** www.squareriggerlodge.com), has its own Lake Michigan beach access. Accommodations include motel-style rooms with fridges (doubles begin at $103) and cottages (beginning at $170 per night or $770 per week).

7 Minneapolis & St. Paul

The Twin Cities, set on opposite sides of the Mississippi River, initially established themselves in the agricultural business. Waves of Scandinavians and Germans farmed the fertile prairie, then shipped their grain to the cities to be milled and transported to the rest of the nation. These days Minneapolis and St. Paul are more likely associated with arts and culture than farming; they are home to terrific museums and one of the finest and most active theater and fine arts communities in the nation. Minneapolis is also fast becoming a hot spot for architectural gems, including the Weisman Art Museum, the Walker Art Center, and the new Guthrie Theatre.

And lest Minnesota's reputation for harsh weather trouble you, not to worry. Both cities incorporate miles of climate-controlled skyway systems enabling residents and visitors to work, shop, and dine without stepping outdoors.

ESSENTIALS

GETTING THERE   By Plane   Minneapolis/St. Paul International Airport (www. mspairport.com), located between the cities, is 16 and 12 miles south of each downtown, respectively, and is a hub for Northwest Airlines. The **Metropolitan Transit Commission** runs buses to both cities (© **612/373-3333;** www.metrotransit.org), and light rail service to Minneapolis for $2 in off-peak hours and $2.75 during rush hour. **SuperShuttle** (© **612/827-7777;** www.supershuttle.com) vans run to downtown Minneapolis hotels for $14, downtown St. Paul for $13; other metro areas vary in price. Taxi fares to downtown Minneapolis begin at $28; the trip to downtown St. Paul begins at $22.

By Train   Amtrak (© **800/USA-RAIL;** www.amtrak.com) provides service from Chicago (trip time: 8 hr.), Milwaukee (6½ hr.), and Seattle (36 hr.) to its station at 730 Transfer Rd., St. Paul (© **651/644-6012**).

By Car   Major routes into the Twin Cities are **I-94** from the east (Milwaukee and Chicago) and west (Fargo), and **I-35** from the south (Des Moines) and north (Duluth).

VISITOR INFORMATION   The **Minneapolis Convention & Visitors Bureau** is at 250 Marquette Ave. S., Suite 1300, Minneapolis, MN 55401 (© **888/676-MPLS;**

www.minneapolis.org). The **St. Paul Convention & Visitors Bureau** is at 175 W. Kellogg Blvd., Suite 502, St. Paul, MN 55102 (© **800/627-6101;** www.stpaulcvb.org).

GETTING AROUND   The **Metropolitan Transit Commission** (© **612/373-3333;** www.metrotransit.org) operates buses between the Twin Cities. The **Hiawatha Light Rail** runs along Hiawatha Avenue from Minneapolis's Warehouse District to the Minneapolis/St. Paul Airport and the Mall of America with a dozen stops in between. Fares for the bus or train system are the same: Rush-hour fare is $2.75; off-peak fare is $2. A day pass good for both buses and trains costs $6.

Both Minneapolis and St. Paul have an extensive skyway system (a godsend during below-zero winters) that makes it easy to explore downtown areas on foot. But you'll need a car to reach many attractions outside downtown and in the suburbs.

FAST FACTS   There's an emergency room at the **University of Minnesota Medical Center, Fairview,** 500 Harvard St., Minneapolis (© **612/273-3000). St. Joseph's Hospital** operates an emergency room at 69 W. Exchange St., in St. Paul (© **651/232-3000**).

There is no sales tax on clothing or shoes in Minnesota. Both Minneapolis and St. Paul are among the safest large cities in the country, and crime rates are extremely low; exercise the same caution you would in any other major city and you should have no problems.

WHAT TO SEE & DO
IN MINNEAPOLIS

Frederick R. Weisman Art Museum   Set on a bluff overlooking the Mississippi River, the Weisman Art Museum is part of the University of Minnesota campus. You won't miss the trademark Frank Gehry–designed building; its fluid form defies conventional architectural lines, and its metallic finish gleams in the sunlight. The permanent collection is especially strong in American modernist paintings, ceramics, Mimbres pottery, and Korean furniture. Allow 1 hour.

333 E. River Rd., Minneapolis. © 612/625-9494. www.weisman.umn.edu. Free admission. Tues–Wed and Fri 10am–5pm; Thurs 10am–8pm; Sat–Sun 11am–5pm. Head southeast on Washington Ave. and take the "Washington Ave. SE" ramp downhill and across the Mississippi. E. River Rd. is immediately to your right.

Mill City Museum   Minneapolis's Mill City Museum recounts the history of the flour industry that earned the city the nickname "Mill City" in the late 19th century. Set in the ruins of what was once the world's largest flour mill, and one of over two dozen such Minneapolis mills, the museum re-creates old milling techniques with period equipment, railroad cars, and interactive exhibits. Visitors also learn the impact of the nation's first high-quality, finely milled flour on the gastronomy of the Twin Cities and the country. Allow 1 hour.

704 S. 2nd St., Minneapolis. © 612/341-7555. www.millcitymuseum.org. Admission $8 adults, $6 children 4–17, free for children under 4. Tues–Wed and Fri–Sat 10am–5pm; Thurs 10am–9pm; Sun noon–5pm. Closed Mon except select holidays: Martin Luther King, Jr., Day, Presidents' Day, Memorial Day, July 4, and Labor Day.

Minneapolis Institute of Arts *Best*   In 2006 the already stellar MIA unveiled a new 113,000-square-foot museum expansion and renovation that increased its exhibition space by nearly 40% and added 34 new galleries. The new space allows the MIA to host more temporary art exhibits, and to display a larger portion of its nearly 100,000-piece permanent collection of fine and decorative art. More than 5,000 years of history are represented in the new museum space, including a 2,000-year-old mummy, European masters (Rembrandt, Titian, and Monet, among others), and a

Downtown Minneapolis

ACCOMMODATIONS ■
Graves 601 Hotel **3**
Minneapolis Marriott
City Center **5**
Nicollet Island Inn **7**
Doubletree Park Place **1**

DINING ◆
Café Lurcat **2**
Chino Latino **10**
D'Amico Cucina **3**
Goodfellow's **5**
Hell's Kitchen **9**
Murray's **6**
The News Room **8**
Solera **4**

comprehensive photography exhibit. If you're short on time, ask for the "Highlights" brochure. Allow 2 hours.

2400 S. 3rd Ave., Minneapolis. © **888/MIA-ARTS** or 612/870-3131. www.artsmia.org. Free admission (excludes select special exhibits). Tues–Wed and Fri–Sat 10am–5pm; Thurs 10am–9pm; Sun 11am–5pm.

Minnesota Zoo *(Kids)*   You'll see most of the exotic animals you expect at the 485-acre Minnesota Zoo, including tigers, camels, dolphins, and monkeys. But this zoo includes an especially nice array of North American animals, including wolves, bison, pumas, and wolverines. During the summer the zoo's working Wells Fargo Family Farm engages visitors with hands-on exhibits and teaches how food travels from the farm to the grocery store shelves. There's also an IMAX theater and a monorail offering great aerial views. Allow 2 hours.

13000 Zoo Blvd., Apple Valley. © **800/366-7811** or 952/431-9500. www.mnzoo.com. Admission to zoo $12 adults, $7 children 3–12. Zoo/IMAX combo $19 adults, $13 children 3–12. Monorail $3.50. Always free for children under 3. Parking $5. Memorial Day to Labor Day daily 9am–6pm; May and Sept Mon–Fri 9am–4pm, Sat–Sun 9am–6pm; Oct–Apr daily 9am–4pm.

University of Minnesota   One of the Midwest's oldest (1851) and most important universities, with 50,000 students on the Twin Cities campus, the UMN offers three significant museums—the **James Ford Bell Museum of Natural History, the University Art Gallery,** and the **Frederick R. Weisman Art Museum** (see above). The 4,800-seat Northrop Auditorium has been a home for distinguished performances since 1929, and the University Theatre has four separate stages.

Located between Mississippi and University aves. and 10th Ave. and Oak St. SE, Minneapolis. © **612/625-5000.** www.umn.edu.

Walker Art Center/Minneapolis Sculpture Garden   The Walker Art Center reopened with great fanfare in early 2005 with a striking new addition that nearly doubled its exhibition space. A fine dining restaurant and cafe, both by Wolfgang Puck, and gift shop are also new. Unchanged is the museum's reputation for edgy, contemporary art: paintings, sculptures, drawings, photographs, and multimedia installations. Across the street is the **Minneapolis Sculpture Garden,** the largest urban sculpture garden in the country. A variety of 20th-century sculpture shares space with horticultural plantings, including the famous "Spoonbridge and Cherry." Allow 2 hours for both.

1750 Hennepin, Minneapolis. © **612/375-7600.** www.walkerart.org. Admission to museum $8 adults, $5 seniors and students, free for children under 12, free to all Thurs 5–9pm and 1st Sat of every month. Free admission to sculpture garden. Museum Tues–Wed 11am–5pm; Thurs–Sat 11am–9pm; Sun 11am–6pm. Sculpture garden daily 6am–midnight.

IN ST. PAUL
Cathedral of St. Paul   Built in 1915 on the highest point in the city, this cathedral is one of the largest in the country. A replica of St. Peter's in Rome, the building boasts a newly restored 175-foot-high copper dome, a massive rose window, and granite-and-travertine construction. Allow 30 minutes.

239 Selby Ave., St. Paul. © **651/228-1766.** www.cathedralsp.org. Free admission. Mon–Thurs 7:30am–6pm; Fri 7:30am–4pm; Sat 8am–8pm; Sun 8am–6pm. Guided tours Mon, Wed, and Fri 1pm.

Historic Fort Snelling   This living history museum commemorates the establishment of a fort here in the wilderness in 1819 by Col. Josiah Snelling and his troops,

Downtown St. Paul

ACCOMMODATIONS ■
Best Western Kelly Inn **2**
Crowne Plaza
Riverfront Hotel **7**
Saint Paul Hotel **6**

DINING ◆
A Rebours **5**
Cossetta's **3**
Great Waters Brewing Co. **4**
St. Paul Grill **6**
WA Frost & Co. **1**

523

who opened the area for homesteaders. Costumed guides are the focus of a living history reenactment during the summer months, re-creating the activities of everyday army life during the 1820s. Allow 1 to 2 hours.

Highways 5 and 55, St. Paul. © 612/726-1171. www.mnhs.org/fortsnelling. Admission $8 adults, $7 seniors, $4 children 6–17, free for children under 6. Memorial Day to Labor Day Mon–Sat 10am–5pm, Sun noon–5pm; May and Sept–Oct Sat 10am–5pm, Sun noon–5pm. Closed Nov–Apr.

Minnesota History Center *Kids*   An impressive array of artifacts is housed in this three-story museum, including photographs, music, and videos, all of it celebrating Minnesota history. Kids enjoy sitting in the re-created basement of a Minnesota farmhouse while a simulated tornado passes overhead. Adults enjoy listening to recordings of Minnesota musicians, including Bob Dylan, Steven Greenberg, and Prince. Allow 1½ hours.

345 Kellogg Blvd. W., St. Paul. © 800/657-3773 or 651/296-6126. www.minnesotahistorycenter.org. Admission $8 adults, $6 seniors, $4 children 6–17, free for children under 6. Tues 10am–8pm; Wed–Sat 10am–5pm; Sun noon–5pm.

Minnesota Museum of American Art   The Twin Cities' only museum dedicated solely to American art, the MMAA has been around for over 30 years, but its new Riverfront Gallery, which opened in 2004, makes the museum feel new. Works range from the mid–19th century to the present with a special emphasis on Minnesota and regional artists. Frequent special exhibitions are popular and also focus on American and regional themes. Allow 1 hour.

50 Kellogg Blvd. W. (at Market St.), St. Paul. © 651/266-1030. www.mmaa.org. Free admission. Tues–Wed and Fri–Sat 11am–4pm; Thurs 11am–8pm; Sun 1–5pm.

Minnesota State Capitol   Built in 1905 on a hill overlooking downtown St. Paul, the capitol is crowned by the world's largest unsupported marble dome (modeled after the one Michelangelo created for St. Peter's Basilica in Rome). The interior is equally impressive, with its marble stairways, chambers, and halls, and its oil paintings. Allow 1 hour.

75 Rev. Dr. Martin Luther King Jr. Blvd., St. Paul. © 651/296-2881. www.mnhs.org/statecapitol. Free admission. Mon–Fri 9am–5pm; Sat 10am–4pm; Sun 1–4pm. Guided tours offered on the hour, last tour departs 1 hr. before closing.

Mississippi River Visitor Center   Located inside the entrance to the Science Museum of Minnesota (see below), the Mississippi River Visitor Center is operated by the National Park Service and designed to educate visitors about the Mississippi National River & Recreation Area. Park rangers can assist travelers with planning outdoor excursions, including canoe and riverboat trips, hiking, biking, and birding. If you're at all outdoorsy, it's worth a stop.

120 W. Kellogg Blvd., St. Paul. © 651/293-0200. www.mississippirivervisitorcenter.org. Free admission. Mon–Wed 9:30am–5pm; Thurs–Sat 9:30am–9pm; Sun noon–5pm. Extended hours during the summer.

Science Museum of Minnesota *Best*   Hands-on exhibits introduce visitors to natural history, science, and technology in this massive museum. Highlights include the Human Body Gallery, navigating a virtual towboat down the Mississippi River, and the dinosaur lab in the Hall of Paleontology. There's also an Omnitheater. Allow 2 to 3 hours.

120 W. Kellogg Blvd., St. Paul. © 651/221-9444. www.smm.org. Admission to exhibits $9.50 adults, $6.50 children. Omnitheater $7.50 adults, $5.50 children, free for children under 4. Combination tickets available. Mon–Wed 9:30am–5pm; Thurs–Sat 9:30am–9pm; Sun noon–5pm. Extended hours in summer.

MORE TO SEE & DO

ARCHITECTURAL HIGHLIGHTS   Minneapolis is quickly developing a reputation for attracting some of the most interesting architecture in the country. Jean Nouvel's new **Guthrie Theater,** 818 S. 2nd St., is a 2006 addition; its dark blue steel exterior is illuminated with visions of past productions. Other gems include Herzog and de Meuron's **Walker Art Center,** 1750 Hennepin; Cesar Pelli's **Minneapolis Central Library,** 300 Nicollet Mall; and Frank Gehry's Frederick R. Weisman Art Museum, 333 E. River Rd.

In St. Paul, don't miss a stroll down **Summit Avenue,** just west of St. Paul Cathedral, one of the finest collections of Victorian residential architecture in the nation. The area has been home to such authors as F. Scott Fitzgerald, Sinclair Lewis, and Garrison Keillor. Take a quiet stroll on your own, or join a guided walking tour. Tours depart from the James J. Hill House, 240 Summit Ave. (© **651/297-2555**).

PARKS   The **Eloise Butler Wildflower Garden and Bird Sanctuary,** inside Theodore Wirth Park at Glenwood Avenue (© **612/370-4903**), is the nation's oldest public wildflower garden, crisscrossed by hiking and bicycle trails. Guided tours are available. It's open April through October daily from 7:30am to sunset. **Minnehaha Park,** Minnehaha Parkway at Hiawatha Avenue (© **612/230-6400**), on the Mississippi, is the site of the famed Minnehaha Falls, the "laughing water" Longfellow celebrated in his poem *Song of Hiawatha.* Other attractions include 15 miles of jogging and bicycle trails, picnic facilities, and a historic frame house that was the first built west of the Mississippi. The park is open daily from 6am to 10pm. Information on both parks as well as dozens of others is available online at **www.minneapolisparks.org**.

St. Paul's **Como Park,** 1250 Kaufman Dr. (© **651/487-8200**), is one of the busiest and most beautiful parks in the Twin Cities, best known for its free zoo and its flower conservatory with a half-acre domed botanical garden. There's also a golf course, ski trails, and footpaths, as well as paddle boats, canoes, bikes, and skates for rent. It's open daily from 10am to 6pm April through September, from 10am to 4pm off season. St. Paul's **Landmark Plaza,** adjacent to the Landmark Center at 5th and Washington streets, is home to four bronze statues of the *Peanuts* comic book characters. The statues pay homage to hometown artist Charles Schulz.

BEST BETS FOR KIDS   **In Minneapolis**   The **Minnesota Zoo** (see above; © **952/431-9500**; www.mnzoo.com), in Apple Valley, houses more than 2,300 animals. The **Children's Theater Company,** 2400 3rd Ave. S. (© **612/874-0400**; www.childrens theatre.org), presents plays for all age groups in one of America's best regional theaters. The Mall of America (see below) houses **The Park at MOA** (© **952/883-8600;** www.theparkatmoa.com), the nation's largest indoor amusement park, **Underwater Adventures Aquarium** (© **888/348-3846;** www.sharky.tv), and **NASCAR** (© **952/854-7700**), an indoor race-car simulator, among other attractions.

In St. Paul   The **Minnesota Children's Museum,** 10 W. 7th St. (© **651/225-6000;** www.mcm.org), offers popular features such as papermaking, a music studio, and a Rooftop ArtPark scheduled to open in 2006. **Como Zoo,** 1250 Kaufman Dr. (© **651/487-8200**), inside Como Park, is Minnesota's only free zoo.

SHOPPING

Nicollet Mall, a pedestrian avenue in downtown Minneapolis, has Neiman Marcus, Macy's, and two malls, upscale **Gaviidae Common** and **City Center.** Hip galleries and antiques stores abound in the restored **Warehouse District,** north of Hennepin

The Mother of All Malls

The **Mall of America,** 60 E. Broadway, Bloomington (© **952/883-8800;** www. mallofamerica.com), the nation's largest shrine to consumerism, has everything—restaurants, major department stores such as Bloomingdale's and Nordstrom, more than 520 specialty stores and boutiques, movie theaters, nightclubs, bowling, even a NASCAR racing experience. **The Park at MOA** (formerly Camp Snoopy) is America's largest indoor theme park.

The mall is in Bloomington, about a 20-minute drive from the city center. Follow I-35W south to I-494 east, and exit onto 24th Ave. Follow the signs to the mall. To get here by public transportation, take the light rail service from the airport, Nicollet Mall, or a dozen other stops along the Hiawatha Line (Rte. 55) for $1.50 ($2 during rush hour). The mall is open Monday through Saturday from 10am to 9:30pm, and Sunday 11am to 7pm. During the summer months, the mall opens at 9:30am Saturdays. Hours for the restaurants, nightclubs, and theaters may vary.

between North 1st and 7th streets. **Uptown,** near Hennepin and Lake streets, is the place to find trendy shops and boutiques. In St. Paul, good shopping can be found all along **Grand Avenue,** just west of the downtown.

WHERE TO STAY

In addition to the choices listed below, you'll find many chain hotels near shopping malls (especially the Mall of America) and along I-494 in the suburbs.

Near the airport, the **Hilton Minneapolis/St. Paul Airport** (© **800/HILTONS** or 952/854-2100; www.hilton.com) offers extensive facilities and services, including free shuttle service to the airport and the Mall of America. Doubles begin at $100. Also near the airport are the **Courtyard Minneapolis Bloomington** (© **800/321-2211** or 952/876-0100; www.courtyard.com), with doubles from $99; and the **Embassy Suites Airport** (© **800/EMBASSY** or 952/854-1000; www.embassysuites.com), with doubles from $149.

IN MINNEAPOLIS

Doubletree Park Place   Located 3½ miles west of downtown, this hotel boasts a five-story pool atrium and reasonable rates outside the hubbub of the busy downtown area. The spacious guest rooms were designed with business travelers in mind, but are perfectly comfortable for leisure travelers as well.

1500 Park Place Blvd., Minneapolis, MN 55416. © **800/222-TREE** or 952/542-8600. Fax 612/542-8063. www.double tree.com. 297 units. $99–$229 double; $239–$304 suite. Children under 18 stay free in parent's room. AE, DC, DISC, MC, V. Free parking. Pets permitted with refundable $15 deposit. **Amenities:** Restaurants; indoor pool; fitness center.

Graves 601 Hotel *(Best*   Formerly a Le Meridien Art + Tech hotel, Graves 601 is widely thought to be the most stylish, sophisticated hotel in Minneapolis. This addition to Minneapolis's downtown hotel scene is designed to immerse guests in an environment marrying contemporary design and top-of-the-line technology. Amenities include custom, etched-glass headboards; modern artworks; in-room entertainment systems; Hermès toiletries; bathrobes; and 42-inch plasma TV screens.

601 First Ave. N., Minneapolis, MN 55403. (℃) 866/523-1100 or 612/677-1100. Fax 612/677-1200. www.graves601 hotel.com. 255 units. $179–$349 double; $454 suite. Children under 12 stay free in parent's room. AE, DC, MC, V. Valet parking $28; self-parking $18. **Amenities:** Restaurant; fitness room.

Minneapolis Marriott City Center   Conveniently located in the heart of downtown, this facility adjoins the three-story City Center shopping mall and is within walking distance of the Target Center and much of the city's nightlife. The hotel caters to the convention crowds and the rooms are standard business hotel issue. The staff is friendly and attentive.

30 S. 7th St. (between Hennepin and Nicollet), Minneapolis, MN 55402. (℃) 800/228-9290 or 612/349-4000. Fax 612/332-7165. www.marriott.com. 583 units. $139–$249 double; $159–$329 suite. Children under 18 stay free in parent's room. AE, DC, DISC, MC, V. Valet parking $25; self-parking $18. Pets permitted with refundable $75 deposit. **Amenities:** Restaurant; health club.

Nicollet Island Inn   Just across from the Mississippi River, this lovely inn was once an 1893 window shade and blind company; it was converted into an inn in the 1970s. The individually decorated rooms are furnished with offbeat originality. All rooms offer plasma TVs, free Wi-Fi, and freshly baked cookies, and some have Jacuzzis. The Nicollet Island Inn Restaurant is highly recommended (make a reservation), featuring contemporary American cuisine and a selection of over 350 wines; it also serves an excellent Sunday brunch ($30 adults, $12 children ages 6–12, free for children 5 and under). Ask about weekend B&B packages.

95 Merriam St., Minneapolis, MN 55401. (℃) 612/331-1800. Fax 612/331-6528. www.nicolletislandinn.com. 24 units. $200–$265 double. Children stay free in parent's room; rollaway beds $25. AE, DC, DISC, MC, V. Free parking. **Amenities:** Restaurant; smoking not permitted.

IN ST. PAUL

Best Western Kelly Inn (Value) (Kids)   This older, plain facility is a good bet for families on a tight budget—the affordable inn features basic but comfortable accommodations. All of the city's downtown attractions are less than a mile away and an indoor pool means there's always something fun to do, whatever the weather. Some rooms offer scenic views and some units have whirlpools.

161 St. Anthony Ave., St. Paul, MN 55103. (℃) 800/780-7234 or 651/227-8711. Fax 651/227-1698. www.bestwestern. com. 126 units. $89–$119 double. Children under 18 stay free in parent's room. AE, DC, DISC, MC, V. Free parking. Pets permitted. **Amenities:** Restaurant; indoor pool; health club.

Crowne Plaza St. Paul Riverfront Hotel   Formerly the Radisson Riverfront, a $9.2-million renovation has spruced up this hotel considerably. Its terrific downtown location, views over the Mississippi River, and the Twin Cities' only revolving restaurant remain unchanged. The St. Paul RiverCentre convention center adjoins the hotel, making it popular with business travelers and conventions. It's also an easy walk to the Science Museum of Minnesota and the Mississippi River Visitor Center for those more interested in leisure pursuits.

11 E. Kellogg Blvd., St. Paul, MN 55101. (℃) 877/227-6963 or 651/292-1900. Fax 651/605-6966. www.ichotelsgroup. com. 489 units. $129–$219 double; $299–$355 suite. Children under 18 stay free in parent's room. AE, DC, DISC, MC, V. Self-parking $13. **Amenities:** 2 restaurants; indoor pool; fitness center.

Saint Paul Hotel (Best)   This beautiful, exquisitely decorated hotel, housed in a 1910 building, makes for a great romantic getaway. The historic property has welcomed many a famous guest over the years, including Calvin Coolidge and Ma Barker. A number of rooms offer great views; all are decorated in elegant European style and feature

Aveda toiletries. The hotel is famous for its afternoon tea and the landmark St. Paul Grill (see "Where to Dine," below).

350 Market St. (at 5th St.), St. Paul, MN 55102. ℂ 800/292-9292 or 651/292-9292. Fax 651/228-9506. www.stpaul hotel.com. 254 units. $149–$299 double; $349–$389 suite. Discount packages available. AE, DC, DISC, MC, V. Parking $18. **Amenities:** 2 restaurants; fitness center.

WHERE TO DINE
IN MINNEAPOLIS

Café Lurcat AMERICAN   Café Lurcat makes its home in a restored urban building just off Loring Park. A hip crowd dines and passes the time here, perhaps before or after an event at the nearby Walker Art Center. A simple but stylish decor pairs beautifully with the restaurant's simple but sophisticated menu that includes apple, cheese, and chive salad; prime rib with béarnaise; and sea bass marinated in miso. The adjoining Bar Lurcat offers a variety of small plates, a 200-bottle wine list, and eclectic live music every evening ($5 cover on weekends).

1624 Harmon Place on Loring Park. ℂ 612/486-5500. www.cafelurcat.com. Reservations recommended. Main courses $20–$35. AE, DISC, MC, V. Cafe Sun–Thurs 5–10pm; Fri–Sat 5–11pm. Bar Sun–Thurs 4:30pm–midnight; Fri–Sat 4:30pm–1am.

D'Amico Cucina ITALIAN   The perfect restaurant for a romantic dinner out, this beautifully appointed restaurant has a distinctive atmosphere, enhanced by warm golden hues, whitewashed wood beams, and French doors. One hundred fifty Italian wines complement the menu's Italian dishes, including house-made ravioli with black truffle butter; and grilled pork loin chop with figs and Gorgonzola polenta.

100 N. 6th St. (in Butler Sq.). ℂ 612/338-2401. www.damico.com. Reservations recommended. Main courses $25–$36. AE, DC, DISC, MC, V. Mon–Thurs 5:30–9pm; Fri–Sat 5:30–10pm.

Chino Latino ASIAN/LATIN   If it's hot, Chino Latino serves it. This restaurant's menu spotlights the spicy cuisines of the world, from Thai coconut shrimp curry to Montego Bay jerked chicken to Argentine tenderloin steaks. You'll also find small plate servings and sizable sushi, taco, and satay selections. Cool your palate with one of three dozen tequilas; a creative martini; sake; or a "hot zone" beer from Cuba, Kenya, India, or Thailand

2916 Hennepin Ave. S. ℂ 612/824-7878. www.chinolatino.com. Reservations recommended. Main courses $13–$39. AE, DC, DISC, MC, V. Mon–Thurs 4:30pm–1am; Fri–Sat 4:30pm–2am.

Goodfellow's 🅑ₑₛₜ AMERICAN   This Art Deco–inspired restaurant serves an American menu amid a polished ambience with impressive table settings. The menu changes seasonally. All pastas, breads, stocks, and pastries are made from scratch, and the extensive wine list—consistently honored by *Wine Spectator*—highlights American vintages.

City Center, 40 S. 7th St. ℂ 612/332-4800. www.restaurant.com/goodfellows. Reservations recommended. Main courses $30–$45. AE, DC, DISC, MC, V. Mon–Fri 11:30am–1:30pm; Mon–Thurs 5:30–9pm; Fri–Sat 5:30–10pm.

Hell's Kitchen AMERICAN   Inventive breakfast and lunch entrees make for very long lines at this popular downtown restaurant. The restaurant's signature breakfast dishes include lemon ricotta hotcakes and Minnesota wild rice porridge with dried blueberries, cranberries, and hazelnuts. Lighter offerings include homemade lemon yogurt with fresh berries and breakfast bruschetta, topped with homemade lemon oil, mascarpone cheese, and berries. Breakfast is served up until closing time, as well as lunchtime sandwiches, soups, and salads.

89 S. 10th St. just off Nicollet Mall. ℂ 612/332-4700. www.HellsKitchenInc.com. Reservations recommended Sat–Sun. Main courses $10–$17. MC, V. Mon–Fri 6:30am–2pm; Sat–Sun 8am–2pm.

Murray's AMERICAN   Since 1946, this classy establishment has delighted guests with steaks so tender they were awarded the "Silver Butter Knife" award. (You'll recognize it by the old neon sign out front.) The equally impressive wine list features over 500 wines. Located in the heart of downtown, Murray's is also known for its strolling violinist and is a good spot for a romantic dinner.

26 S. 6th St. ℂ 612/339-0909. www.murraysrestaurant.com. Reservations required Fri–Sat. Main courses $20–$45. AE, DC, DISC, MC, V. Mon–Fri 11am–2pm and 5–10:30pm; Sat–Sun 5–10:30pm.

The News Room AMERICAN   Here's an original if somewhat manic spin on the traditional theme restaurant: This one's newspaper-themed, with each dining room dedicated to a different section of the paper, such as Sports (catch the hottest game on multiple screens) or Entertainment (films play on wall monitors). The decor is wild and definitely memorable. The food—the lineup features American standards with the occasional twist—is not precisely headline-worthy; the atmosphere's the attraction. There's a deli area for quick lunches, and a full ship-themed bar for after-dinner or after-theater drinks. Go ahead and indulge your inner Deep Throat.

990 Nicollet Mall (at 10th St.). ℂ 612/343-0073. Main courses $11–$26. AE, DC, DISC, MC, V. Daily 11am–1am.

Solera SPANISH   This chic Spanish-inspired restaurant offers over 40 hot and cold tapas—small, savory samplings that encourage guests to try a little of several dishes—and one of the largest sherry menus you've ever seen. Located in the heart of the theater district, the restaurant features an interior as appealing as its food, with mosaic tiles and colorful art glass fixtures. There's an actual dining room and a tapas bar (used mainly after the dining room closes), but both serve the same menu.

900 Hennepin Ave. ℂ 612/338-0062. www.solera-restaurant.com. Tapas $3–$9. AE, MC, V. Dining room Sun–Thurs 5–10pm; Fri–Sat 5–11pm. Tapas bar Sun 5–11pm; Mon–Thurs 4pm–1am; Fri 4pm–2am; Sat 5pm–2am.

IN ST. PAUL

A Rebours FRENCH   This upscale eatery has all the look of a modern French bistro—zinc bar, high ceilings, tile floors, lots of mirrors and wood. The restaurant's personality changes with the time of day: Business execs lunch at midday; pre- and postdinner guests add an air of elegance; and by evening, the crowd becomes younger, hipper, and louder. Entrees range from tempura-fried soft-shell crab with vanilla and tomato; to cocoa-dusted duck with fig sauce; to the heavier, classic lamb cassoulet.

410 St. Peter St. ℂ 651/665-0656. Main courses $18–$30. MC, V. Sun–Thurs 7:30am–10pm; Fri–Sat 7:30am–10pm.

Cossetta's Italian Market & Pizzeria ITALIAN   This enterprise began in 1911 as an Italian market; later it expanded to include this simple, fun, and charming restaurant. Food is served deli-style in a noisy atmosphere reminiscent of an Italian grandmother's house. The menu features great traditional dishes such as eggplant parmigiana and mostaccioli, but Cossetta's is most famous for its award-winning pizza, which is served by the very-large slice.

211 W. 7th St. (between Kellogg Blvd. and Chestnut). ℂ 651/222-3476. Main courses $8–$16. MC, V. Mon–Thurs 11am–9pm; Fri–Sat 11am–10pm; Sun 11am–8pm.

Great Waters Brewing Co. AMERICAN   This restaurant is known for its beers, of course, including cask-conditioned ales (common in Britain, rare in the U.S.) as well as the standard pilsners and IPAs. Five homemade beer selections are offered daily. Great Waters' menu gives reason to visit for more than just a drink. In addition to the traditional pub fare, you'll find interesting sandwiches (try the brie and green apple grilled chicken) and dinners, such as the London broil or pasta.

426 St. Peter St. (✆ 651/224-BREW. www.greatwatersbc.com. Main courses $9–$20. MC, V. Mon–Sat 11am–1am; Sun noon–midnight.

St. Paul Grill (Best) AMERICAN This multiple-award-winner is popular with pretheater diners and is the top choice in town for adults seeking an upscale night out. The elegant interior is enhanced by views of the hotel's lovely English garden and nearby Rice Park; the atmosphere is sophisticated but not stuffy. Juicy steaks, bourbon grilled pork chops, and excellent pastas top a stellar menu. The award-winning bar features a huge collection of single-malt scotches and martinis, as well as a *Wine Spectator*-honored wine list.

In the Saint Paul Hotel, 350 Market St. (✆ 651/224-7455. www.stpaulgrill.com. Reservations recommended. Main courses $16–$45. MC, V. Daily 11am–2pm; Sun–Mon 5–10pm, Tues–Sat 5–11pm.

W.A. Frost & Co. AMERICAN Since 1975, W.A. Frost has served dinner in the shadow of the state capitol's historic Cathedral Hill district. The restaurant's patio is popular during the summer; in cool weather months fireplaces warm guests in a Victorian-style dining area. W.A. Frost prides itself in serving dishes prepared with locally grown produce and artisanal cheeses whenever possible; most of the menu is prepared with organic ingredients. Entrees include grilled Atlantic salmon with crème fraîche and cardamom-glazed duck breast with potato gratin and blackberry sauce. The wine list includes over 900 labels, and vintages throughout the world.

374 Selby Ave. (✆ 651/224-5715. www.wafrost.com. Reservations recommended. Main courses $18–$38. AE, DC, DISC, MC, V. Mon–Sat 11:15am–1:30pm, Sun 10:30am–2pm; Mon–Thurs 5:30–10pm, Fri–Sat 5–11pm, Sun 5–10pm.

THE TWIN CITIES AFTER DARK

The best place to find out what's happening in the Twin Cities is the free newsweekly *City Pages*, which lists all events. Other good sources of information are the local papers (*Star Tribune* and *St. Paul Pioneer Press*), the calendar in *Minneapolis–St. Paul* magazine, and the monthly *Twin Cities Directory*. On the Web, check out **www.minneapolis.org** or **www.stpaulcvb.org** for the most up-to-date information.

THE PERFORMING ARTS There are more theater seats per capita in Minneapolis than anywhere outside New York City. The famous **Guthrie Theater,** 818 S. 2nd St. (✆ 877/44-STAGE or 612/377-2224; www.guthrietheater.org), is one of the nation's premier classical repertory companies and opened its new architecturally stunning venue on the Mississippi in 2006. **Théâtre de la Jeune Lune,** 105 N. 1st St. (✆ 612/333-6200; www.jeunelune.org), in the Warehouse District, is a strong and innovative acting company with a varied performance repertoire. Three historic, renovated theaters, **State,** 805 Hennepin (✆ 612/339-7007), **Orpheum,** 910 Hennepin (✆ 612/339-7007), and **Pantages,** 710 Hennepin (✆ 612/339-7007), feature a variety of entertainment, from pop music to comedy to adult and children's theater. Information for all three can be found at **www.hennepintheatredistrict.org**. The **Children's Theater Company,** 2400 3rd Ave. S. (✆ 612/874-0400; www.childrens theatre.org), presents plays for all age groups in one of America's best regional theaters.

For more than 20 years, **Orchestra Hall,** 1111 Nicollet Mall (✆ 800/292-4141 or 612/371-5656; www.minnesotaorchestra.org), has been home to the internationally acclaimed **Minnesota Orchestra.**

In St. Paul, the **Schubert Club,** 302 Landmark Center (© **651/292-3268;** www. schubert.org), brings celebrated artists to perform, provides music lessons, and commissions new works. The **St. Paul Chamber Orchestra** (© **651/291-1144;** www.the spco.org) makes its home in the **Ordway Center for the Performing Arts,** 345 Washington St. (© **651/224-4222;** www.ordway.org). Opera, recitals, pop and classical concerts, and dance are also presented here. **Fitzgerald Theater,** 10 E. Exchange St. (© **651/290-1221;** http://fitzgeraldtheater.publicradio.org), has been home to Garrison Keillor's wildly popular radio show, *A Prairie Home Companion,* for 25 years. Touring companies also perform in this lovely restored historic building.

THE CLUB & MUSIC SCENE The **Warehouse District** has always been considered the heart of Minneapolis nightlife, but **Block E,** bordered by 6th and 7th streets and by Hennepin and 1st avenues, has its fair share of dining and dancing. **First Avenue,** 701 1st Ave. N. (© **612/338-8388;** www.first-avenue.com), is where Prince got his start (*Purple Rain* was filmed here). Connected to it is **7th Street Entry,** a small, loud venue for local music. **Empire,** 319 1st Ave. N. (© **612/659-9192**), is an upscale gay-friendly dance club, but straights won't feel out of place. The interior is Cuban-inspired, and offers a good mix of techno and pop.

For interesting music and great food to boot, try **Martini Blu,** 615 2nd Ave. S. (© **612/752-9595;** www.martiniblu.com). The elegant nightclub is furnished with blue glass, brushed stainless steel, and lacquered black tables. Expect European dance music as well as dining—sushi, pasta, steaks, hors d'oeuvres, and martinis. **Babalú,** 800 Washington Ave. N. (© **612/746-3158;** www.babalu.us), serves up Latin American and Spanish music (think bossa nova, Afro-Cuban jazz, flamenco) and food along with a classy, pre-Castro Cuban decor. Cuban entrees are available, as are over 70 rums.

St. Paul has a big Irish neighborhood, and many Irish bars and clubs. **Chang O'Hara's Bistro,** 498 Selby Ave. (© **651/290-2338**), is a bar/restaurant popular with the locals. There's live music almost every night, including jazz and blues. **Great Waters Brewing Co.,** 426 St. Peter St. (see "Where to Dine," above), specializes in crafting the best English ales in the Twin Cities, and in the summer, its outdoor patio is the place to be.

8 Kansas City

Established as a trading post in 1821, Kansas City served as the starting point for wagon trains heading over the Santa Fe, California, and Oregon trails and later emerged as the nation's center for cattle stockyards and slaughterhouses. Today, greater Kansas City is a sprawling metropolis of 1.8 million straddling the Kansas-Missouri state line. Yet it retains something of a small-town atmosphere, with tree-lined boulevards, bubbling fountains, and a large number of parks spread over gently rolling hills. Need further incentive to visit? Kansas City is famous for its steaks, barbecue, jazz, rich frontier history, and unique attractions.

ESSENTIALS

GETTING THERE By Plane Kansas City International Airport (© **816/243-5237;** www.flykci.com) is 25 minutes northwest of downtown. **KCI Shuttle buses** (© **816/243-5000;** www.kctg.com) service more than 50 hotels for $16 (downtown) to $55 (outlying suburbs) one-way. The average taxi fare to downtown is $45. **The Metro bus no. 129** travels weekdays between the airport and downtown (10th & Main Transit Plaza) for $1.25 (© **816/221-0660;** www.kcata.org).

By Train Amtrak (𝄇 **800/USA-RAIL;** www.amtrak.com) provides daily service from Chicago (trip time: 8 hr.) and St. Louis (trip time: 5½ hr.) to Kansas City's historic Union Station at 30 W. Pershing Rd. (𝄇 **816/842-4409**). Take a taxi from the station to your hotel.

By Car Major routes into Kansas City are **I-70** from the east (St. Louis) and west (Denver); **I-35** from the north (Des Moines) and southwest (Wichita); and **I-29** from the northwest (Omaha).

VISITOR INFORMATION The **Kansas City Convention and Visitors Association** is downtown at City Center Square, 1100 Main St., Suite 2200, Kansas City, MO 64105 (𝄇 **800/767-7700** or 816/221-5242; www.visitkc.com), open Monday through Friday from 8:30am to 5pm. More convenient are the Visitor Information Centers at Country Club Plaza, 4709 Central, open Monday through Saturday from 10am to 6pm and Sunday from noon to 5pm; and at Union Station, Main and Pershing, open Monday to Saturday 9:30am to 5:30pm.

GETTING AROUND A car is extremely useful in Kansas City; although the downtown is compact, attractions are located throughout the city. Main Street connects to many city attractions. Despite its name, **The Metro** (𝄇 **816/221-0660;** www.kcata.org) is the city's public bus system, with many buses departing from downtown's 10th & Main Transit Plaza. Most convenient for sightseeing is the **MAX** (Metro Area Express), which runs daily 5am to 1am from City Market to Country Club Plaza and stops at downtown, the Crossroads Arts District, Union Station, Crown Center, and Westport. Fares start at $1.25; a day pass costs $3.

FAST FACTS For physician referrals and walk-in urgent care facilities in Kansas City, call 𝄇 **816/751-3751.** A major hospital is **Saint Luke's Hospital,** 4400 Wornall Rd. (𝄇 **816/932-2000**). **Walgreens** is a 24-hour pharmacy located at 39th Street and Broadway (𝄇 **816/561-6980**). Sales tax is 6%; the hotel tax is 7.5%.

SPECIAL EVENTS Around since 1899, the **American Royal** celebration in October or November (𝄇 **816/221-9800;** www.americanroyal.com) features a livestock show, parades, horse shows, a rodeo, big-name entertainment, and the world's largest barbecue competition. The **Kansas Speedway** (𝄇 **913/328-3300;** www.kansasspeedway.com) attracts NASCAR fans with races several times a year.

WHAT TO SEE & DO

Downtown Kansas City, a blend of Art Deco buildings, brick warehouses dating from the 1880s, and modern skyscrapers, is also home to the new **Power & Light District,** a 9-square-block development of shopping, dining, and entertainment venues.

In addition to the attractions listed in this section, baseball fans will be treated to one of the world's largest video boards if the home team **Kansas City Royals** are playing at Kauffman Stadium, I-70 and Blue Ridge Cut-off (𝄇 **816/921-8000;** www.kc royals.com).

Arabia Steamboat Museum This cargo steamboat, laden with 220 tons of merchandise destined for settlers out west, sank in the Missouri River in 1856, where it remained preserved in cold mud until it was excavated in the 1980s. A virtual time capsule of the 1850s and one of the best collections of pre–Civil War artifacts in the world, the museum provides a fascinating look at frontier life, with displays of the steamboat's cargo, from china and hardware to jewelry and leather boots (900 shoes

ACCOMMODATIONS ■
Hilton President Kansas City 4
Hotel Phillips 3
Westin Crown Center 7

DINING ◆
American Restaurant 8
Arthur Bryant's 5
Golden Ox 1
Lidia's 6
Savoy Grill 2

and boots alone are on display). Tours begin with a film of the excavation and restoration of parts of the boat (which are now on display); plan on 1½ hours here.

400 Grand Ave., City Market. (©) **816/471-1856.** www.1856.com. Admission $13 adults, $12 seniors, $4.75 children 4–12. Mon–Sat 10am–4pm (last tour); Sun noon–3:30pm (last tour).

Negro Leagues Baseball Museum/American Jazz Museum These two unique museums, housed under one roof, are in the historic 18th and Vine Jazz District. The Negro Leagues Baseball Museum tells the compelling story of segregated baseball, from the founding of the Negro National League just a few blocks away in 1920, until Jackie Robinson, who played for the Kansas City Monarchs, signed with the Brooklyn Dodgers in 1947. The Jazz Museum pays tribute to jazz greats ranging from Louis Armstrong and Duke Ellington to Ella Fitzgerald and Charlie Parker, with listening stations throughout. Be sure to see the gallery with changing exhibits relating to jazz, baseball, and African-American life, as well as the film in the visitor center highlighting the golden days of the 1930s, when this very district boasted more than 60 jazz clubs and served as the commercial heart of Kansas City's African-American community. The Blue Room, attached to the complex, stages jazz concerts with local musicians 4 nights a week; historic Gem Theater across the street features national acts. Plan on 2 hours here.

18th and Vine. © **816/221-1920** and www.nlbm.com for Baseball Museum; © **816/474-8463** and www.american jazzmuseum.org for Jazz Museum. Admission to either $6 adults, $2.50 children under 12; combination ticket to both $8 adults, $4 children. Both museums Tues–Sat 9am–6pm; Sun noon–6pm.

Nelson-Atkins Museum of Art (*Best*)   Kansas City's premier museum, undergoing massive expansion that will increase its size by 71% upon completion in mid-2007, is especially noted for its Asian art, including Tang dynasty bowls and Ming dynasty furniture; an outdoor sculpture garden with the largest U.S. collection of bronzes by Henry Moore; one of the country's largest collections of American photography; the largest public collection of works by Missouri native Thomas Hart Benton; a collection of 17th- and 18th-century European paintings; Impressionist and post-Impressionist pieces; and American art. The museum includes works by Caravaggio, Titian, Rembrandt, Renoir, Monet, Picasso, Gauguin, van Gogh, Andy Warhol, and Willem

---

(*Kids*) **Best Bets for Kids**

Kansas City's most centrally located attraction for kids is **Science City,** in the restored 1914 Union Station, cater-cornered from Crown Center at 30 Pershing Rd. (© **816/460-2020;** www.sciencecity.com). At this multilevel, interactive museum, open daily, kids can create a personal newspaper front page, anchor a TV news program, bicycle across a tightrope, train as an astronaut, solve a crime, play minigolf, take a tour through the human body, dig for fossils, explore Kansas City's history, view the stars at a planetarium, catch a movie in a five-story theater, climb aboard vintage trains at the KC Rail Experience exhibit, and more. Admission to everything is $14 (children 3 and under are free).

For outdoor fun, there's the 175-acre theme park **Worlds of Fun,** I-435 and Parvin Road (© **816/454-4545;** www.worldsoffun.com), open daily in summer and weekends in April, May, September, and October, with six roller coasters, including the Patriot, the longest, tallest, and fastest full-circuit inverted roller coaster in the Midwest; dozens of other thrill rides like the tumble-and-spin Thunderhawk; and Camp Snoopy for younger kids, featuring attractions based on the comic strip. Admission is $37 adults, $9.95 children under 48 inches and seniors. Next door is Worlds of Fun's water-themed counterpart, the 60-acre **Oceans of Fun** (same contact information as Worlds of Fun, above), open June through August and featuring 18 water slides and various pools (including a wave pool). Admission costs $26 adults, $9.95 children under 48 inches and seniors. Discounts are provided for combined passes and evening admission.

The revitalized **Kansas City Zoo,** at I-435 and 63rd St. in Swope Park (© **816/513-5700;** www.kansascityzoo.org), is open year-round and features animals of Australia, Africa, and more in their natural habitats, as well as the Sprint IMAX Theater. Admission to the zoo and IMAX during high season costs $14 adults, $8 children 3 to 11; on Tuesday, zoo-only admission costs $5 for all.

A Side Trip to Independence

For more about Kansas City area history, visit the town of **Independence** (📞 800/748-7323; www.visitindependence.com), a 20-minute drive east, with its **Harry S. Truman Home National Historic Site,** 219 N. Delaware, which remains virtually unchanged since the Trumans lived here (tickets sold at the Truman Home Ticket & Information Center, Truman and Main sts.; 📞 816/254-9929; www.nps.gov/hstr); the **Truman Presidential Museum & Library,** U.S. 24 and Delaware (📞 816/268-8200; www.trumanlibrary.org), with objects from Truman's presidency, including gifts from foreign heads of state and a reproduction of the Oval Office; the **National Frontier Trails Center,** 318 W. Pacific (📞 816/325-7575; www.frontiertrailsmuseum.org), an excellent museum documenting the Santa Fe, Oregon, and California trails; and the **Bingham-Waggoner Estate,** 313 W. Pacific (📞 816/461-3491; www.bwestate.org), a 22-room, 1885 mansion and former home of Missouri artist George Caleb Bingham that's open April to October.

de Kooning. The airy Rozelle Court Restaurant has extended dinner hours on Friday, with live jazz. Plan on 2 hours or more here.

4525 Oak St. (just east of Country Club Plaza). 📞 816/751-1278. www.nelson-atkins.org. Free admission (special exhibitions cost extra). Tues–Thurs 10am–4pm; Fri 10am–9pm; Sat 10am–5pm; Sun noon–5pm.

Liberty Memorial Museum and Monument   The nation's only public museum and memorial dedicated to World War I features the 217-foot-tall Memorial Tower, which opened in 1926 and offers great views of downtown Kansas City from its top, and a newly completed museum which documents the "Great War" with interactive displays and the largest collection of World War I artifacts in the United States, including photographs, weaponry, uniforms, and letters from the field. Exhibits document the history of the war, including the events leading up to it, U.S. involvement, and new weapons and tactics.

100 W. 26th St. 📞 816/784-1918. www.libertymemorialmuseum.org. Admission $5 adults, $3.50 seniors and children 6–11. Tues–Sun 10am–5pm.

Toy and Miniature Museum _Kids_   Occupying a 1911 mansion, this 33-room museum houses an extensive collection of antique dolls, more than 100 furnished dollhouses, marbles, and toys ranging from model trains to games, as well as perfect scale miniatures of houses, rooms, and furniture. The miniatures are fully functional—scissors cut, clocks run, and musical instruments can be played, making it a fascinating experience for adults and kids alike. You can easily spend an hour or more here.

5235 Oak St. (southeast of Country Club Plaza). 📞 816/333-9328. www.umkc.edu/tmm. Admission $6 adults, $5 seniors and students, $4 children 5–12. Wed–Sat 10am–4pm; Sun 1–4pm. Closed holidays and part of Sept (check website for specific dates).

SHOPPING

Kansas City's premier shopping district (and the country's first suburban shopping center) is **Country Club Plaza,** centered around 47th Street and Ward Parkway (📞 816/753-0100; www.countryclubplaza.com). Built in 1922 to resemble a Spanish marketplace, it's a tree-lined, 15-square-block area with more than 150 shops, restaurants, and nightspots. **Crown Center,** 2450 Grand Ave. (📞 816/274-8444;

www.crowncenter.com), is an 85-acre business and residential complex owned by the world's largest greeting-card company, Hallmark. It contains specialty shops, restaurants, hotels, theaters, and the free Hallmark Visitor Center (closed Sun–Mon), which chronicles 95 years of history with displays of Keepsake Ornaments and other Hallmark products and memorabilia, educational exhibits, and excerpts from Hallmark Hall of Fame television movies. Just northwest of Crown Center is the **Crossroads Arts District (www.kccrossroads.org),** where First Friday lures an artsy crowd to more than 60 galleries and shops the first Friday evening of every month.

City Market, at 5th and Main streets north of downtown and I-70 (© **816/842-1271;** www.kc-citymarket.com), is an outdoor market in operation since the 1850s. It's busiest on Saturday, when 150 vendors offer everything from vegetables and flowers to live chickens and T-shirts, but there are also permanent indoor specialty shops, international groceries, and restaurants occupying an Art Deco building. **Cabela's,** at the intersection of interstates 70 and 435 (© **913/328-0322;** www.cabelas.com), is Kansas's top shopping attraction for its eye-popping wildlife displays and massive showrooms of outdoor equipment. It's located in a new leisure district west of Kansas City that includes the Kansas Speedway, Great Wolf Lodge, and The Legends at Village West, an outdoor shopping and entertainment center.

WHERE TO STAY

In addition to the choices below, consider **Embassy Suites,** conveniently located between Westport and Country Club Plaza at 220 W. 43rd St. (© **800/EMBASSY** or 816/756-1720; www.embassysuites.com). A hit with families, it offers two-room suites with kitchenette, free breakfasts, a nightly cocktail hour, and an indoor pool.

The Elms Resort & Spa *Value*   The Kansas City area's only full-service resort and spa occupies a historic 1912 limestone hotel situated on 16 landscaped acres, about a 30-minute drive from downtown and the airport. Its holistic spa and wellness center offers body and beauty treatments, including Swiss and Vichy showers; mud, seaweed, and aloe body wraps; mineral baths; hydrotherapy; massage (including reflexology and couples massage); and more. Rooms are basic, but the historic lobby, extensive recreational offerings (including an indoor swim track, banked jogging track, hiking and biking trails, badminton, horseshoes, and volleyball), its parklike setting, and rustic grandeur make this a top-choice restorative getaway.

401 Regent St., Excelsior Springs, MO 64024. © **800/843-3567** or 816/630-5500. Fax 816/630-5380. www.elms resort.com. 153 units. Summer $115–$160 double, $165–$250 suite; winter $95–$135 double, $145–$225 suite. Extra person $10. Children under 18 stay free in parent's room. Spa packages available. AE, DC, MC, V. Free outdoor parking. Pets permitted for $50 fee. **Amenities:** 2 restaurants; 2 pools (1 indoor); spa; health club. *In room:* Fridge.

Great Wolf Lodge *Kids*   Geared toward families with its massive indoor/outdoor waterpark (free for hotel guests), huge game arcade, children's activity room, and laundry facilities, this woods-themed lodge combines the adventure of a rustic retreat with the comfort of an upscale hotel. From the moment guests walk into the four-story grand lobby with its overstuffed sofas, huge stone fireplace, and animated clock tower that captivates wee ones, this hotel aims for the "wow" factor. Seven styles of suites, all with patio or balcony and sleeping four to eight persons, are available, including Kid-Cabin Suites that feature a "log cabin" complete with bunk beds. Some suites also have fireplaces and whirlpools.

10401 Cabela Dr. (in Village West at interstates 70 and 435), Kansas City, KS 66111. © **800/608-9653** or 913/299-7001. Fax 913/299-7002. www.greatwolflodge.com. 281 units. $259–$399 suite. Rates include admission to waterpark.

2-night minimum stay required peak periods and some weekends and holidays. Off-season rates available. AE, DC, MC, V. Free outdoor parking. **Amenities:** Restaurant; waterpark; exercise room; spa; smoking not permitted. *In room:* Fridge, microwave.

Hilton President Kansas City

Houdini stayed at the President; Frank Sinatra, Benny Goodman, and Patsy Kline all performed here. But then the 1926 historic landmark shut down and remained empty for 25 years, reopening in 2006 in a prime spot next to the new Power & Light District. It's been restored to its former grandeur, with a stately lobby that closely matches its 1941 former self; the impressive, high-ceilinged Walnut Room offering fine dining; the historic Drum Room offering dinner and entertainment; and comfortable guest rooms adorned with black-and-white photographs of Kansas City. With its history-evoking setting, great location, and lively past, it's a good choice for celebratory occasions.

1329 Baltimore, Kansas City, MO 64105. © **800/433-1426** or 816/221-9490. Fax 816/221-9422. www.president kansascity.hilton.com. 213 units. $279 double; $329–$369 suite. Children under 18 stay free in parent's room. AE, DC, MC, V. Free outdoor parking. **Amenities:** 2 restaurants; fitness room.

Hotel Phillips (*Best*)

Built in 1931 and exalting the Art Deco style (it's listed on the National Register of Historic Places), this classic yet hip downtown boutique hotel has been updated but retains its original woodwork, marble, lighting, and fixtures—including an 11-foot-tall gilded goddess overlooking the lobby. Rooms rise above the ordinary with a mix of contemporary furnishings and vintage touches such as plaster molding on the ceilings. If you opt for a standard room, request a brighter, corner room. The hotel is geared toward business travelers, but its historic charm and downtown location make it a good bet for couples as well.

106 W. 12th St., Kansas City, MO 64105. © **800/433-1426** or 816/221-7000. Fax 816/221-3477. www.hotelphillips. com. 217 units. $109–$249 double. Children under 18 stay free in parent's room. AE, DC, MC, V. Valet parking $15. **Amenities:** 2 restaurants; fitness room.

The Quarterage Hotel Westport (*Value*)

Near Westport's nightlife but far enough away for a good night's sleep, this modest but well-kept locally owned hotel, decorated with copies of Thomas Hart Benton's works, offers small, spotless, comfortable rooms, plus extras such as free local phone calls, a computer with free Internet access, a warm buffet breakfast, an evening cocktail hour (Mon–Sat), and free shuttle service within a 5-mile radius. VIP rooms toss in minifridges and sofa beds.

560 Westport Rd., Kansas City, MO 64111. © **800/942-4433** or 816/931-0001. Fax 816/931-8891. www.quarterage hotel.com. 123 units. $99–$139 double. Children under 17 stay free in parent's room. Rates include buffet breakfast. AE, DC, MC, V. Free outdoor parking. **Amenities:** Sauna and whirlpool; free access to nearby health club.

The Raphael

Overlooking Country Club Plaza with its many shops and restaurants, this intimate, European-style hotel occupies a converted 1927 brick apartment house. Though not as grand as Kansas City's downtown historic hotels, it has a cozy ambience that attracts many repeat guests. Standard rooms vary in size; those facing the back are larger, but preferable are the suites or one of the smaller rooms with views of the plaza.

325 Ward Pkwy., Kansas City, MO 64112. © **800/821-5343** or 816/756-3800. Fax 816/802-2131. www.raphaelkc.com. 123 units. $149–$169 double; $199–$279 suite. Extra person $20. Children under 18 stay free in parent's room. Weekend packages available. AE, DC, MC, V. Free valet parking. **Amenities:** Restaurant. *In room:* Fridge.

Southmoreland on the Plaza

This is a gem of a bed-and-breakfast, located in a 1913 Colonial Revival mansion in a peaceful residential area near the Nelson-Atkins

Museum of Art and Country Club Plaza. The B&B offers well-appointed, themed rooms named after famous Kansas Citians and equipped with one of three extras: a fireplace, Jacuzzi, or outdoor deck—a suite in a carriage house is equipped with all three. Rates include afternoon complimentary wine and appetizers, evening hot beverages and sweets, and gourmet breakfast served in an enclosed veranda or on an outdoor deck. Televisions are available in rooms during the week but are removed on weekends; there are TVs in some of the common rooms along with videos.

116 E. 46th St., Kansas City, MO 64112. (C) **816/531-7979.** Fax 816/531-2407. www.southmoreland.com. 13 units. $135–$250 double. Rates include breakfast. AE, MC, V. Free outdoor parking. No children under 13. **Amenities:** Free access to 2 nearby fitness centers; smoking not permitted. *In room:* No TV on weekends.

Westin Crown Center Connected to the Crown Center with its many shops and restaurants and via walkway to Union Station with its Science City, the Westin incorporates a limestone bluff with a rock garden and 60-foot waterfall in its multilevel lobby. Rooms are endowed with all the comforts, including the Westin's trademark Heavenly Beds (with 250-count sheets and down comforters), tiny balconies, and, on the north side, great views of downtown. The hotel's central location, facilities that include a jogging track and basketball court, and special Heavenly Dog Beds complete with dog dishes, make this a popular choice for families, dog owners, and groups.

One Pershing Rd., Kansas City, MO 64108. (C) **800/WESTIN-1** or 816/474-4400. Fax 816/391-4438. www.westin. com/crowncenter. 729 units. $299 double; from $350 suite. Extra person $25. Children under 16 stay free in parent's room. Packages available. AE, DC, MC, V. Valet parking $16; self-parking $13. Dogs (only under 40 lb.) stay free. **Amenities:** 2 restaurants; heated pool; 2 lighted outdoor tennis courts; health club ($5 usage fee). *In room:* Fridge.

WHERE TO DINE

Kansas City is known for steak and barbecue, but there are plenty of other cuisine possibilities downtown, in Country Club Plaza, and in Westport.

American Restaurant *Best* NEW AMERICAN One of Kansas City's top fine-dining establishments for more than 32 years, this contemporary, high-ceilinged, glass-enclosed restaurant features the best in regional fare (favorite recipes are provided on its website), offers one of the city's most extensive wine lists, and has good views of the downtown skyline. The changing dinner menu offers fixed-price meals with entrees such as grilled Black Angus filet with herbed potato croquette or Hawaiian butterfish with miso soup and crispy shiitake mushrooms. With its gorgeous setting and polished staff, this is a great choice for a celebration.

In Crown Center, 25th and Grand Blvd. (C) 816/545-8000. www.theamericanrestaurantkc.com. Reservations recommended. Fixed-price dinner $50–$80; fixed-price lunch $24. AE, DC, MC, V. Mon–Fri 11:30am–2pm; Mon–Thurs 6–9:30pm; Fri–Sat 6–10pm.

Arthur Bryant's BARBECUE A few blocks east of 18th and Vine, this unpretentious self-serve restaurant, with origins stretching back to the early 1920s, is the most famous—and some swear the best—barbecue joint in town. White bread smothered with tender barbecued meat and barbecued ribs are the specialties, along with Bryant's signature gritty sauce and lard-fried fries.

1727 Brooklyn. (C) 816/231-1123. www.arthurbryantsbbq.com. Main courses $7.65–$11. AE, MC, V. Mon–Thurs 10am–9:30pm; Fri–Sat 10am–10pm; Sun 11am–8:30pm.

Café Sebastienne NEW AMERICAN Art-loving gourmets who can't possibly fit another museum into their tight itinerary, rejoice: This hip venue combines contemporary art and cuisine. Within the confines of the Kemper Museum of Contemporary

Art, it boasts a cheerful setting of art-packed walls and an "outdoor" terrace under a glass ceiling. The menu, which changes weekly to take advantage of local organic produce, may include the likes of pan-seared crab cakes with horseradish slaw and rémoulade. Few can resist a whirl through the free museum with its innovative temporary exhibits and permanent collection that rotates works by Jasper Johns, Pollock, Rauschenberg, Motherwell, de Kooning, Mapplethorpe, and others.

4420 Warwick Blvd. ℂ 816/561-7740. www.kemperart.org/cafe. Main courses $18–$30. AE, DC, MC, V. Tues–Sun 11am–2:30pm; Fri–Sat 5:30–9:30pm.

Classic Cup Cafe CONTEMPORARY CONTINENTAL Restaurants on the Plaza seem to come and go with the swiftness of the changing of the seasons, but this casual cafe with a European atmosphere has proven its staying power as a local favorite. Its glass facade and sidewalk seating make it a perfect spot for people-watching; there's also a backyard patio. Pizzas, sandwiches, pasta, steaks, and seafood are listed on a changing menu that may include such entrees as pan-seared salmon stuffed with Alaskan snow crab. Make reservations early for Sunday brunch, which has its own menu of breakfast and lunch items.

301 W. 47th St. ℂ 816/753-1840. www.classiccup.com. Reservations recommended. Main courses $9–$27. AE, MC, V. Mon–Thurs 7am–10pm; Fri 7am–11pm; Sat 8am–11pm; Sun 10am–10pm.

Golden Ox STEAKS This popular steakhouse was established in 1949 by the founder of the Kansas City Stockyards Company to feed hungry ranchers. The stockyards are now history, but the Golden Ox retains its 1950-ish clubby atmosphere and is still the place for high-powered business lunches (when burgers and daily specials are also available) and some of the best, yet affordably priced, steaks in town, aged and cut on the premises and broiled over a hickory-charcoal flame. Entrees come with a soup or salad, vegetable, and garlic bread.

1600 Genessee. ℂ 816/842-2866. www.goldenox.com. Reservations recommended. Main courses $15–$39. AE, DC, MC, V. Mon–Tues 11am–9pm; Wed–Fri 11am–10pm; Sat 4–10:30pm; Sun 4–9pm.

Lidia's ITALIAN Located in a renovated railway freight house behind Union Station and sporting exposed ceiling beams, brick walls, and an outdoor patio, this very popular restaurant (owned by TV culinary star Lidia Bastianich) specializes in excellent yet affordable Northern Italian cuisine. Try the three-pasta sampler, delivered to your plate straight from the kitchen via a frying pan (you can have as much as you wish) or the very popular veal shanks. There are two wine lists, one with about 40 choices of bottles all priced at $25.

101 W. 22nd St. ℂ 816/221-3722. www.lidiasitaly.com. Reservations recommended. Main courses $15–$28; Sat/Sun brunch $20. AE, DC, MC, V. Daily 11am–2pm; Mon–Thurs 5:30–9pm; Fri–Sat 5–10pm; Sun 5–9pm.

Savoy Grill AMERICAN Located in downtown's historic Hotel Savoy and established in 1903, this well-known landmark exudes turn-of-the-20th-century Kansas City with Art Deco stained-glass windows, dark wainscoting, murals depicting the Santa Fe Trail, and white-coated waiters with black bow ties. The menu, which has hardly changed over the centuries, is unabashedly straightforward American cuisine, primarily steaks and seafood. Although some dishes fall short of the venue, you can't go wrong with the steaks or lobster. In any case, you're dining here mainly for the old-fashioned ambience, so be sure to make reservations for a booth in the main dining room; it's in the smoking section, but few of the largely older clientele smoke.

In the Hotel Savoy, 219 W. 9th St. (© 816/842-3890. Reservations recommended. Main courses $17–$42. AE, DC, MC, V. Mon–Thurs 11am–11pm; Fri–Sat 11am–midnight; Sun 4–10pm.

Stroud's Oak Ridge Manor CHICKEN   In northeast Kansas City, not far from Worlds of Fun, this casual family restaurant is located in an expanded 1829 log cabin and farmhouse. It specializes in pan-fried chicken served with all the trimmings, but it also offers steaks, catfish, and sandwiches. There's a children's menu, a piano player obliges with old-time favorites, and portions are so hearty that few leave without doggie bags. Expect a long wait on weekends.

5410 NE Oak Ridge Rd. (take the Brighton or Vivion exit off I-35). Reservations not accepted. (© 816/454-9600. www.stroudsrestaurant.com. Meals $13–$25. AE, MC, V. Mon–Thurs 5–9:30pm; Fri 11am–10:30pm; Sat 2–10:30pm; Sun 11am–9:30pm.

Winstead's *Kids* DINER   Just east of Country Club Plaza, this Art Deco–style diner has been going strong since 1940 and now has almost a dozen branches. Hamburgers made from steak (ground daily on the premises) are served in tissue paper, the jukebox plays golden oldies, there's a kids' menu, and the milkshakes are the best in town.

101 Cleaver Blvd. (© **816/753-2244.** Sandwiches $2–$3.80. MC, V. Sun–Thurs 6:30am–midnight; Fri–Sat 6:30am–1am.

KANSAS CITY AFTER DARK

Much of the city's nightlife can be found downtown, in Westport, and at Country Club Plaza. For information about what's going on in jazz and blues clubs, pick up the free weekly *Pitch;* or call the **Jazz Hotline** (© **816/753-5277**). For tickets to main events, call **Ticketmaster** (© **816/931-3330;** www.ticketmaster.com).

THE PERFORMING ARTS   The Lyric Theater, 1029 Central, is the venue for both the **Lyric Opera of Kansas City** (© 816/471-7344; www.kcopera.org), which presents four productions yearly in the original language with projected translations, and the **Kansas City Symphony** (© 816/471-1100; www.kcsymphony.org). The **Kansas City Ballet** (© 816/931-2232; www.kcballet.org) performs at the Lyric Theater and at the **Midland Theater,** 1228 Main St. (© 816/471-9703), a lavishly decorated 1927 theater that also stages musicals, concerts, and other performances. The turn-of-the-20th-century **Folly Theater,** 300 W. 12th St. (© 816/474-4444; www. follytheater.com), is known for its Jazz and Children's series. In summer, open-air **Starlight Theatre** in Swope Park (© 816/363-7827; www.kcstarlight.com) has presented Broadway musicals and concerts for more than 50 years.

THE CLUB & BAR SCENE   **Phoenix Piano Bar & Grill,** downtown at 302 W. 8th St. (© 816/472-0001; www.phoenixjazz.net), specializes in Kansas City–style jazz, seafood, and steaks, while the nearby **Majestic Steakhouse,** 931 Broadway (© 816/471-8484; www.magesticsteakhouse.com), offers dining and jazz nightly in a historic setting. **Jardine's Restaurant & Jazz Club,** 45436 Main St., near Country Club Plaza (© 816/561-6480; www.jardines4jazz.com), offers live jazz nightly and New American regional cuisine.

In the historic 18th and Vine District, the best spots offering live blues and jazz include the **Blue Room,** 1600 E. 18th St. (© 816/474-8463; www.americanjazz museum.com), a smoke-free venue (the better to protect its displays of jazz memorabilia) featuring jazz on Monday, Thursday, Friday, and Saturday; and the **Mutual Musicians Foundation,** 1823 Highland Ave. (© 816/471-5212), a National Historic Landmark where musicians have been meeting for decades to jam after midnight—Fridays it's blues, Saturdays it's jazz.

In Westport, **Blayney's,** 415 Westport Rd. (© **816/561-3747;** www.blayneys.com), offers blues, jazz, R&B, and rock Monday to Saturday in a pub setting; while farther south, barbecue meets the blues at the casual **B. B.'s Lawn Side Bar-B-Que,** at 1205 E. 85th St. east of Troost (© **816/822-7427;** www.bbslawnsidebbq.com), with live blues Wednesday to Sunday nights.

RIVERBOAT GAMBLING Riverboat gambling takes place on non-cruising boats along the banks of the Missouri River, including **Harrah's Casino,** U.S. 210 and Chouteau Trafficway, North Kansas City (© **816/472-7777;** www.harrahs.com); **Ameristar Casino,** I-435 and Route 210 (© **816/414-7000;** www.ameristarcasinos.com); and the **Isle of Capri Casino,** off I-35 at 1800 E. Front St. (© **816/855-7777;** www.isle ofcapricasino.com).

9 St. Louis

Established as a French trading post in 1764, St. Louis served as a gateway to the west after the Louisiana Purchase and as a major port for steamboats traveling the Mississippi. Today the city's landmark is the soaring, shining steel **Gateway Arch,** designed by Eero Saarinen in 1966 to commemorate Thomas Jefferson's vision of westward expansion. Though visitors often make it their first stop, there's plenty more beckoning, including expansive Forest Park with its first-rate museums, one of the nation's top botanical gardens, and numerous attractions geared toward children, many of them free, making St. Louis a prime family destination.

ESSENTIALS

GETTING THERE By Plane Flights arrive at **Lambert–St. Louis International Airport** (© **314/426-8000;** www.lambert-stlouis.com), about 20 minutes northwest of downtown. The **MetroLink** light rail (© **314/231-2345**) connects the airport with downtown for $3.25. **Taxis** cost about $30 to $45.

By Train Amtrak (© **800/USA-RAIL;** www.amtrak.com) provides daily service from Chicago and Kansas City (trip time for both: 5½ hr.) to its station at 550 S. 16th St., 2 blocks southeast of Union Station (© **314/331-3309**).

By Car The major routes into St. Louis are **I-70** from the east (Indianapolis) and west (Kansas City), **I-55** from the north (Chicago) and south (Memphis), **I-64** from the southeast (Louisville), and **I-44** from the southwest (Springfield).

VISITOR INFORMATION St. Louis Visitor Information Centers, both open Monday to Friday 9am to 5pm and Saturday 9am to 2pm, are located at America's Center, 7th Street and Washington Avenue (MetroLink: Convention Center); and at Kiener Plaza, 6th and Chestnut streets behind the Old Courthouse (closed Jan–Feb; MetroLink: 8th St. and Pine). There's also a **Visitor Information Center** at the airport's main terminal (open Mon–Fri 10am–6pm; Sat–Sun 1–5pm) and its east terminal (open Mon–Fri 10am–3pm; Sat–Sun 1–5pm). **The Fun Phone** (© **314/421-2100**) is a recording of special events. For more information, call © **800/916-0092** or check www.explorestlouis.com.

GETTING AROUND The **MetroLink** (© **314/231-2345;** www.metrostlouis. org) travels between the airport and east St. Louis, with stops at Delmar Loop, Forest Park, Central West End, Union Station, Busch Stadium, downtown (at 8th and Pine and Convention Center), Laclede's Landing, and other neighborhoods. A one-way ticket costs $1.75 for the entire zone (except for the airport, which costs $3.25); a day pass costs $4.25. Travel is free on weekdays from 11:30am to 1:30pm in the downtown area between Union Station and Laclede's Landing. In Forest Park, where many of St. Louis's top sights are located, the Forest Park Shuttle travels from the Forest Park MetroLink Station to 14 attractions. The service runs daily beginning Memorial Day weekend to Labor Day and is included in the $4.25 MetroLink day pass.

If you're driving a car, be aware that parking is costly. Most hotels and upper-end restaurants offer valet parking. Hotels almost always charge a fee for this service and restaurants sometimes charge as well, though occasionally only a tip is expected.

FAST FACTS A major hospital is **Saint Louis University Hospital,** 3635 Vista Ave., at Grand Avenue (✆ **314/577-8000**). **Walgreens** is open 24 hours at 4140 S. Broadway (✆ **314/832-4995**). Sales tax is 7.6% and the hotel tax is 7.25%.

WHAT TO SEE & DO

Many of St. Louis's top attractions are spread in or around expansive Forest Park, site of the 1904 World's Fair and one of the nation's largest parks (it beats New York City's Central Park by 500 acres).

WHAT TO SEE & DO

Anheuser-Busch Brewery
Anheuser-Busch, one of the world's largest beer brewers, was established at this site in the 1860s, and many architectural gems from that time period remain. Tours of the brewing process take in the 1885 Clydesdale stable, the historic 1892 Brew House, and the packaging plant, ending with free drinks. Allow 1½ hours. Tours begin at 12th and Lynch streets (I-55 at Arsenal).

12th and Lynch sts. ✆ **314/577-2626.** www.budweisertours.com. Free admission. June–Aug Mon–Sat 9am–5pm, Sun 11:30am–5pm; Sept–May Mon–Sat 9am–4pm (Nov–Feb from 10am), Sun 11:30am–4pm. Tours are several times an hour on first-come, first-served basis. Frequency depends on demand (as often as every 10 min. in summer and about every 30 min. in winter).

Cathedral Basilica of Saint Louis
Built after the turn of the 20th century and something of a curiosity, this cathedral combines a Romanesque exterior with a brilliant Byzantine interior and boasts the largest collection of mosaics in the world—42 million pieces of glass used in 83,000 square feet of mosaic art, created by 20 artists over a span of 75 years. Plan at least 15 minutes for this must-see.

4431 Lindell Blvd. (at Newstead Ave.), in Central West End. ✆ **314/533-2824.** www.cathedralstl.org. Free admission. Daily 6am–5pm. MetroLink: Central West End.

Gateway Arch/Jefferson National Expansion Memorial (Best)
America's tallest national park monument, this graceful rainbow of shining steel soars 630 feet above downtown and the Mississippi River, commemorating westward expansion in the 1800s. Tram rides to the top (with great views on clear days) can involve lengthy waits in summer and on weekends; come first thing in the morning to purchase tickets (or order tickets in advance for an additional $3 fee at www.gatewayarch.com), then take in the **Museum of Westward Expansion,** which traces the journey of Lewis and Clark and those who followed. Extra fees are charged for both the Arch Odyssey Theatre, which features changing, 45-minute movies on a giant IMAX screen, and the Monument to the Dream film documenting the Arch's construction. Plan on spending at least 2 hours here.

St. Louis

Mississippi River

M.L. King Jr.
Memorial Bridge
Eads
Bridge

Leonore K. Sullivan Blvd.

Commercial St.
1st St.
Waddingham St.
2nd St.

Pinnacle Casino

Jefferson
National
Expansion
Memorial
N.H.S.

Gateway
Arch

Old
Cathedral

Memorial Drive

Information
Post Office

1/8 mile
100 meters

4th St.

Broadway
Cole St.
6th St.
Delmar Blvd.
Lucas Ave.
Washington Ave.
St. Charles St.
Pine St.

Old
Courthouse

Kiener
Plaza

Broadway
4th St.
Spruce St.

7th St.
Locust St.
Olive St.
Chestnut St.
Market St.
Walnut St.
Clark Ave.
8th St.
Spruce St.

Cervantes
Convention
Center

8th St.
9th St.
10th St.
11th St.

Busch
Memorial
Stadium

10th St.

13th St.

Martin Luther King Blvd.
Delmar
Blvd.
Tucker Blvd.

Memorial
Plaza

City
Hall

Clark Ave.
Belmont St.
Spruce St.

14th St.
Cole St.
Kansas City
St. Louis
Jefferson
City
MISSOURI

Lucas Ave.
Washington Ave.
St. Charles St.
Locust St.
Olive St.
Pine St.

Chestnut St.
Market St.

Savvis
Center

Union
Station

18th St.
20th St.

Poplar St.

ACCOMMODATIONS ■
Chase Park Plaza Hotel **1**
Drury Inn Union Station **5**
Drury Plaza Hotel **11**
Embassy Suites Hotel
  St. Louis Downtown **15**
Hampton Inn Gateway Arch **13**
Hilton St. Louis Downtown **7**
Hyatt Regency St. Louis **3**
Omni Majestic Hotel **7**
Westin St. Louis **8**

DINING ◆
Copia Urban Winery **6**
Hard Rock Cafe **4**
Mike Shannon's Steaks
  and Seafood **9**
Old Spaghetti Factory **14**
Schlafly Tap Room **2**
Tony's **10**

St. Louis Riverfront (between Memorial Dr. and Lenore K. Sullivan Blvd., on the riverfront). ✆ 877/982-1410. www.gatewayarch.com. Admission for tram and 1 movie $14 adults, $11 children 13–15, $5.50 children 3–12. Memorial Day to Labor Day daily 8am–10pm (tram until 9pm); rest of year daily 9am–6pm (tram until 5pm). MetroLink: Laclede's Landing.

Missouri Botanical Garden   Opened in 1859, this is the country's oldest and one of the world's top-rated botanical gardens: a 79-acre delight featuring the nation's largest Japanese strolling garden, a Chinese garden, the world's first geodesic-domed greenhouse, a scented garden for the visually impaired, a hedge maze, a home-gardening resource center, and themed gardens ranging from a Turkish Ottoman garden to an English woodland garden. A must-see for gardeners, who can easily spend 2 or 3 hours of bliss here. A new children's garden, designed to resemble a mid-1800s Missouri river town, opened in 2006. Combining fun and education, it features paths leading through woodlands and over streams to a pioneer village, tree house, fort, rope bridge, cave, splash area, Osage Indian camp, and more.

4344 Shaw Blvd. (Vandeventer exit off I-44). ✆ 314/577-9400. www.mobot.org. Admission $8 adults, free for children 12 and under (children's garden free for adults, $3 for children). Daily 9am–5pm (Memorial Day to Labor Day grounds close Wed 9pm and are open Wed and Sat 7–9am for walkers). MetroLink: Central West End, no. 13 Union Garden bus (weekdays only).

Missouri History Museum   St. Louis's history is presented through photographs, memorabilia, first-person narratives, portraits, and more, with displays featuring the city's role in westward expansion, the Dred Scott case (which upheld slavery), famous St. Louisans such as Chuck Berry and Tennessee Williams, the 1904 World's Fair held at Forest Park, a replica of Charles Lindbergh's *Spirit of St. Louis* plane and other items relating to his life and solo transatlantic flight, and exhibits of the city's past. Allow 1 hour for the permanent exhibits, more for special exhibits.

Jefferson Memorial Building, Forest Park (at Lindell and DeBaliviere). ✆ 314/746-4599. www.mohistory.org. Free admission; special exhibitions cost extra (but are free on Tues). Tues 10am–8pm; Wed–Mon 10am–6pm. MetroLink: Forest Park.

Museum of Transportation   Founded in 1944 but only now getting the attention it deserves with newly expanded grounds, this unique museum "houses one of the largest and best collections of transportation vehicles in the world" (according to the Smithsonian). Certainly, with more than 70 locomotives, the museum boasts one of the most complete collections of American rail power anywhere, including an 1858 wood-burning locomotive, a Big Boy (the world's largest steam locomotive), and a 1920s Pullman sleeping car. Automobiles on display range from a 1915 Ford Model T to Bobby Darin's 1960 dream car. Other highlights include a miniature passenger train and a trolley circulating the museum's 129 acres. Allot at least 2 hours to explore.

3015 Barrett Station Rd. (west of I-270, at the Dougherty Ferry Rd. exit). ✆ 314/965-7998. www.museumoftransport. org. Admission $4 adults, $2 seniors and children 5–12. Summer (May 1 to Labor Day) Mon–Sat 9am–5pm (to 7pm Thurs); Sun 11am–5pm. Winter Tues–Sat 9am–4pm; Sun 11am–4pm.

Saint Louis Art Museum   Housed in a Beaux Arts–style building constructed for the 1904 World's Fair, this great museum is a buffet of the arts, where visitors can sample as much as they like of the displays from around the globe and from virtually all time periods. It contains works ranging from ancient and medieval art to European old masters, French Impressionists, American art from 1800 to 1945, and contemporary art. Its pre-Columbian, Asian, and German expressionist collections are ranked among the best in the world (it owns more paintings by Max Beckmann than any

Destination Union Station

Once the nation's busiest passenger-rail terminal, the restored **St. Louis Union Station** at 1820 Market St. (℡ **314/421-6655**; MetroLink: Union Station) is a popular destination for shopping and dining; it even has a small lake with paddle boats. Be sure to take a peek at the Grand Hall, now the lobby of the Hyatt Regency.

museum on the planet). Other galleries feature Islamic and ancient art; an Egyptian collection (including three mummies); arms and armor; media art; and art from Africa, Oceania, and the Americas. There are also displays of Chinese, European, and American decorative arts. You should spend at least 2 hours here.

Fine Arts Dr., Forest Park. ℡ 314/721-0072. www.slam.org. Free admission; special exhibitions cost extra (but are free on Fri). Tues–Sun 10am–5pm (Fri to 9pm). MetroLink: Forest Park, then Forest Park Shuttle (summers only) or Hampton no. 90 Metrobus.

MORE HIGHLIGHTS

HISTORIC HOMES The **Campbell House Museum**, 1508 Locust St. (℡ **314/421-0325**; www.campbellhousemuseum.org), is an elegant, 10,000-square-foot 1851 Victorian mansion, with most of its original family furnishings remarkably intact. Tours cost $6. The Romanesque Revival–style 1889 **Samuel Cupples House**, 3673 W. Pine Blvd. (℡ **314/977-3575**; http://cupples.slu.edu), is a gem of the Gilded Age on the campus of Saint Louis University, containing 42 rooms, a glass collection, and other fine and decorative arts. Tours cost $5. The **Chatillon-DeMenil Mansion**, 3352 DeMenil Place (℡ **314/771-5828**; www.demenil.org), was a four-room farmhouse in 1848, later expanded to 14 rooms in the Greek Revival style. It contains period furnishings, a collection of 1904 World's Fair memorabilia, and two paintings by Missouri artist George Caleb Bingham. Admission here is $4.

From 1900 to 1903, the **Scott Joplin House State Historic Site**, 2658A Delmar Blvd. (℡ **314/340-5790**; www.mostateparks.com/scottjoplin.htm), was the modest four-family antebellum home of the musician and composer known as the "King of Ragtime." Now a National Historic Landmark, it offers guided tours for $2.50 that include Joplin's second-floor apartment with furnishings representative of the times and a player-piano that rags out renditions of Joplin's best-known tunes, including "The Entertainer."

MAJOR LEAGUE FUN Watch the **St. Louis Cardinals** hit some homers at the new downtown Busch Stadium, Broadway and Clark streets (℡ **314/349-9000**; www.stlcardinals.com).

BEST BETS FOR KIDS St. Louis is a children's town, with more than enough to keep them amused, much of it absolutely free (though there is generally a charge for parking). The top-rated **St. Louis Zoo**, Forest Park (℡ **314/781-0900**; www.stlzoo.org), with its Big Cat Country, Fragile Forest for the zoo's great apes, River's Edge with elephants and hippos, and Penguin and Puffin Coast is free (fees charged for the fascinating Insectarium with everything from giant cockroaches to a butterfly house and an animal-contact area called Children's Zoo). Another freebie is the **St. Louis Science Center**, 5050 Oakland Ave. (℡ **800/456-7572** or 314/289-4444; www.slsc.org), with full-size, animated dinosaurs and 750 hands-on exhibits covering DNA and genetics, health, aviation, the environment, and more (admission charged for special exhibitions, planetarium, and OMNIMAX Theater). Another free attraction is **Grant's Farm,** 10501 Gravois (© **314/843-1700;** www.grantsfarm.com), once farmed by Ulysses S. Grant and now part of the Busch family estate, open mid-April through October and featuring a tram ride through an exotic game preserve, a small zoo, animal shows, a Clydesdale stable, a carriage collection, and a free glass of Anheuser-Busch beer.

Older kids—and adults—love the whimsical, one-of-a-kind **City Museum,** 701 N. 15th St. (© **314/231-2489;** www.citymuseum.org), created by artists and housed in a former shoe factory. The adventure land features a huge indoor play area filled with imaginative caves, slides, and crawling tubes; a circus performance; train rides; art workshops; a collection of oddities; a funky aquarium; and a five-story outdoor climbing contraption called MonstroCity. With a school bus teetering on its roof (and plans to add a rooftop waterpark), this museum is like no other. Admission is $12, plus $6 for the aquarium. At the education-oriented **Magic House** children's museum, 516 S. Kirkwood Rd. (© **314/822-8900;** www.magichouse.org), children 10 and under have a blast experimenting with magnets, water, and tools; testing their fitness; role-playing in a kid-size village; zooming down a three-story slide; and watching their hair stand on end as they touch an electrically charged ball. Special sections are geared toward younger children and toddlers. Admission is $7.

The biggest attraction for kids is the huge amusement park, **Six Flags St. Louis,** 30 miles west of St. Louis on I-44 (© **636/938-4800;** www.sixflags.com), with thrill rides such as Xcalibur (a slinging, rotating catapult), plus Looney Tunes Town for younger visitors, live entertainment, and even a waterpark with a wave pool, slides, and more. Admission is $45 adults, $27 kids under 48 inches tall; 3 years and younger are free. Discount tickets are often available on the park's website. It's open weekends April, May, September, and October and daily in summer.

WHERE TO STAY

Downtown St. Louis has an impressive number of hotel chains ensconced in renovated historic buildings. In addition to the choices below, consider the **Westin St. Louis,** located next to Busch Stadium at 811 Spruce St. (© **314/621-2000;** www.westin.com/stlouis), which gave new life to a group of former 19th-century railroad warehouses with a gorgeous, smoke-free contemporary interior; and the upscale **Hilton St. Louis Downtown,** 400 Olive St. (© **314/436-0002;** www.stlouisdowntown.hilton.com), in the historic Merchants-Laclede building with many of its original features intact (a former vault is now a gift shop). **Sheraton St. Louis City Center Hotel & Suites,** within walking distance of Union Station and Busch Stadium at 400 S. 14th St. (© **314/231-5007;** www.sheraton.com/stlouis), occupies four floors of the renovated Edison Brothers warehouse, distinctive for a *trompe l'oeil* mural that draws its imagery from St. Louis landmarks and the 1904 World's Fair.

Chase Park Plaza Hotel *Best* Located across from Forest Park in the elegant Central West End, with its antiques shops, sidewalk cafes, and sophisticated restaurants, this restored, 1920s historic hotel is one of the city's poshest, offering luxuriously appointed rooms and one- and two-bedroom suites, the latter two featuring minikitchens with microwaves, two-burner stoves, and small fridges. The hotel's many facilities, including a five-screen movie complex, and its proximity to the attractions of Forest Park, make it a winner with the business and leisure set.

212–232 N. Kingshighway (at Lindell Blvd.), St. Louis, MO 63108. © 877/587-2427 or 314/633-3000. Fax 314/633-1144. www.chaseparkplaza.com. 251 units. $246 double; $269–$369 suite. No charge for additional room occupants. AE, DC, MC, V. Valet parking $22; self-parking $14. **Amenities:** 4 restaurants; outdoor heated pool; state-of-the-art health club. *In room:* Kitchen (suites only).

Drury Plaza Hotel

Here's a great location for both business and leisure travelers. Part of a St. Louis–based chain but more upscale than sister Drury Inns, this downtown hotel, situated just minutes from the Arch, opened in 2000 in three renovated buildings, including the 1919 Fur Exchange Building, and boasts Italian marble, massive support columns, and Waterford crystal chandeliers in its lobby. Rooms with the best views face the Arch and river. A less expensive choice is **Drury Inn Union Station,** across from Union Station at 201 S. 20th St. (📞 **314/231-3900**), housed in a restored former YMCA built in 1907. With its indoor pool, exercise room, free parking, and laundry facilities, it's a great choice for families. Like all Drury properties, both offer free breakfasts, free local and long-distance calls, free evening beverages and snacks, and free Internet access.

4th and Market sts., St. Louis, MO 63102. 📞 **800/378-7946** or 314/231-3003. Fax 314/231-2952. www.druryhotels. com. 367 units. $129–$142 double; from $142 suite. Children under 18 stay free in parent's room. Rates include hot breakfast buffet. AE, DC, MC, V. Parking $15. MetroLink: 8th and Pine. Pets permitted free. **Amenities:** 2 restaurants; indoor pool; exercise room. *In room:* Fridge, microwave.

Embassy Suites Hotel St. Louis–Downtown *Kids*

Located near the Arch and downtown, in the Laclede's Landing riverfront nightlife district, this all-suite hotel features a sky-lit, eight-story atrium as its focal point and offers two-room suites equipped with two TVs and Wi-Fi access. Ask for a room facing the Arch or the Mississippi on a higher floor to get the best views. Guests enjoy such extras as cooked-to-order breakfasts, free evening cocktails, a game room, and the very good St. Louis Fish Market restaurant, making it a good choice for couples and families alike.

901 N. 1st St., St. Louis, MO 63102. 📞 **800/362-2779** or 314/241-4200. Fax 314/241-6513. www.embassysuites.com. 297 units. $169–$189 suite. Extra person $20. Children under 18 stay free in parent's room. Rates include free breakfast. Off-season rates available. AE, DC, MC, V. Parking $10. MetroLink: Laclede's Landing. **Amenities:** Restaurant; indoor pool; exercise room. *In room:* Fridge, microwave.

Hampton Inn Gateway Arch *Value*

This new property boasts better-than-average service for its price range, a great downtown location near Laclede's Landing and the Arch, a comfy lobby with plenty of seating, laundry facilities, a game room, free local calls, and free Internet access in its business center and rooms, some of which boast views of the Arch and all of which have recliners and queen- or king-size beds.

333 Washington Ave., St. Louis, MO 63102. 📞 **800/HAMPTON** or 314/621-7900. Fax 314/421-6468. www.hampton innstlouis.com. 190 units. $119–$159 double. Extra person $10. Children under 18 stay free in parent's room. Rates include free breakfast. AE, DC, MC, V. Parking $10. MetroLink: Laclede's Landing or Convention Center. **Amenities:** Indoor pool; exercise room. *In room:* Fridge.

Hyatt Regency St. Louis

Located in restored Union Station with its many shops and restaurants, this hotel boasts Missouri's most spectacular lobby—the station's former Grand Hall, with a six-story vaulted ceiling and gold-leaf frescoes. Most of the spacious (and quiet) rooms are in a modern addition beneath the trusses of the former train shed and feature such luxuries as bathroom TVs. For more pampering, stay in the Regency Club in the historic part of the station, which has the added perks of its own lounge and complimentary breakfast and evening appetizers. Everyone from business travelers to families stays here.

One St. Louis Union Station (18th and Market sts.), St. Louis, MO 63103. 📞 **800/233-1234** or 314/231-1234. Fax 314/923-3970. www.stlouis.hyatt.com. 538 units. $179–$259 double. Children under 18 stay free in parent's room.

Packages available. AE, DC, MC, V. Valet parking $18; self-parking $12. MetroLink: Union Station. **Amenities:** 2 restaurants; outdoor pool; 24-hr. health club.

Omni Majestic Hotel   Built in 1914, this National Historic Landmark and boutique hotel appeals to business travelers and celebrities alike with its old-world charm, downtown location, complimentary downtown shuttle, and excellent service. Comfortable rooms have more character than most and are equipped with triple-sheeted beds, free Wi-Fi connections, and bathrobes. The Get Fit rooms sport treadmills.

1019 Pine St., St. Louis, MO 63101. ℂ 800/THE-OMNI or 314/436-2355. Fax 314/436-0223. www.omnihotels.com. 91 units. $129–$189 double. Extra person $10. Children under 12 stay free in parent's room. Rates include free breakfast. AE, DC, MC, V. Parking $18. MetroLink: 8th and Pine. Pets up to 25 lb. accepted with security deposit. **Amenities:** Restaurant; 24-hr. health club. *In room:* Fridge.

WHERE TO DINE

Dining in one of St. Louis's distinctive neighborhoods ranks high on a short list of must-dos. Clustered around Forest Park are trendy **Central West End** with its grand residences, antiques stores, and fashionable eateries (many with sidewalk seating); **The Loop,** named after an old streetcar turnaround and home to funky shops, art galleries, ethnic restaurants, and the St. Louis Walk of Fame; and **The Hill,** an Italian district famous for its many Italian restaurants (a perennial favorite is **Charlie Gitto's,** 5226 Shaw Ave.; ℂ **314/772-8898;** www.charliegittos.com).

For children, good bets include **The Old Spaghetti Factory,** housed in an old warehouse in Laclede's Landing at 727 N. 1st St. (ℂ **314/621-0276;** www.osf.com), and **Hard Rock Cafe** (ℂ **314/621-7625;** www.hardrockcafe.com) in Union Station, which also has a food court.

It's a St. Louis tradition to drop by **Ted Drewes Frozen Custard,** 6726 Chippewa (ℂ **314/481-2652;** www.teddrewes.com), after a night on the town. Founded more than 75 years ago and open daily except January, this roadside stand and Route 66 attraction specializes in frozen custards, including the Concrete, available in a range of flavors and so thick that it's served upside down. An additional location is open summers only at 4224 S. Grand (ℂ **314/352-7376**).

Blueberry Hill *Kids* SANDWICHES/BURGERS   Located in the lively Loop district, this St. Louis institution is a treasure-trove of pop-culture memorabilia, including vintage posters and more Chuck Berry memorabilia than you can shake a stick at. The digital jukebox, with limitless selections, is rated one of the best in the country, and the hamburgers are among the best in town. Live music is staged in the Elvis Room and Duck Room several nights a week (Chuck Berry still performs here), and outside on the sidewalk is the St. Louis Walk of Fame honoring famous St. Louisans, including Chuck Berry, Josephine Baker, Tennessee Williams, Ulysses S. Grant, and Tina Turner.

6504 Delmar. ℂ 314/727-4444. www.blueberryhill.com. Main courses $5–$9.75. AE, DC, MC, V. Mon–Sat 11am–1am; Sun 11am–midnight. MetroLink: Delmar, then bus 97.

Chez Léon *Value* FRENCH   One of the hip Central West End's friendliest restaurants, this neighborhood bistro has a relaxed atmosphere, sidewalk seating, a staff that aims to please, and standard French fare served in hearty portions. Its 3 Plats dinner for $35 is a popular choice, giving diners a choice of entree (like seared duck breast with figs, currants, and raisins, or veal scallops with a white-wine and mushroom sauce) and two other dishes from the regular menu.

4580 Laclede Ave. (at Euclid). ℂ **314/361-1589**. www.chezleon.com. Main courses $22–$36. AE, DC, MC, V. Tues–Thurs 5:30–10pm; Fri–Sat 5:30–11pm; Sun 5–9pm. MetroLink: Central West End.

Copia Urban Winery AMERICAN   Wine is the raison d'être of this upscale yet casual establishment in the trendy Washington Avenue Loft District in downtown St. Louis. A glass-enclosed "wine cellar" separates a cozy bar from the dining room, where classic American cuisine with a progressive twist reigns, including house-smoked rack of ribs, prime rib, and a popular surf-and-turf combo. The wine list is extensive and includes wine aged on-site, but guests can also peruse the adjoining wine shop and enjoy their purchase with a meal for an additional $8 corkage fee.

1122 Washington Ave. ℂ **314/621-7275**. www.copiawine.com. Main courses $15–$26. AE, DC, MC, V. Mon–Sat 11am–11pm (bar open to 1am). MetroLink: Convention Center.

Meriwether's NEW AMERICAN   On the second floor of the Missouri History Museum, this light and airy casual restaurant overlooking Forest Park offers soups, salads, sandwiches (like a bison burger), quiche, and main dishes (grilled salmon topped with barbecued shrimp), as well as a children's menu. This is a good place for lunch if you're visiting the many sights in Forest Park, but other recommendations include the casual **Boathouse** with its sandwiches, pizzas, and rental paddle boats (ℂ **314/367-2224**; www.boathouseforestpark.com); and **Puck's**, in the Saint Louis Art Museum (ℂ **314/655-5490**; www.wolfgangpuck.com), with its innovative American cuisine and popular Sunday brunch.

Missouri History Museum, Forest Park. ℂ **314/361-7313**. Main courses $7–$9; Sun brunch $20. AE, MC, V. Mon–Sat 11am–2pm; Sun 10am–2pm. MetroLink: Forest Park.

Mike Shannon's Steaks and Seafood STEAKS/SEAFOOD   Owned by a former Cardinals baseball great (and current sportscaster—whose radio show is broadcast live from a table in the restaurant after Fri evening home games), this downtown fine-dining venue is formal yet relaxed, with white tablecloths in a glass-enclosed dining room, an adjoining sports bar, and displays of sports memorabilia. It caters to a business crowd with a menu that concentrates on aged steaks and fresh seafood, plus sandwiches for lunch. With Busch Stadium just a couple of minutes' walk away, it's a popular stop for a meal before or after a Cardinals game.

620 Market St. ℂ **314/421-1540**. www.shannonsteak.com. Main courses $16–$42. AE, DC, MC, V. Mon–Fri 11am–11pm; Sat 5–11pm; Sun 5–10pm. MetroLink: 8th and Pine.

The Schlafly Tap Room AMERICAN   A few blocks north of Union Station, in a 1904 brick building that used to house a printing company, this microbrewery brews more than 30 kinds of Schlafly brand beer on the premises (eight or so are usually on offer) and serves a variety of sandwiches and entrees, many of which include beer in their recipes, including beer-battered shrimp, Oatmeal Stout steak-and-mushroom pie, and beer-and-cheddar soup. An upstairs bar offers live music every Friday, Saturday, and Sunday evening.

2100 Locust St. ℂ **314/241-2337**. www.schlafly.com. Main courses $6.25–$17. AE, DC, MC, V. Mon–Thurs 11am–10pm; Fri–Sat 11am–midnight; Sun noon–9pm.

Tony's *Best* ITALIAN   If you want to splurge on one meal in St. Louis, do it here. Agreement is near unanimous that Tony's is the finest restaurant in the city. Open since 1946, it offers impeccable service, sublime Italian cuisine, an extensive wine selection, one of the cleanest and quietest kitchens on earth, and sophisticated, elegant dining.

Star entrees include the lobster Albanello (served in a heavy, white-wine cream sauce with mushrooms and shallots) and various veal dishes, but everything is fabulous.

410 Market St. (€ 314/231-7007. www.tonysstlouis.com. Reservations recommended. Jackets required for men. Main courses $20–$40. AE, DC, MC, V. Mon–Fri 5:30–10:30pm (last order); Sat 5–10:30pm. MetroLink: 8th and Pine.

ST. LOUIS AFTER DARK

To find out what's on, look for the free weekly *Riverfront Times* at restaurants, bars, and venues around town, buy the Thursday edition of the *St. Louis Post-Dispatch* for its entertainment section, or check the constantly updated *St. Louis Calendar of Events* online at **www.explorestlouis.com**.

THE PERFORMING ARTS   Grand Center (MetroLink: Grand) is the premier performing arts district, with the 1920s-era **Powell Symphony Hall,** 718 N. Grand Blvd. (© **314/534-1700**), home of the **St. Louis Symphony Orchestra** (www.slso.org), founded in 1880 and America's second-oldest symphony orchestra. The **Fabulous Fox Theatre,** 527 N. Grand Blvd. (© **314/534-1111;** www.fabulousfox.com), is a lavish, 1929 Byzantine venue for musicals, dance, and concerts. The **Grandel Theater,** 3610 Grandel Sq. (© **314/534-3810;** www.stlouisblackrep.org), is the home of the St. Louis Black Repertory Company, which stages contemporary works by African-American playwrights. **The Muny,** in Forest Park (© **314/361-1900;** www.muny.org), which opened in 1916 and is the nation's oldest and largest outdoor musical theater, features Broadway musicals in summer.

THE CLUB & CASINO SCENE   St. Louis's nightlife is concentrated around Laclede's Landing, The Loop, and in Soulard on the south edge of downtown. Good bets for live music virtually every night of the week include **BB's Jazz, Blues & Soups,** near Busch Stadium at 700 S. Broadway (© **314/436-5222;** www.bbsjazz bluessoups.com), and the Broadway Oyster Bar, 736 S. Broadway (© **314/621-8811;** www.broadwayoysterbar.com), home to live blues, R&B and Cajun/Creole cuisine. The **Big Bang,** featuring dueling piano players who lead the audience in high-energy singalongs, is a popular hangout in Laclede's Landing at 807 N. 2nd St. (© **314/241-2264;** www.thebigbangbar.com), while in Soulard, the **1860 Hard Shell Cafe & Bar,** 1860 S. 9th St. (© **314/231-1860**), offers blues, R&B, rock, and more nightly. In The Loop, 1,500-seat **The Pageant,** 6161 Delmar (© **314/726-6161;** www.the pageant.com), and **Blueberry Hill,** 6504 Delmar (© **314/727-0880;** www.blueberry hill.com), bring in the hottest national acts. Among the several places to gamble, most convenient is the **President Casino,** docked at Laclede's Landing (© **800/772-3647** or 314/622-1111; www.presidentcasino.com).

10 Branson & the Ozarks

With a population of slightly more than 6,000 and a quaint, historic downtown, Branson attracts more than seven million visitors a year, primarily retirees, families, and RVers drawn by the irresistible lure—and improbable pairing—of outdoor recreation and big-time entertainment. Surrounded by three pristine lakes in the scenic, wooded, mountainous region of the Ozarks in southern Missouri, Branson offers fishing, swimming, golfing, and boating, and is also home to big-name entertainers who present everything from country music to comedy and magic acts in more than 100 live shows daily. If that's not enough, Branson also boasts theme parks such as Silver Dollar City, some unique museums, and a new shopping and dining complex called Branson Landing.

ESSENTIALS

GETTING THERE & GETTING AROUND   The nearest airport is **Springfield-Branson Regional Airport** (© 417/869-0300; www.sgf-branson-airport.com) in Springfield, 43 miles to the north. You really need a car when visiting Branson, and all the major car-rental agencies have desks at the airport. The major highway into Branson, which is 3½ hours from Kansas City and 4 hours from St. Louis, is U.S. 65 from the north, where it intersects with I-44 at Springfield. Be forewarned that traffic on "The Strip" or "76 Country Boulevard" (W. Hwy. 76) in Branson is notorious for traffic jams, but a number of relief roads help.

VISITOR INFORMATION   Contact the **Branson/Lakes Area Chamber of Commerce** (© 800/214-3661 or 417/334-4084; www.explorebranson.com) or stop by one of two Welcome Centers for brochures and maps: north of Branson at the junction of highways 65 and 160, and in town at the junction of highways 65 and 248. Both are open Monday through Saturday from 8am to 5pm (to 6pm in summer) and Sunday from 10am to 4pm.

WHAT TO SEE & DO

In addition to the suggestions below be sure to stroll through **Branson Landing,** a lakefront downtown development featuring shops (including a Bass Pro Shop and Belk department store), restaurants, and a Lake Tanycomo promenade.

THE SHOWS

It all started in 1959 with the **Baldknobbers Jamboree** (© 417/334-4528; www.baldknobbers.com), when four brothers began performing twice a week in a converted building by Lake Taneycomo. In 1968, the **Presleys' Country Jubilee** (© 417/334-4874; www.presleys.com) opened the first theater on West Highway 76, after years of performing to sell-out crowds in cool underground venues—Ozark caves. Both are still going strong, offering wholesome, family-oriented country music, dancing, and comedy.

They're joined by 49 other theaters, most with performances from mid-March or April to December and with two shows a day in peak season. Ticket prices average $22 to $40 for adults (more for dinner shows) and are half-price or free for children. It's a Branson tradition for many performers to sign autographs after the show.

Branson was once known as *the* place for live country music. Although **Roy Clark, Mel Tillis,** the **Oak Ridge Boys,** and other country greats still return for engagements at Branson theaters, the past 10 years have witnessed an explosion in Las Vegas–style production shows. **Andy Williams** was the first major noncountry star to build a venue here, the **Moon River Theatre** (© 800/666-6094 or 417/334-4500; www.andywilliams.com), in 1994. Nowadays, entertainment includes everything from magic shows such as the **Kirby VanBurch Show** (© 417/334-7140) to nostalgia-inducing shows such as **Lost in the '50s** and **Stuck in the '70s** (© 417/337-9333; www.starlite-entertainment.com for both). For comedy, **Yakov Smirnoff** (© 866/559-2568 or 417/339-2568; www.yakov.com) leads the pack with his unique insights into the quirks of everyday life and relationships between men and women.

One of the hottest shows in town is that provided by violinist **Shoji Tabuchi** (© 417/334-7469; www.shoji.com), whose repertoire ranges from country and jazz to classical and Broadway and whose shows include elaborate production numbers, lasers and other stunning visual effects, an 18-piece orchestra, and gorgeous costumes. A great hit with families is the high-energy comedian/musician **Jim Stafford** (© 417/335-8080; www.jimstafford.com), with his fun-filled, action-packed show full of music, spectacular special effects (including a 3-D virtual thrill ride made in-house), and hilarious comedy.

For amazing physical feats, there's the **Incredible Acrobats of China** (© 887/212-4462 or 417/336-8888; www.acrobatsofchina.com) with their gravity-defying performances, and the visually stunning **Cirque** (© 800/884-4536 or 417/336-1220; www.remingtontheatre.com) with its fantasy-provoking theatrical sets and costumes and incredible displays of athleticism onstage and in the air.

The **Dixie Stampede Dinner & Show** (© 800/520-5544 or 417/336-3000; www.dixiestampede.com), owned by Dolly Parton and billed as "Branson's Most Fun Place To Eat," is one of Branson's most popular dinner shows, featuring roast chicken, potato wedges, corn on the cob, and other dishes served without silverware (you're supposed to eat with your fingers), along with a buffalo stampede, horses, trick riders, races, singing, and dancing. Audience participation in friendly competition between Confederate and Yankee rivals, however, may offend some.

Branson's oldest and most widely beloved theater is the **Shepherd of the Hills Homestead and Outdoor Theater** (© 800/653-6288 or 417/334-4191; www.the shepherdofthehills.com), an outdoor amphitheater which for more than 45 years has presented evening reenactments of Harold Bell Wright's 1907 novel, *The Shepherd of the Hills*, which introduced the Ozarks to the world. The mystery/love drama unfolds on a football-field-size dirt stage with 80 performers, 30 horses, a fire, a shootout, a hoedown, comedy, and, essentially, entertainment for the whole family. During the day, the grounds are open for homestead tours of Old Matt's Cabin (the original home of the main characters in the book), a trip up Inspiration Tower for fine views of the Ozarks, and horseback trail rides.

THEME PARKS

Celebration City *Kids*   Branson's newest theme park centers on the top events and eras of 20th-century America, with areas based on such themes as historic Route 66 and a boardwalk harking back to the days of arcades and amusement rides. Mostly, however, it's a place for evening family fun, with more than 30 rides and attractions (including a wooden roller coaster eight stories high), an extreme mountain-boarding stunt show, and a nightly must-see outdoor laser and fireworks display that takes viewers on a visual tour of important events of the 20th century.

Hwy. 376. © 800/831-4-FUN or 417/336-7171. www.bransoncelebrationcity.com. Admission $22 adults, $18 seniors and children 4–11. Weekends May and Sept and daily June–Aug 3–10pm.

Silver Dollar City *Best Kids*   About 5 miles west of Branson, this is the biggest and best of the area's theme parks, featuring more than 20 thrill rides (such as the Wildfire roller coaster with its 15-story vertical drop and speeds up to 66 mph), imaginative playgrounds, 40 live shows daily at a dozen arenas (from gospel to country and bluegrass), restaurants featuring traditional cuisine, about 60 specialty shops, and nearly 100 resident craftspeople practicing their trades, all in a wooded, 1880s mountain-town setting. **Marvel Cave,** the site's original attraction, has 32 miles of passages, which you can explore with a guide on a 1-hour tour (included in the admission price to Silver Dollar City). Plan on arriving first thing in the morning to avoid traffic jams, and spend all day here. Kids of all ages love this place.

W. Hwy. 76. © 800/831-4-FUN or 417/336-7100. www.silverdollarcity.com. Admission $46 adults, $44 seniors, $35 children 4–11. Mid-May to mid-Aug daily 9:30am–7pm; Sept–Dec and Apr Wed–Sun varying hours.

Value **For Theme Park Fanatics**

Those who plan on visiting all three parks—Silver Dollar City, Celebration City, and White Water—can save money with a CityHopper Pass costing $79 for adults and $69 for children. You can buy the pass at any of the three parks (it's good for 4 days), order it online at **www.silverdollarcity.com**, or call © **800/ 475-9370**. Three-day, two-park passes are also available.

White Waterpark *(Kids)* This 12-acre waterpark features a half-dozen rides and slides, a float down Lazy River, a wave pool, lots of water blasters, geysers, and shower shooters at Raintree Island. For little ones, there's Little Squirts Water Works slides, nozzles, and sprays.

3501 W. Hwy. 76. © **800/831-4-FUN** or 417/336-7100. www.bransonwhitewater.com. Admission $33 adults, $29 children 4–11. End of May to mid-June and end of Aug daily 10am–6pm; mid-June to mid-Aug daily 10am–8pm.

MORE HIGHLIGHTS

MUSEUMS Branson bills itself as a year-round home for America's veterans, and nowhere is the city's commitment to veterans more apparent than at the **Veterans Memorial Museum,** 1250 W. Hwy. 76 (© **417/336-2300;** www.veteransmemorial branson.com), which honors those who served in both world wars, Korea, Vietnam, and the Persian Gulf. Uniforms, personal histories, weapons, photographs, and thousands of memorabilia ranging from Adolf Hitler's World War I dog tag to a bicycle used on the Ho Chi Minh Trail are on display. Those who remember one of America's most beloved couples might want to pay their respects at the **Roy Rogers–Dale Evans Museum,** Highway 376 and Green Mountain Drive (© **417/339-1900;** www.roy rogers.com), packed with photographs and the couple's eclectic collection of memorabilia and personal effects, including guns, cowboy clothing and boots, cars, and guitars. Trigger and Buttermilk are preserved here, two 45-minute films document the stars' lives and careers, and Roy "Dusty" Rogers, Jr., performs twice daily at the adjoining Happy Trails Theater.

Visitors to **Titanic: The World's Largest Titanic Museum Attraction,** 3235 W. Hwy. 76 and (© **417/334-9500;** www.titanicbranson.com), can walk a replica of the ship's grand staircase, see the difference between first- and third-class staterooms, view 400 artifacts (each with a personal story), and learn about the fateful last hours of the doomed journey. Kids are drawn to **Ripley's Believe It or Not!,** 3325 W. Hwy. 76 (© **417/337-5300;** www.ripleysbranson.com), like moths to a flame for its collection of oddities from around the world, optical illusions, TV shows (both old and new), and world records.

TRAIN & BOAT TRIPS Departing from downtown Branson's century-old depot March to December, the **Branson Scenic Railway,** 206 E. Main (© **417/334-6110;** www.bransontrain.com), revives the romance of classic rail travel with 40-mile round-trips through the wooded Ozark hills aboard restored vintage 1940s and 1950s dome and passenger cars. These trips appeal to a mostly older crowd. For a lunch or dinner cruise on Table Rock Lake, board the *Showboat Branson Belle,* 4800 Mo. 165 (© **800/831-4-FUN** or 417/336-7171; www.showboatbransonbelle.com), a luxury paddle-wheeler boat offering 2-hour cruises with dining, music, comedy, and entertainment April through December. For a land and water tour, **Ride the Ducks,** 2320

W. Hwy. 76 (© **417/334-DUCK;** www.bransonducks.com), is a wacky 80-minute tour aboard World War II amphibious military assault vehicles that appeals to kids with corny jokes and a cruise of Table Rock Lake March through December.

OUTDOOR ACTIVITIES   Fisherfolk favor Table Rock Lake for bass and Lake Taneycomo for trout. **State Park Marina,** on Highway 165 inside Table Rock State Park (© **417/334-BOAT;** www.stateparkmarina.com), is Branson's closest marina and offers everything from pontoons and ski boats to fish boats and WaveRunners. Table Rock Lake also has several public swimming areas. Outdoor enthusiasts should head to **Dogwood Canyon Nature Park** (© **417/779-5983;** www.dogwoodcanyon.com), a beautiful 10,000-acre private wilderness refuge for elk, bison, Texas longhorns, deer, and other wildlife, accessible by hiking and biking paths (rental bikes are available), 2-hour wildlife tram tours, horseback rides, and kayak trips (fees charged for each activity). Some of the Branson area's seven 18-hole golf courses, open to the public year-round, are described in the brochure "Branson Golf" available at the Welcome Center. A favorite is the 9-hole par 3 **Top of the Rock,** 150 Top of the Rock Rd. (© **417/339-5312**). It's owned by Big Cedar Lodge (which does everything to perfection), was designed by Jack Nicklaus, has great views of Table Rock Lake, includes an Arnold Palmer–designed practice facility and a good restaurant, and is one of the few courses in the nation to be recognized as an Audubon Signature Cooperative. Eighteen-hole **Branson Creek Golf Club** (© **417/339-4653;** www.bransoncreekgolf. com) is one of Missouri's top public courses.

WHERE TO STAY

Branson offers resorts, countless motels and hotels, bed-and-breakfasts, and many camping facilities. In addition to the choices here, consider **Hilton Promenade at Branson Landing** (© **417336-5500;** www.promenadebransonlanding.hilton.com), which opened in October 2006 with 243 rooms overlooking Lake Tanycomo or downtown Branson. For something unique, try a stay in a houseboat; contact **Tri-Lakes Houseboat Rentals** (© **800/982-2628** or 417/739-2370; www.tri-lakeshouseboat. com) on Table Rock Lake.

All the hotels below offer free outdoor parking.

Big Cedar Lodge *Best*   Spread over 800 beautifully cultivated acres on a hill overlooking Table Rock Lake and owned by Bass Pro Shop, Branson's most impressive and classiest resort is a lovely refuge from Branson's congested Strip and is great for families, reunions, and romantic getaways. It offers a wide range of accommodations, from rooms in a rustic and majestic Northwest-style lodge to luxurious log cabins that sleep two to six adults and come with wood-burning fireplace, outdoor grill, kitchen, VCR (free videos available), and Jacuzzi. Facilities are extensive and first class, including a spring-fed pool, outdoor hot tubs, jogging and hiking trails, a children's center (ages 4–12), miniature golf, boat rentals, horseback riding, a playground, and laundry facilities.

612 Devil's Pool Rd. (10 miles south of Branson at Table Rock Lake), Ridgedale, MO 65739. © **417/335-2777.** Fax 417/335-2340. www.bigcedar.com. 247 units, 61 cottages and cabins. $119–$299 double; $179–$699 cottage/cabin. Children under 12 stay free in parent's room. 2-night minimum stay weekends (3-night minimum stay weekends in summer). Off-season rates and packages available. AE, DC, MC, V. **Amenities:** 4 restaurants; 3 pools (1 indoor) and 2 children's pools; 9-hole golf course; 2 outdoor lighted tennis courts; health club; spa.

Grand Country Inn *Kids*   Families that want to be in the thick of 76 Country Boulevard's never-ending string of theaters, go-cart tracks, restaurants, shops, and motels will find this property to their liking. It includes **Splash Country Indoors,** a large indoor/outdoor waterpark free to hotel guests, as well as two buffet restaurants, a theater with a variety of music shows throughout the day, and indoor minigolf. There's so much to do, most guests don't care that rooms are rather basic and ordinary. Local telephone calls are free. To find it, just look for the world's largest banjo.

Grand Country Sq., 1945 W. Hwy. 76, Branson, MO 65616. (℃) 800/828-9068 or 417/335-3535. Fax 417/334-1647. www.grandcountry.com. 319 units. $80–$100 double. Children under 18 stay free in parent's room. Packages available. AE, DC, MC, V. **Amenities:** 3 restaurants; indoor/outdoor waterpark; 3 pools (1 indoor).

Indian Point Resorts *Value* Situated on a wooded point on Table Rock Lake 2½ miles from Silver Dollar City and 6 miles from Branson, this casual, low-key lakefront resort appeals mainly to families with its recreational facilities (playgrounds; volleyball and badminton; game room; free paddle boats; and marina with rentals for fishing and ski boats, pontoons, and WaveRunners) and wide range of accommodations, all equipped with stocked kitchens and barbecue grills. These include comfortable if rather standard motel-like units, ranging from one-room efficiencies for two people to four-bedroom units that sleep 10, free-standing cottages, and log cabins of various sizes with fireplaces and decks. Slightly more upscale condos offer the additional luxuries of laundry facilities, dishwashers, fireplaces, and decks overlooking the lake. An RV park is also here, with rental RVs and mobile homes.

Indian Point Rd., Branson, MO 65616. (℃) 800/888-1891 or 417/338-2250. Fax 417/338-3507. www.indianpoint. com. 92 units, 32 cottages and cabins. $69–$108 double; $62–$98 cottages for 2 people; $95–$135 cabins for 2 people; $99–$170 condo double. Off-season rates and packages available. AE, DC, MC, V. **Amenities:** 3 outdoor pools. *In room:* Kitchen.

WHERE TO DINE

Branson Café *Value* AMERICAN This casual, busy, friendly diner in downtown Branson—a real regulars' hangout—has been the place to go since 1910 for down-home country cooking, including fried chicken, catfish, and sandwiches. Leave room for one of the famous pies.

120 W. Main St. (℃) 417/334-3021. Reservations accepted. Main courses $4.50–$9.95. AE, DC, MC, V. Mon–Sat 6am–8pm (also Sun 7am–2pm in peak season).

BT Bones Steakhouse AMERICAN/STEAKS Popular with an older crowd and also welcoming families, this dimly lit restaurant/bar is one of the few places offering free live country music nightly from 6pm. You can chow down on dinner as you listen, with choices ranging from sandwiches and buffalo burgers to steaks, prime rib, chicken, and barbecue ribs. There's also a children's menu and a lunch menu until 4pm with all entrees costing $6.95.

2280 Shepherd of the Hills Expwy. (at Roark Valley Rd.). (℃) 417/335-2002. www.btbones.com. Reservations not accepted. Main courses $6.95–$23. MC, V. Sun–Thurs 11am–10pm; Fri–Sat 11am–11pm.

Candlestick Inn *Best* STEAKS/SEAFOOD On the other side of Lake Taneycomo, on a bluff with fine views over downtown Branson, this upscale restaurant with an outdoor deck (and live music most nights) is perfect for romantic dining or a special occasion. In business since 1962, it specializes in fresh seafood like lobster tail and aged Black Angus beef, but other great choices include the trout amandine (boneless trout encrusted with maple-roasted almonds) and beef Wellington. Lunch features sandwiches, salads, quiche, and daily specials.

E. Hwy. 76. (℃) 417/334-3633. www.candlestickinn.com. Reservations recommended. Main courses $23–$48. AE, MC, V. Wed–Fri 11am–3pm; Sun–Thurs 5–9pm; Fri–Sat 5–10pm (closed Mon in winter).

Top of the Rock CALIFORNIAN   Perched atop a mountain with one of the Ozarks' best views, this casual, relaxed lodge overlooks a golf course and Table Rock Lake. Sunsets are especially spectacular from the outdoor patio. Owned by Big Cedar Lodge and decorated in rustic woods and stone, it specializes in wood-fired pizzas, homemade pasta creations, and rotisserie half chicken, but also offers grilled salmon, Kansas City strip steak, hamburgers, and sandwiches. *Note:* At press time, Top of the Rock was closed due to fire and was scheduled to reopen in 2007.

150 Top of the Rock Rd. (at Mo. 65 and 86). ⓒ 417/339-5320. Reservations recommended (request a window seat). Main courses $8–$28. AE, MC, V. Summer daily 11am–9:30pm; off season Sun and Wed–Thurs 11am–8pm, Fri–Sat 11am–9:30pm.

A SIDE TRIP TO EUREKA SPRINGS, ARKANSAS

Named one of America's Dozen Distinctive Destinations by the National Trust for Historic Preservation, **Eureka Springs** first drew interest because of its natural springs with purported healing powers. It was settled in the late 1800s as a spa destination and today its entire downtown district is on the National Register of Historic Places. While baths and spa treatments are still available, the city is now nationally renowned for its art and well-preserved Victorian-era architecture. It's actually a charming Victorian hillside village with historic homes, winding roads, and antiques and crafts shops.

For information, contact the **Eureka Springs Chamber of Commerce,** 137 W. Van Buren (ⓒ **866/566-9387;** www.eurekasprings.org), and request their free visitor's guide. *Tip:* For more information on Arkansas, check out appendix A, "The Best of the Rest," on p. 1024.

GETTING THERE   Eureka Springs is a scenic drive across the Missouri border to Arkansas. From Branson, take U.S. 65 south 30 miles to Bear Creek Springs, then U.S. 62 west 37 miles to Route 23.

WHAT TO SEE & DO

Eureka Springs' biggest attraction is the **Great Passion Play,** U.S. 62 East (ⓒ **866/ 882-7529** or 479/253-9200; www.greatpassionplay.com), a religious extravaganza about the life of Jesus. It takes place in an outdoor theater with a cast of 250 people and live animals, and is watched over by the seven-story Christ of the Ozarks statue. Also on the grounds is the New Holy Land, with 35 reproductions of structures referred to in the Bible, and the Museum of Earth History, which presents earth's history from a biblical view.

Other attractions worth seeking out are the **Abundant Memories Heritage Village,** 2½ miles north of Branson at 2434 Hwy. 23 N. (ⓒ **479/253-6764;** www.abundant memories.com), with 25 village buildings packed with artifacts of yesteryear; and the **Eureka Springs and North Arkansas Railway,** 299 N. Main St. (ⓒ **479/253-9623;** www.esnarailway.com), a restored 1906 steam passenger train that takes a scenic route through the Ozark Hills. Architecture buffs should check out **Thorncrown Chapel,** off U.S. 62 West (ⓒ **479/253-7401;** www.thorncrown.com), a church whose design, incorporating wood beams and glass in a woodland setting, was chosen in 2001 as one of the "Top 10 Designs of the 20th Century" by The American Institute of Architecture.

The Northern Rockies & Great Plains

Welcome to Middle America, stretching from the grassy plains of Oklahoma and Nebraska to the wild mountains of the Rockies and the desolation of the Badlands. Montana, Wyoming, and South Dakota proudly stand with one cocksure foot rooted in their Wild West past and the other firmly fixed in a setting of unparalleled splendor and majesty. Whether you come to this region to play cowboy on a guest ranch, or to stay in one of the classic lodges in the region's national parks, you'll experience firsthand nature's magnanimity: Yellowstone's wild abundance, the less-traveled vastness of Glacier National Park, the towering peaks of the Grand Tetons, the eerie desolation of the Badlands. Few ski buffs have to be told twice about the allure of the mountains in Idaho's famous Sun Valley. Opt for the prairies and the grasslands of Nebraska and Oklahoma and you'll be treated to loads of historical sites, top-flight museums, and scenic routes that are among the most storied in the nation. (Rte. 66 anyone?)

But that's not all. People come here to experience the area's back-to-basics way of life, an attitude that makes these states so endearing to visitors and enduring to residents. The residents of these states are self-reliant, hardy folks who are still America's pioneers. They like to fish with flies, hike with bears, and ride horses that buck. They've tried mining, logging, farming, and ranching and still believe that no matter what they have to do to live here, the land here makes it all worthwhile.

Tip: For information on Iowa and North Dakota, two other states in the Great Plains, see "appendix A: The Best of the Rest," on p. 1024.

1 The Flathead & Montana's Northwest Corner

If it's mountains, lakes, and streams you've come for, you'll find them in northwestern Montana. The area, almost empty in the spring and fall, encompasses Flathead Lake, majestic Glacier National Park (see later in this chapter), and Missoula.

ESSENTIALS
GETTING THERE   A number of major airlines offer flights to the **Missoula International Airport** (© **406/728-4381;** www.msoairport.org), northwest of downtown Missoula on U.S. 93.

I-90 leads into Missoula from the west (Washington state and Idaho) and the east (Billings and Bozeman). Two major roads will get you around this area: **U.S. 93** runs north to south (from the Bitterroot Valley south of Missoula to the state's nether regions), and **U.S. 2** runs east to west. **Mont. 200** follows the Clark Fork, Blackfoot, and Flathead rivers and is one of the state's most scenic highways.

The Northern Rockies & Great Plains

VISITOR INFORMATION The Missoula Convention and Visitors Bureau, 1121 E. Broadway, Suite 103, Missoula, MT 59802 (© **800/526-3465** or 406/532-3250; www.missoulacvb.org), has brochures, city maps, and area maps for outdoor activities, shopping, dining, and tours for most of northwestern Montana.

MISSOULA

Missoula has been growing by leaps and bounds for a decade, and the reason is clear: The city is in a beautiful valley along the Clark Fork River, with a relatively mild climate more influenced by the Pacific Northwest than the high Rockies. You could say the same about the local culture.

Since this is the home of the University of Montana, the crowds in Missoula's vibrant downtown are more often young and Birkenstocked than grizzled and cowboy-booted. **Global Village World Crafts,** 519 S. Higgins Ave. (© **406/543-3955**), is a project of the Jeannette Rankin Peace Resource Center, selling jewelry, clothing, and musical items from communities around the world. **Butterfly Herbs,** 232 N. Higgins Ave. (© **406/728-8780**), features an eclectic collection of items, including fresh herbs, jewelry, coffee mugs, teapots, and handmade paper and candles. If you begin to feel the bohemian spirit and suddenly want your own pair of Birkenstocks, just go next door to **Hide & Sole,** 236 N. Higgins Ave. (© **406/549-0666**), for reshodding.

Missoula is home to an impressive literary community, and the city's bookstores are among the state's best, including **Fact and Fiction,** 220 N. Higgins Ave. (© **406/721-2881**). The largest newsstand in Missoula is the **Garden City News,** 329 N. Higgins Ave. (© **406/543-3470**), which specializes in daily newspapers from both coasts, as well as from the Rocky Mountain area. Vintage, rare, and first-edition books are available from **Bird's Nest Books** at 219 N. Higgins Ave. (© **406/721-1125**).

The great outdoors—be it fly-fishing on Rock Creek, skiing at Snowbowl, hiking in the Selway-Bitterroot, or cross-country skiing on Lolo Pass—is probably what most attracts these types to the area. **Pipestone Mountaineering,** 129 W. Front St. (© **406/721-1670**), has an excellent range of outdoor gear for serious climbers, river runners, and campers. **The Trail Head,** 221 E Front St. (© **406/543-6966;** www.trailhead montana.net), is another good outdoors store, with gear for snowshoers, kayakers, and just about everybody in between. The outdoors figures heavily in Missoula-area politics as well. There is a strong pro-environment sentiment among the populace.

WHERE TO STAY & DINE

You won't find a whole lot of lodging variety within Missoula's city limits. For a distinctive night's sleep, try roughing it in a historic cabin. Information on rental of **old-fashioned miners' cabins** at the ghost town of Garnet is available by contacting the **Garnet Preservation Association,** 3255 Fort Missoula Rd., Missoula, MT 59804 (© **406/329-1031;** www.garnetghosttown.org).

Among the list of mostly chain lodgings, there are a couple of standouts. The beautiful 1911 brick home known as **Goldsmith's Inn** (© **866/666-9945;** www.goldsmiths inn.com) is Missoula's only riverside B&B, right on the Clark Fork River just across from the University of Montana. The Goldsmith's fabulous ice cream is a Missoula favorite, and you can get some right next door at Goldsmith's Waterfront Pasta House. **The Fort at Lolo Trail Center and Lolo Hot Springs** (© **406/273-2201;** www.lolo trailcenter.com), 25 miles west of Lolo, provides a stunning resort setting for the rejuvenating powers of the hot springs. Doubles range from $79 to $139.

Thanks to the university and a relatively cultured populace, Missoula is blessed with an excellent variety of restaurants, ranging from organic vegetarian to full-blown carnivorous. In addition to perennial favorites like the **Red Bird** (✆ **406/549-2906**) and **Bernice's Bakery** (✆ **406/728-1358**), we suggest **Two Sisters,** 127 W. Adler (✆ **406/ 327-8438**), for standout dinner dishes such as chipotle barbecue chicken and linguine with clams, and simple breakfast and lunch offerings, including eggs Benedict and sandwiches. A stone's throw from the carousel, **Nap's,** 231 W. Front St. (✆ **406/829-1207**), is a burger fanatic's dream, frying up enormous 12-ouncers, as well as steaks, salads, and sandwiches.

SIDE TRIPS FROM MISSOULA

Founded in the early 1850s by Jesuit priests, the town of **St. Ignatius** (32 miles north of Missoula on U.S. 93), nestled in the heart of the Mission Valley, has one of Montana's most prized architectural treasures, the **St. Ignatius Mission,** P.O. Box 667, St. Ignatius, MT 59865 (✆ **406/745-2768**). Established in 1854, the mission contains 58 unique murals by Brother Josephy Carignano on its walls and ceilings.

The **Ninepipe National Wildlife Refuge** (✆ **406/644-2211;** www.fws.gov/bison range/ninepipe), just off U.S. 93 about 10 miles north of St. Ignatius, is home to a huge waterfowl population. Southwest off U.S. 93 on County Road 212 is the **National Bison Range,** a protected open range for buffalo, deer, bighorn sheep, and pronghorn located on reservation land.

FLATHEAD LAKE

This is one of the most beautiful areas in Montana. Towering peaks rise from the valley floor on the east, and the mountains of the Flathead National Forest define the edge of the valley to the west. This is a land of forests, cattle, and alfalfa—with a velvet-green valley floor, green and granite mountains, and, on a sunny day, a dramatic deep-blue ceiling.

This part of Montana seems to offer something for everyone, whether your interests lie indoors or out. There are watersports on the lake and hikes that lead to sparkling mountain streams with views. But if you want to shop or see a play, you can easily spend your day inside the boutiques, galleries, and theater of Bigfork.

With much of this area lying within tribal lands, there is also a long-standing American Indian heritage. The Confederated Salish and Kootenai Tribes make their home on the Flathead Indian Reservation, with tribal headquarters for the 1.2-million-acre reservation in Pablo.

Your best bet for information on the south end of the lake is the **Port Polson Chamber of Commerce,** P.O. Box 667, Polson, MT 59860 (✆ **406/883-5969;** www. polsonchamber.com). For goings-on north, contact the **Bigfork Chamber of Commerce,** P.O. Box 237, Bigfork, MT 59911 (✆ **406/837-5888;** www.bigfork.org). The **Flathead Convention and Visitor Bureau** (✆ **406/756-9091;** www.fcvb.org), **Travel Montana** (✆ **800/847-4868**), and **Glacier Country** (✆ **800/338-5072**) can supplement this information.

The Flathead is one of those rare places where you see the serious golfer and the serious backpacker in the same spot, sometimes in the same body. The golfing is excellent on several courses, and the backpacking, hiking, and fishing are even better. Fishing, boating, and "yachting" are popular sports for those who can afford to practice them. If your plans take you to one of the lakes or trails on the Salish-Kootenai Reservation, don't forget to buy a tribal permit.

Boat rentals are available at the **Bigfork Marina and Boat Center** (© 406/837-5556), **Kwa Taq Nuk Resort** (© 800/882-6363), **Bayview Resort and Marina** (© 406/837-4843), and **Marina Cay Resort** (© 406/837-5861).

The brochure *Fishing the Flathead,* available from the **Flathead Convention and Visitor Bureau** (© 406/756-9091; www.fcvb.org), provides information on 14 different fishing opportunities, as well as an outline of the licensing and catch-and-release regulations. To increase your odds of snagging something besides a log, contact **Glacier Fishing Charters** (© 406/892-2377). Also, "Shorty" George's **A-Able Fishing** (© 800/231-5214 or 406/257-5214; www.aablefishing.com) will outfit a fishing trip with guides who know the area.

Eagle Bend Golf Club (© 406/837-7300; www.golfmt.com), a challenging Jack Nicklaus–designed track with views of Flathead Lake and the surrounding mountains, is located in Bigfork just off the highway on Holt Drive. The 18-hole course is only 6,200 yards from the white tees, but it's harder than Chinese arithmetic.

Hikers, welcome to bear country. With a little effort, avoiding grizzly confrontations is as easy as making noise and being watchful. Like your mama said, don't surprise them and they won't surprise you. Besides strolling by the lake at one of the marinas or state parks, the best bet for trekking is in the **Jewel Basin,** a designated hiking area north of Bigfork. More than 30 miles of trails make it a great place for day hiking as well as overnights.

WHERE TO STAY & DINE

There are five campgrounds in Flathead Lake state parks, each located at a different point around the lake: Big Arm (© 406/849-5255) and West Shore (© 406/844-3066) on the west side of the lake; and Finley Point (© 406/887-2715), Yellow Bay (© 406/752-5501), and Wayfarers (© 406/837-4196) on the east shore. The phone numbers are operational only in summer.

Accommodations on and near the lake include guest ranches, water-oriented resorts with the gamut of recreational opportunities, and basic motels that offer clean but modest rooms. For an all-around vacation experience, **Averill's Flathead Lake Lodge,** P.O. Box 248, Bigfork, MT 59911 (© 406/837-4397; www.averills.com), is the best on the lake. A beautiful log lodge surrounded by thousands of acres of forest serves as your home base for all activities, which include horseback riding, boating, and fishing. The Western experience is done up right at this place, complete with singalongs, campfires, and barn dances.

Tucked away on 10 acres of pine forest at the foot of the Swan Mountains, **The Candlewycke Inn,** 311 Aero Lane, Bigfork, MT 59911 (© 888/617-8805 or 406/837-6406; www.candlewyckeinn.com), is a luxurious and large modern home that innkeeper Megan Vandegrift converted into a first-rate inn. There's a trail system on the property, an immaculate lawn, and all sorts of little touches (such as antlers converted to back scratchers). The breakfasts, anything from salmon quiche to oatmeal-rice porridge, are tailored to the tastes of guests.

La Provence, 408 Bridge St., Bigfork (© 406/837-2923; www.bigforkla provence.com), is one of the best restaurants in the area, serving French-Mediterranean cuisine. In Somers, the locals like **Tiebuckers Pub and Eatery,** 75 Somers Rd. (© 406/857-3335), for the fresh fish and steamed clams, but they also offer beef, pasta, chicken, and ribs.

WHITEFISH: A GATEWAY TO GLACIER

Whitefish has boomed as a resort community, attracting people from all over the country and making it Montana's fastest growing area. Longtime residents have feared it will become another Aspen or Jackson Hole, but that hasn't quite happened yet. In fact, Whitefish is still relatively sedate.

Whitefish is almost two different towns—the town itself and the Big Mountain ski area. The busy season in town is the summer, and room rates are correspondingly higher there during warm weather. This may seem odd for a ski town, but Glacier National Park attracts about two million visitors a year, while the ski area brings in only about 300,000.

Up on the mountain, however, the peak season is winter, especially during Christmas vacation. So if you don't mind the winding 5-mile drive up (or down) the Big Mountain road, you can find slightly less expensive accommodations in the appropriate season.

Whitefish is extremely accessible. It's easier to get to than virtually any other Montana vacation town. It's a quick drive up U.S. 93 from Kalispell.

The **Whitefish Chamber of Commerce** is located downtown at 520 E. 2nd St. (© **877/862-3548** or 406/862-3501; www.whitefishchamber.com). Here you'll find just about everything you need in the way of brochures, area maps, and travel information.

Whitefish is truly a paradise for outdoors enthusiasts, with ski slopes, hiking trails, watersports opportunities, and Glacier National Park just down the road. For all kinds of outdoor equipment or apparel, check out **Sportsman & Ski Haus** at the Mountain Mall (© **406/862-3111**), or **Ski Mountain Sports,** 238 Central Ave. (© **406/862-7541**).

Just 12 miles north of Whitefish is one of the best-kept ski resort secrets in the country. **The Big Mountain Resort** (© **800/858-5439** or 406/862-2900; www.big-mountain.com) offers lots of powder, lots of skiing in the trees, and plenty of runs for every level of skier. With an annual snowfall of 300 inches, night skiing for $14 (Fri–Sat mid-Dec to mid-Mar), a vertical drop of 2,500 feet, and virtually no lines, the Big Mountain is one of the best resorts in the northwestern United States. More than half the mountain is geared to the intermediate skier, but there is plenty of terrain for experts and beginners. The expert runs are pretty steep—not as steep as those at Wyoming's Jackson Hole Ski Area, but steep enough. There are never any crowds at Big Mountain, even in the holiday seasons, so although the prices have gone up over the years, at least you can spend your time skiing rather than waiting in lift lines.

During the summer months, bikes are nearly as prevalent as cars in the north part of the Flathead Valley. Another Whitefish operation shares the expertise for mountain bikers seeking adventure on seemingly undiscovered paths. **Glacier Cyclery and Fitness,** 326 E. 2nd St. (© **406/862-6446**), provides excellent service and maintenance as well as rentals, area maps, and up-to-date information for the serious mountain biker. This outfit has been ranked among the 100 best cycle shops in a pool of 6,800 independent dealers. For a less challenging ride, you can make the 20-mile round-trip on paved roads from downtown Whitefish to the head of Whitefish Lake.

It's not the Madison Valley, but Whitefish does have some hot spots for anglers wanting to try their hand. **Tally Lake** is a deep hole located north of Whitefish off U.S. 93. Five miles north of town, turn left onto the Tally Lake Road (signs will direct you). You can expect cutthroat, rainbow, kokanee, brook trout, and whitefish. In town, across the viaduct toward the Big Mountain, lies **Whitefish Lake.** If you can handle all the recreationists hovering about like flies, the lake offers some pretty good lake trout. Northern pike can be found here, and rainbow and cutthroat can be nabbed on dry flies in the evening. The **Lakestream Flyshop,** 334 Central Ave. (© **406/862-1298;** www.lakestream.com), is the best resource in town for information about fly-fishing the Flathead River and local streams.

The **Whitefish Lake Golf Club,** U.S. 93 North (© **406/862-4000;** www.golf whitefish.com), is the only 36-hole golf course in the state. Built in the 1930s, the golf club's trees have grown up considerably in the time since. While not especially long, the course offers a wide variety of shots that will require you to use all the clubs in your bag (and maybe some you forgot). Almost all the fairways are lined with trees. There are few fairway bunkers, but they are strategically placed around the greens. Both 18-hole setups measure a little more than 6,500 yards from the tips. There is also a driving range and putting green.

WHERE TO STAY & DINE

Whitefish might just have the best range of accommodations in all of Montana, with everything from mom-and-pop motels to graceful inns to slope-side condos. There's a **Super 8,** 800 Spokane Ave. (© **800/800-8000** or 406/862-8255), with doubles for $65 to $100 nightly. **The Pine Lodge,** 920 Spokane Ave. (© **800/305-7463** or 406/862-7600; www.thepinelodge.com), is a good independent option, with doubles for $75 to $125.

While it's right on the main Whitefish drag, the **Garden Wall Inn,** 504 Spokane Ave. (© **888/530-1700** or 406/862-3440; www.gardenwallinn.com), is a world of its own. The owners clearly take pride in providing all of the little luxurious extras. Every detail is just about perfect, right down to the towels, which are large and fluffy enough to dry two adults.

Grouse Mountain Lodge, 2 Fairway Dr., Whitefish (© **800/321-8822** or 406/862-3000; www.grousemountainlodge.com), is one of Montana's premier vacation lodge properties, with a variety of rooms from standard hotel-like rooms—called the executive rooms—to loft rooms with kitchens. The lodge has two outdoor Jacuzzis and three places to eat: a casual grill, an outdoor patio, and the fine-dining **Wine Room.**

The Big Mountain is a full-service ski area, working to attract local skiers, Canadian and American vacationers, and families. It provides a wide variety of accommodations to fit almost every pocketbook. You can reach central reservations at © **800/858-5439.**

A good cup of organic coffee and a selection of baked goods are available at the **Montana Coffee Traders,** located at 110 Central Ave. (© **406/862-7667**), which also houses a nifty used bookstore and a nice place to sprawl on a couch and read a book. **Loula's Café,** located downstairs at 300 E. 2nd St. (© **406/862-5614**), serves traditional American breakfasts and salads and sandwiches for lunch in an attractive setting. **The Buffalo Cafe,** 514 3rd St. (© **406/862-2833**), is Whitefish's best breakfast spot—try their legendary bacon-and-egg-filled pies. And for plump subs, try **Quickee,** 28 Lupfer Ave. (© **406/862-9866**)—just look for the house with the gas pump above the door.

If it's a dressy night out that you're after, the **Whitefish Lake Restaurant,** U.S. 93 North at the Whitefish Golf Club (© **406/862-5285**), is known as "the best restaurant in the state" to many locals. Housed in a building that was constructed in 1936 as a WPA project, the dining room has an almost churchlike atmosphere: dark and quiet, with log beams and a stone fireplace providing warmth on chilly evenings. The food at **Corner House Grille,** 147 Central Ave. (© **406/863-2323**), blends French and Continental influences, Asian sauces, and regional ingredients for dishes such as sesame moo shu duck and fennel-dusted Florida grouper.

2 Glacier National Park

ESSENTIALS

GETTING THERE   The closest cities to the park with airline service are **Kalispell,** 29 miles southwest of the park, **Missoula,** 150 miles south, and **Great Falls,** 143 miles southeast. If you're driving, you can reach the park from U.S. highways 2 and 89. **Amtrak's Empire Builder** (© 800/872-7245; www.amtrak.com), a Chicago-Seattle round-trip route, makes daily stops at West Glacier and Essex year-round and East Glacier from May 1 to October 1.

ACCESS/ENTRY POINTS   There are six paved entrances that provide vehicular access to Glacier National Park, but if you are traveling by car, you will most likely use **West Glacier** and **St. Mary.** These entrances are located at either end of Going-to-the-Sun Road, with West Glacier on the southwest side and St. Mary on the east. Visitor entrances passes are sold only at these two entrances. The four other entrances include: Camas Creek and Polebridge on the west, and Many Glacier and Two Medicine on the east. *Caution:* Entrance to the park is severely restricted during winter months when the Alpine section of Going-to-the-Sun Road is closed.

VISITOR INFORMATION   For information about the park before your trip, contact **Glacier National Park,** West Glacier, MT 59936 (© **406/888-7800;** www.nps. gov/glac). For up-to-date information on park activities once you arrive, check in at visitor centers located at **Apgar** (open May–Oct and weekends during the winter), **Logan Pass** (open mid-June to late Sept), and **St. Mary** (from mid-May to mid-Oct). Park information may also be obtained from the **Many Glacier Ranger Station** or park headquarters in **West Glacier.**

FEES   Admission to the park for up to 7 days costs $25 per vehicle or $12 per person for those on foot, bicycles, and motorcycles. A season pass costs $30 and allows unlimited entry to Glacier National Park for 1 year. The National Park, Golden Age, and Golden Access passes are also honored. A separate entrance fee is charged for visitors to Waterton Lakes National Park.

SEASONS   In winter, Glacier shuts itself off from the motorized world: Even snowmobiles are forbidden. All unplowed roads—and very little is plowed—become trails for snowshoers and cross-country skiers, who rave about the vast powdered wonderland that exists here. Guided trips into the backcountry are a great way to experience the park in winter.

TOURS   From mid-June to mid-September, **Glacier Park Boat Company,** P.O. Box 5262, Kalispell, MT 59903 (© **406/257-2426;** www.glacierparkboats.com), offers daily **narrated boat tours,** often including hikes and picnics, from Lake McDonald, St. Mary, Two Medicine, and Many Glacier.

GOING-TO-THE-SUN ROAD

One of the most important Glacier things to do is to drive **Going-to-the-Sun Road,** the 50-mile road that bisects the park between West Glacier and St. Mary. Points of interest are clearly marked along this road, and correspond to the park brochure *Points of Interest Along the Going-to-the-Sun Road,* which is available at visitor centers. Bring plenty of film.

The road gains more than 3,400 feet in 32 miles, and is very narrow in places. Visitors with a fear of heights should take a van tour or shuttle. Because of the road's narrowness, oversize vehicles and trailers must use U.S. 2.

As you begin the drive from the West Glacier entrance, you'll pass the largest of the 653 lakes in Glacier—**Lake McDonald.** Numerous turnouts along the way present opportunities to photograph the panoramic views of the lake with its mountainous backdrop. You can see **Sacred Dancing Cascade** and **Johns Lake** after an easy, half-mile hike from the roadside through a hemlock and red cedar forest. The trail head for this hike is 2 miles north of the Lake McDonald Lodge along Going-to-the-Sun Road.

The **Trail of the Cedars** is a short, wheelchair-accessible boardwalk trail through terrain thickly carpeted in vibrant, verdant hues. This is also the beginning of the Avalanche Lake Trail, a 2.1-mile hike (one-way) to the foot of Avalanche Lake, one of the most popular day hikes in the park. The trail head is about 5½ miles north of Lake McDonald Lodge, just past the Avalanche Creek Campground.

Almost exactly halfway along Going-to-the-Sun is the overlook for Heaven's Peak, the massive snow-covered mountain to the south that you've just driven around. This is also the jumping-off point for **The Loop Trail,** which can take you to the Granite Park Chalet. Just 2 miles farther is the **Bird Woman Falls Overlook.** Bird Woman Falls drops in a wondrous bounty of water from a hanging valley above the road. Next along the road is the oft-photographed **Weeping Wall,** which is a wall of rock with water pouring forth.

At the 32-mile mark from West Glacier is **Logan Pass,** one of the park's busiest areas and the starting point for the hike to **Hidden Lake,** likely the park's most popular trail. There's a visitor center here atop the Continental Divide, with a bookstore and a small display about the wildlife, flora, and geology of the area.

As you continue the drive downhill, you'll reach the turnout for **Jackson Glacier,** the most recognizable glacier in the entire park, followed by **Sunrift Gorge** and **Sun Point,** which are accessible via two short trails rife with wildlife.

OUTDOOR ACTIVITIES

FISHING   Glacier's streams and lakes are habitat for whitefish, kokanee salmon, arctic grayling, and five kinds of trout. Try the North Fork of the Flathead to fish for cutthroat and bull trout, and any of the park's three larger lakes (Bowman, St. Mary, and McDonald) for rainbow, brook trout, and whitefish. State of Montana fishing licenses are generally not required within the park's boundaries, although you will need one on the North Fork and Middle Fork of the Flathead River. Also, keep in mind that since the eastern boundary of the park abuts the Blackfeet Indian Reservation, you may find yourself fishing in their territorial waters. To avoid a problem, purchase a $10 use permit from businesses in the gateway towns; the permit covers fishing, hiking, and biking in the reservation. Fishing outside the park in Montana waters requires a state license; check in at a local fishing shop to make certain you're within the law.

HIKING   Glacier is a park that is best seen on foot. Its 1,600 square miles have more than 150 trails, totaling more than 750 miles. You can hike more than 100 miles along the Continental Divide alone. **Trail maps** are available at outdoor stores in Whitefish and Kalispell, as well as at the major visitor centers and ranger stations in the park. Before striking off into the wilderness, however, check with the nearest ranger station to determine the accessibility of your destination, trail conditions, and recent bear sightings.

Among the park's shorter and easier trails is the **Trail of the Cedars Nature Trail** (.25 mile round-trip; access is across from the Avalanche Campground Ranger Station), an easy, level trail that's wheelchair accessible. It has interpretive signs along the way. The **Hidden Lake Nature Trail** (3 miles round-trip; accessed from the Logan

Pass Visitor Center) is an easy-to-moderate interpretive trail that climbs 460 feet to an overlook of scenic Hidden Lake. It's a popular trail, but by hiking all the way to the overlook, you'll avoid some of the crowds, and you might even see a mountain goat.

The Loop (8 miles round-trip; access is on Going-to-the-Sun Rd., about halfway between Avalanche Campground and Logan Pass Visitor Center) offers a moderate hike that climbs to Granite Park Chalet and back. Many people use it as a continuation of the Highline Trail, but this is the section to do if you're not quite so adventurous (the Highline Trail is almost 8 miles long). If you want to spend the night in the chalet, contact **Glacier Wilderness Guides** for reservations (© **800/521-7238**).

The very easy **Running Eagle Falls Trail** (.6 mile round-trip; access is 1 mile west of the Two Medicine entrance) winds through a heavily forested area to a large, noisy waterfall. The popular **Twin Falls Trail** (7.6 miles round-trip; accessed from Two Medicine Campground) is an easy hike to scenic Twin Falls. Hikers can walk the entire distance to Twin Falls on a clearly identified trail, or boat across Two Medicine Lake to the foot of the trail head, and hike the last mile. The **St. Mary Falls Trail** (1.6 miles round-trip; accessed from Jackson Glacier Overlook) is a fairly easy walk that takes you to rushing falls of the St. Mary River. The roar of the cascade is prodigious and satisfying.

HORSEBACK RIDING   Guided horseback riding at East Glacier is provided by **Glacier Gateway Outfitters** (© **406/226-9220**), located a stone's throw from the front door of the lodge; the company offers rides into the nearby wilderness that range in length from an hour to a full day. **Mule Shoe Outfitters** (© **406/888-5121** or 406/732-4203; www.mule-shoe.com) offers similar rides from corrals at Lake McDonald and the Many Glacier Corral. Mule Shoe has hourly and full-day rides through the varied terrain of Glacier.

RAFTING   The **Montana Raft Company** (© **800/521-RAFT** or 406/387-5555; www.glacierguides.com) is an arm of Glacier Wilderness Guides that offers rafting trips in Glacier and the surrounding area. Prices for an adult range from a half-day for $46 to a 3-day trip for $471 per person.

WHERE TO CAMP & STAY

There are a variety of camping opportunities for RV enthusiasts and tent campers alike. Campgrounds accessible by paved roads include **Apgar,** near the West Glacier entrance; **Avalanche Creek,** just up from the head of Lake McDonald; **Fish Creek,** on the west side of Lake McDonald; **Many Glacier,** in the northeast part of the park; **Rising Sun,** on the north side of St. Mary Lake; **St. Mary,** on the east side of the park; and **Two Medicine,** in the southeast part of the park near East Glacier. **Sprague Creek,** near the West Glacier entrance, offers a paved road but does not allow towed vehicles. There are also five campgrounds accessed by narrow dirt roads. Though utility connections are not provided at these sites, fireplaces, picnic tables, washrooms (with sinks and flush toilets), and cold running water are available. Campsites range from $12 to $17 and are available on a first-come, first-served basis. Stop at any ranger station for information on closures and availability.

Glacier Park Inc. (GPI), P.O. Box 2025, Columbia Falls, MT 59912 (© **406/892-2525;** fax 406/892-1375; www.glacierparkinc.com), operates the hostelries in Glacier National Park. **Lake McDonald Lodge, Glacier Park Lodge,** and **Many Glacier Hotel** are first-tier properties that have been popular destinations since early in the 20th century. **Swiftcurrent Motor Inn** is typical of the casual motel-style properties at the other end of the spectrum, providing decent but undistinguished accommodations for less money. Although the lodges have a considerable charm, they don't have spas, air-conditioning, or in-room televisions. Reserve well in advance.

Outside the park, the **Mountain Pine Hotel,** Mont. 49, East Glacier, MT (© **406/ 226-4403**), is a 1950s-type motel with inexpensive, clean, well-furnished rooms. Originally housing railway workers, the historic, moderately priced **Izaak Walton Inn,** 290 Izaak Walton Inn Rd., Essex, MT (© **406/888-5700;** www.izaakwaltoninn. com), maintains a railroad ambience. Situated at the end of Going-to-the-Sun Road, **The Resort at Glacier** (© **800/368-3689** or 406/732-4431) has motel-style units with two single beds or a queen-size, but the nicest units are the cabins, with living areas, kitchenettes, and separate sleeping areas. The **Vista Motel** in West Glacier (© **406/888-5311**) boasts tremendous views of the mountains.

3 Bozeman & South-Central Montana

Relatively unspoiled, yet one of the most heavily touristed areas in the state, south-central Montana is a world-class playground for the outdoor recreational enthusiast. Its biggest draws are the surrounding mountains that are a haven for hikers and campers, and, without a doubt, the fly-fishing waters of the four major rivers that flow through its valleys (the Madison, Jefferson, Gallatin, and Yellowstone), all of which double as recreation areas for rafting, kayaking, and canoeing.

Bozeman, home of Montana State University, provides the hip, intellectual charm and culture of a college town—good bookstores and restaurants, charming shops, even a brewpub—as well as cultural events that appeal to both the cosmopolitan and cowboy cultures.

BOZEMAN

A college town and tourism hot spot with a friendly, semibohemian vibe, Bozeman was first settled in the 1860s as a ranching hub. Today, its cowboy edge has been mostly chipped away, revealing a sophisticated Western chic. The vibrant downtown strip is filled with independent shops and restaurants. The area bustles year-round—whatever the season, the locals always seem to be out and about.

Bozeman has experienced its greatest growth since 1990, and it shows little sign of slacking off. (In fact, longtime residents worry that the town may be getting a little too hip.) The city probably has more nice restaurants per capita than any other town in Montana. The university, Montana State, is a good one, and the students gravitate here for the excellent downhill skiing at nearby Bridger Bowl. The fact that Bozeman is less than 100 miles from Yellowstone National Park certainly hasn't hurt its popularity either.

ESSENTIALS
GETTING THERE   Bozeman's **Gallatin Field** (© 406/388-8321) serves a wide region in this part of the state. Daily service is available from **Delta** (© **800/221-1212**), **Northwest** (© **800/225-2525**), **Horizon Air** (© **800/547-9308**), and **United Express** (© **800/241-6522**).

By car, Interstate 90 handles most of the traffic. It is 140 miles along I-90 from Billings to the east and 202 miles from Missoula to the west.

VISITOR INFORMATION   The **Bozeman Area Chamber of Commerce** is located at 2000 Commerce Dr. (© **800/228-4224** or 406/586-5421; www.bozeman chamber.com). From Memorial Day to Labor Day, there's an information kiosk at 1001 N. 7th Ave., and there's a **Downtown Bozeman Visitor Center** at 224 E. Main

St. (© **406/586-4008**). The chamber publishes an extensive visitors guide, and also leads groups on tours of downtown and local cemeteries during the summer.

WHAT TO SEE & DO

Many of the outdoor activities discussed in this section take place in the **Gallatin National Forest.** For additional information, including current road and trail conditions, contact the Bozeman Ranger District, 3710 Fallon St., Suite C, Bozeman, MT 59718 (© **406/522-2520** or 406/587-6701; www.fs.fed.us/r1/gallatin).

Ski enthusiasts will find **Bridger Bowl** just 16 miles north of town, on Mont. 86 (15795 Bridger Canyon Rd., Bozeman; © **800/223-9609** or 406/587-2111; www. bridgerbowl.com). Although not as steep as Teton Village in Jackson Hole, Bridger Bowl is plenty steep for most of us, and a great hill for good skiers. With 20 feet of snowfall annually, Bridger sees a lot of powder days. It's usually open from the second Friday in December to mid-April, daily from 9am to 4pm. Oh, and there are seldom any lift lines.

At **The River's Edge,** 2012 N. 7th Ave. (© **406/586-5373;** www.theriversedge.com), Dave and Sally Rogers operate a highly professional fly-fishing specialty shop "in the heart of Montana's blue-ribbon trout streams." They offer guided fishing trips year-round—including float fishing and walking or wading trips, plus equipment rental and shuttle service. Wading trips are excellent learning experiences, because guides can focus on your fly-fishing skills. A guided trip for two costs $400 per day and includes lunch.

Two outfitters offer anglers memorable, albeit expensive, **fly-fishing** outings. A full-line Orvis shop, **Montana Troutfitters,** 1716 W. Main St. (© **800/646-7847** or 406/587-4707; www.troutfitters.com), has been operating guide services since 1978. **The Bozeman Angler,** 23 E. Main St. (© **800/886-9111** or 406/587-9111; www. bozemanangler.com), provides guided trips in the Madison, Gallatin, Yellowstone, Jefferson, and Missouri rivers plus numerous creeks, reservoirs, and lakes.

There's a beautiful and popular hiking area near Bozeman, known as the **Hyalite drainage,** in the Gallatin National Forest. The area includes Hyalite Canyon and reservoir, Palisades Falls Trail, and many trail heads for access to the national forest. A lot of the trails here are steep and difficult, though. An excellent introductory hike to get the lay of the land is the half-mile **Palisades Falls National Recreational Trail.**

Hyalite Reservoir is a wonderful place to hike, scale small peaks, and take in some of the Bozeman area's scenic wealth. **The Grotto Falls Trail** is a "difficult" 1.25-mile graveled trail to Grotto Falls located 13 miles up the West Fork Road in Hyalite Canyon. For a longer hike, go the 7.25 miles up the **Hyalite Peak Trail** to the peak. There is a 3,300-foot elevation gain on this hike.

As well as being a center for outdoor activities, Bozeman offers a surprising number of indoor education experiences for the whole family. The unique **American Computer Museum,** 2304 N. 7th Ave., Suite B, in the Bridger Park Mall (© **406/582-1288;** www.compuseum.org), traces the history of computing technologies from the abacus to the Apple. The **Emerson Center for the Arts and Culture,** 111 S. Grand Ave. (© **406/587-9797;** www.theemerson.org), is the home base for Bozeman's art scene, with gallery space and studios for more than 80 artists. The **Gallatin County Pioneer Museum,** 317 W. Main St. (© **406/522-8122;** www.pioneermuseum.org), gives an excellent perspective on early pioneer life in Montana, from its home in an old jail building—a murderer was hanged here in 1924—to the authentic homestead cabin on the premises.

The **Museum of the Rockies,** 600 W. Kagy Blvd. (© **406/994-2251;** www.museum oftherockies.org), on the campus of Montana State University, provides an interesting look into the past and continues to be an important center for studying the many fossils in the area. Kids will like the newly renovated dinosaur exhibits, the **Hall of Horns and Teeth** and the **Mesozoic Media Center.** The **Hall of Giants,** populated with animatronic dinosaurs, is set to open in 2007. Other exhibits explore Native American history, state history, and local art. Also on the premises is the **Taylor Planetarium,** a state-of-the-art, 40-foot domed multimedia theater.

Main Street offers an Old West feel and New West selection, starting at about 7th Avenue and running out to I-90. The chief part of the shopping district is easily accessible on foot. Among our favorite stops here are **Vargo's Jazz City and Books,** 6 W. Main (© 406/587-5383), which sells an eclectic mass of new, used, and out-of-print books, CDs, and LPs (or the elusive, vanishing vinyl); **The Montana Gift Corral,** 237 E. Main (© 406/585-8625), which offers a wide selection of made-in-Montana gifts, in case you need a moose clock to take home; **Thomas Nygard Gallery,** 135 E. Main (© 406/586-3636), which sells pre-1950 artwork from the Northern Plains; **The Country Bookshelf,** 28 W. Main (© 406/587-0166), a terrific bookstore; and **Barkenhowell's,** 777 E. Main (© 406/586-6160), a chic dog boutique.

WHERE TO STAY & DINE

Bozeman has a full complement of chain motels, most just off I-90: You can stay at the **Best Western GranTree Inn,** 1325 N. 7th Ave. (© 800/624-5865 or 406/587-5261); the **Fairfield Inn,** 828 Wheat Dr. (© 406/587-2222); the **Hampton Inn,** 75 Baxter Lane (© 406/522-8000); or the **Hilton Garden Inn,** 2023 Commerce Way (© 877/782-9444 or 406/582-9900). In addition, consider checking out **Lehrkind Mansion,** 719 N. Wallace Ave. (© 800/992-6932 or 406/585-6932; www.bozeman bedandbreakfast.com), the former home of Julius Lehrkind, a Swiss-born brewer who wanted to live next door to his brewery. Ninety-nine years later, the 1897 Queen Anne mansion was turned into a bed-and-breakfast by former national park rangers, who have done a remarkable job of capturing the house in 1890s amber: Everything, from the rare 1897 Regina music box in the parlor to the many original fixtures in the bathrooms to the amazingly preserved original carpet in the Muir Room, is from Lehrkind's day—with the exception of the hot tub out back.

The folks at the **Mackenzie River Pizza Co.,** 232 E. Main St. (© 406/587-0055), do pizza with a decidedly new twist. **Casa Sanchez,** 719 S. 9th Ave. (© 406/586-4516), located in the 100-year-old house near the MSU campus, is home to the best Mexican food in Bozeman—and it's all homemade. A popular local favorite is **John Bozeman's Bistro,** 125 W. Main St. (© 406/587-4100), with buffalo, beef, and chicken plus vegetarian dishes. Beyond these restaurants, we're firm believers in the restorative powers of the breakfast burritos at **Soby's,** in the Bozeman Hotel at 321 E. Main St. (© 406/587-8857), a favorite student haunt for breakfast and lunch. For a burger and a beer on an outdoor deck, you can't beat the **Garage,** 451 E. Main St. (© 406/585-8558). In the winter, the town compensates for the cold weather with the **Soup Shack,** serving seven hot soups and an array of toppings, from a space that houses the ice-cream-oriented **Scoop Shack** in summer.

THE MADISON RIVER VALLEY

The Madison Valley is an almost mythical place surrounded by spectacular mountain scenery where anglers from all over gather to fish. The main attraction is the Madison River, which flows through the valley at the base of the Madison Range, a stretch of peaks that runs toward Yellowstone Park.

Besides the phenomenal fishing, the Madison Valley has tourist-worthy historical sites. **The Missouri Headwaters State Park** is at the confluence of the Jefferson, Madison, and Gallatin rivers, where Lewis and Clark paused to take shelter; **Lewis and Clark Caverns State Park,** with its spectacular underground peaks, is just up the road; and **Madison Buffalo Jump State Park** is nearby.

Contact the **Three Forks Chamber of Commerce** (✆ **406/285-4753;** www.three forksmontana.com), or the **Ennis Chamber of Commerce** (✆ **406/682-4388;** www. ennischamber.com). **Yellowstone Country** (✆ **800/736-5276;** www.yellowstone.visit mt.com) is the Montana tourism office for the region that includes the Madison Valley.

WORLD-CLASS FISHING

There is plenty of fishing water along the road from Three Forks to Quake and Heb-gen lakes along U.S. 287. The first fishing access is **Cobblestone,** just a few miles south of Three Forks on the right side of U.S. 287. If you plan to base yourself in Ennis, the **Valley Garden, Ennis Bridge, Burnt Tree,** and **Varney Bridge** fishing accesses are within minutes of town along U.S. 287. Between Ennis and Quake Lake, the accesses begin popping up frequently. **McAtee Bridge, Wolf Creek, West Fork,** and **Reynolds Pass** are all accessible from the roadside. Hebgen Lake, just south of the dam, and Quake Lake are also great fishing spots.

On Ennis's Main Street, it seems that every second door houses a fly-fishing outfit-ter. The **Madison River Fishing Company,** 109 Main St. (✆ **800/227-7127** or 406/ 682-4293; www.mrfc.com), has a good stock of fishing supplies and a guide service. Guided trips, for one or two people, cost $245 for a half-day and $365 for a full day; full-day trips include lunch. They also offer a free brochure that contains a map of the Madison from Ennis to Quake Lake, listing fishing spots and camping and toilet facilities along the way. Other guide services, with similar rates, include **Clark's Guide Service** (✆ **406/682-7474**); **Howard Outfitters** (✆ **406/682-4834**); and **The Tackle Shop Outfitters** (✆ **800/808-2832** or 406/682-4263; www.thetackleshop.com).

WHAT TO SEE & DO

The lovely limestone **Lewis & Clark Caverns,** located 19 miles west of Three Forks (midway between Butte and Bozeman) on Mont. 2 (✆ **406/287-3541;** www.fwp. state.mt.us), are named for the famous explorers, but there is no evidence that their party ever saw or visited them. Discovered in the late 19th century, these caverns are a succession of vaulted chambers and passageways, thickly decorated with stalactites and stalagmites, as well as other underground formations such as massive, gleaming organ pipes; silky, delicate soda straws; intricate filigrees; and weirdly hung draperies. Plan at least 2 hours for the 2-mile guided tour through the caverns; and aboveground there are hiking trails, several picnic areas, and a large campground. A Christmas can-dlelight tour is held on 2 weekends in December. Reservations should be made in early December for one of the 200 or so spots available. There are three cabins on the premises with electric heat; rates are $39 in summer and $25 in winter.

You can easily spend an hour just exploring the interpretive signage at **Missouri Headwaters State Park,** 4 miles northeast of Three Forks (✆ **406/994-4042;** www.fwp.state.mt.us). Begin by following the Missouri River out from Three Forks. The headwaters themselves are no great shakes—just another river—but the sunsets from the bank of the river are breathtaking. From the headwaters, drive back toward Three Forks where, on the opposite side of the road, you'll see a parking area with interpretive markers. Allow plenty of time to read about Lewis and Clark and the young Shoshone guide Sakakawea (which is the correct spelling of her Hidatsa name, and not the more commonly seen Sacagawea), as well as early American Indians, trappers, traders, and settlers. Camping and RV sites are available as well as access to hiking, boating, and fishing.

WHERE TO STAY & DINE

Tucked deep in the Tobacco Root Mountains, **Potosi Hot Springs,** 1 S. Willow Creek Rd. (© **888/685-1695** or 406/685-3330; www.potosiresort.com), is geared toward romance, relaxation, and outdoor recreation. Accommodating guests in comfy cabins with kitchens and plush furnishings, the resort provides a sea of recreational activities. Then there are the hot springs from which the place draws its name, which fill an idyllic outdoor pool, a creek-side tub, and a private, gazebo-enclosed tub on the banks of Willow Creek. Also on-site is the Mountain Flower Spa, a creek-side yurt used as a setting for massages and herbal wraps. More affordable is **El Western Cabins & Lodges,** 4787 U.S. 287 N. (© **800/831-2773** or 406/682-4217; www.elwestern.com), with a choice in accommodations from simple duplex-style cabins to large three-bedroom lodges.

The **Willow Creek Café and Saloon** (© **406/285-3698**) is a find, if you can find it—it's located 7 miles southwest of Three Forks on the Old Yellowstone Trail. It's worth the search, though, because Willow Creek is the best restaurant in the area (don't let the bullet holes in the ceiling scare you off).

THE GALLATIN VALLEY

According to legend, the Sioux and Nez Perce once engaged in a bloody battle in the lower Gallatin Valley. On the third day of fighting, the sun was blotted out and a booming voice told the warriors to forget old wrongs and stop fighting, because they were in the Valley of Peace and Flowers.

Since those days, the sun still mostly shines around here, but the only booming voices heard are those calling you for your tee time or your dinner reservation. The transition of Big Sky from peace and flowers to year-round resort was not entirely without dissension, however. When legendary NBC newsman Chet Huntley—a Montana native—proposed the Big Sky ski resort, there was an outcry from the budding environmental movement. But Huntley's dream was realized in 1973, and the resort has blossomed into a world-class facility.

Big Sky Resort, P.O. Box 160001 (© **800/548-4486** or 406/995-5000; www.bigskyresort.com), handles a wide variety of lodgings—from economy to full-fledged luxury scattered among some 15 properties. The three-story **Huntley Lodge,** with 205 units, was the beginning of late NBC newsman Chet Huntley's original vision for Big Sky. It offers rooms that can sleep up to four, and several loft rooms that can accommodate six. The 97-unit **Shoshone Condominium Hotel** combines the living quarters of a condo with the amenities and services of a hotel, with sleeping for four to six. Weight-training centers, saunas, an outdoor pool, gift shops, and ski storage are included at both places. **The Summit at Big Sky,** with 213 luxury condominiums, offers European sophistication in a Western style. All three properties are slope-side and offer ski-in/ski-out convenience.

Moonlight Basin, P.O. Box 160040 (© **877/822-0430** or 406/993-6000; www.moonlightbasin.com), offers properties ranging from condos to private residences to luxurious penthouses. **The Moonlight Lodge and Spa** (© **800/845-4428**) is a magnificent mountain lodge offering luxurious penthouse suites and secluded, mid-mountain cabins; plus a sophisticated yet down-home restaurant, a relaxed-atmosphere bar, and a deli. There's also a full-service spa with treatment rooms, complete fitness center, steam rooms, heated pool, and a cascading waterfall hot tub; a concierge ready and able to organize everything from fly-fishing trips, to backcountry skiing, to dog-sled adventures; and even an ice-skating rink just outside in winter. In 2005, Big Sky Resort and Moonlight Basin connected their trail systems for a combined 5,300 acres of terrain— making it the largest ski area in the United States.

4 Little Bighorn Battlefield National Monument

Perhaps there is no phrase in the English language that serves as a better metaphor for an untimely demise than "Custer's Last Stand." It was on this battlefield, on the dry sloping prairies of southeastern Montana, that George Armstrong Custer met his end. Though the details of the actual battle that took place on June 25, 1876, are sketchy at best, much remains for the visitor to explore and ponder in this mysterious place. The **Little Bighorn Battlefield National Monument** chronicles the history of this world-famous engagement, offering a coherent look at how the battle developed, where the members of Custer's contingent died, and how it might have looked to the swarming warriors.

ESSENTIALS

GETTING THERE   The monument is located 56 miles east of Billings. Take **I-94** East to **I-90** South; just past Crow Agency take Exit 510 for **U.S. 212.** The battlefield is located a few hundred yards east.

ADMISSION & HOURS   The park and visitor center are open daily 8am to 9pm from Memorial Day to Labor Day, 8am to 6pm in spring and fall, and 8am to 4:30pm in winter. The visitor center is closed on Christmas, New Year's Day, and Thanksgiving. Admission costs per vehicle $10; $5 for those on foot.

VISITOR INFORMATION   At the **Visitor Center** (© **406/638-2224**) just inside the park entrance, you'll see actual uniforms worn by Custer, read about his life, and view an eerie reenactment of the battles on a small-scale replica of the battlefield. For advance information, contact the Superintendent, Little Bighorn Battlefield National Monument, P.O. Box 39, Crow Agency, MT 59022 (© **406/638-3204;** www.nps.gov/libi).

TOURING THE MONUMENT   It's possible to view the site in less than a half-hour, but you'll shortchange yourself with that approach. Instead, plan to spend enough time to explore the visitor center, listen to interpretive historical talks presented by rangers there, and then tour the site. You'll leave with a greater appreciation for the monument and an understanding of the history that led up to the battle.

After stopping at the **visitor center,** drive 4½ miles to the **Reno-Benteen Monument Entrenchment Trail,** at the end of the monument road, and double back. Interpretive signs at the top of this bluff show the route followed by the companies under Custer, Benteen, and Reno as they approached the area from the south, and the positions from which they defended themselves from their Indian attackers.

As you proceed north along the ridge, you'll pass **Custer's Lookout,** the spot from which the general first viewed the Indian village. This was the spot at which Custer sent for reinforcements, though he continued marching north.

Captain Thomas Weir led his troops to **Weir Point** in hopes of assisting Custer but was immediately discovered by the Indian warriors and forced to retreat to the spot held by Reno.

The **Medicine Trail Ford,** on the ridge, overlooks a spot well below the bluffs in the Medicine Trail Coulee on the Little Bighorn River, where hundreds of warriors who had been sent from the Reno battle pushed across the river in pursuit of Custer and his army.

Farther north, the Cheyenne warrior Lame White Man led an attack up **Calhoun Ridge** against a company of the Seventh Cavalry that had charged downhill into the coulee. When Indian resistance overwhelmed the army, troops retreated back up the hill, where they were killed.

As you proceed to the north, you will find detailed descriptions of the events that occurred on the northernmost edges of the ridge, as well as white markers that indicate the places where army troops fell in battle. The bodies of Custer, his brothers Tom and Boston, and nephew Autie Reed were found on Custer Hill.

Indian casualties during the rout are estimated at 60 to 100 warriors. Following the battle, which some say began early in the morning and ended within 2 hours, the Indians broke camp in haste and scattered to the north and south. Within a few short years they were all confined to reservations.

The survivors of the Reno-Benteen armies buried the bodies of Custer and his slain army where they fell. In 1881, the graves that could be located were reopened, and the bones re-interred at the base of a memorial shaft found overlooking the battlefield. Custer's remains were eventually reburied at the U.S. Military Academy at West Point in 1877.

The adjacent **National Cemetery,** established in 1879, incorporates a self-guided tour to some of the more significant figures buried there. In 2003, there was a dedication for a new Indian memorial, a sculpture garden dubbed "Peace Through Unity." There are also three **walking trails** within the monument for visitors wishing to explore the battle in greater depth.

A SPECIAL EVENT   The **Hardin Area Chamber of Commerce** (I-90 exits 497 and 503) sponsors **Little Bighorn Days,** around June 25 each year, but not at the monument. The events include a reenactment, parade, symposiums, and, of course, food. For information, call ℭ **406/665-1672.**

5 Jackson Hole & Grand Teton National Park

Grand Teton National Park may be smaller than Yellowstone, but in many ways it's no less spectacular—and it's far less crowded. The park encompasses towering mountain spires reaching almost 14,000 feet and the picturesque, glacier-fed waters of Jackson Lake and the Snake River. Jackson Hole, close to the end of the Grand Teton National Park and within an easy drive of Yellowstone, is one of the nation's premier ski resorts and offers many other kinds of outdoor recreation year-round.

JACKSON HOLE

Of the few communities in the Rockies that have successfully toed the line between promoting themselves as resort towns and retaining some semblance of indigenous character, Jackson is a standout. The million-dollar homes are sprouting all over the valley, but there is still open space, a memory of the cowboy past, and some resistance to letting in too much commercial glitz.

The remaining open spaces allow visitors to imagine what it was like early in the 19th century, when fur trappers first camped here. They were followed by ranchers, who soon became *dude* ranchers. Today, the community holds an interesting mixture of ski bums, blue bloods, nouveau riche, avid outdoor types, and even a few old-time cowboys. The cosmopolitans of this motley crew came not just with a hunger for scenery, but also with a taste for music, art, and good restaurants, too, and the selection here is unrivaled in Wyoming. The big ski hill lures a younger crowd, with the final ingredient for resort status—celebrities—supplied by transplants such as Harrison Ford.

ESSENTIALS

GETTING THERE   The **Jackson Airport** (© 307/733-7682) is located north of town at the southern end of Grand Teton National Park. If you're getting here on your own wheels, come north from **I-80** at Rock Springs on **U.S. 189/191;** or come east from **I-15** at Idaho Falls on **U.S. 26** and either come through Snake River Canyon on that highway or veer north over Teton Pass on **Wyo. 32.** If you are coming south from Yellowstone National Park, you can stay on **U.S. 89,** which runs north and south through both parks and into town.

VISITOR INFORMATION   The **Jackson Hole Chamber of Commerce** is a source of information concerning just about everything in and around Jackson. Along with the U.S. Forest Service and National Park Service, representatives of the chamber can be found at the informative **Visitors Center,** 532 N. Cache St., about 3 blocks north of Town Square with a view of the National Elk Refuge. For information on lodging, events, and activities, contact the chamber at P.O. Box 550, Jackson, WY 83001 (© **307/733-3316;** www.jacksonholechamber.com).

WHAT TO SEE & DO

Beyond its role as a staging area for explorations of Grand Teton and Yellowstone national parks, Jackson is a place to relax, shop, golf, or simply check out the sights.

Jackson Hole Aerial Tram Rides, at Jackson Hole Mountain Resort, 7658 Teewinot, Teton Village (© 307/739-2753; www.jacksonhole.com), take you above 10,000 feet for a tremendous view of the Tetons. **The National Museum of Wildlife Art,** 2820 Rungius Rd. (© **307/733-5771;** www.wildlifeart.org), is a 50,000-square-foot castle that houses some of the best wildlife art in the country.

If you don't have the time, money, or inclination for the full guest ranch experience, a fun alternative is to make a beeline for the nearest guest ranch around mealtime to enjoy Western cuisine served up to the strains of yodelin' cowpokes. The **Bar-T-5 Covered Wagon Cookout and Wild West Show,** 790 E. Cache Creek Dr., Jackson (© **800/772-5386** or 307/733-5386), offers a covered-wagon ride through Cache Creek Canyon to the "dining room" for an evening of Western victuals and after-dinner songs from the Bar-T-5's singing cowboys. The covered-wagon dinner runs around $31 for adults, $24 for youngsters 6 to 12; children 5 and under enjoy the night free. Reservations are recommended for both.

There are more than 20 **galleries** in downtown Jackson alone, with, of course, an excellent representation of Western art, although a growing number of galleries are showing a variety of styles.

SUMMER ACTIVITIES   Grand Teton National Park has incredible fishing. The Snake River, which flows through the park, is beaten to a froth every summer by hordes of fly-fishermen. **High Country Flies,** 185 N. Center St. (© **877/732-7210** or 307/733-7210; www.highcountryflies.com), has all the goods and offers guided fishing trips and schools as well as the best in angling fashion. The most renowned fishing experts assemble at the **Jack Dennis Outdoor Shop** on the Town Square at 50 E. Broadway (© **800/570-3270** or 307/733-3270; www.jackdennis.com).

Adventure Sports, at Dornan's in the town of Moose (© 307/733-3307), has a small selection of mountain-bike, kayak, and canoe rentals, and advice on where to go with the gear. When snowboards are put away for the summer, the **Boardroom** switches to BMX bikes and skateboards, at 225 W. Broadway (© 307/733-8327).

Some hotels, including those in Grand Teton National Park, have stables and operate trail rides for their guests. For details, contact **Jackson Hole Trail Rides** (© 307/733-6992), **Spring Creek Ranch Riding Stables** (© 800/443-6139), or the **Mill Iron Ranch** (© 307/733-6390). Rides cost around $50 for 2 hours.

The **Jackson Hole Golf and Tennis Club,** north of Jackson off U.S. 89 (© 800/628-9988 or 307/733-3111), has an 18-hole course that's recently been rated one of the nation's top resort courses. The **Teton Pines Resort and Country Club,** 3450 N. Clubhouse Dr. (© 800/238-2223 or 307/733-1005), designed by Arnold Palmer and Ed Seay, is a challenging course and prime real estate; greens fees are $170 to $190 for 18 holes. Both courses are open to the public.

There are two parts to the Snake River—the smooth water north of Jackson, and the white water of the canyon, to the south and west. A rafting trip down the upper Snake, usually from Jackson Lake Dam or Pacific Creek to Moose, is not about wild water but about wildlife: Moose, bald eagles, osprey, and other creatures come to the water just like we do. Several operators provide scenic float trips. Ask at **Barker-Ewing** (© 800/365-1800), **Grand Teton Lodge Company** (© 800/543-2811), and **Signal Mountain Lodge** (© 307/543-2831).

WINTER ACTIVITIES   This is one of the premier destinations for skiers in the entire country. **Jackson Hole Mountain Resort,** 3395 W. Village Dr., Teton Village (© 888/DEEP-SNO or 307/733-2292, 307/733-2291 for snow conditions, 800/443-6931 for central reservations; www.jacksonhole.com), has one of the best hills in North America and is constantly upgrading its facilities. Here's the trade-off: Prices are approaching those of Colorado resorts, although aficionados of the sport keep coming back for more. Cross-country skiers should contact the attached **Jackson Hole Nordic Center,** 7658 Teewinot, Teton Village (© 307/733-2629); or **Teton Pines Cross Country Skiing Center** (© 307/733-1005).

If your idea of mushing is not oatmeal but a pack of yipping dogs, you might want to try your hand at dog-sledding. **Jackson Hole Iditarod Sled Dog Tours,** P.O. Box 1940, Jackson (© 800/554-7388 or 307/733-7388; www.jhsleddog.com), associated with Iditarod racer Frank Teasley, offers both half- and full-day trips in five-person sleds (the fifth companion is your guide) and you can take a turn in the driver's stand. These trips fill up quickly; call at least 3 to 4 days in advance to reserve a spot.

WHERE TO STAY

Jackson lodgings these days come with palatial trappings and, in some cases, prices that start at $500 a night. Prices are generally discounted in the off season (spring/fall), but not during ski season. For lodging information and reservations, call **Jackson Hole Central Reservations** (© 888/838-6606; www.jacksonholewy.com).

Amangani *Best*   Cut into the side of East Gros Ventre Butte, Amangani's rough rock exterior blends in so incredibly well that the lights from its windows and pool appear at night to glow from within the mountain. The style is understated and rustic, but expensive. Walking through the high-ceilinged corridors or lounging by the outdoor pool, you know not to strike up a casual conversation with your neighbor—this place is all about class and privacy. Hotelier Adrian Zecha has resorts like this around the world, from Bali to Bora Bora, and while the designs are tailored to the landscape, the approach is the same: personal service, luxury, and all the little touches. To name a few of the latter, there are CD players in every bedroom, cashmere throws on the day beds, and stunning slate and redwood interiors.

1535 NE Butte Rd., Jackson, WY 83002 (on top of East Gros Ventre Butte). © **877/734-7333** or 307/734-7333. www.amanresorts.com. 40 units. $750–$1,300 double. AE, DC, DISC, MC, V. **Amenities:** Restaurant; outdoor pool; spa.

Bentwood Inn   This B&B is an architectural marvel. Built from 200-year-old timber cleared from Yellowstone to make room for a rest area, the inn is a 6,000-square-foot log mansion with 43 corners. The rooms themselves, all with remote-controlled gas fireplaces, private balconies, and Jacuzzi tubs, are extensions of the innovative design, with touches equally urban and rural, from the ornate tiles to the longhorn skulls above the bed. Innkeepers Bill and Nell Fay (the former designed the inn himself) pay a great deal of attention to detail, and it shows. The breakfasts are simultaneously hearty and gourmet, and the fridge is always stocked with a wide range of soft drinks and libations. One room is pet-friendly.

4 miles west of Jackson on Teton Village Rd., P.O. Box 561, Jackson Hole, WY 83001. © **307/739-1411.** Fax 307/739-2453. www.bentwoodinn.com. 5 units. $195–$295 double; $245–$325 suite. Rates include complimentary full breakfast and evening cocktails. AE, DISC, MC, V.

Four Seasons Resort Jackson Hole   The newest—and most deluxe—lodging option in Teton Village, the ultrastylish Four Seasons opened in December 2004 and immediately set a new standard for ski-in, ski-out luxury. From a year-round slope-side pool (landscaped to resemble a mountain creek), to the cowboy-hatted doorman, to the rooms, stately, luxurious, and definitively Western, this is one of the top slope-side properties in the country. The range of rooms starts at the high end and goes up from there, but even the standard kings are large and plush, and every unit has a balcony or a fireplace. One especially notable perk: the hotel's "Base Camp," a full-service outdoor activity concierge who can arrange customizable outings involving mountain biking, hiking, fishing, and ballooning, and outfit you in style. In the winter, the service transforms into a first-rate ski concierge, and s'mores and hot chocolate are served alongside heated towels outside at the pool. The eating and drinking facilities are also a cut above, and range from casually hip to extraordinarily extravagant.

7680 Granite Loop, P.O. Box 544, Teton Village, WY 83025. © **307/732-5000.** Fax 307/732-5001. www.fourseasons.com. 140 units. $400–$750 double; $700–$4,000 suite; lower rates spring and fall. AE, DC, DISC, MC, V. Valet parking $18 daily. **Amenities:** 2 restaurants; year-round outdoor pool; exercise room; spa.

Jackson Hole Lodge *(Kids)*   Although it sits near one of the busiest intersections in Jackson and it's packed into a small space, this lodge is quiet and well designed, so its location in the heart of town becomes a plus. The pool is not just for splashing—you can lap its 40-foot length, sit in one of the whirlpools, take a sauna, or sit out on your own sun deck. The rooms are more comfortable and complete than what you'll find at a chain property, blending Western ambience with scads of in-room options. Best of all are the condo lodgings, with two upstairs bedrooms, a full kitchen, and a living room with foldout couch. This gives families a little space, and it's also affordable.

420 W. Broadway, Jackson, WY 83001. © **800/604-9404** or 307/733-2992. Fax 307/739-2144. www.jacksonhole lodge.com. 59 units. $79–$139 double; $129–$309 condo. AE, DC, DISC, MC, V. **Amenities:** Indoor pool. *In room:* Kitchen.

Rusty Parrot Lodge and Spa   The name sounds like an out-of-tune jungle bird, but since 1990 the Rusty Parrot has shown excellent pitch, cultivating a country lodge and spa right in the heart of busy Jackson. Located across from Miller Park, the Parrot is decorated in the nouveau Western style of peeled log, with an interior appointed with elegant furnishings and river-rock fireplaces. One very attractive lure is The Body Sage Spa, where you can get yourself treated to all sorts of scrubs, wraps, massages, and facials. The breakfast that comes with your room includes omelets, fresh pastries, fruits, cereals, and freshly ground coffee; food also appears later in the day, but the lodge likes to make that a surprise (sorry). Rooms are gigantic, and several have private balconies.

175 N. Jackson St. (P.O. Box 1657), Jackson, WY 83001. © **800/458-2004** or 307/733-2000. www.rustyparrot.com. 31 units. $275–$385 double; $550–$650 suite. Rates include full breakfast. AE, DC, DISC, MC, V. **Amenities:** Restaurant; spa.

Spring Creek Ranch   Perched atop East Gros Ventre Butte, 1,000 feet above the Snake River and minutes from both the airport and downtown Jackson, this resort commands a panoramic view of the Grand Tetons and 1,500 acres of land populated by deer, moose, and the horses at its riding facility in the valley below. It seems a little less exclusive now that Amangani has opened next door. But Spring Creek still has much going for it: The rooms, divided among nine buildings with cabinlike exteriors, all have fireplaces, Native American floor and wall coverings, and balconies with views of the Tetons. Most rooms have a king- or two queen-size beds, and the studio units boast kitchenettes. In addition to its own rooms, the resort arranges accommodations in the privately owned condominiums that dot the butte—large, lavishly furnished, and featuring completely equipped kitchens and sleeping accommodations.

1800 Spirit Dance Rd. (on top of the East Gros Ventre Butte), Jackson, WY 83001. © **800/443-6139** or 307/733-8833. www.springcreekranch.com. 125 units. $310 double; $375–$1,200 condo; $2,000–$2,200 home. AE, MC, V. **Amenities:** Restaurant; outdoor pool; tennis court; spa. *In room:* Kitchenette (in condos only), fridge.

Trapper Inn   The employees here are some of the most helpful you'll find in Jackson, and they'll tip you off on the best deals in the valley. Just 2 short blocks from the town square, the Trapper is hard to miss if you're walking north on Cache from the town square. On the west side of Cache, you'll notice the Trapper on the bronze sign. You can walk anywhere downtown within minutes. The rooms are spacious, featuring cozy quilts and stately lodgepole pine furnishings. There are two structures here: Fittingly, the newest building, erected in 1991, features rooms with a more modern feel.

235 N. Cache St., Jackson, WY 83001. © **888/771-2648**, or 307/733-2648 for reservations. www.trapperinn.com. 54 units. $100–$179 double. AE, DC, MC, V. *In room:* Fridge, microwave.

Virginian Lodge *Value*   It's not brand-new. It's not a resort, it doesn't have a golf course, and the highway is right outside the door. Since its overhaul in 1995, however, the Virginian is one of the better motels in Jackson: The prices remain reasonable, the interior courtyard (with a large grassy play area and central pool) is a world away from the Broadway-facing exterior, and it's a busy, cheerful place to stay. You can get a room with a private Jacuzzi or a kitchenette, and many have "dry" bars and sofa sleepers.

750 W. Broadway, Jackson, WY 83001. © **800/262-4999** or 307/733-2792. Fax 307/733-4063. www.virginianlodge.com. 170 units. $95–$109 double; $125–$185 suite. AE, DC, DISC, MC, V. **Amenities:** Restaurant; outdoor pool. *In room:* Kitchenette (in some rooms).

Wort Hotel   Located on Broadway just off the town square—an area constantly in flux with new buildings and new shops—the Wort stands like an old tree, although its Tudor-style two-story building was largely rebuilt after a 1980 fire. Opened in the early 1940s by the sons of Charles Wort, an early-20th-century homesteader, it has an old-fashioned style to it, both in the noisy and relaxed **Silver Dollar Bar** (distinctively graced with

2,032 silver dollars) and the quiet, formal dining room (there's also a new Starbucks out-let on-site). The Wort labels their rooms "New West," and recently has totally renovated each of them. Brass number plates and doorknobs welcome you into comfortable, air-conditioned guest rooms with modern decor, thick carpeting, and armoires.

50 N. Glenwood St., Jackson, WY 83001. © 307/733-2190. www.worthotel.com. 60 units. $165–$275 double; $325–$550 suite. AE, DISC, MC, V. Valet parking $10 daily. **Amenities:** Restaurant; exercise room.

WHERE TO DINE

The Blue Lion *Best* ECLECTIC   In the fast-moving, high-rent world of Jackson din-ing, The Blue Lion stays in the forefront by staying the same. On the outside, it's a two-story blue clapboard building across from the town park that looks like a comfy family home. On the inside, in intimate rooms accented with soft lighting, diners enjoy slow-paced and elegant meals. The menu features rack of lamb and wild game specialties, such as grilled elk loin in a peppercorn sauce. Fresh fish is flown in daily for dishes such as the herb-crusted rainbow trout.

160 N. Millward St. © 307/733-3912. Reservations recommended. Main courses $15–$33. AE, DC, DISC, MC, V. Summer daily 6–10pm; winter daily 6–9pm.

Burke's Chop House STEAKS/GAME/SEAFOOD   Formerly the chef at the steakhouse under the Million Dollar Cowboy Bar, Michael Burke struck out on his own and opened this ambitious eatery in downtown Jackson in February 2004. The sleek dining room, punctuated by plenty of dark wood, a few antique car parts and scenic photographs, and a sweeping bar, provides an understated setting for the unpre-tentious but excellent fare. The menu includes smoked baby back pork ribs with homemade bourbon barbecue sauce, cornmeal-crusted trout, and a nice selection of steaks and chops. The buffalo tenderloin and filets are particularly satisfying.

72 S. Glenwood St. © 307/733-8575. Reservations recommended. Main courses $16–$36. AE, DC, DISC, MC, V. Daily 6–10pm.

Jedediah's House of Sourdough *Kids* AMERICAN   You feel like you've walked into the kitchen of some sodbuster's log cabin home when you enter Jedediah's—the structure was built in 1910 and now resides on the National Register of Historic Places. Bring a big appetite for breakfast, and a little patience—you might have to wait for a table, then you might have to wait for food while you stare at the interesting old photos on the wall. But it's worth it, especially for the rich flavor of the sour jacks (sourdough pancakes) served with blueberries. During summer months, Jedediah's also serves dinners: steaks, barbecue chicken, rainbow trout, and the like.

135 E. Broadway. © 307/733-5671. Reservations not accepted. Breakfast $3–$9; lunch $5–$8. AE, DC, DISC, MC, V. Daily 7am–2pm.

Nani's Genuine Pasta House ITALIAN   The setting is simple, but the food is extraor-dinary at Nani's, where you are handed two menus: *a carta classico* featuring pasta favorites, and a list of specialties from a different featured region of Italy, which might include veal seared in a Marsala sauce or swordfish stuffed with bread crumbs, Parmigiano-Reggiano cheese, capers, and garlic. Your only problem with this restaurant might be finding it—it's tucked away behind a rather run-down motel, and rarely does it fill to the rafters.

242 N. Glenwood St. © 307/733-3888. Reservations recommended. Main courses $13–$33. MC, V. Daily 5–10pm.

Snake River Brewery *Value* MICROBREWERY   One of the West's best micro-breweries, this industrial-meets-contemporary-looking establishment offers a menu of pasta, applewood-fired pizzas and paninis, and salads. The real standouts are the beers, especially Custer's Last Ale and Snake River Pale Ale. This place is a local's favorite and a great lunch spot, with daily $6 specials like turkey-and-brie wraps and chipotle barbecue sandwiches.

265 S. Millward St. (C) 307/739-BEER. Reservations not accepted. Most dishes $6–$12. AE, DISC, MC, V. Daily 11:30am–11pm. Bar open later.

Snake River Grill CONTEMPORARY AMERICAN   This is a popular drop-in spot for locals, including some of the glitterati who sojourn in the area—Harrison Ford and Uma Thurman, to name a few. The front-room dining area overlooks the busy Town Square, but there's a more private, romantic room in the back. It's an award-winning restaurant for its wine list and its menu, which features regular fresh-fish dishes, crispy pork shank, some game entrees, and Idaho trout. The pizzas—cooked in a wood-burning oven—are topped with exotic ingredients such as duck sausage or eggplant with portobello mushrooms.

Town Sq., Jackson. (C) 307/733-0557. Reservations recommended. Main courses $20–$40. AE, MC, V. Summer daily 5:30–10pm; shorter hours rest of year. Closed Nov and Apr.

AFTER DARK
Head down to the **Silver Dollar Bar,** 50 N. Glenwood in the Wort Hotel (C) 307/ 733-2190), for a drink with one of the real or wannabe cowpokes at the bar. And, yes, those 1921 silver dollars are authentic. At the very famous **Million Dollar Cowboy Bar** on the Town Square, 25 N. Cache St. (C) 307/733-2207), you can dance the two-step to live bands. If you want some high-octane dancing fun led by talented local hoofers, head west to Wilson and the **Stagecoach Bar** (C) 307/733-4407) on Wyo. 22 on a Sunday night. It's the only night there's live music in this scruffy bar and hamburger joint, and the place is jammed wall to wall. You'll see some folks who really know how to dance, fueled by a lively band, often with drop-in guitar aces and occasional celebrities (but don't count on Bob Dylan showing up *again*).

GRAND TETON NATIONAL PARK
Yellowstone may have its geysers, but only this park can boast the bare, towering spires of the Cathedral Group, "Le Trois Tetons" (or "the three breasts," as cheeky French trappers named them). The Grand Teton, the largest of the three (known as "The Grand" by locals), is a mountaineer's dream, and hiking throughout the park draws hundreds of thousands each year. In addition to unparalleled mountain views, wildlife watching is also immensely popular; elk, bison, bald eagles, moose, and beavers are just some of the critters with whom you'll be sharing park land.

ESSENTIALS
ACCESS/ENTRY POINTS   There are really only three ways to enter the park. From the **north,** you can enter the park from Yellowstone National Park, which is connected to Grand Teton by a wilderness corridor called the **John D. Rockefeller Jr. Memorial Parkway** through which U.S. 89/191/287 runs for 8 miles. You can also approach the park from the **east,** via U.S. 26/287. This route comes from Dubois, 55 miles east on the other side of the Absaroka and Wind River mountains, and crosses **Togwotee Pass,** where you'll get your first—and one of the best—views of the Tetons towering above the valley. Finally, you can enter Grand Teton from Jackson in the **south,** driving about 13 miles north on U.S. 26/89/191 to the Moose turnoff and the

park's south entrance. Here you'll find the park headquarters, a visitor center, and a small community that includes dining, rental cabins, and shops.

VISITOR INFORMATION   There are three visitor centers in Grand Teton National Park. The **Moose Visitor Center** (© 307/739-3399) is a half-mile west of Moose Junction at the southern end of the park; it's open from 8am to 7pm daily from June to Labor Day, and 8am to 5pm the rest of the year. The **Colter Bay Visitor Center** (© 307/739-3594), the northernmost of the park's visitor centers, is open 8am to 8pm from early June to Labor Day, and from 8am to 5pm after Labor Day to early October. There is also **Jenny Lake Visitor Center** (© 307/739-3343), open from 8am to 7pm daily from early June to Labor Day and from 8am to 5pm after Labor Day to early October. Maps and ranger assistance are available at all three, and there are bookstores and exhibits at Moose and Colter Bay.

FEES & BACKCOUNTRY PERMITS   There are no park gates on U.S. 26/89/191, so you get a free ride through the park on that route. But if you want to get off the highway and explore, you'll pay $20 per automobile for a 7-day pass for entry into both Grand Teton and Yellowstone national parks. If you expect to visit the parks more than once within a year, you can buy a $40 annual permit, but we consider the various national park passes, which are also honored here, to be a better deal. **Backcountry permits** are required from the Park Service for overnight use of backcountry campsites. The permits are free, but they can be reserved only from January 1 to May 15 (and the reservation itself costs $15); thereafter, all backcountry permits are issued on a first-come, first-served basis up to 24 hours before your first night out.

SEEING THE GRAND TETON HIGHLIGHTS

Just viewing the spectacularly beautiful peaks is one of the main reasons to visit the park. Grand Teton National Park is famous for its mountains, and rightly so. The Cathedral Group is composed of **Grand Teton** (elevation 13,770 ft.), **Teewinot** (elevation 12,325 ft.), and **Mount Owen** (elevation 12,928 ft.). Nearby, almost as impressive, are **South Teton** (elevation 12,514 ft.) and **Middle Teton** (elevation 12,804 ft.). The best views of the Cathedral Group are along the trails and roads that ring **Jenny Lake.**

COLTER BAY   **Colter Bay** is a busy outpost of park services where you can get groceries, postcards and stamps, T-shirts, and advice. If this is your first stop in the park, get maps and information at the **Colter Bay Visitor Center.** Here you can view park and wildlife videotapes and attend a park-orientation slide program throughout the day. Ranger-led activities include museum tours, park-orientation talks, natural history hikes, and evening amphitheater programs. Colter Bay has lots of overnight options, from its cabins to its old-fashioned tent camps to its trailer park and campground. There are also a general store and do-it-yourself laundry, two restaurants, a boat launch and boat rentals, and tours. You can take pleasant short hikes in this area, including a walk around the bay or out to **Hermitage Point.**

DORNAN'S   This is a small village area just south of the visitor center on some private land owned by one of the area's earliest homesteading families. There are a few shops and a semi-gourmet grocery store, a post office, a bar where there is sometimes live music, and, surprisingly, a first-rate wine shop.

JACKSON LAKE   The north end of the park is dominated by giant **Jackson Lake,** a huge expanse of water that fills a deep gorge left 10,000 years ago by retreating glaciers. Though it empties east into the Snake River, curving around in the languid

Oxbow Bend—a favorite wildlife-viewing float for canoeists—the water from Jackson Lake eventually turns south, then west through Snake River Canyon and into Idaho.

JENNY LAKE Along Teton Park Road, you move into the park's southern half, where the tallest peaks rise abruptly above a string of smaller lakes strung together in the foothills—**Leigh Lake, String Lake,** and **Jenny Lake,** which is the favorite of many park visitors. At North Jenny Lake Junction you can take a turnoff west to **Jenny Lake Lodge**—the road then continues as a one-way scenic loop along the lakeshore before rejoining Teton Park Road about 4 miles later.

SIGNAL MOUNTAIN If you're here to enjoy the park, you'd probably turn west on **Teton Park Road** at Jackson Lake Junction, and arrive after only 5 miles at **Signal Mountain.** Like its counterpart at Colter Bay, this developed recreation area, on Jackson Lake's southeast shore, offers camping sites, accommodations in cabins and multiplex units, two restaurants, and a lounge with one of the few live televisions in the park. This is also the place to fill up on gasoline and provisions from the small convenience store. Boat rentals and scenic cruises of the lake also originate here.

SPORTS & OUTDOOR ACTIVITIES

For lovers of outdoor recreation, Grand Teton National Park offers one of the most accessible play lands of rock and water in the Lower 48. In addition to hiking, mountaineers and technical climbers can attack the highest hills; paddlers glide across the smooth waters of the lakes or splash along the livelier flow of the Snake River; and there are also waters open to motorized vessels and sailboats.

WHERE TO CAMP & STAY

Since Grand Teton is so much smaller than its counterpart to the north, the mileage between campgrounds is much shorter. As a consequence, selecting a site in one of the five National Park Service campgrounds within the park becomes a matter of preference (rather than geography) and availability. Fees in all campgrounds are $15 per night, and all have modern comfort stations. Campgrounds operate on a first-come, first-served basis, but reservations are available to groups of 10 or more by contacting the **Grand Teton Lodge Co.,** P.O. Box 240, Moran, WY 83013 (© **307/543-3100**). You can get recorded information on site availability by calling © **307/739-3603.**

All the campgrounds but Jenny Lake can accommodate tents, RVs, and trailers, but there are no utility hookups at any of them. **Jenny Lake Campground,** a tents-only area with 51 sites, is situated in a quiet, wooded area near the lake. You have to be here first thing in the morning to get a site. The largest campground, **Gros Ventre,** is the last to fill, if it fills at all—probably because it's located on the east side of the park, a few miles from Kelly on the Gros Ventre River Road. It has 372 sites, a trailer dump station, a tents-only section, and no showers. If you arrive late in the day and you have no place to stay, go here first. **Signal Mountain Campground,** with views of the lake and access to the beach, is another popular spot that fills first thing in the morning. It has 86 sites overlooking Jackson Lake and Mount Moran, as well as a pleasant picnic area and boat launch. No showers or laundry, but there's a store and service station nearby. **Colter Bay Campground and Trailer Village** has 350 sites (some with RV hookups), a general store, showers, and a laundromat. The area has access to the lake but is far enough from the hubbub of the village to offer a modicum of solitude; spaces are usually gone by noon. **Lizard Creek Campground,** at the north end of Grand Teton National Park near Jackson Lake, offers an aesthetically pleasing wooded area near the lake. It's only 8 miles from facilities at Colter Bay and has 60 sites that usually fill by 2pm.

For those who don't want to camp, the premier destination is the pricey **Jenny Lake Lodge** (© **800/628-9988** or 307/543-3100; www.gtlc.com), offering seclusion, award-winning food, and the individual attentions that come with a cabin resort kept intentionally small. Another top choice is **Jackson Lake Lodge** (© **800/628-9988** or 307/543-3100; www.gtlc.com), which is to Grand Teton what Old Faithful is to Yellowstone. The moderately priced **Signal Mountain Lodge** (© **307/543-2831;** www.signalmountainlodge.com) is the only resort on the shores of Jackson Lake inside the park.

6 Yellowstone National Park

What other national park boasts such an assortment of thermal geysers and hot springs that their total exceeds the number found on the rest of the planet? On top of that, there's a waterfall that's twice as tall as Niagara Falls. Not to mention a canyon deep and colorful enough to fall into the "grand" category.

Wildlife? Ever focus your telephoto lens on a wild, untamed grizzly bear? Or a bald eagle? What about a wolf? Thousands of visitors have these experiences here every year.

ESSENTIALS

GETTING THERE   If interstate highways and international airports are the measure of accessibility, then Yellowstone is as remote as Alaska's Denali National Park or the Serengeti Plains of Africa. But three million people make it here every year, on tour buses, in family vans, on bicycles, and astride snowmobiles.

The closest airport to Yellowstone is in **West Yellowstone,** Montana, which sits just outside the park's west entrance. Also, visitors can reach the park from the south by flying into **Jackson,** Wyoming (only 14 miles from the southern entrance to Grand Teton), then driving 56 miles through Grand Teton to the southern entrance of Yellowstone.

American (© 800/433-7300), **Continental** (© 800/523-3273), **Delta** (© 800/221-1212), **Northwest** (© 800/225-2525), and **United** (© 800/241-6522) all have flights to and from **Jackson Airport** (© 307/733-7682).

To the north, **Bozeman,** Montana, is 87 miles from the West Yellowstone entrance on **U.S. 191.** Or you can drive east from Bozeman to Livingston, a 20-mile journey on **Interstate 90,** and then south 53 miles on **U.S. 89** to the northern entrance at Gardiner. Bozeman's airport, **Gallatin Field** (© 406/388-8321), provides daily service via **Delta** (© 800/221-1212), **Northwest** (© 800/225-2525), and **United** (© 800/241-6522), as well as **Horizon** (© 800/547-9308). If you're driving to West Yellowstone from Bozeman, take U.S. 191 south to its junction with **U.S. 287** and continue south into town.

Also to the north, **Billings,** Montana, is 129 miles from the Cooke City entrance. Billings is home to Montana's busiest airport, **Logan International** (© 406/247-8609), 2 miles north of downtown. Daily intrastate service is provided by **Big Sky Airlines** (© 800/237-7788 or 406/245-2300); and regional daily service is provided by **America West** (© 800/235-9292), **Delta** (© 800/221-1212), **Horizon** (© 800/547-9308), **Northwest** (© 800/225-2525), and **United** (© 800/241-6522). From Billings, it's a 65-mile drive south on **U.S. 212** to Red Lodge, then 30 miles on the Beartooth Highway to the northeast entrance to the park. Keep in mind that the Beartooth Highway (U.S. 212), which takes you on a high, twisting journey over a spectacular pass, is open only from Memorial Day weekend until late October.

VISITOR CENTERS & INFORMATION   There are five major visitor and information centers in the park, and each has something different to offer. Unless otherwise indicated, summer hours are from 8am to 7pm.

The **Albright Visitor Center** (© 307/344-2263), at Mammoth Hot Springs, is the largest and is open year-round. It provides visitor information and publications about the park, has exhibits depicting park history from prehistory through the creation of the National Park Service, and houses a wildlife display on the second floor.

The **Old Faithful Visitor Center** (© 307/545-2750) is another large facility. A film on Yellowstone's thermal features is shown throughout the day in an indoor auditorium. Rangers dispense various park publications and post projected geyser eruption times here. The Park Service plans to open a state-of-the-art $15-million visitor-education center in place of the current architecturally maligned building; at press time, the hope was to cut the ribbon on a new facility by 2008.

The **Canyon Visitor Center** (© 307/242-2550), in Canyon Village, is the place to go for books and an informative display about bison in the park. It's staffed with friendly rangers used to dealing with crowds.

The **Fishing Bridge Visitor Center** (© 307/242-2450), near Fishing Bridge on the north shore of Yellowstone Lake, has an excellent display that focuses on the park's bird life. You can get information and publications here as well.

The **Grant Village Visitor Center** (© 307/242-2650) has information, publications, a video program, and a fascinating exhibit that examines the role of fire in Yellowstone.

Helpful staff and park literature can also be found at several small information stations: the **Madison Information Station** (© 307/344-2821); the **Museum of the National Park Ranger** (no phone; open daily in summer 9am–6pm) and the **Norris Geyser Basin Museum and Information Station** (© 307/344-2812; open daily in summer 10am–5pm), both at Norris; the **West Thumb Information Station** (no phone; open daily in summer 9am–5pm); and the **Public Lands Desk** at the West Yellowstone Visitors Information Center, 30 Yellowstone Ave. (© 406/646-7701; open daily 8am–8pm in summer, limited hours the rest of the year).

FEES & PERMITS   Entrance for up to 7 days costs $25 per vehicle and covers both Yellowstone and Grand Teton national parks. A snowmobile or motorcycle pays $20 for 7 days, and someone who comes in on bicycle, skis, or foot pays $12. You can buy an **annual permit** for $40, but the various national park passes are a better deal.

Backcountry permits are free, but you have to have one for any overnight trip, on foot, on horseback, or by boat. Camping is allowed only in designated campsites, many of which are equipped with food-storage poles to keep wildlife away. These sites are primitive and well situated, and you won't feel at all like you're in a campground. If designated campsites in a particular area have already been reserved, you're out of luck. So while you can make a reservation as few as 48 hours before beginning a trip, you would be wise during peak season to make a reservation well in advance (you can contact the park for reservations for the upcoming year beginning Apr 1), although it costs $20. The **Yellowstone Backcountry Office** (P.O. Box 168, Yellowstone National Park, WY 82190) will send you a useful *Backcountry Trip Planner* with a detailed map showing where the campsites are. Call the office for more information at © 307/344-2160.

EXPLORING THE PARK

MAMMOTH HOT SPRINGS   At the park's north entrance, 5 miles south of Gardiner, Mammoth Hot Springs is home to spectacular limestone terraces, historic park buildings, and the Mammoth Hot Springs Hotel. It's one of the older park settlements, with stone buildings dating from the late 19th century, when the army was stationed here at Fort Yellowstone.

There are no geysers at **Mammoth Hot Springs Terraces,** but this cascading staircase of hillside hot pools, among the oldest in the park, offers a boardwalk tour of gorgeous pastels in shades of white, yellow, orange, and green, the unintentionally artistic work of microscopic bacteria in the sediments. The mineral-rich springs constantly bubble to the surface, depositing travertine as the water cools in contact with the air. It's a vivid illustration of the park's unusual geological situation: a rare geologic hot spot of seismic activity in the middle of the continent, where molten rock nearly makes it to the earth's surface.

Whether or not you spend the night at the **Mammoth Hot Springs Hotel**—not the most distinguished lodging in the park, but it has historic character—you should drop by the **Albright Visitor Center.** This building once housed Fort Yellowstone's bachelor officers, but you won't find a pool table here today; rather, you'll find displays on park history, wildlife and photography exhibits, smiling rangers dispensing advice, and numerous park publications and maps. Films on the park's origin and the art it inspired are shown throughout the day. A special treat for international visitors is the opportunity to get their visas stamped with the official Yellowstone National Park document stamp. For more information, call © **307/344-2263.**

TOWER-ROOSEVELT AREA   East of Mammoth Hot Springs you enter a delicious mix of high plains, deep forest, and twisting rivers. Toward the northeast corner lies one of the most beautifully serene valleys in the Rockies, the **Lamar Valley.** This glacier-carved swath of grassy bottom and forested flanks sits apart from the vehicular chaos at the center of the park, a good thing because the traffic here is not automobiles, but the bison, bears, wolves, and elk whose presence has earned the valley the nickname, "The Serengeti of the United States." If you continue east and leave Yellowstone via the park's northeast entrance, you'll be heading up to the spectacular views of the **Beartooth Highway.**

The area around the Tower-Roosevelt Junction was once a favorite spot of U.S. president Theodore Roosevelt. At **Roosevelt Lodge,** visitors can enjoy the kind of simple accommodations that fit the tastes of the Bull Moose himself: those with the rustic flavor of the Old West. This is the most relaxed of the park's villages, and a great place to take a break from the more crowded attractions. Get into the cowboy spirit by taking a **guided trail ride, stagecoach ride,** or **wagon ride.** You can skip the dining room and ride out for an **Old West cookout,** served from a chuck wagon to patrons who arrive by either horseback or wagon. The nearby 132-foot **Tower Falls** is named for the looming volcanic pinnacles at its brink and provides an excellent photo opportunity. While in the area, take time to view the petrified forests on **Specimen Ridge,** where a wide variety of fossilized plants and trees date back millions of years. All things considered, Roosevelt is a great place to escape the hordes.

Farther south, **Pelican and Hayden valleys** are the two most prominent remnants of large, ancient lakebeds in the park. They are now vast, sub-alpine meadows, thriving with plant life that provides feed for sizable bison and elk populations. You might see a bear here, too.

THE GRAND CANYON OF YELLOWSTONE   Hayden Valley flanks the featured attraction of the park's center: the **Grand Canyon of the Yellowstone River,** a colorful, 1,000-foot-deep, 24-mile-long gorge that some can't resist comparing to its larger counterpart in Arizona. Okay, then: This canyon is greener, the water clearer, the air cooler, and it has two dramatic waterfalls, the big one taller than Niagara. As it drops through this gorge, the Yellowstone River in some places moves at 64,000 cubic feet of water per second.

Volcanic explosions and glaciers surging and receding shaped the canyon. The geological story is told in the canyon itself, where hard lava flows formed the lip of the falls next to softer quartz-rich rock that gave way, allowing the river to cut deeply through the layers of red, orange, tan, and brown hue. Plumes of steam pinpoint vents along the canyon's rock spires, where viewing opportunities are extensive and varied. There are many hikes along and down into the canyon, which is 24 miles long and up to 1,200 feet deep, and you'll be surprised at how few people you encounter away from the parking areas. Many do trek down to a view of the Lower Falls on **Uncle Tom's Trail** from the South Rim, and a short path from a parking area for Upper Falls View also offers breathtaking views. Two other favorite trails are **Inspiration Point** and **Artist Point;** both are wheelchair accessible.

Canyon Village has a sprawling 1950s look, which puts off some visitors. It's usually crowded, but you can find many useful services there, and some of the newer lodging is an improvement.

NORRIS GEYSER BASIN If you travel south from Mammoth on the west side of the park, you pass some interesting rock formations, **Obsidian Cliff** and **Roaring Mountain,** before coming to **Norris Geyser Basin.** Norris is not nearly as famous as the Mammoth terraces or the crowd of geysers around Old Faithful, but there's a lot going on here, from the steaming pools of the **Porcelain Basin** to the eruptions of **Echinus Geyser.** If you're the patient type, you can sit by the blowhole of **Steamboat Geyser** and hope that this, the largest of park geysers with a maximum height of 400 feet, will erupt. But be prepared to wait: It has erupted only twice in the last 15 years, once in 2000 and once in 1991. This is one of the hottest, most active thermal areas on the plateau, at the intersection of three faults in the earth's crust; when they shift, new geysers pop up and old ones disappear. The **Norris Geyser Basin Museum** explains geothermal features, and the nearby **Museum of the National Park Ranger** tracks the history of the park's stewards.

OLD FAITHFUL About a quarter of the world's geysers are crowded into hills, valleys, and riverbanks around **Old Faithful,** where the hot pools and spouts are divided into three areas: the **Lower, Midway,** and **Upper geyser basins.** Here you'll find burbling mud pots, radiant pools like **Chromatic Spring,** and geysers with a variety of tricks, from the angled shots of **Daisy Geyser** to the witches' cauldron of **Crested Pool.**

But the grande dame of geysers, the star of the show, is **Old Faithful.** Over the past 100 years, its eruptions have been remarkably consistent, blowing 15 to 23 times daily with a column averaging about 134 feet and a duration of about 40 seconds. Recent seismic activity has elongated the intervals (to about 92 min.) between eruptions a tad, but it's still the most predictable geyser in the world. Estimates posted at the visitor centers are give-or-take 10 minutes; if the last eruption was a long one, you might have to wait 2 hours for the next burst. (No big deal—there's plenty else to see here.)

Since the geyser is one of the key park attractions, the **Old Faithful Visitor Center** (© **307/545-2750**) is larger than most of its counterparts. An excellent film describing the geysers and their microscopic inhabitants is shown throughout the day in an air-conditioned auditorium—quite a relief on hot July afternoons. The Park Service hopes to close the existing visitor center by 2008 and cut the ribbon on a new state-of-the-art building, which will feature interactive exhibits and an environmentally integrated architectural style.

A National Historic Landmark, the shingled, steep-roofed **Old Faithful Inn** was built of local stone and hand-hewn timber, including a pair of interior balconies above the lobby floor.

YELLOWSTONE LAKE

West of Old Faithful, over Craig Pass, or south of Canyon, through the wildlife-rich **Hayden Valley,** is gigantic **Yellowstone Lake,** another natural wonder unique to Yellowstone. At 20 miles long, 14 miles wide, and more than 300 feet deep in places, it's the largest lake in the world above 7,000 feet in elevation. If you took a dip in the frigid water (not recommended), you could hardly guess that the caldera underneath the lake is filling with hot liquid magma, actually tilting the lake northward at a measurable pace. The caldera is the sunken remainder of a huge volcanic blast 600,000 years ago, and another about 700,000 years before that. Experts believe it's due to blow again sometime in the next 100,000 years—any day now, at least in geologic time. Volcanic underpinnings aside, grizzlies work the tributary streams in the spring when fish spawn (some campgrounds are closed), and lots of other wildlife congregate here, including moose and osprey.

The lake has long been a favorite fishing spot, but recent regulations have made cutthroat trout a catch-and-release species parkwide. This is part of a desperate attempt by park biologists to help the cutthroat come back against the planted Mackinaw or lake trout, which dine on small cutthroat and therefore are not to be released alive. You'll see some big sailboats braving the quirky winds of the lake, and experienced paddlers may want to **kayak** or **canoe** into the south and southeast arms of the lake, which are closed to motorboats. These deep bays are true wilderness, and great areas to fish and view wildlife. When you pick up a boating permit, you'll also get a stern warning from rangers to watch out for the changeable weather if you get out on the lake's open water. They're right to urge caution; even the best paddlers risk their lives in a sudden afternoon storm.

Lake Village, on the north shore of the lake, offers a large range of amenities, including fine restaurants at either the rustic cabins at **Lake Lodge** or the majestic 100-year-old **Lake Yellowstone Hotel.** This hotel has Greek columns and a spacious solarium overlooking the lake, the best place for a cocktail or a romantic dinner within park boundaries. It's very different from the Old Faithful Inn, but a rival for its beauty and history. Just south of Lake Village is **Bridge Bay Marina,** the park's water-activity center. Here you can obtain guided fishing trips, small-boat rentals, and dock rentals; there's also a store and tackle shop.

WEST THUMB & GRANT VILLAGE   On the south end of the lake, at **West Thumb,** the boiling thermal features extend into the lake. You can see steaming cones and churning water created by the action of the underwater hot springs. **Fishing Cone** is rumored to be the place where fishermen once used the "hook and cook" method, immediately tossing their catch into a hot pot for instant meal preparation. Don't try it—it's illegal to drop anything into a thermal feature, and the geyser water has traces of mercury and arsenic. You can walk among the lakeshore pools at the **Central Basin** and look at the colorful, thick fudge of the **Thumb Paint Pots.**

Grant Village, named for President Ulysses S. Grant, was completed in 1984 and is the newest of Yellowstone's villages. It has some of the most modern facilities in the park, but it's also the least inspired. On the plus side, this area is a great vantage point for watching sunrises and afternoon squalls move across the lake, and you may see **river otters** and **cutthroat trout** in the old marina's waters. (Come wintertime, the otters like to use holes melted by the underwater thermal features as base camps for ice-fishing escapades.) The **Grant Visitor Center** plays a video that explores the role of fire in the Yellowstone ecosystem.

SPORTS & OUTDOOR ACTIVITIES

HIKING　If you have time for only one hike, hit the **Mount Washburn Trail** (trail heads are at the end of Old Chittenden Rd. and at Dunraven Pass). The rises are fairly gradual, and they're interspersed with long, fairly level stretches. The views are of the Absoraka Mountains, Yellowstone Lake to the south, and the Gallatin Mountains to the west. You might even see mountain sheep. The hike to the summit is an easy 90-minute walk at a steady pace, or 2 hours with breaks. Bring several layers of clothing—it can get cold at the top.

The **Lonestar Geyser Trail** (start at the parking lot opposite Kepler Cascades) is another great walk; it's an easy 5-mile outing, and its popularity is its only disadvantage. From the trail head you'll wend your way through a forested area along a trail that parallels the Firehole River. The payoff for your effort is the arrival at the geyser—a vanilla-chocolate ice-cream cone near the middle of a vast meadow partially covered by grass and tress, exposed rock, gravel, and volcanic debris. Surrounding it are small, bubbling geysers and steam vents.

SUMMER SPORTS & ACTIVITIES　The best place to enjoy **boating** in Yellowstone is on **Yellowstone Lake,** which has easy access and panoramic views. The lake is one of the few areas where powerboats are allowed; you can rent rowboats and outboard motorboats at **Bridge Bay Marina** (© **307/242-3876**). Motorboats, canoes, and kayaks can be used on Lewis Lake (about 15 miles north of the south entrance) also.

In June, one of the best **fishing** spots is on the **Yellowstone River** downstream from Yellowstone Lake, where the cutthroat trout spawn. Anglers head to **Madison River** near the west entrance in July and then again in late fall for rainbow and some brown trout; in late summer, the **Lamar River** and **Soda Butte Creek** in the park's beautiful northeast corner are popular spots to hook cutthroats. You'll find more isolation at **Trout Lake,** a small backcountry lake about 10 miles west of the northeast entrance. Don't forget to pick up your **required Yellowstone fishing permit,** available at any ranger station, visitor center, or Yellowstone Park General Store in the park. Anyone older than 16 needs a fishing permit, which costs $15 for 3 days or $20 for 7 days, and $35 for the season. Fishers aged 12 to 15 also need a permit, but it's free. Casters under 12 can fish without a permit when supervised by an adult.

People who want to pack their gear on a **horse,** llama, or mule must get permits to enter the Yellowstone backcountry, or hire an outfitter with a permit. If you're looking for just a short ride, Xanterra Parks and Resorts offers 1- and 2-hour guided trail rides daily aboard well-broken, tame animals. Stables are located at Canyon Village, Roosevelt Lodge, and Mammoth Hot Springs. Roosevelt Lodge also offers **evening rides** from June into September.

WINTER SPORTS & ACTIVITIES　In winter, Yellowstone is transformed into a surreal wonderland of snow and ice. The geyser basins take on a more dominant role, with the air's temperature in stark contrast to their steaming waters. Nearby trees are transformed into "snow ghosts" by frozen thermal vapors.

Transportation into the park is mainly by snowmobiles and tracked vehicles called snow coaches. **Old Faithful Snow Lodge** and the **Mammoth Hot Springs Hotel,** the park's two winter lodging options, are open December through March. The only road that's open for cars is the **Mammoth Hot Springs–Cooke City Road.**

The best **cross-country** trails in Yellowstone are the **Lonestar Geyser Trail,** a fairly level 5-mile round-trip through a remote setting, starting at the Old Faithful Snow Lodge; and the **Fern Cascades Trail,** which begins in the Old Faithful housing area on the south side of the road and winds for 3 miles through a rolling wooded landscape. Energetic skiers can tackle the 12-mile **Mallard Lake Trail,** though it may take them all day—it departs north of the Old Faithful Lodge area along the north side of the Upper Geyser Basin, then loops north and east to Mallard Lake and back to Old Faithful.

Equipment rentals, ski instruction, ski shuttles to various locations, and guided ski tours are all available at the park's two winter lodgings. Discounts are available for multiday rentals of skis or snowshoes. Ski instruction costs around $25 per person for a 2-hour group lesson. A full-day guided excursion costs $65 to $115 per person (lunch may or may not be included).

The **Mammoth Hot Springs ice rink** is located behind the old Mammoth Hot Springs Recreation Center. On a winter's night you can rent a pair of skates ($1 an hour; $4 per day) and glide across the ice of this outdoor rink, while seasonal melodies are broadcast over the PA system. It's cold out there, but there's a warming fire at the rink's edge.

Roads that are jammed with cars during the summer fill up with **snowmobiles** (assuming that they haven't been banned) and bison during the winter. In deference to the shaggier road warriors, moderate speed limits are strictly enforced, but this is still an excellent way to sightsee at your own pace. A driver's license is required for rental ($170 for a single rider, $180 per day for two at **Mammoth Hot Springs Hotel** or **Old Faithful Snow Lodge**), as is a guide ($215 per group for a custom day trip, rentals not included, or $210 per person for a regularly scheduled trip, rental included). A helmet is included with the snowmobile, and you can rent a clothing package for protection against the bitter cold.

For additional information on winter activities and accommodations, as well as snow coach transportation and equipment rentals, contact **Xanterra Parks and Resorts** (© 307/344-7311).

WHERE TO CAMP & STAY IN THE PARK

The National Park Service has shifted management of five major campgrounds to Xanterra Parks and Resorts, the park concessionaire, which means, predictably, higher fees, but also allows you to make reservations ahead of arrival. The other seven campgrounds still managed by the park are available only on a first-come, first-served basis. These lower-cost campgrounds ($12–$14 per night) are located at Indian Creek, Lewis Lake, Mammoth, Norris, Pebble Creek, Slough Creek, and Tower Fall. We like Lewis Lake and Indian Creek, which tend to be available when others are full. Check with rangers about campsite availability when you enter the park; some campgrounds fill up as early as 8am.

Xanterra Parks and Resorts (© 307/344-7311; www.travelyellowstone.com) operates the large campgrounds at Bridge Bay, Canyon, Grant Village, Madison, and Fishing Bridge, where the fees are $17 per night. The **Fishing Bridge RV Park** is the only campground equipped with water, sewer, and electrical hookups for RVs and trailers, though it accepts hard-sided vehicles only (no tents or tent trailers), and the fees are $33 per night. The **Madison campground** is the first to open in early May, while **Grant Village** is closed until mid-June to avoid bear conflicts during trout-spawning season. These campgrounds are usually busier, and some, like Bridge Bay, are rather barren of trees unless you get a site on the fringes. Most campgrounds close in September, but Madison is open until mid-October.

To book a campsite or a room within any Yellowstone lodging, you also need to contact **Xanterra Parks and Resorts** (see above). If you plan to travel in July or August, *make your reservations 6 months ahead of time.*

The crown jewel of the park's hotels, the **Old Faithful Inn** is 30 miles from West Yellowstone and 39 miles from the South Entrance. The lazy geyser-watcher can avoid the crowds by watching the show from a comfortable second-floor terrace with excellent views of eruptions. The original rooms are well appointed but may not have private bathrooms, while the new-wing rooms offer better facilities and more privacy.

A "new" **Old Faithful Snow Lodge and Cabins** near the original location recently reopened. The modern rooms are spacious and comfortable and there's also the usual selection of cabins. This is only one of two facilities in the park open during winter months.

In the Mammoth Hot Springs area, on the site of old Fort Yellowstone, 5 miles from the north entrance, is the old-fashioned **Mammoth Hot Springs Hotel and Cabins** (at Mammoth Hot Springs). This is one of two hotels that is open during both summer and winter seasons. Suites measure up to those at the Old Faithful Inn and Lake Yellowstone Hotel (see below). Standard rooms and cabins offer minimal but adequate appointments. If you need a tub, make your request when you reserve. The cottage-style cabins are viable alternatives, some having private hot tubs and sun decks. There's also a formal dining room and a fast-food restaurant.

In the Canyon Village area, the newish **Canyon Lodge and Cabins** is a half-mile from the Grand Canyon of Yellowstone and Inspiration Point, one of the busiest spots in the park. The lodge offers tastefully appointed but ordinary motel-style accommodations in the three-story lodge building and in cabins.

The **Roosevelt Lodge Cabins** were built in the wake of one of Teddy Roosevelt's legendary treks west, although he didn't sleep here (he opted instead for a tent in the woods). It is a rugged but charming stone edifice with a building-long porch. Services here include horseback riding, Western trail cookouts, and stagecoach rides. The bare-bone cabins, called Roughriders, are aptly named, with showers nearby. More attractive Frontier cabins have showers.

At the affordable **Lake Lodge Cabins** (on Lake Yellowstone), the cabins are most suitable for outdoor types. The lodge is an old Western longhouse fronted by a porch and rockers that invite visitors to sit and gaze out across the waters. On the other hand, **Lake Yellowstone Hotel & Cabins** (Grand Loop Rd., on the north side of the lake) is one of the most attractive hotels in the park, although still pretty moderately priced. Accommodations are in the hotel, in a motel-style annex, and in cabins. Opt for one of the free-standing cabins decorated with knotty-pine paneling. Request a single cabin, rather than a duplex, because the walls are paper thin.

WHERE TO STAY & DINE IN THE GATEWAY TOWNS

COOKE CITY   Lodging here will be less expensive than in other gateway towns, ranging from $60 to $90 a night. The **Soda Butte Lodge,** 209 Main St. (© **800/527-6462** or 406/838-2251; www.cookecity.com), is the biggest motel in Cooke City, and it includes the **Prospector Restaurant** and a small casino; or, you can go to the cheaper, bare-bones **Alpine Motel,** 105 Main St. (© **406/838-2262;** www.ccalpine motel.com). For a bite to eat and a great selection of beers, try the funky **Beartooth Cafe** (© **406/838-2475**), also on Main Street.

GARDINER   Dinky, personable, and a bit eccentric, Gardiner has long had ultra-friendly lodging—thin-walled motels where, if you show up late, they've gone to bed and left a key in the door. Inexpensive motels fill up quickly during the summer months: The **Yellowstone Park Travelodge** (109 Hellroaring Rd.; (ℂ **406/848-7520**) and **Super 8** (702 U.S. Hwy. 89; (ℂ **800/800-8000** or 406/848-7401) are open year-round, while the **Best Western by Mammoth Hot Springs,** on U.S. Hwy. 89 (ℂ **800/828-9080** or 406/848-7311), is another option, with doubles for $119 to $129 in the summer. The **Absaroka Lodge** (ℂ **800/755-7414** or 406/848-7414; www.yellowstonemotel.com) offers well-appointed rooms with private balconies offering views into Yellowstone Park.

An indication that Gardiner has kept in touch with its mining-town roots is the relative dearth of fancy restaurants—you'll find mostly steakhouse fare, hearty breakfasts, and travelers' food. A few upscale eateries have shown up in recent years, but the dish-clattering local color of the park-side coffee shops is hard to beat. My favorite Gardiner lunch spot is the **Sawtooth Deli,** 270 W. Park St. (ℂ **406/848-7600**), serving up overstuffed, New York–style subs and eclectic specials.

WEST YELLOWSTONE West Yellowstone Central Reservations handles booking for many of the hotels (ℂ **888/646-7077**). Among the newer ones, you'll find chains like the **Marriott Fairfield Inn,** 105 S. Electric St. (ℂ **800/565-6803**), and the **Days Inn,** 301 Madison Ave. (ℂ **800/548-9551**). There are three **Best Western** affiliates, ranging from $80 to $140 a night during the summer. Call ℂ **800/528-1234** for information and reservations. With two different levels of rooms, the **Stage Coach Inn,** 209 Madison Ave. (ℂ **800/842-2882** or 406/646-7381), is another good choice.

All things considered, there is no finer hotel in the area than the moderately priced **Holiday Inn SunSpree Resort,** 315 Yellowstone Ave. (ℂ **800/HOLIDAY** or 406/646-7365; www.doyellowstone.com). From its rooms to its restaurant to its conference facilities, this resort is first-rate. A heated indoor pool, exercise room, sauna, children's program, and activities desk round out the amenities.

Firehole Ranch, 11500 Hebgen Lake Rd. (ℂ **406/646-7294;** www.fireholeranch.com), is a perennial favorite among serious fly-fishers. The resort is surrounded by thousands of acres of national forest, where guests can hike, canoe, ride horses, or bike. Cocktails are served in a cozy nook followed by exquisite meals prepared by a French chef. Lodging is in 10 cabins, perfect for two, although several have sofa beds. Rates are high, but include meals and activities (except guided fishing). A 4-day minimum stay is required.

A good inexpensive option (with more character than the chains to boot), the 1912 **Madison Hotel,** 139 Yellowstone Ave. (ℂ **800/838-7745** or 406/646-7745), has historic rooms for $37 to $56 for a double and newer motel doubles for $50 to $80.

Just as the chain motels have arrived, so have garden-variety fast-food joints; West Yellowstone is a good place to stop for a quick bite on your way into the park. **Uncle Laurie's Riverside Café,** 237 U.S. Hwy. 20 (ℂ **406/646-7040**), is a small but excellent alternative to steak-and-eggs breakfast joints. The menu migrates from breakfast calzones and huckleberry cinnamon rolls in the morning to a lunch menu of cold sandwiches, wraps, and "stinky burgers," so named for their garlic content. For the best variety of coffee drinks and baked goods, visit the espresso bar at the excellent **Book Peddler** in Canyon Square (ℂ **406/646-9358**). **Beartooth BBQ,** 111 Canyon St. (ℂ **406/646-0227**), is a fun place with a nice selection of local microbrews and top-notch slow-smoked ribs. **Bullwinkle's Saloon, Gambling and Eatery,** 19 Madison Ave. (ℂ **406/646-7974**), has a traditional menu full of burgers, salads, steaks, and ribs. The saloon also features video poker machines.

7 The Black Hills & the Badlands of South Dakota

The **Black Hills** area, with its wooded mountains, waterfalls, and rushing streams, is a natural delight. This is where you'll find Wind Cave, one of the country's most beautiful natural caverns; Custer State Park, with its herds of bison, elk, and deer; and the imposing visages carved on Mount Rushmore, as well as the dramatic and still-developing **Crazy Horse Memorial.**

To the east of the Black Hills lie the **Badlands,** a strange and mysterious place. From the ragged ridges and saw-toothed spires to the wind-ravaged desolation of Sage Creek Wilderness Area, Badlands National Park is an awe-inspiring sight and an unsettling experience. Few leave here unaffected by the vastness of this geologic anomaly, spread across 381 square miles of moonscape in western South Dakota. Steep canyons, towering spires, and flat-topped tables are all found among Badlands buttes.

AREA ESSENTIALS

GETTING THERE   The gateway to this area is the **Rapid City Regional Airport** (*©* **605/393-9924**), 10 miles southeast of Rapid City on U.S. 44. Northwest Airlines from Minneapolis, Minnesota; Delta SkyWest from Salt Lake City, Utah; and United Express from Denver, Colorado, serve the airport with daily flights that connect to every major U.S. city. Rental cars from the major chains are available at the airport.

VISITOR INFORMATION   For information about the area, call or write **South Dakota Tourism,** 711 E. Wells Ave., Pierre, SD 57501-3369 (*©* **800/S-DAKOTA** or 605/773-3301; www.state.sd.us).

MOUNT RUSHMORE NATIONAL MEMORIAL

Widely regarded as one of the man-made wonders of the world, Mount Rushmore is as much a work of art as it is an engineering marvel. The faces of Washington, Jefferson, Lincoln, and Theodore Roosevelt carved into granite make up one of America's most enduring icons.

To get to Mount Rushmore, take I-90 to Exit 57 at Rapid City, and then take U.S. 16 (Mt. Rushmore Rd.) southwest for about 23 miles to the entrance. For information before you go, contact **Mount Rushmore National Memorial,** P.O. Box 268, Keystone, SD 57751-0268 (*©* **605/574-2523;** www.nps.gpve/moru). The **visitor center,** just inside the entrance to the memorial, is open every day of the year (except Dec 25) from 8am to 5pm in winter and 8am to 10pm in summer. Mount Rushmore has no admission charge, but there's an $8 fee for parking. Limited free parking is available across from the main parking lot as you arrive at Rushmore from Keystone.

You really need only 2 to 3 hours to see everything. Particularly in summer, try to come at the very beginning or end of your day. Excellent light at daybreak, coupled with its scenic setting and great breakfasts in the **Buffalo Dining Room,** make Mount Rushmore hard to beat for the first stop of the day. The patriotic ranger program and dramatic lighting ceremony, held nightly at 9pm mid-May through September, also make the memorial memorable at night.

While Mount Rushmore is best enjoyed on foot, many visitors overlook an impressive view of the sculpture that can be reached by car. After leaving the park's parking lot, turn right on S. Dak. 244 and proceed west, then northwest, around the memorial. Less than a mile from the parking lot, you'll discover the proud profile of George Washington in the upper-right corner of your windshield. While surveying the scene, keep an eye out for Rocky Mountain goats that frequent the memorial and the Black Elk Wilderness Area to the west.

Note: Though it's an American icon, be advised that some Native Americans consider the monument an intrusion on sacred landscapes that were swiped from them. We know a member of the Illini tribe who calls the monument "the Ugly Faces." She's not alone.

CUSTER STATE PARK

There's little doubt that, had not thoughtful state leaders preserved 83 square miles of the Black Hills as Custer State Park, the area would have become a national park. Its natural attractions are that outstanding. Perhaps the park's main draw is its 1,500-head herd of bison, along with its many elk, deer, and antelope.

The park is right between Mount Rushmore and Wind Cave. It's accessible via S. Dak. 79 and S. Dak. 36 from the east, U.S. 16A from the north and west, and S. Dak. 87 from the north and south. For advance information, contact the park directly at HC83, Box 70, Custer, SD 57730-9705 (© **605/255-4515;** www.state.sd.us/state/ executive/tourism/sdparks/custer/custer.htm). Once in the park, head to the **Peter Norbeck Visitor Center,** between the State Game Lodge and the Coolidge Inn Store on U.S. 16A; it offers informational brochures, interpretive exhibits, and a variety of educational displays. Also, the **Wildlife Station Visitor Center,** on the southeast part of the Wildlife Loop, offers shade, information, and exhibits. An annual park pass is $23; a temporary license (valid for 7 days) is $5 per person or $12 per vehicle; an off-season temporary license is $2.50 per person or $6 per vehicle; and a motorcoach license is $2 per person per visit.

For memorable sightseeing, pick any of the park's three scenic drives: the Needles Highway, the Wildlife Loop Road, or the Iron Mountain Road. Each of these winding drives is enjoyed at a slower pace—generally 25 mph or slower.

The **Needles Highway** is a mesmerizing 14-mile journey through pine and spruce forests, meadows surrounded by birch and quaking aspen, and giant granite spires that reach to the sky. Visitors pass the picturesque waters of Sylvan Lake, walk through tunnels, and pass a unique rock formation called the "Needle's Eye."

The **Wildlife Loop Road** is an 18-mile drive through open grasslands and pine-clad hills—an area that is home to most of the park's wildlife. Count pronghorn, bison, white-tailed deer and mule deer, elk, coyote, begging burros, prairie dogs, eagles, hawks, and other birds. The best wildlife viewing time is early morning and evening, when animals are most active. Stop by the Wildlife Station Visitor Center on the southeast part of the loop for information and interesting exhibits.

Although only a portion of the scenic **Iron Mountain Road** rests in Custer State Park, it ranks as a must-see on any South Dakota visit. The winding road runs between Mount Rushmore and the junction of U.S. 16A and S. Dak. 36. Along the route are wildfire exhibits, wooden pig-tail bridges, pullouts with wonderful views, and tunnels that frame the four presidents at Mount Rushmore. Some of the tunnels have vehicle height and width limits, so RV drivers should check restrictions ahead of time.

Custer State Park is home to a wide variety of **hiking** experiences, ranging from short nature walks to backcountry treks through some of the grandest scenery anywhere. A 22-mile segment of the South Dakota Centennial Trail, the **Harney Peak Summit Trail,** extends through Custer State Park. The **Cathedral Spires Trail** is also a popular choice. Most trails are open to mountain bikers, too.

CRAZY HORSE MEMORIAL

The world's largest mountain carving is so big that all four heads on Mount Rushmore would fit inside the chief's head. Begun in 1947 by the late Polish-American sculptor Korczak Ziolkowski in response to a request from Lakota chief Henry Standing Bear, the monument is being carried on by Korczak's large family with donations and private funding (the sculptor refused to accept federal funding, and all admission fees get funneled into the project). The finished sculpture will be 641 feet long and 563 feet high. The carving is in Crazy Horse, north of Custer on U.S. 385.

At the base of the mountain, the **Indian Museum of North America** features exhibits focusing on the history and tribal life of numerous Native American cultures. Numerous lectures, concerts, and other special events are held here in summer. The building itself—a wonder of natural wood and light—is worth a look; it was designed by Korczak himself to fit in with the landscape. The museum and memorial are open year-round from 8am to 6pm in winter; in summer 8am to 10pm with a laser light show beginning when dark. Admission is $10 adults and children or $24 per carload. Children under 6 are admitted free. For more information, call ℭ **605/673-4681** or go online to **www.crazyhorse.org**.

WIND CAVE NATIONAL PARK

The rolling prairies of western South Dakota run smack into the ponderosa pine forests of the Black Hills in Wind Cave National Park. The park is home to prairie dog towns, large herds of elk and pronghorn antelope, and over 300 bison—and that's just aboveground. Below lies the eighth-longest cave in the world.

Wind Cave is about an hour's drive south of Mount Rushmore on Route 87. From points south or west, you can also take U.S. 385. For advance information, contact **Wind Cave National Park,** R.R. 1, P.O. Box 190, Hot Springs, SD 57747-9430 (© **605/745-4600;** www.nps.gov/wica). The **visitor center** (right off U.S. 385) is open year-round from 8am to 4:30pm (except Thanksgiving and Christmas) and has books, brochures, exhibits, and slide programs about the cave and other park resources. It also has tickets for cave tours and a posted schedule of activities, including talks and nature walks. Wind Cave National Park has no entrance fee, but it does charge for cave tours, ranging from $7 adults, $3.50 ages 6 to 16 (half-price with a Golden Age Passport) for a simple guided tour, to $23 for a 4-hour introduction to basic caving techniques; most tours are $9. The park's highways and backcountry roads provide the scenic backdrop for some of the best **wildlife viewing** opportunities in the region. Wildlife abounds in this rugged preserve, and you may be able to see some of it as you drive down through Custer State Park on S. Dak. 87 to Wind Cave.

No visitor should leave the park without taking a **cave tour.** Five are offered in the summer (fewer in the off season); call ahead for departure times, as they vary. They range from the easy 1-hour **The Garden of Eden Tour** to the adventuresome 4-hour **Caving Tour,** where participants must be 16 or older and wear long pants and boots. The **Candlelight Tour** is one of the most popular. Participants trek through a less-developed, unlighted part of the cave to experience the cave by candlelight. This strenuous tour covers 1 mile of rugged trail and lasts 2 hours. Reservations, available up to 1 month beforehand, are strongly advised. Most tours, even the easiest, involve climbing lots of steps, but all give you an excellent perspective on a unique underground world.

Visitors with more time should get out on the trail. The park hosts a 6-mile stretch of the **Centennial Trail,** which goes through the heart of the Black Hills and offers a taste of everything the area has to offer. There's also usually a ranger-led **prairie hike** in summer mornings at 9am.

WHERE TO STAY IN RAPID CITY & THE BLACK HILLS

Hotels in Rapid City include the **Alex Johnson Hotel,** 523 Sixth St. (© **800/888-2539** or 605/342-1210; www.alexjohnson.com), a restored hotel with moderate prices listed on the National Historic Register; and the **Econo Lodge,** 625 E. Disk Dr. on I-90 at Exit 59 (© **800/214-1971** or 605/342-6400; www.choicehotels.com/hotel/sd010), with an indoor water slide, cable TV, Jacuzzi suites, and guest laundry facilities.

Custer State Park has four mountain resorts and seven campgrounds. **The State Game Lodge,** on U.S. 16A near the park's main visitor center (© **605/255-4541**), features historic decor and pine-shaded cabins. The **Sylvan Lake Lodge,** on S. Dak. 87 at its junction with S. Dak. 89 in the northeast corner of Custer State Park (© **605/574-2561**), overlooking scenic Sylvan Lake and the Harney Range, provides cozy lodge rooms and rustic family cabins. The **Blue Bell Lodge & Resort,** on S. Dak. 87, just before the turnoff for the Wildlife Loop Road (if you're traveling south; © **605/255-4531**), offers handcrafted log cabins as well as lodge rooms, the Buffalo Willow Lounge, and hayrides and chuck wagon cookouts. The **Legion Lake Resort,** near the junction of the Needles Highway (S. Dak. 87) and U.S. 16A, dates from 1913 and features 25 cottages nestled in the pines on the lakeshore. Rates at these lodges range from around $95 for a sleeping cabin at Legion Lake, to $410 for a four-bedroom cabin at the State Game Resort. All are near outdoor activities such as fishing, hiking, and animal watching; some offer excursions into the backcountry. For more information or to make reservations at any of Custer State Park's resorts, call © **605/255-4521** or surf over to **www.custerresorts.com**.

WHERE TO DINE IN RAPID CITY & THE BLACK HILLS

Dining in the Black Hills tends to be a casual affair, but the selection can be wide, ranging from homemade pies and ranch-raised buffalo to hearty steaks and local pheasant.

The **Buffalo Dining Room,** at Mount Rushmore National Memorial (© **605/574-2515**), open daily 8am to 4:30pm, offers cafeteria breakfasts named for the presidents carved into the mountain: Washington is continental, Jefferson is French toast, Lincoln is scrambled eggs, and Roosevelt is biscuits and gravy. Lunch is also served. Near Mount Rushmore, in Keystone, you'll find **The Ruby House Restaurant,** Main Street (© **605/666-4404**), which offers steaks, seafood, and other specialties in a richly appointed Victorian dining room. Open daily 11:30am to 8:30pm. It's closed in winter.

There's no dining at Wind Cave National Park; in Custer State Park, the **Pleasant Pheasant Dining Room** in the State Game Lodge serves great breakfasts, such as buffalo sausages with hot biscuits. Also in summer, a lunch buffet and dinners are served.

In Rapid City, try the **1915 Firehouse Brewing Co.,** 610 Main St. (© **605/348-1915**), where brats, burgers, buffalo, and chicken wings accompany the hearty microbrews on tap Open 11am to 10pm daily, except Sunday when it opens at 4pm. The **Fireside Inn,** 7 miles west of Rapid City on U.S. 44 (© **605/342-3900**), with prime rib and an intimate fireside (and nonsmoking) setting, makes a romantic choice for dinner. Open daily 5 to 9pm for dinner only.

BADLANDS NATIONAL PARK

The Badlands offers not only an unforgettably eerie landscape, but also a wealth of plant and animal life. You'll find 56 different types of grasses here—and almost no trees. Wildflowers abound in a good year. As for animals, you're likely to see bison and Rocky Mountain bighorn sheep (the native Audubon's bighorn is now extinct), as well as pronghorns and mule deer, if you travel at dawn and dusk. You can also see desert and eastern cottontail rabbits darting in and out of the grass. And prairie dogs thrive in the area; there's a prairie dog town just beyond the end of the Badlands Loop Road.

ESSENTIALS

GETTING THERE   Badlands National Park is easily accessed by car either on U.S. 44 east of Rapid City, or off Interstate 90 at Wall or Cactus Flat. Westbound I-90 travelers take Exit 131 south (Cactus Flat) onto S. Dak. 240, which leads to the park boundary and the Ben Reifel Visitor Center at Cedar Pass. This roadway becomes Badlands Loop Road, the park's primary scenic roadway. After passing through the park, S. Dak. 240 rejoins I-90 at Exit 110 at Wall.

VISITOR INFORMATION   For information in advance, call © **605/433-5361** or check out the park's website at **www.nps.gov/badl**. Once you're in the park, head to the visitor center at Cedar Pass or White River. The **Ben Reifel Visitor Center** at Cedar Pass is open daily year-round (7am–8pm June 10–Aug 15, and 9am–4pm the rest of the year) and features exhibits on the park's natural and cultural history. The nearby Cedar Pass Lodge has cabins, a gift shop, and a restaurant; there's a campground (first-come,

---

Warnings in the Badlands

Water in the Badlands is too full of silt for humans to drink and will quickly clog a water filter. When hiking or traveling in the park, always carry an adequate supply of water. Drinking water is only available at the Cedar Pass area, the White River Visitor Center, and the Pinnacles Ranger Station.

Climbing Badlands buttes and rock formations is allowed, but can be extremely dangerous due to loose, crumbly rock. Watch for rattlesnakes and cacti hidden in the prairie grass.

Finally, Badlands **weather** is often unpredictable. Heavy rain, hail, and high, often damaging winds are possible, particularly during spring and summer. Lightning strikes are also common. And winters are simply brutal. But what were you expecting from a place called the Badlands?

---

first-served, $10; no hookups and 14-day limit) here as well. The **White River Visitor Center** (© 605/455-2878) is open during the summer season only (late May through Aug) and houses exhibits about Oglala Sioux history.

ENTRANCE FEES   There is an entrance fee of $10 per passenger vehicle, which allows admission for up to 7 days. The single-person entry fee is $5 per motorcycle, bicycle, or person on foot, plus $5 for each additional passenger.

SEEING THE HIGHLIGHTS

It's relatively easy to see the highlights of the North Unit of Badlands National Park in a day. A few miles south of the park's northeast entrance (on S. Dak 240, the closest entrance to I-90) is the **park headquarters,** open year-round, which includes the Ben Reifel Visitor Center, Cedar Pass Lodge, a campground, an amphitheater, and a dump station. After stopping at the visitor center exhibits, bookstore, information desk, and restrooms, and watching an orientation video (which we recommend), it's time to hit the trail.

The visitor center is within 5 miles of several trail heads, scenic overlooks, and three self-guided nature trails. Each of the seven trails in the area offers an opportunity to view some of the formations for which the Badlands is famous. The **Fossil Exhibit Trail** is wheelchair accessible. The **Cliff Shelf Nature Trail** and the **Door Trail** are moderately strenuous and provide impressive glimpses of Badlands formations. But none is longer than a mile, and any one of them can be hiked comfortably in less than an hour.

Leading directly from the visitor center is the 30-mile-long **Badlands Loop Road,** the park's most popular scenic roadway. Angling northwest toward the town of Wall, this road passes numerous overlooks and trail heads, each of which commands inspiring views of the Badlands and the prairies of the Buffalo Gap National Grassland that forms its backdrop. Binoculars will increase your chances of spotting bison, pronghorn, bighorn sheep, or coyote.

The paved portion of the Loop Road ends at the turnoff for the **Pinnacles Entrance.** Beyond this point the pavement ends and the road becomes the Sage Creek Rim Road, a 30-mile gravel road, at the end of which is the **Sage Creek Campground,** although this one is primitive and does not offer drinking water. Five miles west of the end of the pavement, a visit to the **Roberts Prairie Dog Town** gives you a chance to watch black-tailed prairie dogs "barking" their warnings and protecting their "town." The Sage Creek Basin is the best spot to see bison and bighorn sheep.

Highway 27 leads from the town of Scenic south to the **White River Visitor Center** (© **605/455-2878**), open from late May to August. The visitor center has drinking water, restrooms, information, Lakota exhibits, and a video program.

WHERE TO STAY & DINE IN THE BADLANDS

The night sky in the Badlands is an unforgettable sight, so we recommend staying overnight if you have time. **Camping** is available inside Badlands National Park at either the Cedar Pass Campground or the Sage Creek Primitive Campground (no reservations). Camping in pullouts, parking areas, or picnic grounds is not permitted. The park also provides free permits for backcountry camping.

The only other accommodations in the park is adjacent to the Ben Reifel Visitor Center, with 25 cabins, at **Cedar Pass Lodge Cabins,** P.O. Box 5, Interior, SD 57750 (© **605/433-5460;** fax 605/433-5560). The lodge also has an inexpensive restaurant, whose menu includes buffalo burgers, Indian tacos, and trout, as well as ice-cold soft drinks, beer, and wine.

You'll find a few more restaurants and two motels a few miles north of the park in the small town of Wall, home of the world-famous **Wall Drug Store,** 510 Main St. (© **605/279-2175;** www.walldrug.com). The **Super 8 Motel,** 711 Glenn St., 2 blocks north of I-90 at Exit 110 (© **800/800-8000** or 605/279-2688), has clean rooms at reasonable rates and is open year-round. The **Best Western Plains Motel,** 712 Glenn St., 2 blocks north of I-90 at Exit 110 (© **800/528-1234** or 605/279-2145; www.bestwesternplains.com), is another reliable choice.

A SIDE TRIP TO DEADWOOD

Deadwood was once known as the wildest, wickedest, woolliest town in the West, where Wild Bill Hickok was gunned down and where Calamity Jane Canary claimed she could out-drink, out-swear, and out-spit any man. At the same time, the city's merchants, bankers, and saloonkeepers invested their money in beautiful Victorian buildings and residences that still stand as solid testaments to civic pride.

Today, legalized gambling has revitalized the old town, with more than 80 casinos. Plan to park in one of the edge-of-town lots and take a trolley shuttle into town.

Deadwood is northwest of Rapid City off I-90 and U.S. 14. For more information on accommodations, walking tours, museums, attractions, special events, and gaming packages, contact the **Deadwood Chamber of Commerce & Visitor Bureau,** 735 Main St. (© **800/999-1876;** www.deadwood.org), or stop by the **History and Information Center** in the classic train depot at 3 Siever St.

The **Adams Museum,** 54 Sherman St. (© **605/578-1714;** www.adamsmuseum andhouse.org), is a treasure-trove of local history and memorabilia including a stuffed two-headed calf. The **Broken Boot Gold Mine** (© **605/578-1876**) has guided tours of a gold mine and offers gold-panning. Wild Bill Hickok, Calamity Jane, and other notorious residents are buried in **Mount Moriah Cemetery.**

Deadwood restaurants are more upscale than what you'll generally find in the rest of the area. **Jakes,** upstairs from the casual dining room, **Midnight Star,** 677 Main St. (© **800/999-6482** or 605/578-1555), owned by Kevin Costner and his brother Dan, offers a menu ranging from pheasant quesadillas to buffalo carpaccio. Locals consider it the best dining in the region. If you're not hungry, drop in anyhow to peruse the displays of movie costumes and props from *Dances with Wolves* at Diamond Lil's bar, adjacent to Jakes.

In nearby Lead (pronounced Leed), **Homestake** is the oldest gold mine in continuous operation in the Western Hemisphere, with a visitor center open year-round at 160 W. Main St. (© **888/701-0164** or 605/584-3110; www.homestakevisitorcenter.com).

8 Idaho

Think Idaho and imagine a state bursting with natural beauty. Within its borders you will find vast stretches of sage-covered high desert, white-water rivers rolling and roaring through Rocky Mountain canyons, eerie volcanic landscapes, jagged snowy mountain peaks, glacier lakes, and green pine woods. Most of all, Idaho is home to welcoming and friendly people who will help make your visit a memorable one. For information on the state, call © **800/VISIT-ID**, or go to **www.visitid.org**.

BOISE

Boise is one of the nation's fastest growing metropolitan areas. A remarkably sophisticated and culturally active city of 210,000, Boise offers a variety of scenery, indoor and outdoor activity, and great restaurants. The modern cityscape is nestled up against mainly undeveloped foothills and offers a moderate four-season climate with easy access to year-round activities.

ESSENTIALS

GETTING THERE By Plane Boise Airport (© **208/383-3110;** www.cityofboise. org/transportation/airport), located about 3 miles south of the city center, serves much of southern Idaho with frequent service from most western and some midwestern hubs.

By Car The major route into Boise is **I-84** from the southeast (Salt Lake City) and northwest (Portland and Seattle). Twenty-four-hour road conditions are available at © **208/336-6600.**

VISITOR INFORMATION For advance information, contact the **Boise Convention and Visitors Bureau,** P.O. Box 2106, Boise, ID 83701 (© **800/635-5240** or 208/344-7777; www.boise.org). **Visitor Information Centers** are located in the Boise Centre on the Grove, 850 W. Front St. (© **208/344-5338**); and near the airport at 2676 Airport Way, near I-84 at the Vista Avenue exit (© **208/385-0362**). Hours at both centers vary seasonally, so call before you go.

GETTING OUTSIDE

Boise offers a huge variety of outside activities. Whether you ski, bike, swim, jog, or just like to enjoy the out-of-doors from your favorite sidewalk cafe table, you will find something year-round here.

Twenty-five miles of Greenbelt, mostly paved, have been established along the Boise River and provide recreation for Boiseans and visitors of all ages. The Greenbelt connects most of the city's large downtown parks as well. You can access the Greenbelt from anywhere downtown—just head for the river.

For slightly more strenuous hiking or biking activity, check out the **Ridge to Rivers Trail System (www.ridgetorivers.org)** in the foothills above Boise. This 85-mile system has been established by connecting public land and right-of-ways through private property to provide several multiuse nonmotorized trails around the foothills.

While not a big spot for watersports, a Boise tradition is floating the Boise River. You can float on almost anything but tubes, and rafts can be rented at **Barber Park** (© **208/343-6564**). Book a guided river tour with **Boise River Tours** (© **208/333-0003;** www.boiserivertours.com). The Boise River is also a great place to fish. For fishing information pick up the **Idaho Department of Fish & Game**'s *Official Guide to Fishing in Idaho* and *General Fishing Seasons and Rules* in local shops, or contact the department at 600 S. Walnut St., P.O. Box 25, Boise, ID 83707 (© **208/334-3700;** http://fishandgame.idaho.gov).

Though it doesn't quite have the reputation of other ski areas in the state, **Bogus Basin** (© **800/367-4397** or 208/332-5100; www.bogusbasin.com) is located about a 45-minute drive (16 miles north) from Boise. With 2,600 acres of skiable terrain, 52 runs, and 37 miles of Nordic trails, Bogus offers deep powder, short lift lines, and great night skiing. It's open, on average, for 140 days beginning Thanksgiving Day.

WHAT TO SEE & DO

Boise is home to more people of Basque ancestry than anywhere outside the Basque Country in Europe. You can learn more by visiting the **Basque Museum and Cultural Center,** 611 Grove St. (© **208/343-2671;** www.basquemuseum.com). Just a few blocks away you can wander Julia Davis Park, which houses the **Idaho Historical Museum** (© **208/334-2120;** www.idahohistory.net/museum.html), the **Boise Art Museum** (© **208/345-8330;** www.boiseartmuseum.org), **Zoo Boise** (© **208/384-4260;** www.cityofboise.org/parks/zoo), and the **Discovery Center of Idaho** (© **208/343-9895;** www.scidaho.org), a family-oriented science and activities center.

Head up to the **Idaho State Capitol** (© **208/334-5174**), the nation's only state capitol building heated with geothermal water. Travel east of town on Warm Springs Avenue and take a tour of the **Old Idaho Penitentiary** (© **208/334-2844;** www.idahohistory.net/oldpen.html), built in territorial times and holding prisoners until 1973. Also part of the Old Pen complex are the History of Electricity in Idaho Museum, the Idaho Transportation Museum, and the Museum of Mining & Geology.

Farther out, 6 miles south of I-84 Exit 50, don't miss the **World Center for Birds of Prey** (© **208/362-3716;** www.peregrinefund.org), with a visitor center and injured-bird recovery area that serves as an introduction to the 500,000-acre **Snake River Birds of Prey National Conservation Area** (© **208/384-3300;** www.birdsofprey.blm.gov), home to one of the nation's densest concentrations of nesting raptors along with over 250 other wildlife species.

WHERE TO STAY

For the best digs in town try the **Grove Hotel,** 245 S. Capitol Blvd. (© **888/961-5000** or 208/333-8000; www.grovehotelboise.com), which has all the amenities you could want and high-season doubles starting at $139—plus, it's connected to the Bank of America Centre, a sports and entertainment arena. Downtown's historic hotel is the lovingly refurbished **Owyhee Plaza,** 1109 Main St. (© **800/233-4611** or 208/343-4611; www.owyheeplaza.com), with doubles starting at $145. The **Statehouse Inn,** 981 Grove St. (© **800/243-4622** or 208/342-4622; www.statehouse-inn.com), is near the convention center; double rooms start at $129. Nearby, and with similar rates, is the **Courtyard by Marriott,** 222 S. Broadway (© **800/321-2211** or 208/331-2700). The airport area, only 3 miles from downtown, offers a large number of moderately priced hotels, with doubles that run about $65. Try the **Inn America** (© **800/469-4667** or 208/389-9800; www.innamerica.com), the **Comfort Inn Airport** (© **800/228-5150** or 208/336-0077; www.comfortinn.com/hotel/id011), and **Extended Stay America** (© **800/398-7829** or 208/363-9040; www.extendedstayhotels.com).

WHERE TO DINE

At the following fine-dining restaurants, entrees range between $18 and $25. For a unique dining experience, try **Mortimer's Idaho Cuisine,** 110 S. 5th St. (© **208/338-6550**), featuring inventive regional cuisine based on locally sourced produce and meats. One of Boise's favorites and right on the Greenway, **Cottonwood Grille,** 913 W. River St. (© **208/333-9800**), offers French via Northwest cuisine in a lodgelike dining room dominated by a massive stone fireplace. **The Milky Way,** 205 N. 10th St. (© **208/343-4334**), features fun, sophisticated dining from a pair of chefs who got their start in California with Wolfgang Puck. For old-fashioned elegance (think Steak Diane) and fine service try **The Gamekeeper,** in the Owyhee Plaza Hotel (© **208/343-4611**). In a city known for steaks, try **Lock, Stock and Barrel,** 205 N. 10th St. (© **208/343-4334**), for hand-cut steaks and old-fashioned atmosphere. To experience Basque cooking, drive a dozen miles west of Boise to the town of Meridian, where cozy family-oriented **Epi's Basque Restaurant,** 1115 N. Main St., Meridian (© **208/884-0142**), serves fantastic northern Spanish country-style cooking that many consider the best Basque cooking outside of Europe.

Boise's pubs are popular for lunch and inexpensive dinners ($8–$12) and locally brewed beer. **TableRock Brew Pub,** 705 Fulton St. (© **208/342-0944**), has classic pub fare, while **Bittercreek Ale House,** 246 N. 8th St. (© **208/345-1813**), verges on gourmet. **Gernika Basque Pub & Eatery,** 202 S. Capitol Blvd. (© **208/344-2175**), features Basque cooking in addition to traditional soup and sandwiches; and **Ha'Penny Bridge Pub,** 855 Broad St. (© **208/343-5568**), is the local Irish pub. For a truly unique experience try **Bardenay,** 610 Grove (© **208/426-0538**), the first "distillery-pub" in the United States, featuring its own rum, vodka, and gin in addition to excellent food. For Boise's favorite breakfast spot, don't miss **Goldy's,** 108 S. Capitol Blvd. (© **208/345-4100**).

SUN VALLEY & KETCHUM

The nation's first destination ski resort, Sun Valley was developed near the small town of Ketchum in 1936 by Averell Harriman and immediately attracted the Hollywood set. Still a hangout for the stars, it has been named the number-one ski resort by *Condé Nast Traveler, Ski Magazine,* and *Gourmet Magazine.* It has received numerous other honors as one of the top resorts in the nation.

ESSENTIALS

GETTING THERE By Plane The closest airport to Sun Valley is **Friedman Memorial Airport** (© 208/788-4956), 12 miles south in Hailey. There are direct flights from Salt Lake City, Los Angeles, and Seattle. You can also fly into Boise and take a **Sun Valley Express** bus (© 877/622-8267; www.sunvalleyexpress.com). Be sure to check availability ahead of time and save by booking your bus ticket in advance.

By Car The major route into Sun Valley is **Highway 75,** which runs south from **I-90** at Missoula, Montana, and north from **I-84** at Twin Falls.

VISITOR INFORMATION You can get a vacation planner from the **Sun Valley–Ketchum Chamber of Commerce,** P.O. Box 2420, Sun Valley, ID 83353 (© **866/305-0408**; www.visitsunvalley.com). A **Visitor Information Center** for the area is located on the corner of 4th and Main in Ketchum. You can also check out the seasonally updated *Official Sun Valley Guide* at **www.sunvalleycentral.com**.

GETTING OUTSIDE

Sun Valley's claim to fame is undoubtedly its world-class ski resort (© **800/786-8259** or 208/622-2151; www.sunvalley.com). You can choose from two mountains with over 2,000 skiable acres with 78 ski runs (the longest 3 miles), 149 miles of cross-country trails, and 17 chairlifts. High season lift tickets are $67 adult. For backcountry skiing, try **Sun Valley Trekking Company** (© **208/788-1966;** www.svtrek.com). In summer, they offer day hikes and guided mountain-biking trips. For sleigh rides, try the **Sun Valley Horsemen's Center** (© 208/622-2387). You can enjoy ice-skating year-round at the Sun Valley Resort Lodge's two rinks. Saturday nights during the summer, Olympic skaters perform on the outdoor ice rink adjoining the lodge (© **208/622-2135** for reservations).

In addition to the resort's trails, cross-country skiers and snowshoers can explore the 75-mile North Valley Trails system, which meanders through the Big Wood River Valley north of town and leads to the gold-rush ghost town of Galena, where the **Galena Lodge** (© **208/726-4010**) serves up meals to skiers.

Summer in Sun Valley brings even more outdoor adventure. Almost anything you could ask for is available—from paragliding to white-water rafting to skeet shooting. Ketchum is filled with outfitters, and you'll have no trouble lining up activities even at the last minute. Trail systems around Ketchum offer miles of paved and unpaved trails for biking, hiking, skating, or walking. Information is available from the **Blaine County Recreation District** (© **208/788-2117;** www.bcrd.org) or at the Ketchum Visitor Center. In summer, you can ride the Sun Valley Resort **chairlift** (© **208/622-6136**) to the top of Bald Mountain and hike in wildflower meadows; or bring along a mountain bike and ride down the slopes on two wheels. If you want to really get away, try a llama trek with **Venture Outdoors** (© **800/528-5262;** www.venout.com).

The **Sun Valley Resort Golf Course** (© **208/622-2251**) offers an 18-hole Robert Trent Jones, Jr.–designed course, rated the number-one course in Idaho by *Golf Digest.* There are also two 9-hole courses in the area: **Warm Springs Golf Course** (© **208/726-3715**) and **Bigwood Golf Course** (© **208/726-4024;** www.bigwoodgolf.com).

Other activities include tennis at the **Sun Valley Resort Tennis Club** (© **208/622-2156**) and **Warm Springs Tennis Club** (© **208/726-4040**), horseback riding at **Sun Valley Resort Horsemen's Center** (© **208/622-2387**), trail rides with **Super Outfitter Adventures** (© **208/788-7731**), and fishing. A guide to area fishing is available at the Ketchum visitor center.

WHAT TO SEE & DO

Take a drive north of Ketchum to the **Sawtooth National Recreation Area** (© **208/727-5013;** www.fs.fed.us/r4/sawtooth) to view spectacular jagged peaks. The headquarters is located 8 miles north of Ketchum on Highway 75.

Southeast of Ketchum you will find the **Craters of the Moon National Monument,** a relatively recent (only 2,000 years old) lava bed. This eerie landscape will make you feel as if you've landed on the moon. There is a **visitor center** off Highway 20/26/93 (© **208/527-3257**), which has maps of the area.

Closer to Ketchum you can visit **Ernest Hemingway's grave** in the Ketchum Cemetery on Route 75 North at 10th Street East, or the **Ernest Hemingway Memorial** alongside Trail Creek just north of Sun Valley Lodge. Check out the **Heritage and Ski Museum** in Ketchum to see artifacts from Idaho's ski history (© **208/726-8118**). For a history of Sun Valley and its famous visitors, check out the Sun Valley Lodge lobby to see dozens of photos dating from the 1930s picturing visitors from the shah of Iran to Lucille Ball.

WHERE TO STAY

The **Sun Valley Resort** (© 800/786-8259 or 208/622-2151; www.sunvalley.com) offers over 500 rooms ranging from the original lodge and inn and to more than 100 separate apartments and condominiums. High season rates in winter are higher on weekends and much higher over the holidays; a basic hotel double starts around $169 and goes up quickly. Minimum stays may apply. Off-season rates (spring and fall) are roughly one-quarter less expensive. There are not many bargain rates in the Sun Valley area, but a couple of lower-priced hotels offer high-season rooms between $130 and $160, and discounted off-season rates. **Best Western Kentwood Lodge,** 180 S. Main St. (© 800/805-1001 or 208/726-4114; www.bestwestern.com/kentwood lodge), is in the heart of Ketchum; and the **Best Western Tyrolean Lodge,** 260 Cottonwood St. (© 800/333-7912 or 208/726-5336; www.bestwestern.com/tyrolean), is by the River Run chairlift.

WHERE TO DINE

Sun Valley and Ketchum offer a huge variety of restaurants for a community their size. Top-end choices for fine dining include two Continental restaurants, the **Lodge Dining Room** at the Sun Valley Lodge (© 208/622-2150), and **Michel's Christiania Restaurant,** 309 Walnut Ave. N. (© 208/726-3388), where dinner for two will easily top $120. The **Sawtooth Club,** 231 Main St. N. (© 208/726-5233), and the vintage **Pioneer Saloon,** 308 N. Main St. (© 208/726-3139), are favorites for steaks and seafood in the $18-to-$25 range. Other more casual possibilities are **Whiskey Jacques,** 251 N. Main St. (© 208/726-5297); the **Roosevelt Tavern,** 280 N. Main St. (© 208/726-0051)—also featuring live music nightly—and the **Kneadery,** 260 Leadville Ave. N. (© 208/726-9462), a favorite for breakfast. For a funky Old West bar, check out the **Casino,** 220 N. Main St. (© 208/726-9901).

COEUR D'ALENE

Idaho's northern resort town, Coeur d'Alene, sits amid sparkling lakes and green pines and offers year-round recreation and one of the world's top resort hotels and golf courses.

ESSENTIALS

GETTING THERE   The closest major airport is **Spokane International Airport** (© 509/455-6455; www.spokaneairports.net) in Spokane, Washington, 40 miles west. Major highways into Coeur d'Alene are **I-90** from the west (Spokane) and east (Missoula, MT), and **Highway 95** from the south (Boise).

VISITOR INFORMATION   Contact the **Coeur d'Alene Visitor and Convention Services,** P.O. Box 850, Coeur d'Alene, ID 83816 (© 877/782-9232; www.coeur dalene.org).

GETTING OUTSIDE

Coeur d'Alene is a true outdoor playground. Twenty-five miles long, glacier-dug **Lake Coeur d'Alene** is the center of activities. Boating, sailing, jet-skiing, water-skiing, fishing, and anything else you can do on water are available. In fact, the world's first water skis were used on Lake Coeur d'Alene in the 1920s. Today you can also jet-ski, take a seaplane tour with **Brooks Seaplane Service** (© 208/664-2842), or parasail with **Coeur d'Alene Parasail** (© 208/765-5367) on the lake. **Lake Coeur d'Alene**

Cruises offers a variety of lake cruises, including a sunset dinner cruise (© **800/ 365-8338**).

A summer visit means you can tee up on the **Coeur d'Alene Golf Course** (© **800/ 688-5253;** www.cdaresort.com/golf), one of only 16 golf resorts in America to receive the "five-star" designation by *Golf Digest* and one of 20 with a *Golf Magazine* Gold Medal. The course is unique for its famous Floating Green, anchored to the lake bottom and reachable only by boat.

Winter in northern Idaho means skiing. A short 30-mile drive east of Coeur d'Alene brings you to **Silver Mountain Ski Resort,** near Kellogg (© **800/204-6428** or 208/783-1111; www.silvermt.com), with the world's longest gondola operating year-round. Summer concerts are also held at Silver Mountain. **Schweitzer Mountain Resort** (© **800/831-8810;** www.schweitzer.com), 44 miles north in Sandpoint, offers stunning views of Lake Pend Oreille. Schweitzer also offers golf packages in summer.

WHAT TO SEE & DO

Coeur d'Alene has a variety of historical and natural sites for the visitor. The **Museum of North Idaho** (© **208/664-3448;** www.museumni.org) covers the long history of the area with exhibits and photos. Part of that history goes back to the **Cataldo Mission,** 28 miles east on I-90 (© **208/682-3814**), originally built in 1842 and the oldest standing building in Idaho. Climb **Tubbs Hill** in town for a great view of the area. For family fun, check out **Silverwood Theme Park** (© **208/683-3400;** www.silverwoodtheme park.com), 15 minutes north on Highway 95, with 60 rides and a new waterpark. Right in town, **Wild Waters,** 2119 N. Government Way (© **208/667-6491;** www.wildwaters waterpark), offers a towering water slide and other aqua activities.

WHERE TO STAY

Dominating the shoreline in Coeur d'Alene is the **Coeur d'Alene Resort** (© **800/ 688-5253** or 208/765-4000; www.cdaresort.com), at the western edge of downtown, named by the readers of *Condé Nast Traveler* as America's number-one mainland resort. High season summer rates begin at $169 double. Find cheaper rates, but no lake views, at **La Quinta Inn & Suites,** 2209 E. Sherman Ave. (© **800/531-5900** or 208/667-6777); the **Best Western Coeur d'Alene Inn,** 414 W. Appleway (© **800/523- 2464;** www.cdainn.com); and the **Shilo Inn,** 702 W. Appleway (© **800/222-2244** or 208/664-2300; www.shiloinns.com).

WHERE TO DINE

Downtown is lined with dining possibilities, including **Coeur d'Alene Brewing,** 209 Lakeside Ave. (© **208/664-2739**), with good pub fare; the **Wine Cellar,** 313 Sherman Ave. (© **208/664-9463**), with Mediterranean cuisine and nightly jazz; and **Brix,** 317 Sherman Ave. (© **208/665-7407**), an upscale dining room featuring New American cuisine, with main dishes costing $14 to $24. Eight miles east on East Frontage Road is the local's favorite for steak and prime rib, the venerable, lakeside **Wolf Lodge Steak- house** (© **208/664-6665**). For elegant dining, dress up and make reservations at award-winning **Beverly's** (© **208/765-4000**) in the Coeur d'Alene resort, with great views, refined service, and Northwest regional cuisine. Main dishes range from $20 to $34.

9 Oklahoma City

Oklahoma City was born in a single day, when the Great Land Run of April 22, 1889, allowed tens of thousands of people to race across the border on foot, horseback, wagon, and even bicycle to settle unclaimed land: What was just a solitary railroad station grew to a tent city of 10,000 residents overnight. In 1907, Oklahoma became a state, and 3 years later, Oklahoma City became its capital. But it was a tragic event—the April 1995 bombing of a federal building that claimed 168 lives—that catapulted the city to headline status on the international news front. Since then, Oklahoma City, with a population of more than 500,000 people, has reinvented itself with ongoing revitalization projects (such as the Bricktown entertainment district) that have transformed it into one of the state's most exciting destinations. Yet despite its push to modernity, its frontier heritage remains evident in attractions such as the must-see National Cowboy & Western Heritage Museum and the Oklahoma History Center, and in annual events such as Red Earth, the largest Native American festival in the world.

ESSENTIALS

GETTING THERE   By Plane   Will Rogers Airport (© 405/680-3200; www.fly okc.com) is 10 miles southwest of downtown. The **Airport Shuttle** (© 405/681-3311; www.taxivan.com) charges $17 for one person or $19 for two to downtown hotels, though many hotels provide free airport shuttles. A cab ride downtown costs about $18.

By Train   Amtrak (© 800/USA-RAIL or 405/297-0236; www.amtrak.com) provides daily service from Fort Worth, Texas (trip time: 4 hr.), to the historic downtown Santa Fe Depot at 100 E. K. Gaylord.

By Car   Major routes into Oklahoma City are **I-35** from the northeast (Kansas City, 353 miles) and south (Dallas, 205 miles); **I-40** from the east (Little Rock, 344 miles) and west (Albuquerque, 540 miles); and **I-44** from the northeast (St. Louis, 500 miles).

VISITOR INFORMATION   The **Oklahoma City Convention & Visitors Bureau** is located downtown at 189 S. Sheridan (© 800/225-5652 or 405/297-8912; www.visitokc.com) and is open Monday through Friday from 8:30am to 5pm. In addition, the state operates an Oklahoma City Welcome Center in the northeast part of the city at 12229 N. I-35 Service Rd., near Frontier City amusement park. It's open daily 8:30am to 5pm.

GETTING AROUND   Metro Transit (© 405/235-RIDE; www.gometro.org) operates bus service to most Oklahoma City destinations Monday through Saturday; bus no. 22 is useful for traveling between downtown and the Oklahoma City Zoo and National Cowboy & Western Heritage Museum. The fare is $1.25. Otherwise, the best option for tourists is Metro Transit's rubber-tire Spirit Trolleys, with two routes (the Blue and Red lines) circling through the downtown area and a third (the Orange Line) making runs between downtown and hotels along Meridian to Stockyards City. Fares are 25¢ for the Red and Blue lines and $1 for the Orange. A pass for all trolley lines is $2 for 1 day or $3 for 3.

SPECIAL EVENTS   Red Earth (© 405/427-5228; www.redearth.org), a celebration of Native American cultures and traditions held every June, features a downtown parade, juried art competitions, an art market, and performing arts. From April to December, Oklahoma hosts nine major **horse shows,** more than any other city in the world (contact the Oklahoma City Convention & Visitors Bureau for more information).

WHAT TO SEE & DO

In the past decade, Oklahoma City's downtown has blossomed into a prime vacation destination with new hotels, lively restaurants, the Bricktown entertainment district with a river canal and boat rides, and several worthy attractions. One of downtown's oldest attractions is the lovely **Myriad Botanical Gardens,** at Reno and Robinson avenues (© **405/297-3995;** www.myriadgardens.com), a 17-acre landscaped oasis centered on a sunken lake. Spanning the lake—and the centerpiece of the gardens— is Crystal Bridge, a seven-story, 224-foot-long cylindrical conservatory filled with exotic plants ranging from tropical to desert and set in a wonderland of cliffs, water-falls, and ponds. Lizards, fish, and butterflies also call the Crystal Bridge home. Crys-tal Bridge is open Monday to Saturday 9am to 6pm, and Sunday noon to 6pm. Admission costs $6 adults; $5 seniors, children ages 13 to 18, and students; and $3 children ages 4 to 12.

Nearby is the **Oklahoma City Museum of Art,** 415 Couch Dr. (© **405/236-3100;** www.okcmoa.com), which opened in 2002 and boasts one of the most stun-ning collections you'll see anywhere: 18 installations and ensembles created by Dale Chihuly, representing 3 decades of the glass master's whimsical and color-saturated works. It's worth visiting the museum for the Chihuly exhibition alone, though visi-tors will also want to take a spin through galleries featuring European and American art. A theater screens independent, foreign, and classic films Thursday through Sun-day, while a rooftop outdoor lounge is open for cocktails Thursday evenings. The museum is open Tuesday to Saturday 10am to 5pm (Thurs to 9pm) and Sunday noon to 5pm. Admission costs $7 for adults, $5 for children, students, and seniors.

Located a few blocks to the northeast is the **Oklahoma City National Memorial and Museum,** 620 N. Harvey Ave. (© **405/235-3313;** www.oklahomacitynational memorial.org), which honors the victims, survivors, and rescuers of the April 19, 1995, bomb that destroyed the Alfred P. Murrah Federal Building and took 168 lives. The museum recounts that fateful day and the days, weeks, and years that followed with eyewitness accounts, actual news footage, and exhibitions that document every-thing from rescue missions to how the explosion impacted families and the city. The most moving room in the museum is filled with photographs of the 168 victims, who are honored again in an outside memorial by 168 empty chairs lined in rows; smaller chairs represent the 19 children who died in the blast. A fence on the west perimeter of the memorial gives visitors a place to leave tokens of remembrance. The museum is open Monday to Saturday 9am to 6pm and Sunday 1 to 6pm (you must purchase tickets 1 hr. before closing), while the outdoor memorial is open free 24 hours a day. Admission is $8 for adults, $7 for seniors, and $6 for children and students.

A 5-minute drive northeast of downtown is the state capitol, as well as the new **Oklahoma History Center,** 2401 N. Laird Ave. (© **405/522-5248;** www.okhistory center.org), which explores Oklahoma's history through interactive and visual exhibits that include firsthand accounts, photographs, and artifacts. Memorable events, such as the 1889 Land Run, Wild West shows, and horrific droughts and resultant Dust Bowl of the 1930s are covered, while other displays chronicle the history and traditions of Oklahoma's African Americans and 39 American Indian tribes. Visitors can listen to American Indian languages, view a map depicting Oklahoma's former All-Black Towns (founded from the mid–19th c. to 1920 and numbering more than 50, more than any other region in the U.S.), watch movies filmed in or about Oklahoma, and learn about such Oklahoma greats as Mickey Mantle, Olympic gold medallist Jim Thorpe, and musicians Woody Guthrie and Gene Autry. It's open Monday to Saturday 9am to 5pm and Sunday noon to 5pm. Admission is $5 adults, $4 seniors, and $3 children.

Best   Ride 'em Cowboy

Oklahoma City's top attraction is the outstanding **National Cowboy & Western Heritage Museum**, 1700 NE 63rd St. (✆ **405/478-2250;** www.national cowboymuseum.org), which celebrates the life of the cowboy and the Old West with historic artifacts and one of the country's finest collections of Western art. Works by Charles Russell, Frederick Remington, and contemporary artists who have won top prize in the museum's annual Prix de West invitational exhibition (held every June) are on display, along with a Western Performers Gallery which honors Gene Autry, John Wayne, Gary Cooper, and others who contributed to the myths and legends of the West.

Other features include a lifelike rodeo arena with displays on bull riding, calf roping, and other activities; and a re-created cattle town complete with livery stable, saddle maker, saloon, and other buildings. More exhibits display Native American crafts, saddles, guns, boots, and hats, as well as explore related subjects such as the U.S. cavalry and trail drives. The museum is open daily 9am to 5pm; plan on spending at least 2 hours here. Admission costs $8.50 adults, $7 seniors, and $4 children ages 6 to 12.

Two miles west of downtown is Oklahoma City's most authentic signpost of its cowboy past: **Stockyards City** (✆ **405/235-7267;** stockyardscity.org), founded in 1910, is listed on the National Historic Register, and is centered on Agnew and Exchange streets. Popular for its restaurants and shops specializing in Western wear, custom-made boots, and saddles, it's located next to the **Oklahoma National Stockyards,** which claims to be the largest live cattle market in the world. Cattle auctions, open to the public, are held all day Monday and Tuesday.

The rolling hills of northeast Oklahoma City, nicknamed the Adventure District and easily accessible via I-35 and I-44, are home to several of Oklahoma's top attractions, including the National Cowboy & Western Heritage Museum (see "Ride 'em Cowboy," above). For families, nothing beats a trip to the **Oklahoma City Zoo,** east of Martin Luther King Boulevard on NE 52nd Street (✆ **405/424-3344;** www.okczoo.com), which celebrated its 100th anniversary in 2004. Consistently ranked one of the nation's best zoos (it's accredited as both a zoo *and* a botanical garden), it houses more than 1,500 animals, including more than 50 endangered or threatened species, in innovative, enchanting habitats such as the Great EscApe with its lowland gorilla troops, orangutans, and chimpanzees; Cat Forest/Lion Overlook; and Oklahoma Trails featuring native animals. A kid's-dream playground, aquarium, and all the usual exotic animals—including orphaned grizzly cubs from Alaska—make this one of the city's hottest attractions. Tickets ($7 adults, $4 children 3–11 and seniors) go on sale daily at 9am (7:30am July 1 to Labor Day) until 6pm Memorial Day to Labor Day (grounds stay open until 8pm) and until 5pm the rest of the year (grounds close at dusk).

Next to the zoo is **Omniplex,** 2100 NE 52nd St. (✆ **405/602-OMNI;** www.omniplex. org), a hangarlike building housing hands-on science exhibits that appeal to children ages 12 and younger, a space gallery, vintage aircraft, a toy train collection, the Red Earth Museum with its impressive collection of Native American cradleboards, a planetarium, and a dome-shaped theater. Although newer, more technically advanced museums make this one seem rather old-fashioned (plans call for a gradual overhaul), there's plenty to warrant a 2- or 3-hour visit here, especially in inclement weather. It's open Monday to Friday 9am to 5pm, Saturday 9am to 6pm, and Sunday 11am to 6pm. Admission costs $9.50 adults, $6.75 seniors and children 3 to 12. The planetarium and Omnidome theater cost extra.

Also for children, two popular seasonal attractions are **Frontier City,** located in northeast Oklahoma City just off I-35 at the NE 122nd Street exit (② **405/478-2412;** www.sixflags.com; $33 adults, $25 children), an Old West theme park with 50 thrill rides (its 250-ft. free-fall Eruption is Oklahoma's tallest ride), attractions, and action-packed shows set against a colorful backdrop of log cabins and Wild West storefronts; and **White Water Bay,** a waterpark with raft rides, a wave pool, slides, and more, located west of downtown just off I-40 (take the Meridian Ave. exit) at 3908 W. Reno (② **405/943-9687;** www.sixflags.com; $25 adults, $21 children).

SHOPPING   Wranglers and would-be cowboys should head to **Sheplers,** 812 S. Meridian Ave. (② **405/947-6831;** www.sheplers.com), and **Langston's,** in Stockyards City at 2224 Exchange Ave. (② **405/235-9536;** www.langstons.com), for the city's largest selection in Western wear, hats, and boots. **Bass Pro Shop,** in Bricktown at 200 Bass Pro Dr. (② **405/218-5200;** www.basspro.com), is an outdoor enthusiast's paradise with departments devoted to camping, fishing, hunting, archery, and other pursuits.

WHERE TO STAY

A top choice downtown for both business and leisure travelers is the **Renaissance Oklahoma City Hotel,** located on the edge of Bricktown at 10 N. Broadway (② **800/ HOTELS-1** or 405/228-8000; www.renaissancehotels.com). With a dramatic, 15-story glass-topped atrium lobby complete with waterfalls, ponds, and plants, it offers a 24-hour fitness room, indoor pool, full-service spa, and 311 rooms ($199–$239 double) that face Bricktown or downtown (many with balcony), including club-level rooms with extra privileges. Those with more limited expense accounts can try the nearby **Courtyard by Marriott,** 2 W. Reno Ave. (② **800/321-2211** or 405/232-2290; www.courtyard.com/okcdt). Opened in 2004, it's a smart-looking property decorated in bright contemporary colors and offering a 24-hour exercise room, indoor pool, and chic rooms ($139–$169 double) that rise above the ordinary in decor and comfort.
• Couples searching for a romantic getaway might consider the **Grandison Inn at Maney Park,** just a few minutes' drive from downtown at 1200 N. Shartel (② **888/799-4667** or 405/232-8778; www.bbonline.com/ok/grandison). Built in 1904, this Victorian bed-and-breakfast with a wraparound porch and original woodwork retains all its turn-of-the-20th-century charm and offers nine rooms ($89–$169 double), each one different but decorated with antiques and with private bathroom (most have whirlpool tubs as well). Travelers on a budget can try **Best Western Saddleback Inn,** 4300 SW 3rd St. (② **800/228-3903** or 405/947-7000; www.bestwestern. com/saddlebackinn), one of many motels on or near Meridian Avenue west of downtown with easy access to I-40. Built by the owner's father more than 20 years ago, it's decorated in a Native American/Western theme and has more character than most hotels. It targets business travelers, but families, too, appreciate the rooms with fridge ($69–$109 double) or the extralarge suites ($129) which add a microwave, as well as the free buffet breakfast, full-service restaurant, outdoor pool, exercise room, hot tub,

Feeding the Meter

The eternal quest for change to feed the country's ubiquitous and ever-loathed parking meters started in, of all places, Oklahoma, when the first meter in the U.S. was installed here in 1935.

---

sauna, free cocktail hour Monday through Thursday, and free shuttle service to the airport and within a 3-mile radius of the hotel, including nearby White Water Bay. The Orange Line trolley to downtown stops in front of the hotel.

WHERE TO DINE

Oklahoma City's most famous restaurant is probably **Cattlemen's Steakhouse,** located in Stockyards City at 1309 S. Agnew (© **405/236-0416,** but no reservations accepted; www.cattlemensrestaurant.com). Established in 1910 and catering to tourists and cowboys alike, it serves steaks hand-cut and aged on the premises, then broiled to perfection and served with salad, baked potato, and rolls for $15 to $25. Popular also for its hearty breakfasts, it opens daily at 6am.

Western Avenue, a short drive west of the many attractions in the Adventure District, is lined with restaurants, bars, and one-of-a-kind shops. For a romantic splurge or celebratory meal, **The Metro Wine Bar & Grill,** 6418 N. Western Ave. (© **405/840-9463;** www.metrowinebar.com), fits the bill with its drawing-room ambience, subdued lighting, and eclectic cuisine that blends American fare with French and Asian influences, with most dishes priced between $15 and $20. True to its name, it also offers more than 400 bottles of wine, including half-bottles and more than 20 choices of wine by the glass. For families, a popular neighborhood choice is **The Hideaway,** 6616 N. Western Ave. (© **405/840-4777;** www.hideawaypizza.com), known for its build-your-own pizzas made with fresh dough and signature thick, slightly sweet tomato sauce. Medium-size pizzas (eight slices) start at $14.

OKLAHOMA CITY AFTER DARK

Bricktown, a renovated warehouse district a stone's throw east of downtown, is the city's premier nightlife district. Its focal point is a mile-long, landscaped canal, with **Water Taxi** boat tours (© **405/234-8294;** www.watertaxi.com) offering the most entertaining introduction to the area's history. Alongside the canal are waterfront restaurants and larger-than-life-size bronze statues commemorating the 1889 Land Run; a total of 45 figures will grace the waterway by Oklahoma's 2007 state centennial.

A good watering hole is **Bricktown Brewery,** 1 N. Oklahoma Ave. (© **405/232-2739;** www.bricktownbrewery.com), a microbrewery famous for its barbecued meats and live music on weekends. Down the street is **Citywalk,** 70 N. Oklahoma (© **405/232-9255;** www.citybrickwalk.com), which offers seven clubs and bars under one roof, Friday through Sunday nights. On Western Avenue, a good choice for live music on weekends is **VZD's,** 4200 N. Western Ave. (© **405/524-4203;** www.vzds.com), which offers rock, country, reggae, and other kinds of music in addition to salads, soups, and burgers. For families, **Rodeo Opry,** in Stockyards City at Agnew & Exchange Avenue (© **405/297-9773;** www.ohfo.org), showcases up-and-coming country-and-western entertainers every Saturday evening.

10 Omaha

Located on the western bank of the Missouri River, Omaha was founded in 1854 to outfit those traveling the Oregon and Mormon trails. It wasn't until 1863, when President Lincoln made Omaha the eastern terminus of the first transcontinental railroad, that the city began to grow. Today, Nebraska's largest city, with a population of 400,000, comes as something of a surprise to first-time visitors or those returning after many years. While its zoo—one of the nation's most unique—has long been a top draw as Nebraska's number-one tourist attraction, Omaha boasts several other outstanding attractions too, including a drive-through wildlife park, a museum devoted to U.S. military aircraft and missiles, and Boys Town, made famous in a 1938 film starring Spencer Tracy and Mickey Rooney.

In recent years, Omaha's riverfront has enjoyed a renaissance, with newly created footpaths and parks linking it to the Old Market district, 12 square blocks of former warehouses now enjoying new life as restaurants and shops. Omaha is the Midwest at its best: friendly, casual, and unpretentious. Apparently, those traits are a perfect match for one of the world's richest men; the so-called "Oracle of Omaha," investor Warren Buffett, was raised in Omaha and continues to call it home.

ESSENTIALS

GETTING THERE   By Plane   Eppley Airfield, 4501 Abbott Dr. (© **402/422-6817;** www.eppleyairfield.com), is 5 miles northeast of downtown. Most hotels provide free shuttle service from the airport.

By Train   Amtrak (© **800/USA-RAIL** or 402/342-1501; www.amtrak.com) provides daily service from Chicago and Denver (8½ hr. from both destinations) to its station at S. 9th and Pacific streets.

By Car   Major routes into Omaha are **I-29** from the south (Kansas City, 180 miles) and **I-80** from the east (Des Moines, 125 miles) and west (Denver, 530 miles).

VISITOR INFORMATION   The **Greater Omaha Convention & Visitors Bureau** is located in the Old Market at 1001 Farnam St. (© **866/YES-OMAHA** or 402/444-4660; www.visitomaha.com). It's open June through August Monday to Saturday 9am to 4:30pm and Sunday 1:30 to 4:30pm; the rest of the year it's open Monday to Saturday 9am to 4:30pm.

GETTING AROUND   Metro Area Transit (© **402/341-0800;** www.metroarea transit.com) operates bus service Monday through Saturday; bus no. 10 is useful for traveling between downtown and Omaha's Henry Doorly Zoo. The fare is $1.25. In addition, vintage buses provide limited downtown circular service on weekdays for 25¢.

SPECIAL EVENTS   Every June, fans from across the nation converge at Rosenblatt Stadium next to the zoo to watch collegiate baseball teams vie to win the **NCAA College World Series** (© **402/554-4404**). In September, **River City Roundup** (© **402/554-9610**) features rodeos, concerts, and a parade.

WHAT TO SEE & DO

First on a tour of Omaha should be the **Durham Western Heritage Museum,** 801 S. 10th St. (© **402/444-5071;** www.dwhm.org), an easy walk from the Old Market. Housed in a restored 1931 Union Station, this Art Deco landmark (and Smithsonian Institute affiliate) chronicles Omaha's history, displays train cars (kids love the caboose), and boasts an authentic soda fountain overlooking the elaborately decorated

---

(Best) It's All Happening at the Zoo

Most zoos nowadays give animals free reign of the outdoors, and **Omaha's Henry Doorly Zoo**, 3701 S. 10th St. (℗ **402/733-8401**; www.omahazoo.com), is no exception. What sets this zoo apart is its indoor habitats, for this is truly a fantasyland of interiors, making it a great destination year-round. (Indeed, *Reader's Digest* named it the best zoo in America in 2004.)

The zoo's **Desert Dome**, the world's largest geodesic dome, is a journey of discovery through changing vistas of desert plants and animals, culminating in an underground exploration of caves (lots of bats) and other nocturnal habitats, including the world's largest—and wholly believable—indoor swamp, filled with alligators and other creatures of the night.

The **Lied Jungle** houses the world's largest indoor rainforest, with footpaths leading past waterfalls, ponds, and lush vegetation that provide home to monkeys, tapirs, and other exotic animals; while the **Scott Aquarium** provides an up-close view of sharks through its underwater tunnel. Other highlights include the **Hubbard Gorilla Valley,** where the massive creatures roam free while humans are confined to indoor passageways and bubble windows; **Hubbard Orangutan Forest,** an outdoor habitat where primates hang out in 65-foot-high concrete trees and swing on man-made vines; and a huge free-flight aviary that encompasses natural woods.

Plan on spending 5 hours here; more if you wish to include a show at the zoo's IMAX 3-D theater ($8.25 adults, $6.25 children 3–11). Ticket windows open daily 9:30am to 5pm (8:30am–6pm weekends in summer), with zoo grounds closing 1 hour later. Zoo admission is $11 adults and $6.75 children ages 5 to 11; discount zoo/IMAX tickets are available.

Main Waiting Room. It's open Tuesday 10am to 8pm, Wednesday to Saturday 10am to 5pm, and Sunday 1 to 5pm. Admission is $6 for adults, $5 for seniors, and $4 for children. Just west of downtown is another Art Deco gem, the **Joslyn Art Museum,** 2200 Dodge St. (℗ **402/342-3300;** www.joslyn.org). Although its collection is rather limited, concentrating on 19th- and 20th-century art from Europe and America, it's noted for its art of the American West, including Swiss artist Karl Bodmer's watercolors and prints documenting his journey in the 1830s across North America and up the Missouri River. Check the museum's website for information on special exhibits and on free entertainment, such as its outdoor Jazz on the Green Thursday evenings in July and August. Otherwise, consider this museum only if you have 2 hours to spare. It's open Tuesday to Saturday 10am to 4pm and Sunday noon to 4pm. Admission is $7 for adults, $5 for seniors and students, and $4 for children.

Unique to Omaha is **Boys Town,** on the west end of town at 137th Street and West Dodge Road (℗ **402/498-1140;** www.visitboystown.org). Founded in 1917 by Irish-born immigrant Father Flanagan, Boys Town today is a well-tended, 900-acre village housing more than 500 at-risk boys and girls between the ages of 9 and 18, most of whom stay an average of 18 to 24 months (girls have been accepted since 1979 and now account for half of the residents). Stop by the visitor center to pick up a map and

(Kids) **Best Bets for Kids**

Omaha's Henry Doorly Zoo, the city's top attraction, maintains **Wildlife Safari** ((✆ 402/944-WILD; www.omahazoo.com), near the Strategic Air & Space Museum off I-80 at Exit 426. This 4-mile, drive-through park of scenic prairie, woods, and wetlands takes visitors past herds of buffalo, elk, pronghorn, deer, wolves, and cranes. It's open daily April through October ($5 adults, $4 seniors, $3 children 5–11).

The **Omaha Children's Museum,** located on the south edge of downtown at 500 S. 20th St. ((✆ 402/342-6164; www.ocm.org), is a shoo-in for children 10 and younger with its colorful toddler room; make-believe town with grocery store, post office, farm, and other areas where children can pretend they're in control; a creative center where children can play musical instruments, make art, and stage puppet shows; and a science and technology center with plenty of hands-on activities. It's open Tuesday to Sunday, and admission is $7.50.

Fun-Plex, farther south of downtown at 70th and Q streets ((✆ 402/331-8436; www.fun-plex.com), is a small waterpark that opened in 1978 and is reminiscent of county fairs with its handful of old-fashioned thrill rides, bumper cars, and go-carts in addition to its wave pool, slides, and other pools. It's open Memorial Day to Labor Day. Admission options vary; call or check the website before you go.

audio guide for a self-guided tour of the campus; in the afternoon, resident children are available as tour guides. Must-sees include Father Flanagan's 1920s home, Protestant and Catholic chapels, and the Hall of History, which describes how Father Flanagan changed the way America cares for its children and how the children live and work (all children live with on-campus families and have after-school jobs), and displays artifacts such as the Oscar Spencer Tracy won for his performance in *Boys Town.* Admission to Boys Town is free (donations are appreciated); it's open daily.

About 40 minutes southwest of downtown Omaha, just off I-80 at Exit 426, is the **Strategic Air & Space Museum** ((✆ 402/827-3100; www.strategicairandspace.com), which displays more than 40 military aircraft, missiles, and spacecraft in two massive hangars, including bombers, cargo and troop transporters, jet fighters, and rescue helicopters. Standouts include an SR-71 Blackbird (the world's fastest and highest-flying plane, capable of flying from New York to London in 1 hr. and 55 min.), a B-52 (the principal air force bomber), a B-25 (similar to the one used in the Doolittle bombing raid over Tokyo), and the Apollo 9 launched in 1966. The museum is open daily 9am to 5pm. Admission costs $7 for adults, $6 for seniors, and $3 for children ages 5 to 12.

SHOPPING In addition to the downtown **Old Market's** specialty stores, antiques shops, and Farmer's Market held Saturday mornings and Wednesday afternoons, Omaha boasts two originals: **Borsheim's,** 120 Regency Pkwy. ((✆ 402/391-0400; www.borsheims.com), founded in 1870 and today the country's largest single jewelry store under one roof (Bill Gates bought his wife's engagement ring here); and **Nebraska**

Furniture Mart, 700 S. 72nd St. (℗ **402/397-6100;** www.nebraskafurnituremart. com), America's largest furniture store. Both are owned by Berkshire Hathaway, which is headed by Warren Buffett.

WHERE TO STAY

Omaha's most luxurious hotel is the **Hilton Omaha,** opened in 2004 and located next to the Qwest Center Omaha (a state-of-the-art convention center and 17,000-seat arena) and within easy walking distance of Old Market at 1001 Cass St. (℗ **800/ HILTONS** or 402/998-3400; www.omaha.hilton.com). With a striking contemporary design and adorned with art by regional artists, it's Omaha's only hotel with both doormen and bellmen and a full-service health club. Its 450 rooms ($179–$259 double), decorated in rich, earth-tone colors, offer all the amenities you'd expect. Another good downtown choice is **Embassy Suites,** located across from Old Market at 555 S. 10th St. (℗ **800/EMBASSY** or 402/346-9000; www.embassysuitesomaha.com). Its seven-story, glass-topped atrium, filled with plants, waterfalls, and streams full of goldfish, is surrounded by 249 two-room suites ($149–$189) complete with fridge and microwave, making them a hit with families, who also like the indoor pool and fitness room.

Another good bet with families is the **Regency Lodge,** located west of downtown at 909 S. 107th St. (℗ **800/617-8310** or 402/397-8000; www.regencylodge.com). Decorated with natural stone and fixtures reminiscent of Frank Lloyd Wright, it evokes the atmosphere of a rustic mountain lodge but with all the creature comforts, including an indoor pool, fitness room, game room, laundry facilities, and restaurant. In addition to standard rooms ($119–$140 double), all with fridge and microwave, there are suites ($200–$300) that boast a full kitchen and gas fireplace. Travelers on a budget can try **Comfort Inn at the Zoo,** 2920 S. 13th Court (℗ **800/4-CHOICE** or 402/342-8000; www.choicehotels.com), 2 miles from downtown near the zoo and offering a glass-enclosed indoor pool, 79 basic rooms ($80–$100 double), and complimentary continental breakfast.

Couples searching for a romantic getaway might consider the **Cornerstone Mansion,** west of downtown at 140 N. 39th St. (℗ **888/883-7745** or 402/558-7600; www.cornerstonemansion.com). Built in 1894 and on the National Register of Historic Places, this bed-and-breakfast offers seven rooms ($85–$150 double), each one different but decorated with antiques and with private bathroom. There's also a sitting room with a piano, a library, and a pleasant patio lined with flowers.

WHERE TO DINE

The most atmospheric place to dine is undoubtedly **Rick's Café Boatyard,** located beside the Missouri River at 345 Riverfront Dr. (℗ **402/345-4545;** www.rickscafe boatyard.com). A bustling, airy restaurant seating 1,000 diners both inside and on a huge deck overlooking the river, it's known for its live nightly jazz and fresh seafood but also offers wood-fired pizzas, sandwiches, pastas, and steaks, all priced between $8 and $40. In the Old Market, **The French Café,** 1017 Howard St. (℗ **402/341-3547;** www.frenchcafe.com), is a refined restaurant that opened in 1969 as the warehouse district's first restaurant. It serves fusion American/French cuisine renowned for its presentation, with many dishes, such as the chateaubriand, prepared tableside. Dinner entrees run $28 to $47.

For a taste of Omaha's famous steaks, head to **Gorat's,** 4917 Center St. (℗ **402/ 551-3733**). This family-owned, unpretentious Omaha institution has been serving steaks hand-cut and aged on the premises since 1944 and is a popular hangout of investor Warren Buffet. Seafood, sandwiches, pastas, daily specials, and a children's menu round out the extensive offerings, with steaks and all the trimmings ranging from $16 to $25. Another popular choice is **Dundee Dell,** located in the quaint Dundee neighborhood west of downtown at 5007 Underwood (© **402/533-9501;** www.dundeedell.com). Established in 1934, it's famous for its fish and chips and large assortment of sandwiches, all priced below $9, but also available are steaks, low-carb dishes, a children's menu, and one of the largest selections of single-malt Scotch and liquors in the world.

OMAHA AFTER DARK

Omaha is home to the nation's largest community theater, the **Omaha Community Playhouse,** 6915 Cass St. (© **402/553-0800;** www.omahaplayhouse.com), founded in 1925 with the help of Marlon Brando's mother and where Henry Fonda made his acting debut. It's also home to one of the nation's oldest children's theater companies, the **Omaha Theater Company for Young People,** 2001 Farnam St. (© **402/345-4849;** www.rosetheater.org), founded in 1949. The opulent 1927 **Orpheum Theater,** 409 S. 16th St. (© **402/345-0202;** www.omahaperformingarts.org), restored to its French Renaissance splendor, is home to Broadway hits and **Opera Omaha** (© **402/346-4398;** www.operaomaha.org), while the **Holland Performing Arts Center,** 13th and Douglas streets (© **402/345-0202;** www.omahaperformingarts.org) hosts the **Omaha Symphony** (© **402/342-3560;** www.omahasymphony.org) and other musical events.

Old Market, a renovated warehouse district located between downtown and the Missouri River, is a good place for a nighttime stroll. The **Upstream Brewing Company,** 11th and Jackson (© **402/344-0200;** www.upstreambrewing.com), housed in a renovated, turn-of-the-20th-century firehouse and with outdoor seating, offers handcrafted beers and root beer on tap, as well as New American pub fare ranging from steaks and sandwiches to pizzas and pastas. A good place to hear local music is **Sokol Underground,** 13th and Martha streets (© **402/346-9802;** www.sokolunderground. com), where many Omaha bands get their start.

9

Texas

Texas has an identity and mystique that no other state can match. It fought its own war for independence and remained an independent country for several years. Its history is full of stories of wild characters and unlikely events: the Alamo and its courageous defenders, such as Davy Crockett and James Bowie; reckless and gritty Texas Rangers, such as John Coffee Hayes; empire-building ranchers such as Richard King; flamboyant wildcatters such as Glen McCarthy; and plenty of desperadoes such as Sam Bass or Bonnie and Clyde. Today, Texas is as much a land of modern cities and high-tech industries as of small towns and open prairies. But both places share a lot in common: Pickup trucks and cowboy boots abound, the menu favorites are the same—steaks, chili con carne, fajitas, barbecue, and Tex-Mex enchiladas (beef being the common denominator)—and a good honky-tonk is thought to offer an agreeable way to pass the evening. And, of course, Texas is big. Driving through the state can be taxing; it's more than 800 miles from the Louisiana border in the east to El Paso in the west and the same going north to south. But if you're not in a hurry, you can enjoy one more thing Texas is famous for—its hospitality.

1 Dallas

Dallas is situated in the northeast part of the state, where the Trinity River cuts through a gently undulating prairie. The city was born in the 1840s and became the commercial and financial center for the surrounding region. First cotton was king, and then oil. Now it's a mix of high-tech, financial, and service industries. Dallas is the ninth-largest city in the United States. A modern, attractive city, it offers visitors fine restaurants, fashionable stores and boutiques, and a wide range of entertainment possibilities, including concerts, plays, club acts, golf, and sporting events.

ESSENTIALS

GETTING THERE   By Plane   Dallas–Fort Worth International Airport (DFW; *©* **972/574-8888;** www.dfwairport.com) is a 40-minute drive from downtown Dallas. It is a hub for American Airlines. From DFW, a cheap and quick way to get to either downtown Dallas or Fort Worth is to catch the free shuttle to the CentrePort station of the **Trinity Railway Express** (*©* **214/979-1111;** www.trinityrailwayexpress. org). The trains are frequent but don't run after midnight or on Sunday; the fare is $4.50. **SuperShuttle** (*©* **800/258-3826** or 817/329-2000; www.supershuttle.com) offers van service to anywhere in town. Rates vary with length of trip; for downtown the fare is $16 to $23 for one person. A taxi into central Dallas will cost around $40. **Love Field (DAL;** *©* **214/670-6073;** www.dallas-lovefield.com) is closer to the center of town and is a hub for Southwest Airlines. It is a $20 taxi ride from downtown. A few other airlines offer limited service from Love Field. SuperShuttle offers van service from Love Field at rates slightly lower than from DFW for downtown destinations.

By Train   The Trinity Railway Express (see above) has several trains per day to/from Fort Worth. **Amtrak** (© **800/USA-RAIL** or 214/653-1101; www.amtrak.com) serves **Union Station,** 400 S. Houston St., with daily trains from Austin (trip time: 6¼ hr.), San Antonio (9½ hr.), St. Louis (15 hr.), and Chicago (21 hr.).

By Car   The principal routes into Dallas are **I-35E** from the north (Oklahoma City) and southwest (Austin and San Antonio); **I-30** from the northeast (Little Rock) and west (Fort Worth); **I-20** from the east (Shreveport) and west (Abilene); and **I-45** from the south (Houston). The **I-635** ring road (LBJ Fwy.) circles most of the city.

VISITOR INFORMATION   Contact the **Dallas Convention and Visitors Bureau** (© **800/232-5527;** www.visitdallas.com). Go to the **Dallas Tourist Information Center,** in the Old Red Courthouse, 100 S. Houston St. (© **214/571-1300**), in the West End Historic District. Here you'll find touch-screen computer kiosks, Internet access stations, brochures and coupons, and a helpful staff. It's open daily from 9am to 5pm.

GETTING AROUND   Public transportation in Dallas is good for Texas, but having a car helps considerably. The **Dallas Area Regional Transit (DART;** © **214/979-1111;** www.dart.org) operates a light-rail system and citywide bus service. A local day pass is $2.50 for an adult; $1 for seniors, persons with disabilities, and children 5 to 14. This is good for both buses and the light rail. Single-trip fares are half price but are good for only the bus or the train, but not both. Tickets can be purchased at vending machines at each light-rail station. The restored **McKinney Avenue Trolley** (© **214/855-0006;** www.mata.org) runs 3½ miles from the downtown Arts District up through lower McKinney Avenue. This is a genuine old streetcar that is operated solely by volunteers. The trolley runs every 20 minutes during the day, with slightly reduced hours on the weekends. The ride is free.

It's almost impossible to hail a cab; call the dispatch, or look for a hotel cabstand. Call **Yellow Checker Cab Co.** (© **817/534-5555** or 214/426-6262). The initial charge is $2 per passenger plus $1.80 per mile.

FAST FACTS   **Baylor University Medical Center,** 3500 Gaston Ave. (© **214/820-0111**), provides world-class healthcare. Dallas has three area codes—214, 972, and 469—with 10-digit dialing for all local numbers. The local hotel tax is 15%; the sales tax is 8.25%.

SPECIAL EVENTS   The **State Fair of Texas** (© **214/565-9931;** www.bigtex.com), the largest state fair in the nation, takes place from late September to mid-October in Fair Park. The **Cotton Bowl Classic Football Game** (Jan 1) and **Parade** (Dec 31; © **888/792-BOWL** or 214/634-7764; www.attcottonbowl.com) get a lot of local attention.

WHAT TO SEE & DO

Downtown Dallas is clean and attractive. Its two biggest draws are the **6th Floor Museum** and the **Nasher Sculpture Center.** To the east of downtown is **Deep Ellum,** to the north is the **McKinney Avenue District** (also called Uptown). These are both important restaurant and club districts where the visitor will have no problem finding the necessities, like food and nightlife. To draw a broad distinction between them, Deep Ellum is more bohemian, while McKinney Avenue is more society. East of Deep Ellum is **Fair Park,** an enclosed area of several city blocks (see below), which is a popular attraction for families. Also popular with families is the city of Arlington, which lies to the west between Dallas and Fort Worth and is home to the **Six Flags** amusement park; its

Texas

Dallas–Fort Worth Area

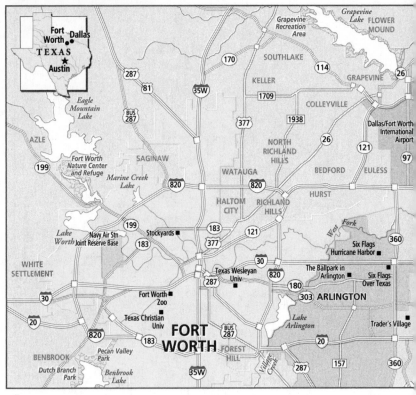

sister waterpark, **Hurricane Harbor;** and the **Ballpark in Arlington,** home of the Texas Rangers baseball team.

Dallas Arboretum & Botanical Garden   Bordering the eastern shore of White Rock Lake, just 10 minutes from downtown, are 66 acres of gardens, woods, and trails. It's the best urban green space in Texas. In springtime the 2,000 varieties of azaleas explode in gaudy colors, while during the rest of the year there's always something blooming. You'll find lots of trails, including the wildflower trail and an 11-mile path around the lake. Seeing just the park without lollygagging takes about an hour (but why rush?).

8525 Garland Rd. (east Dallas). (C) **214/515-6500.** www.dallasarboretum.org. Admission $8 adults, $7 seniors, $5 children 3–12. Parking $5. Daily 9am–5pm.

Fair Park *Kids*   This is an enclosed area of several blocks that holds nine museums, the Cotton Bowl, and two concert halls. Built in 1936, the grand pavilion and several of the museums are bold examples of Art Deco architecture. Each fall the very popular Texas State Fair is held here. During the rest of the year, Fair Park attracts lots of families. Of the nine museums here, the highlights are the following: **The Women's Museum** ((C) **214/915-0860;** www.thewomensmuseum.org) honors American women and their achievements with a panoply of high-tech, visually striking exhibits. The **Museum of Science & Nature** ((C) **214/428-5555;** www.scienceplace.org) is an especially good museum for kids because it offers plenty of interactive exhibits that demonstrate principles of physics, electricity, space, and ecology in imaginative ways. It also has a planetarium and an IMAX theater. The **African-American Museum** (© **214/565-9026;** www.aamdallas.org) is one of few museums in the country to present aspects of the African-American experience in the U.S., which it does in part through exhibitions of folk art (with a fascinating look at connections with African art) and fine art. **The Dallas World Aquarium** (© **214/670-8443;** www.dwazoo. com), specializes in displays of some of the strangest aquatic life forms on the planet and has a 10,000-gallon tank re-creating the Amazon environment.

3809 Grand Ave. © **214/670-8400.** www.fairpark.org. **Women's Museum** Tues–Sun noon–5pm; **Museum of Science & Nature** Mon–Sat 10am–5pm, Sun noon–5pm; **African-American Museum** Tues–Fri noon–5pm, Sat 10am–5pm, Sun 1–5pm; **Aquarium** daily 10am–5pm. Admission fees vary.

Meadows Museum This is probably the best collection of Spanish art on this side of the Atlantic. Paintings by the Spanish masters of the 16th, 17th, and 18th centuries, as well as works by the more modern artists from Goya to Picasso to Miró, are all on display in serene and spacious surroundings. Classic Spanish painting, as represented by Velázquez, Murillo, and others, was inventive in style, and intriguing in subject matter. Many of the works displayed here are breathtaking.

Sporting Options

Dallas is a sports town. Golfers can contact **Golf Guys** (✆ 800/470-9634; www. golfguys.net) to schedule a round at one of the city's local clubs. The company works with several courses. You should schedule in advance. Professional team sports include the NFL **Dallas Cowboys** football team (✆ 972/785-5000); the NBA **Mavericks** basketball team (✆ 214/747-6287); the MLB **Texas Rangers** baseball team (✆ 817/273-5100); and the NHL **Stars** hockey team (✆ 214/GO-STARS). Other sporting events include horse racing at **Lone Star Park** (✆ 972/263-7669) and auto racing at **Texas Motor Speedway** (in Fort Worth; ✆ 817/215-8500).

5900 Bishop Blvd. at Mockingbird Lane (SMU campus). ✆ 214/768-2516. www.meadowsmuseumdallas.org. Admission $8 (free after 5pm Thurs). Tues–Sat 10am–5pm (until 8pm Thurs); Sun noon–5pm.

Nasher Sculpture Center *Best* Now the centerpiece of Dallas's "Arts District," the Nasher Sculpture Center opened in 2003 to wide acclaim. Raymond Nasher, a rich local developer, has collected modern sculpture for decades, assembling, according to some, the finest collection in the world. (No need for a recitation of names; we can't think of any major sculptor that Nasher neglected.) Renzo Piano was chosen to create the space for viewing these pieces, and he's done an admirable job of situating the building and garden within the downtown skyline, while at the same time creating a feel of separation.

Note: Across Harwood Street from the Nasher—and with the same admission charges and hours—is the **Dallas Museum of Art,** 1717 N. Harwood St. (✆ 214/922-1200; www.dm-art.org). The building, designed by Edward Larrabee Barnes, upstages the collection, which is small, but has a few great pieces. And across Flora Street is the small but lovely **Crow Collection of Asian Art,** 2010 Flora St. (✆ 214/979-6430; www.crowcollection.org). Hours are identical to those at Nasher and the Museum of Art, but admission here is free.

2001 Flora St. (Arts District). ✆ 214/242-5100. www.nashersculpturecenter.org. Admission $10 adults, $7 seniors, $5 students, free for children under 12. Tues–Sun 11am–5pm (until 9pm Thurs).

Six Flags Over Texas *Kids* In Arlington, halfway between Dallas and Fort Worth, is this large amusement park with lots of roller coasters and thrill rides. It is one of the largest parks in the country and the most visited attraction in Texas. Nearby is its sister park, **Hurricane Harbor,** 1800 E. Lamar Blvd. (✆ 817/265-3356; www.sixflags. com), a waterpark with pretty much the same thing in mind. In addition there are shows, theme rides, and other amusements.

I-30 at Hwy. 360 (Arlington). ✆ 817/607-6150. www.sixflags.com. Admission to Six Flags $45 adults, $35 children under 4 ft. and seniors, free for children 2 years and under; Hurricane Harbor $30 adults, $20 children under 4 ft., free for children 2 years and under. Daily mid-May to Aug; weekends only in late spring and early fall. Parking $10.

Sixth Floor Museum The museum is in the old Texas School Book Depository. Does this ring a bell? It was from here that Lee Harvey Oswald assassinated JFK (or did he?). This and many issues surrounding the Kennedy presidency and the events leading up to that fateful day are effectively portrayed through the use of film, photographs, artifacts, and interpretive displays. The corner window from which Oswald is said to have fired the fatal shots is part of the exhibit. The museum does a good job of presenting the different findings on the assassination and lets visitors draw their own conclusions. If you're interested in modern history, you can spend 2 hours here. A counterpoint to this museum is the nearby **Conspiracy Museum,** 110 S. Market St. (© 214/741-3040), across from the JFK Memorial (adults $9). It pulls the visitor into the off-centered world of conspiracy theorists and boasts its own "assassinologists."

411 Elm St. (West End). © 214/747-6660. www.jfk.org. Admission $10 adults, $9 seniors and kids 6–18; audio tour $3.50. Daily 9am–6pm.

SHOPPING

Shopping has been called Dallas's number-one indoor sport. Most of the city's shopping malls are north of downtown. **Highland Park Village** (www.hpvillage.com), opened in 1931, was the first mall built in Dallas and is still one of *the* fashionable shopping centers, with many boutiques and small shops catering to its well-heeled clientele. It's not far from downtown, in a lovely part of the city. **NorthPark Center** (www.northparkcenter.com), anchored by a Neiman Marcus, is doubly notable because developer Raymond Nasher displays pieces from his famous modern art collection throughout the mall. You can get there by taking the light rail's Red Line to the Park Lane station, where you can catch a free shuttle to the mall. **The Galleria,** LBJ Freeway and Dallas North Tollway **(www.galleriadallas.com),** is one of Dallas's largest upscale malls, with more than 200 shops—including Nordstrom, Tiffany, and Saks Fifth Avenue. It has the advantage of activities to amuse those not interested in shopping, including a skating rink, race car simulators, and high-tech arcades.

Many shoppers frequent the **uptown** area, just north of downtown. A mixed-use development here, called **West Village** (McKinney Ave. at Lemmon Ave.), is all the rage. It offers 4 square blocks of shops, boutiques, restaurants, and bars. If you're **downtown** (or even if you're not), you might want to visit the original **Neiman Marcus,** a popular destination for many visitors to Dallas.

WHERE TO STAY

Convenient to DFW Airport is the **Hyatt Regency DFW Airport,** International Parkway, at terminal C inside the airport (© **800/233-1234** or 972/453-1234). Easier on the budget are the **Embassy Guest Suites,** 4650 W. Airport Fwy., Irving (© **800/362-2779** or 972/790-0093), near the south entrance to DFW; and the **Holiday Inn Select North,** 4441 Hwy. 114, Irving (© **800/465-4329** or 972/929-8181), 2 miles away.

For a hotel in Arlington, close to the Six Flags and Hurricane Harbor amusement parks, you have 50 choices representing just about every chain of hotels and motels in America. Many of these properties pay for trolley service to and from their hotel and the amusement parks and the ballpark. This will save you a little money on parking and is a real convenience; ask about it when making reservations. The nicest lodgings in the area are at the **Wyndham Arlington,** 1500 Convention Center Dr. (© **800/442-7275**), which is located close by both Six Flags and the ballpark. We also like the **Courtyard by Marriott,** 1500 Nolan Ryan Expwy. (© **800/321-2211**), for its location and rooms.

Fairmont Dallas Combine elegance and comfort with a great location (downtown between the Arts District and the West End), and the result is the Fairmont. The hotel occupies two towers with a terrace pool and patio in between. Rooms, thoughtfully furnished to make them equally suitable for business or pleasure, are large and attractive in a modern, uncluttered style, with a few flourishes such as granite tabletops. All beds are extra long.

1717 N. Akard St., Dallas, TX 75201 (downtown). (℃ **800/527-4727** or 214/720-2020. Fax 214/720-7403. www.fairmont. com/dallas. 551 units. $149–$350 double; $250–$550 suite. AE, DC, DISC, MC, V. Valet parking $19. Children not permitted. Small pets allowed for $25 fee. **Amenities:** Restaurant; outdoor pool; health club.

Four Seasons Resort and Club   Attention to detail and an amazing array of recreational facilities highlight this impressive resort. The main golf course is considered to be the best in the Dallas area, while the full European spa wins high praise from guests. In addition, the resort offers racquetball courts, 40 different exercise classes per week, and lovely settings for just relaxing. Rooms are spacious and well furnished. Bathrooms are large, especially in the deluxe rooms and villas, which come with a large soaking tub and separate shower.

4150 N. McArthur Blvd., Irving, TX 75038 (west of Dallas off Hwy. 114). (℃ **800/332-3442** or 972/717-0700. Fax 972/ 717-2550. www.fourseasons.com/dallas. 357 units. $395–$480 double; $505 villa; $750 and up suite. Children 17 and under stay free in parent's room. Golf packages available. AE, DC, DISC, MC, V. Valet parking $17; free self-parking. Pets 15 lb. and under accepted. **Amenities:** 3 restaurants; 4 pools (1 indoor); 2 18-hole golf courses; 12 tennis courts (4 indoor); health club; spa.

Hotel Adolphus *(Best*   The Adolphus is Dallas's original grand hotel—a classic skyscraper, built in 1912 in the exuberant Beaux Arts style by beer mogul Adolphus Busch. The lobby holds a collection of furniture, tapestries, and paintings plundered from Europe during a shopping trip by the owner's wife. Large guest rooms offer separate sitting areas, fresh flowers, and understated furnishings with large marble bathrooms. The level of service could not be better. If you stay here, or even if you don't, try the hotel's restaurant, the French Room, which was recently selected as America's best hotel restaurant by Zagat.

1321 Commerce St., Dallas, TX 75202. (℃ **800/221-9083** or 214/742-8200. Fax 214/651-3588. www.hoteladolphus. com. 428 units. $175–$385 double; $215–$415 junior suite; $500 and up suite. Children under 12 stay free in parent's room. AE, DC, DISC, MC, V. Valet parking $20. **Amenities:** 3 restaurants; health club.

Hotel ZaZa   This is Dallas's hot property, and it's easy to see why—it's the guest rooms. Instead of taking the bland-but-safe approach, the designers took chances— lots of color, texture, dramatic furniture arrangements, and accent lighting. This is especially true of the suites, which come in several motifs that provide the perfect mise-en-scène for a weekend getaway, or for the executive who wants to feel like there's more to travel than business. All rooms feature marble bathrooms with bathrobes, CD players, and flatscreen TVs; some rooms offer balconies. The hotel's restaurant and courtyard are "in" with the Uptown crowd.

2332 Leonard St., Dallas, TX 75201. (℃ **800/597-8399** or 214/468-8399. Fax 214/468-8397. www.hotelzaza.com. 153 units. $259–$329 deluxe; $459 and up suite. AE, DC, DISC, MC, V. Valet parking $18. **Amenities:** Restaurant; pool; fitness center; spa.

The Mansion on Turtle Creek   This is the hotel of choice for moguls, celebrities, and CEOs. Its flawless accommodations and world-class pampering get it regularly named as one of the top hotels in the country. The large, plush rooms exude comfort and coolness, and the bathrooms are very large, with double sinks and/or separate shower and tub. The original mansion (built by an old cotton baron in 1925) is the most visually striking part of the hotel, but what impresses us most about this hotel is the service.

2821 Turtle Creek Blvd., Dallas, TX 75219. © 800/767-3966 or 214/559-2100. Fax 214/528-4187. www.mansionon turtlecreek.com. 143 units. $415–$500 double; $800 and up suite. AE, DC, DISC, MC, V. Valet parking $20. Pets accepted for a $100 fee. **Amenities:** Restaurant; heated outdoor pool; health club.

Stoneleigh Hotel   This 1923 hotel in the McKinney Avenue area near downtown is a national historic landmark and offers large, well-furnished rooms at good prices. Bathrooms are medium to large and attractively furnished. Some suites come with kitchens. Dallas never looks as good as it does from the hotel's penthouse bar at sunset. We've seen big discounts for rooms at this hotel on the Internet reservation sites. Get a room facing away from the street.

2927 Maple Ave., Dallas, TX 75201. © 800/255-9299 or 214/871-7111. Fax 214/871-9379. www.stoneleighhotel. com. 153 units. $149 double; $200–$330 suite. Children under 18 stay free in parent's room. AE, DC, DISC, MC, V. Valet parking $16; self-parking $8. **Amenities:** Restaurant. *In room:* Kitchen (some suites only).

Westin Hotel Galleria Dallas *Kids*   If you're the type to shop until you drop, think about dropping in here. It's part of the Galleria complex, so you're only a short elevator ride from the mall. And the hotel has more to offer than just its location: Rooms are large and attractive, with big windows and little extra touches; the beds' thick, plush mattresses will certainly get you rested for another day's grueling shopping. Bathrooms are fine but nothing special.

13340 Dallas Pkwy., Dallas, TX 75240. © 800/228-3000 or 972/934-9494. Fax 972/851-2869. www.westin. com/dallas. 432 units. $169–$309 double; $480–$1,275 suite. AE, DC, DISC, MC, V. Valet parking $18; free outdoor parking at connected Galleria shopping mall. Pets allowed (ask about the "Heavenly Pet" package). **Amenities:** Restaurant; outdoor pool.

WHERE TO DINE

Bob's Steak & Chop House STEAKS   In Dallas, a great steak is mightily appreciated. Here, they are served in a classic steakhouse dining room—lots of dark wood and crisp white tablecloths. Bob's is known for its perfectly aged and beautifully grilled, corn-fed, prime beef, and for its hearty side dishes. Good salads, too.

4300 Lemmon Ave. © 214/528-9446. www.bobs-steakandchop.com. Reservations recommended. Main courses $23–$50. AE, DC, DISC, MC, V. Mon–Thurs 5–10pm; Fri–Sat 5–11pm.

The Green Room ECLECTIC   Restaurants in Deep Ellum, even expensive ones such as this, have to look askew of the Dallas mainstream. The Green Room hits the mark by mixing highbrow and lowbrow trappings in its cozy, softly lit dining room. The menu changes nightly, offering surprising combinations of southwestern, Pacific Rim, and Mediterranean flavors. The chef also offers a popular four-course wine-and-dinner combination called "Feed me—Wine me."

2715 Elm St., Deep Ellum. © 214/748-7666. www.thegreenroom.com. Reservations recommended. Main courses $24–$34. "Feed me" dinner with wine $70, without $45. AE, DC, DISC, MC, V. Mon–Wed 5:30–10pm; Thurs–Sat 5:30–11pm.

Jeroboam URBAN BRASSERIE   This restaurant is one of the bold and the few to open in Dallas's downtown area, which up until now has not been known for its nightlife. But success breeds change, and right now Jeroboam succeeds by offering a relatively simple menu of sophisticated dishes and a large selection of wines in a chic urban setting converted from the lobby of an old office building. The menu often changes, but representative dishes are roast chicken stuffed with black truffles and prosciutto or a veal chop with lemon-caper beurre blanc.

1501 Main St. ⓒ **214/748-7226.** Reservations recommended. Main courses $24–$35. AE, DC, DISC, MC, V. Mon–Fri 11am–2:30pm and 5:30–10pm; Sat 5:30–11pm.

The Mansion on Turtle Creek *Best* NEW AMERICAN   If you really want to splurge while in Dallas, this restaurant in the dining room of the original 1920s mansion is the place to do it. It has captured attention for its inventive menu of American and southwestern dishes. Chef Dean Fearing offers his signature dishes, such as the tortilla soup and the lobster tacos, but the specials always seem tantalizing. Consider the multicourse tasting menu for $90. The dining room is an opulent fantasy full of carved stone and marble from Italy and can be enjoyed for a lot less money by going for lunch instead of dinner.

2821 Turtle Creek Blvd. ⓒ **214/559-2100.** www.mansiononturtlecreek.com. Reservations recommended. Jacket required for men. Main courses $35–$55. AE, DC, DISC, MC, V. Mon–Sat 11:30am–2pm; Mon–Thurs 6–10pm; Fri–Sat 6–11pm; Sun 6–9:30pm; brunch Sun 11am–2pm.

Monica's Aca y Alla MEXICAN   The contemporary decor doesn't attempt to hide the warehouse origins of this restaurant's large dining room, which is perfectly appropriate for Deep Ellum. So is the menu. Alongside Mexican and Tex-Mex standards such as green enchiladas and chile con queso, you have unlikely hybrids such as the green pasta with chicken and black beans, pumpkin ravioli, and Mexican lasagna. Always popular and sometimes noisy. Thursdays and weekends you can dine to the sounds of live flamenco, and occasionally there will be some salsa and mambo, too.

2914 Main St. ⓒ **214/748-7140.** www.monicas.com. Reservations accepted for parties of 5 or more. Main courses $8–$20. AE, DISC, MC, V. Mon–Fri 11am–2pm; Tues–Thurs 5–10pm; Fri–Sat 5pm–midnight; Sun 11am–11pm; Sat–Sun brunch 11am–3pm.

Nuevo León MEXICAN/TEX-MEX   Don't pass through Texas without trying the local version of Mexican food. This restaurant is an excellent source for the real thing. Choose from several kinds of enchiladas (the green and the mole were both good). The slow-cooked pork *carnitas* in a chipotle sauce is one of the house specialties. Also, the seviche (marinated fish) was fresh and not too citrusy. The same could be said for the delectable margaritas. The dining area is roomy with high ceilings and comfortable furniture.

2013 Greenville Ave. ⓒ **214/887-8148.** Reservations recommended. Main courses $8–$16. AE, DISC, MC, V. Sun–Thurs 11am–10pm; Fri–Sat 11am–midnight. Valet parking on weekends.

Sonny Bryan's Smokehouse *Kids* BARBECUE   This chain is the first place people think of for barbecue in Dallas. There are several locations. A lot of people consider the original site, at 2202 Inwood Rd. (ⓒ **214/357-7120**), as special, but we found the food just as good at other locations such as this one in the West End. Sonny Bryan's is known for its brisket especially, but the ribs and sausage are also good, as are the classic sides of potato salad and coleslaw. The surroundings are simple and the service is friendly.

302 N. Market. ⓒ **214/744-1610.** www.sonnybryans.com. Sandwiches $4–$5; plates $11–$15. AE, DC, MC, V. Sun–Thurs 11am–9pm; Fri–Sat 11am–10pm.

Stoneleigh P GRILL   Across the street from the Stoneleigh Hotel, in the McKinney Avenue area, you'll find this neighborhood burger joint, bar, and grill, which is a good place to relax over drinks and food. The dining room, with high pressed-tin ceiling, whirring fans, and prominent bar (leftovers from the original pharmacy) has a casual, homey feel. The burgers are made from all-natural beef from the B3R ranch and are top-notch, as are the daily specials such as the crab cakes.

2926 Maple. ⓒ **214/871-2346.** www.stoneleighp.com. Sandwiches $6–$8; main courses $11–$15. AE, DC, DISC, MC, V. Daily 11am–midnight.

DALLAS AFTER DARK

THE PERFORMING ARTS   The **Dallas Symphony Orchestra** (© 214/692-0203; www.dallassymphony.com) performs at the beautiful Meyerson Symphony Center, 2301 Flora St. (© 214/670-3600), designed by I. M. Pei. The **Texas Ballet Theater** (© 214/369-5200; www.texasballettheater.org) gives performances in both Fort Worth and Dallas. If you want to see a play while you're here, the **Dallas Theater Center,** 3636 Turtle Creek Blvd. (© 214/522-8499; www.dallastheatercenter. org), designed by Frank Lloyd Wright, presents a 7-month season of productions ranging from Shakespeare to contemporary works.

THE CLUB & BAR SCENE   **Deep Ellum** was once the city's blues and jazz center. It became popular again in the '80s and now has the best club scene in Dallas, with the widest variety of musical acts. Outside of a lunchtime infusion of downtown office workers, this area is sleepy for much of the day, but come nighttime, its restaurants and nightclubs spring to life. Your best bet is to stroll down the street until you see a club that suits your tastes. Indicative of what you'll find is **Blue Cat Blues,** 2612 Commerce St. (© 214/744-CATS), just what it sounds like; **Club Dada,** 2720 Elm St. (© 214/744-3232), offering a variety of live acts from blues to hip-hop; the **Art Bar & Cafe** (© 214/939-0077), which gets an older crowd; **Trees,** 2709 Elm St. (© 214/748-5009), a cavernous club that hosts the larger alternative rock touring acts; and **Sons of Hermann Hall,** 3414 Elm St. (© 214/747-4422), a dance hall (and real fraternal organization) that has live country music on weekends—often Texas pickers—and attracts everyone from Grandpa to the kids, from straight-ahead country types to alternative club dabblers.

In the Uptown area along McKinney Avenue you can find a lot of bars that attract the fashionable crowd. For live music over drinks and good food, try **Sambuca,** at 2120 McKinney Ave. (© 214/744-0820). It offers some great jazz, blues, and other acts in a stylish club/restaurant (good menu and wine list). It's popular, so make reservations. Also, the restaurant and bar at **Hotel ZaZa** (see above) packs the same crowd in for drinks and dinner. Just a bit farther up McKinney, at 2601, is a **Hard Rock Cafe** (© 214/855-0007). And then there's the **West Village** development, which occupies a few blocks of McKinney between Lemmon Avenue and Blackburn. It has a few bars that are highly popular, including **Paris Vendôme** (© 469/533-5663) and **Nikita** (© 214/520-6454).

2 Fort Worth

Fort Worth is a city of two tales. One is that of the cattle business, which drove herds from south Texas up to Fort Worth's stockyards to be shipped back East by rail. The cowboys who drove these herds were only too happy to celebrate the end of their trail ride, so a number of saloons and other establishments sprang up to cater to their wants. This made Fort Worth a rough-and-tumble place and earned it the nickname "Cowtown." Today you can visit the historic stockyards district and see saloons, boardinghouses, Western-wear stores, a small cattle drive, and the biggest honky-tonk bar in the world.

The other tale is the story of rich philanthropists who have made their city a delightful place to visit, preserving many of the Art Deco buildings downtown and funding some great museums (three of the finest in Texas) that belie the town's nickname. With all it has going for it, Fort Worth is a fun place to visit, possessing all the cosmopolitan pleasures of a bigger city with none of the drawbacks.

ESSENTIALS

GETTING THERE   By Plane   Flights to Fort Worth arrive at the **Dallas–Fort Worth International Airport (DFW);** see "Essentials" under "Dallas," earlier in this chapter, for details. The **Trinity Railway Express** (© **817/215-8600;** www.trinity railwayexpress.org) can get you to the downtown area for $4.50, but it doesn't run on Sunday or late at night. **SuperShuttle** (© **800/258-3826** or 817/329-2000; www. supershuttle.com) offers 24-hour service to downtown for $16 to $29.

By Train   The Trinity Railway Express offers several trains to and from Dallas Monday through Saturday. **Amtrak** (© **800/USA-RAIL** or 817/332-2931; www.amtrak. com) serves the old **Santa Fe Depot,** 1501 Jones St., with daily trains to and from Oklahoma City (trip time: 4 hr.), Austin (4 hr.), San Antonio (7 hr.), St. Louis (16 hr.), and Chicago (22 hr.).

By Car   The principal routes into Fort Worth are **I-35W** from the north (Oklahoma City) and southwest (Austin and San Antonio); **I-30** from the east (Dallas) and west (Abilene); and **I-45** from the south (Houston).

VISITOR INFORMATION   The **Fort Worth Convention and Visitors Bureau** has its main office at 415 Throckmorton St., Fort Worth, TX 76102 (© **800/433-5747** or 817/336-8791; www.fortworth.com), open Monday through Friday from 8:30am to 5pm, Saturday from 10am to 4pm. There are also **visitor information centers** at the Stockyards National Historic District, 130 E. Exchange Ave. (© **817/624-4741**), open Monday through Friday from 9am to 6pm, Saturday from 9am to 7pm, Sunday from noon to 5pm; and in the Cultural District/Zoo at 3401 W. Lancaster Ave. (© **817/882-8588**), open Monday through Thursday from 9am to 5pm, Friday and Saturday from 9am to 6pm, Sunday from noon to 4pm.

GETTING AROUND   Many people find Fort Worth a more manageable city to visit than Dallas because it's smaller and most of its attractions are located in three places (downtown, the Stockyards Historic District, and the Cultural District). **Taxi** service is by dispatch or hotel stand only (© **817/534-5555**). The initial charge is $2 per passenger plus $1.80 per mile.

FAST FACTS   **John Peter Smith Hospital** (© **817/921-3431**) provides 24-hour emergency services at 1500 S. Main St. The downtown area, especially around Sundance Square, has a lot of officers on bikes and is safe at all times. The local hotel tax is 15%; the local sales tax is 8.25%.

SPECIAL EVENTS & FESTIVALS   The Stockyards District holds all kinds of special events, from cowboy gatherings to rodeos. Information on all of these can be found on the Fort Worth CVB's comprehensive website at **www.fortworth.com**.

EXPLORING THE CITY

Fort Worth's **downtown** has shopping, dining, and a fun and relaxed nightlife. Most of the restaurants, shops, clubs, and the Bass Concert Hall are located in the **Sundance Square** section of downtown, which occupies 16 square blocks. It's a lively scene with crowds of pedestrians.

The **Stockyards National Historic District** (www.fortworthstockyards.org) is 2 miles northwest of downtown, across the Trinity River. The old stockyards and surrounding buildings bring to mind the days of the Old West. Several stores sell Western wear. For high-quality boots, try **M. L. Leddy's Boot and Saddlery,** 2455 Main St. (© **817/624-3149**). In memory of the cattle drives of yore, each morning professional cowboys drive

12 longhorns from the stockyards to the nearby Trinity River to graze, and return them in the midafternoon to coincide with the arrival of an excursion train. The **Grapevine Vintage Railroad** (℄ 817/410-3123; www.grapevinesteamrailroad.com) offers steam-engine train rides from the Stockyards Station to 8th Avenue and back most of the year Thursday through Sunday. Fares are $10 adults, $9 seniors, and $6 children. The same company offers a longer train ride that goes round-trip from the town of Grapevine to the Stockyards Station, but to take this train, you must start and finish in Grapevine.

The **Cultural District** is home to the Amon Carter Museum, the Kimbell Art Museum, the Modern Art Museum of Fort Worth, and a few others. The district also holds the Fort Worth zoo and the botanical garden. Any of these are worth the short trip from downtown or the stockyards area. For attractions in nearby Dallas and Arlington, see the "Dallas" section, earlier in this chapter.

Amon Carter Museum *Value*   With its large collection of American and Western art, this museum ranks among the premier museums of the state. Holdings include works of 19th- and early-20th-century American paintings, sculpture, and prints from artists such as Frederic Remington, Charles M. Russell, Georgia O'Keeffe, and Winslow Homer. There is also an impressive collection of photographs from the likes of Ansel Adams and Eliot Porter.

3501 Camp Bowie Blvd. (Museum District). ℄ 817/738-1933. http://cartermuseum.org. Free admission to perma-nent collection. Audio tour $4 adults, $2 seniors and kids under 12. Free docent-guided tour daily at 2pm. Tues–Sat 10am–5pm (Thurs until 8pm); Sun noon–5pm.

Fort Worth Botanic Garden   The gardens showcase 150,000 plants representing 2,500 species, displayed in both formal and natural settings. A 10,000-square-foot glass conservatory houses more than 2,500 tropical plants native to Central and South America. Especially lovely is the Japanese Garden. A leisurely tour of the grounds and conservatory requires 2 hours.

3220 Botanic Garden Blvd. (Cultural District). ℄ 817/871-7686. www.fwgb.org. Japanese Garden $3.50 adults, $2.50 children; conservatory $1 adults, 50¢ children. Japanese garden daily 9am–6pm. Conservatory Mon–Sat 10am–7pm; Sun 1–6pm.

Fort Worth Museum of Science and History *Kids*   This museum has a lot of exhibits that will interest most everyone and is consequently great for families. All but the Omni Theater will close in late 2007 to allow for construction of a new building designed by Ricardo Legorreta. The new building should open sometime in 2009. During construction the major exhibits will be moved to the nearby **National Cow-girl Museum (www.cowgirl.net).**

1501 Montgomery St. (Cultural District). ℄ 817/255-9300. www.fwmuseum.org. Museum $8 adults, $7 seniors and children 3–12; Omni theater $7 adults, $6 seniors and children 3–12; planetarium $3.50 for all; combination tickets available. Mon–Thurs 9am–5:30pm; Fri–Sat 9am–8pm; Sun noon–5:30pm.

Kimbell Art Museum *Best*   A small but nationally acclaimed museum, the Kimbell thrills visitors with a collection of masterpieces ranging in scope from Fra Angelico and El Greco to Matisse and Mondrian. The collection includes some beautiful works from the ancient world as well. The museum also attracts many of the finest traveling exhibitions in the country; make a point of finding out what will be showing when you are in town. Allow 2 hours.

3333 Camp Bowie Blvd. (Cultural District). ℄ 817/332-8451. www.kimbellart.org. Free admission. Tues–Thurs 10am–5pm; Fri noon–8pm; Sat 10am–5pm; Sun noon–5pm.

Modern Art Museum of Fort Worth This museum is located in an eye-catching creation of Japanese architect Tadao Ando. The building, opened in 2002, built mostly of concrete and glass, is light, airy, and serene. It has greatly increased the museum's exhibition space, allowing more of the permanent collection to be displayed, including works from such artists as Picasso and Rothko. The majority of the collection dates from no earlier than the '40s.

3200 Darnell St. (Cultural District). ✆ **866/824-5566**. www.themodern.org. $8 adults, $4 seniors and students. Tues–Sat 10am–5pm; Fri 10am–5pm (until 8pm on the 1st Fri of every month); Sun 11am–5pm.

WHERE TO STAY

See the "Dallas" section, earlier in this chapter, for hotels near the DFW Airport. Of the chain hotels in Fort Worth, Marriott (and all its affiliate brands) has the most properties to choose from.

The Ashton Hotel *Best* Inside two national landmark buildings, The Ashton offers spacious, distinctive guest rooms with lots of comforts such as plush mattresses, refrigerators, and large bathrooms. Rooms and suites vary quite a bit. Some come with Jacuzzis; others come with large sitting areas or larger bathrooms with separate shower and tub, such as the L-shaped "Signature Executive King" rooms, which are quite attractive. The service is excellent, and so is the location.

610 Main St., Fort Worth, TX 76102 (downtown). ✆ **866/327-4866** or 817/332-0100. Fax 817/332-0110. www. theashtonhotel.com. 39 units. $220–$280 double; $320–$370 junior suite. AE, DC, DISC, MC, V. Valet parking $15. Small pets with $100 deposit. **Amenities:** Restaurant; exercise room; smoking not permitted. *In room:* Fridge.

Courtyard by Marriott Downtown—Blackstone Opened in 1929 as the Blackstone, this 20-story hotel offers comfortable rooms for a reasonable price. The location couldn't be better, next to the entertainment district and within easy walking distance of everything. Rooms are large (corner rooms are larger still and go for the same price) and the bathrooms are medium to large, with separate vanities. Four rooms on the 16th floor include balconies where guests can take in the view of downtown. It's a popular hotel, so make reservations in advance.

601 Main St., Fort Worth, TX 76102 (downtown). ✆ **800/321-2211** or 817/885-8700. Fax 817/885-8303. www. marriott.com/dfwms. 203 units. $139–$189 double; $199–$299 suite. AE, DC, DISC, MC, V. Valet parking $10. **Amenities:** Heated outdoor pool; exercise room.

Etta's Place Named for Etta Place, the Sundance Kid's girlfriend, this B&B offers comfortable lodging and feels more like a small hotel than a B&B. The common areas are large and attractive and mostly modern. Guest rooms are large and comfortable and come with period furniture and either one king- or one queen-size bed. Service is good and the staff is helpful.

200 W. Third St., Fort Worth, TX 76102 (downtown). ✆ **866/355-5760** or 817/255-5760. Fax 817/878-2560. www.ettas-place.com. 10 units. $125–$160 double; $170–$240 suite. Rates include full breakfast. AE, DC, DISC, MC, V. Self-parking $5. Children under 10 not accepted. Pets under 25 lb. accepted for $20 fee per night, restrictions apply. **Amenities:** Smoking not permitted. *In room:* Kitchen (in suites only).

Hotel Texas *Value* A comfortable, no-frills hotel with a good location in the Stockyards District, this retains a good bit of the feel of an old "Cowtown" hotel. This is a better choice than the chain hotels in this price range. Rooms are medium in size, with plain, standard-size bathrooms.

2415 Ellis Ave., Fort Worth, TX 76106 (Stockyards District). ✆ **817/624-2224**. Fax 817/624-7177. 20 units. Weekends $79–$99 double; weekdays $69 double. AE, DC, DISC, MC, V.

Miss Molly's   Charming and different, Miss Molly's has preserved the floor plan of the original second-story boardinghouse/bordello built in 1910. Stairs lead from the street up to a large common room around which all the guest rooms are situated. Rooms are decorated in period furniture. Each depicts a different aspect of turn-of-the-20th-century Fort Worth society. All except one share the three bathrooms in back, and robes are provided for guests.

109½ W. Exchange Ave., Fort Worth, TX 76106 (Stockyards District). ℂ 817/626-1522. Fax 817/626-2589. www.missmollyshotel.com. 7 units. $125–$140 with shared bathroom; $200 with private bathroom. Rates include breakfast. AE, DC, DISC, MC, V. Free parking. **Amenities:** Smoking not permitted. *In room:* No TV.

Stockyards Hotel *Kids*   This historic hotel (Bonnie and Clyde once hid out in room no. 305) has medium-size rooms decorated in several styles, all of which take their inspiration from the Old West. If cowhide chairs and mounted longhorn heads are your thing, you'll like it here. A saloon-style restaurant serves breakfast, lunch, and dinner.

109 E. Exchange Ave., Fort Worth, TX 76106 (Stockyards District). ℂ 800/423-8471 or 817/625-6427. Fax 817/624-2571. www.stockyardshotel.com. 52 units. $159–$189 double; $189–$425 suite. AE, DC, DISC, MC, V. Valet parking $8. Pets accepted for a $50 fee. **Amenities:** Restaurant.

WHERE TO DINE

Angelo's Barbecue BARBECUE   The emphasis at Angelo's is on the food, certainly not the decor. Step inside and you'll find a dimly lit large room with concrete floor, cheap tables and chairs, and remarkably lazy ceiling fans. But the barbecue is cooked to perfection and the beer is as cold as it can be. The ribs and the brisket are especially noteworthy.

2533 White Settlement Rd. (between Henderson and University, near downtown). ℂ 817/332-0357. Reservations not accepted. Barbecue plates $7–$12; sandwiches $3–$6. No credit cards. Mon–Sat 11am–10pm.

Cattlemen's Steak House *Kids* STEAK   This old-style steakhouse is a Fort Worth institution. It has the cowboy feel of many of the establishments of the Stockyards District but seems less self-conscious about it. There's a lot of rough-cut wood paneling; plain, solid wood furniture; and some vivid cowboy murals for fun to brighten the place up. The steaks are great, and this place is known for the Texas delicacy known as chicken-fried steak.

2458 N. Main St. (Stockyards District). ℂ 817/624-3945. www.cattlemenssteakhouse.com. Reservations accepted. Main courses $13–$36. AE, DC, DISC, MC, V. Mon–Thurs 11am–10:30pm; Fri–Sat 11am–11pm; Sun 1–9pm.

Lonesome Dove Western Bistro *Best* SOUTHWESTERN   For fine dining in Fort Worth, this small restaurant in the Stockyards District is the place. The dining room is comfortable and attractive with solid-looking furniture and white tablecloths. A bar runs the length of the room adding to the Western flavor of the decor. The intriguing menu includes ingredients from all over the world in bold combinations that tell of "New Cuisine" influences and often include a Mexican touch. The wine list has racked up numerous awards. For lunch, the bargain is the Stockyards Special; it changes every day but costs just $7.

2406 N. Main St. (Stockyards District). ℂ 817/740-8810. www.lonesomedovebistro.com. Reservations recommended. Main courses $6–$17 lunch, $18–$31 dinner. AE, DISC, MC, V. Tues–Sat 11:30am–2:30pm and 5–10pm.

Reata WESTERN   The plucky menu characterizes the food here as Texas cowboy cuisine, which is a tad misleading. Certainly the chicken-fried steak and the rib-eye topped with a pat of butter qualify, and perhaps even the smoked shrimp enchiladas, but what about the pecan-crusted chicken breast with a tomato and raspberry sauce?

Or the angel-hair pasta with Gulf shrimp? The food is excellently prepared, and the margaritas are outstanding. There's a large main dining room, a rooftop section, and a quieter basement room.

310 Houston St. (downtown). ℂ 817/336-1009. Reservations recommended. Main courses $14–$29. AE, DISC, MC, V. Daily 11am–2:30pm and 5–10:30pm.

Joe T. Garcia's MEXICAN   Behind the small, nondescript entrance of this 70-year-old restaurant is a patio that seats 300 people amid fountains, a swimming pool, and a small garden. Seating is also available indoors, but it's not quite the same. The friendly and casual service remains unaffected by celebrity patrons. The menu is simple: either beef or chicken fajitas, or a Tex-Mex enchilada dinner. The margaritas are especially renowned.

2201 N. Commerce St. (Stockyards District). ℂ 817/626-4356. www.joets.com. Reservations accepted for groups of 20 or more. Main courses $11–$15. No credit cards. Mon–Thurs 11am–2:30pm and 5–10pm; Fri–Sat 11am–11pm; Sun 11am–10pm.

FORT WORTH AFTER DARK

The **Sundance Square Downtown Entertainment District** is grabbing the lion's share of city nightlife these days. Dozens of dining and entertainment options abound. The most spectacular venue is the **Bass Performance Hall** (ℂ 817/212-4325), the 2,056-seat, acoustically amazing theater designed by David M. Schwartz, which serves as home for the **Fort Worth Symphony** (ℂ 817/665-6000; www. fwsymphony.org), **Texas Ballet Theater** (ℂ 877/212-4280; www.texasballettheater. org), and **Fort Worth Opera** (ℂ 817/731-0726; www.fwopera.org).

Sundance Square's other options include the **Circle Theater** (ℂ 817/877-3040) and the **Jubilee Theatre** (ℂ 817/338-4411), as well as two multicinemas. For bars and clubs, you have quite a few to choose from and might do well just to walk through the area until you find one to your taste. For dancing, the main venue is **City Streets** (ℂ 817/335-5400), a collection of four clubs at 425 Commerce St. offering pop music and tunes from the '70s and '80s. **The Flying Saucer Beer Emporium** (ℂ 817/336-7468) offers a variety of music and libations. Also very popular is **The Fox & Hound** at 604 Main St. (ℂ 817/338-9200), a large, lively, publike bar.

For cowboy entertainment, go to the **Stockyards District.** There you'll find one of Fort Worth's most popular attractions, the 127,000-square-foot **Billy Bob's Texas,** 2520 Rodeo Plaza (ℂ 817/624-7117; www.billybobstexas.com), which bills itself as "the world's largest honky-tonk." But before going to Billy Bob's, try the **Cowtown Coliseum,** 121 E. Exchange Ave. (ℂ 817/625-1025), which has a small rodeo on Friday and Saturday nights, usually starting at 8pm.

3 Houston

Situated on a flat, nearly featureless Gulf Coast plain, Houston spreads out from its center in vast tracts of subdivisions, freeways, and shopping malls covering an area larger than half the state of Rhode Island. It is the largest, most cosmopolitan city in Texas, and like its terrain, Houston is wide open both economically and socially. This has made it the land of opportunity for many who have come here, which includes a large and varied immigrant population. Houston is also a seaport, the second busiest in the country thanks to a ship channel that cuts inland from Galveston Bay.

A few years back, residential construction shifted away from the suburbs and toward the downtown and inner-city areas as many Houstonians changed their minds about living in the suburbs. Many were lured in by Houston's performing arts and cultural scene, such as its excellent symphony orchestra, highly respected ballet and opera companies, a dynamic theater scene that few cities can equal, and some tiptop museums. Of less interest to them, but always the most popular attraction for visitors, is NASA's Johnson Space Center, which teamed up with Disney to create Space Center Houston. Aside from NASA, Houston is best known for its oil industry and for the Texas Medical Center, arguably the best in the country.

ESSENTIALS

GETTING THERE   **By Plane**   **George Bush Intercontinental/Houston Airport (IAH)** is 45 minutes north of downtown, with taxi fare around $45. It is a hub for Continental Airlines. **Hobby Airport (HOU)** is closer to downtown, 30 minutes to the southeast; taxi fare is about $25. Fares to hotels in the Galleria shopping area run $50 from IAH and $45 from Hobby. Information on both airports is available online at www.fly2houston.com.

Shuttle service from either airport to different parts of the city is operated by **Texans Shuttle** (© 877/770-1655; www.texansshuttle.com) and **Airport Shuttle America** (© 281/530-4000). The second company offers service between the two airports. The fare between downtown and Houston Intercontinental Airport costs $22. **City bus service** (© 713/635-4000) from IAH (terminal C) to downtown costs $1.50 (route 102). It runs daily until about midnight.

By Train   **Amtrak** (© 800/USA-RAIL; www.amtrak.com) serves the **Southern Pacific Station,** 902 Washington Ave. (© 713/224-1577), with trains from San Antonio (trip time: 4 hr.) and New Orleans (9 hr.).

By Car   The principal routes into Houston are **I-45** from the north (Dallas) and southeast (Galveston), and **I-10** from the east (New Orleans) and west (San Antonio and El Paso). The outermost loop, known as **Beltway 8** (Sam Houston Pkwy.), circles the outer city. **Loop 610** circles the central city.

VISITOR INFORMATION   The **Greater Houston Convention and Visitors Bureau** (© 800/4-HOUSTON; www.visithoustontexas.com) has a **Visitors Center** at City Hall, 901 Bagby St., Houston, TX 77002 (© 713/437-5556), open Monday to Saturday from 9am to 4pm, and Sunday 11am to 4pm. While you're there, make sure to see the Art Deco lobby of the city hall proper.

GETTING AROUND   In 2003, the **Metropolitan Transportation Authority (MTA;** © 713/635-4000; www.ridemetro.org) christened a **light-rail train service,** which connects downtown with the Museum District, the Medical Center, and the Reliant Stadium complex. This route is handy for the visitor. Tickets can be purchased at vending machines at every station. A day pass is $2 and is good for bus service, too. Citywide bus service costs $1 for most fares; express service costs $1.50. Seniors and riders with disabilities pay 40¢; children under 4 ride free.

Taxis are plentiful in the city, but trying to hail one on the street can be an exercise in frustration. Call ahead or use hotel taxi stands. The principal companies are **Yellow Cab** (© 713/236-1111; www.yellowcabhouston.com), **Fiesta Cab** (© 713/225-2666), **Liberty Cab** (© 713/695-6700), and **United Cab** (© 713/699-0000). Cabs run $4 for the first mile, $1.85 for each mile thereafter.

FAST FACTS   **Ben Taub General Hospital,** 1502 Taub Loop (© 713/793-2000), is a nationally recognized emergency center. The local hotel tax is 17%; the local sales tax is 8.25%. Houston has three area codes: **713, 281,** and **832.** Local calls require dialing the 10-digit number.

SPECIAL EVENTS & FESTIVALS   The **Houston Livestock Show and Rodeo** (✆ 713/791-9000; www.rodeohouston.com), which runs from late February to mid-March, is the largest rodeo in the world. In April the city celebrates the **Houston International Festival** (✆ 713/654-8808; www.ifest.org), which highlights a particular country each year. It takes place downtown for two weekends and gets more than a million celebrants. Houston is also famous for its **Art Car Parade** (www.orange show.org/artcar.html), which is usually scheduled for the second weekend in May.

EXPLORING THE CITY
THE TOP ATTRACTIONS
Battleship *Texas* & San Jacinto Monument and Museum   It was here, in 1836, that Sam Houston and his Texas army attacked and defeated the Mexican army and won Texas its independence. The site is marked by an obelisk the size of the Washington Monument but topped with a lone star. You can take the elevator up to the observation room, but the view is mostly of the Houston Ship Channel. In the base of the obelisk is an interesting museum and a movie theater with shows describing the battle. Next to the battlefield is the USS *Texas*. Built in 1914, it's the world's last remaining dreadnought battleship. You can clamber up to its small-caliber guns or onto the navigation bridge, inspect the crew's quarters, or check out the engine room. It can take as much as 3 hours to see both museum and battleship.

3527 Battleground Rd. (La Porte, off Hwy. 225). ✆ 281/479-2421. www.sanjacinto-museum.org. Admission to battleship $10 adults, $5 seniors, free for kids under 13. Monument and museum free admission; observation room $3 adults, $2 children; movie $3.50 adults, $2.50 children. Daily 10am–5pm.

Bayou Bend Collection & Gardens   Twenty-eight rooms of the mansion built for Ima Hogg, daughter of a former governor of Texas, who obviously had a cruel sense of humor when he named his offspring, hold an important collection of American furniture and paintings from the 17th, 18th, and 19th centuries. These are seen by guided or audio tour. Fourteen acres of gardens surrounding the estate can be viewed without a guide; children under 10 are not admitted. Allow 2½ hours.

1 Westcott St. (off Memorial Dr.). ✆ 713/639-7750. www.mfah.org/bayoubend. Admission $10 adults, $8.50 seniors, $5 ages 10–18. Tues–Fri 10–11:30am and 1–2:45pm; Sat 10–11:15am. Reservations required.

Houston Museum of Natural Science *(Kids)*   Much better than your average natural history museum, this one is on a roll and has had success attracting important traveling exhibitions. The permanent collection is large and impressive. A special attraction is the Cockrell Butterfly Center, which houses 2,000 real butterflies flying freely in a six-story glass cone. (Next to it is the "bug zoo" with live specimens of enormous insects from the world's tropical forests.) There is also a planetarium and an IMAX theater. A casual stroll through the permanent exhibition and the butterfly center can take 3 hours.

1 Hermann Circle Dr. (in Hermann Park). ✆ 713/639-4629. www.hmns.org. Admission $6 adults, $3.50 seniors and children 3–11; Dome Theater and Butterfly Center each $5 adults, $3.50 seniors and children; IMAX tickets $7 adults, $4.50 seniors and children. Multivenue ticket packages available. General hours daily 9am–5pm (until 9pm Tues); hours for planetarium and IMAX can differ. Parking $8.

Menil Collection *(Value)*   The collections of this private museum, one of the world's most highly regarded, break down roughly into four sections: antiquity, Byzantine, tribal art, and the 20th century. This last section, with its large holdings of works by the modern masters, is what garners most of the attention. Besides the main building (designed by Renzo Piano), there are satellite galleries holding works by Mark Rothko, Cy Twombly, and a Byzantine Fresco ransomed from art thieves. Because it's free and has easy access, it's perfect for a quick stop, but it's also easy to get sucked in for a couple of hours.

1515 Sul Ross St. (Montrose). ℂ 713/525-9400. www.menil.org. Free admission. Wed–Sun 11am–7pm.

Museum of Fine Arts Houston *(Best)* This is the best and biggest public art museum in Texas. It occupies two large buildings connected by a tunnel (make a point of seeing it): an earlier building largely designed by Mies van der Rohe, and a newer, more conservative building by Spanish architect Rafael Moneo. The museum's collection of over 40,000 pieces is wide and varied, but it is perhaps strongest in the areas of Impressionist and post-Impressionist works; baroque and Renaissance art; and 19th- and 20th-century American art. The museum attracts important traveling exhibits, so look for them.

1001 Bissonnet St. (at the intersection of S. Main and Montrose Blvd.). ℂ 713/639-7300. www.mfah.org. Admission $7 adults, $3.50 seniors and children 6–18; free general admission Thurs. Tues–Wed 10am–5pm; Thurs 10am–9pm; Fri–Sat 10am–7pm; Sun 12:15–7pm.

The Orange Show *(Kids)* Former postman Jeff Mckissack spent 25 years assembling a collection of found objects and mundane artifacts to "encourage people to eat

. . . But It's a Wet Heat

Hot and humid, Houston has earned the unofficial title of "Air-Conditioning Capital of the World." If you are unaccustomed to high humidity and its consequences (profuse sweating, bad-hair days), you might want to take it easy at first and work on acquiring some degree of philosophical acceptance. One more thing—bopping around Houston in summertime means jumping from the frying pan into the freezer (to mangle yet another cliché). You'll be repeatedly going from steamy outdoors into superchilled shops, restaurants, and so on. The natives are used to it, but many visitors complain . . . to deaf ears, we might add.

oranges, drink oranges, and be highly amused." The fruits of his labor form a unique urban folk-art park, preserved by The Orange Show Foundation. Great for kids and anyone who enjoys seeing a little outlandishness—the place can easily be seen in an hour and is on the way to the space center from central Houston. *Note:* For the last couple of years The Orange Show has closed for restoration during the month of August—this might become a yearly practice.

2402 Munger St. (off the Gulf Fwy., exit Telephone Rd.). (℃ 713/926-6368. www.orangeshow.org. Admission $1 adults, free for children under 12. Memorial Day to Labor Day Wed–Fri 9am–1pm; Sat–Sun noon–5pm. Open only on weekends rest of the year.

Space Center Houston *(Kids)*   Space Center Houston is the product of the joint efforts of NASA and Disney Imagineering. It is the most popular attraction in Houston, and there's nothing quite like it anywhere else in this sector of the galaxy. It's heavy on interactive displays and simulations on the one hand, and actual access to the real thing on the other. For instance, the Feel of Space gallery simulates working in the frictionless environment of space by using an air-bearing floor (something like a giant air hockey table). Another simulator shows what it's like to land the lunar orbiter. For a direct experience of NASA, the 1½-hour tram tour takes you to the International Space Station Assembly Building and NASA control center. A visit lasts an average of 4 hours.

Johnson Space Center, 1601 NASA Rd. 1 (in Clear Lake, 20 miles south of downtown, off Gulf Fwy.). (℃ 281/244-2100. www.spacecenter.org. Admission (including tours and IMAX theater) $19 adults, $18 seniors, $15 children 4–11. Daily 9am–7pm in summer; otherwise Mon–Fri 10am–5pm, Sat–Sun 10am–6pm. Parking $5.

MORE TO SEE & DO

SPORTS   In recent years, Houston has built modern venues for each of its big three sports teams. The MLB **Astros** (℃ **877/9-ASTROS;** www.astros.com) are enjoying their downtown ballpark with retractable roof, Minute Maid Field (formerly Enron Field). The NFL **Texans** (℃ **866/GO-TEXANS;** www.houstontexans.com) have Reliant Stadium, also with a retractable roof. It's located in south Houston on the light rail line. And the NBA **Rockets** (℃ **877/622-7625;** www.nba.com/rockets) perform at the Toyota Center downtown.

The easiest way to play a round of golf is to call **Golf Guys** (℃ **800/470-9634;** www.golfguys.net). You can consult with the people there about local courses and reserve tee times.

PARKS & ZOOS   The city's playground is **Hermann Park,** a 545-acre park minutes from downtown. It has an 18-hole golf course, picnic areas, the Garden Center, the Miller Outdoor Theater, and many other recreational facilities. It is also home to the **Houston Zoo**, 1513 N. MacGregor (© 713/523-5888; www.houstonzoo.org), open daily 9am to 6pm March through September; 9am to 5pm daily October to February. This 50-acre zoo features a gorilla habitat, rare albino reptiles, a cat facility, a huge aquarium, and vampire bats that eat lunch every day at 2:30pm. Admission to the zoo is $8.50 adults, $5 seniors, $4 children 2 to 11.

ESPECIALLY FOR KIDS The **Children's Museum of Houston,** 1500 Binz (© 713/522-1138; www.cmhouston.org), does a wonderful job of grabbing the attention and engaging the imaginations of children up to 12 years old. It blurs the distinction between museum and playhouse, and there always seems to be something special going on here. It's open Tuesday to Saturday 9am to 5pm, and Sunday noon to 5pm; during summer, it's also open Monday 9am to 5pm. Admission is $5.

Houston is also home to **Six Flags SplashTown** (© 281/355-3300; www.sixflags. com), 40 minutes north of downtown off I-45 (Exit 70A), a waterpark with amusement rides. General admission is $33 (often $5 cheaper if purchased online), children under 48 inches are $25. The park is open only during the summer and on some weekends after the schools open.

SHOPPING

The main shopping area in Houston is called uptown, which includes the **Galleria** (www.simon.com), home to 320 shops, and a few nearby shopping centers, along Post Oak Boulevard and Westheimer Road. Also worth visiting are the stores in the **River Oaks Shopping Center** (www.riveroaksshoppingcenter.com), Houston's first shopping strip, at Shepherd Drive and Gray Street. And, in **The Village,** near Rice University (www.ricevillageonline.com), you'll find several blocks of mixed retail/restaurant space, including a number of boutiques and small shops. The **Parks Shops in Houston Center,** 1200 McKinney St., is the only downtown mall. The **Montrose** area, along Westheimer from Woodward Street to Mandell Street, is a jumble of dealers hawking antiques. Let the buyer beware.

WHERE TO STAY

A number of good hotels are at or near IAH, including the **Houston Airport Marriott,** 18700 John F. Kennedy Blvd. (© 800/228-9290 or 281/443-2310), between terminals B and C; and the **Wingate Inn,** 15615 JFK Blvd. (© 800/228-1000 or 281/987-8777). Near Hobby Airport there is a **Days Inn Hobby Airport,** 1505 College Ave. (© 800/DAYS-INN or 713/946-5900), which is also close to the Astrodome and the Texas Medical Center.

Best Western Downtown Inn and Suites   Located in the shadow of downtown's skyline, this hotel offers convenient location and extralarge rooms with one king-size or two queen-size beds. On the downside, style takes a back seat to comfort and convenience, and there's no restaurant or room service. The greatest savings are had during the week; for a weekend, consider paying a bit extra to stay at one of the fancy hotels.

915 W. Dallas St., Houston, TX 77019. © 800/528-1234 or 713/571-7733. Fax 713/571-6680. www.bestwestern.com. 77 units. $129 double; $139 suite. Rates include continental breakfast. AE, DC, DISC, MC, V. Free guarded parking. **Amenities:** Covered outdoor pool; fitness room. *In room:* Fridge, microwave.

Four Seasons Hotel Houston *Best*   This hotel has lots of space so that you can stretch out in the oversize guest rooms and large health club, but it also offers excellent service so that you don't have to stretch too far. Close to the city's theater and entertainment district, and even closer to the downtown ballpark and basketball arena, the Four Seasons is conveniently located. Rooms are beautifully furnished, and those facing west have great views.

1300 Lamar St., Houston, TX 77010 (downtown). © 800/332-3442 or 713/650-1300. Fax 713/652-6220. www.four seasons.com/houston. 406 units. $330–$415 double; $425 and up suite. Children under 18 stay free in parent's room. AE, DC, DISC, MC, V. Valet parking $23. Pets accepted. **Amenities:** Restaurant; pool; health club; spa.

Hilton University of Houston   This is unlike any other Hilton Hotel as it is part of the Conrad Hilton College of Hotel and Restaurant Management and is staffed not only by professional full-timers, but also by students performing their lab work. It deserves consideration because its rates often drop very low. The location between downtown and the attractions on Houston's southeast side is excellent. Rooms have large L-shaped layouts with modern furnishings. The University Center next door has a health club, and a large pool that guests have access to. Note that the parking garage has a low ceiling and cannot accommodate vehicles such as large SUVs and pickup trucks.

4800 Calhoun Rd., Houston, TX 77004. © 800/HOTEL-UH or 713/741-2447. Fax 713/743-2498. www.hilton.com. 86 units. $70–$140 double. AE, DC, DISC, MC, V. Parking $5. **Amenities:** Restaurant.

Hotel Derek   This modern hotel's namesake, Derek, is a fictitious aging rock star and owner of the hotel. Given the premise, it would have been easy to lapse into cliché and stereotype, but it doesn't. There are nods to the 1960s, but these are blended with unexpected touches and the playful use of materials new and old into a thoughtful design. Guest rooms are functional but with the feel of a "pad." Beds, mostly king-size, are on platforms; and the sitting area is a wonderful mohair velvet built-in sofa stretching the width of the room.

2525 W. Loop S., Houston, TX 77027. © 866/292-4100 or 713/961-3000. Fax 713/297-4392. www.hotelderek.com. 314 units. $280 standard; $310 studio; $375 and up suite. AE, DC, DISC, MC, V. Valet parking $14. Pets allowed for a $50 fee. **Amenities:** Restaurant; fitness center.

Hotel Icon   Lots of texture, ornament, and a definite boudoir feel to the rooms makes staying at this downtown hotel a lot of fun. In renovating the old Union National Bank Building (1911), the designers sought to capture something of the feel of that golden age of refinement and exuberance. The most fun is to be had in the suites on the top floor, each named after a glorious old hotel. These are extra large and extra plush and touched by a bit of idiosyncrasy. Location is excellent.

220 Main St., Houston, TX 77002. © 800/323-7500 or 713/224-4266. Fax 713/223-3223. www.hotelicon.com. 135 units. $295–$350 double; $450 and up suite. Weekend special rates and Internet packages available. AE, DC, DISC, MC, V. Valet parking $20. **Amenities:** Restaurant; spa; fitness center.

La Colombe d'Or   If you enjoy the small scale of a B&B and rooms that don't look like hotel rooms, but you want more space, more service, and more privacy, this is the hotel for you. The five suites are extremely large, with hardwood floors, area rugs, antiques, king-size beds, and large bathrooms built of marble tile. Some suites come with separate dining rooms, and the in-room dining is one of the things this hotel is known for. The original mansion that the hotel occupies was built in the 1920s for oilman Walter Fondren.

3410 Montrose Blvd., Houston, TX 77006. © 713/524-7999. Fax 713/524-8923. www.lacolombedor.com. 6 units. $195–$275 suite; $575 penthouse. AE, DC, DISC, MC, V. Free valet parking. Small pets allowed with $150 deposit. **Amenities:** Restaurant.

Lancaster Hotel   There is no better place to stay for those who enjoy the performing arts and nightlife in general. Within 1 block you have the symphony, the ballet, the opera, and the theater, and, when reserving a room, you can have the concierge buy tickets for performances at any of these venues. The hotel occupies a small 12-story landmark building that dates from the 1920s. Rooms are smaller than their counterparts at other downtown hotels, but they have character and a host of amenities (Frette bathrobes, VCRs, and so on). Service at the hotel is excellent and includes lots of personal touches.

701 Texas Ave., Houston, TX 77002 (downtown). © **800/231-0336** or 713/228-9500. Fax 713/223-4528. www.the lancasterhouston.com. 93 units. $250–$350 double; $350 and up suite. AE, DC, DISC, MC, V. Valet parking $22. Pets allowed with $75 fee. **Amenities:** Restaurant.

Lovett Inn *Value*   Located 1 block off Westheimer and 3 blocks from Montrose Boulevard, the Lovett Inn is on a quiet street right in the middle of the busy restaurant and club district of the Montrose Area. The house dates from the early 1900s. Most rooms are large (well above the usual size for B&Bs). The four rooms in the main house and two rooms in the carriage house are attractive and well furnished with period pieces, wood floors, and area rugs, yet without the cutesiness that so many B&Bs feel obliged to deliver. Almost all have private balconies. There are also four town-house units around the corner (two per house), which have separate entrances and greater privacy. These are comfortable but modern.

501 Lovett Blvd., Houston, TX 77006. © **800/779-5224** or 713/522-5224. Fax 713/528-6708. www.lovettinn.com. 10 units. $115–$175 traditional doubles; $90–$125 town-house doubles. Rates include continental breakfast. AE, DC, DISC, MC, V. Free parking. **Amenities:** Outdoor pool.

WHERE TO DINE

Brennan's SOUTHERN/CREOLE   Fine dining New Orleans–style, Brennan's is a perennial favorite of Houstonians. The various dining rooms are elegant, perhaps the most elegant settings in Houston, and the service is superb. The selection of dishes varies daily, but a few classic Creole specialties such as a roux-less seafood gumbo or its well-known turtle soup are always on the menu.

3300 Smith St. © **713/522-9711.** www.brennanshouston.com. Reservations recommended. Main courses $27–$32. AE, DISC, MC, V. Mon–Fri 11:30am–1:30pm; Sun–Thurs 5:45–9pm; Fri–Sat 5:45–9:30pm; brunch Sat 11am–2pm, Sun 10am–2pm.

Cafe Annie *Best* SOUTHWESTERN   No restaurant in Houston has received more coverage, more acclaim, and more awards from the press than Cafe Annie. The softly lit dining room has lots of dark woodwork and a quiet atmosphere. Dinner here is expensive, but you can save money by going for lunch or ordering from the *botanitas* menu (tapas), served at the bar. One of the restaurant's signature dishes, the crabmeat tostadas, is available on the dinner, lunch, and *botanitas* menus. Also notable is the risotto of Maine lobster and Gulf shrimp in a broth lightly flavored with *chile cascabel* and cream.

1728 Post Oak Blvd. (just south of San Felipe). © **713/840-1111.** www.cafe-annie.com. Reservations recommended. Main courses $28–$50. AE, DC, DISC, MC, V. Tues–Fri 11:30am–2pm; Mon–Fri 6:30–10pm, Sat 6:30–10:30pm.

Churrascos SOUTH AMERICAN/STEAKS   The signature dish at this elegant dining spot is the beef tenderloin butterflied and served with *chimichurri* sauce, the Argentine condiment that accompanies steak. Popular, too, are the fried plantain chips served at every table, the Cuban-style black-bean soup, and the Peruvian-style seviche. Grilled vegetables come "family style" with every entree. Tables are well separated and the decor is in the simple style of an Argentine *estancia*.

2055 Westheimer. © **713/527-8300.** www.churrascos.com. Reservations recommended. Main courses $16–$25; lunch $10–$13. AE, DC, DISC, MC, V. Mon–Thurs 11am–10pm; Fri 11am–11pm; Sat 5–11pm; Sun 11am–9pm.

Goode Company Texas Barbeque _Kids_ BARBECUE   Buffalo trophies, snake skins, and stuffed armadillos adorn this very popular cowboy barbecue joint—a prime destination for those who love good, honest barbecue. Jim Goode's crew smokes delicious duck, chicken, links, and ribs. Try the brisket sandwich on jalapeño bread and see if you don't think you're on to something special. The pecan pie is a must for dessert. _Note:_ An additional location is at 8911 Katy Fwy. (© **713/464-1901**).

5109 Kirby Dr. (near the Village shopping center). © **713/522-2530.** www.goodecompany.com. Barbecue plates $8–$13. AE, DC, DISC, MC, V. Daily 11am–10pm.

Hugo's MEXICAN   Serving the best interior Mexican food in Houston, this restaurant enjoys a strong local following. Main courses include duck in a mole poblano (the classic dark red, bittersweet sauce of the Mexican highlands) and a chile relleno with roasted chicken smothered in a _pipián_ (a spicy sauce in a base of ground roasted pumpkin seeds). Keep an eye out for daily specials; the chef/owner, Hugo Ortega, enjoys seasonal cooking. The dining room is large and airy, owing to a very high ceiling—the building dates from 1935 and was once a drugstore.

1602 Westheimer Rd. (at Mandell St.). © **713/524-7744.** www.hugosrestaurant.net. Reservations recommended. Main courses $13–$30. AE, DC, DISC, MC, V. Sun–Thurs 11am–10pm; Fri–Sat 11am–11pm.

La Mexicana Restaurant MEXICAN   Once a little Mexican grocery store, La Mexicana started serving tacos and such before gradually turning exclusively to the restaurant business. It's well known for delicious Mexican breakfasts and classic enchilada plates (red or green are good choices). There is an extensive menu of tacos a la carte, and good fajitas as well. Service is good, and there's a choice of dining outside or in.

1018 Fairview (at Montrose). © **713/521-0963.** www.lamexicanarestaurant.com. Reservations not accepted. Main courses $7–$13. AE, DC, DISC, MC, V. Daily 7am–11pm.

Mark's American Cuisine NEW AMERICAN   Formerly chef at the renowned Tony's, Mark Cox now sets a formidable table inside a refurbished former church. The ever-changing menu keeps regulars delighted; selections might include lamb in a basil sauce with white cheddar potatoes or bourbon-glazed pork with yams and an apple compote. Many dishes are elegant variations of American classics that can be satisfying while at the same time providing a sensation of newness.

1658 Westheimer (in the Montrose area). © **713/523-3800.** www.marks1658.com. Reservations recommended. Main courses $15–$32. AE, DC, DISC, MC, V. Mon–Fri 11am–2pm; Mon–Thurs 6–11pm; Fri–Sat 5pm–midnight; Sun 5–10pm.

Thai Bistro THAI   Houston is particularly rich in Thai restaurants, having more than 70. This one, in a strip center along the Southwest Freeway, is particularly good. If you have an appetite, do yourself a favor and order the assorted appetizer platter. From there you can go in any number of directions: healthy (barbecued lemon-grass tofu or lettuce wraps), spicy (tiger cries or blazing noodles), classic (pad Thai), or curry (Panang). These are all favorites. Also on the menu are some Vietnamese-style vermicelli dishes, which are there through historical accident.

3241 Southwest Fwy. © **713/669-9375.** Reservations not accepted. Main courses $7–$16. AE, DC, DISC, MC, V. Mon–Fri 11am–3pm and 5–10pm; Sat 11am–10:30pm; Sun 11am–9pm.

Treebeards _Value_ CAJUN/CREOLE   A downtown tradition for lunch that's both good and economical. Try out red beans and rice, jambalaya, étouffée, and chicken and shrimp gumbo that'll fly with the best of them. Service is cafeteria-style. Go early or late to beat the rush of office workers.

315 Travis St. (©) **713/228-2622.** www.treebeardsrestaurant.com. Reservations not accepted. Main courses $6–$8.50. AE, DC, MC, V. Mon–Fri 11am–2pm.

HOUSTON AFTER DARK

THE PERFORMING ARTS The performing arts venues listed here are located within a small area of a few blocks in the northwest part of downtown. This is quite a convenience for visitors. **Jesse H. Jones Hall for the Performing Arts,** 615 Louisiana St. (© **713/227-3974),** is the home of the noted **Houston Symphony Orchestra** (© **713/224-7575;** www.houstonsymphony.org). The **Wortham Theater Center,** 510 Preston (© **713/237-1439;** www.worthamtheaterhouston.com), opened in 1987, is home to the innovative **Houston Grand Opera** (© **713/228-6737;** www.houstongrandopera.org), whose season runs October through May. The **Houston Ballet** (© **800/828-ARTS;** www.houstonballet.org) also performs here. The **Society for the Performing Arts (SPA),** 615 Louisiana St. (© **713/632-8100),** sponsors distinguished artists and productions from all areas of the performing arts. The **Alley Theatre,** 615 Texas Ave. (© **713/228-8421;** www.alleytheatre.org), is one of the few companies to own its own venue, a futuristic theater complex, designed by Ulrich Fransen. The Alley presents about 10 different productions a year, both modern plays and the classics.

THE CLUB & MUSIC SCENE Downtown is the hottest place to be. **Bayou Place,** 530 Texas Ave., is a large multivenue nightclub and restaurant complex in the heart of the Theater District, with live-music spots, a movie theater, and a good concert hall that gets a variety of acts—Verizon Wireless Theater (© **713/230-1666).** A few blocks away, in the city's oldest commercial building, **La Carafe,** 813 Congress Ave. (© **713/229-9399),** is one of the city's most interesting bars, a place to drink and relax and perhaps chat with some of the regulars. Also a couple of blocks away are a few jazz clubs: **Red Cat Jazz Café** is at 924 Congress (© **713/226-7870)** and **Sambuca Jazz Café** is at 909 Texas Ave. (© **713/224-5299).** A number of clubs are springing up overnight in this area, so you might want to take a spin around this part of downtown.

Outside of downtown, you can go to an old Houston institution known as **Fitzgerald's,** 2706 White Oak (© **713/862-3838).** It occupies an old Polish dance hall near the Heights neighborhood and gets talented local and touring bands, mostly rock acts. For country, the best place to go is **Blanco's** (© **713/439-0072),** a Texas-style honkytonk that packs 'em in Mondays through Fridays, attracting all sorts, from yuppies to tool pushers. Lots of good Texas bands like to play here, so it's a good opportunity to see a well-known local band in a small venue. There's a midsize dance floor. Monday through Wednesday is open-mic night, usually with one or another local band. Thursday and Friday offer live music, and the club is closed on Saturdays for private parties. It's located at 3406 W. Alabama, between Kirby Drive and Buffalo Speedway. When there's live music, the cover ranges from $5 to $15.

4 Galveston

Galveston is on the barrier island directly across from the mainland coast closest to Houston. Older than Houston, it was a prosperous port throughout most of the 19th century and is once again being used as a home port by the cruise industry. One of its main attractions is the downtown historic district with its Victorian commercial buildings and houses. Another attraction—the beaches—draws Houstonians and other Texans down in droves. Its leading claim to historical fame, however, lies in tragedy: Galveston was the site of the worst natural disaster ever to strike the United States—the 1900 Galveston Storm, which killed 6,000 people.

ESSENTIALS

GETTING THERE Most visitors arrive here via Houston (50 miles away). The **Gulf Freeway** (I-45) leads directly into Galveston. Houston's Hobby Airport, just off this freeway, is the most convenient airport, though the island does have its own small airport called Scholes Field.

VISITOR INFORMATION If you're planning a trip, contact the **Galveston Convention and Visitors Bureau** (© 888/GAL-ISLE; www.galveston.com). If you're in town already, check out their **Visitor Information Center,** 2027 61st St., open daily from 8:30am to 5pm during the summer.

GETTING AROUND After entering Galveston, I-45 becomes Broadway, Galveston's principal street. Instead of crossing straight to the water, it cuts across the island diagonally, heading eastward until it comes to the coastline at Stewart Beach. Streets crossing Broadway are numbered; those parallel to Broadway have letters, and many have names as well. The East End Historic District and the historic Strand District are north of Broadway between 25th and 9th streets. Galveston has a restored **trolley line** that loops through the Strand District before heading down 25th Street to the beach and the sea wall. After the 1900 storm, Galveston built miles of sea wall along its seaward shore; here you'll find many of Galveston's hotels, motels, and restaurants. **Taxis** are not commonly seen; if you need one, call **Yellow Cab** (© 409/763-3333). Rates run $4 for the first mile, $1.70 for each additional mile.

FAST FACTS Galveston's hospital is the **University of Texas Medical Branch** (© 409/772-1011). The physician referral line is © 409/763-4111. Sales tax is 8.25% and hotel tax is 13%.

SPECIAL EVENTS & FESTIVALS In February/March, Galveston holds an immensely popular 12-day **Mardi Gras (www.mardigrasgalveston.com)** with parades, masked balls, and a live entertainment district. The first weekend in June is the annual **American Institute of Architects Sandcastle Competition (www.aiasandcastle.com)** on East Beach. About 60 architectural firms take the building of sandcastles and sand sculptures to a new level. There are a lot of food and drink stalls, and everybody has a good time. During the first weekend in December, Galveston hosts **Dickens on The Strand** (© 409/765-7834; www.dickensonthestrand.org), a street party in the historic district to celebrate the Victorian age (Galveston's heyday) and the upcoming Christmas holiday with parades, entertainers, lots of the locals in Victorian costume, and street vendors.

WHAT TO SEE & DO

Popular activities among visitors and locals alike are to walk, skate, or ride a bike atop the **sea wall,** which extends 10 miles along the coast. The **beaches** are always Galveston's most popular attraction. They may not measure up to those of the most popular beach destinations; the sand is a light tan color instead of white (but it's pure sand without rocks), and the water isn't turquoise (but it's a wonderful temperature). **East Beach** and **Stewart Beach,** operated by the city, have pavilions with dressing rooms, showers, and restrooms, ideal for day-trippers. There's a $5-per-vehicle entrance fee. Most other beaches are free.

Many tours are offered on the island: **Galveston Harbour Tours** (© 409/765-1700) offers a Saturday-morning dolphin-watch tour and a frequent harbor tour;

Duck Tours (© **409/621-4771**) offers tours of the island in their amphibious buses; **Ghost Tours** (© **409/949-2027**) offers a walking tour of the Strand District. On Broadway there are a few massive 19th-century mansions that offer tours: **Ashton Villa,** 2328 Broadway (© **409/762-3933**); the **Bishop's Palace,** 1402 Broadway (© **409/762-2475**); and the **Moody Mansion,** 2618 Broadway (© **409/762-7668**).

MUSEUMS   Except for Moody Gardens and its neighbor, the Lone Star Flight Museum (see below), all of Galveston's museums are in and around the Strand (the old commercial center). These include the **Pier 21 Theater** (© **409/763-8808**), which shows short films: one about the 1900 storm that devastated the town, and another about a one-time Galveston resident, the pirate Jean Laffite. On the same pier are the **Texas Seaport Museum** (© **409/763-1877;** www.tsm-elissa.org) and the *Elissa,* a restored tall ship. Admission to both attractions is $6 adults, $4 children.

Next door, at Pier 19, is a one-of-a-kind museum about offshore drilling rigs. These mammoth constructions often come to the Port of Galveston to be reconditioned. Since they spend most of their time far offshore, you don't see them often, but here in Galveston you have an opportunity to get up close to one, the **Ocean Star** (© **409/766-STAR;** www.oceanstaroec.com), a rig converted into a museum. Through a short film, scale models, actual drilling equipment, and interactive displays, every aspect of the drilling process is explored, including the many rather daunting engineering challenges. Hours for this and the other museums around the Strand are roughly the same: daily from 10am to 4pm (to 5pm in summer). Admission is $6 adults, $5 seniors, $4 students ages 7 to 18.

The **Texas Aviation Hall of Fame and the Lone Star Flight Museum,** 2002 Terminal Dr. (© **888/354-4488;** www.lsfm.org), just down the road from the Moody Gardens (see below), features restored historical aircraft. Admission is $6 adults, $5 students ages 13 to 17, $4 children ages 5 to 12.

Moody Gardens (© **800/582-4673;** www.moodygardens.com) is across from the aviation museum. It is a large complex easily recognizable by its three big glass pyramids, which hold a rainforest habitat, an ocean habitat, and an exhibition on space exploration. It also has a couple of IMAX theaters (one is 3-D and the other is a Ridefilm), a pool, a white-sand beach, and an old paddle-wheel boat that journeys out into the bay. Admission prices for the individual attractions run from $8 to $15 adults, $6 to $8 kids ages 4 to 12; they are a bit overpriced.

WHERE TO STAY

All the economical hotel/motel chains have properties in Galveston, with higher prices for lodgings along the sea wall. Of the big chains, **La Quinta Galveston,** at 1402 Seawall Blvd. (© **800/531-5900**), ranks highly. Galveston also has a dozen B&Bs, most of which are in Victorian-era houses. For a dependable B&B, go to the Galveston Bed and Breakfast Association website at **www.galvestonbedandbreakfast.com**.

Harbor House   A different hotel for Galveston, the Harbor House is built on a pier overlooking the harbor instead of a beach. It's actually an excellent location. Rooms are large and well appointed in the modern taste without a lot of clutter. Bleached wood floors, Berber carpets, and exposed wood and steel superstructure are design highlights. There's no restaurant, but there are many restaurants within 2 blocks of the hotel.

No. 28, Pier 21, Galveston, TX 77550. © **800/874-3721** or 409/763-3321. Fax 409/765-6421. www.harborhouse Pier21.com. 42 units. Weekdays $115–$135 double; weekends $135–$195 double. Rates include continental breakfast. AE, DC, DISC, MC, V. Self-parking $10.

Hotel Galvez *(Best)*   Galveston's historic grand hotel (it opened in 1911 and has hosted such luminaries as Theodore Roosevelt and Frank Sinatra), the Hotel Galvez is located on the sea wall and has been thoroughly renovated. The spacious, well-furnished, and conservatively decorated rooms come with marble bathrooms with bathrobes and lots of amenities. You have a choice of "gulf view" (about $30 extra) or "city view" rooms. Prices fluctuate a lot depending on the season.

2024 Seawall Blvd., Galveston, TX 77550. © 800/WYNDHAM or 409/765-7721. Fax 409/765-5780. www.wyndham.com. 231 units. $115–$245 double. AE, DC, DISC, MC, V. Valet parking $9; free self-parking. **Amenities:** Restaurant; outdoor pool.

WHERE TO DINE

Seafood is what people come to Galveston for, and there's quite a variety. For the best of Galveston's seafood, try one of the places listed below. If you hanker after steak, the best in town is **The Steakhouse** in the San Luis Resort, 5222 Seawall Blvd. (© **409/744-1500**).

Gaido's *(Best)* SEAFOOD   This is a Galveston tradition that has been owned and operated by the Gaido family, now in its fourth generation. The Gaidos have maintained quality by staying personally involved in all the aspects of the restaurant; thus the seafood is fresh and the service attentive. The soups and side dishes are traditional recipes cooked southern-style and have become comfort food for all the longtime customers. The seasonally changing menu includes a few chicken, pork, and beef items, but seafood rules for the most part.

3800 Seawall Blvd. © **409/762-9625.** Reservations not accepted. Main courses $15–$33; complete dinners $19–$29. AE, DISC, MC, V. Daily 11:45am–10:30pm. Closes 1–2 hr. earlier during low season.

Saltwater Grill SEAFOOD   The restaurant's seafood is fresh, and the preparation shows a light touch. The menu is printed up daily and generally includes some inventive seafood pasta dishes, perhaps a Gulf red snapper pan-sautéed and topped with lump crabmeat, a fish dish with an Asian bent, gumbo or bouillabaisse, and a few non-seafood options. Situated in an old building on Post Office Street (near the Strand), the dining room offers a pleasant mix of past and present, formal and informal.

2017 Post Office St. © **409/762-FISH.** www.galveston.com/saltwatergrill. Reservations recommended. Main courses $14–$29. AE, MC, V. Mon–Fri 11am–2pm and 5–10pm; Sat 5–11pm; Sun 5–9pm. Parking in rear.

GALVESTON AFTER DARK

This city isn't known for its nightlife. Your best bet is the so-called **Post Office Street Arts and Entertainment District,** which is the area around Post Office Street between 25th and 19th streets.

5 San Antonio

Remember the Alamo? Have you heard about the River Walk or the Mission Trail? Or SeaWorld? There's a lot to see and do in San Antonio. And even without the attractions, you would still be left with a city that is fascinating in its own right. It was settled in the early 1700s by Canary Islanders, sent there by the king of Spain and at the invitation of the local Indians who were feeling the depredations of the Apache. The city lies on the edge of south Texas, with Laredo and the Mexican border a scant 3 hours away, and has always been linked to the Mexican world. But it is also on the edge of Texas Hill Country, which ties it to the frontier culture and to the culture of the German settlers who migrated here in large numbers in the mid–19th century. On top of this, San Antonio is Texas through and through, all of which makes it an intriguing multifaceted city that surprises and delights.

ESSENTIALS

GETTING THERE **By Plane** The two-terminal **San Antonio International Airport** (© **210/207-3411;** www.sanantonio.gov/aviation) sits about 13 miles north of downtown. Among the many carriers serving the city, **Southwest Airlines** (© **800/ 435-9792**) offers direct flights from a number of cities.

If you're renting a car, it should take about 15 to 20 minutes to drive downtown via U.S. 281 South. VIA Metropolitan Transit's bus no. 2 is the cheapest (75¢) way to get downtown but also the slowest at 40 to 45 minutes. A taxi should cost about $30 to get downtown.

By Train Amtrak (© **800/USA-RAIL** or 210/233-3226; www.amtrak.com) provides daily service to its station at 250 Hoefgen St. from Austin (trip time: 2 hr.), Fort Worth (7 hr.), Dallas (9 hr.), and Chicago (30 hr.); there is less frequent service from New Orleans (14 hr.) and Los Angeles (29 hr.).

By Car Major routes into San Antonio are **I-35** from the north (Austin) and south (Laredo), and **I-10** from the east (Houston) and west (El Paso).

VISITOR INFORMATION Contact the **San Antonio Convention and Visitors Bureau (SACVB),** P.O. Box 2277, San Antonio, TX 78298 (© **800/447-3372;** www.sanantoniovisit.com), for an information packet. The **City of San Antonio Visitor Information Center,** 317 Alamo Plaza, across the street from the Alamo, is open daily from 9am to 5pm. There are two unstaffed satellite offices at the airport.

GETTING AROUND The **VIA Metropolitan Transit Service** (© **210/362-2020;** www.viainfo.net) has bus routes that cost 80¢ for regular lines and $1.60 for express lines (15¢ for transfers). You'll need exact change. VIA also offers five convenient downtown streetcar routes that cover all the most popular tourist stops for 80¢ a ride (exact change only).

Taxis are next to impossible to hail on the street; call **Yellow Checker Cab** (© **210/ 222-2222**). The base charge is $1.70; add $1.80 per mile.

FAST FACTS For a doctor referral, contact the **Bexar County Medical Society** at 202 W. French Place (© **210/734-6691**). The main downtown hospital is **Baptist Medical Center,** 111 Dallas St. (© **210/297-7000**). Sales tax is 8.25%; the city surcharge on hotel rooms is 16.75%.

SPECIAL EVENTS & FESTIVALS The third week of April brings **Fiesta San Antonio** (© **210/227-5191;** www.fiesta-sa.org), a huge celebration marking Texas independence with an elaborately costumed royal court presiding over 10 days of revelry: parades, balls, food fests, sporting events, concerts, and art shows all over town.

The **Tejano Conjunto Festival,** at Rosedale Park and Guadalupe Theater, is an annual festival in mid-May that celebrates the lively and unique blend of Mexican and German music born in South Texas.

WHAT TO SEE & DO

It goes without saying that the River Walk (see below) is the place to take a stroll in San Antonio, but if you want to see a little more of town, stroll through **La Villita National Historic District,** which is bounded by Durango, Navarro, and Alamo streets and the River Walk. Boutiques, crafts shops, and restaurants occupy this historic district, which resembles a Spanish-Mexican village. Another good walking area is the **King William Historic District,** on the east bank of the river just south of downtown (within walking distance of the convention center). It has beautifully landscaped lawns and several mansions.

The river tours offered by **Yanaguana Cruises** (© 210/244-5700) go more than 2 miles down the most built-up sections of the Paseo del Rio. There are several places along the River Walk where you can buy a ticket and catch a boat; just look for where the boats pull up to the bank. The cost is $6.50 general admission, $4.50 seniors, $1.50 for children 1 to 5. Boats leave every half-hour from 10am for the 40-minute cruise.

The Alamo   Inevitably, the first thing visitors think when they see the Alamo is "Hmmm, I thought it would be bigger." Such a reaction, of course, only underscores the heroic and desperate actions of the Alamo's defenders who in 1836 held off their attackers for 13 days against overwhelming odds. More shrine than museum, the Alamo doesn't do the best job of explaining the battle. If you want to understand more, see the IMAX show *Alamo . . . The Price of Freedom,* presented several times a day at the IMAX theater around the corner from the Alamo in the Rivercenter Mall (© 210/247-4629; www.imax-sa.com).

300 Alamo Plaza. © 210/281-0710. http://thealamo.org. Free admission (donations welcome). Mon–Sat 9am–5:30pm; Sun 10am–5:30pm. Streetcar: Red, Brown, and Blue lines.

Market Square   Market Square will transport you south of the border. Stalls in El Mercado sell everything from onyx chess sets and cheap serapes to beautifully made crafts from the interior of Mexico. Every weekend food stalls hawk specialties such as *gorditas* (thick tortillas topped with a variety of goodies) and funnel cakes. Some of the buildings date from the late 1800s.

Between Dolorosa and Commerce sts. © 210/207-8600. Free admission. El Mercado and Farmer's Market Plaza June–Aug daily 10am–8pm; Sept–May daily 10am–6pm. Restaurants and some of the shops open later. Streetcar: Red and Yellow lines.

The River Walk/Paseo Del Rio *(Best*   The quieter areas of these 2½ paved miles of winding riverbank, shaded by cypresses, oaks, and willows, exude a tropical, exotic aura; the Big Bend section, filled with sidewalk cafes, popular restaurants and bars, high-rise hotels, and even a shopping mall, has a festive, sometimes frenetic feel. Tour boats, water taxis, and floating picnic barges regularly ply the river, and local parades and festivals fill its banks with revelers.

Downtown from the Municipal Auditorium on the north end, to the King William Historic District on the south end. All streetcar lines.

For Art Lovers

Art aficionados should check out the **Marion Koogler McNay Art Museum,** 6000 N. New Braunfels Ave. (© 210/824-5368; www.mcnayart.org), a gem of a small museum. It is particularly strong in French post-Impressionist and early-20th-century European painting, and the building and grounds are lovely. Admission is free. The **San Antonio Museum of Art,** 200 W. Jones Ave. (© 210/978-8100; www.samuseum.org), houses the Rockefeller Center for Latin American Art. The center exhibits pre-Columbian, colonial, folk, and contemporary works from all over Latin America. Admission is $8 adults, $7 seniors, $5 students, and $3 children 4 to 11.

TEXAS
Austin
San Antonio

W. Cypress

San Antonio Museum of Art ■

Convent

DOWNTOWN
Travis Park

Riverwalk

San Fernando Cathedral

Alamo

Market Square

City Hall
Main Plaza

Rivercenter Mall

LA VILLITA NATIONAL HISTORIC DISTRICT

Convention Center

Villita Assembly Hall

Tower of the Americas

Beethoven Hall

HemisFair Park

KING WILLIAM HISTORIC DISTRICT

Institute of Texan Cultures

SOUTHTOWN

Church ✝

SAN ANTONIO
Downtown

ACCOMMODATIONS ■
Emily Morgan Hotel **5**
The Fairmont **9**
Havanna Riverwalk Inn **2**
Menger Hotel **6**
Omni La Mansión del Rio Hotel **4**

DINING ◆
Boudro's **7**
Liberty Bar **1**
Mi Tierra **3**
Rosario's **11**
Schilo's **8**

San Antonio Missions National Historical Park   The Alamo was originally just the first of five missions established by the Franciscans along the San Antonio River. The four missions that now fall under the aegis of the National Park Service are still active parishes, run in cooperation with the Archdiocese of San Antonio. **Concepción,** 807 Mission Rd. at Felisa, is the oldest unrestored Texas mission, and looks much as it did 200 years ago. **San José,** 6707 Roosevelt Ave., established in 1720, was the largest, best known, and most beautiful of the Texas missions. It has been reconstructed. Moved from an earlier site in east Texas to its present location in 1731, **San Juan Capistrano,** 9102 Graf at Ashley, doesn't have the grandeur of the missions to the north. **San Francisco de la Espada,** 10040 Espada Rd., also has an ancient, isolated feel, although the beautifully kept-up church shows just how vital it still is to the local community.

Headquarters: 2202 Roosevelt Ave. ℭ 210/534-8833. Visitor center: 6707 Roosevelt Ave. ℭ 210/932-1001. www. nps.gov/saan. Free admission; donations accepted. All the missions are open daily 9am–5pm.

SeaWorld San Antonio (Kids   Leave it to Texas to provide Shamu, the performing killer whale, with his most spacious digs: At 250 acres, this is the largest marine theme park in the world. The walk-through habitats where you can watch penguins, sea lions, sharks, tropical fish, and flamingos do their thing are endlessly fascinating, but the aquatic acrobatics at the stadium shows are even more fun. The Lost Lagoon has a huge wave pool and there are water slides aplenty.

10500 SeaWorld Dr. (16 miles northwest of downtown San Antonio at Ellison Dr. and Westover Hills Blvd.). ℭ 210/ 523-3611. www.seaworld.com. $42 adults, $32 children ages 3–9, free for children under 3. Schedule varies with season; generally open weekends and some weekdays in spring and fall, daily during summer (through mid-Aug) 10am–9pm. Parking $8.

Six Flags Fiesta Texas   A large amusement park with a San Antonio motif, it has all the roller coasters and thrill rides, plus cartoon characters, shops, and so forth. The attractions are organized into four local themes: Mexican fiesta, German village, country and western, and vintage rock 'n' roll (remember, Buddy Holly was from Texas).

17000 I-10 W. (corner of I-10 W. and Loop 1604; about 15 min. from downtown). ℭ 210/697-5050. www.sixflags. com. Admission $47 adults, $32 children under 48 in., free for children under 3. Prices do not include tax. The park is generally open daily late May to late Aug, Fri–Sun Mar–May and Sept–Nov, closed Nov–Feb. It opens at 8 or 10am, depending on the season, and closes at 10pm. Call ahead or check the website, since times often vary. Parking $10.

Witte Museum   The Witte focuses on Texas history, natural science, and anthropology, but often ranges as far afield as the Berlin Wall or the history of bridal gowns in the United States. An EcoLab is home to live Texas critters ranging from tarantulas to tortoises; the wonderful HEB Science Treehouse is a science center with hands-on activities for all ages. Outside are a butterfly and hummingbird garden, as well as three restored historic homes.

3801 Broadway (at the edge of Brackenridge Park). ℭ 210/357-1900. www.wittemuseum.org. $7 adults, $6 seniors, $5 children 4–11, free for children 3 and under. Mon 10am–5pm; Tues 10am–8pm; Wed–Sat 10am–5pm; Sun noon–5pm.

GOLF

As San Antonio has cemented its reputation as a vacation destination, golf has acquired a bigger presence here, and more and more visitors are deciding to shoot a round or two during their stay. The easiest way to play a round of golf is to call **Golf Guys** (ℭ 800/470-9634; www.golfguys.net). You can consult with the people there about local courses and reserve tee times. You don't pay any more for this service than you would if you were to reserve your own tee times.

SHOPPING

Most out-of-town shoppers will find all they need downtown, between the large **Rivercenter Mall** (www.shoprivercenter.com); the boutiques and crafts shops of **La Villita** (www.lavillita.com); **Market Square,** with its colorful Mexican wares; and assorted souvenir retailers and galleries on and around **Alamo Plaza.**

In the Southtown section near King William, the **Blue Star Arts Complex,** 1400 S. Alamo St. (© **210/227-6960;** www.bluestarcomplex.com), is the up-and-coming place to buy art. More and more galleries are opening downtown as well. You'll find a slew of **antiques shops** on Hildebrand between Blanco and San Pedro, and McCullough between Hildebrand and Basse.

Many of San Antonio's countless small *botánicas* specialize in articles used in the practice of *curandería,* a Latin American fusion of African and Native American magical practices. **Papa Jim's,** 5630 S. Flores St. (© **210/922-6665;** www.papajimsbotanica.com), is the best known of all the *botánicas.* Can't make it to the shop? Order online or get a copy of the more comprehensive print catalog by phoning or ordering through the Papa Jim's website.

WHERE TO STAY

For information about bed-and-breakfasts around the city, contact the **San Antonio Bed & Breakfast Association** (www.sanantoniobb.org). Don't expect to find any bargains right on the River Walk. Several moderate and affordable chain properties are near Market Square, on the west side of downtown, about 6 blocks from the river and easily accessible to it via the trolley. The closest is **La Quinta Market Square,** 900 Dolorosa (© **866/725-1661** or 210/271-0001), offering a swimming pool. A little farther south, but equipped with restaurant, pool, exercise room, and room service, are the **Holiday Inn Market Square,** 318 W. Durango (© **800/HOLIDAY** or 210/225-3211), and **Courtyard by Marriott,** 600 S. Santa Rosa (© **800/648-4462** or 210/229-9449).

Emily Morgan Hotel   Centrally located right next to the Alamo, this hotel is set in a beautiful 1926 Gothic Revival skyscraper that was thoroughly renovated in 2002. Rooms are modern, bright, and immaculate. Corner rooms are called plaza suites and come with a separate sitting area, a minifridge, a CD player, a good view overlooking the Alamo, and an oversize Jacuzzi. All rooms offer such luxe amenities as Aveda toiletries, feather-topped beds, and bathrobes; many of the standard rooms also have Jacuzzis, and some offer views of the Alamo.

705 E. Houston St., San Antonio, TX 78205. © 800/824-6674 or 210/225-5100. Fax 210/225-7227. www.emilymorgan hotel.com. 177 units. $209–$239 standard; $309 executive room; $409 plaza suite. AE, DC, DISC, MC, V. Valet parking $18. **Amenities:** Restaurant; pool; fitness center. *In room:* Fridge (plaza suites only).

The Fairmount   If you're looking for a small hotel with attentive service, this Victorian-era, downtown hotel is your place. Rooms are decorated in a predominantly European style, with rich wood furniture, lots of textured fabrics, antiques, and some great detail work. Many rooms have balconies. The bathrooms are large and come with lots of amenities. The downtown location is excellent.

401 S. Alamo St., San Antonio, TX 78205. © 877/365-0500 or 210/224-8800. Fax 210/475-0082. www.thefairmount hotel-sanantonio.com. 37 units. $159–$179 double; $189–$229 suite. AE, DISC, MC, V. Valet parking $18. **Amenities:** Restaurant; pool; fitness center.

Havana Riverwalk Inn   This small inn, built in 1914 in a Mediterranean Revival style, avoids all the standard hotel room appointments and is the hippest place to stay on the river. Lots of dark wood trim and window shutters in the guest rooms provide soft lighting, and soften the harsh Texas sunlight coming through the windows. Worn wood floors, antique furnishings, and objects usually referred to as "conversation pieces" make staying here fun, and touches such as fresh flowers and free bottled water add to the charm. But all this character and charm come at a price—the standard rooms don't have closets.

1015 Navarro, San Antonio, TX 78205. (C) **888/224-2008** or 210/222-2008. Fax 210/222-2717. www.havanariverwalk inn.com. 27 units. $159–$209 double; $199–$209 deluxe; $249–$599 suite. AE, DC, DISC, MC, V. Self-parking $10. **Amenities:** Restaurant.

Hyatt Regency Hill Country Resort *(Kids)*   Okay, perhaps the hotel does look as if it had been designed by Albert Speer in Texas vernacular. Still, there's no place in San Antonio with such lovely grounds: 200 acres of rolling ranchland complete with a stream for tubing. There are lots of facilities for being active (and quite a few for being lazy, too—the spa is first-rate). Rooms are cheerfully decorated in a modern country style. *A plus:* SeaWorld's just a hop, skip, and a jump away.

9800 Hyatt Resort Dr., San Antonio, TX 78251. (C) **210/223-1234** or 210/647-1234. Fax 210/681-9681. www.hyatt. com. 500 units. $285–$400 double; $450 and up suite. Special family packages available. AE, DC, DISC, MC, V. Valet parking $10; free self-parking. **Amenities:** 4 restaurants; pool; golf course; 3 tennis courts; health club; spa. *In room:* Fridge.

Menger Hotel   Its location, between the Alamo and the Rivercenter Mall, a block from the River Walk, is perfect. Its history—it was built in 1859—is fascinating. A self-guided tour pamphlet will take you to halls, ballrooms, and gardens through which Ulysses S. Grant, Sarah Bernhardt, and Oscar Wilde have walked. Its guest rooms are charming, ranging in decor from ornate 19th-century style to modern but with character. The rooms that are not part of the original building go for significantly less. Some rooms offer kitchenettes and balconies. The Menger Bar is one of San Antonio's great historic taverns.

204 Alamo Plaza, San Antonio, TX 78205. (C) **800/345-9285** or 210/223-4361. Fax 210/228-0022. www.mengerhotel. com. 316 units. $195 double; $345–$439 suite. AE, DC, DISC, MC, V. Valet parking $19. **Amenities:** Restaurant; pool; spa. *In room:* Kitchenettes (some rooms only).

Omni La Mansión del Rio *(Best)*   This place is pure San Antonio and is the favorite choice of visiting Texans. The building, built in 1852, was once a seminary and has been meticulously renovated over the years. Rooms have more character than at the Hyatt, and many feature Mexican tile floors, beamed ceilings, and wrought-iron balconies. Unlike the city's other big hotels, this one is not a skyscraper (six floors). Rooms with a river view are level with the tall cypress trees, and the hotel's location on a central, yet relatively quiet, section of the River Walk is perfect. Guests can use the health club and spa at the hotel's sister property, the Watermark Hotel.

112 College St., San Antonio, TX 78205. (C) **888/444-6664** or 210/518-1000. Fax 210/226-0389. www.lamansion. com. 337 units. $249–$349 double; $575 and up suite. AE, DC, DISC, MC, V. Children under 18 stay free in parent's room. Valet parking $21. Small pets accepted. **Amenities:** Restaurant; pool.

WHERE TO DINE

Boudro's NEW AMERICAN   Locals tend to look down their noses on River Walk restaurants, but Boudro's has always won their respect. And for good reason. The kitchen uses fresh local ingredients—Gulf Coast seafood, Texas beef, Hill Country produce—and the preparations and presentations do them justice. The setting is also out of the ordinary: If you've entered from the river, be sure to turn around and look inside the turn-of-the-20th-century limestone building to see its hardwood floors and handmade mesquite bar.

421 E. Commerce St./River Walk. © 210/224-8484. www.boudros.com. Reservations strongly recommended. Main courses $15–$32. AE, DC, DISC, MC, V. Sun–Thurs 11am–11pm; Fri–Sat 11am–midnight.

La Calesa *Value* REGIONAL MEXICAN   Tucked away in a small house just off Broadway—look for Earl Abel's large sign across the street—this family-run restaurant features several dishes from the southern Yucatán, as well as those from the northern areas that influenced the Tex-Mex style. The difference is mainly in the sauces, and they're done to perfection. The mole, for example, strikes a fine balance between its rich chocolate base and the picante spices. The *conchinita pibil*, a classic pork dish, has a marvelous texture and taste. A separate margarita menu adds even more zest.

2103 E. Hildebrand St. (just off Broadway). © 210/822-4475. www.lacalesa.com. Reservations not accepted. Main courses $7–$18. AE, DC, DISC, MC, V. Mon–Thurs 11am–9:30pm; Fri 11am–10:30pm; Sat 11:30am–10:30pm; Sun 11:30am–8pm.

Liberty Bar AMERICAN/SOUTHERN/MEXICAN   You'd be hard-pressed to guess from the outside that this ramshackle former brothel (opened in 1890) near the Highway 281 underpass hosts one of the hippest haunts in San Antonio. But as every foodie in town can tell you, it's bright and inviting inside, and you'll find everything here from comfort food (pot roast, say, or a ham-and-Swiss sandwich) to regional Mexican cuisine (the *chiles rellenos en nogada* are super).

328 E. Josephine St. © 210/227-1187. www.liberty-bar.com. Reservations accepted. Main courses $8–$19. AE, MC, V. Sun–Thurs 11:30am–10:30pm; Fri–Sat 11:30am–midnight; Sun brunch 10:30am–2pm. Bar open until midnight Sun–Thurs, until 2am Fri–Sat.

Mi Tierra MEXICAN   This Market Square restaurant has been open since 1946. Much expanded and gussied up since then, it still draws a faithful clientele of Latino families and businesspeople along with busloads of tourists. Where else can you come at 2am and order anything from chorizo and eggs to an 8-ounce charbroiled rib-eye— and be serenaded by mariachis? Mi Tierra is justly renowned for its *panadería* (bakery) and its wide variety of margaritas.

218 Produce Row. © 210/225-1262. www.mitierracafe.com. Reservations accepted for large groups only. Main courses $6.95–$15. AE, MC, V. Open 24 hr.

Rosario's MEXICAN   Modern and colorful with lots of neon, glass blocks, and a concrete/metal bar that mixes killer margaritas, this restaurant draws a crowd that is intent on having a good time. Main courses such as the pork *carnitas* in cascabel pepper sauce or the excellent mole enchiladas are favorites. The bargain weekday lunch specials draw a sizable local crowd. Evenings, especially on weekends, the place can be a little noisy.

910 S. Alamo. © 210/223-1806. Reservations not accepted. Main courses $8–$16. AE, DC, DISC, MC, V. Mon 11am–3pm; Tues–Thurs 11am–10pm; Fri–Sat 11am–11pm.

Schilo's *Kids* GERMAN/DELI   You can't leave town without stopping at this San Antonio institution, if only for a hearty bowl of split-pea soup or a piece of the famous cherry cheesecake. The large, open room with its worn wooden booths is evidence of the city's German past. An oompah band plays on Saturday from 5 to 8pm. It's a great place to come for refueling when you're sightseeing near Alamo Plaza; for under $5, a good Reuben sandwich or a bratwurst plate should keep you going for the rest of the day.

424 E. Commerce St. ℂ **210/223-6692.** Reservations not accepted. Sandwiches $4–$7; hot or cold plates $6–$9; main dishes (served after 5pm) $9–$11. AE, DC, DISC, MC, V. Mon–Sat 7am–8:30pm.

Silo *(Best)* NEW AMERICAN   Silo is regularly top-listed by San Antonio foodies, and deservedly so. More than the other chic restaurants in town, it has concentrated on food rather than on attitude, consistently presenting a small but well-balanced menu using fresh ingredients in fresh combinations. Starters such as the spicy Angus beef tenderloin lettuce wrap with chile and mint or a salad of roasted figs, spicy pecans, and goat cheese get the mix of textures and tastes just right, as do entrees such as seared yellowfin tuna au poivre with soba noodle salad or chipotle marinated pork tenderloin on white cheddar andouille grits.

1133 Austin Hwy. ℂ **210/824-8686.** www.siloelevatedcuisine.com. Reservations recommended. Main courses $17–$35. AE, DC, DISC, MC, V. Daily 11am–2:30pm; Sun–Thurs 5:30–10pm; Fri–Sat 5:30–11pm.

SAN ANTONIO AFTER DARK

A Latin flavor lends spice to some of the best local nightlife in San Antonio—this is America's capital for Tejano music, a unique blend of German polka and northern Mexico ranchero sounds, with a dose of pop for good measure. **Southtown,** with its many Hispanic-oriented shops and galleries, celebrates its art scene with the monthly First Friday, a kind of extended block party.

For the most complete listings of what's happening, pick up a free copy of the weekly alternative newspaper, the *Current,* or the Friday "Weekender" section of the *San Antonio Express-News.* You can also call the **San Antonio Arts Hotline** (ℂ **210/ 222-ARTS**).

If you're visiting San Antonio in the summer, try seeing something at the **Arneson River Theatre,** 418 La Villita, on the River Walk (ℂ **210/207-8610**), which stages shows on one side of the river while the audience watches from an amphitheater on the other.

The closest San Antonio comes to having a club district is the stretch of North St. Mary's between Josephine and Magnolia—just north of downtown and south of Brackenridge Park—known as **the Strip.**

Boots, hats, and antique farm equipment hang from the ceiling of the typical Texas roadhouse known as **Floore Country Store,** 14664 Bandera Rd./Hwy. 16, Helotes, 2 miles north of Loop 1604 (ℂ **210/695-8827**), where there's always live music on weekends.

The history at the **Menger Bar** at the Menger Hotel, 204 Alamo Plaza (ℂ **210/ 223-4361**), dates from more than 100 years ago, when Theodore Roosevelt recruited men for his Rough Riders unit at this dark, wooded bar. It moved to its current location in 1956, but 90% of its historic furnishings remain intact. Just below the observation-deck level, the **Tower of the Americas Restaurant bar,** 600 HemisFair Park (ℂ **210/223-3101**), affords dazzling views of the city at night.

6 Austin

Austin, the state's capital, lies in an area of hills and lakes in the middle of Texas. It has a comfortable mix of cyberpunks and honky-tonkers, environmentalists and hedonists. With its leafy intellectual enclave and large university community, Austin is often compared to Berkeley or Seattle, but its Texas flavor belies such comparisons. The city has now passed the half-million population mark and is feeling its growing pains, but society here retains a leisurely, small-town quality.

ESSENTIALS

GETTING THERE   By Plane   Austin-Bergstrom International Airport (℗ 512/530-ABIA; www.ci.austin.tx.us/austinairport) is just off Highway 71, some 8 miles southwest of the center of town. Many hotels offer complimentary shuttle service from the airport. The taxi ride between the airport and downtown generally costs $25. **SuperShuttle** (℗ **800/258-3826;** www.supershuttle.com) charges $10 to $14. A city bus called the Airport Flyer (Rte. 100) runs every day and costs 50¢.

By Train   Amtrak (℗ **800/USA-RAIL;** www.amtrak.com) provides daily service from Fort Worth (trip time: 4 hr.), Dallas (6 hr.), and San Antonio (2 hr.) to its station at 250 N. Lamar Blvd.

By Car   Major routes into Austin are **I-35** from the southwest (San Antonio) and northeast (Dallas–Fort Worth), and **Highway 71** (Ben White Blvd.) from the southeast (Houston).

VISITOR INFORMATION   Contact the **Austin Convention and Visitors Bureau,** 201 E. Second St., Austin, TX 78701 (℗ **866/GO-AUSTIN** or 512/478-0098; www.austintexas.org), located down the street from the convention center downtown; or stop by Monday through Friday from 9am to 5pm, Saturday and Sunday from 9am to 6pm. Or try the **Austin-Bergstrom International Airport Visitors Center** (℗ **512/530-6810**), on the baggage claim level.

GETTING AROUND   There are two north-south freeways: I-35 on the east, and Mo-Pac on the west. The east-west freeways are Ben White Boulevard (Hwy. 71) in the south and Highway 183 in the north. The central city is bicycle-friendly—many streets have separate bicycle lanes.

   Capital Metro (℗ **512/474-1200;** www.capmetro.org) provides bus service throughout the Austin area. A day pass is $1. Free 'Dillo trolley buses circulate through downtown, the Capitol Complex, and the University of Texas campus; the orange 'Dillo is a good choice for seeing the sights of central Austin.

   Among the major cab companies are **Austin Cab** (℗ **512/478-2222**) and **Roy's Taxi** (℗ **512/482-0000**). The flag drops at $2.05 and it's $2.05 per additional mile.

FAST FACTS   Brackenridge Hospital, 601 E. 15th St. (℗ **512/324-7000**), has emergency-care facilities. **Walgreens** at Capitol Plaza, I-35 and Cameron Road (℗ **512/452-9452**), is open 24 hours. The tax on hotel rooms is 15%. Sales tax, added to restaurant bills as well as to other purchases, is 8.25%.

SPECIAL EVENTS & FESTIVALS   Around the third week of March, the Austin Music Awards kick off the acclaimed **South by Southwest (SXSW) Music & Media Conference** (℗ **512/467-7979;** www.sxsw.com). The event schedules dozens of concerts at a variety of venues—all in a 5-day period.

   Around June 19, Austin celebrates the **Juneteenth Freedom Festival,** a celebration of African-American emancipation featuring parades, a jazz and blues festival, gospel singing, a rap competition, and a children's rodeo and carnival.

   Mariachis and folk dancers, Tex-Mex *conjunto* and Tejano music, as well as fajitas, piñatas, and clowns, help celebrate **Mexican Independence Day** at the Fiesta Gardens on the 4 days around September 16.

WHAT TO SEE & DO

A lot of Austin life revolves around the local campus of the **University of Texas,** roughly bounded by Guadalupe; I-35; Martin Luther King, Jr., Boulevard; and 26th

Hanging Out at the Bat Bridge

In the evening hours between March and November, you're likely to see crowds of people standing on or under the Congress Avenue Bridge waiting for one of the city's star attractions to begin. At some point in the 1980s, a Mexican free-tail bat discovered that the underside of the bridge made a good resting place during daylight hours. He invited a million of his closest friends and—*voilà!*—an instant tourist attraction, as well as an easy way of keeping the local mosquito population under control. The bats time their flights according to weather and feeding conditions. Call the **Bat Hotline** (© **512/416-5700,** ext. 3636) for their projected departure time.

Street (© **512/471-3434;** www.utexas.edu). With 50,000 students, it is the largest university in the country. The special collections of the **Harry Ransom Center (HRC),** on 21st and Guadalupe streets (© **512/471-8944**), contain approximately a million rare books, 36 million manuscripts, 5 million photographs, and more than 100,000 works of art, including a Gutenberg Bible, paintings by Diego Rivera and Frida Kahlo, and the original manuscript of *Death of a Salesman.* Another great museum worth visiting is the **Blanton Museum of Art,** having opened at its new location in mid-2006, at the corner of Martin Luther King, Jr., Boulevard and Congress Avenue (© **512/471-7324;** www.blantonmuseum.org), right across the street from The Bob Bullock Texas History Museum (see below). It is one of the best university art museums in the United States, with an especially good Latin American collection. Another thing to do while on campus is to take in the sights from atop the University of Texas Tower. The only way to do so is by guided tour, which costs $3. Hours for the tour are irregular; call © **877/475-6633** to book the tour in advance.

PBS's longest-running show, *Austin City Limits,* has showcased major country-and-western talent. It's taped live August through February at KLRU-TV (© **512/475-9077;** www.pbs.org/klru/austin). Free tickets are distributed on a first-come, first-served basis, on the day of the taping.

Barton Springs Pool   The Native Americans who settled near here believed these waters had spiritual powers, and today's residents still place their faith in them. Each day approximately 32 million gallons of water from the underground Edwards Aquifer flow to the surface. Although the original limestone bottom remains, concrete was added to the banks to form uniform sides to what is now a swimming pool of about 1,000 feet by 125 feet. A large bathhouse offers changing facilities.

Zilker Park, 2201 Barton Springs Rd. © 512/476-9044. www.ci.austin.tx.us/parks/bartonsprings.htm. Admission $3 adults, $2 teens 12–17, $1 children and seniors. Free to all Nov to mid-Mar. Daily 5am–10pm except during pool maintenance (mid-Mar to Oct Mon and Thurs from 7:30pm; Nov to mid-Mar Mon 10am–5pm). Lifeguard on duty Sept–May 9am–dusk; June–Aug 9am–10pm.

The Bob Bullock Texas State History Museum (Kids   To enjoy this museum you must make allowances for Texas chauvinism. Our first impression of it had us worried. The building looks grandiose for a history museum—with lots of polished granite, a mammoth lone star of bronze in front, and a dramatic domed entrance chamber. Yet another act of self-aggrandizement of the state? No. Actually, the collection (all three floors of it) is thoughtfully put together and focuses on social history rather than the spinning of myths and the worship of heroes. Also in the museum are a 3-D IMAX

0   1/4 mi
0   0.25 km

Shoal Creek
Greenbelt

UNIVERSITY
OF TEXAS

LBJ Library
& Museum

W. 26th St.

E. Campus Dr.

Red River

San Gabriel

Nueces

Guadalupe

Speedway

San Jacinto Blvd.

Waller Creek

W. 24th St.

Harry Ransom
Center

Pearl

David St.

San Gabriel

W. 21st St.

Blanton
Museum
of Art

35

Shoal Creek

Pease
Park

Martin Luther King Jr. Blvd.

West Ave

Rio Grande

Nueces

San Antonio

Bob Bullock
Texas State
History Museum

Red River

Enfield Rd.

House
Park

W. 15th St.

W. 14th St.

Guadalupe

Lavaca

Colorado

Congress

Brazos

San Jacinto

Trinity

E. 15th St.

Waterloo
Park

W. 12th St.

W. 11th St.

State
Capitol

E. 12th St.

E. 11th St.

W. Lynn St.

Lamar Blvd.

Duncan
Park

West Ave

Rio Grande

Nueces

San Antonio

Guadalupe

Lavaca

Colorado

Congress

Brazos

San Jacinto

Trinity

Neches

Red River

W. 6th St.

W. 5th St.

Shoal Creek
Greenbelt

W. 6th St.

W. 5th St.

E. 6th St.

E. 5th St.

W. 1st St.

W. 1st St.

Cesar Chavez

Zilker Park

Barton Creek

Colorado River

Auditorium Shores

Butler
Park

E. Riverside Dr.

Town
Lake

35

Barton Springs Rd.

S. Lamar Blvd.

S. 1st St.

S. Congress Ave.

E. Riverside Dr.

Newning

TEXAS

Austin ★

ACCOMMODATIONS ■
Austin Folk House **1**
Austin Motel **11**
Driskill Hotel **5**
Four Seasons Austin **8**
Hyatt Regency Austin on Town Lake **9**
La Quinta Inn—Capitol **4**
Mansion at Judges' Hill **2**

DINING ◆
Castle Hill Cafe **7**
Chez Nous **6**
Curra's Grill **12**
Jeffrey's **3**
Shady Grove **10**

theater and a special effects theater called the Texas Spirit Theater, which is more along the lines suggested by the building's architecture.

1800 N. Congress Ave. ℂ 512/936-4649. www.thestoryoftexas.com. Admission to exhibits: $5.50 adults, $4.50 seniors, free for ages 18 and under. IMAX: $7 adults, $6 seniors, $5 youths 18 and under. Texas Spirit Theater: $5 adults, $4 seniors, $3.50 youths 18 and under. Combination ticket to all 3 attractions $14 adults, $11 seniors, $6.50 youths 18 and under. Mon–Sat 9am–6pm; Sun noon–6pm. Check website for IMAX showtimes.

Lady Bird Johnson Wildflower Center   Founded by Lady Bird Johnson in 1982, the center is dedicated to the study and preservation of native plants. The main attractions are naturally the display gardens—including one designed to attract butterflies—and the wildflower-filled meadow, but the native stone architecture of the visitor center and observation tower is attention grabbing, too.

4801 La Crosse Ave. ℂ 512/292-4100. www.wildflower.org. Admission $7 adults, $6 seniors 60 and older and students, $3 children 5–12. Tues–Sat 9am–5:30pm; Sun noon–5:30pm. Take Loop 1 (Mo-Pac) south to Slaughter Lane; drive ⅔ mile to La Crosse Ave.

LBJ Library and Museum *Value*   Set on a hilltop commanding an impressive campus view, the LBJ Library contains some 45 million documents relating to the colorful 36th president, along with gifts, memorabilia, and other historical objects. Johnson's large cartoon collection (even with him as the target) is one of the museum's most interesting rotating exhibits. Adults and kids alike are riveted by an animatronic version of LBJ, which looks eerily alive from afar.

University of Texas, 2313 Red River. ℂ 512/721-0200. www.lbjlib.utexas.edu. Free admission. Daily 9am–5pm.

State Capitol *Best*   Constructed of pink granite in the usual Renaissance Revival style, this is the largest state capitol building in the country. It has an impressive dome that, though smaller than the U.S. Capitol's dome, is still a few feet taller. A striking underground annex, which connects the capitol and four other state buildings by tunnels, was added in the mid-1990s. Take the tour, which is engaging for some of the oddities and tidbits you learn.

11th and Congress sts. ℂ 512/463-0063. www.capitol.state.tx.us. Free admission. Mon–Fri 7am–10pm; Sat–Sun 9am–8pm. Free 45-min. guided tours every 15 min. on weekdays, every 30 min. on weekends.

SHOPPING

Specialty shops and art galleries are slowly filtering back to the renovated 19th-century buildings along **Sixth Street** and **Congress Avenue.** Little enclaves offering more intimate retail experiences can be found in the **West End** on Sixth Street west of Lamar and, nearby, north of 12th Street and West Lynn. Below Town Lake, **South Congress Avenue,** from Riverside south to Annie Street, has long been a fun place to seek vintage clothing and antiques. Bargain hunters head out to the two factory-outlet malls in **San Marcos** (26 miles south of Austin, Exit 200 on I-35) and **New Braunfels** (16 miles south of San Marcos).

WHERE TO STAY

Favorite affordable chain hotel deals in town include **La Quinta Inn—Capitol,** 300 E. 11th St. (ℂ **800/NU-ROOMS** or 512/476-1166), practically on the grounds of the state capitol.

Austin Folk House *Value*   Located in the West Campus part of town, this B&B offers attractive, comfortable, slightly offbeat rooms for a good price. As you might imagine, there are folk art pieces scattered throughout the house. This adds a light, playful feel to the place. Room size varies, but none of them are cramped; all have plush mattresses, bathrobes, and VCRs. The owner-manager is helpful and obliging. She and her husband also run a B&B, the **Star of Texas Inn** (http://staroftexasinn.com), which is along more normal lines and is located a block from this one.

506 W. 22nd St., Austin, TX 78705. ℂ 866/472-6700 or 512/472-6700. www.austinfolkhouse.com. 9 units. $95–$185 double. Rates include full breakfast. AE, DISC, MC, V. Free parking. **Amenities:** Smoking not permitted.

Austin Motel *(Value)*   A convenient (but not quiet) location in the hip area just south of downtown, along with reasonable rates, are the reasons to stay at this motel, which has been run by the same family for more than 5 decades. Others are a classic kidney-shaped pool, a coin-op laundromat, free coffee in the lobby (donuts too, on Sun), and El Sol y La Luna, a good Mexican restaurant that's popular on weekend mornings. Ask to see the rooms—all are different and some are in better shape than others; some suites have Jacuzzis.

1220 S. Congress Ave., Austin, TX 78704. ℂ/fax 512/441-1157. www.austinmotel.com. 41 units. $60–$90 double; $128–$137 suite. AE, DC, DISC, MC, V. Free parking. Pets accepted for a $15 fee. **Amenities:** Restaurant; pool. *In room:* Fridge (suites), microwave (some suites).

Driskill Hotel   Austin's original grand hotel, the Driskill is a national historic landmark (Lady Bird and Lyndon Johnson had their first date in the hotel dining room) that has been renovated with a loving touch and is easily the most eye-catching hotel in town. It offers guests a choice between rooms in the original 1886 building (labeled "historic") or in the 1928 addition ("traditional"); the latter are the better deal, especially those on the 12th floor, which have higher ceilings. Rooms are well lit, distinctively decorated, and furnished with period pieces. Bathrooms in both buildings are attractive and come with several amenities, including plush bathrobes. This hotel is on Austin's lively Sixth Street, and some of the rooms with balconies can be noisy.

604 Brazos St., Austin, TX 78701. ℂ 800/252-9367 or 512/474-5911. Fax 512/474-2214. www.driskillhotel.com. 188 units. $300–$320 double; $320–$340 deluxe; $465 and up suite. AE, DC, DISC, MC, V. Valet parking $18. Pets accepted for $50 fee. **Amenities:** 2 restaurants; health club.

Four Seasons Austin *(Best)*   Polished sandstone floors, a cowhide sofa, horn lamps, and an elk head hanging over the fireplace in the lobby remind you you're in Texas, but airy, well-equipped rooms look European country elegant, with amenities such as CD players, terry bathrobes, and DVD players on request. Some rooms offer balconies. You can gaze out at the lake over cocktails in the Lobby Lounge, which serves hors d'oeuvres from midday until the wee hours. Some of the best bat-watching in the city draws diners to vie for seating at dusk. Work off your meals at one of the best health clubs in town.

98 San Jacinto Blvd., Austin, TX 78701. ℂ 800/332-3442 or 512/478-4500. Fax 512/478-3117. www.fourseasons.com/austin. 291 units. $360–$455 double; $515 and up suite. AE, DC, DISC, MC, V. Valet parking $20; self-parking $16. Small pets accepted. **Amenities:** Restaurant; pool; health club; spa.

Hyatt Regency Austin on Town Lake *(Kids)*   You'll enjoy lake views with city backdrops at this choice on Town Lake's south shore, but it's the outdoor recreation that makes the hotel tick. Bat tours and other Town Lake excursions depart from the hotel's dock, which also rents canoes; guests can rent mountain bikes for the hike-and-bike trail, right outside the door. Guest rooms are large and modern in decoration, with medium-size bathrooms; the most sought-after rooms are on the upper floors facing the lake.

208 Barton Springs Rd., Austin, TX 78704. © **800/233-1234** or 512/477-1234. Fax 512/480-2069. www.hyatt.com. 447 units. $180–$230 double; $345 and up suite. AE, DC, DISC, MC, V. Valet parking $12; self-parking $8. Pets accepted for a $25 fee. **Amenities:** Restaurant; pool; health club.

Mansion at Judges' Hill All the rooms in this boutique hotel are furnished and decorated with much more character than you'll find at any of the local chain hotels. This is as true of the modern rooms in the north building as it is for the ones in the mansion. The rooms that are the most fun are the second-story signature rooms, which all open onto a sweeping upstairs porch and have tall ceilings and large bathrooms with special amenities (including L'Occitane toiletries and bathrobes). Beds have particularly good mattresses and linens. The West Campus location is convenient to the university and to downtown.

1900 Rio Grande., Austin, TX 78705. © **800/311-1619** or 512/495-1800. Fax 512/495-1869. www.judgeshill.com. 48 units. $139–$199 standard in north wing; $169 3rd-floor standard in mansion; $299 signature rooms in mansion. Children under 12 stay free in parent's room. AE, DC, DISC, MC, V. Free covered parking. Pets allowed with $150 deposit. **Amenities:** Restaurant; smoking not permitted.

WHERE TO DINE

Castle Hill Cafe ECLECTIC A smart, attractive restaurant that eschews showiness and focuses on the food, Castle Hill's dining room is comfortable and understated. The menus change every few weeks, but there's almost always something from Mexico, some kind of pasta dish, something Italian inspired, and a few tantalizing crossover dishes. The lunch menu is a bargain. After your meal, stroll over to the "Treaty Oak," which is cater-cornered to the restaurant. It was under this ancient oak tree that Stephen F. Austin signed the original land grant agreement with the Mexicans, or so it is said.

1101 W. 5th St. © **512/476-0728.** www.castlehillcafe.com. Reservations for parties of 5 or more. Main courses $15–$24; lunch $7–$10. AE, DISC, MC, V. Mon–Fri 11am–2:30 and 6–10pm; Sat 6–10pm.

Chez Nous FRENCH Just around the corner from the Sixth Street action is this intimate little restaurant with lace curtains, fresh flowers in anisette bottles, and Folies Bergère posters. The owners have maintained consistency and quality throughout the years. The most popular choice here is the prix-fixe dinner with a choice of soup, salad, or pâté; one of three designated entrees; and crème caramel, chocolate mousse, or brie for dessert. Everything from the pâtés to the profiteroles is made on the premises.

510 Neches St. © **512/473-2413.** Reservations accepted only for 6 or more. Main courses $16–$27; prix fixe $24. AE, DC, MC, V. Tues–Fri 11:45am–2pm and 6–10:30pm; Sat–Sun 6–10:30pm.

Curra's Grill *Value* INTERIOR MEXICAN This crowded restaurant serves up the best regional Mexican food in south Austin. A couple of breakfast tacos and a cup of special Mexican dark roast coffee are a great way to jump-start your day. The chiles rellenos topped with cream pecan sauce make a super dinner entree, but if you would like something lighter, try one of the fish dishes. The tamales are excellent here, and the margaritas are tops.

614 E. Oltorf. © **512/444-0012.** www.lascurras.com. Reservations not accepted. Main courses $7–$15. AE, DC, DISC, MC, V. Sun–Thurs 7am–10pm; Fri–Sat 7am–11pm.

Fonda San Miguel MEXICAN This restaurant's beautifully lit dining room, with its carved wooden doors, bold paintings, and soft light, is a gorgeous backdrop to the food. Chef Miguel Ravago easily handles several styles of regional Mexican cooking. For appetizers you might try the Veracruz-style seviche. For an entree the *conchinita* *pibil,* a Yucatán dish of pork baked in banana leaves, is very good. The restaurant is famous for its mammoth Sunday brunches.

2330 W. North Loop. © 512/459-4121. www.fondasanmiguel.com. Reservations recommended. Main courses $15–$40. AE, DC, DISC, MC, V. Mon–Thurs 5–9:30pm; Fri–Sat 5–10:30pm. Sun brunch 11am–2pm.

Jeffrey's *(Best)* NEW AMERICAN   In a setting of soft tones and soft lighting, executive chef David Garrido creates dishes known for their creative combinations of flavors and textures. Among the appetizers are his signature crisp oysters and crunchy yucca chips topped with habanero honey aioli—a must if you come here. The main courses are along the same vein, combining disparate ingredients in the search for original tastes.

1204 W. Lynn. © 512/477-5584. www.jeffreysofaustin.com. Reservations recommended. Main courses $26–$40. AE, DC, DISC, MC, V. Mon–Thurs 6–10pm; Fri–Sat 5:30–10:30pm; Sun 5–9:30pm.

The Salt Lick BARBECUE   Driftwood is just a wide spot on the road outside of Austin, but it attracts barbecue aficionados from far and wide. Moist spareribs, brisket, sausage, and chicken, as well as terrific homemade pickles, make for a glorious meal. Bring a cooler and your own drinks. In warm weather, seating is outside at picnic tables under live oak trees; in winter, fireplaces blaze in a series of large, rustic rooms. The Salt Lick prides itself on its sauce, which has a sweet-and-sour tang.

18300 FM 1826, Driftwood. © 512/858-4959, or 888/SALT-LICK (mail order). Reservations not accepted. Main courses $15 for the all-you-can-eat "family style"; $10 for barbecue plates. No credit cards. Daily 11am–10pm.

Shady Grove *(Kids)* TEX-AMERICAN   When you crave something spicy, Shady Grove's Airstream chili might be just the thing. Try a Frito pie (chili in a corn-chip bowl), a burger, or the tortilla-fried queso catfish. Large salads—among them noodles with Asian vegetables—or the hippie sandwich (grilled eggplant, veggies, and cheese) will satisfy less hearty appetites. The inside dining area, with its Texas kitsch roadhouse decor and cushy booths, is plenty comfortable, but most people head for the large, tree-shaded patio when the weather permits.

1624 Barton Springs Rd. © 512/474-9991. www.theshadygrove.com. Reservations not accepted. Main courses $7–$12. AE, DC, DISC, MC, V. Sun–Thurs 11am–10:30pm; Fri–Sat 11am–11pm.

AUSTIN AFTER DARK

Austin enjoys lots of live venues with low cover charges. The best sources for what's happening around town are the *Austin Chronicle* and *XLent,* the entertainment supplement of the *Austin-American Statesman;* both are free and available in hundreds of outlets every Thursday. If all you want to do is explore the nightlife, you should try two places: the well-known **Sixth Street,** which attracts patrons of all ages to bars and clubs with all kinds of music; and, across Congress and just a couple of blocks south, the **Warehouse District,** where you'll find large numbers of young professionals and an eclectic collection of bars.

The **Ticketmaster** number for the University of Texas, the locus for most of the city's performing-arts events, is © 512/477-6060. **The Box Office** (© 512/454-8497; www.austix.com) handles phone charges for many of the smaller theaters in Austin as well as half-price ticket sales (© 512/454-4253).

The **Continental Club,** 1315 S. Congress Ave. (© 512/441-2444; www.continentalclub.com), is a not-to-be-missed Austin classic. Although Willie Nelson and crossover C&W bands such as the Austin Lounge Lizards have been known to turn up at **Antone's,** 213 W. Fifth St. (© 512/474-5314; www.antones.net), the club owner's name has always been synonymous with the blues. The **Broken Spoke,** 3201 S. Lamar

Blvd. (© **512/442-6189;** www.brokenspokeaustintx.com), is the genuine item, a Western honky-tonk with a wood-plank floor and a cowboy-hatted, two-steppin' crowd.

A terrific sound system and a casual country atmosphere make **The Backyard,** on Highway 71 West at R.R. 620, Bee Cave (© **512/263-4146,** or 512/469-SHOW for tickets; www.thebackyard.net), a hot venue, attracting acts that range from John Fogerty to Heart to Norah Jones. Come early and enjoy some barbecue. Another Austin classic, **La Zona Rosa,** 612 W. Fourth St. (© **512/263-4146;** www.lazonarosa. com), mixes a Tex-Mex menu with high-quality music, from Latino and alternative country to punk rock.

Since 1866, when councilman August Scholz first opened his tavern near the state capitol, every Texas governor has visited Texas's oldest operating *biergarten,* **Scholz Garten,** 1607 San Jacinto Blvd. (© **512/474-1958**). Chow down on some barbecue while a state-of-the-art sound system cranks out the polka tunes; patio tables as well as a few strategically placed TV sets help Longhorn fans cheer on their team.

7 The Hill Country

The interstate highway that runs between San Antonio and Austin parallels a geological feature called the Balcones Escarpment, a fault zone that divides the coastal plains from the Hill Country and was produced when the Edwards Plateau was pushed up about 1,500 feet above the plains. This plateau is a thick shelf of limestone that extends for hundreds of miles north and west of San Antonio and Austin, but the part closest to these cities is called the Hill Country. The extra elevation makes the climate a little milder, and the water pouring through the limestone creates an abundance of natural springs (and lots of caverns and caves, too).

These features attracted many German and Czech settlers in the mid–19th century, who were fleeing the social upheavals in Europe. They established small towns that now dot the area and add a little contrast to the prevailing cowboy culture. The mild climate, rolling hills, and abundant springs continue to attract visitors to this part of the state, with summer camps, guest ranches, and resorts serving a public that comes here to enjoy the outdoors.

NEW BRAUNFELS & GRUENE

New Braunfels, a town of 40,000, and the attached village of Gruene (pronounced *Green*) are off I-35 between Austin and San Antonio. They mostly attract visitors seeking fun in the water. This can be done in a number of ways: First, there is the highly popular **Schlitterbahn** waterpark, 305 W. Austin St. (© **830/625-2351;** www.schlitterbahn.com). It is Texas's largest waterpark, which the *Travel Channel* recently rated tops in the country.

A much mellower option is what the locals call "tubing," floating down the Guadalupe River in an inner tube. This is a popular and enjoyable activity. There are a number of companies that will rent you a tube, haul you to a drop-off point, and then pick you up downstream. The quality of the experience depends on the amount of water that is being released from the dam upstream. Two organizers of this activity are **Rockin "R" River Rides** (© **800/553-5628**) and **Gruene River Raft Company** (© **830/625-2800**), both on Gruene Road just south of the bridge. An even simpler option, if you're just passing through, is to go for a swim at the city's **Landa Park** (© **830/608-2160**), which has the second-largest spring-fed pool in Texas.

Other activities include shopping for antiques in the New Braunfels historic downtown or taking in some country music at the landmark Gruene Hall (© **830/606-1281**; www.gruenehall.com), the state's oldest dance hall.

CASTROVILLE

West of San Antonio, on U.S. 90, is the quaint town of **Castroville** (www.castroville.com), originally settled by the Alsatians. It has conserved much of its early small-town feel. If you want to find everything open, come on Thursday, Friday, or Saturday. Almost 100 of the original settlers' uneven slope-roofed houses remain in Castroville. The oldest standing structure, the **First St. Louis Catholic Church,** went up in 1846 on the corner of Angelo and Moy. A gristmill and wood-and-stone dam are among the interesting artifacts at the **Landmark Inn State Historical Park,** 402 Florence St. (© **830/931-2133**).

Get a delicious taste of the past at **Haby's Alsatian Bakery,** 207 U.S. 90 East (© **830/931-2118**), which offers apple fritters, strudels, breads, and coffeecakes. Among the specialties of the **Alsatian Restaurant,** 403 Angelo St. (© **830/931-3260**), set in an atmospheric 19th-century house, is the delicious boneless Strasbourg chicken seasoned with curry.

BANDERA

North of Castroville, on Highway 16, you'll find the town of Bandera. Here, you can get some of the feel of the Old West. Pick up a self-guided tour brochure and information about roping and rodeos at the **Bandera County Convention and Visitors Bureau,** 1808 Hwy. 16 South (© **800/364-3833** or 830/796-3045; www.banderacowboycapital.com). Most people take advantage of the town's living traditions by strolling along Main Street, where craftspeople work in the careful, hand-hewn styles of yesteryear.

You and your horse can canter through the **Hill Country State Natural Area,** 10 miles southwest of Bandera (© **830/796-4413**), the largest state park in Texas allowing horseback riding. The nearest outfitter is the helpful and reliable **Running-R Ranch,** Route 1 (© **830/796-3984**; www.rrranch.com).

If you want to stay overnight at a ranch, try the affordable **Dixie Dude Ranch** (© **800/375-Y'ALL** or 830/796-4481; www.dixieduderanch.com), where you're likely to see white-tailed deer or wild turkeys as you trot on horseback through a 725-acre spread. Tubing on the Medina River and swimming in an Olympic-size pool are among the many things you might do during the day at the moderately priced **Mayan Ranch** (© **830/796-3312** or 830/460-3036; www.mayanranch.com). Rates at both ranches (about $800 per adult per week) include three home-cooked meals, two trail rides, and other activities.

Main Street's **O.S.T.** (© **830/796-3836**) serves down-home Texas and Tex-Mex fare. For a more upscale setting, but similarly down-home cooking, head to **Billy Gene's,** 1105 Main St. (© **830/460-3200**). **Arkey Blue & The Silver Dollar Bar** (© **830/796-8826**) is a genuine spit-and-sawdust cowboy honky-tonk on Main Street.

LYNDON B. JOHNSON COUNTRY

Welcome to Johnson territory, where the forebears of the 36th president settled almost 150 years ago. Try to make a day out of a visit to LBJ's boyhood home and the sprawling ranch that became known as the Texas White House.

Take U.S. 290 west of Austin. Before arriving at Johnson City you'll see a sign for Pedernales State Park on Ranch Road 3232. This is a beautiful state park, with lots of limestone ledges and the Pedernales River flowing through it. The road that leads to the park continues on to Johnson City by a scenic back route. **Johnson City** is a pleasant agricultural town named for founder James Polk Johnson, LBJ's first cousin once removed. The **Boyhood Home**—the house on Elm Street where Lyndon was raised after age 5—is the centerpiece of this unit of the National Historic Park. To get to the visitor center, take F Street to Lady Bird Lane and you'll see the signs.

The **Lyndon B. Johnson State and National Historical Parks at LBJ Ranch** (© **830/868-7128** or 830/644-2252; www.tpwd.state.tx.us) is 14 miles west of Johnson City. Tour buses depart regularly from the visitor center to the still-operating Johnson Ranch. A reconstructed version of the former president's modest birthplace lies close to his final resting place, shared with five generations of Johnsons. On the side of the river sits the **Sauer-Beckmann Living History Farm,** which gives visitors a look at typical Texas-German farm life at the turn of the 20th century. Farm animals roam freely or in large pens, while family members go about their chores. Nearby are nature trails, a swimming pool (open only in summer), and lots of picnic spots. Admission is $3 per person for bus tours; all other areas are free.

FREDERICKSBURG

Farther west on U.S. 290 lie the towns of Stonewall and Fredericksburg. This area produces sweet, delicious peaches and, during the season from May to July, you'll see lots of roadside stands set up by different orchards. Try to stop and get a taste of their crop. Fredericksburg offers good shopping, lots of historic sites, and some of the most unusual accommodations around, all in a pretty rural setting. Many homes were built in the Hill Country version of the German *fachwerk* design, made out of limestone with diagonal wood supports. Fredericksburg became and remains the seat of Gillespie County. The **Visitor Information Center** is on 302 E. Austin, Fredericksburg, TX 78624 (© **888/997-3600** or 830/997-6523).

More than 100 specialty shops, many of them in mid-19th-century houses, feature work by Hill Country artisans. The family-run **Fredericksburg Winery,** 247 W. Main St. (© **830/990-8747;** www.fbgwinery.com), sells its own hand-bottled, hand-corked, and hand-labeled wines. Becoming increasingly well known via its mail-order business is the **Fredericksburg Herb Farm,** 402 Whitney St. (© **800/259-HERB** or 830/997-8615; www.fredericksburgherbfarm.com). There's an outlet on Main Street, but a short trip south of town will take you to the flower beds that produce salad dressings, teas, fragrances, and air fresheners.

Lots of well-known performers turn up in the dance hall of **Luckenbach** (11 miles southeast on R.R. 1376), immortalized in a song by Waylon Jennings and Willie Nelson. It's a great place to hang out on a weekend afternoon, when someone's almost always strumming the guitar.

Fredericksburg is known for its *gastehauses* (guest cottages). Many historic homes have been converted into romantic havens replete with robes, fireplaces, and even spas. To get a booklet detailing some of the most interesting *gastehauses,* contact **Gastehaus Schmidt,** 231 W. Main St. (© **830/997-5612;** www.ktc.com/GSchmidt).

The **Altdorf Biergarten,** 301 W. Main St. (© **830/997-7865**), and **Friedhelm's Bavarian Inn,** 905 W. Main St. (© **830/997-6300**), both feature hearty German schnitzels, dumplings, and sauerbraten, and large selections of beer.

8 The Trans-Pecos

As you drive west from Bandera or Fredericksburg, you start leaving the Hill Country behind. By small degrees, the many little roads become few, the vegetation thins out, the vistas become wide and distant, and the rounded hills are replaced by flat-topped buttes and mesas. You are now entering the "West," which in the U.S. is simultaneously a place and an idea. And being both, it charges what we view with mythic significance. Or, to put it another way, we cannot help but see the land with both our eyes and our imaginations.

Whether coming from Austin or San Antonio, by the time you get to the town of Junction, you'll be traveling on I-10. When you get to the town of Sonora, make a point of seeing the famous **Sonora Caverns (www.cavernsofsonora.com),** which are close by the highway (billboards point the way). These caverns are world famous among speleologists for their wealth of delicate crystalline formations, a few of which defy explanation. The chambers do not impress with their size, in the manner of Carlsbad Caverns (p. 804), but with their beauty. There is so much living rock that some rooms look like jewel boxes.

Farther west, after you pass the town of Ozona, you'll see on a mesa to the right the spinning propellers of giant windmills as they convert the West Texas wind into electricity for Austin and other cities to the east. Once you reach the town of Fort Stockton, you will have entered the Trans-Pecos, home to Texas's tallest mountain ranges and most spectacular views.

DAVIS MOUNTAINS

Viewed as they usually are, against the clear blue sky of the desert, these mountains, with their stark lines and sculpted palisades, offer some of the most dramatic landscapes in Texas. Things to do in this part of the world include stargazing at the University of Texas's **McDonald Observatory** (© 432/426-3640; www.mcdonald observatory.org). The observatory sits on Mount Locke at an elevation of 6,791 feet. The visitor center arranges solar viewing sessions twice a day, and star parties 3 nights a week. Also in the area is **Balmorhea** (bal-mo-*ray*) **State Park** (© 432/375-2370), which is a veritable oasis in the West Texas desert and home to the largest spring-fed pool in the state. Swimming in the crystal-clear water is like swimming in an aquarium full of fish.

If you want to do some hiking, the **Davis Mountains State Park** (© 432/426-3337) has several trails. The longest goes from the park to the historic Fort Davis and is 7.5 miles round-trip. Should you want a little mystery in your vacation, try viewing the **"Marfa mystery lights"** which can be seen most nights from the official Texas Department of Transportation viewing area, on U.S. 90, 9 miles out of Marfa in the

Bad Food Next Exit

If, for any segment of your trip, you were considering economizing on food costs by packing peanut-butter-and-jelly sandwiches and the like, this part of Texas would be the perfect place to do it. West Texas does not have a food culture. What you are served here runs the gamut from horrid to just a notch below mediocre. There are a couple of places in the town of Alpine that do a good job, but otherwise, keep to simple dishes—something grilled, for instance.

Don't Get Sidetracked

Coming from the west, you'll see signs for Big Bend Ranch State Park. Though large, too, and interesting for a couple of reasons, this park doesn't have the variety and grandeur nor the visitor infrastructure that the national park enjoys. Keep right on going.

direction of Alpine. These lights appear along the horizon. They move around and can be of different hues, but are mostly white. They have been observed since the 19th century, but have yet to be explained.

Marfa has another claim to fame. It attracted minimalist artist Donald Judd as a permanent resident for the last 2 decades of his life. He was looking for someplace beautiful and desolate, and he found it here. He also established the **Chinati Foundation** (© 432/729-4362; www.chinati.org), which displays hundreds of works, including Judd's and those of fellow minimalist Dan Flavin.

There are three small towns in the area that can provide food and lodging: Alpine, Fort Davis, and Marfa. But, if you're coming to these parts to get away from civilization (but aren't enamored of camping), your first choice for a hotel should probably be the **Indian Lodge** inside the Davis Mountains State Park. It was built during the Depression as a works project. The construction makes use of local materials and Pueblo Indian designs, with thick adobe walls covered in stucco. You should make reservations as far in advance as possible by calling © **432/426-3254.** Rates range from $80 to $115 and include the admission fee to the state park. The historic rooms are slated for extensive renovation and may be closed for a while, but the standard rooms are comfortable and attractive. Another option is the **Prude Guest Ranch** (© **800/458-6232;** www.prude-ranch.com). It's near the park, at least 6 miles outside of town. Rates run from $70 to $80 a night. Both of these places get you closer to nature than staying in town. You also have the option of camping in the Davis Mountains State Park—first-come, first-served.

BIG BEND NATIONAL PARK

Big Bend National Park (© **432/477-2251;** www.nps.gov/bibe), among the greatest of the national parks, is beautiful, dramatic, and rugged. Do not consider it for a quick day's side trip. It's too far away from everything else and too vast (more than a million acres) to enjoy in anything less than 2 days.

The park gets its name from the Rio Grande, which divides Texas from Mexico. The river flows southeast toward the Gulf above the park, but then makes a big turn northeast, forming the distinctive notch on Texas's southern border. Big Bend Park is in the hollow of the turn. The water, in its course through the mountains, has carved out rugged, spectacular canyons that can be viewed while rafting down the river.

If you come from either Alpine or Marfa, you will arrive at the western side of the park, where the rafting trips begin.

Just west of the park are three settlements (they're too small to call towns): **Lajitas** (rhymes with fajitas), an old trading post that is now an overpriced development being marketed to rich Texans; **Terlingua** (www.terlinguatx.com), a ghost town that in its heyday was one of the largest mines for cinnabar (mercury) in the world; and **Study Butte** ("Study" rhymes with Judy). There are several river outfitters here. You need to contact them ahead of time. Two that I can recommend are **Far Flung Adventures** (✆ 800/359-2627; www.farflung.com) and **Big Bend River Tours** (✆ 800/545-4240; www.bigbendrivertours.com). There is lodging to be had here, too: **Big Bend Motor Inn** (✆ 800/848-2363), and **Chisos Mining Co. Motel** (✆ 432/371-2254; www.cmcm.cc). You should avoid this area in November when around 7,000 crazy Texans gather here for the annual **Terlingua Chili Cook-off,** and lodging becomes impossible to find.

By far the most dramatic sight on the western side of the park is the Santa Elena Canyon and the Sierra Ponce. Viewed from the Santa Elena overlook, the Sierra Ponce mountain range looks like a wall rising straight up from the desert floor. It would be one continuous wall if not for a sharp and deep cleft that is the Santa Elena Canyon. A hiking path leads into the canyon above the river.

The other entrance to the park is from the north, passing through the town of Marathon (rhymes with paraffin). Here is the closest lodging north of the park. There is a grand old hotel that is beautifully kept, called the **Gage Hotel** (✆ 800/884-4243; www.gagehotel.com). It's moderately priced, and one of a kind. From this town, it's still about 60 miles to the park, but it's a straight shot from there to the park's main attraction—the rugged Chisos Mountains, where the park has lodging and camping sites at a refreshing 5,400-foot elevation. Call ✆ 432/477-2291 for reservations. There are three categories of lodging: motel, lodge, and stone cottages, with the last being the favorite. Rates run from $80 to $120 for two people. There is also a **campground** with 65 lots that go for $14 per night and should be reserved ahead of time during the park's busy season (Nov 15–Apr 15), but for the rest of the year are had on a first-come, first-served basis. To reserve a camping space call ✆ 877/444-6777 or go to **www.reserveusa.com**. In the Chisos there are several beautiful trails that vary in length from 1.5 to 15 miles.

Entrance fees to the park are $15 per vehicle. For advance information, contact the **Big Bend Travel Association** (✆ 432/477-2236; www.visitbigbend.com).

GUADALUPE MOUNTAINS NATIONAL PARK

The Guadalupe Mountain Range is the highest in Texas. Its most distinctive peak is El Capitan, with its massive white south face, the remains of ancient coral reef. **Guadalupe Mountains National Park** isn't as big as Big Bend, but it is still quite large. The National Park Service has kept development in this park to a minimum. Hence, it is a favorite place for those who enjoy primitive camping. The park is located on the New Mexico border, only about 35 miles from Carlsbad Caverns. From I-10, take Highway 54 north from the town of Van Horn. It's a pretty road, as it runs between two ranges, the Diablo and the Delaware mountains. From quite a long distance, you'll see the white cliffs of El Capitan. The road leads straight to the visitor center, which offers a limited number of camping sites but no lodging inside the park. The closest lodging is on the New Mexico side by the caverns (p. 804). Entrance fees for the park are $3 per person and are good for several days. For more information call ✆ 915/828-3251 or see **www.nps.gov/gumo**.

Colorado & Utah

These two states contain some of the most gorgeous scenery in the West, from the glorious peaks of the Rockies to the spectacular red-rock formations of Zion, Bryce Canyon, Capitol Reef, and Arches national parks. If you're interested in skiing, rafting, mountain biking, hiking, or wildlife viewing—or experiencing something with the flavor of the Old West—this area is for you.

1 Denver

Denver is the biggest city between the Great Plains and the Pacific, with about 500,000 residents in the city itself and another 1.8 million in the metro area. Today, it's a sprawling city, extending from the Rocky Mountain foothills in the west, far into the plains to the south and east. It's also a major destination for both tourists and business travelers. Denver is noted for its dozens of tree-lined boulevards; 200 city parks comprising more than 20,000 acres; and its architecture, which ranges from Victorian to sleek contemporary.

ESSENTIALS

GETTING THERE **By Plane** **Denver International Airport** (© 800/AIR-2-DEN** or 303/342-2000; www.flydenver.com) is 23 miles northeast of downtown, usually a 35- to 45-minute drive. A city bus ride can take you downtown for $8. The **SuperShuttle** (© 800/525-3177 or 303/370-1300; www.supershuttle.com) has frequent scheduled service between the airport and downtown hotels for $18 one-way; door-to-door service is also available. Expect to spend anywhere from $30 to $50 if you take a taxi downtown, and you can often share a cab and split the fare by calling the cab company ahead of time. **Yellow Cab** (© 303/777-7777) will take up to five people from DIA to most downtown hotels for a flat rate of $45. **Metro Taxi** (© 303/333-3333) is the other service in Denver. All major car-rental agencies have desks at the airport.

By Train **Amtrak** (© 800/USA-RAIL; www.amtrak.com) has two routes through Colorado.

By Car The principal highway routes into Denver are **I-25** from the north (Fort Collins and Wyoming) and south (Colorado Springs and New Mexico); **I-70** from the east (Burlington and Kansas) and west (Grand Junction and Utah); and **I-76** from the northeast (Nebraska). If you're driving into Denver from Boulder, take **U.S. 36;** from Salida and the southwest, **U.S. 285.**

VISITOR INFORMATION The **Denver Metro Convention and Visitors Bureau** (© 800/233-6837; www.denver.org) operates a visitor center on the 16th Street Mall at 1600 California St. (© 303/892-1505). It's open Monday through Friday from 9am to 5pm. In summer, it's open an hour later on weekdays, Saturday from 9am to

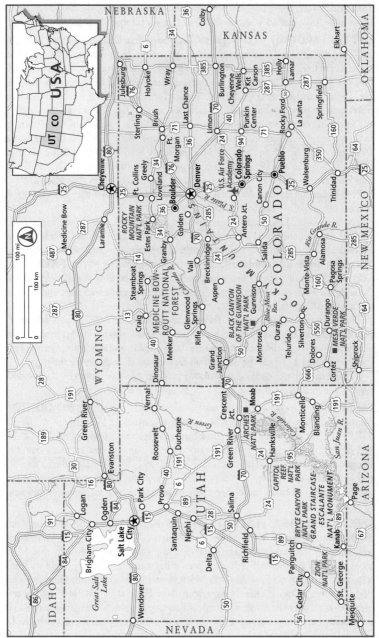

5pm, and Sunday from 11am to 3pm. Be sure to get a copy of the useful *Official Visitors Guide*. Information is also available at Denver International Airport.

GETTING AROUND The **Regional Transportation District (RTD;** © **800/366-7433** or 303/299-6000; www.rtd-denver.com) runs buses and a light-rail system; transfers are free. The local one-way fare is $1.50; seniors and passengers with disabilities pay 75¢, and children 5 and under travel free. Regional bus fares vary (for example, Denver to Boulder costs $3.75). Exact change is required for buses, and train tickets can be purchased at vending machines beneath light-rail station awnings.

Depending on the route, the departure time of the last bus or train varies from 9pm to 2am. Maps for all routes are available at any time at the RTD **Civic Center Station,** 16th Street and Broadway; and the **Market Street Station,** Market and 16th streets. RTD also provides special service to Colorado Rockies (baseball) and Denver Broncos (football) games. All RTD buses and trains are completely wheelchair accessible.

Free buses run up and down the 16th Street Mall between the Civic Center and Market Street, daily from 6am to 1am.

The light-rail **C Line** stops at Invesco Field at Mile High, the Pepsi Center, and Six Flags Elitch Gardens before chugging into Union Station at 17th and Wynkoop streets in lower downtown. The D Line continues along northeast through the east side of downtown before its terminus at 30th Avenue and Downing Street. **T-REX,** a major road and light-rail project, was completed in 2006, making for a wider highway through the south end of town and a light-rail line alongside I-25 from the Broadway exit south to County Line Road.

The main taxi companies are **Yellow Cab** (© **303/777-7777**) and **Metro Taxi** (© **303/333-3333**). Taxis can be hailed on the street, though it's preferable to telephone for a taxi or wait for one at a taxi stand outside a major hotel. On weekends, however, hailing a taxi can be difficult when the bars close down for the night.

Because cars are not necessary downtown, visitors can save money by staying downtown while in Denver, then renting a car to leave the area.

FAST FACTS Doctor and dentist referrals are available by calling © **800/DOCTORS.** Among Denver-area hospitals are **St. Joseph Hospital,** 1835 Franklin St. (© **303/837-7111**), just east of downtown; and **Children's Hospital,** 1056 E. 19th Ave. (© **303/861-8888**), which expects to move east to the Fitzsimons area by year's end 2007. **Walgreens,** at 2000 E. Colfax Ave. (© **303/331-0917**), is open 24 hours a day. State and local **sales tax** in Denver is about 7% (it varies slightly in neighboring counties and suburbs). The **hotel tax** is about 8%, bringing the total tax on accommodations to nearly 15%.

SPECIAL EVENTS & FESTIVALS The second and third weeks of January bring the **National Western Stock Show and Rodeo** (© **303/297-1166;** www.national western.com), the world's largest livestock show and indoor rodeo. In mid-March, more than 1,500 American Indians, representing some 85 tribes, perform traditional music and dances in the **Pow Wow** (© **303/934-8045;** www.denvermarchpowwow.org). Early October brings the **Great American Beer Festival** (© **303/447-0816;** www. beertown.org), where hundreds of American beers are available for sampling, and seminars are presented at what is considered the largest and most prestigious beer event in the U.S.

WHAT TO SEE & DO

Black American West Museum & Heritage Center Nearly one-third of the cowboys in the Old West were black, and this museum chronicles their little-known history,

Breathe Easier

Colorado's high elevation means there's less oxygen and lower humidity than elsewhere in the West. You can ease the transition to a higher elevation by changing altitude gradually. For instance, spend a couple of nights in Colorado Springs (elevation 6,012 ft.) before heading to the top of Pikes Peak (elevation 14,110 ft.). Help yourself adjust by getting sufficient rest, avoiding large meals, and drinking plenty of nonalcoholic fluids. Prescription drugs can help prevent altitude problems and relieve symptoms if they occur; consult your doctor.

along with those of black doctors, teachers, miners, farmers, newspaper reporters, and state legislators. The extensive collection occupies the Victorian home of Dr. Justina Ford, the first black woman licensed to practice medicine in Denver. The museum is loaded with artifacts, memorabilia, photographs, and oral histories. Allow 1 hour.

3091 California St. (at 31st St.). (C) 303/292-2566. www.blackamericanwestmuseum.com. Admission $6 adults, $5 seniors, $4 children 5–12, free for children under 5. June–Aug Tues–Sat 10am–5pm; Sept–May Wed–Fri 10am–2pm, Sat–Sun 10am–5pm. Light Rail: 30th and Downing.

Colorado State Capitol   Built to last 1,000 years, the capitol was constructed in 1886 of granite from a Colorado quarry; its dome, rising 272 feet above the ground, is sheathed in gold. The first-floor rotunda offers a splendid view upward to the underside of the dome; the west lobby offers changing exhibits; and to the west of the main lobby is the governor's reception room. The second floor has main entrances to the House, Senate, and old Supreme Court chambers, and the third floor has entrances to the public and visitor galleries for the House and Senate. The Colorado Hall of Fame is near the top of the dome. On clear days, the views from the dome are spectacular. Allow about an hour.

Lincoln St. and Colfax Ave. (C) 303/866-2604. Free admission. 1-hr. tours offered year-round (more frequently in summer), Memorial Day to Labor Day Mon–Fri 9am–3:30pm; rest of year Mon–Fri 9:15am–2:30pm. Bus: 2, 7, 8, 12, or 15.

Denver Art Museum   Founded in 1893, this seven-story museum has two distinct buildings. The main 1972 building is wrapped by a thin, 28-sided wall faced with one million sparkling tiles, while the second, a jagged, avant-garde addition, was finished in fall 2006, doubling the size of the museum. The museum's collection of Western and regional works is its cornerstone. Included are Frederic Remington's bronze *The Cheyenne,* Charles Russell's painting *In the Enemy's Country,* and 19th-century photography and historical pieces. The American Indian collection represents 150 North American tribes, spanning nearly 2,000 years. Child-oriented and family programs are scheduled regularly. Allow 2 to 3 hours.

100 W. 14th Ave. (at Civic Center Park). (C) 720/865-5000. www.denverartmuseum.org. Admission $8 adults, $6 students and seniors, free for children under 12; free for Colorado residents Sat. Tues–Sat 10am–5pm (Wed until 9pm); Sun noon–5pm. Bus: 5, 7, 8, 9, or 50.

Denver Botanic Gardens   Twenty-three acres of outstanding indoor and outdoor gardens display plants native to the desert, plains, mountain foothills, and Alpine zones; there's also a traditional Japanese garden, a garden to attract songbirds, and "Romantic Gardens" with a waterway, fragrance garden, and courtyard garden. The "Gardens of the World" contains plants from Asia, Europe, Africa, Australia, and the

Downtown Denver

CAPITOL HILL

E. 16th Ave.

E. Colfax Ave.

Civic Center Station (RTD)

Cheyenne Pl.

Cleveland Pl.

State Capitol

E. 14th Ave.

E. 13th Ave.

E. 12th Ave.

E. 11th Ave.

E. 10th Ave.

E. 9th Ave.

Pennsylvania St.

Logan St.

Grant St. **9**

Sherman St.

Lincoln St.

Broadway

Colorado History Museum

CIVIC CENTER PARK

Denver Public Library

Denver Art Museum

Acoma St.

Bannock St.

GOLDEN TRIANGLE

US Mint

Denver City & County Building

Cherokee St.

Delaware St.

Elati St.

Fox St.

Cherry Creek

Speer Blvd.

W. 14th Ave.

8

70

225

76

76

25

70

DENVER

area of detail

0   5 mi
0   5 km

N

RTD Light Rail

C line ---D line

10TH-OSAGE

NINTH ST. PARK

COLFAX-AURARIA

W. Colfax Ave.

Boulder ○   ○ Denver ★
               ○ Colorado Springs

COLORADO

ACCOMMODATIONS ■

Brown Palace Hotel **6**
The Burnsley All Suite Hotel **9**
Hotel Teatro **3**
Hyatt Regency Denver **4**
Jet Hotel **1**
Queen Anne Bed & Breakfast Inn **7**

DINING ◆

Buckhorn Exchange **8**
Duffy's Shamrock **5**
Red Square Euro Bistro **2**

Tropics. Even in the cold of winter, the dome-shaped conservatory houses more than 1,000 species of exotic plants from around the world. Allow 1 or 2 hours.

1005 York St. ℂ 720/865-3500. www.botanicgardens.org. Admission May to mid-Sept $8.50 adults, $5.50 seniors, $5 children 4–15; mid-Sept to Apr $7.50 adults, $4.50 seniors, $4 children 4–15; free for children under 4 year-round. May to mid-Sept Sat–Tues 9am–8pm, Wed–Fri 9am–5pm; mid-Sept to Apr daily 9am–5pm. Bus: 2, 6, or 10.

Denver Museum of Nature & Science *(Best* *Kids)* Exquisitely fashioned figures in numerous dioramas depict the history of life on earth on four continents. Displays explore ancient cultures, prehistoric American peoples, Colorado wildlife, and Australian ecology. The "Prehistoric Journey" traces the history of life over 3.5 billion years, with fossils, interactive exhibits, and dioramas. At "Space Odyssey," visitors experience a carefully crafted mix of exhibits about space exploration. The state-of-the-art Gates Planetarium has an advanced computer graphics and video system unlike any other in the world. The **IMAX Theater** (ℂ **303/322-7009**) presents science, nature, or technology-oriented films on a giant screen. Allow 2 to 4 hours.

City Park, 2001 Colorado Blvd. ℂ 800/925-2250 outside Metro Denver, or 303/322-7009; 303/370-8257 for the hearing impaired. www.dmns.org. Admission to museum $10 adults, $6 children 3–18 and seniors 65 and older; IMAX $8 adults, $6 children and seniors; planetarium $5 additional adults, $4 additional children and seniors. Daily 9am–5pm. Closed Dec 25. Bus: 24, 32, or 40.

Denver Zoo *(Kids)* Some 4,000 animals representing more than 700 species call the zoo home. Feeding times are posted near the entrance. "Northern Shores" allows you to see polar bears and sea lions underwater, while "Tropical Discovery" re-creates an entire tropical ecosystem under glass, complete with crocodiles, piranhas, and king cobras, plus the rare Komodo dragon. The "Primate Panorama" is a 7-acre world-class primate exhibit with 29 species, ranging from a 6-ounce marmoset to a 581-pound gorilla. The newest (and most ambitious) habitat here is "Predator Ridge," a re-created African savanna with lions, hyenas, and other African predators. Allow from 2 hours to a whole day.

City Park, 23rd Ave. and Steele St. (main entrance between Colorado Blvd. and York St.). ℂ 303/376-4800. www. denverzoo.org. Admission summer $11 adults, $9 seniors 62 and older, $7 children 3–12 (accompanied by an adult), free for children under 3; winter $9 adults, $7 seniors, $5 children 3–12 (accompanied by an adult), free for children under 3. Apr–Sept daily 9am–5pm; Oct–Mar daily 10am–4pm. Bus: 24 or 32.

Molly Brown House Museum This is a neat, old house, which from 1894 to 1932 was the residence of James and Margaret (Molly) Brown. The "unsinkable" Molly Brown became a national heroine in 1912 when the *Titanic* sank: She took charge of a group of immigrant women in a lifeboat and later raised money for their benefit. Restored to its 1910 appearance, the Molly Brown House has a large collection of turn-of-the-20th-century furnishings and art objects, many of which belonged to the Brown family. Allow 1 hour.

1340 Pennsylvania St. ℂ 303/832-4092. www.mollybrown.org. Guided tour $6.50 adults, $5 seniors over 65, $3 children 6–12, free for children under 6. June–Aug Mon–Sat 10am–4pm, Sun noon–4pm; Sept–May Tues–Sat 10am–4pm, Sun noon–4pm. Guided tours every 30 min.; last tour of the day begins at 3:30pm. Closed major holidays. Bus: 2 on Logan St. to E. 13th, then 1 block east to Pennsylvania.

U.S. Mint The Denver Mint, one of four in the United States, stamps 10 billion coins a year, and each has a small D on it. Video monitors along the visitors' gallery through the mint provide a close view of the actual coin-minting process. *Note:* Due to increased security, tours must be arranged in advance and have stringent parameters. Check the website for specific instructions.

320 W. Colfax Ave. (between Cherokee and Delaware sts.). (© **303/405-4757** or 303/405-4761. www.usmint.gov. Free admission. Tours Mon–Fri 8am–3pm. Gift shop 8am–3:30pm. Reservations recommended. Closed 1–2 weeks in summer for audit; call for exact date. Bus: 7.

SHOPPING

Most visitors do their shopping along the **16th Street Mall** (the mile-long pedestrian walkway between Market St. and Tremont Place) and adjacent areas, including **Larimer Square, The Shops at Tabor Center, Writer Square,** and the newest retail development downtown, **Denver Pavilions.**

Outside the downtown area there are more options, primarily the huge **Cherry Creek Shopping Center**—a shopper's dream—south of downtown.

Denver claims the world's largest sporting-goods store: the five-story **Gart Sports Castle,** 1000 Broadway (© **303/861-1122;** www.gartsports.com). There are also a number of Gart outlets in the Denver area. The rental department at the **REI** Flagship store, 1416 Platte St. (© **303/756-3100**), is stocked with tents, stoves, kayaks, and other gear. A good source for area maps and hiking guides is **Mapsco Map and Travel Center,** 800 Lincoln St., Denver (© **303/623-4299**).

WHERE TO STAY

Denver is home to a host of chain properties. Reliable chain hotels in the downtown area include: **Comfort Inn,** 401 17th St., Denver, CO 80202 (© **800/228-5150** or 303/296-0400), with a convenient location and rates of $139 double and $189 to $289 suite; **La Quinta Inn Downtown,** 3500 Park Ave. W. (at I-25 Exit 213), Denver, CO 80216 (© **800/531-5900** or 303/458-1222), charging $90 to $100 for a double; and **Red Lion Hotel at Invesco Field,** 1975 Bryant St. (at I-25 Exit 210B), Denver, CO 80204 (© **800/388-5381** or 303/433-8331), with rates of $79 to $129 double.

Brown Palace Hotel (Best For more than 100 years, this National Historic Landmark has been *the* place to stay in Denver—if you're looking to celebrate a special occasion in relaxed elegance, then look no further. Designed in an odd triangular shape, it was built of Colorado red granite and Arizona sandstone. Elaborate cast-iron grillwork surrounds six tiers of balconies up to the stained-glass ceiling high above the lobby. Rooms are either Victorian or Art Deco–style and have all the amenities of a modern luxury hotel. In-room massage is available for an extra charge. A full English tea served in the lobby.

321 17th St., Denver, CO 80202. (© **800/321-2599** or 303/297-3111. Fax 303/312-5900. www.brownpalace.com. 241 units. $280–$350 double; $350–$1,190 suite. Lower weekend rates. AE, DC, DISC, MC, V. Valet parking $24 overnight. Pets up to 20 lb. accepted. **Amenities:** 3 restaurants; exercise room. *In room:* Fridge (in some rooms only).

The Burnsley All Suite Hotel This small, elegant hotel (convenient to the Cherry Creek shopping areas, and only 5 blocks from downtown) offers handsomely furnished suites with private balconies, fully stocked kitchens, and antique furnishings. The suites are expansive (averaging 700 sq. ft.) and popular with travelers who prefer to be away from the hubbub of downtown.

1000 Grant St. (at E. 10th Ave.), Denver, CO 80203. (© **800/231-3915** or 303/830-1000. Fax 303/830-7676. www. burnsley.com. 80 suites. $119–$219 suite. Weekend rates available. AE, DC, MC, V. Free covered parking. **Amenities:** Restaurant; pool; access to a nearby health club. *In room:* Kitchen.

Hotel Teatro One of Denver's most luxurious hotels, Hotel Teatro is also the most dramatic: The Denver Center for the Performing Arts (across the street) inspired the decor, which features masks, playbills, and wardrobe from past productions of its resident theater company. The exquisitely furnished guest rooms feature Indonesian marble, cherrywood furnishings, Frette linens, and Aveda toiletries. The nine-story building is a historic landmark, constructed as the Denver Tramway Building in 1911. The $18-million restoration brought cutting-edge perks like free high-speed Wi-Fi access throughout the property and a combo fax/scanner/copier/printer in each room.

1100 14th St. (at Arapahoe St.), Denver, CO 80202. ℂ 303/228-1100. Fax 303/228-1101. www.hotelteatro.com. 111 units. $225 double; $345–$1,400 suite. AE, DC, DISC, MC, V. Valet parking $24 overnight. Pets accepted. **Amenities:** 2 restaurants. *In room:* Fridge.

Hyatt Regency Denver   Opened in late 2005, the 37-story Hyatt Regency is the city's crisp new convention center hotel, one of the biggest and best such properties in the Rockies and the first skyscraper to rise in downtown Denver since the early 1980s. The hotel, adjacent to the newly expanded Colorado Convention Center, boasts the biggest suites downtown (from 500 to 5,000 sq. ft.) and a thorough, modern list of amenities. Guest rooms are contemporary but comfortable, with plush furnishings and an ergonomic work station. Showcasing a terrific contemporary art collection with a local bent, the sleek lobby features automated check-in kiosks and the Strata bar. On the 27th floor, another bar, Altitude, offers the best views downtown.

650 15th St., Denver, CO 80202. ℂ **800/233-1234** or 303/436-1234. Fax 303/436-9102. www.denverregency.hyatt. com. 1,100 units. $165–$319 double; $550–$5,000 suite. AE, DC, DISC, MC, V. Underground valet parking $24; self-parking $20. **Amenities:** Restaurant; heated indoor pool; health club; spa. *In room:* Fridge.

Jet Hotel   This contemporary boutique hotel is one of the few lodging options in the lively LoDo neighborhood. Formerly the LoDo Inn, the property changed hands and underwent a metamorphosis to the Luna Hotel in 2002, then a rebranding to the Jet in 2006. It remains sleek and smart, combining the personal service of a B&B with the conveniences of a full-service hotel. The guest rooms are spare studies in efficiency, with perks like CD and DVD players, unique art prints, and large armoires. Some rooms have private balconies and others have jetted tubs; the suite has a copper-topped table and a small kitchen. The hotel is entirely nonsmoking.

1612 Wazee St., Denver, CO 80202. ℂ **303/572-3300**. Fax 303/623-0773. www.thejethotel.com. 19 units. $129–$189 double; $249–$299 suite. AE, DC, DISC, MC, V. Parking $10. **Amenities:** 2 restaurants; exercise room. *In room:* Kitchenette.

Queen Anne Bed & Breakfast Inn   A favorite of both business travelers and couples, the Queen Anne might be considered the perfect bed-and-breakfast in the perfect home (actually, the B&B encompasses two Victorian homes). Innkeeper Tom King provides piped-in chamber music and fresh flowers, but no televisions. Each of the 10 double rooms in the 1879 Pierce House is unique, decorated with period antiques (three of the rooms boast original murals). The entire property is nonsmoking.

2147–51 Tremont Place, Denver, CO 80205. ℂ **800/432-4667** or 303/296-6666. Fax 303/296-2151. www.queenanne bnb.com. 14 units. $85–$185 double; $175–$185 suite. Rates include hot breakfast and Colorado wine each evening. AE, DC, DISC, MC, V. Free off-street parking. **Amenities:** Smoking not permitted. *In room:* No TV.

WHERE TO DINE

Buckhorn Exchange *(Best)* ROCKY MOUNTAIN   In the same rickety premises where it was established in 1893, this landmark restaurant displays its Colorado Liquor License No. 1 above the 140-year-old bar in the upstairs saloon. On the first level, the densely decorated dining room dishes out the best game dishes (slow-roasted buffalo prime rib, lean and served medium rare; elk; pheasant; and quail) in the city. The beefsteaks, ranging from 8-ounce tenderloins to 64-ounce table steaks for five, are also quite good. Portions are large. A mile southwest of the State Capitol, the Buck-horn sits adjacent to a light-rail stop, making it an easy trip from downtown.

1000 Osage St. (at W. 10th Ave.). © 303/534-9505. www.buckhorn.com. Reservations recommended. Main courses $8–$16 lunch, $18–$44 dinner. AE, DC, DISC, MC, V. Mon–Fri 11am–2pm; Mon–Thurs 5:30–9pm; Fri–Sat 5–10pm; Sun 5–9pm. Bar open all day. Light rail: Osage.

Casa Bonita *(Kids* MEXICAN/AMERICAN   A west Denver landmark, Casa Bonita is more theme park than restaurant. The 52,000-square-foot restaurant is said to be the largest in the Western Hemisphere. A pink Spanish cathedral-type bell tower greets visitors, and inside are divers plummeting into a pool beside a 30-foot water-fall, puppet shows, a video arcade, and strolling mariachi bands. Food—enchiladas, tacos, fajitas, country-fried steak, and fried chicken—is served cafeteria-style. Hot *sopaipillas* (deep-fried sweet dough) served with honey are included with each meal.

In the JCRS Shopping Center, 6715 W. Colfax Ave., Lakewood. © 303/232-5115. www.casabonitadenver.com. Reservations not accepted. Main courses $7–$13; children's meals around $3. DISC, MC, V. Mon–Thurs 11am–9:30pm; Fri–Sat 11am–10pm.

Duffy's Shamrock *(Value* AMERICAN   This traditional Irish bar and restaurant with fast, cheerful service has been thriving since the late 1950s. Drink specialties include Irish coffees and imported Irish beers, but the food is mostly American. Daily specials may include prime rib, fried Louisiana prawns, low-carb plates, or grilled liver and onions. Sandwiches, on practically every kind of bread imaginable, include corned beef, Reuben, roast beef with gravy, and BLT.

1635 Court Place. © 303/534-4935. Main courses $2–$6 breakfast, $5–$9 lunch, $5–$11 dinner. AE, DC, DISC, MC, V. Mon–Fri 7am–1:30am; Sat 7:30am–1:30am.

Elway's STEAKS/SEAFOOD   Owned by retired Denver Broncos quarterback John Elway, this popular Cherry Creek eatery—unlike many celebrity restaurants—is no flash in the pan. Dim but lively, the restaurant is a model of "New West" design, with a menu that melds swank and comfortable. On the swank side: hand-cut USDA prime steaks, bone-in swordfish chops, and veggies served a la carte. And the comfy: creamed corn, steak loaf, and a dessert menu that includes Ding Dongs and warm chocolate-chip cook-ies and cold milk. But it's the little details, such as buttonholes in the napkins, milk bot-tles full of water, and tiramisu cones, that won us over in the end. Service is smooth and business is brisk, in both the cavernous dining room and the bustling bar. If you're lucky, you might bump into Elway himself here—he's not just the owner, but a regular, too.

2500 E. 1st Ave. (immediately west of the Cherry Creek Shopping Center). © 303/399-5353. www.elways.com. Reservations recommended. Main courses $9–$24 lunch and brunch, $19–$40 dinner. AE, DC, DISC, MC, V. Daily 11am–2pm; Mon–Thurs 5–10pm; Fri–Sat 5–11pm; Sun 5–9pm.

Red Square Euro Bistro RUSSIAN/CONTEMPORARY   This restaurant has a rich red interior, contemporary Russian art, and a vodka bar stocked with infusions made in-house (ranging from raspberry to garlic) and about 100 brands from 17 countries. Chef Maxim Ionikh's excellent entrees are not purely Russian: The steak stroganoff has a salmon counterpart, but there is cold borscht and *golubtsi* (a meat-filled cabbage roll), and vodka. Lots and lots of vodka.

1512 Larimer St. at Writer Sq. © 303/595-8600. www.redsquarebistro.com. Main courses $13–$20. AE, DC, DISC, MC, V. Daily 5–10pm. Bar open later.

Rioja CONTEMPORARY MEDITERRANEAN   Chef-owner Jennifer Jasinski has emerged as Denver's most creatively inspired restaurateur since opening Rioja in 2004.

In two short years, the slick Larimer Square eatery has emerged as a national standout, a critical darling, and our pick for dinner in downtown Denver. With a copper-topped bar and an atmosphere that's formal without being stuffy, Rioja is the perfect vehicle for Jasinski's menu of contrasting flavors and textures. Offerings range from curried cauliflower soup served with fresh apple salad to expertly grilled leg of Colorado lamb on a bed of goat-cheese polenta. Jasinski keeps the menu fresh, but you'll always get a selection of her delectable handmade pastas for dinner—the artichoke tortellini is our pick—and truly transcendent beignets for dessert.

1431 Larimer Sq. (Ⓒ 303/820-2282. www.riojadenver.com. Reservations recommended. Main courses $9.50–$18 brunch and lunch, $16–$30 dinner. AE, DISC, MC, V. Wed–Fri 11:30am–2:30pm; Sat–Sun 11am–2:30pm; Sun–Thurs 5–10pm; Fri–Sat Sat 5–11pm.

T-Wa Inn *Value* VIETNAMESE   Denver's oldest Vietnamese restaurant is still the best. With simple, pleasant decor and relics from the Far East on display, it looks the part, but the food is what makes it work. Everything is excellent, but we especially like the succulent shrimp, perfect pork tenderloin, and the attention to authentic Vietnamese flavors. T-Wa also serves several spicy Thai dishes, as well as Asian beers and a whole rainbow of neon-colored specialty drinks.

555 S. Federal Blvd. (2 blocks south of Alameda Ave.) (Ⓒ 303/922-2378. Most main courses $6–$13. AE, DISC, MC, V. Sun–Thurs 11am–9:30pm; Fri–Sat 11am–10pm.

DENVER AFTER DARK

Current entertainment listings appear in special Friday-morning sections of the two daily newspapers, the *Denver Post* and *Rocky Mountain News. Westword,* a weekly newspaper distributed free throughout the city every Wednesday, has perhaps the best listings: It focuses on the arts, entertainment, and local politics.

You can get tickets for nearly all major entertainment and sporting events from **Ticketmaster** (Ⓒ 303/830-TIXS), which has several outlets in the Denver area.

THE PERFORMING ARTS   Denver's performing-arts scene is anchored by the 4-square-block **Denver Center for the Performing Arts,** located downtown just a few blocks from major hotels at 14th and Curtis streets (Ⓒ 800/641-1222 or 303/893-4100; www.denvercenter.org). The complex houses nine theaters, a concert hall, and what may be the nation's first symphony hall in the round. It's home to the **Colorado Symphony Orchestra** (Ⓒ 303/623-7876; www.coloradosymphony.org), **Colorado Ballet** (Ⓒ 303/837-8888; www.coloradoballet.org), **Opera Colorado** (Ⓒ 877/475-4833 for tickets, or 303/468-2030; www.operacolorado.org), and more.

Quite possibly the country's best and most beautiful venue for top-name outdoor summer concerts, **Red Rocks Amphitheatre,** I-70 Exit 259 South, 16351 County Rd. 93, Morrison (Ⓒ 303/295-4444; www.redrocksonline.com), is set in the foothills of the Rocky Mountains, 15 miles west of the city. Four-hundred-foot-high red sandstone rocks flank the 9,000-seat amphitheater, a product of the Civilian Conservation Corps; at night, with the lights of Denver spread across the horizon, the atmosphere is magical.

THE BAR SCENE   More beer is brewed in Denver than in any other city in the country, so finding a bar won't be a problem. The hip place for barhopping is **LoDo,** which attracts all manner of Gen-Xers and yuppies. Its trendy nightspots are often noisy and crowded, but if you're looking for action, this is where to find it, in spots like **Falling Rock Tap House,** 1919 Blake St. (Ⓒ 303/293-8338), which has the best selection of beers in Denver, darts and pool, and occasional live music.

A Golden Side Trip

Golden, 15 miles west of downtown Denver via U.S. 6 or Colo. 58 off I-70, is one of the fabled Gold Circle towns that boomed with the first strikes of the gold rush in 1859. History aside, most folks head here to see the **Coors Brewing Company,** at 13th and Ford streets (© **303/277-2337** or 303/277-2337; www.coors. com), the world's largest single-site brewery, producing 1.5 million gallons of beer each day. Free tours leave the central parking lot, where visitors board a bus for a short drive through historic Golden before arriving at the brewery. Yes, you'll get free samples. Call for directions and tour times.

For more information on things to do in Golden, contact the **Greater Golden Area Chamber of Commerce,** 1010 Washington Ave. (© **303/279-3113;** www. goldencochamber.org).

Denver's first modern microbrewery, the **Wynkoop Brewing Co.,** 1634 18th St., at Wynkoop Street (© 303/297-2700), offers tours Saturday from 1 to 5pm. Housed in the renovated 1898 J.S. Brown Mercantile Building across from Union Station, the Wynkoop is also a popular restaurant. Ten beers are always on tap, and "tasters" provide a nice sampling. On the second floor is a top-notch pool hall with billiards, snooker, and darts.

You'll find an excellent selection of fine cigars, single-malt Scotches, and after-dinner drinks at the refined **Churchill Bar,** 321 17th St., in the Brown Palace Hotel (© 303/297-3111).

THE CLUB & MUSIC SCENE The historic **Bluebird Theater,** 3317 E. Colfax Ave. (at Adams St.; © 303/322-2308; www.nipp.com), built in 1913 to show silent movies, has been restored and now offers a diverse selection of jazz, rock, alternative, and other live music, as well as films. The **Mercury Cafe,** 2199 California St., at 22nd Street (© 303/294-9281; www.mercurycafe.com), has a wide array of live offerings, from avant-garde jazz to progressive rock.

The Grizzly Rose, 5450 N. Valley Hwy., at I-25 Exit 215 (© 303/295-1330 or 303/295-2353; www.grizzlyrose.com), has a 5,000-square-foot dance floor and draws nationally known country performers offering live music every night.

2 Boulder

Set at the foot of the Flatirons of the Rocky Mountains, just 30 miles northwest of downtown Denver, Boulder is a college town. With close to 27,000 students, the University of Colorado (C.U.) dominates the city. Sophisticated and artsy, Boulder is home to numerous high-tech companies; it has also attracted countless outdoor enthusiasts who have been drawn by the delightful climate, vast open spaces, and proximity to Rocky Mountain National Park. Boulder has 30,000 acres of open space within its city limits, 56 parks, and 200 miles of trails—on any given day, most of the population is outside making great use of this land, generally from the vantage point of a bicycle seat. The city has done such a good job of managing itself that The National Trust for Historic Preservation has named Boulder one of the nation's "dozen distinctive destinations" for preserving historic sites, managing growth, and maintaining a vibrant downtown.

ESSENTIALS

GETTING THERE **By Plane** Air travelers must fly into **Denver International Airport,** then make ground connections to Boulder. Buses operated by the **Regional Transportation District,** known locally as **RTD** (© 800/366-7433 or 303/299-6000, or 303/299-6089 TTY; www.rtd-denver.com), charge $10 for a one-way trip to the airport (exact change required). Buses leave from, and return to, the main terminal at 14th and Walnut streets daily every hour from before 4am to after midnight.

By Car The Boulder Turnpike **(U.S. 36)** branches off **I-25** north of Denver and passes through several suburbs before reaching Boulder. The trip takes about 30 minutes. If you are coming from Denver International Airport, **E-470 West** to **I-25 South** is the best route to U.S. 36.

VISITOR INFORMATION The **Boulder Convention and Visitors Bureau,** 2440 Pearl St. (at Folsom St.), Boulder, CO 80302 (© 800/444-0447 or 303/442-2911; www.bouldercoloradousa.com), is open Monday through Thursday from 8:30am to 5pm, Friday from 8:30am to 4pm, and can provide excellent maps, brochures, and general information on the city.

SPECIAL EVENTS & FESTIVALS In the wacky, crowd-pleasing **Boulder Kinetic Fest** (© 303/444-5600), held in early May at Boulder Reservoir, some 70 teams race over land and water in a variety of imaginative human-powered, handmade machines.

One of the best in the country, the annual **Colorado Shakespeare Festival** (© 303/492-0554; www.coloradoshakes.org) takes place from late June to late August, with more than a dozen performances each of four Shakespeare plays. Tickets run $5 to $52 for single performances and previews, with series packages available.

EXPLORING THE AREA

The tree-lined, pedestrian-only **Pearl Street Mall,** along Pearl Street from 11th to 15th streets, is the city's hub for dining, shopping, strolling, and people-watching. Musicians, mimes, jugglers, and other street entertainers hold court on the landscaped mall day and night, year-round.

Boulder maintains more than 200 miles of hiking trails and long stretches of bike paths. Several canyons lead down from the Rockies directly into Boulder, attracting mountaineers and rock climbers. Families enjoy picnicking and camping in the beautiful surroundings. Everywhere you look, people of all ages are running, walking, biking, skiing, or engaged in other active sports.

On some days, you can see more bikes than cars in Boulder. For current information on biking events, tips on the best places to ride, and equipment sales and repairs, check with **University Bicycles,** 839 Pearl St., about 2 blocks west of the Pearl Street Mall (© 303/444-4196; www.ubikes.com); and with **Full Cycle,** 1211 13th St., near the campus (© 303/440-7771; www.fullcycleboulder.com).

The **Boulder Creek Path,** 55th Street and Pearl Parkway to the mouth of Boulder Canyon (© 303/413-7200), provides a 16-mile-long oasis and recreation area through the city and west into the mountains. The C.U. campus and several city parks are linked by the path. Near the east end, watch for deer, prairie dog colonies, Canada geese, spotted sandpipers, owls, and woodpeckers.

I. M. Pei designed the striking pink-sandstone building that houses the **National Center for Atmospheric Research,** 1850 Table Mesa Dr. (© 303/497-1174; www.ncar.ucar.edu), high atop Table Mesa in the southwestern foothills. Here, scientists study the greenhouse effect, wind shear, and ozone depletion. Among the technological tools on display are satellites, weather balloons, robots, and supercomputers that can simulate the world's climate. There are also hands-on, weather-oriented exhibits and the outdoor, interpretive Walter Orr Roberts Nature and Weather Trail (.4 mile long and wheelchair accessible).

Celestial Seasonings, 4600 Sleepytime Dr., off Spine Road at Colo. 119, Longmont Diagonal (© **303/581-1202;** www.celestialseasonings.com), the nation's leading producer of herbal teas, offers free 45-minute tours (and some sample tastings) on the hour every day.

WHERE TO STAY

Major chains and franchises that provide reasonably priced lodging in Boulder include **Best Western Boulder Inn,** 770 28th St., Boulder, CO 80303 (© **800/223-8469** or 303/449-3800), and **Boulder Creek Quality Inn and Suites,** 2020 Arapahoe Ave., Boulder, CO 80302 (© **888/449-7550** or 303/449-7550; www.qualityinnboulder.com).

We also recommend **The Alps,** a beautiful B&B housed in a historic log lodge, 38619 Boulder Canyon Dr. (© **800/414-2577** or 303/444-5445; www.alpsinn.com), and the series of pleasant log cabins near the east gate of Boulder Canyon at **Foot of the Mountain Motel,** 200 Arapahoe Ave. (© **866/773-5489** or 303/442-5688; www.footofthemountainmotel.com).

At the top of the class of hotels in Boulder is the elegant and historic **Hotel Boulderado,** 2115 13th St. (© **800/433-4344** or 303/442-4344; www.boulderado.com), which boasts a cantilevered, cherrywood staircase and rich woodwork. The original five-story hotel, just a block off the Pearl Street Mall, has 42 bright and cozy rooms, all with a Victorian flavor. The newer North Wing rooms also capture the turn-of-the-20th-century feel with reproduction antiques. Some rooms have refrigerators and a few have jetted tubs. Rates run $150 to $280 double.

The posh $24-million **St. Julien,** 900 Walnut St. (© **877/303-0900** or 720/406-9696; www.stjulien.com), instantly raised the bar for lodging in Boulder when it opened in 2005. The flagstone and Norman brick exterior (accented by patina copper and red roof tiles) sheaths a sumptuous lobby and exquisite guest rooms, averaging a healthy 400 square feet each. Everything from the luxurious linens to the premium bath amenities is first-rate. Honeyed tones and French doors accent the guest rooms, which feature either one California king or two queens. The bathrooms are the best in town; there are separate tubs and showers in every granite-laden one. Perks include guided hikes on weekends ($10 for about 3 hr.), a two-lane lap pool, and a spa that offers "indigenous therapies" using local minerals and plants.

WHERE TO DINE

Note: A Boulder city ordinance prohibits smoking inside restaurants.

An institution for almost 40 years, **Tom's Tavern,** 1047 Pearl St. (© **303/443-3893**), is Boulder's most popular place for a good burger. Nothing on the menu costs more than $12.

Frasca, 1738 Pearl St. (© **303/442-6966;** www.frascafoodandwine.com) is the critical darling in Boulder for its impeccable service and peerless cuisine, drawn exclusively from the culinary traditions of Friuli-Venezia Giulia, a sub-alpine region in northeastern Italy. **The Kitchen,** 1039 Pearl St. (© **303/544-5973;** www.thekitchencafe.com), has also emerged as a standout with its fresh, often organic food, expert service, and the casual atmosphere that melds metropolitan flair with Boulder funkiness.

Amu (℃ **303/440-0807**), a traditional sake bar with its own menu of artfully prepared sashimi and other Japanese staples, translates approximately to "everything/nothing," and requires patrons to leave their shoes at the door.

Head to the **Flagstaff House Restaurant,** 1138 Flagstaff Rd. (℃ **303/442-4640;** www.flagstaffhouse.com), for excellent American cuisine and a spectacular nighttime view of the lights of Boulder, spread out 1,000 feet below. This family-owned and -operated restaurant has an elegant, candlelit dining room with glass walls to maximize the view. The menu, which changes daily, offers an excellent selection of seafood and Rocky Mountain game prepared with a creative flair, plus the state's best wine cellar. Main courses run $25 to $60.

Located at the far east end of the Pearl Street Mall, **Illegal Pete's,** 1447 Pearl St. (℃ **303/440-3955;** www.illegalpetes.com), is renowned locally for its creative, healthy burritos, packed with chicken, steak, veggies, or fish. The menu also includes a similar range of tacos, as well as salads, quesadillas, and chili. Menu items run $4 to $6.

BOULDER AFTER DARK

The Catacombs, in the basement of the Hotel Boulderado, 13th and Spruce streets (℃ **303/443-0486**), offers live blues and jazz by local and regional performers. The **West End Tavern,** 926 Pearl St. (℃ **303/444-3535**), is a great neighborhood bar with a wide-ranging selection of jazz, blues, and other live music.

Boulder's leading sports bar is the **Lazy Dog,** 1346 Pearl St. (℃ **303/440-3355;** www.thelazydog.com), with a great rooftop deck and a plethora of TVs tuned into games of all kinds.

The best local brewpub is the **Walnut Brewery,** 1123 Walnut St., near Broadway (℃ **303/447-1345**), in a historic brick warehouse a block from the Pearl Street Mall. The spacey wall murals make **The Sink,** 1165 13th St. (℃ **303/444-SINK;** www.thesink.com), one of Boulder's funniest nightspots. There's a full bar with more than a dozen regional microbrews, live music, and light fare.

3 Rocky Mountain National Park

ESTES PARK: THE GATEWAY

Estes Park is the eastern gateway to Rocky Mountain National Park, and Grand Lake is the closest town to the park's western entrance. Of the two, Estes Park is more developed, with more lodging and dining choices, plus lots of galleries and shopping. If you're driving to Rocky Mountain National Park via Boulder or Denver, you'll want to make the resort town of Estes Park your base camp. (The town of Grand Lake is more rustic, with plenty of spots to camp, a number of motels, and a few guest ranches. If you're coming from Steamboat Springs or Glenwood Springs, Grand Lake is a more convenient base.)

ESSENTIALS

GETTING THERE   The most direct route is **U.S. 36** from Denver and Boulder. At Estes Park, U.S. 36 joins **U.S. 34,** which runs up the Big Thompson Canyon from **I-25** and Loveland, and continues through Rocky Mountain National Park to Grand Lake and Granby.

VISITOR INFORMATION   The **Estes Park Convention and Visitors Bureau** (℃ **800/443-7837;** www.estesparkcvb.com) has a visitor center on U.S. 34, just east of its junction with U.S. 36, with access from both highways.

GETTING AROUND   In summer, a free national park **shuttle bus** runs from Moraine Park Campground, Moraine Park Museum, and the Glacier Basin parking area to Bear Lake, with departures every 10 to 20 minutes.

WHERE TO STAY

For help in finding accommodations, call the **Estes Park Convention and Visitors Bureau** (*©* **800/443-7837;** www.estesparkcvb.com). National chains here include **Best Western Silver Saddle,** 1260 Big Thompson Ave. (U.S. 34), Estes Park, CO 80517 (*©* **800/WESTERN** or 970/586-4476), with rates of $99 to $199 double from June to mid-September, $79 to $149 double during of the rest of year; **Super 8,** 1040 Big Thompson Ave., Estes Park, CO 80517 (*©* **800/800-8000** or 970/586-5338), charging $89 to $120 double in summer, $50 to $99 double during the rest of the year; and **Travelodge,** 1220 Big Thompson Ave., Estes Park, CO 80517 (*©* **800/578-7878** or 970/586-4421), charging $109 to $220 double in summer, $69 to $107 double during the rest of the year.

Glacier Lodge, Colo. 66 (P.O. Box 2656), Estes Park, CO 80517 (*©* **800/523-3920** or 970/586-4401; www.glacierlodge.com), frequently counts deer and elk among its visitors. The lovely cottages are spread across 19 acres of woodland along the Big Thompson River. Rates for a double early June to late August are $80 to $218; mid-May to early June and late August to late September $60 to $150; late September to mid-October $50 to $130.

Both tent and RV sites are available at **Estes Park KOA,** 2051 Big Thompson Ave. (*©* **800/562-1887** or 970/586-2888; www.estesparkkoa.com), where RV rates for two are $32 to $42.

Alpine Trail Ridge Inn *(Value)*   This top-notch independent motel, right next to the entrance to Rocky Mountain National Park, offers nicely maintained rooms, many with private balconies, with basic Western decor and plenty of functionality. There are rooms with kings and queens, two doubles, as well as a few two-room family units.

927 Moraine Ave., Estes Park, CO 80517. *©* **800/223-5023** or 970/586-4585. Fax 970/586-6249. www.alpinetrail ridgeinn.com. 48 units. Summer $70–$130 double, $130–$192 family unit. Closed mid-Oct to Apr. AE, DC, DISC, MC, V. **Amenities:** Restaurant; outdoor heated pool. *In room:* Fridge.

Baldpate Inn   Located 7 miles south of Estes Park, the Baldpate was built in 1917 and named for the novel *Seven Keys to Baldpate,* a murder mystery in which seven visitors believe each possesses the only key to the hotel (guests today can contribute to the hotel's collection of more than 30,000 keys). Each of the early-20th-century-style rooms is unique, with handmade quilts on the beds. Several rooms are a bit small, and although most of the lodge rooms share bathrooms (five bathrooms for nine units), each room does have its own sink. Among our favorites are the Mae West Room (yes, she was a guest here), with a red claw-foot tub and wonderful views of the valley; and the Pinetop Cabin, with a whirlpool tub, canopy bed, and gas fireplace.

4900 S. Colo. 7 (P.O. Box 700), Estes Park, CO 80517. *©* **866/577-5397** or 970/586-6151. www.baldpateinn.com. 14 units (5 with bathroom), 4 cabins. $100 double with shared bathroom, $120 double with private bathroom; $195–$250 cabin. Rates include full breakfast. DISC, MC, V. Closed Nov–Apr. **Amenities:** Restaurant. *In room:* No phone.

Boulder Brook   It would be hard to find a more beautiful setting for lodging than this. Surrounded by tall pines and cradled in a ruggedly majestic valley 2 miles from the park entrance, all suites face the Fall River, and all have private riverfront decks, VCRs, and full or partial kitchens. The spa suites are equipped with two-person spas, fireplaces, sitting areas with cathedral ceilings, and king-size beds. One-bedroom suites hold king-size beds, window seats, two TVs, and bathrooms with whirlpool tub/ shower combinations.

1900 Fall River Rd., Estes Park, CO 80517. ℂ **800/238-0910** or 970/586-0910. Fax 970/586-8067. www.boulderbrook. com. 19 units. $109–$225 double. DISC, MC, V. **Amenities:** Smoking not permitted. *In room:* Kitchen.

ROCKY MOUNTAIN NATIONAL PARK

One of the most beautiful spots in America, Rocky Mountain National Park should top your list for your trip to Colorado. The scenery is stupendous: Snow-covered peaks—17 mountains above 13,000 feet—stand over lush valleys and shimmering Alpine lakes in the 415 square miles (265,727 acres) that comprise the park.

In relatively low areas, from about 7,500 to 9,000 feet, a lush forest of ponderosa pine and juniper cloaks the sunny southern slopes, with Douglas fir on the cooler northern slopes. Thirstier blue spruce and lodgepole pine cling to stream sides, with occasional groves of aspen. Elk and mule deer thrive. On higher slopes, a sub-alpine ecosystem exists, dominated by forests of Engelmann spruce and sub-alpine fir, but interspersed with wide meadows alive with wildflowers during spring and summer. This is also home to bighorn sheep, which have become unofficial symbols of the park. Above 11,500 feet, the trees become increasingly gnarled and stunted, until they disappear altogether and Alpine tundra predominates.

Trail Ridge Road, the park's primary east-west roadway, is one of America's great Alpine highways. It cuts west through the middle of the park from Estes Park, then south down its western boundary to Grand Lake. Climbing to 12,183 feet near Fall River Pass, it's the highest continuous paved highway in the United States. The road is usually open from sometime in May into October, depending on the snowfall. The 48-mile scenic drive from Estes Park to Grand Lake takes about 3 hours, allowing for stops at numerous scenic outlooks. Exhibits at the **Alpine Visitor Center** at Fall River Pass, 11,796 feet above sea level, explain life on the Alpine tundra.

Fall River Road, the original park road, leads to Fall River Pass from Estes Park via Horseshoe Park Junction. West of the Endovalley picnic area, the road is one-way uphill, and closed to trailers and motor homes. As you negotiate its gravelly switch-backs, you get a clear idea of what early auto travel was like in the West. This road, too, is closed in winter.

One of the few paved roads in the Rockies that leads into a high mountain basin is **Bear Lake Road;** it's kept open year-round, with occasional half-day closings to clear snow. Numerous trails converge at Bear Lake, southwest of the park headquarters/ visitor center, via Moraine Park.

PARK ESSENTIALS

ENTRY POINTS   Entry into the park is from the east (through Estes Park) or the west (through Grand Lake). **Trail Ridge Road** connects the two sides. Most visitors enter the park from the Estes Park side. The **Beaver Meadows entrance,** west of Estes Park on U.S. 36, is the national park's main entrance. U.S. 34 west from Estes Park takes you to the **Fall River entrance** (north of the Beaver Meadows entrance). Those entering the park from the west side should take U.S. 40 to Granby, then follow U.S. 34 north to the **Grand Lake entrance.**

Park admission for up to 7 days is $20 per vehicle; $10 per person for bicyclists, motorcyclists, and pedestrians.

VISITOR CENTERS & INFORMATION   The **Beaver Meadows Visitor Center,** U.S. 36 on the park's east side, has interpretive exhibits including a relief model of the park, an audiovisual program, and books and maps for sale. It's open daily from 8am to 9pm in summer and from 8am to 5pm the rest of the year. Outside the park, on U.S. 34 on the park's east side, the **Fall River Visitor Center** is staffed by park rangers and volunteers from the nonprofit Rocky Mountain Nature Association. It contains exhibits on park wildlife, a children's activity room, an information desk, and a bookstore. It's open daily from 9am to 5pm (until 6pm in summer).

Near the park's west side entrance is the **Kawuneeche Visitor Center** (✆ **970/586-1513**), open daily from 8am to 6pm in summer, from 8am to 5pm in late spring, and 8am to 4:30pm in fall and winter. Located high in the mountains (11,796 ft. above sea level) is the **Alpine Visitor Center,** at Fall River Pass, open from late spring through early fall, daily from 10:30am to 4:30pm; exhibits here explain life on the Alpine tundra. Visitor facilities are also available at the **Moraine Park Museum** on Bear Lake Road, open late June to late August daily from 9am to 4:30pm.

For more information, contact **Rocky Mountain National Park,** 1000 U.S. 36, Estes Park, CO 80517-8397 (✆ **970/586-1206,** or 970/586-1333 for recorded information; www.nps.gov/romo). You can also get information from the **Rocky Mountain Nature Association** (✆ **800/816-7662** or 970/586-0108; www.rmna.org), which sells a variety of maps, books, and videos.

WHEN TO GO   Because large portions of the park are closed half the year due to snowfall, practically everyone visits in spring and summer. The busiest period is from mid-June to mid-August (during school vacations). To avoid the largest crowds, try to visit just before or just after that period. For those who don't mind chilly evenings, late September and early October are less crowded and can be beautiful, although there's always the chance of an early winter storm. Regardless of when you visit, the best way to avoid crowds is by putting on a backpack or climbing onto a horse. Rocky Mountain has almost 350 miles of trails leading into all corners of the park.

SPORTS & OUTDOOR ACTIVITIES

HIKING & BACKPACKING   Park bookstores sell topographic maps and guidebooks, and rangers can direct you to lesser-used trails.

One particularly easy park hike is the **Alberta Falls Trail** from the Glacier Gorge Parking Area (.6 mile one-way), which rises in elevation only 160 feet as it follows Glacier Creek to pretty Alberta Falls.

A slightly more difficult option is the **Bierstadt Lake Trail,** accessible from the north side of Bear Lake Road about 6.4 miles from Beaver Meadows. This 1.4-mile (one-way) trail climbs 566 feet through an aspen forest to Bierstadt Lake, where you'll find excellent views of Longs Peak.

Starting at Bear Lake, the trail up to **Emerald Lake** offers spectacular scenery en route, past Nymph and Dream lakes. The .5-mile hike to Nymph Lake is easy, climbing 225 feet; from there the trail is rated moderate to Dream Lake (another .6 mile) and then on to Emerald Lake (another .7 mile), which is 605 feet higher than the starting point at Bear Lake. Another moderate hike is the relatively uncrowded **Ouzel Falls Trail,** which leaves from Wild Basin Ranger Station and climbs about 950 feet to a picture-perfect waterfall. The distance one-way is 2.7 miles.

Among our favorite moderate hikes is the **Mills Lake Trail,** a 2.5-mile (one-way) hike, with a rise in elevation of about 700 feet. Starting from Glacier Gorge Junction, the trail goes up to a picturesque mountain lake, nestled in a valley among towering mountain peaks. This lake is an excellent spot for photographing dramatic Longs Peak, especially in late afternoon or early evening, and it's the perfect place for a picnic.

Backcountry permits (required for all overnight hikes) can be obtained at Park Headquarters and ranger stations (in summer) for $20 May through October, free November through April. For information, call © **970/586-1242.** There is a 7-night backcountry camping limit from June to September, with no more than 3 nights at any one spot.

HORSEBACK RIDING   Many of the national park's trails are open to horseback riders. Several outfitters provide guided rides inside and outside the park, ranging from 1 hour (about $30) to all day (about $100–$125), plus breakfast and dinner rides and multiday pack trips. Recommended companies include **S. K. Horses (www. cowpokecornercorral.com),** which operates **National Park Gateway Stables,** at the Fall River entrance of the national park on U.S. 34 (© **970/586-5269). Hi Country Stables (www.colorado-horses.com)** operates two stables inside the park: **Glacier Creek Stables** (© 970/586-3244) and **Moraine Park Stables** (© 970/586-2327).

WILDLIFE VIEWING & BIRD-WATCHING   Rocky Mountain National Park is a premier wildlife-viewing area; fall, winter, and spring are the best times, but summer's pretty good, too. Large herds of elk and bighorn sheep can often be seen in the meadows and on mountainsides. In addition, you might spot mule deer, beavers, coyotes, and river otters. Watch for moose among the willows on the west side of the park. In the forests are lots of songbirds and small mammals; particularly plentiful are gray and Steller's jays, Clark's nutcrackers, chipmunks, and golden-mantled ground squirrels. There's a good chance of seeing bighorn sheep, marmots, pikas, and ptarmigan along Trail Ridge Road.

WHERE TO CAMP
The park has five campgrounds with a total of almost 600 sites. About half are at **Moraine Park;** about 150 are at **Glacier Basin.** Moraine Park, **Timber Creek** (98 sites), and **Longs Peak** (26 tent sites) are open year-round; Glacier Basin and **Aspenglen** (54 sites) are seasonal. Camping is limited to 3 days at Longs Peak and 7 days at other campgrounds; the limit is 14 days at all the park's campgrounds in winter. Arrive early in summer if you hope to snare one of these first-come, first-served campsites. Moraine Park and Glacier Basin require reservations from Memorial Day to early September. Make reservations with the **National Park Reservation Service** (© **800/365-2267;** http://reservations.nps.gov). Campsites cost $20 per night during the summer, $14 in the off season when water is turned off. No showers or RV hookups are available.

4 More Highlights of the Northern Colorado Rockies
The northern Rockies begin just outside Denver and extend on either side of the meandering Continental Divide, down saw-toothed ridgelines, through precipitous river canyons, and across broad Alpine plains. Here, snowfall is measured in feet, not inches. And when spring's sun finally melts away the walls of white, a whole new world opens up amid the brilliantly colored Alpine wildflowers. Skis are replaced by mountain bikes, and summer festivals fill the mountains with music.

STEAMBOAT SPRINGS
In this state-of-the-art ski resort town, ranchers still go about their business in cowboy boots and Stetsons, seemingly unaware of the fashion statement they're making to city-slicker visitors.

ESSENTIALS

GETTING THERE   By Plane   The **Yampa Valley Regional Airport,** 22 miles west of Steamboat Springs (© 970/276-5004; www.co.routt.co.us), is served by several major airlines, with the most flights in winter. Car rentals are available at the airport.

By Car   The most direct route to Steamboat Springs from Denver is via **I-70** west 68 miles to Silverthorne, **Colo. 9** north 38 miles to Kremmling, and **U.S. 40** west 52 miles to Steamboat. For statewide **road-condition reports,** call © 303/639-1111.

VISITOR INFORMATION   The **Steamboat Springs Chamber Resort Association,** 1255 S. Lincoln Ave. (P.O. Box 774408), Steamboat Springs, CO 80477 (© 877/ 754-2269 or 970/879-0880; www.steamboatchamber.com and www.steamboatsummer. com), operates a visitor center, open in summer from 8am to 5pm Monday through Friday and from 10am to 4pm Saturday.

SPECIAL EVENTS & FESTIVALS   The first full week in February brings the **Steamboat Springs Winter Carnival** (© 970/879-0695), with races, jumping, broomball, and skijoring street events. Mid-June through August, you'll hear top-notch classical, jazz, country, and pop musicians perform at the **Strings in the Mountains Festival of Music** (© 970/879-5056; www.stringsinthemountains.org).

SKIING & OTHER WINTER ACTIVITIES

When devoted skiers describe Steamboat, they practically invent adjectives to describe its incredibly light powder. Six peaks make up the ski area (mounts Werner, Christie, Storm, Sunshine, Pioneer Ridge, and Thunderhead) and provide slopes for skiers of all ability levels. The 3,668-foot vertical drop here is among the highest in Colorado. There are 143 trails, served by 20 lifts, and it's also a great mountain for snowboarders. For further information, contact **Steamboat Ski & Resort Corporation** (© 877/ 237-2658 or 970/879-0740; www.steamboat.com). For daily **ski reports,** check the resort's website (listed above) or dial © 970/879-7300.

Seasoned cross-country skiers swear by the **Steamboat Ski Touring Center** at the Sheraton Steamboat Resort (© 970/879-8180; www.nordicski.net), with some 30km of groomed cross-country trails near the foot of the mountain.

One of the best snowmobile trails in the Rockies, offering spectacular scenery, is the **Continental Divide Trail,** which runs more than 50 miles from Buffalo Pass north of Steamboat to Gore Pass, west of Kremmling. You can choose from a variety of guided tours from **High Mountain Snowmobile Tours** (© 877/879-6500 or 970/879- 6500; www.stmbtsnowmobiletours.com).

WARM-WEATHER & YEAR-ROUND ACTIVITIES

Most outdoor recreation is enjoyed in 1.1-million-acre Routt National Forest, which virtually surrounds Steamboat Springs. For trail maps and information, contact **Medicine Bow–Routt National Forest,** Hahns Peak/Bears Ears Ranger District Office, 925 Weiss Dr. (© 970/879-1870; www.fs.fed.us/r2/mbr).

The Steamboat Springs Chamber Resort Association produces a **Trails Map,** available at the information center on Lincoln Avenue, showing which trails are open to what sport: biking, horseback riding, hiking, 4WDs, or ATVs. On the reverse side of the map are descriptions of several trails in the area.

BIKING & MOUNTAIN BIKING   The 5-mile, dual-surface **Yampa River Trail** connects downtown Steamboat Springs with Steamboat Village, and links area parks and national forest trails. The **Mount Werner Trail** links the river to the ski area,

Hitting Colorado's Slopes

For current ski conditions and general information, contact **Colorado Ski Country USA** (© **303/837-0793** or 303/825-7669 for snow conditions; www.colorado ski.com).

The slopes are most crowded over Christmas and New Year's, and on the Martin Luther King, Jr., and Presidents' Day holiday weekends, when lodging rates are at their highest. Those who can ski midweek will find more elbowroom on the slopes, and the beginning and end of the season are the best times to avoid crowds—assuming snow conditions are good.

Expect to spend $65 to $75 a day for an adult lift ticket at a Colorado ski resort, but this can vary from less than $50 at the smaller ski areas to more than $80 at the glitzier resorts such as Vail. Kids and seniors usually get hefty discounts, and seniors over 70 and very young kids often ski free. Always ask about multiday passes, which can save you serious money, as well as multiresort passes. Most skiers buy packages that often include lift tickets for a certain number of days, but might also include rental equipment, lessons, lodging and/or meals, transportation, and lift tickets for other nearby ski areas.

which has numerous slopes open to mountain bikers in summer. **Spring Creek Trail** climbs from Yampa River Park into Routt National Forest. Touring enthusiasts can try their road bikes on the 110-mile loop over Rabbit Ears and Gore passes, rated 1 of the 10 most scenic rides in America by *Bicycling* magazine.

Stop at **Sore Saddle Cyclery,** 1136 Yampa St. (© **970/879-1675**), for information on the best local trails (maps are on display), accessories, repairs, and rentals ($20 per day and up).

HOT SPRINGS   More than 150 mineral springs are located in and around the Steamboat Springs area. Heart Spring is part of the **Steamboat Springs Health & Recreation complex,** 136 Lincoln Ave. (© **970/879-1828;** www.sshra.org), in downtown Steamboat Springs. In addition to the man-made pools into which the spring's waters flow, there's a lap pool, water slide, spa, whirlpool, fitness center, and massage therapy.

The **Hot Springs at Strawberry Park,** 44200 C.R. 36 (© **970/879-0342;** www. strawberryhotsprings.com), are 7 miles north of downtown (from Seventh St., follow the signs). It's a wonderful experience to spend a moonlit evening in a sandy-bottomed, rock-lined soaking pool, kept between 101°F and 106°F (38°C–41°C).

MORE TO SEE & DO

You can learn about Steamboat's history at **Tread of Pioneers Museum,** 800 Oak St. (© **970/879-2214**), a beautifully restored Victorian home that features exhibits on pioneer ranch life, the Utes, and 100 years of skiing history. Admission is $5 adults, $4 seniors 62 and older, and $1 children under 12. The museum is open Tuesday through Saturday from 10am to 5pm (opens at 11am Oct–Apr).

Just 4 miles from downtown in Routt National Forest is **Fish Creek Falls** (© **970/ 879-1870**). A footpath leads to a historic bridge at the base of this breathtaking 283-foot waterfall. There's also a special overlook with a short .13-mile trail and ramp designed for those with disabilities, as well as a picnic area and hiking trails. Turn right off Lincoln Avenue onto Third Street, go 1 block, and turn right again onto Fish Creek Falls Road.

WHERE TO STAY

Steamboat Central Reservations (© **877/237-2628** or 970/879-0740; www.steamboat. com) can book your lodging and make virtually all your travel arrangements. Be sure to ask about special packages and programs. **Resort Quest Steamboat** (© **800/ 228-2458** or 970/879-8811; www.resortqueststeamboat.com) and **Steamboat Resorts** (© **800/525-5502** or 970/879-8000; www.steamboatresorts.com) rent everything from ski-in/ski-out condos and town houses to lodge rooms.

Our favorite lodging choices include the impressive **Sheraton Steamboat Resort,** 2200 Village Inn Court (© **800/848-8878** or 970/879-2220; www.sheraton.com/steamboat; $109–$399 double), offering a host of facilities; **Steamboat Bed & Breakfast,** 442 Pine St. (© **877/335-4321** or 970/879-5724; www.steamboatb-b.com; $109–$209 double); and the relatively affordable **Rabbit Ears Motel,** 201 Lincoln Ave. (© **800/ 828-7702** or 970/879-1150; www.rabbitearsmotel.com; $79–$169 double).

BRECKENRIDGE & SUMMIT COUNTY

Summit County is a major recreational sports center, with skiing in winter and fishing, hiking, and mountain biking in summer. Breckenridge is a good place to base yourself, as the entire Victorian core of this 19th-century mining town has been carefully preserved, with colorfully painted shops and restaurants occupying the old buildings, most dating from the 1880s and 1890s.

ESSENTIALS

GETTING THERE   By Plane   You can fly into Denver International or Colorado Springs and continue to Breckenridge, Frisco, Keystone, and/or Copper Mountain via rental car or shuttle, such as the **Colorado Mountain Express** (© **800/525-6363** or 970/926-9800; www.cmex.com).

By Car   I-70 runs through the middle of Summit County. For Keystone, exit on U.S. 6 at Dillon; the resort is 6 miles east of the interchange. For Breckenridge, exit on **Colo. 9** at Frisco and head south 9 miles to the resort. Copper Mountain is right on I-70 at the **Colo. 91** interchange.

VISITOR INFORMATION   The **Breckenridge Resort Chamber** has a new welcome center at 203 S. Main St. (open daily 9am–9pm summer and winter, with shorter hours in spring and fall), and administrative offices at 311 S. Ridge St., Breckenridge, CO 80424 (© **800/221-1091** or 970/453-2913; www.gobreck.com). A source of visitor information for the entire region is the **Summit County Chamber of Commerce,** P.O. Box 2010, Frisco, CO 80443 (© **800/530-3099** or 970/668-2051; www. experiencethesummit.com).

SPECIAL EVENTS & FESTIVALS   The **Breckenridge Music Festival** (© **970/453-9142** or 970/547-3100; www.breckenridgemusicfestival.com) presents dozens of classical and nonclassical music performances mid-June through mid-August. The **Breckenridge Festival of Film** (© **970/453-6200;** www.breckfilmfest.com), held in mid-September, attracts Hollywood directors and actors to town to discuss some two dozen films representing all genres.

SKIING & OTHER WINTER ACTIVITIES

Arapahoe Basin, 28194 U.S. 6, between Keystone and Loveland Pass (© **888/272-7246** or 970/496-0718; www.arapahoebasin.com), is one of Colorado's oldest ski areas. Most of its 490 skiable acres are intermediate and expert terrain, and it's often the last Colorado ski area to close for the season—sometimes not until mid-June.

Spread across four large mountains on the west side of the town, **Breckenridge** ranks third in size among Colorado's ski resorts. Once known for its wealth of open, groomed beginner and intermediate slopes, Breckenridge has, in recent years, expanded its acreage for expert skiers as well. The resort has 146 trails served by 28 lifts. Contact **Breckenridge Ski Resort** (© **800/789-7669** or 970/453-5000, or 970/453-6118 for snow conditions; http://breckenridge.snow.com).

Other notable ski areas in Summit County include **Copper Mountain** (© **866/841-2481;** www.coppercolorado.com); **Keystone,** a superb mountain for intermediate skiers, but also one of the best spots for night skiing in America (© **800/468-5004** or 970/496-4386; www.keystone.snow.com); and **Loveland Ski Area** (© **800/736-3754** or 303/571-5580; www.skiloveland.com).

Frisco Nordic Center, on Colo. 9 south of Frisco (© **970/668-0866;** www.breckenridgenordic.com), sits on the shores of Dillon Reservoir. Its trail network includes 43km of set tracks and groomed skating lanes, and access to backcountry trails. From the Frisco Nordic Center you can ski to the **Breckenridge Nordic Center,** on Willow Lane near the foot of Peak 8 (© **970/453-6855;** www.breckenridgenordic.com), with its own 30km of groomed trails. The **Gold Run Nordic Center** (© **970/547-7889**), at Breckenridge Golf Club, offers more than 20km of groomed trails.

Snowboarding is permitted at all local resorts.

WARM-WEATHER & YEAR-ROUND ACTIVITIES

Two national forests—**Arapahoe** and **White River**—overlap the boundaries of Summit County. These recreational playgrounds offer opportunities not only for downhill and cross-country skiing and snowmobiling in winter, but also for hiking and backpacking, horseback riding, boating, fishing, hunting, and bicycling in summer.

The **U.S. Forest Service's Dillon Ranger District,** in the town of Silverthorne at 680 Blue River Pkwy., just north of I-70 Exit 205 (© **970/468-5400;** www.fs.fed.us/r2), has unusually good information on outdoor recreation, including maps and guides. You can also get information on a wide variety of outdoor activities from the **Breckenridge Resort Chamber Welcome Center,** 203 S. Main St. (© **877/864-0868**).

BIKING   There are more than 40 miles of paved bicycle paths in the county, including a path from Breckenridge (with a spur from Keystone) to Frisco and Copper Mountain, continuing across Vail Pass to Vail. This spectacularly beautiful two-lane path is off-limits to motorized vehicles of any kind.

BOATING   Dillon Reservoir, a beautiful mountain lake along I-70 between Dillon and Frisco, is the place to go. At 9,017 feet in elevation, it claims to have America's highest-altitude yacht club and holds colorful regattas most summer weekends. No swimming. The full-service **Dillon Marina,** 150 Marina Dr. (© **970/468-5100;** www.dillonmarina.com), is open late May to late October.

FISHING   Major fishing rivers within an hour of Breckenridge include the South Platte, Arkansas, Eagle, Colorado, and Blue rivers. For lake fishing, try Dillon Reservoir and Spinney Mountain Reservoir. The Blue River, from Lake Dillon Dam to its confluence with the Colorado River at Kremmling, is rated a gold-medal fishing stream. For tips on where they're biting, as well as supplies, fishing licenses, and all the rest, stop at **Mountain Angler,** 311 S. Main St., in the Main Street Mall (© **800/453-4669** or 970/453-4665; www.mountainangler.com).

MOUNTAIN BIKING   Numerous trails beckon mountain bikers as they wind through the mountains, often following 19th-century mining roads and burro trails and ending at ghost towns. Energetic fat-tire fans can try the **Devil's Triangle,** a difficult 80-mile loop that begins and ends in Frisco after climbing four mountain passes (including 11,318-ft. Fremont Pass). Check with the U.S. Forest Service or Activity Center for directions and tips on other trails. For mountain bikers who prefer not to work so hard, check with the Activity Center on times and costs for taking your bike up the mountain on the Breckenridge chairlift.

WHERE TO STAY

Throughout Summit County, condominiums prevail. While they often offer the best value, they're sometimes short on charm. If you're planning to spend much time in one, it pays to ask about views and fireplaces before booking. Local reservation services include **Summit County Central Reservations** (© **800/525-3682;** www.skierlodging.com) and **Breckenridge Central Reservations** (© **877/593-5260;** www.gobreck.com). Our favorite B&B is **Allaire Timbers Inn Bed & Breakfast,** 9511 Colo. 9, Breckenridge (© **800/624-4904** or 970/453-7530; www.allairetimbers.com; $145–$265 double).

VAIL

Vail is the *big one.* In fact, it's hard to imagine a more celebrated spot to schuss. Off the slopes, Vail is an incredibly compact Tyrolean village, frequented by almost as many Europeans as Americans, a situation which lends its restaurants, lodgings, and trendy shops a more cosmopolitan feel than other Colorado resorts. But the mountain's size and its exciting trails are still what draw the faithful.

ESSENTIALS

GETTING THERE   By Plane   Visitors can fly into **Denver International Airport** or directly into **Eagle County Regional Airport,** 35 miles west of Vail between I-70 exits 140 and 147 (© **970/524-9490;** www.eaglecounty.us/airport), on major national carriers. **Colorado Mountain Express** (© **800/525-6363** or 970/926-9800; www.cmex.com) offers shuttles from Denver and Eagle for about $65 a person.

By Car   Vail is right on the **I-70** corridor, so it's easy to find. Just take Exit 176, whether you're coming from the east (Denver) or the west (Grand Junction). A more direct route from the south may be **U.S. 24** through Leadville; this Tennessee Pass road joins I-70 5 miles west of Vail.

VISITOR INFORMATION   For information or reservations in the Vail Valley, contact the **Vail Valley Chamber and Tourism Bureau,** 100 E. Meadow Dr., Suite 34, Vail, CO 81657 (© **800/525-3875** or 970/476-1000; www.visitvailvalley.com), or **Vail Mountain Resort,** P.O. Box 7, Vail, CO 81658 (© **800/525-2257** or 970/476-5601; www.vail.com or www.beavercreek.com). You can also get information on year-round activities and events by calling the **Resort Information and Activities Center** (© **970/476-9090**).

GETTING AROUND   Vail is one of only a few Colorado communities where you really don't need a car. The Town of Vail runs a free **shuttle-bus** service daily from 6am to 2am.

SPECIAL EVENTS & FESTIVALS   The summer season's big cultural event is the **Bravo! Vail Valley Music Festival** (© 877/812-5700 or 970/827-5700; www.vail musicfestival.org), from late June to early August, featuring everything from classical orchestra and chamber music to baroque and modern jazz. The **Vail International Dance Festival** features both classes and performances. The World Masters Ballet Academy at Vail teaches the Russian style of artistic expression and other techniques, and presents a series of performances each summer. For information, contact the **Vail Valley Foundation** (© 888/883-8245 or 970/949-1999; www.vvf.org).

SKIING & OTHER WINTER ACTIVITIES

Vail is a place that all serious skiers must experience at least once. You can arrive at the base village, unload and park your car, and not have to drive again until it's time to go. You'll find all the shops, restaurants, and nightlife you could want within a short walk of your hotel or condominium.

Ski area boundaries stretch 7 miles from east to west along the ridge-top, from Outer Mongolia to Game Creek Bowl, and the skiable terrain is measured at 5,289 acres. Virtually every lift on the front (north-facing) side of the mountain has runs for every level of skier, with a predominance of novice and intermediate terrain. The world-famous Back Bowls are decidedly not for beginners, and there are few options for intermediates. All told, there are 193 conventional trails served by 34 lifts. Vail also has a highly respected children's program. For further information, contact **Vail Mountain**, P.O. Box 7, Vail, CO 81658 (© 800/404-3535 or 970/476-5601; 970/476-4888 for snow report; www.vail.com).

Vail Resorts, Inc. also owns nearby **Beaver Creek Resort** (© 800/404-3535 or 970/845-9090, or 800/427-8308 for snow reports; www.beavercreek.com), an outstanding resort in its own right, with a more secluded atmosphere. Located in a valley 1½ miles off the I-70 corridor, Beaver Creek combines European château-style elegance in its base village with expansive slopes for novice and intermediate skiers. The Grouse Mountain Express lift reaches expert terrain. Currently, 16 lifts serve 162 trails. Snowboarding is permitted, and there is a snowboarding park with a half-pipe located off the Moonshine Trail. There are seven mountain restaurants, including the highly praised **Beano's Cabin.**

Paragon Guides (© 877/926-5299 or 970/926-5299; www.paragonguides.com) is one of the country's premier winter guide services, offering backcountry ski trips on the Tenth Mountain Trail and Hut System between Vail and Aspen. A variety of trips are available, lasting from 3 to 6 days and designed for all ability levels. Costs start at start around $1,000 per person for the 3-day trip.

Cross-country skiers won't feel left out here, with trails at both resorts as well as a system of trails through the surrounding mountains. **Vail's Nordic Center** (© 970/476-8366) has 33km of trails, and offers guided tours, lessons, and snowshoeing. The **Beaver Creek Nordic Center** (© 970/845-5313) has a 32km mountaintop track system with a skating lane in 9,840-foot McCoy Park. Most of the high-altitude terrain here is intermediate. For general information on backcountry trails, contact the **Holy Cross Ranger District Office** (© 970/827-5715; www.fs.fed.us/r2). Of particular note is the system of trails known as the **10th Mountain Division Hut System** (© 970/925-5775; www.huts.org). Generally following the World War II training network of the Camp Hale militia, the trails cover 300 miles and link Vail with Leadville and Aspen. There are a number of overnight cabins ($20–$40 per person per night), and hikers and mountain bikers also use this trail.

WARM-WEATHER & OTHER YEAR-ROUND ACTIVITIES

Nova Guides (© 888/949-6682 or 719/486-2656; www.novaguides.com) offers guided fishing, mountain-bike and off-road tours, and white-water rafting.

FISHING   The streams and mountain lakes surrounding Vail are rich with trout. Gore Creek through the town of Vail is a popular anglers' venue, especially toward evening from its banks along the Vail Golf Course. Also good are the Eagle River, joined by Gore Creek 5 miles downstream near Minturn; the Black Lakes near the summit of Vail Pass; and 60-acre Piney Lake. The **Lazy J Ranch** in Wolcott (© 970/926-3472; www.lazyjranch.net) offers guided fly-fishing trips on 4 miles of private Eagle River frontage and to stocked lakes. For fishing supplies plus guided trips, contact **Fly Fishing Outfitters, Inc.** (© 800/595-8090 or 970/476-3474; www.flyfishing outfitters.net).

HIKING & BACKPACKING   The surrounding White River National Forest has a plethora of trails leading to pristine lakes and spectacular panoramic views. The Holy Cross Wilderness Area, southwest of Vail, encompasses 14,005-foot Mount of the Holy Cross and is an awesome region with more than 100 miles of trails. Eagle's Nest Wilderness Area lies to the north, in the impressive Gore Range. For information on these and other hiking areas, consult the **Holy Cross Ranger District Office** (see "Skiing & Other Winter Activities," above).

MOUNTAIN BIKING   Summer visitors can take their bikes up the Eagle Bahn Gondola to Adventure Ridge on Vail Mountain and cruise downhill on a series of trails. There are many other choices for avid bikers, both on backcountry trails and road tours. A popular trip is the 13-mile Lost Lake Trail along Red Sandstone Road to Piney Lake. The 30-mile Vail Pass Bikeway goes to Frisco, with a climb from 8,460 feet up to 10,600 feet. Pick up a trail list (with map) at an information center.

Mountain bike repairs and rentals are available at a number of shops, including **Vail Bike Tech,** 555 E. Lionshead Circle, Vail (© 800/525-5995 or 970/476-5995; www. vailbiketech.com), which also offers guided tours; and **Wheel Base,** 610 W. Lionshead Circle (© 970/476-5799).

WHERE TO STAY

Like most of Colorado's ski resorts, Vail has an abundance of condominiums, and it seems that more are built every day. The **Vail Valley Chamber and Tourism Bureau** (© 800/525-3875 or 970/476-1000; www.visitvailvalley.com) can provide additional lodging information or make reservations for you.

Our favorite luxury resorts in the area are the very posh **Vail Cascade Resort & Spa,** 1300 Westhaven Dr., Vail (© 800/420-2424 or 970/476-7111; www.vailcascade. com; $129–$519 double), which seems to get better every time we visit; and the **Park Hyatt Regency Beaver Creek Resort and Spa,** 50 W. Thomas Place, Avon (© 800/55-HYATT or 970/949-1234; www.beavercreek.hyatt.com; $135–$875 double), an architecturally unique hotel at the foot of the Beaver Creek lifts. Other deluxe options include **The Charter at Beaver Creek,** 120 Offerson Rd., Beaver Creek (© 800/525-6660 or 970/949-6660; www.thecharter.com; $99–$445 double); and **The Lodge & Spa at Cordillera,** 2205 Cordillera Way, Edwards (© 800/877-3529 or 970/926-2200; http://cordillera.rockresorts.com; $150–$400 double).

More affordable options include the **Inn & Suites at Riverwalk,** 27 Main St., Edwards (© 888/926-0606 or 970/926-0606; www.innandsuitesatriverwalk.com; $64–$230 double).

ASPEN

Aspen's glitzy, celebrity-studded reputation precedes it. But if you dig beneath the hype, you'll find a real town with a fascinating history, some great old buildings, and spectacular mountain scenery. If you're a serious skier, you owe yourself at least a few days of hitting the slopes. However, if you've never strapped on boards, and you're thinking of visiting in summer, you'll be doubly pleased: Prices are significantly lower, and the crowds thin out. The surrounding forests teem with great trails for hiking, biking, and horseback riding, and Aspen becomes one of the best destinations in the country for summer festivals.

ESSENTIALS

GETTING THERE   By Plane   Visitors who want to fly directly into Aspen can arrange to land at **Aspen/Pitkin County Airport,** 5 miles northwest of Aspen on Colo. 82 (© **970/920-5384;** www.aspenairport.com). **Colorado Mountain Express** (© **800/525-6363** or 970/926-9800; www.cmex.com) offers shuttle service from Denver International Airport.

By Car   Aspen is on **Colo. 82,** halfway between **I-70** at Glenwood Springs (42 miles northwest) and **U.S. 24** south of Leadville (44 miles east). In summer, it's a scenic 3½-hour drive from Denver: Leave I-70 west at Exit 195 (Copper Mountain); follow **Colo. 91** south to Leadville, where you pick up U.S. 24; turn west on Colo. 82 through Twin Lakes and over 12,095-foot Independence Pass. In winter, the Independence Pass road is closed, so you'll have to take I-70 to Glenwood Springs, and head east on Colo. 82. In optimal winter driving conditions, it takes about 4 hours from Denver.

VISITOR INFORMATION   Contact the **Aspen Chamber Resort Association,** 425 Rio Grande Place, Aspen, CO 81611 (© **800/670-0792** or 970/925-1940; www. aspenchamber.org), which operates a **Visitor Center** at the same location (open Mon–Fri 8am–5pm), and another at the Wheeler Opera House, located at Hyman Avenue and Mill Street (usually open daily 10am–6pm). You can also get information from the **Snowmass Village Resort Association** (© **800/766-9627;** www.snowmassvillage.com).

SPECIAL EVENTS & FESTIVALS   The **Aspen Music Festival and School** (© **970/925-9042;** www.aspenmusicfestival.com) originated in 1949. Lasting 9 weeks from mid-June to late August, it offers more than 350 events, including symphonic and chamber music, opera, choral, and children's programs. **Jazz Aspen at Snowmass** (© **970/920-4996;** www.jazzaspen.com) takes place at Snowmass Village in late June, and again on Labor Day weekend.

SKIING & OTHER WINTER ACTIVITIES

Skiing Aspen really means skiing the four Aspen area resorts—Aspen Mountain, Aspen Highlands, Buttermilk, and Snowmass. All are managed by the Aspen Skiing Company, and one ticket gives access to all. For further information, contact the **Aspen Skiing Company** (© **800/525-6200** or 970/925-1220; www.aspensnowmass.com).

Aspen Mountain is not for the timid. It's the American West's original hard-core ski mountain, with no fewer than 23 of its named runs double diamond—for experts only. There are mountain-long runs for intermediate as well as advanced skiers, but beginners should look to one of the other Aspen areas.

Aspen Highlands has the most balanced skiable terrain—novice to expert, with lots of intermediate slopes—in the Aspen area. Freestyle Friday, a tradition at Highlands for almost 3 decades, boasts some of the best freestyle bump and big air competitors in the state of Colorado every Friday from early January to mid-April.

Buttermilk is a premier beginners' mountain that's also home of the ESPN Winter X Games (at least through 2007). But there's plenty of intermediate and ample advanced terrain as well. Special features include the ski and snowboard school's Powder Pandas program for 3- to 6-year-olds; and a snowboard park with a 23% grade.

A huge, intermediate mountain with something for everyone, **Snowmass** has 33% more skiable acreage than the other three Aspen areas combined. It's actually four distinct self-contained areas, each with its own lift system and restaurant, and its terrain varies from easy beginner runs to the pitches of the Cirque and the Hanging Valley Wall, the steepest in the Aspen area. The renowned Snowmass ski school has hundreds of instructors, as well as Snow Cubs and Big Burn Bears programs for children 18 months and older. The area also caters to snowboarders with three terrain parks, one super pipe, and a rail yard.

The **Aspen/Snowmass Nordic Council** operates a free Nordic trail system with nearly 60km of groomed double track extending throughout the Aspen-Snowmass area and incorporating summer bicycle paths. Instruction and rentals are offered along the trail at the **Aspen Cross-Country Center,** Colo. 82 between Aspen and Buttermilk (© **970/925-2145;** www.utemountaineer.com), and the **Snowmass Cross Country Center,** Snowmass Village (© **970/923-9180**), both of which provide daily condition reports and information on the entire trail system.

WARM-WEATHER & YEAR-ROUND ACTIVITIES

Among the best one-stop outfitters is **Blazing Adventures,** Snowmass Village (© **800/282-7238** or 970/923-4544; www.blazingadventures.com), which offers river rafting, mountain biking, four-wheeling, and horseback riding.

Your best source of information on a wide variety of outdoor activities in the mountains around Aspen is the **White River National Forest,** 806 W. Hallam St. (© **970/925-3445;** www.fs.fed.us/r2).

FISHING Perhaps the best trout fishing is in the Roaring Fork and Frying Pan rivers, both considered gold-medal streams. The Roaring Fork follows Colo. 82 through Aspen from Independence Pass; the Frying Pan starts near Tennessee Pass, northeast of Aspen, and joins the Roaring Fork at Basalt, 18 miles down the valley. Stop at **Taylor Creek Fly Shop** in Aspen Sports, 408 E. Cooper Ave., Aspen (© **970/927-4374;** www.taylorcreek.com), for your fishing needs.

HORSEBACK RIDING Several stables in the Aspen valley offer rides, and some outfitters even package gourmet meals and country-western serenades with their expeditions.

Photo Op

The two sheer, pyramidal peaks called **Maroon Bells,** on Maroon Creek Road 10 miles west of Aspen, are among the most photographed mountains in the Rockies. They're a beautiful scene any time, but especially in the fall, when their reflection in Maroon Lake is framed by the changing colors of the aspen leaves. During summer and into early fall, you can take a 20- to 30-minute narrated bus tour from Aspen Highlands up the Maroon Creek Valley (© **970/925-8484;** www.rfta.com). Cost for the bus trip is $6 adults, $3 for kids 6 to 16, $4 for seniors, and it's free for children under 6.

Rates start at about $50 per person for an hour's ride. Inquire at **Aspen Wilderness Outfitters** (© 970/963-0211; www.aspenwilderness.com), **Capitol Peak Outfitters** (© 970/963-4402; www.capitolpeak.com), and **OutWest Guides** (© 970/984-3801; www.outwestguides.net).

MOUNTAIN BIKING There are hundreds of miles of trails through the White River National Forest that are perfect for mountain bikers, offering splendid views of the mountains, meadows, and valleys. Check with the Forest Service (see above) and local bike shops for tips on the best trails. Among full-service bicycle shops, with rentals, are **Aspen Velo Bike Shop,** 465 N. Mill St. (© 970/925-1495; www.aspenvelo.com); and **Aspen Sports,** 408 E. Cooper Ave. (© 970/925-6331; www.aspensports.com).

RIVER RAFTING Rafting trips are offered on the Roaring Fork, Arkansas, and Colorado rivers with several companies, including **Colorado Riff Raft** (© 800/282-7238 or 970/923-4544; www.riffraft.com), **Up Tha Creek Expeditions** (© 877/982-7335 or 970/947-0030; www.upthacreek.com), and **Blazing Adventures** (see above).

WHERE TO STAY

It's essential to make reservations as early as possible. The easiest way to book your lodgings is to call **Stay Aspen Snowmass** central reservations (© 888/649-5982; www.stayaspensnowmass.com). You can also find lodging through **Aspen Resort Accommodations** (© 800/727-7369; www.aspenreservations.net).

Our favorite choice for luxury accommodations is the historic **Hotel Jerome,** 330 E. Main St. (© 800/331-7213 or 970/920-1000; www.hoteljerome.com; $265–$1,080 double), with its period antiques and lovingly preserved Eastlake Victorian architecture. However, the Jerome will be closed for renovations from April 2007 until late November 2007, so a very worthy alternative is the **St. Regis Resort,** 315 E. Dean St. (© 888/454-9005 or 970/920-3300; www.stregisaspen.com; $495–$1,800 double). Less expensive options include the **Hotel Lenado,** 200 S. Aspen St. (© 800/321-3457 or 970/925-6246; www.hotellenado.com; $90–$540 double); and the **Limelite Lodge,** 228 E. Cooper Ave. (© 800/433-0832 or 970/925-3025; www.limelite-lodge.com; $200–$350 double), scheduled to reopen in late 2007 following a complete renovation.

5 Colorado Springs

Colorado Springs is a growing city of 380,000, with more than half a million people in the metropolitan area. It's a conservative city, and in recent years, it has developed a reputation for right-wing political activism. To many visitors it retains the feel of a small Western town, but it also has some of the best lodging and dining in the state. Most tourists come to see the Air Force Academy, marvel at the scenery at Garden of the Gods and Pikes Peak, and explore the history of America's West.

ESSENTIALS

GETTING THERE By Plane Major airlines offer nearly 100 daily flights to **Colorado Springs Airport** (© 719/550-1972; www.flycos.com). Call © 719/550-1930 for information on ground transportation from the airport to local hotels and Denver. We recommend you rent a vehicle; all major rental-car agencies have desks at the airport.

By Car The principal artery to and from the north (Denver: 70 miles) and south (Pueblo: 42 miles), **I-25** bisects Colorado Springs. **U.S. 24** is the principal east-west route through the city. Visitors arriving via **I-70** from the east can take Exit 359 at

Limon and follow U.S. 24 into the Springs. If you arrive on I-70 from the west, the most direct route is Exit 201 at Frisco, then **Colo. 9** through Breckenridge 53 miles to U.S. 24 (at Hartsel), and then east 66 miles to Colorado Springs. This route is mountainous, so check road conditions before setting out in winter (© **303/639--1111;** www.cotrip.org).

VISITOR INFORMATION The **Colorado Springs Convention and Visitors Bureau** is at 515 S. Cascade Ave., Colorado Springs, CO 80903 (© **800/888-4748** or 719/635-7506; www.coloradosprings-travel.com). Ask for the free *Official Visitor Guide to Colorado Springs and the Pikes Peak Region,* a booklet with a comprehensive listing of accommodations, restaurants, and other area visitor services, as well as a basic but efficient map. The **Visitor Information Center** (© **719/635-1723** for recorded info), at the southeast corner of Cascade Avenue and Cimarron Street, is open from 8:30am to 5pm daily in summer, Monday through Friday in winter.

EXPLORING THE AREA

The **Colorado Springs Pioneers Museum,** 215 S. Tejon St. (© **719/385-5990;** www.cspm.org), is an excellent place to begin your visit. Exhibits depict the community's rich history, including its beginning as a fashionable resort, the railroad and mining eras, and its growth and development into the 20th century.

One of the West's unique geological sites, the **Garden of the Gods,** 1805 N. 30th St. (I-25 Exit 146; © **719/634-6666;** www.gardenofgods.com), is a beautiful giant rock garden, composed of spectacular red sandstone formations sculpted by rain and wind over millions of years. Located where several life zones and ecosystems converge, the city-run park harbors a variety of plant and animal communities. Hiking maps for the 1,300-acre park are available at the visitor center.

Colorado Springs' pride and joy, the **United States Air Force Academy,** off I-25 Exit 156B (© **719/333-8723;** www.usafa.af.mil), is open to the public daily. Soon after entering the grounds, you'll see an impressive outdoor B-52 bomber display. After another mile or so, look to your left to see the Parade Ground, where cadets can sometimes be spotted marching. Six miles from the entrance, signs mark the turnoff to the visitor center. Nearby is the Cadet Chapel, whose 17 gleaming aluminum spires soar 150 feet skyward. After leaving the visitor center, you will pass Falcon Stadium, and then Thunderbird Airmanship Overlook, where you might be lucky enough to see cadets parachuting, soaring, and practicing takeoffs and landings in U.S. Air Force Thunderbirds.

There is perhaps no view in Colorado equal to the 360-degree panorama from the 14,110-foot summit of Pikes Peak (but it's not for anyone with heart or breathing problems or a fear of heights). One way to get there is by taking a ride on the **Pikes Peak Cog Railway,** 515 Ruxton Ave., Manitou Springs (© **719/685-5401;** www.cog railway.com), after you've acclimated to Colorado's high elevations. The 9-mile route, with grades up to 25%, takes 75 minutes to reach the top of Pikes Peak, and the round-trip requires 3 hours and 10 minutes (including a 40-min. stopover at the top). Take a jacket or sweater—it can be cold and windy on top, even on warm summer days. The fare is $29 to $31 adults, $16 to $17 children under 12 (those under 3 held on an adult's lap ride free). There are several departures daily, and reservations are required.

Another way to take in this spectacular view is to drive the **Pikes Peak Highway,** off U.S. 24 at Cascade; take I-25 Exit 141 west on U.S. 24 about 10 miles (© **800/318-9505** or 719/385-7325; www.pikespeakcolorado.com). This 19-mile road (paved for 7 miles, graded gravel thereafter) starts at 7,400 feet, some 4 miles west of Manitou

Springs, with numerous photo stops as you head up the mountain. There's a toll of $10 per person, $5 for kids ages 6 to 15, or $35 per car.

The **United States Olympic Complex,** 1 Olympic Plaza, at the corner of Boulder Street (entrance) and Union Boulevard (© **888/659-8687** or 719/866-4618; www.us olympicteam.com), houses a sophisticated training center for numerous U.S. Olympic sports. Free guided tours, available daily, show off the center's state-of-the-art training facilities, where you may see athletes sharpening their skills. The visitor center includes the U.S. Olympic Hall of Fame, interactive kiosks on Olympic subjects, various other displays, and a gift shop that sells Olympic-logo merchandise. *Tip:* If you want even more sports immersion, the **World Figure Skating Museum & Hall of Fame,** 20 1st St. (© **719/635-5200;** www.worldskatingmuseum.org), is also located in Colorado Springs.

WHERE TO STAY

In addition to the listings below, we highly recommend **The Cliff House at Pikes Peak,** 306 Cañon Ave., Manitou Springs (© **888/212-7000** or 719/685-3000; www. thecliffhouse.com), a beautifully restored historic hotel with an outstanding restaurant. Our favorite B&Bs are the **Old Town GuestHouse,** 115 S. 26th St. (© **888/ 375-4210** or 719/632-9194; www.oldtown-guesthouse.com); the **Holden House 1902 Bed & Breakfast Inn,** 1102 W. Pikes Peak Ave. (© **888/565-3980** or 719/ 471-3980; www.holdenhouse.com); and the **Two Sisters Inn,** 10 Otoe Place, Manitou Springs (© **800/2-SIS-INN** or 719/685-9684; www.twosisinn.com). Bargain hunters should try the simple, well-maintained rooms at the **Travel Inn,** 512 S. Nevada Ave. (© **719/636-3986**). There are also numerous chain options available in the area.

The Broadmoor *Best Kids* The best of the best, The Broadmoor is a sprawling, family-friendly resort complex of historic pink Italian Renaissance–style buildings, built in 1918 upon magnificently landscaped 3,000-acre grounds at the foot of Cheyenne Mountain. A $75-million renovation and restoration project was completed in early 2002, and the hotel's marble staircase, chandeliers, Italian tile, carved-marble fountain, and art collection are quite a spectacle. The spacious and luxurious rooms are beautifully decorated in European style, with Italian fabrics, rich wood, and original works of art. Service is impeccable. There's an array of bars and restaurants of every level of formality, including the outstanding Charles Court, plus the number of recreational activities, from horseback riding to fly-fishing, is extensive.

Lake Circle, at Lake Ave. (P.O. Box 1439), Colorado Springs, CO 80901. © 800/634-7711 or 719/634-7711. Fax 719/ 577-5700. www.broadmoor.com. 700 units. May–Oct $385–$550 double, $550–$900 standard suite; Nov–Apr $280–$425 double, $420–$740 standard suite; year-round up to $3,500 large suite. AE, DC, DISC, MC, V. Self-parking $12; valet $15. **Amenities:** 12 restaurants; 3 swimming pools (1 indoor); 3 18-hole golf courses; 9 all-weather tennis courts; state-of-the-art fitness center; full-service spa.

Eastholme in the Rockies Nestled in the quaint Pikes Peak mountain village of Cascade, 10 miles west of downtown Colorado Springs, this Victorian B&B gives guests an opportunity to see the city and get away from it all in the same day. Originally built in 1885 as a resort hotel, this property has a storied history that includes a stint as a boarding house before becoming a guest inn in 1988.

Most of the inn's large rooms feature 10-foot ceilings, and all provide plush quilts and remarkable views. The Marriott and Eisenhower suites feature original furnishings and a plethora of antiques, and the cottages offer VCRs, fireplaces, and spacious bathrooms with whirlpool tubs. Breakfasts include freshly baked breads, pastries, and entrees such as

soufflés or frittatas; gourmet dinners are available with advance reservations. Guest amenities include a wedding gazebo, shared kitchen, and library. Smoking is not permitted.

4445 Hagerman Ave. (P.O. Box 98), Cascade, CO 80809. ☎ 800/672-9901 or 719/684-9901. www.eastholme.com.
8 units (6 with bathroom), including 2 cottages. $85–$135 double; $135 suite; $150 cottage. Rates include full breakfast. AE, DISC, MC, V. Free parking. 10 miles west of I-25, about 1 mile off U.S. 24. **Amenities:** Hot tub. *In room:* Fridge.

WHERE TO DINE

In addition to the listings below, we recommend any of the restaurants at **The Broadmoor** or the **Cliff House at Pikes Peak.**

Craftwood Inn *(Best)* COLORADO CUISINE   Ensconced in an English Tudor
building with beamed ceilings, stained-glass windows, and a copper-hooded fireplace,
the Craftwood Inn specializes in regional game, including antelope and wild boar, plus
seafood, steak, chicken, and vegetarian dishes. Save room for one of the superb
desserts. The outdoor patio provides wonderful views of Pikes Peak.

404 El Paso Blvd., Manitou Springs. ☎ 719/685-9000. Reservations recommended. Main courses $18–$38. AE, DC,
DISC, MC, V. Daily 5:30–8:30pm. Turn north off Manitou Ave. onto Mayfair Ave., go uphill 1 block, and turn left onto
El Paso Blvd.; the Craftwood is on your right.

Margarita at PineCreek ECLECTIC   This delightful restaurant, with a tree-
shaded outdoor patio and simply decorated dining room, offers the perfect spot to sit
and watch the sun setting over Pikes Peak. Six-course dinners offer three choices of
entrees, often including a seafood selection, with an emphasis on fresh ingredients.
The food is top-notch.

7350 Pine Creek Rd. ☎ 719/598-8667. Reservations recommended. Fixed-price lunch $9.50; fixed-price dinner
$25–$35; brunch $10–$15. AE, DISC, MC, V. Tues–Fri 11:30am–2pm; Tues–Sat 5:30–9pm; Sun 10:30am–2pm.

Phantom Canyon Brewing Co. AMERICAN   This popular brewpub is in the
Cheyenne Building, home to the Chicago, Rock Island & Pacific Railroad from 1902
to 1909. On any given day, 8 to 10 of Phantom Canyon's specialty beers are on tap,
including their homemade root beer. Selections here are typical brewpub at lunch,
when you might get wood-fired pizzas, salads, burgers, and fish and chips. Dinner is
more ambitious, with offerings such as charbroiled garlic chicken breast with three-
grain rice and honey-beer mustard.

2 E. Pikes Peak Ave. ☎ 719/635-2800. Main courses $7.50–$11 lunch, $9.95–$20 dinner. AE, DC, DISC, MC, V.
Mon–Thurs 11am–10pm; Fri–Sat 11am–midnight; Sun 9am–10pm.

COLORADO SPRINGS AFTER DARK

Current weekly entertainment schedules can be found in the Friday *Gazette*. Also look
at the listings in *Springs* magazine and the *Independent* (free entertainment tabloids).
Tickets for many major entertainment and sporting events can be obtained from
Ticketmaster (☎ **719/520-9090;** www.ticketmaster.com).

THE PERFORMING ARTS   Pikes Peak Center, the Colorado Springs Fine Arts
Center, City Auditorium, Colorado College, and the various facilities at the U.S. Air
Force Academy are all venues for the performing arts. The city's newest facility is the
8,000-seat **Colorado Springs World Arena,** 3185 Venetucci Blvd., at I-25 Exit 138
(☎ **719/477-2100;** www.worldarena.com), which hosts big-name country and rock
concerts as well as a variety of sporting events.

THE BAR & CLUB SCENE   Two-steppers and country-western music lovers flock
to **Cowboys,** 3910 Palmer Park Blvd. (☎ **719/596-1212**), which has the largest

dance floor in the area and offers dance lessons. There's an eclectic offering of live music at **Poor Richard's Restaurant,** 324½ N. Tejon St. (© **719/632-7721**). **Bijou Bar and Grill,** 2510 W. Bijou Ave. (© **719/473-5718**), is Southern Colorado's longest-standing gay and lesbian bar. **15C,** located just off Bijou Street in the alley between Cascade Avenue and Tejon Street (© **719/635-8303**), is a slick martini and cigar bar with an upscale ambience accented by dim lighting and leather couches.

6 Southwestern Colorado

A land apart from the rest of the state, southwestern Colorado is set off by the spectacular mountain wall of the San Juan Range. The Ancestral Puebloans (also called Anasazi) who once lived here created spectacular cliff dwellings, which you can see at Mesa Verde National Park.

This area is also John Wayne country, where the Duke slugged it out and shot it out as he tamed the West on movie screens from the late 1920s through the 1970s. It was also the location shoot for *Butch Cassidy and the Sundance Kid,* and for *City Slickers,* with Billy Crystal as a hapless city dweller on an Old West–style cattle drive.

DURANGO

Born as a railroad town more than a century ago, Durango remains a railroad town to this day, as thousands of visitors take a journey back in time aboard the Durango & Silverton Narrow Gauge Railroad.

ESSENTIALS

GETTING THERE   Durango is at the crossroads of east-west U.S. 160 and north-south U.S. 550. By plane, there's frequent service from several major airlines to **Durango/La Plata County Airport,** 14 miles southeast of Durango off Colo. 172 (© **970/247-8143;** www.durangoairport.com).

VISITOR INFORMATION   Contact the **Durango Area Tourism Office,** 111 S. Camino del Rio, Durango, CO 81302 (© **800/463-8726;** www.durango.org). The **Durango visitor center** is just south of downtown, on U.S. 160/550 opposite the intersection of East Eighth Avenue. June through October, it's open Monday through Saturday from 8am to 5pm, and Sunday from 10am to 4pm; the rest of the year, hours are from 8am to 5pm Monday through Friday.

SPECIAL EVENTS & FESTIVALS   Mid-July through the first week of August, the **Music in the Mountains** classical music festival (© **970/385-6820;** www.musicinthe mountains.com) takes place at locations in and around Durango.

EXPLORING THE AREA

Colorado's most famous train (and Durango's best attraction), the **Durango & Silverton Narrow Gauge Railroad,** 479 Main Ave. (© **888/872-4607** or 970/247-2733; www.durangotrain.com), has been in continual operation since 1881. In all that time, its route has never varied: up the Rio de las Animas Perdidas (River of Lost Souls), through 45 miles of mountains and San Juan National Forest wilderness to the historic mining town of Silverton, and back. The coal-fired steam locomotives pull strings of gold-colored Victorian coaches on the 3,000-foot climb, past relics of mining and railroad activity from the last century. In summer, the spectacular trip takes 3¼ hours each way, with a 2-hour stopover in the picturesque town of Silverton before the return trip. Summer round-trip fare is $62 for adults, $31 for children ages 5 to 11. Winter trips are shorter and fares are less. Parking is $7 per day per car.

The **Durango & Silverton Narrow Gauge Railroad Museum,** 479 Main Ave. (*©* **970/247-2733**), contains exhibits on steam trains, historic photos, and railroad art. It also has restored railroad cars and a locomotive that can be entered. Hours correspond to the train depot hours, and museum admission is included with train excursion tickets. Admission to the museum only is $5 adults, $2.50 children under 12.

Those interested in a close-up view of Durango's numerous historic buildings can pick up free walking-tour brochures from the visitor center. There are particularly interesting banks, saloons, churches, and fine homes along Main and Third avenues.

OUTDOOR ACTIVITIES

The varied terrain and myriad trails of **San Juan National Forest** have made Durango a nationally known mountain-biking center. The Colorado Trail, Hermosa Creek Trail (beginning 11 miles north of Durango off U.S. 550), and La Plata Canyon Road (beginning 11 miles west of Durango off U.S. 160) are favorite jaunts. You can also get information and rent mountain bikes at **Hassle Free Sports,** 2615 Main Ave. (*©* **800/835-3800** or 970/259-3874; www.hasslefreesports.com), which rents full suspension mountain bikes for $30 per half-day or $40 for a full day.

The three stages of the Animas River provide excitement for rafters of all experience and ability levels. Most of the many outfitters in Durango offer a wide variety of rafting excursions, such as 2- to 4-hour raft trips that cost $25 to $45 for adults and $20 to $35 for kids; and full-day river trips, which include lunch, costing $75 for adults and $65 for kids. Local rafting companies include **Durango Rivertrippers** (*©* **800/ 292-2885** or 970/259-0289; www.durangorivertrippers.com) and **AAM's Mild to Wild Rafting** (*©* **800/567-6745** or 970/247-4789; www.mild2wildrafting.com).

Some 25 miles north of Durango on U.S. 550, **Durango Mountain Resort,** 1 Skier Place, Durango, CO 81301 (*©* **800/982-6103** or 970/247-9000; www.durango mountainresort.com), has a reputation of getting more sunshine than any other Colorado ski area, although the average annual snowfall is 260 inches. There are 85 trails for all levels, served by 11 lifts. Snowboarders are welcome on all lifts and trails, and a snowboard park offers jumps, slides, and a quarter-pipe. The Durango Nordic Center has 16km of trails for Nordic skiers for both classic and skate skiing.

WHERE TO STAY

An easy way to book accommodations is to contact the **Durango Central Reservations** (*©* **866/294-5187;** www.durangoreservations.org). Room taxes add 9.4% to lodging bills.

Durango's most famous lodging is the 1887 **Strater Hotel,** 699 Main Ave. (*©* **800/ 247-4431** or 970/247-4431; www.strater.com), a wonderful place to relax and soak up the ambience of the real Old West (at least the real Old West for those who had money). It's an exceptional example of American Victorian architecture, with one of the world's largest collections of American Victorian walnut antiques, and home to a superb restaurant plus the Diamond Belle Saloon, where prolific author Louis L'Amour gave life to his Western heroes. Service is superb. Doubles run $99 to $249.

Another National Historic Landmark, the 1892 **Rochester Hotel,** 726 E. Second Ave. (*©* **800/664-1920** or 970/385-1920; www.rochesterhotel.com), also captures the feel of the Old West, and is among our favorite places to stay in Durango. Rates run $109 to $199 double.

The **Wit's End Guest Ranch & Resort,** 254 C.R. 500, Bayfield (*©* **800/236-9483** or 970/884-4113; www.witsendranch.com), is a delightful if pricey dude ranch encompassing 550 acres on Vallecito Lake, surrounded by the peaks of the Weminuche Wilderness; it's a unique combination of rustic outdoors and sophisticated luxury. Rates start at $4,906 per week for two guests.

THE SAN JUAN SKYWAY

The San Juan Skyway, a 233-mile circuit that crosses five mountain passes, takes in the magnificent San Juan Mountains, as well as the cities and towns of the region. It can be accomplished in a single all-day drive from Durango or divided into several days, incorporating stops in Cortez, Telluride, and Ouray. Check for closed passes in winter and early spring. The route can be driven either clockwise (heading west from Durango on U.S. 160) or counterclockwise (heading north from Durango on U.S. 550). We'll describe the clockwise route.

Leaving Durango, 11 miles west you'll pass through the village of Hesperus, from which a county road runs 10 miles north into **La Plata Canyon,** with its mining ruins and ghost towns.

Farther west, U.S. 160 passes the entrance road to **Mesa Verde National Park.** About 45 miles west of Durango, just before Cortez, turn north on Colo. 145, which traverses the historic town of Dolores, site of the **Anasazi Heritage Center and Museum,** then proceed up the Dolores River Valley, a favorite of trout fishermen.

Sixty miles from Cortez, the route crosses 10,222-foot **Lizard Head Pass,** named for a startling rock spire looming above the roadside Alpine meadows. It then descends 13 miles to the resort town of **Telluride,** set in a beautiful box canyon 4 miles off the main road.

Follow Colo. 145 west from Telluride down the San Miguel River valley to Placerville, then turn north on Colo. 62, across 8,970-foot Dallas Divide, to Ridgway, a historic railroad town and home of **Ridgway State Park (© 970/626-5822;** www.parks.state.co.us), with a sparkling mountain reservoir.

From Ridgway, turn south, and follow U.S. 550 to the scenic and historic town of Ouray. Here begins the remarkable **Million Dollar Highway,** so named for all the mineral wealth that passed over it.

The 23 miles from Ouray over 11,008-foot **Red Mountain Pass** to Silverton is an unforgettable drive. The drive shimmies up the sheer sides of the Uncompahgre Gorge, goes through tunnels and past cascading waterfalls, then follows a historic toll road built in the 19th century. Mining equipment and log cabins are in evidence on the slopes of the iron-colored mountains, many of them more than 14,000 feet in elevation. Along this route you'll pass a monument to the snowplow operators who died trying to keep the road open during winter storms.

From Silverton, U.S. 550 climbs over the **Molas Divide** (elevation 10,910 ft.), then more or less parallels the track of the Durango & Silverton Narrow Gauge Railroad as it follows the Animas River south to Durango, passing en route the Durango Mountain Resort ski area (see above).

CORTEZ: GATEWAY TO THE ARCHAEOLOGICAL SITES OF THE FOUR CORNERS REGION

Cortez is surrounded by a vast complex of ancient villages that dominated the Four Corners region—where Colorado, New Mexico, Arizona, and Utah meet—1,000 years ago. The inhabitants of those ancient villages, called Ancestral Puebloans, have long been known as the Anasazi, but that Navajo word, considered offensive to some modern Pueblo peoples, is being phased out.

ESSENTIALS

GETTING THERE   By Plane   Cortez Airport, off U.S. 160 and 491, southwest of town (© **970/565-7458;** www.cityofcortez.com), is served by **Great Lakes Airlines** (© **800/554-5111** or 970/565-9510), with direct daily flights to Denver.

By Car   Cortez is at the junction of north-south **U.S. 666** and east-west **U.S. 160,** 45 miles west of Durango. As it enters Cortez from the east, **U.S. 160** crosses Dolores Road (Colo. 145, which goes north to Telluride and Grand Junction), then runs due west through town for about 2 miles as Main Street. The city's main thoroughfare, Main Street, eventually intersects U.S. 666 (Broadway) at the west end of town.

VISITOR INFORMATION   Stop at the **Colorado Welcome Center at Cortez,** Cortez City Park, 928 E. Main St. (© **970/565-4048;** www.swcolo.org), open daily from 8am to 6pm in summer and from 8am to 5pm the rest of the year; or contact the **Mesa Verde Country Visitor Information Bureau,** P.O. Box HH, Cortez, CO 81321 (© **800/253-1616;** www.mesaverdecountry.com).

THE MAJOR ARCHAEOLOGICAL SITES

MESA VERDE NATIONAL PARK   The largest archaeological preserve in the United States, Mesa Verde National Park, located about 10 miles east of Cortez, has some 4,000 known sites dating from A.D. 300 to 1300, including the most impressive cliff dwellings in the Southwest.

The earliest known inhabitants of Mesa Verde (Spanish for "green table") built subterranean pit houses on the mesa tops. During the 13th century they moved into shallow caves and constructed complex cliff dwellings. Although a massive construction project, these homes were occupied for only about a century; their residents left around 1300 for unknown reasons.

The **Cliff Palace,** the park's largest and best-known site, is a four-story apartment complex with stepped-back roofs forming porches for the dwellings above. Accessible by guided tour only, it is reached by a quarter-mile downhill path. Its towers, walls, and kivas (large circular rooms used for ceremonies) are all set back beneath the rim of a cliff. Another ranger-led tour takes visitors up a 32-foot ladder to explore the interior of **Balcony House.** Each tour is given only in summer and into fall (call for exact dates).

Two more important sites—**Step House** and **Long House,** both on Wetherill Mesa— can be visited in summer only. Rangers lead tours to **Spruce Tree House,** another of the major cliff-dwelling complexes, only in winter, when other park facilities are closed. Visitors can also explore Spruce Tree House on their own at any time. Three-hour and 6-hour guided park tours are offered from Far View Lodge (see below) during the summer.

For those who want to avoid hiking and climbing, the 12-mile **Mesa Top Road** makes a number of pit houses and cliff-side overlooks easily accessible by car.

Chapin Mesa, site of the park headquarters, the museum, and a post office, is 21 miles from the park entrance on U.S. 160. **Morefield Village,** site of Mesa Verde's 477-site campground, is 4 miles in from U.S. 160. The **Far View Visitor Center,** site of Far View Lodge (see below), has a restaurant, gift shop, and other facilities; it's 15 miles off U.S. 160. Open from mid-April to mid-October, **Morefield Campground** (© **800/449-2288** or 970/529-4421; www.visitmesaverde.com), 4 miles south of the park entrance, has 435 sites, including 15 with full RV hookups.

Admission to the park costs $10 per vehicle. Tours of Cliff Palace and Balcony House are $3. The **Far View Visitor Center** (© **970/529-4465;** www.nps.gov/meve) is open from early April to mid-October; the **Chapin Mesa Museum** is open year-round.

Located in the park, **Far View Lodge** (© **800/449-2288** or 970/529-4421; www.visit mesaverde.com) is open from late April to late October. Rooms aren't fancy, but the views are magnificent. The lodge serves three meals daily, with two restaurants and a bar. Rooms run $119 to $149 double.

UTE MOUNTAIN TRIBAL PARK If you liked Mesa Verde but would have enjoyed it more without the crowds, you'll love the **Ute Mountain Tribal Park,** in Towaoc (© **800/847-5485** or 970/565-3751, ext. 330; www.utemountainute.com/ tribalpark.htm). Set aside by the Ute Mountain tribe to preserve its heritage, the 125,000-acre park—which abuts Mesa Verde National Park—includes wall paintings, ancient petroglyphs, and hundreds of surface sites and cliff dwellings that compare in size and complexity with those in Mesa Verde.

Accessibility to the park is strictly limited to guided tours, which are offered April through October. Full- and half-day tours begin at the **Ute Mountain Tribal Park Visitor Center** at the junction of U.S. 666 and U.S. 160, 20 miles south of Cortez. Mountain-biking and backpacking trips are also offered. No food, lodging, gasoline, or other services are available within the park. Some climbing is necessary. Charges for tours in your vehicle are $22 per person for a half-day, $42 for a full day; there are extra charges for use of a tour guide's vehicle. Reservations are required.

WHERE TO STAY

Summer is the busy season and brings the highest rates. Among the major chains providing comfortable, reasonably priced lodging in Cortez are **Holiday Inn Express,** 2121 E. Main St. (© **888/465-4329** or 970/565-6000), with rates for two from $89 to $159; and **Best Western Turquoise Inn & Suites,** 535 E. Main St. (© **800/547-3376** or 970/565-3778), with rates for two from $59 to $159.

TELLURIDE

This was one seriously rowdy town a century ago—in fact, this is where Butch Cassidy robbed his first bank, in 1889. Telluride became a National Historic District in 1964, and in 1968 entrepreneur Joe Zoline set to work on a "winter recreation area second to none." Today, Telluride is a year-round outdoor recreation destination and hosts world-renowned film and music festivals.

ESSENTIALS

GETTING THERE By Car From Cortez, follow **Colo. 145** northeast for 73 miles. From the north (Montrose), turn west off **U.S. 550** at Ridgway, onto **Colo. 62.** Proceed 25 miles to Placerville, and turn left (southeast) onto **Colo. 145.** Thirteen miles ahead is a junction—a right turn will take you to Cortez, but for Telluride, continue straight ahead 4 miles to the end of a box canyon. From Durango, in summer take U.S. 550 north to Colo. 62 and follow the directions above; in winter it's best to take the route through Cortez and avoid Red Mountain Pass above Silverton.

By Plane Telluride Regional Airport (© **970/728-5313;** www.tellurideairport. com) is served by several major domestic carriers. National and Budget have car rental desks at the airport.

VISITOR INFORMATION Contact **Telluride & Mountain Village Visitor Services/ Telluride Central Reservations,** 630 W. Colorado Ave. (P.O. Box 1009), Telluride, CO 81435 (© **888/605-2578;** www.visittelluride.com). The **Telluride Visitor Information Center,** open daily from 9am to 6pm, can be found with the visitor services and central reservations offices.

SPECIAL EVENTS & FESTIVALS   The **Telluride Film Festival** (© **970/728-4640;** www.telluridefilmfestival.com), an influential event that takes place over Labor Day weekend, has premiered award-winners such as *Crouching Tiger, Hidden Dragon* and *Sling Blade.* What truly sets it apart, however, is the casual interaction between stars and attendees. Open-air films and seminars are free. The **Telluride Bluegrass Festival** (© **800/624-2422;** www.bluegrass.com) is one of the most renowned bluegrass, folk, and country jam sessions in the U.S. It's held over 4 days in late June.

WHAT TO SEE

To get a glimpse of Telluride's wild and wicked past, stop at the **Telluride Historical Museum,** 201 W. Gregory Ave. (© **970/728-3344;** www.telluridemuseum.com). It was built in 1888 as the community hospital. The museum houses artifacts, historical photos, and exhibits that show what Telluride was like in its Wild West days, when the likes of Butch Cassidy stalked the streets. There are also exhibits on the area's Indian heritage, mining, and even Telluride's ski boom of the 1970s. Admission is $5 adults, $3 seniors and students 6 to 17; the museum is open Tuesday through Saturday from 11am to 5pm, Sunday 1 to 5pm (closed Sun Sept–May).

The best way to see the Telluride National Historic District and get a feel for the West of the late 1800s is to take to the streets, following the excellent **walking tour** described in the *Telluride Visitor's Guide,* available at the Telluride Visitor Information Center (see "Visitor Information," above).

OUTDOOR ACTIVITIES

The elegant European-style Mountain Village offers a fascinating contrast to the laid-back community of artists, shopkeepers, and dropouts in the 1870s Victorian mining town of Telluride below. Located midmountain at an elevation of 9,450 feet, the Mountain Village offers ski-in/ski-out accommodations; eight slope-side restaurants including Gorrono Ranch, a historic homestead; spectacular scenery; and, of course, great skiing for all ability levels. There are 84 trails served by 16 lifts. For snow reports and additional information, contact **Telluride Ski and Golf Company** (© **800/801-4832** or 970/728-6900; www.tellurideskiresort.com).

The Mountain Village at Telluride Ski Resort (see above) has 30km of **Nordic trails,** which connect with 20km of groomed trails at Town Park and River Corridor Trail, giving cross-country skiers a total of 50km. Telluride also has one of the top **snowboarding parks** in Colorado, offering more than 13 acres of terrain.

In addition to splendid skiing and snowboarding, there are numerous outdoor recreation opportunities year-round. The major outfitter and arranger of summertime outdoor activities here is the versatile and dependable **Telluride Outside,** 121 W. Colorado Ave. (© **800/831-6230** or 970/728-3895; www.tellurideoutside.com).

Town Park, at the east end of town (© **970/728-3071;** www.town.telluride.co.us), is home to the community's various festivals. It also has a public outdoor pool, open in summer, plus tennis courts, sand volleyball courts, a small outdoor basketball court, a skateboarding ramp, playing fields, a picnic area, and a fishing pond.

There's excellent **fishing** in the San Miguel River through Telluride, but it's even better in nearby Alpine lakes, including Silver Lake, reached by foot in Bridal Veil Basin, and Trout and Priest lakes, about 12 miles south via Colo. 145.

Telluride is a major **mountain-biking** center. The **San Juan Hut System** (© **970/626-3033;** www.sanjuanhuts.com) links Telluride with Moab, Utah, via a 206-mile-long network of backcountry dirt roads. Every 35 miles is a primitive cabin, with bunks, a woodstove, a propane cooking stove, and cooking gear. The route is appropriate for intermediate-level riders in good physical condition. Cost for those making the whole trip is about $550, which includes use of the six huts, three meals a day, sleeping bags at each hut, and maps and trail descriptions. Shorter trips, guide services, and vehicle shuttles are also available.

WHERE TO STAY

A good way to book lodging is with **ResortQuest Telluride** (© 866/538-7731; www.resortquesttelluride.com). The best way to book lodging, however, is with the **Telluride & Mountain Village Convention & Visitors Bureau** (© 888/605-2578; www.visittelluride.com). Room tax adds a bit over 12%.

Among the top luxury choices is the **Camel's Garden Resort Hotel,** 250 W. San Juan Ave. (© 888/772-2635 or 970/728-9300; www.camelsgarden.com), which has a perfect location—it's ski-in/ski-out and only steps from the town gondola, and also within 2 short blocks of the main shopping and dining section of historic Telluride. Doubles run $155 to $675.

More moderately priced is the **New Sheridan Hotel,** 231 W. Colorado Ave. (© 800/200-1891 or 970/728-4351; www.newsheridan.com), a delightfully restored and modernized 1895 Victorian hotel, where William Jennings Bryan delivered his famous "Cross of Gold" speech in 1902. Rooms run $100 to $300. The **Victorian Inn,** 401 W. Pacific Ave. (© 800/611-9893 or 970/728-6601; www.tellurideinn.com), is an affordable B&B-style alternative to renting a condo. Rates run $99 to $249 double.

7 Salt Lake City

Nestled between the Wasatch Mountains on the east and the Great Salt Lake on the west, at an elevation of 4,330 feet, lies Salt Lake City. Utah's capital is relatively small, with a population of less than 200,000. But travelers come from around the world to visit magnificent Temple Square, world headquarters of the Church of Jesus Christ of Latter-Day Saints (LDS), and to hear the inspired voices of the Mormon Tabernacle Choir.

Exhilarating outdoor recreation possibilities are only about an hour's drive from the city, and include some of the country's best ski resorts; miles of terrific mountain trails for hiking, biking, and horseback riding; and the intriguing Great Salt Lake.

ESSENTIALS

GETTING THERE   By Plane   Direct flights connect Salt Lake City to almost 70 cities in the United States and Canada. **Salt Lake City International Airport** (© 800/595-2442 or 801/575-2400; www.slcairport.com) is located just north of I-80 at Exit 115, on the west side of the city.

By Train   Amtrak has several trains arriving daily from both coasts. The station is at 340 S. 600 W. (© 800/872-7245; www.amtrak.com).

By Car   Salt Lake City is 303 miles north of St. George, 238 miles northwest of Moab, 45 miles north of Provo, and 35 miles south of Ogden. You can reach it via **I-80** from the east (Cheyenne) or west (Reno), or from the north (Pocatello) or south (Las Vegas) via **I-15.**

VISITOR INFORMATION   The **Salt Lake Convention and Visitors Bureau** has an information center downtown in the Salt Palace, 90 S. West Temple (© 800/541-4955 or 801/521-2822; www.visitsaltlake.com). It's open Monday through Friday from 8:30am to 5pm (until 6pm from Memorial Day to Labor Day), Saturday and

Sunday from 9am to 5pm. Additional information centers, staffed 9am to 9pm daily, can be found in the baggage areas in Salt Lake City International Airport Terminals I and II. There is another information center just off I-80 at 7200 West, open Wednesday through Sunday from 9:30am to 5pm.

GETTING AROUND   Salt Lake is a fairly easy city in which to drive, with wide streets and abundant parking. There are many public parking lots in the downtown area, costing from $1 to $7 per day. Parking on streets downtown is metered, costing 25¢ per half-hour, and usually limited to 130 minutes or 2 hours.

The **Utah Transit Authority** (℃ **888/743-3882** or 801/743-3882; www.utabus. com or www.rideuta.com) provides **bus service** throughout the city, with a free-fare zone in the downtown area. **Traxx,** a light-rail system also operated by the Utah Transit Authority, runs 15 miles from the Sandy Civic Center in the Salt Lake City suburb of Sandy north to Delta Center in downtown Salt Lake City. The trains are wheelchair accessible and bicycles are permitted. Route schedules and maps for both the buses and light rail are available at malls, libraries, and visitor centers.

For a taxi, contact **City Cab** (℃ **801/363-5550**), **Yellow Cab** (℃ **801/521-2100**), or **Ute Cab** (℃ **801/359-7788**), all available 24 hours a day.

FAST FACTS   For physician referrals, contact the **Utah Medical Association** (℃ **801/355-7477**) during normal business hours. Hospitals include **LDS Hospital,** 8th Avenue and C Street (℃ **801/408-1100**), and **Salt Lake Regional Medical Center,** 1050 E. South Temple (℃ **801/350-4111**); both have 24-hour emergency rooms. **Sales tax** is 6.6%, and **lodging taxes** total 11.2%.

EXPLORING TEMPLE SQUARE

This is mecca for members of the Church of Jesus Christ of Latter-day Saints, also known as Mormons. The 10-acre square is enclosed by 15-foot walls, with a gate in the center of each. In addition to the church buildings, the square is home to the North and South visitor centers as well as lovely gardens and statuary. Even if you start at the **South Visitor Center,** you may want to stop into the **North Visitor Center** for a look at its murals and 11-foot replica of Thorvaldsen's *Christus.*

The **Temple** is used only for the Mormons' most sacred services and is not open to the public. Early church leader Brigham Young chose the site within 4 days of entering the valley, and work was begun on the six-spired granite structure in 1853. It took 40 years to complete.

The oval **Tabernacle** seats 6,500 people and has one of the West's largest unsupported domed roofs. Boasting unbelievable acoustics, it has served as the city's cultural center for over a century.

Thursday evenings at 8pm, you can listen to the **Mormon Tabernacle Choir** rehearse (except when they're on tour; call ℃ **801/240-3221** or visit www.mormon tabernaclechoir.org to check), and on Sunday mornings you can attend their broadcast from 9:30 to 10am (you must be seated by 9:15am). The choir, composed entirely of volunteers, was formed shortly after the first pioneers arrived; many husband-and-wife members and families participate, sometimes over several generations. The Tabernacle organ has been rebuilt several times over the years, and has grown from the original 1,600 pipes and two manuals to 11,623 pipes and five manuals. Half-hour organ recitals take place year-round Monday through Saturday at noon and Sunday at 2pm. At peak times, an additional 2pm recital is often scheduled Monday through Saturday. Admission to these performances is free.

The Gothic-style **Assembly Hall** was constructed in 1880 from leftover granite from the Temple, and is often the site of concerts and lectures. Inquire at one of the visitor centers for schedules. Two monuments stand in front of the Assembly Hall: One depicts a pioneer family arriving with a handcart filled with their belongings, and the second commemorates the salvaging of the first crops from a plague of crickets (seagulls swooped down and ate the insects).

Guided tours of the square, lasting approximately 45 minutes and available in 30 languages, leave every few minutes from the flagpole in front of the Tabernacle; personnel in the visitor center can direct you. Tour guides provide a general history of the church (touching upon the church's doctrine) and take you around the square, briefly explaining what you are seeing. Our favorite part of the tour is in the Tabernacle: To demonstrate the incredible acoustics, the group is ushered to the back of the seats while someone stands at the podium and drops three pins—the sound is as clear as a bell! (*Note:* The tour ends at the North Visitor Center with a short film on Mormon beliefs. You are then asked to fill out a card with your name and address, indicating whether you would like to receive a visit from Mormon missionaries.)

The square is bounded by Main Street on the east, and by North, South, and West Temple streets. Tours are given daily from 9am to 8pm. Call ✆ **800/537-9703** or 801/240-4872 for more information, or browse www.visittemplesquare.com or www.lds.org.

MORE ATTRACTIONS

Beehive House   Brigham Young built this house in 1854 as his family home, but he also kept an office and entertained church and government leaders here. Young, who loved New England architecture, used much of that style, even including a widow's walk for keeping an eye on the surrounding desert. Today, visitors can get a glimpse of the lifestyle of this famous Mormon leader by taking a guided half-hour tour of the house. It has been decorated with period furniture (many pieces original to the home) to resemble its appearance when Young lived here. Allow 1 hour.

67 E. South Temple. ✆ **801/240-2671**. www.lds.org/placestovisit. Free admission. Mon–Sat 9am–9pm. Trax: Temple Sq.; walk a half-block east.

Capitol Building   Built between 1912 and 1915 of unpolished Utah granite and Georgia marble, the capitol rests on a hill in a beautifully landscaped 40-acre park. The state symbol, the beehive (representing industry and cooperation), is a recurring motif both inside and out. The Rotunda, which stretches upward 165 feet, is decorated with WPA murals and houses several busts of prominent historical figures, including Brigham Young and Philo T. Farnsworth, the man who brought us television. The chandelier is astounding—it weighs 6,000 pounds and hangs from a 7,000-pound chain. Allow 1 to 2 hours.

Note: At press time, the capitol was in the midst of a multi-year restoration project and closed to the public until 2008. Call for current information.

Capitol Hill, at the north end of State St. ✆ **801/538-3000**. Free admission and tours. Building daily 8am–8pm; guided tours every half-hour Mon–Fri 9am–4pm. Bus: 23 up Main St.

Family History Library   This incredible facility contains what is probably the world's largest collection of genealogical records under one roof. Most date from 1550 to 1920, and are from governments, churches, other organizations, and individuals. The collection is composed of a substantial number of records from around the United States, fairly comprehensive data from Scotland and England, and information from many other countries. When you enter the library, you'll find people ready to

Downtown Salt Lake City

assist with your research. They'll offer forms you can fill out with any and all data you already know (so come prepared with copies of whatever you have), and can direct you from there. Allow at least 2 hours.

35 N. West Temple. (© 800/346-6044 or 801/240-2584. www.familysearch.org. Free admission. Mon 8am–5pm; Tues–Sat 8am–9pm. Closed major holidays and July 24. Trax: Temple Sq.

This Is the Place Heritage Park Brigham Young and the first group of pioneers got their first glimpse of the Salt Lake Valley here. A tall granite and bronze sculpture was erected in 1947 to commemorate the centennial of their arrival. Old Deseret is a village made up of original pioneer buildings from across the state. In the summer, it becomes a living history museum of the years 1847 to 1869, featuring people in period garb living and working the way their forefathers did. Pioneer events and demonstrations are offered throughout the year. The 1,600-acre park also offers hiking along part of the trail used by the pioneers, plus picnicking, bird-watching, and cross-country skiing. Allow 1 to 3 hours.

2601 E. Sunnyside Ave. (© 801/582-1847. www.thisistheplace.org. Free admission to park and visitor center. Admission to Deseret Village $6 adults, $4 children 3–11 and seniors 62 and over. Park daily dawn–dusk; visitor center Mon–Sat 9am–6pm; Deseret Village summer Mon–Thurs 10am–6pm, Fri–Sat 10am–9pm, call for off-season hours.

WHERE TO STAY

In addition to the properties discussed below, we recommend the **Hotel Monaco,** 105 W. 200 South (© **800/294-9710** or 801/595-0000; www.monaco-saltlakecity.com), housed in the 14-story former Continental Bank Building. The lobby and rooms are a mix of classic and contemporary, pets are welcome (the pet-less are provided with goldfish), and Sweet Tarts replace the usual pillow mints. The Monaco is also home to an excellent restaurant, **Bambara,** and pumps complimentary Wi-Fi Internet access throughout the building, guest rooms included. The **Little America Hotel,** 500 S. Main St. (© **800/453-9450** or 801/363-6781; www.littleamerica.com/slc), is among Salt Lake City's best hotels, offering a wide variety of rooms, all individually decorated, that range from standard courtside rooms in the two-story motel-like buildings to extralarge deluxe tower suites in the 17-story high-rise.

More affordable is the comfortable, completely renovated **Metropolitan Inn,** 524 S. West Temple (© **801/531-7100;** www.metropolitaninn.com), a former chain hotel turned first-rate independent; the **Econo Lodge,** 715 W. North Temple (© **877/233-2666** or 801/363-0062); and the **Hampton Inn Downtown,** 425 S. 300 West (© **800/426-7866** or 801/741-1110).

The huge **Salt Lake KOA/VIP,** 1400 W. North Temple (© **800/562-9510** or 801/355-1214; www.slckoa.com), is the closest camping and RV facility to downtown Salt Lake City. Sites are $22 to $38, cabins $44 to $50.

Anton Boxrud Bed & Breakfast Inn This former boardinghouse, built in 1901, is now a lovely, comfortable bed-and-breakfast inn. Each room is individually decorated with a mix of antiques and reproductions; all have queen-size beds with down comforters. Pocket doors and stained-glass windows grace the sitting room, where guests gather to enjoy evening refreshments. The homemade full breakfast includes a hot dish, and a continental breakfast is available for early risers. The entire property is nonsmoking.

57 S. 600 East, Salt Lake City, UT 84102. (© **800/524-5511** or 801/363-8035. Fax 801/596-1316. www.antonboxrud. com. 7 units, 2 single rooms with shared bathroom. $78–$140 double. Rates include full breakfast. AE, DC, DISC, MC, V. *In room:* No phone.

Inn at Temple Square   Centrally located, the Inn at Temple Square is a gem. It feels like the grand hotels of old, but with a warm, homey touch. The lobby is like a living room, with fine artwork, couches, and chairs you can sink into. Rooms are spacious, with a comfortable, old-world feel. The property is nonsmoking.

71 W. South Temple, Salt Lake City, UT 84101. ℂ 800/843-4668 or 801/531-1000. Fax 801/536-7272. www.theinn. com. 95 units. $135–$155 double; $170–$270 suite. Rates include full breakfast. AE, DC, DISC, MC, V. **Amenities:** Restaurant; free passes to a nearby health club.

Peery Hotel *Best*   The 1910 Peery is one of the few truly historic hotels left in Salt Lake City. It has been fully renovated and restored to its former understated European elegance, offering comfortable, tastefully decorated accommodations. Each of the comfortable and tastefully decorated rooms is unique. Several suites have whirlpool tubs. The entire hotel is nonsmoking.

110 W. 300 South (Broadway), Salt Lake City, UT 84101. ℂ 800/331-0073 or 801/521-4300. Fax 801/575-5014. www.peeryhotel.com. 73 units. $99–$159 double; $189 and up suite (suite rates include breakfast for 2). AE, DC, DISC, MC, V. Parking fee $9 per day self-parking, $12 per day valet. **Amenities:** 2 restaurants; exercise room.

WHERE TO DINE

In-the-know locals say that **Crown Burgers,** 3190 S. Highland Dr. (ℂ **801/467-6633**), serves the best fast-food burger in town. The upscale European hunting lodge decor sets it apart from your average hamburger joint. Additional locations include 377 E. 200 South (ℂ **801/532-1155**) and 118 N. 300 West (ℂ **801/532-5300**).

Café Trang VIETNAMESE/CHINESE   Serving the best Vietnamese food in the state, this family-run restaurant also serves Cantonese dishes with some Vietnamese influences. A popular vegetarian specialty is the fried bean curd with grilled onions and crushed peanuts, served with rice papers, a vegetable platter, and peanut sauce. The dining room is decorated with Vietnamese paintings, and two large aquariums give you something to watch while waiting for your food.

818 S. Main St. ℂ 801/539-1638. Reservations recommended in winter. Main courses $5–$15. AE, DISC, MC, V. Mon–Thurs 11am–9:30pm; Fri–Sat 11am–10pm; Sun noon–9:30pm.

Lamb's Grill Cafe AMERICAN/CONTINENTAL   Lamb's has been here since 1939, offering very good food at reasonable prices, with friendly, efficient service. Decorated with antiques and furnishings from the 1920s and 1930s, Lamb's is comfortable and unpretentious. The extensive menu offers mostly basic American and Continental fare, although the restaurant's Greek origins are also evident. Several lamb dishes appear on the menu, including broiled French-style lamb chops and barbecued lamb shank. You'll also find a good selection of sandwiches and salads, daily pasta and salad specials, and a variety of desserts, including an extra-special rice pudding. Full liquor service is available.

169 S. Main St. ℂ 801/364-7166. Main courses $5–$21. AE, DC, DISC, MC, V. Mon–Fri 7am–9pm; Sat 8am–9pm.

The New Yorker *Best* AMERICAN   Among Salt Lake's finest restaurants, the elegant New Yorker is noted for quiet sophistication, excellent food, and impeccable service. As it's technically a private club (and thus able to offer complete liquor service even without a food purchase), you'll have to buy a membership to enter (a well-spent $5). Sit either in the dining room or in the less formal cafe, where you'll dine under the original stained-glass ceiling from the old Hotel Utah. From the dining-room dinner menu, you might choose the superb Dungeness crab cakes; or the roasted rack of American lamb with rosemary cream sauce. The cafe menu offers lighter choices.

60 W. Market St. ℭ 801/363-0166. www.gastronomyinc.com. Reservations recommended. Dining room main courses $8–$15 lunch, $20–$35 dinner; cafe main courses $7–$20. AE, DC, DISC, MC, V. Dining room Mon–Thurs 11:30am–2:30pm and 5:30–10pm; Fri 11:30am–2:30pm and 5:30–10:30pm; Sat 5:30–10:30pm. Cafe Mon–Thurs 11:30am–2:30pm and 4:30–10:30pm; Fri 11:30am–2:30pm and 4:30–11pm; Sat 5:30–11pm.

SALT LAKE CITY AFTER DARK

THE PERFORMING ARTS   The historic **Capitol Theatre,** 50 W. 200 South (ℭ **801/355-2787**), is home to several local performing-arts companies. It's the place to go for dance, theater, and musical productions.

The highly acclaimed **Utah Symphony & Opera** (ℭ **801/533-6683;** www.utah symphonyopera.org) combines one of the country's top symphony orchestras and the well-respected Utah Opera Company. They present four operas a year plus a year-round symphony season at Abravanel Hall, 123 W. South Temple, an elegant 2,800-seat venue known for its excellent acoustics.

THE CLUB & BAR SCENE   One of the city's more with-it and cosmopolitan nightspots is **Mynt Lounge,** 63 W. 100 South (ℭ **801/355-6968**), an upscale bar with an extensive martini menu. This place attracts one of Salt Lake City's hippest crowds. Established in 1965, the **Dead Goat Saloon,** 119 S. West Temple, in Arrow Press Square (ℭ **801/328-4628;** www.deadgoat.com), is a fun, funky bar featuring live blues bands. **Squatter's Pub Brewery,** 147 W. Broadway (ℭ **801/305-2739**), brews top-notch suds and thumbs its nose at local conservatism with such beer names as Provo Girl and Chasing Tail.

NEARBY SKIING

You say you want snow? Here it is, some 500 inches of it every year, just waiting for powder-hungry skiers to make that short drive from Salt Lake City. You'll find Brighton and Solitude ski resorts in Big Cottonwood Canyon, and Alta and Snowbird in its sister canyon, known as Little Cottonwood.

If you're skiing on a budget, you might want to stay in Salt Lake City, where lodging is much cheaper, rather than at the resorts themselves. The resorts are so close—less than an hour's drive—that city dwellers sometimes hit the slopes after a hard day at the office. Full-day adult lift ticket prices at these resorts range from $44 to $51, with Alta and Brighton offering the best bargains.

But this area is more than just a winter playground. Big Cottonwood Canyon, cut by ancient rivers over centuries, is a spectacular setting for warm-weather picnicking, camping, mountain-biking, and hiking. Rugged, glacier-carved Little Cottonwood Canyon is filled with lush fields of wildflowers in the summer; that rainbow of color later takes a back seat to the brilliant hues of autumn.

Brighton Ski Resort (ℭ **800/873-5512** or 801/532-4731; www.brightonresort.com) is a low-key, family-friendly resort. The ski school is highly regarded, children 10 and under stay and ski free with their parents, and teens enjoy the bumps of Lost Maid Trail as it winds through the woods. Brighton's slopes are graced with a full range of terrain, all the powder you can ski, and virtually no crowds. Brighton is also one of the best snowboarding destinations in the state.

Solitude Mountain Resort (ℭ **800/748-4754** or 801/534-1400; www.skisolitude. com) is another friendly, family-oriented ski area that hasn't been "discovered" yet, so lift lines are virtually nonexistent. Solitude enjoys excellent powder. Its 1,200-plus acres of skiable terrain range from well-groomed, sunny beginner and intermediate trails to gently pitched bowls and glades. Intermediates also have several excellent forest runs and some great bumpy stretches on which to hone their mogul skills. Advanced skiers will also find plenty to keep them happy. Solitude boasts a world-class Nordic center, which connects to Brighton Ski Resort.

Alta Ski Area (© 801/359-1078; www.alta.com) is famous for its snow—over 500 inches annually of some of the lightest powder in the world—and its lift tickets are one of the best skiing bargains in the country. This is an excellent choice for serious skiers of all levels. Intermediates will find plenty of open cruising ground, forested areas, and long arcing chutes to glide through; experts will find an abundance of the Cottonwood Canyons' famous powder and spectacular runs, like steep, long Alf's High Rustler. Alta has chosen to limit its uphill capacity by not installing high-speed quads, and people are turned away on those occasions when the ski gods determine there are already enough skiers on the mountain. There's a highly regarded ski school here, too. Snowboarding is not permitted.

Snowbird Ski & Summer Resort (© 800/232-9542 or 801/742-2222; www. snowbird.com) offers super skiing and super facilities. Consistently rated among America's top-10 ski resorts, Snowbird has been called Alta's "younger, slicker sister." You'll find the same wonderful snow here, but with a wider range of amenities, including Snowbird's extremely popular spa and salon—worth the trip even if you don't ski. Some, however, find its dense, modern village and resort atmosphere cold compared to Alta's historic, European-style lodges and ruggedly Western attitude. Snowbird gives over almost half of its skiable terrain to the expert skier. There's not a lot for beginners and intermediates, but enough to keep them happy—what is here is top-notch. The entire mountain is open to snowboarders.

GETTING THERE   From Salt Lake City, take **I-215** south to Exit 7; follow **Utah 210** south. Turn east onto **Utah 190** to reach Solitude and Brighton in Big Cottonwood Canyon; continue on Utah 210 south and east to Snowbird and Alta in Little Cottonwood Canyon. From Salt Lake City International Airport, it'll take about an hour to reach any of the four ski areas.

8 Park City: Utah's Premier Resort Town

Utah's most sophisticated resort community, Park City reminds us of Aspen, Colorado, a historic Western town that has made the most of excellent ski terrain while evolving into popular year-round vacation destination, offering a casual Western atmosphere with a touch of elegance—for those willing to pay for it. Visitors will find three separate ski areas; lodgings that range from basic to luxurious; some of the state's most innovative restaurants and best shops; an abundance of fine performing-arts events; many of Utah's liveliest nightspots; and plenty of hiking, mountain biking, fishing, and other outdoor opportunities.

ESSENTIALS

GETTING THERE   Park City is 32 miles east of Salt Lake City via **I-80.** At Exit 145, take **Utah 224** into Park City. Driving time from Salt Lake City International Airport is about 35 minutes.

VISITOR INFORMATION   The **Park City Chamber of Commerce/Convention and Visitors Bureau,** 1910 Prospector Ave. (P.O. Box 1630), Park City, UT 84060 (© 800/453-1360 or 435/649-6100; www.parkcityinfo.com), maintains an information center in the Park City Museum at 528 Main St. and at a visitor information center at 1826 W. Olympic Pkwy. at the entrance to the Utah Olympic Park near I-80.

GETTING AROUND   Parking in Park City is tough, especially in the historic Main Street area. The best plan is to park your car once and ride the free city bus. Park City's efficient transit system connects Deer Valley, Main Street, The Canyons, the factory store area, and the Park City Mountain Resort. The **Main Street Trolley** links Main Street and Park City Mountain Resort, and **public buses** travel to the outlying areas. Pick up the *Transit System Guide* brochure for a good route map and specific schedules. The weekly booklet *This Week in Park City* contains helpful info plus several area maps, including one of Main Street. Both are available at the visitor centers and many lodgings.

SPECIAL EVENTS & FESTIVALS   Throughout the summer, free concerts are presented each Wednesday evening from 6 to 8pm at City Park. One week you might hear bluegrass; the next, classical; and yet another it might be rock or jazz.

The **Deer Valley Music Festival** (© 801/533-6683; www.deervalleymusicfestival. org) takes place in July and August. The program includes classical masterpieces like Tchaikovsky's *1812 Overture,* plus jazz and popular works by composers such as Gilbert and Sullivan and John Philip Sousa. There are also concerts by acts such as Air Supply and the Gatlin Brothers. The stage faces the mountainside; bring a chair or blanket and relax under the stars.

The **Park City International Music Festival** (© 435/649-5309; www.pcmusic festival.com) presents classical performances year-round, and goes all out for its summer concert series from early July to early August. Classical musicians from around the world attend, and programs feature soloists, chamber music, and full orchestras.

In January, the **Sundance Film Festival** takes place, with numerous film showings in Park City (see "Sundance," later in this chapter).

SKIING THE PARK CITY AREA RESORTS

The three area ski resorts, all within a few minutes' drive of Park City, are vastly different. Lift tickets range from $69 to $76, making this a pricier place to ski than the Cottonwood Canyon resorts. Snowboarders are welcome at Park City Mountain Resort and The Canyons, but not Deer Valley.

Many skiers try all three resorts, and if you're going to do so, it will pay to do a bit of advance planning. The three resorts offer what they call a **Silver Passport,** which is a discounted multiday package for use at all three resorts. There are various restrictions, though, including that it MUST be purchased before your arrival in Park City, and that it must be purchased in conjunction with lodging. Contact the resorts or area lodging properties for details.

Unquestionably Utah's most elegant and sophisticated ski area, **Deer Valley** (© 800/ 424-3337 or 435/649-1000; www.deervalley.com) offers perfectly manicured slopes, ski valet service, heated sidewalks, and some of the state's finest dining and lodging. Along with all this, you get great skiing—especially if you crave long, smooth, perfectly groomed cruising runs that let you enjoy the spectacular mountain scenery around you.

Park City Mountain Resort (© 800/222-7275 or 435/649-8111; www.parkcity mountain.com), one of Utah's largest and liveliest resorts, is where the U.S. Olympic ski team comes to train. What brings them here? Plenty of dependable, powdery snow and a variety of terrain and runs that offer something for everyone, from novices to experts. Surveys continually rank Park City among the country's top resorts for both its terrain and its challenging runs. There's even a triple-chair access lift directly from the Old Town onto the mountain, as well as two runs that lead back into town, so those staying in Park City proper don't have to ride back and forth to the base resort every day. Snowboarding is allowed.

The **Canyons Resort** (© **888/CANYONS** or 435/649-5400; www.thecanyons.com), America's fifth-largest ski area, offers skiing and snowboarding on eight peaks served by 16 lifts. In the past few years, intermediate and expert terrains have been greatly expanded. The resort boasts 146 runs on more than 3,500 skiable acres. **White Pine Touring Center** (© **435/649-8701** or 435/615-5858; www.whitepinetouring.com), Park City's cross-country ski center, has 11 miles of groomed trails.

WARM-WEATHER ACTIVITIES IN & AROUND PARK CITY

Getting into the mountains above Park City in summer couldn't be easier for hikers and mountain bikers, thanks to the chairlifts at two resorts. **Deer Valley Resort** offers more than 50 miles of trails, and **Park City Mountain Resort**'s chairlifts provide access to more than 30 miles of trails. As you might expect, the terrain is steep but beautiful.

FLY-FISHING   There are numerous fishing opportunities in the mountains surrounding Park City. For tips on where they're biting, stop at **Jans Mountain Outfitters,** 1600 Park Ave. (© **800/745-1020** or 435/649-4949; www.jans.com), and at the **Park City Fly Shop,** 2065 Sidewinder Dr., Prospector Square (© **800/324-6778** or 435/645-8382; www.pcflyshop.com). Both companies offer guided trips and equipment rentals, and Park City Fly Shop has a sales outlet.

HIKING & MOUNTAIN BIKING   The mountains around Park City offer numerous trails for hiking and mountain biking. For a short hike with a variety of terrain and good views of both mountains and town, try the 1.5-mile **Sweeny Switchbacks Trail,** accessible from the base of the town lift.

The 30-mile **Historic Union Pacific Rail Trail State Park** hiking and biking path follows the old Union Pacific railroad bed from Park City to Echo Reservoir. It offers wonderful views of meadows, the volcanic crags of Silver Creek Canyon, the Weber River, Echo Reservoir, and the steep walls of Echo Canyon. You might spot deer, elk, moose, and bald eagles along the trail. An end-of-the-trail pickup service is available from **Daytrips** (© **888/649-8294;** www.daytrips.com).

More than 30 miles of dirt roads and single-track trails at **Park City Mountain Resort** (p. 710; © **800/222-7275** or 435/649-8111; www.parkcitymountain.com) are open to hikers and mountain bikers, who can ride the PayDay chairlift up and then bike or hike down. Tickets cost $11 for a single ride, or $18 for an all-day pass. **Deer Valley Resort** (p. 710; © **800/424-3337** or 435/649-1000; www.deervalley.com) offers more than 50 miles of panoramic trails for both hikers and bikers, with chairlift access in summer ($12 a ride or $20 a day). As you might expect, the terrain is steep and beautiful.

For a good description of several other area trails, pick up a copy of the free *Park City Hiking & Biking Trail Map* at either visitor center and at sporting goods shops.

MORE TO SEE & DO IN & AROUND PARK CITY

The **Park City Museum of History & Territorial Jail,** 528 Main St. (© **435/615-9559;** www.parkcityhistory.org), is a must-see—the dark, tiny cells were state-of-the-art in 1886! The upstairs is a bit more civilized, with a stagecoach, 19th-century mining equipment, and early ski gear.

Historic **Main Street** is lined with galleries, boutiques, and a wide variety of shops, with transportation conveniently provided by the Main Street Trolley. Although you won't find many bargains, prices aren't too far out of line for a tourist and ski town, and are downright reasonable compared to places such as Aspen and Santa Fe.

Park City also makes a good base for exploring the area's state parks and other attractions. The Jordanelle State Park's two recreation areas provide access to **Jordanelle Reservoir** (© 435/649-9540; www.stateparks.utah.gov) in the beautiful Wasatch Mountains. Both areas are great for boating, fishing, picnicking, and camping. The Rock Cliff area of the park offers great bird-watching, with more than 160 species either living here or passing through, including eagles and other raptors that often nest in the area.

Wasatch Mountain State Park (© 435/654-1791; www.stateparks.utah.gov) is a year-round destination. It's terrific for camping, has trails for hikers and mountain bikers, and boasts two scenic golf courses. Tee times should be reserved the preceding Monday for weekends, and the preceding Thursday for weekdays. Call © **435/654-0532,** or 801/266-0068 for reservations. In the winter, a network of groomed cross-country skiing and snowmobiling trails leads from the park into the surrounding forest, and both cross-country ski and snowmobile rentals are available.

Nestled in Heber Valley, **Heber City** retains its small-town atmosphere, despite its proximity to Salt Lake City. Here you can ride the **Heber Valley Historic Railroad** (© **435/654-5601;** www.hebervalleyrr.org). The diversity of the landscape along the route is unparalleled, especially in fall, when the mountainsides are blanketed with colorful foliage. The round-trip fare is $20 to $26 adults, $12 to $15 children ages 3 to 12, and $15 to $21 seniors 60 and older. Rates are higher for special events, and one-way tickets are also available (call for rates). There are four daily runs in summer, and fewer the rest of year.

WHERE TO STAY

Rates are almost always higher—sometimes dramatically so—during ski season, and rates during Christmas week can be absurd. You'll find the best bargains in spring and fall. Sales and lodging taxes in Park City total just over 10%. Pets are not allowed, unless otherwise noted.

Although it's possible to book reservations directly with individual lodges, many people find it more convenient to go the one-stop shopping route, making all their arrangements directly with one of the resorts. **Deer Valley Resort** (© 800/424-3337 or 435/649-1000; www.deervalley.com) and **Park City Mountain Resort** (© 800/222-7275 or 435/649-8111; www.parkcitymountain.com) both have central reservation offices that can reserve lodging for you at a nearby condo or lodge, and can also make airline, car rental, and lift-ticket reservations.

Goldener Hirsch Inn This château-style inn combines warm hospitality with European charm. Austrian antiques dot the common areas and decorate the walls. The spacious rooms are elegantly furnished with hand-painted and hand-carved furniture from Austria and king-size beds with down comforters. Suites have wood-burning fireplaces and small private balconies. The excellent restaurant is Austrian in decor, and features international cuisine.

7570 Royal St. East, Silver Lake Village, Deer Valley (P.O. Box 859), Park City, UT 84060. © **800/252-3373** or 435/649-7770. Fax 435/649-7901. www.goldenerhirschinn.com. 20 units. Winter (including continental breakfast) $250–$975 double; summer $100–$250 double. AE, MC, V. Closed mid-Apr to mid-June and Oct–Nov. **Amenities:** Restaurant.

Hotel Park City Opening January 2003, this instantly became one of the most posh places to hang your hat in the area, if not the entire state. Drawing inspiration from the grand lodges of the national park system, the brain trust behind Hotel Park City spared no expense, from the masculine guest rooms, all with sublime mountain views, to the year-round pool in the central courtyard. The rooms feature king-size beds, two TVs, kitchenettes, washers and dryers, and Western decor; bathrooms are superb, with big jetted tubs and separate three-headed showers. There's also a top-rate spa and a new Park City Mountain Resort lift on the way to the property in late 2006.

2001 Park Ave. (P.O. Box 683120), Park City, UT 84068. (©) **435/200-2000.** Fax 435/940-5001. www.hotelparkcity. com. 100 suites. Winter $299–$999 suite; summer $1,599–$3,000 governor's or presidential suite. AE, DC, DISC, MC, V. **Amenities:** Restaurant; outdoor heated pool; spa. *In room:* kitchenette.

Old Town Guest House   This cozy little B&B is perfect for outdoor enthusiasts— the innkeeper is a backcountry ski guide in winter and avid hiker and biker in summer. The inn is within easy walking distance of both the Park City Mountain Resort and Main Street. The delightfully homey living room retains its original 1910 fireplace. The decor is country, with lodgepole pine furniture and hardwood floors throughout, but as with most historic bed-and-breakfasts, each guest room is unique. The hearty breakfasts will sustain your energy throughout a day of hiking, biking, or skiing.

1011 Empire Ave. (P.O. Box 162), Park City, UT 84060. (©) **800/290-6423,** ext. 3710, or 435/649-2642. Fax 435/649-3320. www.oldtownguesthouse.com. 4 units. Winter (including breakfast) $109–$250 double; summer $79–$119 double. AE, MC, V. *In room:* No phone in some rooms.

Stein Eriksen Lodge (Best)   This luxurious, full-service lodge features a warm, friendly atmosphere and Scandinavian decor and charm. The lobby is most impressive, with a magnificent three-story stone fireplace. There are 13 rooms in the main lodge, with the remaining units in nearby buildings. The connecting sidewalks are heated, and the grounds are beautifully landscaped with aspen trees, manicured lawns, and flowers cascading over rock gardens and retaining walls. The spacious deluxe rooms, each individually decorated, contain whirlpool tubs, vaulted ceilings, and tasteful, solid wood furniture.

Stein Way (P.O. Box 3177), Park City, UT 84060. (©) **800/453-1302** or 435/649-3700. Fax 435/649-5825. www.stein lodge.com. 170 units. Winter (including buffet breakfast) $700–$1,000 double, from $1,310 suite; mid-Apr to late Nov $200–$225 double, from $275 suite. AE, DC, DISC, MC, V. **Amenities:** 2 restaurants; outdoor heated pool; exercise room; full-service spa.

Washington School Inn   Housed in an 1889 limestone schoolhouse nestled against the Wasatch Mountains, this lovely country inn has preserved its original charm even through modernization. Rooms are individually decorated, many in country style, with antiques and reproductions. Two suites have wood-burning fireplaces. Though the inn has no televisions or air-conditioning, there are ski lockers, a sauna, and a whirlpool area. The inn provides a full breakfast buffet each morning, afternoon tea in the summer, and hearty après-ski refreshments in the winter.

543 Park Ave. (P.O. Box 536), Park City, UT 84060. (©) **800/824-1672** or 435/649-3808. Fax 435/649-3802. www. washingtonschoolinn.com. 15 units. Winter $145–$265 double, $245–$410 suite; summer $95–$150 double, $150–$175 suite. Rates include breakfast. AE, DISC, MC, V. *In room:* No TV, no A/C.

WHERE TO DINE

The Eating Establishment AMERICAN   The Eating Establishment, probably the oldest continuously operating restaurant on Park City's historic Main Street (since 1972), is casual and comfortable, a great choice for families or anyone who wants a heaping serving of comfort food at very reasonable prices. The dining room is brick and light-colored wood, with several fireplaces. The menu offers a variety of salads, excellent barbecued baby back ribs, a certified Black Angus Kansas City strip steak (charbroiled and served with sautéed whole mushrooms), and several pasta selections. There's full liquor service.

317 Main St. ℂ 435/649-8284. Main courses $6–$11 breakfast and lunch, $8–$23 dinner. AE, DISC, MC, V. Daily 8am–10pm. Closed 3:30–5pm on weekdays spring–fall. Main St. Trolley.

Glitretind Restaurant (Best) CONTEMPORARY INTERNATIONAL Located in the elegant Stein Eriksen Lodge, this equally stylish restaurant is our pick for the very best dining in the Park City area, and possibly the entire state. The Glitretind serves innovative, impeccably prepared meals in a modern, airy dining room with views of the spectacular Wasatch Mountains. Great breakfast offerings include the Glitretind omelet, filled with grilled onions, bacon, cheddar, and potatoes. At dinner, you might start with the grilled vegetable and lentil strudel or the seared buffalo carpaccio, then choose for your main course the Tea and Szechuan Pepper Crusted Duck Breast—Muscovy duck breast crusted with a floral spiced mixture of ground jasmine tea and Szechuan peppercorns, then pan-seared and briefly roasted.

Stein Eriksen Lodge, Deer Valley. ℂ 435/649-3700. www.steinlodge.com. Reservations requested. Main courses $10–$20 breakfast, $8–$18 lunch, $22–$47 dinner. AE, DC, DISC, MC, V. Mon–Sat 7–10am and 11:30am–2:30pm; brunch Sun 10:30am–2:30pm; daily 6–9pm. Bus: Deer Valley Loop.

Grappa Italian Restaurant ITALIAN Grappa feels like a Tuscan farmhouse. The restaurant has three floors, with a small patio on the ground floor and a larger second-floor deck with a delightful view. Everything's made from scratch, using the freshest herbs and vegetables. Dishes include grilled chicken and spinach lasagna, and open-spit-roasted guinea fowl. The meats and fowl are seasoned, then grilled or cooked rotisserie-style over a wood fire. There's full liquor service.

151 Main St. ℂ 435/645-0636. www.grapparestaurant.com. Reservations required. Main courses $22–$34. AE, DISC, MC, V. Winter daily 5–10pm; summer Wed–Mon 5:30–10pm. May close several weeks in Nov and Apr. Main St. Trolley.

Wahso—An Asian Grill ASIAN This distinctively elegant restaurant boasts an Art Deco and Victorian interior furnished with authentic Asian screens, an ebony fireplace, and carvings and pictures from around the world. The food is equally unique, an amalgamation of traditional Asian ingredients with French cooking style, which gives rise to deliciously light and healthy offerings. Entrees change frequently, but might include specialties such as Szechuan-style grilled filet mignon, soy- and ginger-glazed sea bass, and spicy Balinese stir-fry of shrimp. Be sure to save room for the dessert specialty—crème brûlée in a coconut shell. Premium sake, imported beer, and an extensive wine list are available.

577 Main St. ℂ 435/615-0300. www.wahso.com. Main courses $24–$35. AE, DISC, MC, V. Winter daily 5–10pm; spring–fall Sun–Thurs 6–9pm, Fri–Sat 6–10pm. Main St. Trolley.

PARK CITY AFTER DARK: THE CLUB SCENE

Known as Utah's Party Town, Park City probably has the best nightlife in the state. If you're looking to drink and dance, join a private club (memberships are available on a short-term basis, usually for $4, and entitle you to bring several guests). The following are busiest during ski season, with fewer nights of live music at other times.

The Spur, 350½ Main St. (ℂ 435/615-1618; www.350main.com), is a contemporary Western joint that's smoke-free and has regular live music. **Cisero's,** downstairs at 306 Main St. (ℂ 435/649-6800), with a large dance floor, hosts good bands. **J.B. Mulligan's Club & Pub,** 804 Main St. (ℂ 435/658-0717), also has live music, including a variety of jazz, reggae, bluegrass, and funk; and you can get food—try their peppercorn burger—between 5 and 10pm. Another nightspot for live jazz, funk, or acoustic is **Mother Urban's Ratskeller,** 625 Main St. (ℂ 435/615-7200). The **No**

Name Saloon, 447 Main St. (© **435/649-6667**), another fun place to drink, is old and oddly furnished.

Harry O's, 427 Main St. (© **435/647-9494**), is very popular, with a huge dance floor and live band or DJ nightly. Romantic and dimly lit, **Bacchus Wine Bar,** 442 Main St. (© **435/940-9463**), pours 100 different wines by the glass and serves a scrumptious menu of light fare.

SUNDANCE

Situated in beautiful Provo Canyon, at the base of 12,000-foot Mount Timpanogos, Sundance is a year-round resort that emphasizes its arts programs as much as its skiing and other outdoor activities. That should come as no surprise—it's owned by actor/director Robert Redford, who bought the property in 1969 and named it after his character in the classic film *Butch Cassidy and the Sundance Kid.* You might recognize the area: Redford's 1972 film *Jeremiah Johnson* was set here.

The goal for Sundance was to create a place where the outdoors and the arts could come together in a truly unique mountain community, and it seems to be a success. The rustic yet elegant, environmentally friendly retreat is a full-service ski resort in winter. During the summer, you'll find great hiking trails and other outdoor activities, as well as the Sundance Institute, which Redford founded in 1980 to support and encourage independent American filmmaking and playwriting.

For information on all facilities and activities, plus lodging reservations, contact **Sundance Resort,** R.R. 3, Box A-1, Sundance, UT 84604 (© **800/892-1600** or 801/225-4100; www.sundanceresort.com).

OUTDOOR ACTIVITIES

Sundance is known for its quiet, intimate setting and lack of lift lines. It offers runs for all levels—some quite challenging—including several delightfully long cruising trails for novices. The area is gaining a reputation as a good place to learn to ski or snowboard. The two levels of skiing are pretty well separated from each other: The beginner and some of the intermediate terrain are on the front mountain, whereas the prime blue runs and all of the expert slopes are on the back mountain. The expert crowd will be pleased with the steep glades, precipitous bump runs (due to the general lack of traffic, the mountain never really bumps up too high, though), and untracked snow on the back mountain, where you'll have to work at it to run into another skier.

The terrain is rated 20% beginner, 40% intermediate, and 40% advanced, with a total of 41 runs over 450 skiable acres. One quad and two triple chairlifts, plus a handle tow, serve the mountain, which has a vertical drop of 2,150 feet, from a base elevation of 6,100 feet to the top at 8,250 feet. Sundance is usually open from mid-December to early April, and has state-of-the-art snow-making equipment on the entire front mountain. Lifts operate daily from 9am to 4:30pm.

Bearclaw's Cabin, the only mountaintop day lodge in Utah, offers snacks, hot drinks, and stupendous views. **Creekside** day lodge, at the base of the ski area, serves excellent quick lunches during ski season. Equipment rental and sales are available.

The Provo River provides great **fly-fishing** just 10 minutes away. Sundance offers guided fishing trips, including equipment rentals. Rates start at $155 for group, $195 for private, half-day fly-fishing trips.

THE FESTIVAL, FILM & PERFORMING ARTS SCENE

The next Tarantino has to start somewhere—and that somewhere might just be the **Sundance Film Festival.** For more than 20 years, the hottest independent films have been discovered at this weeklong January event, hosted by Robert Redford's Sundance Institute. (The festival doesn't actually take place at Sundance, however; it's held 30 miles away, in Park City, covered above.)

Admission to the festival is nonexclusive, so you can rub shoulders with the rich and famous and the up-and-coming. To receive a free guide, or to reserve tickets, contact the **Sundance Institute** (© 877/733-7829 or 801/924-0882 for tickets; www.sundance.org).

Past **Sundance films** are screened in City Park on summer Friday nights. The **Park City Film Series** (www.parkcityfilmseries.com) screens a different independent movie every weekend at the Park City Library for $6.

WHERE TO STAY

Sundance offers standard rooms, studios, and cottage suites that range from $225 to $365 per night, as well as larger mountain suites and several luxury mountain homes that cost from $315 to more than $1,000 per night. Each suite is outfitted with well-crafted handmade furnishings that match the rustic luxury of the entire resort, as well as American Indian crafts, stone fireplaces, and outdoor decks; most have fully equipped kitchens. All accommodations come complete with Sundance's own natural bath products, such as ecosensitive oatmeal soap.

9 Zion National Park

Early Mormon settler Isaac Behunin is credited with naming his homestead "Little Zion" because it seemed to be a bit of heaven on earth. Today, 150 years later, Zion National Park will cast a spell over you as you gaze upon its sheer multicolored walls of sandstone, explore its narrow canyons, hunt for hanging gardens of wildflowers, or listen to the roar of the churning, tumbling Virgin River.

Because of its extremes of elevation (3,666 to almost 9,000 ft.) and climate (temperatures soar over 100°F/38°C in summer, and the landscape is carpeted in snow in winter), Zion harbors a vast array of plants and animals. About 800 native species of plants have been found: cactus, yucca, and mesquite in the hot, dry desert areas; ponderosa pine trees on the high plateaus; and cottonwoods and box elders along the rivers and streams. And Zion is a veritable zoo, with mammals ranging from pocket gophers to mountain lions, hundreds of birds, and lizards of all shapes and sizes.

ESSENTIALS

Zion National Park has three sections: Zion Canyon, the main part of the park, where everyone goes, and the less-visited Kolob Terrace and Kolob Canyons. The main east-west road through Zion Canyon is the park-owned extension of Utah 9, from which you can access a 14-mile round-trip scenic drive/shuttle bus route that leads to most scenic overlooks and trail heads.

GETTING THERE/ACCESS POINTS   St. George and Cedar City are the closest towns with airport service. From either airport, it's easy to rent a car and drive to Zion. Utah 9 crosses Zion National Park, giving the main section of the park two entry gates—south and east. The drive into Zion Canyon (the main part of the park) from I-15 on the park's western side—following Utah 9 or Utah 17 and Utah 9 to the south entrance at Springdale, is by far the more popular, with two-thirds of park visitors arriving there. Most area lodgings and restaurants are found in Springdale, and the park's two campgrounds and the Zion Canyon Visitor Center are located just inside the south entrance. This approach has the added advantage of avoiding possible delays at the Zion–Mount Carmel Tunnel. However, this approach is much less scenic than the eastern approach.

From the east, it's a spectacularly scenic 24-mile drive from Mount Carmel on Utah 9, reached from either the north or south via U.S. 89. However, be aware that this route into the park drops over 2,500 feet in elevation, passes through the mile-long Zion–Mount Carmel Tunnel, and winds down six steep switchbacks. The tunnel is too small for two-way traffic that includes vehicles larger than standard passenger cars and pickup trucks. Buses, trucks, and most recreational vehicles must be driven down the center of the tunnel; therefore, all oncoming traffic must be stopped. This applies to all vehicles over 7 feet 10 inches wide (including mirrors) or 11 feet 4 inches tall (including luggage racks, and so on). March through October, large vehicles are permitted in the tunnel only from 8am to 8pm daily; during other months, arrangements can be made at park entrances or by calling park headquarters (🕿 **435/772-3256**). Affected vehicles must pay a $15 fee, good for two trips through the tunnel during a 7-day period. All vehicles over 13 feet 1 inch tall and certain other particularly large vehicles are prohibited from driving anywhere on the park road between the east entrance and Zion Canyon.

You'll find Kolob Terrace Road, with additional viewpoints and trail heads, heading north off Utah 9 from the village of Virgin, about 15 miles west of the park's southern entrance. This road is closed in winter.

The Kolob Canyons section, in the park's northwest corner, can be reached via the short Kolob Canyons Road off I-15 Exit 40.

Some helpful distances: The park is 83 miles southwest of Bryce Canyon National Park; 120 miles northwest of the north rim of Grand Canyon National Park, in northern Arizona; 309 miles south of Salt Lake City; and 158 miles northeast of Las Vegas, Nevada.

VISITOR INFORMATION   Contact Zion National Park, Utah 9, Springdale, UT 84767-1099 (🕿 **435/772-3256;** www.nps.gov/zion). You can also purchase books, maps, and videos related to the park from the nonprofit **Zion Natural History Association,** Zion National Park, Springdale, UT 84767 (🕿 **800/635-3959** or 435/772-3264; www.zionpark.org).

The park has two visitor centers. The **Zion Canyon Visitor Center** (🕿 **435/772-3256**), near the south entrance, has outdoor exhibits on the many resources available in the park and provides information on the shuttle operation. You can ask rangers questions, get backcountry permits, pick up free brochures, and purchase books, maps, videos, postcards, and posters. The smaller **Kolob Canyons Visitor Center** (🕿 **435/586-9548**), in the northwest corner of the park off I-15, provides information, permits, books, and maps. Both visitor centers are open daily from 8am to 5pm in summer, with shorter varying hours the rest of the year (call to find out when).

WHEN TO GO   The park is open year-round, 24 hours a day, although weather conditions such as extreme heat or icy trails may limit some activities at certain times.

If possible, try to avoid June, July, and August, when Zion receives almost half of its annual visitors. The quietest months are December, January, and February, but of course it's cold and snowy then. A good compromise is to visit in April, May, September, or October, when the weather is usually good but the park is less crowded than in the summer.

The best way to avoid crowds is to simply walk away from them. It's sad but true—most visitors never venture far from their cars, and you can enjoy a wonderful solitary experience if you're willing to expend a little energy. You can also avoid hordes of tourists by spending time in Kolob Canyons, in the far northwest section of the park; it's spectacular and gets surprisingly little use. In the summer, head to Kolob Terrace.

SEEING THE HIGHLIGHTS

If you have only a day or two at the park, we recommend making one of the visitor centers your first stop. Then, if your visit is during the shuttle bus operating season, we suggest the following:

Hop on the free **shuttle bus,** which takes you to the major roadside viewpoints. You'll be able to get off, look at the formations, take a short walk if you like, and then catch the next shuttle for a ride to the next stop.

We particularly recommend getting off the shuttle at the **Temple of Sinawava** and taking the easy 2-mile round-trip **Riverside Walk,** which follows the Virgin River through a narrow canyon past hanging gardens. Then take the shuttle back to the lodge (total time: 2–4 hr.). At the lodge, stop by the gift shop and perhaps have lunch in the excellent restaurant.

Near the lodge, you'll find the trail head for the **Emerald Pools.** Especially pleasant on hot days, this easy walk through a forest of oak, maple, fir, and cottonwood trees leads to a waterfall, hanging garden, and the shimmering lower pool. This part of the walk should take about an hour round-trip, but those with a bit more time may want to add another hour and another mile to the loop by taking the moderately strenuous hike on a rocky, steeper trail to the upper pool. If you still have time and energy, head back to the south park entrance and stop at **Watchman** (east of Watchman Campground), for the 2-mile, 2-hour round-trip, moderately strenuous hike to a plateau with beautiful views of several rock formations and the town of Springdale. In the evening, try to take in a campground amphitheater program.

HIKING

Zion offers a wide variety of hiking trails, ranging from easy half-hour walks on paved paths to grueling overnight hikes over rocky terrain along steep drop-offs. Hikers with a fear of heights should be especially careful when choosing trails; many include steep, dizzying drop-offs. What follows are our hiking suggestions:

The **Weeping Rock Trail,** among the park's shortest and easiest rambles, is a .5-mile round-trip walk to a rock alcove with a spring and hanging gardens of ferns and wildflowers. Although paved, the trail is steep and not suitable for wheelchairs.

Another short hike is the **Lower Emerald Pools Trail,** which can be an easy 1-hour walk or a moderately strenuous 2-hour hike, depending on how much of the loop you choose to do. A .6-mile paved path from the Emerald Pools Parking Area, through a forest of oak, maple, fir, and cottonwood, leads to a waterfall, a hanging garden, and the Lower Emerald Pool, and is suitable for those in wheelchairs, with assistance. From here, a steeper, rocky trail continues past cactus, yucca, and juniper another .5 mile to Upper Emerald Pool, with another waterfall. A third pool, just above Lower Emerald Pool, offers impressive reflections of the cliffs.

A moderately strenuous but relatively short hike is the **Watchman Trail,** which starts near the Zion Canyon Visitor Center. This 3-mile round-trip hike gets surprisingly light use, possibly because it can be very hot in the middle of the day. Climbing to a plateau near the base of the formation called The Watchman, it offers splendid views of lower Zion Canyon, the Towers of the Virgin, and West Temple formations.

Hiking the **Narrows** is not hiking a trail at all, but walking or wading along the bottom of the Virgin River, through a spectacular 1,000-foot-deep chasm that, at a mere 20 feet wide in spots, definitely lives up to its name. Hikers pass fancifully sculptured sandstone arches, hanging gardens, and waterfalls. This moderately strenuous hike can be completed in 1 day or several. However, the Narrows are subject to flash flooding and can be very treacherous. Park Service officials remind hikers that they are responsible for their own safety and should check on current water conditions and weather forecasts. This hike is *not* recommended when rain is forecast or threatening. Permits are required for full-day and overnight hikes in the Narrows, but are not required for easy, short day hikes, which you can access from just beyond the end of the Riverside Walk, a 2-mile trail that starts at the Temple of Sinawava parking area.

WHERE TO CAMP

There are two large and one small **national park campgrounds.** Both of the main campgrounds, just inside the park's south entrance, have paved roads, well-spaced sites, lots of trees, and that national park atmosphere you came here to enjoy. Facilities include restrooms with flush toilets but no showers, a dump station, and a public telephone. The fee is $16 per night for basic sites, or $18 to $20 per night for sites with electric hookups. **South Campground** has 126 sites (no hookups), first-come, first-served, and is usually open from mid-March through October only; **Watchman Campground** (② 800/365-2267 or http://reservations.nps.gov for reservations) has 168 sites, with electric hookups on two loops, and is open year-round (reservations available spring through early fall only).

Lava Point, with only six sites, is located on the Kolob Terrace. It has fire grates, tables, and toilets, but no water, and there's no fee. Vehicles are limited to 19 feet, and it's usually open from June through mid-October.

WHERE TO STAY

The only lodging actually in Zion National Park is at **Zion Lodge** (② 435/772-7700). For information and reservations, contact **Xanterra Parks & Resorts,** 6312 S. Fiddlers Green Circle, Suite 600N, Greenwood Village, CO 80111 (② 888/297-2757 or 303/297-2757; www.zionlodge.com). Situated in a forest, with spectacular views of the park's rock cliffs, the charming cabins each have a private porch, stone (gas-burning) fireplace, two double beds, pine-board walls, and log beams. The comfortable motel units are basically just that.

Springdale, a village of some 350 people at the park's south entrance, has literally become the park's bedroom. Comfortable, affordable motel rooms are available at the **Canyon Ranch Motel,** 668 Zion Park Blvd. (② 866/946-6276 or 435/772-3357; www.canyonranchmotel.com), where the rooms have spectacular views. More upscale are the moderately priced **Cliffrose Lodge & Gardens,** 281 Zion Park Blvd. (② 800/243-8824 or 435/772-3234; www.cliffroselodge.com), and the **Harvest House Bed & Breakfast at Zion,** 29 Canyon View Dr. (② 800/719-7501 or 435/772-3880; www.harvesthouse.net).

We especially like **Flanigan's Inn,** 428 Zion Park Blvd. (② 800/765-7787 or 435/772-3244; www.flanigans.com), a very attractive complex just outside the park entrance. Parts of the inn date to 1947, but all rooms were completely renovated in the early 1990s, with southwestern decor, wood furnishings, and local art. Flanigan's has a heated outdoor swimming pool and its own nature trail leading to a hilltop vista.

10 Bryce Canyon National Park

If you could visit only one national park in your lifetime, we'd send you to Bryce Canyon. Here you'll find magic, inspiration, and spectacular beauty. The main draw of the park is the thousands of intricately shaped hoodoos: those silent rock sentinels and congregations gathered in colorful cathedrals, arranged in formations that invite your imagination to run wild.

Hoodoos, geologists tell us, are simply pinnacles of rock, often oddly shaped, left standing by the forces of millions of years of water and wind erosion. But perhaps the truth really lies in a Paiute legend. These American Indians, who lived in the area for several hundred years before being forced out by Anglo pioneers, told of a "Legend People" who lived here in the old days; because of their evil ways, they were turned to stone by the powerful Coyote, and even today they remain frozen in time.

Although the colorful hoodoos are the first things to grab your attention, it isn't long before you notice the deep amphitheaters that enfold them, with their cliffs, windows, and arches—all colored in shades of red, brown, orange, yellow, and white—that change and glow with the rising and setting sun. Beyond the rocks and light are the other faces of the park: three separate life zones, each with its own unique vegetation that changes with the elevation; and a kingdom of animals, from the busy chipmunks and ground squirrels to the stately mule deer and their archenemy, the mountain lion.

ESSENTIALS

GETTING THERE/ACCESS POINTS Bryce Canyon Airport (© 435/834-5239; www.brycecanyoncountry.com/county/airport.html) is located several miles from the park entrance on **Utah 12.** There are no regularly scheduled direct flights to the airport, but charter service is available from **Bryce Canyon Airlines** (© 435/834-5341). Car rentals are available from **Hertz,** which is located at Ruby's Inn Chevron Station, 1 mile south of Utah 12 on **Utah 63** (© 800/654-3131).

Situated in the mountains of southern Utah, the park is traversed east-west by Utah 12, with the bulk of the park, including the visitor center, accessible via Utah 63, which branches off from Utah 12 and goes south into the main portions of the park. Utah 89 runs north to south, west of the park, and Utah 12 heads east to Tropic and eventually Escalante.

Entry into the park (for up to 7 days) costs $20 per private vehicle, which includes unlimited use of the park shuttle (when it's operating). Campsites cost $10 per night. Backcountry camping permits ($5 per trip), available at the visitor center, are required for all overnight trips into the backcountry.

VISITOR INFORMATION Contact **Bryce Canyon National Park,** P.O. Box 170001, Bryce Canyon, UT 84717 (© 435/834-5322; www.nps.gov/brca).

The visitor center, at the north end as you enter the park, has exhibits and presents a short introductory slide show. Rangers can answer questions and provide backcountry permits. You can stock up on brochures, books, maps, videos, and postcards. The visitor center is open daily year-round except major holidays.

WHEN TO GO Although Bryce Canyon National Park gets only two-thirds the number of annual visitors that pour into Zion, the park can still be crowded, especially from June to September. If you have to visit then, head for some of the lesser-used trails (ask rangers for recommendations), and start your hike as soon after sunrise as possible.

A better time to visit, if your schedule allows, is spring or fall, and if you don't mind a bit of cold and snow, the park is practically deserted from December through February—and the sight of bright red hoodoos capped with fresh white snow is something you won't soon forget.

SEEING THE HIGHLIGHTS

Start at the visitor center, of course, and watch the short slide show that explains some of the area's geology. Then drive the 18-mile (each way) dead-end park road, stopping at viewpoints to gaze down into the canyon. You can also take a guided tour (see below), or see the main section of the park on the shuttle bus, which operates from mid-to-late May to early September. The shuttles run every 10 to 15 minutes, and you can get on and off as frequently as you want.

Whichever way you choose to get around, be sure to spend at least a little time at **Inspiration Point,** which offers a splendid (and yes, inspirational) view into **Bryce Amphitheater** and its hundreds of statuesque pink, red, orange, and brown hoodoo stone sculptures. After seeing the canyon from the top down, it's time to walk at least partway down the **Queen's Garden Trail.** If you can spare 3 hours, hike down the Navajo Loop and return to the rim via Queen's Garden Trail. Those not willing or able to hike into the canyon can enjoy a leisurely walk along the **Rim Trail,** which provides spectacular views down into the canyon, especially just after sunrise and about an hour before sunset.

Bryce Canyon Area Tours & Adventures (© 800/432-5383 or 435/834-5200; www.brycetours.com) offers 1½- to 2-hour tours year-round, leaving from Bryce Canyon Resorts next to the shuttle parking area outside the park entrance, at the intersection of the park entrance road and Utah 12, 3 miles from the park boundary. A general tour, stopping at several viewpoints, costs $26 for adults, $12 for children 5 to 15, free for children under 5. Sunrise/sunset and other specialized tours are also available.

HIKING

One of the things we like best about Bryce Canyon is that you don't have to be an advanced backpacker to really get to know the park. All trails below the rim have at least some steep grades, so you should wear hiking boots with a traction tread and good ankle support to avoid ankle injuries, the most common accidents in the park. During the hot summer months you'll want to hike either early or late in the day; it gets hotter the deeper you go into the canyon.

The **Rim Trail,** which does not drop into the canyon but offers splendid views from above, meanders along the rim for over 5 miles. An easy-to-moderate walk, it includes a .5-mile section between two overlooks—Sunrise and Sunset—that is suitable for wheelchairs. Overlooking Bryce Amphitheater, the trail offers excellent views almost everywhere and is a good choice for an after-dinner walk, when you can watch the changing evening light on the rosy rocks below.

Your best bet for getting down into the canyon and seeing the most with the least amount of sweat is to combine two popular trails—**Navajo Loop** and **Queen's Garden.** The total distance is just less than 3 miles, with a 521-foot elevation change, and it takes most hikers from 2 to 3 hours. It's best to start at the Navajo Loop trail head at Sunset Point and leave the canyon on the less-steep Queen's Garden Trail, returning to the rim at Sunrise Point, .5 mile to the north. The Navajo Loop section is considered fairly strenuous, while Queen's Garden is rated moderate. Along the Navajo Loop section, you'll pass Thor's Hammer, wonder why it hasn't fallen, and ponder the towering skyscrapers of Wall Street. Turning onto the Queen's Garden Trail, you'll see some of the park's most fanciful formations, including majestic Queen Victoria herself, for whom the trail was named, plus the Queen's Castle and Gulliver's Castle.

WHERE TO CAMP

The two campgrounds in the park offer plenty of trees with a genuine "forest camping" experience, easy access to trails, and limited facilities. **North Campground** has 107 sites and **Sunset Campground** has 101 sites. A section of North Campground is open year-round, but Sunset Campground is open from May to September only. We prefer North Campground because it's closer to the Rim Trail—making it easier to rush over to catch those amazing sunrise and sunset colors. Neither has RV hookups or showers, but you will find modern restrooms with running water. North Campground accepts reservations through **National Recreation Reservation Service** (✆ 877/444-6777; www.reserveusa.com), with a $9 booking fee. Sunset Campground does not accept reservations, so get to the campground early to claim a site (usually by 2pm in summer). Cost is $10 per night at both campgrounds.

Showers ($2), a coin-operated laundry, a snack bar, bundles of firewood, food and camping supplies, and souvenirs, are located at the **General Store** (for information, contact Bryce Canyon Lodge ✆ 435/834-5361), which is usually open daily from mid-April through October. The store is a healthy walk from either campground. The Park Service operates an RV dump station ($2 fee) in the summer. Tables on a covered porch run along one side of the building.

WHERE TO STAY

Our preferred lodging choice here is right in the park at the delightful **Bryce Canyon Lodge** (✆ 435/834-5361). For information and reservations contact **Xanterra Parks & Resorts,** Central Reservations, 6312 S. Fiddlers Green Circle, Suite 600N, Greenwood Village, CO 80111 (✆ 888/297-2757 or 303/297-2757; www.brycecanyon lodge.com). There's no denying that this is the perfect place to stay, allowing easy access to the trails and spectacular views. The handsome sandstone and ponderosa pine lodge, which opened in 1924, contains a busy lobby, with information desks for horseback riding and other activities. The luxurious lodge suites are wonderful, with white wicker furniture, ceiling fans, and separate sitting rooms. The motel rooms are just that, but they're pleasant and quite spacious. Our choice would be the "rustic luxury" of one of the cabins, which have been restored to their 1924 decor.

Nearby choices include **Best Western Ruby's Inn,** Utah 63, just outside the park entrance (✆ 866/866-6616 or 435/834-5341; www.rubysinn.com), where you'll also find a large general store, a post office, and tour desks where you can arrange excursions of all sorts. Outside are two gas stations. More basic (and less expensive) motel units can be found at **Bryce View Lodge,** Utah 63, across from Best Western Ruby's Inn (✆ 888/279-2304 or 435/834-5180; www.bryceviewlodge.com); and **Bryce Valley Inn,** 199 Scenic Byway 12, Tropic (✆ 866/679-8811 or 435/679-8846; www.brycevalleyinn.com).

11 Capitol Reef National Park

A relatively unknown gem, Capitol Reef offers more of that spectacular southern Utah scenery, but with a unique twist and a personality all its own. This is a place to let your imagination run wild, where you'll see the appropriately named Hamburger Rocks, sitting atop a white sandstone table; the tall, rust-red Chimney Rock; and the silent and eerie Temple of the Moon.

But Capitol Reef is more than just brilliant rocks and barren desert. Here the Fremont River has helped create a lush oasis in an otherwise unforgiving land, with cottonwoods and willows along its banks. In fact, 19th-century pioneers found the land so inviting and the soil so fertile that they established a community here, planting orchards that have been preserved by the Park Service.

ESSENTIALS

GETTING THERE   Capitol Reef National Park is about 224 miles south of Salt Lake City. It straddles **Utah 24,** which connects with **I-70** both to the northeast and northwest. Entry into the park (for up to 7 days) costs $5 per vehicle or $2 per person on motorcycle, bicycle, or foot.

VISITOR INFORMATION   Contact **Capitol Reef National Park,** HC 70 Box 15, Torrey, UT 84775-9602 (© **435/425-3791;** www.nps.gov/care). The visitor center is on the park access road at its intersection with Utah 24. A trail alongside the access road connects the visitor center and campground.

SEEING THE HIGHLIGHTS

Start at the visitor center, and watch the short slide show explaining the park's geology and early history. From the visitor center, a 25-mile round-trip scenic drive leads into the park, offering good views of its dramatic canyons, colorful cliffs, and commanding rock formations.

If the weather is dry, drive down the unpaved Capitol Gorge Road at the end of the paved scenic drive for a look at what many consider the best backcountry scenery in the park. It's a 6-mile round-trip drive. If you're up for a short walk, the relatively flat 2-mile (round-trip) **Capitol Gorge Trail,** which starts at the end of Capitol Gorge Road, takes you to the historic Pioneer Register, a rock wall where traveling pioneers "signed in."

FROM PETROGLYPHS TO A PIONEER SCHOOLHOUSE: CAPITOL REEF'S HISTORIC SITES

Throughout the park, you'll find evidence of man's presence through the centuries. The Fremont people lived along the river as early as A.D. 700, staying until about 1300. Primarily hunters and gatherers, the Fremont also grew corn, beans, and squash. They lived in pit houses dug into the ground, and the remains of one can be seen from the Hickman Bridge Trail. Many of the Fremont's **petroglyphs** (images carved into rock) and some **pictographs** (images painted on rock) are still visible on the canyon walls. If we could read them, they might even tell us why these early Americans left the area, a puzzle that continues to baffle archaeologists.

Prospectors and other travelers passed through the Capitol Gorge section of the park in the late 1800s, leaving their names on the **Pioneer Register.** You can reach the Pioneer Register via an easy 2-mile (round-trip) hike.

Mormon pioneers established the community of **Fruita** in 1880. A tiny **schoolhouse,** built in 1896, also served as a church, social hall, and community-meeting hall. The school closed in 1941 but was restored by the National Park Service and is furnished with old wood and wrought-iron desks, a woodstove, a chalkboard, and textbooks. The orchards planted by the Mormon settlers continue to flourish, tended by park workers who invite you to sample the fruits of their labors.

SPORTS & ACTIVITIES

FOUR-WHEELING & MOUNTAIN BIKING   Capitol Reef has several so-called roads—actually little more than dirt trails—that provide exciting opportunities for those using 4×4s or pedal-power.

One recommended trip, the **Cathedral Valley Loop,** covers about 60 miles on a variety of road surfaces, including dirt, sand, and rock, and requires the fording of the

Fremont River, where water is usually 1 to 1½ feet deep. But you'll be rewarded with beautiful, unspoiled scenery, including bizarre sandstone monoliths and majestic cliffs, in one of the park's most remote areas. Access to this loop is from Utah 24, just outside the park, 12 miles east of the visitor center, or 19 miles east of the visitor center on the Caineville Wash Road.

For information on guided backpacking, hiking, mountain biking, and four-wheel-drive excursions (many with an emphasis on photo opportunities), contact **Wild Hare Expeditions** (© **888/304-HARE** or 435/425-3999; www.color-country.net/~thehare). Wild Hare also rents mountain bikes.

HIKING   Trails through Capitol Reef National Park offer sweeping panoramas of colorful cliffs and domes, eerie journeys through desolate steep-walled canyons, and cool oases along the tree-shaded Fremont River. Watch carefully for petroglyphs and other reminders of this area's first inhabitants. This is also the real Wild West, little changed from the way cowboys, bank robbers, settlers, and gold miners found it in the late 1800s.

Among our favorite short hikes here is the 2-mile round-trip **Capitol Gorge Trail.** It's easy, mostly level walking along the bottom of a narrow canyon, but looking up at the tall, smooth walls of rock conveys a strong sense of what the pioneers saw and felt 100 years ago. Starting at the end of the dirt Capitol Gorge Road, the hiking trail leads past the Pioneer Register, where early travelers carved their names.

Another short hike, but quite a bit more strenuous, is the 3.5-mile round-trip **Cassidy Arch Trail.** This offers spectacular views as it climbs steeply from the floor of Grand Wash to high cliffs overlooking the park. From the trail, you'll also get several perspectives of Cassidy Arch, a natural stone arch named for outlaw Butch Cassidy, who is believed to have occasionally used the Grand Wash as a hide-out. The trail is off the Grand Wash Road, which branches off the east side of the highway about halfway down the park's scenic drive.

WHERE TO CAMP

The 71-site **Fruita Campground,** open year-round, offers modern restrooms, drinking water, picnic tables, fire grills, and an RV dump station, but no showers or RV hookups. It's located along the main park road, 1 mile south of the visitor center. Water may be turned off in winter, leaving only pit toilets. Camping costs $10; reservations are not accepted. The park also has two primitive campgrounds, free and open year-round on a first-come, first-served basis. Both have tables, fire grills, and pit toilets, but no water. Check road conditions before going, as unpaved roads may be impassable in wet weather. **Cedar Mesa Campground,** with five sites, is located in the southern part of the park, and **Cathedral Valley Campground,** with six sites, is located in the northern part of the park.

WHERE TO STAY

There are no lodging or dining facilities in the park itself, but the town of Torrey, just west of the park entrance, can take care of most needs.

Affordable accommodations include **Austin's Chuck Wagon Lodge,** 12 W. Main St. (© **800/863-3288** or 435/425-3335; www.austinschuckwagonmotel.com); **Best Western Capitol Reef Resort,** 2600 E. Utah 24 (© **888/610-9600** or 435/425-3761), which is only a mile from the park entrance; the **Capitol Reef Inn & Cafe,** 360 W. Main St. (Utah 24; © **435/425-3271;** www.capitolreefinn.com); **Comfort Inn,** 2424 Utah 24 (© **800/424-6423** or 435/425-3866); and the **Super 8,** 600 E. Utah 24 (© **800/800-8000** or 435/425-3688). The **Skyridge Inn Bed & Breakfast,** on Utah 24, just east of its intersection with Utah 12 (© **800/448-6990** or 435/425-3222; www.bbiu.org/skyridge), offers a delightful alternative to the standard motel.

12 Arches National Park

Natural stone arches and fantastic rock formations, which look as if they were sculpted by an artist's hand, are the defining features of this park, and they exist in remarkable numbers and variety. Just as soon as you've seen the most beautiful, most colorful, most gigantic stone arch you can imagine, walk around the next bend and there's another—bigger, better, and more brilliant than the last. It would take forever to see them all, with more than 2,000 officially listed and more being discovered or "born" every day.

Exploring the park is a great family adventure. The arches seem more accessible and less forbidding than the spires and pinnacles at Canyonlands and other southern Utah parks. Just down the road from Canyonlands National Park, Arches is much more visitor-friendly, with relatively short, well-maintained trails leading to most of the park's major attractions.

ESSENTIALS

GETTING THERE   From Moab, drive 5 miles north on **U.S. 191.** Arches National Park is located 27 miles east of Canyonlands National Park's Island in the Sky Visitor Center, 233 miles southeast of Salt Lake City, and 371 miles west of Denver, Colorado.

INFORMATION/VISITOR CENTERS   For advance information, contact **Arches National Park,** P.O. Box 907, Moab, UT 84532-0907 (© **435/719-2299;** www.nps.gov/arch).

The **Arches National Park Visitor Center,** located just inside the park entrance gate, provides maps, brochures, and other information. It's open daily 8am to 4:30pm in winter, with extended hours spring through fall. Entry into the park (for up to 7 days) costs $10 per vehicle or $5 per motorcycle, bicycle, or pedestrian. Free permits, available at the visitor center, are required for all overnight trips into the backcountry. The best time to visit, especially for hikers, is spring or fall, when daytime temperatures are usually between 60°F and 80°F (16°C and 27°C) and nights are cool.

March through October, rangers lead **guided hikes** on the Fiery Furnace Trail twice daily, as well as daily nature walks at various park locations. Evening campfire programs, April through October, are held on topics such as rock art, geological processes, and wildlife. A schedule of events is posted at the visitor center.

SEEING THE PARK'S HIGHLIGHTS BY CAR

Arches is the easiest of Utah's national parks to see in a day, if that's all you can spare. An 18-mile (one-way) **scenic drive** offers splendid views of countless natural rock arches and other formations, and several easy hikes reveal additional scenery. Allow 1½ hours for the round-trip drive, adding time for optional hikes. The main road is easy to navigate, even for RVs, but parking at some viewpoints is limited.

Start out by viewing the short slide show at the **visitor center** to get a feel for what lies ahead. Then drive north past the Moab Fault to the overlook parking for **Park Avenue,** a solid rock "fin" that reminded early visitors of the New York skyline.

From here, your next stop is **La Sal Mountain Viewpoint,** where you look southeast to the La Sal Mountains, named by early Spanish explorers who thought the snow-covered mountains looked like huge piles of salt. In the overlook area is a "desert scrub" ecosystem, composed of sagebrush, saltbush, blackbrush, yucca, and prickly pear cactus. Animals that inhabit the area include the kangaroo rat, the black-tailed jackrabbit, the rock squirrel, several species of lizards, and the coyote.

Continuing on the scenic drive, you'll begin to see some of the park's major formations at **Courthouse Towers,** where large monoliths such as Sheep Rock, the Organ, and the Three Gossips dominate the landscape. Leaving Courthouse Towers, watch for the **Tower of Babel** on the east (right) side of the road, then proceed past the petrified sand dunes to **Balanced Rock,** a huge boulder weighing about 3,600 tons, perched on a slowly eroding pedestal.

Continue down a side road to the east (right) to **The Windows.** Created when erosion penetrated a sandstone fin, they can be seen after a short walk from the parking area. Also in this area are **Turret Arch** and the **Cove of Caves.** Erosion is continuing to wear away at the back of the largest cave, which means it will probably become an arch one day. A short walk from the parking lot takes you to **Double Arch,** which looks exactly like what its name implies. From the end of this trail, you can also see the delightful **Parade of Elephants.**

Return to the main park road, turn north (right) and drive to **Panorama Point,** which offers an expansive view of Salt Valley and the Fiery Furnace, which can really live up to its name at sunset.

Next, turn east (right) off the main road onto the Wolfe Ranch Road and drive to the **Wolfe Ranch** parking area. A very short walk leads to what's left of this ranch. John Wesley Wolfe and his son Fred moved here from Ohio in 1898, and in 1907 were joined by John's daughter Flora, her husband, and their two children. The cabin seen here was built for Flora's family (John's cabin was later destroyed by a flash flood). In 1910, the family decided that this was not the greatest location for a ranch, and they packed up and returned to Ohio. If you follow the trail a bit farther, you'll see some Ute petroglyphs.

More ambitious hikers can continue for a moderately difficult 3-mile round-trip excursion to **Delicate Arch,** with a spectacular view at trail's end. If you don't want to take the hike, you can still see this lovely arch, albeit from a distance, by getting back in your car, continuing down the road for 1 mile, and walking a short trail (about 5 min.) to the **Delicate Arch Viewpoint.**

Returning to the park's main road, turn north (right) and go to the next stop, the **Salt Valley Overlook.** The various shades of color in this collapsed salt dome are caused by differing amounts of iron in the rock, as well as other factors.

Continue now to the viewpoint for **Fiery Furnace,** which offers a dramatic view of colorful sandstone fins. This is the starting point for 2-hour ranger-guided hikes in summer.

From here, drive to a pullout for **Sand Dune Arch,** located down a short path from the road, where you'll find shade and sand along with the arch. This is a good place for kids to play. The trail leads across a meadow to Broken Arch (which isn't broken at all—it just looks that way from a distance).

Back on the road, continue to **Skyline Arch,** whose opening doubled in size in 1940 when a huge boulder tumbled out of it. The next and final stop is the often crowded parking area for the **Devils Garden Trail Head.** From here, you can hike to some of the most unique arches in the park, including **Landscape Arch,** which is among the longest natural rock spans in the world. It's a pretty easy 1.6-mile round-trip hike. From the trail head parking lot, it's 18 miles back to the visitor center.

HIKING IN THE PARK

Most trails here are short and relatively easy, although because of the hot summer sun and lack of shade, it's wise to carry a good amount of water on any jaunt of more than 1 hour.

One easy walk is to **Sand Dune Arch,** a good place to take kids who want to play in the sand. It's only .3 mile (round-trip). Sand Dune Arch is hidden among and shaded by rock walls, with a naturally created giant sandbox below the arch. Resist the temptation to climb onto the arch and jump down into the sand: Not only is it dangerous, but it can also damage the arch. Allow about 30 minutes to Sand Dune Arch and back.

From the **Devils Garden Trail,** you can see about 15 to 20 arches on a fairly long, strenuous, and difficult hike, or view some exciting scenery by following only part of the route. We suggest taking at least the easy-to-moderate 1.6-mile round-trip hike to **Landscape Arch,** a long, thin ribbon of stone that's one of the most beautiful arches in the park. Watch for mule deer along the way, and allow about an hour.

Considered by many to be the park's best and most scenic hike, the 3-mile round-trip **Delicate Arch Trail** is a moderate-to-difficult hike, with slippery slickrock, no shade, and some steep drop-offs along a narrow cliff. Hikers are rewarded with a dramatic and spectacular view of Delicate Arch. You'll see the John Wesley Wolfe ranch and have an opportunity to take a side trip to a Ute petroglyph panel that includes drawings of horses and what may represent a bighorn sheep hunt.

Continuing along the trail, watch for **Frame Arch,** off to the right. Its main claim to fame is that numerous photographers have used it to "frame" a photo of Delicate Arch in the distance. Just past Frame Arch, the trail gets a little weird, having been blasted out from the cliff. Allow 2 to 3 hours.

The **Fiery Furnace Guided Hike** is a difficult and strenuous 2-mile round-trip naturalist-led hike to some of the most colorful formations in the park. Guided hikes are given into this restricted area twice daily, March through October, by reservation, and last from 2¼ to 3 hours. The cost is $8 for adults and $4 for children 6 to 12 and seniors 62 and over; reservations must be made in person, up to 7 days in advance. Permits are required to enter the Fiery Furnace on your own ($2 adults, $1 children 6–12), but special restrictions apply and there are no marked trails, so you must first speak with a ranger at the visitor center. Unless you're an experienced hiker, it's best to join a guided hike.

CAMPING IN THE PARK

Located at the north end of the park's scenic drive, **Devils Garden Campground** is Arches' only developed camping area. The 52 well-spaced sites are nestled among rocks, with plenty of pinyon and juniper trees. March through October, the campground accepts reservations for some sites through **National Recreation Reservation Service** (© 877/444-6777; www.reserveusa.com), with an extra $9 booking fee. In summer, the campground fills early, often by 9am, with people trying to garner the first-come, first-served sites, so either make reservations or get to the campground early. Sites cost $10 per night.

11

The Southwest

From the rugged drama of the Grand Canyon and the haunting ruins of centuries-old cliff dwellings to the manicured fairways of some of the country's best golf courses and the neon-laden Las Vegas Strip, the Southwest is a land of extremes. The stunning landscapes of fanciful red-rock formations, the harsh and delicate beauty of the desert, the wild thrills of America's premiere pleasure cities, and the vestiges of the Wild West are irresistible to many travelers. Whether you're a foodie seeking chic restaurants, a spa buff looking for luxurious pampering, a frustrated cowboy, or an art aficionado looking for the perfect piece, you'll hit the jackpot (possibly literally in Reno and Vegas) in the American Southwest. Even for the pickiest travelers, the attractions in this part of the country have become the stuff of the classic road-trip vacation.

1 Las Vegas

Las Vegas is a true original; there is nothing like it in America or arguably the world. In other cities, hotels are built near the major attractions. Here, the hotels *are* the major attractions. And if you tire of hotel-hopping, you can enjoy great works of art, five-star world-renowned chefs, and rock clubs and arenas that attract significant and still-current acts. With so many options available, you don't have to gamble at all!

As if. Vegas is first and foremost a gambling destination. And though the hotels aren't undercharging for everything anymore in an effort to lure you into gambling round-the-clock, they still do their best to separate you from your cash. The cheap buffets and meal deals still exist, as do some cut-rate rooms, but both are likely to prove the old adage about getting what you pay for. Nevertheless, free drinks are handed to anyone lurking near a slot, and if show tickets aren't in the budget, you won't lack for entertainment. Free lounge shows abound, and the people-watching opportunities alone never pall.

In its own way, Vegas is every bit as amazing as the nearby Grand Canyon and every bit as much a must-see. It's one of the Seven Wonders of the Artificial World. And everyone should experience it at least once—you might find yourself coming back for more.

ESSENTIALS

GETTING THERE By Plane Almost every major domestic airline, and some international airlines, fly into **McCarran International Airport** (© **702/261-5211,** or 702/261-3111 TTY; www.mccarran.com), just a few minutes' drive from the southern end of the Strip.

Bell Trans (© **800/274-7433** or 702/739-7990; www.bell-trans.com) runs 20-passenger minibuses daily between the airport and all major Las Vegas hotels and motels all day (7:45am–midnight). The cost is $5 per person each way to Strip- and Convention Center–area hotels, $6.50 to Downtown or other off-Strip properties (anyplace north of the Sahara Hotel and west of I-15).

Adults Only!

Las Vegas is not a great place to take kids. Many hotels actively discourage guests from bringing children and won't allow nonguests to bring strollers on the premises. Some casino hotels will not allow the children of nonguests on the premises after 6pm—and this policy is seriously enforced. And, of course, kids are not allowed in casinos. If you must bring the kids along on a short trip, you'll survive; but if you're planning a major family excursion, look elsewhere.

Taxis are plentiful and a ride to the Strip costs around $20, though we recommend you rent a car while you're in town; the major rental agencies have desks at the airport.

By Car The main highway connecting Las Vegas with the rest of the country is **I-15** from the northeast (Salt Lake City) and southwest (Los Angeles and San Diego). Lots of folks drive up from Los Angeles, and thanks to the narrow two-lane highway, it can get very crowded on Friday and Sunday afternoons. Other major routes are **U.S. 93** from the southeast (Phoenix) and **U.S. 95** from the northwest (Reno).

VISITOR INFORMATION For advance information, call or write the **Las Vegas Convention and Visitors Authority,** 3150 Paradise Rd., Las Vegas, NV 89109 (© **877/VISIT-LV** or 702/892-0711; www.visitlasvegas.com). They can send you a comprehensive information packet, map, show guide, events calendar, and attractions list; help you find a hotel that meets your specifications (and even make reservations); and tell you if a major convention is scheduled during the time you would like to visit Las Vegas. Or stop by when you're in town. They're open daily from 8am to 5pm.

Another excellent information source is the **Las Vegas Chamber of Commerce,** 3720 Howard Hughes Pkwy., #100, Las Vegas, NV 89109 (© **702/735-1616;** www.lvchamber.com). Ask them to send you their *Visitor's Guide,* which contains extensive information about accommodations, attractions, excursions, children's activities, and more. They're open Monday through Friday from 8am to 5pm.

GETTING AROUND We highly recommend that visitors rent a car. The Strip is too spread out for walking (and Las Vegas is often too hot or too cold to make strolls pleasant), and public transportation is often ineffective in getting you from Point A to Point B. All the major hotels offer free parking, so finding a spot won't be an issue. If, however, you plan to confine yourself to one part of the Strip or to Downtown, your feet will probably suffice. All the major rental-car agencies have desks at the airports and rates are generally pretty good.

By Bus & Trolley The no. 301 bus operated by **CAT** (© **702/CAT-RIDE;** www.rtcsouthernnevada.com/cat) plies a route between the Downtown Transportation Center (at Casino Center Blvd. and Stewart Ave.) and a few miles beyond the southern end of the Strip. The fare is $2 for adults, 60¢ for seniors (62 and older) and children 5 to 17, and free for those under 5. CAT buses run 24 hours a day and are wheelchair accessible. Exact change is required.

Las Vegas Strip Trolley (© **702/382-1404**) operates a classic streetcar replica that runs northward from Hacienda Avenue, stopping at all major hotels en route to the Sahara, and then looping back via the Las Vegas Hilton. They do not, however, go to the Stratosphere Casino Hotel & Tower or Downtown. Trolleys run about every 15 minutes daily between 9:30am and 2am. The fare is $2 for a single one-way ride or $5 (free for children under age 5) for an all-day pass, and exact change is required.

The Southwest

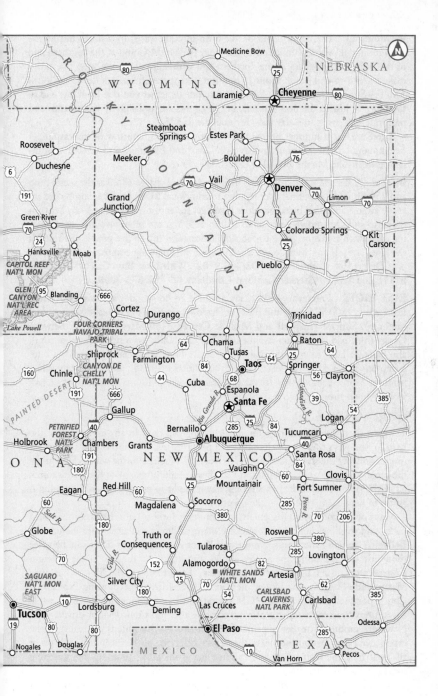

By Monorail   The major debut on the Strip in 2004 wasn't by a hotel, but by the Strip monorail, whose 4-mile route runs from the MGM Grand at the southern end of the Strip to the Sahara at the northern end with stops along the way. The trains make the end-to-end run in about 15 minutes, and operate from 7am until 2am (until 3am Fri–Sun). Fares are $5 (!!!) for a one-way ride (whether you ride from one end to the other or just to the next station), but discounts are available for round-trips and multiride/day passes (a 3-day pass, for example, is $25).

There are also a number of free transportation services, courtesy of the casinos. A free monorail connects Mandalay Bay with Luxor and Excalibur, and a free tram shuttles between The Mirage and TI at the Mirage.

By Taxi   Cabs line up in front of all major hotels and charge $3.20 at the meter drop and 25¢ for each additional ⅛ mile, plus an additional $1.20 fee for being picked up at the airport and time-based penalties if you get stuck in a traffic-jam. A taxi between the Strip and Downtown costs about $10 to $15. You can often save money by sharing a cab with someone going to the same destination (up to five people can ride for the same fare). If you want to call a taxi, any of the following companies can provide one: **Desert Cab Company** (© 702/386-9102), **Whittlesea Blue Cab** (© 702/384-6111), and **Yellow/Checker Cab/Star Company** (© 702/873-2000).

FAST FACTS   Emergency services are available 24 hours a day at **University Medical Center,** 1800 W. Charleston Blvd., at Shadow Lane (© 702/383-2000; www.umc-cares.org). **Sunrise Hospital and Medical Center,** 3186 Maryland Pkwy., between Desert Inn Road and Sahara Avenue (© 702/731-8080; www.sunrisehospital.com), also has a 24-hour emergency room. There's a 24-hour **Walgreens** (which has a 1-hr. photo service) at 3765 Las Vegas Blvd. S. (© 702/739-9638), almost directly across from the Monte Carlo. The **sales tax** on meals, goods, and some services is 7%. Clark County hotel **room tax** is 9%.

WHAT TO SEE & DO

You can't sit at a slot machine forever. (Or maybe you can.) In any event, it's not too hard to find ways to fill your time between poker hands. The **hotels and casinos** are unquestionably the star attractions in Las Vegas. Where else in the world can you sail the canals of Venice, take in a joust at a medieval castle, and explore King Tut's tomb, all in the space of 1 block? Just strolling down the Strip at night when everything is awash in neon is an experience like no other.

Many of the hotels offer free entertainment in the form of light shows, animal-filled parks, and strolling musical performers. Can't-miss shows and attractions include the **Bellagio's dancing fountains,** a musical ballet of water and light that is the best free show in town, bar none; the almost always stunning floral displays at the **Bellagio Conservatory;** the **talking statues in Caesars' Forum Shops;** the Mardi Gras–style **Masquerade Show in the Sky** at the Rio; and the **Mirage's exploding "volcano."** Couch potatoes can watch the MGM Grand's 80-foot outdoor video screens, while adventurers head for a roller coaster celebrating that most daredevil of drivers—the New York cabbie. (This last one's not free, but that only heightens the reality of the experience.) And last but not least, the casinos offer one of the greatest free thrills of all—watching the high rollers win and lose big at the tables (nothing like watching someone else lose fifty grand).

Nevertheless, when you finally tire of Strip-gazing (or your brain shuts down from the overload), there are plenty of other things to see and do in Las Vegas.

The Atomic Testing Museum   From 1951 until 1992, the Nevada Test Site was this country's primary location for testing nuclear weapons. Aboveground blasts in the early days were visible to the tourists and residents of Las Vegas. This well-executed museum, library, and gallery space offers visitors a fascinating glance at the test site from ancient days through modern times, with memorabilia, displays, official documents, videos, interactive displays, motion-simulator theaters (like sitting in a bunker, watching a blast), and emotional testimony from the people who worked there. It respectfully treads that tricky line between honoring the work done at the site and understanding its terrible implications. Not to be missed.

755 E. Flamingo Rd. ⓒ 702/794-5151. www.atomictestingmuseum.org. $10 adults; $7 seniors, military, and students with ID; free for children 6 and under. Mon–Sat 9am–5pm; Sun 1–5pm.

Fremont Street Experience   The Fremont Street Experience in the heart of Downtown is a 5-block open-air pedestrian mall, a landscaped strip of outdoor cafes, vendor carts, and colorful kiosks purveying food and merchandise. Overhead is a 90-foot-high steel-mesh "celestial vault"; at night, it is the newly revamped **Viva Vision,** a high-tech light-and-laser show (the canopy is equipped with more than 12.5 million lights) enhanced by a concert-hall-quality sound system that takes place five times nightly. Not only does the canopy provide shade, it cools the area through a misting system in summer and warms you with radiant heaters in winter. It's a place where you can stroll, eat, or even dance to the music under the lights. The crowd it attracts is more upscale than in years past, and of course, it's a lot less crowded than the hectic Strip.

Fremont St. (between Main St. and Las Vegas Blvd.), Downtown. www.vegasexperience.com. Free admission. Shows nightly.

Liberace Museum *(Best)*   You can keep your Louvres and Vaticans and Smithsonians; *this* is a museum. Housed, like everything else in Vegas, in a strip mall, this is a shrine to the glory and excess that was the art project known as Liberace. You've got your costumes (bejeweled), your many cars (bejeweled), your many pianos (bejeweled), and many jewels (also bejeweled). It just shows what can be bought with lots of money and no taste. This is a one-of-a-kind place, that's better than ever after a recent renovation to make it even more gaudy and over-the-top. Unless you have a severely underdeveloped appreciation for camp or take your museum-going very seriously, you shouldn't miss it.

1775 E. Tropicana Ave. (at Spencer St.). ⓒ 702/798-5595. www.liberace.org. Admission $13 adults, $8.50 seniors over 64 and students, free for children 10 and under. Mon–Sat 10am–5pm; Sun noon–4pm. Closed Thanksgiving, Dec 25, and Jan 1.

Madame Tussaud's Celebrity Encounter *(Kids)*   Even if you aren't a fan of wax museums, this one is probably worth a stop—if you can stomach the ridiculous price. Figures here are state of the art, although some reproductions are considerably better than others. All the waxworks are free-standing, allowing—and indeed encouraging— guests to get up close and personal. Go ahead; lay your cheek next to Elvis's or Sinatra's and have your photo taken. The emphasis is on film, television, music, and sports celebrities, plus some Vegas icons, all housed in five themed rooms. There's also a behind-the-scenes look at the lengthy process involved in creating these figures.

In The Venetian, 3355 Las Vegas Blvd. S. ⓒ 702/862-7800. www.madametussaudslv.com. Admission $23 adults, $15 seniors and students, $13 children 6–12, free for children 5 and under, $50 family pass for 2 adults and 2 students or children. Daily 10am–10pm, but hours vary seasonally.

MGM Grand Lion Habitat *(Value) (Kids)*   Hit this attraction at the right time—when the crowds aren't here—and it's one of the best freebies in town. Lions frolic during various times of day in its large, multilevel glass enclosure. In addition to regular viewing spots, you can walk through a glass tunnel and get a worm's-eye view of the underside of a lion (provided one is in position); note how very big Kitty's paws are.

In MGM Grand, 3799 Las Vegas Blvd. S. ✆ **702/891-7777.** Free admission. Daily 11am–10pm.

Secret Garden of Siegfried & Roy and Mirage Dolphin Habitat (Kids)

Get up close and personal with some of the famed duo's white tigers, lions, and plain old gray elephants, here at this minizoo; or better still, watch dolphins frolic in the neighboring Dolphin Habitat. There is nothing quite like the kick you get from seeing a baby dolphin play. If the knowledgeable staff isn't already, ask them to play ball with the dolphins; they toss large beach balls into the pools, and the dolphins hit them out with their noses; sometimes you can join in, too.

In The Mirage, 3400 Las Vegas Blvd. S. ✆ **702/791-7111.** www.mirage.com. Admission $15 adults, $10 children 4–10, free for children under 4 if accompanied by an adult. Mon–Fri 11am–5:30pm; Sat–Sun and major holidays 10am–5:30pm. Hours subject to change and vary by season.

SPEED: The Ride/Las Vegas Cyber Speedway

This popular stop has two attractions. The first is a remarkable 8-minute virtual-reality ride, **Cyber Speedway,** featuring a three-quarter-size replica of a NASCAR race car. In a separate **3-D motion theater,** you don goggles to view a film that puts you inside another race car for yet another stomach-churning ride (even more dizzying than the virtual-reality portion). **SPEED: The Ride** is a roller coaster that blasts riders out through a hole in the wall by the NASCAR Cafe, then through a loop, under the sidewalk, through the hotel's marquee, and finally straight up a 250-foot tower. At the peak, you feel a moment of weightlessness, and then you do the whole thing backward! Not for the faint of heart.

In the Sahara, 2535 Las Vegas Blvd. S. ✆ **702/737-2111.** www.nascarcafelasvegas.com. $20 for all-day pass on both rides. Cyber Speedway (simulator) $10 (you must be at least 48 in. tall to ride); SPEED: The Ride (roller coaster) $10 for single ride. Sun–Thurs 11am–midnight; Fri–Sat 11am–1am. Hours may vary.

Star Trek: The Experience and Borg Invasion 4-D (Kids)

This is the undisputed champ in the Vegas motion-simulator ride category. Your long wait in line will be somewhat entertaining, thanks to memorabilia and TVs showing various *Trek* clips. The story line involves time travel and evil doings by the Borg, and if all doesn't work out, the very history of *Star Trek* could be affected. Do expect to be beamed aboard the *Enterprise* (really kind of cool), and know that if you have a sensitive stomach, you can skip the actual motion-simulator part, a wild chase through space. *Borg Invasion 4-D* is a 3-D film (with some surprise sensory effects) starring several *Star Trek Voyager* cast members. Both rides will send most Trekkers into orbit with happiness.

In Las Vegas Hilton, 3000 Paradise Rd. ✆ **888/GO-BOLDLY.** www.startrekexp.com. All-day pass including both attractions and museum: $39 adults, $36 seniors and children 12 and under. Purchase tickets online for discounts. Daily 11:30am–7:30pm or 9:30pm, depending on the season.

Stratosphere Thrill Rides (Kids)

Atop the 1,149-foot Stratosphere Tower are three marvelous thrill rides. The **Big Shot** is a breathtaking free-fall ride that thrusts you 160 feet in the air along a 228-foot spire at the top of the tower, then plummets back down again. Sitting in an open car, you seem to be dangling in space over Las Vegas. Amping up the terror factor is **X-Scream,** a giant teeter-totter-style device that propels you in an open car off the side of the 100-story tower and lets you dangle there weightlessly before returning you to relative safety. And now they have the aptly named **Insanity,** a spinning whirly-gig of a contraption that straps you into a seat and twirls you around 1,000 feet or so above terra firma. Insanity is right. *Note:* The rides are shut down in inclement weather and high winds.

Atop Stratosphere Las Vegas, 2000 Las Vegas Blvd. S. ☎ **702/380-7777**. Admission: Big Shot $8; X-Scream $8; Insanity $8; plus fee to ascend Tower: $10 for adults; $6 for locals, seniors, hotel guests, and children 4–12; free for children 3 and under and those dining in the buffet room or Top of the World. Multiride and all-day packages also available for varying costs. Sun–Thurs 10am–1am; Fri–Sat 10am–2am. Hours vary seasonally. Minimum height requirement for all rides is 48 in.

WHERE TO ROLL THE DICE

What? You didn't come to Las Vegas for the Liberace Museum? We are shocked. *Shocked.* Yes, there are gambling opportunities in Vegas. Let's not kid ourselves; gambling is what Vegas is about. The bright lights, shows, showgirls, and food—they are all there just to lure you in and make you open your wallet. You should casino-hop at least once to marvel (or get dizzy) at the decor/spectacle and the sheer excess of it all. Beyond decoration, there isn't too much difference. All the casinos have slot and video poker machines and offer games such as blackjack, roulette, craps, poker, Pai Gow, keno, and baccarat. If you're a novice, many casinos offer free gambling lessons that include low stakes games, so you won't lose much while you learn.

Some notable places to gamble include the **MGM Grand,** the largest casino on the planet (you will get lost); the light and airy **Mandalay Bay,** which has the lowest claustrophobia factor in town; the tasteful **Venetian;** the **Las Vegas Hilton,** where the space-themed casino has light-beam-activated slots; **Harrah's,** where the "party pits" offer the most fun in town; **Paris–Las Vegas,** where you'll find a kitschy Disneyesque atmosphere; and **Binion's Horseshoe,** where all serious gamblers head, thanks to low minimum bets and the highest betting limits in town. *Tip:* Whichever casino you pick, sign up for its free slot club and you'll be eligible for perks, including meals, shows, discounts on rooms, gifts, tournament invitations, discounts at hotel shops, VIP treatment, and (more and more) cash rebates.

Remember that gambling is supposed to be entertainment. Pick a gaming table where the other players are laughing, slapping each other on the back, and generally enjoying themselves. Sometimes you can have a better time at one of the older places Downtown, where stakes are lower, pretensions are nonexistent, and the clientele are often friendlier. You don't have to be a high roller. You would not believe how much fun you can have with a nickel slot machine. You won't get rich, but neither will most of those guys playing the $5 slots, either.

WHERE TO STAY

If there's one thing Vegas has in spades, it's hotels. Big hotels. You'll find the 10 largest hotels in the United States, if not in the world, right here. And you'll find a whole lot of rooms: 140,000 rooms, to be exact—or at least exact at this writing. The hotels are the city's biggest tourist attraction, and they pack in the crowds accordingly. (Las Vegas usually has an occupancy rate of about 90%.) A last-minute Vegas vacation can turn into a housing nightmare. If possible, plan in advance so that you can have your choice: Ancient Egypt or Ancient Rome? New York or New Orleans? Strip or Downtown? Luxury or economy? Vegas has all that and way too much more.

First-time visitors will most likely stay on the Strip, although Downtown is a lot nicer than it used to be, and the rates there are cheaper. The **Las Vegas Convention and Visitors Authority** runs a room reservations hot line (☎ **877/VISIT-LV** or 702/892-0711; www.visitlasvegas.com) that can be helpful. They can apprise you of room availability, quote rates, contact a hotel for you, and tell you when major conventions are in town.

Vegas does have hotels that eschew the theme scheme. Unlike many of the casino hotels, they are far more likely to cater to kids, making them good choices for families. One great selection is the luxurious **Four Seasons** (✆ **877/632-5000** or 702/632-5000; www.fourseasons.com), inside the Mandalay Bay, although it has its own entrance and facilities. It offers a temporary respite from the Vegas hype since there's no casino, but guests who need a numbers fix can use Mandalay's with no problems. The same goes for **THEhotel at Mandalay Bay** (✆ **877/632-7800** or 702/632-7777; www.thehotelatmandalaybay.com), a decidedly chic and sophisticated all-suite part of the casino hotel with its own entrance.

All the usual budget chains have properties in Las Vegas. (See appendix D for their toll-free phone numbers and websites.)

Note: The following are a representative slice of the city's hotels (most of them on the Strip, which is where most first-timers stay) in various price categories. Most of them take Vegas's excess to heart, because, as one traveler who could afford the Four Seasons or Ritz-Carlton, but never stays there when in Vegas told us, "Why would I want to stay in a hotel in Vegas that looks like it could be anywhere else in the U.S.?"

Many hotels offer fridges on request for an extra fee (usually $10–$20 per day); ask when you reserve if this is important to you. For the lowdown on all of the city's fabulous hotels (which would take dozens of pages), check out *Frommer's Las Vegas.*

Bellagio   This $1.6-billion luxury resort ushered in the post-Vegas-is-for-families elegance epoch. Bellagio is not so much a romantic Italian village as its theme would suggest, but it's a big, grand, state-of-the-art Vegas hotel (with all the pluses and minuses therein). Here you'll find fabulous fountains, a magnificent floral conservatory, an art gallery, and the best collection of restaurants in town. There is even an 8-acre Lake Como stand-in out front, complete with a dazzling choreographed water ballet extravaganza (the best free show in town). Rooms are nicely decorated and the roomy bathrooms are even more luxurious. Service is surprisingly good given the size of the place. The pool area is exceptional and the spa is marvelous, if overpriced. This is not much like a getaway to a peaceful, romantic Italian village. It's not the best value in town, but it's still the ultimate Vegas luxury resort experience.

3600 Las Vegas Blvd. S. (at the corner of Flamingo Rd.), Las Vegas, NV 89109. ✆ 888/987-6667 or 702/693-7111. Fax 702/693-8546. www.bellagio.com. 3,933 units. $149 and up double. Extra person $35; no discount for children. AE, DC, DISC, MC, V. Free self- and valet parking. **Amenities:** 14 restaurants; 6 pools; health club; spa.

Caesars Palace   Caesars is the spectacle that every Vegas hotel should be. A combination of Vegas luxury and a good dose of kitsch, the hotel is graced by Roman colonnades, marble fountains, and staff members attired in gladiator outfits and togas. But the hotel has a confusing layout, and it takes forever to get anywhere—especially out to the Strip. Accommodations occupy four towers; art in the rooms keeps to the Greco-Roman theme (some have classical sculptures in niches). The newest rooms are handsome, if not as giggle-inducingly overwhelming as the classic ones, and have floor-to-ceiling windows that offer a hypnotizing panoramic view. You'll likely enjoy a lavish bathroom with marble floor, European fixtures, and oversize marble tubs (about half are whirlpools). The pool area, the $100-million **Garden of the Gods,** is a tasteful, undeniably "Caesar-esque" masterpiece.

3570 Las Vegas Blvd. S. (just north of Flamingo Rd.), Las Vegas, NV 89109. ✆ 877/427-7243 or 702/731-7110. Fax 702/697-5706. www.caesars.com. 3,348 units. $129 and up double; $549 and up suite. Extra person $35. Children under 18 stay free in parent's room. AE, DC, DISC, MC, V. Free self- and valet parking. **Amenities:** 24 restaurants; 4 pools; health club; spa.

Circus Circus Hotel/Casino *Kids*   The last bastion of family-friendly Las Vegas; but even *it* isn't what it ought to be, thanks to a reconfiguration that took the Jumbo the Clown decorating scheme and turned it into somewhat more tasteful, more commedia dell'arte Harlequins. Nevertheless, the world's largest permanent circus and indoor theme park are still here (right by that casino!), and kids will love it. Tower rooms have just slightly better-than-average furnishings; the Manor section comprises five white three-story buildings out back, fronted by rows of cypresses. These rooms are usually among the least expensive in town, but we've said it before and we'll say it again: You get what you pay for. The hotel also has its own RV park.

2880 Las Vegas Blvd. S. (between Circus Circus and Convention Center drives), Las Vegas, NV 89109. ✆ 877/434-9175 or 702/734-0410. Fax 702/734-5897. www.circuscircus.com. 3,774 units. $59 and up double. Extra person $12. Children under 17 stay free in parent's room. AE, DC, DISC, MC, V. Free self- and valet parking. **Amenities:** 7 restaurants; 2 outdoor pools.

The Flamingo Las Vegas   It may be the Strip's senior citizen, but renovations and expansions over the years have freshened up Bugsy Siegel's "real class joint." A recent addition is a branch of singer Jimmy Buffett's Margaritaville nightclub. The Flamingo's exceptional pool area encompasses fishponds, two water slides, five gorgeous swimming pools, two whirlpools, waterfalls, and a flamingo enclave—plus its spa and tennis courts are a big draw. The guest rooms occupy six towers and sport various styles of decor, most with pretty fabrics and the usual array of room amenities.

3555 Las Vegas Blvd. S. (between Sands Ave. and Flamingo Rd.), Las Vegas, NV 89109. ✆ 800/732-2111 or 702/733-3111. Fax 702/733-3353. www.flamingolv.com. 3,999 units. $79 and up double; $249 and up suite. Extra person $30. Children under 18 stay free in parent's room. Timeshare suites available. AE, DC, DISC, MC, V. Free self- and valet parking. **Amenities:** 8 restaurants; 5 outdoor pools; 4 night-lit tennis courts; health club and spa.

Golden Nugget   Thanks to new ownership, this deserving property, the grande dame of Downtown, is getting some much-needed attention, with new restaurants, remodeled rooms and public spaces, a big new pool, and even a entire new hotel tower going in across the street. At press time, much of this work was in the beginning phases, but we think that by the time you read this, the Nugget could be well on her way to reclaiming her Downtown glory. The presence of a pool (which is getting a makeover destined to turn it into a party spot/aquarium where you can get up close and personal with various marine life), and general overall quality, makes this the best hotel Downtown for families; though it's not what we'd call family-friendly.

129 E. Fremont St. (at Casino Center Blvd.), Las Vegas, NV 89101. ✆ 800/846-5336 or 702/385-7111. Fax 702/386-8362. www.goldennugget.com. 1,907 units. $59 and up double; $275 and up suite. Extra person $20, no discount for children. AE, DC, DISC, MC, V. Free self- and valet parking. **Amenities:** 5 restaurants; outdoor pool; health club; spa.

Harrah's Las Vegas   Though parts of Harrah's benefited from a remodeling a few years ago, the rest of it evokes the worst of old Las Vegas—as in, dark, dated, and claustrophobic. Still, there is much to like here, and occasional good rates might make the so-so bits worth overlooking. All the rooms (ask for a recently refurbished one) are larger than average. Spacious minisuites, offering large sofas and comfortable armchairs, are especially desirable. The hotel's health club is one of the better ones on the Strip, but the pool is underwhelming. The casino is one of the friendliest in town.

3475 Las Vegas Blvd. S. (between Flamingo and Spring Mountain roads), Las Vegas, NV 89109. ✆ 800/HARRAHS (427-7247) or 702/369-5000. Fax 702/369-5283. www.harrahs.com. 2,579 units. $99 and up double; $199 and up suite. Extra person $20; no discount for children. AE, DC, DISC, MC, V. Free self- and valet parking. **Amenities:** 9 restaurants; pool; health club; spa.

Luxor Las Vegas   It would be hard to miss the Luxor's 30-story pyramid, even without the 315,000-watt light beam at the top; the hotel thrills us to our very kitsch-worshipping souls with its Egyptian relic copies and talking animatronic camels. The hotel is, despite appearances, inviting and functional. The Egyptian Revival lobby, done up in marble and cherrywood, is one of the nicest lobbies in town, and the rooms are among the few that really stand out in Vegas. They feature fine Art Deco and Egyptian furnishings and have excellent marble bathrooms, although the Pyramid rooms have showers only. High-speed "inclinator" elevators run on a 39-degree angle, making the ride up to the Pyramid rooms a bit of a thrill.

3900 Las Vegas Blvd. S. (between Reno and Hacienda aves.), Las Vegas, NV 81119. (C) **888/777-0188** or 702/262-4000. Fax 702/262-4478. www.luxor.com. 4,400 units. $59 and up double; $149 and up whirlpool suite; $249–$800 other suites. Extra person $25. Children under 12 stay free in parent's room. AE, DC, DISC, MC, V. Free self- and valet parking. **Amenities:** 7 restaurants and a food court; 5 outdoor pools; health club; spa.

Main Street Station   The Main Street Station, one of the best bargains in the city, is 2 short blocks away from Fremont Street in Downtown, barely a 3-minute walk. The overall look is turn-of-the-20th-century San Francisco, and the details, from the ornate chandeliers to the wood-paneled lobby, are outstanding. The long and narrow rooms are possibly the largest in Downtown, though the ornate decorating downstairs does not extend up here. A 2005 overhaul gave them positively modern furnishings, new carpet and wall coverings, updated fixtures in the bathrooms, and more. The bathrooms are small but well appointed. If you're a light sleeper, request a room on the south side.

200 N. Main St. (between Fremont St. and I-95), Las Vegas, NV 89101. (C) **800/465-0711** or 702/387-1896. Fax 702/386-4466. www.mainstreetcasino.com. 406 units. $59 and up double. AE, DC, DISC, MC, V. Free self- and valet parking. **Amenities:** 3 restaurants; use of outdoor pool next door at California Hotel.

Mandalay Bay *(Best*   It doesn't really evoke Southeast Asia, but the Mandalay Bay actually looks like a resort hotel rather than just a Vegas version of one, and we find a hotel whose theme doesn't bop you over the head refreshing. You don't have to walk through the casino to get to the public areas or guest room elevators, the pool area is spiffy, and the whole complex is less confusing and certainly less overwhelming than some neighboring behemoths. Rooms are among the finest on the Strip, spacious and subdued in decor. The large bathrooms, stocked with a host of fabulous amenities, are certainly the best on the Strip and maybe the best in Vegas. The hotel's highly touted wave pool (set in a veritable waterpark) offers a nice afternoon's relaxation.

3950 Las Vegas Blvd. S. (at Hacienda Ave.), Las Vegas, NV 89119. (C) **877/632-7000** or 702/632-7000. Fax 702/632-7228. www.mandalaybay.com. 3,309 units. $99 and up double; $149 and up suite; $149 and up House of Blues Signature Rooms. Extra person $35; children 14 and under free in parent's room. AE, DC, DISC, MC, V. Free self- and valet parking. **Amenities:** 22 restaurants; 4 outdoor pools; health club; spa.

MGM Grand Hotel/Casino   Set on 114 acres, the massive MGM Grand has a green exterior and a casino the size of four football fields (you will get lost at least once). More importantly, almost all traces of a failed movement to turn this into a child-friendly venue have been summarily wiped out (can you say striptease lounge acts?). However, the lion habitat and the fabulous pool area make this place popular with families. The standard guest rooms are blandly upscale, generously proportioned, and equipped with pretty much everything you might need. The West Wing rooms are much smaller, but more memorable and stylish, with lots of mirrors and frosted green glass in the bathroom, at least two flatscreen TVs (one in the bedroom, one in the bathroom), and electronic gizmos like lamps that turn on and off if you touch them.

3799 Las Vegas Blvd. S. (at Tropicana Ave.), Las Vegas, NV 89109. ℂ **800/929-1111** or 702/891-7777. Fax 702/891-1030. www.mgmgrand.com. 5,034 units. $99 and up standard double; $159 and up suite. Extra person $30. Children under 13 stay free in parent's room. AE, DC, DISC, MC, V. Free self- and valet parking. **Amenities:** 15 restaurants; 5 outdoor pools; fitness center; spa.

The Mirage   The mother of all modern Vegas hotels has been somewhat eclipsed by the very hotels whose presence it made possible, but we still really like this place. The hotel, fronted by waterfalls and tropical foliage, centers on a very "active" volcano that erupts every 15 minutes after dark. Inside, you'll find a verdant rainforest, complete with habitats for Siegfried and Roy's white tigers, and a bunch of Atlantic bottlenose dolphins. The rooms are handsome, but there are nicer—and larger—ones all over town now, and the bathrooms are a little too cramped for what's supposed to be a swanky hotel. The staff is genuinely helpful; any problems that may arise are quickly smoothed out. The pool is one of the best in Vegas.

3400 Las Vegas Blvd. S. (between Flamingo Rd. and Spring Mountain Rd.), Las Vegas, NV 89109. ℂ **800/627-6667** or 702/791-7111. Fax 702/791-7446. www.mirage.com. 3,044 units. $119 and up double; $249 and up suite. Extra person $30; no discount for children. AE, DC, DISC, MC, V. Free self- and valet parking. **Amenities:** 11 restaurants; outdoor pool; fitness center; spa.

New York–New York Hotel & Casino   Here's one you'll either love or loathe (reactions tend to be strong on either side of the fence). The hotel looks like the New York City skyline (complete with a taxi-cab themed roller coaster running through it). Subtle it isn't. You can gamble in a casino done up as Central Park or play games in the Coney Island arcade. You'll experience a true taste of the Big Apple—including the noise and the (often claustrophobia-inducing) crowds. Rooms come in 64 different styles and are decorated in a sophisticated modern color scheme of earth tones and pale pastels; some are downright tiny and suffocating (just like New York). Light sleepers should request a room away from the roller coaster. If you're a pool person, go elsewhere—the one here is pretty mediocre.

3790 Las Vegas Blvd. S. (at Tropicana Ave.), Las Vegas, NV 89109. ℂ **800/693-6763** or 702/740-6969. Fax 702/740-6920. www.nynyhotelcasino.com. 2,023 units. $79 and up double. Extra person $30; no discount for children. AE, DC, DISC, MC, V. Free self- and valet parking. **Amenities:** 9 restaurants and a food court; outdoor pool; fitness center; spa.

Paris Las Vegas Casino Resort   *Sacre bleu!* The City of Light comes to Sin City in this Strip fantasy hotel. It's theme-run-amok time again, and we are so happy about it. You can stroll down a mini–Rue de la Paix, ride an elevator to the top of the Eiffel Tower, stop at an overpriced bakery for a baguette, take your photos by several very nice fountains, and snicker at dubious French signage ("le car rental"). Rooms are nice enough but disappointingly uninteresting, with furniture that only hints at mock French Regency, and with small but pretty bathrooms that have deep tubs. Try to get a Strip-facing room so you can see the Bellagio's fountains across the street; north-facing rooms give you nice Peeping Tom views right into neighboring Bally's. Overall, not a bad place to stay, but a great place to visit—*quelle hoot!*

3655 Las Vegas Blvd. S., Las Vegas, NV 89109. ℂ **888/BONJOUR** (266-5687) or 702/946-7000. www.parislv.com. 2,916 units. $119 and up double; $350 and up suite. Extra person $30. Children under 18 stay free in parent's room. AE, DC, DISC, MC. V. Free self- and valet parking. **Amenities:** 12 restaurants; outdoor pool; health club; spa.

Rio All Suite Hotel & Casino   Rio bills itself as a "carnival" atmosphere hotel, which in this case means hectic, crowded, and noisy, and the recent edict requiring the already Most Scantily Clad Waitresses in Town to burst into song and dance in between delivering beers. In addition to its tropically themed resort, the Rio has an immensely popular 41-story tower and Masquerade Village that simulate a European village, complete with shops, restaurants, and a bizarre live-action show in the sky. The "suites" are actually one rather large room with a sofa and coffee table. Rooms feature floor-to-ceiling windows that offer panoramic views of the Strip. Note that the hotel actively discourages guests from bringing children.

3700 W. Flamingo Rd. (just west of I-15), Las Vegas, NV 89103. ✆ **888/752-9746** or 702/777-7777. Fax 702/777-7611. www.playrio.com. 2,582 units. $99 and up double-occupancy suite. Extra person $30; no discount for children. AE, DC, MC, V. Free self- and valet parking. **Amenities:** 12 restaurants; 4 pools; golf course; health club and spa. *In room:* Fridge.

Stratosphere Las Vegas *(Kids)* At 1,149 feet, the Stratosphere is the tallest building west of the Mississippi; it's also in the middle of nowhere on the Strip, which explains the lack of crowds. But if you are looking for a friendly place to hang your hat and don't need frills, it's a good choice. The panoramic views available from the top of the tower and some amazing thrill rides (see "What to See & Do," earlier in this chapter) are the big attractions here. The smaller-size rooms here are basically motel rooms—really nice motel rooms, but with that level of comfort and style. Perfect if you are coming to Vegas with no plans to spend time in your room except to sleep (if even that). That isn't to say there aren't other elements to like here, including a midway area with kiddie-oriented rides, a pool with a view, and some of the friendliest, most accommodating staff in town.

2000 Las Vegas Blvd. S. (between St. Louis and Baltimore aves.), Las Vegas, NV 89104. ✆ **800/99-TOWER** (998-6937) or 702/380-7777. Fax 702/383-5334. www.stratospherehotel.com. 2,444 units. $39 and up double; $69 and up suite. Extra person $15. Children under 13 stay free in parent's room. AE, DC, DISC, MC, V. Free self- and valet parking. **Amenities:** 9 restaurants; pool.

TI at the Mirage *(Value)* Originally the most modern family-friendly hotel on the Strip, the former Treasure Island was a blown-up version of Disneyland's Pirates of the Caribbean. But that's all behind them now, and the name change is there to make sure you understand this is a grown-up, sophisticated resort. Even its famous pirate stunt show out front has been revamped so that the pirates now "battle" scantily clad "strippers"—er, "sirens." The refit has admittedly spruced up the resort so much that we now rank it ahead of its sister, The Mirage, and tops in value for all the MGM MIRAGE properties. The large rooms are decorated in modified French Regency and monochromatic colors; the good bathrooms feature large soaking tubs. The pool, alas, is not particularly memorable.

3300 Las Vegas Blvd. S. (at Spring Mountain Rd.), Las Vegas, NV 89109. ✆ **800/944-7444** or 702/894-7111. Fax 702/894-7446. www.treasureisland.com. 2,885 units. $89 and up double; $129 and up suite. Extra person $30; no discount for children. Inquire about packages. AE, DC, DISC, MC, V. Free self- and valet parking. **Amenities:** 6 restaurants; pool; fitness center; spa.

The Venetian The Venetian falls squarely between an outright adult Disneyland experience and the luxury resort sensibility of other Vegas hotels. The hotel impressively re-creates the city of Venice, including the artwork, the marble pillars and arches, and—unfortunately—the outrageous prices. Rooms are the largest and probably the most handsome in town. They are all "suites," with a good-size bedroom giving way to steps down to a sunken living area, complete with pullout sofa bed. Other touches include half-canopied beds, and exceptional marble bathrooms with glassed-in showers, deep soaking tubs, double sinks, fluffy towels, and lots of space. Rooms in the **Venezia Tower** are even more lush—a plasma TV in the bathroom!—and worth the extra bucks. A branch of the famous Canyon Ranch SpaClub is on-site. If there's a weak point, it's the hotel's pool area, which is disappointing and bland.

3355 Las Vegas Blvd. S., Las Vegas, NV 89109. ℭ 888/2-VENICE (283-6423) or 702/414-1000. Fax 702/414-4805. www.venetian.com. 4,029 units. $149 and up double. Extra person $35. Children under 13 stay free in parent's room. AE, DC, DISC, MC, V. Free self- and valet parking. **Amenities:** 18 restaurants; 6 pools; health club; spa.

WHERE TO DINE

The dining scene in Las Vegas is a melting pot of midnight steak specials, cheap buffets, and gourmet rooms that rival those found in New York or Los Angeles. *One word of warning:* You can eat well in Vegas, and you can eat cheaply in Vegas, but because the dining renaissance in Vegas seems to have hit only the high-end joints in town, it hard to do both at the same time. We list a few of the city's best bets in town, but the inexpensive ones can be hard to find.

Theme-restaurant buffs can chow down at **House of Blues,** in Mandalay Bay, 3950 Las Vegas Blvd. S. (ℭ **702/632-7607**); the **Hard Rock Cafe** at 4475 Paradise Rd., at Harmon Avenue (ℭ **702/733-8400**); **ESPN** at 3790 Las Vegas Blvd. S., in New York–New York Hotel & Casino (ℭ **702/933-3776**); the **Harley Davidson Cafe,** 3725 Las Vegas Blvd. S., at Harmon Avenue (ℭ **702/740-4555**); or the **Rainforest Café** in the MGM Grand, 3799 Las Vegas Blvd. S. (ℭ **702/891-8580**).

For those wanting to sample one of the many hotel buffets—and it's an essential part of the Las Vegas vacation—some of the better bets include **Luxor's Pharaoh's Pheast Buffet,** 3900 Las Vegas Blvd. S. (ℭ 702/262-4000); **Bellagio Buffet,** 3600 Las Vegas Blvd. S. (ℭ 877/234-6358); **Rio's Carnival World Buffet,** 3700 W. Flamingo Rd. (ℭ 702/252-7777); **Paris Le Village Buffet,** 3665 Las Vegas Blvd. S. (ℭ 888/266-5687); **Palms Festival Market Buffet,** in the Palms Resort, 4321 W. Flamingo Rd. (ℭ 702/942-7777); and **Main Street Station Garden Court,** 200 N. Main St. (ℭ 702/387-1896). The best Sunday brunch buffet in Vegas is **Bally's Sterling Sunday Brunch,** 3645 Las Vegas Blvd. S. (ℭ 702/967-7999), which costs $65 per person.

Gourmands will also find plenty of dining options. Celebrity chefs Wolfgang Puck and Emeril Lagasse have half a dozen restaurants in town between them; multi-Michelin-starred chef Joël Robuchon opened two restaurants in the MGM Grand; deservedly famed chef Julian Serrano reigns at Bellagio's **Picasso;** Thomas Keller, the brains behind Napa Valley's French Laundry, has a branch of his **Bouchon** bistro; legendary chef Alain Ducasse is behind **Mix** at THEhotel; and branches of L.A., New York, San Francisco, and Boston high-profile names such as **Pinot Brasserie, Le Cirque, Aqua, Aureole, Olives, Lutèce, Border Grill, Nobu,** and others have all rolled into town.

Border Grill MEXICAN   For our money, here's the best Mexican food in town. This big cheerful space—like a Romper Room for adults—houses a branch of the much-lauded L.A. restaurant, conceived and run by the Food Network's "Two Hot Tamales," Mary Sue Milliken and Susan Feniger. This is truly authentic Mexican home cooking. Consequently, don't expect precisely the same food you would encounter in your favorite corner joint, but do expect fresh and fabulous food, arranged as brightly on the plates as the decor on the walls. Don't miss the dense but fluffy Mexican chocolate cream pie (with a meringue crust).

In Mandalay Bay, 3950 Las Vegas Blvd. S. ℭ **702/632-7403.** www.bordergrill.com. Reservations recommended. Main courses $15–$28. AE, DC, DISC, MC, V. Sun–Thurs 11:30am–10:30pm; Fri–Sat 11:30am–11pm.

Bouchon BISTRO   Here is where the whole celebrity chef concept bursts into full glory. Thomas Keller made his name with his Napa Valley restaurant, The French Laundry, considered by many to be the best restaurant in the United States. His Vegas restaurant is superlative as well. We tried nearly everything on the menu and can report that in almost every case they are gold-standard versions of classics. The sweet and supremely fresh Snow Creek oysters seem to melt on contact with your tongue. The beef bourguignon is exactly as you expect it to be, in the divine perfection sense.

In The Venetian, 3355 Las Vegas Blvd. S. ℂ **702/414-6200.** Reservations strongly recommended. Main courses $8–$22 at breakfast, $14–$29 at lunch, $22–$45 at dinner. AE, DC, DISC, MC, V. Daily 7–10:30am and 5–11pm; Sat–Sun 11:30am–2:30pm; oyster bar daily 3–11pm.

Bougainvillea *Value* DINER   Oh, how we love a Vegas coffee shop. You've got your all-day breakfasts, your graveyard-shift specials, your prime rib, and, of course, your full Chinese menu. And it's all hearty and well priced; we're talkin' build your own three-egg, three-ingredient omelet for around $5. You can get a full dinner entree or a nice light lunch of a large half-sandwich and soup, also for around $5. And 24-hour specials, which include a slab of meat, plus potato or rice, veggies, soup or salad, and a 12-ounce draft beer, run between $8 and $13. Yep. That's the ticket.

In Terrible's, 4100 Paradise Rd. ℂ **702/733-7000.** Entrees $5–$13. AE, MC, V. Daily 24 hr.

Capriotti's SANDWICHES   It looks like a dump but there's a reason that Capriotti's is one of the fastest growing businesses in town. They roast their own beef and turkeys on the premises and stuff them (or Italian cold cuts, or whatever) into sandwiches mislabeled "small," "medium," and "large"—the latter clocks in at 20 inches, easily feeding two for under $10 total. And deliciously so; the "Slaw B Joe" (roast beef, coleslaw, and Russian dressing) is fabulous. They even have veggie varieties. We never leave town without a stop here, and you shouldn't, either.

324 W. Sahara Ave. (at Las Vegas Blvd. S.). ℂ **702/474-0229.** www.capriottis.com. Most sandwiches under $10. No credit cards. Mon–Fri 10am–5pm; Sat 11am–5pm.

Circo ITALIAN   Ignore the bright primary-color scheme, in favor of watching the dancing fountains outside. And then order the *mista di Campo,* a lovely little salad, both visually and in terms of taste; it's a creative construction of vegetables bound with cucumber and topped with a fab balsamic vinaigrette. Follow that with a perfect tagliatelle with rock shrimp—it comes loaded with various crustacean bits in a light sauce. Note that appetizer portions of pastas are plenty filling and cheaper than full-size servings. Entrees usually include more elaborate dishes, such as breast of Muscovy duck with dried organic fruit in port-wine sauce. Save room for desserts such as *panna cotta* (Italian cream-filled donuts) or *tutto cioccolato,* consisting of chocolate mousse, ice cream, and crumb cake.

In Bellagio, 3600 Las Vegas Blvd. S. ℂ **702/693-8150.** Reservations recommended. Main courses $14–$45. AE, DC, DISC, MC, V. Daily 5:30–10:30pm.

Commander's Palace CREOLE   This is an offshoot of the famous New Orleans restaurant, so we did expect a lot, and they came through. Service is nearly as good as at the original; no group of waiters hovering to fulfill every whim and remove every crumb, but we hardly felt neglected. And not one thing on the menu, from appetizer to dessert, disappointed our palates. Your best bet is probably the $39 three-course Creole favorite, featuring Commander's justly legendary turtle soup with sherry, Louisiana pecan-crusted fish, and signature bread pudding soufflé, three things they do very well indeed. Overall, this is a really nice restaurant, run by people who sincerely care about the restaurant business.

In the Desert Passage in the Planet Hollywood Resort & Casino, 3663 Las Vegas Blvd. S. ℂ **702/892-8272.** www. commanderspalace.com. Reservations suggested. Breakfast $6–$11; brunch $21–$36; lunch $12–$25; dinner $23–$39. AE, DISC, MC, V. Mon–Fri 9–11am, 11:30am–2pm, 5:30–10pm; Sat–Sun 10:30am–2pm, 5:30–10pm.

Grand Wok and Sushi Bar *Value* PAN-ASIAN   A Pan-Asian restaurant runs the risk of attempting to be a jack of all trades and master of none, but somehow, this MGM eatery pulls it off. We didn't try every cuisine offered (Japanese, Chinese, Korean, Vietnamese, and maybe more!), but a random sampling (including lovely fresh sushi, fat dumplings, and a huge Vietnamese combo soup full of noodles and different kinds of meat) produced really superb food, delicately prepared. Note that soup portions are most generous—four people could easily split one order and have a nice light (or even heavier) and very cheap lunch.

In MGM Grand, 3799 Las Vegas Blvd. S. ℂ 702/891-7777. Reservations not accepted. Main courses $9–$19; sushi rolls and pieces $4.50–$15. AE, DC, DISC, MC, V. Restaurant Sun–Thurs 11am–10pm, Fri–Sat 11am–midnight; sushi bar Mon–Thurs 5–10pm, Fri–Sat 11am–midnight, Sun 11am–10pm.

Lawry's The Prime Rib STEAK/SEAFOOD   Yes, you can get prime rib all over town for under $5, but why (to mix food metaphors) have tuna when you can have caviar? If you love prime rib, head straight for this meat-lover's institution, with a 1930s-style dining room with Art Deco touches and big-band music on the sound system. Giant metal carving carts come to your table, and you name your cut (the regular Lawry's, the extralarge Diamond Jim Brady for serious carnivores, and the wimpy thin English cut) and specify how you'd like it cooked. Flavorful, tender, perfectly cooked, and lightly seasoned, this will be the best prime rib you will ever have. We kid you not! It comes with terrific Yorkshire pudding, and some creamed horseradish that is combined with fluffy whipped cream, simultaneously sweet and tart.

4043 Howard Hughes Pkwy. (at Flamingo Rd., between Paradise Rd. and Koval Lane). ℂ 702/893-2223. www.lawrys online.com. Reservations recommended. Main courses $20–$43. AE, DC, DISC, MC, V. Sun–Thurs 5–10pm; Fri–Sat 5–11pm.

Lotus of Siam *Value* THAI   We don't feel guilty about dragging you out to a strip mall in the east end of Nowhere because here is what critic Jonathan Gold of *Gourmet* magazine called no less than the best Thai restaurant in North America. In addition to all the usual beloved Thai favorites, they have a separate menu featuring lesser-known dishes from northern Thailand—they don't routinely hand this one out (since most of the customers are here for the more pedestrian, if still excellent, $6 lunch buffet). Standouts include the Issan sausage, a grilled sour pork number; and *Sua Rong Hai* ("weeping tiger"), a dish of soft sliced and grilled marinated beef. If you insist on more conventional Thai, you certainly won't be disappointed.

In the Commercial Center, 953 E. Sahara Ave. ℂ 702/735-3033. www.saipinchutima.com. Reservations strongly recommended for dinner. Lunch buffet $6; other dishes $6–$18. AE, MC, V. Mon–Fri 11:30am–2:30pm and 5:30–9:30pm; Sat–Sun 5:30–10pm.

Monte Carlo Pub & Brewery *Kids* PUB FARE   Lest you think we are big, fat foodie snobs who can't appreciate a meal unless it comes drenched in truffles and caviar, we direct you to this lively (and we mean lively) working microbrewery and its hearty, not-so-highfalutin' food. There's no romantic atmosphere thanks to the 40 TV sets sprinkled around the room—but no fancy French frills and, best of all, no inflated prices. Earning recent raves were the short ribs, in a fine barbecue sauce, and cooked just right; the excellent chicken fingers and shrimp-fried-in-beer appetizers; and the garlic pizza with mounds of our favorite aromatic herb. After 9pm, only pizza is served, and dueling pianos provide dance music and entertainment.

In Monte Carlo Resort & Casino, 3770 Las Vegas Blvd. S. ℂ 702/730-7777. Reservations not accepted. Main courses $6–$15. AE, DC, DISC, MC, V. Sun–Thurs 11am–3am; Fri–Sat 11am–4am.

Picasso FRENCH   Madrid-born chef Julian Serrano's cooking stands proudly next to the $30 million worth of Picassos that pepper the dining room's walls, making a meal here a truly memorable experience. This may well be the best restaurant in Vegas, and given the serious competition for such a title, that says a lot. The menu changes nightly and is always a choice between a four- or five-course fixed-price dinner or tasting menu. We were bowled over by roasted Maine lobster with a "trio" of corn—kernels, sauce, and flan. Hudson Valley foie gras was crusted in truffles and went down smoothly. For dessert, a molten chocolate cake leaves any other you may have tried in the dust.

In Bellagio, 3600 Las Vegas Blvd. S. ✆ **877/234-6358**. Reservations recommended. Fixed-price 4-course dinner $90; 5-course menu degustation $100. AE, DC, DISC, MC, V. Wed–Mon 6–9:30pm.

Rosemary's Restaurant *Best* AMERICAN   A 15-minute (or so) drive down Sahara is all it takes to eat what the *Vegas-Review Journal* calls the best food in Las Vegas (and we do, too). The brainchild of Michael and Wendy Jordan, both veterans of the New Orleans food scene, Rosemary's cuisine covers most regions of the U.S., though southern influences dominate. Interesting sides include ultrarich bleu cheese slaw and perfect cornmeal jalapeño hush puppies. A recent visit found the crispy striped bass fighting it out with the pan-seared honey-glazed salmon for the best fish dish I've ever had. Desserts are most pleasant. The restaurant, unusually, will give beer suggestions to pair with courses, including some fruity Belgian numbers; this is such a rare treat that if you drink, you must try some of their suggestions.

8125 W. Sahara. ✆ **702/869-2251**. www.rosemarysrestaurant.com. Reservations strongly recommended. Lunch $14–$17; dinner $24–$39. AE, MC, V. Mon–Fri 11:30am–2:30pm and 5:30–10:30pm; Sat–Sun 5:30–10:30pm.

Stage Deli DELI   Las Vegas's branch of New York City's legendary Stage Deli retains the original's brightly lit Big Apple essence, and comics and celebrities often drop by whenever they're in town. Most of the fare—including fresh-baked pumpernickel and rye, meats, chewy bagels, lox, spicy deli mustard, and pickles—comes in daily from New York. The Stage dishes up authentic 5-inch-high sandwiches stuffed with pastrami, corned beef, brisket, or chopped liver. Unless you have a hearty appetite, are feeding two, or have a fridge in your room for leftovers, you might want to try the half-sandwich and soup or salad combos. Other specialties here include matzo-ball soup, knishes, kasha varnishkes, cheese blintzes, kreplach, pirogen, and smoked-fish platters accompanied by bagels and cream cheese. The huge menu means it's easy to find something for even the pickiest of eaters.

In the Forum Shops at Caesars Palace, 3570 Las Vegas Blvd. S. ✆ **702/893-4045**. Reservations accepted for large parties only. Main courses $10–$14; sandwiches $6–$14. AE, DC, DISC, MC, V. Sun–Thurs 8am–10:30pm; Fri–Sat 8am–11:30pm (takeout stays open 30 min. later).

LAS VEGAS AFTER DARK

Night is when it's happening in this 24-hour town. In fact, most bars and clubs don't even get going until close to midnight. You certainly won't lack for things to do when the sun sets. In addition to the free street shows (see "What to See & Do," earlier in this chapter), the hotels all have lounges, usually featuring live music, and you haven't truly done Vegas if you don't hit at least one showroom.

For up-to-date listings, contact the **Las Vegas Convention and Visitors Authority** (✆ **877/VISIT-LV** or 702/892-0711; www.visitlasvegas.com) and ask for a free copy of *Showguide* or *What's On in Las Vegas* (one or both of which will likely be in your hotel room). Plan well ahead if you have your heart set on seeing one of the most popular shows or a major headliner. Admission to shows runs the gamut, from about $42

Nighttime Is the Right Time

For a great selection of nightlife on the Strip, head for Mandalay Bay; **Aureole, Red Square, rumjungle,** and the **House of Blues** are all popular. You might also check out the incredible nighttime view at the bar atop the **Stratosphere**—nothing beats it. And the **Petrossian Bar** in Bellagio offers class along with its cocktails (to say nothing of caviar and other delicacies)—but come for the cocktails, as those in the know claim it's not only the best bar in Vegas for such matters, but maybe the best bar in the West.

for *American Superstars* (an impersonator show at the Stratosphere) to $200 and more for top headliners. Prices may include drinks or, in rare instances, dinner.

THE SHOWS

There are shows all over town, ranging from traditional magic shows to cutting-edge acts such as *Mystère*. The showgirls remain, topless and otherwise. The trend in Vegas as we wrote this is toward celebrity showpieces (Céline Dion anyone?); sex (striptease-style shows and Cirque du Soleil's disappointing *Zumanity*); and Broadway productions—*Avenue Q* and *Phantom of the Opera* debuted on the Strip in 2005.

You won't go wrong seeing one of **Cirque du Soleil**'s productions—the best of that august group are **O,** at the Bellagio (© **888/488-7111** or 702/693-7722), which is a breathtaking mix of artistry and acrobatics over a 1.5-million-gallon pool; and *Mystère,* at TI (© **800/963-9634** or 702/796-9999), a sophisticated and surreal circus extravaganza. The most intelligent show in Vegas is definitely *Penn & Teller* at the Rio (© **888/746-7784**); it's got magic, juggling, acerbic comedy, mean stunts, and great quiet beauty. The **Blue Man Group** at The Venetian is performance art for the masses, but don't let that prevent you from going and laughing your head off (© **877/833-6423**). And if you want to see a classic Vegas topless revue—oh, why not?—check out *Jubilee!* at Bally's (© **800/237-7469** or 702/739-4567).

Magic fans will love **Lance Burton: *Master Magician,*** at the Monte Carlo (© **877/386-8224** or 702/730-7160), whose sleight-of-hand tricks are extraordinary. **Danny Gans: *The Man of Many Voices,*** at The Mirage (© **800/963-9634**), is a first-rate impressionist whose uncanny one-man act is a refreshing change of pace and a consistent crowd-pleaser. And for great afternoon (and cheap) entertainment, head straight for the magic and comedy of *Mac King* at Harrah's (© **800/427-7247**).

THE CLUB & BAR SCENE

Most Las Vegas bars and clubs don't even get going until close to midnight. To find out what's going on where, consult the *Las Vegas Weekly* (great club and bar descriptions in its listings) and *City Life* (weekly, with comprehensive listings of what's playing where all over town). You can pick up both at local restaurants, bars, record and music stores, and hep retail stores.

One of the hottest clubs in Vegas is **Rain,** 4321 W. Flamingo Rd. (© **702/940-7246**), featuring a pulse-thumping tempo, thousands of size-two Juicy-Couture-jeans-clad 20-somethings, and a snooty door policy. **The Beach,** 365 S. Convention Center Dr., at Paradise Road (© **702/731-1925;** www.beachlv.com), is an immense two-story club that caters to the young and pretty who are looking to party. **Body English,** in the Hard Rock Hotel, 4455 Paradise Rd. (© **702/693-5000;** www.

bodyenglish.com), is another hot nightspot; a clash of Anne Rice and Cher Gothic–themed wacky decadence that's exactly what a Las Vegas club should be. **Light,** at the Bellagio, 3600 Las Vegas Blvd. S. (© **702/693-8300**), is a grown-up nightclub that caters to the silver-spoon crowd but has a party atmosphere that doesn't feel exclusive.

Gipsy, 4605 Paradise Rd. (© **702/731-1919**), is the gay dance club that draws the biggest crowds. For other gay nightlife, check out **www.gaylasvegas.com** or **www.gay vegas.com.**

It's still an honor for a comedian to play Vegas, and a number of good comedy clubs are on the Strip. The best of the bunch is **The Improv,** at Harrah's, 3475 Las Vegas Blvd. S. (© **800/392-9002**), which presents the top comics on the circuit, ones you're likely to see on Leno and Letterman.

2 Reno

"The Biggest Little City in the World" has grown from the days in the 1920s and 1930s when it was the destination for hundreds of ladies looking for *Reno-vation,* a "quickie" divorce that required only 6 weeks of residence before "freedom." As a result, a goodly number of small Western "dude" ranches made a specialty of the 6-week stay, providing outdoor activities such as horseback riding, hiking, and swimming, and the nighttime excitement of rustic casinos. The town remained pretty much the same, even after the divorce boom petered out, until the late 1970s, when large casino-hotel resorts were built and the city grew to its present population of 207,000, with the adjacent town of Sparks adding another 90,000. The gambling may have arrived in force, but don't mistake this area for Las Vegas; if you're looking for a fantasy world of exotic casino-hotels you're in the wrong end of the state. In Reno the gaming action is only a part of the experience. Sure, you can have a great time gambling here 24 hours a day year-round, but it's the heady combination of hotel bargains, great restaurants, outdoor activities, and close proximity to Lake Tahoe (p. 870) that make Reno a fun and affordable tourist destination.

ESSENTIALS

GETTING THERE **By Air** Most major airlines offer service into **Reno-Tahoe International Airport** (© 775/328-6400; www.renoairport.com). A downtown casino shuttle service runs from the airport every half-hour. Look for the white minibuses outside of baggage claim marked DOWNTOWN HOTELS. Fare is $2.65. Rental cars from the major chains are available at the airport.

By Train Amtrak (© **800/USA-RAIL;** www.amtrak.com) trains pull into the station at 280 North Center St. The company's scenic California Zephyr train connects Reno to Chicago (trip time: 45 hr.), Omaha (35 hr.), Denver (26 hr.), and Salt Lake City (10 hr.).

By Car From San Francisco, take **I-80** East to Sacramento and on to Reno; from Salt Lake City, take I-80 WestFrom Los Angeles, take **I-5** through central California to Sacramento and then I-80 to Reno. Be prepared for winter snowstorms that can make I-80 a chain-required highway. For road conditions, contact the Nevada Department of Transportation's 24-hour **Road Reporting Service** (© **877/687-6237;** http://safetravelusa.com/nv).

VISITOR INFORMATION For information on lodging, attractions, and more, contact the **Reno/Sparks Convention and Visitors Authority (RSCVA),** 4590 S. Virginia St., P.O. Box 837, Reno, NV 89502 (© **800/FOR-RENO** or 775/827-7600; www.visitrenotahoe.com).

GETTING AROUND   Pedestrian-friendly downtown Reno is easily navigable on foot. If you head out of the downtown area and don't want to rent a car, try **Yellow Cab** (© 775/355-5555), **Reno-Sparks Cab Co.** (© 775/333-3333), or **Whittlesea Checker Taxi** (© 775/322-2222). A number of the larger hotels and motels have free courtesy buses on call. Check with your hotel or motel for information.

FAST FACTS   St. Mary's Regional Medical Center, 235 W. 6th St. (© 775/770-3000), is downtown just off I-80 near Circus Circus Reno Hotel Casino. There's a 24-hour Walgreens pharmacy at 750 N. Virginia St. (© 775/337-8703). **Sales tax** in Reno is 7.375%; **hotel tax** is 13.5%.

WHAT TO SEE & DO

The **Historic Reno Preservation Society (HRPS),** P.O. Box 14003, Reno, NV 89533 (© 775/747-4478; www.historicreno.org), offers a series of architectural and historical walking tours of the city. You can stroll through the city's ethnic neighborhoods or bike through some of Reno's historic zones, each loaded with many examples of classic American architectural styles. Schedules change, so check the website for dates and times.

The Truckee River winds through downtown Reno, and the **Arts District (www.renoriver.org)** that's sprung up along its banks is worth a stroll. A walk beginning at Wingfield Park will lead you over the bridge onto West Street Plaza, where concerts are regularly held. Shops line First Street with cinemas, coffeehouses, and art galleries. Follow Virginia Street to find the Riverside Hotel Artist Lofts, and the Pioneer Center for the Performing Arts. The third Saturday of each month the Downtown Merchants Association hosts **Wine Walk on the Riverwalk** from 2 to 5pm. For $15 participants get a commemorative glass and wine tastings at more than a dozen art galleries, specialty shops, restaurants, and theaters in the Riverwalk area.

Fleischmann Planetarium and Science Center   Located at the north end of the University of Nevada Reno campus, the planetarium houses the Star Theater's Sky-Dome large-format movie system, as well as a free public observatory and the Hall of the Solar System featuring many fascinating exhibits including a meteorite found in Nevada weighing in at a whopping ton.

900 N. Virginia St. © 775/784-4811. www.planetarium.unr.nevada.edu. Admission $7 adults, $5 seniors and children 13 and under. Mon–Fri 11am–7pm; Sat–Sun 11:30am–7pm.

The National Automobile Museum   Travel back through time as you stroll through a century of automobiles. More than 220 antique, vintage, classic, special interest, and "cars-of-the-stars" vehicles from the Harrah Collection are displayed in surroundings appropriate to their period. The museum's collection includes educational and historical exhibits relating to the automobile. Notable cars here include an 1892 Philion Road Carriage, James Dean's 1949 Mercury Coupe from *Rebel Without a Cause,* and a gold-plated 1981 De Lorean LK Sport Coupe.

10 S. Lake St. © 775/333-9300. www.automuseum.org. Admission $9 adults, $7 seniors, $3 children 6–18, free for children 5 and under. Mon–Sat 9:30am–5:30pm; Sun 10am–4pm. Tours Mon–Sat at 10:30am and 1:30pm.

Nevada Historical Society   The state's oldest museum (it celebrated its 100th anniversary in 2004) displays memorabilia and historical information about Nevada. It's also home to the largest collection of Nevada-related library material in the country. Special programs augment the regular exhibits.

1650 N. Virginia St. © 775/688-1190. Admission $3 adults, $2 seniors, free for 18 and under. Galleries Mon–Sat 10am–5pm.

Getting Married in Reno

Quickie weddings have replaced the quickie divorce business in Reno. That's hardly a shock when you consider that marriage licenses can be obtained daily from 8am to midnight, inexpensive wedding chapels abound, no blood test is required, there's no waiting period, and anyone 18 or older doesn't need parental consent. You can obtain a marriage license at the Washoe County Courthouse, 75 Court St., Room 131 (© **775/328-3275**), for a fee of $55. Legal ID, such as a driver's license, is required.

When you're ready to tie the knot, the Commissioner of Civil Marriages performs marriages at 350 S. Center St. (© **775/337-4575**), or you can always make an reservation (or not) at any of the city's wedding chapels. Call © **800/FOR-RENO** for a complete list or visit **www.renolaketahoe.com/weddings** on the Web.

The Nevada Museum of Art *(Best* You can't miss the museum's new and very distinctive headquarters downtown. The four-level structure inspired by the state's Black Rock Desert is a work of art in its own right. The permanent collection focuses on works depicting nature and the environment; there's also a rooftop sculpture garden. Traveling exhibitions are scheduled throughout the year.

160 W. Liberty St. © 775/329-3333. www.nevadaart.org. Admission $10 adults, $8 seniors, $1 children 6–12, free for children 5 and under. Tues–Sun 10–5pm (Thurs until 8pm); closed Mon.

OUTDOOR ACTIVITIES

The Reno/Tahoe area abounds in winter and summer outdoor activities, with the major winter snow scene being centered around nearby Lake Tahoe (p. 870) The long spring, summer, and fall seasons provide ample opportunity to stretch the muscles with some adrenaline-pumping thrills to fill the daytime hours. For information on adventure tours and packages, contact the RSCVA (see above).

For those looking for a scenic and leisurely bike ride, the **Truckee River Trail** provides 14 miles of paved trails through downtown Reno/Sparks bordering the crystal-clear Truckee River.

For hikers, on the northwest side of Reno, **Peavine Mountain,** located in the Humboldt-Toiyabe National Forest (© **775/331-6444;** www.fs.fed.us/r4/htnf), is an area of solitude within minutes of paved city streets. Peavine Mountain features former mining roads and trails on Forest Service land that have been converted into a web of hiking and mountain biking routes with extensive views of Reno and Sparks. The trails are of moderate difficulty and varied distances.

Sierra Adventures, 254 W. First St. (© **775/323-8928;** www.wildsierra.com), offers a variety of Reno-area adventure activities including hot-air ballooning, rock climbing, horseback riding, mountain biking, rafting, and more.

The **Truckee River Whitewater Park** (© **800/367-7366**) is a $1.5-million white-water and kayak park that's the first of its kind in Nevada, and is located between First and Arlington streets in the heart of Reno's bustling downtown. More than 2,600 feet long, the Class 3 white-water course includes north and south channels that surround a city park on an island in the river. It features 11 "drop pools," boulders for kayaking maneuvers, a slalom racing course, and 7,000 tons of smooth flat rocks along the shores for easy river access. Best of all, the park is free and open to the public. **Different Strokes Kayaking** (© **775/250-2997;** www.dskadventures.com), offers professional kayak instruction for all levels. Packages include an orientation pool class and a day on the river honing in kayaking techniques and maneuvers.

GOLF   Golf is extremely popular in this mountain area (where the high altitude will put a little more zing in your drive). Reno's golf courses include the oldest in Nevada, the **Washoe County Golf Course,** 2601 W. Arlington Ave. (© 775/828-6640; greens fees $31–$36), a par-72 course that was established in 1934. There are 50 other courses within a 90-minute drive of downtown Reno (many of them public courses with very reasonable greens fees); for course and golf package information, check out **www.visitrenotahoe.com/plan_your_trip/golf.**

SKIING   Skiing and snowboarding tops the list of popular winter activities with 18 ski resorts within a 90-mile radius. In fact, Reno-Tahoe boasts the highest concentration of resorts in North America. For resort and ski package information, check out **www.visitrenotahoe.com/plan_your_trip/ski.**

WHERE TO STAY

The casino hotels are the places to stay when in Reno. They are big, modern, and glitzy, with upscale dining rooms, bars, and showrooms. If you want something a little less busy and easier on the budget, there are numerous smaller motels and chain hotels in town. *Note:* Hotel rates here change almost daily and discounts are almost always available. In addition to the mainstream hotel discounters, **Reno Hotels** (© 888/682-0283; www. renohotels.com) is a good option for obtaining discount hotel rooms.

Atlantis Casino Resort Spa   Located just outside of the downtown district, this deluxe resort is notable for its friendly service and comfortable rooms with high-rise views of the city and mountains. The tropical-theme resort doesn't exactly resemble its namesake, but it makes for a good stay—provided you stick to rooms in the high-rise tower and avoid the cheap Motor Lodge rooms. Splurge on a Concierge Tower room (floors 21–27), which offers 20% more space, oversize tubs, terry robes, and butler service. Free live-music plays from 4pm to 4am at the Center Stage Cabaret, where various performers run the musical gamut from the '40s to the present. The casino also claims Reno's only four-star, smoke-free poker room.

3800 S. Virginia St., Reno, NV 89502. © 800/723-6500 or 775/825-4700. Fax 775/825-1170. www.atlantiscasino.com. 980 units. $46–$150 double; $125–$850 suite. Discounts available. Golf packages start at $89. Free self-parking. AE, DISC, MC, V. Pets allowed. **Amenities:** 7 restaurants; 2 pools (1 indoor); health club; spa.

Circus Circus Reno Hotel Casino (Value) (Kids)   If you're traveling with kids, this is the place to stay. The circus theme so popular in Las Vegas is carried over to this resort, where clowns and acrobats from China augment visiting headline acts from renowned companies such as Cirque du Soleil and Ringling Brothers. The high-flying acts perform for free above a midway housing carnival-style games and a video arcade. Don't let the circus theme fool you, however—there's a 65,000-square-foot casino, so your kids aren't the only ones feeding quarters into machines. The Victorian-style rooms are clean and comfortable; some offer mountain views. Jacuzzi suites feature a separate sitting area with a sofa bed and are good for families. On the downside, there is no pool, though for a fee you can use the one at a neighboring hotel.

500 N. Sierra St., Reno, NV 89503. © 800/648-5010 or 775/329-0711. Fax 775/328-9652. www.circusreno.com. 1,572 units. $39–$169 double; $69–$275 suite. Discount packages available. AE, DC, DISC, MC, V. Free self-parking. **Amenities:** 6 restaurants; exercise room.

Eldorado Hotel and Casino   Attached by a walkway to Circus Circus and the Silver Legacy, this hotel sports an upscale atmosphere with a relaxed vibe and a convenient location in the heart of downtown Reno. The Tower rooms feature a simple yet sophisticated decor, mountain views, and Judith Jackson toiletries in the bathrooms. The deluxe whirlpool suites toss in marble bathrooms, a Jacuzzi tub in the living area, and pop-up TVs. For the budget-minded traveler, the economy and standard rooms are a steal. The hotel casino also boasts nine award-winning restaurants, 24-hour casino action, and a Broadway-style showroom that features a series of excellently produced and performed production shows alternating with headline artists. The Brew Brothers pub with eight custom microbrews swings with live rock and blues nightly beginning at 9:30pm, and Roxy's Bar & Lounge, with its old-world charm and 102 versions of stiff martinis, is a popular gathering place with locals and tourists alike.

345 N. Virginia St., Reno, NV 89501. ℂ **800/648-5966** or 775/786-5700. Fax 775/348-7513. www.eldoradoreno.com. 816 units. $70–$80 double. 2-night golf packages from $115. AE, DISC, MC, V. Free valet and self-parking. **Amenities:** 9 restaurants; heated pool.

Harrah's Reno   This branch of Harrah's, long a dominant player in the casino hotel market, is smack in the middle of downtown. The rooms are modern, clean, and comfortable; suites toss in Jacuzzi tubs and good views. The service, long a Harrah's hallmark, is excellent. Guests enjoy a variety of touches such as 24-hour room service, an extensive health club, pool, and in-house massage. Evening entertainment centers around Sammy's (named for Sammy Davis, Jr.), where Vegas-type shows feature topless gals and special guest entertainers. During the summer, Harrah's presents free concerts at The Plaza, a 65,000-square-foot outdoor venue.

219 N. Center St., Reno, NV 89501 ℂ **800/HARRAHS** or 775/786-3232. Fax 775/788-3703. www.harrahsreno.com. 952 units. $39–$159 double; $175–$375 suite. Golf packages start at $79. AE, DISC, MC, V. Free self-parking. Pet kennel service available. **Amenities:** 7 restaurants; pool; health club; spa.

Peppermill Hotel Casino *(Best)*   Located adjacent to a quiet park and lake about 2 miles south of downtown, this fun hotel consistently racks up awards as the city's best. The Tower rooms are clean and spacious; king rooms feature a sofa. The suites come in eight different configurations (each one better than the next), but all include great views, steam showers, fridges, and Jacuzzi tubs. The health club is free to all guests, and you may need the workout as the dining here is very good. Free cabaret entertainment flows throughout the night and there are 14 themed bars on the premises. The casino was recently named one of the Top 10 Casinos in America by Citysearch and one of Gaming's Top 20 Resorts by *Casino Player Magazine*. In late 2007 the Peppermill will open a $300-million Tuscan-themed expansion.

2707 S. Virginia St., Reno, NV 89502. ℂ **866/821-9996** or 775/826-2121. Fax 775/826-5205. www.peppermillreno.com. 1,070 units. $73–$140 double; $89–$249 suite. Golf packages start at $79. AE, DISC, MC, V. Free self-parking. **Amenities:** 8 restaurants; heated pool; health club; spa.

Siena Hotel Spa and Casino   Set on the banks of the Truckee River near downtown, this hotel offers a bit of Italian elegance and the best beds in the city. Come here if you want more intimate surroundings than the mammoth casino resorts. Rooms are decorated in modern Tuscan style and have views of the river or the mountains. The bathrooms feature Bath & Body Works toiletries, but it's the beds you'll remember—ultracomfy mattresses topped with Egyptian cotton linens and down comforters. Suites toss in more space and Jacuzzi tubs. The spa and rooftop pool are divine, the dining is grand (especially at the smoke-free Enoteca wine bar, which offers more than 35 wines by the glass), and the fitness center is free to guests.

One S. Lake St., Reno, NV 89501. ✆ **877/SIENA-33** or 775/32-SIENA. Fax 775/321-5870. www.sienareno.com. 214 units. $90–$250 double; $200–$460 suite. AE, DISC, MC, V. Free self-parking. **Amenities:** 3 restaurants; pool; fitness center; spa. *In room:* Fridge.

Silver Legacy Resort Casino *(Value)*   The Silver Legacy Resort Casino is a Victorian-themed tour de force, with the largest center for gaming and entertainment in northern Nevada. The resort boasts six restaurants and eateries, Catch a Rising Star comedy club, 85,000 square feet of gaming space, and the world's largest overhead dome. In the unlikely event you can't get your casino fix here, skywalks connect the hotel to Circus Circus on the north and to the Eldorado on the south.

407 N. Virginia St., Reno, NV 89501. ✆ **800/687-8733** or 775/325-7401. Fax 775/325-7177. www.silverlegacy.com. 1,720 units. $55–$250 double; $100–$800 suite. AE, DISC, MC, V. Free self-parking. **Amenities:** 6 restaurants; pool; health spa.

WHERE TO DINE

Even though you'll find a seemingly endless array of restaurants inside the casino hotels, you're likely to have a better dining experience at these local favorites, most of which are far from the maddening din of the slot machines.

Beaujolais Bistro *(Best)* FRENCH   Reno lays claim to its own little corner of France in this small, charming bistro, located near the Truckee River in downtown. With its exposed brick walls, parquet floors, and dreamy atmosphere, Beaujolais Bistro is the perfect spot for an intimate dinner. Expect modern twists on classic French dishes such as beef Bourguignon and roasted duck a l'orange, and be sure to save room for one of the decadent dessert selections. The bistro also offers an extraordinary selection of fine French and domestic wines.

130 West St. ✆ **775/323-2227.** www.beaujolaisbistro.com. Reservations recommended. Main courses $17–$27. AE, MC, V. Tues–Fri 11:30–2pm; Tues–Sun 5–10pm.

Bertha Miranda's *(Kids)* MEXICAN   On the east side of town, this popular Mexican restaurant offers plenty of atmosphere in a three-tiered dining room lined with stone walls. Choose a booth or a table and try the Tamale Special or El Rancho Steak. In the evening there is live music in the bar/cocktail lounge.

336 Mill St. ✆ **775/786-9697.** www.berthamirandas.com. Reservations accepted Sun–Thurs only. Main courses $9–$15. MC, V. Daily 10am–10pm.

Café Bella Sera ITALIAN   Café Bella Sera is unlike anything else Reno has to offer. Serving high-end East Coast Italian dishes with an atmosphere that is both cool and classy, Café Bella Sera is in a class all its own. Many of the high-quality ingredients are imported from Italy, like the aromatic olive oil drizzled on the light-as-air garlic rolls. The chef artfully prepares familiar Italian dishes with his own flair like the pasta Bolognese, which includes chunks of New York strip, filet mignon, Italian sausage, ground beef, ground veal, and merlot cooked slowly in a fresh marinara sauce. The portions are hefty and night owls can rejoice too—the full menu is available until 5am, unheard of even in a 24-hour town.

121 Vesta St. ✆ **775/322-2300.** www.cafebellaserareno.com. Reservations recommended. Main courses $16–$42. AE, MC, V. Daily 4pm–5am.

Golden Fortune CHINESE   Serving up authentic high-style Hong Kong cuisine, Golden Fortune inside the Eldorado Hotel Casino is easily the best Asian fare in town. The extensive menu features more than 90 different specialties including exotic dishes like braised sea cucumber with black mushrooms. The honey-glazed walnut prawns, a house specialty, is divine, as is the Peking duck. For the bold, allow the chef to present several dishes of his choosing and skip the menu altogether—it's well worth it.

Inside the Eldorado Hotel Casino. © 775/786-5700. www.eldoradoreno.com. Reservations recommended. Main courses $10–$25. AE, DISC, MC, V. Thurs–Mon 5–10pm.

Johnny's Ristorante Italiano ITALIAN   A 10-minute drive west from downtown is this sprawling restaurant where in-the-know locals gather to relax at the bar at cocktail time and to enjoy lavish Italian dinners in a casual but spiffy atmosphere. Start your meal off with the yummy bruschetta. The pastas and sauces are all homemade and the desserts are heavenly. Portions are hearty and the service is great. Wine is available by the glass or bottle.

4245 W. 4th St. © 775/747-4511. Reservations recommended. Main courses $15–$35. AE, MC, V. Tues–Sat 5–9:30pm.

Little Nugget Diner *Value* BURGERS/DINER   Pretty much every casino hotel in Reno has a 24-hour diner and this one (inside the Little Nugget Hotel) serves pretty good coffee-shop fare, but that's not why it's always packed to the rafters. The crowds flock here for one reason: the burgers, which are the undisputed champs in town. Practically a Reno institution is the Awful-Awful—a juicy $3.50 cheeseburger served with hot, crispy fries that's been giving carnivores their burger fix for more than 5 decades. If you're a burger fan, this diner a must.

Inside Nugget Hotel, 233 N. Virginia St. © 775/323-0716. Reservations not accepted. Main courses $3.50–$12. No credit cards. Daily 24 hr.

Mi Casa Too! MEXICAN   A few minutes' drive west of town is this large and friendly restaurant, which is broken up into smaller, more intimate rooms with booths and tables. Authentic decor includes piñatas and mariachi music. Relax and enjoy the huge portions of tasty enchiladas, tacos, and grilled meats. Save room for the fried ice cream (hey, you're on vacation). The margaritas are also worth sampling.

205 W. 4th St. © 775/323-6466. Reservations not accepted. Main courses $10–$15. AE, MC, V. Daily 11am–11pm.

Rapscallion Seafood House & Bar SEAFOOD   Reno's local paper has named this charming brick oasis the city's best seafood restaurant so many times, they might as well retire the award. There are pasta and beef dishes on the daily-changing menu, but it's the aquatic cuisine here that's truly memorable, from a perfectly grilled salmon to fresh oysters and prawns. A large mahogany bar with a scenic stained-glass backdrop along with the fireplace also makes this a warm and cozy place to enjoy a predinner cocktail. Wine is offered by the glass or bottle. Live music is offered Wednesday through Saturday in the evenings.

1555 S. Wells Ave. © 775/323-1211. www.rapscallion.com. Reservations recommended. Main courses $15–$50. AE, MC, V. Mon–Fri 11:30am–4pm; Sun–Thurs 5–10pm; Fri–Sat 5–10:30pm; Sun 10am–2pm.

Silver Peak Grill and Tap Room *Value* BREWERY   Silver Peak Grill and Tap Room is as popular for its ales and lagers as it is for its pub fare. With items such as salmon fish and chips dipped in Red Ale batter, grilled-lamb burger with kalamata olives and goat cheese, and their signature barley-crusted chicken breast sandwich with applewood-smoked bacon, this isn't your average bar menu. Located on the corner of First and Sierra streets, across from the Century movie theater, Silver Peak is a popular meeting spot, and the outdoor seating on the patio is a great place for people-watching.

First and Sierra sts. © 775/284-3300. Reservations not accepted. Main courses $7–$10. AE, MC, V. Daily 11am–midnight.

Thai Chili _Value_ THAI   This tiny restaurant south of the downtown area has already made a big splash on the local restaurant scene. Decorated in true Thai fashion, with loads of lacquered wood, bamboo, and rich fabrics, it offers a serene and atmospheric dining experience at a very reasonable price. The seafood dumplings are spiced perfectly, and the stir-fried Prik Khing plate of meat, garlic, bell peppers, Thai chile paste, and string beans is excellent. The service and presentation are first-rate.

1030 S. Virginia St. ℭ 775/786-7878. Reservations recommended. Main courses $6–$14. MC, V. Daily 11am–3pm and 5–9pm.

White Orchid CONTINENTAL   A fresh orchid on every table greets diners as they enter this award-winning haven of tranquillity, perfect for a romantic night out. The menu changes every 2 weeks in order to take advantage of fresh seasonal produce, but typical entrees include elk medallions served with Maine lobster and winter vegetables, and Thai-barbecued salmon with Chinese long beans. A special five-course chef's menu (opt for the wine pairings) is the best way to sample it all and offers the most bang for your buck. _Wine Spectator_ bestowed its Award of Excellence on the long and varied wine list.

Inside Peppermill Hotel & Casino, 2707 S. Virginia St. ℭ 800/648-6992. www.peppermillreno.com. Reservations recommended. Main courses $30–$47; 5-course chef's menu $55, $75 with wine pairings. AE, DISC, MC, V. Daily from 5pm until closing.

RENO AFTER DARK

Reno's big action is in the casinos, and the major resorts have enough showrooms, cabaret lounges, and intimate bars to keep you entertained all night long. If you're staying in one of the big ones, you can usually find all the entertainment you want without leaving the premises. Since its completion in December 2005, the **Reno Events Center** has brought in such A-list entertainers as the Black Eyed Peas, Brooks & Dunn, and Tom Petty & The Heartbreakers. The Reno Events Center is located 1 block north of National Bowling Stadium, bounded by Fourth and Fifth streets, and Center and Lake streets in downtown Reno. Check the RSCVA website at **www.visitrenotahoe.com** for up-to-date information about what's playing at the casino hotels and at the Reno Events Center.

PERFORMING ARTS   The Theater Coalition (ℭ 775/786-2278; www.theater coalition.org) gathers information about area theater, ballet, opera, and musical performances and lists them on its website.

The **Reno Philharmonic Orchestra,** 925 Riverside Dr. (ℭ 775/323-6393; www. renophilharmonic.com), presents a fall and winter concert season plus summer concerts in the park. On a smaller scale but no less talented is the **Reno Chamber Orchestra,** 925 Riverside Dr. (ℭ 775/348-9413; www.renochamberorchestra.org), which presents concerts at various times during the year. **The Pioneer Center,** 100 S. Virginia St. (ℭ 775/686-6610; www.pioneercenter.com), is the home for traveling Broadway companies as well as the ballet and opera. The **Nevada Shakespeare Company,** 1 Booth St. (ℭ 775/324-4198; www.nevada-shakespeare.org), presents modern renditions of the Bard's famous plays, as well as original works.

CLUB & MUSIC SCENE   The 24-hour **Alturas Bar & Nightclub,** 1044 E. 4th St. (ℭ 775/324-5050), is the place for the blues, and also features top R&B entertainment and pool tables. The hottest club on the local scene is the always-packed **BuBinga Lounge,** inside the Eldorado Hotel (ℭ 775/786-5700), where DJs spin everything from electronica to rap and where the young and stylish congregate. Also burning up the late-night scene is **Tonic,** 231 W. 2nd St. (ℭ 775/337-6868). A down-tempo lounge with an urban/chic decor, Tonic has overstuffed lounge chairs and banquettes, local artists' work adorning the walls, and a large dance floor. It's a popular late-night spot with live jazz and DJs Thursday through Saturday, so expect the crowds on the weekends, particularly after 11pm.

Scruples Bar & Grill, 91 W. Plumb Lane (© 775/322-7171), features a huge menu with the best bar food in town, indoor/outdoor dining, live music on the patio in the summer (and a jukebox the rest of the week), and the requisite big-screen TV for watching sports.

Tronix, 303 Kietzke Lane (© 775/333-9696), caters mainly to the gay/lesbian community, while the **1099 Club,** 1099 S. Virginia St. (© 775/329-1099), caters to Reno's drag set.

3 Phoenix & Scottsdale

Phoenix is one of the fastest-growing cities in the country today, and has become a sort of Los Angeles of the desert. The only thing missing is an ocean. The abundance of sunshine has made Phoenix a hot winter vacation spot, and adjacent Scottsdale has become one of the nation's top resort destinations, with dozens of challenging golf courses, rejuvenating health spas, and luxurious resorts, many of which boast sprawling pool complexes complete with waterfalls. Downtown Phoenix has become something of a sports and entertainment district, with several museums, the America West Arena (home of the Phoenix Suns), and the Arizona Diamondbacks' Bank One Ballpark, one of the country's few baseball stadiums with a retractable roof.

ESSENTIALS

GETTING THERE   By Plane   Major domestic and some international carriers fly into **Phoenix Sky Harbor International Airport** (© 602/273-3300; www.phxsky harbor.com), 3 miles from downtown Phoenix.

SuperShuttle (© 800/BLUE-VAN or 602/244-9000) offers 24-hour door-to-door van service to resorts, hotels, and homes throughout the valley. Per-person fares average $7 to $12 to the downtown and Tempe area, $16 to downtown Scottsdale, and $30 to $35 to north Scottsdale.

By Car   The major routes into Phoenix are **I-10** from the west (Los Angeles) and southeast (Tucson), and **I-17** from the north (Flagstaff).

VISITOR INFORMATION   The **Greater Phoenix Convention & Visitors Bureau,** 50 N. Second St. (© 877/225-5749 or 602/254-6500; www.visitphoenix.com), is on the corner of Adams Street in downtown Phoenix. If you're staying in Scottsdale, you may want to drop by the **Scottsdale Convention & Visitors Bureau Visitor Center,** Galleria Corporate Center, 4343 N. Scottsdale Rd., Suite 170 (© 800/782-1117 or 480/421-1004; www.scottsdalecvb.com).

GETTING AROUND   If you want to make the best use of your time in this sprawling area, a car is a must. Outside downtown Phoenix, there's almost always plenty of free parking wherever you go. Rental-car rates tend to be relatively low.

Valley Metro (© 602/253-5000; www.valleymetro.org), the Phoenix public bus system, is not very useful to tourists. Instead, try the free **Downtown Area Shuttle (DASH),** which provides bus service within the downtown area Monday through Friday from 6:30am to 11pm. Attractions along the route include the state capitol and Heritage and Science Park. In Tempe, **Free Local Area Shuttle (FLASH)** buses provide a similar service on a loop around Arizona State University. For information on both, call

C **602/253-5000.** In Scottsdale, the **Scottsdale Trolley** (*C* **480/421-1004;** www. valleymetro.org) shuttle buses run between Scottsdale Fashion Square, the Fifth Avenue shops, the Main Street Arts and Antiques district, and the Old Town district. These buses run Monday through Saturday 11am to 6pm (until 9pm Thurs).

Cab companies include **Yellow Cab** (*C* **602/252-5252**) and **Scottsdale Cab** (*C* **480/994-1616**).

FAST FACTS   If you need a doctor, call the **Banner Health Physician & Resource Line** (*C* **602/230-2273**) for a referral. The **Banner Good Samaritan Regional Medical Center,** 1111 E. McDowell Rd. (*C* **602/239-2000**), is one of the largest hospitals in the valley. Call *C* **800/WALGREENS** for a pharmacy near you; some are open 24 hours.

SPECIAL EVENTS & FESTIVALS   The **FBR Open Golf Tournament** (*C* **602/ 870-0163;** www.fbropen.com) is a prestigious PGA event held in Scottsdale in late January. The **Heard Museum Guild Indian Fair and Market** (*C* **602/252-8848;** www.heard.org), held in March, includes performances of traditional dances and demonstrations of arts and crafts. **Cinco de Mayo** is celebrated in a big way, with food, music, and dancing.

In October, the **Arizona State Fair** (*C* **800/343-FAIR** or 602/268-FAIR; www.az statefair.com) gets underway, with rodeos, entertainment, and ethnic food. Also that month, the Phoenix Art Museum hosts the **Cowboy Artists of America Annual Sale & Exhibition** (*C* **602/257-1222;** www.phxart.org), the most prestigious Western-art show in the region. The old year is ushered out on December 31 with the **Fiesta Bowl Parade,** followed on New Year's Day by the **Fiesta Bowl,** a college football classic (*C* **800/635-5748;** www.tostitosfiestabowl.com).

WHAT TO SEE & DO

Arizona Science Center *Kids*   In this large facility you'll find state-of-the-art interactive exhibits covering a variety of topics, from the human body to coping with living in the desert. There's a huge ant farm, a virtual-reality game that puts you inside a video game, a flight simulator, and a cloud maker—plus a planetarium and a large-screen theater.

600 E. Washington St. *C* 602/716-2000. www.azscience.org. Admission $9 adults, $7 seniors and children 3–12. Planetarium and film combination tickets also available. Daily 10am–5pm. Closed Thanksgiving and Christmas. Bus: Red (R), 0, 1, or DASH downtown shuttle.

Desert Botanical Garden   Devoted exclusively to cacti and other desert plants, this botanic garden displays more than 20,000 plants from all over the world. The "Plants and People of the Sonoran Desert" trail is the state's best introduction to eth-nobotany (human use of plants) in the Southwest. If you come late in the day, you can stay after dark and see night-blooming flowers and dramatically lit cacti. A cafe on the grounds serves surprisingly good food.

At Papago Park, 1201 N. Galvin Pkwy. *C* 480/941-1225. www.dbg.org. Admission $10 adults, $9 seniors, $5 students 13–18, $4 children 3–12. Oct–Apr daily 8am–8pm; May–Sept daily 7am–8pm. Closed July 4 and Christmas. Bus: 3.

Heard Museum *Best*   This is one of the nation's finest museums dealing exclusively with Native American cultures, and the *Native Peoples of the Southwest* exhibit examines the culture of each of the region's major tribes. The Crossroads Gallery offers a fascinating look at contemporary Native American art. On many weekends there are performances by Native American singers and dancers, and throughout the week artists demonstrate their work.

Phoenix, Scottsdale & the Valley of the Sun

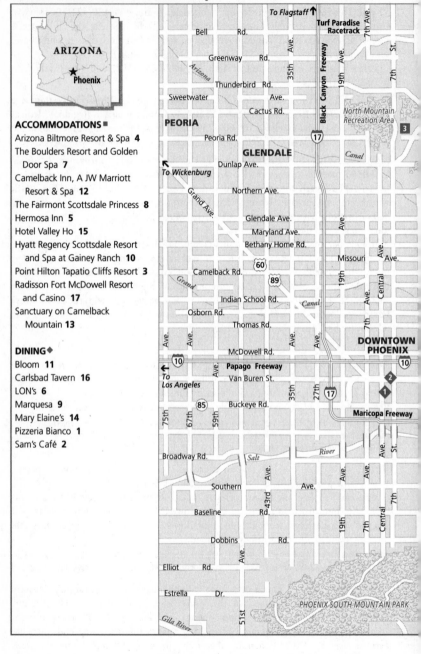

ARIZONA

★ **Phoenix**

ACCOMMODATIONS ■

Arizona Biltmore Resort & Spa **4**

The Boulders Resort and Golden
  Door Spa **7**

Camelback Inn, A JW Marriott
  Resort & Spa **12**

The Fairmont Scottsdale Princess **8**

Hermosa Inn **5**

Hotel Valley Ho **15**

Hyatt Regency Scottsdale Resort
  and Spa at Gainey Ranch **10**

Point Hilton Tapatio Cliffs Resort **3**

Radisson Fort McDowell Resort
  and Casino **17**

Sanctuary on Camelback
  Mountain **13**

DINING ◆

Bloom **11**

Carlsbad Tavern **16**

LON's **6**

Marquesa **9**

Mary Elaine's **14**

Pizzeria Bianco **1**

Sam's Café **2**

To Flagstaff
Turf Paradise Racetrack

Bell   Rd.

Greenway Rd.

Thunderbird Rd.

Sweetwater   Ave.

Cactus Rd.

PEORIA

Peoria Rd.

GLENDALE

Dunlap Ave.

To Wickenburg

Northern Ave.

Glendale Ave.

Maryland Ave.

Bethany Home Rd.

Missouri   Ave.

Camelback Rd.

Indian School Rd.

Osborn Rd.

Thomas Rd.

DOWNTOWN PHOENIX

McDowell Rd.

Papago Freeway

To Los Angeles

Van Buren St.

Buckeye Rd.

Maricopa Freeway

Broadway Rd.

Salt   River

Southern   Ave.

Baseline

Dobbins   Rd.

Elliot   Rd.

Estrella   Dr.

Gila River

PHOENIX SOUTH MOUNTAIN PARK

Black Canyon Freeway

North Mountain Recreation Area

Canal

Grand Ave.

Grand

Arizona

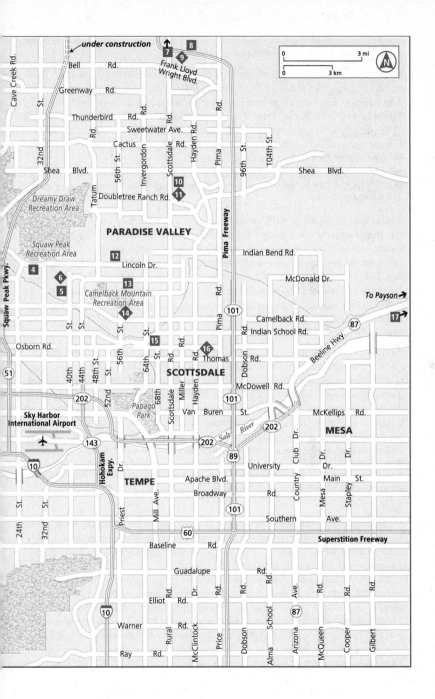

2301 N. Central Ave. ☎ 602/252-8848. www.heard.org. Admission $10 adults, $9 seniors, $5 students, $3 children 6–12. Daily 9:30am–5pm. Closed major holidays. Bus: Blue (B), Red (R), or O.

Phoenix Art Museum   This is the largest art museum in the Southwest, with a collection spanning the major artistic movements from the Renaissance to the present. The selection of modern and contemporary art is particularly good, with works by Diego Rivera, Frida Kahlo, Pablo Picasso, Alexander Calder, Henry Moore, Georgia O'Keeffe, Henri Rousseau, and Auguste Rodin. Other exhibits include decorative arts, historic fashions, Asian art, Spanish colonial furnishings and religious art, and works by members of the Cowboy Artists of America.

1625 N. Central Ave. (at McDowell Rd.). ☎ 602/257-1222. www.phxart.org. Admission $9 adults, $7 seniors and students, $3 children 6–17; free on Thurs. Tues–Wed and Fri–Sun 10am–5pm; Thurs 10am–9pm. Closed major holidays. Bus: Blue (B), Red (R), or O.

Scottsdale Museum of Contemporary Art   Scottsdale may be obsessed with art featuring lonesome cowboys and solemn Indians, but this boldly designed museum makes it clear that patrons of contemporary art are also welcome here. Cutting-edge art, from the abstract to the absurd, fills the galleries. In addition to the main building, there are several galleries in the adjacent Scottsdale Center for the Arts, which also has a pair of Dale Chihuly art-glass installations. The museum shop is excellent.

7374 E. Second St., Scottsdale. ☎ 480/994-ARTS. www.smoca.org. Admission $7 adults, $5 students, free for children under 15; free on Thurs. Tues–Wed and Fri–Sat 10am–5pm; Thurs 10am–8pm; Sun noon–5pm. Closed major holidays. Bus: 41, 50, or 72. Also accessible via Scottsdale Trolley shuttle bus.

Taliesin West   Frank Lloyd Wright fell in love with the Arizona desert and, in 1937, opened a winter camp here that served as his office and school. Today, Taliesin West is the headquarters of the Frank Lloyd Wright Foundation and School of Architecture. Tours explain the campus buildings and include a general introduction to Wright and his theories of architecture. Wright used local stone for the foundations and developed a number of innovative methods for dealing with the extreme desert climate.

12621 Frank Lloyd Wright Blvd. (at Cactus/114th St.), Scottsdale. ☎ 480/860-8810 for information, or 480/860-2700, ext. 494 or 495, for reservations. www.franklloydwright.org. Basic tours: Nov–Apr $18 adults, $16 seniors and students, $5 children 4–12; May–Oct $14 adults, $12 students and seniors, $4.50 children 4–12. Nov–Apr daily 9am–4:15pm; May–Oct daily 9am–4pm. Closed Tues–Wed July–Aug, Easter, Thanksgiving, Christmas, New Year's Day, and occasional special events. From Scottsdale Rd., go east on Shea Blvd. to 114th St., then north 1 mile to the entrance road.

GOLF

With around 200 courses in the Valley of the Sun, golf is just about the most popular sport in Phoenix and one of the main reasons people flock here in winter. Sunshine, spectacular views, and the company of coyotes, quails, and doves make playing a round of golf here a truly memorable experience.

The only thing harder than getting a winter or spring tee time in the valley is facing the bill at the end of your 18 holes. Greens fees at most public and resort courses range from $90 to $170, with the top courses often charging $200 to $250 or more. Municipal courses, on the other hand, charge under $40. You can save money on many courses by opting for twilight play, which usually begins between 1 and 3pm.

You can get more information on Valley of the Sun golf courses from the **Greater Phoenix Convention & Visitors Bureau,** 50 N. Second St. (☎ 877/225-5749 or 602/452-6282; www.visitphoenix.com).

It's a good idea to make reservations well in advance. You can avoid the hassle of booking tee times yourself by contacting **Golf Xpress** (☎ 888/679-8246 or 602/404-

GOLF; www.azgolfxpress.com), which can make reservations farther in advance than you could if you called the golf course directly, and can sometimes get you lower greens fees as well. This company also makes hotel reservations, rents golf clubs, and provides other assistance to golfers visiting the valley. For last-minute reservations, call **Stand-by Golf** (℗ **800/655-5345;** www.discountteetimes.com).

The many resort courses are the favored fairways of valley visitors. For spectacular scenery, the two Jay Morrish–designed 18-hole courses at the **Boulders,** North Scottsdale Road and Carefree Highway, Carefree (℗ **800/553-1717** or 480/488-9009), just can't be beat. Given the option, play the South Course, and watch out as you approach the tee box on the 7th hole—it's a real heart-stopper. Tee times for nonresort guests are very limited in winter and spring (try making reservations a month in advance if you aren't staying at the resort).

Jumping over to Litchfield Park, on the far west side of the valley, there's **The Wigwam Golf Resort & Spa,** 300 Wigwam Blvd. (℗ **800/SAY-PUTT** or 623/935-3811), which has, count 'em, three championship 18-hole courses. The Gold Course is legendary, but even the Blue and Red courses are worth playing. These are traditional courses for purists who want vast expanses of green rather than cactuses and boulders. Reservations for nonguests can be made no more than 7 days in advance.

Way over on the east side of the valley, at the foot of the Superstition Mountains, is the **Gold Canyon Golf Resort,** 6100 S. Kings Ranch Rd., Gold Canyon (℗ **800/ 827-5281** or 480/982-9449; www.gcgr.com), which has been rated the best public course in the state and has three of the state's best holes—the 2nd, 3rd, and 4th on the visually breathtaking, desert-style Dinosaur Mountain course. The Sidewinder course is more traditional and less dramatic, but much more economical. Reserve a week in advance. It's well worth the drive.

If you want to swing where the pros do, beg, borrow, or steal a tee time on the Tom Weiskopf and Jay Morrish–designed Stadium Course at the **Tournament Players Club (TPC) of Scottsdale,** 17020 N. Hayden Rd. (℗ **888/400-4001** or 480/585-4334; www.playatpc.com), which hosts the FBR Open. The 18th hole has standing room for 40,000 spectators, but hopefully there won't be that many around the day you double-bogey this hole. The TPC's second 18, the Desert Course, is a municipal course, thanks to an agreement with the landowner, the Bureau of Land Management.

If you want a traditional course that has been played by presidents and celebrities alike, try to get a tee time at one of the two 18-hole courses at the **Arizona Biltmore Country Club,** 24th Street and Missouri Avenue (℗ **602/955-9655;** www.arizona biltmore.com). The courses here are more relaxing than challenging, good to play if you're not yet up to par. Reservations can be made up to a month in advance. There's also a championship 18-hole putting course.

Of the Valley's many daily-fee courses, it's the two 18-hole courses at **Troon North Golf Club,** 10320 E. Dynamite Blvd., Scottsdale (℗ **888/TROON-US** or 480/585-7700; www.troonnorthgolf.com), seemingly just barely carved out of raw desert, that garner the most local accolades. This is the finest example of a desert course that you'll find anywhere in the state, and with five tee boxes on each hole, golfers of all levels will be thoroughly challenged. Reservations are taken up to 30 days in advance.

If you want to take a crack at a desert-style course or two but don't want to take out a second mortgage, try Dove Valley Ranch Golf Club or Rancho Mañana Golf Club. **Dove Valley Ranch Golf Club,** 33244 N. Black Mountain Pkwy., Cave Creek (℗ **480/488-0009;** www.dovevalleyranch.com), designed by Robert Trent Jones, Jr., was voted Arizona's best new public course when it opened in 1998. It's something of a merger of desert and traditional styles.

Of the municipal courses in Phoenix, **Papago Golf Course,** 5595 E. Moreland St. (© 602/275-8428), at the foot of the red-sandstone Papago Buttes, offers fine views and a killer 17th hole. This is such a great course that it's used for FBR Open qualifying. **Encanto Golf Course,** 2605 N. 15th Ave. (© 602/253-3963), is the third-oldest course in Arizona and, with its wide fairways and lack of hazards, is very forgiving. **Cave Creek Golf Course,** 15202 N. 19th Ave., in north Phoenix (© 602/866-8076), is another good, economical choice. For details on these courses, go to www.ci.phoenix.az.us/SPORTS/golf.html.

OTHER OUTDOOR ACTIVITIES

HIKING The city's largest nature preserve, **South Mountain Park/Preserve,** said to be the largest city park in the world, contains miles of hiking, mountain-biking, and horseback-riding trails, and the views of Phoenix from the Buena Vista Overlook are spectacular, especially at sunset. To reach the park, simply drive south on Central Avenue or 48th Street.

Perhaps the most popular hiking trail in the city is the trail to the top of **Camelback Mountain,** in Echo Canyon Recreation Area, near the boundary between Phoenix and Scottsdale. This is the highest mountain in Phoenix, and the 1.25-mile trail to the summit is very steep. Don't attempt it in the heat of the day, and take at least a quart of water with you. The reward for your effort is the city's finest view. To reach the trail head, drive up 44th Street until it becomes McDonald Drive, then turn right on East Echo Canyon Drive and continue up the hill until the road ends at a large parking lot.

HORSEBACK RIDING Even in the urban confines of the Phoenix metro area, people like to play at being cowboys. On the south side of the city, try **Ponderosa Stables,** 10215 S. Central Ave. (© 602/268-1261; www.arizona-horses.com), or the affiliated **South Mountain Stables,** 10005 S. Central Ave. (© 602/276-8131), both of which lead rides into South Mountain Park and charge $25 for a 1-hour ride.

HOT-AIR BALLOONING The still morning air of the Valley of the Sun is perfect for hot-air ballooning, and because of the stiff competition, prices are among the lowest in the country—between $125 and $185 per person for a 1- to 1½-hour ride. Companies to try include **Over the Rainbow** (© 602/225-5666; www.letsgoballooning.com), **Zephyr Balloon/A Aerozona Adventure** (© 888/991-4260 or 480/991-4260; www.azballoon.com), and **Adventures Out West** (© 800/755-0935 or 602/991-3666; www.adventuresoutwest.com).

WATERPARKS At **Phoenix Waterworld Safari,** 4243 W. Pinnacle Peak Rd. (© 623/581-8446; www.golfland.com), you can free-fall down the Kilimanjaro speed slide or catch a gnarly wave in the wave pool. **Mesa Golfland Sunsplash,** 155 W. Hampton Ave., Mesa (© 480/834-8319; www.golfland.com), has a wave pool and a water roller coaster. **Big Surf,** 1500 N. McClintock Rd., Tempe (© 480/947-2477; www.golfland.com), has the country's original wave pool and more.

WHITE-WATER RAFTING & TUBING In the mountains to the northeast of Phoenix, the **Upper Salt River** flows wild and free and offers some exciting rafting. Most years from late February to late May, snowmelt from the White Mountains turns the river into a Class III and IV river filled with exciting rapids. Companies operating full-day, overnight, and multiday rafting trips include **Wilderness Aware Rafting** (© 800/462-7238; www.inaraft.com), **Canyon Rio Rafting** (© 800/272-3353; www.

canyonrio.com), and **Mild to Wild Rafting** (© 800/567-6745; www.mild2wildrafting. com). Prices range from $99 to $115 for a day trip.

Tamer river trips can be had from **Salt River Tubing & Recreation** (© 480/984-3305; www.saltrivertubing.com), which has its headquarters 20 miles northeast of Phoenix on Power Road at Usery Pass Road in Tonto National Forest. For $12, the company will rent you a large inner tube and will shuttle you upriver for the float down. The season runs from mid-May to September.

SHOPPING

Along the streets of Old Scottsdale, you'll find dozens of **art galleries.** On Main Street, you'll find primarily cowboy art, while on North Marshall Way, you'll find much more imaginative and daring contemporary art.

For contemporary art, try **Art One,** 4120 N. Marshall Way, Scottsdale (© 480/946-5076), specializing in work by art students and cutting-edge artists; or the **Lisa Sette Gallery,** 4142 N. Marshall Way, Scottsdale (© 480/990-7342), which represents international and local artists working in a wide mix of media.

The **Heard Museum Gift Shop,** in the Heard Museum, 2301 N. Central Ave. (© 602/252-8344), has an awesome collection of extremely well-crafted and very expensive Native American jewelry, art, and crafts of all kinds. For one of the finest selections of Navajo rugs in the valley, visit **John C. Hill Antique Indian Art,** 6962 E. First Ave., Scottsdale (© 480/946-2910).

WHERE TO STAY

During the winter, the Phoenix metro area has some of the highest room rates in the country. But keep in mind that most resorts offer a variety of weekend, golf, and tennis packages—it always pays to ask. Most places drop their rates in spring and fall, and prices really plummet for those who can take the summer heat.

While most people dreaming of a Phoenix vacation have visions of luxury resorts dancing in their heads, there are also plenty of bed-and-breakfast inns around the valley. **Mi Casa Su Casa** (© 800/456-0682 or 480/990-0682; www.azres.com) can book you into dozens of different homes in the Valley of the Sun, as can **Arizona Trails Bed & Breakfast Reservation Service** (© 888/799-4284 or 480/837-4284; www.arizonatrails.com), which also books tour and hotel reservations.

Arizona Biltmore Resort & Spa *(Best)*   For timeless elegance, a prime location, and historical character, no other resort in the valley can touch the Biltmore, which was partly designed by Frank Lloyd Wright. While the golf courses and spa are the main draws, the children's center also makes this a popular choice for families. The "resort rooms" are comfortable and have balconies or patios; villa suites are the most spacious and luxurious of all. Afternoon tea, a Phoenix institution, is served in the lobby.

2400 E. Missouri Ave., Phoenix, AZ 85016. © 800/950-0086 or 602/955-6600. Fax 602/381-7600. www.arizonabiltmore. com. 738 units. Jan to mid-May $445–$645 double, from $695 suite; mid-May to early Sept $195–$295 double, from $325 suite; early Sept to Dec $375–$575 double, from $675 suite. Rates do not include a $20 daily service fee. Children under 18 stay free in parent's room. AE, DC, DISC, MC, V. Pets under 20 lb. accepted in cottage rooms ($250 deposit, $50 nonrefundable). **Amenities:** 5 restaurants; 8 pools; 2 18-hole golf courses, plus 18-hole putting course; 7 tennis courts; health club and full-service spa.

The Boulders Resort and Golden Door Spa   Set amid a jumble of giant boulders 45 minutes north of Scottsdale, this prestigious golf resort epitomizes the southwestern aesthetic. Adobe buildings blend unobtrusively into the desert, as do the two noted golf courses. Rooms continue the pueblo styling with stucco walls, beehive fireplaces, and beamed ceilings. Bathrooms are large and luxuriously appointed, with tubs for two and separate showers. If you can tear yourself away from the fairways, you can take advantage of the Golden Door Spa or even try rock climbing. In addition to the on-site restaurants, several dining options are at the adjacent El Pedregal Festival Marketplace.

34631 N. Tom Darlington Dr. (P.O. Box 2090), Carefree, AZ 85377. ℂ 866/397-6520 or 480/488-9009. Fax 480/488-4118. www.theboulders.com. 215 units. Late Dec to May $549 double, from $999 villa; May to early Sept $199 double, from $499 villa; early Sept to early Dec $349 double, from $799 villa; early to late Dec $299 double, from $699 villa. (For all rates add a $29–$33 nightly service charge.) Children under 17 stay free in parent's room. AE, DC, DISC, MC, V. Pets accepted ($100). **Amenities:** 6 restaurants; 4 pools; 2 18-hole golf courses; 8 tennis courts; exercise room; full-service spa.

Camelback Inn, A JW Marriott Resort & Spa

Set at the foot of Mummy Mountain and overlooking Camelback Mountain, the Camelback Inn is one of the grande dames of the Phoenix hotel scene and abounds in traditional southwestern character. Although the two 18-hole golf courses are the main attraction, the spa is among the finest in the state. Rooms are decorated with southwestern furnishings and art, and all have balconies or patios. Some rooms even have their own private pools.

5402 E. Lincoln Dr., Scottsdale, AZ 85253. ℂ 800/24-CAMEL or 480/948-1700. Fax 480/951-8469. www.camelback inn.com. 453 units. Jan to early June $299–$489 double, $570–$1,750 suite; early June to early Sept $179–$199 double, $260–$675 suite; early Sept to Dec $349–$399 double, $595–$1,250 suite. Children under 18 stay free in parent's room. AE, DC, DISC, MC, V. Small pets accepted. **Amenities:** 7 restaurants; 3 pools; 2 18-hole golf courses; pitch-and-putt green; 6 tennis courts; exercise room; full-service spa.

The Fairmont Scottsdale Princess

This modern rendition of a Moorish palace offers an exotic atmosphere unmatched by any other valley resort. It plays host to the FBR Open golf tournament and the city's top tennis tournament, and is also home to the Willow Stream spa and an impressive water playground. Located a 20-minute drive north of Old Town Scottsdale, this resort makes a good romantic hideaway as well as a family destination. Rooms have southwestern decor and private balconies.

7575 E. Princess Dr., Scottsdale, AZ 85255. ℂ 800/441-1414 or 480/585-4848. Fax 480/585-0091. www.fairmont. com/scottsdale. 651 units. $159–$589 double; $319–$3,800 suite. Children under 12 stay free in parent's room. AE, DC, DISC, MC, V. Pets accepted. **Amenities:** 4 restaurants; 4 pools; 2 18-hole golf courses; 7 tennis courts; exercise room; full-service spa.

Hermosa Inn

If you don't like the crowds of big resorts but do enjoy the luxury, this is the spot for you. This boutique hotel in a quiet residential neighborhood is one of the few lodgings in the area to offer a bit of Old Arizona atmosphere. Rooms vary from cozy to spacious and are decorated in tastefully contemporary western and southwestern decor. The dining room, LON's (p. 764), located in the original adobe home, serves excellent cuisine in a rustic, upscale setting.

5532 N. Palo Cristi Rd., Paradise Valley, AZ 85253. ℂ 800/241-1210 or 602/955-8614. Fax 602/955-8299. www.hermosa inn.com. 35 units. Jan–May $299–$369 double, $399–$699 suite; June–Aug $159–$189 double, $269–$469 suite; Sept–Dec $219–$349 double, $419–$639 suite. Rates do not include daily hospitality fee of $12. Rates include full breakfast. Children 12 and under stay free in parent's room. AE, DC, DISC, MC, V. Take 32nd St. north from Camelback Rd., turn right on Stanford Rd., and turn left on N. Palo Cristi Rd. From Lincoln Dr., turn south on N. Palo Cristi Rd. (east of 32nd St.). Pets accepted ($50 fee). **Amenities:** Restaurant; pool; tennis court; access to nearby health club.

Hotel Valley Ho

This Scottsdale grande dame dates from the 1950s, but in 2005, the hotel got a complete face-lift. What a looker she is now. The Valley Ho is hip and convenient, and has loads of outdoor space for soaking up the sun. Its big rooms are done in a bold contemporary style. The studio rooms have curtains to partition off the vanity area and an ultracool free-standing tub. Big balconies and patios provide plenty of space for lounging outdoors. When it's time to get even more relaxed, grab one of the plush, circular lounge chairs at the pool. Cool!

6850 E. Main St., Scottsdale, AZ 85251. © 866/882-4484 or 480/248-2000. Fax 480/248-2002. www.hotelvalleyho. com. 194 units. Jan–Apr $289–$394 double, $389–$519 suite; May and Sept $199–$314 double, $299–$439 suite; June–Aug $139–$234 double, $239–$359 suite; Oct–Dec $259–$364 double, $359–$489 suite. Children under 18 stay free in parent's room. Free valet parking. AE, DC, DISC, MC, V. Pets accepted. **Amenities:** 2 restaurants; pool; exercise room; full-service spa.

Hyatt Regency Scottsdale Resort & Spa at Gainey Ranch   With its gardens full of stately palm trees and an extravagant water playground that encompasses 10 swimming pools, a water slide, a sand beach, a water-volleyball pool, waterfalls, and a huge whirlpool spa, this luxurious resort is designed to astonish. A beautiful new lobby and lobby bar and the big new Spa Avania only enhance the resort's ability to awe. Guest rooms are luxurious and are designed to reflect the desert location. Vu, the resort's premier restaurant, has a sunken waterside gazebo, while Ristorante Sandolo features after-dinner gondola rides. The resort's Native American and Environmental Learning Center provides a glimpse into Sonoran Desert culture and ecology.

7500 E. Doubletree Ranch Rd., Scottsdale, AZ 85258. © 800/55-HYATT or 480/444-1234. Fax 480/483-5550. www. scottsdale.hyatt.com. 490 units. Jan to late May $365 double, from $979 suite and casita; late May to early Sept $189 double, from $548 suite and casita; early Sept to Dec $365 double, from $979 suite and casita. Children under 18 stay free in parent's room. AE, DC, DISC, MC, V. Valet parking $20. **Amenities:** 4 restaurants; 10 pools; 27-hole golf course; 4 tennis courts; health club; full-service spa.

Pointe Hilton Tapatio Cliffs Resort   If you love to lounge by the pool, then this resort is a great choice. The Falls, a 3-acre water playground, includes two pools, a 138-foot water slide, 40-foot cascades, a whirlpool tucked into an artificial grotto, and rental cabanas. If you're a hiker, you can head out on the trails of the adjacent North Mountain Recreation Area. All rooms are spacious suites with southwestern-inspired furnishings; corner units are particularly bright. This resort has steep walkways, so you need to be in good shape to stay here. At the top of the property is Different Pointe of View, a restaurant with one of the finest views in the city.

11111 N. Seventh St., Phoenix, AZ 85020. © 800/947-9784 or 602/866-7500. Fax 602/993-0276. www.pointe hilton.com. 585 units. Jan to mid-Apr $199–$299 double; mid-Apr to late May and mid-Sept to Dec $109–$249 double; late May to mid-Sept $99–$139 double; year-round $1,300 grande suite. Rates do not include $9 daily resort fee. Children under 18 stay free in parent's room. AE, DC, DISC, MC, V. Pets accepted. **Amenities:** 5 restaurants; 8 pools; golf course; 2 tennis courts; fitness center (extra charge); small full-service spa.

Radisson Fort McDowell Resort & Casino   You just can't stay any closer to the desert than at this beautiful new resort that's a 30-minute drive from downtown Scottsdale but with a location that's hard to beat if you've come to the area to experience the desert. The resort is on the Fort McDowell Yavapai Nation and, consequently, the tribe's Fort McDowell Casino is a big draw for many guests. However, the two 18-hole courses at the adjacent We-Ko-Pa Golf Club are also a major draw here.

10438 N. Fort McDowell Rd., Scottsdale/Fountain Hills, AZ 85264. © 800/333-3333 or 480/789-5300. Fax 480/789-5333. www.radisson.com/ftmcdowellaz. 246 units. Jan–Mar $269–$299 double; Apr $199–$210 double; May, Sept, and Dec $169–$189 double; June–Aug $109–$139 double; Oct–Nov $219–$239 double. Children under 12 stay free in parent's room. AE, DC, DISC, MC, V. Pets accepted. **Amenities:** 2 restaurants; 2 pools; 2 18-hole golf courses; health club; full-service spa.

Sanctuary on Camelback Mountain   High on the northern flanks of Camelback Mountain is this lushly landscaped spa resort. Rooms are divided between the more conservative deluxe casitas and the contemporary spa casitas. These latter rooms are the only truly hip lodging option at any valley resort. With their cement floors, kidney-shaped daybeds, and streamline-moderne cabinetry, these units are absolutely stunning (but certainly not for everyone). Some bathrooms have private outdoor soaking tubs. The spa is one of the prettiest in the valley.

5700 E. McDonald Dr., Paradise Valley, AZ 85253. ✆ **800/245-2051** or 480/948-2100. Fax 480/483-7314. www. sanctuaryaz.com. 98 units. Late Dec to early May $425–$795 double; early May to early June and early Sept to mid-Dec $310–$695 double; early June to early Sept and mid-Dec to late Dec $165–$425 double. Children under 16 stay free in parent's room. AE, DC, DISC, MC, V. Pets accepted. **Amenities:** Restaurant; 4 pools; 5 tennis courts; fitness center; full-service spa.

WHERE TO DINE

The Valley of the Sun boasts hundreds of excellent restaurants, with most of the best dining options concentrated in the Scottsdale Road and Biltmore Corridor areas. If you want to splurge on only one expensive meal while you're here, consider a resort restaurant that offers a view of the city lights.

Phoenix is a sprawling city, and can be a real pain to have to drive around in search of a good lunch spot. If you happen to be visiting the Phoenix Art Museum, the Heard Museum, or the Desert Botanical Garden anytime around lunch, stay put for your noon meal. All three of these attractions have cafes serving decent, if limited, menus.

Bloom NEW AMERICAN   Bloom is big and always full of energy. The minimalist decor emphasizes flowers, an elegant wine bar serves a wide range of flights (tasting assortments), and the bistro-style menu has lots of great dishes in a wide range of prices. Among the entrees, the roast duck with a crisp potato nest and drunken cherry sauce is excellent.

8877 N. Scottsdale Rd. ✆ **480/922-5666.** Reservations recommended. Main courses $8–$14 lunch, $15–$29 dinner. AE, DC, DISC, MC, V. Mon–Thurs 11am–3pm and 5–10pm; Fri–Sat 11am–3pm and 5–10:30pm; Sun 5–9:30pm.

Carlsbad Tavern NEW MEXICAN   Carlsbad Tavern blends the fiery tastes of New Mexican cuisine with a hip and humorous bat-theme atmosphere (a reference to Carlsbad Caverns). The menu lists traditional New Mexican dishes such as *carne adovada,* pork simmered in a fiery red-chile sauce, as well as contemporary southwestern specialties such as poblano chiles stuffed with crab, and pasta with an unusual chipotle stroganoff. Cool off your taste buds with a prickly-pear margarita.

3313 N. Hayden Rd. (south of Osborn). ✆ **480/970-8164.** www.carlsbadtavern.com. Reservations accepted for 5 or more. Main courses $7.50–$23. AE, DISC, MC, V. Mon–Sat 11am–1am; Sun 1pm–1am (limited menu daily 10 or 11pm–1am).

LON's AMERICAN REGIONAL   This old adobe hacienda surrounded by colorful gardens is one of the most "Arizonan" places in the Phoenix area. Entrees at both lunch and dinner are reliable, and if you peruse the menu closely, you'll turn up some interesting southwestern ingredients, including prickly pear. Also be sure to ask about dishes made with Arizona-farmed shrimp. The bar is cozy and romantic, and the patio affords beautiful views of Camelback Mountain.

At the Hermosa Inn, 5532 N. Palo Cristi Rd. ✆ **602/955-7878.** www.lons.com. Reservations recommended. Main courses $11–$15 lunch, $21–$34 dinner. AE, DC, DISC, MC, V. Mon–Fri 11:30am–2pm and 6–10pm; Sat 6–10pm; Sun 10am–2pm (brunch) and 6–10pm.

Marquesa MEDITERRANEAN   Thoroughly romantic, the Marquesa has an ambience reminiscent of an 18th-century Spanish villa. The offerings are ripe with exotic ingredients imported from around the world. Contemporary interpretations of Mediterranean cuisine are the focus here; count on almost every dish being an intensive labor of love. For dessert, be sure to order the Salvador Dalí–inspired edible work of chocolate art. The Sunday brunch is one of the best in the valley.

At The Fairmont Scottsdale Princess, 7575 E. Princess Dr. (about 12 miles north of downtown Scottsdale). © 480/ 585-4848. Reservations recommended. Main courses $33–$48; prix-fixe dinner $80–$110; brunch $70. AE, DC, DISC, MC, V. Wed–Sat 6–9pm; Sun 10am–2pm. Closed July–Sept.

Mary Elaine's *Best* FRENCH   Mary Elaine's represents the pinnacle of Arizona dining for its haute cuisine, exemplary service, and superb table settings. The chef focuses on classic French cuisine with an emphasis on impeccably fresh ingredients. You're almost certain to encounter foie gras, truffles, lobster, and caviar. Menus change seasonally, and there are also themed tasting menus. Try to make a reservation that allows you to take in the sunset.

At The Phoenician, 6000 E. Camelback Rd. © 480/423-2530. Reservations highly recommended. Jackets suggested for men. Main courses $43–$58; 7-course tasting menu $125 (plus $85 for matched wines). AE, DC, DISC, MC, V. Tues–Thurs 6–10pm; Fri–Sat 6–11pm.

Pinnacle Peak Patio Steakhouse & Microbrewery *Kids* STEAKHOUSE   Once located miles out in the desert, this "Hollywood Western" steakhouse is now surrounded by some of the valley's poshest suburbs. Although you can indulge in mesquite-broiled steaks with all the traditional trimmings, a meal here is more an event than just an opportunity to put on the feed bag. The real draw is all the entertainment—gunfights, cowboy bands, two-stepping, and cookouts.

10426 E. Jomax Rd., Scottsdale. © 480/585-1599. www.pppatio.com. Reservations accepted only for parties of 8 or more. Main courses $8–$35. AE, DISC, MC, V. Mon–Thurs 4–10pm; Fri–Sat 4–11pm; Sun noon–10pm. Take 101 to Exit 36 (Pima Rd./Princess Dr.). Go north on Pima Rd., east on Happy Valley Rd., north on Alma School Pkwy., and watch for the sign on the left.

Pizzeria Bianco PIZZA   Even though this historic brick building is smack-dab in the center of downtown Phoenix, the atmosphere is so cozy it feels like your neighborhood local. The wood-burning oven turns out deliciously rustic pizzas. Try one with red onion, Parmesan, rosemary, and crushed pistachios. Don't miss the fresh mozzarella, which can be ordered as an appetizer or on a pizza.

At Heritage Sq., 623 E. Adams St. © 602/258-8300. www.pizzeriabianco.com. Reservations accepted for 6–10 people. Pizzas $9–$13. AE, MC, V. Tues–Sat 5–10pm.

Sam's Cafe *Value* SOUTHWESTERN   Sam's Cafe, one of only a handful of decent downtown restaurants, offers food that's every bit as imaginative, but not nearly as expensive, as that served at other southwestern restaurants in Phoenix. Breadsticks with picante-flavored cream cheese, grilled vegetable tacos, and angel-hair pasta in a spicy jalapeño sauce with shrimp and mushrooms all have a nice balance of flavors. The downtown Sam's has a large patio. There's another Sam's in Biltmore Fashion Park, 2566 E. Camelback Rd. (© 602/954-7100).

At the Arizona Center, 455 N. Third St. © 602/252-3545. www.canyoncafe.com. Reservations recommended. Main courses $8–$14. AE, DISC, MC, V. Thurs–Sat 11am–10pm; Sun–Wed 11am–9pm.

PHOENIX AFTER DARK

The best place to look for nightlife listings is in the *Phoenix New Times*, a weekly newspaper that tends to have the most comprehensive listings.

THE PERFORMING ARTS   Phoenix's premier performance venue is **Symphony Hall**, 225 E. Adams St. (© 602/262-7272), which recently had a major renovation and remodeling, making it a much more user-friendly performance hall for its resident companies, the Phoenix Symphony and the Arizona Opera Company.

Out in the east Valley, the new **Mesa Arts Center,** 1 E. Main St. (© **480/644-6500;** www.mesaartscenter.com), is now one of the finest places in the Phoenix metro area for live theater and music performances.

THE CLUB & MUSIC SCENE   **Mill Avenue** in Tempe is a good place to wander around in search of your favorite type of music. Packed into a couple of dozen blocks surrounding Old Town Scottsdale, near the corner of Camelback and Scottsdale roads, there are dozens of trendy dance clubs and chic bars. Clubs in this neighborhood tend to be the places to see and be seen.

At **Handlebar-J,** 7116 E. Becker Lane, Scottsdale (© **480/948-0110;** www.handlebarj.com), you'll hear live git-down two-steppin' music and can even get free dance lessons on Wednesday, Thursday, and Sunday. The beautiful **e4,** 4282 N. Drinkwater Blvd., Scottsdale (© **480/970-3325;** www.e4-az.com), is a nightclub with different spaces that are based on the four elements—earth, air, fire, and water.

THE BAR SCENE   The **Hyatt Regency Scottsdale Lobby Bar,** 7500 E. Doubletree Ranch Rd., Scottsdale (© **480/991-3388**), is a romantic spot for nightly live music. The **Squaw Peak Lounge,** in the Arizona Biltmore, 2400 E. Missouri Ave. (© **602/381-7632**), is a terrific spot for a cocktail at sunset. For the ultimate sports and rock bar, check out downtown Phoenix's **Alice Cooper'stown,** 101 E. Jackson St. (© **602/253-7337**), run by none other than Alice Cooper himself.

CASINOS   **Casino Arizona at Salt River,** U.S. 101 and Indian Bend Road and U.S. 101 and McKellips Road (© **480/850-7777**), is a pair of casinos that together comprise the newest and most conveniently located casinos in the area. **Fort McDowell Casino,** on Fort McDowell Road off Ariz. 87, 2 miles northeast of Shea Boulevard, Fountain Hills (© **800/THE-FORT**), is the oldest in the state.

4 Tucson

Melding Hispanic, Anglo, and Native American roots, Tucson is a city with a strong sense of identity—aware of its desert setting, confident in its style. Tucson supports an active cultural life, but it's the city's natural surroundings that set it apart. Four mountain ranges ring the city, and in those mountains and their foothills are giant saguaro cacti, a national park, an oasis, one of the finest zoos in the world, a ski area, and miles of hiking and horseback-riding trails.

ESSENTIALS

GETTING THERE   By Plane   Tucson International Airport (© **520/573-8000;** www.tucsonairport.org) is 6 miles south of downtown. Many resorts and hotels provide airport shuttle service. **Arizona Stagecoach** (© **520/889-1000;** www.azstagecoach.com) operates 24-hour van service to downtown Tucson and the foothills resorts. One-way fares range from $21 to $35. A taxi to downtown costs around $22, to the resorts about $25 to $45.

Sun Tran (© **520/792-9222;** www.suntran.com), the local public transit, operates a bus service to and from the airport, though you'll have to make a transfer to reach downtown. The fare is $1. Day passes are available on buses for $2.

By Train Amtrak (© **800/USA-RAIL;** www.amtrak.com) provides service from Los Angeles (trip time: 10 hr.), San Antonio (18 hr.), and New Orleans (32 hr.) to its station at 400 E. Toole St.

By Car The major routes into Tucson are **I-10** from the northwest (Phoenix) and east (El Paso). **I-19** connects Tucson with the Mexican border at Nogales. If you're headed downtown, take the Congress Street exit off I-10. If you're headed for one of the foothills resorts north of downtown, take the Ina Road exit.

VISITOR INFORMATION The **Metropolitan Tucson Convention and Visitors Bureau (MTCVB),** 100 S. Church St. (at Broadway), Suite 7199 (© **800/638-8350** or 520/624-1817; www.visitTucson.org), is open Monday through Friday from 8am to 5pm, Saturday and Sunday from 9am to 4pm.

GETTING AROUND Unless you plan to stay by the pool or on the golf course, you'll probably want to rent a car. Rates tend to be low. Downtown Tucson is still a relatively easy place to find a parking space, and parking fees are low. There are two huge parking lots on the south side of the Tucson Convention Center and plenty of metered parking on the smaller downtown streets. Almost all Tucson hotels and resorts provide free parking.

Though they don't go very far, the restored electric streetcars of **Old Pueblo Trolley** (© **520/792-1802;** www.oldpueblotrolley.org) are a fun way to get from the Fourth Avenue shopping district to the University of Arizona. The trolleys run Friday from 6 to 10pm, Saturday from noon to midnight, and Sunday from noon to 6pm. The fare is $1 for adults and 50¢ for children 6 to 12. The fare on Sunday is only 25¢ for all riders. Friday and Saturday all-day passes are $2.50 for adults and $1.25 for children.

For a taxi, phone **Yellow Cab** (© **520/624-6611**) or **Discount Cab** (© **520/ 388-9000**).

FAST FACTS For a doctor referral, call **University Medical Center** (© **520/694-8888**). The **University Medical Center** is at 1501 N. Campbell Ave. (© **520/694-0111**). Call © **800/WALGREENS** for the Walgreens pharmacy that's nearest you or that's open 24 hours.

WHAT TO SEE & DO

Arizona-Sonora Desert Museum *(Best (Kids* The full spectrum of Sonoran Desert life—from plants to insects to fish to reptiles to mammals—is on display in natural settings at this world-class zoo. Coyotes and javelinas (peccaries) seem very much at home in their compounds, which are surrounded by almost invisible wire mesh fences that make it seem as though there is nothing between you and the animals. These display areas are along the Desert Loop Trail, which is also where you'll find the museum's newest exhibits. There are black bears, mountain lions, beavers, otters, frogs, fish, tarantulas, scorpions, prairie dogs, and desert bighorn sheep. Our favorite exhibit is the walk-in hummingbird aviary. The museum has two dining options, which both serve good food.

2021 N. Kinney Rd. © 520/883-2702. www.desertmuseum.org. Admission Nov–Apr $12 adults, $4 children 6–12; May–Oct $9 adults, $2 children 6–12. Oct–Feb daily 8:30am–5pm; Mar–Sept daily 7:30am–5pm (June–Aug Sat until 10pm). From downtown Tucson, go west on Speedway Blvd., which becomes Gates Pass Rd., and follow the signs.

Mission San Xavier del Bac Called the White Dove of the Desert, Mission San Xavier de Bac, a blindingly white adobe building rising from a sere, brown landscape, is considered the finest example of mission architecture in the Southwest. The beautiful church, which was built between 1783 and 1797, incorporates Moorish, Byzantine, and Mexican Renaissance architectural styles. The church was never actually

Tucson

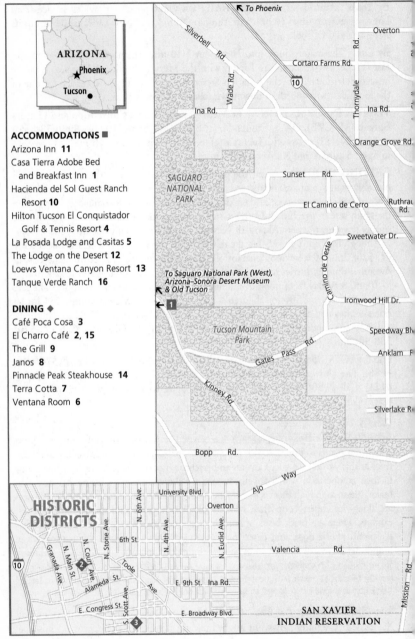

ACCOMMODATIONS ■
Arizona Inn **11**
Casa Tierra Adobe Bed
  and Breakfast Inn **1**
Hacienda del Sol Guest Ranch
  Resort **10**
Hilton Tucson El Conquistador
  Golf & Tennis Resort **4**
La Posada Lodge and Casitas **5**
The Lodge on the Desert **12**
Loews Ventana Canyon Resort **13**
Tanque Verde Ranch **16**

DINING ◆
Café Poca Cosa **3**
El Charro Café **2, 15**
The Grill **9**
Janos **8**
Pinnacle Peak Steakhouse **14**
Terra Cotta **7**
Ventana Room **6**

ARIZONA
Phoenix
Tucson

To Phoenix

Overton
Cortaro Farms Rd.
Silverbell Rd.
Wade Rd.
Rd.
Thornydale
Ina Rd.
Ina Rd.
Orange Grove Rd.
SAGUARO
NATIONAL
PARK
Sunset   Rd.
El Camino de Cerro
Ruthrau
Rd.
Sweetwater Dr.
Camino de Oeste
To Saguaro National Park (West),
Arizona–Sonora Desert Museum
& Old Tucson
Ironwood Hill Dr.
1
Tucson Mountain
Park
Speedway Blv
Gates   Pass   Rd.
Anklam   F
Kinney Rd.
Silverlake R
Bopp   Rd.
Ajo   Way

HISTORIC
DISTRICTS
University Blvd.
N. 6th Ave.
Overton
N. Stone Ave.
6th St.
N. 4th Ave.
N. Euclid Ave.
Granada Ave.
N. Main St.
N. Court Ave.
Toole
Valencia   Rd.
Alameda   St.
E. 9th St.   Ina Rd.
S. Scott Ave.
E. Congress St.
E. Broadway Blvd.
Mission   Rd.
SAN XAVIER
INDIAN RESERVATION

CORONADO   NATIONAL   FOREST

4

Hardy Rd.

Magee Rd.

Tohono Chul
Park

La Canada Dr.

Ina Rd.

6

Orange Grove Rd.

Skyline Dr.

7

8

5

9

10

River   Rd.

Hacienda del Sol Rd.

Wetmore Rd.

Roger   Rd.

Prince   Rd.

Miracle Mile

Flowing Wells Rd.

Romero Rd.

Grant   Rd.

Oracle

Stone

Euclid

Campbell   Ave.

Ft.

Ave.

Ave.

Lowell

Blvd.

Rd.

Tucson

Country

Club

Way

Alvernon

Swan Rd.

Craycroft Rd.

Sunrise Dr.

Kolb   Rd.

13

Kolb   Rd.

Sabino

Canyon   Rd.

Sabino
Canyon
Park

Rd.

Snyder   Rd.

Bear   Canyon Rd.

To Mount
Lemmon

Catalina
Hwy.

River   Rd.

Ft. Lowell
Park

Grant Rd.

Rd.

14

Tanque Verde Rd.

10

Historic
Districts

See Inset at
Bottom Left

Congress

entinel
Peak
Park

Tucson
Greyhound
Park

Ajo   Way

Irvington   Rd.

12th

6th

Ave.

Ave.

Kino Blvd.

Drexel Rd.

Valencia Rd.

To Nogales

19

11

6th   St.

12

Broadway Blvd.

Reid
Park

Randolph
Park

22nd St.

210

36th St.

10

Speedway Blvd.

5th St.

Swan Rd.

Craycroft Rd.

Wilmot Rd.

15

Kolb   Rd.

16

To Saguaro National
Park (East)

22nd St.

Golf   Links   Rd.

Escalante

Pantano Rd.

Camino Seco   Rd.

Irvington   Rd.

Kolb   Rd.

DAVIS
MONTHAN
AFB

Palo Verde Rd.

Kolb   Rd.

Los Reales Rd.

Tucson
International
Airport

10

0   2 mi
0   2 km

N

769

completed, which becomes apparent when the two bell towers are compared. One is topped with a dome, while the other has none. Restored murals cover the walls, and behind the altar are colorful and elaborate decorations.

1950 W. San Xavier Rd. ✆ 520/294-2624. www.sanxaviermission.org. Free admission; donations accepted. Daily 8am–5pm. Take I-19 south 9 miles to Exit 92 and turn right.

Old Tucson Studios *Kids*   Old Tucson was built as the set for the 1939 movie *Arizona* and since then has been used in the filming of countless movies, including *Tombstone* and *Geronimo*. Today, Old Tucson is far more than just a movie set; it's a Wild West theme park with family-oriented activities and entertainment. Throughout the day, there are staged shootouts in the streets, stunt shows, a cancan revue, and other performances. Train rides, stagecoach rides, kiddie rides, educational shows, restaurants, and gift shops round out the experience.

201 S. Kinney Rd. ✆ 520/883-0100. www.oldtucson.com. Admission $15 adults, $9.45 children 4–11. Daily 10am–6pm. Closed Thanksgiving, Christmas, and occasional special events. Take Speedway Blvd. west, continuing in the same direction when it becomes Gates Pass Blvd., and turn left on S. Kinney Rd.

Sabino Canyon Recreation Area   Sabino Canyon is a desert oasis that has attracted people and animals for thousands of years. This spectacular and accessible corner of the desert contains not only impressive scenery, but also hiking trails and a stream. Many visitors come to splash in the canyon's waterfalls and pools, but for those who prefer just to gaze at the beauty of crystal-clear water flowing through a rocky canyon guarded by saguaro cacti, there are narrated tram rides through the lower canyon. There are also many trails and picnic tables. (Bring water if you want to hike.)

5900 N. Sabino Canyon Rd. ✆ 520/749-8700, 520/749-2861 for shuttle information, or 520/749-2327 for moonlight shuttle reservations. www.fs.fed.us/r3/coronado or www.sabinocanyon.com. Parking $5 (also good for driving the Catalina Hwy.). Sabino Canyon tram ride $7.50 adults, $3 children 3–12; Bear Canyon tram ride $3 adults, $1 children 3–12. Park daily dawn–dusk. Sabino Canyon tram rides daily 9am–4:30pm; Bear Canyon tram rides daily 9am–4pm (both trams operate shorter hours in summer). Take Grant Rd. east to Tanque Verde Rd., continuing east; at Sabino Canyon Rd., turn north and watch for the sign.

Saguaro National Park   The massive, treelike saguaro cactus is the quintessential symbol of the American desert. Since 1933, saguaros (and all the other inhabitants of this part of the Sonoran Desert) have been preserved in the two sections of what is now Saguaro National Park. The most impressive stands of saguaros are to be found in the western district, near the Arizona–Sonora Desert Museum. In the area near the Red Hills Information Center is a water hole that attracts wild animals. The eastern section of the park contains an older area of forest at the foot of the Rincon Mountains. Both sections have visitor centers, loop roads, nature trails, hiking trails, and picnic grounds.

Rincon Mountain District visitor center: 3693 S. Old Spanish Trail. ✆ 520/733-5153. Tucson Mountain District visitor center: 2700 N. Kinney Rd. ✆ 520/733-5158. www.nps.gov/sagu. Entry fee $10 per car, $5 per hiker or biker. Daily 7am–sunset; visitor centers daily 9am–5pm; open to hikers 24 hr. a day. Visitor centers closed Christmas.

Tucson Botanical Gardens   Set amid residential neighborhoods in midtown Tucson, these gardens are an oasis of greenery and, though small, are worth a visit if you're interested in desert plant life, landscaping, or gardening. On the 5½-acre grounds are several small gardens that not only have visual appeal but are also historical and educational.

2150 N. Alvernon Way. ✆ 520/326-9686. www.tucsonbotanical.org. Admission $5 adults, $2.50 children 6–12. Daily 8:30am–4:30pm. Closed New Year's Day, July 4th, Thanksgiving, and Christmas. Bus: 11.

OUTDOOR ACTIVITIES

BICYCLING   Tucson is one of the best bicycling cities in the country, and the dirt roads and trails of the surrounding national forest and desert are perfect for mountain biking. Rentals at **Fair Wheel Bikes,** 1110 E. Sixth St. (© **520/884-9018**), go for $40 per day for road bikes and $30 to $50 per day for mountain bikes.

If you'd rather confine your pedaling to paved surfaces, there are some great options around town. The number-one choice in town for cyclists in halfway decent shape is the road up **Sabino Canyon.** Keep in mind, however, that bicycles are allowed on this road only 5 days a week and then only before 9am and after 5pm (the road's closed to bikes all day on Wed and Sat). For a much easier ride, the **Rillito River Park path** currently has a 1-mile paved section between Swan and Craycroft roads and a 6-mile paved section between Campbell Avenue and I-10. The trail parallels River Road and the usually dry bed of the Rillito River, and if you've got knobby tires, you can link the two paved sections or continue west past La Cholla Road after the pavement ends.

BIRD-WATCHING   Southern Arizona has some of the best bird-watching in the country, and although the best spots are south of Tucson, there are a few places around the city that birders will enjoy seeking out. Call the **Tucson Audubon Society's Rare Bird Alert** (© **520/798-1005**) to find out which birds have been spotted lately.

Roy P. Drachman Agua Caliente Park, 12325 Roger Rd. (off N. Soldier Trail), in the northeast corner of the city, is just about the best place in Tucson to see birds. The year-round warm springs here are a magnet for dozens of species, including waterfowl, great blue herons, black phoebes, soras, and vermilion flycatchers. To find the park, follow Tanque Verde Road east 6 miles from the intersection with Sabino Canyon Road and turn left onto Soldier Trail. Watch for signs.

The best area for bird-watching is **Madera Canyon National Forest Recreation Area** (© **520/281-2296;** www.fs.fed.us/r3/coronado), about 40 miles south of the city in the Coronado National Forest. Because of the year-round water here, Madera Canyon attracts a surprising variety of bird life. Avid birders flock to this canyon from around the country in hopes of spotting more than a dozen species of hummingbirds and an equal number of flycatchers, warblers, tanagers, buntings, grosbeaks, and many rare birds not found in any other state. However, before birding became a hot activity, this canyon was popular with families looking to escape the heat down in Tucson, and the shady picnic areas and trails still get a lot of use by those who don't carry binoculars. If you're heading out for the day, arrive early—parking is very limited. To reach Madera Canyon, take the Continental Road/Madera Canyon exit off I-19; from the exit, it's another 12 miles southeast. The canyon is open daily from dawn to dusk for day use; there is a $5 day-use fee.

GOLF   Although there aren't quite as many golf courses in Tucson as in Phoenix, this is still a golfer's town. For last-minute tee-time reservations, contact **Standby Golf** (© **800/655-5345;** www.discountteetimes.com). No fee is charged for this service.

In addition to the public and municipal links, there are numerous resort courses that allow nonguests to play. Perhaps the most famous of these are the two 18-hole courses at **Ventana Canyon Golf and Racquet Club,** 6200 N. Clubhouse Lane (© **520/577-4015**). These Tom Fazio–designed courses offer challenging desert target–style play that is nearly legendary. The 3rd hole on the Mountain Course is one of the most photographed holes in the West.

As famous as Ventana Canyon courses are, it's the 27-hole **Omni Tucson National Golf Resort and Spa,** 2727 W. Club Dr. (© **520/575-7540;** www.tucsonnational.com), a traditional course that is perhaps more familiar to golfers as the site of the annual Tucson Open.

El Conquistador Country Club, 10555 N. La Cañada Dr., Oro Valley (℗ 520/ 544-1800; www.elconquistadorcc.com), with two 18-hole courses and a 9-hole course, offers stunning (and very distracting) views of the Santa Catalina Mountains.

There are many public courses around town. The **Arizona National,** 9777 E. Sabino Greens Dr. (℗ 520/749-3636; www.arizonanationalgolfclub.com), incorporates stands of cacti and rocky outcroppings into the course layout. **Heritage Highlands Golf & Country Club,** 4949 W. Heritage Club Blvd., Marana (℗ 520/579-7000; www.heritagehighlands.com), is a championship desert course at the foot of the Tortolita Mountains.

Tucson Parks and Recreation operates five municipal golf courses, of which the **Randolph** and **Dell Urich,** 600 S. Alvernon Way (℗ 520/791-4161), are the premier courses. The former has been the site of Tucson's LPGA tournament. Other municipal courses include **El Rio,** 1400 W. Speedway Blvd. (℗ 520/791-4229); **Silverbell,** 3600 N. Silverbell Rd. (℗ 520/791-5235); and **Fred Enke,** 8251 E. Irvington Rd. (℗ 520/791-2539). This latter course is the city's only desert-style golf course. For general information and tee-time reservations for any of the municipal courses, visit **www.tucsoncitygolf.com**.

HIKING   Tucson is nearly surrounded by mountains, most of which are protected as city and state parks, national forest, or national park, and within these public areas are hundreds of miles of hiking trails. See the listings for Saguaro National Park and Sabino Canyon Recreation Area, above.

Tucson Mountain Park, at the end of Speedway Boulevard, is adjacent to Saguaro National Park and preserves a similar landscape. The parking area at Gates Pass, on Speedway, is a favorite sunset spot.

With Tucson's city limits pushing right out to the boundary of the Coronado National Forest, there are some excellent hiking options in Tucson's northern foothills. The **Ventana Canyon Trail** begins at a parking area adjacent to the Loews Ventana Canyon Resort (off Sunrise Dr., west of Sabino Canyon Rd.) and leads into the Ventana Canyon Wilderness. Over near the Westward Look Resort is the **Pima Canyon Trail,** which leads into the Ventana Canyon Wilderness and is reached off Ina Road just east of Oracle Road. Both of these trails provide classic desert canyon hikes of whatever length you feel like hiking (a dam at 3 miles on the latter trail makes a good turnaround point).

Catalina State Park, 11570 N. Oracle Rd. (℗ 520/628-5798), is set on the rugged northwest face of the Santa Catalina Mountains, between 2,500 and 3,000 feet high. Hiking trails here lead into the Pusch Ridge Wilderness; however, the favorite park day hike is the 5.5-mile round-trip to **Romero Pools,** a refreshing destination on a hot day. Admission to the park is $6 per vehicle ($3 between Memorial Day and Labor Day). There are horseback-riding stables adjacent to the park, and within the park is an ancient Hohokam ruin.

One of the reasons Tucson is such a livable city is the presence of the cool (and, in winter, snow-covered) pine forests of 8,250-foot Mount Lemmon. Within the **Mount Lemmon Recreation Area,** at the end of the Catalina Highway (also now called the Sky Island Scenic Byway), are many miles of trails, and the hearty hiker can even set out from down in the lowland desert and hike up into the Alpine forests. For a more leisurely excursion, drive to the top to start your hike. Keep in mind that in winter, when the weather is pleasant in Tucson, people may be skiing up here. There is a $5-per-vehicle charge to use any of the sites within this recreation area. Even if you only plan to pull off at a roadside parking spot and ogle the view, you'll need to stop at the roadside ticket kiosk at the base of the mountain and pay your fee.

HORSEBACK RIDING   In addition to renting horses and providing guided trail rides, the stables below offer sunset rides with cookouts. Reservations are a good idea.

Pusch Ridge Stables, 13700 N. Oracle Rd. (℃ **520/825-1664;** www.puschridge stables.com), is adjacent to Catalina State Park and Coronado National Forest. Rates are $30 for 1 hour, $45 for 2 hours, and $35 for a sunset ride.

Over on the east side of Tucson, there's **Spanish Trail Outfitters** (℃ **520/749-0167;** www.spanishtrailoutfitters.com), which leads rides into the foothills of the Santa Catalina Mountains off Sabino Canyon Road. Rates are $35 for a 1-hour ride, $55 for a 2-hour or sunset ride.

HOT-AIR BALLOONING   The ballooning season in Tucson runs October through April. **Balloon America** (℃ **520/299-7744;** www.balloonridesusa.com) offers flights over the desert ($225) or a more adventurous trip over the foothills of the Santa Catalina Mountains ($475). **Fleur de Tucson Balloon Tours** (℃ **520/529-1025;** www.fleurdetucson.net) offers rides over the Tucson Mountains, Saguaro National Park, and the Avra Valley. Rates are $210 to $230 per person, including brunch or hors d'oeuvres and a champagne toast.

WILDFLOWER VIEWING   Bloom time varies from year to year, but April and May are good times to view native wildflowers in the Tucson area. While the crowns of white blossoms worn by saguaro cacti are among the most visible blooms in the area, other cacti are far more colorful. **Saguaro National Park** and **Sabino Canyon Recreation Area** are among the best local spots to see saguaros, other cacti, and various wildflowers in bloom. If you feel like heading farther afield, the wildflower displays at **Picacho Peak State Park,** between Tucson and Casa Grande, are considered the most impressive in the state.

SHOPPING

El Presidio Historic District around the Tucson Museum of Art is the city's center for crafts shops. This area is home to Old Town Artisans and the Tucson Museum of Art museum shop. The **"Lost Barrio"** on the corner of Southwest Park Avenue and 12th Street (a block off Broadway) is a good place to look for Mexican imports and southwestern-style home furnishings.

Mark Sublette Medicine Man Gallery, Santa Fe Square, 7000 E. Tanque Verde Rd. (℃ **520/722-7798**), has the best and biggest selection of old Navajo rugs in the city, as well as Mexican and other Hispanic textiles, Acoma pottery, basketry, and artwork by cowboy artists. With its museum-quality goods (antique Navajo rugs, kachinas, furniture, and a huge selection of old Native American jewelry), **Morning Star Traders,** 2020 E. Speedway Blvd. (℃ **520/881-2112**), just may be the best store of its type in the entire state.

WHERE TO STAY

If you're looking to stay in a B&B, several agencies can help. The **Arizona Association of Bed and Breakfast Inns** (℃ **800/752-1912;** www.arizona-bed-breakfast.com) has several members in Tucson. **Mi Casa Su Casa** (℃ **800/456-0682** or 480/990-0682; www.azres.com) will book you into one of its many home-stays (informal B&Bs) in the Tucson area or elsewhere in the state, as will **Arizona Trails Travel Services** (℃ **888/799-4284** or 480/837-4284; www.arizonatrails.com), which also books tour and hotel reservations.

Best **Two World-Class Spas**

Two of the world's greatest spas are located in and around Tucson. If you want to be pampered by the best, you can't go wrong at either of the following:

Canyon Ranch Health Resort, 8600 E. Rockcliff Rd. (© **800/742-9000** or 520/749-9000; www.canyonranch.com), offers the sort of complete spa experience that's available at only a handful of places around the country. On staff are doctors; psychotherapists; fitness instructors; massage therapists; and tennis, golf, and racquetball pros. Services offered include everything from health and fitness assessments and sports activities to facials and cooking demonstrations. Guests stay in a variety of spacious and very comfortable accommodations. Three gourmet, low-calorie meals are served daily with options for total daily caloric intake (don't worry, you won't go hungry). All this pampering does not come cheap—4-night packages here start at $5,380 double—but the rates do include all meals and a variety of spa services and programs.

Focusing on what it calls "life balancing," **Miraval Life in Balance,** 5000 E. Via Estancia Miraval, Catalina (© **800/232-3969**; www.miravalresorts.com), one of the country's most exclusive health spas, emphasizes stress management, self-discovery, and relaxation rather than facials and mud baths. To this end, activities at the all-inclusive resort include meditation, tai chi, Pilates, and yoga; more active types can go hiking, mountain biking, and rock climbing (on an outdoor climbing wall). Of course, such desert classics as horseback riding, tennis, and swimming are also available. Miraval also offers fitness/nutrition consultations, cooking demonstrations, exercise classes, and skin care and facials. Guest rooms, many of which have views of the Santa Catalina Mountains, are done in a southwestern style. While very large, most of the bathrooms have showers but no tubs. Rates start at $890 double and include all meals, classes, and a $110 per-person per-day credit for spa service, a round of golf, or private consultation.

Arizona Inn   With its pink-stucco buildings and immaculately tended gardens, the historic Arizona Inn is an absolute oasis. If you're searching for Old Arizona charm but also demand modern levels of comfort, then look no further. Most rooms have original or reproduction period furniture; some also have fireplaces. Most suites have private patios or enclosed sun porches. The main dining room is a casually elegant hall with plenty of outdoor seating as well.

2200 E. Elm St., Tucson, AZ 85719. © **800/933-1093** or 520/325-1541. Fax 520/881-5830. www.arizonainn.com. 95 units. Mid-Jan to mid-Apr from $289 double, from $389 suite; mid-Apr to May and Oct to mid-Dec from $199 double, from $299 suite; June–Sept from $149 double, from $249 suite; mid-Dec to mid-Jan $239 double, from $339 suite. Summer rates include full breakfast and complimentary evening ice-cream fountain. Children 2 and under stay free in parent's room (10 and under during summer). AE, DC, MC, V. **Amenities:** 3 restaurants; pool; 2 tennis courts; well-equipped exercise room; access to nearby health club. *In room:* Fridge.

Casa Tierra Adobe Bed & Breakfast Inn   If you've come to Tucson to be in the desert, this modern adobe B&B is worth considering. Built to look as though it has been here since Spanish colonial days, Casa Tierra is surrounded by 5 cactus-studded acres on the west side of Saguaro National Park. Sunsets are enough to take your breath away. Rooms open onto a landscaped courtyard, which is surrounded by a covered seating area. The outdoor whirlpool makes a perfect stargazing spot.

11155 W. Calle Pima, Tucson, AZ 85743. © 866/254-0006 or 520/578-3058. www.casatierratucson.com. 4 units. $135–$195 double; $200–$325 suite. Rates include full breakfast. 2-night minimum stay. AE, DISC, MC, V. Closed June 16–Aug 14. **Amenities:** Exercise room. *In room:* Fridge.

Hacienda del Sol Guest Ranch Resort With its colorful southwestern styling, historical character, desert gardens, and ridge-top setting, Hacienda del Sol is one of the most distinctive hotels in Tucson. Rooms have rustic and colorful Mexican character, with a decidedly artistic flair. If you prefer more modern accommodations, ask for a suite; if you want loads of space, ask for a casita. **The Grill** (see below) is one of Tucson's best restaurants.

5601 N. Hacienda del Sol Rd., Tucson, AZ 85718. © 800/728-6514 or 520/299-1501. www.haciendadelsol.com. 30 units. Early Jan to May $175–$280 double, $345–$355 suite, $395–$495 casita; June–Sept $99–$154 double, $165–$185 suite, $185–$300 casita; Oct to early Jan $155–$250 double, $320–$330 suite, $360–$485 casita. 2-night minimum stay weekends and holidays. Children under 6 stay free in parent's room. AE, DC, DISC, MC, V. **Amenities:** Restaurant; pool. *In room:* Fridge.

Hilton Tucson El Conquistador Golf & Tennis Resort (Kids) With the Santa Catalina Mountains as a backdrop, this resort in Tucson's northern foothills boasts a spectacular setting. Keep in mind that if you stay here, you'll be at least 30 minutes from downtown. Most guest rooms are built around a central courtyard with manicured lawns and a large oasis of swimming pools, one of which has a long water slide. Consequently, this place is a great choice for families. All units feature southwestern-influenced furniture, marble bathrooms, and balconies or patios.

10000 N. Oracle Rd., Tucson, AZ 85704. © 800/325-7832 or 520/544-5000. Fax 520/544-1222. www.hiltonelconquistador. com. 428 units. Jan to late May $259–$490 double, from $339 suite; late May to early Sept $119–$290 double, from $179 suite; early Sept to Dec $219–$420 double, from $299 suite. Rates do not include $10 daily service fee. Children under 18 stay free in parent's room. AE, DC, DISC, MC, V. Valet parking $11. Pets accepted ($50 deposit). **Amenities:** 5 restaurants; 4 pools; 1 9-hole and 2 18-hole golf courses; 31 tennis courts; 2 exercise rooms; spa.

La Posada Lodge and Casitas There are several different types of rooms here, but the best are the "Western"-style rooms, which have a sort of retro south-of-the-border decor that includes headboards painted with classic Mexican scenes. Casitas, which are the largest and most expensive rooms here, have a similar decor. There are also some fun rooms with a 1950s retro feel. The attractive rooms, pleasant pool area, and on-site Mexican restaurant together make this an excellent and economical choice.

5900 N. Oracle Rd., Tucson, AZ 85704. © 800/810-2808 or 520/887-4800. Fax 520/293-7543. www.laposadalodge. com. 72 units. $89–$149 double. Rates include continental breakfast. Children under 18 stay free in parent's room. AE, DC, DISC, MC, V. Pets accepted. **Amenities:** Restaurant; pool; exercise room.

The Lodge on the Desert This restored romantic getaway in central Tucson dates from 1936. It offers a lush and relaxing retreat comparable in many ways to the Arizona Inn (though certainly not as deluxe). Numerous hacienda-style adobe buildings are tucked amid the cactus and orange trees. Inside the rooms, you'll find a mix of contemporary and southwestern furnishings; many units have beamed ceilings or fireplaces, and some are carpeted while others have tile floors.

306 N. Alvernon Way, Tucson, AZ 85711. © 800/456-5634 or 520/325-3366. Fax 520/327-5834. www.lodgeonthe desert.com. 35 units. Mid-Jan to mid-Apr $189–$299 double; mid-Apr to mid-May and mid-Sept to mid-Jan

$129–$204 double; mid-May to mid-Sept $89–$154 double. Rates include full breakfast. Children under 12 stay free in parent's room. AE, DC, DISC, MC, V. Pets accepted ($50 deposit plus $20 per night). **Amenities:** Restaurant; pool.

Loews Ventana Canyon Resort *Best*   For breathtaking scenery and superb facilities, no other Tucson accommodations can compare. The Santa Catalina Mountains rise behind the property, and despite its many amenities, the resort is firmly planted in the desert. Flagstone floors in the lobby give the public rooms a rugged but luxurious appeal. Guest rooms have balconies overlooking city lights or mountains; some have fireplaces. Bathrooms include tubs built for two. The **Ventana Room** (see below) is one of Tucson's finest restaurants. There are jogging and nature trails and a playground on the property.

7000 N. Resort Dr., Tucson, AZ 85750. © 800/234-5117 or 520/299-2020. Fax 520/299-6832. www.loewshotels. com/hotels/tucson. 398 units. Early Jan to late May from $365 double, from $750 suite; late May to early Sept from $150 double, from $295 suite; early Sept to early Jan from $325 double, from $700 suite. Children under 18 stay free in parent's room. AE, DC, DISC, MC, V. **Amenities:** 5 restaurants; 2 pools; 2 18-hole golf courses; 8 tennis courts; exercise room; full-service spa. *In room:* Fridge.

Tanque Verde Ranch   Tanque Verde, the most luxurious guest ranch in Tucson, borders both Saguaro National Park and the Coronado National Forest. The bird-watching here is excellent, and other activities include guided hikes, horseback rides, guided mountain-bike rides, and nature walks. Rooms are spacious and comfortable; many have fireplaces, patios, and fridges, but don't expect a TV. The casitas are absolutely huge and are among the most luxurious accommodations in the state.

14301 E. Speedway Blvd., Tucson, AZ 85748. © 800/234-DUDE or 520/296-6275. Fax 520/721-9426. www.tanque verderanch.com. 74 units. Mid-Dec to Apr $380–$510 double; May–Sept $300–$385 double; Oct to mid-Dec $315–$405 double. Rates include all meals and ranch activities. Children 3 and under $15 extra. AE, DC, DISC, MC, V. **Amenities:** Dining room; 3 pools (1 indoor); 5 tennis courts; exercise room; small full-service spa. *In room:* Fridge.

WHERE TO DINE

Foodies fond of the latest culinary trends will find plenty of spots to satisfy their cravings. Concentrations of creative restaurants can be found along East Tanque Verde Road and at foothills resorts and shopping plazas. On the other hand, if you're on a tight dining budget, look for early-bird dinners, which are quite popular with retirees.

Café Poca Cosa NEW MEXICAN   The food here is not just *any* Mexican food; it's imaginative and different and is served in a bold and angular space that belies the location on the ground floor of a parking garage. The cuisine consists of creations such as chicken with a dark mole sauce made with Kahlúa, chocolate, almonds, and chiles. The staff is courteous and friendly. This lively restaurant is an excellent value, especially at lunch.

110 E. Pennington St. © 520/622-6400. Reservations highly recommended. Main courses $10–$12 lunch, $16–$20 dinner. DISC, MC, V. Tues–Thurs 11am–9pm; Fri–Sat 11am–10pm.

El Charro Café SONORAN MEXICAN   Located in an old stone building in El Presidio Historic District, El Charro is Tucson's oldest family-operated Mexican restaurant. Its specialty is *carne seca,* an air-dried beef similar to jerky. The cafe can be packed at lunch, so arrive early or late. The adjacent ¡**Toma!,** a colorful bar/cantina, is under the same ownership. There are other El Charro locations at 6310 E. Broadway (© **520/745-1922**), 4699 E. Speedway Blvd. (© **520/325-1922**), and 100 W. Orange Grove (© **520/615-1922**).

311 N. Court Ave. © 520/622-1922. www.elcharrocafe.com. Reservations recommended for dinner. Main courses $6–$18. AE, DC, DISC, MC, V. Sun–Thurs 11am–9pm; Fri–Sat 11am–10pm.

The Grill REGIONAL   Located in a 1920s hacienda-style former dude ranch, The Grill is known for its classic southwestern styling and great views of the city. For openers, consider the delicious wild-mushroom bisque, which comes with ancho chile–truffle crème fraîche. Despite the price, the dry-aged New York strip steak is deservedly the most popular entree on the menu and is big enough for two people to share. Sunday brunch here is a treat.

At the Hacienda del Sol Guest Ranch Resort, 5601 N. Hacienda del Sol Rd. ⓒ 520/529-3500. www.haciendadelsol.com. Reservations recommended. Main courses $26–$38; Sun brunch $32. AE, DC, DISC, MC, V. Mon–Sat 5:30–10pm; Sun 10am–2pm and 5:30–10pm.

Janos ⟨Best⟩ SOUTHWESTERN/REGIONAL   Janos Wilder is the city's most celebrated chef. The menu changes both daily and seasonally, with such complex offerings as Guaymas shrimp with morel cream sauce, beef tournedos with foie gras butter and truffle sauce, and lamb chops with a complex spicy southwestern rub. This is about as formal a restaurant as you'll find in this otherwise very casual city. Janos's adjacent J Bar dishes up equally memorable fare at much more moderate prices.

At The Westin La Paloma, 3770 E. Sunrise Dr. ⓒ 520/615-6100. www.janos.com. Reservations highly recommended. Main courses $28–$50; 5-course tasting menu $80 ($115 with wine). AE, DC, MC, V. Mon–Thurs 5:30–9pm; Fri–Sat 5:30–9:30pm.

Pinnacle Peak Steakhouse ⟨Kids⟩ STEAKHOUSE   The Pinnacle Peak Steakhouse specializes in family dining in a fun cowboy atmosphere. Once through the doors, you'll be surprised at the authenticity of the place, which really does resemble a dining room in Old Tombstone. Be prepared for crowds—this place is very popular with tour buses. Oh, and by the way, wear a necktie into this place, and it will be cut off! Actually, lots of people wear ties just so they can have them added to the collection tacked to the ceiling.

6541 E. Tanque Verde Rd. ⓒ 520/296-0911. www.pinnaclepeaktucson.com. Reservations not accepted. Main courses $8–$19. AE, DC, DISC, MC, V. Mon–Fri 5–10pm; Sat–Sun 4:30–10pm.

Terra Cotta SOUTHWESTERN   Terra Cotta is Arizona's original southwestern restaurant, offering a combination of creative cooking, casual atmosphere, and local artwork. A brick oven is used to make pizzas, while salads, sandwiches, small plates, and main dishes flesh out the long menu. With so many choices, it's often difficult to decide, but the must-have signature dish is garlic custard, served with a warm salsa vinaigrette and herbed hazelnuts. The poblano chiles rellenos stuffed with either shrimp or adobo pork are another can't-miss choice.

3500 E. Sunrise Dr. ⓒ 520/577-8100. www.dineterracotta.com. Reservations recommended. Main courses $8–$13 lunch, $13–$30 dinner. AE, DC, DISC, MC, V. Daily 11:30am–10pm.

Ventana Room NEW AMERICAN   *Ventana* means "window" in Spanish, and the views through the windows of this restaurant are every bit as memorable as the food that comes from the kitchen. Whether you're seated overlooking the resort's waterfall or the lights of Tucson far below, you'll likely have trouble concentrating on your food, but do try; you wouldn't want to miss any of the subtle nuances of such dishes as the velvety Dover sole or grilled buffalo tenderloin with seared foie gras.

At Loews Ventana Canyon Resort, 7000 N. Resort Dr. ⓒ 520/615-5494. www.ventanaroom.com. Reservations highly recommended. Jackets recommended for men. Prix-fixe menus $75–$105. AE, DC, DISC, MC, V. Tues–Thurs 6–9pm; Fri–Sat 6–10pm.

TUCSON AFTER DARK

The best place to look for entertainment listings is in the free *Tucson Weekly.*

The **Downtown Arts District** is home to the Temple of Music and Art, the Tucson Convention Center Music Hall, and several nightclubs. The **University of Arizona campus,** only a mile away, is another hot spot for entertainment.

THE PERFORMING ARTS   Tucson's largest performance venue is the **Tucson Convention Center (TCC) Music Hall,** 260 S. Church Ave. (© **520/791-4266**). It's the home of the **Tucson Symphony Orchestra** (© **520/882-8585** or 520/792-9155; www.tucsonsymphony.org) and is where the Arizona Opera Company and Ballet Arizona usually perform.

Downtown Tucson's **Fox Theatre,** 17 W. Congress St. (© **520/624-1515;** www.fox tucsontheatre.org), a recently restored old movie palace, is the city's newest performance hall. Originally opened in 1930, the Fox is the city's most beautiful place to catch some live music, a play, or even a classic or independent film.

THE CLUB & MUSIC SCENE   Tucson is the mariachi capital of the United States, and no one should visit without spending at least one evening listening to some of these strolling minstrels. **La Fuente,** 1749 N. Oracle Rd. (© **520/623-8659**), serves up good Mexican food, but what really draws the crowds is the live nightly mariachi music. If you just want to listen and not have dinner, you can hang out in the lounge.

Club Congress, 311 E. Congress St. (© **520/622-8848**), is Tucson's main alternative-music venue, with usually a couple of nights of live music each week. With its tropical decor and overabundance of potted plants setting the mood, **El Parador** restaurant and dance club, 2744 E. Broadway (© **520/881-2808**), is Tucson's favorite spot for lively Latin jazz and salsa performances (salsa lessons on Fri nights).

THE BAR SCENE   ¡Toma!, 311 N. Court Ave. (© **520/622-1922**), always has a festive atmosphere and serves good margaritas. If you can't afford the lap of luxury, you can at least pull up a chair at **Flying V Bar & Grill,** in the Loews Ventana Canyon Resort, 7000 N. Resort Dr. (© **520/299-2020**). Set next to a waterfall, this watering hole has a grand view over the golf course and Tucson.

CASINOS   **Casino del Sol,** 7406 S. Camino de Oeste (© **800/344-9435;** www.casino delsol.com), is southern Arizona's largest casino and offers slot machines, keno, bingo, and a card room. **Desert Diamond Casino,** 7350 S. Nogales Hwy. (© **866/DDC-WINS** or 520/393-2700; www.desertdiamondcasino.com), operated by the Tohono O'odham tribe and located 3 miles from Mission San Xavier del Bac, has similar offerings.

5 Central Arizona & Sedona

THE VERDE VALLEY

The Verde Valley has long been a magnet for both wildlife and people. With its headwaters in the Juniper Mountains of the Prescott National Forest, the Verde River flows down through a rugged canyon before meandering slowly across the Verde Valley. Contact the **Cottonwood Chamber of Commerce,** 1010 S. Main St., Cottonwood (© **928/634-7593;** http://cottonwood.verdevalley.com).

The **Verde Canyon Railroad,** 300 N. Broadway, Clarkdale (© **800/320-0718;** www. verdecanyonrr.com), traverses unspoiled desert that's inaccessible by car. The views of the rocky canyon walls and green waters of the Verde River are quite dramatic, and if you look closely along the way, you'll see ancient Sinagua cliff dwellings. Tickets are $55 for adults, $50 for seniors, and $35 for children 2 to 12.

Consisting of two impressive stone pueblos, **Montezuma Castle National Monument,** Exit 289 off I-17 (© **928/567-3322;** www.nps.gov/moca), is among the best preserved of Arizona's **cliff dwellings.** The more intriguing pueblo is set in a shallow cave 100 feet up in a cliff overlooking Beaver Creek. Construction on this five-story, 20-room village began sometime in the early 12th century.

The **Hacienda de la Mariposa,** 3875 Stagecoach Rd., Camp Verde (© **888/520-9095** or 928/567-1490; www.lamariposa-az.com; $195–$225 double), is a modern Santa Fe–style inn set on the banks of Beaver Creek and is just up the road from Montezuma Castle National Monument. The almond croissants at **Old Town Café,** 1025 "A" N. Main St., downtown Cottonwood (© **928/634-5980**), are the best we've ever had. If that isn't recommendation enough for you, there are also good salads and sandwiches, such as a grilled panini of smoked turkey, spinach, and tomatoes.

GETTING THERE   Take I-17 north from Phoenix or south from Flagstaff to Camp Verde. Then take Ariz. 260 north through the Verde Valley for 12 miles to Cottonwood.

JEROME

Clinging to the slopes of Cleopatra Hill high on Mingus Mountain, Jerome looks much as it did when it was an active mining town, and has been designated a National Historic Landmark. For information, contact the **Jerome Chamber of Commerce** (© **928/634-2900;** www.jeromechamber.com).

Wandering the streets, soaking up the atmosphere, and shopping are the main pastimes in Jerome. However, you can also learn about the town's past at the **Jerome State Historic Park,** off U.S. 89A on Douglas Road in the lower section of town (© **928/634-5381**). Located in a 1916 mansion, the Jerome State Historic Park has exhibits on mining and a few of the mansion's original furnishings. Admission is $3.

For that classic mining-town tourist-trap experience, follow the signs up the hill from downtown Jerome to the **Gold King Mine** (© **928/634-0053;** www.goldking mine.net), where you can see lots of old, rusting mining equipment and maybe even catch a demonstration.

The **Raku Gallery,** 250 Hull Ave. (© **928/639-0239;** www.rakugallery.com), has gallery space on two floors and walls of glass across the back, with views of the red rocks of Sedona in the distance. The **Jerome Gallery,** 240 Hull Ave. (© **928/634-7033**), has good-quality ceramics, jewelry, and home furnishings. **Sky Fire,** 140 Main St. (© **928/634-8081**), features an interesting collection of southwestern and ethnic gifts and furnishings.

The **Connor Hotel of Jerome,** 164 Main St. (© **800/523-3554** or 928/634-5006; www.connorhotel.com; $95–$155 double), is a renovated historic hotel, with spacious rooms having large windows. The tiny **Flatiron Café,** at Main Street and Hull Avenue (© **928/634-2733**), serves breakfast and light meals.

GETTING THERE   Follow directions to the Verde Valley, above. Jerome is 8 miles west of Cottonwood on Ariz. 89A.

SEDONA & OAK CREEK CANYON

The town of Sedona claims the most beautiful setting in the Southwest. Red-rock buttes, eroded canyon walls, and mesas rise into blue skies. Off in the distance, the Mogollon Rim looms, its forests of juniper and ponderosa pine dark against the red rocks. With this drop-dead scenery and a plethora of resorts and good restaurants, Sedona makes an excellent base for exploring central Arizona.

ESSENTIALS

GETTING THERE   Sedona is 116 miles north of Phoenix. Take **I-17** North, then **Ariz. 179** north to Sedona. From Jerome and the Verde Valley, take **Ariz. 89A** east to Sedona. From Flagstaff, take scenic **Ariz. 89A** south.

VISITOR INFORMATION   The **Sedona–Oak Creek Canyon Chamber of Commerce Visitor Center,** 331 Forest Rd. (© **800/288-7336** or 928/282-7722; www.sedonachamber.com), operates a visitor center at the corner of Ariz. 89A and Forest Road near uptown Sedona.

SPECIAL EVENTS & FESTIVALS   In late September, **Sedona Jazz on the Rocks** (© **928/282-1985;** www.sedonajazz.com) brings world-class jazz to Sedona. From mid-November until early January, more than a million lights illuminate Los Abrigados Resort (© **800/521-3131** or 928/282-1777; www.redrockfantasy.com) in a **Red-Rock Fantasy.**

RED-ROCK COUNTRY

Just south of Sedona, on Ariz. 179, you'll see the aptly named **Bell Rock** on the east side of the road. From Bell Rock, you can see **Cathedral Rock** to the west. Adjacent to Bell Rock is **Courthouse Rock,** and not far from Bell Rock and visible from Chapel Road are **Eagle Head Rock,** the **Twin Nuns,** and **Mother and Child Rock** (to the left of the Twin Nuns).

If you head west through Sedona on Ariz. 89A and turn left onto Airport Road, you'll drive up onto **Airport Mesa.** The views from here are among the best in the region, and there are some easy hiking trails.

One of the most beautiful areas around Sedona is **Boynton Canyon.** Drive west out of Sedona on Ariz. 89A, turn right on Dry Creek Road, take a left at the T intersection, and at the next T intersection take a right. On the way to Boynton Canyon, look north from Ariz. 89A and you'll see **Coffee Pot Rock,** rising 1,800 feet above Sedona. Three pinnacles, known as the **Three Golden Chiefs** by the Yavapai tribe, stand beside Coffee Pot Rock. As you drive up Dry Creek Road, on your right you'll see **Capitol Butte.** Just outside the gates of Enchantment Resort is a parking area for the **Boynton Canyon Trail.** From the parking area, the trail leads 3 miles up into the canyon.

In this same area, you can visit the Sinagua cliff dwellings at **Palatki Ruins.** To reach the ruins, follow the directions to Boynton Canyon, but instead of turning right at the second T intersection, turn left onto unpaved Boynton Pass Road (Forest Rd. 152). Follow this road to another T intersection and go right onto F.R. 125, then veer right onto F.R. 795. To visit the ruins, you'll need a Red Rock Pass, which costs $5 per car for a 1-day pass. Don't try this if the roads are at all muddy.

South of Ariz. 89A and a bit west of the turnoff for Boynton Canyon is Upper Red Rock Loop Road, which leads to **Crescent Moon Recreation Area** (formerly known as Red Rock Crossing), a National Forest Service recreation area that has become a must-see spot. Hiking trails beginning here lead up to Cathedral Rock. Park admission is $7 per vehicle.

If you continue on Upper Red Rock Loop Road, it turns into Lower Red Rock Loop Road and reaches **Red Rock State Park** (© **928/282-6907**), which flanks Oak Creek. The views here take in many of the rocks above, and you have the additional bonus of being right on the creek. Park admission is $6 per vehicle.

OAK CREEK CANYON

The **Mogollon Rim** is a 2,000-foot escarpment cutting diagonally across central Arizona and on into New Mexico. Of the many canyons cutting down from the rim, Oak

Creek Canyon is the best known. Ariz. 89A runs through the canyon from Flagstaff to Sedona, winding its way down from the rim and paralleling Oak Creek. If you have a choice of how first to view Oak Creek Canyon, come at it from the north. Your first stop after traveling south from Flagstaff will be the **Oak Creek Canyon Vista,** which gives you a view far down the valley to Sedona and beyond.

The most popular spot in all of Oak Creek Canyon is **Slide Rock State Park** (© **928/282-3034**). Located 7 miles north of Sedona on the site of an old homestead, this park preserves a natural water slide. Admission is $8 per vehicle ($10 during summer).

By far the most spectacular and popular hike in the canyon is the 6-mile round-trip up the **West Fork of Oak Creek.** Stop by the Sedona–Oak Creek Chamber of Commerce to pick up a free map.

WHAT TO SEE & DO AROUND TOWN

Sedona's most notable architectural landmark is the **Chapel of the Holy Cross,** located south of town just off Ariz. 179 (© **928/282-4069**). The chapel sits high above the road and is built right into the red rock.

The **Sedona Arts Center,** 15 Art Barn Rd., at Ariz. 89A (© **888/954-4442** or 928/282-3809; www.sedonaartscenter.com), near the north end of uptown Sedona, serves both as a gallery for work by local and regional artists and as a theater for plays and music performances.

You'll find the greatest concentration of galleries and shops in the uptown area of Sedona (along Ariz. 89A just north of the Y) and at **Tlaquepaque** (© **928/282-4838;** www.tlaq.com), the arts-and-crafts village on Ariz. 179, at the bridge over Oak Creek on the south side of town.

With a large collection of contemporary and antique Navajo rugs, **Garland's Navajo Rugs,** 411 Hwy. 179 (© **928/282-4070;** www.garlandsrugs.com), is the premier Navajo rug shop in Sedona. **Hoel's Indian Shop,** 9589 N. Hwy. 89A, 10 miles north of Sedona (© **928/282-3925;** www.hoelsindianshop.com), is one of the finest Native American arts-and-crafts galleries in the region.

WHERE TO STAY & DINE

If you're searching for tranquillity or a romantic retreat amid the cool shade of Oak Creek Canyon, the **Briar Patch Inn,** 3190 N. Hwy. 89A (© **888/809-3030** or 928/282-2342; www.briarpatchinn.com; $179–$379 double), is the place and offers good value. This inn's cottages are set amid beautiful shady grounds where bird songs and a babbling creek set the mood.

The **Enchantment Resort,** 525 Boynton Canyon Rd. (© **800/826-4180** or 928/282-2900; www.enchantmentresort.com; $295–$425 double), is pricey, but more than lives up to its name. The setting is breathtaking, and the pueblo-style architecture of the hotel blends in with the canyon landscape. There are plenty of ways to keep busy—pools, tennis courts, a fitness center, hiking trails, and a putting green. The affiliated **Mii amo** spa is one of the finest in the state.

Saddle Rock Ranch, 255 Rock Ridge Dr. (© **866/282-7640** or 928/282-7640; www.saddlerockranch.com; $169–$209 double), offers not only stunning views, but also classic Western ranch styling. **Sky Ranch Lodge,** Airport Road (© **888/708-6400** or 928/282-6400; www.skyranchlodge.com; $75–$189 double), a motel atop Airport Mesa, is another good, inexpensive place with fantastic views.

The **Cowboy Club Grille & Spirits,** 241 N. Hwy. 89A (© **928/282-4200**), may look like an ordinary steakhouse, but it's more than your average meat-and-potatoes joint. You can have fried cactus strips with black-bean caramel gravy, followed by grilled salmon with chipotle hollandaise. Because the view of Boynton Canyon is so much a part of the experience of dining at **Yavapai Restaurant,** at the Enchantment Resort, 525 Boynton Canyon Rd. (© **928/204-6000**), we recommend lunch or a sunset dinner. The menu focuses on southwestern flavors and changes regularly.

6 Flagstaff & the Grand Canyon

FLAGSTAFF: EN ROUTE TO THE GRAND CANYON

Perhaps best known as the jumping-off point for trips to the South Rim of the Grand Canyon, Flagstaff also has a wide variety of accommodations and restaurants, one of the state's finest museums, and a lively cultural community.

ESSENTIALS

GETTING THERE   By Plane   America West serves **Pulliam Airport,** 3 miles south of town off I-17.

By Train   Amtrak (© **800/USA-RAIL;** www.amtrak.com) provides daily service from Los Angeles (11 hr.) and Chicago (32 hr.) to its station at 1 E. Rte. 66. There are direct bus connections to the Grand Canyon (see below).

By Car   The main routes into Flagstaff are **I-40** from the east (Albuquerque) and west (Los Angeles), and **I-17** from the south (Phoenix). **Ariz. 89A** connects Flagstaff to Sedona by way of Oak Creek Canyon, and **U.S. 180** connects Flagstaff with the South Rim of the Grand Canyon.

VISITOR INFORMATION   Contact the **Flagstaff Visitor Center,** 1 E. Rte. 66 (© **800/842-7293** or 928/774-9541; www.flagstaffarizona.org).

WHAT TO SEE & DO

Flagstaff is northern Arizona's center for outdoor activities. Chief among them is snow skiing at **Arizona Snowbowl** (© **928/779-1951;** www.arizonasnowbowl.com) on the slopes of Mount Agassiz, from which you can see all the way to the North Rim of the Grand Canyon. All-day lift tickets are $44 for adults, $25 for children 8 to 12. In summer, you can ride a chairlift almost to the summit and enjoy the expansive views

---

Get Your Kicks on Route 66

The roadside establishments that survive on Route 66 are strange time capsules from another era, vestiges of this old highway's legendary past. Fans of retro architecture, design, and memorabilia shouldn't miss it. As you pass through Holbrook, look for the **Wigwam Motel** and the life-size concrete dinosaurs. West of Winslow, watch for the **Twin Arrows** truck stop. In Seligman, you'll find both the **Delgadillo's Snow Cap Drive-In,** where fast food is served amid outrageous decor, and **Angel & Vilma Delgadillo Memorabilia,** something of a Route 66 information center and souvenir shop. In Kingman, check out **Mr. D'z Route 66 Diner,** a modern rendition of a 1950s diner (housed in an old gas station/cafe). Across the street is the restored powerhouse, which dates from 1907 and is home to the Kingman Area Chamber of Commerce Visitor Center, a 1950s-style malt shop, and the **Historic Route 66 Association of Arizona** (© **928/753-5001;** www.azrt66.com).

across seemingly all of northern Arizona. The round-trip lift-ticket price is $10 for adults, $6 for children 8 to 12.

When there's no snow on the ground, there are plenty of hiking trails throughout the San Francisco Peaks, and many national forest trails in the area are open to mountain bikes as well as to hikers. For information on the trails in the Coconino National Forest, contact the **Peaks Ranger District,** 5075 N. Hwy. 89, Flagstaff (© **928/526-0866;** www.fs.fed.us/r3/coconino).

Downtown Flagstaff along Route 66, San Francisco Street, Aspen Avenue, and Birch Avenue is the city's **historic district,** filled with interesting little shops. It's worth a walk even if you aren't shopping.

The small but thorough **Museum of Northern Arizona,** 3101 N. Fort Valley Rd. (© **928/774-5213;** www.musnaz.org), is the ideal first stop on an exploration of northern Arizona. Here you'll learn about the archaeology, ethnology, geology, biology, and fine arts of the region. Admission is $5 adults, $2 children 7 to 17.

Lowell Observatory, 1400 W. Mars Hill Rd. (© **928/774-3358;** www.lowell.edu), is one of the oldest astronomical observatories in the Southwest. The facility consists of several observatories, a large visitor center with fun and educational exhibits, and outdoor displays. Admission is $5 for adults, $2 for children 5 to 17.

WHERE TO STAY & DINE

The **Inn at 410,** 410 N. Leroux St. (© **800/774-2008** or 928/774-0088; www.inn 410.com; $150–$210 double), is one of the best B&Bs in Arizona and provides convenience, pleasant surroundings, comfortable rooms, and delicious breakfasts. One of Arizona's most unusual little B&Bs is in the middle of nowhere along the road from Flagstaff to the Grand Canyon. The **Shooting Star Inn,** 27948 N. Shooting Star Lane, Flagstaff (© **928/606-8070;** www.shootingstarinn.com; $150 double), a large log house, produces its own electricity from photovoltaic panels and offers guests a chance to gaze at the stars through a number of different telescopes.

For great food in a casual atmosphere, try **Cottage Place Restaurant,** 126 W. Cottage Ave. (© **928/774-8431**), which most people in Flagstaff agree serves the best food in town. From a chair by the woodstove at **Beaver Street Brewery,** 11 S. Beaver St. (© **928/779-0079**), you can enjoy several good brews and great pizzas and burgers. People come to Flagstaff's counterculture hangout, **Macy's European Coffee House & Bakery,** 14 S. Beaver St. (© **928/774-2243**), for the espresso and baked goodies, but there are also decent vegetarian pasta dishes, soups, and salads.

The **Museum Club,** 3404 E. Rte. 66 (© **928/526-9434;** www.museumclub.com), is a Flagstaff institution and one of America's classic roadhouses. There's live music, predominantly country and western, most nights.

THE GRAND CANYON SOUTH RIM

A mile deep, 277 miles long, and up to 18 miles wide, the Grand Canyon is truly one of the great natural wonders of the world. By raft, by mule, on foot, and in helicopters and small planes—more than four million people each year come to gaze into this great chasm. You can expect parking problems and traffic congestion, but don't let these inconveniences dissuade you from visiting. Despite the crowds, the Grand Canyon more than lives up to its name and is one of the most amazing sights on earth.

ESSENTIALS

GETTING THERE   By Plane   Grand Canyon Airport, 6 miles south of Grand Canyon Village in Tusayan, primarily handles sightseeing tours and charters.

By Train   Amtrak (© 800/USA-RAIL; www.amtrak.com) provides daily service to Flagstaff (see above) and Williams. From Flagstaff, there's a bus directly to Grand Canyon Village; from Williams, the Grand Canyon Railway excursion train (see below) takes you to Grand Canyon Village.

By Bus   Bus service between Phoenix, Flagstaff, and Grand Canyon Village is provided by **Open Road Tours** (© 800/766-7117 or 602/997-6474; www.openroadtours. com). It charges $27 one-way or $54 round-trip between Flagstaff and the Grand Canyon. **Grand Canyon Coaches** (© 866/235-9422 or 928/638-0821; www.grand canyoncoaches.com) provides a similar service.

By Car   If at all possible, travel into the park by some means *other* than car and avoid the traffic. From Flagstaff, 78 miles away, you can take U.S. 180 directly to the South Rim or U.S. 89 to Ariz. 64 and the east entrance to the park.

VISITOR INFORMATION   You can get advance information by contacting **Grand Canyon National Park,** P.O. Box 129, Grand Canyon, AZ 86023 (© 928/638-7888; www.nps.gov/grca). When you arrive at the park, stop by the **Canyon View Visitor Center,** at Canyon View Information Plaza, 6 miles north of the south entrance. The center is open daily 8am to 5pm. Unfortunately, the information plaza has no adjacent parking, so you'll have to park where you can and then walk or take a free shuttle bus. The nearest places to park are at Mather Point, Market Plaza, park headquarters, and Yavapai Observation Station. If you're parked anywhere in Grand Canyon Village, you'll want to catch the Village Route bus. If you happen to be parked at Yaki Point, you can take the Kaibab Trail Route bus.

GETTING AROUND   Taxi service is available to and from the airport, trail heads, and other destinations (© 928/638-2822). The fare from the airport to Grand Canyon Village is $10 for up to two adults ($5 for each additional person).

March through November, free shuttle buses operate on three routes within the park. The **Village Route** bus circles through Grand Canyon Village throughout the day with frequent stops at the Canyon View Information Plaza, Market Plaza, hotels, campgrounds, and restaurants. The **Hermit's Rest Route** bus takes visitors to eight canyon overlooks west of Bright Angel Lodge. The **Kaibab Trail Route** bus, which stops at the Canyon View Information Plaza, the South Kaibab trail head, Yaki Point, Mather Point, and Yavapai Observation Station, provides the only access to Yaki Point, the trail head for the South Kaibab Trail to the bottom of the canyon. Hikers needing transportation to or from Yaki Point when the bus is not running can use a taxi (© 928/638-2822).

Trans Canyon (© 928/638-2820) offers shuttle service between the South Rim and the North Rim. The fare is $70 one-way; reservations are required.

FEES   The park entry fee is $25 per car and is good for 1 week. Remember not to lose the little paper receipt that serves as your admission pass.

GRAND CANYON VILLAGE & VICINITY: YOUR FIRST LOOK

Grand Canyon Village is the most crowded place in the park, but it also has the most overlooks and visitor services. **Mather Point** is the first overlook you reach if you enter the park through the south entrance, although just before Mather Point, you should now come to the Canyon View Information Plaza. Continuing west, you'll come to **Yavapai Point,** a favorite spot for sunrise and sunset photos and the site of the **Yavapai Observation Station.** This historic building houses a small museum and has excellent views.

Continuing west from Yavapai Point, you'll come to a parking lot at park headquarters and a side road that leads to parking at the Market Plaza, which is one of the closest parking lots to the Canyon View Information Plaza.

In the historic district, in addition to numerous canyon viewpoints, you'll find **El Tovar Hotel** and **Bright Angel Lodge,** both of which are worth brief visits. Adjacent to El Tovar are two historic souvenir and curio shops. **Hopi House Gift Store and Art Gallery,** the first shop in the park, was built in 1905 to resemble a Hopi pueblo and now sells Hopi and Navajo arts and crafts. The nearby **Verkamps Curios** is the main place to look for souvenirs and crafts.

To the west of Bright Angel Lodge, two buildings cling precariously to the rim of the canyon. These are the **Lookout** and **Kolb studios,** both of which are listed on the National Register of Historic Places.

HERMIT ROAD

Hermit Road leads 8 miles west from Grand Canyon Village to Hermit's Rest. Because it is closed to private vehicles March through November, it is also one of the most pleasant places to do a little canyon viewing or easy hiking during the busiest times of year. Free shuttle buses stop at most of the overlooks. From December to February, you can drive your own vehicle along this road, but keep in mind that winters usually mean a lot of snow.

The first two stops are **Trailview Overlook** and **Maricopa Point.** From both, you have a view of the Bright Angel Trail winding down into the canyon from Grand Canyon Village.

Powell Point, the third stop, is the site of a memorial to John Wesley Powell, the first person to navigate the Colorado River through the Grand Canyon.

Next along the drive is **Hopi Point,** from which you can see a long section of the Colorado River, and **Mohave Point,** where you can see Hermit Rapids.

The next stop is at the **Abyss,** the appropriately named 3,000-foot drop created by the Great Mojave Wall. This vertiginous view is one of the most awe-inspiring in the park. Layers of erosion-resistant sandstone have formed the free-standing pillars that are visible from here.

From **Pima Point,** it's possible to see the remains of Hermit Camp on the Tonto Plateau. At the end of Hermit Road stands **Hermit's Rest,** a log-and-stone building that is listed on the National Register of Historic Places.

DESERT VIEW DRIVE

Desert View Drive extends for 25 miles from Grand Canyon Village to Desert View. The first stop is **Yaki Point;** the spectacular view from here encompasses a wide section of the central canyon.

The next stop, **Grandview Point,** affords a view of Horseshoe Mesa, another interesting feature of the canyon landscape. Next along the drive is **Moran Point,** from which you can see a bright-red layer of shale in the canyon walls.

The **Tusayan Museum** (free admission) is the next stop. This small museum is dedicated to the Hopi tribe and ancient Anasazi people who inhabited this region 800 years ago.

At **Lipan Point,** you get one of the park's best views of the Colorado River. From here you can even see a couple of major rapids. From **Navajo Point,** the Colorado River and Escalante Butte are visible.

Desert View, with its trading post, general store, snack bar, service station, information center, bookstore, and watchtower, is the end of this scenic drive. The views are breathtaking from anywhere at Desert View, but the best lookout is from atop the Desert View Watchtower.

OTHER WAYS TO SEE THE CANYON

MULE RIDES   Mule rides into the canyon are one of the most popular activities at Grand Canyon Village. Trips of various lengths and to different destinations are offered. There are 1-day trips to Plateau Point and overnight trips to Phantom Ranch, the only lodge actually in the canyon. Make a reservation through **Xanterra Parks & Resorts** (© **888/297-2757** or 303/297-2757; www.grandcanyonlodges.com). If at the last minute (5 days or fewer from the day you want to ride) you decide you want to go on a mule trip, contact Grand Canyon National Park Lodges at its Arizona phone number (© **928/638-2631**) for the remote possibility that there may be space available. If you arrive at the canyon without a reservation and decide that you'd like to go on a mule ride, stop by the Bright Angel Transportation Desk to get your name put on the next day's waiting list.

RIDING THE RAILS   The **Grand Canyon Railway** (© **800/843-8724** or 928/ 773-1976; www.thetrain.com), which runs from Williams to the South Rim of the Grand Canyon at Grand Canyon Village, uses early-20th-century steam engines (during the summer) and 1950s-vintage diesel engines (during other months) to pull 1920s passenger cars and a dome coach car. The fun trip offers great scenery and a trip back in time, and allows you to avoid the traffic in Grand Canyon Village.

A BIRD'S-EYE VIEW   Airplane and helicopter flights over the Grand Canyon remain one of the most popular ways to see these natural wonders. Companies offering tours by small plane include **Air Grand Canyon** (© **800/247-4726** or 928/638-2686; www.airgrandcanyon.com) and **Grand Canyon Airlines** (© **866/235-9422** or 928/638-2359; www.grandcanyonairlines.com). Helicopter tours are available from **Maverick Airstar Helicopters** (© **866/689-8687** or 702/262-6199; www.airstar.com) and **Grand Canyon Helicopters** (© **800/541-4537** or 928/638-2764; www.grand canyonhelicoptersaz.com).

HIKING THE CANYON

No visit to the canyon is complete without journeying below the rim. While the views don't get any better than they are from the top, they do change considerably. This is some of the most rugged and strenuous hiking anywhere in the United States, and for this reason anyone attempting even a short walk should be well prepared. Wear sturdy footgear and carry at least 1 to 2 quarts of water for even a short hike. A long hike into or out of the canyon in the heat can require drinking more than a gallon of water. Remember while hiking that mules have the right of way. Don't attempt to hike from the rim to the Colorado River and back in a day; many who have tried this have died.

DAY HIKES   Loop-trail day hikes are not possible in the Grand Canyon. The easiest day hikes are those along the **Rim Trail.** Head out early and get off at the Abyss shuttle stop. From here, it's a 4-mile hike to Hermit's Rest, which makes a great place to take a break. You can catch a shuttle bus back to the village.

Trails leading down into the canyon include the **Bright Angel Trail, South Kaibab Trail, Grandview Trail,** and **Hermit Trail.** If you plan to hike for more than 30 minutes, carry 2 quarts of water per person.

BACKPACKING   There are many miles of trails deep in the canyon and several established campgrounds for backpackers. The best times of year to backpack in the canyon are spring and autumn. Be sure to carry at least 2 quarts, and preferably 1 gallon, of water.

A **Backcountry Use Permit** is required of all hikers planning to overnight in the canyon unless you'll be staying at Phantom Ranch. Make reservations as soon as possible. Reservations are taken in person, by mail, by fax (but not by phone), and over the Internet. Contact the **Backcountry Information Center,** Grand Canyon National Park, P.O. Box 129, Grand Canyon, AZ 86023 (© **928/638-7875** Mon–Fri 1–5pm for information; fax 928/638-2125; www.nps.gov/grca). The office begins accepting reservations on the first of every month for the following 5 months.

There are **campgrounds** at Indian Garden, Bright Angel Campground (near Phantom Ranch), and Cottonwood, but hikers are limited to 2 nights per trip at each of these campgrounds (except Nov 15–Feb 28, when 4 nights are allowed at each campground).

The *Backcountry Trip Planner* contains information to help you plan your itinerary. It's available through the Backcountry Information Center (see contact information, above). Maps are available through the **Grand Canyon Association,** P.O. Box 399, Grand Canyon, AZ 86023 (© **800/858-2808** or 928/638-2481; www.grandcanyon. org), and at bookstores and gift shops within the national park.

WHERE TO STAY

Keep in mind that the Grand Canyon is one of the most popular national parks in the country; make reservations as far in advance as possible.

INSIDE THE PARK Xanterra Parks & Resorts, 6312 S. Fiddlers Green Circle, Suite 600N, Greenwood Village, CO 80111 (© **888/297-2757** or 303/297-2757; www.grandcanyonlodges.com), operates the hotels inside the park. Reservations are taken up to 13 months in advance. It is *sometimes* possible, due to cancellations and no-shows, to get a same-day reservation by calling © **928/638-2631.**

El Tovar Hotel, completely renovated in 2005, is the park's premier lodge. Built of local rock and Oregon pine, it's a rustic yet luxurious mountain lodge that perches on the edge of the canyon, and has awe-inspiring views from some rooms. If you want modern amenities and a fairly large room, **Thunderbird & Kachina Lodges** should be your in-park choice. **Bright Angel Lodge & Cabins** is the most affordable lodge in the park, but you'll pay more for a private bathroom. The rim cabins are the most popular and are usually booked a year in advance. **Phantom Ranch** (© **928/638-3283** for reconfirmations) is the only lodge at the bottom of the Grand Canyon and is very popular. The accommodations are in rustic stone-walled cabins or gender-segregated dormitories. Prices include meals, which must also be reserved ahead.

IN TUSAYAN (OUTSIDE THE SOUTH ENTRANCE)   If you can't get a room in the park, this is the next closest place to stay. If you want lots of resort-style amenities, head to the **Best Western Grand Canyon Squire Inn** (© **800/622-6966** or 928/638-2681; www.grandcanyonsquire.com; $75–$190 double), which has extensive recreational options, including a bowling alley. With its mountain-lodge styling, Native American cultural shows, modern guest rooms, and large restaurant, the **Grand Hotel** (© **888/634-7263** or 928/638-3333; www.visitgrandcanyon.com; $99–$223 double) is the best choice in Tusayan.

Fifty-four miles north of Flagstaff on U.S. 89, the **Cameron Trading Post Motel** (© **800/338-7385** or 928/679-2231; www.camerontradingpost.com; $49–$99 double), offers some of the most attractive rooms anywhere in the vicinity of the Grand Canyon. Most have balconies and some have views of the Little Colorado River.

CAMPGROUNDS   **Mather Campground,** in Grand Canyon Village, has more than 300 campsites. Reservations can be made up to 5 months in advance and are required for stays between April and November (reservations not accepted for other months). Contact the **National Park Reservation Service** (© **800/365-2267** or 301/722-1257; http://reservations.nps.gov). **Desert View Campground,** with 50 sites, is 25 miles east of Grand Canyon Village and open from mid-May to mid-October only. No reservations are accepted. The **Trailer Village RV park,** with 80 RV sites, is in Grand Canyon Village. Reservations can be made up to 13 months in advance by contacting **Xanterra Parks & Resorts** (© **888/297-2757** or 303/297-2757).

Two miles south of Tusayan is the U.S. Forest Service's **Ten-X Campground,** open May through September.

You can also camp just about anywhere within the **Kaibab National Forest,** which borders Grand Canyon National Park, as long as you are more than a quarter-mile away from Ariz. 64/U.S. 180. For more information, contact the **Tusayan Ranger District,** Kaibab National Forest, P.O. Box 3088, Grand Canyon, AZ 86023-3088 (© **928/638-2443;** www.fs.fed.us/r3/kai).

WHERE TO DINE

You'll find several restaurants just outside the south entrance in Tusayan. The best of these is the **Canyon Star** (© **928/638-3333**) at the Grand Hotel, and the **Coronado Room** (© **928/638-2681**) at the Best Western Grand Canyon Squire Inn. You'll also find a steakhouse and a pizza place, as well as familiar chains such as McDonald's, Taco Bell, Pizza Hut, and Wendy's.

For quick, inexpensive meals, try Grand Canyon Village's **Bright Angel Fountain,** at the back of the Bright Angel Lodge, which serves hot dogs, sandwiches, and ice cream. **Hermit's Rest Snack Bar** is at the west end of Hermit Road. At Desert View (near the east entrance to the park), there's the **Desert View Trading Post Cafeteria.**

El Tovar Dining Room, in El Tovar Hotel (© **928/638-2631,** ext. 6432), has one of the most awe-inspiring views in the world and serves up good, spicy southwestern food. Book early.

THE GRAND CANYON NORTH RIM

If Grand Canyon Village sounds like it's going to be more human zoo than the wilderness experience you had expected, the North Rim will probably be much more to your liking. The North Rim is on the Kaibab Plateau, more than 8,000 feet high on average. The higher elevation of the North Rim means you'll find dense forests of ponderosa pines, Douglas firs, and aspens interspersed with large meadows.

ESSENTIALS

GETTING THERE   From Flagstaff, take **U.S. 89** north to Bitter Springs, then **U.S. 89A** to Jacob Lake. From there take **Ariz. 67** (the North Rim Pkwy.) to the end at the North Rim.

Trans Canyon (© **928/638-2820**) operates a shuttle between the North Rim and the South Rim. The trip takes 5 hours; the fare is $70 one-way (reservations required).

VISITOR INFORMATION   For information before leaving home, contact **Grand Canyon National Park,** P.O. Box 129, Grand Canyon, AZ 86023 (© **928/638-7888;** www.nps.gov/grca). At the entrance gate, you'll be given a copy of *The Guide,* a small newspaper with information on park activities. There's also an **information desk** in the lobby of the Grand Canyon Lodge.

Note: Visitor facilities at the North Rim are open only from mid-May to mid-October. From mid-October to November (or until snow closes the road to the North Rim), the park is open for day use only. The campground may be open after mid-October, weather permitting.

For more information, see "Essentials" under "The Grand Canyon South Rim," earlier in this chapter.

EXPLORING THE AREA

The best spots for viewing the canyon are Bright Angel Point, Point Imperial, and Cape Royal. **Bright Angel Point** is the closest to Grand Canyon Lodge, and from here you can see and hear Roaring Springs, 3,600 feet below the rim and the North Rim's only water source. At 8,803 feet, **Point Imperial** is the highest point on the North Rim. A short section of the Colorado River can be seen far below, and off to the east the Painted Desert is visible.

Cape Royal, however, is the most spectacular setting on the North Rim, and along the 23-mile road to Cape Royal are several scenic overlooks. Across the road from the **Walhalla Overlook** are the ruins of an Ancestral Puebloan structure, and just before reaching Cape Royal you'll come to the **Angel's Window Overlook,** which gives you a breathtaking view of the natural bridge that forms Angel's Window. Once at Cape Royal, you can follow a trail across this natural bridge to a towering promontory overlooking the valley.

After simply taking in the views, hiking along the rim is the most popular activity. Day hikes of varying lengths are possible here.

If you want to see the canyon from a saddle, contact **Grand Canyon Trail Rides** (© **435/679-8665;** www.canyonrides.com), which offers mule rides varying in length from 1 hour to a full day.

WHERE TO STAY & DINE

Perched right on the canyon rim, **Grand Canyon Lodge,** operated by Xanterra Parks & Resorts (© **303/297-2757,** or 928/638-2611 for same-day reservations; www.grandcanyonnorthrim.com), is listed on the National Register of Historic Places and is one of the most impressive lodges in the national park system. A large dining hall serves straightforward American food. A saloon and a snack bar are outside the lodge's front entrance, and there's a tour desk in the lobby.

Outside the park, you'll find numerous budget motels in Fredonia, Arizona (30 miles west of Jacob Lake), and Kanab, Utah (37 miles west of Jacob Lake). Located 5 miles north of the entrance to the North Rim, **Kaibab Lodge** (© **800/525-0924** or 928/526-0924; www.canyoneers.com) is on the edge of a large meadow where deer can often be seen grazing. The lodge's dining room serves all meals, and the kitchen also prepares box lunches.

CAMPGROUNDS   Located just north of Grand Canyon Lodge, the **North Rim Campground,** with 75 sites and no hookups for RVs, is the only campground at the North Rim. The campground opens in mid-May and may stay open past the mid-October closing of other North Rim visitor facilities. Reservations can be made up to 5 months in advance by contacting the **National Park Reservation Service** (© **800/365-2267** or 301/722-1257; http://reservations.nps.gov).

There are two nearby campgrounds outside the park in the Kaibab National Forest. **DeMotte Park Campground,** the closest to the park entrance, has 23 sites, while **Jacob Lake Campground,** 30 miles north of the park entrance, has 53 sites. Neither takes reservations. You can also camp anywhere in the Kaibab National Forest as long as you're more than a quarter-mile from a paved road or water source.

7 Monument Valley & Canyon de Chelly

MONUMENT VALLEY NAVAJO TRIBAL PARK

You may not be aware of it, but you have almost certainly seen Monument Valley before. This otherworldly landscape has been an object of fascination for years and has served as a backdrop for countless commercials and movies.

Monument Valley is a vast flat plain punctuated by natural cathedrals of sandstone. These huge monoliths rise from the sagebrush with sheer walls that capture the light of the rising and setting sun and transform it into fiery hues. A 17-mile unpaved loop road winds among these 1,000-foot-tall buttes and mesas.

Human habitation has also left its mark. Within the park are more than 100 ancient Anasazi archaeological sites, ruins, and petroglyphs dating from before A.D. 1300. The Navajo have been living in the valley for generations, herding their sheep through the sagebrush scrublands, and some families continue to live here today.

ESSENTIALS

GETTING THERE From Flagstaff, take **U.S. 89** north, then **U.S. 160** east, then **U.S. 163** north. Monument Valley is 200 miles northeast of Flagstaff.

VISITOR INFORMATION & FEES For information, contact **Monument Valley Navajo Tribal Park** (© 435/727-5870; www.navajonationparks.org). May through September, the park is open daily from 6am to 8pm; between October and April, it's open daily from 8am to 5pm. Admission to the park is $5 per adult (free for kids 9 and under). *Note:* Because this is a tribal park and not a federal park, neither the National Park Service's National Park Pass nor its Golden Eagle Pass are valid here.

EXPLORING THE AREA

This is big country and, like the Grand Canyon, primarily a point-and-shoot experience. Because this is reservation land and people still live in Monument Valley, backcountry or off-road travel is prohibited unless you have a licensed guide. So basically the only way to see the park is from the overlook at the visitor center; by driving the park's scenic (but very rough) dirt road; or by taking a four-wheel-drive, horseback, or guided hiking tour.

At the valley overlook parking area in Monument Valley Navajo Tribal Park, you'll find a small museum, gift shop, restaurant, snack bar, campground, and numerous local Navajo guides who offer tours of the park.

Sacred Monument Tours (© 435/727-3218 or 928/380-4527; www.monument valley.net), offers a variety of ways to tour the park. Four-wheel-drive adventures cost from $46 for a 2-hour jeep tour to $82 for a 4-hour tour. To get away from the rumble of engines, a guided hike will run between $57 and $124 per person for hikes of different lengths. Keep in mind that summers can be very hot here. But if nothing but the cowboy thing will do for you in this quintessential Wild West landscape, you can pay $46 for a 1-hour horseback ride up to $267 for an all-day ride.

If you happen to be staying at Goulding's Lodge, then your best bet is to go out with **Goulding's Tours** (© 435/727-3231; www.gouldings.com), which has its office right at the lodge (see "Where to Stay & Dine," below), just a few miles from the park entrance. Goulding's offers 3½-hour jeep tours ($42 for adults, $27 for children under 8) and full-day tours ($75 for adults, $57 for children).

Before leaving the area, you might want to visit **Goulding's Museum and Trading Post,** at Goulding's Lodge. This old trading post was the home of the Gouldings for many years and is set up as they had it back in the 1920s and 1930s. There are also displays about the many movies that have been shot here. The trading post hours vary with the seasons; admission is by donation.

WHERE TO STAY & DINE
In addition to the lodgings listed here, you'll find numerous budget motels 22 miles north of Monument Valley in Mexican Hat, Utah.

Goulding's Lodge, Monument Valley, Utah (© 435/727-3231; www.gouldings.com; $73–$170 double), is the only lodge actually in Monument Valley, and it offers superb views from the balconies of its rooms, which are furnished with southwestern decor. A restaurant serves Navajo and American dishes.

Hampton Inn—Navajo Nation, U.S. 160, in Kayenta (© 800/HAMPTON or 928/697-3170; www.hampton-inn.com; $56–$134 double), is built in a modern Santa Fe style and has spacious rooms.

CANYON DE CHELLY NATIONAL MONUMENT
Canyon de Chelly National Monument consists of two major canyons—**Canyon de Chelly** (pronounced "canyon duh *shay*" and derived from the Navajo word *tsegi,* meaning "rock canyon") and **Canyon del Muerto** (Spanish for "Canyon of the Dead")—as well as several smaller canyons. The canyons extend for more than 100 miles through the rugged slick-rock landscape of northeastern Arizona, draining the seasonal runoff from the snowmelt of the Chuska Mountains.

Canyon de Chelly's smooth sandstone walls of rich reds and yellows contrast sharply with the deep greens of corn, pasture, and cottonwood on the canyon floor. Vast stone amphitheaters form the caves in which the ancient Anasazi built their homes, and today there are more than 100 prehistoric dwelling sites in the area. With its mysteriously abandoned cliff dwellings and breathtaking natural beauty, Canyon de Chelly is certainly as worthy of a visit as the Grand Canyon.

ESSENTIALS
GETTING THERE   Canyon de Chelly is 222 miles northeast of Flagstaff and 110 miles southeast of Monument Valley Navajo Tribal Park. From Flagstaff, the easiest route to Canyon de Chelly is to take **I-40** east to Chambers, then **U.S. 191** north to Chinle. If you're coming down from Monument Valley or Navajo National Monument, **Indian Route 59,** which connects U.S. 160 and U.S. 191, is an excellent road with plenty of beautiful scenery. Take U.S. 191 south to Chinle.

VISITOR INFORMATION   Before leaving home, you can contact **Canyon de Chelly National Monument** (© 928/674-5500; www.nps.gov/cach) for information. The visitor center is open daily, May through September from 8am to 6pm (MST), and October through April from 8am to 5pm. The monument itself is open daily from sunrise to sunset; admission is free.

SEEING THE CANYON
Your first stop at Canyon de Chelly should be the **visitor center,** in front of which is an example of a traditional crib-style hogan, a hexagonal structure of logs and earth that Navajo use both as a home and as a ceremonial center. Inside, a small museum acquaints visitors with the history of Canyon de Chelly, and there's often a silversmith demonstrating Navajo jewelry-making techniques. From here most people tour the canyon by car.

The North and South Rim drives offer very different views of the canyon. The North Rim Drive overlooks Canyon del Muerto, and the South Rim Drive overlooks Canyon de Chelly. Each of the rim drives is around 20 miles in each direction, and with stops it can easily take 3 hours to visit each rim.

THE NORTH RIM DRIVE   The first stop on the North Rim is the **Ledge Ruin Overlook.** On the opposite wall, about 100 feet up from the canyon floor, you can see the Ledge Ruin. The Anasazi occupied this site between A.D. 1050 and 1275. Nearby, at the **Dekaa Kiva Viewpoint,** you can see a lone kiva (circular ceremonial building). This structure was reached by means of toeholds cut into the soft sandstone cliff wall.

The second stop is the **Antelope House Overlook.** The Antelope House ruin takes its name from the paintings of antelopes on a nearby cliff wall. It's believed that the paintings were done in the 1830s. Beneath the ruins, archaeologists have found the remains of an earlier pit house dating from A.D. 693. Though most of the Anasazi cliff dwellings were abandoned sometime after a drought began in 1276, Antelope House had already been abandoned by 1260, possibly because of flood damage. Across the wash from Antelope House, the Tomb of the Weaver was discovered in the 1920s by archaeologists. The ancient tomb contained the well-preserved body of an old man wrapped in a blanket of golden eagle feathers and accompanied by cornmeal, shelled and husked corn, pinyon nuts, beans, salt, and thick skeins of cotton. Also visible from this overlook is **Navajo Fortress,** a red-sandstone butte that the Navajo once used as a refuge from attackers. A steep trail leads to the top of Navajo Fortress, and through the use of log ladders that could be pulled up into the refuge, the Navajo were able to escape their attackers.

The third stop is at **Mummy Cave Overlook,** named for two mummies found in burial urns below the ruins. Archaeological evidence indicates that this giant amphitheater consisting of two caves was occupied from A.D. 300 to 1300. In the two caves and on the shelf between them there are 80 rooms, including three kivas. The central structure between the two caves is interesting because it includes a three-story building characteristic of the architecture in Mesa Verde, New Mexico. Archaeologists speculate that a group of Anasazi migrated here from New Mexico. Much of the original plasterwork of these buildings is still intact and indicates that the buildings were colorfully decorated.

The fourth and last stop on the North Rim is at the **Massacre Cave Overlook.** The cave got its name after an 1805 Spanish military expedition killed more than 115 Navajo at this site. The Navajo at the time had been raiding Spanish settlements that were encroaching on Navajo territory. Accounts of the battle at Massacre Cave differ. One claims that there were only women, children, and old men taking shelter in the cave, although the official Spanish records claim 90 warriors and 25 women and children were killed. Also visible from this overlook is Yucca Cave, which was occupied about 1,000 years ago.

THE SOUTH RIM DRIVE   The South Rim Drive climbs slowly but steadily, and at each stop you're a little bit higher above the canyon floor.

Near the mouth of the canyon, you'll find the **Tunnel Overlook** and, nearby, the **Tsegi Overlook.** *Tsegi* means "rock canyon" in Navajo, and that's just what you'll see when you gaze down from this viewpoint. A short narrow canyon feeds into Chinle Wash, formed by the streams cutting through the canyons of the national monument.

The next stop is **Junction Overlook,** so named because it overlooks the junction of Canyon del Muerto and Canyon de Chelly. Visible here is the Junction Ruin, with its 10 rooms and one kiva. The Anasazi occupied this ruin during the Great Pueblo Period, which lasted from around 1100 until the Anasazi disappeared shortly before

1300. Also visible is First Ruin, perched precariously on a long, narrow ledge. In this ruin are 22 rooms and two kivas.

The next stop, at **White House Overlook,** provides the only opportunity for descending into Canyon de Chelly without a guide or ranger. The **White House Ruins Trail** descends 600 feet to the canyon floor, crosses Chinle Wash, and approaches the White House Ruins. These buildings were constructed both on the canyon floor and 50 feet up the cliff wall in a small cave. You cannot enter the ruins, but you can get close enough to get a good look. You're not allowed to wander off this trail, and please respect the privacy of the Navajo living here. The 2.5-mile round-trip hike takes about 2 hours. Be sure to carry water. If you aren't inclined to hike the trail, you can view the ruins from the overlook. This is one of the largest ruins in the canyon and contains 80 rooms. It was inhabited between 1040 and 1275. Notice the black streaks on the sandstone walls above the White House Ruins. These streaks were formed by seeping water that reacted with the iron in the sandstone. Iron gives the walls their reddish hue. Anasazi artists used to chip away at this black patina to create petroglyphs. Later the Navajo would use paints to create pictographs, painted images of animals, and records of historic events such as the Spanish military expedition that killed 115 Navajo at Massacre Cave. Many of these petroglyphs and pictographs can be seen if you take one of the guided tours into the canyon.

The next stop is at **Sliding House Overlook.** These ruins are built on a narrow shelf and appear to be sliding down into the canyon. Inhabited from about 900 until 1200, Sliding House contained between 30 and 50 rooms. This overlook is already more than 700 feet above the canyon floor, with sheer walls giving the narrow canyon a foreboding appearance.

The **Face Rock Overlook** provides yet another dizzying glimpse of the ever-deepening canyon. Here you gaze 1,000 feet down to the bottom of the canyon. The last stop on the South Rim is one of the most spectacular: **Spider Rock Overlook.** This viewpoint overlooks the junction of Canyon de Chelly and Monument Canyon, and at this wide spot in the canyon stands the monolithic pinnacle called Spider Rock. Rising 800 feet from the canyon floor, the free-standing twin towers of Spider Rock are a natural monument, a geologic wonder. Across the canyon from Spider Rock stands the similarly striking **Speaking Rock,** connected to the far canyon wall.

ALTERNATIVE WAYS OF SEEING THE CANYON   Access to the floor of Canyon de Chelly is restricted, so to enter the canyon *you must be accompanied by either a park ranger or an authorized guide* (unless you're on the White House Ruins Trail). **Navajo guides** charge $20 per hour with a 3-hour minimum and will lead you into the canyon on foot or in your own four-wheel-drive vehicle. **De Chelly Tours** (© **928/674-3772;** www.dechellytours.com) charges $20 per hour, with a 3-hour minimum, to go out in your four-wheel-drive vehicle; if it supplies the vehicle, the cost goes up to $125 for three people for 3 hours.

Another way to see Canyon de Chelly and Canyon del Muerto is on what locals call **shake-and-bake tours,** via six-wheel-drive truck. In summer, these excursions really live up to the name. (In winter, the truck is enclosed to keep out the elements.) The trucks operate out of **Thunderbird Lodge** (© **800/679-2473** or 928/674-5841; www.tbirdlodge.com) and are equipped with seats in the bed. Tours make frequent stops for photographs and to visit ruins, Navajo farms, and rock art. Half-day trips cost $41 per person ($31 for children 12 and under).

If you'd rather use a more traditional means of transportation, you can go on a guided horseback ride. Stables offering horseback tours into the canyon include **Totsonii Ranch** (© **928/755-6209;** www.totsoniiranch.com), which charges $15 per group per hour for the guide and $15 per person per hour.

WHERE TO STAY & DINE

The **Holiday Inn—Canyon de Chelly,** Indian Route 7, Chinle (© **800/HOLIDAY** or 928/674-5000; www.holiday-inn.com/chinle-garcia; $56–$144 double), is the top choice in Chinle. Rooms come with patios or balconies, most facing the cottonwood-shaded pool courtyard. The restaurant serves the best food in town.

Thunderbird Lodge (© **800/679-BIRD** or 928/674-5841; www.tbirdlodge.com; $65–$106 double), built on the site of an early trading post at the mouth of Canyon de Chelly, is the most appealing of the hotels in Chinle and the closest to the national monument. The red-adobe construction is reminiscent of ancient pueblos. American and Navajo meals are served.

Adjacent to the Thunderbird Lodge is the free **Cottonwood Campground,** which doesn't take reservations. In summer, the campground has water and restrooms, but in winter, you must bring your own water, and only portable toilets are available. On South Rim Drive 10 miles east of the Canyon de Chelly Visitor Center, you'll also find the private **Spider Rock Campground** (© **877/910-CAMP** or 928/674-8261; http://home.earthlink.net/~spiderrock), which charges $10 to $15 per night. This campground also has a couple of hogans for rent for $25 per night. The next nearest campgrounds are at **Tsaile Lake** and **Wheatfields Lake,** both south of the town of Tsaile on Indian Route 12. Tsaile is at the east end of the North Rim Drive.

8 The Petrified Forest & Painted Desert

Though petrified wood can be found in almost every state, the "forests" of downed logs here in northeastern Arizona are by far the most spectacular. A 27-mile scenic drive winds through the petrified forest and a small corner of the Painted Desert, providing a fascinating high desert experience.

It may be hard to believe when you drive across this arid landscape, but at one time this was a vast, humid swamp. That was 225 million years ago, when dinosaurs and huge amphibians ruled the earth and giant now-extinct trees grew on the high ground around the swamp. Fallen trees were washed downstream, gathered in piles in still backwaters, and were eventually covered over with silt, mud, and volcanic ash. As water seeped through this soil, it dissolved the silica in the volcanic ash and redeposited this silica inside the cells of the logs. Eventually the silica recrystallized into stone to form petrified wood.

This region was later inundated with water, and thick deposits of sediment buried the logs ever deeper. Eventually, the land was transformed yet again as a geologic upheaval thrust the lake bottom up above sea level. This upthrust of the land cracked the logs into the segments we see today. Wind and water gradually eroded the landscape, once again exposing the now-petrified logs and creating the Painted Desert and the many other colorful and fascinating landscape features of northern Arizona.

Throughout the region you'll see petrified wood in all sizes and colors, natural and polished, being sold in gift stores. This petrified wood comes from private land, *not* the national park. No piece of petrified wood, no matter how small, may be removed from Petrified Forest National Park.

ESSENTIALS

GETTING THERE   Take **I-40** east from Flagstaff or west from Albuquerque. The north entrance to Petrified Forest National Park is 25 miles east of Holbrook on I-40. The south entrance is 20 miles east of Holbrook on **U.S. 180.**

VISITOR INFORMATION & FEES   For further information on the Petrified Forest or the Painted Desert, contact **Petrified Forest National Park,** P.O. Box 2217, Petrified Forest, AZ 86028 (*✆* **928/524-6228;** www.nps.gov/pefo). For information on Holbrook and the surrounding region, contact the **Holbrook Chamber of Commerce,** 100 E. Arizona St. (*✆* **800/524-2459** or 928/524-6558; www.ci.holbrook.az.us). The park is open daily from 8am to 5pm (7am–7pm in summer). The entry fee is $10 per car.

EXPLORING A UNIQUE LANDSCAPE

Petrified Forest National Park has both a north and a south entrance (and visitor centers at both entrances). Connecting the two park entrances is a 27-mile scenic road with more than 20 overlooks. For the most enjoyable visit, start at the southern entrance and work your way north. This way, you'll see the most impressive displays of petrified logs early in your visit.

At the south entrance, you'll find the **Rainbow Forest Museum** (*✆* **928/524-6228**), which has exhibits on the geology and human history of the park. A snack bar here serves sandwiches and ice cream. Just outside the museum is the **Giant Logs self-guided trail,** which winds across a hillside strewn with logs. Almost directly across the parking lot from the museum is the entrance to the **Long Logs** and **Agate House** areas. On the Long Logs trail, you can see more big trees, while at Agate House you will see the ruins of a pueblo built from colorful agatized wood.

Heading north, you pass by the unusual formations known as the **Flattops.** These structures are caused by the erosion of softer soil deposits from beneath a harder and more erosion-resistant layer of sandstone. This is one of the park's wilderness areas (both of the park's visitor centers issue the free permits necessary to backpack into the park's wilderness areas). The **Crystal Forest** is the next stop to the north, named for the beautiful amethyst and quartz crystals that were once found in the cracks of petrified logs.

At the **Jasper Forest Overlook,** you can see logs that include petrified roots, and a little bit farther north, at the **Agate Bridge** stop, you can see a petrified log that forms a natural agate bridge. Continuing north, you'll reach **Blue Mesa,** where pieces of petrified wood form capstones over easily eroded clay soils. As wind and water wear away at the clay beneath a piece of stone, the balance of the stone becomes more and more precarious until it eventually comes toppling down. A 1-mile loop trail here leads into the park's badlands.

Erosion has played a major role in the formation of the Painted Desert, and to the north of Blue Mesa you'll see some of the most interesting erosional features of the area. It's quite evident why these hills of sandstone and clay are known as the **Teepees.** The layers of different color are due to different types of soils and stone and to minerals dissolved in the soil.

Human habitation of the area dates from more than 2,000 years ago, and at **Newspaper Rock,** you can see petroglyphs left by generations of Native Americans. At nearby **Puerco Pueblo,** which was probably constructed around 1400, you can see the remains of homes built by the people who created the park's petroglyphs.

North of Puerco Pueblo, the road crosses I-40. From here to the Painted Desert Visitor Center, there are eight overlooks onto the southernmost edge of the **Painted Desert.** Named for the vivid colors of the soil and stone that cover the land here, the Painted Desert is a dreamscape of pastel colors washed across a barren expanse of eroded hills. At Kachina Point, you'll find the historic **Painted Desert Inn,** open daily from 8am to 4pm. Just inside the park's northern entrance is the **Painted Desert Visitor Center,** which shows a short film explaining the process by which wood becomes fossilized. Adjacent to the visitor center are a cafeteria and a gas station.

WHERE TO STAY

Holbrook is the nearest town to Petrified Forest National Monument, and here you'll find lots of budget chain motels.

Although nearly 50 miles from the park, **La Posada,** 303 E. Second St., Winslow (© **928/289-4366;** www.laposada.org; $89–$129 double), a restored historic railroad hotel, is this region's best and most memorable hotel. The hotel is a reproduction of a Spanish colonial hacienda. If you're willing to sleep on a sagging mattress for the sake of reliving a bit of Route 66 history, consider the concrete wigwams at the **Wigwam Motel,** 811 W. Hopi Dr., Holbrook (© **800/414-3021** or 928/524-3048; www.galerie-kokopelli.com/wigwam; $42–$48 double). This unique motel was built in the 1940s, when unusual architecture was springing up all along Route 66.

9 Albuquerque

Albuquerque may initially strike visitors as nothing more than one big strip mall. But look closely and you'll see ranchers, Native Americans, and Hispanic villagers stocking up on goods to take back to the New Mexico boot heel or the Texas panhandle. Climbing out of the valley is the legendary Route 66, a major route from the East to California before the interstates were built. It's well worth a drive, if only to see the rust time has left. Old court hotels still line the street, many with their funky 1950s signage. One enclave on this route is the University of New Mexico district, with a number of hippie-ish cafes and shops.

Farther downhill is downtown Albuquerque. During the day, this area is all suits and heels, but after dark it becomes a hip nightlife scene. Old Town is also worth a visit; though touristy, it's a unique southwestern village with a graceful, intact Plaza.

ESSENTIALS

GETTING THERE   By Plane   Albuquerque International Sunport (© **505/842-4366**) is in the south-central part of the city, between I-25 on the west and Kirtland Air Force Base on the east, only about 4 miles from downtown. Most hotels have courtesy airport vans, and many car-rental agencies have desks here. In addition, **Checker Airport Express** (© **505/765-1234**) runs to and from city hotels. **ABQ Ride** (© **505/243-7433**), Albuquerque's public bus system, also makes airport stops; it takes about 20 minutes. There is also efficient taxi service to and from the airport.

By Train   Amtrak (© **800/USA-RAIL;** www.amtrak.com) provides daily service from Chicago (trip time: 26 hr.), Flagstaff (5–6 hr.), and Los Angeles (26 hr.) to its station at 214 First St. SW.

By Car   The major routes into Albuquerque are **I-40** from the east (Amarillo) and west (Flagstaff), and **I-25** from the north (Santa Fe and Denver) and south (El Paso).

Central Albuquerque

VISITOR INFORMATION The main office of the **Albuquerque Convention and Visitors Bureau** is at 20 First Plaza NW (℃ **800/284-2282** or 505/842-9918). It's open Monday to Friday 8am to 5pm. There are information centers at the airport, on the lower level at the bottom of the escalator, open daily 9:30am to 8pm; and in Old Town at 303 Romero St. NW (Suite 107), open daily 9am to 5pm.

GETTING AROUND ABQ Ride (℃ **505/243-7433**) cloaks the arterials with its city bus network. Call for information on routes and fares. **Yellow Cab** (℃ **505/247-8888**) serves the city and surrounding area 24 hours a day.

Parking is generally not difficult. Only the large downtown hotels charge for parking. Traffic is a problem only at rush hours. Avoid I-25 and I-40 at the center of town around 5pm.

FAST FACTS For a doctor, call the **Greater Albuquerque Medical Association** (℃ **505/821-4583**). **Presbyterian Hospital** is at 1100 Central Ave. SE (℃ **505/841-1234,** or 505/841-1111 for emergency services). **Walgreens,** 5001 Montgomery St. (℃ **505/881-5210**), runs a 24-hour pharmacy. In Albuquerque, the **sales tax** is 6.75%. An additional **hotel tax** of 6% will be added to your bill.

SPECIAL EVENTS & FESTIVALS The last weekend in June brings the **New Mexico Arts and Crafts Fair** (℃ **505/884-9043;** www.nmartsandcraftsfair.org) to the State Fairgrounds. The fairgrounds also host the **New Mexico State Fair and Rodeo** (℃ **505/265-1791;** http://exponm.com), one of America's top state fairs, for 17 days in early September. In mid-October, there's the **Albuquerque International Balloon Fiesta** (℃ **800/733-9918;** www.balloonfiesta.com), the world's largest balloon rally, with races, contests, and special events.

WHAT TO SEE & DO

Albuquerque Museum of Art and History *Kids* In this museum on the outskirts of Old Town, you can take an interesting journey into New Mexico's past. Drawing on the largest U.S. collection of Spanish colonial artifacts, displays here include Don Quixote–style helmets, swords, and horse armor. You can wander through an 18th-century house compound with adobe floor and walls, and see gear used by *vaqueros,* the original cowboys who came to the area in the 16th century. Kids can spin wool or touch pelts in the hands-on exhibits. Upper floors house permanent art collections and a huge exhibit space where you'll find some extraordinary shows.

2000 Mountain Rd. NW. ℃ 505/243-7255. www.albuquerquemuseum.com. Admission $4 adults, $2 seniors 65 and older, and $1 children 4–12. Tues–Sun 9am–5pm. Closed major holidays.

Balloon Museum *Kids* With the Albuquerque International Balloon Fiesta drawing hundreds of brilliantly colored and imaginatively shaped balloons to the city each October, this new museum's time has come. Opened in 2005, it tells the history of ballooning, from the first flight in France in 1783, with a rooster, sheep, and duck as passengers, to the use of balloons in military, science, and aerospace research. Most poignant are displays of Albuquerque balloonists Maxie Anderson and Ben Abruzzo, who, with Larry Newman, completed the first manned crossing of the Atlantic Ocean in 1978. Kids will enjoy the flight simulator, which tests their ability to fly and land a balloon on target.

9201 Balloon Museum Dr. NE. ℃ 505/768-6020. www.balloonmuseum.com. Admission $4 adults, $2 seniors 65 and older, $1 children 4–12, free for children 3 and under. Tues–Sun 9am–5pm.

Indian Pueblo Cultural Center *Kids* Owned and operated as a nonprofit organization by the 19 pueblos of New Mexico, this is a fine place to begin an exploration of Native American culture. A permanent exhibit depicts the evolution from prehistory to the present of the various pueblos, including displays of the distinctive crafts of each community. The Pueblo House Children's Museum, in a separate building, gives kids a hands-on opportunity to learn about Pueblo culture. On weekends, look for Native American dancers and artisans demonstrating their skills. A restaurant serves traditional Native American foods.

2401 12th St. NW. ℃ 800/766-4405 or 505/843-7270. www.indianpueblo.org. Admission $6 adults, $5 seniors, $3 students, free for children 4 and under. AE, DISC, MC, V. Daily 9am–5:30pm; restaurant 8am–3pm. Closed New Year's Day, Memorial Day, July 4, Labor Day, Thanksgiving, and Christmas.

National Atomic Museum   This is a good introduction to the nuclear age. The 51-minute film *Ten Seconds That Shook the World* is shown several times daily and is well worth seeing. There's a permanent Marie Curie exhibit, full-scale models of the "Fat Man" and "Little Boy" bombs, and displays on the peaceful application of nuclear technology.

1905 Mountain Rd. NW (P.O. Box 5800, MS1490). ℃ **505/245-2137**. Fax 505/242-4537. www.atomicmuseum.com. Admission $5 adults, $4 seniors and children 7–18, free for children 6 and under. Children under 12 not admitted without adult. Group rates available. Daily 9am–5pm. Closed New Year's Day, Easter, Thanksgiving, and Christmas.

New Mexico Museum of Natural History and Science *Kids*   A trip through this museum will take you through 12 billion years of natural history. Highlights include dinosaur skeletons; the Evolator (kids love this!), a simulated time-travel ride that moves and rumbles through 38 million years of history; a walk-in cave showing the inner workings of a volcano; FossilWorks, where paleontologists work behind glass excavating bones of a seismosaurus; and the LodeStar Astronomy Center, a sophisticated planetarium with Virtual Voyages, a simulation theater.

1801 Mountain Rd. NW. ℃ **505/841-2800**. www.nmnaturalhistory.org. Admission $6 adults, $5 seniors, $3 children 3–12, free for children under 3. DynaTheater, Planetarium, and Virtual Voyages cost extra. Buying ticket combinations qualifies you for discounts. Daily 9am–5pm. Jan and Sept closed on Mon except major holidays, when it's open Mon; also closed Thanksgiving and Christmas.

Sandia Peak Tramway *Best*   This is a fun half-day or evening outing with incredible views of the Albuquerque landscape and wildlife. The Sandia Peak tram is a "jigback"; in other words, as one car approaches the top, the other nears the bottom. The two pass halfway through the trip, in the midst of a 1½-mile "clear span" of unsupported cable between the second tower and the upper terminal. There are several hiking trails; La Luz Trail travels to the top of the Sandias and is very steep and scenic. *Note:* The trails on Sandia may not be suitable for children.

10 Tramway Loop NE. ℃ **505/856-7325**. Fax 505/856-6335. www.sandiapeak.com. Admission $15 adults, $13 seniors, $10 children 5–12, free for children under 5. Memorial Day to Labor Day daily 9am–9pm; spring and fall Thurs–Tues 9am–8pm, Wed 5–8pm; ski season Thurs–Tues 9am–8pm, Wed noon–8pm. Closed 2 weeks each spring and fall for maintenance; check the website for details. Parking $1 daily. AE, DISC, MC, V. To reach the base of the tram, take I-25 north to Tramway Rd. (Exit 234), then proceed east about 5 miles on Tramway Rd. (N.M. 556); or take Tramway Blvd., Exit 167 (N.M. 556), north of I-40 approximately 8½ miles.

EXPLORING OLD TOWN

A maze of cobbled courtyard walkways leads to hidden patios and gardens, where many of Old Town's 150 galleries and shops are located. Adobe buildings, many refurbished in the Pueblo Revival style in the 1950s, are grouped around the tree-shaded **Plaza,** created in 1780. Pueblo and Navajo artisans often display their pottery, blankets, and jewelry on the sidewalks lining the Plaza. (Look especially for silver bracelets and strung turquoise. For something cheaper, buy a dyed corn necklace.)

When Albuquerque was established in 1706, the first building erected by the settlers was the cozy **Church of San Felipe de Neri,** with wonderful stained-glass windows and vivid *retablos* (religious paintings). Next door to the church is the **Rectory,** built about 1793. Also on the north Plaza is **Loyola Hall,** the Sister Blandina Convent, built originally of adobe in 1881 as a residence for Sisters of Charity teachers who worked in the region. When the Jesuit fathers built **Our Lady of the Angels School,** 320 Romero St., in 1877, it was the only public school in Albuquerque.

The **Antonio Vigil House,** 413 Romero St., is an adobe-style residence with traditional viga ends sticking out over the entrance door. The **Florencio Zamora Store,** 301 Romero St., was built in the 1890s of "pugmill" adobe for a butcher and grocer. The **Jesus Romero House,** 205 Romero St., was constructed by another grocer in 1915. Just down the street, the **Jesus Romero Store,** built in 1893, has Territorial and Queen Anne structural features. On the south Plaza, the **Manuel Springer House**'s hipped roof and bay windows are still visible under its present-day commercial facade. The adjacent **Cristobal Armijo House,** a banker's two-story adobe, combines Italianate and Queen Anne architectural styles.

Casa Armijo, in the 200 block of San Felipe Street, dates from before 1840; it was a headquarters for both Union and Confederate troops during the Civil War. The nearby **Ambrosio Armijo House and Store,** also on San Felipe, an 1882 adobe structure, once had the high false front of wooden boards so typical of Old West towns in movies. The **Herman Blueher House,** 302 San Felipe St., built by a businessman in 1898, is a three-story Italianate mansion with fancy porches on two levels, now obscured by storefronts.

An excellent Old Town historical walking tour starts at the Albuquerque Museum of Art and History (see above) at 11am Tuesday through Sunday during spring, summer, and fall. The museum also publishes a brochure for a self-guided walking tour.

SHOPPING

The best buys in Albuquerque are southwestern regional items, including arts and crafts of all kinds—traditional Native American and Hispanic as well as contemporary works. If you want a real bargain in Native American arts and crafts, **Skip Maisel's,** 510 Central Ave. SW (© **505/242-6526**), is the place to shop. You'll find a broad range of quality and price here in goods such as pottery, weavings, and kachinas. Fifty artisans show their talents at the lovely cooperative **Amapola Gallery,** 205 Romero St. (© **505/242-4311**), off a cobbled courtyard. You'll find pottery, paintings, textiles, carvings, baskets, jewelry, and other items.

WHERE TO STAY

Hacienda Antigua Hacienda Antigua, a 200-year-old adobe home that's a 20-minute drive from the airport, was once the first stagecoach stop out of Old Town in Albuquerque. Now, it's one of Albuquerque's most elegant inns, with an artistically landscaped courtyard. Rooms are gracefully outfitted with antiques, fireplaces, custom toiletries, and VCRs. *Tip:* Light sleepers, beware—the Santa Fe Railroad runs by this inn, with one to three trains passing by each night.

6708 Tierra Dr. NW, Albuquerque, NM 87107. © **800/201-2986** or 505/345-5399. Fax 505/345-3855. www.hacienda ntigua.com. 8 units. $129–$209 double. Additional person $25. Rates include gourmet breakfast. AE, MC, V. Free parking. Pets welcome with $30 fee. **Amenities:** Pool.

Hotel Albuquerque at Old Town   This completely renovated hotel just 5 minutes from Old Town offers artfully decorated rooms with views and excellent service. No Albuquerque hotel is closer to top tourist attractions than this former Sheraton, which recently underwent a $16-million makeover. The cathedral-style lobby has Spanish colonial furnishings and art, a theme that carries into the guest rooms. They're medium-size, with comfortable beds and medium-size bathrooms with outer vanities.

800 Rio Grande Blvd. NW, Albuquerque, NM 87104. ✆ **877/901-ROOM** or 505/843-6300. Fax 505/842-8426. www.hotel abq.com. 188 units. $99–$209 double; $149–$350 junior suite double. Children stay free in parent's room. AE, DC, DISC, MC, V. Free parking. **Amenities:** 2 restaurants; pool.

Hotel Blue *Value*   If you like the bustle of a city stay but your bank balance prohibits the Hyatt, this is your place. A total remodel in 2001 turned this five-story 1960s hotel into a comfortable Art Deco inn with the color blue as a theme. It's nothing fancy but neither are the prices. Rooms are medium-size with a small bathroom that has a two-sink outer vanity. Beds are awesomely comfortable. A hot breakfast greets you in the mornings. Old Town is a brisk 20-minute walk away.

717 Central Ave. NW. ✆ **877/878-4868** or 505/924-2400. Fax 505/924-2465. www.thehotelblue.com. 134 units. $69 double; $99 suite. Price includes hot breakfast. AE, DC, DISC, MC, V. Free parking. **Amenities:** Pool.

Hyatt Regency Albuquerque *Kids*   For a luxury stay right downtown, this is the place, pure shiny gloss and Art Deco. The lobby features a sky-lit and palm-shaded fountain, and the hotel's public areas feature an extensive art collection, including original Frederic Remington sculptures. Rooms are spacious, with views of the mountains. The hotel is located right next door to the Galeria, a shopping area, and has a number of shops itself.

330 Tijeras Ave. NW, Albuquerque, NM 87102. ✆ **800/233-1234** or 505/842-1234. Fax 505/843-2710. www.hyatt. com. 395 units. Weekdays $225 double, weekends $105 double; $350–$700 suite. AE, DC, DISC, MC, V. Self-parking $12; valet $16. **Amenities:** Restaurant; pool; health club.

Hyatt Regency Tamaya Resort and Spa *Best*   It's 15 minutes outside of the city, in the hills above the lush Rio Grande Valley, but this pueblo-style resort is *the* spot for a get-away-from-it-all luxury vacation. It offers a 16,000-square-foot full-service spa and fitness center, an 18-hole Twin Warriors Championship Golf Course designed by Gary Panks, and views of the Sandia Mountains. Rooms are spacious, with large tile bathrooms. Request one that faces the mountains for one of the state's more spectacular vistas.

1300 Tuyuna Trail, Santa Ana Pueblo, NM 87004. ✆ **800/55-HYATT** or 505/867-1234. www.tamaya.hyatt.com. 350 units. May–Oct $245–$415; Nov–Apr $199–$305, depending on the type of room. Suite rates available upon request. Inquire about spa, horseback riding, golf, and family packages. AE, DC, DISC, MC, V. Free parking. From I-25 take Exit 242, following U.S. 550 west to Tamaya Blvd.; drive 1½ miles to the resort. **Amenities:** 2 restaurants; 3 pools; golf course; 2 tennis courts; health club and spa. *In room:* Fridge.

WHERE TO DINE

Artichoke Cafe CONTINENTAL   An art gallery as well as a restaurant, this popular spot has modern paintings and sculptures set against azure walls. Start with an artichoke steamed with three dipping sauces or roasted and stuffed with forest mushrooms and rock shrimp. For lunch, there are a number of salads and gourmet sandwiches, as well as dishes such as garlic and lime prawns with orzo. At dinner, try the pumpkin ravioli with butternut squash, spinach, and ricotta filling.

424 Central Ave. SE. ✆ **505/243-0200.** www.artichokecafe.com. Reservations recommended. Main courses $7–$12 lunch, $13–$24 dinner. AE, DC, DISC, MC, V. Mon–Fri 11am–2:30pm; Mon 5:30–9pm; Tues–Sat 5:30–10pm; Sun 5–9pm.

Graze (Best) NEW AMERICAN   The place offers a chance to sample the divine creations of chef Jennifer James. Be aware that this isn't a chicken-fried-steak kind of place, though I wouldn't be surprised to see some refined version of that on this inventive menu. Set in a minimalist room, with hardwood floors and sunny colored walls, it's a fun spot for a culinary adventure. The portion sizes here are intentionally small, with the notion that diners will order many and share, though they're larger than tapas, so will suffice for a meal for a medium-size appetite. You might try the "piccolo frito," flash-fried calamari, with baby tomatoes, garbanzo beans, and basil; or the grilled tuna, with nori, daikon salad, and nicely sweet ponzu sauce.

3128 Central Ave. SE. (✆) 505/268-4729. www.grazejj.com. Reservations recommended on weekend nights. Individual plates $2–$25. AE, DISC, MC, V. Mon–Thurs 11am–10pm; Fri–Sat 11am–11pm; Sun noon–9pm.

Range Cafe (Kids) NEW MEXICAN/AMERICAN   This cafe, about 15 minutes north of Albuquerque, is a perfect place to stop on your way out of town. However, the food's so good you may just want to make a special trip. Housed in what was once an old drugstore, the restaurant has a pressed-tin ceiling and is decorated with Western touches. The cuisine ranges from enchiladas to chicken-fried steak to elegantly prepared meals. Taos Cow ice cream is a must for dessert. Two other branches of the restaurant in Albuquerque have similar food offerings (4200 Wyoming Blvd. NE, (✆) **505/293-2633;** and 2200 Menaul Blvd. NE, (✆) **505/888-1660**).

925 Camino del Pueblo (P.O. Box 1780), Bernalillo. (✆) 505/867-1700. www.rangecafe.com. Reservations accepted for 8 or more. Breakfast and lunch $5–$10; dinner $9–$25. AE, DISC, MC, V. Summer Sun–Thurs 7:30am–10pm; winter Sun–Thurs 7:30am–9:30pm; a half-hour later on Fri–Sat. Closed Thanksgiving and Christmas.

Sadie's (Value) (Kids) NEW MEXICAN   Many New Mexicans lament the lost days when this restaurant was in a bowling alley. Though the current dining room is a little too big and the atmosphere a little too bright, the food is simply some of the best in New Mexico, with tasty sauces and large portions. Try the enchilada, either chicken or beef, or the stuffed sopaipilla dinner. There's a full bar, with excellent margaritas (and TV screens for you sports fans).

6230 4th St. NW. (✆) 505/345-5339. Main courses $7–$15. AE, DC, DISC, MC, V. Mon–Sat 11am–10pm; Sun 10am–9pm.

ALBUQUERQUE AFTER DARK

Current listings appear in the two daily newspapers; detailed weekend arts calendars can be found in the Thursday *Tribune* and the Friday *Journal.* The monthly *On the Scene* also carries entertainment listings.

THE PERFORMING ARTS   The **New Mexico Symphony Orchestra** ((✆) **800/ 251-6676** for tickets and information, or 505/881-9590; www.nmso.org) performs at Popejoy Hall, on the University of New Mexico campus; it also presents highly recommended outdoor concerts at the Rio Grande Zoo band shell. The **New Mexico Ballet Company** ((✆) **505/292-4245;** www.nmballet.org) has several performances a year at Popejoy Hall.

THE CLUB & MUSIC SCENE   Top acts from each coast, including nationally televised comedians, are booked at **Laffs Comedy Cafe,** San Mateo Boulevard and Osuna Road ((✆) **505/296-5653;** www.laffscomedy.com).

   O'niell's Pub, 3211 Central NE. ((✆) **505/256-0564**), a favorite club in the University of New Mexico area, serves up good pub fare as well as live local music on Saturday nights and Celtic and bluegrass on Sunday evenings. **Burt's Tiki Lounge,** 313

Gold Ave. (© **505/243-BURT**), has the city's best variety of drinks. The club offers live music Thursday through Sunday.

OASIS IN THE DESERT: A SIDE TRIP TO BOSQUE DEL APACHE NATIONAL WILDLIFE REFUGE

Bosque del Apache National Wildlife Refuge is a haven for migratory waterfowl such as snow geese and cranes. Particularly if you're here November through March, the experience is thrilling, not only for the variety of birds—more than 300 species—but also for the sheer numbers of them. Huge clouds of snow geese and sandhill cranes take flight at dawn and dusk, the air filling with the sounds of their calls and their wings flapping. In early December, the refuge may harbor as many as 45,000 snow geese, 57,000 ducks of many different species, and 18,000 sandhill cranes. There are also plenty of raptors about, including numerous red-tailed hawks and northern harriers (sometimes called marsh hawks), Cooper's hawks and kestrels, and even bald and golden eagles. The refuge has a 15-mile auto tour loop; drive very slowly. Dawn is the best time to be here.

GETTING THERE   Bosque del Apache is about a 1½-hour drive from Albuquerque. Follow **I-25** to the San Antonio exit. At the main intersection, turn south onto N.M. 1. In 3 miles you'll be on refuge lands, and another 4 miles will bring you to the excellent **visitor center** (© **505/835-1828**). The refuge is open daily year-round.

10 White Sands National Monument

Arguably the most memorable natural area in this part of the Southwest, White Sands National Monument preserves the best part of the world's largest gypsum dune field, an area of 275 square miles of pure white gypsum sand reaching out over the floor of the Tularosa Basin in wavelike dunes. Plants and animals have evolved in special ways to adapt to the bright white environment here. Some creatures have a bleached coloration to match the whiteness all around them, and some plants have evolved means for surviving the smothering pressures of the blowing sands.

The surrounding mountains—the Sacramentos to the east, with their forested slopes, and the serene San Andres to the west—are composed of sandstone, limestone, sedimentary rocks, and pockets of gypsum. Over millions of years, rains and melting snows dissolved the gypsum and carried it down into Lake Lucero. Here the hot sun and dry winds evaporate the water, leaving the pure white gypsum to crystallize. Then the persistent winds blow these crystals, in the form of minuscule bits of sand, in a northeastern direction, adding them to growing dunes. As each dune grows and moves farther from the lake, new ones form in what seems an endless procession.

The dunes are especially enchanting at sunrise and under the light of a full moon, but you'll have to camp to experience this extraordinary sight (see below). If you're not camping, you'll probably want to spend only a couple of hours here.

ESSENTIALS

GETTING THERE   The visitor center is 15 miles southwest of Alamogordo on **U.S. 70/82** (*Note:* Due to missile testing on the adjacent White Sands Missile Range, this road is sometimes closed for up to 2 hr. at a time.) The nearest major airport is El Paso International, 90 miles away. You can drive from there or take a commuter flight from Albuquerque to Alamogordo–White Sands Regional Airport. By car, take **I-25** south from Albuquerque or north from El Paso to Las Cruces. From there, take **U.S. 70** east to White Sands.

VISITOR INFORMATION   Contact **White Sands National Monument,** P.O. Box 1086, Holloman AFB, NM 88330-1086 (© **505/479-6124;** www.nps.gov/whsa). When driving near or in the monument, tune your radio to 1610 AM for information on what's happening.

ADMISSION FEES & HOURS   Admission is $3 for adults age 17 and over (free for children 16 and under). Memorial Day to Labor Day, the visitor center is open from 8am to 7pm, and Dunes Drive is open from 7am to 9pm. The rest of the year, the visitor center is open from 8am to 5pm, and Dunes Drive is open from 7am to sunset.

SEEING THE HIGHLIGHTS

The 16-mile **Dunes Drive** loops through the "heart of sands" from the visitor center. Information available at the center tells you what to look for on your drive. Sometimes the winds blow the dunes over the road, which must then be rerouted. The dunes are, in fact, all moving slowly to the northeast, pushed by prevailing southwest winds, some at the rate of as much as 20 feet a year.

In the center of the monument, the road itself is made of hard-packed gypsum (it can be especially slick after an afternoon thunderstorm, so drive cautiously!). Visitors are invited to get out of their cars at established parking areas and explore a bit; some like to climb a dune for a better view of the endless sea of sand. If you'd rather experience the park by hiking instead of the long drive, a good option right near the entrance is the **Big Dune Trail.** It takes you on a 45-minute loop along the edges of the dunes and then into their whiteness, ending atop a 60-foot-tall one.

The National Park Service emphasizes that (1) tunneling in this sand can be dangerous, for it collapses easily and could suffocate a person; (2) sand-surfing down the dune slopes, although permitted, can also be hazardous, so it should be undertaken with care, and never near an auto road; and (3) hikers can get lost in a sudden sandstorm should they stray from marked trails or areas.

We strongly recommend camping here, especially to see the dunes at sunrise or under a full moon. If you don't camp, you'll miss both because the park closes at dusk and doesn't reopen until after dawn. There are no campgrounds and no facilities, however, so this is strictly a backcountry adventure. Only tent camping is allowed, and you must register and get clearance from monument headquarters before you pitch yours. Call © **505/479-6124** for information.

11 Carlsbad Caverns National Park

One of the largest and most spectacular cave systems in the world, Carlsbad Caverns encompasses some 80 known caves that snake through the porous limestone reef of the Guadalupe Mountains. Fantastic and grotesque formations fascinate visitors, who find every shape imaginable sculpted in this underground world—frozen waterfalls, strands of pearls, soda straws, miniature castles, ice-cream cones, and everything in between.

ESSENTIALS

GETTING THERE   Take **U.S. 62/180** from either Carlsbad, New Mexico, which is 23 miles to the northeast, or El Paso, Texas (150 miles west). The scenic entrance road to the park is 7 miles long and originates at the park gate at Whites City. Van service to Carlsbad Caverns National Park from Whites City, south of Carlsbad, is provided by **Sun Country Tours/Whites City Services** (© **505/785-2291**).

VISITOR INFORMATION   For more information about the park, contact **Carlsbad Caverns National Park,** 3225 National Parks Hwy., Carlsbad, NM 88220 (✆ **800/967-CAVE** for tour reservations, 505/785-2232 for information about guided tours, or 505/785-3012 for bat flight information; www.nps.gov/cave).

ADMISSION FEES & HOURS   General admission to the park is $6 for adults, $3 for children ages 6 to 15, and free for children under age 6. Admission is good for 3 days and includes entry to the two self-guided walking tours. Guided tours range in price from $7 to $20 depending on the type of tour, and reservations are required. The visitor center and park are open daily from Memorial Day to mid-August from 8am to 7pm; the rest of the year they're open from 8am to 5pm. Closed December 25.

WHAT TO SEE & DO

Two caves, Carlsbad Cavern and Slaughter Canyon, are open to the public. The National Park Service has provided facilities, including elevators, to make it easy for everyone to visit the cavern, and there is wheelchair access.

In addition to the options described below, ask at the visitor center about other ranger-guided tours, including climbing and crawling "wild" cave tours. Be sure to call in advance—some tours are offered only 1 day per week. Spelunkers require special permission from the park superintendent.

CARLSBAD CAVERN TOURS   You can tour the caverns in one of three ways, depending on your time, interest, and level of ability. The first, and least difficult, option is to take the elevator from the visitor center down 750 feet to the start of the self-guided tour of the Big Room. More difficult and time-consuming, but vastly more rewarding, is the 1-mile self-guided tour along the Natural Entrance route, which follows the traditional explorer's route, entering the cavern through the large historic natural entrance. The paved walkway through the natural entrance winds into the depths of the cavern and leads through a series of underground rooms; this tour takes about an hour. Parts of it are steep. At its lowest point, the trail reaches 750 feet below the surface, ending finally at an underground rest area.

Visitors who take either the elevator or the Natural Entrance route begin the self-guided tour of the spectacular Big Room near the rest area. The floor of this room covers 14 acres; the tour, over a relatively level path, is 1¼ miles in length and takes about an hour.

The third option is the 1½-hour ranger-guided Kings Palace tour, which also departs from the underground rest area. This tour descends 830 feet beneath the surface of the desert to the deepest portion of the cavern open to the public. Reservations are required and an additional fee is charged.

TOUR TIPS   Wear flat shoes with rubber soles and heels because of the slippery paths. A light sweater or jacket feels good in the constant temperature of 56°F (13°C), especially when it's 100°F (38°C) outside in the sun. The cavern is well lit, but you

The Bat Cave!

Every sunset from May to October, a crowd gathers at the natural entrance of the cave to watch a quarter of a million bats take flight for a night of insect feasting. (The bats winter in Mexico.) All day long the Mexican free-tailed bats sleep in the cavern; at night they all strike out on an insect hunt.

may want to bring along a flashlight as well. Rangers are stationed in the cave to answer questions.

SLAUGHTER CANYON CAVE TOUR Slaughter Canyon Cave was discovered in 1937 and was mined for bat guano commercially until the 1950s. It consists of a corridor 1,140 feet long with many side passageways. The lowest point is 250 feet below the surface, and the passage traversed by the ranger-guided tours is 1¾ miles long, but more strenuous than hiking through the main cavern. There is also a strenuous 500-foot-rise hike from the parking lot to the cave mouth. The tour lasts about 2½ hours. No more than 25 people may take part in a tour, and then by reservation only. Everyone needs a flashlight (make sure that you have fresh batteries), hiking boots or shoes, and a container of drinking water. Slaughter Canyon Cave is reached via U.S. 180 south 5 miles from Whites City, to a marked turnoff that leads 11 miles into a parking lot.

OTHER GUIDED TOURS Be sure to ask about the Left Hand Tunnel, Lower Cave, Hall of the White Giant, and Spider Cave tours. They vary in degree of difficulty and adventure, from **Left Hand,** which is an easy half-mile lantern tour; to **Spider Cave,** where you can expect tight crawlways and canyonlike passages; to **Hall of the White Giant,** a strenuous tour in which you're required to crawl long distances, squeeze through tight crevices, and climb up slippery flow-stone-lined passages. Call in advance for times of each tour. All depart from the visitor center.

OTHER PARK ACTIVITIES There's a 10-mile one-way scenic loop drive through the Chihuahuan Desert to view **Rattlesnake** and **Upper Walnut canyons.** Picnickers can head for Rattlesnake Springs Picnic Area, on County Road 418 near Slaughter Canyon Cave, a water source for hundreds of years for the Native Americans of the area. Backcountry hikers must register at the visitor center before going out on any of the trails.

12 Santa Fe

With a strong local flavor that's made rich by vibrant Native American and Hispanic communities, Santa Fe has become increasingly sophisticated in recent decades. Visitors flock here for cutting-edge cuisine, world-class opera, first-run art films, and some of the finest artwork in the world, seen easily while wandering on foot from gallery to gallery, museum to museum. They're also enchanted by the city's setting, backed by rolling hills and the blue peaks of the Sangre de Cristo Mountains.

Santa Fe, the oldest capital city in the country, was founded by Spanish governor Don Pedro de Peralta, who built the Palace of the Governors as his capitol on the north side of the central Plaza, where it stands today as an excellent museum of the city's 4 centuries of history. The Plaza, once the terminus of the Santa Fe Trail from Missouri and of the earlier Camino Real from Mexico, is the focus of numerous bustling art markets and Santa Fe's early September fiesta, celebrated annually since 1770. It's also one of the major attractions in the Southwest, and under its portico, Native Americans sit cross-legged, selling their crafts to eager tourists, as they have done for decades.

ESSENTIALS

GETTING THERE **By Plane** Although you can fly to **Santa Fe Municipal Airport** (© 505/955-2900), it's easier to fly to **Albuquerque International Sunport** (© 505/842-4366) and drive from there. From the Santa Fe Municipal Airport, **Roadrunner Shuttle** (© 505/424-3367) meets every flight and takes visitors anywhere in Santa Fe. Car-rental options are also available.

Downtown Santa Fe

0 1/10 mi
0 100 meters

Church
Information
Post Office

Rio Grande Ave.
Griffin St.
Arroyo de las Lovantos
Paseo de la Cuma
Old Taos Highway
Washington Ave.
Sunset St.
Arroyo Mascras
Paseo de Peralta
Artist Rd.
N. Guadalupe St.
Jefferson St.
Catron St.
Staab St.
McKenzie St.
Grant Ave.
N. Federal Pl.
S. Federal Pl.
Paseo de Peralta
Kearney Ave.
Otero St.
W. San Francisco St.
Johnson St.
Sheridan St.
W. Marcy St.
Lincoln Ave.
E. Marcy St.
Old Fort Marcy Park
Georgia O'Keefe Museum 6
Museum of Fine Arts
San Francisco St.
Plaza
Palace of the Governors 10 11
Palace Ave.
14 Hillside Park
Santa Fe River Park
W. Alameda St.
Water St.
7
W. De Vargas St.
St. Francis Cathedral
Guadalupe St.
Aztec St.
Montezuma St.
Garfield St.
Sandoval St.
Shelby St.
Loretto Chapel Museum
Cathedral Pl.
E. Alameda St.
Santa Fe River
Read St.
S. Capitol St.
9
De Vargas Park
E. De Vargas St.
Cerrillos Rd.
3
W. Manhattan Ave.
State Capitol Complex 8
Paseo de Peralta
Garcia St.
Delgado St.
4
5
Galisteo St.
Don Gaspar Ave.
Webber St.
Old Santa Fe Trail
W. Santa Fe Ave.
E. Santa Fe Ave.
W. Booth St.
Acequia Madre

Taos
Santa Fe
Albuquerque
NEW MEXICO

ACCOMMODATIONS ■
Bishop's Lodge
  Ranch Resort and Spa **1**
El Rey Inn **4**
Hacienda Nicholas **14**
Inn of the Anasazi **10**
Water Street Inn **6**

DINING ◆
Anasazi Restaurant **12**
Coyote Cafe **7**
Guadalupe Cafe **8**
La Choza **3**
mu du noodles **5**
Santacafé **13**
The Shed **11**
Upper Crust Pizza **9**

By Train Amtrak (📞 **800/USA-RAIL;** www.amtrak.com) provides service from Albuquerque (trip time: 2 hr.), Chicago (24 hr.), and Los Angeles (19 hr.) to its station at nearby Lamy (approximately 20 miles from downtown Santa Fe).

By Car The major route into Santa Fe is **I-25** from the south (Albuquerque) and north (Denver and Colorado Springs). For those coming from the northwest, the most direct route is via Durango, Colorado, on **U.S. 160** east, then **U.S. 84** south to Santa Fe.

VISITOR INFORMATION The **Santa Fe Convention and Visitors Bureau** is at 125 Lincoln Ave. (P.O. Box 909), Santa Fe, NM 87504-0909 (📞 **800/777-CITY** or 505/955-6200; www.santafe.org).

GETTING AROUND The best way to see downtown Santa Fe is on foot. Street parking is difficult to find during summer months. You can pick up a wallet-size guide to parking areas at the visitor center. There's a metered parking lot near the federal courthouse, 2 blocks north of the Plaza; a city lot behind Santa Fe Village, a block south of the Plaza; and a another city lot at Water and Sandoval streets.

The public bus system, **Santa Fe Trails** (📞 **505/955-2001**), has seven routes. You can pick up a map from the visitor center. Buses operate Monday through Friday from 6am to 11pm and Saturday from 8am to 8pm. **Capital City Cab** (📞 **505/438-0000**) is the main taxi company.

FAST FACTS **St. Vincent Hospital** is at 455 St. Michael's Dr. (📞 **505/983-3361,** or 505/995-3934 for emergency services). **Del Norte Pharmacy,** 1691 Galisteo St. (📞 **505/988-9797**), offers delivery and emergency service. A **sales tax** of 7.625% is added to all purchases, with an additional 5% **hotel tax** for lodging bills.

Warning: Although the tourist district appears very safe, Santa Fe is not on the whole a safe city; theft and the number of reported rapes have risen. Though the city's overall crime statistics do appear to be falling, when walking the streets, guard your purse carefully because there are many bag-grab thefts, particularly during the summer tourist months.

SPECIAL EVENTS & FESTIVALS Santa Fe Plaza is often the site of special events. The last weekend in July brings the **Spanish Markets** (📞 **505/982-2226**), when more than 300 Hispanic artists from New Mexico and southern Colorado exhibit and sell their work. In August, there's the **Annual Indian Market** (📞 **505/983-5220**), with artisans' booths, musical entertainment, tribal dancing, and crafts demonstrations. Beginning Thursday night after Labor Day is **Fiesta de Santa Fe** (📞 **505/988-7575**), the oldest community celebration in the United States. Events include Masses, parades, mariachi concerts, and dances.

EXPLORING THE CITY

One of the oldest cities in the United States, Santa Fe has long been a center for the creative and performing arts, so it's not surprising that most of the city's major sights are related to local history and the arts. The city's Museum of New Mexico, art galleries and studios, historic churches, and cultural sights associated with local Native American and Hispanic communities all merit a visit.

El Rancho de las Golondrinas This 200-acre ranch was once the last stopping place on the 1,000-mile El Camino Real from Mexico City to Santa Fe. Today, it's a living 18th- and 19th-century Spanish village, comprising a hacienda, a village store, a schoolhouse, and several chapels and kitchens. There's also a working molasses mill, wheelwright and blacksmith shops, shearing and weaving rooms, a threshing ground, a winery and vineyard, and four water mills, as well as dozens of farm animals. Costumed volunteers demonstrate traditional trades. The Spring Festival (in June) and the Harvest Festival (in Oct) are the year's highlights.

334 Los Pinos Rd. ℭ 505/471-2261. www.golondrinas.org. Admission $5 adults, $4 seniors and teens, $2 children 5–12, free for children under 5. Festival weekends $7 adults, $5 seniors and teens, $3 children 5–12. June–Sept Wed–Sun 10am–4pm; Apr–May and Oct open by advance arrangement. Closed Nov–Mar. From Santa Fe, drive south on I-25, taking Exit 276, which leads to N.M. 599 going north; turn left on W. Frontage Rd.; drive ½ mile; turn right on Los Pinos Rd.; travel 3 miles to the museum.

Georgia O'Keeffe Museum   This museum contains the largest collection of O'Keeffes in the world: 117 oil paintings, drawings, watercolors, pastels, and sculptures. It's the only museum in the United States dedicated solely to one woman's work. The rich and varied collection includes such works as *Jimson Weed* (1932) and *Evening Star No. VII* (1917).

217 Johnson St. ℭ 505/946-1000. www.okeeffemuseum.org. Admission $8, free for students, free for all Fri 5–8pm. July–Oct daily 10am–5pm (Fri until 8pm); Nov–June Thurs–Tues 10am–5pm (Fri until 8pm).

Museum of Fine Arts   The museum's permanent collection of more than 20,000 works emphasizes regional art and includes landscapes and portraits by all the Taos masters, *los Cincos Pintores* (a 1920s organization of Santa Fe artists), and contemporary artists. The museum also has a collection of photographic works by such masters as Ansel Adams, Edward Weston, and Elliot Porter.

107 W. Palace (at Lincoln Ave.). ℭ 505/476-5072. www.mfasantafe.org. Admission $8 adults, free for children 11 and under, free for all Fri 5–8pm. 4-day passes (good at all 4 branches of the Museum of New Mexico, plus the Museum of Spanish Colonial Art) $18 for adults. Tues–Sun 10am–5pm (Fri until 8pm). Closed New Year's Day, Easter, Thanksgiving, and Christmas.

Museum of Indian Arts and Culture *Best*   A permanent interactive exhibit here makes this one of the most exciting Native American museum experiences in the Southwest. "Here, Now and Always" takes visitors through thousands of years of Native American history. More than 70,000 pieces of basketry, pottery, clothing, carpets, and jewelry—much of it quite old—are on continual rotating display. The rest of the museum houses a lovely pottery collection as well as changing exhibits. Call for information on demonstrations of traditional skills, lectures on native traditions and arts, and performances of Native American music and dancing.

710 Camino Lejo. ℭ 505/476-1250. www.miaclab.org. Admission $8 adults, free for kids 16 and under. 4-day passes (good at all 4 branches of the Museum of New Mexico, plus the Museum of Spanish Colonial Art) $18 for adults. Tues–Sun 10am–5pm. Drive southeast on Old Santa Fe Trail (**beware:** Old Santa Fe Trail takes a left turn; if you find yourself on Old Pecos Trail, you missed the turn). Look for signs pointing right onto Camino Lejo.

Museum of International Folk Art *Kids*   With a collection of some 130,000 objects from more than 100 countries, this museum is the largest of its kind in the world. The special collections include Spanish colonial silver, traditional and contemporary New Mexican religious art, Mexican tribal costumes, Mexican majolica ceramics, Brazilian folk art, European glass, African sculptures, the marvelous Morris Miniature Circus, and American weather vanes and quilts. Children love to look at the hundreds of toys on display throughout the museum.

706 Camino Lejo. ℭ 505/476-1200. www.moifa.org. Admission $8 adults, free for kids 11 and under. 4-day passes (good at all 4 branches of the Museum of New Mexico, plus the Museum of Spanish Colonial Art) $18 for adults. Tues–Sun 10am–5pm (open Mon 10am–5pm summer only). The museum is about 2 miles southeast of the Plaza. Drive southeast on Old Santa Fe Trail (**Beware:** Old Santa Fe Trail takes a left turn; if you find yourself on Old Pecos Trail, you missed the turn). Look for signs pointing right onto Camino Lejo.

Palace of the Governors Built in 1610 as the original capitol of New Mexico, the palace has been in continuous public use longer than any other structure in the United States. Today, this museum chronicles 400 years of New Mexico's history. Highlights include a world-class collection of pre-Columbian art objects, with ceramics, gold, and stone work; a stagecoach and tools used by early Hispanic residents; a replica of a mid-19th-century chapel; and restored Mexican and 19th-century U.S. governors' offices.

North Plaza. © 505/476-5100. www.palaceofthegovernors.org. Admission $8 adults, free for children 11 and under, free for all 5–8pm Fri. 4-day passes (good at all 4 branches of the Museum of New Mexico, plus the Museum of Spanish Colonial Art) $18 for adults. Tues–Sun 10am–5pm (until 8pm Fri). Closed New Year's Day, Thanksgiving, and Christmas.

St. Francis Cathedral Santa Fe's grandest religious structure, built in the style of the great cathedrals of Europe, is an architectural anomaly here. The small adobe Our Lady of the Rosary chapel on the northeast side is the only portion that remains from the original church, founded in 1610. Look for Our Lady of Peace, the oldest representation of the Madonna in the United States; and for the cathedral's front doors, featuring 16 carved panels memorializing the 38 Franciscan friars who were martyred during New Mexico's early years.

Cathedral Place at San Francisco St. © 505/982-5619. Donations appreciated. Open daily. Visitors may attend Mass Mon–Sat 7am and 5:15pm; Sun 8am, 10am, noon, and 5:15pm. Free parking in city lot next to the cathedral to attend church services.

SHOPPING

Some call Santa Fe one of the top art markets in the world, and it's no wonder. Galleries speckle the downtown area, and as an artists' thoroughfare, Canyon Road is preeminent. Still, the greatest concentration of Native American crafts is displayed beneath the portal of the Palace of the Governors.

LewAllen Contemporary, 129 W. Palace Ave. (© **505/988-8997**), stocks bizarre and beautiful contemporary works in a range of media from granite to clay to twigs. **Shidoni Foundry, Gallery, and Sculpture Gardens,** Bishop's Lodge Road, Tesuque (© **505/988-8001**), is one of the area's most exciting spots for sculptors and sculpture enthusiasts. **Gerald Peters Gallery,** 1011 Paseo de Peralta (© **505/954-5700**), features the art of Georgia O'Keeffe, William Wegman, and the founders of the Santa Fe and Taos artists' colonies.

WHERE TO STAY

Year-round reservation assistance is available from **Santa Fe Hotels.com** (© 800/745-9910), the **Accommodation Hot Line** (© 800/338-6877), **All Santa Fe Reservations** (© 877/737-7366), and **Santa Fe Stay,** which specializes in casitas (© 800/995-2272). **Emergency Lodging Assistance** is available free after 4pm daily (© 505/986-0038).

Bishop's Lodge Ranch Resort & Spa *Kids* The 1,000-acre Bishop's Lodge is an active resort, and its many outdoor opportunities, including riding lessons, nature walks, and cookouts, make it an ideal place for families. Rooms, spread through many buildings, feature handcrafted furniture and regional artwork. Many have balconies; deluxe units have traditional kiva fireplaces and private decks or patios. Some offer spectacular views of the Jemez Mountains.

Bishop's Lodge Rd. (P.O. Box 2367), Santa Fe, NM 87504. © 505/983-6377. Fax 505/989-8939. www.bishopslodge. com. 111 units. Summer $399–$459 double; fall and spring $299–$399 double; midwinter $189–$269 double. Resort fee $15 per person per day. Additional person $15. Children 3 and under stay free in parent's room. Ask about packages that include meals. AE, DC, DISC, MC, V. Free parking. **Amenities:** Restaurant; pool; tennis courts; spa.

El Rey Inn   The two stories of suites around the Spanish colonial courtyard are a sweet deal. They feel like a Spanish inn, with carved furniture and cozy couches, and some have kitchenettes. Ten newer units offer more upscale amenities and gas log fireplaces. The oldest section feels a bit cramped, although the rooms have style, with Art Deco tile in the bathrooms. Some have little patios. Be sure to request a room as far back as possible from Cerrillos Road.

1862 Cerrillos Rd. (P.O. Box 4759), Santa Fe, NM 87502. ℂ 800/521-1349 or 505/982-1931. Fax 505/989-9249. www.elreyinnsantafe.com. 85 units. $95–$165 double; $120–$225 suite. Rates include continental breakfast. AE, DC, DISC, MC, V. Free parking. **Amenities:** Pool; exercise room. *In room:* Fridge.

Hacienda Nicholas   This inn, a few blocks from the Plaza, has a delightful southwestern hacienda feel. Rooms surround a sunny patio. All beds are comfortable and bathrooms range from small with showers only to larger with tub/showers. A full breakfast—including such delicacies as house-made granola and red and green breakfast burritos—and afternoon wine and cheese are served in the lovely Great Room or on the patio, both with fireplaces. Service in this inn is excellent.

320 E. Marcy St., Santa Fe, NM 87501. ℂ 888/284-3170 or 505/992-8385. Fax 505/982-8572. www.hacienda nicholas.com. 7 units. $110–$210 double. Additional person $25. Rates include breakfast and afternoon wine and cheese. AE, DISC, MC, V. Free parking. Pets accepted with $20 deposit.

Inn of the Anasazi *Best*   This fine luxury hotel, built in 1991 right off the Plaza, manages to suggest a feeling of grandness in a very limited space, and in 2006 a remodel added even finer touches, including new bedding and decor in the rooms, with bold splashes of color from indigenous rugs and hand-woven fabrics. The spacious rooms feature pearl-finished walls, cream-toned decor, iron sconces, four-poster beds, kiva gas fireplaces, and humidifiers. All rooms are quiet, though none have dramatic views. The Anasazi Restaurant (see below) serves creative southwestern cuisine.

113 Washington Ave., Santa Fe, NM 87501. ℂ 800/688-8100 or 505/988-3030. Fax 505/988-3277. www.innofthe anasazi.com. 56 units. Jan 5–Feb 26 $269–$469 double; Feb 27–Apr 28 $325–$525 double; Apr 29–June 23 $325–$525 double; June 24–Jan 4 $325–$525 double. AE, DC, DISC, MC, V. Valet parking $15 per day. **Amenities:** Restaurant.

La Quinta Inn *Value*   Though it's a good 15-minute drive from the Plaza, this is our pick of the Cerrillos Road chain hotels. Rooms in the three-story white-brick buildings have an unexpectedly elegant feel, with lots of deep colors and Art Deco tile in the bathrooms. The kidney-shaped pool has a nice lounging area. If you're a shopper, you'll enjoy the proximity to the Santa Fe Place mall.

4298 Cerrillos Rd., Santa Fe, NM 87507. ℂ 800/531-5900 or 505/471-1142. Fax 505/438-7219. www.lq.com. 130 units. June to mid-Oct $89–$110 double; late Oct to May $60–$66 double. Children 18 and under stay free in parent's room. Discount for AAA members. Rates include continental breakfast. AE, DC, DISC, MC, V. Free parking. Maximum 2 pets stay free. **Amenities:** Pool.

Water Street Inn   An award-winning adobe restoration 4 blocks from the Plaza, this friendly inn features beautiful Mexican-tile bathrooms, several kiva fireplaces and woodstoves, and antique furnishings. A happy hour with quesadillas and margaritas, is offered. Rooms are decorated in a Moroccan/southwestern style and come with balconies or terraces, flatscreen TVs, DVD/VCR players, and CD players. Four suites have private patios with fountains.

427 West Water St., Santa Fe, NM 87501. ℂ 800/646-6752 or 505/984-1193. Fax 505/984-6235. www.waterstreet inn.com. 12 units. $100–$250 double. Rates include continental breakfast and afternoon hors d'oeuvres and refreshments. AE, DISC, MC, V. Free parking. Children and pets welcome with prior approval.

WHERE TO DINE

Anasazi Restaurant CREATIVE SOUTHWESTERN/NATIVE AMERICAN
This is one of Santa Fe's more interesting dining experiences. All the food is inventive, and organic meats and vegetables are used whenever available. For breakfast, try the breakfast burrito with homemade chorizo, green-chile potatoes, and refried Anasazi beans. Among the moderate-size lunches, consider crispy ahi tuna tacos with mango salsa. For dinner, try cinnamon-chile-rubbed beef tenderloin with potato bone-marrow purée, oyster mushrooms, and asparagus. A favorite dessert is the almond milk panna cotta parfait.

At the Inn of the Anasazi, 113 Washington Ave. ℂ **505/988-3236.** Reservations recommended. Main courses $7.50–$12 breakfast, $9.50–$15 lunch, $25–$36 dinner. AE, DISC, MC, V. Daily 7–10:30am, 11:30am–2:30pm, and 5:30–10pm.

Coyote Cafe CREATIVE SOUTHWESTERN/LATIN   Chef Mark Miller's trendy restaurant offers cutting-edge cuisine in a fun atmosphere (but can be quite noisy on a busy night). The menu changes seasonally, but look for delights such as chipotle tiger prawns with griddled corn cakes or a duck tamale for appetizers. Move on to a braised-ancho lamb shank or horseradish-crusted Maine haddock.

132 Water St. ℂ **505/983-1615.** www.coyotecafe.com. Reservations highly recommended. Main courses $19–$36. AE, DC, DISC, MC, V. Daily 5:30–9pm.

Guadalupe Cafe NEW MEXICAN   This casually elegant cafe is in a white-stucco building that's warm and friendly, with a nice-size patio for dining in warmer months. For dinner, start with fresh roasted ancho chiles (filled with a combination of Montrachet and Monterey Jack cheese and pinyon nuts) and move on to the sour-cream chicken enchilada or any of the other southwestern dishes. Order both red and green chile ("Christmas") so that you can sample some of the best sauces in town.

422 Old Santa Fe Trail. ℂ **505/982-9762.** Breakfast $4.50–$8.75; lunch $6–$12; dinner $7–$15. DISC, MC, V. Tues–Fri 7am–2pm; Sat–Sun 8am–2pm; Tues–Sat 5:30–9pm.

La Choza *Value* NEW MEXICAN   This warm, casual spot offers some of the best New Mexican food in town. The menu features enchiladas, tacos, and burritos on blue-corn tortillas, as well as green chile stew, chile con carne, and carne adovada. The portions are medium-size, so if you're hungry, start with guacamole or nachos. The cheese or chicken enchiladas are reliable favorites, though you might check out the blue-corn burritos served with *posole*. Vegetarians and children get their own menus.

905 Alarid St. ℂ **505/982-0909.** Lunch or dinner $7.95–$10. AE, DISC, MC, V. Summer Mon–Sat 11am–9pm; winter Mon–Thurs 11am–8pm, Fri–Sat 11am–9pm.

mu du noodles PACIFIC RIM   If you're ready for a light, healthy meal with lots of flavor, head to this small restaurant, about an 8-minute drive from downtown. Of the two rooms, the back room is cozier, and the woodsy-feeling patio is worth requesting during warmer months. We recommend the Malaysian *laksa*, thick rice noodles in a blend of coconut milk, hazelnuts, onions, and red curry, stir-fried with chicken or tofu and julienne vegetables and sprouts. Wash it all down with the ginseng ginger ale.

1494 Cerrillos Rd. ℂ **505/983-1411.** Reservations for parties of 3 or larger only. Main courses $9–$18. AE, DC, DISC, MC, V. Mon–Sat 5:30–9pm (sometimes 10pm in summer).

Santacafé *Best* CREATIVE SOUTHWESTERN   Be prepared for spectacular bursts of flavor. The southwestern food here has an Asian flair, and is served amid a minimalist decor that accentuates the graceful architecture of the 18th-century Padre

Gallegos House. The dishes change to take advantage of seasonal specialties: Shiitake and cactus spring rolls are served with green chile salsa, while achiote-marinated halibut comes with orange salsa and green rice.

231 Washington Ave. © 505/984-1788. www.santacafe.com. Reservations recommended. Main courses $9–$15 lunch, $19–$40 dinner. AE, DISC, MC, V. Mon–Sat 11:30am–2pm; daily 5:30–10pm. Sun brunch served in summer, Easter Sunday, and Mother's Day.

The Shed NEW MEXICAN   During lunch, lines often form outside The Shed, a local institution since 1953. It occupies several rooms and the patio of a rambling hacienda built in 1692. Festive folk art adorns the doorways and walls. The food, like the cheese enchilada and the tacos and burritos, is some of the best in the state. All are served on blue-corn tortillas. The green chile soup is a local favorite. Vegetarian and low-fat dishes are available, as is full bar service.

113½ E. Palace Ave. © **505/982-9030.** Reservations accepted at dinner. Lunch $5.75–$9.50; dinner $8–$17. AE, DC, DISC, MC, V. Mon–Sat 11am–2:30pm and 5:30–9pm.

Upper Crust Pizza *Kids* PIZZA/ITALIAN   Upper Crust serves Santa Fe's best pizzas, in an adobe house near the old San Miguel Mission. Try the Grecian gourmet (feta and olives) or the whole-wheat vegetarian pizza (topped with sesame seeds). You can either eat here or request free delivery to your downtown hotel. Beer and wine are available, as are salads, calzones, sandwiches, and stromboli.

329 Old Santa Fe Trail. © 505/982-0000. Pizzas $7.95–$16. DISC, MC, V. Summer daily 11am–midnight; winter Sun–Thurs 11am–10pm, Fri–Sat 11am–11pm.

SANTA FE AFTER DARK

Current listings on all major cultural events are published each Friday in the "Pasatiempo" section of the *New Mexican,* the city's daily newspaper, and in the *Santa Fe Reporter,* published every Wednesday.

For tickets to select events, try **Nicholas Potter, Bookseller,** 211 E. Palace Ave. (© **505/983-5434**); **Candyman,** 851 St. Michaels Dr. (© **505/983-5906**); and **CD Café,** 301 N. Guadalupe (© **505/986-0735**). You can also order by phone from **Ticketmaster** (© **505/883-7800**).

THE PERFORMING ARTS   Many rank the **Santa Fe Opera** (© **800/280-4654** or 505/986-5900; www.santafeopera.org) second only to the Metropolitan Opera of New York as the finest company in the United States today. The company performs in an open-sided venue on a wooded hilltop 7 miles north of the city off U.S. 84/285. It consistently attracts famed conductors, directors, and singers. The 8-week season runs from late June to late August.

The **Santa Fe Symphony Orchestra and Chorus** (© **800/480-1319** or 505/983-1414; www.sf-symphony.org) performs classical and popular works from October to May. An extraordinary group of international artists comes to Santa Fe every summer for the **Santa Fe Chamber Music Festival** (© **505/983-2075** or 505/982-1890; www.sfcmf.org).

The oldest extant theater group in New Mexico, **Santa Fe Playhouse,** 142 E. de Vargas St. (© **505/988-4262;** www.santafeplayhouse.org), attracts thousands to its dramas, avant-garde theater, and musical comedy. The outstanding offerings at the **Santa Fe Stages,** 100 N. Guadalupe St. (© **505/982-6683;** www.santafestages.org), play to an intimate gathering.

You won't want to miss a performance of the **María Benitez Teatro Flamenco,** in the Maria Benitez Theater at the Radisson Hotel (© **888/435-2636** or 505/982-1237; www.mariabenitez.com).

THE BAR, CLUB & MUSIC SCENE **El Farol,** 808 Canyon Rd. (© **505/983-9912**), is the place to head for Santa Fe's largest and most unusual selection of tapas. Jazz, swing, folk, and ethnic musicians, some of national note, perform most nights.

There's live entertainment nightly at the **Cowgirl Hall of Fame,** 319 S. Guadalupe St. (© **505/982-2565**): folk, rock, blues guitar, comedy, and cowboy poetry. In the summer, this is a great place to sit under the stars and listen to music.

You'll find everyone from businesspeople to bikers at **Evangelo's,** 200 W. San Francisco St. (© **505/982-9014**), a raucous downtown hangout with tropical decor and a mahogany bar. More than 60 varieties of imported beer are available, and pool tables are an added attraction. You might catch live rock, jazz, or reggae.

TOURING SOME PUEBLOS AROUND SANTA FE

The pueblos described in this section can easily be visited in a single day's round-trip from Santa Fe. Certain rules of etiquette should be observed in visiting the pueblos: These are personal dwellings and/or important historic sites, and must be respected as such. Don't climb on the buildings or peek into doors or windows. Don't enter sacred grounds, such as cemeteries and kivas. If you attend a dance or ceremony, remain silent while it's taking place and refrain from applause when it's over. Many pueblos prohibit photography or sketches; others require you to pay a fee for a permit.

Ohkay Owingeh (San Juan Pueblo) This largest (pop. 1,950) and northernmost of the Tewa-speaking pueblos is on the east side of the Rio Grande—opposite the 1598 site of San Gabriel, the first Spanish settlement west of the Mississippi River and the first capital of New Spain. The annual **San Juan Fiesta** is held here on June 23 and 24, and the **turtle dance** is on December 26. The **Matachine dance,** performed Christmas Day, vividly depicts the subjugation of the Native Americans by the Catholic Spaniards. A crafts shop, **Ohkay Owingeh Arts and Crafts Cooperative** (© **505/852-2372**), specializes in local wares. This is a fine place to seek out San Juan's distinctive red pottery. Also for sale are seed, turquoise, and silver jewelry; wood and stone carvings; weavings; embroidery; and paintings.

On N.M. 74 about 4 miles north of Española. © 505/852-4400 or 505/852-4210. Free admission. Photography or sketching may be allowed with prior permission from the governor's office. Fishing $8 adults, $5 children and seniors. Daily during daylight hours.

San Ildefonso Pueblo This pueblo has a broad, dusty Plaza, with a kiva on one side, ancient dwellings on the other, and a church at the far end. It's nationally famous for its matte-finish black-on-black pottery, developed by tribeswoman María Martinez in the 1920s. A few shops surround the Plaza, and the **San Ildefonso Pueblo Museum** is tucked away in the governor's office beyond the Plaza. It's especially memorable to visit during ceremonial days. **San Ildefonso Feast Day,** on January 23, features the buffalo and Comanche dances in alternate years. **Corn dances,** held in late August or early September, commemorate a basic element in pueblo life, the importance of fertility in all creatures—humans as well as animals—and plants. The pueblo has a half-acre fishing lake surrounded by woodlands, open from April to October. Picnicking is encouraged, but camping is not allowed.

Rte. 5. © 505/455-3549. Admission $5 per car. Still camera $10; video camera $20; sketching $25. Fishing $10 adults, $5 for kids under 12. Summer daily 8am–5pm; call for weekend hours. Winter Mon–Fri 8am–4:30pm. Closed for major holidays and tribal events.

Santa Clara Pueblo   Close to Española, Santa Clara, with a population of about 1,800, is one of the largest pueblos. You'll see the village sprawling across the river basin near the beautiful Black Mesa, rows of tract homes surrounding an adobe central area. Within the village are lots of little pottery and crafts shops. There are corn and harvest dances on **Santa Clara Feast Day** (Aug 12).

On N.M. 5, close to Española. © 505/753-7326. Free admission. Still camera $5; video cameras and sketching are not allowed. Daily 9am–4pm.

13 Taos

Located about 70 miles north of Santa Fe, this town of 5,000 residents combines 1960s hippiedom (thanks to communes set up in the hills back then) with the ancient culture of Taos Pueblo (some people still live without electricity and running water, as their ancestors did 1,000 years ago). It can be an odd place, where some completely eschew materialism and live "off the grid" in half-underground houses called earth ships.

But take a moment longer to look and you'll see a thriving art colony, not glitzy like Santa Fe, but very real and down-to-earth, often with artists selling work straight out of their studios. You'll wander through amazing galleries, many displaying the town's rich history in a variety of art forms. And you'll eat some of the most inventive food in the Southwest, at very affordable prices.

Taos is just 40 miles south of the Colorado border, about 70 miles north of Santa Fe, and 135 miles from Albuquerque. In addition to its collection of artists and writers, it's famous for the pueblo and for the nearby ski area, one of the most highly regarded in the Rockies.

ESSENTIALS

GETTING THERE   By Plane   The **Taos Municipal Airport** (© 505/758-4995) is about 8 miles northwest of town on U.S. 64. However, it's easier to fly into **Albuquerque International Sunport** (© 505/842-4366), rent a car, and drive from there (trip time: 2½ hr.). If you'd rather be picked up at Albuquerque International Sunport, call **Faust's Transportation, Inc.** (© 505/758-3410), which offers daily service, as well as taxi service between Taos and Taos Ski Valley.

By Car   From Santa Fe, take **U.S. 84/285** north, then **N.M. 68** to Taos. From Denver, take **I-25 South** to **U.S. 64,** then continue west about 95 miles to Taos.

VISITOR INFORMATION   The **Taos County Chamber of Commerce,** at the junction of N.M. 68 and N.M. 585 (P.O. Drawer I), Taos, NM 87571 (© 800/732-TAOS or 505/758-3873; www.taoschamber.com), is open in summer, daily 9am to 5pm. It's closed on major holidays.

GETTING AROUND   Chile Line Town of Taos Transit (© 505/751-4459) operates local bus service on the half-hour Monday to Saturday 7am to 7pm in summer, 7am to 6pm in winter, and on the hour Sunday 8am to 5pm. There are two simultaneous routes running southbound from Taos Pueblo and northbound from the Ranchos de Taos Post Office on the half-hour. Each route makes stops at the casino and at various hotels in town, as well as Taos RV Park. Bus fares are 50¢ one-way, $1 round-trip, and $5 for a 7-day pass.

Faust's Transportation (℃ 505/758-3410) has a taxi service linking town hotels and Taos Ski Valley, shuttle service, and on-call taxi service daily from 7am to 8:30pm, with fares of about $10 anywhere within the city limits for up to two people.

Parking can be difficult in summer. If you can't find a spot on the street or in the Plaza, check out some of the nearby roads. *Safety tips:* En route to many recreation sites, reliable paved roads can lead to poorer forest roads. Once you get off the main roads, you won't find gas stations or cafes. Four-wheel-drive vehicles are recommended on snow and much of the otherwise unpaved terrain of the region. If you're doing off-road adventuring, it's wise to go with a full gas tank, extra food and water, and warm clothing. Sudden summer snowstorms are not unheard of.

FAST FACTS You can get information on road conditions from the **State Highway Department** (℃ 800/432-4269); if you have a highway emergency, contact the Taos area state police at ℃ 505/758-8878. **Holy Cross Hospital,** 1397 Weimer Rd., off Paseo del Canyon (℃ 505/758-8883), has 24-hour emergency service. **Raley's Pharmacy** (℃ 505/758-1203), **Smith's Pharmacy** (℃ 505/758-4824), and **Wal-Mart Pharmacy** (℃ 505/758-2743) are all on Pueblo Sur and are easily seen from the road.

Sales tax for the city of Taos is 7%, and for Taos County it's 6.31%. There is an additional local **hotel tax** of 4.5% in the city of Taos and 5% in Taos County.

SPECIAL EVENTS & FESTIVALS May brings the **Taos Spring Arts Festival,** with gallery openings, studio tours, performances by visiting theatrical and dance troupes, musical events, traditional ethnic entertainment, readings, and more. For dates and tickets, contact the **Taos County Chamber of Commerce** (℃ 800/732-TAOS or 505/758-3873; www.taoschamber.com). From mid-August to early September, there's **Music from Angel Fire** (℃ 505/377-3233; www.angelfirenm.com), an acclaimed program of chamber music.

WHAT TO SEE & DO

If you'd like to visit five museums that comprise the Museum Association of Taos—Blumenschein Home, Martinez Hacienda, Harwood Museum, Millicent Rogers Museum, and Taos Art Museum—you'll save money by purchasing a **combination ticket** for $20.

Given the town's historical associations with the arts, it isn't surprising that many visitors come to Taos to buy fine art. Some 50-odd galleries are within easy walking distance of the Plaza. The best-known modern artist in Taos is R. C. Gorman. His **Navajo Gallery,** 210 Ledoux St. (℃ 505/758-3250), is a showcase for his widely varied works.

Millicent Rogers Museum of Northern New Mexico
This museum is small enough to introduce some of the Southwest's finest arts and crafts without being overwhelming. Included are Navajo and Pueblo jewelry, Navajo textiles, Pueblo pottery, Hopi and Zuni kachina dolls, paintings from the Rio Grande Pueblo people, and basketry from a wide variety of southwestern tribes. The permanent collection also includes Anglo arts and crafts and Hispanic religious and secular arts and crafts.

Off U.S. 64, 4 miles north of Taos Plaza, on Millicent Rogers Rd. ℃ 505/758-2462. www.millicentrogers.org. Admission $8 adults, $6 students and $7 seniors, $2 children 6–16, $18 family rate. Daily 10am–5pm. Closed Mon Nov–Mar, Easter, Thanksgiving, Christmas, and New Year's Day.

San Francisco de Asis Church
From N.M. 68, about 4 miles south of Taos, this famous church looks like a modern adobe sculpture with no doors or windows. Visitors

ACCOMMODATIONS ■
Adobe Sun God Lodge **7**
Best Western Kachina Lodge
& Meeting Center **4**
Casa de las Chimeneas **6**
Little Tree Bed & Breakfast **2**

DINING ◆
Joseph's Table **5**
Orlando's New Mexican Cafe **1**
Taos Pizza Out Back **3**
Trading Post Café **8**

must walk through the garden on the east side of this remarkable two-story church to enter and get a full perspective of its massive walls, authentic adobe plaster, and beauty. A video presentation is given in the church office every hour on the half-hour. A few crafts shops surround the square.

Ranchos de Taos Plaza. ℂ **505/758-2754**. Admission $3 for video and mystery painting. Mon–Sat 9am–4pm. Visitors may attend Mass Mon–Fri 5pm, Sat 6pm (Mass rotates from this church to the 3 mission chapels), Sun 7 (Spanish), 9, and 11:30am. Closed to the public 1st 2 weeks in June, when repairs are done; however, services still take place.

Taos Historic Museums   Two historic homes are operated as museums, affording visitors a glimpse of early Taos lifestyles.

The **Martinez Hacienda,** Lower Ranchitos Road, Highway 240, is remarkably beautiful, with thick, raw adobe walls and no exterior windows, to protect against raids by Plains tribes. The 21 rooms built around two interior courtyards give you a glimpse of the austerity of frontier lives. You'll see bedrooms, servants' quarters, stables, a kitchen, and a large fiesta room. The hacienda is also a living museum, with weavers, blacksmiths, and woodcarvers demonstrating their trades daily, more often during the **Taos Trade Fair** (in late Sept).

The **Ernest L. Blumenschein Home & Museum,** 222 Ledoux St., 1½ blocks southwest of the Plaza, re-creates the lifestyle of one of the founders of the Taos Society of Artists (founded 1915). Period furnishings include European antiques and handmade Taos furniture in Spanish colonial style. An extensive collection of works by early-20th-century Taos artists is on display in several rooms of the home.

222 Ledoux St. ℂ 505/758-0505 (information for both museums can be obtained at this number). www.taos historicmuseums.com. Admission for each museum $7 adults, $3 children ages 6–16, free for children under 6; $15 families. Summer daily 9am–5pm; call for winter hours.

Taos Pueblo (Best About 150 residents of Taos Pueblo live much as their ancestors did 1,000 years ago, and the village looks much as it did when a regiment from Coronado's expedition first came upon it in 1540. When you enter the pueblo, you'll see two large buildings, each with rooms piled on top of each other, forming structures that mimic Taos Mountain nearby. Here, a portion of Taos residents live without electricity and running water. The remaining residents of Taos Pueblo (nearly 2,000) live in conventional homes on the pueblo's 95,000 acres. In your explorations, you can visit the residents' studios, look into the **San Geronimo Chapel,** and wander past the fascinating ruins of the old church and cemetery. Ask permission from individuals before taking their photos; some will ask for a small payment. Kivas and other ceremonial underground areas are restricted.

The **Feast of San Geronimo** (the patron saint of Taos Pueblo), on September 29 and 30, is filled with dances, footraces, and artists and craftspeople. The **Taos Pueblo Powwow,** which brings together tribes from throughout North America, is held in July on tribal lands. Call for information on other special events.

Veterans Hwy. (P.O. Box 1846), Taos Pueblo. ℂ 505/758-1028. www.taospueblo.com. Admission cost, as well as camera, video, and sketching fees, subject to change on a yearly basis; be sure to ask about telephoto lenses and digital cameras; photography not permitted on feast days. Daily 8am–4:30pm, with a few exceptions. Guided tours available. Closed for 45 consecutive days every year late winter or early spring (call ahead). Also, because this is a living community, you can expect periodic closures. From Paseo del Pueblo Norte, travel north 2 miles on Veterans Hwy.

WHERE TO STAY

About 1,500 of Taos County's beds are in condominiums and lodges at or near Taos Ski Valley. The **Taos Valley Resort Association** (ℂ 800/776-1111 or 505/776-2233; www.visitnewmexico.com) can book these, as well as rooms in Taos and the rest of northern New Mexico, and private home rentals. **Reservations of Taos** (ℂ 505/751-1292) helps with accommodations from bed-and-breakfasts to home rentals, hotels, RV parks, and cabins throughout Taos and the rest of northern New Mexico.

Adobe Sun God Lodge (Value For an economical stay with a New Mexico ambience, this is your best choice. This hotel, a 5-minute drive from the Plaza, has three distinct parts spread across 1½ acres of landscaped grounds. The oldest has some court-motel charm with a low ceiling and large windows. In a recently remodeled section, rooms are small but have little touches that make them feel cozy. The newest buildings have portal-style porches and balconies. Some rooms have kitchenettes; others have kiva fireplaces.

919 Paseo del Pueblo Sur, Taos, NM 87571. ℂ 800/821-2437 or 505/758-3162. Fax 505/758-1716. www.sun godlodge.com. 53 units. $61–$111 double; $91–$161 suite. AE, DISC, MC, V. Pets allowed for $10 per day. *In room:* Kitchenette (in some).

(Best) Hitting the Slopes of Taos

Five Alpine resorts are within an hour's drive of Taos; all offer complete facilities, including equipment rentals. Although exact opening and closing dates vary according to snow conditions, the season usually begins around Thanksgiving and continues into early April.

Taos Ski Valley (© 505/776-2291; www.skitaos.org) is the preeminent ski resort in the southern Rockies, internationally renowned for its light, dry powder (320 in. annually), its superb ski school, and its personal, friendly service. Experienced skiers will most appreciate Taos Ski Valley's steep, high-Alpine, high-adventure skiing. The mountain is more intricate than it might seem at first glance, and it holds many surprises and challenges—even for the expert.

The area has an uphill capacity of 15,000 skiers per hour on its five double chairs, one triple, four quads, and one surface tow. Full-day lift tickets, depending on the season, cost $33 to $57 for adults, $21 to $35 for children 12 and under, $22 to $45 for teens ages 13 to 17, $43 for seniors ages 65 to 79, and are free for seniors over 80 and for children 6 and under with an adult ticket purchase. Taos Ski Valley is open daily 9am to 4pm from Thanksgiving to around the second week of April. *Note:* Taos Ski Valley has one of the best ski schools in the country, specializing in teaching people how to negotiate steep and challenging runs.

Best Western Kachina Lodge & Meeting Center (Kids) This lodge on the north end of town, within walking distance of the Plaza, has a lot of charm despite the fact that it's really a motor hotel. The southwestern-style rooms surrounding a grassy courtyard are solidly built and quiet, and there's plenty of outdoor space for the kids. On summer nights, a family from Taos Pueblo builds a bonfire and performs, explaining the significance of the dances—a real treat.

413 Paseo del Pueblo Norte (P.O. Box NM), Taos, NM 87571. © 800/522-4462 or 505/758-2275. Fax 505/758-9207. www.kachinalodge.com. 118 units. $59–$139 double. Additional person $10. Children under 12 stay free in parent's room. AE, DC, DISC, MC, V. **Amenities:** 2 restaurants; pool.

Casa de las Chimeneas (Best) This 82-year-old adobe home is a full-service luxury inn and a model of southwestern elegance. The Rio Grande and Territorial rooms have heated saltillo-tile floors and Jacuzzi tubs. If you prefer a more antique-feeling room, the older section is delightful, and renovation in the Library Suite has made it worth recommending. All have elegant bedding, private entrances, kiva fireplaces, and fridges stocked with complimentary beverages. Most look out onto flower and herb gardens.

405 Cordoba Rd., at Los Pandos Rd. (mailing address: 5303 NDCBU), Taos, NM 87571. © 877/758-4777 or 505/758-4777. Fax 505/758-3976. www.visittaos.com. 8 units. $180–$290 double; $325 suite. Rates include breakfast and evening supper. AE, DC, DISC, MC, V. **Amenities:** Small exercise room; spa. *In room:* Fridge.

Little Tree Bed & Breakfast Little Tree is one of our favorite Taos B&Bs, partly because it has a beautiful, secluded setting (midway between Taos and the ski area), and partly because it's constructed with real adobe that's been left in its raw state, lending the place an authentic hacienda feel. The charming and cozy rooms have radiant heat under the floors, queen-size beds (one with a king-size), nice medium-size bath-rooms (one with a Jacuzzi tub), and access to the portal and courtyard garden, at the center of which is the little tree for which the inn is named. Some units are equipped with fireplaces and private entrances.

County Rd. B-143 (P.O. Box 509), Taos, NM 87513. ℂ **800/334-8467** or 505/776-8467. www.littletreebandb.com. 4 units. $125–$185 double. Rates include breakfast and afternoon snack. MC, V.

Snakedance Condominiums and Spa   A recent $3.5-million renovation has transformed the rooms of this former hotel into comfortable condominiums. Skiers appreciate the inn's location, just steps from the lift, as well as amenities such as ski storage and boot dryers. All units have balconies with French doors and kitchens with granite counters and a range, fridge, dishwasher, and microwave. Many feature wood-burning fireplaces. Shuttle service is offered to and from nearby shops and restaurants.

110 Sutton Place (P.O. Box 89), Taos Ski Valley, NM 87525. ℂ **800/322-9815** or 505/776-2277. Fax 505/776-1410. www.snakedancecondos.com. 33 units. 1-bedroom condo $225–$475 double in winter, $95 in summer; 2-bedroom condo $285–$600 for 4 people in winter, $120 in summer; 2-bedroom loft condo $345–$725 for 6 people in winter, $150 in summer. Extra person $30 in winter, $10 in summer. AE, DC, DISC, MC, V. Free parking at Taos Ski Valley parking lot. Closed mid-Apr to Memorial Day and mid-Oct to mid-Nov. **Amenities:** Restaurant; bar; exercise room; spa; smoking not permitted. *In room:* Kitchen.

WHERE TO DINE

Joseph's Table *Best* NEW AMERICAN/MEDITERRANEAN   This notable eatery serves some of the most imaginative and precisely prepared food in northern New Mexico. The setting is unique, with hand-hewn vigas (beams) on the ceiling and hard-wood floors and some Asian-style tables along the back. Chef/owner Joseph Wrede creates such delicacies as a juicy green-chile buffalo burger served with homemade sweet potato chips or Mediterranean mussels in a pesto broth and Tuscan bread for lunch. Dinner is equally inventive, if not for the faint of palate. It might start with marlin sashimi on fried kale and move on to steak au poivre with mashed potatoes and a Madeira mushroom sauce.

In the Hotel La Fonda de Taos, 108-A South Taos Plaza. ℂ **505/751-4512.** www.josephstable.com. Reservations recommended. Main courses $8–$18 lunch, $18–$35 dinner. AE, DISC, MC, V. May–Aug Mon–Sat 11:30am–2:30pm; daily 5:30–10pm; Sun brunch 10:30am–2:30pm. Hours are abbreviated in winter; call first.

Orlando's New Mexican Café *Value* NEW MEXICAN   Festivity reigns in this spicy little cafe on the north end of town. Serving some of northern New Mexico's best chili, this place has colorful tables set around a bustling open kitchen, as well as airy patio dining during warmer months. Try Los Colores, their most popular dish, with three enchiladas (chicken, beef, and cheese) smothered in chile and served with beans and *posole.* The taco salad is another favorite. Portions are big, and you can order a Mexican or microbrew beer, or a New Mexican or California wine.

114 Don Juan Valdez Lane (1¾ miles north of the Plaza, off Paseo del Pueblo Norte). ℂ **505/751-1450.** Reservations not accepted. Main courses under $10. No credit cards. Daily 10:30am–9pm.

Taos Pizza Out Back *Kids* PASTA/GOURMET PIZZA   At this raucous old adobe restaurant, the level of informality is high, the food is great, and the portions are huge. What to order? One word: *Pizza.* All come with a delicious thin crust. The variations are broad: From Thai chicken pizza (pineapple, peanuts, and a spicy sauce) to our favorite, the Florentine (spinach, basil, sun-dried tomatoes, chicken, mushrooms, capers, and garlic sautéed in white wine). Don't leave without trying the Taos Yum (a "mongo" chocolate-chip cookie with ice cream, whipped cream, and chocolate sauce).

712 Paseo del Pueblo Norte (just north of Allsup's). ℂ **505/758-3112.** Reservations recommended weekends and holidays. Pizzas $12–$26; pastas and calzones $7–$12. MC, V. Summer daily 11am–10pm; winter Sun–Thurs 11am–9pm, Fri–Sat 11am–10pm.

Trading Post Café ITALIAN/INTERNATIONAL   Ask folks in town where they most like to eat, and they'll probably name the Trading Post. What draws them is a gallery atmosphere, where rough plastered walls are set off by sculptures, paintings, and photographs from the Lumina Gallery. Be prepared to wait for a table, and don't expect quiet, unless you come at an off-time. Although the focus is on the fine food, diners feel comfortable trying three appetizers and skipping the main course. You've probably never had a Caesar salad as good as the one here, and if you like pasta, you'll find a nice variety on the menu. There's also fresh fish, and stews and soups.

4179 Paseo del Pueblo Sur, Ranchos de Taos. ℂ **505/758-5089.** Reservations accepted. Menu items $6–$28. AE, DC, DISC, MC, V. Tues–Sat 11:30am–9:30pm; Sun 5–9pm.

TAOS AFTER DARK

You can get information on current events in the *Taos News,* published every Thursday.

For a small town, Taos has its share of top entertainment. Performers are attracted to Taos because of the resort atmosphere and the arts community, and the city enjoys annual programs in music and literary arts. State troupes, such as the New Mexico Repertory Theater and New Mexico Symphony Orchestra, make regular visits. Many events are scheduled by the **Taos Center for the Arts (TCA),** 133 Paseo del Pueblo Norte (ℂ **505/758-2052;** www.taoscenterforthearts.org), at the **Taos Community Auditorium** (ℂ **505/758-4677**). The TCA imports local, regional, and national performers in theater, dance, and concerts.

A favorite gathering place for locals and visitors, the **Adobe Bar,** in the Historic Taos Inn, 125 Paseo del Pueblo Norte (ℂ **505/758-2233**), often hosts live music—classical, jazz, folk, Hispanic, and acoustic. The bar features a wide selection of international beers, wines by the glass, light New Mexican dining, desserts, and an espresso menu.

The **Alley Cantina,** 121 Teresina Lane (ℂ **505/758-2121**), is a hot late-night spot with a kitchen open until 11pm and games such as pool, chess, and backgammon. The **Sagebrush Inn,** Paseo del Pueblo Sur (ℂ **505/758-2254**), has pure Old West atmosphere, with a rustic wooden dance floor and plenty of smoke. Dancers generally two-step to country performers nightly. The **Anaconda Bar,** in the new ecoresort El Monte Sagrado (ℂ **505/758-3502**), is Taos's most happening nightspot, with live entertainment—jazz, blues, Native American flute, or country—playing nightly. An anaconda sculpture snaking across the ceiling and an 11,000-gallon fish tank set the contemporary tone of the place, where a variety of delectable tapas are served.

A SCENIC DRIVE AROUND THE ENCHANTED CIRCLE

If you're in the mood to explore, take this 90-mile loop north of Taos through the old Hispanic villages of Arroyo Hondo and Questa, into a pass the Apaches, Kiowas, and Comanches once used to cross through the mountains to trade with the Taos Indians. Although you can drive the entire loop in 2 hours from Taos, most folks prefer to take a full day, and many take several days.

ARROYO HONDO   Traveling north from Taos via N.M. 522, it's a 9-mile drive to this village, the remains of an 1815 land grant along the Rio Hondo. Along the dirt roads that lead off N.M. 522, you may find a windowless *morada* or two, marked by plain crosses in front—places of worship for the still-active Penitentes, a religious order known for self-flagellation. This is also the turnoff point for trips to the Rio Grande Box, an awesome 1-day, 17-mile **white-water** run for which you can book trips in Santa Fe, Taos, Red River, and Angel Fire. En route north, the highway passes near **San Cristobal,** where a side road turns off to the **D. H. Lawrence Ranch** (© 505/776-2245) and **Lama,** site of an isolated spiritual retreat.

Next, N.M. 522 passes through **Questa.** If you turn west onto N.M. 378 about 3 miles north of Questa, you'll drive 8 miles on a paved road to the edge of the Bureau of Land Management–administered **Wild Rivers Recreation Area** (© 505/770-1600). Here, where the Red River enters the gorge, are over 20 miles of hiking and biking trails, some of which take you down to the Rio Grande. Information and hikers' trail maps can be obtained at the visitor center here.

The village of **Costilla,** near the Colorado border, is 20 miles north of Questa. This is the turnoff point for **four-wheel-drive** jaunts and hiking trips into **Valle Vidal,** a huge U.S. Forest Service–administered reserve with 42 miles of roads and many hiking trails. A day hike in this area can bring you sightings of hundreds of elk.

RED RIVER To continue on the Enchanted Circle loop, turn east at Questa onto N.M. 38 for a 12-mile climb to Red River, a rough-and-ready 1890s gold-mining town that has parlayed its Wild West ambience into a pleasant resort village.

This community is a center for skiing, snowmobiling, fishing, hiking, off-road driving, horseback riding, mountain biking, river rafting, and other outdoor pursuits. Frontier-style celebrations, honky-tonk entertainment, and even staged shootouts are held throughout the year.

Although it can be a charming, fun place, Red River's food and lodging are mediocre at best. If you do decide to stay, try the **Lodge at Red River** (© 800/91-LODGE or 505/754-6280; www.redrivernm.com/lodgeatrr; $84–$225 double), in the center of town. If you're passing through and want a quick meal, the **Mountain Treasures,** 212 W. Main St. (© 505/754-2700), a gallery, bistro, and espresso coffee bar, offers excellent sandwiches.

For more information, contact the **Red River Chamber of Commerce,** P.O. Box 870, Red River, NM 87558 (© 800/348-6444 or 505/754-2366; www.redrivernew mexico.com).

EAGLE NEST About 16 miles east of Red River, on the other side of 9,850-foot Bobcat Pass, is the village of Eagle Nest, resting on the shore of Eagle Nest Lake in the Moreno Valley. Gold was mined in this area as early as 1866, starting in what is now the ghost town of **Elizabethtown,** about 5 miles north. The 4-square-mile lake is considered one of the top trout producers in the United States and attracts ice fishers in winter as well as summer anglers. Sailboats and windsurfers also use the lake, although swimming, water-skiing, and camping are not permitted.

If you're heading to Cimarron or Denver, proceed east on U.S. 64 from Eagle Nest. But if you're circling back to Taos, continue southwest on U.S. 38 and U.S. 64 to Agua Fría and Angel Fire.

Shortly before the Agua Fría junction, you'll see the **Vietnam Veterans Memorial State Park** (© 505/377-6900). It's a stunning structure with curved white walls soaring high against the backdrop of the Sangre de Cristo Range.

ANGEL FIRE If you like the clean efficiency of a resort complex, you may want to plan a night or two here. Opened in the late 1960s, the **Angel Fire Resort,** North Angel Fire Road (© 800/633-7463 or 505/377-6401; www.angelfireresort.com), is a

155-unit hotel with spacious, comfortable rooms, some with fireplaces and balconies. Rates range from $90 to $200. The area also has condos and cabins.

The medium-size beginner and intermediate mountain is an excellent place for families to ski and roam about. The views of the Moreno Valley are awe-inspiring. During spring, summer, and fall, the resort offers golf, tennis, hiking, mountain biking, fly-fishing, river rafting, and horseback riding. Visitors can also go horseback riding with **Roadrunner Tours** (© **505/377-6416;** www.rtours.com).

For more information on the Moreno Valley, contact the **Angel Fire Chamber of Commerce** (© **800/446-8117** or 505/377-6661; fax 505/377-3034; www.angelfire chamber.org).

12

California

California's allure is understandable. It really is warm and sunny most of the year, movie stars do abound in Los Angeles, and you can't swing a cat by its tail without hitting a rollerblading hottie in Venice Beach. This part of the California mystique—however exaggerated it may be—does exist, and it's not hard to find.

But there's more—a lot more—to California that isn't scripted, sanitized, and broadcast to the world's mesmerized masses. Beyond the glitter and glamour is an incredibly diverse state that, if it ever seceded from the Union, would be a productive and powerful nation. This state has it all: redwood forests, an incredibly verdant Central Valley, the Sierra Nevada mountains, deserts, a host of world-renowned cities, and hundreds of miles of stunning coastline.

And despite the crime, pollution, traffic, and earthquakes for which California is famous, it's still the golden child of the United States: America's spoiled rich kid everyone else either loves or loathes. But, truth be told, natives really don't care. Californians *know* they live in one of the most diverse and interesting places in the world, and they're proud of the state they call home.

1 San Francisco

Consistently rated one of the top tourist destinations in the world, San Francisco abounds in multiple dimensions. Its famous, thrilling streets go up, and they go down; its multifarious citizens—and their adopted cultures, architectures, and cuisines—hail from San Antonio to Singapore; and its politics range from hyper-liberalism to an ever-encroaching wave of conservatism. Even something as mundane as fog takes on a new dimension as it creeps from the ocean and slowly envelops San Francisco in a resplendent blanket of mist.

In a city so multifaceted, so enamored with itself, it's hard not to find what you're looking for. Feel the cool blast of salt air as you stroll across the Golden Gate. Stuff yourself on dim sum in Chinatown. Browse the Haight for incense and crystals. Walk along the beach, pierce your nose, see a play, rent a Harley—the list is endless. It's all happening in San Francisco, and everyone's invited.

ESSENTIALS
GETTING THERE   By Plane   San Francisco International Airport (SFO; © 650/877-0118; www.flysfo.com), 14 miles south of downtown directly on U.S. 101, is served by almost four dozen major scheduled carriers and several budget airlines (AirTran, Independence Air, and WestJet). Travel time to downtown during rush hours is about 40 minutes; at other times, it's about 20 to 25 minutes.

The airport offers a ground transportation information hot line available Monday through Friday from 7:30am to 5pm (© 415/817-1717). Each of the three main terminals also has a desk where you can get the same information.

California

USA

CALIFORNIA

OREGON

CRATER LAKE NP

Upper Klamath Lake

Goose Lake

REDWOOD NP

Klamath

KLAMATH NAT'L FOREST

97

LAVA BEDS NM

Eureka

Klamath R.

Ferndale

SHASTA NAT'L FOREST

395

Garberville

Sacramento R.

CASCADE RANGE

Redding

LASSEN VOLCANIC NP

Pyramid Lake

Humboldt R.

Quinn R.

COAST RANGE

Eel R.

5

Chico

Fort Bragg

Mendocino

Ukiah

Clear Lake

1

Sacramento R.

Yuba City

Auburn

80

Reno

80

POINT REYES NS

Napa

Sacramento

Placerville

★

Carson City

Lake Tahoe

Carson R.

50

Oakland

SIERRA NEVADA

395

San Francisco

49

Reese R.

1

Modesto

NEVADA

San Jose

49

YOSEMITE NP

Santa Cruz

Merced

Mammoth Lakes

6

Monterey

Salinas

SIERRA NAT'L FOREST

▲ *Mammoth Mtn.*

Carmel

Fresno

Big Sur

KINGS CANYON NP

Bishop

LOS PADRES NAT'L FOREST

Kings R.

95

SEQUOIA NP

Cambria

101

SAN JOAQUIN VALLEY

SEQUOIA NAT'L FOREST

San Luis Obispo

5

93

Arroyo Grande

Kern R.

Santa Maria

Bakersfield

DEATH VALLEY NM

Solvang

395

Las Vegas

Santa Barbara

101

Ojai

MOJAVE DESERT

Lake Mead

CHANNEL ISLANDS NP

Simi Valley

Barstow

15

LAKE MEAD NRA

Oxnard

Burbank

15

Los Angeles

40

Lake Mohave

Long Beach

Anaheim

San Bernardino

Santa Ana

Palm Springs

Lake Havasu

Laguna Beach

JOSHUA TREE NM

PACIFIC OCEAN

Salton Sea

10

San Diego

Colorado R.

USA MEXICO

8

Mexicali

Imperial Reservoir

0   100 mi

0   100 km

N

A cab from the airport to downtown costs $30 to $35, plus tip. **SuperShuttle** (© **415/ 558-8500;** www.supershuttle.com) will take you anywhere in the city, charging $15 to a residence or business, plus $8 for each additional person. Keep in mind that this shuttle demands they pick you up 2 hours before your flight (3 hr. during holidays).

For budget travelers, **BART** (Bay Area Rapid Transit; © **415/989-2278;** www.bart. gov) runs from the airport to downtown. Rates are about $5 per person, depending on where you're bound, and the trip takes less than half an hour.

The San Mateo County Transit system, **SamTrans** (© **800/660-4287** in Northern California, or 650/508-6200; www.samtrans.com), runs two buses between the airport and Transbay Terminal (First and Mission sts.). Bus no. 292 is $1.50 and takes 55 minutes. The KX bus is $4 and takes 35 minutes but permits only one carry-on bag. Both buses run daily.

Oakland International Airport (© **800/247-6255** or 510/563-3300; www.oakland airport.com), about 5 miles south of downtown Oakland, at the Hegenberger Road exit off Calif. 17 (U.S. 880), is used primarily by passengers with East Bay destinations. Some San Franciscans, however, prefer this less-crowded, accessible airport when flying during busy periods.

Taxis from the Oakland airport to downtown San Francisco are expensive, costing approximately $50, plus tip. **Bayporter Express** (© **877/467-1800** or 415/467-1800; www.bayporter.com) shuttle service is $26 for the first person, $12 for each additional person, to downtown San Francisco; it costs more to the city's outlying neighborhoods. Children under 12 ride for $7.

The cheapest way to downtown San Francisco (and the easiest during traffic snarls) is the shuttle bus from the airport to **BART.** The **AirBART** shuttle bus runs about every 15 minutes Monday through Saturday from 6am to 11:30pm, and Sunday from 8:30am to 11:30pm. It makes pickups in front of terminals 1 and 2 near the ground transportation signs. Passengers must purchase tickets from airport vending machines before boarding. The 10-minute ride to BART's Coliseum station in Oakland is $2. BART fares vary, depending on your destination; the trip to downtown San Francisco costs $3.15 and takes 15 minutes once you're on board. The entire excursion should take around 45 minutes.

By Train   San Francisco–bound **Amtrak** trains (© **800/USA-RAIL;** www.amtrak. com) leave from New York and cross the country via Chicago. The journey takes about 3½ days, and seats sell quickly. At press time, the lowest round-trip fare starts at $294 from New York and $270 from Chicago. Round-trip tickets from Los Angeles cost as little as $108. Trains arrive in Emeryville, just north of Oakland, and connect with regularly scheduled buses to San Francisco's Ferry Building and Caltrain station downtown.

Caltrain (© **800/660-4287** or 415/546-4461; www.caltrain.com) operates train service between San Francisco and other towns on the peninsula. The city depot is at 700 Fourth St., at Townsend Street.

By Car   Major routes into San Francisco are **U.S. 101** and **Highway 1** from the north (Sonoma and the Napa Valley) and south (San Jose), and **I-80** and **I-580** from the northeast (Sacramento) and east, respectively.

VISITOR INFORMATION   The **San Francisco Visitor Information Center,** Hallidie Plaza, 900 Market St. (at Powell St.), Lower Level, San Francisco, CA 94102 (© **415/391-2000;** www.sfvisitor.org), is the best source for any kind of specialized information about the city. Even if you don't have a specific question, you may want to request the free *Visitors Planning Guide* or the *San Francisco Visitors Kit.*

GETTING AROUND   The San Francisco Municipal Railway, better known as **Muni** (© **415/673-6864;** www.sfmuni.com), operates the city's cable cars, buses, and Metro streetcars. Bus and streetcar fares are $1.50 for adults, 50¢ for children ages 5 to 17 and seniors over 65. Cable cars cost $5 for people over 5 years old ($1 for seniors after 9pm). Exact change is required on all but the cable cars.

    BART, an acronym for **Bay Area Rapid Transit** (© **650/992-2278**), is a high-speed rail network that connects San Francisco with the East Bay. Fares range from $1.45 to $7.45. Trains run Monday through Friday from 4am to midnight, Saturday from 6am to midnight, and Sunday from 8am to midnight.

FAST FACTS   **Saint Francis Memorial Hospital,** 900 Hyde St., between Bush and Pine streets, Nob Hill (© **415/353-6000**), provides 24-hour emergency-care service. The hospital also operates a physician-referral service (© **800/333-1355**). The **Walgreens** on Divisadero Street at Lombard (© **415/931-6415**) has a 24-hour pharmacy.

    San Francisco, like any large city, has its fair share of crime and a serious homelessness problem. Exercise extra caution, particularly at night, in the Tenderloin, the Mission District (especially around 16th and Mission sts.), the lower Fillmore area, around lower Haight Street, and SoMa (south of Market St.).

    An 8.5% **sales tax** is added to all goods and services purchased in San Francisco. The city **hotel tax** is a whopping 14%.

WHAT TO SEE & DO

Alcatraz Island   The sheer cliffs, treacherous tides and currents, and frigid temperatures of the surrounding water supposedly made "the Rock" a totally escape-proof prison. Among the famous gangsters who did time here were Al Capone, Robert Stroud (the Birdman of Alcatraz), and Machine Gun Kelly. In 1963, after an apparent escape in which no bodies were recovered, the government closed the prison, and in 1972 it became part of the Golden Gate National Recreation Area. Tours of Alcatraz include the ferry ride, an audio tour of the prison block, and a slide show. It's a popular excursion and space is limited, so purchase tickets as far in advance as possible. The tour is operated by **Blue & Gold Fleet** (© **415/705-5555;** www.blueand goldfleet.com), and you can buy tickets in advance from the Blue & Gold ticket office on Pier 41. Wear comfortable shoes (there are a lot of steps) and take a jacket.

Pier 41, near Fisherman's Wharf. © **415/773-1188** (info only); www.nps.gov/alcatraz. Admission (includes ferry trip and audio tour) $16 adults with headset, $12 without; $15 seniors 62 and older with headset, $9.75 without; $11 children 5–11 with headset, $8.25 without. Night tours cost $24 adults, $21 seniors 62 and older, $14 children 5–11. Fall, winter, and spring daily 9:30am–4:30pm; summer daily 9:30am–6:30pm. Ferries depart 15 and 45 min. after the hour. Arrive at least 20 min. before sailing time. Night tours leave Thurs–Sun at 4:20 and 5:10pm.

Cable Cars   Designated official historic landmarks by the National Park Service, the city's beloved cable cars clank across the hills like mobile museum pieces. Each weighs about 6 tons and is hauled along by a steel cable, enclosed under the street. They move at a constant 9½ mph. This may strike you as slow, but it doesn't feel that way when you're cresting an almost perpendicular hill and looking down at what seems like a bobsled dive straight into the ocean. But in spite of the thrills, they're perfectly safe.

Powell-Hyde and Powell-Mason lines begin at the base of Powell and Market sts.; California St. line begins at the foot of Market St. $5 per ride.

The Legion of Honor   Designed as a memorial to California's World War I casualties, the neoclassical structure is an exact replica of the Legion of Honor Palace in Paris, right down to the inscription HONNEUR ET PATRIE above the portal. Reopened

San Francisco

San Francisco Bay

Golden Gate Bridge

Area of detail

PRESIDIO

GOLDEN GATE PARK

SAN FRANCISCO

Bay Bridge

ACCOMMODATIONS ■
Argonaut Hotel **4**
Campton Place Hotel **16**
The Fairmont Hotel & Tower **11**
Golden Gate Hotel **15**
King George Hotel **19**
The Marina Inn **3**
Ritz-Carlton **12**
St. Regis Hotel **21**
The Savoy Hotel **17**
Westin St. Francis **20**
The Wharf Inn **6**

DINING ◆
Ame **21**
Aqua **13**
Boulevard **14**
Brandy Ho's Hunan Food **9**
Grand Café **18**
Greens Restaurant **2**
Kokkari **10**
L'Osteria del Forno **8**
Restaurant Gary Danko **5**
Swan Oyster Depot **7**
Ton Kiang **1**
Zuni Café **22**

CABLE CAR LINES
California Line ———
Powell-Mason Line – – – ·
Powell-Hyde Line ———
Cable Car Turnaround ◎

GOLDEN GATE NATIONAL RECREATION AREA

FORT MASON

THE MARINA

Bay St.
Francisco St.
Chestnut St.
Lombard St.
Greenwich St.

COW HOLLOW

PACIFIC HEIGHTS

Divisadero St.
Scott St.
Pierce St.
Steiner St.
Fillmore St.
Webster St.
Buchanan St.
Laguna St.
Octavia St.
Gough St.

Washington St.
Clay St.
Sacramento St.
California St.
Pine St.
Bush St.
Sutter St.
Post St.
Geary St.
O'Farrell St.
Ellis St.
Eddy St.
Turk St.
Golden Gate Ave.
McAllister St.
Fulton St.
Grove St.
Hayes St.
Fell St.
Oak St.

Pacific Medical Center

Lafayette Park

Japan Center

Alamo Square

Ivy St.

HAYES VALLEY

Fell St.

Octavia St.

To Haight-Ashbury (see inset top right)

Page St.
Haight St.
Waller St.
Hermann St.

Duboce Park

Duboce Ave.

THE CASTRO

Market St.

Duboce Ave.

McCopp

Gough

Castro St.
Noe St.
Sanchez St.
Church St.
Dolores St.
14th St.
15th St.
16th St.
Guerrero St.
Valencia St.

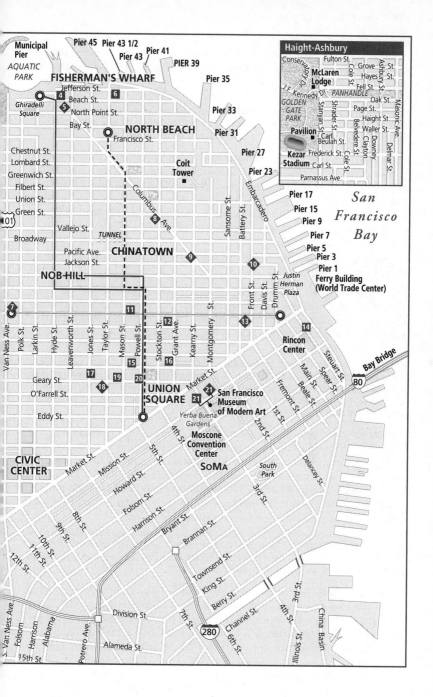

Municipal Pier

AQUATIC PARK

Pier 45 Pier 43 1/2 Pier 43 Pier 41

PIER 39

FISHERMAN'S WHARF

Pier 35

Jefferson St.

4

Beach St.

Ghiradelli Square

5

North Point St.

6

Pier 33

Bay St.

NORTH BEACH

Pier 31

Francisco St.

Pier 27

Chestnut St.

Coit Tower

Pier 23

Lombard St.

Greenwich St.

Filbert St.

Union St.

Green St.

101

Vallejo St.

TUNNEL

8

Broadway

Pacific Ave.

CHINATOWN

Jackson St.

9

NOB HILL

10

7

11

12

13

14

Rincon Center

Geary St.

17

19

20

O'Farrell St.

18

UNION SQUARE

Eddy St.

21

15

16

San Francisco Museum of Modern Art

21

Yerba Buena Gardens

CIVIC CENTER

Moscone Convention Center

Market St.

SoMa

Mission St.

South Park

Howard St.

Folsom St.

Harrison St.

Bryant St.

Brannan St.

Townsend St.

King St.

Berry St.

Channel St.

China Basin

280

Division St.

Alameda St.

15th St.

Haight-Ashbury

Conservatory Fulton St.

McLaren Lodge

Grove St.

Hayes St.

Fell St.

J.F. Kennedy Dr.

PANHANDLE

GOLDEN GATE PARK

Oak St.

Page St.

Haight St.

Waller St.

Pavilion

Carl Beulah St.

Kezar Stadium

Frederick St.

Carl St.

Parnassus Ave.

Pier 17

Pier 15

Pier 9

Pier 7

Pier 5

Pier 3

Pier 1

Ferry Building (World Trade Center)

Justin Herman Plaza

San Francisco Bay

Bay Bridge

80

Columbus Ave.

Sansome St.

Battery St.

Front St.

Davis St.

Drumm St.

Embarcadero

Van Ness Ave.

Polk St.

Larkin St.

Hyde St.

Leavenworth St.

Jones St.

Taylor St.

Mason St.

Powell St.

Stockton St.

Grant Ave.

Kearny St.

Montgomery St.

Market St.

Main St.

Spear St.

Beale St.

Fremont St.

1st St.

2nd St.

3rd St.

Delancey St.

Steuart St.

4th St.

5th St.

8th St.

9th St.

10th St.

11th St.

12th St.

7th St.

6th St.

Van Ness Ave.

Folsom

Harrison

Alabama

Potrero Ave.

Conservatory

Cole St.

Shrader St.

Stanyan St.

Clayton St.

Belvedere St.

Cole St.

Ashbury St.

Masonic Ave.

Downey

Delmar St.

after a 2-year, $29-million renovation and seismic upgrading project that was stalled by the discovery of almost 300 coffins, the museum's collection contains paintings, sculpture, and decorative arts. The display of more than 800 years of European art includes a fine collection of Rodin sculpture. The expansive, grassy surroundings afford astounding views of the Golden Gate.

In Lincoln Park (34th Ave. and Clement St.). $\textcircled{C}$ **415/750-3600,** or 415/863-3330 (recorded information). www.thinker.org. Admission $10 adults, $7 seniors 65 and over, $6 youths 13–17 and college students with ID, free for children 12 and under. Fees may be higher for special exhibitions. Free 1st Tues of each month. Tues–Sun 9:30am–5pm. Bus: 18.

Coit Tower   In a city known for its panoramic views and vantage points, Coit Tower is "The Peak." If it's a clear day, it's wonderful to get here by walking up the Filbert Steps. Inside the base of the tower are the impressive WPA murals titled *Life in California, 1934,* which were completed during the New Deal by more than 25 artists, many of whom had studied under master muralist Diego Rivera. You can see the murals for free, so we recommend not paying the admission to go to the top; the view is just as good from the parking area.

Telegraph Hill. $\textcircled{C}$ **415/362-0808.** Admission is free to enter; to go to the top $3.75 adults, $2.50 seniors, $1.50 children 6–12. Daily 10am–6pm. Bus: 39 (Coit).

The Exploratorium   This fun, hands-on science fair contains more than 650 permanent exhibits that explore everything from color theory to Einstein's theory of relativity. Every exhibit is designed to be used. You can whisper into a concave reflector and have a friend hear you 60 feet away, or you can design your own animated abstract art—using sound.

3601 Lyon St., in the Palace of Fine Arts (at Marina Blvd.). $\textcircled{C}$ **415/563-7337,** or 415/561-0360 (recorded information). www.exploratorium.edu. Admission $13 adults; $10 seniors, youth 13–17, visitors with disabilities, and college students with ID; $8 children 4–12; free for children under 4. Groups of 10 or more must make advance reservations. AE, MC, V. Tues–Sun 10am–5pm. Closed Mon except MLK, Jr., Day, Presidents' Day, Memorial Day, and Labor Day. Free parking. Bus: 28, 30, or Golden Gate Transit.

Golden Gate Bridge   With its spidery bracing cables and sky-high twin towers, the bridge looks more like a work of abstract art than one of the greatest engineering feats of the 20th century. The mile-long steel link reaches a height of 746 feet above the water, and is an awesome bridge to cross. Millions of pedestrians brave the cold, wind, and vibrations each year; it's one of the best ways to experience the bridge's immense scale. You can walk out onto the span from either end. From Marin's Vista Point, you can look back on one of the most famous cityscapes in the world.

Hwy. 101 N. www.goldengatebridge.org. $5 cash toll collected when driving south. Bridge-bound Golden Gate Transit buses (($\textcircled{C}$ **415/923-2000)** depart hourly during the day for Marin County, starting from Mission and First sts. (across from the Transbay Terminal), stopping at Market and Seventh sts., at the Civic Center, along Van Ness Ave., at Lombard and Fillmore sts., and at Francisco and Richardson sts.

Golden Gate Park *(Best*   From the Conservatory of Flowers near the eastern end to Ocean Beach on the western border, Golden Gate Park is an interactive, 1,017-acre botanical symphony—and anyone who likes can play in the orchestra. Spend a sunny day lounging on the grass along JFK Drive, have a good read in the Shakespeare Garden, stroll around Stow Lake, or check out the M. H. de Young Museum's spectacular new home.

The park is made up of hundreds of gardens and attractions linked by wooded paths and roads, so make your first stop the **McLaren Lodge and Park Headquarters** ($\textcircled{C}$ **415/831-2700)** for a detailed overview of information.

The best gardens, among dozens in the park, are the aforementioned Conservatory of Flowers, Rhododendron Dell, the Rose Garden, the Strybing Arboretum and, at the western edge in spring, the thousands of tulips and daffodils around the Dutch windmill. The AIDS Memorial Grove is a special, low-key place for reflection, near the northeastern side of the park.

The park also contains recreational facilities such as tennis courts; playing fields for baseball, soccer, and polo; a golf course; riding stables; and fly-casting pools.

Between Fulton St. and Lincoln Way; main entrance at Fell and Stanyan sts. ℭ 415/831-2700. Bus: 16AX, BX, 5, 6, 7, 66, or 71.

Lombard Street

Known (erroneously) as the "crookedest street in the world," the whimsically winding block of Lombard Street puts smiles on the faces of thousands of visitors each year. The elevation is so steep that the road has to snake back and forth to make a descent possible. This short stretch is one-way, downhill, and fun to drive. You can also take staircases up or down on either side of the street.

Between Hyde and Leavenworth sts.

Mission Dolores

This is the oldest structure in the city, built on order of Franciscan Father Junípero Serra by Father Francisco Palou. It was constructed of 36,000 sunbaked bricks and dedicated in 1776 at the northern terminus of El Camino Real, the Spanish road from Mexico to California. It's a moving place to visit, with its cool, serene buildings and the cemetery and gardens where the early settlers were buried.

16th St. (at Dolores St.). ℭ 415/621-8203. www.missiondolores.org. $3 adults, $2 children. Daily 9am–4pm winter; 9am–4:30pm spring; Good Friday 9am–noon. Closed Thanksgiving, Easter, and Dec 25. Bus: 14, 26, or 33 to Church and 16th sts. Streetcar: J.

San Francisco Museum of Modern Art (SFMOMA)

MOMA's collection consists of more than 23,000 works, including close to 5,000 paintings and sculptures by artists such as Henri Matisse, Jackson Pollock, and Willem de Kooning. Other artists represented include Diego Rivera, Georgia O'Keeffe, Paul Klee, the Fauvists, and exceptional holdings of Richard Diebenkorn. MOMA was also one of the first to recognize photography as a major art form; its extensive collection includes more than 12,000 photographs by such notables as Ansel Adams, Alfred Stieglitz, Edward Weston, and Henri Cartier-Bresson. Whatever you do, check out the fabulous MuseumStore and cafe.

151 Third St. (2 blocks south of Market St., across from Yerba Buena Gardens). ℭ 415/357-4000. www.sfmoma.org. Admission $13 adults, $8 seniors, $7 students over 12 with ID, free for children 12 and under. Half price for all Thurs 6–9pm; free to all 1st Tues of each month. Thurs 11am–8:45pm; Fri–Tues 11am–5:45pm. Closed Wed and major holidays. Bus: 15, 30, or 45. Streetcar: J, K, L, or M to Montgomery.

Yerba Buena Center for the Arts & Yerba Buena Gardens *Kids*

This urban interactive wonderland could keep you busy all day with its 5-acre garden (www.yerba buenagardens.org; open daily 6am–10pm; free admission), cafes, and art-related attractions. The **Center for the Arts** presents music, theater, dance, and visual arts; and **Zeum** (ℭ 415/777-2800; www.zeum.org) is the children's addition, with a cafe, interactive cultural center, ice-skating rink, fabulous 1906 carousel, and interactive play and learning garden. You'll also find retail-and-entertainment mecca **The Metreon** (ℭ 415/537-3400; www.metreon.com), a 350,000-square-foot complex of cinemas, an **IMAX** theater, food court, shops, and interactive attractions.

Yerba Buena Center for the Arts: 701 Mission St. ℭ 415/978-ARTS (box office). www.ybca.org. Admission for gallery $6 adults; $4 seniors, teachers, and students. Free to all 1st Tues of each month; every Thurs free for seniors and students with ID. Tues–Wed and Sun noon–5pm; Thurs–Sat noon–8pm. Streetcar: Powell or Montgomery. Bus: 5, 9, 14, 15, 30, or 45.

GOLDEN GATE NATIONAL RECREATION AREA & THE PRESIDIO

One could easily contend that no urban shoreline is as stunning as San Francisco's. Wrapping around the northern and western edges of the city, the Golden Gate National Recreation Area is run by the National Park Service, which lets visitors fully enjoy it as a park. Several landmarks line the shore, from which visitors have views of both the bay and the ocean. Muni runs service to most sites, including Aquatic Park, the Cliff House, and Ocean Beach. For more information, contact the **National Park Service** (© 415/561-4700; www.nps.gov/goga).

At the northern end of Fillmore Street, **Marina Green** is a favorite spot for flying kites or watching the sailboats on the bay. Just west of here begins the 3.5-mile paved **Golden Gate Promenade,** a favorite biking and hiking path, which leads to the fantastic, recently reestablished marshland preserve **Crissy Field,** one of the city's favorite natural playgrounds. Make a point of seeing this spectacular destination with sandy beach, lots of native birds, and jogging paths.

A national historic site under the Golden Gate Bridge, **Fort Point** (© 415/556-1693; www.nps.gov/fopo) was built in 1853 to protect the entrance to the harbor. Film buffs will recognize it from Alfred Hitchcock's *Vertigo*.

Lincoln Boulevard sweeps around the western edge of the bay to two of the most popular beaches in San Francisco. **Baker Beach,** a small and beautiful strand just outside the Golden Gate, is a fine spot for sunbathing (nudists flock here), walking, or fishing. It's usually packed, but if the cold water doesn't deter you from swimming here, the roaring currents will. Here you can pick up the **Coastal Trail,** which leads through the Presidio, and a short distance from Baker, **China Beach** is a small cove where swimming is permitted. Changing rooms, showers, a sun deck, and restrooms are available. But be warned: The water is crazy-cold!

A little farther around the coast, **Land's End** looks out to Pyramid Rock. A lower and upper trail provide varied hiking options amid wind-swept cypress trees and pines on the cliffs above the Pacific.

Point Lobos, the **Sutro Baths,** and the **Cliff House** lie still farther along the coast. The Cliff House, which underwent major renovations in 2004, has been serving refreshments to visitors since 1863. Here you can view the **Seal Rocks,** home to a colony of sea lions and marine birds. Only traces of the Sutro Baths remain today, northeast of the Cliff House. This popular swimming facility accommodated as many as 24,000 people before it burned down in 1966. A little farther inland, at the western end of California Street, **Lincoln Park** is home to a golf course and The Legion of Honor.

From the Cliff House, the Esplanade continues south along the 4-mile-long **Ocean Beach,** which is unsuitable for swimming, but popular with brave surfers. At the southern end of Ocean Beach, around **Fort Funston,** an easy loop trail runs across the cliffs; for information, call the ranger station (© 415/239-2366).

Farther south along I-280, **Sweeney Ridge** is accessible only by car but affords sweeping views of the coastline from the many trails that crisscross these 1,000 acres of land.

The Presidio, a 1,480-acre former military base, is now an urban park that combines historical, architectural, and natural aspects. It's adjacent to the Golden Gate National Recreation Area, but you could wander from one area to the other without knowing it. The Presidio is especially popular with hikers, bikers, bird-watchers, golfers, and joggers. On the 2-mile **Ecology Loop Trail,** walkers can see more than 30 different species of trees, including redwood, spruce, cypress, and acacias. Hikers can follow the 2.5-mile **Coastal Trail** from Fort Point along this part of the coastline all the way to Land's End. For schedules, maps, and updates on ongoing developments in the Presidio, contact the **Golden Gate National Recreation Area Headquarters** (© 415/556-0560).

SHOPPING

UNION SQUARE   San Francisco's most congested and popular shopping mecca is home to big department stores and many high-end specialty shops. Be sure to venture to Grant Avenue, Post and Sutter streets, and Maiden Lane.

If you're into art, pick up the *San Francisco Gallery Guide*, a comprehensive, bimonthly publication listing the city's current shows. One of our favorite galleries is the **Catharine Clark Gallery,** on the second floor at 49 Geary St., between Kearny and Grant streets (© **415/399-1439;** www.cclarkgallery.com). It exhibits up-and-coming contemporary artists, mainly from California, and nurtures beginning collectors by offering an unusual interest-free purchasing plan.

CHINATOWN   When you pass under the gate to Chinatown on Grant Avenue, say goodbye to the world of fashion and hello to a swarm of cheap tourist shops selling everything from linen and jade to plastic toys and $2 slippers. Grant Avenue is the main thoroughfare, but the real gems are found on the side streets between Bush Street and Columbus Avenue, in small, one-person shops selling Chinese herbs, original art, and jewelry.

SOMA   Though this area isn't suitable for strolling, you'll find almost all the discount shopping in warehouse spaces south of Market. You can pick up a discount-shopping guide at most major hotels. At the **SFMOMA MuseumStore,** 151 Third St. (© 415/357-4035; www.sfmoma.org), the array of cards, books, jewelry, housewares, and knickknacks makes it one of the locals' favorite shops. It also offers far more tasteful mementos than most Fisherman's Wharf options. Fashionable bargain hunters head to **Jeremys,** 2 South Park, at Second Street between Bryant and Brannan streets (© **415/882-4929;** www.jeremys.com), where top designer fashions from shoes to suits go for rock-bottom prices.

THE CASTRO   You could easily spend all day wandering through the home and men's-clothing shops of the Castro. We also come here to visit our favorite chocolate shop, **Joseph Schmidt Confections,** 3489 16th St., at Sanchez Street (© **415/861-8682;** www.josephschmidtconfections.com), where sinfully luscious sweets take on sculptural shapes so exquisite you'll be reluctant to bite into them. Prices are remarkably reasonable.

FISHERMAN'S WHARF & ENVIRONS   The tourist-oriented malls—Ghirardelli Square, PIER 39, the Cannery at Del Monte Square, and the Anchorage—run along Jefferson Street and include hundreds of shops, restaurants, and attractions. Standing out from the usual T-shirt shops and fudge emporiums is **Cost Plus World Market,** 2552 Taylor St., between North Point and Bay streets (© **415/928-6200**), a vast warehouse crammed to the rafters with Chinese baskets, Indian camel bells, Malaysian batik scarves, and innumerable other items from Algeria to Zanzibar.

FILLMORE STREET   Some of the best shopping in town is packed into 5 blocks of Fillmore Street in Pacific Heights. **Zinc Details,** 1905 Fillmore St., between Bush and Pine streets (© **415/776-2100;** www.zincdetails.com), has an amazing collection of locally handcrafted glass vases, pendant lights, ceramics, and furniture.

HAIGHT STREET   The shopping in the 6 blocks of upper Haight Street, between Central Avenue and Stanyan Street, reflects its green-haired, spiked-haired, and no-haired clientele, offering everything from incense and European and American street styles to furniture and antique clothing. **Recycled Records,** 1377 Haight St., between Central and Masonic streets (© **415/626-4075;** www.recycled-records.com), easily one of the best used-record stores in the city, has a good selection of promotional CDs and used, classic rock LPs.

NORTH BEACH   Along with a great cup of coffee, Grant and Columbus avenues cater to their hip clientele with a small but worthy selection of boutiques and specialty shops. For a dose of local color, join the brooding literary types who browse **City Lights Booksellers & Publishers,** 261 Columbus Ave., at Broadway (© **415/362-8193;** www.citylights.com), the famous bookstore owned by renowned Beat-generation poet Lawrence Ferlinghetti. The shelves here are stocked with a comprehensive collection of art, poetry, and political paperbacks, as well as more mainstream books.

WHERE TO STAY

Most of the hotels listed below are within easy walking distance of Union Square, the city's premier shopping and tourist district. Prices listed below do not include state and city taxes, which total 14%.

 San Francisco Reservations, 360 22nd St., Suite 300, Oakland, CA 94612 (© **800/ 677-1500** or 510/628-4450; www.hotelres.com), arranges reservations at more than 150 of San Francisco's hotels and often offers discounted rates.

 In addition to the hotels below, we also recommend those represented by the reasonably priced and fashionable **Joie de Vivre** chain (© **800/SF-TRIPS;** www.sftrips. com) and **Personality Hotels** (© **800/553-1900;** www.personalityhotels.com), which spiffs up older buildings in central locales.

Argonaut Hotel *Kids*   This historic gem, the best hotel on the wharf, opened in 2003. Half a block from the action on the bay (though miraculously quiet), the four-story timber-and-brick landmark building features comfortable rooms and suites whimsically decorated in cheerful nautical colors. Luxurious touches include flatscreen TVs, DVD and CD players, and Aveda toiletries. Suites have killer views, telescopes, and spa tubs. Get a "view" room, which peers onto the wharf or bay (some overlook Alcatraz). Argonaut's friendly staff goes out of their way to make little ones feel at home, making this a great choice for families. All guests are welcome at nightly weekday wine receptions.

495 Jefferson St (at Hyde St.), San Francisco, CA 94109. © **866/415-0704** or 415/563-0800. Fax 415/563-2800. www.argonauthotel.com. 252 units. $179–$379 double; $479–$1,079 suite. Rates include evening wine in the lobby, daily newspaper, and kid-friendly perks such as cribs and strollers. AE, DC, DISC, MC, V. Parking $39. Bus: 10, 30, or 47. Streetcar: F. Cable car: Powell-Hyde line. **Amenities:** Restaurant; exercise room.

Campton Place Hotel   This fabulous Union Square boutique hotel offers some of the best accommodations in town—not to mention the most expensive. Management recently replaced the furnishings with limestone, pear wood, and more Italian-modern and Asian-influenced decor. Guests will still find superlative service, robes, slippers, fax machines, and every necessity and whim that's made Campton Place a favored address.

340 Stockton St. (between Post and Sutter sts.), San Francisco, CA 94108. © **800/235-4300** or 415/781-5555. Fax 415/955-5536. www.camptonplace.com. 110 units. $340–$475 double; from $575–$2,000 suite. American breakfast $18. AE, DC, MC, V. Valet parking $38. Bus: 2, 3, 4, 30, 38, or 45. Cable car: Powell-Hyde or Powell-Mason lines (1 block west). BART and underground: Market St. **Amenities:** Restaurant; health club.

The Fairmont Hotel & Tower   The granddaddy of Nob Hill's ritzy hotels, the historic Fairmont was designed by the same architect who dreamed up Hearst Castle and wins top honors for the most awe-inspiring lobby in town. Even if you're not staying here, come gape at its massive marble columns, vaulted ceilings, velvet chairs, gilded mirrors, and spectacular wraparound staircase. Thanks to an $85-million renovation in 2001, everything in the guest rooms is new, opulent, and in good taste. In addition to the expected luxuries, you'll find goose-down pillows, electric shoe buffers, and walk-in closets.

950 Mason St. (at California St.), San Francisco, CA 94108. ℂ 800/441-1414 or 415/772-5000. Fax 415/772-5086. www.fairmont.com. 591 units. Main building $229–$349 double; from $500 suite. Tower $289–$469 double; from $750 suite. Penthouse $12,500. Extra person $30. AE, DC, DISC, MC, V. Parking $43. Cable car: California St. line (direct stop). **Amenities:** 2 restaurants; health club ($15 daily). *In room:* Kitchenette (in some units).

Golden Gate Hotel   The family-run Golden Gate Hotel, occupying a historic building, is a real gem, just 2 blocks north of Union Square. The hospitable innkeepers take obvious pleasure in making their guests comfortable. Each individually decorated room has handsome antiques (plenty of wicker), quilted bedspreads, and fresh flowers; some have claw-foot tubs. Guests are welcome to complimentary afternoon tea, served daily from 4 to 7pm, and free use of the house fax and computer with wireless DSL.

775 Bush St. (between Powell and Mason sts.), San Francisco, CA 94108. ℂ 800/835-1118 or 415/392-3702. Fax 415/392-6202. www.goldengatehotel.com. 25 units, 14 with bathroom. $95 double without bathroom; $130 double with bathroom. Rates include continental breakfast and afternoon tea. AE, DC, MC, V. Self-parking $18. Bus: 2, 4, 30, 38, or 45. Cable car: Powell-Hyde or Powell-Mason lines (1 block east). BART: Powell and Market. **Amenities:** Access to health club 1 block away.

The Hotel California *Value*   This European-style hotel (formerly the Savoy Hotel) is one of our favorite moderately priced downtown hotels (the Warwick Regis is our other top pick). Given the cozy, apartment-like feel of each room, appointed with featherbeds and goose-down pillows, it's easy to relax here. Rooms can be small, but each has 18th-century period furnishings, 400-thread-count sheets, full-length mirrors, two-line telephones, and clean bathrooms with original tile work. Guests also enjoy round-the-clock concierge service and access to the **Millennium** restaurant, the city's only gourmet vegan dining room.

580 Geary St. (between Taylor and Jones sts.), San Francisco, CA 94102. ℂ 800/227-4223 or 415/441-2700. Fax 415/441-0124. www.thesavoyhotel.com. 82 units. $119–$289 double; $129–$399 suite. Complimentary wine and cheese 4–6pm daily. Ask about packages; continental breakfast $7. AE, DC, DISC, MC, V. Valet parking $30. Bus: 2, 3, 4, 27, or 38. **Amenities:** Restaurant; fitness center.

King George Hotel *Value*   This utterly delightful hotel has fared well over the years, continuing to draw a mostly European clientele. The location—surrounded by cable-car lines, the Theater District, and Union Square—is superb. The small but very clean guest rooms are surprisingly quiet for such a busy area, and new mattresses, desks, and textiles add to the handsome studylike ambience. The English afternoon tea is a big hit, served in the Windsor Tea Room Saturday, Sunday, and holidays from 1 to 4:30pm. Recent additions include a pub, 24-hour business center, and an upgraded "executive" level.

334 Mason St. (between Geary and O'Farrell sts.), San Francisco, CA 94102. ℂ 800/288-6005 or 415/781-5050. Fax 415/835-5991. www.kinggeorge.com. 153 units. $165 double; $185 suite. Breakfast $9.95–$13. Special-value packages available seasonally. AE, DC, DISC, MC, V. Valet parking $26; self-parking $23. Bus: 1, 2, 3, 4, 5, 7, 30, 38, 45, 70, or 71. Cable car: Powell-Hyde or Powell-Mason lines (1 block west). **Amenities:** Tearoom.

The Marina Inn *(Value)*   This is the best value among the city's low-priced hotels. How this 1924 four-story Victorian offers so much for so little is mystifying. Each room looks as though it's been culled from a country-furnishings catalog, complete with four-poster bed topped by a silk-soft comforter. Extra perks include new TVs discreetly hidden in pine cabinetry, nightly turndown service, afternoon sherry, friendly service, and an armada of nearby shops and restaurants. (*Note:* Traffic can be noisy here, so the hotel added double-paned glass on windows facing the street.)

3110 Octavia St. (at Lombard St.), San Francisco, CA 94123. ℂ 800/274-1420 or 415/928-1000. Fax 415/928-5909. www.marinainn.com. 40 units. Nov–Feb $65–$105 double; Mar–May $75–$125 double; June–Oct $85–$135 double. Rates include continental breakfast. AE, DC, DISC, MC, V. Bus: 28, 30, 43, or 76.

Ritz-Carlton *(Best)*   Ranked among the top hotels in the world by readers of *Condé Nast Traveler,* the Ritz-Carlton has been the benchmark of Nob Hill's luxury hotels since it opened in 1991, and it's the best in town. It's outfitted with the finest furnishings, fabrics, and artwork, and the rooms offer every possible amenity, from Italian-marble bathrooms to plush terry robes. The more expensive rooms offer good views of the city. Club rooms have a dedicated concierge, separate elevator-key access, and complimentary buffet meals. Services include a courtesy car and in-room massage.

600 Stockton St. (between Pine and California sts.), San Francisco, CA 94108. ℂ 800/241-3333 or 415/296-7465. Fax 415/986-1268. www.ritzcarlton.com. 336 units. $425–$460 double; $580–$830 club-level double; from $730–$830 executive suite. Buffet breakfast $32; Sun champagne brunch $65. Weekend discounts and packages available. AE, DC, DISC, MC, V. Parking $55. Cable car: California St. cable car line (direct stop). **Amenities:** 2 restaurants; pool (indoor); health club.

St. Regis Hotel   The latest in full-blown high-tech luxury is yours at this new superchic 40-story SoMa tower near Yerba Buena Gardens. A shrine to urban luxury living, it welcomes guests with a trendy lobby bar; minimalist-chic rooms with touch-screen control panels that work everything; sexy touches such as Barcelona benches, 42-inch plasma TVs, deep soaking tubs, 13-inch LCD TVs, and fancy toiletries; the superposh two-floor Remède Spa; and restaurant Ame, where chef Hiro Sone, who also owns Terra in Napa Valley, presides over an Asian-influenced luxury menu that has been heralded as the hottest new restaurant of the past year.

125 Third St. (at Mission St.), San Francisco, CA 94103. ℂ 877/787-3447 or 415/284-4000. Fax 415/284-4100. stregis.com/sanfrancisco. 260 units. From $529–$679 double; from $1,050–$8,500 suite. AE, DC, DISC, MC, V. Parking $45 per day. Bus: 15, 30, or 45. Streetcar: J, K, L, or M to Montgomery. **Amenities:** 2 restaurants; health club w/heated lap pool; spa.

Westin St. Francis *(Kids)*   Although the St. Francis is too massive to offer the personal service found at smaller Nob Hill accommodations, few hotels can match its majestic aura. Stroll through the ornate lobby and you can feel 100 years of history oozing from its hand-carved redwood paneling. Rooms in the Tower, which was built in the 1970s and renovated in 2001, evoke a contemporary design in the vein of W Hotel style. The main building accentuates its history with traditional, more elegant ambience. Unfortunately, the tearoom closed, but **Michael Mina**—one of the town's fanciest dining experiences—debuted on the premises in 2004. The Westin Kids Club program entitles children to a goodie bag.

335 Powell St. (between Geary and Post sts.), San Francisco, CA 94102. ℂ 800/WESTIN-1 or 415/397-7000. Fax 415/774-0124. www.westin.com. 1,195 units. Main building: $199–$499 double; Tower (Grand View): $219–$549 double; from $650 suite (in either building). Extra person $30. Continental breakfast $15–$18. AE, DC, DISC, MC, V. Valet parking $42. Bus: 2, 3, 4, 30, 38, 45, or 76. Cable car: Powell-Hyde or Powell-Mason lines (direct stop). Pets under 40 lb. accepted (dog beds available on request). **Amenities:** 2 restaurants; health club and spa.

The Wharf Inn *(Kids)*   Our top choice for good-value lodging at Fisherman's Wharf, The Wharf Inn boasts newly refurbished rooms with all of the necessary amenities, free parking (almost unheard of in this city), and no charge for an extra person in the room. Its main calling card, however, is its location—smack-dab in the middle of the wharf and within walking distance of North Beach.

2601 Mason St. (at Beach St.), San Francisco, CA 94133. C 800/548-9918 or 415/673-7411. Fax 415/776-2181. www.wharfinn.com. 51 units. $99–$209 double; $299–$439 penthouse. AE, DC, DISC, MC, V. Free parking. Bus: 10, 15, 39, or 47. Streetcar: F. Cable car: Powell-Mason or Powell-Hyde lines. **Amenities:** Access to nearby health club ($10 per day).

WHERE TO DINE

San Francisco's dining scene is one of the best in the world. Since our space is limited, we had to make tough choices, but the end result is a cross section of the best in every cuisine and price range. Remember, for top restaurants, make your reservation weeks in advance.

Ame ECLECTIC   Hiro Sone and Lissa Doumani, the owners of Napa Valley's special-occasion restaurant Terra, are behind the hottest opening of the past year. On the ground level of the new and *très* chic St. Regis Hotel, Ame fits right in with dark woods, red accents, and long striped curtains hiding the street scene. But what makes it the new destination restaurant is the menu. Crafted by Sone, a master of Japanese, French, and Italian cuisine, it offers exotic selections ranging from pristine and creative sashimi to Japanese egg custard with lobster and urchin to wildly decadent mushroom risotto topped with foie gras and barbecued eel. And if those are too esoteric, there's always lobster, scallops, and cuttlefish dressed in decidedly Italian lemon-garlic-parsley butter. The neighboring superswank bar offers equally delicious food orchestrated by Sone.

689 Mission St. (at 3rd St.). C 415/284-4040. www.amerestaurant.com. Reservations recommended. Main courses lunch $19–$25, dinner $22–$35. AE, DC, DISC, MC, V. Daily 11:30am–2pm and 6–10pm. Bus: 15, 30, or 45. Streetcar: J, K, L, or M to Montgomery.

Aqua SEAFOOD   At San Francisco's finest seafood restaurant, heralded chef Laurent Manrique dazzles customers with a bewildering juxtaposition of earth and sea treats. Under his care, the artfully composed dishes are delicately decadent. The sommelier pairs wines to perfection with dishes such as Alaskan black cod wrapped in smoked bacon and accompanied by tomato-and-date chutney and glazed carrots. Desserts are not quite as impressive.

252 California St. (near Battery). C 415/956-9662. www.aqua-sf.com. Reservations recommended. Main courses $29–$39; 3-course menu $68; 6-course tasting menu $95; vegetarian tasting menu $65. AE, DC, DISC, MC, V. Mon–Fri 11:30am–2pm; Mon–Sat 5:30–10:30pm; Sun 5:30–9:30pm. Bus: All Market St. buses.

Boulevard *(Best)* AMERICAN   This SoMa spot is already an all-time favorite and our pick for the best in the city. Why? The dramatic Belle Epoque interior combined with well-sculpted, mouthwatering dishes. Creative main courses might include fire-roasted Angus filet with crispy Yukon gold potatoes, béarnaise sauce, sautéed spinach and crimini mushrooms, and red-wine jus. Vegetarian items, such as wild-mushroom risotto with fresh chanterelles and Parmesan, are also offered.

1 Mission St. (between The Embarcadero and Steuart sts.). C 415/543-6084. www.boulevardrestaurant.com. Reservations recommended. Main courses $14–$22 lunch, $28–$39 dinner. AE, DC, DISC, MC, V. Mon–Fri 11:30am–2:15pm; Sun–Thurs 5:30–9:30pm; Fri–Sat 5:30–10:30pm. Bus: 12, 15, 30, 32, or 41. BART: Embarcadero.

Brandy Ho's Hunan Food *(Kids)* CHINESE   Fancy black-and-white granite table-tops and a large, open kitchen are the first clues that the food at this casual, fun restaurant is a cut above the usual Hunan fare. Take my advice and start immediately with fried dumplings (in sweet-and-sour sauce) or cold chicken salad, and then move on to fish-ball soup with spinach, bamboo shoots, noodles, and other goodies. The best main course is Three Delicacies, a combination of scallops, shrimp, and chicken with onion, bell pepper, and bamboo shoots, seasoned with ginger, garlic, and wine, and served with black-bean sauce. Most dishes are hot and spicy, but the kitchen will adjust the level of heat to your specifications. A full bar includes Asian food–friendly libations such as plum wine and sake from 11:30am to 11pm.

217 Columbus Ave. (at Pacific Ave.). (C) 415/788-7527. www.brandyhos.com. Reservations recommended. Main courses $8–$13. AE, DISC, MC, V. Sun–Thurs 11:30am–11pm; Fri–Sat 11:30am–midnight. Bus: 15 or 41.

Grand Café FRENCH   If you want a huge dose of atmosphere with your seared salmon, Grand Café is your best bet. Its claims to fame? The most *grand* dining room in San Francisco, an enormous turn-of-the-20th-century grand ballroom–like dining oasis that's a magnificent combination of old Europe and Art Nouveau; and a festive (read: crowded) cocktail area. To match the surroundings, newly appointed chef Ron Boyd, a San Francisco native and Domaine Chandon alum, serves dressed-up French-inspired California dishes such as sautéed salmon with French lentils and house-cured bacon or salade niçoise. You can drop by for a lighter meal in the casual front room, the Petit Café, with a raw bar and similar dishes for about half the price.

501 Geary St. (at Taylor St., adjacent to the Hotel Monaco). (C) 415/292-0101. www.grandcafe-sf.com. Reservations recommended. Main courses $18–$28. AE, DC, DISC, MC, V. Mon–Fri 7–10:30am and 11:30am–2:30pm; Sat 8am–2:30pm; Sun 9am–2:30pm; Sun–Thurs 5:30–10pm; Fri–Sat 5:30–11pm. Bus: 2, 3, 4, 27, or 38.

Greens Restaurant VEGETARIAN   Knowledgeable locals swear by Greens, where executive chef Annie Somerville cooks with the seasons, using produce from local organic farms. Located in an old warehouse, with enormous windows overlooking the bridge and the bay, the restaurant is both a pioneer and a legend. Entrees run the gamut from pizza with wilted escarole, red onions, lemon, and Parmesan to Vietnamese yellow curry. Those interested in the whole shebang should make reservations for the $48 four-course dinner served on Saturday only. The adjacent Greens To Go bakery sells breads, sandwiches, soups, salads, and pastries.

Building A, Fort Mason Center (enter Fort Mason opposite the Safeway at Buchanan and Marina sts.). (C) 415/771-6222. www.greensrestaurant.com. Reservations recommended. Main courses $9.50–$14 lunch, $15–$20 dinner; fixed-price dinner $48; Sun brunch $8–$14. AE, DISC, MC, V. Tues–Sat noon–2:30pm; Sun 10:30am–2pm; Mon–Sat 5:30–9pm. Greens To Go Mon–Thurs 8am–8pm; Fri–Sat 8am–5pm; Sun 9am–4pm. Bus: 28 or 30.

Kokkari *(Value)* GREEK   Kokkari (Ko-*car*-ee) takes Greek food to delicious contemporary heights—both in decor and flavor. The dining area is like a rustic living room, with a commanding fireplace and oversize furnishings. Delicious, traditional Aegean dishes include a moussaka (eggplant, lamb, potato, and béchamel) that's to die for, or the quail stuffed with winter greens served on oven-roasted leeks, orzo, and wild-rice *pilafi*.

200 Jackson St. (at Front St.). (C) 415/981-0983. www.kokkari.com. Reservations recommended. Main courses $14–$23 lunch, $19–$35 dinner. AE, DC, DISC, MC, V. Mon–Thurs 11:30am–10pm, Fri 11:30am–11pm, Sat 5–11pm. Bus: 12, 15, 41, or 83.

L'Osteria del Forno ITALIAN   It's not much bigger than a closet, but L'Osteria del Forno is one of the top Italian restaurants in North Beach. Peer in the window, and you'll probably see two Italian women sweating from the heat of the brick-lined oven, which cranks out the best focaccia in the city. There's no pomp or circumstance: Locals come here strictly to eat. The menu features a variety of pizzas, salads, soups, and pastas, plus daily specials. Good news for folks on the go: You can get pizza by the slice.

519 Columbus Ave. (between Green and Union sts.). © 415/982-1124. Reservations not accepted. Sandwiches $6–$7; pizzas $10–$18; main courses $6–$14. No credit cards. Sun–Mon and Wed–Thurs 11:30am–10pm; Fri–Sat 11:30am–10:30pm. Bus: 15, 30, 41, or 45.

Restaurant Gary Danko MODERN CLASSIC   Gary Danko, who received the James Beard Foundation award for best chef in California, presides over this romantic yet unfussy dining room. The three- to five-course menu is freestyle, so whether you want a sampling of appetizers or a flight of meat courses, you need only ask. Top picks? Glazed oysters, which are as creamy as the light accompanying sauce graced with leeks and intricately carved "zucchini pearls"; and seared foie gras with peaches, caramelized onions, and verjuice sauce. Diners at the bar have the option of ordering a la carte.

800 North Point St. (at Hyde St.). © 415/749-2060. www.garydanko.com. Reservations required except at walk-in bar. 3- to 5-course fixed-price menu $61–$89. AE, DC, DISC, MC, V. Daily 5:30–10pm; bar open 5pm. Bus: 10. Streetcar: F. Cable car: Hyde.

Swan Oyster Depot SEAFOOD   Opened in 1912, this Russian Hill hole in the wall boasts only 20 or so seats, jammed cheek-by-jowl along a long marble bar. The menu is limited to fresh crab, shrimp, oyster, clam cocktails, Maine lobster, and Boston-style clam chowder, all of which are exceedingly fresh. Don't let the lunchtime line dissuade you—it moves fast.

1517 Polk St. (between California and Sacramento sts.). © 415/673-1101. Reservations not accepted. Seafood cocktails $7–$15; clams and oysters on the half shell $7.95 per half-dozen. No credit cards. Mon–Sat 8am–5:30pm. Bus: 1, 19, 47, or 49.

Ton Kiang (Kids) CHINESE/DIM SUM   Ton Kiang is the number-one place in the city to do dim sum. From stuffed crab claws, roast Peking duck, and a gazillion dumpling selections to the delicious and hard-to-find *doa miu* (snow-pea sprouts, flash-sautéed with garlic and peanut oil) and a mesmerizing mango pudding, every tray of morsels coming from the kitchen is an absolute delight. The full menu of Hakka cuisine is worth investigation as well.

5821 Geary Blvd. (between 22nd and 23rd aves.). © 415/387-8273. www.tonkiang.net. Reservations accepted for parties of 8 or more. Dim sum $2–$5.50; main courses $9–$25. AE, DC, DISC, MC, V. Mon–Thurs 10am–10pm; Fri 10am–10:30pm; Sat 9:30am–10:30pm; Sun 9am–10pm. Bus: 38.

Zuni Café MEDITERRANEAN   Trend-setting Zuni Café is, and probably always will be, a local favorite. Its expanse of windows and prime lower Castro location guarantee good people-watching, but even better is the incredibly satisfying menu. Stand at the bustling bar, order a glass of wine and a few oysters, and then take a seat amid the exposed-brick maze of little dining rooms. The proven winners are the brick-oven-roasted chicken for two with Tuscan-style bread salad, and the hamburger on grilled rosemary focaccia bread.

1658 Market St. (at Franklin St.). © 415/552-2522. Reservations recommended. Main courses $10–$19 lunch, $15–$29 dinner. AE, MC, V. Tues–Sat 11:30am–midnight; Sun 11am–11pm. Bus: 6, 7, or 71. Streetcar: All Market St. streetcars.

SAN FRANCISCO AFTER DARK

For up-to-date nightlife information, turn to the *San Francisco Weekly* and the *San Francisco Bay Guardian,* which contain comprehensive, current listings. They're free at bars and restaurants, and from street-corner boxes around the city. *Where,* a free tourist monthly, also details programs and performance times; it's available in most fine hotels. The Sunday edition of the *San Francisco Chronicle* also features a "Date-book" section, on pink paper, with information and listings.

Tix Bay Area (© 415/433-7827; www.tixbayarea.org) sells half-price tickets to theater, dance, and music performances on the day of the show only. Tix also sells advance, full-price tickets, as does **City Box Office,** 180 Redwood St., Suite 100, between Golden Gate and McAllister streets off Van Ness Avenue (© 415/392-4400; www.city boxoffice.com). **Tickets.com** (© 800/225-2277; www.tickets.com) sells computer-generated tickets to concerts, sporting events, plays, and special events. Beware, though, that this service imposes a hefty service charge of $3 to $19 per ticket.

For information on local theater, check out **www.bayareatheatre.org**.

THE PERFORMING ARTS   The **American Conservatory Theater** (© 415/749-2-ACT; www.act-sfbay.org), one of the nation's premier theater ensembles, performs at the Geary Theater, 415 Geary St., at Mason Street, and features both classical and experimental works. The highly acclaimed **Magic Theatre** (© 415/441-8822; www.magictheatre.org) has nurtured the talents of such modern playwrights as Sam Shepard and Jon Robin Baitz. Performances are held at Building D, Fort Mason Center, Marina Boulevard at Buchanan Street.

The well-regarded **San Francisco Symphony** (© 415/864-6000; www.sfsymphony.org) performs at Davies Symphony Hall, 201 Van Ness Ave., at Grove Street.

The War Memorial Opera House, 301 Van Ness Ave., at Grove Street, is home to performances of both the **San Francisco Ballet** (© 415/865-2000; www.sfballet.org), the oldest professional ballet company in the nation, and the **San Francisco Opera** (© 415/864-3330; www.sfopera.org), the first municipal opera in the United States.

COMEDY & CABARET   A San Francisco tradition for more than 3 decades, *Beach Blanket Babylon,* Club Fugazi, 678 Green St. (© 415/421-4222), is best known for its outrageous costumes and oversize headdresses. Almost every performance sells out, so get tickets at least 3 weeks in advance.

JAZZ & BLUES CLUBS   **Biscuits & Blues,** 401 Mason St. (© 415/292-2583; www.biscuitsandblues.com), boasts a blow-your-eardrums-out sound system in a New Orleans–style basement speak-easy. **Lou's Pier 47 Club,** 300 Jefferson St. (© 415/771-5687; www.louspier47.com), attracts few locals, but hosts decent jazz, blues, rock, and country bands near the Wharf. If there's one good-time destination that's an anchor for the party people, it's Embarcadero's **Pier 23,** at The Embarcadero and Greenwich Street (© 415/362-5125; www.pier23cafe.com). Part ramshackle patio spot and part dance floor with a heavy dash of dive bar, here it's all about fun for a startlingly diverse clientele. Expect to boogie down shoulder-to-shoulder to live bands playing blues or funk. **Cafe du Nord,** 2170 Market St. (© 415/861-5016), has been around since 1907, but only recently convinced a younger generation to appreciate it as a respectable jazz venue, with American fare, live music, and a front-room bar.

SUPPER CLUBS   If you can eat dinner, listen to live music, and dance in the same room, we call it a supper club, and **Harry Denton's Starlight Room,** at the Sir Francis Drake Hotel, 450 Powell St., 21st floor (© 415/395-8595; www.harrydenton.com), is one of the best. Tourists and locals come to this 1930s-era lounge-turned-nightclub to sip drinks at sunset and boogie down to live swing and big-band tunes after dark. A change of ownership in 2003 converted **Jazz at Pearls,** 256 Columbus

Ave. (© **415/291-8255;** www.jazzatpearls.com), from one of the best jazz venues in the city into one of the best supper clubs. Jazz at Pearl's combines a 1930s vibe, Spanish tapas, and great live music. With only 25 tables, advance tickets are recommended if you want to sit; general admission tickets are available as well, but don't guarantee seating.

DANCE CLUBS   The **Endup,** 401 Sixth St. (© **415/357-0827;** www.theendup. com) is where the sleepless dance-all-day crowd comes after other clubs close (it's open Sat morning from 6am–noon and then nonstop from Sat night around 10pm until Sun night/Mon morning at 4am). Every night hosts a different theme, but you can always count on a huge heated outdoor deck (with waterfall and fountain), an indoor fireplace, and an eclectic clientele. **Suite one8one,** 181 Eddy St. (© **415/345-9900;** www.suite 181.com), may be in one of the sketchiest parts of town, but this tri-level club is a fantastic place to work up a sweat on the dance floors. Chic, softly lit, and *très* fashionable, it's where the velvet rope set gets their groove on to house, funk, and hip-hop grooves.

Within an 1890s Victorian playhouse previously known as The Stage Door, **Ruby Skye,** 420 Mason St. (© **415/693-0777;** www.rubyskye.com), hosts hundreds of partyers who dance on the ballroom floor, mingle on the mezzanine, and puff freely in the smoking room. DJs or live music bring the dancing house down Thursdays through Saturdays. Big spenders should book the VIP lounge, which offers a glitzy place to hang, and bird's-eye views of the whole club scene.

THE BAR SCENE   **Bambuddha Lounge,** 601 Eddy St. (© **415/885-5088;** www. bambuddhalounge.com), adjoins the rock-'n'-roll Phoenix Hotel and is the hottest place for the young and the trendy to feast, flirt, or just be fabulous. The **Bubble Lounge,** 714 Montgomery St. (© **415/434-4204;** www.bubblelounge.com), serves 300 kinds of champagne (30 of them by the glass).

Over in North Beach, **Vesuvio,** 255 Columbus Ave. (© **415/362-3370**), has been catering to local writers, artists, and musicians since Beatnik days (it's no coincidence that City Lights Bookstore is just across Jack Kerouac Alley).

Thirsty Bear Brewing Company, 661 Howard St. (© **415/974-0905;** www. thirstybear.com), serves seven superb, handcrafted varieties of beer and excellent Spanish food. The **San Francisco Brewing Company,** 155 Columbus Ave. (© **415/434-3344;** www.sfbrewing.com), is one of the city's few remaining old saloons, aglow with stained-glass windows, skylights, and a mahogany bar.

For cocktails with a view, try the **Carnelian Room,** 555 California St., in the Bank of America Building (© **415/433-7500;** www.carnelianroom.com). The restaurant has the most extensive wine list in the city, with 1,600 selections, and due to the recent appointment of a new chef, the food may just be impressive soon, too. Jacket and tie are required for men. **Top of the Mark,** in the Mark Hopkins Intercontinental, 1 Nob Hill (© **415/616-6916**), is the most famous cocktail lounge in the city. During World War II, thousands of Pacific-bound servicemen toasted their farewells to the States here.

THE GAY & LESBIAN SCENE   **Twin Peaks Tavern,** 401 Castro St. (© **415/864-9470**), is considered the first gay bar in America. Because of its notoriety and its small size, the place becomes fairly crowded and convivial by 8pm. The **Stud,** 399 Ninth St. (© **415/863-6623;** www.studsf.com), around for 40 years and one of the most successful gay establishments in town, is mellow enough for straights as well as gays. Music varies from cabaret nights and oldies to disco. The **Café,** 2367 Market St. (© **415/861-3846;** www.cafesf.com), started out as a lesbian dance club on Saturday nights, but once the guys found out how much fun the girls were having, they joined the party. **The EndUp,** 401 Sixth St. ((C) **415/357-0827**), is a different club every night, but the place is always jumping with the DJs blasting tunes.

2 The Wine Country

California's Napa and Sonoma valleys are two of the most famous winegrowing regions in the world. Hundreds of wineries are nestled among the vines, and most are open to visitors. But even if you don't want to wine-taste, the fresh country air, beautiful rolling countryside, and world-class restaurants and spas are reason enough to come. If you can, plan on spending more than a day here; you'll need a couple of days just to get to know one of the valleys (don't try to do both unless you've got several days free).

NAPA VALLEY

Napa Valley dwarfs Sonoma Valley in both population and number of wineries. It also has more spas (some at far cheaper rates), a far superior selection of fine restaurants and hotels, and, of course, more traffic jams. But if your goal is to really learn about the wonderful world of winemaking, world-class wineries such as Sterling and Robert Mondavi offer the most edifying wine tours in North America, if not the world.

Napa Valley is just 35 miles long; you can venture from one end to the other in less than a half-hour (traffic permitting). Conveniently, most of the large wineries—as well as most of the hotels, shops, and restaurants—are located along a single road, **Highway 29.** The beauty of the valley is striking any time of the year, but it's most memorable in September and October when the grapes are being pressed and the wineries are in full production.

VISITOR INFORMATION   Once in Napa Valley, stop first at the **Napa Valley Conference & Visitors Bureau (NVCVB),** 1310 Town Center Mall, Napa, CA 94559 ((C) **707/226-7459**), and pick up the *Napa Valley Guide.* Or call ahead and order the $10 package—the guide plus a bunch of brochures, a map, and *Four Perfect Days in the Wine Country* itinerary. If you don't want to pay for the official publications, point your browser to **www.napavalley.com**, the NVCVB's official site, which has much of the same information for free.

TOURING THE TOP WINERIES

No place in the valley brings together art and wine better than the **Hess Collection,** 4411 Redwood Rd., Napa ((C) **707/255-1144;** www.hesscollection.com). After acquiring the old Christian Brothers winery in 1978, Swiss art collector Donald Hess also funded a huge restoration and expansion project to honor wine and the fine arts. The result is a working winery interspersed with gloriously lit rooms that exhibit his truly stunning art collection. The self-guided tour is free, but the tasting fee is $10.

Domaine Chandon, 1 California Dr., at Highway 29, Yountville ((C) **707/944-2280;** www.chandon.com), is the valley's most renowned sparkling winery. It was founded in 1973 by French champagne house Moët et Chandon. Stroll the manicured gardens, sip sparkling wine on the patio, and then glide into the dining room for lunch. Bubbly is sold by the glass ($9–$14); the comprehensive tour of the facilities is worth the time.

At the magnificent mission-style **Robert Mondavi Winery,** 7801 St. Helena Hwy. (Hwy. 29), Oakville ((C) **800/MONDAVI** or 707/226-1395; www.robertmondavi winery.com), almost every variable in the winemaking process is controlled by computer. After the hour tour ($25), you can sample the results in selected current wines, free of charge. If you don't tour, you have to pay to taste. Reserve at least a week in advance in summer.

PlumpJack Winery, 620 Oakville Cross Rd., Oakville (© **707/945-1220;** www. plumpjack.com), stands out as the Todd Oldham of wine tasting—chic, colorful, a little wild, and popular with a young and old crowd. This playfully medieval winery is a welcome diversion from the same old, same old. But there's some serious winemaking going on here, too, and for $5 you can sample the impressive cabernet, chardonnay, and sangiovese. There are no tours or picnic spots, but this refreshingly friendly facility will make you want to linger nonetheless.

Hollywood meets Napa Valley at the **Rubicon Estate,** 1991 St. Helena Hwy. (Hwy. 29), Rutherford (© **800/RUBICON** or 707/968-1100; www.rubiconestate.com), owned by director Francis Ford Coppola. Amid the Oscars and other Tinseltown glitz, you'll find some decent wine, produced on spectacular grounds. You'll have to fork over $25 to visit the estate, but that includes a tasting of five wines, a tour of various historic properties, and valet parking. **V. Sattui Winery,** 1111 White Lane, at Highway 29, St. Helena (© **707/963-7774;** www.vsattui.com), is a combination winery and enormous gourmet deli, which stocks sandwich meats, breads, and exotic salads, while the wine bar in the back offers everything from chardonnay to a tasty Madeira. The expansive, lively picnic facilities make this a favorite for families.

Joseph Phelps Vineyards, 200 Taplin Rd., St. Helena (© **800/707-5789** or 707/ 963-4831; www.jpvwines.com), is a favorite stop for serious wine lovers. The winery was founded in 1973 and has since become a major player in both the region and the worldwide wine market. The intimate tour and knockout tasting are available only by reservation, and the location—a quick and unmarked turn off the Silverado Trail in Spring Valley—makes it impossible to find unless you're looking for it.

Schramsberg, 1400 Schramsberg Rd., off Highway 29, Calistoga (© **707/942-2414;** www.schramsberg.com), is one of our all-time favorite places. Schramsberg is the label that U.S. presidents serve when toasting foreign dignitaries, and there's plenty of memorabilia to prove it. The unintimidating tour of the 2-mile champagne caves ends in a charming tasting room, where you can sample surprisingly varied selections of bubbly. Tasting prices are a bit dear at $25 per person, but it's money well spent. Tastings are offered only to those who take the free tour; you must reserve a spot in advance.

Architect Michael Graves designed the incredible oasis known as **Clos Pegase,** 1060 Dunaweal Lane, off Highway 29 or the Silverado Trail, Calistoga (© **707/942-4981;** www.clospegase.com), which integrates art, 20,000 square feet of aging caves, and a luxurious private hilltop home on its 450 acres. Viewing the art here is as much the point as tasting the wines. Tasting current releases costs $10 for samples of three wines.

You don't need climbing shoes to reach **Sterling Vineyards,** 1111 Dunaweal Lane, off Highway 29, Calistoga (© **707/942-3344;** www.sterlingvineyards.com), a dazzling white Mediterranean-style winery, perched 300 feet up on a rocky knoll. Just hand over $15 ($10 for kids, which includes a goodie bag), and you'll arrive via aerial tram, which offers dazzling bucolic views along the way. Once on land, follow the valley's most comprehensive self-guided tour of the winemaking process. Samples at the panoramic tasting room are included in the tram fare.

BEYOND THE WINERIES: WHAT TO SEE & DO IN NAPA VALLEY

ART GALLERIES   Anyone with an appreciation for art absolutely must visit the **di Rosa Preserve,** 5200 Sonoma Hwy., Napa (© 707/226-5991). Rene and Veronica di Rosa's world-renowned collection of contemporary American art—more than 2,000 works by more than 900 Bay Area artists—is displayed practically everywhere throughout their 53-acre estate. Visits are by appointment only and last about 2 hours.

Find the New You—in a Calistoga Mud Bath

The one thing you should do while you're in Calistoga is what people have been doing here for the last 150 years: Take a mud bath. The natural baths are composed of local volcanic ash, imported peat, and naturally boiling mineral hot-springs water, all mulled together to produce a thick mud that simmers at a temperature of about 104°F (40°C). Follow your soak in the mud with a warm mineral-water shower, a whirlpool bath, a visit to the steam room, and a relaxing blanket-wrap. The outcome: a rejuvenated, revitalized, squeaky-clean new you.

Indulge yourself at any of these Calistoga spas: **Dr. Wilkinson's Hot Springs,** 1507 Lincoln Ave. (© 707/942-4102); **Golden Haven Hot Springs Spa,** 1713 Lake St. (© 707/942-6793); **Calistoga Spa Hot Springs,** 1006 Washington St. (© 707/942-6269); **Calistoga Village Inn & Spa,** 1880 Lincoln Ave. (© 707/942-0991); **Indian Springs Resort,** 1712 Lincoln Ave. (© 707/942-4913); or **Roman Spa Motel,** 1300 Washington St.

NATURAL WONDERS   Old Faithful Geyser of California, 1299 Tubbs Lane (© **707/942-6463;** www.oldfaithfulgeyser.com), is one of only three "old faithful" geysers in the world. It's been blowing off steam at regular intervals for as long as anyone can remember. The 350°F (176°C) water spews to a height of about 60 feet every 40 minutes, day and night. The performance lasts about 3 minutes, and you can watch the show as many times as you wish. Bring along a picnic lunch to munch on between spews.

You won't see thousands of trees turned into stone, but you'll still find many petrified specimens at the **Petrified Forest,** 4100 Petrified Forest Rd., just north of Calistoga off Highway 128 (© **707/942-6667;** www.petrifiedforest.org). Volcanic ash blanketed this area after an eruption near Mount St. Helena three million years ago. You'll find redwoods that have turned to rock through the slow infiltration of silicas and other minerals, as well as petrified seashells, and marine life indicating that water covered this area before the redwood forest appeared.

GOLF   South of downtown Napa, 1⅓ miles east of Highway 29 on Highway 12, is the **Chardonnay Golf Club** (© **707/257-8950;** chardonnaygolfclub.com), a challenging 36-hole land-links golf complex with first-class service. There are three 9s of similar challenge, all starting at the clubhouse so that you can play the 18 of your choice. You pay just one fee ($45–$79, depending on day and time), which includes cart and practice balls. Tee times can be reserved up to 2 weeks in advance.

SHOPPING   Vanderbilt and Company, 1429 Main St., in St. Helena (© **707/ 963-1010**), purveyor of gorgeous cookware and fine housewares, is a must for gourmands. So is **Napa Valley Olive Oil Manufacturing Company,** 835 Charter Oak Rd. (© **707/963-4173**). This tiny market presses and bottles its own oils and sells them at a fraction of the price you'll pay elsewhere. Shopaholics won't be able to avoid at least one sharp turn off Highway 29 for a stop at the **St. Helena Premier Outlets,** 2 miles north of downtown St. Helena (© **707/963-7282;** www.sthelenapremier outlets.com), whose stores include Tumi, Coach, Movado, Escada, and more.

WHERE TO STAY

While we recommend shacking up in the more romantically pastoral areas such as St. Helena, there's no question you're going to find better deals in the towns of Napa or laid-back Calistoga.

Calistoga Ranch, 580 Lommel Rd., Calistoga (© **707/254-2800;** www.calistoga ranch.com), Napa Valley's hottest new luxury resort, is tucked into the eastern mountainside, on 157 pristine hidden-canyon acres. It's beautifully decorated and packed with every conceivable amenity (including fireplaces, outdoor patios along a wooded area, and cushy outdoor furnishings). Reasons not to leave include a giant swimming pool, reasonably large gym, beautifully designed indoor-outdoor spa with a natural thermal pool and individual pavilions with private-garden soaking tubs, and a breathtaking restaurant with stunning views of the property's petite Lake Lommel.

Meadowood Napa Valley, 900 Meadowood Lane, St. Helena (© **800/458-8080** or 707/963-3646; www.meadowood.com), is summer camp for wealthy grown-ups. Rooms, furnished with American country classics, have beamed ceilings, patios, stone fireplaces, and wilderness views. Many are individual suite-lodges so far removed from the common areas that you must drive to get to them. With golf, tennis, croquet, pools, hiking trails, and a spa on-site, you might never leave.

The 1892 **Cedar Gables Inn,** 486 Coombs St., Napa (© **800/309-7969** or 707/ 224-7969; www.cedargablesinn.com), is a cozy, romantic, moderately priced B&B in Old Town Napa. Rooms contain rich tapestries and stunning gilded antiques; four units have fireplaces.

The **Cottage Grove Inn,** 1711 Lincoln Ave., Calistoga (© **800/799-2284** or 707/ 942-8400; www.cottagegrove.com), is our top pick for couples looking to do the Calistoga spa scene in comfort and style. This complex of cottages is well removed from the action once you step across the threshold. Each compact guesthouse comes complete with a wood-burning fireplace, cozy quilts, CD player, VCR, wet bar, and an enormous bathroom with a skylight and a deep, two-person Jacuzzi tub. **Maison Fleurie,** 6529 Yount St., Yountville (© **800/788-0369** or 707/944-2056; www. maisonfleurienapa.com), is one of the prettiest hotels in the Wine Country, a trio of 1873 brick-and-fieldstone buildings overlaid with ivy. Some rooms feature private balconies, patios, Jacuzzis, and fireplaces. A basic breakfast is served in the little dining room; afterward, you're welcome to wander the landscaped grounds or hit the wine-tasting trail, returning in time for afternoon hors d'oeuvres and wine.

If your idea of the ultimate vacation is a cozy cabin set among 330 acres of creeks, waterfalls, hot springs, hiking trails, and redwood trees, paradise is a short drive away from St. Helena. Established in 1852, **White Sulphur Springs Retreat & Spa,** 3100 White Sulphur Springs Rd., St. Helena (© **800/593-8873** or 707/963-8588; www. whitesulphursprings.com), claims to be the oldest resort in California. The large creek-side cabins are decorated with simple but homey furnishings; no. 9 has two queen-size beds and a kitchenette. If the solitude alone isn't relaxing enough, you can schedule a day of aromatherapy, massage, and other spa treatments.

The Art Deco **El Bonita Motel,** 195 Main St., St. Helena (© **800/541-3284** or 707/963-3216; www.elbonita.com), was built a bit too close to Highway 29 for comfort, but the 2½ acres of beautifully landscaped gardens help even the score. The affordable rooms, while small, are spotlessly clean and decorated with comfy furnishings; some have kitchens or whirlpool tubs. Families like the larger bungalows with kitchenettes, but everybody loves the heated pool, Jacuzzi, and spa facility.

Best The Finest Eating in the Land

Plainly put, **The French Laundry,** 6640 Washington St., at Creek Street, Yountville (*C* 707/944-2380; www.thefrenchlaundry.com), is unlike any other dining experience. Part of its appeal has to do with intricate preparations, often finished table-side and always presented with uncommon artistry and detail, from the food itself to the surface it's delivered on.

Technically, the prix-fixe menu ($210, including service) offers a choice of nine courses (including a vegetarian menu), but after several presentations from the kitchen, everyone starts to lose count. Signature dishes include Keller's "tongue in cheek" (a marinated and braised round of sliced lamb tongue and tender beef cheeks) and "macaroni and cheese" (sweet butter-poached Maine lobster with creamy lobster broth and orzo with mascarpone cheese). Portions are small, but only because Keller wants his guests to taste as many things as possible. Trust me, nobody leaves hungry. The staff is well acquainted with the wide selection of regional wines; there's a $50 corkage fee if you bring your own bottle, which is only welcome if it's not on the list. Reserve at least 2 months in advance; jackets are required for men.

WHERE TO DINE

To best enjoy Napa's restaurant scene, keep one thing in mind: *Reserve*—especially for seats in a more renowned room.

Ultrafresh food, gorgeous patio seating, all-day service, and "reasonable" prices make **Tra Vigne Restaurant,** 1050 Charter Oak Ave., St. Helena (*C* 707/963-4444; www.travignerestaurant.com), a long-standing favorite. Try irresistible oven-roasted polenta with cheese, mushrooms, and balsamic reduction, and then move on to the outstanding whole roasted fish. The adjoining **Cantinetta** offers sandwiches, pizzas, and lighter meals.

ZuZu, 829 Main St., Napa (*C* 707/224-8555), serves delicious affordable tapas for $3 to $13. The kitchen cranks out fantastic paella, sizzling prawns, and Moroccan barbecue lamb chops guaranteed to make you swoon.

Chef Richard Reddington's **Redd,** 6480 Washington St., Yountville (*C* 707/944-2222), is one the best fine-dining experiences in the valley. Expect exceptional appetizers such as a delicate sashimi *hamachi* with *edamame,* cucumber, ginger, and sticky rice, and a cold foie gras trio with pistachios and brioche. For entrees, the Atlantic cod with chorizo, clams, and curry sauce manages to be rich *and* light. Desserts aren't quite as celestial, but they are lovely, with Meyer lemon *panna cotta* and rose water crème brûlée.

SONOMA VALLEY

Sonoma is often thought of as the "other" Wine Country, forever in the shadow of Napa Valley. Truth is, it's a very different experience. Sonoma still manages to maintain a backcountry ambience thanks to its much lower density of wineries, restaurants, and hotels; because it's far less traveled than its neighbor to the east, it offers a more genuine "escape from it all" experience. Small, family-owned wineries are its mainstay, and tastings and tours are usually free and low-key, and come with plenty of friendly banter between the winemakers and their guests.

While you're in Sonoma, stop by the **Sonoma Valley Visitors Bureau,** 453 First St. E. (© **707/996-1090;** www.sonomavalley.com), and pick up the free *Sonoma Valley Visitors Guide,* which lists most every lodging, winery, and restaurant in the valley (or order it from the bureau in advance of your trip).

TOURING THE VALLEY & WINERIES

Sonoma Valley is currently home to about 40 wineries. They tend to be a little more spread out than those in Napa, so decide where you're going before you get on the road.

A visit to the **Benziger Family Winery,** 1883 London Ranch Rd., off Arnold Drive, Glen Ellen (© **888/490-2739** or 707/935-3000; www.benziger.com), confirms that this is indeed a "family" winery. At any given time, three generations of Benzigers may be running around tending to chores. The pastoral, user-friendly property features an exceptional self-guided tour. Tastings of the standard-release wines are $5. The winery has several scenic picnic spots.

Buena Vista Winery, 18000 Old Winery Rd., Sonoma (© **800/926-1266** or 707/265-1472; www.buenavistawinery.com), is the granddaddy of all California wineries, founded in 1857 by Count Agoston Haraszthy, the Hungarian émigré who returned from Europe in 1861 with 100,000 of the finest vine cuttings. The winery's tasting room is inside the restored 1862 Press House—a beautiful stone-crafted room brimming with wines, wine-related gifts, and accessories. Tastings are $5 for four wines; $10 for a flight of three of the really good stuff.

When you've had it with chardonnays and pinots, visit **Gloria Ferrer Champagne Caves,** 23555 Carneros Hwy. (Calif. 121), Sonoma (© **707/996-7256;** www.gloria ferrer.com), home of Freixenet, the largest producer of sparkling wine in the world. If you're unfamiliar with the term *méthode champenoise,* take the free tour of the fermenting tanks, bottling line, and caves brimming with yeast-laden bottles. Afterward, retire to the elegant tasting room, order a glass of one of seven sparkling wines ($4–$10 a glass) or tastes of their eight still wines ($2–$3 per taste). There are picnic tables outside, but it's usually too windy for comfort. You must buy a bottle (from around $18–$40) or glass of sparkling wine to reserve a table.

Viansa Winery and Italian Marketplace, 25200 Arnold Dr. (Hwy. 121), Sonoma (© **800/995-4740** or 707/935-4700; www.viansa.com), is the brainchild of Sam and Vicki Sebastiani, who left the family dynasty to create their own temple to food and wine. The marketplace is crammed with a cornucopia of high-quality gourmet foods; the winery has quickly established a favorable reputation for its cabernet, sauvignon blanc, and chardonnay. Guided tours, held at 11am and 2pm, will set you back $5.

WHERE TO STAY

If you're having trouble finding a vacancy, contact the **Sonoma Valley Visitors Bureau** (© **707/996-1090;** www.sonomavalley.com). They'll try to refer you to establishments with a room to spare, but they won't make reservations for you. Another option is the **Bed and Breakfast Association of Sonoma Valley** (© **800/969-4667**), which will refer you to a member B&B and make reservations for you.

The century-old, buttercup-yellow **Beltane Ranch,** 11775 Sonoma Hwy./Hwy. 12, Glen Ellen (© **707/996-650;** www.beltaneranch.com), has been everything from a bunkhouse to a brothel to a turkey farm. Rooms are decorated with American and European antiques, and all have sitting areas and separate entrances. A big country breakfast is served, and the 105-acre estate has hiking trails and a private tennis court.

The **Gaige House Inn,** 13540 Arnold Dr., Glen Ellen (© **800/935-0237** or 707/935-0237; www.gaige.com), is the best B&B we've ever stayed in. The service, amenities, and decor are what you'd expect from an outrageously expensive resort, but without the snobbery. All rooms have private bathrooms and king- or queen-size beds; two rooms have Jacuzzi tubs, and several have fireplaces. The eight new, superfancy spa garden suites have, among other delights, granite soaking tubs. There's even a pool and outdoor hot tub on the manicured lawn out back.

Victorian Garden Inn, 316 E. Napa St. (© **800/543-5339** or 707/996-5339; www.victoriangardeninn.com), is easily the cutest B&B in Sonoma Valley. The themed guest units—three in the century-old water tower, one in the main building (an 1870s Greek Revival farmhouse), and a cottage—each have their own entrance and a garden view; the cottage has a sofa and armchairs in front of the fireplace. A porch and pool are appealing after a long day of wine tasting. Note that young kids are not permitted.

The honey-colored Italian-style buildings and pastoral views of vineyard-covered hills at the **Kenwood Inn & Spa,** 10400 Sonoma Hwy., Kenwood (© **800/353-6966** or 707/833-1293; www.kenwoodinn.com), are enough to make any Italian homesick for Tuscany. Spacious rooms are exquisitely decorated with imported tapestries, velvets, and antiques, plus a fireplace, balcony (except on the ground floor), feather bed, CD player, and down comforter. Start your morning with a three-course gourmet breakfast, and spend the rest of the day at the spa or pool.

The **Best Western Sonoma Valley Inn,** 550 Second St. W. (© **800/334-5784** or 707/938-9200; www.sonomavalleyinn.com), is perfect for families. Kids will love the large heated outdoor saltwater pool and in-room satellite TV, while perks for parents include continental breakfast delivered to your room and a gift bottle of Sonoma Valley wine (chilling in the fridge). Most rooms have either a balcony or a deck overlooking the inner courtyard.

Set on 12 meticulously groomed acres, the **Fairmont Sonoma Mission Inn & Spa,** 101 Boyes Blvd. (© **800/441-1414** or 707/938-9000; www.fairmont.com/sonoma), is the Wine Country's most extensive super resort and spa, and a popular retreat for the wealthy. The spa and the slew of attendant luxury amenities—massages, facials, tennis courts, hot tub, and two pools—are the main event.

WHERE TO DINE

Though Sonoma Valley has far fewer visitors than Napa Valley, its restaurants are often equally as crowded, so be sure to make reservations in advance.

The girl & the fig, 110 W. Spain St. (© **707/938-3634;** www.thegirlandthefig.com), draws crowds nightly to its downtown digs. Figs are sure to be on the menu in one form or another, as in the wonderful winter fig salad made with arugula, pecans, dried figs, goat cheese, and fig-and-port vinaigrette.

If you just can't take another expensive, chichi meal, follow the locals to **Della Santina's,** 133 E. Napa St., just east of the square (© **707/935-0576;** www.dellasantinas.com). Every classic Tuscan dish is refreshingly authentic and well flavored—without overbearing sauces or one *hint* of California pretentiousness. Don't worry about breaking the bank on a bottle of wine, as most of the choices here go for under $40.

Eclectic food, friendly owners, soothing atmosphere, and moderate prices make **Cafe La Haye,** 140 E. Napa St., Sonoma (© **707/935-5994**), a favorite. The small, straightforward menu offers just enough options, such as a risotto special; creative salads; and pan-roasted chicken breast with caramelized shallot jus and fennel mashed potatoes.

If you're looking for picnic fare, head to the venerable **Sonoma Cheese Factory,** on the plaza at 2 Spain St. (© **707/996-1000**), which offers award-winning house-made cheeses and imported meats and cheeses. Also available are caviar, gourmet salads, pâté, and homemade Sonoma Jack cheese. Pick up some good, inexpensive sandwiches, such as fire-roasted pork loin or New York steak.

3 The Northern Coast

North of San Francisco, you can forget about California's fabled surf-and-bikini scene; instead, you'll find miles and miles of rugged coastline with broad beaches and tiny bays harboring dramatic rock formations carved by the ocean waves. The best time to visit is in the spring or fall. In spring, the headlands are carpeted with wildflowers—golden poppy, iris, and sea foam—and in fall, the sun shines clear and bright. Summers are typically cool and windy, with the ubiquitous fog burning off by the afternoon. The water's too cold for much swimming this far north, but that doesn't mean you can't enjoy the beaches, whether by strolling along the water or taking in the panoramic views of towering cliffs and seascapes.

POINT REYES NATIONAL SEASHORE

This preserve is a 71,000-acre hammer-shaped peninsula jutting 10 miles into the Pacific and backed by Tomales Bay. It encompasses several surf-pounded beaches, bird estuaries, open swaths of land with roaming elk, and the Point Reyes Lighthouse, which offers spectacular views.

The infamous San Andreas Fault separates Point Reyes—the northernmost landmass on the Pacific Plate—from the rest of California, which rests on the North American Plate. In 1906, Point Reyes jumped north almost 20 feet in an instant, leveling San Francisco and jolting the rest of the state. The half-mile **Earthquake Trail,** near the Bear Valley Visitor Center, illustrates this geological drama with a loop through an area torn by the slipping fault. Shattered fences, rifts in the ground, and a barn knocked off its foundation by the quake illustrate how alive the earth is here.

Point Reyes is only 30 miles northwest of San Francisco, but it takes at least 90 minutes to reach by car (it's all the small towns, not the topography, that slow you down). The easiest route is via Sir Francis Drake Boulevard from U.S. 101 south of San Rafael. For a much longer but more scenic route, take the Stinson Beach/Highway 1 exit off U.S. 101 just south of Sausalito and follow Highway 1 north.

As soon as you arrive at Point Reyes, stop at the **Bear Valley Visitor Center** (© 415/464-5100; www.nps.gov/pore) on Bear Valley Road (look for the small sign posted just north of Olema on Hwy. 1) and pick up a free Point Reyes trail map. The rangers here are extremely friendly and helpful. Be sure to check out the great natural-history and cultural displays as well. It's open Monday through Friday from 9am to 5pm, Saturday and Sunday from 8am to 5pm. Websites with information about Point Reyes include www.pointreyes.net and www.pointreyes.org.

Entrance to the park is free. Camping is $15 per site per night, and permits are required; reservations can be made up to 3 months in advance by calling © 415/663-8054, Monday through Friday from 9am to 2pm.

WHAT TO SEE & DO

The most popular attraction is the venerable **Point Reyes Lighthouse,** at the westernmost tip. Even if you plan to forego the 308 steps down to the lighthouse, it's worth the visit just to marvel at the scenery, which includes thousands of common murres and prides of sea lions basking on the rocks far below (binoculars come in handy). The lighthouse visitor center (© **415/669-1534**) is open Thursday through Monday from 10am to 4:30pm, weather permitting; admission is free.

The lighthouse is also the top spot on the California coast to see **gray whales** as they make their southward and northward migrations along the coast from January to April. The annual round-trip is 10,000 miles—one of the longest mammal migrations known. The whales head south in December and January, and return north in March. *Tip:* If you plan to drive out to the lighthouse to whale-watch, arrive early as parking is limited. If possible, come on a weekday. On a weekend or holiday from December to April (weather permitting), it's wise to park at the Drake's Beach Visitor Center and take the shuttle bus to the lighthouse, which is $5 for adults and free for kids age 12 and under. Dress warmly—it's often quite cold and windy—and bring binoculars.

North and South **Point Reyes Beach** face the Pacific and withstand the full brunt of ocean tides and winds—the water is far too rough for even wading. Until a few years ago, entering the water was illegal, but persistent surfers went to court for their right to shred the mighty waves. Today the Park Service strongly advises against taking on the tides, so play it safe and content yourself to stroll the coastline. Along the southern coast, the waters of **Drake's Beach** can be as tranquil and serene as Point Reyes's are turbulent.

Some of the park's best—and least crowded—highlights can only be approached on foot, such as **Alamere Falls,** a freshwater stream that cascades down a 40-foot bluff onto Wildcat Beach; or **Tomales Point Trail,** which passes through the Tule Elk Reserve, a protected haven for roaming herds of tule elk that once numbered in the thousands.

One of our favorite things to do in Point Reyes is paddle through placid **Tomales Bay,** a haven for migrating birds and marine mammals. **Blue Water Kayaking** (© **415/669-2600;** www.bwkayak.com) organizes kayak trips, including 3-hour morning or sunset outings, oyster tours, day trips, and longer excursions. Instruction, clinics, and boat delivery are available, and all ages and levels are welcome. Prices for tours start at $68. Rentals begin at $30 for one person, $50 for a double kayak. The two launching points are on Highway 1 at the Marshall Boatworks in Marshall, 8 miles north of Point Reyes Station, and on Sir Francis Drake Blvd. in Inverness, 5 miles east of Point Reyes Station. Blue Water is open daily April to October from 9am to 5pm and by appointment.

WHERE TO STAY & DINE

If you're having trouble finding a vacancy, **Inns of Marin** (© **800/887-2880** or 415/663-2000; www.innsofmarin.com), **Point Reyes Lodging Association** (© **800/539-1872** or 415/663-1872; www.ptreyes.com), and **West Marin Network** (© **415/663-9543**) are reputable services that will help you find accommodations, from one-room cottages to inns and vacation homes.

If there were ever a reason to pack your bags and leave San Francisco for a day or two, **Manka's Inverness Lodge,** 30 Callendar Way, Inverness (© **415/669-1034;** www.mankas.com), is it. A former hunting-and-fishing lodge, it's all romantic in a Jack London sort of way, and tastefully done. Accommodations consist of rooms in the main lodge and an annex, as well as ultraromantic secluded cabins. There's an excellent restaurant on the first floor.

Finding an inexpensive place to stay in Point Reyes is next to impossible, but **Motel Inverness,** 12718 Sir Francis Drake Blvd. (© **888/669-6909** or 415/669-1081; www.motelinverness.com), is one exception. The homey, well-maintained property fronts Tomales Bay, and a giant great room with a fireplace and pool table is attached to the hotel. The two-bedroom suite with a kitchenette is ideal for families, as is the Dacha cottage, on the water, with three bedrooms.

The **Point Reyes Country Inn & Stables,** 12050 Hwy. 1, Point Reyes Station (© 415/663-9696; www.ptreyescountryinn.com), is a ranch-style home on 4 acres that offers pastoral accommodations for two- and four-legged guests (horses only), plus access to plenty of trails. Each room has either a balcony or a garden. Also available are two studios (with kitchens) above the stables, plus two Tomales Bay cottages with decks, kitchens, fireplaces, and a shared dock.

The **Station House Café,** Main Street, Point Reyes Station (© 415/663-1515; ww.stationhousecafe.com), has been a low-key favorite for more than 2 decades, thanks to its open kitchen, garden seating, and live music on weekends. Breakfast dishes range from a hangtown fry with local Johnson's oysters to mashed-potato pancakes. Dinner specials might include fettuccine with fresh local mussels or two-cheese polenta served with fresh spinach sauté—all made from local produce, seafood, and organically raised Niman-Schell Farms beef.

Fresh, fast, good, and cheap: What more could you ask for in a restaurant? **Taqueria La Quinta,** 11285 Hwy. 1, at Third and Main streets (© 415/663-8868), has been one of our favorite lunch stops in downtown Point Reyes for years. Try the chile verde in a spicy tomatillo sauce with a side of handmade corn tortillas.

BODEGA BAY

Beyond the tip of the Point Reyes peninsula, the road curves around toward the coastal village of Bodega Bay, which supports a fishing fleet of around 300 boats. It's a good place to stop for lunch or a stroll around town. **Bodega Head State Park** is a great vantage point for whale-watching during the annual migration season from January to April. At **Doran Beach,** there's a large bird sanctuary, home to willets, curlews, godwits, and more.

The **Bodega Harbour Golf Links,** 21301 Heron Dr. (© 800/503-8158 or 707/875-3538; www.bodegaharbourgolf.com), enjoys a panoramic ocean-side setting. It's an 18-hole Scottish-style course designed by Robert Trent Jones, Jr. A warm-up center and practice facility are free of charge to registered golfers. Rates are $60 to $90. If golfing isn't your thing, you can go horseback riding through some spectacular coastal scenery by contacting **Chanslor Horse Stables** (© 707/875-3333; www.chanslor.com), which also has pony rides for the kids. Open daily from 9am to 5pm.

One of the bay's major events is the **Fisherman's Festival** in April. Local fishing boats, decorated with ribbons and banners, sail out for a Blessing of the Fleet, while up to 25,000 landlubbers enjoy music, a lamb-and-oyster barbecue, and an arts-and-crafts fair.

For more information about these festivals and other goings-on in Bodega Bay, call or stop in at the **Bodega Bay Area Visitors Center,** 860 Hwy. 1, Bodega Bay, CA 94923 (© 707/875-3866; www.bodegabay.com or www.visitsonomacoast.com), which has lots of information about the area, including maps of the beaches and the best local fishing spots.

If you'd like to stay over, the upscale **Bodega Bay Lodge & Duck Club Restaurant,** 103 Hwy. 1 (© 800/368-2468 or 707/875-3525; www.bodegabaylodge.com), is easily the best choice. Each room has a fireplace and a balcony with sweeping views. Guests have access to a beautiful fieldstone spa and heated pool perched above the bay. The lodge's Duck Club Restaurant also enjoys a reputation as Bodega Bay's finest.

The larger **Inn at the Tides,** 800 Coast Hwy. 1 (© 800/541-7788 or 707/875-2751; www.innatthetides.com), consists of a cluster of condolike complexes perched on the side of a gently sloping hill. The selling point here is the view; each unit is staggered just enough to guarantee a view of the bay across the highway. In summer, as many as 1,000 diners a day pass through the inn's **Tides Wharf Restaurant,** 835 Hwy. 1 (© **707/875-3652**). Back in the 1960s, it served as one of the settings for Hitchcock's *The Birds,* but renovation has enlarged and redecorated the place beyond recognition. The best tables offer views overlooking the ocean, and the bill of fare includes clam chowder and fish fresh from the cold blue waters offshore.

THE SONOMA COAST STATE BEACHES, JENNER & FORT ROSS STATE HISTORIC PARK

Along 13 winding miles of Calif. 1—from Bodega Bay to Goat Rock Beach in Jenner—stretch the Sonoma Coast State Beaches, ideal for walking, tide-pooling, abalone picking, fishing, and bird-watching. Each beach is clearly marked from the road, and numerous pullouts are available for parking. Even if you don't stop at any of the beaches, the drive alone is spectacular.

At **Jenner,** the Russian River empties into the ocean. **Penny Island,** in the river's estuary, is home to otters and many species of birds; a colony of harbor seals lives out on the ocean rocks. **Goat Rock Beach** is a popular breeding ground for the seals; pupping season is March through June.

From Jenner, a 12-mile drive along some very dramatic coastline will bring you to **Fort Ross State Historic Park** (© 707/847-3286; www.parks.sonoma.net/fortross. html), a reconstruction of the fort that was established here in 1812 by the Russians as a base for seal and otter hunting. At the visitor center, you can view the silver samovars and elaborate table services that the Russians used. The fenced compound contains several buildings, including the first Russian Orthodox church ever built in North America outside Alaska. The park offers beach trails and picnic grounds on more than 1,000 acres. Admission to the park costs $6 per car.

North from Fort Ross, the road continues to **Salt Point State Park** (© **707/847-3221**). This 3,500-acre expanse contains 30 campsites, 14 miles of trails, tide pools, a pygmy forest, and old Pomo village sites. Your best bet is to pull off the highway any place that catches your eye and start exploring on foot. At the north end of the park, head inland on Kruse Ranch Road to the **Kruse Rhododendron Reserve** (© 707/847-3221), where the wild purple and pink *Rhododendron californicum* grow to a height of 18 feet under the redwood-and-fir canopy.

MENDOCINO

Mendocino is, to our minds, *the* premier destination on California's north coast. Despite (or because of) its relative isolation, it emerged as one of Northern California's major centers for the arts in the 1950s. It's easy to see why artists were—and still are—attracted to this idyllic community, a cluster of New England–style sea captains' homes and small stores set on headlands overlooking the ocean.

At the height of the logging boom, Mendocino became an important and active port. Its population was about 3,500, and eight hotels were built, along with 17 saloons and more than a dozen bordellos. Today, it has only about 1,000 residents, most of whom reside at the north end of town. On summer weekends, the population seems more like 10,000, as hordes of tourists drive up from the Bay Area—but despite the crowds, Mendocino manages to retain its small-town charm.

ESSENTIALS

GETTING THERE   The fastest route from San Francisco is via **U.S. 101** north to Cloverdale, then **Highway 128** west to **Highway 1,** then north along the coast. It's about a 4-hour drive. The most scenic route from the Bay Area, if you have the time and your stomach doesn't mind the twists and turns, is to take Highway 1 north along the coast the entire way; it's at least a 5- to 6-hour drive.

VISITOR INFORMATION   Stock up on brochures and maps at the **Fort Bragg/ Mendocino Coast Chamber of Commerce,** 332 N. Main St. (P.O. Box 1141), Fort Bragg, CA 95437 (© **800/726-2780** or 707/961-6300; www.mendocinocoast.com). Pick up a copy of the center's monthly magazine, *Arts and Entertainment,* which lists upcoming events. It's available at numerous stores and cafes, including the Mendocino Bakery, Gallery Bookshop, and Mendocino Art Center.

WHAT TO SEE & DO

Stroll through town, enjoy the architecture, and browse through the dozens of galleries and shops. Our favorites include the **Highlight Gallery,** 45052 Main St. (© **707/937-3132**), for its handmade furniture, pottery, and other crafts; and the **Gallery Bookshop & Bookwinkle's Children's Books,** at Main and Kasten streets (© **707/937-2665;** www.gallerybooks.com), one of the best independent bookstores in Northern California. Another popular stop is **Mendocino Jams & Preserves,** 440 Main St. (© **800/708-1196** or 707/937-1037; www.mendojams.com), which offers free tastings of its locally made gourmet wares.

After exploring the town, walk out on the headlands that wrap around the town and constitute **Mendocino Headlands State Park.** The visitor center is in Ford House on Main Street (© 707/937-5397). Three miles of trails wind through the park, giving visitors panoramic views of sea arches and hidden grottoes. If you're here at the right time of year, the area will be blanketed with wildflowers. The headlands are home to many unique species of birds, including black oystercatchers. Behind the Mendocino Presbyterian Church on Main Street is a trail leading to stairs that take you down to the beach, a small but picturesque stretch of sand where driftwood formations have washed ashore.

In town, stop by the **Mendocino Art Center,** 45200 Little Lake St. (© **707/937-5818;** www.mendocinoartcenter.org), the town's unofficial cultural headquarters. It's also known for its gardens, galleries, and shops that sell local crafts. Open daily from 10am to 5pm.

For a special treat, go to **Sweetwater Spa & Inn,** 955 Ukiah St. (© **800/300-4140** or 707/937-4140; www.sweetwaterspa.com), which offers group and private saunas and hot-tub soaks by the hour, along with massages. Reservations are recommended. Private tub prices are $12 per person per half-hour, $16 per person per hour; group prices are $10 per person with no time limit. Special discounts are available on Wednesdays. The spa is open Sunday through Friday from noon to 10pm and Saturday from noon to 11pm.

OUTDOOR ACTIVITIES

Explore the Big River by renting a canoe, kayak, or outrigger from **Catch a Canoe & Bicycles Too** (© **707/937-0273;** www.stanfordinn.com), located on the grounds of the Stanford Inn by the Sea. If you're lucky, you'll see osprey, blue herons, harbor seals, deer, and wood ducks. These same folks will also rent you a mountain bike so you can head up Highway 1 and explore the nearby state parks on two wheels.

Horseback riding on the beach and into the redwoods is offered by **Ricochet Ridge Ranch,** 24201 N. Hwy. 1, Fort Bragg (© **888/873-5777** or 707/964-7669; www. horse-vacation.com). Prices range from $45 for a 1½-hour beach ride to $250 for an all-day private beach-and-redwoods trail ride.

In addition to Mendocino Headlands State Park, there are several other nearby state parks; all are within an easy drive or bike ride and make for a good day's outing. Information on all the parks' features, including maps, is found in a brochure called *Mendocino Coast State Parks,* available from the visitor center in Fort Bragg. These areas include **Manchester State Park,** located where the San Andreas Fault sweeps to the sea; **Jughandle State Reserve;** and **Van Damme State Park,** with a sheltered, easily accessible beach.

Our favorite of these parks, on Highway 1 just north of Mendocino, is **Russian Gulch State Park.** It's one of the region's most spectacular parks, where roaring waves crash against the cliffs that protect the coastal redwoods. The most popular attraction is the **Punch Bowl,** a collapsed sea cave that forms a tunnel through which waves crash, creating throaty echoes. Inland, there's a scenic paved bike path, and visitors can also hike along miles of trails. Admission is $6; camping costs $14. Call © **800/444-7275** for reservations; for general state park information, call © **707/937-5804** or visit **www.cal-parks.ca.gov.**

WHERE TO STAY

Just south of town, the rustic but ever-so-sumptuous **Stanford Inn by the Sea,** North Highway 1 and Comptche Ukiah Road (© **800/331-8884** or 707/937-5615; www. stanfordinn.com), has captivating grounds, with tiers of elaborate gardens, a pond for ducks and geese, and fenced pastures containing horses, llamas, and gnarled old apple trees. There's a gorgeous solarium-style indoor hot tub and pool. Rooms offer down comforters, fresh flowers, fireplaces or stoves, stereos and VCRs, and private decks from which you can look out onto the Pacific. The inn has the only totally vegetarian restaurant on the Mendocino coast, a big hit with both guests and locals.

Less expensive is the small **Agate Cove Inn,** 11201 N. Lansing St. (© **800/527-3111** or 707/937-0551; www.agatecove.com), with a sweeping vista of the waves crashing onto the dramatic bluffs. All but one of the 10 spacious units have views of the ocean, down comforters, CD players, VCRs, fireplaces, and private decks.

Right in the heart of town, the **Mendocino Hotel & Garden Suites,** 45080 Main St. (© **800/548-0513** or 707/937-0511; www.mendocinohotel.com), was built in 1878 and evokes California's gold-rush days. Rooms feature hand-painted French porcelain sinks with floral designs, quaint wallpaper, old-fashioned beds and armoires, and photographs of historic Mendocino. About half are located in four handsome small buildings behind the main house. Many of the deluxe rooms have fireplaces.

The moderately priced **Joshua Grindle Inn,** 44800 Little Lake Rd. (© **800/ GRINDLE** or 707/937-4143; www.joshgrin.com), is housed in a stately 1879 Victorian with a wraparound porch and large emerald lawns. Another affordable Victorian B&B choice is the **Mendocino Village Inn & Spa,** 44860 Main St. (© **800/882-7029** or 707/937-0246; www.mendocinoinn.com). A garden of flowers, plants, and frog ponds fronts the large blue-and-white guesthouse, built in 1882 and later occupied by famed local artist Emmy Lou Packard.

In the nearby town of Albion is the modern, upscale **Albion River Inn and Restaurant,** North Highway 1 (© **800/479-7944** or 707/937-1919; www.albion riverinn.com), perched on a bluff some 90 feet above the Pacific. Most rooms have decks; all have ocean views, fireplaces, down comforters, fridges, and CD players. The restaurant serves up stellar cuisine and stellar views.

WHERE TO DINE

Note: In addition to the following, see "Where to Stay," above, for hotel restaurants.

Café Beaujolais, 961 Ukiah St. (© 707/937-5614; www.cafebeaujolais.com), is one of Mendocino's—if not Northern California's—top dining choices. The venerable French country–style tavern is set in a century-old house; rose-colored chandeliers add a burnish to the wood floors and the heavy oak tables adorned with flowers. On warm nights, request a table at the enclosed deck overlooking the gardens. The menu usually lists about six main courses, such as roast free-range duck with wild-huckleberry sauce.

Large but surprisingly cozy, **The 955 Ukiah Street Restaurant,** 955 Ukiah St. (© 707/937-1955; www.955restaurant.com), is accented with massive railway ties and vaulted ceilings. Ask for a window table overlooking the gardens. The cuisine is creative and reasonably priced, a worthy alternative to the perpetually booked Café Beaujolais next door.

The moderately priced **Bay View Café,** 45040 Main St. (© 707/937-4197), is one of the most popular restaurants in town and serves a good breakfast. From the second-floor dining area, there's a sweeping view of the Pacific and faraway headlands. You'll find a menu with southwestern selections, a good array of sandwiches, and the fresh catch of the day.

You'd be surprised what $7 will get you for lunch if you know where to go. **Garden Bakery** (© 707/937-3140), at the corner of Albion and Lansing streets, has a carry-out booth serving gourmet sandwiches, pizzas, focaccia, and pastries.

Regardless of preference—beef, chicken, turkey, or veggie—burger lovers won't be let down at **Mendo Burgers** (© 707/937-1111), arguably the best burger joint on the north coast. Hidden behind the Mendocino Bakery and Café at 10483 Lansing St., it's a little hard to find, but well worth searching out.

THE AVENUE OF THE GIANTS & FERNDALE

From Fort Bragg, Highway 1 continues north along the shoreline for about 30 miles before turning inland to Leggett and the Redwood Highway (U.S. 101), which runs north to Garberville. Six miles beyond Garberville, the **Avenue of the Giants** (Hwy. 254) begins around Phillipsville. It's an alternate route that roughly parallels U.S. 101, and there are about a half-dozen interchanges between the two roads if you don't want to drive the whole thing. This stretch of Highway 254 is one of the most spectacular scenic routes in the West, cutting along the Eel River through the 51,000-acre **Humboldt Redwoods State Park.** The Avenue ends just south of Scotia; from here, it's only about 10 miles to the turnoff to Ferndale, about 5 miles west of U.S. 101. Since Redwoods National Park is so remote, we recommend this outing as a more convenient way to see California's majestic giants.

For more information or a detailed map of the area, go to the **Humboldt Redwoods State Park Visitor Center** in Weott (© 707/946-2263; www.humboldt redwoods.org), in the center of the Avenue of the Giants.

Thirty-three miles long, the Avenue of the Giants was left intact for sightseers when the freeway was built. The giants, of course, are the majestic coast redwoods *(Sequoia sempervirens);* more than 50,000 acres of them make up the most outstanding display in the redwood belt. Their rough-bark columns climb 100 feet or more without a branch and soar to a total height of more than 340 feet. With their immunity to insects and fire-resistant bark, they have survived for thousands of years.

A few miles north of Weott is **Founders Grove,** named in honor of those who established the Save the Redwoods League in 1918. Farther north, close to the end of the Avenue, stands the 950-year-old **Immortal Tree,** just north of Redcrest. Near Pepperwood at the end of the Avenue, the **Drury Trail** and the **Percy French Trail** are two good short hikes. The park itself is also good for mountain biking. Ask the rangers for details. For more information, contact **Humboldt Redwoods State Park** (© 707/ **946-2409;** www.humboldtredwoods.org).

The state park has three **campgrounds** with 248 campsites: Hidden Springs, half a mile south of Myers Flat; Burlington, 2 miles south of Weott, near park headquarters; and Albee Creek State Campground, 5 miles west of U.S. 101 on the Mattole Road north of Weott. You'll also come across picnic and swimming facilities, motels, resorts, restaurants, and numerous rest and parking areas.

Near the southern entrance to the Avenue of the Giants is the **Benbow Inn,** 445 Lake Benbow Dr., Garberville (© **800/355-3301** or 707/923-2124; www.benbowinn. com), a National Historic Landmark overlooking the Eel River and surrounded by marvelous gardens. The sumptuous lobby has a huge fireplace surrounded by cushy sofas, grandfather clocks, and Oriental carpets. Rooms are tastefully decorated with period antiques; the deluxe units have fireplaces, Jacuzzis, private entrances and patios, and VCRs. Bicycles are available, and beautiful Benbow Lake State Park is right out the front door. Complimentary afternoon tea and scones are served in the lobby at 4pm, hors d'oeuvres in the lounge at 5pm, and port wine at 9pm—all very proper, of course. The dramatic high-ceilinged dining room opens onto a spacious terrace.

The landmark village of **Ferndale,** beyond the Avenue of the Giants and west of U.S. 101, has many Victorian homes and storefronts (which include a smithy and a saddlery). Despite its unbearably cute shops, it is nonetheless a vital part of the northern coastal tourist circuit.

The small town has a number of artists in residence and is also home to one of California's oddest events, the **World Championship Great Arcata to Ferndale Cross-Country Kinetic Sculpture Race,** a bizarre 3-day event held every Memorial Day weekend. The race, which draws more than 10,000 spectators, is run over land and water in whimsically designed human-powered vehicles. Stop in at the museum at 780 Main St. if you want to see some race entries.

If you'd like to stay over in Ferndale, try the **Gingerbread Mansion,** 400 Berding St. (© **800/952-4136** or 707/786-4000; www.gingerbread-mansion.com), a beautiful antiques-filled Victorian built in 1899. Some of the large rooms have claw-foot tubs for two; others offer fireplaces.

4 The Monterey Peninsula & the Big Sur Coast

MONTEREY

Monterey was one of the West Coast's first European settlements, and the capital of California under the Spanish, Mexican, and American flags. A major whaling center in the 1800s, Monterey eventually became the sardine capital of the Western Hemisphere. By 1913, the boats were bringing in 25 tons of sardines a night to the 18 canneries. The gritty lives of the mostly working-class residents were captured by local hero John Steinbeck in his 1945 novel *Cannery Row.*

After the sardines disappeared, Monterey was forced to fish for tourist dollars, hence the array of boutiques, knickknack stores, and theme restaurants that now reside along the bay. The city's saving grace is its historic architecture, world-class aquarium, and beautiful Monterey Bay, where sea lions and otters still frolic in abundance. More important, Monterey is only a short drive from Pacific Grove, Carmel, Pebble Beach, and Big Sur, and the lodgings here are far less expensive, which makes it a great place to set up base while exploring the coast.

ESSENTIALS
GETTING THERE   By Plane   Monterey Peninsula Airport (© 831/648-7000) is 3 miles east of Monterey on Highway 68. Many area hotels offer free airport shuttle service. If you take a taxi, it will cost about $10 to $15 to get to a peninsula hotel.

By Car   The major routes into Monterey are **Highway 1** from the north (Santa Cruz) and south (Carmel and Big Sur), and **Highway 68** from the east, which connects with **U.S. 101** (San Francisco).

VISITOR INFORMATION   The **Monterey Peninsula Visitors and Convention Bureau** (© 888/221-1010 or 831/649-1770; www.montereyinfo.org) has two visitor centers: one in Maritime Museum at Custom House Plaza near Fisherman's Wharf, and the other at Lake El Estero on Camino El Estero. Both locations, open daily, offer good maps and free publications, including the magazine *Coast Weekly.*

GETTING AROUND   The free **Waterfront Area Visitor Express (WAVE)** operates from Memorial Day weekend to Labor Day and takes passengers to and from the aquarium and other waterfront attractions. Stops are located at many hotels and motels in Monterey and Pacific Grove. For further information call **Monterey Salinas Transit** (© 831/899-2555).

WHAT TO SEE & DO
The enormous **Monterey Bay Aquarium,** 886 Cannery Row (© 831/648-4800 or 831/648-4888; www.mbayaq.org), is home to more than 350,000 marine animals and plants. One of the main exhibits is a three-story, 335,000-gallon tank with clear acrylic walls; inside, hundreds of leopard sharks, sardines, anchovies, and other fish play hide-and-seek in a towering kelp forest. The outstanding Outer Bay exhibit features yellowfin tuna, large green sea turtles, barracuda, sharks, very cool giant ocean sunfish, and schools of bonito. The Outer Bay's jellyfish exhibit is guaranteed to amaze, and kids will love Flippers, Flukes, and Fun, a learning area for families. Mysteries of the Deep is the largest collection of live deep-sea species in the world. Everyone falls in love with the playful sea otters, and there's a petting pool where you can touch living bat rays and handle sea stars. Admission is $22 for adults, $20 for students and seniors over 65, and $13 for visitors with disabilities children 3 to 12. Avoid lines by calling the above numbers and ordering tickets in advance. Open daily from 10am to 6pm.

 Fisherman's Wharf, at 99 Pacific St. (© 831/649-6544; www.montereywharf.com) is a wooden pier jampacked with gift shops, fish markets, and seafood restaurants. The natural surroundings are so beautiful that if you cast your view toward the bobbing boats and surfacing sea lions, you might not even notice the hordes of tourists around you. Grab some clam chowder in a sourdough bread bowl and find a perch along the pier. **Chris' Fishing Trips,** 48 Fisherman's Wharf (© 831/375-5951; www.chrissfishing. com), offers fishing excursions for cod, salmon, and whatever else is running.

 Kayaks can be rented from several outfitters for a spin around the bay. Contact **Monterey Bay Kayaks,** 693 Del Monte Ave. (© 800/649-5357 or 831/373-5357; www.montereykayaks.com), north of Fisherman's Wharf, which offers instruction as well as natural-history tours. Prices start at $45 for tours, $30 for rentals. For bikes and in-line skates as well as kayak tours and rentals, contact **Adventures by the Sea,** 299 Cannery Row (📞 **831/372-1807;** www.adventuresbythesea.com). Bikes cost $6 per hour or $24 a day; kayaks are $30 per person or $50 for a 2½-hour tour; and skates are $12 for 2 hours. Adventures by the Sea has another location at 201 Alvarado Mall (📞 **831/648-7235**), at the Doubletree Hotel.

Once the center for an industrial sardine-packing operation immortalized by John Steinbeck, **Cannery Row,** between David and Drake avenues (📞 **831/373-1902;** www.canneryrow.com), is now a congested strip of tacky gift shops, overpriced seafood restaurants, and an overall parking nightmare. Curious tourists continue to visit Steinbeck's fabled area, and where there are tourists, there are capitalists.

The dozen or so historic buildings clustered around Fisherman's Wharf and the adjacent town collectively form the "Path of History," a tour that examines 1800s architecture and lifestyle (pick up a brochure detailing the route at the visitor center). Many of the buildings are a part of the **Monterey State Historic Park,** 20 Custom House Plaza (📞 **831/649-7118**).

The Monterey area has become an increasingly important and acclaimed winemaking region. Stop by **A Taste of Monterey,** 700 Cannery Row (📞 **831/646-5446** or 831/646-5446; www.tastemonterey.com), daily between 11am and 6pm, to learn about and taste locally produced wines in front of huge bayfront windows. This is also the place to get a map and winery touring information.

STROLLING THROUGH NEARBY PACIFIC GROVE

Just next door to Monterey, Pacific Grove is a town to be strolled, so park the car, put on your walking shoes, and make an afternoon of it.

An excellent shorter alternative, or complement, to the 17-mile Drive is the scenic drive or bike ride along Pacific Grove's **Ocean View Boulevard.** This coastal stretch starts near Monterey's Cannery Row and follows the Pacific around to the lighthouse point. Here it turns into Sunset Drive, which runs along secluded **Asilomar State Beach** (📞 **831/648-3130**). Park on Sunset and explore the trails, dunes, and tide pools of this sandy stretch of shore. You might find purple shore crabs, green anemone, sea bats, starfish, and limpets.

Marine Gardens Park, a stretch of shoreline along Ocean View Boulevard on Monterey Bay and the Pacific, is renowned not only for its ocean views and colorful flowers, but also for its fascinating tide-pool seaweed beds. Walk out to Lover's Point and watch the sea otters playing in the kelp beds and cracking open an occasional abalone for lunch.

Thousands of **monarch butterflies** migrate here from November to February, traveling from as far away as Alaska. Many settle in the Monarch Grove sanctuary, a eucalyptus stand on Grove Acre Avenue off Lighthouse Avenue.

Just as Ocean View Boulevard serves as an alternative to the 17-mile Drive, the **Pacific Grove Municipal Golf Course,** 77 Asilomar Ave. (📞 **831/648-5777**), is a reasonably priced alternative to the courses at Pebble Beach. Views are panoramic, and the fairways and greens are better maintained than those of most semiprivate courses. Greens fees are $35 to $40. Optional carts cost $30.

WHERE TO STAY

If you're having trouble finding a vacancy, try calling **Resort 2 Me** (📞 **800/757-5646;** www.resort2me.com), a local reservations service that offers free recommendations of Monterey Bay–area hotels in all price ranges.

Although it's not waterfront (it's close to the wharf and across the street from the Monterey Conference Center), the **Hotel Pacific,** 300 Pacific St. (© **800/554-5542** or 831/373-5700; www.hotelpacific.com), is our favorite upscale choice in Monterey. Rooms are clustered around courtyards and gardens complete with spas and fountains. The cozy southwestern-style suites have fluffy down comforters atop four-poster beds, terra-cotta floors, and fireplaces surrounded by cushy couches.

The **Old Monterey Inn,** 500 Martin St., off Pacific Avenue (© **800/350-2344** or 831/375-8284; www.oldmontereyinn.com), is an intimate, vine-covered, Tudor-style country inn. Though it's away from the surf, it's romantic, with rose gardens, a bubbling brook, and brick-and-flagstone walkways shaded by a panoply of oaks. Breakfast is stellar, and at 5pm guests retire to the living room for wine and hors d'oeuvres in front of a blazing fire.

In neighboring Pacific Grove is the opulent **Seven Gables Inn,** 555 Ocean View Blvd. (© **831/372-4341;** www.pginns.com), a compound of Victorian buildings constructed in 1886 by the Chase family (as in Chase Manhattan Bank). Everything here is luxurious and gilded, including the oceanview rooms, which are linked by verdant gardens. If the hotel's booked, ask about the Grand View Inn, a slightly less ornate but comparable B&B next door that's run by the same owners.

Also in Pacific Grove is the former Methodist minister boardinghouse, **Gobsy House,** 643 Lighthouse Ave. (© **800/527-8828** or 831/375-1287; www.gosbyhouseinn.com), with individually decorated rooms, a separate dining room and parlor, and amenities including a complimentary newspaper, twice-daily maid service, and bicycles.

WHERE TO DINE

A historic 1833 adobe house has been converted into **Stokes Restaurant and Bar,** 500 Hartnell St., at Madison Street (© **831/373-1110;** www.stokesrestaurant.com). The rustic yet stylish interior is the perfect showcase for chef Brandon Miller's carefully crafted California-Mediterranean fare.

The enormous dining room at **Montrio,** 414 Calle Principal, at Franklin (© **831/ 648-8880;** www.montrio.com), is definitely the sharpest in town, awash with the buzz of well-dressed diners. Enjoy crispy Dungeness crab cakes with spicy rémoulade, or succulent grilled pork chops with apple, pear, and currant compote.

On sunny afternoons, patrons at **Tarpy's Roadhouse,** 2999 Monterey-Salinas Hwy., at Highway 68 and Canyon del Rey near the airport (© **831/647-1444;** www.tarpys. com), relax under umbrellas on the huge outdoor patio, sipping margaritas and munching on Tarpy's legendary Caesar salad. Come nightfall, the place fills quickly with tourists and locals who pile in for the hefty plate of bourbon-molasses pork chops or Dijon-crusted lamb loin, all moderately priced.

If you want to take in the views at Fisherman's Wharf, avoid the many tourist traps overcharging for mediocre food. Stick with **Cafe Fina,** 47 Fisherman's Wharf (© **800/ THE-FINA** or 831/372-5200; www.cafefina.com), where mesquite-grilled meats, well-prepared fresh fish, brick-oven pizzas, and delicious salads and pastas give even locals a reason to head here.

In nearby Pacific Grove, **Joe Rombi's,** 208 17th St. (© **831/373-2416;** www.joe rombi.com), offers an intimate dining room and very fresh Italian cuisine (pastas are made that day). At **Fandango,** 223 17th St. (© **831/372-3456;** www.fandango restaurant.com), provincial Mediterranean specialties from Spain to Greece to North Africa spice up the menu. The five upstairs and downstairs dining rooms have roaring fires, wood tables, and antiqued walls. There's an award-winning international wine list. The **Fishwife at Asilomar Beach,** 1996½ Sunset Dr. (© **831/375-7107;** www. fishwife.com), is a casual, affordable, family-friendly spot offering terrific seafood.

PEBBLE BEACH & THE 17-MILE DRIVE

Pebble Beach is a world unto itself, a pricey, elite golfers' paradise where endless grassy fairways are interrupted only by a few luxury resorts and cliffs where the ocean meets the land.

But even if you can't afford to stay here, come and check out the beautiful **17-mile Drive** (which is also a great bike ride). You'll have to fork over $9 to enter the drive, but you'll get to see some of the most exclusive coastal real estate in California. The drive can be entered from any of five gates: two from Pacific Grove to the north, one from Carmel to the south, or two from Monterey to the east. The most convenient entrance from Highway 1 is just off the main road at the Holman Highway exit. You may beat traffic by entering at the Carmel Gate and doing the tour backward.

Admission to the drive includes an informative map that lists 26 points of interest along the way. Aside from homes of the ultrarich, highlights include **Seal and Bird Rocks,** where you can see countless gulls, cormorants, and other offshore birds as well as seals and sea lions; and **Cypress Point Lookout,** which gives you a 20-mile view all the way to the Big Sur Lighthouse on a clear day. From afar, you can also admire the famous **Lone Cypress** tree that has inspired many artists and photographers (although it's no longer accessible on foot). The drive also traverses the **Del Monte Forest,** thick with tame blacktailed deer and often described as a "billionaire's private game preserve." *Note:* One of the best ways to see 17-mile Drive is by bike. For more information and an interactive map, see **www.pebblebeach.com** and click on "17-mile Drive" at the bottom of the page.

Pebble Beach is synonymous with golf; guests of the posh resorts get first crack at preferred tee times. The most famous of all is the **Pebble Beach Golf Links** (© **800/ 654-9300;** www.pebblebeach.com) at The Lodge at Pebble Beach. Each year it hosts the AT&T Pebble Beach National Pro-Am, a celebrity-laden tournament televised worldwide. Jack Nicklaus has claimed, "If I could play only one course for the rest of my life, this would be it." Built in 1919, this 18-hole course is 6,799 yards and par 72; it's precariously perched over a rugged ocean. Greens fees are a staggering $450, and that doesn't include the cart fee for nonguests.

Also frequented by celebrities is the **Spyglass Hill Golf Course,** at Stevenson Drive and Spyglass Hill Road (© **800/654-9300;** www.pebblebeach.com), one of the toughest courses in California. It's justifiably famous at 6,859 yards and par 72 with five oceanfront holes. The rest reach deep into the Del Monte Forest. Greens fees are $300 plus cart. Reservations for nonguests should be made a month in advance. The excellent Grill Room restaurant is on the grounds.

Poppy Hills (© **831/622-8239;** www.poppyhillsgolf.com), an 18-hole, 6,219-yard course designed by Robert Trent Jones, Jr., on the 17-mile Drive, was named one of the world's top 20 by *Golf Digest.* Fees are $130 Monday through Thursday and $160 Friday through Sunday, plus $32 for the cart rental. You can make reservations 30 days in advance.

Lying on the north end of 17-mile Drive at the Pebble Beach Resort and Inn at Spanish Bay, the **Links at Spanish Bay** (© **800/654-9300;** www.pebblebeach.com) is the most easily booked course and perhaps the most challenging. Robert Trent Jones, Jr., Tom Watson, and Frank Tatum designed it to duplicate a Scottish links course. Greens fees are $240 plus a cart fee. Reservations accepted 60 days in advance.

The **Del Monte Golf Course,** 1300 Sylvan Rd. (© **831/373-2700;** www.pebble beach.com), is the oldest course west of the Mississippi, charging some of the most "reasonable" greens fees: $105 per player, plus a cart rental of $20. The course, often cited in magazines for its "grace and charm," is relatively short—only 6,339 yards. This seldom-advertised course, which is at the Hyatt east of Monterey, is part of the Pebble Beach complex, but is not along 17-mile Drive.

WHERE TO STAY & DINE

The **Inn at Spanish Bay,** 2700 17-mile Dr. (© **800/654-9300** or 831/647-7500; www.pebblebeach.com), surrounded by its world-renowned golf course, is a plush, super-expensive low-rise set on 236 manicured acres. Half the rooms face the ocean and are more expensive than their counterparts, which overlook the forest. Each spacious unit has a fireplace, four-poster bed with down comforter, and deck or patio. Roy Yamaguchi, Hawaii's celebrity chef, offers a Eurasian menu at Roy's, the best restaurant in Pebble Beach. A bagpiper strolls the terrace at dusk. Guests enjoy eight tennis courts, pro shops, a superb fitness center, an equestrian center, and a heated pool.

For the combined cost of greens fees and a room at the **Lodge at Pebble Beach,** 1700 17-mile Dr. (© **800/654-9300** or 831/624-3811; www.pebblebeach.com), you could easily create a professional putting green in your own backyard. But if you're a dedicated hacker, you've got to play here at least once. Your ultraplush room will have every conceivable amenity, including a wood-burning fireplace. Amenities include 12 tennis courts, a fitness room, horseback riding, a pool, and hiking trails.

CARMEL-BY-THE-SEA

Once a bohemian artists' village, Carmel is today an adorable (albeit touristy) town that knows how to celebrate its surroundings. Vibrant wildflower gardens flourish along each residential street, and gnarled cypress trees reach up from white sandy beaches. It's still intimate enough that there's no need for street numbers. But a few hints such as Saks Fifth Avenue, intolerable traffic, and lofty B&B rates indicate we're not in Kansas anymore, but rather a well-preserved upscale tourist haven. If the prices here are too high, you can easily stay in nearby Monterey or Pacific Grove.

The **Carmel Business Association,** P.O. Box 4444, Carmel (© **831/624-2522;** www.carmelcalifornia.org), is on San Carlos Street between Fifth and Sixth streets. It distributes local maps, brochures, and publications. Pick up the *Guide to Carmel* and a schedule of events. Hours are Monday through Friday from 9am to 5pm. On weekends, an information booth is set up from 11am to 3pm at Carmel Plaza, on Ocean Avenue between Junipero and San Carlos streets.

WHAT TO SEE & DO

A wonderful stretch of white sand backed by cypress trees, **Carmel Beach City Park** is a wee bit o' heaven (although the jammed parking lot can feel more like a visit to a car rally). There's plenty of room for families, surfers, and dogs with their owners (pooches are allowed to run off-leash here). If the parking lot is full, there are some spaces on Ocean Avenue, but take heed: They're generally good for 90-minute parking only. Farther south around the promontory, **Carmel River State Beach** is a less crowded option, with white sand and a bird sanctuary.

If the tourists aren't lying on the beach, then they're probably shopping. This small town packs in more than 500 boutiques and a veritable cornucopia of art galleries. Most of the commercial action is along the small stretch of Ocean Avenue between Junipero and San Antonio.

The **Mission San Carlos Borromeo del Rio Carmelo,** on Basilica Rio Road at Lasuen Drive, off Highway 1 (© **831/624-1271;** www.carmelmission.org), is the burial ground of Father Junípero Serra and the second oldest of the 21 Spanish missions he established. The stone church, with its gracefully curving walls and Moorish bell tower, was begun in 1793. The old mission kitchen, the first library in California, the high altar, and the flower gardens are all worth visiting. More than 3,000 Native Americans are buried in the adjacent cemetery; their graves are decorated with seashells. The mission is open Monday through Saturday from 9:30am to 5pm, Sunday from 10:30am to 5pm. Admission is $5 for adults, $4 for seniors, and $1 for children under 17. Docent-led tours are $7. Call the tour office (© **831/624-1271,** ext. 213) for schedules.

One of Carmel's prettiest homes and gardens is **Tor House,** 26304 Ocean View Ave. (© **831/624-1813;** www.torhouse.org), built by poet Robinson Jeffers. On Carmel Point, the house dates from 1918. Its 40-foot tower has stones embedded in the walls from around the world (including the Great Wall of China). Inside, an old porthole is reputed to have come from the ship on which Napoleon escaped from Elba in 1815. No photography is allowed. Admission is by guided tour only on Friday and Saturday from 10am to 3pm, and reservations are requested. It's $7 for adults, $4 for college students, and $2 for high-school students (no children under 12).

WHERE TO STAY

The pricey, intimate **Carriage House Inn,** Junipero Street, between Seventh and Eighth avenues (© **800/433-4732** or 831/625-2585; www.ibts-carriagehouse.com), offers a luxurious atmosphere and lots of pampering in the heart of "downtown." Each room comes with a VCR, fireplace, fridge, and king-size bed with down comforter. While most other choices in town are of the frill-and-lace variety, the Carriage House has a more mature, formal, yet cozy ambience.

If you want to stay a bit off the beaten track, consider **Mission Ranch,** 26270 Dolores St. (© **800/538-8221** or 831/624-6436), a converted 1850s dairy farm that was purchased and restored by Clint Eastwood. The accommodations are scattered amid different structures, both old and new, and surrounded by wetlands and grazing sheep. As befits a ranch, rooms are decorated in a provincial style, with carved wooden beds bedecked with handmade quilts. Most are equipped with whirlpool tubs, fireplaces, and decks or patios. The restaurant is terrific.

Inland from Carmel, in sunny Carmel Valley, is the superplush, superexpensive **Quail Lodge Resort and Golf Club,** 8205 Valley Greens Dr. (© **888/828-8787** or 831/624-2888; www.quaillodge.com). Lying in the foothills of the Santa Lucia Range, Quail Lodge is set on 850 acres of sparkling lakes, secluded woodlands, and rolling meadows. Rooms have balconies or terraces; some have fireplaces and wet bars. Guests enjoy an excellent 18-hole golf course, four tennis courts, two outdoor pools, a full-service spa, and hiking and jogging trails.

Back in Carmel itself, more moderately priced choices (for Carmel, anyway) include the **Normandy Inn,** Ocean Avenue, between Monte Verde and Casanova streets, 3 blocks from the beach (© **800/343-3825** or 831/624-3825; www.normandy inncarmel.com). Rooms show their age a little, but are well appointed with French country decor and down comforters. The tiny heated pool is banked by a sweet flower garden. The three large family-style units are an especially good deal.

The **Cobblestone Inn,** on Junipero Street, between Seventh and Eighth avenues, 1½ blocks from Ocean Avenue (© **800/833-8836** or 831/625-5222; www.cobblestone

inncarmel.com), is flowery, well kept, and cute, with hand-stenciled wall decorations and an abundance of teddy bears. Rooms vary in size; some can be small, and most have showers only, but the largest units include a wet bar, sofa, and separate bedroom.

A flower garden welcomes visitors to the **Sandpiper Inn by the Sea,** 2408 Bay View Ave. (© **800/590-6433** or 831/624-6433; www.sandpiper-inn.com), a quiet, midscale standby that's been in business for more than 60 years. Rooms are decorated with handsome country antiques and fresh flowers, and Carmel's white-sand beaches are a mere 300 feet away.

The **Carmel Sands Lodge,** San Carlos and Fifth streets (© **800/252-1255** or 831/624-1255; www.carmelsandslodge.com), and the **Carmel Village Inn,** Ocean Avenue and Junipero Street (© **800/346-3864** or 831/624-3864; www.carmel villageinn.com), are both well-maintained motor lodges with excellent locations. If you're traveling with Fido, your best bet is the **Cypress Inn,** Lincoln and Seventh (© **800/443-7443** or 831/624-3871; www.cypress-inn.com), a moderately priced option owned by actress Doris Day.

WHERE TO DINE

Though you may not spot owner Clint Eastwood, the **Restaurant at Mission Ranch,** 26270 Dolores St. (© **831/625-9040;** www.missionranchcarmel.com), delivers quality food and a merry atmosphere. Large windows accentuate the view of the marshlands and bay beyond. At happy hour, you'll find some of the cheapest drinks around (and Clint often stops by when he's in town). Prime rib with twice-baked potato and vegetables is the favored dish. At the piano bar, locals and tourists croon their favorites. The Sunday buffet brunch with live jazz piano is hugely popular.

Dark and romantic, the moderately priced **Flying Fish Grill,** in Carmel Plaza, Mission Street between Ocean and Seventh avenues (© **831/625-1962**), features fresh seafood with exquisite Japanese accents. Prepare for seriously sensational main courses, like a savory rare peppered ahi, blackened and served with mustard-and-sesame-soy vinaigrette and angel-hair pasta.

Il Fornaio, Ocean Avenue at Monte Verde (© **831/622-5100**), offers a great selection of salads, pastas, and pizzas, as well as rotisserie chicken, duck, and rabbit fresh from the brick oven. Start with the decadent grilled polenta with sautéed wild mushrooms, provolone, and Italian truffle oil. The airy dining room and sunny terrace offer charming atmosphere.

The food and the festive atmosphere at the **Rio Grill,** in the Crossroads Shopping Center, 101 Crossroads Blvd. (© **831/625-5436;** www.riogrill.com), have won over even the locals. The whimsical Santa Fe–style dining room belies the kitchen's serious preparations, which include homemade soups; a rich quesadilla with almonds, cheeses, and smoked-tomato salsa; and barbecue baby back ribs from a wood-burning oven.

BIG SUR

Though there is an actual Big Sur Village approximately 25 miles south of Carmel, "Big Sur" refers to the entire 90-mile stretch of coastline between Carmel and San Simeon, blessed on one side by the majestic Santa Lucia Range and on the other by the rocky Pacific coastline. It's one of the most romantic and relaxing places on earth, often misty and mysterious, and if you need respite from the rat race, we can recommend no better place.

Contact the **Big Sur Chamber of Commerce** (© **831/667-2100;** www.bigsur california.org) for specialized information on places and events in Big Sur.

Most of this stretch is state park, and **Highway 1** runs its entire length, hugging the ocean the whole way. Restaurants, hotels, and sights are easy to spot—most are situated directly on the highway—but without major towns as reference points, their addresses can be obscure. For the purposes of orientation, we'll use the River Inn as our mileage guide. Located 29 miles south of Monterey on Highway 1, the inn is generally considered to mark the northern end of Big Sur.

EXPLORING THE BIG SUR COAST

Big Sur offers visitors tranquillity and natural beauty—ideal for hiking, picnicking, camping, fishing, and beachcombing. The inland **Ventana Wilderness,** maintained by the U.S. Forest Service, contains 167,323 acres straddling the Santa Lucia Mountains and is characterized by steep-sided ridges separated by V-shaped valleys. The streams that cascade through the area are marked by waterfalls, deep pools, and thermal springs. The wilderness offers 237 miles of hiking trails that lead to 55 designated trail camps—a backpacker's paradise. One of the easiest trails to access is the **Pine Ridge Trail** at Big Sur station (© **831/667-2315**).

From Carmel, the first stop along Highway 1 is **Point Lobos State Reserve** (© **831/ 624-4909**), 3 miles south of Carmel. Sea lions, harbor seals, sea otters, and thousands of seabirds reside in this 1,276-acre reserve. Between December and May, you can also spot migrating California gray whales just offshore. Trails follow the shoreline and lead to hidden coves. Parking is limited; on weekends especially, arrive early.

From here, cross the Soberanes Creek, passing **Garrapata State Park** (© **831/624-4909**), a 2,879-acre preserve with 4 miles of coastline. It's unmarked and undeveloped, though the trails are maintained. To explore them, you'll need to park at one of the turnouts on Highway 1 near Soberanes Point and hike in.

Ten miles south of Carmel, you'll arrive at North Abalone Cove. From here, Palo Colorado Road leads back into the wilderness to the first of the Forest Service camping areas at **Bottchers Gap** (© **805/434-9199;** www.campone.com). It costs $12 to camp, $5 to park overnight.

Continuing south, about 13 miles from Carmel, you'll cross the **Bixby Bridge** and see the **Point Sur Lighthouse** off in the distance. The Bixby Bridge, one of the world's highest single-span concrete bridges, towers nearly 270 feet above Bixby Creek Canyon, and offers gorgeous canyon and ocean views from several observation alcoves at regular intervals along the bridge. The lighthouse, which sits 361 feet above the surf on a volcanic rock promontory, was built in 1889, when only a horse trail provided access to this part of the world. Lighthouse tours, which take 2 to 3 hours and involve a steep half-mile hike, are scheduled on most weekends. For information call © **831/625-4419** or go to **www.pointsur.org**. Admission is $8 for adults, $4 for youths 6 to 17, and free for kids 5 and under.

About 3 miles south of the lighthouse is **Andrew Molera State Park** (© **831/667-2315;** www.bigsurcalifornia.org), which is much less crowded than Pfeiffer–Big Sur. Miles of trails meander through meadows and along beaches and bluffs. **Molera Big Sur Trail Rides** (© **800/942-5486** or 831/625-5486; www.molerahorsebacktours. com) offers coastal trail rides for riders of all levels of experience. The 2½-mile-long beach is accessible via a mile-long path flanked in spring by wildflowers and offers excellent tide-pooling. The park also has campgrounds.

Back on Highway 1, you'll soon reach the village of Big Sur, where commercial services are available.

About 26 miles south of Carmel you'll come to **Big Sur Station** (© **831/667-2315**), where you can pick up maps and other information about the region. It's located a quarter-mile past the entrance to **Pfeiffer–Big Sur State Park** (© **831/667-2315**), an 810-acre park that offers 218 camping sites along the Big Sur River (© **800/444-7275** for camping reservations), picnicking, fishing, and hiking. It's a scenic park of redwoods, conifers, oaks, and open meadows, but often gets crowded. **The Big Sur Lodge** in the park has cabins with fireplaces and other facilities. Admission to the park is $5 per car, and it's open daily from dawn to dusk.

A mile south of the entrance to Pfeiffer–Big Sur State Park is the turnoff to Sycamore Canyon Road (unmarked), which will take you 2 winding miles down to beautiful **Pfeiffer Beach,** a great place to soak in the sun on the wide expanse of golden sand. It's open for day use only, there's no fee, and it's the only beach accessible by car (but not motor homes).

Back on Highway 1, the road travels 11 miles past Sea Lion Cove to Julia Pfeiffer Burns State Park. High above the ocean is the famous **Nepenthe** restaurant, the retreat bought by Orson Welles for Rita Hayworth in 1944. A few miles farther south is the **Coast Gallery** (© **800/797-6869** or 831/667-2301; www.coastgalleries.com), which shows lithographs of works by Henry Miller. The gallery's casual Coast Cafe offers simple serve-yourself lunches of soup, sandwiches, baked goods, and coffee drinks. Miller fans will also want to stop at the **Henry Miller Memorial Library** on Highway 1 (© **831/667-2574;** www.henrymiller.org), 30 miles south of Carmel and ¼ mile south of Nepenthe restaurant. The library displays and sells books and artwork by Miller and houses a permanent collection of first editions. Admission is free; hours are from 11am to 6pm daily in the summer and 11am to 6pm Thursday through Sunday in the winter.

Julia Pfeiffer Burns State Park (© **831/667-2315;** www.bigsurcalifornia.org) encompasses some of Big Sur's most spectacular coastline. To get a closer look, take the trail from the parking area at McWay Canyon, which leads under the highway to a bluff overlooking 80-foot-high McWay Waterfall dropping directly into the ocean. It's less crowded here than at Pfeiffer–Big Sur, and there are miles of trails to explore in the 3,580-acre park. Scuba divers can apply for permits to explore the 1,680-acre underwater reserve.

From here, the road skirts the Ventana Wilderness, passing Anderson and Marble Peaks and the Esalen Institute, before crossing the Big Creek Bridge to Lucia and several campgrounds farther south. **Kirk Creek Campground,** about 3 miles north of Pacific Valley, offers camping with ocean views and beach access. Beyond Pacific Valley, the **Sand Dollar Beach** picnic area is a good place to stop and enjoy the coastal view and take a stroll. Two miles south of Sand Dollar is **Jade Cove,** a popular spot for rockhounds. From here, it's about another 27 miles past the Piedras Blancas Light Station to San Simeon.

WHERE TO CAMP

Big Sur is one of the most spectacular places in the state for camping. One of the most glorious settings can be found at **Pfeiffer–Big Sur State Park,** on Highway 1, 26 miles south of Carmel (© **831/667-2315**), with hundreds of secluded sites in the redwood forest. Hiking trails, streams, and the river are steps away from your sleeping bag, and the most modern amenities are the 25¢ showers. Water faucets are located between sites, and each spot has its own picnic table and fire pit. There are, however, no RV hookups or electricity. At the entrance are a store, gift shop, restaurant, and cafe. Fees are $25 for family sites. Call © **800/444-7275** or go to **www.reserveamerica. com** to make reservations.

The entrance to **Ventana Campground,** Highway 1, 28 miles south of Carmel, 4 miles south of the River Inn (© **831/667-2712;** www.ventanawildernesscampground. com), is adjacent to the entrance of the resort of the same name, but the comparison stops there. This is pure rusticity. The 80 campsites, on 40 acres of a redwood canyon, are set along a hillside and spaced well apart for privacy. Each is shaded by towering trees and has a picnic table and fire ring, but offers no electricity, RV hookups, or river access. There are, however, three bathhouses with hot showers (25¢). Rates are $29 for a site for two with one vehicle, $35 on weekends. It'll cost $5 to bring Fido. Open April through October. Call ahead to reserve a space.

The sites at the **Big Sur Campground and Cabins,** Highway 1, 26 miles south of Carmel, half a mile south of the River Inn (© **831/667-2322;** www.bigsurcalifornia. org/camping.html), are cramped, so the feel is more like a camping village than an intimate retreat. However, it's well maintained and perfect for families, who love the playground, river swimming, and inner-tube rentals. Each campsite has its own fire pit, picnic table, and freshwater faucet within 25 feet of the pitching area. RV water and electric hookups are available. Facilities include bathhouses with showers, laundry, an aged volleyball/basketball court, and a grocery store. There are 81 tent sites (30 RV-ready with electricity and water hookups), plus 13 cabins (all with showers). The cabins are absolutely adorable, with country furnishings, wood-burning ovens, patios, and full kitchens. Rates are $28 for a tent site for two or an RV hookup (plus $4 extra for electricity and water), $58 for a tent cabin (bed, but no heat or plumbing), or $105 to $221 for a cabin for two. Pets cost $4 for campsites and $12 for tent cabins; pets are not allowed in the other cabins.

WHERE TO STAY

Only a handful of Big Sur's accommodations offer the kind of pampering and luxury you'd expect in a fine urban hotel; even direct-dial phones and TVs (often considered gauche in these parts) are rare. Big Sur hotels are especially busy in summer, when advance reservations are required. If you're having trouble securing a room or a site, contact the **chamber of commerce** (© **831/667-2100;** www.bigsurcalifornia.org) for other options.

In a class by itself is the incredibly expensive **Post Ranch Inn,** on Highway 1 (© **800/527-2200** or 831/667-2200; www.postranchinn.com), one of our very favorite places to stay on the planet. Perched on 98 acres of pristine seaside ridges 1,200 feet above the Pacific, the wood-and-glass cottages are built around existing trees—some are elevated on stilts to avoid damaging native redwood root structures— and the ultraprivate Ocean and Coast cottages are so close to the edge of the earth that you get the impression you've joined the clouds. Each room has a fireplace, terrace, massage table, CD player, and wet bar filled with complimentary goodies. There's also a small workout room, the best Jacuzzi we've ever encountered (it's on a cliff and seems to join the sky), a mediocre pool, spa services, and sun decks. The only drawback is that the vibe can be stuffy, which is due more to the clientele than the staff. The Sierra Mar restaurant is open to the public nightly for dinner. It's one of the best (and most expensive) dining choices in the area.

Equally as expensive, but perhaps not delivering quite as much for your money, is the luxuriously rustic **Ventana Inn and Spa,** Highway 1 (© **800/628-6500** or 831/ 667-2331; www.ventanainn.com). Located on 243 mountainous oceanfront acres, Ventana has an elegance that's atypical of the region, and continually attracts famous guests. The accommodations, in one- and two-story, natural-wood buildings along winding, wildflower-flanked paths, blend in with the magical Big Sur countryside. Rooms are divinely decorated in warm, cozy luxury, with such amenities as VCRs, fridges, and terraces or balconies overlooking the ocean or forest. Most offer fireplaces; some have hot tubs and cathedral ceilings. A small fitness center offers the basics—but you'll be more inspired to hike the pastoral grounds, where you'll find a pool, a rustic library, and clothing-optional tanning decks and spa tubs.

Affordable choices include the family-friendly **Big Sur Lodge,** in Pfeiffer–Big Sur State Park, Highway 1, 26 miles south of Carmel (© **800/424-4787** or 831/667-3100; www.bigsurlodge.com). The rustic motel-style cabins are huge, clean, and heated. Some have fireplaces or kitchenettes. All offer porches or decks with views of the redwoods or the Santa Lucia Range. In addition, the lodge has its own pool, grocery store, and laundry facilities.

Deetjen's Big Sur Inn, Highway 1 (© **831/667-2377**; www.deetjens.com), is affordable and very cute. Folks either love or hate the accommodations, which are set in a redwood canyon. They're rustic and adorable with their old-fashioned furnishings and down-home feel. But those who want extensive creature comforts should go elsewhere. Rooms are far from soundproof, so children under 12 are allowed only if families reserve both rooms of a two-room building; and not all of the units have private bathrooms. There's no insulation, so prepare to crank up the fire or wood-burning stove. The cabins near the river offer the most privacy. The restaurant is a local favorite.

WHERE TO DINE

Cielo Restaurant, at the Ventana Inn and Spa (© **831/667-4242;** www.ventanainn.com), is woodsy but extravagant. The airy cedar interior is divided into two spaces: the lounge, where a wooden bar and cocktail tables look onto a roaring fire and through picturesque windows; and the dining room, which overlooks the mountains and ocean. But in summer it's the patio, with its views of the Big Sur coast, that's the coveted spot. Lunch offers sandwiches, burgers, and an array of gourmet salads; dinner includes oak-grilled Kansas City steak au poivre and caramelized Maine Diver scallops in a red Thai curry–coconut milk broth.

Stop by **Nepenthe,** on Highway 1, 29 miles south of Carmel, 5 miles south of the River Inn (© **831/667-2345;** www.nepenthebigsur.com), for the outrageous views. Sitting 808 feet above sea level along the cliffs overlooking the ocean, Nepenthe is naturally celestial. On a warm day, join the crowds on the terrace. On colder days, go the indoor route—the redwood-and-adobe structure offers an equally magical view, and with its fireplace, redwood ceilings, and bayfront windows, the atmosphere is something you can't find anywhere else. Unfortunately, that's not been our experience with the overpriced fare, so just come for lunch and spend big dinner bucks elsewhere.

One level below Nepenthe, **Café Kevah** (© **831/667-2345;** www.nepenthebigsur.com) offers the same celestial view (at a fraction of the price), a more casual environment, and better food. Seating is entirely outdoors—a downside when the biting fog rolls in (bring a jacket), but perfect on a clear day. Fare here is more eclectic than Nepenthe's, with such choices as homemade granola, baby greens with broiled salmon and papaya, chicken brochettes, and new-potato hash.

The **Big Sur River Inn,** on Highway 1, 2 miles north of Pfeiffer–Big Sur State Park (© **831/667-2700;** www.bigsurriverinn.com), is an unpretentious, rustic, down-home restaurant that's got something for all tastes. In winter, the wooden dining room is the prime spot; on summer days, some folks grab their patio chair and a cocktail and hang out literally midstream. Along with the local color, attractions include a full bar and good ol' American fare.

With the feel of an English farmhouse, **Deetjen's Big Sur Inn Restaurant,** on Calif. 1 (© **831/667-2377;** www.deetjens.com), is the perfect venue for delicious comfort food and friendly service, including great breakfasts.

The **Big Sur Bakery and Restaurant,** on Highway 1, just past the post office and a mile south of Pfeiffer–Big Sur State Park (© **831/667-0520;** www.bigsurbakery. com), offers healthy fare, ranging from wood-fired pizzas and portobello burgers at lunch to salmon, tuna, and chicken selections at dinner. Pastries are baked on the premises.

5 San Simeon: Hearst Castle

Few places on earth compare to **Hearst Castle.** The 165-room estate of publishing magnate William Randolph Hearst, situated high above the coastal village of San Simeon, is an ego trip par excellence. One of the last great estates of America's Gilded Age, it's an astounding, completely over-the-top monument to wealth—and to the power that money brings.

Hearst Castle is a sprawling compound, constructed over 28 years in a Mediterranean Revival architectural style, set in undeniably magical surroundings. The focal point of the estate is the you-have-to-see-it-to-believe-it **Casa Grande,** a 100-plus-room mansion brimming with priceless art and antiques. Hearst acquired most of his vast European collection via New York auction houses, where he bought entire rooms (including walls, ceilings, and floors) and shipped them here. Each week, railroad cars carrying fragments of Roman temples, lavish doors and carved ceilings from Italian monasteries, Flemish tapestries, ancient Persian rugs, and antique French furniture arrived—5 tons at a time—in San Simeon. The result is an old-world castle done in a priceless mix-and-match style.

Three opulent "guesthouses" also contain magnificent works of art. A lavish private movie theater was used to screen first-run films twice nightly—once for employees, and again for the guests and host. The ranch soon became a playground for the Hollywood crowd as well as dignitaries like Winston Churchill and George Bernard Shaw, who is said to have wryly remarked of the estate, "This is the way God would have done it if He had the money."

And then there are the swimming pools. The Roman-inspired indoor pool has intricate mosaic work, Carrara-marble replicas of Greek gods and goddesses, and alabaster globe lamps that create the illusion of moonlight. The breathtaking outdoor Greco-Roman Neptune pool, flanked by marble colonnades that frame the distant sea, is one of the mansion's most memorable features.

In 1957, in exchange for a massive tax write-off, the Hearst Corporation donated the estate to the state of California (while retaining ownership of approximately 80,000 acres). The California Department of Parks and Recreation now administers it as a State Historic Monument.

ESSENTIALS

GETTING THERE Hearst Castle is on **Highway 1,** about 42 miles north of San Luis Obispo, 94 miles south of Monterey, 250 miles north of Los Angeles, and 250 miles south of San Francisco. From San Francisco or Monterey, take U.S. 101 south to Paso Robles, then Highway 46 west to Highway 1, and Highway 1 north to the castle. From Los Angeles, take U.S. 101 north to San Luis Obispo, then Highway 1 north to the castle. Park in the visitor center lot; a bus takes guided tour guests up the hill to the estate. The movie theater and visitor center adjoin the parking lot and are easily accessible without heading up to the actual estate.

VISITOR INFORMATION   To get information about Hearst Castle, call ℂ **800/ 444-4445** or 805/927-2020, or log on to **www.hearstcastle.org**. For more information on nearby Cambria (see below), check out **www.cambria-online.com** or stop into the **Cambria Chamber of Commerce**'s visitor center at 767 Main St., in the west village (ℂ **805/927-3624;** www.cambriachamber.org).

TOURING THE ESTATE

Hearst Castle can be visited only by guided tours, which are conducted daily beginning at 8:20am, except on New Year's Day, Thanksgiving, and Christmas. Two to six tours leave every hour, depending on the season. Allow 2 hours between starting times if you plan on taking more than one tour. Reservations are recommended and can be made up to 8 weeks in advance. Tickets can be purchased by phone or online at California Reservations (ℂ **800/444-4445;** www.hearstcastle.org). If you're ordering tickets from outside the United States, call ℂ **916/414-8400,** ext. 4100. Tickets for the daytime tours are $24 for adults and $12 for kids 6 to 17. The Evening Tour is $30 for adults and $15 for kids. Children under 6 are free. Prices are a few bucks cheaper during the off season, September 16 to May 14.

The Experience Tour (Tour 1) is ideal for first-time visitors and is the first to get filled up. In addition to the swimming pools, this tour visits several rooms on the ground floor of Casa Grande, including Hearst's private theater, where you'll see some home movies taken during the castle's heyday.

Tour 2 focuses on Casa Grande's upper floors, including Hearst's opulent library, private suite of rooms, and lots of fabulous bathrooms. Tour 2 is a perfectly fine choice for first-timers if you're planning to take only one tour, particularly if your interest lies more in the home's private areas.

Tour 3, which delves into the construction and subsequent alterations of Hearst Castle, is fascinating for architecture buffs and detail hounds, but it shouldn't be the first and only tour if you've never visited the castle before.

From April to October, **Tour 4** is dedicated to the estate's gardens, terraces, and walkways, the Casa del Mar guesthouse, the wine cellar of Casa Grande, and the dressing rooms at the Neptune Pool. This tour does not visit any of the interiors of the main house.

Evening tours are held most Friday and Saturday nights during spring and fall, and usually nightly around Christmas (when the house, decked out for the holidays, is magical). Thirty minutes longer than the daytime tours, they visit highlights of the main house, the most elaborate guesthouse, and the illuminated pools and gardens.

No matter how many tours you take in a day, you must return to the visitor center each time and ride the bus back to the top of the hill with your tour group, so allow at least 2 hours between tours when you buy your tickets. You'll find plenty to keep you busy at the visitor center before, after, and in between tours: an observation deck of the Enchanted Hill, two gift shops, ballpark-quality food vendors, and a good small museum. The permanent William Randolph Hearst Exhibit focuses on the castle's history, art, and architecture.

Tip: Wear comfortable shoes—you'll walk about a half-mile per tour, each of which includes 150 to 400 steps. (Wheelchair tours are available by calling ℂ **800/444-4445** or 805/927-2020, with 10 days notice.)

You can visit the giant-screen **Hearst Castle National Geographic Theater** regardless of whether you take a tour. Larger-than-life films include the 40-minute *Hearst*

Castle: Building the Dream and other films in five-story-high iWERKS format (just like IMAX) with seven-channel surround sound. Shows begin every 45 minutes throughout the day. The movie is included in the price of Tour One; by itself it's $8 for adults, $6 for kids 6 to 17. For current information, call © **805/927-6811** or visit their website at **www.ngtheater.com**.

STAYING IN NEARBY CAMBRIA

Just south of San Simeon, Cambria, known as an artists' colony, is a charming town with little more than 4 blocks of art and antiques shops, restaurants, and a handful of B&Bs. It's the perfect escape and an ideal place to stay when visiting Hearst Castle.

Gray whales pass through the area from late December to early February, and since 1990, thousands of **elephant seals** have made the shore just north of the Hearst Castle entrance their year-round playground—much to the delight of locals and nature enthusiasts. Keep your distance from these mammoth mammals: They're a protected species and can be dangerous if approached. There is a parking lot, and docents are usually on hand to answer questions. The beaches and coves are also wonderful places for humans to frolic. For more information on Cambria, check out **www.cambria-online.com**.

Our favorite B&B in the area is the **Olallieberry Inn,** 2476 Main St., Cambria (© **888/927-3222** or 805/927-3222; www.olallieberry.com), an 1873 Greek Revival house whose rates are on the high side of moderate. A countrified berry motif reigns, and the guest rooms are lovingly and individually appointed. The grounds are perfectly manicured but bloom whimsically, in the afternoon the aromas of baked brie and homemade bread waft through the main house, and the staff does everything imaginable to make your stay special.

Other reliable lodging choices include the **Best Western Cavalier Oceanfront Resort,** 9415 Hearst Dr. (Hwy. 1), San Simeon (© **800/826-8168** or 805/927-4688; www.cavalierresort.com), a family-friendly place that is indeed the only true oceanfront resort in the area; and the **Ragged Point Inn,** 19019 Hwy. 1, 21 miles north of Cambia, with sweeping ocean views from each basic motel-style room.

6 Lake Tahoe

Lake Tahoe has long been California's most popular recreational playground. In summer, you can enjoy boating and watersports, in-line skating, camping, ballooning, horseback riding, biking, parasailing—the list is endless. In winter, Lake Tahoe becomes one of the nation's premier ski destinations.

And then there's the lake. It's disputable whether Lake Tahoe is the most beautiful lake in the world, but it's certainly near the top of the list. It's famous for its pure water (a white dinner plate at a depth of 75 ft. would be clearly visible from the surface) and its size (at 22 miles long and 12 miles wide, it's the largest Alpine lake in North America).

The north and south shores have about as much in common as snow cones and sand castles. The scenery is absolutely stunning on the less developed north shore, although the lake isn't quite as accessible on this side. South Lake Tahoe is brimming with developments: high-rise casinos, condos, and minimalls. Which side you choose to stay on is important, as driving from one end of the lake to the other is a 1- to 2-hour affair on summer weekends and downright treacherous during snowstorms. So which side is for you? If you're here to gamble, stay south: The selection of casinos is better and the lodging more abundant. The south is also the place for families that are watching their wallets, as this is where you'll find the greatest concentration of affordable motels. The north shore offers a better selection of upscale lodgings and restaurants, and the scenery is more pristine.

ESSENTIALS

GETTING THERE **By Plane** **Reno-Tahoe International Airport** (45 min. to the north shore, 90 min. to the south shore; www.renoairport.com) is served by major airlines. Rent a car or take a shuttle up to the lake: **No Stress Express** (© 888/4-SHUTTLE; www. nostressexpress.com) serves the north and west shores; **Tahoe Casino Express** (© 866/ 89-TAHOE; www.southtahoeexpress.com) serves the south shore (1-day advance reservations recommended). *Note:* For more on the airport and nearby Reno, see p. 746.

By Train Amtrak (© 800/USA-RAIL; www.amtrak.com) stops in Truckee, 10 miles north of the lake. Public transportation (TART or Truce Trolley) is available, or you can take a taxi to the north shore.

By Car It's a 4-hour drive from San Francisco; take **I-80 east** to Sacramento, then **U.S. 50** to the south shore, or I-80 east to **Calif. 89** or **Calif. 267** to the north shore. Be prepared for snow in the winter. During heavy storms, you won't be permitted to pass the checkpoints without four-wheel-drive or chains. From Los Angeles, it's a 9-hour drive; take **I-5** through the Central Valley to Sacramento, and then follow the directions above.

VISITOR INFORMATION In Tahoe City, stop by the **Tahoe City Visitor Information Center,** 380 North Lake Blvd. (© 800/824-6348; www.PureTahoeNorth. com). In Incline Village, go to the Incline **Village/Crystal Bay Visitors Center,** 969 Tahoe Blvd. (© 800/468-2463 or 775/832-1606; www.gotahoe.com). In South Lake Tahoe, go to the **Lake Tahoe Visitors Authority,** 1156 Ski Run Blvd. (© 800/ 288-2463 or 530/544-5050; www.bluelaketahoe.com), or to the **South Lake Tahoe Chamber of Commerce,** 3066 Lake Tahoe Blvd. (© 530/541-5255; www.tahoe info.com). Many other websites offer information about Lake Tahoe, including www. virtualtahoe.com, www.skilaketahoe.com, www.laketahoeconcierge.com, and www. tahoevacationguide.com.

LAKE CRUISES

Tahoe Queen (© 800/238-2463; www.zephyrcove.com), departing from the Marina Village at Ski Run Boulevard in South Lake Tahoe, is an authentic paddle-wheeler offering Emerald Bay sightseeing tours ($33 adults, $9 children) and dinner/dance cruises ($61 adults, $31 children). Live music, buffet breakfast, dinner, and appetizers are all available onboard.

The *Tahoe Gal* (© 800/218-2464 or 530/583-0141; www.tahoegal.com), departing from the Lighthouse Marina (behind Safeway) in Tahoe City, is the only cruise boat on the north shore. Cruises include the Scenic Brunch Cruise ($26 adults, $14 children), Emerald Bay ($31 adults, $16 children), Happy Hour (4:30–6pm; $15 adults, $11 children), and Sunset Dinner ($28 adults, $14 children). *Note:* Prices are for the cruise only; food and beverages cost extra.

Woodwind Sailing Cruises (© 888/867-6394; www.sailwoodwind.com) runs daily sightseeing tours ($28 adults, $12 children 3–12), and a Sunset Champagne Cruise ($36). The Woodwind fleet includes the *Woodwind I,* a 30-passenger Searunner trimaran sailing to Emerald Bay from Camp Richardson Marina in South Lake Tahoe, and the *Woodwind II,* a 50-passenger Searunner catamaran sailing from Zephyr Cove Marina.

Tahoe Sailing Charters (© 530/583-6200; www.tahoesail.com) offers scenic 2-hour afternoon ($40) or sunset cruises ($50) aboard the *Tahoe Cruz,* a sleek 50-foot

Santa Cruz-class yacht with a 12-foot beam and plenty of elbow room. Guests can take turns on the helm or just sit back, relax, and let captain and crew sail the deep blue. Complimentary refreshments and snacks are included with every voyage. The *Tahoe Cruz* sails daily from the Tahoe City Marina on Lake Tahoe's north shore.

A DRIVE AROUND THE LAKE

We'll start at the California–Nevada border in South Lake Tahoe and loop around the western shore on Highway 89 to Tahoe City and beyond. U.S. 50, which runs along the south shore, is an overdeveloped strip that obliterates any view of the lake, but keep heading west.

First stop is the **Tallac Historic Site,** a cluster of rustic 100-year-old mansions that provide a glimpse into Tahoe's past. Throughout the summer, the **Valhalla Festival of Arts and Music** (© 530/541-4975; www.valhalla-tallac.com) showcases jazz, bluegrass, rock, mariachi, and classical music.

From here, Highway 89 climbs northward. Soon you'll be peering down into beautiful **Emerald Bay,** a 3-mile-long inlet containing tiny Fanette Island, which has an old stone teahouse clearly situated at its peak. Across Highway 89 from Emerald Bay, there's another parking area. From here, it's a short, steep, quarter-mile hike to a footbridge above **Eagle Falls,** then about a mile to **Eagle Lake.**

It's not surprising that someone chose to build a mansion right here overlooking the bay—**Vikingsholm** (© 530/541-3030; www.vikingsholm.com), a 38-room replica of a medieval Viking castle. Tours of this unique structure are available from mid-June to Labor Day every half-hour between 10am and 4pm.

From here, it's only about 2 miles to **D. L. Bliss State Park** (© 530/525-7982), where you'll find one of the lake's best beaches, though it's crowded in summer. The park also contains 168 campsites and several trails, including one along the shoreline.

About 7 miles farther on, **Sugar Pine State Park** (© 530/525-7232) is the largest of the lake's parks and also the only one that has year-round camping. In summer, you can visit the beaches in the park plus a nature trail; in winter, there's cross-country skiing on well-maintained trails.

It's a clear drive through the small town of Homewood (site of the ski resort of the same name) to Tahoe City, which is smaller and more appealing than South Lake Tahoe, although it, too, has its share of strip development.

At Tahoe City, Highway 89 turns off to Truckee and to Alpine Meadows and Squaw Valley ski resorts. Squaw Valley is only 5 miles out, and a ride on the **Squaw Valley cable car** (© 530/583-6985) will reward you with incredible vistas from 2,000 feet above the valley floor. It operates year-round and costs $20 for adults, $16 for seniors, and $5 for children under 13.

If you continue around the lake on Highway 28, you'll reach Carnelian Bay, Tahoe Vista, and Kings Beach before crossing the state line into Nevada to Crystal Bay, Incline Village, the Ponderosa Ranch, and Sand Harbor Beach. **Kings Beach State Recreation Area** (© 530/546-7248), 12 miles east of Tahoe City, is a long, wide beach and picnic area, jammed in summer with sunbathers and swimmers.

As you approach **Crystal Bay,** you will immediately know, by the string of small casinos that suddenly appear, that you have crossed the state line. The **Cal-Neva Resort, Spa & Casino** on the right was once owned by Frank Sinatra and has a celebrity-studded history. The state line goes right through the lodge, and gambling is allowed only on the Nevada side (it's worth stopping to see). The east shore of the lake is largely undeveloped and very scenic. Drive about 4 miles south of Incline Village to

Sand Harbor (© 775/831-0494), one of the lake's best-loved beaches, home to the very popular **Lake Tahoe Shakespeare Festival** (© 800/747-4697; www.tahoebard. com) every mid-July to August. In addition to turquoise water dotted with big boulders and a wide sandy beach, you'll find nature trails, picnic areas, and boating.

South of Sand Harbor, if you wish, you can turn inland to Spooner Lake and Carson City, or continue south along Highway 28 to an outcropping called **Cave Rock,** where the highway passes through 75 feet of solid stone. Farther along is **Zephyr Cove,** from which the tour boats depart. You'll then return to Stateline and South Lake Tahoe, your original starting point.

SUMMER ACTIVITIES

MOUNTAIN BIKING   Biking is big at Lake Tahoe. For serious bikers, there is a dizzying choice of trails. At both **Northstar-at-Tahoe Resort** (© 530/562-0321; p. 874) and **Squaw Valley USA** (© 530/583-6985; p. 875), you can take the cable car (Squaw) or chairlift (Northstar) up with your bike and ride the trails all the way down. For other trails, check with one of the bicycle rental shops for maps and information. In North Tahoe, try **The Back Country,** 255 N. Lake Blvd., Tahoe City (© 530/ 581-5861); **Olympic Bike Shop,** 620 N. Lake Blvd., Tahoe City (© 530/581-2500); **Tahoe Bike & Ski,** 8499 N. Lake Blvd., Kings Beach (© 530/546-7437); or **Porter's Sports Shop,** 885 Tahoe Blvd., Incline Village (© 775/831-3500). In South Tahoe, try **Anderson's Bike Rental,** 645 Emerald Bay Rd. (© 530/541-0500), or **Lakeview Sports,** 3131 Hwy. 50 at El Dorado Beach (© 530/544-0183).

Another great choice is **Cyclepaths Mountain Bike Adventures,** 1785 W. Lake Blvd. in Tahoe Park, a few miles south of Tahoe City (© 800/780-BIKE or 530/581-1171; www.cyclepaths.com), where you can arrange a guided off-road tour. Whether you're into hard-core downhill single track or easygoing scenic outings, the expert guides will provide you with the necessary gear, food, and transportation.

BOAT RENTALS, WATERSPORTS & PARASAILING   Nothing beats actually getting out on the water. Take a guided tour, go off on your own, or just paddle around. Here are a few reliable choices: **Zephyr Cove Marina** (© 800/238-2463; www.zephyrcove.com) is the lake's largest marina. Here you can parasail, charter sport-fishing trips, or take guided tours. You can also rent motorized boats, pedal boats, kayaks, canoes, water-ski equipment, and jet skis. **Tahoe City Marina,** 700 N. Lake Blvd., Tahoe City (© 530/583-1039), rents motorized boats, sailboats, and fishing boats. Sailboat cruises are available. This is also the location for **Lake Tahoe Parasailing** (© 530/583-7245). **Camp Richardson Marina,** 1900 Jameson Beach Rd., off Highway 89 on the south shore (© 530/542-6570; www.camprichardson.com), rents power and ski boats, kayaks, and paddle boats. It also offers fishing charters, cruises, and raft and kayak tours to Emerald Bay.

FISHING   The cold, clear waters of Lake Tahoe are home to kokanee salmon and rainbow, brown, and Mackinaw trout. With lots of hiding places in the deep water, fishing here is a challenge, and many anglers opt to use a guide or charter boat. There are dozens of charter companies offering daily excursions. Rates run about $65 for a half-day to $95 for a whole day (bait, tackle, fish cleaning, and food included). On the north shore, try **Mickey's Big Mack Charters** at the Sierra Boat Company in Carnelian Bay (© 800/877-1462 or 530/546-4444; www.mickeysbigmack.com); or **Reel Deal Sportfishing,** Tahoe City (© 530/581-0924). On the south shore, try **Avid Fisherman,** Zephyr Cove (© 775/588-7675); **Blue Ribbon Fishing Charters,** Tahoe

Keys Marina (© 530/544-6552; www.blueribbonfishing.com); or **Tahoe Sportfishing,** 900 Ski Run Blvd. (© 800/696-7797 or 530/541-5448).

If you'd rather try your hand at fly-fishing, the **Northstar-at-Tahoe** resort (© **530/ 582-5393;** www.northstarattahoe.com) has a private 10-acre reservoir stocked with hundreds of rainbow trout, reserved for catch-and-release fly-fishing only. Equipment is available for guests at no extra cost and there's a guide on-site daily to provide helpful hints.

GOLF With its world-class golf courses, mild summer weather, and magnificent scenery, Lake Tahoe is a golfer's paradise. All of the following courses are very busy in the summer so call *far* in advance for tee times. For more information about Tahoe-area golf courses, log on to **www.tahoesbest.com/Golf.**

Starting at the north end of the lake, there are four highly rated courses: **Incline Village Championship Course,** 955 Fairway Blvd., and the smaller **Incline Village Mountain (Executive) Course,** 690 Wilson Way (© 775/832-1144 for both); **Northstar-at-Tahoe** (© 530/562-2490); and **The Resort at Squaw Creek** (© 800/327-3353).

In the south, **Edgewood,** U.S. 50 at Lake Parkway, Stateline (© 775/588-3566), is home of the Celebrity Golf Championship; **Lake Tahoe Golf Course,** 2500 Emerald Bay Rd., South Lake Tahoe (© 530/577-0788), also has some good 9-hole municipal courses. There's also **Old Brockway Golf Course,** 7900 N. Lake Blvd., Kings Beach (© 530/546-9909); **Tahoe City Golf Course,** 251 N. Lake Blvd., Tahoe City (© 530/ 583-1516); and **Bijou Municipal Golf Course,** 3436 Fairway Ave., South Lake Tahoe (© 530/542-6097).

HORSEBACK RIDING Most stables offer a variety of guided trail rides and lessons for individuals, families, and groups. Choose the one that appeals to your sense of adventure: 1- to 2-hour trail rides; breakfast, lunch, or dinner rides; half-day, full-day, overnight, and extended pack trips. Expect to pay $20 to $25 for a 1-hour ride, $6 for a half-hour pony ride. Saddle up and savor the scenery. Try **Alpine Meadows Stables,** Alpine Meadows Road, Tahoe City (© 530/583-3905); **Northstar Stables,** Highway 267, 6 miles north of Kings Beach (© 530/562-2480); **Squaw Valley Stables,** 1525 Squaw Valley Rd., north of Tahoe City (© 530/583-7433); **Camp Richardson Corral,** Highway 89, South Lake Tahoe (© 530/541-3113); or **Zephyr Cove Stables,** Zephyr Cove Resort, U.S. 50 at Zephyr Cove (© 775/588-5664).

RIVER RAFTING For a swift but gentle ride down the Truckee River (the lake's only outlet), try **Truckee River Raft Rental,** 185 River Rd., Tahoe City (© **530/583-0123;** www.truckeeriverraft.com). Only available in the summer, the rates are $32 for adults and $27 for children 6 to 12 (kids under 5 are free). If you prefer a more exciting white-water experience, **Tributary Whitewater Tours (800/672-3846;** www.whitewatertours.com) offers daily excursions (in season) down the Truckee River on Class II to III-plus rapids. For a half-day trip rates range from $68 to $78 for adults and $60 to $70 for kids 7 and older.

SKIING

With the largest concentration of ski resorts in North America, Lake Tahoe offers California's best skiing. The ski season typically lasts from November to May and frequently extends into the summer. Lift tickets during peak season currently range from $40 to $70 per day for adults and from free to $35 for children. Ticket prices go up every year, but bargains are available, particularly midweek. Many resorts, hotels, and motels offer ski packages. Contact the visitor centers or visit the websites listed in "Visitor Information," above, to look for these values. The resorts offer instruction for adults and children, equipment rental, special courses for snowboarding, and restaurants. Most have free shuttles.

Six miles from Tahoe City, midsize **Alpine Meadows** (© 530/583-4232; www.ski alpine.com) is a great all-around performer, with something for everyone: unique kids' programs and a family ski zone, as well as its "wild side," for the double black diamond crowd.

Site of the 1960 Olympic Winter Games, **Squaw Valley USA** (© 800/545-4350 or 530/583-6985; www.squaw.com) offers the most challenging array of runs. Squaw's terrain is 70% for beginners and intermediates, 30% for the advanced, expert, and/or insane. The Cross-Country Ski Center at the Resort at Squaw Creek (© 530/583-6300) has 400 acres of groomed trails.

Heavenly Resort (© 775/586-7000; www.skiheavenly.com), which straddles the California–Nevada border, has the highest elevation (10,067 ft.) of any ski area at the lake. Skiers of all levels will find something here to challenge them, including 3 snowboard parks, 4,800 skiable acres, 30 lifts (including a 50-passenger aerial tram), and 86 runs. The Heavenly Gondola takes passengers from the south shore downtown area up to an observation deck at 9,200 feet.

Great choices for families include **Diamond Peak** (© 775/832-1177; www.diamondpeak.com), which is smaller, less crowded, and less expensive than many of the other choices. It's primarily a mountain for intermediates; kids love the snowboard park and sledding area. There's also cross-country skiing and snow shoeing, as well as dining and lodging in nearby Incline Village. Another good family option is **Homewood Mountain Resort** (© 530/525-2992; www.skihomewood.com), a homey little resort with gorgeous views of the lake. There's child care for 2- to 6-year-olds and ski schools for kids 4 to 12. It's 6 miles south of Tahoe City and 19 miles north of South Lake Tahoe. **Northstar-at-Tahoe** (© 800/466-6784 or 530/562-1010; www.northstarattahoe.com) also has a highly touted full-time kids' program. It offers 2,420 acres of downhill skiing with 70 runs, plus sleigh rides, snowmobiling, and various snow toys.

The only real drawback of **Kirkwood**, off Highway 88 (© 209/258-6000; www.kirkwood.com), is that it's 30 miles from South Lake Tahoe. Otherwise, this is one of the top ski areas in Tahoe, with lots of snow and excellent spring skiing on its 2,300 acres.

WHERE TO STAY & DINE

ON THE SOUTH SHORE MontBleu Resort Casino & Spa, 55 U.S. 50 (© 888/829-7630 or 775/588-3515; www.montbleuresort.com), took over the Caesars Tahoe in May 2006. Makeovers designed to attract a younger clientele include a chic new lobby that makes the other hotels on the strip look frumpy, seven stylin' new restaurants (tapas anyone?), two hip new nightclubs, the 1,500-seat MontBleu Theatre featuring celebrity performers, a new outdoor sports arena hosting pro volleyball tournaments, a lagoon-style indoor pool, a Starbucks, and the new Onsen Spa.

In hot competition with MontBleu is **Harrah's Lake Tahoe,** U.S. 50 at Stateline Avenue (© 800/427-7247 or 775/588-6611; www.harrahstahoe.com), a glitzy, modern, Vegas-style palace. Rooms are among the largest in Tahoe, and most have bay windows overlooking the lake or the mountains. With families in mind, the casino has an enormous fun center with the latest in video and arcade games, virtual reality, and an indoor "playscape" for young children. Big names in showbiz headline at the casino's South Shore Room.

Harvey's Lake Tahoe Casino & Resort, U.S. 50 at Stateline Avenue (© 800/427-7247 or 775/588-2411; www.harrahs.com), is the largest (and possibly the ugliest) hotel in Tahoe, boasting an enormous casino, eight restaurants (including a Hard Rock Cafe), and a cabaret with glittering entertainment. Harvey's (owned by Harrah's) is like a city unto itself, with a pool, spa, salon, children's day camp, even a wedding chapel.

Perched near the state line, **Embassy Suites Resort,** 4130 Lake Tahoe Blvd., South Lake Tahoe (© **877/497-8483** or 530/544-5400; www.embassytahoe.com), competes for the upscale gambling crowd and the convention business with Nevada's glittering casino hotels across the way. A château-style hotel of character, it offers an indoor pool and a basic gym. Accommodations are typical Embassy Suites, with fridges, microwaves, and VCRs. The resort's fine-dining restaurant, **Echo,** serves New American cuisine for lunch and dinner. In summer, guests have access to a private beach.

Big, modern, and loaded with luxuries, the all-suites **Tahoe Seasons Resort,** 3901 Saddle Rd., off Ski Run Boulevard, South Lake Tahoe (© **800/540-4874** or 530/541-6700; www.tahoeseasons.com), lies in a relatively uncongested residential neighborhood at the base of the Heavenly Valley Ski Resort, 2 miles from Tahoe's casinos. Most suites have gas fireplaces, and all have huge whirlpools, VCRs, and fridges. Play a round of tennis on the roof or hop aboard the free casino shuttles.

More moderately priced choices include the **Best Western Station House Inn,** 901 Park Ave., South Lake Tahoe (© **800/822-5953** or 530/542-1101; www.stationhouseinn.com), one of the few hotels in town that has its own private "gated" beach on the lake. It offers free shuttle service to the casinos and most ski resorts. There's also an array of condo options at the **Lakeland Village Beach & Mountain Resort,** 3535 Lake Tahoe Blvd., South Lake Tahoe (© **800/822-5969** or 530/544-1685; www.lakeland-village.com).

ON THE NORTH SHORE   Part ski chalet, part boutique hotel, the **PlumpJack Squaw Valley Inn,** 1920 Squaw Valley Rd., off Highway 89, Olympic Valley (© **800/323-7666** or 530/583-1576; www.plumpjack.com), is easily Tahoe's most refined hotel and restaurant. Swirling sconces and sculpted metal accents are candy for the eyes, while the rest of your body parts are soothingly enveloped in thick hooded robes, slippers, and down comforters atop expensive mattresses. Rooms have mountain views. The sleek and sexy PlumpJack Cafe has a wonderful wine list and terrific food. Guests also enjoy ski rentals and storage, a pool, and two Jacuzzis.

The most deluxe resort on the lake, the **Resort at Squaw Creek,** 400 Squaw Creek Rd., Olympic Valley (© **800/327-3353** or 530/583-6300; www.squawcreek.com), boasts ski-in/ski-out access to Squaw Valley skiing (in fact, a chairlift lands just outside the door). Rooms are not particularly spacious, but they're well equipped. There are several dining options, including a steakhouse/sports bar with a pool table and live entertainment. Other perks include children's activities, an 18-hole golf course, three pools, two outdoor tennis courts, a fitness center, 20 miles of groomed cross-country skiing trails (marked for hiking and biking in the summer), an ice-skating rink, and an equestrian center with riding stables.

The fancy new **Village at Squaw Valley,** 1985 Squaw Valley Rd., Olympic Valley (© **866/818-6963;** www.thevillageatsquaw.com), may look expensive, but it's actually one of the best deals in Tahoe. For as little as $140 per night you can score a fully furnished condominium—fireplace, full kitchen, deck, huge TV, sofa bed, DVD player—right next to the ski lifts. And the lodge's free perks are superb: covered underground parking, eight whirlpool spas, ski and snowboard lockers, a billiards lounge, and three fitness centers with saunas. And you'll never need to use your car during your stay because the best restaurants, bars, and shops are all within walking distance, including **Auld Dubliner** (© **530/584-6041;** www.aulddubliner.com), an authentic Irish Pub straight from Ireland (literally—the pub was built in Ireland, then dismantled, shipped over, and reassembled).

If you're looking for a romantic little B&B right on Lake Tahoe's shoreline, the **Shore House,** 7170 N. Lake Blvd., Tahoe Vista (© **800/207-5160** or 530/546-7270; www.shorehouselaketahoe.com), is a real charmer. Each room has its own entrance, handmade log furniture, fridge, gas-log fireplace, and blissfully comfortable feather bed. All guests have access to a private beach and landscaped lawn, as well as a common hot tub.

Situated alongside the Truckee River, the rustic **River Ranch Lodge & Restaurant,** on Highway 89, at Alpine Meadows Road, Tahoe City (© **800/535-9900** or 530/583-4264; www.riverranchlodge.com), is a terrific bargain. It's minutes away from the Alpine Meadows and Squaw Valley ski resorts. All rooms have a handsome mountain-home decor; the best feature private balconies overlooking the river. In summer, guests relax on the patio, downing burgers while watching rafters float by. During ski season, the circular lounge and dining area, which cantilevers over the river, is a popular après-ski hangout. Also a big hit is the River Ranch Lodge Restaurant, which serves fresh seafood, steaks, and rack of lamb.

Built as a private home in 1908, the moderately priced **Sunnyside Lodge,** 1850 W. Lake Blvd., off Highway 89, Tahoe City (© **800/822-2754** or 530/583-7200; www. sunnysideresort.com), is one of the few grand old lodges still left on the lake and has a popular restaurant. It looks very much like a giant wooden cabin, complete with dormers and steep pitched roofs; a large deck fronts a tiny marina. The place is rustic but fairly sophisticated.

The 14 reasonably priced cabins at the **Tahoma Meadows Bed & Breakfast,** 6821 W. Lake Blvd., on Highway 89, 8½ miles from Tahoe City in Homewood (© **866/525-1553** or 530/525-1553; www.tahomameadows.com), are perched on a gentle forest slope. The largest cabins, Treehouse and Sugar Pine, sleep six and are ideal for families. In the main lodge is the highly recommended Stoneyridge Cafe, serving breakfast, lunch, and dinner. Nearby activities include skiing at Ski Homewood (including shuttle service), fly-fishing at a private trout-stocked lake, and sunbathing at the lakeshore just across the street.

TAHOE AFTER DARK

Tahoe is not known for its nightlife, although something is always going on in the showrooms of the major casinos on the south shore. Call **Harrah's** (© 775/588-6611), **Harveys** (© 775/588-2411), **MontBleu Resort Casino & Spa** (© 775/588-3515), and the **Horizon** (© 775/588-6211) for current show schedules and prices. Most cocktail shows cost $15 to $45. On the north shore, **Bullwhackers Pub,** at the Resort at Squaw Creek (© 530/583-6617), hosts live music nightly. The **Pierce Street Annex,** 850 N. Lake Blvd. (© 530/583-5800), behind the Safeway in Tahoe City, has pool tables, shuffleboard, and DJ dancing every night. It's one of the livelier places around. If it's just a casual cocktail you're after, my favorite spot is the cozy fireside lounge at **River Ranch Lodge,** which cantilevers over a turbulent stretch of the Truckee River, on Highway 89 at the entrance to Alpine Meadows (© 530/583-4264).

7 Yosemite National Park

It was in Yosemite that naturalist John Muir found "the most songful streams in the world . . . the noblest forests, the loftiest granite domes, the deepest ice sculpted canyons." Even today, despite the impact that hordes of people and cars have made, few visitors would disagree with Muir's early impressions as they explore this land of towering cliffs, Alpine lakes, river beaches, and fields of snow in winter.

YOSEMITE'S GATEWAYS

Towns on each gateway's periphery are virtually built around the tourism industry. They offer plenty of places to stay and eat and have natural wonders of their own. The bad news: If you stay here, reaching any point within the park requires at least a half-hour drive (usually closer to an hour), which is especially frustrating during high season, when motor homes and overall congestion cause traffic to move at a snail's pace.

But there's no shortage of options to encourage you to help the environment by leaving your car at your lodging or a parking area and entering the park on convenient, inexpensive buses (and then moving around the valley floor on free, readily available shuttles). The **Yosemite Area Regional Transit System (YARTS; ℂ 877/989-2787;** www.yarts.com) provides round-trip transit service from communities within Mariposa, Merced, and Mono counties to Yosemite. Fares vary, but generally range from $7 to $15 round-trip for adults, including entrance to the park.

BIG OAK FLAT ENTRANCE

Among the string of small communities along the way is charming **Groveland** (24 miles from the park's entrance), a throwback to gold-mining days complete with the oldest saloon in the state. It'll take about an hour to reach the park entrance from Groveland, but at least there's some extracurricular activity should you choose to hang around. (Big Oak Flat has a few hotels as well, but no town.) If you're driving from San Francisco, take **I-580** (which turns into I-205) to Manteca, then **Highway 120 East.** For information, contact the **Highway 120 Chamber of Commerce (ℂ 800/**

Burgers & Bullets at the Iron Door Saloon

Walk through the English iron doors that were shipped around the Horn, and you'll step into a saloon that has been serving shots of whiskey to thirsty travelers for more than 150 years. Built from solid blocks of granite, the Iron Door Saloon is a must-stop on your way to Yosemite, if only to gawk at the thousands of dollar bills tacked to the ceiling. They say the infamous Black Bart enjoyed a tumbler here now and again, and even put a few bullet holes in the walls to keep the locals jumpy (keep looking). A stuffed buffalo's head hangs on the wall to remind guests of the house special—a thick, juicy, charbroiled buffalo burger served with pickles, tomato, onions, and house-made coleslaw. Espressos, cappuccinos, and lattes are available as well, in case you need a boost from the long drive. At 18761 Main St. in downtown Groveland, it's open daily for lunch and dinner and for breakfast Friday through Sunday (ℂ 209/962-8904; www.iron-door-saloon.com). Live music acts (with both local and national artists) regularly play at the saloon—a remnant perk from the days when the owners used to work for concert promoter Bill Graham.

449-9120 or 209/962-0429; www.groveland.org) for a list of hotels, motels, cabins, RV parks, and camping in the area.

Our favorite accommodations here are the affordable, rustic cabins at **Evergreen Lodge,** 33160 Evergreen Rd., at Highway 120, Groveland (© **800/935-6343** or 209/379-2606; www.evergreenlodge.com). It's only 8 miles from Yosemite's entrance. There are endless hiking trails and, in summer, access to Camp Mather's tennis courts, pool, and horseback riding. Though officially in Groveland, the lodge is 40 minutes east of downtown.

The moderately priced **Groveland Hotel,** 18767 Main St., Groveland (© **800/ 273-3314** or 209/962-4000; www.groveland.com), is a historic choice that complements the surroundings of the Wild West–like town. Rooms are sweetly appointed with antiques as well as modern amenities; the suite has a spa tub and fireplace. The staff is accommodating, and the restaurant (the best and most expensive in town) is surprisingly sophisticated for its remote location.

Yosemite National Park gets crowded during summer months, so it's wise to stay outside the park at a quiet B&B like the **Berkshire Inn Bed & Breakfast,** 19950 Hwy. 120, Groveland (© **888/225-2064** or 209/962-6744; www.berkshireinn.net), then make day trips into the park. This sprawling open-beam lodge sits on 20 wooded acres just outside Groveland, and consists of six spacious and pleasantly decorated guest rooms and four minisuites, all with private entrances and bathrooms.

ARCH ROCK ENTRANCE

Arch Rock is 75 miles northeast of Merced. If you're driving from central California, take I-5 to Highway 99 to Merced, then Highway 140 east.

The **Yosemite View Lodge,** 11136 Hwy. 140, El Portal (© **888/742-4371** or 209/379-2681; www.yosemite-motels.com), is a gargantuan compound set amid the otherwise awesome natural surroundings. This 279-room megamotel is scheduled to eventually offer around 500 rooms. The motel-style units include fridges and microwaves; some offer river views, balconies, and fireplaces. There's also a general store, two restaurants, two pools, four hot tubs, and more public areas in the works.

SOUTH ENTRANCE

The South Entrance is 332 miles north of Los Angeles and 190 miles east of San Francisco. Fish Camp and Oakhurst are the closest towns to the south entrance at Wawona. If you're driving from Los Angeles, take **I-5** to **Highway 99 North,** then **Highway 41 North.** For more options, contact the **Yosemite Sierra Visitors Bureau,** 40637 Hwy. 41, Oakhurst (© **559/683-4636;** www.yosemitethisyear.com). Ask for the helpful brochure on the area, and be sure to check out the excellent online guide.

The estate of **Château du Sureau,** 48688 Victoria Lane, Oakhurst (© **559/683-6860;** www.chateaudusureau.com), is the sine qua non of luxurious lodging, decadent dining, and exclusivity. The main house resembles a French château, with turret and terra-cotta-tile roof. The interior is exquisitely furnished with antiques, rugs, and fabrics. Each individually decorated room has a wood-burning fireplace and a wrought-iron balcony. Canopy beds are covered in Italian linens and goose down comforters; several rooms have whirlpool tubs. The restaurant, **Erna's Elderberry House** (© **559/ 683-6800**), is famous in its own right, offering impeccable food, ambience, and service. The six-course prix-fixe menu changes daily.

Folks looking for moderately priced accommodations might check out the **Narrow Gauge Inn,** 48571 Hwy. 41, Fish Camp (© **888/644-9050** or 559/683-7720;

www.narrowgaugeinn.com), just 4 miles south of the park entrance. All of the super-clean motel-style units have a rustic cabin feel, complete with little balconies or decks, antiques, quilts, and lace curtains. On the property are a pool, a hot tub, and hiking trails, as well as a wonderfully old-fashioned, lodge-style restaurant.

The **Tenaya Lodge,** 1122 Hwy. 41, Fish Camp (© **888/514-2167** or 559/683-6555; www.tenayalodge.com), is idyllic for families, as it's set on 35 acres of forest a few miles outside of the national park. The decor is a cross between an Adirondack hunting lodge and a southwestern pueblo, with a lobby dominated by a massive river-rock fireplace rising three stories; rooms are ultramodern. Extras include restaurants, two pools, and a spa.

YOSEMITE NATIONAL PARK

Yosemite is a place of record-setting statistics: the highest waterfall in North America and three of the world's 10 tallest (Upper Yosemite Fall, Ribbon Fall, and Sentinel Falls); the tallest and largest single granite monolith in the world (El Capitan); the most recognizable mountain (Half Dome); one of the world's largest trees (the Grizzly Giant in the Mariposa Grove); and literally thousands of rare plant and animal species. But trying to explain its majesty is impossible: This is a place you simply must experience firsthand.

Bears, too, are at home in the valley. Grizzlies are gone from the park now, but black bears are plentiful—and hungry for your food. They don't actually come begging by daylight, but they make their presence known through late-night ransacking of ice chests and have been known to rip into cars that have even the smallest treats inside.

Right in the middle of the valley's thickest urban cluster is the **Yosemite Valley Visitor Center** (© **209/372-0200;** www.nps.gov/yose), with exhibits that will teach you about glacial geology, history, and the park's flora and fauna. Check out the **Yosemite Museum** next door for insight into what life in the park was once like. Excellent exhibits highlight the Miwok and Paiute cultures that thrived here. The **Ansel Adams Gallery** (© 209/372-4413; www.adamsgallery.com) displays the famous photographer's prints as well as other artists' works. You'll also find much history and memorabilia from the career of nature writer John Muir, one of the founders of the conservation movement.

Tenaya Lake and Tuolumne Meadows are two of the most popular high-country destinations, as well as starting points for many great trails to the backcountry. Since this area of the park is under snow November through June, summer is really more like spring. From snowmelt to the first snowfall, the high country explodes with wildflowers and long-dormant wildlife trying to make the most of the short season.

ESSENTIALS

ENTRY POINTS There are four main entrances to the park. Most valley visitors enter through the **Arch Rock Entrance** on Highway 140. The best entrance for Wawona is the **South Entrance** on Highway 41 from Oakhurst. If you're going to the high country, you'll save a lot of time by coming in through the **Big Oak Flat Entrance,** which puts you straight onto Tioga Road without forcing you to deal with the congested valley. The **Tioga Pass Entrance** is only open in summer and is only really relevant if you're coming from the east side of the Sierra (in which case it's your only choice). A fifth, little-used entrance is the **Hetch Hetchy Entrance,** in the euphonious Poopenaut Valley, on a dead-end road. *Note:* There are no gas stations in Yosemite Valley, so be sure to fill up your tank before entering the park.

It costs $20 per car per week to enter the park, or $10 per person per week. Annual Yosemite Passes are a steal at only $40. Wilderness permits are free, but reserving them requires a $5 fee per person.

VISITOR CENTERS & INFORMATION   There's a central, 24-hour recorded information line for the park (☎ **209/372-0200;** www.nps.gov/yose). All visitor-related service lines, including hotels and information, can be accessed by touch-tone phone at ☎ **209/372-1000,** or at www.yosemitepark.com. Another good resource is **Yosemite Area Travelers Information** (☎ **209/723-3153;** www.yosemite.com). For details on much of the lodging within Yosemite National Park, contact **Yosemite Reservations,** 5410 E. Home Ave., Fresno, CA 93727 (☎ **559/252-4848;** www.yosemitepark.com).

The biggest visitor center is the **Valley Visitor Center** (☎ **209/372-0200**). The **Wawona Information Station** (☎ **209/375-9501**) gives general park information (closed in winter). For biological and geological displays about the High Sierra, as well as trail advice, the **Tuolumne Meadows Visitor Center** (☎ **209/372-0263**) is great (closed in winter). All can provide you with maps, plus more newspapers, books, and photocopied leaflets than you'll ever read.

Yosemite's wonderful rangers also take time to lead a number of educational and interpretive programs ranging from backcountry hikes to fireside talks to snow-country survival clinics. Call the main park-information number with specific requests for the season and park area you'll be visiting.

WHEN TO GO   Winter is one of the nicest times to visit the valley. It isn't crowded, as it is during summer, and a dusting of snow provides a stark contrast to all that granite. To see the waterfalls at their best, come in spring when snowmelt is at its peak. Fall can be cool, but it's beautiful and much less crowded than summer. Sunshine seekers will love summer—if they can tolerate the crowds. The high country is under about 20 feet of snow November through May, so unless you're snow camping, summer is pretty much the only season to pitch a tent. Even in summer, thundershowers are a frequent occurrence, sometimes with a magnificent lightning show. Mosquitoes can be a plague during the peak of summer but the plague gets better after the first freeze.

Unfortunately, popularity isn't always the greatest thing for wild places. Over the last 20 years, tourist-magnet Yosemite Valley has set records for the worst crowding, noise, crime, and traffic in any California national park. Our best advice is to try to come before Memorial Day or after Labor Day. If you must come in summer, do your part to help out. Once you're here, park your car, then bike, hike, or ride the shuttle buses. **Curry Village** (☎ **209/372-8319**) and **Yosemite Lodge** (☎ **209/372-1208**) both offer bicycle rentals in summer. It may take longer to get from point A to point B, but you're in one of the most gorgeous places on earth—so why hurry?

SEEING THE HIGHLIGHTS
The Valley
First-time visitors are often completely dumbstruck as they enter the valley from the west. The first two things you'll see are the delicate and beautiful **Bridalveil Fall** and the immense face of **El Capitan,** a stunning and anything-but-delicate 3,593-foot-tall solid-granite rock. A short trail leads to the base of Bridalveil, which at 620 feet tall is only a medium-size fall by park standards, but one of the prettiest.

It's a good idea to buy the excellent *Map and Guide to Yosemite Valley* for $2.50; it describes many hikes and short nature walks. Then go take a look. Walking and biking are the best ways to get around. To cover longer distances, the park shuttles run frequently around the east end of the valley.

A variety of **guided tram and bus tours** are also available. You can buy tickets at Yosemite Lodge, The Ahwahnee, Curry Village, or beside the Village Store in Yosemite

Village. Advanced reservations are suggested for all tours; space can be reserved in person or by phone (© **209/372-1240**). Prices range from about $20 for adults for a 2-hour tour, to about $50 for adults for full-day trips. Children's rates are usually 40% to 50% less, and most tours offer discounts for seniors. The 2-hour **Valley Floor Tour** is a great way to get acclimated to the park, with a good selection of photo ops, including El Capitan, Tunnel View, and Half Dome.

The best single view in the valley is from **Sentinel Bridge** over the Merced River. At sunset, Half Dome's face functions as a projection screen for all the sinking sun's hues from yellow to pink to dark purple, and the river reflects it all. Ansel Adams took one of his most famous photographs from this very spot.

VALLEY WALKS & HIKES   Yosemite Falls is within a short stroll of the visitor center. You can actually see it better elsewhere in the valley, but it's really impressive to stand at the base of all that falling water. The wind, noise, and blowing spray generated when millions of gallons catapult 2,425 feet through space onto the rocks below are sometimes so overwhelming you can barely stand on the bridge.

If you want more, the **Upper Yosemite Fall Trail** zigzags 3.5 miles from Sunnyside Campground to the top of Upper Yosemite Fall. This trail gives you an inkling of the weird, vertically oriented world entered by climbers when they head up Yosemite's sheer walls. As you climb this narrow switchback trail, the valley floor drops away until people below look like ants, but the top doesn't appear any closer. It's a little unnerving at first, but braving it promises indescribable rewards. Plan on spending all day on this 7-mile round-trip because of the incredibly steep climb.

A mile-long trail leads from the Valley Stables (take the shuttle; no car parking) to **Mirror Lake.** The already-tiny lake is gradually becoming a meadow as it fills with silt, but the reflections of the valley walls and sky on its surface remain one of the park's most memorable sights.

Also accessible from the Valley Stables or nearby Happy Isles is the best valley hike of all—the **John Muir Trail** to Vernal and Nevada falls. It follows the Sierra crest 200 miles south to Mount Whitney, but you only need go 1.5 miles round-trip to get a great view of 317-foot **Vernal Fall.** Add another 1.5 miles and 1,000 vertical feet for the climb to the top of Vernal Fall on the **Mist Trail,** where you'll get wet as you climb directly alongside the falls. On top of Vernal and before the base of Nevada Fall is a beautiful little valley and deep pool. For a truly outrageous view of the valley and one heck of a workout, continue on up the Mist Trail to the top of Nevada Fall. From 2,000 feet above Happy Isles where you began, it's a dizzying view straight down the face of the fall. To the east is an interesting profile perspective of Half Dome. Return either by the Mist Trail or by the slightly easier John Muir Trail for a 7-mile round-trip hike.

Half Dome may look insurmountable to anyone but an expert rock climber, but thousands every year take the popular cable route up the backside. It's almost 17 miles round-trip and a 4,900-foot elevation gain from Happy Isles on the John Muir Trail. Many do it in a day, starting at first light and rushing home to beat nightfall. A more relaxed strategy is to camp in the backpacking campground in Little Yosemite Valley just past Nevada Fall. From here the summit is within easy striking distance of the base of Half Dome. If you plan to spend the night, you must have a Wilderness Pass (see "Where to Camp," below). You must climb up a very steep granite face using steel cables installed by the Park Service. In summer, boards are installed as crossbeams, but they're still far apart. Wear shoes with lots of traction and bring your own leather gloves for the cables (your hands will thank you). The view from the top is an unbeatable vista of the high country, Tenaya Canyon, Glacier Point, and the awe-inspiring abyss of the valley below. When you shuffle up to the overhanging lip for a look down the face, be extremely careful not to kick rocks or anything else onto the climbers below, who are earning this view the hard way.

The Southwest Corner

This corner of the park is densely forested and gently sculpted in comparison to the stark granite that makes up so much of Yosemite. Coming from the valley, Highway 41 passes through a long tunnel. Just before the entrance is **Tunnel View,** the subject of another famous Ansel Adams photograph, and the best scenic outlook of the valley accessible by car. Virtually the whole valley is laid out below: Half Dome and Yosemite Falls straight ahead in the distance, Bridalveil to the right, and El Capitan to the left.

A few miles past the tunnel, Glacier Point Road turns off to the east. Closed in winter, this winding road leads to a picnic area at **Glacier Point,** site of another fabulous view of the valley, this time 3,000 feet below. Schedule at least an hour to drive here from the valley and an hour or two to absorb the view. This is a good place to study the glacial scouring of the valley below; the Glacier Point perspective makes it easy to picture the valley filled with sheets of ice.

Some 30 miles south of the valley on Highway 41 are the **Wawona Hotel** and the **Pioneer Yosemite History Center.** The Wawona was built in 1879 and is the oldest hotel in the park. Its Victorian architecture evokes a time when travelers spent several days in horse-drawn wagons to get here. The Pioneer Center is a collection of early homesteading log buildings across the river from the Wawona.

One of the primary reasons Yosemite was first set aside as a park was the **Mariposa Grove** of giant sequoias. (Many good trails lead through the grove.) These huge trees have personalities that match their gargantuan size. Single limbs on the biggest tree in the grove, the Grizzly Giant, are 10 feet thick. The tree itself is 209 feet tall, 32 feet in diameter, and more than 2,700 years old. Totally out of proportion with the size of the trees are the tiny cones of the sequoia. Smaller than a baseball and tightly closed, the cones won't release their cargo of seeds until opened by fire.

The High Country

The high country of Yosemite is stunning: Dome after dome of beautiful crystalline granite reflects the sunlight above deep-green meadows and ice-blue rivers.

Tioga Pass is the gateway to the high country. At times it clings to the side of steep rock faces; in other places it weaves through canyon bottoms. Several good campgrounds make it a pleasing overnight alternative to fighting summertime crowds in the valley, although use is increasing here, too.

Near the top of Tioga Pass is beautiful **Tuolumne Meadows.** This enormous meadow covering several square miles is bordered by the Tuolumne River on one side and spectacular granite peaks on the other. The meadow is cut by many stream channels full of trout, and herds of mule deer are almost always present. The **Tuolumne Meadows Lodge** and store is a welcome counterpoint to the overdeveloped valley. In winter, the canvas roofs are removed and the buildings fill with snow. You can buy last-minute backpacking supplies here, and there's a basic burgers-and-fries cafe.

TUOLUMNE MEADOWS HIKES & WALKS   So many hikes lead from here into the backcountry that it's impossible to do them justice. A good trail passes an icy-cold spring and traverses several meadows.

On the far bank of the Tuolumne from the meadow, a trail leads downriver, eventually passing through the grand canyon of the Tuolumne and exiting at Hetch Hetchy. Shorter hikes will take you downriver past rapids and cascades.

An interesting geological quirk is the **Soda Springs** on the far side of Tuolumne Meadow from the road. This bubbling spring gushes carbonated water from a hole in the ground; a small log cabin marks its site.

For a great selection of Yosemite high-country hikes and backpacking trips, consult some of the specialized guidebooks to the area. Two of the best are published by Wilderness Press: *Tuolumne Meadows*, a hiking guide by Jeffrey B. Shaffer and Thomas Winnett; and *Yosemite National Park*, by Thomas Winnett and Jason Winnett.

SPORTS & OUTDOOR ACTIVITIES

BICYCLING   With 10 miles of bike paths in addition to the valley roads, biking is the perfect way to go. You can rent bicycles at the **Yosemite Lodge** (*℃* **209/372-1208**) or **Curry Village** (*℃* **209/372-8319**) for $6 per hour or $20 per day. You can also rent bike trailers for little kids at $11 per hour or $33 per day. All trails in the park are closed to mountain bikes.

FISHING   Trout season begins on the last Saturday in April and continues through November 15. The Merced River from Happy Isles downstream to the Pohono Bridge is catch-and-release only for native rainbow trout, and barbless hooks are required. Everyone 16 years old or more must display a California license to fish. Get licenses at the Yosemite Village Sport Shop (*℃* **209/372-1286**). Guided fly-fishing trips in Yosemite for all levels are available from **Yosemite Guides** (*℃* **877/425-3366** or 209/379-2231; www.yosemiteguides.com).

HORSEBACK RIDING   Three stables offer scenic day rides and multiday pack excursions. **Yosemite Valley Stables** (*℃* **209/372-8348**) is open spring through fall. The other two—**Wawona** (*℃* **209/375-6502**) and **Tuolumne Stables** (*℃* **209/372-8427**)—operate only in summer. Day rides run $55 to $95, depending on length. Multiday backcountry trips cost roughly $100 per day and must be booked almost a year in advance. The park wranglers can also be hired to make resupply drops at any of the backcountry High Sierra Camps if you want to arrange for a food drop while on an extended trip. See www.yosemiteparktours.com (click on "Activities") for more information.

ICE-SKATING   In winter, the outdoor **Curry Village Ice Rink** (*℃* **209/372-8341**) is a lot of fun. Rates are $6.50 for adults and $5 for children. Skate rentals are available for $3.25.

ROCK CLIMBING   Much of the most important technical advancement in climbing came out of the competitive Yosemite Valley climbing scene of the 1970s and 1980s. Yosemite is still one of the most desirable climbing destinations in the world. The **Yosemite Mountaineering School** (*℃* **209/372-8344**; www.yosemitemountaineering. com) runs classes for beginning through advanced climbers. Considered one of the best climbing schools in the world, it offers private lessons that will teach you basic body moves and rappelling, and will take you on a single-pitch climb. Classes run from early spring to early October in the valley, and during summer in Tuolumne Meadows.

SKIING & SNOWSHOEING   Opened in 1935, **Badger Pass** (*℃* **209/372-8430**; www.yosemitepark.com) is the oldest operating ski area in California. It's nice for families. Four chairs and one rope tow cover a compact mountain of beginner and intermediate runs. At $37 for adults and $21 for children under 12, it's a great place to learn how to ski or snowboard. There are naturalist-led winter children's programs and even babysitting.

Both the Badger Pass ski school and the mountaineering school run cross-country and snow shoeing trips and lessons. There are two ski huts available on guided cross-country tours, including the spiffy **Glacier Point Hut** (✆ **209/372-8444**) with its massive stone fireplace, beamed ceilings, and bunk beds; and the **Ostrander Hut** (✆ **209/372-0740**) with 25 bunks. You have to pack in your own supplies, however.

WHERE TO CAMP

Campgrounds in Yosemite can be reserved up to 5 months in advance through the **National Park Reservation Service** (✆ **800/436-7275;** http://reservations.nps.gov). During the busy season, all valley campsites sell out within hours of becoming available on the service.

Backpacking into the wilderness and camping is always the least crowded option and takes less planning than reserving a campground. If you plan to backpack and camp in the wilderness, you must get a free **Wilderness Pass** (and still pay the park entrance fee). At least 40% of each trail head's quota is allocated up to 24 hours in advance; the rest is available by mail. Write to the Wilderness Center, P.O. Box 545, Yosemite, CA 95389, and specify the dates and trail heads of entry and exit, principal destination, number of people, and any accompanying animals; include a $5-per-person advance-registration fee. You may also call ✆ **209/372-0740** for a pass.

VALLEY CAMPGROUNDS

Until 1997, the park had five car campgrounds that were always full except in the dead of winter. Now the park has half the number of campsites available, and getting a reservation on short notice takes a minor miracle. (Yosemite Valley lost almost half of its 900 camping spaces in a freak winter storm that washed several campsites downstream and buried hundreds more beneath a foot of silt.)

The 2½ campgrounds that remain—**North Pines, Upper Pines,** and half of **Lower Pines**—charge $20 per night. All have drinking water, flush toilets, pay phones, fire pits, and a heavy ranger presence. Showers are available for a small fee at Curry Village. Upper Pines, North Pines, and Lower Pines allow small RVs (less than 40 ft. long). If you're expecting a real nature experience, skip camping in the valley unless you like doing so with 4,000 strangers.

Camp 4 (previously named Sunnyside Campground) is a year-round, walk-in campground in the valley and fills up with climbers since it's only $5 per night. Hardcore climbers used to live here for months at a time, but the Park Service has cracked down on that. It still has a much more bohemian atmosphere than any of the other campgrounds.

CAMPGROUNDS ELSEWHERE IN THE PARK

Outside the valley, things start looking up for campers. Two car campgrounds near the south entrance of the park, **Wawona** and **Bridalveil Creek,** offer a total of 210 sites with all the amenities. Wawona is open year-round, and reservations are required May through September; otherwise, it's first-come, first-served. Family sites at Wawona are $20 per night. Because it sits well above snow line at more than 7,000 feet, Bridalveil is open in summer only. Rates are $12 per night for first-come, first-served sites, and $40 for group sites.

Crane Flat, Hodgdon Meadow, and Tamarack Flat are all in the western corner of the park near the Big Oak Flat Entrance. **Crane Flat** is the nearest to the valley, about a half-hour drive, with 166 sites, water, flush toilets, and fire pits. Rates are $20 per night; it's open June through September. **Hodgdon Meadow** is directly adjacent to the Big Oak Flat Entrance at 4,800 feet in elevation. It's open year-round, charges $20 per night, and requires reservations May through September through the National Park Reservation Service. Facilities include flush toilets, running water, a ranger station, and pay phones. It's one of the least crowded low-elevation car campgrounds, but there's not a lot to do here. **Tamarack Flat** is a waterless, 52-site campground with pit toilets. Open June through October, it's a bargain at $8 per night.

Tuolumne Meadows, White Wolf, Yosemite Creek, and Porcupine Flat are all above 8,000 feet and open in summer only. **Tuolumne Meadows** is the largest campground in the park, with more than 300 spaces, but it absorbs the crowd well and has all the amenities, including campfire programs and slide shows in the outdoor amphitheater. You will, however, feel sardine-packed between hundreds of other visitors. Half of the sites are reserved in advance; the rest are set aside on a first-come, first-served basis. Rates are $15.

White Wolf, west of Tuolumne Meadows, is the other full-service campground in the high country, with 87 sites available for $20 per night. It offers a drier climate than the meadow and doesn't fill up as quickly. Sites are available on a first-come, first-served basis.

Two primitive camps, **Porcupine Flat** and **Yosemite Creek,** are the last to fill up in the park. Both have pit toilets but no running water, and charge $8 per night on a first-come, first-served basis.

WHERE TO STAY IN THE PARK

All hotel reservations can be made exactly 366 days in advance. Call **Yosemite Concessions Services** at © **559/252-4848** in the morning 366 days before your intended arrival for the best chance of securing your reservation. If you don't plan far in advance, it's good to call anyway—cancellations may leave new openings. Online reservations may be booked through **www.yosemitepark.com.** The reservations office is open Monday through Friday from 7am to 6pm, Saturday and Sunday from 8am to 5pm (PST).

An intriguing option bridging the gap between backpacking and staying in a hotel is Yosemite's five backcountry **High Sierra Camps** (© **559/253-5674**). Due to the popularity of these camps, reservations are booked by lottery. Applications are accepted from October 15 to November 30. The lottery is then held in December and the winning applicants are notified by the end of March.

The Ahwahnee Hotel (Best) A National Historic Landmark noted for its granite-and-redwood architecture and soaring lobby, the six-story Ahwahnee is one of the most romantic and beautiful hotels in California; it's definitely a special-occasion sort of affair. Try to reserve one of the more spacious cottages, which cost the same as rooms in the main hotel. For the price you're paying, the hotel's guest rooms, although pleasant in warm woods and Indian motif fabrics, may seem simple to the point of austerity. On the other hand, where else in the world can you look out your window and see Half Dome, Yosemite Falls, or Glacier Point? The **Ahwahnee Restaurant** is a colossal and impressive chamber highlighted by 50-foot-tall, floor-to-ceiling leaded windows. It's more noteworthy, however, for its ambience than for its expensive cuisine.

© **559/253-5635.** www.yosemitepark.com. 99 units, 24 cottages. $393–$863 double. Children 12 and under stay free in parent's room. Extra person $21. AE, DC, DISC, MC, V. Pets are not accepted, but they can board in the kennel at the park stables. **Amenities:** Restaurant; heated outdoor pool; nearby golf course; 2 tennis courts. *In room:* No A/C in cottages, fridge in cottages.

Wawona Hotel   If The Ahwahnee doesn't fit your plans or your pocketbook, the Wawona is the next best thing. Also a National Historic Landmark, the Wawona is a romantic throwback to another century. However, old-world charm has its ups and downs. Private bathrooms were not a big hit in the 19th century, rooms were small to hold in heat, there were no TVs or phones, and walls were thin—and all of the above still applies today. Still, the Wawona is less commercial than other accommodations on the valley floor.

© 559/253-5635. www.yosemitepark.com. 104 units, 52 with private bathroom. $126 double without private bathroom; $183 double with private bathroom. Children 12 and under stay free in parent's room. Extra person $16. AE, DC, DISC, MC, V. **Amenities:** Restaurant; pool; golf course; tennis court. *In room:* No phone.

Yosemite Lodge   The next step down in valley accommodations, Yosemite Lodge is not actually a lodge but a large, more modern complex with two types of accommodations. The larger "Lodge" rooms with balconies have striking views of Yosemite Falls. Indeed, the largest bonus—and curse—is that every room's front yard is the valley floor, which means you're near glorious larger-than-life natural attractions and equally gargantuan crowds.

© 559/253-5635. www.yosemitepark.com. 245 units. $113–$170 double. Children 12 and under stay free in parent's room. Extra person $10–$12. AE, DC, DISC, MC, V. **Amenities:** 2 restaurants; food court; pool; nearby golf course.

8 Santa Barbara

Nestled between palm-lined Pacific beaches and gently sloping foothills, this prosperous resort community presents a mosaic of red-tile roofs and a gracious, relaxed attitude.

ESSENTIALS
GETTING THERE   By Car   U.S. 101 runs right through Santa Barbara; it's the fastest and most direct route from north or south (1½ hr. from Los Angeles, 6 hr. from San Francisco).

By Train   Amtrak (© 800/USA-RAIL; www.amtrak.com) offers daily service to Santa Barbara. Trains arrive and depart from the **Santa Barbara Rail Station,** 209 State St. (© 805/963-1015). Fares can be as low as $40 (round-trip) from Los Angeles's Union Station.

VISITOR INFORMATION   The **Santa Barbara Visitor Information Center,** 1 Garden St. (off Cabrillo Blvd., across from the beach; © 805/966-9222; www. santabarbaraca.com), distributes maps, brochures, an events calendar, and information. It's open Monday through Saturday from 9am to 5pm, and Sunday from 10am to 5pm.

WHAT TO SEE & DO
State Street is the city's main thoroughfare and has the largest concentration of cafes, boutiques, antiques stores, and more. Electric shuttle buses (25¢) run up and down State Street. At the harbor end is the city's 1872-vintage Stearns Wharf, offering a small collection of souvenir shops, attractions, and restaurants, plus terrific inland views and fishing.

The town has an array of beaches. **Arroyo Burro Beach County Park,** aka **Hendry's Beach,** at the end of Cliff Drive, is popular with families, Boogie boarders, and sunset strollers. **East Beach** is a wide swath of clean white sand that hosts beach umbrellas, sand-castle builders, and spirited volleyball games.

A relatively flat, palm-lined, 2-mile coastal pathway runs along the beach and is perfect for biking and skating. More adventurous riders can pedal through town, up to the mission, or to Montecito, the next town over. For bike or skate rentals, head to

Wheel Fun Rentals, 101 State St. (just off Cabrillo Blvd.; © **805/966-2282;** www.wheelfunrentals.com).

Santa Barbara's most distinctive attraction is the 1786 **Santa Barbara Mission,** at Laguna and Los Olivos streets (© **805/682-4149;** www.sbmission.org), whose graceful Spanish-Moorish style earned it the title "Queen of the Missions." It overlooks the town and the sea beyond. Admission is $4 for adults, free for children 11 and under; open daily from 9am to 5pm.

The **Red Tile Tour** of downtown (ask for details at the visitor center) passes many historic and architectural highlights, including the exquisite 1929 **Santa Barbara County Courthouse,** 1100 Anacapa St. (© **805/962-6464;** www.santabarbaracourthouse.org), the most flamboyant example of Spanish Colonial Revival architecture in the entire city. The observation deck atop the clock tower affords great views of the ocean, the mountains, and the courthouse's outstanding gardens.

WHERE TO STAY

The Convention and Visitors Bureau's free reservations service, **Hot Spots** (© **800/793-7666** or 805/564-1637; www.hotspotsusa.com), keeps an updated list of availability for the area's hotels, motels, inns, and B&Bs. Call Monday through Saturday from 9am to 9pm and Sunday from 9am to 4pm.

In addition to the listings below, there are moderately priced rooms at the **Casa del Mar Inn at the Beach,** 18 Bath St. (© **800/433-3097** or 805/963-4418; www.casadelmar.com); and at the **Franciscan Inn,** 109 Bath St. (© **800/663-5288** or 805/963-8845; www.franciscaninn.com).

Four Seasons Biltmore *Best*   This grand Spanish-style hacienda, once patronized by such Hollywood golden age celebs as Greta Garbo and Errol Flynn, manages to adhere to the most elegant standards of hospitality without making anyone feel unwelcome. Rooms have an airy feel, heightened by white plantation shutters and marble bathrooms with all the modern amenities. Guests can amuse themselves with a putting green, shuffleboard, and croquet courts, plus numerous treatments, a fitness center, and pool at The Spa, a multimillion-dollar, 10,000-square-foot Spanish-style annex. In addition to two acclaimed dining rooms, the Biltmore offers a no-holds-barred Sunday brunch. As of press time, the hotel is nearing completion of a massive 4-year, $145-million renovation to all of its guest rooms and landscaping.

1260 Channel Dr. (at the end of Olive Mill Rd.), Santa Barbara, CA 93108. © 800/819-5053 or 805/969-2261. Fax 805/565-8323. www.fourseasons.com/santabarbara. 207 units. Superior rooms from $600 double; from $1,650 suite. Extra person $55. Children age 18 and under stay free in parent's room. Special midweek and package rates available. AE, DC, MC, V. Valet parking $20; free self-parking. **Amenities:** 4 restaurants; 2 pools; 3 tennis courts (lit for night play); spa.

Hotel Oceana   The 2½-acre Spanish mission–style property consists of four adjacent motels built in the 1940s that have been merged and renovated into one sprawling hotel. The result is a wide range of charmingly old-school accommodations—everything from apartments with real day beds (great for families) to inexpensive courtyard rooms and deluxe oceanview suites—with bright modern furnishings. Each guest room is smartly appointed with soft Frette linens, down comforters (the beds are fantastic), ceiling fans, CD players, cozy duvets, and Aveda bath products.

202 W. Cabrillo Blvd., Santa Barbara, CA 93101. © 800/965-9776 or 805/965-4577. Fax 805/965-9937. www.hoteloceana.com. 122 units. $185–$360 double. 2-night minimum for weekend reservations. AE, DC, DISC, MC, V. **Amenities:** Denny's restaurant adjacent; 2 swimming pools; fitness room; spa.

Simpson House Inn Bed & Breakfast Simpson House is truly something special. Rooms in the 1874 Historic Landmark house are decorated to Victorian perfection, with extras ranging from a claw-foot tub to French doors; cottages are nestled throughout the grounds. Accommodations have everything you could possibly need (including VCRs), but most impressive are the extras: the Mediterranean hors d'oeuvres and Santa Barbara wines, the enormous video library, and the heavenly gourmet breakfast.

121 E. Arrellaga St. (between Santa Barbara and Anacapa sts.), Santa Barbara, CA 93101. ① 800/676-1280 or 805/963-7067. Fax 805/564-4811. www.simpsonhouseinn.com. 15 units. $235–$615 double; $595–$605 suite and cottage. 2-night minimum on weekends. Rates include full gourmet breakfast, evening hors d'oeuvres, and wine. AE, DISC, MC, V.

The Upham Victorian Hotel and Garden Cottages This conveniently located inn combines the intimacy of a B&B with the service of a small hotel. Built in 1871, The Upham is the oldest continuously operating hostelry in Southern California. Somewhere the management made time for upgrades, though, because guest accommodations are complete with all the modern comforts. The hotel is constructed of redwood, with sweeping verandas and a Victorian cupola on top. It also has a warm lobby and a cozy restaurant.

1404 De La Vina St. (at Sola St.), Santa Barbara, CA 93101. ① 800/727-0876 or 805/962-0058. Fax 805/963-2825. www.uphamhotel.com. 50 units. $195–$255 double; from $265 suite and cottage. Rates include continental breakfast and afternoon wine and cheese. AE, DC, MC, V. **Amenities:** Restaurant.

WHERE TO DINE

bouchon ☞*Best* CALIFORNIA This warm and inviting restaurant serves a seasonal menu inspired by the wines of the Santa Barbara countryside—*bouchon* is French for "wine cork." Past delights have included smoked Santa Barbara albacore "carpaccio," luscious sweetbread and chanterelle ragout cradled in a potato-leek basket, and monkfish saddle fragrant with fresh herbs and accompanied by a creamy fennel-Gruyère gratin. Request a table on the romantic patio, and don't miss the chocolate soufflé.

9 W. Victoria St. (off State St.). ① 805/730-1160. www.bouchonsantabarbara.com. Reservations recommended. Main courses $22–$30. AE, DC, MC, V. Daily 5:30–10pm.

Brophy Bros. Clam Bar & Restaurant SEAFOOD This place is most known for its unbeatable view of the marina, but the dependable fresh seafood keeps tourists and locals coming back. Favorites include New England clam chowder and cioppino. The scampi-and-garlic-baked clams are consistently good, as is all the fresh fish, which comes with soup or salad, coleslaw, and pilaf or french fries. A great deal is the hot-and-cold shellfish combo platter for $13. Ask for a table on the narrow deck overlooking the harbor. *Be forewarned:* The wait at this small place can be up to 2 hours on a weekend night.

119 Harbor Way (off Cabrillo Blvd. in the Waterfront Center). ① 805/966-4418. www.brophybros.com. Reservations not accepted. Main courses $9–$19. AE, MC, V. Sun–Thurs 10am–10pm; Fri–Sat 10am–11pm.

La Super-Rica Taqueria ☞*Value* MEXICAN Looking at this street-corner shack, you'd never guess it's blessed with the Nobel Prize of cuisine: an endorsement by the late Julia Child. The tacos here are no-nonsense, generous portions of filling piled onto fresh, grainy corn tortillas. Sunday's special is *pozole*, a stew of pork and hominy in red chile sauce. On Friday and Saturday, the specialty is freshly made tamales.

622 N. Milpas St. (between Cota and Ortega sts.), Santa Barbara. ① 805/963-4940. Most menu items $3–$7. No credit cards. Sun–Thurs 11am–9pm; Fri–Sat 11am–9:30pm.

Wine Cask CALIFORNIA/ITALIAN Take an 18-year-old wine shop, a 1920s landmark dining room, outstanding Italian fare, and an attractive clientele, and you've got the Wine Cask. Heavenly creations include lamb sirloin with twice-baked au gratin potatoes, or perhaps potato- and prosciutto-wrapped halibut in cioppino sauce. The wine list reads like a novel, and has deservedly received the *Wine Spectator* award for excellence.

In El Paseo Center, 813 Anacapa, Santa Barbara. © **800/436-9463** or 805/966-9463. www.winecask.com. Reservations recommended. Lunch $12–$17; dinner main courses $29–$36. AE, DC, MC, V. Mon–Thurs 11:30am–2pm and 5:30–10pm; Fri 11:30am–2pm and 5:30–11pm; Sat 5:30–11pm; Sun 5:30–10pm.

9 Los Angeles & Environs

The allure of L.A.—for better or for worse—is undeniable. Los Angelenos know their city will never have the sophisticated style of Paris or the historical riches of London, but they cheerfully lay claim to living in the most entertaining city in the country, if not the world.

This part of the L.A. mystique—however exaggerated it may be—truly does exist, and it's not hard to find. In fact, it's fitting that L.A. is home to the world's first amusement park, because it feels like one, as the line between fantasy and reality is often obscured. From the unattainable, anachronistic glamour of Beverly Hills to the vibrant street energy of Venice, each of the city's neighborhoods is like a mini–theme park, offering its own kind of adventure. Drive down Sunset Boulevard and you'll see what we mean: the billboards are racier, the fashions trendier, the cars fancier, the bodies sexier, and the energy higher than anyplace you've ever been. Darlin,' you ain't in Kansas anymore—you're in La-La Land.

ESSENTIALS

GETTING THERE   By Plane   Most visitors fly into **Los Angeles International Airport** (© **310/646-5252;** www.lawa.org/lax), almost universally known as LAX. Situated ocean-side just off I-405, LAX is minutes away from the city's beach communities, and about a half-hour from Westside, Hollywood, or downtown. **Travelers Aid of Los Angeles** (© **310/646-2270;** www.travelersaid.org) operates booths in each terminal.

For a **taxi,** expect to pay about $35 to Hollywood and downtown, $25 to Beverly Hills, $20 to Santa Monica, and $45 to $60 to the Valley and Pasadena, *including* a $2.50 service charge for rides originating at LAX.

For some travelers, one of the area's smaller airports might be more convenient than LAX. **Bob Hope Airport** (2627 N. Hollywood Way, Burbank; © **818/840-8840;** www.bobhopeairport.com) is the best place to land if you're headed for Hollywood or the valleys—and it's even closer to downtown L.A. than LAX. The small airport has especially good links to Las Vegas and other southwestern cities. **Long Beach Municipal Airport,** 4100 Donald Douglas Dr., Long Beach (© **562/570-2600;** www.lgb.org), south of LAX, is the best place to land if you're visiting Long Beach or northern Orange County and want to avoid L.A. **John Wayne Airport,** 19051 Airport Way N., Anaheim (© **949/252-5200;** www.ocair.com), is closest to Disneyland, Knott's Berry Farm, and other Orange County attractions.

By Train   Amtrak (© **800/USA-RAIL;** www.amtrak.com) serves **Union Station,** 800 N. Alameda St. (© **213/617-0111**), on downtown's northern edge. There's frequent service from San Diego (trip time: 3 hr.), as well as daily service from Santa Barbara (3 hr.), Oakland (12 hr.), and Chicago (30 hr.).

By Car   Los Angeles is well connected to the rest of the United States by several major highways. Among them are **I-5,** which enters the state from the north; **I-10,**

which originates in Jacksonville, Florida, and terminates in Los Angeles; and **U.S. 101,** a scenic route that follows the western seaboard from Los Angeles north to the Oregon state line.

VISITOR INFORMATION   The **Los Angeles Convention and Visitors Bureau** (aka **LA Inc.;** © **800/366-6116** or 213/689-8822; www.visitLAnow.com) is the city's main source for information. In addition to offering an informative website, answering phone inquiries, and sending free visitor's kits, the bureau provides a **walk-in visitor center** at 685 S. Figueroa St., downtown (open Mon–Fri 9am–5pm).

Many Los Angeles–area communities also have their own visitor centers, including the **Beverly Hills Visitors Bureau** (© **800/345-2210** or 310/248-1015; www.beverly hillscvb.com); the **Pasadena Convention and Visitors Bureau,** 171 S. Los Robles Ave. (© **626/795-9311;** www.pasadenacal.com); and the **Santa Monica Convention and Visitors Bureau** (© **800/544-5319** or 310/393-7593; www.santamonica.com).

Cybersurfers should visit **At L.A.'s** website, **www.at-la.com**; its exceptional search engine (one of our favorite tools) provides links to more than 23,000 sites relating to the L.A. area.

GETTING AROUND   Forget about trying to get around the city by the slow and inconvenient public transportation system. Despite its hassles (L.A.'s traffic problems are the stuff of legend), driving is still the only way to go. L.A. is one of the cheapest places in the United States to rent a car. All car-rental agencies have locations at LAX.

FAST FACTS   The centrally located (and world-famous) **Cedars-Sinai Medical Center,** 8700 Beverly Blvd., Los Angeles (© **310/423-3277**), has a 24-hour emergency room staffed by some of the country's finest MDs. Chances are good that there's either a **Walgreens** (www.walgreens.com) or **Rite Aid** (www.riteaid.com) within a mile of where you're staying.

The combined Los Angeles County and California state **sales taxes** amount to 8.25%; **hotel taxes** range from 12% to 17%, depending on the municipality you're in.

SPECIAL EVENTS & FESTIVALS   New Year's Day is greeted by the spectacular **Tournament of Roses** (© **626/449-4100;** www.tournamentofroses.com) parade in Pasadena, with lavish floats, music, and extraordinary equestrian entries, followed by the Rose Bowl Game.

In early May, **Cinco de Mayo** (© **213/485-6855**) ushers in a weeklong celebration throughout the city. The fiesta's carnival-like atmosphere is created by large crowds, live music, dances, and food. The main festivities are held in El Pueblo de Los Angeles State Historic Park, downtown, with other events around the city.

The **Los Angeles County Fair** (© **909/623-3111;** www.fairplex.com), held at the Los Angeles County Fair and Exposition Center in Pomona, usually runs throughout September, with horse racing, arts, agricultural displays, celebrity entertainment, and carnival rides. It's the largest county fair in the world.

WHAT TO SEE & DO

California Science Center *Kids*   Using high-tech sleight-of-hand, the center stimulates kids of all ages with lessons about the world. One of the museum's highlights is Tess, a 50-foot animatronic woman whose muscles, bones, organs, and blood vessels are revealed, demonstrating how the body reacts to a variety of conditions. The **Air and Space Gallery** is a seven-story space where real air- and spacecraft are suspended overhead. There are nominal fees, ranging from $2 to $5, to enjoy the science center's more thrilling attractions—try the high-wire bicycle ride or the zero-gravity Space

Los Angeles

Docking Simulator. The IMAX theater screens breathtaking surround-sound movies in 2-D and 3-D throughout the day until 9pm.

700 State Dr., Exposition Park. © **323/724-3623**, or 213/744-7400 IMAX theater. www.casciencectr.org. Free admission to the museum; IMAX theater $8 adults, $5.75 seniors over 60 and children 13–17, $4.75 ages 4–12. Multishow discounts available. Daily 10am–5pm. Closed Thanksgiving, Dec 25, and Dec 31. Parking $6.

Farmers Market & The Grove *(Kids)*   The original Depression-era farmers' stands have slowly grown into permanent buildings topped by a trademark clock tower and have evolved into a sprawling marketplace with a carnival atmosphere. About 100 restaurants, shops, and grocers cater to a mix of locals and visitors. Retailers sell greeting cards, kitchen implements, candles, and souvenirs, but everyone comes for the food stands, which offer oysters, Cajun gumbo, fresh-squeezed orange juice, fresh-pressed peanut butter, and all kinds of international fast foods. Don't miss **Kokomo Café** (© **323/933-0773**), a "gourmet" outdoor coffee shop that has become a power breakfast spot for showbiz types. At the eastern end of the Farmers Market is **The Grove,** a massive 575,000-square-foot Vegas-style retail complex composed of various architectural styles ranging from Art Deco to Italian Renaissance.

6333 W. 3rd St. (at Fairfax Ave.), Hollywood. © **323/933-9211.** www.farmersmarketla.com or www.thegrovela.com. Mon–Fri 9am–9pm; Sat 9am–8pm; Sun 10am–7pm.

The Getty Villa Malibu *(Kids)*   After 8 years and $275 million, the magnificent Getty Villa is receiving guests again. This former residence of oil tycoon J. Paul Getty, built in 1974 on the edge of a Malibu bluff with dazzling views of the ocean, was modeled after a first-century Roman country house buried by the eruption of Mt. Vesuvius in A.D. 79—the Villa dei Papiri in Herculaneum, Italy. The museum's permanent collection of Greek, Roman, and Etruscan artifacts—from 6500 B.C. to A.D. 400—includes more than 1,200 works in 23 galleries arranged by theme, and five additional galleries for changing exhibitions. Highlights include the *Statue of a Victorious Youth,* a large-scale bronze discovered in an Adriatic shipwreck. Admission to the Getty Villa is free, but advance tickets are required; they can be obtained online or by phone.

17985 Pacific Coast Hwy. (1 mile N. of Sunset Blvd.), Malibu. © **310/440-7300.** www.getty.edu. Free admission, but tickets required. Thurs–Mon 10am–5pm. Closed major holidays. Parking $7.

Grauman's Chinese Theatre   One of the world's great movie palaces, the Chinese Theatre was opened in 1927 by entertainment impresario Sid Grauman, a brilliant promoter who's credited with originating the idea of the paparazzi-packed movie premiere. Original Chinese heavenly doves top the facade, and two of the theater's columns once propped up a Ming Dynasty temple. Visitors flock to the theater for its famous entry court, where stars like Elizabeth Taylor, Ginger Rogers, Humphrey Bogart, Frank Sinatra, Marilyn Monroe, and about 160 others set their signatures and hand- and footprints in concrete.

6925 Hollywood Blvd. (between Highland and La Brea Ave.). © **323/464-8111.** www.manntheatres.com. Movie tickets $11. Call for showtimes.

Griffith Observatory   Made world-famous in the film *Rebel Without a Cause,* Griffith Observatory's bronze domes have been Hollywood Hills landmarks since 1935. Most visitors don't go inside; they come to this spot on the south slope of Mount Hollywood for unparalleled city views. The main dome houses a **planetarium,** and the adjacent **Hall of Science** holds exhibits on galaxies, meteorites, and other cosmic objects. On clear nights, you can gaze at the heavens through the powerful 12-inch telescope. *Please note:* At press time, a 4-year major renovation and expansion of the Griffith Observatory area was nearing completion, with reopening scheduled for November 2006. Check website or call for new hours and admission fees.

2800 E. Observatory Rd. (in Griffith Park, at the end of Vermont Ave.). © 323/664-1181, or 323/663-8171 for the Sky Report, a recorded message on current planet positions and celestial events. www.griffithobs.org.

The Hollywood Sign   These 50-foot-high, white sheet-metal letters have come to symbolize both the movie industry and the city itself. Erected in 1923 as an advertisement for a real-estate development, the full text originally read HOLLYWOODLAND. A thorny hiking trail leads to the sign from Durand Drive near Beachwood Drive, but the best view is from down below, at the corner of Sunset Boulevard and Bronson Avenue. For more information, call the Griffith Park headquarters at © 323/913-4688.

Huntington Library, Art Collections & Botanical Gardens   The Huntington Library is the jewel in Pasadena's crown. Industrialist and railroad magnate Henry E. Huntington collected such rarities as Shakespeare first editions, Benjamin Franklin's handwritten autobiography, and a Gutenberg Bible. If you prefer canvas to parchment, Huntington also put together a terrific 18th-century British and French art collection, including Gainsborough's *The Blue Boy.* These and other works are displayed in a stately Italianate mansion, so you can also get a glimpse of its splendid furnishings. But it's the botanical gardens that draw most locals to the Huntington. The Japanese Garden comes complete with a koi-filled stream and serene Zen garden. The cactus garden is exotic, the jungle garden is intriguing, the lily ponds are soothing—and there are many benches scattered about so you can sit and enjoy the surroundings. A popular English high tea (© 626/683-8131 for reservations) is served in the charming tearoom overlooking the Rose Garden.

1151 Oxford Rd., San Marino. © 626/405-2100. www.huntington.org. Admission $15 adults, $12 seniors 65 and over, $10 students and children age 12 and over, $6 children ages 5–11, free to children under 5; free to all the 1st Thurs of each month. Sept–May Tues–Fri noon–4:30pm, Sat–Sun 10:30am–4:30pm; June–Aug Tues–Sun 10:30am–4:30pm. Closed major holidays.

The Getty Center Los Angeles *(Best* *(Kids*   Since opening in 1997, the Richard Meier–designed Getty Center has quickly assumed its place as a cultural cornerstone and international mecca. Museum galleries display J. Paul Getty's enormous art collection, which includes antiquities, Impressionist paintings, French decorative arts, illuminated manuscripts, contemporary photography, and graphic arts. One of the museum's finest holdings is van Gogh's *Irises.* Realizing that fine-art museums are usually dreadfully boring for kids, the center also provides several clever programs for kids, including exploratory games such as *Perplexing Paintings* and *The Getty Art Detective;* and a Family Room filled with puzzles, computers, picture books, and games. Visitors park at the base of the hill and ascend via an electric tram. On clear days, the sensation is of being in the clouds, gazing across Los Angeles and the Pacific Ocean. *Tip:* Avoid the crowds by visiting in the late afternoon or evening.

1200 Getty Center Dr., Los Angeles. © 310/440-7300. www.getty.edu. Free admission. Tues–Thurs and Sun 10am–6pm; Fri–Sat 10am–9pm. Closed major holidays. Parking $7.

La Brea Tar Pits & Page Museum *(Kids*   The La Brea Tar Pits are an awesome, primal sight right on Museum Row, where hot tar has been bubbling from the earth for more than 40,000 years. The glistening pools have enticed thirsty animals throughout history. Thousands of mammals, birds, amphibians, and insects mistakenly crawled into the sticky sludge and stayed forever. In 1906, scientists began a systematic removal and classification of entombed specimens, including ground sloths, giant vultures, mastodons, camels, and even prehistoric relatives of today's superrats. The best finds are on display in the adjacent George C. Page Museum of La Brea Discoveries, which also shows an entertaining 15-minute film documenting the recoveries.

5801 Wilshire Blvd. (east of Fairfax Ave.), Los Angeles. ℂ 323/934-PAGE. www.tarpits.org. Museum admission $7 adults, $4.50 seniors 62 and older and students with ID, $2 children ages 5–12, free for kids under 5; free for everyone the 1st Tues of every month. Mon–Fri 9:30am–5pm; Sat–Sun 10am–5pm (museum). Parking $6 with validation.

Los Angeles County Museum of Art This vast complex (the largest visual arts museum west of the Mississippi) was designed by three very different architects and houses works by Degas, Rembrandt, Hockney, and Monet. The **Japanese Pavilion** contains a collection of Edo paintings rivaled only by the holdings of the emperor of Japan. The **Anderson Building** is home to 20th-century painting and sculpture by Matisse, Magritte, and a number of dada artists. The **Ahmanson Building** houses the rest of the museum's permanent collections, everything from 2,000-year-old pre-Columbian Mexican ceramics to a unique glass collection spanning the centuries, plus one of the nation's largest holdings of costumes and textiles along with important Indian and Southeast Asian art. The **Hammer Building** is primarily used for major special-loan exhibitions. Free guided tours covering the museum's highlights depart on a regular basis from here.

5905 Wilshire Blvd. ℂ 323/857-6000. www.lacma.org. Admission $9 adults, $5 students and seniors age 62 and over, free for children 17 and under; regular exhibitions free for everyone after 5pm and all day the 2nd Tues of each month. Mon–Tues and Thurs noon–8pm; Fri noon–9pm; Sat–Sun 11am–8pm. Parking $5.

Museum of the American West Located north of downtown in Griffith Park, this is one of the country's finest and most comprehensive museums of the American West. More than 78,000 artifacts showcasing the history of the region west of the Mississippi River are intelligently displayed. Evocative exhibits illustrate the everyday lives of early pioneers, not only with antique firearms, tools, saddles, and the like, but with many hands-on displays that successfully stir the imagination and the heart, including footage from Buffalo Bill's Wild West Show, movie clips from the silent days, contemporary films, the works of Wild West artists, and plenty of memorabilia from Gene "The Singing Cowboy" Autry's film and TV projects. Docent-led tours are generally scheduled on Saturday at 11am and noon.

4700 Western Heritage Way (in Griffith Park). ℂ 323/667-2000. www.autrynationalcenter.org. Admission $7.50 adults, $5 seniors 60 and over and students 13–18, $3 children 2–12, free for kids under 2; free to all Thurs after 4pm. Tues–Sun 10am–5pm (Thurs until 8pm). Parking free.

Norton Simon Museum of Art Architect Frank Gehry helped remodel the galleries at what has become one of California's most important museums. The Norton Simon displays one of the finest private collections of European, American, and Asian art in the world. Comprehensive collections of masterpieces by Degas, Picasso, Rembrandt, and Goya are augmented by sculptures by Henry Moore and Auguste Rodin. The "Blue Four" collection of works by Kandinsky, Jawlensky, Klee, and Feininger is impressive, as are the superb Southeast Asian sculptures. One of the most popular pieces is *The Flower Vendor/Girl with Lilies* by Diego Rivera.

411 W. Colorado Blvd., Pasadena. ℂ 626/449-6840. www.nortonsimon.org. Admission $8 adults, $4 seniors, free for students and kids 17 and under. Free for everyone the 1st Fri of each month 6–9pm. Wed–Mon noon–6pm (Fri until 9pm). Free parking.

Universal Studios Hollywood *Kids* Universal is more than just one of the largest movie studios in the world—it's one of the biggest amusement parks. The main attraction is the **Studio Tour,** a 1-hour guided tram ride that gives you a peek at stars' dressing rooms, production offices, and back-lot sets that include the famous town square from the *Back to the Future* films. Along the way, the tram encounters several staged "disasters," which we won't divulge here lest we ruin the surprise. On **Back to the Future—The Ride,** you're seated in a mock time-traveling DeLorean and thrust into a fantastic multimedia roller-coasting extravaganza. The newest ride, **Revenge of the Mummy,** is a high-tech indoor roller coaster that's enhanced with animatronics, motion picture technology, and lots of creepy Warrior Mummies. Other high-tech fun can be found at **Terminator 2 3-D** and **Shrek 4-D,** virtual adventures utilizing giant-screen technology and surprise special effects to hit all the senses. The **Animal Planet Live!** stars trained monkeys and other animals doing various tricks. It's all fun, but lines can be brutally long; skip weekends and school vacations if possible.

Hollywood Fwy. (Universal Center Dr. or Lankershim Blvd. exits), Universal City. (C) 800-UNIVERSAL or 818/662-3801. www.universalstudioshollywood.com. Admission $56 adults, $46 children under 48 in. tall, free for kids under 3. Parking $10. Winter 10am–6pm; summer 9am–7pm.

Venice Beach's Ocean Front Walk *Kids*   No visit to Los Angeles would be complete without a stroll along Venice's famous beach path, an almost surreal assemblage of every L.A. stereotype—and then some. Among stalls and stands selling cheap sunglasses and Mexican blankets swirls a carnival of humanity that includes bikini-clad in-line skaters, tattooed bikers, muscle-bound pretty boys, panhandling vets, beautiful wannabes, and plenty of tourists and gawkers. On any given day, you're bound to come across all kinds of performers: mimes, buskers, chain-saw jugglers, talking parrots, and the occasional apocalyptic evangelist.

On the beach, between Venice Blvd. and Rose Ave., Venice. www.venicebeach.com.

MORE HIGHLIGHTS
TV TAPINGS
Being part of the audience for the taping of a television show might be the quintessential L.A. experience. Timing is important here—remember that most series productions go on hiatus from March to July. Tickets to the top shows are in greater demand than others, so getting your hands on them usually takes advance planning—and possibly some time waiting in line.

Request tickets as far in advance as possible. In addition to the suppliers listed below, tickets are sometimes given away to the public outside popular tourist sites like Grauman's Chinese Theatre in Hollywood and Universal Studios in the Valley; L.A.'s visitor centers in downtown and Hollywood often have tickets as well. But if you're determined to see a particular show, contact the following sources.

Audiences Unlimited, Inc. ((C) **818/753-3470;** www.tvtickets.com), is a good place to start. It distributes tickets for most of the top sitcoms, including *The King of Queens, Two and a Half Men,* and many more. This service is organized and informative (as is its website), and fully sanctioned by production companies and networks. ABC no longer handles ticket distribution directly, but refers all inquiries to Audiences Unlimited, Inc. **TVTIX.COM** ((C) **323/653-4105;** www.tvtix.com) also distributes tickets for numerous talk and game shows, including *The Tonight Show with Jay Leno* and *Jeopardy!*

HITTING THE BEACH
Los Angeles County's 72-mile coastline sports over 30 miles of beaches, most of which are operated by the **Department of Beaches & Harbors,** 13837 Fiji Way, Marina del Rey ((C) **310/305-9503**). County-run beaches usually charge for parking; alcohol,

bonfires, and pets are prohibited. For recorded surf conditions (and coastal weather forecast), call ✆ **310/457-9701.** The following are the county's best beaches, listed from north to south.

Jampacked on warm weekends, L.A. County's largest beach park, **Zuma Beach County Park,** is located off the Pacific Coast Highway (Hwy. 1), a mile past Kanan Dume Road. While it can't claim to be the loveliest beach in the Southland, Zuma has the most comprehensive facilities: plenty of restrooms, lifeguards, playgrounds, volleyball courts, and snack bars. The southern stretch, toward Point Dume, is Westward Beach, separated from the noisy highway by sandstone cliffs. A trail leads over the point's headlands to Pirate's Cove, once a popular nude beach.

Malibu Lagoon State Beach is not just a pretty white-sand beach, but an estuary and wetlands area as well. The entrance is on the Pacific Coast Highway (Hwy. 1), south of Cross Creek Road, and there's a small admission charge. Marine life and shorebirds teem where the creek empties into the sea, and the waves are always mild. The historic Adamson House is here, a showplace of Malibu tile now operating as a museum.

Without a doubt, L.A.'s best waves roll ashore at **Surfrider Beach.** One of the city's most popular surfing spots, this beach is located between the Malibu Pier and the lagoon. Few "locals-only" wave wars are ever fought here—surfing is not as territorial here as it can be in other areas, where out-of-towners can be made to feel unwelcome. Surfrider is surrounded by all of Malibu's hustle and bustle, so don't come here for peace and quiet.

Three miles along the Pacific Coast Highway (Hwy. 1), between Sunset Boulevard and the Santa Monica border, are named for the American humorist, whose ranch-turned-state-historic-park is nestled above the palisades that provide the backdrop for the popular **Will Rogers State Beach.** Facilities include a pay parking lot, restrooms, lifeguards, and a snack hut in season. While the surfing is not the best, the waves are friendly for swimmers and there are always competitive volleyball games to be found.

Santa Monica State Beach, encompassing the beaches on either side of the Santa Monica Pier, is popular for its white sands and easy accessibility. There are big parking lots, eateries, and lots of restrooms. A paved beach path runs along here, allowing you to walk, bike, or skate to Venice and points south. Colorado Boulevard leads to the pier; turn north on the Pacific Coast Highway (Hwy. 1) below the coastline's bluffs, or south along Ocean Avenue.

Moving south from Santa Monica, the paved pedestrian Promenade along **Venice Beach** becomes Ocean Front Walk and gets progressively weirder until it reaches an apex at Washington Boulevard and the Venice fishing pier. Although there are people who swim and sunbathe, Venice Beach's character is defined by the sea of humanity that gathers here, plus the bevy of boardwalk vendors and old-fashioned pedestrian streets a block away. Park on the side streets or in the plentiful lots west of Pacific Avenue.

A very wide white-sand beach with tons to recommend it, **Hermosa City Beach** extends to either side of the pier and includes "The Strand," a pedestrian lane that runs its entire length. Main access is at the foot of Pier Avenue, which is lined with interesting shops. There's plenty of street parking, as well as restrooms, lifeguards, volleyball courts, a fishing pier, playgrounds, and good surfing.

ORGANIZED TOURS

STUDIO TOURS   Universal Studios offers daily tram tours of their studio lot as part of the general admission price to their amusement park. See the listing on p. 896 above for more information.

Seeing the Stars at Work

It's not uncommon for star-studded movie productions to use L.A.'s diverse cultural landscape for **location shots;** in fact, it's such a regular occurrence that locals are usually less impressed with an A-list presence than perturbed about the precious parking spaces lost to all those equipment trucks and dressing-room trailers. On-the-street movie shoots are part of what makes L.A. unique, and onlookers gather wherever hastily scrawled production signs point to a hot site.

For the inside track on where the action is, check the **"Daily Shoot Sheet"** at **www.eidc.com.** This isn't some word-of-mouth groupie posting—it's a strictly legit online listing of every filming permit applied for within the city limits. Entries are classified by type (commercial advertisement, feature film, student film, TV program) and working title, and the site lists production hours and exact street addresses.

If you're really intent on seeing as many stars as possible, log onto **www.seeing-stars.com,** a website that keeps tabs on where all the stars shop, eat, stay, and play in L.A.

Paramount Pictures, 5555 Melrose Ave., Hollywood (© **323/956-1777;** www. paramount.com), the only studio still in Hollywood, offers a 2-hour "cart" tour that's both a historical ode to filmmaking and a real-life look at a working studio. Chances of spotting a celebrity are pretty good, though every tour is different. The $35 tours depart Monday through Friday by advance reservations only. Cameras, recording equipment, and children under 12 are not allowed.

NBC Studios, 3000 W. Alameda Ave., Burbank (© **818/840-3537**), offers guided 70-minute tours Monday through Friday from 9am to 3pm that feature a behind-the-scenes look at *The Tonight Show with Jay Leno* set, wardrobe, makeup, and set-building departments, and several sound studios. The tour includes some cool video demonstrations of high-tech special effects. Prices are $7.50 for adults, $6.75 for seniors, and $4 children ages 5 to 12.

Warner Brothers Studios, 3400 Riverside Dr., Burbank (© **818/972-8687;** www. wbstudiotour.com), has the most comprehensive—and the least theme-park-like—of the studio tours. The 2-hour drive-and-walk jaunt goes around the studio's faux streets, including stops (whenever possible) at working film and television sets. Whether it's an orchestra scoring a film or a TV show being taped or edited, you'll get a glimpse of how it's all done. Tours are $39 (kids under 8 not admitted), and are offered Monday through Friday from 8:30am to 4pm. Reservations are required.

SIGHTSEEING TOURS   **L.A. Tours'** (© **323/460-6490;** www.latours.net) plush shuttle buses pick up riders from major hotels for morning or afternoon tours of Sunset Strip, the movie studios, the Farmers Market, Hollywood, and homes of the stars. Tours vary in length from a half-day Beaches & Shopping tour to a full-day Grand City tour. Advance reservations are required.

GREAT SHOPPING AREAS

Serious shoppers often make Santa Monica their first stop; the seaside end of L.A. offers many diverse shopping neighborhoods, including **Third Street Promenade** (www.third st.com), a pedestrians-only outdoor mall boasting trendy chain stores and boutiques as well as dozens of restaurants and a large movie theater. The Promenade bustles on into the evening with a seemingly endless assortment of street performers and shoppers.

Main Street, between Pacific Street and Rose Avenue, is another good strip for strolling, boasting a healthy combination of mall standards as well as left-of-center boutiques and casually hip cafes; Main Street's relaxed, beach-community vibe sets it apart, straddling the fashion fence between upscale trendy and beach-bum edgy.

And there's **Montana Avenue,** between Seventh and 17th streets, a breezy, slow-traffic stretch where specialty shops still outnumber the chains. Look around and you'll see upscale moms with strollers shopping for designer fashions, country-home decor, and gourmet takeout.

Elsewhere in L.A., check out **West Third Street,** between Fairfax Avenue and Robertson Boulevard: You can shop till you drop on this trendy strip, anchored on the east end by the Farmers Market. "Fun" is more the catchword here than "funky," and the shops (including the vintage-clothing stores) tend a bit more to the refined. Nearby, **La Brea Avenue,** north of Wilshire Boulevard, is L.A.'s artsiest shopping strip. Anchored by the giant **American Rag, Cie** alterna-complex (© 323/935-3157), La Brea is home to lots of great urban antiques stores dealing in Deco, Arts and Crafts, 1950s modern, and the like. You'll also find vintage clothiers, furniture galleries, and other warehouse-size stores, as well as some of the city's hippest restaurants, such as Campanile.

Everyone knows about **Rodeo Drive,** the city's most famous shopping street. Couture shops from high fashion's old guard—like Gucci and Hermès—are here, along with plenty of newer high-end labels. The 16-square-block area surrounding Rodeo is known as Beverly Hills' **"Golden Triangle."** Shops off Rodeo are generally not as name-conscious as those on the strip, but they're nevertheless plenty upscale.

Although stretches of **Melrose Avenue** are showing some wear, this is still one of the most exciting shopping streets in the country for cutting-edge fashions—and some eye-popping people-watching to boot. There are scores of shops selling the latest in clothes, gifts, jewelry, and accessories. Melrose is a playful stroll, dotted with plenty of hip restaurants and funky shops that are sure to shock. Where else could you find green patent-leather cowboy boots, a working 19th-century pocket watch, an inflatable girlfriend, and glow-in-the-dark condoms in the same shopping spree?

If you're a shopping rookie, you might consider an outing with **Urban Shopping Adventures** (© 213/683-9715; www.urbanshoppingadventures.com), which offers custom guided shopping tours to the Fashion District—90 sprawling blocks loaded with wholesale and retail venues—and the trendy Melrose Heights Shopping District.

WHERE TO STAY

In sprawling Los Angeles, location is everything. Choosing the right neighborhood as a base can make or break your vacation. If you plan to spend your days at the beach but stay downtown, for example, you're going to lose a lot of valuable relaxation time on the freeway. But wherever you stay, count on doing a good deal of driving—no hotel in Los Angeles is convenient to everything.

In addition to the listings below, other good bets near the beach include the **Cal Mar Hotel Suites,** 220 California Ave., Santa Monica (© 800/776-6007 or 310/395-5555; www.calmarhotel.com), whose garden apartments are lovingly cared for and deliver a lot of bang for your vacation buck; and the **Best Western Marina Pacific Hotel & Suites,** 1697 Pacific Ave., Venice (𝒞 **800/786-7789** or 310/452-1111; www.mphotel.com), a haven of smart value just off the newly renovated Venice Boardwalk.

The **Beverly Laurel Motor Hotel,** 8018 Beverly Blvd. (𝒞 **800/962-3824** or 323/ 651-2441), is a great choice for wallet-watching travelers who want a central location and a room with more style than your average motel.

Beach House at Hermosa Beach   Sporting a Cape Cod style that suits the on-the-sand location, this luxurious, romantic inn is comprised of beautifully designed and outfitted split-level studio suites. Every bright, sunny unit comes with a plush, furnished living room with wood-burning fireplace (Duraflame logs provided) and entertainment center; a microkitchen with china and flatware for four; an elevated sleeping niche with a down-dressed king-size bed; an extralarge bathroom with extradeep soaking tub, a separate shower, cotton robes, and Aveda products; and a furnished balcony, many of which overlook the beach (and believe us—it's worth the extra money to score a beach-front room).

1300 The Strand, Hermosa Beach, CA 90254. 𝒞 **888/895-4559** or 310/374-3001. Fax 310/372-2115. www.beachhouse.com. 96 units. $224–$349 double. Rates include continental breakfast. AE, DC, DISC, MC, V. Valet parking $17. *In room:* Kitchenette.

Beverly Hills Hotel and Bungalows   Behind the famous facade of the "Pink Palace" (pictured on the cover of the Eagles' *Hotel California*) lies this star-studded haven where legends were, and still are, made. The hotel's grand lobby and impeccably landscaped grounds retain their over-the-top glory, while the lavish rooms boast state-of-the-art luxuries such as marble bathrooms, CD players, VCRs, and butler service at the touch of a button. Many units feature private patios, Jacuzzis, and kitchens. Dining options include the iconic Polo Lounge, the famous Fountain Coffee Shop, and the alfresco Cabana Club Cafe.

9641 Sunset Blvd. (at Rodeo Dr.), Beverly Hills, CA 90210. 𝒞 **800/283-8885** or 310/276-2251. Fax 310/887-2887. www.beverlyhillshotel.com. 203 units. $440–$545 double; from $900 suite or bungalow. AE, DC, MC, V. Parking $23. Pets accepted in bungalows only. **Amenities:** 3 restaurants; pool; 2 outdoor tennis courts (lit for night play); fitness center. *In room:* Kitchens (in some).

Casa del Mar   Housed in a former 1920s Renaissance Revival beach club, this Art Deco stunner is a real dream of a resort hotel, radiating period glamour. The villalike building's shape awards ocean views to most of the guest rooms, whose abundant luxuries include sumptuously dressed beds, big Italian marble bathrooms with extralarge whirlpool tubs and separate showers, CD players, VCRs, and playful treats such as rubber duckies. The Oceanfront restaurant has earned justifiable kudos (and more than a few celebrity fans) for its lovely setting and seafood-heavy California cuisine.

1910 Ocean Way (next to the Santa Monica Pier), Santa Monica, CA 90405. 𝒞 **800/898-6999** or 310/581-5533. Fax 310/581-5503. www.hotelcasadelmar.com. 129 units. $450–$725 double; from $1,075 suite. AE, DC, DISC, MC, V. Valet parking $26. **Amenities:** Restaurant; pool; health club w/spa services.

Casa Malibu   Evoking the heyday of Malibu's golden age, this modest, low-rise inn on the beach is a refreshing alternative to sleek, impersonal resorts. Wrapped around a palm-studded inner courtyard, the rooms are comfortable, charming, and thoughtfully outfitted in a timeless "California beach cottage" look. Many have been upgraded with air-conditioning and VCRs, but even the older ones are in great shape and boast top-quality bedding, robes, and fridges. Some units have fireplaces, kitchenettes, and

CD players. A handsome brick sun deck faces the blue Pacific, while wooden stairs lead to the hotel's private beach.

22752 Pacific Coast Hwy. (about ¼ mile south of Malibu Pier), Malibu, CA 90265. (C) **800/831-0858** or 310/456-2219. Fax 310/456-5418. 21 units. $129–$229 garden or oceanview double; $289–$299 beachfront double; $269–$429 suite. Rates include continental breakfast. Extra person $15. AE, MC, V. Free parking. *In room:* Fridge.

Chamberlain West Hollywood
This four-story boutique hotel, in a tree-lined, residential West Hollywood neighborhood, looks and feels much like a high-quality Manhattan apartment building. The location is reason enough to stay here, 2 blocks from the Sunset Strip and Santa Monica Boulevard. Each guest room is a suite with a separate living and sleeping area, a plush king-size bed with Mascioni 250-count sheets, gas-log fireplace, small balcony, flatscreen TV, DVD/VCR combo, CD player, and large desk with Internet access. The rooftop pool and cabana is ideal for sunbathing with a great view of the city, and the small restaurant and bar is good for drinks and appetizers before you hit the town.

1000 Westmount Dr. (1 block west of La Cienega Blvd.), West Hollywood, CA 90069. (C) **800/201-9652** or 310/657-7400. Fax 310/854-6744. www.chamberlainwesthollywood.com. 112 units. $169–$269 junior or 1-bedroom suite. AE, DC, DISC, MC, V. Valet parking $24 with in/out privileges. **Amenities:** Heated rooftop pool; fitness center.

Figueroa Hotel (Value)
With an artistic eye and a heartfelt commitment to budget travelers—particularly from Europe and Japan—this former 1925-vintage YWCA residence has been transformed into L.A.'s best budget hotel. This enchanting 12-story property sits in an increasingly gentrified corner of downtown. The big, airy lobby exudes a romantic Spanish Colonial–Gothic vibe with beamed ceilings and soaring columns, tile flooring, ceiling fans, Moroccan chandeliers, and medieval-style furnishings. Elevators lead to equally artistic guest rooms, which, though a bit dark and small, are very comfortable.

939 S Figueroa St. (at Olympic Blvd.), Los Angeles, CA 90015. (C) **800/421-9092** or 213/627-8971. Fax 213/689-0305. www.figueroahotel.com. 285 units. $124 double; $175–$195 suite; $245 Casablanca suite. AE, DC, MC, V. Parking $8. **Amenities:** Restaurant; pool w/lounge. *In room:* Fridge.

Hotel Angeleno Los Angeles
This L.A. landmark—the last of a vanishing breed of circular hotels from the 1960s and 1970s—is destined to become the next "in" hotel in Los Angeles. Formerly a Holiday Inn, it's the first L.A. venture of the Joie de Vivre hotel group, which made its name in San Francisco by revamping tired hotels into hip, modern destinations. The location alone is a good reason to stay here: It's beside the city's busiest freeway, a short hop from the popular Getty Center and centrally located between the beaches, Beverly Hills, and the San Fernando Valley. Each pie-shape room comes with a private balcony and double-paned glass to keep most of the freeway din at bay, while comfort comes in the form of 300-count Italian linens, feather duvets, and pillow-top mattresses. Little extras like 30-inch plasma TVs, wireless Internet access, ergonomic workstations, and great views add to the panache. Also destined to be a hot spot is the 17-story hotel's penthouse-level **West** supper club and cocktail lounge, the city's first Italian steakhouse.

170 N. Church Lane (at intersection of Sunset Blvd. and I-405), Los Angeles, CA 90049. (C) **800/264-3536** or 310/476-6411. Fax 310/472-1157. www.hotelangeleno.com. 209 units. $179–$229 double; from $285 suite. AE, DC, DISC, MC, V. Valet parking $18. **Amenities:** Rooftop restaurant; heated outdoor pool and fireplace; fitness center.

Magic Castle Hotel (Value) (Kids)
Located a stone's throw from Hollywood Boulevard's attractions, this bargain offers newly refurbished units that are spacious and well kept. Named for the Magic Castle, the illusionist club just uphill, the former apartment building retains a sense of privacy. Situated around a pool courtyard, all units

boast full kitchens; several have balconies overlooking the large pool. It's ideal for wallet-watching families or long-term stays. *Tip:* The Magic Castle Club is renowned throughout the world as a magician's mecca and is very exclusive—you can get in only by invitation from a member (for example, you better know a really well-connected magician) . . . or if you happen to be a guest of the hotel.

7025 Franklin Ave. (between La Brea and Highland aves.), Hollywood, CA 90028. (C) **800/741-4915** or 323/851-0800. Fax 323/851-4926. www.magiccastlehotel.com. 49 units. $129 double; $149–$239 suite. Extra person $10. Off-season and other discounts available. AE, DC, DISC, MC, V. Parking $8. **Amenities:** Pool. *In room:* Kitchen (suites only).

The Mosaic Hotel Beverly Hills (Best)
Few properties have impressed us as much as this Beverly Hills boutique hotel. New owners pumped $3 million into redoing the former Beverly Hills Inn, and the result is spectacular. The lobby is a showcase of functional art, with tile mosaics, fabrics in deep rich tones, and a profusion of artfully arranged orchids. The guest rooms are equally impressive, with 300-count Frette linens, goose-down comforters and piles of pillows, and sparkling bathrooms with Bulgari bath products and huge Rain Forest showerheads. *Tip:* The corner deluxe rooms are worth the extra $15.

125 S. Spalding Dr., Beverly Hills, CA 90212. (C) **800/463-4466** or 310/278-0303. Fax 310/278-1728. www.mosaic hotel.com. 49 units. $265–$500 double; from $600 2-bedroom suite. AE, DC, MC, V. Parking $15. Small pets accepted. **Amenities:** Restaurant; pool; exercise room. *In room:* Fridge.

Sheraton Universal Hotel
The 21-story Sheraton is considered *the* Universal City hotel of choice for tourists, businesspeople, and industry folks visiting the studios. It has a spacious 1960s feel, with updated styling and amenities. Choose a Lanai room for balconies that overlook the pool area, or a Tower room for stunning views and solitude. The hotel is very close to the Hollywood Bowl, and you can practically roll out of bed and into the theme park (via free shuttle).

333 Universal Hollywood Dr., Universal City, CA 91608. (C) **800/325-3535** or 818/980-1212. Fax 818/985-4980. www.sheraton.com/universal. 436 units. $149–$219 double; from $400 suite. Children stay free in parent's room. Ask about AAA, AARP, and corporate discounts; also inquire about packages that include theme-park admission. AE, DC, DISC, MC, V. Valet parking $21; self-parking $16. **Amenities:** Restaurant; pool; health club.

Shutters on the Beach
This Cape Cod–style luxury hotel is directly on the beach, a block from Santa Monica Pier. The beach-cottage rooms are more desirable than those in the towers. All units have balconies, VCRs, and CD players; some have fireplaces and/or whirlpool tubs; and all have floor-to-ceiling windows that open. The elegant marble bathrooms come with waterproof radios and toy whales. Despite this welcome whimsy, there's a relaxed and elegant ambience throughout the contemporary art-filled hotel. The small pool and the sunny lobby lounge are two great celebrity-spotting perches.

1 Pico Blvd., Santa Monica, CA 90405. (C) **800/334-9000** or 310/458-0030. Fax 310/458-4589. www.shuttersonthe beach.com. 198 units. $480–$775 double; from $1,075 suite. AE, DC, DISC, MC, V. Valet parking $26. **Amenities:** 2 restaurants; pool; health club; spa.

Wyndham Bel Age Hotel (Value) (Kids)
This high-rise West Hollywood all-suite hotel has it all: lots of room, excellent service, terrific rooftop deck, and an A-1 location just off the Sunset Strip. And thanks to an excellent art collection, the place has far more personality than your average chain hotel. The monster-size suites boast plush bedding, Herman Miller desk chairs, VCRs, PlayStations, CD players, and robes. The best rooms face south; on a clear day, you can see all the way to the Pacific.

1020 N. San Vicente Blvd. (between Sunset and Santa Monica boulevards), West Hollywood, CA 90069. (C) **800/ WYNDHAM** or 310/854-1111. Fax 310/854-0926. www.belagehotel.com. 200 units. $210–$340 suite (accommodates up to 4 at no extra charge). Ask about weekend rates, holiday specials, and discounts on longer stays. AE, DC, DISC, MC, V. Valet parking $18. **Amenities:** 2 restaurants; pool; exercise room.

WHERE TO DINE

The Apple Pan *Value* SANDWICHES/AMERICAN   There are no tables, just a U-shaped counter, at this classic American burger shack and L.A. landmark. Open since 1947, The Apple Pan is a diner that looks—and acts—the part. It's famous for juicy burgers, speedy service, and authentic frills-free atmosphere. The hickory burger is best, though the tuna sandwich also has its share of fans. Definitely order fries and, if you're in the mood, the home-baked apple pie.

10801 Pico Blvd. (east of Westwood Blvd.). ℂ 310/475-3585. Most menu items under $6. No credit cards. Tues–Thurs and Sun 11am–midnight; Fri–Sat 11am–1am.

El Cholo MEXICAN   El Cholo has been serving up south-of-the-border comfort food in this festive hacienda since 1927, even though the surrounding mid-Wilshire neighborhood has become Koreatown. Their expertly blended margaritas, invitingly messy nachos, and classic combination dinners don't break new ground, but the kitchen has perfected these standards over 70 years (we wish they bottled their rich enchilada sauce). The creative sizzling vegetarian fajitas go way beyond just eliminating the meat. The atmosphere is festive, as people from all parts of town dine happily in the many rambling dining rooms.

1121 S. Western Ave. (south of Olympic Blvd.). ℂ 323/734-2773. www.elcholo.com. Reservations suggested. Main courses $8–$15. AE, DC, DISC, MC, V. Mon–Thurs 11am–10pm; Fri–Sat 11am–11pm; Sun 11am–9pm.

Jar MODERN CHOP HOUSE   Jar offers everything you could hope for in a restaurant: a warm and relaxed setting, excellent service, and generous servings of reliably fantastic food. Flavorful meat dishes such as braised Kurobuta pork shank and Kobe filet of beef are perfectly cooked, simply seasoned, and divinely flavorful. Among the most popular dishes are the Neiman Ranch Char Sui pork chops and an unparalleled pot roast with caramelized onions and carrots. An extensive wine list and martini menu are two good reasons to arrive early and stay for a nightcap at the beautiful Parisian-style bar. *Tip:* Sunday brunch is one of the best in the city.

8225 Beverly Blvd. (at Harper Ave.), Los Angeles. ℂ 323/655-6566. www.thejar.com. Reservations recommended. Main courses $32–$38. AE, DC, DISC, MC, V. Mon–Thurs 5:30–10pm; Fri–Sat 5–11pm; Sun brunch 10am–2pm.

The Wolfgang Puck Experience

Already a household word, Puck has a culinary empire that keeps growing. For perhaps the quintessential L.A. dining experience, be sure to try at least one of the master's L.A. restaurants. Of course, there's **Spago Beverly Hills,** 176 N. Canon Dr. (ℂ **310/385-0880**). Puck also has two terrific restaurants near the beach. **Chinois on Main,** 2709 Main St., Santa Monica (ℂ **310/392-9025**), serves terrifically quirky East-meets-West Franco-Chinese cuisine. If you're dining on a budget, try one of the several **Wolfgang Puck Cafe** branches around town, where Puck's cuisine is interpreted in an affordable style and served up in colorful surroundings. There's one in Los Angeles at 630 W. 6th St., at the Library Court Building (ℂ **213/614-1900**), and one in Santa Monica, 1315 Third St. Promenade (ℂ **310/576-4770**). And cybergourmets can always get a foodie fix online at **www.wolfgangpuck.com.**

Joe's Restaurant *Value* AMERICAN ECLECTIC   This is one of L.A.'s best dining bargains. Chef/owner Joseph Miller excels in simple cuisine, particularly grilled fish and roasted meats accented with piquant herbs. Formerly a tiny, quirky storefront, the restaurant has been gutted and completely remodeled (the best tables are on the patio complete with waterfall). Entrees are sophisticated: fallow deer wrapped in bacon, served in a black currant sauce; monkfish in a saffron broth; wild striped bass with curried cauliflower coulis. Four-course prix-fixe menus are offered as well—a real bargain for under $40.

1023 Abbot Kinney Blvd., Venice. © **310/399-5811.** www.joesrestaurant.com. Reservations required. Main courses dinner $18–$25, lunch $8–$15. AE, MC, V. Tues–Thurs noon–2:30pm and 6–10pm; Fri noon–2:30pm and 6–11pm; Sat 11am–2:30pm and 6–11pm; Sun 11:30am–2:30pm and 6–10pm.

Koi *Best* ASIAN-FUSION   If your goal is to spot Hollywood's A-list of celebrities, make a reservation at Koi: Stars from George Clooney to Madonna are all spotted here regularly. Or just make a reservation because the food—brilliant fusions of Japanese and California cuisine—is so damn good. Either way, you won't be disappointed. Incorporating feng shui elements of trickling water, votive candles, open-air patios, and soft lighting, the minimalist earthen-hued interior has a calming ambience that is a relief from the hectic Melrose scene outside the ornately carved gates.

730 N. La Cienega Blvd. (between Melrose Ave. and Santa Monica Blvd.), West Hollywood. © **310/659-9449.** www. koirestaurant.com. Reservations recommended. Main courses $13–$27. AE, MC, DC, DISC, V. Mon–Thurs 6–11pm; Fri–Sat 6pm–midnight; Sun 6–10pm.

Lucques FRENCH/MEDITERRANEAN   Pronounced *Luke,* this quietly sophisticated restaurant has a clubby style and handsome enclosed patio. Chef Suzanne Goin cooks with bold flavors, fresh-from-the-farm produce, and an instinctive feel for the food of the Mediterranean. The short menu makes the most of unusual ingredients, such as salt cod and oxtail. Lucques's bar menu and tantalizing hors d'oeuvres are a godsend for late-night diners. *Insider Tip:* On Sunday, Lucques offers a $40 prix-fixe three-course dinner from a weekly changing menu.

8474 Melrose Ave. (east of La Cienega), West Hollywood. © **323/655-6277.** www.lucques.com. Reservations recommended. Main courses $18–$30. AE, DC, MC, V. Mon 6–11pm; Tues–Sat noon–2:30pm and 6–11pm; Sun 5:30–10pm.

Matsuhisa JAPANESE/PERUVIAN   Chef/owner Nobuyuki Matsuhisa is a true master of fish cookery, creating fantastic dishes by combining Japanese flavors with South American spices and salsas. Broiled sea bass with black truffles is one example of the masterfully prepared delicacies that are available, in addition to nigiri and creative sushi rolls. Matsuhisa is popular with celebrities and foodies, so reserve early. *Tip:* If you're feeling adventurous, ask for *omakase* and the chef will personally compose a selection of eclectic dishes.

129 N. La Cienega Blvd. (north of Wilshire Blvd.), Beverly Hills. © **310/659-9639.** www.nobumatsuhisa.com. Reservations recommended. Main courses $15–$50; sushi $4–$13 per order; full *omakase* dinner from $65. AE, DC, MC, V. Mon–Fri 11:45am–2:15pm; daily 5:30–10:15pm.

The Palm STEAKS/LOBSTER   Every great American city has a renowned steakhouse; in Los Angeles it's The Palm. The child of the famous New York restaurant of the same name, The Palm is widely regarded by local foodies as one of the best traditional American eateries in the city. The glitterati seem to agree, as stars and their handlers are regularly in attendance. In both food and ambience, this West Coast apple hasn't fallen far from the proverbial tree. The restaurant is brightly lit, bustling with energy, and playfully decorated with dozens of celebrity caricatures on the walls.

9001 Santa Monica Blvd. (between Doheny Dr. and Robertson Blvd.), West Hollywood. ℂ 310/550-8811. www.the palm.com. Reservations recommended. Main courses dinner $17–$41; lobsters $18 per pound; lunch $10–$19. AE, DC, MC, V. Mon–Fri noon–10:30pm; Sat 5–10:30pm; Sun 5–9:30pm.

Pink's Hot Dogs (Value) (Kids) SANDWICHES/BURGERS/HOT DOGS   This crusty corner stand isn't your typical hot dog shack; name another stand that has its own valet parking attendant. This L.A. icon grew around the late Paul and Betty Pink, who opened for business in 1939 selling 10¢ wieners from a used hot dog cart. Now 2,000 of them are served every day on Pink's soft steamed rolls. There are 24 varieties of dogs available, many of the them coined by the celebrities who order them (try the Martha Stewart). Even though the dogs are churned out every 30 seconds, expect to wait in line even at midnight—you'll invariably meet a true crossroads of Los Angeles cultures.

709 N. La Brea Ave. (at Melrose Ave.). ℂ 323/931-4223. www.pinkshollywood.com. Chili dog $2.65. No credit cards. Sun–Thurs 9:30am–2am; Fri–Sat 9:30am–3am.

Providence MODERN AMERICAN SEAFOOD   After 6 years at Water Grill, chef Michael Cimarusti and his multilingual Italian compatriot, Donato Poto, have fulfilled their dream to create the city's preeminent seafood experience. Relax in this sleek, modern space, which, like the sauces used, is not overpowering. Cimarusti visits the fish market daily for the choicest seafood available; think striped sea bass in a pea tendril broth, wild king salmon with truffle vinaigrette, kelp-marinated fluke. If you're in a mood to splurge, go with the $140 Market Menu: nine memorable courses paired with superb wines (the sommelier is a wizard). And order anything Cimarusti makes with sea urchin—especially if you don't like it. He'll convert you.

5855 Melrose Ave. (at N. Cahuenga Blvd), Los Angeles. ℂ 323/460-4170. www.providencela.com. Reservations recommended. Main courses $32–$38. AE, MC, V. Wed–Fri noon–2:30pm; Mon–Sat 6–10pm, Sun 5:30–9pm.

Sofi (Value) GREEK   Look for the simple black awning that leads to this hidden Aegean treasure. Ask for a table on the romantic patio amid twinkling lights, and immediately order a plate of the thick, satisfying *tzatziki* (yogurt-cucumber-garlic spread) accompanied by a basket of warm pitas for dipping. Other specialties include herbed rack of lamb with rice, fried calamari salad, *saganaki* (kasseri cheese flamed with ouzo), and other hearty taverna favorites.

8030¾ W. 3rd St. (between Fairfax Ave. and Crescent Heights Blvd.). ℂ 323/651-0346. Reservations recommended. Main courses $7–$14. AE, DC, MC, V. Mon–Sat 11:30–2:30pm; daily 5:30–11pm.

LOS ANGELES AFTER DARK

Your best bet for current entertainment info is the *L.A. Weekly* (www.laweekly.com), a free weekly paper available at sidewalk stands, shops, and restaurants. It has all the most up-to-date news on what's happening in Los Angeles's playhouses, cinemas, museums, and live-music venues. The Sunday **"Calendar"** and Thursday **"Weekend"** sections of the *Los Angeles Times* (www.calendarlive.com) are also good sources of information on what's going on throughout the city. **Ticketmaster** (ℂ 213/480-3232; www.ticketmaster.com) is L.A.'s major charge-by-phone ticket agency, selling tickets to concerts, sporting events, plays, and special events, but beware of the absurdly high processing fees.

THE PERFORMING ARTS   It's a little-known fact that on any given night, there's more live theater to choose from in Los Angeles than in New York. The all-purpose **Music Center of Los Angeles County,** 135 N. Grand Ave., downtown, houses the

---

(*Value* Free Morning Music at Hollywood Bowl

It's not widely known, but the Bowl's morning rehearsals are open to the public and absolutely free. On Tuesday, Thursday, and Friday from 9:30am to 12:30pm you can see the program scheduled for that evening. So bring some coffee and doughnuts (the concession stands aren't open) and enjoy the best seats in the house (© 323/850-2000; www.hollywoodbowl.org).

Ahmanson Theatre and **Mark Taper Forum** (© 213/628-2772; www.taperahmanson. com). You've probably already heard of the **Kodak Theatre,** 6834 Hollywood Blvd. (© 323/308-6300; www.kodaktheater.com), home of the Academy Awards. And the recently restored **Pantages Theatre,** 6233 Hollywood Blvd. between Vine and Argyle streets (© 323/468-1770), reflects the full Art Deco glory of L.A.'s theater scene.

The city is also home to nearly 200 small- and medium-size theaters and theater companies. Across town, the **Geffen Playhouse,** 10886 Le Conte Ave., Westwood (© 310/208-5454; www.geffenplayhouse.com), presents work by prominent and emerging writers. One of L.A.'s most venerable landmarks, the **Orpheum Theatre,** 842 S. Broadway (at 9th St.; © 877/677-4386; www.laorpheum.com), reopened after a 75-year hiatus. **Actors Circle Theater,** 7313 Santa Monica Blvd., West Hollywood (© 323/882-8043), is a 47-seater that's as acclaimed as it is tiny.

The world-class **Los Angeles Philharmonic** (© 323/850-2000; www.laphil.org), led by Finnish-born Esa-Pekka Salonen, just moved into its breathtaking new Frank Gehry–designed home—the **Walt Disney Concert Hall,** 111 S. Grand Ave. (© 213/ 972-7200), with a summer season at the **Hollywood Bowl,** 2301 N. Highland Ave., Hollywood (© 323/850-2000; www.hollywoodbowl.org), an elegant Greek-style natural outdoor amphitheater. The Hollywood Bowl also hosts jazz, pop, and virtuoso performances in summer.

Slowly but surely, the **Los Angeles Opera** (© 213/972-8001; www.losangeles opera.com), which performs at the **Dorothy Chandler Pavilion,** is gaining respect and popularity with inventive stagings of classic and modern operas.

Finally, the **UCLA Center for the Performing Arts** (© 310/825-2101; www. performingarts.ucla.edu) has presented music, dance, and theatrical performances of unparalleled quality for more than 60 years, and continues to be a major presence in the local and national cultural landscape.

THE CLUB & MUSIC SCENE   Veteran record producer/executive Lou Adler opened the **Roxy,** 9009 W. Sunset Blvd., West Hollywood (© 323/276-2222; www.theroxy onsunset.com), in the mid-1970s, and it's remained among the top showcase venues in Hollywood ever since. There are plenty of reasons music fans and industry types keep coming back to the **House of Blues,** 8430 Sunset Blvd., West Hollywood (© 323/ 848-5100; www.hob.com). Night after night, audiences are dazzled by hot acts of national acclaim, ranging from Soul Coughing to Eric Clapton.

Nearby is **The Troubadour,** 9081 Santa Monica Blvd. (© 310/276-6168; www. troubadour.com), the infamous West Hollywood mainstay that radiates rock history. This beer- and sweat-soaked club likes it loud. Louder still is the hip **Viper Room,** 8852 Sunset Blvd., West Hollywood (© 310/358-1881; www.viperroom.com), owned by Johnny Depp. With an often star-filled scene, the club is known for late-night surprise performances from such powerhouses as Iggy Pop, Tom Petty, and Everclear.

In south central L.A.'s up-and-coming Leimert Park, **Babe's & Ricky's Inn,** 4339 Leimert Blvd., Leimert Park (© **323/295-9112;** www.bluesbar.com), stands out as an original, a place where we can imagine B. B. King himself would have played before he became famous. Mama Laura Gross is the cultivator of the fabulous, endangered sound and the house goddess of this intimate bar. Great guitarists are the rule, not the exception here.

The legendary bi-level **Whisky A Go-Go,** 8901 Sunset Blvd., West Hollywood (© **310/652-4202,** ext. 15; www.whiskyagogo.com), personifies L.A. rock 'n' roll, from Jim Morrison and X to Guns N' Roses and Beck. Every trend has passed through this club, and it continues to be the most vital venue of its kind. With the hiring of an in-house booker a few years ago, the Whisky began showcasing local talent on free-admission Monday nights.

Straight from New York, a West Coast branch of the famous **Knitting Factory,** 7021 Hollywood Blvd., Hollywood (© **323/463-0204;** www.theknittingfactory.com), sees such diverse bookings as Kristin Hersh, Pere Ubu, and Jonathan Richman. On the fringe of east Hollywood, **Spaceland,** 1717 Silver Lake Blvd., Silver Lake (© **323/ 661-4380;** www.clubspaceland.com), has become one of the most important clubs on the L.A. circuit, with performances by Pavement, Mary Lou Lord, Elliott Smith, and the Eels.

When you've just gotta dance, head for **The Conga Room,** 5364 Wilshire Blvd. (© **323/938-1696;** www.congaroom.com), which attracts Latin-music luminaries and is *the* nightspot for live salsa and merengue. **El Floridita,** 1253 N. Vine St., Hollywood (© **323/871-8612;** www.elfloridita.com), is a Cuban restaurant and salsa joint that's hot, hot, hot. **The Derby,** 4500 Los Feliz Blvd., Los Feliz (© **323/663-8979;** www.the-derby.com), attracts dancers who come dressed to the nines to swing the night away to such musical acts as Big Bad Voodoo Daddy and the Royal Crown Revue.

COMEDY CLUBS You can't go wrong at the **Comedy Store,** 8433 Sunset Blvd., West Hollywood (© **323/650-6268;** www.comedystore.com). New comics develop their material, and established ones work out the kinks, at this landmark venue owned by Mitzi Shore (Pauly's mom). The talent here is always first-rate and includes comics who regularly appear on *The Tonight Show.*

For more edgy fare, head to the **Groundling Theater,** 7307 Melrose Ave. (© **323/ 934-4747;** www.groundlings.com), the most innovative group in town. The Groundlings were the springboard to fame for former *Saturday Night Live* stars Jon Lovitz, the late Phil Hartman, and Julia Sweeney.

The Improv, 8162 Melrose Ave., West Hollywood (© **323/651-2583;** www.improvclubs.com), a showcase for top stand-ups since 1975, features the likes of Jay Leno and Billy Crystal more often than you'd expect. But even if the comedians on the bill are all unknowns, they won't be for long.

10 The Disneyland Resort

There are newer and larger Disneyland parks in Florida, Tokyo, and even France, but the original and inspiration for all of them still opens its gates in Anaheim, California, every day, proudly proclaiming itself "The Happiest Place on Earth." Smaller than Walt Disney World (see "Walt Disney World & Orlando," p. 332), Disneyland—which opened in 1955 on a 107-acre tract surrounded almost exclusively by orange groves—has always capitalized on being the world's first family-oriented mega-theme park. The Disney difference—the one that keeps the park fresh and fantastic, whether you're 6 or

60—is *imagination*. Disneyland is about more than rides and shows . . . it's fantasy elevated to an art form.

In 2001, Disney unveiled a brand-new theme park, Disney's California Adventure, and revamped its own name to "The Disneyland Resort," reflecting a greatly expanded array of entertainment options.

ESSENTIALS

GETTING THERE   Disneyland is about an hour's drive south of Los Angeles, or 90 minutes north of San Diego. Follow **I-5** until you see signs for Disneyland; off-ramps from both directions lead into parking lots and surrounding streets.

VISITOR INFORMATION   For information on **The Disneyland Resort,** log onto its official website at **www.disneyland.com**. For general information on the entire Anaheim region, contact the **Anaheim/Orange County Visitor and Convention Bureau,** 800 W. Katella Ave., inside the Anaheim Convention Center (📞 **714/765-8888;** www.anaheimoc.org). They can fill you in on area activities and shopping, as well as send you their *Official Visitors Guide* and the AdventureCard, which offers discounts at dozens of local attractions, hotels, restaurants, and shops.

ADMISSION & HOURS   Admission to *either* Disneyland or Disney's California Adventure, including unlimited rides and all festivities and entertainment, is $59 for adults and children over 10, $49 for children 3 to 9, and free for children under 3. Parking is $10. Two-day Park Hopper tickets, which allow you to go back and forth as much as you'd like each day, are $116 for adults and children over 10, $96 for children 3 to 9. Other multiday, multipark combination passes are available as well.

Disneyland and Disney's California Adventure are open every day of the year from morning until after nightfall, but operating hours vary (with extended summer and holiday hours), so we recommend that you call ahead (📞 **714/781-7290**). Hours, ride closures, and show schedules can also be found online at **www.disneyland.com**.

DISNEYLAND

Though many visitors tackle Disneyland systematically, beginning at the entrance and working their way clockwise around the park, the most effective method is to arrive early and run to the most popular rides first—the Indiana Jones Adventure, Star Tours, Big Thunder Mountain Railroad, Splash Mountain, the Haunted Mansion, and Pirates of the Caribbean rides in Disneyland; and Twilight Zone Tower of Terror, Soarin' Over California, California Screamin', Grizzly River Run, and It's Tough to Be a Bug rides in Disney's California Adventure—where midday lines can last an hour or more.

This time-honored plan of attack may eventually become obsolete, however, thanks to the new **FASTPASS** system. Say you want to ride Space Mountain, but the line is long—*so* long the wait sign indicates a 75-minute standstill. Now you can head to the Automated FASTPASS ticket dispensers, which allow you to swipe the magnetic strip of your Disneyland entrance ticket, get a free FASTPASS for later that day, and return to use the reduced-wait FASTPASS entrance (to the envy of everyone in the slowpoke line). At press time, more than a dozen Disneyland rides were equipped with FAST-PASS; several more will be added by the time you read this. The hottest features at Disney's California Adventure had FASTPASS built in from the start; for a complete list for each park, check your official map/guide when you enter.

Only 1 day in the park? Then start by riding the most popular rides (see above) first—or obtaining a FASTPASS early—so you don't waste precious time in line. If you've got smaller children with you, concentrate on Fantasyland (behind Sleeping

Beauty's Castle), a kids' paradise with fairy-tale-derived rides like **King Arthur Carousel, Dumbo the Flying Elephant, Mr. Toad's Wild Ride, Peter Pan's Flight, Alice in Wonderland, Pinocchio's Daring Journey,** and the Disney signature ride, **It's a Small World,** a boat ride through a saccharine nightmare of all the world's children singing the song everybody loves to hate. (It's a major rite of passage for all Disney-goers.) Elsewhere in the park, little ones will enjoy clambering through **Tarzan's Treehouse** and singing along with the audio-animatronic **Country Bear Jamboree. Mickey's Toontown** is a wacky, gag-filled world inspired by the *Roger Rabbit* films, featuring endless amusement for young imaginations.

If high-speed thrills are your style, then follow the **Indiana Jones Adventure** into the Temple of the Forbidden Eye, or jump on one of Disneyland's "mountain"-themed action roller coasters. There's perennial favorite **Space Mountain,** a pitch-black indoor roller coaster; **Splash Mountain,** a water flume ride (with a big, wet splash at the end) based on the Disney movie *Song of the South;* the **Matterhorn Bobsleds,** a zippy coaster through the landmark mountain's chilled caverns and drifting fog banks; and **Big Thunder Mountain Railroad,** where runaway railroad cars careen through a deserted 1870s gold mine. **Star Tours** is a *Star Wars*–inspired Tomorrowland simulation ride.

Disneyland highlights that have stood the test of time include the more-funny-than-scary **Haunted Mansion,** which showcases the brilliant eye for details of the Disney "imagineers"; and **Pirates of the Caribbean,** a wild world of swashbuckling, rum-running, and buried treasure (but, drat, no Johnny Depp!).

If you've got more than 1 day, you'll have the luxury of enjoying some Disney extras not essential enough to pack into a single day. For example, avoid the midday crush by strolling along **Main Street U.S.A.,** shopping for Disney souvenirs, enjoying a sweet treat of ice cream or candy, and ducking into **Great Moments with Mr. Lincoln,** the patriotic look at America's 16th president that was Walt Disney's first foray into audio-animatronics.

The **parades and shows** within the park draw huge crowds. There's also a nighttime **fireworks** spectacular above Sleeping Beauty's Castle, and the after-dark pyrotechnic show **Fantasmic!**

DISNEY'S CALIFORNIA ADVENTURE

Disneyland's new "sister" theme park consists of four distinct themed areas. The **Golden State** represents California's history, heritage, and physical attributes. Sound boring? Actually, the park's splashiest attractions are here. The ride **Soarin' Over California** combines suspended seats with a spectacular IMAX-style movie (take advantage of FAST-PASS for this one), while the **Grizzly River Run** is a wet gold-country ride through caverns and mine shafts. **Pacific Wharf,** inspired by Monterey's Cannery Row, features mouthwatering demonstration attractions by Boudin Sourdough Bakery and Mission Tortillas.

A Bug's Land encompasses **Flik's Fun Fair, Bountiful Valley Farm,** and *It's Tough to Be a Bug,* a interactive 3-D film that takes *A Bug's Life* characters on an underground romp with bees, termites, grasshoppers, spiders, and a few surprises that keep everyone laughing along. **Bountiful Farm** pays tribute to California's agriculture, and includes the park's most upscale eatery, the **Vineyard Room,** a great place to sip champagne and watch Disney's Electrical Parade.

At the fantasy boardwalk **Paradise Pier,** highlights include the **California Screamin'** roller coaster; the **Maliboomer,** a trio of towers that catapults riders to the tiptop bell, then lets them down bungee-style; the **Orange Stinger,** a whooshing swing ride inside an enormous orange; and **Mulholland Madness,** a wacky wild trip along L.A.'s precarious hilltop street.

The **Hollywood Pictures Backlot** features the **Disney Animation** building, where visitors can learn how stories become animated features, and the **Hyperion Theater,** which presents a live-action tribute to classic Disney films. Across the way, step aboard the **Superstar Limo,** where you're cast as a hot new star being chauffeured around Hollywood. **Who Wants To Be A Millionaire—Play It!** is an interactive, high-energy mock-up of the game show. **Jim Henson's MuppetVision 3D** is a blast from the past featuring Kermit, Miss Piggy, Gonzo, and Fozzie Bear. But the major star of this area is the spooky **Twilight Zone Tower of Terror**—this truly scary ride (if you're scared of heights or free-falling elevators, don't even think about getting on it) debuted in 2004 and has been a huge hit ever since.

WHERE TO STAY NEAR THE PARK

The **Disneyland Hotel,** 1150 W. Magic Way (© **714/956-MICKEY**), is across the street and linked to the park by monorail. While the hotel's grounds are a theme park unto themselves, the 990 rooms are plainer, like those of a good-quality business hotel. Disney's new **Grand Californian Hotel,** 1600 S. Disneyland Dr. (© **714/956-MICKEY**), is an Arts and Crafts–style high-rise hotel with 745 spacious rooms that are smartly designed. *Tip:* Ask for a free upgrade to a room with a view of the park when you check in at this hotel—they're pretty generous about this. Rates at both hotels start at around $205, but you can almost always get a money-saving package that includes park admission.

Other nearby hotels in the lower price range are the **Candy Cane Inn,** 1747 S. Harbor Blvd. (© **800/345-7057** or 714/774-5284; www.candycaneinn.net), where doubles run $82 to $159; and the **Anaheim Stardust Inn,** 1057 W. Ball Rd. (© **800/-222-3639** or 714/774-7600; www.anaheimstardustinn.com), where rates run $70 to $95 double.

11 San Diego

San Diego, California's first city, is best known for its benign climate and fabulous beaches. On sunny days, the city is one big outdoor playground—you can choose from swimming, snorkeling, windsurfing, kayaking, bicycling, skating, and tons of other fun in or near the water. The city is also home to top-notch attractions, including three world-famous animal parks and splendid Balboa Park. Once dismissed as a conservative navy town, San Diego now boasts an almost Los Angeles–like diversity of neighborhoods and residents. Several charming restored historic districts draw a stylish young crowd that's updating the face of San Diego dining, shopping, and entertainment. So pack a laid-back attitude along with your sandals and swimsuit; welcome to California's grown-up beach town.

ESSENTIALS

GETTING THERE   By Plane   San Diego International Airport, 3707 N. Harbor Dr. (© **619/231-2100;** www.san.org), locally known as Lindbergh Field, is just 2 miles from downtown. If you're driving into the city from the airport, take Harbor Drive south to Broadway and turn left. All the major car-rental agencies have offices at the airport and we recommend renting a car if you plan to explore the city in any depth.

If you don't want to rent a car, several **shuttles** run regularly from the airport to downtown hotels, charging around $8 per person. **Taxis** line up outside both terminals and charge around $10 (plus tip) to take you to a downtown location.

By Train Amtrak (© **800/USA-RAIL;** www.amtrak.com) trains connect San Diego to Los Angeles (trip time: 3 hr.) and the rest of the country, arriving at **Santa Fe Train Depot,** 1850 Kettner Blvd., at Broadway, within walking distance of many downtown hotels and 1½ blocks from the Embarcadero.

By Car From Los Angeles, you'll enter San Diego via coastal route **I-5.** From points northeast of the city, you'll come down on **I-15** and **Highway 163** south to drive into downtown (where 163 turns into 10th Ave.), or hook up with **I-8** west for the beaches.

VISITOR INFORMATION There are staffed information booths at the airport terminals and train station. Downtown, the **San Diego Convention & Visitor Bureau** (© **800/350-6205** or 619/236-1212; www.sandiego.org) is at 1040⅓ W. Broadway at Harbor Drive (across the street from the cruise ship terminal). The *Official Visitors Planning Guide* includes information on accommodations, dining, activities, attractions, tours, and transportation. Be sure to ask for the *San Diego Travel Values* pamphlet, which is full of discount coupons for hotels, restaurants, and attractions. Daily summer hours are from 9am to 5pm; 9am to 4pm Thursday through Tuesday, the remainder of the year; the office is closed on major holidays.

Other sources of information include *San Diego Reader* (www.sdreader.com), a free weekly newspaper available all over the city; and the Thursday entertainment supplement called **"Night & Day"** in the *San Diego Union-Tribune* (www.signonsandiego.com).

GETTING AROUND San Diego has its fair share of traffic downtown, heaviest during the morning and evening commute. Aside from that, it's a very car-friendly town, and easy to navigate. Finding a parking space can be tricky—but some reasonably priced parking lots are centrally located. Two large parking structures (on Sixth Ave. at Market and K sts.) have eased parking problems in the busy Gaslamp Quarter, while free parking is the rule in Balboa Park and Old Town. Because of the city's widespread layout, cabs are a very expensive proposition—a rental car is far more cost-effective.

Both city buses and the San Diego Trolley are operated by the **San Diego Metropolitan Transit System** (MTS; © **800/266-6883** or 619/233-3004; www.sdcommute.com). The website offers timetables, maps, and fares online, and provides information on how the transit system accommodates travelers with disabilities. Or visit the system's **Transit Store,** 102 Broadway, at First Avenue (© **619/234-1060**), a complete public-transportation information center, supplying travelers with passes, tokens, timetables, maps, and brochures. The store is open Monday through Friday from 9am to 5pm.

The **San Diego Trolley** runs south to the Mexican border (a 40-min. trip), north to Old Town, and east to the city of Santee. Trolleys stop at many popular locations; fares range from $1.25 to $3.

FAST FACTS The most conveniently located hospital emergency room is at **UCSD Medical Center—Hillcrest,** 200 W. Arbor Dr. (© **619/543-6222**).

Of the 10 largest cities in the United States, San Diego historically has had the lowest incidence of violent crime, per capita. Still, it never hurts to take precautions. Caution is advised in Balboa Park, in areas not frequented by regular foot traffic. Parts of the city that are usually safe on foot at night include the Gaslamp Quarter, Hillcrest, Old Town, Mission Valley, La Jolla, and Coronado.

San Diego Area

0 1 mi
0 1 km

N

UCSD

La Jolla Shores

La Jolla Cove

Torrey Pines Rd.

LA JOLLA

Pearl St. High Ave.
Rushville St.
Nautilus

La Jolla Village Dr.

5

805

La Jolla Shores Dr.

Ardath Rd.

Miramar Rd.

15

7

MIRAMAR NAVAL AIR STAION

52

Claremont Mesa Blvd.

La Jolla Blvd.

Dawes

Soledad Mountain

Lamo

Crown Point Dr.

Ingraham St.

PACIFIC BEACH

Garnet Ave.
Grand Ave.

Mission Blvd.

MISSION BEACH

Mission Bay Dr.

Mission Bay

Fiesta Island

5

Sea World

5

Pacific Highway

Claremont Dr.

Balboa Ave.

274

Genesee Ave.

163

Linda Vista Rd.

Qualcomm Stadium ■

805

6

Friars Rd.

15

Ocean Beach Fwy.

Midway Dr.

209

OCEAN BEACH

Sunset Cliffs Blvd.

Nimitz Blvd.

Point Loma

209

Rosecrans

San Diego International Airport ✈

Harbor Dr.

Harbor Island Dr.
Harbor Island

Shelter Island

Cabrillo Memorial Dr.

209

OLD TOWN

4

El Cajon Blvd.

University Ave.

Washington St.

163

UPTOWN/ HILLCREST

1st Ave.
6th Ave.

See "Balboa Park" map

3

BALBOA PARK

2

DOWNTOWN Market St.
Petco Park

Broadway

94

San Diego Bay

San Diego Bay

282

CORONADO

Orange Ave.

1

75

30th St.

15

Imperial Ave.

Ocean View Blvd.

28th St.

Harbor Dr.

5

Sacramento ★
CALIFORNIA

San Diego ●

🏖 Beach

Coronado Beach

Gaslamp Quarter **2**
Hotel Del Coronado **1**
LEGOLAND California **8**
Mission Basilica San Diego de Alcala **6**
Old Town State Historic Park **4**

San Diego Wild Animal Park **7**
San Diego Zoo **3**
SeaWorld San Diego **5**
Torrey Pines Golf Course **9**

A 7.75% **sales tax** is added at the register for all goods and services purchased in San Diego. The **city hotel tax** is 10.5%.

SPECIAL EVENTS & FESTIVALS From mid-June to early July, the whole county heads to the Del Mar Fairgrounds for the **San Diego County Fair** (© 858/755-1161; www.sdfair.com), a 3-week event with livestock competitions, rides, flower and garden shows, food and crafts booths, carnival games, and home-arts exhibits; concerts by name performers are included with admission.

The first weekend after Labor Day, the **San Diego Street Scene** (© 619/557-0505; www.street-scene.com) transforms the historic Gaslamp Quarter with a 3-day extravaganza featuring food, dance, international character, and live music on six separate stages. The festival is all-ages, with certain shows restricted to the 21-and-older crowd. Call © 800/260-9985 for more information.

WHAT TO SEE & DO

The **Old Town Trolley** (© 619/298-TOUR; www.historictours.com) isn't a trolley at all; it's a privately operated open-air tour bus that travels in a continuous loop around the city. You can hop on and off at will throughout the day. Major stops include Old Town, Presidio Park, Bazaar del Mundo, Balboa Park, the San Diego Zoo, the Embarcadero, Seaport Village, and the Gaslamp Quarter. Tours operate daily from 9am to 4pm (until 5pm in summer); they cost $30 for adults and $15 for children 4 to 12.

LEGOLAND California *(Kids)* The ultimate monument to the world's most famous plastic building blocks, LEGOLAND opened in 1999. In addition to 5,000 LEGO models, the Carlsbad park is beautifully landscaped with 1,360 bonsai trees and other plants from around the world, and features more than 50 rides, shows, and attractions. Attractions include hands-on interactive displays; a life-size menagerie of animals; and scale models of international landmarks (the Eiffel Tower, Sydney Opera House, and so on)—all constructed of real LEGO bricks. There are three relatively tame coaster rides (don't worry, they're built from steel), but the park is geared toward children ages 2 to 12.

1 Legoland Dr. © 877/534-6526 or 760/918-5346. www.legoland.com. $53 adults, $43 seniors and kids 3–12, free for children under 3. AE, DISC, MC, V. Summer (late June to Aug) daily 10am–8pm; off season Thurs–Mon 10am–5 or 6pm. Closed Tues–Wed Sept–May, but open daily during winter and spring vacation periods. Parking $8. From I-5 take Cannon Rd. exit east, following signs for Legoland Dr.

San Diego Wild Animal Park *(Best)* *(Kids)* Located 34 miles north of San Diego, outside of Escondido, this 1,800-acre park features 3,500 animals, many of them endangered species, roaming freely—it's the humans who are enclosed. This living arrangement encourages breeding colonies, so it's not surprising that you'll find the largest crash of rhinos at any zoological facility in the world here. Several other species that had vanished from the wilds have been reintroduced to their natural habitats from stocks bred here. The best way to see the animals is by riding the 5-mile **monorail** (included in the price of admission), a 50-minute ride through areas resembling Africa and Asia. Other exhibits bring you closer to the animals, like the three self-guided **walking tours,** which visit various habitats. The San Diego Zoo may be more famous, but we actually enjoy this park more. For a real up-close experience, take one of the park's **Photo Caravans** (call for details and current prices).

15500 San Pasqual Valley Rd., Escondido. © 760/747-8702. www.wildanimalpark.org. Admission $29 adults, $26 seniors 60 and over, $18 children 3–11, free for children under 3 and military in uniform. AE, DISC, MC, V. Daily 9am–4pm (grounds close at 5pm); extended hours during summer and Festival of Lights (2 weekends in Dec). Parking $8. Take I-15 to Via Rancho Pkwy.; follow signs for about 3 miles.

(Value) Now That's What I Call a Deal!

Always aware of what side their tourism bread is buttered on, San Diego's three main animal attractions have joined forces with combo ticket deals that reward big savings to visitors with recreational stamina. Here's how it works: If you plan to visit both the zoo and Wild Animal Park, a two-park ticket (the "Best Value" zoo package, plus Wild Animal Park admission) is $55 adults, $34 children 3 to 11 (a $61/$38 value). You get one visit to each attraction, to be used within 5 days of purchase. Or throw in SeaWorld within the same 5 days—this combo works out to $100 adults, $77 children ages 3 to 9 (a $114/$81 value).

San Diego Zoo *(Kids)*   More than 4,000 animals reside at this world-famous zoo. The zoo is one of only four in the U.S. with giant pandas, but there are many other animals worth seeing here: cuddly koalas from Australia, wild Przewalski's horses from Mongolia, lowland gorillas from Africa, and giant tortoises from the Galápagos. The usual lions, elephants, giraffes, and tigers are present, too, housed in barless, moated enclosures designed to resemble their natural habitats. There's a **Children's Zoo,** with a nursery for baby animals and a petting area where kids can cuddle up to sheep, goats, and the like. The zoo offers **bus tours,** which provide a narrated overview and show you about 75% of the park. You can get an aerial perspective via the **Skyfari.**

2920 Zoo Dr., Balboa Park. ℂ 619/234-3153 (recorded info), or 619/231-1515. www.sandiegozoo.org. Admission $22 adults, $15 children 3–11, free for military in uniform. The "Best Value" package (admission, guided bus tour, round-trip Skyfari aerial tram) $32 adults, $29 seniors, $20 children. AE, DISC, MC, V. Sept to mid-June daily 9am–5pm (last ticket sold at 4pm); mid-June to Aug daily 9am–9pm (last ticket sold at 8pm). Bus: 7 or 7A/B. I-5 south to Pershing Dr., follow signs.

SeaWorld San Diego *(Kids)*   This 165-acre, multimillion-dollar aquatic playground may be your main reason for visiting California. Several successive 4-ton black-and-white killer whales have functioned as the park's mascot, Shamu. At its heart, Sea-World is a family entertainment center where the performers are dolphins, otters, sea lions, walruses, and seals. Shows run continuously throughout the day, while visitors can rotate through the various theaters. The 2-acre hands-on area called **Shamu's Happy Harbor** encourages kids to handle things—and features everything from a pretend pirate ship to tube crawls, slides, and chances to get wet. There is also a small collection of rides, led by **Journey to Atlantis,** a 2004 arrival that combines a roller coaster and log flume with Atlantis mythology and a simulated earthquake. **Shipwreck Rapids** is a splashy adventure on raftlike inner tubes through caverns, and **Wild Arctic** is a motion-simulator helicopter trip to the frozen North.

500 Sea World Dr., Mission Bay. ℂ 800/257-4268 or 619/226-3901. www.seaworld.com. Admission $53 adults, $43 children 3–9, free for children under 3. AE, DISC, MC, V. Daily 10am–5pm; most weekends and in summer the park opens at 9am and stays open until 11pm during peak periods. Parking $8. Bus: 9 or 27. From I-5, take Sea World Dr. exit; from I-8, take W. Mission Bay Dr. exit to Sea World Dr.

EXPLORING BALBOA PARK

Balboa Park is one of the nation's largest and loveliest city parks, boasting walkways, gardens, historic buildings, a restaurant, an ornate pavilion with one of the world's largest outdoor organs, and the world-famous San Diego Zoo. Stroll along **El Prado,** the park's main street, and admire the distinctive Spanish/Mediterranean buildings, which house an amazing array of museums. El Prado is also popular with musicians and other performers whose busking provides an entertaining backdrop.

Entry to the park is free, but most of its museums have admission charges and varying open hours. A free tram transports you around the park. Get details from the **Balboa Park Visitor Center,** in the House of Hospitality (© **619/239-0512;** www.balboapark.org). *Note:* Most Balboa Park attractions are open free of charge one Tuesday each month; there's a rotating schedule so two or three participate each Tuesday (the visitor center has a schedule). If you plan to visit more than three of the park's museums, buy the **Passport to Balboa Park,** a coupon booklet that allows entrance to 13 major museums and is valid for 1 week for $30.

The **San Diego Aerospace Museum,** 2001 Pan American Plaza (© **619/234-8291;** www.aerospacemuseum.org), celebrates great achievers and achievements in the history of aviation and aerospace with a superb collection of aircraft and artifacts.

The impressive painting and sculpture collections at the **San Diego Museum of Art,** 1450 El Prado (© **619/232-7931;** www.sdmart.com), include outstanding Italian Renaissance and Dutch and Spanish baroque art, along with an impressive collection of works by Toulouse-Lautrec.

The **Museum of Contemporary Art San Diego,** 700 Prospect St. (© **858/454-3541;** www.mcasd.org), focuses on works produced since 1950, and is known internationally for its permanent collection and thought-provoking exhibitions. The 3,000-plus holdings represent every major art movement of the past half-century, with a strong showing by California artists. The MCASD recently opened its third facility, directly across the street from its 1993 downtown annex, 1001 Kettner Blvd. (© **619/234-1001**). The new complex takes over what was once historic Santa Fe Depot's "baggage building," and it will provide an additional 10,000 square feet of gallery space.

The **Museum of Photographic Arts,** 1649 El Prado (© **619/238-7559;** www.mopa.org), is one of few in the United States. If the names of Ansel Adams, Margaret Bourke-White, Imogen Cunningham, Edward Weston, and Henri Cartier-Bresson stimulate your interest, then don't miss this 7,000-plus image collection.

The best exhibits in the **San Diego Natural History Museum,** 1788 El Prado (© **619/232-3821;** www.sdnhm.org), focus on the plants, animals, and minerals of the Southwest. In 2006 the museum opened the largest, most detailed exhibit in its history, *Fossil Mysteries.* The interactive installation also includes life-size models of pre-historic animals, including the megalodon shark, the largest predator the world has ever known.

The **Reuben H. Fleet Science Center,** 1875 El Prado (© **619/238-1233;** www.rhfleet.org), features five galleries with hands-on exhibits as intriguing for grown-ups as for kids, plus SciTours, a simulator ride that voyages into space and the worlds of science and biology. Equally popular is the OMNIMAX movie theater, surrounding viewers with breathtaking adventure travelogues.

The graceful **Botanical Building** shelters more than 1,000 varieties of tropical and flowering plants, and the lily pond out front attracts the occasional street performer.

The ornate **Spreckels Organ Pavilion** (© **619/702-8138;** www.sosorgan.com) houses a fantastic organ with more than 4,000 individual pipes. Free concerts are given Sunday at 2pm year-round and on summer evenings. In the nearby **Japanese Friendship Garden** (© **619/232-2721;** www.niwa.org), visitors can sample the tranquillity of traditional elements like a koi-filled stream, pastoral meadow, and ancient *sekitei* (sand-and-stone garden). Visit the tearoom/snack bar for udon, sushi, or Pokémon candies.

0   1/4 mi
0   0.25 km

Parking **P**

SAN DIEGO ZOO

Richmond Dr.

Zoo Dr.

Skyfari

Quince

Balboa Dr.

(one way)

(one way)

Florida Dr.

Zoo Pl.

Zoo Pl.

Park Blvd.

Freeway

Cabrillo Bridge

El Prado

Laurel St.

Pedestrian Mall

Plaza de Balboa

6th Ave.

Juniper St.

Ivy St.

U.S. Naval Hospital

Grape St.

Pan-American Plaza

President's Way

Park Blvd.

Florida Dr.

Elm St.

Old Town

Uptown/Hillcrest

BALBOA PARK

Downtown

Embarcadero

Coronado

Gaslamp Quarter

Balboa Park Municipal Golf Course **28**
Botanical Building and Lily Pond **8**
Carousel **4**
Casa de Balboa **15**
  Model Railroad Museum
  Museum of Photographic Arts
  San Diego Historical Society Museum
Casa del Prado **7**
The Old Globe Theatres **11**
Hall of Nations **20**
House of Charm **13**
  Mingei International Museum
  SDAI Museum of the Living Artist
House of Hospitality **14**
  Balboa Park Visitors Center
  Prado Restaurant
House of Pacific Relations
   International Cottages **22**
Japanese Friendship Garden **18**

Marie Hitchcock Puppet Theatre **23**
Marston House **1**
Reuben H. Fleet Science Center **16**
Rose & Desert Gardens **17**
San Diego Aerospace Museum **25**
San Diego Automotive Museum **24**
San Diego Hall of Champions
  Sports Museum **27**
San Diego Miniature Railroad **3**
San Diego Museum of Art **10**
San Diego Museum of Man **12**
San Diego Museum
  of Natural History **6**
San Diego Zoo entrance **2**
Spanish Village Art Center **5**
Spreckels Organ Pavilion **19**
Starlight Bowl **26**
Timken Museum of Art **9**
United Nations Building **21**

OLD TOWN & BEYOND: A LOOK AT CALIFORNIA'S BEGINNINGS

The birthplace of San Diego is Old Town, the hillside where the Spanish Presidio and Father Junípero Serra's mission (the first in California) were built. By protecting the remaining adobes and historic buildings, **Old Town State Historic Park** brings to life Mexican California, which existed here until the mid-1800s. Much of the surrounding area, however, has become a mini–Mexican theme park. Free walking tours leave daily at 11am and 2pm from **Robinson-Rose House** (© **619/220-5422;** www. parks.ca.gov)

In nearby Mission Valley lies **Mission Basilica San Diego de Alcala,** 10818 San Diego Mission Rd. (© **619/281-8449;** www.missionsandiego.com). Established in 1769, Mission San Diego was the first link in the chain of 21 missions founded in California by Spanish missionary Junípero Serra. Mass is held regularly in this still-active Catholic parish. Admission is $3 for adults, $2 for seniors and students, and $1 for children 12 and under (free on Sun and for daily services). It's open daily from 9am to 4:45pm, with Mass daily at 7am and 5:30pm. To get here, take I-8 to Mission Gorge Road to Twain Avenue.

BEACHES & OUTDOOR ACTIVITIES
HITTING THE BEACH

San Diego County is blessed with 70 miles of sandy coastline. The following are some of our favorite San Diego beaches, arranged geographically from south to north.

Lovely, wide, and sparkling white, **Coronado Beach** is conducive to strolling and lingering, especially in the late afternoon. It fronts Ocean Boulevard and is especially pretty in front of the Hotel del Coronado.

The northern end of **Ocean Beach** is known as "Dog Beach," and is one of only two in San Diego where your pooch can roam freely on the sand. Surfers congregate around the Ocean Beach Pier. Rip currents are strong here and discourage most swimmers from venturing beyond waist depth. To get here, take West Point Loma Boulevard all the way to the end.

In the 4,600-acre aquatic playground of **Mission Bay Park,** you'll find 27 miles of bay front; 17 miles of oceanfront beaches; picnic areas; playgrounds; and paths for biking, roller skating, and jogging. The bay lends itself to windsurfing, sailing, water-skiing, and fishing. One of the most popular access points is off I-5 at Clairemont Drive, where there's a visitor center.

Pacific Beach is the home of Tourmaline Surfing Park, where the sport's old guard gathers to surf waters where swimmers are prohibited; and there's always some action along Ocean Front Walk, a paved promenade featuring a human parade akin to that at L.A.'s Venice Beach boardwalk. It runs along Ocean Boulevard (just west of Mission Blvd.), north of Pacific Beach Drive.

The protected, calm waters of **La Jolla Cove**—praised as the clearest along the California coast—attract swimmers, snorkelers, divers, and families. There's a small sandy beach and, on the cliffs above, the Ellen Browning Scripps Park. The cove's "look but don't touch" policy protects the colorful marine life in this Underwater Park. La Jolla Cove can be accessed from Coast Boulevard.

The wide, flat mile of sand at **La Jolla Shores Beach** is popular with joggers, swimmers, and beginning body- and board surfers, as well as with families. Weekend crowds can be enormous, though, quickly occupying both the sand and the metered parking spaces in the beach's lot.

MORE PLACES TO PLAY

Mission Bay and Coronado are especially good for leisurely biking. The boardwalks in Pacific Beach and Mission Beach can get very crowded, especially on weekends. For rentals, call **Bike Tours San Diego,** 509 Fifth Ave. (✆ **619/238-2444**), which offers free delivery ($5) as far north as Del Mar. Rates for a city/hybrid bike start at $20 a day, and include helmets, locks, maps, and roadside assistance. Other rental outlets include **Mission Beach Club,** 704 Ventura Place, off Mission Boulevard at Ocean Front Walk, for one-speed beach cruisers (✆ 858/488-8889); and **Cheap Rentals** on Mission Boulevard for mountain bikes and more (✆ **858/488-9070**).

San Diego's extensive waterways are popular for boating. If you have sailing or boating experience, there are options for nonchartered rentals. **Seaforth Boat Rental,** 1641 Quivira Rd., Mission Bay (✆ **888/834-2628** or 619/223-1681; www.seaforth boatrental.com), has a variety of boats for bay or ocean. **Mission Bay Sportcenter,** 1010 Santa Clara Place (✆ **858/488-1004;** www.missionbaysportcenter.com), rents sailboats, catamarans, sailboards, kayaks, and motorboats. Prices range from $18 to $100 an hour, with discounts for 4-hour and full-day rentals.

With 90-plus courses, more than 50 of them open to the public, San Diego County offers golf enthusiasts endless opportunities to play. For a full listing of area courses, visit **www.golfsd.com**, or request the *Golf Guide* from the San Diego Convention and Visitors Bureau (✆ **619/236-1212;** www.sandiego.org). **San Diego Golf Reservations** (✆ **866/701-4653** or 858/964-5980; www.sandiegogolf.com) can arrange tee times for you at San Diego's premiere golf courses. They will consult with you on the courses, charging a $10 per person/per tee time coordination fee. In La Jolla, **Torrey Pines Golf Course** (✆ **800/985-4653** or 858/452-3226) comprises a pair of gorgeous championship cliff-top courses overlooking the ocean. Greens fees range from $75 to $135 depending on the course and tee time; twilight rates are available.

If you prefer to watch other people play, in 2004 the city completed the $474-million **PETCO Park.** The 42,000-seat ballpark incorporates seven historic structures into the stadium, including the Western Metal Supply building, a four-story brick edifice dating from 1909 that now sprouts left field bleachers from one side. The San Diego Padres play April through September. PETCO parking is limited and costly—take the San Diego Trolley. For schedules, information, and tickets, call ✆ 877/374-2784 or 619/795-5000, or visit www.padres.com.

SHOPPING

Horton Plaza (✆ 619/238-1596; www.westfield.com/hortonplaza) is the Disneyland of shopping malls, set in the heart of the revitalized city center. Within a rambling, colorful, and often confusing series of paths and bridges, the complex has tons of shops, including galleries, several fun shops for kids, a 14-screen cinema, three major department stores, and a variety of restaurants. Other downtown shopping opportunities include **Seaport Village,** on Harbor Drive (✆ 619/235-4014; www.seaportvillage.com), a Cape Cod–style "village" of cutesy shops snuggled alongside San Diego Bay; it's worth a visit for the 1890 carousel imported from Coney Island, New York.

In Old Town State Historic Park, **Plaza del Pasado,** 2754 Calhoun St. (✆ 619/297-3100; www.plazadelpasado.com), maintains the park's old *Californio* theme and has 11 specialty shops, 3 restaurants, and a boutique hotel. Costumed employees, special events and activities, and strolling musicians heighten the festive atmosphere.

San Diego's greatest concentration of antiques stores is in the **Ocean Beach Antique District,** along the 4800 block of Newport Avenue. Several stores are mall-style, with multiple dealers. **Newport Ave. Antique Center,** 4864 Newport Ave. (© **619/222-8686**), has 18,000 square feet of retail and a small espresso bar. Most of the O.B. antiques stores are open daily from 10am to 6pm, with reduced hours Sunday.

Shopping in **La Jolla** tends toward the conservative and costly; women's fashion boutiques include Ann Taylor, Armani Exchange, Polo/Ralph Lauren, and Talbots; and Swiss watches, tennis bracelets, and pearl necklaces sparkle at you from windows along every street.

WHERE TO STAY

The **San Diego Convention & Visitors Bureau** is a good place to start looking for hotel deals (© **800/350-6205;** www.sandiego.org), while the **San Diego Bed & Breakfast Guild** (© **800/619-7666;** www.bandbguildsandiego.org) is a helpful resource if you are interested in staying someplace cozy.

Near Old Town there's the exquisite **Heritage Park Bed & Breakfast Inn,** 2470 Heritage Park Row (© **800/995-2470** or 619/299-6832; www.heritageparkinn.com). The **La Jolla Village Lodge,** 1141 Silverado St. (© **877/551-2001** or 858/551-2001; www.lajollavillagelodge.com), is a basic motel that's a good value in tony La Jolla. Well-located and terrifically priced, the **Village Inn,** 1017 Park Place (© **619/435-9318;** www.coronadovillageinn.com), is within walking distance all of Coronado's sights.

For those on a budget: Room rates at properties on Hotel Circle in Mission Valley (an area loaded with chain properties) are significantly cheaper than those in many other parts of the city. One good choice with some character is the **Red Lion Hanalei Hotel,** 2270 Hotel Circle N. (© **800/733-5466** or 619/297-1101; www.hanaleihotel.com), a comfort-conscious yet sophisticated Polynesian-themed hotel whose rooms sport contemporary furnishings and conveniences.

The **Grand Del Mar Resort & Spa,** 5200 Grand Del Mar Way (© **858/350-7600;** www.thegranddelmar.com), will up the luxury quotient in the North County. This 261-room property, designed in a Mediterranean-cum-South-Beach style, sits on 24 acres, and cozies up to one of San Diego's top golf courses, created by Tom Fazio. Scheduled to open in early 2007, The Grand Del Mar will offer the largest standard guest rooms (610 sq. ft.) in San Diego, as well as a 12-room, full-service spa.

Crystal Pier Hotel *Kids*   This historic, charming, and utterly unique cluster of cottages sits literally over the surf on the vintage Crystal Pier. Each self-contained hideaway has a living room, bedroom, full kitchen, and private patio with breathtaking ocean views. The sound of waves is soothing, but the boardwalk action is only a few steps away. Guests drive right out and park beside their cottages, a real boon on crowded weekends. Boogie boards, fishing poles, beach chairs, and umbrellas are all available.

4500 Ocean Blvd. (at Garnet Ave.), San Diego, CA 92109. © 800/748-5894 or 858/483-6983. Fax 858/483-6811. www.crystalpier.com. 29 units. $225–$320 double; $270–$400 for larger units sleeping 4 or 6. 3-night minimum in summer. DISC, MC, V. Free parking. Bus: 27, 30, or 34. Take I-5 to Grand/Garnet exit; follow Garnet to the pier. *In room:* Kitchen.

Hilton San Diego Gaslamp Quarter   With a location at the foot of the Gaslamp Quarter, the Hilton is a great place for guests who want to be close to the action (which includes loads of restaurants, nightlife, and the ballpark within a few blocks) but not get lost in the shuffle. The hotel opened in 2001 on the site of the old Bridgeworks building; much of the brick facade was incorporated into the hotel's polished design. Standard rooms boast upmarket furniture, down comforters, and pillow-top mattresses. The snazziest picks are rooms in the intimate Enclave wing, which features 30 oversize guest rooms (the handsomest in town) with towering ceilings, custom furnishings, Frette linens, and lavish bathrooms sporting whirlpool tubs.

401 K St. (at Fourth Ave.), San Diego, CA 92101. 📞 800/445-8667 or 619/231-4040. Fax 619/231-6439. 282 units. $329 double; from $399 suite. Children under 12 stay free in parent's room. AE, DC, DISC, MC, V. Valet parking $21. Trolley: Gaslamp Quarter. **Amenities:** 2 restaurants; pool; health club; spa.

Holiday Inn on the Bay *(Kids)*   Renovated in 2001, this better-than-average Holiday Inn is reliable and nearly always offers great deals. Rooms, while basic, always seem to sport clean new furnishings and plenty of thoughtful comforts. Although rooms are identical inside, choose carefully; the bay views are marvelous, while city views can be depressing. In either case, request the highest floor possible.

1355 N. Harbor Dr. (at Ash St.), San Diego, CA 92101-3385. 📞 800/465-4329 or 619/232-3861. Fax 619/232-4924. www.holiday-inn.com/san-onthebay. 600 units. $171 double; from $299 suite. Children under 18 stay free in parent's room. AE, DC, MC, V. Self-parking $18; valet $22. Bus: All Pacific Hwy. routes. Trolley: American Plaza. Pets accepted with $25 fee and $100 deposit. **Amenities:** 4 restaurants; pool; exercise room.

Horton Grand   A cross between an elegant hotel and a charming inn, the Horton Grand combines two historic 1880s hotels connected by an airy atrium lobby. Each room is utterly unique; all were renovated in 2000 with vintage furnishings, gas fireplaces, and business-savvy features. Rooms overlook either the city or the fig tree–filled courtyard. The suites (really just large studio-style rooms) are located in a newer wing; choosing one means sacrificing historical character for a sitting area/sofa bed and minibar with microwave.

311 Island Ave. (at Fourth Ave.), San Diego, CA 92101. 📞 800/542-1886 or 619/544-1886. Fax 619/239-3823. www.hortongrand.com. 132 units. $169–$199 double; from $269 suite. Extra person $20. Children under 18 stay free in parent's room. AE, DC, MC, V. Valet parking $20. Bus: 1, 4, 5, 16, or 25. Trolley: Convention Center. **Amenities:** Restaurant.

Hotel del Coronado *(Best) (Kids)*   Opened in 1888 and designated a National Historic Landmark, the "Hotel Del" is the last of California's grand old seaside hotels. Legend has it that the Duke of Windsor met his duchess here, and Marilyn Monroe frolicked here in *Some Like It Hot*. This monument to Victorian grandeur boasts cupolas, turrets, and gingerbread trim, all spread over 26 acres (including some contemporary tower additions). Rooms run the gamut from compact to extravagant, and all are packed with antique charm. The best have balconies fronting the ocean. Even if you don't stay here, take a stroll through the grand, wood-paneled lobby or along the pristine beach.

1500 Orange Ave., Coronado, CA 92118. 📞 800/468-3533 or 619/435-6611. Fax 619/522-8238. www.hoteldel. com. 688 rooms. $305–$580 double; from $780 suite. Children under 18 stay free in parent's room. Additional person $25. Minimum-stay requirements apply most weekends. AE, DC, DISC, MC, V. Valet parking $23; self-parking $18. Bus: 901 or 902. From Coronado Bridge, turn left onto Orange Ave. **Amenities:** 9 restaurants/bars; 2 pools; 3 tennis courts; health club and spa.

Keating House   This grand 1880s Bankers Hill mansion, located between downtown and Hillcrest and 4 blocks from Balboa Park, has been meticulously restored by two energetic innkeepers with a solid background in architectural preservation. Doug Scott and Ben Baltic not only know old houses, but are also neighborhood devotees filled with historical knowledge. Breakfast is served in a sunny, friendly setting; special dietary needs are cheerfully considered. The classy, not frilly, inn draws guests ranging from Europeans to businesspeople avoiding the cookie-cutter ambience of a chain hotel.

2331 Second Ave. (between Juniper and Kalmia sts.), San Diego, CA 92101. ℂ 800/995-8644 or 619/239-8585. Fax 619/239-5774. www.keatinghouse.com. 9 units. $115–$165 double. Rates include full breakfast. AE, DISC, MC, V. Bus: 1, 3, 11, or 25. From the airport, take Harbor Dr. toward downtown; turn left on Laurel St., then right on Second Ave. *In room:* No phone.

La Pensione Hotel (*Value*)

Offering modern amenities, remarkable value, a convenient location, and a friendly staff, the three-story La Pensione feels like a small European hotel. The decor throughout is modern and streamlined, with minimal furniture and plenty of sleek black and metallic surfaces. Rooms, while not overly large, make the most of their space. Try for a bay or city view rather than the view of the concrete courtyard. La Pensione is in Little Italy, within walking distance of eateries and nightspots.

606 W. Date St. (at India St.), San Diego, CA 92101. ℂ 800/232-4683 or 619/236-8000. Fax 619/236-8088. www.la pensionehotel.com. 80 units. $90 double. AE, DC, DISC, MC, V. Limited free underground parking. Bus: 5 or 16. Trolley: Little Italy. *In room:* No A/C in some rooms, fridge.

Pacific Terrace Hotel

The best modern hotel on the boardwalk sports a soothing South Seas ambience and upscale atmosphere that make it stand apart from the casual beach pads in the area. Large guest rooms come with balconies or terraces; about half have kitchenettes. Management keeps cookies, coffee, and iced tea at the ready throughout the day; the lushly landscaped pool and hot tub overlook a relatively quiet stretch of beach. Several local restaurants allow meals to be billed to the hotel, but there's no restaurant on the premises.

610 Diamond St., San Diego, CA 92109. ℂ 800/344-3370 or 858/581-3500. Fax 858/274-3341. www.pacificterrace. com. 75 units. $309–$415 double; from $485 suite. Rates include continental breakfast. AE, DC, DISC, MC, V. Parking $15; limited free parking in off-street lot. Bus: 30 or 34. Take I-5 to Grand/Garnet exit and follow Grand or Garnet west to Mission Blvd., turn right (north), then left (west) onto Diamond. **Amenities:** Pool. *In room:* Kitchenette (in some rooms).

Paradise Point Resort & Spa (*Kids*)

This Mission Bay hotel complex is as much a theme park as its closest neighbor, SeaWorld (a 3-min. drive). Single-story accommodations are spread across 44 acres of lagoons, gardens, and swim-friendly beaches; all have private patios and plenty of thoughtful conveniences like fridges and coffeemakers. Recently updated to keep its 1960s charm but lose tacky holdovers, the resort offers so much fun and recreation you may never want to leave! And despite daunting high-season rack rates, there's usually a deal to be had here. In 2001, the resort unveiled a stunning Indonesian-inspired spa that offers cool Asian treatments.

1404 Vacation Rd. (off Ingraham St.), San Diego, CA 92109. ℂ 800/344-2626 or 858/274-4630. Fax 858/581-5924. www.paradisepoint.com. 462 units. $279–$455 double; from $479 suite. Extra person $20. Children 17 and under stay free in parent's room. AE, DC, DISC, MC, V. Parking $20. Bus: 9. Follow I-8 west to Mission Bay Dr. exit; take Ingraham St. north to Vacation Rd. **Amenities:** 3 restaurants; 6 pools; 18-hole putting course; tennis courts; fitness center. *In room:* Fridge.

WHERE TO DINE

If you've got a sweet tooth, the city's top dessert emporium is aptly monikered **Extraordinary Desserts,** with locations in Little Italy, 1430 Union St. (ℂ 619/294-7001), and adjacent to Balboa Park, 2929 Fifth Ave. (ℂ 619/294-2132). Both locations stay open late (midnight Fri–Sat, 11pm Sun–Thurs). Proprietor Karen Krasne produces exquisite cakes and pastries garnished with edible gold and flowers.

Noteworthy in the Gaslamp for those on a budget is the hip, bohemian **Café Lulu,** 419 F St. (ℂ 619/238-0114), a coffee bar with light meals; the spot is open until 1am (3am Fri–Sat). **Alambres,** 756 Fifth Ave. (ℂ 619/233-2838), serves cheap, tasty Mexican food to famished club-goers until 3am daily.

Cafe Pacifica CALIFORNIA   Inside this cozy Old Town casita, the decor is cleanly contemporary (but still romantic) and the food anything but Mexican. Cafe Pacifica serves upscale, imaginative seafood. Signature items include Hawaiian ahi with shiitake mushrooms and ginger butter, and the "Pomerita," a pomegranate margarita. Patrons tend to dress up, though it's not required.

2414 San Diego Ave., Old Town ⓒ 619/291-6666. www.cafepacifica.com. Reservations recommended. Main courses $16–$29. AE, DC, DISC, MC, V. Mon–Sat 5–10pm; Sun 4:30–9:30pm. Bus: 5/5A. Trolley: Old Town.

Chez Loma FRENCH   You'd be hard-pressed to find a more romantic dining spot than this intimate Victorian cottage filled with antiques and candlelight. Tables are scattered throughout the house and on the enclosed terrace; an upstairs wine salon is a cozy spot for coffee. Among the creative entrees are salmon with smoked-tomato vinaigrette and roast duckling with green-peppercorn sauce. Chez Loma's service is attentive, the herb rolls addictive, and early birds enjoy specially priced meals.

1132 Loma (off Orange Ave.), Coronado. ⓒ 619/435-0661. www.chezloma.com. Reservations recommended. Main courses $21–$34. AE, DC, DISC, MC, V. Daily 5–10pm. Bus: 901, 902, or 904.

Chive CALIFORNIAN   This big-city-style Gaslamp venue introduced San Diego to the sleek and chic dining rooms of the East Coast, and to daring culinary adventures. Start off with a fashionable cocktail: The local martini is embellished with Gorgonzola-stuffed olives, and Chive's twist on the *mojito* adds a gingery splash to the Cuban trademark. The menu changes every 6 to 8 weeks, but popular dishes are found more often than not. The always-evolving wine list offers many intriguing selections by "cork" or "stem."

558 Fourth Ave. (at Market St.), Gaslamp Quarter. ⓒ 619/232-4483. www.chiverestaurant.com. Reservations recommended. Main courses $20–$32. AE, DC, DISC, MC, V. Daily 5–11pm. Live jazz Sat. Bus: 3, 5, 16, or 25. Trolley: Convention Center.

Crest Cafe AMERICAN/BREAKFAST   This long-popular Hillcrest diner is a great refuge from sleek designer food and swank settings. The cheery pink interior announces 1940s style, and the room bubbles with upbeat waiters and comfort food doled out on Fiestaware. No matter: Burger lovers will fall in love with the "butter burger"—a dollop of herb butter is buried in the patty before cooking. During the early evening, the joint brims with neighborhood bohemians in search of a cholesterol fix, while later the club contingent swoops in; the breakfast of omelets or crème brûlée French toast is a happy eye-opener.

425 Robinson Ave. (between Fourth and Fifth aves.), Hillcrest. ⓒ 619/295-2510. www.crestcafe.net. Reservations not accepted. Main courses $5–$14. AE, DISC, MC, V. Daily 7am–midnight. Bus: 1, 3, 25, or 908.

El Agave Tequileria MEXICAN   Don't be misled by this restaurant's less-than-impressive location above a liquor store—this warm, bustling eatery offers the best regional Mexican cuisine in the city and a rustic elegance that leaves the touristy fajitas-and-*cerveza* joints of Old Town far behind. If you like tequila, the restaurant boasts more than 850 boutique and artisan tequilas from throughout the Latin world. But even teetotalers will enjoy the restaurant's authentically flavored mole sauces or the signature beef filet with goat cheese and dark tequila sauce. Lunches are simpler affairs without the exotic sauces, and inexpensive.

2304 San Diego Ave., Old Town. ⓒ 619/220-0692. www.elagave.com. Reservations recommended. Main courses $8–$11 lunch, $16–$32 dinner. AE, MC, V. Daily 11am–10pm. Bus: 5. Trolley: Old Town.

Filippi's Pizza Grotto *Value* *Kids* ITALIAN   To get to the dining area of this "Little Italy" tradition, which is decorated with chianti bottles and red-checked tablecloths, you walk through a "cash and carry" Italian grocery store and deli. The intoxicating smell of pizza wafts into the street; Filippi's has more than 15 varieties (including vegetarian), plus pasta. Children's portions are available. The Friday- and Saturday-evening line to get in can look intimidating, but it moves quickly. This is the original of a dozen branches throughout the county; the other locations include one in **Pacific Beach** at 962 Garnet Ave. (© **858/483-6222**).

1747 India St. (between Date and Fir sts.), Little Italy. © 619/232-5095. No reservations accepted on weekends. Main courses $5–$13. AE, DC, DISC, MC, V. Sun–Mon 9am–10pm; Tues–Thurs 9am–10:30pm; Fri–Sat 9am–11:30pm. Bus: 5. Trolley: Little Italy.

The Fish Market _(Value_ SEAFOOD   Ask any San Diegan where to go for the biggest selection of the freshest fish, and they'll send you to the bustling Fish Market on the end of the G Street Pier on the Embarcadero. Chalkboards announce the day's catches—be it Mississippi catfish, Maine lobster, Canadian salmon, or Mexican yellowtail—sold by the pound or available in a number of classic, simple preparations in the casual restaurant. Upstairs, the related Top of the Market offers similar fare at jacked-up prices; we recommend having a cocktail in Top's posh clubby atmosphere with stupendous bay views—then head downstairs for affordable fare and/or treats from the sushi and oyster bars.

750 N. Harbor Dr., Embarcadero. © 619/232-3474. www.thefishmarket.com. Reservations not accepted. Main courses $10–$25 lunch, $13–$32 dinner (Top of the Market main courses $13–$35 lunch, $18–$45 dinner). AE, DC, DISC, MC, V. Daily 11am–9:30pm (10pm Fri–Sat). Bus: 7/7B. Trolley: Seaport Village.

George's at the Cove CALIFORNIA   A beloved La Jolla tradition, George's wins consistent praise for impeccable service, gorgeous views of the cove, and outstanding California cuisine. Dishes combine flavors with practiced artistry, ranging from the Asian-tinged grilled swordfish atop gingered vegetables to a Provençal-inspired rack of lamb in aromatic spices. George's signature smoked chicken, broccoli, and black-bean soup is still a mainstay. As an alternative to dinner's pricey main courses, try the tasting menu, which offers a seasonally composed five-course sampling for $62 per person ($86 with wine). The informal **Ocean Terrace Cafe** is upstairs.

1250 Prospect St., La Jolla. © 858/454-4244. www.georgesatthecove.com. Reservations strongly recommended. Main courses $12–$15 lunch, $26–$45 dinner. AE, DC, DISC, MC, V. Daily 11:30am–2:30pm; Sun–Thurs 5:30–10pm; Fri–Sat 5–10:30pm. Bus: 34.

Jack's La Jolla AMERICAN   Jack's La Jolla is a three-floor Epicurean fun house that rises from sidewalk coffee stop to rooftop oyster bar, with a fine dining component and a couple of bars and lounges (with live music and DJs) thrown in for good measure. Jack's is built around an open-air courtyard that can take full advantage of sunny days and mild nights. Jack's is also built around the talents and modern American cuisine of chef/owner Tony DiSalvo, formerly executive chef at Jean-Georges in New York City. The middle level features the chic Wall Street Bar and The Dining Room at Jack's. Jack's Grille provides more casual, less expensive dining.

7863 Girard Ave., La Jolla. © 858/456-8111. www.jackslajolla.com. Reservations recommended for dinner. Main courses $9–$14 lunch, $28–$42 dinner. AE, DC, DISC, MC, V. Daily 11:30–1:30am; Sidewalk Cafe daily 8:30am–10pm (serving baked goods only before 11:30am). Bus: 34.

Laurel _(Best_ FRENCH/MEDITERRANEAN   Given its stylish decor, pedigreed chefs, prime Balboa Park location, and well-composed menu of country French dishes with a Mediterranean accent, it's no wonder this restaurant is at the top of its game. It's a rewarding splurge for a special occasion. Tantalizing choices include mouthwatering crisp duck confit with applewood bacon and green lentil, and New Zealand lamb loin with Japanese eggplant and wild rice. If you're overwhelmed by the choices, succumb to the $35 three-course tasting menu ($55 with wine).

505 Laurel St. (at Fifth Ave.), Hillcrest. © 619/239-2222. www.laurelrestaurant.com. Reservations recommended. Main courses $22–$34. AE, DC, DISC, MC, V. Daily 5–10pm.

SAN DIEGO AFTER DARK

For a rundown of major events, check out **www.sandiegoartandsol.com**. Half-price tickets to theater, music, and dance events are available at the **ARTS TIX** booth, in Horton Plaza Park, at Broadway and Third Avenue. For a daily listing of offerings, call © 619/497-5000 or see **www.sandiegoperforms.com**. The San Diego Performing Arts League produces *What's Playing?*, a performing arts guide, every 2 months. You can pick one up at the ARTS TIX booth or write to 110 W. C St., Suite 1414, San Diego, CA 92101 (© **619/238-0700**; www.sandiegoperforms.com).

THE PERFORMING ARTS   Near the entrance to Balboa Park, the Tony Award–winning **Old Globe** (© 619/234-5623; www.theoldglobe.org) is fashioned after Shakespeare's, and has billed such notable performers as Jon Voight and Christopher Walken. Another Tony winner, the **La Jolla Playhouse,** 2910 La Jolla Village Dr. (© **858/550-1010;** www.lajollaplayhouse.com), has staged such productions as *How to Succeed in Business Without Really Trying* before it went on to Broadway fame and fortune.

The **San Diego Repertory Theatre** offers professional, culturally diverse productions at the Lyceum Theatre in Horton Plaza (© **619/544-1000;** www.sandiegorep. com). In Coronado, **Lamb's Players Theatre** (© **619/437-0600;** www.lambsplayers. org), is a professional repertory company that stages shows in the historic Spreckels Building, where no seat is more than seven rows from the stage.

THE CLUB & BAR SCENE   The **Casbah,** 2501 Kettner Blvd., near the airport (© 619/232-4355; www.thecasbah.com), is a divey joint with a rep for breakthrough alternative and rock bands. **Croce's Nightclubs,** 802 Fifth Ave., at F Street (© **619/ 233-4355;** www.croces.com), are attached to one of the Gaslamp Quarter's most popular restaurants, and feature jazz and rhythm and blues. **Humphrey's,** 2241 Shelter Island Dr. (© **619/523-1010;** www.humphreysconcerts.com), is a 900-seat outdoor venue set on the water, and has a seasonal lineup that ranges from rock to folk to international.

The Gaslamp Quarter is the epicenter for the city's hottest dance clubs including **Olé Madrid,** 751 Fifth Ave. (© **619/557-0146**), a loud, energetic club with tapas and sangria from the adjoining Spanish restaurant; and **Sevilla,** 555 Fourth Ave. (© **619/233-5979**), where you can salsa and merengue to Brazilian dance music. **belo** (© **619/231-9200;** www.belosandiego.com), below street level in the Gaslamp on E St., between Fourth and Fifth avenues, is a huge three-room space with retro design.

Stingaree, 454 Sixth Ave. at Island Street (© **619/544-0867**), has three levels, a cool rooftop lounge, and 22,000 square feet of party space. **The Beach,** the rooftop bar of the W Hotel at 421 B St., downtown (© **619/231-8220**), features a heated sand floor and a fire pit—very popular among trendoids, but don't forget your flip-flops, shovel, and pail. The **Onyx Room,** 852 Fifth Ave., Gaslamp Quarter (© **619/ 235-6699**), is an underground (literally) club where the atmosphere is lounge, the drinks are up, and the music is cool. San Diego's ultimate bar with a view, **Top of the Hyatt,** 1 Market Place, at Harbor Drive (© **619/232-1234**), is the 40th floor of the West Coast's tallest waterfront building—you'll get a wide view of the city, harbor, and Coronado. Hyper-modern **Thin** and its downstairs sister club, **The Onyx Room,** 852

Fifth Ave., Gaslamp Quarter (© **619/235-6699**), let you to move from a contemporary vibe to classic lounge. The Onyx Room also has a live jazz on Tuesdays.

12 Palm Springs

Palm Springs, once known for polyester-clad golfing retirees and college-age spring breakers, has been quietly changing its image and attracting a whole new crowd. These days, the city fancies itself a European-style resort with a dash of good ol' American small town thrown in for good measure, and Hollywood's young glitterati are returning to "the Springs." One thing hasn't changed: Swimming, sunbathing, golfing, and playing tennis are still the primary pastimes in this convenient little oasis.

ESSENTIALS

GETTING THERE   By Plane   You can fly into **Palm Springs Regional Airport,** 3400 E. Tahquitz Canyon Way (© **760/323-8161**). Flights from LAX take about 40 minutes.

By Car   Most visitors drive to Palm Springs, a trip that takes about 2 hours from either Los Angeles (via **I-10 East** and **Hwy. 111**) or San Diego (via **I-15 North** to connect with **I-10 East**).

VISITOR INFORMATION   Be sure to pick up *Palm Springs Life* magazine's free monthly *Desert Guide,* which contains tons of information and a calendar of events. Copies are distributed in hotels and newsstands and by the **Palm Springs Desert Resorts Convention & Visitors Authority,** 70–100 Hwy. 111, Rancho Mirage, CA 92270 (© **800/967-3767** or 760/770-9000; www.palmspringsusa.com), open Monday through Friday from 8:30am to 5pm.

The **Palm Springs Visitors Information Center,** 2901 N. Palm Canyon Dr. (© **800/34-SPRINGS;** www.palm-springs.org), offers maps, brochures, advice, souvenirs, and a free hotel reservation service. The office is open Monday through Saturday from 9am to 5pm and Sunday from 8am to 4pm.

SPECIAL EVENTS & FESTIVALS   Golf takes center stage in the desert at two high-profile events each year: January's **Bob Hope Chrysler Classic** (© **888/MR-BHOPE;** www.bhcc.com), which features a celebrity-studded Pro-Am; and March's **Kraft Nabisco Championship** (© **760/324-4546;** www.kncgolf.com), an LPGA event that coincides with a legendary lesbian convention in the desert. Other only-in-the-desert happenings include the 2-week **National Date Festival** (© **800/811-3247;** www.datefest.org) in February, an Arabian Nights–esque pageant and fair celebrating the area's most abundant fruit.

WHAT TO SEE & DO

GOLF   The Palm Springs area is a world-famous mecca for golfers, with 115 courses. If you're planning a golf vacation, you're best off staying at one of the valley's many golf resorts (most are outside Palm Springs), where you can enjoy the proximity of your hotel's facilities as well as smart package deals that can give you a taste of country club membership. See "Where to Stay," below.

Tee times at many resort courses cannot be booked more than a few days in advance for nonguests, but several companies are able to make arrangements several months earlier and even construct a custom package for you with accommodations, golf, meals, and other extras. Among them is **Golf à la Carte** (© **877/887-6900** or 760/772-9330; www.palmspringsgolf.com).

One of our favorite desert courses is the **PGA West TPC Stadium Course,** La Quinta Resort & Club, 49499 Eisenhower Dr., La Quinta (℗ 760/564-7111), which received *Golf* magazine's 1994 Gold Medal Award for the total golf-resort experience. The par-3 17th has a picturesque island green where Lee Trevino made Skins Game history with a spectacular hole-in-one. The rest of Pete Dye's 7,261-yard design is flat, with huge bunkers, lots of water, and severe mounding throughout. Also open for semiprivate play is the **Mountain Course at La Quinta,** another Dye design that regularly appears on U.S. top-100 lists. It's set dramatically against the rocky mountains, which thrust into fairways to create tricky doglegs, and its small Bermuda greens are well guarded by boulders and deep bunkers. Greens fees for nonguests vary seasonally, from $180 to $199.

Recommended public courses include **Tommy Jacobs' Bel-Air Greens,** 1001 El Cielo, Palm Springs (℗ 760/322-6062; www.tommyjacobsbelairgreens.com), a scenic 9-hole, par-32 executive course well suited for beginners and high-handicappers; greens fees range from $15 to $19.

Slightly more advanced amateurs will like **Tahquitz Creek Golf Resort,** 1885 Golf Club Dr., Palm Springs (℗ 760/328-1005), whose two diverse courses both appeal to mid-handicappers; greens fees, including cart, range from $69 to $95, depending on the day of the week.

The **Palm Springs Country Club,** 2500 Whitewater Club Dr. (℗ 760/323-2626), is the oldest public-access golf course within the city of Palm Springs, and is especially popular with budget-conscious golfers; greens fees are only $35 to $45, including cart.

OTHER OUTDOOR ACTIVITIES   Within an hour's drive of Palm Springs is **Joshua Tree National Park,** named for the curious shaggy succulent found only in California's Mojave Desert. A mecca for hikers, campers, and rock climbers, the park's intriguing geology and abundant spring wildflowers can also be easily appreciated by car and make for a wonderful day's outing. For more information, contact the **Park Superintendent's Office,** 74485 National Park Dr., Twentynine Palms, CA 92277 (℗ 760/367-5525; www.nps.gov/jotr).

Desert Adventures (℗ 888/440-JEEP or 760/324-JEEP; www.red-jeep.com) offers four-wheel-drive off-road eco-tours led by experienced naturalist guides; destinations include ancient Cahuilla grounds, San Andreas Fault ravines, and more. Tours range from 2 to 4 hours and cost $75 to $115. Reservations are required.

Elite Land Tours (℗ 800/514-4866 or 760/318-1200; www.elitelandtours.com) offer a new way to visit the desert region—eco-exploration of the greater Palm Springs backcountry from the air-conditioned comfort of an all-terrain Hummer H2. Tours can include desert and mountain regions, exploration of ancient cultures, wildlife, and geological wonders. The Night Discovery Tour lets you view the desert wildlife after dark with special night-vision equipment. Tours run from $129 to $159 per person.

OTHER ATTRACTIONS   The **Living Desert Zoo & Gardens,** 47–900 Portola Ave., Palm Desert (℗ 760/346-5694; www.livingdesert.org), is a 1,200-acre desert reserve designed to acquaint visitors with the unique habitats of California deserts. You can walk or take a tram, learning about bighorn sheep, mountain lions, rattlesnakes, lizards, owls, golden eagles, and the ubiquitous roadrunner. Admission is $12 for adults, $11 for seniors, and $7.50 for children 3 to 12. Open in summer daily from 8am to 1:30pm, the rest of the year daily from 9am to 5pm.

To gain a bird's-eye perspective of the Coachella Valley, try the **Palm Springs Aerial Tramway,** off Highway 111 (℗ 888/515-TRAM or 760/325-1391; www.pstramway. com), a 14-minute, 2½-mile ascent to the top of Mount San Jacinto. At the top you'll

Gay Life in Palm Springs

The Palm Springs area is a major destination for gay travelers, who will want to check out *The Bottom Line* (www.psbottomline.com), the desert's free biweekly magazine of articles, events, and community guides for the gay reader; it's available at hotels and newsstands and from select merchants.

Throughout the year, events are held that transcend the gay community to include everyone. In March, the **Desert AIDS Walk** benefits the Desert AIDS Project, while one of the world's largest organized gatherings of lesbians—the **Dinah Shore Weekend** (www.clubskirts.com)—coincides with the LPGA's **Kraft Nabisco Championship** in mid-March. The predominantly men's **White Party** (www.jeffreysanker.com), the area's largest circuit party event, takes place Easter weekend. **Greater Palm Spring Pride** occurs the first weekend in November, with a parade and 2-day cultural fair (© 760/416-8711; www.pspride.org).

find Alpine scenery, a ski-lodge-style restaurant and gift shop, and temperatures typically 40° cooler than the desert floor. Guided mule rides and cross-country ski equipment are available. Tickets are $22 for adults, $20 for seniors, and $15 for children 3 to 12; a Ride 'n' Dine combination is available. It runs Monday through Friday from 10am to 8pm, Saturday and Sunday from 8am to 8pm.

Unlikely though it may sound, the well-endowed **Palm Springs Desert Museum,** 101 Museum Dr. (© 760/325-7186; www.psmuseum.org), is a must-see. Exhibits include world-class Western and Native American art, plus extensive artifacts of the local Cahuilla tribe. Plays, lectures, and other events are presented in the museum's Annenberg Theater. Admission is $13 for adults, $11 for seniors, and $5 for children 6 to 17. Open Tuesday through Saturday from 10am to 5pm, Sunday from noon to 5pm.

SHOPPING   Downtown Palm Springs revolves around **North Palm Canyon Drive;** many art galleries, souvenir shops, and restaurants are here, along with a couple of large-scale hotels and shopping centers. This wide, one-way boulevard is designed for pedestrians, with many businesses set back from the street itself—don't be shy about poking around the little courtyards you'll encounter. The northern section of Palm Canyon is becoming known for vintage collectibles and is being touted as the **Antique and Heritage Gallery District.**

Down in Palm Desert lies the delicious excess of **El Paseo,** a glitzy cornucopia of high-rent boutiques, salons, and upscale restaurants reminiscent of Rodeo Drive in Beverly Hills, along with a dozen or more major shopping malls just like back home.

WHERE TO STAY

Some of the best golf resorts in the country are in the resort towns just beyond Palm Springs. We've listed La Quinta below, but other equally fabulous choices, all with great golf, tennis, and complete resort services, include **Marriott's Desert Springs Spa & Resort** in Palm Desert (© 760/341-2211), **Marriott's Rancho Las Palmas Resort & Spa** in Rancho Mirage (© 760/568-2727), the **Hyatt Grand Champions** in Indian Wells (© 760/341-1000), and the **Westin Mission Hills Resort** in Rancho Mirage (© 800/WESTIN-1 or 760/328-5955).

Casa Cody   Once owned by "Wild" Bill Cody's niece, this 1920s casa with a double courtyard has been restored to fine condition. It now sports a vaguely southwestern decor and peaceful grounds marked by large lawns and mature fruit trees. You'll feel more like a houseguest than a hotel client here, in a residential area a couple of blocks from Palm Canyon Drive. All units have fridges; many have fireplaces and kitchens. Breakfast is served poolside.

175 S. Cahuilla Rd. (between Tahquitz Way and Arenas Rd.), Palm Springs, CA 92262. ℰ **800/231-2639** or 760/320-9346. Fax 760/325-8610. www.casacody.com. 23 units. $69–$159 double; $139–$199 suite; $359 2-bedroom house. Rates include expanded continental breakfast. AE, DC, DISC, MC, V. Pets accepted for $10 extra per night. **Amenities:** 2 pools. *In room:* Fridge.

La Quinta Resort & Club *(Best)*   A luxury resort set amid citrus trees, towering palms, and cacti at the base of the rocky Santa Rosa Mountains, La Quinta is *the* place to be if you're serious about your golf or tennis game. Rooms are in single-story, Spanish-style buildings; each unit has a VCR, patio, and access to one of several dozen small pools, enhancing the feeling of privacy. Some rooms have fireplaces or Jacuzzis. The tranquil lounge in the original hacienda hearkens back to the early days of the resort, when Clark Gable, Greta Garbo, and other luminaries chose La Quinta as their hideaway. The resort is renowned for its five championship golf courses. Spa La Quinta has 35 treatment rooms for every pampering luxury.

49499 Eisenhower Dr., La Quinta, CA 92253. ℰ **800/598-3828** or 760/564-4111. Fax 760/564-7656. www.laquinta resort.com. 800 units. $455–$560 double; from $1,000 suite. $20 resort fee per night. Extra person $25. Children 17 and under stay free in parent's room. Packages available. AE, MC, V. Free self-parking; valet parking $15. **Amenities:** 5 restaurants; 41 pools; 23 tennis courts (10 night-lit); spa.

Movie Colony Hotel   Take one classic 1930s hotel designed by prolific and renowned area architect Albert Frey, newly remodeled with black-and-white 1935 Moderne suites, some two-storied, but all with DVD players and bathrobes, and you've got a flashback into the "reel" world.

726 N. Indian Canyon Dr., Palm Springs, CA 92262. ℰ **888/953-5700** or 760/320-6340. Fax 760/320-1640. www.moviecolonyhotel.com. 16 units. Double Jan–May $199–$309, June–Aug $129–$229, Sept–Dec $189–$289. Rates include continental breakfast and evening wine. AE, MC, V. Free parking. **Amenities:** Heated pool. *In room:* Fridge.

Palm Mountain Resort and Spa *(Kids)*   Within easy walking distance of Palm Springs's main drag, this former Holiday Inn welcomes kids under 18 free in their parent's room, making it a good choice for families. The rooms are in the two- or the three-story wing, and many have a patio or balcony, with a view of the mountains or the large Astroturf courtyard. Midweek and summer rates can be as low as $99. For the best rates, book online or ask for "Great Rates."

155 S. Belardo Rd., Palm Springs, CA 92262. ℰ **800/622-9451** or 760/325-1301. Fax 760/323-8937. www.palm mountainresort.com. 119 units. Double June–Apr $119–$189, May–Sept $69–$139, Oct–Dec $99–$169. Rates include continental breakfast. Children 17 and under stay free in parent's room. AE, DC, DISC, MC, V. Free parking. **Amenities:** Restaurant; heated pool. *In room:* Fridge.

Spa Resort Casino   One of the more unusual choices in town, this resort is on Indian-owned land above the city's eponymous mineral springs, believed by the Cahuilla to have healing properties. Today's travelers still come here to pamper both body and soul in this sleekly modern facility. There are three pools—one a conventional outdoor swimming pool, the other two filled from the underground natural springs. Inside the extensive spa are private marble baths and many pampering treatments. Despite the addition of an adjoining Vegas-style casino, the Cahuilla have truly managed to integrate modern hotel comforts with the ancient healing and Indian spirit this land represents.

100 N. Indian Canyon Dr., Palm Springs, CA 92263. © **888/999-1995** or 760/325-1461. Fax 760/325-3344. www.spa resortcasino.com. 228 units. $169–$239 double; $269–$379 suite. AE, DC, MC, V. Free parking. **Amenities:** 3 restaurants; 3 pools; fitness center; spa. *In room:* Fridge.

Villa Royale   This charming inn, 5 minutes from downtown Palm Springs, evokes a European cluster of villas, complete with climbing bougainvillea and antiques-filled rooms. Uniform luxuries (down comforters and other pampering touches) appear throughout. Rooms vary widely in size and ambience; larger isn't always better, as some of the most appealing rooms are in the more affordable range. Many rooms have fireplaces, patios with Jacuzzis, or kitchens. The inn's Europa Restaurant (see "Where to Dine," below) is the finest in the area.

1620 Indian Trail (off E. Palm Canyon), Palm Springs, CA 92264. © **800/245-2314** or 760/327-2314. Fax 760/ 322-3794. www.villaroyale.com. 31 units. $100–$250 double; $150–$275 suite; $200–$450 villa. Rates include full breakfast. AE, DC, DISC, MC, V. Free parking. **Amenities:** Restaurant; 2 pools.

WHERE TO DINE

Europa Restaurant *(Best* CALIFORNIA/CONTINENTAL   Long advertised as the "most romantic dining in the desert," Europa is a sentimental favorite of many regulars among an equally gay and straight clientele. Whether you sit on the garden patio or in subdued candlelight indoors, you'll savor dinner prepared by one of Palm Springs's most dedicated kitchens. Standouts are filet mignon on a bed of crispy onions with garlic butter, and a show-stopping salmon baked in parchment with crème fraîche and dill. For dessert, don't miss the signature chocolate mousse.

1620 Indian Trail (at the Villa Royale). © **760/327-2314.** Reservations recommended. Main courses $22–$34. AE, DC, DISC, MC, V. Tues–Sat 6–9pm; Sun 11:30am–2pm and 6–9pm..

Las Casuelas Terraza CLASSIC MEXICAN   The original Las Casuelas, a tiny storefront several blocks away, is still open, but the bougainvillea-draped front patio here is a much better place to people-watch. You can order Mexican standards such as quesadillas, enchiladas, and mountainous nachos, as well as equally super-size margaritas. Inside, the action heats up with live music and raucous happy-hour crowds. During hot weather, the patio and even sidewalk passersby are cooled by the restaurant's well-placed misters.

222 S. Palm Canyon Dr. © **760/325-2794.** www.lascasuelas.com. Reservations recommended on weekends. Main courses $8–$20. AE, DC, DISC, MC, V. Mon–Fri 11am–10pm; Sat–Sun 10am–10pm.

Simba's BARBECUE   For the best barbecue ribs in the desert, check out Simba's Ribhouse in Palm Springs. You'll also find down-home versions of chicken and dumplings, black-eyed peas, barbecued beans, cornbread, hush puppies, and sweet-potato pie.

190 N. Sunrise Way, in a former bank building. © **760/778-7630.** $11–$15. MC. V. Tues–Fri 11am–2pm and 5–9pm; Sat–Sun 3–10pm. Closed Mon.

PALM SPRINGS AFTER DARK

Good sources for nightlife information are *The Desert Guide* (the official visitor publication) and *The Bottom Line* (a biweekly gay magazine). On Thursday nights, **VillageFest** turns Palm Canyon Drive into an outdoor party with vendors and colorful entertainment.

The **Fabulous Palm Springs Follies,** at Plaza Theatre, 128 S. Palm Canyon Dr., Palm Springs (© **760/327-0225;** www.psfollies.com), is a vaudeville-style show filled with lively production numbers. The season runs November through May; call for exact schedule.

13 Death Valley National Park

The forty-niners, whose suffering gave the valley its name, would have howled at the notion of Death Valley National Park. Americans looking for gold in California's mountains in 1849 were forced to cross the burning sands to avoid severe snowstorms in the nearby Sierra Nevada. Some perished along the way, and the land became known as Death Valley.

Mountains stand naked, unadorned. The bitter waters of saline lakes evaporate into bizarre, razor-sharp crystal formations. Jagged canyons jab deep into the earth. Oven-like heat, frigid cold, and the driest air imaginable combine to make this one of the most inhospitable locations in the world.

Human nature being what it is, however, it's not surprising that people have long been drawn to challenge the power of Mother Nature. Man's first foray into tourism began in 1925. It probably would have begun sooner, but the valley had been consumed with lucrative borax mining since the late 1880s.

Today's visitor drives in air-conditioned comfort, stays in comfortable hotel rooms or at well-maintained campgrounds, orders meals and provisions at park concessions, even quaffs a cold beer at the local saloon. You can take a swim in the Olympic-size pool, tour a Moorish castle, shop for souvenirs, and enjoy the desert landscape while hiking along a nature trail with a park ranger.

ESSENTIALS

ACCESS POINTS   There are several routes into the park, all of which involve crossing one of the steep mountain ranges that isolate Death Valley from, well, everything. Perhaps the most scenic entry to the park is via **Calif. 190,** east of **Calif. 178** from Ridgecrest. Another scenic drive to the park is by way of **Calif. 127** and **Calif. 190** from Baker. You'll be required to pay a $10-per-car entrance fee, valid for 7 days.

VISITOR CENTER & INFORMATION   The **Furnace Creek Visitor Center & Museum,** 15 miles inside the eastern park boundary on Calif. 190 (© **760/786-3200**), offers interpretive exhibits and an hourly slide program. Ask at the information desk for ranger-led nature walks and evening naturalist programs. The center is open daily from 8am to 6pm in winter (to 5pm in summer).

SEEING THE HIGHLIGHTS

A good first stop after checking in at the main park visitor center in Furnace Creek is the **Harmony Borax Works**—a rock-salt landscape as tortured as you'll ever find. Death Valley prospectors called borax "white gold"; this profitable—though unglamorous—substance was mined here until 1928. The famous 20-mule teams hauled huge loaded wagons 165 miles to the rail station at Mojave.

Badwater—at 282 feet below sea level, the lowest point in the Western Hemisphere—is also one of the hottest places in the world, with regularly recorded summer temperatures of 120°F (38°C).

Salt Creek is the home of the **Salt Creek pupfish,** found nowhere else on earth. This little fish, which has made some amazing adaptations to survive in this arid land, can be glimpsed from a wooden-boardwalk nature trail.

Before sunrise, photographers set up their tripods at **Zabriskie Point** and aim their cameras down at the magnificent panoramic view of Golden Canyon's pale mudstone hills and the great valley beyond. For another grand vista, check out **Dante's View,** a 5,475-foot viewpoint looking out over the shimmering Death Valley floor, backed by the high Panamint Mountains.

Just south of Furnace Creek is the 9-mile loop of **Artists Drive,** an easy must-see for visitors (except those in RVs, which can't negotiate the sharp, rock-bordered curves in the road). From the highway, you can't see the splendid palette of colors splashed on the rocks behind the foothills; once inside, continue through to aptly named **Artists Palette,** where an interpretive sign explains the source of nature's rainbow.

Scotty's Castle & the Gas House Museum (© 760/786-2392), the 1930s Mediterranean hacienda in the northern part of the park, is Death Valley's premier tourist attraction. Visitors are wowed by the elaborate Spanish tiles, well-crafted furnishings, and innovative construction that included solar water heating. The 1-hour walking tour is excellent, both for its inside look at the mansion and for what it reveals about the eccentricities of the millionaire who built the "castle." Tours fill up quickly; arrive early for the first available spots ($11 adult, $9 senior, and $6 child).

Near Scotty's Castle is **Ubehebe Crater.** It's known as an explosion crater—one look and you'll know why. When hot magma rose from the depths of the earth to meet the groundwater, the resultant steam blasted out a crater and scattered cinders.

WHERE TO CAMP & STAY

The park's nine campgrounds are at elevations ranging from below sea level to 8,000 feet. In Furnace Creek, **Sunset** offers 1,000 spaces with water and flush toilets. **Furnace Creek Campground** has 200 similarly appointed spaces. **Stovepipe Wells** has 200 spaces with water and flush toilets. Reservations can be made online at **http://reservations.nps.gov** or by calling © **800/365-2267.**

Like an oasis in the middle of Death Valley, the **Furnace Creek Inn**'s (© **800/236-7916** or 760/786-2345; www.furnacecreekresort.com) red-tiled roofs and sparkling blue mineral-spring-fed swimming pool hint at the elegance within. The hotel has equipped its 66 deluxe rooms and suites with every modern amenity while successfully preserving the charm of this 1930s resort. Rates run $250 to $375 double.

The **Furnace Creek Ranch** (© **760/786-2345;** www.furnacecreekresort.com), a private in-holding within the park, has 224 no-frills cottage units ($105–$182) with air-conditioning and showers. The swimming pool is a popular hangout. Nearby are a coffee shop, saloon, steakhouse, and general store. **Stove Pipe Wells Village** (© **760/786-2387**) has 74 modest rooms with air-conditioning and showers, plus a casual dining room that closes between meals.

The only lodging within the park not operated by the official concessionaire is the **Panamint Springs Resort** (© **775/482-7680;** www.deathvalley.com), a charming rustic motel, cafe, and snack shop about an hour east of Furnace Creek.

Because accommodations in Death Valley are both limited and expensive, you might consider the money-saving (but inconvenient) option of spending a night at one of the two gateway towns: **Lone Pine,** on the west side of the park, or **Baker,** on the south. **Beatty, Nevada,** which has inexpensive lodging, is an hour's drive from the park's center. The restored **Amargosa Hotel** (© **760/852-4441**) in Death Valley Junction offers 14 rooms in a historic, out-of-the-way place, 40 minutes from Furnace Creek ($50–$65).

Tip: Meals and groceries are exceptionally costly at Death Valley due to the remoteness of the park. If possible, consider bringing a cooler with some snacks, sandwiches, and beverages to last the duration of your visit. Ice is easily obtainable, and you'll also be able to keep water chilled.

The Pacific Northwest

Washington and Oregon, situated in the upper left-hand corner of the nation, are an amalgam of American life and landscapes; within their boundaries, these two states reflect a part of almost every region of the country. Take a bit of New England's rural beauty: covered bridges, steepled churches, and familiar place names such as Portland and Springfield. Temper the climate to that of the upper South to avoid harsh winters. Now bring in some low rolling mountains similar to the Appalachians; rugged, glaciated mountains like those in the Rockies; and even volcanoes, as in Hawaii. Add a river as large and important as the Mississippi. Toss in a coastline as rugged as California's, and an island-filled inland sea that offers as many sailing and kayaking opportunities as the coast of Maine. Even the deserts of the Southwest and wheat fields of the Midwest could be added. The wine country of California would be a nice touch, and so would some long sandy beaches. On top of all this, there should be a beautiful city, one with hills and a waterfront like those in San Francisco. Mix all these things together, and you have a portrait of the Northwest.

1 Seattle

Imagine yourself seated at a table on the Seattle waterfront, a double tall latte and an almond croissant close at hand. The snowy peaks of the Olympic Mountains shimmer on the far side of Puget Sound, and the ferryboats come and go across Elliott Bay. It just doesn't get much better than this, unless of course you swap the latte for a microbrew and catch a 9:30pm summer sunset. No wonder people love this town so much.

ESSENTIALS
GETTING THERE   By Plane   Seattle–Tacoma International Airport (© 206/433-5388; www.portseattle.org/seatac), most commonly referred to simply as Sea-Tac, is located about 14 miles south of Seattle.

Inside the arrivals terminal, you'll find a **Visitor Information Desk** (© 206/433-5218) in the baggage-claim area across from carousel no. 11. It's open daily from 9am to 5pm. You'll also find branches of all the major car-rental companies (for further details see "Getting Around," below).

A **taxi** into downtown Seattle will cost you about $34 to $36 ($28 for the return ride to the airport). There are usually plenty of taxis around, but if not, call **Yellow Cab** (© 206/622-6500) or **Farwest Taxi** (© 206/622-1717). The flag-drop charge is $2.50; after that, it's $2 per mile.

Gray Line Airport Express (© 800/426-7532 or 206/626-6088; www.graylineofseattle.com) is your best bet for getting downtown. These shuttle vans provide service between the airport and downtown Seattle daily, every 30 minutes from 5:30am (5am from downtown) to 11pm. Fares are $10 one-way for adults and $7.25 one-way for children 2 to 12. **Shuttle Express** (© **800/487-7433** or 425/981-7000; www.shuttle express.com) provides 24-hour service between Sea-Tac and the Seattle, north Seattle, and Bellevue areas. Rates to downtown Seattle are $28 for one or two adults, $32 for three, and $35 for four. Children 12 and under ride free.

Metro Transit (© **800/542-7876** in Washington, or 206/553-3000; http://transit. metrokc.gov) operates two public buses between the airport and downtown. Bus trips to downtown take 40 to 50 minutes, depending on conditions. The fare is $1.25 during off-peak hours, $2 during peak hours.

By Train   Amtrak (© **800/872-7245** or 206/382-4125; www.amtrak.com) trains stop at King Street Station, 303 S. Jackson St., within a few blocks of the historic Pioneer Square neighborhood. Any bus running north on First, Second, Third, or Fourth avenues will take you to within a few blocks of most downtown hotels. The Waterfront Streetcar also stops within a block of King Street Station and can take you to The Edgewater hotel. Although the streetcar is currently scheduled to be out of service until sometime in mid-2007, a bus has temporarily replaced its route.

By Car   The major routes into Seattle are **I-5** from the north (Vancouver) and south (Portland), and **I-90** from the east (Spokane). **I-405,** Seattle's east-side bypass, leads to the cities of Bellevue, Redmond, and Kirkland on the east side of Lake Washington; **Wash. 520** connects I-405 with Seattle just north of downtown; and **Wash. 99,** the Alaskan Way Viaduct, is another major north-south highway through downtown and the waterfront.

VISITOR INFORMATION   Visitor information on Seattle and the surrounding area is available by contacting **Seattle's Convention and Visitors Bureau Citywide Concierge Center,** Washington State Convention and Trade Center, Eighth Avenue and Pike Street, main level (© **206/461-5888;** www.seeseattle.org). To find it, walk up Pike Street to the Convention Center (the street is covered by a huge arched glass ceiling in front of the convention center).

GETTING AROUND   Seattle's **Metro** buses (© **800/542-7876** in Washington, or 206/553-3000; http://transit.metrokc.gov) are free if you ride only in the downtown area between 6am and 7pm. The Ride Free Area is between Alaskan Way (the waterfront) in the west, Sixth Avenue and I-5 in the east, Battery Street in the north, and South Jackson Street in the south. Within this area are Pioneer Square, the waterfront attractions, Pike Place Market, the Seattle Art Museum, and almost all of the city's major hotels. The Ride Free Area also encompasses the Metro Tunnel, which extends from the International District in the south to the Convention Center in the north and allows buses to drive underneath downtown Seattle.

Outside the Ride Free Area, fares range from $1.25 to $2, depending on distance and time of day. (The higher fares are incurred during commuter hours.) *Note:* When traveling out of the Ride Free Area, you pay when you get off the bus; when traveling into the Ride Free Area, you pay when you get on the bus. Exact change is required; dollar bills are accepted.

In addition to the bus system, **Metro** also operates old-fashioned streetcars that follow a route along the waterfront from Pier 70 to Pioneer Square and then east to the corner of Fourth Avenue South and South Jackson Street, which is on the edge of the International District. One-way fare for adults is $1.25 in off-peak hours and $1.50 in peak hours; youths 5 to 17 pay 50¢. Exact change is required. If you plan to transfer to a Metro bus, you can get a transfer good for 90 minutes. Streetcars are wheelchair

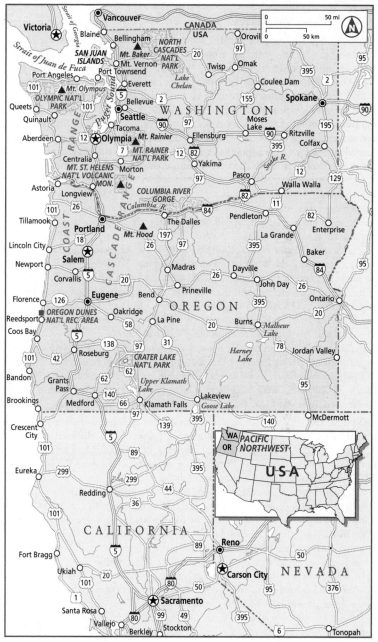

The Pacific Northwest

(Value **Discount Passes**

On Saturday, Sunday, and holidays, you can purchase an **All-Day Pass** for $2.50; it's available on any Metro bus as well as the Waterfront Streetcar, and it's good for anywhere outside the Ride Free Area. On other days of the week, you can purchase a **Visitor Pass** for $5. These passes can be used on buses, the water taxi, and the Waterfront Streetcar. Visitor Passes are available at Metro Customer Service offices at King Street Center, 201 S. Jackson St., and at Rainier Square's Transportation Connection, which can be entered from Fourth Avenue, between University and Union streets. These passes can also be purchased at Seattle's Convention and Visitors Bureau Citywide Concierge Center, Seventh Avenue and Pike Street. For more information, contact **Metro.**

---

accessible. At press time, the streetcar is not running, but is scheduled to be back in service sometime in mid-2007. Call or check the website for operating hours when you're visiting.

The **Seattle Monorail** (© **206/905-2600;** www.seattlemonorail.com) connects Seattle Center with the Westlake Center shopping mall (Fifth Ave. and Pine St.). The elevated train covers the 1¼ miles in 2 minutes and passes right through the middle of the Experience Music Project, the Frank Gehry–designed rock-music museum. The monorail operates Monday through Friday from 7:30am to 11pm, Saturday and Sunday from 9am to 11pm. Departures are every 10 minutes. The one-way fare is $1.50 for adults and 75¢ for seniors and children ages 5 to 12.

Between May and September, a water taxi runs between the downtown Seattle waterfront (Pier 55) and Seacrest Park in West Seattle, providing access to West Seattle's popular Alki Beach and adjacent paved path. For a service schedule, check with Metro (© **206/205-3866;** http://transit.metrokc.gov). The one-way fare is $3 (free for children under 6); $1 with a valid bus transfer; free with all-day pass.

FAST FACTS Hospitals convenient to downtown include **Swedish Medical Center,** 747 Broadway (© **206/386-6000**); and **Virginia Mason Hospital and Clinic,** 925 Seneca St. (© **206/583-6433** for emergencies, or 206/624-1144 for information). For 24-hour service, try **Bartell Drug Store,** 600 First Ave. N. (© **206/284-1353**), in the Lower Queen Anne neighborhood.

Although Seattle is a relatively safe city, it has its share of crime. The most questionable neighborhood you're likely to visit is the Pioneer Square area, which is home to more than a dozen bars and nightclubs. By day, this area is quite safe, but late at night, when the bars are closing, keep your wits about you. And keep an eye on your wallet or purse when you're in the crush of people at Pike Place Market. Whenever possible, try to park your car in a garage, instead of on the street, at night.

In Seattle you'll pay an 8.8% **sales tax,** and in restaurants you'll pay an additional .5% **food-and-beverage tax** on top of the sales tax. **Hotel tax** in the Seattle metro area ranges from around 10% to 16%. On rental cars, you'll pay not only an 18.5% **car-rental tax,** but also, if you rent at the airport, an additional 10% to 12% **airport concession fee** (plus other fees for a whopping total of around 45%!).

SPECIAL EVENTS & FESTIVALS Memorial Day weekend brings the **Northwest Folklife Festival** (© **206/684-7300;** www.nwfolklife.org), with dozens of national and regional folk musicians, crafts, and plenty of good food and dancing. All perform-ances take place at Seattle Center.

By far the city's biggest event of the year is **Seafair** (© **206/728-0123;** www.seafair.org), with festivities occurring daily from early July to early August: parades, hydroplane boat races, the navy's Blue Angels, a Torchlight Parade, ethnic festivals, sporting events, and open house on naval ships.

The city's second-most-popular festival is **Bumbershoot, the Seattle Arts Festival** (© **206/281-7788;** www.bumbershoot.org). Rock, folk, jazz, rap, and world music performances draw crowds into Seattle Center and other venues over Labor Day week-end. You'll also find arts and crafts, film, theater, and more.

WHAT TO SEE & DO

The Seattle waterfront, which lies along Alaskan Way between Yesler Way in the south and Bay Street and Myrtle Edwards Park in the north, is the city's most popular attrac-tion. Yes, it's very touristy, with tacky gift shops, saltwater taffy, T-shirts galore, and lots of overpriced restaurants, but it's also home to the Seattle Aquarium, Odyssey Maritime Discovery Center, and Ye Olde Curiosity Shop (king of the tacky gift shops).

Burke Museum   Located on the University of Washington campus, the Burke Museum features exhibits on the natural and cultural heritage of the Pacific Rim. It's noteworthy for its Northwest Native American art collection as well as its displays (with lots of fossils) on 500 million years of the region's history.

17th Ave. NE and NE 45th St. © 206/543-5590. www.burkemuseum.org. Admission $8 adults, $6.50 seniors, $5 children 5–18, free for children under 5. Free 1st Thurs of each month. Daily 10am–5pm (1st Thurs of each month until 8pm). Closed New Year's Day, July 4th, Thanksgiving, and Christmas. Bus: 43, 70, 71, 72, or 73.

Experience Music Project   The brainchild of Microsoft co-founder Paul Allen and designed by architect Frank Gehry, this rock-'n'-roll museum is a massive multi-colored blob at the foot of the Space Needle. The museum encompasses all of the Northwest's rock scene (from "Louie Louie" to grunge) and the general history of American popular music. The most popular exhibits here (after the Jimi Hendrix room) are the interactive rooms. In one room you can play guitars, drums, keyboards, or even DJ turntables. In another, you can experience what it's like to be onstage per-forming in front of adoring fans. Another exhibit focuses on the history of guitars and includes some of the first electric guitars, which date from the early 1930s. In the museum's main hall, known as the Sky Church, there are regularly scheduled concerts. Expect long lines in the summer and leave plenty of time to see this unusual museum.

Seattle Center, 325 Fifth Ave. N. © 877/EMP-LIVE or 206/EMP-LIVE. www.emplive.com. Admission $20 adults, $16 seniors and youths 13–17, $15 children 7–12, free for children 6 and under. Memorial Day to Labor Day daily 10am–8pm; rest of year Tues–Thurs 10am–5pm, Fri–Sat 10am–9pm, Sun 10am–6pm. Bus: 1, 2, 3, 4, 8, 13, 15, 16, 18, 19, 24, 33, 81, or 82. Monorail: From Westlake Center at Pine St. and Fourth Ave.

Hiram M. Chittenden Locks   Locks don't provide panoramic views and aren't nearly as dramatic as waterfalls, but for some strange reason, a lot of people are intrigued by the concept of two side-by-side bodies of water on two different levels and these locks are one of the city's most popular attractions. From June through September (July–Aug are the peak months), you can view salmon both as they leap up the locks' fish ladder and through underwater observation windows. These locks, used primarily by small boats, connect Lake Union and Lake Washington with the waters of Puget Sound.

3015 NW 54th St. © 206/783-7059. Free admission. Daily 7am–9pm (visitor center: May–Sept daily 10am–6pm; Oct–Apr Thurs–Mon 10am–4pm). Bus: 17.

Downtown Seattle

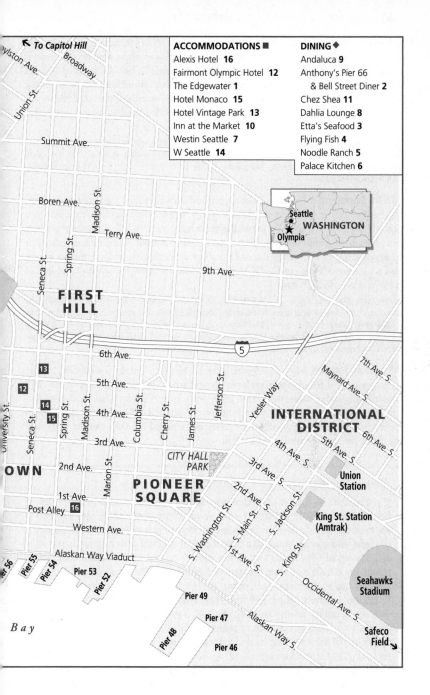

ACCOMMODATIONS ■
Alexis Hotel **16**
Fairmont Olympic Hotel **12**
The Edgewater **1**
Hotel Monaco **15**
Hotel Vintage Park **13**
Inn at the Market **10**
Westin Seattle **7**
W Seattle **14**

DINING ◆
Andaluca **9**
Anthony's Pier 66
   & Bell Street Diner **2**
Chez Shea **11**
Dahlia Lounge **8**
Etta's Seafood **3**
Flying Fish **4**
Noodle Ranch **5**
Palace Kitchen **6**

Seattle
Olympia
WASHINGTON

← *To Capitol Hill*

Broadway
ylston Ave.
Union St.
Summit Ave.
Boren Ave.
Madison St.
Terry Ave.
Spring St.
Seneca St.
9th Ave.

**FIRST
HILL**

6th Ave.
5
5th Ave.
4th Ave.
3rd Ave.
2nd Ave.
1st Ave.
Post Alley **16**
Western Ave.
Alaskan Way Viaduct

University St.
Seneca St.
Spring St.
Madison St.
Columbia St.
Cherry St.
James St.
Marion St.
Jefferson St.

OWN

**PIONEER
SQUARE**

CITY HALL
PARK

Yesler Way
Maynard Ave. S.
7th Ave. S.
4th Ave. S.
5th Ave. S.
6th Ave. S.
3rd Ave. S.
2nd Ave. S.
S. Washington St.
S. Main St.
S. Jackson St.
1st Ave. S.
S. King St.
Occidental Ave. S.
Alaskan Way S.

**INTERNATIONAL
DISTRICT**

Union
Station

King St. Station
(Amtrak)

Seahawks
Stadium

Safeco
Field ↘

Pier 56
Pier 55
Pier 54
Pier 53
Pier 52
Pier 49
Pier 47
Pier 48
Pier 46

B a y

13
12
14
15

Odyssey Maritime Discovery Center *(Kids)*   Sort of an interactive promotion for modern fishing and shipping, this facility at the north end of the Seattle waterfront is aimed primarily at kids and has more than 40 hands-on exhibits highlighting Seattle's modern working waterfront and its links to the sea. Exhibits include a kid-size fishing boat, a virtual kayak trip through Puget Sound, and a live radar center that allows you to track the movement of vessels in Elliott Bay. In another exhibit, you can use a simulated crane to practice loading a scale model of a cargo ship.

Pier 66 (Bell St. Pier), 2205 Alaskan Way. *(C)* **206/374-4000.** www.ody.org. Admission $7 adults, $5 seniors and students 5–18, $2 children 2–4, free for children under 2. Tues–Thurs 10am–3pm; Fri 10am–4pm; Sat 11am–5pm. Closed New Year's Day, day before Thanksgiving, Thanksgiving, and Dec 24–25. Bus: 15, 18, 21, 22, or 56 to Bell St. Waterfront Trolley: Bell St. Station.

Pacific Science Center *(Kids)*   Although its exhibits are aimed primarily at children, the Pacific Science Center is fun for all ages. There are life-size robotic dinosaurs, a butterfly house and insect village (with giant robotic insects), a **Tech Zone** where kids can play virtual-reality soccer or play tic-tac-toe with a robot, and dozens of other fun hands-on exhibits addressing the biological sciences, physics, and chemistry. There's also a planetarium and an IMAX theater. Be sure to check the schedule for special exhibits when you're in town.

Seattle Center, 200 Second Ave. N. *(C)* **206/443-2001;** 206/443-IMAX for IMAX information, or 206/443-2850 for laser show information. www.pacsci.org. Admission $10 adults, $8.50 seniors, $7 ages 3–12, free for children under 3. IMAX $8–$10 adults, $7.50–$9 seniors, $7–$8 ages 3–12, free for children under 3. Laser show $5–$7.50. Various discounted combination tickets available. Mon–Fri 10am–5pm; Sat–Sun and holidays 10am–6pm. Closed Thanksgiving and Christmas. Bus: 1, 2, 3, 4, 13, 15, 16, or 18. Monorail: Seattle Center.

Pike Place Market *(Best)*   This 9-acre National Historic District is a bustling market with farmers and fishmongers, craftspeople and artists, restaurants, some of the city's best specialty shops, and entertaining street performers. Pick up a free market map at the information booth almost directly below the large Pike Place Market sign. Watch for *Rachel,* the giant piggy bank that's raised more than $100,000 over the years, and the flying fish at the Pike Place Fish stall.

Value **Saving Money on Sightseeing**

If you're a see-it-all, do-it-all kind of person, you'll definitely want to buy a **City-Pass** (*(C)* **888/330-5008** or 208/787-4300; www.citypass.com), which gets you into the Pacific Science Center, Seattle Aquarium, Woodland Park Zoo, and the Museum of Flight, and also lets you take a boat tour of the harbor with Argosy Cruises, all at a savings of 50% if you visit all five attractions and do the harbor tour. The passes, good for 9 days from the date of first use, cost $36 for adults and $22 for children 4 to 13. Purchase your CityPass at any of the participating attractions.

The **Go Seattle Card** (*(C)* **800/887-9103;** www.goseattlecard.com) is another interesting option for the see-it-all, do-it-all travelers who are able to plan out a daily tour route in advance. It takes careful planning to get your money's worth out of this card, but it can be done. The way this card works is that you pay $49 ($39 for children ages 3–12) for a card that will get you into as many participating attractions as you can visit in 1 day. There's a discount for 2-, 3-, 5-, and 7-day cards, and your best bet would probably be the 3-day card.

For a glimpse behind the scenes at the market and to learn all about its history, you can take a 1-hour guided **Market Heritage Tour** (✆ 206/774-5249 for information and reservations). Tours are offered Wednesday through Sunday at 11am and 2pm; the cost is $8 for adults and $6 for seniors and children under 18. Tours depart from the market's **Information Booth** at the corner of Pike Street and First Avenue.

Between Pike and Pine sts. at First Ave. ✆ 206/682-7453. www.pikeplacemarket.org. Pike Place/First Ave. businesses Mon–Sat 10am–6pm, Sun 11am–5pm; Down Under stores daily 11am–5pm; many produce vendors open at 8am in summer; restaurant hours vary. Closed New Year's Day, Easter, Thanksgiving, and Christmas. Bus: 10, 12, 15, 18, 21, or 22. Waterfront Streetcar: Pike St. Station.

Seattle Aquarium   Although it's not nearly as large and impressive as the Oregon Coast Aquarium (p. 979), the Seattle Aquarium has just undergone a major remodel and expansion, and by summer 2007, the new "Window on Washington Waters" exhibit should be open to the public. This aquarium's main focus is on the water worlds of the Puget Sound region, but there are also fascinating exhibits of sea life from around the world. The star attractions are the playful river otters and the sea otters, as well as the giant octopus. There's also an underwater viewing dome, and each September, you can watch salmon return up a fish ladder to spawn. A beautiful large coral-reef tank, as well as many smaller tanks that exhibit fish from distant waters, are also worth seeing.

Pier 59, 1483 Alaskan Way. ✆ 206/386-4300. www.seattleaquarium.org. Admission $13 adults, $8.50 children 6–12, $5.50 children 3–5. Early Sept to Mar daily 10am–5pm; Apr to late May daily 9:30am–5pm; late May to early Sept daily 9:30am–7pm. Bus: 10, 12, 15, 16, or 18 and then walk through Pike Place Market to the waterfront. Waterfront Streetcar: Pike St. Station.

Seattle Art Museum   By the time you get to Seattle, the newly expanded Seattle Art Museum may be the biggest news in town. Currently scheduled to reopen in spring 2007, SAM is the largest and most impressive art museum in the Northwest. The museum is a repository for everything from 18th-century masters to works by Andy Warhol, but is especially noteworthy for its Northwest Coast Indian art and artifacts, African collection, and Northwest contemporary art. Outside stands Jonathon Borofsky's *Hammering Man,* an animated three-story steel sculpture that hammers unceasingly. Free guided tours of the different collections are offered.

100 University St. ✆ 206/654-3100. www.seattleartmuseum.org. Call for new admission prices and hours. Closed Thanksgiving and Christmas (open some holiday Mon). Bus: 10, 12, 15, 18, 21, 22, 39, or 42.

Seattle Asian Art Museum   Housed in the renovated Art Deco building that once served as the city's main art museum, the Asian art collection emphasizes Chinese and Japanese art but also includes objects from Korea, Southeast Asia, South Asia, and the Himalayas. Collections of Chinese terra-cotta funerary art, snuff bottles, and Japanese netsukes (belt decorations) are among the museum's most notable. There are frequent lectures and concerts.

Volunteer Park, 1400 E. Prospect St. ✆ 206/654-3100. www.seattleartmuseum.org. Admission $5 adults, $3 seniors and youths 13–17, free for children 12 and under. Free to all 1st Thurs and 1st Sat of each month. Tues–Wed and Fri–Sun 10am–5pm; Thurs 10am–9pm. Closed New Year's Day, Columbus Day, Thanksgiving, and Christmas. Bus: 10.

Space Needle   From a distance it resembles a flying saucer on top of a tripod, and when it was built for the 1962 World's Fair, the 605-foot-tall Space Needle was meant to suggest future architectural trends. Today the Space Needle is the quintessential symbol of Seattle, and at 520 feet above ground level, its observation deck provides superb views of the city and its surroundings. If you don't mind standing in line and paying quite a bit for an elevator ride, make this your first stop in Seattle so you can orient yourself.

Seattle Center, 400 Broad St. ℂ 206/905-2100. www.spaceneedle.com. Admission $14 adults ($17 for day and night ticket), $12 seniors ($15 for day and night ticket), $7 ages 4–13 ($10 for day and night ticket), free for children under 4. No charge if dining in the SkyCity restaurant. Sun–Thurs 9am–11pm; Fri–Sat 9am–midnight. Valet parking $11 for all-day parking. Bus: 1, 2, 3, 4, 13, 15, 16, or 18. Monorail: From Westlake Center at Pine St. and Fourth Ave.

Woodland Park Zoo *Kids*   Located in north Seattle, this sprawling zoo has outstanding exhibits focusing on Alaska, tropical Asia, the African savanna, and the tropical rainforest. The brown bear enclosure, one of the zoo's best exhibits, is a very realistic reproduction of an Alaskan stream and hillside. A large walk-through butterfly house ($1 additional fee) is open during the summer months. A farm animal area and petting zoo are big hits with the little ones.

750 N. 50th St. ℂ 206/684-4800. www.zoo.org. Admission $11 adults, $8.50 seniors, $7.50 children 3–12, free for children under 3. Mar 15–Apr 30 and Sept 15–Oct 14 daily 9:30am–5pm; May 1–Sept 14 daily 9:30am–6pm; Oct 15–Mar 14 daily 9:30am–4pm. Parking $4. Bus: 5.

PARKS & PUBLIC GARDENS

For serious communing with nature, nothing will do but **Discovery Park,** 3801 W. Government Way (ℂ **206/386-4236**). Occupying a high bluff and sandy point jutting into Puget Sound, this is Seattle's largest and wildest park. You can easily spend a day wandering the trails and beaches here. The park's visitor center is open Tuesday through Sunday from 8:30am to 5pm. To reach the park, follow the waterfront north from downtown Seattle toward the Magnolia neighborhood and watch for signs to the park.

Up on Capitol Hill, at East Prospect Street and 14th Avenue East, you'll find **Volunteer Park,** 1247 15th Ave. E. (ℂ **206/684-4075**), which is surrounded by the elegant mansions of Capitol Hill. It's a popular spot for sunning and playing Frisbee, and it's home to the Seattle Asian Art Museum (p. 941), an amphitheater, a water tower with a superb view of the city, and a conservatory filled with tropical and desert plants.

Any avid gardener should be sure to make a trip across one of Seattle's two floating bridges to the city of Bellevue and the **Bellevue Botanical Garden,** Wilburton Hill Park, 12001 Main St. (ℂ **425/452-2750;** www.bellevuebotanical.org). This 36-acre garden has become one of the Northwest's most talked-about perennial gardens. The summertime displays of flowers, in expansive mixed borders, are absolutely gorgeous. Admission is free; take the Northeast Fourth Street exit off I-405.

Situated on 3½ acres of land, the **Japanese Garden,** Washington Park Arboretum, 1075 Lake Washington Blvd. E., north of East Madison Street (ℂ **206/684-4725;** bus: 11), is a perfect little world unto itself, with babbling brooks, a lake rimmed with Japanese irises and filled with colorful koi (Japanese carp), and a cherry orchard (for spring color). A special tea garden encloses a teahouse where, on the third Saturday of each month between April and October, you can attend a traditional tea ceremony ($10). Unfortunately, noise from a nearby road can be distracting at times. Admission is $5 adults, $3 seniors, persons with disabilities, and children 6 to 17. It's closed December through February.

Acres of trees and shrubs stretch from the far side of Capitol Hill all the way to the Montlake Cut, a canal connecting Lake Washington to Lake Union. Within the 230-acre **Washington Park Arboretum,** 2300 Arboretum Dr. E. (ℂ **206/543-8800;** http://depts.washington.edu/wpa/general.htm; bus: 11, 43, or 48), there are 4,600 varieties of plants and quiet trails that are pleasant throughout the year but are most beautiful in spring, when the azaleas, cherry trees, rhododendrons, and dogwoods are all in flower. The north end of the arboretum, a marshland that is home to ducks and herons, is popular with kayakers, canoeists (see "Outdoor Activities," below, for places

Value **Money-Saving Tip**

The **Ticket/Ticket** booth under the big clock at Pike Place Market sometimes has boat tour tickets available at discounted prices. If your schedule is flexible, be sure to check here first.

to rent a canoe or kayak), and bird-watchers. Free tours are offered the first and third Sundays of each month at 1pm. Admission is free. Enter on Lake Washington Boulevard off East Madison Street; or follow Wash. 520 off I-5 north of downtown, take the Montlake Boulevard exit, and go straight through the first intersection.

ORGANIZED TOURS

If you have an appreciation for off-color humor and are curious about the seamier side of Seattle history, the **Underground Tour,** 608 First Ave. (© **206/682-4646;** www. undergroundtour.com), will likely entertain and enlighten you. The tours lead down below street level in the Pioneer Square area, where you can still find the vestiges of Seattle businesses built before the great fire of 1889. Tours are held daily. The cost is $11 for adults, $9 for seniors and students 13 to 17 or with college ID, and $5 for children 7 to 12; children 6 and under are discouraged.

For an insider's glimpse of life in Seattle's International District, hook up with **Chinatown Discovery Tours** (© **425/885-3085;** www.seattlechinatowntour.com). On these walking tours, which last from 1½ to 3¼ hours, you'll learn the history of this colorful and historic neighborhood; some tours include a six-course lunch or eight-course banquet. Rates (for four or more on a tour) range from $17 to $44 per person (slightly higher for fewer than four people).

Seattle is a city surrounded by water; if you'd like to see it from this perspective, contact **Argosy Cruises** (© **800/642-7816** or 206/623-1445; www.argosycruises.com), which offers everything from a 1-hour harbor jaunt to a cruise around Lake Washington that will take you past Bill Gates's fabled waterfront Xanadu.

Tillicum Village Tours, Pier 55 (© **800/426-1205** or 206/933-8600; www.tillicum village.com), takes you across Puget Sound to Blake Island State Park, where you'll enjoy a salmon dinner and Northwest Coast Indian masked dances in a "village" built in conjunction with the 1962 Seattle World's Fair. The "village" is actually just a large restaurant and performance hall fashioned after a traditional Northwest Coast longhouse, but with the totem poles standing vigil out front, the forest encircling the longhouse, and the waters of Puget Sound stretching out into the distance, Tillicum Village is a beautiful spot.

OUTDOOR ACTIVITIES

See "Parks & Public Gardens," above, for a rundown of great places to play.

BIKING   Gregg's Greenlake Cycle, 7007 Woodlawn Ave. NE (© **206/523-1822;** www.greggscycles.com), and the **Bicycle Center,** 4529 Sandpoint Way NE (© **206/ 523-8300;** www.bicyclecenterseattle.com), both rent bikes by the hour, day, or week. Rates range from $5 to $7 per hour and $18 to $50 per day. These shops are both convenient to the **Burke-Gilman/Sammamish River Trail,** a 27-mile paved pathway created mostly from an old railway bed. This path is immensely popular and is a great place for a family bike ride or to get in a long, vigorous ride without having to deal with traffic. The Burke-Gilman portion of this trail starts in the Ballard neighborhood of north Seattle, but the most convenient place to start a ride is at **Gas Works Park** on the north shore of Lake Union. From here you can ride north and east to **Kenmore Logboom Park** at the north end of Lake Washington. There are lots of great picnicking spots along both trails. The West Seattle bike path along **Alki Beach** is another good place to ride and offers great views of the sound and the Olympics.

IN-LINE SKATING   The city has dozens of miles of paved paths perfect for skating. You can rent in-line skates at **Gregg's Greenlake Cycle,** 7007 Woodlawn Ave. NE (© **206/523-1822**), for $5 per hour. The trail around **Green Lake** and the **Burke-Gilman/Sammamish River Trail** (see the description under "Biking," above) are both good places for skating that are convenient to Gregg's. Other favorite skating spots to try include the paved path in **Myrtle Edwards Park** just north of the Seattle waterfront, the paved path along **Lake Washington Boulevard** north of Seward Park, and the **Alki Beach** pathway in west Seattle.

SEA KAYAKING   If you'd like to try your hand at **sea kayaking,** check out the **Northwest Outdoor Center,** 2100 Westlake Ave. N. (© **800/683-0637** or 206/281-9694; www.nwoc.com), located on the west side of Lake Union. Here you can rent a sea kayak for between $12 and $17 per hour. You can also opt for guided tours lasting from a few hours to several days, and there are plenty of classes available for those who are interested.

SHOPPING

The heart of Seattle's shopping district is the corner of **Pine Street** and **Fifth Avenue.** Within 2 blocks of this intersection are two major department stores (**Nordstrom** and **Macy's**) and two upscale urban shopping malls (**Westlake Center** and **Pacific Place**). The most famous shopping area is **Pike Place Market** (see "What to See & Do," above). **Pioneer Square,** Seattle's historic district, is filled with art galleries and antiques stores. **Capitol Hill** is the center of both the gay community and the city's youth culture, and has the most eclectic selection of shops in the city. Even funkier is the **Fremont** neighborhood just north of Lake Union, filled with retro stores selling vintage clothing, collectibles, and curious crafts.

A couple of miles east of Fremont there's the **Wallingford** neighborhood, which is anchored by an old schoolhouse that has been converted into a shopping arcade with interesting crafts, fashions, and gifts. The **University District,** also in north Seattle, has everything necessary to support a student population and also goes upscale at the University Village shopping center.

If antiques are your passion, you won't want to miss the opportunity to spend a day browsing the many antiques stores in the historic farm town of **Snohomish,** located roughly 30 miles north of Seattle off I-5. The town has more than 400 antiques dealers and is without a doubt the antiques capital of the Northwest.

In business since 1933, **The Legacy Ltd.,** 1003 First Ave. (© **800/729-1562** or 206/624-6350; www.thelegacyltd.com), is Seattle's oldest and finest gallery of contemporary and historic Northwest Coast Indian and Alaskan Eskimo art and artifacts.

REI (Recreational Equipment, Inc.), 222 Yale Ave. N. (© **888/873-1938** or 206/223-1944; www.rei.com), was founded in Seattle back in 1938 and today is the nation's largest co-op selling outdoor gear. Its awesome flagship store, just off I-5, is a cross between a high-tech warehouse and a mountain lodge, with a 65-foot climbing pinnacle, a rain room for testing rain gear, a trail for test-riding mountain bikes, even a play area for kids.

For the way-offbeat shopping experience, **Ye Olde Curiosity Shop,** Pier 54, 1001 Alaskan Way (© **206/682-5844;** www.yeoldecuriosityshop.com), is a cross between a souvenir store and *Ripley's Believe It or Not!* It's weird! It's wacky! It's tacky! The collection of oddities was started in 1899 by Joe Standley, who developed a more-than-passing interest in strange curios. See Siamese-twin calves, a natural mummy, the Lord's Prayer on a grain of rice, a narwhal tusk, shrunken heads, a 67-pound snail, fleas in dresses—all the stuff that may have fascinated you as a kid.

WHERE TO STAY

If you're willing to head out a bit from downtown (usually booked solid in July–Aug), you'll find prices a little easier to swallow. Room rates are almost always considerably lower October through April (the rainy season), and downtown hotels often offer substantially reduced prices on weekends.

If you're having a hard time finding a room in your price range, consider using the services of **Pacific Northwest Journeys** (© **800/935-9730** or 206/935-9730; www.pnw journeys.com). It charges $45 per reservation, but you can usually make that up in savings on just a 2-night stay. You might also want to check with **Seattle Super Saver** (© **800/535-7071** or 206/461-5882; www.seattlesupersaver.com), a reservation service operated by Seattle's Convention and Visitors Bureau. Rates are comparable to what you might find at online booking sites.

We list some of our favorite Seattle B&Bs (often less expensive than downtown hotels) in the pages that follow, but to find out about other good B&Bs in Seattle, contact the **Seattle Bed & Breakfast Association** (© **800/348-5630** or 206/547-1020; www.seattlebandbs.com) or **A Pacific Reservation Service** (© **800/684-2932** or 206/439-7677; www.seattlebedandbreakfast.com), which represent dozens of accommodations in the Seattle area, including B&Bs and houseboats on Lake Union.

Alexis Hotel   Listed on the National Register of Historic Places, this century-old building is a sparkling gem in an enviable location halfway between Pike Place Market and Pioneer Square. The Alexis is dedicated to the visual, performance and literary arts, and throughout the hotel, both in guest rooms and in public space, are numerous original works of art. The cheerful, personalized service and the pleasant mix of contemporary and antique furnishings give the Alexis a very special atmosphere. Almost half of the classically European-flavored rooms here are suites, including very comfortable fireplace suites with whirlpool tubs. The spa suites are the real winners, offering whirlpool tubs in exceedingly luxurious bathrooms. The hotel also has complimentary evening wine tastings and an Aveda day spa.

1007 First Ave. (at Madison St.), Seattle, WA 98104. © **800/426-7033** or 206/624-4844. Fax 206/621-9009. www.alexis hotel.com. 109 units. $299–$319 double; $355–$549 suite. Children under 18 stay free in parent's room. AE, DC, DISC, MC, V. Valet parking $26. Pets accepted. **Amenities:** Restaurant; exercise room; access to nearby health club; Aveda day spa.

The Edgewater   Located on a pier at the north end of the waterfront, The Edgewater is Seattle's only hotel situated directly on the bay and was designed to resemble a deluxe mountain or fishing lodge. It's one of our very favorites in the city because of the views, which are among the best in Seattle—check out one of the memorable sunsets. Rooms feature rustic fireplaces, lodgepole-pine furniture, and cool touches such as Ralph Lauren bedding, rubber duckies in the bathrooms, and Wi-Fi access; it's worth the extra money to spring for a water view. The rooms with balconies are a bit smaller than other rooms, but are a top choice, although the new premium water-view rooms, with claw-foot tubs and walls that open out to those great views, are hard to beat.

Pier 67, 2411 Alaskan Way, Seattle, WA 98121. ℂ 800/624-0670 or 206/728-7000. Fax 206/441-4119. www.edgewater hotel.com. 223 units. $269–$589 double; $629–$2,500 suite. Children under 18 stay free in parent's room. AE, DC, DISC, MC, V. Valet parking $24. Pets accepted. **Amenities:** Restaurant; exercise room and access to nearby health club.

Fairmont Olympic Hotel (*Best*)   If nothing but classically elegant surroundings will do, then head straight for the Fairmont Olympic Hotel, a national historic landmark that's a gorgeous facsimile of an Italian Renaissance palace. For plush surroundings, excellent service, and great amenities, this hotel can't be beat. Without a doubt, this hotel has the grandest lobby in Seattle. Gilt-and-crystal chandeliers hang from the arched ceiling, while ornate moldings grace the glowing hand-burnished oak walls and pillars. Although many of the guest rooms tend to be rather small, all are very elegant and include luxe touches such as bathrobes and CD players.

411 University St., Seattle, WA 98101. ℂ 800/223-8772, 800/821-8106 (in Washington), 800/268-6282 (in Canada), or 206/621-1700. Fax 206/682-9633. www.fairmont.com/seattle. 450 units. $339–$349 double; $369–$3,000 suite. Children 18 and under stay free in parent's room. AE, DC, DISC, MC, V. Valet parking $30. Small pets accepted. **Amenities:** 2 restaurants; indoor pool; health club; spa.

The Gaslight Inn   Anyone enamored of Craftsman bungalows and the Arts and Crafts movement of the early 20th century should enjoy a stay in this 1906 home. The common rooms are spacious and attractively decorated with a combination of western and northwestern flair, and throughout the inn are lots of art-glass pieces. In summer, guests can swim in the backyard pool or lounge on the deck. Guest rooms continue the design themes of the common areas, with lots of oak furnishings and heavy, peeled-log beds in some units. The innkeepers here can provide a wealth of information about the surrounding Capitol Hill neighborhood, which is the center of Seattle's gay scene.

1727 15th Ave., Seattle, WA 98122. ℂ 206/325-3654. Fax 206/328-4803. www.gaslight-inn.com. 8 units, 3 with shared bathroom. $88–$98 double with shared bathroom; $108–$158 double with private bathroom. Rates include continental breakfast. AE, MC, V. No children allowed. **Amenities:** Small heated outdoor pool.

Hotel Deca (*Value*)   Despite the location away from downtown in the city's University District, the Hotel Deca (formerly the University Tower Hotel) is one of Seattle's hippest hotels and offers excellent value—it's considerably cheaper than comparable downtown options and is one of our favorites in the city. You'll be surrounded by modern Art Deco style as soon as you arrive, and the retro look is both elegant and playful. Every room here is a corner unit, which means plenty of space to spread out and plenty of views from the higher floors. Small bathrooms are the biggest drawback.

4507 Brooklyn Ave. NE, Seattle, WA 98105. ℂ 800/899-0251 or 206/634-2000. Fax 206/547-6029. www.hoteldeca. com. 158 units. June–Sept $149–$199 double; Oct–May $119–$159 double. Children under 16 stay free in parent's room. AE, DC, DISC, MC, V. Free parking. **Amenities:** Restaurant; exercise room. *In room:* Fridge.

Hotel Monaco   The Monaco is one of downtown Seattle's hippest business hotels, attracting a young and affluent clientele. If you appreciate cutting-edge style, you'll go for the eclectic, over-the-top, retro-contemporary design here. The lobby has reproductions of ancient Greek murals; in the guest rooms, you'll find wild color schemes, bold striped wallpaper, flat-panel LCD TVs, DVD and CD players, and leopard-print terry-cloth robes. Miss your pet back home? Call the front desk, and a staff member will send up a pet goldfish for the night.

1101 Fourth Ave., Seattle, WA 98101. ℂ 800/945-2240 or 206/621-1770. Fax 206/621-7779. www.monaco-seattle. com. 189 units. $179–$319 double; $229–$349 suite. Rates include evening wine and beer tasting. Children under 18 stay free in parent's room. AE, DC, DISC, MC, V. Valet parking $27. Pets accepted. **Amenities:** Restaurant; exercise room and access to nearby health club.

Hotel Vintage Park   Small, classically elegant, and exceedingly romantic, the Vintage Park is a must for both lovers and wine lovers. Guests stay in rooms named for Washington wineries and enjoy a complimentary wine tasting each evening. Rooms vary quite a bit here, but when you see the plush draperies framing the beds and the neo-Victorian furnishings in the deluxe units, you'll likely want to spend your days luxuriating amid the sumptuous surroundings. Deluxe rooms have the best views. Standard rooms, though smaller, are still very comfortable.

1100 Fifth Ave., Seattle, WA 98101. Ⓒ 800/624-4433 or 206/624-8000. Fax 206/623-0568. www.hotelvintage park.com. 126 units. $139–$319 double; $475–$595 suite. Children under 18 stay free in parent's room. AE, DC, DISC, MC, V. Valet parking $30. Pets accepted. **Amenities:** Restaurant; access to nearby health club.

Inn at the Market   For romance, convenience, and the chance to immerse yourself in the Seattle aesthetic, it's hard to beat this small, European-style hotel located right in Pike Place Market. To make the most of a stay here, be sure to ask for one of the water-view rooms, which overlook Puget Sound. But even if you don't get a water-view room, you'll still find spacious accommodations, with mold-to-your-body Tempur-Pedic beds, large bathrooms, and elegant decor that gives the feel of an upscale European beach resort.

86 Pine St., Seattle, WA 98101. Ⓒ 800/446-4484 or 206/443-3600. www.innatthemarket.com. 70 units. $220–$375 double; $595 suite. Children 18 and under stay free in parent's room. AE, DC, DISC, MC, V. Parking $23. **Amenities:** 3 restaurants; access to nearby health club.

Silver Cloud Inn—Lake Union (Value (Kids   Located across the street from Lake Union, this moderately priced hotel offers good views and a great location. The rooms are big and filled with lots of amenities, which makes them convenient for long stays and family vacations. The two swimming pools also appeal to kids. Although the hotel doesn't have a restaurant of its own, plenty of waterfront options are within walking distance.

1150 Fairview Ave. N., Seattle, WA 98109. Ⓒ 800/330-5812 or 206/447-9500. Fax 206/812-4900. www.silvercloud. com. 184 units. June–Sept $139–$269 double; Oct–May $119–$189 double. Rates include continental breakfast. Children under 18 stay free in parent's room. AE, DC, DISC, MC, V. Free parking. **Amenities:** 2 pools (1 indoor); exercise room. In room: Fridge, microwave.

Westin Seattle (Kids   With its distinctive cylindrical towers, the 47-story Westin is the tallest hotel in Seattle, and consequently, rooms on the upper floors offer breathtaking vistas of the city and surrounding mountains. Guest rooms here are some of the nicest in town, and both the north and south towers of the hotel have undergone extensive renovations. Couple those great views (seen through unusual curved walls of glass) with the Westin's plush "Heavenly Beds," and you'll be sleeping on clouds both literally and figuratively. The hotel, unlike most downtown properties, has a pool, making it a good choice for families.

1900 Fifth Ave., Seattle, WA 98101. Ⓒ 800/WESTIN-1 or 206/728-1000. Fax 206/728-2007. www.westin.com/seattle. 891 units. $169–$345 double; from $419 suite. Children under 18 stay free in parent's room. AE, DC, DISC, MC, V. Valet parking $29; self-parking $26. Pets accepted ($50 deposit). **Amenities:** 2 restaurants; large indoor pool; exercise room.

W Seattle   The W hotel chain has won plenty of national attention and devoted fans for its oh-so-hip accommodations, and here in the land of espresso and high tech, the W is a natural (and definitely the coolest hotel in town). Sleek guest rooms (larger than at most W hotels) are full of the usual amenities, as well as great perks such as Bliss Spa bath products, goose-down comforters, plasma HDTVs, and CD players (there's a CD library from which you can borrow discs). Although the -09 and -02 "Cool Corner" rooms cost a bit more than regular units, they are worth requesting.

A Sporting Town

With professional football, baseball, and basketball teams, Seattle is definitely a city of sports fans and it's a great place to take in a game.

Of all of Seattle's major league sports teams, none are more beloved than baseball's **Seattle Mariners** (*©* 206/346-4000 or 206/346-4001; www.seattle mariners.com). The Mariners' beautiful, retro-style **Safeco Field** is one of only a handful of stadiums with a retractable roof, allowing the Mariners a real grass field without the worry of getting rained out.

The NBA's **Seattle SuperSonics** (*©* 800/4NBA-TIX or 206/283-3865; www. supersonics.com) play in the Key Arena at Seattle Center, and generally put in a good showing every season.

Although the NFL's **Seattle Seahawks** (*©* 888/NFL-HAWK or 206/381-7816; www.seahawks.com) didn't win the Superbowl in 2006, they came close, and best of all they developed a little respect in their hometown. The Seahawks play at **Qwest Field,** Occidental Avenue South, on the site of the old Kingdome.

Ticketmaster (*©* **206/628-0123**; www.ticketmaster.com) sells tickets to almost all sporting events in the Seattle area. You'll find Ticketmaster outlets at area Fred Meyer stores and Tower Records.

1112 Fourth Ave., Seattle, WA 98101. *©* **877/W-HOTELS** or 206/264-6000. Fax 206/264-6100. www.whotels. com/seattle. 426 units. $299–$439 double; from $959 suite. Children under 18 stay free in parent's room. AE, DC, DISC, MC, V. Valet parking $29. Pets accepted ($100 nonrefundable cleaning fee plus $25 per day). **Amenities:** Restaurant; exercise room; access to nearby health club.

WHERE TO DINE

As everyone on earth must know by now, Seattle takes coffee very seriously. This is where **Starbucks** got its start, and though the stylish espresso bars are now ubiquitous all across the country, there was a time when there was only one Starbucks—if you feel the need to make a pilgrimage, the first-ever store is still located at Pike Place Market.

Andaluca NORTHWEST/MEDITERRANEAN   The sumptuous Andaluca mixes traditional and contemporary like few other restaurants in town. The menu changes frequently, but you'll usually find a traditional Spanish *zarazuela* (shellfish stew), *cabrales*-crusted beef tenderloin (made with blue cheese, grilled pears, and Marsala glaze), and the artful Dungeness crab tower, made with avocado, palm hearts, and gazpacho salsa.

In the Mayflower Park Hotel, 407 Olive Way. *©* **206/382-6999.** www.andaluca.com. Reservations recommended. Small plates $6–$15; main courses $13–$15 at lunch, $19–$38 at dinner. AE, DC, DISC, MC, V. Mon–Thurs 6:30–11am, 11:30am–2:30pm, and 5–10pm; Fri 6:30–11am, 11:30am–2:30pm, and 5–11pm; Sat 7–11am and 5-11pm; Sun 7am–noon and 5–10pm.

Anthony's Pier 66 & Bell Street Diner SEAFOOD   There are lots of mediocre restaurants on the waterfront, but if you head up to the north end you'll find not only excellent food but also a stylish decor featuring lots of art glass. The upstairs dining room serves the likes of applewood-grilled salmon; downstairs, the Bell Street Diner offers meals easier on the wallet. There's also a walk-up window out front. In summer, the decks are the place to be.

2201 Alaskan Way. ⓒ **206/448-6688.** www.anthonys.com. Reservations recommended at Pier 66, not taken at Bell Street Diner. Pier 66 main courses $9–$24; Bell Street Diner main courses $7–$19. AE, MC, V. Pier 66 Mon–Thurs 5–9:30pm, Fri–Sat 5–10pm, Sun 5–9pm; Bell Street Diner Mon–Thurs 11:30am–10pm, Fri–Sat 11:30am–10:30pm, Sun 11:30am–9pm.

Canlis NORTHWEST   A local tradition since 1950, the rather formal Canlis offers Northwest cuisine with Asian and Continental influences, keeping both traditionalists and adventurous diners happy. This is the perfect place to close a big deal or celebrate a special occasion over steaks from the copper grill or spicy Peter Canlis prawns. To finish, go for the Grand Marnier soufflé. Canlis also has one of the best wine lists in Seattle.

2576 Aurora Ave. N. ⓒ **206/283-3313.** www.canlis.com. Reservations highly recommended. Main courses $27–$70; chef's tasting menu $80 ($125 with wines). AE, DC, DISC, MC, V. Mon–Thurs 5:30–9pm; Fri–Sat 5:30–10pm.

Chez Shea *(Best)* NORTHWEST   Dark, romantic, and intimate, this is one of Seattle's finest restaurants and the best bet for a romantic meal. Candlelit tables and views across Puget Sound to the Olympic Mountains provide the setting for the seasonally changing menu, prepared with ingredients fresh from the market below. The eight-course tasting menu is the best way to go. On a recent spring evening, dinner started with oysters on the half shell, followed by a Dungeness crab, leek, and camembert tart; an asparagus bisque with roasted-tomato oil; seared foie gras with blueberry-pistachio compote; salmon with morel butter; Kobe-style beef tenderloin wrapped in prosciutto; and finally a cheese course and chilled lemon soufflé.

Corner Market Building, 94 Pike St., Suite 34. ⓒ **206/467-9990.** www.chezshea.com. Reservations highly recommended. Main courses $18–$29; 8-course tasting menu $65 ($95 with wine). AE, MC, V. Tues–Sun 5–10pm.

Dahlia Lounge PAN-ASIAN/NORTHWEST   One bite of any dish here will convince you that this is one of Seattle's finest restaurants. Mouthwatering and succulent Dungeness crab cakes are the house specialty and should not be missed. The menu, influenced by the far side of the Pacific Rim, changes regularly, with the lunch menu featuring many of the same offerings at slightly lower prices. For dessert, try the crème caramel.

2001 Fourth Ave. ⓒ **206/682-4142.** www.tomdouglas.com. Reservations highly recommended. Main courses $12–$25 at lunch, $22–$35 at dinner. AE, DC, DISC, MC, V. Mon–Fri 11:30am–2:30pm; Mon–Thurs 5–10pm; Fri–Sat 5–11pm; Sun 5–9pm.

Etta's Seafood SEAFOOD   Located smack in the middle of the Pike Place Market area, this stylish, contemporary restaurant is as popular with locals as it is with tourists. The kitchen dishes out signature crab cakes (crunchy on the outside, creamy on the inside), which are not to be missed (if they're not on the menu, just ask), plus other great seafood dishes.

2020 Western Ave. ⓒ **206/443-6000.** www.tomdouglas.com. Reservations recommended. Main courses $11–$25 at lunch, $12–$34 at dinner. AE, DC, DISC, MC, V. Mon–Thurs 11:30am–9:30pm; Fri 11:30am–10pm; Sat 9am–3pm and 4–10pm; Sun 9am–3pm and 4–9pm.

Flying Fish NORTHWEST/SEAFOOD   This hip Belltown restaurant offers bold combinations of vibrant, Asian-influenced flavors—and serves dinner until 1am nightly, keeping late-night partyers from going hungry. Diners can choose from small plates, large plates, and platters for sharing. The menu changes almost daily and every dish here is a work of art. Don't miss the smoked rock-shrimp spring rolls. There's also a huge wine list.

2234 First Ave. ⓒ **206/728-8595.** www.flyingfishseattle.com. Reservations recommended. Main courses $7.50–$15 at lunch, $18–$37 at dinner. AE, DC, MC, V. Mon–Fri 11:30am–2pm; daily 5pm–1am.

Noodle Ranch PAN-ASIAN   This Belltown hole in the wall serves Pan-Asian for the hip-but-financially-challenged crowd. It's a lively, boisterous scene, and the food is packed with intense, and often unfamiliar, flavors. The Mekong grill—rice noodles with a rice-wine/vinegar-and-herb dressing topped with grilled pork, chicken, beef, or tofu—should not be missed. You'll also find Laotian cucumber salad, Japanese-style eggplant, and many other vegetarian options. Although the place is frequently packed, you can usually get a seat without having to wait too long.

2228 Second Ave. ⓒ 206/728-0463. Reservations not accepted. Main courses $7.25–$12. AE, MC, V. Mon–Thurs 11am–10pm; Fri 11am–11pm; Sat noon–10pm.

Palace Kitchen AMERICAN REGIONAL/MEDITERRANEAN   Chef Tom Douglas's Palace Kitchen has an urban chic atmosphere, with cement pillars, simple wood booths, a few tables in the window, and a popular bar. The short menu features a nightly selection of unusual cheeses and different preparations from the applewood grill. Entrees are usually simple and delicious, ranging from the Palace burger royale (a strong contender for best burger in Seattle) to such unusual dishes as braised oxtail with polenta, chard, and green peppercorns. For dessert, the coconut cream pie is an absolute must.

2030 Fifth Ave. ⓒ 206/448-2001. www.tomdouglas.com. Reservations accepted only for parties of 6 or more. Main courses $12–$30. AE, DC, DISC, MC, V. Daily 5pm–1am.

Palisade NORTHWEST   If we were to splurge on dinner at a waterfront restaurant, we'd make it Palisade, which offers panoramic views of the city and Olympic Mountains. It also happens to have fine food and inventive interior design (a fish-laden saltwater pond sits in the middle of the dining room). The menu features both fish and meats prepared in a wood-fired oven and in a wood-fired rotisserie. The three-course sunset dinners, served before 6pm, cost $30 and are a great way to enjoy this place on a budget. *Tip:* Call for exact directions as it can be hard to find.

Elliott Bay Marina, 2601 W. Marina Place. ⓒ 206/285-1000. www.palisaderestaurant.com. Reservations recommended. Main courses $9–$17 at lunch, $19–$45 at dinner; Sun brunch $20–$26. AE, DC, DISC, MC, V. Mon–Fri 11:15am–2pm; Mon–Thurs 5–9pm; Fri 4:30–10pm; Sat 4–10pm; Sun 9:30am–2pm and 4–9pm.

Rover's NORTHWEST   Tucked away in a quaint clapboard house behind a chic little shopping plaza is one of Seattle's most acclaimed restaurants. Award-winning Chef Thierry Rautureau received classic French training before falling in love with the Northwest and the wonderful ingredients available here. The fixed-price menus change frequently, but may include venison with caramelized turnips and Armagnac sauce. You won't often find a vegetarian feast that can compare with the ones served here.

2808 E. Madison St. ⓒ 206/325-7442. www.rovers-seattle.com. Reservations required. Main courses $17–$20 at lunch; $35 prix-fixe 3-course lunch; 5-course menu degustation $80 (vegetarian) and $90; chef's 8-course grand menu $125. AE, DC, MC, V. Fri noon–1:30pm; Tues–Thurs 5:30–9:30pm; Fri–Sat 5:30–9:30pm.

Serafina ITALIAN   Off the beaten tourist track, Serafina is one of our favorite Seattle dining spots. It has a nice touch of sophistication, but overall, it's a relaxed neighborhood place where the rustic, romantic atmosphere underscores the earthy, country-style dishes. It's hard to resist ordering at least one of the bruschetta appetizers, which come with any of three different toppings. Among the pasta offerings, don't pass up the delicious veal meatballs in a green olive–tomato sauce served over penne. There's live music (mostly jazz and Latin) Friday through Sunday nights.

2043 Eastlake Ave. E. ⓒ 206/323-0807. www.serafinaseattle.com. Reservations recommended. Main courses $10–$17 at lunch, $17–$22 at dinner. AE, DISC, MC, V. Mon–Fri 11:30am–2:30pm; Sun 10am–2pm; Sun–Thurs 5:30–10pm; Fri–Sat 5:30–1am.

SEATTLE AFTER DARK

To find out what's going on when you're in town, pick up a free copy of *Seattle Weekly* (www.seattleweekly.com), Seattle's arts-and-entertainment newspaper. You'll find it in bookstores, convenience stores, grocery stores, newsstands, and newspaper boxes around downtown and other neighborhoods. On Friday, the *Seattle Times* includes a section called "Ticket," a guide to the week's arts-and-entertainment offerings.

Ticketmaster (© 206/292-ARTS; www.ticketmaster.com) sells tickets to a wide variety of performances and events in the Seattle area. Half-price, day-of-show tickets to musical and theatrical performances are available at **Ticket/Ticket** (© 206/324-2744), with sales booths at Pike Place Market's information booth; downtown at Pacific Place mall's information booth; in Capitol Hill's Broadway Market, 401 Broadway E., 2nd floor; and in Bellevue at Meydenbauer Center, Northeast Sixth Street and 112th Avenue. Ticket/Ticket charges a small service fee, the amount of which depends on the ticket price.

THE PERFORMING ARTS   The **Seattle Opera** (© 800/426-1619 or 206/389-7676; www.seattleopera.org), which performs at Seattle Center's Marion Oliver McCaw Hall, is considered one of the finest opera companies in the country, and *the* Wagnerian opera company in the United States. In addition to classical operas such as *The Magic Flute* and *The Barber of Seville,* the season usually includes a more contemporary production.

The 90-musician **Seattle Symphony** (© 866/833-4747 or 206/215-4747; www. seattlesymphony.org), which performs in the acoustically superb Benaroya Hall, offers an amazingly diverse musical season that runs from September to July.

The **Seattle Repertory Theatre** (© 877/900-9285 or 206/443-2222; www.seattle rep.org), which performs at the Bagley Wright and Leo K. theaters, Seattle Center, 155 Mercer St., is Seattle's top professional theater. The Rep's season runs from September to May and productions range from classics to world premieres.

With a season that runs from April to December, the **Intiman Theatre** (© 206/269-1900; www.intiman.org), which performs at the Intiman Playhouse, Seattle Center, 201 Mercer St., fills in the gap left by those months when the Seattle Rep's lights are dark. Performing in the historic Eagles Building theater adjacent to the Washington State Convention and Trade Center, **A Contemporary Theater (ACT),** Kreielsheimer Place, 700 Union St. (© 206/292-7676; www.acttheatre.org), offers slightly more adventurous productions than the other major theater companies in Seattle, though it's not nearly as avant-garde as some of the smaller companies. The season runs from March to December.

The **Pacific Northwest Ballet,** Marion Oliver McCaw Hall, 301 Mercer St. (© 206/441-2424; www.pnb.org), is Seattle's premier dance company. During the season, which runs from September to June, the company presents a wide range of classics, new works, and (the company's specialty) pieces choreographed by George Balanchine. This company's performance of *The Nutcracker,* with outstanding dancing and sets and costumes by children's book author Maurice Sendak, is the highlight of every season. **On the Boards,** Behnke Center for Contemporary Performance, 100 W. Roy St. (© 206/217-9888; www.ontheboards.org), is the area's best modern-dance venue.

THE CLUB & MUSIC SCENE   If you want to go clubbing and barhopping, there's no better place to start than **Pioneer Square.** Good times are guaranteed, whether you want to hear a live band, hang out in a good old-fashioned bar, or dance. Keep in mind that this neighborhood tends to attract a very rowdy crowd (lots of frat boys) and can be pretty rough late at night. **Belltown,** north of Pike Place Market, is another good place to club-hop. Clubs here are way more style-conscious than those in Pioneer Square and tend to attract 20- and 30-something trendsetters.

For alternative rock, head to **The Crocodile Cafe** in Belltown, 2200 Second Ave. (© **206/441-5611;** www.thecrocodile.com), a combination bar/club/restaurant that played a big role in Seattle's grunge movement. The **Showbox,** 1426 First Ave. (© **206/ 628-3151;** www.showboxonline.com), books a variety of rock acts, many with a national following. Cool and sophisticated, **Dimitriou's Jazz Alley,** 2033 Sixth Ave. (© **206/441-9729;** www.jazzalley.com), has been Seattle's premier jazz club for more than 25 years, featuring only the best performers. The classic **Century Ballroom,** 915 E. Pine St. (© **206/324-7263;** www.centuryballroom.com), plays host to some of the best touring acts to come to town. This is Seattle's top spot for swing and salsa dancing. Established in 1892, **The Central Saloon,** 207 First Ave. S. (© **206/622-0209;** www.centralsaloon.com), is a Seattle institution. It's a must-stop during a night out in Pioneer Square. You might catch sounds ranging from funk to reggae.

THE BAR SCENE   Belltown's **Virginia Inn,** 1937 First Ave. (© **206/728-1937**), has a decidedly old Seattle feel, due in large part to the fact that this place has been around since 1903. Best of all, this is a nonsmoking bar and it serves French food! **Oliver's,** located in the Mayflower Park Hotel, 405 Olive Way (© **206/623-8700**), is martini central for Seattle.

You might see members of the Seahawks or Mariners at Pioneer Square's **FX McRory's,** 419 Occidental Ave. S. (© **206/623-4800;** www.fxmcrorys.com), an upscale sports bar with an oyster bar and a large selection of bourbons and microbrews. For good stout and strong ales at a local brewpub, try Capitol Hill's **Elysian Brewing Company,** 1221 E. Pike St. (© **206/860-1920;** www.elysianbrewing.com). South of Pioneer Square and popular before or after sports events is **Pyramid Ale House,** 1201 First Ave. S. (© **206/682-3377;** www.pyramidbrew.com), part of the brewery that makes Thomas Kemper lagers and Pyramid ales.

THE GAY & LESBIAN SCENE   Capitol Hill is Seattle's main gay neighborhood, where you'll find the greatest concentration of gay and lesbian bars and dance clubs. Look for the readily available *Seattle Gay News* (© **206/324-4297;** www.sgn.org), where you'll find ads for many of the city's gay bars and nightclubs. **Thumpers,** 1500 Madison St. (© **206/328-3800**), is a classy restaurant/bar with a fireplace and two decks with great views. For dancing, head to **Neighbours,** 1509 Broadway Ave. (© **206/324-5358;** www. neighboursonline.com). A longtime favorite of the lesbian community is **Wildrose,** 1021 E. Pike St. (© **206/324-9210;** www.thewildrosebar.com), a friendly restaurant/bar.

2 The San Juan Islands

There's something magical about traveling to the San Juans. Some people say it's the light, some say it's the sea air, some say it's the weather (temperatures are always moderate, and rainfall is roughly half what it is in Seattle). Whatever it is that so entrances, the San Juans have become the favorite getaway of urban Washingtonians, and if you make time to visit these idyllic islands, we think you, too, will fall under their spell. On the downside, the islands have been discovered by tourists and, in summer, there can be waits of several hours to get on a ferry with your car. One solution is to come over on foot or with a bicycle. You can then get around by renting a car or bike, hopping on the island shuttle buses, or calling taxis.

The San Juans consist of at least 175 named islands, or up to 786 if you include all the rocks and reefs that poke above the water at low tide. Only three (San Juan, Orcas, and Lopez) have anything in the way of tourist accommodations. *Warning:* Don't expect to find a place to stay in summer if you come out here without a room reservation.

ESSENTIALS

GETTING THERE   By Boat   Washington State Ferries (© 800/84-FERRY or 888/808-7977 in Washington, or 206/464-6400; www.wsdot.wa.gov/ferries) operates ferries between Anacortes and four of the San Juan Islands (Lopez, Shaw, Orcas, and San Juan) and Sidney, British Columbia (on Vancouver Island near Victoria). Foot passengers are welcome to ride as well. There are also passenger-ferry services from several cities around the region. **Victoria Clipper** (© 800/888-2535, 206/448-5000, or 250/382-8100; www.victoriaclipper.com) operates excursion boats between Seattle and Friday Harbor on San Juan Island. There are also boats that go to Victoria, British Columbia.

By Plane   Kenmore Air (© 800/543-9595 or 425/486-1257; www.kenmoreair. com) offers floatplane flights that take off from either Lake Union or the north end of Lake Washington. Flights go to Friday Harbor and Roche Harbor on San Juan Island; Rosario Resort, Deer Harbor, and West Sound on Orcas Island; and the Lopez Islander on Lopez Island. You can also get from Sea-Tac Airport to the San Juan Islands ferry terminal in Anacortes on the **Airporter Shuttle** (© 866/235-5247 or 360/380-8800; www.airporter.com).

VISITOR INFORMATION   For information on all the islands, contact the **San Juan Islands Visitor Information Service,** P.O. Box 1330, Friday Harbor, WA 98250 (© 888/468-3701 or 360/378-9551; www.guidetosanjuans.com).

GETTING AROUND   Cars, scooters, and mopeds are available on San Juan Island from **Susie's Mopeds,** at the top of the ferry lanes in Friday Harbor (© 800/532-0087 or 360/378-5244; www.susiesmopeds.com). **San Juan Transit** (© 800/887-8387, or 360/378-8887 on San Juan Island; www.sanjuantransit.com) operates a shuttle bus on San Juan during the summer.

To rent a car on Orcas Island, contact **M&W Auto Sales** (© 800/323-6037 or 360/378-2886; www.interisland.net/mandw), which charges between $50 and $80 per day during the summer.

SAN JUAN ISLAND

San Juan Island is the most populous and touristy of the islands. **Friday Harbor,** where the ferry docks, is the county seat for San Juan County and the only real town on all the islands. Friday Harbor's simple wood-frame buildings date back to the turn of the 20th century and now house numerous shops, restaurants, motels, and inns.

Whale-watching is one of the most popular summer activities in the San Juans. Before you head out, stop by the **Whale Museum,** 62 First St. N. (© 360/378-4710; www.whale-museum.org), where you can see whale skeletons and models of whales and learn all about the area's pods of orcas (aka killer whales).

San Juan Vineyards, 3136 Roche Harbor Rd. (© 360/378-9463; www.sanjuan vineyards.com), makes wines both from grapes grown off the island and from its own estate-grown Siegrebbe and Madeline Angevine grapes. The tasting room is housed in an old schoolhouse built in 1896. It's open daily in summer.

A little farther north, you'll come to **Roche Harbor,** once the site of large limestone quarries that supplied lime to much of the West Coast. Many of the quarries' old structures are still visible, giving this area a decaying industrial look, but amid the abandoned machinery stands the historic **Hotel de Haro,** a simple whitewashed wooden building with verandas across its two floors. Stop to admire the old-fashioned marina and colorful gardens; the deck of the hotel's lounge is one of the best places on the island to linger over a drink. In an old pasture on the edge of the resort property, you'll find the **Westcott Bay Sculpture Park** (✆ **360/370-5050;** www.wbay.org), a park that includes more than 100 works of art set in grassy fields and along the shores of a small pond. Back in the woods near the resort is an unusual **mausoleum,** which was erected by the founder of the quarries and the Hotel de Haro.

South of Roche Harbor, on West Valley Road, you'll come to the **English Camp** unit of **San Juan Island National Historical Park** (✆ **360/378-2902;** www.nps.gov/ sajh). The park commemorates San Juan Island Pig War, one of North America's most unusual and least remembered confrontations. San Juan Island nearly became the site of a battle between the British and the Americans in 1859, when a British pig on San Juan Island decided to have dinner in an American garden while the two countries were having a border dispute.

The English Camp unit of the park is set amid shady trees and spacious lawns; the camp is the picture of British civility. There's even a formal garden surrounded by a white picket fence. You can look inside the reconstructed buildings and imagine the days when this was one of the most far-flung corners of the British Empire. If you're full of energy, hike up to the top of 650-foot **Mount Young** for a beautiful panorama of the island. An easier hike is out to the end of **Bell Point.**

South of English Camp, watch for the Mitchell Bay Road turnoff. This connects to the Westside Road, which leads down the island's west coast. Along this road, you'll find **San Juan County Park,** a great spot for a picnic. A little farther south, you'll come to **Lime Kiln Point State Park** (✆ **360/378-2044;** www.parks.wa.gov), the country's first whale-watching park and a great place to spot these gentle giants in summer.

OUTDOOR ACTIVITIES

BIKING   Winding country roads are ideal for leisurely trips. If you didn't bring your own wheels, you can rent a bike in Friday Harbor from **Island Bicycles,** 380 Argyle St. (✆ **360/378-4941;** www.islandbicycles.com), which charges $7 to $14 per hour (2-hr. minimum) or $35 to $70 per day.

SEA KAYAKING   Three- and 5-hour sea-kayak tours out of Roche Harbor are offered by **San Juan Safaris** (✆ **800/450-6858** or 360/378-1323; www.sanjuansafaris. com), which also operates out of Friday Harbor. Tours run mid-April through early October and cost $59 to $75. **Crystal Seas Kayaking** (✆ **877/SEAS-877** or 360/ 378-4223; www.crystalseas.com) does anything from 3-hour tours ($59), to sunset tours ($59), to all-day tours ($79). Three- and 4-day trips are offered by **San Juan Kayak Expeditions** (✆ **360/378-4436;** www.sanjuankayak.com), which charges $399 and $499, respectively, for its outings.

WHALE-WATCHING   The best months to see orcas are June through September, but it's possible to see them throughout the year. In the summer, 3-hour whale-watching cruises from Roche Harbor, on the north side of the island, are offered by **San Juan Safaris** (✆ **800/450-6858** or 360/378-1323; www.sanjuansafaris.com), which charges $59 for adults and $39 for children 12 and under. This company also offers tours from Friday Harbor. Similar cruises are offered by **San Juan Excursions** (© 800/ **80-WHALE** or 360/378-6636; www.watchwhales.com), which operates out of Friday Harbor. Cruises are $59 for adults and $39 for children 2 to 12. For a speedier and more personalized whale-watching excursion, book a tour with **Maya's Whale Watch Charters** (© 360/378-7996; www.mayaswhalewatch.biz), which operates the fastest whale-watching boat in the islands and takes out only six people at a time. A 3-hour tour costs $65 ($55 for children 12 and under).

WHERE TO STAY & DINE

Friday Harbor House, 130 West St., Friday Harbor (© **866/722-7356** or 360/378- 8455; www.fridayharborhouse.com), is a luxurious contemporary hotel. The bluff-top location ensures excellent views, and rooms contain fireplaces, whirlpool tubs, and balconies. In 2006, three spacious new suites were added, but they have only partial harbor views. The dining room is one of the best on the island, offering a seasonal menu with an emphasis on Northwest cuisine. Rates run $135 to $340 double and include continental breakfast.

   Olympic Lights Bed & Breakfast, 146 Starlight Way, Friday Harbor (© **888/ 211-6195** or 360/378-3186; www.olympiclights.com), on San Juan's dry southwestern tip, is a Victorian farmhouse surrounded by windswept meadows. The Ra Room has a bay window with a glorious view. Rates ($99–$140 double) include full breakfast; the B&B doesn't take credit cards.

   The Place Bar & Grill, 1 Spring St. (© **360/378-8707**), is the island's finest waterfront restaurant. It aims to attract the upscale Seattle market with its regularly changing seafood menu. Main courses run $20 to $34. Located in the luxurious Friday Harbor House boutique hotel, **Friday Harbor House Dining Room,** 130 West St. (© **360/378-8455**), is the most sophisticated restaurant on San Juan Island, boasting a great harbor view. The menu is short and relies heavily on local ingredients, including island-grown greens and Westcott Bay oysters. Main courses cost $19 to $34.

ORCAS ISLAND

Shaped like a horseshoe and named for an 18th-century Mexican viceroy (not for the area's orca whales, as is commonly believed), Orcas Island has long been a popular summer-vacation spot and is the most beautiful of the San Juan Islands. Orcas is a particular favorite of nature lovers, who come to enjoy the views of green rolling pastures, forested mountains, and fjordlike bays. **Eastsound** is the largest town on the island, with several interesting shops and good restaurants.

   Several pottery shops are located around the island. A few miles west of Eastsound off Enchanted Forest Road is **Orcas Island Pottery,** 338 Old Pottery Rd. (© **360/ 376-2813;** www.orcasislandpottery.com), the oldest pottery studio in the Northwest. Between Eastsound and Orcas on Horseshoe Highway is **Crow Valley Pottery,** 2274 Orcas Rd. (© **360/376-4260;** www.crowvalley.com), housed in an 1866 log cabin. And on the east side of the island in the community of Olga, you'll find **Orcas Island Artworks,** Horseshoe Highway (© **360/376-4408;** www.orcasisland.com/artworks), which is full of beautiful work by island artists.

OUTDOOR ACTIVITIES

Covering 5,252 acres of the island, **Moran State Park** (© **360/902-8844;** www. parks.wa.gov) is the largest park in the San Juans and the main destination for most island visitors. If the weather is clear, you'll enjoy great views from the summit of Mount Constitution, which rises 2,409 feet above Puget Sound. There are also five lakes, 33 miles of hiking trails, and an environmental learning center. Popular park activities include fishing, hiking, boating, mountain biking, and camping (for campsite reservations, contact **Washington State Parks** at © 888/226-7688; www.parks. wa.gov/reserve.asp). The park is off Horseshoe Highway, approximately 13 miles from the ferry landing.

BIKING Although Orcas is considered the most challenging of the San Juan Islands for biking, plenty of cyclists pedal the island's roads. **Dolphin Bay Bicycles** (© 360/ 376-4157; www.rockisland.com/~dolphin), located just to the right as you get off the ferry, has long been our favorite place in the islands to rent a bike. Bikes rent for $30 per day, $70 for 3 days, and $100 per week. Guided bike rides are also sometimes available.

WHALE-WATCHING If you want to see some of the orca whales for which the San Juans are famous, you can take a whale-watching excursion with **Deer Harbor Charters** (© 800/544-5758 or 360/376-5989; www.deerharborcharters.com), which operates out of both Deer Harbor and Rosario Resort and charges $49 to $55 for adults and $32 to $37 for children; or with **Orcas Island Eclipse Charters** (© 800/ 376-6566 or 360/376-6566; www.orcasislandwhales.com), which operates out of the Orcas Island ferry dock and charges $59 for adults and $35 for children.

WHERE TO STAY & DINE

The **Spring Bay Inn,** Olga (© 360/376-5531; www.springbayinn.com), is one of the only waterfront B&Bs in the San Juans. Innkeepers Sandy Playa and Carl Burger, both retired park rangers, make a stay here both fun and educational. You can soak in the hot tub on the beach, spot bald eagles, hike on the nature trails, and go for a guided sea-kayak tour. Four rooms have fireplaces, two have views from their tubs, and two have balconies; all have fridges. Rates ($220–$260 double) include continental breakfast, brunch, and a daily kayak tour. The **Turtleback Farm Inn,** 1981 Crow Valley Rd., Eastsound (© 800/376-4914 or 360/376-4914; www.turtlebackinn.com), is a restored farmhouse overlooking 80 idyllic acres of farmland at the foot of Turtleback Mountain. Simply furnished with antiques, the rooms range from cozy to spacious. The four rooms in the Orchard House are among the biggest and most luxurious on the island (with gas fireplaces, claw-foot tubs, balconies, wood floors, and fridges). Rates ($100–$245 double) include full breakfast.

Café Olga, Horseshoe Highway, Olga (© 360/376-5098), is the best place for breakfast or lunch. Everything here is homemade, using fresh local produce whenever possible. Try the blackberry pie with Lopez Island Creamery ice cream. This building also houses Orcas Island Artworks, a gallery representing more than 70 local artists. Main courses run $10 to $18. **Christina's,** Main Street and North Beach Road, Eastsound (© 360/376-4904; www.christinas.ne), has a beautiful view down the sound. The deck is *the* place on the island for sunset dinners. The short menu changes regularly and features innovative cuisine prepared with an emphasis on local ingredients. Desserts can be heavenly. Main courses average $27 to $34.

3 The Olympic Peninsula & Olympic National Park

Olympic National Park is unique in the contiguous United States for its temperate rainforests, which are found in the valleys of the Hoh, Queets, Bogachiel, Clearwater, and Quinault rivers. Rainfall here can exceed 150 inches per year, trees grow nearly 300 feet tall, and mosses hang from every limb. Trails lead from these valleys (and other points around the peninsula) into the interior of the park, providing access to hundreds of miles of hiking trails. In fact, trails are the only access to most of the park, which has fewer than a dozen roads, none of which lead more than a few miles into the park.

Within a few short miles of the park's rainforests, the jagged, snowcapped Olympic Mountains rise to the 7,965-foot peak of Mount Olympus and produce an Alpine zone where no trees can grow. Together, elevation and heavy rainfall combine to form 60 glaciers within the park. It is these glaciers that have carved the Olympic Mountains into the jagged peaks that mesmerize visitors and beckon to hikers and climbers. Rugged and spectacular sections of the coast have also been preserved as part of the national park, and offshore waters have been designated the Olympic Coast National Marine Sanctuary. June through September are much less wet than the other months. In winter, the road to Hurricane Ridge can be iffy, as it's plowed only Saturday through Monday.

ESSENTIALS

GETTING THERE   By Plane   Kenmore Air Express (© **800/543-9595;** www. kenmoreair.com) flies between Seattle's Boeing Field and Port Angeles's William R. Fairchild International Airport (with a free shuttle from Seattle-Tacoma International Airport to Boeing Field). Rental cars are available in Port Angeles from **Budget** (© **800/527-0700;** www.budget.com).

By Car   U.S. 101 circles Olympic National Park with main park entrances south of Port Angeles, at Lake Crescent, at Sol Duc, and at the Hoh River. The Port Angeles park entrance is 48 miles west of Port Townsend and 55 miles east of Forks.

VISITOR INFORMATION   For information on the national park, contact **Olympic National Park,** 600 E. Park Ave., Port Angeles, WA 98362-6798 (© **360/565-3131** or 360/565-3130; www.nps.gov/olym). For information on Port Angeles and the rest of the northern Olympic Peninsula, contact the **North Olympic Peninsula Visitor and Convention Bureau,** 338 W. First St., Suite 104 (P.O. Box 670), Port Angeles, WA 98362 (© **800/942-4042** or 360/452-8552; www.olympicpeninsula. org); or the **Port Angeles Chamber of Commerce Visitor Center,** 121 E. Railroad Ave., Port Angeles, WA 98362 (© **360/452-2363;** www.portangeles.org).

The **Olympic National Park Visitor Center,** 3002 Mt. Angeles Rd. (© **360/565-3130**), is on the south edge of Port Angeles on the road leading to Hurricane Ridge. In addition to offering lots of information, maps, and books about the park, the center has exhibits on the park's flora and fauna, old-growth forests, and whaling by local Native Americans. It's open daily from 9am to 4:30pm in summer (shorter hours fall through spring). The park entry fee is $15 per motor vehicle or $5 per person for pedestrians, motorcyclists, and bicyclists.

SEEING THE HIGHLIGHTS
THE NORTH SIDE

From the **Olympic Park National Visitor Center,** continue 17 miles up to Hurricane Ridge, which offers breathtaking views of the park. Several trails lead into the park from here, and several day hikes are possible. The 3-mile **Hurricane Hill Trail** and the 1-mile **Meadow Loop Trail** are the most scenic. Stop by the **Hurricane Ridge Visitor Center** to see its exhibits on plants and wildlife; this is a good place to learn about the fragile nature of this beautiful Alpine landscape.

West of Port Angeles on U.S. 101 lies **Lake Crescent,** a glacier-carved lake. Near the east end of the lake, you'll find the 1-mile trail to 90-foot-high **Marymere Falls** and the **Storm King Ranger Station** (© **360/928-3380**). At the west end, you'll find

Fairholm General Store (© 360/928-3020), which rents kayaks (and sometimes canoes, rowboats, and motorboats) between May and October.

Continuing west from Lake Crescent, watch for the turnoff to **Sol Duc Hot Springs** (© 866/4-SOLDUC; www.visitsolduc.com). For 14 miles the road follows the Soleduck River, passing the Salmon Cascades along the way. Sol Duc Hot Springs were for centuries considered healing waters by local Indians, and after white settlers arrived in the area, the springs became a popular resort. In addition to the hot swimming pool and soaking tubs, you'll find cabins, a campground, a restaurant, and a snack bar. The springs are open daily from early March to late October; admission is $11 for adults, $8 for children ages 4 to 12, and $3 for children 3 and under. A 4.5-mile loop trail leads from the hot springs to **Sol Duc Falls,** which are among the most photographed falls in the park.

THE WEST SIDE

The western regions of Olympic National Park can be roughly divided into two sections—the rugged coastal strip and the famous rainforest valleys. Of course, these are the rainiest areas within the park, and many a visitor has called short a vacation here because of rain. Well, what do you expect? It is, after all, a *rainforest.* Come prepared to get wet.

Located just outside the northwest corner of the park on U.S. 101, the timber town of Forks serves as the gateway to Olympic National Park's west side. It is the largest community in this northwest corner of the Olympic Peninsula. For more information on the Forks area, contact the **Forks Chamber of Commerce,** 1411 S. Forks Ave. (P.O. Box 1249), Forks, WA 98331 (© 800/443-6757 or 360/374-2531; www.forkswa.com). The Forks area is home to quite a few artists' studios and galleries. You can pick up an **Olympic West Arttrek** guide and map to these studios and galleries at the chamber office.

Just west of Forks is the first place you can drive to the Pacific Ocean. At the end of a spur road you come to the **Quileute Indian Reservation** and the community of La Push. Right in town there's a beach at the mouth of the Quillayute River; however, before you reach La Push, you'll see signs for **Third Beach** and **Second Beach,** which are two of the prettiest beaches on the peninsula. Third Beach is a 1.5-mile walk and Second Beach is just over half a mile from the trail head. **Rialto Beach,** just north of La Push, is another beautiful and rugged beach; it's reached from a turnoff east of La Push. On any of these beaches, keep an eye out for bald eagles, seals, and sea lions.

HOH RIVER VALLEY & RUBY BEACH

Roughly 8 miles south of Forks is the turnoff for the Hoh River Valley. It's 17 miles up this side road to the **Hoh Rain Forest Visitor Center** (© 360/374-6925), campground, and trail heads. This valley receives an average of 140 inches of rain per year—and as much as 190 inches per year—making it the wettest region in the continental United States. At the visitor center, you can learn all about the natural forces that cause this tremendous rainfall.

To see the effect of so much rain on the landscape, walk the .8-mile **Hall of Mosses Trail,** where the trees (primarily Sitka spruce, western red cedar, and western hemlock) tower 200 feet tall. Here you'll see big-leaf maple trees with limbs draped in thick carpets of mosses. If you're up for a longer walk, try the **Spruce Nature Trail.** If you've come with a backpack, there's no better way to see the park and its habitats than by hiking the **Hoh River Trail,** which is 17 miles long and leads to Glacier Meadows and Blue Glacier on the flanks of Mount Olympus. A herd of elk calls the Hoh Valley home and can sometimes be seen along these trails.

Continuing south on U.S. 101, but before crossing the Hoh River, you'll come to a secondary road (Oil City Rd.) that heads west from the Hoh Oxbow campground. From the end of the road, it's a hike of less than a mile to a rocky beach at the **mouth of the Hoh River.** You're likely to see sea lions or harbor seals feeding just offshore here, and to the north are several haystack rocks that are nesting sites for numerous seabirds. Primitive camping is permitted on this beach, and from here backpackers can continue hiking for 17 miles north along a pristine wilderness of rugged headlands and secluded beaches.

U.S. 101 finally reaches the coast at **Ruby Beach,** noted for its pink sand. The highway parallels the wave-swept coastline for another 17 miles. Along this stretch are pull-offs and short trails down to six numbered beaches. Near the south end, you'll find Kalaloch Lodge, which also has a gas station, and the **Kalaloch Ranger Station** (② **360/962-2283**), which is usually open only in summer.

Shortly beyond Kalaloch, the highway turns inland again, passing through the community of **Queets** on the river of the same name. If you'd like to do some rainy valley hiking away from the crowds, head up the gravel road to the **Queets campground** to find the trail leading up the valley.

A long stretch of clear-cuts and tree farms, mostly on the Quinault Indian Reservation, will bring you to **Lake Quinault.** Surrounded by forested mountains, this deep lake offers boating and freshwater fishing as well as more rainforests to explore. This is also a good area for spotting Roosevelt elk.

OUTDOOR ADVENTURES & GUIDED TOURS

With its rugged beaches, rainforest valleys, Alpine meadows, and mountaintop glaciers, the park offers a variety of **hiking** opportunities. Day hikes, overnight trips, and longer backpacking trips are all possible. For several of the most popular backpacking destinations in Olympic National Park (the Ozette Coast Loop, Grand Valley, Royal Basin, Badger Valley, Flapjack Lakes, and Lake Constance), advance-reservation hiking permits are required or highly recommended between May 1 and September 30 and can be made up to 30 days in advance. Reservations can be made by contacting the **Wilderness Information Center** (② **360/565-3100**). If you'd like to have a llama carry your gear, contact **Kit's Llamas,** P.O. Box 116, Olalla, WA 98359 (② **253/857-5274;** www.northolympic.com/llamas).

If you want to hire a guide to take you out on the rivers to where the park's big salmon and steelhead are biting, try **Sol Duc River Lodge Guide Service** (② **866/868-0128** or 360/327-3709; www.solducriverfishing.com). If you're more interested in heading out on open water to do a bit of salmon or deep-sea fishing, numerous charter boats operate out of Sekiu and Neah Bay. In Neah Bay, try **King Fisher Charters** (② **888/622-8216;** www.kingfisherenterprises.com). Expect to pay from $140 to $180 per person for a day of fishing.

Olympic Raft & Kayak (② **888/452-1443** or 360/452-1443; www.raftandkayak.com) offers sea-kayak tours on Freshwater Bay and Lake Aldwell, and at Dungeness National Wildlife Refuge.

WHERE TO STAY
IN & AROUND PORT ANGELES

As the peninsula's biggest town and a base for families exploring the national park, Port Angeles abounds in budget hotels. You'll find dozens along U.S. 101 east of downtown.

Beyond town, accommodations are scarce, and those places worth recommending tend to be popular. It's wise to reserve before heading west from Port Angeles.

Domaine Madeleine, 146 Wildflower Lane, 7 miles east of Port Angeles (𝒞 **888/811-8376** or 360/457-4174; www.domainemadeleine.com), is a secluded B&B with a waterfront setting. Rooms are in several different buildings surrounded by colorful gardens, and all have views of the Strait of Juan de Fuca and the mountains beyond. All units have fireplaces and VCRs; four have whirlpool tubs. Rates ($160–$265 double) include full breakfast.

The historic **Lake Crescent Lodge,** 416 Lake Crescent Rd. (𝒞 **360/928-3211;** www.lakecrescentlodge.com), 20 miles west of Port Angeles on picturesque Lake Crescent, contains rustic wood paneling, a stone fireplace, and a sunroom. Rooms in the main lodge are the oldest, with shared bathrooms. More modern motel-style rooms and cottages are available, some with fireplaces and all with a lake or mountain view. None of the rooms have phones, but the lodge does offer free Wi-Fi access. The lodge features a dining room, a lobby lounge, and rowboat rentals. Rates run $68 to $85 for a double without bathroom, $106 to $145 for a double with bathroom, and $132 to $211 for a cottage.

Long a popular family vacation spot, the **Sol Duc Hot Springs Resort,** Sol Duc Road (𝒞 **866/4-SOLDUC;** www.visitsolduc.com), 40 miles west of Port Angeles, attracts campers, day-trippers, and resort guests to its three hot spring–fed swimming pools. The grounds are grassy and open, but the forest is at arm's reach. The modern cabins are comfortable if not spacious. There's an excellent restaurant, a poolside deli, an espresso bar, a grocery store, and massage service. Closed late October to early March. Rates run from $125 to $155 for a cabin for two.

IN THE FORKS AREA

The town of Forks has several inexpensive motels and is a good place to look if you happen to be out this way without a reservation.

Perched on a bluff above the thundering Pacific Ocean, the **Kalaloch Lodge,** 157151 U.S. 101 (𝒞 **866/525-2562;** www.visitkalaloch.com), 35 miles south of Forks, has a breathtaking setting and is the national park's only waterfront hotel. Rooms in the old cedar-shingled lodge are the least expensive, but the oceanview bluff cabins are the most in demand. For modern comforts, there are motel-like rooms in the Sea Crest House. You'll find a coffee shop, dining room, general store, and gas station. Book at least 4 months ahead. Rates run from $149 to $159 for a double and $169 to $279 for a cabin in season.

Set on Lake Quinault in the southwest corner of the park, **Lake Quinault Lodge,** 345 South Shore Rd., Quinault (𝒞 **800/562-6672** or 360/288-2900; www.visitlakequinault.com), is the grande dame of the Olympic Peninsula. It possesses an ageless tranquillity, with towering firs and cedars shading the rustic lodge and deck. Some rooms have balconies or fireplaces, but none have TVs or phones. There's a dining room, an indoor pool, a sauna, lawn games, boat rentals, and massages. Rates run from $81 to $196 double.

WHERE TO CAMP

In addition to the lodgings listed here, there are numerous campgrounds in or near Olympic National Park. For general information on national park campgrounds, contact **Olympic National Park** (𝒞 **360/565-3130**). Make reservations by contacting the **National Park Reservation Service** (𝒞 **800/365-2267** or 301/722-1257; http://reservations.nps.gov).

The national park's **Heart o' the Hills Campground** (105 campsites), on Hurricane Ridge Road 5 miles south of the Olympic National Park Visitor Center, is the most convenient campground for exploring the Hurricane Ridge area. On Olympic Hot Springs Road up the Elwha River, you'll find both **Elwha Campground** (40 campsites) and **Altaire Campground** (30 campsites). The only campground on Lake Crescent is **Fairholm** (88 campsites), at the west end of the lake. The nearby **Sol Duc Campground** (82 campsites), set amid impressive stands of old-growth trees, is adjacent to the Sol Duc Hot Springs. The national park's remote **Ozette Campground** (15 campsites), on the north shore of Lake Ozette, is a good choice for people wanting to day-hike out to the beaches on either side of Cape Alava.

The national park's **Mora Campground** (94 campsites) is on beautiful Rialto Beach at the mouth of the Quillayute River west of Forks. If you want to say you've camped at the wettest campground in the contiguous United States, head for the park's **Hoh Campground** (88 campsites), in the Hoh River Valley. South of the Hoh River, along the only stretch of U.S. 101 right on the beach, you'll find **Kalaloch Campground** (175 campsites), the national park's largest campground and the only one that takes reservations.

WHERE TO DINE

The casual **Bella Italia,** 118 E. First St. (© **360/457-5442;** www.bellaitaliapa.com), is located in the basement of a natural foods store in downtown Port Angeles and serves reliable Italian food. Local seafood makes it onto the menu in a few places, including smoked salmon ravioli and steamed mussels and clams. There are also some interesting individual pizzas, a good selection of wines, and plenty of excellent Italian desserts. Main courses cost $8 to $28.

You can't miss the strikingly painted **C'est Si Bon,** 23 Cedar Park Rd. (© **360/452-8888;** www.cestsibon-frenchcuisine.com), 4 miles south of Port Angeles off U.S. 101. Inside, you'll find classic decor, European artwork, chandeliers, and deftly prepared Gallic standards such as French onion soup and escargot. Whatever you have, it will likely be tasty and fresh. Main courses run $24 to $36.

On the west side of Port Angeles, your best bets are inside the dining rooms and restaurants of the hotels listed in "Where to Stay," above.

4 Mount Rainier National Park

At 14,410 feet, Mount Rainier is the highest point in Washington, and to the sun-starved residents of Seattle, the dormant volcano is a giant weather gauge. Either "the Mountain" is out and the weather is good, or it isn't (out or good). And when the Mountain is out, all eyes turn to admire its broad slopes, which remain snow-covered year-round. The region's infamous moisture-laden air has made Mount Rainier one of the snowiest spots in the country; record snowfalls have created numerous glaciers on the mountain's flanks, and one of these, the Carbon Glacier, is the lowest-elevation glacier in the continental United States.

Snow and glaciers notwithstanding, Rainier has a heart of fire. Steam vents at the mountain's summit are evidence that, although this volcanic peak has been dormant for more than 150 years, it could erupt again at any time. However, scientists believe that Rainier's volcanic activity occurs in 3,000-year cycles—and luckily we have another 500 years to go before there's another big eruption.

ESSENTIALS

For advance information, contact **Mount Rainier National Park,** Tahoma Woods, Star Route, Ashford, WA 98304-9751 (© **360/569-2211,** ext. 3314; www.nps.gov/mora). We recommend visiting the park as early in the day as possible, especially on summer weekends, when traffic and crowds can be daunting. Keep in mind that during the winter, only the Henry M. Jackson Memorial Visitor Center at Paradise is open, and then only on weekends and holidays. Park entrances other than the Nisqually entrance are closed by snow throughout the winter.

The entry fee to Mount Rainier National Park is $15 per motor vehicle or $5 per person for pedestrians, motorcyclists, and bicyclists.

EXPLORING THE PARK

Just past the main southwest (Nisqually) entrance, you'll come to **Longmire,** site of the National Park Inn, the Longmire Museum (with exhibits on the park's natural and human history), a hiker information center that issues backcountry permits, and a ski-touring center where you can rent cross-country skis and snowshoes in winter.

The road then climbs to **Paradise** (elevation 5,400 ft.), the aptly named mountainside aerie that affords a breathtaking close-up view of the mountain. Paradise, 110 miles southeast of Seattle and 150 miles northeast of Portland, is the park's most popular destination, so expect crowds. In July and August, the meadows here are ablaze with wildflowers. The circular **Henry M. Jackson Memorial Visitor Center** provides 360-degree panoramic views, and includes exhibits on the flora, fauna, and geology of the park, as well as a display on mountain climbing. (*Note:* It's not unusual to find plenty of snow at Paradise as late as July. In 1972, the area set a world's record for snowfall in 1 year: 94 ft.!)

A 1.2-mile walk from the visitor center leads to a spot from which you can look down on the **Nisqually Glacier.** Many miles of other trails lead out from Paradise, looping through meadows and up onto snowfields above timberline.

In summer, you can continue beyond Paradise to the **Ohanapecosh Visitor Center,** where you can walk through a forest of old-growth trees, some more than 1,000 years old.

Continuing around the mountain, you'll reach the turnoff for **Sunrise.** At 6,400 feet, Sunrise is the highest spot in the park accessible by car, and a beautiful old log lodge serves as the visitor center. From here you can see not only Mount Rainier, seemingly at arm's length, but also Mount Baker and Mount Adams. Some of the park's most scenic trails begin here at Sunrise. This area is usually less crowded than Paradise.

If you want to avoid the crowds and see a bit of dense old-growth forest, head for the park's **Carbon River entrance** in the northwest corner. This is the least visited region of the park because it offers views only to those willing to hike several miles uphill. At 3 miles, there's a glacier plowing through the middle of the rainforest, and at about 5 miles, you reach meadows and in-your-face views of the northwest flank of Mount Rainier. The road into this area is in bad shape and has washed out twice in recent years. Currently, high-clearance vehicles are recommended, but regular passenger vehicles have been getting through by driving very slowly.

OUTDOOR ACTIVITIES

Hikers have more than 240 miles of trails to explore within the park. The 5-mile **Skyline Trail** is the highest trail at Paradise and climbs above the tree line, with views of Mount Adams, Mount St. Helens, and the Nisqually Glacier. The **Lakes Trail,** of similar length, heads downhill to the Reflection Lakes, which have picture-perfect views of the mountain reflected in their waters. The park's single most memorable low-elevation hike is the **Grove of the Patriarchs Trail.** This 1.5-mile round-trip trail is fairly flat (good for kids) and leads through a forest of huge old trees to a grove of 1,000-year-old red cedars on an island in the Ohanapecosh River. The trail head for this hike is near the Steven Canyon park entrance (southeast entrance).

If you'd like to do some horseback riding, contact **EZ Times Trail Rides,** 18703 Wash. 706, in Elbe (© **360/569-2449**); or **Indian Creek Corral,** east of White Pass on U.S. 12 near the shore of Rimrock Lake (© **509/672-2400**). Expect to pay around $20 to $25 for a 1-hour ride, $40 for 2 hours.

In winter, miles of trails are open for **snowshoeing** and **cross-country skiing,** but there is limited access because of road closures. At Longmire, you'll find a **rental shop** at the National Park Inn (© **360/569-2411**) with skis and snowshoes. There are also guided snowshoe walks at Paradise. Just outside the northeast corner of the park, off Wash. 410, **Crystal Mountain** (© **360/663-2265** for information, or 888/754-6199 for snow conditions; www.skicrystal.com) is the state's best all-around downhill ski area. Experienced backcountry skiers will also find some challenging cross-country skiing here at Crystal Mountain. Call for hours and current lift-ticket prices.

WHERE TO STAY & CAMP

Currently, Paradise Inn, the national park's premiere historic lodge, is closed for a major restoration and rehabilitation. The lodge is scheduled to reopen for the 2008 summer season. Until then, your only options within the park are the inn listed below and several **campgrounds.** Two of these—Cougar Rock and Ohanapecosh—take reservations, which should be made several months in advance for summer weekends. To make reservations, contact the **National Park Reservation Service** (© **800/365-2267** or 301/722-1257; http://reservations.nps.gov).

The 25-room **National Park Inn** (© **360/569-2275**) is in Longmire, at the southwest corner of the park. The inn's front veranda does have a view of the mountain, and guests often gather here at sunset on clear days. Because this lodge stays open year-round, it's popular with cross-country skiers. Guest rooms vary in size and contain rustic furnishings, but are definitely not the most memorable part of a stay here. Rates ($100 double with shared bathroom; $134–$185 double with private bathroom) from late October to late April include breakfast.

5 Mount St. Helens National Volcanic Monument

Mount St. Helens was once considered the most perfect of the Cascade peaks, a snow-covered cone rising above lush forests. Then on May 18, 1980, a violent eruption blew out the side of the volcano and removed the top 1,300 feet of the peak, causing the largest landslide in history. More than 540 million tons of ash traveled nearly 16 miles into the atmosphere, raining down as far away as Denver, and laid waste to the immediate area. Although today the volcano is quiet and life has returned to the once devastated landscape, this volcano and much of the land surrounding it has been designated the Mount St. Helens National Volcanic Monument.

ESSENTIALS

The monument is located roughly 160 miles south of Seattle, off I-5 (take the Castle Rock exit). Admission to one monument visitor center is $3 for adults; to two or more visitor centers, it's $6 for adults. If you just want to park at one of the monument's trail heads and go for a hike, all you need is a valid Northwest Forest Pass, which costs $5 per day. In winter you'll need a Sno-Park permit, which costs $8 to $9 per day. For more information, contact **Mount St. Helens National Volcanic Monument (© 360/449-7800;** www.fs.fed.us/gpnf/mshnvm).

EXPLORING THE PARK

The best place to begin is the **Mount St. Helens Silver Lake Visitor Center** at Silver Lake, 5 miles east of Castle Rock on Wash. 504 (© **360/274-0962;** www.parks.wa.gov/mountsthelens.asp), which houses extensive exhibits on the eruption and its effects on the region. Before reaching this center, you can stop and watch a 28-minute, 70mm film about the eruption at the **Mount St. Helens Cinedome Theater (© 360/274-9844;** www.thecinedome.com), at Exit 49 off I-5; tickets cost $6 for adults, $5 for seniors and children.

Continuing east, you'll come to the **Hoffstadt Bluffs Visitor Center,** at milepost 27 (© **360/274-7750;** www.mt-st-helens.com), which has a snack bar and is home to the takeoff site for 25-minute helicopter flights over Mount St. Helens ($129 with a three-person minimum). Just past milepost 33, you'll reach the **Charles W. Bingham Forest Learning Center** (© **360/414-3439**), open mid-May through mid-October. This is primarily a promotional center for the timber industry; in a theater designed to resemble an ash-covered landscape, you can watch a short, fascinating video about the eruption. Outside either of these centers you can usually see numerous elk on the floor of the Toutle River valley far below.

The **Coldwater Ridge Visitor Center,** at milepost 47 on Wash. 504 (© **360/274-2114**), only 8 miles from the crater, features interpretive displays on the events leading up to the eruption and the subsequent slow regeneration of life around the volcano. You'll also find a picnic area, interpretive trail, restaurant, and boat launch at Coldwater Lake.

The **Johnston Ridge Observatory** (© 360/274-2140), is 10 miles past the Coldwater Ridge Visitor Center. This observatory houses the equipment currently used to monitor activity within Mount St. Helens. The view from here is stupendous. The observatory is open daily from early May to October. The best trail on this side of the monument is the **Boundary Ridge Trail,** which heads east from the Johnson Ridge Observatory.

Drive around to the monument's east side for a close-up view of how the eruption affected the surrounding lands. For the best views, take U.S. 12 east from Exit 68 off I-5. In Randle, head south on Local Route 25 and then take Local Route 26. The **Woods Creek Information Station,** on Route 25 just before the junction with Route 26, has information on this part of the monument. At Meta Lake, Route 26 joins Route 99, which continues to the **Windy Ridge Viewpoint,** where visitors get their closest look at the crater. Below Windy Ridge lies Spirit Lake, which was once one of the most popular summer vacation spots in the Washington Cascades. Today the lake is desolate and lifeless.

On the south side of the monument, you can explore the **Ape Cave,** a 2-mile lava tube formed 1,900 years ago when lava poured from the volcano. At Ape Headquarters, open from late June to early September, you can join a regular ranger-led exploration of the cave or rent a lantern to explore on your own.

WHERE TO STAY & CAMP

You'll find nearly a dozen campgrounds near the monument. For reservations at state campgrounds, contact **Washington State Parks Reservations** (© **888/226-7688;** www.parks.wa.gov). For information on national forest campgrounds in the area, contact the **Cowlitz Valley Ranger District,** 10024 U.S. 12 (P.O. Box 670), Randle (© **360/ 497-1100**). For national forest campground reservations, contact the **National Recreation Reservation Service** (© **800/280-CAMP;** www.reserveusa.com).

Blue Heron Inn Bed & Breakfast, 2846 Spirit Lake Hwy., Castle Rock (© **800/ 959-4049** or 360/274-9595; www.blueheroninn.com), is a modern B&B on the road to the Coldwater and Johnston Ridge visitor centers. It has an excellent view of Mount St. Helens and is by far the best choice for accommodations in the area. Rates run $159 to $205 double.

6 Portland

Situated at the confluence of the Willamette and Columbia rivers, Portland is a city of discreet charms. Strolling through the tranquil Japanese Garden on a misty May morning; people-watching at Pioneer Courthouse Square; perusing the acres of books at Powell's; shopping for arts and crafts at the Saturday Market; beer sampling at one of the many brewpubs; kayaking around Ross Island; or leaving the city for a quick trip to the beach or Oregon wine country—these are the quintessential Portland experiences to seek out and savor.

ESSENTIALS

GETTING THERE   By Plane   Portland International Airport (PDX; © **877/ 739-4636** or 503/460-4040; www.flypdx.com) is 10 miles northeast of downtown, adjacent to the Columbia River. Many hotels near the airport provide courtesy shuttle service; be sure to ask when you make a reservation.

If you're driving to central Portland from the airport, follow signs for downtown, which will take you first onto **I-205** and then **I-84** west. Take the Morrison Bridge exit to cross the Willamette River. The trip into town takes about 20 minutes.

If you haven't rented a car at the airport, the best way to get into town is to take the **Airport MAX (Red Line)** light-rail system, which operates daily every 15 minutes between 5am and midnight (11:30pm on Sun) and takes about 40 minutes to make the trip from the airport to downtown Portland. The fare is $2. For information on this service, contact **TriMet** (© **503/238-7433;** www.trimet.org).

A taxi to downtown generally costs between $20 and $25.

By Train   Amtrak (© **800/872-7245;** www.amtrak.com) serves **Union Station,** 800 NW Sixth Ave., about 10 blocks from the heart of downtown, with daily service from Seattle (trip time: 3½ hr.), Spokane (8 hr.), Chicago (37 hr.), Oakland (19 hr.), and Los Angeles (31 hr.).

By Car   The major routes into Portland are **I-5** from the north (Seattle) and south (Sacramento), and **I-84** from the east (Boise). **I-405** arcs around the west and south of downtown; **I-205** bypasses the city to the east; and **U.S. 26** runs west to the coast.

VISITOR INFORMATION   The **Portland Oregon Visitors Association (POVA) Information Center,** 701 SW Sixth Ave., Portland, OR 97205 (© **877/678-5263** or 503/275-8355; www.travelportland.com), is underneath Pioneer Courthouse Square near Starbucks. Hours are Monday through Friday from 8:30am to 5:30pm and Saturday from 10am to 4pm. There are also two information booths in the baggage-claim area at Portland Airport.

GETTING AROUND   City blocks in Portland are about half the size of average blocks elsewhere, and because the entire downtown area covers only about 15×32 blocks, it's easy to explore on foot. Because the city is committed to keeping this area uncongested, it has invested heavily in its public transportation system. **TriMet public buses,** the **MAX (Metropolitan Area Express) light-rail system,** and the **Portland Streetcar** are all free within Fareless Square, the area between I-405 on the south and west, Hoyt Street on the north, and the Willamette River on the east. There is also a Fareless Square extension that allows free rides across the Willamette River (on buses and the MAX) to the Lloyd Center area, which is the site of a large shopping mall, the Portland Convention Center, and the Rose Garden arena.

Outside Fareless Square, adult fares on both TriMet buses and MAX are $1.70 or $2, depending on distance. A $4.25 all-day ticket, available from any MAX ticket-vending machine or bus driver, is good for travel to all zones and is valid on buses, streetcars, and MAX. Transfers between the bus, the streetcar, and MAX are free. Pick up bus route and schedule information at the **TriMet Customer Assistance Office** (② **503/238-7433;** www.trimet.org), behind the waterfall fountain at Pioneer Courthouse Square, open Monday through Friday from 8:30am to 5:30pm. The Portland Streetcar runs from the waterfront south of downtown, through downtown and the trendy Pearl District, to the Northwest shopping and restaurant district. It costs $1.75 outside of Fareless Square.

Because Portland is fairly compact, getting around by taxi is not prohibitively expensive. Wait at a taxi stand at one of the major hotels, or call **Broadway Cab** (② **503/227-1234**) or **Radio Cab** (② **503/227-1212**). Fares are $2.50 for the first mile, $1.80 for each additional mile, and $1 for additional passengers.

FAST FACTS Three conveniently located area hospitals are Legacy Good Samaritan, 1015 NW 22nd Ave. (② **503/413-7711**); Providence Portland Medical Center, 4805 NE Glisan St. (② **503/215-1111**); and the Oregon Health Sciences University Hospital, 3181 SW Sam Jackson Park Rd. (② **503/494-8311**), just southwest of the city center. If you need a physician referral, call the Medical Society of Metropolitan Portland (② **503/222-0156**).

A pharmacy convenient to most downtown hotels is **Central Drug,** 538 SW Fourth Ave. (② **503/226-2222**), open Monday through Friday from 9am to 6pm, Saturday from 10am to 4pm.

Portland is a relatively safe city. Take extra precautions, however, if you venture into the entertainment district along West Burnside Street or into Chinatown at night. If you plan to go hiking in Forest Park, don't leave anything valuable in your car. This holds true in the Skidmore Historic District (Old Town) as well.

Portland is a shopper's paradise—there's no sales tax. However, there is a 12.5% tax on hotel rooms in the city. (Outside the city limits, the room tax varies.) On car rentals, there is a 12.5% tax, and if you pick your car up at the airport, there is an additional airport concession fee of around 10%. You can avoid all of these car-rental taxes by renting your car over on the west side of the metro area in Beaverton, Tigard, or Hillsboro.

SPECIAL EVENTS & FESTIVALS Celebrated annually since 1888, the **Portland Rose Festival** (② **503/227-2681;** www.rosefestival.org) has blossomed into the city's biggest celebration. The festivities span 2½ weeks and include a rose show, two parades, a rose queen contest, an art festival, and dragon boat races. Most events take place during the first 2 weeks of June. Contact **Ticketmaster** (② **503/224-4400;** www.ticketmaster.com) for tickets to specific events.

The last full weekend in July brings the **Oregon Brewers Festival** (② **503/778-5917;** www.oregonbrewfest.com) to Tom McCall Waterfront Park. This is one of the country's largest festivals of independent craft brewers and features plenty of local and international microbrews, as well as food and music.

WHAT TO SEE & DO

Pioneer Courthouse Square, at the corner of Southwest Broadway and Yamhill Street, is the heart of downtown Portland and acts as an outdoor stage for everything from flower displays to protest rallies. The square, with its tumbling waterfall fountain and free-standing columns, is the city's favorite gathering spot, especially at noon when the Weather Machine, a mechanical sculpture, forecasts the weather for the upcoming 24 hours. Keep your eyes on the square's brick pavement for some surprising names.

A few blocks away, at 1120 SW Fifth Ave., stands *Portlandia,* the symbol of the city and the second-largest hammered bronze statue in the country, second only to the Statue of Liberty.

International Rose Test Garden Covering 4½ acres of hillside in the West Hills above downtown Portland and planted with nearly 8,000 rose bushes, this garden was established in 1917 and is one of the largest and oldest rose test gardens in the United States. The American Rose Society uses the garden as a testing ground for new varieties of roses. Although you will likely see some familiar roses in the Gold Medal Garden, most of the 400 varieties on display are new hybrids. These acres of roses give Portland its nickname: "City of Roses." Allow 1 hour.

400 SW Kingston Ave., Washington Park. ℂ **503/823-3636.** Free admission (donations accepted). Daily 7:30am–9pm. Bus: 63.

Japanese Garden *Best* Considered the finest example of a Japanese garden in North America, Portland's Japanese Garden is one of the city's most popular attractions. Don't miss it. There are five different styles of Japanese gardens scattered over 5½ acres, and a view of volcanic Mount Hood, which has a strong resemblance to Mount Fuji. This is a very tranquil spot and is even more peaceful on rainy days when the crowds stay away, so don't pass up a visit just because it's drizzling. Many special events, exhibits, and demonstrations are held here throughout the year. Allow 2 hours.

611 Kingston Ave. (in Washington Park). ℂ **503/223-1321.** www.japanesegarden.com. Admission $8 adults, $6.25 seniors, $5.25 students, free for children under 6. Apr–Sept Mon noon–7pm, Tues–Sun 10am–7pm; Oct–Mar Mon noon–4pm, Tues–Sun 10am–4pm. Closed Thanksgiving, Christmas, and New Year's Day. Bus: 63. MAX: Washington Park Station (late May to Sept, take the shuttle bus).

Oregon Historical Society If you're going to explore the state, this museum is a great introduction to Oregon. The state's history, from before the arrival of the first Europeans to contemporary times, is chronicled in fascinating exhibits including "Oregon my Oregon," which utilizes two theaters and lots of interactive displays to make the state's history accessible. Temporary exhibits change frequently and might include a display of contemporary art by Oregon artists or a traveling exhibit on loan from the Smithsonian Institution. Museum docents are often on hand to answer questions. Allow 2 hours.

1200 SW Park Ave. ℂ **503/222-1741.** www.ohs.org. Admission $10 adults, $8 seniors and students, $5 youths 6–18, free for children under 6. Mon–Sat 10am–5pm. Bus: 63. MAX: Library Station. Portland Streetcar: Art Museum (northbound); 11th Ave. and Jefferson St. (southbound).

Oregon Museum of Science and Industry (OMSI) Located on the east bank of the Willamette River, this modern science museum has six huge halls filled with exhibits aimed at youngsters but often of interest to adults as well. This is a hands-on museum, and the motion simulator and tornado-like air vortex are perennial favorites.

Portland

NW Upshur St.
NW Upshur St.
NW Thurman St.
NW Thurman St.
Fremont Bridge

NW Savier St.
NW Raleigh St.
NW Quimby St.

NW 27th Ave.
NW 26th Ave.
NW 25th Ave.
NW 24th Ave.

NW Pettygrove St.
NW Overton St.
1 **2** NW Northrup St.

NW Cornell Rd.
NW Westover Rd.

Main Post Office

NORTHWEST

NW Marshall St.
NW Lovejoy St.
NW Kearney St.
NW Johnson St.
NW Irving St.
NW Hoyt St.

NW Albemarle
NW Melinda

NOB HILL

NW Westover Rd.

NW 23rd Ave.
NW 22nd Ave.
NW 21st Ave.
NW 20th Ave.
NW Trinity Pl.
NW 19th Ave.
NW 18th Ave.

405

NW Glisan St.
NW Flanders St.

PEARL DISTRICT

NW Everett St.
NW Davis St.
NW Couch St.

NW 9th Ave.
NW Park Ave.
NW 8th Ave.

NW Maywood Dr.
Tichner Dr.

W. Burnside St.

Lewis & Clark Cir.

W. Burnside St.

SW Washington St.
SW Alder St

6

7

SW Vista Ave.
SW Clair St.
SW Park Pl.
King Ave.

SW 20th Ave.
SW 19th Ave.
SW 18th Ave.
SW 17th Ave.
SW 16th Ave.
SW 15th Ave.
SW 14th Ave.

Pioneer Courthouse Square

SW Morrison St.
SW Yamhill St.
SW Taylor St.
SW Salmon St.

SW Main St.
SW Kings Ct.
SW Madison Dr.

SW Main
Madison St.

SW Broadway
SW 6th Ave.

5

SW Kingston Ave.
SW Sacajawea Blvd.
SW Rutland
Sherwood Blvd

SW Market St. Dr.

Portland Art Museum

Oregon Historical Society

Japanese Garden

International Rose Test Garden

TUNNEL

26

4 SW Jefferson St.

SW Columbia St.

DOWNTOWN SW

WASHINGTON PARK
Kingston Dr.

26 Sunset Hwy.

SW Montgomery Dr.
SW Carter Lane
Harrison St.
SW Upper Hall St.
SW Jackson
SW College St.

SW Market St.
SW Clay St.
SW Mill St.
SW Montgomery St.
SW Harrison St.

SW 11th Ave.
SW 10th Ave.

To Oregon Zoo

ⓘ Information
✉ Post Office
Fareless Square

SW Montgomery Dr.
SW Vista Ave.
SW Clifton
SW Myrtle St.
SW Laurel St.
SW Elm St.
SW Spring St.

SW Cardinell Dr.
SW Rivington Dr.
SW Clifton

PORTLAND STATE UNIVERSITY

SW Hall St.
SW College St.
SW Jackson St.
SW Lincoln St.

3

0   1/2 mi
0   0.5 km

N

★ **Portland**
★ Salem

OREGON

ACCOMMODATIONS ■

The Benson **7**
Embassy Suites Portland Downtown **10**
Inn @ Northrup Station **1**
Hotel Lucia **8**

Hotel Vintage Plaza **9**
The Lion and the Rose **14**
McMenamins Edgefield **1**
RiverPlace Hotel **11**

DINING ◆

Caprial's Bistro and Wine **13**

Chart House **3**

Genoa **16**

Higgins **4**

Jake's Famous Crawfish **6**

Newport Bay RiverPlace Marina **12**

Southpark Seafood Grill & Wine Bar **5**

Wildwood **2**

Hitting the Water

If you want to check out the Portland skyline from water level, arrange for a sea-kayak tour through the **Portland River Company,** 0315 SW Montgomery St. (✆ **888/238-2059** or 503/229-0551; www.portlandrivercompany.com). A 2½-hour tour ($43) circles nearby Ross Island. The company also rents sea kayaks for independent use and offers raft trips.

The museum also has an OMNIMAX theater and the Kendall Planetarium, which features laser-light shows and astronomy presentations. The USS *Blueback* submarine is docked here, and tours are given daily. Allow 2 to 3 hours.

1945 SE Water Ave. ✆ **800/955-6674** or 503/797-6674. www.omsi.edu. $9 adults, $7 seniors and children 3–13; $8.50 adults, $6.50 seniors and children OMNIMAX shows; $5.50 submarine tours, planetarium shows, or laser light show matinees; $7.50 evening laser light shows; $4 motion simulator; discounted combination tickets available. Mid-June to Labor Day daily 9:30am–7pm; the rest of the year Tues–Sun 9:30am–5:30pm (open holiday Mon). Closed Dec 25. Bus: 33.

Oregon Zoo   The Oregon Zoo is best known for its large breeding herd of elephants. It also has an excellent Africa exhibit, which includes a rainforest and a savanna. The Cascade Crest exhibit includes mountain goats, while the Steller Cove exhibit has endangered sea lions and sea otters. The Eagle Canyon exhibit focuses on eagles and salmon, and the Amazon Flooded Forest displays everything from poisonous dart frogs to two-toed sloths. In the summer, there are outdoor concerts. A scaled-down train connects the zoo with the International Rose Test Garden and the Japanese Garden.

4001 SW Canyon Rd., Washington Park. ✆ **503/226-1561**. www.oregonzoo.org. Admission $9.50 adults, $8 seniors, $6.50 children ages 3–11, free for children under 3; $2 admission for all on 2nd Tues of each month. Apr 15–Sept 15 daily 9am–6pm; Sept 16–Apr 14 daily 9am–4pm. Closed Dec 25. Bus: 63. MAX: Washington Park Station.

Portland Art Museum   This oldest art museum in the Northwest added a new wing in 2005 that gives the museum much more space for displaying its collection of modern and contemporary art. This collection begins with European Impressionists and moves right up to the present. Although the museum also has respectable collections of European, Asian, and American art, the best reason to visit is to see the extensive collection of Native American art and artifacts. There's also a good collection of Northwest contemporary art. Blockbuster exhibits often stop here.

1219 SW Park Ave. ✆ **503/226-2811**. www.portlandartmuseum.org. Admission $10 adults, $9 seniors, $6 ages 5–18, free for children under 5. Tues–Wed and Sat 10am–5pm; Thurs–Fri 10am–8pm; Sun noon–5pm. Bus: 4, 6, or 63. MAX: Library Station. Portland Streetcar: Art Museum (northbound); 11th Ave. and Jefferson St. (southbound).

Portland Classical Chinese Garden   With its rare plants and unusual imported limestone rocks, this classically styled Chinese garden is designed to evoke the wild mountains of China. The garden, located in Portland's Chinatown, takes up an entire city block and is surrounded by walls that separate the tranquil, timeless Chinese oasis from the buzz of 21st-century urban life that surrounds it. To fully appreciate this garden, quietly stroll the winding paths, stop in the many viewing pavilions, and gaze at the reflections in the garden's tiny lake. It's easy to imagine that you have been transported to China. Try to visit as soon as the gardens open in the morning, before the crowds descend and the guided tours start circulating; also be sure to stop and have a cup of tea and maybe a snack in the garden's tearoom. Allow 2 hours.

NW. Everett St. and NW Third Ave. ℂ **503/228-8131.** www.portlandchinesegarden.org. Admission $7 adults, $6 seniors, $5.50 students, free for children 5 and under. Apr–Oct daily 9am–6pm; Nov–Mar daily 10am–5pm. Bus: 1, 4, 5, 8, 10, 16, 33, 40, or 77. MAX: Skidmore Fountain.

Portland Saturday Market   For decades, the Northwest has attracted artists and craftspeople, and on Saturday and Sunday throughout most of the year, hundreds of them can be found selling their creations at this outdoor market. Most of the art and crafts sold here are fairly inexpensive and small enough to fit into a suitcase. These days the market seems to appeal primarily to teenagers and 20-somethings. There are also food vendors and performances by local bands.

108 W. Burnside St. (underneath the west end of the Burnside Bridge between SW First Ave. and SW Naito Pkwy). ℂ **503/222-6072.** www.portlandsaturdaymarket.com. Free admission. 1st weekend in Mar to Christmas Eve, Sat 10am–5pm, Sun 11am–4:30pm. Bus: 12, 19, or 20. MAX: Skidmore Fountain.

SHOPPING
The blocks around **Pioneer Courthouse Square** are Portland's main upscale shopping streets. Here you'll find Nordstrom, Saks Fifth Avenue, the upscale Pioneer Place shopping mall, and numerous boutiques. The city's prettiest shopping area is the **Nob Hill/Northwest** neighborhood along Northwest 23rd Avenue beginning at West Burnside Street. Here you'll find block after block of interesting boutiques. For art galleries and shops with a hip, urban aesthetic, head to the **Pearl District,** which is north of West Burnside Street between Northwest 9th Avenue and Northwest 15th Avenue. For funkier shops, head out to the **Hawthorne District,** the city's main counterculture shopping area, on the east side of the Willamette River along Hawthorne Boulevard between 17th and 43rd avenues.

No visit to Portland is complete without a stop at the humongous **Powell's City of Books,** 1005 W. Burnside St. (ℂ **800/878-7323** or 503/228-4651; www.powells.com), the bookstore to end all bookstores. Covering an entire city block three floors deep, Powell's is unusual in that it shelves new and used books together. You can easily spend hours browsing here.

WHERE TO STAY
The largest concentration of hotels is downtown, which is the most convenient for visitors, and near the airport. Be sure to reserve as far in advance as possible. If you're having trouble booking a room, contact the **Portland Oregon Visitors Association** (ℂ **877/678-5263;** www.travelportland.com), which offers a reservations service for the Portland metro area as well as information on B&Bs.

The Benson   Built in 1912, The Benson exudes old-world sophistication and elegance. In the French baroque lobby, walnut paneling frames a marble fireplace, Austrian crystal chandeliers hang from the ornate plasterwork ceiling, and a marble staircase allows for grand entrances. These are the poshest digs in Portland, and guest rooms are luxuriously furnished in a plush Euro-luxe styling. Rooms vary considerably in size, but most of the deluxe kings are particularly spacious. The corner junior suites, which are large and have lots of windows, are the hotel's best deal. All the guest rooms have Tempur-Pedic mattresses.

309 SW Broadway, Portland, OR 97205. ℂ **888/523-6766** or 503/228-2000. Fax 503/471-3920. www.benson hotel.com. 287 units. $140–$230 double; $215–$280 junior suite; $500–$900 suite. AE, DC, DISC, MC, V. Valet parking $25. Pets accepted for $75 fee. **Amenities:** 2 restaurants; exercise room.

Embassy Suites Portland Downtown   Located in the restored 1912 Multnomah Hotel, the Embassy Suites rivals The Benson hotel for the plushness of its lobby. This is a historic hotel in the grand style, with gilded plasterwork and potted palms in the lobby. Units are primarily two-room suites with classically styled furnishings and lots of space, a rarity in downtown hotels. The location is only a couple of blocks from the waterfront and the Portland Saturday Market. You'll find everyone from couples to families to business travelers here.

319 SW Pine St., Portland, OR 97204-2726. ✆ **800/EMBASSY** or 503/279-9000. Fax 503/220-0206. www.embassy portland.com. 276 units. $139–$209 double. Rates include full breakfast. AE, DC, DISC, MC, V. Valet parking $22; self-parking $15. **Amenities:** Restaurant; indoor pool; spa. *In room:* Fridge, microwave.

Hotel Lucía   With guest rooms and public spaces decorated with colorful contemporary art and black-and-white photos by former White House photographer David Hume Kennerly, this is downtown Portland's only truly hip hotel, and it attracts stylish young visitors and business travelers. Guest rooms boast dreamy beds with luxurious down comforters and bathrooms with gorgeous modern sinks, Aveda toiletries, and bathrobes. Try to get one of the corner rooms, which have lots of big windows and a bit more space than other rooms. The location puts you within walking distance of most of the city's top attractions.

400 SW Broadway, Portland, OR 97205. ✆ **877/225-1717** or 503/225-1717. Fax 503/225-1919. www.hotellucia. com. 127 units. $189–$729 double. AE, DC, DISC, MC, V. Valet parking $24. Pets accepted ($35 fee). **Amenities:** Restaurant; exercise room.

Hotel Vintage Plaza   This 1894 National Historic Landmark hotel is the place to stay in Portland if you're a wine lover. A wine theme predominates in the decor, and there are complimentary evening tastings of Northwest wines. Although the standard rooms have much to recommend them (free Wi-Fi access, Aveda toiletries, bathrobes), the starlight rooms and bi-level suites are the real scene-stealers. The starlight rooms, though small, have greenhouse-style windows that provide romantic views at night and let in tons of light during the day. The bi-level suites, some with Japanese soaking tubs, are equally impressive.

422 SW Broadway, Portland, OR 97205. ✆ **800/263-2305** or 503/228-1212. Fax 503/228-3598. www.vintageplaza. com. 107 units. $139–$239 double; $189–$339 suite. Children under 18 stay free in parent's room. AE, DC, DISC, MC, V. Valet parking $25. Pets accepted. **Amenities:** Restaurant; exercise room.

Inn @ Northrup Station   This hotel in the trendy Nob Hill neighborhood is located on the Portland Streetcar line, which makes it convenient for exploring the city's most interesting neighborhoods. The colorful retro decor also sets this all-suite hotel apart from other hotels around town. If you appreciate bright colors and contemporary styling, this should be your first choice in town. Many of the suites here have full kitchens, and all have balconies and Wi-Fi access. The hotel's location in a quiet residential neighborhood is a plus, and the hotel is also within a few blocks of some of Portland's top restaurants.

2025 NW Northrup St., Portland, OR 97209. ✆ **800/224-1180** or 503/224-0543. Fax 503/273-2102. www.northrup station.com. 70 units. $109–$179 double. Rates include continental breakfast. Children under 12 stay free in parent's room. AE, DISC, MC, V. Free parking. *In room:* Kitchen (in some), fridge and microwave.

Lion and the Rose   This imposing Queen Anne–style Victorian inn is located in the Irvington District 1 block off Northeast Broadway, and restaurants, cafes, eclectic boutiques, and a huge shopping mall are all within 4 blocks. In the Lavonna Room, there's a turret sitting area, while in the Starina Room you'll find an imposing Edwardian bed and armoire. Both the Garden Room and the Lavonna Room's bathroom have claw-foot tubs. If you have problems climbing stairs, ask for the ground floor's Rose Room, which has a whirlpool tub.

1810 NE 15th Ave., Portland, OR 97212. © **800/955-1647** or 503/287-9245. Fax 503/287-9247. www.lionrose.com. 6 units. $119–$179 double. AE, DISC, MC, V. Children 10 and older welcome.

McMenamins Edgefield   Ideally situated for exploring the Columbia Gorge and Mount Hood, this flagship of the McMenamin microbrewery empire is the former Multnomah County poor farm. Today, the property includes not only tastefully decorated guest rooms with antique furnishings, but a brewery, a pub, a beer garden, a restaurant, a movie theater, a winery, a wine-tasting room, a distillery, a golf course, a cigar bar in an old shed, and extensive gardens. With so much in one spot, this makes a great base for exploring the area. The beautiful grounds give this inn the feel of a remote retreat, though you are still within a 30 miles of Portland.

2126 SW Halsey St., Troutdale, OR 97060. © **800/669-8610** or 503/669-8610. www.mcmenamins.com. 114 units (100 with shared bathroom). $50–$99 double with shared bathroom; $95–$133 double with private bathroom; $30 per person for a bed in the hostel. Children under 7 stay free in parent's room. AE, DC, DISC, MC, V. **Amenities:** 3 restaurants; 9-hole golf course. *In room:* No TV, no phone.

RiverPlace Hotel *Best*   With the Willamette River at its back doorstep and the sloping lawns of Waterfront Park to one side, the recently renovated RiverPlace (in summer 2004) is one of Portland's only waterfront hotels and is hands-down the best place to stay if you're in Portland for a luxurious vacation. The quiet boutique-hotel atmosphere tends to attract affluent couples and business travelers. There are standard river-view rooms, as well as slightly more expensive junior suites that provide a bit more space. Some rooms come with fireplaces and whirlpool tubs; all feature bathrobes and special toiletries.

1510 SW Harbor Way, Portland, OR 97201. © **800/227-1333** or 503/228-3233. Fax 503/295-6161. www.riverplace hotel.com. 84 units. $179–$219 double; $209–$499 suite. Children under 18 stay free in parent's room. AE, DC, DISC, MC, V. Valet parking $24. Pets accepted ($45 nonrefundable cleaning fee). **Amenities:** Restaurant; access to nearby athletic club and spa. *In room:* Fridge.

WHERE TO DINE

Caprial's Bistro and Wine NORTHWEST   If you're a foodie, you're probably already familiar with celebrity chef Caprial Pence, who has written several cookbooks and hosted TV and radio food shows. That her eponymous restaurant is tucked away in a quiet residential neighborhood in southeast Portland may come as a surprise. Entrees are distinctive for their unusual pairings of ingredients (pork-loin chop with a savory doughnut and rhubarb compote). While there is an excellent wine list here, there are also lots of interesting cocktails that are made with fresh fruits and juices.

7015 SE Milwaukie Ave. © **503/236-6457.** www.caprialandjohnskitchen.com. Dinner reservations highly recommended. Main courses $8.50–$13 lunch, $19–$28 dinner. AE, MC, V. Tues–Thurs 11:30am–2:30pm and 5–9pm; Fri–Sat 11:30am–2:30pm and 5–10pm.

Chart House SEAFOOD   Although this place is part of a national restaurant chain, it also happens to boast the finest view of any restaurant in Portland. While you savor the best New England clam chowder in Portland, you can marvel at the views of the Willamette River, Mount Hood, Mount St. Helens, and nearly all of Portland's east side. Fresh fish (grilled, baked, or blackened) is the house specialty.

5700 SW Terwilliger Blvd. © **503/246-6963.** Reservations recommended. Main courses $11–$25 lunch, $17–$43 dinner. AE, DC, DISC, MC, V. Mon–Fri 11:30am–2pm and 5–10pm; Sat–Sun 5–10pm.

Genoa REGIONAL ITALIAN   This has long been the best Italian restaurant in Portland, and with fewer than a dozen tables, it's also one of the smallest. Everything, from the breads to the luscious desserts, is made fresh in the kitchen with the best of locally available seasonal ingredients. This is an ideal setting for a romantic dinner. Service is attentive. The menu (fixed-price only) changes every couple of weeks.

2832 SE Belmont St. ✆ **503/238-1464**. www.genoarestaurant.com. Reservations required. Fixed-price 3-course dinner (Sun–Thurs only) $45, 4-course dinner $60, 7-course dinner $75. AE, DC, DISC, MC, V. Daily 5:30–9:30pm.

Higgins (*Best* NORTHWEST/MEDITERRANEAN   Higgins has long been one of Portland's top restaurants and strikes a balance between contemporary and classic in both its decor and its cuisine. The menu, which changes frequently, explores the contemporary culinary landscape, with the flavors of Asia and the Mediterranean emphasized. Dishes here are inventive, yet homey and satisfying. Be sure to leave room for dessert. Although the main dining room is quite formal, the bar in the back is a casual spot with its own less expensive menu (you can also order off the main menu in the bar).

1239 SW Broadway. ✆ **503/222-9070**. Reservations recommended. Main courses $8–$16 lunch, $20–$32 dinner. AE, DC, DISC, MC, V. Mon–Fri 11:30am–midnight; Sat 4pm–2:30am; Sun 4pm–midnight.

Jake's Famous Crawfish SEAFOOD   This place is a Portland institution and has been serving up crawfish since 1909 at an address that has housed a restaurant or bar since 1892. The noise level after work, when the bar is packed, can be high, and the wait for a table can be long if you don't have a reservation. However, don't let these obstacles dissuade you from visiting. A daily menu lists a dozen or more specials, but there's really no question about what to eat here: crawfish, which are served a variety of ways.

401 SW 12th Ave. ✆ **888/344-6861** or 503/226-1419. www.jakesfamouscrawfish.com. Reservations recommended. Main courses $6.50–$17 lunch, $13–$34 dinner. AE, DC, DISC, MC, V. Mon–Thurs 11am–11pm; Fri 11am–midnight; Sat noon–midnight; Sun 3–11pm.

Newport Bay RiverPlace Marina SEAFOOD   This downtown Portland restaurant isn't just on the waterfront, it's on the water. The building floats in the middle of the Willamette River at the end of a floating dock. This fact alone makes this a not-to-be-missed Portland restaurant. The food is also pretty good, with lots of fresh Northwest seafood available throughout the year. In summer, try to get a seat on the deck.

RiverPlace Marina, 0425 SW Montgomery St. ✆ **503/227-3474**. www.newportbay.com. Reservations recommended. Main courses $7–$15 lunch, $8–$28 dinner. AE, DC, DISC, MC, V. Summer Mon–Thurs 11am–11pm, Fri–Sat 11am–midnight, Sun 9am–11pm; other months restaurant closes 1 hr. earlier.

Southpark Seafood Grill & Wine Bar MEDITERRANEAN/SEAFOOD   The wine bar here is a contemporary interpretation of late-19th-century Paris, and the main dining room is both comfortable and classy. For a starter, don't pass up the fried calamari and vegetables served with spicy aioli. Equally delicious is the butternut squash and ricotta-filled ravioli with toasted hazelnuts, which comes in a rich sauce that begs to be sopped up with the crusty bread. An extensive wine list presents some compelling choices, and the desserts are consistently delicious.

901 SW Salmon St. ✆ **503/326-1300**. www.southpark.citysearch.com. Reservations recommended. Main courses $9–$20 lunch, $15–$23 dinner. AE, DC, DISC, MC, V. Mon–Thurs 11:30am–3pm and 5–10pm; Fri 11:30am–3pm and 5–11pm; Sat 11am–3pm and 5–11pm; Sun 11am–3pm and 5–10pm.

Wildwood AMERICAN REGIONAL   With a menu that changes daily and an elegant and spare interior decor straight out of *Architectural Digest,* Wildwood has for many years now been one of the best, most talked-about restaurants in Portland. Fresh seasonal ingredients are the basis for chef Cory Schreiber's simple yet imaginative dishes; often no more than four ingredients are used in order to let the flavors shine through. While entrees are always quite good, salads and sorbets are exceptional.

1221 NW 21st Ave. (℗ 503/248-9663. www.wildwoodrestaurant.com. Reservations highly recommended. Main courses $12–$16 lunch, $17–$34 dinner. AE, MC, V. Mon–Thurs 11:30am–2:30pm and 5:30–9pm; Fri–Sat 11:30am–2:30pm and 5:30–10pm; Sun 5–8:30pm (family-style dinner).

PORTLAND AFTER DARK

To find out what's going on, pick up a copy of *Willamette Week* or the "A&E" section of Friday's *Oregonian*. Tickets for many events can be purchased through **Ticketmaster** (℗ **503/224-4400;** www.ticketmaster.com) or **Tickets West** (℗ **800/992-TIXX** or 503/224-TIXX).

THE PERFORMING ARTS   For the most part, the Portland performing arts scene revolves around the **Portland Center for the Performing Arts,** 1111 SW Broadway (℗ **503/248-4335;** www.pcpa.com), which is comprised of four theaters in three different buildings.

Founded in 1896, the **Oregon Symphony** (℗ **800/228-7343** or 503/228-1353; www.orsymphony.org) is the oldest symphony orchestra on the West Coast. The diverse season runs September through May. Performances are held at the Arlene Schnitzer Concert Hall, 1037 SW Broadway at Main Street, an immaculately restored 1920s Italian Rococo Revival movie palace. The **Oregon Ballet Theatre** (℗ **888/922-5538** or 503/222-5538; www.obt.org), which performs at the Portland Civic Auditorium, is best loved for its December performances of *The Nutcracker.*

Portland Center Stage (℗ **503/274-6588;** www.pcs.org), which performs at the Diana Gerding Theater in the newly renovated Historic Portland Armory, is the city's largest professional theater company. The season runs October through early June.

THE CLUB & MUSIC SCENE   The **Crystal Ballroom,** 1332 W. Burnside St. (℗ **503/225-0047;** www.danceonair.com), has over the years seen everyone from James Brown to the Grateful Dead. The theater is noted for its "floating" dance floor (set on hidden rollers so that it bounces). The **Aladdin Theater,** 3017 SE Milwaukie Ave. (℗ **503/233-1994;** www.aladdin-theater.com), is one of the city's main venues for touring performers such as Richard Thompson and Brian Wilson. A diverse performance calendar usually includes blues, rock, country, folk, and jazz.

THE BAR SCENE   At the **Rogue Ales Public House,** 1339 NW Flanders St. (℗ **503/222-5910;** www.rogue.com), you can sample the beers of one of Oregon's most diverse and eclectic breweries. Don't miss the Old Crustacean ale. With two levels of brewpubs, a restaurant, and a bakery, **Bridgeport Brewpub and Bakery,** 1313 NW Marshall St. (℗ **503/241-3612;** www.bridgeportbrew.com), in the trendy Pearl District, is Portland's oldest microbrewery. A recent remodel has turned this into the swankiest brewpub in the state.

If you want to taste some Oregon pinot noirs, drop by **Oregon Wines on Broadway,** 515 SW Broadway (℗ **800/943-8858** or 503/228-4655; www.oregonwineson broadway.com), which usually has 30 red wines available for tasting or by the glass. For the best cocktails with a view (and a great happy hour), head to the bar at **Portland City Grill,** 111 SW Fifth Ave. (℗ **503/450-0030;** www.portlandcitygrill.com), which is located on the 30th floor of the Unico/US Bancorp Tower.

7 The Oregon Coast

One of the most beautiful coastlines in the United States, the spectacular Oregon coast is this state's top tourist destination. Beginning less than 2 hours from Portland, the coast has everything from rugged coves to long sandy beaches, from artists' communities to classic family beach towns.

The quickest route from Portland to the coast is via **U.S. 26,** also called the Sunset Highway. Just before reaching the coast and the junction with U.S. 101, watch for a sign for the **world's largest Sitka spruce tree.** This giant, over 750 years old, is in a small park just off the highway.

ASTORIA

If you're interested in history and historic towns, turn north at the junction with U.S. 101 and proceed 20 minutes to Astoria. Situated on the banks of the Columbia River just inland from the river's mouth, this is the oldest American community west of the Mississippi. More a river town than a beach town, Astoria boasts hillsides of restored Victorian homes and scenic views across the Columbia to the hills of southwestern Washington. However, the town's biggest claim to fame is that it was here Lewis and Clark's Corps of Discovery spent the winter of 1805–06 at a log structure they named Fort Clatsop. A restoration of their "fort" can be seen a few miles out of town at **Lewis and Clark National and State Historical Parks** (© 503/861-2471; www.nps.gov/lewi). Not far from Fort Clatsop, near the mouth of the Columbia River, there are miles of wide sand beaches and bike trails at **Fort Stevens State Park** (© 503/861-1671; www.oregonstateparks.org).

In downtown Astoria, you'll find the impressive **Columbia River Maritime Museum,** 1792 Marine Dr. (© 503/325-2323; www.crmm.org), several smaller historical museums, and numerous art galleries, boutiques, and good restaurants.

Astoria's most striking lodging choice is the **Cannery Pier Hotel,** 10 Basin St. (© **888/325-4996** or 503/325-4996; www.cannerypierhotel.com; $179–$269 double), which is built at the end of a 600-foot-long pier on the Columbia River. For historic accommodations, try the stylish **Hotel Elliott,** 357 12th St. (© **877/378-1924** or 503/325-2222; www.hotelelliott.com; $109–$375).

CANNON BEACH

Cannon Beach is the artsiest town on the Oregon coast and lies just off U.S. 101 just a few miles south of the junction of with U.S. 26. Before you reach the town, detour to **Ecola Beach State Park** for some of the most spectacular views on the coast. Several trails lead through the park's lush forest, which contains stands of old-growth spruce, hemlock, and Douglas fir. The park's Indian Beach is popular with surfers.

What makes Cannon Beach truly memorable are the views of offshore rocks, most of which are protected as nesting grounds for colorful **tufted puffins** and other seabirds. The most famous of these monoliths is the massive, 235-foot-tall **Haystack Rock,** the most photographed rock on the coast. At low tide, Haystack Rock is popular with beachcombers and tide-pool explorers.

In mid-June, **Sand Castle Day** attracts sand sculptors and thousands of appreciative viewers, and throughout the year, the winds here are ideal for kite flying. However, for many visitors, **shopping** is the town's greatest attraction. You'll find dozens of galleries and shops along Hemlock Street, selling everything from fine crafts to casual fashions.

Three miles south of town on U.S. 101, watch for the pretty little **Arcadia Beach Wayside.** Another mile farther south, you'll come to **Hug Point State Recreation Site,** which has picnic tables and a sheltered beach. Rugged and remote **Oswald West State Park,** 10 miles south of Cannon Beach, is one of our favorites. A short trail takes you through dense forest to a driftwood-strewn beach on a small cove. Hiking trails lead to headlands on either side of the cove. The waves here are popular with surfers, and there are plenty of picnic tables and a walk-in campground.

The **Stephanie Inn,** 2740 S. Pacific St. (© **800/633-3466** or 503/436-2221; www. stephanie-inn.com; $179–$369 double), is one of the most classic and romantic inns on the Oregon coast; rooms have fireplaces, Jacuzzi tubs, and DVD players. **Cannon Beach Hotel Lodgings,** 1116 S. Hemlock St. (© **800/238-4107;** www.cannonbeach hotel.com; $85–$230 double), has a wide variety of rooms that fit a broad range of budgets.

TILLAMOOK COUNTY

U.S. 101 continues south from Oswald West State Park and climbs over **Neahkahnie Mountain.** Legend has it that the survivors of a wrecked Spanish galleon buried a fortune in gold at the base of this ocean-side mountain. Keep your eyes open for elk, which frequently graze in the meadows here.

Just below this windswept mountain is the quiet resort village of **Manzanita.** Tucked under the fir, spruce, and hemlock trees are attractive summer homes. There's not much to do here except walk along the sandy beach, which is precisely the appeal of the place.

Just before reaching the busy town of **Tillamook,** which lies inland from the Pacific at the south end of Tillamook Bay, you'll come to the **Tillamook Cheese Factory,** 4175 U.S. 101 N. (© **503/815-1300;** www.tillamookcheese.com). Since 1851, this cheese factory has turned out a substantial portion of the cheese consumed in the Northwest. Each year, hundreds of thousands of visitors watch the cheese-making process through large windows. The store sells an assortment of tasty cheeses and ice creams.

From Tillamook, the **Three Capes Scenic Route** leads to Cape Meares, Cape Lookout, and Cape Kiwanda, all of which provide stunning vistas of rocky cliffs, misty mountains, and booming surf.

Cape Meares State Park is the site of the Cape Meares Lighthouse, built in 1890 and open to the public. Continuing around the cape, you'll come to the village of Oceanside. If you walk north along the beach, you'll find a pedestrian tunnel through the headland that protects this hillside community. Through the tunnel is another beautiful stretch of beach.

A few miles south of Oceanside is **Cape Lookout State Park.** A breathtaking trail leads to the end of Cape Lookout, which is an excellent spot for whale-watching in the spring and fall. **Cape Kiwanda,** which lies just outside the town of Pacific City, is the last of the three capes on this scenic loop. This sandstone headland, backed by a huge sand dune, is popular with hang gliders. At the base of the cape is the staging area for Pacific City's beach-launched dory fishing fleet. Located right on the beach and boasting a terrific view, the **Pelican Pub & Brewery,** 33180 Cape Kiwanda Dr. (© **503/965-7007;** www.pelicanbrewery.com), is a good spot to grab a burger and a beer.

With its artfully designed modern cabins, **Coast Cabins,** 635 Laneda Ave. (© **800/435-1269** or 503/368-7113; www.coastcabins.com; $125–$355 double), is our favorite lodging in Manzanita. There's also the romantic **Inn at Manzanita,** 67 Laneda Ave. (© **503/368-6754;** www.innatmanzanita.com; $120–$170 double), where double whirlpool tubs sit between the fireplace and the bed in every room, and balconies look out through shady pines to the ocean. In Pacific City, the **Inn at Cape Kiwanda,** 33105 Cape Kiwanda Dr. (© **888/965-7001;** www.innatcapekiwanda.com; $159–$249 double), a cedar-shingled modern (and romantic) hotel, has rooms with great views of Pacific City's Haystack Rock.

LINCOLN CITY

Lincoln City, 44 miles south of Tillamook, is not really a city, but a collection of five small towns that stretch for miles along the coast. Over the years, these towns all grew together as this area became a popular beach destination.

Family vacationers will love Lincoln City's 7½-mile-long sandy beach. The water may be too cold for swimming, but the steady winds here offer the best **kite flying** on the Oregon coast. The Summer Kite Festival takes place in late June, while the Fall International Kite Festival is held in early October.

Adding to the appeal of the Lincoln City beach area is **Devil's Lake,** which drains across the beach by way of the D River, the world's shortest river. Boating, sailing, waterskiing, boardsailing, swimming, fishing, and camping are all popular activities here.

Nearby Gleneden Beach is home to the largest full-service resort on the coast, the **Salishan Spa & Golf Resort,** 7760 U.S. 101 N. (© **800/452-2300** or 541/764-2371; www.salishan.com; $179–$249 double), which has a fine-dining room and excellent golf course. For oceanfront rooms, try **The Inn at Spanish Head,** 4009 SW U.S. 101 (© **800/452-8127** or 541/996-2162; www.spanishhead.com; $185–$199 double), which is 10 stories high but is built into the side of an oceanfront bluff. Consequently, the lobby is at the top of the hotel.

Prices are moderate for the inventive seafood dishes at **Kyllo's Seafood Grill,** 1110 NW First Court (© **541/994-3179**), where the decor has a touch of urban chic. On the drive down from Portland, don't miss the perfect pies and other terrific diner staples at the **Otis Cafe,** 1259 Salmon River Hwy. (Ore. 18), Otis (© **541/994-2813**).

DEPOE BAY

Depoe Bay, 13 miles south of Lincoln City, calls itself the smallest harbor in the world, and although the tiny harbor covers only 6 acres, it's home to more than 100 fishing boats. Just outside the harbor mouth, storm waves cause the impressive fountains of Depoe Bay's famous spouting horns. These geyserlike fountains are produced when waves break in the narrow fissures of the area's rocky coastline, sending plumes of water into the air.

On U.S. 101, you'll find a row of garish souvenir shops, plus several family restaurants as well as charter-fishing and whale-watching companies.

The road south from Depoe Bay winds its way through grand, rugged scenery and passes small, picturesque coves. Several miles south of town, watch for signs to the **Otter Crest State Scenic Viewpoint,** atop Cape Foulweather. Keep an eye out for sea lions sunning themselves on offshore rocks.

Just south of Cape Foulweather, you'll find **Devil's Punchbowl State Natural Area.** The site of a collapsed sea cave becomes a cauldron of churning foam during high tides or stormy seas. A short path here leads to the Marine Gardens, where you can explore numerous tide pools containing various sea creatures.

Channel House Inn, 35 Ellingson St., Depoe Bay (© **800/447-2140** or 541/765-2140; www.channelhouse.com; $100–$310 double), is a luxurious small inn built above the narrow channel into Depoe Bay; all accommodations have whirlpool tubs and fireplaces.

NEWPORT

As coastal towns go, Newport has a split personality. Dockworkers unloading fresh fish mingle with vacationers licking ice-cream cones as freeloading sea lions wait for their next meal from the processing plants along the waterfront. Many of the town's old cottages and late-19th-century buildings still stand, and despite downtown's souvenir shops, galleries, and restaurants, Newport is still home to the largest commercial fishing fleet on the Oregon coast.

Newport is home to the **Oregon Coast Aquarium,** 2820 SE Ferry Slip Rd. (© **541/ 867-3474;** www.aquarium.org), the Oregon coast's top attraction. There are seals, otters, sea lions, tufted puffins, jellyfish, a giant octopus, and a huge walk-through tank. Admission is $12 adults, $10 seniors, and $7 children 3 to 13. It's open Memorial Day to Labor Day daily from 9am to 6pm, the rest of the year daily from 10am to 5pm.

Beaches in the Newport area range from tiny, rocky coves where you can search for agates, to long, wide stretches of sand perfect for kite flying. Right in town, north and west of the Yaquina Bay Bridge, you'll find **Yaquina Bay State Park,** which borders both the ocean and the bay. North of Newport is **Agate Beach,** which has a stunning view of Yaquina Head. This latter spot has a historic lighthouse and is preserved as the **Yaquina Head Outstanding Natural Area.** Two miles south of Newport, you'll find **South Beach State Park,** a wide, sandy beach with picnic areas and a large campground that rents yurts (if you haven't brought your own tent).

Six miles south of Newport, you'll find **Ona Beach State Park,** a sandy beach with a picnic area under the trees. Beaver Creek, a fairly large stream, flows through the park and across the beach to the ocean. **Seal Rock State Recreation Site** is another 2 miles south. Here, a long wall of rock rises from the waves and sand, creating numerous tide pools and fascinating nooks and crannies to explore.

Located north of town in a grove of fir trees on the edge of a cliff, the condos at **Starfish Point,** 140 NW 48th St. (© **800/870-7795** or 541/265-3751; www.starfish point.com; $125–$200 double), are our favorite rooms in the area. The bathrooms here are extravagant affairs with double whirlpool tubs and skylights or big windows. For unique accommodations, book a stateroom on the *Newport Belle,* Newport Marina (© **800/348-1922** or 541/867-6290; www.newportbelle.com; $125–$145 double), a reproduction paddle-wheeler moored near the Oregon Coast Aquarium. The **Sylvia Beach Hotel,** 267 NW Cliff St. (© **888/795-8422** or 541/265-5428; www.sylviabeachhotel.com; $68–$183 double), has rooms named for different authors, and in each you'll find memorabilia, books, and decor that reflects these writers' lives, times, and works. The hotel's restaurant is a local favorite.

YACHATS

Located 26 miles south of Newport, the village of Yachats (pronounced *Yah*-hots) is known as something of an artists' community—small but sophisticated and a little bit funky. The town is set on a pretty little cove with adjoining rocky beaches and the tiny Yachats River flowing into the surf. To the east, steep, forested mountains rise up on the edge of town.

Looming over the town is the impressive bulk of **Cape Perpetua,** which, at 800 feet, is the highest spot on the Oregon coast. The **Cape Perpetua Interpretive Center** (© **541/547-3289;** www.fs.fed.us/r6/siuslaw), located up a steep road off U.S. 101, houses displays on the cape's natural history and the Native Americans who harvested its bountiful seafood for hundreds of years. Within the Cape Perpetua Scenic

---

Barking Up a Storm with the Sea Lions

Approximately 10 miles south of Yachats, you'll find **Sea Lion Caves**, 91560 U.S. 101 North (© 541/547-3111; www.sealioncaves.com), the only year-round mainland home for Steller sea lions, hundreds of which reside here. Admission is $8 adults, $4.50 children 6 to 15, free for children under 6. The cave is open daily from 9am to 1 hour before dark.

Area are more than 20 miles of hiking trails, tide pools, ancient forests, scenic overlooks, and a campground.

If you're looking for wide, sandy **beaches,** continue south to the Stonefield Beach State Recreation Site, Muriel O. Ponsler Memorial State Scenic Viewpoint, or Carl G. Washburne Memorial State Park. Washburne offers 2 miles of beach, plus hiking trails and a campground. At Heceta Head State Scenic Viewpoint you'll find a pretty little cove, a historic lighthouse, and miles of hiking trails.

The **Shamrock Lodgettes,** 105 U.S. 101 South (© **800/845-5028** or 541/547-3312; www.shamrocklodgettes.com; $59–$179 double), classic log cabins set amid spacious lawns and old fir trees at the mouth of the Yachats River, are just bewitching. We also recommend the romantic **Overleaf Lodge,** 280 Overleaf Lodge Lane (© **800/338-0507** or 541/547-4880; www.overleaflodge.com; $105–$450 double). South of Yachats, there's the **Heceta Lighthouse Keeper's House,** 92072 U.S. 101 South (© **866/547-3696;** www.hecetalighthouse.com; $133–$251 double), a B&B housed in a historic lighthouse keeper's home in Heceta Head State Scenic Viewpoint. Just south of this park, there is a stupendous view of Heceta Head Lighthouse.

FLORENCE

Florence (www.florencechamber.com), 50 miles south of Newport, has long been a popular vacation spot for families. However, with few roads providing access to the ocean's shore, this area is known more for its lakes than for its beaches. Sand dunes, the Siuslaw River, and 17 freshwater lakes offer an abundance of recreational opportunities. Many area lakes are ringed with summer homes and public campgrounds. Popular activities include water-skiing, four-wheeling through the sand dunes, and fishing.

Florence's **Old Town,** on the north bank of the Siuslaw River, has quite a bit of charm, with many restored wood and brick buildings, interesting boutiques and galleries, and waterfront seafood restaurants.

THE OREGON DUNES NATIONAL RECREATION AREA

The Oregon Dunes National Recreation Area, more than 14,000 acres of sand dunes, stretches for more than 40 miles along the coast between Florence and Coos Bay. Within this vast area of shifting sands are dunes more than 500 feet tall, numerous lakes both large and small, living forests, and skeletal forests of trees that were long ago "drowned" beneath drifting sands. It is here that you'll find the longest unbroken, publicly owned stretches of Oregon's coast.

Jessie M. Honeyman Memorial State Park (www.oregonstateparks.org), 3 miles south of Florence, is a unique spot with a beautiful forest-bordered lake and towering sand dunes. The park offers camping, picnicking, hiking trails, and access to Cleawox and Woahink lakes. Cleawox Lake has a swimming area and boat rentals, and adjacent dunes are open to off-road vehicles.

On the **Taylor Dunes Trail,** which begins at the Carter Lake Campground, 7½ miles south of Florence, a platform overlooks the dunes. It's an easy half-mile walk to the platform. If you want to get your shoes full of sand but have time for only a quick walk, you can continue on to the beach, which is less than a mile beyond the viewing platform; roughly half this distance is through dunes.

At the **Dunes Overlook,** 10 miles south of Florence, you'll find viewing platforms high atop a forested sand dune overlooking a vast expanse of bare sand. A 3.5-mile loop trail leads from this overlook out to the beach by way of Tahkenitch Creek. Another mile south of the Dunes Overlook, you'll find the trail head for the **Tahkenitch Trail,** which gives you access to an 8-mile network of trails that wander through dunes, forest, marshes, and meadows.

For truly impressive dunes, the best route is the **John Dellenback Dunes Trail;** its trail head is half a mile south of **Eel Creek Campground,** which is 11 miles south of Reedsport (32 miles south of Florence). This 2.5-mile round-trip trail leads through an area of dunes 2 miles wide by 4 miles long. Don't get lost!

BANDON

Once known primarily as the cranberry capital of Oregon, **Bandon (www.bandon.com)** is a quaint seaside village set on one of the most spectacular pieces of coastline in the Northwest. The beach here is littered with boulders, monoliths, and haystack rocks that seem to have been strewn by some giant hand. About 20 miles north of town, near the town of Coos Bay, three state parks together preserve more breathtaking shoreline. The Coquille River empties into the Pacific here at Bandon, and at the river's mouth stands a picturesque little lighthouse.

Coquille Point, at the end of 11th Street, is one of the best places to view Bandon's famous rocks. Here you'll find a short, paved, interpretive trail atop a bluff overlooking the beach, rock monoliths, and the river's mouth. From the nearby **Face Rock Viewpoint** you can see the area's most famous rock, which resembles a face gazing skyward.

At **Sunset Bay State Park,** 20 miles north of Bandon, you'll find a small bay almost completely surrounded by sandstone cliffs. The entrance to the bay is narrow, which means the waters here stay fairly calm. This is one of the few beaches in Oregon where the water gets warm enough for swimming. Picnicking and camping are available in the park, and there are lots of tide pools to explore.

Another 3 miles southwest brings you to **Shore Acres State Park,** once the estate of a local shipping tycoon who spent years developing his gardens. The park includes formal English and Japanese gardens. The gardens are atop sandstone cliffs overlooking the Pacific and a tiny cove. Here, rock walls rise from the water and have been sculpted by the waves into unusual shapes.

Continue a little farther along the same road and you'll come to **Cape Arago State Park.** Just offshore from the rugged cape are the rocks and small islands of Simpson Reef, which offers sunbathing spots for hundreds of seals (including elephant seals) and sea lions. Their barking can be heard from hundreds of yards away. The best viewing point is the **Simpson Reef Viewpoint.** *Tip:* Information on all three state parks is available online at **www.oregonstateparks.org**.

The **Bandon Dunes Golf Resort,** 57744 Round Lake Dr. (© **888/345-6008** or 541/347-4380; www.bandondunesgolf.com; $105–$320 double), is the most tasteful and luxurious accommodations on the Oregon coast. However, the emphasis is so entirely on the golf course that anyone not interested in the game will most certainly feel like an interloper. Dozens of Bandon's famous monoliths rise from the sand and waves in front of the **Sunset Motel,** 1865 Beach Loop Dr. (📞 **800/842-2407** or 541/347-2453; www.sunsetmotel.com; $50–$150 double), making sunsets from the Sunset truly memorable. Although many of the rooms are dated, the view can't be beat.

8 The Columbia River Gorge & Mount Hood

Formed when 1,000-foot-high ice-age floodwaters raged down the Columbia River, the Columbia River Gorge is a landscape of rare beauty that has been preserved as the Columbia River Gorge National Scenic Area. Within this flood-carved landscape, sheer basalt cliffs rise from the river and diaphanous waterfalls cascade down dark, forested heights. The Gorge is the only sea-level gap along the entire length of the Cascade Range, which stretches from California to Canada, and consequently, this massive opening in the mountains serves as a sort of natural wind tunnel that funnels air between the cool, moist coastal regions and the hot, dry interior.

Although I-84 runs beside the river on the Oregon side, and Wash. 14 follows the Washington shore, a leisurely drive along U.S. 30, the **Historic Columbia River Highway,** is the preferred way to see the Gorge. This winding highway parallels I-84 for 22 miles at the west end of the Gorge and for 15 miles at the east end. Along the way there are close-up views of numerous waterfalls, unequaled scenic vistas, and opportunities for hiking.

Rising to the south of the Gorge is 11,235-foot **Mount Hood,** Oregon's highest peak and a popular destination in both summer and winter. A drive up the Gorge can easily be combined with a loop around the mountain, and from Timberline, on the southern flanks of the mountain, you can get close-up views of Mount Hood, do a bit of hiking, and visit the historic Timberline Lodge.

From Portland, head east on I-84. At Troutdale, take the exit marked HISTORIC COLUMBIA RIVER HIGHWAY. This winding highway is an engineering marvel, but it's dwarfed by the spectacular vistas that present themselves at every turn. To learn more about the road and how it was built, stop at **Vista House** (📞 **503/695-2230;** www. vistahouse.com), 733 feet above the river on Crown Point, for displays and a spectacular view that includes Beacon Rock, an 800-foot-tall monolith on the far side of the river.

There are some 77 waterfalls in the Columbia Gorge, but **Multnomah Falls** is by far the most impressive and best known. At 620 feet from the lip to the pool, it's also the tallest waterfall in Oregon and the fourth tallest in the United States. A paved trail leads to the top of the falls and a dizzying view from an observation platform.

Near **Ainsworth State Park** (📞 **503/695-2301;** www.oregonstateparks.org), the western segment of the Historic Columbia River Highway comes to an end. Five miles east of here on I-84, you'll come to **Bonneville Lock and Dam** (📞 **541/374-8820;** www.nwp.usace.army.mil/op/b/home.asp). In operation since 1938, this is the oldest dam on the river. Thousands of visitors come each year to see its fish ladder, which allows salmon and other fish to migrate upstream. June and September are the best months to observe salmon.

Just east of the dam is the **Bridge of the Gods,** which connects Oregon and Washington at the site where an old Indian legend says a natural bridge once stood. Geologists believe that the legend has its basis in fact. There is evidence that 500 years ago a massive rock slide blocked the river at this point.

On the Washington side of the Columbia, east of the Bridge of the Gods, is the **Columbia Gorge Interpretive Center,** 990 SW Rock Creek Dr., Stevenson (📞 **800/ 991-2338** or 509/427-8211; www.columbiagorge.org). This museum is the single best introduction to the natural and human history of the Columbia Gorge; it also boasts an awesome view. Admission is $6 adults, $5 seniors and students, and $4 children 6 to 12. Hours are daily from 10am to 5pm.

Just beyond Bridge of the Gods on the Oregon side is **Cascade Locks** where, in 1896, navigational locks were built so that river traffic could avoid the treacherous passage through the cascades that once existed at this spot. There are two small museums here, one of which also holds the ticket office for the stern-wheeler *Columbia Gorge* (℮ **800/224-3901** or 503/224-3900; www.sternwheeler.com), which makes regular trips on the river all summer. Sightseeing excursions are $25 for adults and seniors, and $15 for children. Dinner and brunch cruises are also offered.

Anyone who windsurfs has likely heard of the town of Hood River. Because of the strong winds that blow through the gorge in summer, the Hood River section of the Columbia River is one of the most popular windsurfing spots in the world. If you want to try this thrilling sport, stop by one of the many board shops downtown for rental and instruction information. In recent years, kite-surfing, which uses a kite instead of a sail, has become very popular here.

The **Mount Hood Railroad** excursion train, 110 Railroad Ave., Hood River (℮ **800/872-4661** or 541/386-3556; www.mthoodrr.com), runs from mid-April to late December, and uses vintage rail cars to carry passengers up the Hood River Valley from the town of Hood River to Parkdale and back. Fares for the 4-hour excursion are $23 to $26 adults, $21 to $24 seniors, and $15 to $18 children 2 to 12. In July and August, the train runs Tuesday through Sunday. From mid-April to late June, and September to October, it runs Wednesday through Sunday; in November and December, the schedule varies.

If you continue heading east on I-84 from Hood River, you'll come to **The Dalles,** which was an important stop on the Oregon Trail. Here in The Dalles, you can learn more about the Columbia Gorge at the **Columbia Gorge Discovery Center,** 5000 Discovery Dr. (℮ **541/296-8600;** www.gorgediscovery.org). Among the displays here are reproduced historic storefronts and Native American artifacts. Admission is $8 adults, $7 seniors, and $4 children ages 6 to 16. Hours are daily from 9am to 5pm.

If you turn south on Ore. 35 at Hood River, you'll pass through thousands of acres of apple, pear, and cherry orchards. Shortly after Ore. 35 merges into U.S. 26, turn right onto the road to **Timberline Lodge.** As the name implies, this lodge is at the timberline, and a July or August walk on one of the trails in the vicinity will lead you through wildflower-filled meadows. Because of the glacier and snowfields above the lodge, you can ski and snowboard here all summer long.

WHERE TO STAY & DINE

The **Columbia Gorge Hotel,** 4000 Westcliff Dr., just west of Hood River (℮ **800/ 345-1921** or 541/386-5566; www.columbiagorgehotel.com), which perches 200 feet above the Columbia River atop a cliff, opened in 1921 and is the grande dame hotel of the gorge. While the rooms are a bit eclectically furnished and tend to look a bit dated, the gardens and the view from the guest room windows make this one of your best options in the area. Rates run $159 to $299 double.

Constructed during the Depression as a WPA project, the classic Alpine-style **Timberline Lodge,** Timberline (℮ **800/547-1406** or 503/622-7979; www.timberline lodge.com), boasts a grand stone fireplace, exposed beams, wide plank floors, wood-carvings, wrought-iron fixtures, hand-hooked rugs, and handmade furniture. Rooms vary in size considerably, with the smallest lacking private bathrooms ($95 double);

some have fireplaces. The Cascade Dining Room serves pricey (but good) Northwest cuisine; however, service can be glacially slow. Rates for rooms with bathroom run $145 to $250.

On the Washington side, **Skamania Lodge,** 1131 SW Skamania Lodge Way (© **800/221-7117** or 509/427-7700; www.skamania.com), in Stevenson, has the most spectacular vistas of any hotel in the Gorge, plus the only golf course. The interior features a cathedral-ceilinged lobby, stone fireplace, and Native American artwork and artifacts. The dining room serves good Northwest cuisine amid stupendous views of the Gorge. Facilities include a full-service spa, tennis courts, an indoor pool, whirlpools, a sauna, an exercise facility, nature trails, and bike rentals. Guest rooms not facing the parking lot feature wonderful views. Rates run $189 to $309 double.

9 Willamette Valley Wine Country

Although it is not nearly as well known as Napa Valley, Oregon's Willamette Valley, which stretches south from Portland, is one of the country's premier wine-producing regions. Pinot noir, some of which rivals that of France's Burgundy region, is what has put Oregon on the world's wine map, but area wineries also produce pinot gris, pinot blanc, chardonnay, and even sparkling wines.

Oregon wineries remain, for the most part, small establishments. Even the new wineries that are opening up right on Ore. 99W (and that seem calculated to provide beach-bound vacationers with a bit of distraction and some less-than-impressive wine for the weekend) are still small affairs compared to the wineries of Napa Valley. Although in recent years more and more "corporate" wineries have opened with the sole purpose of producing high-priced pinot noir, many of the region's wineries are still family-owned and -operated and produce moderately priced wines.

Wine country begins less than an hour southwest of Portland near the town of Newberg, and all along Ore. 99W, which runs through the heart of wine country, you'll see blue road signs directing you to nearby wineries. At most wineries in the region, you can pick up a map of Willamette Valley wineries. Alternatively, you can get a copy of this map by contacting **Willamette Valley Wineries,** P.O. Box 25162, Portland, OR 97298 (© **503/646-2985;** www.willamettewines.com).

In between visiting wineries, you can visit McMinnville's **Evergreen Aviation Museum,** 500 NE Capt. Michael King Smith Way (© **503/434-4180;** www.sprucegoose.org), which is home to Howard Hughes's famous "Spruce Goose" flying boat.

The town of McMinnville makes the best base for exploring the north Willamette Valley wine country. Although it is part of a regional microbrew empire, the simply furnished yet artistically designed **McMenamins Hotel Oregon,** 310 NE Evans St. (© **888/472-8427** or 503/472-8427; www.mcmenamins.com; $50–$105 double), with its rooftop bar overlooking the valley, is a good place to stay. For more luxurious all-suite accommodations surrounded by the vineyards above the town of Dundee, try the **Black Walnut Inn,** 9600 NE Worden Hill Rd. (© **866/429-4114** or 503/429-4114; www.blackwalnut-inn.com; $180–$430 double).

10 Crater Lake National Park

At 1,943 feet deep, Crater Lake is the deepest lake in the United States and the seventh deepest in the world. But depth alone is not what makes this one of the most visited spots in the Northwest—it's the startling sapphire-blue waters that are truly mesmerizing.

Two World-Class Festivals in Southern Oregon

Each year, hundreds of thousands of people flock to the town of Ashland for the internationally acclaimed **Oregon Shakespeare Festival** (© 541/482-4331; www.osfashland.org). The season runs February through October, and typically includes four works by Shakespeare plus another six or seven classic or contemporary plays. In addition to theater, Ashland has galleries, interesting shops, fine restaurants, and dozens of B&Bs.

Nearby Jacksonville is home to the **Britt Festivals** (© 800/882-7488 or 541/773-6077; www.brittfest.org), which run mid-June through mid-September. Jacksonville, a gold boomtown in the mid-1800s, became a forgotten backwater after the Depression, inadvertently preserving its many historic buildings. Today, more than 80 of the town's buildings have been restored. A pine-shaded amphitheater on the grounds of 19th-century photographer Peter Britt's estate is now home to folk, pop, country, jazz, and classical music concerts, as well as modern dance performances. Past performers have included Shawn Colvin, Kenny G, Blues Traveler, Lyle Lovett, and The Temptations. If you opt for lawn seating, bring a blanket and a picnic.

The caldera (crater) that today holds the serene lake was born in an explosive volcanic eruption 7,700 years ago. When the volcano now known as Mount Mazama erupted, its summit (thought to have been around 12,000 ft. high) collapsed, leaving a crater 4,000 feet deep. Thousands of years of rain and melting snow created cold, clear Crater Lake, which today is surrounded by walls nearly 2,000 feet high.

Don't despair as you drive through uninteresting forest en route to the lake. The drive into the park winds through forests that don't provide a single glimpse of the spectacular lake. With no warning except the signs leading to Rim Village, you'll suddenly find yourself gazing down into a vast bowl full of blue water. Toward one end of the lake rises the cone of Wizard Island, the tip of a volcano that has been slowly building since the last eruption of Mount Mazama.

pPark admission (good for 7 days) is $10 per vehicle. For information, contact **Crater Lake National Park,** P.O. Box 7, Crater Lake, OR 97604 (© **541/594-3100;** www.nps.gov/crla).

After your first breathtaking view of the lake, you may want to stop by one of the park's two visitor centers—**Steel Information Center** and **Rim Village Visitor Center.** The park is open year-round, but in winter, when deep snows blanket the region, only the road to **Rim Village** is kept clear. In summer (beginning roughly in late June), the 39-mile Rim Drive provides stunning views.

Boat trips around the lake are the park's most popular activity. These tours last 2 hours and begin at Cleetwood Cove, at the bottom of a very steep 1-mile trail that descends 700 feet from the rim to the lakeshore. Be sure you're in good enough physical condition to make the steep climb back up to the rim. Bring warm clothes, as it can be quite a bit cooler on the lake than on the rim. A naturalist on each boat provides a narrative on the ecology and history of the lake; all tours include a stop on Wizard Island. Tours are offered from early July to mid-September and cost $25 for adults ($30 if you want to get dropped off on Wizard Island) and $15 for children 3 to 11 ($18 for drop off on Wizard Island).

Many miles of **hiking trails** can be found in the park, but the Cleetwood Trail is the only one that leads down to the lakeshore. The trail to the top of Mount Scott, although a rigorous 2.5 miles, is the park's most rewarding hike. Shorter trails with good views include the .8-mile trail to the top of the Watchman, which overlooks Wizard Island, and the 1.7-mile trail up Garfield Peak. The short Castle Crest Wildflower Trail is best hiked in late July and early August when the wildflowers are at the height of their glory. Backpackers can hike the length of the park on the Pacific Crest Trail.

In winter, **cross-country skiing** is popular on the park's snow-covered roads. Skiers in good condition can usually make the entire circuit of the lake in 2 days, but must be prepared to camp in the snow. Spring, when the weather is warmer and there are fewer severe storms, is actually the best time to ski around the lake.

WHERE TO STAY & CAMP

The park contains two lodging options. Overlooking the lake from the rim, **Crater Lake Lodge** (© 541/830-8700; www.craterlakelodges.com) has the look and feel of a historic mountain lodge, and though it boasts many modern conveniences, guest rooms do not have telephones, televisions, or air-conditioning. About half the rooms overlook the lake. The dining room serves creative Northwest cuisine and provides a view of both Crater Lake and the Klamath River basin. Rates run $129 to $248 double. A short drive away, **The Cabins at Mazama Village** (© 541/830-8700; www. craterlakelodges.com) is, despite the name, a collection of motel-style rooms in 10 buildings that are designed to resemble traditional mountain cabins. Once again, there are no TVs, telephones, or air-conditioning. Rates are $111 double. Both lodges are closed from mid-October to late May.

Tent camping and RV spaces are available on the south side of the park at the **Mazama Village Campground,** which is open mid-June through early October. There are also tent sites at **Lost Creek Campground** on the park's east side. This latter campground is open mid-July through mid-September. Reservations are not accepted at either campground.

Alaska & Hawaii

The last two states to enter the Union, Alaska and Hawaii, have, by the very fact that they aren't part of the contiguous 48, secured reputations as exotic destinations. And those reputations are deserved. Both offer an abundance of natural beauty—admittedly of different types—not found anywhere else in the country.

Alaska, geographically the largest state in the country (twice the size of Texas!), has more unexplored wilderness and arctic beauty than any other state in the nation. Few won't gasp in amazement when they see a chunk of ice the size of a building fall from a glacier, a bear or caribou grazing in one of the numerous state parks, or an orca feeding in the waters off the southeast coast. It's the ultimate destination for those who like their terrain rugged and unspoiled.

If it's arctic glaciers and rugged outdoor sports that attract visitors to Alaska, then it's sun-soaked beaches, loads of water fun, and breathtaking, lush greenery that lure travelers (seven million of them each year) to **Hawaii.** There's no place quite like this handful of sun-drenched mid-Pacific islands, remote no matter what continent you live on. The possibilities for adventure—and relaxation—are endless, whether you want to surf a wave, snorkel in pristine waters, or hike a volcano.

Note: We discuss many of the best spots for the first-time visitor in this chapter, but it's admittedly the tip of the iceberg—covering the cream of the crop in each state would take an entire book. If you plan to visit either state, we recommend getting detailed guidebooks such as *Frommer's Alaska* and *Frommer's Hawaii.*

1 Southeast Alaska

The Southeast Panhandle is the relatively narrow strip of mountains and islands between Canada and the Gulf of Alaska. It's a land of huge rainforest trees, glacier-garbed mountains, and countless islands, all of it reachable by the ferry system or cruise ships along the waterway known as the **Inside Passage.** This land of ice and forest may not look as large on the map as other parts of Alaska, but the better you know it, the bigger it becomes, until you have to surrender to its immensity. Nearly all of Southeast Alaska, stretching 500 miles from Ketchikan to Yakutat, is in **Tongass National Forest.** The towns sit in small pockets of private land surrounded by 17 million acres of land controlled by the U.S. Forest Service—an area nearly as large as the state of Maine, and considerably larger than any other national forest or any national park in the U.S. Southeast contains **Juneau,** Alaska's capital and third-largest city; and **Ketchikan,** next in size to Juneau. Southeast's towns are as quaint and historic as any in Alaska, especially **Sitka,** which preserves the story of Russian America and its conflict with the indigenous Native people. Alaska **Native culture**—Tlingit and Haida—is rich and close at hand, as is the history of the region's **gold rush,** which towns have

Arriving by Cruise Ship

Most visitors to Southeast Alaska (and many visitors headed to Anchorage) arrive by cruise ship, stopping at the port towns by day and allowing the ship to do the traveling for them by night. It's by far the easiest and most comfortable way of seeing the state, though what you save in convenience you obviously give back in lack of control and spontaneity. Where the ship goes, you go, and on shore you're rarely out of a crowd.

Covering all of the cruise options available for Alaska would literally take an entire book, so if you're interested in visiting Alaska in this manner, contact the **Alaska Travel Industry Association,** 2600 Cordova St., Suite 201, Anchorage, AK 99503 (© **907/929-2842;** www.travelalaska.com), the state's official visitor information agency. Or get a dedicated guidebook, such as *Frommer's Alaska Cruises & Ports of Call.*

turned into perpetual performance art. No other region is richer in opportunities for boating or seeing marine wildlife. The weather is wet and temperate.

ESSENTIALS

GETTING THERE   By Plane   Since most of Southeast Alaska's towns are not linked by road, anyone traveling to or around the region does so by plane or boat. Major towns without road access have jet service, provided by **Alaska Airlines** (© **800/252-7522;** www.alaskaair.com), the region's only major airline. **Juneau International Airport (www.juneau.org/airport)** is Southeast Alaska's travel hub. Ketchikan and Sitka each have a few flights a day.

By Ferry   The state-run **Alaska Marine Highway System** (© **800/642-0066** or 907/465-3941, or 800/764-3779 TTY; www.ferryalaska.com) is a subsidized fleet of big, blue-hulled ferries whose mission is to connect the roadless coastal towns of Alaska for roughly the same cost you'd pay if there were roads and you were driving. Call for a free schedule, or download it from the website. If you're bringing a vehicle or need a cabin, be sure to make reservations as early as possible. Rates vary widely depending on your destination, if you're bringing a vehicle or not, whether you're reserving a cabin, and so on. Call or consult the website to get current rates.

The ferry system's strengths are its frequent summer sailings, inexpensive stopovers, exceptional safety, and the fact that kids love it. In the summer, on-board Forest Service guides offer interpretive talks in Southeast's Inside Passage and in Prince William Sound. The system's weaknesses are the crowds during the July peak season, the fact that if they're late they can be many hours late (although they're usually on time), and a shortage of cabins, which means that most people have to camp on deck or in chairs during overnight passages.

VISITOR INFORMATION   The **Southeast Alaska Discovery Center,** 50 Main St., Ketchikan, AK 99901 (© **907/228-6220,** or 907/288-6237 TTY; fax 901/228-6234; www.fs.fed.us/r10/tongass), is a great resource for planning your trip. The center is open May through September daily from 8am to 5pm, October through April Tuesday through Saturday from 10am to 4:30pm.

Alaska

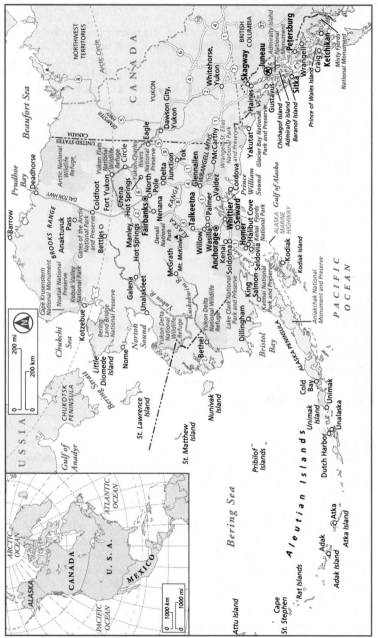

Fishing in Southeast

There is great fishing in Southeast Alaska. The best fishing is away from the roads. The **Alaska Department of Fish and Game,** 2030 Sea Level Dr., Suite 205, Ketchikan, AK 99901 (© **907/465-4100;** www.alaska.gov/adfg, click on "Sport Fishing," then on the Southeast region on the map), produces fishing guides for most of Southeast Alaska's major towns, including Ketchikan and Sitka. The guides detail where to find fish in both fresh and salt water, and include maps of favorite fishing areas. You can pick up a copy at the Southeast Alaska Discovery Center (see "Visitor Information," above).

The **Alaska Travel Industry Association,** 2600 Cordova St., Suite 201, Anchorage, AK 99503 (© **907/929-2842;** www.travelalaska.com), is the state's official visitor information agency.

GETTING AROUND   Planes and boats are your two options. See "By Ferry" under "Getting There," earlier in this chapter, for information on the ferry. **Wings of Alaska** (© **907/789-0790;** www.ichoosewings.com) offers many flights to surrounding communities and an active flightseeing operation.

KETCHIKAN

Not so long ago, Ketchikan was a rugged and exotic intersection of cultures built on the profits of logging Southeast's rainforest, but in a decade it has transformed itself into a tourist center. The rough waterfront streets and boardwalk red-light district of rainy Ketchikan have been prettified and packaged for the cruise ship crowds, who cram streets of gift shops when the ships dock. But when the ships leave, history's ghosts still lurk in the twisting, mountainside streets, and the totem poles look on with their forbidding magic. Tlingit and Haida culture are close at hand, as well as outdoor water attractions.

WHAT TO SEE & DO

Tip: Pick up a copy of the **Official Historic Ketchikan Walking Tour Map,** available all over town, which gives you three different routes through town and loads of information about sites of interest on the way.

Stop first at the **Southeast Alaska Discovery Center,** 50 Main St., Ketchikan, AK 99901 (© **907/228-6220,** or 907/288-6237 TTY; fax 907/228-6234; www.fs.fed.us/r10/tongass). This exceptional museum of the region's natural and cultural history and contemporary society costs $5 (free in winter). You can also get free guidance for planning outdoor activities.

Creek Street was Ketchikan's red-light district; now it's a quaint tourist mall. **Dolly's House** (© **907/225-6329**), a museum dedicated to a prostitute who had a long career here, is amusing, mildly racy, and a little sad. Admission is $5; it's open daily from 8am to 4pm during the summer. The attractively situated **Tongass Historical Museum** (© **907/225-5600**) presents the history and Native heritage of Ketchikan ($2 admission, free in winter).

Following the creek upstream, take a look at the **fish ladder** at the Park Avenue bridge, then continue to the **Deer Mountain Tribal Hatchery & Eagle Center,** 1158 Salmon Rd. (© **800/252-5158** or 907/225-6760), a small king and silver salmon hatchery where you can see fry swimming in large tubs and even feed them. The eagle center exhibits captive bald eagles and other raptors in indoor cages and a large outdoor eagle enclosure. Admission costs $9 adults, kids 12 and under free.

Beyond the hatchery is **City Park,** where Ketchikan Creek splits into a maze of ornamental pools and streams once used as a hatchery. You'll find the **Totem Heritage Center** (© **907/225-5900**) here. Admission is $5 in summer to see the largest collection of original 19th-century totem poles in existence.

Two major totem pole sites that shouldn't be missed will require you to have transportation or join a tour. The excellent **Totem Bight State Historical Park,** 10 miles out of town on North Tongass Highway (© **907/247-8574**), presents poles and a clan house carved since 1938 by elders working with traditional tools to copy fragments of historic poles that had mostly rotted away. The setting, the site of a traditional fish camp, is a peaceful spot on the edge of Tongass Narrows, at the end of a short walk through the woods, so the experience is both aesthetic and educational. Admission is free. The **Saxman Native Village Totem Pole Park,** 2½ miles south of Ketchikan on the South Tongass Highway (© **907/225-4846**), has artifacts similar to those at Totem Bight Park, but with an added resource: You can watch carvers work in the building to the right of the park. The park offers 2-hour tours ($35 adults, $18 children 12 and under), which include entry to the clan house, a short performance of a Tlingit legend, and traditional dance and song by the Cape Fox Dancers. Or, you can buy a pamphlet ($1.50) and tour the park yourself for free, though this is the kind of place that warrants a guided tour.

The islands, coves, and channels around Ketchikan create protected waters rich with life and welcoming for exploration by kayak. **Southeast Sea Kayaks** (© **800/287-1607** or 907/225-1258; www.kayakketchikan.com) rents kayaks and guides day trips and overnights. Tours start at $79 adults for a 2½-hour paddle.

WHERE TO STAY & DINE

In addition to the hotels and B&Bs listed below, the **Ketchikan Reservation Service,** 412 D-1 Loop Rd., Ketchikan, AK 99901 (© **800/987-5337** or ©/fax 907/247-5337; www.ketchikan-lodging.com), books many bed-and-breakfasts and outfitted apartments online.

Salmon Falls Resort, 16707 N. Tongass Hwy. (P.O. Box 5700), Ketchikan, AK 99901 (© **800/247-9059** or 907/225-2752; www.salmonfallsresort.net), a huge fishing lodge, has its own waterfall where salmon spawn in August, plus a dock on Clover Passage with boats for guests. The large, quiet rooms at **Captain's Quarters Bed &**

Best Lodging in Luxury

The **Westcoast Cape Fox Lodge,** 800 Venetia Way, Ketchikan (© **800/325-4000** or 907/225-8001; www.westcoasthotels.com), is the most beautiful hotel in Southeast Alaska. A sheer drop-off and tall rainforest trees create the lofty feeling of a treehouse in the rooms and restaurant (also the best in town, with great views and a menu of steak and seafood ranging from $17–$37). The hotel has an understated but inspired design; masterpieces of Tlingit art lend a sense of the peace and spirit of the rainforest. Rooms are large and airy, appointed in rich-toned wood, and have attractively tiled bathrooms. All but a dozen share a view of Ketchikan and the sea and islands beyond. Rates for doubles run $190 to $200 in high season.

Breakfast, 325 Lund St., Ketchikan, AK 99901 (© **907/225-4912;** www.ptialaska. net/~captbnb), rival the best hotel rooms in Ketchikan, but cost half as much. All have a sweeping view of the city and the ocean.

The **New York Hotel/The Inn at Creek Street,** 207 Stedman St., Ketchikan, AK 99901 (© **800/225-0246;** www.thenewyorkhotel.com), have the perfect central location just off Creek Street. Both properties are operated by the same family. The quirky hotel building has antiques-furnished rooms that look out on a small boat harbor. The inn consists of spacious, modern luxury suites with kitchens, excellent amenities, and lots of privacy

Ocean View Restaurante, 1831 Tongass Ave. (© **907/225-7566**), is a lively local favorite, with a long menu featuring reasonably priced, tasty dishes. The restaurant offers Mexican and Italian cuisine (and an occasional Greek item). Service is friendly and efficient. The pizza, delivered free, is the best in town.

SITKA

Sitka's history is Alaska's richest, and there's more of real interest in this town than any other you might visit. Once the capital of Russian America—and the site of a historic battle between the Russian colonists and the proud Tlingit tribe—Sitka retains much of the influence of both of its formative cultures. Historical photographs bear a surprising resemblance to today's city. Even a superficial exploration of the attractions takes a day, and that's without time for the out-of-the-way points of interest or the outdoors. Besides its historical significance, Sitka is fun to visit. Somehow it has retained a friendly, authentic feel, despite the crush of thousands of visitors (though there are fewer than in many other Alaska towns because cruise ships can't get easy access to its harbor).

GETTING AROUND   Unless you have mobility problems, we recommend walking in this town. You can hoof it to all the sites, and it's a beautiful place to explore. The Visitor Transit Bus, operated by the Sitka Tribe, makes a continuous circuit of the sites from May to September, Monday through Friday from 12:30 to 4:30pm, with added morning hours when cruise ships are in. The all-day fare is $7.

WHAT TO SEE & DO

A kiosk in the city-operated **Harrigan Centennial Hall,** 330 Harbor Dr., next to the Crescent Boat Harbor (© **907/747-3225**), is staffed by volunteers who distribute information only when cruise ships are in town, although you may be able to ask questions of staff at other times. The hall is open Monday through Friday from 8am to 10pm, Saturday 8am to 5pm, and sometimes Sunday. The **Sitka National Historic Park Visitor Center,** 106 Metlakatla St., Sitka, AK 99835 (© **907/747-0110;** www.nps.gov/sitk), run by the National Park Service, maintains the key historic sites in Sitka, and is an essential stop for gathering information and learning about the town's history. The center is open daily from 8am to 5pm in summer, Monday through Saturday from 8am to 5pm in winter.

At the **Sitka Tribe of Alaska's Community House,** you can sign up for walking or bus tours, kayaking, trail hikes, and other outdoor activities. **Sitka Tribe Dance Performances** presents traditional dances by members of the tribe at 200 Katlian St. (© **888/270-8687** or 907/747-7290; www.sitkatribe.org). Tickets cost $7 adults, $5 kids.

Most of Alaska's historic buildings are within walking distance. Up the road to your left, at Lincoln and Cathedral streets, **St. Michael's Cathedral** (© **907/747-8120**) is the first Russian Orthodox cathedral built in the New World—or at least a facsimile of the 1848 building, which burned in 1966. The icons, saved from the fire, date from the 16th century. A $2 donation is requested.

Continue on Lincoln Street to **Castle Hill,** where the American flag first rose over Alaska in 1867. In the opposite direction on Lincoln Street, at Monastery Street, **The Bishop's House** is Alaska's most interesting historic site. Downstairs is a self-guided museum; upstairs, the bishop's quarters are furnished with original and period pieces. It's an extraordinary window into an alternate stream of American history, from a time before the founding of Seattle or San Francisco, when Sitka was the most important city on North America's Pacific Coast. The tour concludes with a visit to a beautiful little chapel with many original icons from Russia. Admission is $4.

Farther on, at Lincoln Street and College Drive, the **Sheldon Jackson Museum** (© 907/747-8981; www.museums.state.ak.us) houses one of the best collections of Alaska Native art to be found anywhere. Admission is $4. A few more blocks down Lincoln Street you reach the must-see **Sitka National Historical Park** (© 907/747-0110), the site of the 1804 battle in which the Russians won Southeast Alaska from its Tlingit owners. The visitor center contains a museum explaining the history and the art of totem carving and a series of workshops in which to see Native artisans at work. Outside, explore the rainforest battlefield on trails lined with an extraordinary collection of totem poles.

At 1000 Raptor Way, not far from the park, the nonprofit **Alaska Raptor Center** (© 907/747-8662; www.alaskaraptor.org) heals bald eagles, owls, and other injured birds of prey. You'll have the opportunity to see the impressive birds up close in large enclosures; the highlight is an extraordinary flight-training center, built in 2003 at a cost of $3 million. Admission is $12 for adults, $6 for kids 12 and under.

The **Sitka Wildlife Quest,** operated by Allen Marine Tours (© 888/747-8101 or 907/747-8100; www.allenmarinetours.com), does terrific wildlife boat tours, guided by well-trained naturalists. Cruises start at $59 adults, $30 children. Sitka's waters and intricate shorelines are perfect for sea kayaking. Various companies offer guided paddles. Beginners will do well with **Sitka Ocean Adventures** (© 907/747-6375; www. ssoceanadventures.com).

WHERE TO STAY & DINE

Ebullient Carol and Bill Denkinger have a passion for making the **Alaska Ocean View Bed & Breakfast,** 1101 Edgecumbe Dr. (© 907/747-8310; www.sitka-alaska-lodging. com), a place you'll remember. They've thought of everything, from the covered outdoor Jacuzzi to games for the kids. The inn has a view of the Gulf of Alaska and is about a mile from the historic district.

The **Westmark Atika,** 330 Seward St. (© 800/544-0970 or 907/747-56241; www. westmarkhotels.com), overlooks Crescent Harbor in the heart of the historic district. The lobby suggests the building style of Northwest Native Americans, but the more anonymous rooms will be familiar to any business traveler, with furniture of warm wood and all the expected amenities.

The **Bayview Restaurant,** 407 Lincoln St. (© 907/747-5440), though sometimes noisy and a bit cramped, offers a great view of the boat harbor, reasonable prices, and good food (especially the burgers and chowder). The **Channel Club,** 2906 Halibut Point Rd. (© 907/747-9916), serves amazing steak. The salad bar, which comes with every meal, is legendary. **Pizza Express,** 236 Lincoln St. (© 907/966-2428), has a Mexican menu, but they also serve and deliver good pizza.

JUNEAU

Impossibly tucked into the mountains along the Gastineau Channel, Juneau (*June*-oh) is the nation's most remote state capital and surely its most beautiful. Eagles wheel over downtown streets and land on mountainside rainforest roosts just blocks from the capitol building. Yet the town also bustles like no other Alaskan city, the downtown streets echoing with the mad shopping sprees of cruise-ship passengers in the summer tourist season and the whispered intrigues of the politicians during the winter legislative session.

Downtown, the crush of visitors can be overwhelming when numerous cruise ships are in port at once. The streets around the docks have been entirely taken over by shops and other touristy businesses, but only a few blocks away are quiet mountainside neighborhoods of houses with mossy roofs, and the woods and mountains, populated by bears, eagles, and salmon. The city's many government workers make it the most cosmopolitan town between Vancouver and Anchorage, a place where you can get a great meal at the end of a day's mountain hike or kayak paddle.

GETTING AROUND   A car is a hindrance in compact downtown Juneau, but if you're going to the Mendenhall Glacier or to any of the attractions out the road or on Douglas Island, renting a car for a day or two is a good idea. Hertz, Avis, Budget, Alamo, and National are based at Juneau's airport (see "Getting There," on p. 998).

WHAT TO SEE & DO

The **Visitor Information Center** is in the Centennial Hall at 101 Egan Dr., near the State Museum (© **888/581-2201** or 907/586-2201; fax 907/586-6304; www.travel juneau.com). Volunteers also staff a **visitor information desk** at the airport, near the door in the baggage-claim area, and at the Auke Bay ferry terminal. During summer, centers are staffed at the cruise-ship terminal and at Marine Park.

You can see a good many of Juneau's sights, and some of its nature, within walking distance of the downtown cruise-ship dock. The bronze statue of **Patsy Ann** on the dock represents a beady-eyed bull terrier famous in the 1930s for greeting all arriving boats. To the right, as you face the mountains, the **Mount Roberts Tramway,** 490 S. Franklin St. (© **888/461-8726** or 907/463-3412; www.goldbelttours.com), whisks passengers from tourist-clogged Franklin Street to clear air, expansive trails, and overwhelming views at the tree line. It costs $25 adults, $14 children ages 6 to 12, and free for kids under 5. Don't bother spending the money, however, if it's a cloudy day, as the views will be nonexistent. Closed October through April.

The interesting **Alaska State Museum,** below the state office building at 395 Whittier St. (© **907/465-2901;** www.museums.state.ak.us), puts the whole state in context with its huge collection of Alaskan art and Alaska Native artifacts. Summer admission is $5 adults, free for ages 18 and under. After tackling the museum, head to the intersection of Fourth and Main streets, the center of the city, where you'll find the state capitol, courthouse, state office building, and **Juneau–Douglas City Museum** (© **907/ 586-3572;** www.juneau.org/parksrec/museum). This fun little museum is worth a visit to learn about Tlingit culture and the city's pioneer and mining history. The plaza in front is where the 49-star U.S. flag was first raised in 1959, when Alaska got its statehood before Hawaii did. Summer admission is $4. About 3 blocks away, at Fifth and Gold, the tiny, octagonal **St. Nicholas Russian Orthodox Church** is a landmark built in 1893 by local Tlingits who, under pressure to convert to Christianity, chose the only faith that allowed them to keep their language. Admission $2.

The **Macaulay Salmon Hatchery,** 2697 Channel Dr., 3 miles from downtown (© **877/463-2486** or 907/463-4810; www.dipac.net), was ingeniously designed to allow visitors to watch from outdoor decks the entire process of harvesting and fertilizing eggs. From mid-June to October, salmon swim up a 450-foot fish ladder, visible through a window. Inside, large saltwater aquariums show off the area's marine life as it looks in the natural environment. Admission is $3.25 adults, $1.75 kids 12 and under.

A truly impressive sight is the state's third-most-visited attraction, **Mendenhall Glacier,** at the head of Glacier Spur Road (from Egan Dr., turn right on Mendenhall Loop Rd. to Glacier Spur; visitor center © **907/789-0097**). Mendenhall is the most easily accessible glacier in Alaska, with great views from the parking lot across the lake to the glacier's face, and a wheelchair-accessible trail that leads to the water's edge. Simply standing in front of the blue ice and feeling its cool breath is worth the stop, but also check out the visitor center, a sort of glacier museum with excellent explanatory models, computerized displays, and ranger talks. Excellent hiking trails start from here, too, ranging from a half-mile nature trail loop to two fairly steep, 3.5-mile hikes approaching each side of the glacier. Those with experience and the proper equipment can hike on the glacier. Admission is $3 for adults, free for children under 12.

WHERE TO STAY & DINE

Hotel rooms can be scarce in the summer, so book ahead. Bed-and-breakfasts are a good option. The Juneau Convention and Visitors Bureau's *Juneau Travel Planner* and website contain listings of and links to hotels and B&Bs (© **888/581-2201;** www.travel juneau.com). You also can find a B&B in Juneau, or anywhere in Southeast Alaska, through **www.accommodations-alaska.com.**

Set in a historic building that once functioned as a branch of the state capitol, the **Baranof Hotel,** 127 N. Franklin St. (© **800/544-0970** or 907/586-2660; www. westmarkhotels.com), has the feel of a grand hotel, although some rooms are a bit small. The upper-floor rooms have great views on the water side. Its restaurant offers the best fine dining in Juneau. The business-oriented **Goldbelt Hotel Juneau,** 51 W. Egan Dr. (© **888/478-6909** or 907/586-6900; www.goldbelttours.com), is decorated with masterpieces of Tlingit art, including a totem pole out front and a huge yellow cedar bas-relief by Nathan Jackson in the lobby-restaurant area. The large rooms are noticeably silent and immaculate. **Pearson's Pond Luxury B&B Inn and Adventure Spa,** 4541 Sawa Circle (© **888/658-6328** or 907/798-3772; www.pearsonspond.com), has every amenity from yoga, laptops, and fishing rods to VCRs, a separate hot tub in the garden (and maybe one in your room, too), and kitchenettes stocked with food, wine, and the owner's home-baked bread.

You'll find comfortable, private rooms in a house downtown at **Gold Street Inn** (© **907/586-9863;** www.juneauinn.com). All five rooms come with full kitchens; continental breakfast is included. **The Driftwood Lodge,** 435 Willoughby Ave. (© **800/ 544-2239** or 907/586-2280; www.driftwoodalaska.com), offers modernized two-bedroom suites with full kitchens for the same price that other hotels charge for a regular room (though the lodge has standard rooms, too).

At **DiSopra,** 429 W. Willoughby Ave. (© **907/586-3150**), classically trained chefs turn out flawless Mediterranean cuisine in a quiet and airy dining room with a great view. A cheaper cafe and bakery, **The Fiddlehead Restaurant and Bakery** (© **907/ 586-3150**) shares the same owners and building as DiSopra. **The Hangar,** handy to the docks at 2 Marine Way (© **907/586-5018**), is a fun bar and grill with great sea views. Literally across the hall from The Hangar, **Pizzeria Roma** (© **907/723-4658**) serves fantastic pizza—the best in Southeast Alaska—and tasty Italian cuisine.

SOUTHEAST ALASKA'S NATURAL WONDERS
GLACIER BAY NATIONAL PARK

What you can see in Glacier Bay you can see few other places. Humpback whales often frequent the waters right in front of the visitor center and lodge, jumping out of the water as if putting on performances for sea kayakers, and glaciers of bright blue drop immense hunks of ice into the ocean at the head of the bay. And there's the land itself. Crushed under a mile-thick wall of ice less than 2 centuries ago, today it's an impossibly rugged 65-mile-long fjord. Mankind has left no mark on this new land; there are no roads or buildings beyond the edge of the park.

Most of the cruise ships on Inside Passage itineraries visit Glacier Bay, although the National Park Service limits their number to protect the whales, so some lines skip it. Independent travelers can visit by day boat, fly over in a small plane, or join a sea kayaking adventure.

Exploring the Park

Glacier Bay Lodge (© **888/229-8687** or 907/697-4000; www.visitglacierbay.com) is the only place to stay in the park, and a new concessionaire upgraded the rooms in 2005. In general, they are comfortable but unmemorable, although the setting is pleasant. The buildings are set amid the soothing quiet of large rainforest trees and are reached from the main lodge by boardwalks and steps. Laundry facilities and rental of bikes and fishing gear are available. The company offers all-inclusive packages starting at $399 per person, which include lodging, meals, activities, and transfers from the airport.

VISITOR INFORMATION For advance information, contact the **Glacier Bay National Park and Preserve** at P.O. Box 140, Gustavus, AK 99826 (© **907/697-2230;** www.nps.gov/glba). The Park Service interprets the park mainly by placing well-prepared rangers on board most cruise and tour vessels entering the bay. The park also maintains a modest visitor center with displays on the park on the second floor of the lodge at wooded Bartlett Cove. Pick up the park map and handy guide, *The Fairweather.* Nearby are the park's offices, a free campground, a backcountry office, a few short hiking trails, a dock, sea kayak rental, and other park facilities. Rangers lead daily nature walks and present an evening slide show.

BY TOUR BOAT A day boat is the main way for independent travelers to see the park. It is operated by a park concessionaire, a joint venture of ARAMARK and Huna Totem, with offices at 241 W. Ship Creek Ave., Anchorage, AK 99501 (© **888/229-8687** or 907/264-4600; www.visitglacierbay.com), or, locally, in the summer only, at 199 Bartlett Cove (P.O. Box 179), Gustavus, AK 99826 (© **907/697-4000;** fax 907/697-4001). The boat leaves from the dock in Bartlett Cove and sails to the fjords' very head and the Grand Pacific Glacier. The 8-hour voyage is too long for many children. There's a snack bar, and a simple lunch is provided. Bring good rain gear and layers of warm clothing. Binoculars, a necessity, are provided. A Park Service ranger does the commentary, so you can count on accuracy and a didactic approach missing from most commercial tours. The fare is $160 for adults, half price for children.

The company offers a same-day trip from Juneau, but it makes for too long a day, and the schedule leaves no shore time in Glacier Bay or Gustavus, or time for whale-watching in Icy Strait. A better choice is to book one of their multiday packages, which may save money over separate transportation and room rates, and include all the transfers and details.

BY SEA KAYAK You won't forget seeing a breaching humpback whale from a sea kayak, sitting just inches off the water. It happens around here. When we breathlessly told our innkeepers about the experience, they smiled politely. They hear the same descriptions all the time.

Inexperienced paddlers should choose a guided trip. **Alaska Discovery,** 5310 Glacier Hwy., Juneau (© **800/586-1911** or 907/780-6226; www.akdiscovery.com), is Alaska's best large sea-kayak guide organization. They offer paddles ranging from 6 hours to 8 days in Glacier Bay. A 6-hour guided paddle from Bartlett Cove is the best choice for beginners. Although the trip goes nowhere near the glaciers, the paddlers stand a good chance of seeing whales, sometimes quite close up. The guides are well trained and know how to teach and make the trip an adventure. Any fit person can enjoy the trip. It costs $140, including a tasty lunch and a ride from your lodgings or the airport. Longer tours are available as well.

TRACY ARM & ENDICOTT ARM

About 50 miles due south of Juneau, these long, deep, and almost claustrophobically narrow fjords reach back into the coastal mountains to active glaciers—the **Sawyer Glacier** in Tracy Arm and **Dawes Glacier** in Endicott. Both calve ice constantly, sometimes discarding blocks of such size that they clog the narrow fjord passages, making navigation difficult. A passage up either fjord offers stunning views of high, cascading waterfalls; tree- and snow-covered mountain valleys; and wildlife that might include Sitka black-tailed deer, bald eagles, sea lions, harbor seals, and possibly even the odd black bear or whale.

The scenery and wildlife viewing in Tracy Arm easily rival the more widely known Glacier Bay, and for those not riding a cruise ship, Tracy Arm has a significant advantage: It's much easier and less expensive to visit. The largest operator is the Native-owned **Goldbelt,** 76 Egan Dr., Juneau (© **800/820-2628** or 907/586-8687; www.goldbelttours.com). They offer daylong glacier trips to Tracy Arm Fjord daily, with the exact destination somewhat contingent on tides; at times they go to Fords Terror and Dawes Glacier. Tours start at 8am in the summer (check for schedule changes). A naturalist provides commentary on the high-speed catamaran. Light meals are for sale, and the use of binoculars is included in the adult price of $139, $90 children ages 2 to 10, free under 2. The family-operated **Adventure Bound Alaska,** 215 Ferry Way, Juneau (© **800/228-3875** or 907/463-2509; www.adventureboundalaska.com), prides itself on slower tours that allow more time to soak up the sights. They charge $120 adults, $80 ages 17 and younger.

MISTY FJORDS NATIONAL MONUMENT

President Jimmy Carter set aside these 2.3 million acres of inviolate wilderness as a national monument in 1978, and they're still waiting to be discovered. The monument's **Rudyerd Bay** is like a place where the earth shattered open: The cliffs in its Punchbowl Cove rise vertically 3,150 feet from the surface of water that's 900 feet deep—topography in a league with the Grand Canyon. Waterfalls pound down out of the bay's granite. The glaciers of the northern part of the monument are also impressive, although they require a plane to visit.

Visits to the monument are by tour boat, floatplane, or sea kayak. It isn't a cheap place to go, and you don't see much wildlife. By boat, you don't see glaciers, although glaciated mountains are a spectacular feature of the flights. Unlike Glacier Bay or

Tracy Arm—places with more wildlife and more glaciers at sea level—the experience at Misty is pure geology: You go for the scenery.

The main tour boat operation to Misty is **Alaska Cruises,** owned by Juneau's Goldbelt Native corporation, 57 Main St., Suite 201, Ketchikan (© **800/228-1905** or 907/225-6044; www.goldbelttours.com). The company offers the opportunity see the fjords from above by float plane and return to Ketchikan by water; the price—$150 adults, $125 children 2 to 10, free 1 and under—is a bargain with the inclusion of the flightseeing.

Visiting the fjords by kayak is a real expedition, advisable only for those who already know they enjoy this mode of travel. **Southeast Exposure** (© **907/225-8829;** www.southeastexposure.com) has done guided paddles here for 20 years, earning a good reputation. Their 6-day trip is $950 per person.

2 Denali National Park

Denali (Den-*al*-ee) National Park gives regular people easy access to real wilderness. This is Alaska's most visited—environmentalists say overvisited—wilderness area, with almost one million people a year entering annually to soak up the park's scenic splendor. It's got sweeping tundra vistas, abundant wildlife, and North America's tallest mountain, **Mount McKinley** (commonly known to Alaskans by its original Native name, Denali, which means the "Great One"), all in a pristine natural environment where truly wild animals live in a complete ecosystem pretty much without human interference. A single National Park Service decision makes this possible: The only road through the park is closed to the public. This means that to get into the park, you must ride a crowded bus over a dusty gravel road hour after hour, but it also means that the animals are still there to watch, and their behavior remains essentially normal. From the window of the bus, you're likely to see grizzly bears doing what they would be doing even if you weren't there.

What's even more unique is that you can get off the bus whenever you want to and walk away across the tundra, out of sight of the road, to be alone in this primeval wilderness. When you're ready to return to civilization, you can just walk to the road and catch the next bus—they come every half-hour.

VISITOR INFORMATION

The most important resource for setting up a trip is the concessionaire: **Doyon/ARAMARK Joint Venture,** 241 W. Ship Creek Ave., Anchorage, AK 99501 (© **800/622-7275** or 907/272-7275; fax 907/264-4684; at Denali, May 15 through the visitor season, the number is © 907/683-8200; www.reservedenali.com). The concession is operated by a joint venture of ARAMARK and the Doyon Native corporation; for the purposes of visitors, any of those names refer to the same outfit. They handle the reservations system for the campgrounds and shuttle buses, as well as two hotels, bus tours, a rafting operation, and a dinner theater.

The easiest place to make in-person contact with the concessionaire or the Park Service itself is the **Wilderness Access Center** on Denali Park Road, ½ mile from the park entrance (P.O. Box 9), Denali National Park, AK 99755 (© **907/683-2294;** www.nps.gov/dena). It's closed October through April. Here you will find the Denali Park Resorts reservation and ticketing desks and the park backcountry desk. Since there's no park entrance station, this center is also the stop for the park map, a copy of the *Alpenglow* park newspaper, and other handouts.

Getting to the Park by Train

The **Alaska Railroad** (℗ **800/544-0552** or 907/265-2494; www.alaskarailroad.com) pioneered tourism to the park before the George Parks Highway was built in 1972. All the cars are luxurious; the rail line follows a historic, unspoiled route through beautiful countryside; the commentary by well-trained Alaska high school students is fresh and engaging; and the food is good.

In summer, trains leave both Anchorage and Fairbanks daily at 8:15am, arriving at the park from Anchorage at 3:45pm and from Fairbanks at noon, crossing and going on to the opposite city for arrival at 8:15pm in each. The fare from Anchorage to Denali is $129 one-way for adults, from Fairbanks $59, half price for children. The full train runs only from mid-May to mid-September, with somewhat lower fares in the first and last few weeks of the season. During the winter, the Alaska Railroad runs a single passenger car from Anchorage to Fairbanks and back once a week—a truly spectacular, truly Alaskan experience.

Park entrance fees are $20 per family (up to eight) or $10 per person, good for 7 days. There is no entrance station to collect the fee, but it is automatically added to your bill when you make shuttle or campground reservations. If you have a National Parks Pass or a Golden Age or Golden Access pass, mention it when you reserve to get your discount. Entrance fees are now in place year-round, and are collected at the Murie Science and Learning Center during winter months.

Warning: Reserving shuttle-bus seats and a space at one of the campground sites in advance is essential if you want to guarantee yourself entrance into the park. Only 35% of shuttle seats and any leftover car-camping sites are opened to walk-ins, 2 days before date of entrance. You could easily get shut out of a visit. For information on reserving ahead of time, as well as walk-in procedures, contact Denali Park Resorts (see above), or check out the park's website (**www.nps.gov/dena**).

WHAT TO SEE & DO

There are no reserved seats on the park buses, but if you arrive early, choose a place on the left side, which has the best views on the way out. Most buses will see grizzly bears, caribou, Dall sheep, moose, and, occasionally, wolves.

Here are some of the highlights along the road (check the visitor center or the Park Service information handouts to confirm times of the guided walks):

Mile 9: In clear weather, this is the closest spot to the park entrance with a view of Mount McKinley. This section also is a likely place to see moose, especially in the fall rutting season.

Mile 29: An hour and 10 minutes into the drive, a large rest stop overlooks the Teklanika River. The Teklanika, like many other rivers on Alaska's glacier-carved terrain, is a braided river—a stream wandering in a massive gravel streambed that's much too big for it.

Mile 34: Craggy Igloo Mountain is a likely place to see Dall sheep. Without binoculars, they'll just look like white dots. Manageable climbs on Igloo, Cathedral, and Sable mountains take off along the road in the section from Igloo Creek to Sable Pass.

Miles 38–43: Sable Pass, a critical habitat area for bears, is closed to people. A half-eaten sign helps explain why. Bears show up here mostly in the fall. This is the start of the road's broad Alpine vistas.

Mile 46: The top of 5-mile-wide Polychrome Pass, the most scenic point on the ride, and a toilet break, is 2 hours and 25 minutes into the trip. Caribou look like specks when they pass in the great valley below you. Note how the mountains of colored rock on either side of the plain match up—they were once connected before glacial ice carved this valley. Huge rocks on its floor are glacial erratics, plucked from the bedrock by moving ice and left behind when it melted.

Mile 53: The Toklat River, another braided river, is a flat plain of gravel with easy walking. The glaciers that feed the river are 10 miles upstream. The river bottom is habitat for bears, caribou, and wolves, and a good place for picnics.

Mile 58: Highway Pass is the highest point on the road. In good weather, dramatic views of Mount McKinley start here. The Alpine tundra from here to the Eielson Visitor Center is inviting for walking, but beware: Tundra is soft underfoot and can conceal holes and declivities that can twist an ankle.

Mile 64: Thorofare Pass, where the road becomes narrow and winding, is a good area to look for bears and caribou.

Mile 68.5: The incredibly rugged terrain to the north is the earth and vegetation covering Muldrow Glacier. The ice extends to McKinley's peak, and was the early and arduous route for climbers. McKinley's glaciers, falling 15,000 vertical feet and extending up to 45 miles in length, are among the world's greatest. The Ruth Glacier has carved the Great Gorge on the south side, which is almost 6,000 feet deep above the ice and another 4,000 below—almost twice the depth of the Grand Canyon. The park road comes within a mile of the Muldrow's face, then continues through wet, rolling terrain past beaver ponds, and finally descends into a small spruce patch near Mile 82.

Mile 86: Wonder Lake campground is the closest road point to Mount McKinley, 27 miles away. The fact that McKinley looks so massive from this considerable distance, dominating the sky, is a testament to its stupendous size. You'll likely never see a larger object on this planet. From its base (elevation here is only 2,000 ft.) to its top is an elevation gain greater than that of any other mountain on earth. Other mountains are taller overall, but they stand on higher ground.

WHERE TO CAMP, STAY & DINE

There are a number of campgrounds in and around Denali, bookable through ARA-MARK (see "Visitor Information," above). **Riley Creek campground,** near the visitor center, is best for those who want to be in the middle of things, near the store, showers, a bus stop for the free front-country shuttle, and a pay phone. **Savage River,** on Denali Park Road, 13 miles from the entrance, is a wonderful campground with unforgettable views.

The **Denali Bluffs Hotel,** at Mile 238.4 on the Parks Highway (© 866/683-8500 or 907/683-8500; www.denalialaska.com), looks down on the Nenana Canyon area from above the highway. Rooms are light and tastefully decorated. **Denali Crow's Nest Log Cabins,** at Mile 238.5 on the Parks Highway (© 888/917-8130 or 907/683-2723; www.denalicrowsnest.com), is a series of roomy and comfortable cabins perched in five tiers on the side of a mountain above the Nenana Canyon area.

You can't miss the tacky highway frontage of the **Denali Salmon Bake** (© 907/683-2733; www.thebakerocks.com) in the Nenana Canyon area. It can be a fun place to eat in a picnic setting, and the food is fine. **The Overlook Bar and Grill,** at Mile 238.5 on the Parks Highway (© 907/683-2641), is a fun, noisy place with the feeling of a classic bar and grill. A huge variety of craft beers is available, with several on tap. **The Perch,** at Mile 224 on the Parks Highway (© 888/322-2523 or

©/fax 907/683-2523; www.denaliperchresort.com), is a friendly place serving a simple steak and seafood menu. The home-baked bread is noteworthy.

3 Anchorage

Anchorage, which started as a tent camp for workers building the Alaska Railroad in 1914, stands between the Chugach Mountains and the waters of upper Cook Inlet. It was a sleepy railroad town until World War II, when a couple of military bases opened and livened things up. Even with that, though, Anchorage did not start becoming a city in earnest until the 1950s, when the Cold War (and Alaska's proximity to the ol' Evil Empire) spurred a huge investment in infrastructure. Today, Anchorage boasts good restaurants, good museums, and a nice little zoo; fancy ski resorts such as Mount Alyeska; and cultural attractions such as the world-class Alaska Native Heritage Center, a 26-acre celebration of the region's five major Native groups. And always, of course, there is wilderness, so close that moose regularly annoy gardeners, and bears sometimes amble though town.

Anchorage's downtown area is about 8×20 blocks near Ship Creek, but the rest of the city spreads some 5 miles east and 15 miles south. Most visitors spend a day or two in town before going somewhere more remote. The downtown area is pleasant, but we recommend you try to see more than just the streets of tourist-oriented shops. Check out the **Coastal Trail** and the **museums,** and if you have time, plan a day trip about 50 miles south along the incredibly scenic inlet known as **Turnagain Arm.**

ESSENTIALS

GETTING THERE   By Plane   If you're arriving or leaving by plane, you'll land at the **Ted Stevens Anchorage International Airport.** The facility is located within the city limits, a 15-minute drive from downtown. Taxis, the best way to get downtown, run about $15 for the trip. The **People Mover** city bus also has an airport route, for those whose priority is saving money; fares are $1.50 adults, 75¢ ages 5 to 18, 35¢ over age 60, free ages 4 and under.

By Car   By car, there is only one road into Anchorage from the rest of the world: the **Glenn Highway.** The other road out of town, the **Seward Highway,** leads to the Kenai Peninsula.

VISITOR INFORMATION   The **Anchorage Convention and Visitor Bureau,** 524 W. 4th Ave., Anchorage, AK 99501-2212 (© **907/276-4118;** fax 907/278-5559; www.anchorage.net), offers information on the whole state at its centers and extensive website. The main location is the **Log Cabin Visitor Information Center,** downtown at 4th Avenue and F Street (© **907/274-3531;** open daily June–Aug 7:30am–7pm, May and Sept 8am–6pm, Oct–Apr 9am–4pm). If it's crowded, go to the storefront office right behind it.

For an extensive listing of the city's major events and festivals (there's something happening in town almost every day of the year), check **www.anchorage.net.**

FAST FACTS   There's no sales tax in Anchorage. The **bed tax** is 12%.

GETTING AROUND   Most **car-rental** companies operate at the airport. A compact car costs about $50 a day, with unlimited mileage. Advanced bookings are recommended. It takes a long time to go far using the **People Mover** bus system (© **907/ 343-6543;** www.peoplemover.org), but if you have the time it's inexpensive and covers most of the city.

WHAT TO SEE & DO

At the **Anchorage Museum of History and Art,** 121 W. Seventh Ave. (© **907/343-4326;** www.anchoragemuseum.org), the Alaska Gallery offers an informative and enjoyable walk through the state's history and anthropology. In the art galleries, you can see what's happening in art in Alaska today; Alaska art isn't all scenery and walrus ivory, but the grandeur of the place does influence almost every work. Admission is $6.50 adults, $6 seniors 65 and older, free for children 17 and under.

Alaska Native Heritage Center, near the intersection of the Glenn Highway and Muldoon Road (© **800/315-6608** or 907/330-8000; www.alaskanative.net), is Alaska's best cultural site. Alaska Natives built this extraordinary center to bring their cultures to visitors. What makes it so memorable is not the graceful building or the professional and informative displays, but the Native people themselves, real village people, who make a personal connection with visitors. The center takes most of a day to absorb. Attractions include storytellers, dance performances, and a series of workshops where artisans practice traditional crafts. Finally, there's a pond surrounded by five traditional Native dwellings representing each cultural group, each hosted by a member of that group. Admission is $24 adults, $16 children ages 7 to 16. Open daily from 8:30am to 5:30pm in summer.

At the **Alaska Zoo,** 4731 O'Malley Rd. (© **907/346-3242;** www.alaskazoo.org), gravel paths wander through the woods past large enclosures with natural flora for bears, seals, otters, musk oxen, mountain goats, moose, caribou, and waterfowl. Admission is $10 adults, $8 seniors, $6 children 12 to 17, $4 children 3 to 12, free under 3. Drive out the New Seward Highway to O'Malley Road, then turn left and go 2 miles; it's 20 minutes from downtown, without traffic.

Earthquake Park, on the west end of Northern Lights Boulevard, offers a sculpture and excellent interpretive signs commemorating and explaining the 1964 Good Friday earthquake (North America's largest earthquake ever) and pointing out its few remaining marks on the land. It is also a good access point to the **Coastal Trail,** which leads 10 miles from the western end of Second Avenue along the shore to **Kincaid Park.** It's a unique pathway to a natural environment from the heart of downtown. You can join the wide, paved trail at various points; downtown, **Elderberry Park,** at the western end of Fifth Avenue, is the most popular. From there, you might see beluga whales swimming along the trail at high tide. Moose are sometimes spotted toward the Kincaid Park end of the trail.

The **Eklutna Historical Park,** about 26 miles out the Glenn Highway (© **907/688-6026;** www.eklutna.com), has a fascinating old cemetery, still in use, in which each

---

Big State, Big Movie

The **Alaska Experience Theatre** (© 907/272-9076; www.alaskaexperience theatre.com) is on the northwest corner of 6th Avenue and G Street, partly in a dome tent. A 40-minute Omnivision wraparound movie about Alaska costs $8 for adults, $4 for children, showing hourly. It's certainly spectacular—too much so for some people, who get motion sickness. Sit toward the center at the back. An Alaska Earthquake display that really shakes is $6 for adults and $4 for children ages 5 to 12. Combination tickets are discounted. The theater is open in summer daily from 9am to 9pm, in winter noon to 6pm.

grave is enclosed by a decorated spirit house the size of a large dollhouse. The unique practice evolved in the melding of Athabascan and Russian Orthodox beliefs. There are two Russian Orthodox churches on the site, including the **St. Nicholas Orthodox Church.** Built north of here sometime before 1870, it is among the oldest buildings in the Southcentral region. Walk through the park by yourself or take an informative 30-minute tour for the same price: $5 adults, $2.50 children ages 10 to 18 and seniors over 65, free under 10. Take the Glenn Highway to the Eklutna exit, then go left across the overpass.

For information on outdoors options from Anchorage, stop by the **Alaska Public Lands Information Center,** located at 605 W. 4th Ave., Suite 105, in the 1930s concrete federal building across the intersection from the log cabin at 4th Avenue and F Street (✆ **907/271-2737;** www.nps.gov/aplic), where staff can offer guidance for anyone planning to spend time in the outdoors anywhere in Alaska. You can buy ferry tickets from the Alaska Marine Highway System, there's an excellent selection of trail and field guides, and the rangers behind the desk know what they're talking about.

WHERE TO STAY

Rooms can be hard to come by in Anchorage in the summer, so be sure to arrange lodging as far in advance as possible. Note that rates quoted in this section represent the average rack rates during high season; low-season rates are usually about half the price. About 50 B&Bs link through a website maintained by the cooperative **Anchorage Alaska Bed and Breakfast Association** (✆ **888/584-5147** or 907/272-5909; www. anchorage-bnb.com).

The **Hotel Captain Cook,** 4th Avenue and K Street (✆ **800/843-1950** or 907/ 276-6000; www.captaincook.com), is Alaska's great, grand hotel, where royalty and rock stars stay. Rates run $240 to $250 double. The rooms in the **Aspen Hotel Anchorage,** 108 E. 8th Ave. (✆ **907/868-1605;** www.aspenhotelsak.com), right across from the museum and federal building, attain such a level of luxury that it's hard to think of anything they could improve upon. Summer rates are $179 double, including breakfast.

The small, unpretentious, and centrally located **Voyager Hotel,** 501 K St. (✆ **800/ 247-9070** or 907/277-9501; www.voyagerhotel.com), has large, light rooms with kitchens, and gets consistent raves from travelers. Rooms go for $179 double; smoking is not permitted. The owners of the **Parkwood Inn,** 4445 Juneau St. (✆ **800/ 478-3590** or 907/563-3590; www.parkwoodinn.net), have turned apartments into trim standard hotel rooms. Every unit has a full kitchen and a private balcony, and even the least expensive rooms have large sitting areas and dining room tables. Rates are $130 to $140.

WHERE TO DINE

The **Marx Brothers Cafe,** 627 W. 3rd Ave. (✆ **907/278-2133;** www.marxcafe.com), began as a hobby among three friends and sets the standard of excellence in the state. The cuisine is varied and creative, ranging from Asian to Italian, but everyone orders the Caesar salad, prepared tableside. The decor and style are studied casual elegance. Main courses run $18 to $36. Despite its Italian name, **Orso,** 737 W. 5th Ave. (✆ **907/ 222-3232;** www.orsoalaska.com), offers superb wood-grilled steaks and locally caught seafood as well as excellent pastas, all in an elegant, comfortable setting. Main courses cost $12 to $33. For an active, hardy experience, the **Glacier Brewhouse,** 737 W. 5th Ave. (✆ **907/274-BREW;** www.glacierbrewhouse.com), offers a tasty, eclectic, and ever-changing menu served in a large dining room with lodge decor, where the pleasant scent of the wood-fired grill hangs in the air. They brew five hearty beers behind a glass wall. Main courses cost $9 to $34.

The best pizza and beer in Anchorage undoubtedly come from the fun and friendly **Moose's Tooth Pub and Pizzeria,** 3300 Old Seward Hwy. (© **907/258-2537;** www. moosestooth.net). The microbrewery came first, but the pizza really is the greater accomplishment. It has a soft, light crust like Italian pizza but with the oomph of the American version. Dine inside (perhaps in the "hippie pad"), or at picnic tables outside in a tent that's open year-round. A large pie will run you between $13 and $25.

Simon and Seafort's Saloon and Grill, 420 L St. (© **907/274-3502**), is one of Anchorage's great dinner houses with a turn-of-the-20th-century decor, a cheerful atmosphere, and fabulous sunset views of Cook Inlet. Prime rib and seafood are the specialties. To enjoy the place on a budget, order a sandwich and soup for lunch in the well-stocked bar. Main courses run $18 to $42.

4 Honolulu & Oahu

It's astounding to spend hours flying across the barren blue of the Pacific and then suddenly see below you the 26-mile-long metropolis of Honolulu, with its bright city lights, five-star restaurants, world-class shopping, and grand old hotels. Most visitors end up along the canyonlike streets of Waikiki, Honolulu's well-known hotel district and its most densely populated neighborhood. Some days, it seems like the entire world is sunning itself on Waikiki's famous beach.

Out in the country, the island of Oahu can be as down-home as a slack-key guitar. Here's where you'll find a big blue sky, perfect waves, empty beaches, rainbows, waterfalls, sweet tropical flowers, and fiery Pacific sunsets.

ESSENTIALS

GETTING THERE **Honolulu International Airport** sits on the south shore of Oahu, west of downtown Honolulu and Waikiki near Pearl Harbor. The cheapest shuttle service is **Airport Waikiki Express** (© **808/566-7333;** www.hawaii.gov/dot/ airports/hnl/hnl_ground_trans.htm), with 24-hour service in air-conditioned vans for just $8 from the airport to Waikiki ($14 round-trip). You'll find the shuttle at street level outside baggage claim. **TheBus** nos. 19 and 20 (Waikiki Beach and Hotels) take about an hour from the airport to downtown Honolulu and Waikiki. The one-way fare is $2 for adults and $1 for students ages 6 to 19; exact change only. You can bring a small suitcase, as long as it fits under your seat. **Taxi** fare is about $18 to downtown Honolulu, $25 to $30 to Waikiki.

VISITOR INFORMATION The **Oahu Visitors Bureau,** 735 Bishop St., Suite 1872, Honolulu, HI 96813 (© **877/525-OAHU** or 808/524-0722; www.visit-oahu. com), distributes a free travel planner and map. For general state information, contact the **Hawaii Visitors and Convention Bureau (HVCB),** 2270 Kalakaua Ave., 7th floor, Honolulu, HI 96815 (© **800/GO-HAWAII** or 808/923-1811; www.gohawaii. com). You can request a helpful accommodations guide, brochures, maps, and the *Islands of Aloha* magazine.

GETTING AROUND Traffic can be extremely heavy on Oahu's mostly two-lane roads. You can avoid gridlock by driving between 9am and 3pm or after 6pm.

Taking **TheBus** (© **808/848-5555,** or 808/296-1818 for recorded information; www.thebus.org) is often easier than parking your car. One of the best deals anywhere,

Hawaii

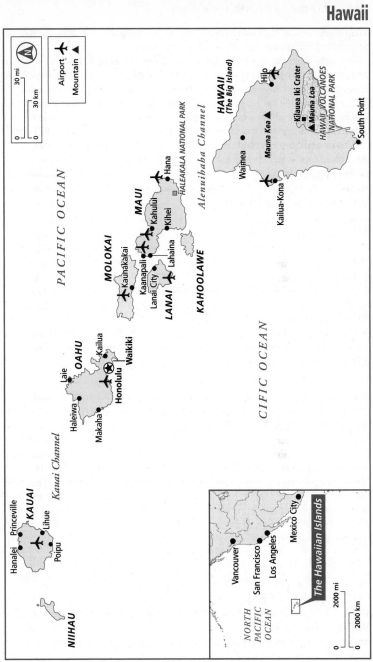

TheBus goes around the whole island for $2. The most popular route is no. 8, which shut-tles between Waikiki and Ala Moana Center every 10 minutes (trip time: 15–20 min.).

The fun, open-air, motorized **Waikiki Trolley** (© **800/824-8804** or 808/593-2822; www.waikikitrolley.com) loops around Waikiki and downtown Honolulu, stop-ping every 40 minutes at 12 key places, with commentary along the way. A 1-day pass ($25 for adults, $12 for kids 4–11) allows you to jump on and off all day long.

The major cab companies offer islandwide service; vehicles with wheelchair lifts (there's a $5 charge for wheelchairs) are available. **Star Taxi** (© **800/671-2999** or 808/942-STAR; www.hawaiistartaxi.net) offers a discount taxi service at the fixed price of $22 to Waikiki for up to five passengers, and no charge for baggage.

FAST FACTS   Hospitals with 24-hour emergency care include **Queens Medical Center,** 1301 Punchbowl St. (© **808/538-9011**), and **Moanalua Medical Center,** 3288 Moanalua Rd. (© **808/834-5333**). Central Oahu has **Wahiawa General Hospital,** 128 Lehua St. (© **808/621-8411**). **Straub Doctors on Call** (© **808/971-6000**) can dispatch a van if you need help getting to any of its numerous clinics.

Although Oahu is generally safe, there has been a series of purse-snatching incidents there. Thieves in slow-moving cars or on foot have snatched handbags from female pedestrians (in some instances, dragging women who refuse to let go of their purses down the street). The most common crime against tourists is rental-car break-in. Never leave any valuables in your car, not even in your trunk. Be especially leery of high-risk areas, such as beaches and resorts. And don't carry valuables or large amounts of cash in Waikiki and other tourist zones, including the USS *Arizona,* a high-theft area.

The **general excise tax** is 4%. **Hotel and room taxes** total about 11.42%.

HITTING THE BEACH

No beach anywhere is as famous as **Waikiki Beach,** a narrow, 1½-mile-long crescent of sand at the foot of a string of high-rise hotels. Home to the world's longest-running beach party, Waikiki is fabulous for swimming, board- and bodysurfing, diving, sail-ing, and snorkeling. Go early—it gets crowded.

Gold-sand **Ala Moana Beach Park,** on sunny Mamala Bay, stretches for more than a mile between downtown and Waikiki. This 76-acre midtown park has spreading lawns, a lagoon, a yacht harbor, tennis courts, and more. The water is calm almost year-round. Oahu's most popular snorkeling spot is **Hanauma Bay,** a marine-life conserva-tion district with a small, gold-sand beach that's packed with people year-round. TheBus runs frequent shuttles from Waikiki. Closed Tuesdays. Two-mile-long **Kailua Beach** is a 35-acre golden strand with dunes, palms, and panoramic views. The waters are great for swimming, windsurfing, bodysurfing, and kayaking. Best of all, the crowds haven't found it yet. Postcard-perfect **Lanikai Beach** is good for sailing, windsurfing, and kayaking, and perfect for swimming in the crystal-clear lagoon. Because it's in a residen-tial neighborhood, Lanikai has fewer crowds. There are no facilities or lifeguards.

OUTDOOR ACTIVITIES

GOLF   For last-minute and discount tee times, call **Stand-by Golf** (© **888/645-BOOK;** www.stand-bygolf.com), which offers discounted tee times for same-day or next-day golfing. Call between 7am and 11pm for a guaranteed tee time with up to a 50% discount off greens fees.

The **Makaha Resort Golf Club,** 84–627 Makaha Valley Rd., Waianae, 45 miles west of Honolulu (© **800/695-7111** or 808/695-5239; www.makahavalleyycc.com; greens fees $100), is "The Best Golf Course on Oahu," according to *Honolulu* magazine. The

Into the Deep: Submarine Rides

Want to play Jules Verne and experience Hawaii's underwater world from the comfort of a submarine? **Atlantis Submarines** (© **800/548-6262** or **808/973-9811;** www.go-atlantis.com) offers visitors the chance to explore the state's aquatic life in their natural habitat by plunging 100 feet below the surface of the sea in a state-of-the-art, high-tech submarine. Tours are offered in Oahu, Maui, and the Big Island, and cost $84 for adults, $42 for kids 12 and under (children must be at least 36 in. tall). Book online for discount rates of $76 adults and $38 kids. *Warning:* Though the ride is safe for everyone, skip it if you suffer from claustrophobia.

challenging par-72, 7,091-yard course meanders toward the ocean before turning and heading into the valley; sheer volcanic walls tower above.

The North Shore's **Turtle Bay Resort** (© **808/293-8574** or 808/293-9094; www.turtlebayresort.com; greens fees $155–$160) is home to two of Hawaii's top courses. The challenging 18-hole **Arnold Palmer Course** was designed by Arnold Palmer and Ed Seay. The front 9 holes play like a British Isles course, with rolling terrain and lots of wind. The back 9 have narrower, tree-lined fairways and water. A more forgiving choice is the **George Fazio–designed 9-hole course,** which can be played twice for a regulation par-71, 6,200-yard course. The course has two sets of tees, one designed for men and one for women, so you can get a slightly different play if you decide to tackle 18 holes.

HIKING   A moderate but steep, 1½-hour, 1.4-mile walk leads to the summit of Hawaii's most famous landmark: **Diamond Head Crater,** a 760-foot volcanic cone that affords 360-degree views of Oahu. The hike, which costs $1 per person, starts at Monsarrat and 18th avenues on the crater's inland side. Take TheBus no. 58 from the Ala Moana Shopping Center, or drive to the intersection of Diamond Head Road and 18th Avenue. Follow the road through the tunnel and park in the lot. The trail head proceeds along a paved walkway as it climbs the slope. You'll pass old World War I and II pillboxes, gun emplacements, and tunnels built as part of the Pacific defense network. Several steps take you up to the top observation post on Point Leahi. The views are indescribable. Wear decent shoes (sneakers are fine) and bring a flashlight (for the tunnels you'll walk through), water, a hat, and binoculars. Try to head out just after the 6:30am opening, before the noonday sun starts beating down.

WATERSPORTS   Because Oahu's best dives are offshore, your best bet for scuba diving is to book a two-tank dive from a dive boat. In Waikiki, try **South Sea Aquatics** (© **808/922-0852;** www.ssahawaii.com), which features two-tank boat dives, with transportation to and from Waikiki hotels, for $85 to $95 without gear and $16 extra for equipment. **Aaron's Dive Shop** (© **808/262-2333;** www.hawaii-scuba.com), Hawaii's oldest and largest, offers boat-dive excursions from $125 per person, including two tanks and transportation from the Kailua shop.

For snorkelers, Hanauma Bay has clear, warm, protected waters and an abundance of friendly fish. The bay has two reefs, an inner and an outer—the first for novices, the other for experts. Closed on Tuesday. The uninitiated can take a lesson and a 2-hour snorkel tour with **Surf-N-Sea** (© **808/637-9887**). Snorkel rentals are available at most dive shops and beach activity centers.

Summer is surf season in Waikiki, the best place on Oahu to learn how to surf. For lessons, go early to **Aloha Beach Service,** next to the Sheraton Moana Surfrider (© **808/ 922-3111**). Surfboards are available for rent at **Surf-N-Sea,** 62–595 Kamehameha Hwy., Haleiwa (© **808/637-9887;** www.surfnsea.com), for $5 to $7 an hour; they also offer lessons.

More experienced surfers should drop by any surf shop or call the **Surf News Network Surfline** (© **808/596-SURF**) to get the latest conditions. A good spot for advanced surfers is **The Cliffs,** at the base of Diamond Head.

In winter, you can watch the serious surfers at the beach near **Kalalua Point.**

THE TOP ATTRACTIONS

The forbidding, four-story Romanesque lava-rock structure that houses the **Bishop Museum,** 1525 Bernice St. (© **808/847-3511;** www.bishopmuseum.org), holds a vast collection of natural and cultural artifacts from Hawaii and the Pacific, including insect specimens, ceremonial spears, and pre-industrial Polynesian art. Daily cultural shows and demonstrations enrich the experience. Admission is $15 adults, $12 kids 4 to 12 and seniors. *Note:* A "mini" version of the Bishop Museum, at 2005 Kalia Rd. (© **808/946-9478**), is just right for visitors who want to get an insider's view of Hawaiian culture but are pressed for time (1½ hr. will do). You can participate in a variety of interactive, hands-on activities, from lei making to playing a Hawaiian instrument. Admission costs $7 adults, $5 seniors, and is free to kids 12 and under.

You can experience the natural beauty and culture of the vast Pacific at the **Polynesian Cultural Center,** 55–370 Kamehameha Hwy. (© **800/367-7060,** 808/293-3333, or 808/923-2911; www.polynesia.com), a living museum of seven islands. You "travel" through the 42-acre park by foot or canoe on a man-made freshwater lagoon. Each re-created village is "inhabited" by native students from Polynesia, who attend Hawaii's Brigham Young University. The park, which is operated by the Mormon Church, also features a variety of stage shows celebrating the music, dance, history, and culture of Polynesia; there's a luau every evening. Since a visit can take up to 8 hours, it's a good idea to arrive before 2pm. Basic admission costs $50 adults, $34 children 3 to 11.

At **Pearl Harbor** (© **808/422-0561** or 808/422-2771; www.nps.gov/usar), you can't miss the **USS *Arizona* Memorial,** built right above the shallow water where the ship was sunk on December 7, 1941; or the battleship **USS *Missouri*** (© **808/423-2263;** www.ussmissouri.com), on the decks of which peace was declared. Admission is free to the USS *Arizona* Memorial, but costs $16 adults, $8 kids 4 to 12 for the USS *Missouri.* What you may not notice, and should, is the **USS *Bowfin* Submarine Museum & Park** (© **808/423-1341;** www.bowfin.org). This National Historic Landmark offers a rare glimpse into the thrill and danger of life aboard a submarine. Admission is $8 adults, $3 kids 4 to 12.

WHERE TO STAY

The moderately priced **Ohana Hotels & Resorts** offer dependable, clean, well-appointed rooms and terrific deals for budget travelers. The chain's price structure (from $159) is based entirely on location, room size, and amenities. Check the Internet site where "best available rates" start at $79 (true bargain in Waikiki!). They also offer other deals, including air and car-rental packages; for information, call © **800/ 462-6262,** or visit www.ohanahotels.com.

You should also consider using the top reservations service in the state: **Hawaii's Best Bed & Breakfasts** (© **800/262-9912** or 808/985-7488; fax 808/967-8610;

www.bestbnb.com). This service charges $20 and is well worth the money. The owners personally select the traditional home stays, cottages, and inns, based on each one's hospitality and charm. They also book vacation rentals, hotels, and resorts.

The 80-room **Aston Coconut Plaza,** 450 Lewers St. (© **800/92-ASTON** or 808/923-8828; www.aston-hotels.com), is an island of integrity in a sea of tourist schlock. Calling itself a "studio-apartment boutique hotel," the recently renovated property offers personalized service and a tropical-plantation feel, with airy, island-style rooms, terracotta tile, and lots of greenery. Rooms have private lanais; most offer views of the Ala Wai Canal and the mountains. The rooms with kitchenettes are especially good deals.

For the ultimate heavenly Hawaii vacation, **Halekulani,** 2199 Kalia Rd. (© **800/367-2343** or 808/923-2311; www.halekulani.com), is *the* best place on the island. The luxury resort features five buildings spread out over 5 acres of prime Waikiki beachfront interconnected by courtyards and lush, tropical gardens. Rooms, 90% of which face the ocean, are huge, with separate sitting areas, furnished lanais, and fridges. Bathrooms have deep soaking tubs, separate showers, and luxurious robes.

At the intimate low-rise **Hawaiiana Hotel,** 260 Beach Walk (© **800/367-5122** or 808/923-3811; www.hawaiianahotelatwaikiki.com), you'll find a pineapple waiting for you at check-in, complimentary Kona coffee and tropical juice served poolside each morning, and flower leis at checkout. Each concrete hollow-tiled room contains a kitchenette, two beds (a double and a single), a fridge, and a view of the gardens and pools.

The best place to stay with the kids, the **Hilton Hawaiian Village Beach Resort & Spa,** 2005 Kalia Rd. (© **800/HILTONS** or 808/949-4321; www.hiltonhawaiian village.com), is Waikiki's biggest resort, with nearly 3,000 rooms spread over 20 acres. You'll find tropical gardens dotted with exotic birds, award-winning restaurants, a secluded lagoon, and a gorgeous stretch of Waikiki Beach. Accommodations in the four towers range from simply lovely to ultradeluxe; rooms are large and beautifully furnished. Its two spas—**Holistica Hawaii** (a wellness center with high-tech body-scanning equipment) and the more traditional **Mandara Spa**—are top-notch.

For people looking for a quieter stay, the elegant 25-story **Royal Garden at Waikiki,** 440 Olohana St. (© **800/367-5666** or 808/943-0202; www.royalgardens.com), is tucked away on a quiet, tree-lined side street. Each plush room contains a kitchenette, lots of closet space, and a lanai. The beach is a few blocks away, but at these prices ($150–$250 double), it's worth the hike. The hotel offers a free shuttle to shopping areas.

Step back in time at Waikiki's first hotel, the **Sheraton Moana Surfider,** 2365 Kalakaua Ave. (© **800/325-3535** or 808/922-3111; www.moana-surfrider.com), a National Historic Landmark that dates from 1901. The aloha spirit pervades this classy and charming place. You'll even see female employees wearing traditional Victorian-era muumuus. Most rooms have ocean views; all come with fridges and plush robes. The hotel sits on a prime stretch of beach. Daily activities include Hawaiian arts and crafts.

The **Waikiki Joy,** 320 Lewers St. (© **800/92-ASTON** or 808/923-2300; www.aston-hotels.com), is a hidden jewel that offers not only outstanding personal service but also a Bose entertainment system and a Jacuzzi in every room. The marble-accented open-air lobby and the tropical veranda set the tone for the beautifully decorated rooms. All rooms come with a fridge and lanai. A downside: The beach is a 10- to 15-minute walk away.

WHERE TO DINE

Cozy, busy, casual, and occasionally smoky, with a tiny tatami room for small groups, **Akasaka,** 1646B Kona St. (© **808/942-4466**), wins high marks for sushi, sizzling tofu and scallops, miso-clam soup, and the overall quality of its cuisine. During soft-shell crab season, you can order these spiny delicacies in sushi—a novel, tasty treat. Ordering specials, noodles, or other less-expensive a la carte items helps ease the bite of the bill.

Chef/owner George Mavrothalassitis, a native of Provence, runs the warm and elegant **Chef Mavro Restaurant,** 1969 S. King St. (© **808/944-4714;** www.chefmavro. com), in an accessible, nontouristy neighborhood in McCully. Hints of Tahitian vanilla, lemon grass, ogo, rosemary, and Madras curry add exotic flavors to the French-inspired cooking and fresh island ingredients.

Named after fabled surfer Duke Kahanamoku, the casual, all-day, upbeat, ocean-front **Duke's Canoe Club,** in the Outrigger Waikiki on the Beach at 2335 Kalakaua Ave. (© **808/922-2268**), buzzes with diners and Hawaiian-music lovers throughout the day. Open-air dining gives a front-row view of the sunset. Dinner fare is steak and seafood, with high marks for the prime rib, macadamia-crab wontons, and several preparations of the daily catch. Duke's is also loved for its barefoot bar with top-notch island entertainment and its island-style ambience.

Honolulu's most sumptuous and expensive dining takes place at **La Mer,** in the Halekulani hotel, 2199 Kalia Rd. (© **808/923-2311**), the only AAA Five-Diamond restaurant in the state. Classical French influences meld with fresh island ingredients in this second-floor, open-sided ocean-side room with views of Diamond Head and the sunset. Samplings from the rarefied world of Michelin-award-winning chef Yves Garnier include masterful *onaga* (ruby snapper) filets, skin crisped, with truffle juice and fried basil. The wine list, desserts, and service are formal without being stiff.

Roy's Restaurant, 6600 Kalanianaole Hwy. (© **808/396-7697;** www.roysrestaurant. com), was the first of Roy Yamaguchi's six signature restaurants in Hawaii. It is still the flagship and many people's favorite, true to its Euro-Asian roots and Yamaguchi's winning formula: open kitchen, fresh ingredients, and a good dose of nostalgia mingled with European techniques. The menu changes nightly, but you can generally count on individual pizzas, and entrees such as lemon grass–roasted chicken and several types of fresh fish.

Sam Choy's Breakfast, Lunch, Crab & Big Aloha Brewery, 580 Nimitz Hwy. (© **808/545-7979;** www.samchoy.com), is a happy, carefree eatery—elegance and cholesterol be damned. The menu assures delightfully messy dining such as beef stew and fried rice at breakfast, the Hawaiian plate and fresh fish at lunch, and the featured attraction—crab—at dinner. A 2,000-gallon live-crab tank lines the open kitchen. The eight varieties of "Big Aloha Beer," brewed on-site, go well with the crab and poke.

The **Sushi Sasabune,** 1419 S. King St. (© **808/947-3800**), serves "trust-me" sushi: Obey the chef, eat what's served, and may God help you if you drop a grain of rice or dip something in wasabi without permission. There is no California roll, no avocado, nothing that's not authentically Japanese. If you wish to order from the menu, grab a table; if you're brave enough to sit at the sushi bar, you'll receive what the chef serves. This is an extraordinary experience for sushi aficionados, and well worth the expense.

5 Maui

On a map, Maui doesn't look like much, but this 727-square-mile island has three peaks more than a mile high, thousands of waterfalls, 120 miles of shoreline, more than 80 golden-sand beaches, great seaside hotels, and a historic port town teeming with fine restaurants, B&Bs, and art galleries. Next to Waikiki, Maui is Hawaii's most popular destination, welcoming 2.5 million people each year to its sunny shores.

Maui's microclimates offer distinct variations on the tropical-island theme: It's as lush as an equatorial rainforest in Hana; as dry as the Arizona desert in Makena; as hot as Mexico in Lahaina; and cool and misty, like Oregon, up in Kula.

ESSENTIALS

GETTING THERE Several major carriers offer direct service from the U.S. mainland to **Kahului Airport.** Other major carriers fly to Honolulu, where you'll have to pick up an interisland flight. You can avoid Kahului altogether by taking Island Air to **Kapalua–West Maui Airport,** which is only a 10- to 15-minute drive to most hotels in West Maui, as opposed to an hour from Kahului. All of the airports have car-rental desks.

SpeediShuttle (© **800/977-2605** or 808/661-6667; www.speedishuttle.com) runs between Kahului Airport and all major resorts. Rates vary, but figure on $30 one-way to Wailea, $41 one-way to Kaanapali, and $57 one-way to Kapalua.

VISITOR INFORMATION The **Maui Visitors Bureau** is at 1727 Wili Pa Loop, Wailuku, Maui, HI 96793 (© **800/525-MAUI** or 808/244-3530; fax 808/244-1337; www.visitmaui.com).

GETTING AROUND The only way to really see Maui is by rental car. All of the major rental firms have offices on the island.

FAST FACTS **Maui Memorial Hospital,** in central Maui, is at 221 Mahalani, Wailuku (© **808/244-9056**). East Maui's **Hana Medical Center** is on Hana Highway (© **808/248-8924**). In upcountry Maui, **Kula Hospital** is at 204 Kula Hwy., Kula (© **808/878-1221**).

HITTING THE BEACH

Four-mile-long **Kaanapali Beach** is one of Maui's best, with grainy gold sand as far as the eye can see. A paved beach walk links hotels, open-air restaurants, and the Whalers Village shopping center, but the beach is crowded only in pockets. Summertime swimming is excellent; the best snorkeling is around Black Rock, in front of the Sheraton.

Kapalua Beach, the cove that fronts the Kapalua Bay Hotel and the Coconut Grove Villas, is the stuff of dreams and one of the best in Hawaii: a golden crescent bordered by two palm-studded points. Protected from strong winds and currents, Kapalua's calm waters are great for snorkelers and swimmers of all ages and abilities.

Wailea Beach is the best gold-sand crescent on Maui's sunny south coast. It's big, wide, and protected on both sides by black-lava points. The view out to sea, framed by the islands of Kahoolawe and Lanai, is magnificent. The waves are just the right size for gentle riding, with or without a board.

The hard, constant wind and endless waves at **Hookipa Beach Park,** 2 miles past Paia, make it one of the most famous windsurfing sites in the world. A grassy cliff provides a natural amphitheater for spectators. Weekdays are the best time to watch the daredevils fly over the waves; winter weekends host regular competitions.

OUTDOOR ACTIVITIES

GOLF   Weekdays are your best bet for tee times. For last-minute and discount tee times, call **Stand-by Golf** (© **888/645-BOOK** or 808/874-0600; www.standby golf.com) from 7am to 9pm. It offers discounted (up to 50%) guaranteed tee times for same-day or next-day golfing.

Golf Club Rentals (© **808/665-0800;** www.mauiclubrentals.com) has custom-built clubs for men, women, and juniors (both right- and left-handed); the rates are just $20 to $25 a day. The company also offers lessons with pros starting at $150 for 9 holes plus greens fees.

The views from the championship **Kapalua Resort Courses,** off Highway 30 (© **877/KAPALUA;** ww.kapsluamaui.com; greens fees $185–$250), are worth the greens fees alone. The par-72, 6,761-yard **Bay Course** (© **808/669-8820**), designed by Arnold Palmer and Ed Seay, is a bit forgiving, but its greens are difficult to read. The par-71, 6,632-yard **Village Course** (© **808/669-8830**), another Palmer/Seay design, is the most scenic. The par-73, 6,547-yard **Plantation Course** (© **808/669-8877**), a Ben Crenshaw/Bill Coore design set on a rolling hillside, is excellent for developing your low shots and precise chipping.

At the **Makena Courses,** Makena Alanui Drive, just past the Maui Prince Hotel (© **808/879-3344;** www.maui.net/~makena; greens fees $170–$180), you'll find 36 holes of "Mr. Hawaii Golf"—Robert Trent Jones, Jr.—at its best, with great views of Molokini and humpback whales. The par-72, 6,876-yard South Course has a couple of holes you'll never forget, while the par-72, 6,823-yard North Course is more difficult and even more spectacular.

Wailea Courses, Wailea Alanui Drive (© **888/328-MAUI** or 808/875-7540; www.waileagolf.com; greens fees $175–$185), offers three courses to choose from, two designed by Robert Trent Jones, Jr. The par-72 Gold Course is the toughest, with narrow fairways and several tricky dogleg holes.

WATERSPORTS   Activity Warehouse (© **800/343-2087;** www.travelhawaii.com), which has branches in Lahaina at 578 Front St., near Prison Street (© **808/661-1970**), and in Kihei at Azeka Place II, on the mountain side of Kihei Road near Lipoa Street (© **808/875-4050**), rents everything from beach chairs and coolers to kayaks, Boogie boards, and surfboards.

Snorkel Bob's (www.snorkelbob.com) has snorkel gear, Boogie boards, and other ocean toys at four locations: 1217 Front St., Lahaina (© **808/661-4421**); Napili Village, 5425-C Lower Honoapiilani Hwy., Napili (© **808/669-9603**); Azeka Place II, 1279 S. Kihei Rd. #310 (© **808/875-6188**); and Kamaole Beach Center, 2411 S. Kihei Rd., Kihei (© **808/879-7449**). All locations are open daily from 8am to 5pm. If you're island hopping, you can rent from a Snorkel Bob's location on one island and return to a branch on another.

Maui's largest diving retailer, with rentals, instruction, and boat charters, is **Maui Dive Shop** (www.mauidiveshop.com), with locations in Kihei at Azeka Place II Shopping Center (© **808/879-3388**), Kamaole Shopping Center (© **808/879-1533**), and Shops at Wailea (© **808/875-9904**); in Lahaina Cannery Mall (© **808/661-5388**); and the Honokowai Market Place (© **808/661-6166**).

Trilogy (© **888/MAUI-800** or 808/TRILOGY; www.sailtrilogy.com) offers our favorite Hawaiian boat trip: a sail to Lanai for snorkeling, swimming, and whale-watching (in season). This is the only cruise that offers a personalized ground tour of the island of Lanai.

Ed Robinson's Diving Adventures (© **800/635-1273** or 808/879-3584; www. mauiscuba.com), one of the best on Maui, offers specialized charters for small groups. If Ed is booked, call **Mike Severns Diving** (© **808/879-6596;** www.mikeseverns diving.com), for small, personal tours. Mike and his wife are both biologists who make diving in Hawaii not only fun but educational.

If fishing is more your thing, marlin, tuna, ono, and mahimahi await you in Maui's coastal and channel waters. No license is required; just book a sportfishing vessel out of Lahaina or Maalaea harbors. The best booking desk in the state is **Sportfish Hawaii** (© **877/388-1376** or 808/396-2607; www.sportfishhawaii.com), which books boats not only on Maui but on all islands. These fishing vessels have been inspected and must meet rigorous criteria. Prices range from $850 to $950 for a full-day exclusive charter (you, plus five friends, get the entire boat to yourselves); it's $599 to $750 for a half-day exclusive.

Want to catch a wave? Experts visit Maui in winter, when the surf's really up. The best beaches include **Honolua Bay,** north of Kapalua Resort; **Maalaea,** just outside the breakwater of Maalaea Harbor; and **Hookipa Beach,** where surfers get the waves until noon (after that, the windsurfers take over). The **Nancy Emerson School of Surfing,** 358 Papa Place, Suite F, Kahului (© **808/244-SURF** or 808/662-4445; www.surfclinics.com), offers lessons. Nancy has pioneered a new instructional technique called "Learn to Surf in One Lesson"—you can, really. It's $75 per person for a 2-hour group lesson; private 2-hour classes are $160. In Hana, **Hana-Maui Sea Sports** (© **808/248-7711;** www.hana-maui-seasports.com) has 2-hour long-board lessons taught by a certified ocean lifeguard for $89.

The best time to **whale-watch** is from mid-December to April: Just look out to sea. For a close-up look, take a whale-watching cruise; try **Maui Classic Charters** in Maalaea Harbor (© **800/736-5740** or 808/879-8188; www.mauicharters.com), which offers a 3½-hour whale-watching trip for $42 for adults and $30 for children ages 3 to 12; price includes beverages.

Maui has Hawaii's best **windsurfing** beaches. In winter, windsurfers from around the world flock to **Hookipa Beach,** site of several world-championship contests. **Hawaiian Island Surf and Sport,** 415 Dairy Rd., Kahului (© **800/231-6958** or 808/871-4981; www.hawaiianisland.com), offers lessons (from $79), rentals, and repairs.

HOUSE OF THE SUN: HALEAKALA NATIONAL PARK

Haleakala National Park, extending from the summit of Mount Haleakala down the volcano's southeast flank to Maui's eastern coast, is Maui's main natural attraction. More than 1.3 million people a year go up the 10,023-foot-high mountain to peer down into the crater of the world's largest dormant volcano—a hole that would hold Manhattan. Just going up the mountain is an experience in itself. Where else can you climb from sea level to 10,000 feet in just 37 miles, or a 2-hour drive? The snaky road passes through puffy cumulus clouds to offer magnificent views of the isthmus of Maui, the West Maui Mountains, and the Pacific Ocean.

ACCESS POINTS   There are actually two separate and distinct destinations within the park: Haleakala Summit and the Kipahulu coast. No road links the summit and the coast; you have to approach them separately. **Haleakala Summit** is 37 miles, or a 1½- to 2-hour drive, from Kahului. Take Highway 37 to Highway 377 to Highway 378. (See "Driving to the Summit," below.) The **Kipahulu** section of the park is on

Maui's east end near Hana, 60 miles from Kahului on Highway 36 (the Hana Hwy.). Due to traffic and rough road conditions, plan on 4 hours, one-way.

At both entrances to the park, the admission fee is $5 per person or $10 per car, good for a week of unlimited entry.

INFORMATION & VISITOR CENTERS For advance information, contact **Haleakala National Park,** Box 369, Makawao, HI 96768 (© **808/572-4400;** www.nps. gov/hale). A mile from the park entrance, at 7,000 feet, is **Haleakala National Park Headquarters** (© **808/572-4400**), which provides information on park programs and activities, camping permits, restrooms, a pay phone, and drinking water. It's open daily from 7:30am to 4pm. The **Haleakala Visitor Center,** open daily from sunrise to 3pm, is near the summit, 11 miles from the park entrance. It offers a panoramic view, exhibits on the area, restrooms, and water. Rangers offer excellent, informative, and free naturalist talks at 9:30, 10:30, and 11:30am daily.

DRIVING TO THE SUMMIT Highway 378, also known as **Haleakala Crater Road,** is one of the few roads in the world that climbs from sea level to 10,000 feet, in just 37 miles. It has at least 33 switchbacks; passes through numerous climate zones; goes under, in, and out of clouds; and offers a view that extends for more than 100 miles.

Going to the summit takes 1½ to 2 hours from Kahului. Follow Highway 37 (Haleakala Hwy.) to Pukalani, where you'll pick up Highway 377 (also Haleakala Hwy.), which you'll take to Highway 378. Along the way, expect fog, rain, and wind. Fill up your gas tank before you go—Pukalani is the last town with services. There are no facilities beyond the ranger stations. Bring your own food and water.

Remember, you're entering a high-altitude wilderness area. Some people get dizzy due to the lack of oxygen; you may also suffer lightheadedness, shortness of breath, nausea, and headaches. People with asthma, pregnant women, heavy smokers, and those with heart conditions should be especially careful. Bring water and a jacket or a blanket, especially if you go up for sunrise.

Beyond headquarters are two scenic overlooks. Stop at **Leleiwi Overlook,** just beyond mile marker 17, to stretch and get accustomed to the heights. If you feel dizzy or drowsy, consider heading back down. A short trail leads to a panoramic view of the crater.

Two miles farther is **Kalahaku Overlook,** the best place to see a rare silversword. You can turn into this overlook only when you are descending from the top. The silversword, which grows only in Hawaii, has silvery bayonets displaying tiny, purple bouquets; it takes from 4 to 50 years to bloom.

Continue on and you'll quickly reach **Haleakala Visitor Center,** which offers spectacular views. But don't turn around here; the actual summit's a little farther on, at

---

A Word of Warning about the Weather

The weather at nearly 10,000 feet can change suddenly and without warning. Come prepared for cold, high winds, rain, and even snow in winter. Temperatures can range from 77°F down to 26°F (25°C to –3°C), and high winds are frequent. Rainfall varies from 40 inches a year on the western end of the crater to more than 200 inches on the eastern side. Bring boots, waterproof gear, warm clothes, extra layers, and lots of sunscreen—the sun shines very brightly up here. For the latest weather information, call © **808/871-5054.**

Puu Ulaula Overlook (also known as Red Hill), the volcano's highest point. If you do go up for the sunrise, the building at Puu Ulaula Overlook is the best viewing spot.

Tip: When driving down the Haleakala Crater Road, be sure to put your car in low gear; that way, you won't destroy your brakes by riding them the whole way down.

HIKING IN THE PARK Hiking into Maui's dormant volcano is really the way to see it. There are some 27 miles of hiking trails, two camping sites, and three cabins, which are so popular that requests for them must be made 3 months in advance—and that only gets you into a lottery system. For more on camping in the park, contact the park directly (© **808/572-4400;** www.nps.gov/hale).

Park rangers offer free guided hikes several times a week. If you opt to take one (and they're great), wear sturdy shoes and be prepared for wind, rain, and intense sun. Bring water and a hat. Options include full-moon hikes and star program hikes. *Always call in advance:* The hikes and briefing sessions may be canceled, so check first. For details and program schedules, call the park at © **808/572-4400,** or visit **www.nps.gov/hale**.

For those venturing out on their own, the best route takes in two trails: into the crater along **Sliding Sands Trail,** which begins on the rim at 9,800 feet and descends to the valley floor at 6,600 feet; and back out along **Halemauu Trail.** Hardy hikers can consider making the 11-mile, one-way descent, which takes 9 hours, and the equally long return ascent, in a day. The rest of us will need to extend this steep hike to 2 days. The descending and ascending trails aren't loops; the trail heads are miles apart, so you'll need to make transportation arrangements in advance. Before you set out, stop at park headquarters to get camping and hiking updates.

A shorter, easier option is the half-mile walk down the **Hosmer Grove Nature Trail,** or a mile or two down **Sliding Sands Trail** for a hint of what lies ahead. A good day hike is Halemauu Trail to Holua Cabin and back, an 8-mile, half-day trip.

WHERE TO STAY

See "Where to Stay" under "Honolulu & Oahu" earlier in this chapter for information on reservation services that will help you book accommodations in Maui.

You'll get your money's worth at **The Fairmont Kea Lani Maui,** 4100 Wailea Alanui Dr. (© **800/659-4100** or 808/875-4100; www.fairmont.com/kealani), plus a few extras. This all-suite luxury hotel has 840-square-foot suites with kitchenettes; a living room with high-tech media center and pullout sofa bed (great if you have the kids in tow); a marble wet bar; an oversize bathroom with separate shower big enough for a party; a separate spacious bedroom; and a large lanai overlooking the pools and lawns, right down to the white-sand beach.

If money's not a factor, the **Four Seasons Resort Maui at Wailea,** 3900 Wailea Alanui Dr. (© **800/334-MAUI** or 808/874-8000; www.fourseasons.com/maui), a Hawaiian palace by the sea, is the place to spend it. The spacious (about 600 sq. ft.) rooms feature furnished lanais with ocean views, along with grand bathrooms containing deep marble tubs, showers for two, hair dryers, and plush terry robes. Service is attentive but not cloying.

The **Kahana Sunset,** 4909 Lower Honoapiilani Hwy. (© **800/669-1488** or 808/ 669-8011; www.kahanasunset.com), a series of wooden condo units, stair-steps down the side of a hill to a postcard-perfect white-sand beach. The location, nestled between the coastline and road above, makes it very private. In the midst of the buildings lies a small pool and Jacuzzi; down by the sandy beach are gazebos and picnic areas. The units are great for families, with full kitchens, washer/dryers, large lanais with terrific views, and sofa beds.

Just across the street from the ocean, **Koa Resort,** 811 S. Kihei Rd. (© **800/541-3060** or 808/879-3328; www.bellomaui.com), consists of five two-story wooden buildings on 5½ acres of landscaped grounds. The spacious, privately owned one-, two-, and three-bedroom units come fully equipped with kitchens, large lanais, ceiling fans, and washer/dryers. For maximum peace and quiet, ask for a unit far from Kihei Road.

The spacious condo units at the **Maui Eldorado Resort,** 2661 Kekaa Dr. (© **800/688-7444** or 808/661-0021; www.outrigger.com), feature full kitchens, washer/ dryers, and daily maid service. The Outrigger chain has managed to keep prices down to reasonable levels, especially if you come in spring or fall. This is a great choice for families, with grassy areas and a beachfront that's usually safe for swimming.

If you can't decide between the privacy of a condominium and the conveniences of a hotel, try the **Maui Hill,** 2881 S. Kihei Rd. (© **800/92-ASTON** or 808/879-6321; www.aston-hotels.com). Managed by the respected Aston chain, this large, Spanish-style resort is set on a hill above the heat of Kihei town. It combines all the amenities of a hotel—large pool, hot tub, tennis courts, putting green, Hawaiiana classes, daily maid service—with the luxury of large condos that have full kitchens, lots of space, and plenty of privacy. Nearly all units offer ocean views, washer/dryers, sofa beds, and big lanais.

One of Maui's best secret bargains is the small, two-story **Napili Bay,** 33 Hui Dr. (© **877/782-5642**; www.alohacondos.com), right on Napili's beautiful white-sand beach. The place is great for a romantic getaway. The compact studio apartments have everything you need, from full kitchens to roomy lanais. Though there is no air-conditioning, louvered windows and ceiling fans keep the units cool during the day. Book early.

The oceanfront **Noelani Condominium Resort,** 4095 Lower Honoapiilani Rd. (© **800/367-6030** or 808/669-8374; www.noelani-condo-resort.com), is a great value. Everything is first class, from the furnishings to the location—on the ocean with a sandy cove next door at the new county park. There's good snorkeling off the cove, which is frequented by spinner dolphins and turtles in summer and humpback whales in winter. All units feature complete kitchens, entertainment centers, and spectacular views. Our favorites are in the Anthurium Building, where the one-, two-, and three-bedrooms have oceanfront lanais just 20 feet from the water.

A lovingly restored 1924 former plantation manager's home, **Old Wailuku Inn at Ulupono,** 2199 Kahookele St. (© **800/305-4899** or 808/244-5897; www.mauiinn. com), offers a genuine Old Hawaii experience. The theme centers around 1920s and 1930s Hawaii, with decor, design, and landscaping to match. The spacious rooms are gorgeously outfitted with exotic ohia-wood floors, high ceilings, and traditional Hawaiian quilts. Some of the mammoth bathrooms have claw-foot tubs; others have Jacuzzis. In the recently added "Vagabond House," rooms feature all the modern amenities you can imagine (TV/VCR, air-conditioning, and an ultraluxurious multihead shower).

The **Ritz-Carlton Kapalua,** 1 Ritz-Carlton Dr. © **800/262-8440** or 808/669-6200; www.ritzcarlton.com), may be the best Ritz-Carlton in the world. It rises proudly on a knoll, in a spectacular setting between the rainforest and the sea. The public spaces are open, airy, and graceful. Rooms have private lanais. Hospitality is the keynote here; you'll find exemplary Ritz service seasoned with good old-fashioned Hawaiian aloha.

Terrific facilities and the best location on Kaanapali Beach make the beautiful **Sheraton Maui,** 2605 Kaanapali Pkwy. (© **800/782-9488** or 808/661-0031; www.sheraton. com/maui), a great place to stay. It's built into the side of the cliff on the white-sand cove next to Black Rock (an 80-ft.-high lava formation); a new lagoonlike pool features lava-rock waterways and an open-air spa. The new emphasis is on family appeal, with a class of rooms dedicated to those traveling with kids. Every unit is outfitted with amenities galore.

In the heart of Kaanapali, right on the world-famous beach, lies **The Whaler on Kaanapali Beach,** 2481 Kaanapali Pkwy. (© 800/922-7866 or 808/661-4861; www. astonhotels.com), an oasis of elegance, privacy, and luxury. Each of the gorgeous units has a full kitchen, washer/dryer, 10-foot beamed ceilings, and lanai. The spectacular views take in Kaanapali's gentle waves and the peaks of the West Maui Mountains.

WHERE TO DINE

More than a decade after opening the **Haliimaile General Store,** Haliimaile Road (© 808/572-2666; www.haliimailegeneralstore.com), Bev Gannon, one of the 12 original Hawaii regional cuisine chefs, is still going strong at her foodie haven in the pineapple fields. You'll dine at tables set on old wood floors under high ceilings (sound ricochets fiercely here), in a room emblazoned with works by local artists. The food, a blend of eclectic American with ethnic touches, puts an innovative spin on Hawaii regional cuisine. Sip the lilikoi lemonade and nibble the notable sashimi napoleon.

Mañana Garage, 33 Lono Ave. (© 808/873-0220), serves incomparable Latin American fare and has introduced exciting new flavors to Maui's dining scene. The restaurant's industrial motif features table bases like hubcaps, blown-glass chandeliers, and gleaming chrome and cobalt walls with orange accents. The menu is brilliantly conceived and executed. The seviche perfectly balances flavors and textures: lime, cilantro, chile, coconut, and fresh fish.

Nick's Fishmarket Maui, in the Fairmont Kea Lani Hotel at 4100 Wailea Alanui (© 808/879-7224; www.tri-star-restaurants.com), has a perfect balance of visual sizzle and memorable food. Stefanotis vines create shade on the terrace, where the sunset views are superb. We love the onion vichyssoise with taro swirl and a hint of *tobiko* (flying-fish roe). Bow-tied waiters and almond-scented cold towels add an extra touch to this ocean-side phenomenon—not to mention the lavish wine list and torch lighting at sunset.

Despite the lack of dramatic view and an upstairs location in a shopping mall, **Roy's Kahana Bar & Grill,** in the Kahana Gateway Shopping Center at 4405 Honoapiilani Hwy. (© 808/669-6999; www.roysrestaurant.com), remains crowded and extremely popular for one reason—fabulous food. Young, hip, impeccably trained servers deliver Euro-Asian fare such as blackened ahi, rack of lamb, and fresh seafood (usually eight or nine choices) to tables of satisfied customers.

Best A Night to Remember: Maui's Top Luau

The nightly **Old Lahaina Luau** (© 800/248-5828 or 808/667-1998; www.old lahainaluau.com), staged at a 1-acre site just ocean side of the Lahaina Can-nery, is the indisputable champ of Maui's luaus. Local craftspeople display their wares. Seating is provided on lauhala mats for those who wish to dine as the traditional Hawaiians did, but there are tables for everyone else.

The luau begins at sunset and features Tahitian and Hawaiian entertain-ment, including ancient, missionary-era and modern hula. The entertainment is riveting. The food is as much Pacific Rim as authentically Hawaiian. No watered-down mai tais, either; these are the real thing. The cost is $89 for adults, $59 for children 12 and under.

Furiously fusion, part Hawaii regional cuisine, and all parts sushi, **Sansei Seafood Restaurant and Sushi Bar,** Kapalua Shops, 115 Bay Dr. (© **808/669-6286;** www.sanseihawaii.com), is tirelessly creative, with a menu that scores higher with the adventurous than the purists. Maki is the mantra here. Other choices include panko-crusted ahi sashimi and traditional Japanese tempura. There's also simpler fare, such as pastas and wok-tossed vegetables. Desserts, including the macadamia nut tempura fried ice cream, are not to be missed.

The best Italian food on Maui is served at the exquisite **Vino Italian Tapas & Wine Bar,** at the Kapalua Resort (© **808/661-VINO**), overlooking the rolling hills of the Kapalua Golf Course and run by famed chef D. K. Kodama and master sommelier Chuck Furuya. The menu changes constantly, but it's always pure Italian—lots of homemade pastas, classic and contemporary preparations of poultry and meat, and special fish and seafood dishes nightly. And every dish is perfectly paired with wine (the list is exceptional).

6 The Big Island

The Big Island of Hawaii—the island that lends its name to the entire 1,500-mile-long Hawaiian archipelago—is where Mother Nature pulled out all the stops. Simply put, it's spectacular. The island looks like the inside of a barbecue pit on one side and a lush jungle on the other, with fiery volcanoes and sparkling waterfalls, black-lava deserts and snowcapped mountain peaks, tropical rainforests and Alpine meadows, a glacial lake and miles of beaches filled with a rainbow of black, green, and golden sands. A 50-mile drive will take you from snowy winter to sultry summer, passing through spring or fall along the way. Five volcanoes—one still erupting—have created this continental island, which is expanding every day.

The Big Island is not for everyone, however. Some tourists are taken aback at the sight of stark fields of lava or black-sand beaches, and you may have to go out of your way if you're looking for traditional tropical beauty, such as a quintessential white-sand beach.

ESSENTIALS

GETTING THERE   The Big Island has two major airports: **Kona International Airport,** on the west coast, and **Hilo International Airport,** on the east. The Kona Airport receives direct overseas flights from Japan as well as direct mainland flights from Los Angeles and San Francisco. Otherwise, you'll have to pick up an interisland flight in Honolulu. All major rental companies have cars available at both airports.

VISITOR INFORMATION   The **Big Island Visitors Bureau** has two offices on the Big Island: one at 250 Keawe St., Hilo, HI 96720 (© **808/961-5797**); and one on the other side of the island at 250 Waikoloa Beach Dr., Waikoloa, HI 96738 (© **808/886-1652**). Its website is **www.bigisland.org**. The Big Island's best free tourist publications are *This Week,* the *Beach and Activity Guide,* and *101 Things to Do on Hawaii the Big Island.* All three offer lots of useful information, as well as discount coupons on a variety of island adventures. Copies are easy to find all around the island.

GETTING AROUND   You'll need a rental car here, where taxis can take you anywhere but are prohibitively expensive. All the major car-rental firms have agencies at both the airports and at the Kohala Coast resorts.

FAST FACTS   Kona Community Hospital, on the Kona Coast in Kealakekua (© **808/322-9311**), has a 24-hour urgent-care facility. If you need a doctor, call **Hualalai Urgent Care,** 75–1028 Henry St., Kona (© **808/327-HELP**).

BEACHES

Too young geologically to have many great beaches, the Big Island instead has an odd collection of unusual ones: brand-new black-sand beaches, green-sand beaches, salt-and-pepper beaches, and even a rare white-sand beach.

Just off Queen Kaahumanu Highway, south of the Hapuna Beach Prince Hotel, lies the golden crescent of **Hapuna Beach**—big, wide, and a half-mile long. In summer, when the beach is widest, the ocean calmest, and the crowds biggest, this is the island's best beach for swimming, snorkeling, and bodysurfing. But beware of Hapuna in winter, when its thundering waves, strong rip currents, and lack of lifeguards can be dangerous.

A coconut grove sweeps around **Kaunaoa Beach (Mauna Kea Beach),** at the foot of Mauna Kea Beach Hotel, where the water is calm and protected by two black-lava points. The sandy bottom slopes gently into the bay, which often fills with schools of tropical fish, green sea turtles, and manta rays. Swimming is excellent year-round, except in rare winter storms. Snorkelers prefer the rocky points, where fish thrive in the surge.

The Big Island makes up for its dearth of beaches with a few spectacular ones, such as **Anaehoomalu Bay** (or **A-Bay,** as the locals call it). This peppered, gold-sand beach, fringed by palms and backed by royal fishponds, fronts the Outrigger Waikoloa Beach Resort. The beach slopes gently from shallow to deep water; swimming, snorkeling, diving, kayaking, and windsurfing are all excellent. At the far edge of the bay is a turtle cleaning station, where snorkelers and divers can watch endangered green sea turtles line up, waiting their turn to have small fish clean them.

OUTDOOR ACTIVITIES

The not-for-profit group **Friends for Fitness,** P.O. Box 1671, Kailua-Kona, HI 96745 (© **808/322-0033**), offers a free brochure on physical activities (from aerobic classes to dancing to yoga) in West Hawaii; they will gladly mail it to you upon request.

GOLF For last-minute and discount tee times, call **Stand-by Golf** (© **888/645-BOOK** or 808/322-BOOK) between 7am and 11pm. Stand-by Golf offers discounted (10%–40%), guaranteed tee times for same-day or next-day golfing.

Designed by Arnold Palmer and Ed Seay, the 18-hole championship **Hapuna Golf Course,** Hapuna Prince Beach Resort, off Highway 19 near mile marker 69 (© **808/880-3000;** www.hapunabeachprincehotel.com; greens fees $145), has been named the most environmentally sensitive course by *Golf* magazine. The 6,027-yard links-style course extends from the shoreline to 700 feet above sea level, with views of the pastoral Kohala Mountains and sweeping vistas of the Kohala coastline.

The breathtakingly beautiful, par-72, 7,114-yard **Mauna Kea Golf Course,** Mauna Kea Beach Resort, Highway 19 near mile marker 68 (© **808/882-5400;** www.maunakeabeachhotel.com; greens fees $195), designed by Robert Trent Jones, Jr., is consistently rated one of the top courses in the U.S. The signature 3rd hole is 175 yards long (and a shocking par 3); the Pacific Ocean and shoreline cliffs stand between the tee and the green, giving every golfer a real challenge.

The **Mauna Lani Frances I'i Brown Championship Courses** are on Mauna Lani Drive, off Highway 19, 20 miles north of Kona Airport (© **808/885-6655;** www.maunalani.com; greens fees $195). The par-72, 7,029-yard, Mauna Lani South Course has an unforgettable ocean hole: the downhill, 221-yard, par-3 7th, which is bordered by the sea, a salt-and-pepper sand dune, and lush kiawe trees. The North Course's more extensive indigenous vegetation gives it a Scottish feel.

WATERSPORTS   If you want to rent beach toys (snorkel gear, Boogie boards), the beach concessions at all the big resorts, as well as tour desks and dive shops, offer equipment rentals and sometimes lessons for beginners. The cheapest place to get great rental equipment is **Snorkel Bob's,** in the parking lot of Huggo's Restaurant at 75–5831 Kahakai Rd., at Alii Drive, Kailua-Kona (© **808/329-0770;** www.snorkelbob.com).

There are nearly two dozen dive operators on the west side of the island, offering everything from certification courses to guided boat dives. The newly opened **Bottom-Time,** 74–5590 Luhia St. (© **866/GO-DIVEN** or 808/331-1858; www.bottomtime hawaii.com) takes their 34-foot catamaran (complete with showers, TV, and restrooms) to unusual dive sites, and also offers free introductory dives in enriched air (Nitrox) for $130 and two-tank dives for $120.

One of Kona's oldest dive shops, **Jack's Diving Locker,** 75–5819 Alii Dr. (© **800/ 345-4807** or 808/329-7585; www.jacksdivinglocker.com), offers the classic two-tank for $105, advanced dives for $145, and three-tank dives for $185.

The year-round calm waters along the Kona and Kohala coasts are home to spectacular marine life. Some of the best areas include the secret little **Hapuna Beach Cove,** at the foot of the Hapuna Beach Prince Hotel. If you're a first-time snorkeler, you can simply wade in and look down at **Kahaluu Beach Park.** The best snorkeling for all levels is in **Kealakekua Bay.** The calm waters of this underwater preserve teem with a wealth of marine life. Kealakekua is reachable only by boat or kayak.

If you want to fish, it doesn't get any better than the Kona Coast, known internationally as the marlin capital of the world. Nearly 100 charter boats with professional captains and crew offer fishing charters out of **Keauhou, Kawaihae, Honokohau,** and **Kailua Bay harbors.** If you're not an expert angler, the best way to arrange a charter is through a booking agency such as the **Charter Desk at Honokohau Marina** (© **888/KONA-4-US** or 808/329-5735; www.charterdesk.com) or **Charter Services Hawaii** (© **800/567-2650** or 808/334-1881; www.konazone.com).

Most surfing off the Big Island is for the experienced only. **Ocean Eco Tours** (© **808/324-SURF;** www.oceanecotours.com) is the only company on the Big Island that teaches surfing. Your only choice for surfboard rentals is **Pacific Vibrations,** 75–5702 Likana Lane, just off Alii Dr., across from the pier, Kailua-Kona (© **808/ 329-4140;** www.laguerdobros.com/pacvib/pacificv.html).

HAWAII VOLCANOES NATIONAL PARK

Hawaii Volcanoes National Park is a work in progress, thanks to Kilauea volcano, which pours red-hot lava into the sea and adds land to the Big Island every day. Hawaii's eruptions produce slow-moving, oozing lava that provides excellent, safe viewing most of the time. You can see the highlights by car (the park has 50 miles of good roads, some of them often covered by lava flows) if you have only a day to spare, or allow at least 3 days to fully explore the park, which has hiking trails, rainforests, and campgrounds in addition to some of the world's weirdest landscapes.

ACCESS POINTS   Hawaii Volcanoes National Park is 29 miles from Hilo, on **Hawaii Belt Road** (Hwy. 11). From Kailua-Kona, it's 100 miles, or about a 2½-hour drive. Entry is $10 per vehicle (good for 7 days). Hikers and bicyclists pay $5; bikes are allowed on roads and paved trails only.

INFORMATION & VISITOR CENTERS   For advance information, contact **Hawaii Volcanoes National Park,** P.O. Box 52, Hawaii Volcanoes National Park, HI 96718 (© **808/985-6000;** www.nps.gov/havo). If you want to camp or hike in the

Dressing for Volcano-Watching

Thanks to its higher elevation and windward (rainier) location, the volcanic area is always colder than it is at the beach. In the winter months, expect temperatures to be in the 40s or 50s (5°–15°C), and dress accordingly. Always have rain gear on hand, especially in winter.

park, be sure to inquire about them in advance or check out *Frommer's Hawaii* for detailed information. **Kilauea Visitor Center** is at the entrance to the park, just off Highway 11; it's open daily from 7:45am to 5pm.

Get the latest **eruption update** and information on volcanic activity in the park by visiting **http://hvo.wr.usgs.gov** or calling the **park's 24-hour hot line** (© **808/985-6000**).

SEEING THE HIGHLIGHTS

Your first stop should be **Kilauea Visitor Center,** just inside the park entrance, where you can get up-to-the-minute reports on the volcano's activity and learn how volcanoes work. Then walk across the street to **Volcano House;** go through the lobby and out the other side, where you can have a good look at **Kilauea Caldera,** a 2½-mile-wide, 500-foot-deep pit. It used to be a bubbling pit of lava; today, you can still see wisps of steam.

Now, get out on the highway and drive by the **Sulphur Banks,** which smell like rotten eggs, and the **Steam Vents,** where trails of smoke, once molten lava, rise from within the inner reaches of the earth. It's one of the few places where you can feel that the volcano is truly alive. Stop at the **Thomas A. Jaggar Museum** (daily 8:30am–5pm; free admission), which shows eruption videos, explains the Pele legend, and monitors earthquakes (a precursor of eruptions).

Next, drive around the caldera to the other side, park, and take the short walk to Halemaumau Crater's edge to stand at the overlook and stare in awe at this once-fuming and bubbling old fire pit, which still generates ferocious heat out of vestigial vents. If you feel the need to cool off, go to the Thurston Lava Tube, the coolest place in the park. You'll hike down into a natural bowl, a forest preserve the lava didn't touch, and see a black hole in the earth; step in. It's dripping and cool, with bare roots hanging down.

A BIRD'S-EYE VIEW OF THE VOLCANO   The best way to see the volcano is from up high, in a helicopter. This view puts the enormity of it all into perspective. The best outfitter is **Blue Hawaiian Helicopter** (© **800/745-BLUE** or 808/886-1768; www.bluehawaiian.com), a professionally run, locally based company with an excellent safety record, comfortable copters, and extremely knowledgeable pilots. The 45-minute **Circle of Fire** flight from Hilo takes you over the boiling volcano and then on to a bird's-eye view of the destruction the lava has caused and remote beaches ($165 per person). Our favorite trip, from Waikoloa, is the 2-hour **Big Island Spectacular,** starring the volcano, tropical valleys, Hamakua Coast waterfalls, and the Kohala Mountains (from $340 and worth every penny).

WHERE TO STAY

See "Where to Stay," under "Honolulu & Oahu," earlier in this chapter, for information on reservation services that will help you book accommodations on the Big Island.

Relax in the lap of luxury at **Four Seasons Resort Hualalai at Historic Kaupulehu,** Kailua-Kona (© **888/340-5662** or 808/325-8000; www.fourseasons. com/hualalai), the best hotel on the island. Low-rise clusters of villas nestle between the sea and the greens of a fabulous new golf course. The rooms are furnished in Pacific tropical style; some have bathrooms with private outdoor gardens (surrounded by black-lava rock), so you can shower under the sun or the stars.

Those seeking a peaceful, low-key atmosphere find refuge at the expensive-but-worth-it **Kona Village Resort,** Kailua-Kona (© **800/367-5290** or 808/325-5555; www.konavillage.com), where the thatched-roof bungalows lack air-conditioning, TVs, and phones (they do have fully stocked fridges and some have an outdoor hot tub). Rates include meals, tennis, watersports, walking tours, and a fabulous Friday-night luau. There are seasonal children's programs, live entertainment most nights, two pools, and a petroglyph field.

The serene, luxurious **Mauna Lani Bay Hotel & Bungalows,** 68–1400 Mauna Lani Dr., Kohala Coast (© **800/367-2323** or 808/885-6622; www.maunalani.com), offers sandy beaches and lava tide pools, plus gracious hospitality. The plush rooms, each with lanai, are arranged to capture the best ocean views. The posh, two-bedroom, 4,000-square-foot bungalows come with private pools and spas.

The elegant, upscale **Fairmont Orchid,** 1 N. Kaniku Dr., Kohala Coast (© **800/845-9905** or 808/885-2000; www.fairmont.com/orchid), is *the* place for watersports nuts, families, or those who just want to relax. The spacious rooms feature ocean views (all have lanais), sitting areas, and marble bathrooms. The beach and watersports facilities are extensive, and the excellent Hawaiiana program covers everything from paddling a canoe to strumming a ukulele.

The inexpensive, 60-unit **Kona Billfisher,** Alii Drive (across from Royal Kona Resort), Kailua-Kona (© **800/622-5348** or 808/329-3333; www.konahawaii.com), is our favorite of all the affordable condos on this coast. Each well-maintained unit comes with a full kitchen and a balcony, and features new furnishings and king-size beds. Book well in advance.

The comfortable, spacious condos at **Kanaloa at Kona,** 78–261 Manukai St., Kailua-Kona (© **800/688-7444** or 808/322-9625; www.outrigger.com), border the rocky coast beside Keauhou Bay, 6 miles south of Kailua-Kona. They're ideal for families; the huge bathrooms have whirlpool bathtubs and spacious lanais.

If you're going to Volcanoes National Park, you'll really need to stay 3 days to take in the park properly. The best way to do this is to rent a cottage or house, and the best rental agency is **Hawaii Volcano Vacations,** P.O. Box 913, Volcano, HI 96785 (© **800/709-0907** or 808/967-7271; www.hawaiivolcanovacations.com). Manager Aurelia Gutierrez selects only the top cottages, cabins, and houses in Volcano and makes sure that they are perfect for you. Very reasonably priced, her units range from $109 to $200, and each one is outfitted with a full kitchen, plus an outdoor grill, cooler, flashlight, umbrella, and fresh flower arrangement.

WHERE TO DINE

Huggo's on the Rocks, a mound of thatch, rock, and grassy, sandy ground right next to **Huggo's,** 75–5828 Kahakai Rd. (© **808/329-1493;** www.huggos.com), is a sunset-lover's nirvana. At sundown, it's choked with people either on chaises or at the 50-seat thatched bar, sipping mai tais and noshing on salads, poke, sandwiches, plate lunches, sashimi, and fish and chips.

Coffee Farms

Notable among the island's famous coffee farms is the **Kona Blue Coffee Company,** in Holualoa (© 877/322-1700 or 808/322-1700; www.kona blueskycoffee.com), which handles its own beans exclusively. The Christian Twigg–Smith family and staff grow, handpick, sun-dry, roast, grind, and sell their coffee, whole or ground.

Also in Holualoa, 10 minutes above Kailua-Kona, **Holualoa Kona Coffee Company** (© 800/334-0348 or 808/322-9937; www.konalea.com) purveys organic Kona: unsprayed, handpicked, sun-dried, and carefully roasted. You can witness the hulling, sorting, roasting, and packaging of beans on a farm tour, Monday through Friday from 8am to 4pm.

In Waimea, the **Waimea Coffee Company,** Parker Square, Highway 19 (© 808/885-4472; www.waimeacoffeeandco.com), a deli/coffee farm/retail operation, is a whirl of activity. Coffee is heady stuff here: pure Kona from Rooster Farms, pure organic from Sakamoto Estate—an impressive selection of the island's best estate-grown coffees.

The **Beach Tree Bar and Grill,** Four Seasons Resort Hualalai, Queen Kaahumanu Highway, Kaupulehu-Kona (© 808/325-8000), is an example of outstanding cuisine in a perfect setting—without being fancy, expensive, or fussy. The bar on the sand is a sunset paradise, and the sandwiches, seafood, and grilled items at the casual outdoor restaurant (a few feet from the bar) are simple, excellent, and prepared with imagination and no shortcuts.

Great food, crisp air, and a sweeping ocean view make **The Coffee Shack,** Highway 11, 1 mile south of Captain Cook (© 808/328-9555), one of South Kona's great finds. Besides trying its fabulous breakfasts, come here for lunch: imported beers, excellent sandwiches on home-baked breads, and fresh, hearty salads made with organic lettuces.

Local favorite **Keei Cafe,** at mile marker 113 on Highway 11, in Kalakekua (© 808/322-9992), is in a new location but its friendly ambience, great food, and affordable prices are still intact. The menu roams the globe, from spicy fajitas (chicken or tofu) to excellent vegetarian black-bean soup. Everything is made from scratch, and virtually everything is grown or harvested in the Honaunau Valley area.

When it comes to dining on the Big Island, **Merriman's,** Opelu Plaza, Highway 19 in Waimea (© 808/885-6822), is peerless. At dinner, choose from the signature wok-charred ahi, lamb from nearby Kahua Ranch, and a noteworthy vegetarian selection. The restaurant's famous platters of seafood and meats are among the many reasons this is the best dining spot in Waimea.

Appendix A:
The Best of the Rest

The attractions of the states listed in this section may not have caught on with the masses yet (with a couple of notable exceptions), but that hardly means there's nothing worth seeing or doing in Arkansas, Iowa, Kansas, North Dakota, and West Virginia. On the contrary, these states offer excellent attractions and boast some of the best scenery in the United States. And you'll find lots of friendly natives eager for you to enjoy their home territory. Best of all, the current lack of major crowds in these areas means you can explore in relative peace and quiet, and you won't get hit with the high prices so common in major tourist zones.

1 Arkansas

Once on the eastern edge of the American frontier, Arkansas was once a rough-and-ready territory comprised of plantations and settlements of poor immigrants from nearby Appalachia. The Civil War brought an end to slavery, but racial tensions remained until desegregation was forced on the state in 1957. Industrialization improved the economic plight of residents somewhat during the same time period. Today, the Natural State is best known for its fabulous outdoor recreational opportunities, exceptional hot springs, and glorious mountain scenery. For history buffs, there are many sites and attractions dealing with the civil rights movement, rural Ozark mountain culture, and Bill Clinton (who remains a favorite son, whether he inhaled or not). All in all, the state offers a good deal of variety—and a lot of good value.

ESSENTIALS

VISITOR INFORMATION Contact the **Arkansas Department of Parks & Tourism,** 1 Capitol Mall, Little Rock, AR 72201 (✆ **800/NATURAL** or 501/682-7777; www.arkansas.com), and request the state's comprehensive vacation kit, which includes a map, visitor's guide, and calendar of events.

Fourteen tourist information centers are located at strategic entry points and long major road routes within the state. The centers are open 8am to 5pm daily (they are closed on several major holidays; summer hours extended by 1 hr.) and are staffed by travel counselors who will gladly dispense attractions and sightseeing information.

GETTING THERE **By Plane** Arkansas's largest commercial airport, **Little Rock National Airport** (✆ 501/372-3439; www.lrn-airport.com), spent $170 million upgrading facilities in the 1990s, is served by nine major domestic and discount carriers. Most of the major car-rental agencies have desks at the airport.

By Train **Amtrak**'s *Texas Eagle* train (✆ 800/872-7245; www.amtrak.com) makes stops at several cities in Arkansas, including Little Rock and Texarkana, as it travels from Chicago to Dallas.

By Car **I-40** enters the state out of Tennessee and continues west into Little Rock, then shifts slightly northward and heads in the direction of the Ozark region and Oklahoma. **I-30** enters the southwest corner of the state from Texas and ends in Little Rock. **I-540** and **U.S. 71** both offer lots of scenery as they run through the Ozarks. *Note:* A major portion of the state's 655-mile interstate network is currently undergoing a $950-million renovation (see www.arkansasinterstates.com for progress updates).

SPECIAL EVENTS Held in mid-October, the **Arkansas State Fair and Livestock Show,** at the State Fairgrounds and Barton Coliseum in Little Rock (© **501/372-8341;** www.arkansasstate fair.com), celebrated its 65th anniversary in 2004. The festivities include educational exhibits, concerts, a rodeo, a carnival, a midway with rides and games, arts and crafts, clowns, magicians, strolling musicians, and talent contests.

WHERE TO STAY The state offers a host of accommodations, ranging from full-scale resorts to park lodges to motels to quaint inns. An online directory of available accommodations in cities throughout the state is available at www.arkansas.com. Noteworthy hotels in the state include Eureka Springs's historic **1886 Crescent Hotel and Spa** (© **877/342-9766** or 479/253-9766; www.crescent-hotel.com), which recently underwent a multimillion-dollar renovation; and Little Rock's **Peabody Hotel** (© **501/906-4000;** www.peabody littlerock.com), a branch of the famous luxury hotel group that opened in 2002 and features its famous marching ducks.

Arkansas features a plethora of bed-and-breakfasts, many of them situated in historic buildings and woodsy cabins. **The Bed & Breakfast Association of Arkansas (www.bedandbreakfast arkansas.com)** publishes a free directory listing all 63 of its member inns.

HIGHLIGHTS OF ARKANSAS

Dubbed "The Natural State," Arkansas features first-class parks and recreation areas. Outdoor enthusiasts will find more activities than anyone could hope to fit into one vacation. For information on all of the state's outdoor and recreational opportunities, contact the **Arkansas Department of Parks & Tourism** (see above), the **Division of State Parks** (© **888/287-2757;** www.arkansasstate parks.com), or the **National Park Service** (www.nps.gov).

In November 2004, the $160-million **Clinton Presidential Center & Library** (© **501/374-4242;** www.clintonfoundation.org) opened inside downtown Little Rock's revitalized River Market District off I-30. America's 12th presidential library contains the largest collection of presidential papers and artifacts in U.S. history. The **River Market District** (© **501/375-2552**) itself is worth a stop. The city took an abandoned warehouse district and turned it into an area that is now home to numerous restaurants, businesses, museums, shops, and galleries; a riverside park and amphitheater; and vibrant nightlife.

Located in Little Rock's historic MacArthur Park, the **Arkansas Art Center,** at 9th and Commerce streets (© **501/ 372-4000;** www.arkarts.com), is the state's largest cultural institution and features exhibits spread over seven galleries. It encompasses the **Arkansas Museum of Art,** whose noteworthy collection includes some Renaissance-era drawings, and the **Arkansas Children's Theater.**

Do visit the **State Capitol,** at Woodlane Drive and Capitol Avenue (© **501/ 682-5080;** www.sosweb.state.ar.us), a striking neoclassical structure of limestone and marble, whose six brass doors—ordered from Tiffany's—are worth an estimated $250,000 each. Organized and self-guided tours are available.

A major U.S. civil rights landmark, the **Little Rock Central High School National Historic Site,** 2125 W. Daisy L. Gatson Bates Dr. (© **501/374-1957**), is still a working school. In 1957, when the state's governor tried to block the school's first African-American students—the

Best   **Soaking in Hot Springs**

A remarkable array of thermal springs in a valley of the Ouachita Mountains in western Arkansas prompted Congress in 1832 to set aside the valley known today as **Hot Springs** as a federal reservation. People have used the hot-spring-water therapeutic baths here for more than 200 years to treat rheumatism and other ailments. The reservation eventually developed into a well-known resort nicknamed "The American Spa" because it attracted not only the famous (Al Capone and Harry S Truman) but also indigent health seekers from around the world.

Though it officially became America's 18th national park in 1921, **Hot Springs National Park,** off I-70 and Highway 7 (© 501/624-2701; www.nps.gov/hosp), is actually the oldest in the national park system protected by law. On Bathhouse Row, the park's most celebrated feature, the **Fordyce Bathhouse,** serves as the park's visitor center and a museum of the thermal bathing industry. The park also features a working bathhouse, the **Buckstaff Bathhouse;** a mountain observation tower; an open cascade spring; and hiking trails. Stop in at the visitor center, located in downtown Hot Springs on Highway 7 North (Central Ave.). They distribute a pamphlet detailing the city's associations with former President Bill Clinton, who spent much of his childhood in Hot Springs.

For more information on the park and the many sights and activities available in Hot Springs, contact the **Hot Springs Convention & Visitors Bureau** (© 800/543-2284; www.hotsprings.org), and request their free visitor's guide.

famous Little Rock Nine—from being admitted, President Eisenhower sent federal troops to intervene. The **Central High Museum and Visitor Center,** located in a renovated Mobil Service Station across the street from the school, features a permanent exhibit, detailing the events of the 1957 desegregation crisis at the school.

Fans of *Gone With the Wind* should head to the **Old Grist Mill** (© 501/758-1424), a National Historic Landmark at McCain Boulevard and Lakeshore Drive in north Little Rock. An authentic reproduction of an old water-powered grist mill, this striking structure, built in 1933 but designed to look as if it were constructed in the 1800s, appears in the opening scene of the classic film and is believed to be the only building used in the movie that's still standing.

If diamonds are a girl's best friend, then **Crater of Diamonds State Park,** off Ark. 301 near Murfreesboro (© 870/285-3113; www.craterofdiamondsstatepark.com), is a bastion of female goodwill. The world's only public diamond mine lets visitors prospect for their own shiny souvenirs; if you find one (more than 25,000 have gotten lucky since 1972), you can keep it. Exhibits at the park trace the history of Arkansas's diamonds.

On U.S. 278, just northwest of Hope, is **Old Washington Historic State Park** (© 870/983-2684; www.oldwashingtonstatepark.com), a National Historic Landmark established on the site of the town of Washington, which came into being in 1824. Today visitors can explore over 30 carefully restored historic structures, including classic examples of southern

Greek Revival and Federal architecture, as well as hand-hewn timber framed cottages. Tour the public buildings and homes; see the remarkable collections of antiques, guns, and knives (the blacksmith shop here was where the famous Bowie knife was first forged); and visit with guides in period attire who will greet you at each stop.

Off Ark. 14, you'll find **Blanchard Springs Cavern,** a limestone formation located deep in the Ozark National Forest, 15 miles north of Mountain View. It is operated by the U.S. Forest Service and is open throughout the year. Lighted walkways lead to stunning formations and massive rooms, one as large as six football fields. Nearby, Blanchard Springs Recreational Use Area provides scenic campgrounds, picnic areas, hiking trails, a massive natural spring, and a trout lake. For information, call the U.S. Forest Service at © **202/205-8333** or head online to **www.fs.fed.us**.

For information on the historic and charming city of **Eureka Springs,** see "A Side Trip to Eureka Springs, Arkansas," on p. 239.

2 Iowa

No, it isn't heaven, no matter what the Oscar-nominated *Field of Dreams* may imply. But the 29th state admitted to the Union is a pretty cool place to visit. The movie's famous baseball field is here (and you can play on it), as are cornfields galore, one of the country's oldest and most celebrated state fairs, and the famous covered bridges of Madison County. Forget New Hampshire; this is square one for aspiring presidential candidates on the political caucus trail (only one native's managed to make it all the way—Herbert Hoover, whose unfortunate presidency dovetailed with the Great Depression). It's also the home state of Grant Wood, the artist whose *American Gothic* is one of the most famous pieces of art on the planet (that particular work isn't in Iowa, but 5,000 or so of his other works are scattered throughout the state).

Love the great outdoors? Iowans do, and visitors reap the benefits of the local passion for recreation. Iowa offers a wide variety of outdoor activities, including an abundance of fishing, hiking, hunting, camping, and biking. The state even has the largest number of golfers per capita in the country, and they tee up on some of America's best public courses. Native minigolfers are so devoted to getting in their strokes, they even play on ice in the winter (bring spikes!). And before the snow starts falling, the state offers some beautiful fall foliage-watching (and prices that aren't as sky-high as those in states better known for their seasonal coloring). In other words, Iowa is a hidden bargain that hasn't truly been discovered yet. Which *is* pretty heavenly when you think about it.

ESSENTIALS

VISITOR INFORMATION For a calendar of events, map, and comprehensive travel guide, contact the **Iowa Tourism Office,** 200 E. Grand Ave., Des Moines, IA 50309 (© **888/472-6035** or 515/242-4705; www.traveliowa.com). A good website featuring lots of information on the state can be found at **www.iowa.com**.

The Tourism Office runs 19 welcome centers dispensing tourist information at strategic points along major roads and border crossings, and in small towns throughout the state. For locations, check **www.traveliowa.com**.

GETTING THERE By Plane The state's major airport is **Des Moines International** (© **515/256-5100;** www.dsmairport.com), just 10 minutes outside of Des Moines. It's serviced by most domestic carriers and car-rental agencies.

By Car The major east-west route through the state is **I-80,** which enters from Illinois and passes through Des Moines before heading southwest toward Omaha. **I-35** runs from the northern Minnesota border before intersecting with I-80 just above Des Moines and continuing southward to Kansas City. I-29 weaves through the state's western border with Nebraska. Road conditions, especially during the winter, can change in a hurry. Before setting out on a long drive, call © **511** in Iowa, or 800/288-1047 from outside the state. You can also go online to **www.511ia.org.**

SPECIAL EVENTS Iowa's largest event, the **Iowa State Fair,** in Des Moines (© **800/545-3247** or 515/262-3111; www.iowastatefair.org), is one of the oldest (it celebrated its 150th anniversary in 2004) in the country, and one of the best (both *Esquire* and *USA Today* named it one of the country's best summer experiences in 2004). Highlights include a livestock show, the state's largest arts show, tons of wacky contests, performances by nationally renowned artists (ranging from Kid Rock to Fabian), tons of food, fireworks, and more.

WHERE TO STAY The majority of the state's accommodations are of the chain variety; consult the Iowa Tourism Office (see above) for information on lodging and reservations. Noteworthy hotels in Iowa include Des Moines's **Suites of 800 Locust Hotel & Spa** (© **515/288-5800;** www.800locust.com), the city's only boutique property and its best hotel; and, just 40 minutes north of Des Moines in the city of Perry, the **Hotel Pattee** (© **888/424-4268** or 515/465-3511; www.hotelpattee.com), a luxury property and National Historic Landmark whose 40 rooms and suites are individually decorated to pay tribute to historical figures from the Midwest.

Iowa's B&Bs range in style from historic properties to farmhouses. For information

on available options, contact the **Iowa Bed & Breakfast Guild,** 9001 Hickman Rd., Suite 220, Des Moines, IA 50322 (© **800/743-4692;** www.ia-bednbreakfast-inns.com). One especially lovely choice in Des Moines is the multi-award-winning **Butler House on Grand** (© **866/455-4096** or 515/255-4096; www.butlerhouseongrand.com), whose romantic and exquisitely decorated rooms have been picked one of the 2006 Top Ten Most Romantic Inns by *American Historic Inns.*

HIGHLIGHTS OF IOWA

In the capital city of Des Moines, the **Des Moines Art Center,** 4700 Grand Ave. (© **515/277-4405;** www.desmoinesart center.org), is a masterpiece designed not by one, but three renowned architects: I. M. Pei, Eliel Saarinen, and Richard Meier. It houses a world-class collection of contemporary modern art featuring works by Matisse, O'Keeffe, Rothko, and Richter, and sculptures by Rodin. It's hard to miss the gold-leaf-covered dome of the century-old **Iowa State Capitol,** East 12th Street and Grand Avenue (© **515/281-5129;** www.legis.state.ia.us). Do go on one of the hour-long tours of the premises, which take in, among other things, an absolutely delightful collection of First Lady dolls. On the grounds you'll find several monuments and memorials to armed forces personnel who fell during various wars. For the lowdown on the state's history, check out the **State Historical Building,** 600 E. Locust St. (© **515/281-5111;** www.iowahistory.org), whose ultramodern building houses interactive exhibits on native wildlife, American Indian and pioneer artifacts, military history, and an extensive collection of Iowa's historical records. A favorite exhibit traces the history of the woolly mammoth; the highlight of the exhibit is a complete skeleton of one of the extinct creatures.

Cedar Rapids, just north of Iowa City off I-380, is home to the **Cedar Rapids**

Museum of Art, 410 Third Ave. SE (© **319/366-7503;** www.crma.org). It's home to the world's largest collection of works by native Iowan artist Grant Wood (1892–1942), best known for the iconic *American Gothic.* (Wood's studio and home opened to the public under the auspices of the museum in 2005.) The city is also home to the **National Czech & Slovak Museum & Library,** 30 16th Ave. SW (© **319/362-8500;** www.ncsml. org), the country's foremost museum covering Czech and Slovak history and culture, which is set in Czech Village, an area along the Cedar River that is loaded with old-world European charm. The state is home to a large population of Czech immigrants; a highlight of the museum is a restored 19th-century immigrant home.

About 10 miles west of Iowa City in the small community of West Branch is the **Herbert Hoover Presidential Library, Museum, and National Historic Site,** 210 Parkside Dr. (© **319/643-5301;** www. hoover.archives.gov), where you can tour the birthplace cottage of former president Hoover, his father's blacksmith shop, a Quaker meetinghouse, a pioneer schoolhouse, and the president's gravesite. Other exhibits detail the life of former First Lady Lou Henry Hoover, and President Hoover's diminishing reputation during the days of the Great Depression.

In the city of West Bend (2½ hr. from Des Moines), the dream of Catholic priest Father Paul Dobberstein, the **Grotto of the Redemption** (© **515/887-2371;** www.westbendgrotto.com) is a religious shrine composed of nine exceptionally designed grottos depicting the life of Christ. It has been hailed by critics as "a miracle in stone," and took 45 years to build. The on-premises museum includes a large display of precious and semiprecious stones from throughout the world (its geological value is approximately $4.3 million). Tours are given daily May 1 through October 16.

Set alongside the Iowa River, you'll find the **Amana Colonies,** settled in the 19th century (they celebrated their 150th anniversary in 2005) by Inspirationists, a German religious sect. Though the original colonists' descendants voted to end their communal lifestyle in 1932, they left behind seven colonies, a virtually intact district of 500 historical buildings (including barns, kitchens, a mill, and factories—among them the famous appliance factory that bears the colonies' name) that's a National Historic Landmark. To begin your visit, head for the **Amana Colonies Welcome Center,** 622 46th Ave. in Amana (© **800/579-2294** or 319/622-7622; www.amanacolonies. com).

Fans of Robert James Waller's novels should head to picturesque Winterset in **Madison County,** off U.S. 92 (© **515/ 462-1185;** www.madisoncounty.com).

A Little Piece of Baseball Heaven

Okay, so there really is a little piece of heaven in Iowa. Baseball heaven, that is. In the town of Dyersville, Iowa, you'll find the famous cornfield-based baseball diamond immortalized in the Oscar-nominated film *Field of Dreams.* The **Field of Dreams Movie Site,** 28963 Lansing Rd., off Highway 136 South (© **888/875-8404;** www.fieldofdreamsmoviesite.com), was opened to the public in 1989 and, true to form, they built it and fans came. The field is open for play April through November, 9am to 6pm, and admission is free. If you're a baseball fan, it's worth going the distance to come here—just don't forget to bring your bat and glove.

Its five covered bridges date from the 1880s and are National Historic Landmarks. The best time to visit is October, when fall foliage is at its peak and the Covered Bridge Festival takes place. Also notable in Winterset is the **birthplace of** **John Wayne,** 216 S. 2nd St. (© **515/462-1044;** www.johnwaynebirthplace.org). You can visit the four-room house in which the legendary actor was born; it's loaded with memorabilia and rare photos.

3 Kansas

Rightly or wrongly, no state has come to signify the American heartland in the way that Kansas does. This picturesque land of rolling prairies and wheat fields is where all-American Superman grew up (sorry, there is no actual Smallville) and the place the *Wizard of Oz*'s Dorothy Gale called home. But there's more to Kansas than Aunt Em and apple pie. This is the state of Bleeding Kansas, where pro- and antislavery forces fought long and hard against each other before Kansas finally joined the Union as a free state in 1860; it was also a major battleground for civil rights when desegregation was challenged here in 1954. It's the home of the Chisholm Trail, the Santa Fe Trail, the pioneers, and the Pony Express; of plains and grasslands that saw many an Indian skirmish and relocation; and of Dodge City, where many of the gunslingers of the Old West made their reputations. The state is also a major center of aviation and features several top-notch space- and aeronautics-related attractions. It may not be home, but Kansas has got a ton of interesting options for visitors.

ESSENTIALS

VISITOR INFORMATION   For the state's comprehensive *Visitors' Guide,* contact the **Kansas Department of Commerce's Travel & Tourism Development Division** (© 785/296-2009; www.travel KS.com). For information on the state's many parks and outdoor facilities, try the **Kansas Department of Wildlife & Parks** (© 620/672-5911; www.kdwp. state.ks.us). History buffs can get the scoop

on the state's many historical sites from the **Kansas State Historical Society** (© 785/272-8681; www.kshs.org). Golfers can get the inside scoop on the state's best courses from the **Kansas Golf Association** (© 785/842-4833; www.kansasgolf.org).

If you're driving, you'll find two visitor centers scattered along some of the state's major travel corridors: along I-35, just north of the Oklahoma border (© **620/ 326-5123**), and off I-70, east of the Colorado state line (© **785/899-6695**). The friendly staff dispenses travel and touring advice, as well as maps and brochures.

GETTING THERE   By Plane   The state's major airport is **Kansas City International Airport (www.flykci.com);** it's serviced by several major domestic carriers. For general information call © **816/ 243-5237.** Most major car-rental agencies have desks at the airport.

By Train   Amtrak (© 800/872-7245; www.amtrak.com) trains stop at several cities, including Topeka, Lawrence, and Kansas City.

By Car   The major road route is **I-70,** which runs west from St. Louis, Missouri, passing through the entire state before moving on to Colorado and Denver. **I-35** runs north to Kansas City out of Oklahoma City. Two scenic and historic routes in the state that originate in Dodge City are **U.S. 50** (moving west along the old Santa Fe Trail) and **U.S. 56** (heading north). Note that road conditions can change at a whim; call the **Road & Weather Conditions Hotline** (© 877/511-5368) before setting out on a long drive.

SPECIAL EVENTS The **Kansas City Renaissance Festival** (© 800/373-0357 or 913/721-2110; www.kcrenfest.com), one of the largest of its kind in the country, kicks off on 16 acres in Bonner Springs (15 min. outside Kansas City) on Labor Day, runs for 7 consecutive weekends, and then ends on Columbus Day. Each weekend features its own theme, lots of food, a mock-up of a 16th-century English village, live entertainment, tons of shopping, and 500 costumed characters. It's a royal hoot.

Cowboys and wannabes shouldn't miss one of the state's many rodeos. Dates vary, so consult **www.travelKS.com** for up-to-the-minute event information.

HIGHLIGHTS OF KANSAS

Most of Kansas's major sights are set along the state's historic I-70 corridor.

In Topeka, stop in at the **Brown vs. Board of Education National Historic Site,** 1515 Monroe St. (© 785/354-4273; www.nps.gov/brvb), a National Historic Site commemorating the landmark 1954 Supreme Court decision that originated in the city's Monroe school, and ended segregation in the United States. The site opened in 2004 in time for the decision's 50th anniversary. While you're in town, also check out the **Kansas State Capitol,** 300 SW 10th St. (© 785/296-3966; www.kshs.org), noted for its impressive dome and famous mural of abolitionist John Brown. Free tours of the building are offered on weekdays.

A former cow town on the Chisholm Trail, Wichita is now home to some of the state's best cultural attractions. The newly renovated **Wichita Art Museum,** 1400 W. Museum Blvd. (© 316/268-4921; www.wichitaartmuseum.org), features an excellent collection of American art. Don't miss the stunning Dale Chihuly Persian Seafoam Installation hanging in the lobby. For a look at the Native American experience in Kansas, take in

the **Mid-America All-Indian Center & Museum,** 650 N. Seneca (© 316/262-5221; www.theindiancenter.org), which allows visitors to experience Native American culture and cuisine, artwork exhibitions, and artifacts.

Architecture aficionados should head over to the **Allen Lambe House Museum,** 255 N. Roosevelt St. (© 316/687-1027), the last of the prairie houses designed by Frank Lloyd Wright; the interior and many of the furnishings are still intact. Kansas has always been a major player in the aviation industry, and Wichita's **Kansas Aviation Museum,** 3350 George Washington Blvd. (© 316/683-9242; www.kansasaviationmuseum.org), is a must for any airplane buff. Set inside Wichita's old municipal airport building (built in 1935), the museum showcases over 40 of the aircraft built by many of the state's famous manufacturers, including Cessna, Boeing, and Learjet. For an out-of-this-world experience, head 60 miles northwest out of Wichita to Hutchinson's **Kansas Cosmophere and Space Center,** 1100 N. Plum St. (© 800/397-0330 or 620/662-2305; www.cosmo.org). The Smithsonian-affiliated center has an impressive array of space- and aeronautics-related exhibits, including the only Soviet *Vostok* craft in the West, the *Apollo 13* spacecraft ("Houston, we have a problem . . ."), and the gloves Neil Armstrong wore on the moon. There's also an IMAX theater.

The city of Abilene is home to the **Eisenhower Center,** 200 SE 4th St. (© 877/746-4453 or 785/263-6700; www.eisenhower.archives.gov), which celebrates native son Dwight D. Eisenhower's presidency. The complex includes the family home where the Eisenhowers lived from 1898 to 1946; the burial site of the president, his First Lady, and their son; the Eisenhower Presidential Library; a museum; and a visitor center. Also in

Best   Rising from the Ashes

The historic **Eldridge Hotel,** 701 Massachusetts St., in Lawrence, Kansas (© 800/527-0909 or 785/749-5011; www.eldridgehotel.com), has a never-die attitude. It began life in 1855 as the Free State Hotel, its name a clear statement by its New England–born owners about their preference for Kansas's admittance to the Union as a nonslave state. It didn't take long for proslavery forces to express their own inclination—by burning the building to the ground in 1856. That same year, Colonel Shalor Eldridge vowed to rebuild—again and again if he had to. This time, the building managed to last until 1863, when Quantrill's raiders did the hotel in, along with pretty much everything else in the city. Not one to be cowed, Colonel Eldridge did indeed rebuild, and his hotel stood until 1926, when the structure was torn down due to deterioration. It was rebuilt again and remained a hotel until 1970, when it was closed and converted into apartments. A massive renovation campaign begun in 1985 restored it to its former glory as a fitting symbol of a city whose motto is "From ashes to immortality."

A stay at this National Landmark will steep you in history. The all-suite hotel's lobby evokes it with its old-style lighting, dark woods, and rich fabrics. Each of the 48 suites offers separate sitting areas, old-style elegance, and refrigerators. The hotel's spa offers a full range of treatments, as well as in-room spas. Rates run $125 to $315 double, including breakfast. Stay here in early December to catch the hotel's famed Christmas Parade featuring nearly 100 old-fashioned horse-drawn buggies, wagons, and carriages.

the area is the **Dickinson County Heritage Center,** 412 S. Campbell St. (© 785/263-2681; www.heritagecenterdk.com), which features exhibits on prairie life, the Chisholm Trail, and the area's Native Americans—and also has a splendid (and must-ride) 1901 C. W. Parker carousel that's a National Historic Landmark.

The tallgrass prairies of the Great Plains are rapidly disappearing, and one of the few places you still see them in all of their natural glory is **Tallgrass National Prairie Preserve,** Highway 177, Strong City (© 620/273-8494; www.nps.gov/tapr). The only preserve of its kind encompasses the remains of a 19th-century ranch and its surrounding grassland. There are several self-guided and ranger-led hikes to choose from, and a number of interesting living history programs are offered several times a year.

The city of Lawrence was founded by abolitionists in 1854 and eventually became an important stop on the underground railroad. Most of the city was destroyed in 1863 by Quantrill's Raiders, but today's Lawrence is home to the University of Kansas and offers a beautiful downtown historic district loaded with 19th-century architecture that's well worth a stroll. Be sure to stop in at the **Spencer Art Museum,** 1301 Mississippi St. (© 785/864-4710; www.ku.edu/~sma), whose varied collections include works by Dale Chihuly, Claude Monet, Jean Fragonard, Georgia O'Keeffe, and Ansel Adams. It's one of the best university art museums in the country.

Historic Dodge City is renowned for its Old West roots (Wyatt Earp and Bat Masterson both made their reputations here during the city's rough-and-tumble heyday during the late 19th c.). Head first to the **Boot Hill Museum,** Front Street (© 620/227-8188; www.boothill. org), a living-history reconstruction of Dodge City's notorious Front Street in 1876, with lots of authentic artifacts, the infamous Boot Hill Cemetery, exhibits on several Indian tribes, and historical reenactments.

4 North Dakota

Quick: Name the state whose scenic landscape so inspired Teddy Roosevelt that he went on to do his darnedest to preserve America's great parklands by creating the National Forest Service. If you answered North Dakota, pat yourself on the back; the rest of you can take solace in the fact that most people didn't get it right either. This sparsely populated corner of the Great Plains has a lot going for it—picturesque farmland and wheat fields, the stark beauty of the Badlands, numerous historic sites, and so on—but it also has something of an identity problem: Even the movie that put one of its major cities on the map, the Coen brothers' Oscar-winning *Fargo,* was filmed elsewhere. So impassioned have North Dakotans become about forging their own path that it seems to be a sport for residents to try and rename the state every couple of years to prevent it from being that "other Dakota" (no luck so far). Still, outside of Alaska, the Rough Rider State has more unexplored and untainted wilderness than any other. Forget the Wild West; this is truly the final frontier.

ESSENTIALS

VISITOR INFORMATION Contact the **North Dakota Tourism Division,** 1600 E. Century Ave., Suite 2, P.O. Box 2057, Bismarck, ND 58502-2057 (© 800/ 435-5663 or 701/328-2525; www.nd tourism.com), and request a free visitor travel guide. Several welcome centers are scattered at strategic points along the state's major road routes; for operating hours and exact locations, contact the Tourism Division. *Note:* Road conditions can change at whim; call © 701/328-7623 (or 511 when in North Dakota) before heading out on a long drive.

GETTING THERE By Plane The two major airports are **Bismarck Municipal Airport** (© 800/453-4244; www. bismarckairport.com) and **Minot International Airport** (© 701/857-4724; http://web.ci.minot.nd.us/airport). **Northwest** is the domestic airline that offers the most service to North Dakota.

By Train **Amtrak**'s *Empire Builder* (© 800/872-7245; www.amtrak.com) services six cities in North Dakota, including Grand Forks, Devils Lake, and Minot on its way from Chicago to Seattle.

By Car The major east-west corridor is **I-94,** which enters the state from Minnesota at Fargo and runs through Bismarck and on to Medora before exiting into Montana. **I-29** enters from Canada along the eastern edge of the state and runs south through Grand Forks and Fargo into South Dakota.

SPECIAL EVENTS The **North Dakota State Fair (www.ndstatefair.com)** is held annually in Minot in late July. Visitors will enjoy live entertainment from top national artists (Keith Urban and the Steve Miller Band performed here in 2006), a parade, rodeo events, a car show, a carnival, lots of local and native cuisine, and a host of juried competitions involving everything from wine to rabbits. The **United Tribes International Pow Wow** (© 701/255-3285; www.unitedtribes powwow.com), held annually in Bismarck on the weekend after Labor Day, is one of the largest powwows in the United States. Representatives from over 70 tribes, including more than 1,500 dancers

Best   **The Park That Launched Them All**

Theodore Roosevelt once claimed, "I never would have been President if it had not been for my experiences in North Dakota." Roosevelt, who spent a great deal of time in the North Dakota Badlands, was appalled by the increasing amount of destruction being inflicted upon the land and its wildlife habitats. His subsequent conservation efforts as president led to the founding of the National Park Service. North Dakota's best attraction, **Theodore Roosevelt National Park (www.nps.gov/thro),** was created in 1947 as a memorial to the man responsible for its very existence.

The park is actually comprised of two distinct areas—the North Unit and the South Unit—separated by about 70 miles of highway. The **South Unit** is the most-visited of the two and lies along I-94 in Medora. It features a 36-mile scenic driving route, numerous wildlife and hiking trails, a petrified forest, and the absolutely spectacular Painted Canyon (check out the scenic overlook at Exit 32). A small visitor center with restrooms, picnic shelters, tables, and water is open at the canyon April through October. Be sure to stop in at the main **Medora Visitor's Center,** at Exit 24 (© **701/623-4466**), year-round, where rangers can advise you on your various touring and activity options. A small museum there exhibits some of Roosevelt's personal items, ranching artifacts, and natural history displays.

The more isolated **North Unit,** off U.S. Highway 85, 16 miles south of Watford City (© **701/842-2333**), is usually less crowded, giving it a more serene feel. It, too, features lots of wildlife viewing, as well as several hiking trails. Stop in at the **North Unit Visitor Center** at the park's entrance to get maps and park information and to see a movie on the park's famous badlands. Be sure to take the 14-mile Scenic Drive that runs from the entrance to the Oxbow Overlook, with turnouts and interpretive signs along the way.

No matter where you go in each park, you'll see tons of wildlife—bison, mule deer, coyote, bighorn sheep, elk, and dozens of bird species. There are also several campgrounds, ranger-led programs, and biking trails.

and drummers, take part in numerous concerts and performances.

WHERE TO STAY   Most of the accommodations in the state are of the chain variety. For information on North Dakota B&Bs, check out the website of the **North Dakota Bed & Breakfast Association (www.ndbba.com).**

HIGHLIGHTS OF NORTH DAKOTA

Lewis and Clark spent more time in North Dakota than in any other state; it was here that they met up with an Indian woman named Sakakawea (note the correct spelling of her Hidatsa name), who would end up on the back of the country's current dollar coin. The State Historical Society of North Dakota has identified and marked 27 locations of significance to Lewis and Clark's expedition. For details on visiting these preserved sites on the Lewis & Clark Trail, contact the Tourism Division (see "Visitor Information," above).

The **North Dakota Heritage Center,** 612 E. Boulevard Ave., Bismarck (© **701/328-2666;** www.state.nd.us/hist/hcenter.htm), is the state's largest museum and features an exceptional collection of Plains Indian artifacts and interpretive exhibits that feature North Dakota's varied American Indian, military, and agricultural history. A statue of Sakakawea is located near the entrance. The 19-story Art Deco **North Dakota State Capitol,** 600 E. Boulevard Ave. (*℗* **701/328-2471;** www.nd.gov), was constructed in 1933 and contains unique woods and materials from many states and countries.

Fort Abraham Lincoln State Park, 4480 Fort Lincoln Rd. (*℗* **800/807-4723** or 701/667-6340; www.ndparks.com), 7 miles south of Mandan on Highway 1806, is a former cavalry post that is rich in both military and early Native American history. It was from here that Custer and the Seventh Cavalry rode out on their ill-fated expedition against the Sioux at Little Big Horn. Portions of the military post, including the Custer House, have been reconstructed, and there is also a reconstructed Indian village. Visitors have a panoramic vista of the Missouri River from the park's nature and historic trails.

The **Dakota Dinosaur Museum,** 200 Museum Dr., Dickinson (*℗* **701/225-3466;** www.dakotadino.com), about 100 miles west of Bismarck, features 14 full-scale dinosaur skeletons (including a triceratops), numerous fossils (check out the new Great White Shark tooth!), and mineral exhibits.

The historic city of **Medora (www.medorand.com)** is a restored cow town founded by a French nobleman, the Marquis de Mores, in 1883. The most popular attraction in North Dakota, the city still offers a lot of Western flavor; stroll its streets and soak up the atmosphere, then go see the *Medora Musical* (*℗* **800/633-6721;** www.Medora.com), an entertaining and patriotic Broadway-quality musical extravaganza about Roosevelt and the Wild West (it's staged only in summer in the Burning Hills Badlands Amphitheater).

Château De Mores State Historic Site, on the southwestern edge of Medora (*℗* **701/623-4355;** www.state.nd.us/hist/sites), is a 26-room two-story frame building that was built in 1883 as the summer residence of the Marquis de Mores family. The château is now a historic house museum. The historic von Hoffman House, on the National Register of Historic Places, is home to the **Medora Doll House** (*℗* **800/633-6721** or 701/623-4444; www.medora.com), which features unique exhibits of antique dolls and toys. The **Badlands Museum,** 195 Third Ave. (*℗* **800/633-6721**), features numerous Native American artifacts and exhibits on the area's wildlife and pioneer heritage.

Knife River Indian Villages National Historic Site, Stanton **(www.nps.gov/knri),** is the only National Park Service site that preserves and protects the heritage of the Northern Plains Indians. There are the remains of three Hidatsa village sites within the park boundaries. A state-of-the-art museum dedicated to preserving the culture of the Hidatsa, Mandan, and Arikara tribes is located at the visitor center.

Devils Lake, 152 S. Duncan Rd., Devils Lake State Park (*℗* **701/766-4015,** or 800/807-4723 for camping reservations; www.ndparks.com), is one of North Dakota's most scenic regions. The sprawling lake with its hidden bays is an angler's paradise, and the surrounding woodlands are home to numerous forms of wildlife. It's also known for its incredible ice fishing in winter.

Want to see what life was like for the pioneers of the prairies? **Bonanzaville USA,** 1351 Main Ave. W., West Fargo (*℗* **701/282-2822;** www.bonanzaville.org), is a living history museum and village that shows what life was like in the Dakota Territory during the late 19th century. The village is home to over 400,000 artifacts, several museums, and

40 historic or re-created buildings gathered here from points in the Midwest and Great Plains. While in Fargo, do check out the fully restored 1926 Art Moderne **Fargo Theatre,** 314 Broadway (© 701/ 239-8385; www.fargotheatre.com), and the superb collections at the **Plains Art Museum,** 704 First Ave. (© 701/232-3821; www.plainsart.org), the region's largest fine arts museum.

5 West Virginia

Yes, this is the land of the *Deliverance* and the Hatfields and the McCoys. But to chalk up West Virginia as a punch line to a hillbilly joke is to do the state an incredible disservice. For those who love the great outdoors, there are few states that can match this corner of Appalachia for scenic beauty and challenging terrain (the state's nickname, "the Mountain State," is well earned). Indeed, West Virginia ranks just behind Colorado in the quality of its white-water rapids, and offers splendid skiing—and it's a whole lot cheaper than Colorado to visit. You'll find plenty of history, too. Harpers Ferry, site of one of the most famous raids in American history, is located here; the raid helped chart West Virginia's course of secession from Virginia and its entrance as a separate state into the Union in 1863. And if you prefer relaxation, the state is home to one of the country's most renowned resorts, The Greenbrier, and to the historic spa city of Berkeley Springs, where the Founding Fathers liked to get away from all—and you can, too. For sheer value, few states in the country can beat this one.

ESSENTIALS

VISITOR INFORMATION Contact the **West Virginia Division of Tourism** (© 800/CALL-WVA or 304/558-2200; www.callwva.com), for its very comprehensive travel guide as well as maps and other travel information. Very knowledgeable travel counselors will offer advice, suggest travel ideas, and make reservations for you if you so desire.

Eight welcome centers, staffed daily from 9am to 5pm November to April and 8am to 6pm May to October, are strategically placed along major road routes and state borders. For exact locations, contact the Division of Tourism.

For information on the state's myriad outdoor recreational activities, contact the Division of Tourism or head to the website of **West Virginia State Parks** (www.wvstateparks.com).

GETTING THERE **By Plane** West Virginia has nine commercial airports. For more information on flying into the state, consult the **West Virginia Department of Transportation Aeronautics Commission** (© 304/558-3436; www. wvdot.com).

By Train Amtrak (© 800/872-7245; www.amtrak.com) provides service to several major cities, including White Sulphur Springs and Charleston, via its *Cardinal* train. **MARC commuter rail service** (© 866/743-3682; www.mtamaryland. com) is available from Washington, D.C., to Harpers Ferry.

By Car The major north-south interstate is the four-lane **I-77** which runs south out of Cleveland, through West Virginia, and down to Charlotte. The other major interstate is **I-79,** which enters the state just north of Morgantown from Pittsburgh and runs southwest until Charleston, where it intersects with **I-64,** which runs from Virginia to Charleston, and on into Kentucky. **I-81** runs from Maryland through the northeast corner of the state and into Virginia.

SPECIAL EVENTS The annual **State Fair of West Virginia** (© 304/645-1090; www.wvstatefair.com) has featured family-friendly livestock exhibits, a carnival,

Best A Hotel Fit for Congress

Since 1778, visitors have trooped to the town of White Sulphur Springs to restore their health in the curative waters that flow from the town's spring. Today, the spring in question is the centerpiece of **The Greenbrier,** 300 W. Main St. (© 800/453-4858; www.greenbrier.com), a magnificent 6,500-acre resort that is rich in both history (it's hosted 26 presidents) and luxury.

Once the most fashionable summer resort in the South where Robert E. Lee built a summer home, it was forced to close during the Civil War when, depending on which side was occupying the property, it served as a hospital or as a military headquarters. At the end of the war the resort once again rose to prominence, only to switch identities once more during World War II, when it was purchased by the U.S. Army and turned into a hospital. Following the war, the building was transformed into a luxury resort by noted designer Dorothy Draper (the exterior of the magnificent Georgian main building strongly resembles the White House), and counted the legendary Sam Snead as its golf pro (establishing the resort as a premiere golf destination) until his death in 2002.

But perhaps the most interesting bit of Greenbrier history is this: In the 1950s, the government built a secret underground Emergency Relocation Center under the resort that, for nearly 30 years, was maintained to serve as the emergency location of Congress should an international crisis ever force the legislative branch out of Washington. The shelter was finally closed down in 1995 (you can tour it along with other notable portions of this National Historic Landmark's interior and grounds on guided tours).

Today a stay at The Greenbrier features luxurious accommodations, unbelievable service, first-class dining, and an amazing array of recreational activities, ranging from the Falconry Academy and *Golf Digest* Academy to state-of-the-art fitness and tennis centers and a world-renowned spa. There's also a specialized diagnostic and health evaluation clinic. The resort renovates each of its guest rooms at least once every 4 years, which means that all of them—from the small but elegant standard rooms to the two-bedroom cottages—are exquisitely decorated and kept in tiptop condition. Don't miss having at least one meal in the elegant main dining room, renowned for its classical cuisine.

concerts, food, and other fun for over 80 years. It's staged in mid-August at the State Fairgrounds in Lewisburg. On **West Virginia Day,** commemorating the date the state was granted admittance to the Union (June 20, 1863), celebrations, concerts, parades, and fireworks are staged in various cities all over the state. For more information, check out **www.callwva.com.**

WHERE TO STAY For information on B&Bs throughout the state, contact the **Mountain State Association of Bed & Breakfasts** (www.wvbedandbreakfasts.com).

HIGHLIGHTS OF WEST VIRGINIA

The top historical attraction in the state is **Harpers Ferry National Historic Park**

(© **304/535-6029;** www.nps.gov/hafe), whose 2,300 acres actually cover three states, though the primary historic sites are in West Virginia, in the historic town of Harpers Ferry. It was here that ardent abolitionist John Brown launched a raid of the federal arsenal (which supplied guns for Lewis and Clark's famous expedition), as an attack on slavery. It was also here that Stonewall Jackson secured the largest surrender of Union troops (over 12,000 of them) during the Civil War. The town still looks as it did in the 19th century, and many of the historic buildings are open to the public; there are lots of quaint shops and restaurants on the premises as well. Stop in at the **Cavaliers Visitors Center,** off U.S. 340 (© **304/535-6298**), for assistance in planning your visit.

Hikers should head for the **Appalachian Trail Conference,** 799 Washington St., Harpers Ferry (© **304/535-6331;** www.appalachiantrail.org), the headquarters for the Appalachian Trail, for information, maps, and advice on hiking the famous trail.

Once you've worked your muscles into a frenzy, head to historic **Berkeley Springs** (© **800/447-8797** or 304/258-9147; www.berkeleysprings.com), a quirky town that's a haven for artists, and where massage therapists outnumber lawyers three to one. George Washington was among the first of many visitors who came to "take the waters" at the first spa town in the country. Today it's still a popular a place to kick back and relax. **Berkeley Springs Historic State Park** (© **304/258-2711;** www.berkeleyspringssp.com), whose bathhouse opened in 1930, is still a working mineral spa today. Luxuriate in the Roman-style baths or take advantage of the health treatments; prices are extremely reasonable. Once you've soaked and relaxed, browse the town's many art galleries and antiques shops.

For those of a more scientific bent, the state's Potomac Highlands region is home to the **National Radio Astronomy Observatory,** Route 92/28 in Green Bank (© **304/456-0211;** www.nrao.edu/epo), which houses the world's largest radio telescope and several hands-on exhibits dealing with radio waves and space exploration. Tours of the facility are offered daily in summer.

When it comes to outdoor recreation, West Virginia offers more activities and opportunities than most outdoor enthusiasts can hope to take advantage of. More than three million visitors a year take advantage of some of the best wildlife viewing, hiking, mountain biking, and horseback riding in the state at the exceptional **Monongahela National Forest,** 200 Sycamore St., Elkins (© **304/636-1800;** www.fs.fed.us/r9/mnf). Civil War buffs can also drive the park's **Auto Tour,** featuring stops at historic sites such as Fort Summit and Camp Allegheny. Be sure to stop at the park's **Seneca Rocks Discovery Center** (© **304/567-2827**), at the base of the exceptionally scenic Seneca Rocks cliffs off I-33, which attract rock climbers from all over the country.

Two state parks just north of the National Forest on Highway 32—**Canaan Valley Resort** (© **800/622-4121** or 304/866-4121; www.canaanresort.com) and **Backwater Falls State Park** (© **304/259-5216;** www.blackwaterfalls.com)— offer first-class downhill and cross-country skiing in winter, and fabulous mountain biking and hiking trails in summer. The best skiing in the Southeast and Mid-Atlantic states, as well as superior mountain biking trails, can be found at **Snowshoe Mountain,** 10 Snowshoe Dr., Snowshoe (© **877/441-4386;** www.snowshoemtn.com), an 11,000-acre resort in the scenic Allegheny Mountains.

If you prefer watersports, head straight for the southeast section of the state to the **New River Gorge National River Recreation Area,** off I-64 (© **304/574-2115** or 304/466-0417; www.nps.gov/neri). Here you'll find the best whitewater rapids in the eastern U.S., as well as numerous other recreational activities, from horseback riding and hiking, to fishing and boating. Be sure to stop at the year-round **Canyon Rim Visitor Center,** off Route 19 just north of the New River Gorge Bridge, where you'll find exhibits on the natural and cultural history of the area, and several rangers who dispense valuable information and offer guided walks several times a year. Contact the Tourism Division (see "Visitor Information," above) for information on the numerous reputable outfitters who service the region if you're interested in a guided raft trip or other organized tour.

For a different sort of scenic tour, head over to **Cass Scenic Railroad State Park,** Route 66 (© **304/456-4300;** www.cassrailroad.com), which encompasses a historic early-20th-century logging town, but whose prime attraction is a vintage steam train ride amid the West Virginia mountains. Head here in the fall for breathtaking foliage.

Appendix B:
State Tourism Offices

Alabama Bureau of Tourism & Travel
P.O. Box 4927
Montgomery, AL 36103-4927
☎ 800/ALABAMA
☎ 334/242-4169
www.touralabama.org

Alaska Travel Industry Association
2600 Cordova St., Suite 201
Anchorage, AK 99503
☎ 800/862-5275
www.travelalaska.com

Arizona Office of Tourism
1110 W. Washington St., Suite 155
Phoenix, AZ 85007
☎ 866/275-5816
www.arizonaguide.com

**Arkansas Department
of Parks & Tourism**
1 Capitol Mall
Little Rock, AR 72201
☎ 800/NATURAL
☎ 501/682-7777
www.arkansas.com

**California Travel and Tourism
Commission**
P.O. Box 1499
Sacramento, CA 95812-1499
☎ 800/GO-CALIF
☎ 916/444-4429
www.visitcalifornia.com

Colorado Tourism Office
1625 Broadway, Suite 2700
Denver, CO 80202
☎ 800/COLORADO
www.colorado.com

**Connecticut Commission
on Culture & Tourism**
1 Financial Plaza
755 Main St.
Hartford, CT 06103
☎ 888/CT-VISIT (288-4748)
☎ 860/270-8080
www.ctvisit.com

Delaware Tourism Office
99 King's Hwy.
Dover, DE 19901
☎ 866/284-7483
☎ 302/739-4271
www.visitdelaware.net

**Washington, DC Convention &
Tourism Corporation**
901 7th St. NW, 4th Floor
Washington, DC 20001
☎ 800/422-8644
www.washington.org

Visit Florida
661 E. Jefferson St., Suite 300
Tallahassee, FL 32301
☎ 888/7-FLA-USA
☎ 850/488-5607
www.visitflorida.com

**Georgia Department of Economic
Development**
75 5th St. NW, Suite 1200
Atlanta, GA 30308
☎ 800/VISIT-GA
☎ 404/962-4000
www.georgia.org

Hawaii Visitors & Convention Bureau
2270 Kalakaua Ave., Suite 801
Honolulu, HI 96815
℃ 800/464-2924
www.gohawaii.org

Idaho Department of Commerce
700 W. State St.
Boise, ID 83720
℃ 800/842-5858
℃ 208/334-2470
www.visitid.org

Illinois Bureau of Tourism
100 W. Randolph, Suite 3-400
Chicago, IL 60601
℃ 800/2-CONNECT
℃ 312/814-4732
www.enjoyillinois.com

Indiana Department of Commerce/Tourism
1 N. Capitol Ave., Suite 100
Indianapolis, IN 46204
℃ 800/677-9800
www.in.gov/enjoyindiana

Iowa Division of Tourism
200 E. Grand Ave.
Des Moines, IA 50309
℃ 888/472-6035
℃ 515/242-4705
www.traveliowa.com

Kansas Travel & Tourism Division
Department of Commerce and Housing
1000 SW Jackson St., Suite 100
Topeka, KS 66612
℃ 800/2-KANSAS
℃ 785/296-2009
www.travelks.com

Kentucky Department of Tourism
Capital Plaza Tower, 22nd Floor
500 Metro St.
Frankfort, KY 40601
℃ 800/225-8747
℃ 502/564-4930
www.kentuckytourism.com

Louisiana Office of Tourism
P.O. Box 94291
Baton Rouge, LA 70804
℃ 800/677-4082
℃ 225/342-8100
www.louisianatravel.com

Maine Office of Tourism
59 State House Station
Augusta, ME 04333
℃ 888/624-6345
www.visitmaine.com

Maryland Office of Tourism Development
217 E. Redwood St., 9th Floor
Baltimore, MD 21202
℃ 866/639-3526
www.mdisfun.org

Massachusetts Office of Travel & Tourism
10 Park Plaza, Suite 4510
Boston, MA 02116
℃ 800/227-MASS
www.massvacation.com

Travel Michigan
300 N. Washington Sq., 2nd Floor
Lansing, MI 48913
℃ 888/784-7328
http://travel.michigan.org

Explore Minnesota Tourism
100 Metro Sq., 121 7th Place E.
St. Paul, MN 55101
℃ 888/TOURISM
℃ 651/296-5029
www.exploreminnesota.com

Mississippi Division of Tourism Development
P.O. Box 849
Jackson, MS 39205
℃ 866/733-6477
℃ 601/359-3297
www.visitmississippi.org

Missouri Division of Tourism
Box 1055
Jefferson City, MO 65102
✆ 800/519-2100
✆ 573/751-4133
www.missouritourism.org

Travel Montana
301 South Park
P.O. Box 200533
Helena, MT 59620
✆ 800/VISIT-MT
✆ 406/841-2870
http://visitmt.com

Nebraska Division of Tourism & Travel
P.O. Box 98907
Lincoln, NE 68509-8907
✆ 877/NEBRASKA
www.visitnebraska.org

Nevada Commission on Tourism
401 N. Carson St.
Carson City, NV 89701
✆ 800/NEVADA-8
www.travelnevada.com

New Hampshire Office of Travel & Tourism
172 Pembroke Rd.
P.O. Box 1856
Concord, NH 03302-1856
✆ 800/386-4664
✆ 603/271-2665
www.visitnh.gov

New Jersey Division of Travel & Tourism
P.O. Box 820
Trenton, NJ 08625-0820
✆ 800/VISIT-NJ
✆ 609/777-0885
www.visitnj.org

New Mexico Department of Tourism
491 Old Santa Fe Trail
Santa Fe, NM 87501
✆ 800/733-6396
✆ 505/827-7400
www.newmexico.org

New York State Division of Tourism
30 S Pearl St.
Main Concourse, Room 110
Albany, NY 12246
✆ 800/CALL-NYS
✆ 518/474-4116
www.iloveny.com

North Carolina Division of Travel & Tourism
301 N. Wilmington St.
Raleigh, NC 27699-4301
✆ 800/VISIT-NC
www.visitnc.com

North Dakota Tourism Division
Century Center
1600 E. Century Ave., Suite 2
P.O. Box 2057
Bismarck, ND 58502-2057
✆ 800/HELLO-ND
www.ndtourism.com

Ohio Division of Travel & Tourism
P.O. Box 1001
Columbus, OH 43216-1001
✆ 800/BUCKEYE
www.discoverohio.com

Oklahoma Travel & Tourism Division
P.O. Box 52002
Oklahoma City, OK 73152
✆ 800/652-6552
✆ 405/230-8400
www.travelok.com

Oregon Tourism Commission
670 Hawthorne SE, Suite 240
Salem, OR 97301
✆ 800/378-8850
✆ 503/378-8850
www.traveloregon.com

Pennsylvania Tourism Marketing Office
400 North St., 4th Floor
Harrisburg, PA 17120-0225
✆ 800/VISIT-PA
✆ 717/787-5453
www.visitpa.com

Rhode Island Tourism Division
1 W. Exchange St.
Providence, RI 02903
✆ 800/556-2484
✆ 401/222-2601
www.visitrhodeisland.com

South Carolina Department of Parks, Recreation, and Tourism
1205 Pendleton St.
Columbia, SC 29201
✆ 866/224-9339
✆ 803/734-1700
www.discoversouthcarolina.com

South Dakota Department of Tourism
711 E. Wells Ave.
Pierre, SD 57501-5070
✆ 800/S-DAKOTA
✆ 605/773-3301
www.travelsd.com

Tennessee Department of Tourism Development
Wm. Snodgrass/Tennessee Tower
312 8th Ave. N., 25th Floor
Nashville, TN 37243
✆ 800/GO-2-TENN
✆ 615/741-2159
www.tnvacation.com

Texas Department of Commerce, Tourist Division
P.O. Box 12428
Austin, TX 78711
✆ 800/888-8TEX
www.traveltex.com

Utah Travel Council
P.O. Box 147420
Salt Lake City, UT 84114-7420
✆ 800/200-1160
✆ 801/538-1030
www.utah.com

Vermont Department of Tourism
National Life Building, 6th Floor,
Drawer 20
Montpelier, VT 05620-0501
✆ 800/VERMONT
✆ 802/828-3237
www.vermontvacation.com

Virginia Tourism Corporation
901 E. Byrd St.
Richmond, VA 23219
✆ 800/VISIT-VA
✆ 804/545-5500
www.virginia.org

Washington State Tourism
128 10th Ave. SW
Olympia, WA 98504
✆ 800/544-1800
✆ 360/753-4470
www.experiencewashington.com

West Virginia Division of Tourism
90 MacCorkle Ave. SW
South Charleston, WV 25303
✆ 800/CALL-WVA
✆ 304/558-2200
www.callwva.com

Wisconsin Division of Tourism
201 W. Washington Ave.
P.O. Box 8690
Madison, WI 53708
✆ 800/432-TRIP outside Wisconsin
✆ 608/266-2161
www.travelwisconsin.com

Wyoming Tourism
I-25 at College Dr., Dept. WY
Cheyenne, WY 82002
✆ 800/225-5996
✆ 307/777-7777
www.wyomingtourism.org

Appendix C:
For International Visitors

ENTRY REQUIREMENTS

Check at any U.S. embassy or consulate for current information and requirements. You can also obtain a visa application and other information online at the **U.S. State Department**'s website, at **http://travel. state.gov**.

VISAS The U.S. State Department has a **Visa Waiver Program** allowing citizens of certain countries to enter the United States without a visa for stays of up to 90 days (check **http://travel.state.gov** for the most current list of participating countries). Citizens of these countries need only a valid passport and a round-trip air or cruise ticket in their possession upon arrival.

Citizens of all other countries must have (1) a valid passport that expires at least 6 months later than the scheduled end of their visit to the United States, and (2) a tourist visa, which may be obtained without charge from any U.S. consulate.

MEDICAL REQUIREMENTS If you have a medical condition that requires **syringe-administered medications,** carry a valid signed prescription from your physician—the **Federal Aviation Administration (FAA)** no longer allows airline passengers to pack syringes in their carry-on baggage without documented proof of medical need. If you have a disease that requires treatment with **narcotics,** you should also carry documented proof with you—smuggling narcotics aboard a plane is a serious offense that carries severe penalties in the U.S.

For **HIV-positive visitors,** requirements for entering the United States are somewhat vague and change frequently. For up-to-the-minute information, contact **AIDSinfo** (© **800/448-0440,** or 301/519-6616 outside the U.S.; www.aids info.nih.gov) or the **Gay Men's Health Crisis** (© **212/367-1000;** www.gmhc.org).

DRIVER'S LICENSES Foreign driver's licenses are mostly recognized in the U.S., although you may want to get an international driver's license if your home license is not written in English.

CUSTOMS
WHAT YOU CAN BRING IN

Every visitor more than 21 years of age may bring in, free of duty, the following: (1) 1 liter of wine or hard liquor; (2) 200 cigarettes, 100 cigars (but not from Cuba), or 3 pounds of smoking tobacco; and (3) $100 worth of gifts. These exemptions are offered to travelers who spend at least 72 hours in the United States and who have not claimed them within the preceding 6 months. It is altogether forbidden to bring into the country foodstuffs (particularly fruit, cooked meats, and canned goods) and plants (vegetables, seeds, tropical plants, and the like). Foreign tourists may bring in or take out up to $10,000 in U.S. or foreign currency with no formalities; larger sums must be declared to U.S. Customs on entering or leaving, which includes filing form CM 4790. For more specific information regarding U.S. Customs and Border Protection, contact your nearest U.S.

embassy or consulate, or the **U.S. Customs** office (© **202/927-1770;** www.customs. ustreas.gov).

WHAT YOU CAN TAKE HOME

U.K. citizens should contact **HM Customs & Excise** at © **0845/010-9000,** or 020/8929-0152 from outside the U.K.), or consult its website at www.hmce.gov. uk for Customs information.

For a clear summary of Canadian rules, write for the booklet *I Declare,* issued by the **Canada Border Services Agency** (© **800/461-9999** in Canada, or 204/ 983-3500; www.cbsa-asfc.gc.ca).

A helpful brochure available from **Australian** consulates or Customs offices is *Know Before You Go.* For more information, call the **Australian Customs Service** at © **1300/363-263,** or log on to www. customs.gov.au.

Most **New Zealand** Customs questions are answered in a free pamphlet available at New Zealand consulates and Customs offices: *New Zealand Customs Guide for Travellers, Notice no. 4.* For more information, contact **New Zealand Customs,** The Customhouse, 17–21 Whitmore St., Box 2218, Wellington (© **0800/428-786** or 04/473-6099; www.customs.govt.nz).

HEALTH INSURANCE

Although it's not required of travelers, health insurance is highly recommended. Unlike many European countries, the United States does not usually offer free or low-cost medical care to its citizens or visitors. Doctors and hospitals are expensive, and in most cases will require advance payment or proof of coverage before they render their services. Packages such as **Europ Assistance's "Worldwide Healthcare Plan"** are sold by European automobile clubs and travel agencies at attractive rates. **Worldwide Assistance Services, Inc.** (© **800/777-8710;** www. worldwideassistance.com), is the agent for Europ Assistance in the United States.

Though lack of health insurance may prevent you from being admitted to a hospital in nonemergencies, don't worry about being left on a street corner to die: The American way is to fix you now and bill the living daylights out of you later.

INSURANCE FOR BRITISH TRAVELERS Most big travel agents offer their own insurance and will probably try to sell you their package when you book a holiday. Think before you sign. **Britain's Consumers' Association** recommends that you insist on seeing the policy and reading the fine print before buying travel insurance. **The Association of British Insurers** (© **020/7600-3333;** www.abi.org.uk) gives advice by phone and publishes *Holiday Insurance,* a free guide to policy provisions and prices. You might also shop around for better deals: Try **Columbus Direct** (© **0870/033-9988;** www.columbusdirect.net).

INSURANCE FOR CANADIAN TRAVELERS Canadians should check with their provincial health plan offices or call **Health Canada** (© **866/225-0709;** www.hc-sc.gc.ca) to find out the extent of their coverage and what documentation and receipts they must take home in case they are treated in the United States.

MONEY

CURRENCY The most common **bills** are the $1 (colloquially, a "buck"), $5, $10, and $20 denominations. There are also $2 bills (seldom encountered), $50 bills, and $100 bills (the last two are usually not welcome as payment for small purchases). There are seven denominations of coins: 1¢ (1 cent, or a penny); 5¢ (5 cents, or a nickel); 10¢ (10 cents, or a dime); 25¢ (25 cents, or a quarter); 50¢ (50 cents, or a half dollar); the new gold-colored "Sacagawea" coin worth $1; and, prized by collectors, the rare, older silver dollar.

Leave any currency other than U.S. dollars at home—"foreign-exchange bureaus" common in Europe are rare even at airports in the United States and it's best not to change foreign money at local banks.

CREDIT CARDS & ATMS Credit cards are the most widely used form of payment in the United States: **Visa** (Barclaycard in Britain), **MasterCard** (Eurocard in Europe, Access in Britain, Chargex in Canada), **American Express, Diners Club,** and **Discover.** There are, however, a handful of stores and restaurants that do not take credit cards, so be sure to ask in advance. (*Note:* Businesses may require a minimum purchase, usually around $10, to use a credit card.)

It is strongly recommended that you bring at least one major credit card. You must have a credit or charge card to rent a car. Hotels and airlines usually require a credit card imprint as a deposit against expenses, and in an emergency a credit card can be priceless.

You'll find **automated teller machines (ATMs)** on just about every block across the country. Some ATMs will allow you to draw U.S. currency against your bank and credit cards. Check with your bank before leaving home, and remember that you will need your personal identification number (PIN) to do so. Most accept Visa, MasterCard, and American Express, as well as ATM cards from other U.S. banks. The **Cirrus** (© 800/424-7787; www. mastercard.com) and **PLUS** (© 800/843-7587; www.visa.com) networks span the country; you can find them even in remote regions. Look at the back of your bank card to see which network you're on, then call or check online for ATM locations at your destination. Expect to be charged up to $3 per transaction, however, if you're not using your own bank's ATM.

ATM cards with major credit card backing, known as "debit cards," are now a commonly acceptable form of payment in most stores and restaurants. Debit cards draw money directly from your checking account. Some stores enable you to receive "cash back" on your debit-card purchases as well.

TRAVELER'S CHECKS Though traveler's checks are widely accepted, foreign-currency checks are often difficult to exchange. The most popular traveler's checks are offered by **American Express** (© 800/807-6233, or 800/221-7282 for card holders—this number accepts collect calls, offers service in several foreign languages, and exempts Amex gold and platinum cardholders from the 1% fee); **Visa** (© 800/732-1322)—AAA members can obtain Visa checks for a $9.95 fee (for checks up to $1,500) at most AAA offices or by calling © 866/339-3378; and **MasterCard** (© 800/223-9920). Most businesses are pretty good about taking traveler's checks, but you're better off cashing them at a bank and paying in cash.

SAFETY

GENERAL SUGGESTIONS Although tourist areas are generally safe, U.S. urban areas tend to be less safe than those in Europe or Japan. This is particularly true of large American cities. If you're in doubt about which neighborhoods are safe, don't hesitate to make inquiries with the hotel front desk staff or the local tourist office. Avoid deserted areas, especially at night, and don't go into public parks after dark unless there's a concert or similar occasion that will attract a crowd.

Avoid carrying valuables with you on the street, and keep expensive cameras or electronic equipment bagged up or covered when not in use. If you're using a map, try to consult it inconspicuously. Hold onto your pocketbook, and place your billfold in an inside pocket. In theaters, restaurants, and other public places, keep your possessions in sight.

DRIVING SAFETY If you have an accident, even on the highway, stay in your car with the doors locked until you

Prepare to Be Fingerprinted

As of January 2004, many international visitors traveling on visas to the United States will be photographed and fingerprinted at Customs in a new program created by the Department of Homeland Security called **US-VISIT.** Non-U.S. citizens arriving at airports and on cruise ships must undergo an instant background check as part of the government's ongoing efforts to deter terrorism by verifying the identity of incoming and outgoing visitors. Exempt from the extra scrutiny are visitors entering by land or those from the 28 countries (mostly in Europe) that don't require a visa for short-term visits. For more information, go to the Homeland Security website at **www.dhs.gov/dhspublic.**

assess the situation or until the police arrive. If you're bumped from behind on the street or are involved in a minor accident with no injuries, and the situation appears to be suspicious, motion to the other driver to follow you. Never get out of your car in such situations. Go directly to the nearest police precinct, well-lit service station, or 24-hour store.

Park in well-lit and well-traveled areas whenever possible. Always keep your car doors locked, whether the vehicle is attended or unattended. Never leave any packages or valuables in sight. If someone attempts to rob you or steal your car, don't try to resist the thief/carjacker. Report the incident to the police department immediately by calling ✆ **911.**

Many car-rental agencies now offer the option of renting a cellphone for the duration of your car rental; check with the rental agent when you pick up the car. Otherwise, contact **InTouch USA** at ✆ **800/872-7626** or www.intouchusa. com for short-term cellphone rental.

2 Getting to the U.S.

AIRLINE DISCOUNTS Overseas visitors can take advantage of the APEX (advance purchase excursion) reductions offered by all major U.S. and European carriers. For the best rates, compare fares and be flexible with the dates and times of travel.

IMMIGRATION & CUSTOMS CLEARANCE Getting through immigration control can take as long as 2 hours on some days, especially on summer weekends. People traveling by air from Canada, Bermuda, and certain countries in the Caribbean can sometimes clear Customs and Immigration at the point of departure, which is much quicker.

3 Getting Around the U.S.

BY PLANE Some large airlines (for example, Northwest and Delta) offer travelers on their transatlantic or transpacific flights special discount tickets under the name **Visit USA,** allowing mostly one-way travel from one U.S. destination to another at very low prices. These discount tickets are not on sale in the United States and must be purchased abroad in conjunction with your international ticket. This system is the best, easiest, and fastest way to see the United States at low cost. You should obtain information well in advance from your travel agent or the office of the airline concerned, since the conditions attached to these discount tickets can be changed without advance notice.

BY TRAIN International visitors (excluding Canada) can also buy a **USA Rail Pass,** good for 15 or 30 days of unlimited travel on Amtrak (© **800/ USA-RAIL;** www.amtrak.com). The pass is available through many overseas travel agents and at Amtrak offices nationwide. See Amtrak's website for the cost of travel within the western, eastern, or northwestern United States. With a foreign passport, you can also buy passes direct from some Amtrak locations, including San Francisco, Los Angeles, Chicago, New York, Miami, Boston, and Washington, D.C. Reservations are generally required and should be made as early as possible. Regional rail passes are also available.

BY BUS Although bus travel is often the most economical form of public transit for short hops between U.S. cities, it can also be slow and uncomfortable—certainly not an option for everyone (particularly when Amtrak, which is far more luxurious, offers similar rates). **Greyhound/ Trailways** (© **800/231-2222;** www. greyhound.com) offers an **International Ameripass** that must be purchased before coming to the United States, or by phone through the Greyhound International Office at the Port Authority Bus Terminal in New York City (© 212/971-0492). The pass can be obtained from foreign travel agents or through Greyhound's website (order at least 21 days before your departure to the U.S.) and costs less than the domestic version.

BY CAR Unless you plan to spend the bulk of your vacation time in a city where walking is the best and easiest way to get around, the most cost-effective, convenient, and comfortable way to travel around the United States is by car. A list of the major rental-car companies in the United States can be found in appendix D, "Useful Toll-Free Numbers & Websites." Foreign driver's licenses are usually recognized in the U.S., but you should get an international one if your home license is not in English.

If you plan to rent a car in the United States, you probably won't need the services of an additional automobile organization. If you're planning to buy or borrow a car, automobile-association membership is recommended. **AAA,** the **American Automobile Association** (© **800/222-4357;** http://travel.aaa.com), is the country's largest auto club and supplies its members with maps, insurance, and, most importantly, emergency road service. The cost of joining runs from $67 for singles to $91 for two members, but if you're a member of a foreign auto club with reciprocal arrangements, you can enjoy free AAA service in America.

FAST FACTS: For the International Traveler

Business Hours Offices are usually open weekdays from 9am to 5pm. Banks are open weekdays from 9am to 3pm or later and sometimes Saturday mornings. Stores typically open between 9 and 10am and close between 5 and 6pm Monday through Saturday. Stores in shopping complexes or malls tend to stay open late: until about 9pm on weekdays and weekends. Many malls and larger department stores are open on Sunday.

Drinking Laws The legal age for purchase and consumption of alcoholic beverages is 21; proof of age is required and often requested at bars, nightclubs, and restaurants, so it's always a good idea to bring ID when you go out. Beer and wine often can be purchased in supermarkets, but liquor laws vary from state to state.

Do not carry open containers of alcohol in your car or any public area that isn't zoned for alcohol consumption. The police can fine you on the spot. And nothing will ruin your trip faster than getting a citation for DUI ("driving under the influence"), so don't even think about driving while intoxicated.

Electricity Like Canada, the United States uses 110–120 volts AC (60 cycles), compared to 220–240 volts AC (50 cycles) in most of Europe, Australia, and New Zealand. If your small appliances use 220–240 volts, you'll need a 110-volt transformer and a plug adapter with two flat parallel pins to operate them here. Downward converters that change 220–240 volts to 110–120 volts are difficult to find in the United States, so bring one with you.

Embassies & Consulates All embassies are located in the nation's capital, Washington, D.C. Some consulates are located in major U.S. cities, and most nations have a mission to the United Nations in New York City. If your country isn't listed below, call for directory information in Washington, D.C. (✆ **202/555-1212**) or log on to **www.embassy.org/embassies**.

The embassy of **Australia** is at 1601 Massachusetts Ave. NW, Washington, DC 20036 (✆ **202/797-3000**; www.austemb.org). There are consulates in New York, Honolulu, Houston, Los Angeles, and San Francisco.

The embassy of **Canada** is at 501 Pennsylvania Ave. NW, Washington, DC 20001 (✆ **202/682-1740**; www.canadianembassy.org). Other Canadian consulates are in Buffalo (NY), Detroit, Los Angeles, New York, and Seattle.

The embassy of **Ireland** is at 2234 Massachusetts Ave. NW, Washington, DC 20008 (✆ **202/462-3939**; www.irelandemb.org). Irish consulates are in Boston, Chicago, New York, San Francisco, and other cities. See website for complete listing.

The embassy of **Japan** is at 2520 Massachusetts Ave. NW, Washington, DC 20008 (✆ **202/238-6700**; www.embjapan.org). Japanese consulates are located in many cities including Atlanta, Boston, Detroit, New York, San Francisco, and Seattle.

The embassy of **New Zealand** is at 37 Observatory Circle NW, Washington, DC 20008 (✆ **202/328-4800**; www.nzemb.org). New Zealand consulates are in Los Angeles, Salt Lake City, San Francisco, and Seattle.

The embassy of the **United Kingdom** is at 3100 Massachusetts Ave. NW, Washington, DC 20008 (✆ **202/588-7800**; www.britainusa.com). Other British consulates are in Atlanta, Boston, Chicago, Cleveland, Houston, Los Angeles, New York, San Francisco, and Seattle.

Emergencies Call ✆ **911** to report a fire, call the police, or get an ambulance anywhere in the United States. This is a toll-free call.

If you encounter serious problems, contact **Traveler's Aid International** (✆ **202/546-1127**; www.travelersaid.org). This nationwide, nonprofit, social-service organization geared to helping travelers in difficult straits offers services that might include reuniting families separated while traveling, providing food and/or shelter to people stranded without cash, or even emotional counseling. If you're in trouble, seek them out.

Gasoline (Petrol) Petrol is known as gasoline (or simply "gas") in the United States, and petrol stations are known as both gas stations and service stations. At press time, in the U.S., the cost of gasoline (also known as gas, but never petrol), is abnormally high. Taxes are already included in the printed price. One U.S. gallon equals 3.8 liters or .85 imperial gallons.

Holidays Banks, government offices, post offices, and many stores, restaurants, and museums are closed on the following legal national holidays: January 1 (New Year's Day), the third Monday in January (Martin Luther King, Jr., Day), the third Monday in February (Presidents' Day, Washington's Birthday), the last Monday in May (Memorial Day), July 4 (Independence Day), the first Monday in September (Labor Day), the second Monday in October (Columbus Day), November 11 (Veterans Day/Armistice Day), the fourth Thursday in November (Thanksgiving Day), and December 25 (Christmas).

Legal Aid If you are "pulled over" for a minor infraction (such as speeding), never attempt to pay the fine directly to a police officer; this could be construed as attempted bribery, a much more serious crime. Pay fines by mail, or directly into the hands of the clerk of the court. If accused of a more serious offense, say and do nothing before consulting a lawyer. Here the burden is on the state to prove a person's guilt beyond a reasonable doubt, and everyone has the right to remain silent, whether he or she is suspected of a crime or actually arrested. Once arrested, a person can make one telephone call to a party of his or her choice. Call your embassy or consulate.

Mail Generally found at intersections, mailboxes are blue with a red-and-white stripe and carry the inscription U.S. MAIL.

At press time, domestic postage rates were 24¢ for a postcard and 39¢ for a letter. For international mail, a first-class letter of up to 1 ounce costs 84¢ (63¢ to Canada and Mexico); a first-class postcard costs 75¢ (55¢ to Canada and Mexico); and a preprinted postal aerogramme costs 75¢. For more information go to www.usps.com and click on "Calculate Postage."

Passports **For Residents of Australia:** You can pick up an application from your local post office or any branch of Passports Australia, but you must schedule an interview at the passport office to present your application materials. Call the **Australian Passport Information Service** at © 131-232, or visit the government website at www.passports.gov.au.

For Residents of Canada: Passport applications are available at travel agencies throughout Canada or from the central **Passport Office,** Department of Foreign Affairs and International Trade, Ottawa, ON K1A 0G3 (© **800/567-6868;** www.ppt.gc.ca). *Note:* Canadian children who travel must have their own passport. However, if you hold a valid Canadian passport issued before December 11, 2001, that bears the name of your child, the passport remains valid for you and your child until it expires.

For Residents of Ireland: You can apply for a 10-year passport at the **Passport Office,** Setanta Centre, Molesworth Street, Dublin 2 (© **01/671-1633;** www.irl gov.ie/iveagh). Those under age 18 and over 65 must apply for a 3-year passport. You can also apply at 1A South Mall, Cork (© **021/272-525**) or at most main post offices.

For Residents of New Zealand: You can pick up a passport application at any New Zealand Passports Office or download it from their website. Contact the **Passports Office** at © **0800/225-050** in New Zealand, or 04/474-8100, or log on to www.passports.govt.nz.

For Residents of the United Kingdom: To pick up an application for a standard 10-year passport (5-year passport for children under 16), visit your nearest passport office, major post office, or travel agency or contact the **United Kingdom Passport Service** at © **0870/521-0410** or search its website at www.ukpa.gov.uk.

Taxes The United States has no value-added tax (VAT) or other indirect tax at the national level. Every state, county, and city has the right to levy its own local tax on all purchases, including hotel and restaurant checks, airline tickets, and so on. These taxes will not appear on price tags.

Telephone, Telegraph, Telex & Fax Generally, hotel surcharges on long-distance and local calls are astronomical, so you're usually better off using your **cellphone** or a **public pay telephone,** which you'll find clearly marked in most public buildings and private establishments as well as on the street. Many convenience groceries and packaging services sell **prepaid calling cards** in denominations up to $50; these can be the least expensive way to call home. Many public phones now accept American Express, MasterCard, and Visa credit cards. **Local calls** made from public pay phones in most locales cost either 25¢ or 35¢.

Most long-distance and international calls can be dialed directly from any phone. **For calls within the United States and to Canada,** dial 1 followed by the area code and the seven-digit number. **For other international calls,** dial 011 followed by the country code, city code, and the telephone number of the person you are calling.

Calls to area codes **800, 888, 877,** and **866** are toll-free. However, calls to numbers in area codes **700** and **900** (chat lines, bulletin boards, "dating" services, and so on) can be very expensive—usually a charge of 95¢ to $3 or more per minute, and they sometimes have minimum charges that can run as high as $15 or more.

For **reversed-charge or collect calls,** and for person-to-person calls, dial 0 (zero, not the letter O) followed by the area code and number you want; an operator will then come on the line, and you should specify that you are calling collect, or person-to-person, or both. If your operator-assisted call is international, ask for the overseas operator.

For **local directory assistance** ("Information"), dial 411; for long-distance information, dial 1, then the appropriate area code and 555-1212.

Telegraph and telex services are provided primarily by Western Union. You can bring your telegram into the nearest Western Union office (there are hundreds across the country) or dictate it over the phone (© **800/325-6000**). You can also telegraph money, or have it telegraphed to you, very quickly over the Western Union system, but this service can cost as much as 15% to 20% of the amount sent.

Most hotels have **fax machines** available for guest use (be sure to ask about the charge to use it). Many hotel rooms are even wired for guests' fax machines.

Time   The continental United States is divided into **four time zones:** Eastern Standard Time (EST), Central Standard Time (CST), Mountain Standard Time (MST), and Pacific Standard Time (PST). Alaska and Hawaii have their own zones. For example, when it's 9am in Los Angeles (PST), it's 7am in Honolulu (HST),10am in Denver (MST), 11am in Chicago (CST), noon in New York City (EST), 5pm in London (GMT), and 2am the next day in Sydney.

Daylight saving time takes effect at 2am the first Sunday in April until 2am the last Sunday in October, except in Arizona, Hawaii, the U.S. Virgin Islands, and Puerto Rico. Daylight saving moves the clock 1 hour ahead of standard time. (In 2007, a new law extending daylight saving time took effect; clocks now change the second Sun in May and the first Sun in Nov.)

Tipping   In hotels, tip **bellhops** at least $1 per bag ($2–$3 if you have a lot of luggage) and tip the **chamber staff** $1 to $2 per day (more if you've left a disaster area for him or her to clean up). Tip the **doorman** or **concierge** only if he or she has provided you with some specific service (for example, calling a cab for you or obtaining difficult-to-get theater tickets). Tip the **valet-parking attendant** $1 every time you get your car.

In restaurants, bars, and nightclubs, tip **service staff** 15% to 20% of the check, tip **bartenders** 10% to 15%, tip **checkroom attendants** $1 per garment, and tip **valet-parking attendants** $1 per vehicle.

As for other service personnel, tip **cabdrivers** 15% of the fare; tip **skycaps** at airports at least $1 per bag ($2–$3 if you have a lot of luggage); and tip **hairdressers** and **barbers** 15% to 20%.

Toilets   You won't find public toilets or "restrooms" on the streets in most U.S. cities, but they can be found in hotel lobbies, bars, restaurants, museums, department stores, railway and bus stations, and service stations. Large hotels and fast-food restaurants are probably the best bets for good, clean facilities.

Appendix D:
Useful Toll-Free Numbers
& Websites

AIRLINES

Air Canada
© 888/247-2262
www.aircanada.com

AirTran Airways
© 800/247-8726
www.airtran.com

Alaska Airlines/Horizon Air
© 800/252-7522
www.alaskaair.com

American Airlines
© 800/433-7300
www.aa.com

America West Airlines
© 800/235-9292
www.americawest.com

ATA Airlines
© 800/I-FLY-ATA (435-9282)
www.ata.com

British Airways
© 800/247-9297
© 0870/850-9850 in Britain
www.british-airways.com

Cape Air and Nantucket Airlines
© 800/352-0714
www.flycapeair.com

Continental Airlines
© 800/525-0280
www.continental.com

Delta Air Lines
© 800/221-1212
www.delta.com

Frontier Airlines
© 800/432-1359
www.frontierairlines.com

JetBlue Airways
© 800/538-2583
www.jetblue.com

Midwest Airlines
© 800/452-2022
www.midwestairlines.com

North American Airlines
© 800/371-6297
www.northamericanair.com

Northwest Airlines
© 800/225-2525
www.nwa.com

Qantas
© 800/227-4500
© 13 13 13 in Australia
www.qantas.com

Ryanair
© 353/249-7700
© 0818 30 30 30 in Ireland
© 0871 246 0000 in the U.K.
www.ryanair.com

Song
© 800/359-7664
www.flysong.com

Southwest Airlines
© 800/435-9792
www.southwest.com

Spirit Airlines
© 800/772-7117
www.spiritair.com

United Airlines
© 800/241-6522
www.united.com

US Airways
📞 800/428-4322
www.usairways.com

Virgin Atlantic Airways
📞 800/862-8621
📞 0870 380 2007 in the U.K.
www.virgin-atlantic.com

CAR-RENTAL AGENCIES

Advantage
📞 800/777-5500
www.advantagerentacar.com

Alamo
📞 800/GO-ALAMO (462-5266)
www.alamo.com

Auto Europe
📞 888/223-5555
www.autoeurope.com

Avis
📞 800/230-4898
📞 800/272-5871 outside the U.S.
www.avis.com

Budget
📞 800/527-0700
www.budget.com

Dollar
📞 800/800-4000
www.dollar.com

Enterprise
📞 800/325-8007
www.enterprise.com

Hertz
📞 800/654-3131
www.hertz.com

Kemwel (KHA)
📞 800/678-0678
📞 877/820-0668
www.kemwel.com

National
📞 800/CAR-RENT
www.nationalcar.com

Payless
📞 800/PAYLESS
www.paylesscarrental.com

Rent-A-Wreck
📞 800/535-1391
www.rentawreck.com

Thrifty
📞 800/367-2277
www.thrifty.com

MAJOR HOTEL & MOTEL CHAINS

Best Western International
📞 800/528-1234
📞 800/780-7234
www.bestwestern.com

Clarion Hotels
📞 800/CLARION
📞 877/424-6423
www.choicehotels.com

Comfort Inns
📞 800/228-5150
www.choicehotels.com

Courtyard by Marriott
📞 800/321-2211
www.marriott.com/courtyard

Crowne Plaza Hotels
📞 888/303-1746
www.ichotelsgroup.com

Days Inn
📞 800/325-2525
www.daysinn.com

Doubletree Hotels
📞 800/222-TREE
www.doubletree.com

Econo Lodges
📞 800/55-ECONO
www.choicehotels.com

Embassy Suites
📞 800/EMBASSY
www.embassysuites.hilton.com

Fairfield Inn by Marriott
© 800/228-2800
www.marriott.com/fairfieldinn

Four Seasons
© 800/819-5053
www.fourseasons.com

Hampton Inn
© 800/HAMPTON
www.hamptoninn.hilton.com

Hilton Hotels
© 800/HILTONS
www.hilton.com

Holiday Inn
© 800/HOLIDAY
www.ichotelsgroup.com

Howard Johnson
© 800/654-2000
www.hojo.com

Hyatt
© 800/228-9000
www.hyatt.com

InterContinental Hotels & Resorts
© 888/567-8725
www.ichotelsgroup.com

La Quinta Inns and Suites
© 800/531-5900
© 866/725-1661
www.lq.com

Loews Hotels
© 800/23-LOEWS
www.loewshotels.com

Marriott
© 800/228-9290
www.marriott.com

Motel 6
© 800/4-MOTEL-6 (466-8356)
www.motel6.com

Omni Hotels
© 800/THE-OMNI
www.omnihotels.com

Quality
© 877/424-6423
www.choicehotels.com

Radisson Hotels & Resorts
© 800/333-3333
www.radisson.com

Ramada Worldwide
© 800/2-RAMADA
www.ramada.com

Red Carpet Inns
© 800/251-1962
www.bookroomsnow.com

Red Lion Hotels
© 800/RED-LION
www.redlion.rdln.com

Red Roof Inns
© 888/RED-ROOF
www.redroof.com

Renaissance
© 888/236-2427
www.renaissancehotels.com
www.marriott.com/renaissancehotels

Residence Inn by Marriott
© 800/331-3131
www.marriott.com/residenceinn

Ritz-Carlton
© 800/241-3333
www.ritzcarlton.com

Rodeway Inns
© 800/228-2000
www.choicehotels.com

Sheraton Hotels & Resorts
© 800/325-3535
www.starwoodhotels.com/sheraton

Super 8 Motels
© 800/800-8000
www.super8.com

Travelodge
© 800/255-3050
© 800/578-7878
www.travelodge.com

Vagabond Inns
© 800/522-1555
www.vagabondinn.com

Westin Hotels & Resorts
© 800/937-8461
www.starwoodhotels.com/westin

Wyndham Hotels & Resorts
© 800/822-4200
www.wyndham.com

Index